Diagnostic Histopathology of Tumors
Third Edition

VOLUME 1

Diagnostic Histopathology of Tumors

THIRD EDITION

VOLUME 1

EDITED BY

Christopher D.M. Fletcher MD FRCPath

Director of Surgical Pathology
Brigham and Women's Hospital;
Chief of Onco-Pathology
Dana-Farber Cancer Institute;
Professor of Pathology
Harvard Medical School
Boston, Massachusetts, USA

CHURCHILL LIVINGSTONE
ELSEVIER

An imprint of Elsevier Limited

First edition 1995
Second edition 2000
Third edition 2007

ISBN-13: 978-0-443-07434-9
ISBN-10: 0-443-07434-8

British Library Cataloguing in Publication Data
A catalogue record for this book is available from the British Library

Library of Congress Cataloging in Publication Data
A catalog record for this book is available from the Library of Congress

Notice
Medical knowledge is constantly changing. Standard safety precautions must be followed, but as new research and clinical experience broaden our knowledge, changes in treatment and drug therapy may become necessary or appropriate. Readers are advised to check the most current product information provided by the manufacturer of each drug to be administered to verify the recommended dose, the method and duration of administration, and contraindications. It is the responsibility of the practitioner, relying on experience and knowledge of the patient, to determine dosages and the best treatment for each individual patient. Neither the Publisher nor the author assume any liability for any injury and/or damage to persons or property arising from this publication.

The Publisher

ELSEVIER your source for books, journals and multimedia in the health sciences
www.elsevierhealth.com

Working together to grow libraries in developing countries

www.elsevier.com | www.bookaid.org | www.sabre.org

ELSEVIER BOOK AID International Sabre Foundation

Printed in China
Last digit is the print number: 9 8 7 6 5 4 3 2

For Elsevier

Commissioning Editor: Michael Houston
Project Development Manager: Sheila Black
Editorial Assistant: Liz Brown
Project Manager: Bryan Potter
Design Manager: Stewart Larking
Illustration Manager: Gillian Richards
Illustrators: Oxford Illustrators • Ian Ramsden
Marketing Managers: John Canelon (NL/UK), Katherine Neely (USA)

Contents

VOLUME 2

List of Contributors

Mahul B. Amin MD
Chairman, Department of Pathology & Laboratory Medicine
Professor of Pathology at UCLA School of Medicine
Cedars-Sinai Medical Center
Los Angeles, CA, USA

Alberto G. Ayala MD
Deputy Chief of Service
Professor of Pathology, Weill Medical College of Cornell University
The Methodist Hospital;
Ashbel-Smith Professor Emeritus of Pathology
The University of Texas M.D. Anderson Cancer Center
Houston, TX, USA

Anton E. Becker MD PhD
Emeritus Professor of Cardiovascular Pathology
Academic Medical Center
University of Amsterdam
Netherlands

Eduardo Calonje MD DipRCPath
Director of Diagnostic Dermatopathology
Department of Dermato-Histopathology
St John's Institute of Dermatology
St. Thomas's Hospital
London, UK

Fiona Campbell BSc(Hons) MD FRCPath
Consultant Gastrointestinal Pathologist
Department of Pathology
Royal Liverpool University Hospital
Liverpool, UK

John K. C. Chan MBBS FRCPath FRCPA
Consultant Pathologist
Department of Pathology
Queen Elizabeth Hospital
Kowloon, Hong Kong

Wah Cheuk MD
Associate Consultant
Department of Pathology
Queen Elizabeth Hospital
Kowloon, Hong Kong

Philip B. Clement MD
Professor of Pathology
Department of Pathology
Vancouver General Hospital
Vancouver, BC, Canada

Christopher P. Crum MD
Professor of Pathology
Harvard Medical School;
Director, Women's and Perinatal Pathology
Brigham and Women's Hospital
Boston, MA, USA

John N. Eble MD FRCPA
Nordschow Professor of Laboratory Medicine
Professor & Chairman,
Department of Pathology & Laboratory Medicine
Indiana School of Medicine
Indianapolis, IN, USA

Ian O. Ellis BMedSci BM BS FRCPath
Professor of Cancer Pathology and Honorary Consultant Pathologist
Department of Histopathology
Nottingham University Hospitals NHS Trust
Nottingham, UK

Linda D. Ferrell MD
Professor and Vice Chair of Pathology
Director of Surgical Pathology
Department of Pathology
University of California,
San Francisco, CA, USA

Christopher D.M. Fletcher MD FRCPath
Director of Surgical Pathology
Brigham and Women's Hospital;
Chief of Onco-Pathology
Dana-Farber Cancer Institute;
Professor of Pathology
Harvard Medical School
Boston, MA, USA

Jonathan A. Fletcher MD
Director, Solid Tumor Cytogenetics
Department of Pathology
Brigham and Women's Hospital;
Associate Professor of Pathology and Pediatrics
Harvard Medical School
Boston MA, USA

Robert Folberg MD
Frances B. Geever Professor and Head
Department of Pathology
University of Illinois College of Medicine
Chicago, IL, USA

David R. Genest MD
Associate Professor of Pathology
Harvard Medical School;
Division of Women's and Perinatal Pathology
Brigham and Women's Hospital
Boston, MA, USA

Philipp U. Heitz MD
Emeritus Professor of Pathology
Department of Pathology
University of Zürich
Zürich, Switzerland

Tan A. Ince MD PhD
Instructor in Pathology
Harvard Medical School;
Associate Pathologist
Division of Women's and Perinatal Pathology
Department of Pathology
Brigham and Women's Hospital
Boston, MA, USA

Carrie Y. Inwards MD
Assistant Professor of Pathology and
Consultant, Division of Anatomic Pathology
Mayo Clinic College of Medicine
Rochester MN, USA

Jeremy R. Jass MD DSc FRCPath FRCPA
Canada Research Chair in Gastrointestinal Pathology
Department of Pathology
McGill University
Montreal, QC, Canada

Sanjay Kakar MD
Assistant Professor
Department of Pathology
UCSF and Veterans Administration Medical Center,
San Francisco, CA, USA

Kyu-Rae Kim MD PhD
Associate Professor
Department of Pathology
Asan Medical Center,
The University of Ulsan College of Medicine
Seoul, Korea

David S. Klimstra MD
Attending Pathologist and Chief of Surgical Pathology
Memorial Sloan-Kettering Cancer Center
Professor of Pathology and Laboratory Medicine
Weill Medical College of Cornell University
New York, NY, USA

Günter Klöppel MD PhD
Professor of Pathology and
Director of Department of Pathology
University of Kiel
Kiel, Germany

Jeffery L. Kutok MD PhD
Associate Professor of Pathology
Harvard Medical School;
Hematopathologist
Brigham and Women's Hospital
Boston, MA, USA

Ernest E. Lack MD
Director of Anatomic Pathology
Department of Pathology
Washington Hospital Center
Washington, DC, USA

Gregory Y. Lauwers MD
Director, Gastrointestinal Pathology Service
Department of Pathology
Massachusetts General Hospital;
Associate Professor of Pathology
Harvard Medical School
Boston, MA, USA

Andrew H. S. Lee MB BChir MRCP MRCPath
Consultant Histopathologist
Department of Histopathology
Nottingham University Hospitals
Nottingham, UK

Kenneth R. Lee MD
Associate Professor of Pathology
Harvard Medical School;
Boston, MA, USA

Yonghee Lee MD
Associate Professor of Pathology
Pochon CHA University College of Medicine
Bundang CHA General Hospital
Kyonggi-do, Korea

Janina A. Longtine MD
Chief, Molecular Diagnostics
Department of Pathology
Brigham & Women's Hospital;
Associate Professor of Pathology
Harvard Medical School
Boston, MA, USA

M. Beatriz S. Lopes MD
Professor of Pathology and Neurological Surgery
Department of Pathology - Neuropathology
University of Virginia School of Medicine
Charlottesville, VA, USA

The late D. Gordon MacDonald BDS PhD FRCPath FDSRCPS(G)
Formerly Professor in Oral Pathology and Honorary
Consultant
Department of Oral Medicine & Pathology
Glasgow Dental Hospital
Glasgow, UK

Bruce Mackay MD PhD
Emeritus Professor of Pathology
University of Texas MD Anderson Cancer Center
Missouri City, TX, USA

Leslie Michaels MD FRCPath FRCP(C) FCAP
Professor Emeritus
Department of Histopathology
Royal Free and UCL Medical School
London, UK

Cesar A. Moran MD
Professor of Pathology, Director of Thoracic Pathology
and Deputy Chairman
Department of Pathology
The University of Texas
MD Anderson Cancer Center
Houston TX, USA

George L. Mutter MD
Associate Professor of Medicine
Harvard Medical School;
Pathologist, Division of Women's and Perinatal
Pathology
Department of Pathology
Brigham and Women's Hospital
Boston, MA, USA

Marisa R. Nucci MD
Associate Pathologist
Divisions of Women's and Perinatal Pathology and
Surgical Pathology
Department of Pathology
Brigham and Women's Hospital;
Assistant Professor of Pathology
Harvard Medical School
Boston, MA, USA

Ben Z. Pilch MD
Associate Pathologist
Massachusetts General Hospital;
Associate Professor of Pathology
Harvard Medical School
Boston, MA, USA

Sarah E. Pinder MBChB FRCPath
Consultant Breast Pathologist
Histopathology Department
Addenbrooke's NHS Trust
Cambridge, UK

Jae Y. Ro MD PhD
Professor of Pathology
Department of Pathology
The Methodist Hospital
Weill Medical College of Cornell University
Houston, TX, USA

Daniel J. Santa Cruz MD
Cutaneous Pathology
WCP Laboratories Inc.
St Louis, MO, USA

Paul M. Speight BDS FDSRCPS(Glas) PhD FRCPath FDS RCS(Edin)
Professor of Oral and Maxillofacial Pathology
Department of Oral and Maxillofacial Pathology
School of Clinical Dentistry
University of Sheffield
Sheffield, UK

Saul Suster MD
Professor and Vice Chair
Director of Anatomic Pathology
The Ohio State University Hospital
Columbus, OH, USA

K. Krishnan Unni MB BS
Professor of Pathology and Orthopedics and
Consultant, Division of Anatomic Pathology and
Division of Orthopedic Oncology
Mayo Clinic College of Medicine
Rochester, MN, USA

Scott R. VandenBerg MD PhD
Professor of Pathology and Neurological Surgery
University of California School of Medicine,
San Francisco
San Francisco, CA, USA

Bruce M. Wenig MD
Chairman
Department of Pathology and Laboratory Medicine
Beth Israel Medical Center;
Professor of Pathology
Albert Einstein College of Medicine
New York, NY, USA

Geraint T. Williams BSc MD MRCR FRCP(Lond) FRCPath FMedSci
Professor of Pathology
Department of Pathology
Wales College of Medicine
Cardiff University
Cardiff, UK

Robert H. Young MD FRCPath
Director of Surgical Pathology
Department of Anatomic Pathology
Massachusetts General Hospital
Boston, MA, USA

Charles F. Zaloudek MD
Professor of Pathology
Department of Pathology
University of California, San Francisco
San Francisco, CA, USA

Preface

In the seven year interval since publication of the Second Edition, conventional morphologic and immuno-histochemical assessment has continued to hold sway as the pre-eminent, most reliable and most cost-effective means by which to provide a diagnosis, prognostic assessment and, in most cases, determination of the adequacy of excision for human tumors, which remain so prevalent. The continued utility of such 'traditional' technologies and interpretive skills is somewhat reassuring in the setting of the ever widening disparities in the availability of more expensive modern technologies, such as molecular genetic diagnosis, gene expression profiling and proteomics, not only (to an appalling degree) between the developed and still developing (or underdeveloped) areas of the world, but even between different developed countries or regions thereof. Furthermore, many of the latter technologies have yet to fulfil their promise as potential clinical tools.

For sure, the role of molecular diagnosis is now firmly established. In more recent years, it has expanded to include: susceptibility testing, for example in carcinomas of breast and colon; prognostication in glial neoplasms; more sensitive tracking of minimal residual disease, principally in hematolymphoid malignancies. This expanded and important role is reflected throughout this new edition and is particularly highlighted in Chapter 32 by Janina Longtine and Jonathan Fletcher. Perhaps the most high profile molecular advance has been the increasing implementation of rational targeted therapies, based upon reproducible identification of the relevant target molecule. Notably, most such targets, at least initially, are identified immunohistochemically (e.g. HER2/neu, c-kit and EGFR). However, as treatment resistance very often develops and resistance mechanisms are being characterized, then increasing reliance will likely be placed on mutational analysis in order to facilitate optimal treatment selection. As attention in recent years has been focussed on tyrosine kinases,

optimists envisage broad-based screening of any given tumor's 'kinome' with the goal of identifying suitable activated targets or signalling pathways susceptible to intervention. Such technology is highly unlikely to become widely available in the foreseeable future and, furthermore, until the therapeutic relevance of the varied and quite different mechanisms of kinase overexpression or activation are better understood, then optimism should best be cautious.

Remarkably, and seemingly with no evident slowing of the pace, morphologic tumor classifications and methods of prognostication continue to evolve and be ever more refined, constantly enhancing the value of high quality anatomic pathology. Many of these advances have been codified in the new WHO classifications which have been issued over the past five years or so. Furthermore, 'new' tumor types (or subtypes) of clinical or therapeutic relevance continue to be recognized in a seemingly limitless fashion. This Third Edition has been substantially revised and updated to incorporate this broad range of new information and some chapters have been entirely rewritten, notably those dealing with tumors of the hepatobiliary system, many components of the female reproductive tract, the hematopoietic system and the eye (and its adnexa).

As always, any and all errors or omissions are entirely the responsibility of the Editor and I remain deeply indebted to the Contributors for the unfailingly high quality of the material which they provide, as well as the enthusiasm with which they do so. Finally I should like to warmly acknowledge, with considerable gratitude, the hard work and unfailing support of my outstanding secretary, Kathleen Radzikowski, and also of the 'key players' at Elsevier – Michael Houston, Sheila Black and Bryan Potter.

Christopher D.M. Fletcher
Boston, 2006

Introduction

Christopher D. M. Fletcher

In no area of surgical pathology, possibly even in all diagnostic histopathology, does the pathologist play a more important and crucial role than in the diagnosis of tumors. Although patients or laypersons are often entirely ignorant of this role and fondly imagine that their surgeon, other clinician, or oncologist is the true diagnostician – a misapprehension which some of our colleagues do not always dispel! – the reality is that the histology report is the principal determinant of diagnosis, likely clinical course, and therapy in any patient found to have a swelling or mass, with the possible exception of patients with an abscess or hematoma.

The need for timely, accurate, and detailed reports has never been greater, especially in our increasingly subspecialized and litigious society. This need comes at a time when the fields of tumor pathology and surgical pathology in general are expanding at an unprecedented rate, as reflected in the constant characterization of previously unrecognized tumor types or variants and the advancing delineation and application of new technologies which provide objective aids, not only to diagnosis, but also to prognostication and to the understanding of pathogenetic mechanisms. This almost daily expansion in the surgical pathologist's "database" is manifest in the perceived need for ever more numerous journals and textbooks, which of themselves become more and more subspecialized. It is against this background that we have attempted to put together a book dealing solely with the diagnostic histopathology of tumors in all systems, employing contributors who are all recognized specialists in their own areas of this field. I use the term "we" to underline the close nature of the collaboration between editor, contributor, and publisher in a project of this scale, but all errors and omissions, as in prior editions, are the sole responsibility of the editor. It should also be admitted that the rate at which surgical pathology is progressing will be reflected in the fact that some small parts of this book will inevitably be outdated or superseded by the time of publication!

The philosophy of this book has been to use the word "tumor" in its traditionally descriptive sense; in other words, to encompass neoplastic and, in some cases, non-neoplastic swellings. In this regard, it is commonly impossible, or at least a source of unresolved argument, to know whether certain lesions should be classified as hamartomatous, hyperplastic, or neoplastic and, most often, this text has adopted a pragmatically neutral role. It is of interest to note that there is currently no generally accepted definition of a neoplasm, since clonality alone is viewed as insufficient in this regard: some processes traditionally regarded as reactive, for example in lymphoid tissue and synovium, have been shown to be clonal or oligoclonal. The capacity for growth in a transplanted (xenograft) model is perhaps the most convincing criterion, but is not readily applicable in a routine setting! While the focus of this book is inevitably on histomorphology, basic clinical data, as well as molecular genetic data where relevant, are also provided for most lesions, since these contribute significantly to accurate classification. Guidelines to differential diagnosis (with appropriate cross-references where necessary) are described for those tumors that pose a particular or common problem.

This introductory chapter provides an opportunity to put forward, with due modesty, some personal approaches and views regarding the routine practice of diagnostic tumor pathology. The philosophy propounded hereinafter is individual and should not be construed as representing any policy agreed among the contributors. Some of the suggestions put forward below undoubtedly are unoriginal but represent simply the "folklore" of surgical pathology. Within Europe at least, I am aware that some of these ideas (although I'm not sure which ones!) originated from Professor John Azzopardi, one of the great teachers in this field. In some quarters today, the passage of such valuable information is regarded as being of little value and we, as practicing histopathologists, are often encouraged to concentrate upon purportedly more objective or "scientific" assessments of diagnosis or prognosis. This is reflected in the remarkable extent to which the content of some large academic meetings worldwide is governed by fashionable, but often transient, techniques, antibodies, genes, or mutational analyses. For as long as human tumors remain more varied, unpredictable, and idiosyncratic than their hosts, in terms of both morphology and behavior, then there will be a clear and unassailable need for good surgical pathology, based principally on careful and experienced light microscopic examination, supported, where appropriate or necessary, by more modern techniques. For the time being at least, such skilled morphologic examination remains the gold standard in anatomic pathology and it is unlikely to be surpassed in terms of either reliability or cost-effectiveness in the near future. While it is true that some aspects of diagnostic pathology are subjective to a troubling degree and while we should all work towards diagnostic reproducibility and objectivity by whatever means are most effective, it is a simple fact (at least in tumor medicine) that surgical pathology has never played a more important and pivotal role than at the present time. This is largely due to the central role of histopathologic parameters in determining therapy and hence the wish of clinicians to obtain (and often discuss) detailed pathology reports. The manner in which expertise in surgical pathology is often taken for granted in some academic centers, especially in Europe and the USA, is reprehensible and, if it continues, may lead to the progressive loss of important diagnostic skills, due to erosion of experiential training and realignment of priorities within academic departments. In part this trend reflects an increasing tendency to shorten training time prior to certification, as well as the importance attached to grant-raising by MD/PhDs and PhDs engaged in basic research, one outcome of which has been to widen the gap between much of the research undertaken in academic medical centers and the primary clinical mission of a hospital environment. There is a clear need for increased numbers of true physician scientists, increased funding for clinical and translational research, and greater mutual respect and collaboration between physicians and laboratory scientists. No one is better placed to take advantage of such collaborative opportunities than pathologists.

The guidelines that follow are set out in an order which corresponds, as far as possible, to the events in a surgical pathology laboratory from receipt of a specimen to the issuance of a report.

To diagnose a tumor in the absence of clear and complete clinical data is foolhardy, dangerous, and sometimes impossible. Many of our clinical colleagues often need to be reminded of this fact; even simple information concerning age, sex, or location may be missing on the request form. This may raise compliance issues in addition to the potentially negative impact on patient care. If a specimen arrives in the laboratory without such data then a medically qualified member of staff should not hesitate to contact the errant clinician or his/her staff; sometimes it may be appropriate to withhold the report until the pathologist is fully apprised of the necessary information. If there is a history of any previous neoplasm, especially at the same anatomical location, then the date of biopsy, diagnosis, and laboratory reference (when available) should be requested and recorded. If ancillary data, such as the radiologic findings or serum chemistry in a bone tumor, are necessary to make a diagnosis these should be requested, if not demanded!

Accurate and careful macroscopic description of a tumor specimen, particularly the definitive resection, is vital to diagnosis, prognosis, and retrospective data analysis for pathological or clinical studies. The first occasion upon which a resection specimen is examined in the pathology laboratory is usually the one and only time at which tumor size, weight, approximate extent of necrosis, and distance to resection margins can be gauged properly; once the specimen has been dissected, cut up, fixed, and otherwise distorted then such valuable parameters often cannot be assessed. Similarly, features such as the type of margin (encapsulated, circumscribed, or infiltrative), the presence of satellite nodules, the presence (or involvement) of lymph nodes, the extent of spread or invasion of adjacent structures are often best determined at the time of specimen cut-up. The macroscopic description of the tumor in the final report should be sufficiently detailed to enable any other pathologist to conjure up a clear mental image of the neoplasm. If this is done well, then often, in combination with the clinical data, it is possible to have a good idea of the final diagnosis, even before seeing the slides, especially in the more common tumor types. The other important role of good macroscopic examination is to ensure that a tumor is adequately sampled. The type or extent of sampling varies according to the size and anatomic location of

the neoplasm but, as a general rule of thumb, all lesions of appreciable size (perhaps > 2 cm) should be sliced serially and all areas showing a differing appearance should be examined histologically. In the appropriate organ systems, care should be taken to obtain blocks at the most likely site of muscular, serosal, or capsular invasion, as determined by naked-eye examination. Given the currently prevailing fashion for inking specimen margins, I would like to make a plea in this regard – think before you ink! The indiscriminate inking of specimens, almost irrespective of type, has led in some contexts to the time-wasting and often irrelevant examination of margins in lesions which either have no potential to recur, or else have been so obviously marginally or incompletely excised that the positive (or at least oncologically inadequate) margins can be recorded grossly. In some cases, lesions (or biopsies) which are so small that they are embedded and sectioned in their entirety in one block are still inked, yet it is hardly a challenge to assess the margins (without inking) in such cases. This trend in specimen-handling is almost anti-intellectual, often obliterates the benefit of examining a specimen in a thoughtful manner, and taints the validity of inking, which can be invaluable in an appropriate context.

Turning now to histologic evaluation, clearly this is a complex, often organ-specific process, the details of which are described in the separate chapters of this book. However, one or two pertinent generalizations can be made. Generalizations admittedly are dangerous and stand only to be shot down by exceptions to each rule; however, I believe that they provide useful guidelines. In any patient with a previous primary (or recurrent) neoplasm, the slides should always be reviewed. This serves four main purposes: (1) it provides a simple but useful form of audit; (2) it enables comment to be made as to whether a tumor has advanced (or sometimes decreased) in histologic grade, thereby possibly influencing clinical outcome; (3) it is the only way of determining with certainty if a patient has developed two separate primary neoplasms, whether of the same or different types; and (4) sometimes such review provides a vital clue to diagnosis since recurrent or metastatic neoplasms, especially of mesenchymal type, show a remarkable capacity to alter their phenotype or to lose evidence of specific differentiation. What appears to be a weird or undiagnosable neoplasm, on occasion, can suddenly become a simple case when the previous histology is reviewed! In this regard, the principle of Occam's razor should be remembered: a patient is always more likely to have a single primary neoplasm with an odd pattern of recurrence than to have two separate primaries.

A second generalization, which, although possibly a philosophical point, I personally regard to be of paramount importance, is that strict histologic criteria should be employed for all tumor diagnoses. With rare exceptions, usually relating to specialist expertise based upon experience, it is not acceptable to make an arbitrary diagnosis founded on personal whim. If a colleague or trainee asks how a diagnosis was reached, one should be able to enumerate reasons or criteria, be they positive or negative findings; hopefully, the days of saying "It is what it is because I say it is" are gone! The merits of this practice are: (1) that uniformity in diagnosis is increased, thereby facilitating treatment decisions; (2) when analyzing published data or initiating new studies (whether clinical or pathological), one can hopefully compare like with like – a vital step towards understanding tumor morphology and behavior, especially if large multicenter studies are required; and (3) the provision of clear diagnostic criteria is the only reliable means by which trainee pathologists can be taught. In this regard we need to introduce morphologic objectivity whenever possible, even though surgical pathology, by necessity, remains a subjective art, at least in part.

The third, hopefully well-known, generalization applicable to light microscopic examination of tumors using hematoxylin and eosin (H&E)-stained sections is that, in most (but not all!) cases, low-power appearances often provide the best guide to the separation of benign from malignant lesions. Features such as the preservation of normal (often lobular) architecture, lesional symmetry, and the general impression of overall cellularity and nuclear atypia are exceedingly helpful in this distinction. Conversely, if one rushes straight to the high-power lenses, it is remarkably easy to find (and be misled by) cells with atypical or worrisome features in a very wide range of tumors or pseudoneoplastic lesions. Good examples of this phenomenon are the bizarre, often multinucleate, stromal cells found in the submucosa or lamina propria of reactive, often polypoid lesions at almost any mucosal or cutaneous location and the densely hyperchromatic, irregular, degenerative ("ancient") nuclei encountered in a variety of soft tissue neoplasms. Similarly, the presence of single, or very rare, abnormal mitotic figures need not equate with malignancy: I will always remember being shown such a mitosis in an otherwise normal proliferative endometrium during my first year in pathology!

With regard to the application of more modern techniques to diagnostic practice, this is mentioned (where relevant) in each chapter and is discussed in more detail in Chapter 32. Immunohistochemistry, which now is more than 25 years old and therefore no longer regarded as modern by the arbiters of fashion, is indeed very useful but must always be interpreted in context. A seemingly aberrant result, especially if this is a negative result, should never be allowed to overrule an obvious morphologic diagnosis. Quality control is vital if immunohistochemistry is to have any worthwhile role and often this requires that any given laboratory should have a "minimum throughput," albeit this level of work activity is poorly defined. Laboratories that perform a large number of immunostains on a daily basis and do not change the staff around unnecessarily almost invariably produce more consistent and better-quality results than their smaller, intermittently utilized counterparts. The value of using large antibody panels or complex algorithms for immunodiagnosis is somewhat controversial but, in these days of cost-effectiveness, it is my view that the choice of immunostains, where necessary, should be governed (and limited) by a carefully assessed differential diagnosis, based on H&E morphology, through which specific questions need to be answered. The broader and more mindless a panel of antibodies becomes, the greater is the likelihood of obtaining inexplicable, misleading, or aberrant results. Equally, if reliance is placed upon an algorithm (especially one generated by a laboratory other than your own), then a single aberrant or false-positive (or negative) result can lead to an irrational diagnosis, as well as a lengthy and costly trail of immunostains. A separate point of contemporary importance is the increasing trend of using immunohistochemistry for identification of potential therapeutic targets (e.g., *c-kit* or various growth factor receptors). Pathologists must not allow themselves to be bullied into undertaking such testing unless the protein in question has been proven to have biologic relevance (usually activation or mutation) in the given tumor type and unless there are well-validated, reliable, and reproducible antibodies available for this purpose.

With regard to many of the more recent molecular genetic techniques, some of which undoubtedly have proved (and will continue to prove) to be valuable in tumor pathology, two points should be borne in mind. First, the published results concerning a pattern of gene expression or karyotypic abnormality in a given tumor type are only as meaningful (or as valid) as the corresponding morphologic diagnoses. If the diagnoses upon which these results are based happen to be inconsistent or even wrong, then the conclusions made are rendered worthless. Therefore collaboration and mutual respect between histopathologists and basic scientists are absolute prerequisites for continued progress in this setting. As chip technology has begun to allow rapid and detailed molecular profiling of large numbers of tumors, such professional interactions will be crucial in validating such data and in extracting maximal clinical value from this new information. In this regard, it is important to note that the majority of genomic expression profiling studies in recent years, trumpeting new-found diagnostic or prognostic accuracy, have failed (with a few notable exceptions) to improve upon the daily achievements of routine light microscopic techniques. This may in part reflect the fact that many such studies have not included expert pathologists in the research team. Thus, the second key point, despite initial optimism, is that many of the molecular and genetic parameters assessed in recent years, with important exceptions (e.g., *N-myc* amplification in neuroblastoma, cytogenetic and molecular characterization of many leukemias and sarcomas, and the detection of minimal residual disease in hematolymphoid neoplasms), have not improved upon careful (or expert) light microscopic examination for diagnosis and prognosis. The latter therefore remains the gold standard against which all new technology needs to be assessed; claims that newer modalities provide greater objectivity should be weighed not only against financial cost and problems of reproducibility in non-specialized laboratories, but also against the frequency with which such claims seem to be proved wrong, as witness previous descriptions of so-called cancer-specific antigens or mutations, or the short-lived misapprehension that expression of *p53* was a reliable marker of the malignant phenotype.

Once a diagnosis has been reached, then a report must be formulated, guidelines for which are well beyond the remit of a book of this type. However it is important to ensure that any report provides as much useful information to the clinician as possible and, in this context, there are increasingly good reasons to use synoptic (or template) reporting formats, especially for common tumor types. In this way, key elements of information are not forgotten and the clinician's ability to interpret a report is maximized. Not only does this mean the inclusion of clear statements regarding tumor type, grade, or stage (where applicable) and status of resection margins, but the report offers a unique opportunity to provide general data concerning clinical features, likely behavior, and ideal management, supported by references to the published literature where appropriate. The transmission of such information may only be appropriate in the case of uncommon or unusual neoplasms and the extent to which a surgical pathologist will feel able or comfortable to offer advice on therapy will depend greatly on local circumstances and the tolerance or insight of clinical colleagues. In my view, however, surgical pathologists should never forget that they are providing a clinical, often subjective opinion quite different from the type of report required of some other specialties in pathology, and in this circumstance we should not shy away from offering whatever expertise or background data that are available to us. It is an extraordinary but undoubted fact that the key papers describing clinical features and therapeutic outcome in many tumor types are published, at least initially, in pathological, rather than clinical, journals. Often, therefore, surgical pathologists are more likely to have received (and hopefully read!) the latest published studies on the general aspects of a given neoplasm than their clinical colleagues. However, any tendency to try and achieve "one-upmanship" in this relation-ship should be carefully curbed until such time as pathologists can feel sure that they have also scanned the relevant clinical literature!

To conclude this introductory chapter, I would like to offer some simple truisms applicable to diagnostic tumor pathology. Many of these are self-evident and most likely are widely known; the frequency with which they are forgotten is there-fore all the more remarkable and regrettable:

1. By virtue of simple statistical probability, common things remain common; therefore do not be tempted into an esoteric (or exciting!) diagnosis until you have confidently excluded a more probable diagnosis. A good example that typifies this pitfall is the characterization of spindle-celled malignant neoplasms arising in epithelial-lined viscera, such as the upper aerodigestive tract or urinary bladder; sarcomatoid (or spindle cell) carcinomas are a far more likely prospect than some unusual sarcoma or carcinosarcoma.

2. Pathologists should never be afraid to request a larger (or repeat) biopsy if they are having difficulty in coming to a firm diagnosis prior to definitive therapy. It is a matter of fact that some tumor biopsies are inadequate or unrepresentative. In fact the increasing trend for our clinical and radiological colleagues to provide smaller and smaller biopsies (in the names of cost-effectiveness and convenient patient care) is not only limiting our ability to make definitive diagnoses but is also diminishing the opportunity to provide valuable prognostic information. This tide needs to be stemmed, or at least challenged and first validated, especially since the use of preoperative neoadjuvant therapy is also increasing and often renders the ultimate resection specimen relatively useless for diagnostic or prognostic purposes. Painful hours, or even days, of indecision followed by an inconclusive or, worse, inappropriately confident report are far better avoided by a clear request for more tissue. On occasion this undoubtedly prevents the institution of inappropriate therapy. Any attempt to hedge (or spread) one's bets in a diagnostic report should be avoided whenever possible.

3. Pathologists should never be afraid to admit that they cannot diagnose or classify a given neoplasm. There is no pathologist on this planet who does not sometimes benefit from a second opinion, however intermittent this need may be. Pathologists who believe that they never need a second or specialist opinion are dangerous. Increasingly this becomes true in surgical pathology which is ever more subspecialized and in which the days of the true generalist are numbered. Conversely, there will always remain a subset of human tumors that defy rational classification by anyone. In this context there may be (but there are not always) clues to the likely clinical behavior of such a neoplasm, even if the line of differentiation is obscure, but such clues should be interpreted only tentatively; the reality is that if one cannot categorize a neoplasm reliably on morphologic grounds then any attempt at prognostication is inevitably unreliable and only amounts to more or less sophisticated guesswork!

4. The (possibly obvious) corollary of the point above is that pathologists can only diagnose what they have seen, read, or heard about previously. This sets clear limitations on the interpretative skills of any pathologist and underlines the need to keep abreast of recent continued developments, either by regular attendance at postgraduate meetings or the routine perusal of major journals in our specialty. Those (increasingly few) who insist on regarding the recognition or recategorization of diagnostic entities as worthless "splitting" do so at their peril; those who attempt to force all tumor diagnoses into categories with which they are already familiar do likewise.

5. A further point which is related, at least peripherally, to the "don't know" situation, is that a pathologist (or, for that matter, any other practising physician) should never be afraid to admit a mistake. Every pathologist has made at least an occasional error, however trivial or clinically insignificant, and anyone who suggests otherwise is probably deluded. Our specialty is an interpretative skill or art, not a black-or-white measurement, and therefore human error is unfortunately inevitable. Far more trouble can be generated by concealment or dishonesty in this regard than by admitting a suboptimal diagnosis.

6. Prognostication in cancer management, especially among clinical oncologists, is often believed to rely largely upon tumor grade and stage, both of which the pathologist may be instrumental in assessing. There are some clinicians who believe that such parameters (particularly grade) can be determined in the absence of a specific diagnosis. In the light of the foregoing discussion, this is clearly nonsensical and it is up to surgical pathologists to resist this trend. In very many organ systems, the principal determinant of likely outcome is accurate histologic typing and the importance of an unequivocal diagnosis should never be underestimated. Equally there are some types of cancer in which substratification by grade is meaningless because a given tumor type may invariably be biologically low-grade (e.g., infantile fibrosarcoma) or high-grade (e.g., pleural malignant mesothelioma), irrespective of histologic appearances. Therefore it is important to recognize that grading (and often also staging) systems need to be tailored, in many cases, to the individual tumor type and this is one

circumstance in which generalizations can undoubtedly be dangerous. In parallel, we need to take care that the rush to incorporate mutational analysis as a prognostic component of clinical care (as, for example, in gastrointestinal stromal tumors and non-small cell lung carcinomas) does not bypass careful validation studies, remains confined to the tumor types for which such validation has been achieved, and has demonstrable clinical impact. For the relative lack of significant therapeutic advances in some tumor types to hide behind the use of ever more sophisticated (and expensive) diagnostic or prognostic technologies is not a desirable outcome. This discussion also begs the question of what constitutes a high-grade neoplasm; there are no easy or clear answers to this question but the following examples provide food for thought and should prompt careful appraisal of the manner in which we, as doctors, assess malignant neoplasms. Consider the following three patients: the first is a 60-year-old man with an inoperable small cell carcinoma of bronchus; we know that his tumor is likely to disseminate rapidly and his prospects of surviving more than 12 months are very slim. The second is a 25-year-old female with localized alveolar soft-part sarcoma of the thigh; we know that her 5-year survival probability is 60–70% and, with this information, she may well form a stable relationship and start a family – but we also know that her chances of surviving beyond the age of 45 are no more than 15%,

because most patients with this type of tumor eventually develop distant metastases. The third is a 45-year-old with a grade 2 astrocytoma in the frontal lobe; we know that the risk of extracranial spread (metastasis) is very small but that the chances of postsurgical recurrence are high; we also know that such recurrences are likely to be progressively fatal over a 5–10-year period. I believe that all three patients would be justified in claiming that they had a biologically high-grade neoplasm, yet the perception of the physician, pathologist, or scientist in each case would undoubtedly be different, particularly with regard to the inherent biology of these tumors. This variability underlines the need to treat tumors on the basis of biologic, rather than histologic, grade, at least in those circumstances in which our therapeutic options allow any flexibility.

7. The last, and perhaps most straightforward, truism is that histology reports, whether on specimens from one's own hospital or from a patient thousands of miles away, should be as prompt as is feasible and safe. The surgical pathology report is not simply a matter of record or a means of rubber-stamping a clinical suspicion; in the context of tumor pathology, almost always it is the diagnostic arbiter and one of the major determinants of therapy. It impinges enormously on patients, even if they are commonly unaware of this fact. Any pathologist who fails to recognize or shoulder this responsibility might best be advised to consider alternative employment!

Tumors of the heart and pericardium

Anton E. Becker

2

Introduction

Primary tumors of the heart and pericardium are rare. This statement is best exemplified by referring to the experience of the Armed Forces Institute of Pathology (AFIP), which in 1977 had registered only 444 primary tumors of the heart and pericardium, excluding cysts.[1] A more recent update from the same institution recorded 386 primary tumors of the heart in the period 1976–1993.[2] Hence, these are a rather esoteric subject, even in large referral centers for cardiovascular disease.

To put this in perspective, a comparison between three institutions, each with a different background, may be helpful. Table 2.1 shows the relative incidence of cardiac tumors as they were referred to the AFIP, based on the figures produced by Burke and Virmani in 1996.[2] The 25-year experience with the surgical treatment of cardiac tumors, covering the period

| Table 2.1 | A survey of primary tumors of the heart (excluding cysts and tumors of the pericardium) registered in the Armed Forces Institute of Pathology from 1976 to 1993 (adapted from Burke & Virmani[2]) |

Infants and children[a] ($n = 55$)				Adults ($n = 319$)			
Benign	($n = 44$)	**Malignant**	($n = 11$)	**Benign**	($n = 193$)	**Malignant**	($n = 126$)
Rhabdomyoma	20 (19)	Rhabdomyosarcoma	3 (1)	Myxoma	110	Angiosarcoma	32
Fibroma	13 (8)	Angiosarcoma	1 (0)	Papillary fibroelastoma	31	Malignant fibrous histiocytoma	15
Myxoma	4 (0)	Malignant fibrous histiocytoma	1 (0)	Hemangioma	15	Osteosarcoma	13
Hemangioma	2 (1)	Leiomyosarcoma	1 (1)	Lipomatous hypertrophy (atrial septum)	12	Leiomyosarcoma	11
Mesothelioma of the atrioventricular node	2 (1)	Fibrosarcoma	1 (0)	Mesothelioma of the atrioventricular node	8	Fibrosarcoma	8
Purkinje cell tumor	2 (2)	Myxosarcoma	1 (0)	Fibroma	7	Myxosarcoma	7
Teratoma	1 (1)	Unclassified	3 (1)	Lipoma	2	Rhabdomyosarcoma	3
				Paraganglioma	2	Synovial sarcoma	4
				Miscellaneous	6	Liposarcoma	2
						Malignant schwannoma	1
						Unclassified	30

[a]Age at time of presentation < 16 years.
The number of patients < 1 year of age is shown in parentheses.

between 1964 and 1989, reported from the Texas Heart Institute and the MD Anderson Cancer Institute, Houston, Texas,[3] is shown in Table 2.2. All primary tumors of the heart and pericardium filed in the cardiovascular pathology registry of the Academic Medical Center, Amsterdam, including specimens referred for consultation, are shown in Table 2.3.

The bottom line is that primary tumors of the heart are rare indeed, and that the bias of the institution involved has a tremendous effect, not only regarding the absolute numbers, but also with respect to ranking of the various tumors. Nevertheless, a few items are undisputed. First, the most common primary tumor of the heart by far is the cardiac myxoma (Table 2.4). In infants and children, however, the most common primary tumor of the heart is the rhabdomyoma. Second,

Table 2.2	The 25-year experience with the surgical treatment of primary cardiac tumors (adapted from Murphy et al. with permission from The Society of Thoracic Surgeons[3])		
Benign	**(n = 102)**	**Malignant**	**(n = 12)**
Myxoma	63	Angiosarcoma	4
Purkinje cell tumor	14	Malignant fibrous histiocytoma	2
Rhabdomyoma	9	Fibromyosarcoma	1
Fibroma	7	Myxosarcoma	1
Lipoma	4	Leiomyosarcoma	1
Other[a]	5	Fibrosarcoma	1
		Undifferentiated sarcoma	2

[a]Hemangioma, angiomatous hamartoma, venous malformation, mitral valve cyst, granuloma.

Table 2.3	Primary tumors of the heart and pericardium in the cardiovascular pathology registry of the Academic Medical Center, Amsterdam		
Benign	**(n = 118)**	**Malignant**	**(n = 18)**
Myxoma	73	Angiosarcoma	7
Lipoma	11	Leiomyosarcoma	3
Rhabdomyoma	8	Rhabdomyosarcoma	3
Papillary fibroelastoma	8	Myxofibrosarcoma	2
Hemangioma	6	Mesothelioma	1
Fibroma	5	Lymphoma	1
Purkinje cell tumor	2	Malignant nerve sheath tumor	1
Paraganglioma	2		
Other[a]	3		

[a]Fibroelastic hamartoma mitral valve, angiolipofibroma mitral valve, mesothelioma of the atrioventricular node.

malignant primary cardiac tumors, in the sense of invasive destructive growths with the potential to metastasize, are extremely rare, particularly in infants and children.

Clinical aspects

It is important for the pathologist to know that the clinical manifestations of cardiac tumors are often non-specific. Indeed, many other diseases may be mimicked. The clinical presentation is usually subdivided under three major headings: (1) systemic; (2) embolic; and (3) cardiac.[4] Although largely based on clinical experience with cardiac myxomas, this approach to the clinical manifestations of primary cardiac tumors is also useful in a general sense.

Systemic manifestations

The systemic manifestations of tumors of the heart are manifold and include findings such as fever, cachexia, and malaise. Abnormal laboratory findings are an elevated erythrocyte sedimentation rate, hypergammaglobulinemia, thrombocytosis or thrombocytopenia, polycythemia, leukocytosis, and anemia. The mechanisms that underlie these systemic manifestations are not as yet fully understood, but it is likely that they relate to release of cytokines as part of an inflammatory reaction.

Embolic manifestations

These events can be due either to embolization of fragments of the tumor itself or of thrombi aggregated on the surface of the tumor. Embolization of tumor fragments can only occur when the tumor itself has an intracavitary extension. Thromboemboli, on the other hand, can also occur with intramural tumors, which compromise the function of the heart and thus may lead to intracavitary thrombosis.

The pathologist can play an important role in this situation simply by being aware of the fact that systemic emboli may be the first manifestation of a cardiac tumor. Sudden occlusion of a peripheral artery should always raise this possibility. An embolectomy specimen, therefore, should be examined most carefully for the presence of tumor fragments. But, even when only recent thrombotic material is found, the pathology report should refer to the possibility of a cardiac tumor as the source of the thromboembolus. Moreover, multiple systemic emboli may mimic systemic vasculitis or infective endocarditis, particularly when associated with systemic manifestations.

Primary tumors of the right heart chambers may cause pulmonary emboli, which may be indistinguishable from those occurring secondary to venous thrombosis.

Cardiac manifestations

The cardiac events are mainly determined by the location and size of the tumor. Tumors that are localized within the myocardium usually lead to impaired myocardial function through either substantial replacement of the myocardium by tumor or because of compression of a cardiac cavity. Moreover, intramural location may lead to a wide variety of rhythm disturbances, including atrial fibrillation and ventricular fibrillation. Sudden death may thus be the first manifestation

Table 2.4	Distribution of cardiac myxomas as reported in various series					
	Left atrium	Right atrium	Left ventricle	Right ventricle	Valvar[a]
Armed Forces Institute of Pathology series[2] (114 myxomas – 29% of benign tumors; biatrial in 2 (2%), multiple chambers in 3 (3%)	83 (73%) (MV 2) (LA + RA 2) (LA + LV 1) (LA + RA +MV 1)	22 (19%)	2 (2%) (LV + RV1)	2 (2%) (TV 1)	4 (3.5%)
Mayo Clinic series[5] (1954–1979) (68 myxomas, multiple myxomas in 3)	48 (70.6%)	12 (17.6%)	–	1 (1.5%)	7 (10.3%)
"Texas" series[3] (1964–1989) (63 myxomas – 61.8% of benign tumors)	57 (90.5%)	6 (9.5%)	–	–	–
University of Minnesota series[6] (1959–1989) (51 myxomas – 50% of benign tumors)	45 (88.3%)	4 (7.8%)	–	2 (3.9%) -	
"French" joint study[7] (1961–1988) (444 myxomas – 92% of benign tumors; multiple myxomas in 5)	368 (82.9%) (LA + RA 3) (LA + LV 1)	47 (10.6%)	2 (0.4%)	11 (2.7%) (RV + RA 1)	11 (2.7%)
"Japanese" survey[8] (1984–1989) (74 myxomas – 89.1% of benign tumors; no multiple myxomas)	66 (89.2%)	7 (9.3%)	1 (1.3%)	–	–
"Chinese" survey[9] (1962–1988) (633 myxomas reported in Chinese literature – 97.8% of benign tumors; multiple myxomas in 26)	566 (93.2%)	31 (5.6%)	4 (0.6%)	9 (1.5%)	–
Cardiovascular Pathology Registry; Academic Medical Center, Amsterdam (56 myxomas – 56.5% of benign tumors; multiple myxomas in 3)	61 (83.5%)	8 (11%)	1 (1.4%)	3 (4.1%)	–

[a]For further details, see p. 16–17.
MV, mitral valve; LA, left atrium; RA, right atrium; LV, left ventricle; RV, right ventricle, TV, tricuspid valve.

of a tumor of the heart. Primary tumors of the heart with an intracavitary extension may cause obstruction and may interfere with valve function. The signs and symptoms are highly dependent upon the chamber involved and the size of the tumor.

Pericardial effusion, eventually with signs and symptoms of cardiac tamponade, usually relates to either epicardial extension or else a primary pericardial tumor.

Pathology

In this section a distinction is made between benign and malignant primary tumors of the heart. However, the designation "benign" has a similar connotation to benign primary tumors of the brain. Biologic behavior and the salient histopathologic features may be those of a non-invasive and non-metastasizing tumor, but the tumor's location and size may have serious clinical consequences. Moreover, the category "benign" also contains lesions that do not necessarily represent neoplasms in the strict sense. In fact, some of these lesions are presently considered to be hamartomas rather than true neoplasms. This is more than a matter of semantics, since some of these lesions may regress spontaneously if the clinical situation permits a conservative approach.

Benign tumors of the heart and pericardium

Cardiac myxoma

This is the most frequent primary heart tumor (Tables 2.1–2.3). The vast majority of cases (approximately 90% or more) originate in the atria, with a significant preference for the left atrium (Table 2.4).

Cardiac myxomas usually originate from the atrial septum, in the neighborhood of the oval fossa, but other locations within the atria have been reported.[5–11] A ventricular location is rare. The unusually high incidences reported from the AFIP[1] and from our own cardiovascular pathology registry (7.4% and 5.5%) without doubt relate to the bias of referral material. Myxomas may also originate from cardiac valves (see also p. 16–17). The high incidence (10.3%) reported from the Mayo Clinic[5] is out of proportion compared to other reports.[6–9] Whether this is purely coincidental or whether other lesions, such as papillary fibroelastomas, have been included in this category remains uncertain (see also p. 24). Multiple myxomas are uncommon. On the other hand, the incidence is such that multiplicity cannot be ignored (6 of 130 patients in the initial AFIP series;[1] 5 of 114 patients in the updated series;[2] 3 of

Fig. 2.1 • A 70-year-old woman admitted with sudden onset of severe pain in one leg, who shortly after admission developed right-sided hemiplegia and died in coma.[10] The left atrium shows multiple myxomas of relatively small size (the right atrium contained a large pedunculated myxoma – not shown).

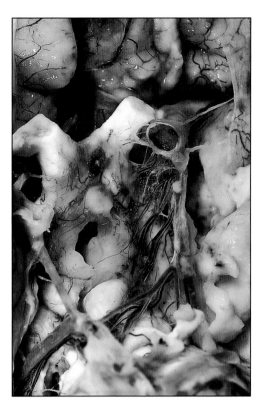

Fig. 2.2 • Same patient as shown in Figure 2.1. The undersurface of the brain shows the internal carotid artery obstructed by a myxoma embolus.

59 patients in the Mayo Clinic series;[5] 3 of 73 in the "Amsterdam series"). It is important also to realize that multiplicity is not necessarily confined to one cardiac chamber and may be part of the myxoma syndrome (see p. 16). A striking example is shown in Figures 2.1 and 2.2, which at the same time shows the dramatic consequences of tumor embolization.[10]

Gross pathology

Cardiac myxomas are either pedunculated or sessile, but, irrespective of the presence or absence of a well-defined stalk, they usually show distinct mobility. The tumor usually presents as a polypoid mass with multiple fronds (Fig. 2.3). Some myxomas present as globular, almost round masses with a smooth surface (Fig. 2.4). They show a range in color from pale grayish to dark red. Transitions from one aspect to the other are common. Occasionally surface thrombosis can be seen. They are usually soft and friable with a distinctive gelatinous appearance. The base is usually of a firm consistency with a smooth surface and pale grayish color, while the bulk of the tumor is soft and friable with spotty hemorrhagic discolorations increasing in size and intensity towards the periphery. Some myxomas have an overall firm consistency and occasionally gross calcifications can be observed, even to the extent that the bulk of the tumor consists of a calcified mass. This condition is known also as "petrified cardiac myxoma" (Figs 2.5–2.7) and may be mistaken for an atrial thrombus clinically.[12]

The surgeon, aware of the possibility of recurrence after excision, will remove the tumor together with its site of origin. Thus, in atrial myxoma, the surgical specimen almost certainly

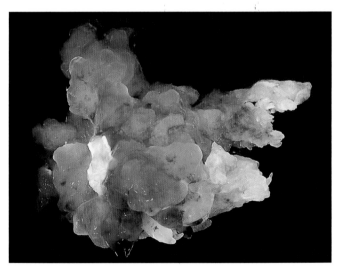

Fig. 2.3 • Left atrial myxoma originating from the atrial septum excised surgically presents as a polypoid mass with multiple fronds.

will contain a through-and-through segment of the atrial septum or of the atrial wall. Histologic study of these sites is indicated, although it is extremely rare not to find the margins of resection free of tumor. Moreover, in the case of incomplete resection, there is no pressing need for reoperation since the development of a recurrent myxoma can be detected most reliably with echocardiographic follow-up studies.

The cut surface of a cardiac myxoma shows a gelatinous, in part almost mucoid, and shiny aspect, with a similar color palette as observed on the outside (Fig. 2.8). The more peripheral parts usually appear dark and hemorrhagic. Sections for

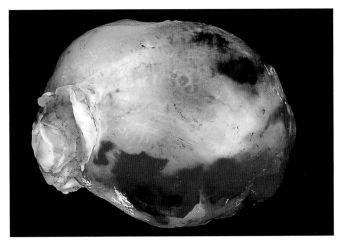

Fig. 2.4 • A left atrial myxoma originating from the atrial septum presents as a globular mass with a smooth surface.

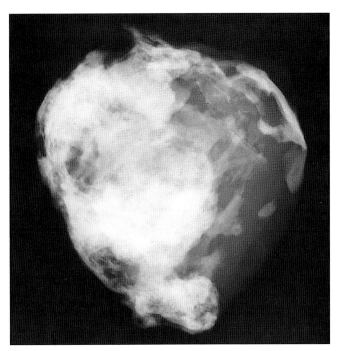

Fig. 2.6 • Roentgenogram of the same specimen as in Figure 2.5, showing heavy calcifications.

Fig. 2.5 • The gross aspect of a surgically excised specimen of a "petrified cardiac myxoma" removed from the left atrium in a 48-year-old male.

Fig. 2.7 • A histological section of the specimen shown in Figure 2.5 reveals a calcified mass adjacent to nests of myxoma cells, thus revealing the myxomatous nature of this lesion.

microscopic studies should always be taken from different areas in order to obtain a reliable impression of the overall histopathologic features and, hence, the correct diagnosis. This is of major importance since really the only major differential diagnostic option is a primary malignant tumor with myxomatous features (see later).

Histopathology

Microscopically, the overall picture of cardiac myxomas is dominated by a myxomatous matrix and a dispersed cellular component. The latter consists of different types of cells.[13] The principal cell type, known as the "myxoma cell," is considered the true neoplastic cell.[13–15] These cells may appear elongated and fusiform, polyhedral or stellate (Fig. 2.9). The cytoplasm is mostly homogeneous, sometimes finely vacuolated, and is usually slightly eosinophilic. The nucleus may be elongated,

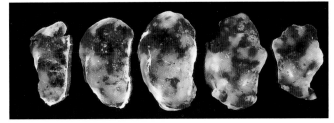

Fig. 2.8 • Surgically excised globular myxoma sectioned longitudinally in parallel slices. The cut surface shows a gelatinous, in part almost mucoid, and glistening aspect, with extensive patches of hemorrhage.

rounded, or oval and its staining characteristics may vary from pale to intensely hyperchromatic. Mitoses are virtually absent. The large polyhedral myxoma cells are occasionally referred to also as "lepidic cells" (from the Greek *lepis* meaning "scale," and based on a rather fanciful resemblance to the scales on

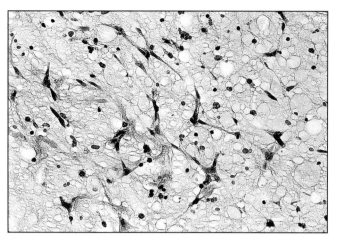

Fig. 2.9 • Microscopic section showing diversity in morphology of the myxoma cells.

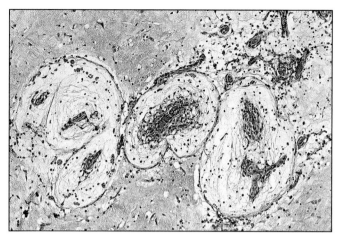

Fig. 2.11 • Micrographs showing the typical arrangement of myxoma cells. They appear as complex interlacing networks, which often clearly surround capillaries lined by endothelial cells, albeit not always that obviously.

butterfly wings). The term was introduced by Orr[16] in 1942, who at the time considered these cells to be of endocardial origin. At the ultrastructural level the cytoplasm of a "typical" myxoma cell is characterized by scantness of cell organelles (Fig. 2.10). There are variable numbers of mitochondria, elements of smooth and rough endoplasmic reticulum and cytoplasmic filaments. The latter consist of two types. The majority consist of thick (10 nm) non-branching filaments, often arranged in parallel bundles coursing in various directions. The second type are smaller (6–8 nm) and more irregular in outline.

The myxoma cells are arranged in various patterns. A common variety is an arrangement in single or multiple layers surrounding vascular channels, themselves lined by endothelium (Fig. 2.11). This may appear as complex interlacing networks or single strands. These clusters of myxoma cells are often associated with an extensive halo of myxoid extracellular matrix, almost empty optically, which contrasts with the surrounding and slightly more condensed matrix which stains palely eosinophilic (Fig. 2.12). Other possible arrangements of myxoma cells include the formation of small nests (Fig. 2.13) and a singular arrangement dispersed throughout the myxoid

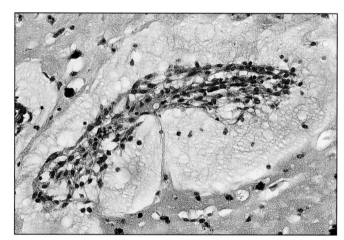

Fig. 2.12 • This arrangement, as shown in Figure 2.11, is usually accompanied by an extensive halo of myxoid tissue which contrasts with the surrounding more eosinophilic matrix.

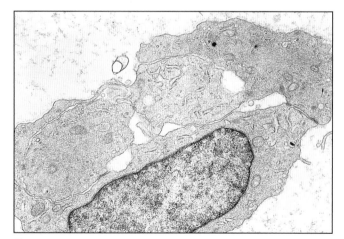

Fig. 2.10 • Electron micrograph of closely apposed "typical" myxoma cells with paucity of organelles. The cytoplasmic ground substance contains numerous intermediate filaments. Intercellular junctions are present.

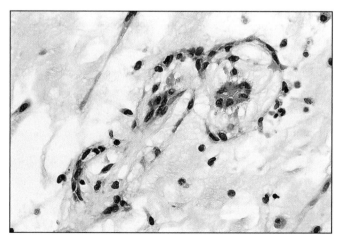

Fig. 2.13 • Micrograph showing an arrangement of myxoma cells varying from perivascular cuffing to small nests.

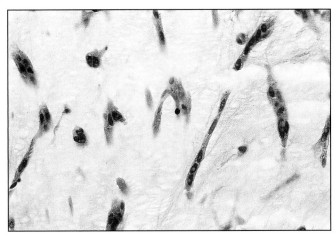

Fig. 2.14 • This micrograph shows an almost singular arrangement of myxoma cells dispersed throughout the myxoid stroma.

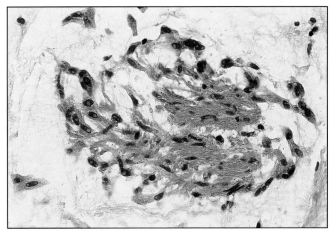

Fig. 2.15 • Micrograph showing "typical" myxoma cells in conjunction with elongated spindle-shaped cells that resemble smooth muscle cells.

stroma (Fig. 2.14). Myxoma cells with an appearance of multinucleated cells can occur, but ultrastructurally they are composed of small groups of closely apposed cells with single nuclei.[13] Occasionally, gland-like spaces may be encountered, lined by cells of a different nature (see below). The surface of the tumor may be covered by a single layer of endothelial cells or may be absent, almost certainly an artifact consequent upon the surgical procedure.

The histo- and cytologic appearance of the myxoma cells is thus highly variable within one and the same tumor. This point needs to be emphasized, since the pathologist is trained to consider tumor cells in terms of various degrees of atypia, often with a connotation of malignant transformation. In cardiac myxomas the overall picture is much more important in deriving a proper diagnosis than is the high-power observation of the cellular characteristics of a few cells only. It is important also to re-emphasize that mitoses are exceptional (I have not seen a single unequivocal mitosis in 56 myxomas) and, hence, for practical purposes can be considered as non-existent. In fact, if mitoses are identified, one should be extremely cautious about a diagnosis of (benign) cardiac myxoma (see below).

Apart from myxoma cells, a range of other cell types can be encountered in cardiac myxomas. It is likely that this range of mesenchymal cells is an expression of differentiation rather than histogenesis.[13] The most striking example is the occurrence of elongated, spindle-shaped cells that resemble fibroblasts, myoblasts, or smooth muscle cells (Fig. 2.15). These cells are usually seen in close association with undisputed myxoma cells and vascular spaces lined by distinct endothelial cells.

Immunohistochemical studies[11,14] also clearly indicate differences in the phenotypic expression of the various cell types encountered. The vascular channels are lined by endothelial cells that stain positively with anti-von Willebrand factor or with antibodies against *Ulex europaeus* agglutinin I.[14,15,17,18] Myxoma cells show distinct staining for vimentin, but do not stain with anti-von Willebrand factor, although fine fibrillar positivity may occur in the myxoid stroma in between these cells. It is not uncommon, moreover, to obtain positive staining with a monoclonal antibody directed against smooth muscle actin in cells that immediately surround the endothelial

cells. Desmin staining is positive in the walls of larger vessels, usually in the base of the tumor, and occasionally some of the spindle-shaped stromal cells may show positivity with the desmin stain. Our own observations, with the use of different monoclonal antibodies used as markers for actin filaments, show that some of these cells stain positively, a finding that lends further support to the ultrastructural observations of thin cytoplastic filaments in some of the cells.[13] Similarly, the dense staining with vimentin (a 57-kDa intermediate filament) may relate to the thicker filaments observed with the electron microscope.

In approximately 5% of all cardiac myxomas gland-like structures occur, lined by cells that may vary from flat to cuboidal or columnar (Figs 2.16–2.18). These cells stain positive with alcian blue, mucicarmine, and periodic acid–Schiff (PAS) (diastase-resistant) and show positive immunoreactivity with antibodies to cytokeratins.[14,15] The ultrastructural features of these cells are characteristic for mucin-secreting epithelium[14] (see section on histogenesis, below).

Macrophages are an almost universal finding in myxomas, often diffusely dispersed throughout the myxoid stroma,

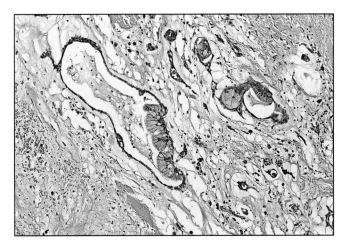

Fig. 2.16 • Micrograph of gland-like structures in a cardiac myxoma. Tubules are lined by alternating flat and cylindrical cells. (Courtesy of Dr R. J. van Suylen, Department of Pathology, Academic Hospital, Maastricht, The Netherlands.)

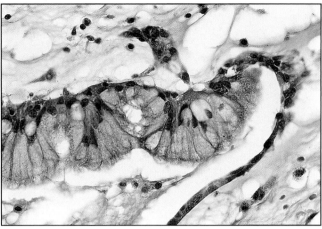

Fig. 2.17 • A detail from Figure 2.16 reveals the mucin-secreting nature of the cylindrical cells, resembling gut epithelium.

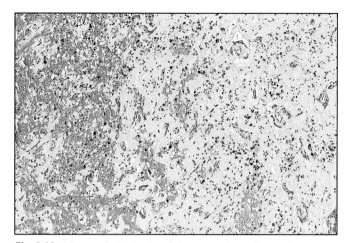

Fig. 2.19 • Micrograph showing iron-laden macrophages dispersed throughout the myxoid stroma adjacent to a recent hemorrhage.

Fig. 2.18 • The myxoma cells show positive staining with an antibody to cytokeratins.

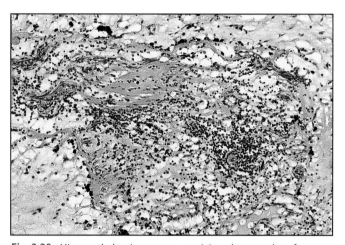

Fig. 2.20 • Micrograph showing an area containing a large number of lymphocytes.

although generally condensed towards the base and at sites of hemorrhage (Fig. 2.19).

Other cell types frequently observed in cardiac myxomas are lymphocytes and plasma cells (Fig. 2.20). These cellular aggregates occur predominantly in the base of the tumor and can also be found in the adjacent myocardium. Mast cells and foci of extramedullary hematopoiesis[10] are seen occasionally.

The myxoid stroma itself stains strongly with alcian blue, unaffected by predigestion with hyaluronidase, and may show patchy positivity with mucicarmine and the PAS stain, resistant to diastase. It contains variably prominent connective tissue fibers having characteristics of reticulin, collagen, and elastin. Fibrous tissue is most pronounced in the stalk of the tumor, a site often dominated by the presence of large, thick-walled arteries. The "tumor blush" occasionally observed at coronary angiography has its anatomic substrate in this vascular tuft. The media of these arteries is often "moth-eaten" by myxoma cells (Fig. 2.21).

Hemorrhages within the stroma are an almost universal finding in myxomas. Although slightly more pronounced in surgical specimens than in autopsy cases,[5] these foci are most likely the consequence of trauma secondary to the mobile nature of the intracavitary tumor. Histologic evidence of old and recent episodes of hemorrhage is the rule; areas with

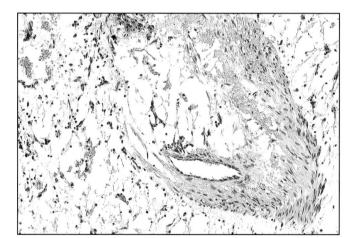

Fig. 2.21 • Large-caliber muscular artery at the base of a myxoma. The media appears "moth-eaten" by myxoma cells.

hemosiderin-laden macrophages (Fig. 2.19) and connective tissue fibers encrusted with iron and calcium (so-called Gamna–Gandy bodies; Fig. 2.22) provide evidence in this respect. It has been suggested that these fibrosclerotic nodules in cardiac myxomas may have a causal relationship with anti-coagulant and/or antiplatelet therapy.[19] I doubt whether this is

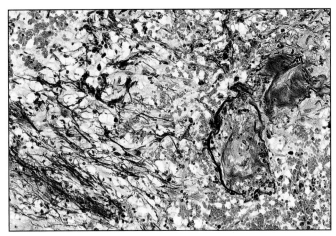

Fig. 2.22 • Gamna–Gandy body within the stroma of a myxoma. The encrustation of connective tissue fibers with iron and calcium provides evidence for previous breakdown of hemorrhages.

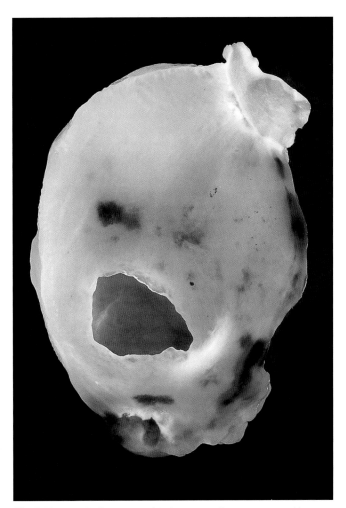

Fig. 2.23 • Cyst-like formation within the stroma of a myxoma caused by liquefaction of the extracellular matrix is evident in this surgically excised myxoma with a large "cyst" which was filled with clear fluid.

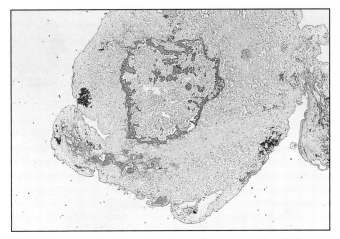

Fig. 2.24 • Micrograph of the peripheral part of a myxoma with multiple superficial and recent hemorrhages reveals a cyst-like structure lined by a rim of fibrinoid material.

so (an opinion also expressed by Lie[20]) since these nodules are not at all infrequent, once carefully looked for, irrespective of prior treatment.

Apart from these particular encrustations, microscopic foci of calcification are not uncommon. Occasionally the dystrophic calcifications within the tumor may become so extensive that the tumor is almost completely transformed to a calcified mass (Figs 2.5–2.7).

It is important to emphasize that, like the cellular components, the stroma may also show extensive variability from one part of the tumor to the other. Distinct fibrous areas and parts showing liquefaction of the myxoid stroma, leading to cyst-like areas, may occur in one and the same tumor (Fig. 2.23). Some of these "cysts" appear to be caused by hemorrhage, leading to a fibrinoid stromal change and subsequently fibrinoid degeneration (Fig. 2.24). These latter changes should not be confused with necrosis (see also section on recurrent and "malignant" cardiac myxomas, below).

Aspects of special interest

Some particular aspects of cardiac myxomas are of additional interest to the pathologist and warrant a brief discussion.

Recurrent and "malignant" cardiac myxomas Recurrence of a cardiac myxoma, after surgical excision, is relatively rare but undisputed as an occasional phenomenon (see Loire & Thermet[21] for review). It is for this reason that excision of the entire area of attachment of myxoma is recommended.[22,23] The mechanism involved in cases of recurrence, however, remains largely a matter of speculation. Of course, incomplete excision of the primary tumor, with subsequent regrowth and tumor spill with implantation into the tissues of the heart, has been suggested. Recurrence of a cardiac myxoma has also been put forward as evidence that myxomas are not necessarily benign in nature.[24] However, other mechanisms may play a role. A detailed analysis, based on personal experience and a review of the literature, has led Loire & Thermet[21] to conclude that recurrent myxomas in young adults appear to be familial and occur because of multicentric onset in the context of the so-called "myxoma syndrome," known also as Carney's

syndrome[25] or the Swiss syndrome[26] (see below). Under these circumstances the recurrence rate is much higher than among patients with "sporadic" cardiac myxomas (21% versus 1%).[25] Moreover, recurrences tend to show a more rapid growth[27] and more pronounced local invasiveness.[28] The multicentric onset is also expressed by the fact that recurrences in these patients may grow in more than one heart chamber at the same time (Fig. 2.1).

Awareness of the myxoma syndrome may also shed light on some instances of "metastasizing" cardiac myxomas (see Kotani et al.[29] for a case report and review of the literature). For instance, the appearance of cutaneous myxomas after surgical removal of a cardiac myxoma is more likely to be part of the myxoma syndrome than interpreted as "skin metastases."[30]

Indeed, the potential malignancy of cardiac myxomas is highly controversial. A critical review by Loire[31] of cases of so-called malignancy reported in the literature endorses earlier statements that such cases most likely represent "mistaken identity."[1,5] Almost all reported instances of a malignant cardiac myxoma could be categorized as a histopathological diagnostic error, through either a cardiac sarcoma not being recognized and reported as a myxoma instead, or the inclusion of false metastases based on "invasiveness" of fragments of myxoma which had embolized, causing ischemic infarction and subsequent infiltration of the arterial wall. The few cases which Loire could not fit into these categories were explained logically and malignancy was excluded. Nevertheless, the possibility of sequential malignant transformation of cardiac myxomas remains a matter of concern.[32] The case reported by Kasugai et al.[32] showed the typical findings of a benign cardiac myxoma originating from the left atrial wall, while several metastatic lesions that developed afterwards and a recurrent atrial tumor showed features very suggestive of a myxoid variant of so-called malignant fibrous histiocytoma (myxo-fibrosarcoma). The latter is a well-known potential diagnostic problem in cases of cardiac myxoma.[33] The major histo-pathologic features to distinguish between a benign cardiac myxoma and the myxoid variant of so-called malignant fibrous histiocytoma, according to Laya et al.,[33] are foci of hyper-cellularity with pleomorphism, mitotic figures, necrosis, and extensive vascularity in myxofibrosarcoma, features that are strikingly absent in cardiac myxomas. Kasugai et al.,[31] how-ever, explicitly state that multiple sections were taken from the first cardiac tumor, none of which showed evidence of malig-nancy, in contrast to the microscopic features in the follow-up specimens. Scarpelli and coworkers documented a case of an atrial myxoma with glandular elements, lined by cytokeratin-positive cells, which had metastasized to the brain 12 years (!) after removal of the original tumor.[34] The histologic appear-ance of the brain tumor was dominated by irregularly shaped glands lined by mucus-secreting cells. The case is presented as the first report of brain metastases from a cardiac myxoma with glandular elements, but certainly one may wonder whether the two are truly related.

The dispute between "malignancy" and "mistaken identity" in cases of cardiac myxomas will almost certainly not be laid to rest in the immediate future, and it is sobering to realize that the cases reported are exceedingly rare and tend to be published several times by different authors, while in each instance alter-native explanations for the unusual biologic behavior are readily provided. For practical purposes the pathologist should be alerted to the fact that an intracavitary tumor in an adult is not necessarily a cardiac myxoma. Primary malignant tumors of the heart may present in similar fashion and, once the histologic features appear to confirm the diagnosis of a myxoma, extra effort should be made to exclude the possibility of "mistaken identity." To this end the most important tumors to be considered in the differential diagnosis are the myxoid variants of soft tissue sarcomas such as myxoid malignant fibrous histiocytoma (myxofibrosarcoma) and liposarcoma (see also Ch. 24).

The myxoma syndrome In 1980 Schweizer-Cagianut et al.[35] reported the familial occurrence of Cushing's syndrome with an unusual bilateral microadenomatosis of the adrenal glands. Two years thereafter they reported the follow-up of 1 of these patients who had had an eyelid "fibroma" diagnosed, became hemiparetic at age 4, and died.[36] Autopsy revealed a cardiac myxoma (previously already diagnosed at autopsy in a sibling), a "myxoma" rather than a fibroma of the eyelid, multiple small benign fibroadenomas with myxomatous change in both breasts, and "finely freckled pigmentation around the mouth and on the lips." Credit should be given to Carney et al.,[37] who have studied in detail this unusual combination, which they presented as a complex of myxomas, spotty pigmentation, and endocrine overactivity. On the basis of a family study, an autosomal dominant mode of inheritance was considered most likely.[38]

At present this peculiar syndrome is known by a variety of names, including "Swiss syndrome"[26] (because of the initial publication by Schweizer-Cagianut et al. from Zurich, Switzerland) and Carney's syndrome,[25] as well as the acronyms NAME syndrome (nevi, atrial myxoma, myxoid neurofibroma and neurofibromata, and ephelides) and LAMB syndrome (lentigines, atrial myxoma, mucocutaneous myxoma, blue nevi). As pointed out by Carney et al.,[38] however, the latter two designations "are more indicative of ingenious contrivance of acronyms than of clinicopathologic precision." The syndrome is also known as "familial endocrine myxolentiginosis," which is descriptive of the major components of the syndrome.[39] Indeed, the syndrome consists of a variable complex of muco-cutaneous, visceral, and endocrine disorders, not all of which are necessarily present in a single patient. The lesions to be considered in these cases are cardiac myxomas (with a strong tendency to multiplicity; see above), cutaneous myxomas (single or multiple), mammary myxoid fibroadenomas (single or multiple), spotty mucocutaneous pigmentation (including lentigines and blue nevi and combinations), psammomatous melanotic schwannomas, primary pigmented nodular adreno-cortical disease (including patients who are symptomatic with Cushing's syndrome), testicular tumors (characteristically Sertoli cell tumors, usually bilateral and multicentric), and pituitary growth hormone-secreting tumors (which may cause acromegaly or gigantism).[38,40] Pathologists should be aware of this peculiar syndrome since they may be in a position to make the diagnosis first. Particularly in the case of a recurrent cardiac myxoma the possible presence of this syndrome should be discussed with the clinician, who may not necessarily be aware of this complex. The occurrence of myxomas, spotty pigmentation, and endocrine overactivity in three successive generations of one family, as reported by Carney et al.,[38] has led them to recommend that first-degree relatives of affected persons should be thoroughly examined for this syndrome.

Myxomas originating from heart valves As outlined previously, the origin of myxomas from cardiac valves has been disputed, mainly because McAllister & Fenoglio in their authoritative compilation of cardiac tumors[1] state that "true myxomas do not occur on the cardiac valves"; they categorize papillary tumors of cardiac valves as papillary fibroelastomas. However, the description of the latter tumors, which resemble sea anemones with multiple papillary fronds attached to the endocardium by a short pedicle (see also p. 24), is not always consistent with the occasional report of a myxoma of a heart valve. Indeed, the more recent update from AFIP includes two myxomas originating from the anterior leaflet of the mitral valve and one from the septal leaflet of the tricuspid valve (see also Becker[10]).

Recently transesophageal echocardiography has been advocated as a useful tool to differentiate between a papillary fibroelastoma and a true valve myxoma.[41] At the same time the pathologist has to be cautious not to interpret nodular valvar (or endocardial) dysplastic tissue, which appears highly myxomatous, as a myxoma. The case report of a "myxoma" of the aortic valve in a child 4 years of age may serve to exemplify this point.[42]

Be that as it may, Wold & Lie[5] reported seven myxomas originating from heart valves, each in their autopsy group of 29 cases. Four of these originated from the pulmonary valve. The remaining three myxomas originated from the aortic, mitral, and tricuspid valve leaflets, respectively. According to these authors the morphologic characteristics are indistinguishable from atrial myxomas, although valve myxomas tend to have fewer cellular clusters, fewer syncytial tumor giant cells, and infrequent perivascular cuffing of tumor cells. A tricuspid valve myxoma in a 10-year-old boy, who was successfully operated without valve replacement, is on record[43] and unequivocal clinical documentation of a tricuspid valve myxoma, albeit without a display of tumor histology, together with a review of the literature, is provided by Cole et al.[44] and by Sharma et al.[45] They report (in a 74-year-old man and a 45-year-old man) a solid mass or tumor, measuring 4×6 cm and 6×7 cm, respectively, attached by a short stalk or a small pedicle to the atrial surface of the septal leaflet of the tricuspid valve. Similarly, a mitral valve myxoma was described as a mass of 3.3×3.2 cm attached by a short wide stalk to the atrial side of the posterior leaflet of the mitral valve[41] and such a tumor arising from the aortic leaflet of the mitral valve has been documented in a 50-year-old woman.[46] In each instance the histopathologic diagnosis was myxoma.

There is strong evidence, therefore, that at least occasional myxomas may originate from a heart valve. It is of additional interest that among the reported cases of such myxomas a right heart location appears to be more common than a left-sided one and that the tumors may be attached either to the atrial or to the ventricular side of the atrioventricular valve leaflets.

Histogenesis In the past it has been suggested that myxomas develop from organized thrombi – an old concept[47,48] revived[49] and buried[50] every now and then. Most investigators today consider cardiac myxomas as true neoplasms.

It has been suggested for a long time that these tumors originate from primitive multipotential mesenchymal cells, which may be present in the heart wall as embryonic remnants.[15,51–58] Indeed, studies have shown unequivocally a range of differentiation patterns highly suggestive of a process of cellular adaptation or maturation from a primitive mesenchymal cell to cells with specialized functions. Immunohistochemical and cytochemical studies of cardiac myxomas support this concept.[16,17,19,54] With immunostaining techniques a distinction can be made between endothelial cells and myxoma cells. This suggests, contrary to findings previously reported,[55] that myxoma cells are not endothelial in origin, but rather derive from primitive subendocardial cells which may show the capacity for CD31-positive endothelial differentiation.[56] The differences in phenotypic expression of the stromal cells strongly suggest a process of differentiation, well known from wound-healing;[57] a concept promoted also by the finding of numerous factor XIIIa-positive dendrophages, suggesting abnormal organizing thrombus-like differentiation.[56] Since some myxomas contain stellate cells that express Schwann cell and neuroendocrine differentiation markers (S-100 protein, protein gene product (PGP) 9.5, neuron-specific enolase, synaptophysin), it has been suggested that myxomas originate from endocardial sensory nerve tissue.[58]

Cytogenetic analysis of cardiac myxomas, thus far, has shown a variety of clonal and non-clonal abnormalities. As it stands now, cytogenetic analysis is of little or no value in the differential diagnosis of cardiac myxomas, although these studies may eventually contribute to understanding the molecular genetics of their histogenesis.[59,60]

Myxomas with gland-like spaces need special consideration. The cells may appear as mucus-secreting cells and immunohistochemical analysis reveals positivity for cytokeratins.[16,61,62] These observations suggest that the cells from which myxomas originate have the potential for epithelial as well as mesenchymal differentiation. On that basis some have classified cardiac myxomas as hamartomas.[61–64] This concept finds support in a study evaluating proliferative activity, metastatic potential, and expression of oncogene/tumor suppressor gene products, which concluded that the results were in keeping with a reactive/hamartomatous process.[65]

Cardiac rhabdomyoma

This is one of the more frequent primary tumors of the heart and by far the most common in infants and children (Tables 2.1–2.3). Cardiac rhabdomyomas have a close association with tuberous sclerosis (see below). The clinical profile varies considerably. In some instances, the tumor may have led to stillbirth or perinatal death.[66,67] Intrauterine myocardial infarction due to coronary arterial compression by a large adjacent rhabdomyoma has been documented.[67]

In other patients the clinical history is dominated by cardiac manifestations such as cardiomegaly, congestive heart failure, or cardiac arrhythmias. Sudden and unexpected death has also been reported.[68,69] The clinical significance of cardiac rhabdomyomas is largely determined by their size, whether they are solitary or multiple, and whether or not they expand into a chamber cavity. The vast majority of rhabdomyomas are multiple, although this is not necessarily immediately apparent. The lesion has a distinct preference for the ventricles, with left ventricular involvement in almost 100% and right ventricular involvement in approximately 80%.[66] Involvement of the atria is much less common (11 of 36 patients, 30%[66]) or even rare (1 of 77 rhabdomyomas (1.3%) in 33 patients (3%)[70]).

Multiple small rhabdomyomas originating from the ventricular aspect of the mitral valve have been documented.[71] Diffuse rhabdomyomatosis of the heart, first described by Schmincke[72] in 1922, does occur but is exceedingly rare. In this situation the myocardium is diffusely replaced by cells that show the characteristics of rhabdomyoma cells (see below), although small strands and islands of normal-looking myocardium are still present.[73] The condition most likely represents an extreme in the spectrum of multiplicity of rhabdomyomatous lesions.

It is generally accepted that any infant who presents with findings suggestive of an intracavitary mass most likely has a rhabdomyoma (myxomas in that age group are extremely rare; see Table 2.1). This is clinically important because once the diagnosis of cardiac rhabdomyoma has been established, surgical intervention is no longer indicated unless there are clinical manifestations from the heart (see below).

Gross pathology

Rhabdomyomas present as circumscribed but not encapsulated lesions, easily distinguished from the surrounding myocardium. They have a wax-like consistency and a white to yellowish-gray coloration. The size may vary from millimeters to several centimeters. Occasionally the lesions may grow to bizarre proportions, with intracavitary extension almost totally obliterating the pre-existing cavities (Fig. 2.25).

Histopathology

The histopathologic features of cardiac rhabdomyomas are distinct. The tissue is composed of grotesquely swollen myocytes, showing an almost "empty" cytoplasm often with a centrally placed cytoplasmic mass and nucleus (Fig. 2.26). Strands of cytoplasm extend to the periphery of the cell, thus providing the architectural basis for the term "spider cell" (Fig. 2.27). At high magnification, striations are often seen in the tiny strands. The cells contain glycogen, best demonstrated with the PAS method on alcohol-fixed tissue or on frozen-tissue sections. The type of polysaccharide involved is rather labile, a striking contrast with that present in glycogen storage disease.[74] Immunohistochemical studies reveal positivity for myoglobin, actin, desmin, and vimentin, with negative results for S-100 protein, similar to that of normal heart muscle.[75] Ultrastructural studies, furthermore, confirm the myogenic nature of the cells involved.[66]

The stromal component is usually scanty, although occasionally, areas with distinct collagen may occur. In some cases calcifications can be seen associated with necrosis of cells (Fig. 2.28). The older the patient, the more likely that extensive calcification has occurred.[76]

Aspects of special interest

Tuberous sclerosis A close association between tuberous sclerosis and cardiac rhabdomyomas has been established. Echocardiographic studies of patients with tuberous sclerosis reveal a high incidence of cardiac rhabdomyomas.[77] However, a significant difference exists between children and infants (58% versus 18%). These observations may support the concept of spontaneous regression of cardiac rhabdomyomas (see below). Fenoglio and coworkers[66] reported a 37% incidence of

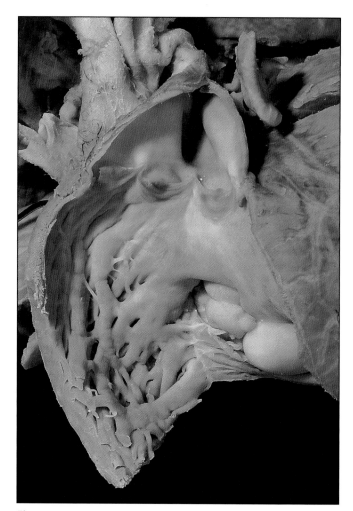

Fig. 2.25 • Gross aspect of a large right atrial rhabdomyoma extending from the right atrial cavity through the tricuspid orifice into the right ventricular inlet part.

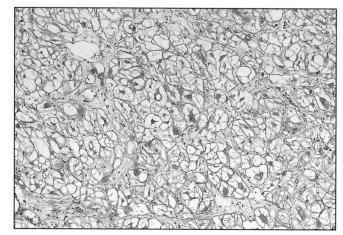

Fig. 2.26 • Micrograph of a cardiac rhabdomyoma characterized by grotesquely swollen myocytes.

associated tuberous sclerosis in their autopsy series of patients with cardiac rhabdomyomas. However, a good proportion of their cases were stillborns or newborns and the histologic diagnosis in these age groups is difficult. A retrospective study of 33 infants and children collected from three pediatric cardiology centers showed that 30 (90.9%) had associated

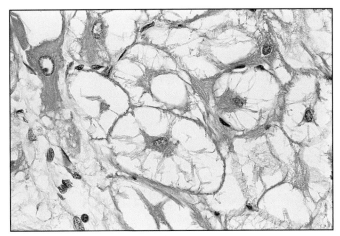

Fig. 2.27 • Cardiac rhabdomyoma. A high-power view of the specimen in Figure 2.26 shows the typical "spider cells," characterized by a centrally placed cytoplasmic mass and nucleus connected to the perimeter of the cell by strands of cytoplasm.

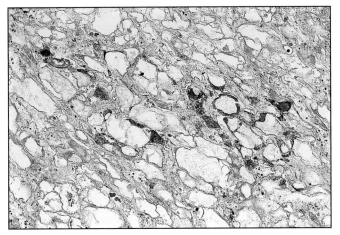

Fig. 2.28 • Necrobiosis of rhabdomyoma cells associated with calcification.

tuberous sclerosis.[70] It seems fair to state that the precise incidence of tuberous sclerosis in patients who have cardiac rhabdomyomas will remain uncertain, which in part relates to the fact that some of these patients will die before signs and symptoms of tuberous sclerosis may have become manifest, but nevertheless the incidence will be high. Indeed, Davies[78] suggested that cardiac rhabdomyomas are always accompanied by tuberous sclerosis of the brain, whether or not the latter condition is clinically manifest. This is further strengthened by the observation that in each of 5 infants, in whom fetal or early postnatal echocardiography revealed a cardiac tumor, tuberous sclerosis was subsequently diagnosed.[79]

Spontaneous regression As long ago as 1923 Steinbiss suggested that rhabdomyomas of the heart, in patients who also suffered from tuberous sclerosis, could regress and eventually disappear altogether.[74] This has now been confirmed and is of the utmost clinical relevance.[80–82] A retrospective evaluation of patients with tuberous sclerosis, over a 10-year period (1984–1994), revealed that 10 of 16 (62.5%) patients had a cardiac rhabdomyoma identified at the time of the initial study. However, the number of rhabdomyomas steadily declined with follow-up: 23 in 10 patients at the first study,

16 in 8 patients at the time of the second study, 12 in 5 patients at the third study, and 4 in 2 patients at the fourth investigation.[83] In fact, complete spontaneous regression of cardiac rhabdomyomas, based on echocardiographic evaluation, was seen by the age of 6 years. Hence, once an intracardiac tumor mass has been detected in an infant who otherwise has no signs or symptoms from the heart, the tendency is not to operate but to wait and see whether or not the tumor will regress.

Such biologic behavior supports the concept that cardiac rhabdomyomas, whether or not associated with tuberous sclerosis, are basically hamartomas rather than true neoplasms. There are several arguments that favor such a concept, particularly the preponderance of multiple as opposed to solitary cardiac rhabdomyomas and their most frequent occurrence in infants. Furthermore, Fenoglio et al.[84] demonstrated extensive intercellular junctions, with the characteristics of desmosomes and nexuses, randomly distributed throughout the cell surfaces, contrasting with the more regular arrangement of these structures in normal myocardium. They suggested that the cells had undergone arrest of development and lost the ability to differentiate fully. This view was endorsed by Bruni et al.,[85] who demonstrated two varieties of cells: typical "spider cells," and cells with more myofibrils, less glycogen and vacuoles containing membrane-bound glycogen. They interpreted these observations as two successive stages in the early maturation of normal myocytes. It is of interest along these lines that genetic studies have linked tuberous sclerosis to loss of heterozygosity mapped to chromosome 9q34 and, more recently, 16q13.3; it has been suggested, on the basis of similar allelic losses in the associated hamartomas, that these genes may act as growth suppressors.[86,87]

Differential diagnosis

The histopathologic diagnosis should not normally be a problem because of the bizarre appearance of the swollen myocytes. Nevertheless, distinction from glycogen storage disease may occasionally pose a problem. However, in the latter, the myocardial histology is rather monotonous, in the sense that the shape of the myocytes is usually well preserved, although they appear empty with a peripheral rim of myofibrils. In rhabdomyomas the overall picture is chaotic: the myocytes are bizarre and sometimes reach monstrous sizes of up to 80 mm in diameter (Fig. 2.29).

In addition, cardiac rhabdomyomas should not be confused with a rare condition known as "Purkinje cell tumor" or "foamy myocardial transformation" (see below), nor with the more recently described and rare hamartoma of mature cardiac myocytes,[88] which lacks the cytoplasmic vacuolation of a rhabdomyoma.

Cardiac fibroma

This is a rare tumor, although among the most frequent tumor types encountered in infants and children (Table 2.1). A survey of the clinicopathologic correlates in 23 patients registered in the AFIP, Washington, DC, revealed a mean patient age of 13 years, with a range of 1 day to 56 years.[89] The eldest patient – to the best of my knowledge – was a male 77 years of age.[90] The clinical signs and symptoms are largely dependent

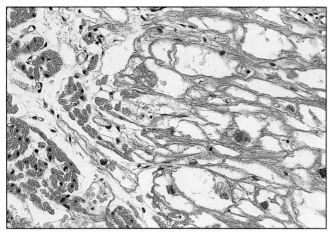

Fig. 2.29 • Micrograph to emphasize the monstrous size of rhabdomyoma cells compared to adjacent normal myocytes.

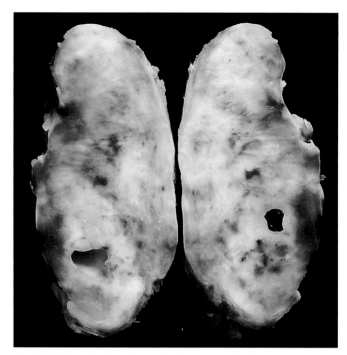

Fig. 2.30 • The cut surface of a cardiac fibroma reveals a fibromatous nature with focal hemorrhages (probably artifactual due to the surgical procedure) and cyst-like degeneration.

on the location and size of the tumor. The leading sign is cardiomegaly, but symptoms may include heart failure, arrhythmias, sudden death, cyanosis, and chest pain.[89] Patients in whom the fibroma is located in the ventricular septum (10 out of 17 patients initially documented from the files of the AFIP[1]) appear to be either symptomatic (documented ventricular fibrillation in 2, congestive heart failure in 2) or die suddenly and unexpectedly. Fibromas located in the ventricular free wall or in the atrium tend to be asymptomatic for a long time. Eventually, symptoms of valvar or intracavitary obstruction may appear. However, some free wall fibromas may be extremely large, almost the size of the entire heart, while the patient may still be asymptomatic.[91]

Gross pathology

Cardiac fibromas present as circumscribed solid, firm, and whitish lesions, which are clearly demarcated from the surrounding myocardium. Occasionally, however, there may be extensive spread amidst the myocardium to an extent that resection cannot be accomplished.[92] In other instances complete resection may not be feasible because of the location and the size of the tumor, as, for example, when almost all of the ventricular septum is replaced by the fibroma.

The cut surface reveals the fibromatous nature of the lesion (Fig. 2.30). Occasionally calcifications may be apparent at gross inspection.

Histopathology

Fibromas are composed of connective tissue, often with a mixture of different elements (Figs 2.31–2.33). The peripheral parts intermingle with the surrounding myocardium, thus rendering the fibroma less well demarcated than the gross aspect would suggest. The central area is often composed of a hyalinized type of acellular collagen (Fig. 2.32), whereas the more peripheral parts of the lesion may exhibit more pronounced cellularity (Fig. 2.33). Elastin fibers may occur, sometimes even in abundance. The term "fibroelastic hamartoma" is based on this particular observation.[93] Occasionally, myocytes amidst fibrous tissue are encountered and small aggregates of immature cells, most probably of hematopoietic nature, are

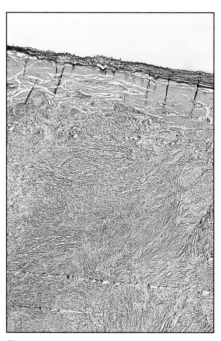

Fig. 2.31 • Micrograph illustrating the salient features of a cardiac fibroma. The perimeter of the fibroma shows intermingling of the fibroma with pre-existing myocardium. The overlying endocardial layer shows slight fibroelastic thickening. (Elastic tissue stain.)

seen. Microscopic foci of calcification are often observed (Fig. 2.34). Cystic degeneration, particularly in the more central parts of the lesion, is common. This feature may relate to a paucity of capillaries. Mitotic figures are extremely rare, even in parts that are distinctly cellular. Cellularity itself, furthermore, cannot be considered an indication of malignancy.

These histopathologic features are highly characteristic for the diagnosis of cardiac fibroma.

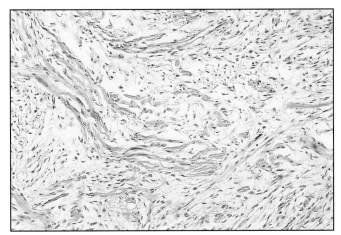

Fig. 2.32 • The peripheral parts of a cardiac fibroma often show spindle-shaped cells organized in differently oriented bundles. (Hematoxylin and eosin stain.)

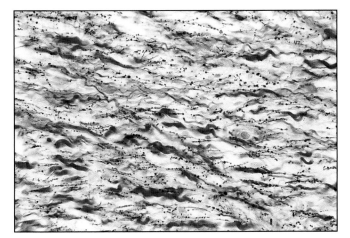

Fig. 2.33 • The central part of a cardiac fibroma is often dominated by coarse collagen and fragmented clumps of elastin. (Elastic tissue stain.)

Fig. 2.34 • Micrograph of a cardiac fibroma showing an extensive zone of calcific degeneration.

Aspects of special interest

Histogenesis Ultrastructural studies have shown clearly that the principal cellular component of the cardiac fibroma is the fibroblast, set in a matrix composed of glycosaminoglycans and collagen.[93,94] Turi et al.[94] also demonstrated that cells of intermediate differentiation were present, containing both myofilaments and abundant rough endoplasmic reticulum. These cells had previously been designated myofibroblasts[95] and are a familiar constituent of proliferative fibrous lesions. Because of the similarities between fibromatoses and cardiac fibromas, with regard both to the natural history of the lesion and to their light microscopic and ultrastructural characteristics, Turi et al.[94] suggested that they are identical disease processes. These authors, therefore, consider the term "cardiac fibromatosis" a more appropriate designation than cardiac fibroma.

These considerations have clinical implications, since the question may be raised whether or not to intervene surgically in cases of asymptomatic presentation. Partial resection of a fibroma, histologically confirmed as a fibroma, located in the interventricular septum in a baby approximately 6 months of age, revealed no further growth 14 months after the operation.[96] Another case report of subtotal resection of a cardiac fibroma, which originated from the posterior left ventricular free wall in an infant of 22 months of age, revealed that the child was free of symptoms and doing well 7 years after the operation.[97] One may argue, therefore, that in a case where the patient is symptomatic and surgical intervention is considered necessary, there is no indication to remove a cardiac fibroma as radically as possible if the procedure endangers postoperative heart function.

Associated syndromes A few cases have been reported of cardiac fibroma associated with the nevoid basal cell carcinoma syndrome, known also as the Gorlin syndrome;[97–101] this was seen in just 1 out of 23 patients reported by Burke and associates.[89] This syndrome consists of a range of abnormalities, such as rib and vertebral anomalies, a large head with a characteristic appearance, calcification of the falx cerebri, odontogenic keratocysts of the mandible, and multiple basal cell carcinomas.[102] An accurate diagnosis, however, is difficult because of the variable clinical features.

Cardiac lipoma

This is a rare lesion in the heart. McAllister & Fenoglio[1] documented an incidence of 18.6% among benign primary heart tumors in adults and the updated AFIP series shows an incidence of 6.2%[2] (Table 2.1). Our own series contains 11 lipomas (9.3%; see also Table 2.3). This high incidence may again relate to the bias of a referral center like the AFIP; however, some nosologic considerations should be introduced at this point.

First, it is well known that epicardial fat stores increase with advancing age.[103] They have a characteristic distribution on the anterior surface of the right ventricle, the atrioventricular groove, on both the right and the left side, and along the epicardial course of coronary arteries. Moreover, an excessive increase of epicardial fat is usually accompanied by fatty infiltration of the right ventricular myocardium and the interatrial groove. Thus, the question may arise as to at what stage, if any, an increase in adipose tissue should lead to a diagnosis of "lipoma."

Second, the classification of benign lipomatous tumors includes a variety of conditions[104] such as solitary well-delineated lipomas and their variants, intra- and intermuscular lipomas (also known as infiltrating lipomas) as well as the group of diffuse lipomatoses (see also Ch. 24). This varied tableau is also seen in "cardiac lipomas." Solitary lipomas of the heart, defined as well-circumscribed and thinly encapsulated tumors, composed of mature fat cells, are very rare. Tumors that fit this definition have been described both in the myocardium and in the epicardium. The latter localization is usually an incidental finding at surgery or autopsy,[105] although occasionally large tumors in this location may cause left ventricular dysfunction,[106,107] or problems at surgery because of coronary artery involvement.[108] A highly unusual case has been reported of sudden death in a 15-year-old girl in whom multiple large lipomas encased the whole heart, compromising all cardiac chambers.[109] The files of the AFIP contain 14 cases of lipoma. In the majority of these cases the lipomas were not associated with cardiac symptoms. However, in some instances patients may become symptomatic; the size and localization of the tumor are the determining factors. Subendocardial lipomas with intracavitary expansion can cause valve stenosis or insufficiency, whereas an intramyocardial location may cause abnormalities in rhythm or conduction.[110–117] An association with tuberous sclerosis has been documented.[1,118,119]

Another type of cardiac lipoma, very much like the "infiltrating lipoma" of skeletal muscle (see Ch. 24), is known as "lipomatous hypertrophy of the atrial septum."[120–122] This condition was first reported by Prior[120] and has been studied methodically in an unselected series of 50 autopsy hearts by Page.[121] Page concluded that the condition most likely relates to an increase in interatrial fat deposits, as part of an overall increase in fat deposition with advancing age; others have shown an association with increased body mass.[122] Extreme examples of this phenomenon may then be identified as "lipomatous hypertrophy," but should not necessarily be considered a nosologic entity. This point of view has been challenged on the grounds that the lesion is well demarcated from the neighboring epicardial fat deposits, contains hypertrophic myocytes with an irregular distribution, and is quantitatively different from the usual structural composition of the atrial septum.[123] Inoue et al. therefore propose the term "lipomatous hamartoma of the heart."[123] Be that as it may, the presence of excessive fat within the interatrial groove has a definite tendency to be associated with cardiac arrhythmias.[1,119] This cardiac irritability may be the result of myocardial atrophy and fibrosis, which accompany the local deposition of large amounts of fat. The condition may be encountered as an incidental finding at autopsy or at surgery.[124]

Lipomatous hamartoma of an atrioventricular valve is another extremely rare condition with which the pathologist may be confronted. To the best of my knowledge fewer than 10 examples have been documented;[125] these affected both the mitral and the tricuspid valve, with a spread in age from 2 to 76 years. Valvar insufficiency may occur, as in the case reported by Behman et al.,[126] in which the lipomatous change also involved the papillary muscle. Finally, at least 2 cases of hibernoma of the heart and pericardium are on record.[127,128]

Gross pathology

It is immediately obvious from the introduction above that the gross pathology depends highly on the type of "lipoma."

In the case of an encapsulated collection of fat cells, the gross morphology will be identical to that seen with lipomas in other locations (Figs 2.35 and 2.36).

In cases of so-called lipomatous hypertrophy of the interatrial septum the lesion is usually first seen from the right atrial aspect. It presents as a distinct bulge of the superior limbus, directly above the oval fossa (Fig. 2.37). The fossa may occasionally be hardly visible as it may be masked by the protruding atrial wall. On the cut surface the interatrial groove appears extremely thickened and composed of yellow-gray adipose tissue, often with a brown tinge, infiltrating into adjacent atrial myocardium. Close inspection will usually reveal strands of pre-existing heart muscle amidst the adipose tissue. In cases of valvar involvement the chances are that the valve will show a deformity with localized thickening, which on the cut surface will appear as adipose tissue (Fig. 2.38).

Histopathology

The histopathology of lipomas, defined as circumscribed encapsulated tumors, is not different from that encountered in lipomas elsewhere in the body. Amidst the dominant feature of mature adipose tissue, occasional muscle cells may be encountered and various degrees of connective tissue involvement and vascularity may occur. The various terms, such as myolipoma, fibrolipoma, angiolipoma, etc., relate directly to these features.

In cases of so-called lipomatous hypertrophy of the atrial septum the histology is dominated by massive infiltration of mature fat cells with displacement and atrophy of pre-existing myocardial cells (Fig. 2.39). Usually the best-preserved parts of the myocardium are subendocardial in position, but islands of myocytes are trapped in the lipoma and often appear to be totally surrounded by fatty tissue. A subset of cases appear to be iatrogenic in origin and such lesions more often occur on

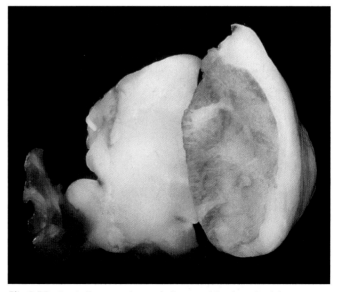

Fig. 2.35 • Surgically resected part of a lipoma arising from the right ventricular free wall, extending to the ventral part of the interventricular septum and protruding into the right ventricular cavity.[117] The gross specimen shows a peripheral rim of solid fat tissue bordering myocardium heavily infiltrated with adipose tissue. (Courtesy of Dr J. R. J. Elbers, Department of Pathology, St. Antonius Ziekenhuis, Nieuwegein, Utrecht, The Netherlands.)

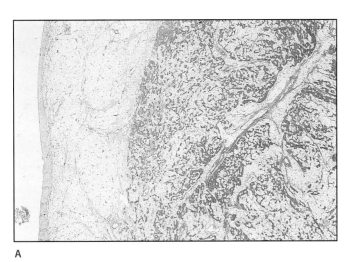
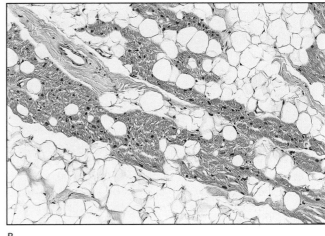

A   B

Fig. 2.36 • Lipoma. A micrograph shows the surface area composed of mature adipose cells and the underlying zone of "infiltrating lipoma" of cardiac muscle.

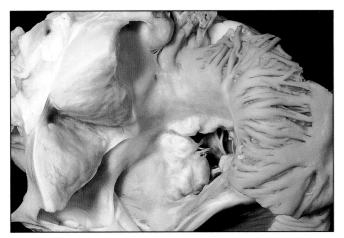

Fig. 2.37 • Lipomatous hypertrophy of the interatrial septum. Heart specimen with opened right atrium and an incision through the bulging interatrial septum. The cut surface reveals adipose tissue.

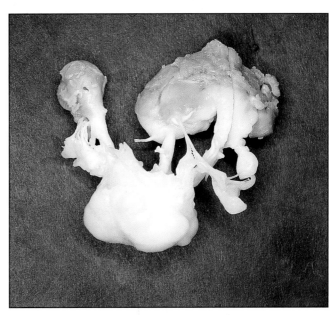

Fig. 2.38 • Lipomatous hamartoma of mitral valve and part of the chordae and posteromedial papillary muscle group. Gross specimen showing the lipomatous hamartoma prominent at the atrial aspect of the anterior mitral valve leaflet and the lipomatous change of part of the chords and papillary muscle. (Courtesy of Dr Leon M. Gerlis, Department of Paediatrics, National Heart & Lung Institute, London, UK.)

non-valvular endocardium.[129] Occasionally, areas can be traced where mature fat cells intermingle with vacuolated, multiglobular fat cells (Fig. 2.40). In addition, granular cells may occur, which resemble fetal fat cells by light and electron microscopy.

Lipomatous hamartomas of cardiac valves show diffuse infiltration of mature fat cells, with almost complete replacement of the pre-existing tissue architecture of the valve leaflet.

Aspects of special interest

Clinical correlates As mentioned above, "true" lipomas usually remain asymptomatic, but may nevertheless be detected at routine examination. In infants and children such tumors are extremely rare, but when present may cause thickening of the myocardial wall and subsequent narrowing of a cardiac cavity, even to the extent that surgical resection is indicated. Incomplete resection under these circumstances may be dictated by the anatomy, but the late follow-up may still be satisfactory.[130] In addition, the possible association with tuberous sclerosis should always be kept in mind.

The association of cardiac arrhythmias and sudden cardiac death in cases of so-called lipomatous hypertrophy of the

interatrial septum is well established.[1,121,131] Knowledge of this particular association is important when confronted with cases of sudden unexpected death, but at the same time the pathologist should be extremely careful not to overdiagnose this condition. Accumulation of fat tissue in the interatrial groove with gradual fatty infiltration of the atrial walls occurs with advancing age and relates to an increase in overall epicardial fat deposition,[121] and it is extremely difficult, if not impossible, to determine in any given individual whether or not the fat deposition may have contributed to a fatal dysrhythmia. At the same time, the pathologist may be confronted with surgical specimens from the atrial septum so called, either in a patient known to have rhythm disturbances and lipomatous hypertrophy of the interatrial septum, or as an incidental finding which has left the surgeon puzzled and confused.[124,132]

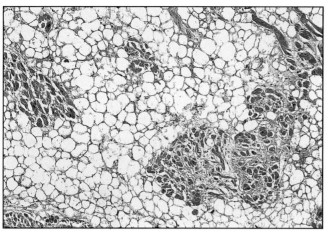

Fig. 2.39 • The histology in a case of lipomatous hypertrophy of the interatrial septum (gross specimen shown in Fig. 2.37) reveals massive infiltration of mature fat cells with focal remnants of myocytes.

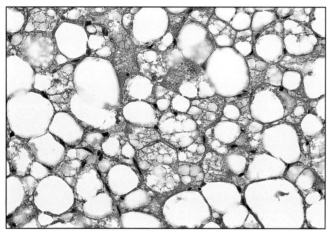

Fig. 2.40 • Lipomatous hypertrophy. Histology of same specimen shown in Figure 2.39 reveals areas of mature fat cells intermingled with vacuolated, multiglobular fat cells.

Papillary fibroelastoma

This lesion is also known as fibroelastic papilloma, papillary tumor of the cardiac valve, or giant Lambl's excrescence (see below).

Surgical and clinical experience, particularly relevant since the introduction of two-dimensional echocardiography, indicates that papillary fibroelastoma is a relatively rare lesion. Nevertheless, these lesions rank third among the primary benign heart tumors in adults filed in the AFIP[1] (17.4% of all benign tumors; Table 2.1) as well as in our own registry (6.8% of all benign tumors; Table 2.3). The "Texas experience,"[3] recently expanded by including cases from 1957 onwards,[133] does not mention this lesion. Similarly, the reviews from France,[7] Japan,[8] and China[9] do not mention its occurrence. On the other hand, the experience reported from the University of Minnesota[6] with primary cardiac tumors does include "papilloma" as a frequently encountered primary tumor, ranking third in order of frequency (12 of 124 (9.7%) of all primary heart tumors, 12 of 103 (11.6%) of all histologically benign cardiac tumors). It appears that centers that include "outside"

cases in the registry produce higher figures, thus reflecting referral bias rather than the true incidence.

Be that as it may, these papillary tumors occur on all heart valves and may be an incidental finding at echocardiography (see review of echocardiographic characteristics[134,135]), surgery, or autopsy. A subset of cases appear to be iatrogenic in origin and such lesions occur more often on non-valvular endocardium.[129] Occasionally they may produce clinical signs and symptoms, including cerebral embolization,[136,137] or cardiac-related symptoms (see review of papillary fibroelastoma as a "not-so-benign" cardiac tumor).[138] It is suggested that left-sided lesions are more likely to be symptomatic and therefore may be detected more readily by echocardiography.[139] The location on the aortic valve is potentially hazardous with respect to obstruction of coronary ostia or coronary arterial embolization and, in fact, may cause acute myocardial infarction.[140–144]

Two cases have been documented in which a fibroelastoma was attached to the right ventricular outflow tract.[135,145] Papillary fibroelastomas occur in adults, without preference for any particular age. There is only an occasional report documenting a fibroelastoma in an infant or child.[144–146] In this context a precise description of the gross pathology and histopathology is mandatory to ensure that papillary fibroelastoma is not confused with myxomatous and other valvar lesions that may occur in childhood.

Gross pathology

These tumors have the appearance of sea anemones[147] (Fig. 2.41). They consist of a bouquet of filiform threads attached to the endocardium, being either sessile or connected by a distinct but short pedicle. They may be very small, not more than a few millimeters in diameter, or huge, with a diameter expressed in centimeters rather than millimeters (Fig. 2.42). The tumors most frequently arise on the valves, with a distinct preference for the aortic valve, but may also arise from mural endocardium of both atria and ventricles. On the mitral and tricuspid valves the lesions are always found on the atrial aspect, usually at about the midportion. On the aortic and pulmonary valves these papillary tumors occur with near-equal frequency on the ventricular and the arterial side of the leaflet, without further preference for the base or the tip. Occasionally, a patient may develop multiple fibroelastomas.

Histopathology

The microscopic appearance is highly characteristic. The threads consist of a central core of dense, almost acellular collagen, occasionally surrounded by a myxomatous matrix. One case has been reported with chondroid metaplasia of the fibrous core.[148] The peripheral rim often contains coarse and fragmented elastin fibrils (Fig. 2.43). The surface lining consists of a layer of endothelial cells, which may appear hyperplastic.[148] The central core of collagen is continuous with that of the valve leaflet. The amount and distribution of elastin vary considerably among the various threads in one tumor.

The histopathologic features are typical and there is no real differential diagnostic problem. The similarities with cardiac myxoma are limited to the collar of loose connective tissue surrounding the central cores of dense collagen and its prominent

Fig. 2.41 • Surgically excised papillary fibroelastoma in a male, 49 years of age, who first presented with severe chest pain not typical of angina pectoris. Echocardiography revealed a tumor associated with the mitral valve apparatus. Surgery showed the tumor to be attached to mitral valve chordae. The gross specimen (partially resected) reveals its papillary nature (when floating in water) resembling a sea anemone.

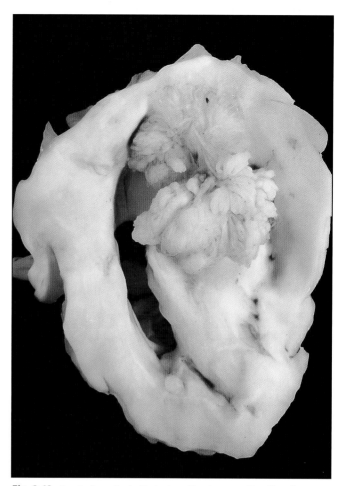

Fig. 2.42 • Surgically excised mitral valve with a large papillary fibroelastoma arising from the atrial aspect of the anterior leaflet. (Reproduced with permission from Becker A E, Anderson R H 1983 Cardiac pathology. An integrated text and colour atlas. Gower, London, Fig. 7.4.)

lining with endothelial cells (Fig. 2.44), but this should not pose a differential diagnostic problem once the overall picture is taken into account.

Aspects of special interest

The lesion is of interest because, at present, it is most frequently diagnosed by two-dimensional echocardiography in patients who may be asymptomatic. Once it has been identified clinically the question arises as to what to do. This introduces the question of the nature of this papillary proliferation.

McAllister & Fenoglio[1] consider papillary fibroelastoma to be either a true tumor or a hamartoma. They argue that, since the histologic appearance is very much like that of normal chordae tendineae, so that basically all components of normal endocardium are replicated, the lesion should be considered as a hamartoma. At the same time they also argue that papillary fibroelastomas are found in older individuals and not in children (which, strictly, should be "rarely" rather than "not"), which goes against a hamartomatous nature. These considerations and the histologic resemblance with so-called Lambl's excrescences have led some authors to consider a similar histogenesis, i.e. a proliferative response of the endocardium related to mechanical injury and associated with advancing age; hence the alternative term "giant Lambl's excrescence" for papillary fibroelastoma.[149] Indeed, immunohistochemistry suggests active participation of surface endothelial cells, with

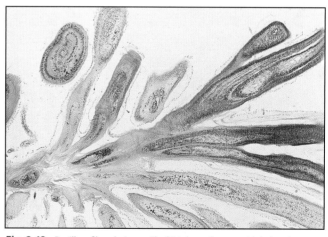

Fig. 2.43 • Papillary fibroelastoma. The histology shows multiple fronds composed of acellular collagen with irregular clumping of fragmented elastin fibrils along the surface. The surface lining consists of endothelial cells. (Elastic tissue stain.)

excessive formation of basal membrane material.[150] Although many features of distinction with the usual Lambl's excrescences occur,[1] the fact remains that many transitional stages exist where the similarities between these two lesions are striking and a distinction between the two fades.

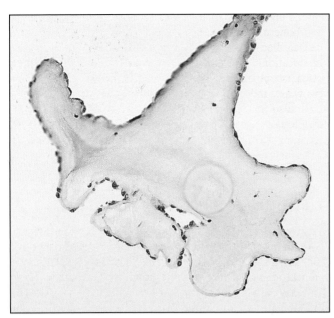

Fig. 2.44 • Peripheral part of one of the fronds of a papillary fibroelastoma showing the myxoid stroma and a surface lining composed of crevices, lined by prominent endothelial cells. This picture shows some resemblance to the peripheral parts of a cardiac myxoma, but the overall picture would easily reveal this to be part of a papillary fibroelastoma.

ing concept, since at an earlier stage James et al.[160] reported sudden death in infancy associated with "multifocal Purkinje cell tumors of the heart." With advances in techniques of electrophysiologic mapping and the increasing attention given to arrhythmias in children, the clinical relevance of this particular lesion for inducing incessant ventricular tachycardia in infants has been demonstrated. Garson et al.[161] were able to trace at surgery 14 lesions of this particular nature, 9 of which were discrete and 4 diffusely dispersed throughout both ventricles. These 14 "Purkinje cell tumors" are the ones referred to in the surgical series from the Texas Heart Institute and the MD Anderson Cancer Institute, Houston, Texas[3] (Table 2.2). This surprisingly high incidence undoubtedly relates to the bias of referral patterns, given the interest in cardiac arrhythmias in infancy in these institutions, and the fact that some centers will not include these lesions under the heading "primary heart tumors." I have seen this condition twice, both times at autopsy. The first case was a baby girl, 7 months of age, seen in 1980 (see Figs 30.12 and 30.13 in Becker & Anderson[158]); the second case, seen in 1991, was also a baby girl, 4 weeks of age (Figs 2.45 and 2.46).

This is not without clinical relevance, since it has been shown unequivocally that papillary fibroelastoma, particularly when located in the left side of the heart, may produce serious clinical consequences because of systemic thromboemboli.[138,151–153] Papillary fibroelastoma should therefore be included in the list of diagnostic options in cases of sudden and unexpected cardiac death. Thus far, I am unaware of any recurrence of a papillary fibroelastoma after surgical excision, despite the fact that the lesion is usually removed locally from the valve leaflet without valve replacement.

Purkinje cell tumor

This is a peculiar and rare lesion which thus far has only been described in young infants, with a distinct preference for females, and in association with tachyarrhythmias. The nature of the lesion remains uncertain. In fact, one may argue that this is not a tumor and not derived from Purkinje cells, but a cardiomyopathy of unknown etiology and pathogenesis. These uncertainties are reflected in the jumble of terms for this abnormality, the most popular being foamy myocardial transformation of infancy,[154] infantile xanthomatous cardiomyopathy,[155] infantile cardiomyopathy with histiocytoid change,[156] and histiocytoid cardiomyopathy in infancy[157] (see Becker & Anderson[158] for a review). Ferrans et al.[156] suggested, on ultrastructural evidence, that the disorder represents persistence of an early developmental stage of myocytes. Silver et al.[159] have suggested that the myocytes have not differentiated beyond a primitive stage where they have been changed into oncocytes. They consider a viral infection, such as rubella, early in gestation as a possible mechanism.

Amini et al.[157] first suggested that this disease should not be considered as a cardiomyopathy but as a specific condition involving the peripheral Purkinje network. This is an interest-

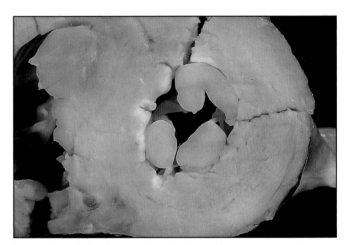

Fig. 2.45 • Purkinje cell tumor. Case of sudden and unexpected death in a baby girl 4 weeks of age. A cross-section through the heart reveals tan-white patches in subendocardial position.

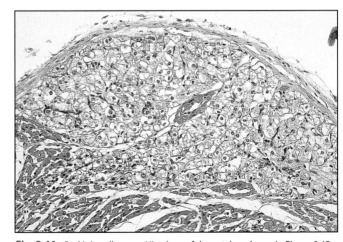

Fig. 2.46 • Purkinje cell tumor. Histology of the patches shown in Figure 2.45 reveals that these areas are composed of slightly swollen cells with a vacuolated cytoplasm.

Gross pathology

Purkinje cell tumors present as circumscribed or diffuse lesions, tan-white or yellowish in color, and usually in either a subendocardial (Fig. 2.45) or a subepicardial location.[162] They appear randomly distributed throughout the ventricles. Atrial myocardium may also be involved.

Histopathology

The histopathologic features are distinctive and readily recognized, once one is familiar with this peculiar lesion.[163] The areas involved show clusters or sheaths of myocardial cells transformed into swollen (up to twice the size of adjacent myocardial cells), rounded, or polyhedral cells with a slightly granular eosinophilic and often abundantly vacuolated cytoplasm (Fig. 2.46). There are no mitotic figures. The cells thus give a foamy appearance, hence the use of terms such as "lipoid" and "histiocytoid."

Ultrastructural study shows that the granularity is due to an increase in the number of mitochondria, often swollen, with distorted cristae showing intramitochondrial vacuoles. All cells so affected contain sparse and usually peripherally placed myofibrils with Z-bands, desmosomes, and leptofibrils. The concept of a myocytic origin of the transformed cells is based on these observations in particular, but at the same time warrants the analogy with peripheral Purkinje cells. The parallel with oncocytic transformation, known from other sites, is founded particularly on the massive accumulation of mitochondria.

Aspects of special interest

Apart from its histogenesis, which will almost certainly remain a matter of controversy for some time to come, clinical and surgical experience with infants in whom a "Purkinje cell tumor" could be correlated with incessant ventricular tachycardia strongly suggests that the lesion is not a progressive cardiomyopathy. On the basis of the present knowledge of these lesions it is not far-fetched to consider them as a form of "cardiac hamartoma."[162]

The close association with cardiac arrhythmias in very young infants is an important aspect also for pathologists. One is unlikely to be called upon to examine a biopsy unless one is affiliated with a center that specializes in this type of infant heart disease. However, every now and then, the pathologist may be confronted with a case of sudden death in a young infant in whom a correct diagnosis can be made once alerted to this possibility.

Cardiac teratoma

By far the largest series of cardiac teratomas was documented by McAllister & Fenoglio[1] (11 of 78 benign tumors, 9 of which were in patients aged 1 year or less). In contrast, the later AFIP update[2] reports only 1 cardiac teratoma in infants and children (Table 2.1) and only 3 among 47 benign pericardial tumors. There is a distinct preference for infants and children, as expected, and the vast majority of cardiac teratomas have been described in females.

Teratomas are usually intrapericardial tumors attached to the root of the aorta and pulmonary trunk, but the heart wall can be involved (as in the case described from the University of Minnesota)[6] and occasionally the tumor may present as an intracardiac mass.[163] The clinical signs and symptoms relate to the location.[163] Cardiac enlargement is the dominant feature, often accompanied by signs and symptoms of compression of the heart. Indeed, these tumors may grow rapidly to a large size, also involving the anterior mediastinum. Accurate diagnosis is usually provided through echocardiography and scanning techniques, and surgical removal is often feasible. Thus far, excision has yielded favorable results, even in cases of subtotal resection.[6]

Gross pathology

Teratomas are usually intrapericardial and attached, with or without a well-defined stalk, to the great arteries arising from the heart. They may vary in size, but those that come to clinical attention have usually grown to an appreciable size and may even be several times larger than the heart itself. They are lobulated with a smooth surface. Once incised, the tumor presents as a multilocular cyst with fluid-filled cavities of varying sizes, intermingling with solid areas, as seen usually in cases of ovarian teratomas.

Histopathology

By definition, teratomas contain elements derived from all three germ layers. Teratomas of the heart are very much like those that occur elsewhere in the body, such as those in the ovaries (see Ch. 13A). Diagnosing these tumors is not a real problem for the pathologist, except that malignancy has to be excluded (see below).

Aspects of special interest

Teratomas of the heart seldom occur within the myocardium. Their intrapericardial localization usually makes them easily accessible to the surgeon and successful removal is usually feasible. The follow-up, moreover, appears to be good. Why this tumor shows such a predilection for the female sex remains puzzling.

As far as the pathologist is concerned there are two items of additional interest. First, be sure to differentiate teratomas from cysts or cyst-like structures. Pericardial cysts usually remain asymptomatic and, although they are usually multiloculated, the histology is strikingly different from that seen in teratomas. The wall of the cyst is composed of connective tissue and the cavities are lined by a single layer of flat mesothelial cells. Bronchogenic cysts, another potential diagnostic error, are usually located intramyocardially and microscopically show the classical picture of cysts lined by ciliated columnar or cuboidal epithelium, occasionally with squamous metaplasia, lining a wall which contains variable amounts of collagen, smooth muscle, and cartilage. Seromucinous glands may occur as well as occasional foci of aggregated lymphocytes. The lack of other tissue components provides a distinction with teratomas.

Second, once the diagnosis of teratoma is made, a careful search should be made to exclude the (remote) possibility of malignancy. For this purpose several sections should be taken from different parts of the tumor, very much like that indicated in cases of teratomas elsewhere in the body.

Cardiac angioma

Of the soft tissue tumors, benign hemangiomas are one of the most common (see Ch. 3), but in the heart these lesions are much less frequent (Tables 2.1–2.3). Lymphangiomas, which will not be discussed further, are truly exceptional (2 cardiac lymphangiomas are in the collection of the AFIP: 1 in the parietal pericardium and 1 in the left ventricular myocardium[1]).

The clinical presentation of cardiac hemangiomas depends on the location and size of the tumor. They may occur at any site in the heart. They show preference for the visceral layer of the pericardium, where they may produce hemopericardium.[164] Within the myocardium hemangiomas show preference for the interventricular septum and anterior wall of the ventricles, while subendocardial hemangiomas have been described in all four heart chambers.[165] In both locations the tumor may cause myocardial dysfunction with congestive heart failure as a consequence or may mimic valvar heart disease.[166] An odd case has been documented of a 15-year-old girl who presented with signs and symptoms of pulmonary outflow tract obstruction, with secondary polycythemia, and in whom an inoperable right ventricular hemangioma was found.[167] An intramural location, furthermore, may cause atrioventricular block.[51] In a subendocardial position, once the tumor has extensive intra-cavitary growth, it may mimic a cardiac myxoma, particularly when the hemangioma originates from the interatrial septum.[51]

Cardiac hemangiomas can usually be classified as localized, although occasionally the lesion may present as an angiomatosis with extensive and diffuse involvement of a large part of the heart (Fig. 2.47).

Cardiac hemangiomas may be detected at almost any age (the 15 patients presented by McAllister & Fenoglio ranged in age from 7 months to 80 years), although cardiac hemangiomas that are symptomatic in infancy are exceptional.[168] There is no preference for gender.

Gross pathology

The gross aspect of cardiac hemangiomas is not different from that seen with hemangiomas arising in other parts of the body. An intracavitary location initially may give the impression of a myxoma.

Histopathology

The histologic appearance is not different from hemangiomas in general (see Ch. 3). The most common variants are capillary (Fig. 2.48) and cavernous hemangiomas. In endomyocardial biopsies the density of vascular channels, often accompanied by interstitial fibrosis, should alert the pathologist to the diagnosis (Fig. 2.49). The epithelioid variants of vascular tumors appear to be extremely rare; I am aware of only 2 well-documented cases originating in the heart. One is a case of epithelioid hemangioma in a 62-year-old male who, at routine cardiovascular check-up for long-lasting idiopathic hypertension, was noticed to have an echographic mass attached to the interatrial septum, protruding into the right atrium.[169] The preoperative diagnosis was cardiac myxoma, but pathologic examination showed the typical features of an epithelioid

Fig. 2.47 • Extensive diffuse hemangiomatosis involving the heart and pericardium in a 4-month-old baby boy. The opened left atrium, left ventricle, and aorta are fully enwrapped by the hemangioma.

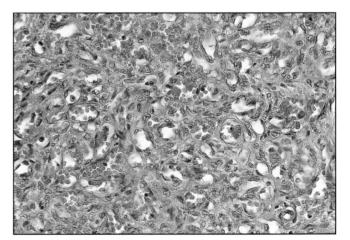

Fig. 2.48 • The typical histology of a basically benign capillary hemangioma (section taken from the specimen shown in Fig. 2.47).

hemangioma (see also Ch. 3, p. 51). This tumor has been known under a variety of names ("histiocytoid hemangioma" is one commonly encountered), but presently is categorized as part of a family of vascular tumors with epithelioid endothelial cells as a common characteristic.[170] Epithelioid hemangioma is

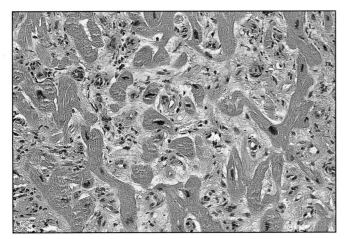

Fig. 2.49 • Endomyocardial biopsy in a 22-year-old male who was asymptomatic until 1 week before admission when he developed progressive dyspnea. Clinical studies revealed pericarditis (more than 1 liter of serosanguineous fluid), an unusual ground-glass appearance of a large part of the myocardium of the inferior heart wall on echocardiography, and vascular convolutions on coronary angiography. The right ventricular endomyocardial biopsy (from the septal aspect) revealed a hemangioma of the capillary type. Hypertrophic myocardial cells are separated by the diffuse capillary hemangioma.

considered to represent the benign end of a spectrum, whereas epithelioid angiosarcoma (see p. 33) represents its malignant counterpart.[171] The "in-between" variant in this family, presently known as epithelioid hemangioendothelioma, was initially considered a low-grade malignant vascular neoplasm,[172] but the occurrence of systemic metastases in 21% and the fact that 4 of 20 patients (17%) died of tumor has led to the conclusion that epithelioid hemangioendothelioma "is better regarded as a fully malignant, rather than borderline, vascular neoplasm."[173] Predicting the behavior of epithelioid hemangioendothelioma may be difficult[174] and some cases may overlap morphologically with epithelioid hemangioma. It is of interest that a case report exists of a left atrial tumor in a 65-year-old male, again diagnosed preoperatively as a myxoma, which at pathologic examination was shown to be a "histiocytoid hemangioma" but exhibited the borderline microscopic features alluded to above.[175] In retrospect this tumor most likely represents an example of an epithelioid hemangioendothelioma.

It is clinically important to differentiate between these epithelioid vascular lesions and the rather bizarre "histiocytoid" lesions, resembling "histiocytoid hemangioma," described by Luthringer et al.[176] (see section on differential diagnosis, below).

Aspects of special interest

Biologic behavior The biologic behavior of cardiac hemangiomas is similar to that seen with hemangiomas in general. They may possess a limited growth potential and will persist if not surgically excised, although spontaneous involution has been documented.[177] Once the tumor has been totally removed by the surgeon the prognosis appears excellent.[178]

Differential diagnosis There is hardly any serious differential diagnostic problem in cases of cardiac hemangioma. Nevertheless, these benign lesions should be distinguished from

dilated blood vessels. The latter may occur anywhere in the heart, but show preference for the subendocardium. Histologic examination will reveal a cluster of dilated vessels, often thrombosed, resembling that seen in hemorrhoids.

Another potential error may occur in misdiagnosing a blood cyst as a hemangioma. Blood cysts are almost exclusively seen in the hearts of newborns and infants, with particular preference for the tricuspid and mitral valves. Basically, these so-called blood cysts are not cysts in the true sense of the word, but represent crevices in the valve leaflets with trapped blood, thus mimicking a varicose lesion.

Finally, lesions have been documented attached to mural endocardium, heart valves, and "free-floating" within the pericardial sac (one was part of the contents of a dissecting aneurysm of the ascending aorta!), which bear some resemblance to "histiocytoid" (or epithelioid) hemangioma.[176] The lesions consisted of solid cell clusters contained within a meshwork of fibrin (Fig. 2.50). The cells were round to polygonal with an eosinophilic and sometimes mildly foamy or vacuolated cytoplasm and distinct cell borders, thus providing a histiocytoid or epithelioid appearance (Fig. 2.51).

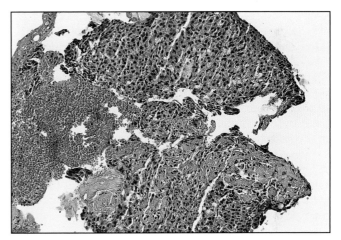

Fig. 2.50 • Endomyocardial biopsy in a male, 23 years of age, with non-specific chest pain, echocardiographically diminished left ventricular contractility, and a normal coronary angiogram, suspected to have myocarditis. The histology reveals myocardium and relatively large solid clusters of cells amidst blood and fibrin.

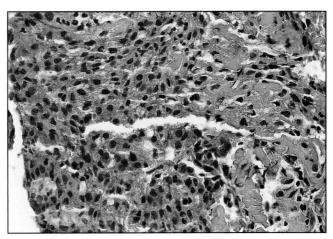

Fig. 2.51 • Higher magnification of the specimen in Figure 2.50 reveals these clusters to be composed of polygonal cells with a finely granular, slightly eosinophilic cytoplasm, sometimes vacuolated and with distinct cell borders.

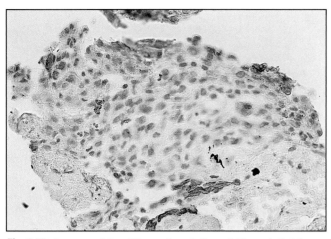

Fig. 2.52 • Immunostaining of the specimen in Figure 2.50 reveals that the cells stained positive with a cytokeratin marker. The lesion resembles nodular mesothelial hyperplasia, although its presence in an endomyocardial biopsy remains puzzling, and should not be mistaken for a primary or metastatic malignancy.

Immunostaining reveals that these cells do not stain with endothelial markers, in contrast to the cells of epithelioid hemangioma, but instead show immunoreactivity for keratin (Fig. 2.52). I have seen this lesion once in an endomyocardial biopsy; I diagnosed it at the time as an aggregate of mesothelial cells, although its origin left me puzzled (Figs 2.50–2.52). The original authors[176] also considered the option of nodular mesothelial hyperplasia, but remained vague as to its possible genesis. Subsequent data suggested that these lesions are predominantly histiocytic, and the term "mesothelial/monocytic incidental cardiac excrescence" (cardiac MICE) was proposed.[179] It seems that all of the reported cases occurred following a cardiovascular surgical procedure. Be that as it may, these lesions should not be mistaken for a primary or metastatic malignancy.

Other benign cardiac tumors

Mesothelioma (so called) of the atrioventricular node

To the best of my knowledge this rare lesion was first reported by Armstrong & Mönckeberg[180] in 1911. In 1942 Mahaim[181] considered this particular tumor to be derived from invaginations of epicardial mesothelium within the atrioventricular canal during embryogenesis of the heart. Prior to Mahaim's concept, which was almost universally accepted, Rezek[182] had proposed that this lesion was of endodermal origin, rather than lymphatic, as suggested by Armstrong & Mönckeberg.[180] Immunohistochemical studies of these lesions have demonstrated that the principal cells stain positively for carcinoembryonic antigen (CEA) and keratin, suggesting an endodermal origin.[183,184] On that basis the lesion could represent displaced endodermal foregut tissue and, hence, may be pathogenetically similar to bronchogenic cysts.[183] These observations endorse a concept previously proposed by Sopher & Spitz[184] and Travers.[186] More recently, other authors have demonstrated a neuroendocrine component and have suggested that these lesions represent ultimobranchial

heterotopia.[187] The histogenesis will almost certainly remain a matter of debate for many years to come.

From a clinical viewpoint it is worthwhile emphasizing that the cases documented thus far have ranged in age from 11 months to 89 years and that partial or complete atrioventricular heart block has been the dominating feature. Indeed, sudden death may be the first sign of this tumor.[188,189] In a 66-year-old patient the tumor, which had almost completely replaced the atrioventricular node, was associated with an intra-atrial conduction defect, paroxysmal atrial arrhythmia, and spontaneous intermittent pre-excitation; the latter was facilitated by multiple left-sided accessory pathways.[190]

The gross pathology consists of thickening of the atrial septum, with or without slightly elevated nodules, in the region of the atrioventricular node. Gross inspection usually reveals the multicystic nature of the lesion.

The histopathology is dominated by a polycystic lesion, replacing the atrioventricular node, composed of cysts, ducts, and solid nests of cells (Figs 2.53 and 2.54). The cysts vary in size considerably. The cells lining the cavities are either single or multilayered and flat or cuboidal in shape, often in a palisaded arrangement along the innermost lining. The cells stain with PAS, diastase-resistant, and with alcian blue, which remains unchanged by prior digestion with hyaluronidase. Moreover, these cells also stain with anti-CEA. Some cell nests fail to show mucin staining and exhibit prominent eosinophilic cytoplasm, resembling squamous or transitional epithelium. The cell nests are embedded in a dense tissue stroma which contains collagen and elastin fibers; remnants of an atrioventricular node are rarely identifiable.

Electron microscopically there are two principal cell types.[183] One population of cells is characterized by an almost oval shape, numerous desmosomes and cytoplasm containing many tonofibrillar bundles circumferentially arranged around

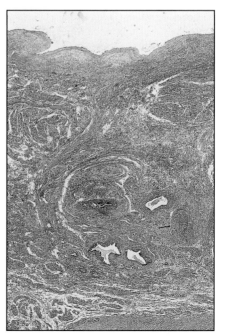

Fig. 2.53 • Mesothelioma of the atrioventricular node. The lesion is composed of small cysts. (Courtesy of Dr J. E. Edwards, Cardiovascular Registry, United Hospital, St. Paul, MN, USA.)

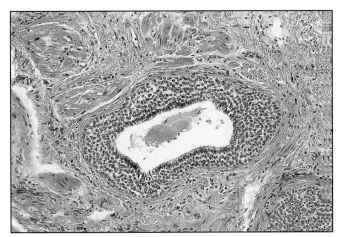

Fig. 2.54 • Higher magnification of the specimen in Figure 2.53 reveals a multilayered lining of cuboidal cells with clear cytoplasm and with a palisading arrangement on the inner surface.

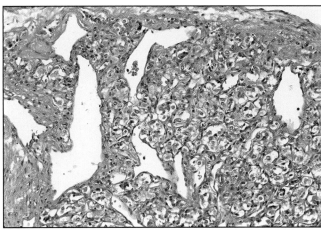

Fig. 2.55 • Cardiac paraganglioma. A 71-year-old woman presented with a history of atrial fibrillation, hypertension, and myocardial infarction. Coronary angiography revealed three-vessel coronary artery disease and a highly vascularized area in the atrial septum. Transesophageal echocardiography showed a tumor (5 cm in diameter) in the region of the atrial septum. Bypass surgery was performed and the tumor was resected, but the patient died due to excessive blood loss from the atrial septal area. The hematoxylin and eosin stain shows wide vascular spaces and clusters of pale-staining eosinophilic cells, grouped together in Zellballen surrounded by capillaries. (Courtesy of Dr R. J. van Suylen, Department of Pathology, Academic Hospital, Maastricht, The Netherlands.)

the nucleus. The second cell type contains intermediate filaments and dense granules limited by a single membrane, in part fused with the surface membrane, suggesting secretory activity.

Cardiac paraganglioma

These tumors originate from chromaffin paraganglia localized at the base of the heart, in close association with the aorta and pulmonary trunk and nourished by branches of the main coronary arteries. On that basis the name "coronary glomera" has been introduced.[191] These tumors are included among the extra-adrenal paraganglia dealt with in the AFIP atlas.[192] The first case of an intrapericardial paraganglioma (also known as pheochromocytoma or chemodectoma) was reported by Besterman et al.[193] in 1974. Most patients are young adults. The clinical presentation is usually dominated by signs and symptoms of excessive norepinephrine secretion, with hypertension as the principal sign, although the clinical manifestations may be rather diverse.[194–198]

Cardiac paragangliomas are usually positioned intra-epicardially, with a preference for the epicardial surface of the left atrial inferoposterior wall, the interatrial groove and the root of the great arteries, but they may occur in other locations, such as the proximal parts of either the right or the left coronary artery and protrude into the atrial cavities from a primary location within the interatrial groove.[199] In the latter position these tumors may mimic an atrial myxoma on two-dimensional echocardiography. Coronary angiography, moreover, may show a "tumor blush," consequent upon the localized vascular density. Despite the fact that such a "blush" is non-specific, since an intracavitary hemangioma may show a similar picture, the angiographic appearance may easily be misleading as it is commonly considered "typical" for myxoma. Histologic studies, however, readily provide the correct diagnosis.

The gross pathology is that of a homogeneous, brown mass of tissue, which microscopically reveals the characteristic pattern of a paraganglioma. The lesions are composed mainly of so-called chief cells, which are grouped together in cell clusters or "Zellballen" surrounded by a capillary network with varying degrees of connective tissue (Fig. 2.55; see also

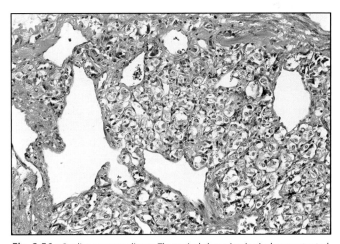

Fig. 2.56 • Cardiac paraganglioma. The typical clustering is nicely accentuated with a Gomori stain for reticulin.

Ch. 28). These features, if not already conspicuous in a routine hematoxylin and eosin stain, can be accentuated with the use of a stain for reticulin (Fig. 2.56). If necessary, specific markers for neuroendocrine differentiation, such as chromogranin, can be used (Fig. 2.57).

The biologic behavior of cardiac paragangliomas is probably comparable to that of carotid body paragangliomas (see Ch. 28), but the rarity of the lesion prohibits firm statements in this respect. Nevertheless, 2 of the 15 cases reviewed in the literature had developed metastases[190] and thus may well come into the range of incidence of metastases reported for carotid body tumors.[200] At the same time it is worth mentioning that one of the major hazards is surgery without a preconceived notion of the nature of the lesion. Intraoperative massive hemorrhage and death, under such conditions, are possibilities[199] (see also case documented in Fig. 2.55).

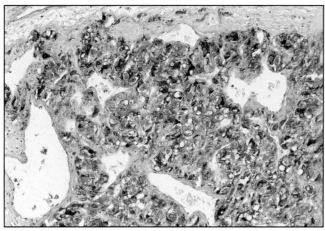

Fig. 2.57 • Cardiac paraganglioma. The cells stain intensely positive for chromogranin.

Granular cell tumor

This tumor, identical to granular cell tumors in other locations in the body (see Ch. 27), was described in 3 adult patients by McAllister & Fenoglio,[1] and 4 additional cases have since been added to the AFIP registry.[2] In each of the cases described by McAllister & Fenoglio[1] the tumor was originally diagnosed as a rhabdomyoma. The pictures provided (their Fig. 66) readily clarify that this truly is a matter of mistaken identity. At the same time, the pictures are vaguely reminiscent of a lesion previously described under the heading of "Purkinje cell tumor" (see p. 26). Histochemical and ultrastructural studies should easily solve such a differential diagnostic problem: the principal cell in the so-called Purkinje cell tumor shows an abundance of mitochondria, whereas the cells of a granular cell tumor contain large (PAS-positive) autophagic granules within the cytoplasm.

McAllister & Fenoglio[1] explicitly state that they have included these tumors only as "mere oddities of no clinical significance," apart from being mistaken for rhabdomyomas.

Neurofibroma

Neurofibromas in the heart are extremely rare, but when present are usually part of von Recklinghausen's disease (see Ch. 27). The condition may lead to right ventricular outflow tract obstruction.[201]

Heterotopic tissues

The odd case can be encountered in which the heart and pericardium contain islands of thymic or thyroid tissue.[202,203] These are usually incidental findings, either at surgery or at autopsy. I include under this heading the rare case of an adenomatoid tumor, found incidentally at cardiac surgery and infiltrating the right atrial myocardium.[204]

Malignant tumors of the heart and pericardium

A survey of the malignant tumors indigenous to the heart reveals a varied tableau (Tables 2.1–2.3). Malignant tumors

accounted for approximately 37% of all primary tumors of the heart and pericardium filed in the AFIP between 1976 and 1993.[2] The "Texas experience" adds up to a total of 11.7%,[3] whereas our own cardiovascular pathology registry contains 18 primary malignancies of the heart and pericardium, together accounting for 13.2% of all primary tumors. There is no doubt that the considerable range in the incidence of malignant tumors is strongly biased by the differences in background of the three institutions. Burke et al.,[205] updating the AFIP series[1] of 1978, have collected another 75 primary cardiac sarcomas (40 surgical cases), which provides the overall impression that angiosarcomas are the most frequent primary cardiac sarcomas, although other surveys report an equal incidence of so-called malignant fibrous histiocytomas.[206,207] The latter series contains 21 primary cardiac sarcomas, diagnosed between 1964 and 1989, of which 7 were identified as angiosarcoma and 7 as malignant fibrous histiocytoma. (As far as one can judge, this represents basically the series previously reported by Murphy et al.[3] (see Table 2.2) with probably some adjustments in diagnoses and expanded with the experience from the Department of Thoracic Surgery of the University of Texas.) The remaining 7 tumors were diagnosed as rhabdomyosarcoma (2), leiomyosarcoma (2), undifferentiated sarcoma (1), fibromyxosarcoma (1), and myxosarcoma (1).[206] It thus appears that malignant fibrous histiocytoma has found recognition amidst primary sarcomas of the heart, just at the time when such lesions are under re-examination and reclassification in the arena of soft tissue sarcomas[208] (see Ch. 24).

This section on malignant primary cardiac tumors also includes primary pericardial mesotheliomas and primary cardiac lymphomas. In the following paragraphs only salient details are provided with respect to cardiac involvement. For a detailed description of the histopathology of each of the tumors, the reader is referred to the appropriate chapters in this book.

Angiosarcoma

Angiosarcoma is probably the most common primary malignant heart tumor.[209–212] The clinical presentation is variable, but outstanding features are congestive heart failure and dyspnea.[1,210] There is a tendency for primary cardiac angiosarcomas to arise from the right side of the heart, with preference for a primary atrial location.[1,206] A review of the clinicopathologic spectrum under these circumstances reveals two major forms: a large obstructing mass with associated clinical signs and symptoms and a less common, less symptomatic, locally infiltrative tumor.[213] Pericardial lesions simulate pericarditis in their clinical presentation.

The mean age at presentation is approximately 40 years, but a range of 10–76 years is thus far on record. The natural history is usually reflected in a short clinical course, with most patients being dead of their disease within 10 months of the onset of symptoms. The cause of death almost always relates directly to cardiac effects of the tumor, such as cardiac tamponade or intracavitary obstruction. Occasionally more prolonged survival can occur; 2 patients have been reported[214,215] who had large tumors which could not be resected completely on cardiac pulmonary bypass, and neither had evidence of distant metastases at the time of operation. Both patients received radiation therapy, and 1 received an incomplete course of chemotherapy. There were no signs of recurrence 36 and 34 months after tumor resection, respectively. In one instance complete excision without cardiopulmonary bypass of an angiosarcoma located in the left atrium was performed and the patient was reported clinically well 3 years after the procedure.[216]

At the time of clinical presentation the tumor is usually extensive, often to the extent that radical surgery is no longer feasible. The diagnosis can be made on surgical biopsy specimens or on pericardial fluid cytology.[211] Angiosarcoma of the heart has also been diagnosed on an endomyocardial biopsy.[217]

The histopathology may vary considerably, from well-differentiated areas showing neoplastic blood vessels to poorly differentiated sites with solid tumor growth of spindle-shaped and anaplastic cells with no vasoformative pattern. In cases of poorly differentiated or undifferentiated growth, factor VIII-related antigen is usually negative, but other endothelial cell markers (such as CD31 and CD34) usually show positivity. In negative cases electron microscopic studies may be more helpful than immunohistochemical and cytochemical studies. A rare case of a primary cardiac epithelioid angiosarcoma is shown in Figures 2.58 and 2.59 (see Ch. 3, p. 66).

In general, once large areas of the tumor are available for histologic evaluation, there is usually no major problem in diagnosing the tumor as an angiosarcoma. The main differential diagnostic problem, particularly in cases of poorly differentiated angiosarcomas, is with other poorly differentiated sarcomas, fibrous (sarcomatoid) mesotheliomas and, of course, metastatic tumors to the heart.

Malignant fibrous histiocytoma (unclassified pleomorphic sarcoma)

To the best of my knowledge, primary malignant fibrous histiocytoma (so called) of the heart was first reported in 1978.[218] This tumor has often been regarded as one of the most common soft tissue sarcomas, but is generally reported as

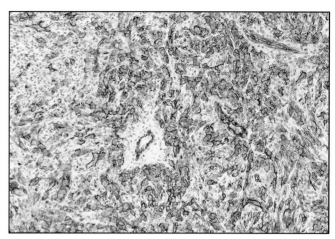

Fig. 2.59 • Epithelioid angiosarcoma. Immunostaining with CD34 shows marked positivity.

being rare as a primary heart tumor. The term is contentious, and the so-called myxoid variant of malignant fibrous histiocytoma is probably better named "myxofibrosarcoma" (see Ch. 24 for a discussion of malignant fibrous histiocytoma).

The vast majority of primary pleomorphic sarcomas of the heart have been localized in the left atrium (in one instance with a location in the left ventricle also[206]). Burke et al.[205] mention a right atrial and a right ventricular location in one instance each. Because of its preference for the left atrium the tumor may easily be mistaken clinically for an atrial myxoma.[35,219–221] This is relevant information to the pathologist as well, since the tumor may arrive as a surgical specimen at the pathologist's desk with the firm label "myxoma." For the less experienced the differential diagnosis with myxofibrosarcoma (the myxoid variant of so-called malignant fibrous histiocytoma) may be troublesome, because of the overwhelming presence of a myxoid stroma separating strands and clusters of predominantly spindle-shaped cells (see also Ch. 24). However, thus far I have not seen a single case where the histologic features of a myxofibrosarcoma truly mimic those of a cardiac myxoma. The myxoid variant of malignant fibrous histiocytoma contains foci of hypercellularity with pleomorphism, mitotic figures, necrosis, and extensive vascularity and lacks any of the characteristic features of a cardiac myxoma (other than the myxomatous matrix).[35,221] I have seen 2 cases in which the initial pathologic diagnosis was "cardiac myxoma," both arising from unusual sites (1 from the pulmonary valve and 1 from the mitral valve) and both showing the typical features of myxofibrosarcoma with nuclear pleomorphism, mitoses, and necrosis. It is only because these tumors were "cardiac and myxomatous" that otherwise experienced pathologists were led astray. Nevertheless, if in doubt, sampling from several sites of the tumor may be helpful.

Tumors in the left atrium usually arise from the posterior wall or the septum, but other locations may also be involved. Multiple tumors can be encountered.[220] The overall prognosis is poor, also following surgically radical resection, and varies from approximately 10 to 60 months after surgery as far as has been recorded.[222] The response to radiation therapy and chemotherapy has been variable and most authors report uniform fatality despite therapy.[35,219] Local recurrence is common and the tumor has a marked tendency for local invasion.[33,223] The average age of patients (36 years in the

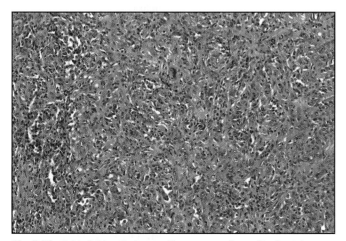

Fig. 2.58 • Epithelioid angiosarcoma. The tumor was located in the right atrium and had extended intracavitarily. The tumor shows an almost solid nodular growth pattern composed of strands and cords of epithelioid tumor cells with eosinophilic cytoplasm and distinct nuclear pleomorphism. (Courtesy of Dr P. Pauwels, Laboratory of Pathology (Stichting PAMM), Catharina Ziekenhuis, Eindhoven, The Netherlands.)

review report by Laya et al.[33]) at presentation is younger than the usual age of presentation of so-called malignant fibrous histiocytoma of the soft tissues.

Rhabdomyosarcoma

Cardiac rhabdomyosarcoma was the second most frequent malignant primary tumor of the heart in adults originally reported from the AFIP,[1] whereas the 1976–1993 series contains only 3 such tumors, likely representing a shift in diagnostic criteria.[2] These tumors have been reported at almost any age and show no definite preference for gender, although they are relatively rare in the pediatric age group. A survey of reported cases of primary cardiac rhabdomyosarcoma revealed 17 cases under 16 years of age, 6 of whom were 1 year or less.[224] In this age group, Burke & Virmani[2] registered 3 primary cardiac rhabdomyosarcomas, 1 of which presented in the first year of life. A rare case of a botryoid embryonal rhabdomyosarcoma, originating from the ventricular aspect of the aortic leaflet of the mitral valve, in an 8-year-old boy has been documented.[225] I am aware of only one report of a *malignant rhabdoid tumor* of the heart, in a 6-month-old girl.[226] The tumor, which extended throughout the left ventricular inferolateral wall and obliterated the pericardial cavity, was composed of large polygonal cells with eosinophilic cytoplasm, pleomorphic nuclei, and frequent single eosinophilic intracytoplasmic inclusions. Electron microscopic evaluation revealed that these consisted of masses of intermediate filaments, as reported by Hass et al.,[227] who coined the term "malignant rhabdoid tumor," and it is now well recognized that these lesions are unrelated to rhabdomyosarcoma.

The clinical signs and symptoms relate to the location of the tumor. General malaise is a common phenomenon, often accompanied by cardiac murmurs and arrhythmias. The tumors may extend intracavitarily, and if so usually have a polypoid appearance; they may also involve the visceral and parietal layers of the pericardium. In both instances these extensions are almost always due to growth from an intramyocardial location. In the pediatric age group the tumor preferentially originates from the atrial or ventricular septum (35% altogether), whereas in adults the tumor frequently arises from the left atrium or right ventricle.[224] The morphology of cardiac rhabdomyosarcoma is similar to that encountered in the soft tissues elsewhere in the body (see Ch. 24); an example of a primary cardiac pleomorphic rhabdomyosarcoma is shown in Figure 2.60.

The natural history of these tumors is dismal. To the best of my knowledge there are no long-term survivors once the diagnosis has been made. Most patients die within 1 year of diagnosis (with an average survival of 1.5 months under 16 years of age and of 6 months in adults[224]).

Fibrosarcoma

As in sarcomas of soft tissue, the diagnosis "fibrosarcoma" has been seriously challenged over the past decades. This relates to ongoing efforts and modern techniques used to categorize soft tissue tumors more precisely according to cell type and, in particular, regarding their distinction from malignant fibrous histiocytoma as a specific entity (see above). These trends are reflected in the reported series of malignant primary heart

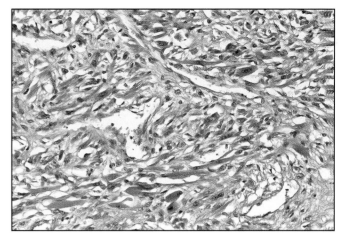

Fig. 2.60 • Pleomorphic rhabdomyosarcoma. A 40-year-old woman with a large tumor in the left atrial wall extending into the left atrial cavity and on to the aortic mitral valve leaflet. The characteristic features of a pleomorphic rhabdomyosarcoma are evident; note the large bizarre rhabdomyoblasts. (Courtesy of Dr C. H. Heijmans, Laboratory of Pathology, Enschede, The Netherlands.)

tumors. The series reported from the AFIP[1] in 1978 documents 14 primary cardiac fibrosarcomas and no malignant fibrous histiocytoma, while a recent update based on newly collected cases documents 6 fibrosarcomas and 6 malignant fibrous histiocytomas[205] (see also Table 2.1). Nevertheless, McAllister & Fenoglio[1] do mention that the histopathology in 5 of their 14 cases diagnosed as a fibrous sarcoma showed a "storiform or whorled pattern of the spindle cells and the presence of giant cells" suggestive of so-called malignant fibrous histiocytoma. A recent surgical series, moreover, documents no tumor under the heading fibrosarcoma, but instead produces 7 cases of malignant fibrous histiocytoma.[206] Our own series contains 2 cases of myxofibrosarcoma (see also Table 2.3), dealt with under the heading "malignant fibrous histiocytoma" (see p. 33).

The diagnosis of a fibrosarcoma otherwise is based on the same criteria applied to tumors that arise in the soft tissues elsewhere in the body (see Ch. 24).

Undifferentiated sarcoma

By far the largest series is reported by Burke et al.[205] They classified 18 of 75 primary cardiac sarcomas as "undifferentiated." These tumors were located in both right ($n = 4$) and left atria ($n = 5$) and in both right ($n = 2$) and left ventricles ($n = 3$), and in the pericardium ($n = 4$); in one instance diffuse spread had occurred. Immunohistochemical techniques revealed positive staining for smooth muscle actin and vimentin and an occasional cell showed positive staining for cytokeratin, but more helpful markers remained negative.

The overall survival of these patients is poor and it appeared that there was no statistically significant difference between those with a differentiated (classified) sarcoma and those with an undifferentiated sarcoma (with undifferentiated ($n = 18$) and malignant fibrous histiocytoma ($n = 6$) grouped together[205]). A more recent large French series,[228] in which undifferentiated sarcomas predominated, also found that histologic type had little effect on prognosis in cardiac sarcomas.

Other rare primary sarcomas of the heart

Leiomyosarcoma

There was only one such tumor in the files of the AFIP, reported in 1978,[1] while the 1976–1993 data included 12 new cases, 1 of which presented in the first year of life.[2] Among the 143 surgically treated patients reported from the Texas Heart Institute by Murphy et al.,[3] only 1 case occurred, while the follow-up of this series[206] revealed 2 leiomyosarcomas among a total of 21 primary sarcomas of the heart. The fact that our series of 18 malignant primary tumors of the heart contains 3 leiomyosarcomas undoubtedly reflects the referral bias alluded to in the introductory paragraphs of this chapter, and this also applies to the recent French series, which included 6 cases.[228] One of these is a primary pleomorphic mitral valve sarcoma in a 7-month-old male[229] in which, contrary to the authors, we could demonstrate immunoreactivity of tumor cells with the anti-smooth muscle-actin antibody 1A4 and CD34.[230] Because of these signs of (smooth) muscle cell differentiation we argued that this tumor could be classified as a leiomyosarcoma. Occasional cases of cardiac leiomyosarcoma have epithelioid morphology.[231]

The tumors are highly aggressive and locally invasive and the outcome is almost inevitably fatal.[232,233] The histopathologic diagnosis is based on the same criteria as at other sites (see Ch. 24).

Liposarcoma

True primary cardiac liposarcomas are exceptional neoplasms, with only 1 such case being reported from the files of the AFIP[1] and only 11 illustrated cases reported in the literature (see Paraf et al.[234]). Thus far the reported cases show a distinct preference for an atrial location and the cardiac manifestations relate directly to the position of the tumor mass. The progosis is dismal, with a mean survival of 8.3 months. Metastases are common and involve mostly lungs and bones.

The histopathologic diagnosis is based on the same criteria as those applied to liposarcomas in other parts of the body (see Ch. 24).

Osteosarcoma

A review from the files of the AFIP[235] revealed 9 primary cardiac sarcomas with osteosarcomatous differentiation among 81 primary sarcomas of the heart from which slides were available; the most recent AFIP fascicle[2] enumerates 13 cases (9% of all primary cardiac sarcomas). The interesting observation is that each of these 9 tumors was localized in the left atrium, including 1 which appeared to have originated from the mitral valve. Because of its location the tumor was often mistaken clinically for a myxoma, despite the fact that the echocardiographic findings were atypical. This observation is important since it further highlights the potential danger of accepting each and every left atrial tumor as a cardiac myxoma. The prognosis of these tumors is uniformly bad, although prolonged survival may occur after surgical palliation. All patients thus far reported with a primary cardiac osteosarcoma have died.

The histologic diagnosis of cardiac osteosarcoma is no different from that of osteosarcomas elsewhere in the body (see Ch. 25).

Chondrosarcoma

I am aware of only 3 case reports of a primary chondrosarcoma of the heart.[236–238] The best-documented case is the one reported by Muir & Seah.[236] They described a 50-year-old woman with a primary cardiac chondrosarcomatous mesenchymoma of the mitral valve. The precise origin of the tumor remains unclear, but the autopsy description favors a left ventricular site of origin. Histologically the bulk of the tumor consisted of chondrosarcoma, but other areas exhibited characteristics of fibrosarcoma, and parts were interpreted as hemangiosarcomatous.

The clinical course from the time of onset of symptoms (dyspnea) to death was about 6 months.

Synovial sarcoma

Primary cardiac synovial sarcomas showing the typical biphasic pattern are exceptional.[1] A case has been documented in a 13-year-old boy who presented with a large tumor in the right atrium attached by a stalk to the atrioventricular ring.[239] Postoperative microscopic examination revealed a biphasic malignant tumor composed of epithelial glandular structures and a cellular spindle-celled stroma. Immunohistochemical markers confirmed the diagnosis, mainly by excluding mesothelioma. There is room for doubt, to this end, with respect to the initial case documented from the files of the AFIP,[1] which could well fit a biphasic mesothelioma, as well as to the report of a synovial sarcoma of the heart, arising from a so-called mesothelioma of the atrioventricular node.[240] Be that as it may, primary synovial sarcoma of the heart is an exceedingly rare tumor. Nicholson and coworkers[239] present a brief survey of the 6 published cases (including their own, as well as both cases critically alluded to above). The ages ranged from 13 to 53 years; the prognosis is evidently poor, with all previously published patients dying within 1 year.

Malignant peripheral nerve sheath tumor (MPNST)

This term is used synonymously with terms such as "neurogenic sarcoma", "neurofibrosarcoma" and "malignant schwannoma".

The histopathologic diagnosis of these tumors in the heart is based on the same criteria as applied to neurogenic soft tissue sarcomas elsewhere in the body (see Ch. 27). The initial series from the AFIP[1] documented 4 patients with such a malignancy, but without ultrastructural or immunohistochemical evidence. In 3 of these 4 patients the bulk of the tumor was located over the outflow tract of the right ventricle and in the remaining patient the main tumor mass was situated over the right atrium. Two additional cases were later included in the AFIP registry,[2] one of which contained heterologous rhabdomyosarcoma. A case of multiple MPNSTs of the heart, with intracardiac expansion, has been reported in a 51-year-old woman.[241] We have seen 1 case (courtesy of Dr P. Pauwels, Pathology Laboratory, Catharina Hospital, Eindhoven, The Netherlands) diagnosed as a malignant peripheral nerve sheath tumor, located in the right ventricle of a 75-year-old woman.

Other primary malignant tumors of the heart and pericardium

Mesothelioma

Primary malignant cardiac mesothelioma accounts for fewer than 5% of mesotheliomas diagnosed. Chun et al.[242] collected some 120 cases from the literature, and the AFIP files from 1970 contain 240 thoracic mesotheliomas, of which only 8 were limited to the heart and pericardium.[2] The incidence of antemortem diagnosis is low due to a paucity of clinical signs and symptoms, which in themselves are non-specific.[1,242–244] Although dyspnea and pericardial effusion are often the leading clinical findings, the possibility of metastatic disease is much more likely than primary pericardial mesothelioma. The differential diagnosis in such circumstances will rely heavily on exfoliative cytology and tissue biopsy studies. A correct diagnosis will usually be established with these means, but the diversity in cell forms and histologic patterns may occasionally hamper the differentiation between malignant mesothelioma and metastatic deposits. Basically, however, the diagnosis of mesothelioma at a primary pericardial location is not different from that in other sites in the body (see Ch. 5).

According to McAllister & Fenoglio,[1] superficial myocardial invasion of a primary pericardial mesothelioma is a common feature in the end-stage of the disease, but massive extension into the endocardium is considered an important feature to differentiate at autopsy a primary pericardial mesothelioma from various types of sarcoma. Our own experience is contradictory to this statement (Fig. 2.61). The tumor had massively invaded both the right and the left ventricular myocardium, with extension into the endocardium, although without intracavitary extension.

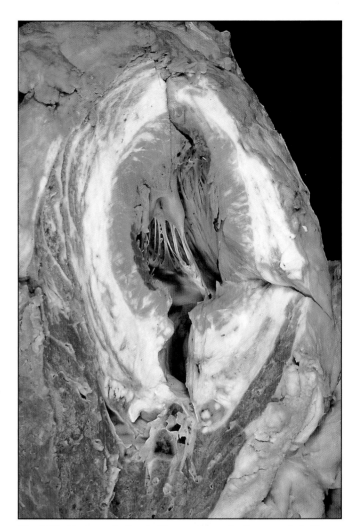

Fig. 2.61 • The heart of a female, 30 years of age, who first presented with signs of pericardial effusion, diagnosed as a mesothelioma by cytology and biopsy. The heart is fully encapsulated by the mesothelioma, with involvement of the left lung and massive invasion of the myocardium. The illustration shows the opened left ventricle.

Malignant teratoma

The original collection of the AFIP[1] contained 4 cases of malignant teratoma, each occurring in a child ranging in age from 1 to 4 years of age. At the time of diagnosis the tumor had already extensively invaded the heart, making radical surgery impossible. All 4 children died within 3 months of onset of symptoms. The more recent fascicle[2] added an endodermal sinus tumor occurring in a 14-month-old girl.

The diagnosis is based on the identification of malignant change in one type of tissue in an otherwise benign teratoma.

Primary cardiac lymphoma

Cardiac involvement as part of disseminated malignant lymphoma, late in the course of the disease, appears to be rather common and has been observed in almost 20% of cases when taken to autopsy.[245] On the other hand, primary cardiac lymphoma, defined as a lymphoma first originating in the heart, appears extremely rare, certainly in immunocompetent patients.[246–248] A review of the literature reveals that primary cardiac lymphomas include types of low, intermediate, and high grade, mostly of B-cell nature. The lymphomatous process usually arises in the right chambers as a mass, often with pericardial effusion.[248,249] Cytology of the latter is diagnostic in the majority of patients. The overall prognosis is poor, which in part relates to diagnostic delay, with patients presenting with unresponsive heart failure. Treatment should be as for other aggressive lymphomas.

The histopathologic diagnosis is based on the same criteria as applied to lymphomas in general (see Ch. 21). A word of caution should be introduced at this stage when it comes to the diagnosis of "lymphoma" after cardiac transplantation. Experience has shown thus far that a variety of bizarre lymphocytic proliferations may occur, most likely consequent upon viral infection and not necessarily recognized as such; these should not be diagnosed erroneously as a lymphoma. The pathologist aware of the intricacies of post-transplant pathology may play a vital role in this setting.

References

1. McAllister H A, Fenoglio J J Jr 1978 Tumors of the cardiovascular system. Atlas of tumor pathology, series 2, fascicle 15. Armed Forces Institute of Pathology, Washington, DC

2. Burke A, Virmani R 1996 Tumors of the heart and great vessels. Atlas of tumor pathology, series 3, fascicle 16. Armed Forces Institute of Pathology, Washington, DC

3. Murphy M C, Sweeney M S, Putnam J B Jr et al. 1990 Surgical treatment of cardiac tumours: a 25-year experience. Ann Thorac Surg 49: 612–618

4. Colucci W S, Braunwald E 1980 Primary tumors of the heart. In: Braunwald E (ed) Heart disease. A textbook of cardiovascular medicine. Saunders, Philadelphia, p 1502–1504

5. Wold L E, Lie J T 1980 Cardiac myxomas: a clinicopathologic profile. Am J Pathol 101: 219–234

6. Molina J E, Edwards J E, Ward H B 1990 Primary cardiac tumours: experience at the University of Minnesota. Thorac Cardiovasc Surg 38 (suppl. 2): 183–191

7. Blondeau Ph 1990 Primary cardiac tumours – French study of 533 cases. Thorac Cardiovasc Surg 38 (suppl. 2): 192–195

8. Sezai Y 1990 Tumours of the heart. Incidence and clinical importance of cardiac tumours in Japan and operative technique for left atrial tumours. Thorac Cardiovasc Surg 38 (suppl. 2): 201–204

9. Li G Y 1990 Incidence of clinical importance of cardiac tumours in China. Review of the literature. Thorac Cardiovasc Surg 38 (suppl. 2): 205–207

10. Becker A E 1973 Cardiac myxoma. Eur J Cardiol 1: 119–122

11. Burke A P, Virmani R 1993 Cardiac myxoma. A clinicopathologic study. Am J Clin Pathol 100: 671–680

12. Lie J T 1989 Petrified cardiac myxoma masquerading as organized atrial mural thrombus. Arch Pathol Lab Med 113: 742–745

13. Ferrans V J, Roberts W C 1973 Structural features of cardiac myxomas. Histology, histochemistry, and electron microscopy. Hum Pathol 4: 111–146

14. Goldman B I, Frydman C, Harpaz N et al. 1987 Glandular cardiac myxomas. Histologic, immunohistochemical, and ultrastructural evidence of epithelial differentiation. Cancer 59: 1767–1775

15. Johansson L 1989 Histogenesis of cardiac myxomas. An immunohistochemical study of 19 cases, including one with glandular structures, and review of the literature. Arch Pathol Lab Med 113: 735–741

16. Orr J W 1942 Endothelioma (pseudomyxoma) of heart. J Pathol Bacteriol 54: 125–128

17. Abenoza P, Sibley R K 1986 Cardiac myxoma with glandlike structures. An immunohistochemical study. Arch Pathol Lab Med 110: 736–739

18. Landon G, Ordoñez N G, Guarda L A 1986 Cardiac myxomas. An immunohistochemical study using endothelial, histiocytic, and smooth muscle cell markers. Arch Pathol Lab Med 110: 116–120

19. Kawano H, Sueyoshi N, Kawai S et al. 1993 The Gamna–Gandy body in cardiac myxoma. Cardiovasc Pathol 2: 93–96

20. Lie J T 1993 Gamna–Gandy body of the heart: petrified cardiac myxoma mimicking atrial thrombus. Cardiovasc Pathol 2: 97–98

21. Loire R, Thermet H 1991 Les récidives des myxomes intracardiaques. A propos de 6 patients sur 85 opérés. Ann Cardiol Angéiol 40: 1–7

22. Gerbode F, Keith W J, Hill J D 1967 Surgical management of tumours of the heart. Surgery 61: 94–101

23. Kabbani S S, Cooley D A 1973 Atrial myxoma. Surgical considerations. J Thorac Cardiovasc Surg 65: 731–737

24. Read R C, White H J, Murphy M L et al. 1974 The malignant potentiality of left atrial myxoma. J Thorac Cardiovasc Surg 68: 857–868

25. McCarthy P M, Piehler J M, Schaff H V et al. 1986 The significance of multiple, recurrent, and "complex" cardiac myxomas. J Thorac Cardiovasc Surg 91: 389–396

26. Hedinger C 1987 Kombination von Herzmyxomen mit primärer nodulärer Dysplasie der Nebennierenrinde, fleckenförmigen hauptpigmentierungen und myxomartigen Tumoren anderer Lokalisation – ein eigenartiger familiärer Symptomenkomplex ("Swiss syndrome"). Schweiz Med Wochenschr 117: 591–594

27. Meyer B J, Weber R, Jenzer H R et al. 1990 Rapid growth and recurrence of atrial myxomas in two patients with Swiss syndrome. Am Heart J 120: 220–222

28. Martin L W, Wasserman A G, Goldstein H et al. 1987 Multiple cardiac myxomas with multiple recurrences: unusual presentation of a "benign" tumour. Ann Thorac Surg 44: 77–78

29. Kotani K, Matsuzawa Y, Funahashi T et al. 1991 Left atrial myxoma metastasizing to the aorta, with intraluminal growth causing renovascular hypertension. Cardiology 78: 72–77

30. Oemus K, Rath F W 1990 Subkutane Metastasen eines Vorhofmyxoms? Fallbericht und Literaturübersicht. Zentralbl Allg Pathol 136: 189–197

31. Loire R 1991 Existe-t-il une malignité carcinologique des myxomes cardiaques? Arch Mal Coeur 84: 395–399

32. Kasugai T, Sakurai M, Yutani C et al. 1990 Sequential malignant transformation of cardiac myxoma. Acta Pathol Jpn 40: 687–692

33. Laya M B, Mailliard J A, Bewtra C et al. 1987 Malignant fibrous histiocytoma of the heart. A case report and review of the literature. Cancer 59: 1026–1031

34. Scarpelli M, Montironi R, Ricciuti R et al. 1997 Cardiac myxoma with glandular elements metastatic to the brain 12 years after the removal of the original tumor. Clin Neuropathol 16: 190–194

35. Schweizer-Cagianut M, Froesh E R, Hedinger C 1980 Familial Cushing's syndrome with primary adrenocortical microadenomatosis (primary adrenocortical nodular dysplasia). Acta Endocrinol 94: 529–535

36. Schweizer-Cagianut M, Salomon F, Hedinger C E 1982 Primary adrenocortical nodular dysplasia with Cushing's syndrome and cardiac myxomas. A peculiar familial disease. Virchows Arch [A] 397: 183–192

37. Carney J A, Gordon H, Carpenter P C et al. 1985 The complex of myxomas, spotty pigmentation, and endocrine overactivity. Medicine 64: 270–283

38. Carney J A, Hruska L S, Beauchamp G D et al. 1986 Dominant inheritance of the complex of myxomas, spotty pigmentation, and endocrine overactivity. Mayo Clin Proc 61: 165–172

39. Panossian D H, Marais G E, Marais H J 1995 Familial endocrine myxolentiginosis. Clin Cardiol 18: 675–678

40. Carney J A 1995 Carney complex: the complex of myxomas, spotty pigmentation, endocrine overactivity, and schwannomas. Semin Dermatol 14: 900–908

41. Zamorano J, Vilacosta I, Almeria C et al. 1993 Diagnosis of mitral valve myxoma by transesophageal echocardiography. Eur Heart J 14: 862–863

42. Görlach G, Hagel K J, Mulch J et al. 1986 Myxoma of the aortic valve in a child. J Cardiovasc Surg 27: 679–680

43. Pessotto R, Santini F, Piccin C et al. 1994 Cardiac myxoma of the tricuspid valve: description of a case and review of the literature. J Heart Valve Dis 3: 344–346

44. Cole D J, Hendren W G, Sink J D et al. 1989 Myxoma attached solely to the tricuspid valve. Am J Cardiol 64: 546–547

45. Sharma S C, Kulkarni A, Bhargava V et al. 1991 Myxoma of tricuspid valve. J Thorac Cardiovasc Surg 101: 938–939

46. Kulshrestha P, Rousou J A, Tighe D A 1995 Mitral valve myxoma: a case report and review of the literature. J Heart Valve Dis 4: 196–198

47. Thorel C 1915 Geschwülste des Herzens. Ergeb Allg Pathol Anat 17: 667–687

48. Husten K 1922 Über Tumoren und Pseudotumoren des Endocards. Beitr Pathol Anat 71: 132–169

49. Salyer W R, Page D L, Hutchins G M 1975 The development of cardiac myxomas and papillary endocardial lesions from mural thrombus. Am Heart J 89: 4–17

50. Lie J T 1989 The identity and histogenesis of cardiac myxomas. A controversy put to rest. Arch Pathol Lab Med 113: 724–726

51. Prichard R W 1951 Tumours of the heart: review of the subject and report of one hundred and fifty cases. Arch Pathol 51: 98–128

52. Stein A A, Mauro J, Thibodeau L et al. 1969 The histogenesis of cardiac myxoma: relation to other proliferative diseases of subendothelial vasoformative reserve cells. In: Sommers SC (ed) Pathology annual. Appleton-Century-Crofts, New York, vol 4, p 293–312

53. Feldman P S, Horvath E, Kovacs K 1977 An ultrastructural study of seven cardiac myxomas. Cancer 40: 2216–2232

54. Deshpande A, Venugopal P, Kumar A S et al. 1996 Phenotypic characterization of cellular components of cardiac myxoma: a light microscopy and immunohistochemistry study. Hum Pathol 27: 1056–1059

55. Morales A R, Fine G, Castro A et al. 1981 Cardiac myxoma (endocardioma). An immunocytochemical assessment of histogenesis. Hum Pathol 12: 896–899

56. Berrutti L, Silverman J S 1996 Cardiac myxoma is rich in factor XIIIa positive dendrophages: immunohistochemical study of four cases. Histopathology 28: 529–535

57. Gabbiani G, Ryan G B, Majno G 1971 Presence of modified fibroblasts in granulation tissue and their possible role in wound contraction. Experientia 27: 549–550

58. Krikler D M, Rode J, Davies M J et al. 1992 Atrial myxoma: a tumour in search of its origins. Br Heart J 67: 89–91

59. Richkind K E, Wason D, Vidaillet H J 1994 Cardiac myxoma characterized by clonal telomeric association. Genes Chromos Cancer 9: 68–71

60. Dijkhuizen T, van den Berg E, Molenaar W M et al. 1995 Rearrangements involving 12p12 in two cases of cardiac myxoma. Cancer Genet Cytogenet 82: 161–162

61. Schultrich S 1990 Zur Histogenese der kardialen Myxome an hand eines Myxoms mit drüsenartigen Strukturen. Pathologe 11: 220–223

62. Pucci A, Bartoloni G, Tessitore E et al. 2003 Cytokeratin profile and neuroendocrine cells in the glandular component of cardiac myxoma. Virchows Arch 443: 618–624

63. Mohr H J, Kolmeier K H 1959 Fibro-adenomatöses, schleimbildendes Hamartom in der rechten Herzkamer. Zentralbl Allg Pathol 100: 142–149

64. Vacek R 1963 Das intrakardiale Hamartoblastom. Zentralbl Allg Pathol 104: 383–391

65. Suvarna S K, Royd J A 1996 The nature of the cardiac myxoma. Int J Cardiol 57: 211–216

66. Fenoglio J J Jr, McAllister H A Jr, Ferrans V J 1976 Cardiac rhabdomyoma: a clinicopathologic and electron microscopic study. Am J Cardiol 38: 241–251

67. Geva T, Santini F, Pear W et al. 1991 Cardiac rhabdomyoma. Rare cause of fetal death. Chest 99: 139–143

68. Bohm N, Krebs G 1980 Solitary rhabdomyoma of the heart: clinically silent case with sudden, unexpected death in an 11-month-old boy. Eur J Pediatr 144: 167–173

69. Grellner W, Henssge C 1996 Multiple cardiac rhabdomyoma with exclusively histological manifestation. Forensic Sci Int 78: 1–5

70. Bosi G, Lintermans J P, Pellegrino P A et al. 1996 The natural history of cardiac rhabdomyoma with and without tuberous sclerosis. Acta Pediatr 85: 928–931

71. Pillai R, Kharma N, Brom A G et al. 1991 Mitral valve origin of pedunculated rhabdomyomas causing subaortic stenosis. Am J Cardiol 67: 663–664

72. Schmincke A 1922 Kongenitale Herzhypertrophie, bedingt durch diffuse Rhabdomyobildung. Beitr Pathol Anat 70: 513–515

73. Shrivastava S, Jacks J J, White R S et al. 1977 Diffuse rhabdomyomatosis of the heart. Arch Pathol Lab Med 101: 78–80

74. Fine G 1974 Primary tumors of the pericardium and heart. In: Edwards J E, Lev M, Abell M R (eds) The heart. Williams & Wilkins, Baltimore, p 189–210

75. Burke A P, Virmani R 1991 Cardiac rhabdomyomas: a clinicopathologic study. Mod Pathol 4: 70–74

76. Steinbiss W 1923 Zur Kenntnis der Rhabdomyome des Herzens und ihrer Beziehungen zur tuberösen Gehirnsklerose. Virchows Archiv [A] 243: 22–38

77. Smith H C, Waston G H, Patel R G et al. 1989 Cardiac rhabdomyomata in tuberous sclerosis: their course and diagnostic value. Arch Dis Child 64: 196–200

78. Davies M J 1975 Tumours of the heart and pericardium. In: Pomerance A, Davies M J (eds) The pathology of the heart. Blackwell, Oxford, p 423–440

79. Wallace G, Smith H C, Watson G H et al. 1990 Tuberous sclerosis presenting with fetal and neonatal cardiac tumours. Arch Dis Child 65: 377–379

80. Matsuoka Y, Nakati T, Kawaguchi K et al. 1990 Disappearance of a cardiac rhabdomyoma complicating congenital mitral regurgitation as observed by serial two-dimensional echocardiography. Pediatr Cardiol 11: 98–101

81. Farooki Z Q, Ross R D, Paridon S M et al. 1991 Spontaneous regression of cardiac rhabdomyoma. Am J Cardiol 67: 897–899

82. Nir A, Tajik A J, Freeman W K et al. 1995 Tuberous sclerosis and cardiac rhabdomyoma. Am J Cardiol 76: 419–421

83. DiMario F J Jr, Diana D, Leopold H et al. 1996 Evolution of cardiac rhabdomyoma in tuberous sclerosis complex. Clin Pediatr 35: 615–619

84. Fenoglio J J Jr, Diana D J, Bowen T E et al. 1977 Ultrastructure of cardiac rhabdomyoma. Hum Pathol 8: 700–706

85. Bruni C, Prioleau P G, Ivey H H et al. 1980 New fine structural features of cardiac rhabdomyoma. Report of a case. Cancer 46: 2068–2073

86. Green A J, Johnson P H, Yates J R 1994 The tuberous sclerosis gene on chromosome 9q34 acts as a growth suppressor. Hum Mol Genet 3: 1833–1834

87. Green A J, Smith M, Yates J R 1994 Loss of heterozygosity on chromosome 16p13.3 in hamartomas from tuberous sclerosis patients. Nat Genet 6: 193–196

88. Burke A P, Ribe J K, Bajaj A K et al. 1998 Hamartoma of mature cardiac myocytes. Hum Pathol 29: 904–909

89. Burke A P, Rosado-de-Christenson M, Templeton P A et al. 1994 Cardiac fibroma: clinicopathologic correlates and surgical treatment. J Thorac Cardiovasc Surg 108: 862–870

90. Sakata K, Ohtaki A, Aiba M et al. 1997 Left ventricular fibroma in an aged patient: report of a case. Surg Today 27: 88–89

91. Tahernia A C, Bricker J T, Ott D A 1990 Intracardiac fibroma in an asymptomatic infant. Clin Cardiol 13: 506–512

92. Van der Hauwaert L G, Corbeel L, Maldague P 1965 Fibroma of the right ventricle producing severe tricuspid stenosis. Circulation 32: 451–456

93. Feldman P S, Meyer M W 1976 Fibroelastic hamartoma (fibroma) of the heart. Cancer 38: 314–323

94. Turi G K, Albala A, Fenoglio J J Jr 1980 Cardiac fibromatosis: an ultrastructural study. Hum Pathol 11: 577–579

95. Churg A M, Kahn L B 1977 Myofibroblasts and related cells in malignant fibrous and fibrohistiocytic tumours. Hum Pathol 8: 205–218

96. Bertolini P, Meisner J, Paek S U et al. 1990 Special considerations on primary cardiac tumours in infancy and childhood. Thorac Cardiovasc Surg 38: 164–167

97. Cotton J L, Kavey R E W, Palmier C E et al. 1991 Cardiac tumours and the nevoid basal cell carcinoma syndrome. Pediatrics 87: 725–727

98. Littler B O 1979 Gorlin's syndrome and the heart. Br J Oral Surg 17: 135–146

99. Harris S A, Large D M 1984 Gorlin's syndrome with a cardiac lesion and jaw cysts with some unusual histologic features: a case report and review of the literature. Int J Oral Surg 13: 59–64

100. Jones K L, Wolf P L, Jensen P et al. 1986 The Gorlin syndrome: a genetically determined disorder associated with cardiac tumour. Am Heart J 111: 1013–1015

101. Coffin C M 1992 Case I congenital cardiac fibroma associated with Gorlin syndrome. Pediatr Pathol 12: 255–262

102. Gorlin R J 1987 Nevoid basal-cell carcinoma syndrome. Medicine 66: 98–113

103. Reiner L, Mazzoleni A, Rodriguez F L 1955 Statistical analysis of epicardial fat weight in human hearts. Arch Pathol 60: 369–373

104. Enzinger F M, Weiss S W 1988 Soft tissue tumours, 2nd edn. Mosby, St Louis, p 301–345

105. Harjola P T, Ala-Kulju K, Ketonen P 1985 Epicardial lipoma. Scand J Thorac Cardiovasc 19: 181–183

106. Rokey R, Mulvagh S L, Cheirif J et al. 1989 Lipomatous encasement and compression of the heart: antemortem diagnosis by cardiac nuclear magnetic resonance imaging and catheterization. Am Heart J 117: 952–953

107. Verkkala K, Kupari M, Maamies T et al. 1989 Primary cardiac tumors – operative treatment of 20 patients. Thorac Cardiovasc Surg 37: 361–364

108. Reece I J, Cooley D A, Frazier O H et al. 1984 Cardiac tumors. J Thorac Cardiovasc Surg 66: 439–446

109. Li J, Ho S Y, Becker A E, Jones H 1998 Multiple cardiac lipomas and sudden death: a case report and literature review. Cardiovasc Pathol 7: 51–55

110. Estevez J M, Thompson D S, Levinson J P 1964 Lipoma of the heart. Arch Pathol 77: 638–642

111. Harada K, Seki I, Kobayashi H et al. 1980 Lipoma of the heart in a child. Clinical, echocardiographic, angiographic, and pathological features. Jpn Heart J 21: 903–910

112. Pansard Y, Hvass U, de Brux J L et al. 1985 Lipome du ventricule droit. Ann Chir 39: 403–407

113. Pilichowski P, Wolf J E, Delgove L et al. 1987 Lipome du ventricule gauche. Ann Chir 41: 85–88

114. Bellin M, Lermuziaux J N, Fabiani J N et al. 1987 Lipome du coeur. Ann Chir 41: 405–410

115. Anderson D R, Gray M R 1988 Mitral incompetence associated with lipoma infiltrating the mitral valve. Br Heart J 60: 169–171

116. Reynen K, Rein J, Wittekind C et al. 1993 Surgical removal of a lipoma of the heart. Int J Cardiol 40: 67–68

117. Wajon E M C J, Jaarsma W, Knaepen P J et al. 1992 Lipoma of the heart. Neth J Cardiol 2: 63–67

118. Murphy E S, Fujii Y, Yasuda A et al. 1958 The tuberous sclerosis complex: a study of a new case. Arch Pathol 65: 166–173

119. Lie J T 1991 Cardiac, pulmonary, and vascular involvements in tuberous sclerosis. Ann NY Acad Sci 615: 58–70

120. Prior J T 1964 Lipomatous hypertrophy of the cardiac interatrial septum. A lesion resembling hibernoma, lipoblastomatosis and infiltrating lipoma. Arch Pathol 78: 11–15

121. Page D L 1970 Lipomatous hypertrophy of the cardiac interatrial septum. Its development and probable clinical significance. Hum Pathol 1: 151–163

122. Burke A P, Litovsky S, Virmani R 1996 Lipomatous hypertrophy of the atrial septum presenting as a right atrial mass. Am J Surg Pathol 20: 678–685

123. Inoue T, Mohri N, Nagahara T et al. 1988 A case report of "lipomatous hypertrophy of the cardiac interatrial septum," with a proposal for a new term "lipomatous hamartoma of the cardiac atrial septum." Acta Pathol Jpn 38: 1588–1589

124. Bhattacharjee M, Neligan M C, Dervan P 1991 Lipomatous hypertrophy of the interatrial septum: an unusual intraoperative finding. Br Heart J 65: 49–50

125. Crotty T B, Edwards W D, Oh J K et al. 1991 Lipomatous hamartoma of the tricuspid valve: echocardiographic–pathologic correlations. Clin Cardiol 14: 262–266

126. Behman R, Williams G, Gerlis L et al. 1983 Lipoma of the mitral valve and papillary muscle. Am J Cardiol 51: 1459–1460

127. Kindblom L G, Svensson U 1977 Multiple hibernomas of the heart. A case report. Acta Pathol Microbiol Scand 85: 122–126

128. Heifetz S A, Parikh S R, Brown J W 1990 Hibernoma of the pericardium presenting as pericardial effusion in a child. Pediatr Pathol 10: 575–580

129. Kurup A N, Tazalaar H D, Edwards W D et al. 2002 Iatrogenic cardiac papillary fibroelastoma: a study of 12 cases (1990–2000). Hum Pathol 33: 1165–1169

130. Arciniegas E, Hakimi M, Farooki Z Q et al. 1980 Primary cardiac tumours in children. J Thorac Cardiovasc Surg 79: 582–591

131. Heggtveit H A, Fenoglio J J, McAllister H A 1976 Lipomatous hypertrophy of the interatrial septum. An assessment of 41 cases. Lab Invest 34: 318 (abstract)

132. Corbi P, Jebara V, Fabiani J N et al. 1990 Les tumeurs bénignes du coeur (à l'exception des myxomes). Expérience de neuf cas opérés. Ann Cardiol Angéiol 39: 433–436

133. Cooley D A 1990 Surgical treatment of cardiac neoplasms: 32 year experience. Thorac Cardiovasc Surg 38: 176–182

134. Klarich K W, Enriquez-Sarano M, Gura G M et al. 1997 Papillary fibroelastoma: echocardiographic characteristics for diagnosis and pathologic correlation. J Am Coll Cardiol 30: 784–790

135. Sun J P, Asher C R, Yang X S et al. 2001 Clinical and echocardiographic characteristics of papillary fibroelastomas: a retrospective and prospective study in 162 patients. Circulation 203: 2687–2693

136. McFadden P M, Lacy J R 1987 Intracardiac papillary fibroelastoma: an occult cause of embolic neurologic deficit. Ann Thorac Surg 43: 667–669

137. Gowda R M, Khan J A, Nair C K et al. 2003 Cardiac papillary fibroelastoma: a comprehensive analysis of 725 cases. Am Heart J 146: 404–410

138. Valente M, Basso C, Thiene G et al. 1992 Fibroelastic papilloma: a not-so-benign cardiac tumour. Cardiovasc Pathol 1: 161–166

139. Wolfe J T III, Finck S J, Safford R E et al. 1991 Tricuspid valve papillary fibroelastoma: echocardiographic characterization. Ann Thorac Surg 51: 116–118

140. Etienne Y, Jobic Y, Houel J F et al. 1994 Papillary fibroelastoma of the aortic valve with myocardial infarction: echocardiographic diagnosis and surgical excision. Am Heart J 127: 443–445

141. Grote J, Mugge A, Schafers H J et al. 1995 Multiplane transoesophageal detection of a papillary fibroelastoma of the aortic valve causing myocardial infarction. Eur Heart J 16: 426–429

142. Eckstein F S, Schafers H J, Grote J et al. 1995 Papillary fibroelastoma of the aortic valve presenting with myocardial infarction. Ann Thorac Surg 60: 206–208

143. Pasteuning W H, Zijnen P, van der Aa M A et al. 1996 Papillary fibroelastoma of the aortic valve in a patient with an acute myocardial infarction. J Am Soc Echocardiogr 9: 897–900

144. Deodhar A P, Tometzki A J, Hudson I N et al. Aortic valve tumor causing acute myocardial infarction in a child. Ann Thorac Surg 64: 1482–1484

145. Chang Y-S, Chu P-H, Jung S-M et al. 2005 Unusual cardiac papillary fibroelastoma in the right ventricular outflow tract. Cardiovasc Pathol 14: 104–106

146. de Menezes I C, Fragata J, Martins F M 1996 Papillary fibroelastoma of the mitral valve in a 3-year-old child: case report. Pediatr Cardiol 17: 194–195

147. Heath D, Thompson I M 1965 Papillary "tumours" of the left ventricle. Br Heart J 29: 950–954

148. Fishbein M C, Ferrans V J, Roberts W C 1975 Endocardial papillary elastofibromas. Histologic, histochemical, and electron microscopical findings. Arch Pathol Lab Med 99: 335–341

149. Pomerance A 1961 Papillary "tumours" of the heart valves. J Pathol Bacteriol 81: 135–140

150. Rubin M A, Snell J A, Tazelaar H D et al. 1995 Cardiac papillary fibroelastoma: an immunohistochemical investigation and unusual clinical manifestations. Mod Pathol 8: 402–407

151. Butterworth J S, Poindexter C A 1973 Papilloma of cusp of the aortic valve: report of a patient with sudden death. Circulation 48: 213–215

152. Topol E J, Biern R O, Reitz B A 1986 Cardiac papillary fibroelastoma and stroke. Echocardiographic diagnosis and guide to excision. Am J Med 80: 129–132

153. Kasarskis E J, O'Connor W, Earle G 1988 Embolic stroke from cardiac papillary fibroelastomas. Stroke 19: 1171–1173

154. Witzleben C L, Pinto M 1978 Foamy myocardial transformation in infancy. Arch Pathol Lab Med 102: 306–311

155. MacMahon E H 1971 Infantile xanthomatous cardiomyopathy. Pediatrics 48: 312–315

156. Ferrans V J, McAllister H A Jr, Haese W H 1976 Infantile cardiomyopathy with histiocytoid change in cardiac muscle cells: report of six patients. Circulation 53: 708–719

157. Amini M, Bosman C, Marino B 1980 Histiocytoid cardiomyopathy in infancy: a new hypothesis. Chest 77: 556–558

158. Becker A E, Anderson R H 1981 Pathology of congenital heart disease. Butterworths, London, p 407–412

159. Silver M M, Burns J E, Sethi R K et al. 1980 Oncocytic cardiomyopathy in an infant with oncocytosis in exocrine and endocrine glands. Hum Pathol 11: 598–605

160. James T N, Beeson C W II, Sherman E B et al. 1975 De subitaneis mortibus. XIII. Multifocal Purkinje cell tumors of the heart. Circulation 52: 333–344

161. Garson A Jr, Smith R T Jr, Moak J P et al. 1987 Incessant ventricular tachycardia in infants: myocardial hamartomas and surgical cure. J Am Coll Cardiol 10: 619–626

162. Kearney D L, Titus J L, Hawkins E P et al. 1987 Pathologic features of myocardial hamartomas causing childhood tachyarrhythmias. Circulation 75: 705–710

163. Farooki Z Q, Chang C H, Jackson W L et al. 1988 Intracardiac teratoma in a newborn. Clin Cardiol 11: 642–644

164. Stoupel E, Primo G, Kahn R J 1979 Cardiac tamponade with renal failure due to haemangioma of the heart. Acta Cardiol 34: 345–351

165. Chao J C, Reyes C V, Hwang M H 1990 Cardiac hemangioma. South Med J 83: 44–47

166. Weir I, Mills P, Lewis T 1987 A case of left atrial haemangioma: echocardiographic, surgical, and morphological features. Br Heart J 58: 665–668

167. Case records of the Massachusetts General Hospital. Weekly clinicopathological exercises 1983. Case 4 – 1983. A 15-year-old girl with a right ventricular mass. N Engl J Med 308: 206–214

168. Chang J S, Young M L, Chuu W M et al. 1992 Infantile cardiac hemangioendothelioma. Pediatr Cardiol 13: 52–55

169. de Nictolis M, Brancorsini D, Goteri G et al. 1996 Epithelioid haemangioma of the heart. Virchows Arch 428: 119–123

170. Rosai J, Gold J, Landy R 1979 The histiocytoid hemangiomas: a unifying concept embracing several previously described entities of skin, soft tissue, large vessels, bone and heart. Hum Pathol 10: 707–730

171. Fletcher C D M, Beham A, Bekir S et al. 1991 Epithelioid angiosarcoma of deep soft tissue: a distinctive tumor readily mistaken for an epithelial neoplasm. Am J Surg Pathol 15: 915–924

172. Weiss S W, Ishak K G, Dail D H 1986 Epithelioid hemangioendothelioma and related lesions. Semin Diagn Pathol 3: 259–287

173. Mentzel T, Beham A, Calonje E et al. 1997 Epithelioid hemangioendothelioma of skin and soft tissues: clinicopathologic and immunohistochemical study of 30 cases. Am J Surg Pathol 21: 363–374

174. Weiss S W, Enzinger F M 1982 Epithelioid hemangioendothelioma: a vascular tumor often mistaken for a carcinoma. Cancer 50: 970–981

175. Kuo T, Hsueh S, Su I et al. 1985 Histiocytoid hemangioma of the heart with peripheral eosinophilia. Cancer 55: 2854–2861

176. Luthringer D J, Virmani R, Weiss S W et al. 1990 A distinctive cardiovascular lesion resembling histiocytoid (epithelioid) hemangioma. Evidence suggesting mesothelial participation. Am J Surg Pathol 14: 993–1000

177. Palmer T E, Tresch D D, Bonchek L I 1986 Spontaneous resolution of a large, cavernous hemangioma of the heart. Am J Cardiol 58: 184–185

178. Tabry I F, Nassar V H, Rizk G et al. 1975 Cavernous haemangioma of the heart: case report and review of the literature. J Thorac Cardiovasc Surg 69: 415–420

179. Veinot J P, Tazelaar H D, Edwards W D, Colby T V 1994 Mesothelial/monocytic incidental cardiac excrescences: cardiac MICE. Mod Pathol 7: 9–16

180. Armstrong H, Mönckeberg J G 1911 Herzblock, bedingt durch primären Herztumor bei einem 5-jährigen Kinde. Dtsch Arch Klin Med 102: 144–166

181. Mahaim I 1942 Le coelethéliome tawarien bénin. Une tumeur sui generis du noeud de Tawara, avec bloc du coeur. Cardiologia 6: 57–82

182. Rezek P 1938 Über eine primäre epitheliale Geschwülst in der Gegend des Reizleitungssystems beim Menschen (Zugleich ein Beitrag zur Histiogenese seltener Herzgeschwülste). Virchows Arch [A] 301: 305–320

183. Linder J, Shelburne J D, Sorge J P et al. 1984 Congenital endodermal heterotopia of the atrioventricular node: evidence for the endodermal origin of so-called mesotheliomas of the atrioventricular node. Hum Pathol 15: 1093–1098

184. Burke A P, Anderson P G, Virmani R et al. 1990 Tumors of the atrioventricular nodal region. A clinical and immunohistochemical study. Arch Pathol Lab Med 114: 1057–1062

185. Sopher I M, Spitz W E 1971 Endodermal inclusion of the heart. So-called mesotheliomas of the atrioventricular node. Arch Pathol 92: 180–186

186. Travers H 1982 Congenital polycystic tumour of the atrioventricular node: possible familial occurrence and critical review of reported cases with special emphasis on histogenesis. Hum Pathol 13: 25–35

187. Cameselle-Teijeiro J, Abdulkader I, Soares P et al. 2005 Cystic tumor of the atrioventricular node of the heart appears to be the heart equivalent of the solid cell nests (ultimobranchial rests) of the thyroid. Am J Clin Pathol 123: 369–375

188. Wolf P L, Bing R 1965 The smallest tumor which causes sudden death. JAMA 194: 674–675

189. James T N, Galakhov I 1977 De subitaneis mortibus XXVI. Fatal electrical instability of the heart associated with benign congenital polycystic tumour of the atrioventricular node. Circulation 56: 667–678

190. Bharati S, Bauernfeind R, Josephson M 1995 Intermittent preexcitation and mesothelioma of the atrioventricular node: a hitherto undescribed entity. J Cardiovasc Electrophysiol 6: 823–831

191. Becker A E 1966 The glomera in the region of the heart and great vessels. A microscopic-anatomical and histochemical study. Pathol Eur 1: 410–424

192. Lack E E 1997 Tumors of the adrenal gland and extra-adrenal paraganglia. Atlas of tumor pathology, series 3, fascicle 19. Armed Forces Institute of Pathology, Washington DC

193. Besterman E, Bromley L L, Peart W S 1974 An intrapericardial phaeochromocytoma. Br Heart J 36: 318–320

194. Johnson T L, Shapiro B, Beierwaltes W H et al. 1985 Cardiac paragangliomas. A clinicopathologic and immunohistochemical study of four cases. Am J Surg Pathol 9: 827–834

195. Hui G, McAllister H A, Angelini P 1987 Left atrial paraganglioma: report of a case and review of the literature. Am Heart J 114: 1230–1234

196. Stowers S A, Gilmore P, Stirling M et al. 1987 Cardiac pheochromocytoma involving the left main coronary artery presenting with exertional angina. Am Heart J 114: 423–427

197. Shimoyama Y, Kawada K, Imamura H 1987 A functioning intrapericardial paraganglioma (pheochromocytoma). Br Heart J 57: 380–383

198. Chang C H, Lin P J, Chang J P et al. 1991 Intrapericardial pheochromocytoma. Ann Thorac Surg 51: 661–663

199. Aravot D J, Banner N R, Cantor A M et al. 1992 Location, localization and surgical treatment of cardiac pheochromocytoma. Am J Cardiol 69: 283–285

200. Gaylis H, Mieny C J 1977 The incidence of malignancy in carotid body tumours. Br J Surg 64: 885–889

201. Rosenquist G C, Krovetz L J, Haller J A Jr et al. 1970 Acquired right ventricular outflow obstruction in a child with neurofibromatosis. Am Heart J 79: 103–108

202. Lanks K W, Lautsch E V 1966 Pathogenesis of intramyocardial epithelial inclusion cysts. Arch Pathol 81: 365–367

203. Rose A G, Novitzky D, Price S K 1988 Heterotopic thyroid tissue in the heart. Am J Cardiovasc Pathol 1: 401–404

204. Natarajan S, Luthringer DJ, Fishbein MC 1997 Adenomatoid tumor of the heart: report of a case. Am J Surg Pathol 21: 1378–1380

205. Burke A P, Cowan D, Virmani R 1992 Primary sarcomas of the heart. Cancer 69: 387–395

206. Putnam J B Jr, Sweeney M S, Colon R et al. 1991 Primary cardiac sarcomas. Ann Thorac Surg 51: 906–910

207. Tazelaar H A, Locke T J, McGregor CGA 1992 Pathology of surgically excised primary cardiac tumors. Mayo Clin Proc 67: 957–965

208. Fletcher C D M 1992 Pleomorphic malignant fibrous histiocytoma: fact or fiction? A critical reappraisal based upon 159 tumors diagnosed as pleomorphic sarcoma. Am J Surg Pathol 16: 213–228

209. McAllister H A 1979 Primary tumours of the heart and pericardium. Pathol Ann 14: 325–355

210. Chitwood W R Jr 1988 Cardiac neoplasms: current diagnosis, pathology, and therapy. J Cardiac Surg 3: 119–154

211. Randall M B, Geisinger K R 1990 Angiosarcoma of the heart: pericardial fluid cytology. Diagn Cytopathol 6: 58–62

212. Löffler H, Grille W 1990 Classification of malignant cardiac tumours with respect to oncological treatment. Thorac Cardiovasc Surg 38 (suppl. 2): 196–199

213. Makhoul N, Bode F R 1995 Angiosarcoma of the heart: review of the literature and report of two cases that illustrate the broad spectrum of the disease. Can J Cardiol 11: 423–428

214. Sorlie D, Myhre E S, Stalsberg H 1984 Angiosarcoma of the heart. Unusual presentation and survival after treatment. Br Heart J 51: 94–97

215. Percy R F, Perryman R A, Amornmarn R et al. 1987 Prolonged survival in a patient with primary angiosarcoma of the heart. Am Heart J 113: 1228–1230

216. Hager W, Kremer K, Müller W 1970 Angiosarkom des Herzens. Dtsch Med Wochenschr 95: 680

217. Poletti A, Cocco P, Valente M et al. 1993 In vivo diagnosis of cardiac angiosarcoma by endomyocardial biopsy. Cardiovasc Pathol 2: 89–91

218. Shah A A, Churg A, Sbarbaro J A et al. 1978 Malignant fibrous histiocytoma of the heart presenting as an atrial myxoma. Cancer 42: 2466–2471

219. Weiss S W, Enzinger F M 1977 Myxoid variant of malignant fibrous histiocytoma. Cancer 39: 1672–1685

220. Ouzan J, Joundi A, Chapoutot L et al. 1990 Histiocytofibrome malin du coeur simulant un myxome de l'oreillette gauche. Arch Mal Coeur 83: 1011–1014

221. Pasquale M, Katz N M, Caruso A C et al. 1991 Myxoid variant of malignant fibrous histiocytoma of the heart. Am Heart J 122: 248–250

222. Korbmacher B, Doering C, Schulte H D et al. 1992 Malignant fibrous histiocytoma of the heart – case report of a rare left-atrial tumour. Thorac Cardiovasc Surg 40: 303–307

223. Wahba A, Liebold A, Birnbaum D E 1993 Recurrent malignant fibrous histiocytoma of the left atrium in a 27-year-old male. Eur J Cardiothorac Surg 7: 387–389

224. Hui K S, Green L K, Schmidt W A 1988 Primary cardiac rhabdomyosarcoma: definition of a rare entity. Am J Cardiovasc Pathol 2: 19–29

225. Hajar R, Roberts W C, Folger G M Jr 1986 Embryonal botryoid rhabdomyosarcoma of the mitral valve. Am J Cardiol 57: 376

226. Small E, Gordon G J, Barrett Dahms B 1985 Malignant rhaboid tumor of the heart in an infant. Cancer 55: 2850–2853

227. Haas J E, Palmer N F, Weinberg A G et al. 1981 Ultrastructure of malignant rhabdoid tumor of the kidney: a distinctive renal tumor in children. Hum Pathol 12: 646–657

228. Donsbeck A-V, Ranchere D, Coindre J M et al. 1999 Primary cardiac sarcomas: an immunohistochemical and grading study with long-term follow-up of 24 cases. Histopathology 34: 295–304

229. Itoh K, Matsumura T, Egawa Y et al. 1998 Primary mitral valve sarcoma in infancy. Pediatr Cardiol 19: 174–177

230. Becker A E, van der Wal A C 1998 Leiomyosarcoma on an infant's mitral valve. Pediatr Cardiol 19: 193

231. Pins M R, Ferrell M A, Madsen J C et al. 1999 Epithelioid and spindle cell leiomyosarcoma of the heart. Report of two cases and review of the literature. Arch Pathol Lab Med 123: 782–788

232. Antunes M J, Vanderdonck K M, Andrade C M et al. 1991 Primary cardiac leiomyosarcomas. Ann Thorac Surg 51: 999–1001

233. Fyfe A I, Huckell V F, Burr L H et al. 1991 Leiomyosarcoma of the left atrium: case report and review of the literature. Can J Cardiol 7: 193–196

234. Paraf F, Bruneval P, Balaton A et al. 1990 Primary liposarcoma of the heart. Am J Cardiovasc Pathol 3: 175–180

235. Burke A P, Virmani R 1991 Osteosarcomas of the heart. Am J Surg Pathol 51: 289–295

236. Muir C S, Seah C S 1966 Primary chondrosarcomatous mesenchymoma of the mitral valve. Thorax 21: 254–262

237. Tsai F C, Lin P J, Wu W J 1996 Primary chondrosarcoma of the heart: a case report. Chang Keng I Hsueh 19: 348–351

238. Miwa S, Konishi Y, Matsumoto M et al. 1997 Primary cardiac chondrosarcoma – a case report. Jpn Circ J 61: 795–797

239. Nicholson A G, Rigby M, Lincoln C et al. 1997 Synovial sarcoma of the heart. Histopathology 30: 349–352

240. Sheffield E A, Corrin B, Addis B J et al. 1988 Synovial sarcoma of the heart arising from a so-called mesothelioma of the atrioventricular node. Histopathology 12: 191–202

241. Guschmann M, Weng Y 1996 Primare multiple maligne Schwannome im Herzen – eine Raritat. Pathologe 17: 222–226

242. Chun P K C, Leeburg W T, Coggin J T et al. 1980 Primary pericardial epithelial mesothelioma causing acute myocardial infarction. Chest 77: 559–561

243. Sytman A L, MacAlpin R B 1971 Primary pericardial mesothelioma: report of 2 cases and review of the literature. Am Heart J 81: 760–769

244. Klima M, Spjut H J, Seybold W D 1976 Diffuse malignant mesothelioma. Am J Clin Pathol 65: 583–600

245. McDonnell P J, Mann R B, Bulkley B H 1982 Involvement of the heart by malignant lymphoma. A clinicopathologic study. Cancer 49: 944–951

246. Curtsinger C R, Wilson M J, Yoneda K 1989 Primary cardiac lymphoma. Cancer 64: 521–525

247. Zaharia L, Gill S 1991 Primary cardiac lymphoma. Am J Clin Oncol 14: 142–145

248. Chalabreysse L, Berger F, Leire R et al. 2002 Primary cardiac lymphoma in immunocompetent patients: a report of three cases and review of the literature. Virchows Arch 441: 456–461

249. Ceresoli G L, Ferreri A J, Bucci E et al. 1997 Primary cardiac lymphoma in immunocompetent patients: diagnostic and therapeutic management. Cancer 80: 1497–1506

Vascular tumors 3

Eduardo Calonje   Christopher D. M. Fletcher

Introduction

There are few groups of tumors which can show such a broad spectrum of morphologic appearances and clinical behavior as vascular tumors. Classification is a problem, not only because the line between neoplasia and malformation (or so-called "hamartoma") remains undefined but also, and more importantly, because it is frequently difficult to distinguish benign from malignant lesions. It is interesting that, in comparison to other soft tissue tumors (see Ch. 24), cytogenetic and molecular genetic analysis has provided very little useful information in vascular lesions, principally because these tumors are very hard to grow or maintain in culture and also because available material is often inextricably admixed with non-neoplastic tissue components. In this chapter, an updated classification of vascular tumors is used, including recently described entities and reclassifying some better-known entities in the light of recent developments in the understanding of their biology (Table 3.1). Emphasis is placed upon lesions presenting in soft tissue and skin as vascular tumors are more common in these locations. Distinctive vascular tumors in other organs are dealt with in the appropriate chapters.

Benign tumors

Reactive vascular proliferations

Intravascular papillary endothelial hyperplasia (Masson's tumor)

Clinical features

Intravascular papillary endothelial hyperplasia[1-5] is a relatively common reactive condition representing an unusual form of organizing thrombus. It presents in three different settings: (1) as a pure form involving an isolated dilated blood vessel (primary); (2) as a focal change in a variety of pre-existing vascular lesions including hemangiomas, hemorrhoidal veins, and varices (secondary); and, rarely, (3) in an extravascular location in association with a hematoma.[5] Trauma does not appear to be related consistently to any of these forms. In the primary type the lesion typically presents as an asymptomatic bluish nodule in the finger or head and neck region of young adults; there is no sex predilection. Presentation in the breast has also been described and in this setting, distinction from

Table 3.1	Classification of vascular tumors

Blood vessels

Benign tumors and tumor-like conditions

Reactive vascular proliferations
    Papillary endothelial hyperplasia (Masson's tumor)
    Reactive angioendotheliomatosis
    Glomeruloid hemangioma
    Bacillary angiomatosis

Vascular ectasias
    Nevus flammeus (salmon patch, port-wine stain)
    Nevus araneus
    Venous lake
    Angioma serpiginosum
    Hereditary hemorrhagic telangiectasia (Osler–Weber–Rendu)
    Angiokeratoma

Capillary hemangioma
    Variants: Tufted angioma
                Verrucous hemangioma
                Cherry angioma
                Lobular hemangioma (pyogenic granuloma)
Cavernous hemangioma
    Variant: Sinusoidal hemangioma
Arteriovenous hemangioma
    Variants: Superficial (cirsoid aneurysm)
                Deep
Microvenular hemangioma
Hobnail ("targetoid hemosiderotic") hemangioma
Acquired elastotic hemangioma
Cutaneous epithelioid angiomatous nodule
Epithelioid hemangioma (angiolymphoid hyperplasia with eosinophilia)
Venous hemangioma
Spindle cell hemangioma ("hemangioendothelioma")
Deep hemangiomas
    Variants: Intramuscular
                Synovial
                Neural
                Nodal
Angiomatosis

Intermediate vascular tumors

Locally aggressive
    Kaposi-like hemangioendothelioma
    Giant cell angioblastoma
Rarely metastasizing
    Retiform hemangioendothelioma
    Malignant endovascular papillary angioendothelioma (Dabska tumor)
    Composite hemangioendothelioma
    Polymorphous hemangioendothelioma
    Kaposi sarcoma

Malignant vascular tumors

Epithelioid hemangioendothelioma
Angiosarcoma
    Variants: Idiopathic (head and neck)
                Associated with lymphedema ("lymphangiosarcoma")
                Postirradiation
                Soft tissue
                Epithelioid
"Intimal" sarcomas

Lymph vessels

Lymphangioma
    Variants: Lymphangioma circumscriptum
                Cavernous lymphangioma/cystic hygroma
                Benign lymphangioendothelioma (acquired progressive lymphangioma)
Lymphangiomatosis
Lymphangiomyoma
Lymphangiomyomatosis

Tumors of perivascular cells

Glomus tumor
Glomangiomatosis
    Variant: Infiltrating glomus tumor
Glomangiosarcoma
"Hemangiopericytoma", so called
Myopericytoma

---

angiosarcoma may be difficult.[6] Lesions are generally less than 2 cm in diameter and, following excision, recurrence is rare. Multiple lesions are uncommon and have been exceptionally described in association following treatment with interferon-beta.[7,8] When papillary endothelial hyperplasia arises in a pre-existing vascular lesion, clinical findings are related to the primary vascular abnormality and lesions tend to be larger. These secondary lesions theoretically can present in any vascular tumor and in any anatomic site, but are particularly common in association with deep-seated hemangiomas, especially of the cavernous type.

Histologic appearances

Primary forms appear as well-circumscribed hemorrhagic lesions, which on closer examination reveal a pre-existing dilated vascular space, most commonly a thin-walled vein. The appearances of secondary cases depend on the nature of the pre-existing primary lesion. In extravascular lesions no obvious vascular structure is identified even after serial sectioning. All forms are typified by the presence of multiple small papillary structures, covered by a single layer of attenuated endothelial cells showing little or no atypia (Fig. 3.1). Mitoses are usually absent. The papillary core is composed of hypocellular, hyaline collagen with occasional small capillaries. In the earliest lesions, papillae appear to be composed of fibrin. Although most papillae seem to be lying free in the vascular lumina, some of them appear to be attached to the vascular wall. Numerous red blood cells surround the papillae and usually there is associated thrombus, which may be organized to a variable degree; at the edge of the thrombus one may identify the early stages of the formation of fibrinoid papillae.

Differential diagnosis

Well-differentiated angiosarcoma occurs in a different clinical setting and is generally an extravascular process characterized by an infiltrative or dissecting growth pattern, moderate to

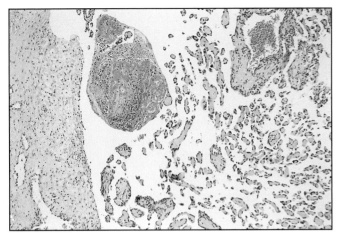

Fig. 3.1 • Masson's tumor. Note the typically hyaline papillae and adjacent thrombus.

prominent cytologic atypia, endothelial multilayering, and mitotic activity.

Reactive angioendotheliomatosis

Clinical features

Until the early 1980s, angioendotheliomatosis was traditionally classified into malignant and benign variants, which were thought, in some cases, to be difficult to separate from each other on clinical and histologic grounds. However, it has become clear that the malignant variant is a systemic angiotropic lymphoma (associated with a poor prognosis; see Ch. 21), not related at all to the reactive variant which is truly endothelial, self-limiting, and generally confined to the skin.[9,10] Clinically, reactive angioendotheliomatosis is a very rare condition that presents as erythematous macules, papules, or plaques, which can be associated with petechiae and ecchymoses and more rarely with a livedo-like pattern. It has no age predilection and most cases occur in adults, children being only exceptionally affected.[11] It can be idiopathic or associated with a wide range of systemic diseases including paraproteinemia, renal disease, amyloidosis, antiphospholipid syndrome, rheumatoid arthritis, cirrhosis, polymyalgia rheumatica, and sarcoidosis.[10,12–16] However, the association with systemic disease, particularly bacterial endocarditis, is not as strong as previously believed. A variant of reactive angioendotheliomatosis has been described as angiomatosis with luminal cryoprotein deposition in patients with cryoglobulinemia.[17] The clinicopathologic spectrum of the disease has recently been expanded to include rare localized forms of the disease, including a variant associated with peripheral vascular atherosclerotic disease and iatrogenic arteriovenous fistulas, described as diffuse dermal angiomatosis.[18–21]

Histologic appearances

In the dermis and superficial subcutis there are multiple clusters of very closely packed capillaries (Fig. 3.2) lined by larger than normal endothelial cells, which show no cytologic atypia and are surrounded by pericytes. Many cases have a rather lobular architecture. These endothelial cells may occlude the vascular lumina but there is no multilayering. Focal extravasation of red blood cells and occasional fibrin

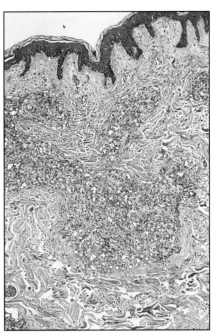

Fig. 3.2 • Reactive angioendotheliomatosis. Note the irregular clusters of closely packed variably canalized capillaries in the dermis.

thrombi are also seen. Adjacent dermis shows mild chronic inflammation, sometimes associated wtih fasciitis-like changes. In angiomatosis with luminal cryoprotein deposition, many capillaries appear occluded by refractile eosinophilic thrombi. In diffuse dermal angiomatosis there is proliferation of poorly canalized capillaries.

Glomeruloid hemangioma

Glomeruloid hemangioma is a distinctive reactive vascular proliferation that occurs in patients with multicentric Castleman's disease and POEMS syndrome (polyneuropathy, organomegaly, endocrinopathy, M-protein, skin changes).[22–25] Clinically, patients present with numerous cutaneous angiomas, which on histologic examination can show features of cherry angioma or, less frequently, those of glomeruloid hemangioma. Histologically, multiple dilated vascular spaces are seen, especially in the superficial dermis, and these contain in their lumina clusters of capillaries with a striking resemblance to renal glomeruli (Fig. 3.3). Around the capillaries there are pericytes and larger cells with clear cytoplasm and occasional periodic acid–Schiff (PAS)-positive hyaline globules, probably representing deposits of immunoglobulin. These large cells are positive for endothelial markers. Human herpesvirus 8 (HHV-8) has not been detected in lesions of glomeruloid hemangioma.[26]

Vascular ectasias

As opposed to true hemangiomas, vascular ectasias[27–29] do not show an increase in the number of blood vessels, but rather they are composed of dilated pre-existing normal blood vessels. However, some vascular ectasias may be associated with an underlying cavernous hemangioma or arteriovenous malformation.[30] Vascular ectasias include nevus flammeus (port-wine stain and salmon patch), spider nevus (nevus araneus), venous lakes, angioma serpiginosum, and angiokeratomas.

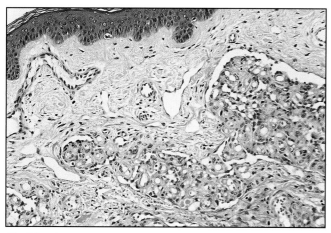

Fig. 3.3 • Glomeruloid hemangioma. Capillary lobules protrude into pre-existing vessels. Note the eosinophilic droplets.

Nevus flammeus

Nevus flammeus includes salmon patch and port-wine stain. Both lesions are also known as the common birthmark and may occur in as many as 50% of infants.[31] The salmon patch is characterized by a red-pink macule, located in the head and neck area, which tends to involute with time. By contrast, the port-wine stain shows progressive growth with no tendency to regress and can acquire an elevated surface. Most lesions are congenital but rare acquired cases have been documented, including a case presenting after trauma.[32] Familial cases also occur and in such cases the gene has been mapped to chromosome 5q.[33,34] Port-wine stains may be associated with vascular malformations of the meninges, brain, or retina in the Sturge–Weber syndrome, and with limb hypertrophy, varicosities, and partial venous agenesis in the Klippel–Trenaunay syndrome. If the latter is associated with an arteriovenous fistula, it is known as Parke–Weber syndrome. Other vascular lesions, particularly pyogenic granuloma and, exceptionally, tufted angioma, may occur within a port-wine stain.[35–37] Histologically, both conditions show ectatic dermal blood vessels of differing size (Fig. 3.4), with usually deeper subcutaneous involvement in the port-wine stain.

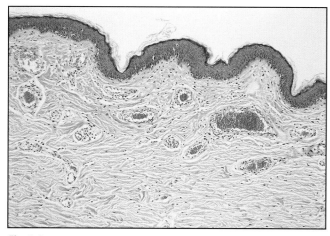

Fig. 3.4 • Port-wine stain. Dilated thin-walled vessels are evenly distributed in the upper dermis.

Nevus araneus (spider nevus)

Spider nevi are very common acquired lesions. They present over a wide age range as tiny, red, pinhead papules from which tortuous blood vessels radiate. They are commonly associated with pregnancy, chronic liver disease, and hyperthyroidism. Typical histologic findings are the presence of a thick-walled, dilated arteriole in the superficial dermis communicating with a number of anastomosing capillaries.

Venous lake

Venous lakes[38] are common vascular ectasias that occur in elderly people; sun-exposed areas are affected, especially the face, with predilection for the lips and ears. Histologically, a markedly dilated and congested vein is seen in the superficial dermis and is surrounded by an irregular layer of smooth muscle.

Angioma serpiginosum

Angioma serpiginosum[39–42] is an uncommon, slowly progressive lesion that mainly affects the lower limbs of children, especially females. It presents as tiny punctate red-purple papules in a gyrate or serpiginous arrangement. A linear pattern is exceptionally seen.[43] Involvement of the eye and the central nervous system may rarely occur.[44,45] Familial cases are very rare.[46] Histology of individual lesions shows small, dilated blood vessels in the dermal papillae.

Hereditary hemorrhagic telangiectasia (Osler–Weber–Rendu)

Hereditary hemorrhagic telangiectasia[47] is an autosomal dominant inherited condition characterized by numerous telangiectasias involving skin, mucosae, and internal organs, especially gastrointestinal tract and lungs. There may be an association with arteriovenous malformations. Histologically, dilated capillaries and venules are seen in the affected organs.

Angiokeratoma

Angiokeratomas[48] are not true vascular neoplasms but represent superficial vascular ectasias with overlying warty epidermal changes. There are four clinical types of angiokeratoma:

1. Angiokeratoma corporis diffusum in association with Fabry's disease, in which multiple angiokeratomas appear late in childhood. Fabry's disease is associated with inherited deficiency of the lysosomal enzyme alpha-galactosidase A. However, not all patients with angiokeratoma corporis diffusum have Fabry's disease. Identical lesions have been described in patients with other enzyme deficiencies, including alpha-L-fucosidase,[49] B-mannosidase,[50] alpha-N-acetylgalactosaminidase,[51,52] beta-galactosidase,[53] and exceptionally in a patient with normal enzyme activities[54]
2. Angiokeratoma of Mibelli, characterized by bilateral papules on dorsum of fingers and toes[55]
3. Angiokeratoma of Fordyce, characterized by lesions on the scrotum or, more rarely, the vulva[56,57]
4. Solitary angiokeratoma[58]

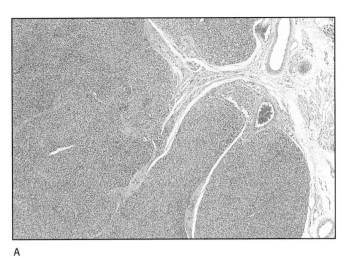 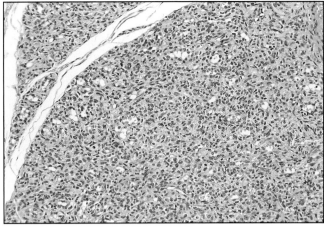

A   B

Fig. 3.5 • Capillary hemangioma (infantile hemangioendothelioma). Note the lobular growth pattern (A) and closely packed, largely uncanalized capillaries (B).

The histological features are identical in all forms. In Fabry's disease, the epidermal changes tend to be minimal and lipid deposits in the form of cytoplasmic vacuoles can be detected in skin lesions in the endothelial cells, pericytes, and fibroblasts.[59] Distinction from verrucous hemangioma is discussed below.

Capillary hemangioma

Clinical features

Capillary hemangioma[27–29,60] is the most common benign vascular tumor of infancy, affecting as many as 1 in every 100 live births[29] and comprising between 32% and 42% of all vascular tumors.[27,60] It can affect almost any organ but by far the commonest location is the skin and soft tissues, especially in the head and neck area.

In infants, the lesion is also known as cellular hemangioma of infancy, infantile hemangioendothelioma, strawberry nevus, or juvenile hemangioma. Females are affected slightly more often than males. The tumor presents at birth or shortly thereafter as a red-purple macule that slowly becomes raised and then tends to regress in over 70% of cases after a period of months to years.[61] Large lesions are usually disfiguring and can be associated with high morbidity if located near vital structures.

Histologic appearances

The histologic features change as the lesion evolves. The overall low-power architecture in all cases, regardless of the organ involved, is that of a multilobular tumor (Fig. 3.5). In early lesions the lobules are highly cellular and composed of mitotically active, plump endothelial cells forming tiny, rounded, often uncanalized vascular spaces (Fig. 3.5). For this reason, in very early lesions the endothelial nature of the tumor might not be immediately apparent. As lesions mature the vessels become canalized and more easily recognized, then often showing congested lumina and flat endothelial cells. A small feeding vessel is often found in the vicinity of the tumor. Older lesions become progressively fibrotic with almost

complete regression or absence of the vascular elements. Perineurial invasion is not uncommon in infantile cases but this does not imply malignant behavior.[62,63]

A reticulin stain is useful, especially in immature solid lesions, to highlight the tubular vascular architecture (Fig. 3.6). Although histologically immature tumors appear to be composed only of endothelial cells, ultrastructural and immunohistochemical studies have demonstrated a prominent number of other cells, including fibroblasts, pericytes, and mast cells.[64–66] The demonstration of an almost consistent layer of actin-positive pericytes around individual vascular channels may be helpful in excluding malignancy.

Tumors have a unique immunophenotype that is shared by placental microvessels and is characterized by expression of GLUT1 and LeY. GLUT1, the erythrocyte-type glucose transporter protein, is expressed in these lesions at all the stages of their evolution.[67,68] Since GLUT1 is not expressed in other vascular tumors usually occurring in children, expression of this marker is a valuable aid in differential diagnosis, particularly in the setting of vascular malformations, which do not express this marker. Recent studies have suggested that these lesions are composed, at least in part, of CD133-positive

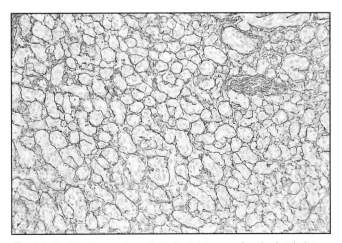

Fig. 3.6 • Capillary hemangioma. Reticulin staining reveals a clearly tubular architecture even in the least canalized examples (same case as in Fig. 3.5).

endothelial progenitor cells.[69] In addition, juvenile capillary hemangiomas have been shown to be clonal.[70,71]

Variants of capillary hemangioma

Tufted angioma ("angioblastoma of Nakagawa")

Tufted angioma[72–77] is a highly distinctive benign vascular tumor closely related to capillary hemangioma. Although it was first recognized as an entity in the English literature in 1976,[72] identical cases had been described in the Japanese literature since 1949 under the name "angioblastoma."[78]

Clinically, tufted angioma presents as an acquired lesion, most often on the neck or trunk of small children but rarely at mucosal sites;[79] there is no sex predilection. Rare cases can occur in adults. Congenital presentation is very rare.[80] Familial predisposition has been documented exceptionally.[81] Lesions progress slowly over the years as ill-defined red or brown macules, papules, and nodules, which are commonly tender. Spontaneous regression has been reported only occasionally.[82,83] Although the clinical course is benign, complete excision is not usually possible because of the extensive nature of the disease process. Furthermore, local recurrence beyond the apparent disease margin is quite common. Rarely, the Kasabach–Merritt syndrome may occur[84,85] and may indicate a relationship or similarity with kaposiform hemangioendothelioma (see p. 56). Association with a vascular malformation has also been documented.[86]

Histologic appearances The cardinal feature of tufted angioma is the presence of scattered round or ovoid lobules of closely packed capillaries in the dermis and superficial subcutis in a typically discohesive "cannonball" distribution (Fig. 3.7). Individual lobules are very similar to those seen in the early stages of strawberry nevus and consist of varying proportions of poorly canalized bloodless capillaries surrounded by pericytes. The endothelial cells are bland and mitotic figures are rare. Focally, cytoplasmic crystalline inclusions can be seen in the endothelial cells. The nature of these inclusions is unknown.[87] A distinctive feature is the presence of dilated, crescent-shaped, lymphatic-like vascular channels at the periphery of some of the tumor lobules. Intravascular location

has been described[88] and in rare cases there is histologic overlap between kaposiform hemangioendothelioma and tufted angioma.[89,90]

Differential diagnosis A common source of confusion is nodular Kaposi sarcoma (KS), from which tufted angioma is easily distinguished by its "cannonball" pattern, lack of a significant spindle cell population, and vasoformative reticulin pattern. Kaposiform hemangioendothelioma is generally a larger or more extensive lesion in which the lobules are more confluent.

Verrucous hemangioma

Verrucous hemangioma[91–93] usually presents as a warty blue-black lesion in the lower extremities of children. Due to its warty appearance, clinical misdiagnosis is not uncommon. Histologically, most lesions consist of numerous dilated capillaries and occasional cavernous-like vascular spaces in the superficial dermis, extending into the deep dermis and subcutaneous tissue (Fig. 3.8). Overlying epidermis shows very marked acanthosis and hyperkeratosis. Wide excision is necessary in order to avoid local recurrence, which is common. Although verrucous hemangiomas have a superficial resemblance to angiokeratomas, the latter represent vascular ectasias, involve only the papillary dermis, and are cured by simple excision.

Cherry angioma (senile angioma, Campbell de Morgan spot)

Cherry angiomas[27] are very common and present as red papules on the trunk and upper limbs of middle-aged and elderly adults. They increase in number with age and are characterized histologically by dilated and congested capillaries, with a lobular architecture, situated in the papillary dermis.

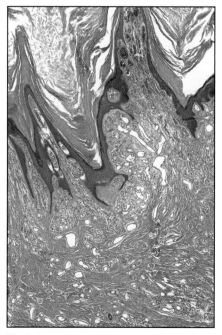

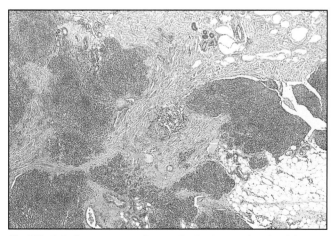

Fig. 3.7 • Tufted angioma. Note the irregular distribution of capillary lobules and semilunar vascular spaces at their periphery (top right).

Fig. 3.8 • Verrucous hemangioma. Beneath a markedly hyperkeratotic epidermis, thin-walled vessels fill the papillary and deep dermis.

Lobular capillary hemangioma (pyogenic granuloma)

Clinical features Pyogenic granuloma[94,95] is a very common vascular lesion of the skin and mucous membranes, which for many years was considered to be a reactive or infective process. This was based on the presence of extensive superficial secondary inflammatory changes (due to frequent ulceration) and an apparent association with trauma in up to a third of cases.[96,97] The underlying process, however, is a lobular vascular proliferation, which appears to be neoplastic, has deep and intravascular counterparts (see below), and has been redesignated, appropriately, as lobular capillary hemangioma.[98] Lesions can appear at any age, in either sex, and with special predilection for the fingers and head and neck area, especially the nasal and oral mucosae. Congenital lesions have been described rarely.[99,100] The classical appearance is that of a solitary, rapidly growing, ulcerated, bleeding, polypoid blue-red nodule which is usually less than 2 cm in diameter. Rare cases of disseminated ("eruptive") pyogenic granuloma have been reported.[101–103] Complete spontaneous regression does not occur and local recurrence is seen in up to 10% of cases, especially after incomplete excision. This is especially notable in lesions of the nasal septum. An unusual phenomenon, that tends to occur mainly on the trunk of children and young adults, is the development of recurrence characterized by multiple sessile nodules ("satellitosis").[104,105] Lesions may rarely occur within port-wine stains[106,107] and pyogenic granuloma-like lesions have been described in association with therapy with capecitabine,[108] topical tretinoin,[109] and isotretinoin.[110,111]

Histologic appearances Most lesions are exophytic, ulcerated, and surrounded by an acanthotic epidermal collarette. Near the surface, if ulcerated, there is a prominent acute inflammatory cell infiltrate and exuberant, often edematous granulation tissue, but the core of the tumor shows lobules of small capillaries, with or without discernible lumina, lined by prominent endothelial cells (Fig. 3.9). The stroma is loose and edematous and normal mitotic figures can be numerous, especially in mucosal lesions (Fig. 3.10). Moderate cytologic atypia can be present, especially in lesions arising in the

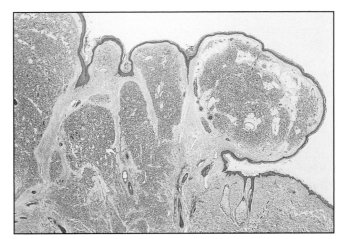

Fig. 3.9 • Pyogenic granuloma. This low-power view of an early non-ulcerated lesion shows the typical lobular architecture.

mouth[112] and conjunctiva; such atypia is often most striking adjacent to an ulcerated surface and is likely reactive in nature. Rarely, epithelioid endothelial cells are seen focally lining the vascular spaces. Older lesions can show marked fibrosis. The resemblance to granulation tissue is lost in deep or intravascular lesions. Satellite nodules show similar histologic findings with involvement of the reticular dermis and even the subcutis. Immunostaining with actin highlights a layer of pericytes surrounding each individual blood vessel.

Variants

Granuloma gravidarum refers to identical lesions occurring in the gingivae of pregnant women; these usually involute after delivery. *Subcutaneous pyogenic granuloma* presents as an asymptomatic nodule, mainly in the upper limb, and shows identical histologic features without the secondary changes associated with classical pyogenic granuloma.[113] *Intravenous pyogenic granuloma* is a rare variant presenting predominantly in adults, especially in the neck and upper extremity.[114] Secondary inflammatory changes are not seen and the clinical behavior is benign.

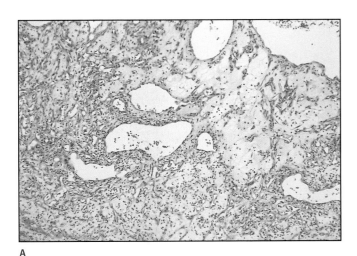

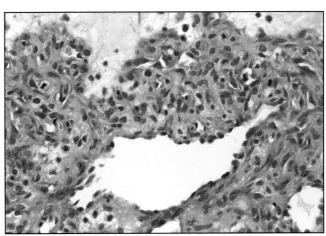

A   B

Fig. 3.10 • Pyogenic granuloma. (**A**) Ulcerated lesions show stromal edema and acute inflammatory cells. (**B**) Despite considerable cellularity and frequent mitoses, there is no endothelial nuclear atypia or multilayering.

Differential diagnosis The traditional differential diagnosis is from well-differentiated angiosarcoma and nodular KS. In the first, there is usually poor circumscription, cellular atypia, and dissection of collagen bundles. In the second, there is invariably a prominent spindle cell component with formation of slit-like spaces. The main differential diagnosis in recent years has been with *bacillary angiomatosis*, an infectious vascular proliferation caused by a Gram-negative organism, *Bartonella henselae* (formerly *Rochalimaea henselae*) and much less commonly by *B. quintana*.[115,116] This condition occurs almost exclusively in patients with acquired immune deficiency syndrome (AIDS) or other immunosuppressive conditions and rarely in normal individuals. Its recognition is important because of the dramatic response to antibiotic therapy, especially erythromycin. The incidence of this condition has diminished dramatically in the last few years because of the sensitivity of the causative organism to the prophylactic anti-tuberculous treatment routinely received by human immuno-deficiency virus (HIV)-positive individuals. The architecture of both conditions is very similar, the main difference being the presence in bacillary angiomatosis of pale epithelioid endo-thelial cells, focal cytoplasmic vacuolation, clusters of poly-morphs with leukocytoclasis throughout the lesion, and granular basophilic or amphophilic material in relation to the inflammatory cells (Fig. 3.11). When stained with Warthin–Starry or Giemsa this material is shown to contain aggregates of short bacilli.

Cavernous hemangioma

Clinical features Although less common, cavernous hemangioma[27–29,60] has the same age, sex, and anatomic distribution as capillary hemangioma. As opposed to capillary hemangioma, however, these lesions tend to be larger, deeper, and less well circumscribed; very few, if any, show a tendency to regress. Virtually any organ in the body can be affected by cavernous hemangioma. Associated clinical syndromes include Mafucci's syndrome, with multiple enchondromas, occasional lymphangiomas and often spindle cell hemangiomas, Kasabach–Merritt syndrome with consumption coagulopathy,[117] and blue rubber bleb nevus syndrome with numerous hemangiomas in the skin and gastrointestinal tract.[118,119]

Histologic appearances Cavernous hemangiomas consist of poorly circumscribed, irregularly dilated blood vessels lined by flat endothelium and with walls of varying thickness (Fig. 3.12). Areas resembling capillary hemangioma can often be found focally, especially in the superficial portion, and many lesions represent combined capillary and cavernous hemangiomas. Thrombosis, secondary dystrophic calcification, and mild inflammation are frequently found.

Variants of cavernous hemangioma

Sinusoidal hemangioma

Clinical features Sinusoidal hemangioma is a more recently described distinctive variant of cavernous hemangioma.[120] It has a wide anatomic distribution with special predilection for the subcutaneous tissue of the breast. In this anatomic location it can be confused with angiosarcoma. Most lesions occur in middle-aged adults, predominantly females, as a superficially located blue nodule. Simple excision is curative.

Histologic appearances Typically, lesions are lobular, relatively circumscribed, and composed of irregular, dilated and congested, thin-walled gaping blood vessels with a typical sinusoidal or sieve-like appearance (Fig. 3.13). Cross-sectioning

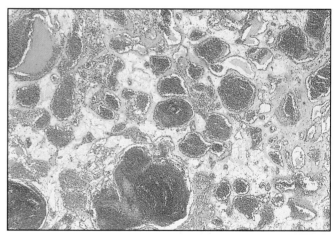

Fig. 3.12 • Cavernous hemangioma. The blood vessels are dilated, congested, and focally thrombosed.

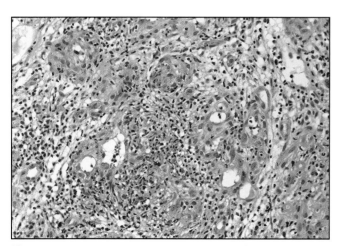

Fig. 3.11 • Bacillary angiomatosis. Note the epithelioid endothelium along with inflammatory and karyorrhectic debris (center).

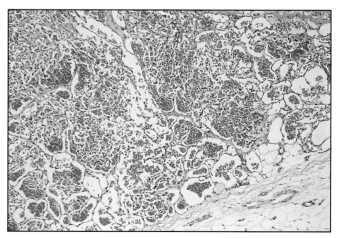

Fig. 3.13 • Sinusoidal hemangioma. Note the delicate vessel walls producing a sieve-like pattern.

of back-to-back blood vessels with little intervening stroma results in prominent pseudopapillary structures, reminiscent of Masson's tumor. The vascular spaces are lined mainly by an attenuated monolayer of endothelial cells, which can be focally prominent with mild reactive nuclear hyperchromasia. An outer layer of actin-positive pericytes can also often be discerned. As in ordinary cavernous hemangioma, thrombosis with dystrophic calcification is commonly seen and this may be the cause of abnormality on mammographic screening. Rarely, central infarction is present. Old lesions show fibrosis and hyalinization of blood vessels.

Differential diagnosis The main differential diagnosis is from well-differentiated angiosarcoma, especially in lesions occurring in the breast. Mammary angiosarcoma is intraparenchymal, rather than dermal or subcutaneous, and shows a clearly infiltrative or dissecting pattern with at least focal nuclear pleomorphism and endothelial multilayering.

Arteriovenous hemangioma

Clinical features Arteriovenous hemangioma (arteriovenous malformation)[121–124] is an uncommon lesion. It is divided into two distinctive variants according to the depth of involvement. The deep type usually presents in the head and neck or limbs of adolescents and young adults and can be associated with severe degrees of arteriovenous shunting and soft tissue hypertrophy. These deep lesions probably represent congenital malformations. Symptoms can be severe and patients may present with heart failure or Kasabach–Merritt syndrome. Clinicopathologic correlation, including arteriographic studies, is very important in establishing the diagnosis. Persistent growth and symptoms are common after incomplete excision.

The superficial type, which is also known as cirsoid aneurysm or acral arteriovenous tumor,[123] typically presents in the skin of the head and neck (especially the lip) of middle-aged or elderly adults (often males) as a small red-blue papule. A variant presenting on the digits has been documented.[125] Some cases have been associated with chronic liver disease.[126] Symptoms are minimal and include pain and intermittent bleeding. Shunting is not usually a major feature. Superficial

cutaneous changes associated with deep arteriovenous hemangiomas can mimic KS clinically and histologically and have been named pseudo-KS or acroangiodermatitis.[127] However, similar changes can be seen associated with any cause of venous insufficiency.

Histologic appearances The histologic features are very variable, especially in the deep variant of arteriovenous hemangioma. Superficial lesions tend to be better circumscribed than deep lesions. Both variants show a mixture of thick- and thin-walled blood vessels that correspond to arteries and veins of varying caliber with a predominance of the latter (Fig. 3.14), as can be demonstrated by the use of elastic stains (Fig. 3.15). Focally, some tumors can resemble capillary or cavernous hemangiomas. Serial sections are helpful in demonstrating arteriovenous anastomosis. Focal

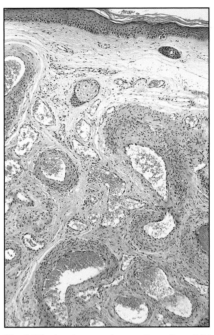

Fig. 3.14 • Arteriovenous hemangioma. Superficial examples are often known as cirsoid aneurysm.

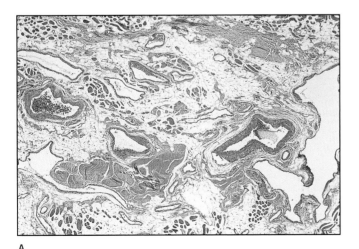

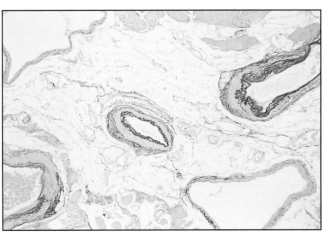

A   B

Fig. 3.15 • Arteriovenous hemangioma. This deep lesion is composed of large vessels (**A**) which are distinguishable by the distribution of their elastic laminae (**B**). (Elastic van Gieson.)

thrombosis and stromal calcification are sometimes seen. Convincing demonstration of arteries in superficial lesions is often very difficult. Conceivably these vessels can represent arterialized veins and it is likely that many superficial lesions are true venous hemangiomas.[128]

Microvenular hemangioma

Microvenular hemangioma is a distinctive cutaneous hemangioma proposed to be a form of acquired venous hemangioma.[129,130] Lesions most often present in young adults as red or bluish papules, especially on the limbs. Occurrence in children is very rare.[131] There is no apparent tendency to recur. A case has been documented in a patient with POEMS syndrome.[132] Histologically (Fig. 3.16), the tumor is composed of irregular branching, thin-walled venules, lined by a monolayer of endothelial cells with plump nuclei, occupying the superficial and deep dermis, and surrounded by sclerotic collagen bundles. The vessels show angular ramification through the dermis and generally have an easily identified outer layer of pericytes. A more lobular component may be evident at the base of the lesion.

Hobnail hemangioma (targetoid hemosiderotic hemangioma)

Hobnail hemangioma,[133–135] first described under the rubric targetoid hemosiderotic hemangioma,[133] is a distinctive cutaneous vascular tumor that usually presents on the trunk or extremities of young or middle-aged adults, with male predilection. Its original descriptive name refers to what was regarded as the distinctive clinical presentation of a small round lesion with a purple center, surrounded by successive pale and ecchymotic haloes. However, it has become clear that relatively few lesions have this appearance and, furthermore,

the same appearance may be associated with other pathologies, including trauma.[136] Some patients have described cyclic changes in the lesion.[137] Simple excision is curative.

Histologically, in the superficial dermis, there are irregular dilated thin-walled vascular channels lined by distinctive, bland, hobnail endothelial cells with focal papillary projections (Fig. 3.17). As the lesion extends deeper into the dermis, the endothelial cells become flatter and narrower vascular channels dissect between collagen bundles. The surrounding stroma frequently shows extravasated red blood cells and hemosiderin deposition. We consider this lesion to be at the benign end of the spectrum of vascular tumors characterized by hobnail endothelial cells, which includes papillary intralymphatic angioendothelioma (PILA: Dabska tumor) and retiform hemangioendothelioma.[138] The differential diagnosis is discussed in the section on Papillary intralymphatic angioendothelioma (see below), but it should also be noted that histologic changes almost identical to hobnail hemangioma may be seen after radiation therapy (see p. 69). Immunohistochemistry for HHV-8 is consistently negative in these lesions.[139]

Acquired elastotic hemangioma

Acquired elastotic hemangioma is a rare lesion which develops in sun-exposed skin of the forearms and neck, with predilection for middle-aged and elderly women.[140] It presents as a small, solitary, asymptomatic erythematous plaque. Histologically, in the background of dermal solar elastosis there is a band-like superficial dermal proliferation of capillaries.

Cutaneous epithelioid angiomatous nodule

Clinical features Cutaneous epithelioid angiomatous nodule is a recently described lesion in the spectrum of epithelioid

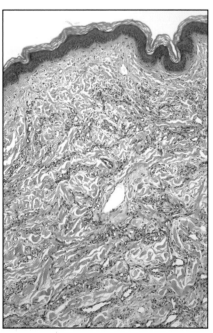

Fig. 3.16 • Microvenular hemangioma. Note the angular ramification of vessels between dermal collagen bundles.

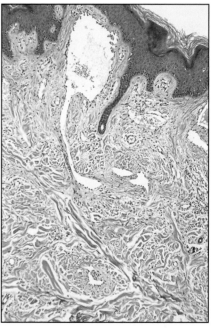

Fig. 3.17 • Hobnail hemangioma. The vascular channels are lined by protuberant endothelial nuclei; note the focal papillae (top).

vascular tumors.[141] It presents as a papule or nodule in adults, of usually short duration, with predilection for the trunk, followed by the limbs and face.[141] Multiple lesions are exceptional. There is no tendency for recurrence.

Histopathology Histology shows a single, usually circumscribed lobule composed of plump, pink epithelioid endothelial cells with intracytoplasmic lumina and only very focal formation of vascular channels (Fig. 3.18). Despite the worrisome solid growth, there is no nuclear hyperchromasia or pleomorphism. In the background there may be mild fibrosis, hemosiderin deposition, and scattered inflammatory cells, including some eosinophils.

Differential diagnosis Distinction from epithelioid hemangioma can be made based on the different clinical presentation and the presence of a single lobule of poorly vasoformative epithelioid endothelial cells and fewer inflammatory cells in cutaneous epithelioid angiomatous nodule. In bacillary angiomatosis, the endothelial cells are pale pink and form small vascular channels in a lobular architecture. Furthermore, throughout the lesion, aggregates of neutrophils with nuclear dust and clumps of amorphous basophilic material representing bacteria are seen.

Epithelioid hemangioma (angiolymphoid hyperplasia with eosinophilia)

Epithelioid hemangioma is also sometimes known as angiolymphoid hyperplasia with eosinophilia,[142] pseudo- or atypical pyogenic granuloma,[143] inflammatory angiomatous nodule,[143] papular angioplasia,[144] intravenous atypical vascular proliferation,[145] and histiocytoid hemangioma.[146] Although accurately descriptive, the term "histiocytoid hemangioma" is controversial[147–150] and has gradually been abandoned since, as originally formulated, it included a broader group of tumors.[146] Epithelioid hemangioma represents the benign end of the spectrum of a family of vascular tumors characterized by epithelioid endothelial cells, which includes the recently described cutaneous epithelioid angiomatous nodule (see above), and, at the malignant end of the spectrum, epithelioid

hemangioendothelioma and epithelioid angiosarcoma. Although separation between these tumor types is usually possible, rare cases show a degree of overlap, especially within the two latter categories. There is still some controversy whether epithelioid hemangioma represents a true vascular neoplasm or a reaction to various stimuli, especially trauma,[151] but the former is generally favored.

Clinical features Epithelioid hemangioma typically presents as single or multiple cutaneous red nodules in the head and neck area (especially around the ear) of middle-aged adults, with slight predilection for males.[152,153] Lesions can also occur in the trunk and limbs and involve deeper soft tissues. Cases have also been reported in the oral mucosa,[154–156] tongue,[157,158] breast,[159] lymph node,[160] bone,[161] testis,[162] and even in an ovarian teratoma.[163] A group of morphologically similar lesions in the heart, considered in the past to be epithelioid hemangiomas, are probably mesothelial or histiocytic in origin (see Ch. 2).[164,165] Circulating eosinophilia is infrequent but has been reported to occur in up to 15% of patients.[150,152] In contrast to Kimura's disease, there is generally no lymph node involvement. In up to a third of the cases there is local recurrence, but metastasis does not occur.[149,150,152,153] Transient angiolymphoid hyperplasia and KS has been reported after primary infection with HHV-8 in a patient with HIV infection.[166] However, HHV-8 has not been found in lesions of epithelioid hemangioma.[167] Lesions with similar histologic features to those seen in epithelioid hemangioma have been described rarely in association with vascular malformations.[168]

Histologic appearances Most lesions are fairly well circumscribed and composed of numerous small to medium-sized, thin-walled blood vessels lined by plump cells with copious eosinophilic cytoplasm and oval vesicular nuclei with inconspicuous nucleoli. Often there is at least a partially lobular architecture (Fig. 3.19). Frequently the epithelioid endothelial cells protrude into the vascular lumina in a "hobnail" or "tombstone" fashion (Fig. 3.20). These cells may show cytoplasmic vacuoles that, if confluent, can form vascular lumina. Mitotic figures are uncommon and pleomorphism is not a feature. Occasional thicker blood vessels, with muscular walls

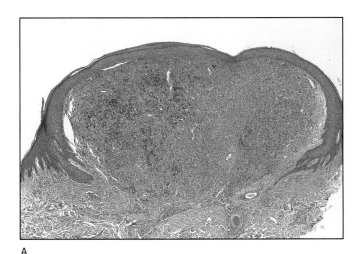

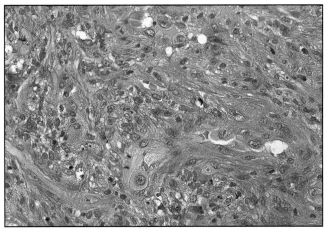

A   B

Fig. 3.18 • Epithelioid angiomatous nodule. This characteristically exophytic nodule (**A**) is composed of close-packed epithelioid endothelial cells (**B**).

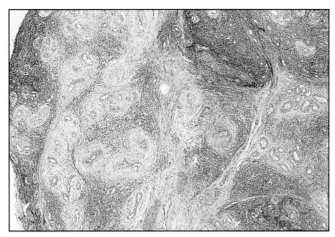

Fig. 3.19 • Epithelioid hemangioma. Note the somewhat lobular architecture and prominent lymphoid infiltrate.

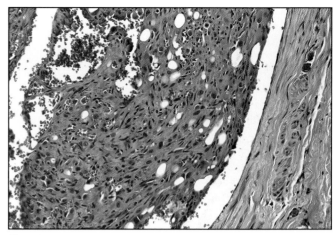

Fig. 3.21 • Intravenous atypical vascular proliferation. The lesion in this vein lumen is composed of epithelioid cells and spindle cells.

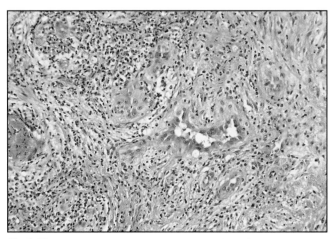

Fig. 3.20 • Epithelioid hemangioma. Note the very plump, focally vacuolated endothelial cells and prominent stromal eosinophils.

showing myxoid change, and solid aggregates of epithelioid cells can be seen. Demonstrable origin from a small artery or a vein is common and the entire lesion quite often can be intravascular. Origin from a large peripheral artery has occasionally been described.[169,170] Surrounding the blood vessels, there is often a prominent inflammatory infiltrate composed of histiocytes, lymphocytes, plasma cells, mast cells, and eosinophils. Occasionally there is germinal center formation but this is less frequent than in Kimura's disease. Tumor cells stain for endothelial markers and, although keratin positivity is not generally seen in cutaneous lesions, it has been reported in cases arising in bone.[161]

The intravascular lesions described as "*intravenous atypical vascular proliferation*"[145] have been thought to represent a variant of epithelioid hemangioma. They occur predominantly in young to middle-aged adults as a solitary nodule, most often in the head and neck region or upper limb. They differ somewhat from conventional epithelioid hemangioma in that they usually have a prominent spindle cell (pericytic) component (closely admixed with the epithelioid endothelial channels), which enhances the pseudomalignant appearance of these lesions (Fig. 3.21). However, at least in our experience

(and in the original paper[145]), there is no evident tendency to recur.

Differential diagnosis Kimura's disease is no longer considered synonymous with epithelioid hemangioma,[171–175] as the former clinically affects mainly young oriental males and more commonly is associated with lymphadenopathy, eosinophilia, and other systemic features of an immunologically mediated disorder. Histologically, lesions are deeper, show more fibrosis, and, most importantly of all, do not show epithelioid endothelial cells lining the blood vessels. Eosinophil microabscesses are common. In injection-site granuloma, epithelioid cells are absent.[176,177] Bacillary angiomatosis shows epithelioid cells with pale cytoplasm and numerous neutrophils and is associated with basophilic clusters of bacteria. Epithelioid hemangioendothelioma has a prominent myxoid or hyaline stroma and tumor cells are arranged in cords or nests, generally lacking formation of overt vascular channels.

Venous hemangioma

Venous hemangioma has been described as a distinctive entity in the mesentery, retroperitoneum, and skeletal muscle of the limbs in adults.[178] Although it has been described formally only in deep soft tissues, in our experience similar lesions present with equal incidence in superficial locations and also occasionally at visceral locations. Sometimes the designation "venous" hemangioma is rendered on radiologic grounds but the histopathologic correlate of such a diagnosis is unclear. Many of those cases occurring in skeletal muscle are probably best classified as examples of intramuscular hemangioma (see below). Tumors are composed of numerous, irregular, dilated or congested muscular veins (Fig. 3.22), which are occasionally thrombosed. Dystrophic calcification is sometimes seen within thrombi. Focally, the tumor resembles a cavernous hemangioma.

Spindle cell hemangioma (formerly "spindle cell hemangioendothelioma")

Clinical features Spindle cell hemangioma is a distinctive vascular tumor, which was first described in 1986 under the

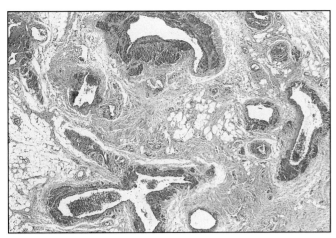

Fig. 3.22 • Venous hemangioma. This subcutaneous lesion is composed of large thick-walled veins.

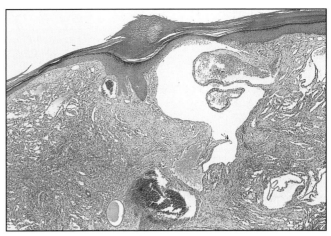

Fig. 3.23 • Spindle cell hemangioma. The typical combination of solid spindle cell areas and cavernous foci (associated with pseudopapillary structures) is evident.

rubric spindle cell hemangioendothelioma, at which time it was regarded as a low-grade variant of angiosarcoma.[179] Typically, the lesion presents as solitary, or often multiple, red-blue nodules in the dermis or subcutis of the distal extremities, especially the hands; the nodules may be painful. Extremely rarely, lesions may occur in skeletal muscle. There is no sex predilection and the tumor may present over a wide age range with a tendency to cluster in the second and third decades. The clinical course is indolent and patients with multiple lesions tend to develop new lesions over a period of many years.[179–181] These new lesions, which were originally interpreted as recurrences, appear to be lesions arising *de novo* in normal neighboring skin. Spontaneous regression occurs only infrequently. Association with other anomalies such as lymphedema, early-onset varicose veins, Klippel–Trenaunay syndrome, or Mafucci's syndrome is seen in up to 10% of cases.[179–183] It seems likely that the association between these lesions and Mafucci's syndrome is stronger than was previously realized.[183] The basis for considering spindle cell hemangioendothelioma as a form of angiosarcoma was the development of lymph node metastasis in a patient from the original series.[179] However, this patient appears to have developed a separate radiation-induced high-grade sarcoma. Mounting evidence in recent years suggests that spindle cell hemangioma is a non-neoplastic lesion, associated with either abnormalities of local blood flow or else a vascular malformation,[180,181,184,185] hence the more appropriate revised nomenclature.[181,186]

Histologic appearances Histologically the lesion is poorly circumscribed and consists of irregular, cavernous thin-walled vascular spaces intermixed with solid areas composed mainly of spindle-shaped cells (Fig. 3.23). In perhaps 40–50% of cases the process is predominantly intravascular, affecting mainly medium-sized veins. In the periphery of the tumor, thick-walled muscular vessels which often show fibrointimal thickening, reminiscent of an arteriovenous malformation, are commonly seen. The cavernous spaces are lined by an attenuated monolayer of endothelial cells and show organizing thrombus with frequent phleboliths. Papillary projections, superficially resembling Masson's tumor but clearly more cellular, are often present. The solid areas are composed of bland spindle cells

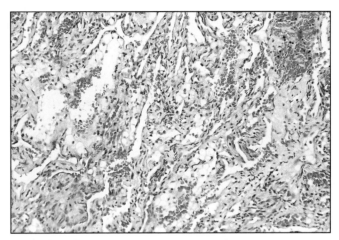

Fig. 3.24 • Spindle cell hemangioma. Note the strikingly vacuolated endothelial cells.

with scanty eosinophilic cytoplasm and elongated or plump rounded nuclei, along with small numbers of more epithelioid cells, variable numbers of which show large intracytoplasmic vacuoles (Fig. 3.24). Slit-like vascular spaces are also commonly found in these solid areas. Bundles of smooth muscle cells are often present, not only around some of the dilated vascular spaces, but also in the solid areas. Very rarely there is focal degenerative endothelial atypia. Immunohistochemically, only the cells lining the vascular spaces and the epithelioid cells in the solid areas stain for endothelial markers. Most spindle cells stain only for vimentin and a smaller percentage for actin and/or desmin. Rare cases showing combined features with epithelioid hemangioendothelioma have been described,[180,187] but it is most likely that these represent examples of the recently described composite hemangioendothelioma (see p. 58).

Differential diagnosis Nodular KS generally lacks either cavernous vascular spaces or epithelioid vacuolated cells and shows cytoplasmic hyaline globules in the spindle cell population. Moreover the spindle cells in KS invariably express HHV-8, which is negative in the spindle cells of spindle cell hemangioma.

Deep hemangiomas

Intramuscular angioma

Clinical features Intramuscular angioma, although relatively uncommon, is one of the most frequent deeply located soft tissue tumors (Fig. 3.25). It presents at any age but has a tendency to manifest in adolescents and young adults; there is no sex predilection.[188–190] The lower limbs are most commonly affected, followed by the head and neck area, upper limbs, and trunk. A typical lesion develops as a slowly growing mass, which is often painful, especially after exercise. Trauma does not appear to play a role in its pathogenesis and most cases are probably congenital in origin. Radiologically, there is frequently soft tissue calcification, corresponding either to phleboliths or metaplastic ossification. Recurrence rates are high, ranging from 30% to 50%,[188,190] usually as a result of incomplete primary excision.

Histologic appearances Traditionally, intramuscular angiomas have been classified histologically, according to vessel size and predominant blood vessel type, into small (capillary), large

(cavernous), and mixed types.[188] In practice, however, most lesions appear to be of the mixed type and can consist of capillaries, veins, small arteries, and even lymphatic-like channels,[190] making reliable subclassification difficult, if not impossible (Fig. 3.26). However, pure intramuscular capillary hemangiomas are mainly seen in the head and neck area, while intramuscular lymphangioma is most common in the trunk. All intramuscular angiomas are associated with variable amounts of mature fat, explaining why these lesions have in the past sometimes been called infiltrating angiolipomas[191] (Fig. 3.27). Degenerative or reactive sarcolemmal nuclei are a common feature in the stroma. Earlier reports suggesting a correlation between histologic subtype and risk of recurrence have not been confirmed and it seems that recurrence correlates only with adequacy of excision, reflecting the infiltrative nature of all intramuscular angiomas, regardless of histologic subtype.[190]

Differential diagnosis Although histologic diagnosis is usually easy, intramuscular angioma has to be distinguished from intramuscular lipoma which has a more indolent course with

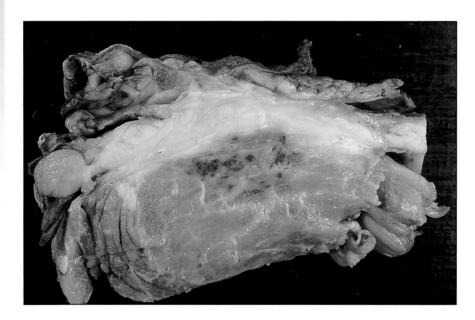

Fig. 3.25 • Intramuscular hemangioma. Note the obviously thrombosed vessels centrally and the diffuse fatty pallor of the adjacent muscle, all of which is irregularly infiltrated by tumor.

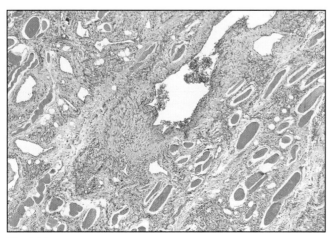

Fig. 3.26 • Intramuscular hemangioma. Note the complex admixture of vessels of varying size.

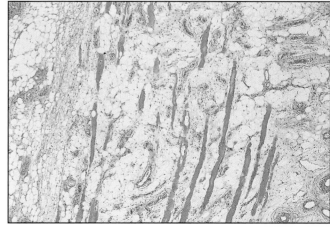

Fig. 3.27 • Intramuscular hemangioma. Most cases have a very prominent adipocytic component.

less tendency to recur. In the latter, however, a prominent vascular component is never found. Pure intramuscular capillary hemangioma is occasionally confused with angiosarcoma, but the usual presence of a lobular architecture and the absence of endothelial atypia or multilayering in the former should make distinction easy.

Synovial hemangioma

Synovial hemangiomas are uncommon lesions that have traditionally included tumors arising in the intra-articular space, bursae, and even tendon sheath. However, it has been proposed that this name should be reserved for lesions occurring in the first two sites.[192] Synovial hemangioma presents in young adults or children, especially males, as a slowly growing asymptomatic or painful mass, affecting especially the knee and elbow and, rarely, the finger.[192] Lesions which affect surrounding soft tissue or bone are best regarded as examples of angiomatosis. The behavior of purely synovial lesions is benign; there is no tendency to recur. About half of the cases of synovial hemangioma represent cavernous lesions and the rest are examples of capillary hemangioma, arteriovenous hemangioma, and pure venous hemangioma.

Intraneural hemangioma

Neural hemangiomas are extremely uncommon and very few true cases have been reported.[193–195] Symptoms are related to the nerve involved and include pain, paresthesiae, and numbness. Extensive epineurial, perineurial, and endoneurial involvement can occur and is associated with significant morbidity.[195] The cases described have involved large nerves from the limbs and, in one case, the trigeminal nerve.[195] Histologically, most lesions are cavernous hemangiomas.

Angiomatosis

Angiomatosis is an uncommon condition that presents exclusively in childhood or adolescence and is characterized by the diffuse proliferation of blood vessels affecting large contiguous areas of the body.[196] Familial cases occur rarely.[197] Typically this process involves the limbs, affecting multiple tissue planes, including dermis, subcutis, muscle, and even bone. Commonly, hypertrophy of the affected limb occurs and some patients present clinically with the features of angiokeratoma.[198] Rare cases have been associated with visceral and central nervous system hemangiomas. In view of the extensive disease, surgical treatment is difficult and recurrences are common (varying from 60% to 90% of cases in different series).[197,198]

Two histologic patterns have been described.[197] In both types abundant mature fat is seen surrounding the proliferating vessels, a feature that seems to confirm the probably hamartomatous nature of angiomatosis. The most common pattern consists of a mixture of veins, cavernous vascular spaces, and capillaries, the first of which show irregular walls with a variable incomplete muscle layer. Frequently, clusters of small vessels are present in the walls of larger vessels.[197] The second pattern consists of small capillaries and sparse larger feeding vessels (Fig. 3.28). In both patterns, perineural invasion can be seen.

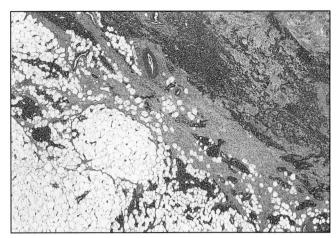

Fig. 3.28 • Capillary angiomatosis. Note the diffuse infiltration of fat and fascia.

Intramuscular angioma, although very similar histologically to angiomatosis, is usually limited to one muscle group and clinicopathologic correlation is therefore necessary to allow confident distinction. Deep arteriovenous malformations usually show clinical evidence of shunting and a histologic admixture of veins and arteries, of which the latter are only occasionally seen in angiomatosis.

Vascular tumors of intermediate malignancy

Although the concept of tumors of low-grade or borderline malignancy is well established in other fields of pathology, it has only been introduced more recently in the classification of soft tissue neoplasms and, in particular, in that of vascular tumors (reviewed by Fletcher[199]). The term hemangioendothelioma, originally used very loosely to refer to a number of benign (i.e., infantile capillary hemangioma) and malignant (i.e., angiosarcoma) vascular tumors, has been chosen to denote many of the lesions in this new category. Strictly, the concept of borderline tumors refers to neoplasms that have very low but definite metastatic potential (e.g., retiform hemangioendothelioma). Less commonly, it has been used to refer to tumors whose biologic behavior cannot be predicted accurately on histologic grounds. In the most recent World Health Organization (WHO) classification of soft tissue tumors, the concept has been expanded to include tumors that do not have potential for metastatic spread but may be locally aggressive.[200] In this classification, low-grade or borderline malignant tumors are classified as of intermediate potential. Tumors classifed as locally aggressive include kaposiform hemangioendothelioma and giant cell angioblastoma. The latter tumor and polymorphous hemangoioendothelioma were not included by the WHO working group in the classification of vascular neoplasms because it was considered that, due to the very small number of cases reported, the available data were insufficient for definitive classification of these lesions. In this chapter we describe them in the intermediate category group. Epithelioid hemangioendothelioma has been moved to the category of malignant vascular tumors, as it is associated with high morbidity and mortality (see below). The controversy continues whether KS represents a reactive or a neoplastic process but we have decided to keep it in the category of intermediate tumors. It is likely that in future years the classification of borderline vascular tumors will undergo further changes as our understanding of this fascinating group of neoplasms evolves.

Kaposiform hemangioendothelioma

Clinical features

Kaposiform hemangioendothelioma is a distinctive but rare neoplasm that was originally described in the retroperitoneum of infants, but appears to present more often in subcutaneous or deep soft tissue of the extremities, chest wall, and head and neck area.[201–204] Pure cutaneous involvement also occurs.[205,206] Most cases present in the first decade of life, especially during the first 2 years, but tumors in adults have also been described.[207] There is no sex predilection. In some cases morbidity and mortality are associated with complications arising from the tumor as a result of its destructive and infiltrative growth. Retroperitoneal tumors are usually associated with intestinal obstruction and jaundice. A common association with these tumors at almost any site is Kasabach–Merritt syndrome. A few cases have been associated with lymphangiomatosis of bone and soft tissue. These lesions may be hard to resect properly (because of their anatomic location) but it seems that true recurrence is infrequent. Rare perinodal/nodal metastasis has been described,[204] but distant metastasis has not been reported to date.

Histologic appearances

Histologically, the tumor is composed of lobules of differing size, which infiltrate surrounding tissues in an irregular manner and are separated by fibrous septa. Retroperitoneal tumors frequently show involvement of adjacent structures such as the pancreas, small intestine, and lymph nodes. Tumor lobules are composed of different proportions of short fascicles of bland spindle cells, slit-like vascular spaces, and congested capillaries with scattered fibrin thrombi (Fig. 3.29). Rarely, especially in cases from skin and soft tissues, small nests of epithelioid cells can be found. These cells can contain hemosiderin granules, hyaline globules, and even cytoplasmic vacuoles. Rare hyaline globules are also seen in the spindle cells. Inflammatory cells are usually sparse and mitotic figures are rare. Ectatic blood vessels are found in the periphery of the tumor lobules. Cases arising in association with lymphangiomatosis show transition between both conditions. Endothelial cells in the tumor are positive for CD31, CD34, and FLI-1 but negative for GLUT-1 and LeY (juvenile hemangioma-associated antigens).[204] Von Willebrand factor is only very focally positive. The spindle-shaped cells are variably positive for endothelial cell markers and may be focally positive for actin. HHV-8 has not been demonstrated.

Differential diagnosis

The histologic resemblance to nodular KS is striking. Clinically, however, KS is very rare in children, tends to be multicentric, and shows predilection for lymph nodes in this age group. Morphologically, nodular KS has a more prominent chronic inflammatory cell infiltrate, lacks a lobular architecture, and individual lobules are not surrounded by dense fibrous bands. Infantile capillary hemangioma ("juvenile hemangioendothelioma," see p. 45) is composed of solid nodules of incompletely canalized capillaries without a spindle cell component. Kaposiform hemangioendothelioma can be distinguished from angiosarcoma by its lack of cytologic atypia and the absence of individually infiltrative, anastomosing channels.

Giant cell angioblastoma

Very rare examples of what appears to be a distinctive vascular tumor with aggressive local behavior have been described under the name giant cell angioblastoma.[208,209] These have presented as infiltrative congenital or neonatal lesions at a variety of sites.

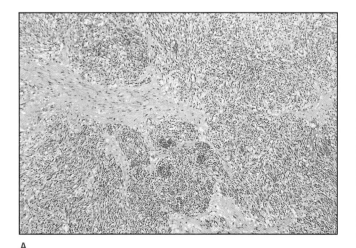

A

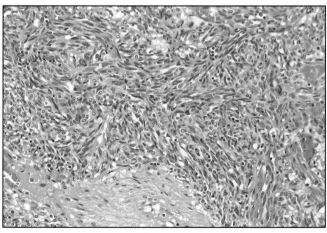

B

Fig. 3.29 • Kaposiform hemangioendothelioma. This spindle-celled vascular tumor has a lobular architecture (**A**); at higher power, note the resemblance to Kaposi sarcoma, as well as fibrin microthrombi (**B**).

Histologically, they are composed of bundles and nodules of spindle-shaped and plump histiocyte-like cells intermixed with multinucleate giant cells, simulating granulomas, generally oriented around ramifying vascular spaces lined by plump endothelial cells.

Retiform hemangioendothelioma

Clinical features

Retiform hemangioendothelioma is an uncommon lesion which falls into the intermediate, rarely metastasizing category.[138,210,211] It is significantly more common than PILA (Dabska tumor). It presents as a slowly growing cutaneous tumor, most often in young adults; there is no sex predominance. Tumors show predilection for the distal extremities, especially the lower limb. Very rarely, these lesions can arise after radiotherapy or in the setting of chronic lymphedema. A patient with multiple lesions has been described.[212] Persistent local recurrences are common but metastatic spread to regional lymph nodes has been described in only one case and a further case has metastasized to soft tissues close to the primary tumor.[213] Distant spread or tumor-related death has not been reported to date.

Histologic appearances

Retiform hemangioendothelioma is an ill-defined dermal and/or subcutaneous tumor with a striking histologic resemblance to normal rete testis. This appearance is conferred by the presence of elongated, arborizing blood vessels (Fig. 3.30) lined by monomorphic, strikingly protuberant (hobnail) endothelial cells (Fig. 3.31). A prominent stromal and intraluminal lymphocytic infiltrate is present in perhaps 50% of cases. These endothelial cells have limited, usually basal, cytoplasm and vacuolation is rare. The vascular lumina may contain occasional papillae with hyaline collagenous cores. Most tumors show focally solid areas composed of monomorphic spindle or epithelioid cells, which usually stain positively for endothelial markers.

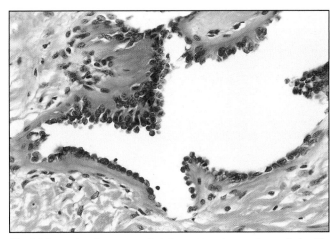

Fig. 3.31 • Retiform hemangioendothelioma. Note the protuberant "hobnail" endothelial nuclei.

Differential diagnosis

The differential diagnosis of retiform hemangioendothelioma is described under PILA (see below).

Papillary intralymphatic angioendothelioma (endovascular papillary angioendothelioma, Dabska tumor)

Clinical features

PILA is a rare vascular tumor, described by Dabska in 1969 as a locally invasive neoplasm with low malignant potential, occurring in infants and children.[214] In a recent series, however, 25% of the cases occurred in adults.[215] There is no sex predilection and the topographic distribution is wide, with a slight predominance on the limbs and trunk.[214,215] Local recurrence, metastatic spread to regional lymph nodes, and death in at least 1 patient was reported in the original series. Recently, however, follow-up in 8 of 12 reported cases revealed neither local recurrences nor metastatic spread.[215] It now appears that Dabska tumor is part of a family of vascular neoplasms typified by the presence of characteristic cells with a hobnail appearance, possibly indicating high endothelial cell differentiation.[216] This group of neoplasms includes retiform hemangioendothelioma[138] and a group of benign lesions initially described as targetoid hemosiderotic hemangioma and now known as hobnail hemangioma.[136] It seems likely that at least some of Dabska's original cases would nowadays be classified as retiform hemangioendothelioma. Therefore, the issue about the true malignant potential of this tumor will remain unsolved until further series are reported. While this doubt remains, complete excision of the tumor should be advised.

Histologic appearances

Using stringent diagnostic criteria, our experience and that of others[215] suggests that these tumors are usually composed of

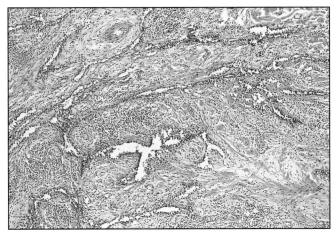

Fig. 3.30 • Retiform hemangioendothelioma. Typical arborizing channels are associated with a prominent lymphoid infiltrate.

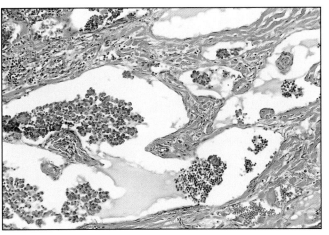

Fig. 3.32 • Dabska tumor. Cavernous lymphatic-like spaces contain prominent endothelial papillae and clusters of lymphocytes.

dilated, irregular vascular channels resembling a cavernous lymphangioma, although some cases have smaller, irregularly branching vascular channels. Tumors usually involve subcutaneous tissue. Numerous lymphocytes are seen not only in the surrounding stroma but also within the vascular channels. The endothelial cells lining some of the spaces have a prominent atypical nucleus and inconspicuous cytoplasm, giving a typical hobnail or matchstick appearance. Most characteristic is the presence of prominent endothelial intraluminal papillary tufts (Fig. 3.32) with hyaline cores surrounded by lymphocytes. These hyaline cores appear to be composed of basement membrane material synthesized by the tumor cells. Recent immunohistochemical evidence has suggested lymphatic endothelial differentiation,[215] although the specificity of VEGFR3 in this context is questionable.

Differential diagnosis

PILA shares with retiform hemangioendothelioma similar clinical and histologic features, to the point that it has been proposed that retiform hemangioendothelioma might be the adult counterpart of PILA. However, although very similar cytologically, PILA lacks the arborizing architecture of retiform hemangioendothelioma and shows prominent papillary tufts, which are, at best, only poorly developed in the latter. Hobnail hemangioma occurs mainly in children and young adults and in a wide range of anatomic sites, including the oral cavity. Histologically, the lesions tend to be superficial and circumscribed, with a sparse inflammatory infiltrate and only focal hobnail endothelial cells. Large papillary structures are not seen. Angiosarcoma usually occurs in a different clinical setting and is characterized by irregularly infiltrative vascular channels, lined by atypical endothelial cells, which usually show multilayering.

Composite hemangioendothelioma

Composite hemangioendothelioma[217] is the term recently coined for a remarkable group of vascular lesions usually arising in the hands and feet of adult patients. Associated lymphedema is sometimes seen. A single congenital case has

been documented.[218] These lesions behave similarly to retiform hemangioendothelioma, being characterized by frequent local recurrence, while metastasis is rare. However, we have seen occasional cases progress to high-grade angiosarcoma over a period of many years. Histologically, composite hemangioendothelioma generally consists of admixed components of benign, intermediate, and morphologically malignant vascular elements. A combination of epithelioid and retiform hemangioendothelioma is most common. Many cases also have areas indistinguishable from low-grade angiosarcoma (which, in other circumstances, might have heralded more aggressive behavior) and some examples additionally show features of spindle cell hemangioma. In cases with a benign component, areas with features of a lymphangioma may be seen.

Polymorphous hemangioendothelioma

Polymorphous hemangioendothelioma[219,220] is an extremely rare vascular neoplasm, which occurs more often in lymph node than soft tissue. Prolonged follow-up has revealed its ability to metastasize and to pursue a fatal clinical course, suggesting that it may in fact represent an unusual variant of angiosarcoma. Histologically it consists of an unusual admixture of solid, angiomatous, and primitive vascular patterns. Whether this tumor represents a discrete entity remains uncertain.

Kaposi sarcoma (KS)

KS,[221–227] a fascinating entity first described more than 100 years ago, has in the last two decades been the subject of renewed interest in view of its common association with AIDS. Although the cell of origin remains controversial, most evidence points towards endothelial cells, particularly lymphatic endothelium, as the principal cellular component;[228–232] increasingly, however, it would seem that these lesions comprise a mixed-cell population. For many years epidemiologic and clinicopathologic findings suggested that an etiologic association with an infectious organism was likely, and several viral organisms, including cytomegalovirus, were initially implicated as the culprit.[227,233,234] In 1994 there was finally a breakthrough with the identification by polymerase chain reaction of herpesvirus-like sequences in AIDS-associated KS.[235] Since then, this finding has consistently been reproduced in all types of KS, including both the classic and endemic variants.[236,237] The virus, which has been isolated in culture and visualized by electron microscopy, has been designated as HHV-8.[236,238–240] Other neoplasms in which the virus has been reported include AIDS-related body cavity lymphoma,[236] multicentric Castleman's disease,[236] non-melanoma skin cancer in immunocompromised organ transplant patients,[241] and other vascular tumors, including some angiosarcomas.[242] However detection of the virus in the latter tumors has been inconsistent[243,244] and it is unlikely that there is an etiologic association. The isolation of this novel virus in all types of KS seems to give some support to the epidemiologic and clinical evidence that KS is a reactive multifocal vascular process.[245] On the other hand, however, the reported finding of monoclonality in multifocal lesions of KS[246] argues in favor of KS being a neoplastic process in which the virus might have an oncogenic role, although findings in other studies have been contradictory,[247,248] suggesting the possibility that this disease might evolve through a preneoplastic phase. Clearly, more research in this area is needed before this intriguing problem is solved.

Clinical features

KS can be classified into the following clinical groups.[223,225–227]

Classic endemic KS

This presents as indolent tumors in the distal extremities of elderly patients, especially males of Mediterranean or Jewish Ashkenazic origin. Females are very infrequently affected. In this setting, rare familial cases have been reported.[223] Progression to systemic disease is rare but a proportion of cases are associated with hemopoietic neoplasms, especially non-Hodgkin's lymphoma, suggesting the possibility of immune dysregulation in this group of patients also.

AIDS-related KS

This was originally characterized by the presence of disseminated aggressive disease especially, but not exclusively, in young men with AIDS.[223,225,226] In western (as opposed to African) AIDS patients, most cases occur in the homosexual risk group. Organs commonly involved include the skin (Fig. 3.33), gastrointestinal tract, lymph nodes, lungs, and spleen and, less frequently, organs as diverse as liver, kidney, eye, prostate, heart, bladder, gallbladder, thyroid, pancreas, and bone marrow.[249,250] Involvement of muscle, bone, and central nervous system, if existent, must be vanishingly rare. Skin involvement is usually extensive and not confined to the lower limbs; it is characterized by the presence of bluish-brown macules, plaques, or nodules. Mucosal, especially oral, involvement is frequent. Improved treatment of HIV infection has been associated with a markedly reduced incidence of KS in certain populations.

Immunosuppression-associated KS[225,226,251,252]

This rare form of KS presents as an indolent or, rarely, aggressive disease in patients receiving immunosuppressive therapy, especially in relation to kidney transplantation. Regression of lesions is sometimes seen after withdrawal or reduction of immunosuppression.

African KS

For many years, well before the AIDS epidemic, this form of KS has been endemic in sub-Saharan Central Africa, accounting for up to 9% of "malignancies" in some countries, such as Uganda.[225,226] There are two principal categories of endemic African KS: one arises in young children, with generalized lymphadenopathy and a generally fatal course;[245,253,254] another arises in middle-aged adults, especially males, and commonly follows an indolent course, favoring the lower limbs. At least some aggressive cases described in the past might have been related to HIV infection and the commonest form of KS in sub-Saharan Africa is now AIDS-related (see above).

Histologic appearances Regardless of the clinical subgroup, all cases show similar histologic features. Three distinctive stages, which can overlap, are described according to the evolution of a particular lesion: patch, plaque, and nodular stage. The first two stages are seen most often in the context of AIDS, as early lesions are more likely to be biopsied in these patients. Early changes in the patch stage can be very subtle: confusion with an inflammatory dermatosis is possible. In the reticular dermis, especially near the surface and around pre-existing blood vessels and adnexal structures, there is a proliferation of irregular, small, jagged vascular channels lined by a single layer of mildly atypical endothelial cells (Fig. 3.34). These vascular spaces tend to be oriented parallel to the epidermis. Surrounding these vessels there are extravasated red blood cells associated with hemosiderin deposition, and a sparse inflammatory infiltrate composed of lymphocytes and plasma cells (Fig. 3.35). The latter, although not invariably present, are a helpful diagnostic clue. Normal blood vessels

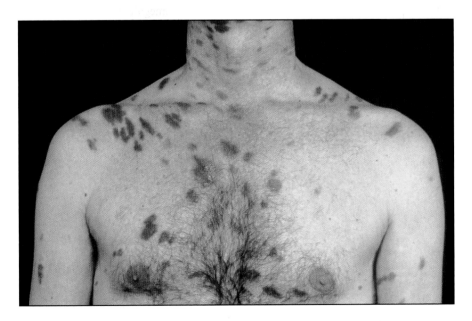

Fig. 3.33 • Kaposi sarcoma. Extensive patch and plaque disease in a young homosexual male with acquired immunodeficiency syndrome (AIDS). (Courtesy of St John's Institute of Dermatology, London, UK.)

and adnexal structures may protrude into the neoformed blood vessels in a fashion described as the "promontory sign." This change, however, is not specific for KS and can be seen in other benign and malignant conditions, including benign lymphangioendothelioma and angiosarcoma. Focally, there is often striking collagen dissection, very similar to that in angiosarcoma. Spindle cells are only occasionally seen around blood vessels. The plaque stage represents an exaggeration of the patch stage with involvement of the whole reticular dermis and even the subcutis. The spindle cell component is more pronounced and hemosiderin deposition becomes more prominent (Fig. 3.36); eosinophilic globules are easily found.

Nodular KS is characterized by a well-circumscribed, most often dermal, tumor composed of intersecting fascicles of uniform spindle cells, which show only mild cytologic atypia and frequent mitotic figures. Between the spindle cells there are numerous slit-like vascular spaces containing extravasated red blood cells (Fig. 3.37). In the periphery of the nodules, ectatic blood vessels may be present. Intra- or extracellular hyaline (eosinophilic) globules (Fig. 3.38), measuring from 0.4 to 10 mm and probably representing degenerate red blood cells, are commonly seen.[223,226,255] These globules, although present in all types of KS, are more frequent in AIDS-related KS.

While the blood vessels in KS show variable reactivity for different endothelial markers, the spindle cell population is usually negative for factor VIII-related antigen but consistently

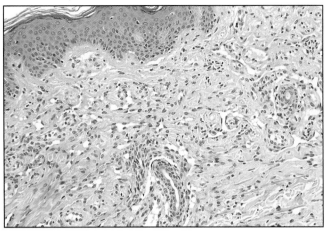

Fig. 3.34 • Patch-stage Kaposi sarcoma. Numerous jagged vascular spaces dissect through the dermis and around skin adnexa.

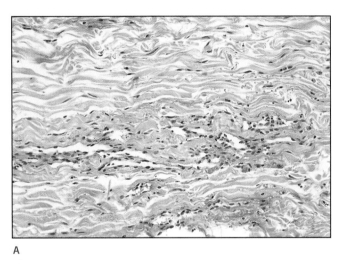

A

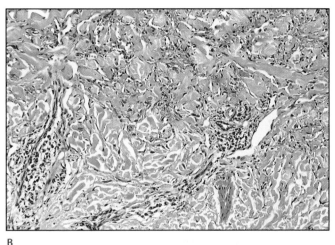

B

Fig. 3.35 • Patch-stage Kaposi sarcoma. The vascular channels tend to be parallel to the epidermis (A) and are commonly associated with extravasated red blood cells, plasma cells, and hemosiderin deposition (B).

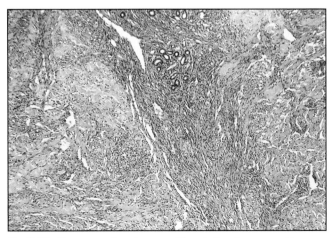

Fig. 3.36 • Plaque-stage Kaposi sarcoma. The spindle cell component is now much more obvious.

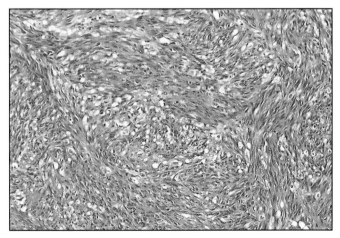

Fig. 3.37 • Nodular Kaposi sarcoma. Monomorphic spindle cells are arranged around slit- or sieve-like spaces.

and extensively positive for CD34 (Fig. 3.39) and also often CD31. Pleomorphism and necrosis are generally not features of nodular KS; vascular or perineural invasion, if they occur, are exceedingly rare. The so-called "lymphangiomatous" variant of KS[256,257] represents classical patch/plaque-stage KS in which proliferating vascular channels dissecting between collagen bundles appear moderately dilated, resembling focally a benign lymphangioendothelioma (Fig. 3.40). The existence of an anaplastic variant of KS, mainly reported in African cases some years ago,[221,258] is controversial and it seems likely that most cases represent other types of tumor, showing clear evidence of malignancy. We have, however, encountered very rare but convincing examples of pleomorphic KS in African patients and a small series on anaplastic transformation of classic KS has been reported.[259]

Recently, a monoclonal antibody against the latent nuclear antigen-1 of HHV8 has become available for use in paraffin-embedded biopsies.[260,261] This represents an invaluable tool in the histologic diagnosis of KS, as this marker is consistently positive in all clinical variants of the disease (Fig. 3.41). Furthermore, other vascular tumors are only exceptionally positive for HHV8.

Differential diagnosis Histologically, the differential diagnosis includes benign lymphangioendothelioma, hobnail hemangioma, spindle cell hemangioma, kaposiform hemangioendothelioma, cutaneous angiosarcoma, acroangiodermatitis, aneurysmal benign fibrous histiocytoma, and so-called multinucleate cell angiohistiocytoma. Clinically, bacillary angiomatosis and pyogenic granuloma can simulate KS but histologic distinction is usually not a problem.

Although it shares with KS the dissection of collagen bundles by newly formed vascular spaces, angiosarcoma shows endothelial multilayering and more cytologic atypia. Aneurysmal benign fibrous histiocytoma is more polymorphic with foam cells, multinucleate giant cells, and absence of vascular clefts. Features of acroangiodermatitis[262] comprise proliferation of small blood vessels of the superficial vascular plexus, commonly in a nodular arrangement, accompanied by fibrosis, hemosiderin deposition, and very few inflammatory cells. As opposed to patch-stage KS, the newly formed blood vessels are smaller and not irregular, there is no involvement of adnexal structures, and plasma cells are not conspicuous. In multinucleate cell angiohistiocytoma, the lesion is more circumscribed and contains giant cells and scattered non-irregular

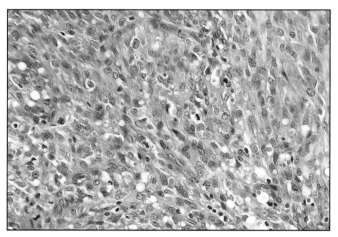

Fig. 3.38 • Nodular Kaposi sarcoma. Note the numerous eosinophilic hyaline globules.

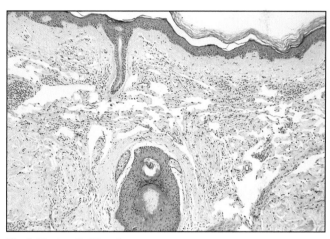

Fig. 3.40 • So-called "lymphangiomatous" Kaposi sarcoma. Note the resemblance to benign lymphangioendothelioma except for the stromal spindle and inflammatory cells.

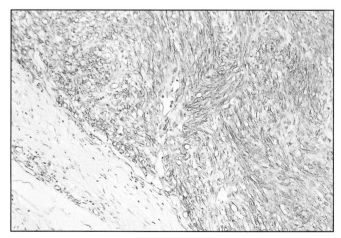

Fig. 3.39 • Nodular Kaposi sarcoma. The spindle cell component is consistently CD34-positive.

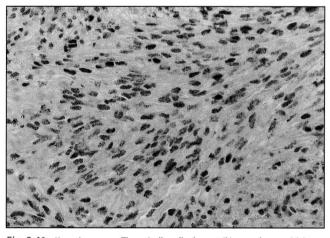

Fig. 3.41 • Kaposi sarcoma. The spindle cells show striking nuclear positivity for human herpesvirus 8.

blood vessels, which are not located around pre-existing normal blood vessels.

Malignant vascular tumors

Epithelioid hemangioendothelioma

Clinical features

Epithelioid hemangioendothelioma, described as a distinctive entity in soft tissues in 1982,[263] is a low-grade malignant vascular neoplasm in the spectrum of epithelioid endothelial tumors.[150,264] We regard this tumor, however, as fully malignant in view of its significant morbidity and mortality (see below).[265] Previously, similar cases were classified with other epithelioid lesions under the term histiocytoid hemangioma.[146,266] Identical tumors occur in other organs, including the lung (where they were formerly known as intravascular bronchiolo-alveolar tumor),[267] liver,[268] bone,[269] pleura and peritoneum,[270] skin,[271–274] lymph node,[219] and even stomach,[275] brain, and meninges.[264] In lung, liver, and bone, multicentricity is common (see Chs 5, 10, and 25). In soft tissue, 30–50% of the lesions arise from a large or medium-sized blood vessel, especially a vein,[264–266,276] and this tumor can therefore arise potentially from any organ. Epithelioid hemangioendothelioma occurs over a wide age range, but is commonest in middle-aged adults; it is distinctly rare in children.[277] Soft tissue lesions have no sex predilection, as opposed to those in the lung and liver, where females predominate. Tumors in soft tissue are usually solitary, in contrast to the multicentricity at other sites, which can be mistaken for metastasis. Clinical presentation varies according to the organ involved; in soft tissue, as well as a mass, symptoms such as intractable pain can be related to the effects of vascular occlusion by tumor. Up to 30% of soft tissue cases are associated with metastasis. Reported mortality rates vary from 17% in soft tissue[265] to 43% in liver,[268] and 65% in lung.[264]

Histologic appearances

Macroscopically, these tumors typically have a pale, very firm, and sometimes rather hyaline appearance, especially when arising in deep soft tissue. Most tumors are ill defined and infiltrative and are composed of round polygonal, or less commonly, short spindle-shaped endothelial cells with variable amounts of glassy pink cytoplasm and a vesicular nucleus with inconspicuous nucleolus. Tumor cells are arranged in cords, small nests, or short trabeculae surrounded by a variably hyaline or myxoid stroma, which commonly has a rather chondroid appearance (Fig. 3.42). Prominent cytoplasmic vacuoles containing occasional erythrocytes, reminiscent of primitive vascular channels, are frequently seen (Fig. 3.43), but well-formed blood vessels are, at best, only focally present. When the tumor arises from a blood vessel, the cells fill the lumen and extend centrifugally through the wall into the surrounding tissue. Complete occlusion or obliteration of the pre-existing vessel is common. A reticulin stain shows a tubular pattern, highlighting the vascular architecture (Fig. 3.44). In

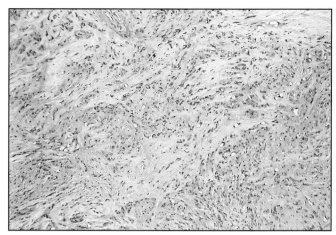

Fig. 3.42 • Epithelioid hemangioendothelioma. Typically cord-like growth pattern in a hyaline stroma.

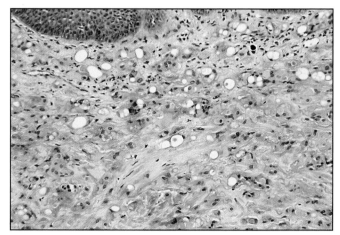

Fig. 3.43 • Epithelioid hemangioendothelioma. Note the prominent intracytoplasmic lumina and intraluminal red blood cells in this dermal lesion.

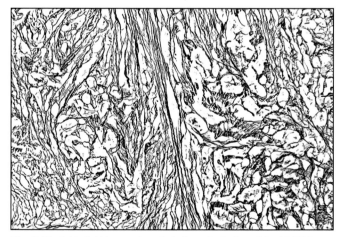

Fig. 3.44 • Epithelioid hemangioendothelioma. Reticulin staining highlights the vasoformative architecture.

some cases, dystrophic calcification and metaplastic ossification are prominent features.[265,278] Stromal inflammation is generally not a prominent feature but some cases are associated with a prominent osteoclast-like giant cell reaction.[278–280] What appears possibly to be a variant of epithelioid hemangioendothelioma has been described as spindle and histiocytoid (epithelioid) hemangioendothelioma. Cases have so far only been described in lymph node and spleen.[150,219,281,282]

Although tumor cells are usually only mildly atypical, with a low mitotic count, there is a spectrum of morphology, sometimes within the same lesion; a small proportion of cases show larger nests of cells with prominent cytologic atypia and high mitotic count[264,265] (Fig. 3.45), and even areas indistinguishable from epithelioid angiosarcoma can be seen. Cases with such features are usually associated with a poor prognosis and have been labeled malignant.[264,265] Although there is no clear correlation between histologic features and prognosis, there is a trend for striking nuclear atypia, mitotic count, and angiosarcoma-like foci to be associated with poor clinical outcome.

Immunohistochemically, most epithelioid hemangio-endotheliomas show a typical vascular phenotype with expression of endothelial markers, most notably CD31 (Fig. 3.46) and von Willebrand factor. Up to 45% of cases show positivity for α-smooth muscle actin and 26% show positivity for cytokeratin[265,283,284] (Fig. 3.47). As opposed to epithelial tumors, epithelial membrane antigen (EMA) is usually negative. The keratin positivity, which is most frequent in lesions arising in bone, most likely reflects the high intermediate filament content of the cell cytoplasm. Cytogenetic studies in two cases of epithelioid hemangioendothelioma have shown a translocation t(1;3)(p36.3;q25).[285]

Differential diagnosis

The main differential diagnosis, especially in parenchymal organs and bone, is with metastatic or primary carcinoma. Helpful distinguishing features are the presence of erythrocytes and absence of mucin in the cytoplasmic vacuoles of epithelioid hemangioendothelioma, coupled with the immunopositivity for vascular markers. Also, the degree of nuclear pleomorphism in carcinomas is usually more pronounced. In soft tissues, the differential diagnosis also includes epithelioid sarcoma.[286] The latter generally shows a more sheet-like growth pattern (at least in areas), only occasional cytoplasmic vacuoles, and is positive for both keratin and EMA, often CD34-positive, but negative for more specific endothelial markers such as CD31 or von Willebrand factor. Cases with a very prominent myxoid stroma can be confused with myxoid liposarcoma or myxoid chondrosarcoma but the latter has a lobular architecture, lacks cytoplasmic vacuoles, and is S-100 protein-positive. Myxoid liposarcoma is best distinguished by identification of the typical branching vascular pattern and small multivacuolated lipoblasts.

Angiosarcoma

This term covers lesions previously known as lymphangiosarcoma and malignant hemangioendothelioma, as there are no currently reliable means of distinguishing blood vascular from lymphatic endothelial differentiation (or origin). It is likely that individual cases of angiosarcoma may differentiate in either or both directions. We will refer here mainly to cutaneous and soft tissue angiosarcomas, as visceral lesions are described in their relevant chapters. Interestingly, angiosarcomas of deep soft tissue were formerly regarded as exceedingly rare but they are more often recognized nowadays, perhaps because their

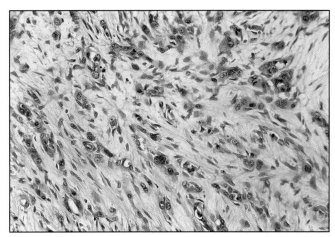

Fig. 3.45 • "Malignant" epithelioid hemangioendothelioma. This lesion shows more cytologic atypia and small, solid clusters of cells.

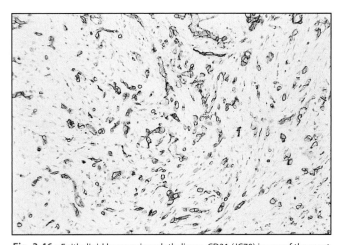

Fig. 3.46 • Epithelioid hemangioendothelioma. CD31 (JC70) is one of the most sensitive immunohistochemical markers of endothelial differentiation.

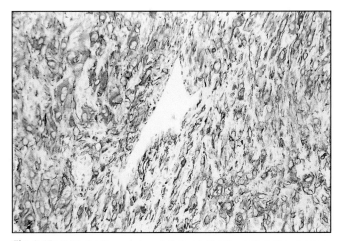

Fig. 3.47 • Epithelioid hemangioendothelioma. Keratin positivity is a common finding, although this is not as consistent as in epithelioid angiosarcoma. Note the negatively stained normal endothelium.

predominant epithelioid cytomorphology was easily mistaken for epithelial or mesothelial differentiation in the past.

Cutaneous angiosarcoma[287-292] almost always occurs in one of three different clinical settings: (1) idiopathic angiosarcoma of the head and neck; (2) lymphedema-associated angiosarcoma; and (3) postirradiation angiosarcoma. Vinyl chloride exposure, an association frequently considered in hepatic angiosarcoma, has been reported only exceptionally in cutaneous angiosarcoma.[293] Very rarely angiosarcoma can arise within a large blood vessel,[294] a hemangioma, or a vascular malformation,[295] nerve,[296] a plexiform neurofibroma in a patient with neurofibromatosis,[297] a schwannoma,[296,298] or as part of a malignant peripheral nerve sheath tumor.[296,299] It may also rarely develop as the sarcomatous component in a malignant germ-cell tumor. Angiosarcoma in children is very rare[300,301] and exceptionally can be associated with xeroderma pigmentosum.[302,303] Exceptional cases of angiosarcoma have also been documented with epidermolysis bullosa,[304] chronic venous ulceration,[305] in association with morbid obesity,[306] and in a gouty tophus.[307] An association with immunosuppression in transplant patients has also been reported, however HHV-8 plays no evident role in the pathogenesis of angiosarcomas.[308,309,309a]

Idiopathic angiosarcoma of the face, neck, and scalp

Idiopathic angiosarcoma typically presents in elderly patients, with a higher incidence in males, as multifocal bruise-like erythematous-purplish areas, plaques, and nodules, especially on the scalp and central face (Fig. 3.48).[287–292,310] The clinical diagnosis may be missed in atypical cases presenting as diffuse facial edema. The prognosis is very poor, with a 5-year survival rate of between 12% and 33%.[310,311] A study combining angiosarcoma of the face and scalp with angiosarcomas occurring in internal organs has reported an overall 5-year survival of 24%.[312] Death is usually due to extensive local disease or widespread metastasis, especially to the lungs. Younger patients appear to have a better prognosis and radiation therapy appears to improve survival.[313,314]

Lymphedema-associated angiosarcoma[315–322]

This type of tumor has often been known as lymphangiosarcoma. Classically, it arises in the arm of females 1–30 years after mastectomy with removal of axillary lymph nodes, with or without radiation therapy (Stewart–Treves syndrome). Although there may be overlap with radiation-induced angiosarcoma, most cases occur outside the radiation field. Clinically gross lymphedema is not always apparent. More rarely this type of angiosarcoma can also occur in other types of chronic lymphedema, including congenital lymphedema, iatrogenic lymphedema, lymphatic malformations, and filarial lymphedema. The clinical appearances consist of bluish plaques, nodules, and vesicles involving large areas of the affected limb. Prognosis is similar to that of idiopathic angiosarcoma.

Postradiation angiosarcoma[323–326]

This was formerly rare but is an increasingly common variant and usually presents many years after radiation therapy for benign or malignant conditions. By far the most frequent are lesions arising in skin or less often parenchyma of the breast after breast-conserving therapy for carcinoma. In cutaneous postirradiation angiosarcoma of the breast there is usually no associated lymphedema and the latency period is shorter than that in Stewart–Treves syndrome.[327] Some cases of postradiation angiosarcoma of the breast may be associated with chronic lymphedema and this may contribute to the development of the disease.[328] The prognosis generally appears to be just as ominous as in other types of angiosarcoma, although the cause may be somewhat more indolent.

Soft tissue angiosarcoma[291,329,330]

As mentioned above, although angiosarcomas in deep soft tissue were regarded in the past as rare, they are nowadays diagnosed with increasing frequency, perhaps due to altered diagnostic criteria and sensitivity, since the majority of cases show epithelioid cytomorphology (see below). These tumors are most common in older adults, with a predilection for males, and arise most often in the lower limb or abdominal cavity (including retroperitoneum). Some are associated with prior radiation. Five-year survival, as for cutaneous lesions, is at best 20–30%.

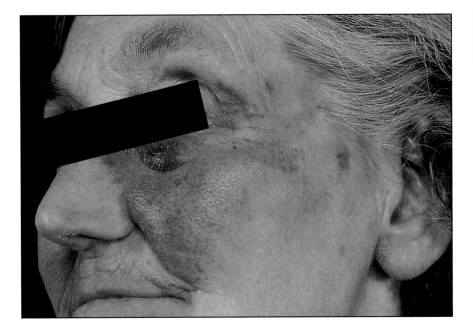

Fig. 3.48 • Cutaneous angiosarcoma. Typical bruise-like head lesion in an elderly patient. (Courtesy of St John's Institute of Dermatology, London, UK.)

Histologic appearances The histologic features of cutaneous angiosarcoma occurring in each clinical setting are very similar and show a wide spectrum of appearances, ranging from clearly vasoformative to poorly differentiated solid tumors in which the vascular nature is not readily apparent. The typical case is an infiltrative dermal tumor, composed of numerous, irregular, anastomosing vascular spaces with a distinctive dissecting pattern between collagen bundles (Fig. 3.49). Invasion of the subcutis and even skeletal muscle and periosteum can be seen. The vascular channels are lined by variably pleomorphic, hyperchromatic endothelial cells which frequently show multilayering and papillary growth (Fig. 3.50). Normal and abnormal mitoses are easily found. Solid areas are not uncommon and poorly differentiated lesions can be predominantly solid with no obvious suggestion of a vascular architecture (Fig. 3.51). A reticulin stain is very useful, especially in the latter tumors, to highlight better differentiated areas in which the neoformed blood vessels are encircled by a reticulin sheath. In perhaps 5% of tumors epithelioid cells predominate (Fig. 3.52).[331] A very rare variant of angiosarcoma composed predominantly of granular cells has been reported.[332,333] An inflammatory infiltrate is usually present and can be prominent. It has been suggested that a heavy mononuclear inflammatory infiltrate correlates with a better prognosis[310] and that a high mitotic rate correlates with poor prognosis,[334,335] although, in our experience, histologic features (including grade) do not correlate reliably with outcome, and tumor size or resectability seems more important.

In poorly differentiated tumors, immunohistochemistry may be helpful as angiosarcoma is variably positive for different endothelial markers. While many cases are factor VIII-related antigen-negative, a higher proportion stain for CD31, von Willebrand factor (monoclonal) (Fig. 3.53), or, less specifically, CD34. Recently, Fli-1, a marker of Ewing's sarcoma, has been described as having similar sensitivity and specificity to CD31 in the diagnosis of vascular neoplasms,[336] but in our experience is less specific. The demonstration of endothelial cell features by electron microscopy, especially Weibel–Palade bodies, is also occasionally useful, but these are often very hard to find in cutaneous lesions. Cytogenetic analysis in a few

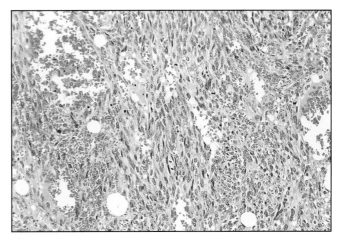
Fig. 3.51 • Poorly differentiated angiosarcoma. Solid spindle-celled lesions may be hard to diagnose.

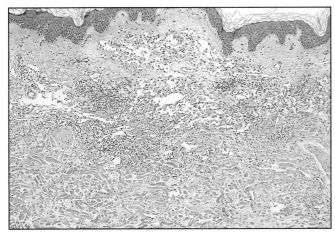
Fig. 3.49 • Cutaneous angiosarcoma. Note the numerous vascular channels dissecting between collagen bundles.

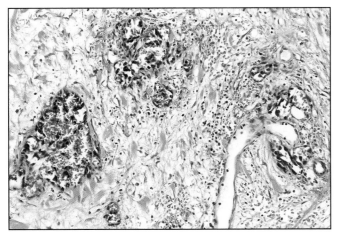
Fig. 3.50 • Cutaneous angiosarcoma. Endothelial multilayering and marked nuclear atypia are evident in this case.

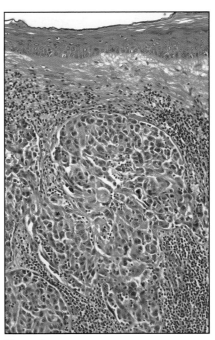
Fig. 3.52 • Cutaneous epithelioid angiosarcoma. Cases such as this in the skin may easily be mistaken for melanoma or carcinoma.

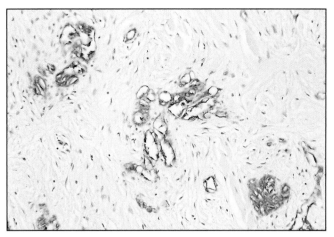

Fig. 3.53 • Lymphedema-associated angiosarcoma. This tumor from the foot is positive for von Willebrand factor.

deep and superficial angiosarcomas has shown complex chromosomal abnormalities mainly involving chromosomes 5, 7, 8, 13, 15, 20, 22, and Y.[337]

Differential diagnosis The distinction between angiosarcoma and benign vascular tumors has already been described elsewhere in this chapter. Atypical vascular lesions (see p. 69) can develop in the skin of the breast after radiotherapy for breast cancer and can be misdiagnosed as angiosarcoma.[324] The former, however, consist of focal proliferation of dilated vascular spaces with a single layer of hyperchromatic endothelial cells with no multilayering or mitotic figures. Poorly differentiated angiosarcoma can simulate other spindle cell sarcomas, melanoma, and carcinoma. In these cases the use of reticulin stains, immunohistochemistry, and (more rarely) electron microscopy is very helpful in reaching the correct diagnosis. It is important to remember that, among endothelial markers, *Ulex europaeus* lectin type I is also positive in many carcinomas.

Epithelioid angiosarcoma

Clinical features Epithelioid angiosarcoma is a distinctive but uncommon tumor, representing the malignant end of the spectrum of epithelioid vascular neoplasms.[150,329] This term is reserved for neoplasms composed almost exclusively of epithelioid cells, as conventional angiosarcomas may also show epithelioid foci. This histologic variant was originally recognized in the thyroid gland, particularly in association with endemic goiter.[338,339] Although its occurrence in skin and soft tissue has been acknowledged in the past, it was only fairly recently delineated as a distinctive entity.[329] While the majority of cases occur in deep soft tissue (see above), occasional cases also occur in the adrenal gland,[340] and individual cases have been described arising in sites such as pleura,[270] pulmonary artery,[341] breast,[342] bone,[343] and vagina.[344] Cutaneous[331,345] and the more common soft tissue examples usually present in middle age to late adult life; there is a marked male predominance. Lesions generally grow rapidly and have no distinctive clinical features other than the development of hemorrhagic cutaneous satellite lesions in some patients. Some cases arise as a type of malignant change in schwannomas[298] and rare cases have been associated with a foreign body,[346] an arteriovenous

fistula,[330,347,348] or previous irradiation.[329,330,349] Exceptionally epithelioid angiosarcoma originating in another organ may metastasize to the skin.[350] Most cases have a very aggressive clinical course, with the development of systemic metastasis and death within 2–3 years of presentation in most patients. Claims by some that cutaneous examples have an improved prognosis await independent verification.

Histologic appearances Epithelioid angiosarcoma commonly shows necrosis and hemorrhage. It is composed of solid sheets (Fig. 3.54) of large, oval or rounded, epithelioid cells with abundant eosinophilic or amphophilic cytoplasm, having a large, pale vesicular nucleus with a conspicuous eosinophilic nucleolus. Pleomorphism is not marked but mitoses are frequent. Focally, some cells show intracytoplasmic vacuoles, occasionally containing red blood cells. At least focal blood vessel formation can be identified in most cases and this is associated rarely with a papillary arrangement. Origin from a large blood vessel is evident in some cases. A reticulin stain typically reveals a tubular vasoformative architecture (Fig. 3.55). Immunohistochemically, tumor cells are positive for factor VIII-related antigen and CD31 in almost all cases. Positivity for cytokeratin is also a feature in around 50% of cases, while only rare cases are focally positive for EMA.

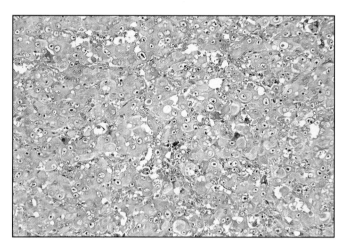

Fig. 3.54 • Epithelioid angiosarcoma. Note the sheet-like growth pattern and very prominent nucleoli.

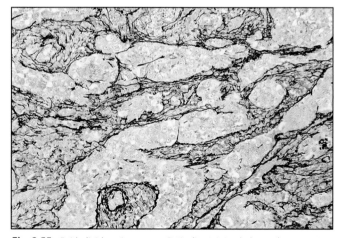

Fig. 3.55 • Epithelioid angiosarcoma. Reticulin staining helps to demonstrate the tubular vasoformative architecture.

Differential diagnosis Epithelioid angiosarcoma has to be included in the differential diagnosis of almost any epithelioid malignant neoplasm, including metastatic carcinoma, mesothelioma, melanoma, epithelioid sarcoma, and epithelioid malignant schwannoma, especially when located in skin and soft tissues. Recognition is usually possible by the identification of intracytoplasmic lumina, vasoformative areas, and, most importantly, positivity of tumor cells for specific endothelial markers (especially factor VIII-related antigen and CD31).

"Intimal" sarcomas

Primary sarcomas of major blood vessels are rare, altogether fewer than 200 cases have been reported in the literature.[351–360] Although most mural sarcomas, especially those presenting in large veins such as the inferior vena cava, are leiomyosarcomas,[355] there is a group of luminal sarcomas which appear to arise from the intima and are therefore known as intimal sarcomas. Most of these cases present in the aorta or pulmonary artery as poorly differentiated spindle cell sarcomas. They may rarely show immunohistochemical evidence of endothelial differentiation but are more commonly positive for smooth muscle actin.[360] Most recently, positivity for osteopontin has also been documented.[358] However a large proportion are only positive for vimentin. Based on these findings it has been proposed that intimal sarcomas arise from intimal endothelial cells, fibroblasts, or myofibroblasts. These lesions are virtually confined to adulthood and are associated with a very poor prognosis. A study of a small number of cases by comparative genomic hybridization has shown that the most consistent cytogenetic abnormality consists of gains and amplifications 12q13-14.[360]

Tumors of lymph vessels

Tumors of lymphatic vessels are much less common than hemangiomas and comprise about 4% of all vascular tumors.[18] The great majority of tumors are benign and it is believed that most of them represent developmental malformations rather than true neoplasms. Distinction between tumors of lymphatic vessels and blood vessels is not always possible, even with the use of immunohistochemistry or electron microscopy, and in some lesions there is a combination of both vessel types as, for example, in intramuscular angioma (see above). Lymphangiomas can be classified into five main types: (1) cavernous lymphangioma; (2) cystic hygroma; (3) lymphangioma circumscriptum; (4) the more recently characterized acquired progressive lymphangioma (benign lymphangioendothelioma); and (5) lymphangiomatosis. It is doubtful whether capillary lymphangioma exists.

Cavernous lymphangioma and cystic hygroma

Clinical features

Both conditions are described together, as cystic hygroma appears simply to be a variant of cavernous lymphangioma in which there is macroscopic dilatation of the vascular channels. It seems that cystic hygromas develop at anatomic sites in which there is less resistance to expansion from surrounding structures.[361] Most lesions present at birth or in the first years of life, with an equal sex incidence;[362–364] a minority of cases are detected in adults.[365] Cystic hygromas tend to occur more commonly in the neck, axillae, and groins, while cavernous lymphangioma also occurs in the oral cavity (especially the tongue), limbs, and abdomen (principally the mesentery and less often the retroperitoneum). Although both lesions are prone to local recurrence, this is more common in cavernous lymphangioma.

Histologic appearances

The dermis, subcutis, or deeper tissues contain dilated thin-walled lymphatic channels lined by attenuated, bland endothelial cells (Fig. 3.56), which rarely can be plump or cuboidal. Vascular lumina may be empty or contain proteinaceous lymph, lymphocytes, and occasional erythrocytes. In the surrounding stroma there are variable numbers of lymphocytes and, rarely, lymphoid follicles. Around larger channels there is often an incomplete layer of smooth muscle (Fig. 3.57). Long-standing lesions can show prominent stromal fibrosis. For reasons that are somewhat unclear, intra-abdominal examples may present acutely and histologically such cases are associated with

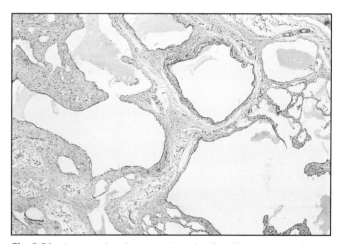

Fig. 3.56 • Cavernous lymphangioma. Note the dilated lymphatic vessels with variably thick walls.

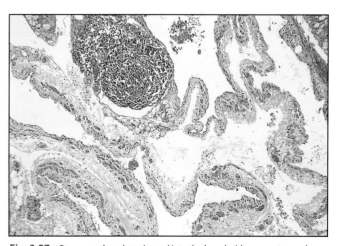

Fig. 3.57 • Cavernous lymphangioma. Note the lymphoid aggregates and prominent smooth muscle in some of the vessel walls.

marked inflammation, adjacent fat necrosis, and reactive changes.[366]

Differential diagnosis

Distinction from cavernous hemangioma may sometimes be impossible, especially in the presence of hemorrhage and intraluminal erythrocytes. The finding of lymphoid aggregates tends to favor the diagnosis of lymphangioma. Lesions in the peritoneum have to be distinguished from cystic mesothelioma, which usually shows more variation in the size of the cystic spaces and in which the lining cells are positive for keratin and negative for endothelial markers.

Lymphangioma circumscriptum

Clinical features

Lymphangioma circumscriptum presents as a developmental malformation in infancy, often in association with cavernous lymphangioma, cystic hygroma, or lymphangiomatosis, or as an acquired lesion in adults, usually in relation to radiotherapy or chronic lymphedema.[367–369] This latter form is better regarded as lymphangiectasia. There is an equal sex incidence and lesions can occur at any site, with predilection for the limbs. Clinically, they are characterized by the presence of numerous asymptomatic, circumscribed vesicles containing clear fluid or blood. Recurrence after excision is common only in those lesions developing in childhood.

Histologic appearances

The lesions are composed of numerous dilated lymphatic vessels in the superficial and papillary dermis, associated with overlying epidermal hyperplasia (Fig. 3.58) and a lymphocytic infiltrate in the surrounding stroma. Often the lymphatic channels appear almost to be intraepidermal, due to crosscutting. Some lesions, especially those in children, are connected with a deep muscular lymphatic, which, if not ligated when the lesion is excised, is associated with a high rate of local recurrence.[370]

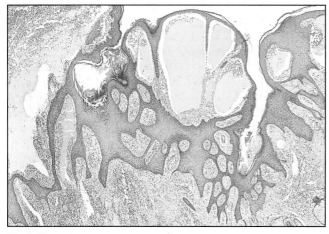

Fig. 3.58 • Lymphangioma circumscriptum. Note the dilated lymphatics in the papillary dermis and the associated inflammation, a common secondary feature.

Benign lymphangioendothelioma (acquired progressive lymphangioma)

Clinical features

Benign lymphangioendothelioma (acquired progressive lymphangioma) is a rare, benign lymphatic abnormality. Although it was described as early as 1970 under the name angioendothelioma (lymphatic type),[371] relatively few cases have been reported in the literature since that time.[372–375] While any age group may be affected, there is a predilection for middle-aged to older adults. The incidence is equal in males and females. Most lesions are located on the extremities, especially the lower limb, but this lesion also occurs on the face, back, and abdomen. Clinically, it presents as a solitary, well-defined erythematous macule or plaque that can mimic a bruise but which slowly enlarges over a period of years. A published report of multifocal progressive lymphangioma is more likely to represent an example of lymphangiomatosis.[376] Lesions only very rarely recur after simple excision, and focal, but subtotal, spontaneous regression has been described.[377] Exceptional cases have been said to occur after radiotherapy[378] and after arteriography.[379]

Histologic appearances

The typical lesion consists of horizontal, irregular thin-walled vascular channels, showing dissection of collagen bundles and an anastomosing growth pattern; these spaces are lined by a single layer of flat endothelial cells with, at most, only very mild cytologic atypia (Fig. 3.59). Their lumina often appear empty or contain a few red blood cells and/or proteinaceous material. Although most channels are located in the superficial dermis, extension into the deep dermis and subcutaneous tissue is sometimes seen. Involvement of the papillary dermis is not

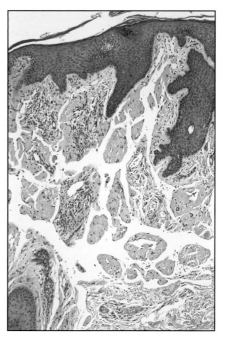

Fig. 3.59 • Benign lymphangioendothelioma ("progressive lymphangioma"). Note the dissection of collagen but complete absence of endothelial atypia.

present and there is no connection with deep large muscular lymphatics, as seen in lymphangioma circumscriptum.

Differential diagnosis

In view of the presence of collagen dissection by vascular channels, the main differential diagnosis is with well-differentiated angiosarcoma, despite the differences in clinical setting. Distinction from the latter is based on the absence of significant endothelial atypia, multilayering, or mitotic activity in progressive lymphangioma. Patch-stage KS is clinically multifocal and shows histologically irregular vascular channels around pre-existing dermal vessels and adnexa, associated with plasma cells and extravasation of red blood cells with hemosiderin deposition. Although clinically different, benign lymphangioendothelioma may show a striking architectural resemblance to hobnail hemangioma. The former, however, generally lacks prominent hobnail cells, intraluminal red cells are sparse, and hemosiderin deposition is usually less conspicuous.

Lymphangiomatosis

Lymphangiomatosis is a very rare developmental abnormality characterized by diffuse involvement of parenchymal organs, bone, and/or soft tissue.[380,381] In a significant proportion of cases, the disease is confined to one limb with or without bone involvement.[382] Typically, it presents in children, sometimes from birth, with no sex predilection.[381,382] There may be clinical overlap with conventional angiomatosis or other vascular malformations and in some cases a firm diagnosis cannot be made without angiography. Cases in soft tissue present as diffuse, boggy, fluctuant swellings, which can be associated with a cutaneous fistula or, less often, as lesions indistinguishable from lymphangioma circumscriptum. Involvement of visceral organs, as opposed to soft tissues and bone, is associated with a poor prognosis.[381]

Histologic appearances in soft tissue can simulate those of cavernous lymphangioma or, more commonly, those of benign lymphangioendothelioma, with typically extensive dissection of collagen reminiscent of angiosarcoma. However, the lymphatic channels are far more extensive and involve dermis and subcutis widely (Fig. 3.60). An additional finding, especially in lymphangiomatosis of soft tissues, is the presence of abundant hemosiderin in the interstitium despite the relative absence of red blood cells in the vascular lumina. Long-standing cases show prominent stromal fibrosis.

Atypical vascular lesions after radiotherapy

Angiomatous lesions rarely present in the field of prior radiation therapy, most often in the skin of the breast.[324,383–385] Histology of some of these lesions may display atypical features, raising the possibility of a postirradiation angiosarcoma, and these are the ones described here.

Lesions usually develop a few years after radiotherapy for breast cancer. The time elapsed between radiotherapy and development of the lesions is usually shorter than that for angiosarcomas.[385] The clinical presentation is not distinctive and varies from skin-coloured to red, usually multiple macules and papules.

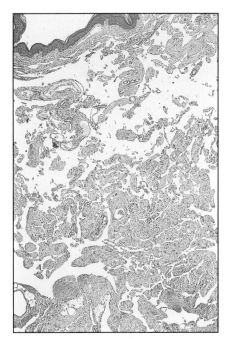

Fig. 3.60 • Lymphangiomatosis. Note the very extensive, diffuse dissection between normal structures.

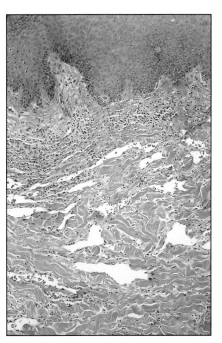

Fig. 3.61 • Atypical postradiation vascular proliferation. This skin lesion from the breast is composed of architecturally atypical lymphatic-like channels but there is no endothelial multilayering or pleomorphism.

The histologic features vary and occasional lesions may resemble lymphangioma circumscriptum[368] or benign lymphangioendothelioma.[378] Most biopsies show irregular, variably dilated lymphatic-like vascular channels lined by a single layer of endothelial cells in the superficial and/or deep dermis. The lesions are usually fairly circumscribed but may have a dissecting growth pattern. The endothelial cells lining the channels are flat or have a somewhat hyperchromatic hobnail appearance and papillary projections may occasionally be seen (Fig. 3.61). There is no nuclear pleomorphism or endothelial multilayering and mitoses are usually absent.

The differential diagnosis includes well-differentiated angiosarcoma, hobnail hemangioma, and KS. As opposed to hobnail hemangioma, the lesion is not symmetrical, and the vascular channels do not always have a predominantly superficial dermal location. However, in some cases this distinction may be impossible on morphologic grounds and may best be predicated on the history of radiation. The clinical setting, the absence of inflammation, and the presence of hobnail endothelial cells with focal papillary projections should allow distinction from KS. Careful examination of multiple sections is recommended to make sure that there are no mitotic figures and cytologic atypia to distinguish it from a well-differentiated angiosarcoma.

Lymphangiomyomatosis

Lymphangiomyomatosis is a very rare hamartomatous condition characterized by diffuse proliferation of smooth muscle within lymphatics and lymph nodes of the retroperitoneum, mediastinum, and, in up to 70% of cases, the lung parenchyma.[386–388] When the condition is localized, it is usually referred to as lymphangiomyoma. It presents exclusively in women, mainly during the reproductive years, suggesting a hormonal role in its pathogenesis. However, this relationship is controversial.[388–390] Patients present with dyspnea, pneumothorax, and chylothorax and, when involvement is extensive, the disease commonly pursues a fatal course unless lung transplantation is performed.[386–388] There is a well-recognized association with renal angiomyolipoma and some patients with tuberous sclerosis develop lymphangiomyomatosis.[388,391] It has now also been demonstrated that sporadic lymphangiomyomatosis is tightly linked to a mutation of one of the tuberous sclerosis complex genes (*TSC2*) on chromosome 16.[392,393]

Histologically, the lesions are composed of lymphatic channels surrounded by clusters of bland smooth muscle cells, often with somewhat granular cytoplasm, arranged in short fascicles (Fig. 3.62). Immunohistochemically, these cells express a typical smooth muscle phenotype and are also positive consistently for HMB-45, a melanoma-associated marker that reacts with a premelanosome-associated glycoprotein;[394] similar staining may also be seen for MART-1.[395] This

reactivity is shared with the smooth muscle component in angiomyolipomas (but not with any other type of smooth muscle) and also with clear cell (sugar) tumors of the lung and other locations. Although this may reflect cross-reaction with a different protein, it identifies a distinctive subtype of perivascular smooth muscle cells (referred to as perivascular epithelioid cells[396] – see Ch. 24), and this phenotype may be helpful in differential diagnosis.

Tumors of perivascular cells

Glomus tumor

Clinical features

Glomus tumors[397–399] arise from a modified smooth muscle cell located in the walls of specialized arteriovenous anastomoses (the Sucquet–Hoyer canal) involved in temperature regulation. These lesions are relatively common and occur most often in young adults; there is no sex predilection except for digital and subungual lesions, which tend to predominate in females. Most tumors are less than 1 cm in diameter and develop in the dermis or subcutis of the upper and lower extremities, especially the hands; any site, however, including mucosae and visceral locations, can be affected. Cutaneous lesions present as red-blue nodules and may be associated with paroxysmal pain in relation to tactile stimulation. Pain is most often a feature of the histologically solid type of lesion (see below).

Multiple lesions are seen occasionally, most often in children, and most are thought to be inherited in an autosomal dominant fashion.[400,401] The genetic aberration associated with multiple inherited glomangiomas has been linked to chromosome 1p21-22.[402,403] The gene has been named glomulin.[404] When multiple, these lesions often simulate cavernous hemangiomas and can be confused clinically with the lesions seen in the blue rubber bleb nevus syndrome. Rare cases of glomus tumor can occur at a wide variety of sites, including the trachea, lung, mediastinum, stomach, small bowel, colon, rectum, mesentery, bone, vagina, cervix, pterygoid fossa, liver, pancreas, ovary, and even in an ovarian teratoma.[405–416] Very rarely a glomus tumor can originate within a blood vessel[417,418] or a nerve.[419] An association between subungual glomus tumors and von Recklinghausen's disease (neurofibromatosis type 1) has also been described.[420–422] Multiple gastric lesions with intravascular spread and benign behavior have been described exceptionally.[423] It is important to be aware of a normal prominent glomus body, the glomus coccygeum located near the tip of the coccyx, that can measure up to several millimeters; if found incidentally, this can be confused with a neoplasm.[424]

The majority of glomus tumors are entirely benign and local recurrence is very uncommon.[399,425] Despite worrying histologic features in occasional cases (see below), malignant glomus tumors (or glomangiosarcomas) are very rare.[426–430]

Histologic appearances

Histologically, most glomus tumors are well circumscribed and composed of varying proportions of glomus cells, blood vessels, and smooth muscle. Glomangiomas are by far the most common, accounting for up to 60% of glomus tumors

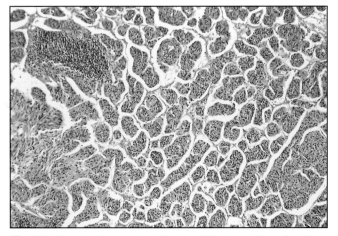

Fig. 3.62 • Lymphangiomyomatosis. Nodules of bland smooth muscle cells arranged around numerous lymphatic channels.

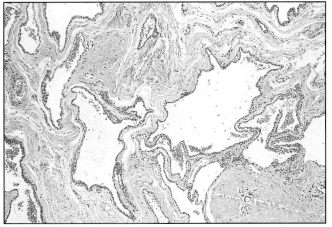

Fig. 3.63 • Glomangioma. In this commonest variant of glomus tumor, attenuated layers of glomus cells are sometimes overlooked.

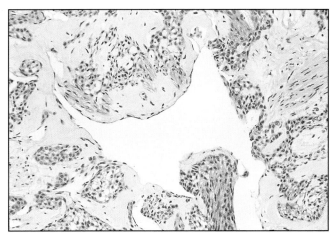

Fig. 3.65 • Glomangiomyoma. Many of the tumor cells are eosinophilic and spindle-shaped.

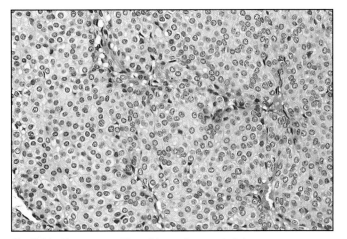

Fig. 3.64 • Glomus tumor. The solid type shows typical glomus cytomorphology with well-defined cell margins.

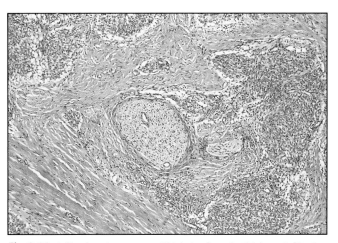

Fig. 3.66 • Infiltrating glomus tumor. This lesion from the thigh was infiltrating in and around the femoral nerve. (Courtesy of Dr W.K. Blenkinsopp.)

(Fig. 3.63). They are followed by solid glomus tumors (Fig. 3.64; 25% of cases) and glomangiomyomas (Fig. 3.65; 15% of cases). A typical solid glomus tumor is composed of numerous monotonous, rounded glomus cells with palely eosinophilic cytoplasm and a large central round or oval punched-out uniform nucleus. Cell borders are typically sharply defined and can be highlighted by PAS positivity. The surrounding stroma often appears edematous and can show extensive myxoid degeneration. Small blood vessels are scattered between the tumor cells but they are usually difficult to detect in the absence of special stains. Rare variants of glomus tumor showing oncocytic change[431] or composed predominantly of epithelioid cells[432] have been described. In glomangiomas and glomangiomyomas the proportion of glomus cells varies and in some cases they are only seen as a thin rim around blood vessels. In glomangiomyomas, the proportion of tumor composed of well-formed smooth muscle bundles is also variable. In the vicinity of glomus tumors it is common to find groups of glomus cells surrounding normal blood vessels.

Glomangiomatosis is defined as a tumor with features of angiomatosis and excess glomus cells.[430,433]

The so-called "infiltrating glomus tumor" (Fig. 3.66) is a rare variant of histologically otherwise typical glomus tumor that is usually deep-seated and shows diffuse infiltration of surrounding soft tissues.[434,435] Its recognition is important because it is associated with a high local recurrence rate.

Glomus tumor cells are typically immunopositive for smooth muscle actin (Fig. 3.67) and muscle-specific actin, and are occasionally focally positive for desmin.[436–438] Positivity for CD34 may also be seen.[439]

The diagnosis of glomangiosarcoma is usually based on the histologic presence of a benign glomus tumor associated with a frankly sarcomatous component;[426–430,440,441] most such cases have either a round-cell or leiomyosarcomatous appearance. The histologic diagnosis is difficult and, only recently, refined criteria have been proposed to define malignant lesions.[430] The proposed criteria for malignancy are: deep location and a size of more than 2 cm, or atypical mitotic figures, or moderate to high nuclear grade and 5 or more mitotic figures per 50 high-power field. Lesions with marked nuclear atypia but no other malignant features are termed symplastic. Glomus tumors of uncertain malignant potential are defined as lesions that lack criteria for the diagnosis of malignant glomus tumor or symplastic glomus tumor but have high mitotic activity and superficial location, or large size only, or deep location only.[430] Thirty-eight percent of cases fulfilling criteria for malignancy metastasized in the largest series published.[430]

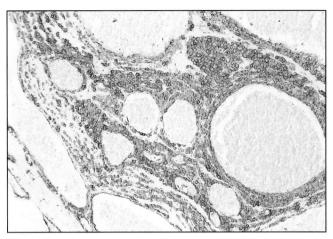

Fig. 3.67 • Glomangioma. The tumor cells are strongly and uniformly smooth muscle actin-positive.

Differential diagnosis

Distinction between solid glomus tumor and cutaneous adnexal neoplasms, especially eccrine spiradenoma, is based on the presence of focal ductal differentiation, two populations of cells, and positivity for epithelial markers in the latter. Intradermal nevus with pseudovascular spaces shows at least focal nesting, evidence of maturation, and positivity for S-100 protein.

Hemangiopericytoma

So-called hemangiopericytoma was described by Stout in 1942 as a vascular tumor originating from the pericyte, a perivascular modified smooth muscle cell.[442] This proposal was mainly based on the architectural pattern with tumor cells surrounding branching blood vessels, and was supported to some extent (at least in the past) by ultrastructural studies.[443–445] However, immunohistochemistry has failed to support this theory, as most tumors (at least in adulthood) stain only (and non-specifically) for vimentin and CD34,[446] but not for actin or other myoid markers.[437,445,447]

Traditionally, hemangiopericytoma has been classified into adult and infantile variants which have little in common, either clinically or histologically, except for the presence of a branching "pericytomatous" vascular pattern, a feature that is also shared with many other tumors.[448–450] Most common among those tumors, which consistently share this pattern are solitary fibrous tumor, synovial sarcoma, infantile myofibromatosis, low-grade endometrial stromal sarcoma, mesenchymal chondrosarcoma, deep benign fibrous histiocytoma, and infantile fibrosarcoma. In recent years it has become clear that infantile and adult hemangiopericytoma are two completely independent entities, the former being closely related to infantile myofibromatosis and the latter being of disputed nature and most likely synonymous with solitary fibrous tumor (see Ch. 24).

Among the lesions traditionally diagnosed as hemangiopericytoma in adults there seems to be considerable inhomogeneity, likely reflecting the absence of reproducible diagnostic criteria. In fact the personal opportunity to review some of Stout's original cases has suggested that this entity may have been heterogeneous and relatively non-cohesive from the outset,

as is easy to understand given the absence of more modern diagnostic techniques at that time. As a consequence, this has become (like so-called "malignant fibrous histiocytoma") something of a wastebasket diagnosis, yet there remain discrete subsets (detailed below) for which there is no better name. In parallel with this realization, it is also increasingly appreciated that there probably exists a group of truly pericytic lesions (examples of which were included in Stout's early work on this topic[442,451]). These lesions, which include examples of so-called "myofibromatosis" occurring in adults,[452] are best categorized as *myopericytoma* and are described in more detail below.

Clinical features

Adult hemangiopericytoma is said to occur in middle to late adult life with an equal sex distribution.[453,454] Probably the majority of the cases so classified in the past would nowadays be regarded as examples of solitary fibrous tumor at the more cellular end of that morphologic spectrum (see Ch. 24). This would also include the cellular lesions located in pelvis and retroperitoneum, seemingly most often in adult females, which may be associated with hypoglycemia due to secretion of insulin-like growth factor.[455] A supposedly distinct group comprises those lesions which arise in the meninges (formerly often known as angioblastic meningioma: see Ch. 26).[456,457] However, many would argue that these are also cellular examples of solitary fibrous tumor and certainly there seem to be no convincing criteria for distinguishing these tumour types. Although histologic grading of these so-called meningeal hemangiopericytomas is unreliable, many seem ultimately to pursue an aggressive course: a distinctive feature of considerable relevance to general pathologists is the propensity of meningeal lesions to give rise to osseous, intra-abdominal, or (less often) pulmonary metastases, often after a prolonged latent period.

Sinonasal hemangiopericytoma, which is discussed in more detail in Chapter 4, is a histologically distinct subset composed of more obviously myoid (actin-positive) cells. It occurs principally in adults and is characterized by the tendency for local recurrence but not metastasis.[458,459]

Infantile hemangiopericytoma can be congenital or present in the first years of life as a solitary, most often deep, dermal or subcutaneous mass.[453,460,461] Some patients have multiple lesions,[461] further underlining the overlap with infantile myofibromatosis. Recurrence is common but the ultimate behavior is generally benign. Rare cases with metastasis have been reported;[462] however this might represent an unusual manifestation of multicentricity rather than true metastasis. The clinicopathologic features are virtually identical to those of infantile myofibromatosis and it is nowadays generally agreed that they represent different stages or patterns of the same entity.[460,461,463]

Myopericytoma is the term we currently prefer to use to embrace lesions described as myofibromatosis in adults – glomangiopericytoma and myopericytoma.[452,463a] We also believe that this is usually a more appropriate term for infantile myofibromatosis (see Ch. 24) and solitary myofibroma in adults,[464] although general adoption of such changes in terminology has been gradual to date. As a group, these lesions most commonly develop in superficial soft tissue of the extremities (particularly the distal lower limb) of adults, although often they have been noticed since birth or early childhood. The lesions may be solitary or multiple, are sometimes painful, and appear to recur locally in 10–20% of patients, although this probably represents multifocal (or "field change") disease. A case of glomangiopericytoma associated with oncogenic osteomalacia has been described.[465] Examples of malignant myopericytoma are very rare.[463a,466]

Histologic appearances

Adult hemangiopericytomas (so called) are indistinguishable from cellular examples of solitary fibrous tumor (see Ch. 24). They are usually well circumscribed, often lobulated, and are composed of cytologically uniform small, basophilic, ovoid to spindled cells with an oval nucleus and ill-defined cytoplasm. These cells are arranged in a patternless fashion around numerous thin-walled ramifying blood vessels, which often adopt a typical staghorn configuration (Fig. 3.68). Focal or diffuse myxoid change and stromal fibrosis can be a feature. A silver stain shows that the tumor cells are located outside the vascular spaces and are each surrounded by a reticulin sheath.

Features that have been said to indicate malignancy are the presence of increased cellularity, necrosis, hemorrhage, and more than 4 mitotic figures per 10 hpf,[453] the latter being the most important feature – these are essentially the same criteria as are nowadays employed in solitary fibrous tumor.[467]

Infantile hemangiopericytoma is a multinodular tumor in which the lesional cells tend to be more polymorphic and focally spindle-shaped or myoid in appearance (Fig. 3.69). Mitotic figures and focal necrosis are common findings, as is subendothelial proliferation, which may simulate vascular invasion. In essentially all cases it is possible to distinguish a second tumor cell population composed of micronodules and fascicles of plump spindle-shaped cells with myoid features that stain positively for α-smooth muscle actin. This creates a subtle zoning phenomenon, indistinguishable from (but often less marked than) that seen in myofibromatosis.

Myopericytoma encompasses a morphologic continuum of lesions ranging from those with the appearance of myofibromatosis (Fig. 3.70) to those that almost resemble glomus tumor (Fig. 3.71) (but often with "pericytoma-like" vessels) or angioleiomyoma. All are composed of actin-positive perivascular contractile cells showing a variable degree of myoid

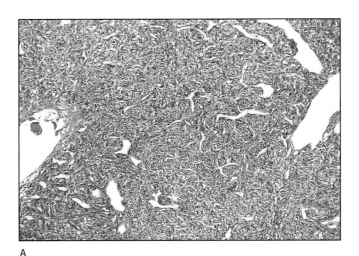

A

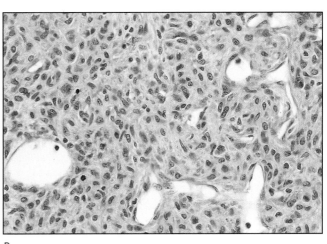

B

Fig. 3.68 • So-called hemangiopericytoma. (**A**) Typical branching, staghorn vessels, patternless architecture, and nondescript fibroblastic cytology. (**B**) Pleomorphism is usually minimal, even in malignant lesions: this case showed up to 15 mitoses per 10 high-power fields. The appearances are indistinguishable from cellular examples of solitary fibrous tumor.

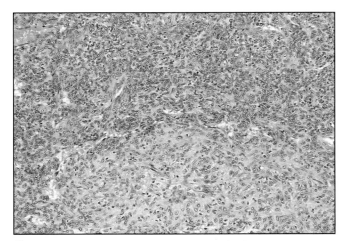

Fig. 3.69 • Infantile hemangiopericytoma. Note the focal transition to a more spindle-shaped, myoid morphology.

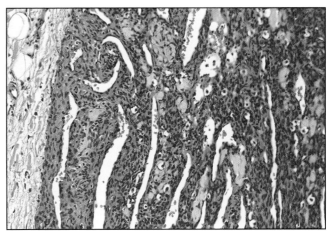

Fig. 3.70 • Myopericytoma. This lesion closely resembles myofibromatosis. Note the perivascular orientation of the spindle cells.

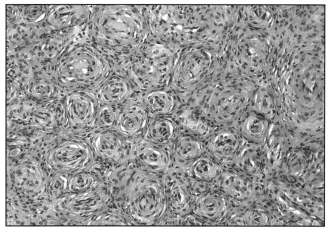

Fig. 3.71 • Myopericytoma. At the most glomoid end of the spectrum, myoid spindle cells are arranged concentrically around small vessels – the appearances are truly pericytic.

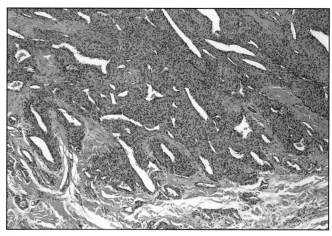

Fig. 3.72 • Myopericytoma. Lesions with intermediate morphology are composed of eosinophilic spindle cells arranged around prominent branching vessels.

(spindle-celled or glomoid) cytomorphology. In many cases there are admixed patterns that closely resemble myofibromatosis and so-called "hemangiopericytoma," except that the perivascular spindle cells in these lesions are eosinophilic and clearly myogenic (Fig. 3.72). It is common, particularly at the periphery of these lesions, to find perivascular proliferation of similar spindle-shaped cells (outside the main tumor nodule) and these cells may proliferate in either the adventitial or subendothelial layers. The latter closely mimics true vascular invasion, except for the intact overlying layer of endothelium, and this is the feature which has previously been well described in both infantile myofibromatosis and infantile hemangiopericytoma (which in reality are points on this same morphologic spectrum). Examples of true intravascular myopericytoma are rarely seen.[463a,468]

Differential diagnosis

With the advent of immunohistochemistry, the diagnosis of so-called hemangiopericytoma has become one of exclusion since many neoplasms can show, at least focally, a pericytoma-like pattern.[448,449] Most particularly these include:

- synovial sarcoma, which may show a biphasic pattern and is EMA and keratin-positive
- mesenchymal chondrosarcoma, which shows islands of mature cartilage
- deep benign fibrous histiocytoma, which is more polymorphic (showing a storiform pattern and inflammatory cells)
- phosphaturic mesenchymal tumor, which has a variety of histologic patterns and is often associated with calcification and osteoclast-like giant cells

Other tumors which commonly show this vascular pattern are solitary fibrous tumor and infantile fibrosarcoma (see Ch. 24) and, in truth, almost any type of sarcoma may show focally a perfect resemblance to so-called "hemangiopericytoma" on occasion. Hence this diagnostic term is falling into disuse and should only be employed with great caution.

References

1. Salyer W R, Salyer D C 1975 Intravascular angiomatosis: development and distinction from angiosarcoma. Cancer 36: 995–1001
2. Clearkin K P, Enzinger F M 1976 Intravascular papillary endothelial hyperplasia. Arch Pathol Lab Med 100: 441–444
3. Kuo T T, Sayers C P, Rosai J 1976 Masson's "vegetant intravascular hemangioendothelioma": a lesion often mistaken for angiosarcoma. Study of seventeen cases located in the skin and soft tissues. Cancer 38: 1227–1236
4. Hashimoto H, Daimaru Y, Enjoji M 1983 Intravascular papillary endothelial hyperplasia. A clinicopathologic study of 91 cases. Am J Dermatopathol 5: 539–545
5. Pins M R, Rosenthal D I, Springfield D S et al. 1993 Florid extravascular papillary endothelial hyperplasia (Masson's pseudoangiosarcoma) presenting as a soft tissue sarcoma. Arch Pathol Lab Med 117: 259–263
6. Branton P A, Lininger R, Tavassoli F A 2003 Papillary endothelial hyperplasia of the breast: the great impostor for angiosarcoma: a clinicopathologic review of 17 cases. Int J Surg Pathol 11: 83–87
7. Reed C N, Cooper P H, Swerlick R A 1984 Intravascular papillary endothelial hyperplasia. Multiple lesions simulating Kaposi's sarcoma. J Am Acad Dermatol 10: 110–113.
8. Durieu C, Bayle-Lebey P, Gadroy A et al. 2001 Intravascular papillary endothelial hyperplasia: multiple lesions appearing in the course of treatment with interferon beta. Ann Dermatol Venereol 128: 1336–1338
9. Wick M R, Rocamora A 1988 Reactive and malignant "angioendotheliomatosis": a discriminant clinicopathological study. J Cutan Pathol 15: 260–271
10. McMenamin M E, Fletcher C D M 2002 Reactive angioendotheliomatosis: a study of 15 cases demonstrating a wide clinicopathologic spectrum. Am J Surg Pathol 26: 685–697
11. Brazzelli V, Baldini F, Vassallo C et al. 1999 Reactive angioendotheliomatosis in an infant. Am J Dermatopathol 21: 42–45
12. Ortonne N, Vignon-Pennamen M D, Majdalani G et al. 2001 Reactive angioendotheliomatosis secondary to dermal amyloid angiopathy. Am J Dermatopathol 23: 315–319
13. Creamer D, Black M M, Calonje E 2000 Reactive angioendotheliomatosis in association with the antiphospholipid syndrome. J Am Acad Dermatol 45: 903–906
14. Thai K E, Barrett W, Kossard S 2003 Reactive angioendotheliomatosis in the setting of antiphospholipid syndrome. Australas J Dermatol 44: 151–155
15. Tomasini C, Soro E, Pippione M 2000 Angioendotheliomatosis in a woman with rheumatoid arthritis. Am J Dermatopathol 22: 334–338
16. Shyong E Q, Gorevic P, Lebwohl M et al. 2002 Reactive angioendotheliomatosis and sarcoidosis. Int J Dermatol 41: 894–897
17. Le Boit P E, Solomon A R, Santa Cruz D J et al. 1992 Angiomatosis with luminal cryoprotein deposition. J Am Acad Dermatol 27: 969–973
18. Krell J M, Sánchez R L, Solomon A R 1994 Diffuse dermal angiomatosis: a variant of reactive cutaneous angioendotheliomatosis. J Cutan Pathol 21: 363–370
19. Kim S, Elenitsas R, James W D 2002 Diffuse dermal angiomatosis: a variant of reactive angioendotheliomatosis associated with peripheral vascular atherosclerosis. Arch Dermatol 138: 456–458

20. Kimyai-Asadi A, Nousari H C, Ketabchi N et al. 1999 Diffuse dermal angiomatosis: a variant of reactive angioendotheliomatosis associated with atherosclerosis. J Am Acad Dermatol 40: 257–259

21. Requena L, Farina M C, Renedo G et al. 1999 Intravascular and diffuse dermal reactive angioendotheliomatosis secondary to iatrogenic arteriovenous fistulas. J Cutan Pathol 26: 159–164

22. Chan J K C, Fletcher C D M, Hicklin G A et al. 1990 Glomeruloid hemangioma. A distinctive cutaneous lesion of multicentric Castleman's disease associated with POEMS syndrome. Am J Surg Pathol 14: 1036–1046

23. Yang S G, Cho K H, Bang Y-J et al. 1998 A case of glomeruloid hemangioma associated with multicentric Castleman's disease. Am J Dermatopathol 20: 266–270

24. Tsai C Y, Lai C H, Chan H L et al. 2001 Glomeruloid hemangioma – a specific marker of POEMS syndrome. Int J Dermatol 40: 403–406

25. Scheers C, Kolivras A, Corbisier A et al. 2002 POEMS syndrome revealed by multiple glomeruloid angiomas. Dermatology 204: 311–314

26. Obermoser G, Larcher C, Sheldon J A et al. 2003 Absence of human herpesvirus-8 in glomeruloid haemangioma associated with POEMS syndrome and Castleman's disease. Br J Dermatol 148: 1276–1278

27. MacCollum D W, Martin L W 1956 Hemangiomas in infancy and childhood. A report based on 6479 cases. Surg Clin North Am 36: 1647–1663

28. Watson W L, McCarthy W B 1940 Blood and lymph vessel tumors. A report of 1056 cases. Surg Gynecol Obstet 71: 569–588

29. Edgerton M T, Hiebert J M 1978 Vascular and lymphatic tumors in infancy, childhood and adulthood: challenge of diagnosis and treatment. Curr Probl Cancer 2: 4–44

30. Finley J L, Noe J M, Arndt K A et al. 1984 Port-wine stains. Morphologic variations and developmental lesions. Arch Dermatol 120: 1453–1455

31. Johnson S C, Hanke C W 2001 Unilateral acquired nevus flammeus in women. Cutis 67: 225–228

32. Adams B, Lucky A W 2000 Acquired port-wine stains and antecedent trauma: case report and review of the literature. Arch Dermatol 136: 897–899

33. Berg J N, Quaba A A, Georgantopoulou A et al. 2000 A family with hereditary port wine stain. J Med Genet 37: E12

34. Breugem C C, Alders M, Salieb-Beugelaar G B et al. 2002 A locus for hereditary capillary malformations mapped on chromosome 5q. Hum Genet 110: 343–347

35. Askar I, Kilinc N, Yucetas A 2003 Pyogenic granuloma appearing on port-wine stain: a case report. Acta Chir Plast 45: 51–54

36. Valeyrie L, Lebrun-Vignes B, Descamps V et al. 2002 Pyogenic granuloma within port-wine stains: an alarming clinical presentation. Eur J Dermatol 12: 373–375

37. Kim H T, Choi E H, Ahn S K et al. 1999 Vascular tumors arising in port-wine stains: two cases of pyogenic granuloma and a case of acquired tufted angioma. J Dermatol 26: 813–816

38. Bean W B, Walsh J R 1956 Venous lakes. Arch Dermatol 74: 459–463

39. Stevenson J R, Lincoln C S 1967 Angioma serpiginosum. Arch Dermatol 95: 16–22

40. Frain-Bell W 1957 Angioma serpiginosum. Br J Dermatol 69: 251–268

41. Stevenson J R, Lincoln C S 1967 Angioma serpiginosum. Arch Dermatol 95: 16–22

42. Kumakiri M, Katoh N, Miura Y 1980 Angioma serpiginosum. J Cutan Pathol 7: 410–421

43. Al Hawsawi K, Al Aboud K, Al Aboud D et al. 2003 Linear angioma serpiginosum. Pediatr Dermatol 20: 167–168

44. Erbagci Z, Erbagci I, Erkilic S et al. 2004 Angioma serpiginosum with retinal involvement in a male: a possible role of continuous cold exposure. J Eur Acad Dermatol Venereol 18: 238–239

45. Gautier-Smith P C, Sanders M D, Sanderson K V 1971 Ocular and nervous system involvement in angioma serpiginosum. Br J Ophthalmol 55: 433–443

46. Marriot P J, Munro D D, Ryan T (1975) Angioma serpiginosum – familial incidence. Br J Dermatol 93: 701–706

47. Johnson W C 1976 Pathology of cutaneous vascular tumors. Int J Dermatol 15: 239–270

48. Imperial R, Helwig E B 1967 Angiokeratoma. A clinicopathological study. Arch Dermatol 95: 166–175

49. Epinette W W, Norins A L, Drew A L et al. 1973 Angiokeratoma corporis diffusum with α-L fucosidase deficiency. Arch Dermatol 107: 754–757

50. Rodríguez-Serna M, Botella-Estrada R, Chabás A et al. 1996 Angiokeratoma corporis diffusum associated with B-mannosidase deficiency. Arch Dermatol 132: 1219–1222

51. Kanzaki T, Yokota M, Irie F et al. 1993 Angiokeratoma corporis diffusum with glycopeptiduria due to deficient lysosomal α-N-acetylgalactosaminidase activity. Arch Dermatol 129: 460–465

52. Kodama K, Kobayashi H, Abe R et al. 2001 A new case of α-N-acetylgalactosaminidase deficiency with angiokeratoma corporis diffusum, with Meniere's syndrome amd without mental retardation. Br J Dermatol 144: 363–368

53. Ishibashi A, Tsuboi R, Shinmei M 1984 β-galactosidase and neuraminidase deficiency associated with angiokeratoma corporis diffusum. Arch Dermatol 120: 1344–1346

54. Holmes R C, Fensom A H, McKee P H et al. 1984 Angiokeratoma corporis diffusum in a patient with normal enzyme activities. J Am Acad Dermatol 10: 384–387

55. Haye K R, Rebello D J A 1961 Angiokeratoma of Mibelli. Acta Dermat Venereol 41: 56–60

56. Imperial R, Helwig E B 1967 Angiokeratoma of the scrotum (Fordyce type). J Urol 98: 379–387

57. Imperial R, Helwig E B 1967 Angiokeratoma of the vulva. Obstet Gynecol 29: 307–312

58. Lynch P J, Kosanovich N 1967 Angiokeratoma circumscriptum. Arch Dermatol 96: 665–668

59. Tarnowski W M, Hashimoto K 1969 New light microscopic findings in Fabry's disease. Acta Derm Venereol 49: 386–389

60. Coffin C M, Dehner L P 1993 Vascular tumors in children and adolescents: a clinicopathologic study of 228 tumors in 222 patients. Pathol Annu 28: 97–120

61. Lister W A 1938 The natural history of strawberry naevi. Lancet 1: 1429–1434

62. Perrone T 1985 Vessel-nerve intermingling in benign infantile hemangioendothelioma. Hum Pathol 16: 198–200

63. Calonje E, Mentzel T, Fletcher C D M 1995 Pseudomalignant perineural invasion in cellular ("infantile") capillary hemangiomas. Histopathology 26: 159–164

64. Taxy J B, Gray S R 1979 Cellular angiomas of infancy. An ultrastructural study of two cases. Cancer 43: 2322–2331

65. Gonzalez-Crussi F, Reyes-Mugica M 1991 Cellular hemangiomas ("hemangioendotheliomas") in infants. Light microscopic immunohistochemical and ultrastructural observations. Am J Surg Pathol 15: 769–778

66. Smoller B R, Apfelberg D B 1993 Infantile (juvenile) capillary hemangioma: a tumor of heterogeneous cellular elements. J Cutan Pathol 20: 330–336

67. North P E, Waner M, Mizeracki A et al. 2001 A unique microvascular phenotype shared by juvenile hemangiomas and human placenta. Arch Dermatol 137: 559–570

68. North P E, Waner M, Mizeracki A et al. 2000 GLUT1: a newly discovered immunohistochemical marker for juvenile hemangiomas. Hum Pathol 31: 11–22

69. Yu Y, Flint A F, Mulliken J B et al. 2004 Endothelial progenitor cells in infantile hemangioma. Blood 103: 1373–1375

70. Boye E, Yu Y, Paranya G et al. 2001 Clonality and altered behavior of endothelial cells from hemangiomas. J Clin Invest 107: 745–752

71. Walter J W, North P E, Waner M et al. 2002 Somatic mutation of vascular endothelial growth factor receptors in juvenile hemangioma. Genes Chromos Cancer 33: 295–303

72. Wilson-Jones E 1976 Malignant vascular tumours. Clin Exp Dermatol 1: 287–312

73. Wilson-Jones E, Orkin M 1989 Tufted angioma (angioblastoma). A benign progressive angioma, not to be confused with Kaposi's sarcoma or low-grade angiosarcoma. J Am Acad Dermatol 20: 214–225

74. Padilla R S, Orkin M, Rosai J 1987 Acquired "tufted" angioma (progressive capillary hemangioma). Am J Dermatopathol 9: 292–300

75. Herron M D, Coffin C M, Vanderhooft S L 2002 Tufted angiomas: variability of clinical morphology. Pediatr Dermatol 19: 394–401

76. Wong S N, Tay Y K 2002 Tufted angioma: a report of five cases. Pediatr Dermatol 19: 388–393

77. Okada E, Tamura A, Ishikawa O et al. 2000 Tufted angioma (angioblastoma): case report and review of 41 cases in the Japanese literature. Clin Exp Dermatol 25: 627–630

78. Cho K H, Kim S H, Park K C et al. 1991 Angioblastoma (Nakagawa) – is it the same as tufted angioma? Clin Exp Dermatol 16: 110–113

79. Kleinegger C L, Hammond H L, Vincent S D et al. 2000 Acquired tufted angioma: a unique vascular lesion not previously reported in the oral mucosa. Br J Dermatol 142: 794–799

80. Satter E K, Graham B S, Gibbs N F 2002 Congenital tufted angioma. Pediatr Dermatol 19: 445–447

81. Tille J C, Morris M A, Brundler M A et al. 2003 Familial predisposition to tufted angioma: identification of blood and lymphatic vascular components. Clin Genet 63: 393–399

82. Miyamoto T, Mihara M, Mishima E et al. 1992 Acquired tufted angioma showing spontaneous regression. Br J Dermatol 127: 645–648

83. Lam W Y, Mac-Moune Lai F, Look C N et al. 1994 Tufted angioma with complete regression. J Cutan Pathol 21: 461–466

84. Maguiness S, Guenther L 2002 Kasabach–Merritt syndrome. J Cutan Med Surg 6: 335–339

85. Enjolras O, Mulliken J B, Wassef M et al. 2000 Residual lesions after Kasabach–Merritt phenomenon in 41 patients. J Am Acad Dermatol 42: 225–235

86. Michel S, Hohenleutner U, Stolz W et al. 1999 Acquired tufted angioma in association with a complex cutaneous vascular malformation. Br J Dermatol 141: 1142–1144

87. Kumakiri M, Muramoto F, Tsukinaga I et al. 1983 Crystalline lamellae in the endothelial cells of a type of hemangioma characterised by the proliferation of immature endothelial cells and pericytes – angioblastoma (Nakagawa). J Am Acad Dermatol 8: 68–75

88. Fukunaga M 2000 Intravenous tufted angioma. APMIS 108: 287–292

89. Brasanac D, Janic D, Boricic I et al. 2003 Retroperitoneal kaposiform hemangoendothelioma with tufted angioma-like features in an infant with Kasabach–Merritt syndrome. Pathol Int 53: 627–631

90. Chu C Y, Hsiao C H, Chiu H C 2003 Transformation between Kaposiform hemangioendothelioma and tufted angioma. Dermatology 206: 334–337

91. Imperial R, Helwig E 1967 Verrucous hemangioma. A clinicopathologic study of 21 cases. Arch Dermatol 96: 247–253
92. Chan J K C, Tsang W Y W, Calonje E et al. 1995 Verrucous hemangioma. A distinctive but neglected variant of cutaneous hemangioma. Int J Surg Pathol 2: 171–176
93. Calduch L, Ortega C, Navarro V et al. 2000 Verrucous hemangioma: report of two cases and review of the literature. Pediatr Dermatol 17: 213–217
94. McGeoch A H 1961 Pyogenic granuloma. Aust J Dermatol 6: 33–40
95. Bhaskar S M, Jacoway J R 1961 Pyogenic granuloma. Clinical features, incidence, histology and result of treatment: report of 242 cases. J Oral Surg 24: 391–398
96. Patrice S J, Wiss K, Mulliken J B 1991 Pyogenic granuloma (lobular capillary hemangioma): a clinicopathologic study of 178 cases. Pediatr Dermatol 8: 267–276
97. Harris M N, Desai R, Chuang T Y et al. 2000 Lobular capillary hemangiomas: an epidemiologic report, with emphasis on cutaneous lesions. J Am Acad Dermatol 42: 1012–1016
98. Mills S E, Cooper P H, Fechner R E 1980 Lobular capillary hemangioma. The underlying lesion of pyogenic granuloma. A study of 73 cases from the oral and nasal mucous membranes. Am J Surg Pathol 4: 471–479
99. Ogunleye A O, Nwaorgu O G 2000 Pyogenic granuloma, a cause of congenital nasal mass: case report. Ann Trop Paediatr 20: 137–139
100. Willies-Jacobo L J, Isaacs H Jr, Stein M T 2000 Pyogenic granuloma presenting as a congenital epulis. Arch Pediatr Adolesc Med 154: 603–605
101. Nappi O, Wick M R 1986 Disseminated lobular capillary hemangioma (pyogenic granuloma). A clinicopathologic study of two cases. Am J Dermatopathol 8: 379–385
102. Wilson B B, Greer K E, Cooper P H 1989 Eruptive disseminated lobular capillary hemangioma (pyogenic granuloma). J Am Acad Dermatol 21: 391–394
103. Behne K, Robertson I, Weedon D 2002 Disseminated lobular capillary hemangioma. Australas J Dermatol 43: 297–300
104. Warner J, Wilson-Jones E 1968 Pyogenic granuloma recurring with multiple satellites. A report of 11 cases. Br J Dermatol 80: 218–227
105. Tursen U, Demirkan F, Ikizoglu G 2004 Giant recurrent pyogenic granuloma on the face with satellitosis responsive to systemic steroids. Clin Exp Dermatol 29: 40–41
106. Kim T H, Choi E H, Ahn S K et al. 1999 Vascular tumors arising in port-wine stains: two cases of pyogenic granuloma and a case of acquired tufted angioma. J Dermatol 26: 813–816
107. Askar I, Kilinc N, Yucetas A 2003 Pyogenic granuloma appearing on port-wine stain: a case report. Acta Chir Plast 45: 52–54
108. Piguet V, Borradori L 2002 Pyogenic granuloma-like lesions during capecitabine therapy. Br J Dermatol 147: 1270–1272
109. MacKenzie-Wood A R, Wood G 1998 Pyogenic granuloma-like lesions in a patient using topical tretinoin. Australas J Dermatol 39: 248–250
110. Exner J H, Dahod S, Pochi P E 1983 Pyogenic granuloma-like acne lesions during isotretinoin therapy. Arch Dermatol 119: 808–811
111. Hagler J, Hodak E, David M et al. 1992 Facial pyogenic granuloma-like lesions under isotretinoin therapy. Int J Dermatol 31: 199–200
112. Renshaw A A, Rosai J 1993 Benign atypical vascular lesions of the lip. A study of 12 cases. Am J Surg Pathol 17: 557–565
113. Cooper P H, Mills S E 1982 Subcutaneous granuloma pyogenicum. Lobular capillary hemangioma. Arch Dermatol 118: 30–33
114. Cooper P H, McAllister H A, Helwig E B 1979 Intravenous pyogenic granuloma. A study of 18 cases. Am J Surg Pathol 3: 221–228
115. LeBoit P E, Berger T G, Egbert B M et al. 1989 Bacillary angiomatosis. The histopathology and differential diagnosis of a pseudoneoplastic infection in patients with human immunodeficiency virus disease. Am J Surg Pathol 13: 909–920
116. Slater L N, Welch D F, Min K W 1992 Rochalimaea henselae causes bacillary angiomatosis and peliosis hepatis. Arch Intern Med 152: 602–606
117. Kasabach H H, Merritt K K 1961 Capillary hemangioma with extensive purpura. Report of a case. Am J Dis Child 59: 1063–1070
118. Fine R M, Derbes V J, Clark W H Jr 1961 Blue rubber bleb nevus. Arch Dermatol 84: 802–805
119. Rice S J, Fischer D S 1962 Blue rubber bleb nevus syndrome. Arch Dermatol 86: 502–511
120. Calonje E, Fletcher C D M 1991 Sinusoidal hemangioma: a distinctive benign vascular neoplasm within the group of cavernous hemangiomas. Am J Surg Pathol 15: 1130–1135
121. Girard C, Graham J H, Johnson W C 1974 Arteriovenous hemangioma (arteriovenous shunt): a clinicopathologic and histochemical study. J Clin Pathol 1: 73–87
122. Rusin L J, Harrel E 1976 Arteriovenous fistula. Cutaneous manifestations. Arch Dermatol 112: 1135–1138
123. Connelly M G, Winkelmann R K 1985 Acral arteriovenous tumor. Am J Surg Pathol 9: 15–21
124. Angervall L, Nielsen J M, Stener B et al. 1979 Concomitant arteriovenous vascular malformation in skeletal muscle. A clinical, angiographic and histologic study. Cancer 44: 232–238
125. Kadono T, Kishi A, Onishi Y et al. 2000 Acquired digital arteriovenous malformation: a report of six cases. Br J Dermatol 142: 362–365
126. Akiyama M, Inamoto N 2001 Arteriovenous haemangioma in chronic liver disease: clinical and histopathological features in four cases. Br J Dermatol 144: 604–609

127. Strutton G, Weedon D 1987 Acro-angiodermatitis: a simulant of Kaposi's sarcoma. Am J Dermatopathol 9: 85–89
128. Koutlas I G, Jessurun J 1994 Arteriovenous hemangioma: clinicopathological and immunohistochemical study. J Cutan Pathol 21: 343–349
129. Hunt S J, Santa Cruz D J, Barr R J 1991 Microvenular hemangioma. J Cutan Pathol 18: 235–240
130. Aloi F, Tomasini C, Pippione M 1993 Microvenular hemangioma. Am J Dermatopathol 15: 534–538
131. Sánz-Trelles A, Ojeda-Martos A, Jiménez-Fernández A et al. 1998 Microvenular hemangioma: a new case in a child. Histopathology 32: 89–90
132. Hudnall S D, Chen T, Brown K et al. 2003 Human herpesvirus-8-positive microvenular hemangioma in POEMS syndrome. Arch Pathol Lab Med 127: 1034–1036
133. Santa Cruz D J, Aronberg J 1988 Targetoid hemosiderotic hemangioma. J Am Acad Dermatol 19: 550–558
134. Guillou L, Calonje E, Speight P et al. 1999 Hobnail hemangioma: a pseudomalignant vascular lesion with a reappraisal of targetoid hemosiderotic hemangioma. Am J Surg Pathol 23: 97–105
135. Mentzel T, Partanen T A, Kutzner H 1999 Hobnail hemangioma ("targetoid hemosiderotic hemangioma"): clinicopathologic and immunohistochemical analysis of 62 cases. J Cutan Pathol 26: 279–286
136. Christenson L J, Stone M S 2001 Trauma-induced simulator of targetoid hemosiderotic hemangioma. Am J Dermatopathol 23: 221–223
137. Carlson J A, Daulad S, Godheart H P 1999 Targetoid hemosiderotic hemangioma – a dynamic vascular tumor: report of 3 cases with episodic and cyclic changes and comparison with solitary angiokeratomas. J Am Acad Dermatol 41: 215–224
138. Calonje E, Fletcher C D M, Wilson-Jones E et al. 1994 Retiform hemangioendothelioma: a distinctive form of low-grade angiosarcoma delineated in a series of 15 cases. Am J Surg Pathol 18: 115–125
139. Gutzmer R, Kaspari M, Herbst R A et al. 2002 Absence of HHV-8 DNA in hobnail hemangioma. J Cutan Pathol 29: 154–158
140. Requena L, Kutzner H, Mentzel T 2002 Acquired elastotic hemangioma: a clinicopathologic variant of hemangioma. J Am Acad Dermatol 47: 371–376
141. Brenn T, Fletcher C D M 2004 Cutaneous epithelioid angiomatous nodule: a distinct lesion in the morphologic spectrum of epithelioid vascular tumors. Am J Dermatopathol 26: 14–21
142. Wells G C, Whimster I W 1969 Subcutaneous angiolymphoid hyperplasia with eosinophilia. Br J Dermatol 81: 1–15
143. Wilson-Jones E, Bleehen S S 1969 Inflammatory angiomatous nodules with abnormal blood vessels occurring about the ears and scalp (pseudo or atypical pyogenic granuloma). Br J Dermatol 81: 804–816
144. Wilson-Jones E, Marks R 1970 Papular angioplasia. Vascular papules of the face and scalp simulating malignant vascular tumors. Arch Dermatol 102: 422–427
145. Rosai J, Akerman L R 1974 Intravenous atypical vascular proliferation. A cutaneous lesion simulating a malignant blood vessel tumor. Arch Dermatol 109: 714–717
146. Rosai J, Gold J, Landy R 1979 The histiocytoid hemangiomas. A unifying concept embracing several previously described entities of skin, soft tissue, large vessels, bone and heart. Hum Pathol 10: 707–730
147. Cooper P H 1988 Is histiocytoid hemangioma a specific pathologic entity? (editorial) Am J Surg Pathol 12: 815–817
148. Rosai J 1982 Angiolymphoid hyperplasia with eosinophilia of the skin. Its nosological position in the spectrum of histiocytoid hemangioma. Am J Dermatopathol 4: 175–184
149. Allen P W, Ramakrishna B, MacCormac L B 1992 The histiocytoid hemangiomas and other controversies. Pathol Annu 27 (part 1): 51–87
150. Tsang W Y W, Chan J K C 1993 The family of epithelioid vascular tumors. Histol Histopathol 8: 187–212
151. Fetsch J F, Weiss S W 1991 Observations concerning the pathogenesis of epithelioid hemangioma (angiolymphoid hyperplasia). Mod Pathol 4: 449–455
152. Olsen T G, Helwig E B 1985 Angiolymphoid hyperplasia with eosinophilia. A clinicopathologic study of 116 patients. J Am Acad Dermatol 12: 781–796
153. Castro C, Winkelmann R K 1974 Angiolymphoid hyperplasia with eosinophilia in the skin. Cancer 34: 1696–1705
154. Razquin S, Mayayo E, Citores M A et al. 1991 Angiolymphoid hyperplasia with eosinophilia of the tongue: report of a case and review of the literature. Hum Pathol 22: 837–839
155. Park Y, Chung J, Cho C G 2002 Angiolymphoid hyperplasia with eosinophilia of the tongue: report of a case and review of the literature. Oral Oncol 38: 103–106
156. Bartralot R, García-Patos V, Hueto J et al. 1996 Angiolymphoid hyperplasia with eosinophilia affecting the oral mucosa: report of a case and a review of the literature. Br J Dermatol 134: 744–748
157. Mariatos G, Gorgoulis V G, Laskaris G et al. 1999 Epithelioid hemangiomas (angiolymphoid hyperplasia with eosinophilia) in the oral mucosa. A case report and review of the literature. Oral Oncol 35: 435–438
158. Tsuboi H, Fujimura T, Katsuoka K 2001 Angiolymphoid hyperplasia with eosinophilia in the oral mucosa. Br J Dermatol 145: 365–366
159. Nair M, Aron M, Sharma M C 2000 Angiolymphoid hyperplasia with eosinophilia (epithelioid hemangioma) of the breast: report of a case. Surg Today 30: 747–749
160. Suster S 1987 Nodal angiolymphoid hyperplasia with eosinophilia. Am J Clin Pathol 88: 236–239

161. O'Connell J X, Kattapuram S V, Mankin H J et al. 1993 Epithelioid hemangioma of bone. A tumor often mistaken for low-grade angiosarcoma or malignant hemangioendothelioma. Am J Surg Pathol 17: 610–617

162. Banks E R, Mills S E 1990 Histiocytoid (epithelioid) hemangioma of the testis. The so-called vascular variant of "adenomatoid tumor." Am J Surg Pathol 14: 584–589

163. Madison J F, Cooper P H 1989 A histiocytoid (epithelioid) vascular tumor of the ovary: occurrence within a benign cystic teratoma. Mod Pathol 2: 55–58

164. Luthringer D J, Virmani R, Weiss S W et al. 1990 A distinctive cardiovascular lesion resembling histiocytoid/epithelioid hemangioma, evidence suggesting mesothelial participation. Am J Surg Pathol 14: 993–1000

165. Chan J K, Loo K T, Yau B K et al. 1997 Nodular histiocytic/mesothelial hyperplasia: a lesion potentially mistaken for a neoplasm in transbronchial biopsy. Am J Surg Pathol 21: 658–663

166. Oksenhendler E, Cazals-Hatem D, Schulz T F et al. 1998 Transient angiolymphoid hyperplasia and Kaposi's sarcoma after primary infection with human herpesvirus 8 in a patient with human immunodeficiency virus infection. N Engl J Med 338: 1585–1590

167. Jang K A, Ahn S J, Choi J H et al. 2001 Polymerase chain reaction (PCR) for human herpesvirus 8 and heteroduplex PCR for clonality assessment in angiolymphoid hyperplasia with eosinophilia and Kimura's disease. J Cutan Pathol 28: 363–367

168. Onishi Y, Ohara K 1999 Angiolymphoid hyperplasia with eosinophilia associated with arteriovenous malformation: a clinicopathological correlation with angiography and serial estimation of serum levels of renin, eosinophilic cationic protein and interleukin 5. Br J Dermatol 140: 1153–1156

169. Reed R J, Terazakis N 1972 Subcutaneous angiolymphoid hyperplasia with eosinophilia (Kimura's disease). Cancer 29: 489–497

170. Morton K, Robertson A J, Hadden W 1987 Angiolymphoid hyperplasia with eosinophilia: report of a case arising from the radial artery. Histopathology 11: 963–969

171. Kung I T, Gibson J B, Bannatyne P M 1984 Kimura's disease: a clinicopathological study of 21 cases and its distinction from angiolymphoid hyperplasia with eosinophilia. Pathology 16: 39–44

172. Urabe A, Tsuneyoshi M, Enjoji M 1987 Epithelioid hemangioma versus Kimura's disease. A comparative clinicopathologic study. Am J Surg Pathol 10: 758–766

173. Googe P B, Harris N L, Mihm M C J 1987 Kimura's disease and angiolymphoid hyperplasia with eosinophilia: two distinct clinicopathological entities. J Cutan Pathol 15: 263–271

174. Kuo T T, Shih L Y, Chan H L 1988 Kimura's disease, involvement of regional lymph nodes and distinction from angiolymphoid hyperplasia with eosinophilia. Am J Surg Pathol 12: 843–854

175. Chan J K C, Hui P K, Ng C S et al. 1989 Epithelioid haemangioma (angiolymphoid hyperplasia with eosinophilia) and Kimura's disease in Chinese. Histopathology 15: 557–574

176. Fawcett H A, Smith N P 1984 Injection site granuloma due to aluminium. Arch Dermatol 120: 1318–1322

177. Miliauskas J R, Mukherjee T, Dixon B 1993 Postimmunization (vaccination) injection-site reactions. A report of four cases and review of the literature. Am J Surg Pathol 17: 516–524

178. Weiss S W, Goldblum J R 2001 Soft tissue tumors, 4th edn. CV Mosby-Harcourt, Philadelphia, p 593

179. Weiss S W, Enzinger F M 1986 Spindle cell hemangioendothelioma, a low grade angiosarcoma resembling a cavernous hemangioma and Kaposi's sarcoma. Am J Surg Pathol 10: 521–530

180. Fletcher C D M, Beham A, Schmid C 1991 Spindle cell hemangioendothelioma: a clinicopathological and immunohistochemical study indicative of a non-neoplastic lesion. Histopathology 18: 291–301

181. Perkins P, Weiss S W 1996 Spindle cell hemangioendothelioma: an analysis of 78 cases with reassessment of its pathogenesis and biologic behavior. Am J Surg Pathol 20: 1196–1204

182. Scott G A, Rosai J 1988 Spindle cell hemangioendothelioma. Report of seven additional cases of a recently described vascular neoplasm. Am J Dermatopathol 10: 281–288

183. Fanburg J C, Meis-Kindblom J M, Rosenberg A C 1995 Multiple enchondromas associated with spindle-cell hemangioendotheliomas. An overlooked variant of Mafucci's syndrome. Am J Surg Pathol 19: 1029–1038

184. Imayama S, Murakamai Y, Hashimoto H et al. 1992 Spindle cell hemangioendothelioma exhibits the ultrastructural features of reactive vascular proliferation rather than of angiosarcoma. Am J Clin Pathol 97: 279–287

185. Ding J, Hashimoto H, Imayama S et al. 1992 Spindle cell hemangioendothelioma: probably a benign vascular lesion not a low-grade angiosarcoma. A clinicopathological, ultrastructural and immunohistochemical study. Virchow's Arch [A] 420: 77–85

186. Fletcher C D M 1996 Vascular tumors: an update with emphasis on the diagnosis of angiosarcoma and borderline vascular neoplasms. In: Weiss SW, Brooks JSJ (eds) Soft tissue tumors. Monographs in pathology. Williams & Wilkins, Baltimore, p 181–206

187. Zoltie N, Roberts P F 1989 Spindle cell haemangioendothelioma in association with epithelioid haemangioendothelioma. Histopathology 15: 544–546

188. Allen P W, Enzinger F M 1972 Hemangioma of skeletal muscle. An analysis of 89 cases. Cancer 29: 8–22

189. Fergusson I L 1972 Haemangiomata of skeletal muscle. Br J Surg 59: 634–637

190. Beham A, Fletcher C D M 1991 Intramuscular angioma: a clinicopathological analysis of 74 cases. Histopathology 18: 53–59

191. Lin J J, Lin F 1974 Two entities in angiolipoma. A study of 459 cases of lipoma with review of the literature on infiltrating angiolipoma. Cancer 34: 720–727

192. Devaney K, Vinh T Z, Sweet D E 1993 Synovial hemangioma: a report of 20 cases with differential diagnostic considerations. Hum Pathol 24: 737–745

193. Losli E J 1952 Intrinsic hemangioma of the peripheral nerves: a report of two cases and a review of the literature. Arch Pathol 53: 226–232

194. Wood M B 1980 Intraneural hemangioma: report of a case. Plast Reconstr Surg 65: 74–76

195. Vigna P A, Kusior M F, Collins M B et al. 1994 Peripheral nerve hemangioma. Potential for clinical aggressiveness. Arch Pathol Lab Med 118: 1038–1041

196. Rao V K, Weiss S W 1992 Angiomatosis of soft tissue. An analysis of the histologic features and clinical outcome in 51 cases. Am J Surg Pathol 16: 764–771

197. Howat A J, Campbell P E 1987 Angiomatosis: a vascular malformation of infancy and childhood. Report of 17 cases. Pathology 19: 377–382

198. Kraus M D, Lind A C, Alder S L et al. 1999 Angiomatosis with angiokeratoma-like features in children: a light microscopic and immunophenotypic examination of four cases. Am J Dermatopathol 21: 350–355

199. Fletcher C D M 1998 Borderline malignancy in soft tissue neoplasia – a meaningful concept? Pathol Case Rev 3: 100–104

200. Fletcher C D M, Unni K K, Mertens F 2002 World Health Organization classification of tumours. Pathology and genetics. Tumours of soft tissue and bone. IARC Press, Lyon

201. Tsang W Y W, Chan J K C 1991 Kaposi-like infantile hemangioendothelioma. A distinctive vascular neoplasm of the retroperitoneum. Am J Surg Pathol 15: 982–989

202. Tsang W Y W, Chan J K C, Fletcher C D M 1991 Recently characterized vascular tumours of skin and soft tissues. Histopathology 19: 489–501

203. Zukerberg L R, Nickoloff B J, Weiss S W 1993 Kaposiform hemangioendothelioma of infancy and childhood. An aggressive neoplasm associated with Kasabach–Merritt syndrome and lymphangiomatosis. Am J Surg Pathol 17: 321–328

204. Lyons L L, North P E, Lai F M M et al. 2004 Kaposiform hemangioendothelioma. A study of 33 cases emphasizing its pathologic, immunophenotypic, and biologic uniqueness from juvenile hemangioma. Am J Surg Pathol 28: 559–568

205. Vin-Christian K, McCalmont T H, Frieden I J 1997 Kaposiform hemangioendothelioma. An aggressive, locally invasive vascular tumor that can mimic hemangioma of infancy. Arch Dermatol 133: 1573–1578

206. Lai F M M, Choi P C L, Leung P C et al. 2001 Kaposiform hemangioendothelioma: five patients with cutaneous lesions and long follow-up. Mod Pathol 14: 1087–1092

207. Mentzel T, Mazzoleni G, Dei Tos A P et al. 1997 Kaposiform hemangioendothelioma in adults. Clinicopathologic and immunohistochemical analysis of three cases. Am J Clin Pathol 108: 450–455

208. Gonzalez-Crussi F, Choud P, Crawford S E 1991 Congenital infiltrating giant cell angioblastoma, a new entity? Am J Surg Pathol 15: 175–183

209. Vargas S O, Pérez-Atayde A R, Gonzalez-Crussi F et al. 2001 Giant cell angioblastoma: three additional occurrences of a distinct pathologic entity. Am J Surg Pathol 25: 185–196

210. Dufau J P, Pierre C, De SaintMaur P P et al. 1997 Hemangioendothelioma retiforme. Ann Pathol 17: 47–51

211. Fukunaga M, Endo Y, Masui F et al. 1996 Retiform haemangioendothelioma. Virchows Arch 428: 301–304

212. Duke D, Dvorak A, Harris T J et al. 1996 Multiple retiform hemangioendotheliomas. A low-grade angiosarcoma. Am J Dermatopathol 18: 606–610

213. Mentzel T, Stengel B, Katenkamp D 1997 Retiform hemangioendothelioma. Clinico-pathologic case report and discussion of the group of low-grade malignancy vascular tumors. Pathologe 18: 390–394

214. Dabska M 1969 Malignant endovascular papillary angioendothelioma of the skin in childhood. Clinicopathologic study of 6 cases. Cancer 24: 503–510

215. Fanburg-Smith J C, Michal M, Partanen T et al. 1999 Papillary intralymphatic angioendothelioma (PILA). A report of twelve cases of a distinctive vascular tumor with phenotypic features of lymphatic vessels. Am J Surg Pathol 23: 1004–1010

216. Manivel J C, Wick M R, Swanson P E et al. 1986 Endovascular papillary angioendothelioma of childhood: a vascular lesion possibly characterized by "high" endothelial cell differentiation. Hum Pathol 17: 1240–1244

217. Nayler S J, Rubin B P, Calonje E et al. 2000 Composite hemangioendothelioma: a complex low-grade vascular lesion mimicking angiosarcoma. Am J Surg Pathol 24: 352–361

218. Reis-Filho J S, Paiva M E, Lopes J M 2002 Congenital composite hemangioendothelioma: case report and reappraisal of the hemangioendothelioma spectrum. J Cutan Pathol 29: 226–231

219. Chan J K C, Frizzera G, Fletcher C D M et al. 1992 Primary vascular tumors of lymph nodes other than Kaposi's sarcoma. Analysis of 39 cases and delineation of two new entities. Am J Surg Pathol 16: 335–350

220. Nascimento A G, Keeney G L, Sciot R et al. 1997 Polymorphous hemangioendothelioma: a report of two cases, one affecting extranodal soft tissues, and review of the literature. Am J Surg Pathol 21: 1083–1089

221. Templeton A C 1981 Kaposi's sarcoma. Pathol Annu 16: 315–336

222. Gottlieb G J, Ackerman A B 1982 Kaposi's sarcoma: an extensively disseminated form in young homosexual men. Hum Pathol 13: 882–892

223. Gottlieb G J, Ackerman A B 1988 Kaposi's sarcoma: a text and an atlas. Lea & Febiger, Philadelphia

224. Dorfman R F 1984 Kaposi's sarcoma revisited. Hum Pathol 15: 1013–1017

225. Krigel R L, Friedman-Kien A E 1990 Epidemic Kaposi's sarcoma. Semin Oncol 17: 350–360

226. Chor P J, Santa Cruz D J 1992 Kaposi's sarcoma. A clinicopathologic review and differential diagnosis. J Cutan Pathol 19: 6–20

227. Tappero J W, Conant M A, Wolfe S F et al. 1993 Kaposi's sarcoma. Epidemiology, pathogenesis, histology, clinical spectrum, staging criteria and therapy. J Am Acad Dermatol 28: 371–395

228. Beckstead J H, Wood G S, Fletcher V 1985 Evidence for the origin of Kaposi's sarcoma from lymphatic endothelium. Am J Pathol 119: 294–300

229. Russell Jones R, Spaull J, Spry C et al. 1986 Histogenesis of Kaposi's sarcoma in patients with and without acquired immune deficiency syndrome (AIDS). J Clin Pathol 39: 742–744

230. Rutgers J L, Wieczorek R, Bonetti F et al. 1986 The expression of endothelial cell surface antigens by AIDS-associated Kaposi's sarcoma. Evidence for a vascular endothelial cell origin. Am J Pathol 122: 493–499

231. Regezi J A, MacPhail L A, Daniels T E et al. 1993 Human immunodeficiency virus-associated oral Kaposi's sarcoma. A heterogeneous cell population dominated by spindle-shaped endothelial cells. Am J Pathol 143: 240–249

232. Weninger W, Partanen T A, Breiteneder-Geleff S et al. 1999 Expression of vascular endothelial growth factor receptor-3 and podoplanin suggests a lymphatic endothelial cell origin of Kaposi's sarcoma tumor cells. Lab Invest 79: 243–251

233. Grody W W, Lewin K J, Naeim F 1988 Detection of cytomegalovirus DNA in classic and epidemic Kaposi's sarcoma by in situ hybridization. Hum Pathol 19: 524–528

234. Ioachim H L, Dorsett B, Melamed J et al. 1992 Cytomegalovirus, angiomatosis, and Kaposi's sarcoma: new observations of a debated relationship. Mod Pathol 5: 169–178

235. Chang Y, Cesarman E, Pessin M S et al. 1994 Identification of herpesvirus-like DNA sequences in AIDS-associated Kaposi's sarcoma. Science 266: 1865–1869

236. Cesarman E, Knowles D M 1997 Kaposi's sarcoma-associated herpesvirus: a lymphotropic human herpesvirus associated with Kaposi's sarcoma, primary effusion lymphoma and multicentric Castleman's disease. Semin Diagn Pathol 14: 54–66

237. Kennedy M M, Lucas S B, Jones R R et al. 1997 HHV-8 and Kaposi's sarcoma: a time cohort study. J Clin Pathol Mol Pathol 50: 96–100

238. Renne R, Zhong W, Herndier B et al. 1996 Lytic growth of Kaposi's sarcoma-associated herpesvirus (human herpesvirus 8) in culture. Nature Med 2: 342–346

239. O'Leary J J, Kennedy M M, McGee J O 1997 Kaposi's sarcoma associated herpes virus (KSHV/HHV8): epidemiology, molecular biology and tissue distribution. Molec Pathol 5: 4–8

240. Cesarman E, Knowles D M 1997 Kaposi's sarcoma-associated herpesvirus: a lymphotropic human herpesvirus associated with Kaposi's sarcoma, primary effusion lymphoma and multicentric Castleman's disease. Semin Diagn Pathol 14: 54–66

241. Boshoff C, Talbot S, Kennedy M et al. 1996 HHV-8 and skin cancers in immunosuppressed patients. Lancet 347: 338–339

242. McDonagh D P, Liu J, Gaffey M J et al. 1996 Detection of Kaposi's sarcoma-associated herpes virus-type DNA sequences in angiosarcoma. Am J Pathol 149: 1363–1368

243. Lebbe C, Pellet C, Avril M F et al. 1997 Sequences of human herpesvirus 8 are not detected in various non-Kaposi sarcoma vascular lesions. Arch Dermatol 133: 919–920

244. Lasota J, Miettinen M 1999 Absence of Kaposi's sarcoma-associated virus (human herpes virus-8) sequences in angiosarcoma. Virchow's Arch 434: 51–56

245. Bayley A C, Lucas S B 1990 Kaposi's sarcoma or Kaposi's disease? A personal reappraisal. In: Fletcher CDM, McKee PH (eds) The pathobiology of soft tissue tumours. Churchill Livingstone, Edinburgh, Ch. 7

246. Rabkin C S, Janz S, Lash A et al. 1997 Monoclonal origin of multicentric Kaposi's sarcoma lesions. N Engl J Med 336: 988–993

247. Delabesse E, Oksenhendler E, Lebbe C et al. 1997 Molecular analysis of clonality in Kaposi's sarcoma. J Clin Pathol 50: 664–668

248. Gill P S, Tsai Y C, Rao A P et al. 1998 Evidence for multiclonality in multicentric Kaposi's sarcoma. Proc Natl Acad Sci USA 95: 8257–8261

249. Moskowitz L B, Hensley G T, Gould E W et al. 1985 Frequency and anatomic distribution of lymphadenopathic Kaposi's sarcoma in the acquired immunodeficiency syndrome: an autopsy series. Hum Pathol 16: 447–456

250. Lemlich G, Schwam L, Lebwohl M 1987 Kaposi's sarcoma and acquired immunodeficiency syndrome: postmortem findings in twenty-four cases. J Am Acad Dermatol 16: 319–325

251. Gange R W, Wilson Jones E 1978 Kaposi's sarcoma and immunosuppressive therapy: an appraisal. Clin Exp Dermatol 3: 135–146

252. Stribling J, Weitzner S, Smith G V 1978 Kaposi's sarcoma in renal allograft recipients. Cancer 42: 442–446

253. Dutz W, Stout A P 1960 Kaposi's sarcoma in infants and children. Cancer 13: 684–693

254. Dorfman R F 1986 Kaposi's sarcoma. With special reference to its manifestations in infants and children and to the concepts of Arthur Purdy Stout. Am J Surg Pathol 10 (suppl. 1): 68–77

255. Kao G F, Johnson F B, Sulica V I 1990 The nature of hyaline (eosinophilic) globules and vascular slits of Kaposi's sarcoma. Am J Dermatopathol 12: 256–267

256. Gange R W, Wilson Jones E 1979 Lymphangioma-like Kaposi's sarcoma. A report of three cases. Br J Dermatol 100: 327–334

257. Cossu S, Satta R, Cottoni F et al. 1997 Lymphangioma-like variant of Kaposi's sarcoma. Clinicopathologic study of seven cases with review of the literature. Am J Dermatopathol 19: 16–22

258. O'Connell K M 1977 Kaposi's sarcoma: histopathological study of 159 cases from Malawi. J Clin Pathol 30: 687–695

259. Satta R, Cossu S, Massarelli G et al. 2001 Anaplastic transformation of classic Kaposi's sarcoma: clinicopathological study of five cases. Br J Dermatol 145: 847–849

260. Cheuk W, Wong K O, Wong C S et al. 2004 Immunostaining for human herpesvirus 8 latent nuclear antigen-1 helps distinguish Kaposi sarcoma from its mimickers. Am J Clin Pathol 121: 335–342

261. Robin Y M, Guillou L, Michels J J et al. 2004 Human herpesvirus 8 immunostaining: a sensitive and specific method for diagnosing Kaposi sarcoma in paraffin-embedded sections. Am J Clin Pathol 121: 330–334

262. Wilson Jones E, Cerio R, Smith N P 1990 Multinucleate cell angiohistiocytoma: an acquired vascular anomaly to be distinguished from Kaposi's sarcoma. Br J Dermatol 122: 651–653

263. Weiss S W, Enzinger F M 1982 Epithelioid hemangioendothelioma. A vascular tumor often mistaken for a carcinoma. Cancer 50: 970–981

264. Weiss S W, Ishak K G, Dail D H et al. 1986 Epithelioid hemangioendothelioma and related lesions. Semin Diagn Pathol 3: 259–287

265. Mentzel T, Beham A, Calonje E et al. 1997 Epithelioid hemangioendothelioma of skin and soft tissues: clinicopathologic and immunohistochemical study of 30 cases. Am J Surg Pathol 21: 363–374

266. Angervall L, Kindblom L-G, Karlsson K et al. 1985 Atypical hemangioendothelioma of venous origin. A clinicopathologic, angiographic, immunohistochemical and ultrastructural study of two endothelial tumors within the concept of histiocytoid hemangioma. Am J Surg Pathol 9: 504–516

267. Dail D H, Liebow A A, Gmelich J T et al. 1983 Intravascular, bronchiolar and alveolar tumor of the lung (IVBAT). Cancer 51: 452–464

268. Makhlouf H R, Ishak K G, Goodman Z D 1999 Epithelioid hemangioendothelioma of the liver: a clinicopathologic study of 137 cases. Cancer 85: 562–582

269. Tsuneyoshi M, Dorfman H D, Bauer T W 1986 Epithelioid hemangioendothelioma of bone. A clinicopathologic, ultrastructural and immunohistochemical study. Am J Surg Pathol 10: 754–764

270. Lin B T, Colby T, Gown A M et al. 1996 Malignant vascular tumors of the serous membranes mimicking mesothelioma. A report of 14 cases. Am J Surg Pathol 20: 1431–1439

271. Quante M, Patel N K, Hill S et al. 1998 Epithelioid hemangioendothelioma presenting in the skin. A clinicopathologic study of eight cases. Am J Dermatopathol 20: 541–546

272. Tyring S, Guest P, Lee P et al. 1989 Epithelioid hemangioendothelioma of the skin and femur. J Am Acad Dermatol 20: 362–366

273. Resnik K S, Kantor G R, Spielvogel R L et al. 1993 Cutaneous epithelioid hemangioendothelioma without systemic involvement. Am J Dermatopathol 15: 272–276

274. Polk P, Webb J M 1997 Isolated cutaneous epithelioid hemangioendothelioma. J Am Acad Dermatol 36: 1026–1028

275. Lee K C, Chan J K C 1988 Epithelioid haemangioendothelioma presenting as a gastric polyp. Histopathology 16: 335–337

276. Suster S, Moran C A, Koss M N 1994 Epithelioid hemangioendothelioma of the anterior mediastinum. Clinicopathologic, immunohistochemical and ultrastructural analysis of 12 cases. Am J Surg Pathol 18: 871–881

277. Roh H S, Kim Y S, Suhr K B et al. 2000 A case of childhood epithelioid hemangioendothelioma. J Am Acad Dermatol 42: 897–899

278. Kiryu H, Hashimoto H, Hori Y 1996 Ossifying epithelioid hemangioendothelioma. J Cutan Pathol 23: 558–561

279. Lamovec J, Sobel H, Zidon A et al. 1990 Epithelioid hemangioendothelioma of the anterior mediastinum with osteoclast-like giant cells. Am J Clin Pathol 93: 813–817

280. Williams S B, Bulter C B, Gilkey G W et al. 1993 Epithelioid hemangioendothelioma with osteoclast like giant cells. Arch Pathol Lab Med 117: 315–318

281. Silva E G, Philips M J, Langer B et al. 1986 Spindle and histiocytoid (epithelioid) haemangioendothelioma, primary in lymph node. Am J Clin Pathol 85: 731–735

282. Suster S 1992 Epithelioid and spindle-cell hemangioendothelioma of the spleen, report of a distinctive splenic vascular neoplasm of childhood. Am J Surg Pathol 16: 785–792

283. Van Haelst U J G M, Pruszczynski M, Ten Cate L N et al. 1990 Ultrastructural and immunohistochemical study of epithelioid

hemangioendothelioma of bone: coexpression of epithelial and endothelial markers. Ultrastruct Pathol 14: 141–149

284. Gray M F, Rosenberg A E, Dickersin G R et al. 1990 Cytokeratin expression in epithelioid vascular neoplasms. Hum Pathol 21: 212–217

285. Mendick M R, Nelson M, Pickering D et al. 2001 Translocation t(1;3)(p36.3;q25) is a nonrandom aberration in epithelioid hemangioendothelioma. Am J Surg Pathol 25: 684–687

286. Billings S D, Folpe A L, Weiss S W 2003 Epithelioid sarcoma-like hemangioendothelioma. Am J Surg Pathol 27: 48–57

287. Wilson Jones E 1964 Malignant angioendothelioma of skin. Br J Dermatol 76: 21–39

288. Girard C, Johnson W C, Graham J H 1970 Cutaneous angiosarcoma. Cancer 26: 868–883

289. Rosai J, Summer H W, Kostianovsky M et al. 1976 Angiosarcoma of the skin. A clinicopathologic and fine structural study. Hum Pathol 7: 83–109

290. Wilson Jones E 1976 Malignant vascular tumours. Clin Exp Dermatol 1: 287–312

291. Maddox J C, Evans H L 1981 Angiosarcoma of skin and soft tissues: a study of forty-four cases. Cancer 48: 1907–1921

292. Cooper P H 1987 Angiosarcomas of the skin. Semin Diagn Pathol 4: 2–17

293. Ghandur-Mnaymneh L, Gonzales M S 1981 Angiosarcoma of the penis with hepatic angiomas in a patient with low vinyl chloride exposure. Cancer 47: 1318–1324

294. Abratt R P, Williams M, Raff M et al. 1983 Angiosarcoma of the superior vena cava. Cancer 52: 740–743

295. Rossi S, Fletcher C D M 2002 Angiosarcoma arising in hemangioma/vascular malformation: report of four cases and review of the literature. Am J Surg Pathol 26: 1319–1329

296. Mentzel T, Katenkamp D 1999 Intraneural angiosarcoma and angiosarcoma arising in benign and malignant peripheral nerve sheath tumours: clinicopathological and immunohistochemical analysis of four cases. Histopathology 35: 114–120

297. Chaudhuri B, Ronan S G, Manaligod J R 1980 Angiosarcoma arising in a plexiform neurofibroma. Cancer 46: 605–610

298. McMenamin M E, Fletcher C D M 2001 Expanding the spectrum of malignant change in schwannomas: epithelioid malignant change, epithelioid malignant peripheral nerve sheath tumor and epithelioid angiosarcoma: a study of 17 cases. Am J Surg Pathol 25: 13–25

299. Morphopoulos G D, Banerjee S S, Ali H H et al. 1996 Malignant peripheral nerve sheath tumour with vascular differentiation: a report of four cases. Histopathology 28: 401–410

300. Kauffman S L, Stout A P 1961 Malignant hemangioendothelioma in infants and children. Cancer 14: 1186–1196

301. Lezana-del Valle P, Gerald W L, Tsai J et al. 1998 Malignant vascular tumors in young patients. Cancer 83: 1634–1639

302. Leake J, Sheehan M P, Rampling D et al. 1992 Angiosarcoma complicating xeroderma pigmentosum. Histopathology 21: 179–181

303. Marcon I, Collini P, Casanova M 2004 Cutaneous angiosarcoma in a patient with xeroderma pigmentosum. Pediatr Hematol Oncol 21: 23–26

304. Schmutz J L, Kue E, Baylac F et al. 1998 Angiosarcoma complicating Hallopeau–Siemens-type epidermolysis bullosa. Br J Dermatol 138: 910–912

305. Al-Najjar A-W, Harrington C I, Slater D N 1986 Angiosarcoma: a complication of varicose leg ulceration. Acta Derm Venereol 66:167–170

306. Folpe A L, Johnston C A, Weiss S W 2000 Cutaneous angiosarcoma arising in a gouty tophus: report of a unique case and a review of foreign material-associated angiosarcomas. Am J Dermatopathol 22: 418–421

307. Azam M, Saboorian H, Bieligk S et al. 2001 Cutaneous angiosarcoma complicating morbid obesity. Arch Pathol Lab Med 125: 531–533

308. Kibe Y, Kishimoto S, Katoh N et al. 1997 Angiosarcoma of the scalp associated with renal transplantation. Br J Dermatol 136: 752–756

309. Ahmed I, Hamacher K L 2002 Angiosarcoma in a chronically immunosuppressed renal transplant recipient: report of a case and review of the literature. Am J Dermatopathol 24: 330–335

309a. Schmid H, Zeitz C 2005 Human herpesvirus 8 and angiosarcoma: analysis of 40 cases and review of the literature. Pathology 37: 284–287

310. Holden C A, Spittle M F, Wilson Jones E 1987 Angiosarcoma of the face and scalp, prognosis and treatment. Cancer 59: 1046–1057

311. Lydiatt W M, Shaha A R, Shah J P 1994 Angiosarcoma of the head and neck. Am J Surg 168: 451–454

312. Mark R J, Poen J C, Tran L M et al. 1996 Angiosarcoma. A report of 67 patients and a review of the literature. Cancer 77: 2400–2406

313. Pawlik T M, Paulino A F, McGinn C J et al. 2003 Cutaneous angiosarcoma of the scalp: a multidisciplinary approach. Cancer 98: 1716–1726

314. Morrison W H, Byers R M, Garden A S et al. 1995 Cutaneous angiosarcoma of the head and neck. A therapeutic dilemma. Cancer 76: 319–327

315. Stewart F W, Treves N 1948 Lymphangiosarcoma in postmastectomy lymphedema. A report of six cases in elephantiasis chirurgica. Cancer 1: 64–81

316. Woodward A H, Ivins J C, Soule E H 1972 Lymphangiosarcoma arising in chronic lymphedematous extremities. Cancer 30: 562–572

317. Alessi E, Sala F, Berti E 1986 Angiosarcomas in lymphedematous limbs. Am J Dermatopathol 8: 371–378

318. Capo V, Ozzello L, Fenoglio C M et al. 1985 Angiosarcomas arising in edematous extremities: immunostaining for factor VIII related antigen and ultrastructural features. Hum Pathol 16: 144–150

319. Danese C A, Grishman E, Oh C et al. 1967 Malignant vascular tumors of the lymphedematous extremity. Ann Surg 166: 245–253

320. Mackenzie D H 1971 Lymphangiosarcoma arising in chronic congenital and idiopathic lymphoedema. J Clin Pathol 24: 524–529

321. Woodward A H, Ivins J C, Soule E H 1972 Lymphangiosarcoma arising in chronic lymphedematous extremities. Cancer 30: 562–572

322. Krasagakis K, Hettmannsperger U, Tebbe B et al. 1995 Cutaneous metastatic angiosarcoma with a lethal outcome, following radiotherapy for a cervical carcinoma. Br J Dermatol 133: 610–614

323. Goette D K, Detlefs R L 1985 Postirradiation angiosarcoma. J Am Acad Dermatol 12: 922–926

324. Fineberg S, Rosen P P 1994 Cutaneous angiosarcoma and atypical vascular lesions of the skin and breast after radiation therapy for breast carcinoma. Am J Clin Pathol 102: 757–763

325. Karlsson P, Holmberg E, Johansson K A et al. 1996 Soft tissue sarcoma after treatment for breast cancer. Radiother Oncol 38: 25–31

326. Cafiero F, Gipponi M, Peressini A et al. 1996 Radiation-associated angiosarcoma. Diagnostic and therapeutic implications – two case reports and a review of the literature. Cancer 77: 2496–2502

327. Billings S D, McKenney J K, Folpe A L et al. 2004 Cutaneous angiosarcoma following breast-conserving surgery and radiation. Am J Surg Pathol 28: 781–788

328. Majeski J, Austin R M, Fitzgerald R H 2000 Cutaneous angiosarcoma in an irradiated breast after breast conservation therapy for cancer: association with chronic breast lymphedema. J Surg Oncol 74: 208–212

329. Fletcher C D M, Beham A, Bekir S et al. 1991 Epithelioid angiosarcoma of deep soft tissue: a distinctive tumor readily mistaken for an epithelial neoplasm. Am J Surg Pathol 15: 915–924

330. Meis-Kindblom J M, Kindblom L-G 1998 Angiosarcoma of soft tissue. A study of 80 cases. Am J Surg Pathol 22: 683–697

331. Marrogi A J, Hunt S J, Santa Cruz D J 1990 Cutaneous epithelioid angiosarcoma. Am J Dermatopathol 12: 350–356

332. McWilliam L J, Harris M 1985 Granular cell angiosarcoma of the skin: histology, electron microscopy and immunohistochemistry of a newly recognised tumor. Histopathology 9: 1205–1216

333. Hitchcock M G, Hurt M A, Santa Cruz D J 1994 Cutaneous granular cell angiosarcoma. J Cutan Pathol 21: 256–262

334. Naka N, Ohsawa M, Tomita Y et al. 1996 Prognostic factors in angiosarcoma: a multivariate analysis of 55 cases. J Surg Oncol 61: 170–176

335. Morgan M B, Swann M, Somach S et al. 2004 Cutaneous angiosarcoma: a case series with prognostic correlation. J Am Acad Dermatol 50: 867–874

336. Folpe A L, Chand E M, Goldblum J R et al. 2001 Expression of Fli-1, nuclear transcription factor, distinguishes vascular neoplasms from potential mimics. Am J Surg Pathol 25: 1061–1066

337. Schuborg C, Mertens F, Rydholm A et al. 1998 Cytogenetic analysis of four angiosarcomas from deep and superficial soft tissue. Cancer Genet Cytogenet 100: 52–56

338. Eckert F, Schmid U, Gloor F et al. 1986 Evidence of vascular differentiation in anaplastic tumours of the thyroid: an immunohistochemical study. Virchow's Arch [A] 410: 203–215

339. Eusebi V, Carcangiu M L, Dina R et al. 1990 Keratin positive epithelioid angiosarcoma of thyroid. A report of four cases. Am J Surg Pathol 14: 737–747

340. Wenig B M, Abbondanzo S L, Heffer C S 1994 Epithelioid angiosarcoma of the adrenal glands. Am J Surg Pathol 18: 62–73

341. Goldblum J R, Rice T W 1995 Epithelioid angiosarcoma of the pulmonary artery. Hum Pathol 26: 1275–1277

342. Macias-Martínez V, Murrieta-Tiburcio L, Molina-Cárdenas H et al. 1997 Epithelioid angiosarcoma of the breast. Clinicopathological, immunohistochemical and ultrastructural study of a case. Am J Surg Pathol 21: 599–604

343. Hasegawa T, Fujii Y, Seki K et al. 1997 Epithelioid angiosarcoma of bone. Hum Pathol 28: 985–989

344. McAdam J A, Stewart F, Reid R 1998 Vaginal epithelioid angiosarcoma. J Clin Pathol 51: 928–930

345. Prescott R J, Banerjee S S, Eyden B P et al. 1994 Cutaneous epithelioid angiosarcoma: a clinicopathological study of four cases. Histopathology 25: 421–429

346. Jennings T A, Peterson L, Axiotis C A et al. 1988 Angiosarcoma associated with foreign body material. Cancer 62: 2436–2444

347. Byers R J, McMahon R F T, Freemont A J et al. 1992 Epithelioid angiosarcoma arising in an arteriovenous fistula. Histopathology 21: 87–89

348. Wehrli B M, Janzen D L, Shokeir O et al. 1998 Epithelioid angiosarcoma arising in a surgically constructed fistula: a rare complication of chronic immunosuppression in the setting of renal transplantation. Am J Surg Pathol 22: 1154–1159

349. Seo I S, Min K W 2003 Postirradiation epithelioid angiosarcoma of the breast: a case report with immunohistochemical and electron microscopic study. Ultrastruct Pathol 27: 197–203

350. Val-Bernal J F, Figols J, Arce F P et al. 2001 Cardiac epithelioid angiosarcoma presenting as cutaneous metastases. J Cutan Pathol 28: 265–270

351. Sebenik M, Ricci A Jr, DiPasquale B et al. 2005 Undifferentiated intimal sarcoma of large systemic blood vessels: report of 14 cases with immunohistochemical profile and review of the literature. Am J Surg Pathol 29: 1184–1193

352. Herzberg A J, Pizzo S V 1988 Primary undifferentiated sarcoma of the thoracic aorta. Histopathology 13: 571–574

353. Haber L M, Truong L 1988 Immunohistochemical demonstration of the endothelial nature of aortic intimal sarcoma. Am J Surg Pathol 12: 798–802

354. Seelig M H, Klinger P J, Oldenburg W A et al. 1998 Angiosarcoma of the aorta: report of a case and review of the literature. J Vasc Surg 28: 732–737

355. Burke A P, Virmani R 1993 Sarcomas of the great vessels. A clinicopathologic study. Cancer 71: 1761–1773

356. Johansson L, Carlen B 1994 Sarcoma of the pulmonary artery: report of four cases with electron microscopic and immunohistochemical examinations, and review of the literature. Virchows Arch 424: 217–224

357. Nonomura A, Kurumaya H, Kono N et al. 1988 Primary pulmonary artery sarcoma. Report of two autopsy cases studied by immunohistochemistry and electron microscopy, and review of 110 cases reported in the literature. Acta Pathol Jpn 38: 883–896

358. Gaumann A, Petrow P, Mentzel T et al. 2001 Osteopontin expression in primary sarcomas of the pulmonary artery. Virchows Arch 439: 668–674

359. Santonja C, Martin-Hita A M, Dotor A et al. 2001 Intimal angiosarcoma of the aorta with tumour embolisation causing mesenteric ischaemia. Report of a case diagnosed using CD31 immunohistochemistry in an intestinal resection specimen. Virchows Arch 438: 404–407

360. Bode-Lesniewska B, Zhao J, Speel E J et al. 2001 Gains of 12q13-14 and overexpression of mdm2 are frequent findings in intimal sarcomas of the pulmonary artery. Virchows Arch 438: 57–65

361. Bill A H, Sumner D S 1965 A unified concept of lymphangioma and cystic hygroma. Surg Gynecol Obstet 120: 79–86

362. Gross R E, Goeringer C F 1939 Cystic hygroma of the neck. Report of twenty-seven cases. Surg Gynecol Obstet 69: 48–60

363. Harkin G A, Sabiston D C 1960 Lymphangioma in infancy and childhood. Surgery 47: 811–822

364. Chervenak F A, Isaacson G, Blakemore K J et al. 1983 Fetal cystic hygroma. Cause and natural history. N Engl J Med 309: 822–825

365. De Perrot M, Rostan O, Morel P et al. 1998 Abdominal lymphangioma in adults and children. Br J Surg 85: 395–397

366. Hornick J L, Fletcher C D M 2005 Intra-abdominal cystic lymphangiomas obscured by marked superimposed reactive changes: clinicopathologic analysis of a series. Hum Pathol 36: 426–432

367. Peachey R D G, Lim C-C, Whimster I W 1970 Lymphangioma of the skin. A review of 65 cases. Br J Dermatol 83: 519–527

368. Flanagan B P, Helwig E B 1977 Cutaneous lymphangioma. Arch Dermatol 113: 24–30

369. Prioleau P G, Santa Cruz D J 1978 Lymphangioma circumscriptum following radical mastectomy and radiation therapy. Cancer 42: 1989–1991

370. Whimster I W 1976 The pathology of lymphangioma circumscriptum. Br J Dermatol 94: 473–486

371. Gold S C 1970 Angioendothelioma (lymphatic type). Br J Dermatol 82: 92–93

372. Wilson Jones E, Winkelmann R K, Zachary C B et al. 1990 Benign lymphangio-endothelioma. J Am Acad Dermatol 23: 229–235

373. Guillou L, Fletcher C D M 2000 Benign lymphangioendothelioma (acquired progressive lymphangioma): a lesion not to be confused with well-differentiated angiosarcoma and patch stage Kaposi's sarcoma. Am J Surg Pathol 24: 1047–1057

374. Grunwald M H, Amichai B, Avinoach I 1997 Acquired progressive lymphangioma. J Am Acad Dermatol 37: 656–657

375. Sevila A, Botella-Estrada R, Sanmartín O et al. 2000 Benign lymphangioendothelioma of the thigh simulating a low grade angiosarcoma. Am J Dermatopathol 22: 151–154

376. Watanabe M, Kishiyama K, Ohkawara A 1983 Acquired progressive lymphangioma. J Am Acad Dermatol 8: 663–667

377. Mehregan D R, Mehregan A H, Mehregan D A 1992 Benign lymphangioendothelioma: report of two cases. J Cutan Pathol 19: 502–505

378. Rosso R, Gianelli U, Carnevali L 1995 Acquired progressive lymphangioma of the skin following radiotherapy for breast carcinoma. J Cutan Pathol 22: 164–167

379. Kato H, Kadoya A 1996 Acquired progressive lymphangioma following femoral arteriography. Clin Exp Dermatol 21: 159–162

380. Asch M J, Cohen A H, Moore T C 1974 Hepatic and splenic lymphangiomatosis with skeletal involvement: report of a case and review of the literature. Surgery 76: 334–339

381. Ramani P, Shah A 1992 Lymphangiomatosis. Histological and immunohistochemical analysis of four cases. Am J Surg Pathol 16: 764–771

382. Singh Gomez C, Calonje E, Ferrar D W et al. 1995 Lymphangiomatosis of the limbs: clinicopathologic analysis of a series with a good prognosis. Am J Surg Pathol 19: 125–133

383. Díaz-Cascajo C, Borghi S, Weyers W et al. 1999 Benign lymphangiomatous papules of the skin after radiotherapy: a report of five new cases and review of the literature. Histopathology 35: 319–327

384. Requena L, Kutzner H, Mentzel T et al. 2002 Benign vascular proliferations in irradiated skin. Am J Surg Pathol 26: 328–337

385. Brenn T, Fletcher C D M 2005 Radiation-induced cutaneous atypical vascular lesions and angiosarcoma: Clinicopathologic analysis of 42 cases. Am J Surg Pathol 29: 983–996

386. Frack M D, Simon S, Dawson B H 1968 The lymphangiomyomatosis syndrome. Cancer 22: 428–437

387. Wolff M 1973 Lymphangiomyoma: clinicopathologic study and ultrastructural confirmation of its histogenesis. Cancer 31: 988–1007

388. Johnson S 1999 Rare diseases. I. Lymphangioleiomyomatosis: clinical features, management and basic mechanisms. Thorax 54: 254–264

389. Berger U, Khaghani A, Pomerance A et al. 1990 Pulmonary lymphangioleiomyomatosis and steroid receptors. An immunocytochemical study. Am J Clin Pathol 93: 609–614

390. Ohori N P, Yousem S A, Sonmez-Alpan E et al. 1991 Estrogen and progesterone receptors in lymphangioleiomyomatosis, epithelioid hemangioendothelioma, and sclerosing hemangioma of the lung. Am J Clin Pathol 96: 529–535

391. Torres V E, Bjornsson J, King B F et al. 1995 Extrapulmonary lymphangioleiomyomatosis and lymphangiomatous cysts in tuberous sclerosis complex. Mayo Clin Proc 70: 641–648

392. Smolarek T A, Wessner L L, McCormack F X et al. 1998 Evidence that lymphangiomyomatosis is caused by TSC2 mutations: chromosome 16p13 loss of heterozygosity in angiomyolipomas and lymph nodes from women with lymphangiomyomatosis. Am J Hum Genet 62: 810–815

393. Pacheco-Rodríguez G, Kristof A S, Stevens L A et al. 2002 Giles F. Filley lecture. Genetics and gene expression in lymphangioleiomyomatosis. Chest 121: 56S–60S

394. Chan J K C, Tsang W Y W, Pau M Y et al. 1993 Lymphangiomyomatosis and angiomyolipoma: closely related entities characterized by hamartomatous proliferation of HMB-45 positive smooth muscle. Histopathology 22: 445–455

395. Fetsch P A, Fetsch J F, Marincola F M et al. 1998 Comparison of melanoma antigen recognized by T cells (MART-1) to HMB-45: additional evidence to support a common lineage for angiomyolipoma, lymphangiomyomatosis and clear cell sugar tumor. Mod Pathol 11: 699–703

396. Pea M, Martignoni G, Zamboni G et al. 1996 Perivascular epithelioid cell. Am J Surg Pathol 20: 1149–1153

397. Bailey O T 1935 The cutaneous glomus and its tumors – glomangiomas. Am J Pathol 11: 915–935

398. Kohout E, Stout A P 1961 The glomus tumor in children. Cancer 14: 555–565

399. Tsuneyoshi M, Enjoji M 1982 Glomus tumor: a clinicopathologic and electron microscopic study. Cancer 50: 1601–1607

400. Pepper M C, Laubenheimer R, Cripps D J 1977 Multiple glomus tumours. J Cutan Pathol 4: 244–257

401. Happle R, Konig A 1999 Type 2 segmental manifestation of multiple glomus tumors: a review and reclassification of 5 case reports. Dermatology 198: 270–272

402. Boon L M, Brouillard P, Irrthum A et al. 1999 A gene for inherited cutaneous venous anomalies ("glomangiomas") localizes to chromosome 1p21-22. Am J Hum Genet 65: 125–133

403. Calvert J T, Burns S, Riney TJ et al. 2001 Additional glomangioma family link to chromosome 1p: no evidence for genetic heterogeneity. Hum Hered 51: 180–182

404. Brouillard P, Boom L M, Mulliken J B et al. 2002 Mutations in a novel factor, glomulin, are responsible for glomuvenous malformations ("glomangiomas"). Am J Hum Genet 70: 866–874

405. Kanwar Y S, Manaligod J R 1975 Glomus tumor of the stomach. An ultrastructural study. Arch Pathol 99: 392–397

406. Kim Y I, Kim J H, Suh J et al. 1989 Glomus tumor of the trachea. Report of a case with ultrastructural observations. Cancer 64: 881–886

407. Sunderraj S, Al-Kahalifa A A, Pal A K et al. 1989 Primary intra-osseous glomus tumour. Histopathology 14: 532–536

408. Geraghty J M, Everitt N J, Blundell J W 1991 Glomus tumour of the small bowel. Histopathology 19: 287–289

409. Harvey J A, Walker F 1987 Solid glomus tumor of the pterygoid fossa: a lesion mimicking an epithelial neoplasm of low-grade malignancy. Hum Pathol 18: 965–966

410. Koss M N, Hochholzer L, Moran C A 1998 Primary pulmonary glomus tumor: a clinicopathologic and immunohistochemical study of two cases. Mod Pathol 11: 253–258

411. Gaertner E M, Steinberg D M, Huber M et al. 2000 Pulmonary and mediastinal glomus tumors – report of five cases including a pulmonary glomangiosarcoma: a clinicopathologic study with literature review. Am J Surg Pathol 24: 1105–1114

412. Hirose T, Hasegawa T, Seki K et al. 1996 Atypical glomus tumor in the mediastinum: a case report with immunohistochemical and ultrastructural studies. Ultrastruct Pathol 20: 451–456

413. Jaiswal V R, Champine J G, Sharma S et al. 2004 Primary glomangioma of the liver: a case report and review of the literature. Arch Pathol Lab Med 128: 46–49

414. Miliauskas J R, Worthley C, Allen P W 2002 Glomangiomyoma (glomus tumor) of the pancreas: a case report. Pathology 34: 193–195

415. Gokten N, Peterdy G, Philpott T et al. 2001 Glomus tumor of the ovary: report of a case with immunohistochemical and ultrastructural observations. Int J Gynecol Pathol 20: 390–394

416. Silver S A, Tavassoli F A 2000 Glomus tumor arising in a mature teratoma of the ovary: report of a case simulating a metastasis from cervical squamous carcinoma. Arch Pathol Lab Med 124: 1373–1375

417. Beham A, Fletcher C D M 1991 Intravascular glomus tumour: a previously undescribed phenomenon. Virchow's Arch [A] 418: 175–177

418. Googe P B, Griffin W C 1993 Intravenous glomus tumor of the forearm. J Cutan Pathol 20: 359–363

419. Calonje E, Fletcher C D M 1995 Cutaneous intraneural glomus tumor. Am J Dermatopathol 17: 395–398

420. Sawada S, Honda M, Kamide R et al. 1995 Three cases of subungual glomus tumors with von Recklinghausen neurofibromatosis. J Am Acad Dermatol 32: 277–278

421. Okada O, Demitsu T, Manabe M et al. 1999 A case of multiple subungual glomus tumors associated with neurofibromatosis type 1. J Dermatol 26: 535–537

422. De Smet L, Sciot R, Legius E 2002 Multifocal glomus tumours of the fingers in two patients with neurofibromatosis type 1. J Med Genet 39: 45

423. Haque S, Modlin I M, West A B 1992 Multiple glomus tumors of the stomach with intravascular spread. Am J Surg Pathol 16: 291–299

424. Albrecht S, Zbieranowski J 1990 Incidental glomus coccygeum. When a normal structure looks like a tumor. Am J Surg Pathol 14: 922–924

425. Van Geertruyden J, Lorea P, Goldschmidt D et al. 1996 Glomus tumours of the hand. A retrospective study of 51 cases. J Hand Surg (Br) 21: 257–260

426. Brathwaite C D, Poppiti R J Jr 1996 Malignant glomus tumor. A case report of widespread metastases in a patient with multiple glomus body hamartomas. Am J Surg Pathol 20: 233–238

427. Watanabe K, Sugino T, Saito A et al. 1998 Glomangiosarcoma of the hip: report of a highly aggressive tumour with widespread distant metastases. Br J Dermatol 139: 1097–1101

428. Kayal J D, Hampton R W, Sheehan D J et al. 2001 Malignant glomus tumor: a case report and review of the literature. Dermatol Surg 27: 837–840

429. Park J H, Oh S H, Yang M H et al. 2003 Glomangiosarcoma of the hand: a case report and review of the literature. J Dermatol 30: 827–833

430. Folpe A L, Fanburgh-Smith J C, Miettinen M et al. 2001 Atypical and malignant glomus tumors: analysis of 52 cases, with a proposal for the reclassification of glomus tumors. Am J Surg Pathol 25: 1–12

431. Slater D N, Cotton D W K, Azzopardi J G 1987 Oncocytic glomus tumour: a new variant. Histopathology 11: 523–531

432. Pulitzer D R, Martin P C, Reed R J 1995 Epithelioid glomus tumor. Hum Pathol 26: 1022–1027

433. Jalali M, Netscher D T, Connelly J H 2002 Glomangiomatosis. Ann Diagn Pathol 6: 326–328.

434. Wood W S, Dimmiek J E 1977 Multiple infiltrating glomus tumours in children. Cancer 40: 1680–1685

435. Gould E W, Manivel J C, Albores-Saavedra J et al. 1990 Locally infiltrative glomus tumors and glomangiosarcoma. A clinical, ultrastructural and immunohistochemical study. Cancer 65: 310–318

436. Dervan P A, Tobbin I N, Casey M et al. 1989 Glomus tumours: an immunohistochemical profile of 11 cases. Histopathology 14: 483–491

437. Porter P L, Bigler S A, McNutt M et al. 1991 The immunophenotype of hemangiopericytomas and glomus tumors with special reference to muscle protein expression: an immunohistochemical study and review of the literature. Mod Pathol 4: 46–52

438. Liapi-Avgeri G, Karabela-Bouropoulou X, Agnanti N 1994 Glomus tumor. A histological, histochemical and immunohistochemical study of the various types. Pathol Res Pract 190: 2–10

439. Mentzel T, Hugel H, Kutzner H 2002 CD34-positive glomus tumor: clinicopathologic and immunohistochemical analysis of six cases with myxoid stromal changes. J Cutan Pathol 29: 421–425

440. Hiruta N, Kameda N, Tokudome T et al. 1997 Malignant glomus tumor: a case report and review of the literature. Am J Surg Pathol 21: 1096–1103

441. López-Rios F, Rodríguez-Peralto J L, Castaño E et al. 1997 Glomangiosarcoma of the lower limb: a case report with a literature review. J Cutan Pathol 24: 571–574

442. Stout A P, Murray M R 1942 Hemangiopericytoma: a vascular tumor featuring Zimmermann's pericytes. Ann Surg 116: 26–33

443. Battifora H 1973 Hemangiopericytoma: ultrastructural study of five cases. Cancer 31: 1418–1432

444. Nunnery E W, Khan L B, Reddick R L et al. 1981 Hemangiopericytoma: a light microscopic and ultrastructural study. Cancer 47: 906–914

445. Dardick I, Hammar S P, Scheithauer B W 1989 Ultrastructural spectrum of hemangiopericytoma: a comparative study of fetal, adult, and neoplastic pericytes. Ultrastruct Pathol 13: 111–154

446. Middleton L P, Duray P H, Merino M J 1998 The histologic spectrum of hemangiopericytoma: application of immunohistochemical analysis including proliferative markers to facilitate diagnosis and predict prognosis. Hum Pathol 29: 636–640

447. Schurch W, Skalli O, Lagace R et al. 1990 Intermediate filament proteins and actin isoforms as markers for soft tissue tumor differentiation and origin III. Hemangiopericytomas and glomus tumors. Am J Pathol 136: 771–786

448. Tsuneyoshi M, Daimaru Y, Enjoji M 1984 Malignant hemangiopericytoma and other sarcomas with hemangiopericytoma-like pattern. Pathol Res Pract 178: 446–453

449. Fletcher C D M 1994 Haemangiopericytoma – a dying breed? Reappraisal of an "entity" and its variants. Curr Diagn Pathol 1: 19–23

450. Nappi O, Ritter J H, Pettinato G et al. 1995 Hemangiopericytoma: histopathological pattern or clinicopathologic entity? Semin Diagn Pathol 12: 221–232

451. Stout A P 1949 Hemangiopericytoma. A study of twenty-five new cases. Cancer 2: 1027–1035

452. Granter S R, Badizadegan K, Fletcher C D M 1998 Myofibromatosis in adults, glomangiopericytoma and myopericytoma. A spectrum of tumors showing perivascular myoid differentiation. Am J Surg Pathol 22: 513–525

453. Enzinger F M, Smith B H 1976 Hemangiopericytoma. An analysis of 106 cases. Hum Pathol 7: 61–82

454. Angervall L, Kindblom L G, Moller Nielsen J M et al. 1978 Hemangiopericytoma, a clinicopathologic, angiographic and microangiographic study. Cancer 42: 2412–2427

455. Pavelic K, Cabrijan T, Hrascan R et al. 1998 Molecular pathology of hemangiopericytomas accompanied by severe hypoglycemia: oncogenes, tumor-suppressor genes and the insulin-like growth factor family. J Cancer Res Clin Oncol 124: 307–314

456. Guthrie B L, Ebersold M J, Scheithauer B W et al. 1989 Meningeal hemangiopericytoma: features, treatment and long-term follow-up of 44 cases. Neurosurgery 25: 514–522

457. Mena H, Ribas J L, Pezeshkpour G H et al. 1991 Hemangiopericytoma of the central nervous system: a review of 94 cases. Hum Pathol 22: 84–91

458. Compagno J, Hyams V J 1976 Hemangiopericytoma-like intranasal tumors. A clinicopathologic study of 23 cases. Am J Clin Pathol 66: 672–683

459. Eichhorn J H, Dickersin G R, Bhan A K et al. 1990 Sinonasal hemangiopericytoma. A reassessment with electron microscopy, immunohistochemistry, and long-term follow-up. Am J Surg Pathol 14: 856–866

460. Coffin C M, Dehner L P 1991 Fibroblastic-myofibroblastic tumors in children and adolescents: a clinicopathologic study of 108 examples in 103 patients. Pediatr Pathol 11: 569–588

461. Mentzel T, Calonje E, Nascimento A G et al. 1994 Infantile haemangiopericytoma versus infantile myofibromatosis: a study of a series suggesting a spectrum of infantile myofibroblastic lesions. Am J Surg Pathol 18: 922–930

462. Dictor M, Elner A, Andersson T et al. 1992 Myofibromatosis-like hemangiopericytoma metastasising as differentiated vascular smooth muscle and myosarcoma. Myopericytes as a subset of "myofibroblasts." Am J Surg Pathol 16: 1239–1247

463. Variend S, Bax N M, Van Gorp J 1995 Are infantile myofibromatosis, congenital fibrosarcoma and congenital haemangiopericytoma histogenetically related? Histopathology 26: 57–62

463a. Mentzel T, Dei Tos A P, Sapi Z, Kutzner H 2006 Myopericytoma of skin and soft tissues: clinicopathologic and immunohistochemical study of 54 cases. Am J Surg Pathol 30: 104–113

464. Requena L, Kutzner H, Hugel H et al. 1996 Cutaneous adult myofibroma: a vascular neoplasm. J Cutan Pathol 23: 445–457

465. Sakamoto A, Oda Y, Nagayoshi Y et al. 2001 Glomangiopericytoma causing oncogenic osteomalacia. A case report with immunohistochemical analysis. Arch Orthop Trauma Surg 121: 104–108

466. McMenamin M E, Fletcher C D M 2002 Malignant myopericytoma: expanding the spectrum of tumors with myopericytic differentiation. Histopathology 41: 450–460

467. Vallet-Decouvelaere A V, Dry S M, Fletcher C D M 1998 Atypical and malignant solitary fibrous tumors in extrathoracic locations: evidence of their comparability to intra-thoracic tumors. Am J Surg Pathol 22: 1501–1511

468. McMenamin M E, Calonje E 2002 Intravascular myopericytoma. J Cutan Pathol 29: 557–561

Nasal cavity, paranasal sinuses, and nasopharynx

Bruce M. Wenig

The nasal cavity and paranasal sinuses – including the maxillary, ethmoid, sphenoid, and frontal sinuses – are collectively referred to as the sinonasal tract. The sinonasal tract is anatomically and embryologically distinct from the nasopharynx. Although the sinonasal tract and nasopharynx have identical-appearing ciliated respiratory epithelium, the epithelium of the sinonasal tract is ectodermally derived, while that of the nasopharynx is endodermally derived. This embryologic difference may be a factor in the development of certain epithelial lesions unique to these surfaces (e.g., schneiderian papillomas of the sinonasal tract and nasopharyngeal carcinomas (NPCs)). Despite these differences, the sinonasal tract and nasopharynx are comprised of similar structures such as minor salivary glands and connective tissue. These structures may give rise to identical neoplasms that differ only in their location and resulting clinical symptomatology. The classification of neoplasms of the nasal cavity and paranasal sinus is listed in Table 4A.1 and the neoplasms of the nasopharynx are listed in Table 4A.2.

Benign epithelial and neuroectodermal neoplasms

Sinonasal-type (Schneiderian) papillomas

The ectodermally derived lining of the sinonasal tract, termed the Schneiderian membrane, may give rise to three morphologically distinct benign papillomas collectively referred to as schneiderian or sinonasal-type papillomas. The three morphologic types are inverted, oncocytic (cylindrical or columnar cell), and fungiform (exophytic, septal) papillomas (Table 4A.3).

Collectively, Schneiderian papillomas represent fewer than 5% of all sinonasal tract tumors.[1] The literature indicates that, among sinonasal-type papillomas, the septal papilloma is the most common type. However, practical experience indicates that the inverted type is the most common subtype seen. The oncocytic type is the least common. In general, the sinonasal-type papillomas occur over a wide age range but are rare in children.[1-8] Inverted papillomas are most common in the fifth to eighth decades; cylindrical papillomas occur in a somewhat older age range (greater than 50 years) and are uncommon in patients younger than the fourth decade of life; septal papillomas tend to occur in a younger age group.[1,2] The septal papillomas are almost invariably limited to the nasal septum. Inverted papillomas occur along the lateral nasal wall (middle turbinate or ethmoid recesses) with secondary extension into the paranasal sinuses (maxillary and ethmoid, and less often sphenoid and frontal); less frequently, inverted papillomas may originate in a paranasal sinus. Oncocytic papillomas also are most often seen along the lateral nasal wall but may originate within a paranasal sinus (maxillary or ethmoid). The inverted and oncocytic subtypes rarely occur on the nasal septum. Typically, the Schneiderian papillomas are unilateral; bilateral papillomas, in particular the inverted subtype, may occur with a reported incidence of up to 10%.[1,7-9] In the presence of bilaterality, clinical evaluation to exclude the possibility of extension from unilateral disease (i.e., septal perforation) should be undertaken. Inverted papillomas may occur in a paranasal sinus without involvement of the nasal cavity.[10]

Table 4A.1 Classification of nasal cavity and paranasal sinus neoplasms

Benign
Epithelial
  Schneiderian papillomas
  Squamous papilloma (nasal vestibule)
  Minor salivary gland tumors
Neuroectodermal
  Ectopic pituitary adenoma
  Paraganglioma
  Meningioma
Mesenchymal
  Lobular capillary hemangioma (pyogenic granuloma)
  Solitary fibrous tumor
  Ossifying and non-ossifying fibromyxoid tumor
  Peripheral nerve sheath tumors
  Fibrous histiocytoma
  Fibromatosis
  Osteoma
  Fibro-osseous lesions (ossifying fibroma, psammomatoid ossifying fibroma)
  Leiomyoma
  Myxoma/fibromyxoma/chondromyxoid fibroma
  Lipoma
  Ameloblastoma
  Others
Indeterminant for malignancy/low-grade malignant potential
  Sinonasal-type hemangiopericytoma
  Epithelioid hemangioendothelioma

Malignant
Epithelial
  Squamous cell carcinoma:
  • Keratinizing squamous cell carcinoma
  • Non-keratinizing squamous cell carcinoma
  • Variants of squamous cell carcinoma (verrucous carcinoma, papillary squamous cell carcinoma, spindle cell squamous carcinoma, basaloid squamous cell carcinoma, lymphoepithelial carcinoma, adenosquamous carcinoma)
  Sinonasal undifferentiated carcinoma
  Adenocarcinoma:
  • Intestinal types
  • Non-salivary, non-intestinal types
  Minor salivary gland neoplasms
Mesenchymal/neuroectodermal
  Mucosal malignant melanoma
  Olfactory neuroblastoma
  Non-Hodgkin malignant lymphomas
  Extraosseous Ewing's sarcoma/primitive neuroectodermal tumor
  Undifferentiated pleomorphic sarcoma (malignant fibrous histiocytoma)
  Fibrosarcoma
  Malignant peripheral nerve sheath tumor
  Leiomyosarcoma
  Angiosarcoma
  Osteosarcoma
  Chondrosarcoma
  Teratocarcinosarcoma
  Others
Secondary tumors

Table 4A.2 Classification of neoplasms of the nasopharynx

Benign
Epithelial
  Squamous papilloma
  Minor salivary gland tumors
Mesenchymal/neuroectodermal
  Angiofibroma
  Granular cell tumor
  Lymphangioma/cystic hygroma
  Hemangiomas
  Neurilemmoma/neurofibroma
  Lipoma
  Paraganglioma
  Fibrous histiocytoma
  Leiomyoma
  Rhabdomyoma
  Teratomas
  Others

Malignant
Epithelial
  Nasopharyngeal carcinoma
  • Keratinizing
  • Non-keratinizing:
      Differentiated type
      Undifferentiated type
  Low-grade papillary adenocarcinoma
  Minor salivary gland tumor
Mesenchymal/neuroectodermal
  Mucosal malignant melanoma
  Lymphomas (non-Hodgkin's and Hodgkin's)
  Rhabdomyosarcoma
  Undifferentiated pleomorphic sarcoma (malignant fibrous histiocytoma)/fibrosarcoma
  Malignant peripheral nerve sheath tumor
  Chordoma
  Angiosarcoma
  Kaposi's sarcoma
  Liposarcoma
  Synovial sarcoma
  Leiomyosarcoma
  Others
Secondary tumors

Schneiderian papillomas have a tendency to spread along the mucosa into adjacent areas. Symptoms vary according to site of occurrence and include airway obstruction, epistaxis, an asymptomatic mass, and pain. Schneiderian papillomas may occur simultaneously with nasal inflammatory polyps. The radiologic appearance varies with extent of disease: a soft tissue density is seen early in the disease; opacification and mucosal thickening are present with more extensive disease. Evidence of pressure erosion of bone may be seen.

Human papillomavirus (HPV) types 6/11, less often 16/18, and rarely other HPV types (e.g., HPV 57) have been found in septal and inverted papillomas by molecular biologic analysis (in-situ hybridization (ISH), and/or polymerase chain reaction (PCR)).[11–15] In a review of the literature, Barnes reported that

Table 4A.3	Sinonasal (Schneiderian) papillomas: clinicopathologic features		
	Septal	**Inverted**	**Oncocytic**
Percentage	20–50%	47–73%	3–8%
Gender, age	M > F; 20–50 years	M > F; 40–70 years	M = F; > 50 years
Location	Nasal septum	Lateral nasal wall in region of middle turbinates with extension into sinuses (maxillary or ethmoid)	Lateral nasal wall and sinuses (maxillary or ethmoid)
Focality	Unilateral	Typically unilateral; rarely, bilateral	Unilateral
Histology	Papillary fronds composed of a predominantly squamous (epidermoid) epithelium; mucocytes (goblet cells) and intraepithelial mucous cysts are present; delicate fibrovascular cores	Endophytic or "inverted" growth consisting of thickened squamous epithelium composed of squamous, transitional, and columnar cells (all three may be present in a given lesion) with admixed mucocytes (goblet cells) and intraepithelial mucous cysts; mixed chronic inflammatory cell infiltrate is characteristically seen within all layers of the surface epithelium	Multilayered epithelial proliferation composed of columnar cells with abundant eosinophilic and granular cytoplasm; outer surface of the epithelial proliferation may demonstrate cilia; intraepithelial mucous cysts, often containing polymorphonuclear leukocytes
Incidence of human papillomavirus (HPV)	Approximately 50% positive; HPV 6 and 11; less frequently HPV 16, 18; rarely HPV 57	Approximately 38% positive; HPV 6 and 11; less frequently HPV 16, 18; rarely HPV 57	Typically absent
Incidence of malignant transformation	Rare	2–27%	4–17%

38% (131/341) of inverted papillomas were positive for HPV.[16] Whether there is a cause and effect relationship between the presence of HPV and the development of Schneiderian papillomas remains to be determined. Molecular biologic analysis to date on oncocytic papillomas has not identified the presence of HPV. There is no association with the development of additional papillomas elsewhere in the upper respiratory tract. Epstein–Barr virus (EBV) has also been identified in inverted papillomas, possibly implicating EBV in the development of

these tumors;[17] however, other studies failed to confirm the presence of EBV in tumor cells.[18]

Septal papillomas are papillary, exophytic, verrucoid lesions with a pink to tan appearance and a firm to rubbery consistency. They are often attached to the mucosa by a narrow or broad-based stalk. Histologically, papillary fronds are seen and are composed of a thick epithelium which is predominantly squamous (epidermoid) and, less frequently, of respiratory type (Fig. 4A.1). Surface keratinization is uncommon. Mucocytes

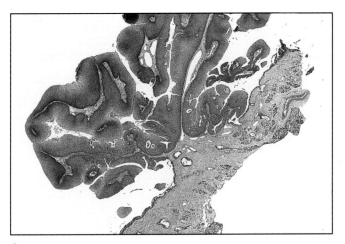

A

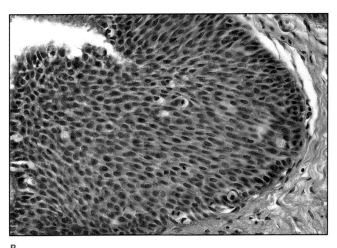

B

Fig. 4A.1 • Schneiderian papilloma, exophytic (septal) type. (**A**) The tumor shows exophytic and papillary growth from the surface respiratory epithelium and is composed of a thickened non-keratinized squamous (epidermoid) epithelium; note the presence of minor salivary glands in the submucosa, indicative of mucosal rather than cutaneous origin. (**B**) At higher magnification the epithelium is bland with retention of cellular polarity, absence of cytologic atypia, presence of scattered mucous cysts, and intraepithelial inflammatory cells; residual non-neoplastic ciliated respiratory epithelium is seen along the surface.

(goblet cells) and intraepithelial mucous cysts are present. The stromal component is composed of delicate fibrovascular cores.

Inverted papillomas are large, bulky, translucent masses with a red to gray color, varying from firm to friable in consistency. Histologically, these tumors have an endophytic or "inverted" growth pattern consisting of markedly thickened squamous epithelial proliferation growing downward into the underlying stroma (Fig. 4A.2). The epithelium varies in cellularity and is composed of squamous, transitional, and columnar cells (all three may be present in a given lesion) with admixed muco-cytes (goblet cells) and intraepithelial mucous cysts. A mixed chronic inflammatory cell infiltrate is characteristically seen within all layers of the epithelium. The cells are generally bland in appearance with uniform nuclei and no piling up.

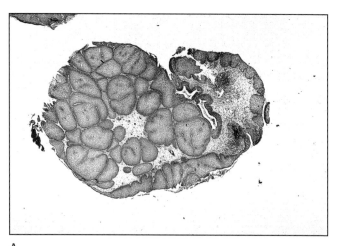

A

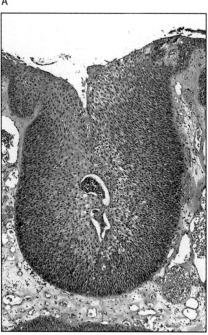

B

Fig. 4A.2 • Schneiderian papilloma, inverted type. **(A)** In contrast to the exophytic type, in the inverted type the squamous epithelial cell proliferation grows in a downward trajectory into an underlying edematous stroma. **(B)** Bulbous downward (inverted) growth of benign epithelium taking origin from squamous metaplasia of the normally respiratory epithelial-lined schneiderian mucosa; an intraepithelial cyst with inflammatory cells is present.

However, pleomorphism and cytologic atypia may be present. The epithelial component may demonstrate extensive clear cell features indicative of abundant glycogen content. Mitotic figures may be seen in the basal and parabasal layers but atypical mitotic figures are not identified. Surface keratinization may be present. The stromal component varies from myxoid to fibrous with admixed chronic inflammatory cells and variable vascularity.

Schneiderian papillomas, oncocytic type, are dark red to brown papillary or polypoid lesions. Histologically, there is a multilayered epithelial proliferation composed of columnar cells with abundant eosinophilic and granular cytoplasm (Fig. 4A.3). The nuclei vary from vesicular to hyperchromatic; nucleoli are usually indistinct. The outer surface of the epithelial proliferation may demonstrate cilia. Intraepithelial mucin cysts, often containing polymorphonuclear leukocytes, are seen; cysts are not identified in the submucosa. The stromal component varies from myxoid to fibrous with admixed chronic inflammatory cells and variable vascularity.

The differential diagnosis for septal papillomas includes verruca vulgaris and squamous papilloma. In contrast to all of the sinonasal-type papillomas, squamous papilloma of the nasal vestibule does not have mucocytes as part of the neoplastic proliferation. The differential diagnosis for inverted papillomas includes inflammatory sinonasal polyps, non-keratinizing respiratory ("transitional") carcinoma, and verrucous carcinoma (VC). The differential diagnosis for oncocytic papilloma includes rhinosporidiosis and (low-grade) papillary adenocarcinoma.

The treatment for all sinonasal-type papillomas is complete surgical excision, including adjacent uninvolved mucosa. The latter is necessary as growth and extension along the mucosa results from the induction of squamous metaplasia in the adjacent sinonasal mucosa.[2,3] Adequate surgery includes a lateral rhinotomy or medial maxillectomy with en bloc excision.[19] This group of neoplasms will recur if incompletely resected; recurrence probably represents persistence of disease rather than multicentricity of the neoplasm. In general, prognosis is good following complete surgical excision; however, if left unchecked, these neoplasms have the capability of continued growth with extension along the mucosal surface with destruction of bone and invasion of vital structures. Adjuvant therapy (chemo- and radiotherapy) has not been shown to be of benefit in sinonasal papilloma. However, radiation may prove beneficial in a select population of patients with unresect-able tumors due to locally advanced disease.[20]

Complications associated with Schneiderian papillomas include recurrence and malignant transformation. Inverted papillomas and oncocytic papillomas can undergo malignant transformation. The incidence of malignant transformation varies per subtype: malignant transformation reported for the inverted subtype ranges from from 2 to 27%;[1,3,16,21–24] malignant transformation reported for the oncocytic subtype ranges from 4 to 17%;[1,3,17–20] malignant transformation of septal papilloma rarely, if ever, occurs. The majority of the malignancies occurring in association with Schneiderian papillomas are squamous cell carcinomas (keratinizing and non-keratinizing), varying in appearance from well to poorly differentiated. Less frequently, other carcinomas may occur, including VC, muco-epidermoid carcinoma, small cell carcinoma, adenocarcinoma, and sinonasal undifferentiated carcinoma (SNUC). The

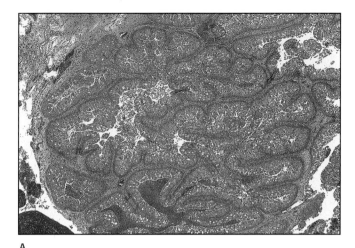

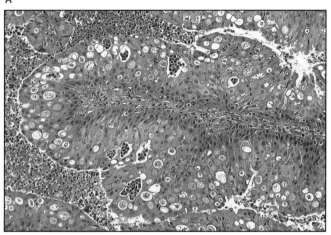

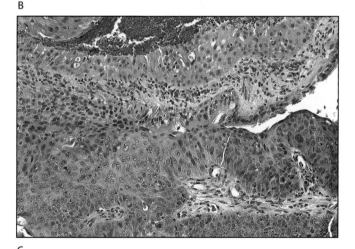

Fig. 4A.3 • Schneiderian papilloma, oncocytic type. (**A**) Exophytic epithelial proliferation with readily apparent eosinophilic appearance. (**B**) At higher magnification the epithelium is multilayered, being composed of columnar cells with abundant eosinophilic and granular cytoplasm; intraepithelial mucin cysts, some with polymorphonuclear leukocytes, are present. (**C**) Malignant transformation of an oncocytic-type papilloma showing residual benign epithelium (top) with areas of carcinoma in situ (lower). Invasive keratinizing squamous cell carcinoma was present in this case (not shown).

carcinoma may occur synchronously or metachronously with the papilloma; metachronous carcinomas develop with a mean interval of 63 months (range 6 months to 13 years) from the onset of the papilloma to the development of the carcinoma.[16] The carcinomatous foci may be limited or extensive and may show epithelial dysplasia as well as carcinoma in situ or invasive carcinoma. Possibilities include a tumor that is predominantly benign (papilloma) with only limited foci of malignancy or a tumor that is predominantly a carcinoma with very limited residual papilloma. In some cases, there may be no residual evidence of a pre-existing benign tumor and only by history was the patient known to have had a previous benign sinonasal papilloma. There are no reliable histologic features that predict which papillomas are likely to become malignant. Papillomas with increased cellularity, pleomorphism, and increased mitotic activity do not necessarily become malignant. The presence of moderate to severe epithelial dysplasia is a potential indicator of malignant transformation. Similarly, surface keratinization and dyskeratosis have anecdotally been considered as possible predictors of malignant transformation. Any sinonasal papilloma that shows moderate to severe dysplasia or has surface keratinization should prompt thorough histologic examination of all resected tissue to exclude the presence of malignancy. There is no correlation between the number of recurrences and the development of carcinoma.

The treatment for malignant transformation of a sinonasal papilloma includes surgery and radiotherapy. The prognosis varies. In some patients the carcinomas are only locally invasive with favorable prognosis following treatment. In other patients there may be extensive invasion with involvement of vital structures and/or metastatic disease; these patients generally have a poor clinical outcome irrespective of therapeutic intervention.

Squamous papillomas

Squamous papillomas represent the most common benign neoplasms of the upper aerodigestive tract (UADT) mucosa and are commonly seen in the oral cavity and larynx. Less often, squamous papillomas occur in the nasopharynx and nasal vestibule.[25,26] The nasal vestibular squamous papillomas are of cutaneous origin. In contrast to the sinonasal-type papillomas, cutaneous squamous papillomas lack intraepithelial mucocytes and cartilage and they are endodermally derived. Squamous papillomas are exophytic, warty, or cauliflower-like tumors ranging in size from a few millimeters up to 3.0 cm in greatest dimension. Histologically, these tumors are composed of benign squamous epithelium arranged in multiple finger-like projections with prominent fibrovascular cores. The squamous epithelium is free of any dysplastic change. In general, these tumors lack surface keratin but in any tumor there may be (hyper)keratosis, as well as para- and ortho-keratosis. The presence of surface keratin carries no additional risk for the development of carcinoma. Although uncommon, the sinonasal-type (Schneiderian) papillomas may originate in the nasopharynx without any connection to the sinonasal tract, probably arising from misplaced ectodermal-derived epithelial rests from the sinonasal tract.[27] Surgical excision is the treatment of choice and is curative. Recurrences occur infrequently and relate to inadequate excision.[27] Malignant transformation does not occur.

Benign neoplasms of minor salivary glands

Benign salivary gland tumors of the sinonasal region and nasopharynx are uncommon. In general, minor salivary gland tumors occur most often in the nasal cavity and rarely in the paranasal sinuses. Pleomorphic adenoma (benign mixed tumor) is the dominant histologic type seen;[28] less often, monomorphic adenomas such as myoepithelioma and oncocytoma occur.

Pleomorphic adenomas tend to originate along the nasal septum (bony or cartilaginous component) more than any other site.[28] Although these tumors may arise from within the paranasal sinus, more often paranasal sinus involvement occurs secondary to extension from an intranasal lesion. These tumors appear as polypoid or exophytic growths, usually covered by an intact mucosa, and vary in size from 1 to 7 cm. As is true of all UADT minor salivary gland tumors (benign or malignant), the pleomorphic adenomas are unencapsulated. However, in contrast to malignant minor salivary gland tumors, these tumors are relatively circumscribed without invasive growth; involvement of surface epithelium does not constitute invasion. Histologically, these tumors are identical to those of major salivary glands (see Ch. 7), including an admixture of ductular or tubular structures, spindle-shaped myoepithelial cells, and a myxochondroid stroma. There is a tendency for pleomorphic adenomas of the nasal cavity to be cellular, showing a predominant myoepithelial component. The latter is usually in the form of plasmacytoid (hyaline cell) rather than spindle-shaped myoepithelial cells (Fig. 4A.4). Given the presence of ductular or tubular structures and myxochondroid stroma, these tumors would not be considered as myo-epitheliomas. Myoepitheliomas represent a type of monomorphic adenoma composed only of myoepithelial cells. Typically, myoepitheliomas are of the spindle cell type and rarely the tumor cells are of the plasmacytoid type. Myoepithelial differentiation can be shown by immunoreactivity for cytokeratin, S-100 protein, and smooth muscle actin,[29] as well as more specific markers of myoepithelial differentiation, including *p63* and calponin (Fig. 4A.4). Surgical excision is the treatment of choice for all types of benign minor salivary gland tumors. Surgery is usually curative: local recurrence is seen in fewer than 10% of patients.[28]

Benign neuroectodermal tumors

Pituitary adenoma

Pituitary neoplasms originating from the sella turcica (see also Ch. 17) may occasionally extend into the sinonasal tract or nasopharynx and appear to present as a primary neoplasm of those regions. Ectopic pituitary adenomas without any continuity with the sella turcica may arise in various UADT sites from remnants of Rathke's pouch. In these locations, misdiagnosis with other neuroendocrine tumors or with malignant epithelial neoplasms may occur. Ectopic pituitary adenomas occur in adults with no gender predilection and present with airway obstruction, chronic sinusitis, visual field

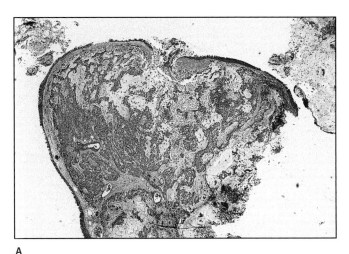

A

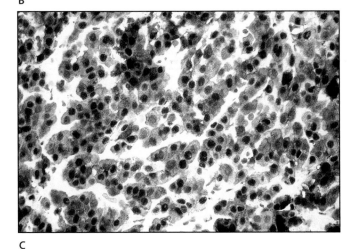

B

C

Fig. 4A.4 • Intranasal myoepithelial-predominant pleomorphic adenoma. **(A)** Submucosal unencapsulated cellular proliferation with associated myxochondroid stroma. **(B)** Admixture of glands, myxochondroid stroma, and prominent plasmacytoid myoepithelial cells; the presence of the ductular structures, glands, and myxochondroid stroma allows categorization as a pleomorphic adenoma, myoepithelial predominant, and not as a myoepithelioma, which is better regarded as a monomorphic adenoma. **(C)** In addition to cytokeratin staining, myoepithelial cells are immunoreactive for S-100 protein (nuclear and cytoplasmic).

defects, cerebrospinal fluid leakage, and endocrinopathic manifestations (e.g., Cushing's syndrome, hirsutism).[30,31] The most common ectopic sites of occurrence are the sphenoid sinus followed by the nasopharynx. Other less common sites include the nasal cavity and ethmoid sinus. The tumors may be polypoid in appearance. Histologically, there is a submucosal epithelioid neoplastic proliferation with solid, organoid, and trabecular growth patterns (Fig. 4A.5). The epithelioid cells have round nuclei with a dispersed chromatin pattern and granular eosinophilic-appearing cytoplasm. Pleomorphism, necrosis, or mitotic activity is not seen. There is no evidence of glandular or squamous differentiation. Immunophenotype and variability of hormone expression parallel that seen in primary pituitary lesions (see Ch. 17). Wide surgical resection is the treatment of choice. Complete removal is curative without recurrent or progressive tumor, and with resolution of endocrinopathies.[31] Rarely, malignant transformation of ectopic pituitary adenoma may occur.[32]

Paraganglioma

Extra-adrenal paragangliomas are identified throughout the body and are classified according to the anatomic site of occurrence. Paragangliomas in the head and neck region include those of carotid body, jugulotympanic, and vagal origin (see Ch. 28). Paragangliomas may rarely occur in other mucosal sites of the UADT, including the nasal cavity, where they produce nasal obstruction and/or epistaxis. Parasympathetic paraganglia are found throughout the body and give rise to almost all of the paragangliomas of the UADT.[33] Most paragangliomas in this location are non-functional, although rare cases exist of adrenocorticotropic hormone-producing nasal paraganglioma associated with Cushing's syndrome.[34] Irrespective of the site of origin, the histologic appearance of all extra-adrenal paragangliomas is the same (see Ch. 28). As at other sites, the hallmark histologic feature is the presence of a cell nest or "Zellballen" pattern, composed of variably atypical chief cells surrounded by sustentacular cells. The immunohistochemical profile of paragangliomas in this region[35,36] is also the same as at other sites. Only rare cases

have been cytokeratin-reactive.[36] Surgical excision is the treatment of choice. The prognosis is excellent following complete resection. While the majority of these tumors are benign and behave in an indolent manner, they may recur locally and be invasive. Rarely, these tumors are malignant.[37] The histology is not reliably predictive of malignant behavior and malignancy in any paraganglioma should be determined by the presence of metastatic disease.

Meningioma

Meningiomas are benign neoplasms of meningothelial cells, representing 13–18% of all intracranial tumors.[38] Occurrence outside the central nervous system is considered ectopic; these meningiomas are divided into those with no identifiable central nervous system connection (primary) and those with central nervous system connection (secondary). The most common sites of occurrence of the ectopic meningiomas of the head and neck region include the middle ear and temporal bone, sinonasal cavity, orbit, oral cavity, and parotid gland.[39] Sinonasal tract meningiomas most often involve the nasal cavity, or a combination of nasal cavity and paranasal sinuses;[40] less frequently, involvement may be isolated to the nasopharynx, frontal sinus, or sphenoid sinus.[40] In the sinonasal cavity, symptoms include nasal obstruction, epistaxis, headache, pain, visual disturbances, and facial deformity. The tumors may erode the bones of the sinuses with involvement of surrounding soft tissues, the orbit, and occasionally the base of the skull.[40] These tumors appear as a polypoid mass. Often, the tumor is curetted out and received as fragments of solid, white tissue. A gritty consistency may be noted. The histology is similar to that of their intracranial counterparts (see Ch. 26). Among the histologic subtypes of meningioma, the meningotheliomatous type is the most common in the sinonasal cavity. The histologic features include a lobular growth pattern with tumor nests separated by a variable amount of fibrous tissue (Fig. 4A.6). Characteristically, the nuclei have a punched-out appearance resulting from intra-nuclear cytoplasmic inclusions. Psammoma bodies, typical and numerous in intracranial meningothelial meningiomas,

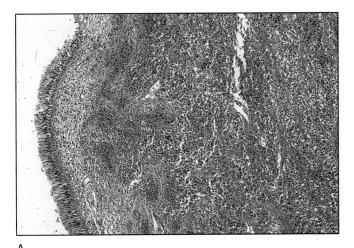

A

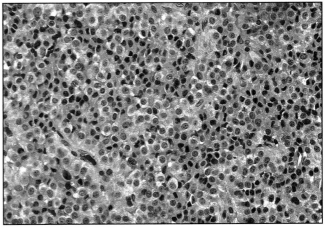

B

Fig. 4A.5 • Ectopic (nasopharyngeal) pituitary adenoma. **(A)** The neoplastic infiltrate is submucosal and is composed of an epithelioid neoplastic proliferation with an organoid growth pattern. **(B)** The epithelioid cells have round nuclei with dispersed chromatin pattern and granular eosinophilic cytoplasm. Immunohistochemical stains confirmed a pituitary neoplasm.

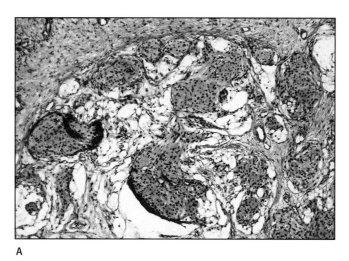

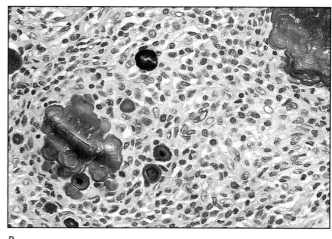

A

B

Fig. 4A.6 • Sinonasal tract (ectopic) meningioma. (A) This submucosal cellular proliferation shows a lobular growth pattern with tumor nests separated by a variable amount of fibroconnective tissue and with a whorled arrangement. (B) The neoplastic cells have round to oval nuclei with pale-staining cytoplasm, indistinct cell borders, and characteristic punched-out or empty appearance resulting from intranuclear cytoplasmic inclusions; several psammoma bodies are present.

may be seen but are not as common in the ectopically located meningiomas. The immunohistochemical antigenic profile of meningiomas includes reactivity with epithelial membrane antigen (EMA) and vimentin, with absence of cytokeratin or neuroendocrine markers (chromogranin and synaptophysin). Surgical removal is the treatment of choice. However, complete surgical excision may be difficult to achieve resulting in recurrence; recurrence rates range up to 30%.[39–41] Following the histologic diagnosis, it is essential to exclude spread from a primary intracranial neoplasm.

Benign mesenchymal neoplasms

Hemangiomas

Lobular capillary hemangiomas (LCH), which were formerly often known as pyogenic granulomas, are benign vascular tumors representing the polypoid form of capillary hemangioma primarily occurring on skin and mucous membranes (see Ch. 3). Aside from the LCH, other types of hemangiomas of the sinonasal cavity and nasopharynx are rare.[42,43] Hemangiomas of the sinonasal tract tend to be mucosally based but may also arise from within the osseous components of this region (intraosseous hemangiomas).

LCH occurs equally in both genders. There is a wide age range but these lesions are most commonly seen in the fourth to fifth decades of life and are uncommon under 16 years of age. LCH is most often found in the anterior portion of the nasal septum[42,44] in an area referred to as Little's area or Kisselbach's triangle; the second most common sinonasal location is the turbinates.[42,44] The most common clinical complaint is epistaxis; an obstructive painless mass may be present.

The pathogenesis remains unclear. A minority of cases may be associated with prior trauma. LCH may occur in association with pregnancy and in association with oral contraceptive use, suggesting that hormonal factors may be involved. However, in an immunohistochemical study of 21 cases of

LCH, Nichols et al.[45] did not identify estrogen or progesterone receptors in any of these tumors. The mechanism for the occasional regression of pregnancy-related pyogenic granuloma after parturition remains unclear. Recently, Yuan & Lin evaluated the role of vascular endothelial growth factor (VEGF) and angiopoietin-2 (Ang-2) in the regression of pregnancy pyogenic granuloma.[46] They found that the amount of VEGF was high in the granulomas in pregnancy and almost undetectable after parturition and concluded that a lack of VEGF is associated with apoptosis of endothelial cells and lesional regression. They found no role for Ang-2 alone in regression.

The gross appearance of LCH is a smooth lobulated, polypoid red mass measuring up to 1.5 cm in diameter. Histologically, LCH is characterized by a submucosal vascular proliferation arranged in lobules or clusters composed of central capillaries and smaller ramifying tributaries (Fig. 4A.7). The central capillaries vary in caliber, as well as in shape, and in more "mature" lesions may show a "staghorn" appearance. The endothelial cell lining may be prominent and may display

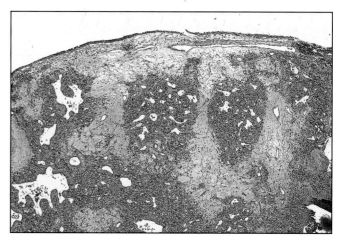

Fig. 4A.7 • Sinonasal lobular capillary hemangioma. Submucosal lobular proliferation in which variable-sized vascular spaces are present, including some with irregular to staghorn shapes.

endothelial tufting, as well as mitoses. However, there is no intercommunication of vascular spaces as seen in angiosarcomas, nor is there true cytologic atypia or atypical mitoses. Surrounding and intimately associated with the vascular component is granulation tissue and a mixed chronic inflammatory cell infiltrate. The surface epithelium is often ulcerated with associated necrosis. The diagnosis of LCH and its differentiation from other lesions is usually accomplished by light microscopic evaluation and immunohistochemical staining is generally not required. In contrast to Kaposi's sarcoma, no immunoreactivity is present for human herpesvirus 8 (HHV-8) latent nuclear antigen-1 (LNA-1) in LCH.[47]

The treatment for LCH is conservative but complete surgical excision. The prognosis following excision is excellent. Recurrences are relatively infrequent.

Cavernous hemangiomas occur less frequently in the upper respiratory tract when compared to capillary hemangioma. In general, cavernous hemangiomas have a similar clinical presentation to capillary hemangiomas but are more often identified in the turbinates, lateral nasal wall, or within bone (intraosseous) than in the nasal septum.[48] Similar to cavernous hemangiomas of other sites (see Ch. 3), those of the sinonasal tract are comprised of multiple, variably sized, dilated and thin-walled, endothelial cell-lined vascular spaces. Surgical resection is curative.

Nasopharyngeal angiofibroma

Nasopharyngeal angiofibroma is a relatively rare neoplasm accounting for fewer than 1% of all head and neck tumors.[42,49–52] This tumor occurs almost exclusively in men and some believe that it is a tumor limited to the male population.[53] Nasopharyngeal angiofibromas occur over a wide age range but are most common in the second decade of life. They are uncommon over the age of 25 years. However, these tumors may occur in older ages, thereby negating the use of the designation "juvenile" angiofibroma. The most common clinical complaints are persistent nasal obstruction and epistaxis.[50] Late signs and symptoms include facial swelling or deformity (swelling of the cheek), nasal discharge, proptosis, diplopia, headache, sinusitis, cranial nerve palsies, anosmia and hearing deficits.[50] Pain may occur but is considered an unusual finding. Typically, symptoms have been present for more than 1 year prior to diagnosis. The site of occurrence is usually the posterolateral portion of the roof of the nasal cavity in the area of the sphenopalatine foramen. Large tumors may extend anteriorly into the nasal cavity, causing nasal obstruction and simulating a primary intranasal or paranasal sinus tumor. Extension posteriorly may fill the nasopharynx and extend into the oropharynx, causing displacement of the soft palate. Extension can occur through the sphenopalatine foramen with involvement of the pterygomaxillary fossa and infratemporal fossa, resulting in facial deformities.[54] Extension into the middle cranial fossa can occur if the tumor involves and destroys the pterygoid process.

As a result of the overwhelming occurrence in males, this tumor has been thought to be hormonally driven, being dependent on testosterone and inhibited by estrogen.[55] Androgen receptors have been found in these tumors,[56] but not estrogen receptors.[55,57] A familial predisposition for nasopharyngeal angiofibromas has been suggested in patients with familial adenomatous polyposis (FAP).[58,59] Patients with FAP develop nasopharyngeal angiofibroma 25 times more frequently than an age-matched population.[58,59] A role for the *APC*-β-catenin pathway has been suggested in patients with nasopharyngeal angiofibroma with the *APC* gene mutation. Activating β-catenin mutation without the *APC* gene mutation has been reported in sporadic nasopharyngeal angiofibroma.[60,61] An immunohistochemical study by Zhang et al.[62] supports a role for beta-catenin in nasopharyngeal angiofibromas. These authors found that expression of beta-catenin, *c-kit* (CD117), and nerve growth factor (NGF) was higher and more frequent in stromal cells of nasopharyngeal angiofibromas than those of nasal polyps. In a limited number of patients, consumption coagulopathy has been a complication of nasopharyngeal angiofibromas, suggesting that preoperative coagulation studies may be useful in ensuring perioperative hemostasis.[63]

Routine radiographs show characteristic bowing of the posterior wall of the maxillary antrum,[64] as well as distortion and posterior displacement of the pterygoid plates (Holman–Miller sign). Arteriographic findings are usually diagnostic[50,52] and show a tumor with marked vascular hypertrophy and an increased number of arteries without beading, dilatation, segmental narrowing, or aneurysmal dilatation. The blood supply may be uni- or bilateral and typically comes from branches of the external carotid artery (internal maxillary or ascending pharyngeal branches). Intracranial extension should be considered in cases where the internal carotid artery is the dominant vascular supply. Radiographic staging of nasopharyngeal angiofibroma based on extent of disease has been proposed.[65–68]

Angiofibromas appear as sessile or lobulated masses but may occasionally be polypoid or pedunculated. Histologically, angiofibromas are unencapsulated and are characterized by a fibrocollagenous stromal proliferation with an admixture of variably sized vascular spaces (Fig. 4A.8). The vascular component is made up of thin-walled, small to large vessels varying in appearance from stellate or staghorn to inconspicuous due to marked compression by stromal fibrous tissue. The endothelial cells form a single layer and are flat or plump in appearance. The vessel walls lack elastic fibers and are distinctive in having a smooth muscle layer which may be incomplete or discontinuous and which shows marked variation in thickness.[69] Central aspects of the tumor may be relatively hypovascular. The stroma is composed of fibrous tissue with fine or coarse collagen fibers and may be focally myxoid. The stromal cells are spindle-shaped and stellate with plump nuclei and they tend to radiate around vessels. Nuclear pleomorphism and multinucleated giant cells (MGCs) may be seen. Mitotic figures are rare. Mast cells are common; however other inflammatory cells are absent except near areas of surface ulceration. Evidence of preoperative embolization may be seen in tissue sections in the form of intravascular fibrin thrombi containing foreign material, and tumor infarction. Tumors of longer duration tend to be more fibrous and less vascular. Immunohistochemical staining shows smooth muscle actin-positive cells around the circumference of the vascular spaces.[69] The spindle-shaped and stellate stromal cells are vimentin-positive. In addition, Hwang and colleagues[56] found the stromal cells to be strongly reactive for testosterone receptors.

In uncomplicated cases (with tumor limited to the nasopharynx), surgical excision via a transverse palatal approach

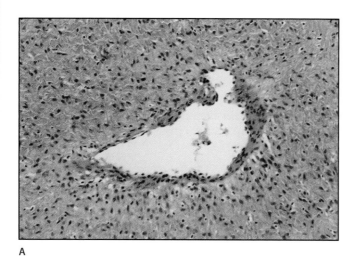
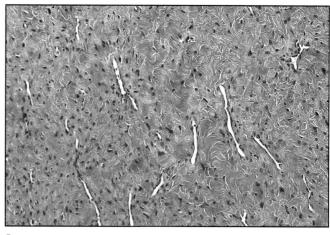

A   B

Fig. 4A.8 • Nasopharyngeal angiofibroma. These tumors are composed of a variable admixture of fibrocollagenous stroma with variably sized vascular spaces. The vascular component includes thin-walled structures varying in appearance from **(A)** readily apparent to **(B)** less conspicuous due to marked compression from the collagenized stroma. Note that the vascular walls have an incomplete or absent smooth muscle layer.

is the treatment of choice. Vascular embolization usually precedes surgical intervention in order to control bleeding.[70] Successful management using less invasive techniques has been achieved with reduction in morbidity and without increasing the chance of recurrence.[71] Non-surgical management has been proposed, including estrogen therapy,[57] use of testosterone receptor blockers such as flutamide,[72] or irradiation.[73–75] These treatment modalities reduce the angiomatous component of the tumor and may be utilized in patients whose tumors are deemed unresectable. Complications associated with angiofibromas include excessive bleeding, recurrence of tumor, and extension of the tumor beyond the nasopharynx to involve adjacent anatomic compartments (sinonasal cavities, oropharynx, pterygomaxillary fossa, superior buccal sulcus, orbit, infratemporal fossa, and cranial cavity).[54] Given their propensity to bleed, biopsies of the tumor should be performed with extreme caution.[76] Recurrence rates vary from 6% to as high as 24%.[77] High recurrence rates and early recurrence may occur in nasopharyngeal angiofibromas involving the skull base. Recurrences are more common in cases with intracranial extension. Tumor recurrence in cases without intracranial extension usually occurs within 2 years of treatment. In general, the prognosis is excellent following surgical removal; mortality rates range from 3[51] to 9%.[50] Rarely, spontaneous regression may occur.[78,79] Malignant (sarcomatous) transformation is a rare event and has been linked to treatment with radiotherapy (post-irradiation sarcoma).[80–83]

Solitary fibrous tumor

Solitary fibrous tumor (SFT) is a distinctive neoplasm comprised of CD34-positive fibroblasts (see Ch. 24).[84,85] SFTs are rare but do occur in the UADT, primarily involving the nasal cavity and paranasal sinuses.[86–88] Patients with tumors in these sites present with nasal obstruction. Usually, the symptoms have been present for an extended period of time (a year or more).

These tumors are typically polypoid. Histologically, they are circumscribed but unencapsulated and are composed of a variably cellular proliferation of bland spindle-shaped cells

lacking any distinct pattern of growth and with ropey, keloidal collagen bundles and associated thin-walled vascular spaces (Fig. 4A.9). The latter may be focally prominent and often have a branching pericytomatous appearance. Most cases at this site show a low mitotic rate and no necrosis. Immunohistochemical analysis will show CD34, *bcl-2*, and CD99 reactivity but absence of S-100 protein, desmin, or actin.

Given their tendency to be polypoid, SFTs of the sinonasal tract are amenable to complete surgical resection, which is usually curative.[86,87] SFTs of the nasopharynx may be more difficult to excise completely.

Fibromatosis (aggressive fibromatosis; extra-abdominal desmoid, desmoid-type fibromatosis)

Fibromatosis is a locally infiltrative/aggressive, non-metastasizing cytologically bland, fibroblastic neoplasm (see Ch. 24).[89,90] Involvement of the head and neck region occurs

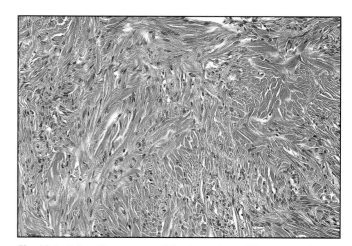

Fig. 4A.9 • Solitary fibrous tumor of the sinonasal tract. This unencapsulated tumor is composed of a variably cellular proliferation of bland spindle-shaped cells lacking any pattern of growth with associated hyaline collagen.

primarily in the soft tissues of the neck.[91] Excluding the neck, the common sites of occurrence are the sinonasal tract, nasopharynx, tongue, and oral cavity.[92,93] In the sinonasal tract, the maxillary sinus is the most common site.[94] This lesion is seen in both children and adults but most commonly occurs in the third to fourth decades of life. Symptoms vary according to site. In the sinonasal tract and nasopharynx, the clinical presentation includes a painless enlarging mass or nasal obstruction.[92,93] With progression of disease, other symptoms, including epistaxis, facial deformity, proptosis, and dysphagia, may occur.

The gross and histologic appearances are the same as those in fibromatoses at more common locations (see Ch. 24).

The differential diagnosis primarily includes reactive fibrosis and fibrosarcoma.[93] In contrast to fibrosarcoma, fibromatoses lack a herringbone growth pattern, hypercellularity, and increased mitotic rate. Other differential diagnostic considerations include peripheral nerve sheath tumors, myxoma and fibromyxoma, SFT, myofibromatosis, nodular fasciitis, fibro-osseous lesions, and myofibroblastic tumors (inflammatory myofibroblastic tumor, low-grade myofibroblastic sarcoma).

The treatment of choice is wide surgical excision. In general, the prognosis is good.[93] However, these lesions may present difficulties in management due to insinuation of the lesion into adjacent structures without clear demarcation, making complete excision difficult. As a result of the difficulties in completely excising the lesion, recurrent disease is common.[94] Recurrence usually occurs within the first few years following surgery. Radiotherapy has been used with some success in patients with residual tumor and/or recurrent disease.[95,96] Hormonal therapy has been used with varying results.[97,98] Death due to uncontrolled local disease may occur but is an exceptional occurrence.

Benign peripheral nerve sheath tumors (benign schwannoma and neurofibroma)

Benign peripheral nerve sheath tumors of the head and neck are common, perhaps accounting for as many as 45% of all soft tissue lesions. However, benign peripheral nerve sheath tumors of the sinonasal tract and nasopharynx are uncommon, accounting for fewer than 4%.[99–101] In this location schwannomas are substantially more common than neurofibromas. Adults are most commonly affected, with no gender predilection. Patients present with symptoms related to nasal obstruction and epistaxis. Nasopharyngeal involvement may result in unilateral serous otitis media.[101] In two of the cases reported by Hasegawa et al.,[101] visual disturbances were present due to intracranial extension of the tumor. These tumors may cause pressure erosion of bone.[99,100]

Unlike their soft tissue counterparts, benign schwannomas of the UADT are unencapsulated (Fig. 4A.10). Aside from this finding, the histologic features are similar to those described for benign peripheral nerve sheath tumors at other sites (see Ch. 27). These tumors may be very cellular but significant pleomorphism is not seen. The mitotic rate is usually low and atypical mitoses are not present. Diffuse and intense S-100 protein immunoreactivity (cytoplasmic and nuclear pattern) is present. Cytokeratin, actins, desmin, CD34, and EMA staining are absent. Proliferation rate (i.e., MIB-1 staining) is low, with

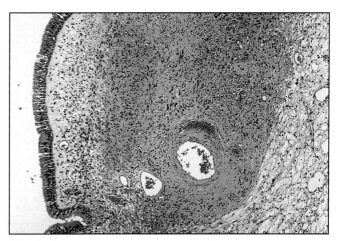

Fig. 4A.10 • Sinonasal benign peripheral nerve sheath tumor (benign schwannoma). The tumor is submucosal, unencapsulated, and composed of a bland spindle cell proliferation with wavy or buckled-appearing nuclei, admixed inflammatory cells, and perivascular hyalinization.

staining of 1–5% of tumor cell nuclei.[102] Surgical resection is the treatment of choice and is curative.

Neurofibromas at this site are submucosal, relatively circumscribed tumors composed of spindle-shaped cells with "wavy" or buckled, hyperchromatic nuclei, and indistinct cytoplasm. An associated collagenized and/or myxoid stromal component is present. Neoplastic cells are S-100 protein-positive but the extent of staining is less than that seen in schwannomas. Surgical resection is curative.

Leiomyoma

In general, leiomyomas are one of the least common mesenchymal tumors in the head and neck area. The most frequent sites of occurrence are the skin and oral cavity (lips, tongue, and palate). Less often, leiomyomas may arise from within the sinonasal cavity, presenting as a painless mass with nasal obstruction.[103,104] This is a tumor of adults with a peak incidence in the sixth decade of life. Within the sinonasal tract, leiomyomas most often involve the turbinates. Histologically, these tumors are localized to the submucosa, appearing well delineated and characterized by the presence of interlacing bundles or fascicles of cells composed of blunt-ended or "cigar-shaped" nuclei with abundant eosinophilic cytoplasm. The nuclei may appear rounded. The neoplastic cells are often seen in intimate association with vascular spaces. Degenerative-type changes, including stromal fibrosis and myxoid change, may be present. Hypercellular tumors, referred to as cellular leiomyoma, characterized by an absolute increase in cells but lacking significant pleomorphism, mitotic activity, necrosis, or invasive growth may be identified. Another suggested category among sinonasal tract smooth muscle tumors is the so-called smooth muscle tumors of uncertain malignant potential (SMTUMP).[104] SMTUMP is histologically characterized by increased cellularity, moderate nuclear pleomorphism, and the presence of no more than 4 mitoses per 10 high-power fields (hpf).[104] Locally, infiltrative growth (i.e., into bone) may occur in association with SMTUMP.[104] The neoplastic cells in leiomyoma and SMTUMP are immunoreactive with actin (smooth muscle and muscle-specific) and desmin; S-100

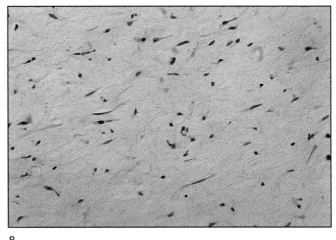

A   B

Fig. 4A.11 • Sinonasal myxoma. **(A)** Submucosal loose cellular proliferation with compressed but identifiable vascularity. **(B)** The cells are spindle-shaped or stellate-appearing with uniform small, hyperchromatic nuclei, embedded in a copious mucinous stroma.

protein reactivity is absent. MIB-1 index for both leiomyoma and SMTUMP is low (≤ 5%).[104] Simple surgical excision is curative.

Rhabdomyoma

Adult or fetal types of rhabdomyoma (see Ch. 24) rarely occur in the sinonasal tract or nasopharynx.[105–107] The cellular features of fetal rhabdomyomas show rhabdomyoblasts in different stages of differentiation, including spindle-shaped and strap cells. These findings may be worrisome for a diagnosis of rhabdomyosarcoma (RMS), however, in contrast to RMS, fetal rhabdomyomas tend to be circumscribed and lack nuclear atypia or mitotic activity.[107]

Sinonasal myxoma and fibromyxoma

Myxomas and fibromyxomas are benign neoplasms of uncertain histogenesis with a characteristic histologic appearance and which often behave in an aggressive (infiltrating) manner. When a relatively greater amount of stromal collagen is present, the term fibromyxoma (or myxofibroma) is used. In the sinonasal tract, these tumors appear to be of osseous derivation. There is no gender predilection; these tumors occur over a wide age range but are most frequently seen in the second and third decades of life.[108,109] In general, these are gnathic tumors, the mandible (posterior and condylar regions) being involved more often than the maxilla (zygomatic process and alveolar bone). Extragnathic tumors are uncommon and primarily involve the sinonasal tract; specifically, the maxillary sinus (antrum) is most often involved with secondary extension into the nasal cavity. The presentation is usually as a painless swelling of the affected area. Localization to the jaw bones has led to the belief that these tumors take origin from the primordial odontogenic mesenchyme or from osteogenic embryonic connective tissue.

The radiologic appearance is that of a unilocular or multilocular radiolucency with a "honeycomb" or "soap-bubble" appearance. Grossly, these are delineated but unencapsulated multinodular, gelatinous-appearing lesions. Histologically,

these tumors show a scant, loosely cellular proliferation consisting of spindle-shaped or stellate-appearing cells embedded in an abundant mucinous stroma (Fig. 4A.11). The nuclei are small and hyperchromatic. Cellular pleomorphism, mitotic figures, and necrosis are absent. The amount of collagenous fibrillary material varies between cases and, depending on the extent, its presence may lead to the designation "fibromyxoma" (Fig. 4A.12). The periphery of the tumor appears circumscribed but local infiltration with replacement of bone can be seen. A vascular component is present but is limited in extent. The mucinous stroma stains positively for acid mucopolysaccharides. Conservative but wide local excision is the treatment of choice. These tumors tend to be slow-growing and usually follow a benign course, but may have the potential for local destruction following inadequate excision. Recurrence or metastasis does not occur. Metastasis from a presumptive sinonasal myxoma or fibromyxoma should place that diagnosis in serious doubt and the lesion probably represents a myxoid sarcoma of some type.

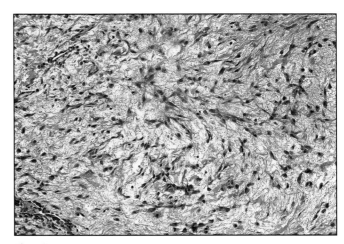

Fig. 4A.12 • Sinonasal fibromyxoma. As compared to myxomas the stromal component includes greater collagenous fibrillary material and the lesion is often more cellular. The absence of specific immunoreactivity excludes other diagnoses and is required to make the diagnosis of fibromyxoma.

The differential diagnosis includes dental papillae, nasal inflammatory polyps, peripheral nerve sheath tumors, low-grade fibromyxoid sarcoma,[110] other myxoid sarcomas, and chondroid tumors.

Osseous, fibro-osseous, and cartilaginous lesions

Osteoma

Osteomas are benign bone-forming tumors that are identified almost exclusively in the craniofacial skeleton. In the sinonasal tract, osteomas may be found in all sites but are most common in the frontal and ethmoid sinuses.[111,112] These tumors are most often asymptomatic, being found only by radiographic studies. Symptoms associated with paranasal sinus osteomas include headaches, facial swelling or deformity, and ocular disturbances.[113] Sinonasal osteomas are more common in men and occur over a wide age range but are most often encountered in the second to fourth decades of life. Sinonasal osteomas usually occur as a single lesion but may be associated with Gardner's syndrome, an inherited autosomal dominant trait characterized by intestinal (colorectal) polyposis, soft tissue lesions (fibromatosis, cutaneous epidermoid cysts, lipomas, leiomyomas), and multiple craniofacial osteomas.[114] The radiographic appearance is that of a sharply delineated radiopaque lesion confined to bone or protruding into a sinus. Histologically, osteomas are well circumscribed and are composed of dense, mature predominantly lamellar bone, sometimes rimmed by osteoblasts. Interosseous spaces may be composed of fibrous, fibrovascular, or fatty tissue, and hematopoietic elements may be present. Unless symptomatic, osteomas require no treatment. Complete surgical excision is curative.

Benign fibro-osseous lesions

Ossifying fibroma

In contrast to fibrous dysplasia (see below; Table 4A.4), ossifying fibromas are commoner in women and tend to occur in older age groups, being most frequently seen in the third and fourth decades of life, although any age may be affected.[115] A predilection to occur in black women has been reported.[116] Sinonasal tract involvement is generally asymptomatic and is often diagnosed incidentally following radiographic examination. Symptomatic tumors are manifest by displacement of teeth or as an expansile mass. Radiologic features include the presence of a well-circumscribed or sharply demarcated lesion with smooth contours.

Ossifying fibromas appear as tan/gray to white, gritty and firm, varying in size from 0.5 to 10 cm. Histologically, ossifying fibromas are composed of randomly distributed mature (lamellar) bone spicules rimmed by osteoblasts admixed with a fibrous stroma (Fig. 4A.13). While the osseous component is generally described as mature, the central portions may be woven bone with lamellar bone at the periphery. Complete bone maturation is seldom seen. The fibrous stroma may be densely cellular; mitotic figures are rare to absent. Secondary changes, including hemorrhage, inflammation and giant cells,

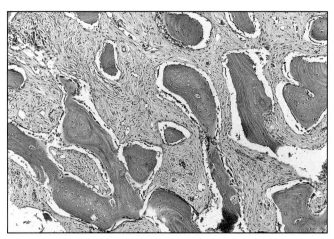

Fig. 4A.13 • Ossifying fibroma of the paranasal sinuses composed of mature (lamellar) bone spicules rimmed by osteoblasts with an admixed fibrous stroma.

may be seen. The differential diagnosis of ossifying fibroma is primarily with fibrous dysplasia (see below; Table 4A.4). For ossifying fibromas, surgical excision is the treatment of choice and the well-circumscribed nature of this lesion allows for relatively easy removal. The prognosis is excellent following complete excision. Recurrences are rare.

Psammomatoid (active) ossifying fibroma (cementifying or cemento-ossifying fibroma)

This is a variant of ossifying fibroma that typically occurs in the sinonasal tract and potentially may behave aggressively with locally invasive and destructive capabilities.[117] There is no gender predilection and, while generally occurring in younger age groups (first and second decades), this lesion can occur over a wide age range, including older individuals.[117] Presenting symptoms include facial swelling, nasal obstruction, pain, sinusitis, headache, and proptosis. These lesions may occur in any area of the sinonasal tract but are most frequent in the ethmoid sinus and supraorbital frontal region.[117,118] There may be involvement of a single site or multiple sinuses; the orbit may also be involved. The radiologic appearance is that of a lytic or mixed lytic/radiopaque osseous and/or soft tissue mass, varying from well demarcated to invasive with bone erosion. Ossifying fibroma has been suggested as arising from the mesenchyme of the periodontal ligament and, as such, is related to the cementifying fibroma and cemento-ossifying fibroma.[118]

The histology is that of a benign fibro-osseous proliferation composed of bony spicules and spherules admixed with a fibrous stroma. The most distinctive component is the presence of mineralized or calcified "psammomatoid" bodies or ossicles (Fig. 4A.14). These ossicles vary from a few in number to a dense population of innumerable spherical bodies. The ossicles are demarcated with a central blue to black appearance surrounded by a pink-appearing rim and with concentric laminations. The ossicles vary from small, with a round to oval shape, to being larger and irregularly shaped, and are present within the bony trabeculae as well as within the adjacent cellular stroma. Osteoclasts are present within the ossicles,

Table 4A.4 Benign fibroosseous lesions: clinicopathologic comparison

	Ossifying fibroma	Psammomatoid ossifying fibroma	Fibrous dysplasia
Gender, age	F > M; 3rd–4th decades	F = M; younger age groups (first and second decades), but may occur in older individuals	F = M; first two decades of life
Location	No specific site of involvement	Ethmoid sinus; supraorbital frontal region	No specific site of involvement
Focality	Single site	Single site or involvement of multiple (contiguous) sites/sinuses	Monostotic (75–80%); Polyostotic (20–25%)
Radiology	Well-circumscribed or sharply demarcated lesion with smooth contours	Lytic or mixed lytic/radiopaque osseous and/or soft-tissue mass varying from well-demarcated to invasive with bone erosion	Poorly defined expansile osseous lesion with a thin intact cortex; predominantly fibrous lesions are radiolucent; predominantly osseous lesions are radiodense; lesions with an equal admixture of fibrous and osseous components have a ground-glass appearance
Histology	Randomly distributed mature (lamellar) bone spicules rimmed by osteoblasts admixed with a fibrous stroma; central portions may be woven bone with lamellar bone at the periphery	Bony spicules and distinctive mineralized or calcified "psammomatoid" bodies or ossicles admixed with a fibrous stroma; psammomatoid bodies vary from a few in number to a dense population of innumerable spherical bodies; osteoclasts are present within the ossicles, and osteoblasts can be seen along their peripheral aspects; bony trabeculae vary in appearance and include odd shapes with a curvilinear pattern	Fibrous tissue component is nondescript and of variable cellularity; osseous component includes irregularly shaped trabeculae of osteoid and immature (woven) bone that is poorly oriented with misshapen bony trabeculae with odd geometric patterns, including "C"- or "S"-shaped configurations; the trabeculae typically lack osteoblastic rimming
Syndromes	No known association	No known association	Albright syndrome (1–3%)
Treatment	Surgical resection	Surgical resection	Disease may stabilize at puberty and, in children, therapy should be delayed if possible until after puberty; surgical resection indicated in cases with compromise of function, progression of deformity, associated pathologic fracture(s) or the development of a malignancy
Prognosis	Excellent	Good following complete excision; recurrence(s) often occur due to incomplete excision; may behave in an aggressive manner with local destruction and potential invasion into vital structures	Good prognosis; recurrence rates are low and death due to extension into vital structures rarely occurs
Malignant transformation	Not known to occur	Not known to occur	Malignant transformation (osteosarcoma) occurs in fewer than 1%

and osteoblasts can be seen along their surfaces. The bony trabeculae vary in appearance and include odd shapes with a curvilinear pattern. The trabeculae are composed of lamellar bone with associated osteoclasts and osteoblastic rimming. Transition zones between the spherical ossicles and bony trabeculae can be seen. The non-osseous component includes a cellular stroma with a fascicular to storiform growth composed of round to polyhedral to spindle-shaped cells with prominent basophilic nuclei and inapparent cytoplasmic borders. Mitotic figures can be seen but mitotic activity is not prominent and atypical mitoses are not present. Giant cells can be seen among the psammomatoid ossicles or scattered throughout the non-osseous stromal component. Osteoid formation may be focally present.

Complete surgical excision is the treatment of choice. The prognosis is good following complete excision but, if margins are involved, recurrences quite often occur and the tumors may behave in an aggressive manner with local destruction and potential invasion into vital structures.[117]

Fibrous dysplasia

Fibrous dysplasia is an idiopathic non-neoplastic bone disease in which normal medullary bone is replaced by structurally

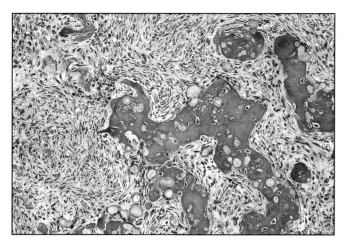

Fig. 4A.14 • Psammomatoid ossifying fibroma. The most distinctive component is the presence of mineralized or calcified "psammomatoid" bodies or ossicles.

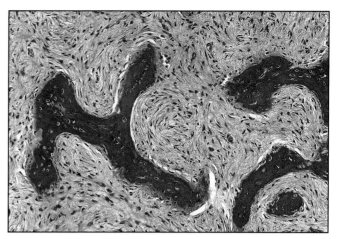

Fig. 4A.15 • Sinonasal fibrous dysplasia includes irregularly shaped immature (woven) bone, typically lacking osteoblastic rimming, with an associated nondescript fibrous tissue component.

weak fibrous and osseous tissue (see Ch. 25). Fibrous dysplasia may be monostotic (only a single osseous site is involved) or polyostotic (involvement of two or more bones). The majority of patients affected by fibrous dysplasia are under 30 years of age, usually in the first two decades of life. Craniofacial symptoms of fibrous dysplasia include painless, asymmetric swelling associated with functional disturbances. In the sinonasal tract, signs and symptoms may include headaches, proptosis, and nasal obstruction. Involvement of the craniofacial or jaw regions occurs in up to 50% of patients with polyostotic lesions and in up to 25% of patients with monostotic lesions.[119,120] A small percentage (1–3%) of fibrous dysplasia lesions are associated with Albright syndrome (or McCune–Albright syndrome), characterized by the triad of polyostotic fibrous dysplasia, endocrine dysfunction (hyperthyroidism and/or sexual precocity, the latter predominantly identified in females), and cutaneous hyperpigmentation.

The radiologic appearance is that of a poorly defined expansile osseous lesion with a thin intact cortex. Predominantly fibrous lesions are radiolucent while predominantly osseous lesions are radiodense. Lesions with an equal admixture of fibrous and osseous components have a ground-glass appearance. Histologically, the fibrous tissue component is nondescript and of variable cellularity. The osseous component includes irregularly shaped trabeculae of osteoid and immature (woven) bone arising in a fibrous stroma, is poorly oriented with misshapen bony trabeculae, increased cellularity and irregular margins, and forms odd geometric patterns including "C"- or "S"-shaped configurations (so-called Chinese characters) (Fig. 4A.15). The trabeculae typically lack osteoblastic rimming. Multinucleate giant cells, macrophages, increased vascularity, and calcification may be seen.

Gnathic fibro-osseous lesions (fibrous dysplasia and ossifying fibromas) may be histologically indistinguishable; therefore the diagnosis and differentiation rests on clinical–radiologic–histopathologic correlation. The differentiation of ossifying fibromas from fibrous dysplasia is important since the therapeutic rationale differs for these lesions. For fibrous dysplasia, conservative surgical excision is the preferred treatment and is only indicated in cases with compromise of function, progression of deformity, pain, associated patho-

logic fracture(s), or the development of a malignancy. The disease may stabilize at puberty and, in children, therapy should be delayed if possible until after puberty.[121] Recurrence rates are low and death due to extension into vital structures rarely occurs. Malignant transformation occurs in fewer than 1% of cases[122,123] and, when it occurs, is most often to an osteosarcoma. Radiation treatment is not utilized because of the risk of inducing malignant change.[111]

Giant cell reparative granuloma

Giant cell reparative granuloma is a benign reactive fibro-osseous proliferation. Giant cell reparative granuloma shares many features with aneurysmal bone cyst and, in many regards, these lesions may be indistinguishable.[124] In the head and neck area, the maxilla and mandible are the most common sites of occurrence. Sinonasal tract or nasopharyngeal involvement is uncommon. Those lesions predominantly confined to intraosseous sites (e.g., jaws) are referred to as central giant cell reparative granulomas and those primarily involving soft tissues (e.g., sinonasal or oral) are termed peripheral giant cell reparative granulomas.[125,126] Sinonasal tract involvement is associated with pain and swelling. Head and neck giant cell reparative granulomas are more common in women and occur in patients under 30 years of age (most are under 20 years old).[127] Hormonal factors may influence the growth of giant cell reparative granulomas.[128,129]

The central and peripheral giant cell reparative granulomas are histologically identical and are composed of a cellular fibroblastic stroma that includes multinucleate giant cells. The giant cells tend to aggregate in and around foci of hemorrhage; less often, the giant cells are diffusely distributed in the fibroblastic stroma. Mitotic figures are seen in the fibroblasts but not the giant cells. Cyst formation and reactive new bone may be present. Peripheral giant cell reparative granulomas are submucosal lesions lying beneath an intact and uninvolved respiratory or squamous epithelium. Surgical curettage is the treatment of choice. Up to 15% of gnathic lesions will recur[127] but sinonasal tract lesions are less likely to recur following curettage. Since the giant cell reparative granulomas are histologically identical to brown tumor of hyperparathyroidism, prudent management includes laboratory evaluation of parathyroid gland function.

Giant cell tumor

Giant cell tumors of bone are potentially aggressive but benign tumors that uncommonly occur in the head and neck (see Ch. 25).[125,130,131] Sinonasal tract and nasopharyngeal involvement is rare. In contrast to giant cell reparative granulomas, giant cell tumors are characterized by the presence of abundant multinucleate giant cells that are more diffusely distributed, larger, have more numerous nuclei (50–100) and are associated with a mononuclear cell stromal component rather than a fibroblastic background. Mitoses are seen in the stromal mononuclear cells but atypical mitoses are not present. The presence of atypical mitoses has been proposed as an indicator of malignancy.[132] Telomeric associations represent the most frequent chromosomal abnormality.[132] Malignant giat cell tumor of the sphenoid arising in a patient with Paget's disease has been reported.[133]

Chondroma

Chondromas of the sinonasal tract and nasopharynx are rare. The most frequent sites of occurrence include the nasal septum and the nasopharynx.[134,135] Sinus opacification or a circumscribed radiolucent lesion can be seen by radiographic studies. Sinonasal chondromas appear as a polypoid, firm, smooth-surfaced nodule measuring usually 0.5–2.0 cm and rarely being greater than 3.0 cm. Histologically, these are lobulated tumors composed of chondrocytes recapitulating the normal histology of cartilage. Cellular pleomorphism, binucleate chondrocytes, or increased mitotic activity are not present. Conservative but complete surgical excision is the treatment of choice. Recurrences are uncommon.

Ameloblastoma

Ameloblastomas are locally aggressive jaw tumors with a high propensity for recurrence that are thought to arise from remnants of odontogenic epithelium, lining of odontogenic cysts, and the basal layer of the overlying oral mucosa (see Ch. 6).[136] Ameloblastomas can occur in either the maxilla or mandible at almost any age, but are most frequently discovered as a painless expansion in the mandible of patients in their third to fifth decades.[137] Sinonasal tract involvement is uncommon and usually occurs by secondary extension from the maxilla. However, true primary sinonasal ameloblastomas without connection to gnathic sites uncommonly occur. Schafer and colleagues[138] reported a series of 24 primary sinonasal ameloblastomas. In their series there was a decided male predilection of 3.8:1, with a mean age at presentation of 59.7 years (approximately 15–25 years later than in patients with ameloblastoma occurring within the jaws). The patients usually presented with a mass lesion and nasal obstruction. Symptoms ranged from 1 month to several years in duration. Sites of involvement included either the nasal cavity only, the paranasal sinuses only, or both. In contrast to the characteristic multilocular, radiolucent presentation of ameloblastomas within the jaws, sinonasal ameloblastomas are described radiographically as solid masses or opacifications.[138] Bone

destruction, erosion, and remodeling (remnant of bony shell delimiting the lesion as it grew) may be present.

Histologically, sinonasal ameloblastomas are similar in appearance to their gnathic counterparts. The plexiform pattern, composed of a network of long anastomosing cords of odontogenic epithelium, represents the predominant histologic pattern (Fig. 4A.16).[138] The epithelial strands are bounded at the periphery by a layer of columnar cells exhibiting hyperchromatic, palisaded, and reverse polarized nuclei, along with subnuclear cytoplasmic vacuolization. The stellate reticulum-like component associated with the other patterns of ameloblastoma is often less conspicuous in association with the plexiform histologic type.[139] The acanthomatous pattern, characterized by squamous metaplasia and keratin formation in the central portions of the epithelial islands, can also be seen but is limited to a secondary or focal component. The ameloblastomatous proliferation can be seen arising in direct continuity with the intact sinonasal surface mucosal epithelium. The latter finding, in conjunction with the absence of continuity with gnathic sites, supports the histogenesis of these sinonasal tumors from totipotential cells of the sinonasal mucosal epithelium.[138]

Surgical excision is the treatment of choice in all cases. Schafer and colleagues reported a 22% recurrence rate.[138] Recurrence of the tumor generally occurred within 1–2 years of the initial procedure but, in one of their patients, recurrence occurred 13 years after initial surgery. Overall treatment success correlated most positively with complete surgical eradication when performed in conjunction with thoroughly detailed radiographic imaging. No tumor deaths, metastases, or malignant transformation have been reported.[138]

Craniopharyngioma

Craniopharyngiomas arise from Rathke's pouch in the area of the pituitary gland (sella turcica) or along the developmental tract leading to Rathke's pouch and the pituitary gland (see Ch. 17). Extrasellar craniopharyngiomas may occur in the sinonasal tract or nasopharynx, either by direct extension from a sellar tumor or independently of sellar involvement.[140-143] Symptoms include nasal obstruction, epistaxis, headache, and impaired vision. Most patients are in the first decade of life.[140] Histologically, craniopharyngiomas are epithelial neoplasms composed of centrally situated stellate cells with small nuclei and clear cytoplasm surrounded by a row of basaloid-appearing columnar cells with polarized nuclei in a palisaded arrangement. Degenerative necrobiotic changes, such as ghost cells and calcification, can be identified in the tumor. These features closely resemble the appearance of gnathic ameloblastomas. However, the clinical features of craniopharyngiomas markedly contrast with those of sinonasal tract ameloblastomas so that the lesions should be readily separable. Complete surgical removal is the treatment of choice and generally is curative.[140]

Benign teratoma

Teratomas in the UADT are rare neoplasms, accounting for fewer than 2% of all teratomas.[144] There is no gender predilection. Teratomas may be seen in the adult population but the majority occur in newborns or infants and are rarely

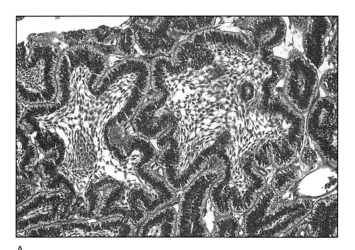

A

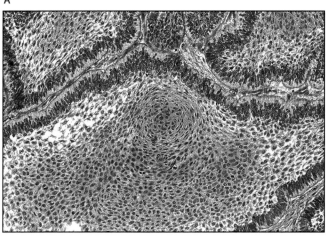

B

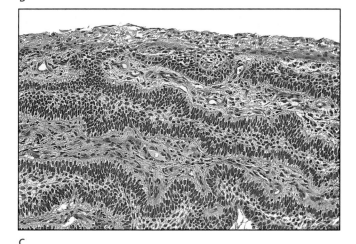

C

Fig. 4A.16 • Sinonasal ameloblastoma. **(A)** This unencapsulated tumor is composed of proliferating nests or islands of odontogenic epithelium, including a central area of loosely arranged cells similar to the stellate reticulum of the enamel organ and a peripheral area of palisading columnar or cuboidal cells with hyperchromatic small nuclei oriented away from the basement membrane (reverse polarity). **(B)** Acanthomatous changes can be seen as a focal alteration or as the dominant finding. **(C)** Ameloblastomatous proliferation is arising in direct continuity with the intact sinonasal surface mucosal epithelium. This finding in the setting of an isolated sinonasal mass without continuity with gnathic sites supports the histogenesis of these sinonasal tumors from totipotential cells of the sinonasal mucosal epithelium.

seen over the age of 1 year (cervical teratoma) and 2 years (nasopharyngeal teratoma). The most common location for teratomas to be seen within the UADT mucosa is the nasopharynx; other less commonly involved sites include the oral cavity (tonsil, tongue, palate), sinonasal cavity, and the ear and temporal bone. Nasopharyngeal teratoma presents as a mass protruding into the oral cavity or pharynx causing dysphagia and/or airway obstruction. Teratomas may be associated with maternal hydramnios and stillbirth.[145] In contrast to teratomas occurring in the pediatric population, teratomas of the head and neck in adults occur much less frequently but a much larger percentage of these tumors will be malignant.

Teratomas are encapsulated cystic, solid, or multiloculated, measuring 5–17 cm in diameter. The histologic composition of teratomas includes tissues arising from all three germ layers, including epithelia (keratinizing squamous, columnar, ciliated respiratory, or gastrointestinal-type epithelium), cutaneous adnexa, minor salivary glands, neuroectodermal and central nervous system tissue, cartilage, bone, fat, and smooth muscle. Epithelial-lined cystic spaces are prominent. Immature or embryonal tissue components can be identified throughout the tumor, but this is not of any prognostic significance. In nasopharyngeal teratomas, neuroectodermal and neural tissue components predominate. Necrosis and hemorrhage may be seen. In adults with malignant teratomas there is a prominent neural component associated with poorly differentiated carcinoma and/or sarcoma (see later, under malignant teratoma (teratocarcinosarcoma)).

Complete surgical excision is the treatment of choice. Morbidity may be high due to the size and location of the tumors. Mortality rates are low if surgical intervention is initiated early; however, death may ensue in inadequately treated cases and is usually caused by complications of respiratory obstruction. Nasopharyngeal teratomas may extend intracranially. In the pediatric age group, malignant transformation (or behavior) of a head and neck teratoma has not been reported.

The differential diagnosis of nasopharyngeal teratoma includes the nasopharyngeal dermoid (so-called hairy polyp).[146] Nasopharyngeal dermoid is a developmental (congenital) anomaly predominantly comprised of skin (ectodermal-derived) but may also include well-formed cartilage (mesodermal-derived); the absence of endodermal-derived structures and the presence of limited heterogeneity of tissue types argue against inclusion as a teratoma. The fact that these lesions contain skin, a tissue type not normally found in the nasopharynx, suggests that these lesions may be better classified as a choristoma rather than a hamartoma, possibly of first branchial arch origin.[147,148] However, some authors argue that these lesions are best classified as a subset of benign teratoma.[149]

Tumors of indeterminant malignant potential

Sinonasal-type hemangiopericytoma

So-called hemangiopericytoma (HPC) at most locations is nowadays most often reclassified as SFT (see Ch. 3).

Sinonasal-type HPC is a very uncommon tumor, showing perivascular myoid differentiation, and typically behaves in a benign manner.[150–153] Given light microscopic and immuno-histochemical evidence of myoid differentiation and the fact that the light microscopic features of sinonasal-type HPC differ from soft tissue HPC, a more apt designation for the sinonasal tract lesion may be myopericytoma or glomangiopericytoma.[151] Despite the usually indolent behavior of this sinonasal tumor, the most recent World Health Organization (WHO) classification of sinonasal tract tumors has classified the sinonasal-type of HPC as having indeterminant biologic potential.[154]

For sinonasal-type HPC there is no gender predilection; it occurs over a wide age range but is most commonly seen in the sixth to seventh decades of life.[155] These lesions can be identified in virtually any site but the most frequent site of occurrence is the nasal cavity and paranasal sinuses. Sinonasal-type HPC typically presents as a unilateral nasal mass with obstruction and epistaxis. Extension into adjacent paranasal sinuses may occur but isolated involvement of a paranasal sinus is uncommon. The radiologic appearance of sinonasal-type HPC is usually opacification of the involved sinus. Bone erosion due to pressure may be seen. Arteriographic findings reveal a richly vascular neoplasm. There are no known etiologic factors.

The gross appearance of sinonasal-type HPC is that of a red to tan-gray, soft to firm polypoid mass of varying size. Histologically, sinonasal-type HPC is a submucosal, circumscribed, but unencapsulated cellular tumor. In contrast to lobular capillary hemangioma (LCH), sinonasal-type HPC has a diffuse growth pattern and is composed of a single cell type that is situated around endothelial-lined vascular spaces (Fig. 4A.17). The tumor cells are usually arranged in short fascicles, and less often may show storiform, whorled, or even palisaded growth patterns. The tumor cells are uniform and ovoid with round to oval nuclei, vesicular to hyperchromatic-appearing chromatin, and indistinct eosinophilic cytoplasm; occasionally, more spindle-shaped cells are seen. Mild nuclear pleomorphism and an occasional mitotic figure can be seen, but there typically is not a marked increase in the mitotic activity and atypical mitoses are not present. Necrosis is not usually found. The vascular channels range from capillary size to large sinusoidal spaces that may have a "staghorn" or "antler-like" configuration. A characteristic but not pathognomonic feature is the presence of perivascular hyalinization (Fig. 4A.17). The cellular proliferation may compress and obscure blood vessels of smaller size. Extravasated erythrocytes are often identified. An inflammatory cell component, usually including mast cells but also eosinophils, is present scattered throughout the tumor. Multinucleated (tumor) giant cells can be seen in a minority of cases.[151] Fibrosis or a myxoid stroma may be seen, especially in tumors showing degenerative changes. Heterologous metaplastic elements, including bone and cartilage, may occasionally be seen.

Neoplastic cells of so-called HPC at more usual soft tissue sites fail to stain with muscle-specific actin and desmin,[156,157] but the immunophenotype of sinonasal-type HPC includes positivity for vimentin, smooth muscle actin, muscle-specific actin, factor XIIIa, and vascular endothelial growth factor (VEGF).[151,152,158] No immunoreactivity is present with cytokeratin, factor VIII-related antigen, neuron-specific enolase (NSE), KP-1 (CD68), bcl-2, CD99, and CD117 (c-kit). Ultra-

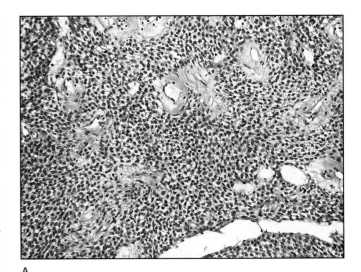

A

B

Fig. 4A.17 • Sinonasal-type hemangiopericytoma. **(A)** The tumor is cellular, diffuse in its growth, and well vascularized. The neoplastic cells are tightly packed with hyperchromatic nuclei and are situated around endothelial-lined vascular spaces. **(B)** A characteristic finding relative to the vascular spaces is the presence of perivascular (peritheliomatous) hyalinization that, in conjunction with the cytomorphology, assists in recognizing this tumor.

structural findings include the presence of pericellular basal lamina, pinocytotic vesicles, intracytoplasmic (thin) filaments, dense bodies, and membranous attachment plaques.[159,160]

The differential diagnosis includes LCH, angiofibroma, glomus tumor (glomangioma), SFT, smooth muscle tumors (leiomyoma and leiomyosarcoma) and synovial sarcoma. Both sinonasal-type HPC and SFT may show CD34 immunoreactivity; however the extent of CD34 immunoreactivity varies. In sinonasal-type HPC there is localized CD34, while in SFTs it tends to be more diffuse. Further, in contrast to the SFT, the sinonasal-type HPC lack the presence of "ropey" keloidal-appearing collagen or amianthoid fibers and bcl-2 staining.

Surgery is the treatment of choice. HPC are considered radioresistant neoplasms. Sinonasal-type HPC are indolent-behaving tumors with overall 5-year survival rates of >90%.[152,156] Local recurrence may occur in as many as 30% of cases and is likely due to inadequate surgical excision. Eichorn et al.[160] and El-Naggar et al.[161] report that recurrence of sinonasal-type HPC can be anticipated over extended follow-up periods (1–2 decades). Aggressively behaving cases of sinonasal-type HPC are uncommon and include tumors that are locally destructive or are metastatic.[155] Findings potentially linked to aggressive behavior include large tumor size (>5 cm), marked nuclear pleomorphism, increased mitotic activity, necrosis, invasive growth (e.g., bone) and proliferation index of >10%.[151,162,163] Metastatic tumor rarely occurs to regional lymph nodes and lung and is usually preceded by local recurrence.[155]

Malignant epithelial and neuroectodermal neoplasms

Carcinoma of the nasal vestibule

Carcinomas of the nasal vestibule are uncommon and are considered to represent cutaneous carcinomas rather than mucosal carcinomas.[164] Of the 5 cases reported by Taxy,[164] 4 were men and 1 was a woman; the cases ranged in age from 52 to 82 years. The tumors were located either in the nasal vestibule or at the mucocutaneous junction. The most common tumor type is squamous carcinoma. The majority of these tumors are well differentiated. Basal cell carcinomas may also occur but are uncommon.[164] The differential diagnosis includes squamous papilloma, schneiderian papillomas, and VC (see below). Treatment includes local excision and/or radiotherapy. Most patients have an excellent prognosis. Five-year survival rates range from 70 to 80%.[164] Invasion of the subjacent nasal septal perichondrium or bone may occur. Metastasis to cervical neck lymph nodes may occur but is uncommon.

Squamous cell carcinoma of the sinonasal tract and nasopharynx

The epithelium lining the sinonasal tract and nasopharynx is capable of differentiating along various cell lines, accounting for the morphologic variety of carcinomas seen to arise from these surfaces. Squamous cell carcinomas of the UADT mucosa are divided according to histologic subtype. The most common type of squamous cell carcinoma of the sinonasal tract is the conventional type, including keratinizing and non-keratinizing squamous cell carcinomas. In addition, there are a number of variants of conventional squamous carcinoma, including exophytic or papillary squamous carcinoma, VC, spindle cell squamous carcinoma (SCSC), basaloid squamous cell carcinoma, and adenosquamous carcinoma (ASC) that are sufficiently different in their pathologic features, biologic behavior and therapeutic approach to merit separate discussion.

Squamous cell carcinoma (conventional type) of the sinonasal tract

Squamous cell carcinoma is the most common type of malignant epithelial neoplasm of the sinonasal tract. However, it represents approximately 3% of all head and neck malignant neoplasms and fewer than 1% of all malignant neoplasms.[165–167]

Sinonasal squamous cell carcinoma affects men more than women and is most frequent in the sixth and seventh decades of life, with 95% of cases arising in patients older than 40 years. In decreasing order of frequency, the sites of occurrence include antrum of the maxillary sinus, the nasal cavity, the ethmoid sinus, and the sphenoid and frontal sinuses.[165–167] Although the frontal and sphenoid sinuses may be the sites of a primary carcinoma, most of the neoplasms involving these sinuses arise from the ethmoid sinus or from the nasopharynx. Clinical presentations include facial asymmetry, unilateral nasal obstruction, epistaxis, a tumor mass palpable or visible in the nasal or oral cavity, pain, persistent purulent rhinorrhea, non-healing sore or ulcer, and exophthalmos. The diagnosis of paranasal sinus carcinomas is often delayed as the clinical signs and symptoms in the earlier stages of disease are similar to those of chronic sinusitis, while the diagnosis of carcinoma of the nasal cavity is usually recognized relatively early as symptoms prompt earlier clinical detection.[168] Risk factors that have been associated with sinonasal tract squamous carcinoma include nickel exposure,[169,170] as well as exposure to textile dust, smoking, prior Thorotrast use, and development of a schneiderian papilloma. In the latter, HPV may be found, but a direct cause and effect has not been definitively found. Patients with nasal cavity squamous carcinomas are at greater risk for a second primary malignancy, either at another mucosal site in the UADT or involving the lung, gastrointestinal tract, or breast.[171]

The gross appearance of sinonasal squamous cell carcinomas varies and includes exophytic, polypoid, papillary, fungating, or inverted growth patterns that may be well circumscribed, with an expansile growth and limited invasion, or necrotic and friable with a hemorrhagic appearance and destructive growth.

Sinonasal squamous cell carcinomas are histologically divided into keratinizing and non-keratinizing subtypes. The keratinizing type is the most common. These tumors can be divided into well-differentiated, moderately differentiated, and poorly differentiated carcinomas. In well-differentiated squamous cell carcinomas there is readily apparent keratinization with keratin pearl formation or individual cell keratinization (Fig. 4A.18). Dyskeratosis (abnormal keratinization)

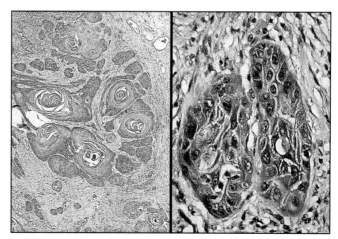

Fig. 4A.18 • Sinonasal squamous cell carcinoma, keratinizing. Left: Infiltrating keratinizing squamous cell carcinoma; right: individual cell keratinization and intercellular bridges are present.

may be prominent. Intercellular bridges are identifiable. The neoplastic cells show mild to moderate nuclear atypia with enlarged, hyperchromatic nuclei and low mitotic activity. As a squamous carcinoma becomes less differentiated (higher histologic grade), the tumor shows less keratinization and more nuclear atypia with increased mitotic activity, including atypical forms. Even in the poorly differentiated carcinomas, evidence of keratinization is usually focally present. Stromal invasion may include cohesive nests or cords of malignant cells or may be represented by isolated invasive malignant cells. The host response to invasive carcinoma (desmoplasia) includes collagen deposition with or without an associated chronic inflammatory cell reaction.

The non-keratinizing subtype may also have a papillary or exophytic growth pattern, but often shows a downward (inverted or endophytic) growth with broad interconnecting bands or nests of neoplastic epithelium (Fig. 4A.19). The tumor nests may have rounded or smooth borders or may be delineated by basement membrane-like material. This pattern of growth is similar to that of bladder cancers, hence the designation of these tumors as transitional-type carcinomas.[172] This tumor type is composed of elongated cells with a cylindrical or columnar appearance, oriented perpendicular to the surface and generally lacking evidence of keratinization. Keratin may be present focally but does not represent a significant component of the tumor. In general, these are hypercellular tumors characterized by nuclear pleomorphism, hyperchromasia, increased nuclear-to-cytoplasmic ratio, loss of cell polarity and increased mitotic activity, including atypical forms (Fig. 4A.19). Given the smooth borders or surrounding basement membrane-like material, these tumors may not be interpreted as invasive and may be underdiagnosed as papillomas with severe dysplasia or as carcinoma in situ. For both types of squamous carcinoma, dysplasia of the adjacent or overlying surface epithelium may be seen. The dysplasia may vary from mild to moderate to severe (i.e., carcinoma in situ). The differential diagnosis of sinonasal squamous cell carcinoma includes sinonasal (schneiderian) papillomas (see above).

The treatment for sinonasal squamous cell carcinoma is complete surgical resection and adjuvant radiotherapy.[173,174] Surgical advances now permit complex tumor removal and reconstruction of surrounding structures, resulting in functional and cosmetic improvements.[174] Recent trends have broadened the indications for chemotherapeutic and radiotherapeutic options in the management of advanced sinonasal squamous carcinomas.[174,175] Local recurrence occurs frequently but metastatic disease is uncommon if the tumor is confined to the involved sinus. Tumor extension beyond the sinus wall results in a higher incidence of regional lymph node metastasis. In general, the prognosis is poor.[168] Clinical stage is of more importance to prognosis than histologic type. Factors portending a poorer prognosis include higher clinical stage disease with involvement of more than one anatomic area, extension beyond the nasal cavity or paranasal sinuses, and regional lymph node metastasis. The pattern of invasion may also impact on prognosis. Tumors with "diffuse spread" or single-cell invasive growth pattern have a decreased survival of 30–40% as compared to 80–90% survival in patients with a more cohesive or "pushing" pattern of invasion.[170] Crissman & Zarbo have discussed the implications of pattern of tumor invasion and correlation with prognosis.[176] These authors

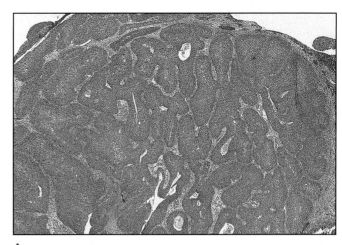

A

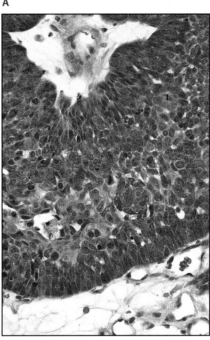

B

Fig. 4A.19 • Sinonasal squamous cell carcinoma, non-keratinizing. **(A)** The tumor invades into the submucosa as broad interconnecting bands of neoplastic epithelium growing down ("inverted") into the stroma. **(B)** Marked cellular pleomorphism with loss of polarity, increased nuclear-to-cytoplasmic ratio, and increased mitotic activity.

indicated that invasive cancers with single-cell or small aggregates of tumor cells invading into the host stroma are much more capable of lymphovascular invasion as compared to large cohesive tumor nests.

Papillary (exophytic) squamous cell carcinoma

Squamous cell carcinomas (keratinizing and non-keratinizing) of the UADT are characterized by an exophytic or papillary growth clinically simulating the appearance of a benign papilloma or a VC, but, in contrast with the latter, the neoplastic cells of the exophytic and papillary squamous cell carcinoma are cytologically malignant.[177–180] Papillary (exophytic) squamous cell carcinoma represents an uncommon but distinct subtype of head and neck squamous cell carcinoma. The demographics are similar to those of conventional squamous cell carcinoma with the tendency to affect men more than women and occurring in adults with a mean age in the seventh decade of life. Papillary squamous cell carcinomas are commonest in the larynx, oral cavity, oro- and hypopharynx, and sinonasal tract. The larynx is the most frequent site of occurrence. Symptoms vary according to the site of involvement. HPV (by ISH and PCR) has been detected in papillary squamous cell carcinoma and pre-existing papillomas have been reported in up to 34% of patients.[180]

Papillary squamous cell carcinoma is most often seen as a solitary lesion with an exophytic or papillary growth. Tumor size may range from 2 mm up to 4 cm. Histologically, papillary squamous cell carcinoma has filiform growth with finger-like projections and identifiable fibrovascular cores or a broad-based bulbous to exophytic growth with rounded projections, resembling a cauliflower-like growth pattern, in which fibrovascular cores can be seen but tend to be limited or absent (Fig. 4A.20). The squamous epithelium is cytologically malignant and this malignant epithelium identifies these tumors as carcinomas, separating them from papillomas. Surface keratinization is generally limited and often absent. Definitive invasion may be difficult to demonstrate in biopsy specimens, with the carcinomatous epithelium suggesting an in-situ process rather than invasive carcinoma. However, the extent of growth with the formation of a clinically appreciable exophytic mass goes beyond the general concept of an in-situ carcinoma. These tumors should be considered as being invasive, even in the absence of definitive stromal invasion.

Papillary squamous cell carcinoma usually arises *de novo* without identification of a coexisting benign lesion such as a papilloma, although association with a precursor papilloma or occurrence in patients with a previous history of a papilloma at the site of the papillary squamous cell carcinoma has been reported.

Surgery is the treatment of choice; adjunctive therapy may be utilized. The majority of papillary squamous cell carcinomas are of low clinical stage (T2). Their behavior overall is similar to conventional squamous cell carcinoma of similar stage, although some authors report a better overall prognosis for papillary squamous cell carcinoma than for conventional squamous cell carcinoma when matched for T-stage.

The differential diagnosis of papillary and exophytic squamous cell carcinoma includes laryngeal papillomatosis (LP), conventional squamous cell carcinoma, and VC. LP is distinguished by its bland epithelial proliferation. Cytologic abnormalities may be seen in LP, but tend to be focal when present and do not approach the level of dysplasia seen in papillary squamous cell carcinoma. VC is characterized by an exophytic growth pattern with marked keratosis in layers or tiers, absent nuclear atypia, absent mitotic activity beyond the basal layer, and a pushing rather than infiltrative pattern of invasion. These features contrast with those seen in papillary and exophytic squamous cell carcinoma.

Verrucous carcinoma (VC)

VC is a highly differentiated variant of squamous cell carcinoma with locally destructive, but not metastatic, capabilities. VC can occur anywhere in the UADT. The most common sites, in descending order, are the oral cavity, larynx, nasal fossa, sinonasal tract, and nasopharynx.[181–184] In the sinonasal tract, the maxillary sinus is the most common paranasal sinus involved (93%).[185,186] Symptoms vary accordingto site. In the sinonasal tract and nasopharynx, the most common presentations include airway obstruction and dysphagia, respectively. The etiology of VC remains speculative and includes the use of tobacco products.[184] Viral induction may be a factor in the development of VC.[187,188] However, there are conflicting data in the literature on the identification of HPV DNA by ISH techniques. Some investigators either failed to identify HPV DNA in any oral cavity VC,[189] or identified HPV DNA in a very limited number of cases.[190–193] Perhaps these discrepancies relate to the difficulties in the interpretation of ISH studies. This may be complicated by problems of non-specific staining or sensitivity of detection[194] and it is unclear that VC has been separated reliably from conventional squamous cell carcinoma. PCR analysis for the presence of HPV in VCs has confirmed the presence of HPV DNA.[195,196] These studies suggest a direct pathogenetic role of HPV, rather than that of an innocent bystander, in the

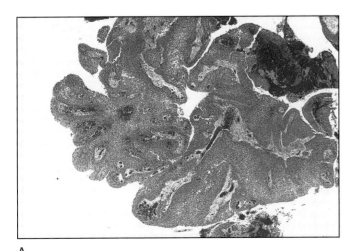
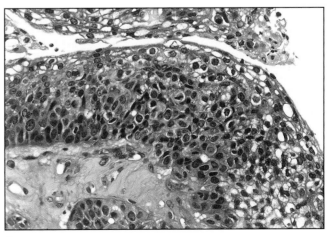

Fig. 4A.20 • Exophytic (papillary) squamous cell carcinoma. **(A)** Prominent exophytic and papillary epithelial growth; **(B)** the entire epithelial component is malignant.

development of VC. The active role of HPV may be as a promoter in the multistep process of carcinogenesis in squamous cells of the UADT. Dyson et al.[197] have shown that a protein product of HPV can bind the retinoblastoma gene product, thereby removing the regulatory block on cell cycle progression from G1 to S-phase.

Irrespective of site, the pathologic appearance of VC is generally the same. The gross appearance of VC is a tan or white, warty, fungating or exophytic, firm to hard mass measuring up to 10 cm in diameter. In general, the tumors have a broad base. The histologic appearance of VC is that of a bland squamous cell proliferation with uniform cells lacking dysplastic features (Fig. 4A.21). There is orderly maturation with retention of polarity. There is no increased nuclear-to-cytoplasmic ratio, nuclear pleomorphism, or dyskeratosis. Mitotic figures can be seen in the basal area but are not present elsewhere. In addition to the bland epithelial cell proliferation, there is marked surface keratinization ("church-spire" keratosis) and, characteristically, broad or bulbous rete pegs push downward into the stroma. Invasive growth into the submucosa as angulated, cohesive tumor nests or individual discohesive neoplastic cells is not a feature. A mixed chronic inflammatory cell infiltrate composed of lymphocytes, plasma cells and histiocytes may be prominent in the stroma. Viral-associated cytopathic changes (koilocytosis) may be present. An adequate biopsy for a diagnosis of VC should include ample epithelial and underlying stromal tissue. In the absence of stroma, the biopsy should be considered as inadequate and a definitive diagnosis of VC should not be made.

The diagnosis of VC does not usually require any special stains (i.e., histochemistry or immunohistochemistry). In certain settings, a florid but bland epithelial proliferation may occur secondary to fungal infection, such as candidiasis. The fungal forms are best seen by silver stains, such as Gomori methenamine silver (GMS). The fungi should be present within the depths of the epithelial proliferation and not limited to the surface keratin or most superficial epithelium. Fungi may secondarily colonize any squamous epithelial proliferation and may occur concomitantly with neoplastic proliferation, including VC.

VC must be differentiated from "conventional" types of squamous cell carcinoma. Both clinically and histopathologically, there may be overlapping features between these tumor types. The histologic differentiation of VC from a "conventional" squamous carcinoma is based on the presence or absence of cytologic abnormalities. Any dysplastic features should exclude a diagnosis of VC. Minimal dysplastic features are limited to the basal zone in VC. Dyskeratosis can be seen in "conventional" squamous cell carcinoma but usually is not a feature of VC. The pathologic diagnosis of VC may be extremely difficult and require multiple biopsies over several years prior to identification of definitively diagnostic features. Both clinicians and pathologists need to be aware of this fact. To this end, adequate initial biopsy material is critical and should include a good epithelial–stromal interface. The pathologist should not overinterpret a verrucoid lesion as carcinoma without seeing the relationship of the lesion to the underlying stroma. Similarly, an adequate epithelial–stromal interface is required in order to exclude invasive carcinoma in the presence of dysplastic squamous epithelial alterations.

Surgical excision is the definitive diagnostic modality for VC.[182,198] Sinonasal tract VC often presents with advanced disease, initially being seen at stage T3 or higher.[185] Cervical adenopathy may be present, but reflects reactive changes and not metastatic disease.[183] Some literature supports the dogma that radiotherapy is contraindicated in the treatment of VC due to the purported induction of anaplastic transformation. However, there are many reasons to doubt the validity of radiation-induced anaplastic transformation of VC. Similar transformations of VC occur following surgery, cryosurgery, and even in the absence of any therapeutic intervention.[183,199] Batsakis et al.[182] point out several factors that weigh against the association of radiation-induced transformation, including the fact that the interval between radiotherapy and the high-grade malignancy may be extremely short (less than 8 months), and that most descriptions and illustrations of "anaplastic transformation" of VCs are inadequate. A more likely scenario is that "host tumors" were not VCs but were conventional squamous carcinomas that may not have been adequately sampled, thus precluding the identification of less differentiated ("anaplastic") foci that were a part of the neoplasm from its inception. Surgery remains the treatment of choice, with local control in 85% of patients.[200] The rate of local control with radiotherapy is less than 50%.[200] Vidyasagar et al.[201] reported a series of 107 irradiated patients in which 31% of tumors recurred. They claim that these figures compare favorably with a similar recurrence rate following surgery. Radiotherapy can be utilized in selected clinical settings for patients with locally advanced disease or in patients who are not good surgical candidates.[202]

Spindle cell squamous carcinoma (sarcomatoid carcinoma)

Squamous carcinomas composed predominantly of spindle cells (SCSC) occur in the sinonasal tract and naso-

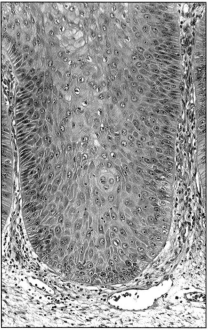

Fig. 4A21 • Verrucous carcinoma. The epithelium is bland, lacking cytologic atypia or mitotic activity.

pharynx.[202–204] In these anatomic sites, SCSCs often appear as fungating, ulcerating masses as compared with a polypoid or exophytic appearance in their more usual UADT locations (i.e., larynx, oral cavity). The histologic features that define SCSC include a malignant undifferentiated spindle cell proliferation in the presence of a differentiated squamous cell component that includes severe dysplasia, carcinoma in situ, or frankly invasive squamous cell carcinoma (Fig. 4A.22). However, not infrequently, the differentiated component is absent and the tumor is composed entirely of the spindle-shaped and pleomorphic (undifferentiated) component. In general, these are hypercellular tumors composed of pleomorphic-appearing spindle and epithelioid cells with large, hyperchromatic nuclei, increased nuclear-to-cytoplasmic ratio, indistinct to prominent eosinophilic nucleoli, inconspicuous to ample eosinophilic to amphophilic cytoplasm, increased mitotic activity (typical and atypical), and necrosis. The growth pattern of SCSC may be fascicular, storiform, or palisading, with or without an associated myxomatous stroma. If the superficial epithelium is intact, the malignant spindle cell component is not separated from the surface but can be seen intimately associated with the surface epithelium. An intact surface epithelium may or may not be dysplastic.

In some SCSCs, the spindle cell proliferation may be sparsely cellular with marked fibrosis or collagenized stroma (Fig. 4A.23). In these hypocellular SCSC, the surface epithelium may be intact without dysplasia or a definitive squamous cell carcinoma. In this situation, the diagnosis of malignancy may be extremely difficult. The hypocellular SCSC is still a polypoid lesion, involving the superficial submucosal compartment, and the spindle or pleomorphic cell proliferation has atypical nuclear features with increased mitotic activity that includes typical and atypical forms. The superficial localization of the tumor and the presence of nuclear atypia assist in differentiating this tumor from mesenchymal neoplasms or reactive proliferations, such as a predominantly myofibroblastic process. Heterologous elements, including bone and cartilage, can be seen. These elements may show features of malignancy (chondrosarcomatous and osteosarcomatous foci).

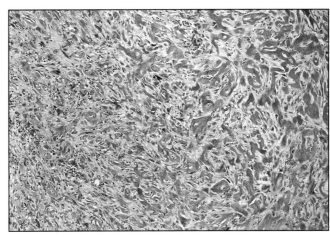

Fig. 4A.23 • Spindle cell squamous carcinoma. This example has a prominent collagenous stroma.

Immunohistochemical evaluation may be helpful in the diagnosis of SCSC (Fig. 4A.22). The spindle cells are keratin-positive in the majority of cases but cytokeratin may be absent in up to 40% of cases.[205] Other authors have identified a similar staining pattern for cytokeratin, ranging from 30 to 50% of cases of SCSC, depending on the antibody used.[203,206–210] Therefore, the absence of cytokeratin staining does not preclude a diagnosis of SCSC. *p63*, a marker of squamous cells and myoepithelial cells, has been shown to be as effective in marking the spindle cells in SCSC as cytokeratin, and should be used in conjunction with cytokeratins in the diagnosis of spindle cell squamous carcinomas.[211] In the absence of cytokeratin reactivity, a diagnosis of SCSC is suggested by the absence of immunoreactivity that may be specific for another diagnosis, such as S-100 protein for a mucosal malignant melanoma (MMM) or reactivity with mesenchymal markers (desmin and myogenin) that might be diagnostic of a sarcoma. However, potentially compounding the diagnostic problem is the presence in some cases of immunoreactivity with markers that have traditionally been felt to be representative

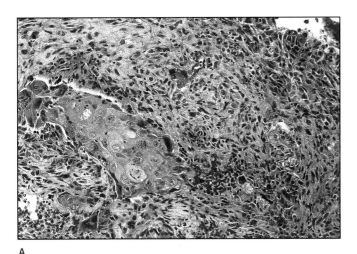

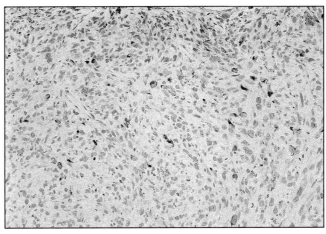

A

B

Fig. 4A.22 • Maxillary sinus spindle cell squamous carcinoma. **(A)** The combination of a differentiated squamous epithelial component (in this illustration, infiltrating squamous carcinoma) and an intimately associated malignant spindle and pleomorphic cell infiltrate is diagnostic of this neoplasm. **(B)** Cytokeratin immunoreactivity is present and is usually focal but may be negative.

of mesenchymal differentiation. Vimentin and various myogenic markers (desmin, actins) have been reported in SCSC.[204,206,210–214] In a study of 26 SCSCs of various UADT sites, 42% of the tumors were reactive with cytokeratin, 100% reactive with vimentin, and 42% reactive with the myogenic markers HHF-35 (pan-actin) and α-smooth muscle actin,[209] as often seen in spindle cell carcinomas in other locations. Twenty-five percent coexpressed cytokeratin and actin. Ultrastructurally, SCSC usually shows evidence of epithelial differentiation, including desmosomes, tonofilaments, and macula adherens, and, on occasion, this may be the most reliable means of making the diagnosis.[204,208,210]

In general, SCSCs are more aggressive than conventional squamous cell carcinomas and are more radioresistant. Sinonasal spindle cell carcinomas specifically have a worse prognosis than similar tumors in other UADT sites. In a comparison of spindle cell carcinomas of various UADT sites, Batsakis and colleagues[215] reported 70% mortality for sinonasal SCSC, as compared with 60% for oral cavity SCSC and 30% for laryngeal SCSC. In addition, local recurrence and metastatic disease are common, the latter primarily to cervical lymph nodes and to lung.[216,217] The histology of the metastatic deposits may include conventional squamous cell carcinoma alone, spindle cell carcinoma alone, or both conventional and SCSC.[216] Etiologic factors associated with sinonasal or nasopharyngeal SCSCs have not been identified. One study failed to identify HPV in oropharyngeal SCSCs.[215]

Basaloid squamous cell carcinoma

Basaloid squamous cell carcinoma is a high-grade variant of squamous cell carcinoma that shows a predilection for the hypopharynx (pyriform sinus), supraglottic larynx, oral cavity, tongue, tonsil, and palate.[218–223] Less frequently, the sinonasal tract may be involved.[222,224,225] In the sinonasal tract, the presentation is as a mass lesion with unilateral nasal obstruction.[225] Etiologic factors linked to non-sinonasal tract sites include excessive alcohol and/or tobacco use[223,226] but specific etiologic factors have not been found for sinonasal tumors.[225]

Basaloid squamous cell carcinomas are firm to hard, tan-white masses often with associated central necrosis, measuring up to 6.0 cm in greatest dimension. Infrequently, they may be exophytic. The histologic appearance is that of an infiltrating tumor arranged in a variety of growth patterns, all of which may be seen within any given tumor and include solid, lobular, cell nests, cribriform, cords, trabeculae, and gland-like or cystic spaces. The tumor originates from the surface epithelium, which may show severe dysplasia and/or direct continuity with the invasive carcinoma. Frequently, comedonecrosis is identified within the center of the neoplastic lobules. One of the distinctive cytologic features is the presence of a basaloid-cell component consisting of small, closely apposed cells with hyperchromatic nuclei, scanty cytoplasm, and marked mitotic activity; large cells and pleomorphism may be seen (Fig. 4A.24). Another important cytologic feature is the intimate association with foci of squamous differentiation, whether dysplastic, in-situ malignant, or invasive. In addition, a neoplastic spindle cell carcinomatous component may be identified in association with the basaloid squamous elements. The presence of intercellular deposition of eosinophilic hyalin or mucohyalin material simulates the appearance of reduplicated basement membrane material associated with tumors of (minor) salivary gland origin. Rosette-like structures can be seen.[227] BSCC are deeply invasive tumors with frequent invasion of soft tissue structures and neurotropism.

The basement membrane-like material is periodic acid–Schiff (PAS) and alcian blue-positive. Immunohistochemistry shows consistent staining with cytokeratin, as well as with other epithelial markers, including EMA and carcinoembryonic antigen (CEA).[224,225] The neuroendocrine markers chromogranin and synaptophysin are typically negative, although chromogranin has been reported in a minority of cases;[227] glial fibrillary acidic protein (GFAP) and the melanocytic marker HMB-45 are consistently negative. There is variable immunoreactivity seen with vimentin, S-100 protein, and actin. Electron microscopy shows the basaloid component to have desmosomes, rare tonofilaments, and loose stellate granules or replicated basal lamina within the cystic

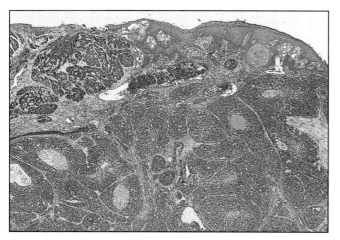

A

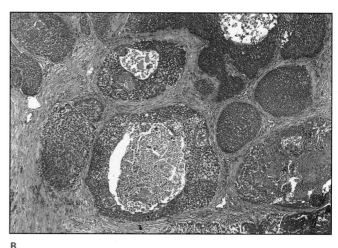

B

Fig. 4A.24 • Basaloid squamous cell carcinoma of the sinonasal tract. **(A)** Invasive carcinoma with lobular growth pattern and associated comedo-type necrosis, foci of trabecular growth (upper right), and a focus of abrupt keratinization (upper left). **(B)** The carcinoma is predominantly composed of a basaloid cell proliferation with limited but identifiable squamous differentiation.

spaces.[218] Hewan-Lowe & Dardick[228] identified ultrastructural features that assist in differentiating basaloid squamous cell carcinoma from adenoid cystic carcinoma (ACC). These authors compared the ultrastructural features of 3 basaloid squamous cell carcinomas and 3 ACCs and found that the basaloid squamous cell carcinomas had features of squamous cell carcinoma, including cell groups with numerous and prominent tonofilament bundles, prominent desmosomes, and epithelial pearls. These features were not present in ACCs.[228] Features of glandular differentiation were exclusively identified in the ACCs but not in basaloid squamous cell carcinoma, including oligocilia and lumina (large lumina and smaller compressed ones).

Because of the propensity for early metastases to regional lymph nodes and visceral locations, the treatment of choice for basaloid squamous cell carcinomas is multimodality therapy, including radical surgical excision, neck dissection, radiotherapy, and often chemotherapy.[218,222,223,226]

Basaloid squamous cell carcinoma of all UADT sites is an aggressive, high-grade tumor with an increased tendency to be multifocal, deeply invasive, and metastatic, even at initial presentation.[218] Shallow biopsies may belie the depth and extent of invasion and may not be representative of the lesion, leading to erroneous staging. Multifocality includes other mucosal sites of the head and neck, as well as in the gastrointestinal tract.[229] Metastases occur via lymphatics and blood vessels, principally to regional and distant lymph nodes. Approximately 64% of patients will have (or will develop) cervical lymph node metastasis.[227] Distant metastasis develops in up to 44% of cases[183] involving the lung, bone, skin, and brain.[218,222,226] Metastases include both basaloid and squamous cell components.

Adenosquamous carcinoma (ASC)

ASC is another high-grade variant of squamous cell carcinoma arising from the surface epithelium and shows histologic features of both adenocarcinoma and squamous cell carcinoma. ASC is an uncommon variant of squamous cell carcinoma. This neoplasm may occur in virtually all UADT sites but is identified most frequently in the larynx, hypopharynx, oral cavity, and sinonasal cavity.[230–235] In the sinonasal tract, these tumors present as a mass, with or without pain, and airway obstruction. The etiology is not clearly defined and may be related to alcohol and/or tobacco use.

These tumors can be exophytic or submucosal, friable, edematous, or granular, with or without surface ulceration, and measure 0.6–5.0 cm. The histologic appearance is that of an infiltrating neoplasm with solid and glandular areas. The squamous cell carcinoma component varies from well to poorly differentiated; often there is in-situ carcinoma of the surface epithelium, extension of the in-situ component to the contiguous minor salivary glands, and/or an invasive carcinoma arising from the surface epithelium. Squamous cell differentiation is evident by individual cell keratinization, intercellular bridges, keratin pearl formation, and/or dyskeratosis (Fig. 4A.25). The adenocarcinomatous component is identified in the submucosa and may be recognized easily by its glandular differentiation (Fig. 4A.25). Mucous cell differentiation may not be seen and is not a prerequisite for diagnosis. Squamous cell carcinoma and adenocarcinoma may be admixed but may also be distinct and separate from one another. Cellular pleomorphism, increased mitoses, foci of necrosis, and perineural invasion may be prominent. Intracellular and intraluminal mucicarmine and diastase-resistant, PAS-positive material is associated with the glandular component. The presence of epithelial mucin in ASC differentiates it from an adenoid squamous cell carcinoma. The neoplastic cells are cytokeratin-positive.

The differential diagnosis of ASC includes basaloid squamous cell carcinoma (see above) and high-grade (poorly differentiated) mucoepidermoid carcinoma. Differentiation is important as the biologic behavior and prognosis of ASC are much worse than those of poorly differentiated mucoepidermoid carcinoma. The treatment of choice for ASC is radical surgical excision. Due to the propensity for this neoplasm to demonstrate early regional lymph node metastasis, radical neck dissection may be necessary as part of the initial management. Radiotherapy is of questionable benefit. Prognosis is poor as this neoplasm is extremely aggressive and

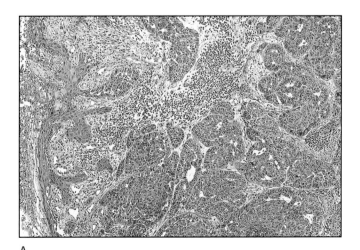

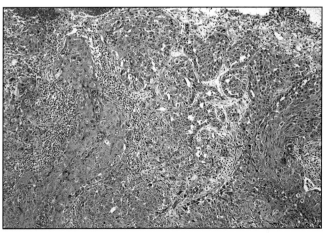

A

B

Fig. 4A.25 • Adenosquamous carcinoma. **(A)** This invasive carcinoma originates from the surface epithelium (left) showing squamous differentiation (surface) and glandular (invasive component); **(B)** admixture of squamous and glandular differentiation is present in the invasive carcinoma.

highly malignant.[230] ASC has a tendency to be multifocal, deeply invasive, and metastatic, even at the initial presentation.[234] Metastatic disease is histologically similar to the primary neoplasm and includes both histologic components. The 5-year survival rate is approximately 22%.[234] These neoplasms behave very aggressively, irrespective of tumor size.

Lymphoepithelial carcinoma

Lymphoepithelial carcinoma of the sinonasal tract is morphologically similar to its better-known histologic counterpart in the nasopharynx (see below). This is a rare sinonasal tract carcinoma primarily affecting men in the fifth to seventh decades of life.[236] Sinonasal lymphoepithelial carcinoma is more common in the nasal cavity than the paranasal sinuses. Clinical presentation includes nasal obstruction, epistaxis, and, in the presence of invasive growth, proptosis and cranial nerve palsies.[237,238] Similar to its nasopharyngeal counterpart, there is a strong association with EBV.[236–240]

The histologic findings are similar to those of NPC (see below). Immunohistochemical reactivity for cytokeratins is present. In most cases there is strong expression of EBV-encoded RNA (EBER).[236–240]

The differential diagnosis includes sinonasal undifferentiated carcinoma (SNUC), MMM, and non-Hodgkin lymphoma (see below). It is imperative to exclude sinonasal involvement from a nasopharyngeal primary tumor and, to this end, detailed clinical evaluation of the nasopharynx is indicated.

The prognosis is favorable owing to a good response to local radiotherapy. Regional cervical lymph node metastasis may be present at presentation. The favorable prognosis is not altered, even in the presence of nodal metastasis.[236,237,240]

General considerations for sinonasal tract squamous cell carcinoma and variants

Precursor lesions

Unlike other UADT sites, in particular the oral cavity and larynx, precursor lesions of the sinonasal tract (i.e., dysplasia and carcinoma in situ) are not clearly defined. As previously detailed under the section on sinonasal-type (schneiderian) papillomas, squamous cell carcinoma and variants thereof may develop from inverted and oncocytic types of schneiderian papillomas. As such, schneiderian papillomas appear to represent a precursor lesion for sinonasal sqaumous-cell carcinoma. HPV can be found in these types of schneiderian papilloma but there is no definitive link between the presence of HPV and the development of sinonasal squamous cell carcinoma. There is no known association between the presence of squamous metaplasia of the sinonasal epithelium and the development of squamous cell carcinoma.

Molecular genetics

For the majority of patients with head and neck squamous cell carcinoma and its variants, there are genetic alterations in the short arm of chromosome 9 regions.[241] Specific types of squamous cell carcinoma demonstrate distinctive molecular alterations.[241] These findings support the early involvement of these chromosomal loci in squamous epithelial carcinogenesis and support their temporal occurrence prior to the phenotypic conversion to malignancy.[241]

Nasopharyngeal carcinoma (NPC) (Table 4A.5)

NPC is a squamous cell carcinoma arising from the surface epithelium and subtyped according to the WHO into two histologic variants: keratinizing and non-keratinizing.[242] The non-keratinizing type is further subdivided as being "differentiated" and "undifferentiated." The current WHO classification retains the terminology of the 1991 classification and adds the category of basaloid squamous cell carcinoma.[243] NPC, by definition, takes origin from the nasopharyngeal mucosa and shows evidence of squamous differentiation by light microscopy, immunohistochemistry, or electron microscopy. Therefore, the use of this term is to the exclusion of all other malignant tumors which may arise in this region, including adenocarcinomas (minor salivary gland origin and non-salivary gland origin). Synonyms for NPC include lymphoepithelioma, Rigaud and Schmincke types of lymphoepithelioma, and transitional carcinoma. The designation lymphoepithelioma is a misnomer. This is a tumor entirely of epithelial origin with a secondary associated benign lymphoid component. Use of the term lymphoepithelioma may result in confusion with a diagnosis of malignant lymphoma. The prior numerical designations of WHO types 1 (squamous cell carcinoma), 2 (non-keratinizing carcinoma), and 3 (undifferentiated carcinoma) are no longer used. It should be noted that, although they share the unfortunate designation of "undifferentiated," there is no relationship between the SNUC (see below) and the nasopharyngeal undifferentiated carcinoma. These tumors are anatomically distinct, with differing therapeutic approaches and biologic outcome.

Overall, NPC is an uncommon neoplasm in the USA, accounting for approximately 0.25% of all cancers.[244,245] In China, it accounts for 18% of all cancers[246] and 1 in 40 men develop NPC before the age of 72 years.[247] NPC affects men more than women and occurs over a wide age range but is most common in the fourth to sixth decades of life. Fewer than 20% of cases occur in pediatric age groups. Pediatric NPC is most common in northern and central Africa, accounting for 10–20% of all cases, while only approximately 2% of NPC in China occur in children.[248–250] Irrespective of the histologic type, the clinical presentation is similar and includes the presence of an asymptomatic cervical neck mass, typically localized to the posterior cervical triangle or the superior jugular nodal chain, with additional clinical signs and symptoms that include nasal obstruction, nasal discharge, epistaxis, pain, serous otitis media, otalgia, hearing loss, and headache.[244–252] The signs and symptoms are often subtle and non-specific, often resulting in clinical presentation at an advanced stage of disease. Up to 25% of patients may experience cranial nerve involvement.[253] The lateral wall of the nasopharynx (fossa of Rosenmüller) is the most common site of occurrence, followed by the superior posterior wall.[251]

Radiologic imaging is an important diagnostic aid in assessing the extent of local disease and the presence of metastatic disease.[254,255] In addition to other imaging studies (e.g., conventional X-ray, ultrasound, computed tomography (CT)), positron emission tomography and computed tomography

Table 4A.5	Nasopharyngeal carcinoma (NPC)		
	Keratinizing[a]	**Non-keratinizing**[b]	**Undifferentiated**[c]
Percent	Approximately 25%	Least common, <15%	Most common, >60%
Sex, age	M > F; fourth–sixth decades	M > F; fourth–sixth decades	M > F; fourth–sixth decades; may occur in children
Histology	Keratinization, intercellular bridges; conventional squamous carcinoma graded as well, moderately or poorly differentiated; desmoplastic response to invasion	Little to absent keratinization, growth pattern interconnecting cords (similar to transitional urothelial carcinoma); typically, limited to absent desmoplastic response to invasion	Absence of keratinization, syncytial growth, cohesive or non-cohesive cells with round nuclei, prominent eosinophilic nucleoli, scant cytoplasm and limited mitoses; prominent non-neoplastic lymphoid component; typically, absence of desmoplastic response to invasion
Epstein–Barr virus	Weak association	Strong association	Strong association
Treatment	Radioresponsiveness is not good	Radioresponsive	Radioresponsive
Prognosis	20–40% 5-year survival	65% 5-year survival	65% 5-year survival

[a]World Health Organization (WHO) designation as NPC, keratinizing.
[b]WHO designation as NPC, non-keratinizing, differentiated.
[c]WHO designation as NPC, non-keratinizing, undifferentiated.

(PET-CT) is used in the detection of locoregional and distant spread of tumor.

Multiple interactive etiologic factors have been linked to the development of NPC. Genetic and geographic factors play an important role in the genesis of NPC. There is an increased incidence of NPC in China, especially in southern (Kwantung province) and northern provinces and Taiwan.[246] Although the incidence among Chinese people decreases after emigration to low-incidence areas, it still remains higher than in non-Chinese populations.[246,256] Human leukocyte antigen (HLA)-A2, HLA-B17, HLA-Bw46, and HLA-BW58 histocompatibility loci have been suggested as the marker for genetic susceptibility to NPC.[246] Perhaps the most important link to the development of NPC is EBV.[246,257,258] There is a strong association between certain NPCs and the presence of EBV, indicating a probable oncogenic role of EBV in the development of NPC.[258] Both the non-keratinizing and undifferentiated types of nasopharyngeal squamous carcinoma are linked with the presence of EBV DNA. Elevated titers of immunoglobulin A (IgA) antibodies (against viral capsid antigen (VCA)) and IgG antibodies (against early antigen (EA)) are seen in patients with NPC,[259–265] with detection rates ranging up to 93%;[243] elevated titers have been used as a marker to screen populations in high-risk areas and as a potential indicator of disease relapse.[260,261,265] Positive serology against EBV in 90% of patients with non-keratinizing carcinoma has been reported.[266] Newer antibody tests based on recombinant EBV antigens (e.g., EBV nuclear antigens (EBNA), membrane antigen (MA), and others) have been utilized in the diagnosis of NPC, as has quantitative PCR to test for elevated circulating EBV DNA in plasma and serum, with reported sensitivity rates in NPC of up to 96%.[267–270] Molecular biologic analysis of NPC by either ISH or PCR detects EBV DNA or RNA in 75–100% of NPC.[271,272] This is not true of the keratinizing subtype, in which the detection of EBV genomes is variable and, if present, is generally limited to scattered dysplastic intraepithelial cells. Pathmanathan et al.[273] report that EBV is an early initiating event in the development of NPC. These authors note that EBV was present in preinvasive (precursor) nasopharyngeal lesions, that the EBV DNA was clonal, suggesting that the preinvasive lesions arose from a single EBV-infected cell, and that these preinvasive lesions progressed to invasive cancer within 1 year.[273] EBV infection in NPC results in expression of EBV nuclear antigen-1 (EBNA-1) and latent membrane protein-1 (LMP-1) with an abundance of EBERs.[243] Hording et al.[274] evaluated 38 cases of NPC for the presence of HPV and reported that 4 of 15 keratinizing squamous carcinomas were HPV-positive but that none of the non-keratinizing or undifferentiated NPC had HPV. HPV may have a pathogenetic role in some nasopharyngeal keratinizing squamous cell carcinomas, but not for the non-keratinizing or undifferentiated types. Other suggested factors implicated in NPC include diet (salted fish high in nitrosamines), poor hygiene, and non-dietary environmental factors, including atmospheric agents such as dust, smoke, chemical fumes, domestic smoke from burning wood, grass, and incense, and inhalation (active or passive) of tobacco smoke, the use of herbal medicines, and the use of nasal inhalants in the treatment of nasal disease.[246]

Consistent non-random deletions and rearrangement of the short arm of chromosome 3 have been found in NPC.[275–278] Genetic instabilities (losses and gains) are common molecular events in NPC, and play an important role in the development and progression of NPC. Loss of heterozygosity (LOH) and comparative genomic hybridization (CGH) studies have shown frequent allelic losses on chromosomes 1p, 3p, 9p, 9q, 11q, 13q, 14q, 16q, and 19q.[279–281] CGH analysis showed that gains on chromosome 1q, 8q, 18q, and loss on 9p were closely related to advanced stage of NPC. LOH analysis also showed

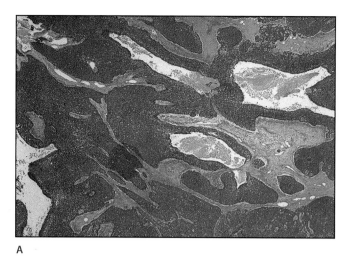

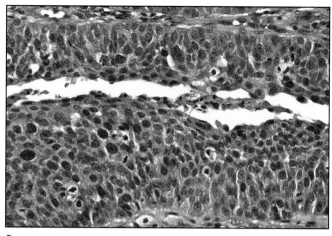

A   B

Fig. 4A.26 • Nasopharyngeal non-keratinizing carcinoma, differentiated type. **(A)** The neoplasm invades in broad anastomosing cords and trabeculae; **(B)** the neoplastic cells have pleomorphic nuclei with increased mitotic activity and lack keratinization.

frequent LOH on 3p in normal nasopharyngeal epithelium (74%) and dysplastic lesions (75%) from the southern Chinese, suggesting that LOH at 3p may be an earlier genetic event of NPC tumorigenesis.[280]

Linkage analysis indicates that the HLA gene and cytochrome p4502E gene may be susceptibility genes for NPC. Through LOH, CGH, linkage analysis, and cDNA microarray analysis, specific biomarkers of NPC can be used for earlier diagnosis and prognosis of NPC.[280] The development of NPC likely involves cumulative genetic and epigenetic changes in a background of predisposing genetic and environmental factors.[282] Genome-wide studies have identified multiple chromosomal abnormalities with involvement of specific oncogenes and tumor suppressor genes, including inactivation of the p16 tumor suppressor gene on 9p21, the most common molecular alteration in NPC tumorigenesis.[283,284] Alterations of genes such as *Ras* association domain family 1A (*RASSF1A*), *p16/INK4A*, *p14/ARF* suggest that multiple cellular pathways are dysregulated in the NPC cells. Studies on the precancerous lesions revealed early genetic changes and a critical role of EBV latent infection in the development of this cancer.[243,282]

The gross appearance of NPC varies from a mucosal bulge with an overlying intact epithelium to a clearly demonstrable infiltrative mass with extensive involvement of the surface epithelium to a totally unidentifiable lesion fortuitously sampled and identified by microscopic evaluation. Three histologic types are recognized based on the predominant appearance.[285] The conventional keratinizing squamous carcinoma is characterized by the presence of keratinization and intercellular bridges and graded as well, moderately, or poorly differentiated. A desmoplastic response is typically found in response to invasive growth by this histologic type of NPC. The keratinizing NPC represents approximately 25% of all NPC, and rarely occurs in patients under 40 years of age.[286]

The non-keratinizing carcinomas show little to absent keratinization and have a growth pattern similar to transitional cell carcinoma of the bladder, including stratified cells with sharp delineation from the surrounding stroma (Fig. 4A.26). Well-defined cell borders and vague intercellular bridges may be present; rarely, an occasional keratinized cell may be identified. Typically, there is no desmoplastic response to invasive growth.

These tumors may undergo cyst formation with associated necrosis and may metastasize with this pattern to the cervical nodes. Further, the primary carcinomatous focus may be small, lie within the submucosa (e.g., in crypt epithelium) with an overlying intact, nondescript surface epithelium, representing an occult primary carcinoma (Fig. 4A.27). This type of NPC is the least common, representing approximately 12% of all NPCs.[286]

The undifferentiated type of NPC represents approximately 60% of all NPCs,[274] and is the most frequent tumor type seen in pediatric age groups.[249] The neoplastic cells are characterized by the presence of round nuclei, prominent eosinophilic nucleoli, dispersed nuclear chromatin, and scant eosinophilic to amphophilic cytoplasm (Fig. 4A.28). Keratinization is absent. Increased mitoses, including atypical forms, are present. A prominent non-neoplastic lymphoid component comprised of mature lymphocytes and plasma cells is seen in association with the malignant epithelial components, although in any given example the lymphoplasmacytic infiltrate may be scanty

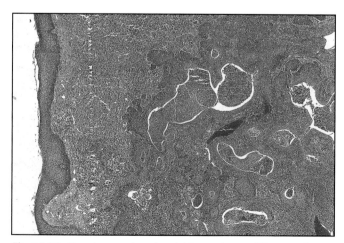

Fig. 4A.27 • Nasopharyngeal non-keratinizing carcinoma, differentiated type, originating in crypt epithelium. The overlying surface epithelium is unremarkable. This may represent the primary (occult) focus for a metastatic carcinoma to a lateral cervical neck lymph node, thereby mimicking a branchial cleft cyst or a carcinoma arising in a branchial cleft cyst (so-called branchiogenic carcinoma).

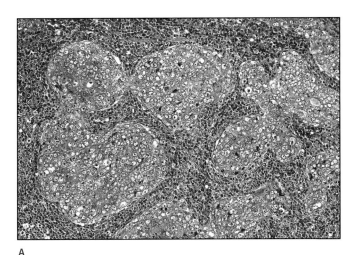
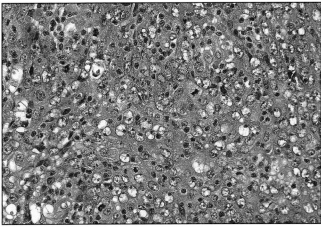

A

B

Fig. 4A.28 • Nasopharyngeal non-keratinizing carcinoma, undifferentiated type. **(A)** Tumor nests are readily apparent and are clearly delineated from the surrounding non-neoplastic lymphocytic cell infiltrate. **(B)** The neoplastic cells are characterized by the presence of enlarged round nuclei, vesicular chromatin, prominent eosinophilic nucleoli, and scant eosinophilic to amphophilic cytoplasm. A non-neoplastic lymphoid component is present.

or absent. Other inflammatory cell types that can be present include eosinophils and neutrophils, and scattered epithelioid granulomas may be present. This tumor type may have a syncytial growth pattern with cohesive or nested cells, or a diffuse pattern composed of non-cohesive cells. The diffuse pattern is the one that is difficult to differentiate from a malignant lymphoma by light microscopy. The Regaud and Schmincke types of NPC refer to those neoplasms with a syncytial versus individual cell growth pattern, respectively. These designations (and their associated growth patterns) have no bearing on the biology of the disease. The infiltrative growth of this tumor generally does not produce a host desmoplastic response. This may be problematic in biopsy samples as the tumor may be overrun by the benign lymphohistiocytic cell infiltrate and thus is easily overlooked (Fig. 4A.29). Similarly, metastasis to cervical lymph nodes may not elicit a desmoplastic response in the involved lymph node.

Since distinction between the non-keratinizing differentiated type and the non-keratinizing undifferentiated type is

of no clinical or prognostic significance, subclassification into differentiated and undifferentiated subtypes is optional.[243] Shanmugaratnam et al.[287] reported that 26% of NPCs had features of more than one tumor type. In such a situation, classification is according to the dominant component. It should be noted that the histologic distinction among the three types of NPC may not always be clear, with overlapping histology in any given tumor.

It is uncommon to identify the presence of a precursor lesion in the form of intraepithelial dysplasia or an in-situ carcinoma. If present, the changes are similar to those of other UADT sites, being characterized by the presence of a variably thickened epithelium with nuclear hyperchromasia, loss of cell polarity with nuclear crowding, increased nuclear-to-cytoplasmic ratio, prominent nucleoli, and increased mitotic activity. These changes can be seen in the surface or crypt epithelium.

All three histologic types of NPC are immunoreactive with cytokeratin, including pan-cytokeratins and high-molecular-

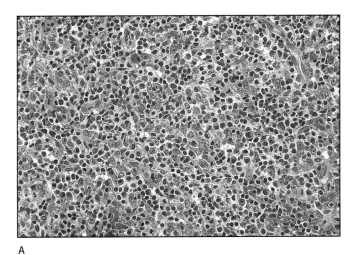
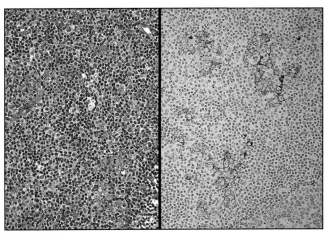

A

B

Fig. 4A.29 • Nasopharyngeal non-keratinizing carcinoma, undifferentiated type. **(A)** In this example the absence of a desmoplastic response coupled with the presence of coexisting non-neoplastic lymphocytic cell infiltrate obscures the neoplastic cells, creating difficulties in the diagnosis. **(B)** Cytokeratin staining (right) delineates the presence of the neoplastic cells (left).

weight cytokeratins; weak immunoreactivity is present for low-molecular-weight cytokeratins (Fig. 4A.29). No immunoreactivity is seen for cytokeratins 7 and 20. Franchi et al. evaluated differential cytokeratin staining in various squamous cell carcinoma types of the head and neck and found NPCs to express CK5/6, CK8, CK13 and CK18 (Table 4A.6).[288] The diagnosis of both the keratinizing and non-keratinizing types of NPC is usually straightforward. Undifferentiated NPC, primarily when it occurs as a diffuse cellular infiltrate composed of discohesive cells, may be difficult to distinguish from non-Hodgkin's malignant lymphoma. Differentiation is readily accomplished by immunohistochemical stains. NPC will be reactive with cytokeratin and not leukocyte common antigen (LCA); non-Hodgkin's malignant lymphomas of the nasopharynx are predominantly of B-cell lineage and will be reactive with LCA and B-cell lineage markers.

As a result of the anatomic constraints imposed by the nasopharynx and the tendency of these neoplasms to present at an advanced stage, supervoltage radiotherapy (6500 to >7000 rads) is considered the treatment of choice. Overall 5-year survival for keratinizing squamous cell carcinoma is 20–40% and for non-keratinizing carcinomas (differentiated and undifferentiated) is approximately 65%.[286] Stage at presentation is the most important prognostic factor. The 5-year disease-specific survival (DSS) is as follows:

- for stage I, 98%
- for stage II A–B, 95%
- for stage III, 86%
- for stage IVA–B, 73%[243]

Factors that may influence prognosis include the clinical stage, patient age and gender, presence of keratinization, lymph node metastasis, and possibly genetic factors. Better prognosis is associated with lower clinical stage, younger patient age, and female gender, while worse prognosis is seen with higher-stage tumors, older patients, and male gender.[246,287] Reddy et al.[289] evaluated 50 patients with NPC and found that the patients with the keratinizing type of NPC had a higher incidence of locally advanced tumor but a lower incidence of lymphatic and/or distant spread. Despite these findings, the patients with the keratinizing NPC had a poorer 5-year survival rate than those with the other histologic subtypes due to a higher incidence of deaths secondary to local uncontrollable disease and nodal metastases.[289] NPC frequently metastasizes to regional lymph nodes and the presence of lymph node metastasis decreases survival by approximately 10–20%.[287] Similarly, a large percentage of NPC, particularly of the undifferentiated type, metastasize to sites below the clavicle, including the lungs, bone (ribs and spine), and liver.[290,291] Poorer prognosis is seen in those patients with the HLA-Aw33-C3-B58/DR3 haplotype, while patients with A2-Cw11-Bw46/DR9 haplotype have longer survival.[246] DNA ploidy has been studied in NPC, with mixed results.[292,293] Prominent tumor angiogenesis and c-erbB2 expression have been suggested as indicators of a poor prognosis.[294]

Newer therapeutic modalities have been evaluated in the treatment of NPC. Chua and colleagues evaluated the long-term outcome in patients with NPC treated with induction chemotherapy and radiotherapy versus radiotherapy alone. While they report a modest (but significant) decrease in relapse and improvement in DSS in advanced-stage NPC with the addition of cisplatin-based induction chemotherapy to radiotherapy, there was no improvement in overall survival.[295] The risk of developing a synchronous or metachronous second primary malignancy in patients with NPC is approximately 4%.[296] The second malignancies tend to occur in the UADT.

Sinonasal undifferentiated carcinoma (SNUC)

The original definition for SNUC was reported by Frierson et al.[297] as a high-grade malignant epithelial neoplasm of the nasal cavity and paranasal sinuses of uncertain histogenesis with or without neuroendocrine differentiation but without evidence of squamous or glandular differentiation. Subsequently, the WHO classification defines SNUC as a highly aggressive and clinicopathologically distinctive carcinoma of uncertain histogenesis that typically presents with locally extensive disease; it is composed of pleomorphic tumor cells with frequent necrosis, and should be differentiated from lymphoepithelial (and other) carcinomas or olfactory neuroblastoma (ONB).[298]

SNUC is a rare tumor, with fewer than 100 reported cases. There is a male predominance (2–3:1).[298,299] SNUCs occur over a wide age range, including the third to ninth decades of life, with a median at presentation in the sixth decade.[297,299] Generally, SNUCs are extensive at presentation and involve multiple sites, including the nasal cavity, one or more paranasal sinuses, orbit, skull base, and the brain.[297,300] Most

Table 4A.6	Cytokeratin expression in various carcinoma types of the sinonasal tract and nasopharynx						
	AE1/AE3	CK5/6	CK7	CK8	CK13	CK14	CK19
Squamous cell carcinoma	+	+ (9/10)	+ (6/10)	+ (9/10)	+ (9/10)	+ (8/10)	+ (9/10)
Non-keratinizing squamous cell carcinoma	+	+ (9/10)	–	+ (9/10)	+ (9/10)	+ (8/10)	+ (9/10)
Sinonasal undifferentiated carcinoma	+	–	+ (3/6)	+ (6/6)	–	–	+ (3/6)
Nasopharyngeal carcinoma, undifferentiated type	+	+ (4/5)	–	+ (4/5)	+ (4/5)	–	+ (5/5)

Reproduced from Franchi et al.[288]

patients have unilateral disease but bilateral disease may occur. Typically, patients present with multiple symptoms of short duration, including nasal obstruction, epistaxis, proptosis, visual disturbances (e.g., diplopia), facial pain, and symptoms of cranial nerve involvement. Radiographic studies (CT scan, magnetic resonance imaging (MRI)) often demonstrate a large (sinonasal) mass typically with locally invasive growth extending beyond its bony confines with involvement of orbital and/or cranial bones.[299] Intracranial extension may occur.

SNUC is a tumor of uncertain histogenesis. It seems likely that SNUC arises from the schneiderian epithelium and, therefore, is of ectodermal derivation. However, while speculative, given overlapping clinical, light microscopic, immunohistochemical and ultrastructural features with ONB and neuroendocrine carcinoma (NEC), the cell of origin may be related to both the schneiderian membrane and olfactory epithelia. On the basis of finding neuroendocrine features by immunohistochemistry and electron microscopy, Mills[301] suggested that SNUC may be an NEC with classification essentially equivalent to the pulmonary large-cell (neuroendocrine) carcinoma. Evidence of very limited foci of squamous differentiation has been reported, a finding that supports surface (schneiderian) epithelial origin.[302]

There are no known etiologic agents. SNUCs are typically negative for EBV,[303,304] even though there have been reports of EBV RNA identified in Asian and Italian patients with SNUC but not in other western patients with SNUC.[305,306] Some cases have been reported to develop following radiation therapy for NPC.[303] Although no specific etiology is linked to the development of SNUC, cigarette-smoking and nickel exposure have been identified in patients with SNUC.[297] Deletion of the retinoblastoma gene has also been implicated in the development of SNUC.[307]

SNUCs are usually large tumors, typically >4 cm in greatest dimension, and tend to be fungating with poorly defined margins, and with invasion into adjacent structures and/or anatomic compartments, including bone destruction. The histologic appearance is characterized by a hypercellular proliferation with varied growth, including trabecular, sheet-like, ribbons, solid, lobular, and organoid patterns (Fig. 4A.30).

Surface involvement may be seen in the form of severe dysplasia/carcinoma in situ, but often there is ulceration which precludes evidence of surface epithelial derivation. The cellular infiltrate consists of polygonal cells composed of medium to large-sized, round to oval, hyperchromatic to vesicular nuclei, inconspicuous to prominent nucleoli and a varying amount of eosinophilic-appearing cytoplasm with poorly defined cell membranes, although in some examples distinct cell borders may be present; occasionally, cells with clear cytoplasm can be identified. The nuclear-to-cytoplasmic ratio is high. Increased mitotic activity is present, including atypical mitoses, and there is often prominent tumor necrosis (confluent areas and individual cells) and apoptosis (Fig. 4A.30). Lymphovascular invasion and neurotropism are often present. Squamous or glandular differentiation is not evident; however, recent evidence indicates that the presence of very focal squamous differentiation is acceptable in SNUC as long as the overwhelming majority of the tumor shows morphologic features associated with SNUC.[302] Neurofibrillary material and true neural rosettes are not identified.

Histochemical studies are non-contributory to the diagnosis of SNUC; stains for epithelial mucin are negative. The immunohistochemical antigenic profile may vary from case to case, but SNUCs are consistently immunoreactive with epithelial markers, including pankeratins and simple keratins (i.e., CK7, CK8, and CK19); reactivity for pankeratins is often intense and diffuse. Staining for CK4, CK5/CK6, and CK14 is reported to be negative (Table 4A.6).[288] Variable reactivity can be identified for *p63*. Fewer than half of the cases have been reported to be positive for EMA, NSE, or *p53*.[304] Reactivity for synaptophysin, chromogranin, S-100 protein, or Leu-7 is only rarely observed. Vimentin, muscle markers (desmin, myoglobin, myf-4, actins) hematolymphoid markers (LCA, B- and T-cell), melanocytic cell markers (HMB-45, melanA) and CD99 (Ewing marker) are usually absent. By electron microscopy, rare membrane-bound, dense core neurosecretory granules have been noted, and poorly formed desmosomes may occasionally be found.[297,301,308]

The differential diagnosis of SNUC includes ONB (high-grade), small cell undifferentiated neuroendocrine carcinoma,

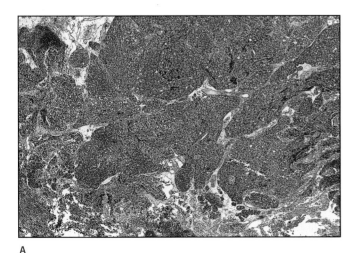

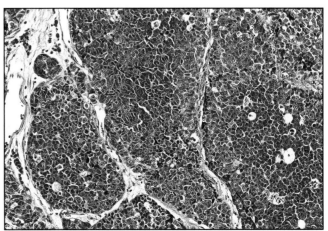

A   B

Fig. 4A.30 • Sinonasal undifferentiated carcinoma. **(A)** Hypercellular and infiltrative neoplasm showing trabecular and lobular growth; **(B)** at higher magnification, the cellular infiltrate includes round to oval, hyperchromatic and pleomorphic nuclei, prominent nucleoli, increased mitotic activity, and individual cell necrosis.

nasopharyngeal-type undifferentiated carcinoma,[303] lympho-epithelial carcinoma, MMM, nasal-type natural killer (NK)/T-cell lymphoma, rhabdomyosarcoma and others. While differences can be identified by light microscopic evaluation, often the differentiation of all these tumor types rests on the immunohistochemical staining profile for a given tumor. Among epithelial malignancies of the sinonasal tract and nasopharynx, cytokeratin-staining differences have been reported between keratinizing squamous cell carcinoma, non-keratinizing squamous cell carcinoma, SNUC, and naso-pharyngeal undifferentiated carcinoma (Table 4A.7).[288]

The treatment of SNUC requires intensive multimodality therapy, including surgical resection and adjuvant therapy (radiotherapy, chemotherapy). However, SNUC is a highly aggressive neoplasm that cannot be completely eradicated by surgery, nor is it responsive to radiation treatment.[309,310] Frierson et al.[297] report a mean survival of 4 months with no disease-free patients. Other studies report median survival of less than 18 months,[254,258,259] with 5-year survival rates of less than 20%.[311] Deutsch et al.[312] reported improved survival following treatment with chemotherapy (cyclophosphamide, doxorubicin, and vincristine), followed by radiotherapy and then radical surgery. These authors, as well as others,[313] recommend this treatment regimen for SNUC regardless of the extent of disease. High-dose chemotherapy and autologous bone marrow transplantation have been used.[314] For patients with good performance status and limited intracranial or intraorbital disease, initial chemoradiotherapy followed by craniofacial resection has been advocated.[315] Patients who are deemed inoperable as a result of advanced disease may nevertheless experience significant palliation with chemoradiotherapy only. More recently, induction chemotherapy followed by concurrent chemoradiation represents a potentially promising treatment strategy for SNUC.[316] Local recurrence is common and is the major cause of morbidity and mortality.[299] Metastatic disease to bone, brain, liver, and cervical lymph nodes may occur.[304]

Olfactory neuroblastoma (ONB)

ONB is a malignant neuroectodermal neoplasm thought to arise from the olfactory membrane of the sinonasal tract. There are a variety of terms for this tumor, including olfactory placode tumor, esthesioneuroblastoma, esthesioneurocytoma, esthesioneuroepithelioma, and esthesioneuroma. It appears that ONB takes origin from the olfactory neuroepithelium found in the upper one-third to one-half of the nasal septum, the cribriform plate, and the superior medial surface of the superior turbinate.[317] With aging, the olfactory epithelium degenerates and is replaced by respiratory epithelium.[317] The olfactory neuroepithelium is composed of bipolar sensory neurons, supporting cells, and reserve (basal) cells. The latter are mitotically active and are the presumed progenitor of ONB.

ONB is an uncommon malignant neoplasm, representing approximately 2–3% of sinonasal tract tumors. There is no gender predilection;[318] ONB occurs over a very wide age range from 3 years to the ninth decade, with a bimodal peak in the second and sixth decades of life.[318–323] The main presenting symptoms are unilateral nasal obstruction and epistaxis; less common manifestations include anosmia, headache, pain,

excessive lacrimation, and ocular disturbances.[320] The most common site of occurrence is the upper nasal cavity in the area of the cribriform plate; often there is involvement of the ethmoid sinus. "Ectopic" origin in the lower nasal cavity, within one of the paranasal sinuses (e.g., maxillary sinus) and nasopharynx may occur.[324] Radiologically, a sinonasal mass causing sinus opacification with or without bone erosion may be seen. ONB may be associated with calcifications, which produce a speckled pattern by radiographic analysis. MRI studies demonstrate the presence of a vascular lesion with enhancement following gadolinium injection, as seen on T1-weighted imaging.[325]

There are no known etiologic agent(s). Administration of diethylnitrosamine to hamsters[326,327] and N-nitrosopiperidine to rats[328] produces nasal tumors that are histologically identical to ONB. There are conflicting data regarding the inclusion of ONB in the category of peripheral neuro-ectodermal tumors (PNET). Classically, PNET shows reactivity with monoclonal antibodies that recognize the Ewing's sarcoma cell surface glycoprotein p30/32[MIC2 329,330] and t(11;22) translocation with $EWS/FL1$ gene fusion.[331] Based on reports of the t(11;22) translocation reported in ONB[332] and the presence of $EWS/FLI1$ gene fusion in ONB,[333] these data would support inclusion of ONB within the spectrum of PNET related to Ewing's sarcoma. However, other studies using immunohistochemistry, fluorescence ISH, and reverse transcriptase PCR have failed to identify these "markers" of PNET, thereby failing to confirm this translocation in ONB.[334–338] As such, ONB, at least for now, should be seen as a distinct entity from PNET and the Ewing sarcoma family of tumors.

The gross appearance of ONB is that of a glistening, mucosa-covered, soft, polypoid mass varying from a small nodule <1 cm to a mass filling the nasal cavity, with possible extension into adjacent paranasal sinuses and nasopharynx. The histologic appearance is classified into four grades, as defined by Hyams (Table 4A.8).[339] Grade I is the most differentiated; the architecture is lobular with intercommunication between lobules. The neoplastic cells are well differentiated with uniform round to vesicular nuclei with or without nucleoli (Fig. 4A.31) and with indistinct borders. The nuclei are surrounded by neurofibrillary material. A pseudorosette pattern (Homer Wright rosettes) is frequently seen. Varying amounts of calcification may be noted. The interlobular fibrous stroma is often extremely vascular. Mitotic activity and necrosis are absent. Grade II tumors share many of the histologic features described for grade I lesions but the neurofibrillary element is less well defined, and the neoplastic nuclei show increased pleomorphism. Scattered mitoses can be seen. Grade III tumors may retain a lobular architecture with an interstitial vascular stroma. These tumors are characterized by a hypercellular neoplastic cell proliferation in which the cells are more anaplastic and hyperchromatic, and have increased mitotic activity as compared to grade I or II tumors. Necrosis is seen. The neurofibrillary component may be focally present, but is much less conspicuous as compared to grades I or II tumors (Fig. 4A.32). True neural rosettes (Flexner–Wintersteiner rosettes) may be seen (Fig. 4A.33); however, in general, these structures are uncommonly identified. Calcification is absent. Grade IV tumors may also retain the overall lobular architecture but the neoplastic element is the most

Table 4A.7 Immunohistochemical (selective) reactivity of sinonasal tract malignancies

	Cytokeratin	Neuron-specific enolase	Chromogranin	Synaptophysin	S-100 protein	HMB	LCA	CD56	CD99	Vimentin	Desmin	Myf4
Squamous cell carcinoma	+	–	–	–	–	–	–	–	–	–	–	–
Sinonasal undifferentiated carcinoma (SNUC)	+	v	–	–	–	–	–	–	–	–	–	–
Olfactory neuroblastoma (ONB)	–	+	v	v	+[a]	–	–	–	–	–	–	–
Small "oat" cell undifferentiated neuroendocrine carcinoma (SCUNC)	+	+	+	+	+	–	–	–	–	–	–	–
Mucosal malignant melanoma (MMM)	–	–	–	–	+	+	–	–	–	+	–	–
Nasal-type natural killer/ T cell lymphoma	–	–	–	–	–	–	v	+	–	v	–	–
Rhabdomyosarcoma (RMS)	–	–	–	–	–	–	–	–	–	+	+	+
Primitive (peripheral) neuroectodermal tumor/extraosseous Ewing's sarcoma (PNET)	R+	v	–	v	v	–	–	–	+	+	–	–

HMB, HMB-45 (as well as other melanocytic markers [melanA]); LCA, leukocyte common antigen; CD99, Ewing marker.

+, positive; –, negative; v, variably positive; R+, rarely positive.

[a]Positive in the peripherally situated sustentacular-like cells.

Table 4A.8	Hyams' histologic grading system for olfactory neuroblastoma[339] © 1982 American Society of Clinical Pathologists			
Microscopic features	**Grade I**	**Grade II**	**Grade III**	**Grade IV**
Architecture	Lobular	Lobular	± Lobular	± Lobular
Pleomorphism	Absent to slight	Present	Prominent	Marked
Neurofibrillary matrix	Prominent	Present	May be present	Absent
Rosettes	Present[a]	Present[a]	May be present[b]	May be present[b]
Mitoses	Absent	Present	Prominent	Marked
Necrosis	Absent	Absent	Present	Prominent
Glands	May be present	May be present	May be present	May be present
Calcification	Variable	Variable	Absent	Absent

[a]Homer Wright rosettes (pseudorosettes).
[b]Flexner–Wintersteiner rosettes (true neural rosettes).

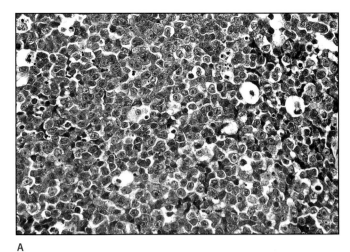

A

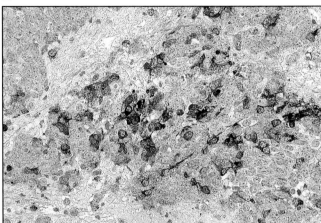

B

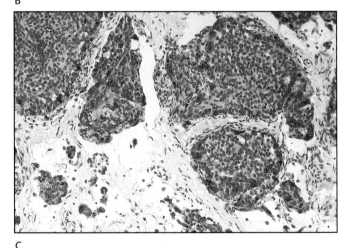

C

Fig. 4A.32 • Olfactory neuroblastoma, grade III. (**A**) In contrast to its lower-grade counterpart, this high-grade neoplasm lacks neurofibrillary matrix and is a pleomorphic cellular infiltrate with increased mitotic activity. In this setting immunohistochemical stains become important in the diagnosis and in differentiation from other malignant neoplasms. (**B**) Olfactory neuroblastomas, irrespective of histologic grade, are consistently immunoreactive for neuron-specific enolase and (**C**) show S-100 protein staining, usually limited to the periphery of tumor nests (sustentacular cell-like pattern).

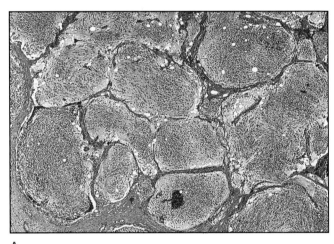

A

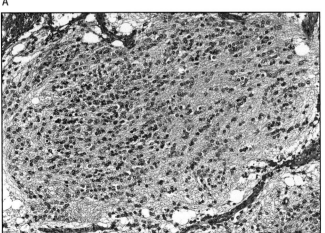

B

Fig. 4A.31 • Olfactory neuroblastoma, grade I. (**A**) Typical lobular pattern of growth; (**B**) uniform-appearing round cells surrounded by a neurofibrillary material.

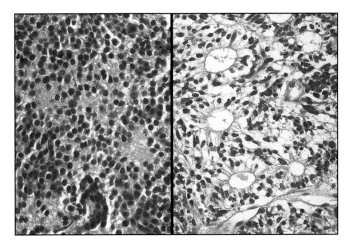

Fig. 4A.33 • Olfactory neuroblastomas are associated with the presence of rosettes. This illustration contrasts (left) Homer Wright pseudorososettes seen in grades I and II olfactory neuroblastomas, characterized by grouping of cells in a circumferential fashion around neurofibrillary matrix but without a defining basement membrane, with (right) Flexner–Wintersteiner true neural rosettes, in which cells align in a glandular fashion around spaces lined by distinct cell membranes.

undifferentiated and anaplastic of all the histologic grades. In these high-grade tumors, the cellular infiltrate is characterized by pleomorphic nuclei, often with prominent eosinophilic nucleoli and indistinct cytoplasm. Necrosis is commonly seen and there is increased mitotic activity, including atypical mitoses. True neural rosettes may be seen but, as in grade III tumors, are uncommon. The neurofibrillary component is generally absent. Calcification is absent.

Rarely, ONB may coexist with foci of adenocarcinoma, squamous carcinoma, or undifferentiated carcinoma, when it is referred to as mixed ONB and carcinoma.[340] Miller and colleagues[340] proposed the basal cells of the olfactory epithelium as the progenitor for these mixed neoplasms. Alternatively, these mixed tumors may originate from the seromucous glands (Bowman's glands) lying subjacent to the olfactory epithelium. This author has seen a limited number of such tumors that we have designated as olfactory carcinomas.

In general, the lower-grade ONB are readily recognizable and diagnosable by light microscopy. Adjunct studies, particularly in the higher histologic grade tumors, may assist in the diagnosis. Histochemical stains have been replaced by immuno-histochemistry in the diagnosis of ONB.

The most consistent marker is NSE (Fig. 4A.32). S-100 protein staining is typically limited to the sustentacular cells situated along the periphery of the neoplastic lobules, although such cells may be sparse in the higher-grade tumors (Fig. 4A.32). Reactivity is also present in a majority of cases for synaptophysin, neurofilament protein, class III beta-tubulin, and microtubule-associated protein, and variable immunoreactivity may be present for chromogranin, GFAP, and Leu-7.[341,342] Cytokeratin is usually negative; some cases can show positive cells in a patchy, punctate fashion or, less often, diffusely. Epithelial markers, including EMA and CEA, are absent. LCA, HMB-45, desmin, and CD99 are absent. Proliferation marker studies using Ki-67 and MIB-1 have shown a high proliferative index of 10–50% and flow cytometric analysis shows a high rate of polyploidy/aneuploidy.[343,344]

Electron microscopic evaluation is a useful adjunct in the diagnosis and reveals the presence of dense-core neuro-secretory granules measuring 80–250 nm in diameter.[324,345,346] In addition, neurofilaments and neurotubules and, occasionally, Schwann-like cells, can be seen.

The differential diagnosis includes a variety of other sinonasal malignant neoplasms discussed in this chapter. While differences can be identified by light microscopic evaluation, often the differentiation of all these tumor types rests on the immunohistochemical staining profile for a given tumor (Table 4A.7).

Complete surgical eradication (craniofacial resection that includes removal of the cribriform plate) followed by full-course radiotherapy is the treatment of choice.[321,322,347] Limited success using chemotherapeutic modalities has been achieved for advanced unresectable tumors and/or for disseminated disease.[348] High-dose chemotherapy, including platinum-based protocols and autologous bone marrow transplantation, has resulted in long-term survival.[349–351] The overall 5-, 10-, and 15-year survival rates have been reported to be 78%, 71%, and 68%, respectively.[349] Initial multimodality therapy is associated with 5-year survival of 80% for low-grade tumors and 40% for high-grade tumors.[347] The majority of the recurrences occur within the first 2 years.[322] The most frequent recurrence is local, with rates around 30%. Prognosis has traditionally been correlated to clinical staging, as defined by Kadish[352] (Table 4A.9), with 5-year survivals of 75%, 68%, and 41% for stage A, B, and C tumors, respectively.[320,352] Complete tumor resection was found to be of more prognostic importance than clinical staging.[323] Other factors purportedly implicated in prognosis include histologic grading, proliferation rate, and ploidy. Histologically lower-grade tumors (grades I and II) have been reported to have a better 5-year survival than higher-grade tumors (grades III and IV).[353] High proliferation indices and a high rate of ploidy/aneuploidy have been correlated with increased morbidity (i.e., tumor recurrence, metastasis) and mortality (i.e., decreased survival).[343,344] The majority of tumors behave as locally aggressive lesions, mainly involving adjacent structures (orbit and cranial cavity). Local recurrence and distant metastasis may occur years after the initial diagnosis. Approximately 15–70% of patients will experience local recurrence, 10–25% will have cervical lymph node metastasis, and approximately 10–60% will experience distant metastasis.[320,327,349,354] The more common sites of metastatic disease include lymph nodes, lungs, and bone. All histologic grades have the capacity to metastasize.

Table 4A.9	Clinical staging for olfactory neuroblastoma	
Stage	**Extent of tumor**	**5-Year survival**
A	Tumor confined to the nasal cavity	75–91%
B	Tumor involves the nasal cavity plus one or more paranasal sinuses	68–71%
C	Extension of tumor beyond the sinonasal cavities	41–47%

Modified from Elkon et al.[320] and Kadish et al.[352]

Neuroendocrine carcinoma (NEC)

NECs represent a heterogeneous group of malignant neoplasms with divergent differentiation along epithelial and neuroendocrine cell lines. The classification of NEC is still being debated. Some divide these tumors into three types: (1) carcinoid tumor; (2) atypical carcinoid tumor; and (3) small cell carcinoma.[355,356] Others classify them according to differentiation: (1) well-differentiated NEC (equated with carcinoid tumor); (2) moderately differentiated NEC (equated with atypical carcinoid); and (3) poorly differentiated NEC (equated with small "oat" cell undifferentiated NEC (SCUNC)).[357] A few authors further subdivide the "group" of small cell NECs into small cell variant and large-cell variant.[358] According to the time-honored terminology and to minimize confusion, the terms carcinoid, atypical carcinoid, and small cell carcinoma, as proposed by the WHO,[355,359] will be used in this section. However, it should be kept in mind that the "atypical" carcinoid tumor is a fully lethal tumor and the term "atypical" should not lull the clinician into a false sense of security that this tumor is only slightly different in its behavior from the relatively indolent "classic" carcinoid tumor.

In general, all three subtypes of NEC are uncommon in the head and neck and even more so in the sinonasal tract. Perhaps the most commonly encountered subtype of NEC in the head and neck is the SCUNC, followed by the atypical carcinoid, with carcinoid tumor being the least common. SCUNC may be identified in virtually all UADT sites but primarily involves the larynx, salivary glands (parotid), and sinonasal tract.[356–362] SCUNC of the sinonasal tract affects men and women equally and occurs over a wide age range from the third to eighth decades of life with a mean of 49 years.[363] Sinonasal tract SCUNC most commonly occurs in the superior or posterior nasal cavity, often with extension into adjacent paranasal sinuses (e.g., maxillary and ethmoid sinuses).[363] Primary paranasal sinus disease in the absence of nasal cavity involvement may occur. Presenting signs and symptoms include nasal obstruction, epistaxis, and pain. Local invasion may result in exophthalmos.

Irrespective of the site of occurrence, the histologic appearance of SCUNC is the same. These tumors are hypercellular with varied growth, including sheets, cords, or ribbons. The cells are small and hyperchromatic with oval to spindle-shaped nuclei, absent nucleoli, and minimal cytoplasm. Cellular pleomorphism, increased nuclear-to-cytoplasmic ratio, increased mitotic activity, confluent necrotic areas, and individual cell necrosis are readily apparent. Characteristically, crush artifact of the neoplastic cells is seen. Squamous cell foci may occasionally be present; glandular or ductal differentiation is rarely seen. Although uncommon, neural-like rosettes can be seen in association with SCUNC.[360,361] SCUNCs are infiltrative tumors frequently associated with lymphovascular and perineural invasion.

SCUNC may have epithelial mucin.[361,364] Argyrophilia can be seen but argentaffin staining is absent. Because of its poor differentiation, the immunohistochemical antigenic profile of SCUNC may be quite variable from case to case. Reactivity with the following antibodies may be present to a varying degree: cytokeratin, chromogranin, synaptophysin, NSE, and S-100 protein.[361,364] Cytokeratin reactivity results in a punctate paranuclear or globoid pattern similar to that characteristically seen in Merkel cell carcinoma. Chan et al.[365] compared the staining pattern of CK20 in SCUNC of various anatomic sites with that of Merkel cell carcinoma and found that CK20 preferentially reacted with Merkel cell carcinomas. Furthermore, those tumors diagnosed as SCUNC of salivary gland origin, including a paranuclear punctate staining pattern for cytokeratin, reacted with CK20. These results suggested that the purported salivary gland SCUNC were in fact Merkel cell carcinomas either arising from a cutaneous site with secondary involvement of the parotid gland or else originating within the parotid gland. Rarely, calcitonin reactivity is present in SCUNC but LCA, CK20, HMB-45, and CD99 are absent. Ultrastructural studies may show the presence of neurosecretory granules measuring 50–200 nm.[361,364] Cellular junctional complexes, including desmosomes and tonofilaments, are scanty, and lumina (inter- and intracellular) are usually absent.

The differential diagnosis includes a variety of other sinonasal malignant neoplasms discussed in this chapter. While differences can be identified by light microscopic evaluation, often the differentiation of all these tumor types rests on the immunohistochemical staining profile for a given tumor (Table 4A.7).

The preferred treatment for SCUNC is multimodality therapy, including systemic chemotherapy and irradiation.[361] Surgery is not considered appropriate therapy due to the high rate of metastatic disease.[361] SCUNCs are highly malignant tumors; median survival rates for head and neck SCUNC are reported to be 14.5 months.[366] Local recurrence and distant metastasis occur frequently, with reported rates of 45% and 35%, respectively.[363] Metastases occur to cervical lymph nodes, lung, liver, and bone.

Mucosal malignant melanoma (MMM)

Malignant melanomas are neural crest-derived neoplasms originating from melanocytes and demonstrating melanocytic differentiation. Approximately 15–25% of all malignant melanomas arise in head and neck sites.[337] Of the head and neck malignant melanomas, over 80% are of cutaneous origin. MMMs of the UADT represent 0.5–3% of malignant melanomas of all sites.[368] Of the non-cutaneous head and neck malignant melanomas, the majority are of ocular origin, and approximately 6–8% originate in the mucous membranes of the UADT.[367] The sinonasal tract is considered to be an uncommon site for the development of MMM, accounting for fewer than 5% of all sinonasal tract neoplasms.[369] Irrespective of the site of occurrence, UADT MMMs are more common in men than women. This is primarily a disease of adults, occurring over a wide age range, but most frequently in the sixth to eighth decades of life.[367,370–372] Most cases of UADT MMM occur in Caucasians but blacks are also affected. Symptoms vary according to the site of occurrence and, in the sinonasal tract and nasopharynx, include airway obstruction, epistaxis, pain, non-healing ulcer, and dysphagia. In the sinonasal tract, nasal cavity involvement is more common than that of the paranasal sinuses. In the nasal cavity, the most frequent site of occurrence is the septum (anterior portion) (Fig. 4A.34) and the lateral nasal wall. In the sinuses, the maxillary sinus is the most common site, followed by the ethmoid, frontal, and sphenoid sinuses. Concurrent nasal cavity and paranasal sinus

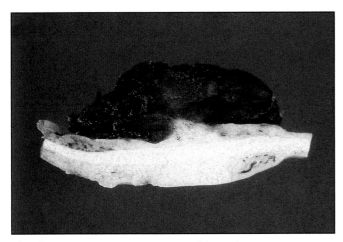

Fig. 4A.34 • Mucosal malignant melanoma of the nasal septum.

growth patterns vary and may be solid, organoid, nested, trabecular, alveolar, or any combination of these patterns. The cells are round to oval, and tend to be markedly pleomorphic, having an increased nuclear-to-cytoplasmic ratio, vesicular to hyperchromatic nuclei, prominent eosinophilic nucleoli, and eosinophilic to clear-appearing cytoplasm. Nuclear pseudo-inclusions and nuclear molding are present. The epithelioid cells may have plasmacytoid features with eccentrically located nuclei and eosinophilic cytoplasm. However, in contrast to plasma cell proliferations, the nuclear chromatin pattern is more densely hyperchromatic and there is no paranuclear clear zone. In predominantly or exclusively spindle cell MMMs, the growth patterns may be storiform or fascicular. The cells are oblong to cigar-shaped and markedly pleomorphic with large vesicular to hyperchromatic nuclei, absent to prominent nucleoli, and scant eosinophilic cytoplasm. Spindle cell MMMs may have an associated myxoid stroma. In both cytomorphologic types of MMM, necrosis and prominent mitoses with atypical mitotic figures are common findings. Uncommon features that may be seen include neoplastic giant cells, and glandular or squamous differentiation.[368]

By light microscopy, MMM may demonstrate heavy melanin deposition, but approximately one-third of cases have only focal, weak pigmentation or are non-pigmented tumors.[372,373] The diagnosis of MMM is facilitated by histochemical and immunohistochemical stains. Histochemistry may be invaluable in the identification of melanin, as seen by argentaffin and argyrophilic-positive staining; however immunohistochemistry remains the diagnostic gold standard. Immunohistochemistry remains the diagnostic parameter of choice with the presence of S-100 protein, HMB-45, and vimentin positivity in both the epithelioid and spindle cells.[368,372] For both S-100 protein and HMB-45, the intensity of staining is strong and the extent of staining is diffuse. Exceptions to this staining pattern may occur in desmoplastic melanomas where HMB-45 may be non-reactive. In addition melanomas express reactivity with T311 (antityrosinase), A103, and D5.[378] No immunoreactivity is seen for cytokeratin, EMA, or myogenic markers. Ultra-structurally, melanosomes and premelanosomes can be seen.[368]

melanomas frequently occur either as a result of direct extension or as multicentric tumors. There are no known etiologic agents linked to the development of MMM. However, Reuter & Woodruff[373] speculated that tobacco-smoking plays an important factor in the development of laryngeal malignant melanomas.

A variety of gross appearances can be seen: tumors may be polypoid or sessile, brown, black, pink, or white friable to rubbery masses measuring from 1.0 cm to large, resulting in obstructive signs and symptoms. In general, surface ulceration is a common finding. In tumors with an intact surface epithelium, continuity of the tumor with the surface epithelium (junctional or pagetoid changes) can usually be identified. The presence of a junctional or in-situ component suggests origin from the surface epithelium but is not a requirement for MMM as melanocytes are found in both the seromucous glands and the submucosa of the UADT.[374–376]

The cytomorphologic features of MMM include most often epithelioid and/or spindled cells (Fig. 4A.35). Tumors with small cell morphology are also relatively frequent.[377] In predominantly or exclusively epithelioid cell MMM, the

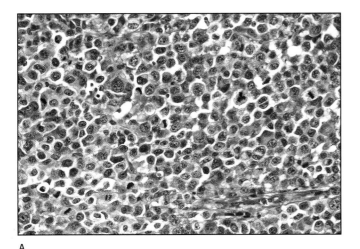

A

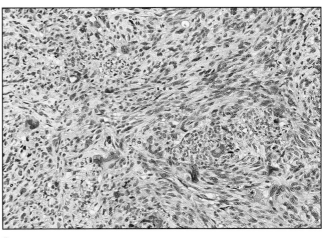

B

Fig. 4A.35 • Sinonasal mucosal malignant melanoma. These tumors may demonstrate cytomorphologic heterogeneity, including: **(A)** pleomorphic epithelioid cells with large nuclei, prominent nucleoli, nuclear molding, and increased mitotic activity; **(B)** pleomorphic spindle-shaped cells with storiform growth reminiscent of mesenchymal tumors.

The differential diagnosis includes a variety of other sinonasal malignant neoplasms discussed in this chapter. While differences can be identified by light microscopic evaluation, often the differentiation of all these tumor types rests on the immunohistochemical staining profile for a given tumor (Table 4A.7).

Irrespective of their site of origin, MMMs as a group represent aggressive and highly lethal tumors. Radical surgical excision is the treatment of choice. Radiotherapy or chemotherapy in the treatment of MMM is felt to have little effect on local or distant disease, and presently is utilized as adjuvant therapy.[379] Overall, the prognosis for MMM of all UADT sites is considered poor: 5-year survival rates are generally <30%.[380] For sinonasal tract MMM, the 5-year DSS ranges from 17 to 46%.[380] There is no time period after which a patient with MMM should be considered as cured. Malignant melanoma is notorious for remaining quiescent for long periods following the initial diagnosis, only to resurface years to decades later. Recurrence, metastasis, and death may occur decades after "curative" therapy. Metastatic disease occurs most frequently to the lungs, lymph nodes, and brain. Before a diagnosis of a primary MMM of the UADT is made, a metastasis from a cutaneous primary malignant melanoma or even another mucosal-based malignant melanoma must be excluded. Cutaneous malignant melanomas are capable of spontaneous regression, lying dormant for many years only to re-emerge as a metastasis (distant from the primary cutaneous site of occurrence) many years later.[381] In the absence of a previous or concurrent malignant melanoma elsewhere, the MMM can be considered as the primary neoplasm.

Sinonasal (mucosal) adenocarcinoma

Adenocarcinomas of the sinonasal tract represent 10–20% of all primary malignant neoplasms of this region[382] but, exclusive of salivary gland types, represent only 6.3% of all malignant sinonasal tract tumors.[383] Two main categories of non-salivary gland-type adenocarcinomas are recognized in the sinonasal tract, including intestinal-type adenocarcinomas (ITACs) and non-intestinal-type adenocarcinomas.

Intestinal-type adenocarcinomas

ITACs are malignant epithelial glandular tumors of the sinonasal tract that histologically resemble intestinal adenocarcinoma and adenoma. ITACs are more common in men than in women, and occur over a wide age range but are most common in the fifth to seventh decades of life. ITACs most frequently involve the ethmoid sinus followed by the nasal cavity (inferior and middle turbinates) and maxillary sinus; however, ITACs may arise anywhere in the sinonasal tract.[382] Early symptoms tend to be non-specific and vary from nasal stuffiness to obstruction that, with persistence, may be associated with epistaxis, prompting further clinical evaluation. Due to the delay in diagnosis, tumors may reach a large size with extensive invasion at the time of presentation. Advanced tumors present with pain, cranial nerve deficits, visual disturbances, and exophthalmos. Etiologic factors associated with the development of ITACs include exposure to hardwood

dust, leather, and softwood; increased incidences of adenocarcinoma are seen in woodworkers and workers in the shoe and furniture industries.[382,384–388] Sporadic ITACs unassociated with occupational exposure occur and tend to affect women more than men, with most tumors involving the maxillary antrum.[382]

These tumors have a variable appearance; they may be well demarcated to poorly defined and invasive, flat to exophytic or papillary growths with a tan/white to pink color and a friable to firm consistency. A mucinous or gelatinous quality may be readily identifiable. Histologically, the ITACs are invasive tumors with various growth patterns, including papillary-tubular, alveolar-mucoid or alveolar-goblet, signet-ring, and mixed.[382,384,389,390] Two classifications of ITAC have been proposed (Table 4A.10). Barnes[382] divided these tumors into five categories: (1) papillary; (2) colonic; (3) solid; (4) mucinous; and (5) mixed. Kleinsasser & Schroeder[384] divided ITACs into four categories: (1) papillary tubular cylinder cell (PTCC) types I–III (I = well-differentiated, II = moderately differentiated, and III = poorly differentiated); (2) alveolar goblet type; (3) signet-ring type; and (4) transitional type. Barnes' papillary, colonic, and solid types correspond to Kleinsasser & Schroeder's PTCC I, PTCC II, and PTCC III, respectively. Either classification is acceptable, but for simplicity the Barnes classification is preferred and is utilized in this text. The most common histologic types seen in association with woodworkers as well as in sporadically occurring cases are the papillary and colonic types.[382,384]

The papillary type (papillary tubular cylinder I or well-differentiated adenocarcinoma), representing approximately 18% of cases, shows a predominantly papillary architecture with occasional tubular glands, minimal cytologic atypia, and rare mitotic figures (Fig. 4A36A).

The colonic type (PTCC II or moderately differentiated adenocarcinoma) shows a mainly tubuloglandular architecture and rare papillae, with increased nuclear pleomorphism and mitotic activity (Fig. 4A.36B).

The solid type (PTCC III or poorly differentiated adenocarcinoma) shows loss of differentiation, characterized by solid and trabecular growth with isolated tubule formation, marked

Table 4A.10	Classification of sinonasal tract intestinal-type adenocarcinoma		
Barnes[382]	Kleinsasser & Schroeder[384]	Percentage of cases	3-year cumulative survival[a]
Papillary type	PTCC I	18%	82%
Colonic type	PTCC II	40%	54%
Solid type	PTCC III	20%	36%
Mucinous type	Alveolar goblet	Uncommon	48%
	Signet-ring	Uncommon	0%
Mixed	Transitional	Rare	71%

PTCC, papillary tubular cylinder cell.
[a]Survival data derived from Klesinsasser & Schroeder.[384]

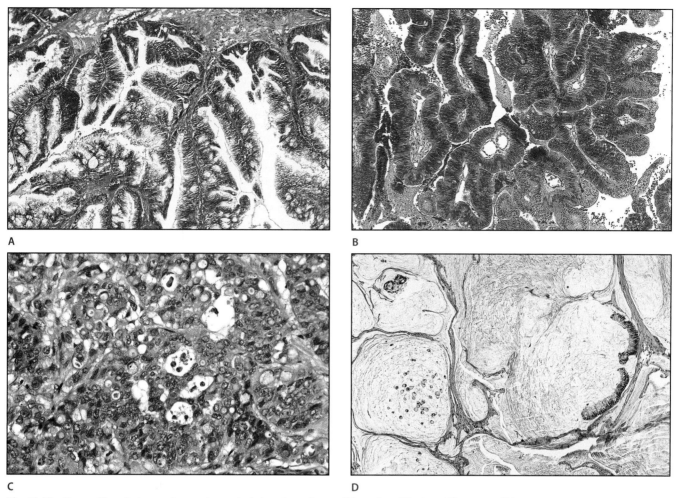

Fig. 4A.36 • Sinonasal intestinal-type adenocarcinomas include various subtypes: **(A)** papillary; **(B)** colonic; **(C)** solid, and **(D)** mucinous.

increase in the number of smaller cuboidal cells with nuclear pleomorphism, round vesicular nuclei, prominent nucleoli, and increased mitotic figures (Fig. 4A.36C).

Analogous to colonic adenocarcinoma, some ITACs are comprised predominantly of abundant mucus and are classified as mucinous-type ITAC (Fig. 4A.36D). The mucinous type (alveolar goblet cell and signet ring) includes two growth patterns. In one pattern there are solid clusters of cells, individual glands, signet-ring cells, and short papillary fronds with or without fibrovascular cores; mucin is predominantly intracellular and a mucoid matrix may be present. The other pattern shows the presence of large, well-formed glands distended by mucus and extracellular mucin pools;[384,390,391] pools of extracellular mucin are separated by thin connective tissue septa, creating an alveolar-type pattern. Predominantly cuboidal or goblet tumor cells are present in single layers at the periphery of mucous lakes. Mucus extravasation may elicit an inflammatory response that may include multinucleate giant cells. Those tumors, where the mucus component predominates (>50%), similar to their gastrointestinal counterparts, may be classified as mucinous adenocarcinomas.[391]

The mixed type (transitional) is composed of an admixture of two or more of the previously defined patterns.

Irrespective of the histologic type, ITACs histologically simulate normal intestinal mucosa and may include villi,

Paneth cells, enterochromaffin cells, and muscularis mucosae. In rare instances, the lesion is composed of well-formed villi lined by columnar cells resembling resorptive epithelium; in such cases, bundles of smooth muscle cells resembling muscularis mucosae may also be identified under the villi.[392]

ITACs are diffusely positive for epithelial markers, including EMA, B72.3, Ber-EP4, BRST-1, Leu-M1, and human milk fat globule (HMFG-2), and are strongly reactive with anti-cytokeratin cocktails.[394] CEA staining is variable, with conflicting results in the literature.[393,394] ITACs show CK20-positivity (73–86%) and variable CK7 reactivity (43–93% of cases).[395–400] CDX-2, a nuclear transcription factor involved in the differentiation of intestinal epithelial cells and diffusely expressed in intestinal adenocarcinomas, can be found in ITACs.[395,397–399] Expression of claudins and villin is also present.[397] Neoplastic cells may express a variety of hormone peptides, including serotonin, cholecystokinin, gastrin, somatostatin, and leu-enkephalin.[401] Chromogranin and synaptophysin-positive cells can be identified.[393,397]

The treatment for ITACs is complete surgical excision, generally via a lateral rhinotomy; depending on the extent and histology of the neoplasm the surgery varies from local excision to more radical procedures (maxillectomy, ethmoidectomy, and additional exenterations). Radiotherapy may be utilized for extensive disease or for higher-grade neoplasms.

All ITACs are considered as potentially aggressive, lethal tumors.

Metastasis to cervical lymph nodes and spread to distant sites are infrequent, occurring in about 10% and 20%, respectively.[384,386,390,391] The 5-year cumulative survival rate is around 40%, with most deaths occurring within 3 years. Death results from uncontrollable local or regional disease with extension and invasion of vital structures and/or metastatic disease. Sinonasal ITACs are generally locally aggressive tumors with frequent local failure (about 50%). Since most patients present with advanced local disease, clinical staging generally is not discriminatory. The histologic subtype has been identified as predictive of clinical behavior, with the papillary type (grade I) lesions behaving more indolently than the other variants (Table 4A.7).[382,384,390,391] There is no difference in behavior between ITACs occurring in occupationally exposed individuals and sporadic ITACs.

Non-intestinal (non-salivary gland) adenocarcinomas

The non-intestinal, non-salivary gland adenocarcinomas are those sinonasal tract tumors that are not of minor salivary gland origin and do not demonstrate histopathologic features of the sinonasal "intestinal" types of adenocarcinoma. These adenocarcinomas are divided into low- and high-grade types.

Sinonasal non-intestinal types of adenocarcinomas occur predominantly in adults but have been identified over a wide age range, from 9 to 80 years.[402] The low-grade adenocarcinomas have an average age at presentation of 53 years, while the high-grade adenocarcinomas have a mean age at presentation of 59 years.[402] There is a slight male predominance for low-grade adenocarcinomas but a much higher male predilection in the high-grade adenocarcinomas.[402] The low-grade non-"intestinal" adenocarcinomas are commonest in the ethmoid sinus (to a lesser extent as compared with the "intestinal" type), and the high-grade non-"intestinal" type

adenocarcinomas are most frequent in the maxillary sinus.[402] Either tumor type may also originate in the nasal cavity, other paranasal sinuses, or (not infrequently) in multiple sinonasal sites in various combinations.[402] Patients with low-grade adenocarcinoma primarily present with nasal obstruction and epistaxis. Pain is an infrequent feature.[402] The duration of symptoms ranges from 2 months to 5 years with a median duration of 5.5 months. For high-grade adenocarcinomas the primary presenting symptoms include nasal obstruction, epistaxis, pain, and facial deformity (e.g., proptosis). The duration of symptoms ranges from 2 weeks to 5 years with a median duration of 2.5 months.[402]

There are no known occupational or environmental factors associated with the non-"intestinal" type of adenocarcinoma.

These tumors have a variable appearance, including well-demarcated to poorly defined and invasive, flat to exophytic or papillary growths with a tan/white to pink color and a friable to firm consistency.

These tumors, whether low- or high-grade, may be confined within the submucosa without surface involvement or may involve the overlying ciliated respiratory epithelium. The low-grade adenocarcinomas have a glandular or papillary growth pattern and may be circumscribed but are unencapsulated tumors. Numerous uniform small glands or acini are seen, often with a back-to-back growth pattern without any intervening stroma (Fig. 4A.37). Occasionally, large, irregular cystic spaces can be seen. The glands are lined by a single layer of non-ciliated, cuboidal to columnar cells with uniform, round nuclei, which may be limited to the basal aspect of the cell or may demonstrate stratification with loss of nuclear polarity, and eosinophilic cytoplasm. Cellular pleomorphism is mild to moderate and occasional mitotic figures are seen, but atypical mitoses and necrosis are absent. Despite the relatively bland histology, the complexity of growth, absence of two cell layers, absence of encapsulation, and presence of invasion into the submucosa confer a diagnosis of adenocarcinoma. Variants include papillary, clear cell, and oncocytic adenocarcinomas.

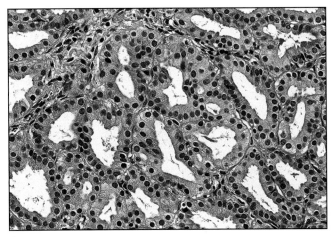

A

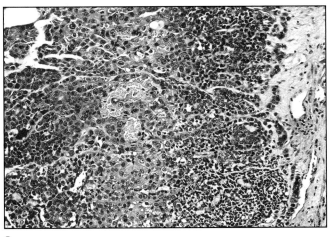

B

Fig. 4A.37 • Sinonasal non-intestinal, non-salivary gland adenocarcinomas include invasive low-grade and high-grade tumors. **(A)** Low-grade adenocarcinoma is characterized by the presence of numerous small glands or acini with a back-to-back growth pattern without intervening stroma; glands are lined by a single layer of non-ciliated, cuboidal to columnar cells with uniform, round nuclei. Cellular pleomorphism is limited. The complexity of growth, absence of two cell layers, absence of encapsulation, and presence of invasion into the submucosa are diagnostic of adenocarcinoma. **(B)** High-grade adenocarcinoma. These tumors are characterized by the presence of moderate to marked cellular pleomorphism, increased mitotic activity, including atypical forms, and necrosis.

Multiple morphologic patterns may be seen in any one neoplasm.

The high-grade sinonasal adenocarcinomas are invasive tumors with a predominantly solid growth pattern but glandular and papillary growth patterns can also be seen. These tumors are characterized by the presence of moderate to marked cellular pleomorphism, increased mitotic activity, including atypical forms, and necrosis (Fig. 4A.37).

The non-intestinal adenocarcinomas are consistently and intensely CK7-reactive but, in contrast to ITACs, are non-reactive for CK20, CDX2, villin, claudins, chromogranin, and synaptophysin.[395–397,399]

The treatment for all the histologic variants of non-intestinal, non-salivary gland sinonasal adenocarcinomas is complete surgical excision, generally via a lateral rhinotomy; depending on the extent and histology of the neoplasm, the surgery varies from local excision to more radical procedures (maxillectomy, ethmoidectomy, and additional exenterations). Radiotherapy may be utilized for extensive disease or for higher-grade neoplasms. The low-grade neoplasms have an excellent prognosis, while high-grade neoplasms have a dismal prognosis with approximately 20% 3-year survival rates.[402]

Malignant salivary gland tumors

The most common malignant salivary gland tumor of the sinonasal tract and nasopharynx is ACC. The more common malignant neoplasms of major salivary glands, including mucoepidermoid carcinoma and acinic cell adenocarcinoma, are uncommon in the sinonasal tract and nasopharynx. The reader is referred to Chapter 7 for a detailed discussion of these and other types of salivary gland malignancies.

Adenoid cystic carcinoma (ACC)

ACC is characterized by a distinctive histologic appearance, a tendency to invade nerves, and its protracted but nonetheless relentless clinical course. Approximately 20% of all ACCs occur in the sinonasal tract.[403] ACC represents approximately 5% of sinonasal malignancies.[383,404]

The most common site of involvement is the maxillary sinus (57%), followed by the nasal cavity (24%), ethmoid sinus (14%), and other sites (5%).[403] ACC of the sinonasal tract is a tumor of adults and rarely occurs in the first two decades of life. Symptoms may include airway obstruction, epistaxis, and pain. These tumors can attain large sizes with extensive infiltrative growth at presentation.

Grossly, ACC is a variably encapsulated, solid, rubbery to firm, tan-white to gray-pink mass measuring 2–4 cm in greatest dimension. The histologic appearance of ACC is that of an unencapsulated, infiltrating neoplasm with varied architecture consisting of cribriform, tubular/ductular, and solid patterns. Individual neoplasms may have a single growth pattern but characteristically they show multiple patterns, any one of which may predominate. The most common pattern is the cribriform type, considered the "classic" pattern, demonstrating arrangement of cells in a "Swiss cheese" configuration with many oval or circular spaces. These spaces contain basophilic mucinous substance or hyalinized eosinophilic material. The tubular type has cells arranged in ducts or

tubules, which contain faintly eosinophilic mucinous material. Cribriform and tubular patterns often occur together. The least common pattern is the solid type, composed of neoplastic cells arranged in sheets or nests of varying size and shape. There is little tendency to form cystic spaces, tubules, or ducts. Irrespective of the growth pattern, the tumors are composed of fairly uniformly sized cells with small, hyperchromatic round to oval or angulated nuclei, scant amphophilic to clear cytoplasm, and indistinct cell borders. The nuclear-to-cytoplasmic ratio is about 1 to 1. The majority of the neoplastic cells are abluminal type myoepithelial cells. The cystic spaces seen in the cribriform or classic type are pseudocysts, which are extracellular and lined by replicated basement membrane. Scattered among these abluminal cells are ductal cells, which surround small true lumens (glands). True duct-like lumens are an infrequent feature of ACC but are seen most frequently in cases with a tubular pattern. In the solid pattern, the cell population is dominated by basaloid myoepithelial cells. The interstitial stroma, from which the epithelial component is sharply demarcated, varies in appearance from myxoid to hyalinized. Cellular and nuclear pleomorphism, necrosis, and mitotic activity are limited in the cribriform and tubular patterns. However, these features are more frequently seen in the solid pattern. Common to all histologic variants is the proclivity for nerve invasion (neurotropism), including peri- and intraneural invasion. However, ACC is not the only salivary gland tumor to show neurotropism.

The histochemical features of ACC include the presence of diastase-resistant, PAS-positive and mucicarmine-positive material within the pseudocysts. Alcian blue staining is also present within the pseudocysts. The immunohistochemistry of ACC varies according to cell type. The myoepithelial cells show cytokeratin, S-100 protein, *p63*, calponin, vimentin, and actin-positivity with variable GFAP reactivity. The ductal cells show cytokeratin, EMA, and CEA-positivity. Ultrastructural studies show the presence of cells with bidirectional differentiation, including luminal or ductal cells and abluminal or myoepithelial/basal cells.[405]

The treatment of choice for ACC is wide local excision and postoperative radiotherapy. Problems in the surgical removal of ACC relate to the infiltrative nature of these neoplasms, with their tendency to extend along nerve segments, which is further compounded by their deceptively circumscribed macroscopic appearance. Recurrence rates are high, ranging from 75 to 90%,[403] and directly related to inadequate surgical excision. ACCs are radiosensitive and radiotherapy is particularly useful in controlling microscopic disease after initial surgery, in treating locally recurrent disease, or as palliation in unresectable tumors. Radiotherapy is not curative. Sinonasal and nasopharyngeal ACCs have similar biologic behavior to ACCs at other locations. The short-term prognosis is generally good, because tumor growth is slow, but the long-term prognosis is poor. These facts are reflected in the 5-year and 20-year survival rates of ACCs of all head and neck sites of 75% and 13% respectively.[406] Tumor location affects prognosis. ACCs located in major salivary glands have a better prognosis than their minor salivary gland counterparts. Clinical staging plays a more decisive role than histologic grading in predicting prognosis in ACC.[407,408] Spiro & Huvos reported a cumulative 10-year survival of 75%, 43%, and 15% for patients with stage I, II, and III and IV, respectively.[407]

Low-grade nasopharyngeal papillary adenocarcinoma

Low-grade nasopharyngeal papillary adenocarcinoma is an uncommon nasopharyngeal surface epithelium-derived malignant tumor with adenocarcinomatous differentiation and indolent biologic behavior.[409] There is no gender predilection and this tumor occurs over a wide age range from the second to seventh decades of life (median, 37 years). The tumor may occur anywhere in the nasopharynx but most often involves the posterior nasopharyngeal wall. The most common symptom is nasal obstruction. There are no known etiologic factors.

These tumors are exophytic, papillary, nodular, or cauliflower-like with a soft to gritty consistency, measuring from a few millimeters to 4.0 cm.[410] Histologically, they are unencapsulated and have papillary and glandular growth patterns. The papillary structures are complex with arborization and hyalinized fibrovascular cores (Fig. 4A.38). Similarly, the glandular pattern is complex and is characterized by back-to-back and cribriform architecture. The cells vary in appearance from pseudostratified columnar to cuboidal. The nuclei are round to oval with vesicular to optically clear-appearing chromatin, indistinct nucleoli and eosinophilic cytoplasm (Fig. 4A.38). There is mild to moderate nuclear pleomorphism. Scattered mitotic figures can be seen but atypical mitoses are not present. Focal necrosis can be found. Psammoma bodies may be present. In adequately sampled material, surface epithelial derivation can be seen in the form of transitional zones from normal nasopharyngeal surface epithelium to neoplastic proliferation.

Histochemical stains for epithelial mucin are positive (intracytoplasmic diastase-resistant, PAS-positive, and intracytoplasmic and luminal mucicarmine). There is diffuse immunoreactivity for cytokeratin and EMA. Focal reactivity is seen with CEA. No immunoreactivity is found with S-100 protein or GFAP. Because of the histologic similarities with thyroid papillary carcinoma, thyroglobulin immunostaining should be performed. The nasopharyngeal papillary adenocarcinomas are thyroglobulin-negative, but thyroid tran-

scription factor 1 (TTF-1) positivity has been reported in these tumors.[410a] There is no association with EBV.

Conservative surgical excision with complete removal is the treatment of choice and is curative.[409,410] Surgery is usually via a transpalatal approach. Adjuvant therapy (radiotherapy) does not-appear to be warranted. These are slow-growing tumors with the potential to recur if incompletely excised; metastatic disease does not occur.

Non-epithelial malignant neoplasms

Non-Hodgkin lymphomas of the sinonasal tract

Non-Hodgkin lymphomas of the sinonasal tract (SNT-ML) are heterogeneous and can be clinically aggressive.[411] Although the terms polymorphic reticulosis, lethal midline granuloma, midline malignant reticulosis, and idiopathic midline destructive disease have been used over the years synonymously with SNT-ML, this is categorically incorrect. Non-neoplastic lesions, inflammatory and infectious diseases, as well as numerous benign and malignant neoplasms of the sinonasal tract may all result in a destructive process occurring in the midline aspect of this region. Therefore, idiopathic midline destructive disease is not a specific term and should never be used to indicate a diagnosis of a malignant lymphoproliferative neoplasm. Other designations for these lesions include angiocentric immunoproliferative lesions and peripheral T-cell lymphoma, the most current designation being angiocentric NK/T-cell lymphoma of nasal type.[412] SNT-MLs also include lymphomas of B-cell lineage, with diffuse large B-cell lymphoma (DLBCL) being the most common type.[413] Other B-cell lymphomas of these sites include Burkitt lymphoma, extranodal marginal B-cell lymphoma of the mucosa-associated lymphoid tissue (MALT) type, and follicular lymphoma.[415] Nasal cavity lymphomas are predominantly of NK/T-cell type while the majority of B-cell lymphomas occur in the paranasal sinuses.[411]

SNT-ML are uncommon and account for only 1.5% of non-Hodgkin malignant lymphomas in the USA.[414,415] The incidence has been reported to be higher, however, in Asian and South American countries where the incidence of primary sinonasal non-Hodgkin malignant lymphoma is approximately 6.7–8.0% of all malignant lymphomas.[414,416,417] Virtually the entire spectrum of morphologic types of lymphoma can be seen (see Ch. 21). The most common type of lymphoma in the sinonasal tract is the extranodal NK/T-cell lymphoma of nasal type.[411,418] The NK/T-cell lymphoma of nasal type primarily affects men and is a disease of adults with a median age in the sixth decade of life.[418] It is most common in Asians and has been reported with significant frequency in South and Central America and Mexico.[419,420] In these populations, the disease is seen primarily in individuals of Native American origin. Although uncommon, NK/T-cell lymphomas of nasal type also occur in western populations and can affect Caucasians.[412] DLBCL of the sinonasal tract also primarily affects men, with a median age in the seventh decade of life.[411,418] The sites of involvement may include the nasal cavity, one or more paranasal sinuses, or multiple regions within the sinonasal tract.[411] The clinical presentations vary according to histologic

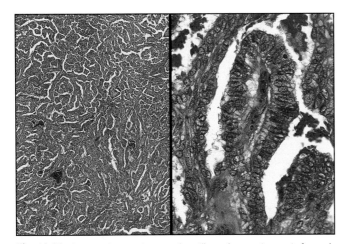

Fig. 4A.38 • Low-grade nasopharyngeal papillary adenocarcinoma. Left panel: these tumors are unencapsulated and infiltrative and show a complex papillary growth with fibrovascular cores. Right panel: papillary frond with fibrovascular core and nuclear features with similarities to thyroid papillary carcinoma markers (e.g., thyroglobulin) is negative.

type and/or immunophenotype. Low-grade lymphomas may present as a nasal cavity or paranasal sinus mass associated with airway obstructive symptoms. High-grade lymphomas are more likely to present with aggressive signs and symptoms, including non-healing ulcer, cranial nerve manifestations, facial swelling, epistaxis, or pain. High-grade B-cell lymphomas tend to present with soft tissue or osseous destruction, particularly of the orbit, with associated proptosis.[411] NK/T-cell lymphoma of nasal type commonly presents as a destructive process of the mid facial region with nasal septal destruction, palatal destruction, orbital swelling, or with obstructive symptoms related to a mass.

Irrespective of ethnic background, NK/T-cell lymphoma of the nasal type is strongly associated with EBV.[413] However, B-cell lymphomas of the sinonasal tract have only a weak association with EBV.[413] An increased risk of sinonasal lymphomas, primarily DLCBL but also NK/T-cell lymphoma of nasal type, is also associated with immunosuppression, including post-transplantation and human immunodeficiency virus (HIV) infection.[421–423]

NK/T-cell lymphoma of nasal type

Histologically, nasal-type NK/T-cell lymphomas may show a broad spectrum but usually cytologically atypical cells are present.[412,424] The atypical cells may vary from small and medium-sized cells to large, hyperchromatic cells. The atypical cells may have irregular and elongated nuclei, prominent nucleoli, or clear cytoplasm (Fig. 4A.39). Epitheliotropism and pseudoepitheliomatous hyperplasia may be present. Prominent admixed inflammatory cell infiltrate, including plasma cells, histiocytes, and eosinophils, may be present. The polymorphous cell population may obscure the atypical cells, causing diagnostic difficulties. Multinucleate giant cells and true granulomas are absent.

In adequately sampled material, the low-power appearance almost invariably includes the presence of geographic necrosis characterized by bluish or so-called "gritty" necrosis (Fig. 4A.39). The zonal pattern of necrosis suggests a vascular pathogenesis. The atypical cells invade and destroy blood vessels (Fig. 4A.40), hence the destruction is responsible for

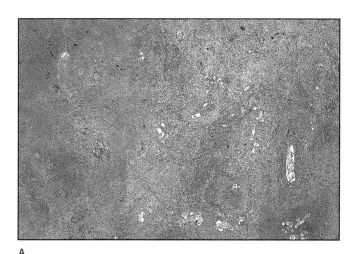

A

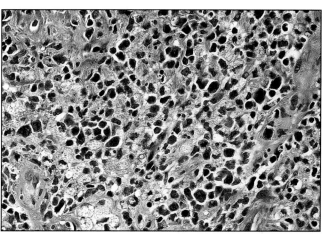

B

Fig. 4A.39 • Extranodal natural killer/T-cell lymphoma of nasal type. **(A)** At low magnification, areas of geographic necrosis are seen (left) with a cellular infiltrate present, focally surrounding vascular spaces (right). **(B)** Diffuse discohesive cellular proliferation comprised of medium to large cells with round to oval to irregular and elongated nuclei, vesicular to hyperchromatic nuclei, and indistinct eosinophilic cytoplasm.

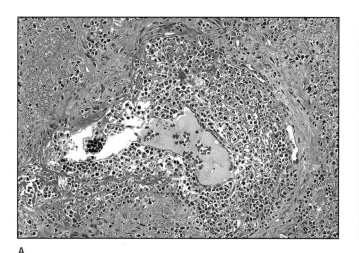

A

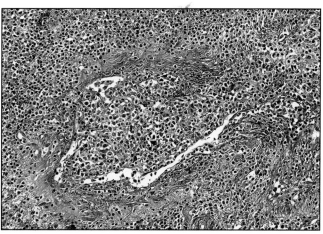

B

Fig. 4A.40 • Extranodal natural killer/T-cell lymphoma of nasal type. **(A)** The neoplastic cells surround and invade vascular spaces (angiocentricity). **(B)** Elastic stain shows disruption of the elastic membranes with tumor invasion through the wall and plugging of the vessel lumen.

Table 4A.11 Clinicopathologic comparison between sinonasal malignant lymphomas, Wegener's granulomatosis, and allergic granulomatosis and vasculitis (Churg–Strauss)

	Angiocentric natural killer/ T-cell lymphoma	Diffuse large cell B-cell lymphoma	Wegener's granulomatosis (WG)	Allergic granulomatosis and vasculitis[a]
Gender, age	M > F; sixth decade; most common in Asians; occurs in western population but with less frequency	M > F; 7th decade	M > F; fourth–fifth decades; laryngeal WG affects F > M	M > F; wide age range (third–sixth decades)
Location	Generally limited to the sinonasal region; extra-sinonasal disease occurs and represents a higher-stage tumor	Nasal cavity and one or more paranasal sinuses	Localized upper aerodigestive tract WG most common in nasal cavity > paranasal sinuses; other sites may include nasopharynx, larynx (subglottis), oral cavity, trachea, ear, salivary glands	Multisystem disease including pulmonary, nasal, renal, cutaneous, cardiac, and nervous system involvement
Symptoms	Destructive process of mid facial region: nasal septal perforation, obstruction, palate destruction, orbital swelling	Non-healing ulcer, epistaxis, facial swelling, pain, cranial nerve manifestations	Sinonasal tract: sinusitis, with or without purulent rhinorrhea, obstruction, pain, epistaxis, anosmia, headaches Larynx: dyspnea, hoarseness; voice changes Oral: ulcerative lesion Ear: hearing loss, pain	Asthma, allergic rhinitis, evidence of eosinophilia, serum and tissue (e.g., eosinophilic pneumonia, eosinophilic gastroenteritis, other), evidence of vasculitis
Systemic involvement	Majority are localized (stage IE/II/E); may progress to disseminated/systemic involvement	Majority are localized (stage IE/II/E); may progress to disseminated/systemic involvement	ELK classification: E: ear, nose, throat L: lung K: kidney E, EL = limited-form WG ELK = systemic WG	Typically multisystem involvement, although limited forms of disease exist
Serology	ANCA-negative; no specific serologic marker(s)	ANCA-negative; no specific serologic marker(s)	ANCA-positive: • increased in both primary disease and recurrent disease; • (C-ANCA more specific than P-ANCA)	ANCA levels may or may not be present; peripheral eosinophilia

the designation "angiocentric lymphomas." Angiocentricity is defined as the presence of tumor cells around and within vascular spaces with infiltration and destruction of the vessel wall. Perivascular localization is not sufficient for the designation of angiocentricity.

Immunohistochemically, tumor cells are typically CD2-positive, surface (membranous) CD3-negative, cytoplasmic CD3e-positive, and CD56 (neural cell adhesion molecule (NCAM))-positive.[412] T-cell markers including CD43 and UCHL1 (CD45RO) are positive. Expression of perforin, TIa1 and granzyme B, indicative of a cytotoxic phenotype, is present.[413] T-cell receptor genes are often in germline configuration.[412] Tumors that are CD56-negative may still be classified as NK/T-cell lymphomas if they express T-cell and cytotoxic markers and are EBV-positive.[413]

NK/T-cell lymphomas are positive for EBV in greater than 95% of cases[413] by ISH for EBER.[425] Since EBV-positive cells are typically absent in the nasal cavity mucosa or in inflammatory diseases of the nasal cavity, the presence of EBV by ISH can be used in conjunction with light microscopy in the diagnosis of nasal cavity NK/T lymphomas. EBV may induce the expression of cytokines (e.g., tumor necrosis factor-α) which could lead to the presence of necrosis, even in those cases without vascular invasion. Expression of Fas and Fas ligand, a frequent finding in NK/T cell lymphomas, may also account for the presence of necrosis.[425,426]

The differential diagnosis includes a variety of other sinonasal malignant neoplasms discussed in this chapter. While differences can be identified by light microscopic evaluation, often the differentiation of all these tumor types rests on the immunohistochemical staining profile for a given tumor (Table 4A.7). The differential diagnosis also includes infectious disease of the sinonasal tract and Wegener's granulomatosis (WG) (Table 4A.11). Identification of microorganisms by special stains or microbiologic cultures will assist in confirming an infectious etiology. The constellation of histologic features associated with WG (see later in chapter) coupled with the presence of elevated antineutrophil cytoplasmic antibodies (ANCA) assists in confirming a diagnosis of WG and differentiating it from NK/T-cell lymphoma.

Table 4A.11	Clinicopathologic comparison between sinonasal malignant lymphomas, Wegener's granulomatosis, and allergic granulomatosis and vasculitis (Churg–Strauss) (Cont'd)			
	Angiocentric natural killer/ T-cell lymphoma	Diffuse large cell B-cell lymphoma	Wegener's granulomatosis (WG)	Allergic granulomatosis and vasculitis[a]
Histology	Overtly malignant cellular infiltrate but in early phases malignant cells may not be easily identifiable; angiocentricity and angioinvasion; ischemic-type necrosis; no giant cells or granulomas; negative cultures and stains for organisms	Diffuse discohesive cellular proliferation of medium to large cells with large round to oval vesicular (non-cleaved) nuclei, prominent nucleoli, increased mitotic acitivity and necrosis	Polymorphous (benign) cellular infiltrate; vasculitis; ischemic-type necrosis; isolated multinucleated giant cells (not well-formed granulomas); negative cultures and stains for organisms	Polymorphous (benign) cellular infiltrate, predominantly eosinophils; vasculitis which may be a granulomatous vasculitis (multinucleated giant cells in the wall of involved blood vessels); eosinophilic microabscesses; negative cultures and stains for organisms
Immuno-histochemistry	CD56, CD2, cytoplasmic CD3e-positive; T-cell markers (CD3, UCHL-1) positive	Leukocyte common antigen and B-cell markers (CD20, CD79) positive	Polymorphous and polyclonal	Polymorphous and polyclonal
Epstein–Barr virus	Strong association	No to weak association	Negative	Negative
Treatment	Radiotherapy for localized disease; chemotherapy for disseminated disease	Radiotherapy and/or chemotherapy	Cyclophosphamide and prednisone	Systemic corticosteroids
Prognosis	Overall survival 30–50%; local recurrence/relapse and systemic failure common	Dependent on stage; survival rates 35–60%	Limited disease associated with a good to excellent prognosis and occasional spontaneous remissions; mortality related to complications of renal and pulmonary involvement	62% 5-year survival; increased morbidity and mortality due to cardiac involvement resulting in congestive heart failure or myocardial infarction

ANCA, antineutrophil cytoplasmic antibodies.
[a]Also known as Churg–Strauss syndrome.

Diffuse large B-cell lymphoma

In DLBCL there is a diffuse submucosal discohesive cellular infiltrate composed of medium to large cells with large, round to oval, vesicular (non-cleaved) nuclei and several membrane-bound small nucleoli or a single centrally located prominent eosinophilic nucleolus. Mitotic activity, necrosis, and apoptotic figures can be seen.

Immunohistochemistry is essential in confirming the diagnosis and in differentiating a malignant lymphoma from carcinoma. Immunoreactivity is seen for LCA (or CD45) and pan B-cell markers, including CD20 and CD79a.

The majority of NK/T-cell lymphomas of nasal type are localized at presentation (stage IE/IIE).[366] NK/T-cell lymphomas are radiosensitive tumors but the prognosis is generally poor once dissemination occurs. The treatment in disseminated disease is aggressive chemotherapy. In some patients, surgical resection may be needed for symptomatic relief (e.g., airway obstruction). The overall survival is 30–50%.[418,427,428] Local recurrence/relapse and systemic failure are common.[427,429] Systemic failure includes increased risk of dissemination to skin, testes, and gastrointestinal tract.[429] A complication seen in some cases of NK/T-cell lymphoma of nasal type is hemo-

phagocytic syndrome, which adversely affects survival.[412,429] Other factors that negatively impact prognosis include advanced-stage disease, poor performance status, B symptoms, and bulky disease.[428]

For B-cell lymphomas, including DLCBL, the prognosis is dependent on the clinical stage. Patients with sinonasal DLCBL usually present with low-clinical-stage disease (IE/IIE).[413,418] Treatment primarily includes radiotherapy and/or chemotherapy. Surgical resection may be needed for symptomatic relief. Survival rates range from 35 to 60%.[418,421] Systemic failure includes increased risk of dissemination to nodal and extranodal sites below the diaphragm (e.g., para-aortic lymph nodes, gastrointestinal tract).[429]

Malignant lymphomas of Waldeyer's tonsillar tissues

Waldeyer's tonsillar ring includes the lymphoid tissues of the nasopharynx, tonsils, and base of tongue. It represents an extranodal but not an extralymphatic site. Waldeyer's ring lymphomas account for approximately 50% of all extranodal non-Hodgkin malignant lymphoma in the head and neck, where the incidence of extranodal non-Hodgkin lymphomas is second only to that in the gastrointestinal tract.[430,431] In western countries Waldeyer's ring lymphomas are overwhelmingly B-cell lymphomas, with the most common subtype being DLCBL. B-cell lymphomas of Waldeyer's ring tend to affect men slightly more than women, and are most common in the fifth to seventh decades of life.[432–435] The most common sites of occurrence (in order of frequency) are the tonsils, nasopharynx, and base of tongue. The most common symptoms include airway obstruction, otalgia, decreased hearing, pain, and sore throat. There is no specific association between Waldeyer's ring lymphoma and EBV.[425]

Grossly, a large submucosal mass with or without surface ulceration may be seen. In the majority of cases involvement is unilateral. Typically, the cellular infiltrate is discohesive but occasionally it may demonstrate syncytial or cohesive growth, simulating an epithelial malignancy. In large-cell lymphoma, the cells are medium to large with a large round to oval vesicular (non-cleaved) nucleus with several nucleoli often located at the periphery of the nucleus. Numerous macrophages (giving a starry-sky appearance) or epithelioid cells may be present. Mitotic activity, necrosis, and apoptotic figures can be seen. In immunoblastic lymphoma, the cells are large with round to oval nuclei and a large, prominent and usually centrally located nucleolus. Necrosis (individual cell or confluent areas) and increased mitotic activity with atypical forms are common features. These tumors may show plasmacytic differentiation.

Immunohistochemistry is essential in confirming the diagnosis and in differentiating a malignant lymphoma from carcinoma. LCA (CD45) will be positive in almost all malignant lymphomas, while cytokeratin is negative. The overwhelming majority of Waldeyer's ring lymphomas are of follicle center cell origin, reflected in their expression of B-cell lineage markers (CD20) and absence of T-cell markers.

In addition to the immunohistochemical features, other findings associated with DLCBL include the presence of immunoglobulin gene rearrangement and EBV and human lymphotropic virus (HTLV-1) in a proportion of cases; the chromosomal translocation t(14;18) is present in many of the B-cell neoplasms.[436]

The most important prognostic factor for patients with Waldeyer's ring lymphoma is the clinical stage.[436,437] Treatment primarily includes radiotherapy and/or chemotherapy. Surgical resection may be needed for symptomatic relief. The majority of patients have localized disease (stage IE/IIE).[413] In patients with DLCBL and stage IE disease reported 5-year survival rates range from 58 to 86%.[432,433,438] Patients with stage IIE or higher have a much worse prognosis.

Extramedullary plasmacytoma (EMP)

EMP comprises approximately 3–5% of all plasma cell neoplasms.[439] Eighty percent of EMP occur in the head and neck, and most cases primarily involve the UADT, including the sinonasal tract and nasopharynx.[439–441] Eighty percent of EMP are primary (solitary) without evidence of tumor elsewhere; 20% are part of the generalized picture associated with multiple myeloma.[439] EMP is more common in men than women; it occurs over a wide age range but the vast majority of patients are over 40 years of age. EMP tends to develop in mucosa-associated sites, including the sinonasal tract, naso-

pharynx, pharynx (including tonsil), larynx, oral cavity, salivary glands, and thyroid gland. The clinical presentation is dependent on the site of occurrence and may include a soft tissue mass, airway obstruction, epistaxis, pain, proptosis, or cranial nerve involvement.[441] Serum immunoelectrophoresis may show monoclonal abnormalities in both the systemic and localized forms of the disease; up to 25% of patients with EMP will have a monoclonal gammopathy (M component).[440] Disappearance of the M component may be indicative of a cure.[440] Radiologic features of EMP include a soft tissue density; bone destruction may be present; in patients with primary EMP, skeletal survey will be negative.[440]

EMP may appear as a sessile or pedunculated, mucosa-covered mass measuring 1–7.5 cm in greatest dimension. The lesions have a soft to rubbery to firm consistency with a variable color. These tumors bleed easily on biopsy. Typically, EMP is submucosal with a diffuse growth pattern which replaces the normal parenchyma. Plasma cell malignancies are composed of plasma cells with varying degrees of maturation and atypicality (see also Ch. 21). Plasma cells are round to oval with an eccentrically situated round nucleus; the nucleus has a characteristic clock-face chromatin pattern but dispersed nuclear chromatin can be seen; a characteristic paranuclear clear zone represents the Golgi apparatus where immunoglobulin is processed and glycosylated for secretion.[440] The cytoplasm is abundant and basophilic. Amyloid deposits may be present in association with the plasma cell infiltrate. Histochemical stains (Congo red or crystal violet) and/or immunohistochemistry (AA protein) assist in confirming the presence of amyloid. Histochemical evaluation includes the presence of cytoplasmic pyroninophilia (methyl green pyronin (MGP)); plasma cells appear red on staining. On immunohistochemistry, monotypic cytoplasmic immunoglobulin heavy- and/or light-chain restriction is present, as are plasma cell-associated antigens (CD38, CD138, VS38); plasma cell malignancies are generally CD45 and CD20-negative.[442]

An anaplastic variant of plasmacytoma may occur in UADT sites and is characterized by cells with enlarged pleomorphic nuclei, indistinct to prominent eosinophilic nucleoli, and a variable amount of eosinophilic cytoplasm. Tumor giant cells may be present and there is increased mitotic activity, including atypical forms. In these anaplastic lesions, the cells may have a plasmacytoid appearance but, by and large, there is loss of the histologic features diagnostic of plasma cell tumor. Differentiation from large-cell (immunoblastic) lymphomas may be extremely difficult. Of assistance would be a previous history of plasmacytoma, residual evidence of a plasma cell neoplasm with transformation to less differentiated (i.e., anaplastic foci), and/or immunohistochemical features supporting a plasma cell neoplasm.

As in non-Hodgkin lymphoma, careful staging is required prior to the initiation of therapy and may necessitate a bone marrow biopsy. The treatment is dependent on the extent of disease and may include radiotherapy alone or, for large tumors, local resection followed by radiotherapy. Many cases of EMP remain localized, and surgical resection with postoperative radiotherapy (30–50 Gy) is curative.[440] Seventy percent of patients with EMP are alive at 10 years, with a median survival of 7–9 years.[440,441] Involvement of a head and neck site may represent dissemination from multiple myeloma, or dissemination may occur to other sites from the primary head and neck site. The prognosis is drastically affected by the presence of disseminated disease – median survival after dissemination is less than 2 years.[440,441]

Other hematolymphoid malignancies and related lesions

Other malignancies of hematolymphoid origin occurring in Waldeyer's ring includes NK/T-cell lymphoma, anaplastic large-cell lymphoma (ALCL), Burkitt lymphoma, and Hodgkin lymphoma (HL).

The B-cell predominance of Waldeyer's ring malignant lymphomas is less true in Asian populations, where B-cell lymphomas comprise up to 60% of cases as a result of a higher proportion of NK/T-cell lymphoma and peripheral T-cell lymphomas.[416] Waldeyer's ring extranodal NK/T-cell lymphoma of nasal type tend to occur more commonly in men than in women with a median age in the sixth decade of life.[416] Extranodal ALCL of the head and neck is rare but may be seen in HIV-infected patients.[442,443] Burkitt lymphoma is a highly aggressive lymphoma composed of B cells that often presents in extranodal sites, including the head and neck (e.g., jaws, sinonasal tract, nasopharynx, other) and tends to occur in children and young adults.[444]

Primary UADT mucosal HL is rare but is often associated with EBV infection.[445,446]

Follicular dendritic cell tumor (FDCT) (sarcoma) is a rare neoplasm of spindled to ovoid cells showing morphologic and phenotypic features of follicular dendritic cells. FDCT is typically a tumor of adults, with equal gender predilection. FDCTs present with painless lymphadenopathy most often in the cervical neck region and, less often, in the axillary region. Extranodal sites of occurrence include the mucosal sites of the UADT, notably the tonsil and pharynx;[447–451] FDCTs occur in association with Castleman's disease, usually hyaline vascular type, in about 10% of patients.[452]

FDCTs in the mucosa of the UADT are usually polypoid with an intact surface epithelium. Growth patterns include diffuse, storiform, fascicular, and whorled. The cellular proliferation includes oval to spindle-shaped cells with round to oval, uniform-appearing, elongated nuclei with vesicular or granular-appearing chromatin, inconspicuous nucleoli, and pale to slightly eosinophilic cytoplasm with indistinct borders. Scattered multinucleate giant cells may be identified; pseudo-nuclear inclusions may be present. Absent to scattered mitotic figures (0–10 mitoses per hpf) can be found but atypical mitoses, significant pleomorphism, and necrosis are infrequent. A background lymphocytic infiltrate either as individual cells or in clusters can be identified throughout the tumor, and often in a perivascular (cuffing) location; occasional germinal centers can be identified.

FDCT typically express CD21, CD35, CD23, and vimentin. In addition, other follicular dendritic cell markers (e.g., R4/23, Ki-M4P, Ki-FDRC1p), fascin, HLA-DR, and EMA are unusually positive, the latter despite the fact that normal follicular dendritic cells are EMA-negative. Variable reactivity is identified for S-100 protein, CD68, CD45, CD20, and smooth muscle actin. FDCTs are consistently EBV-negative and HHV-8-negative. Recently, diffuse strong staining for clusterin was found in 100% of FDCTs, including cases that were negative for traditional markers (CD21, CD23, CD35), but that were

classified based on characteristic ultrastructural features.[453] Ultrastructurally, FDCTs show the presence of complex interdigitating (villous) cytoplasmic processes or extensions, often joined through numerous cell junctions, including well-formed desmosomes. Treatment includes surgical excision with or without adjunctive therapy (i.e., radiotherapy, chemotherapy). The overall behavior is rather indolent and has been likened to that of low-grade sarcomas.[454]

Malignant mesenchymal neoplasms

Malignant peripheral nerve sheath tumor (neurogenic sarcoma; neurofibrosarcoma)

Malignant peripheral nerve sheath tumors (MPNST) of the sinonasal tract and nasopharynx are uncommon neoplasms. Up to 14% of malignant schwannomas (see also Ch. 27) occur in the head and neck, with the neck being the most common site of involvement; all areas may be involved, including the sinonasal cavity and nasopharynx.[455] MPNST may occur *de novo* or in the setting of neurofibromatosis 1 (NF1).[456]

Histologically, MPNSTs of the sinonasal tract may be spindle-celled or epithelioid, and low-grade or high-grade. The majority of sinonasal MPNSTs are low-grade spindle cell-type, appearing as a nondescript fascicular spindle cell proliferation in and around non-neoplastic glands.[455] The nuclei are irregular in contour and are often wavy or buckled in appearance; the cytoplasm is indistinct. As compared to benign schwannomas, there is increased cellularity, nuclear atypia, and increased mitotic activity. Hypocellular areas with a myxoid stroma can be seen alternating with areas of greater cellularity. Heterologous elements, including bone and cartilage, may be present. In contrast to benign schwannomas, S-100 protein reactivity is focal and less intensely positive in low-grade MPNSTs and is only variably present in high-grade MPNSTs.[457] Complete surgical excision is the treatment of choice. Radiotherapy may be utilized in conjunction with surgery or in cases with recurrent disease. Sinonasal MPNSTs generally have a relatively good prognosis. Unfavorable prognosis is associated with occurrence in the setting of NF1, male gender, and higher histologic grade.[455,456]

Fibrosarcoma and so-called malignant fibrous histiocytoma

Sinonasal and nasopharyngeal fibrosarcomas and so-called malignant fibrous histiocytomas (see Ch. 24) are uncommon.[92,455,458] The most common sites of occurrence are the paranasal sinuses. Patients present with signs and symptoms of a mass lesion, including nasal obstruction, epistaxis, facial swelling, and pain. Histologically, fibrosarcomas are composed of spindle-shaped cells in a fascicular or "herringbone" pattern of growth and associated collagen deposition. The tumors lack any specific differentiation on light microscopy and lack immunohistochemical evidence supportive of another tumor type (e.g., S-100 protein in MPNST; cytokeratin in SCSC or monophasic synovial sarcoma). The microscopic grading of these tumors includes low-grade and high-grade forms.[455] In low-grade fibrosarcomas there is mild cellular pleomorphism and readily identifiable mitotic activity (but atypical forms are not seen) and there is retention of the fascicular growth pattern. In contrast to low-grade tumors, the high-grade fibrosarcomas have less distinct fascicular growth, show marked nuclear atypia with marked increase in mitotic activity, including atypical forms, and have associated hemorrhage and necrosis. These tumors, however, lack bizarre or giant neoplastic cells with hyperchromatic nuclei and prominent nucleoli. The presence of the latter would support the diagnosis of undifferentiated pleomorphic sarcoma, often formerly known as malignant fibrous histiocytoma. The immunohistochemical findings in fibrosarcoma and malignant fibrous histiocytoma are non-contributory. Since there are a number of malignant tumors that may share the growth pattern of fibrosarcoma and so-called malignant fibrous histiocytoma, it is important to demonstrate the absence of immunoreactivity with markers that may be diagnostic for another tumor type such as cytokeratins, S-100 protein, or HMB-45. Surgical resection is the treatment of choice. Adjuvant radiotherapy can be used for higher-grade tumors or tumors involving the surgical margins of resection. Chemotherapy is used for patients with extensive local recurrent tumor or metastatic disease. Local tumor recurrence is the most significant cause of morbidity and mortality in these patients.[455,459]

Rhabdomyosarcoma

RMS is a malignant mesenchymal tumor showing skeletal muscle differentiation. In the head and neck, RMS is primarily but not exclusively a disease of the pediatric population.[460] If all ages are considered, RMS comprises up to 50% of all soft tissue sarcomas of the head and neck (see Ch. 24). RMS restricted to pediatric age groups represents up to 75% of all soft tissue sarcomas of the head and neck;[467,461] in this age group, RMS represents the most common aural malignant neoplasm. There is no gender predilection. In the head and neck, the most common sites of occurrence of RMS (in descending order of frequency) include the orbit, nasopharynx, middle ear/temporal bone, and the sinonasal tract.[462–464] If adults only are considered, the most frequent site is the sinonasal tract.[465,466] Symptoms vary according to site. Patients

with sinonasal tract RMS may present with symptoms such as sinusitis, rhinorrhea, nasal obstruction, epistaxis, pain, otalgia, facial swelling, and headaches. In contrast to pediatric patients, RMS in adults often is a more aggressive neoplasm.[465–467] In the sinonasal tract, progression of disease may result in proptosis, facial deformity, visual field disturbances, and/or cranial nerve deficits.

RMS of the sinonasal tract most often appears as a nodular, lobular, or polypoid mass with an appearance similar to that of sinonasal inflammatory polyps. Approximately 25% of nasopharyngeal and sinonasal cavity RMS assume a sarcoma botryoides appearance with a grape-like, multinodular, or polypoid configuration.

The majority of RMS of the head and neck are of the embryonal type, mainly botryoid type (80–85%), followed by alveolar (10–15%) (Fig. 4A.41).[462] The other histologic types, including spindle cell (a variant of embryonal RMS) and pleomorphic, may occur in the head and neck but are considered uncommon. Typically, there is a variation in the cellularity of these tumors with alternating hyper- and hypocellular areas; the latter is often associated with a myxoid stroma. The tumor is composed of primitive mesenchymal cells in various stages of myogenesis. The small undifferentiated cells (primitive-appearing) are round or spindle-shaped cells with hyperchromatic nuclei and indistinct cytoplasm; mild nuclear pleomorphism, increased mitotic activity, and necrosis are present. The differentiated cells are larger, round to oval, with eosinophilic cytoplasm. Uncommonly, embryonal RMS with foci of prominent cellular pleomorphism may occur, being known as the anaplastic variant.

Sarcoma botryoides (botryoid RMS) is a macroscopic variant of embryonal RMS characterized by its gross appearance that includes a polypoid and myxoid mass. Histologically, the tumor may demonstrate a dense layer or aggregate of tumor cells localized beneath the epithelial surface, referred to as a cambium layer.

Alveolar RMS is characterized by ill-defined aggregates of poorly differentiated but relatively uniform small round to oval neoplastic cells (Fig. 4A.42). Often there is central loss of cellular cohesion resulting in "alveolar" spaces, but other areas (or whole tumors) are composed of solid aggregates of tumor

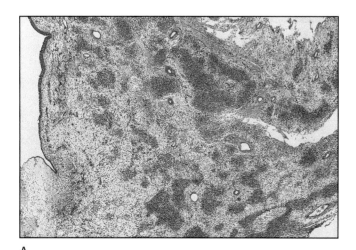

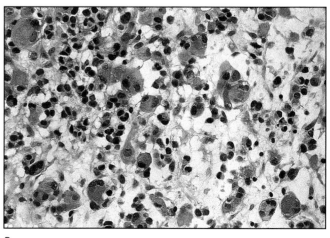

A

B

Fig. 4A.41 • Embryonal rhabdomyosarcoma of the sinonasal tract. **(A)** At low power the submucosal infiltrate shows alternating cellular and myxoid areas. **(B)** At high magnification cells with eosinophilic cytoplasm characteristic of rhabdomyoblasts are present.

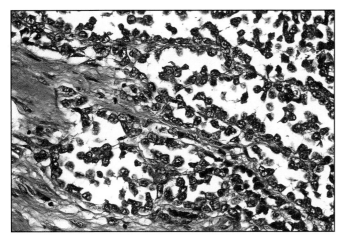

Fig. 4A.42 • Alveolar rhabdomyosarcoma of the nasopharynx. The neoplastic cells adhere to the fibrous septa with central loss of cellular cohesion, giving the appearance of spaces or alveoli and creating an "alveolar" growth.

cells, sometimes arranged in a trabecular pattern. The cellular portions of the tumor are separated by dense fibrous connective tissue forming septa and associated with prominent vascular spaces. The cells at the periphery of the alveolar spaces are best preserved and often adhere to the fibrous septa. Neoplastic rhabdomyoblasts with prominent granular eosinophilic cytoplasm are less common in the alveolar type than in the embryonal type. Wreath-like multinucleate cells with peripheral nuclei are often found in alveolar RMS and represent a diagnostically important clue.

In the presence of a poorly differentiated neoplasm lacking evidence of cross-striations, special stains are invaluable in confirming the diagnosis of RMS. Immunohistochemistry is an important adjunct in the diagnosis of RMS and includes reactivity for desmin, myf-4, actin (muscle-specific), and myoglobin.

Cytogenetic evaluation may play a critical role in the diagnosis and differential diagnosis of RMS (Table 4A.12; see Ch. 24).[468,469]

The differential diagnosis includes a variety of other sinonasal malignant neoplasms discussed in this chapter. While differences can be identified by light microscopic evaluation, often the differentiation of all these tumor types rests on the immunohistochemical staining profile for a given tumor (Table 4A.7).

Table 4A.12	Cytogenetics of rhabdomyosarcoma

Embryonal rhabdomyosarcoma
Loss of heterozygosity at chromosome 11p15.5
Short arm of chromosome 11 abnormalities
PAX3/FKHR and *PAX7/FKHR* fusion transcripts generally absent

Spindle cell rhabdomyosarcoma
No data regarding cytogenetic abnormalities

Alveolar rhabdomyosarcoma
t(2;13)(q36;q14) translocation – majority of cases
t(1;13)(p36;q14) translocation – minority of cases
PAX3/FKHR fusion transcript (80–90% of cases)
PAX7/FKHR fusion transcript (10–20% of cases)

Prior to the efforts of the Intergroup Rhabdomyosarcoma Study (IRS),[460] the treatment for RMS was surgical excision and the 5-year survival rate for RMS of the head and neck was less than 20%. However, the IRS developed a staging system for RMS[460] and showed that multimodality therapy, including surgery, radiotherapy, and chemotherapy (vincristine, dactinomycin, cyclophosphamide, and Adriamycin) enhances survival rates over single-modality therapy. Following biopsy diagnosis, recommendations for treatment depend on several factors, including site of the disease, clinical group of the disease, and stage of the disease.

Tumor staging is an important element in the overall approach to treating the disease. Overall 5-year survival rates based on clinical staging include: groups I, II: 85–88%; group III: 66%; group IV: 26%.[470] The IRS subsequently divided head and neck RMS into three categories for statistical purposes,[471] including: (1) eye-orbit RMS with 5-year survival rates of 92%; (2) parameningeal RMS, including the middle ear-mastoid, external auditory canal, nasopharynx, sinonasal region, and infratemporal fossa with 5-year survival rates of 70%; (3) other head and neck sites, including neck, scalp, oropharyngeal region, larynx, and parotid gland, with 5-year survival rates of 55%. Those patients who remain free of tumor for a 2-year period are probably cured, although the IRS study[460] showed that 8% of their patients who were tumor-free at 2 years subsequently developed recurrences. In addition to clinical stage, the prognosis is also related to patient age and histology.[472] RMSs have a tendency to invade bone, and in the head and neck this tendency may result in extensive meningeal involvement. Inadequately treated tumors result in recurrence. Metastases most frequently involve the lungs, bone, and lymph nodes.

Angiosarcoma

Sinonasal or nasopharyngeal angiosarcomas are rare tumors presenting as a mass lesion with or without epistaxis and airway obstruction.[473,474] Angiosarcomas (see also Ch. 3) tend to be nodular or ulcerative, ill-defined lesions with a bluish red color. Histologically, most of these tumors are low-grade, including a proliferation of ramifying and anastomosing vascular channels which dissect through surrounding structures. The endothelial cells lining the vascular spaces are plump, atypical, increased in number, and pile up along the lumen, creating papillations. They demonstrate mitotic activity, including atypical mitoses. The endothelial cells may appear spindled, epithelioid, or polygonal. Immunohistochemical stains assist in the diagnosis; reactivity is identified with either factor VIII-related antigen, CD31 or CD34. Epithelioid angiosarcomas may be cytokeratin-positive, potentially creating diagnostic problems with carcinoma. Rare examples of epithelioid hemangioendotheliomas may occur in the sinonasal tract.[475] Complete surgical excision is the treatment of choice, especially with well-delineated and solitary tumors. Radiotherapy and chemotherapy may be of benefit in multifocal, ill-defined tumors.

Kaposi's sarcoma

Kaposi's sarcoma is a malignant vascular neoplasm that occurs in three principal forms: (1) classic (endemic); (2) epidemic;

or (3) acquired immunodeficiency syndrome (AIDS)-related, and transplantation-associated (see Ch. 3). Sinonasal or nasopharyngeal involvement is uncommon and usually only occurs in patients with AIDS.[476–478] In this form of Kaposi's sarcoma, the tumor appears as a blue-red or violaceous mucosal papule or nodule, and may simulate the appearance of a benign vascular proliferation.[479] Histologically, the tumor is usually of nodular type, being composed of uniform eosinophilic spindle cells in a fascicular pattern. Scattered mitotic figures can be identified. Separating the spindle cell proliferation are slit-like spaces containing erythrocytes. Intra- and extracellular diastase-resistant, PAS-positive hyaline globules can be seen. Immunoreactivity for CD34 and CD31 is usually present. Immunohistochemical positivity for HHV-8 supports the diagnosis of KS.[480] The presence of HHV-8 in nasal secretions and saliva by PCR indicates frequent shedding of multiple herpesviruses in nasal secretions and saliva, particularly in Kaposi's sarcoma patients.[481,482] Surgery is not generally utilized in treatment other than for diagnostic purposes.

Leiomyosarcoma

Up to 10% of all leiomyosarcomas arise in the head and neck.[483] In the sinonasal tract, leiomyosarcomas occur in adults; there is no gender predilection. These tumors present with nasal obstruction, pain, and epistaxis. Sinonasal leiomyosarcomas are circumscribed but not encapsulated, polypoid, or sessile masses, usually measuring >5 cm in diameter.[484] Histologically, they are cellular neoplasms comparable to leiomyosarcomas at other locations (see Ch. 24). Focal infiltrative growth is seen, as is an increase in mitotic activity (>4/10 hpf) and foci of necrosis.[104] Strong and intense immunoreactivity can be seen with actins (smooth muscle and muscle-specific), desmin and h-caldesmon. Epithelioid morphology and myxomatous change may be seen and occasionally may predominate.[484] Wide surgical resection is the treatment of choice. Adjuvant therapy (radio- and chemotherapy) is of questionable utility. The prognosis is dependent on the site and extent of tumor and is not contingent on the histology.[484] Tumors limited to the nasal cavity are associated with a good prognosis and are cured following complete removal.[104,484] Those tumors involving both the nasal cavity and paranasal sinuses tend to behave aggressively with increased recurrence, morbidity, and mortality rates.[484]

Osteosarcoma (osteogenic sarcoma)

Up to 10% of conventional osteosarcomas occur in the head and neck region.[485,486] Craniofacial osteosarcomas (excluding those arising in the setting of Paget's disease) have an equal gender predilection and occur in patients who are generally a decade or two older than those with extrafacial osteosarcomas.[487,488] The jaws are most commonly affected, the mandible being more often involved than the maxilla.[485–487] The most common clinical complaints include painful swelling of the face, dentition problems, nasal obstruction, and epistaxis. Radiographically, osteosarcomas are destructive, poorly delineated, osteolytic, osteosclerotic, or mixed lesions.

The gross appearance of osteosarcoma depends on the extent of mineralization as compared to the extent of the stromal component. As such, osteosarcomas vary from firm, hard, and gritty to fleshy and fibrous. The histopathologic features of osteosarcoma in the head and neck are comparable to those at other locations (see Ch. 25). The prognosis in osteosarcoma does not correlate with the histologic subclassification.[489,490]

Osteosarcomas of the head and neck are aggressive tumors that are prone to local recurrence and distant metastasis.[488] Multimodality therapy, including complete surgical excision with adjunctive radiation and chemotherapy, offers the best chance to control disease as compared to surgery alone.[488] Craniofacial osteosarcomas are associated with a better prognosis than extrafacial tumors.[486,489] This has been attributed to their tendency to remain localized with metastatic spread only late in the disease course, and a lower histologic grade. In spite of the overall better prognosis of craniofacial osteosarcomas, these are still potentially lethal tumors requiring radical management. The overall 5-year survival rate is no better than 35%.[486,489,491] Osteosarcomas arising in Paget's disease are highly malignant, with negligible 5-year survival rates.

Chondrosarcoma

The proportion of chondrosarcomas arising at head and neck sites varies from 5 to 12%.[492,493] In the head and neck, chondrosarcomas are slightly more common in men than in women and primarily occur in the fourth to seventh decades of life. Approximately 2% of chondrosarcomas occur in patients under 20 years of age.[492–495] The most common site of occurrence in the head and neck is the larynx; chondrosarcomas occur in virtually all other sites in which cartilage is found but primarily occur in the craniofacial area, including the mandible, maxilla, and maxillofacial skeleton (nose and paranasal sinuses), as well as base of skull and the nasopharynx.[492,494,496,497] Symptoms vary according to the site of origin. Craniofacial chondrosarcomas may cause nasal obstruction, epistaxis, changes in dentition (loosening or eruption of teeth), proptosis, visual disturbances, and an expanding mass associated with pain, trismus, headaches, and neurologic deficits. The radiologic appearance of craniofacial chondrosarcomas is that of a destructive lesion with single or multiple radiolucent, radiopaque, or mixed-appearing areas, and coarse calcifications. The radiographic appearance may correlate with histologic grade.[498]

The gross appearance of chondrosarcoma is that of a smooth, lobulated, hard submucosal mass larger than 2 cm in diameter. Histologically, chondrosarcomas are lobulated, hypercellular tumors composed of cells with hyperchromatic, pleomorphic nuclei, which are binucleated or multinucleated, have prominent nucleoli, and have increased mitotic activity. The appearances are comparable to those of chondrosarcomas at other locations (see Ch. 25) and grade I lesions are most common in the head and neck region. Histologic variants of chondrosarcoma, including dedifferentiated chondrosarcoma, mesenchymal chondrosarcoma, and clear cell chondrosarcoma, are rare in the sinonasal tract and nasopharynx.

For maxillofacial chondrosarcomas, radical resection with adequate margins is indicated.[496] In these sites, chondrosarcoma is a slow-growing but persistent tumor characterized by multiple recurrences. Maxillofacial chondrosarcomas are more lethal than laryngeal chondrosarcoma, perhaps because they tend to be of a histologically higher grade,[496] but more likely due to their proximity to vital structures and the difficulty in achieving negative margins. Death is generally due to uncontrolled local disease with invasion and destruction of vital structures, including intracranial extension. The overall 5-year survival rate for head and neck chondrosarcoma is approximately 70%.[493,494]

Chordoma

Chordomas (see Ch. 25) are more common in men than in women and can occur at any age but are generally uncommon below the fourth decade of life. Craniocervical chordomas are identified most frequently in the dorsum sella, clivus, and naso-pharyngeal regions.[499] Symptoms vary according to the site of occurrence and extent of tumor and include diplopia, visual field defects, headaches, pain, nasal obstruction, epistaxis, nasal discharge, soft tissue mass, and endocrinopathies (secondary to destruction of the sella turcica). The radio-graphic appearance is that of an expansile and destructive osteolytic lesion, often associated with a soft tissue mass.

Chordomas are well-demarcated or encapsulated, soft, mucoid or gelatinous tumors with a variegated appearance, including solid and cystic areas. Histologically, chordomas are similar to those at more common spinal locations (see Ch. 25) and most often contain characteristic physaliferous cells (Fig. 4A.43). Immunoreactivity is seen with cytokeratin, EMA, and S-100 protein (Fig. 4A.43).[500,501] Complete surgical excision is the treatment of choice. The 5-year survival rate for patients under 40 years is 100% as compared with 22% for patients over 40 years of age.[501]

Malignant teratoma (teratocarcinosarcoma)

Malignant teratoma of the sinonasal tract is a rare tumor showing combined histologic features of carcinosarcoma and teratoma.[502,503] These tumors occur in adults with a male predominance and median age of 60 years. Sinonasal malig-nant teratomas are rapidly growing neoplasms. The most common site of involvement is the nasal cavity; other sites of involvement include the ethmoid and maxillary sinuses. Symptoms include nasal obstruction and epistaxis. These tumors are friable to firm, red-brown masses. Histologically, malignant teratomas are characterized by a combination of epithelial and mesenchymal tissue components with very variable growth patterns.[502] The epithelial components include glandular or ductal structures lined by benign-appearing partly ciliated columnar epithelium with transitional areas to non-keratinizing squamous epithelium, with or without clear cells. In addition, areas of squamous carcinoma and adeno-carcinoma are present. The mesenchymal components may include fibroblasts or myofibroblasts of variably benign or malignant appearance, RMS, benign cartilage with an imma-ture appearance, and chondrosarcoma, or osteogenic tissue. The teratoid components include "fetal-appearing" clear cell squamous epithelium, organoid structures, or neural tissue in the form of neural rosettes and neurofibrillary matrix. The "fetal-appearing" clear cell squamous epithelium represents a characteristic histologic finding in this entity and is supportive evidence of the teratoid nature of this neoplasm, given its description in teratomas of other organ systems.[502] Foci of seminoma, germinoma, choriocarcinoma, or embryonal carci-

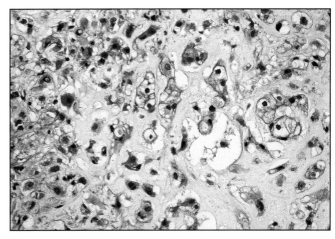

A

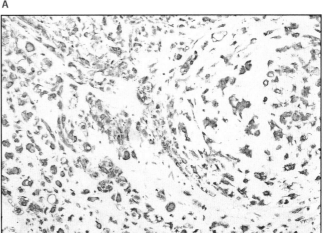

B

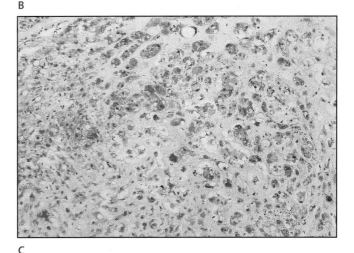

C

Fig. 4A.43 • Nasopharyngeal chordoma. (**A**) The neoplastic cells are epithelioid with vesicular nuclei and abundant granular to vacuolated cytoplasm. The vacuolization corresponds to the presence of glycogen or mucus; when extensive it can produce a soap-bubble appearance, compressing the nucleus and creating the characteristic physaliferous cells; neoplastic cells are immunoreactive for (**B**) cytokeratin and (**C**) S-100 protein.

noma have not been found in association with these tumors. Immunohistochemical staining is dependent on the cell type: epithelial components are cytokeratin and EMA-positive; neural components are NSE, CD99, chromogranin, synapto-physin, GFAP, and S-100 protein-positive; mesenchymal components are vimentin-positive and, depending on cell type, may be reactive for myogenic markers or smooth muscle actin.[503,504] Sinonasal malignant teratomas are highly malignant neoplasms with an average survival of less than 2 years.[502] Aggressive therapy, including radical surgical extirpation and irradiation, is indicated.[505] Recurrence of tumor is common with extensive local invasion. Metastasis occurs, primarily to cervical lymph nodes.

Miscellaneous tumors

Other malignant tumors that may arise from the sinonasal tract or nasopharynx include lipogenic neoplasms,[506,507] synovial sarcoma,[508] alveolar soft-part sarcoma,[509] peripheral (primitive) neuroectodermal tumor/extraosseous Ewing's sarcoma,[510–513] and endodermal sinus tumor.[514,515]

Secondary tumors

Metastatic tumors to the sinonasal tract and nasopharynx may represent the initial manifestation of disease or the first known site of metastatic tumor. More often, metastasis to the UADT is part of widely metastatic disease. While virtually every conceivable malignancy may metastasize to the UADT, the most common primary tumor metastatic to this region is renal cell carcinoma.[516–518]

Pseudoneoplastic lesions

Sinonasal (inflammatory) polyps

Sinonasal inflammatory polyps are non-neoplastic inflammatory swellings of the sinonasal mucosa. There is no gender predilection; sinonasal polyps occur at all ages but are commonly seen in adults over 20 years of age and rarely seen in children less than 5 years of age.[519] The exception to this age restriction occurs in patients with cystic fibrosis, who develop nasal polyps in the first and second decades of life.[520] Most polyps arise from the lateral nasal wall or from the ethmoid recess. Not infrequently, involvement of both the nasal cavity and paranasal sinuses occurs. Polyps may be unilateral or bilateral, single or multiple. Symptoms include nasal obstruction, rhinorrhea, and headaches. The triad of nasal polyps, asthma, and aspirin intolerance is well recognized.[521] The etiology is linked to multiple factors, including allergy, cystic fibrosis, infections, diabetes mellitus, and aspirin intolerance.

Antrochoanal polyps are sinonasal polyps specifically arising from the maxillary sinus antrum.[522] They represent approximately 3–6% of all sinonasal polyps.[523] Antrochoanal polyps are more common in men than in women and primarily occur in younger patients than those with nasal polyps. The majority of antrochoanal polyps are single, unilateral lesions with associated nasal obstruction. Posterior extension from the maxillary sinus toward the nasopharynx may result in obstruction of the nasopharynx and clinical suspicion of a primary nasopharyngeal tumor. Antrochoanal polyps are often associated with bilateral maxillary sinusitis and may also be associated with more typical sinonasal polyps. In up to 40% of cases there may be a documented history of allergies.[523,524]

The radiologic appearance of sinonasal inflammatory polyps includes soft tissue densities, air–fluid levels, mucosal thickening, and opacification of the paranasal sinuses. When extensive, inflammatory polyps may expand and even destroy bone. Antrochoanal polyps appear as a soft tissue density in the posterior choanal region or in the nasopharynx with clouding or opacification of the maxillary sinus.

Sinonasal polyps are soft, fleshy, polypoid lesions with a myxoid or mucoid appearance. Polyps vary in size, ranging up to several centimeters in diameter. Antrochoanal polyps are identical to other nasal polyps except for the presence of a stalk with attachment to the maxillary sinus. Histologically, the surface epithelium is composed of intact respiratory epithelium but may show squamous metaplasia. The basement membrane may be thickened and eosinophilic in appearance. The stroma is markedly edematous and is noteworthy for the absence of mucoserous glands. A mixed chronic inflammatory cell infiltrate is present and is predominantly composed of eosinophils, plasma cells, and lymphocytes. Neutrophils may predominate in polyps of infectious origin. The stroma contains bland-appearing fibroblasts and small to medium-sized blood vessels. Secondary changes include surface ulceration, fibrosis, infarction, granulation tissue, deposition of an amyloid-like stroma, osseous and/or cartilaginous metaplasia, glandular hyperplasia, granuloma formation, and atypical stromal cells. Granulomas result from ruptured mucous cysts, cholesterol granulomas, or as a reaction to medicinal intranasal injections (steroids) or inhalants. Atypical stromal cells can be seen in sinonasal and antrochoanal polyps but tend to be more common in the latter. These atypical cells are bizarre-appearing cells with enlarged, pleomorphic and hyperchromatic nuclei, indistinct to prominent nucleoli, and eosinophilic to basophilic-appearing cytoplasm (Fig. 4A.44). These cells tend to cluster near areas of tissue injury (e.g., near thrombosed vascular spaces). The atypical stromal cells may be confused with malignant cells (e.g., rhabdomyoblasts) but their localization to limited areas of the lesion, coupled with the absence of an increased nuclear-to-cytoplasmic ratio, increased mitoses, or cross-striations, should preclude a diagnosis of malignancy. These cells are of myofibroblastic origin and likely represent a component of wound-healing.[524]

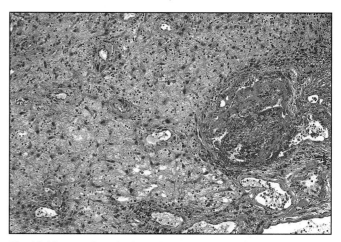

Fig. 4A.44 • Antrochoanal polyp with associated atypical stromal cells. The atypical stromal cells (i.e., myofibroblasts) have enlarged, pleomorphic and hyperchromatic nuclei, indistinct to prominent nucleoli, and eosinophilic to basophilic-appearing fibrillar cytoplasm. These cells are usually focally identified with a tendency to cluster near areas of injury, including thrombosed vascular spaces, as seen at the extreme right of this illustration.

A prominent vascular component, variably termed angio-matous[525] or angioectatic[526] nasal polyps, may clinically and histologically simulate a malignant tumor. These lesions may undergo infarction or be associated with acellular eosinophilic material simulating amyloid deposition.[526]

Identification and treatment of possible etiologic factor(s) is the initial approach in the treatment of sinonasal polyps. Surgical excision includes polypectomy for nasal polyps and medial maxillectomy (Caldwell–Luc procedure) to include removal of the stalk for antrochoanal polyps. Approximately 50% of patients will have recurrence of their nasal polyps following surgery; recurrence rates are highest in patients with aspirin intolerance and asthma.[519] A high recurrence rate also occurs in antrochoanal polyps, especially in patients with a history of allergies; endoscopic removal may result in a higher recurrence rate.[527] Surgical removal of the polyp with its stalk markedly decreases the likelihood of recurrence.

Heterotopic central nervous system tissue (glial heterotopias, nasal glioma)

Heterotopic central nervous system tissue (HCNST) is thought to represent non-neoplastic displacement of neuroglial tissue in extracranial sites (see Ch. 27). Glial heterotopias are generally considered to represent a variant of encephalocele in which the communication to the central nervous system has closed, remains undetected, or has become fibrotic. HCNSTs generally present at birth or within the first few years of life, although any age group may be affected.[528] In the sinonasal tract and nasopharynx, HCNST most commonly occurs in and around the nasal cavity but may involve the ethmoid sinus, nasopharyngeal, and pharyngeal areas.[529] Subcutaneous lesions appear as a blue or red mass along the bridge of the nose. Intranasal lesions present with nasal obstruction, respiratory distress, epistaxis, septal deviation, cerebrospinal fluid rhinorrhea, or meningitis. Intranasal lesions may be con-fused with nasal polyps. Mixed extra- and intranasal HCNST occur and develop via a communication through a defect in the nasal bone. The Furstenberg test, in which there is swelling or pulsation of the lesion following pressure on the ipsilateral jugular vein, is typically positive in an encephalocele and negative in HCNST. Radiographic studies, especially MRI, are indicated in order to rule out a bony defect which may identify communication to the cranial cavity (encephalocele).[530]

Histologically, HCNSTs are composed of astrocytes and neuroglial fibers associated with a fibrous, vascularized con-nective tissue. Reactive astrocytes, including multinucleated or gemistocytic astrocytes, may be present. Neurons are sparse to absent. In long-standing clinically undetected cases, a fibrous stroma may predominate and obscure the astrocytes and neuroglial fibers. In contrast to the nasal lesions, those of the nasopharynx may include the presence of ependymal elements as well as intracytoplasmic melanin.[529] Immunohistochemically, reactivity will be identified with GFAP and S-100 protein.[531] Surgery is the treatment of choice and is curative.

Respiratory epithelial adenomatoid hamartoma

Respiratory epithelial adenomatoid hamartoma is an uncommon benign non-neoplastic overgrowth of indigenous glands of the nasal cavity, paranasal sinuses, or nasopharynx, arising from the surface epithelium and devoid of ectodermal, neuroectodermal, and/or mesodermal elements.[532,533] The majority of hamartomas of this region are of the pure epi-thelial type.[533] Mesenchymal hamartomas or mixed epithelial–mesenchymal hamartomas may occur[532–534] Respiratory epithelial adenomatoid hamartomas predominantly occur in adult patients with a decided male predominance; patients range in age from the third to ninth decades of life, with a reported median age in the sixth decade.[533] The majority of respiratory epithelial adenomoid hamartomas occur in the nasal cavity, in particular the posterior nasal septum; involve-ment of other intranasal sites occurs less often and may be identified along the lateral nasal wall, middle meatus, and inferior turbinate.[533] Other sites of involvement include the nasopharynx, ethmoid sinus, and frontal sinus. The majority of lesions are unilateral but occasionally bilateral lesions may occur. Patients present with nasal obstruction or stuffiness, deviated septum, epistaxis, and chronic (recurrent) rhinosinusitis. The symptoms may occur over months to years.

The hamartoma appears as a polypoid mass lesion with a slightly more indurated quality than an inflammatory polyp.[532] Histologically, these lesions are characterized by a prominent glandular proliferation composed of widely spaced, small to medium-sized glands separated by stromal tissue. In areas the glands are seen arising in direct continuity with the surface epithelium, which invaginates downward into the submucosa (Fig. 4A.45). The glands are round to oval and are composed of multilayered ciliated respiratory epithelium, often with admixed mucin-secreting (goblet) cells. A characteristic find-ing is the presence of stromal hyalinization with envelopment of glands by a thick, eosinophilic basement membrane. Small reactive-appearing seromucinous glands can be seen. The stroma is edematous or fibrous, containing a mixed chronic inflammatory cell infiltrate.

Additional findings that can be found in association with the respiratory epithelial adenomatoid hamartomas include inflammatory sinonasal polyps, hyperplasia, and/or squamous metaplasia of the surface epithelium unrelated to the adenomatoid proliferation, osseous metaplasia, rare associ-ation with inverted-type schneiderian papilloma, and rare association with an SFT.[532]

The differential diagnosis includes schneiderian papilloma of the inverted type and adenocarcinomas. Diagnostic misinterpretation may result in untoward surgical interention. Limited but complete surgical resection is curative.[532]

Teratoid lesions (nasopharyngeal dermoid; nasopharyngeal "hairy polyp")

Teratoid lesions of the nasopharynx are developmental (congenital) anomalies rather than neoplastic lesions; they are predominantly composed of ectodermal structures (e.g., skin) but may also include mesodermal structures (e.g., cartilage) but not endodermal-derived structures.[535] The absence of endodermal-derived structures and the presence of limited heterogeneity of tissue types argue against inclusion as a teratoma. The fact that these lesions contain skin, a tissue type not normally found in the nasopharynx, suggests that they may be better classified as a choristoma rather than a hamartoma, and possibly of first branchial arch origin.[536–538]

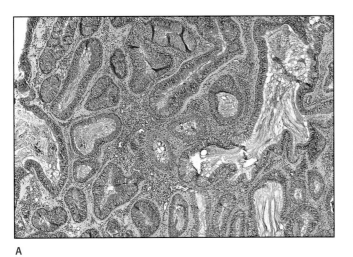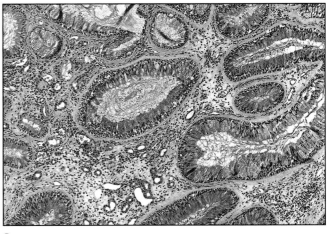

A   B

Fig. 4A.45 • Respiratory epithelial adenomatoid hamartoma. **(A)** These lesions originate from the surface epithelium with invagination and proliferation of glands in the submucosa. **(B)** The glands are lined by ciliated respiratory epithelium with stromal hyalinization characteristically enveloping the adenomatous proliferation; residual minor salivary glands are seen in and around the adenomatoid proliferation.

Some authors argue that these lesions are best classified as a subset of benign teratoma.[539]

Nasopharyngeal dermoids are polypoid, predominantly solid, but partially cystic lesions and may be pedunculated or sessile. Histologically, there is a combination of various ectodermal and mesodermal tissues, including skin (keratinizing squamous epithelium), cutaneous adnexa, cartilage, bone, muscle (striated or smooth), fibrous, or mature adipose tissue. These lesions are polypoid and covered by skin with identification of hair follicles and sebaceous glands within the submucosa. In addition, elastic cartilage is identified. These histologic findings identified in a lesion of the ear have suggested to some authors that these lesions are of branchial cleft origin, representing congenital accessory auricles, akin to accessory tragus.[537] In addition to cartilage, other tissue types found to a varying degree may include muscle (smooth and striated), fibroadipose tissue, and vascular tissue.

Given the definition of these lesions as a non-neoplastic developmental anomaly, the differential diagnosis is primarily with a teratoma. The absence of endodermally derived tissue and absence of the wide variety of tissue types usually seen in teratoma will allow distinction of these lesions. Simple surgical excision is curative.

Nasal chondromesenchymal hamartoma

Nasal chondromesenchymal hamartoma is a tumefactive process of the sinonasal tract comprised of an admixture of chondroid and stromal elements with cystic features, analogous to chest-wall hamartoma.[540] These lesions have some histologic similarities to respiratory epithelial adenomatoid hamartomas and they may be within the spectrum of the same type of lesion. They are distinguished, however, by mostly presenting in the neonatal age group and by a tendency to be larger and more aggressive than the respiratory epithelial adenomatoid hamartomas.[540] Fewer than 20 cases have been reported to date.[540,541] There is a male predilection. Most of these lesions occur in newborns within the first 3 months of life but they may also occur in the second decade of life,[539,539a] or even in adults.[539a] Patients present with respiratory difficulty

and an intranasal mass or facial swelling may be evident. Some of these tumors have eroded into the cranial cavity (through the cribriform plate area), a finding that may simulate the appearance of a meningoencephalocele.[542]

Histologically, these lesions are characterized by the presence of nodules of cartilage, varying in size, shape, and contour. Further, the degree of differentiation varies, with some nodules appearing similar to the chondromyxomatous nodules of chondromyxoid fibroma while others are composed of well-differentiated cartilage. A loose spindle cell stroma or abrupt transition to hypocellular fibrous stroma is present at the periphery of the cartilaginous nodules. Other patterns include a myxoid to spindle cell stroma, fibro-osseous proliferation with cellular stromal component, and ossicles or trabeculae of immature (woven) bone. Additional findings may include focal osteoclast-like giant cells in the stroma, and erythrocyte-filled spaces resembling those of an aneurysmal bone cyst.[540,543] Proliferating epithelial elements are not a prominent feature. The chondromesenchymal elements are relatively cellular and "immature," probably reflecting the immature age of the patients. For these reasons, the lesions deserve recognition as a distinct clinicopathologic subgroup of nasal hamartomas.

Lymphangiomatous polyp of the tonsil (lymphoid polyp)

Lymphangiomatous polyps are non-neoplastic developmental lesions comprised of tissue elements native to the nasopharynx and categorized as a hamartoma.[544] Lymphangiomatous polyps are considered uncommon. There is an equal gender predilection; they occur over a wide age range from the first to the seventh decades, with a mean age of 25 years.[544] The clinical presentation includes dysphagia, sore throat, and the sensation of a mass lesion in the throat. Symptoms may be present from a few weeks to years. These lesions are unilateral without side predilection. The majority are of palatine tonsil origin but occasionally they may originate from the nasopharynx or from the nasopharyngeal tonsil (i.e., adenoids).[544]

The majority of these lesions are polypoid or pedunculated with a smooth external surface, spongy to firm consistency. On cut section they have a white, tan, or yellow appearance measuring 0.5–3.8 cm in greatest dimension. Some lesions are sessile. The polyps are covered by squamous or respiratory epithelium composed of a submucosal proliferation of dilated lymphatic vascular channels and varying amounts of fibrous connective tissue. The vascular components are thin-walled and usually contain proteinaceous fluid and mature lymphocytes. In addition, mature adipose tissue may be present and prominent fibrosis may dominate in any given lesion.

Additional findings that can be identified include epithelial hyperplasia, hyperkeratosis, and dyskeratosis without epithelial dysplasia or intraepithelial lymphocytes.[544]

Special stains are not usually required for the diagnosis. Simple surgical excision usually in the form of a unilateral tonsillectomy is curative. The differential diagnosis includes nasopharyngeal (juvenile) angiofibroma, fibroepithelial polyps, papillomas, and lymphangioma.

Sinonasal and nasopharyngeal infectious diseases

Infectious diseases of the sinonasal tract and nasopharynx may clinically simulate the appearance of a neoplastic disease. Some of the more common infections of these areas include fungal disease such as aspergillosis,[545,546] rhinosporidiosis,[547] and mucormycosis,[548] bacterial diseases such as rhinoscleroma[549] and *Pseudomonas aeruginosa* causing a bacterial ball (botryomycosis),[550] and mycobacterial diseases such as leprosy and tuberculosis. Sarcoidosis, a non-caseating granulomatous disease of uncertain etiology, may involve the nasal cavity as part of systemic involvement or as an isolated occurrence.[551] In the immunocompromised patient, viral diseases such as herpes simplex, cytomegalovirus and HIV,[552] and protozoa such as microsporidiosis[553] may produce ulcerative and/or mass lesions of the sinonasal cavity or nasopharynx that clinically simulate a neoplasm (see below). Infectious mononucleosis is a systemic, benign, self-limiting lymphoproliferative disease that may result in enlargement of the nasopharyngeal tonsils (adenoids) or palatine tonsils that clinically and histologically simulates a neoplasm (i.e., malignant lymphoma). Infectious mononucleosis primarily affects adolescents and young adults. Infectious mononucleosis is usually caused by EBV infection but very similar pathology may be caused by other microorganisms, including *Toxoplasma gondii*, rubella, hepatitis A virus, and adenoviruses.

Myospherulosis, a pseudomycotic mass, is a reactive phenomenon that results from the alteration of red blood cells following interaction with petrolatum-based ointments found in surgical packing material.[554]

Human immunodeficiency virus infection of Waldeyer's tonsillar tissues

HIV infection may first present clinically as enlargement of the lymphoid tissues of Waldeyer's ring, including the tonsils and adenoids.[552] These tissues are a major site of viral replication. Primary HIV infection results in a spectrum of histopathologic changes that may represent the initial manifestation of HIV infection in otherwise asymptomatic patients. The clinical enlargement of tonsillar and particularly nasopharyngeal lymphoid tissue (adenoids) may represent the earliest clinical manifestation of HIV.[552] Clinically the enlargement may be unilateral and raise concern for a possible diagnosis of lymphoma.

The presence of HIV in these tissues causes a unique constellation of diagnostic features, including florid follicular hyperplasia, follicle lysis, and productively HIV-infected multinucleate giant cells. Serologic evaluation is confirmatory of HIV infection. The histomorphologic changes in HIV-induced tonsillar and adenoidal enlargement vary with the progression of disease. In the early stages of infection, the histomorphology may include florid follicular hyperplasia with and without follicular fragmentation, and follicle lysis with areas of follicular involution (Fig. 4A.46). Additional findings include the presence of monocytoid B-cell hyperplasia, paracortical and interfollicular zone expansion with immunoblasts and plasma cells, interfollicular clusters of high endothelial venules, intrafollicular hemorrhage, and the presence of multinucleate giant

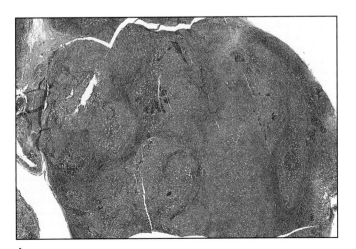

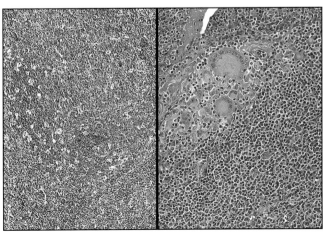

Fig. 4A.46 • Human immunodeficiency virus (HIV) infection of the tonsils. **(A)** Florid follicular hyperplasia; **(B)** left panel: follicle lysis with attenuation and loss of mantle lymphocytes; right panel: clustering of multinucleated giant cells near surface (and/or crypt) epithelium.

cells (Fig. 4A.46). The giant cells characteristically cluster adjacent to or within the adenoidal surface epithelium or the tonsillar crypt epithelium.

The histologic features in patients with more advanced stages of disease contrast with those described above and correlate with the lymphoid obliteration seen in the terminal stages of HIV infection or AIDS. In these cases, there is effacement of nodal architecture, loss of the normal lymphoid cell population with replacement by a benign plasma cell infiltrate, and the presence of increased vascularity. The multinucleate giant cells characteristically seen in the early and chronic stages of disease are not identified in the more advanced stages of HIV infection.

Reactivity for HIV p24 (gag protein), an indicator of active HIV infection, is consistently identified in the early and chronic stages of disease Anti-HIV p24 reactivity is seen within the follicular dendritic cell network of the germinal centers, in scattered interfollicular lymphocytes, in the multinucleate giant cells, and within intraepithelial cells of crypt epithelium. The HIV p24-positive intraepithelial cells are S-100 protein (a dendritic cell marker) positive and their morphologic appearance fits well with the appearance of dendritic cells.

Wegener's granulomatosis (WG)

WG is a systemic necrotizing vasculitis that typically involves the kidneys, lung, and UADT. The classic definition of WG includes involvement of the head and neck region, the lung, and the kidney.[555,556] It should be noted that the majority of WG patients do not exhibit this classic clinical triad simultaneously at the time of initial presentation. WG may present as an isolated disease confined to the sinonasal tract without systemic involvement; sinonasal involvement may represent the initial manifestation of systemic disease.[557,558] The etiology of WG remains unknown.

WG may be systemic or limited (localized). The extent of disease is reflected in the clinical manifestations such that limited or localized disease may be asymptomatic while, in systemic disease, the patient is always sick. WG may progress from limited to systemic involvement or may remain limited or even regress with treatment. The ELK classification[555] of WG includes:

E = ear, nose, and throat involvement
L = lung involvement
K = kidney involvement

Patients with E or EL disease are considered to have the limited form of WG while patients with ELK disease correspond to systemic WG. The incidence of limited WG varies from 29 to 58%.[555] Localized WG of the UADT tends to affect men more than women (except for laryngeal WG which is predominantly a disease of women). WG occurs over a wide age range, with the average age of occurrence in the fourth and fifth decades of life. WG is infrequent in patients less than 10 years of age. In the UADT, the most common site of occurrence is the sinonasal region (nasal cavity > maxillary > ethmoid > frontal > sphenoid); other sites of involvement may include the nasopharynx, larynx (subglottis), oral cavity, ear (external and middle ear, including the mastoid), and salivary glands. WG of the sinonasal tract and nasopharyngeal

region may present with sinusitis with or without purulent rhinorrhea, obstruction, septal perforation, pain, epistaxis, anosmia, and headaches. An important laboratory finding in WG is an elevated ANCA. WG is characteristically associated with cytoplasmic (C-ANCA) and only infrequently with perinuclear (P-ANCA).[557–559] C-ANCA is of greater specificity than P-ANCA. The sensitivity of the test varies with the extent of disease: 50–67% of patients with limited disease are C-ANCA-positive, while 60–100% of those with systemic disease are positive.[558,560] A negative test does not rule out WG. Although identified in other vasculitides[561] and in inflammatory bowel disease and hepatobiliary diseases,[562,563] ANCA titers are elevated in WG but are not elevated in infections or in lymphomas.

The head and neck manifestations of WG are dominated by nasal cavity and paranasal sinus involvement. The clinical appearance is that of diffuse mucosal swelling with ulcerative and crusted lesions and tissue destruction; in advanced cases, septal perforation may be seen, resulting in a "saddle-nose" deformity. In view of the destructive nature of many lesions of WG, a clinical suspicion of malignancy is sometimes raised.

The histologic features include the classic triad of vasculitis, tissue necrosis, and granulomatous inflammation (which may involve vessel walls as well as the supporting tissues) (Fig. 4A.47). In practice, however, it has become apparent that finding all three of these "characteristic" features in a single biopsy or even a series of biopsies is actually very uncommon.[564] Vasculitis involving small to medium-sized arteries consists of a polymorphous inflammatory infiltrate composed of lymphocytes and histiocytes and, less often, eosinophils and polymorphonuclear leukocytes. Necrosis is "ischemic"- or "geographic"-type with a basophilic smudgy appearance. Granulomatous inflammation in the form of scattered multinucleate giant cells is the typical appearance and well-formed granulomas are not a common finding in UADT WG. The parenchymal inflammatory infiltrate in WG is typically mixed, being composed predominantly of lymphocytes, histiocytes, plasma cells, and neutrophils; eosinophils, while generally uncommon, may be numerous in an occasional case.

Elastic stains may assist in the identification of vasculitis. The key histologic differential diagnostic considerations are infectious and neoplastic. A granulomatous response to an infectious process (e.g., fungal, mycobacterial, parasitic) must be ruled out. As a result, the exclusion of infectious agents by tissue stains and culture should form a part of the basic evaluation of all patients with suspected WG. A granulomatous response to some foreign material (e.g., myospherulosis) likewise may be a consideration in some biopsies and so examination of the tissues for polarizable foreign material is recommended in all cases of suspected WG.

Since some sinonasal NK/T-cell lymphomas are angiocentric, the vessel infiltrate can be mistaken for the vasculitis of WG (Table 4A.11). The cytologic characteristics of the lymphoid infiltrate often permit distinction between the two entities. In general, the lymphoid infiltrates in WG lack cytologic atypia. Atypia is characteristic of the tumor cells of malignant lymphoma. In view of the fact that some degree of subjectivity may enter into the recognition of lymphoid atypia by light microscopic features alone, demonstration of monoclonality by immunohistochemical or molecular biologic studies may be helpful. Typically, the inflammatory infiltrate

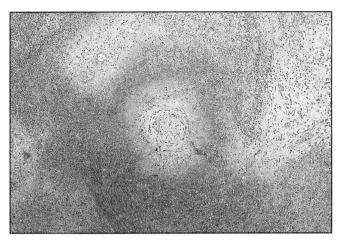

A

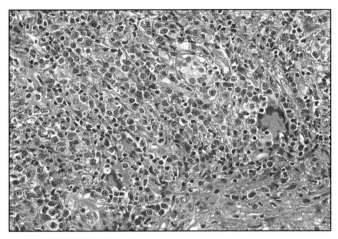

B

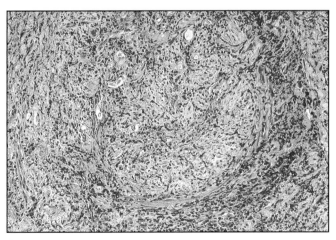

C

Fig. 4A.47 • Wegener's granulomatosis of the sinonasal tract. (A) At low magnification the changes include the presence of multifocal necrosis ("geographic or ischemic-type" necrosis) with a basophilic smudgy appearance surrounding an obliterated vascular space in the center of the illustration. (B) The inflammatory cell infiltrate of Wegener's granulomatosis is polymorphous, composed of a variable admixture of mature lymphocytes, plasma cells, histiocytes, eosinophils, and neutrophils without evidence of atypical or overtly malignant cells; in all the illustrations there are isolated multinucleated giant cells representing the granulomatous component of the disease ("poor man's" granuloma) since well-formed granulomas are typically not identified. (C) Vasculitis, a potentially difficult finding on histology, is seen here with the inflammatory infiltrate concentrically surrounding a blood vessel (angiocentric) and invading through the wall (angioinvasion) with occlusive changes of the endothelial-lined lumen.

of WG will be polymorphic and show reactivity with both B-cell and T-cell lineage markers. In sinonasal malignant lymphomas, a monomorphic infiltrate is usually seen and lineage markers will typically show B- or T-cell lineage specificity. Further, the presence of microabscesses and scattered giant cells of WG and elevated C-ANCA levels would not be expected in malignant lymphoma. Since the inflammatory infiltrate in WG can include appreciable numbers of eosinophils, the question of Churg–Strauss granulomatosis may arise (Table 4A.11). Churg–Strauss disease (allergic granulomatosis and vasculitis) is characterized by asthma, systemic vasculitis, and tissue and peripheral eosinophilia. These findings should assist in the differential diagnosis of WG. Since elevated ANCA levels have been reported in Churg–Strauss disease,[565,566] this finding cannot be used to differentiated Churg–Strauss disease from WG. It should be kept in mind that Churg–Strauss disease is not expected to present clinically as a sinonasal disorder and the chance of this happening is extremely remote.

Extranodal sinus histiocytosis with massive lymphadenopathy (Rosai–Dorfman disease)

Sinus histiocytosis with massive lymphadenopathy (SHML) is an idiopathic, nodal-based histiocytic proliferative disorder that usually resolves spontaneously.[567–569] Immunophenotypic studies support the interpretation that the SHML cells are part of the mononuclear phagocyte and immunoregulatory effector (M-PIRE) system belonging to the macrophage/histiocytic family.[570] SHML may occur as part of a generalized process involving lymph nodes or may involve extranodal sites independent of the lymph node status.[571] The head and neck region is one of the extranodal areas more commonly affected by SHML.[569,571] Within the head and neck, there is predilection for the nasal cavity and paranasal sinuses.[571] Sinonasal tract involvement results in a polypoid, nodular, or exophytic mass producing nasal obstruction and simulating a neoplasm. The histopathologic features include the presence in the submucosa of lymphoid aggregates alternating with pale-appearing areas composed of histiocytes, lymphocytes, and plasma cells diffusely involving the submucosa. The characteristic histiocytes (or SHML cells) are characterized by round to oval, vesicular to hyperchromatic nuclei, with abundant amphophilic to eosinophilic, granular, foamy to clear cytoplasm (Fig. 4A.48). The nuclei do not demonstrate nuclear lobation, indentation, or longitudinal grooving as seen in Langerhans cell histiocytes. The histiocytes demonstrate emperipolesis. The phagocytized cells are usually lymphocytes but plasma cells, erythrocytes, and neutrophils can also be seen engulfed within the histiocytic cell cytoplasm. The SHML cells are diffusely S-100 protein-positive. In addition, they may also demonstrate CD68, lysozyme, and MAC-387 immunoreactivity.[571–573] There is no ideal treatment.[574] Treatment protocols should mirror the clinical manifestations. In cases of airway compromise, treatment should be directed at alleviating the obstruction, requiring surgical intervention. Rare deaths have been reported.[575] The etiology of SHML remains obscure. An infectious etiology has been suggested[567,568] but an infectious agent has never been isolated. Other considerations implicated but never substantiated as the cause of SHML include immunodeficiency, autoimmune disease, or a neoplastic process.[569]

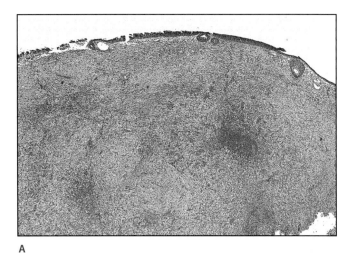
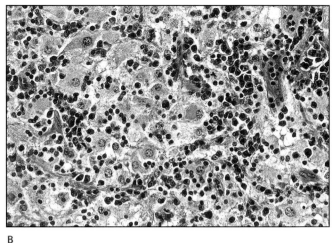

A   B

Fig. 4A.48 • Extranodal sinus histiocytosis with massive lymphadenopathy of the sinonasal tract. **(A)** Submucosal diffuse inflammatory cell infiltrate with effacement of the normal submucosal structures; a benign lymphoid aggregate is present to the right of center that in conjunction with the cellular infiltrate has an architectural appearance reminiscent of that of lymph node parenchyma. **(B)** At higher magnification the infiltrate includes mature lymphocytes and plasma cells that somewhat obscure the histiocytic cell infiltrate; the latter demonstrates phagocytosis of mononuclear cells (emperipolesis).

References

1. Lampertico P, Russel WO, MacComb WS 1963 Squamous papilloma of the upper respiratory epithelium. Arch Pathol 75: 293–302
2. Hyams V J 1971 Papillomas of the nasal cavity and paranasal sinuses: a clinicopathologic study of 315 cases. Ann Otol Rhinol Laryngol 80: 192–206
3. Hyams V J, Batsakis J G, Michaels L 1988 Papilloma of the sinonasal tract. In: Tumors of the upper respiratory tract and ear, series 2, fascicle 25. Armed Forces Institute of Pathology, Washington, DC, p 34–44
4. Joseph M, Carroll E, Goodman M L et al. 1980 Inverted papilloma of the nasal septum. Arch Otolaryngol 106: 767–771
5. Christensen W N, Smith R R L 1986 Schneiderian papillomas: a clinicopathologic study of 67 cases. Hum Pathol 17: 393–400
6. Lawson W, Le Benger J, Som P et al. 1989 Inverted papilloma: an analysis of 87 cases. Laryngoscope 99: 1117–1124
7. Siivonen L, Virolainen E 1989 Transitional papillomas of the nasal cavity and paranasal sinuses. ORL J Otorhinolaryngol Relat Spec 51: 262–267
8. Lawson W, Ho B T, Shaari C M et al. 1995 Inverted papilloma: A report of 112 cases. Laryngoscope 105: 282–288
9. Buchwald C, Franzmann M-B, Tos M 1995 Sinonasal papillomas: a report of 82 cases in Copenhagen county, including a longitudinal clinical study. Laryngoscope 105: 72–79
10. Peters BW, O'Reilly RC, Wilcox TO Jr et al. 1995 Inverted papilloma isolated to the sphenoid sinus. Otolaryngol Head Neck Surg 113: 771–781
11. Brandwein M, Steinberg B, Thung S et al. 1989 Human papillomavirus 6/11 and 16/18 in schneiderian inverted papillomas: in situ hybridization with human papillomavirus RNA probes. Cancer 63: 1708–1713
12. Judd R, Zaki S R, Coffield L M et al. 1991 Sinonasal papillomas and human papillomavirus: human papillomavirus 11 detected in fungiform Schneiderian papillomas by in situ hybridization and polymerase chain reaction. Hum Pathol 22: 550–556
13. Sarkar F H, Visscher D W, Kintanar E B et al. 1992 Sinonasal Schneiderian papillomas: human papillomavirus typing by polymerase chain reaction. Mod Pathol 5: 329–332
14. Buchwald C, Franzmann M-B, Jacobsen G K et al. 1995 Human papillomavirus (HPV) in sinonasal papillomas: a study of 78 cases using in situ hybridization and polymerase chain reaction. Laryngoscope 105: 66–71
15. Harris M O, Beck J C, Terrell J E et al. 1998 Expression of human papillomavirus 6 in inverted papilloma arising in a renal transplant patient. Laryngoscope 108: 115–119
16. Barnes L 2002. Schneiderian papillomas and nonsalivary glandular neoplasms of the head and neck. Mod Pathol 15: 279–297
17. Macdonald M R, Le K T, Freeman J et al. 1995 A majority of inverted sinonasal papillomas carries Epstein–Barr virus genomes. Cancer 75: 2307–2312
18. Gaffey M J, Frierson H F, Weiss L M et al. 1996 Human papillomavirus and Epstein–Barr virus in sinonasal Schneiderian papillomas. An in situ hybridization and polymerase chain reaction study. Am J Clin Pathol 106: 475–482
19. Myers E N, Fernau J L, Johnson J T et al. 1990 Management of inverted papilloma. Laryngoscope 100: 481–490
20. Mendenhall W M, Million R R, Cassisi N J et al. 1985 Biologically aggressive papillomas of the nasal cavity: the role of radiation therapy. Laryngoscope 134: 73–79
21. Klemi P J, Joensu H, Siivonen L et al. 1989 Association of DNA aneuploidy with human papillomavirus-induced malignant transformation of sinonasal transitional papillomas. Otolaryngol Head Neck Surg 100: 563–567
22. Ward B E, Fechner R E, Mills S E 1990 Carcinoma arising in oncocytic Schneiderian papilloma. Am J Surg Pathol 14: 364–369
23. Kapadia S B, Barnes L, Pelzman K et al. 1993 Carcinoma ex oncocytic Schneiderian (cylindrical cell) papilloma. Am J Clin Pathol 14: 1–7
24. Lesperanie M M, Esclamado R M 1995 Squamous cell carcinoma arising in inverted papilloma. Laryngoscope 105: 178–183
25. Norris H J 1962 Papillary lesions of the nasal cavity and paranasal sinuses. Part I: Exophytic (squamous) papillomas. A study of 28 cases. Laryngoscope 72: 1784–1797
26. Batsakis J G 1980 The pathology of head and neck tumors: nasal cavity and paranasal sinuses, part 5. Head Neck Surg 2: 410–419
27. Sulica R L, Wenig B M, Debo R F et al. 1999 Schneiderian papillomas of the pharynx. Ann Otol Rhinol Laryngol 108: 392–397
28. Compagno J, Wong R T 1977 Intranasal mixed tumors (pleomorphic adenomas). A clinicopathologic study of 40 cases. Am J Clin Pathol 68: 213–218
29. Begin L R, Rochon L, Frenkiel S 1991 Spindle cell myoepithelioma of the nasal cavity. Am J Surg Pathol 15: 184–190
30. Lloyd R V, Chandler W F, Kovacs K et al. 1986 Ectopic pituitary adenomas with normal anterior pituitary glands. Am J Surg Pathol 10: 546–552
31. Wenig B, Heffess C, Adair C et al. 1995 Ectopic pituitary adenomas: a clinicopathologic study of 15 cases. Mod Pathol 8: 56A (abstract)
32. Hosaka N, Kitajiri S, Hiraumi H et al. 2002 Ectopic pituitary adenoma with malignant transformation. Am J Surg Pathol 26: 1078–1082
33. Zak F G, Lawson W 1982 The paraganglionic chemoreceptor system: physiology, pathology and clinical medicine. Springer-Verlag, New York
34. Apple D, Kreines K 1982 Cushing's syndrome due to ectopic ACTH production by a nasal paraganglioma. Am J Med Sci 283: 32–35
35. Kliewer K E, Wen D-R, Cancilla P A et al. 1989 Paragangliomas: assessment of prognosis by histologic, immunohistochemical, and ultrastructural techniques. Hum Pathol 20: 29–39
36. Johnson T L, Zarbo R J, Lloyd R V et al. 1988 Paragangliomas of the head and neck: immunohistochemical neuroendocrine and intermediate filament typing. Mod Pathol 1: 216–223
37. Nguyen Q A, Gibbs P M, Rice D H 1995 Malignant nasal paraganglioma: a case report and review of the literature. Otolaryngol Head Neck Surg 113: 157–161
38. Burger P C, Scheithauer B W 1994 Tumors of meningiothelial cells. In: Rosai J, Sobin L H (eds) Tumors of the central nervous system, series 3, fascicle 10. Armed Forces Institute of Pathology, Washington, DC, p 259–286
39. Perzin K H, Pushparaj N 1984 Non-epithelial tumors of the nasal cavity, paranasal sinuses, and nasopharynx: a clinicopathologic study. XIII. Meningiomas. Cancer 54: 1860–1869
40. Thompson L D, Gyure K A 2000 Extracranial sinonasal tract meningiomas: a clinicopathologic study of 30 cases with a review of the literature. Am J Surg Pathol 24: 640–650
41. Ho K L 1980 Primary meningioma of the nasal cavity and paranasal sinuses. Cancer 46: 1442–1447

42. Fu Y S, Perzin K H 1974 Non-epithelial tumors of the nasal cavity, paranasal sinuses, and nasopharynx: a clinicopathologic study. I. General features and vascular tumors. Cancer 33: 1275–1288

43. Sheppard L M, Michaelson S A 1990 Hemangioma of the nasal septum and paranasal sinuses. Henry Ford Hosp Med J 38: 25–27

44. Mills S E, Cooper P H, Fechner R E 1980 Lobular capillary hemangioma: the underlying lesion of pyogenic granuloma. A study of 73 cases from the oral and nasal mucous membranes. Am J Surg Pathol 4: 471–479

45. Nichols G E, Gaffey M J, Mills S E et al. 1992 Lobular capillary hemangioma. An immunohistochemical study including steroid hormone receptor status. Am J Clin Pathol 97: 770–775

46. Yuan K, Lin M T 2004 The roles of vascular endothelial growth factor and angiopoietin-2 in the regression of pregnancy pyogenic granuloma. Oral Dis 10: 179–185

47. Cheuk W, Wong K O, Wong C S et al. 2004 Immunostaining for human herpesvirus 8 latent nuclear antigen-1 helps distinguish Kaposi sarcoma from its mimickers. Am J Clin Pathol 121: 335–342

48. Batsakis J G, Rice D H 1981 The pathology of head and neck tumors. Vasoformative tumors, part 9A. Head Neck Surg 3: 231–239

49. Apostol J V, Frazell E L 1965 Juvenile nasopharyngeal angiofibroma. A clinical study. Cancer 18: 869–878

50. Neel H B, Whicker J H, Devine K D et al. 1973 Nasopharyngeal angiofibroma. Review of 120 cases. Am J Surg 126: 547–556

51. McGavran M H, Dorfman R F, Davis D O et al. 1969 Nasopharyngeal angiofibroma. Arch Otolaryngol 90: 68–78

52. Amedee R, Klaeyle D, Mann W et al. 1989 Juvenile angiofibromas: a 40-year surgical experience. ORL J Otorhinolaryngol Relat Spec 51: 56–61

53. Hyams V J, Batsakis J G, Michaels L 1988 Angiofibroma. In: Tumors of the upper respiratory tract and ear, series 2, fascicle 25. Armed Forces Institute of Pathology, Washington, DC, p 130–134

54. Hazarika P, Nayak R G, Chandran M 1985 Extra-nasopharyngeal extension of juvenile angiofibroma. J Laryngol Otol 99: 813–817

55. Johnson S, Kloster J H, Schiff M 1966 The actions of hormones on juvenile angiofibroma. Acta Otolaryngol 61: 153–160

56. Hwang H C, Mills S E, Patterson K et al. 1998 Expression of androgen receptors in nasopharyngeal angiofibroma: an immunohistochemical study of 24 cases. Mod Pathol 11: 1122–1126

57. Johns M E, MacLeod R M, Cantrell R W 1980 Estrogen receptors in nasopharyngeal angiofibromas. Laryngoscope 90: 628–634

58. Giardello F M, Hamilton S R, Krush A J et al. 1993 Nasopharyngeal angiofibroma in patients with familial adenomatous polyposis. Gastroenterology 105: 1550–1552

59. Ferouz A S, Mohr R M, Paul P 1995 Juvenile nasopharyngeal angiofibroma and familial adenomatous polyposis: an association? Otolaryngol Head Neck Surg 113: 435–439

60. Abraham S C, Montgomery E A, Giardiello F M et al. 2001 Frequent β-catenin mutations in juvenile nasopharyngeal angiofibromas. Am J Pathol 158: 1073–1078

61. Guertl B, Beham A, Zachner R et al. 2000 Nasopharyngeal angiofibroma: an APC-gene-associated tumor? Hum Pathol 31: 1411–1413

62. Zhang P J, Weber R, Liang H-H et al. 2003 Growth factors and receptors in juvenile nasopharyngeal angiofibroma and nasal polyps: an immunohistochemical study. Arch Pathol Lab Med 127: 1480–1484

63. Baguley C, Sandhu G, O'Donnell J et al. 2004 Consumptive coagulopathy complicating juvenile angiofibroma. J Laryngol Otol 118: 835–839

64. Sessions R B, Wills P I, Alford B R et al. 1976 Juvenile angiofibroma: Radiographic aspects. Laryngoscope 86: 2–18

65. Sessions R B, Bryan R N, Naclerio R M et al. 1981 Radiographic staging of juvenile angiofibroma. Head Neck Surg 3: 279–283

66. Fisch U 1983 The infratemporal fossa approach for nasopharyngeal tumors. Laryngoscope 93: 36–44

67. Chandler J R, Goulding R, Moskowitz L et al. 1984 Nasopharyngeal angiofibromas: staging and management. Ann Otol Rhinol Laryngol 93: 322–329

68. Radkowski D, McGill T, Healy G B et al. 1996 Angiofibroma. Changes in staging and treatment. Arch Otolaryngol Head Neck Surg 122: 122–129

69. Beham A, Fletcher C D M, Kainz J et al. 1993 Nasopharyngeal angiofibroma: an immunohistochemical study of 32 cases. Virchows Archiv (A) Pathol Anat 423: 281–285

70. Garcia-Cervigon E, Bien S, Rufenacht D et al. 1988 Pre-operative embolization of nasopharyngeal angiofibromas. Report of 58 cases. Neuroradiology 30: 556–560

71. Mann W J, Jecker P, Amedee R G 2004 Juvenile angiofibromas: changing surgical concept over the last 20 years. Laryngoscope 114: 291–293

72. Gates G A, Rice D H, Koopman C F Jr et al. 1992 Flutamide-induced regression of angiofibroma. Laryngoscope 102: 641–644

73. Fields J N, Halverson K J, Devineni V R et al. 1990 Juvenile nasopharyngeal angiofibroma: efficacy of radiation therapy. Radiology 176: 263–265

74. Gudea F, Vega M, Canals E et al. 1990 Role of radiation therapy for juvenile angiofibroma. J Laryngol Otol 104: 725–726

75. Kaspar M E, Parsons J T, Mancuso A A et al. 1993 Radiation therapy for juvenile angiofibroma: evaluation by CT and MRI, analysis of tumor regression, and selection of patients. Int J Radiat Oncol Biol Phys 25: 689–694

76. Biller H F 1978 Juvenile nasopharyngeal angiofibroma. Ann Otol Rhinol Laryngol 87: 630–632

77. Gullane P J, Davidson J, O'Dwyer T et al. 1992 Juvenile nasopharyngeal angiofibroma: a review of the literature and a case series report. Laryngoscope 102: 928–933

78. Weprin L S, Siemers P 1991 Spontaneous regression of juvenile nasopharyngeal angiofibroma. Arch Otolaryngol Head Neck Surg 117: 796–799

79. Dohar J E, Duvall A J 1992 Spontaneous regression of juvenile nasopharyngeal angiofibroma. Ann Otol Rhinol Laryngol 101: 469–471

80. Batsakis J G, Klopp C T, Newman N 1958 Fibrosarcoma arising in a "juvenile" nasopharyngeal angiofibroma following extensive radiation therapy. Am Surg 21: 786–793

81. Gisselsson L, Lindgren M, Stenram U 1958 Sarcomatous transformation of juvenile nasopharyngeal angiofibroma. Acta Pathol Microbiol Scand 42: 305–312

82. Chen K T K, Bauer F W 1982 Sarcomatous transformation of nasopharyngeal angiofibroma. Cancer 49: 369–371

83. Spagnolo D V, Papadimitiou J M, Archer M 1984 Postirradiation malignant fibrous histiocytoma arising in juvenile nasopharyngeal angiofibroma producing alpha-1-antitrypsin. Histopathology 8: 339–352

84. Hasegawa T, Hirose T, Seki K et al. 1996 Solitary fibrous tumors of soft tissue. An immunohistochemical and ultrastructural study. Am J Clin Pathol 106: 325–331

85. Suster S, Nascimento A G, Miettinen M et al. 1995 Solitary fibrous tumors of soft tissue. A clinicopathologic and immunohistochemical study of 12 cases. Am J Surg Pathol 19: 1257–1266

86. Zukerberg L R, Rosenberg A E, Randolph G et al. 1991 Solitary fibrous tumor of the nasal cavity and paranasal sinuses. Am J Surg Pathol 15: 126–130

87. Witkin G B, Rosai J 1991 Solitary fibrous tumor of the upper respiratory tract. Am J Surg Pathol 15: 842–848

88. Fukunaga M, Ushigome S, Nomura K et al. 1995 Solitary fibrous tumor of the nasal cavity and orbit. Pathol Int 45: 952–957

89. Karlsson I, Mandahl N, Heim S et al. 1988 Complex chromosome rearrangements in an extraabdominal desmoid tumor. Cancer Genet Cytogen 32: 241–245

90. Bridge J A, Sreekantaiah C, Mouron B et al. 1992 Clonal chromosomal abnormalities in desmoid tumors: implications for histogenesis. Cancer 69: 430–436

91. Enzinger F M, Weiss S W 1995 Fibromatoses. In: Enzinger F M, Weiss S W (eds) Soft tissue tumors, 3rd edn. Mosby, St Louis, p 201–229

92. Fu Y S, Perzin K H 1976 Non-epithelial tumors of the nasal cavity, paranasal sinuses, and nasopharynx: a clinicopathologic study. VI. Fibrous tissue tumors (fibroma, fibromatosis, fibrosarcoma). Cancer 37: 2912–2928

93. Gnepp D R, Henley J, Weiss S et al. 1996 Desmoid fibromatosis of the sinonasal tract and nasopharynx. Cancer 78: 2572–2579

94. Batsakis J G, Raslan W 1994 Extra-abdominal desmoid fibromatosis. Ann Otol Rhinol Laryngol 103: 331–334

95. Sherman N E, Romsdahl M, Evans H et al. 1990 Desmoid tumors: a 20-year radiotherapy experience. Int J Radiat Oncol Biol Phys 19: 37–40

96. McCollough W M, Parsons J T, van der Griend R et al. 1991 Radiation therapy for aggressive fibromatosis: the experience of the University of Florida. J Bone Joint Surg 73: 717–725

97. Lanari A 1983 Effect of progesterone on desmoid tumors (aggressive fibromatosis). N Engl J Med 309: 1523

98. Easter D W, Halasz N A 1989 Recent trends in the management of desmoid tumors. Summary of 19 cases and review of the literature. Ann Surg 210: 765–769

99. Shugar J M A, Som P A, Biller H F et al. 1981 Peripheral nerve sheath tumors of the paranasal sinuses. Head Neck Surg 4: 72–76

100. Fu Y S, Perzin K H 1974 Non-epithelial tumors of the nasal cavity, paranasal sinuses, and nasopharynx: a clinicopathologic study. XII. Schwann cell tumors (neurilemmoma, neurofibroma, malignant schwannoma). Cancer 50: 65–69

101. Hasegawa S L, Mentzel T, Fletcher C D M 1997 Schwannomas of the sinonasal tract and nasopharynx. Mod Pathol 10: 777–784

102. Buob D, Wacrenier A, Chevalier D et al. 2003 Schwannoma of the sinonasal tract: a clinicopathologic and immunohistochemical study of 5 cases. Arch Pathol Lab Med 127: 1196–1199

103. Fu Y S, Perzin K H 1976 Non-epithelial tumors of the nasal cavity, paranasal sinuses, and nasopharynx: a clinicopathologic study. IV. Smooth muscle tumors (leiomyoma, leiomyosarcoma). Cancer 35: 1300–1308

104. Huang, H Y, Antonescu C R 2003 Sinonasal smooth muscle cell tumors: a clinicopathologic and immunohistochemical analysis of 12 cases with emphasis on the low-grade end of the spectrum. Arch Pathol Lab Med 127: 297–304

105. Fu Y S, Perzin K H 1976 Non-epithelial tumors of the nasal cavity, paranasal sinuses, and nasopharynx: a clinicopathologic study. V. Skeletal muscle tumors (rhabdomyoma, rhabdomyosarcoma). Cancer 37: 364–376

106. Gale N, Rott T, Kambic V 1984 Nasopharyngeal rhabdomyoma. Report of a case (light and electron microscopic studies) and review of the literature. Pathol Res Pract 178: 454–460

107. Kapadia S B, Meis J M, Frisman D M et al. 1993 Fetal rhabdomyoma of the head and neck: a clinicopathologic and immunophenotypic study of 24 cases. Hum Pathol 24: 754–765

108. Fu Y S, Perzin K H 1977 Non-epithelial tumors of the nasal cavity, paranasal sinuses, and nasopharynx: a clinicopathologic study. VII. Myxomas. Cancer 39: 195–203

109. Heffner D K 1993 Sinonasal myxomas and fibromyxomas in children. Ear Nose Throat J 72: 365–368

110. Evans H 1993 Low-grade fibromyxoid sarcoma. A report of 12 cases. Am J Surg Pathol 17: 595–600

111. Fu Y S, Perzin K H 1974 Non-epithelial tumors of the nasal cavity, paranasal sinuses, and nasopharynx: a clinicopathologic study. II. Osseous and fibro-osseous lesions, including osteoma, fibrous dysplasia, ossifying fibroma, osteoblastoma, giant cell tumor and osteosarcoma. Cancer 33: 1289–1305

112. Earwaker J 1993 Paranasal sinus osteomas: a review of 46 cases. Skeletal Radiol 22: 417–423

113. Atallah N, Jay M M 1981 Osteomas of the paranasal sinuses. J Laryngol Otol 95: 291–304

114. Bulow S, Sondergaard J O, Witt I et al. 1984 Mandibular osteomas in familial polyposis coli. Dis Col Rectum 27: 105–108

115. Waldron C A, Giansati A S 1973 Benign fibro-osseous lesions of the jaws: a clinico-pathologic-histologic review of sixty-five cases. II. Benign fibro-osseous lesions of peridontal ligament origin. Oral Surg 35: 340–350

116. Nevelle B W, Albenesius R J 1986 The prevalence of benign fibro-osseous lesions of the peridontal ligament origin in black women: a radiographic survey. Oral Surg 62: 340–344

117. Wenig B M, Vinh T N, Smirniotopoulos J G et al. 1995 Aggressive psammomatoid ossifying fibromas of the sinonasal region. A clinicopathologic study of a distinct group of fibro-osseous lesions. Cancer 76: 1155–1165

118. Johnson L C, Youssefi M, Vinh T N et al. 1991 Juvenile active ossifying fibroma. Its nature, dynamics and origin. Acta Otolaryngol Suppl 488: 1–40

119. Harris W H, Dudley H R Jr, Barry R J 1962 The natural history of fibrous dysplasia. An orthopedic, pathological and roentenographic study. J Bone Joint Surg (Am) 44A: 207–233

120. Gibson M J, Middlemiss J H 1971 Fibrous dysplasia of bone. Br J Radiol 44: 1–13

121. Henry A 1969 Monostotic fibrous dysplasia. J Bone Joint Surg (Br) 51: 300–306

122. Yabut S M Jr, Kenan S, Sissons H A et al. 1988 Malignant transformation of fibrous dysplasia. A case report and review of the literature. Clin Orthop 228: 281–289

123. Taconis W K 1988 Osteosarcoma in fibrous dysplasia. Skeletal Radiol 17: 1047–1056

124. Oda Y, Tsuneyoshi M, Shinohara N 1993 "Solid" variant of aneurysmal bone cyst (extragnathic giant cell reparative granuloma) in axial skeleton and long bones. A study of its morphologic spectrum and distinction from allied bone lesions. Cancer 70: 2642–2649

125. Smith G A, Ward P H 1978 Giant cell lesions of the facial skeleton. Arch Otolaryngol 7: 366–370

126. Hirsch I S, Katz A 1974 Giant cell reparative granuloma outside the jaw bone. Hum Pathol 5: 171–181

127. Waldron C A, Shafer W G 1966 The central giant cell reparative granuloma of the jaws. An analysis of 38 cases. Am J Clin Pathol 45: 437–447

128. McGowan D A 1969 Central giant cell tumours of the mandible in pregnancy. Br J Oral Med 7: 131–135

129. Littler B O 1979 Central giant cell granuloma of the jaw – a hormonal influence. Br J Oral Surg 17: 43–46

130. Bertoni F, Unni K K, Beabout J W et al. 1992 Giant cell tumor of the skull. Cancer 70: 1124–1132

131. Saleh E A, Taibh A K, Naguib M et al. 1994 Giant cell tumor of the lateral skull: a case report. Otolaryngol Head Neck Surg 111: 314–318

132. Bridge J A, Neff J R, Bhatia P S et al. 1990 Cytogenetic findings and biologic behavior of giant cell tumors of bone. Cancer 65: 2697–2703

133. Chan J, Gannon F H, Thompson L D 2003 Malignant giant cell tumor of the sphenoid. Ann Diagn Pathol 7: 100–105

134. Fu Y S, Perzin K H 1974 Non-epithelial tumors of the nasal cavity, paranasal sinuses, and nasopharynx: a clinicopathologic study. III. Cartilaginous tumor (chondroma, chondrosarcoma). Cancer 34: 453–463

135. Kilby D, Amegaokar A G 1977 The nasal chondroma. J Laryngol Otol 91: 415–426

136. Shafer W G, Hine M K, Levy B M 1983 A textbook of oral pathology, 4th edn. W B Saunders, Philadelphia, p 258–317

137. Waldron C A 1995 Odontogenic cysts and tumors. In: Neville D W, Damm D D, Allen C M et al. (eds) Oral and maxillofacial pathology. W B Saunders, Philadelphia, p 453–540

138. Schafer D R, Thompson L D R, Smith B C et al. 1998 Primary ameloblastoma of the sinonasal tract. A clinicopathologic study of 24 cases. Cancer 82: 667–674

139. Guilemany J M, Ballesteros F, Alos L et al. 2004 Plexiform ameloblastoma presenting as a sinonasal tumor. Eur Arch Otorhinolaryngol 261: 304–306

140. Bryne M N, Sessions D G 1990 Nasopharyngeal craniopharyngioma. Case report and literature review. Ann Otol Rhinol Laryngol 99: 633–639

141. Chakrabarty A, Mitchell P, Bridges LR 1998 Craniopharyngioma invading the nasal and paranasal spaces, and presenting as nasal obstruction. Br J Neurosurg 12: 361–363

142. Taguchi Y, Tanaka K, Miyakita Y et al. 2000 Recurrent craniopharyngioma with nasopharyngeal extension. Pediatr Neurosurg 32: 140–144

143. Buhl R, Nabavi A, Fritsch M 2004 Nasopharyngeal extension of a craniopharyngioma in a 4 year old girl. Acta Neurochir (Wien) 143: 1283–5128

144. Dehner L P 1983 Gonadal and extragonadal germ cell neoplasia of childhood. Hum Pathol 14: 493–511

145. Tharrington C L, Bosen E H 1992 Nasopharyngeal teratomas. Arch Pathol Lab Med 116: 165–167

146. Coppit G L, Perkins J A, Manning S 2000 Nasopharyngeal teratomas and dermoids: a review of the literature and case series. Int J Pediatr Otorhinolaryngol 52: 219–227

147. Heffner D K, Thompson L D R, Schall D G et al. 1996 Pharyngeal dermoids ("hairy polyps") as accessory auricles. Ann Otol Rhinol Laryngol 10: 819–824

148. Heffner D K 1983 Problems in pediatric otorhinolaryngic pathology, III. Teratoid and neural tumors of the nose, sinonasal tract, and nasopharynx. Int J Pediatr Otorhinolaryngol 6: 1–21

149. Ferlito A, Devaney K O 1995 Developmental lesions of the head and neck: terminology and biological behavior. Ann Otol Rhinol Laryngol 104: 913–918

150. Gorenstein A, Facer G W, Weiland L H 1978 Hemangiopericytoma of the nasal cavity. ORL J Otorhinolaryngol Relat Spec 86: 405–415

151. Thompson L D, Miettinen M, Wenig B M 2003 Sinonasal-type hemangiopericytoma: a clinicopathologic and immunophenotypic analysis of 104 cases showing perivascular myoid differentiation. Am J Surg Pathol 27: 737–749

152. Kuo F Y, Lin H C, Eng H L et al. 2005 Sinonasal hemangiopericytoma-like tumor with true pericytic myoid differentiation: a clinicopathologic and immunohistochemical study of five cases. Head Neck 27: 124–129

153. Fletcher C D M 1994 Haemangiopericytoma: a dying breed? Reappraisal of an "entity" and its variants. Curr Diagn Pathol 1: 19–23

154. Fanburg-Smith J, Thompson L D R, Wenig B M 2005 Borderline and LMP tumours of soft tissue. In: Barnes L, Eveson J, Reichart P et al. (eds) World Health Organization classification of tumours. Pathology and genetics of head and neck tumours. IARC Press, Lyon, France, p 44–45

155. Compagno J, Hyams V J 1976 Hemangiopericytoma-like intranasal tumors. A clinicopathologic study of 23 cases. Am J Clin Pathol 66: 672–683

156. Schürch W, Skalli O, Lagace R et al. 1990 Intermediate filament proteins and actin isoforms as markers for soft tissue differentiation and origin: III. Hemangiopericytomas and glomus tumors. Am J Pathol 136: 771–786

157. Porter P L, Bigler S A, McNutt M et al. 1991 The immunophenotype of hemangiopericytomas and glomus tumors, with special reference to muscle protein expression: an immunohistochemical study and review of the literature. Mod Pathol 4: 46–52

158. Kapadia S K, Meis J M, Wenig B M et al. 1993 Sinonasal hemangiopericytoma. Mod Pathol 6: 81A (abstract)

159. Dardick I, Hammar S P, Sheithauer B W 1989 Ultrastructural spectrum of hemangiopericytoma: a comparative study of fetal, adult and neoplastic pericytes. Ultrastruct Pathol 13: 111–154

160. Eichorn J H, Dickerson G R, Bhan A K et al. 1990 Sinonasal hemangiopericytoma: a reassessment with electron microscopy, immunohistochemistry and long term follow-up. Am J Surg Pathol 14: 856–866

161. El-Naggar A, Batsakis J G, Garcia G M et al. 1992 Sinonasal hemangiopericytomas. A clinicopathologic and DNA content study. Arch Otolaryngol Head Neck Surg 118: 134–137

162. Billings K R, Fu Y S, Calcaterra T C et al. 2000 Hemangiopericytoma of the head and neck. Am J Otolaryngol 21: 238–243

163. Kowalski P J, Paulino A F 2001 Proliferation index as a prognostic marker in hemangiopericytoma of the head and neck. Head Neck 23: 492–496

164. Taxy J B 1997 Squamous carcinoma of the nasal vestibule. An analysis of five cases and literature review. Am J Clin Pathol 107: 698–703

165. Bosch A, Vallecillo L, Frias Z 1976 Cancer of the nasal cavity. Cancer 37: 1458–1463

166. Jackson R T, Fitz-Hugh G S, Constable W C 1977 Malignant neoplasms of the nasal cavities and paranasal sinuses. Laryngoscope 87: 726–736

167. Hopkin N, McNicoll W, Dalley V M et al. 1984 Cancer of the paranasal sinuses and nasal cavities. Part I. Clinical features. J Laryngol Otol 98: 585–595

168. Batsakis J G, Rice D H, Solomon A R 1980 The pathology of head and neck tumors: squamous and mucous-gland carcinomas of the nasal cavity, paranasal sinuses, and larynx, part 6. Head Neck Surg 2: 497–508

169. Pedersen E A, Hogetreit A C, Andersen A 1973 Cancer of the respiratory organs among workers at a nickel refinery in Norway. Int J Cancer 12: 32–41

170. Trojussen W, Solberg L A, Hogetveit A C 1979 Histopathologic changes of nasal mucosa in nickel workers. A pilot study. Cancer 44: 963–974

171. Shibuya H, Amagasa T, Hanai A et al. 1986 Second primary carcinomas in patients with squamous cell carcinoma of the maxillary sinus. Cancer 58: 1122–1125

172. Osborn D A 1970 Nature and behavior of transitional tumors in the upper respiratory tract. Cancer 25: 50–60

173. Giri S P G, Reddy E K, Gemer L S et al. 1992 Management of advanced squamous cell carcinomas of the maxillary sinus. Cancer 69: 657–661

174. Day T A, Beas R A, Schlosser R J 2005 Management of paranasal sinus malignancy. Curr Treat Options Oncol 6: 3–18

175. Diaz E M Jr, Kies M S 2001 Chemotherapy for skull base cancers. Otolaryngol Clin North Am 34: 1079–1085

176. Crissman J D, Zarbo R J 1989 Dysplasia, in situ carcinoma, and progression to invasive squamous cell carcinoma of the upper aerodigestive tract. Am J Surg Pathol 13 (suppl.): 5–16

177. Crissman J D, Kessis T, Shah K V et al. 1988 Squamous papillary neoplasia of the adult upper aerodigestive tract. Hum Pathol 19: 1387–1396

178. Ishiyama A, Eversole L R, Ross D A et al. 1994 Papillary squamous neoplasms of the head and neck. Laryngoscope 104: 1446–1452

179. Thompson L D R, Wenig B M, Heffner D K et al. 1999 Exophytic and papillary squamous cell carcinoma of the larynx: a report of 104 cases. Otolaryngol-Head Neck Surg 120: 718–724

180. Suarez P A, Adler-Storthz K, Luna M A et al. 2000 Papillary squamous cell carcinoma of the upper aerodigestive tract: a clinicopathologic and molecular study. Head Neck 22: 360–368

181. Kraus F T, Perez-Mesa C 1966 Verrucous carcinoma. Clinical and pathologic study of 105 cases involving oral cavity, larynx and genitalia. Cancer 19: 26–38

182. Batsakis J G, Hybels R, Crissman J D et al. 1982 The pathology of head and neck tumors: verrucous carcinoma, part 15. Head Neck Surg 5: 29–38

183. Medina J E, Dichtel W, Luna M A 1984 Verrucous-squamous carcinomas of the oral cavity. A clinicopathologic study of 104 cases. Arch Otolaryngol 110: 437–440

184. Luna M A, Tortoledo M E 1988 Verrucous carcinoma. In: Gnepp D R (ed) Pathology of the head and neck. Churchill Livingstone, New York, p 497–515

185. Paleri V, Orvidas LJ, Wight RG et al. 2004 Verrucous carcinoma of the paranasal sinuses: case report and clinical update. Head Neck 26: 184–189

186. Ram B, Saleh H A, Baird A R et al. 1998 Verrucous carcinoma of the maxillary antrum. J Laryngol Otol 112: 399–402

187. Abramson A L, Brandsma J L, Steinberg B M et al. 1985 Verrucous carcinoma of the larynx: possible human papillomavirus etiology. Arch Otolaryngol 111: 709–715

188. Brandsma J L, Steinberg B M, Abramson A L et al. 1986 Presence of HPV-16 related sequences in verrucous carcinoma of the larynx. Cancer Res 46: 2185–2188

189. Young K, Min K W 1991 In situ hybridization analysis of oral papillomas, leukoplakias, and carcinomas for human papillomavirus. Oral Surg Oral Med Oral Pathol 71: 726–729

190. Watts S L, Brewer E E, Fry T L 1991 Human papillomavirus DNA types in squamous cell carcinomas of the head and neck. Oral Surg Oral Med Oral Pathol 71: 701–707

191. Kashima H K, Kutcher M, Kessis T et al. 1990 Human papillomavirus in squamous cell carcinoma, leukoplakia, lichen planus, and clinically normal epithelium of the oral cavity. Ann Otol Rhinol Laryngol 99: 55–61

192. Löning T, Ikenberg H, Becker J et al. 1985 Analysis of oral papillomas, leukoplakias, and invasive carcinomas for human papillomavirus type related DNA. J Invest Dermatol 84: 417–420

193. Löning T 1986 Detection of papillomavirus DNA in oral papillomas and carcinomas: application of in situ hybridization with biotinylated HPV 16 probes. J Oral Path 15: 292–296

194. Shroyer K R, Greer R O, Fanhouser C A et al. 1993 Detection of human papillomavirus DNA in oral verrucous carcinoma by polymerase chain reaction. Mod Pathol 6: 669–772

195. Kasperbauer J L, O'Halloran G L, Espy M J et al. 1993 Polymerase chain reaction (PCR) identification of human papillomavirus (HPV) DNA in verrucous carcinoma of the larynx. Laryngoscope 103: 416–420

196. Fliss D M, Noble-Topham S E, McLachlin M et al. 1994 Laryngeal verrucous carcinoma: a clinicopathologic study and detection of human papillomavirus using polymerase chain reaction. Laryngoscope 104: 146–152

197. Dyson N, Howley P M, Münger K et al. 1989 The human papillomavirus-16 E7 oncoprotein is able to bind the retinoblastoma gene product. Science 243: 934–937

198. Hagen P, Lyons G D, Haindel C 1993 Verrucous carcinoma of the larynx: role of human papillomavirus, radiation, and surgery. Laryngoscope 103: 253–257

199. McDonald J S, Crissman J D, Gluckman J L 1982 Verrucous carcinoma of the oral cavity. Head Neck 5: 22–28

200. Tharp M E II, Shidnia H 1995 Radiotherapy in the treatment of verrucous carcinoma of the head and neck. Laryngoscope 105: 391–396

201. Vidyasagar M S, Fernandes D J, Pai Kasturi D et al. 1992 Radiotherapy and verrucous carcinoma of the oral cavity. A study of 107 cases. Acta Oncol 31: 43–47

202. Leventon G S, Evans H L 1981 Sarcomatoid squamous cell carcinoma of the mucous membranes of the head and neck: a clinicopathologic study of 20 cases. Cancer 48: 994–1003

203. Piscioli F, Aldovini D, Bondi A et al. 1984 Squamous cell carcinoma with sarcoma-like stroma of the nose and paranasal sinuses: report of two cases. Histopathology 8: 633–639

204. Zarbo R J, Crissman J D, Venkat H et al. 1986 Spindle-cell carcinoma of the aerodigestive tract mucosa: an immunohistologic and ultrastructural study of 18 biphasic tumors and comparison with seven monophasic spindle-cell tumors. Am J Surg Pathol 10: 741–753

205. Hyams V J, Batsakis J G, Michaels L 1988 Spindle cell carcinoma of the upper aerodigestive tract. In: Tumors of the upper respiratory tract and ear, series 2, fascicle 25. Armed Forces Institute of Pathology, Washington, DC, p 76–81

206. Ellis G L, Langloss J M, Heffner D K et al. 1987 Spindle-cell carcinoma of the aerodigestive tract: an immunohistochemical analysis of 21 cases. Am J Surg Pathol 11: 335–342

207. Huntington A C, Langloss J M, Hidayat H A 1990 Spindle cell carcinoma of the conjunctiva. An immunohistochemical and ultrastructural study of six cases. Am Acad Opthalmol 97: 711–717

208. Takata T, Ito H, Ogawa I et al. 1991 Spindle cell squamous carcinoma of the oral cavity. An immunohistochemical and ultrastructural study on the histogenesis and differential diagnosis with a clinicopathologic analysis of six cases. Virchows Arch (A) Pathol Anat 419: 177–182

209. Nakleh R E, Zarbo R J, Ewing S et al. 1993 Myogenic differentiation in spindle cell (sarcomatoid) carcinoma of the upper aerodigestive tract. Appl Immunohistochem 1: 58–68

210. Balercia G, Bhan A K, Dickersin G R 1995 Sarcomatoid carcinoma: an ultrastructural study with light microscopic and immunohistochemical correlation of 10 cases from various anatomic sites. Ultrastruct Pathol 19: 249–263

211. Krassilnik N, Gologan O, Ghali V et al. 2004 p63 and p16 expression in spindle cell squamous carcinomas of the head and neck (SCSCHN). Mod Pathol 17: 226A

212. Ellis G, Langloss J M, Enzinger F M 1985 Coexpression of keratin and desmin in a carcinosarcoma involving the maxillary alveolar ridge. Oral Surg Oral Med Oral Pathol 60: 410–416

213. Ophir D, Marshak G, Czernobilsky B 1987 Distinctive immunohistochemical labeling of epithelial and mesenchymal elements in laryngeal pseudosarcoma. Laryngoscope 97: 490–494

214. Smith K J, Skelton H G III, Morgan A M et al. 1992 Spindle cell neoplasms coexpressing cytokeratin and vimentin (metaplastic squamous cell carcinoma). J Cutan Pathol 19: 286–293

215. Batsakis J G, Rice D H, Howard D R 1982 The pathology of head and neck tumors: spindle cell lesions (sarcomatoid carcinomas, nodular fasciitis, and fibrosarcoma) of the upper aerodigestive tracts, part 14. Head Neck Surg 4: 499–513

216. Lambert P R, Ward P H, Berci G 1980 Pseudosarcoma of the larynx: a comprehensive analysis. Arch Otolaryngol 106: 700–708

217. Larsen E T, Duggan M A, Inoue M 1994 Absence of human papilloma virus DNA in oropharyngeal spindle-cell squamous carcinomas. Am J Clin Pathol 101: 514–518

218. Wain S L, Kier R, Vollmer R T et al. 1986 Basaloid-squamous carcinoma of the tongue, hypopharynx and larynx. Hum Pathol 17: 1158–1166

219. Batsakis J G, El Naggar A 1989 Basaloid-squamous carcinomas of the upper aerodigestive tracts. Ann Otol Rhinol Laryngol 98: 919–920

220. McKay M J, Bilous A M 1989 Basaloid-squamous carcinomas of the hypopharynx. Cancer 63: 2528–2531

221. Luna M A, El Naggar A, Parichatikanond P et al. 1990 Basaloid squamous cell carcinoma of the upper aerodigestive tract: clinicopathologic and DNA flow cytometric analysis. Cancer 66: 537–542

222. Banks E R, Frierson H F Jr, Mills S E et al. 1992 Basaloid squamous cell carcinoma of the head and neck: a clinicopathologic and immunohistochemical study of 40 cases. Am J Surg Pathol 16: 939–946

223. Barnes L, Ferlito A, Altavilla G et al. 1996 Basaloid squamous cell carcinoma of the head and neck: clinicopathological features and differential diagnosis. Ann Otol Rhinol Laryngol 105: 75–82

224. Wan S K, Chan J K C, Tse K C 1992 Basaloid-squamous carcinoma of the nasal cavity. J Laryngol Otol 106: 370–371

225. Wieneke J, Thompson L D R, Wenig B M 1999 Basaloid squamous cell carcinoma of the nasal cavity and paranasal sinuses. Cancer 85: 841–854

226. Raslan W F, Barnes L, Krause J R et al. 1994 Basaloid squamous cell carcinoma of the head and neck: a clinicopathologic and flow cytometric study of 10 new cases with review of the English literature. Am J Otolaryngol 15: 204–211

227. Morice W G, Ferreiro J A 1998 Distinction of basaloid squamous cell carcinoma from adenoid cystic and small cell undifferentiated carcinoma by immunohistochemistry. Hum Pathol 29: 609–612

228. Hewan-Lowe K, Dardick I 1995 Ultrastructural distinction of basaloid-squamous carcinoma and adenoid cystic carcinoma. Ultrastruct Pathol 19: 371–381

229. Seidman J, Berman J J, Yost B A et al. 1991 Basaloid squamous carcinoma of the hypopharynx and larynx associated with second primary tumors. Cancer 68: 1545–1549

230. Gerughty R M, Hennigar G R, Brown F M 1968 Adenosquamous carcinoma of the nasal, oral, and laryngeal cavities. Cancer 22: 1140–1155

231. Damiani J M, Damiani K K, Hauck K et al. 1981 Mucoepidermoid-adenosquamous carcinoma of the larynx and hypopharynx: a report of 21 cases and review of the literature. Otolaryngol Head Neck Surg 89: 235–243

232. Siar C H, Ng K H 1987 Adenosquamous carcinoma of the floor of the mouth and lower alveolus: a radiation-induced lesion? Oral Surg Oral Med Oral Pathol 63: 216–220

233. Aden K K, Adams G L, Niehans G et al. 1988 Adenosquamous carcinoma of the larynx and hypopharynx with five new case presentations. Trans Am Laryngol Assoc 109: 216–221

234. Fujino K, Ito J, Kanaji M et al. 1995 Adenosquamous carcinoma of the larynx. Am J Otolaryngol 16: 115–118

235. Napier S S, Gormley J S, Ramsay-Baggs P 1995 Adenosquamous carcinoma. A rare neoplasm with an aggressive course. Oral Surg Oral Med Oral Pathol 79: 607–611

236. Tsang W Y W, Chan J K C 2005 Lympoepithelial carcinoma. In: Barnes L, Eveson J, Reichart P et al. (eds) World Health Organization classification of tumours. Pathology and genetics of head and neck tumours. IARC Press, Lyon, France, p. 18

237. Jeng Y M, Sung M T, Fang C L et al. 2002 Sinonasal undifferentiated carcinoma and nasopharyngeal-type undifferentiated carcinoma: two

clinically, biologically, and histopathologically distinct entities. Am J Surg Pathol 26: 371–376

238. Leung S Y, Yuen S T, Chung L P et al. 1995 Epstein–Barr virus is present in a wide histological spectrum of sinonasal carcinomas. Am J Surg Pathol 19: 994–1001

239. Dubey P, Ha C S, Ang K K et al. 1998 Nonnasopharyngeal lymphoepithelioma of the head and neck. Cancer 82: 1556–1562

240. Zong Y, Liu K, Zhong B et al. 2001 Epstein–Barr virus infection of sinonasal lymphoepithelial carcinoma in Guangzhou. Chin Med J (Engl) 114: 132–136

241. Choi H R, Roberts D B, Johnigan R H et al. 2004 Molecular and clinicopathologic comparisons of head and neck squamous carcinoma variants: common and distinctive features of biological significance. Am J Surg Pathol 28: 1299–1310

242. Shanmugaratnam K, Sobin L H, Barnes L et al. 1991 World Health Organization histological classification of tumours. Histological typing of tumours of the upper respiratory tract and ear, 2nd edn. Springer-Verlag, Berlin, p 32–33

243. Chan J K C, Bray F, McCarron P et al. 2005 Nasopharyngeal carcinoma. In: Barnes L, Eveson J, Reichart P et al. (eds) World Health Organization classification of tumours. Pathology and genetics of head and neck tumours. Lyon, France, IARC Press, p 87–99

244. Easton J M, Levine P H, Hyams V J 1981 Nasopharyngeal carcinoma in the United States. A pathologic study of 177 US and 30 foreign cases. Arch Otolaryngol 106: 88–91

245. Dickson R I, Flores A D 1985 Nasopharyngeal carcinoma: an evaluation of 134 patients treated between 1971–1980. Laryngoscope 95: 276–283

246. Huang D P 1991 Epidemiology and aetiology. In: van Hasselt C A, Gibb A G (eds) Nasopharyngeal carcinoma. The Chinese Free Press, Hong Kong, p 23–35

247. Parkin D M, Whelan S L, Ferlay J et al. 2003 Cancer incidence in five continents, vol VIII. IARC Press, Lyon

248. Jenkin R D T, Anderson J R, Jereb B et al. 1981 Nasopharyngeal carcinoma – a retrospective review of patients less than thirty years of age: A report from children's cancer study group. Cancer 47: 360–366

249. Heffner D K 1983 Problems in pediatric otorhinolaryngic pathology. IV. Epithelial and lymphoid tumors of the sinonasal tract and nasopharynx. Int J Pediatr Otorhinolaryngol 6: 219–237

250. Hawkins E P, Krisher J P, Smith B E et al. 1990 Nasopharyngeal carcinoma in children – a retrospective review and demonstration of Epstein–Barr virus genomes in tumor cell cytoplasm: a report of the pediatric oncology group. Hum Pathol 21: 805–810

251. Batsakis J G, Solomon A R, Rice D H 1981 The pathology of head and neck tumors: carcinoma of the nasopharynx, part 11. Head Neck Surg 3: 511–524

252. Skinner D W, van Hasselt C A, Tsao S Y 1991 Nasopharyngeal carcinoma: a study of the modes of presentation. Ann Otol Rhinol Laryngol 100: 544–551

253. Wang C C, Little J B, Schulz M D 1962 Cancer of the nasopharynx. Its clinical and radiotherapeutic considerations. Cancer 15: 921–926

254. Chong V F, Fan Y F 1996 Skull base erosion in nasopharyngeal carcinoma: detection by CT and MRI. Clin Radiol 51: 625–631

255. Ng S H, Chang T C, Ko S F et al. 1997 Nasopharyngeal carcinoma: MRI and CT assessment. Neuroradiology 39:741–746

256. Buell P 1974 The effect of migration on the risk of nasopharyngeal cancer among Chinese. Cancer Res 34: 1189–1191

257. Vasef M A, Ferlito A, Weiss L M 1997 Nasopharyngeal carcinoma with emphasis on its relationship to Epstein–Barr virus. Ann Otol Rhinol Laryngol 106: 348–356

258. Raab-Traub N 2002 Epstein–Barr virus in the pathogenesis of NPC. Semin Cancer Biol 12: 431–441

259. Henderson B E, Louie E, Jing J S et al. 1976 Risk factors associated with nasopharyngeal carcinoma. N Engl J Med 295: 1101–1106

260. Zeng Y, Zhang L G, Li H Y et al. 1982 Serological mass survey for early detection of nasopharyngeal carcinoma in Wuzhou City, China. Int J Cancer 29: 139–141

261. de-Vaithaire F, Sancho-Garnier H, de-Thé H et al. 1988 Prognostic value of EBV markers in the clinical management of nasopharyngeal carcinoma (NPC): a multicenter follow-up study. Int J Cancer 47: 176–181

262. Young L S, Dawson C W, Clark D et al. 1988 Epstein–Barr virus gene expression in nasopharyngeal carcinoma. J Gen Virol 69: 1051–1065

263. Gasmi J, Bachouchi M, Cvitkovic E et al. 1990 Nasopharyngeal carcinoma: a medical oncology viewpoint: the Gustave Roussy experience. Ann Oncol 1: 245–253

264. Feinmesser R, Miyazaki I, Chueng R et al. 1992 Diagnosis of nasopharyngeal carcinoma by fine-needle aspiration. N Engl J Med 326: 17–21

265. Tam J S 1991 Epstein–Barr virus serologic markers. In: van Hasselt C A, Gibb A G (eds) Nasopharyngeal carcinoma. The Chinese Free Press, Hong Kong, p 147–156

266. Hadar T, Rahima M, Kahan E et al. 1986 Significance of specific Epstein–Barr virus IgA and elevated IgG antibodies to viral capsid antigens in nasopharyngeal carcinoma patients. J Med Virol 20: 329–339

267. Chan K C, Lo Y M 2002 Circulating EBV DNA as a tumor marker for nasopharyngeal carcinoma. Semin Cancer Biol 12: 489–496

268. Lin J C, Chen K Y, Wang W Y et al. 2001 Detection of Epstein–Barr virus DNA in the peripheral-blood cells of patients with nasopharyngeal

carcinoma: relationship to distant metastasis and survival. J Clin Oncol 19: 2607–2615

269. Lo Y M, Chan L Y, Lo K W 1999 Quantitative analysis of cell-free Epstein–Barr virus DNA in plasma of patients with nasopharyngeal carcinoma. Cancer Res 59: 1188–1191

270. Shotelersuk K, Khorprasert C, Sakdikul S et al. 2000 Epstein–Barr virus DNA in serum/plasma as a tumor marker for nasopharyngeal cancer. Clin Cancer Res 6: 1046–1051

271. Akao I, Sato Y, Mukai K et al. 1991 Detection of Epstein–Barr virus DNA in formalin-fixed paraffin-embedded tissue of nasopharyngeal carcinoma using polymerase chain reaction and in-situ hybridization. Laryngoscope 101: 279–283

272. Tsai S-T, Jin Y-T, Su I-J 1996 Expression of EBER1 in primary and metastatic nasopharyngeal carcinoma tissues using in-situ hybridization. A correlation with WHO subtypes. Cancer 77: 231–236

273. Pathmanathan R, Prasad U, Sadler R et al. 1995 Clonal proliferation of cells infected with Epstein–Barr virus in preinvasive lesions related to nasopharyngeal carcinoma. N Engl J Med 333: 693–698

274. Hording U, Nielsen H W, Daugaard S et al. 1994 Human papillomavirus types 11 and 16 detected in nasopharyngeal carcinomas by polymerase chain reaction. Laryngoscope 204: 99–102

275. Huang D P, Ho J H, Chan W K et al. 1989 Cytogenetics of undifferentiated nasopharyngeal carcinoma xenografts from southern Chinese. Int J Cancer 43: 936–939

276. Waghray M, Parhar R S, Taibah K 1992 Rearrangements of chromosome arm 3q in poorly differentiated nasopharyngeal carcinoma. Genes Chromosomes Cancer 4: 326–330

277. Choi P H R, Suen M W M, Huang D P et al. 1993 Nasopharyngeal carcinoma: genetic changes, Epstein–Barr virus infection, or both. A clinical and molecular study of 36 patients. Cancer 72: 2873–2878

278. Wong N, Hui A B, Fan B et al. 2003 Molecular cytogenetic characterization of nasopharyngeal carcinoma cell lines and xenografts by comparative genomic hybridization and spectral karyotyping. Cancer Genet Cytogenet 140: 124–132

279. Shao J Y, Zeng W F, Zeng Y X 2002 Molecular genetic progression on nasopharyngeal carcinoma. Ai Zheng 21: 1–10

280. Shao J Y, Huang X M, Yu X J et al. 2001 Loss of heterozygosity and its correlation with clinical outcome and Epstein–Barr virus infection in nasopharyngeal carcinoma. Anticancer Res 21: 3021–2039

281. Fang Y, Guan X, Guo Y et al. 2001 Analysis of genetic alterations in primary nasopharyngeal carcinoma by comparative genomic hybridization. Genes Chromosomes Cancer 30: 254–260

282. Lo K W, Huang D P 2002 Genetic and epigenetic changes in nasopharyngeal carcinoma. Semin Cancer Biol 12: 451–462

283. Lo K W, Huang D P, Lau K M 1995 p16 gene alterations in nasopharyngeal carcinoma. Cancer Res 55: 2039–2043

284. Lo K W, Cheung S T, Leung S F et al. 1996 Hypermethylation of the p16 gene in nasopharyngeal carcinoma. Cancer Res 56: 2721–2725

285. Nicholls J M 1997 Nasopharyngeal carcinoma: classification and histologic appearances. Adv Anat Pathol 4: 71–84

286. Barnes L 2001 Nasopharyngeal carcinoma. In: Barnes L (ed) Surgical pathology of the head and neck, 2nd edn. Marcel Dekker, New York, p 527–535

287. Shanmugaratnam K, Chan S H, de-The G et al. 1979 Histopathology of nasopharyngeal carcinoma: correlations with epidemiology, survival rates, and other biological characteristics. Cancer 44: 1029–1044

288. Franchi A, Moroni M, Massi D et al. 2002 Sinonasal undifferentiated carcinoma, nasopharyngeal-type undifferentiated carcinoma, and keratinizing and nonkeratinizing squamous cell carcinoma express different cytokeratin patterns. Am J Surg Pathol 26: 1597–1604.

289. Reddy S P, Raslan W F, Gooneratne S et al. 1995 Prognostic significance of keratinization in nasopharyngeal carcinoma. Am J Otolaryngol 16: 103–108

290. Ahmad A, Stefani S 1986 Distant metastases of nasopharyngeal carcinoma: a study of 256 male patients. J Surg Oncol 33: 194–197

291. McGuire L J, Suen M W M 1991 Histopathology. In: van Hasselt C A, Gibb A G (eds) Nasopharyngeal carcinoma. The Chinese Free Press, Hong Kong, p 47–84

292. Cheng D S, Campbell B H, Clowry L J et al. 1990 DNA content in nasopharyngeal carcinoma. Am J Otolaryngol 11: 393–397

293. Costello F, Mason B R, Collins R J et al. 1990 A clinical and flow cytometric analysis of patients with nasopharyngeal carcinoma. Cancer 66: 1789–1795

294. Roychowdhury D F, Tseng A, Fu K K et al. 1996 New prognostic factors in nasopharyngeal carcinoma. Tumor angiogenesis and C-erbB2 expression. Cancer 77: 1419–1426

295. Chua D T, Ma J, Sham J S et al. 2005 Long-term survival after cisplatin-based induction chemotherapy and radiotherapy for nasopharyngeal carcinoma: a pooled data analysis of two phase III trials. J Clin Oncol 20: 1118–1124

296. Cooper J S, Scott C, Marcial V et al. 1991 The relationship of nasopharyngeal carcinomas and second independent malignancies based on radiation therapy oncology group experience. Cancer 67: 1673–1677

297. Frierson H F Jr, Mills S E, Fechner R E et al. 1986 Sinonasal undifferentiated carcinoma. An aggressive neoplasm derived from Schneiderian epithelium and distinct from olfactory neuroblastoma. Am J Surg Pathol 10: 771–779

298. Frierson H F 2005 Sinonasal undifferentiated carcinoma. In: Barnes L, Eveson J, Reichart P et al. (eds) World Health Organization classification of tumours. Pathology and genetics of head and neck tumours. IARC Press, Lyon, France, p 19

299. Righi P D, Francis F, Aron B S et al. 1996 Sinonasal undifferentiated carcinoma: a 10-year experience. Am J Otolaryngol 17: 167–171

300. Helliwell T R, Yeoh L H, Stell P M 1986 Anaplastic carcinoma of the nose and paranasal sinuses. Light microscopy, immunohistochemistry and clinical correlation. Cancer 58: 2038–2045

301. Mills S E 2002 Neuroectodermal neoplasms of the head and neck with emphasis on neuroendocrine carcinomas. Mod Pathol 15: 264–278

302. Ejaz A, Wenig B M 2005 Sinonasal undifferentiated carcinoma. Clinical and pathologic features and a discussion on classification, cellular differentiation, and differential diagnosis. Adv Anat Pathol 12: 134–143

303. Jeng Y M, Sung M T, Fang C L et al. 2002 Sinonasal undifferentiated carcinoma and nasopharyngeal-type undifferentiated carcinoma: two clinically, biologically, and histopathologically distinct entities. Am J Surg Pathol 26: 371–376

304. Cerilli L A, Holst V A, Brandwein M S et al. 2001 Sinonasal undifferentiated carcinoma: immunohistochemical profile and lack of EBV association. Am J Surg Pathol 25: 156–163

305. Lopategui J R, Gaffey M J, Frierson H F Jr et al. 1994 Detection of Epstein–Barr viral RNA in sinonasal undifferentiated carcinoma from western and Asian patients. Am J Surg Pathol 18: 391–398

306. Gallo O, Di Lollo S, Graziani P et al. 1995 Detection of Epstein–Barr virus genome in sinonasal undifferentiated carcinoma by use of in situ hybridization. Otolaryngol Head Neck Surg 112: 659–664

307. Greger V, Schirmacher P, Bohl J et al. 1990 Possible involvement of the retinoblastoma gene in undifferentiated sinonasal carcinoma. Cancer 66: 1954–1959

308. Mills S E, Fechner R E 1989 "Undifferentiated" neoplasms of the sinonasal tract: differential diagnosis based on clinical, light microscopic, immunohistochemical, and ultrastructural features. Semin Diagn Pathol 6: 316–328

309. Kramer D, Durham J S, Sheehan F et al. 2004 Sinonasal undifferentiated carcinoma: case series and systemic review of the literature. J Otolaryngol 33: 32–36

310. Kim B S, Vongtama R, Juillard G 2004 Sinonasal undifferentiated carcinoma: case series and literature review. Am J Otolaryngol 25: 162–166

311. Gallo O, Graziani P, Fini-Storchi O 1993 Undifferentiated carcinoma of the nose and paranasal sinuses. An immunohistochemical and clinical study. Ear Nose Throat J 72: 588–590, 593–595

312. Deutsch B D, Levine P A, Stewart F M et al. 1993 Sinonasal undifferentiated carcinoma: a ray of hope. Otolaryngol Head Neck Surg 108: 697–700

313. Pitman K T, Costantino P D, Lassen L F 1995 Sinonasal undifferentiated carcinoma: current trends in treatment. Skull Base Surg 5: 269–272

314. Stewart F M, Lazarus L M, Levine P A et al. 1989 High-dose chemotherapy and autologous marrow transplantation for esthesioneuroblastoma and sinonasal undifferentiated carcinoma. Am J Clin Oncol 12: 217–221

315. Musy P Y, Reibel J F, Levine P A 2002 Sinonasal undifferentiated carcinoma: the search for a better outcome. Laryngoscope 112: 1450–1455

316. Rischin D, Porceddu S, Peters L et al. 2004 Promising results with chemoradiation in patients with sinonasal undifferentiated carcinoma. Head Neck 26: 435–441

317. Nakashima T, Kimmelman C P, Snow J B Jr 1984 Structure of human fetal and adult olfactory neuroepithelium. Arch Otolaryngol 110: 641–646

318. Wenig B M, Dulguerov P, Kapadia S B et al. 2005 Neuroectodermal tumours. In: Barnes L, Eveson J, Reichart P et al. (eds) World Health Organization classification of tumours. Pathology and genetics of head and neck tumours. IARC Press, Lyon, France, 66–9

319. Baker D C, Perzin N H, Conley J 1979 Olfactory neuroblastoma. Otolaryngol Head Neck Surg 87: 279–283

320. Elkon D, Hightower S I, Lim M L et al. 1979 Esthesioneuroblastoma. Cancer 44: 1087–1094

321. Dulguerov P, Calcaterra T 1992 Esthesioneuroblastoma: the UCLA experience 1970–1990. Laryngoscope 102: 843–849

322. Dulguerov P, Allal A S, Calcaterra T C 2001 Esthesioneuroblastoma: a meta-analysis and review. Lancet Oncol 2: 683–690

323. Mills S E, Frierson H F Jr 1985 Olfactory neuroblastoma. A clinicopathologic study of 21 cases. Am J Surg Pathol 9: 317–327

324. Hirose T, Scheithauer B W, Lopes M B S et al. 1995 Olfactory neuroblastoma. An immunohistochemical, ultrastructural, and flow cytometric study. Cancer 76: 4–19

325. Woodhead P, Lloyd G A 1988 Olfactory neuroblastoma: imaging by magnetic resonance, CT and conventional techniques. Clin Otolaryngol 13: 387–394

326. Herrold K M 1964 Induction of olfactory neuroepithelial tumors in Syrian hamsters by diethylnitrosamine. Cancer 17: 114–121

327. Bailey B J, Barton S 1975 Olfactory neuroblastoma: management and prognosis. Arch Otolaryngol 101: 1–5

328. Vollrath M, Altmannsberger M, Weber K et al. 1986 Chemically induced tumors of rat olfactory epithelium: a model for human esthesioneuroblastoma. JNCI 76: 1205–1216

329. Ambrose I M, Ambros P F, Strehl S et al. 1991 MIC2 is a specific marker for Ewing's sarcoma and peripheral primitive neuroectodermal tumors. Evidence for a common histogenesis of Ewing's sarcoma and peripheral primitive neuroectodermal tumors from MIC2 expression and specific chromosome aberration. Cancer 67: 1886–1893

330. Fellinger E J, Garin-Chesa P, Triche T J et al. 1991 Immunohistochemical analysis of Ewing's sarcoma cell surface antigen p30/32^{MIC2}. Am J Pathol 139: 317–325

331. Ladanyi M 1995 The emerging molecular genetics of sarcoma translocations. Diagn Mol Pathol 4: 162–167

332. Whang-Peng J, Freier R E, Knutsen T 1987 Translocation t(11;22) in esthesioneuroblastoma. Cancer Genet Cytogenet 29: 155–157

333. Sorensen P H B, Wu J K, Berean K W et al. 1996 Olfactory neuroblastoma is a peripheral primitive neuroectodermal tumor related to Ewing sarcoma. Proc Natl Acad Sci USA 93: 1938–1943

334. Nelson R S, Perlman E J, Askin F B 1995 Is esthesioneuroblastoma a peripheral neuroectodermal tumor? Hum Pathol 26: 639–641

335. Devaney K, Wenig B M, Abbondanzo S L 1996 Olfactory neuroblastoma and other round cell lesions of the sinonasal cavity. Mod Pathol 9: 658–663

336. Argani P, Perez-Ordonez B, Xiao H et al. 1998 Olfactory neuroblastoma is not related to the Ewing family of tumors. Absence of EWS/FLI1 gene fusion and MIC2 expression. Am J Surg Pathol 22: 391–398

337. Kumar S, Perlman E, Pack S et al. 1999 Absence of EWS/FLI1 fusion in olfactory neuroblastomas indicates these tumors do not belong to the Ewing's sarcoma family. Hum Pathol 30: 1356–1360

338. Mezzelani A, Tornielli S, Minoletti F et al. 1999 Esthesioneuroblastoma is not a member of the primitive peripheral neuroectodermal tumour – Ewing's group. Br J Cancer 81: 586–591

339. Hyams V J 1982 Olfactory neuroblastoma (case 6). In: Batsakis J G, Hyams V J, Morales A R (eds) Special tumors of the head and neck. ASCP Press, Chicago, p 24–29

340. Miller D C, Goodman M L, Pilch B Z et al. 1984 Mixed olfactory neuroblastoma and carcinoma. A report of two cases. Cancer 54: 2019–2028

341. Frierson H F Jr, Ross G W, Mills S E et al. 1990 Olfactory neuroblastoma. Additional immunohistochemical characterization. Am J Clin Pathol 94: 547–553

342. Choi H S H, Anderson P J 1986 Olfactory neuroblastoma: an immunohistochemical and electron microscopic study of S-100-protein cells. J Neuropathol Exp Neurol 45: 576–587

343. Tatagiba M, Samii M, Dankoweit T et al. 1995 Esthesioneuroblastomas with intracranial extension. Proliferative potential and management. Arq Neuropsiquiatr 53: 577–586

344. Vartanian R K 1996 Olfactory neuroblastoma: an immunohistochemical, ultrastructural and flow cytometric study. Cancer 77: 1957–1959

345. Kahn L B 1974 Esthesioneuroblastoma. A light and electron microscopic study. Hum Pathol 5: 364–371

346. Taxy J B, Hidvegi D F 1977 Olfactory neuroblastoma. An ultrastructural study. Cancer 39: 131–138

347. Morita A, Ebersold M J, Olsen K D et al. 1993 Esthesioneuroblastoma: prognosis and management. Neurosurgery 32: 706–715

348. Wade P M Jr, Smith R E, Johns M E 1984 Response of esthesioneuroblastoma to chemotherapy. Report of five cases and review of the literature. Cancer 53: 1036–1041

349. Eden B V, Debo R F, Larner J M et al. 1994 Esthesioneuroblastoma. Long term follow-up and patterns of failure – the University of Virginia experience. Cancer 73: 2556–2562

350. O'Conor G T Jr, Drake C R, Johns M E et al. 1985 Treatment of advanced esthesioneuroblastoma with high-dose chemotherapy and autologus bone marrow transplanatation. A case report. Cancer 55: 347–349

351. Polin R S, Sheehan J P, Chenelle A G et al. 1998 The role of preoperative adjuvant treatment in the management of esthesioneuroblastoma: the University of Virginia experience. Neurosurgery 42: 1029–1037

352. Kadish S, Goodman M, Wang C C 1976 Olfactory neuroblastoma. A clinical analysis of 17 cases. Cancer 37: 1571–1576

353. Hyams V J, Batsakis J G, Michaels L 1988 Tumors of the upper respiratory tract and ear, 2nd edn. Armed Forces Institute of Pathology, Washington, DC

354. Kapadia S 2001 Olfactory neuroblastoma. In: Barnes L (ed) Surgical pathology of the head and neck. Marcel Dekker, New York, p 841–845

355. Shanmugaratnam K, Sobin L H, Barnes L et al. 1991 World Health Organization histological classification of tumours. Histological typing of tumours of the upper respiratory tract and ear, 2nd edn. Springer-Verlag, Berlin, p 32–33

356. Ferlito A, Rosai J 1991 Terminology and classification of neuroendocrine neoplasms of the larynx. ORL J Otorhinolaryngol Relat Spec 53: 185–187

357. Wenig B M, Hyams V J, Heffner D K 1988 Moderately differentiated neuroendocrine carcinoma of the larynx. A clinicopathologic study of 54 cases. Cancer 62: 2658–2676

358. Woodruff J M, Huvos A G, Erlandson R A et al. 1985 Neuroendocrine carcinomas of the larynx. A study of two types, one of which mimics thyroid medullary carcinoma. Am J Surg Pathol 9: 771–790

359. Ferlito A, Rinaldo A, Barnes L et al. 2005 Neuroendocrine neoplasms. In: Barnes L, Eveson J, Reichart P et al. (eds) World Health Organization classification of tumours. Pathology and genetics of head and neck tumours. IARC Press, Lyon, France, p 139–142

360. Huntrakoon M 1987 Neuroendocrine carcinoma of the parotid gland: a report of two cases with ultrastructural and immunohistochemical studies. Hum Pathol 18: 1212–1217

361. Gnepp D R 1991 Small cell neuroendocrine carcinoma of the larynx. ORL J Otorhinolaryngol Relat Spec 53: 210–219

362. Perez-Ordonez B, Caruana S, Huvos A G et al. 1998 Small cell neuroendocrine carcinoma of the nasal cavity and paranasal sinuses. Hum Pathol 29: 826–832

363. Perez-Ordonez B 2005 Neuroendocrine carcinomas. In: Barnes L, Eveson J, Reichart P et al. (eds) World Health Organization classification of tumours. Pathology and genetics of head and neck tumours. IARC Press, Lyon, France, p 26–27

364. Wenig B M, Gnepp D R 1989 The spectrum of neuroendocrine carcinomas of the larynx. Semin Diagn Pathol 6: 329–350

365. Chan J K C, Suster S, Wenig B M et al. 1997 Cytokeratin 20 immunoreactivity distinguishes Merkel cell (primary cutaneous) neuroendocrine carcinomas and salivary gland small cell carcinomas from small cell carcinomas of various sites. Am J Surg Pathol 21: 226–234

366. Galanis E, Frytak S, Lloyd R V 1997 Extrapulmonary small cell carcinoma. Cancer 79: 1729–1736

367. Barnes L 2001 Malignant melanoma of the nasal cavity and paranasal sinuses In: Barnes L (ed) Surgical pathology of the head and neck, 2nd edn. Marcel Dekker, New York, p 523–527

368. Wenig B M 1995 Laryngeal mucosal malignant melanoma: a clinicopathologic, immunohistochemical and ultrastructural study of four cases and a review of the literature. Cancer 75: 1568–1575

369. Thompson L D, Wieneke J A, Miettinen M 2003 Sinonasal tract and nasopharyngeal melanomas: a clinicopathologic study of 115 cases with a proposed staging system. Am J Surg Pathol 27: 594–611

370. Panje W R, Moran W J 1986 Melanoma of the upper aerodigestive tract: a review of 21 cases. Head Neck Surg 8: 309–312

371. Trapp T K, Fu Y S, Calcaterra T C 1987 Melanoma of the nasal and paranasal sinus mucosa. Arch Otolaryngol Head Neck Surg 113: 1086–1089

372. Franquemont D W, Mills S E 1991 Sinonasal malignant melanoma: a clinicopathologic and immunohistochemical study of 14 cases. Am J Clin Pathol 96: 689–697

373. Reuter V E, Woodruff J M 1986 Melanoma of the larynx. Laryngoscope 94: 389–393

374. Goldman J L, Lawson W, Zak F G et al. 1972 The presence of melanocytes in the human larynx. Laryngoscope 82: 824–835

375. Busuttil A 1976 Dendritic pigmented cells within the human laryngeal mucosa. Arch Otolaryngol 102: 43–44

376. Taira K 1985 Endocrine-like cells in the laryngeal mucosa of adult rabbits demonstrated by electron microscopy and by the Grimelius silver-impregnation method. Biomed Res 6: 377–385

377. Reganer S, Anderhuber W, Richtig E et al. 1998 Primary mucosal melanomas of the nasal cavity and paranasal sinuses. A clinicopathological analysis of 14 cases. APMIS 106: 403–410

378. Prasad M L, Jungbluth A A, Iversen K et al. 2001 Expression of melanocytic differentiation in malignant melanomas of the oral and sinonasal mucosa. Am J Surg Pathol 25: 782–787

379. Harwood A, Stringer S P, Million R 1994 Melanoma of the head and neck. In: Million R R, Cassisi N J (eds) Management of head and neck cancer, 2nd edn. J B Lippincott, Philadelphia, p 705–709

380. Wenig B M, Dulguerov P, Kapadia S B et al. Mucosal malignant melanoma. In: Barnes L, Eveson J, Reichart P et al. (eds) World Health Organization classification of tumours. Pathology and genetics of head and neck tumours. IARC Press, Lyon, France, p 72–75

381. McGovern V J 1982 The nature of melanoma: a critical review. J Cutan Pathol 9: 61–81

382. Barnes L 1986 Intestinal-type adenocarcinoma of the nasal cavity and paranasal sinuses. Am J Surg Pathol 10: 192–202

383. Robin P E, Powell D J, Stansbie J M 1979 Carcinoma of the nasal cavity and paranasal sinuses: incidence and presentation of different histological types. Clin Otolaryngol 4: 432–456

384. Kleinsasser O, Schroeder H G 1988 Adenocarcinoma of the inner nose after exposure to wood dust: morphological findings and relationships between histopathology and clinical behavior in 79 cases. Arch Otorhinolaryngol 245: 1–15

385. Hadfield E H, Macbeth R G 1971 Adenocarcinoma of ethmoids in furniture workers. Ann Otol Rhinol Laryngol 80: 699–703

386. Hadfield E H 1970 A study of adenocarcinoma of the paranasal sinuses in woodworkers in the furniture industry. Ann R Coll Surg Engl 46: 302–319

387. Acheson E D, Cowdell R H, Hadfield E H et al. 1970 Nasal cancer in the Northamptonshire boot and shoe industry. Br Med J 1: 385–393

388. Cecchi F, Buiatti E, Kreibel D et al. 1980 Adenocarcinoma of the nose and paranasal sinuses in shoemakers and woodworkers in the province of Florence, Italy (1963–77). Br J Ind Med 37: 222–225

389. Batsakis J G, Holtz F, Sueper R H 1968 Adenocarcinoma of the nasal and paranasal cavities. Arch Otolaryngol 77: 625–633

390. Franquemont D W, Fechner R E, Mills S E 1991 Histologic classification of sinonasal intestinal-type adenocarcinoma. Am J Surg Pathol 15: 368–375

391. Franchi A, Gallo O, Santucci M 1999 Clinical relevance of the histological classification of sinonasal intestinal-type adenocarcinomas. Hum Pathol 30: 1140–1145

392. Mills S E, Fechner R E, Cantrell R W 1982 Aggressive sinonasal lesion resembling normal intestinal mucosa. Am J Surg Pathol 6: 803–809

393. McKinney C D, Mills S E, Franquemont D W 1995 Sinonasal intestinal-type adenocarcinoma: immunohistochemical profile and comparison with colonic adenocarcinoma. Mod Pathol 8: 421–426

394. Urso C, Ninu M B, Franchi A et al. 1993 Intestinal-type adenocarcinoma of the sinonasal tract: a clinicopathologic study of 18 cases. Tumori 79: 205–210

395. Franchi A, Massi D, Baroni G et al. 2003 CDX-2 homeobox gene expression. Am J Surg Pathol 27: 1390–1391

396. Bashir A A, Robinson R A, Benda J A et al. 2003 Sinonasal adenocarcinoma: immunohistochemical marking and expression of oncoproteins. Head Neck 25: 763–771

397. Amre R, Ghali V, Elmberger G et al. 2004 Sinonasal "intestinal type" adenocarcinomas (SNITAC): an immunohistochemical (IHC) study of 22 cases. Mod Pathol 17: 221A

398. Kennedy M T, Jordan R C, Berean K W et al. 2004 Expression pattern of CK7, CK20, CDX-2, and villin in intestinal-type sinonasal adenocarcinoma. J Clin Pathol 57: 932–937

399. Cathro H P, Mills S E 2004 Immunophenotypic differences between intestinal-type and low-grade papillary sinonasal adenocarcinomas: an immunohistochemical study of 22 cases utilizing CDX2 and MUC2. Am J Surg Pathol 28: 1026–1032

400. Franchi A, Massi D, Palomba A et al. 2004 CDX-2, cytokeratin 7 and cytokeratin 20 immunohistochemical expression in the differential diagnosis of primary adenocarcinomas of the sinonasal tract. Virchows Arch 445: 63–67

401. Batsakis J G, Mackay B, Ordonez N G 1984 Enteric-type adenocarcinoma of the nasal cavity. An electron microscopic and immunocytochemical study. Cancer 54: 855–860

402. Heffner D K, Hyams V J, Hauck K W et al. 1982 Low-grade adenocarcinoma of the nasal cavity and paranasal sinuses. Cancer 50: 312–322

403. Barnes L, Brandwein M 2001 Adenoid cystic carcinoma. In: Barnes L (ed.) Surgical pathology of the head and neck, 2nd edn. Marcel Dekker, New York, p 522–523

404. Eby L S, Johnson D S, Baker H W 1972 Adenoid cystic carcinomas of the head and neck. Cancer 29: 1160–1168

405. Orenstein J M, Dardick I, van Nostrand A W 1985 Ultrastructural similarities of adenoid cystic carcinoma and pleomorphic adenoma. Histopathology 9: 623–638

406. Tomich C E 1991 Adenoid cystic carcinoma. In: Ellis G L, Auclair P L, Gnepp D R (eds) Surgical pathology of the salivary glands. W B Saunders, Philadelphia, p 333–349

407. Spiro R H, Huvos A G 1992 Stage means more than grade in adenoid cystic carcinoma. Am J Surg 164: 623–628

408. Kadish S B, Goodman M L, Wang C C 1972 Treatment of minor salivary gland malignancies of upper food and air passage epithelium. Cancer 29: 1020–1026

409. Wenig B M, Hyams V J, Heffner D K 1988 Nasopharyngeal papillary adenocarcinoma. A clinicopathologic study of a low-grade carcinoma. Am J Surg Pathol 12: 946–953

410. Kuo T T, Chan J K C, Wenig B M et al. Nasopharyngeal papillary adenocarcinoma. In: Barnes L, Eveson J, Reichart P et al. (eds) World Health Organization classification of tumours. Pathology and genetics of head and neck tumours. IARC Press, Lyon, France, p 100

410a. Carrizo F, Luna M A 2005 Thyroid transcription factor-1 expression in thyroid-like nasopharyngeal papillary adenocarcinoma: report of 2 cases. Ann Diagn Pathol 9: 189–192

411. Abbondanzo S L, Wenig B M 1995 Non-Hodgkin's lymphoma of the sinonasal tract: a clinicopathologic and immunophenotypic study of 120 cases. Cancer 75: 1281–1291

412. Jaffe E S, Chan J K C, Su I-H et al. 1996 Report of the workshop on nasal and related extranodal angiocentric T/natural killer cell lymphomas. Definitions, differential diagnosis, and epidemiology. Am J Surg Pathol 20: 103–111

413. Chan A C L, Chan J K C, Cheung M M C et al. 2005 Hematolymphoid tumours. In: Barnes L, Eveson J, Reichart P et al. (eds) World Health Organization classification of tumours. Pathology and genetics of head and neck tumours. IARC Press, Lyon, France, p 59–65

414. Arber D A, Weiss L M, Albujar P F et al. 1993 Nasal lymphomas in Peru: high incidence of T-cell immunophenotype and Epstein–Barr virus infection. Am J Surg Pathol 17: 392–399

415. Fellbaum Chr, Hansmann M-L, Lennert K 1989 Malignant lymphomas of the nasal cavity and paranasal sinuses. Virchows Archiv (A) Pathol Anat 414: 399–405

416. Ho F C S, Loke S L, Ng R P et al. 1984 Clinico-pathological features of malignant lymphomas in 294 Hong Kong Chinese patients, retrospective study covering an eight-year period. Int J Cancer 34: 143–148

417. Ng C S, Chan J K C, Lo S T H et al. 1986 Immunophenotypic analysis of non-Hodgkin's lymphomas in Chinese. A study of 75 cases in Hong Kong. Pathology 18: 419–425

418. Cheung M M, Chan J K, Lau W H et al. 1998 Primary non-Hodgkin's lymphoma of the nose and nasopharynx: clinical features, tumor immunophenotype, and treatment outcome in 113 patients. J Clin Oncol 16: 70–77

419. Anderson J R, Armitage J O, Weisenburger D D 1998 Epidemiology of the non-Hodgkin's lymphomas: distributions of the major subtypes differ by geographic locations. Non-Hodgkin's Lymphoma Classification Project. Ann Oncol 9: 717–720

420. Quintanilla-Martinez L, Franklin J L, Guerrero I et al. 1999 Histological and immunophenotypic profile of nasal NK/T cell lymphomas from Peru: high prevalence of p53 overexpression. Hum Pathol 30: 849–855

421. Cuadra-Garcia I, Proulx G M, Wu C L et al. 1999 Sinonasal lymphoma: a clinicopathologic analysis of 58 cases from the Massachusetts General Hospital. Am J Surg Pathol 23: 1356–1369

422. Pomilla P V, Morris A B, Jaworek A 1995 Sinonasal non-Hodgkin's lymphoma in patients infected with human immunodeficiency virus: report of three cases and review. Clin Infect Dis 21: 137–149

423. Canioni D, Arnulf B, Asso-Bonnet M et al. 2001 Nasal natural killer lymphoma associated with Epstein–Barr virus in a patient infected with human immunodeficiency virus. Arch Pathol Lab Med 125: 660–662

424. Jaffe E S, Krenacs L, Kumar S et al. 1999 Extranodal peripheral T-cell and NK-cell neoplasms. Am J Clin Pathol 111: S46–S55

425. Chan J K C, Yip T T C, Tsang W Y W et al. 1994 Detection of Epstein–Barr viral RNA in malignant lymphomas of the upper aerodigestive tract. Am J Surg Pathol 18: 938–946

426. Ohshima K, Suzumiya J, Shimazaki K et al. 1997 Nasal T/NK cell lymphomas commonly express perforin and Fas ligand: important mediators of tissue damage. Histopathology 31: 444–450

427. Cheung M M, Chan J K, Lau W H et al. 2002 Early stage nasal NK/T-cell lymphoma: clinical outcome, prognostic factors, and the effect of treatment modality. Int J Radiat Oncol Biol Phys 54: 182–190

428. Cheung M M, Chan J K, Wong K F 2003. Natural killer cell neoplasms: a distinctive group of highly aggressive lymphoma/leukemia. Semin Hematol 40: 221–232

429. Kim G E, Koom W S, Yang W I 2004 Clinical relevance of three subtypes of primary sinonasal lymphoma characterized by immunophenotypic analysis. Head Neck 26: 584–593

430. Freeman C, Berg J W, Cutler S J 1972 Occurrence and prognosis of extranodal lymphomas. Cancer 29: 252–260

431. Otter R, Gerrits W B J, Sandt M M V D et al. 1989 Primary extranodal and nodal non-Hodgkin's lymphomas: survey of a population-based registry. Eur J Cancer Clin Oncol 25: 1203–1210

432. Hoppe R T, Burke J S, Glatstein E et al. 1978 Non-Hodgkin's lymphoma: involvement of Waldeyer's ring. Cancer 42: 1096–1104

433. Barton J H, Osborne B M, Butler J J et al. 1984 Non-Hodgkin's lymphoma of the tonsil: a clinicopathologic study of 65 cases. Cancer 53: 86–95

434. Saul S H, Kapadia S B 1985 Lymphoma of Waldeyer's ring: clinicopathologic study of 68 cases. Cancer 56: 157–166

435. Shima N, Kobashi Y, Tsutsui K et al. 1990 Extranodal non-Hodgkin's lymphoma of the head and neck: a clinicopathologic study in the Kyoto-Nara area of Japan. Cancer 66: 1190–1197

436. Medeiros L J, Bagg A, Cossman J 1992 Application of molecular genetics to the diagnosis of hematopoietic neoplasms. In: Knowles D M (ed) Neoplastic hematopathology. Williams & Wilkins, Baltimore, p 263–298

437. Carbone P P, Kaplan H S, Musshoff K et al. 1971 Report of the committee on Hodgkin's disease staging classification. Cancer Res 31: 1860–1861

438. Shimm D S, Dosooretz D E, Harris N L et al. 1984 Radiation therapy of Waldeyer's ring lymphoma. Cancer 54: 426–431

439. Kapadia S, Desai U, Cheng U 1982 Extramedullary plasmacytoma of the head and neck: a clinicopathologic study of 20 cases. Medicine 61: 317–329

440. Grogan T M, Spier C M 1991 The B cell immunoproliferative disorders, including multiple myeloma and amyloidosis. In: Knowles D (ed) Neoplastic hematopathology. Williams & Wilkins, Baltimore, p 1235

441. Kinney M C, Swerdlow S H 2001 Plasma cell neoplasms. In: Barnes L (ed) Surgical pathology of the head and neck. Marcel Dekker, New York, p 1323–1329

442. Carbone A, Vaccher E, Barzan L et al. 1995 Head and neck lymphomas associated with human immunodeficiency virus infection. Arch Otolaryngol Head Neck Surg 121: 210–218

443. Alexanian R 1985 Ten-year survival in multiple myeloma. Arch Intern Med 145: 2073–2074

444. Heffner D K 1983 Problems in pediatric otorhinolaryngic pathology. IV. Epithelial and lymphoid tumors of the sinonasal tract and nasopharynx. Int J Pediatr Otorhinolaryngol 6: 219–237

445. Kapadia S B, Roman L N, Kingma D W et al. 1995 Hodgkin's disease of Waldeyer's ring. Clinical and histoimmunophenotypic findings and association with Epstein–Barr virus in 16 cases. Am J Surg Pathol 19: 1431–1439

446. Moghe G M, Borges A M, Soman C S et al. 2001. Hodgkin's disease involving Waldeyer's ring: a study of four cases. Leuk Lymphoma 41: 151–156

447. Perez-Ordonez B, Erlandson R A, Rosai J 1996 Follicular dendritic cell tumor: report of 13 additional cases of a distinctive entity. Am J Surg Pathol 20: 944–955

448. Perez-Ordonez B, Rosai J 1998 Follicular dendritic cell tumor: review of the entity. Semin Diagn Pathol 15: 144–154

449. Biddle D A, Ro J Y, Yoon G S et al. 2002 Extranodal follicular dendritic cell sarcoma of the head and neck region: three new cases, with a review of the literature. Mod Pathol 15: 50–58

450. Weiss L M, Grogan T M, Müller-Hermelink H-K et al. 2001 Follicular dendritic cell sarcoma/tumour. In: Jaffe ES, Harris NL, Stein H et al. (eds) World Health Classification of tumours. Pathology and genetics. Tumours of haematopoietic and lymphoid tissues. IARC Press, Lyon, p 288–289

451. Dominguez-Malagon H, Cano-Valdez A M, Mosqueda-Taylor A et al. 2004 Follicular dendritic cell sarcoma of the pharyngeal region: histologic, cytologic, immunohistochemical, and ultrastructural study of three cases. Ann Diagn Pathol 8: 325–332

452. Chan A C, Chan K W, Chan J K et al. 2001 Development of follicular dendritic cell sarcoma in hyaline-vascular Castleman's disease of the nasopharynx: tracing its evolution by sequential biopsies. Histopathology 38: 510–518

453. Grogg K L, Lae M E, Kurtin P J et al. 2004 Clusterin expression distinguishes follicular dendritic cell tumors from other dendritic cell neoplasms: report of a novel follicular dendritic cell marker and clinicopathologic data on 12 additional follicular dendritic cell tumors and 6 additional interdigitating dendritic cell tumors. Am J Surg Pathol 28: 988–998

454. Chan J K, Fletcher C D, Nayler S J et al. 1997 Follicular dendritic cell sarcoma. Clinicopathologic analysis of 17 cases suggesting a malignant potential higher than currently recognized. Cancer 79: 294–313

455. Heffner D K, Gnepp D R 1992 Sinonasal fibrosarcomas, malignant schwannomas, and "Triton" tumors. A clinicopathologic study of 67 cases. Cancer 70: 1089–1101

456. Loree T R, North J H Jr, Werness B A et al. 2000 Malignant peripheral nerve sheath tumors of the head and neck: analysis of prognostic factors. Otolaryngol Head Neck Surg 122: 667–672

457. Wick M R, Swanson P E, Scheithauer B W et al. 1987 Malignant peripheral nerve sheath tumor. An immunohistochemical study of 62 cases. Am J Clin Pathol 87: 425–433

458. Barnes L, Kanbour A 1988 Malignant fibrous histiocytoma of the head and neck. A report of 12 cases. Arch Otolaryngol Head Neck Surg 114: 1149–1156

459. Perzin K H, Fu Y S 1980 Non-epithelial tumors of the nasal cavity, paranasal sinuses, and nasopharynx: a clinicopathologic study. XI. Fibrous histiocytomas. Cancer 45: 2616–2626

460. Mauer H M, Beltangady M, Gehan E A et al. 1988 The Intergroup Rhabdomyosarcoma Study – I. A final report. Cancer 61: 209–220

461. Weiss S W, Goldblum J R 2001 Rhabdomyosarcoma. In: Weiss S W, Goldblum J R (eds) Enzinger and Weiss's soft tissue tumors, 4th edn. Mosby, St. Louis, p 785–835

462. Barnes L 2001 Rhabdomyosarcoma. In: Barnes L (ed) Surgical pathology of the head and neck, 2nd edn. Marcel Dekker, New York, p. 960–967

463. Anderson G J, Tom L W C, Womer R B et al. 1990 Rhabdomyosarcoma of the head and neck in children. Arch Otolaryngol Head Neck Surg 116: 428–431

464. Callender T A, Weber R S, JanJan N et al. 1995 Rhabdomyosarcoma of the nose and paranasal sinuses in adults and children. Head Neck Surg 112: 252–257

465. El-Naggar A K, Batsakis J G, Ordonez N G et al. Rhabdomyosarcoma of the adult head and neck: a clinicopathological study and DNA ploidy study. J Laryngol Otol 107: 716–720

466. Nakhleh R E, Swanson P E, Dehner L P 1991 Juvenile (embryonal and alveolar) rhabdomyosarcoma of the head and neck in adults. A clinical, pathologic, and immunohistochemical study of 12 cases. Cancer 67: 1019–1024

467. Nayar R C, Prudhomme F, Parise O Jr et al. 1993 Rhabdomyosarcoma of the head and neck in adults. A study of 26 patients. Laryngoscope 103: 1362–1366

468. Parham D M, Barr F G 2002 Embryonal rhabdomyosarcoma. In: Fletcher C D M, Unni K K, Mertens F (eds) In: World Health Organization classification of tumours. Pathology and genetics. Tumours of soft tissue and bone. IARC Press, Lyon, p 146–149

469. Parham D M, Barr F G 2002 Alveolar rhabdomyosarcoma. In: Fletcher C D M, Unni K K, Mertens F (eds) In: World Health Organization classification of tumours. Pathology and genetics. Tumours of soft tissue and bone. IARC Press, Lyon, p 150–152

470. Maurer H M, Gehan E A, Beltangady M et al. 1993 The Intergroup Rhabdomyosarcoma Study II. Cancer 71: 1904–1922

471. Newton W A Jr, Gehan E A, Webber B L et al. 1995 Classification of rhabdomyosarcoma and related sarcomas. Pathologic aspects and proposal for a new classification – an Intergroup Rhabdomyosarcoma study. Cancer 76: 1073–1085

472. Raney R B, Asmar L, Vassilopoulou-Sellin R et al. 1999 Late complications of therapy in 213 children with localized, nonorbital soft tissue sarcoma of the head and neck: a descriptive report from the Intergroup Rhabdomyosarcoma Studies (IRS)-II and -III. IRS Group of the Children's Cancer Group and the Pediatric Oncology Group. Med Pediatr Oncol 33: 362–371

473. Bankaci M, Myers E N, Barnes L et al. 1979 Angiosarcoma of the maxillary sinus. Head Neck Surg 1: 274–280

474. Panje W R, Moran W J, Bostwick D G et al. 1986 Angiosarcoma of the head and neck: review of 11 cases. Laryngoscope 96: 1381–1384

475. Di Girolamo A, Giacomini P G, Coli A et al. 2003 Epithelioid haemangioendothelioma arising in the nasal cavity. J Laryngol Otol 117: 75–77

476. Goldberg A N 1993 Kaposi's sarcoma of the head and neck in acquired immunodeficiency syndrome. Am J Otolaryngol 14: 5–14

477. Fliss D M, Parikh J, Freeman J L 1992 AIDS-related Kaposi's sarcoma of the sphenoid sinus. J Otolaryngol 21: 235–237

478. Moazzez A H, Alvi A 1998 Head and neck manifestations of AIDS in adults. Am Fam Physician 57: 1813–1822

479. Wyatt M E, Finlayson C J, Moore-Gillon V 1998 Kaposi's sarcoma masquerading as pyogenic granuloma of the nasal mucosa. J Laryngol Otol 112: 280–282

480. Cheuk W, Wong K O, Wong C S et al. 2004. Immunostaining for human herpesvirus 8 latest nuclear antigen-1 helps distinguish Kaposi sarcoma from its mimickers. Am J Clin Pathol 121: 335–342

481. Blackbourn D J, Lennette E T, Ambroziak J et al. 1998 Human herpesvirus 8 detection in nasal secretions and saliva. J Infect Dis 177: 213–216

482. Gandhi M, Koelle D M, Ameli N et al. 2004 Prevalence of human herpesvirus-8 salivary shedding in HIV increases with CD4 count. J Dent Res 83: 639–643

483. Barnes L 2001 Leiomyosarcoma. In: Barnes L (ed) Surgical pathology of the head and neck, 2nd edn. Marcel Dekker, New York, p 979–984

484. Kuruvilla A, Wenig B M, Humphrey D M et al. 1990 Leiomyosarcoma of the sinonasal tract. A clinicopathologic study of nine cases. Arch Otolaryngol Head Neck Surg 116: 1278–1286

485. Dahlin D C, Unni K K 1986 Bone tumors: general aspects and data on 8542 cases, 4th edn. Charles C Thomas, Springfield, p 227–259

486. Batsakis J G 1987 Osteogenic and chondrogenic sarcomas of jaws. Ann Otol Rhinol Laryngol 96: 474–475

487. Waldron C A 1985 Osteosarcoma. In: Neville B D, Damm D D, Allen C M, Bouquot J E (eds) Oral and maxillofacial pathology. W B Saunders, Philadelphia, p 482–485

488. Mark R J, Sercarz J A, Tran L et al. 1991 Osteogenic sarcoma of the head and neck. The UCLA experience. Arch Otolaryngol Head Neck Surg 117: 761–766

489. Garrington G E, Scofield H H, Coryn J et al. 1967 Osteosarcoma of the jaws. An analysis of 56 cases. Cancer 20: 377–391

490. Fechner R E, Mills S E 1993 Conventional intramedullary osteosarcoma. In: Rosai J, Sobin L H (eds) Tumors of the bones and joints, series 3, fascicle 8. Armed Forces Institute of Pathology, Washington, DC, p 38–50

491. Caron A S, Hajdu S I, Strong E W 1971 Osteogenic sarcoma of the facial and cranial bones. A review of forty-three cases. Am J Surg 122: 719–725

492. Ruark D S, Schlehaider U K, Shah J P 1992 Chondrosarcomas of the head and neck. World J Surg 16: 1010–1016

493. Burkey B B, Hoffman H T, Baker S R et al. 1990 Chondrosarcoma of the head and neck. Laryngoscope 100: 1301–1305

494. Mark R J, Tran L M, Sercarz J et al. 1993 Chondrosarcoma of the head and neck. The UCLA experience, 1955–1988. Am J Clin Oncol (CCT) 16: 232–237

495. Huvos A G, Marcove A C 1987 Chondrosarcoma in the young. A clinicopathologic analysis of 79 patients younger than 21 years of age. Am J Surg Pathol 11: 930–942

496. Finn D G, Goepfert H, Batsakis J G 1984 Chondrosarcoma of the head and neck. Laryngoscope 94: 1539–1544

497. Webber P A, Hussain S S, Radcliffe G J 1986 Cartilaginous neoplasms of the head and neck. J Laryngol Otol 100: 615–619

498. Rosenthal D I, Schiller A L, Mankin H J 1984 Chondrosarcoma: correlation of radiological and histological grade. Radiology 150: 21–26

499. Perzin K H, Pushparaj N 1986 Non-epithelial tumors of the nasal cavity, paranasal sinuses, and nasopharynx: a clinicopathologic study. XIV. Chordomas. Cancer 57: 784–796

500. Meis J M, Giraldo A A 1988 Chordoma. An immunohistochemical study of 20 cases. Arch Pathol Lab Med 112: 553–556

501. Mitchell A, Scheithauer B W, Unni K K et al. 1993 Chordoma and chondroid neoplasms of the spheno-occiput. An immunohistochemical study of 41 cases with prognostic and nosologic implications. Cancer 72: 2943–2949

502. Heffner D K, Hyams V J 1984 Teratocarcinosarcoma (malignant teratoma?) of the nasal cavity and paranasal sinuses. A clinicopathologic study of 20 cases. Cancer 53: 2140–2154

503. Pai S A, Naresh K N, Masih K et al. 1998 Teratocarcinosarcoma of the paranasal sinuses: a clinicopathologic and immunohistochemical study. Hum Pathol 29: 718–722

504. Shimazaki H, Aida S, Tamai S 2000 Sinonasal teratocarcinosarcoma: ultrastructural and immunohistochemical evidence of neuroectodermal origin. Ultrastruct Pathol 24: 115–122

505. Chao K K, Eng T Y, Barnes J et al. 2004 Sinonasal teratocarcinosarcoma. Am J Clin Oncol 27: 29–32

506. Fu Y S, Perzin K H 1977 Non-epithelial tumors of the nasal cavity, paranasal sinuses, and nasopharynx: a clinicopathologic study. VIII. Lipoma and liposarcoma. Cancer 40: 1314–1317

507. McCullough T M, Makielski K H, McNutt M A 1992 Head and neck liposarcoma. A histopathologic reevaluation of reported cases. Arch Otolaryngol Head Neck Surg 118: 1045–1049

508. Shmookler B M, Enzinger F M, Brannon R B 1982 Orofacial synovial sarcoma. A clinicopathologic study of 11 new cases and review of the literature. Cancer 50: 269–276

509. Simmons W B, Haggerty H S, Ngan B et al. 1989 Alveolar soft part sarcoma of the head and neck. A disease of children and young adults. Int J Pediatr Otorhinolaryngol 17: 139–153

510. Pontius K I, Sebek B A 1981 Extra-skeletal Ewing's sarcoma arising in the nasal fossa. Light- and electron-microscopic observations. Am J Clin Pathol 75: 410–415

511. Lane S, Ironside J W 1990 Extra-skeletal Ewing's sarcoma of the nasal fossa. J Laryngol Otol 104: 570–573

512. Toda T, Atari E, Sadi A M et al. 1999 Primitive neuroectodermal tumor in sinonasal region. Auris Nasus Larynx 26: 83–90

513. Windfuhr J P 2004 Primitive neuroectodermal tumor of the head and neck: incidence, diagnosis, and management. Ann Otol Rhinol Laryngol 113: 533–543

514. Lack E E 1985 Extragonadal germ cell tumors of the head and neck region: review of 16 cases. Hum Pathol 16: 56–64

515. Manivel C, Wick M R, Dehner L P 1986 Transitional (cylindric) cell carcinoma with endodermal sinus tumor-like features of the nasopharynx and paranasal sinuses. Clinicopathologic and immunohistochemical study of two cases. Arch Pathol Lab Med 110: 198–202

516. Bernstein J M, Montgomery W W, Balogh K Jr 1966 Metastatic tumors to the maxilla, nose, and paranasal sinuses. Laryngoscope 76: 621–650

517. Kent S E, Majumdar B 1985 Metastatic tumours in the maxillary sinus. A report of two cases and a review of the literature. J Laryngol Otol 99: 459–462

518. McClatchey K D, Lloyd R V, Schaldenbard J D 1985 Metastatic carcinoma to the sphenoid sinus. Case report and review of the literature. Arch Otorhinolaryngol 241: 219–224

519. Drake-Lee A B, Lowe D, Swanston A et al. 1984 Clinical profile and recurrence of nasal polyps. J Laryngol Otol 98: 783–793

520. Settipane G A, Chafee F H 1977 Nasal polyps in asthma and rhinitis. A review of 6037 patients. J Allergy Clin Immunol 59: 17–21

521. Patriarca G, Nucera E, Di Rienzo V et al. 1991 Nasal provocation test with lysine acetylsalicylate in aspirin-sensitive patients. Ann Allergy 67: 60–62

522. Killian G 1906 The origin of choanal polypi. Lancet 2: 81–82

523. Sirola R 1966 Choanal polyps. Acta Otolaryngol 61: 42–48

524. Nakayama M, Wenig B M, Heffner D K 1995 Atypical stromal cells in inflammatory nasal polyps: immunohistochemical and ultrastructural analysis in defining histogenesis. Laryngoscope 105: 127–134

525. Sheahan P, Crotty P L, Hamilton S et al. 2005 Infarcted angiomatous nasal polyps. Eur Arch Otorhinolaryngol 262: 225–230

526. Yfantis H G, Drachenberg C B, Gray W et al. 2000 Angiectatic nasal polyps that clinically simulate a malignant process: report of 2 cases and review of the literature. Arch Pathol Lab Med 124: 406–410

527. Orvidas L J, Beatty C W, Weaver A L 2001 Antrochoanal polyps in children. Am J Rhinol 15: 321–325

528. Theaker J M, Fletcher C D M 1991 Heterotopic glial nodules: a light microscopic and immunohistochemical study. Histopathology 18: 255–260

529. Heffner D K 1983 Problems in pediatric otorhinolaryngic pathology. III. Teratoid and neural tumors of the nose, sinonasal tract, and nasopharynx. Int J Pediatr Otorhinolaryngol 6: 1–21

530. Puppala B, Mangurten H H, McFadden J et al. 1990 Nasal glioma presenting as neonatal respiratory distress. Clin Pediatr 29: 49–52

531. Kapadia S B, Popek E J, Barnes L 1994 Pediatric otorhinolaryngic pathology: diagnosis of selected lesions. Pathol Annu 29: 159–209

532. Graeme-Cook F, Pilch B Z 1992 Hamartomas of the nose and nasopharynx. Head Neck 14: 321–327

533. Wenig B M, Heffner D K 1995 Respiratory epithelial adenomatous hamartomas of the sinonasal tract and nasopharynx: a clinicopathologic study of 31 cases. Ann Otol Rhinol Laryngol 104: 639–645

534. Baille E E, Batsakis J G 1974 Glandular (seromucinous) hamartoma of the nasopharynx. Oral Surg 38: 760–762

535. Kapadia S B, Popek E J, Barnes L 1994 Pediatric otorhinolaryngic pathology: diagnosis of selected lesions. Pathol Annu 29: 159–209

536. Burns B V, Axon P R, Pahade A 2001 'Hairy polyp' of the pharynx in association with an ipsilateral branchial sinus: evidence that the 'hairy polyp' is a second branchial arch malformation. J Laryngol Otol 115: 145–148

537. Heffner D K, Thompson L D R, Schall D G et al. 1996 Pharyngeal dermoids ("hairy polyps") as accessory auricles. Ann Otol Rhinol Laryngol 105: 819–824

538. Heffner D K 1983 Problems in pediatric otorhinolaryngic pathology. III. Teratoid and neural tumors of the nose, sinonasal tract, and nasopharynx. Int J Pediatr Otorhinolaryngol 6: 1–21

539. Ferlito A, Devaney K O 1995 Developmental lesions of the head and neck. Terminology and biologic behavior. Ann Otol Rhinol Laryngol 104: 913–918

539a. Ozolek J A, Carrau R, Barnes E L, Hunt J L 2005 Nasal chondromesenchymal hamartoma in older children and adults: series and immunohistochemical analysis. Arch Pathol Lab Med 129: 1444–1450

540. McDermott M B, Ponder T, Dehner L P 1998 Nasal chondromesenchymal hamartoma: an upper respiratory tract analogue of the chest wall mesenchymal hamartoma. Am J Surg Pathol 22: 425–433

541. Norman E S, Bergman S, Trupiano J K 2004 Nasal chondromesenchymal hamartoma: report of a case and review of the literature. Pediatr Dev Pathol 7: 517–520

542. Kim B, Park S H, Min H S 2004 Nasal chondromesenchymal hamartoma of infancy clinically mimicking meningoencephalocele. Pediatr Neurosurg 40: 136–140

543. Shet T, Borges A, Nair C et al. 2004 Two unusual lesions in the nasal cavity of infants – a nasal chondromesenchymal hamartoma and an aneurysmal bone cyst like lesion. More closely related than we think? Int J Pediatr Otorhinolaryngol 68: 359–364

544. Kardon D E, Wenig B M, Heffner D K et al. 2000 Tonsillar lymphangiomatous polyps: a clinicopathologic series of 26 cases. Mod Pathol 13: 1128–1133

545. Friedman G C, Hartwick W J, Ro J Y et al. 1991 Allergic fungal sinusitis: report of three cases associated with dematiaceous fungi. Am J Clin Pathol 96: 368–372

546. Saeed S R, Brooks G B 1995 Aspergillosis of the paranasal sinuses. Rhinology 33: 46–51

547. Satyanarayana C 1960 Rhinosporidiosis with a record of 225 cases. Acta Otolaryngol 51: 348–356

548. Nussbaum E S, Hall W A 1994 Rhinocerebral mucormycosis: changing patterns of disease. Surg Neurol 41: 152–154

549. Hyams V J, Batsakis J G, Michaels L 1988 Rhinoscleroma. In: Tumors of the upper respiratory tract and ear, series 2, fascicle 25. Armed Forces Institute of Pathology, Washington, DC, p 24–26

550. Wenig B M, Smirniotopolous J, Heffner D K 1996 Botryomycosis of the sinonasal tract: a report of two cases. Arch Pathol Lab Med 120: 1123–1128

551. Gordon W W, Cohn A M, Greenberg S D et al. 1976 Nasal sarcoidosis. Arch Otolaryngol 102: 11–14

552. Wenig B M, Thompson L D R, Frankel S S et al. 1996 Lymphoid changes of the nasopharynx and tonsils that are indicative of human immunodeficiency virus infection: a clinicopathologic study of 12 cases with a discussion on the possibility of transmucosal infection. Am J Surg Pathol 20: 572–587

553. Moss R, Beaudet L M, Wenig B M et al. 1997 Microsporidium-associated sinusitis. Ear Nose Throat J 76: 95–101

554. Kyriakos M 1977 Myospherulosis of the paranasal sinuses, nose and middle ear. Am J Clin Pathol 67: 118–130

555. DeRemee R A, McDonald T J, Harrison E G et al. 1976 Wegener's granulomatosis, anatomic correlates, a proposed classification. Mayo Clin Proc 51: 777–781

556. DeRemee R A 1988 Extrapulmonary manifestations of Wegener's granulomatosis and other respiratory vasculitides. Semin Resp Med 9: 403–408

557. Specks U, Wheatley C L, McDonald T J et al. 1989 Anticytoplasmic autoantibodies in the diagnosis and follow-up of Wegener's granulomatosis. Mayo Clin Proc 64: 28–36

558. Nolle B, Specks U, Ludemann J et al. 1989 Anticytoplasmic autoantibodies: their immunodiagnostic value in Wegener's granulomatosis. Ann Intern Med 111: 28–40

559. Fienberg R, Mark E J, Goodman M et al. 1993 Correlation of antineutrophil cytoplasmic antibodies with the extrarenal histopathology of Wegener's (pathergic) granulomatosis and related forms of vasculitis. Hum Pathol 24: 160–168

560. DeRemee R A 1991 Antineutrophil cytoplasmic autoantibody-associated disease: a pulmonologist's perspective. Am J Kidney Dis 18: 180–183

561. Falk R J, Jennette J C 1988 Anti-neutrophil cytoplasmic autoantibodies with specificity for myeloperoxidase in patients with systemic vasculitis and idiopathic necrotizing and crescenteric glomerulonephritis. N Engl J Med 318: 1651–1657

562. Hardarson S, Labrecque D R, Mitros F A et al. 1993 Antineutrophil cytoplasmic antibody in inflammatory bowel and hepatobiliary diseases: high prevalence in ulcerative colitis, primary sclerosing cholangitis, and autoimmune hepatitis. Am J Clin Pathol 99: 221–223

563. Zholudev A, Zurakowski D, Young W et al. 2004 Serologic testing with ANCA, ASCA, and anti-OmpC in children and young adults with Crohn's disease and ulcerative colitis: diagnostic value and correlation with disease phenotype. Am J Gastoenterol 99: 2235–2241

564. Devaney K O, Travis W D, Hoffman G et al. 1990 Interpretation of head and neck biopsies in Wegener's granulomatosis. Am J Surg Pathol 14: 555–564

565. Keogh K A, Specks U 2003 Churg–Strauss syndrome: clinical presentation, antineutrophil cytoplasmic antibodies, and leukotriene receptor antagonists. Am J Med 115: 284–290

566. Barnes L 2001 Midfacial destructive diseases. In: Barnes L (ed) Surgical pathology of the head and neck, 2nd edn. Marcel-Dekker, New York, p 759–786

567. Rosai J, Dorfman R F 1969 Sinus histiocytosis with massive lymphadenopathy: a newly recognized benign clinicopathologic entity. Arch Pathol 87: 63–70

568. Rosai J, Dorfman R F 1972 Sinus histiocytosis with massive lymphadenopathy: a pseudolymphomatous benign disorder. Cancer 30: 1174–1188

569. Foucar E, Rosai J, Dorfman R 1990 Sinus histiocytosis with massive lymphadenopathy (Rosai–Dorfman disease): review of the entity. Semin Diagn Pathol 7: 19–73

570. Foucar K, Foucar E 1990 The mononuclear phagocyte and immunoregulatory effector (M-PIRE) system: evolving concepts. Semin Diagn Pathol 7: 4–18

571. Wenig B M, Abbondanzo S L, Childers E L 1993 Extranodal sinus histiocytosis with massive lymphadenopathy (Rosai–Dorfman disease) of the head and neck. Hum Pathol 24: 483–492

572. Eisen R N, Buckley P J, Rosai J 1990 Immunophenotypic characterization of sinus histiocytosis with massive lymphadenopathy (Rosai–Dorfman disease). Semin Diagn Pathol 7: 74–82

573. Paulli M, Rosso R, Kindl S et al. 1992 Immunophenotypic characterization of the cell infiltrate in five cases of sinus histiocytosis with massive lymphadenopathy (Rosai–Dorfman disease). Hum Pathol 23: 647–654

574. Komp D M 1990 The treatment of sinus histiocytosis with massive lymphadenopathy (Rosai–Dorfman disease). Semin Diagn Pathol 7: 83–86

575. Foucar E, Rosai J, Dorfman R F 1984 Sinus histiocytosis with massive lymphadenopathy: an analysis of 14 deaths occurring in a patient registry. Cancer 54: 1834–1840

Larynx and trachea

Ben Z. Pilch

Benign neoplasms

Squamous papilloma

Squamous papillomas are the most common tumors of the larynx in childhood.[1-4] They are characterized clinically by their multiplicity and repeated recurrences with occasionally long intervening latent periods.[1,3] Laryngeal squamous papillomas have traditionally been divided into juvenile and adult types, but the multiple recurring papillomas, whether presenting in childhood or adulthood, are now generally considered to represent the same basic entity,[5,6] although childhood cases tend clinically to be more aggressive than those occurring initially in adults.[2] These polypoid exophytic lesions can cause significant airway obstruction, especially in children, and, with their recalcitrance to treatment, often present a formidable therapeutic challenge. The standard therapy for recurrent papillomatosis is surgery using the carbon dioxide laser or microdebrider.[2] More recent techniques, such as use of the pulsed dye laser,[7] and intralesional injection of the antiviral drug cidofovir,[8,9] show some therapeutic potential. The true vocal cord is the commonest site for laryngeal papillomas, but subglottic, supraglottic, and tracheal lesions also occur.[1,5] Rarely, squamous papillomatosis can involve the entire respiratory tract, including the tracheobronchial tree to the level of the pulmonary parenchyma.[5,10] This unfortunate occurrence predisposes to obstructive pneumonia and abscess formation, with a potentially fatal outcome. Tracheostomy has been found to be associated with an increased incidence of subglottic and tracheal occurrence of papillomas,[1,3] and thus its use has been frowned upon by some, at least unless absolutely necessary.[2] However, a review by Shapiro et al. suggests that tracheostomy is not associated with a significantly deleterious outcome, and

that it remains a viable treatment option for severe airway compromise in affected children.[11] The former notion that juvenile laryngeal papillomas tend to regress at puberty has been largely replaced by recognition that spontaneous regression can be capricious and unpredictable.[4,12,13]

Laryngeal squamous papillomas are definitely associated with, and appear to be caused by, human papillomavirus (HPV) infection,[1,2,14-16] particularly subtypes 6 and 11.[14-18] These HPV subtypes are commonly also associated with anogenital condylomata and, in fact, infection of an infant during pregnancy or delivery by a mother with condylomas is thought to represent a significant means of acquiring the disease.[1,4,19,20] Fortunately, malignant degeneration of laryngeal squamous papillomas, in the absence of prior irradiation, is quite rare.[5] A reported case of laryngeal squamous papilloma with severe dysplasia/carcinoma in situ (CIS) was shown to be associated with HPV type 16 (a "high-risk" HPV in the uterine cervix) in addition to type 11;[21] however, other cases of carcinoma progressing from papillomatosis were, in fact, associated with HPV type 6/11.[22]

Grossly, squamous papillomas are generally exophytic, friable, cauliflower-like masses presenting either singly or in clusters. Histologically, they are characterized by finger-like or frond-like projections of thickened stratified squamous epithelium around central fibrovascular cores (Fig. 4B.1). Some branching of the papillae may occur. There is typically either a thin parakeratotic layer or no keratin layer on the surface of the papillae, and prominent keratinization generally does not occur, a differential diagnostic clue (see below). The squamous epithelial cells show conspicuous maturational arrest[1,2] with an absence of cell flattening and surface squamous maturation, although a thin uppermost layer may be flattened. Individual cell dyskeratosis occurs commonly, and cellular polarity is at times disturbed, imparting a disorganized appearance to the epithelial cells. Koilocytotic changes, as seen in the female genital tract (cytoplasmic clearing around a dark, wrinkled

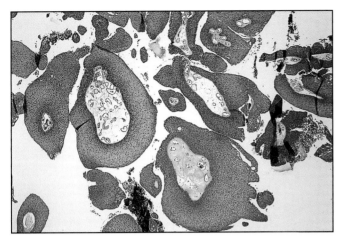

Fig. 4B.1 • Squamous papilloma of the larynx. Finger-like papillae of thickened squamous epithelium contain central fibrovascular cores.

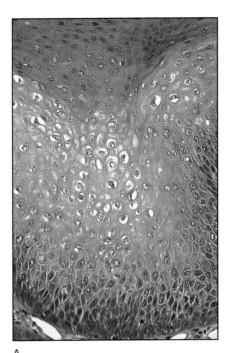

A

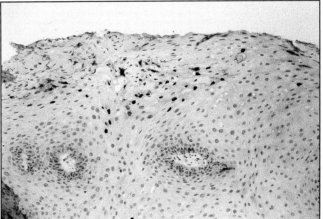

B

Fig. 4B.2 • Squamous papilloma of the larynx. (A) Koilocytosis, as evidenced by perinuclear clearing, nuclear contour irregularity or "wrinkling," and a binucleate cell, slightly above the middle of the photomicrograph. (B) Immunohistochemical stain for pan-human papillomavirus shows positive staining in multiple nuclei.

nucleus, with occasional binucleate or trinucleate cells), are not infrequently observed (Fig. 4B.2A) but tend not to be as prominent as in the cervix.[1,14,23] When laryngeal papillomatosis extends into the subglottis or tracheobronchial tree, the epithelium can be squamous or ciliated columnar and can contain so-called "intermediate cells" – polygonal cells intermediate in appearance between squamous and cuboidal/columnar epithelial cells.[24]

There has been some discussion regarding the histologic "atypicality" of papillomas and its association with aggressive clinical behavior and local recurrence.[25–27] However "premalignant" or dysplastic epithelial changes, such as significant nuclear pleomorphism, hyperchromasia, increased nuclear-to-cytoplasmic ratio, and abnormal mitotic figures, are rarely seen in HPV-associated laryngeal squamous papillomas in my experience, and the "atypical" changes mentioned in most previous literature likely relate to the viral-associated changes of maturational arrest, dyskeratosis, and koilocytosis. While some studies have shown no correlation between histopathology and clinical behavior in both juvenile and adult-onset viral-associated laryngeal squamous papillomas,[1] others have suggested that increased histologic "atypia" is associated with increased severity and/or recurrence in papillomas;[25,26] however, these changes have not been found to be associated with the subsequent occurrence of carcinoma.[26] HPV-related antigens can occasionally be demonstrated by focal staining in papillomas using conventional immunohistochemical techniques (Fig. 4B.2B); however, more recent methods such as in-situ or Southern-blot hybridization or polymerase chain reaction are more consistently successful in identifying lesional HPV DNA.[1,14–18]

Differential diagnosis

So-called "solitary adult papilloma" or "keratinizing papilloma" is a term found in the literature to describe a keratotic papillary solitary lesion in the larynx of an adult.[5] It has been grouped with laryngeal squamous papillomas, but it is not HPV-related and represents a hyperplastic, keratotic, occasionally dysplastic laryngeal lesion that has a papillary configuration, and may be thought of as a papillary leukoplakic lesion. It is generally more keratotic than viral papillomas, is usually solitary, and does not exhibit koilocytosis.

Verrucous carcinoma (see page 161) is a larger, broader-based lesion than squamous papilloma, with a thicker epithelial layer and generally more surface keratin. This lesion tends to infiltrate subjacent tissue in a broad pushing manner, and characteristically has a prominent chronic inflammatory infiltrate at its base. Verruca vulgaris has very rarely been reported in the larynx.[28,29] This lesion mimics the cutaneous verruca, with pointed, spire-like papillae, abundant keratin production, and a prominent granular cell layer. This lesion is also related to HPV infection. Occasionally, the term "condyloma" is applied to a papillary lesion in the upper aerodigestive tract.[14,23] This term may be appropriate to refer to the subset of squamous papillomas that exhibit prominent koilocytotic changes, thus reflecting their analogy to comparable lesions in the anogenital area. *Papillary squamous cell carcinoma* (PSCC) is a malignant lesion that does not have the benign nuclear characteristics of squamous papilloma.[26] Rarely, extensive laryngotracheal papillomas may become aggressive and infiltrate surrounding tissue, although still maintaining a bland cytologic appearance and a sharp stromal interface. Such uncommon lesions have been termed "invasive papillomatosis."[10,24]

Benign epithelial neoplasms of salivary gland type

The seromucinous glands of the upper respiratory tract may be considered as analogues of salivary glands, and thus tumors of salivary gland type may be expected to arise in them (see Ch. 7). Benign neoplasms of salivary gland type are extremely rare in the larynx and trachea. Pleomorphic adenomas, resembling their salivary gland counterparts in morphology and clinical behavior, have been reported in the larynx[30,31] and trachea.[32] Laryngeal oncocytic lesions are more aptly considered cystic glandular hyperplasia and/or metaplasias and are described below. Most laryngotracheal neoplasms of salivary gland type are malignant and will be discussed with the malignant neoplasms.

Granular cell tumor

Granular cell tumors, relatively uncommon tumors of somewhat controversial nature and histogenesis, occur most frequently in the skin and subcutaneous tissue (see Ch. 27).[33,34] The oral cavity, particularly the tongue, is a frequent site,[33,35] and the larynx is a well-recognized although uncommon location.[36–38] Only very occasional cases have been reported in the trachea.[39] Laryngeal granular cell tumors typically present in the fourth or fifth decade of life, but patients aged 5–82 years have been described.[38,40] The characteristic location is the vocal cord,[36,38] particularly posteriorly.[37] Presenting complaints include hoarseness or a sore throat, and some lesions are discovered as asymptomatic incidental findings.[36] The lesions are usually small, rounded, ill-defined submucosal masses.[36] Almost all granular cell tumors in all locations are benign, with laryngeal tumors recurring uncommonly.[33,34,37,41,42] An "atypical" laryngeal tumor with aggressive (although non-metastasizing) clinical behavior and histologic pleomorphism has been described.[41]

Histologically, granular cell tumors are characterized by masses of large, rounded, polygonal, and occasionally fusiform to spindled cells with ample eosinophilic granular cytoplasm (Fig. 4B.3). Cell borders may be ill defined, imparting a syncytial appearance to the cells. The tumor is not well demarcated; the granular cells infiltrate adjacent tissue and are often intimately admixed with the constituent native tissue, including nerve and muscle. Nuclei are usually small and regular, but occasionally larger, more hyperchromatic nuclei may be seen. Mitoses are typically absent or scant.

A distinctive and noteworthy histologic feature of many mucosal granular cell tumors is the presence of pseudo-epitheliomatous squamous epithelial hyperplasia of the mucosa overlying the tumor (Fig. 4B.3). This change can at times be striking, with strands and tongues of cytologically bland surface epithelium extending into the underlying granular cell lesion. Care must be taken not to misinterpret this change as invasive squamous cell carcinoma. Recognition of the under-

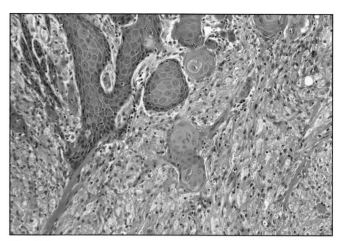

Fig. 4B.3 • Granular cell tumor of the larynx. A sheet of large cells with abundant granular cytoplasm and ill-defined cell borders is associated with pseudoepitheliomatous hyperplasia of overlying mucosal squamous epithelium.

lying granular cell tumor as well as the bland epithelial cytology should serve as clues to the true nature of the lesion.

Although the histiocyte and a primitive mesenchymal cell have been advocated as possible cells of origin, the predominant current opinion is that most granular cell tumors are neurally derived and probably of Schwann cell origin.[33,42,43]

Differential diagnosis

The most significant differential diagnostic issue regarding a granular cell tumor in the head and neck is probably differentiating its associated overlying pseudoepitheliomatous mucosal hyperplasia from squamous cell carcinoma, as has been discussed above. A case of synchronous squamous cell carcinoma and granular cell tumor in the tongue, an extremely rare occurrence, has been reported, and is notable for the fact that the pseudoepitheliomatous mucosal hyperplasia overlying the granular cell tumor was cytologically bland and distinct from the carcinoma.[44] Adult-type rhabdomyomas may resemble granular cell tumors, especially in frozen sections; however, rhabdomyoma cells contain abundant glycogen (diastase-sensitive rather than resistant), have well-defined cell borders, and often have a characteristic "spider-cell" appearance with strands of cytoplasm extending from the nuclear region to the cell membrane, resembling a spider's web. Oncocytomas have large granular eosinophilic cells, but their granularity is due to abundant packed mitochondria and not autophagolysosomes. Oncocytoma cells, like rhabdomyoma cells, have well-defined cell borders rather than a syncytial appearance, and occur predominantly in epithelial, usually glandular, organs rather than in soft tissue.

Paraganglioma

Paragangliomas (see also Ch. 28) are uncommon neoplasms arising from paraganglia, the latter being small neural crest-derived neuroectodermal structures distributed throughout the body, usually in close relation to autonomic nerves and ganglia and/or vascular structures.[45,46] Carotid body tumors are the most common and best known of the paragangliomas.

Laryngeal paragangliomas are quite rare but do occur,[46–49] associated with the superior laryngeal paraganglia located in the false vocal cord region or, more rarely, the less consistently positioned inferior laryngeal paraganglia located subglottically in the cricothyroid or cricotracheal region, in rare instances associated with the capsule of the thyroid gland[46,47,50] (Fig. 4B.4). Tracheal paragangliomas are even more uncommon.[51]

Most paragangliomas (of all sites) are benign, although rare malignant paragangliomas occur. It is difficult, if not impossible, to predict accurately clinical behavior on the basis of morphologic features alone.[46] Laryngeal paragangliomas have classically been reported to include a relatively high percentage of malignant neoplasms, as well as painful tumors. More recent reviews, however, suggest that many of the reported malignant laryngeal paragangliomas may actually have represented neuroendocrine carcinomas,[46,48,49,52–54] an occasionally difficult histologic differential diagnosis but one that is substantially facilitated by immunohistochemical techniques (see below).[55] This interpretation would bring the biologic behavior of most laryngeal paragangliomas more into line with that of paragangliomas at other sites (i.e., predominantly benign).

Histologically, laryngeal and tracheal paragangliomas resemble those in other sites (see Ch. 28). The tumors are highly vascular and are composed of nests of round, occasionally fusiform, chief cells that have ample cytoplasm and central nuclei. Occasionally darker, smaller, and more angulated sustentacular cells may be present, usually at the periphery of the nests of chief cells. The nests are arranged as characteristic "balls of cells" (zellballen), in intimate, at times glomeruloid, relation to capillaries (Fig. 4B.5). Nuclei in chief cells can range from small to large and hyperchromatic. Nuclear pleomorphism appears not to correlate with clinical behavior. Mitoses are generally scant in laryngeal lesions.

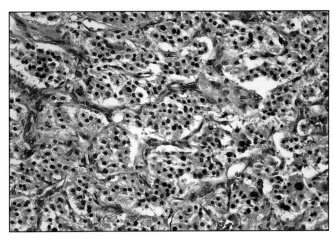

Fig. 4B.5 • Paraganglioma of the larynx. Characteristic "Zellballen" of chief cells in intimate relation to capillaries.

The tumor cells are argyrophilic and stain immunohistochemically with neuroendocrine markers, especially neuron-specific enolase and/or chromogranin.[46,47] Sustentacular cells are S-100 protein-positive.[47,49] An important differential diagnostic point is that paragangliomas are generally keratin-negative, whereas neuroendocrine carcinomas (carcinoids or "atypical" carcinoids) are keratin-positive.[47,54,55] Ultrastructurally, characteristic dense-core neurosecretory-type granules with delimiting membranes are seen in chief cells.

Differential diagnostic considerations include carcinomas, in particular carcinoid-type neuroendocrine carcinomas. The typical zellballen architectural pattern should suggest the appropriate diagnosis. The presence of prominent argyrophilia and chromogranin positivity basically excludes non-neuroendocrine neoplasms, and the absence of keratin positivity and presence of S-100 protein-positive sustentacular cells tends to exclude neuroendocrine carcinomas.

Subglottic hemangioma

Subglottic hemangioma of the larynx is a vasoproliferative lesion of infancy which, although uncommon, is fraught with the potential danger of causing airway obstruction.[56,57] It has not definitely been established whether this lesion represents a vascular malformation or a true neoplasm;[57] however, for convenience it is considered here with the benign tumors.

Subglottic hemangiomas usually present clinically in the first 6 months of life. Symptoms of partial airway obstruction such as stridor or croup of a laryngotracheitis-like nature herald its appearance.[58] Cutaneous angiomatous lesions are concurrently present in about half the cases.[56–58] The degree of respiratory obstruction may wax and wane, increasing during periods of excitability or infection,[57,59] possibly as a result of varying venous pressure within the lesion.[56,60] The usual tendency of juvenile (capillary) hemangiomas of the head and neck, including the subglottic variety, is to involute spontaneously after several years;[56–58] however, obstructing lesions often necessitate more immediate therapeutic intervention.[57]

The endoscopic appearance is characteristic, the lesion manifesting as a soft compressible subglottic mass, usually bluish but occasionally pink, located just below the vocal cords, usually in an asymmetrical posterolateral location.[56,57,59]

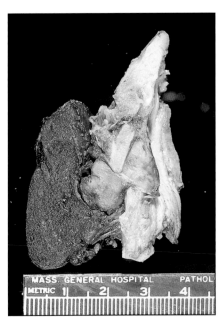

Fig. 4B.4 • Paraganglioma of the inferior laryngeal paraganglion protruding in dumbbell fashion between cartilages to abut the thyroid gland. (Reproduced, with permission of the American Medical Association, from Googe R B, Ferry J A, Bhan A K et al. 1988 A comparison of paraganglioma, carcinoid tumor, and small cell carcinoma of the larynx. Arch Pathol Lab Med 112: 809–815.[47]) © 1988 American Medical Association. All rights reserved.

Significant airway compromise may be present.[56,59] Biopsy is often not required for diagnosis; although some authors are wary of excessive hemorrhage following surgical manipulation,[59] others report few, if any, significant complications from biopsy.[57]

Histologically, the appearance is that of a capillary hemangioma of infantile type (See Ch. 3).[56,58] Numerous blood vessels, which may be largely empty and collapsed or blood-filled and dilated, infiltrate, in a mainly lobular fashion, around and among native structures such as seromucinous glands (Fig. 4B.6). The lesion is infiltrative and unencapsulated.[56] The constituent endothelial cells are plump, and mitoses may be seen. The cellularity may be such as to partially obscure the vascular lumina.[56] The histomorphology is sufficiently characteristic so as to preclude difficulty in differential diagnosis, with the exception that a solid, cellular mitotically active lesion may perhaps raise the possibility of an angiosarcoma; however, this latter condition in an infant is virtually non-existent.

Other benign mesenchymal neoplasms

Benign nerve sheath tumors, both schwannomas and neurofibromas, occur in the larynx and trachea, but they are rare.[60-64] Laryngeal neurofibromas may occur in the context of neurofibromatosis type I and may be of the plexiform variety.[65] A single case of hypopharyngeal cellular neurothekeoma has been reported.[66] Laryngeal nerve sheath tumors pathologically resemble their counterparts elsewhere in the body. Benign muscular neoplasms also rarely occur in the larynx. Leiomyomas, both conventional[67] and vascular (angioleiomyoma or angiomyoma),[68] have been reported, as have rhabdomyomas of both adult[69] and fetal type.[70,71] Laryngeal fibromatosis in infants and children occurs rarely as an example of the childhood fibromatosis syndromes.[72,73] Lipomas of the larynx and hypopharynx are rarely encountered.[74] Case reports of benign neoplastic oddities occurring in the larynx and trachea include

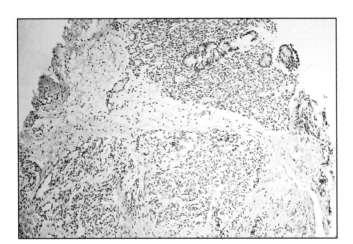

Fig. 4B.6 • Subglottic hemangioma in a 9-month-old child. Numerous capillary structures with small lumina, imparting a highly cellular appearance, infiltrate in and around indigenous structures, such as the gland in the upper portion of the photomicrograph. Reproduced from Shapshay S M and Aretz H T. Benign lesions of the larynx with permission of the American Academy of Otolaryngology – Head and Neck Surgery Foundation, copyright © 1984. All rights reserved.

mention of fibrolipoma,[75] so-called hemangiopericytoma,[76,77] fibrous histiocytoma,[78-80] fibromyxoma,[81] glomangioma/glomus tumor,[82] teratoma,[83] and benign clear cell ("sugar") tumor.[84]

Non-neoplastic tumorous lesions

Vocal cord polyps

Vocal cord polyps are localized non-neoplastic swellings, thought to be induced by vocal abuse or "phonotrauma" and possibly by airborne irritants.[85,86] Because of their functionally significant location on the true vocal cords, they cause symptoms of hoarseness, although they may be small in size. Polyps appear as localized swellings, either unilateral or bilateral, which may be either pale and translucent, or bluish in color, the latter type resembling a vascular structure and referred to in older clinical parlance as "varix of the cord." Histologically, polyps consist of a loose, edematous, often myxoid expansion of the subepithelial connective tissue (Fig. 4B.7A). The vascular variety has prominent endothelial-lined vascular spaces with fibrin deposition, often abundant, both within and outside the vascular spaces (Fig. 4B.7B). Often, polyps display an admixture of the myxoid and vascular patterns. Their histogenesis is thought to relate to increased blood flow and vascular permeability caused by the noxious stimuli of phonotrauma and/or airborne irritants. Edema fluid and fibrin then collect in Reinke's space (the compartment between the mucosal epithelium of the vocal cord and the vocal ligament). Organization of the fibrin may occur, resembling the organization of a thrombus. The term vocal "nodule" has been used to describe a swelling more firm or fibrotic than the classic polyp, but some authors maintain that the two represent essentially the same lesion,[85] and this is also our view.

Contact ulcer/"granuloma"

A contact ulcer is an ulcerative lesion of the larynx, characteristically affecting the posterior vocal cord mucosa overlying the vocal process of the arytenoid cartilage.[87] It is often associated with proliferative granulation tissue, resulting in a mass lesion called a contact "granuloma," although pathologically the lesion is not a true (histiocytic) granuloma. The condition, which may be unilateral or bilateral, results from traumatic injury to the thin mucosa of this region, either from pressure necrosis secondary to intubation[88] (postintubation "granuloma"), reflux of gastric contents ("peptic granuloma"),[89,90] or vocal abuse, e.g., in public speakers.[91,92] The cases involving vocal abuse or gastric acid reflux predominantly affect men.[93] Symptoms include sore throat, hoarseness, sensation of a foreign body in the throat, and dysphagia.[90-93] On examination, a polypoid round sessile mass, usually ulcerated, varying in size from a few millimeters to 3 cm in diameter is seen.[93]

Histologically, granulation tissue is seen, with capillaries oriented radially to the mucosal surface (Fig. 4B.8); the latter is either ulcerated or lined by hyperplastic regenerative squamous epithelium. This lesion is to be differentiated from a pyogenic granuloma, which does not normally occur in this location. A pyogenic granuloma is a lobular capillary hemangioma,[94] in which capillaries are disposed in a lobular

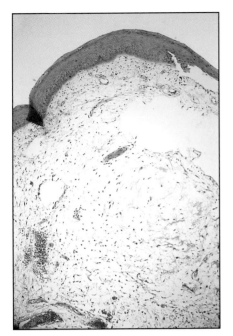

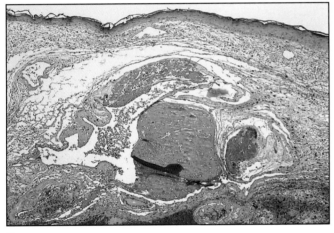

B

Fig. 4B.7 • Vocal cord polyp. **(A)** Myxoid polyp with edematous myxoid stroma. **(B)** Vascular polyp containing prominent vascular spaces and abundant fibrinous material.

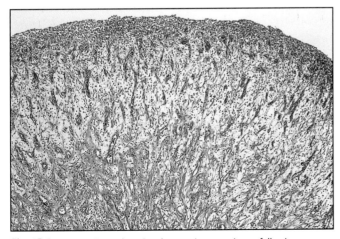

Fig. 4B.8 • Contact "granuloma" at the anterior commissure following instrumentation. Ulcerated polypoid granulation tissue has capillaries oriented radially to the surface.

pattern, often around central larger vessels, rather than in the radial array of a contact "granuloma." In cases of prolonged intubation injury, focal chondritis and chondronecrosis of the arytenoid cartilage, often associated with bacterial infection, may occur.

Idiopathic laryngotracheal stenosis

Although intubation injury, previous surgery, and other specific infections and non-infectious processes (e.g., amyloid deposition, Wegener's granulomatosis) can cause significant laryngotracheal narrowing, a small group of patients exhibit laryngotracheal stenosis, usually involving the cricoid area of the larynx and uppermost trachea, without a known specific etiology. This entity of idiopathic laryngotracheal stenosis[95,96] occurs mainly in females over a broad age range. The presenting symptom is progressively worsening dyspnea; on examination, a narrowing of the subglottic airway, generally involving the cricoid area and uppermost trachea, is seen, resulting from submucosal thickening that is often circumferential. Focal mucosal ulceration occasionally occurs.

Histologically, the lesion is characterized by keloidal dense fibrosis, which is mainly paucicellular.[95] Occasionally, lymphocytes and histiocytes are present, but not usually in profusion. The lesion tends to be non-progressive and usually responds favorably to surgical resection.[95] In some cases of subglottic stenosis, gastroesophageal reflux may be a contributing factor.[97]

Cysts

A *laryngocele* is a dilatation of the saccule (a narrow appendiceal outpouching in the anterior portion of the laryngeal ventricle) that communicates with the laryngeal lumen via the ventricle and is filled with air.[98–100] It may present as a submucosal bulge in the supraglottic larynx or aryepiglottic fold area (internal laryngocele), or it may penetrate the thyrohyoid membrane, through the foramen which contains the superior laryngeal nerve and vessels, to present as a cystic neck mass (external laryngocele). Combined laryngoceles consist of cystic masses in both locations. Laryngoceles may present clinically with hoarseness or as a cystic neck mass that may fluctuate in size due to communication with the laryngeal lumen. They may also be asymptomatic. Onset may be congenital (i.e., a congenitally enlarged dilated saccule) or acquired, with development of the laryngocele abetted by repeated dilatations of the saccule. These result from increased intralaryngeal pressure with relaxed supraglottic muscles against tightened lips, as in brass instrument players or glassblowers.[98,101] Histologically, laryngoceles consist of cystic outpouchings of indigenous ventriculosaccular ciliated columnar mucosa.

Saccular cysts are also saccular dilatations like laryngoceles, but they are filled with mucus and do not communicate with the laryngeal lumen,[99,102] characteristically because of an obstruction to the narrow saccular orifice that may be congenital or acquired. Possible causes of obstruction resulting in saccular cysts/laryngoceles include inflammation, trauma, or tumor. In fact, an association between laryngeal carcinoma and laryngoceles has been noted, and saccular dilatation may be caused by clinically inapparent carcinoma of the ventricular area.

Small laryngeal ductal cysts may arise as a result of obstruction of the ducts of any of the numerous seromucinous glands of the larynx.[102] Occasionally, cysts of ductal or saccular origin are lined by oncocytic cells, often thrown up into papillary folds and associated with cellular proliferation, reminiscent of a Warthin's tumor of the parotid gland[103,104] (Fig. 4B.9). These have been called by various names, including oncocytic cystadenoma, papillary cystadenoma, and oncocytic cyst.[105] We feel, as do others, that such lesions are due to oncocytic metaplasia/hyperplasia and are not true neoplasms.[103,104] A spectrum of changes may be found, ranging from isolated foci of oncocytic metaplasia in seromucinous glands (Fig. 4B.10), to dilatation of ducts lined in whole or in part by oncocytes, to full-blown papillary cystic lesions (Fig. 4B.9). They occur predominantly in middle-aged to elderly people and are mainly innocuous curiosities unless they cause symptoms by attaining considerable size. We prefer the term oncocytic cyst for such metaplastic/hyperplastic cystic lesions.

Chronic infections

Although once a relatively common terminal complication of advanced pulmonary disease, laryngeal tuberculosis currently most often presents, in western countries, as a mass lesion mimicking a neoplasm in patients with only mild or clinically inapparent chest disease.[106–108] It is now much rarer than in the early twentieth century; however, an alarming increase in the incidence of tuberculosis in recent years, due in part to the acquired immune deficiency syndrome (AIDS), and to the development of drug-resistant strains of mycobacteria, may result in increasing encounters with the laryngeal form of the disease.[109] The lesion characteristically presents with hoarseness and an ulcerative or mass lesion in the larynx. Histologically, the classic morphology of necrotizing granulomatous inflammation with giant cells is seen. Rare acid-fast bacilli can usually be found in lesions of untreated patients.

Even more uncommon than laryngeal tuberculosis in the west are fungal infections of the larynx which may also clinically mimic neoplasms. These include histoplasmosis,[110] blastomycosis,[111] coccidioidomycosis,[112] paracoccidioidomycosis,[113] sporotrichosis,[114] aspergillosis,[115] and actinomycosis (technically a bacterial infection).[116] Laryngeal candidiasis may follow pulmonary or disseminated disease, be associated with chronic mucocutaneous candidiasis,[117] or be associated with antibiotic treatment or immunosuppressive states or therapies.[118] Interestingly, some laryngeal fungal infections, including candidiasis, are associated with an accompanying mucosal squamous epithelial hyperplasia that may mimic carcinoma.[118]

Amyloid deposition

The larynx and trachea are rarely involved in generalized amyloidosis to a clinically significant degree; however, the larynx is a well-recognized site of localized amyloid deposition,[119–123] and is reportedly the most common site of localized amyloidosis in the upper aerodigestive tract.[122] The trachea may also be affected by localized disease.[124,125] Patients present with hoarseness, and rarely with stridor, dyspnea, or hemoptysis.[124] Laryngotracheal amyloid may manifest clinically as discrete tumor-like masses or as diffuse submucosal thickening.[120,122,125] Growth of both kinds tends to be quite slow. The supraglottic larynx/false-cord area appears most commonly affected,[121,122] but the vocal cords and subglottic regions may also be sites of amyloid deposition. Multiple sites in the larynx may be involved.[122] Isolated tumorous masses rarely cause significant problems and have a good prognosis. Diffuse submucosal lesions may be more problematic and difficult to eradicate, and very rare cases of diffuse extensive tracheobronchial amyloidosis may be fatal, with obstruction and repeated infections.[124,125]

Histologically, amyloid is seen as an amorphous homogeneous eosinophilic extracellular deposit in the tissues (Fig. 4B.11A). An artifact of tissue-processing often produces small clefts separating masses of amyloid, resulting in a "cracked" appearance.[119] A chronic inflammatory infiltrate, including a prominent plasma cell component, is often present.[122,123] Foreign-body giant cells may occasionally be seen, reacting to the amyloid material. Preferential sites for amyloid deposition include the adventitia of blood vessels, around seromucinous glands (Fig. 4B.11B), "squeezing" them into atrophy, and occasionally as "rings" around fat cells.[119,124] Amyloid is distinguished from other material by its distinctive property of "apple-green" birefringence on staining with congo red when viewed under polarized light. Studies have shown

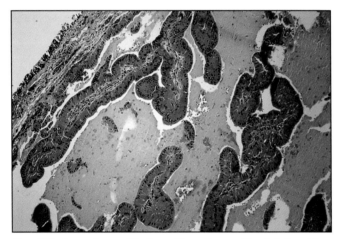

Fig. 4B.9 • Oncocytic cyst of the larynx. View of large multicystic lesion with focal invagination of papillary structures, lined by oncocytic epithelium. Surface mucosa is at upper left.

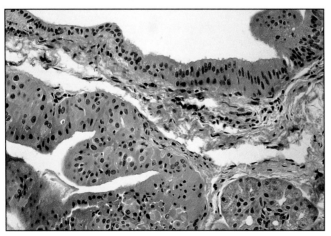

Fig. 4B.10 • Oncocytic laryngeal cyst, showing oncocytic metaplasia of glandular ducts.

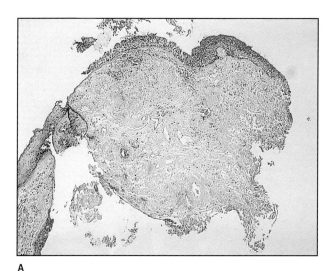

A

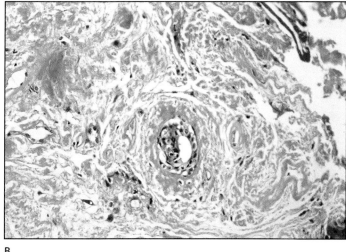

B

Fig. 4B.11 • Amyloid deposition in the larynx. **(A)** Amorphous deposit of homogeneous extracellular eosinophilic amyloid material deep to surface mucosal epithelium. **(B)** Amyloid deposited around a solitary small ductal structure. (Fig. 4B.11B reproduced from Shapshay S M and Aretz H T. Benign lesions of the larynx with permission of the American Academy of Otolaryngology – Head and Neck Surgery Foundation, copyright © 1984. All rights reserved.)

that localized laryngeal amyloid is of the immunoglobulin light chain-derived variety.[121–126]

Two differential diagnoses to consider are a vascular vocal cord polyp and a plasmacytoma. The eosinophilic material in a vocal cord polyp is fibrin, not amyloid, and thus it will not produce the characteristic birefringence with congo red staining. Furthermore, a myxoid component to the polyp is often present. Plasmacytomas may be associated with amyloid production, but in these lesions there is a neoplastic mass consisting of a relatively pure population of plasma cells exhibiting monotypic staining for immunoglobulin light chains. In 12 cases of laryngeal amyloid deposition associated with significant numbers of plasma cells studied by Lewis et al.,[122] the plasma cells showed a polyclonal staining pattern for immunoglobulin light chains. However in a meticulously studied case reported by Berg et al.,[126] the amyloid-associated plasma cells stained for kappa but not lambda immunoglobulin light chain, as did the amyloid material, suggesting that at least some cases of localized amyloidosis may represent a variety of plasma cell dyscrasia, albeit one that is much more benign than a classic plasmacytoma and that does not appear to progress to multiple myeloma.[126] Two other reported cases of localized pulmonary amyloidosis associated with monotypic lymphoplasmacytic proliferation would tend to support such a notion.[127] Further, Thompson et al. found immunoglobulin light-chain restriction in plasma cells associated with laryngeal amyloid deposition in 3 of 10 cases tested.[123]

Tracheopathia osteoplastica

Tracheopathia osteoplastica[128] (or tracheobronchopathia osteochondroplastica[129]) is a condition characterized by the presence of multiple submucosal osteocartilaginous nodules in the trachea and bronchi. In mild cases, patients may be asymptomatic and the condition is diagnosed at autopsy.[128] More extensive involvement, however, may produce symptoms of cough, hemoptysis, exertional dyspnea, or wheezing.[129] The lesions are not well seen on conventional posteroanterior chest radiographs, but lateral views, tomograms, and com-

puted tomography scans may show the characteristic beaded or shell-like calcifications.[128,129] Endoscopically, the lesions present as nodular submucosal firm to hard masses, at times mimicking a neoplasm, and imparting a rigidity to the involved tracheal segment. The condition preferentially involves the distal trachea and proximal bronchi, but the upper trachea[130] and larynx may be involved; rarely, the larynx may be the only site of disease.[131]

Histologically, one sees nodules of hyaline cartilage and lamellar bone, at times containing hematopoietic marrow, in a submucosal location, internal (luminal) to the endogenous tracheal rings (Fig. 4B.12). Collagenous, cartilaginous, and/or osseous connections between the lesional nodules and the inner perichondrium of the tracheal rings may often be identified. The condition spares the posterior membranous portion of the trachea and bronchi. Although there is no universal agreement as to precise etiology and pathogenesis, these latter findings would lend support to the theory of a degenerative ecchondrosis and exostosis of the tracheal rings.[128]

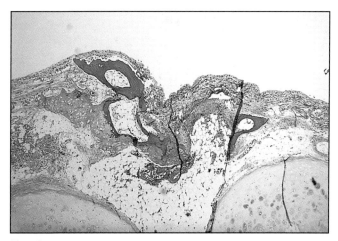

Fig. 4B.12 • Tracheopathia osteoplastica. Deposits of bone lie just deep to mucosal epithelium internal (luminal) to the tracheal rings. (Courtesy of Dr. E. Mark.)

Miscellaneous rarities

Additional conditions that may rarely be encountered as a mass or tumorous lesion in the larynx and/or trachea as rarities or oddities include Wegener's granulomatosis,[132–134] Rosai–Dorfman disease (sinus histiocytosis with massive lymphadenopathy),[135–137] sarcoidosis,[133,138] gout,[139] vocal cord Teflon granuloma,[133,140,141] hamartoma,[142–145] inflammatory pseudotumor,[146] malakoplakia,[147] warty dyskeratoma,[148] schistosomiasis,[149] aneurysmal bone cyst,[150] and Kimura's disease.[151]

Malignant neoplasms

Squamous cell carcinoma

Premalignant/preinvasive lesions (atypicality/carcinoma in situ, precursor lesions)

Reactive changes of the mucosa of the upper aerodigestive tract may include hyperplasia, keratosis, and varying degrees of architectural and cytologic atypicality. Currently it is generally agreed that only those mucosal lesions exhibiting significant atypia or dysplasia should be considered premalignant in the sense of having a relatively high propensity to progress to carcinoma.[152–158]

In general, the degree of dysplasia in the mucosa of the larynx and trachea is considered to increase in severity with increasing cytologic and/or architectural abnormality and with the progression of such changes towards the surface of the mucosal epithelium (Fig. 4B.13). This approach is analogous to that utilized in the oral cavity and uterine cervix. Squamous cell carcinoma in situ (CIS) is traditionally defined as atypicality that occupies the full thickness of the mucosal epithelial layer[152] (Fig. 4B.14). Several classification schemas for precursor lesions have been proposed. The three generally most commonly utilized currently are the World Health

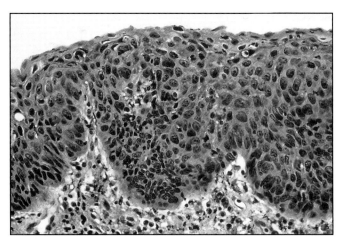

Fig. 4B.14 • Hypopharyngeal squamous cell carcinoma in situ. There is full-thickness atypicality; cells with enlarged nuclei and prominent nucleoli are arranged in a somewhat disorderly fashion and occupy the entire thickness of the mucosal epithelial layer. (Reproduced with permission from Fried M P 1996 The larynx: a multidisciplinary approach, 2nd edn. Mosby, New York, Fig. 40-26.)

Organization (WHO) system, the "squamous intraepithelial neoplasia" (SIN) system, and the Ljubljana classification, commonly utilized in Europe (Table 4B.1).[153] The WHO system is utilized in this chapter.

The classic form of CIS as seen in the uterine cervix (i.e., a uniform mucosal proliferation of immature basaloid cells with no surface maturation) is, in fact, uncommonly seen in the larynx.[157,158] More common is dysplasia characterized by abnormal cellular keratinization, or dyskeratosis, and the presence of large pleomorphic cells with eosinophilic cytoplasm, with surface keratinization being frequent.[159] This change has been called severe keratinizing dysplasia, and is reported to correlate with an increased incidence of subsequent invasive carcinoma.[158] In addition, the distinction between

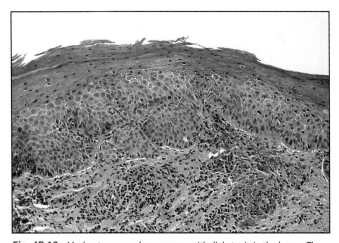

Fig. 4B.13 • Moderate mucosal squamous epithelial atypia in the larynx. The mucosal epithelium is hyperplastic, and there is a maturational abnormality, with immature-appearing cells, some with enlarged and/or hyperchromatic nuclei, extending about halfway to the mucosal surface.

Table 4B.1	Classification schemas that histologically categorize precursor and related lesions	
2005 World Health Organization classification	**Squamous intraepithelial neoplasia (SIN)**	**Ljubljana classification Squamous intraepithelial lesions (SIL)**
Squamous cell hyperplasia		Squamous cell (simple) hyperplasia
Mild dysplasia	SIN 1	Basal/parabasal cell hyperplasia[a]
Moderate dysplasia	SIN 2	Atypical hyperplasia[b]
Severe dysplasia	SIN3[c]	Atypical hyperplasia[b]
Carcinoma in situ	SIN 3[c]	Carcinoma in situ

[a]Basal/parabasal cell hyperplasia may histologically resemble mild dysplasia, but the former is a conceptually benign lesion and the latter the lower grade of precursor lesions.
[b]'Risky' epithelium. Analogy to moderate and severe dysplasia is approximate.
[c]The advocates of SIN combine severe dysplasia and carcinoma in situ. Reproduced from Barnes L, Eveson J W, Reichart P et al.[153]

severe dysplasia and CIS, although still utilized by many, is subtle, often difficult, and subjective, and some (proponents of the SIN system) would combine the two into a category of high-grade intraepithelial neoplasia, again analogous to the situation in the uterine cervix.[157–159]

Clinically, severe dysplasia/CIS may appear as a reddened mucosal patch (erythroplakia), a thickened whitish patch (leukoplakia), or a mixture of the two patterns (speckled leukoplakia). Alternatively, it may be clinically inapparent. Its diagnosis and differentiation from lesser degrees of atypicality depend upon biopsy and histologic interpretation.

The clinical significance and natural history of laryngeal CIS have been difficult to pin down precisely, and various studies have reported a rate of progression to invasive carcinoma varying from 3.5% to 90%.[160] Differences in criteria for diagnosis and patient selection probably contribute to this disparity in results. Furthermore, it is important to remember that CIS often is not an isolated lesion, and may be present near or adjacent to a frank invasive carcinoma. Appropriate clinical and histologic sampling is therefore of extreme importance. It is generally felt that severe dysplasia/CIS, if left untreated, will progress to an invasive carcinoma in a significant number of cases, although perhaps not in every case. Treatment, therefore, is considered necessary; most would advocate a conservative approach of vocal cord stripping or local but complete excision in localized cases. Radiotherapy has been used as well.[161]

The concept of superficially invasive, or microinvasive, squamous cell carcinoma is recognized in the larynx, as in the cervix[157–159,162,163] (Fig. 4B.15). It may be difficult, especially in small biopsy specimens, to identify a focus of microscopic invasion (i.e., penetration through the mucosal basement membrane into the subjacent stroma) in a predominantly intraepithelial carcinoma. The basement membrane of an intraepithelial lesion may be obscured by inflammation; also, nests of carcinoma that invade via a rounded pushing margin may have basement membrane components (laminin and type IV collagen) identifiable immunohistochemically.[158,164] Features

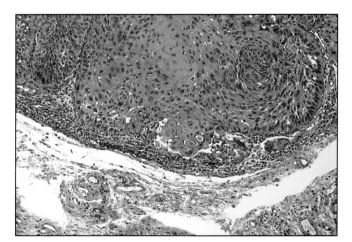

Fig. 4B.15 • Superficially invasive (microinvasive) squamous cell carcinoma of the larynx. In the center of the figure, a focus of epithelium has an irregular border and appears to protrude into underlying connective tissue, as opposed to adjacent epithelium that has a rounded, even base and appears well demarcated from underlying tissue. Several multinucleated giant cells are present adjacent to the microinvasive focus, consistent with foreign-body reaction to keratin that has penetrated the basement membrane.

such as a desmoplastic stromal reaction, foreign-body reaction to keratin in the stroma, and the presence of separate tiny clusters of (or single) neoplastic cells in the stroma are useful as evidence of superficial invasion.[165] It has been suggested that the clinical significance of microinvasion is similar to that of CIS/severe dysplasia,[157,166] and that the prognosis is excellent with appropriate therapy.[166]

Invasive squamous cell carcinoma

Squamous cell carcinoma is by far the most common malignant neoplasm of the larynx. Invasive laryngeal cancer, although not one of the most common malignancies, is not rare, with 10 270 new cases in the USA estimated for 2004.[167] In the USA the larynx is the single most common non-cutaneous organ to harbor a primary cancer in the head and neck.[168] Cancer of the larynx is much more common in men than in women, occurring most commonly in the fifth, sixth, and seventh decades.[169] Estimated new laryngeal cancer cases in the USA for 2004 are 8060 for men and 2210 for women.[167] The discrepancy in incidence between men and women has recently decreased slightly, possibly because of the increased incidence of smoking among women. Smoking and alcohol consumption are considered highly significant etiologic factors in this disease.[165,170,171] Recent evidence has suggested a possible role for HPV infection, *ras* oncogene activation, and gastro-esophageal reflux as well.[165,166,170,172–174] Cancers of the trachea are much more rare, but squamous cell carcinoma is also the most common tracheal malignancy. Its mean age of incidence is about 50 years.[175] The classic symptom of carcinomas of the vocal cord or supraglottic larynx is hoarseness, or a muffled or altered voice. Pain, dysphagia, or hemoptysis may also occur.[161,176] Subglottic carcinomas are more likely to produce stridor or airway obstruction, even when not particularly large, because of the inflexibility imparted to the subglottic space by the cricoid cartilage, the only circumferential cartilage in the respiratory tract.[161] Pyriform sinus cancers are, unfortunately, often large and advanced when discovered because they tend to produce symptoms late. Dysphagia, otalgia, a neck mass secondary to lymph node disease, or general inanition are possible symptoms of hypopharyngeal cancer.[177] Tracheal carcinomas tend to produce stridor or wheezing when sufficient airway compromise develops.

The larynx is divided into supraglottic, glottic, and subglottic compartments. The supraglottis consists of the epiglottis, false vocal cords, laryngeal ventricles, aryepiglottic folds, and arytenoid regions; the glottic portion is composed of the true vocal cords and the anterior and posterior commissures. The subglottic region lies between the true cords and the inferior border of the cricoid cartilage. The dividing line between the glottic and subglottic areas is variously described as being about 5 mm below the true vocal cord[178] and 1 cm inferior to the lateral margin of the ventricle.[179] Perhaps a better division (because it is defined by an anatomic structure) is the conus elasticus, a membrane joining the superior surface of the cricoid cartilage and the ligament of the vocal cord.[165] The glottic compartment would be superolateral to the conus elasticus, and the subglottic compartment inferomedial to it. Glottic cancers are the most common laryngeal cancers, followed in incidence by supraglottic cancers. Primary subglottic carcinomas are rare.[180] Supraglottic tumors are more prone to

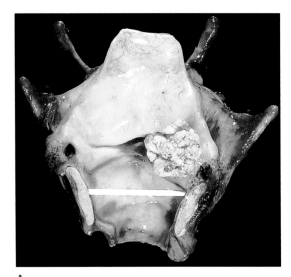

A

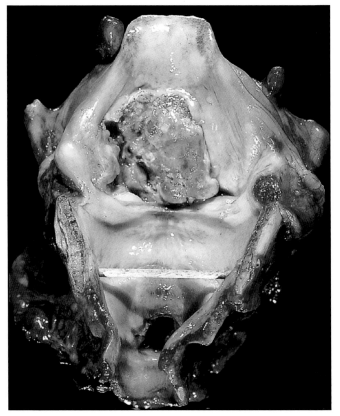

B

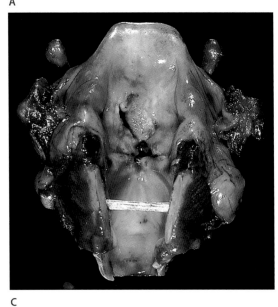

C

Fig. 4B.16 • Squamous cell carcinoma of the larynx. **(A)** Exophytic fungating tumor involving right true vocal cord. **(B)** Raised plaque-like supraglottic tumor with focal ulceration that crosses the midline. **(C)** Ulceroinfiltrative supraglottic tumor.

extend across the midline than glottic lesions. The laryngeal ventricles appear to be a barrier to extension of carcinoma between the glottic and supraglottic compartments, resulting in the successful utilization of horizontal supraglottic laryngectomy to treat some supraglottic cancers. More recent reports, however, indicate that there are pathways for carcinomas to spread between these compartments, notably with spread from the glottis to the arytenoid region posterior to and behind the ventricle, spread in the paraglottic space near the thyroid cartilage lateral to the ventricle, and extension to the anterior commissure area, with invasion of the anterior commissure tendon and/or the thyroid cartilage and spread inferiorly.[181–183] It is not surprising then, that large transglottic tumors, involving both glottic and supraglottic compartments, do occur. These tend to be aggressive neoplasms with a poor prognosis. Glottic cancers extend subglottically more commonly than supraglotically; the conus elasticus acts as a rather imperfect barrier to the spread of tumors.

The hypopharynx, or laryngopharynx, has three components: (1) the pyriform sinus, located between the aryepiglottic folds and the laminae of the thyroid cartilage; (2) the postcricoid region, located on the posterior surface of the cricoid cartilage; and (3) the posterior hypopharynx, located on the posterior pharyngeal wall from the level of the epiglottis (border with the oropharynx) to the level of the inferior border of the cricoid cartilage (border with the esophagus). The majority of hypopharyngeal cancers occur in the pyriform sinus, with carcinomas of the posterior wall occurring next most commonly and primary postcricoid carcinomas being the rarest of hypopharyngeal carcinomas.[184] As with laryngeal cancers, men are more frequently affected than women, and 90% of patients report a history of tobacco use.[184]

Laryngeal squamous cell carcinomas may present grossly as exophytic shaggy-surfaced masses, with or without surface ulceration, or as deeply invasive ulceroinfiltrative masses without a prominent surface mass (Fig. 4B.16).

The histologic appearance of squamous cell carcinoma of the larynx, hypopharynx, and trachea corresponds to that of squamous cell carcinomas in other sites (e.g., oral cavity, lung, esophagus, skin)[165] (Fig. 4B.17). Tumors may be keratinizing or non-keratinizing, although most produce recognizable intracellular or extracellular keratin, and they vary from well to poorly differentiated. Many tumors have associated CIS adjacent to their invasive foci. Efforts to attach prognostic

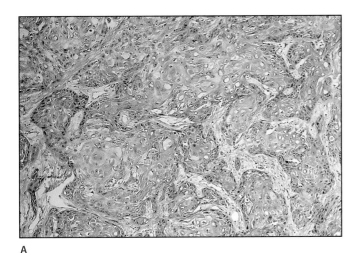
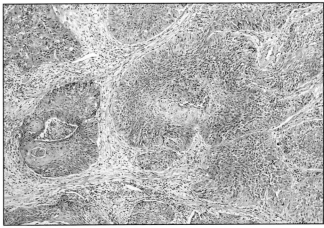

A   B

Fig. 4B.17 • Squamous cell carcinoma of the larynx. (**A**) Well-differentiated carcinoma. (**B**) Moderately differentiated carcinoma.

significance to morphologic features, such as degree of differentiation, have met with varying degrees of success.[185–191] More recently, data involving the morphologic pattern at the advancing tumor front, DNA analysis, oncogenes such as *p53*, and cyclin D1 protein expression have shown promise in predicting the clinical behavior of laryngeal cancers.[192–196] It would appear that evaluation based on multiple factors, such as tumor grade, stage and size, DNA, and oncogene factors, as well as the general status of the patient, might most accurately give an indication of prognosis.

Patients with laryngeal/hypopharyngeal squamous cell carcinomas frequently undergo irradiation therapy; this induces morphologically recognizable effects on the tumor and irradiated tissues. Fibrous obliteration of tumor and increased keratin production by the neoplasm, as well as foreign-body giant cell and/or histiocytic reaction to keratin or other tumor debris, may be seen following irradiation, together with dilatation of lymphatics and atypical mesenchymal cell nuclei in the host stromal tissue. Atrophy of non-neoplastic seromucinous glands in the radiated field often occurs, with enlargement of glandular epithelial nuclei. This appearance can simulate persistent small islands of carcinoma to the unwary observer. Appreciation of the normal glandular architecture and structure may facilitate recognition of the structures as atrophic glands rather than tumor.

The prognosis for patients with a small laryngeal squamous cell carcinoma discovered early is favorable. Overall, more than 60% of patients in the USA with laryngeal cancer are alive after 5 years,[197] with 5-year disease-free rates as high as 90% being reported for T1 (small localized) carcinomas of the vocal cord.[169] As might be expected, survival decreases with advancing stage of disease and the presence of lymph node metastases, especially with extranodal extension of the tumor. The staging system recommended by the American Joint Committee on Cancer is outlined in Table 4B.2. Subglottic and hypopharyngeal tumors generally have a worse prognosis, probably related to their generally more advanced stage at diagnosis. Surgery and radiation therapy, alone or in combination, with or without adjunctive chemotherapy, have been used as treatment modalities in cases of cancer of the larynx and hypopharynx.[180,184]

Variants of squamous cell carcinoma

Verrucous carcinoma

Verrucous carcinoma is a proliferative squamous epithelial lesion that is generally considered a variant of squamous cell carcinoma. It is characterized by an exophytic warty broad-based clinical and gross appearance, very well-differentiated histology and biologic behavior characterized by slow, progressive, expansile, and destructive local growth and virtual absence of metastases. Originally described as a lesion of the oral cavity,[198] where it occurs with greatest frequency, verrucous carcinoma has been reported in the larynx, its next most common location, as well as in other sites, such as the anogenital area and extremities. It is an entity that has engendered controversy and is still, in our opinion, incompletely understood. The lesion is rare in the larynx, with an incidence of about 1–3% of all laryngeal malignancies.[199–204] It tends to occur in individuals over the age of 50 years and is more common in males.[203,204] The vocal cord is the most frequent laryngeal location.[201,205] Clinically, a broad-based surface growth is seen that is keratotic, gray-white in color, exophytic, and wart-like (hence the appellation "verrucous"). If left untreated, it can become quite extensive, and may extend deeply in an expansile, pushing, well-delineated fashion to encroach upon and eventually penetrate underlying structures such as muscle, cartilage, and bone.

Histologically, the lesion consists of an acanthotic squamous epithelial proliferation composed of generally thick papillary folds covered with keratin that protrude into the underlying tissue as bulbous fronds with broad, pushing, well-demarcated borders (Figs 4B.18 and 4B.19). The squamous epithelium is very well differentiated with only slight atypicality (mitoses, enlarged nuclei and nucleoli),[206] confined to the basal zone. A dense chronic inflammatory infiltrate characteristically hugs the base of the lesion (Fig. 4B.19). Keratin may deeply invaginate between adjacent epithelial folds, producing keratotic cysts in the tissue. Jagged infiltration of stromal tissues by individual cells or small stands or clusters of cells does not occur in classic "pure" verrucous carcinoma.

These histologic features can make the diagnosis of verrucous carcinoma in a small biopsy specimen quite difficult.

Table 4B.2   TNM staging of carcinoma of the larynx

Primary tumor (T)

TX	Primary tumor cannot be assessed
T0	No evidence of primary tumor
Tis	Carcinoma in situ

Supraglottis

T1	Tumor limited to one subsite of supraglottis with normal vocal-cord mobility
T2	Tumor invades mucosa of more than one adjacent subsite of supraglottis or glottis or region outside the supraglottis (e.g., mucosa of base of tongue, vallecula, medial wall of pyriform sinus) without fixation of the larynx
T3	Tumor limited to larynx with vocal-cord fixation and/or invades any of the following: postcricoid area, pre-epiglottic tissues, paraglottic space, and/or minor thyroid cartilage erosion (e.g., inner cortex)
T4a	Tumor invades through the thyroid cartilage and/or invades tissues beyond the larynx (e.g., trachea, soft tissues of neck including deep extrinsic muscle of the tongue, strap muscles, thyroid, or esophagus)
T4b	Tumor invades prevertebral space, encases carotid artery, or invades mediastinal structures

Glottis

T1	Tumor limited to the vocal cord(s) (may involve anterior or posterior commissure) with normal mobility
T1a	Tumor limited to one vocal cord
T1b	Tumor involves both vocal cords
T2	Tumor extends to supraglottis and/or subglottis, or with impaired vocal-cord mobility
T3	Tumor limited to the larynx with vocal-cord fixation, and/or invades paraglottic space, and/or minor thyroid cartilage erosion (e.g., inner cortex)
T4a	Tumor invades through the thyroid cartilage and/or invades tissues beyond the larynx (e.g., trachea, soft tissues of neck, including deep extrinsic muscle of the tongue, strap muscles, thyroid, or esophagus)
T4b	Tumor invades prevertebral space, encases carotid artery, or invades mediastinal structures

Subglottis

T1	Tumor limited to the subglottis
T2	Tumor extends to vocal cord(s) with normal or impaired mobility
T3	Tumor limited to larynx with vocal-cord fixation
T4a	Tumor invades cricoid or thyroid cartilage and/or invades tissues beyond the larynx (e.g., trachea, soft tissues of neck, including deep extrinsic muscles of the tongue, strap muscles, thyroid, or esophagus)
T4b	Tumor invades prevertebral space, encases carotid artery, or invades mediastinal structures

Regional lymph nodes (N)

NX	Regional lymph nodes cannot be assessed
N0	No regional lymph node metastasis
N1	Metastasis in a single ipsilateral lymph node, 3 cm or less in greatest dimension
N2	Metastasis in a single ipsilateral lymph node, more than 3 cm but not more than 6 cm in greatest dimension, or in multiple ipsilateral lymph nodes, none more than 6 cm in greatest dimension, or in bilateral or contralateral lymph nodes, none more than 6 cm in greatest dimension
N2a	Metastasis in a single ipsilateral lymph node, more than 3 cm but not more than 6 cm in greatest dimension
N2b	Metastasis in multiple ipsilateral lymph nodes, none more than 6 cm in greatest dimension
N2c	Metastasis in bilateral or contralateral lymph nodes, none more than 6 cm in greatest dimension
N3	Metastasis in a lymph node, more than 6 cm in greatest dimension

Distant metastasis (M)

MX	Distant metastasis cannot be assessed
M0	No distant metastasis
M1	Distant metastasis

Reproduced with permission of the American Joint Committee on Cancer (AJCC), Chicago, Illinois. The original source for this material is the AJCC Cancer Staging Manual, Sixth Edition (2002). Published by Springer-Verlag, New York (www.springeronline.com).

One is understandably reluctant to render a diagnosis of carcinoma in the presence of well-differentiated non-anaplastic tissue and in the absence of obvious tissue infiltration. Careful correlation and close communication between surgeon and pathologist may call attention to the broad base and exophytic nature of the lesion, and an optimal biopsy specimen may demonstrate the extension of the lesion deep to the level of the adjacent uninvolved mucosal epithelium.[202]

It has become apparent that verrucous carcinoma is not always a "pure" lesion, and cases have been recognized wherein foci of conventional infiltrative squamous cell carcinoma are present in lesions otherwise characteristic of classic verrucous

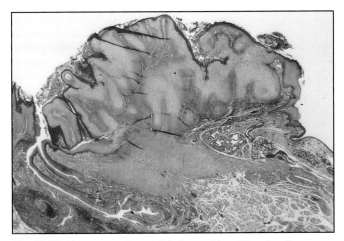

Fig. 4B.18 • Verrucous carcinoma of the larynx. A broad-based, well-differentiated papillary acanthotic tumor of the true vocal cord.

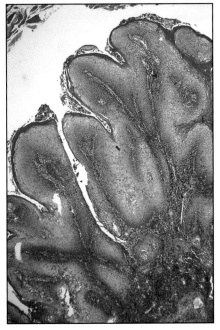

Fig. 4B.19 • Verrucous carcinoma of the larynx, showing bulbous fronds with a pushing border and associated dense chronic inflammatory infiltrate.

carcinoma.[205,207–210] Such "hybrid" or combined verrucous–squamous carcinomas have been noted in both oral and laryngeal sites. In the larynx they have been said to be more aggressive than pure verrucous carcinomas, and to behave (and hence merit treatment) more like comparably staged conventional squamous cell carcinomas.[205] Obviously, then, such foci should be sought and commented upon in specimens of verrucous carcinoma.

One of the controversies surrounding this interesting lesion involves the purported tendency towards irradiation-induced anaplastic transformation of verrucous carcinomas to aggressive malignancies. Although this phenomenon has been reported by some observers,[199,210,211] one must be cautious in accepting this assertion at face value, for areas of more conventional squamous cell carcinoma, as mentioned above, may have been missed on biopsy. Still, an occasional pro-

vocative case may possibly reflect such an association on rare occasions. Surgery is generally considered the treatment of choice for verrucous carcinoma; a favorable prognosis is reported in pure verrucous lesions.[205,211]

Differential diagnosis Verrucous carcinoma may generally be differentiated from benign epithelial hyperplasia by the degree of proliferation combined with the extension of the former lesion into underlying tissue. Verrucous hyperplasia, a lesion described in the oral cavity,[212] is analogous to verrucous carcinoma but does not extend below the level of the adjacent mucosal epithelial layer. Batsakis et al.[201] consider it an early form of verrucous carcinoma. Differentiation from squamous papillomas has been commented upon earlier (see p. 151). esions described as verruca vulgaris of the larynx have been reported very rarely.[28,29] LThese are described as having a more prominent granular layer and narrower papillary fronds than classic verrucous carcinomas, as well as exhibiting koilocytotic changes. Evidence of HPV infection may be found in laryngeal verrucae using immunohistochemical or molecular biologic techniques; however, some studies have also shown HPV to be associated with some cases of verrucous carcinoma as well, and the relationship between verrucous carcinomas and HPV is not definitively settled.[202,213] Conventional squamous cell carcinoma is distinguished by a greater degree of cytologic atypicality and infiltrative properties, but attention must be paid to the "hybrid" or combined lesions referred to above. It is important to remember that some laryngeal squamous cell carcinomas may be papillary or exophytic,[214,215] and that biopsies of such lesions may not reveal frank infiltration into subepithelial stroma. Such tumors, however, are more cytologically atypical than verrucous carcinoma, and a diagnosis of verrucous carcinoma should not be rendered on a biopsy with an appearance of papillary CIS.

From the foregoing it may be appreciated that verrucous carcinoma has some, but not all, of the characteristics of a conventional malignancy (exhibiting progressive local growth and extension into underlying tissue, but lacking significant nuclear atypicality and, probably, metastatic potential). Some[216] maintain that the very term "carcinoma" is a misnomer and would substitute "verrucous acanthosis." Perhaps it is most helpful to view verrucous carcinoma as being intermediate in the spectrum of proliferative mucosal epithelial lesions, occupying a position between benign hyperplasia and frank conventional metastasizing carcinoma.[201]

Spindle cell carcinoma (sarcomatoid carcinoma)

Spindle cell carcinoma is a fascinating tumor of the larynx and hypopharynx that has engendered much controversy and speculation. This is primarily a result of the characteristic bimorphic nature of the lesion, which combines foci of squamous cell carcinoma and/or CIS/severe dysplasia with an often bizarre spindle cell/mesenchymal-type proliferation reminiscent of a sarcoma. This morphology has given rise to several terms and corresponding theories of histogenesis, including spindle cell carcinoma,[217–221] carcinosarcoma,[222] squamous cell carcinoma with sarcoma-like stroma,[223] pseudo-sarcoma,[224,225] pleomorphic carcinoma, polypoid carcinoma,[226] and sarcomatoid carcinoma.[227–229] The tumor, as currently defined, is generally considered to represent a variant of squamous cell carcinoma.[221,230,231] In addition to the upper respiratory tract, the tumor also occurs in the esophagus[222,232] and oral cavity,[233,234] and similar tumors occur in the lung.[235]

The majority of patients with laryngeal tumors are elderly males.[228,229] Most lesions are glottic[217,221] and present with hoarseness, but hypopharyngeal, supraglottic, and subglottic tumors also occur. A significant percentage of patients have had previous irradiation for a carcinoma.[228] The majority of tumors have a polypoid exophytic configuration, with either a broad base or a relatively narrow pedicle[228,229] (Fig. 4B.20). Tumors of this latter type may autoamputate in whole or in part and be expectorated by the patient.[228] Sessile and ulcero-infiltrative tumors occur more rarely.

The prognosis, as well as the histogenesis, of this lesion has been much debated. Most current opinion suggests that this tumor is potentially lethal.[228,229] Superficial polypoid tumors and tumors located on the true vocal cord appear to have a better prognosis than extraglottic and deeply infiltrating lesions.[223,227–229] Histologic appearance and the proportion of conventional squamous cell carcinoma are thought not to have a significant bearing on clinical outcome,[223,227] although keratin immunopositivity of the spindle cell component has been reported to be adversely associated with survival.[236]

The polypoid tumors are often extensively ulcerated, with surface fibrin deposition. The characteristic histomorphology is that of a conventional squamous cell carcinoma admixed with a population of atypical spindled or mesenchymal-appearing cells (Fig. 4B.21). The squamous cell component is usually rather scant, and thorough sampling is often required to demonstrate it. It may be invasive (often only superficially invasive) or in situ, and, according to some authors,[220] only severely dysplastic squamous epithelium may be identified in some cases. The difficulty in finding and identifying the squamous component may be related to the extensive surface ulceration that is frequently encountered. The base of the polypoid tumor has been suggested as a productive location in which to search for and locate the conventional carcinomatous tissue.[217,229] The sarcoma-like portion is characteristically considerably more prominent and extensive. It can assume multiple patterns. Generally, an atypical spindled-cell component resembling fibrosarcoma is present (Fig. 4B.21A). Collagen is generally sparse but may occasionally be more prominent. The sarcoma-like element may be loose and myxoid; a vascular, granulation tissue-like element may be present, especially near the surface, associated with numerous inflammatory and/or histiocytic cells. Mitoses are often abundant and may be atypical. Bizarre, hyperchromatic, and multinucleated cells are common. In my opinion, the diagnosis of spindle cell carcinoma requires the presence of an unequivocal epithelial component. Thus, if the diagnosis is to be made on the basis of conventional light microscopy, recognizable squamous cell carcinoma or CIS or, at the very least, severe squamous epithelial dysplasia must be identified. In the absence of a histologically recognizable component of conventional squamous cell carcinoma, immunohistochemical and/or ultrastructural evidence of epithelial differentiation is required for a definitive diagnosis.

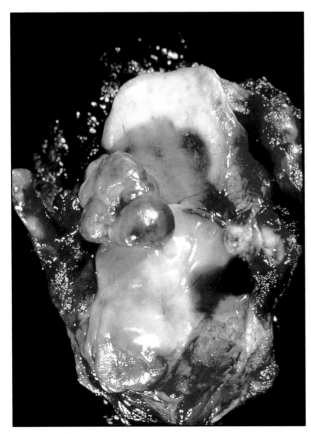

A

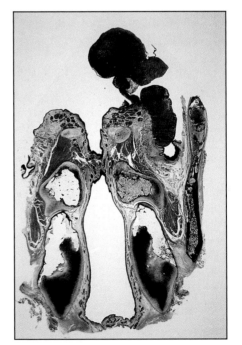

B

Fig. 4B.20 • Spindle cell carcinoma of the larynx. **(A)** Gross photograph of a polypoid tumor in the arytenoid region. **(B)** Whole-organ section of the same tumor, showing much of the tumor connected to the larynx by a pedicle and a portion of the tumor with a broader base. The tumor is not deeply infiltrative. (Reproduced with permission from Fried M P 1996 The larynx: a multidisciplinary approach, 2nd edn. Mosby, New York, Fig. 40-30.)

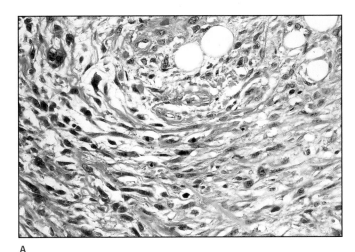
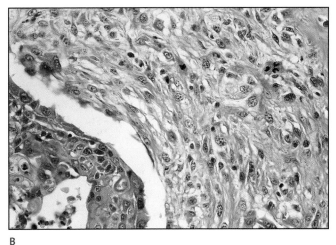

Fig. 4B.21 • Spindle cell carcinoma of the larynx. **(A)** Spindle cell component composed of pleomorphic spindled cells, resembling a sarcoma. **(B)** The same tumor showing the juxtaposition of conventionally appearing squamous cell carcinoma (lower left) and the spindle cell component.

Immunohistochemically, keratin proteins may often be found in the spindled cells of the tumor (Fig. 4B.22); however, not all cases have keratin-positive spindled cells by conventional immunohistochemical techniques,[219,220] and keratin staining may be only focal. The conventional carcinomatous component almost always stains for keratin. The spindled component generally stains for vimentin, and some individual spindled tumor cells have been shown to stain for both keratin and vimentin, using an alkaline phosphatase double-labeling technique.[219] Furthermore, ultrastructural studies have yielded disparate results, with some spindled cells showing mesenchymal features (abundant dilated rough endoplasmic reticulum), some epithelial features (desmosomes and tonofilaments), and some both.[218] These confusing findings may be explained by invoking the currently favored theory of the histogenesis of this remarkable neoplasm: that it is an epithelial neoplasm, a variant of squamous cell carcinoma, in which many of the constituent neoplastic epithelial cells have undergone mesenchymal metaplasia, in some cases so complete as to result in the loss of most, if not all, of their epithelial characteristics.[218,227–229] Such a phenomenon is recognized in tumors in other sites and has been referred to as "homologous neometaplasia" (Scully,

personal communication). The situation is analogous to that of so-called metaplastic or matrix-producing carcinomas of the breast. The concept of the atypical spindle cells representing a reactive non-neoplastic stromal component, originally proposed by Lane[224] and reiterated by Goellner et al.,[225] is contradicted by the presence of metastases containing both spindled and carcinomatous components;[217] the finding of positive immunohistochemical staining for *ras* oncogene *p21* in the spindled cells[226] adds further evidence for the neoplastic nature of these cells. A rare case described as a true carcinosarcoma of the larynx[237] is occasionally reported, but the question arises whether such cases represent the independent concurrent malignant transformation of two progenitor cells, one epithelial and one mesenchymal, or whether they are cases of metaplastic carcinoma or "neometaplasia," as described here. The latter viewpoint is generally favored.

Differential diagnosis

The three principal differential diagnoses to consider are sarcoma, bizarre postirradiation granulation tissue, and so-called inflammatory myofibroblastic tumor. Sarcomas may usually be differentiated from spindle cell carcinoma by the presence of a recognizable carcinomatous component in the latter lesion. An exception is the case of synovial sarcoma (see below). A much more difficult problem is encountered in the absence of a carcinomatous component on hematoxylin and eosin (H&E) microscopy. In such a case, immunohistochemical and/or ultrastructural demonstration of epithelial differentiation is helpful; however, rare sarcomas may show keratin positivity. For example, biphasic synovial sarcomas (rare in the head and neck but occasionally reported) have, in addition to spindled cells, areas of keratin-positive carcinomatous appearance. These are usually gland-like rather than of squamous morphology; moreover, the spindled component is usually more uniform in appearance, compact, cellular, and less pleomorphic than in the classic spindle cell carcinoma.[229] Rare keratin-positive cells have been described in so-called malignant fibrous histiocytomas.[238] Such cases do not have carcinomatous areas on H&E microscopy, nor do they exhibit epithelial differentiation ultrastructurally, but, in the light of

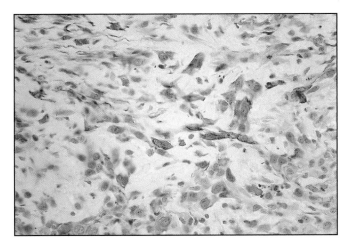

Fig. 4B.22 • Spindle cell carcinoma of the larynx. Immunohistochemical stain for keratin showing spindle cells staining positively.

potential sampling problems, some of these cases may well represent spindle cell (sarcomatoid) carcinomas. Bizarre, highly atypical proliferative granulation tissue reactions can occur following irradiation and may closely mimic the sarcoma-like component of spindle cell carcinoma.[239] Such lesions do not possess a carcinomatous component, and it has been mentioned that the endothelial cells in such lesions share the atypicality of the other constituent mesenchymal cells.[239] Rare cases of laryngeal inflammatory myofibroblastic tumor have been reported.[240] These are benign proliferations of spindled and occasionally stellate cells, disposed in a generally loose arrangement and often associated with chronic inflammatory cells. The tumor cells are bland to slightly atypical, and do not feature severe pleomorphism, a high mitotic rate, an associated component of conventional squamous cell carcinoma, or keratin positivity of spindled cells.[240]

Basaloid squamous cell carcinoma (basaloid squamous carcinoma)

Basaloid squamous cell carcinoma is a variant of squamous cell carcinoma that has relatively recently been described and delineated as a distinct clinicopathologic entity.[241–247] It has been reported in the hypopharynx, larynx, and oral cavity of middle-aged to elderly patients, occasionally in the nasal cavity[244,248] and nasopharynx, and more recently in the trachea.[249] Its recognition is significant in that it is a high-grade aggressive neoplasm with a poor prognosis. Analogous tumors have been reported in the esophagus and uterine cervix in the earlier literature under headings with some reference to adenoid cystic carcinoma.[250–252] More recently, basaloid squamous carcinoma of the esophagus has been recognized as an entity.[253]

Histologically, basaloid squamous carcinoma is a high-grade carcinoma consisting of basaloid and squamous components (Fig. 4B.23). The basaloid carcinomatous element comprises nests, masses, and strands of small basophilic epithelial cells with relatively scant cytoplasm and a high nuclear-to-cytoplasmic ratio. Nuclei are often hyperchromatic with generally inconspicuous nucleoli. The cells are often arranged in lobular nests just deep to the mucosal epithelium. A palisaded peripheral cell layer is not uncommonly present. The basaloid cells characteristically enclose gland-like or pseudoglandular spaces, which at times are cribriform and contain myxoid alcian blue-positive material; the tumor cells themselves, however, are mucin-negative (Figs 4B.23 and 4B.24). The tumor stroma may often assume a hyaline as well as a myxoid appearance (Fig. 4B.24). A comedo pattern of central necrosis in tumor cell nests is a common finding. In addition to the basaloid tumor cells, a squamous carcinomatous component is invariably present. This may manifest as squamous differentiation within tumor nests, distinct foci of frank squamous cell carcinoma, and/or areas of overlying CIS (Figs 4B.23 and 4B.25).

Differential diagnostic considerations include adenoid cystic carcinoma and adenosquamous or mucoepidermoid carcinoma. Basaloid squamous carcinoma shares features with adenoid cystic carcinoma, especially the anaplastic variety, with both exhibiting a cribriform or pseudoglandular arrangement of basaloid cells. Adenoid cystic carcinoma, however, does not characteristically have a squamous component.

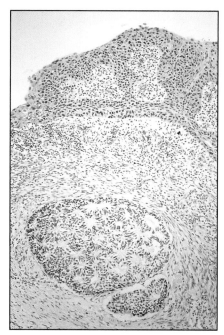

Fig. 4B.23 • Basaloid squamous carcinoma of the larynx/hypopharynx. A nest of basaloid carcinoma with gland-like spaces, reminiscent of adenoid cystic carcinoma, underlies mucosal squamous cell carcinoma in situ.

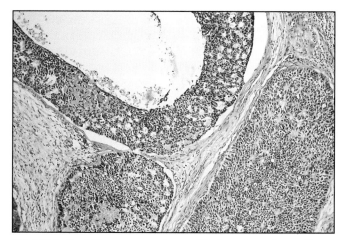

Fig. 4B.24 • Basaloid squamous carcinoma of the larynx/hypopharynx. Nests of basaloid carcinoma with pseudoglandular spaces and focal amorphous hyaline material are seen.

Moreover, the myoepithelial cell element of adenoid cystic carcinomas, occurring as an outer epithelial layer in ductules or tubules present in many tumors, is not seen in basaloid squamous carcinoma. The tumor cells in adenoid cystic lesions are also usually somewhat smaller and less anaplastic in appearance than those of the basaloid squamous lesions. Adenosquamous carcinoma (ASC), as described by Gerughty et al.[254] is a duct-associated neoplasm that may contain areas of ductal CIS and areas of large "glassy" cells; it is not characteristically associated with mucosal squamous cell CIS. Most mucoepidermoid carcinomas are less anaplastic than basaloid squamous carcinoma, and some of their cells contain demonstrable intracytoplasmic mucin. They also tend to be glandular lesions without a primary surface mucosal component.

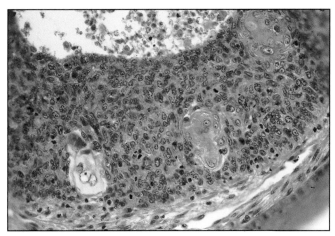

Fig. 4B.25 • Basaloid squamous carcinoma of the larynx, showing a nest of basaloid cells with focal squamous pearls.

Fig. 4B.26 • Pseudovascular adenoid squamous cell carcinoma of the larynx. Acantholysis in carcinoma cell nests creates spaces mimicking glandular or vascular spaces. Focal squamous differentiation is seen (center of figure) as well as degenerating acantholytic carcinoma cells in the spaces.

Lymphoepithelial carcinoma

Undifferentiated carcinoma, lymphoepitheliomatous type, is a variant of squamous cell carcinoma classically occurring in the nasopharynx (see Ch. 4A). It occurs rarely in other sites, such as the parotid gland[255] and thymus.[256] Rare cases have been reported in the larynx/hypopharynx region.[257–261] The morphology of the tumor in these laryngeal/pharyngeal locations is analogous to that in the nasopharynx. Evidence of association of the tumor with the Epstein–Barr virus, as in the nasopharynx, has been found in some, but not all, of these lesions.[260–262]

Adenoid squamous carcinoma (acantholytic squamous cell carcinoma, pseudovascular squamous cell carcinoma)

So-called adenoid or acantholytic squamous cell carcinoma is well known to occur in sun-exposed skin.[263] It is a variant of squamous cell carcinoma in which acantholysis of squamous carcinoma cells in tumor nests creates a gland-like or adenoid appearance, often with the acantholytic cells floating in these spaces; however these tumors are negative with mucin stains. At times the carcinoma cells at the periphery of these spaces can be flattened, resulting in a vascular appearance mimicking angiosarcoma (pseudovascular adenoid squamous cell carcinoma).[263] Although these tumors are characteristically reported in the skin,[263] we have encountered such tumors in the larynx (Fig. 4B.26). Differential diagnosis from adenocarcinoma is accomplished by recognizing the acantholytic nature of the process creating the spaces and by lack of mucin positivity in tumor cells. Differentiation from angiosarcoma is accomplished by identifying a component of conventional squamous cell carcinoma as well as by the lack of tumor immunohistochemical staining for vascular markers such as CD31, von Willebrand factor, or CD34, combined with keratin positivity of the tumor cells.[263]

Papillary squamous cell carcinoma (PSCC)

Within the group of squamous cell carcinomas are a subgroup of carcinomas that are predominantly papillary, and which

have been recently recognized as a distinct clinicopathologic variant of squamous cell carcinoma.[264,265] The tumors are characterized by generally thin papillary fronds or fingers of malignant squamous epithelium surrounding fibrovascular cores (Fig. 4B.27). The appearance of the superficial portion of the tumor is essentially that of papillary CIS, in that, although cellular atypia is great and generally full-thickness, the base of the epithelial layer abutting the central fibrovascular core is usually flat. Conventional infiltrative invasion is often not identified on superficial biopsies, but may be identified deeply. In a recent study, 36% of PSCCs in the head and neck were found to be associated with HPV.[265] PSCC of the larynx is biologically less aggressive than conventional squamous cell carcinoma, including the exophytic variety,[264] with recurrences in about a third of cases, but with very few metastases and a high rate of survival, with no deaths due to tumor reported in the series of Thompson et al.[264] It is useful, therefore, to recognize this variant of squamous cell carcinoma.

Differential diagnosis includes other papillary squamous lesions of the larynx, including squamous papilloma, verrucous carcinoma, the very rare laryngeal verruca vulgaris, and exophytic conventional squamous cell carcinoma. The first three entities may be differentiated from PSCC by their bland cytologic features, whereas PSCC has marked cytologic atypia, resembling CIS. Exophytic squamous cell carcinoma has broader, less finger-like fronds than PSCC.

Adenosquamous carcinoma

Adenosquamous carcinoma of the head and neck was initially considered a type of mucoepidermoid carcinoma (see below). Recently, however, ASC has been recognized as a distinct entity, involving and probably arising from surface squamous mucosal epithelium, with an aggressive biologic course.[266,267] It is thus considered here as a variant of squamous cell carcinoma. In the head and neck, the larynx and floor of mouth are its most common locations.[266] Males are affected significantly more commonly than females. The tumor is an aggressive neoplasm, with frequent local recurrences and lymph

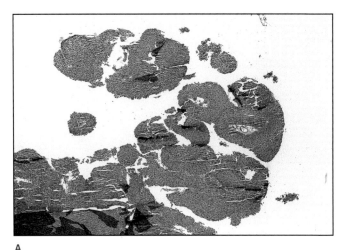

A

B

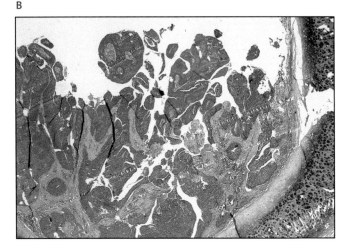

C

Fig. 4B.27 • Papillary squamous cell carcinoma. (**A**) Larynx: multiple neoplastic papillae lined by squamous epithelium surrounding fibrovascular cores. (**B**) Larynx: high-power view showing malignant squamous epithelial lining, giving the picture of papillary carcinoma in situ. (**C**) Trachea: papillary squamous cell carcinoma showing invasion to the level of the tracheal perichondrium.

node metastases, and a 5-year survival rate of only about 15%.[266]

Histologically, the tumor combines areas of conventional squamous cell carcinoma, at times keratinizing, with foci of mucin-containing adenocarcinoma arranged generally as

ducts, ductules, or tubules (Fig. 4B.28). There is a component of surface mucosal squamous cell carcinoma, usually with mucosal severe dysplasia/CIS. The squamous component almost always predominates.[266,267] The adenocarcinomatous component generally is mainly present in deeper areas of the tumor. The carcinoma is usually moderately or poorly differentiated. The lesion should be separated from mucoepidermoid carcinoma, even the high-grade type, because of the more aggressive behavior of ASC. Mucoepidermoid carcinoma of minor salivary/seromucinous glands is a glandular, not a mucosal, neoplasm, is present submucosally, and very rarely (and then generally only minimally) involves the surface. It is histologically of lower grade than ASC, and characteristically does not contain a component of keratin-producing, frankly squamous cell carcinoma, but is "epidermoid," its solid areas being generally composed mainly of intermediate cells. Basaloid squamous cell carcinoma has spaces but not true malignant glands. Tumor cells do not contain mucin, and the basaloid character of much of the neoplasm is in contrast to the conventional squamous appearance present in ASC.

Neuroendocrine carcinomas

Neuroendocrine carcinomas of the larynx have only been delineated as a distinct category fairly recently. Although by no means as common as their counterparts in the bronchi and lung, laryngeal neuroendocrine carcinomas are being recognized with increasing frequency. The development and more widespread utilization of ancillary diagnostic techniques, such as immunohistochemistry and electron microscopy, have contributed to the recognition that laryngeal tumors originally classified in other categories (e.g., adenocarcinoma, undifferentiated carcinoma, paraganglioma) are more likely neuroendocrine carcinomas. Some authors, in fact, consider most non-squamous cell laryngeal carcinomas to be neuroendocrine neoplasms.[52]

The nomenclature of this group of neoplasms has been varied and somewhat confusing, with terms such as carcinoid, atypical carcinoid, oat-cell carcinoma, large-cell neuroendocrine carcinoma, small cell carcinoma, small cell undifferentiated carcinoma, and oncocytic/oncocytoid carcinoid tumors appearing in the literature. As understanding of laryngeal neuroendocrine carcinomas increases, analogies between these laryngeal neoplasms and their pulmonary counterparts are appreciated, and the proposed nomenclature of Gould et al.[268] for pulmonary neuroendocrine neoplasms has been modified and adapted for laryngeal neuroendocrine carcinomas.[53,54] Thus these tumors have been categorized as well-differentiated neuroendocrine carcinoma (carcinoid tumor or typical carcinoid tumor), moderately differentiated neuroendocrine carcinoma (atypical carcinoid or large-cell neuroendocrine carcinoma) and poorly differentiated neuroendocrine carcinoma (oat-cell carcinoma, small cell undifferentiated carcinoma, small cell neuroendocrine carcinoma). Such a taxonomic scheme recognizes these neoplasms as carcinomas (malignant epithelial tumors) which share neuroendocrine features (peptide production, "neurosecretory" granules) and vary along a continuum with respect to degree of histologic differentiation and biologic aggression.

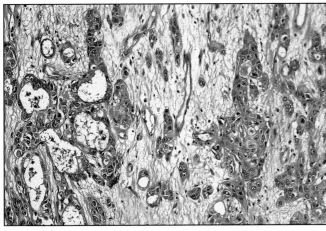

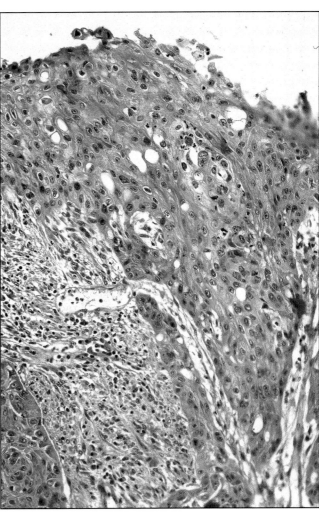

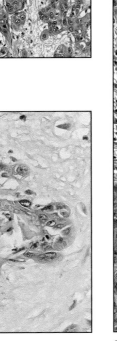

Fig. 4B.28 • Adenosquamous carcinoma of the larynx. **(A)** Adenocarcinomatous gland-forming component to the left of the figure, and squamous component to the right. **(B)** Surface involvement by the squamous component. **(C)** Mucicarmine stain showing mucin production in carcinoma with glandular differentiation adjacent to and involving squamous carcinoma with keratinization.

Well-differentiated neuroendocrine carcinoma (carcinoid tumor, typical carcinoid tumor)

Well-differentiated neuroendocrine carcinoma of the larynx is a very rare neoplasm. Many of the cases reported as laryngeal carcinoids in the literature have most likely been examples of moderately differentiated neuroendocrine carcinoma or atypical carcinoids.[54] Tracheal carcinoid tumors are also quite rare;[175,269] bronchial carcinoids are significantly more common. El-Naggar & Batsakis, in a review in 1991,[270] were able to collect only 13 acceptable cases of laryngeal well-differentiated neuroendocrine carcinoma. The patients were mainly males and ranged in age from 45 to 80 years. The tumors were predominantly supraglottic in location, often in the arytenoid/aryepiglottic fold area. The prognosis is excellent, although metastases may rarely occur.[54]

Histologically, laryngeal well-differentiated neuroendocrine carcinomas resemble typical carcinoid tumors in other locations. They are well-circumscribed neoplasms composed of generally small uniform cells arranged in an organoid pattern of nests, ribbons, trabeculae, and/or acini/gland-like structures (Fig. 4B.29). Nuclei are round to oval with stippled chromatin and inconspicuous nucleoli. Mitoses are scant. Nuclear pleomorphism and tumor necrosis are essentially absent. The tumors stain with argyrophilic stains such as the Grimelius stain.

Immunohistochemically, laryngeal well-differentiated neuroendocrine carcinomas stain positively for neuroendocrine markers, usually neuron-specific enolase and chromogranin. These lesions would be expected to be immunohistochemically positive for epithelial markers such as keratin, but few reports of such staining results are available.[47] Characteristic dense-core neurosecretory granules are seen on electron microscopy.

Differential diagnostic considerations include primarily paraganglioma, moderately differentiated neuroendocrine carcinomas and well-differentiated adenocarcinomas. The differential points between well-differentiated neuroendocrine carcinoma and paraganglioma have been discussed in the section on paraganglioma (see p. 152). Moderately differentiated neuroendocrine carcinoma has an organoid neuroendocrine pattern, but is a higher-grade neoplasm than the well-differentiated type. Thus, nuclear atypicality and pleomorphism, infiltrative properties of the tumor, and necrosis

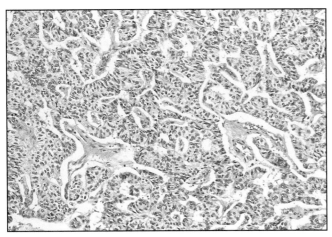

Fig. 4B.29 • Well-differentiated neuroendocrine carcinoma (carcinoid tumor, typical carcinoid tumor) of the larynx. Note the organoid pattern of tumor cells in a trabecular arrangement.

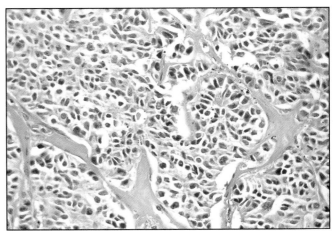

Fig. 4B.30 • Moderately differentiated neuroendocrine carcinoma (atypical carcinoid) of the larynx, showing an organoid pattern of atypical tumor cells, less distinct than in well-differentiated neuroendocrine carcinoma.

and mitotic activity serve to separate these two lesions morphologically (see below). Adenocarcinomas (not otherwise specified) are not argyrophilic, do not stain for neuroendocrine markers (such as chromogranin) immunohistochemically, and do not contain neurosecretory granules ultrastructurally.

Moderately differentiated neuroendocrine carcinoma (atypical carcinoid)

Moderately differentiated neuroendocrine carcinomas of the larynx are more common than well-differentiated neuroendocrine carcinomas. Some of these tumors have been reported in the literature as carcinoid tumors.[271–273] In a review in 1991[274] Woodruff & Senie identified about 200 cases reported in the literature. Patients characteristically present in the sixth or seventh decades, and most lesions are supraglottic. About a third of patients in one series[49] presented with severe pain. In contrast to laryngeal well-differentiated neuroendocrine carcinomas, these tumors are aggressive, with a reported 5-year survival rate of 48%.[274] In Wenig & Gnepp's series,[54] all patients with metastatic disease died. Interestingly, these tumors have a propensity to metastasize to the skin.[274–276]

Histologically, moderately differentiated neuroendocrine carcinoma is an epithelial neoplasm consisting of cells arranged in nests, sheets, glands/acini, trabeculae, and ribbons, reflecting the "organoid" pattern characteristic of neuroendocrine tumors (Fig. 4B.30). Multiple patterns are characteristically present in an individual neoplasm, and glandular structures are almost always in evidence.[53] The cells are round to polygonal with eosinophilic cytoplasm. Occasionally cells with oncocytic properties are described.[272] The nuclei are round to ovoid, with stippled chromatin, occasionally with multiple nucleoli that are rarely prominent, and with occasional hyperchromasia. Mitoses, cellular pleomorphism, and an invasive margin are often present and are more prominent than in well-differentiated neuroendocrine carcinomas. Typically, tumor cells are argyrophilic and are positive for keratin, chromogranin, and neuron-specific enolase (Fig. 4B.31). Interestingly, calcitonin is detected immunohistochemically in many laryngeal moderately differentiated neuroendocrine carcinomas.[49,52,53,275] Neurosecretory granules are seen ultrastructurally.

The differential diagnosis is primarily with well-differentiated neuroendocrine carcinoma, poorly differentiated neuroendocrine carcinoma, adenocarcinoma, "undifferentiated" carcinoma, and medullary carcinoma of thyroid origin. Distinction from well-differentiated neuroendocrine carcinoma has been discussed above. Moderately differentiated neuroendocrine carcinomas do not have as undifferentiated a histologic pattern, generally have more prominent staining for neuroendocrine markers, and have a greater number of neurosecretory granules than the poorly differentiated type. The demonstration of neuroendocrine differentiation, histochemically, immunohistochemically, and/or ultrastructurally, serves to distinguish moderately differentiated neuroendocrine carcinomas from adenocarcinoma or carcinoma not otherwise specified. The neuroendocrine differentiation and calcitonin positivity may pose differential diagnostic problems with medullary thyroid carcinoma. Most moderately differentiated neuroendocrine carcinomas do not have an amyloid-rich stroma (although occasional cases may be associated with amyloid deposition)[49] and primary origin in the thyroid gland is lacking. Furthermore, patients with metastatic medullary

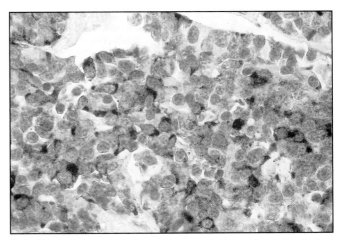

Fig. 4B.31 • Moderately differentiated neuroendocrine carcinoma (atypical carcinoid) of the larynx. Immunohistochemical stain for chromogranin showing marked positivity of tumor cells.

thyroid carcinoma frequently have an elevated serum calcitonin level.

Poorly differentiated neuroendocrine carcinoma (small cell neuroendocrine carcinoma, small cell carcinoma, "oat-cell" carcinoma)

Although small cell carcinoma is a common pulmonary tumor, the analogous poorly differentiated neuroendocrine carcinoma is rare in the larynx/hypopharynx[47,277–279] and extremely rare in the trachea.[175,280] Patients with laryngeal poorly differentiated neuroendocrine carcinoma are mainly elderly male smokers. Like other laryngeal neuroendocrine carcinomas, most lesions are supraglottic.[54,279] Metastases are common, with about half of patients presenting with cervical metastases.[279] Associated paraneoplastic syndromes are reported occasionally.[54,281] The prognosis is very poor: about 70% of patients die of the disease.[52,279] Patients who present with metastatic disease have a worse prognosis,[282] as do patients with tracheal tumors.[280]

The histomorphology of laryngeal poorly differentiated neuroendocrine carcinoma is analogous to that of its pulmonary counterpart. The tumor is composed of small cells arranged in undifferentiated sheets and nests (Fig. 4B.32). Occasionally, ribbons of cells may be seen, as may a rare rosette-like structure.[279] The cells are round and occasionally fusiform with very scant cytoplasm and hyperchromatic nuclei without prominent nucleoli (Fig. 4B.33A). Nuclear smearing and DNA encrustation on vessel walls may be seen. Slightly larger cells with somewhat more cytoplasm may also be seen. Nuclei may contain recognizable, though not especially prominent, nucleoli. The combined type of small cell carcinoma consists of poorly differentiated neuroendocrine carcinoma admixed with squamous cell carcinoma and/or adenocarcinoma[283,284] (Fig. 4B.33B).

Evidence of neuroendocrine differentiation is less prominent than in the well-differentiated or moderately differentiated neuroendocrine carcinomas and may be difficult to document. Tumor cells are only rarely argyrophilic, and neurosecretory

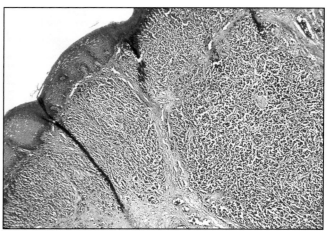

Fig. 4B.32 • Poorly differentiated neuroendocrine carcinoma (small cell carcinoma) of the larynx. Sheets of small undifferentiated tumor cells lie deep to the surface mucosal epithelium.

granules are sparse ultrastructurally. Immunohistochemical staining for neuroendocrine markers such as chromogranin and neuron-specific enolase (the latter not entirely specific for neuroendocrine cells) is often positive, but may not be readily demonstrable in every case.[47] Gnepp[279] asserts that either immunohistochemical or ultrastructural evidence of neuroendocrine differentiation must be present to merit a diagnosis of laryngeal poorly differentiated neuroendocrine carcinoma, whereas Aguilar et al.[285] maintain that laryngeal small cell carcinomas may or may not exhibit definite evidence of neuroendocrine differentiation. It is conceivable that, as the least differentiated of the neuroendocrine carcinomas, some poorly differentiated neuroendocrine carcinomas may have lost neuroendocrine features detectable by conventional techniques, or that some primitive laryngeal tumors with the histologic properties of poorly differentiated neuroendocrine carcinomas, arising from a pluripotential stem cell capable of neuroendocrine and/or non-endocrine epithelial differentiation, have constituent tumor cells that tend to express epithelial

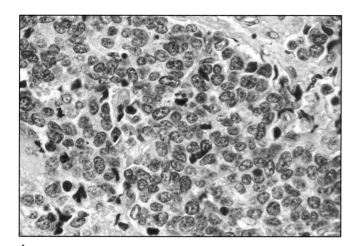

A

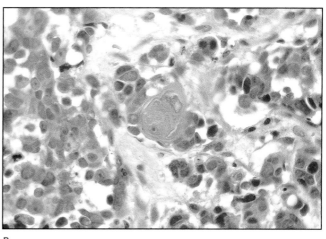

B

Fig. 4B.33 • Poorly differentiated neuroendocrine carcinoma (small cell carcinoma) of the larynx. **(A)** Undifferentiated small tumor cells with scant indistinct cytoplasm and nuclei with finely stippled chromatin and generally inconspicuous nucleoli. **(B)** Focal squamous differentiation (squamous pearl).

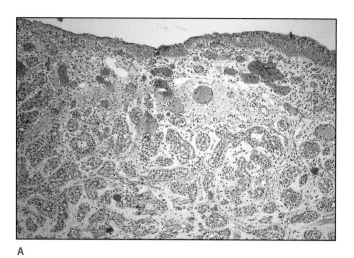

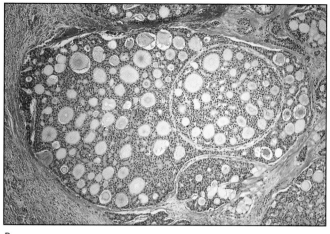

A   B

Fig. 4B.34 • Adenoid cystic carcinoma of the trachea. **(A)** Tumor, predominantly of the tubular pattern, deep to mucosal epithelium. **(B)** Classical cribriform pattern of adenoid cystic carcinoma.

rather than neuroendocrine immunohistochemical and ultra-structural features. At any rate, it seems prudent to classify such neoplasms with the poorly differentiated neuroendocrine carcinomas and to designate those tumors in this group that fail to demonstrate evidence of neuroendocrine differentiation as small cell carcinomas.

Differentiation between poorly differentiated neuroendocrine carcinomas and other neuroendocrine neoplasms has been discussed above. The differential diagnosis with lymphoma/leukemia may be problematic. The latter tumors should stain with hematologic markers such as leukocyte common antigen (CD45), whereas poorly differentiated neuroendocrine carcinomas will not, and should stain with epithelial markers (keratin and/or epithelial membrane antigen).

The histogenesis of laryngeal neuroendocrine carcinomas is controversial. The possibilities include a Kulchitsky-type argyrophilic mucosal cell (very rare mucosal argyrophilic cells have been identified in the human larynx)[286] or a pluripotential epithelial stem cell. The existence of combined poorly differentiated neuroendocrine carcinomas is evidence in support of this latter hypothesis.

Adenocarcinoma

Primary adenocarcinomas of the larynx and trachea are quite rare, with an incidence generally estimated to be about 1% of laryngeal neoplasms.[287–289] As expected, they tend to occur most frequently in areas where seromucinous glands are most plentiful (i.e., the supraglottic and subglottic regions). The majority of tracheal adenocarcinomas are adenoid cystic carcinomas.[175,290] Traditionally, the most common histologic subtype of laryngeal adenocarcinomas has generally been adenocarcinoma, not otherwise specified;[287–289] however, as with salivary gland neoplasms, it is possible that, as more specific subtypes of adenocarcinoma are recognized, more of the laryngeal adenocarcinomas will be subclassified. For example, cases of laryngeal acinic cell carcinoma,[291] salivary duct carcinoma,[292] and epithelial-myoepithelial carcinoma[293] are documented, and some lesions originally diagnosed as

adenocarcinoma not otherwise specified may represent neuroendocrine carcinomas.[53,289]

The most common specific subtype of laryngeal and tracheal adenocarcinoma is *adenoid cystic carcinoma*.[175,294–296] This lesion tends to affect younger individuals more often than the other laryngeal adenocarcinomas, and is often subglottic in location. It shares with its salivary gland counterpart the clinical properties of slowly progressive growth, extensively infiltrative properties, frequently well beyond its clinical gross extent, frequent local recurrence, and a characteristically protracted clinical course over many years, with death often occurring 10 or more years following diagnosis. The histomorphology of laryngotracheal adenoid cystic carcinoma is analogous to that in its more common sites of major salivary and minor oral salivary glands (Fig. 4B.34) (see Ch. 7).

Mucoepidermoid carcinoma (MEC) is another tumor of salivary gland type that occurs in the larynx, although rarely.[297–300] The average age at presentation is about 60 years,[298–300] and the favored location is supraglottic. These tumors also mirror their salivary gland counterparts in morphology and clinical behavior (Fig. 4B.35) (see Ch. 7). Low-grade tumors (prominent cystic pattern, abundant mucin, paucity of solid areas,

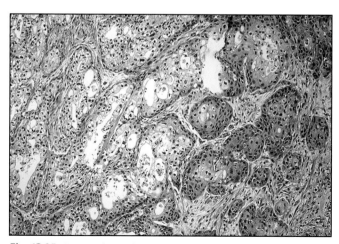

Fig. 4B.35 • Mucoepidermoid carcinoma of the larynx. Tumor with glandular areas on the left of the figure, and more solid, squamoid nests on the right.

little if any cytologic pleomorphism) tend to have a better prognosis than high-grade lesions, with 5-year survival rates reported as 90–100% for low-grade tumors and about 50% for high-grade tumors, with a 77–80% 5-year survival reported for all laryngeal MECs.[298,300] The high-grade tumors generally have less marked cyst formation, more solid squamoid areas, and an increase in nuclear atypicality and mitotic activity. Gerughty et al.[254] described, under the heading of "adeno-squamous carcinoma" a tumor occurring in the nasal and oral cavities and larynx that had a very aggressive clinical course. The tumor is separated by some from MEC by the occurrence of separate foci of adenocarcinoma, squamous cell carcinoma, and ductal CIS in the former lesion.[253,301] Damiani et al.[298] incorporate this entity with high-grade MEC in their material and do not report as dismal an outcome as Gerughty et al. did.[254] More recently, the term "adenosquamous carcinoma" has come to refer to a carcinoma with squamous and glandular components that has a prominent surface mucosal component of squamous cell carcinoma (see above).[302,303] These are generally high-grade lesions. This author views these ASCs as essentially squamous cell carcinomas of mucosal origin with focal glandular differentiation, analogous to ASC of the lung, and considers a MEC to be a tumor of salivary (or in laryngo-tracheal cases, seromucinous) gland origin.

The tumors that traditionally have been subsumed under the rubric of adenocarcinoma not otherwise specified are often advanced when diagnosed and are associated with aggressive behavior and a poor prognosis.[287–289]

Cartilaginous tumors

Cartilaginous tumors are rare laryngeal lesions; they are extremely rare in the trachea.[304] Laryngeal tumors most commonly involve the cricoid cartilage, with the thyroid cartilage being the next most common site.[304–308] Epiglottic and arytenoid tumors are exceptionally rare. Nine lesions reported as "chondromas" of the vocal cord, unattached to the laryngeal cartilaginous skeleton,[309] may actually represent chondroid metaplasia of the vocal cord.[310] Patients with laryngeal cartilaginous tumors tend to be males, mainly over 50 years, with a median age in the mid-60s.[306–308] Symptoms include dysphagia, dyspnea, or wheezing, or a mass in the neck, depending on the location of the neoplasm. Radiographs may show stippled calcification in the neoplasm, a finding virtually pathognomonic of laryngeal cartilaginous tumors.[304,307]

The tumors present as hard, smoothly lobulated sub-mucosal masses that are well demarcated, grayish, and myxoid in appearance on cut section (Figs 4B.36 and 4B.37). Histologically, the chondrocytes tend to cluster in a bluish chondroid and/or myxoid matrix. Cellularity as well as nuclear size and frequency of multinucleate chondrocytes may vary within as well as among tumors[165,304,311] (Fig. 4B.38); however, marked anaplasia, necrosis, and atypicality generally do not occur. Thus, applying conventional diagnostic criteria for cartilaginous neoplasms of the ossicular skeleton, most laryngeal cartilaginous tumors would be classified as low-grade chondrosarcomas (or chondrosarcomas grades 1 or 2).[306,308] An exceptionally rare case of clear cell chondrosarcoma of the larynx has been reported.[312] Despite this histologic appear-

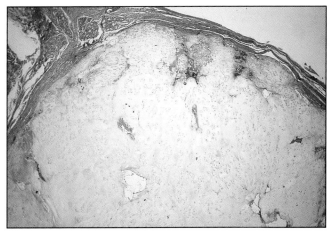

Fig. 4B.36 • Cartilaginous tumor of the larynx. The tumor, with a blue-gray, myxoid cut surface, arises from the cricoid cartilage and significantly narrows the subglottic lumen. (Reproduced from Shapshay S M and Aretz H T. Benign lesions of the larynx with permission of the American Academy of Otolaryngology – Head and Neck Surgery Foundation, copyright © 1984. All rights reserved.)

Fig. 4B.37 • Cartilaginous tumor of the larynx. Low-power photomicrograph showing well-delineated cartilaginous nodule in submucosal laryngeal tissue.

ance, the biologic behavior of laryngeal cartilaginous tumors is less aggressive than that of chondrosarcomas in other sites.[307,313] They are slowly growing neoplasms that tend eventually to recur locally if incompletely excised but very rarely metastasize.[306,307] High-grade chondrosarcomas (chondro-sarcomas grade 3 or dedifferentiated chondrosarcomas) of the larynx do occur,[308,314–316] but these are very rare. It is difficult to generalize about their biologic behavior, as some have been aggressive and some not.[316]

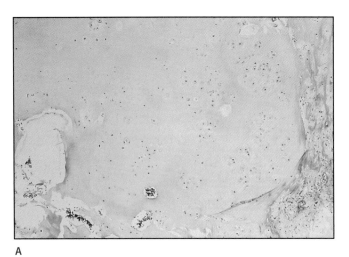 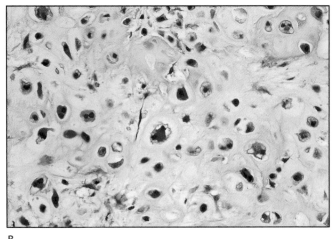

A   B

Fig. 4B.38 • Cartilaginous tumor of the larynx. (**A**) "Chondromatous" area, sparsely cellular with small nuclei. (**B**) "Sarcomatous" appearance of another tumor, showing a more cellular region with larger cells and nuclei and numerous binucleate chondrocytes. (Reproduced from Shapshay S M and Aretz H T. Benign lesions of the larynx with permission of the American Academy of Otolaryngology – Head and Neck Surgery Foundation, copyright © 1984. All rights reserved.)

Other malignant neoplasms

Malignant mesenchymal neoplasms other than primary cartilaginous tumors in the larynx and trachea are so rare as to be curiosities. Fibrosarcoma was originally considered the most common laryngeal malignant mesenchymal tumor;[317,318] however, the development of modern diagnostic techniques has resulted in a decreased incidence of the diagnosis of laryngeal fibrosarcoma.[318] Lesions initially thought to be fibrosarcomas may prove to be other entities, such as spindle cell carcinoma, monophasic synovial sarcoma, or fibromatosis.[318] The designation of laryngeal fibrosarcoma should be reserved for those malignant mesenchymal neoplasms in which no differentiation other than fibroblastic can be detected using available diagnostic techniques such as immunohistochemistry and electron microscopy.

Other malignant mesenchymal neoplasms reported in the larynx (all rare occurrences) include rhabdomyosarcoma,[317,319–321] so-called malignant fibrous histiocytoma,[322] osteosarcoma,[323,324] synovial sarcoma,[318,325–327] liposarcoma (generally well differentiated in the larynx/hypopharynx and consequently often difficult to differentiate histologically from lipomas),[328,329] malignant schwannoma,[330] leiomyosarcoma,[318,331] angiosarcoma,[332] malignant hemangiopericytoma,[333] and extraskeletal Ewing's

sarcoma.[334] There is an unpublished case of laryngeal Kaposi's sarcoma from our institution. Tracheal leiomyosarcomas have also been reported.[335] Malignant lymphomas can involve the trachea,[175] and the larynx may be involved by lymphoma either primarily or as part of generalized disease;[336–338] laryngeal involvement by mycosis fungoides has been described.[339,340] Plasmacytomas occur in the larynx and trachea, at times with progression to, or as part of, multiple myeloma.[175,341,342] Cases of epiglottic granulocytic sarcoma[343] and of laryngeal mast-cell sarcoma[344] have been reported. Malignant melanoma can involve the larynx, rarely as a primary neoplasm, and also as a metastatic lesion,[345–347] and a case of tracheal melanoma is cited by Weber & Grillo.[175] A unique case of laryngeal blastoma has been reported by Eble et al.[348]

Secondary malignant neoplasms can involve the larynx and trachea by direct extension from adjacent neoplasms, such as carcinomas of the thyroid gland or esophagus, or by hematogenous metastases. Clinically significant distant metastases to the larynx are rare occurrences. They are reported most commonly to originate from melanomas and renal cell carcinomas, but other sites of origin (pancreas, colon, ovary) have been reported as well.[349–351] Distant metastases to the trachea have included carcinomas of the endometrium, colon, breast, and uterine cervix.[175]

References

1. Abramson A L, Steinberg B M, Winkler B 1987 Laryngeal papillomatosis: clinical, histopathologic and molecular studies. Laryngoscope 97: 678–685
2. Derkay C S 2001 Recurrent respiratory papillomatosis. Laryngoscope 111: 57–69
3. Cohen S R, Seltzer S, Geller K A et al. 1980 Papilloma of the larynx and tracheobronchial tree in children. A retrospective study. Ann Otol Rhinol Laryngol 89: 497–503
4. Bauman N M, Smith R J H 1996 Recurrent respiratory papillomatosis. Pediatr Clin North Am 43: 1385–1401
5. Batsakis J G, Raymond A K, Rice D H 1983 The pathology of head and neck tumors. Papillomas of the upper aerodigestive tracts, part 18. Head Neck Surg 5: 332–344
6. Kleinsasser O, Oliveira E, Cruz G 1973 "Juvenile" und "adulte" Kehlkopfpapillome. HNO 21: 97–106

7. Franco R A, Zeitels S M, Farinelli W A et al. 2002 585-NM pulsed dye laser treatment of glottal papillomatosis. Ann Otol Rhinol Laryngol 111: 486–492
8. Naiman A N, Ceruse P, Coulombeau B et al. 2003 Intralesional cidofovir and surgical excision for laryngeal papillomatosis. Laryngoscope 113: 2174–2181
9. Pransky S M, Albright J T, Magit A E 2003 Long-term follow-up of pediatric recurrent respiratory papillomatosis managed with intralesional cidofovir. Laryngoscope 113: 1583–1587
10. Fechner R E, Goepfert H, Alford B R 1974 Invasive laryngeal papillomatosis. Arch Otolaryngol 99: 147–151
11. Shapiro A M, Rimell F L, Pou A et al. 1996 Tracheotomy in children with juvenile-onset recurrent respiratory papillomatosis: The Children's Hospital of Pittsburgh experience. Ann Otol Rhinol Laryngol 105: 1–5

12. Lindeberg H, Elbrond O 1989 Laryngeal papillomas: clinical aspects in a series of 231 patients. Clin Otolaryngol 14: 333–342

13. Doyle D J, Gianoli G J, Espinola T et al. 1994 Recurrent respiratory papillomatosis: juvenile versus adult forms. Laryngoscope 104: 523–527

14. Duggan M A, Lim M, Gill M J et al. 1990 HPV DNA typing of adult-onset respiratory papillomatosis. Laryngoscope 100: 639–642

15. Quiney R E, Wells M, Lewis F A et al. 1989 Laryngeal papillomatosis: correlation between severity of disease and presence of HPV 6 and 11 detected by in-situ DNA hybridisation. J Clin Pathol 42: 694–698

16. Terry R M, Lewis F A, Griffiths S et al. 1987 Demonstration of human papillomavirus types 6 and 11 in juvenile laryngeal papillomatosis by in-situ DNA hybridization. J Pathol 153: 245–248

17. Lie E S, Heyden A, Johannesen M K et al. 1996 Detection of human papillomavirus in routinely processed biopsy specimens from laryngeal papillomas: evaluation of reproducibility of polymerase chain reaction and DNA in situ hybridization procedures. Acta Otolaryngol (Stockh) 116: 627–632

18. Shen J, Tate J E, Crum C P et al. 1996 Prevalence of human papillomaviruses (HPV) in benign and malignant tumors of the upper respiratory tract. Mod Pathol 9: 15–20

19. Quick C A, Krzyzek R A, Watts S L et al. 1980 Relationship between condylomata and laryngeal papillomata. Clinical and molecular virological evidence. Ann Otol Rhinol Laryngol 89: 467–471

20. Kosko J R, Derkay C S 1996 Role of cesarean section in prevention of recurrent respiratory papillomatosis – is there one? Int J Pediatric Otorhinolaryngol 35: 31–38

21. Lin K-Y, Westra W H, Kashima H K et al. 1997 Coinfection of HPV-11 and HPV-16 in a case of laryngeal squamous papillomas with severe dysplasia. Laryngoscope 107: 942–947

22. Go C, Schwartz M R, Donovan D T 2003 Molecular transformation of recurrent respiratory papillomatosis: viral typing and p53 overexpression. Ann Otol Rhinol Laryngol 112:298–302

23. Nash M, Lucente F E, Srinivasan K et al. 1987 Condylomatous lesions of the upper aerodigestive tract. Laryngoscope 97: 1410–1416

24. Fechner R E, Fitz-Hugh G S 1980 Invasive tracheal papillomatosis. Am J Surg Pathol 4: 79–86

25. Quick C A, Foucar E, Dehner L P 1979 Frequency and significance of epithelial atypia in laryngeal papillomatosis. Laryngoscope 89: 550–560

26. Crissman J D, Kessis T, Shah K V et al. 1988 Squamous papillary neoplasia of the adult upper aerodigestive tract. Hum Pathol 19: 1387–1396

27. Heffner D K 1984 Problems in pediatric otorhinolaryngic pathology. V. Diseases of the larynx and trachea. Int J Pediatr Otorhinolaryngol 7: 203–219

28. Fechner R E, Mills S E 1982 Verruca vulgaris of the larynx. A distinctive lesion of probable viral origin confused with verrucous carcinoma. Am J Surg Pathol 6: 357–362

29. Barnes L, Yunis E J, Krebs F J III et al. 1991 Verruca vulgaris of the larynx. Demonstration of human papillomavirus types 6/11 by in-situ hybridization. Arch Pathol Lab Med 115: 895–899

30. MacMillan R H III, Fechner R E 1986 Pleomorphic adenoma of the larynx. Arch Pathol Lab Med 110: 245–247

31. Batsakis J G 1972 Neoplasms of the minor and lesser major salivary glands. Surg Gynecol Obstet 135: 289–298

32. Ma C K, Fine G, Lewis J et al. 1979 Benign mixed tumor of the trachea. Cancer 44: 2260–2266

33. Lack E E, Worsham G F, Callihan M D et al. 1980 Granular cell tumour: a clinicopathologic study of 110 patients. J Surg Oncol 13: 301–316

34. Morrison J G, Gray G F, Dao A H et al. 1987 Granular cell tumors. Am Surg 53: 156–160

35. Frable M A, Fischer R A 1976 Granular cell myoblastomas. Laryngoscope 86: 36–42

36. Compagno J, Hyams V J, Ste-Marie P 1975 Benign granular cell tumors of the larynx: a review of 36 cases with clinicopathologic data. Ann Otol 84: 308–314

37. Coates H L, Kevine K D, McDonald T J et al. 1976 Granular cell tumors of the larynx. Ann Otol 85: 504–507

38. Nolte E, Kleinsasser O 1982 Granularzelltumoren des Kehlkopfes. HNO 30: 333–339

39. Burton D M, Heffner D K, Patow C A 1992 Granular cell tumors of the trachea. Laryngoscope 102: 807–813

40. Garud O, Elverland H H, Bostad L et al. 1984 Granular cell tumor of the larynx in a 5-year-old child. Ann Otol Rhinol Laryngol 93: 45–47

41. Brandwein M, LeBenger J, Strauchen J et al. 1990 Atypical granular cell tumor of the larynx: an unusually aggressive tumor clinically and microscopically. Head Neck 12: 154–159

42. Mazur M T, Shultz J J, Myers J L 1990 Granular cell tumor. Immunohistochemical analysis of 21 benign tumors and one malignant tumor. Arch Pathol Lab Med 114: 692–696

43. Nathrath W B J, Remberger K 1986 Immunohistochemical study of granular cell tumours. Demonstration of neuron specific enolase, S100 protein, laminin and alpha-I-antichymotrypsin. Virchows Arch [A] 408: 421–434

44. Said-Al-Naief N, Brandwein M, Lawson W et al. 1997 Synchronous lingual granular cell tumor and squamous carcinoma. A case report and review of the literature. Arch Otolaryngol Head Neck Surg 123: 543–547

45. Lack E E 1997 Tumors of the adrenal gland and extra-adrenal paraganglia. Atlas of tumor pathology, series 3, fascicle 19. Armed Forces Institute of Pathology, Washington, DC

46. Barnes L 1991 Paraganglioma of the larynx. A critical review of the literature. ORL J Otorhinolaryngol Relat Spec 53: 220–234

47. Googe P B, Ferry J A, Bhan A K et al. 1988 A comparison of paraganglioma, carcinoid tumor, and small cell carcinoma of the larynx. Arch Pathol Lab Med 112: 809–815

48. Baugh R F, McClatchey K D, Sprik S A et al. 1987 Laryngeal paraganglioma. J Otolaryngol 16: 167–168

49. Milroy C M, Rode J, Moss E 1991 Laryngeal paragangliomas and neuroendocrine carcinomas. Histopathology 18: 201–209

50. Lawson W, Zak F G 1974 The glomus bodies ("paraganglia") of the human larynx. Laryngoscope 84: 98–111

51. Liew S H, Leong A S-Y, Tang H M K 1981 Tracheal paraganglioma: a case report with review of the literature. Cancer 47: 1387–1393

52. Woodruff J M, Huvos A G, Erlandson R A et al. 1985 Neuroendocrine carcinomas of the larynx. A study of two types, one of which mimics thyroid medullary carcinoma. Am J Surg Pathol 9: 771–790

53. Wenig B M, Hyams V J, Heffner D K 1988 Moderately differentiated neuroendocrine carcinoma of the larynx. A clinicopathologic study of 54 cases. Cancer 62: 2658–2676

54. Wenig B, Gnepp D R 1989 The spectrum of neuroendocrine carcinomas of the larynx. Semin Diagn Pathol 4: 329–350

55. Bosq M J, Micheau C, Nivet P et al. 1991 Paragangliomas of the head and neck. Immunohistochemical analysis of 16 cases in comparison with neuroendocrine carcinoma. Pathol Res Pract 187: 814–823

56. Brodsky L, Yoshpe N, Ruben R J 1983 Clinical pathological correlates of congenital subglottic haemangiomas. Ann Otol Rhinol Laryngol 92 (suppl 105): 4–18

57. Shikhani A H, Marsh B R, Jones M M et al. 1986 Infantile subglottic hemangiomas. An update. Ann Otol Rhinol Laryngol 95: 336–347

58. Meeuwis J, Bos C E, Hoeve L J et al. 1990 Subglottic hemangiomas in infants: treatment with intralesional corticosteroid injection and intubation. Int J Pediatr Otorhinolaryngol 19: 145–150

59. Cotton R T, Richardson M A 1981 Congenital laryngeal anomalies. Otolaryngol Clin North Am 14: 203–218

60. Batsakis J G, Fox J E 1970 Supporting tissue neoplasms of the larynx. Surg Gynecol Obstet 131: 989–997

61. Cummings C W, Montgomery W W, Balogh K Jr 1969 Neurogenic tumors of the larynx. Ann Otol Rhinol Laryngol 78: 76–95

62. Ma C K, Raju U, Fine G et al. 1981 Primary tracheal neurilemoma. Report of a case with ultrastructural examination. Arch Pathol Lab Med 105: 187–189

63. Schaeffer B T, Som P M, Biller H F et al. 1986 Schwannomas of the larynx: review and computed tomographic scan analysis. Head Neck Surg 8: 469–472

64. Al-Otieschan A T, Mahasin Z Z, Gangopadhyay K et al. 1996 Schwannoma of the larynx: Two case reports and review of the literature. J Otolaryngol 25: 412–415

65. Cohen S R, Landing B H, Isaacs H 1978 Neurofibroma of the larynx in a child. Ann Otol Rhinol Laryngol 87 (suppl 52): 29–31

66. Chow L T C, Ma T K F, Chow W H 1997 Cellular neurothekeoma of the hypopharynx. Histopathology 30: 192–194

67. Karma P, Hyrynkangas K, Rasanen O 1978 Laryngeal leiomyoma. J Laryngol Otol 92: 411–415

68. Shibata K, Komune S 1980 Laryngeal angiomyoma (vascular leiomyoma): clinicopathological findings. Laryngoscope 90: 1880–1886

69. Boedts D, Mestdagh J 1979 Adult rhabdomyoma of the larynx. Arch Otorhinolaryngol 224: 221–229

70. Di Sant'Agnese P A, Knowles D M 1980 Extracardiac rhabdomyoma: a clinicopathologic study and review of the literature. Cancer 46: 780–789

71. Granich M S, Pilch B Z, Nadol J B et al. 1983 Fetal rhabdomyoma of the larynx. Arch Otolaryngol 109: 821–826

72. Rosenberg H S, Vogler C, Close L G et al. 1981 Laryngeal fibromatosis in the neonate. Arch Otolaryngol 107: 513–517

73. McIntosh W A, Kassner G W, Murray J F 1985 Fibromatosis and fibrosarcoma of the larynx and pharynx in an infant. Arch Otolaryngol 111: 478–480

74. Wenig B M 1995 Lipomas of the larynx and hypopharynx: a review of the literature with the addition of three new cases. J Laryngol Otol 109: 353–357

75. Jesberg N 1982 Fibrolipoma of the pyriform sinuses: thirty-seven year follow-up. Laryngoscope 92: 1157–1159

76. Ballard R W, Yarington C T Jr 1981 Hemangiopericytoma of the tracheal wall. Arch Otolaryngol 107: 558–560

77. Schwartz M R, Donovan D T 1987 Hemangiopericytoma of the larynx: a case report and review of the literature. Otolaryngol Head Neck Surg 96: 369–372

78. Cohen S R, Landing B H, Isaacs H 1978 Fibrous histiocytoma of the trachea. Ann Otol Rhinol Laryngol 87 (suppl. 52): 2–4

79. Gonzalez-Campora R, Matilla A, Sanchez-Carrillo J J et al. 1981 "Benign" fibrous histiocytoma of the trachea. J Laryngol Otol 95: 1287–1292

80. Van Laer C, Hamans E, Neetens I et al. 1996 Benign fibrous histiocytoma of the larynx: presentation of a case and review of the literature. J Laryngol Otol 110: 474–477

81. Pollak E R, Naunheim K S, Little A G 1985 Fibromyxoma of the trachea. A review of benign tracheal tumors. Arch Pathol Lab Med 109: 926–929

82. Garcia-Prats M D, Sotelo-Rodriguez M T, Ballestin C et al. 1991 Glomus tumour of the trachea: report of a case with microscopic, ultrastructural

and immunohistochemical examination and review of the literature. Histopathology 19: 459–464

83. Cannon C R, Johns M E, Fechner R E 1987 Immature teratoma of the larynx. Otolaryngol Head Neck Surg 96: 366–368

84. Küng M, Landa J F, Lubin J 1984 Benign clear cell tumor ("sugar tumor") of the trachea. Cancer 54: 517–519

85. Kambic V, Radsel Z, Zargi M et al. 1981 Vocal cord polyps: incidence, histology and pathogenesis. J Laryngol Otol 95: 609–618

86. Kleinsasser O 1982 Pathogenesis of vocal cord polyps. Ann Otol Rhinol Laryngol 91: 378–381

87. Holinger P H, Johnston K C 1960 Contact ulcer of the larynx. JAMA 172: 511–515

88. Barton R T 1953 Observation of the pathogenesis of laryngeal granuloma due to endotracheal anesthesia. N Engl J Med 248: 1097–1099

89. Ward P H, Zwitman D, Hanson D et al. 1980 Contact ulcers and granulomas of the larynx: new insights into their etiology as a basis for more rational treatment. Otolaryngol Head Neck Surg 88: 262–269

90. Miko T L 1989 Peptic (contact ulcer) granuloma of the larynx. J Clin Pathol 42: 800–804

91. Al-Dousary S 1997 Vocal process granuloma. ENT – Ear Nose Throat J 76: 382–387

92. Thompson L D R 1997 Diagnostically challenging lesions in head and neck pathology. Eur Arch Otorhinolaryngol 254: 357–366

93. Wenig B M, Heffner D K 1990 Contact ulcers of the larynx. A reacquaintance with the pathology of an often underdiagnosed entity. Arch Pathol Lab Med 114: 825–828

94. Mills S E, Cooper P H, Fechner R E 1980 Lobular capillary hemangioma: the underlying lesion of pyogenic granuloma. A study of 73 cases from the oral and nasal mucous membranes. Am J Surg Pathol 4: 471–479

95. Grillo H C, Mark E J, Mathisen D J et al. 1993 Idiopathic laryngotracheal stenosis and its management. Ann Thorac Surg 56: 80–87

96. Park S S, Streitz J M, Rebeiz E E et al. 1995 Idiopathic subglottic stenosis. Arch Otolaryngol Head Neck Surg 121: 894–897

97. Jindal J R, Milbrath M M, Hogan W J et al. 1994 Gastroesophageal reflux disease as a likely cause of "idiopathic" subglottic stenosis. Ann Otol Rhinol Laryngol 103: 186–191

98. Canalis R F, Maxwell D S, Hemenway W G 1977 Laryngocele – an updated review. J Otolaryngol 6: 191–199

99. Holinger L D, Barnes D R, Smid L J et al. 1978 Laryngocele and saccular cysts. Ann Otol 87: 675–68

100. Baker H L, Baker S R, McClatchey K D 1982 Manifestations and management of laryngoceles. Head Neck Surg 4: 450–456

101. Macfie D D 1966 Asymptomatic laryngoceles in wind-instrument bandsmen. Arch Otolaryngol 83: 270–275

102. DeSanto L W, Devine K D, Weiland L H 1970 Cysts of the larynx – classification. Laryngoscope 80: 145–176

103. Yamase H T, Putman H C III 1979 Oncocytic papillary cystadenomatosis of the larynx. A clinicopathologic entity. Cancer 44: 2306–2311

104. Newman B H, Taxy J B, Laker H I 1984 Laryngeal cysts in adults: clinicopathologic study of 20 cases. Am J Clin Pathol 81: 715–720

105. Oliveira C A, Roth J A, Adams G L 1977 Oncocytic lesions of the larynx. Laryngoscope 87: 1718–1725

106. Hunter A M, Millar J W, Wightman A J A et al. 1981 The changing pattern of laryngeal tuberculosis. J Laryngol Otol 95: 393–398

107. Yarnal J R, Golish J A, Van der Kuypt F 1981 Laryngeal tuberculosis presenting as carcinoma. Arch Otolaryngol 107: 503–505

108. Thaller S R, Gross J R, Pilch B Z et al. 1987 Laryngeal tuberculosis as manifested in the decades 1963–1983. Laryngoscope 97: 848–850

109. Kandiloros D C, Nikolopoulos T P, Ferekidis E A et al. 1997 Laryngeal tuberculosis at the end of the 20th century. J Laryngol Otol 111: 619–621

110. Caldarelli D D, Friedberg S A, Harris A A 1979 Medical and surgical aspects of the granulomatous diseases of the larynx. Otolaryngol Clin North Am 12: 767–781

111. Blair P A, Gnepp D R, Riley R S et al. 1981 Blastomycosis of the larynx. South Med J 74: 880–882

112. Platt M A 1977 Laryngeal coccidioidomycosis. JAMA 237: 1234–1235

113. Maymo Arganaraz M, Luque A G, Tosello M E et al. 2003 Paracoccidioidomycosis and larynx carcinoma. Mycoses 46: 229–232

114. Khabie N, Boyce T G, Roberts G D et al. 2003 Laryngeal sporotrichosis causing stridor in a young child. Int J Pediatr Otorhinolaryngol 67: 819–823

115. Nakahira M, Matsumoto S, Mukushita N et al. 2002 Primary aspergillosis of the larynx associated with CD4+ T lymphocytopenia. J Laryngol Otol 116: 304–306

116. Brandenburg J H, Finch W W, Kirkham W R 1978 Actinomycosis of the larynx and pharynx. Trans Am Acad Ophthalmol Otolaryngol 86: 739–742

117. Kobayashi R H, Rosenblatt H M, Carney J M et al. 1980 Candida esophagitis and laryngitis in chronic mucocutaneous candidiasis. Pediatrics 66: 380–384

118. Pabuçcuoglu U, Tuncer C, Sengiz S 2002 Histopathology of candidal hyperplastic lesions of the larynx. Path Res Pract 198: 675–678

119. Barnes E L Jr, Zafar T 1977 Laryngeal amyloidosis: clinicopathologic study of seven cases. Ann Otol Rhinol Laryngol 86: 856–863

120. Hellquist H, Olofsson J, Sokjer H et al. 1979 Amyloidosis of the larynx. Acta Otolaryngol 88: 443–450

121. Godbersen G S, Leh J F, Rudert H et al. 1992 Organ-limited laryngeal amyloid deposits: clinical, morphological, and immunohistochemical results of five cases. Ann Otol Rhinol Laryngol 101: 770–775

122. Lewis J E, Olsen K D, Kurtin P J et al. 1992 Laryngeal amyloidosis: a clinicopathological and immunohistochemical review. Otolaryngol Head Neck Surg 106: 372–377

123. Thompson L D R, Derringer G A, Wenig B M 2000 Amyloidosis of the larynx: a clinocopathologic study of 11 cases. Mod Pathol 13: 528–535

124. Michaels L, Hyams V J 1979 Amyloid in localised deposits and plasmacytomas of the respiratory tract. J Pathol 128: 29–38

125. Simpson G T II, Skinner M, Strong M S et al. 1984 Localized amyloidosis of the head and neck and upper aerodigestive and lower respiratory tracts. Ann Otol Rhinol Laryngol 93: 374–379

126. Berg A M, Troxler R F, Grillone G et al. 1993 Localized amyloidosis of the larynx: evidence for light chain composition. Ann Otol Rhinol Laryngol 102: 884–889

127. Weirich Ch IG, Gaa A, Schaefer H E 1996 Amyloid tumors of the lung – an immunocytoma? Pathol Res Pract 192: 446–452

128. Young R H, Sandstrom R E, Mark G J 1980 Tracheopathia osteoplastica. J Thorac Cardiovasc Surg 79: 537–541

129. Nienhuis D M, Prakash U B S, Edell E S 1990 Tracheobronchopathia osteochondroplastica. Ann Otol Rhinol Laryngol 99: 689–694

130. Birzgalis A R, Farrington W T, O'Keefe L et al. 1993 Localized tracheopathia osteoplastica of the subglottis. J Laryngol Otol 107: 352–353

131. Paaske P B, Tang E 1985 Tracheopathia osteoplastica in the larynx. J Laryngol Otol 99: 305–310

132. Thomas K 1970 Laryngeal manifestations of Wegener's granuloma. J Laryngol Otol 84: 101–106

133. Wenig B M, Devaney K L, Wenig B L 1995 Pseudoneoplastic lesions of the oropharynx and larynx simulating cancer. Pathol Annu 30: 143–187

134. Matt B H 1996 Wegener's granulomatosis, acute laryngotracheal airway obstruction and death in a 17-year-old female: case report and review of the literature. Int J Pediatr Otorhinolaryngol 37: 163–172

135. Carpenter R J III, Banks P M, McDonald T J et al. 1978 Sinus histiocytosis with massive lymphadenopathy (Rosai–Dorfman disease): report of a case with respiratory tract involvement. Laryngoscope 88: 1963–1969

136. Case records 1981 Case no. 52. N Engl J Med 305: 1572–1580

137. Wenig B M, Abbondanzo S L, Childers E L et al. 1993 Extranodal sinus histiocytosis with massive lymphadenopathy (Rosai–Dorfman disease) of the head and neck. Hum Pathol 24: 483–492

138. Weisman R A, Canalis R F, Powell W J 1980 Laryngeal sarcoidosis with airway obstruction. Ann Otol Rhinol Laryngol 89: 58–61

139. Marion R B, Alperin J E, Maloney W H 1972 Gouty tophus of the true vocal cord. Arch Otolaryngol 96: 161–162

140. Dedo H H, Carlsoo B 1982 Histologic evaluation of Teflon granulomas of human vocal cords. A light and electron microscopic study. Acta Otolaryngol 93: 475–484

141. Varvares M A, Montgomery W W, Hillman R E 1995 Teflon granuloma of the larynx: etiology, pathophysiology, and management. Ann Otol Rhinol Laryngol 104: 511–515

142. Wey W, Torhorst J 1974 Hamartom des Hypopharynx (Verlaufsbeobachtung eines Falles uber 11 Jahre). HNO 22: 217–219

143. Patterson H C, Pilch B Z, Dickersin G R et al. 1981 Hamartoma of the hypopharynx. Arch Otolaryngol 107: 767–772

144. Zapf B, Leymann W B, Snyder G G III 1981 Hamartoma of the larynx: an unusual cause of stridor in an infant. Otolaryngol Head Neck Surg 89: 797–799

145. Fine E D, Dahms B, Arnold J E 1995 Laryngeal hamartoma: a rare congenital abnormality. Ann Oto Rhinol Laryngol 104: 87–89

146. Manni J J, Mulder J J S, Schaafsma H E et al. 1992 Inflammatory pseudotumor of the subglottis. Eur Arch Otorhinolaryngol 249: 16–19

147. Gabrielides C G, Karkavelas G, Triarides C et al. 1981 Malakoplakia of the larynx. Pathol Res Pract 172: 53–57

148. Kambic V, Gale N, Radsel Z 1982 Warty dyskeratoma of the vocal cord. First reported case. Arch Otolaryngol 108: 385–387

149. Manni H J, Lema P N, Van Raalte J A et al. 1983 Schistosomiasis in otorhinolaryngology: review of the literature and case report. J Laryngol Otol 97: 1177–1181

150. Libera D D, Redlich G, Bittesini L et al. 2001 Aneurysmal bone cyst of the larynx presenting with hypoglottic obstruction. A case report and review of the literature. Arch Pathol Lab Med 125: 673–676

151. Cho M S, Kim E S, Kim H J et al. 1997 Kimura's disease of the epiglottis. Histopathology 30: 592–594

152. Fechner R E 1974 Laryngeal keratosis and atypia. Can J Otolaryngol 3: 516–521

153. Barnes L, Eveson J W, Reichart P et al. (eds) 2005 WHO classification of tumors. Pathology and genetics of head and neck tumors, Lyon, France, IARC Press

154. Hellquist H, Olofsson J, Grontoft O 1981 Carcinoma in-situ and severe dysplasia of the vocal cords. A clinicopathologic and photometric investigation. Acta Otolaryngol 92: 543–555

155. Crissman J D 1982 Laryngeal keratosis preceding laryngeal carcinoma. A report of four cases. Arch Otolaryngol 108: 445–448

156. Crissman J D, Fu Y S 1986 Intraepithelial neoplasia of the larynx. A clinicopathologic study of six cases with DNA analysis. Arch Otolaryngol Head Neck Surg 112: 522–528

157. Crissman J D, Zarbo R J, Drozdowicz S et al. 1988 Carcinoma in-situ and microinvasive squamous carcinoma of the laryngeal glottis. Arch Otolaryngol Head Neck Surg 114: 299–307

158. Crissman J D, Zarbo R J 1989 Dysplasia, in situ carcinoma, and progression to invasive squamous cell carcinoma of the upper aerodigestive tract. Am J Surg Pathol 13 (suppl. 1): 5–16

159. Crissman J D 1985 Histopathologic diagnosis of early cancer. In: Chretien P B, Johns M E, Shedd D P et al. (eds) Head and neck cancer. Decker, Philadelphia, vol 1, p 134–140

160. Bouquot J E, Gnepp D R 1991 Laryngeal precancer: a review of the literature, commentary, and comparison with oral leukoplakia. Head Neck 13: 488–497

161. Fried M P, Gopal H 1996 Carcinoma of the glottis and subglottis. In: Fried M P (ed) The larynx: a multidisciplinary approach, 2nd edn. Mosby, St Louis, p 503–517

162. McGavran M H, Stutsman A C, Ogura J H 1974 Superficially invasive epidermoid carcinoma of the true vocal cord. Can J Otolaryngol 3: 526–527

163. Gillis T M, Incze J, Strong M S et al. 1983 Natural history and management of keratosis, atypia, carcinoma in-situ, and microinvasive cancer of the larynx. Am J Surg 146: 512–516

164. Sakr W A, Zarbo R J, Jacobs J R et al. 1987 Distribution of basement membrane in squamous cell carcinoma of the head and neck. Hum Pathol 18: 1043–1050

165. Pilch B Z, Dorfman D M, Brodsky G L et al. 1996 Pathology of laryngeal malignancies. In: Fried M P (ed) The larynx: a multidisciplinary approach, 2nd edn. Mosby, St Louis, p 461–485

166. Nguyen C, Naghibzadeh B, Black MJ et al. 1996 Glottic microinvasive carcinoma: is it different from carcinoma in situ? J Otolaryngol 25: 223–226

167. Jemal A, Tiwari R C, Murray T et al. 2004 Cancer statistics, 2004. CA Cancer J Clin 54: 8–29

168. Muir C, Weiland L 1995 Upper aerodigestive tract cancers. Cancer 75: 147–153

169. Wang C C 1983 Head and neck neoplasms. In: Mansfield C M (ed) Therapeutic radiology: new directions in therapy. Medical Examination Publishing, New Hyde Park, NY, p 144–169

170. Koufman J A, Burke A J 1997 The etiology and pathogenesis of laryngeal carcinoma. Otolaryngol Clin North Am 30: 1–19

171. Talamini R, Bosetti C, La Vecchia C et al. 2002 Combined effect of tobacco and alcohol on laryngeal risk: a case-control study. Cancer Causes Control 13: 957–964

172. McKaig R G, Baric R S, Olshan A F 1998 Human papillomavirus and head and neck cancer: epidemiology and molecular biology. Head Neck 20: 250–265

173. Fischer M, Von Winterfeld F 2003 Evaluation and application of a broad-spectrum polymerase chain reaction assay for human papillomaviruses in the screening of squamous cell tumours of the head and neck. Acta Otolaryngol 123: 752–758

174. Bacciu A, Mercante G, Ingegnoli A et al. 2003 Reflux esophagitis as a possible risk factor in the development of pharyngolaryngeal squamous cell carcinoma. Tumori 89: 485–487

175. Weber A L, Grillo H C 1978 Tracheal tumours. A radiological, clinical and pathological evaluation of 84 cases. Radiol Clin North Am 16: 227–246

176. Maisel R H, Cohen J I 1996 Carcinoma of the supraglottis. In: Fried M P (ed) The larynx: a multidisciplinary approach, 2nd edn. Mosby, St Louis, p 487–501

177. Fabian R L, Varvares M A 1996 Carcinoma of the laryngopharynx and cervical esophagus. In: Fried M P (ed) The larynx: a multidisciplinary approach, 2nd edn. Mosby, St Louis, p 549–560

178. Wang C C 1997 Radiation therapy for head and neck neoplasms, 3rd edn. Wiley-Liss, New York, p 224

179. American Joint Committee on Cancer 1997 AJCC cancer staging manual, 5th edn. Lippincott-Raven, Philadelphia, p 41–42

180. Shah J P, Karnell L H, Hoffman H T et al. 1997 Patterns of care for cancer of the larynx in the United States. Arch Otolaryngol Head Neck Surg 123: 475–483

181. Kirchner J A 1997 Glottic–supraglottic barrier: fact or fantasy? Ann Otol Rhinol Laryngol 106: 700–704

182. Ferlito A, Olofsson J, Rinaldo A 1997 Barrier between the supraglottis and the glottis: myth or reality? Ann Otol Rhinol Laryngol 106: 716–719

183. Weinstein G S, Laccourreye O, Brasnu D et al. 1995 Reconsidering a paradigm: the spread of supraglottic carcinoma of the glottis. Laryngoscope 105: 1129–1133

184. Hoffman H T, Karnell L H, Shah J P et al. 1997 Hypopharyngeal cancer patient care evaluation. Laryngoscope 107: 1005–1017

185. McGavran M H, Bauer W C, Ogura J H 1961 The incidence of cervical lymph node metastases from epidermoid carcinoma of the larynx and their relationship to certain characteristics of the primary tumor. A study based on the clinical and pathological findings for 96 patients treated by primary en bloc laryngectomy and radical neck dissection. Cancer 14: 55–66

186. Jakobsson P A, Eneroth C-M, Killander D et al. 1973 Histologic classification and grading of malignancy in carcinoma of the larynx. Acta Radiol Ther Phys Biol 12: 1–8

187. Fisher H R 1975 Grading of biopsies of laryngeal carcinomas by multiple criteria. Can J Otolaryngol 4: 881–884

188. Helweg-Larsen K, Graem N, Miestrup-Larsen K-I et al. 1978 Clinical relevance of histological grading of cancer of the larynx. Acta Pathol Microbiol Scand Sect A 86: 499–504

189. Jacobs J R, Sessions D G, Ogura J H 1980 Recurrent carcinoma of the larynx and the hypopharynx. Otolaryngol Head Neck Surg 88: 425–433

190. Glanz H K 1984 Carcinoma of the larynx. Growth, p-classification and grading of squamous cell carcinoma of the vocal cords. Adv Otorhinolaryngol 32: 1–123

191. Wiernik G, Millard P R, Haybittle J L 1991 The predictive value of histological classification into degrees of differentiation of squamous cell carcinoma of the larynx and hypopharynx compared with the survival of patients. Histopathology 19: 411–417

192. Cappellari J O 1997 Histopathology and pathologic prognostic indicators of laryngeal cancer. Otolaryngol Clin North Am 30: 251–268

193. Bryne M, Jenssen N, Boysen M 1995 Histological grading in the deep invasive front of T1 and T2 glottic squamous cell carcinomas has high prognostic value. Virchows Arch 427: 277–281

194. Welkoborsky H-J, Hinni M, Dienes H-P et al. 1995 Predicting recurrence and survival in patients with laryngeal cancer by means of DNA cytometry, tumor front grading, and proliferation markers. Ann Otol Rhinol Laryngol 104: 503–510

195. Capaccio P, Pruneri G, Carboni N et al. 1997 Cyclin D1 protein expression is related to clinical progression in laryngeal squamous cell carcinomas. J Laryngol Otol 111: 622–626

196. Narayana A, Vaughan A T M, Gunaratne S et al. 1998 Is p53 an independent prognostic factor in patients with laryngeal carcinoma? Cancer 82: 286–291

197. Cann C I, Rothman K J, Fried M P 1988 Epidemiology of laryngeal cancer. In: Fried M P (ed) The larynx: a multidisciplinary approach, 2nd edn. Mosby, St Louis, p 425–436

198. Ackerman L V 1948 Verrucous carcinoma of the oral cavity. Surgery 23: 670–678

199. Van Nostrand A W P, Olofsson J 1972 Verrucous carcinoma of the larynx. A clinical and pathologic study of 10 cases. Cancer 30: 691–702

200. Burns H P, van Nostrand A W P, Bryce D P 1976 Verrucous carcinoma of the larynx. Management by radiotherapy and surgery. Ann Otol 85: 538–543

201. Batsakis J G, Hybels R, Crissman J D et al. 1982 The pathology of head and neck tumors. Verrucous carcinoma, part 15. Head Neck Surg 5: 29–38

202. Ferlito A 1985 Diagnosis and treatment of verrucous squamous cell carcinoma of the larynx: a critical review. Ann Otol Rhinol Laryngol 94: 575–579

203. Lundgren J A V, van Nostrand A W P, Harwood A R et al. 1986 Verrucous carcinoma (Ackerman's tumor) of the larynx: diagnostic and therapeutic considerations. Head Neck Surg 9: 19–26

204. Ferlito A, Recher G 1980 Ackerman's tumor (verrucous carcinoma) of the larynx. A clinicopathologic study of 77 cases. Cancer 46: 1617–1630

205. Orvidas L J, Olsen K D, Lewis J E et al. 1998 Verrucous carcinoma of the larynx: a review of 53 patients. Head Neck 20: 197–203

206. Biller H F, Ogura J H, Bauer W C 1971 Verrucous cancer of the larynx. Laryngoscope 81: 1323–1329

207. Fisher H R 1975 Verrucous carcinoma of the larynx – a study of its pathologic anatomy. Can J Otolaryngol 4: 270–277

208. Medina J E, Dichtel W, Luna M A 1984 Verrucous-squamous carcinomas of the oral cavity. A clinicopathologic study of 104 cases. Arch Otolaryngol 110: 437–440

209. Niparko J K, Rubinstein M I, McClatchey K D 1988 Invasive squamous cell carcinoma within verrucous carcinoma. J Otolaryngol 17: 38–40

210. Smith R R L, Kuhajda F P, Harris A E 1985 Anaplastic transformation of verrucous carcinoma following radiotherapy. Am J Otolaryngol 6: 448–452

211. Maurizi M, Cadoni G, Ottaviani F et al. 1996 Verrucous squamous cell carcinoma of the larynx: diagnostic and therapeutic considerations. Eur Arch Otorhinolaryngol 253: 130–135

212. Shear M, Pindborg J J 1980 Verrucous hyperplasia of the oral mucosa. Cancer 46: 1855–1862

213. Lopez-Amado M, Garcia-Caballero T, Lozano-Ramirez A et al. 1996 Human papillomavirus and p53 oncoprotein in verrucous carcinoma of the larynx. J Laryngol Otol 110: 742–747

214. Crissman J D, Kessis T, Shaw K V et al. 1988 Squamous papillary neoplasia of the adult upper aerodigestive tract. Hum Pathol 19: 1387–1396

215. Thompson L D R, Wenig B M, Heffner D R et al. 1999 Exophytic and papillary squamous cell carcinomas of the larynx: a clinicopathologic series of 104 cases. Otolaryngol Head Neck Surg 120: 718–724

216. Glanz H, Kleinsasser O 1987 Verrucous carcinoma of the larynx – a misnomer. Arch Otorhinolaryngol 244: 108–111

217. Hyams V J 1975 Spindle cell carcinoma of the larynx. Can J Otolaryngol 4: 307–313

218. Battifora H 1976 Spindle cell carcinoma. Ultrastructural evidence of squamous origin and collagen production by tumor cells. Cancer 37: 2275–2282

219. Zarbo R J, Crissman J D, Venkat H et al. 1986 Spindle-cell carcinoma of the upper aerodigestive tract mucosa. An immunohistologic and ultrastructural study of 18 biphasic tumors and comparison with seven monophasic tumors. Am J Surg Pathol 10: 741–753

220. Ellis G L, Langloss J M, Heffner D K et al. 1987 Spindle-cell carcinoma of the aerodigestive tract. An immunohistochemical analysis of 21 cases. Am J Surg Pathol 11: 335–342

221. Lewis J E, Olsen K D, Sebo T J 1997 Spindle cell carcinoma of the larynx: review of 26 cases including DNA content and immunohistochemistry. Hum Pathol 28: 664–673

222. Miranda F J, Neto J A K, da Costa E A et al. 1980 Carcinosarcoma of the esophagus. Int Surg 65: 463–467

223. Appelman H D, Oberman H A 1965 Squamous cell carcinoma of the larynx with sarcoma-like stroma. A clinicopathologic assessment of spindle cell carcinoma and "pseudosarcoma." Am J Clin Pathol 44: 135–145

224. Lane N 1957 Pseudosarcoma (polypoid sarcoma-like masses) associated with squamous cell carcinoma of the mouth, fauces, and larynx. Report of ten cases. Cancer 10: 19–41

225. Goellner J R, Devine K D, Weiland L H 1973 Pseudosarcoma of the larynx. Am J Clin Pathol 59: 312–326

226. Toda S, Yonemitsu N, Miyabara S et al. 1989 Polypoid squamous cell carcinoma of the larynx. An immunohistochemical study for ras p21 and cytokeratin. Pathol Res Pract 185: 860–866

227. Leventon G S, Evans H L 1981 Sarcomatoid squamous cell carcinoma of the mucous membranes of the head and neck: a clinicopathologic study of 20 cases. Cancer 48: 994–1003

228. Batsakis J G, Rice D H, Howard D R 1982 The pathology of head and neck tumors. Spindle cell lesions (sarcomatoid carcinomas, nodular fasciitis, and fibrosarcoma) of the aerodigestive tracts, part 14. Head Neck Surg 4: 499–513

229. Weidner N 1987 Sarcomatoid carcinoma of the upper aerodigestive tract. Semin Diagn Pathol 4: 157–168

230. Mills SE, Gaffey MJ, Frierson HF Jr 2000 Tumors of the upper respiratory tract and ear. Atlas of tumor pathology, series 3, fascicle 26. Armed Forces Institute of Pathology, Washington, DC, p 98–106

231. Choi H R, Sturgis E M, Rosenthal D I et al. 2003 Sarcomatoid carcinoma of the head and neck. Molecular evidence for evolution and progression from conventional squamous cell carcinoma. Am J Surg Pathol 27: 1216–1220

232. Takubo K, Tsuchiya S, Nakagawa H et al. 1982 Pseudosarcoma of the esophagus. Hum Pathol 13: 503–505

233. Ellis G L, Corio R L 1980 Spindle cell carcinoma of the oral cavity. A clinicopathologic assessment of fifty-nine cases. Oral Surg 50: 523–534

234. Takata T, Ito H, Ogawa I et al. 1991 Spindle cell squamous carcinoma of the oral region. An immunohistochemical and ultrastructural study on the histogenesis and differential diagnosis with a clinicopathological analysis of six cases. Virchows Archiv [A] Pathol Anat 419: 177–182

235. Ro J Y, Chen J L, Lee J S et al. 1992 Sarcomatoid carcinoma of the lung. Immunohistochemical and ultrastructural studies of 14 cases. Cancer 69: 376–386

236. Olsen K D, Lewis J E, Suman V J 1997 Spindle cell carcinoma of the larynx and hypopharynx. Otolaryngol Head Neck Surg 116: 47–52

237. Klijanienko J, Vielh P, Duvillard P et al. 1992 True carcinosarcoma of the larynx. J Laryngol Otol 106: 58–60

238. Litzky L A, Brooks J J 1992 Cytokeratin immunoreactivity in malignant fibrous histiocytoma and spindle cell tumors: comparison between frozen and paraffin-embedded tissues. Mod Pathol 5: 30–34

239. Weidner N, Askin F B, Berthrong M et al. 1987 Bizarre (pseudomalignant) granulation-tissue reactions following ionizing-radiation exposure. A microscopic, immunohistochemical, and flow-cytometry study. Cancer 59: 1509–1514

240. Wenig B M, Devaney K, Bisceglia M 1995 Inflammatory myofibroblastic tumor of the larynx. A clinicopathologic study of eight cases simulating a malignant spindle cell neoplasm. Cancer 76: 2217–2229

241. Wain S L, Kier R, Vollmer R T et al. 1986 Basaloid-squamous carcinoma of the tongue, hypopharynx, and larynx: report of 10 cases. Hum Pathol 17: 1158–1166

242. Batsakis J G, El Naggar A 1989 Basaloid-squamous carcinomas of the upper aerodigestive tracts. Ann Otol Rhinol Laryngol 98: 919–920

243. Luna M A, El Naggar A, Parichatikanond P et al. 1990 Basaloid squamous carcinoma of the upper aerodigestive tract. Clinicopathologic and DNA flow cytometric analysis. Cancer 66: 537–542

244. Banks E R, Frierson H F Jr, Mills S E et al. 1992 Basaloid squamous cell carcinoma of the head and neck. A clinicopathologic and immunohistochemical study of 40 cases. Am J Surg Pathol 16: 939–946

245. Raslan W F, Barnes L, Krause J R et al. 1994 Basaloid squamous cell carcinoma of the head and neck: a clinicopathologic and flow cytometric study of 10 new cases with review of the English literature. Am J Otolaryngol 15: 204–211

246. Barnes L, Ferlito A, Altavilla G et al. 1996 Basaloid squamous cell carcinoma of the head and neck: clinicopathological features and differential diagnosis. Ann Otol Rhinol Laryngol 105: 75–82

247. Bahar G, Feinmesser R, Popovtzer A et al. 2003 Basaloid squamous carcinoma of the larynx. Am J Otolaryngol 24: 204–208

248. Wan S K, Chan J K C, Tse K C 1992 Basaloid-squamous carcinoma of the nasal cavity. J Laryngol Otol 106: 370–371

249. Saltarelli M G, Fleming M V, Wenig B M et al. 1995 Primary basaloid squamous cell carcinoma of the trachea. Am J Clin Pathol 104: 594–598

250. Epstein J I, Sears D L, Tucker R S et al. 1984 Carcinoma of the esophagus with adenoid cystic differentiation. Cancer 53: 1131–1136

251. Ferry J A, Scully R E 1988 "Adenoid cystic" carcinoma and adenoid basal carcinoma of the uterine cervix. A study of 28 cases. Am J Surg Pathol 12: 134–144

252. Tsang W Y W, Chan J K C, Lee K C et al. 1991 Basaloid-squamous carcinoma of the upper aerodigestive tract and so-called adenoid cystic carcinoma of the oesophagus: the same tumour type? Histopathology 19: 35–46

253. Abe K, Sasano H, Itakura Y et al. 1996 Basaloid-squamous carcinoma of the esophagus. A clinicopathologic, DNA ploidy, and immunohistochemical study of seven cases. Am J Surg Pathol 20: 453–461

254. Gerughty R M, Hennigar G R, Brown F M 1968 Adenosquamous carcinoma of the nasal, oral and laryngeal cavities. A clinicopathologic survey of ten cases. Cancer 22: 1140–1155

255. Kott E T, Goepfert H, Ayala A G et al. 1984 Lymphoepithelial carcinoma (malignant lymphoepithelial lesion) of the salivary glands. Arch Otolaryngol 110: 50–53

256. Suster S, Rosai J 1991 Thymic carcinoma. A clinicopathologic study of 60 cases. Cancer 67: 1025–1032

257. Micheau C, Luboinski B, Schwaab G et al. 1979 Lymphoepitheliomas of the larynx (undifferentiated carcinomas of nasopharyngeal type). Clin Otolaryngol 4: 42–48

258. Toker C, Peterson D W 1978 Lymphoepithelioma of the vocal cord. Arch Otolaryngol 104: 161–162

259. Ferlito A 1976 Histological classification of larynx and hypopharynx cancers and their clinical implications. Pathologic aspects of 2052 malignant neoplasms diagnosed at the ORL department of Padua University from 1966 to 1976. Acta Otolaryngol Suppl 342: 1–88

260. Andryk J, Freije J E, Schultz C J et al. 1996 Lymphoepithelioma of the larynx. Am J Otolaryngol 17: 61–63

261. Zbären P, Borisch B, Läng H et al. 1997 Undifferentiated carcinoma of nasopharyngeal type of the laryngopharyngeal region. Otolaryngol Head Neck Surg 117: 688–693

262. Marioni G, Mariuzzi L, Gaio E et al. 2002 Lymphoepithelial carcinoma of the larynx. Acta Otolaryngol 122: 429–434

263. Nappi O, Wick M R, Pettinato G et al. 1992 Pseudovascular adenoid squamous cell carcinoma of the skin. A neoplasm that may be mistaken for angiosarcoma. Am J Surg Pathol 16: 429–438

264. Thompson L D R, Wenig B M, Heffner D K et al. 1999 Exophytic and papillary squamous cell carcinomas of the larynx: a clinicopathologic series of 104 cases. Otolaryngol Head Neck Surg 120: 718–724

265. Suarez P A, Adler-Storthz K, Luna M A et al. 2000 Papillary squamous cell carcinomas of the upper aerodigestive tract: a clinicopathologic and molecular study. Head Neck 22: 360–368

266. Keelawat S, Liu C Z, Roehm P C et al. 2002 Adenosquamous carcinoma of the upper aerodigestive tract: a clinicopathologic study of 12 cases and review of the literature. Am J Otolaryngol 23: 160–168

267. Alos A, Castillo M, Nadal A et al. 2004 Adenosquamous carcinoma of the head and neck: criteria for diagnosis in a study of 12 cases. Histopathology 44: 570–579

268. Gould V E, Linnoila R I, Memoli V A et al. 1983 Neuroendocrine cells and neuroendocrine neoplasms of the lung. Pathol Ann 18: 287–330

269. Briselli M, Mark G J, Grillo H C 1978 Tracheal carcinoids. Cancer 42: 2870–2879

270. El-Naggar A K, Batsakis J G 1991 Carcinoid tumor of the larynx. A critical review of the literature. ORL J Otorhinolaryngol Relat Spec 53: 188–193

271. Tamai S, Iri H, Maruyama T et al. 1981 Laryngeal carcinoid tumor: light and electron microscopic studies. Cancer 48: 2256–2259

272. Stanley R J, DeSanto L W, Weiland L H 1986 Oncocytic and oncocytoid carcinoid tumors (well-differentiated neuroendocrine carcinomas) of the larynx. Arch Otolaryngol Head Neck Surg 112: 529–535

273. Baugh R F, Wolf G T, McClatchey K D et al. 1987 Carcinoid (neuroendocrine carcinoma) of the larynx. Ann Otol Rhinol Laryngol 96: 315–321

274. Woodruff J M, Senie R T 1991 Atypical carcinoid tumor of the larynx. A critical review of the literature. ORL J Otorhinolaryngol Relat Spec 53: 194–209

275. Ereno C, Lopez J I, Sanchez J M 1997 Atypical carcinoid of larynx: presentation with scalp metastases. J Laryngol Otol 111: 89–91

276. Ottinetti A, Colombo E, Dardano F et al. 2003 Cutaneous metastasis of neuroendocrine carcinoma of the larynx: report of a case. J Cutan Pathol 30: 512–515

277. Mills S E, Cooper P H, Garland T A et al. 1983 Small cell undifferentiated carcinoma of the larynx. Report of two patients and review of 13 additional cases. Cancer 51: 116–120

278. Gnepp D R, Ferlito A, Hyams V 1983 Primary anaplastic small cell (oat cell) carcinoma of the larynx. Review of the literature and report of 18 cases. Cancer 51: 1731–1745

279. Gnepp D R 1991 Small cell neuroendocrine carcinoma of the larynx. A critical review of the literature. ORL J Otorhinolaryngol Relat Spec 53: 210–219

280. Baugh R F, Wolf G T, McClatchey K D 1986 Small cell carcinoma of the head and neck. Head Neck Surg 8: 343–354

281. Medina J E, Moran M, Goepfert H 1984 Oat cell carcinoma of the larynx and Eaton–Lambert syndrome. Arch Otolaryngol 110: 123–126

282. Giddings N A, Kennedy T L, Vrabec D P 1987 Primary small cell carcinoma of the larynx: analysis of treatment. J Otolaryngol 16: 157–166

283. Ferlito A, Recher G, Caruso G 1985 Primary combined small cell carcinoma of the larynx. Am J Otolaryngol 6: 302–308

284. Chen D A, Mandell-Brown M, Moore S F et al. 1986 "Composite" tumor – mixed squamous cell and small cell anaplastic carcinoma of the larynx. Otolaryngol Head Neck Surg 95: 99–103

285. Aguilar E A III, Robbins K T, Stephens J et al. 1987 Primary oat cell carcinoma of the larynx. Am J Clin Oncol 10: 26–32

286. Pesce C, Tobia-Gallelli F, Toncini C 1984 APUD cells of the larynx. Acta Otolaryngol 98: 158–162

287. Whicker J H, Weiland L H, Neel H B III et al. 1974 Adenocarcinoma of the larynx. Ann Otol 83: 487–490

288. Fechner R E 1975 Adenocarcinoma of the larynx. Can J Otolaryngol 2: 284–289

289. Spiro R H, Hajdu S I, Lewis J S et al. 1976 Mucus gland tumors of the larynx and laryngopharynx. Ann Otol 85: 498–503

290. Hajdu S I, Huvos A G, Goodner J T et al. 1970 Carcinoma of the trachea. Clinicopathologic study of 41 cases. Cancer 25: 1448–1456

291. Crissman J D, Rosenblatt A 1978 Acinous cell carcinoma of the larynx. Arch Pathol Lab Med 102: 233–236

292. Ferlito A, Gale N, Hvala H 1981 Laryngeal salivary duct carcinoma: a light and electron microscopic study. J Laryngol Otol 95: 731–738

293. Mikaelian D O, Contrucci R B, Batsakis J G 1986 Epithelial-myoepithelial carcinoma of the subglottic region: a case presentation and review of the literature. Otolaryngol Head Neck Surg 95: 104–106

294. Pearson F G, Thompson D W, Weissberg D et al. 1974 Adenoid cystic carcinoma of the trachea. Experience with 16 patients managed by tracheal resection. Ann Thorac Surg 18: 16–29

295. Oloffsson J, van Nostrand A W P 1977 Adenoid cystic carcinoma of the larynx. A report of four cases and a review of the literature. Cancer 40: 1307–1313

296. Ferlito A, Caruso G 1983 Biological behaviour of laryngeal adenoid cystic carcinoma. Therapeutic considerations. ORL J Otorhinolaryngol Relat Spec 45: 245–256

297. Binder W J, Kaneko M, Som P et al. 1980 Mucoepidermoid carcinoma of the larynx. A case report and review of the literature. Ann Otol Rhinol Laryngol 89: 103–107

298. Damiani J M, Damiani K K, Hauck K et al. 1981 Mucoepidermoid-adenosquamous carcinoma of the larynx and hypopharynx: a report of 21 cases and a review of the literature. Otolaryngol Head Neck Surg 89: 235–243

299. Ferlito A, Recher G, Bottin R 1981 Mucoepidermoid carcinoma of the larynx. A clinicopathological study of 11 cases with review of the literature. ORL J Otorhinolaryngol Relat Spec 41: 280–299

300. Ho K-J, Jones J M, Herrera G A 1984 Mucoepidermoid carcinoma of the larynx: a light and electron microscopic study with emphasis on histogenesis. South Med J 77: 190–195

301. Ferlito A 1976 A pathologic and clinical study of adenosquamous carcinoma of the larynx. Report of four cases and review of the literature. Acta Otorhinolaryngol Belg 30: 379–389

302. Ellis G L, Auclair P L, Gnepp D R et al. 1991 Other malignant epithelial neoplasms. In: Ellis G L, Auclair P L, Gnepp D L (eds) Surgical pathology of the salivary glands. Saunders, Philadelphia, p 455–459

303. Heffner D K 1991 Sinonasal and laryngeal salivary gland lesions. In: Ellis G L, Auclair P L, Gnepp D L (eds) Surgical pathology of the salivary glands. Saunders, Philadelphia, p 554–557

304. Weber A L, Shortsleeve M, Goodman M et al. 1978 Cartilaginous tumors of the larynx and trachea. Radiol Clin North Am 16: 261–271

305. Cantrell R W, Jahrsdoerfer R A, Reibel J F et al. 1980 Conservative surgical treatment of chondrosarcoma of the larynx. Ann Otol Rhinol Laryngol 89: 567–571

306. Neel H B III, Unni K K 1982 Cartilaginous tumors of the larynx: a series of 33 patients. Otolaryngol Head Neck Surg 90: 201–207

307. Ferlito A, Nicolai P, Montaguti A et al. 1984 Chondrosarcoma of the larynx: review of the literature and report of three cases. Am J Otolaryngol 5: 350–359

308. Thompson L D R, Gannon F H 2002 Chondrosarcoma of the larynx, a clinicopathologic study of 111 cases with a review of the literature. Am J Surg Pathol 26: 836–851

309. Hyams V J, Rabuzzi D D 1970 Cartilaginous tumors of the larynx. Laryngoscope 80: 755–767

310. Burtner D, Goodman M, Montgomery W 1972 Elastic cartilaginous metaplasia of vocal cord nodules. Ann Otol Rhinol Laryngol 81: 844–847

311. Huizenga C, Balogh K 1970 Cartilaginous tumors of the larynx. A clinicopathologic study of 10 new cases and a review of the literature. Cancer 26: 201–210

312. Kleist B, Poetsch M, Lang C et al. 2002 Clear cell chondrosarcoma of the larynx. A case report of a rare histologic variant in an uncommon location. Am J Surg Pathol 26: 386–392

313. Goethals P L, Dahlin D C, Devine K D 1963 Cartilaginous tumors of the larynx. Surg Gynecol Obstet 117: 77–82

314. Bleiweiss I J, Kaneko M 1988 Chondrosarcoma of the larynx with additional malignant mesenchymal component (dedifferentiated chondrosarcoma). Am J Surg Pathol 12: 314–320

315. Brandwein M, Moore S, Som P et al. 1992 Laryngeal chondrosarcomas: a clinicopathologic study of 11 cases, including two "dedifferentiated" chondrosarcomas. Laryngoscope 102: 858–867

316. Rinaggio J, Duffey D, McGruff H S 2004 Dedifferentiated chondrosarcoma of the larynx. Oral Surg Oral Med Oral Pathol Oral Radiol Endod 97: 369–375

317. Gorenstein A, Neel H B III, Weiland L H et al. 1980 Sarcomas of the larynx. Arch Otolaryngol 106: 8–12

318. Ferlito A, Nicolai P, Barion U 1983 Critical comments on laryngeal fibrosarcoma. Acta Otorhinolaryngol Belg 37: 918–925

319. Winther L K, Lorentzen M 1978 Rhabdomyosarcoma of the larynx. Report of two cases and a review of the literature. J Laryngol Otol 92: 417–424

320. Balazs M, Egerszegi P 1989 Laryngeal botryoid rhabdomyosarcoma in an adult. Report of a case with electron microscopic study. Pathol Res Pract 184: 643–649

321. Libera D D, Falconieri G, Zanella M 1999 Embryonal "botryoid" rhabdomyosarcoma of the larynx: a clinicopathologic and immunohistochemical study of two cases. Ann Diagn Pathol 3: 341–349

322. Ferlito A, Nicolai P, Recher G et al. 1983 Primary laryngeal malignant fibrous histiocytoma: review of the literature and report of seven cases. Laryngoscope 93: 1351–1358

323. Dahm L J, Schaefer S D, Carder H M et al. 1978 Osteosarcoma of the soft tissue of the larynx. Report of a case with light and electron microscopic studies. Cancer 42: 2343–2351

324. Van Laer C G, Atkinson M W A, Helliwell T R et al. 1989 Osteosarcoma of the larynx. Ann Otol Rhinol Laryngol 98: 971–974

325. Quinn H J J Jr 1984 Synovial sarcoma of the larynx treated by partial laryngectomy. Laryngoscope 94: 1158–1161

326. Pruszczynski M, Manni J J, Smedts F 1989 Endolaryngeal synovial sarcoma: case report with immunohistochemical studies. Head Neck 11: 76–80

327. Chew K K, Sethi D S, Stanley R E et al. 1992 View from beneath: pathology in focus. Synovial sarcoma of hypopharynx. J Laryngol Otol 106: 285–287

328. Wenig B M, Heffner D K 1995 Liposarcomas of the larynx and hypopharynx: a clinicopathologic study of eight new cases and a review of the literature. Laryngoscope 105: 747–756

329. Wenig B M, Weiss S W, Gnepp D R 1990 Laryngeal and hypopharyngeal liposarcoma: a clinicopathologic study of 10 cases with a comparison to soft tissue counterparts. Am J Surg Pathol 14: 134–141

330. DeLozier H L 1982 Intrinsic malignant schwannoma of the larynx. A case report. Ann Otol Rhinol Laryngol 91: 336–338

331. Paczona R, Jori J, Tiszlavicz L et al. 1999 Leiomyosarcoma of the larynx. Review of the literature and report of two cases. Ann Otol Rhinol Laryngol 108: 677–682

332. Ferlito A, Nicolai P, Caruso G 1985 Angiosarcoma of the larynx. Case report. Ann Otol Rhinol Laryngol 94: 93–95

333. Ferlito A 1978 Primary malignant haemangiopericytoma of the larynx. A case report with autopsy. J Laryngol Otol 92: 511–519

334. Abramowski C R, Witt W J 1983 Sarcoma of the larynx in the newborn. Cancer 51: 1726–1730

335. Pearson F G, Todd T R J, Cooper J D 1984 Experience with primary neoplasms of the trachea and carina. J Thorac Cardiovasc Surg 88: 511–518

336. Wang C C 1972 Malignant lymphoma of the larynx. Laryngoscope 82: 97–100

337. Ferlito A, Carbone A, Volpe R 1981 Diagnosis and assessment of non-Hodgkin's malignant lymphomas of the larynx. ORL J Otorhinolaryngol Relat Spec 43: 61–78

338. Swerdlow J B, Merl S A, Davey F R et al. 1984 Non-Hodgkin's lymphoma limited to the larynx. Cancer 53: 2546–2549

339. Gordon L J, Lee M, Conley J J et al. 1992 Mycosis fungoides of the larynx. Otolaryngol Head Neck Surg 107: 120–123

340. Kuhn J J, Wenig B M, Clark D A 1992 Mycosis fungoides of the larynx. Report of two cases and review of the literature. Arch Otolaryngol Head Neck Surg 118: 853–858

341. Bjelkenkrantz K, Lundgren J, Olosson J 1981 Extramedullary plasmacytoma of the larynx. J Otolaryngol 10: 28–34

342. Kost K M 1990 Plasmacytomas of the larynx. J Otolaryngol 19: 141–146

343. Ferguson J L, Maragos N E, Weiland L H 1987 Granulocytic sarcoma (chloroma) of the epiglottis. Otolaryngol Head Neck Surg 97: 588–590

344. Horny H-P, Parwaresch M R, Kaiserling E et al. 1986 Mast cell sarcoma of the larynx. J Clin Pathol 39: 596–602

345. El-Barbaray A E-S, Fouad H A, El-Sayed A F-I 1968 Malignant melanoma involving the larynx. Report of two cases. Ann Otol 77: 338–343

346. Reuter V E, Woodruff J M 1986 Melanoma of the larynx. Laryngoscope 96: 389–393

347. Wenig B M 1995 Laryngeal mucosal melanoma. A clinicopathologic, immunohistochemical, and ultrastructural study of four patients and a review of the literature. Cancer 75: 1568–1577

348. Eble J N, Hull M T, Bojrab D 1985 Laryngeal blastoma: a light and electron microscopic study of a novel entity analogous to pulmonary blastoma. Am J Clin Pathol 84: 378–385

349. Freeland A P, van Nostrand A W P, Jahn A F 1979 Metastases to the larynx. J Otolaryngol 8: 448–456

350. Oku T, Hasegawa M, Watanabe I et al. 1980 Pancreatic cancer with metastasis to the larynx. J Laryngol Otol 94: 1205–1209

351. Maung R, Burke R C, Hwang W S 1987 Metastatic renal carcinoma to larynx. J Otolaryngol 16: 16–18

Tumors of the lung and pleura

Cesar A. Moran Saul Suster

Introduction

Carcinomas arising in the lung are currently one of the major causes of death in many countries around the developed world. These tumors have been clearly associated with the use of tobacco, and an increase in their number has been observed in female patients in recent years. However, the etiology of pulmonary carcinoma appears to be multifactorial, with both environmental and genetic conditions playing a role. Proof of this is the occurrence of these tumors in children and in non-smokers. Nevertheless, the vast majority of patients are adults over 35 years of age with a history of tobacco-smoking. Certain trends have also been noted regarding the relative frequency of the different histologic types. For instance, in the USA, adenocarcinomas now represent the most common histologic type of lung cancer, whereas squamous cell carcinoma is the one that statistically has been more frequently associated with cigarette-smoking. Other demographic trends include an increased incidence of lung cancer in black men as compared with whites, and a higher incidence of squamous cell carcinoma in white women as compared with black women. More recently, it has been observed that the incidence of lung carcinoma in the general population may have reached a plateau, and a possible decline is expected.[1–8] Whether this is a correct assumption or not, the fact remains that lung carcinoma continues to represent a serious health problem and a major consideration in the delivery of health care. The prognosis for these neoplasms is still poor and most patients succumb within 5 years of diagnosis. Therefore, more studies regarding treatment and prevention are needed to improve the outcome of patients with this disease.

Classification

The most widely accepted classification of lung tumors is that proposed by the World Health Organization (WHO).[9] Currently, however, this classification is under review due to the numerous recent advances in our understanding of these tumors and the delineation of new histopathologic types. It is therefore likely that significant changes will be incorporated into the WHO scheme in the future. To present a new classification of lung neoplasms is not within the scope of this chapter. However, to facilitate their study, we will follow a scheme that attempts to summarize current trends in our understanding of these tumors and that incorporates recently described entities in pulmonary pathology (Table 5.1).

Bronchogenic ("non-small cell") carcinomas

Bronchogenic carcinomas of non-small cell type represent the most common form of lung cancer; these tumors typically affect individuals in the sixth or seventh decades of life.[10] A number of specific genetic abnormalities, aberrant autocrine production of growth factors, and alterations in growth-promoting and tumor suppressor genes have long been demonstrated in these tumors.[11] A wide spectrum of mutations of the tumor suppressor gene *TP53* has been identified in lung cancer. A common event in lung tumors is the loss of one allele at 17p13, a locus that harbors the *TP53* gene.[12] *p53* mutations in lung cancer have been elicited *in vitro* with carcinogens found in cigarette smoke, supporting that idea that such mutations

Table 5.1	Classification of lung tumors

I. Malignant epithelial neoplasms

  A. Bronchogenic non-small-cell carcinoma

    Adenocarcinoma

    Variants: Bronchioloalveolar carcinoma

                Mucinous (so-called "colloid") carcinoma

                Papillary carcinoma

    Squamous cell carcinoma

    Variants: Spindle cell squamous carcinoma

                Basaloid carcinoma

                Lymphoepithelioma-like carcinoma

    Pleomorphic carcinoma (spindle/giant cell carcinoma)

    Anaplastic large-cell carcinoma

    Mixed

  B. Neuroendocrine carcinomas

    Well-differentiated neuroendocrine carcinoma (carcinoid tumor)

    Moderately differentiated neuroendocrine carcinoma (atypical carcinoid)

    Poorly differentiated neuroendocrine carcinoma

    Variants: Small-cell carcinoma

                Mixed small cell/large-cell carcinoma

                Large-cell neuroendocrine carcinoma

  C. Salivary gland-type tumors

    Adenoid cystic carcinoma

    Acinic cell carcinoma (Fechner tumor)

    Salivary gland-type mixed tumors

    Mucoepidermoid carcinoma

    Epithelial-myoepithelial carcinoma

    Oncocytoma

II. Biphasic epithelial/mesenchymal neoplasms

  A. Carcinosarcoma

  B. Pulmonary blastoma

III. Mesenchymal neoplasms

  Benign mesenchymal tumors and sarcomas (all types)

IV. Lymphoproliferative disorders

  Non-Hodgkin's lymphoma

  Lymphomatoid granulomatosis

  Hodgkin's disease

V. Tumors derived from embryologically displaced or ectopic tissues

  Meningioma

  Thymoma

  Glomus tumor

  Malignant melanoma

  Paraganglioma

  Ganglioneuroblastoma

  Germ-cell tumors

VI. Tumors of uncertain histogenesis

  Granular cell tumor of bronchus

  Sclerosing hemangioma

  Clear cell "sugar" tumor

  Inflammatory pseudotumor

VII. Miscellaneous benign tumors

  Cartilaginous hamartoma

  Endobronchial lipoma

  Alveolar adenoma

  Mucous gland adenoma

  Papillary adenoma

  Adenofibroma

  Minute pulmonary chemodectoma

VIII. Metastatic tumors to the lung

---

may be directly related to the effects of smoking.[13] Promoter genes involved in lung cancer include oncogenes with tyrosine-kinase receptor functions such as epidermal growth factor receptor and the *myc* and *ras* family of oncogenes. Alterations of the *ras* family of oncogenes are frequently present in non-small cell carcinomas, especially adenocarcinoma. The most frequently mutated *ras* gene in lung tumors is K-*ras*; approximately 30% of adenocarcinomas of the lung show a K-*ras* codon 12 mutation. This mutation is most frequently expressed in smokers, highlighting the relationship between tobacco use and the development of these tumors.[14] Aberrant promoter methylation has been found to represent an alternative pathway to genetic loss of a transcriptional silencing gene function by deletion or mutation.[15] Aberrant promoter methylation has thus been demonstrated in a variety of genes in lung tumors, as well as in smoking-damaged non-malignant lung tissue.[16,17] Further studies in this evolving field of cancer research may elucidate additional important pathways in the molecular characterization of the development of lung cancer, as exemplified by recent data that suggest that the presence of *EGFR* mutations may predict response to therapy with gefitinib (a targeted tyrosine kinase inhibitor).[18]

Symptoms of bronchogenic carcinoma will depend on the tumor's anatomic distribution. Centrally located lesions are more likely to elicit symptoms of bronchial obstruction, including cough, hemoptysis, dyspnea, wheezing, or pneumonia; those located peripherally will only give rise to symptoms when the tumor reaches a larger size and invades adjacent structures. The latter tumors are most likely to be diagnosed on routine chest radiographic studies. In certain subtypes of carcinoma, such as bronchioloalveolar carcinoma, the patient may present with bronchorrhea (expectoration of large amounts of mucus).[19] When the tumors reach an advanced stage, they may invade adjacent structures such as the pleura, chest wall, and/or mediastinum, giving rise to symptoms of pleuritic pain, the Pancoast syndrome, or the superior vena cava syndrome.[10,19] Other clinical manifestations include paraneoplastic syndromes such as the syndrome of inappropriate secretion of antidiuretic hormone, Cushing's syndrome, or acromegaly.[10,19,20] In some instances, adenocarcinomas can be associated with other non-neoplastic lung conditions such as fibrotic lung disease, tuberculosis, bronchiectasis, or pneumonia.[21–23] Squamous cell carcinomas may be associated with hypercalcemia.

On imaging studies, adenocarcinoma may present as a solitary pulmonary mass with a well-circumscribed or poorly defined appearance.[8,24] In some instances, the tumors can grow along the pleural surface, thereby resembling a pleural mesothelioma. When the tumor is peripheral and small, thin-section computed tomography scan may prove helpful since it may display air bronchograms or air bronchiolograms in approximately 65% of cases. These features may help distinguish carcinomas from benign lesions.[25] The use of magnetic resonance imaging can also be helpful in assessing chest wall invasion, since there will be an increased signal intensity on T2-weighted images.[26] Squamous cell carcinomas are more often central tumors growing within the main bronchus. The typical radiographic presentation is that of total or partial bronchial obstruction. This clinical presentation may lead to obstructive pneumonia. Intractable pneumonia in an adult should always be closely investigated for the possibility of underlying malignancy.

Grossly, adenocarcinoma more often involves the upper lobes and typically presents as a subpleural mass or nodule with retraction of the pleura. The term "scar cancer," which was applied to subpleural adenocarcinomas associated with scarring, has lost clinical significance since it has been noted that, in the majority of instances, the "scar" is the result of a secondary desmoplastic stromal response to the tumor itself rather than the inciting cause of the lesion. Squamous cell carcinoma, although more often presenting as a central lesion obstructing the bronchial lumen, may also present as a peripheral mass in approximately one-third of cases. Approximately 10% of squamous cell carcinomas undergo central cavitation.

Non-small cell carcinomas in general are treated by surgical resection with additional radiation or chemotherapy depending on the stage of the tumor. The stage of the tumor at the time of diagnosis is the single most important parameter for assessing prognosis. The more advanced the stage, the more guarded the prognosis. In some types of non-small cell carcinomas, such as pleomorphic carcinoma, the behavior of the tumor is very aggressive with a median survival of only 18 months. Adenosquamous carcinomas are also believed to behave more aggressively than conventional squamous or adenocarcinomas. In contrast, bronchioloalveolar carcinoma and mucinous carcinoma more commonly exhibit low-grade malignant behavior. However, when bronchioloalveolar carcinoma presents with diffuse involvement of extensive areas of the lung, the prognosis is more guarded.

Adenocarcinoma

Primary pulmonary adenocarcinoma is defined as a malignant epithelial neoplasm showing features of glandular differentiation. Grading of adenocarcinoma into well, moderately, and poorly differentiated tumors depends on the degree and extent of glandular differentiation present. Well-differentiated neoplasms are characterized by a proliferation of well-formed glands lined by atypical cells that infiltrate the surrounding stroma, whereas poorly differentiated tumors grow as solid sheets of tumor cells with scant or poorly formed glandular structures and are recognized as adenocarcinomas on the basis of the demonstration of intracellular mucin production (Fig. 5.1). The glands in well-differentiated adenocarcinoma are generally composed of tall columnar or mucinous epi-

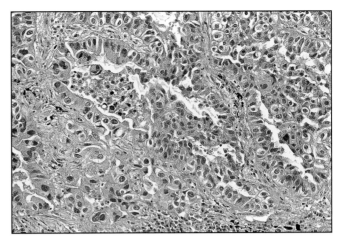

Fig. 5.1 • Moderately differentiated adenocarcinoma of lung.

thelium with ample clear or eosinophilic cytoplasm, basally situated nuclei, prominent nucleoli, and frequent mitotic figures. In moderately differentiated adenocarcinoma, the glandular proliferation is more haphazardly distributed, with more intervening stromal reaction and inflammation, and the tumor cells show more atypia and frequent mitotic figures. A variety of unusual morphologic appearances can be assumed focally by these tumors. The predominance of some of these unusual morphologic features has served as the basis for the creation of several histologic variants of lung adenocarcinoma. In this regard, pulmonary adenocarcinomas with extensive signet-ring cell features have been noted to be especially aggressive.[27] Adenocarcinomas of fetal lung type are discussed under the heading of pulmonary blastoma, below.

Bronchioloalveolar carcinoma

Bronchioloalveolar carcinoma is a distinctive type of tumor characterized by a neoplastic proliferation of cells that grows exclusively along the lining of the alveolar walls, a pattern referred to as "lepidic."[28] The cells are characterized by mild cellular atypia and can display some mitotic activity, but are restricted to the alveolar walls without any evidence of infiltration into the interstitium (Fig. 5.2). Grossly the lesions may

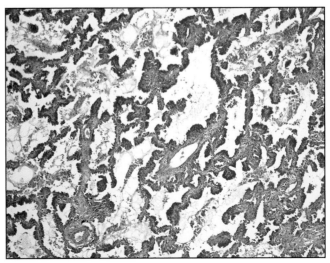

Fig. 5.2 • Bronchioloalveolar carcinoma.

be single, multifocal, or diffuse. When the tumor is diffuse, the lesion may mimic pneumonia both grossly and radiographically. Two principal histologic types have been described: (1) the mucinous type is characterized by a proliferation of fairly uniform columnar, mucin-secreting cells which completely replace the normal alveolar lining; (2) the non-mucinous type is characterized by round to cuboidal cells with scant cytoplasm and prominent, hyperchromatic nuclei which often adopt a "hobnail" configuration. The latter form has been shown to exhibit ultrastructural features of Clara cells or type II alveolar pneumocytes. Intranuclear cytoplasmic inclusions are also a prominent feature in some cases. It is important to mention that a focally bronchioloalveolar pattern can be seen in many cases of otherwise conventional adenocarcinoma; such tumors are best designated as "adenocarcinoma with bronchiolo-alveolar features." To render a diagnosis of bronchioloalveolar carcinoma, it is necessary not only to find the distinctive growth pattern (which includes the absence of well-formed glands) but also for there to be no evidence of infiltration of the tumor into the adjacent lung parenchyma or the inter-stitium. It is also worth noting that, on occasion, metastases of adenocarcinoma from other organs to the lung may adopt a bronchioloalveolar pattern of growth, particularly those from the colon, breast, pancreas, stomach, and kidney.

Mucinous (so-called "colloid") carcinoma

Mucinous carcinoma represents a more recently described variant of adenocarcinoma.[29] The typical growth pattern of mucinous carcinoma of the lung is characterized by the accumulation of abundant pools of mucin destroying the normal lung parenchyma (Fig. 5.3). The alveolar walls can show focally mucinous epithelium with atypia. Another distinctive and diagnostic feature of these tumors is the presence of small clusters of, or singly scattered, mucinous tumor cells lying within the pools of mucin. In the past, tumors with identical histologic features were diagnosed under several designations, including mucinous cystadenoma and mucinous cystic tumors of borderline malignancy, among others. Because of their demonstrated capability for distant metastases and aggressive behavior, we prefer to designate them collectively under the term mucinous carcinoma.[29–33] It should be stressed that the diagnosis of mucinous carcinoma is one of

exclusion; it should not be made unless the presence of a primary lesion at other sites where such tumors are frequently known to arise (such as breast, colon, gallbladder, and urinary bladder) has been thoroughly excluded on clinical and radiographic grounds.

Papillary carcinoma

A papillary growth pattern may be seen in association with otherwise conventional adenocarcinoma, with or without a prominent bronchioloalveolar pattern. In some instances, however, a papillary growth pattern predominates and the lesion qualifies for the designation of papillary carcinoma. In such cases, the tumors are characterized by numerous papillary infoldings with thin fibroconnective tissue stalks that completely fill and distort the air spaces (Fig. 5.4). Psammoma bodies may also be present in the stroma, similar to those observed in ovarian papillary carcinomas. True papillary adenocarcinoma of the lung is believed to exhibit considerably worse morbidity and mortality than bronchioloalveolar carcinoma.[34] Predominantly papillary carcinomas of the lung also require strict clinicopathologic correlation to rule out the possibility of a metastasis from an occult or distant primary.

Squamous cell carcinoma

Squamous cell carcinoma of the lung is defined as a malignant epithelial neoplasm showing features of squamous (epidermoid) differentiation. Grading of squamous cell carcinoma into well, moderately, and poorly differentiated types will depend on the degree of squamous differentiation within the tumor, such as the presence of intercellular bridges and keratinization. Well-differentiated tumors are characterized by sheets of cells that adopt a pavement-like architecture and contain ample eosinophilic cytoplasm, round to oval nuclei, and prominent nucleoli. The cell borders are well defined and show well-formed intercellular bridges (Fig. 5.5A). In the less differentiated tumors, the above features may be only focally observed and the lesions are characterized by more pronounced cytologic atypia, increased mitotic activity, and frequent areas of necrosis and/or hemorrhage. A central, comedo-type pattern of necrosis is typically seen in the higher-grade lesions (Fig. 5.5B). It is of interest to note that in-situ carcinoma is recognized in

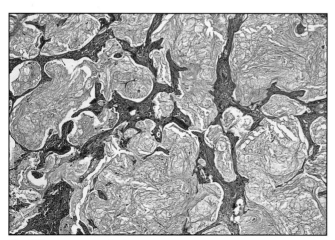

Fig. 5.3 • Mucinous ("colloid") carcinoma.

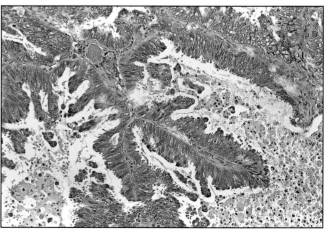

Fig. 5.4 • Papillary carcinoma of the lung.

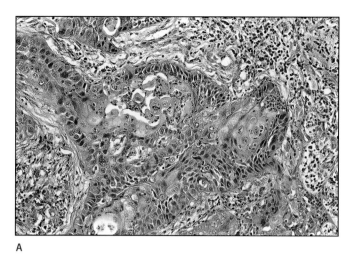

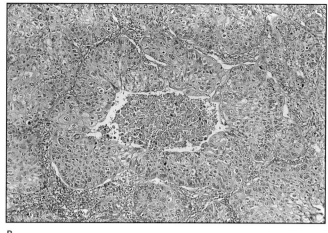

Fig. 5.5 • (A) Well- to moderately well-differentiated squamous carcinoma; **(B)** poorly differentiated squamous carcinoma with central comedo-like areas of necrosis.

association with squamous cell carcinoma but not with adenocarcinoma in the lung. Sections taken from the junction between apparently normal bronchial mucosa and frank squamous cell carcinoma will often display changes that range from squamous metaplasia, to intraepithelial atypia (dysplasia), to carcinoma in situ. Occasional lesions may show prominent clearing of the cytoplasm due to accumulation of glycogen. In the past, such tumors were referred to as clear cell carcinomas of the lung and were identified as a separate category. Squamous cell carcinoma with prominent clear cell changes, however, will behave in the same manner as conventional squamous cell carcinoma; it therefore does not warrant classification as a separate type.[35] Squamous cell carcinoma may rarely grow as an endobronchial polypoid mass somewhat reminiscent of a cutaneous keratoacanthoma, a condition sometimes referred to as exophytic squamous cell carcinoma.[36] Such tumors are usually very well differentiated and show minimal infiltration into the underlying lamina propria. Three other rare histologic variants, however, deserve mention.

Spindle cell squamous carcinoma

Spindle cell squamous carcinoma, also known as sarcomatoid carcinoma, is a tumor characterized by an appearance that mimics sarcoma.[37,38] The tumor is composed predominantly of atypical spindle cells with elongated nuclei, moderate amounts of cytoplasm, and prominent nucleoli. However, focally, the tumor cells are usually seen to blend with areas of more conventional squamous cell carcinoma (Fig. 5.6). The most important distinction is with spindle cell sarcoma, although some cases of sarcomatoid carcinoma may have a prominent chronic inflammatory component and simulate inflammatory pseudotumor.[39] Spindle cell squamous carcinoma is characterized by the presence of keratin reactivity in the tumor cells, as well as by the demonstration of tonofilaments and desmosome-type intercellular junctions on ultrastructural examination.[37] There is some degree of overlap between spindle cell squamous carcinoma and pleomorphic (spindle/giant cell) carcinoma (see p. 186). The latter probably represents a more poorly differentiated variant of the same tumor with more pronounced cytologic atypia and pleomorphism, multi-

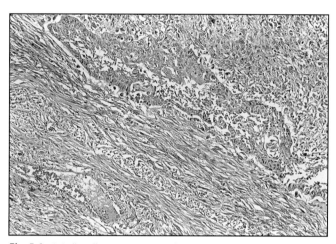

Fig. 5.6 • Spindle cell carcinoma arising from squamous cell carcinoma (top).

nucleated tumor cells, and correspondingly more aggressive behavior.

Basaloid carcinoma

Basaloid carcinoma is a more recently described variant of bronchogenic carcinoma characterized by a proliferation of islands of relatively large, hyperchromatic tumor cells showing prominent peripheral palisading of nuclei (Fig. 5.7). Cellular atypia is common, as are mitotic figures.[40] There has been debate about whether this tumor is another distinctive variant of bronchogenic carcinoma or is simply an unusual but non-specific growth pattern; however, it appears that lesions displaying such features are characterized by a more aggressive clinical behavior than conventional squamous cell carcinoma, thus justifying their recognition as a distinct clinicopathologic entity.[40]

Lymphoepithelioma-like carcinoma

Lymphoepithelioma-like carcinoma[41,42] corresponds to a poorly differentiated squamous carcinoma with prominent lymphoid stroma, similar to those occurring in the nasopharynx. The

Tumors of the lung and pleura

185

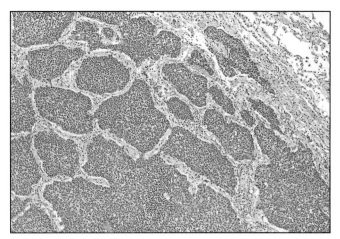

Fig. 5.7 • Basaloid carcinoma showing solid islands of tumor cells with peripheral palisading of nuclei.

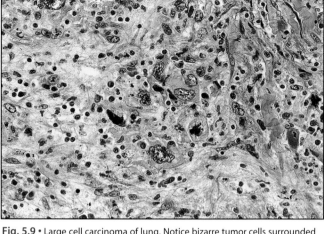

Fig. 5.9 • Large cell carcinoma of lung. Notice bizarre tumor cells surrounded by abundant inflammatory infiltrate.

tumor cells are characterized by large, vesicular nuclei with prominent eosinophilic nucleoli surrounded by a scant rim of cytoplasm. The tumor cell islands are characteristically surrounded by a prominent lymphoplasmacytic host response. Positive serology for Epstein–Barr virus has been demonstrated in only a few instances.[41,42]

Pleomorphic carcinoma

This tumor entity encompasses previous terms such as giant cell carcinoma and carcinoma with pseudosarcomatous stroma.[43,44] These tumors are characterized by a highly pleomorphic, mitotically active giant and spindle tumor cell population with frequent areas of hemorrhage and/or necrosis (Fig. 5.8). The main histologic component of this tumor appears to be the spindle cell component, which is usually admixed in various proportions with a highly pleomorphic malignant giant cell component. In some cases, focal areas of conventional adenocarcinoma or squamous cell carcinoma may be present and, as such, some authors prefer to regard these lesions as a phenotype rather than as an entity.[45] However, it is believed that the tumor arises *de novo* and does not have any relationship with any of the conventional types of carcinoma such as adenocarcinoma or squamous cell

carcinoma.[43,46] As its name implies, this tumor is distinguished from the spindle cell variant of squamous carcinoma by its marked pleomorphism and prominent giant cell component. Cases of this type appear to carry a poor prognosis.[44]

Large cell carcinoma

Also known as undifferentiated large cell carcinoma or anaplastic carcinoma, the designation of large cell carcinoma is reserved for tumors composed of sheets of poorly differentiated large tumor cells which do not show any clear-cut light microscopic features of differentiation towards either adenocarcinoma or squamous cell carcinoma. The older designation of "undifferentiated large cell carcinoma" should be abandoned since the epithelial nature of the neoplasm has been amply demonstrated by immunohistochemical and ultrastructural studies; hence, a more accurate designation would be poorly differentiated anaplastic carcinoma rather than undifferentiated.[9] The lack of a spindle cell component or atypical multinucleated and giant tumor cells separates this group from pleomorphic carcinoma. These tumors are characterized histologically by sheets of large tumor cells with round to oval nuclei, prominent nucleoli, increased mitotic activity, and marked cellular atypia. Another distinctive feature in some cases is the presence of abundant polymorphonuclear leukocytes in the stroma, admixed with the anaplastic tumor cells (Fig. 5.9). We have also encountered examples of these tumors that were characterized by prominent "rhabdoid" features, with abundant, eccentric, deeply eosinophilic cytoplasmic inclusions, composed of whorls of intracytoplasmic intermediate filaments, a pattern which may also be seen in other types of non-small cell carcinoma.[47]

Mixed tumors

Tumors showing admixed features of several of the above categories are encountered not uncommonly in clinical practice. The most common type in this category is *adenosquamous carcinoma*. As the name implies, these tumors show conventional areas of both adenocarcinoma and squamous cell carcinoma (Fig. 5.10). It has been stated that at least 5–10% of either component must be present in order to make this

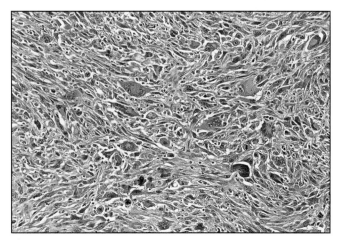

Fig. 5.8 • Pleomorphic (spindle and giant cell) carcinoma.

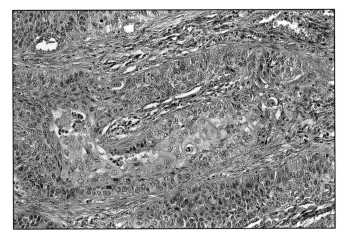

Fig. 5.10 • Adenosquamous carcinoma.

diagnosis.[48–50] In rare cases, there may be a sharp demarcation between the two components while, in other cases, both components will be found intimately admixed. Adenosquamous carcinoma is distinguished from mucoepidermoid carcinoma because, in the latter, well-formed glandular structures are not seen. The clinical significance of this type of tumor is uncertain; adenosquamous carcinoma, however, appears to follow a more aggressive behavior than conventional pure squamous carcinoma or adenocarcinoma.

Another combination that is not infrequently observed is that of adenocarcinoma or squamous cell carcinoma with areas of small cell neuroendocrine carcinoma (see below). Such tumors were referred to as "combined" carcinomas in the old WHO classification of small cell carcinoma of the lung.

Neuroendocrine carcinomas

The term "neuroendocrine," as applied in this section, refers to tumors which form part of a spectrum of lesions displaying evidence of neuroendocrine differentiation and which range from very well-differentiated neuroendocrine neoplasms (traditionally known as carcinoid tumors) to poorly differentiated malignancies with neuroendocrine features, typified by small cell carcinoma. Subclassification of these lesions has been somewhat controversial; nevertheless the presently available system seems to be both reproducible and meaningful clinically.[51] Neuroendocrine differentiation is defined at the morphologic level by the presence of a typical organoid growth pattern, at the ultrastructural level by the demonstration of dense-core neurosecretory granules, and at the immunohistochemical level by the presence of immunoreactivity for neuroendocrine markers such as chromogranin A and synaptophysin, or peptide hormones such as serotonin, adrenocorticotropic hormone, and bombesin.[52] More recently, much controversy was generated by the introduction of a new category of lesions designated as large-cell neuroendocrine carcinoma. It is not certain whether such tumors represent a distinctive clinicopathologic entity or simply correspond to poorly differentiated carcinomas showing spurious or aberrant neuroendocrine differentiation. This category requires further study to determine whether significant differences exist in

prognosis and response to therapy when compared to non-small cell bronchogenic carcinoma.[53–55]

An important clinical association of some neuroendocrine carcinomas is the development of paraneoplastic syndromes due to aberrant expression of peptide hormones, including Cushing's syndrome and the syndrome of inappropriate secretion of antidiuretic hormone. Well-differentiated neuroendocrine carcinoma is associated with the carcinoid syndrome in approximately 10% of cases.[56,57] Clinical symptoms of neuroendocrine carcinomas of the lung depend on the tumor's size, location, and biologic activity. Typically, these tumors present in an endobronchial location, which in turn gives rise to symptoms of wheezing, cough, and hemoptysis. Radiographically, the tumors may partially or almost totally obstruct the bronchial lumen. However, well-differentiated tumors (carcinoid) can also be located peripherally. These tumors most often affect adults between the fifth and seventh decades of life; there is no sex predilection. However, such tumors in younger patients are being diagnosed more often nowadays.

Well-differentiated neuroendocrine carcinoma (carcinoid tumor)

The hallmark of well-differentiated neuroendocrine carcinoma of the lung is the presence of a very bland and monotonous population of tumor cells which characteristically adopt a well-developed "organoid" or neuroendocrine growth pattern, characterized by the formation of well-defined nests of tumor cells separated by thin fibrovascular septa ("zellballen"; Fig. 5.11A). Other growth patterns commonly seen in these tumors include serpiginous cords and strands of tumor cells arranged in ribbons or festoons, or the formation of small, rosette-like microacinar structures (Fig. 5.11B). Cytologically the tumor cells are relatively small, round to polygonal, with central nuclei and abundant lightly eosinophilic, granular cytoplasm. The nuclei usually display a scattered, coarse ("salt-and-pepper") stippling of chromatin and an occasional small nucleolus. Mitotic activity is generally absent but may rarely be present (up to 1–2 mitoses per 10 high-power fields (hpf)). Necrosis and hemorrhage are not features of these tumors. Several unusual histologic variants have been described, including one composed predominantly of cells with prominent oncocytic cytoplasm (oncocytic carcinoid), a pigmented melanotic variant (pigmented carcinoid), carcinoid with metaplastic bone formation, and tumors characterized by gland formation and abundant production of stromal mucins.[58–62] Another unusual variant is one composed predominantly of spindle cells arranged in a fascicular pattern mimicking a sarcoma or other spindle cell tumor; in the lung the latter tumors are often peripheral in location. The presence of a spindle cell growth pattern in a carcinoid tumor, however, should not be considered synonymous with the term "atypical carcinoid." The majority of these tumors are centrally located and present as well-circumscribed, polypoid intrabronchial lesions with an intact overlying bronchial mucosa. They comprise approximately 1–2% of lung tumors and can occur in any age group. The diagnosis in the majority of instances is quite straightforward and can be facilitated by the use of histochemical stains (negative argentaffin and positive argyrophilic reaction), immunohistochemical stains (positive broad-

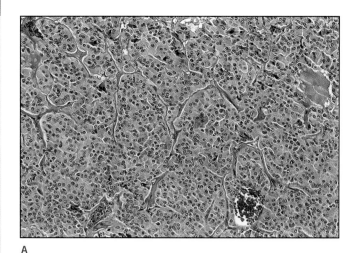
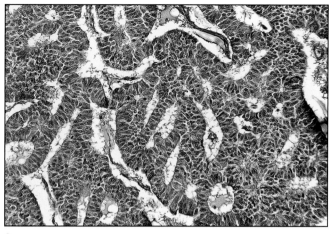

A

B

Fig. 5.11 • **(A)** Well-differentiated neuroendocrine carcinoma (bronchial carcinoid type) showing prominent neuroendocrine (zellballen) growth pattern; **(B)** well-differentiated neuroendocrine carcinoma (bronchial carcinoid type) with ribbon-like, trabecular growth pattern.

spectrum and low-molecular-weight cytokeratin, chromogranin, synaptophysin, neuron-specific enolase (NSE), serotonin, and bombesin), and electron microscopy (demonstration of dense-core neurosecretory granules). The vast majority of these tumors are cured by surgical excision. Approximately 10–15% of cases, however, may present with regional metastases and this is the reason why they are best regarded as low-grade malignant neoplasms. These lesions, as well as atypical carcinoids, are consistently TTF-1-positive, in contrast to extrapulmonary carcinoids.[63]

Moderately differentiated neuroendocrine carcinoma (atypical carcinoid)

Moderately differentiated neuroendocrine carcinoma of the lung was first described in 1972 by Arrigoni et al.,[64] who noted that pulmonary lesions sharing many of the features of carcinoid tumor, but characterized by more pronounced cellular atypia and mitotic activity, showed a greater tendency for metastases and aggressive behavior. These tumors represent moderately differentiated lesions which conceptually occupy an intermediate position in the spectrum of differentiation of neuroendocrine neoplasms of the lung. Histologically, they share many of the features of a conventional pulmonary carcinoid but are distinguished by more pronounced cytologic atypia, increased mitotic activity (>5 mitoses per 10 hpf), and frequent foci of necrosis.[64–67] The tumor cells usually show a higher nuclear-to-cytoplasmic ratio with prominent nucleoli and abnormal mitotic figures. Central, comedo-like areas of necrosis are typically seen (Fig. 5.12). These tumors are more often infiltrative and frequently show foci of vascular and lymphatic invasion. Increasing tumor size, stage, and high mitotic rate degree of cellular atypia and necrosis appear to correlate with a poorer prognosis.[68]

Poorly differentiated neuroendocrine carcinoma

This group of tumors represents the least differentiated end of the spectrum of neuroendocrine neoplasms of the lung and consists of high-grade tumors with a clinically highly aggressive

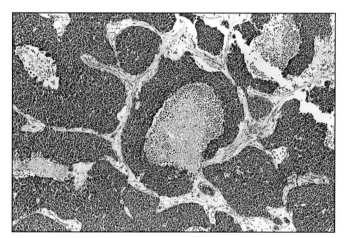

Fig. 5.12 • Moderately differentiated neuroendocrine carcinoma (atypical carcinoid type).

behavior. Features of neuroendocrine differentiation may be difficult to demonstrate in some of these lesions, and not all tumors will give the expected positive reactions with immuno-histochemical stains for neuroendocrine markers. The diagnosis is basically dependent on routine light microscopy and recognition of the characteristic cytologic features. The old WHO terminology recognized three forms: small cell (oat-cell), intermediate, and combined. More recently, a new variant of poorly differentiated neuroendocrine carcinoma has been added to this roster: the large-cell neuroendocrine carcinoma.[53,54] Whether the latter tumor indeed represents a distinct clinico-pathologic entity is at present unresolved; however, it will be included in this section as it has been acknowledged as a novel variant of high-grade lung cancer with neuroendocrine features.

Poorly differentiated neuroendocrine carcinomas of the lung account for approximately 20% of bronchogenic carcinomas and tend to occur most often in patients between 50 and 70 years of age. These tumors are characterized by early and rapid dissemination.[62,63] Recent advances in radiographic detection and chemotherapy, however, have resulted in significant palliation and prolonged survival for some patients. Clinically, these tumors are more often located centrally and present with symptoms of airway obstruction. The tumors commonly spread early into the mediastinum, giving rise to symptoms of superior vena cava syndrome, hoarseness, and dysphagia. Massive metastases to hilar and mediastinal lymph nodes are a common mode of presentation. Common extra-thoracic sites of metastasis include bone, bone marrow, liver, and brain. Paraneoplastic syndromes such as Cushing's syndrome, the syndrome of inappropriate antidiuretic hormone secretion, and the Eaton–Lambert syndrome are characteristically associated with small cell lung cancer.

Small cell carcinoma

Small cell carcinoma is characterized by a proliferation of primitive-appearing, round to oval-shaped tumor cells that average two to three times the size of normal small lymphocytes. In the classical oat-cell variety, the tumor cells form haphazardly arranged sheets of monotonous tumor cells that may be separated by thin fibrous septa and display extensive areas of necrosis (Fig. 5.13A). The cells appear rather small with scant cytoplasm, round to oval nuclei, and granular, dense chromatin. Nucleoli are usually inconspicuous or absent, and the tumor cells are characterized by brisk mitotic activity. Basophilic deposition of DNA material within blood vessel walls, referred to as nuclear encrustation or the Azzopardi phenomenon, is another distinctive feature of these tumors. In small endoscopic biopsies, the tumor cells will show a tendency to become markedly distorted and crushed, a finding that traditionally has been associated with small cell carcinoma but which may also be observed in lymphoid neoplasms. Spindling of the nuclei is another feature that may be observed occasionally in these tumors (Fig. 5.13B). A trabecular or ribbon-like arrangement of tumor cells, peripheral palisading of nuclei, and formation of rosette-like microacinar structures are rarely seen in small cell carcinoma and are features indicative of a higher degree of differentiation (i.e., atypical carcinoid). However, they may be occasionally seen in otherwise predominantly poorly differentiated neuroendocrine carcinomas and are most likely an expression of transition between areas of high-grade and intermediate-grade differentiation within the same tumor. In the "intermediate" subtype of small cell carcinoma, the cells appear larger, oval to polygonal, with more marked nuclear pleomorphism, less stippling of chromatin, more prominent nucleoli, and more abundant cytoplasm (Fig. 5.13C). The latter features are more easily appreciated in well-fixed material. In such cases TTF-1 positivity, combined with *p63* negativity, may facilitate distinction from poorly differentiated squamous cell carcinoma.

Mixed small cell/large-cell carcinoma

Mixed small cell/large-cell carcinomas are characterized by the presence of a subpopulation of large, undifferentiated tumor cells occurring singly or in small clusters within an otherwise conventional small cell carcinoma of the lung.[71,72] The large cells are usually twice the size of the small cell component and show large, hyperchromatic nuclei surrounded by a scant rim of amphophilic to lightly eosinophilic cytoplasm (Fig. 5.14). A continuum of cell types is usually appreciated, ranging from typical small cells (oat cells) to the large cells. A large-cell component admixed with the small cells is also frequently

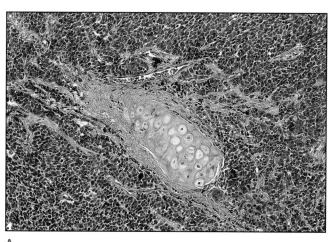

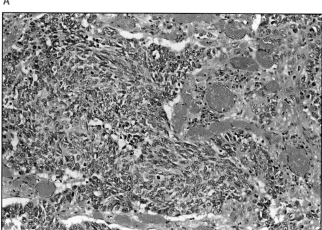

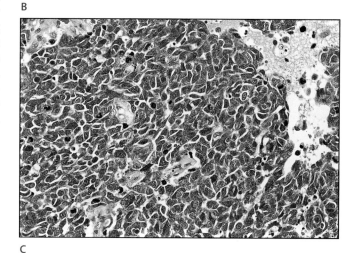

Fig. 5.13 • (A) Poorly differentiated neuroendocrine carcinoma of the lung, small cell type; (B) small cell carcinoma with spindle cell features; (C) small cell carcinoma, intermediate cell type.

observed at metastatic sites of otherwise conventional small cell carcinomas. Mixed small cell/large-cell carcinoma appears to have a poorer survival and a more limited response to treatment than typical small cell carcinoma.[71,73]

Large-cell neuroendocrine carcinoma

Large-cell neuroendocrine carcinoma represents a controversial category for which the true clinical implications as well

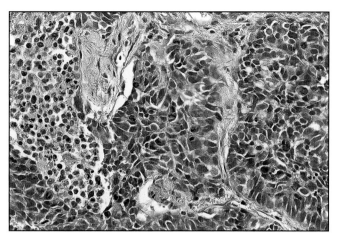

Fig. 5.14 • Poorly differentiated neuroendocrine carcinoma of lung, mixed small cell/large-cell type.

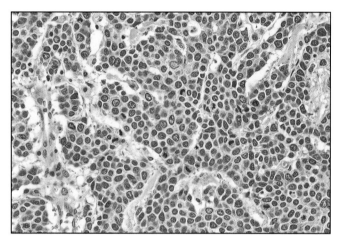

Fig. 5.15 • Large-cell neuroendocrine carcinoma.

as histopathologic criteria for diagnosis are still not fully defined. In general terms, the overall histopathologic appearance of this lesion is that of a poorly differentiated non-small cell carcinoma. However, the cellular proliferation may be focally arranged in ribbons or cords admixed with rosette-like structures, giving the lesion a vaguely neuroendocrine appearance (Fig. 5.15). In addition, the tumor cells may show positive staining with neuroendocrine markers such as synaptophysin or chromogranin.[53–55] Another feature that may also be seen in these tumors is the presence of areas showing a "basaloid" appearance. This latter feature is similar to that described in basaloid carcinoma of the lung, a variant of squamous cell carcinoma. Whether both tumors represent the same entity or not still remains a controversial issue. The issue of whether large-cell neuroendocrine carcinoma should be regarded as a distinct variant of neuroendocrine carcinoma or simply as a variant of non-small cell carcinoma with aberrant expression of neuroendocrine markers remains unsettled.

Salivary gland-type tumors

This is an unusual family of primary neoplasms of the lung, the histology of which recapitulates tumors of the salivary gland (See Ch. 7). Because the histologic features of these tumors are

indistinguishable from those of their salivary gland counterparts, it is imperative, before rendering a diagnosis of this type of tumor in the lung, that a thorough history be obtained to rule out the possibility of a metastasis from a head and neck primary. These tumors most likely originate from submucosal glands of the bronchi; nevertheless, not all of them occur in relationship with a bronchus. In unusual circumstances, they may arise within the pulmonary parenchyma, in the periphery of the lung, without direct connection to a bronchial structure.

In general, primary salivary gland-type tumors of the lung are rare. However, in recent years, several reports addressing their biologic behavior and spectrum of histopathologic features have been presented.[74–83] Although most of the tumors observed in salivary glands can also be seen in the lung, there does not exist a parallel in the incidence of these tumors, when the two sites are compared. For instance, mixed tumors, which represent the most common tumor in salivary gland, are rarely seen in the lung. Other subtle differences in the pathologic features and behavior of these lesions have also been noted. These tumors can occur in any age group without sex predilection. There does not appear to be any predilection for a particular lung or lung segment. Clinically, they most often present as endobronchial lesions that cause symptoms related to bronchial obstruction, including cough, dyspnea, and hemoptysis. Peripheral lesions are more likely to be asymptomatic and hence discovered incidentally on routine chest X-ray.

As a group, salivary gland-type tumors tend to behave as low-grade neoplasms with a good clinical outcome when completely resected. In particular, salivary gland-type mixed tumors, acinic cell carcinoma, low-grade mucoepidermoid carcinoma, and epithelial-myoepithelial carcinoma are curable by surgical excision alone. However there are some exceptions; for example, adenoid cystic carcinomas may follow an aggressive course with distant spread and high mortality, depending on the stage of the disease at the time of initial diagnosis. Tumors found to be at an advanced stage at the time of diagnosis will usually prove fatal, independent of the histologic features. Poorly differentiated salivary gland-type mixed tumors and mucoepidermoid carcinomas of high-grade histology will also show highly aggressive behavior leading to death due to widespread metastases.

Adenoid cystic carcinoma

Adenoid cystic carcinoma of the bronchus may demonstrate a variety of histologic growth patterns: (1) cribriform (cylindromatous); (2) tubular; and (3) solid.[75] Of these, the cribriform growth pattern is the most commonly encountered and is characterized by nests and islands of tumor cells with sharply outlined luminal spaces which are often filled with mucinous material (Fig. 5.16). The islands of tumor cells are separated by fibrous bands and contain cells with round nuclei showing clear nuclear outlines and scant eosinophilic cytoplasm. The cystic areas are composed of two rows of cells, and mitotic figures are usually absent. The solid growth pattern is perhaps the most uncommon and is characterized by similar cells that form diffuse sheets. Mitotic figures are more frequently found in association with the latter growth pattern. Perineurial invasion is another common feature of adenoid cystic carcinoma; this feature, however, is not associated with

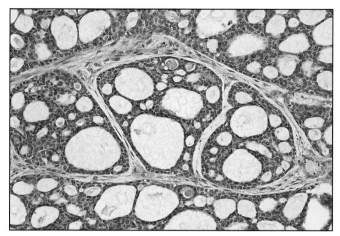

Fig. 5.16 • Adenoid cystic carcinoma, cylindromatous pattern.

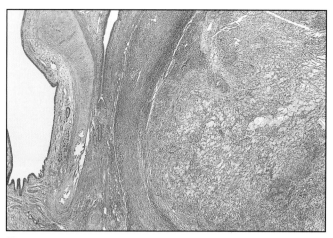

Fig. 5.17 • Salivary gland-type mixed tumor of bronchial glands.

a more ominous prognosis, although it may play a role in local recurrence. The only parameter that has been found to predict the prognosis for these tumors reliably is staging at the time of initial diagnosis. Immunohistochemical stains will identify both a glandular secretory and a myoepithelial component. The glandular component strongly reacts with broad-spectrum keratin stains and carcinoembryonic antigen (CEA); the myoepithelial component shows coexpression of keratin and actin filaments, as well as variable expression of vimentin, S-100 protein, and glial fibrillary acidic protein (GFAP).[75]

Acinic cell carcinoma (Fechner tumor)

This is a rare primary low-grade lung tumor that has been reported in both children and adults.[76,77] Metastasis appears to be very infrequent. Several morphologic growth patterns have been identified in these tumors, including acinar, cystic or papillocystic, nesting, and oncocytic. These lesions are characterized by a neoplastic proliferation of clear cells with displacement of the nuclei towards the periphery (resembling signet-ring cells) and containing ample granular eosinophilic cytoplasm which shows a strongly positive reaction for periodic acid–Schiff (PAS). The tumor may show a nesting arrangement separated by thin fibrous bands. In other areas, the tumor may contain cystic spaces lined by neoplastic cells. Some tumors may be composed predominantly of oncocytic cells showing a strikingly nested growth pattern, thus closely resembling a neuroendocrine neoplasm. The presence of PAS-positive staining in the tumor cells is helpful for diagnosis. The most important feature for diagnosis, however, is the finding of 600–800 nm membrane-bound intracellular zymogen granules by electron microscopy.[76,77] Immunohistochemical stains are of limited value in these tumors, and essentially demonstrate an immunophenotype consistent with secretory epithelial cells. Immunohistochemical stains for pancreatic amylase have been claimed to be of help for diagnosis in the salivary gland counterparts, but in our experience this antibody is rarely positive in lung primaries.

Salivary gland-type mixed tumor

This tumor is defined by a biphasic population of mesenchymal and epithelial elements. The epithelial elements usually take the form of ductal, glandular, and solid areas composed of rather small, eosinophilic or clear cells with round to oval nuclei and inconspicuous nucleoli. In some cases the solid cellular proliferation can adopt a plasmacytoid appearance. In the majority of cases, the predominant component is a solid proliferation of myoepithelial cells. Immunohistochemical stains demonstrate the myoepithelial nature of these cells by showing coexpression of keratin and actin filaments. The myoepithelial tumor cells also strongly express vimentin, and may show positivity for S-100 protein and GFAP to various degrees. The mesenchymal stromal component in mixed tumors is characterized by loose chondromyxoid tissue, and more rarely by the formation of cartilaginous matrix (Fig. 5.17). It is important to note that, although the most prominent mesenchymal component in mixed tumors of the parotid gland is mature cartilage, such differentiation is not commonly seen in salivary gland-type mixed tumors of lung. The tumors may be very solid and show low to moderate mitotic activity, yet still behave in a low-grade fashion with complete surgical excision generally being curative. The presence of increased mitotic activity, necrosis, vascular invasion, and pronounced cellular atypia should alert the pathologist to the possibility of a malignant mixed tumor.[80] Such tumors will behave as high-grade malignancies with capability for widespread metastases and a fatal outcome.

Mucoepidermoid carcinoma

Mucoepidermoid carcinoma represents the most common primary salivary gland-type tumor of the lung, and is one of the most common primary lung tumors in children. These tumors can be divided into those of low and high grade. They are characterized by sheets of cells showing epidermoid differentiation admixed with mucocytes containing intra- and extracellular mucin (Fig. 5.18). The more solid component may be composed predominantly of clear cells embedded in a fibrous stroma. In the low-grade tumors, the solid or epidermoid component is devoid of significant cellular atypia or mitotic activity. The presence of marked cellular atypia and mitotic activity as well as areas of necrosis and hemorrhage are features indicative of a high-grade tumor. Transitions between areas of low- and high-grade malignancy may be seen in any given tumor. High-grade mucoepidermoid carcinoma

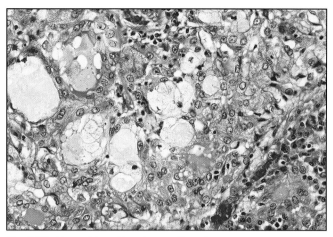

Fig. 5.18 • Mucoepidermoid carcinoma of bronchus.

may be impossible to distinguish from poorly differentiated squamous cell carcinoma in the absence of a well-differentiated mucoepidermoid carcinoma component in the same tumor.[78] Immunohistochemical stains are of limited value for diagnosis. PAS and mucicarmine stains, however, may be useful for identifying scattered mucocytes admixed with the epidermoid cells in the more poorly differentiated cases.

Epithelial-myoepithelial carcinoma

This is an unusual tumor characterized by glandular or tubular structures made up of cells with abundant clear cytoplasm showing characteristic displacement of the nuclei toward the periphery[79] (Fig. 5.19). The tumor cells do not usually display any cellular atypia, pleomorphism, or mitotic activity. Immunohistochemical stains demonstrate the myoepithelial nature of the clear cells; there is coexpression of actin and keratin, as well as focal positivity for vimentin and S-100 protein.

Oncocytoma

Rare cases of oncocytoma resembling those seen in the salivary glands have been reported in the past as primary lung neoplasms.[81–83] The tumors are characterized by a monotonous proliferation of large, round cells with small central nuclei and abundant oxyphilic cytoplasm. We have not, however, seen any *bona fide* case of this type of tumor in our personal practice.

Biphasic epithelial/mesenchymal neoplasms

This term encompasses a group of tumors characterized by the admixture of epithelial and mesenchymal elements within the same lesion.[84–95] They represent fewer than 1% of all primary malignancies of the lung. The two most important lesions in this category are carcinosarcoma and pulmonary blastoma.[84] It is important to note, in this context, that pulmonary blastoma may be composed exclusively or predominantly of epithelial tissue.

Carcinosarcoma

The term as it is applied in this section implies a tumor that is composed of both well-defined epithelial and mesenchymal elements, both of which are morphologically malignant.[94,95] These tumors must be distinguished from carcinomas with benign bony or cartilaginous metaplasia. For the diagnosis of pulmonary carcinosarcoma, both the epithelial and the mesenchymal component must be easily recognized as malignant on routine microscopic examination (Fig. 5.20). Carcinosarcoma must also be distinguished from sarcomatoid or spindle cell carcinoma. In the latter, the tumor is composed entirely of a malignant proliferation of epithelial cells, as demonstrated by immunohistochemical or ultrastructural evidence of epithelial differentiation in the sarcomatoid or spindle cell component, whereas in carcinosarcoma the two separate components display unequivocal features of either epithelial or mesenchymal differentiation by light microscopic, immunohistochemical, and ultrastructural studies.[37,91,93,95] Clinically, carcinosarcomas may present as either peripheral or central (endobronchial) lesions. There appears to be a male predominance as well as a direct correlation with the use of tobacco. The tumor appears to show a predilection for adults, with an average age of 60 years. The clinical symptoms generally correlate with the

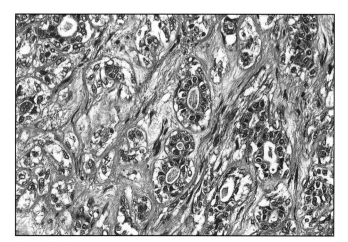

Fig. 5.19 • Epithelial-myoepithelial carcinoma. Notice clear myoepithelial outer cell layer in the glands.

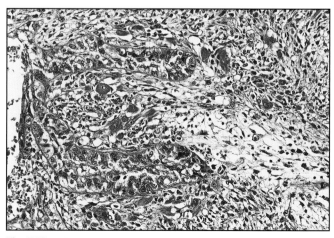

Fig. 5.20 • Pulmonary carcinosarcoma. The stromal component surrounding the gland is composed of rhabdomyoblasts.

anatomic location of the tumor; those located centrally are not only smaller in size but are also more likely to produce early symptoms due to bronchial obstruction. On the other hand, tumors arising in the periphery of the lung are more likely to reach a large size before they produce symptoms. Therefore, the prognosis for these tumors, although poor, is also linked to their anatomic location. Among the most common clinical symptoms are cough, hemoptysis, and obstructive pneumonia for the central lesions, and chest pain for the peripheral lesions.[92,93] Grossly, the tumors appear well-circumscribed and may range in size from 1 cm to over 20 cm in greatest diameter. Although the tumors are generally solitary, satellite nodules can be observed in the vicinity of the main lesion.

Histologically the epithelial component may take the form of an adenocarcinoma, squamous cell carcinoma, small cell carcinoma, or anaplastic large-cell carcinoma. The mesenchymal component usually corresponds to one of the well-defined forms of differentiated soft tissue sarcomas such as chondrosarcoma, osteosarcoma, or rhabdomyosarcoma. As stated previously, these components should be recognized easily by routine light microscopy; the role of immunohistochemistry for diagnosis will usually only be confirmatory.

Pulmonary blastoma

This type of tumor corresponds to a mixed epithelial/mesenchymal neoplasm in which both components appear to correspond to immature or primitive glandular or stromal elements suggestive of embryonal structures.[84] It is an entirely different entity from pleuropulmonary blastoma, which occurs in childhood (see p. 210). Two histologic variants are identified: (1) predominantly epithelial (monophasic); and (2) mixed epithelial/mesenchymal (biphasic blastoma). The predominantly epithelial tumors have also been designated under a variety of other terms, including adenocarcinoma of fetal lung type, well-differentiated fetal adenocarcinoma, pulmonary endodermal tumor resembling fetal lung, and pulmonary embryoma.[84,85,87–89] Such terms reflect the fetal appearance of the tissues in these tumors that are thought to recapitulate the developing lung during the ninth to 11th weeks of gestation.

Clinically, these tumors most often affect adults, with a mean age of 35 years. Tumors located centrally are more likely to produce symptoms of bronchial obstruction, while those located in the periphery of the lung most often remain asymptomatic until the tumor reaches a larger size.

Grossly, the tumors are usually well circumscribed, unencapsulated, and solitary, and may range in size from 1 cm to over 20 cm in diameter. On cut section, these lesions are firm and rubbery, and in about 50% of cases display areas of necrosis. In some instances, the tumor may grow as a polypoid endobronchial mass.

Histologically, the biphasic tumors are characterized by a glandular proliferation composed of tubular structures of different sizes separated by a densely cellular spindle cell stromal component (Fig. 5.21). The tubular structures may resemble endometrial glands, or may show clear cell features with striking subnuclear vacuolization reminiscent of fetal lung. In the monophasic lesions, i.e., well-differentiated fetal adenocarcinoma, the glandular proliferation displays similar histologic features to the biphasic blastoma but is usually accompanied by a minimal or inconspicuous stromal spindle

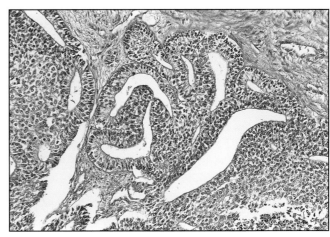

Fig. 5.21 • Pulmonary blastoma. Note the basally oriented nuclei and the abundant clear cytoplasm.

cell component. More recently, a high-grade form of the monophasic epithelial type has been described.[89] Another distinctive feature of pulmonary blastoma is the presence of discrete collections of oval to spindle cells without cellular atypia or mitotic activity adjacent to the glandular structures. These structures have been referred to as "morules." In the biphasic tumors, the spindle cell component may be completely undifferentiated or show features of a conventional sarcoma. Other elements that may occasionally be encountered in pulmonary blastoma include cartilage, bone, and multinucleated trophoblast-like giant cells.[84] PAS stains show moderate amounts of glycogen within the tumor cells; however, mucicarmine and D-PAS are negative for intracellular mucin. Nevertheless, mucicarmine and D-PAS may show mucin deposition in the lumen of the glandular structures. Immunohistochemical stains generally show positivity with epithelial markers such as keratin and epithelial membrane antigen (EMA). Interestingly, the morules may show positive staining for chromogranin.

The prognosis for pulmonary blastoma, as with carcinosarcoma, is poor. However, it has been observed that monophasic tumors have a better prognosis than the biphasic ones.[90]

Pulmonary mesenchymal neoplasms

The existence of pure mesenchymal tumors arising from lung parenchyma is recognized. Theoretically, any given type of tumor affecting the soft tissue may also occur in the lung as a primary tumor.[96] Pulmonary sarcomas can affect both children and adults without predilection for gender or particular pulmonary lobe or lung. Because the lung is a common site of metastases from soft tissue sarcomas, care must be taken to obtain a complete clinical history and examination prior to rendering a diagnosis of primary sarcoma of the lung in order to rule out the possibility of metastasis from a soft tissue primary.

Leiomyosarcoma

Leiomyosarcoma is one of the most commonly encountered mesenchymal tumors of the lung and has been described at all

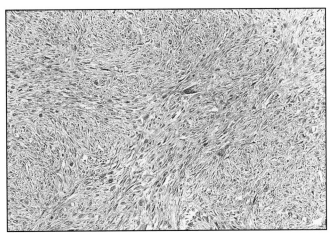

Fig. 5.22 • Leiomyosarcoma of lung composed of fascicles of atypical spindle cells with cigar-shaped nuclei.

ages, including in children.[97–99] Because these tumors can occur in an endobronchial location, patients may present with symptoms of pulmonary obstruction such as cough, hemoptysis, and dyspnea. On the other hand, the patients may be completely asymptomatic when the tumors are peripherally located.

The morphologic features of these tumors recapitulate those seen in soft tissue (see Ch. 24), namely a fascicular proliferation of spindle cells with moderate amounts of eosinophilic cytoplasm, cigar-shaped nuclei, and inconspicuous nucleoli (Fig. 5.22). Pulmonary leiomyosarcoma can show a wide spectrum of differentiation.[96] Low-grade tumors are characterized by a well-developed fascicular arrangement of tumor cells intersecting at right angles, with low mitotic rates (<3 per 10 hpf) and absence of cellular atypia, necrosis, and hemorrhage. Intermediate-grade tumors are characterized by increased cellularity with mild to moderate nuclear atypia and brisk mitotic activity (3–8 mitoses per 10 hpf). High-grade tumors comprise lesions showing marked cellularity with nuclear pleomorphism and atypia, high mitotic activity (average 8–12 mitoses per 10 hpf), abundant necrosis, and hemorrhage.

By immunohistochemistry, the low-grade (well-differentiated) tumors are more likely to show immunoreactivity for muscle markers such as smooth muscle actin and desmin, while the less differentiated (high-grade) tumors can be negative for all muscle markers and may require ultrastructural examination for confirmation of the diagnosis. It is important to note that some smooth muscle tumors may show a positive reaction for cytokeratin. A panel of markers is therefore recommended when evaluating spindle cell neoplasms of the lung to avoid misinterpretation as spindle cell carcinoma.

Surgical resection of the tumor followed by radiation or chemotherapy has been the favored modality of treatment for these tumors. The prognosis appears to correlate directly with tumor grade and degree of differentiation. The low-grade tumors generally follow a less aggressive course than those of intermediate or high-grade histology.[96]

Rhabdomyosarcoma

Rhabdomyosarcoma rarely arises as a primary lung tumor. These tumors have been described in children as well as in adults.[100–104] In children, they occur most often in the setting of a pulmonary cystic lesion.[103,104] Rhabdomyosarcomas may present within lung parenchyma as solid tumor masses, or may also present as endobronchial lesions, giving rise to the classical symptoms of pulmonary obstruction. Histologically, most primary pulmonary rhabdomyosarcomas correspond to the alveolar or embryonal variants. The tumors are characterized by a proliferation of small round "blue" cells and scattered rhabdomyoblasts with abundant deeply eosinophilic cytoplasm. Although traditionally claimed to be important for diagnosis, cytoplasmic cross-striations are extremely difficult to find and are not present in most cases. Immunohistochemical stains are of great value for diagnosis and very useful for separating these lesions from other small "blue" cell tumors. The majority of the lesions will show some degree of positivity for muscle actin, desmin, and myoglobin.[100] The prognosis for these tumors is poor despite surgery and chemotherapy. The tumors usually metastasize widely within and outside the thoracic cavity.

Malignant peripheral nerve sheath tumor

Malignant peripheral nerve sheath tumor (MPNST) is an uncommon primary sarcoma of the lung (see Ch. 27). In the majority of cases, the patients have a history of neurofibromatosis.[105] However, some cases may arise *de novo* in the absence of such a history. These tumors may be seen in patients of any age or sex; however, they seem to be more common in young adults and only rarely affect children.[105–107]

Grossly, the tumors may present as endobronchial masses or as solid nodules within lung parenchyma without any connection to the bronchial tree. They can measure from a few centimeters to over 15 cm and show frequent areas of hemorrhage and/or necrosis.

Histologically, these tumors are composed of a fascicular spindle cell proliferation replacing lung parenchyma. The spindle cell proliferation may show a vague storiform pattern and may have a myxoid or edematous stroma, but most often is characterized by a "herringbone" pattern with the formation of long sweeping fascicles. Cellular atypia and mitotic activity vary from tumor to tumor and may be mild or pronounced. A perivascular distribution of tumor cells is a common finding in the high-grade lesions. Rarely, features of rhabdomyoblastic differentiation may be observed in these tumors in association; as in soft tissue, such tumors are designated malignant "triton" tumors.[108]

The immunohistochemical diagnosis of these tumors is dependent on the demonstration of S-100 protein positivity in the absence of other markers. Unfortunately, only the better differentiated examples of these tumors will demonstrate a positive reaction for this marker; also, S-100 protein positivity is not an exclusive marker for neurogenic tumors. In poorly differentiated examples, and in the absence of a history of neurofibromatosis, ultrastructural examination may be the only means of reliably confirming the diagnosis.

Monophasic synovial sarcoma

Monophasic synovial sarcoma is a comparatively newly recognized entity in the lung that can affect relatively young individuals as well as older patients; there is no gender predilection.[109,110] The tumors may range in size from 1 to 20 cm in greatest dimension, and display grossly a whitish-tan, rubbery, homogeneous cut surface. Areas of hemorrhage and/or necrosis may also be present.

Histologically, these tumors are characterized by a monotonous spindle cell proliferation, frequently adopting a "herringbone" pattern of growth and often showing a prominent hemangiopericytic vascular pattern. The tumor cells have oval nuclei with a rim of scant eosinophilic cytoplasm. In some areas, the tumor cells can assume a more epithelioid appearance with round nuclei and more abundant cytoplasm. Areas of necrosis, hemorrhage, or metaplastic bone formation may be seen in some cases. The mitotic activity can range from 2 to more than 20 mitoses per 10 hpf (Fig. 5.23) Immunohistochemical studies are of value for diagnosis; the tumor cells are usually positive for at least one epithelial marker, such as EMA (which is most sensitive), broad-spectrum keratin, and low-molecular-weight cytokeratin antibodies. These markers are generally coexpressed in the tumor cells with vimentin.[109] S-100 protein positivity may also be seen in 20–30% of these tumors. Another marker that strongly stains the tumor cells of synovial sarcoma is *bcl-2*. This marker has been shown to be strongly expressed in these tumors even when epithelial markers are only weakly or focally positive.[111] However, this antigen has only limited specificity. The biologic behavior of monophasic synovial sarcoma of the lung is similar to that of similar lesions in the soft tissues (see Ch. 24). Essentially, the tumor may follow a protracted clinical course, or it may show aggressive behavior culminating in death of the patient.[109] Although there is no specific treatment for these tumors, complete surgical excision is the preferred treatment. The relative absence of biphasic cases reported to date most likely reflects their overall lower incidence in the context of a rare location.

Fibrosarcoma, solitary fibrous tumor (hemangiopericytoma), and malignant fibrous histiocytoma

This group of fibrous and fibrohistiocytic tumors, of which hemangiopericytoma (currently reclassified as intrapulmonary solitary fibrous tumor) is a part, basically represent diagnoses of exclusion.[96] In the past, fibrosarcoma and malignant fibrous histiocytoma (MFH) used to be the most commonly diagnosed sarcomas of the lung. In today's era of more sophisticated techniques, however, the use of immunohistochemical stains, electron microscopy, and cytogenetics has allowed more precise characterization of such lesions.

Fibrous and fibrohistiocytic tumors may affect any individual, from young children to adults, without predilection for gender, side, or segment of lung. These tumors may also arise in an endobronchial location, producing symptoms of bronchial obstruction.[96,112–118] Currently there is great controversy regarding the diagnosis of hemangiopericytoma; some still accept this as a valid diagnostic category, but there are others who question whether it represents merely a nonspecific growth pattern rather than a true clinicopathologic entity.[96,118] Cases that we have had an opportunity to review which had been coded in the past as pulmonary hemangiopericytomas have all been reclassified as either intrapulmonary solitary fibrous tumors or synovial sarcomas. The lines that separate solitary fibrous tumor from fibrosarcoma, and fibrosarcoma from MFH, can also be very thin. In essence, we conceptualize all these tumors as forming part of a continuum or spectrum of differentiation, with solitary fibrous tumor corresponding to the relatively benign end of the spectrum, fibrosarcoma being an intermediate form, and MFH being the poorly differentiated counterpart of the above.[96]

Grossly the tumors may be small and well circumscribed, or may reach a large size and undergo central cavitation and necrosis. Endobronchial variants have also been described. Histologically, *solitary fibrous tumor* (see also p. 208) is characterized by a bland-appearing spindle cell proliferation which may adopt a variety of growth patterns that simulate other soft tissue spindle cell neoplasms, including fibrosarcoma, fibrous histiocytoma, neural neoplasms, synovial sarcoma, and hemangiopericytoma.[119,120] The solid spindle cell population is characteristically admixed with areas of diffuse stromal sclerosis and contains a prominent vascular component. A distinctive feature of these tumors is the presence of areas containing rope-like strands of keloidal collagen separating the spindle cells (Fig. 5.24). The tumors are generally well

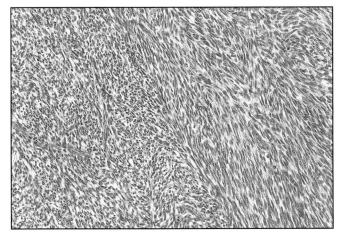

Fig. 5.23 • Primary synovial sarcoma of lung composed of fascicles of monotonous atypical spindle cells with herringbone pattern.

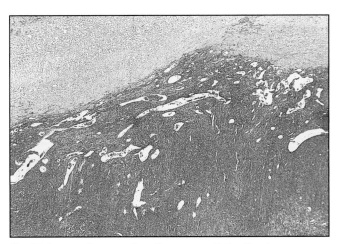

Fig. 5.24 • Intrapulmonary solitary fibrous tumor. Notice dilated, hemangiopericytoma-like vessels.

circumscribed and show a tendency to entrap respiratory epithelium in the periphery, imparting a biphasic (or "fibro-adenomatoid") appearance. Immunohistochemical stains show absence of reactivity for specific differentiation markers such as keratin, desmin, actin, and S-100 protein, but the tumor cells are consistently positive for CD34.[121,122] We have also recently encountered strong and diffuse immunoreactivity in these tumors for *bcl-2*, a feature that may be helpful for diagnosis.[111] However, because both CD34 and *bcl-2* are not specific for this tumor and may be observed in a variety of spindle cell proliferations, the diagnosis still rests on the identification of the characteristic histopathologic features and the absence of reactivity for other markers of more specific differentiation. *Fibrosarcoma* of the lung is defined as a malignant spindle cell proliferation composed of cells showing features of fibroblastic differentiation. Such features are best demonstrated at the ultrastructural level, but can also be inferred from the light microscopic features in a tumor composed of atypical spindle cells with tapered ends, elongated nuclei surrounded by scant amphophilic cytoplasm, prominent collagen matrix deposition in the interstitium, and absence of immunoreactivity for any of the specific markers of differentiation such as keratins, actin, desmin, and S-100 protein.[96] Although the "herringbone" pattern was said to be distinctive for this tumor, this is no longer acceptable as a criterion for diagnosis since this pattern can be observed just as frequently in synovial sarcoma and MPNST. The presence of more marked cellular atypia, multinucleation, nuclear pleomorphism, and bizarre mitotic figures heralds the development of unclassified pleomorphic sarcoma or so-called MFH. Again, the diagnosis is one of exclusion, and is supported by demonstration of lack of immunoreactivity for any of the specific markers of differentiation currently available. The differential diagnosis for the latter includes sarcomatoid (spindle cell) and pleomorphic carcinoma, metastases of malignant melanoma, and poorly differentiated variants of other types of sarcoma.

There is no specific treatment for any of these tumors. Intrapulmonary solitary fibrous tumors respond well to surgical excision alone. However, for high-grade sarcomas, complete surgical excision followed by radiation or chemotherapy may be of value.[112,113,115,117]

Bone- and cartilage-forming sarcomas

This group of primary sarcomas is exceedingly rare in the lung.[123–127] Few well-documented cases have been reported. In any case, the presence of malignant cartilage or bone in any given tumor should alert the pathologist to the possibility of a biphasic neoplasm (i.e., carcinosarcoma), and should prompt a careful search for a malignant epithelial component. This is best accomplished by extensive and thorough sampling of the lesion. It is possible that many of the cases presented in the literature as belonging to this group of tumors may, in fact, have been carcinosarcomas. There is no specific treatment for these tumors and the prognosis is generally poor, with death generally occurring within 12 months.

Kaposi's sarcoma and angiosarcoma

Primary vascular tumors of the lung are rare.[128–132] Kaposi's sarcoma is generally found in the setting of human immuno-

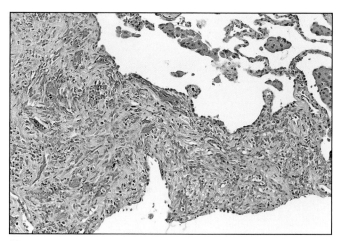

Fig. 5.25 • Kaposi's sarcoma of lung.

deficiency virus (HIV) infection.[128–130] Angiosarcomas, on the other hand, are most often the result of metastases from a cardiac primary or some other distant primary.[132]

Kaposi's sarcoma (see Ch. 3) is characterized by a spindle cell proliferation with mild nuclear atypia and low mitotic activity, and vascular slits with extravasated red blood cells (Fig. 5.25). The tumor tends to grow around large vessels and airways and frequently follows a lymphangitic distribution in the lung that may make it very difficult to diagnose. In general, the tumor cells show moderate to diffuse positivity with CD34, CD31, and HHV-8. Occasional reports have described factor VIII and actin positivity in these tumors, but such reactivity is inconstant and cannot be relied upon for diagnosis.

Angiosarcomas, on the other hand, are characterized by a proliferation of atypical cells lining anastomosing vascular channels that strongly react with vascular endothelial markers such as factor VIII-related antigen, CD31, and CD34. The presence of multiple nodules as opposed to a single dominant mass should raise the possibility of a metastasis and prompt the search for a primary source outside the lungs.[132] The presence of multiple intravascular nodules often suggests a cardiac primary (especially in the right atrium).

Epithelioid hemangioendothelioma

Epithelioid hemangioendothelioma (see Ch. 3) represents a rare form of vascular endothelial neoplasm that has been considered to be intermediate in morphology and behavior between a hemangioma and conventional angiosarcoma. This tumor was initially thought to represent a decidual process in the lung and was later interpreted as intravascular bronchioloalveolar tumor (IVBAT).[133,134] Subsequent immunohistochemical and ultrastructural studies demonstrated the vascular endothelial nature of the tumor cells.[135,136] Clinically, there appears to be a predilection for females in the fourth and fifth decades of life. The classical presentation is that of multiple well-circumscribed pulmonary nodules. Clinically, symptoms of pulmonary obstruction may be seen, such as cough and dyspnea.

Histologically, the tumors are characterized by a proliferation of oval to round epithelioid cells with abundant eosinophilic cytoplasm, oval nuclei, and inconspicuous nucleoli, embedded in a myxoid or hyaline matrix (Fig. 5.26). A distinctive feature is the presence of large intracytoplasmic

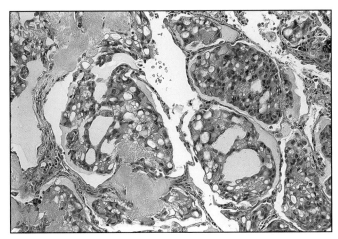

Fig. 5.26 • Epithelioid hemangioendothelioma of lung. Notice glomeruloid clusters of epithelioid cells filling alveolar lumens.

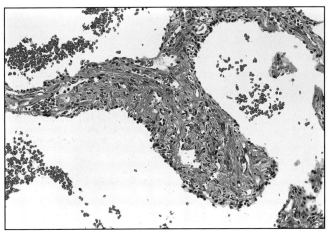

Fig. 5.27 • Thickening of alveolar septum by smooth muscle proliferation characteristic of lymphangioleiomyomatosis.

vacuoles in the tumor cells. In early lesions, tongues of tumor tissue show a tendency to fill the alveoli in a polypoid fashion, creating a distinctive glomeruloid appearance. Older lesions may show prominent stromal hyalinization containing only scant residual neoplastic cells. Necrosis, hemorrhage, and mitotic activity are not generally seen in these tumors. The tumor cells are strongly positive for vascular endothelial markers, including factor VIII-related antigen, CD31, and CD34. Some cases may also show keratin positivity. Electron microscopy shows features of vascular endothelial cells, including tight cell junctions, basal lamina material, pinocytotic activity and, more rarely, Weibel–Palade bodies.

There is no specific treatment for these tumors and the prognosis will depend on the extent of involvement of the lung parenchyma. The majority of the patients die after a period of 10–15 years due to respiratory insufficiency because of the presence of multiple bilateral pulmonary nodules.[134]

Lymphangioleiomyomatosis (see also Ch. 3)

This is a rare pulmonary disease that affects women of reproductive age and generally leads to death due to respiratory failure within 10 years of onset. A minority of cases is associated with tuberous sclerosis. Grossly, the lung displays diffuse honeycombing in the absence of deposition of fibrous tissue between the cystic spaces.[137,138] Histologically, the lesion is characterized by a proliferation of bland-appearing smooth muscle cells distributed around the bronchial lymphatics, interlobular septa, and pleura (Fig. 5.27). The spindle cell proliferation can be quite focal and inconspicuous and is not associated with the formation of recognizable tumor nodules. Immunohistochemical stains for smooth muscle actin and HMB-45 may be quite useful in highlighting the spindle cell proliferation around lymphatics.

Lymphoproliferative disorders

Lymphoproliferative disorders of the lung are distinctly rare and may run the gamut from benign, reversible processes to high-grade malignant lymphomas. Rare examples of pulmonary plasmacytoma also occur.[139] Since the introduction of the concept of bronchus-associated lymphoid tissue (BALT), a better understanding of lymphoproliferative disorders of the lung has been achieved, with the result that many conditions previously thought to represent pseudolymphomatous processes have now been identified as low-grade monoclonal lymphoid malignancies.[140,141] The three most important categories in this group are: (1) low-grade B-cell lymphomas; (2) lymphomatoid granulomatosis; and (3) Hodgkin's disease (HD).

Malignant non-Hodgkin's lymphoma

The vast majority of malignant lymphomas of the lung are of B-cell phenotype and of low-grade malignancy.[142] A term that has been recently coined for some of these lesions is "BALT lymphoma," which stands for bronchus-associated lymphoid tissue lymphoma.[140–143] These tumors occur most often in adults in their sixth decade of life. Radiologically, the tumor may present as pulmonary nodules or as diffuse pulmonary infiltrates. Clinically, the patients may be completely asymptomatic or present with constitutional symptoms such as weight loss, fever, and night sweats. Hilar adenopathy may be seen in some cases.[143–148] Histologically the lesions are characterized by a monotonous proliferation of small lymphocytes with mild nuclear irregularities, admixed with scattered immunoblasts. Features of plasmacytoid differentiation are often seen in the small lymphocytes, and Russell or Dutcher bodies may be present. A distinguishing feature of the lymphoid cell population is the presence of a rim of clear cytoplasm surrounding the nucleus of the cells, resembling that of centrocytes or monocytoid (parafollicular) B cells. Reactive follicles with well-formed germinal centers may be seen in up to 70% of cases. Another important distinctive feature is the presence of so-called "lymphoepithelial lesions," defined by invasion and infiltration of bronchial epithelium by the small lymphocytes (Fig. 5.28). Other features of BALT lymphomas include multinucleated giant cells or sarcoid-like granulomas which are seen in up to 50% of cases. Interestingly, bone marrow involvement and serum monoclonal immunoglobulin spikes occur in only about 20% of the cases, while hilar lymph node involvement may be present in up to 30% of cases.[147] The majority of cases of BALT lymphoma are stage I tumors with survivals of up to 80% after 5 and 10 years.

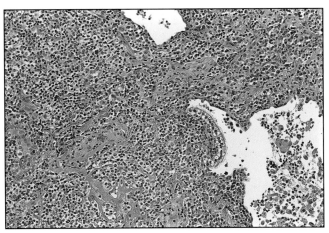

Fig. 5.28 • Bronchus-associated lymphoid tissue (BALT) lymphoma composed of monotonous proliferation of small lymphocytes focally involving bronchial mucosa.

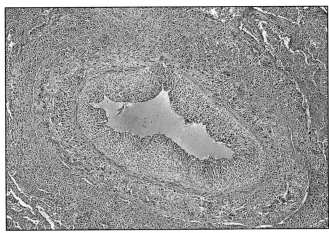

Fig. 5.29 • Lymphomatoid granulomatosis of lung. Notice infiltration and destruction of vessel wall by atypical lymphocytes.

The immunohistochemical diagnosis of these tumors rests on demonstrating monoclonality. This can be achieved using antibodies for kappa and lambda light chains on paraffin sections, by flow cytometry immunophenotyping, or by performing gene rearrangement analysis.

The differential diagnosis includes pseudolymphoma and lymphoid interstitial pneumonia.[144] Pseudolymphoma of the lung, currently designated as *nodular BALT hyperplasia*, most likely represents a precursor lesion of BALT lymphoma, and is characterized by a polyclonal population of small lymphocytes with the formation of prominent germinal centers.[145] Nodular BALT hyperplasia is distinguished from BALT lymphoma histologically by the lesser extent of the lymphoid proliferation, lack of the "monocytoid" features of the lymphocytes, and absence of lymphoepithelial lesions. The *diffuse form of BALT hyperplasia* is synonymous with lymphoid interstitial pneumonia (LIP) of the old literature. This type of BALT hyperplasia may be associated with various immune disorders, including acquired immune deficiency syndrome (AIDS). Radiologically and histologically the lesions are characterized by diffuse interstitial lymphoid infiltrates associated with fibrosis. The infiltrates consist predominantly of small B lymphocytes admixed with plasma cells and occasional histiocytes. Lymphoid follicles are frequently seen, and small granulomas may also be present. Some lesions may progress to lymphoma; others remain localized or regress with time.

Rarely, primary lymphomas of the lung may show features of *large cell lymphoma* of B-cell type. Such lesions usually present as large ill-defined tumor masses with areas of necrosis and infiltration of the overlying pleura, and are usually accompanied by extensive destruction of bronchial cartilage and air spaces.[149] Some of these lesions may remain localized to the lung for some time, a finding that supports the idea that they may represent high-grade transformation of low-grade BALT lymphomas.[143]

Lymphomatoid granulomatosis/angioimmunoproliferative lesion

Another unusual but highly distinctive type of non-Hodgkin's large-cell lymphoma of the lung is the condition initially described as lymphomatoid granulomatosis by Liebow et al.[150]

and which is currently also known as angioimmunoproliferative lesion (AIL).[144] Although conventionally accepted as an angiocentric T-cell lymphoma of the lung, this entity is currently being re-evaluated for the possibility that it may represent a T-cell-rich large B-cell lymphoma. The tumor appears to affect men more often than women and is most commonly seen in the fifth and sixth decades of life. However, cases occurring in children have been reported. Radiographically, the patients may present with multiple pulmonary nodules, reticulonodular infiltrates, or solitary pulmonary tumors. Dermal involvement may be observed in the form of skin nodules, rashes, or ulcers.[150–155] Histologically the tumors are characterized by an atypical lymphoid infiltrate with prominent angiocentricity. Binucleated (Reed–Sternberg-like) cells with prominent eosinophilic nucleoli similar to those seen in HD are a frequent finding. The tumor cells are often admixed with histiocytes, imparting a pseudogranulomatous appearance. These lesions are usually accompanied by extensive necrosis and show prominent infiltration and destruction of vessel walls by the tumor cells (Fig. 5.29). Immunohistochemical studies so far seem to point to a T-cell lineage for the atypical neoplastic cells, although there is still some controversy regarding the exact nature of this lesion. A few studies appear to suggest that some of these cases may represent T-cell-rich large B-cell lymphomas.

Hodgkin's disease

Primary pulmonary HD, defined strictly by the absence of HD elsewhere (including hilar lymph nodes), is extremely rare.[156–158] The lesions can present grossly as either single or multiple well-circumscribed intrapulmonary nodules. Histologically these lesions do not always show the classical features of HD as seen in the more conventional nodal sites and may be difficult to diagnose. A mixed cellular infiltrate is generally seen and contains small lymphocytes, plasma cells, and eosinophils, as well as scattered larger lymphoid cells with single or multiple atypical nuclei and prominent eosinophilic nucleoli (Fig. 5.30). Immunohistochemistry is critical for the diagnosis by showing strong membrane and paranuclear cytoplasmic staining of the atypical cells for CD30 and CD15 antibodies, and negative staining of the same cells for leukocyte common antigen and B- and T-cell markers.

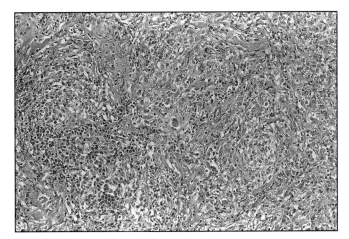

Fig. 5.30 • Hodgkin's disease of the lung showing proliferation of atypical mononuclear and multinucleated cells against a background of small lymphocytes, plasma cells, and eosinophils.

Tumors derived from embryologically displaced or ectopic tissues

Tumors derived from embryologically displaced or ectopic tissues are tumors that are seen normally in other areas of the body, but are not commonly expected to arise within the lung. It has been speculated that the origin of these tumors is from embryologically displaced or ectopic tissues, such as meningothelial rests, thymic epithelium, glomus cells, and neuroectodermal derivaties.[159]

Pulmonary meningioma

Pulmonary meningiomas are relatively uncommon in the lung.[160–163] Radiologically, they present as well-circumscribed intraparenchymal masses that measure up to 10 cm in greatest dimension. The patients are usually adults; there is no predilection for gender, lung, or segment of lung. The morphologic characteristics of meningiomas of the lung recapitulate those of their intracranial counterparts (see Ch. 26). Both transitional and fibrous types are seen. These tumors show a proliferation of bland-appearing spindle cells with a tendency to form whorls (Fig. 5.31). Mitotic figures are rare and cellular atypia

is not marked. The presence of psammoma bodies generally facilitates the diagnosis. Unusual features that may be observed in meningiomas of the lung include metaplastic bone formation and collections of foamy macrophages. The most important combination of immunostains for support-ing the diagnosis is the coexpression of EMA and vimentin within the same tumor cells. Other markers that may be focally positive in these tumors include keratin, S-100 protein, and CD34. The prognosis after complete surgical resection appears to be excellent. Intracranial meningiomas may on occasion metastasize late to the lungs, and a thorough history must therefore be obtained prior to rendering a diagnosis of primary pulmonary meningioma.[160]

Intrapulmonary thymoma

Intrapulmonary thymomas are extremely rare. A pulmonary mass may occasionally represent the initial manifestation of a mediastinal thymoma, so it is imperative that a mediastinal tumor be ruled out by appropriate imaging studies prior to rendering a diagnosis of primary thymoma of the lung. Radiologically, these tumors appear as well-circumscribed nodules measuring up to 10 cm in diameter. Intrapulmonary thymomas are not associated with myasthenia gravis, unlike those in a mediastinal location.[164–166]

Histologically, the tumors show the same morphologic features as those seen in their normal anterior mediastinal location (see Ch. 21), namely, a biphasic population of cells composed of epithelial cells admixed with lymphocytes, with prominent lobulation and fibrosis (Fig. 5.32). In some cases, the histology may be that of a spindle cell proliferation showing a marked fascicular or hemangiopericytic growth pattern. Mitotic activity is generally very low with only sporadic mitotic figures. Thymomas react strongly with keratin antibodies. This marker, however, is non-specific in this setting and will not serve to distinguish these tumors from spindle cell carcinoma, synovial sarcoma, or a metastasis from other epithelial neoplasms. The diagnosis is facilitated by the recognition of the biphasic population of cells (epithelial cells/lymphocytes), the characteristic lobulation as observed under low-power magnification, and the identification of the other organotypical features of thymic differentiation such as perivascular spaces and areas of "medullary" differentiation (see Ch. 21). Intrapulmonary

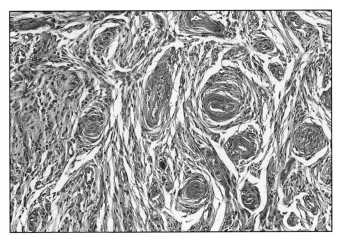

Fig. 5.31 • Pulmonary meningioma.

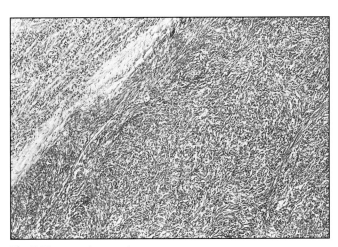

Fig. 5.32 • Intrapulmonary thymoma.

thymomas are slowly growing tumors amenable to complete surgical resection. The prognosis for these patients after complete surgical excision is good.[164]

Glomus tumor

Glomus tumors are thought to be derived from the glomus apparatus or Sucquet–Hoyer canal, a specialized arteriovenous anastomosis involved in blood and temperature control in the skin (see Ch. 3). Interestingly, such structures have not been identified in internal organs such as the lung, yet glomus tumors have also been described in several other organs outside the skin. In the lung, only a few well-documented cases have been recorded.[167,168] The tumors affect mostly adults without gender or lung predilection. Most of the patients are asymptomatic and the lesions are discovered incidentally on routine physical examination. The tumors are grossly well delimited and average 3–4 cm in diameter. Histologically, glomus tumors are characterized by a monotonous proliferation of round to oval cells with a generous rim of eosinophilic or clear cytoplasm, distinct cell membranes, centrally placed nuclei, and inconspicuous nucleoli (Fig. 5.33). Necrosis, hemorrhage, or mitotic activity is not commonly seen. The tumor cells tend to grow in sheets and to arrange themselves around dilated, often cavernous, thick-walled vessels. Glomus cells are characterized at the immunohistochemical level by their strong reactivity for smooth muscle actin. The tumor cells are negative for other markers of differentiation such as keratin, desmin, and S-100 protein. Complete surgical resection of the tumor appears to be curative and the prognosis is excellent.

Primary malignant melanoma of bronchus

This is another unusual primary lung tumor, with fewer than 30 well-documented cases reported in the literature. These tumors occur in adults, and the most important parameter for correctly identifying their primary nature is the absence (or history) of a similar tumor elsewhere. Most cases are centrally located and may grow endobronchially with a polypoid, exophytic appearance.[169–173]

Histologically, bronchial melanomas may show the same wide range of growth patterns as those seen in the skin and other organs. The tumor cells are typically arranged in a promi-nent nesting pattern and show an epithelioid appearance with moderate amounts of eosinophilic cytoplasm, round nuclei with prominent nucleoli, and frequent mitotic figures. Some tumors may be composed predominantly of spindle cells with marked cellular atypia (Fig. 5.34). Melanin pigment is seen in some but not all cases. Melanoma in situ can be observed in the adjacent bronchial mucosa in a few cases. However, when the tumor shows erosion of the bronchial epithelium, the in-situ component may be difficult to appreciate and its absence should not deter one from making the diagnosis.[169] Bronchial melanomas, as with melanomas at other sites, will react strongly with S-100 protein and HMB-45. However, it is important to note that HMB-45 may be negative in tumors composed exclusively of spindle cells. On the other hand, other antibodies, such as CEA, EMA, CD-99, and bcl-2 may occasionally be aberrantly expressed in these tumors.

There is no specific treatment for these tumors and the prognosis is poor, usually leading to death in less than 18 months.

Pulmonary paraganglioma

Pulmonary paragangliomas (see Ch. 28) are rare and still controversial tumors. Some authors believe that all such cases actually represent unusual carcinoid tumors, since normal paraganglia have not been demonstrated in the lung. The tumors are characterized by a proliferation of round to oval cells with large, often hyperchromatic, nuclei with stippled chromatin and abundant amphophilic cytoplasm. The tumor cells often adopt a nested (zellballen) pattern of growth typical of neuroendocrine neoplasms. Rosettes, ribbons, trabeculae, or festoons are not a feature of paragangliomas and serve to differentiate them from bronchial carcinoids. Another distinguishing feature that helps to separate these tumors from carcinoid is the presence of nuclear atypicality with enlarged, occasionally multilobated and hyperchromatic nuclei. The tumor cells of paraganglioma generally react with neuroendocrine markers, such as chromogranin, synaptophysin, NSE, and met-enkephalin, but in the vast majority of instances they will be negative for keratin antibodies. Another distinctive feature is the presence of a network of S-100 protein-positive sustentacular cells surrounding the nests of tumor cells, although such cells have also been described in

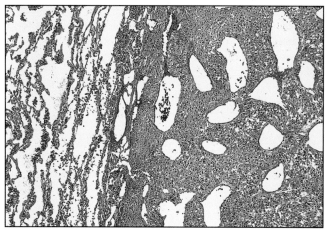
Fig. 5.33 • Intrapulmonary glomus tumor.

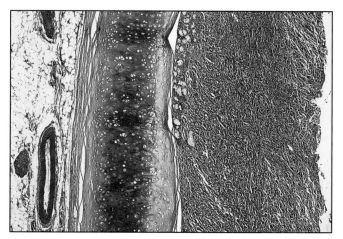
Fig. 5.34 • Primary melanoma of bronchus.

carcinoid tumors. The majority of cases are benign and treated adequately by surgical resection alone.[174,175]

Ganglioneuroblastoma

Ganglioneuroblastoma is an exceedingly rare tumor of lung (see Ch. 28). Only a few well-documented cases have been reported in the literature.[176,177] Pulmonary ganglioneuroblastoma has been described in adults presenting with obstructive symptoms due to an endobronchial lesion. At least in one case, the tumor was associated with the multiple endocrine neoplasia syndrome, but this finding may have been coincidental. Grossly, the tumors are well circumscribed and can measure up to 5 cm in diameter. Histologically, ganglioneuroblastomas are characterized by a proliferation of small cells containing cellular processes, with indistinct cell borders, moderate amounts of eosinophilic cytoplasm, and round to oval nuclei with inconspicuous nucleoli. Larger cells containing ample cytoplasm and round nuclei, some of them with Nissl substance in their cytoplasm, may also be seen, indicative of ganglionic differentiation. The cellular component proliferation is characteristically embedded in a neuropil-rich matrix. Mitotic activity or marked cellular atypia is not a feature seen in these tumors. The tumors may show variable positivity for neurofilament protein, S-100 protein, and GFAP. Epithelial markers such as keratin and EMA are negative. Due to the scarcity of reported cases, it is difficult to determine the clinical behavior of these tumors. However, they have the potential to invade adjacent organs and metastasize to hilar lymph nodes.

Germ-cell tumors

Teratomas, both benign and malignant, can originate within the lung in rare instances.[178,179] The tumors are often large and cystic, and show a predilection for the left upper lobe. They can present with cough, hemoptysis, chest pain, and occasionally with the expectoration of hair. Their histopathologic features are identical to those of teratomas arising in the gonads (see Ch. 14). Rare cases of primary *choriocarcinoma* of the lung have also been described.[180]

Tumors of uncertain histogenesis

This group comprises neoplasms of uncertain or disputed histogenesis, including granular cell tumor of bronchus, sclerosing hemangioma (pneumocytoma), clear cell (sugar) tumor, and inflammatory myofibroblastic tumor.

Granular cell tumor of bronchus

Granular cell tumor of bronchus is an unusual lesion in the lung. It affects predominantly adults, with a median age of 45 years.[181,182] Classically, the tumors present in an endobronchial location and approximately 50% of patients present with symptoms related to bronchial obstruction. The tumors are most often solitary, but in some cases they may be multiple. The presence of extrapulmonary granular cell tumors in association with such a lung tumor has been described.[183,184]

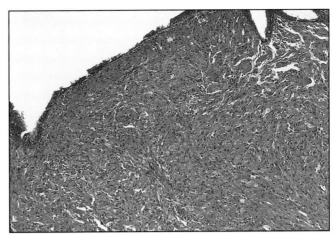

Fig. 5.35 • Granular cell tumor of bronchus.

Histologically (see Ch. 27), granular cell tumors are characterized by a proliferation of relatively large round to oval cells with distinct cell borders and abundant granular cytoplasm, eccentrically placed small round nuclei and absent nucleoli. In some cases, the cells can adopt a signet-ring cell configuration. The tumor may be well delimited or have infiltrative borders. Marked cellular atypia, necrosis, hemorrhage, and mitotic activity are not generally seen. The overlying bronchial epithelium can show squamous metaplasia but there will be no evidence of invasion by tumor cells (Fig. 5.35). The immunohistochemical profile of these tumors can be quite variable. In general, the majority of lesions are strongly positive for S-100 protein. Epithelial markers such as keratin or EMA and neuroendocrine markers are negative. Complete surgical resection of the tumor appears to be curative.

Sclerosing "hemangioma" (pneumocytoma)

Sclerosing hemangioma is a rare benign lung neoplasm that was first described by Liebow & Hubbell in 1956.[185] The tumor shows a marked female predilection and is more common in the fourth to fifth decades of life. In most cases, the tumor is discovered incidentally on a routine chest X-ray, but some patients may present with chest pain. Grossly, these tumors present as relatively small (~5 cm in diameter), well-circumscribed intraparenchymal masses unrelated to bronchial structures, with a finely granular cut surface.

Sclerosing hemangioma is characterized histologically by a variety of growth patterns,[186] including papillary, solid, angiomatous, and sclerotic. Rare examples have been described showing a prominent granulomatous reaction as well as a cystic appearance.[187] The neoplastic cell population is characterized by a monotonous proliferation of round to polygonal, bland-appearing tumor cells with central nuclei without nucleoli, and abundant clear or lightly eosinophilic cytoplasm (Fig. 5.36A). In the papillary areas (Fig. 5.36B), the surface of the papillae will be composed of a single cell layer of smaller, darker cuboidal cells with large, hyperchromatic and immature-appearing nuclei. In the more solid areas, the tumor cells can be admixed with foamy macrophages and often contain entrapped alveolar structures. The more angiomatous areas may resemble capillary or cavernous hemangioma; perivascular

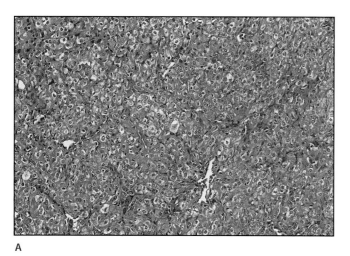
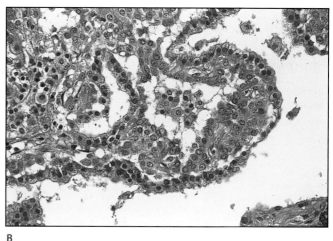

A
B

Fig. 5.36 • Sclerosing hemangioma of lung: **(A)** solid pattern – notice monotonous proliferation of bland-appearing cells with clear cytoplasm; **(B)** papillary pattern.

hyalinization with deposition of abundant collagenous matrix results in the characteristic "sclerosing" appearance. Necrosis, hemorrhage, and mitotic activity are not features seen in these tumors.[185,188–190]

More recent ultrastructural and immunohistochemical studies indicate that the tumor cells are epithelial and most closely correspond to alveolar pneumocytes.[191–193] Immunohistochemical stains for surfactant apoprotein have been strongly positive in the tumor cells in most, but not all,[193] studies. Other markers that consistently label these tumors include EMA and vimentin. Stains for keratin intermediate filaments have been claimed to be positive by some, but such results have not been reproduced by others. One immunohistochemical study also showed positive results with neuroendocrine markers.[194]

Sclerosing hemangiomas are benign tumors. Complete surgical excision of the lesion appears to be the treatment of choice and is curative. There is one reported case, however, of a metastatic deposit in a lymph node in a case of sclerosing hemangioma of the lung.[195]

Clear cell (sugar) tumor

Clear cell tumor is a rare, benign tumor of lung that has been the object of much controversy in the literature due to its as yet undetermined histogenesis. The tumor seems to affect principally adults without any predilection for gender, and most often presents as a solitary peripheral "coin" lesion.[196,197]

Histologically it is characterized by a proliferation of large round to oval cells with round nuclei, inconspicuous nucleoli, and a prominent rim of clear cytoplasm. The tumor contains numerous gaping vessels but there is very little connective tissue in between the cellular proliferation (Fig. 5.37). No necrosis, hemorrhage, cellular atypia, or mitotic activity is seen. PAS histochemical reaction with diastase shows abundant cytoplasmic glycogen in the tumor cells. Studies have shown that these tumors react positively with HMB-45 and HMB-50 antibodies,[198,199] a finding that has been interpreted as indicative of either melanocytic differentiation or of differentiation towards a postulated distinctive perivascular epithelioid cell.[199] Other studies have reported focal positivity for synaptophysin, Leu-7, NSE, S-100 protein, and CD34.[198,200] There are, as yet,

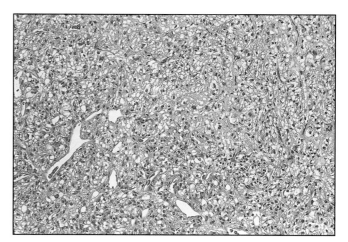

Fig. 5.37 • Clear cell "sugar" tumor of lung.

no good data as to whether these lesions express markers of myogenic differentiation, as they do other anatomic sites. Ultrastructurally, the tumor can show dense-core neurosecretory granules and/or pinocytotic vesicles with intracytoplasmic filaments. Complete surgical resection of the tumor is curative.

Inflammatory myofibroblastic tumor

Inflammatory myofibroblastic tumor, also formerly known as inflammatory pseudotumor, represents a usually benign, slowly growing process of undetermined etiology. It affects predominantly younger individuals, with an equal sex distribution. Other designations employed in the past for these lesions include plasma cell granuloma, histiocytoma, and xanthofibroma.[201–205] The tumors can present with symptoms secondary to obstruction when arising in an endobronchial location, or may be completely asymptomatic and discovered on routine examination as a solitary coin lesion. Grossly they are usually well circumscribed and small, but they may occasionally attain a large size and infiltrate the mediastinum.

Two main histologic variants are seen: (1) the plasma cell granuloma variant is characterized by areas of hyalinized fibroconnective tissue, containing variable numbers of plump fibroblasts, which is diffusely infiltrated by sheets of plasma

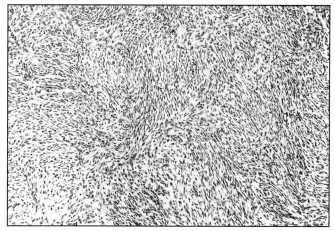

Fig. 5.38 • Inflammatory pseudotumor showing prominent storiform pattern.

cells admixed with histiocytes, mast cells, and lymphocytes; (2) the fibrohistiocytic variant is composed of a dense spindle cell proliferation arranged in a whorled, fascicular, or storiform pattern that may mimic a sarcoma (Fig. 5.38). Mitotic figures can be seen; however, mitotic activity should be low and there should be no abnormal mitoses. In more advanced stages, extensive fibrosis and hyalinization ensue, creating a centrally scarred lesion that may closely resemble the end stage of interstitial fibrosis. Calcifications may be seen in some cases. In unusual circumstances the lesion may coexist with an infectious condition (such as aspergillosis) which may obscure the true nature of the process.

Complete surgical excision is the treatment of choice. However, in some cases, the tumor may recur after several years. Recurrences are seen more often with the fibrohistiocytic variant and exceptional cases have been shown to evolve into a true sarcoma.[201] The existence of occasional recurrent and malignant examples suggests that, in fact, these lesions are neoplastic and are likely related to inflammatory myofibroblastic tumors at other locations (see Ch. 24), as is also supported by the presence of *ALK* gene rearrangement in some cases.[206]

Miscellaneous benign tumors

Cartilaginous hamartoma

Cartilaginous hamartoma is the most common benign tumor of the lung.[207,208] It is more often found in men than in women and is more common in adults. However, cases of hamartoma in children have been reported. The tumors can present as endobronchial lesions or as intraparenchymatous nodules. Histologically they are characterized by a combination of epithelial and mesenchymal elements, with varying amounts of mature cartilage and fatty tissue being present, containing invaginations of respiratory epithelium in the periphery. Interestingly, these lesions have been shown to have distinctive clonal cytogenetic aberrations, essentially identical to those occurring in lipomas, uterine leiomyomas, and other benign tumors, which result in rearrangement of high-mobility group (*HMG*) genes.[209,210] Surgical resection is the treatment of choice and is curative.

Endobronchial lipoma

Endobronchial lipomas are unusual lesions most often seen in adults.[211] Grossly, they present as pedunculated or polypoid endobronchial tumors with a soft yellowish appearance. Histologically they are composed of mature adipose tissue. Surgical resection is the treatment of choice and is curative.

Alveolar adenoma

Alveolar adenoma is a rare lung neoplasm[212–214] that was often misinterpreted in the past as a form of pulmonary lymphangioma. The tumor primarily affects adults and is usually asymptomatic and only found incidentally on routine radiographic examination. Grossly, the lesions are well circumscribed and hemorrhagic with cystic areas, and usually measure less than 3 cm in greatest diameter.

Histologically, at scanning magnification, the tumor appears vascular due to the presence of multiple cystically dilated structures filled with serum-like proteinaceous material (Fig. 5.39). However, the dilated structures are lined by alveolar pneumocytes, some of which exhibit a hobnail appearance. The tumor is benign and surgical resection is curative.

Bronchial "mucous gland" adenoma

Mucous gland adenomas are uncommon benign tumors. They are thought to occur due to exaggerated enlargement of the seromucinous bronchial glands.[215] They are more often seen in adults and do not seem to have a predilection for any particular lung or gender. Because of the endobronchial location of these tumors, the patients usually present with symptoms of bronchial obstruction.

Grossly, these lesions are exophytic and pedunculated, well circumscribed and soft, with a mucoid cut surface; they can measure up to 6 cm in greatest dimension. Histologically, on low power, the tumor usually has a cystic appearance due to the dilation of normal bronchial glands that are filled with mucus (Fig. 5.40). In other areas the tumor may show a papillary appearance admixed with dilated bronchial glands. On closer examination, the tumor is composed of bland-appearing cells without cellular atypia or mitotic activity. Some of the cells may show displacement of the nuclei towards the periphery

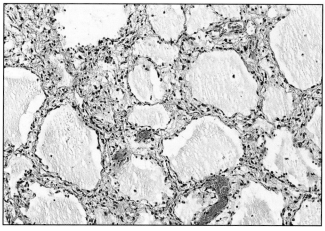

Fig. 5.39 • Alveolar adenoma.

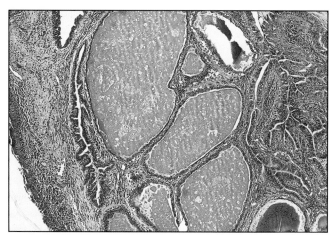

Fig. 5.40 • Mucous gland adenoma showing cystically dilated bronchial glands.

and abundant granular cytoplasm. D-PAS or mucicarmine stains will show abundant intracellular mucin, and a PAS stain will demonstrate scant glycogen content. Surgical resection is the treatment of choice and is curative.

Papillary adenoma

Papillary adenoma is an exceptionally rare neoplasm[216,217] occurring over a wide age range. It is most often small and asymptomatic, presenting as a peripheral solitary coin lesion on X-ray. The clinical course is entirely benign. Histologically, this is a well-circumscribed nodule with a complex branching papillary appearance, consisting of fibrous cores covered by uniform cuboidal to columnar cells. Ultrastructurally these epithelial cells have the features of type 2 pneumocytes.

Pulmonary adenofibroma

Pulmonary adenofibroma represents an uncommon lung lesion seen in adults.[218] The lesions are usually small and well circumscribed and are unrelated to bronchial structures. Histologically, they are characterized by complex branching glandular spaces lined by a single layer of simple cuboidal to columnar epithelium, surrounded by an abundant spindle cell fibrous stroma. The glandular spaces often adopt a characteristic club-like papillary configuration reminiscent of müllerian adenofibromas of the ovary (Fig. 5.41). Immunohistochemically, the epithelial lining cells show positive staining for epithelial markers such as keratin and EMA. The stroma of the lesion is negative for S-100 protein, actin, keratin, EMA, desmin, and CD34. The differential diagnosis is mainly with solitary fibrous tumor. Unlike solitary fibrous tumor, the gland-like areas in pulmonary adenofibroma are evenly distributed throughout the entire lesion, whereas in solitary fibrous tumors entrapped glandular structures are generally observed only in the periphery of the lesion. Surgical resection is the treatment of choice and is curative.

Minute pulmonary 'chemodectoma' (meningothelial-like nodule)

Minute pulmonary chemodectomas, which were initially mistaken for paraganglionic rests, are characterized most often by multiple, small, grayish-pink subpleural nodules, measuring approximately 2 mm in greatest diameter, which are made up of aggregates of circular or oval cells with ill-defined borders and abundant eosinophilic cytoplasm. These cells characteristically tend to adopt a whorled appearance reminiscent of meningiomas.[219,220] By immunohistochemistry, these cells stain strongly positive for vimentin and EMA, but stains for keratin, S-100 protein, chromogranin, NSE, and actin are negative. Ultrastructural observations have shown that the lesions show features of meningothelial cells, including complex cytoplasmic interdigitations joined by frequent desmosomes, and abundant intermediate filaments. Thus, the features of these lesions are closer immunohistochemically and ultrastructurally to those of meningeal arachnoid granulations than to true chemodectoma.[220] Such lesions are most often incidental findings at autopsy or in lungs resected for other reasons, and are therefore of little clinical consequence. They are generally regarded as being reactive in nature, with an entirely different molecular pathogenesis than conventional meningioma.[221]

Metastases to the lungs

The lung is one of the most common visceral sites of metastasis from a wide variety of malignancies. In fact, metastases represent the most frequent type of lung tumor. There is a wide range of tumors that can frequently metastasize to the lungs and so it is important always to obtain a good clinical history when evaluating pulmonary lesions so as to avoid misinterpreting a metastasis for a primary neoplasm. Distinguishing a primary lesion from a solitary metastasis to the lung may be difficult based on morphology alone, and a multidisciplinary approach that involves thorough clinical and radiographic examination, careful scrutiny of the clinical history, and application of special pathologic techniques is indicated.[222,223]

The terminal pulmonary vascular bed is one of those most frequently involved in the arrest of circulating tumor cells; the peripheral subpleural portions of the lungs will therefore be the initial sites for hematogenous metastases. Thus, the classical presentation of metastatic tumors to the lungs is in the form of multiple bilateral peripheral nodules. An isolated

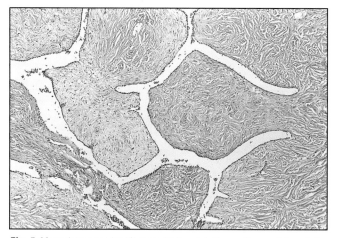

Fig. 5.41 • Pulmonary adenofibroma. Notice club-like papillae reminiscent of ovarian adenofibroma.

metastasis occurring as a solitary coin lesion is much rarer, but can be observed in up to 9% of cases.[224] Endobronchial metastasis simulating primary bronchogenic carcinoma is another unusual growth pattern which has been described with carcinoma of the colon, rectum, biliary tract, pancreas, breast, uterus, and kidney. The latter, in particular, may often adopt a polypoid endobronchial configuration. Another pattern of metastasis to the lungs that may cause difficulties for diagnosis is one characterized by miliary spread of microscopic tumor nodules that may closely simulate an infectious process, such as tuberculosis or sarcoidosis, on clinical and radiographic evaluation. A related form of metastatic spread to the lungs is that of lymphangitis carcinomatosa, in which diffuse tumor emboli are seen plugging thin-walled bronchial vessels. Such a pattern of spread will often present as a bilateral reticulo-nodular infiltrate that can lead to confusion with interstitial lung disease or vascular embolic phenomena on imaging studies. One unusual form of metastatic spread to the lung that may pose serious difficulties for diagnosis is that characterized by growth of the tumor cells along the lining of the alveolar walls, resulting in a picture that closely simulates a primary bronchioloalveolar cell carcinoma of the lung. Such peculiar growth has been described with metastases from the colon, rectum, gallbladder, breast, pancreas, stomach, prostate, thyroid, and kidney. Examination of deeper sections may be necessary in such cases to identify areas in which the tumor loses its bronchioloalveolar-like appearance and displays the more conventional features of the primary lesion.

Another rare phenomenon described in the lung is the occurrence of pulmonary metastases from supposedly "benign" tumors. Such cases are exemplified by "benign metastasizing leiomyoma," which refers to the presence of single, or sometimes multiple, cytologically benign, smooth muscle tumors in the lung.[225,226] In the majority of cases, the patients are women with a history of previous removal of a uterine leiomyoma or multiple benign leiomyomas many years previously. Although the nature of these lesions remains controversial, they have been considered by some to represent late metastases of very low-grade, well-differentiated uterine leiomyosarcomas.[226] A similar occurrence has been observed with other types of "benign" tumors, including meningioma, thymoma, and giant cell tumor of bone (osteoclastoma).[223]

Tumors of the pleura

The pleura can be involved by a number of neoplastic conditions that may range from benign to malignant. In addition, it is a common site of metastases. More recently, it has also been recognized as the site of rare primary *pyothorax-related lymphomas*, which appear to be Epstein–Barr virus-related.[227] For this reason, correct interpretation of pleural biopsies should include not only obtaining adequate material for examination but also appropriate clinical and radiographic information from the clinician.

Malignant mesothelioma

Malignant mesothelioma of the pleura may occur over a wide age range, but is most commonly observed in adults over the age of 50, and shows a strong male predilection (3:1). The majority of pleural mesotheliomas are related to asbestos exposure, although it must be kept in mind, in this context, that lung carcinoma is more often seen as a complication of asbestos exposure than mesothelioma. The tumors usually develop many years after exposure (>20 years); in some cases, a clear history of exposure to asbestos may be difficult to obtain.[228,229] This long latency accounts for the continued significant (and, in many places, increasing) number of new cases of mesothelioma, despite recognition of the dangers of asbestos quite some years ago. The exposure may be occupational or through environmental factors unrelated to the workplace.[230]

The diagnosis of mesothelioma depends on a constellation of findings, including a history of asbestos exposure, clinical signs and symptoms, radiographic findings, histopathologic features, and immunohistochemical and ultrastructural studies.[231–234] There is often a history of insidious onset of pleuritic pain and shortness of breath. Pleural effusions often occur and may be bloody and voluminous. Clinically, there is an overlap between mesothelioma and adenocarcinoma involving the pleural surface. Moreover, adenocarcinoma can closely mimic mesothelioma histologically. For this reason, a multimodal approach to diagnosis will yield the best results, including conventional histology, special stains, and electron microscopy. In addition, since mesotheliomas harbor distinctive karyotypic abnormalities, the cytogenetic analysis of cells obtained from pleural effusions can be diagnostically discriminatory.[235] Thoracotomy with full examination of the pleural space offers the greatest certainty for diagnosis; however, thoracoscopy with visual inspection of the pleural surface and direct biopsy of the lesion will also yield acceptable results.

The biologic behavior of malignant mesothelioma is almost uniformly dismal. The average interval between onset of symptoms and death is 18 months, and current treatment for the disease is generally ineffective, with the exception of a minority of cases amenable to radical surgery.[236] Few factors affect prognosis, but certain histologic subtypes such as the sarcomatoid variant have been associated with more aggressive behavior. Mesotheliomas only rarely give rise to clinically detected metastases (although, due to the increasing incidence, such cases are becoming more frequent) and most often they spread locally within the thoracic cavity. The tumors start as small, raised areas on the surface of the pleura that progress to form coalescent nodules, which eventually turn into large pleural masses. The classical gross picture of mesothelioma is that of a thick layer of fibrocollagenous tissue which totally encases the lung. Fleshy tumors that invade the underlying lung parenchyma may be particularly difficult to differentiate from primary lung adenocarcinomas with a pseudomesotheliomatous growth pattern.[237] In recent years, a rare subset of localized mesothelioma's have been identified and these are associated with more frequent resectability and a notably better prognosis.[237a]

Malignant mesothelioma can assume three basic histologic forms: (1) epithelioid; (2) sarcomatoid; or (3) mixed (biphasic). More often, areas showing features and admixtures of these three types may be encountered within a single tumor. Roughly 70% of mesotheliomas will be predominantly epithelioid, 25% predominantly biphasic, and 5% predominantly sarcomatoid. There also exist very rare well-differentiated papillary mesotheliomas, which carry an improved prognosis.[238]

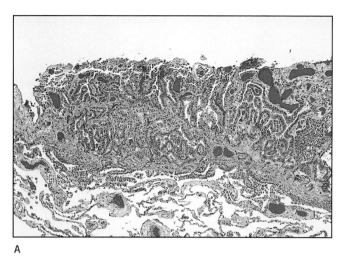
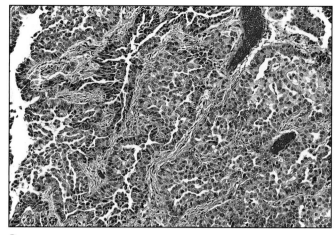

A

B

Fig. 5.42 • (A) Epithelioid mesothelioma with plaque-like growth along the pleural surface; **(B)** higher magnification showing tubulopapillary pattern of growth.

Epithelioid mesothelioma is characterized by a proliferation of round to polygonal tumor cells with abundant densely eosinophilic cytoplasm and bland nuclei that are often devoid of mitotic activity. The tumor cells may adopt a variety of growth patterns, the most common of which is the tubulo-papillary type, characterized by the formation of tubular structures lined by cuboidal cells admixed with papillary structures which contain delicate fibrovascular cores (Fig. 5.42). Psammoma bodies can occasionally be encountered in these areas but are of no diagnostic significance. A microglandular growth pattern can also be observed; this is characterized by a proliferation of small glandular structures lined by a single layer of cuboidal to columnar epithelium. This pattern can be very difficult to distinguish from metastatic pleural spread of adenocarcinoma. The tumor cells can also grow as solid sheets of large polygonal cells with round nuclei and occasionally prominent nucleoli. This variant is known as deciduoid mesothelioma.[239] Other unusual growth patterns include tumors composed predominantly of small dark cells with high nuclear-to-cytoplasmic ratios simulating small cell carcinoma; tumors with large, bizarre cells, including pleomorphic giant cells that may simulate anaplastic carcinoma of the lung or a metastatic sarcoma; tumors containing an abundance of

inflammatory cells admixed with the neoplastic mesothelial component (so-called lymphohistiocytoid mesothelioma[240]); tumors composed of clear cells that may simulate renal cell carcinoma;[240a] tumors showing signet-ring cell features simulating metastases from a gastric malignancy and tumors with prominent rhabdoid cytoplasmic inclusions, these latter cases apparently being associated with an especially aggressive course.[240b] A prominent myxoid stroma containing abundant acid mucopolysaccharides (hyaluronic acid) is another distinctive, albeit infrequent, feature of epithelioid mesothelioma (Fig. 5.43) and this maybe associated with a somewhat better prognosis.[240c]

Sarcomatoid mesothelioma is composed of a fascicular proliferation of spindle cells with oval nuclei, scant amphophilic cytoplasm, and occasionally prominent nucleoli. The tumor cells can display a fibrosarcoma-like appearance with elongated fascicles showing herringbone formations and abundant intercellular collagen deposition, or may adopt a prominent storiform appearance indistinguishable from that of so-called MFH, although pleomorphism is not usually a striking feature (Fig. 5.44). When stromal collagenization becomes more advanced, the tumor will adopt a prominent desmoplastic appearance, a situation that may be difficult to

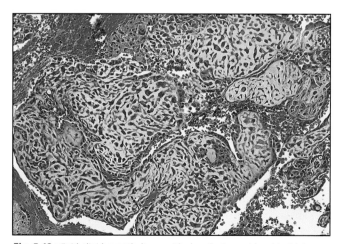

Fig. 5.43 • Epithelioid mesothelioma with abundant myxoid matrix rich in hyaluronic acid.

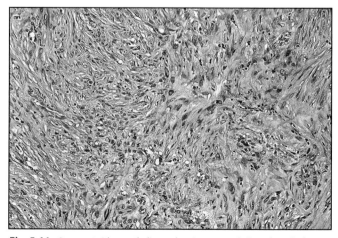

Fig. 5.44 • Sarcomatoid mesothelioma showing a population of atypical spindle cells in a fibrous stroma.

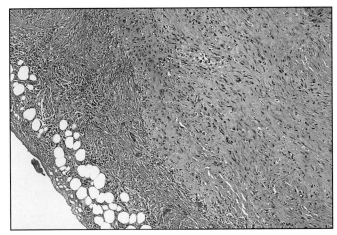

Fig. 5.45 • Desmoplastic mesothelioma. Notice irregular infiltration of fat.

distinguish from fibrous pleurisy on small biopsy samples (Fig. 5.45). In this context, invasion into soft tissues of the chest wall (e.g., adipose tissue) is an important diagnostic clue. In general, sarcomatoid mesotheliomas show more atypia than their epithelioid counterparts, and often display mitotic activity and foci of necrosis. Occasional cases showing foci of osseous and cartilaginous metaplasia have also been described.

Biphasic mesothelioma is characterized by a combination of easily recognizable epithelioid and sarcomatoid elements in varying proportions.

Because mesotheliomas may adopt a variety of morphologic appearances, and because many metastatic neoplasms to the pleura can mimic the clinical, radiographic, and gross appearance of mesothelioma, the diagnosis of this tumor may be very difficult to establish with confidence in many cases. Even distinction from reactive mesothelial proliferation is often very difficult[241] and, while necrosis, cytologic atypia, and pattern of staining for EMA may be helpful, the demonstration of convincing invasion into adjacent subpleural tissue is usually required. Diagnosis is usually achieved by the application of a combination of techniques, including histochemical, immunohistochemical, and ultrastructural examination. The most frequently used histochemical stain is PAS with diastase; the presence of strong PAS positivity within the tumor cells after diastase digestion, indicative of epithelial mucin, strongly argues against a diagnosis of malignant mesothelioma, although rare positive cells are a recognized occasional finding. Alcian blue stains hyaluronic acid positively in mesothelioma; the bluish positive reaction is characteristically removed by digestion with hyaluronidase.

Immunohistochemistry is currently the most widely applied technique for establishing the diagnosis of mesothelioma. Unfortunately, there are no reliable or specific markers that can unequivocally establish the diagnosis of malignant mesothelioma, and the diagnosis is therefore one of exclusion based on the pattern of immunoreactivity for a panel of antibodies.[231–233,242–244] Mesotheliomas are universally positive for keratin and EMA; however, because of the wide distribution of these markers in other epithelial neoplasms, they may be of limited value for diagnosis. Current recommendations for immunostaining of malignant mesothelioma include using a panel of at least two positive and two negative markers. The best discriminators among the antibodies considered to be

"negative" markers for mesothelioma include CEA, MOC31, Ber-EP4, and B72.3, and the best "positive" markers include cytokeratin 5/6 and calretinin.[243] More recently, MUC4 has also been proposed as a valuable discriminant negative marker,[245] while D2-40 and podoplanin have been recognized to be quite specific positive markers.[245a] However, it is important to mention that many of the "negative" markers can be positive in a small percentage of cases of malignant mesothelioma, and several of the "positive" markers have been demonstrated in adenocarcinomas of non-mesothelial origin and other conditions that may enter the differential diagnosis.[244,246] It is also important to note that smooth muscle markers such as actin and desmin can also occasionally be expressed in mesothelioma, particularly in the sarcomatoid elements, potentially leading to confusion with smooth muscle tumors.[247] In fact, immunohistochemistry is quite often not discriminatory in the differential diagnosis of sarcomatoid mesotheliomas.[248] Electron microscopy has been accepted for many years as the "gold standard" for the diagnosis of mesothelioma.[231–233] Mesothelioma cells (at least, those with epithelioid morphology) are characterized by a profusion of markedly elongated surface microvilli in the absence of secretory cytoplasmic granules. Ultrastructural examination, however, may not be feasible in all cases when adequately fixed material is not available for electron microscopy, and the characteristic elongated microvilli may not be apparent in poorly differentiated tumors or in sarcomatoid mesotheliomas. In recent years, a number of purportedly specific mesothelial markers have been introduced for the diagnosis of malignant mesothelioma, including thrombomodulin, calretinin, cadherins, CD44, HBME-1, WT1, and keratin 5/6.[249–253] However, exceptions to the rules and a broad catalogue of cross-reactivity with other tumors, in particular metastatic carcinoma, have been noted (in at least some cases) for all of these markers, rendering their utility somewhat limited.[244] The diagnosis of mesothelioma thus continues to rely on a multimodal approach that incorporates clinical features, gross and microscopic features, immunohistochemistry, and electron microscopy for arriving at a definitive diagnosis.[231,233]

Pseudomesotheliomatous adenocarcinoma

Great attention has been focused in recent years on a form of peripheral lung adenocarcinoma that can mimic clinically, radiologically, and histologically a diffuse malignant mesothelioma. The term pseudomesotheliomatous adenocarcinoma was coined for these lesions by Harwood and associates.[254] These tumors are included here because of their ability to simulate closely a primary malignant mesothelioma, and because of their predominant pleural site of involvement. Several studies delineating this condition have been published in the recent literature.[237,254–256]

Pseudomesotheliomatous adenocarcinoma occurs in older patients and is more frequent in men than women. The clinical symptoms are indistinguishable from those of malignant mesothelioma, and include chest pain, dyspnea, cough, and signs of an infiltrative pleural tumor. The most common chest radiographic finding is pleural effusion with or without pleural masses. A history of asbestos exposure was present in up to 21% of patients in one study.[255] A smoking history is elicited in up to 73% of cases. Grossly, the tumors grow as thick, fleshy

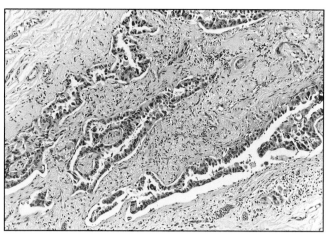

Fig. 5.46 • Pseudomesotheliomatous adenocarcinoma involving the pleura with focal tubulopapillary growth pattern.

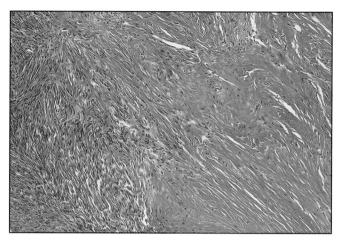

Fig. 5.47 • Solitary fibrous tumor of the pleura showing transitions between solid spindle cell areas and areas of diffuse sclerosis.

pleural plaques and masses that extend along the pleural surface and encase the lung. Histologically, there is infiltration of the pleura by nests or sheets of cells that focally form glands or tubulopapillary structures (Fig. 5.46). Psammoma bodies can also be found, particularly in the papillary areas. Isolated glands lying within a fibrotic stroma are a common finding. The glandular lumens are often filled with PAS-positive, diastase-resistant mucin or intracytoplasmic vacuoles. Immunohistochemical studies show strong positivity for polyclonal CEA and low-molecular-weight cytokeratins in 100% of cases, followed by BER-EP4 (60%), Leu-M1 (53%), and B72.3 (47%).[255] The majority of cases express more than one of these antigens at the same time.

It has been proposed that adenocarcinoma simulating mesothelioma might originate from a relatively small subpleural adenocarcinoma. Such tumors have been identified microscopically or grossly in autopsy cases reported in the literature.[254,255] In some cases, however, the possibility of a metastasis from an occult extrapulmonary site cannot be ruled out as a source of the tumor in the pleura. The prognosis for these tumors is quite poor, and has been shown to be at least as bad as that of mesothelioma. The importance of distinguishing this form of adenocarcinoma from mesothelioma lies mostly in its medicolegal implications, rather than in differences in prognosis or clinical response to treatment.

Mesenchymal tumors of the pleura

Primary mesenchymal tumors of the pleura are relatively rare. The vast majority are benign and characteristically grow as well-circumscribed, polypoid, and pedunculated lesions attached to the parietal or visceral pleura. Primary pleural sarcomas are exceedingly rare; most sarcomatous tumors of the pleura correspond to either metastases or sarcomatoid mesotheliomas.

Solitary fibrous tumor is the most common benign mesenchymal pleural neoplasm. These tumors were first described by Klemperer & Rabin as a form of localized fibrous mesothelioma.[257] Subsequent ultrastructural studies by Scharifker & Kaneko[258] and others demonstrated that the tumor cells did not have features of mesothelial cells and showed fibroblastic features, thus leading to the designation of submesothelial

fibroma, localized fibrous tumor, or solitary fibrous tumor.[259,260] The tumors occur most often in adults between the fifth and sixth decades of life. Most patients are asymptomatic, but symptoms of chest pain, dyspnea, and fever have been reported.[261–263] Some tumors show a rather characteristic association with hypoglycemia. The tumors are grossly well-circumscribed, polypoid, and encapsulated masses that may reach up to 20 cm in diameter, and are often attached to the pleura by a short pedicle. The tumors usually compress the lung and may thus mimic a subpleural lung mass on chest roentgenograms.

Histologically, they are characterized by their variegated morphologic appearance, a feature that often leads to misdiagnosis as other mesenchymal neoplasms. Two basic elements are commonly encountered in varying proportions: a solid spindle cell component, and a diffuse sclerosing component[120] (Fig. 5.47). The solid spindle cell component can adopt a variety of growth patterns that may be mistaken for other types of well-defined mesenchymal neoplasm, including a short storiform pattern reminiscent of fibrohistiocytic tumors, hemangiopericytic, angiofibromatous, and herring-bone patterns, areas showing a wavy neural configuration with

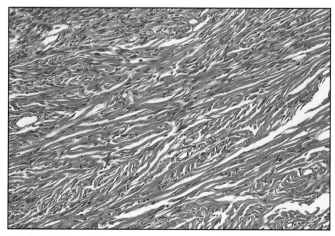

Fig. 5.48 • Solitary fibrous tumor of pleura, solid spindle cell area, with deposition of longitudinal strands of rope-like collagen.

prominent neural-type palisading, and a fascicular growth pattern indistinguishable from monophasic synovial sarcoma. In addition, degenerative stromal changes such as prominent myxoid matrix deposition, degeneration of collagen, metaplastic bone formation, formation of "amianthoid" fibers, and multinucleated stromal cells can be present, introducing added difficulties for diagnosis. The tumor cells are usually oval-shaped and contain bland nuclei with scattered chromatin and inconspicuous nucleoli surrounded by an indistinct rim of amphophilic cytoplasm. The cytoplasm of the tumor cells often shows long dendritic prolongations that are best appreciated with the use of special stains or electron microscopy. A highly distinctive appearance of these tumors is the deposition of rope-like strands of keloidal collagen in parallel distribution alongside the spindle cells (Fig. 5.48). Mitotic activity is absent or minimal in most cases. The diffuse sclerosing pattern consists of paucicellular areas showing prominent collagen fiber deposition and stromal hyalinization, particularly centered around vessels. Admixtures and transitions between the areas of diffuse sclerosis and solid spindle cell proliferation are commonly seen. The diagnosis rests on the identification of the characteristic histopathologic appearance in conjunction with the clinical setting and gross features of the lesion (i.e., pleural-based polypoid and pedunculated tumor mass).

Immunohistochemistry has an important supportive role in diagnosis by helping to rule out alternate lines of differentiation. The tumor cells are uniformly positive for vimentin, but are negative for keratin, EMA, actin, desmin, and S-100 protein. CD34 has been shown to react positively with the spindle cells of solitary fibrous tumor in up to 80% of cases.[121,122] bcl-2 was found to be uniformly and strongly positive in the tumor cells in all cases in two studies.[111,264] In addition, CD99 immunopositivity is a relatively consistent finding.[265] None of these markers is specific, and they may be positive in a variety of other spindle cell tumors, hence they must always be interpreted within the clinical context and in correlation with the histology.

Solitary fibrous tumor is most often a benign neoplasm that is cured by local excision alone. Between 5 and 10% of tumors, however, are characterized by poor circumscription, infiltration of adjacent structures, and high mitotic activity and nuclear pleomorphism, and therefore qualify for a diagnosis of malignancy. Conceptually, a malignant solitary fibrous tumor is best regarded as a fibrosarcoma of the pleura.[266] The cut-off point between a benign solitary fibrous tumor and a malignant one is not clear. England et al. have proposed the presence of hypercellularity, pleomorphism, necrosis, and more than 4 mitoses per 10 hpf as criteria for malignancy in these tumors.[260] However, we have observed cases in which well-circumscribed, polypoid, and encapsulated tumors exhibited morphologic features of malignancy, including necrosis, hypercellularity, nuclear pleomorphism, and mitotic activity, but behaved in an indolent fashion.[120] We therefore personally believe that poor circumscription and infiltration of adjacent structures must be present in addition to cytologic atypia before a diagnosis of malignancy is rendered for these tumors.

Smooth muscle tumors of the pleura have also been recognized more recently.[267,268] These tumors may present as pleural-based masses or as diffuse pleural thickening reminiscent of diffuse malignant mesothelioma. Clinically, the patients present with symptoms of chest pain, cough, dyspnea,

and/or fever in the absence of a history of tumor elsewhere. Histologically, pleural leiomyosarcomas are similar to their soft tissue counterparts. They consist of a spindle cell proliferation of elongated cells with moderate amounts of eosinophilic cytoplasm, and cigar-shaped nuclei with varying degrees of atypia and mitotic activity. Immunohistochemical studies demonstrate reactivity for smooth muscle markers and vimentin, and negative results with epithelial markers, CD34, and *bcl-2*. The diagnosis is dependent on the recognition of the distinctive histopathologic features of smooth muscle tumors at any location, the immunohistochemical or ultrastructural demonstration of smooth muscle phenotype and absence of other differentiation, and the absence of a similar tumor elsewhere in the body on thorough clinical examination.

Synovial sarcomas of the pleura have also been recognized.[269] These tumors occur primarily in children, adolescents, and young adults. The clinical course is characterized by multiple recurrences and metastasis that may lead to the death of the patient. Pleural synovial sarcomas exhibit the same histologic, immunohistochemical, and ultrastructural features as synovial sarcomas in other locations (see Ch. 24). All the tumors described corresponded to the biphasic variant of synovial sarcoma, although monophasic lesions also occur. The main differential diagnosis is with biphasic malignant mesothelioma. In contrast to malignant mesothelioma, pleural synovial sarcomas occur in younger patients, show rapid growth with the formation of a well-circumscribed tumor nodule rather than a diffusely infiltrating mass, and are more amenable to treatment.

Pseudomesotheliomatous (epithelioid) angiosarcoma of the pleura is another recently described condition.[270,271] Such tumors are characterized by a proliferation of large epithelioid vascular endothelial cells that can closely mimic an epithelial neoplasm. The tumors present clinically with diffuse pleural thickening and hemorrhagic effusion. Histologically, the lesions show features that range from those of epithelioid hemangioendothelioma to frank epithelioid angiosarcoma. The tumors are characterized by sheets and clusters of tumor cells showing large vesicular nuclei with occasional prominent nucleoli and abundant eosinophilic cytoplasm containing frequent cytoplasmic vacuoles (Fig. 5.49A). A tubulopapillary growth pattern similar to that in mesothelioma can also be seen (Fig. 5.49B). Immunohistochemical studies showed strong positivity for vimentin and weak, focal positivity for keratin in all cases in one study.[270] The tumor cells also coexpress at least two of the more common endothelial cell markers, including CD31, CD34, factor VIII-related antigen, and *Ulex europaeus* agglutinin-I. The clinical behavior of these tumors is quite aggressive, often with disseminated disease at presentation and death within a few months of diagnosis.

Rare tumors of the pleura

Pleural thymomas are rare lesions that may present as a localized tumor mass or as a diffuse pleural thickening mimicking malignant mesothelioma.[272,273] The patients are generally adult individuals who present with a localized pleural mass in the absence of mediastinal involvement. No association with myasthenia gravis has been noted in such cases. Histologically the tumors are essentially identical to those occurring in the anterior mediastinum (see Ch. 21) and are characterized by a

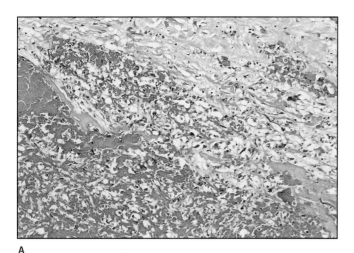 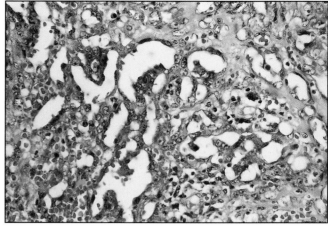

A   B

Fig. 5.49 • **(A)** Pseudomesotheliomatous angiosarcoma of the pleura; **(B)** tubulopapillary formations in pseudomesotheliomatous angiosarcoma of the pleura.

biphasic cell population composed of epithelial cells admixed with lymphocytes, arranged in lobules and separated by thick fibrous bands. A spindle cell morphology has also been described. The epithelial tumor cells are positive for keratin antibodies, a finding that facilitates the diagnosis. In cases of spindle cell thymoma, the differential diagnosis with sarcomatoid mesothelioma and solitary fibrous tumor may arise. Complete surgical resection is the treatment of choice for localized tumors. However, in cases with diffuse pleural involvement or when the tumor is incompletely resected, radiation therapy may be indicated.

Adenomatoid tumors have been described arising in the pleura.[274] The lesions present as small pleural nodules discovered incidentally during surgery for unrelated intrapulmonary masses. The tumors consist of a proliferation of epithelioid cells with prominent vacuoles and tubular spaces in a fibrous stroma similar to that of adenomatoid tumors at other sites. Keratin stains are helpful in demonstrating the epithelial nature of the cells in these lesions.

Mucoepidermoid carcinoma is another recently described type of primary pleural malignancy.[275] These tumors are characterized by the occurrence of a localized pleural-based mass that on histologic examination shows islands of atypical squamous epithelium admixed with scattered mucocytes that are strongly positive for mucicarmine stains. One of the reported cases was characterized by a prominent fibrous stroma containing abundant spindled fibroblasts, raising the diagnostic consideration of a biphasic mesothelioma. The localized nature of the tumor, however, and the presence of tumor islands showing obvious mucoepidermoid features of differentiation should permit proper identification of the lesion.[275]

Pleuropulmonary blastomas are a group of tumors that occur predominantly in children and that encompass various neoplasms previously designated as sarcomas arising in congenital cystic adenomatoid malformations or bronchogenic cysts, and as mesenchymal cystic hamartoma.[276–279] Grossly, the lesions may present as cystic or solid tumors that can vary in size from a few centimeters to more than 20 cm in diameter. Purely cystic lesions are rare. Histologically, the tumors are quite different from pulmonary blastoma of the adult (see p. 193) in that an immature epithelial component is not part of the lesion. Pleuropulmonary blastoma of infancy can show a variegated histologic appearance, with areas of chondrosarcoma, osteosarcoma, leiomyosarcoma, rhabdomyosarcoma, or undifferentiated mesenchymal component. When the tumors are cystic, areas of uninvolved normal epithelium may be seen lining the cystic structures. Immunohistochemical stains will be of value only to confirm the mesenchymal nature of the lesion and to rule out epithelial or mesothelial differentiation. The prognosis for these patients depends largely on the staging at the time of diagnosis and the grading of the sarcomatous elements, but in general these are aggressive neoplasms with a 5-year survival probability of less than 50% in cases with a solid component.[277] The infrequent purely cystic lesions have a better outcome.

References

1. Garfinkel L, Silverberg E 1991 Lung cancer and smoking trends in the United States over the past 25 years. CA 41: 137–145
2. Rubin S A 1991 Lung cancer: past, present, and future. J Thorac Imaging 7: 1–8
3. Stanley K, Stjernsward J 1989 Lung cancer: a worldwide health problem. Chest 96 (suppl): 1s–5s
4. Gritz E R 1993 Lung cancer: now, more than ever, a feminist issue. CA 43: 197–199
5. Aronchick J M 1990 Clinical aspects of lung cancer. Semin Roentgenol 25: 5–11
6. Devesa S S, Shaw G L, Blot W J 1991 Changing patterns of lung carcinoma. Cancer Epidemiol Biomarkers Prev 1: 29–34
7. Travis W D, Travis L B, Devesa S S 1995 Lung cancer. Cancer 75: 191–202
8. Rosado-de-Christenson M L, Templeton P A, Moran C A 1994 Bronchogenic carcinoma: radiologic/pathologic correlation. Radiographics 14: 429–446
9. Sobin L, Yesner R 1981 Histologic typing of lung tumors. International histologic classification of tumors, 2nd edn. World Health Organization, Geneva, vol 1
10. Fraser R G, Pare J A P, Pare P D et al. 1989 Neoplastic diseases of the lung. In: Fraser R G, Pare J A P, Pare P D et al. (eds) Diagnosis of diseases of the chest, 3rd edn. Saunders, Philadelphia, PA, p 1327–1399
11. Viallet J, Minna J D 1990 Dominant oncogenes and tumor suppressor genes in the pathogenesis of lung cancer. Am J Respir Cell Mol Biol 2: 225–237
12. Takahashi T, Takahashi Y, Suzuki H et al. 1991 The *p53* gene is frequently mutated in small cell lung cancer with a distinctive nucleotide substitution pattern. Oncogene 6: 1775–1778

13. Harris C C, Hollstein M 1993 Clinical implications of the *p53* tumor-suppressor gene. N Engl J Med 329: 1318–1327
14. Rodenhuis S, Slebos R J C 1992 Significance of *ras* oncogene activation in human lung cancer. Cancer Res 52: 2665–2669
15. Baylin S B, Herman J G, Graaf J R et al. 1998 Alterations in DNA methylation. A fundamental aspect of neoplasia. Adv Cancer Res 72: 141–196
16. Zuchbauer-Muller S, Fong K M, Virmani A K et al. 2001 Aberrant promoter methylation in multiple genes in non-small cell cancers. Cancer Res 61: 249–255
17. Damman R, Li C, Yoon J-H et al. 2000 Epigenetic inactivation of a RAS associated domain family protein from the lung tumor suppressor locus 3p21.3. Nat Genet 25: 315–319
18. Paez J G, Janne P A, Lee J C et al. 2004. *EGFR* mutations in lung cancer: correlation with clinical reponse to gefitinib therapy. Science 304: 1497–1500
19. Grippi M A 1990 Clinical aspects of lung cancer. Semin Roentgenol 25: 12–24
20. Boyards M C 1991 Clinical manifestations of carcinoma of the lung. J Thorac Imaging 7: 21–28
21. Haque A K 1991 Pathology of carcinoma of the lung: an up-date on current concepts. J Thorac Imaging 7: 9–20
22. Pietra G G 1990 The pathology of carcinoma of the lung. Semin Roentgenol 25: 25–33
23. Yesner R 1988 Histopathology of lung cancer. Semin Ultrasound CT MR 9: 4–26
24. Wilson R W, Frazier A 1998 Pathological and radiological correlation of endobronchial neoplasms: part II, malignant tumors. Ann Diagn Pathol 2: 31–54
25. Kuriyama K, Tateishi R, Doi O et al. 1977 Prevalence of air bronchograms in small peripheral carcinomas of the lung on thin-section CT: comparison with benign lesions. AJR 128: 893–914
26. White C S, Templeton P A 1993 Radiologic manifestations of bronchogenic cancer. Clin Chest Med 14: 56–67
27. Tsuta K, Ishii G, Yoh K et al. 2004 Primary lung carcinoma with signet-ring cell carcinoma components. Clinicopathologic analysis of 39 cases. Am J Surg Pathol 28: 868–874
28. Liebow A A 1960 Bronchiolo-alveolar carcinoma. Advances in internal medicine. Year Book, Chicago, vol 10
29. Moran C A, Hochholzer L, Fishback N F et al. 1992 Mucinous (so-called colloid) carcinoma of lung. Mod Pathol 5: 634–638
30. Graeme-Cook F, Mark E J 1991 Pulmonary mucinous cystic tumors of borderline malignancy. Hum Pathol 22: 185–190
31. Kragel P J, Devaney K O, Meth B M et al. 1990 Mucinous cystadenoma of the lung: a report of two cases with immunohistochemical and ultrastructural analysis. Arch Pathol Lab Med 114: 1053–1056
32. Higashiyama M, Doi O, Kodama K et al. 1992 Cystic mucinous adenocarcinoma of the lung: two cases of cystic variant of mucinous-producing lung adenocarcinoma. Chest 101: 763–766
33. Moran C A 1995 Mucin-rich tumors of the lung. Adv Anat Pathol 2: 299–305
34. Silver S A, Askin F B 1997 True papillary carcinoma of the lung. A distinct clinicopathologic entity. Am J Surg Pathol 21: 43–51
35. Katzenstein A-L A, Prioleau P G, Askin F B 1980 The histologic spectrum and significance of clear cell change in lung carcinoma. Cancer 45: 943–947
36. Dulmet-Brender E, Jaubert F, Huchou G 1986 Exophytic endobronchial epidermoid carcinoma. Cancer 57: 1358–1364
37. Suster S, Huczar M, Herczeg E 1987 Spindle cell squamous carcinoma of lung. A light microscopic, immunohistochemical and ultrastructural study of a case. Histopathology 11: 871–878
38. Nappi O, Glasner S D, Swanson P E et al. 1994 Biphasic and monophasic sarcomatoid carcinomas of the lung. A reappraisal of "carcinosarcomas" and "spindle-cell carcinomas." Am J Clin Pathol 102: 331–340
39. Wick M R, Ritter J H, Nappi O 1995 Inflammatory sarcomatoid carcinoma of the lung. Hum Pathol 26: 1014–1021
40. Brambilla E, Moro D, Veale D et al. 1992 Basal cell (basaloid) carcinoma of the lung. A new morphologic and phenotypic entity with separate prognostic significance. Hum Pathol 23: 993–998
41. Chang Y L, Wu C T, Shih J Y et al. 2002. New aspects in clinicopathologic and oncogene studies of 23 pulmonary lymphoepithelioma-like carcinomas. Am J Surg Pathol 26: 715–723
42. Butler A E, Colby T V, Weiss L M et al. 1989 Lymphoepithelioma-like carcinoma of the lung. Am J Surg Pathol 13: 629–632
43. Fishback N F, Travis W D, Moran C A et al. 1994 Pleomorphic (spindle/giant cell) carcinoma of the lung. Cancer 73: 2936–2945
44. Rossi G, Cavazza A, Sturm N et al. 2003 Pulmonary carcinomas with pleomorphic, sarcomatoid or sarcomatous elements. A clinicopathologic and immunohistochemical study of 75 cases. Am J Surg Pathol 27: 311–324
45. Attanoos R L, Papagiannis A, Suttinont P et al. 1998 Pulmonary giant cell carcinoma: pathological entity or morphological phenotype? Histopathology 32: 225–231
46. Przygodzki R M, Koss M N, Moran C A et al. 1996 Pleomorphic (giant and spindle cell) carcinoma is genetically distinct from adenocarcinoma and squamous cell carcinoma by K-*ras*-2 and *p53* analysis. Am J Clin Pathol 106: 487–492
47. Tamboli P, Toprani T H, Amin M B et al. 2004. Carcinoma of lung with rhabdoid features. Hum Pathol 35: 8–13
48. Sridhar K S, Bounassi M J, Raub W et al. 1990 Clinical features of adenosquamous lung carcinoma in 127 patients. Am Rev Respir Dis 142: 19–23
49. Naunheim K S, Taylor J R, Skosey C et al. 1987 Adenosquamous lung carcinoma: clinical characteristics, treatment and prognosis. Ann Thorac Surg 44: 462–469
50. Fitzgibbons P L, Kern W H 1985 Adenosquamous carcinoma of the lung: a clinical and pathological study of seven cases. Hum Pathol 16: 463–467
51. Travis W D, Gal A A, Colby T V et al. 1998 Reproducibility of neuroendocrine lung tumor classification. Hum Pathol 29: 272–279
52. Gould V E, Linnoila R I, Memoli V A et al. 1983 Neuroendocrine cells and neuroendocrine neoplasms of the lung. Pathol Annu 18: 287–305
53. Mooi W J, Dewar A, Springall D et al. 1988 Non-small cell lung carcinoma with neuroendocrine features. A light microscopic, immunohistochemical, and ultrastructural study of 11 cases. Histopathology 13: 329–334
54. Travis W D, Linnoila R I, Tsokos M G et al. 1991 Neuroendocrine tumors of the lung with proposed criteria for large cell neuroendocrine carcinomas. An ultrastructural, immunohistochemical, and flow cytometric study of 35 cases. Am J Surg Pathol 16: 529–553
55. Jiang S-X, Kameya T, Shoji M 1998 Large cell neuroendocrine carcinoma of the lung. A histologic and immunohistochemical study of 22 cases. Am J Surg Pathol 22: 526–537
56. Ricci C, Patrassi N, Massa R et al. 1973 Carcinoid syndrome in bronchial adenoma. Am J Surg 126: 671–675
57. Minna J D, Pass H I, Gladstein E et al. 1989 Cancer of the lung. In: DeVita V T, Hellman S, Rosenberg S A (eds) Cancer. Principles and practice of oncology, 3rd edn. J B Lippincott, Philadelphia, PA, p 591
58. Cebelin M S 1980 Melanocytic bronchial carcinoid tumor. Cancer 46: 1843–1848
59. Grazer R, Cohen S M, Jacobs J B et al. 1982 Melanin-containing peripheral carcinoid of the lung. Am J Surg Pathol 6: 73–78
60. Gal A A, Koss M N, Hochholzer L et al. 1993 Pigmented pulmonary carcinoid tumor: an immunohistochemical and ultrastructural study. Arch Pathol Lab Med 117: 832–836
61. Sklar J L, Churg A, Bensch K G 1980 Oncocytic carcinoid tumor of the lung. Am J Surg Pathol 4: 287–292
62. Wise W S, Bonder D, Aikawa M et al. 1982 Carcinoid tumor of lung with varied histology. Am J Surg Pathol 6: 261–267
63. Du EZ, Goldstraw P, Zacharias J et al. 2004. TTF-1 expression is specific for lung primary in typical and atypical carcinoids: TTF-1-positive carcinoids are predominantly in peripheral location. Hum Pathol 35: 825–831
64. Arrigoni M G, Woolner L B, Bernatz P E 1985 Atypical carcinoid tumors of the lung. J Thorac Cardiovasc Surg 89: 8–15
65. Paladugu R R, Benfield J R, Pak H Y et al. 1989 Bronchopulmonary Kultchitzky cell carcinomas. A new classification scheme for typical and atypical carcinoids. Cancer 64: 1304–1310
66. El-Naggar A K, Ballance W, Abdul-Karim F W et al. 1991 Typical and atypical bronchopulmonary carcinoids: a clinicopathologic and flow cytometric study. Am J Clin Pathol 95: 828–834
67. Travis W D, Rush W, Flieder D B et al. 1998 Survival analysis of 200 pulmonary neuroendocrine tumors with clarification of criteria for atypical carcinoid and its separation from typical carcinoid. Am J Surg Pathol 22: 934–944
68. Beasley M B, Thunnissen F B J M, Brambilla E et al. 2000 Pulmonary atypical carcinoid: predictors of survival in 106 cases. Hum Pathol 31: 1255–1265
69. Kato Y, Ferguson T B, Bennet D E et al. 1969 Oat cell carcinoma of the lung. A review of 138 cases. Cancer 23: 517–523
70. Spiegelman D, Maurer L H, Ware J H et al. 1989 Prognostic factors in small cell carcinoma of the lung. An analysis of 1521 patients. J Clin Oncol 7: 344–356
71. Adelstein D J, Tomashefski J F, Snow N J et al. 1986 Mixed small cell and non-small cell lung cancer. Chest 89: 699–708
72. Nicholson S A, Beasley M B, Brambilla E et al. 2002 Small cell lung carcinoma (SCLC). A clinicopathologic study of 100 cases with surgical specimens. Am J Surg Pathol 26: 1184–1197
73. Radice P A, Matthews M J, Inde D C et al. 1982 The clinical behavior of "mixed" small cell/large cell bronchogenic carcinoma compared to "pure" small cell subtype. Cancer 50: 2894–2903
74. Moran C A 1995 Primary salivary gland-type tumors of the lung. Semin Diagn Pathol 12: 106–122
75. Moran C A, Suster S, Koss M N 1994 Primary adenoid cystic carcinomas of the lung: a clinicopathologic and immunohistochemical study of 16 cases. Cancer 73: 1390–1397
76. Moran C A, Suster S, Koss M N 1992 Acinic cell carcinoma of the lung (Fechner tumor): a clinicopathologic, immunohistochemical, and ultrastructural study of five cases. Am J Surg Pathol 16: 1039–1050
77. Fechner R E, Bentnick B R, Askew J B Jr 1972 Acinic cell tumor of the lung. A histologic and ultrastructural study. Cancer 29: 501–508
78. Yousem S A, Hochholzer L 1987 Mucoepidermoid tumors of the lung. Cancer 60: 1346–1352
79. Wilson R W, Moran C A 1997 Epithelial-myoepithelial carcinoma of the lung: immunohistochemical and ultrastructural observations and review of the literature. Hum Pathol 28: 631–635
80. Moran C A, Suster S, Askin F B et al. 1994 Benign and malignant salivary gland-type mixed tumors of the lung: a clinicopathologic and immunohistochemical study of eight cases. Cancer 73: 2481–2490

81. Fechner R E, Bentnick B R 1973 Ultrastructure of bronchial oncocytoma. Cancer 31: 1451–1457

82. Nielsen A L 1985 Malignant bronchial oncocytoma: a case report and review of the literature. Hum Pathol 16: 852–854

83. Santos-Briz A, Jenron J, Sastre R et al. 1977 Oncocytoma of the lung. Cancer 40: 1330–1336

84. Berho M, Moran C A, Suster S 1995 Malignant mixed epithelial/mesenchymal neoplasms of the lung. Semin Diagn Pathol 12: 123–139

85. Barnard W G 1952 Embryoma of the lung. Thorax 7: 229–234

86. Spencer H 1961 Pulmonary blastomas. J Pathol Bacteriol 82: 161–165

87. Kodama T, Shimosato Y, Watanabe S et al. 1984 Six cases of well differentiated adenocarcinoma simulating fetal lung tubules in the pseudoglandular stage. Comparison with pulmonary blastoma. Am J Surg Pathol 8: 735–744

88. Nakatani Y, Dickersin R, Mark E 1990 Pulmonary endodermal tumor resembling fetal lung. A clinicopathologic study of five cases with immunohistochemical and ultrastructural characterization. Hum Pathol 21: 1095–1104

89. Nakatani Y, Kitamura H, Inayama Y et al. 1998 Pulmonary adenocarcinomas of the fetal lung type. Am J Surg Pathol 22: 399–411

90. Koss M N, Hochholzer L, O'Leary T 1991 Pulmonary blastomas. Cancer 67: 2368–2381

91. Nappi O, Wick M R 1993 Sarcomatoid neoplasms of the respiratory tract. Semin Diagn Pathol 10: 137–147

92. Ludwigsen E 1977 Endobronchial carcinosarcoma. Virchows Arch [A] Pathol Anat Histopathol 373: 293–302

93. Kakos G S, Williams T E, Assor D et al. 1971 Pulmonary carcinosarcoma: Etiologic, therapeutic, and prognostic considerations. J Thorac Cardiovasc Surg 61: 777–783

94. Davis M P, Eagan R T, Weiland L H et al. 1984 Carcinosarcoma of the lung: Mayo Clinic experience and response to chemotherapy. Mayo Clin Proc 59: 598–603

95. Koss M N, Hochholzer L, Frommelt R A 1999 Carcinosarcomas of the lung. A clinicopathologic study of 66 patients. Am J Surg Pathol 23: 1514–1526

96. Suster S 1995 Primary sarcomas of the lung. Semin Diagn Pathol 12: 140–157

97. Moran C A, Suster S, Abbondanzo S L et al. 1997 Primary leiomyosarcomas of the lung: a clinicopathologic and immunohistochemical study of 18 cases. Mod Pathol 10: 121–128

98. Guccion J G, Rosen S H 1972 Bronchopulmonary leiomyosarcoma and fibrosarcoma: a study of 32 cases and review of the literature. Cancer 30: 836–847

99. Wick M R, Scheithauer B W, Piehler J M et al. 1982 Primary pulmonary leiomyosarcoma: a light and electron microscopy study. Arch Pathol Lab Med 106: 510–514

100. Przygodzki R M, Moran C A, Suster S et al. 1995 Primary pulmonary rhabdomyosarcomas: a clinicopathologic and immunohistochemical study of three cases. Mod Pathol 8: 658–661

101. Drennan J M, McCormack R J M 1960 Primary rhabdomyosarcoma of the lung. J Pathol 79: 1960–1962

102. Lee S H, Rengachary S S, Paramesh J 1981 Primary pulmonary rhabdomyosarcoma. Hum Pathol 12: 92–94

103. Murphy J J, Blair G K, Fraser G C et al. 1992 Rhabdomyosarcoma arising within congenital pulmonary cyst. J Pediatr Surg 27: 1364–1366

104. Ueda K, Gruppo R, Unger F et al. 1977 Rhabdomyosarcoma of the lung arising in congenital cystic adenomatoid malformation. Cancer 40: 383–385

105. Roviaro G, Montorsi M, Varoli F et al. 1983 Primary pulmonary tumors of neurogenic origin. Thorax 38: 942–945

106. Malik S K, Behera D, Kalra S et al. 1987 Intrabronchial schwannoma. Scand J Thor Cardiovasc Surg 21: 281–282

107. Bartley T D, Arean V M 1965 Intrapulmonary neurogenic tumors. J Thorac Cardiovasc Surg 50: 114–123

108. Moran C A, Suster S, Koss M N 1997 Primary malignant "triton" tumour of the lung. Histopathology 30: 140-144

109. Zeren H, Moran C A, Suster S et al. 1995 Primary malignant spindle cell neoplasms of the lung with features of monophasic synovial sarcoma: clinicopathologic, immunohistochemical and ultrastructural study of 25 cases. Hum Pathol 26: 474–480

110. Essary L R, Vargas S O, Fletcher C D M 2002 Primary pleuropulmonary synovial sarcoma: reappraisal of a recently described anatomic subset. Cancer 94: 459–469

111. Suster S, Fisher C, Moran C A 1998 Expression of bcl-2 oncoprotein in benign and malignant spindle cell tumors of soft tissue, skin, serosal surfaces and gastrointestinal tract. Am J Surg Pathol 22: 863–872

112. Carswell J, Kraeft N H 1950 Fibrosarcoma of the bronchus. J Thorac Surg 19: 117–123

113. Nascimento A G, Unni K K, Bernatz P E 1982 Sarcomas of the lung. Mayo Clin Proc 57: 355–359

114. Meade J B, Whitwell F, Bickford J K B 1974 Primary hemangiopericytoma of lung. Thorax 29: 1–15

115. Kern W H, Hughes R K, Meyer B W et al. 1979 Malignant fibrous histiocytoma of the lung. Cancer 44: 1793–1801

116. Bedrossian C W M, Veroni R, Unger K M et al. 1979 Pulmonary malignant fibrous histiocytoma. Chest 75: 186–189

117. Lee J T, Shelburne J D, Linder J 1984 Primary malignant fibrous histiocytoma of the lung: a clinicopathologic and ultrastructural study of five cases. Cancer 53: 1124–1130

118. Yousem S A, Hochholzer L 1987 Primary pulmonary hemangiopericytoma. Cancer 59: 549–555

119. Yousem S A, Flynn S D 1988 Intrapulmonary localized fibrous tumor. Intraparenchymal so-called localized fibrous mesothelioma. Am J Clin Pathol 89: 365–369

120. Moran C A, Suster S, Koss M N 1992 The spectrum of histologic growth patterns in benign and malignant solitary fibrous tumors of the pleura. Semin Diagn Pathol 9: 109–180

121. Van de Rijn M, Rouse R V 1994 CD-34. A review. Appl Immunohistochem 2: 71–80

122. Westra W H, Gerald W L, Rosai J 1994 Solitary fibrous tumor. Consistent CD-34 immunoreactivity and occurrence in the orbit. Am J Surg Pathol 18: 992–998

123. Morgenroth A, Pfeuffer H P, Viereck H J et al. 1989 Primary chondrosarcoma of the left inferior lobar bronchus. Respiration 56: 241–244

124. Nosanchuck J S, Weatherbee L 1969 Primary osteogenic sarcoma of the lung. J Thorac Cardiovasc Surg 58: 242–248

125. Colby T V, Bilbao J E, Battifora H et al. 1989 Primary osteosarcoma of the lung. A reappraisal following immunohistologic study. Arch Pathol Lab Med 113: 1147–1150

126. Reingold I M, Amromin G D 1971 Extraosseous chondrosarcoma of the lung. Cancer 28: 491–498

127. Loose J H, El-Naggar A K, Ro J Y et al. 1990 Primary osteosarcoma of the lung. Report of two cases and review of the literature. J Thorac Cardiovasc Surg 100: 867–873

128. Ognibene F P, Steis R G, Macher A M et al. 1985 Kaposi's sarcoma causing pulmonary infiltrates and respiratory failure in the acquired immunodeficiency syndrome. Ann Intern Med 102: 471–475

129. Moran C A, Suster S, Pavlova Z et al. 1994 The spectrum of pathological changes in the lung in children with AIDS: an autopsy study of 36 cases. Hum Pathol 25: 877–882

130. Meduri G U, Stover D E, Lee M et al. 1986 Pulmonary Kaposi's sarcoma in the acquired immune deficiency syndrome: clinical, radiographic and pathologic manifestation. Am J Med 81: 5–12

131. Spragg R G, Wolf P L, Haghighi P et al. 1983 Angiosarcoma of the lung with fatal pulmonary hemorrhage. Am J Med 74: 1072–1076

132. Yousem S A 1986 Angiosarcoma presenting in the lung. Arch Pathol Lab Med 110: 112–115

133. Farinacci C J, Blauw A S, Jennings E M 1973 Multifocal pulmonary lesions of possible decidual origin (so-called pulmonary deciduosis). Report of a case. Am J Clin Pathol 59: 508–514

134. Dail D H, Liebow A A, Gmelich J T et al. 1983 Intravascular bronchiolar and alveolar tumor (IVBAT). Cancer 51: 452–464

135. Bhagavan B S, Murthy M S N, Dorfman H D et al. 1982 Intravascular bronchioalveolar tumor (IVBAT). A low-grade sclerosing epithelioid angiosarcoma of lung. Am J Surg Pathol 6: 41–52

136. Azumi N, Churg A 1981 Intravascular and sclerosing bronchioloalveolar tumor. A pulmonary sarcoma of probable vascular origin. Am J Surg Pathol 5: 587–596

137. Corrin B, Liebow A A, Friedman P J et al. 1975 Pulmonary lymphangioleiomyomatosis. Am J Pathol 79: 348–368

138. Ramani P, Shah A 1993 Lymphangioleiomyomatosis. Histologic and immunohistochemical analysis of four cases. Am J Surg Pathol 17: 329–335

139. Koss M N, Hochholzer L, Moran C A et al. 1998 Pulmonary plasmacytomas: a clinicopathologic and immunohistochemical study of five cases. Ann Diagn Pathol 2: 1–11

140. Addis B J, Hyjek E, Isaacson P G 1988 Primary pulmonary lymphoma: a reappraisal of its histogenesis and its relationship to pseudolymphoma and lymphoid interstitial pneumonia. Histopathology 13: 1–17

141. Isaacson P G, Spencer J 1983 Malignant lymphoma of mucosa-associated lymphoid tissue. A distinctive type of B-cell lymphoma. Cancer 52: 1410–1417

142. Fiche M, Capron F, Berger F et al. 1995 Primary pulmonary non-Hodgkin's lymphomas. Histopathology 26: 529–537

143. Herbert A, Wright D H, Isaacson P G et al. 1984 Primary malignant lymphoma of the lung. Hum Pathol 15: 415–422

144. Koss M N 1995 Pulmonary lymphoid disorders. Semin Diagn Pathol 12: 158–171

145. Abbondanzo S L, Rush W, Bijwaard K E et al. 2000 Nodular lymphoid hyperplasia of the lung. A clinicopathologic study of 14 cases. Am J Surg Pathol 24: 587–597

146. Nicholson A G, Wotherspoon A C, Diss T C et al. 1995 Pulmonary B-cell non-Hodgkin's lymphomas. Histopathology 26: 395–403

147. Li G, Hansmann M L, Zwingers T et al. 1990 Primary lymphoma of the lung: morphological, immunohistochemical and clinical features. Histopathology 16: 519–531

148. L'Hoste R J, Filippa D A, Lieberman P H et al. 1984 Primary pulmonary lymphomas: a clinicopathologic analysis of 36 cases. Cancer 54: 1397–1406

149. Koss M N, Hochholzer L, Nichols P W et al. 1983 Primary non-Hodgkin's lymphomas and pseudolymphomas of the lung: a study of 161 patients. Hum Pathol 14: 1024–1038

150. Liebow A A, Carrington C B, Friedman P J 1972 Lymphomatoid granulomatosis. Hum Pathol 3: 457–558

151. Fauci A S, Haynes B F, Costa J et al. 1982 Lymphomatoid granulomatosis – prospective clinical and therapeutic experience over 10 years. N Engl J Med 306: 68–74

152. Katzenstein A L, Carrington C B, Liebow A A 1979 Lymphomatoid granulomatosis – a clinicopathologic study of 152 cases. Cancer 43: 360–373

153. Koss M N, Hochholzer L, Langloss J M et al. 1986 Lymphomatoid granulomatosis: a clinicopathologic study of 42 patients. Pathology 18: 283–288

154. Jaffe E S 1988 Pulmonary lymphocytic angiitis: a nosologic quandary. Mayo Clin Proc 63: 411–413

155. Saldana M J, Patchefsky A S, Israel H I et al. 1977 Pulmonary angiitis and granulomatosis: the relationship between histological features, organ involvement, and response to treatment. Hum Pathol 8: 391–409

156. Kern W H, Crepean A G, Jones J L 1961 Primary Hodgkin's disease of the lung: report of four cases and review of the literature. Cancer 14: 1151–1165

157. Yousem S A, Weiss L M, Colby T V 1986 Primary pulmonary Hodgkin's disease: a clinicopathologic study of 15 cases. Cancer 57: 1217–1224

158. Radin A I 1990 Primary pulmonary Hodgkin's disease. Cancer 65: 550–563

159. Marchevsky A M 1995 Lung tumors derived from ectopic tissues. Semin Diagn Pathol 12: 172–184

160. Moran C A, Hochholzer L, Rush W et al. 1996 Primary intrapulmonary meningiomas: a clinicopathologic and immunohistochemical study of ten cases. Cancer 78: 2328–2333

161. Kodama K, Osamu D, Higashiyama M et al. 1991 Primary and metastatic pulmonary meningioma. Cancer 67: 1412–1417

162. Drlicek M, Grisold W, Lorber J et al. 1991 Pulmonary meningioma. Am J Surg Pathol 15: 455–459

163. Flynn S D, Yousem S A 1991 Pulmonary meningioma. Hum Pathol 22: 469–474

164. Moran C A, Suster S, Fishback N F et al. 1995 Primary intrapulmonary thymoma: a clinicopathologic and immunohistochemical study of eight cases. Am J Surg Pathol 19: 304–313

165. Yeoh C B, Ford J M, Lattes R et al. 1966 Intrapulmonary thymoma. J Thorac Cardiovasc Surg 51: 131–136

166. James C L, Iver P V, Leong A S 1992 Intrapulmonary thymoma. Histopathology 21: 175–177

167. Tang C, Toker C K, Foris N P et al. 1978 Glomangioma of the lung. Am J Surg Pathol 2: 103–109

168. Koss M N, Hochholzer L, Moran C A 1998 Primary pulmonary glomus tumor. A clinicopathologic and immunohistochemical study of three cases. Mod Pathol 11: 253–258

169. Wilson R W, Moran C A 1997 Primary melanoma of the lung: a clinicopathologic and immunohistochemical study of eight cases. Am J Surg Pathol 21: 1196–1202

170. Alghanem A A, Mehan J, Hassan A A 1987 Primary malignant melanoma of the lung. J Surg Oncol 34: 109–112

171. Cagle P, Mace M L, Judge D M et al. 1984 Pulmonary melanoma: primary vs metastatic. Chest 85: 125–126

172. Farrell D J, Kashyap A P, Ashcroft T et al. 1996 Primary malignant melanoma of the bronchus. Thorax 51: 223–224

173. Gephart G N 1981 Malignant melanoma of the bronchus. Hum Pathol 12: 671–673

174. Singh G, Lee R E, Brooks D H 1997 Primary pulmonary paraganglioma. Report of a case and review of the literature. Cancer 40: 2286–2289

175. Fawcett F J, Husband E M 1967 Chemodectoma of the lung. J Clin Pathol 20: 260–262

176. Cooney T P 1981 Primary pulmonary ganglioneuroblastoma in an adult: maturation, involution, and the immune response. Histopathology 5: 451–463

177. Hochholzer L, Moran C A, Koss M N 1998 Primary pulmonary ganglioneuroblastoma: a clinicopathologic and immunohistochemical study of two cases. Ann Diagn Pathol 2: 154–158

178. Jamieson M P G, McGowan A R 1982 Endobronchial teratoma. Thorax 37: 157–159

179. Day S W, Taylor S A 1975 An intrapulmonary teratoma associated with thymic tissue. Thorax 30: 582–587

180. Tanimura A, Natsuyama H, Kawano M et al. 1985 Primary choriocarcinoma of the lung. Hum Pathol 16: 1281–1284

181. Deavers M, Guinee D, Koss M N et al. 1995 Granular cell tumors of the lung: clinicopathologic study of 20 cases. Am J Surg Pathol 19: 627–635

182. Alvarez-Fernandez E, Carretero-Albinama L 1987 Bronchial granular cell tumor. Presentation of three cases with tissue culture and ultrastructural study. Arch Pathol Lab Med 111: 1065–1069

183. Roger C L 1965 Multicentric endobronchial myoblastoma. Arch Otolaryngol 82: 652–655

184. Seo I S, Azzarrelli B, Warner T F et al. 1984 Multiple visceral and cutaneous granular cell tumors. Ultrastructural and immunohistochemical evidence of Schwann cell origin. Cancer 53: 2104–2110

185. Liebow A A, Hubbell D S 1972 Sclerosing hemangioma (histiocytoma, xanthoma) of the lung. Cancer 30: 512–518

186. Spencer H, Nambu S 1986 Sclerosing haemangiomas of the lung. Histopathology 10: 477–487

187. Moran C A, Zeren H, Koss M N 1994 Sclerosing hemangioma of the lung: granulomatous variant. Arch Pathol Lab Med 108: 128–130

188. Noguchi M, Kodama T, Morinaga S et al. 1986 Multiple sclerosing hemangiomas of the lung. Am J Surg Pathol 10: 429–435

189. Huszar M, Suster S, Herczer E et al. 1986 Sclerosing hemangioma of the lung: immunohistochemical demonstration of mesenchymal origin using antibodies to tissue-specific intermediate filaments. Cancer 58: 2422–2427

190. Yousem S A, Wick M R, Singh G et al. 1988 So-called sclerosing hemangioma of lung: an immunohistochemical study supporting a respiratory epithelial origin. Am J Surg Pathol 12: 582–590

191. Fukuyama M, Koike M 1988 So-called sclerosing hemangioma of the lung. An immunohistochemical, histochemical and ultrastructural study. Acta Pathol Jpn 38: 627–642

192. Shimosato Y 1995 Lung tumors of uncertain histogenesis. Semin Diagn Pathol 12: 185–192

193. Leong A S-Y, Chan K-W, Seneviratne H S K 1995 A morphological and immunohistochemical study of 25 cases of so-called sclerosing haemangioma of the lung. Histopathology 27: 121–128

194. Xu H M, Li W H, Hou N et al. 1997 Neuroendocrine differentiation in 32 cases of so-called sclerosing hemangioma of the lung: identified by immunohistochemical and ultrastructural study. Am J Surg Pathol 21: 1013–1022

195. Tanaka I, Inoue M, Matsui Y et al. 1986 A case of pneumocytoma (so-called sclerosing hemangioma) with lymph node metastasis. Jpn J Clin Oncol 16: 77–86

196. Liebow A A, Castleman B 1971 Benign clear cell (sugar) tumors of the lung. Yale J Biol Med 43: 213–222

197. Becker N H, Soifer I 1971 Benign clear cell tumor (sugar tumor) of the lung. Cancer 27: 712–719

198. Gaffey M J, Mills S E, Zambo R et al. 1991 Clear cell tumor of the lung. Immunohistochemical and ultrastructural evidence of melanogenesis. Am J Surg Pathol 15: 644–653

199. Bonetti F, Pea M, Martignoni G et al. 1994 Clear cell ("sugar") tumor of the lung is a lesion strictly related to angiomyolipoma. The concept of a family of lesions characterised by the presence of a perivascular epithelioid (PEC) cell. Pathology 26: 230–236

200. Lantuejoul S, Isaac S, Pinel N et al. 1997 Clear cell tumor of lung: an immunohistochemical and ultrastructural study supporting a pericytic differentiation. Mod Pathol 10: 1001–1008

201. Spencer H 1984 The pulmonary plasma cell/histiocytoma complex. Histopathology 8: 903–907

202. Buell R, Wang N S, Seemayer T A et al. 1976 Endobronchial plasma cell granuloma (inflammatory pseudotumor): a light and electron microscopic study. Hum Pathol 7: 411–415

203. Monzon C, Gilchrist G, Burgert E et al. 1982 Plasma cell granuloma of the lung in children. Pediatrics 70: 268–271

204. Berardi R, Lee S, Chen H et al. 1983 Inflammatory pseudotumor of the lung. Surg Gynecol Obstet 36: 108–110

205. Pettinato G, Manivel J C, De Rosa N et al. 1990 Inflammatory myofibroblastic tumor (plasma cell granuloma). Clinicopathologic study of 20 cases with immunohistochemical and ultrastructural observations. Am J Clin Pathol 94: 538–542

206. Coffin C M, Patel A, Perkins S et al. 2001 ALK1 and p80 expression and chromosomal rearrangements involving 2p23 in inflammatory myofibroblastic tumor. Mod Pathol 14: 569–576

207. Tomashevski J F Jr 1982 Benign endobronchial mesenchymal tumors. Am J Surg Pathol 6: 531–540

208. Van Den Bosch J M, Wagenaar S S, Corrin B et al. 1987 Mesenchymoma of the lung (so-called hamartoma): a review of 154 parenchymal and endobronchial cases. Thorax 42: 790–793

209. Dal Cin P, Kools P, de Jonge I et al. 1993 Rearrangement of 12q14-15 in pulmonary chondroid hamartoma. Genes Chromos Cancer 8: 131–133

210. Xiao S, Lux M L, Reeves R et al. 1997 HMG-I(Y) activation by chromosome 6p21 rearrangements in multilineage mesenchymal cells from pulmonary hamartoma. Am J Pathol 150: 901–910

211. Moran C A, Suster S, Koss M N 1994 Endobronchial lipomas: a clinicopathologic study of four cases. Mod Pathol 7: 212–214

212. Yousem S A, Hochholzer L 1986 Alveolar adenoma. Hum Pathol 17: 1066–1070

213. Oliveira P, Nunes J G M, Clode A L et al. 1996 Alveolar adenoma of the lung: further characterization of this uncommon tumor. Virchows Arch 429: 101–108

214. Burke L M, Rush W I, Khoor A et al. 1999 Alveolar adenoma: a histochemical, immunohistochemical and ultrastructural analysis of 17 cases. Hum Pathol 30: 158–167

215. England D M, Hochholzer L 1995 Truly benign "bronchial adenoma:" report of 10 cases of mucous gland adenoma with immunohistochemical and ultrastructural findings. Am J Surg Pathol 19: 887–899

216. Fantone J C, Geisinger K, Appelman H D 1982 Papillary adenoma of the lung with lamellar and electron dense granules. Cancer 50: 2839–2844

217. Hegg C A, Flint A, Singh G 1992 Papillary adenoma of the lung. Am J Clin Pathol 97: 393–397

218. Suster S, Moran C A 1993 Pulmonary adenofibroma: report of two cases of an unusual type of hamartomatous lesion of the lung. Histopathology 23: 547–551

219. Korn D, Bensch K, Liebow A A et al. 1960 Multiple minute pulmonary tumors resembling chemodectoma. Am J Pathol 37: 641–672

220. Gaffey M J, Mills S F, Askin F G 1988 Minute pulmonary meningothelial-like nodules. A clinicopathologic study of so-called pulmonary chemodectoma. Am J Surg Pathol 12: 167–175

221. Ionescu D N, Sasatomi E, Aldeeb D et al. 2004 Pulmonary meningothelial-like nodules: a genotypic comparison with meningiomas. Am J Surg Pathol 28: 207–214

222. Suster S 1994 Pulmonary metastases of extrapulmonary tumors. In: Saldana M J (ed) Pathology of pulmonary disease. J B Lippincott, Philadelphia, p 701–710

223. Suster S, Moran C A 1995 Unusual manifestations of metastatic tumors of the lungs. Semin Diagn Pathol 12: 193–206

224. Toomes H, Delphenial A, Manke H-G et al. 1983 The coin lesion of the lung. A review of 995 resected coin lesions. Cancer 51: 534–537

225. Abell M R, Littler E R 1975 Benign metastasizing uterine leiomyoma. Cancer 36: 2206–2213

226. Wolff M, Kaye G, Silva F 1979 Pulmonary metastases (with admixed epithelial elements) from smooth muscle neoplasms. Am J Surg Pathol 3: 325–342

227. Nakatsuka S, Yao M, Hoshida Y et al. 2002 Pyothorax-associated lymphoma: a review of 106 cases. J Clin Oncol 20: 4255–4260

228. Legha S S, Muggia F M 1977 Pleural mesothelioma: clinical features and therapeutic implications. Ann Intern Med 87: 613–617

229. Whitwell F, Scott J, Grimshaw M 1977 Relationship between occupation and asbestos fiber content of the lungs in patients with pleural mesothelioma, lung carcinoma, and other diseases. Thorax 32: 377–384

230. Selikoff I J, Churg J, Hammond E C 1965 Relation between exposure in asbestos and mesothelioma. N Eng J Med 272: 560–563

231. Bedrossian C M W, Bonsib S, Moran C A 1992 Differential diagnosis between mesothelioma and adenocarcinoma: a multimodal approach based on ultrastructure and immunohistochemistry. Semin Diagn Pathol 9: 124–135

232. Ordonez N G, Mackay B 1996 The role of immunohistochemistry and electron microscopy in distinguishing epithelial mesothelioma of pleura from adenocarcinoma. Adv Anat Pathol 5: 273–282

233. Moran C A, Wick M R, Suster S 2000 The role of immunohistochemistry in the diagnosis of malignant mesothelioma. Semin Diagn Pathol 17: 178–183

234. Bedrossian C W M 1994 Malignant mesothelioma and other pulmonary tumors. In: Saldana M J (ed) Pathology of pulmonary disease. J B Lippincott, Philadelphia, p 657–671

235. Granados R, Cibas E S, Fletcher J A 1994 Cytogenetic analysis of effusions in malignant mesothelioma. Acta Cytol 38: 711–717

236. Sugarbaker D J, Flores R M, Jaklitsch M T et al. 1999 Resection margins, extrapleural nodal status and cell type determine postoperative long-term survival in trimodality therapy of malignant pleural mesothelioma: results in 183 patients. J Thorac Cardiovasc Surg 117: 54–63

237. Koss M N, Hochholzer L, Moran C A et al. 1992 Pseudomesotheliomatous adenocarcinoma. Semin Diagn Pathol 9: 97–105

237a. Allen T C, Cagle P T, Churg A M et al. 2005 Localized malignant mesothelioma. Am J Surg Pathol 29: 866–873

238. Galateau-Salle F, Vigraud J M, Burke L et al. 2004 Well differentiated papillary mesothelioma of the pleura. A series of 24 cases. Am J Surg Pathol 28: 534–540

239. Ordonez N G 2000 Epithelial mesothelioma with deciduoid features. Report of four cases. Am J Surg Pathol 24: 816–823

240. Khalidi H S, Medeiros L J, Battifora H 2000 Lymphohistiocytoid mesothelioma. An often misdiagnosed variant of sarcomatoid malignant mesothelioma. Am J Clin Pathol 113: 649–654

240a. Ordonez N G 2005 Mesothelioma with clear cell features: an ultrastructural and immunohistochemical study of 20 cases. Hum Pathol 36: 465–473

240b. Ordonez N G 2006 Mesothelioma with rhabdoid features: an ultrastructural and immunohistochemical study of 10 cases. Mod Pathol 19: 373–383

240c. Shia J, Qin J, Erlandson R A et al. 2005 Malignant mesothelioma with a pronounced myxoid stroma: a clinical and pathological evaluation of 19 cases. Virchows Arch 447: 828–834

241. Henderson D W, Shilkin K B, Whitaker D 1998 Reactive mesothelial hyperplasia vs mesothelioma, including mesothelioma in situ. A brief review. Am J Clin Pathol 110: 397–404

242. Wick M R, Moran C A, Mills S E et al. 2001 Immunohistochemical differential diagnosis of pleural effusions, with emphasis on malignant mesotheliomas. Curr Opin Pulm Med 7: 187–192

243. Ordoñez N G 2003 The immunohistochemical diagnosis of mesothelioma: a comparative study of epithelioid mesothelioma and lung adenocarcinoma. Am J Surg Pathol 27: 1031–1051

244. Lugli A, Forster Y, Haas P et al. 2003 Calretinin expression in human normal and neoplastic tissue: a tissue microarray analysis of 5233 tissue samples. Hum Pathol 34: 994–1000

245. Llinares K, Escande F, Aubert S et al. 2004 Diagnostic value of MUC4 immunostaining in distinguishing epithelial mesothelioma and lung adenocarcinoma. Mod Pathol 17: 150–157

245a. Ordonez N G 2005 D2-40 and podoplanin are highly specific and sensitive immunohistochemical markers of epithelioid malignant mesothelioma. Hum Pathol 36: 372–380

246. Pan C-C, Paul C-H, Chou T-Y et al. 2003 Expression of calretinin and other mesothelioma-related markers in thymic carcinoma and thymoma. Hum Pathol 34: 1155–1162

247. Mayall F G, Goddard H, Gibbs A R 1992 Intermediate filament expression in mesotheliomas: leiomyoid mesotheliomas are not uncommon. Histopathology 21: 453–457

248. Lucas D R, Pass H I, Madan S K et al. 2003 Sarcomatoid mesothelioma and its histologic mimics: a comparative immunohistochemical study. Histopathology 42: 270–279

249. Ordoñez N G 1997 Value of antibodies 44-3AG, SM3, HBME-1 and thrombomodulin in differentiating epithelial pleural mesotheliomas from lung adenocarcinoma. A comparative study with other commonly used antibodies. Am J Surg Pathol 21: 1399–1408

250. Attanoos L L, Goddard H, Gibbs A R 1996 Mesothelioma-binding antibodies: thrombomodulin, OV 632, and HBME-1 and their use in the diagnosis of malignant mesothelioma. Histopathology 29: 209–215

251. Doglioni C, Dei Tos A P, Laurino L et al. 1996 Calretinin: a novel immunocytochemical marker for mesothelioma. Am J Surg Pathol 20: 1037–1046

252. Clover J, Oates J, Edwards C 1997 Anticytokeratin 5/6: A positive marker for epithelial mesothelioma. Histopathology 31: 140–143

253. Han A C, Peralta-Soler A, Knudsen K A et al. 1997 Differential expression of N-cadherin in pleural mesothelioma and E-cadherin in lung adenocarcinoma in formalin-fixed paraffin-embedded tissues. Hum Pathol 28: 641–645

254. Harwood T R, Gracey D R, Yokoo H 1976 Pseudomesotheliomatous carcinoma of the lung. A variant of peripheral lung cancer. Am J Clin Pathol 65: 159–167

255. Koss M N, Fleming M, Przygodzki R M et al. 1998 Adenocarcinoma simulating mesothelioma: a clinicopathologic and immunohistochemical study of 29 cases. Ann Diagn Pathol 2: 89–98

256. Attanoos R L, Gibbs A R 2003 "Pseudomesotheliomatous" carcinomas of the pleura: a 10-year analysis of cases from the Environmental Lung Disease Research Group, Cardiff. Histopathology 43: 444–452

257. Klemperer P, Rabin C B 1937 Primary neoplasms of the pleura. Report of five cases. Arch Pathol 11: 385–412

258. Scharifker D, Kaneko M 1979 Localized fibrous "mesothelioma" of pleura (submesothelial fibroma): a clinicopathologic study of 18 cases. Cancer 43: 627–635

259. Burrig K-F, Kastendieck H 1984 Ultrastructural observations on the histogenesis of localized fibrous tumors of the pleura (benign mesothelioma). Virchows Arch [A] 403: 413–424

260. Said J W, Nash B, Banks-Schlegel S et al. 1984 Localized fibrous mesothelioma: an immunohistochemical and electron microscopy study. Hum Pathol 15: 440–446

261. England D M, Hochholzer L, McCarthy M J 1989 Localized benign and malignant fibrous tumors of the pleura: a clinicopathologic review of 223 cases. Am J Surg Pathol 13: 640–648

262. Dalton W R, Zollicker A S, McCaughey M T E et al. 1979 Localized primary tumors of the pleura: an analysis of 40 cases. Cancer 44: 1465–1475

263. Briselli M, Mark E J, Dickersin R 1981 Solitary fibrous tumor of the pleura: eight new cases and review of 360 cases in the literature. Cancer 47: 2678–2689

264. Chilosi M, Facchetti F, Dei Tos A P et al. 1997 Bcl-2 expression in pleural and extrapleural solitary fibrous tumors. J Pathol 181: 362–367

265. Renshaw A A 1995 O13 (CD99) in spindle cell tumors. Appl Immunohistochem 3: 250–256

266. Carter D, Otis C N 1988 Three types of spindle cell tumors of the pleura. Fibroma, sarcoma, and sarcomatoid mesothelioma. Am J Surg Pathol 12: 747–753

267. Moran C A, Suster S, Koss M N 1995 Smooth muscle tumors presenting as pleural neoplasms. Histopathology 27: 227–234

268. Proca D M, Ross P Jr, Pratt J et al. 2000 Smooth muscle tumor of the pleura: a case report and review of the literature. Arch Pathol Lab Med 124: 1688–1692

269. Gaertner E, Zeren H, Colby T V et al. 1996 Biphasic synovial sarcomas arising in the pleural cavity: a clinicopathologic study of five cases. Am J Surg Pathol 20: 36–45

270. Falconieri G, Bussani R, Mirra M et al. 1997 Pseudomesotheliomatous angiosarcoma: a pleuropulmonary lesion simulating malignant pleural mesothelioma. Histopathology 30: 419–424

271. Lin B T-Y, Colby T, Gown A M et al. 1996 Malignant vascular tumors of the serous membranes mimicking mesothelioma. Am J Surg Pathol 20: 1431–1439

272. Moran C A, Rosado-de-Christenson M L, Koss M N et al. 1992 Thymomas presenting as pleural tumors. Am J Surg Pathol 16: 138–142

273. Attanoos R L, Galateau-Salle F, Gibbs A R et al. 2002 Primary thymic epithelial tumors of the pleura mimicking malignant mesothelioma. Histopathology 41: 42–49

274. Kaplan M A, Tazellar H D, Hayashi T et al. 1996 Adenomatoid tumors of the pleura. Am J Surg Pathol 20: 1219–1223

275. Moran C A, Suster S 2003 Primary mucoepidermoid carcinoma of the pleura: a clinicopathologic study of three cases. Am J Clin Pathol 120: 381–385

276. Manivel J C, Priest J, Watterson J et al. 1988 Pleuropulmonary blastoma. The so-called pulmonary blastoma of childhood. Cancer 62: 1516–1526

277. Priest J R, McDermott M B, Bhatia S et al. 1997 Pleuropulmonary blastoma. A clinicopathologic study of 50 cases. Cancer 80: 147–161

278. Hedlung G, Bisset M, Bove K 1989 Malignant neoplasms arising in cystic hamartomas of the lung in childhood. Radiology 173: 77–79

279. Hachitanda Y, Aoyama C, Sato J K et al. 1993 Pleuropulmonary blastoma in childhood. A tumor of divergent differentiation. Am J Surg Pathol 17: 382–391

Tumors of the oral cavity

The late D. Gordon MacDonald   Paul M. Speight

Introduction

The most frequent tumors in the mouth arise from the stratified squamous oral epithelium. These are closely similar to tumors of stratified squamous epithelium occurring at other body sites and only infrequently present problems in diagnosis. The mesenchymal tissues of the mouth are less frequently the source of neoplasms, but a number of overgrowths occur in response to chronic irritation and it is important that these are distinguished from true neoplasms. Tumors of the jaws may also be problematic since many are rare or may show features specific to the site. Odontogenic cysts and tumors are derived from the dental tissues and show variable features that may recapitulate stages of tooth development. Odontogenic tumors are rare, but often pose diagnostic problems for the pathologist unfamiliar with dental tissues; hence they receive more emphasis in this chapter. Odontogenic cysts are common and, although rarely neoplastic, they are included since classification may be confusing and they frequently cause diagnostic difficulty.

Tumors of oral epithelium

Squamous cell papilloma and related lesions

Clinical features

Discrete exophytic papillary overgrowths of oral epithelium occur at any intraoral site, mainly in adults. There are probably several variants, although these overlap in clinical and histologic appearance. All are slow-growing and there is no evidence that these lesions are premalignant. The incidence of lesions diagnosed as squamous cell papillomas or warts is increased in patients with human immunodeficiency virus (HIV) infection.

Histologic appearances

In the typical squamous cell papilloma the epithelium is of fairly uniform thickness, with variable keratinization or hyperkeratosis, and covers cores of loose vascular connective tissue. Some cytologic atypia may be present in the deeper cell layers and increased mitotic activity is often present. This may be accentuated if there is infestation by *Candida albicans* in the superficial layers of the epithelium.

The typical histologic appearances of verruca vulgaris are seen in some oral lesions and there may be a clear association with cutaneous warts on the fingers. Condyloma acuminatum, also reported in the mouth, cannot be diagnosed with certainty on histologic grounds.[1] Where a discrete papillary exophytic growth shows acanthosis instead of relatively uniformly thick folds of epithelium (Fig. 6.1) and there is obviously increased mitotic activity, condyloma acuminatum should be suspected.

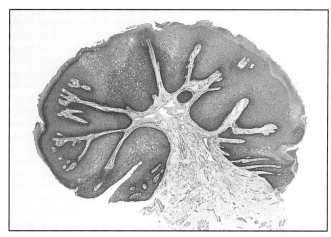

Fig. 6.1 • Exophytic epithelial growth with features suggestive of condyloma acuminatum.

Focal epithelial hyperplasia

Focal epithelial hyperplasia (Heck's disease), caused by human papillomavirus (HPV) 13 and 32,[2] presents as multiple, sessile elevated nodules. Histologically there is fibrous overgrowth covered by irregularly hyperplastic epithelium (Fig. 6.2). Arrested, fragmented metaphases, described as mitosoid cells, may be present in the stratum spinosum.

Squamous cell carcinoma

Clinical features

Squamous cell carcinoma[3] is much the most common malignant neoplasm of the mouth. Tumors arise on the lower lip and at multiple different intraoral sites. Most textbooks quote the lateral margin of the tongue as the most frequent intraoral site, but specific studies of small symptomless neoplasms indicate that the floor of the mouth, especially anteriorly, is the most frequent site for small, presumed "early" tumors. The next most frequent site is the "soft palate complex" consisting of the soft palate, anterior pillar of fauces, and retromolar area.

In parts of the world with a high incidence of oral cancer, such as India, most oral cancers arise in areas of leukoplakia. By contrast, in developed countries, small intraoral carcinomas are almost always red or predominantly red.[4] The majority of the latter arise in clinically apparently normal epithelium.

Histologic appearances

Oral squamous cell carcinomas show the same range of features and variants as such carcinomas at other sites (see Ch. 23) and diagnosis is usually straightforward. The earliest stages of invasion may be difficult to determine and criteria for microinvasion are not adequately defined. This is especially a problem in verrucous, well-differentiated lesions. Fortunately, such lesions are unlikely to metastasize at the stage when the term microinvasive might be used, and the local excision appropriate for a verrucous lesion is also the appropriate treatment for microinvasive carcinoma. Exophytic, verrucous lesions can pose particular problems when there is superimposed infestation with *Candida albicans*. This is often associated with obviously increased mitotic activity and it is important to recognize that this is disproportionate to the degree of dysplasia. It is often wise to defer a diagnosis of malignancy in such cases until fungal infection is treated and the lesion is rebiopsied.

There have been many attempts to devise schemes for predicting the prognosis of oral carcinomas from analysis of histologic features,[5,6] but none of these has found general favor. A tumor-invasive front composed of single cells or small cords is used by some pathologists as a predictor of increased likelihood of metastatic spread to lymph nodes. Vascular and perineural invasion are also important predictors.[7] Several studies have shown the importance of tumor thickness. This should be measured from the actual surface for flat lesions or the presumed original epithelial surface for exophytic or ulcerated lesions. There is a growing consensus that tumor thickness exceeding 5 mm is associated with a significantly increased risk of metastasis.[8]

Variants of squamous cell carcinoma

A number of variants are described[9,10] and their relevance is that they are thought to have differing prognoses. Some tumors are comprised entirely of the variant type, but in many instances lesions show a mixture of conventional squamous cell carcinoma and other patterns. In these cases it is probably best to report the mixed patterns and advise that the behavior is likely to be determined by the most aggressive variant present.

Spindle cell carcinoma

Spindle cell squamous carcinoma is a pleomorphic spindle cell neoplasm most frequently found in the head and neck.[11] Spindle cell tumors of all sorts are uncommon in the mouth, but the full spectrum of soft tissue sarcomas (see Ch. 24) can occur. In any such case, spindle cell carcinoma should always be included in the differential diagnosis. A wide range of histologic appearances is seen in these tumors (Figs 6.3 and 6.4). Immunohistochemical demonstration of cytokeratin in tumor cells strongly supports the diagnosis. Variable results are obtained with different cytokeratin antibodies, but, in our experience, positivity is most frequently demonstrated with AE1/3. In the majority of cases, it is probably wise to insist on finding areas of conventional squamous cell carcinoma or severe epithelial dysplasia, usually at the growing edge of the tumor, before making the diagnosis of spindle cell carcinoma, although mucosal ulceration may preclude this.

Adenoid (or acantholytic) squamous cell carcinoma and adenosquamous carcinoma

The term adenoid squamous cell carcinoma describes cases in which loss of intercellular adhesion in the center of tumor

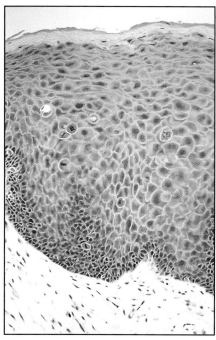

Fig. 6.2 • Focal epithelial hyperplasia, showing acanthotic keratinized epithelium with mitosoid cells in the stratum spinosum.

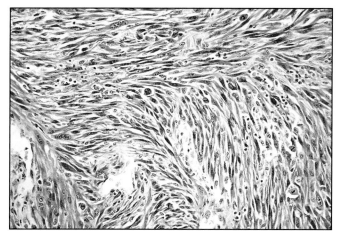

Fig. 6.3 • Spindle cell carcinoma exhibiting a very mesenchymal appearance.

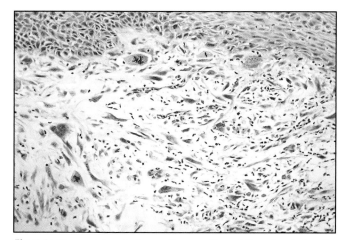

Fig. 6.4 • Bizarre cytology in dispersed tumor cell population of a spindle cell carcinoma. Note the adjacent dysplastic surface epithelium.

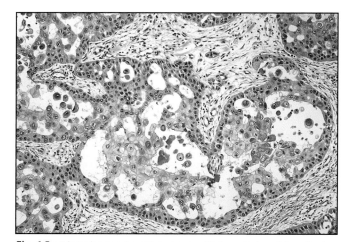

Fig. 6.5 • Adenoid squamous cell carcinoma with loss of intercellular adhesion within tumor islands, resulting in a pseudoglandular appearance.

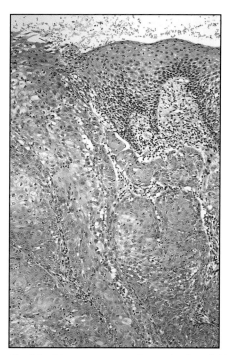

Fig. 6.6 • Adenosquamous carcinoma showing a field of conventional squamous cell carcinoma arising from surface epithelium.

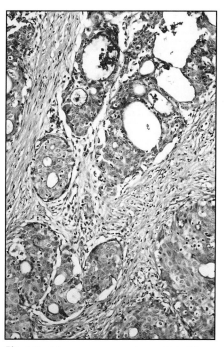

Fig. 6.7 • Adenosquamous carcinoma. Part of the same tumor shown in Figure 6.6 illustrating adenocarcinomatous differentiation. Diastase–periodic acid–Schiff.

islands resembles glandular differentiation (Fig. 6.5). These are poor-prognosis tumors.[12,13] Adenosquamous carcinomas[14] are also poor-prognosis tumors. In these lesions there is involvement of salivary gland ducts, often concurrently with tumor arising from the surface mucosa. The main differential diagnosis is from mucoepidermoid carcinoma and is made by the recognition of discrete areas of adenocarcinoma and of squamous cell carcinoma arising from the surface epithelium (Figs 6.6 and 6.7). A small number of otherwise conventional squamous cell carcinomas may show a few mucus-secreting cells and demonstration of these, in the absence of ductal differentiation (Fig. 6.8), is not sufficient for a diagnosis of

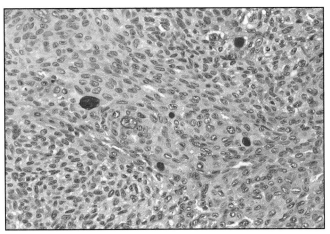

Fig. 6.8 • Squamous cell carcinoma with a small number of mucus-secreting cells. Diastase–periodic acid–Schiff.

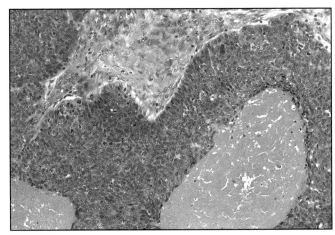

Fig. 6.10 • Basaloid squamous cell carcinoma showing mass of basal cells with comedo necrosis.

adenosquamous carcinoma. It is also important to recognize correctly the potentially confusing presence of invasion by squamous cell carcinoma into salivary gland (Fig. 6.9).

Basaloid squamous carcinoma[15,16]

This uncommon variant of squamous cell carcinoma (see Ch. 4) usually occurs in combination with areas of conventional squamous cell carcinoma. The basaloid areas show demarcated nests of cells with peripheral palisading, basal cell morphology, and numerous mitotic figures. Comedo necrosis is common (Fig. 6.10). These lesions are typically aggressive with early lymph node metastasis. They are most typically seen in the posterior aspect or base of the tongue and must be distinguished from other basaloid lesions, particularly solid adenoid cystic carcinoma or salivary duct carcinoma.

Verrucous carcinoma

This term was first coined for exophytic, massively acanthotic lesions showing minimal cytologic atypia which would not, on strict histologic grounds, be diagnosed as carcinoma. Sub-

sequently the term has been much misused. Verrucous carcinomas have a better prognosis than conventional squamous cell carcinoma.

Clinical features. Verrucous carcinomas are exophytic, keratinized growths with a white papillary or warty surface. They are mainly seen in the elderly and are associated with tobacco usage. They may have surface dimensions of several centimeters, but show a superficial spreading growth rather than invasion into deeper tissues.

Histologic appearances. There is marked acanthosis, often with broad bulbous processes showing central columns of keratin (Fig. 6.11). Although exophytic, with columns of keratin rising

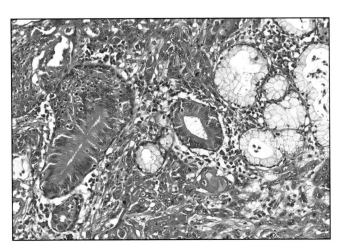

Fig. 6.9 • Squamous cell carcinoma invading minor salivary gland in the tongue. Note that the acinar tissue and the ducts are from existing gland and not part of the tumor, although one duct shows squamous metaplasia.

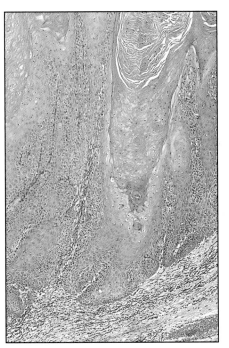

Fig. 6.11 • Exophytic carcinoma showing marked acanthosis and columns of keratin. There is a blunt pushing edge of tumor. Many pathologists would diagnose verrucous carcinoma for lesions of this type, although dysplasia is present.

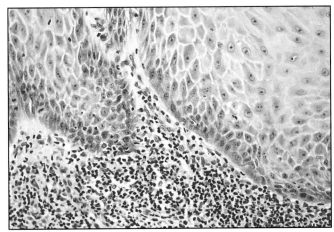

Fig. 6.12 • High-power view of advancing edge of an exophytic carcinoma. This type of lesion is diagnosed as verrucous carcinoma by some pathologists, although others would suggest that even the small degree of dysplasia present precludes that diagnosis.

above the adjacent mucosal surface, there is also an endophytic component. The bulbous rete processes "push" deep into the lamina propria so that the base of the lesion is below the adjacent basement membrane. There is no cytologic evidence of malignancy. Pronounced chronic inflammatory cell infiltration is often present in the lamina propria (Fig. 6.12). The diagnosis of verrucous carcinoma in this location should only be made after clinicopathologic correlation.[17]

Differential diagnosis. The main differential diagnosis is from conventional squamous cell carcinoma. Many oral cancers are exophytic and well differentiated, but show cytologic features of malignancy and invasion. The term verrucous carcinoma, although used by some authors for such lesions, is inappropriate. Some tumors have areas of verrucous carcinoma and areas of conventional squamous cell carcinoma and it is important that the latter be sought for before the diagnosis of verrucous carcinoma is made.

Papillary squamous cell carcinoma

When applied to the oral cavity, this term has often been used for some otherwise conventional squamous cell carcinomas with an exophytic papillary surface. True papillary carcinomas are rare in the mouth but are most frequently encountered in the larynx and hypolarynx.[9] They are composed of exophytic papillary fronds of epithelium overlying a fibrovascular core. There is considerable cytologic atypia of the epithelium, but stromal invasion may not be prominent. Differential diagnosis is from verrucous carcinoma and squamous papilloma, but papillary carcinomas are exophytic and show epithelial dysplasia. Distinction from an exophytic conventional carcinoma is based on the degree of stromal invasion and the clearly defined papillary pattern of true papillary carcinoma.

Oral premalignancy

Leukoplakia and erythroplakia are recognized clinically as potentially malignant lesions. The main reason for biopsying such lesions is to exclude the possibility that a carcinoma is

already present. Thereafter the histopathologist is asked to assess and grade any dysplasia present. This is on the assumption that dysplasia is an indicator of the potential likelihood of progression to malignancy. The rationale for this assumption is that dysplasia is likely to be due to mutations involving the epithelium. It is unlikely that the mutations resulting in dysplasia are the same ones that are responsible for progression to malignancy. Microarray studies indicate substantial genomic change in dysplasia,[18] suggesting that many of the changes are epiphenomena not directly related to malignant change. It is assumed that the more dysplastic an epithelium is, the more likely it is that the critical mutations linked to malignant transformation will be present. Thus, more severely dysplastic lesions have a greater risk of progression. Overall, only a minority of lesions showing epithelial dysplasia progress to malignancy;[19] however malignancy can also arise in epithelium not showing dysplasia, but in which abnormal DNA by ploidy analysis may predict the development of carcinoma.[20]

The new World Health Organization (WHO) classification[9] recognizes that problems exist with the very subjective nature of assessment of dysplasia and the variation in grading, not only between pathologists but also for the same pathologist examining the same material on different occasions. The stratum corneum, if present, is ignored and dysplasia is assessed on the viable cell layers. The recommendation made is that the epithelium should be assessed in terms of change in architecture and then cytologic change (Table 6.1). If the architectural change is confined to the lower third of the epithelium, the dysplasia is mild (Fig. 6.13). Extension into the middle third indicates moderate dysplasia (Fig. 6.14) and involvement of the superficial third indicates severe dysplasia (Fig. 6.15). These preliminary judgments, based on the extent of architectural change, can be modified when consideration is given

Table 6.1	Criteria used in diagnosing dysplasia
Architecture	**Cytology**
Irregular epithelial stratification	Abnormal variation in nuclear size (anisonucleosis)
Loss of polarity of basal cells	Abnormal variation in nuclear shape (nuclear pleomorphism)
Drop-shaped rete ridges	Abnormal variation in cell size (anisocytosis)
Increased number of mitoses	Abnormal variation in cell shape (cellular pleomorphism)
Abnormally superficial mitoses	Increased nuclear–cytoplasmic ratio
Premature keratinization in single cells	Increased nuclear size
Keratin pearls within rete pegs	Atypical mitotic figures
Loss of intercellular attachment	Increased number and size of nucleoli Hyperchromatism

Based on the 2005 World Health Organization classification.[9]

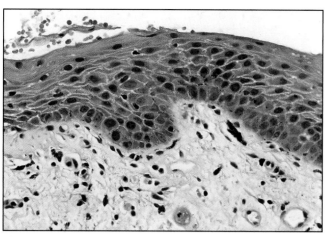

Fig. 6.13 • Mild dysplasia with changes confined to the deepest third of the epithelium and only mild cytologic changes. The pigmentation is reactive melanosis related to smoking in this floor-of-mouth lesion.

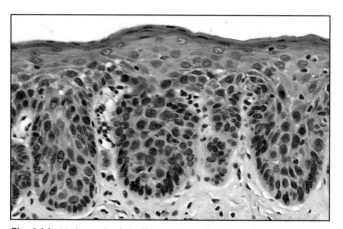

Fig. 6.14 • Moderate dysplasia. The prominent drop-shaped rete ridges show moderate cytologic changes which extend into the middle third of the epithelium.

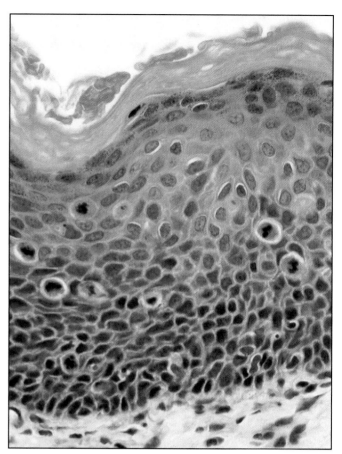

Fig. 6.15 • Severe dysplasia. Architectural change extends into the superficial third of the epithelium with increased and abnormally superficial mitoses.

to the severity of the cytologic features. In Figure 6.16 the initial assessment of moderate dysplasia is upgraded to severe dysplasia on this basis.

In determining whether or not dysplasia is present, it is important to recognize that other situations may mimic dysplasia. These include regenerative and reparative changes which might be related to inflammation, ulceration, or irradiation. Nutritional deficiencies such as iron, folate, or vitamin B₁₂ can also simulate dysplasia.

The concept of carcinoma in situ is that it represents epithelium which has already undergone malignant transformation, but in which invasion has not occurred. Where dysplasia involves the full thickness (or almost the full thickness) of the epithelium, the diagnosis of carcinoma in situ is appropriate (Fig. 6.17).

Proliferative verrucous leukoplakia[21,22] is a particularly aggressive form of leukoplakia which starts as simple hyperkeratosis but pursues a relentless clinical course to malignancy. The clinical features[23] are critical in the diagnosis and emphasize the need for histopathologic interpretation to be made in the proper clinical context. Diagnosis is therefore retrospective, based on a history of multiple and recurrent lesions and increasingly aggressive behavior.

Hairy leukoplakia is the term used to describe a clinically distinctive hyperkeratosis, principally restricted to the lateral aspect of the tongue in HIV-positive patients. It is caused by Epstein–Barr virus infection and less frequently in other immunosuppressed individuals. It does not show dysplasia and there is no evidence that it is premalignant.

Mesenchymal neoplasms and tumor-like lesions

The oral tissues are subject to the same types of mesenchymal neoplasms as are found at other body sites (see Chs 3, 23, and 24). All are uncommon and only a small minority are malignant. Perhaps the most frequently encountered are benign neural tumors, lipomas, and myofibromas. The most frequently encountered lesions submitted for histopathologic diagnosis, however, are various non-neoplastic fibrous overgrowths, usually related to some source of chronic irritation.

Fibrous and vascular overgrowths

Fibrous overgrowths not uncommonly occur as discrete lesions of cheek or tongue related to chronic irritation, usually from some tooth-related cause or from chronic cheek- or tongue-biting.

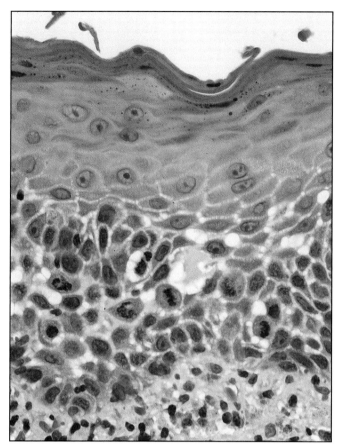

Fig. 6.16 • Moderate epithelial dyspalsia recategorized as severe. Although the architectural change appears restricted to the lower two-thirds of the epithelium, the magnitude of cytologic change justifies this lesion being recategorized as severe dysplasia.

Histologic appearances

Lesions are often pedunculated and consist of relatively cellular collagenous connective tissue covered by epithelium which may be hyperplastic or atrophic but which invariably shows keratinization. Enlarged, angular fibroblasts and occasional multinucleate fibroblasts are seen in some cases. The term giant cell fibroma has been used by some authors for such lesions, but this seems inappropriate as there is no evidence that they are neoplasms.

Pyogenic granuloma

Although the gingiva is the usual site for this lesion, discussed below under epulides, pyogenic granulomas (see Ch. 3) can occur as exuberant overgrowths at any intraoral site. The clinical differential diagnosis may include other hemangiomas and angiosarcoma, as well as bacillary angiomatosis and Kaposi sarcoma.

Histologic appearances

There is usually ulceration of the surface epithelium, which might account for a superficial zone of granulation tissue. The bulk of the lesion consists of loose connective tissue containing lobules of proliferating capillaries, which may be mitotically active.

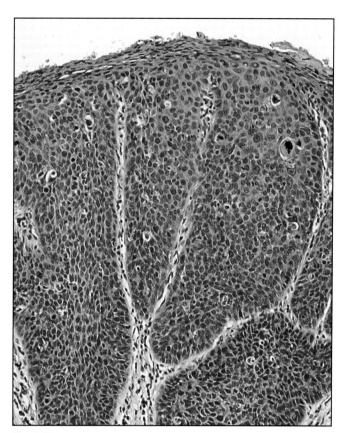

Fig. 6.17 • Carcinoma in situ. Architectural and cytologic changes involve the full thickness of the epithelium.

Differential diagnosis

On histologic grounds alone it may be impossible to differentiate a vascular epulis from a hemangioma with overlying ulceration. The differential diagnosis from rarer vascular neoplasms may require specialist consultation, especially since endothelial nuclear atypia is common in pyogenic granulomas in this region.[24]

Epulides

The term epulis describes a localized swelling on the gingiva. This can very often be related to chronic irritation. Three main types are recognized: (1) fibrous epulis; (2) giant cell epulis; and (3) vascular epulis. There are similarities in clinical presentation. Ulceration of the overlying epithelium is common, resulting in the superficial part of the lesion being granulation tissue. All are liable to recurrence, usually because of persistence of the provoking stimulus.

Fibrous epulis

Histologic appearances. The main mass of the lesion is a non-encapsulated area of very cellular connective tissue (Fig. 6.18) of bland cytologic appearance. Calcification in the form of small, rounded, usually acellular foci is common. Metaplastic bone formation, which is variably mature, is quite frequent. Such lesions are quite often inappropriately labelled as 'peripheral ossifying fibroma.' Small numbers of multinucleate giant cells may be seen. Areas of fibrous epulides can resemble

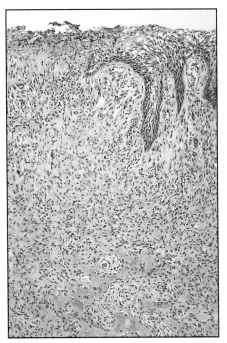

Fig. 6.18 • Fibrous epulis showing a mass of very cellular fibrous tissue and bone formation. Frequently there is ulceration of the surface epithelium, and the superficial parts of the lesion consist of granulation tissue.

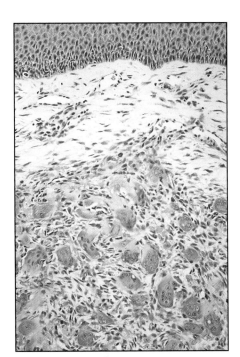

Fig. 6.19 • Giant cell epulis with numerous multinucleate giant cells in a vascular stroma.

fibrous dysplasia or ossifying fibroma, but the distinction from such bone lesions (see Ch. 25) is readily made by the clinically peripheral location of fibrous epulis, which does not arise in bone.

Giant cell epulis (synonym: peripheral giant cell granuloma)

Histologic appearances. The main feature is a non-encapsulated mass of closely packed osteoclast-like multinucleated giant cells lying in a vascular stroma containing plump mononuclear cells which are presumed to be the monocyte precursors of the giant cells (Fig. 6.19). Obvious mitotic activity is not uncommon in these cells.

Differential diagnosis. The main differential diagnosis is from central giant cell lesions extending from the bone to present as soft tissue lesions. The diagnosis of central giant cell granuloma is made after exclusion of hyperparathyroidism.[25] The brown tumors of osteitis fibrosa cystica are usually intra-osseous, but peripheral extension cannot be distinguished histologically from a giant cell epulis. Very occasionally giant cell epulis is a manifestation of hyperparathyroidism. This diagnosis should be considered where giant cell epulides are multiple or are associated with pregnancy, which can potentiate the manifestations of hyperparathyroidism.

Vascular epulides

Vascular epulides are essentially pyogenic granulomas which occur on the gingiva, this being the most frequent intraoral site (see also Ch. 3). The pregnancy epulis is such a lesion occurring during pregnancy; its growth may be quite exuberant, reaching 2 or 3 cm in size.

Histologic appearances. Lesions are identical to pyogenic granulomas seen at other intraoral sites, as described above.

Congenital epulis (synonym: granular cell epulis)

The congenital epulis is a rare but distinctive oral lesion of unknown etiology, found in the alveolus of neonates. Almost all affected patients are female. This lesion shows histologic similarities to granular cell tumor elsewhere but is S-100 protein-negative (see Ch. 27). Immunohistochemical studies have suggested primitive pericytic or myofibroblastic differentiation.[26]

Fibrous overgrowths related to wearing of dentures

Dentures, particularly if old and ill-fitting, are a common source of irritation. This gives rise to mucosal overgrowths to which various names are applied. Recurrence may be a problem following excision if the cause is not removed.

Denture-induced hyperplasia (poor synonyms: denture granuloma, epulis fissuratum, irritation fibroma)

These overgrowths are usually found in the labial or buccal sulci related to the denture periphery. Less frequently they occur at the posterior edge of an upper denture in the palate. "Leaf fibroma" is a descriptive term sometimes used for a pedunculated flattened fibrous overgrowth which may occur in the palate, occupying space between a poorly fitting denture and the palatal mucosa. This term is inappropriate in that the lesion is not a true neoplasm.

Histologic appearances. The lesion consists largely of collagenous connective tissue. The overlying epithelium varies from hyperplastic to ulcerated, in which case part of the tissue bulk may be granulation tissue.

Papillary hyperplasia of the palate

This occurs in the vault of the palate under a denture as a coarsely granular mass of soft tissue.

Histologic appearances. Cores of moderately vascular connective tissue are covered by irregularly hyperplastic epithelium. At low power this can sometimes simulate invasion (Fig. 6.20) with epithelial downgrowths and sometimes apparent keratin pearl formation. Higher-power examination confirms the entirely benign cytologic features.

Odontogenic cysts and tumors

The jaws are the only site in the body where epithelium may be found within bone. The epithelium of the dental lamina is involved in the formation of enamel and maps out the shape of the tooth. On completion of tooth formation, epithelial remnants remain in various areas. These may give rise to a range of lesions, including neoplasms and hamartomas, which should pose no problem with diagnosis when seen to be associated with teeth, but can cause difficulty in other situations. The most frequent epithelial rests are the debris of Malassez, which are found in the periodontal ligament as small clusters and strands of non-keratinizing stratified squamous epithelium, but occasionally as larger nests. These may be left in alveolar bone following tooth extraction. This epithelium gives rise to the most frequent type of odontogenic epithelial cyst, the *radicular cyst*, which is an inflammatory cyst arising as an extension from pulpitis in a tooth. Epithelial rests are also found in the follicles related to the crowns of unerupted teeth, where they may be misdiagnosed as ameloblastic fibroma.[27] Calcification can also occur in hyperplastic follicles, which are sometimes multiple.[28] The soft tissues overlying a partially erupted lower third molar often contain small hamartomatous overgrowths of odontogenic epithelium which may simulate several types of odontogenic tumor.[29,30] Less frequently, odontogenic epithelial hamartomas present as small overgrowths in gingiva and should not be overdiagnosed as peripheral ameloblastomas.

The classification of odontogenic lesions has recently been reviewed[9,31] but can be very complex. The classification used in this chapter is essentially that given by the earlier WHO publication.[32] The majority of lesions fit into this classification, but it is probably appropriate to regard odontogenic tumors as forming clusters of variably well-defined lesions with tumor labels. Several entities can show overlapping features and are best described as such. A key underlying principle in the classification scheme relates to the inductive interactions of the dental tissues, in which tumors mimic normal tooth development. The epithelium of the normal dental lamina arises by downgrowth from the oral epithelium. The formation of the connective tissue of the dental papilla is followed by differentiation of odontoblasts, which commence the formation of dentine, and ameloblasts then start to lay down enamel. Odontogenic tumors may consist entirely of epithelium or of mesenchyme, or may show an admixture of epithelial and mesenchymal components. Hard tissue formation may be variable, from small deposits of dentine-like material, to production of well-formed tooth-like structures seen in odontomes. The histopathology of tumors arising from odontogenic epithelium has been reviewed[33] and a detailed account of this whole subject area has been published.[31] Almost all odontogenic tumors are benign and non-metastasizing, although they can cause substantial local destruction and disfigurement.

A classification of benign tumors is shown in Table 6.2, with an indication of the relative frequency of occurrence of individual lesions.

Table 6.2	Classification of benign odontogenic tumors and relative frequency
	Frequency (%)
Odontogenic epithelium without odontogenic ectomesenchyme	
Ameloblastoma	12
Squamous odontogenic tumor	<1
Calcifying epithelial odontogenic tumor	<1
Odontogenic epithelium with odontogenic ectomesenchyme, with or without dental hard tissue formation	
Ameloblastic fibroma	2
Ameloblastic fibrodentinoma and ameloblastic fibro-odontoma	2
Odontoameloblastoma	<1
Adenomatoid odontogenic tumor	3
Calcifying odontogenic cyst	2
Complex odontoma	41
Compound odontoma	33
Odontogenic ectomesenchyme with or without included odontogenic epithelium	
Odontogenic fibroma	<1
Odontogenic myxoma	3
Cementoblastoma	<1

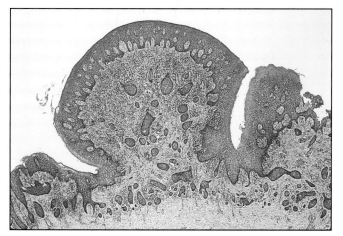

Fig. 6.20 • Papillary hyperplasia of palate with irregular epithelial overgrowth giving a low-power impression of invasion.

Tumor of odontogenic epithelium without odontogenic ectomesenchyme

Ameloblastoma

Clinical features

Ameloblastoma, the most frequent odontogenic neoplasm,[34] occurs most often in the mandible, particularly posteriorly. It may occur at any age, but the peak reported incidence is in the fourth decade. Mandibular tumors are painless, slow-growing swellings, which are said characteristically to produce multicystic or soap-bubble radiolucencies. Unilocular variants occur. Growth is by local expansion and infiltration with destruction of adjacent tissues. Untreated cases may reach a substantial size. Extension of tumor from the bone into adjacent soft tissues is an unfavorable sign.

Ameloblastomas in the maxilla occur in an older age group and have a poorer prognosis. There is a higher recurrence rate after surgery, probably related to the different bone structure in the maxilla and earlier spread into extraosseous soft tissues and the paranasal sinuses.

The most common type of ameloblastoma is the conventional or solid/multicystic type.[31] This type may have a number of histologic variants, but these do not have prognostic significance. Peripheral and unicystic types of ameloblastoma are also recognized (Table 6.3).

Macroscopic appearances

Ameloblastomas range greatly in gross appearance, from entirely solid to variably cystic lesions. When any cystic jaw lesion is being examined it is important to examine histologically any areas of thickening or growth into the cyst cavity for the possible presence of ameloblastoma.

Histologic appearances

Ameloblastomas are composed of epithelium and lack any evidence of induction of dental hard tissues. In the conventional, solid/multicystic type, the epithelium may show a follicular or a plexiform pattern, but a mixture of patterns may be seen within a single tumor. The most common pattern is follicular (Fig. 6.21), characterized by islands of epithelium with peripheral palisading of elongated columnar cells with reversed polarity, in that the nuclei are orientated away from the basement membrane. These cells resemble the pre-ameloblasts of normal tooth development. Centrally the islands contain loosely arranged stellate cells, showing a resemblance to the

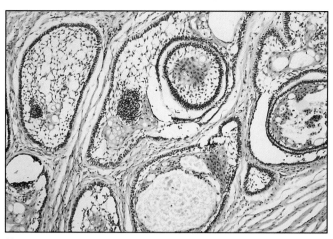

Fig. 6.21 • Follicular ameloblastoma with obvious peripheral palisading and central stellate reticulum areas. Some follicles show squamous differentiation and others show cystic change.

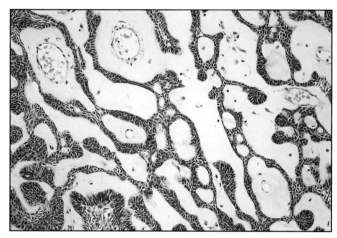

Fig. 6.22 • Plexiform ameloblastoma. The interlacing strands of epithelium often lack the peripheral palisading and stellate reticulum areas typical of follicular ameloblastoma.

stellate reticulum of the tooth germ. The plexiform pattern consists of strands and cords of epithelium (Fig. 6.22), often interconnecting. Columnar ameloblast-like cells are seen at the periphery, but stellate reticulum areas may be difficult to find. Within these two patterns there may be cellular variants. Acanthomatous ameloblastomas show evidence of squamous metaplasia within the tumor follicles, the stellate reticulum-like appearance is lost, and keratinization may be seen. A minority of tumors show areas of eosinophilic granular cells (Fig. 6.23) and very occasionally these may be the dominant feature, making the diagnosis of ameloblastoma difficult,

Table 6.3	Types of ameloblastoma, relative frequency, and key features	
Subtype	**Frequency (%)**	**Characteristics**
Conventional ameloblastoma (solid/multicystic)	85	Intraosseous lesions, may be solid or multicystic. Follicular or plexiform pattern. Most often at angle of mandible. Locally aggressive
Unicystic ameloblastoma	14	Intraosseous, single large unilocular cyst. May have luminal projections. Good prognosis, curettage usually curative
Peripheral ameloblastoma	1	Extraosseous, on the gingiva. Follicular or plexiform pattern. Good prognosis, rarely recurs

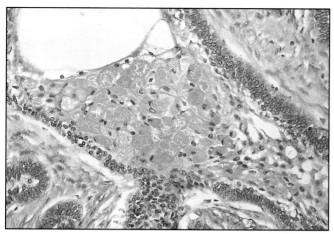

Fig. 6.23 • Granular cell area in a follicular ameloblastoma.

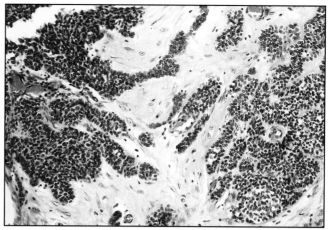

Fig. 6.25 • Basaloid pattern of ameloblastoma. In such cases it is important to look for more typical ameloblastoma in order to make the diagnosis.

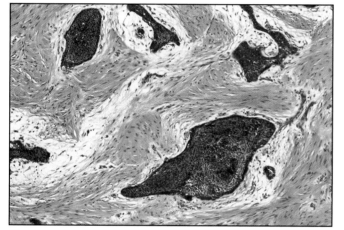

Fig. 6.24 • Desmoplastic ameloblastoma with epithelial elements widely dispersed in a dense collagenous stroma. The largest epithelial island shows the features of acanthomatous ameloblastoma, lacking the formation of stellate reticulum.

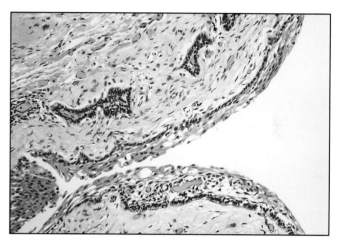

Fig. 6.26 • Cystic ameloblastoma. Part of the lining shows features identifiable as ameloblastoma, but other areas are stratified squamous epithelium lacking ameloblastoma features. Note the nests of plexiform ameloblastoma in the cyst wall.

particularly on small biopsy specimens. Desmoplastic ameloblastomas show extensive stromal desmoplasia characterized by densely collagenous fibrous tissue and, occasionally, bone formation.[35] The epithelial component may be reduced to thin anastomosing strands, although typical follicles with peripherally palisaded cells can usually be found (Fig. 6.24). Other uncommon variants are the basaloid (Fig. 6.25) and papilliferous types. Clear cells are infrequent, but there is a growing consensus that they are a sinister feature associated with aggressive and possibly malignant behavior[36,37] (see Malignant ameloblastoma, below).

Cyst formation in ameloblastomas is common. The cysts are usually lined by epithelium which is readily recognizable as ameloblastomatous, but occasionally cysts may be lined, at least in part, by attenuated squamous epithelium lacking features of ameloblastoma (Fig. 6.26). This can pose diagnostic difficulty in some cases, especially in biopsies, and surgeons should always be encouraged to biopsy solid or multicystic areas in preference to part of a large cyst.

Cytologically, ameloblastomas appear bland. There is variation in nuclear shape between peripheral and central cells in epithelial nests, but there is limited variation in cell and nuclear size and staining intensity. Mitotic activity is often

difficult to demonstrate. If more than a few mitoses are seen, the possibility of malignant ameloblastoma (see below) should be considered.

Unicystic ameloblastoma

A minority of ameloblastomas present as unilocular cysts.[31,38] These are often not diagnosed preoperatively as ameloblastomas, but as other types of odontogenic cyst. They are often treated by enucleation and the diagnosis is made subsequently by the pathologist. Unicystic ameloblastomas have the same site distribution as conventional ameloblastomas, but occur in a younger age group, often in the second decade. Three variants are described. The first shows a simple cystic lesion lined by ameloblastomatous epithelium which may become flattened and resemble a simple squamous epithelial lining. In the second variant, there may be intraluminal proliferations of ameloblastomatous epithelium. The intraluminal variant is usually plexiform[39] (plexiform unicystic ameloblastoma), with strands of epithelium that sometimes lack obvious ameloblastomatous features. Distinguishing this from hyperplastic proliferation in a non-neoplastic cyst may be difficult and is largely dependent upon the magnitude of proliferation. In these two types, the prognosis is good, with low recurrence rates even after conservative surgery. The third variant shows growth into the connective tissue wall of the cyst, so-called intramural proliferation. This variant is not truly unicystic and probably represents cystic change in a conventional follicular ameloblastoma. It has a similar prognosis to conventional ameloblastoma and requires similarly aggressive management.

Peripheral ameloblastoma

Very occasionally, ameloblastomas may arise from the oral epithelium of the gingiva or alveolus rather than within bone. The designation peripheral ameloblastoma[31,40] is used for these lesions. There is a superficial resemblance to basal cell carcinomas of skin. Peripheral ameloblastomas appear less aggressive than intraosseous lesions.

Squamous odontogenic tumor

Clinical features

Squamous odontogenic tumor, derived from debris of Malassez, was described as a distinct entity in 1975,[41] and only a small number of cases have been recorded. It presents as an apparently cystic lesion in the alveolus adjacent to tooth roots, causing tooth mobility and displacement. Multicentric and familial cases are recorded.[42]

Histologic appearances

The tumor consists of islands and strands of bland-looking stratified squamous epithelium lying in a collagenous stroma. Individual cell keratinization and small foci of keratin may be seen; cystic degeneration can occur within the epithelial islands. Calcified, crystalloid structures can occur within the epithelium, but dental hard tissue or amyloid is not found.

Differential diagnosis

The differential diagnosis from ameloblastoma is made by the lack of palisading of elongated cells at the periphery of the epithelial islands and the lack of stellate reticulum areas. The important differential diagnosis from squamous cell carcinoma is made by the lack of any cytologic features of malignancy in the squamous odontogenic tumor. Squamous odontogenic tumor-like proliferations have been described in association with some odontogenic cysts,[43] but these seem to be of no prognostic relevance.

Calcifying epithelial odontogenic tumor

This is also known as the Pindborg tumor, following its original description by that author, first in 1958[44] and later in more detail.[45]

Clinical features

Cases have been reported over a wide age range, although middle-aged adults are most often affected. The mandible is the most common site. The clinical and radiologic features are similar to ameloblastoma. It may present as an ill-defined multi- or unilocular radiolucency, but there is often calcified material which may be associated with unerupted teeth. Occasional extraosseous lesions occur, but these are essentially benign and non-destructive. Calcifying epithelial odontogenic tumor has a local recurrence rate of 10–15%.

Histologic appearances

The tumor shows quite variable histology (Fig. 6.27) and diagnosis is not always easy. Sheets and strands of polyhedral epithelial cells lie in a fibrous, often hyalinized stroma which may contain extensive dystrophic or cementum-like calcifications. The epithelium frequently contains rounded masses of tumor amyloid-like material which may calcify. Cyst formation may be present. A striking feature, often present, is marked anisonucleosis, nuclear pleomorphism, and hyperchromasia (Fig. 6.28). This gives a spurious impression of aggressiveness, but there is absent or minimal mitotic activity.

Differential diagnosis

The lesion is readily distinguishable from ameloblastoma. Clear cell areas may occur[46] (Fig. 6.28) and, when taken in conjunction with the bizarre nuclear features, require to be

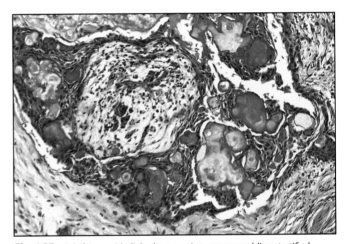

Fig. 6.27 • Calcifying epithelial odontogenic tumor resembling stratified squamous epithelium with areas of amyloid.

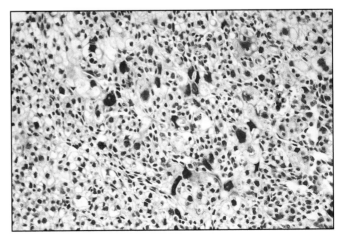

Fig. 6.28 • Calcifying epithelial odontogenic tumor. Focus showing marked cytologic atypia, but no mitotic activity in a clear cell variant.

distinguished from mucoepidermoid carcinoma, a metastatic clear cell neoplasm or from clear cell odontogenic carcinoma.

Tumors of odontogenic epithelium with odontogenic ectomesenchyme

Ameloblastic fibroma, ameloblastic fibrodentinoma, and ameloblastic fibro-odontoma

These tumors have been grouped together by some authors as mixed odontogenic tumors.[31,47] They are rare lesions which share many features but differ in regard to the calcified dental tissue components. Lesions presenting before the age of about 20 may well be part of the spectrum of developing odontomas. However, some ameloblastic fibromas and ameloblastic fibrodentinomas presenting beyond that age behave as benign neoplasms. It is not possible to differentiate between the neoplastic and hamartomatous variants on histologic grounds alone.[47]

Clinical features

Lesions most frequently present in the first two decades of life. The presentation may be similar to ameloblastoma but lesions are less aggressive, slowly growing, and usually less than 4 cm at presentation. Recurrence of ameloblastic fibroma after conservative surgery has been reported.[48]

Histologic appearances

There is a mixture of odontogenic mesenchyme, often myxomatous and similar to primitive dental pulp, and epithelium in strands and small nests (Fig. 6.29). The epithelium characteristically resembles branching strands of dental lamina with small buds resembling the enamel organ. The ameloblastic fibrodentinoma shows, in addition, dysplastic dentine (Fig. 6.30) and the ameloblastic fibro-odontoma shows odontoma formation (see below). Ameloblastic fibromas must

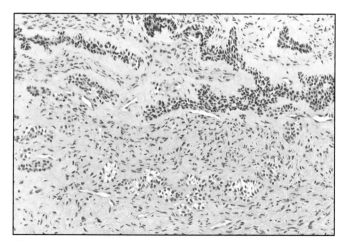

Fig. 6.29 • Ameloblastic fibroma with odontogenic epithelium and cellular connective tissue. The clear cell component seen in this field is not thought to have any prognostic significance.

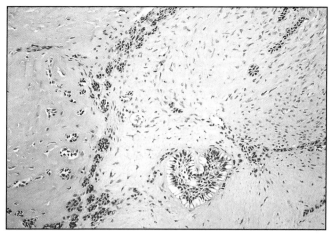

Fig. 6.30 • Ameloblastic fibrodentinoma showing dysplastic dentine in association with proliferating odontogenic epithelium and mesenchyme.

be differentiated histologically from ameloblastomas so as to prevent the risk of inappropriately aggressive management in a young person. Ameloblastomas do not contain dental lamina-like strands and the stroma is collagenous fibrous tissue rather than the loose odontogenic mesenchyme typical of ameloblastic fibroma.

Odontoameloblastoma

This very rare tumor shows odontoma formation in association with an otherwise conventional ameloblastoma.[49] The behavior is that of an ameloblastoma.

Adenomatoid odontogenic tumor

The adenomatoid odontogenic tumor,[50] at one time designated adenoameloblastoma, is a benign lesion, but whether it should be categorized as a hamartoma or a benign neoplasm is still debated.

Clinical features

These tumors most frequently present in the second decade, almost twice as often in the maxilla as in the mandible. About 40% are related to the crowns of unerupted maxillary canine teeth. A useful radiographic feature, strongly indicative of an odontogenic tumor, is the presence of radiopacities within a cyst cavity. Adenomatoid odontogenic tumors are symptomless and slow-growing; they are often discovered incidentally on radiographs, but may be large enough to appear as clinical swellings. Conservative surgical treatment is usually curative; recurrence, even after incomplete removal, is very rare.

Histologic appearances

There is usually a well-circumscribed epithelial proliferation which may have a cystic component. Much of the epithelium consists of small polyhedral cells with little cytoplasm, present in strands, sheets, and whorled areas, not particularly suggestive of odontogenic origin (Fig. 6.31). The adenomatoid elements (Fig. 6.32) are cross-sections of blind-ended infoldings from the periphery of the lesion, lined by more cuboidal

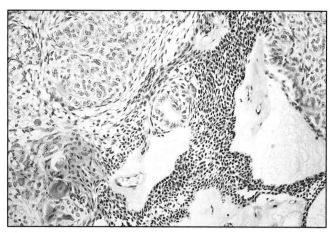

Fig. 6.31 • Adenomatoid odontogenic tumor showing small dark cells and whorls of larger paler cells.

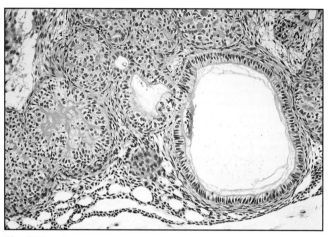

Fig. 6.32 • Adenomatoid components in association with other patterns of epithelium in adenomatoid odontogenic tumor.

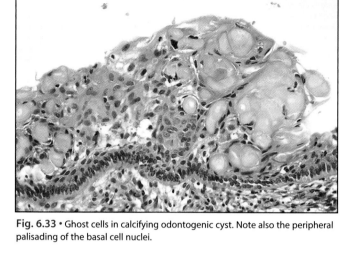

Fig. 6.33 • Ghost cells in calcifying odontogenic cyst. Note also the peripheral palisading of the basal cell nuclei.

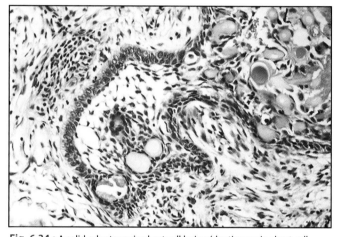

Fig. 6.34 • A solid odontogenic ghost cell lesion (dentinogenic ghost cell tumor) with area closely resembling ameloblastoma.

or columnar cells, and their frequency in any given case is variable. An additional variable feature is matrix formation in the form of small rounded acellular eosinophilic masses, probably a form of enamel protein, or less frequently as larger areas of dysplastic dentine which may calcify. Amyloid may occasionally be demonstrable[51] and melanin pigmentation is present on rare occasions.[52]

Odontogenic ghost cell lesions

Jaw lesions containing ghost cells are rare but well recognized. However their classification is complex and controversial. For a detailed discussion of this topic, readers are referred to specialist texts.[9,31] The most frequently encountered lesion is the calcifying odontogenic cyst which is a simple cystic lesion. Rare neoplastic variants are also recognized and have been designated *calcifying cystic odontogenic tumor* and *dentinogenic ghost cell tumor* for the cystic and solid variants respectively.[9,31,53,54]

Clinical features

Lesions usually present as symptomless unilocular cystic swellings. They are often associated with unerupted teeth or with

an odontoma.[55] Several variants of central lesions[31,56] and less frequent peripheral lesions[57] are recognized.

Histologic appearances

The characteristic feature of this group of lesions is the presence of ghost cells (Fig. 6.33) similar to those seen in pilomatrixoma (see Ch. 23). These are eosinophilic cells with distinct cell boundaries, many of which show a faint shadowy staining of the nucleus. The viable epithelium usually shows areas of peripheral nuclear palisading and looser stellate reticulum-like areas. The resemblance to ameloblastoma can be striking (Fig. 6.34). Calcification of ghost cell areas occurs. Dysplastic dentine or odontomas may be present adjacent to the epithelium. For all practical purposes it is not usually possible to distinguish histologically between a simple calcifying odontogenic cyst and a calcifying cystic odontogenic tumor. A judgment must be made on the basis of clinical behaviour, radiology, and histology. In any case, both lesions appear to be indolent and conservative enucleation is usually curative. The solid variant, dentinogenic ghost cell tumor, may arise in older age groups and be more aggressive. It has been suggested that these should be managed in the same way as ameloblastoma.

Differential diagnosis

Areas showing the features of calcifying odontogenic cyst have been reported in association with a number of other types of odontogenic tumor.[56] Lesions must be differentiated from cystic or solid ameloblastomas, but this is usually straightforward unless ghost cells are sparse. Lesions involving the palate need to be distinguished from craniopharyngiomas.

Odontoma (odontome)

By definition, an odontoma has to include all the calcified dental tissues. These are hamartomas and are the most frequent of the odontogenic tumors[47] (Table 6.2).

Clinical features

Odontomas are either detected as incidental radiologic findings or, less frequently, as slow-growing swellings in adolescence. They are often associated with unerupted teeth and are a cause of failed eruption of permanent teeth in young people. Sometimes ulceration of the overlying mucosa allows access of oral bacteria and the resulting infection causes presentation with pain.

Histologic appearances

Two variants are identified with differing clinical and histologic features. *Complex odontomas* are most frequently found in the posterior mandible and are composed of a mixture of dental hard tissues with no resemblance to a tooth. *Compound odontomas* are most common in the anterior maxilla and consist of numerous small, often irregularly shaped teeth. The dominant tissue is usually dentine, recognizable by the presence of tubules. Enamel matrix (Fig. 6.35) is acellular and pale-staining, with only the prism boundaries being evident. Cementum and loose connective tissue of the dental pulp are present. Areas of odontogenic epithelium are often present, usually associated with the areas of enamel matrix (Fig. 6.36), but forming only a small part of the total tumor mass. Not infrequently, a related dentigerous cyst is present.

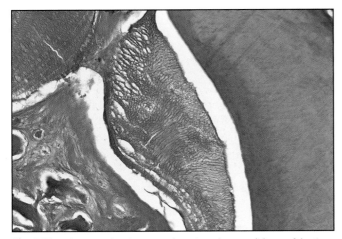
Fig. 6.35 • Odontoma showing enamel matrix and more solid area of dentine.

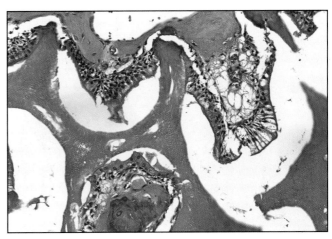
Fig. 6.36 • Odontoma with active odontogenic epithelium.

Differential diagnosis

Odontomas are usually simple, solitary lesions. However, they may be associated with another odontogenic tumor such as a calcifying odontogenic cyst,[55] or, very infrequently, they may be associated with ameloblastomatous proliferation, warranting the diagnosis of odontoameloblastoma. Immature or developing odontomas may be indistinguishable from ameloblastic fibroma or other mixed odontogenic tumors.

Tumors of odontogenic ectomesenchyme with or without included odontogenic epithelium

Odontogenic myxoma (synonym: myxoma of jaw)

Clinical features

Odontogenic myxomas can occur anywhere in the jaws but are most frequent in the mandibular premolar area. They are slow-growing swellings, radiographically seen as multilocular or soap-bubble radiolucencies. These tumors may be infiltrative and locally aggressive and often recur after attempted conservative surgical treatment.[31,58]

Histologic appearances

The tumor consists of dispersed, bland-looking stellate or spindled fibroblastic cells in a myxomatous matrix (Fig. 6.37). Small islands of odontogenic epithelium may be present but are not necessary to make the diagnosis. Bands of collagen may be seen and when present sometimes lead to the term myxofibroma. The tumor is not well defined and infiltrates into marrow spaces beyond the apparent radiographic limits.

Differential diagnosis

The diagnosis of odontogenic myxoma is made after exclusion of other possible myxomatous tumors. These may include myxoid liposarcoma, myxoid chondrosarcoma, chondromyxoid fibroma, myxoid neurofibroma, and neurofibrosarcoma.

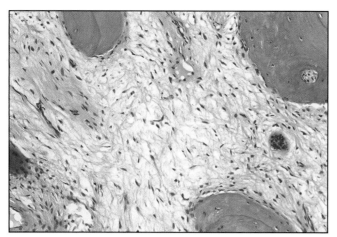

Fig. 6.37 • Odontogenic myxoma infiltrating bone. A small nest of inactive odontogenic epithelium is present.

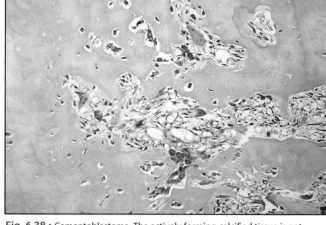

Fig. 6.38 • Cementoblastoma. The actively forming calcified tissue is not obviously recognizable as cementum. Prominent reversal lines may be present, sometimes with a pagetoid appearance.

Odontogenic fibroma

Clinical features

This term has been applied to more than one entity.[59] Enlarged follicles related to unerupted teeth may show relatively immature connective tissue with strands of proliferating odontogenic epithelium. Some authors regard this as an odontogenic fibroma, but most oral pathologists would diagnose it as an enlarged or hyperplastic dental follicle. Apart from such lesions, there exist both intraosseous (central)[59] and peripheral lesions designated as odontogenic fibromas. Central lesions present as relatively well-defined radiolucencies and the more common peripheral lesions present as epulides.[60]

Histologic appearances

Central odontogenic fibromas are well-defined non-infiltrating lesions composed of loosely collagenous fibrous connective tissue resembling a dental follicle. Widely scattered islands of inactive-looking odontogenic epithelium are seen throughout the lesion. Some lesions also contain calcifications resembling cementum, bone, or dentine. Peripheral lesions show similar features, although calcifications are more frequent.[61]

Cementoblastoma

Of the lesions previously designated as types of cemental tumor, only cementoblastoma is now regarded as an odontogenic neoplasm.[9,31] The previously designated cementifying fibroma is now categorized as ossifying fibroma (see Ch. 25). Periapical cemental dysplasia and gigantiform cementoma are no longer regarded as cemental neoplasms, but are thought to be non-neoplastic lesions, although their exact nature is still controversial. Cementoblastoma is analogous to osteoblastoma and can be very locally destructive.

Clinical features

Cementoblastoma usually presents as a tender, sometimes painful swelling of the alveolus in younger adults. Radiographically it is seen as a well-defined radiopaque expansion of a tooth root, most often a mandibular first permanent molar, with a radiolucent margin. Occasionally it presents as a lesion which persists after extraction of the related tooth.

Histologic appearances

The lesion consists of irregular trabeculae and islands of calcified tissue which may fuse into masses. Cementoblasts may be entrapped in the tissue and reversal lines may be prominent. At the tumor periphery there is often abundant matrix formation. Very active-looking plump cementoblasts (Fig. 6.38) can be alarming.

Differential diagnosis

Histologically the lesion may be identical to osteoblastoma, but the clear association with a tooth root allows the diagnosis.[62] It is important that the variable cytologic features are not overdiagnosed as osteosarcoma and it is always essential to take account of the clinical and radiographic features before making such a diagnosis.

Other "cemental" lesions[63]

Cementum is modified bone, altered by its relationship to teeth. Previous attempts to distinguish cementum from osteoid histologically are thought to be unsound. The neoplasm formerly designated as a cementifying fibroma is now regarded as part of the spectrum of ossifying fibroma (see Ch. 25). There are a number of other jaw lesions consisting of a mixture of calcified tissue and cellular connective tissue, thereby falling within the broad category of fibro-osseous lesions. The most frequent of these are thought to be dysplastic in nature rather than neoplasms, and the term cemento-osseous dysplasia covers this group.

Cemento-osseous dysplasias

Three entities are currently identified which share similar histologic features of variably cellular connective tissue and calcified tissue (Fig. 6.39). In practice it is not always easy to

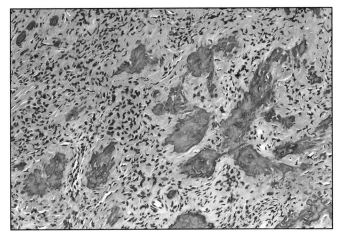

Fig. 6.39 • Cemento-osseous dysplasia. This cellular field with limited calcified material is from a periapical cemental dysplasia.

<table>
</table>

Table 6.4	Classification of malignant odontogenic neoplasms and key features
Odontogenic carcinomas	
Malignant ameloblastoma	An ameloblastoma with evidence of metastasis. The primary lesion and metastasis show similar histologic features of conventional ameloblastoma
Ameloblastic carcinoma	An ameloblastoma showing cytologic evidence of malignancy. May arise *de novo* or in a pre-existing conventional ameloblastoma. May metastasize
Primary intraosseous carcinoma	Squamous cell carcinoma derived from odontogenic epithelial rests. Must be wholly intraosseous and must exclude extension from mucosal lesion or metastasis
Clear cell odontogenic carcinoma	Entirely composed of clear cells. Aggressive and may metastasize. Exclude clear cell variants of other tumors and metastasis
Dentinogenic ghost cell carcinoma	Malignant variant of dentinogenic ghost cell tumour. Well characterized but very rare
Malignant variants of other odontogenic epithelial tumors	Malignant variants have rarely been described for most tumours. Key features are cytologic atypia or evidence of metastasis
Malignant change in odontogenic cysts	Described for most cyst types but for keratocyst most often. Cytologic evidence of malignancy in association with residual areas of the benign cyst
Odontogenic sarcomas	
Ameloblastic fibrosarcoma	Ameloblastic fibroma , but with cell crowding and evidence of cytologic atypia in the mesenchymal component
Ameloblastic fibrodentinosarcoma, ameloblastic fibro-odontosarcoma	Evidence of cytologic atypia in the mesenchymal component

categorize individual cases and they might be better regarded as parts of a morphologic spectrum rather than discrete conditions. These lesions are not distinguishable histologically. Periapical cemental dysplasia occurs at the apices of vital teeth, presenting classically as multiple radiolucencies. These can be mistaken radiographically for periapical inflammatory lesions, but become progressively more calcified over time. Solitary lesions, which may not be related to the teeth, are designated as focal cemento-osseous dysplasia,[64] while multiple lesions are seen in florid cemento-osseous dysplasia.

Malignant odontogenic neoplasms

All of these neoplasms are very rare and do not warrant extended discussion. A classification is shown in Table 6.4. This is based on the WHO classification.[9] Odontogenic carcinomas arise within bone and are much less frequent than involvement of bone by carcinomas of oral mucosa. Where tumors are large and have surface and intraosseous components it may be impossible to determine the site of origin. In general, a diagnosis of odontogenic carcinoma can only be made if a metastasis from a primary lesion elsewhere is first excluded.

Malignant ameloblastoma

Malignant ameloblastoma may arise from an existing ameloblastoma or the tumor may be malignant from the outset. Two types are recognized: those that resemble a conventional ameloblastoma histologically but have metastasized and those that show cytologic evidence of malignancy. The latter lesions have been designated ameloblastic carcinoma.[9,31,65] Areas recognizable as ameloblastoma need to be present, but the areas suggestive of malignancy are more densely cellular (Fig. 6.40), with cytologic features of malignancy. Invasive areas at the tumor periphery may present as undifferentiated carcinoma (Fig. 6.41). Recurrences are common and metastases to the lungs and regional lymph nodes may be seen.

Metastasizing ameloblastomas are very rare, but are characterized histologically by conventional solid/multicystic

ameloblastoma in both the jaw lesion and the metastasis. Many of the original reports of metastases in ameloblastomas were to the lung in patients subjected to multiple episodes of oral surgery. A number of apparent metastases are now thought to have been due to either iatrogenic vascular spread or perhaps even inhalation of tumor. Genuine hematogenous and lymphatic metastases can undoubtedly occur, confirming the malignant nature of these tumors. Metastasizing ameloblastomas are associated with a poor prognosis.

Clear cells appearing in an ameloblastoma (Fig. 6.42) are associated with clinical aggression and there is a growing view that such lesions are low-grade carcinomas.[36,37] The diagnosis

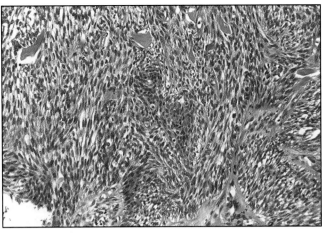

Fig. 6.40 • Densely cellular area within an ameloblastoma, but not showing obvious features of ameloblastoma.

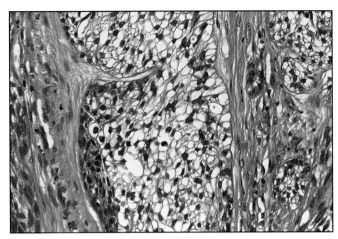

Fig. 6.42 • Clear cell area within an ameloblastoma. The appearance of these areas is closely similar to clear cell odontogenic carcinoma.

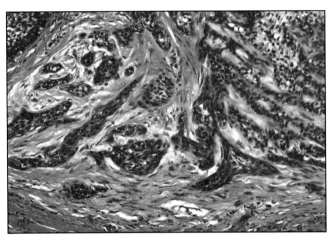

Fig. 6.41 • Undifferentiated invasive carcinoma at the margin of a malignant ameloblastoma.

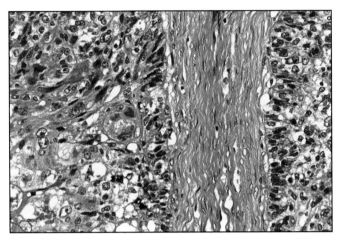

Fig. 6.43 • Primary intraosseous carcinoma with obviously malignant features showing limited palisading of basal cells in one area suggestive of an odontogenic origin.

should be made where the tumor shows areas of identifiable ameloblastoma in addition to the clear cell areas.[66]

Primary intraosseous carcinoma

This is essentially a squamous cell carcinoma arising within bone, presumably from odontogenic epithelial nests (Fig. 6.43). The diagnosis is made after exclusion of possible origin from a mucosal neoplasm invading bone, a neoplasm arising from an odontogenic cyst, or a metastasis.[67] Primary intraosseous carcinomas show a male predominance and are seen most frequently in the mandibular molar area.

Clear cell odontogenic carcinoma

This tumor was originally called clear cell odontogenic tumor,[32,68] but it is now apparent that this is an aggressive lesion with the potential to metastasize. There is a growing perception that clear cells in odontogenic tumors indicate malignancy and the designation of carcinoma is now appropriate.[9,31] Clinically this lesion most often presents as a painful

jaw swelling, associated with an ill-defined radiolucency with tooth mobility and destruction of bone.

Histologic appearances

The dominant cells have clear or faintly stippled cytoplasm (Fig. 6.44) which is rich in glycogen. The cells are arranged in clumps or strands within a collagenous stroma,[69] with wide infiltration of marrow spaces. A more basaloid population may form part of the tumor, but where areas of the tumor show recognizable features of other types of odontogenic tumor, the designation clear cell odontogenic carcinoma should not be used. Some authors dissent from this view and suggest that clear cell odontogenic carcinoma and ameloblastoma with clear cells should be grouped together.[70]

Differential diagnosis

The main differential diagnosis is from other clear cell tumors,[71] including clear cell variants of ameloblastoma, calcifying epithelial odontogenic tumor, and salivary gland tumors such as mucoepidermoid carcinoma and acinic cell carcinoma.

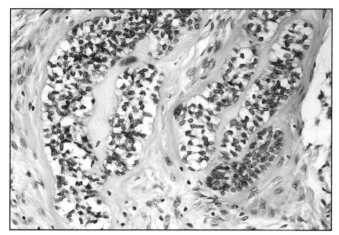

Fig. 6.44 • Clear cell odontogenic carcinoma. The cytologic features vary, but even the bland cytology illustrated belies the aggressive behavior of some of these tumors.

Other more typical areas of such tumors should be sought. Metastatic clear cell tumors, especially from kidney, need to be excluded.

Malignant variants of other odontogenic tumors

These are recorded as case reports and are so infrequent that no definitive pattern of presentation or behavior is yet apparent. The diagnosis depends on the recognition of the features of the benign variant, in association with a tumor identifiable as malignant either on cytologic grounds or by its behavior.[31]

Malignant change in odontogenic cysts

Squamous cell carcinoma arising from an odontogenic cyst is a rare complication, but this is still the most frequent of the malignant odontogenic neoplasms. In order for this diagnosis to be made with confidence, areas of non-neoplastic cyst lining must be identified and incidental involvement of a cyst in a tumor spreading from adjacent oral mucosa must be excluded. Such carcinomas usually arise in long-standing cysts, often with infection and with keratinization of the cyst lining. Sometimes these may be keratocysts, but other cases are probably due to keratinizing metaplasia.

Odontogenic sarcomas and carcinosarcomas

Very rare examples of these tumors have been described,[72,73] mainly as case reports. The histologic features are similar to those of the benign counterparts and the diagnosis of malignancy is made on the basis of cytologic features or the behavior. As such, it seems that these rare lesions most often arise in a pre-existing benign lesion.

Odontogenic cysts

Odontogenic cysts are benign cystic lesions derived from odontogenic epithelial rests within the jaws. Their classifi-

cation can be confusing and some lesions may be mistaken for tumors. For this reason a brief description of the common and important lesions has been included. Some lesions in particular have a potential for being confused as neoplasms because of their size or potential for recurrence. These include the odontogenic keratocyst, glandular odontogenic cyst, and botryoid odontogenic cyst. These will be discussed briefly, but more detail is available in specialized texts.[10,74] A simple classification and key features of odontogenic cysts are given in Table 6.5.

Radicular cyst

This is the most common of the odontogenic cysts and is variably designated as dental cyst, radicular cyst, or periapical cyst. These cysts arise as a result of inflammatory changes at the apex of a tooth and are thus always associated with a non-vital tooth, usually as a result of dental caries. The cyst develops due to proliferation of epithelial rests of Malassez in a pre-existing chronic inflammatory lesion (periapical granuloma). Clinically they present as slow-growing swellings or as a chance finding of a well-demarcated radiolucency at the apex of a tooth. Following extraction of the tooth, occasional cysts remain in the edentulous jaw and are termed residual cysts.

Histologic appearances

Radicular cysts are composed of an inflamed fibrous wall lined by non-keratinized stratified squamous epithelium (Fig. 6.45). In immature cysts the epithelium is proliferative and may form prominent arcades and thin strands, but with time the lining becomes thinned and of even thickness. Cholesterol clefts are often found in the cyst wall and the epithelium may contain small eosinophilic hyaline bodies. Areas of mucous metaplasia are not uncommon.

Dentigerous cyst

These are developmental cysts which arise from the attenuated enamel epithelium around the crown of an unerupted tooth. They are most commonly encountered on impacted third molars (wisdom teeth) or upper canines and present as a well-defined radiolucency enveloping the crown of the unerupted tooth. A superficial dentigerous cyst overlying an erupting tooth is sometimes called an eruption cyst. A cyst which is often confused with dentigerous cyst, but occurs in relation to the crown of a partially erupted tooth, and is inflammatory in origin rather than developmental, is called a paradental cyst.[75]

Histologic appearances

Typically the cyst wall is composed of loosely collagenous fibrous connective tissue without inflammation, lined by thin regular stratified squamous epithelium. In small cysts the lining may still resemble enamel epithelium, which includes a layer of cuboidal or low columnar epithelium and can be misinterpreted as a glandular epithelium (Fig. 6.46). By definition the cyst is attached to the neck of the associated tooth at the cement–enamel junction and examination of the macroscopic specimen is useful to confirm this.

Table 6.5	A simple classification of odontogenic cysts, relative frequency, and key features	
	Frequency (%)	Characteristics
Inflammatory odontogenic cysts		
Radicular cyst	65	Arises at the apex of a tooth root which is always non-vital. Inflamed fibrous wall lined by thickened or proliferative stratifying epithelium. Cholesterol clefts common
Paradental cyst	<5	Arises adjacent to a vital tooth, usually a partially erupted third molar. Due to inflammatory proliferation of follicular epithelium. Similar histologically to radicular cyst
Developmental odontogenic cysts		
Dentigerous cysts	20	Arises from follicular epithelium and embraces the crown of an unerupted tooth. Uninflamed wall lined by thin regular stratified epithelium
Odontogenic keratocyst	5	Arises within the bone from dental lamina rests. May be associated with a tooth. Multilocular radiolucency at angle of mandible. Uninflamed wall lined by thin regular parakeratinized epithelium. Prominent basal layer and folding of the lining. May be associated with nevoid basal cell carcinoma syndrome. A neoplastic variant, keratinizing cystic odontogenic tumor, has been described
Lateral periodontal cyst	<1	Arises from rest cells of Malassez adjacent to a vital tooth. Simple cyst lined by thin regular stratified epithelium with characteristic plaque-like thickenings
Botryoid odontogenic cysts	<1	Multilocular variant of lateral periodontal cyst. May recur because of convoluted nature of lining
Glandular odontogenic cysts	<1	Multilocular cyst, arises adjacent to teeth. Lining shows glandular metaplasia with mucus cells and duct-like structures. May recur
Gingival cysts	1	Small simple cysts (<1 cm) lined by stratified squamous epithelium. May be keratinized. Found on gingival margin in adults or on the alveolus in babies

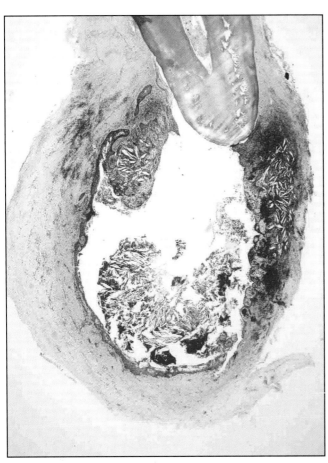

Fig. 6.45 • A typical radicular cyst. The lesion is attached to the apex of a tooth and is lined by variably proliferative stratified squamous epithelium. Cholesterol clefts are common in the inflamed fibrous wall.

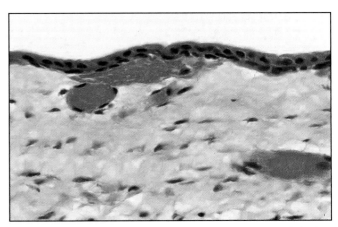

Fig. 6.46 • Dentigerous cyst. In this small cyst the lining is composed of only two cell layers and resembles the reduced enamel epithelium. Note the lack of inflammation in the wall. Inflamed dentigerous cysts may resemble a radicular cyst.

Odontogenic keratocyst

The odontogenic keratocyst has generally been regarded as a developmental cyst, but there is now evidence that at least a subset of these lesions may be benign cystic tumors. In the latest WHO classification, a new entity, the *keratinizing cystic odontogenic tumor*, has been introduced.[9] This is based on the findings that some keratocysts behave aggressively, solid variants have been described,[76] and that some lesions are associated with basal cell carcinomas in the nevoid basal cell carcinoma syndrome (Gorlin's syndrome). Syndromic keratocysts and a minority of spontaneous lesions share a similar *PTCH* gene mutation with basal cell carcinomas,[77] and molecular studies have shown evidence of clonality and multiple losses of tumor suppressor genes.[78,79] Sporadic lesions also frequently show allelic imbalances.[79a] Criteria for histologic differentiation of simple cysts from neoplastic variants remain to be established.

Clinical features

Odontogenic keratocyst presents most typically as a symptomless expansion of the jaw associated with a multilocular radiolucency. The angle of the mandible is the most common site. Lesions are usually solitary except when associated with the nevoid basal cell carcinoma syndrome when multiple and recurrent cysts may be found. Keratocysts may envelop an unerupted tooth and appear dentigerous on a radiograph, or may occasionally replace a tooth. They arise from rests of dental lamina, but the alternative name "primordial cyst" was derived from the erroneous concept that this cyst arises by degeneration of a tooth germ before calcified tissue has formed.

Histologic appearances

The diagnostic feature of this cyst is the keratinized lining. The epithelium is typically thin and tightly folded with a palisaded basal layer and a thin corrugated parakeratinized surface layer (Fig. 6.47). Cysts are often large and multilocular, particularly those located in the posterior mandible. Occasional lesions are multicystic or solid and are thought to represent one end of the neoplastic spectrum.[76] Recurrence is thought to be due either to incomplete removal of cysts or because of growth of daughter cysts adjacent to the main cyst. Ameloblastoma-like proliferation can occasionally be seen in the wall of keratocysts and should not be overdiagnosed. The keratinization can be missing in inflamed areas. Some keratocysts have areas of orthokeratosis in the lining; cysts lined entirely by orthokeratinized epithelium are said to be less aggressive.

Botryoid odontogenic cyst[80]

This cyst is a multilocular variant of the lateral periodontal cyst, which is a developmental cyst arising from epithelial rests in the periodontal ligament. The lining is non-keratinized stratified squamous epithelium and a distinctive feature is the presence of thickened areas called epithelial plaques (Fig. 6.48). Although usually small, the multilocular nature of the lesion may result in residual disease after surgery and recurrence.

Glandular odontogenic cyst (sialo-odontogenic cyst)[81,82]

These are rare multilocular cysts which share many features with botryoid odontogenic cysts. The additional characteristic feature is the presence of areas of glandular epithelium (Fig. 6.49) often with lumina in the epithelial lining and with mucus production. Cuboidal or columnar surface cells may be present and cilia are sometimes seen. An important differential diagnosis is from central mucoepidermoid carcinoma.[83]

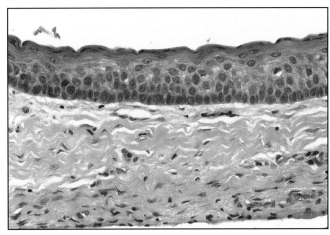

Fig. 6.47 • Odontogenic keratocyst with thin parakeratinized surface layer. The basal layer varies from aligned low columnar cells, as in this case, to more elongated palisaded cells.

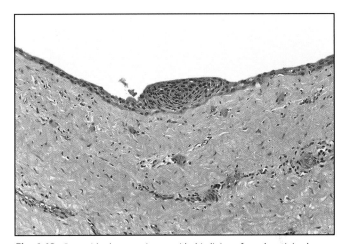

Fig. 6.48 • Botryoid odontogenic cyst with thin lining of non-keratinized stratified squamous epithelium and thickened area known as an epithelial plaque.

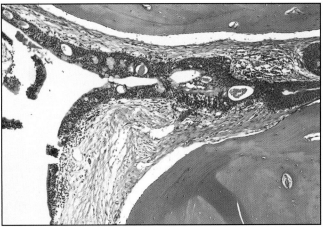

Fig. 6.49 • Recurrent glandular odontogenic cyst within bone.

References

1. Henley J D, Summerlin D-J, Tomich C E 2004 Condyloma acuminatum and condyloma-like lesions of the oral cavity: a study of 11 cases with an intraductal component. Histopathology 44: 216–221

2. Henke R P, Guerin-Reverchon I, Milde-Langosch K et al. 1989 In situ detection of human papillomavirus types 13 and 32 in focal epithelial hyperplasia of the oral mucosa. J Oral Pathol Med 18: 419–421

3. Speight P M, Farthing P M, Bouquot J E 1996 The pathology of oral cancer and precancer. Curr Diagn Pathol 3: 165–176

4. Mashberg A, Feldman L J 1988 Clinical criteria for identifying early oral and oropharyngeal carcinoma: erythroplasia revisited. Am J Surg 156: 273–275

5. Anneroth G, Batsakis J, Luna M 1987 Review of the literature and a recommended system of malignancy grading in oral squamous cell carcinomas. Scand J Dent Res 95: 229–249

6. Bryne M, Koppang H, Lilleng R et al. 1992 Malignancy grading of the deep invasive margins of oral squamous cell carcinomas has high prognostic value. J Pathol 166: 375–381

7. Woolgar J A 1995 Prediction of cervical lymph node metastasis in squamous cell carcinoma of the tongue/floor of mouth. Head Neck 17: 463–472

8. Fukano H, Matsuura H, Hasegawa Y et al. 1997 Depth of invasion a predictive factor for cervical lymph node metastasis in tongue carcinoma. Head Neck 19: 205–210

9. Barnes L, Eveson J W, Reichart P, Sidransky D (eds) 2005 WHO classification of tumours. Pathology and genetics of head and neck tumours. IARC Press, Lyon

10. Odell E W, Morgan P R 1998 Biopsy pathology of the oral tissues. Chapman & Hall Medical, London, p 214–236

11. Ellis G L, Corio R L 1980 Spindle cell carcinoma of the oral cavity. Oral Surg Oral Med Oral Pathol 50: 523–534

12. Batsakis J G, Huser J 1990 Squamous carcinomas with gland-like (adenoid) features. Ann Otol Rhinol Laryngol 99: 87–88

13. Ferlito A, Devaney K O, Rinaldo A et al. 1996 Mucosal adenoid squamous cell carcinoma of the head and neck. Ann Otol Rhinol Laryngol 105: 409–413

14. Izumi K, Nakajima T, Maeda T et al. 1998 Adenosquamous carcinoma of the tongue. Oral Surg Oral Med Oral Pathol 85: 178–184

15. Banks E R, Frierson H F, Mills S E et al. 1992 Basaloid squamous cell carcinoma of the head and neck. Am J Surg Pathol 16: 939–946

16. Barnes L, Ferlito A, Altavilla G et al. 1996 Basaloid squamous cell carcinoma of the head and neck: clinicopathological features and differential diagnosis. Ann Otol Rhinol Laryngol 105: 75–82

17. Luna M A, Tortoledo M E 1988 Verrucous carcinoma. In: Gnepp D R (ed) Pathology of the head and neck. Churchill Livingstone, Edinburgh, p 497–515

18. Hunter K D, Parkinson E K, Harrison P R 2005 Profiling early head and neck cancer. Nat Rev Cancer 5: 127–135

19. Schepman K P, van der Meij E H, Smeele L E et al. 1998 Malignant transformation of oral leukoplakia: a follow-up study of a hospital-based population of 166 patients with oral leukoplakia from The Netherlands. Oral Oncol 34: 270–275

20. Sudbo J, Ried T, Bryne M et al. 2001 Abnormal DNA content predicts the occurrence of carcinomas in non-dysplastic oral white patches. Oral Oncol 37: 558–565

21. Hansen L S, Olson J A, Silverman S 1985 Proliferative verrucous leukoplakia: a long term study of thirty patients. Oral Surg Oral Med Oral Pathol 60: 285–298

22. Batsakis J G, Suarez P, El-Naggar A K 1999 Proliferative verrucous leukoplakia and its related lesions. Oral Oncol 35: 354–359

23. Zakrzewska J M, Lopes V, Speight P et al. 1996 Proliferative verrucous leukoplakia. Oral Surg Oral Med Oral Pathol 82: 396–401

24. Renshaw A A, Rosai J 1993 Benign atypical vascular lesions of the lip. A study of 12 cases. Am J Surg Pathol 17: 557–565

25. MacDonald D G, Boyle I T 1990 Skeletal diseases. In: Jones J H, Mason D K (eds) Oral manifestations of systemic disease, 2nd edn. Bailliere Tindall, London, p 616–659

26. Damm D D, Cibull M L, Geissler R H et al. 1993 Investigation into the histogenesis of congenital epulis of the newborn. Oral Surg Oral Med Oral Pathol 76: 205–212

27. Kim J, Ellis G L 1993 Dental follicular tissue: misinterpretation as odontogenic tumors. J Oral Maxillofac Surg 51: 762–767

28. Gardner D G, Radden B 1995 Multiple calcifying hyperplastic dental follicles. Oral Surg Oral Med Oral Pathol 79: 603–606

29. Philipsen H P, Thosaporn W, Reichert P A et al. 1992 Odontogenic lesions in opercula of permanent molars delayed in eruption. J Oral Pathol Med 21: 38–41

30. Yonemochi H, Noda T, Saku T 1998 Pericoronal hamartomatous lesions in the opercula of teeth delayed in eruption: an immunohistochemical study of the extracellular matrix. J Oral Pathol Med 27: 441–452

31. Reichart P A, Philipsen H P 2004 Odontogenic tumours and allied lesions. Quintessence Publishing, London

32. Kramer I R H, Pindborg J J, Shear M 1992 Histological typing of odontogenic tumors, 2nd edn. Springer-Verlag, Berlin

33. MacDonald D G, Browne R M 1997 Tumours of odontogenic epithelium. In: Anthony P P, MacSween R N M, Lowe D G (eds) Recent advances in histopathology 17. Churchill Livingstone, Edinburgh, p 139–166

34. Reichart P A, Philipsen H P, Sonner S 1995 Ameloblastoma: biological profile of 3677 cases. Eur J Cancer B Oral Oncol 31: 86–99

35. Philipsen H P, Ormiston I W, Reichart P A 1992 The desmo- and osteoplastic ameloblastoma. Int J Oral Maxillofac Surg 21: 352–357

36. Waldron C A, Small I A, Silverman H 1985 Clear cell ameloblastoma – an odontogenic carcinoma. J Oral Maxillofac Surg 43: 707–717

37. Muller H, Slootweg P 1986 Clear cell differentiation in an ameloblastoma. J Maxillofac Surg 14: 158–160

38. Philipsen H P, Reichert P A 1998 Unicystic ameloblastoma. A review of 193 cases from the literature. Oral Oncol 34: 317–325

39. Gardner D G, Corio R L 1984 Plexiform unicystic ameloblastoma. Cancer 53: 1730–1735

40. Gardner D G 1977 Peripheral ameloblastoma: a study of 21 cases including 5 reported as basal cell carcinoma of the gingiva. Cancer 39: 1625–1633

41. Pullon P A, Shafer W G, Elzay R P et al. 1975 Squamous odontogenic tumor. Oral Surg Oral Med Oral Pathol 40: 616–630

42. Leider A S, Jonker L A, Cook H E 1989 Multicentric familial squamous odontogenic tumor. Oral Surg Oral Med Oral Pathol 68: 175–181

43. Unal T, Gomel M, Gunel O 1987 Squamous odontogenic tumor-like islands in a radicular cyst. J Oral Maxillofac Surg 45: 346–349

44. Pindborg J J 1958 A calcifying epithelial odontogenic tumor. Cancer 11: 838–843

45. Franklin C D, Pindborg J J 1976 The calcifying epithelial odontogenic tumor. Oral Surg Oral Med Oral Pathol 42: 753–765

46. Hick M J, Flaitz C M, Wong M E K et al. 1994 Clear cell variant of calcifying epithelial odontogenic tumor: a case report and review of the literature. Head Neck 16: 272–277

47. Philipsen H P, Reichart P A, Praetorius F 1997 Mixed odontogenic tumours and odontomas. Considerations on interrelationship. Review of the literature and presentation of 134 new cases of odontomas. Oral Oncol 33: 86–99

48. Zallen R D, Preskar M H, McClary S A 1982 Ameloblastic fibroma. J Oral Maxillofac Surg 40: 513–517

49. La Briola J D, Steiner M, Bernstein M L et al. 1980 Odontoameloblastoma. J Oral Surg 38: 139–143

50. Philipsen H P, Reichart P A, Zhang K H et al. 1991 Adenomatoid odontogenic tumor: biologic profile based on 499 cases. J Oral Pathol Med 20: 149–158

51. Buchner A, David R 1976 Amyloid-like material in odontogenic tumors. J Oral Surg 34: 320–323

52. Takeda Y 1989 Pigmented adenomatoid odontogenic tumour. Virchows Arch [A] 415: 571–575

53. Hong S P, Ellis G L, Hartman K S 1991 Calcifying odontogenic cyst. Oral Surg Oral Med Oral Pathol 72: 56–64

54. Toida M 1998 So-called calcifying odontogenic cyst: review and discussion on the terminology and classification. J Oral Pathol Med 27: 49–52

55. Hirshberg A, Kaplan I, Buchner A 1994 Calcifying odontogenic cyst associated with odontoma. J Oral Maxillofac Surg 52: 555–558

56. Buchner A 1991 The central (intraosseous) calcifying odontogenic cyst: an analysis of 215 cases. J Oral Maxillofac Surg 49: 330–339

57. Buchner A, Merrill P W, Hansen L S et al. 1991 Peripheral (extraosseous) calcifying odontogenic cyst: a review of 45 cases. Oral Surg Oral Med Oral Pathol 72: 65–70

58. Baker B F 1999 Odontogenic myxoma. Semin Diagn Pathol 16: 297–301

59. Gardner D G 1996 Central odontogenic fibroma – current concepts. J Oral Pathol Med 25: 556–561

60. Buchner A, Ficarra G, Hansen L S 1987 Peripheral odontogenic fibroma. Oral Surg Oral Med Oral Pathol 64: 432–438

61. Slabbert H de V, Altini M 1991 Peripheral odontogenic fibroma: a clinicopathologic study. Oral Surg Oral Med Oral Pathol 72: 86–90

62. Slootweg P J 1992 Cementoblastoma and osteoblastoma: a comparison of histologic features. J Oral Pathol Med 21: 385–389

63. Waldron C A 1993 Fibro-osseous lesions of the jaws. J Oral Maxillofac Surg 51: 828–835

64. Su L, Weathers D R, Waldron C A 1997 Distinguishing features of focal cemento-osseous dysplasias and cemento-osseous fibromas. Oral Surg Oral Med Oral Pathol 84: 301–309

65. Simko E J, Brannon R B, Eibling D E 1998 Ameloblastic carcinoma of the mandible. Head Neck 20: 654–659

66. Mari A, Escutia E, Carrera M et al. 1995 Clear cell ameloblastoma or odontogenic carcinoma. J Cranio Maxillo-Fac Surg 23: 387–390

67. Suei Y, Tanimoto K, Taguchi A et al. 1994 Primary intraosseous carcinoma: review of the literature and diagnostic criteria. J Oral Maxillofac Surg 52: 580–583

68. Hansen L S, Eversole L R, Green T L et al. 1985 Clear cell odontogenic tumor – a new histologic variant with aggressive potential. Head Neck Surg 8: 115–123

69. Eversole L R, Duffey D C, Powell N B 1995 Clear-cell odontogenic carcinoma – a clinicopathological analysis. Arch Otolaryngol Head Neck Surg 121: 685–689

70. Yamamoto H, Inui M, Mori A et al. 1998 Clear cell odontogenic carcinoma. Oral Surg Oral Med Oral Pathol 86: 86–89

71. Maiorano E, Altini M, Favia G 1997 Clear cell tumours of the salivary glands, jaws and oral mucosa. Semin Diagn Pathol 14: 203–212

72. Chomette G, Auriol M, Guilbert F et al. 1983 Ameloblastic fibrosarcoma of the jaws – report of three cases. Pathol Res Pract 178: 40–47

73. Wood R M, Markle T L, Barker B F et al. 1988 Ameloblastic fibrosarcoma. Oral Surg Oral Med Oral Pathol 66: 74–77

74. Cawson R A, Speight P, Binnie W H et al. (eds) 1998 Lucas's pathology of the tumors of the oral tissues, 5th edn. W B Saunders, Philadelphia

75. Craig G T 1976 The paradental cyst. A specific inflammatory odontogenic cyst. Br Dent J 141: 9–14

76. Vered M, Buchner A, Dayan D et al. 2004 Solid variant of odontogenic keratocyst. J Oral Pathol Med 33: 125–128

77. Barreto D C, Gomez R S, Bale A et al. 2000 PTCH gene mutations in odontogenic keratocysts. J Dent Res 79: 1418–1422

78. Shear M 2002 The aggressive nature of the odontogenic keratocyst: is it a benign cystic neoplasm? Part 2. Proliferation and genetic studies. Oral Oncol 38: 323–331

79. Agaram N P, Collins B M, Barnes L et al. 2004 Molecular analysis to demonstrate that odontogenic keratocysts are neoplastic. Arch Pathol Lab Med 128: 313–317

79a. Henley J, Summerlin D J, Tomich C et al. 2005 Molecular evidence supporting the neoplastic nature of odontogenic keratocyst: a laser capture microdissection study of 15 cases. Histopathology 47:582–586

80. Gurol M, Burkes E J, Jacoway J 1995 Botryoid odontogenic cyst: analysis of 33 cases. J Periodontol 66: 1069–1073

81. Hussain K, Edmondson H D, Browne R M 1995 Glandular odontogenic cysts. Oral Surg Oral Med Oral Pathol 79: 593–602

82. Koppang H S, Johannessen S, Haugen L K et al. 1998 Glandular odontogenic cyst (sialo-odontogenic cyst): report of two cases and literature review of 45 previously reported cases. J Oral Pathol Med 27: 455–462

83. Manojlovic S, Grgurvic J, Knezevic G et al. 1997 Glandular odontogenic cyst: a case report and clinicopathologic relationship to central mucoepidermoid carcinoma. Head Neck 19: 227–231

Salivary gland tumors

Wah Cheuk   John K.C. Chan

The normal salivary glands

Applied anatomy

The salivary gland system comprises three pairs of major glands (parotid, submandibular, and sublingual) and about 500–1000 lobules of minor glands dispersed in the submucosa of the oral cavity. The seromucinous glands of the nasal cavity, larynx, and bronchi, although not producing saliva by definition, are histologically similar to the minor salivary glands and share a similar repertoire of neoplasms.

The normal adult parotid gland weighs 15–30 g. The superficial and deep lobes are separated by the facial nerve. Most salivary gland tumors arise from the superficial lobe and present as facial swellings. Tumors that occur in the deep lobe often expand through the parapharyngeal space, manifesting as pharyngeal swelling.[1] The accessory lobe of the parotid gland, situated adjacent to Stenson's duct and separate from the main body of the parotid gland, is found in 21% of normal subjects.[2] Tumors arising in this lobe often present as mid-cheek masses.[3] About 20 lymph nodes and randomly distributed lymphoid aggregates are normally present in the parotid gland, with the latter component representing the mucosa-associated lymphoid tissue (MALT).[4] Conventional types of nodal lymphoma occurring in intraparotid lymph nodes may present as a salivary gland tumor. Conversely, salivary gland tissues can be found in intraparotid, para-parotid, and cervical lymph nodes, and are believed to give rise to Warthin tumor and other salivary gland tumors in lymph nodes mimicking metastatic disease.[5]

The submandibular and sublingual glands weigh approximately 7–15 g and 2–4 g respectively. Unlike the parotid gland, there is no lymph node or large nerve coursing through the parenchyma, although lymph nodes are normally present adjacent to the submandibular gland.

Minor salivary glands can be found in the lateral margins of the tongue, lips, buccal mucosa, palate, and glossopharyngeal area. Among them, the palate is the site of predilection for salivary gland neoplasms.

Histology

Tissue organization

The major salivary glands are enveloped by a thin fibrous capsule, except the sublingual gland, where the capsule is incomplete. The salivary lobules consist of variable proportions of serous and mucous cells. The parotid gland is exclusively serous, the submandibular gland mixed seromucinous, and the sublingual gland predominantly mucous; the minor glands are seromucinous or predominantly mucous, depending on location.

Salivary glands are tubuloacinar exocrine glands. The acini are the secretory units situated at the terminus. The secretion reaches the oral cavity via the conducting unit, consisting of intercalated, striated, interlobular, excretory, and salivary ducts (Fig. 7.1). Preservation of the lobular architecture is an important feature favoring a diagnosis of a non-neoplastic process over a tumor. The entire glandular structure is a

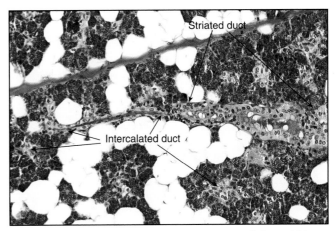

Fig. 7.1 • The normal parotid gland. The acini are composed of pyramidal-shaped serous cells with basally located nuclei and abundant dark-purple zymogen granules. They drain into the narrow intercalated ducts which are lined by cuboidal cells. The intercalated ducts are in continuity with the striated ducts, which have a wider lumen lined by columnar oncocytic cells.

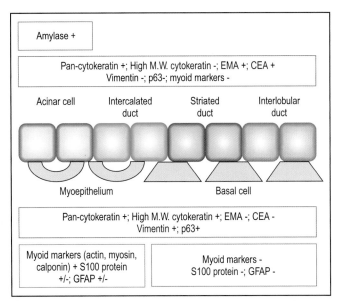

Fig. 7.2 • Schematic drawing depicting the cell types that constitute the serous secretory unit and their immunophenotypic profiles.

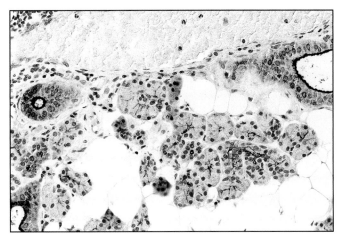

Fig. 7.3 • The normal parotid gland immunostained for epithelial membrane antigen (EMA). The luminal borders of the secretory cells and ducts are highlighted.

two-tiered organization which comprises luminal (acinar and ductal cells) and abluminal (myoepithelial and basal cells). The secretory acini and the intercalated ducts are wrapped by myoepithelial cells (Fig. 7.2). The striated ducts and the downstream conducting units are lined by simple or pseudostratified columnar epithelium which gradually transforms into stratified squamous epithelium in the salivary duct, and they are supported by basal cells.

Cellular morphology and immunophenotypic profile

Serous cells are pyramidal, with basal nuclei and abundant basophilic cytoplasm rich in zymogen granules that are periodic acid–Schiff (PAS)-positive (diastase-resistant) and mucicarmine-negative. The mucous cells are cuboidal to columnar, and have pale, finely vacuolated cytoplasm containing sialomucins. They are PAS-positive (diastase-resistant) and mucicarmine-positive. The luminal cells of the intercalated ducts are cuboidal, with eosinophilic to amphophilic cytoplasm and centrally located nuclei. The striated ducts are lined by columnar cells with granular cytoplasm (mitochondria-rich) and subnuclear vertical striations due to the prominent basal folds in the plasma membrane (Fig. 7.1). The luminal cells are readily highlighted by immunostaining for cytokeratin, carcinoembryonic antigen (CEA), and epithelial membrane antigen (EMA) (Figs 7.2 and 7.3). CD117/c-kit is negative in the normal salivary gland cells, but is interestingly often positive in the luminal (glandular) cells of various types of salivary gland tumors.

Myoepithelial cells are physiologically and functionally modified epithelial cells situated between the luminal cells and the basement membrane. They are stellate-shaped with cytoplasmic processes embracing the acini, or spindle-shaped surrounding the intercalated ducts. However, they cannot be reliably distinguished from basal cells on light microscopy. They possess a dual epithelial and smooth muscle phenotype characterized ultrastructurally by the presence of desmosomes, intermediate filaments, pinocytotic vesicles, and myofilaments.[6]

Myoepithelial cells produce extracellular matrix such as basement membrane materials and myxoid substances, which may account for the diverse morphology of various salivary gland tumors. They may also exert an anti-invasive effect in neoplasms by promoting epithelial differentiation, secreting proteinase inhibitors, and suppressing angiogenesis.[7] Myoepithelial cells are best highlighted by immunostaining for p63, high-molecular-weight cytokeratin (including cytokeratin 14 (CK14)), calponin, actin, and variably glial fibrillary acidic protein (GFAP) (Figs 7.2 and 7.4).

The abluminal cells in the striated ducts, excretory ducts, and salivary ducts are basal cells, which differ ultrastructurally from myoepithelial cells in the absence of myofilaments. They maintain the capacity of multidirectional differentiation and play an important role in the processes of regeneration and metaplastic changes.[8] They are immunoreactive for p63 and high-molecular-weight cytokeratin (Figs 7.2 and 7.4B), but not the myoid markers.

Oncocytic cells, characterized by abundant eosinophilic granular cytoplasm due to accumulation of mitochondria, are uncommon below the age of 50, but increase thereafter until they are almost universal above the age of 70. They show variable replacement of the normal cells of ductoacinar units. Oncocytic metaplasia has been implicated in the development of oncocytic hyperplasia, nodular oncocytosis, and even oncocytoma.[9]

Adipose tissue is normally a conspicuous component of the parotid gland, which increases in proportion with age. Groups of sebaceous glands may occur in the parotid gland, and represent the normal counterpart of the salivary sebaceous neoplasms (Fig. 7.5).

Salivary gland neoplasms

General features

The worldwide annual incidence of salivary gland tumors ranges from 0.4 to 13.5 cases per 100 000 people.[10] In general, salivary gland tumors are most common in older adults and females are more commonly affected than males, except for Warthin tumor and high-grade carcinomas. Epithelial tumors

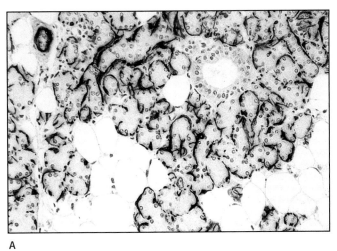

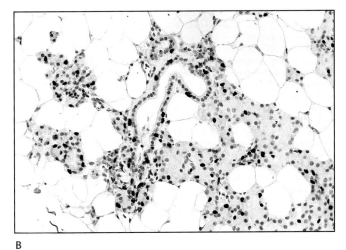

A

B

Fig. 7.4 • Normal salivary gland immunostained for myoepithelial or basal cell markers. (**A**) Calponin is expressed in myoepithelial cells (the cell processes of which wrap around the acini and intercalated ducts), but not in the basal cells that surround the striated ducts. (**B**) p63 is expressed in the nuclei of both myoepithelial and basal cells that surround the secretory ductal units.

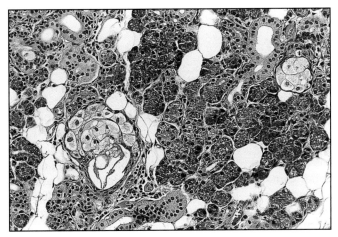

Fig. 7.5 • The normal parotid gland. If sampled extensively, groups of sebaceous cells can often be seen among the serous acini and striated ducts. Note also the typical abundance of adipose cells in the parotid gland.

constitute 80–90% of all salivary gland tumors, with the majority being benign (75%), and pleomorphic adenoma is the commonest (about 65% of all tumors) (Table 7.1). The parotid gland is the commonest site for occurrence of salivary gland tumors. Some tumor types show predilection to occur either in the major or minor salivary glands, and thus knowledge regarding the site of tumor can aid in diagnosis (Table 7.2).

Primary carcinomas of the salivary glands are uncommon, accounting for fewer than 0.3% of all cancers. The sites of occurrence with respect to the number of cases in descending order are: parotid gland, submandibular gland, palate, cheek, and tongue. However, tumors have the highest chance of being malignant if they arise from the retromolar area (89.7%), floor of mouth (88.2%), tongue (85.7%), and sublingual gland (70.2%),[11] while only approximately 20% of all parotid tumors are malignant. Among the salivary gland carcinomas, the commonest histologic types in descending order are: mucoepidermoid carcinoma, adenoid cystic carcinoma, adenocarcinoma not otherwise specified (NOS) and acinic cell carcinoma, with polymorphous low-grade adenocarcinoma (PLGA) replacing adenocarcinoma NOS in the minor salivary glands.[12,13]

The age of presentation of malignant tumors is similar to, or slightly older than, that of benign tumors. In practice, most malignant salivary gland tumors are not clinically distinguishable from benign ones, except when they show rapid increase in size, pain, fixation to adjacent structures, ulceration, or cervical lymph node enlargement. Facial nerve paralysis is a more consistent sign of malignancy, more often seen in high-grade tumors such as squamous cell carcinoma and undifferentiated carcinoma, although it can also rarely occur in Warthin tumor and pleomorphic adenoma.[14]

Salivary gland tumors are generally rare in children. In patients under the age of 18, half of the epithelial tumors are malignant, with low-grade mucoepidermoid carcinoma being the commonest.[14–16] In infants, mesenchymal tumors (hemangioma and lymphangioma) are the commonest, and some unusual tumors such as sialoblastoma and salivary gland anlage tumor occur almost exclusively in this age group.

Behavior of salivary gland carcinomas

Some salivary gland carcinomas are biologically low-grade (e.g., acinic cell carcinoma, PLGA, basal cell adenocarcinoma, epithelial-myoepithelial carcinoma, clear cell carcinoma, cystadenocarcinoma), some are biologically high-grade (e.g., salivary duct carcinoma, most cases of carcinoma ex pleomorphic adenoma, undifferentiated carcinoma, oncocytic carcinoma), while some span a range of behavior according to grade (e.g., mucoepidermoid carcinoma, adenoid cystic carcinoma). The prognosis of an individual tumor type is further influenced by clinical stage and margin status.[12] The TNM staging is listed in Table 7.3.

Some studies have shown high proliferative fraction (Ki67 index), DNA aneuploidy, and expression of p53 protein to be associated with a worse prognosis.[17] Since some salivary gland tumors are notorious for pursuing a protracted clinical course with late recurrence or metastasis, long-term follow-up is usually required to ascertain that cure is truly achieved. The survival curves of the three major types of salivary gland carcinoma, shown in Figure 7.6, are most instructive.[18] The plateau in the curve after an initial drop indicates that a significant proportion of patients with mucoepidermoid carcinoma

Table 7.1	Histologic classification of epithelial tumors of salivary gland (modified from 2005 WHO classification)

Benign epithelial tumors	Malignant epithelial tumors
Pleomorphic/monomorphic adenoma family	**Malignant counterpart**
Pleomorphic adenoma	Carcinoma ex pleomorphic adenoma
	Metastasizing pleomorphic adenoma
	Carcinosarcoma
Basal cell adenoma	Basal cell adenocarcinoma
Myoepithelioma	Myoepithelial carcinoma
Oncocytic tumors	**Malignant counterpart**
Warthin tumor	Carcinoma arising in Warthin tumor
Oncocytoma	Oncocytic carcinoma
Sebaceous tumors	**Malignant counterpart**
Sebaceous adenoma	Sebaceous carcinoma
Sebaceous lymphadenoma	Sebaceous lymphadenocarcinoma
Adenoma with additional stromal component	
Lymphadenoma	
Lipoadenoma (sialolipoma)	
Adenofibroma	
Ductal papillomas	**Malignant counterpart**
Inverted ductal papilloma	Malignant transformation of ductal papilloma
Intraductal papilloma	
Sialadenoma papilliferum	
Other benign tumors	**Malignant counterpart**
Cystadenoma	Cystadenocarcinoma
Canalicular adenoma	
Keratocystoma	
Salivary gland anlage tumor	
Sclerosing polycystic adenosis	
	Other salivary gland-type carcinomas
	Mucoepidermoid carcinoma
	Adenoid cystic carcinoma
	Acinic cell carcinoma
	Polymorphous low-grade adenocarcinoma
	Epithelial-myoepithelial carcinoma
	Clear cell carcinoma (NOS and hyalinizing variant)
	Salivary duct carcinoma
	Intraductal carcinoma
	Sialoblastoma
	Undifferentiated carcinoma
	Small cell carcinoma (Merkel and pulmonary types)
	Large-cell carcinoma
	Lymphoepithelial carcinoma
	"Non-specific" carcinomas
	Adenocarcinoma NOS
	Mucinous adenocarcinoma
	Signet-ring cell adenocarcinoma
	Squamous cell carcinoma

NOS, not otherwise specified.

Table 7.2	Predilection for the major or minor salivary glands as clue to diagnosis

Tumors occurring exclusively or predominantly in major glands	Tumors occurring exclusively or predominantly in minor glands
• Warthin tumor	• Canalicular adenoma (lip, buccal mucosa)
• Acinic cell carcinoma	• Polymorphous low-grade adenocarcinoma (palate)
• Basal cell adenoma/adenocarcinoma	• Cystadenoma/cystadenocarcinoma (lip, buccal mucosa)
• Oncocytoma/oncocytic carcinoma	• Inverted papilloma (lip, buccal mucosa)
• Epithelial-myoepithelial carcinoma	• Intraductal papilloma (lip, buccal mucosa)
• Salivary duct carcinoma	• Sialadenoma papilliferum (palate)
• Lymphoepithelial carcinoma	

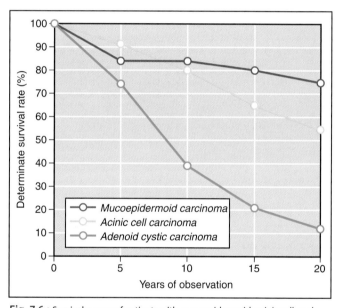

Fig. 7.6 • Survival curves of patients with mucoepidermoid, acinic cell, and adenoid cystic carcinoma of the salivary gland. Note the plateau in the survival curve for mucoepidermoid carcinoma, and poor long-term outcome for adenoid cystic carcinoma. (Adapted from Eneroth CM, Hamberger CA: Principles of treatment of different types of parotid tumors. Laryngoscope 84:1732–40, 1974.[18])

can be cured of their tumors. Acinic cell carcinoma is indolent, but unfavorable events may not become manifest until after 10 years. Although the short-term survival for adenoid cystic carcinoma is good, the long-term outcome is bleak; that is, a high proportion of patients eventually succumb to the tumor.[13]

Making a diagnosis

Salivary gland tumors not uncommonly pose problems in diagnosis due to their rarity, broad morphologic spectrum,

Table 7.3	TNM Staging system for major salivary gland tumors

Primary Tumor (T)

TX Primary tumor cannot be assessed

T0 No evidence of primary tumor

T1 Tumor 2 cm or less in greatest dimension without extraparenchymal extension*

T2 Tumor more than 2 cm but not more than 4 cm in greatest dimension without extraparenchymal extension*

T3 Tumor more than 4 cm and/or tumor having extraparenchymal extension*

T4a Tumor invades skin, mandible, ear canal, and/or facial nerve

T4b Tumor invades skull base and/or pterygoid plates, and/or encases carotid artery

Regional Lymph Nodes (N)

NX Regional lymph nodes cannot be assessed

N0 No regional lymph node metastasis

N1 Metastasis in a single ipsilateral lymph node, 3 cm or less in greatest dimension

N2 Metastasis in a single ipsilateral lymph node, more than 3 cm but not more than 6 cm in greatest dimension, or in multiple ipsilateral lymph nodes, none more than 6 cm in greatest dimension, or in bilateral or contralateral lymph nodes, none more than 6 cm in greatest dimension

    N2a Metastasis in a single ipsilateral lymph node, more than 3 cm but not more than 6 cm in greatest dimension

    N2b Metastasis in multiple ipsilateral lymph nodes, none more than 6 cm in greatest dimension

    N2c Metastasis in bilateral or contralateral lymph nodes, none more than 6 cm in greatest dimension

N3 Metastasis in a lymph node, more than 6 cm in greatest dimension

Distant Metastasis (M)

MX Distant metastasis cannot be assessed

M0 No distant metastasis

M1 Distant metastasis

Stage Grouping

Stage I	T1	N0	M0
Stage II	T2	N0	M0
Stage III	T3	N0	M0
	T1	N1	M0
	T2	N1	M0
	T3	N1	M0
Stage IVA	T4a	N0	M0
	T4a	N1	M0
	T1	N2	M0
	T2	N2	M0
	T3	N2	M0
	T4a	N2	M0
Stage IVB	T4b	Any N	M0
	Any T	N3	M0
Stage IVC	Any T	Any N	M1

*Note: Extraparenchymal extension is clinical or macroscopic evidence of invasion of soft tissues or nerves. Microscopic evidence alone does not constitute extraparenchymal extension for classification purposes.

(Used with the permission of the American Joint Committee on Cancer (AJCC), Chicago, Illinois. The original source of the material is the AJCC Cancer Staging Manual, Sixth Edition (2002) published by Springer-Verlag New York, www.springeronline.com)

and morphologic overlap among the different tumor types. It is important to understand the basic cytoarchitectural features of each tumor type, in particular whether the tumor shows dual luminal–abluminal cell differentiation (Fig. 7.7), so that a diagnosis can be made logically through analysis of the cellular components, cell arrangement, and extracellular components (see section on "Analytic approach to diagnosis," below).

Histochemistry

Histochemical studies have only a limited role in the diagnosis of salivary gland tumors. Although staining for mucosubstances and basement membrane materials in adenoid cystic carcinoma is often mentioned, such stains do not help in the establishment of this diagnosis. Any salivary gland tumor with luminal cell differentiation can have epithelial-type mucin (usually PAS-positive diastase-resistant) in the lumens. Many tumor types are associated with production of basement membrane-like material (PAS-positive diastase-resistant),

especially those showing myoepithelial or basal cell differentiation. Variable amounts of acidic stromal mucin (alcian blue-positive, but PAS-negative) may also be found in many types of salivary gland tumors, such as pleomorphic adenoma and adenoid cystic carcinoma. The limited applications of histochemistry include:

1. Aid in diagnosis of acinic cell carcinoma by PAS-diastase to demonstrate serous cell differentiation.
2. Aid in diagnosis of high-grade mucoepidermoid carcinoma by demonstrating intracytoplasmic mucin. Mucin stains are often not required for the diagnosis of low- to intermediate-grade mucoepidermoid carcinomas because mucin is often obvious in routine histologic sections.
3. PAS-diastase can aid in the detection of focal luminal cell differentiation in a predominantly basal cell or myoepithelial-cell neoplasm, such as the solid type of adenoid cystic carcinoma, or clear cell-rich epithelial-myoepithelial carcinoma.

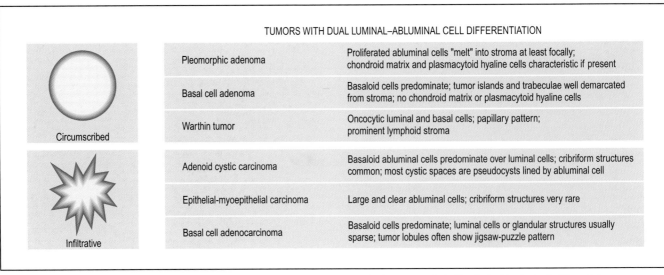

TUMORS WITH DUAL LUMINAL–ABLUMINAL CELL DIFFERENTIATION		
Circumscribed	Pleomorphic adenoma	Proliferated abluminal cells "melt" into stroma at least focally; chondroid matrix and plasmacytoid hyaline cells characteristic if present
	Basal cell adenoma	Basaloid cells predominate; tumor islands and trabeculae well demarcated from stroma; no chondroid matrix or plasmacytoid hyaline cells
	Warthin tumor	Oncocytic luminal and basal cells; papillary pattern; prominent lymphoid stroma
Infiltrative	Adenoid cystic carcinoma	Basaloid abluminal cells predominate over luminal cells; cribriform structures common; most cystic spaces are pseudocysts lined by abluminal cell
	Epithelial-myoepithelial carcinoma	Large and clear abluminal cells; cribriform structures very rare
	Basal cell adenocarcinoma	Basaloid cells predominate; luminal cells or glandular structures usually sparse; tumor lobules often show jigsaw-puzzle pattern

Fig. 7.7 • Schematic diagram showing features helpful in differential diagnosis of salivary gland tumors with dual luminal–abluminal cell differentiation.

4. Phosphotungstic acid hematoxylin stain may help in the diagnosis of the clear cell variant of oncocytoma, by highlighting the mitochondria.

Immunohistochemistry

Currently, immunohistochemical staining has only a limited role in the diagnosis of salivary gland tumors. Its main applications are:

1. To delineate whether there is two-cell-type differentiation in tumors with complex architecture, although results can be disappointing as a result of aberrant immunophenotypes.
2. To confirm the diagnosis of myoepithelioma/myoepithelial carcinoma by demonstrating the appropriate immunophenotype.
3. Ki67 proliferative index may be useful in distinguishing an adenoma from a carcinoma (Ki67 index usually <5% versus >10%).

Genetic studies

Genetic studies have identified several recurrent events in pleomorphic adenoma (rearrangement of chromosomes 8q12 and 12q13-15), mucoepidermoid carcinoma (translocation of chromosomes 11q21 and 19p13), adenoid cystic carcinoma (structural or molecular alterations at 6q, 8q, and 12q), and salivary duct carcinoma (amplification of *HER-2*). Gene expression profiling studies using microarrays have also identified genes that can separate benign salivary gland tissue from neoplasms, and demonstrated differential profiles in pleomorphic adenoma, adenoid cystic carcinoma, mucoepidermoid carcinoma, clear cell carcinoma, acinic cell carcinoma, and salivary duct carcinoma.[19–23] However, currently, molecular studies have no established role in routine diagnosis.

Hybrid tumor

Rare salivary gland tumors show hybrid features. Hybrid tumor refers to a tumor that is composed of two or more histologically distinct components at a single site.[24] The most common components of hybrid carcinomas are salivary duct carcinoma, epithelial-myoepithelial carcinoma, and adenoid cystic carcinoma.[24–28] Others include mucoepidermoid carcinoma, acinic cell carcinoma, squamous cell carcinoma, basal cell adenocarcinoma, and PLGA.[24,26,29,30] Treatment is probably best based on the histologic component with higher-grade malignancy.[28] Rare hybrid adenomas include combinations of basal cell adenoma with canalicular adenoma, Warthin tumor with sebaceous adenoma, and Warthin tumor with onocytoma.[24] Hybrid tumors are postulated to arise through divergent differentiation or collision of two tumor types. However, at least some examples of hybrid carcinomas reported in the literature can be alternatively interpreted as a dedifferentiation process (such as combination of a lower-grade carcinoma with salivary duct carcinoma).

Progression in salivary gland tumors

The majority of salivary gland tumors are benign or low-grade malignant. It is thus not surprising to encounter biologic progression as a result of acquisition of additional genetic alterations (such as *p53* mutation, and *c-erbB2* amplification) in long-standing neoplasms. Tumor progression can manifest as malignant transformation, stromal invasion, high-grade progression, overgrowth, and dedifferentiation (Table 7.4).

Epithelial tumors and tumor-like lesions

Pleomorphic adenoma

Definition

Pleomorphic adenoma is a benign neoplasm consisting of cells with epithelial (luminal) and myoepithelial (abluminal) differentiation, accompanied by variable amounts of characteristic stroma. The diverse morphology results from amalgamation of cellular and stromal components. The coexistence of apparently epithelial and mesenchymal elements gives rise to

Table 7.4	Different modes of tumor progression in salivary gland tumors	
Phenomenon	**Relationship of components**	**Examples**
Malignant transformation	Benign tumor → malignant tumor	• Pleomorphic adenoma → carcinoma *ex* pleomorphic adenoma • Basal cell adenoma → carcinoma (including basal cell adenocarcinoma) • Myoepithelioma → myoepithelial carcinoma • Warthin tumor → carcinoma or lymphoma • Oncocytoma → oncocytic carcinoma
Stromal invasion	In-situ carcinoma → invasive carcinoma	• Intraductal carcinoma → salivary duct carcinoma • In-situ carcinoma arising in pleomorphic adenoma → invasive carcinoma (intracapsular, microinvasive, and frankly invasive carcinoma)
Overgrowth	Carcinoma with dual-cell differentiation → monomorphic carcinoma with one-line of differentiation	• Epithelial-myoepithelial carcinoma → myoepithelial carcinoma
High-grade progression	Same tumor type, from low-grade → high-grade	• Adenoid cystic carcinoma (low-grade → high-grade) • Mucoepidermoid carcinoma (low-grade → high-grade)
Dedifferentiation	Carcinoma → high-grade malignant neoplasm with loss of original line of differentiation	• Dedifferentiated acinic cell carcinoma • Dedifferentiated adenoid cystic carcinoma • Dedifferentiated mucoepidermoid carcinoma • Dedifferentiated epithelial-myoepithelial carcinoma • Dedifferentiated polymorphous low-grade adenocarcinoma • Dedifferentiated salivary duct carcinoma (sarcomatoid variant)

the synonym "mixed tumor." Pleomorphic adenoma is now widely accepted as a pure epithelial tumor with divergent differentiation instead of collision of epithelial and mesenchymal tumors. The monoclonal origin of both the epithelial and mesenchymal elements has also been supported by molecular analysis.[31]

Clinical features

Pleomorphic adenoma occurs more frequently in women than men, and is most prevalent from the fourth to sixth decades, with a mean age of 45 years. It usually presents as a slow-growing and painless swelling. When it occurs in the minor glands, ulceration of the overlying mucosa or apparent fixation to surrounding tissue can be seen rarely. Pleomorphic adenoma can occur in various mucosal sites such as nasal cavity, bronchus, skin (also known as chondroid syringoma), breast, and soft tissues.[32–36]

The treatment of choice is complete surgical excision. The recurrence rates at 5 and 10 years following complete excision are 3.4% and 6.3% respectively.[37] Enucleation alone, rupture or spillage of tumor during removal, presence of protuberances beyond the main tumor, abundance of chondromyxoid stroma, and young age are associated with a higher recurrence rate.[14,38–41] In most instances, the recurrent tumor maintains the original histology; however, with each recurrence, there is an increased possibility of malignant transformation. Factors associated with an increased risk of malignant transformation are: older patient age, long-standing tumor, submandibular location, large tumor size, prominent zones of hyalinization, and at least moderate mitotic activity.[42]

Macroscopic appearances

The size ranges from a few millimeters to several centimeters. The tumor is typically thinly encapsulated and solitary. Intraoral examples, especially those arising from the palate, may lack a well-defined capsule. The cut surface may be rubbery, fleshy, mucoid, or glistening, depending on the amount of stroma in the tumor (Fig. 7.8). In areas where the capsule is deficient, tumor buds may lie in direct contact with the adjacent salivary tissue.[43] Recurrent tumor typically appears as multiple nodules scattered over the field of the previous operation (Fig. 7.9).

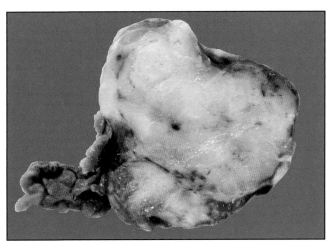

Fig. 7.8 • Gross specimen of pleomorphic adenoma. The cut surface shows tan-colored solid tumor with a glistening quality, the latter being attributable to the presence of chondromyxoid matrix.

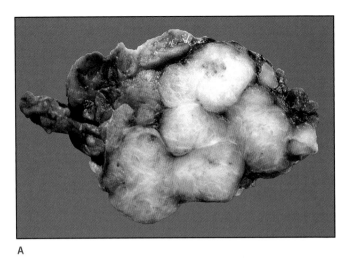

A

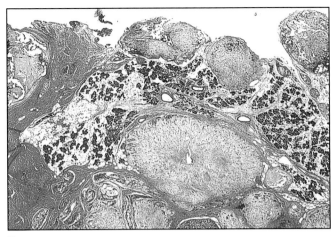

B

Fig. 7.9 • Recurrent pleomorphic adenoma of the parotid gland. Note the typical multinodular growth pattern. Very frequently, as in this case, the tumor is predominantly myxoid. **(A)** Gross specimen. **(B)** Corresponding histologic features.

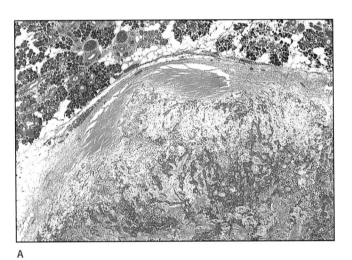

A

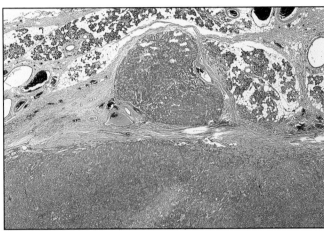

B

Fig. 7.10 • Scanning magnification views of pleomorphic adenoma. **(A)** The tumor is characteristically well circumscribed. The loose myxoid matrix is evident at this magnification. **(B)** There is a small satellite nodule immediately outside the thin capsule of the tumor. This represents a tumor protuberance in which the site of capsular penetration is not evident in this plane of sectioning. This finding is still compatible with a diagnosis of benign pleomorphic adenoma.

Microscopic appearances

Growth pattern Pleomorphic adenoma is thinly encapsulated (Fig. 7.10A). A few small, smooth-contoured buds (protuberances) may protrude through the fibrous capsule. Occasionally, tumor islands may appear outside the capsule at a short distance from the main tumor mass (Fig. 7.10B), but serial sectioning usually demonstrates that such satellites are, in fact, outgrowths continuous with the main tumor mass and should not be regarded as invasion. Rarely, pleomorphic adenoma can grow entirely within a dilated duct. Pleomorphic adenoma is characterized by highly variable growth patterns in different areas of the same tumor (Fig. 7.11).

Basic cellular organization The prototypic histologic appearance consists of tubular structures enveloped by myoepithelial mantles submerging in a chondromyxoid stroma. The interface between the tumor islands and the stroma is usually

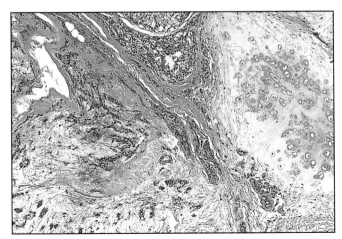

Fig. 7.11 • Pleomorphic adenoma. Note the characteristic regional variations in cellularity, cell arrangement, and quantity of matrix. Chondroid matrix (hyaline cartilage) is seen in the right field.

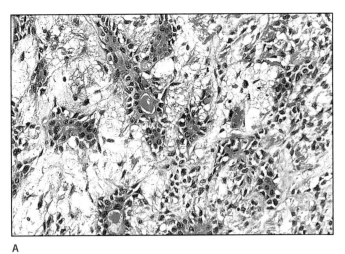

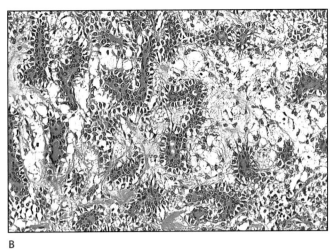

A

B

Fig. 7.12 • Pleomorphic adenoma, showing the basic cytoarchitectural features diagnostic of this tumor type. Tubules are lined by an inner layer of ductal cells, and an outer layer of modified myoepithelial cells of variable thickness. The latter cells disperse into a myxoid matrix, rendering it difficult to define the outer contours of the individual tubules. This pattern is not found in any other type of salivary gland tumor. **(A)** The tubules in this example contain eosinophilic secretion in the lumens. **(B)** In this example, the myoepithelial cells are oriented perpendicular to the axis of the tubules, and show centrifugal dispersion into the stroma.

poorly demarcated. The myoepithelial mantle radiates centrifugally, forming sheets, clusters, lattices, and isolated cells, where they appear to "melt" into the sea of stroma which they produce (Fig. 7.12). While the "melting" phenomenon is characteristic, it can be focal, and some areas of the tumor can be composed of tubules or trabeculae well delineated from the stroma (Fig. 7.13). There may even be foci resembling mucoepidermoid carcinoma or adenoid cystic carcinoma (Fig. 7.14), but carcinoma *ex* pleomorphic adenoma should not be diagnosed unless a discrete expansile lesion is formed.

Luminal cell component The luminal cell component takes the form of anastomosing tubules, cysts, ribbons, and solid sheets (Fig. 7.15). The cells may be columnar, cuboidal, or flat. The duct lumen may be empty or contain eosinophilic colloid-like material, which is PAS-positive diastase-resistant and variably mucicarmine-positive (Figs 7.12 and 7.15). Rarely, metaplastic change to squamous, sebaceous, oncocytic, or clear

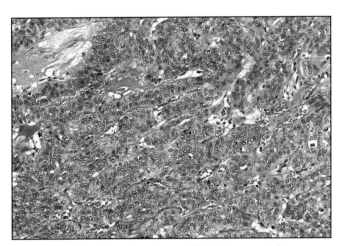

Fig. 7.13 • Cellular pleomorphic adenoma. This cellular tumor shows predominance of trabeculae and scanty stroma.

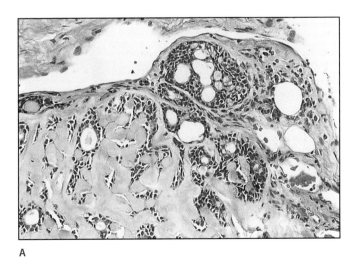

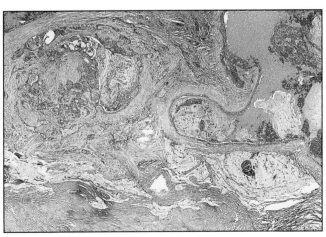

A

B

Fig. 7.14 • Pleomorphic adenoma with focal areas resembling adenoid cystic carcinoma or mucoepidermoid carcinoma. **(A)** There are some cribriform structures and tubules sharply demarcated from the stroma, which shows extensive hyalinization in the left field. These features are not incompatible with a diagnosis of pleomorphic adenoma provided that the tumor is circumscribed and other areas show typical cytoarchitectural features. **(B)** The presence of glandular structures distended with mucus as well as extravasation of mucus into the fibrous stroma results in mimicry of low-grade mucoepidermoid carcinoma.

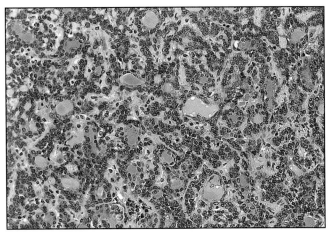

Fig. 7.15 • Cellular pleomorphic adenoma. This cell-rich and stroma-poor tumor is composed of anastomosing tubules. Although there is no obvious "melting" pattern, the intervening stroma contains scattered plump cells. Nonetheless, this field is indistinguishable from a basal cell adenoma with myoepithelium-derived stroma.

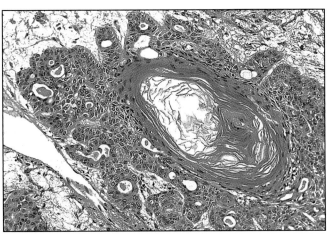

Fig. 7.17 • Pleomorphic adenoma. Focal squamous differentiation with keratinization is seen amidst complex glandular structures. Such an overt degree of squamous differentiation is practically never seen in mucoepidermoid carcinoma.

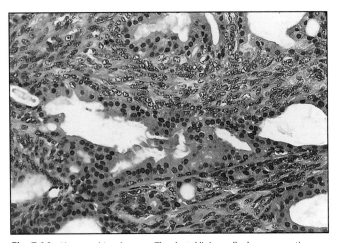

Fig. 7.16 • Pleomorphic adenoma. The ductal lining cells show oncocytic change. The outer layer of polygonal myoepithelial cells merge into compact fascicles of spindly cells.

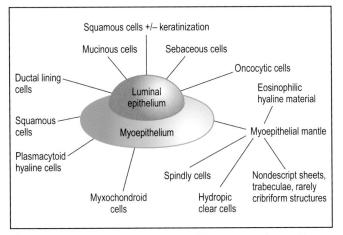

Fig. 7.18 • The multipotentiality of cellular differentiation in pleomorphic adenoma (PA). Possible lines of differentiation and appearances of the luminal ductal cells as well as abluminal cells (myoepithelial cells) are shown.

cells can occur (Figs 7.16–7.18). Very occasionally, the epithelium may form goblet or mucous cells, which, in association with squamous epithelium, can lead to an erroneous interpretation of mucoepidermoid carcinoma.

Myoepithelial component Myoepithelial or modified myoepithelial cells appear as cuboidal, spindle, stellate, plasmacytoid hyaline, nondescript epithelioid, and hydropic clear cells (Fig. 7.18). The spindle or cuboidal cells surround the ducts in a single layer, thick mantle, or radiating corona (Figs 7.12, 7.16, and 7.19). They can form nondescript sheets, trabeculae, and even cribriform structures.

Plasmacytoid hyaline cells represent the most distinctive form of modified myoepithelial cells; they are oval-shaped, with homogeneous eosinophilic hyaline cytoplasm (Fig. 7.20A). The nucleus is round and eccentrically located, with a tendency for peripheral margination of the dense chromatin. Plasmacytoid hyaline cells are so named because of their superficial resemblance to plasma cells, but they are larger, show less coarse clumping of the chromatin, and lack a perinuclear Golgi zone. They are usually arranged in aggregates or sheets, often with

focal areas of non-cohesive growth (Fig. 7.20). Since their occurrence is restricted to pleomorphic adenoma and myoepithelioma, their identification is of great diagnostic value, especially in small biopsies. There can be transitional forms which show overlapping features with other types of myoepithelial cell.

Stellate or spindly myoepithelial cells occur singly, or form anastomosing strands, suspended in an abundant myxoid matrix (Fig. 7.21). Uncommonly, myoepithelial cells may merge into squamous nests or cystic squamous lined structures filled with keratin, suggesting an ability to differentiate towards the squamous lineage. In occasional cases, myoepithelial cells dominate the tumor. Rarely, skeletal muscle differentiation and scattered melanocytes can occur, the latter also imparting a pigmented macroscopic appearance to the tumor.[44,45]

Stroma Extracellular stroma is one of the defining components of pleomorphic adenoma, although it can be scanty to abundant. It is mostly composed of acidic mucosubstances produced by the modified myoepithelial cells, and is positive for alcian blue, but variably positive for PAS. The stroma takes

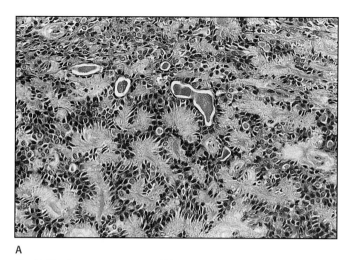

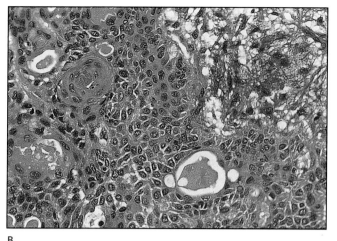

A

B

Fig. 7.19 • Pleomorphic adenoma. (**A**) Anastomosing tubules are separated by stellate fibrillary collagen fibers. (**B**) Extensive coalescence of the tubules creates solid sheets of cells punctuated by some glandular lumens. Many of the polygonal cells seen in this field represent modified myoepithelial cells, which merge into a myxoid matrix in the right upper field.

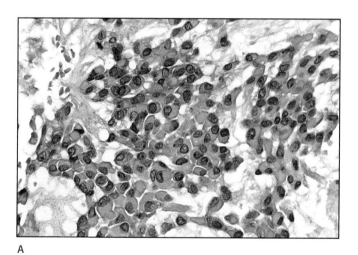

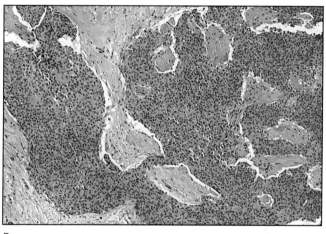

A

B

Fig. 7.20 • Pleomorphic adenoma rich in plasmacytoid hyaline cells. (**A**) Plasmacytoid hyaline cells are typically ovoid, with eccentric-placed nuclei and abundant eosinophilic hyaline cytoplasm. They are not uncommonly dispersed in a myxoid stroma. (**B**) Plasmacytoid hyaline cells can form alarmingly solid sheets.

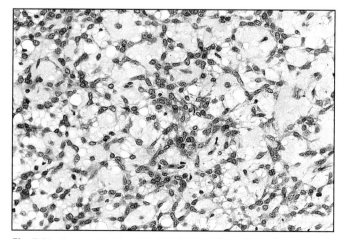

Fig. 7.21 • Pleomorphic adenoma. Spindly and stellate cells are disposed in a lattice-like fashion within the myxoid stroma. These represent modified myoepithelial cells. A myoepithelioma can show a similar appearance.

the form of a mixture of chondroid (hyaline cartilage), myxoid, chondromyxoid, hyaline, and very rarely, osseous and adipose tissues (Figs 7.11, 7.12, and 7.21).[46] Of interest, adipocytic differentiation is uncommon,[46a] except in cutaneous sites. Isolated or groups of stellate, oval, or polygonal cells are suspended in the matrix. The presence of chondromyxoid stroma in a salivary gland tumor is practically pathognomonic of pleomorphic adenoma (Fig. 7.11). In tumors in which chondromyxoid matrix predominates, the ductal structures are most likely found in the peripheral zone immediately beneath the capsule. Tumors with very scanty or no extracellular stroma are often called "cellular pleomorphic adenomas" (Figs 7.13, 7.15, and 7.22); they can be recognized by the focal "melting" of the myoepithelial mantles. It has been suggested that recurrence is more frequent in a stroma-rich tumor, which has a higher chance of spillage of mucoid stroma during operation. Highly cellular tumors, on the other hand, may be more prone to malignant change.

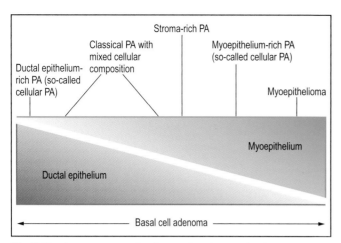

Fig. 7.22 • The continuum in the pleomorphic adenoma–basal cell adenoma–myoepithelioma family. The relative proportions of ductal epithelial and myoepithelial cells as well as the interaction with the stroma will determine into which category the tumor falls.

Homogenous fibrillary, or radiating hyaline material can be interspersed among the epithelial or myoepithelial cells (Figs 7.14A and 7.19A). Crystalloids composed of collagenous substance, tyrosine, and oxalate can develop between the cellular or stromal components. Tyrosine crystals often appear as "daisy-heads" in the myxoid stroma. Elastic fibers are present in variable amounts in most pleomorphic adenomas, and they are particularly abundant in long-standing lesions. They show up as globular masses or irregular bands with fluffy outlines on an elastic stain (Fig. 7.23). These thick elastic fibers are diagnostically helpful because they are uncommon in other salivary gland tumors.

Fine-needle aspiration-associated changes Fine-needle aspiration commonly results in hemorrhagic tracts and micronecrosis, accompanied by variable reparative changes (Fig. 7.24). Complete or incomplete infarction can also occur (Fig. 7.25). There can be florid reactive proliferation of the

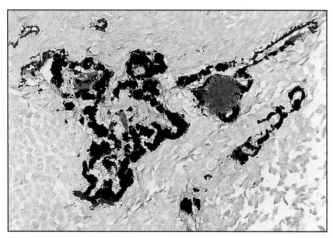

Fig. 7.23 • Pleomorphic adenoma, stained with elastic van Gieson. The thick elastic fibers with fluffy outline are characteristic of pleomorphic adenoma, and are rarely found in other salivary gland tumor types.

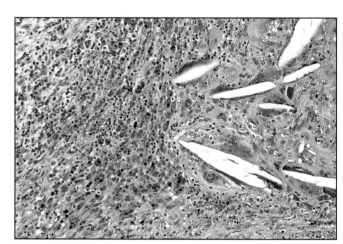

Fig. 7.24 • Pleomorphic adenoma, post fine-needle aspiration changes. Response to tissue injury takes the form of chronic inflammatory cell infiltration, siderophage accumulation, and foreign-body giant cell reaction against cholesterol crystals.

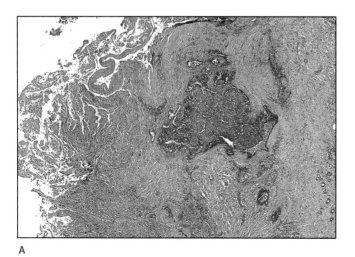

A

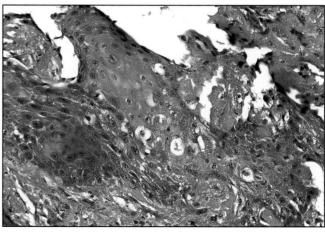

B

Fig. 7.25 • Pleomorphic adenoma, post fine-needle aspiration infarction. **(A)** This tumor has undergone near-total infarction. **(B)** Surviving tumor islands commonly exhibit squamous metaplasia with variable degrees of nuclear atypia, mimicking squamous cell or mucoepidermoid carcinoma.

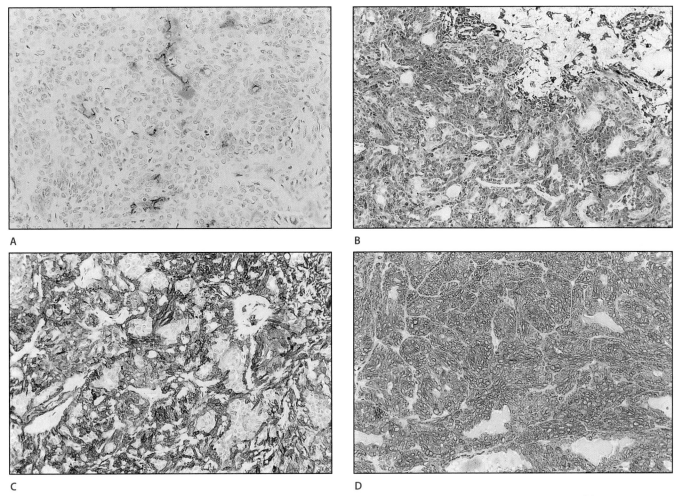

A

B

C

D

Fig. 7.26 • Pleomorphic adenoma: immunohistochemical profile. (**A**) Staining for epithelial membrane antigen highlights the ductal lumens. (**B**) Staining for S-100 protein often highlights the abluminal cells as well as those lying in the matrix. The ductal cells are negative in this case, although variable staining can be observed in some cases. (**C**) Staining for calponin highlights the myoepithelial and modified myoepithelial cells. The staining can be more patchy in some cases. (**D**) Staining for cytokeratin 14 is diffuse in this example. Paradoxically, in contrast to the negative staining of the normal ductal epithelium, the staining is stronger in the ductal cells in this tumor.

myoepithelium, which can protrude into the fibrous capsule or show nodular bulging beneath the endothelium of veins. Atypical squamous metaplasia is also common (Fig. 7.25B).[47]

Immunohistochemistry

The main application of immunohistochemistry is to demonstrate the coexistence of glandular and myoepithelial components when the diagnosis is uncertain. The glandular component, which may be inconspicuous, can be highlighted by EMA, CEA, or c-kit (Fig. 7.26). The myoepithelial and modified myoepithelial cells are positive for cytokeratin, but not EMA and CEA. Although CK14 and various myoid markers (such as actin and myosin) mark the normal myoepithelium nicely, the pattern of staining in neoplasms is anarchic: the staining of neoplastic myoepithelium can be patchy or totally negative, while that in the luminal cells can even be stronger (Fig. 7.26D)! The myoepithelial component is commonly positive for S-100 protein and GFAP, although S-100 immunoreactivity can also variably be observed in the luminal cells (Fig. 7.26). Currently the most reliable markers for the neoplastic myoepithelial component are p63 and calponin (Fig. 7.27).[48]

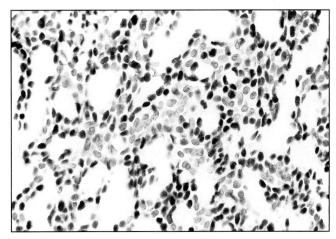

Fig. 7.27 • Pleomorphic adenoma immunostained for p63. The modified myoepithelial cells (abluminal cells) are highlighted, while the luminal cells are negative.

Pleomorphic adenoma shows a low Ki-67 proliferative index (mean 1.6%), rare immunoreactivity for p53 protein (mean 1.2% positive cells); and weak BCL2 staining. These parameters can help to distinguish it from adenoid cystic carcinoma, because the latter tumor shows a mean Ki67 index of 20.5–54% depending on grade, mean p53 protein-positive cells of 4.3–24%, and intense staining for BCL2.[49,50]

Genetic features

Cytogenetic studies demonstrate abnormal findings in approximately 70% of pleomorphic adenomas in one of three patterns:[51]

1. rearrangement of 8q12 (39%), such as t(3;8)(p21;q12), t(5;8)(p13;q12), or
2. rearrangement of 12q13-15 (8%), such as t(9;12)(p24;q14-15), ins(9;12)(p24;q12q15), or
3. sporadic, clonal changes not involving 8q21 or 12q13-15 (23%).[52]

The target genes on chromosome 8q and 12q are *PLAG1* and *HMGA2* (formerly known as *HMGIC*) respectively, which encode for transcription factors.[53,54] Translocation resulting in overexpression of these genes has been postulated to play an important role in the pathogenesis. Since, among salivary tumors, *PLAG1* or *HMGA2* gene translocations have only been identified in pleomorphic adenoma, their detection by reverse transcriptase polymerase chain reaction (RT-PCR) or fluorescence in-situ hybridization (FISH) may potentially aid in the diagnosis of this tumor type.

Major differential diagnoses (see section on "Analytic approach to diagnosis," p. 310)

1. Monomorphic adenoma, e.g., basal cell adenoma, myoepithelioma
2. Adenoid cystic carcinoma
3. PLGA
4. Epithelial-myoepithelial carcinoma
5. Mucoepidermoid carcinoma
6. Various mesenchymal tumors, e.g., nerve sheath tumor, smooth muscle tumor

Metastasizing pleomorphic adenoma

Metastasizing pleomorphic adenoma is a rare complication of pleomorphic adenoma. Generally, metastases occur after a relatively long period (ranging from 1.5 to 51 years, mean 16.3 years), and may develop synchronously with or following local recurrence. Rarely, the metastatic tumor may represent the initial manifestation of an occult pleomorphic adenoma in the salivary gland.[55]

The metastatic tumor characteristically retains the benign histologic features of pleomorphic adenoma. Retrospective analysis and flow cytometry both fail to identify any features that can predict the metastasis.[56] The commonest metastatic sites are bone (50%), lungs (30%), and lymph nodes (30%); scalp, abdominal wall, and liver metastases have also been reported.[57] Despite the bland histology of the metastatic lesions, up to 37% of patients die of the disease. The disease apparently pursues a more rapidly aggressive course in immunocompromised hosts.[58] Malignant transformation of metastatic pleomorphic adenoma has also been reported.[59]

With the exception of one case,[55] most metastasizing pleomorphic adenomas had a history of one or multiple operations.

Vascular permeation secondary to mechanical implantation has been postulated as a probable mechanism for the development of metastasis.[60] The treatment of choice is local excision of both the primary and metastatic tumors.

Carcinoma *ex* pleomorphic adenoma

Definition

Carcinoma *ex* pleomorphic adenoma represents malignant transformation of a pre-existing pleomorphic adenoma, usually in the setting of long-standing pleomorphic adenoma or in a tumor with multiple recurrences. The incidence ranges from 1.9% to 23.3% (mean 6.2%) according to different series.[42] The risk increases with the duration of the tumor, with an incidence of 1.6% for tumors present for less than 5 years, increasing to 9.5% for tumors present for more than 15 years.[61] Malignant transformation may follow a stepwise sequence (Fig. 7.28), manifested as:[62]

1. *Carcinoma in-situ*: in the earliest phase, carcinoma cells replace ductal luminal cells while retaining an intact neoplastic but non-atypical myoepithelial layer (Fig. 7.29).
2. *Intracapsular carcinoma*: stromal invasion develops upon further progression of the carcinoma, but without violation of the fibrous capsule of the parent pleomorphic adenoma (Fig. 7.30).[63,64]
3. *Invasive carcinoma*: extracapsular invasion subsequently follows (Fig. 7.31).

Clinical features

Malignant transformation is heralded by rapid growth after a long period of a minimally perceptible increase in size. Signs of malignancy also include fixation to surrounding tissues, ulceration, facial nerve palsy, and regional lymphadenopathy. The mean age at presentation is 61 years, about one decade older than that of pleomorphic adenoma.[63,65] The majority of patients present with stage III/IV disease (65%). Most patients develop recurrence and metastases, and the overall 5-year survival is only 30%.[63]

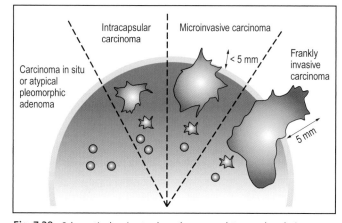

Fig. 7.28 • Schematic drawing to show the nomenclature and evolution steps of carcinoma *ex* pleomorphic adenoma. Deep blue, pleomorphic adenoma; light blue, fibrous capsule; red, carcinoma.

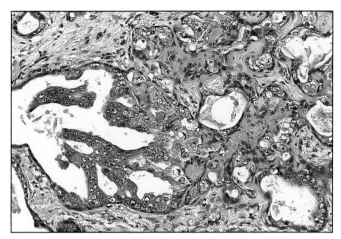

Fig. 7.29 • Carcinoma in situ *ex* pleomorphic adenoma. The pre-existing pleomorphic adenoma is seen in the right field. It merges into an in-situ carcinoma in the left field, where atypical large apocrine-like cells replace the luminal cells. Elsewhere, the carcinoma cells have broken through the myoepithelial layer and invaded into the stroma (not shown).

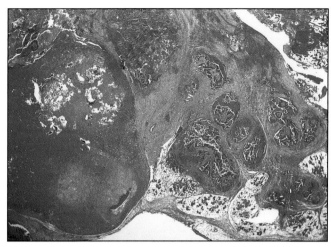

Fig. 7.31 • Frankly invasive carcinoma *ex* pleomorphic adenoma. The circumscribed nodule in the left field represents the parent pleomorphic adenoma. The supervening carcinoma has invaded beyond the confines of the parent tumor, into the surrounding parotid parenchyma. In this example, the tumor has invaded for a distance of 8 mm from the parent tumor.

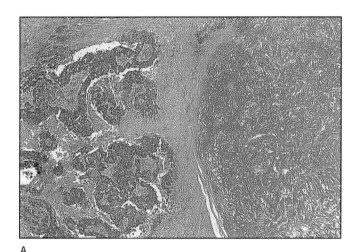

A

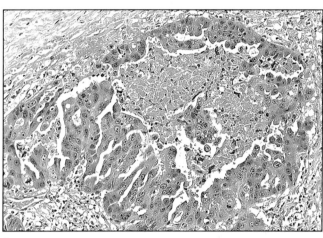

B

Fig. 7.30 • Intracapsular carcinoma *ex* pleomorphic adenoma. (**A**) The right field shows the parent pleomorphic adenoma with extensive deposits of thick elastic fibers. The left field shows the supervening carcinoma accompanied by necrosis. (**B**) This carcinoma is an invasive high-grade adenocarcinoma and has invaded the stroma of the parent pleomorphic adenoma.

Pathology

The tumor is usually larger than its benign counterpart. Most cases are frankly infiltrative; areas of necrosis or hemorrhage are common. Histologically, the malignant component is characterized by widespread significant cellular pleomorphism, a high mitotic count, atypical mitotic figures, coagulative necrosis, and the presence of an expansile or infiltrative nodule within the parent adenoma (Figs 7.30 and 7.31).

In most cases, the malignant component dominates the tumor, and is most frequently a high-grade carcinoma (85% of cases) such as adenocarcinoma NOS or salivary duct carcinoma (Fig. 7.30B) but sometimes maybe adenosquamous carcinoma, undifferentiated carcinoma, or sarcomatoid carcinoma. Low-grade carcinomas such as PLGA, adenoid cystic carcinoma, mucoepidermoid carcinoma, epithelial-myoepithelial carcinoma, and myoepithelial carcinoma can also occur infrequently (Fig. 7.32).[62,63,65] Transitional zones

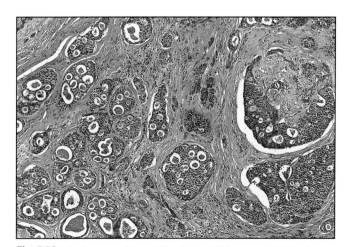

Fig. 7.32 • Carcinoma *ex* pleomorphic adenoma. This supervening invasive carcinoma shows cytoarchitectural features strongly reminiscent of adenoid cystic carcinoma.

with morphologic features intermediate between the malignant and benign components may be present.

Often the residual pleomorphic adenoma is difficult to find and it may appear hypocellular or markedly hyalinized. The clues to its existence are:

1. hyalinized or calcified nodule within or directly adjacent to the carcinoma
2. S-100 protein or actin-positive spindle cells in the nodule
3. thick fluffy elastic fibers (best highlighted by elastic stain)
4. clinical history of recurrent pleomorphic adenoma or long-standing mass[63]

Hence, when a salivary gland carcinoma is not easily classifiable into one of the recognized entities, the possibility of carcinoma *ex* pleomorphic adenoma should be seriously considered.

Prognosis

The most important prognostic factor is the extent of extracapsular invasion. Carcinoma in situ and intracapsular carcinoma have no metastatic potential,[63,64] with the exception of a single reported case with cervical lymph node metastasis.[66] In several large series, excellent prognosis has been found in tumors with extracapsular invasion less than 8 mm,[67] 5 mm,[63] or 1.5 mm[68] beyond the capsule respectively. In other words, the optimal cut-off point to define a category of invasive carcinoma *ex* pleomorphic adenoma with minimal metastatic potential is currently unsettled, but the different findings may reflect difficulties in making reproducible measurements. In addition, poor outcome has been found to be associated with: (1) high histologic grade of malignant component (5-year survival 30% versus 96% for low histologic grade); (2) high pathologic stage; and (3) proportion of carcinoma more than 50% of the tumor.[63,67]

Genetic studies

Alterations or rearrangements of chromosome 8q21 and 12q13-15 are frequent in carcinoma *ex* pleomorphic adenoma, similar to its benign counterpart. In addition, amplification and overexpression of genes in chromosome 12q13-15, including *CDK4*, *HMGIC*, and *MDM2*, may represent important genetic events in the malignant transformation.[69] c-erbB2 overexpression or gene amplification occurs in 21–82% of cases.[63,64,70–72] It has been suggested that c-erbB2 staining may aid in distinguishing carcinoma *ex* pleomorphic adenoma from atypical pleomorphic adenoma.[64] Alterations of *p53* gene are found in 29–67% and p53 protein overexpression in 41–75% of cases, suggesting that the gene may play a role in transformation.[63,73–76] The Ki67 proliferative index is increased (mean 35%) compared with the parent pleomorphic adenoma.[64]

Atypical pleomorphic adenoma

Capsular involvement and vascular tumor plugging are acceptable features in benign pleomorphic adenoma.[77,78] Isolated enlarged or pleomorphic nuclei in a background of bland-looking cells can also be disregarded because they do not signify a worse outcome (Fig. 7.33). However, rare tumors may exhibit atypical features such as diffuse mild nuclear atypia

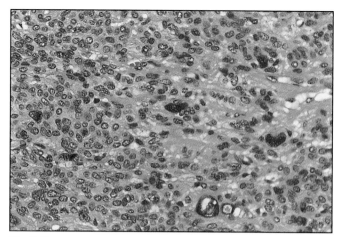

Fig. 7.33 • Pleomorphic adenoma. The presence of occasional enlarged hyperchromatic or even bizarre nuclei among bland-looking cells, especially when not accompanied by mitotic figures, does not signify a more aggressive behavior.

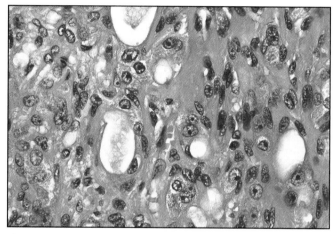

Fig. 7.34 • Atypical pleomorphic adenoma. This tumor is worrisome because of generalized nuclear atypia, including prominence of nucleoli. However, since mitotic figures are rare and there is no invasive growth, a designation of "atypical pleomorphic adenoma" is appropriate.

and the presence of occasional mitotic figures but without coagulative tumor necrosis or formation of an expansile mass (Fig. 7.34). Under such circumstances, the designation "atypical pleomorphic adenoma" may be appropriate. A conservative designation is justified because of an excellent prognosis even if there is already carcinomatous change, as long as there is no invasion beyond the capsule.

Carcinosarcoma

Carcinosarcoma, or true malignant mixed tumor, is very rare.[79] The mean age at presentation is 62 years with no sex predilection. The tumor most frequently affects the major salivary glands. In one-third of cases, there is clinical or histologic evidence of coexisting pleomorphic adenoma.[80] Histologically, the neoplasm comprises frankly malignant epithelial and mesenchymal elements. The epithelial component is most often a squamous cell carcinoma or adenocarcinoma, and the most common malignant mesenchymal component is chondrosarcoma, followed by fibrosarcoma, leiomyosarcoma, osteosarcoma, liposarcoma, and rhabdomyosarcoma (Fig. 7.35).[80,81]

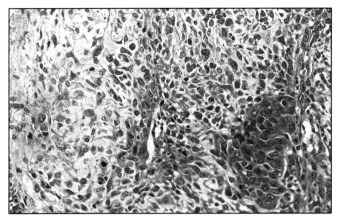

Fig. 7.35 • Carcinosarcoma. The carcinomatous component comprises cohesive polygonal cells (right lower field), and the sarcomatous component comprises loosely dispersed spindly to stellate cells.

It is an aggressive tumor with a mean survival of only 29.3 months.[81]

Basal cell adenoma

Definition

Basal cell adenoma is a benign tumor composed of basaloid cells sharply delineated from the stroma by basement membrane-like material. It usually exhibits a monotonous solid, trabecular, tubular, or membranous growth pattern. Chondromyxoid stroma should, by definition, be absent.

Clinical features

Basal cell adenoma typically presents as a solitary, slow-growing, otherwise asymptomatic mass. Age at presentation peaks in the sixth to seventh decades with a female predilection. About 70% occur in the parotid glands, and 10–20% in the upper lip.

Membranous basal cell adenoma, also known as dermal analogue tumor, is a distinctive variant that may be associated with cutaneous adnexal tumors. It shows no gender predilection.

Surgical excision is the treatment of choice. Recurrence is rare except for the membranous type, which is associated with a recurrence rate of 25% because of its multifocal nature.[82] Basal cell adenoma may rarely undergo malignant transformation (carcinoma *ex* monomorphic adenoma, 4%) to basal cell adenocarcinoma, adenoid cystic carcinoma, salivary duct carcinoma, or adenocarcinoma NOS.[83,84] The transformation rate is much higher in the membranous subtype, up to 28%.[82]

Pathologic features

Basal cell adenoma is well circumscribed, with or without a fibrous capsule. The cut surface is uniform and varies from light tan to brown. The cartilage-like or mucoid quality characteristic of pleomorphic adenoma is lacking. Membranous basal cell adenoma is usually multifocal (50% of cases) and multinodular.

Histologically, the small basaloid cells possess round, uniform, basophilic nuclei and scant cytoplasm (Fig. 7.36). Nuclear pleomorphism and mitoses are not seen. Sometimes, two populations of basaloid cells, dark and light cells, can be discerned. Some ductal structures lined by cells with a greater amount of eosinophilic cytoplasm are commonly interspersed among the basaloid cells (Fig. 7.36B). The tumors are usually dominated by one type of architecture (as detailed below), but a mixture of patterns can sometimes be seen.

Solid type The basaloid cells form broad bands, smooth-contoured jigsaw puzzle-like islands, and solid masses with peripheral palisading, which can be so prominent as to mimic ameloblastoma (Fig. 7.36A). The basaloid cells are sharply demarcated from the loose, often highly vascularized stroma by basement membrane. This feature contrasts with the centrifugal or "melting" growth of pleomorphic adenoma.

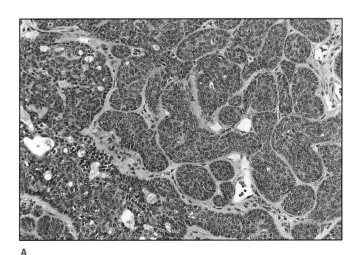

A

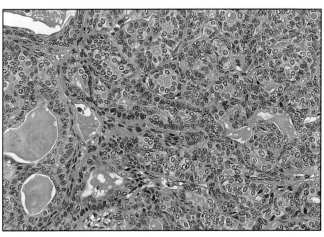

B

Fig. 7.36 • Basal cell adenoma. (A) Islands and broad trabeculae of basaloid cells characterize this tumor. There are some interspersed small glandular spaces. In contrast to pleomorphic adenoma, the cell islands are sharply demarcated from the stroma. (B) Tubular type of basal cell adenoma. The dual luminal–abluminal cell population is evident. This field is indistinguishable from some foci in a pleomorphic adenoma.

Trabecular type The trabecular type consists of interconnected narrow or broad trabeculae of cells, producing a reticular pattern (Fig. 7.37).

Tubular type The tubular type, which is the least common, comprises discrete or anastomosing tubules lined by two distinct layers of cells, with inner cuboidal ductal cells surrounded by an outer layer of basaloid cells (Fig. 7.36B). The lumen frequently contains PAS-positive eosinophilic secretion. Rarely, cribriform structures are formed or constitute the predominant pattern, mimicking adenoid cystic carcinoma (Fig. 7.38).

Basal cell adenoma with myoepithelium-derived stroma
This is an uncommon variant characterized by spindle cell-rich stroma that separates the cords and islands of basaloid cells[85] (Fig. 7.39). These spindle cells are strongly positive for S-100 protein and show ultrastructural features of myoepithelium, although actin and p63 are often negative. This tumor is distinguished from pleomorphic adenoma by the sharp demarcation of the abluminal basaloid cells from the stroma.

Membranous type The membranous type is characterized by the presence of abundant, thick, eosinophilic, and PAS-positive hyaline basal lamina material around the smooth-contoured tumor islands. The hyaline material also insinuates between individual cells in the form of droplets. There can be some interspersed glandular lumens in the tumor islands (Figs 7.40 and 7.41). Focal squamous metaplasia can occur. Since membranous basal cell adenoma grows in a multinodular fashion, with normal salivary gland tissue often entrapped within the tumor, it can be misinterpreted as a malignant lesion.

Membranous basal cell adenoma is histologically identical to dermal cylindroma (Fig. 7.42). Familial cases accompanied by multiple cylindromas, trichoepithelioma, eccrine spiradenoma, and milia constitute an autosomal Brooke–Spriegler syndrome (familial cylindromatosis or Turban tumor syndrome).

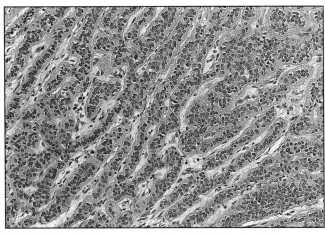

Fig. 7.37 • Basal cell adenoma, trabecular variant. Trabeculae of columnar or cuboidal cells with bland nuclei are separated by a loose stroma.

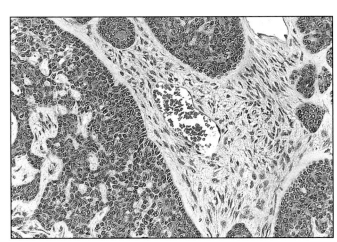

Fig. 7.39 • Basal cell adenoma with myoepithelium-derived stroma. The fibrous stroma between the trabeculae and islands of tumor harbors spindly cells with plump nuclei. These spindly cells are S-100 protein-positive (not shown). In contrast to pleomorphic adenoma, the tumor trabeculae are discrete, show cellular palisading at the periphery, and do not "melt" directly into the stroma.

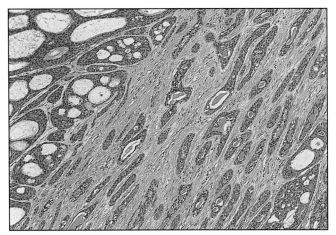

Fig. 7.38 • Basal cell adenoma. This tumor is composed of tubules and cribriform structures associated with a dense stroma. Without the opportunity to assess the borders, a firm distinction from adenoid cystic carcinoma cannot be made.

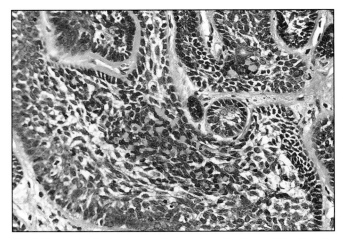

Fig. 7.40 • Basal cell adenoma, membranous type. The islands of basaloid cells are typically surrounded by an eosinophilic hyaline sheath made up of basement membrane material.

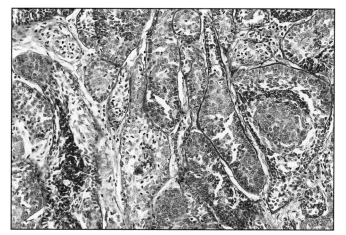

Fig. 7.41 • Basal cell adenoma, membranous type. Periodic acid–Schiff-diastase stain dramatically highlights the thick hyaline sheaths around the tumor islands as well as the interposed hyaline material among the tumor cells.

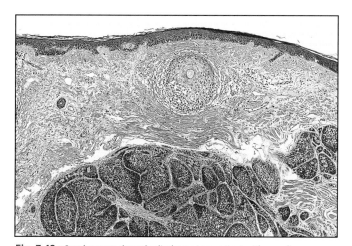

Fig. 7.42 • Synchronous dermal cylindroma in a patient with membranous basal cell adenoma. Note the remarkable identity of histologic appearances of the two tumor types, which explains the alternative name of "dermal analogue tumor" for membranous basal cell adenoma.

Germline mutations of the cylindromatosis gene (*CYLD*), a tumor suppressor gene located at chromosome 16q12-q13, has been implicated in these familial cases. Somatic mutations of this gene are also frequently found in sporadic cases.[86,87]

Immunohistochemistry

The vast majority of basal cell adenomas exhibit dual luminal–abluminal cell differentiation. Epithelial markers (cytokeratin, CEA, EMA) can be demonstrated in the luminal cells. Myoepithelial markers (p63, calponin, actin, GFAP, S-100) can be variably demonstrated in the peripherally located basaloid cells.[48,88,89]

Basal cell adenocarcinoma

Definition

Basal cell adenocarcinoma is a low-grade malignant neoplasm with cytologic resemblance to basal cell adenoma.[90] Diagnosis of malignancy usually rests on demonstration of infiltration of surrounding salivary lobules, nerves, or blood vessels.

Clinical features

The median age is 60 years, with no gender predilection.[91] Most tumors arise *de novo* in the parotid gland,[17] and less commonly, submandibular gland, oral cavity, and upper respiratory tract.[92,93] The tumors may arise from pre-existing basal cell adenoma, particularly the membranous subtype, or other monomorphic adenomas, in approximately 23% of cases.[91,94]

Basal cell adenocarcinomas are generally low-grade carcinomas with local destruction and a tendency for recurrence; regional lymph node or distant metastasis occurs infrequently. The outcome is favorable with adequate surgical treatment. However, tumors arising in minor salivary glands appear to have a higher recurrence rate (71%), metastatic rate (21%), and mortality (29%) compared with those arising in major glands (corresponding figures 37%, 11%, 3%).[84,91,92,94–96]

Pathologic features

Basal cell adenocarcinoma has a predominantly solid growth,[97] characterized by jigsaw puzzle-like islands of basaloid cells with peripheral palisading, usually invading in broad fronts (Fig. 7.43). Small areas with trabecular or membranous arrangement are frequently seen. Rarely, well-defined tubular structures with two-cell-type lining can be identified focally. As in basal cell adenoma, two distinctive basaloid cell populations, small dark cells and large pale cells, are present (Fig. 7.44A). Focal squamous differentiation is seen in 25% of cases, and some tumor cells may assume a spindly appearance (Fig. 7.45).[92] Within the basaloid cell islands, there can be small numbers of interspersed glandular spaces lined by cuboidal cells.

Cases showing nuclear atypia and readily identified mitotic figures are easy to recognize as being malignant (Fig. 7.44B). However, most cases have a relatively bland cytologic appearance, and only identification of infiltrative growth permits a diagnosis of malignancy (Fig. 7.43). Perineural infiltration or vascular invasion is present in 25–35% of cases.[95,97,98] The immunohistologic profile is similar to basal cell adenoma (see above).[99,100]

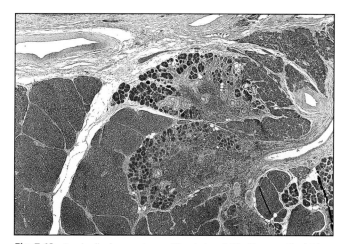

Fig. 7.43 • Basal cell adenocarcinoma. The obvious infiltrative growth of this basal cell neoplasm unequivocally places it into the malignant category. Basal cell adenocarcinoma typically grows in the form of lobules, often with a jigsaw puzzle-like quality.

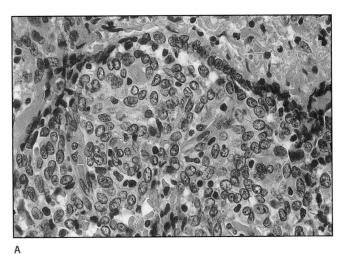

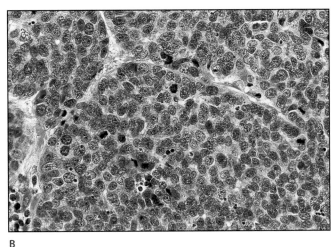

A

B

Fig. 7.44 • Basal cell adenocarcinoma. **(A)** Note the characteristic palisading of cells at the periphery. In this example, the cells are bland-looking, and distinction from basal cell adenoma is based on the presence of unequivocal infiltrative growth. As is typical of basal cell adenocarcinoma, some cells have darker nuclei and some have larger paler nuclei. **(B)** This example shows obvious nuclear atypia and mitotic activity in the basaloid cells.

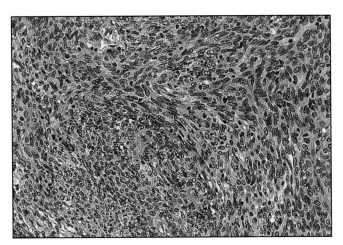

Fig. 7.45 • Basal cell adenocarcinoma. Some examples may have spindle cells in the centers of the tumor islands.

Major differential diagnoses (see sections on "Analytic approach to diagnosis" and "adenoid cystic carcinoma," p. 310)

1. Basal cell adenoma
2. Adenoid cystic carcinoma, solid variant
3. Undifferentiated carcinoma
4. Basaloid squamous cell carcinoma
5. Myoepithelial carcinoma

Myoepithelioma

Definition

Myoepithelioma is a benign tumor composed exclusively, or almost exclusively, of neoplastic cells exhibiting myoepithelial differentiation. While some investigators require total absence of ductal component for this designation,[65] most accept the presence of a minor epithelial component (e.g., less than 5–10%).[101–103]

Pleomorphic adenoma, basal cell adenoma, and myo-epithelioma can be envisaged to lie on a continuum: myo-epithelioma may represent an extreme form of basal cell adenoma without a ductal component, whereas basal cell adenoma is "pleomorphic adenoma minus the characteristic stroma," and pleomorphic adenoma lies in the middle of this continuum (Fig. 7.22).[104] However, given the benign nature of all these lesions, problems in nomenclature are merely a matter of semantics.

Clinical features

Myoepithelioma most frequently affects the parotid gland and palate. Less commonly, it can occur in the skin, breast, or soft tissue.[35,105] Clinically, it presents as a painless mass. The peak age is from the third to fifth decade with no sex predilection.[65,104,106] The treatment of choice is surgical excision.

The prognosis is excellent and recurrence is not expected after complete excision. Nonetheless, it can be difficult to predict the biologic behavior of a myoepithelial tumor on histologic grounds, in that metastasis may unexpectedly develop in an apparently benign-looking lesion (Fig. 7.46).

Pathologic features

Myoepithelioma is often thinly encapsulated, and has a solid, tan or yellow cut surface. The neoplastic myoepithelial cells can be spindly, plasmacytoid hyaline, epithelioid, clear, or oncocytic, with the first two cell types being most common. Either a single cell type predominates in a tumor, or there can be a mixture of cell types. Myoepitheliomas of the minor glands tend to be composed of plasmacytoid cells, and those of the parotid are more often composed of spindle or epithelioid cells. The stroma is usually scanty, but variable amounts of myxoid or hyaline stroma can be present. Collagenous crystalloids in the form of radially arranged and intercellular hyaline materials are variably present (Fig. 7.47).[104,107]

The spindle cells are elongated, with central vesicular nuclei and eosinophilic cytoplasm (Fig. 7.48A). They form variable interlacing fascicles. Myoepithelioma consisting predominantly

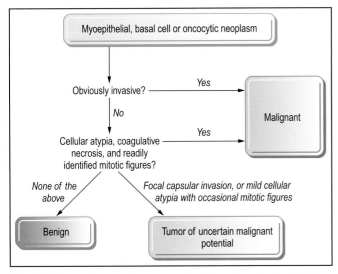

Fig. 7.46 • Practical approach to assessment of the malignant potential of myoepithelial, basal cell, and oncocytic neoplasms of the salivary gland.

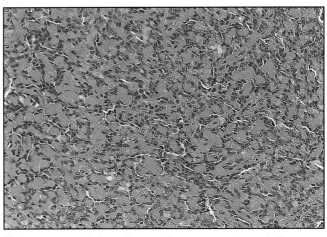

Fig. 7.47 • Myoepithelioma. The tumor forms anastomosing cords. The abundant intercellular hyaline material and vague nuclear palisading produce a schwannoma-like appearance.

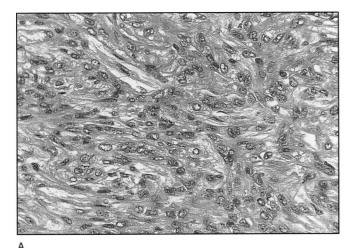

A

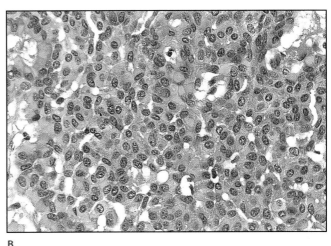

B

Fig. 7.48 • Myoepithelioma. **(A)** This tumor is composed of plump spindly cells with eosinophilic cytoplasm. **(B)** This tumor is composed mostly of plasmacytoid hyaline cells. These cells are identical to those seen in pleomorphic adenoma.

of spindle cells tends to be more cellular, with little fibrous stroma. However, some cases can be collagen-rich, mimicking solitary fibrous tumor (Fig. 7.49).

Plasmacytoid hyaline cells in myoepithelioma are identical to those seen in pleomorphic adenoma (Fig. 7.48B); they are frequently accompanied by a loose myxoid stroma. They form nondescript islands and sheets, or are suspended in myxoid matrix in the form of isolated cells, cords, or aggregates, and in the absence of true chondroid differentiation. Although it has been disputed that plasmacytoid hyaline cells lack immunohistochemical and ultrastructural evidence of myoid differentiation,[108] positive staining for calponin, actin, and p63 indicates that the cells indeed show myoepithelial differentiation.[48,104,109,110]

Epithelioid cells are large polygonal cells with eosinophilic cytoplasm and centrally located bland nuclei. They commonly show a reticular, trabecular, or solid growth pattern (Fig. 7.50).

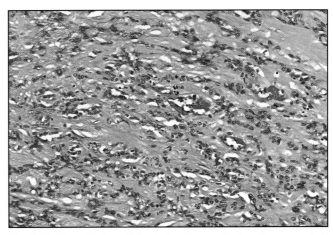

Fig. 7.49 • Myoepithelioma. This spindle cell myoepithelioma is accompanied by abundant collagenous stroma, mimicking solitary fibrous tumor.

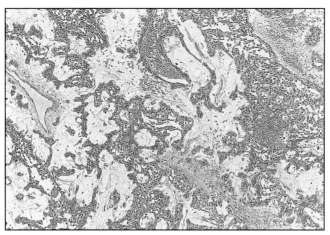

Fig. 7.50 • Myoepithelioma. The myxoid stroma breaks up the sheets of myoepithelial cells, resulting in a trabecular to reticulated pattern. Chondroid matrix, by definition, is absent.

Clear cells are rich in glycogen. They are usually present only focally, but can occasionally be so prominent as to pose difficulties in distinction from other clear cell tumors.

Infiltrative growth, cytologic pleomorphism, easily identified mitotic figures, and coagulative necrosis should not be present. However, the presence of rare enlarged hyperchromatic nuclei in a background of benign-appearing cells is acceptable.

Immunohistochemistry and ultrastructural studies

Pan-cytokeratin as well as myoepithelial markers (calponin, S-100, GFAP, actin, CK14, p63) are generally positive, but the frequency of positivity and percentage positive cells with the individual markers are highly variable. S-100 has been reported to be the most useful marker, but it lacks specificity.[104] Many cases also express EMA, but only rarely CEA. Ultrastructural studies may be useful to confirm myoepithelial differentiation by identifying both epithelial (hemidesmosomes) and myoid features (myofilaments with focal densities, pinocytotic vesicles).

Differential diagnoses

1. Pleomorphic adenoma or basal cell adenoma
2. Myoepithelial carcinoma
3. Various mesenchymal lesions, e.g., nerve sheath tumor, nodular fasciitis, solitary fibrous tumor

Myoepithelial carcinoma (malignant myoepithelioma)

Definition

Myoepithelial carcinoma is a myoepithelial tumor which demonstrates cytologic atypia and a potential for aggressive behavior.[90] All grades between benign myoepithelioma and myoepithelial carcinoma can be seen, and distinction of the latter from the former depends on demonstration of infiltrative growth, cellular atypia, frequent mitoses, and coagulative necrosis. A designation "myoepithelial neoplasm of uncertain malignant potential" may be appropriate for a tumor that exhibits some worrisome features but falls short of frankly infiltrative growth (Fig. 7.46).

Clinical features

The peak age is in the sixth decade, about 10 years older than the benign counterpart. Approximately one-half of cases arise from a pre-existing pleomorphic adenoma or myoepithelioma, particularly in recurrences.[111–113] It most commonly involves the parotid gland, but other major or minor glands and the breast can also be affected.[106,109,111,114,115] Myoepithelial carcinoma is an intermediate- to high-grade carcinoma. Approximately one-third of patients die, another third have recurrences, mostly multiple, and the remaining third are disease-free.[65,106,109,111] The commonest site of distant metastasis is the lung, followed by the liver and vertebra.[65] The diverse clinical outcomes reported in different series probably reflect the variable leniency in rendering a diagnosis of malignancy in a myoepithelial tumor.

Pathologic features

Myoepithelial carcinoma is usually unencapsulated and may exhibit areas of necrosis and cystic degeneration, although rare examples may be encapsulated. According to a series of 25 cases, the size ranges from 2.1 to 5.5 cm.[111] Most tumors show a pushing type of infiltration (Fig. 7.51). The tumor islands exhibit a cellular periphery and frequently a necrotic or myxoid central zone. Like myoepithelioma, it may show one or more of the following cell types: spindle, epithelioid, plasmacytoid hyaline, and clear cells. Nuclear atypia ranges from mild to marked (Fig. 7.52). Solid, fascicular, trabecular, and lace-like growth patterns are common, but glandular structures are not found (Figs 7.51–7.53). There can be variable amounts of myxoid, collagenous, or hyaline stroma (Fig. 7.51). There can be metaplastic changes such as squamous (often with keratinization) or sebaceous features and these cells gradually merge with the surrounding neoplastic cells.

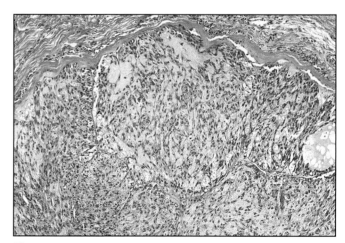

Fig. 7.51 • Myoepithelial carcinoma. This tumor infiltrates in broad fronts into the salivary parenchyma (upper field). The invasion identifies this as a malignant neoplasm. The tumor shows a trabecular-reticulated pattern, accompanied by variable amounts of myxohyaline stroma.

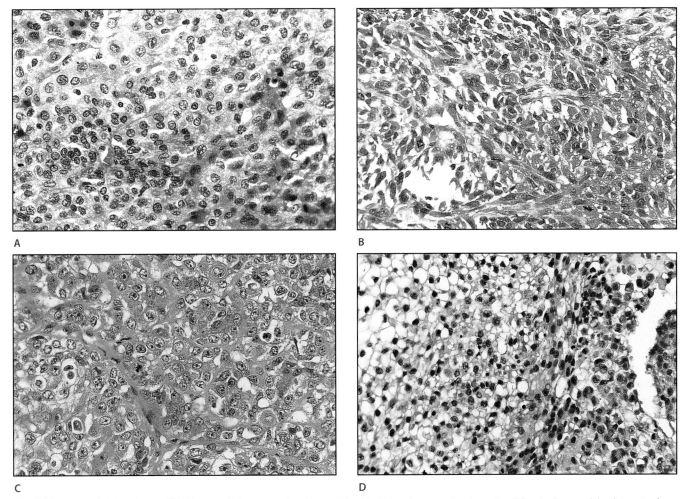

A

B

C

D

Fig. 7.52 • Myoepithelial carcinoma. **(A)** This example is composed of sheets of bland-looking polygonal cells with eosinophilic cytoplasm, and the diagnosis of malignancy is based on the presence of unequivocal invasive growth. **(B)** This example is obviously malignant on cytologic grounds. The plump spindly cells have pleomorphic nuclei and are mitotically active. As characteristic of myoepithelial neoplasms, the cytoplasm is eosinophilic. **(C)** This example is composed purely of polygonal cells with vesicular nuclei, distinct nucleoli, and eosinophilic cytoplasm. A diagnosis of malignancy is possible because of the cytologic atypia and the presence of mitotic figures. In other areas, there is also coagulative tumor necrosis. The problem is to document the presence of myoepithelial differentiation in the tumor cells. **(D)** Clear cells (left field) may constitute a significant population in some myoepithelial carcinomas.

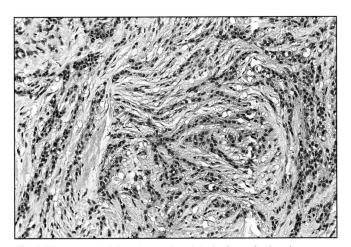

Fig. 7.53 • Myoepithelial carcinoma. Growth in the form of trabeculae separated by variable amounts of fibromyxoid stroma is one of the characteristic architectural features of myoepithelial carcinoma.

According to Nagao et al.,[109] myoepithelial carcinoma can be distinguished from benign myoepithelioma by a mitotic count greater than 7 per 10 high-power fields (hpf) or Ki-67 index greater than 10%. Furthermore, tumors with marked cellular pleomorphism, perineural invasion, high mitotic count (>61/10 hpf), high Ki-67 index (>50%) and p53 protein overexpression are associated with a worse prognosis.[109] On the other hand, rare cases of myoepithelial carcinoma can be bland-looking and exhibit a low mitotic count (Fig. 7.52A); demonstration of invasive growth is essential to establish their malignant nature. There is no difference in prognosis between *de novo* myoepithelial carcinoma and those arising from pleomorphic adenoma or myoepithelioma. Dedifferentiated myoepithelial carcinoma has also rarely been described.[116]

Immunohistochemistry

To render a diagnosis of myoepithelial carcinoma, the myoepithelial differentiation has to be substantiated by

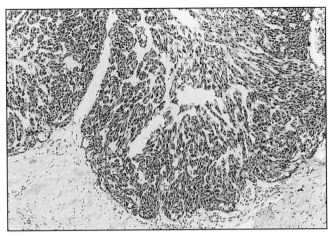

Fig. 7.54 • Myoepithelial carcinoma. This tumor shows strong immunoreactivity for S-100 protein.

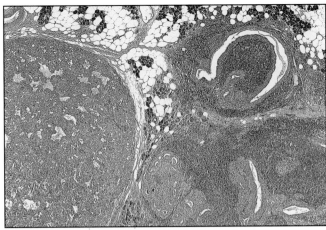

Fig. 7.55 • An unusual tumor showing combined features of oncocytoma (left field) and Warthin tumor (right field). In contrast to the solid glandular component of Warthin tumor, oncocytoma grows in the form of trabeculae and packets.

immunohistochemistry or electron microscopy. The immuno-histochemical profile is similar to that of the benign counterpart. Tumor cells express p63, calponin, S-100 protein, CK14, EMA and, variably, cytokeratin (90%), actin (70–80%), GFAP (50%), but not CEA and HMB-45 (Fig. 7.54).[48,109]

Differential diagnoses

Differential diagnoses include myoepithelioma, various sarcomas (leiomyosarcoma, fibrosarcoma, so-called malignant fibrous histiocytoma, malignant peripheral nerve sheath tumor), interdigitating dendritic cell sarcoma, and melanoma. The latter two tumors also express S-100 protein but not cytokeratin and myoid markers.

Clear cell myoepithelial carcinoma also raises the differential diagnosis of various clear cell tumors in the salivary glands (Table 7.5).[101]

Oncocytoma

Definition and related entities

Oncocytoma is a discrete, encapsulated tumor consisting exclusively of oncocytes and lacking features of other defined tumor types.[117] Oncocytoma, when accompanied by lymphoid stroma, can be indistinguishable from a Warthin tumor. Alternatively, it has been argued that oncocytoma may represent Warthin tumor that lacks lymphoid stroma.[118] The distinction, however, is not significant as both are benign. Occasionally, oncocytoma and Warthin tumor may even coexist (Fig. 7.55).

Oncocytosis is a diffuse oncocytic metaplastic process in the salivary gland, often associated with atrophy of the surrounding parenchyma (Fig. 7.56).[119,120] The lobular architecture is, however, preserved. Nodular oncocytic hyperplasia consists of multiple nodular proliferations of closely packed oncocytes. The nodules are less circumscribed and organized than those of oncocytoma, and a fibrous capsule is lacking.[120,121] Since oncocytosis can be pharmacologically induced in rats and these lesions may subsequently transform into oncocytoma,[9] the various oncocytic lesions described above could represent a spectrum of a single entity.[122] Although distinguishing features have been described for these three conditions, given the

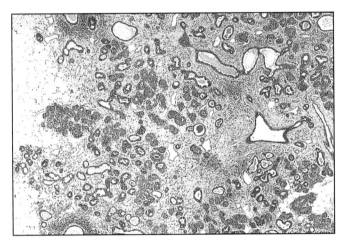

Fig. 7.56 • Diffuse oncocytosis of the submandibular gland. There is extensive oncocytic metaplasia of the ductal cells, accompanied by loss of acinar units. Note the preservation of lobular architecture.

similarly excellent prognosis and treatment modality, it is not worthwhile making great efforts to achieve definite distinction in controversial cases.

Clinical features

Oncocytoma most commonly occurs in the parotid gland of older adults (mean age 58–77 years) without gender predilection,[65,120,123] but the submandibular gland can also be affected.[117] Radiation exposure to the head and neck region has been implicated in the pathogenesis in about 20% of cases; this risk factor is also associated with presentation 20 years younger than those without a history of irradiation.[120] Surgical excision is the treatment of choice and recurrence is uncommon (0–10%).[117,120,123]

Pathologic features and special studies

Oncocytoma is a thinly encapsulated, mahogany brown, solid lesion (Fig. 7.57). The tumor cells form trabeculae, packets, diffuse sheets and, rarely, glands, separated by thin fibrous septa or scanty loose vascularized stroma (Fig. 7.57).

Table 7.5 Differential diagnoses of salivary gland tumors containing prominent clear cells

	Clear cell oncocytoma	Clear cell carcinoma	Mucoepidermoid carcinoma	Epithelial-myoepithelial carcinoma	Clear cell myoepithelioma and myoepithelial carcinoma	Acinic cell carcinoma	Metastatic renal-cell carcinoma
Nature of clear cells	Oncocytes	Ductal cells	Intermediate cells, mucinous cells	Myoepithelial cells	Myoepithelial cells	Acinic cells	Neoplastic renal epithelial cells
Cause of cytoplasmic clearing	Glycogen	Glycogen	Glycogen and mucin respectively	Glycogen	Glycogen	Tissue-processing artifact	Glycogen and lipid
Growth patterns	Encapsulated or circumscribed; trabeculae or packets	Infiltrative; solid or trabecular; sclerotic or hyalinized stroma	Infiltrative; inflamed fibrous stroma; islands of epidermoid, intermediate and mucinous cells; some cystic spaces	Infiltrative; ductal structures lined by inner cuboidal cells and outer clear myoepithelial cells	Lobules, nests, trabeculae, and fascicles; may have collagenous spherules	Infiltration in broad fronts; microcystic pattern	Prominent sinusoids; hemorrhage and hemosiderin deposition; some glandular structures
Cytologic features of clear cells	Centrally located, round nuclei; peripheral rim of cytoplasm may retain pink granularity	Polygonal cells with water-clear cytoplasm; nuclei central or eccentric	Intermediate clear cells are large cells with water-clear cytoplasm; mucinous cells have flocculent cytoplasm	Polygonal cells, with basally located or central nuclei; water-clear cytoplasm	Cells polygonal or spindly; variable degrees of nuclear atypia; often admixed with a population of cells with eosinophilic cytoplasm	Peripherally located nuclei; sparse basophilic granules in some cells	Water-clear cytoplasm; variable nuclear atypia
Staining properties of clear cells	PTAH+, mitochondrial antibody+	CK+, EMA+, myoepithelial markers (actin, calponin, p63)−	PAS+, PASD−, mucin− for intermediate clear cells; PAS+, PASD+, mucin+ for mucinous cells	S-100+, actin+, calponin+, p63+	S-100+, actin+, calponin+, p63+	PASD+ granules, amylase+	Lipid+, PAS+, PASD−, CK+, EMA+, myoepithelial markers−

PTAH, phosphotungstic acid hematoxylin; CK, cytokeratin; EMA, epithelial membrane antigen; PAS, periodic acid–Schiff; PAS-D, PAS with diastase pretreatment.

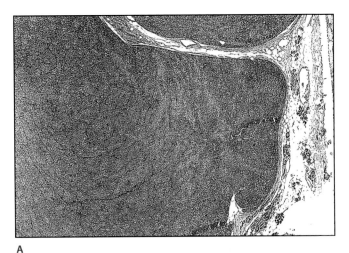

A

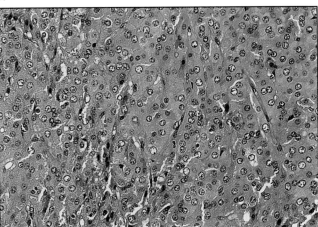

B

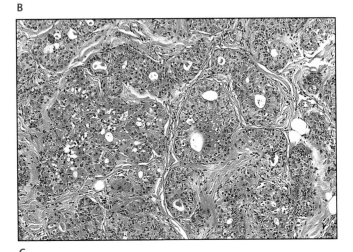

C

Fig. 7.57 • Oncocytoma. (**A**) The tumor has circumscribed contours, and this example consists of two contiguous nodules. (**B**) The tumor is composed of compact trabeculae of polygonal cells with abundant eosinophilic granular cytoplasm. (**C**) Rarely, glandular structures can be formed in oncocytoma.

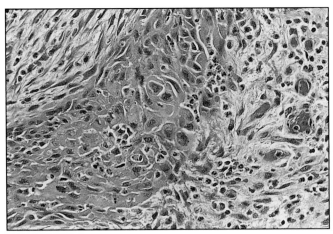

Fig. 7.58 • Oncocytoma complicated by infarction. In the surviving islands of tumor, there is squamous metaplasia. The cellular atypia can lure one to an erroneous diagnosis of squamous cell carcinoma. Note the characteristic reparative/inflammatory background.

Occasionally, the proliferated oncocytes appear to arise from ductal epithelial cells which have undergone oncocytic metaplasia. The oncocytes are polygonal or cuboidal, with abundant eosinophilic granular cytoplasm, central round nuclei, and often distinct nucleoli (Fig. 7.57). The cytoplasm is packed with mitochondria, which can be highlighted by phosphotungstic acid hematoxylin stain or immunostaining with antimitochondrial antibody.[124] Focally, sebaceous, goblet cell, or squamous differentiation and psammoma bodies may be present. Although many studies dispute the presence of myoepithelial or basal cells in oncocytoma,[48,89,125] such cells (with an attenuated appearance) can indeed often be demonstrated by immunostaining for p63 or CK14.

Tyrosine-rich crystals can be found in the tumor and adjacent striated ducts of some oncocytomas.[126] These eosinophilic crystals are needle-shaped or plate-like. They are seen extracellularly as well as within the oncocytic cells. Such crystals can also be found in Warthin tumor and oncocytic cystadenoma.

Oncocytoma is prone to infarction either spontaneously or following fine-needle aspiration. The necrotic cells manifest as ghost shadows or eosinophilic granular material. The residual viable tumor or adjacent salivary epithelium commonly undergoes squamous metaplasia with atypical (reparative) nuclei, mimicking squamous cell carcinoma (Fig. 7.58) (see "Analytic approach to diagnosis," p. 310).[47]

Variant: clear cell oncocytoma

Clear cells are present in 11% of oncocytomas as a dominant or partial component.[123] The architecture is otherwise the same as conventional oncocytoma[127–129] (Fig. 7.59). The cytoplasmic clearing is due to glycogen accumulation, but sparse granularity is still evident. Transition of clear cells to typical oncocytes can often be identified. Clear cell oncocytoma appears to show a higher frequency of bilateral tumors and recurrence in comparison to conventional oncocytoma.[130]

Differential diagnosis

Typical oncocytoma poses no difficulty in diagnosis. The major diagnostic challenge is to distinguish oncocytoma from salivary gland tumors with prominent oncocytic change, most notably Warthin tumor, pleomorphic adenoma, basal cell adenoma, and the oncocytic variant of mucoepidermoid carcinoma (see section on "Analytic approach to diagnosis," p. 310). Sometimes oncocytoma may be mistaken for acinic cell carcinoma

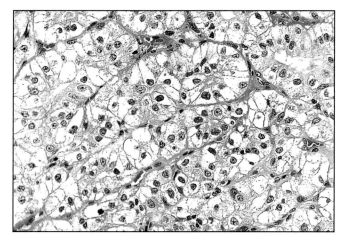

Fig. 7.59 • Clear cell oncocytoma. Like the ordinary oncocytoma, polygonal cells are arranged in compact trabeculae separated by a delicate vasculature. Most cells in this field have clear cytoplasm, while some cells retain a patchy granularity in the cytoplasm.

by virtue of the similar cell arrangement (cellular groups or cords) and cytoplasmic granularity, especially at intra-operative frozen section. However, the nuclei of acinic cell carcinomas are peripherally located, in contrast to the central round nuclei in oncocytoma.[123,131] Clear cell oncocytoma may also be mistaken for other clear cell salivary gland tumors (Table 7.5).

Oncocytic carcinoma (malignant oncocytoma)

Clinical features

Oncocytic carcinoma is an oncocytic tumor that demonstrates malignant histologic features. Most cases occur in the parotid gland of patients aged over 60 years.[65] Some cases may arise from a pre-existing oncocytoma. In contrast to oncocytoma, oncocytic carcinoma is not associated with prior radiation exposure. It is a high-grade neoplasm associated with frequent recurrence (56%) and metastasis (80%), most commonly to

the lung, kidney, liver, thyroid, mediastinum, and bone.[65,132] The average reported survival for patients with metastasis is 3.8 years.[123] Tumors less than 2 cm in diameter are associated with a better prognosis than larger tumors.[132]

Pathologic features

Oncocytic carcinoma is an unencapsulated, single, or multi-nodular tumor. The oncocytic cells, in contrast to their benign counterparts, show variation in size and shape and nuclear pleomorphism, although nuclear atypia may be minimal in some cases. They form trabeculae, sheets, nests, or ducts that infiltrate the salivary gland parenchyma and surrounding connective tissue (Fig. 7.60). Frequent atypical mitoses, and perineural and vascular invasion can be seen (Fig. 7.60A). Coagulative tumor necrosis appears to be specific for oncocytic carcinoma versus oncocytoma, and may confer an ominous prognosis;[123] it must not be confused with tumor infarction, which can also be seen in oncocytoma.

Metastasizing oncocytoma and oncocytic neoplasm of uncertain malignant potential

The malignant nature of most oncocytic carcinomas is easily recognized by their nuclear pleomorphism and infiltrative borders.[65] Some investigators, however, suggest that there may not be a sharp histologic distinction between oncocytoma and oncocytic carcinoma, and an otherwise bland-looking tumor may rarely develop metastasis unexpectedly.[123,132,133] Sugimoto reported a case of encapsulated oncocytoma with minimal nuclear atypia and low mitotic count that had lymph node metastasis at presentation. Multiple distant metastases occurred at 7 months and the patient succumbed at 18 months.[134] These tumors may represent metastasizing oncocytoma, akin to metastasizing pleomorphic adenoma, and both portend a poor clinical outcome.

For tumors showing borderline atypical features, such as cellular atypia alone, occasional mitotic figures, or limited local invasion, use of the designation "oncocytic neoplasm of uncertain malignant potential" may be appropriate to indicate uncertainties about their behavior (Fig. 7.46).

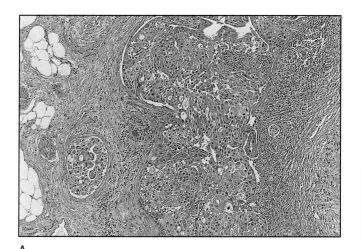

A

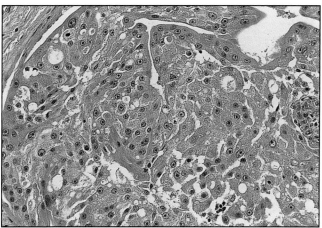

B

Fig. 7.60 • Oncocytic carcinoma. **(A)** The invasive growth distinguishes this tumor from an oncocytoma. Lymphovascular invasion is also evident in the left field. **(B)** The oncocytic tumor cells show mild to moderate nuclear pleomorphism and prominent nucleoli.

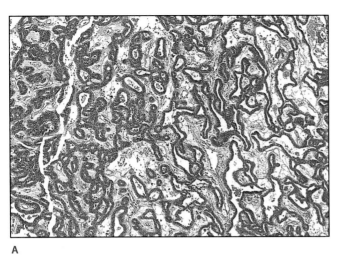
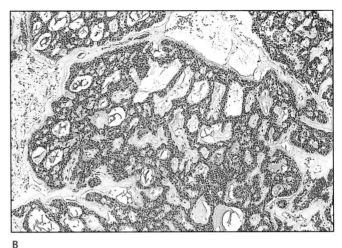

A
B

Fig. 7.61 • Canalicular adenoma. **(A)** Typical low-magnification appearance, featuring tramtrack-like double rows of cells that run in parallel, merge at some knots, and part at other areas to form dilated spaces. Note the characteristic loose stroma. **(B)** A less typical example showing a more complex, anastomosing pattern in the double row of cells.

Canalicular adenoma

Clinical features

Canalicular adenoma occurs most commonly in the elderly, with a mean age of 65 years and mild female predilection.[65] It is primarily an oral lesion. The upper lip is the site of predilection, which accounts for 74% of the cases, followed by the buccal mucosa (12%), palate, and, rarely, major salivary glands. The patients present with a non-ulcerated, painless mass that grows slowly. Infrequently, multifocal nodules, ulceration, necrosis, and bone destruction may be seen.[135-137] Recurrence does not occur after complete excision.[136,138]

Pathologic features

Canalicular adenoma is usually small (<3 cm) and well circumscribed, with or without a capsule. Multifocal lesions are not uncommon.[135] It is composed of bilayered strands of cells which abut and separate haphazardly, giving rise to single files, beads, canaliculi, and pseudopapillae (Fig. 7.61). The epithelial cells that form the strands are cuboidal to columnar, with a moderate amount of amphophilic cytoplasm and regular oval nuclei (Fig. 7.62). Cellular pleomorphism and mitoses are not seen. The stroma is characteristically edematous with many capillaries and sinusoids; it can be so loose that tumor strands may appear to be "floating in the air."[65] Foci of basaloid cells may be present, rendering it difficult to distinguish from basal cell adenoma, particularly the trabecular variant, although the distinction is unimportant for management purposes.

Immunohistochemistry and electron microscopy

Immunohistochemistry and electron microscopy have shown exclusive luminal cell differentiation without myoepithelial or basal cell participation. The tumor cells are positive for cytokeratin, vimentin, S-100 protein, and, infrequently, EMA.[88,139,140]

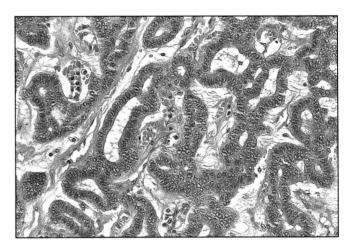

Fig. 7.62 • Canalicular adenoma. The spaces are lined by bland-looking columnar ductal cells. Myoepithelial cells are not seen.

Warthin tumor

Definition

Warthin tumor, also known as adenolymphoma or papillary cystadenoma lymphomatosum, is composed of bilayered oncocytic and basaloid epithelium forming cystic structures, papillae, and glands which are accompanied by a dense lymphoid stroma. Recent molecular studies have shown that the epithelial component is polyclonal and does not exhibit clonal allelic losses, suggesting that this tumor is not a true neoplasm.[141-143]

Clinical features

Warthin tumor is the second most common salivary gland tumor.[144-146] There is almost restricted occurrence in the parotid glands and the periparotid lymph nodes. It commonly presents in the sixth or seventh decade and is rare below the age of 40. There is a definite male predominance (5-26:1).

Interestingly, a decline in the incidence in men and a concurrent increased incidence in women has been observed in recent years. This change is probably due to a decline in the smoking habit, an established risk factor for this tumor,[147] in men, and a reverse trend in women.[148,149] Studies conducted among atomic-bomb survivors suggest that radiation may also be implicated in the tumorigenesis.[150] An earlier claim of a strong association with Epstein–Barr virus (EBV)[151] has not substantiated.[152,153]

This tumor typically presents as a doughy to cystic mass in the inferior pole of the parotid gland. In contrast to other monomorphic adenomas, Warthin tumor can manifest a variety of symptoms. The patients can be asymptomatic or can have pain, facial weakness, and ipsilateral ear symptoms such as earache, tinnitus, and deafness. Sudden painful increase in size associated with acute pain (known as papillary cystadenoma lymphomatosum syndrome) has been postulated to be caused by leakage of fluid into the surrounding tissues and retrograde infection from the oral cavity via the Stensen duct.[154] Rarely, facial nerve palsy may be seen in tumors complicated by inflammation and fibrosis, which may be mistaken clinically or intraoperatively for carcinoma. Warthin tumor is multicentric in 12–20% of patients (either synchronous or metachronous), and bilateral in 5–14%.[155,156] In addition, serial sectioning may reveal additional subclinical lesions in 50% of cases.[157] This tumor is sometimes seen in association with other benign salivary gland tumors, especially pleomorphic adenoma.[158,159]

Superficial parotidectomy or enucleation of tumor is curative. The rare recurrences (<2%) are believed to represent either a second primary or an expression of multifocal tumor.[160–164] In old patients or those with poor surgical risk, observation without surgery may be an option.

Macroscopic appearances

Warthin tumor is a well-circumscribed, spherical to ovoid lesion. The cut surfaces often reveal solid tumor interspersed with cystic spaces containing clear, mucoid, brown, or "caseous" semisolid debris, and the latter may sometimes give a false impression of tuberculous lymphadenitis on gross examination. There are usually fine papillary projections protruding into the cystic spaces (Fig. 7.63A). Prior fine-needle aspiration commonly results in areas of hemorrhage, necrosis, or fibrosis (Fig. 7.63B).

Microscopic appearances

Warthin tumor comprises irregular cystic structures with the lining epithelium thrown into papillary folds (Fig. 7.64A). The epithelium can also show downward extension to form loosely arranged or closely packed tubular glands (Fig. 7.64B). The epithelium consists of two layers: a luminal layer of oncocytic columnar cells supported by a discontinuous layer of oncocytic basal cells (Fig. 7.65). The nuclei of the luminal cells appear uniform and display palisading towards the free surface. Their brightly eosinophilic granular cytoplasm is due to accumulation of mitochondria.[124] The basal cells possess round to oval nuclei and small but conspicuous nucleoli. The lumens of the cysts contain thick proteinaceous secretions, cellular debris, cholesterol crystals, and sometimes laminated bodies that resemble corpora amylacea.[165]

A distinct layer of basement membrane separates the cyst lining from the lymphoid stroma, which consists of small lymphocytes and some plasma cells, histiocytes, and mast cells. Germinal centers and sinusoids can be seen in some cases. Sometimes there may be a granulomatous reaction with Langhans-type giant cells. The intimate relationship between glandular structures and lymphoid stroma earned the designation of "adenolymphoma" for this tumor. The origin of the lymphoid cells is still controversial: residual normal nodal lymphoid tissue versus reactive lymphoid proliferation against the neoplasm. Tumors developing in extraparotid (such as cervical) lymph node can potentially be misinterpreted as metastatic Warthin tumor.

The epithelial component can undergo metaplastic change to squamous, mucous cells or even ciliated cells, especially in response to inflammation or infarction (Fig. 7.66). Sometimes the tumor undergoes infarction, either spontaneously or following fine-needle aspiration, and the tumor cells can be

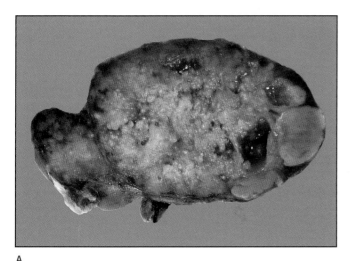

A

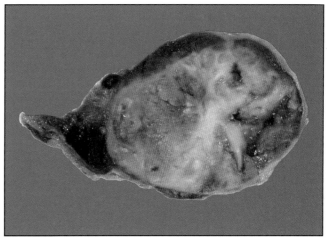

B

Fig. 7.63 • Warthin tumor, gross appearance. **(A)** The cut surface shows a well-encapsulated tumor with some cysts and brown-colored solid areas exhibiting a granular texture. **(B)** This example shows prominent fibrosis, attributable to repair after prior fine-needle aspiration.

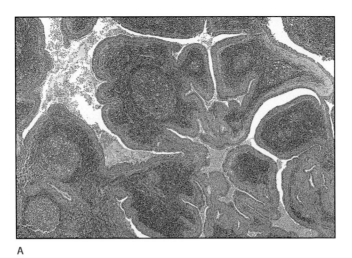

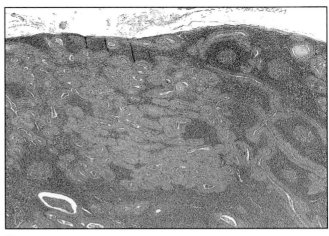

A

B

Fig. 7.64 • Warthin tumor. **(A)** Papillae covered by pink epithelium and densely populated by lymphoid cells project into the cystic spaces. Lymphoid follicles are evident. **(B)** The oncocytic epithelium can proliferate to form closely packed tubules, but is still accompanied by a lymphoid stroma.

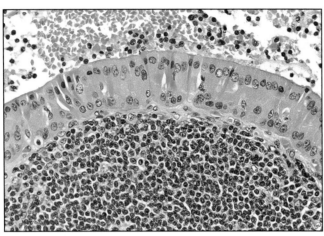

Fig. 7.65 • Warthin tumor. The papillae and glands are typically lined by columnar oncocytic luminal cells in which the nuclei are often polarized towards the lumen. Beneath the luminal cells is a layer of basal cells, which are sharply demarcated from the underlying lymphoid stroma.

obscured by necrosis, granulation tissue, inflammatory reaction, and fibrosis. Worse still, cellular atypia and a pseudoinfiltrative appearance of the metaplastic squamous epithelium in the residual tumor often invite an erroneous diagnosis of squamous cell or mucoepidermoid carcinoma.[166] Lack of true infiltrative growth into the surrounding parenchyma and merging of the atypical squamous islands with oncocytic epithelium should point to the correct diagnosis (Fig. 7.67).[47]

The relative proportions of epithelial and lymphoid components in Warthin tumors vary. Four subtypes are recognized by Seifert: subtype 1 (classic Warthin tumor) is 50% epithelial (77% of all Warthin tumors); subtype 2 (stroma-poor) is 70–80% epithelial (14% of cases); subtype 3 (stroma-rich) is only 20–30% epithelial (2%); and subtype 4 is characterized by extensive squamous metaplasia.[164] Subtype 2 shows morphologic overlap with oncocytoma. In fact, Dardick suggested that Warthin tumor and oncocytoma constitute the two extremes of a spectrum of lesions.[6] This classification does not have clinical importance, but serves to alert pathologists to the variable appearances of this seemingly monotonous tumor.

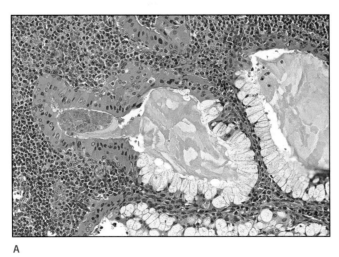

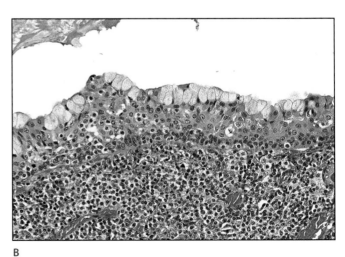

A

B

Fig. 7.66 • Warthin tumor with metaplastic epithelium. **(A)** There is abrupt transition from oncocytic epithelium (left) to mucinous epithelium (right). **(B)** Metaplasia of oncocytic epithelium to mucinous and squamoid cells results in mimicry of mucoepidermoid carcinoma.

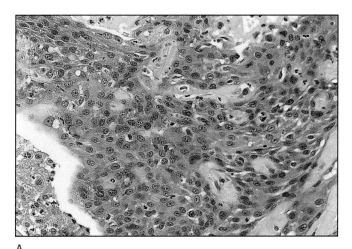

A

B

Fig. 7.67 • Warthin tumor complicated by infarction and squamous metaplasia. **(A)** The residual neoplastic epithelium has undergone squamous metaplasia. The presence of cytologic atypia may lead to a mistaken diagnosis of squamous cell or mucoepidermoid carcinoma. **(B)** Identification of continuity of the squamous epithelium with residual oncocytic epithelium (right field) establishes the metaplastic nature of the squamous proliferation. Note also the inflammatory reaction to the infarction process.

Malignant change in Warthin tumor

Rarely, either the epithelial or lymphoid component of Warthin tumor can undergo malignant transformation,[65] with an estimated incidence of less than 0.1%.[167] In order of frequency, the commonest carcinomas are squamous cell carcinoma, oncocytic carcinoma, adenocarcinoma, undifferentiated carcinoma, mucoepidermoid carcinoma, and Merkel cell carcinoma.[168–172] From the literature, one-third of patients have regional lymph node metastasis, and some may also develop distant metastasis.

Lymphoma arising from the lymphoid stroma is characterized by a relatively monomorphic infiltrate with distortion of the epithelial and lymphoid architecture. Various types of non-Hodgkin lymphoma and Hodgkin lymphoma have been reported.[173–176]

Differential diagnosis

Typical Warthin tumor has a highly distinctive morphology and poses no problem in diagnosis. It differs from oncocytoma

in the presence of a prominent lymphoid component, papillae, and glands rather than trabeculae and packets, and conspicuous basal cells (which are inconspicuous in the latter tumor). The squamous metaplastic Warthin tumor, particularly if infarcted, can be mistaken for squamous or muco-epidermoid carcinoma. Squamous metaplasia of Warthin tumor usually lacks keratinization, which is seen in most squamous cell carcinomas. In contrast to low-grade muco-epidermoid carcinoma, there is no definite infiltrative growth and the tumor cells appear more frankly squamous.

Sebaceous neoplasms

Sebaceous cells can be found normally in the parotid gland, submandibular gland, and oral minor salivary gland. Sebaceous tumors are very rare neoplasms which are believed to arise from these sebaceous-differentiated cells. It should be noted that different types of salivary gland tumors can show focal sebaceous differentiation, such as pleomorphic adenoma, Warthin tumor, and mucoepidermoid carcinoma.[177]

Sebaceous adenoma and lymphadenoma

Clinical features Affected patients are generally in their sixth or seventh decade of life with a slight male predilection. These tumors usually present as an asymptomatic, slow-growing mass. The parotid gland is the commonest site, in keeping with the natural occurrence of sebaceous glands there. Complete excision is curative.

Sebaceous adenoma

Sebaceous adenoma is an encapsulated tumor comprising multiple incompletely differentiated sebaceous lobules accompanied by a fibrous stroma. Each lobule consists of groups of mature sebaceous cells surrounded by basaloid cells. Some cells can show transitional features between the two cell types. The sebaceous cells contain multiple small honey-combed vacuoles of lipid that can be highlighted by oil red O stain on frozen section. Focal squamous, mucous, or oncocytic metaplasia is common. Disintegration of mature sebaceous cells can result in cyst formation in the lobule. There can also be cystic structures lined by squamous, columnar, or cuboidal cells, with or without sebaceous cells. The fibrous stroma can be infiltrated by copious inflammatory cells, including lipogranuloma formation, probably in response to extravasated sebum.

Sebaceous lymphadenoma

Sebaceous lymphadenoma bears a strong resemblance to Warthin tumor. Islands of sebaceous lobules, duct-like structures, or cysts are intimately mixed with a dense lymphoid stroma. The lymphoid stroma often contains many reactive lymphoid follicles. Foreign-body granulomas related to extruded sebum are frequently present (Fig. 7.68). It has been postulated that sebaceous lymphadenoma, similar to Warthin tumor, originates from ectopic salivary gland tissue in parotid lymph node,[90,178] Nonetheless, in parallel to the controversy over Warthin tumor, the lymphoid stroma has alternatively been interpreted as a tumor-associated reaction.[65]

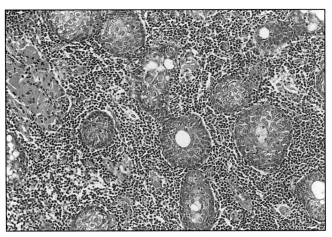

Fig. 7.68 • Sebaceous lymphadenoma. In the epithelial islands disposed in a lymphoid background, basaloid cells are located peripherally, while sebaceous cells are located centrally. In the extreme left field, there is a collection of histiocytes, which probably represents a reaction to extruded sebum from the tumor.

Sebaceous carcinoma and lymphadenocarcinoma

Sebaceous carcinoma Sebaceous carcinoma is a rare, intermediate-grade malignancy. There is a bimodal age distribution, with peaks in the third and seventh to eighth decades. The gender distribution is equal. Patients present with a mass lesion, pain, or facial paralysis. The treatment of choice is wide surgical excision for low-stage carcinomas. Adjunctive radiation therapy is recommended for higher-stage and grade tumours. The overall 5-year survival rate is 62%.[65,177]

These tumors are partially circumscribed but show infiltrative margins at least focally. There are variable-sized islands, sheets, and infiltrative cords of basaloid, squamous, and sebaceous cells. Duct-like and cystic spaces are common. Many cells are undifferentiated, but distinct sebaceous cells with foamy cytoplasm are present in the center of most or some tumor islands. All cases exhibit cellular pleomorphism, nuclear atypia, and frequent mitoses. Tumor necrosis is common and perineural invasion is noted in 20% of cases.[179]

Sebaceous lymphadenocarcinoma Sebaceous lymphadeno-carcinoma is a very rare malignant tumor representing malignant transformation of sebaceous lymphadenoma. All 3 reported cases occurred in patients aged above 70 years.[177,180] One of the patients died of unrelated causes and the other 2 were free of disease at 6 and 14 years. The tumors contain areas of typical sebaceous lymphadenoma juxtaposed to a frankly malignant component; the latter lacks the characteristic lymphoid stroma and can be a sebaceous carcinoma, undifferentiated carcinoma, adenoid cystic carcinoma, or epithelial-myoepithelial carcinoma.[177,178]

Cystadenoma

Definition

Cystadenoma is a rare, non-invasive epithelial tumor characterized by cystic proliferation of benign ductal epithelium.[65,181]

Clinical features

It occurs equally in the major glands and minor glands (most notably the lip, buccal mucosa, palate, and tonsil). The mean age is 55 years, with a female predilection. The tumor usually presents as an asymptomatic, variably fluctuant, slow-growing cyst.[181] Complete excision is curative. Rarely, malignant transformation may occur.[182]

Pathologic features

The cut surface of the tumor reveals multicystic spaces or a single large cyst, into which there may be nodular projections. The tumor is well circumscribed with or without a fibrous capsule. Microscopically, there is a single or multiple variably sized cysts separated by dense fibrous stroma. The cysts are lined by attenuated, cuboidal, or columnar epithelial cells, which may be thrown into papillary folds (Fig. 7.69). The nuclei are bland, and mitoses are extremely rare. Focal or extensive mucous, oncocytic, and, rarely, squamous metaplasia of the epithelial cells can occur. The lumens of the cysts contain proteinaceous fluid.

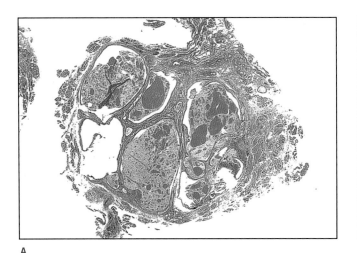

A

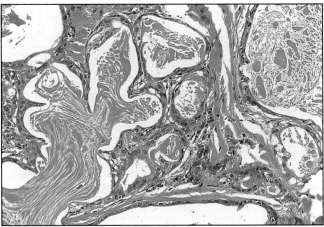

B

Fig. 7.69 • Cystadenoma of the tongue. (**A**) This circumscribed tumor comprises multiple variable-sized cysts that contain thick secretion. (**B**) The cysts are lined by bland-looking attenuated or cuboidal cells. The multiplicity of cell types that characterize low-grade mucoepidermoid carcinoma is lacking.

Since papilla formation is almost a constant feature, cystadenoma is sometimes called papillary cystadenoma.[90] When oncocytic or mucous metaplasia is prominent, designations such as papillary oncocytic cystadenoma or papillary mucous cystadenoma can be applied.[178]

Differential diagnosis

The main differential diagnoses include low-grade mucoepidermoid carcinoma (infiltrative; presence of some solid islands; mixture of cell types), cystadenocarcinoma (presence of definite invasion), duct ectasia, polycystic disease, and sclerosing polycystic adenosis. See "Analytic approach to diagnosis," p. 310.

Cystadenocarcinoma

Clinical features

Cystadenocarcinoma or papillary cystadenocarcinoma is a rare low-grade malignant tumor representing the malignant counterpart of cystadenoma. The majority of patients are above 50 years old (mean age 59). There is no gender predilection. About 65% occur in the major salivary glands, and the rest affect the buccal mucosa, lips, and palate. It manifests as a slowly growing asymptomatic mass. Palatal tumor may erode the bone. Local recurrence and regional lymph node metastasis rates are 7.5% and 10% respectively.[183]

Pathologic features

Similar to the benign counterpart, the cut surfaces of the tumor reveal single or multiple cysts containing clear or brown fluid. The tumor size ranges from 0.4 to 6 cm. Microscopically, the malignant nature of the tumor is manifested by invasion into the surrounding tissue (Fig. 7.70).[180] Perineural invasion occurs in 9% of cases. The tumor comprises numerous variably sized cysts with frequent intraluminal papillary processes. Foci of solid growth and extraluminal extension are evident in some cases. The cysts are lined by small cuboidal, large cuboidal, or columnar cells, or a mixture of these cells. Cellular atypia is

usually mild to moderate, but nucleoli are usually prominent.[65] Tumors composed predominantly of pseudostratified tall columnar cells appear to have a higher rate of metastasis.[183] The stroma ranges from being fibrotic, sclerotic, hyalinized, to desmoplastic.

Low-grade cribriform cystadenocarcinoma

Low-grade cribriform cystadenocarcinoma has been listed as a variant of cystadenocarcinoma in the recent World Health Organization classification.[184] As discussed in a subsequent section (see p. 295), this term is misleading, and the tumor is in fact an intraductal salivary duct carcinoma.

Differential diagnosis

It is important to distinguish cystadenocarcinoma from papillary-cystic acinic cell carcinoma and mucoepidermoid carcinoma because it requires less radical surgery and has a better prognosis. Cystadenocarcinoma is distinguished from cystadenoma by the presence of invasion, foci of solid growth, and, in some cases, cytologic atypia. It can be distinguished from salivary duct carcinoma by the low nuclear grade and lack of comedo necrosis.

Ductal adenomas

Sialadenoma papilliferum, inverted ductal papilloma, and intraductal papilloma belong to a group of rare benign salivary tumors which arise from the excretory ducts or junction between ductal and mucosal epithelium, and are characterized by papillary growth. There is a distinct predilection for the minor salivary glands.

Sialadenoma papilliferum

The mean age of the patients is 59 years, with slight male predilection. The tumor forms an exophytic, papillary, or verrucous growth from the buccal mucosal surface with a broad or pedunculated base. The analogous lesion in the skin is syringocystadenoma papilliferum. Histologically, the tumor comprises multiple papillary processes with convoluted clefts and spaces in between. The superficial portion of the lesion is covered by acanthotic stratified squamous epithelium, in continuity with the adjacent mucosal epithelium. In the deeper levels, there is a transition to ductal epithelium consisting of a layer of luminal columnar cells supported by a layer of basal cuboidal cells. Proliferation of the ductal epithelium beneath the papillary stalks may result in cysts and duct-like structures with irregular luminal contours. The stroma is characteristically rich in plasma cells.

Sialadenoma papilliferum shows a higher rate of recurrence (10–15%) after excision compared with other types of ductal adenoma.[185] A single case of malignant transformation into epithelial-myoepithelial carcinoma and micropapillary carcinoma has been reported.[186]

Inverted ductal papilloma

This tumor presents as a nodular submucosal mass beneath an apparently intact surface. The proliferation of papillae appears

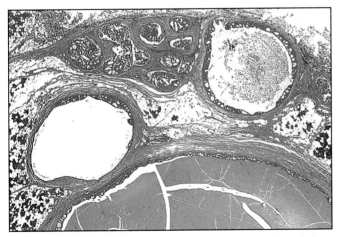

Fig. 7.70 • Cystadenocarcinoma. This cystic neoplasm is categorized as being malignant because of the presence of invasion into the parotid parenchyma (upper field).

to start from a pit on the mucosal surface, and grow inwards into the underlying stroma. The epithelial islands are smooth-contoured and sharply demarcated from the adjacent lamina propria. The lining epithelium of the papillae is largely composed of non-keratinizing squamous cells or transitional epithelium with occasional columnar and goblet cells. This lesion morphologically resembles inverted papilloma of the sinonasal tract. There is no recurrence after complete excision.[185]

Intraductal papilloma

Intraductal papilloma develops within a deeply situated salivary duct, often presenting as unicystic dilatation of a duct. An elaborate papillary proliferation is seen projecting into a cystic lumen. A single or double layer of cuboidal to columnar cells forms the epithelial lining that is supported by thin cores of fibrovascular tissue. There is no invasion of the cyst wall. The analogous lesion in the breast is also known as intraductal papilloma. A single case with malignant transformation characterized by cytologic atypia, intraductal extension, microinvasion, and lymph node metastasis has been reported.[187]

Keratocystoma

Clinical features

Keratocystoma is a rare benign tumor consisting of multiple cystic structures and solid nests formed by benign squamous epithelial proliferation. Only 3 cases have been reported.[188,189] All cases affected the parotid glands of children or young adults (age 8–38 years) as a painless mass. There is no recurrence after complete excision.

Pathologic features

Grossly, the tumor is a multilocular cystic lesion filled with keratin-like substance. Histologically, there are multiple, randomly disposed cystic structures and solid nests of squamous cells. The former are lined by non-dysplastic stratified squamous epithelium with ortho- or parakeratosis

but lacking a granular layer. The cyst lumens are filled with lamellated keratin. The basal layer is demarcated from the stroma by basement membrane. The stroma is fibrotic with moderate amounts of chronic inflammatory cells. Foreign-body reaction against keratin released from the ruptured cysts is also present. The squamous cells express pan-cytokeratin and CK14, but not S-100 protein or actin.

Salivary gland anlage tumor

Clinical features

Salivary gland anlage tumor of the nasopharynx manifests in newborns or within the first few weeks of life with respiratory distress.[190] There is a strong male predilection of 7:1. The tumor is postulated to be a hamartoma because the histologic features are reminiscent of embryonic salivary gland, although some investigators favor a teratomatous interpretation.[191] Recurrence or metastasis has not been reported after excision.[192]

Pathologic features

The tumor produces a smooth or nodular, midline naso-pharyngeal mass, sometimes with a narrow pedicle. The surface is covered by non-keratinizing stratified squamous epithelium, which extends downwards to form squamous nests, branching ducts, and cystic structures (Fig. 7.71A). Interspersed between these epithelial structures are densely cellular nodules consisting of mesenchymal-like plump spindle cells with focal whorling and rudimentary ductoglandular structures (Fig. 7.71B). The epithelial units (cytokeratin-positive) in the internodular stroma blend into the cellular nodules (with highly variable proportions of cells immunoreactive for cytokeratin, vimentin, and actin). Ultrastructurally, the nodules comprise cells with epithelial, myoepithelial, and myogenic features. Chondroid or myxochondroid tissue is not found; hence the previous designation "congenital pleomorphic adenoma" is not appropriate.[193]

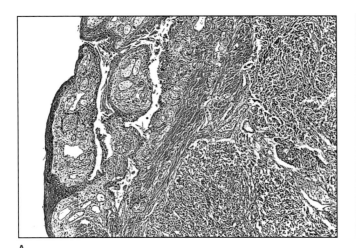

A

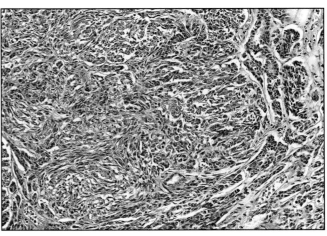

B

Fig. 7.71 • Salivary gland anlage tumor of the nasopharynx. **(A)** Cleft-like glandular structures are in continuity with the surface epithelium. Whorls and fascicles of spindly cells are present in the deeper portion. **(B)** The glands merge into fascicles of bland-looking spindly cells.

Sclerosing polycystic adenosis

Clinical features

Sclerosing polycystic adenosis is a lesion of uncertain nature characterized by a striking morphologic resemblance to fibrocystic changes of the breast.[194–199a] It occurs in patients from 9 to 80 years of age (mean, 33–44.5 years) with a female to male ratio of 22:15. Most cases arise in the major salivary glands, but intraoral minor salivary glands can also be affected. The patients present with a slow-growing mass. Recurrence occurs in almost one-third of cases but most likely reflects multifocal disease. No metastasis or mortality has been reported so far.

Pathologic features

The lesion is well circumscribed and partially encapsulated. There are multiple ducts, glands, and acinar structures arranged in a lobular pattern (Fig. 7.72). The sclerotic stroma

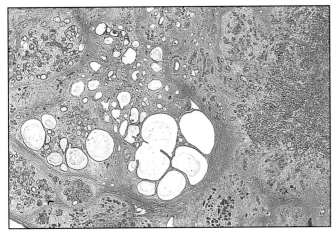

Fig. 7.72 • Sclerosing polycystic adenosis. The lesion is typically well demarcated from the normal salivary parenchyma (not shown). The lobular architecture is preserved. The stroma shows sclerosis, and there are aggregates of cysts. The right field shows a more cellular focus.

shows focal lymphocytic infiltration. The glandular epithelial cells exhibit a spectrum of foamy, apocrine-like granular and mucinous appearances. Some cells contain large, brightly eosinophilic granules (Fig. 7.73A). There can be variable degrees of epithelial hyperplasia forming solid aggregates and cribriform structures. There are also strangulated tubules reminiscent of sclerosing adenosis (Fig. 7.73B). Ductal epithelial atypia ranging from mild dysplasia to carcinoma in situ can be found in 40–75% of cases.[194,199a]

Immunohistochemically, the luminal epithelial cells express CEA, BRST-2, estrogen receptor (20%), and progesterone receptor (80%), but not c-erbB2.[199] A continuous layer of myoepithelial cells can be demonstrated around the ducts and acini.[199a]

Polycystic disease of parotid gland

Polycystic (dysgenetic) disease of parotid gland is a developmental malformation believed to result from defects and dilatation of the intercalated ducts.[200–202] Most patients present in childhood with recurrent parotid swelling. Histologically, the lobular architecture is preserved. The extent of involvement varies from lobule to lobule. The lesion comprises honeycombed, lattice-like cysts of variable sizes and shapes lined by flat cuboidal to low columnar or apocrine-like cells. Occasional striated ducts of acinar units appear to communicate with the cysts. The cyst lumens often contain flocculent secretion and sometimes laminated microliths. A mild chronic inflammatory infiltrate is commonly present in the fibrous septa (Fig. 7.74).

Adenoma with additional stromal components

Lymphadenoma

Lymphadenoma is a rare tumor in which the adenoma is accompanied by a dense lymphoid infiltrate. There is resemblance to sebaceous lymphadenoma minus the sebaceous component. It is likely that lymphadenoma is not a distinctive tumor type, but is merely a basal cell adenoma or cystadenoma accompanied by a heavy lymphoid infiltrate.[203,204] All cases

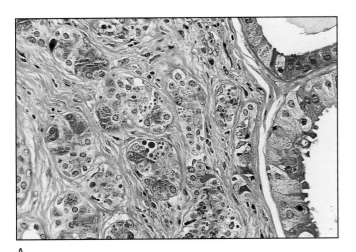

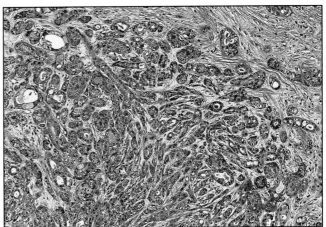

A   B

Fig. 7.73 • Sclerosing polycystic adenosis. **(A)** Some tubuloacinar units are lined by apocrine-like cells stuffed with brightly eosinophilic hyaline globules. **(B)** The cellular focus comprises closely packed narrow tubules resembling sclerosing adenosis of the breast.

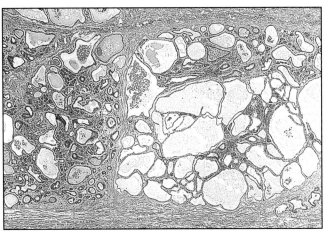

Fig. 7.74 • Polycystic (dysgenetic) disease of the parotid gland. The lobular architecture is preserved, but variable-sized cysts have replaced the normal lobular ductal units. The cysts, formed by dilatation of the ducts, are lined by attenuated epithelial cells.

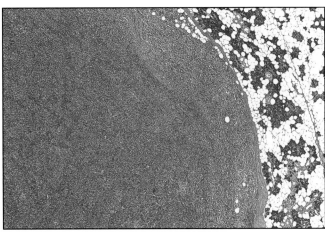

Fig. 7.75 • Lymphadenoma. The tumor is typically circumscribed, and densely infiltrated by lymphocytes and plasma cells.

have occurred in the parotid glands of male patients ranging in age from 17 to 57 years. Complete surgical excision is curative.

Pathologic features The tumor comprises an adenomatous proliferation accompanied by a dense lymphoid background (Fig. 7.75). The latter is generally considered to represent tumor-associated lymphoid proliferation, thus conventional salivary gland adenomas occurring within lymph nodes are excluded. The epithelial component can take the form of anastomosing trabeculae, islands, solid tubules, cystically dilated glands filled with proteinaceous materials, or papillary structures. The cyst or gland lining cells are cuboidal to columnar without significant cytologic atypia. The trabeculae are composed of basaloid cells. In some cases, the epithelial component can be obscured by lymphocytes, and PAS-diastase can be used to highlight the basement membrane-like material around the epithelial islands (Fig. 7.76).

This tumor can be distinguished from lymphoepithelial carcinoma by its lack of invasive growth, lack of frank nuclear atypia or significant mitotic activity, presence of ductal dif-

ferentiation at least focally, and lack of EBV association. In short, lymphadenoma is glandular, whereas lymphoepithelial carcinoma is a squamous-related neoplasm. Lymphadenoma can be distinguished from lymphoepithelial sialadenitis (LESA) by the circumscribed borders and presence of a more proliferative epithelial component.

Lipoadenoma (sialolipoma)

Lipoadenoma, also known as sialolipoma, is a benign tumor consisting predominantly of adipose tissue admixed with variable amounts of an adenomatous component.

It affects patients of a wide age range (20–75 years, mean 54.5) with a male predilection. The clinical presentation is typically a slowly growing asymptomatic mass in the parotid gland, or occasionally the palate. There is no recurrence after complete excision.

Pathologically, it is thinly encapsulated or circumscribed, and consists of mature adipose tissue and benign salivary gland tissue, with the former usually constituting more than 90% of the tumor. The glandular component is sharply demar-

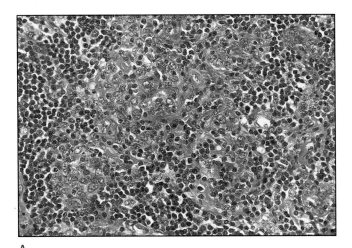

A

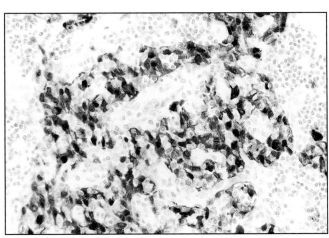

B

Fig. 7.76 • Lymphadenoma. (A) The epithelial component, in the form of solid tubules and trabeculae, is masked by the lymphoid component. (B) The abluminal cells of the epithelial component are remarkably highlighted by immunostaining for S-100 protein.

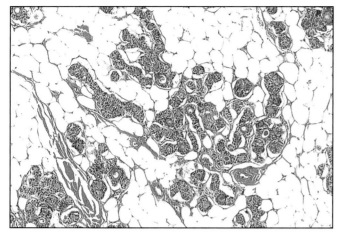

Fig. 7.77 • Lipoadenoma. In this circumscribed tumor, "sertoliform" narrow tubules are intermingled with abundant mature adipose cells.

cated from the fat, and comprises normal duct-acinar units without cytologic atypia or proliferative activity, or exhibits adenomatous features, forming sertoliform tubules. Focal oncocytic change, ductal dilatation with fibrosis, and sebaceous or squamous metaplasia can be seen (Fig. 7.77).[205–208] It is currently unclear whether the glandular component represents entrapped salivary tissue or part of the tumor.

Adenofibroma

Adenofibroma is a very rare neoplasm comprising proliferated adenomatous glands admixed with a prominent cellular stroma in which the delicate spindly cells are CD34+ but lack myoepithelial features (S-100, actin, and p63-negative).

Mucoepidermoid carcinoma

Definition

Mucoepidermoid carcinoma, previously known as "mucoepidermoid tumor," is an invasive malignant neoplasm that comprises mucus-secreting cells, epidermoid cells, and intermediate cells in variable combinations, forming cysts and solid islands. This is the commonest malignant salivary gland neoplasm in adults and childhood.[65]

Clinical features

The tumor typically presents as a slow-growing painless mass. About one-third of patients experience tenderness, pain, drainage from the ipsilateral ear, dysphagia, and trismus. Facial paralysis is uncommon, except in high-grade tumors.[14] Age of presentation spans from the first to the ninth decades, peaking in the fourth decade. There is a slight female predilection. The parotid gland (45%) and palate (21%) are the commonest sites of occurrence.[65]

Mucoepidermoid carcinoma is the principal histologic type of radiation-related salivary gland carcinoma in survivors of the atomic bombings of Hiroshima and Nagasaki.[150] This tumor also occurs with increased frequency among children who received high-dose and low-dose radiotherapy for leukemia and tinea capitis respectively.[209,210]

Mucoepidermoid carcinoma has been described in the nasal cavity, paranasal sinuses, nasopharynx, breast, bronchus, thymus, and skin.[211–216] Central mucoepidermoid carcinoma of the jaw bones probably results from malignant transformation of the epithelial lining of odontogenic cysts. In that context, the tumor typically presents as asymptomatic radiolucent lesion. It usually shows low-grade malignant behavior and histology.

Macroscopic appearances

Mucoepidermoid carcinoma appears as an ill-defined mass which may be partially encapsulated, with firm to hard consistency. There can be interspersed cysts that contain mucus or blood-stained fluid.

Microscopic appearances

Most cases exhibit irregular invasive borders, at least focally (Fig. 7.78). The tumor comprises haphazardly dispersed mucin-filled cysts and tumor nests composed of mucus, squamoid (epidermoid), and nondescript intermediate cells in variable combinations (Fig. 7.79). The stroma is characteristically sclerotic and abundant, with chronic inflammatory cell infiltration and occasional extravasated mucin pools (Figs 7.78 and 7.80). Such stromal changes are most frequently seen in low- and intermediate-grade mucoepidermoid carcinomas. Rarely, there can be a dense lymphoplasmacytic infiltrate admixed with tumor islands, scattered multinucleated giant cells in the stroma, or melanin pigmentation.[203,217,218]

Low-grade mucoepidermoid carcinoma Variable-sized, mucin-filled cystic structures constitute a high proportion of the tumor, and there are abundant mucous cells (Fig. 7.81A). However, irregular-shaped epithelial islands are almost always present (Fig. 7.79). The tumor cells have bland nuclei, and mitotic figures are rarely seen (Fig. 7.79).

Mucous cells are large, columnar, goblet shaped, or polygonal cells with copious mucin, imparting a frosted-glass

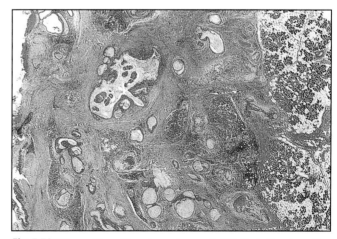

Fig. 7.78 • Mucoepidermoid carcinoma, low-grade. This illustration shows the prototypic low-magnification appearance of this tumor: infiltrative borders (residual parotid tissue present in right field), dense fibrous background with aggregates of chronic inflammatory cells, cystic and solid islands of tumor cells, and presence of mucin.

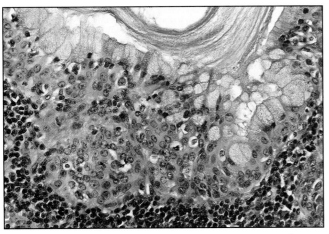

Fig. 7.79 • Mucoepidermoid carcinoma, low-grade. The constituent cells include mucinous cells, intermediate cells, and squamoid cells. The nuclei are typically bland-looking.

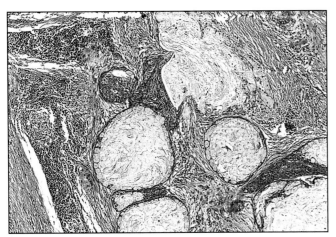

Fig. 7.80 • Mucoepidermoid carcinoma, low-grade. Characteristically, cystic tumor islands lie in a chronically inflamed fibrous stroma. There is extravasation of mucin into the stroma (right upper field); the inflammation and fibrosis are probably elicited by the extravasated mucin.

appearance to the cytoplasm (Fig. 7.81B). The intracellular mucin can be readily demonstrated by mucicarmine or diastase-PAS stain. Mucous cells may form closely packed nests, line cystic structures, or be scattered among islands of squamoid cells.

Another major cell type is the intermediate cell, which ranges from being small to medium-sized, is polygonal, and has a nondescript appearance (Fig.7.79). It represents the putative common precursor of mucous and epidermoid cells.[219] It forms nests and sheets, and often merges into other cell types.

Squamoid (epidermoid) cells occur in nests or line cystic spaces. They have a stratified appearance, but intercellular bridges are often inconspicuous (Fig. 7.79). Keratinization or keratin pearls are practically never seen.

Mucin-containing cysts may rupture, allowing the escape of mucus into the stroma, eliciting an inflammatory response and subsequently sclerosis. The lymphoid infiltrate can be exuberant and accompanied by lymphoid follicles, imparting a resemblance to a metastatic deposit in lymph node (Fig. 7.80).

High-grade mucoepidermoid carcinoma High-grade mucoepidermoid carcinoma contains more solid areas and few cystic spaces, and perineural and intravascular invasion are common. The solid areas are formed by large polygonal squamoid (epidermoid) cells with pale to eosinophilic cytoplasm and distinct cell borders, as well as nondescript intermediate cells (Fig. 7.82). Squamous features are often better developed compared with low-grade tumors – there can be intercellular bridges and even individual cell keratinization, but keratin pearls are rare. Cellular pleomorphism, nuclear hyperchromasia, and mitotic figures are more impressive, and areas of coagulative necrosis may be present. Mucous cells are usually sparse, and staining for mucin may be required to identify them (Fig. 7.83). In general, there is less fibrous stroma or chronic inflammatory infiltrate compared with low-grade tumors. Rarely, a component of low-grade mucoepidermoid carcinoma is present, suggesting that the high-grade tumor arises through progressive loss of differentiation.

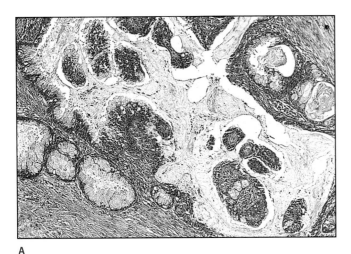

A

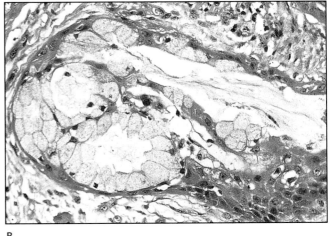

B

Fig. 7.81 • Mucoepidermoid carcinoma, low-grade. **(A)** The cystic tumor islands can form intraluminal papillary folds. The cells that line the cystic spaces are often mucinous cells with lightly basophilic cytoplasm. **(B)** This cystic tumor island is formed by a mixture of mucinous cells and squamoid cells. There are vague intercellular bridges among the latter cell type. As is characteristic of low-grade mucoepidermoid carcinoma, the tumor cells are bland-looking.

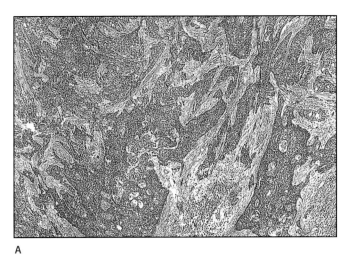

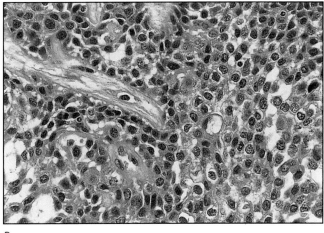

A

B

Fig. 7.82 • Mucoepidermoid carcinoma, high-grade. **(A)** The tumor grows in anastomosing, irregular solid islands with scarcely any interspersed cystic spaces. **(B)** Higher magnification shows epidermoid cells with intercellular bridges, exhibiting moderate nuclear pleomorphism. There are rare interspersed vacuolated cells.

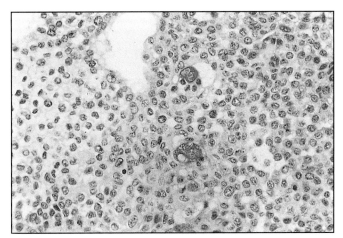

Fig. 7.83 • Mucoepidermoid carcinoma, high-grade, stained with mucicarmine (same case as Fig. 7.82). Mucin stain is often required to confirm the presence of mucin-secreting cells in this predominantly squamoid tumor.

Intermediate-grade mucoepidermoid carcinoma The intermediate-grade tumors lie histologically between the low- and high-grade tumors. Cystic spaces do not constitute a significant portion of the tumor. Some degree of nuclear pleomorphism is observed in the tumor cells (Fig. 7.84). Epidermoid features are generally more obvious than in the low-grade tumors.

Variants of mucoepidermoid carcinoma Large polygonal clear cells with discrete cell membranes, abundant clear cytoplasm, and eccentric nuclei are a minor component of most mucoepidermoid carcinomas (Fig. 7.85A). The clearing of cytoplasm is due to accumulation of glycogen. Occasionally these cells constitute a major portion of the tumor, rendering distinction from other clear cell tumors problematic. The cells located in the peripheral portions of the clear cell islands are often much smaller, with eosinophilic cytoplasm, and a squamoid quality. The clear cell variant appears to be more common in the palate.

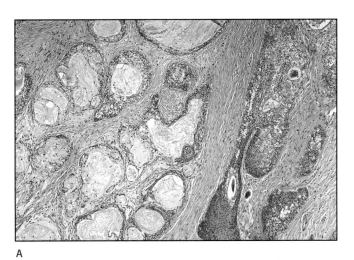

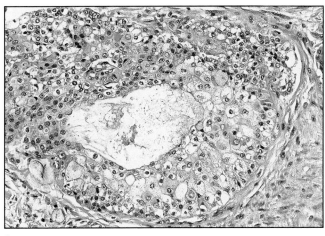

A

B

Fig. 7.84 • Mucoepidermoid carcinoma, intermediate-grade. **(A)** Solid and cystic tumor islands infiltrate a fibrous stroma. Cystic spaces constitute a less prominent component compared with low-grade tumors. **(B)** Intermediate and squamoid cells predominate, with occasional interspersed mucinous cells. There is a mild to moderate nuclear atypia.

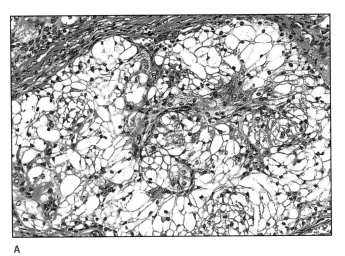
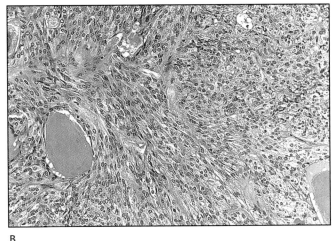

A

B

Fig. 7.85 • Mucoepidermoid carcinoma variants. (**A**) The clear cells have distinct cell membranes and water-clear cytoplasm. (**B**) Fascicles of spindle cells (left field) are interposed among polygonal cells.

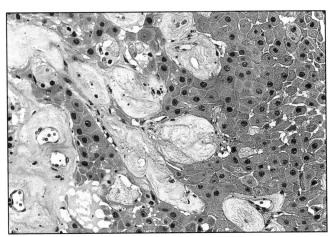

Fig. 7.86 • Oncocytic variant of mucoepidermoid carcinoma. This variant may be mistaken for oncocytoma.

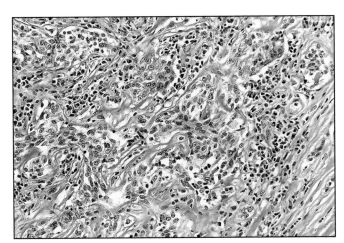

Fig. 7.87 • Sclerosing mucoepidermoid carcinoma with eosinophilia. This parotid tumor comprises islands and trabeculae of squamoid cells that infiltrate a sclerotic stroma rich in lymphocytes and eosinophilia. Mucinous cells are interspersed in some tumor islands (not shown).

Focal spindle cell growth and oncocytic change are uncommon patterns observed in some mucoepidermoid carcinomas (Fig. 7.85B). The rare oncocytic variant (oncocytes accounting for >60% of cell population) can potentially be confused with oncocytoma (Fig. 7.86).[220,221]

The sclerosing variant shows prominent central keloid-like sclerosis and lymphoid infiltration at the periphery. Because of the paucity of tumor islands, which are often confined to the peripheral zone, this variant may be mistaken for an inflammatory lesion.[222–225]

Sclerosing mucoepidermoid carcinoma with eosinophilia is characterized by tumor islands dispersed in a sclerotic stroma densely infiltrated by chronic inflammatory cells and eosinophils (Fig. 7.87).[226] Its relationship with the thyroid counterpart bearing the same name and conventional salivary gland mucoepidermoid carcinoma, if any, remains unclear.[227]

Immunohistochemistry

The tumor cells are positive for cytokeratin. There can be variable staining for EMA, CEA, and S-100. p63 immunoreactivity can be demonstrated in the intermediate, squamous,

and clear cells,[48] but myoepithelial markers such as actin and calponin are negative.[228] In contrast to squamous cell carcinoma, mucoepidermoid carcinoma often expresses CK7.[229]

Genetic features

Translocation involving *mucoepidermoid carcinoma translocated 1 (MECT1)* and *mastermind-like gene family (MAML2)*, located at chromosome 19 and 11 respectively, is the most frequent genetic alteration in mucoepidermoid carcinoma,[230] and disrupts the Notch signaling pathway.[231] The gene fusion can be detected by in-situ hybridization or RT-PCR in up to 70% of cases, and can potentially be utilized to aid in the diagnosis of mucoepidermoid carcinoma.[232] This is not detected in Warthin tumor, despite earlier claims otherwise.[233,234]

Prognostic factors

The behavior of mucoepidermoid carcinoma is strongly correlated with the clinical stage and histologic grade. Cure is possible, especially for low- and intermediate-grade tumors (Fig. 7.6). Several two- or three-tiered grading systems are in

Table 7.6	Mucoepidermoid carcinoma: standard three-tier grading system		
Histologic parameters for grading	Low-grade	Intermediate-grade	High-grade
Cysts	Many macrocysts and microcysts	Some cysts	Few cysts
Mucinous cells	Many	Some	Few
Mitotic figures	Few	Few or some	Many
Cytology	Bland	Some atypia	Significant cellular pleomorphism
Biologic potential	Locally infiltrative; slow-growing	Intermediate	Highly infiltrative; rapid-growing
Recurrence	0–6%	20–39%	61–78%
Metastasis	Very rare	Some cases (lymph node 22%)	Common (44–72%; commonly lymph node; distant metastasis in 33%)
5-year survival rate	92%	70–83%	22–42%

Table 7.7	Mucoepidermoid carcinoma: Armed Forces Institute of Pathology grading system (only applicable to intraoral and parotid tumors)[237,238]
Parameters	Score
Intracystic component <20%	+2
Neural invasion	+2
Necrosis	+3
Mitoses ≥ 4/10 high-power field	+3
Anaplasia (nuclear pleomorphism, increased nuclear-to-cytoplasmic ratio, large nucleoli, anisochromia, hyperchromasia)	+4

Total score	Interpretation	Frequency among all mucoepidermoid carcinomas	Behavior		
			Recurrence rate	Regional lymph node metastasis	Died of tumor
0–4	Low-grade	84%	7.5%	2.5%	0%
5–6	Intermediate-grade	9%	8.3%	0%	8.3%
7–14	High-grade	7%	40%	70%	60%

use (Tables 7.6 and 7.7).[223,235–241] Recently, a new grading system using five histopathologic features has been shown to be reproducible and of prognostic significance.[237,242,243] Nonetheless, a recent Mayo Clinic study shows that grade and stage are less important if radical surgery is performed.[244]

Submandibular mucoepidermoid carcinomas have significant metastatic potential irrespective of histologic grade; for example, 13% of patients with low-grade tumor died of tumor.[237,238] High proliferative index (mitotic count >2/10 hpf or MIB1 index greater than 10%), expression of MUC1, vascular invasion, involved margins, and aneuploidy are also associated with a poor prognosis.[239,245–248]

Differential diagnosis

Mucoceles are extremely rare in the major salivary glands. In a major gland showing unexplained mucin pools associated with fibrosis and chronic inflammation, the most likely diag-

nosis is low-grade mucoepidermoid carcinoma. Extensive sampling will usually reveal the diagnostic tumor islands.

The tumors that should be considered in the differential diagnosis (see section on "Analytic approach to diagnosis," p. 310) are:

1. Warthin tumor with squamous/mucinous metaplasia
2. Pleomorphic adenoma with squamous differentiation
3. Cystadenoma or cystadenocarcinoma
4. Poorly differentiated adenocarcinoma (versus high-grade mucoepidermoid carcinoma)
5. Squamous cell carcinoma. Features favoring a diagnosis of mucoepidermoid carcinoma over squamous cell carcinoma include: identification of interspersed mucinous tumor cells (such as by histochemistry), predominantly sclerotic rather than desmoplastic stroma, presence of a component of low-grade mucoepidermoid carcinoma, immunoreactivity for CK7, and immunoreactivity for MUC5AC.[248]

Adenoid cystic carcinoma

Definition

Adenoid cystic carcinoma is an invasive neoplasm composed predominantly of basaloid cells with myoepithelial/basal cell differentiation, accompanied by interspersed ductal structures. It is characterized by cribriform, tubular, and/or solid patterns of growth and a myxohyaline stroma.[249]

Clinical features

Adenoid cystic carcinoma most commonly presents in the fourth to sixth decades, with a slight female predominance (3:2). The parotid gland, submandibular gland, and palate are most commonly involved. This tumor has also been reported in lacrimal glands, auditory canal, upper respiratory tract, lung, digestive tract, skin, breast, prostate, and lower female genital tract.[250–255]

Clinically, the commonest complaint is a slow-growing swelling. Large tumors often cause fixation to skin or deeper tissues. There may also be tenderness, pain, and facial nerve palsy due to the marked propensity of the tumor for neural invasion.[256] Palatal tumors often ulcerate. Bone invasion may occur without radiographic changes as the tumor infiltrates through the marrow spaces. The tumor has often invaded well beyond the clinically apparent borders.[249,257–264]

Although adenoid cystic carcinoma is generally indolent, the long-term prognosis is poor (Fig. 7.4). The 5-year survival is about 60–75%, but the 10-year survival drops dismally to 30–54%.[12,14,37] The majority of affected patients (80–95%) eventually die of the disease after a protracted clinical course characterized by multiple local recurrences and metastases.[249,265] Distant metastasis (most commonly lung, bone, and soft tissue) is more common than regional lymph node metastasis,[266] and often occurs 5–10 years after initial treatment.[267] Radical excision is the treatment of choice, and the benefit of radiotherapy remains unproven.[256,268]

Pathology

Grossly, the tumor is tan, fleshy, firm, and invasive. Infiltrative growth is usually obvious on histologic examination, and perineural invasion is very common (Fig. 7.88). The three characteristic growth patterns (cribriform, tubular, and solid) are present in variable combinations in an individual case. In contrast to pleomorphic adenoma, there is no "melting" of the basaloid cells into the stroma (Fig. 7.89). The stroma is fibrous with variable amounts of myxohyaline material rather than desmoplastic, and cartilage is not formed. Sometimes extensive hyalinization results in "strangulation" of the tumor islands, to the extent that few tumor cells remain or a lace-like pattern is produced (Fig. 7.90).

Cribriform pattern The cribriform structures are the most characteristic feature of adenoid cystic carcinoma. They are almost always found, albeit very focally sometimes. They are variable-sized, smooth-contoured, discrete to coalescent islands comprising small, uniform basaloid cells punctuated by round rigid spaces, giving rise to a "Swiss-cheese" appearance. The majority of the spaces are not glandular lumens, but represent

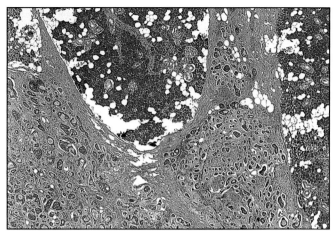

A

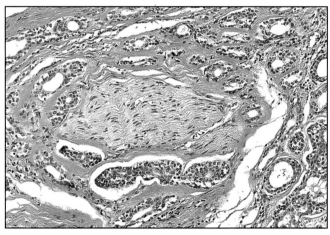

B

Fig. 7.88 • Adenoid cystic carcinoma. **(A)** This figure depicts the prototypic low-magnification appearances of this tumor type: invasive borders, tubules, and cribriform structures, and sclerotic or hyaline stroma. **(B)** Perineural invasion is a common feature.

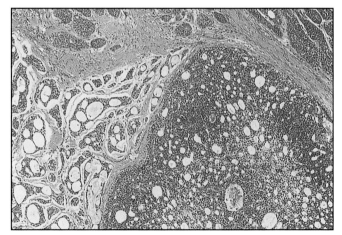

Fig. 7.89 • Adenoid cystic carcinoma. This tumor commonly shows great regional variabilities in pattern. In the left field small cribriform plates predominate, and the right field is occupied by a huge cribriform structure. The upper field shows some solid islands.

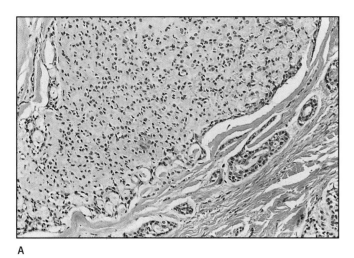

A

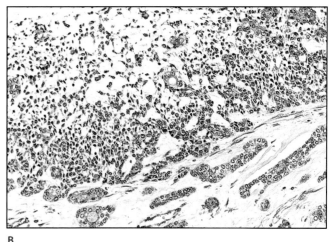

B

Fig. 7.90 • Adenoid cystic carcinoma with hyalinization or myxoid change, mimicking pleomorphic adenoma. **(A)** The cribriform island (upper and left fields) shows deposits of abundant hyaline material, with "strangulation" of the tumor cells. It can be difficult to make a diagnosis if an adenoid cystic carcinoma shows extensive hyalinization such as this. This pattern differs from the hyalinization seen in pleomorphic adenoma in that the process is confined to the cellular island, which itself is sharply delineated from the fibrous stroma. **(B)** The cribriform island (upper field) shows myxoid change, reminiscent of the "melting" pattern seen in pleomorphic adenoma. In contrast to the latter, this change is confined to the large cellular island, and the island itself is well demarcated from the stroma.

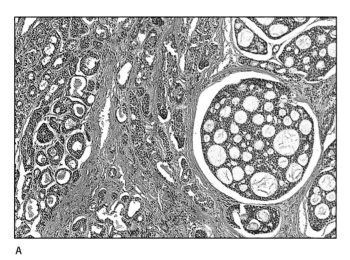

A

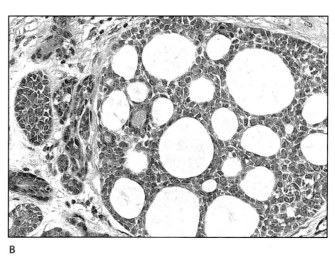

B

Fig. 7.91 • Adenoid cystic carcinoma, cribriform type. **(A)** Cribriform structures (right field) and some tubules (left field) are seen. This field alone is indistinguishable from pleomorphic adenoma or basal cell adenoma. **(B)** In this cribriform structure, practically all spaces are pseudocysts surrounded by basaloid (modified myoepithelial) cells. The spaces are filled with lightly basophilic mucin. A few small true glandular spaces are present towards the left side.

stromal invaginations (pseudocysts); continuity with the stroma can sometimes be demonstrated. These spaces are filled with eosinophilic hyaline material (PAS-positive, diastase-resistant) and/or lightly basophilic myxoid ground substance (Alcian blue-positive) (Figs 7.89, 7.91, and 7.92). Ultrastructurally, these materials represent glycosaminoglycans and duplicated basal lamina. Within these cribriform islands, there are occasional true narrow glands lined by low cuboidal cells with eosinophilic cytoplasm (Fig. 7.91A). A thin eosinophilic cuticle may be present along the luminal border, and the lumen may contain PAS-positive diastase-resistant eosinophilic secretion. Occasionally, the glandular structures are abortive, manifesting as a small collection of vacuolated cells with eosinophilic cytoplasm (Fig. 7.93A). Exceptionally, the luminal cells may exhibit oncocytic changes (Fig. 7.93B).

The neoplastic basaloid cells constitute the major cell population. They possess round or angulated nuclei, and scanty

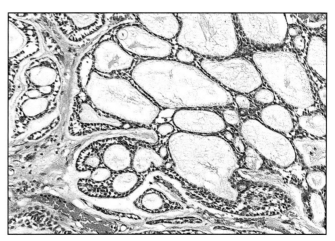

Fig. 7.92 • Adenoid cystic carcinoma. Large cribriform unit in which the spaces are filled with eosinophilic hyaline material or lightly basophilic mucosubstance. Note the continuity of the spaces with the surrounding stroma (left field).

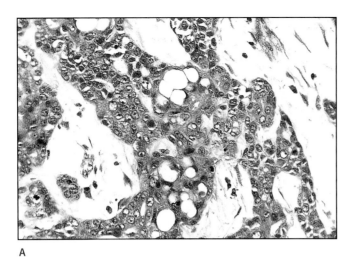

A

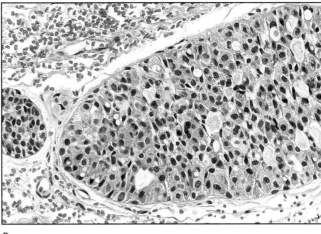

B

Fig. 7.93 • Adenoid cystic carcinoma, uncommon appearances. **(A)** Tubules within the basaloid-cell islands are abortive, being represented by groups of vacuolated cells with eosinophilic cytoplasm. **(B)** Oncocytic change in luminal cells.

cytoplasm with indistinct cell borders (Fig. 7.93A). Some cells may have pale to clear cytoplasm. Nuclear pleomorphism is usually mild, and mitotic figures are usually few or absent.

Tubular pattern The elongated tubules are lined by a single layer of ductal epithelial cells surrounded by a single or multiple layers of basaloid cells. This is the architectural pattern in which glandular lumens are most easily and consistently found. The glandular lumens are empty or contain secretion; rarely they may be dilated (Fig. 7.94). The tubules can be apparently coiled upon themselves, producing a necklace appearance. They are often embedded in abundant hyaline stroma, to the extent that they may appear strangulated.

Solid pattern The solid pattern is characterized by smooth-contoured or focally jagged sheets and islands of closely packed basaloid cells (Fig. 7.95). There are few or no interspersed pseudocysts. Nuclear palisading is absent in contrast to basal cell adenocarcinoma. The basaloid cells, in comparison to those seen in the cribriform and tubular patterns, usually exhibit more significant nuclear pleomorphism and mitotic activity. Coagulative tumor necrosis is not uncommon. There are usually few true glandular lumens (Fig. 7.88). The solid growth pattern is rarely present in a pure form, and if so, may be extremely difficult to recognize.[269]

Dedifferentiated adenoid cystic carcinoma

Dedifferentiation of adenoid cystic carcinoma is associated with bulky disease, frequent local recurrence and metastasis, and rapidly fatal outcome.[270,271] It can occur *ab initio* or in recurrent tumors. The dedifferentiated component is usually represented by poorly differentiated adenocarcinoma, sarcomatoid carcinoma or undifferentiated carcinoma (Fig. 7.96). *p53* gene mutation, Her2/neu overexpression, cyclin D1 overexpression, and loss of Rb expression have been variably demonstrated in the dedifferentiated component in contrast to the parent adenoid cystic carcinoma.[271,272]

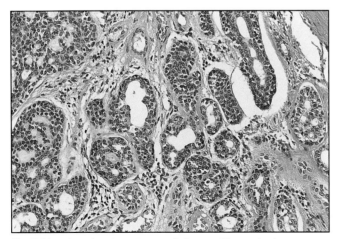

Fig. 7.94 • Adenoid cystic carcinoma, tubular type. Discrete simple or more complex tubules are disposed in a fibrous stroma. The tubules have an inner layer of cells with eosinophilic cytoplasm and an outer layer of basaloid cells. This field alone is indistinguishable from basal cell adenoma (tubular variant) or pleomorphic adenoma.

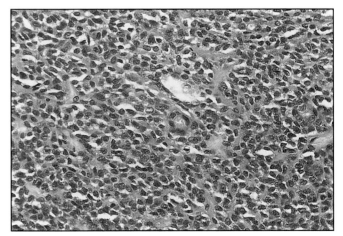

Fig. 7.95 • Adenoid cystic carcinoma, solid variant. The tumor is dominated by large solid islands of basaloid cells. Among the basaloid cells, only rare tubular structures are interspersed (center of field). Note that the basaloid cells in the solid variant exhibit a greater degree of nuclear atypia compared with conventional adenoid cystic carcinoma.

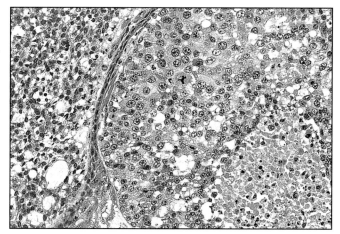

Fig. 7.96 • Dedifferentiated adenoid cystic carcinoma. The left field depicts the pre-existing adenoid cystic carcinoma, comprising basaloid cells with interspersed pseudocystic spaces. The right field shows the poorly differentiated (dedifferentiated) solid tumor composed of much larger, pleomorphic, and mitotically active cells, associated with coagulative necrosis.

Immunohistochemistry

Immunohistochemical staining confirms the predominant myoepithelial differentiation of the basaloid cells. These cells express cytokeratin, vimentin, S-100 protein (usually patchy staining), actin (variably), calponin, and p63,[273] whereas the interspersed ductal epithelial cells express cytokeratin (strongly), CEA, EMA, and c-kit (CD117) (Fig. 7.97). The stromal hyaline material can be highlighted by staining for type IV collagen and laminin. Although c-kit is expressed in ductal cells,[274,275] a clinical trial using a specific tyrosine kinase receptor inhibitor (Imatinib) has shown no beneficial effects,[276] which is not unexpected since these lesions lack activating mutations of the *c-kit* gene.

Genetic features

The most frequent cytogenetic aberrations involve chromosomes 6p, 9p, and 17p12-13, and t(6;9)(q21-24;p13-23), reported in several tumors, has been considered a primary event in at least a subset of adenoid cystic carcinomas.[274,277–280] Microsatellite marker analysis shows frequent losses at 6q23-qter, 12q, 13q21-q22, and 19q.[280] Promoter methylation of *p16* is found in 20% of cases.[281] A study of 25 tumors has found a high frequency of loss of heterozygosity at 6q23-25 and this alteration is correlated with unfavorable clinical outcome.[282,283]

Prognostic factors

The prognosis is significantly influenced by the histologic grade, which is determined by the proportion of the various growth patterns (Table 7.8).[269,284,285] Tumor showing tubular and cribriform patterns represent lower-grade growths.[269,284,285] The solid pattern is associated with large tumor size, earlier and more frequent recurrence, higher incidence of metastasis, and earlier fatal outcome.[263,265] Yamamoto et al. postulate that the solid area arises through transformation from the tubular or cribriform areas in association with mutations in the *p53* and *Rb* genes,[286] and the solid component is also more frequently associated with DNA aneuploidy.[287] On analysis of the long-term survival rates of 79 cases of adenoid cystic carcinoma, Szanto et al. found that carcinomas with significant solid areas (>30% of tumor area) have cumulative 5-year and 15-year survival rates of only 14% and 5% respectively, compared with 92% and 39% for tumors without a significant solid component.[285]

Advanced clinical stage, location in a minor gland, large tumor size (>2–4 cm), bone invasion, positive excision margins, non-diploid DNA content, high S-phase fraction, and high Ki67 index have been reported to be poor prognostic factors.[256,263,265,268,288,289]

Differential diagnosis

Adenoid cystic carcinoma can be difficult to distinguish from other salivary gland tumors with a prominent myoepithelial/basal cell component, such as basal cell adenoma/adenocarcinoma and pleomorphic adenoma, since they exhibit overlapping morphologic features (Fig. 7.7) (see section on "Analytic approach to diagnosis," p. 310) Distinction from

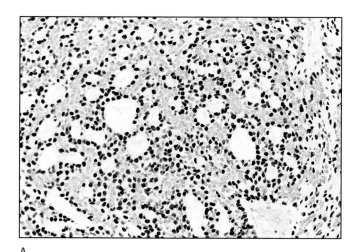

A

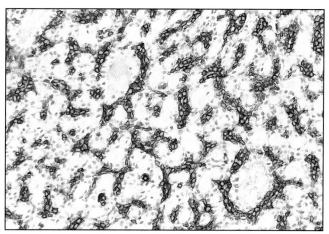

B

Fig. 7.97 • Adenoid cystic carcinoma, immunohistochemical features. **(A)** The nuclei of the abluminal cells are highlighted by immunostaining for p63 protein. The luminal cells are totally negative. **(B)** In contrast, the luminal cells are highlighted by immunostaining for c-kit (CD117).

Table 7.8 Adenoid cystic carcinoma: grading system (MD Anderson Cancer Center and Batsakis et al.[284])

	Grade I	Grade II	Grade III
Criteria for grading	Tubular and cribriform patterns, with no solid areas; cytologically bland; few or no mitoses	Pure cribriform pattern, or mixed pattern but with < 30% solid area; cytologically more atypical than grade I	>30% solid area; usually with necrosis; more cellular atypia, and mitoses
Behavior of tumor	Usually small-sized tumor that may even have a capsule; amenable to complete excision; protracted clinical course	Intermediate behavior	Larger tumor that is difficult to excise completely; frequent early recurrence; often resulting in death within 4 years
15-year survival rate	39%	26%	5%

epithelial-myoepithelial carcinoma and polymorphous low-grade adenocarcinoma is discussed under their corresponding sections. The claimed value of c-kit immunoreactivity for diagnosis of adenoid cystic carcinoma has not been substantiated by recent studies.[274,275]

Adenoid cystic carcinoma can be distinguished from basal cell adenoma and pleomorphic adenoma by invasion of the surrounding parenchyma or nerves, and usual prominence of cribriform structures. It lacks the "melting" myoepithelial pattern and chondroid matrix of pleomorphic adenoma; the occasional hyaline or myxoid change within the larger tumor islands of adenoid cystic carcinoma should not be mistaken for a "melting" phenomenon (Fig. 7.90). The solid type of adenoid cystic carcinoma poses special problems in differential diagnosis from basal cell adenocarcinoma, and basaloid squamous cell carcinoma (Table 7.9).

Acinic cell carcinoma

Definition

Acinic cell carcinoma, previously known as "acinic cell tumor," is a neoplasm demonstrating at least focal differentiation towards serous acinar cells. This neoplasm does not show myoepithelial participation.

Clinical features

The most frequent sites of occurrence are the parotid gland (84%) and submandibular gland (4%), followed by the buccal mucosa, upper lip, and palate.[65] It is the commonest malignant tumor that may present bilaterally (3%).[290] A slight female predominance is observed, and the mean age at presentation is 44 years. Acinic cell carcinoma has also been reported in

Table 7.9 Contrasting features of malignant tumors composed predominantly of basaloid cells: adenoid cystic carcinoma (solid type), basal cell adenocarcinoma, and basaloid squamous cell carcinoma

	Adenoid cystic carcinoma, solid variant	Basal cell adenocarcinoma	Basaloid squamous cell carcinoma
Site of occurrence	Major or minor glands	Major or minor glands	Mucosal sites, such as larynx, hypopharynx, base of tongue
Architectural patterns	Although islands and diffuse sheets predominate, some cribriform structures are almost always present; comedo necrosis may be present in some large solid islands	Discrete jigsaw puzzle-like islands; rarely may show trabecular or tubular pattern; cribriform structures absent or very focal; comedo necrosis rare	Lobules and trabeculae with festooning and frequent comedo necrosis
Intercellular hyaline droplets	Very rare	Common	Occasional
Basophilic mucosubstance in stroma or empty spaces	Common	Rare	Common
Cellular palisading at periphery of tumor islands	Usually not evident	Often a prominent feature	Usually not evident
Predominant cell type	Mostly basaloid cells with dark nuclei and a monotonous appearance; luminal cells very sparse	Basaloid cells include small dark cells and bigger paler cells; luminal cells very sparse	Basaloid cells with pale and atypical nuclei and frequent mitoses; true glandular cells rare
Squamous differentiation	Rare	Sometimes present in the centers of cell islands	Commonly present (often in the form of frank squamous cell carcinoma or carcinoma in situ)

antronasal mucosa,[291] larynx,[292] mandible,[156] breast,[293] lung,[294] and pancreas.[295]

Acinic cell carcinoma typically presents as a slow-growing mass with or without pain. Facial nerve palsy is uncommon (5–10%).[296,297] This indolent tumor pursues a protracted clinical course (Fig. 7.4).[297–299] In the Mayo Clinic series including 65 patients with long follow-up of up to 45 years, 44% of patients had local recurrence, 19% had metastasis, and 25% died of disease.[300] Local recurrence and metastasis are often delayed, sometimes to more than 30 years after the initial presentation. The overall survival probabilities are 90% at 5 years, 83% at 10 years, and 67% at 20 years. Therefore life-long follow-up is imperative, even after apparently complete excision.[300] Acinic cell carcinomas arising from the minor glands appear to be associated with a better prognosis.[65] The treatment of choice is complete surgical excision, supplemented by postoperative radiotherapy if the resection margin is involved.

Macroscopic appearances

Acinic cell carcinoma is often circumscribed with an incomplete capsule, but it can be multinodular or infiltrative. The cut surface is solid with or without cystic areas.

Microscopic appearances

Acinic cell carcinoma typically forms a solitary mass or multiple nodules, and invades in broad fronts. The tumor is compactly cellular with little sclerotic stroma except for occasional traversing fibrous bands (Fig. 7.98). Lymphoid aggregates, with or without lymphoid follicle formation, can be present. The tumor often reveals a mixture of growth patterns comprising a number of cell types that recapitulate the acinar-intercalated duct unit. In general, the nuclei are bland-looking, and mitotic figures are rare.

The tumor cells are most commonly arranged in organoid sheets traversed by ramifying delicate blood vessels, sheets punctuated by microcystic spaces, cords, intertwining solid or near-solid tubules, and coalescent acini (Figs 7.99 and 7.100). The lobular architecture of the normal salivary gland is lacking.

The microcystic pattern is the most characteristic growth pattern, although it is not invariably present. There are multiple small empty spaces, producing a lacy appearance (Fig. 7.100). Formation of these microcysts is thought to result from lack of ducts to conduct away secretions and break down products, causing accumulation of fluid between the cells. Occasionally the microcysts coalesce to form larger cystic cavities. The microcystic spaces differ from microglandular spaces in that the surrounding cells lack orientation around the spaces.

Similar to their benign counterparts, the neoplastic acinar cells possess basophilic granular cytoplasm and basally located nuclei. The cytoplasmic granules are PAS-positive and diastase-resistant, but negative for mucicarmine. In contrast to normal acinar cells, these cells are polygonal instead of triangular, there is a greater variability in size with nuclear hyperchromasia, and they frequently show a range of granularity, even in the same microscopic field, with some cells being so sparsely granulated that they are difficult to recognize

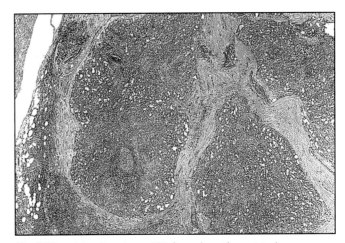

Fig. 7.98 • Acinic cell carcinoma. This figure shows the prototypic appearance of this tumor type: invasion in pushing fronts, scanty stroma except between tumor nodules, violaceous staining quality of the tumor cells, microcystic spaces, and interspersed lymphoid aggregates.

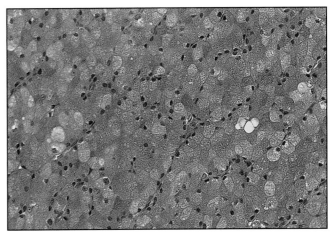

Fig. 7.99 • Acinic cell carcinoma. Solid growth of polygonal cells traversed by very delicate blood vessels. The tumor cells contain very fine basophilic granules, which impart a foamy quality to the cytoplasm. Note regimenting of the nuclei.

as such (Fig. 7.101). Some cells can exhibit a reticulated or foamy quality in the cytoplasm (Fig. 7.99). Not uncommonly, the nuclei are lined up in characteristic "regimented" rows (Fig. 7.99).[131] The finding of cytoplasmic vacuoles of variable sizes is highly characteristic of this tumor.

Some tumor cells resemble intercalated duct cells, being cuboidal cells, with central nuclei and pink cytoplasm. They often form small, closely packed glandular structures (Fig. 7.101). There are also non-specific glandular cells that are generally small, with eosinophilic to amphophilic cytoplasm, often forming sheets (Fig. 7.101). Uncommon cell types include vacuolated cells with a solitary or multiple clear vacuoles (Fig. 7.102)[128] and clear cells (cytoplasmic clearing probably due to tissue-processing artifact or alteration of organelles rather than glycogen accumulation) (Fig. 7.103).[301]

Acinic cell carcinomas possess a peculiar self-destructive quality. They are prone to ischemia and infarction either spontaneously or after fine-needle aspiration, resulting in secondary hemorrhage, lipogranulomatous reaction, and/or cystic degeneration.[47] It is not uncommon to find hemosiderin

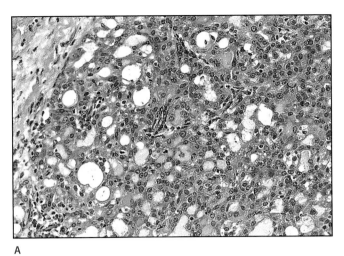

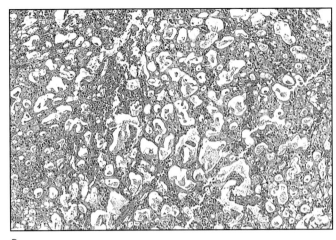

A   B

Fig. 7.100 • Acinic cell carcinoma, depicting the characteristic microcystic pattern. **(A)** The solid island of tumor is punctuated by irregular-shaped small cystic spaces. The cells that surround the spaces do not show specific orientation around the space; this feature distinguishes the microcystic pattern from a microglandular pattern. Note also the violaceous color of the cytoplasm, as commonly observed in acinic cells. **(B)** Larger microcystic spaces are seen in this example.

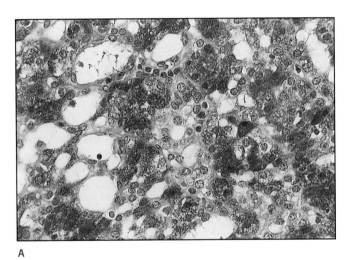

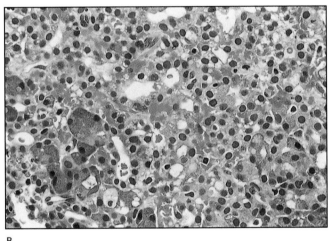

A   B

Fig. 7.101 • Acinic cell carcinoma. The tumor cells commonly exhibit a range of cytoplasmic granularity even in the same microscopic field. Cell types other than acinic cells are also commonly admixed. **(A)** Some cells are heavily granulated, while others are sparsely or not granulated. In the central field, there is apparent differentiation toward an intercalated duct with a small lumen. **(B)** Some tumor cells contain basophilic granules (left lower field). Most cells are polygonal, and many resemble intercalated duct cells. Note the bland appearances of the nuclei.

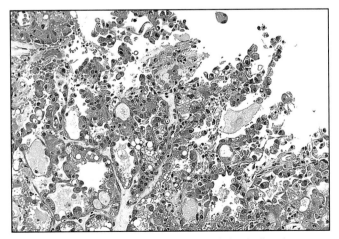

Fig. 7.102 • Acinic cell carcinoma. There are many hobnail cells and some vacuolated cells. Such cells are most commonly found in the papillary-cystic variant.

deposition in the fibrous stroma and even inside the tumor cells.

Papillary-cystic variant This rare variant is characterized by large cystic spaces lined by simple or stratified cuboidal epithelium with some papillary projections (Fig. 7.104). The papillae are covered by hobnailed cells, intercalated duct-like cells, vacuolated cells, non-specific glandular cells, and non-descript cells which possess eosinophilic to amphophilic cytoplasm, central nuclei, and indistinct cell borders (Fig. 7.102). Fibrovascular cores may or may not be found.

Follicular variant This rare variant comprises closely packed round cystic spaces filled with homogeneous eosinophilic colloid-like material, highly reminiscent of thyroid follicles (Fig. 7.105). The colloid-like material is strongly PAS-positive and diastase-resistant. The follicles are lined by intercalated duct-like cells and non-specific glandular cells. Immunostaining

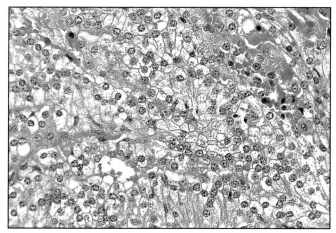

Fig. 7.103 • Acinic cell carcinoma with clear cells. Distinction from other clear cell neoplasms based on this field alone is very difficult; examination of other areas of the tumor will reveal more diagnostic patterns.

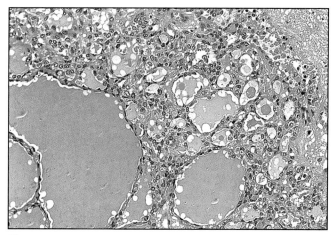

Fig. 7.105 • Acinic cell carcinoma, follicular variant. This rare variant is characterized by follicles containing eosinophilic colloid-like material. Resemblance to thyroid follicles is striking.

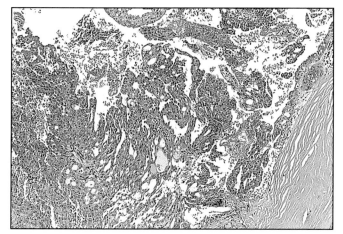

Fig. 7.104 • Acinic cell carcinoma, papillary-cystic variant. This variant is characterized by papillae and pseudopapillae projecting into a cystic cavity.

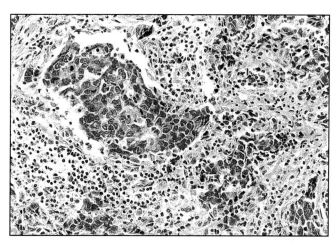

Fig. 7.106 • Dedifferentiated acinic cell carcinoma. This field shows a poorly differentiated carcinoma that is not recognizable as an acinic cell carcinoma. Other areas of the tumor show a typical acinic cell carcinoma (not shown).

for thyroglobulin is helpful for ruling out a thyroid follicular neoplasm.

Dedifferentiated acinic cell carcinoma Dedifferentiation of acinic cell carcinoma to a high-grade adenocarcinoma, poorly differentiated carcinoma, or undifferentiated carcinoma can rarely occur at presentation or in a recurrent tumor (Fig. 7.106). Usually the two components are juxtaposed to each other without transition. Dedifferentiated acinic cell carcinoma is associated with rapid tumor growth, significant pain, facial nerve palsy, bulky tumor, and an extremely poor prognosis.[296,302–304]

Immunohistochemistry and electron microscopy

Most tumor cells exhibit immunohistochemical evidence of differentiation towards acinar cells and ductal cells, such as positivity for cytokeratin (especially low-molecular-weight cytokeratin), CEA, and amylase. However, the value of amylase staining is limited because only 15% of cases are positive.[305] There is no immunohistochemical evidence of myoepithelial/basal cell differentiation.[48,125] Ultrastructural studies reveal zymogen granules in at least some tumor cells.

Prognostic factors

The most important prognostic indicators are clinical stage and resection margin status. Histologic grading has not been found to be a reliable predictor of prognosis, although frequent mitoses or high proliferative index (MIB1 index >5%), focal necrosis, neural invasion, gross invasion, desmoplasia, atypia, and depletion of stromal lymphocytes have been associated with more frequent recurrences and metastases.[65,265,297,299,300,306] One study suggests that tumors accompanied by a dense lymphoid stroma with well-developed germinal centers and showing a microcystic growth pattern throughout have a particularly favorable prognosis (no recurrence or metastasis on follow-up of 19 months to 14 years) (Fig. 7.107).[307]

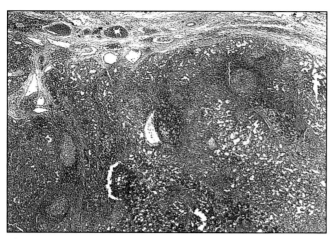

Fig. 7.107 • Acinic cell carcinoma, "favorable-prognosis" variant. This tumor is characterized by circumscription, prominent lymphoid component including many lymphoid follicles, and exclusive microcystic pattern throughout tumor.

Differential diagnosis

1. Oncocytoma
2. Adenoid cystic carcinoma
3. Adenocarcinoma NOS or cystadenocarcinoma
4. Normal salivary gland tissue, especially in biopsies
5. Metastatic thyroid carcinoma
6. Granular cell tumor

Polymorphous low-grade adenocarcinoma (PLGA)

Definition

PLGA is a malignant tumor characterized by infiltrative growth, morphologic diversity, and cytologic uniformity. Other designations include lobular carcinoma,[308] terminal duct carcinoma,[309] and low-grade papillary adenocarcinoma.

Clinical features

PLGA occurs almost exclusively in the minor salivary glands. Only rarely does it occur in the major glands, in that setting most often being the malignant component in carcinoma *ex* pleomorphic adenoma.[65,310–312] The commonest site of occurrence is the palate (60–70%), followed by buccal mucosa (16%), upper lip (12%), retromolar area, base of tongue,[65,313,314] and exceptionally, lacrimal gland.[315] PLGA has also been reported in the nasopharynx,[316] vulva and vagina,[317] maxilla (intraosseous),[318] and lung.[319] The peak age of presentation is in the fifth and sixth decades, but children can also be affected.[320] There is a female predominance. Clinically the tumor presents as an asymptomatic mass with or without ulceration.

PLGA is a low-grade neoplasm, with more than 95% of patients being alive after a mean follow-up of 10 years.[314] Local recurrence and regional metastasis rates are 9–17% and 9–15% respectively, which may occur up to 14 years after initial treatment (mean, 7 years).[314,321,322] Tumors with a predominant papillary configuration have been reported to carry a higher incidence of cervical lymph node metastasis.[322] Complete excision is the treatment of choice.

Macroscopic and microscopic appearances

Grossly, most tumors are circumscribed but non-encapsulated, with a light tan to grey glistening cut surface. Despite the gross circumscription, infiltrative growth is obvious histologically, with invasion of salivary gland lobules, adjacent adipose tissue, or muscle (Fig. 7.108). Perineural invasion is common (76%).[313]

The growth patterns are diverse, including simple tubules, complex or fused tubules, trabeculae, single-cell files, targetoid swirls, solid nests, fascicles, and cribriform, papillary, or papillary-cystic structures (Fig. 7.109). The three most commonly observed patterns are: (1) tubular; (2) trabecular; and (3) solid nests (Fig. 7.110).[313] The variability of growth pattern is the most consistent feature of the tumor.

Tubules are often disposed in lobules or streaming rows. Complex coalesced tubuloglandular structures are common (Fig. 7.110). The cribriform plates appear as islands of tumor cells interrupted by round, rarefied spaces that are empty or filled with mucoid material. A relatively diagnostic feature in PLGA is the targetoid pattern formed by concentrically arranged cords and narrow tubules of cells, reminiscent of sclerosing adenosis of the breast (Fig. 7.111). The papillary or

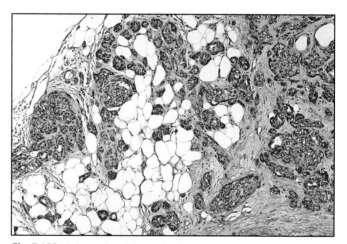

Fig. 7.108 • Polymorphous low-grade adenocarcinoma. The tumor typically shows invasion into the adjacent tissues.

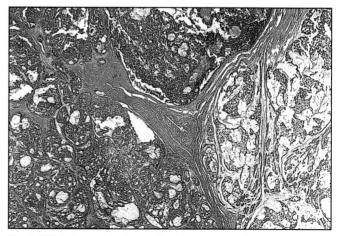

Fig. 7.109 • Polymorphous low-grade adenocarcinoma. There are highly variable growth patterns in different areas of the neoplasm.

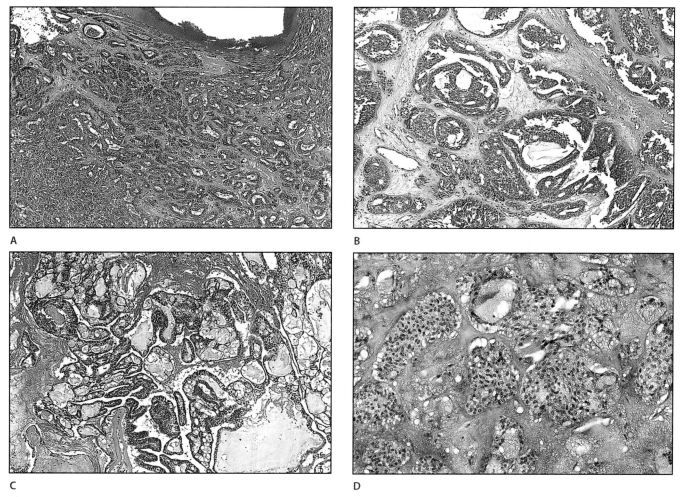

A

B

C

D

Fig. 7.110 • Polymorphous low-grade adenocarcinoma, depicting the multiplicity of growth pattern within the tumor. (A) Simple tubular and more complex glands merge into a solid area in the left lower field. (B) Complex tubulopapillary structures are present. (C) A predominantly papillary pattern is seen. (D) Tumor islands may merge into a mucinous stroma, mimicking pleomorphic adenoma.

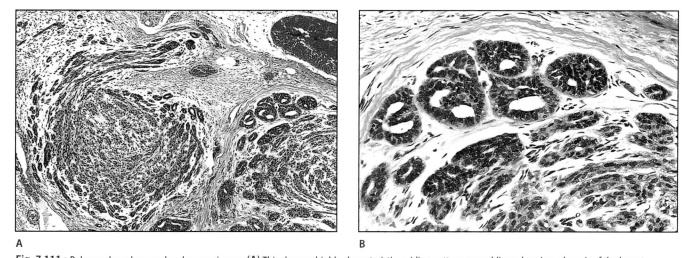

A

B

Fig. 7.111 • Polymorphous low-grade adenocarcinoma. (A) This shows a highly characteristic swirling pattern, resembling sclerosing adenosis of the breast. (B) Tubules with open lumens and strangulated tubules show a streaming growth pattern. The tubules are lined by a single cell type, and myoepithelial cells are not seen.

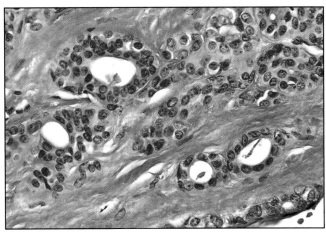

Fig. 7.112 • Polymorphous low-grade adenocarcinoma. The tubules are lined by ductal cells only. The nuclei are typically pale and bland-looking.

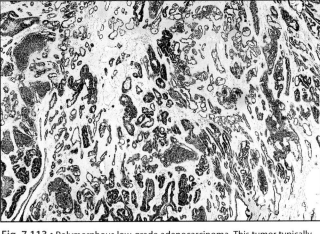

Fig. 7.113 • Polymorphous low-grade adenocarcinoma. This tumor typically shows diffuse and intense immunoreactivity for S-100 protein.

papillary-cystic pattern consists of dilated cysts with small intraluminal papillary projections (Fig. 7.110). The papillae are lined by a single layer of tumor cells.

There is generally one single cell type (ductal cell) that forms all these structures. The tumor cells have round pale nuclei with fine, evenly distributed chromatin and indistinct nucleoli (Fig. 7.112). There is a moderate amount of lightly eosinophilic cytoplasm. The tumor cells may assume cuboidal, columnar, spindly, or polygonal shapes, but the bland cytologic features are always maintained. Mucinous or clear cells are occasionally seen. Necrosis or mitosis is very rare. Although some authors consider myoepithelium to be an integral component of this tumor type,[269,323] myoepithelial cells are absent or at most present very focally at the light microscopic level.[324] The tumor cells are surrounded by a hyalinized eosinophilic stroma that occasionally displays myxoid change. A slate gray-blue stroma is said to be characteristic[325] (Fig. 7.110D). Psammoma bodies and collagenous or tyrosine-type crystalloids can be found in some cases.

Dedifferentiated PLGA can rarely occur many years after the initial diagnosis or at presentation. Such lesions often resemble salivary duct carcinoma,[326,327] with predominantly solid and cystic growth, high nuclear grade, and obvious tumor necrosis.

Immunohistochemistry and special studies

The tumor cells show immunoreactivity for cytokeratin, EMA, and S-100 protein (Fig. 7.113). Staining for GFAP is generally negative, except for occasional positive cells in some cases.[49,111,313,314,328–332] A proportion of the tumor cells can express p63 in a haphazard distribution;[48,88] and markers for myoepithelial differentiation (smooth muscle actin, smooth muscle myosin heavy chains, calponin) are negative.[125] Electron microscopy reveals that most tumor cells exhibit differentiation towards luminal cells, although there may be an inconsistent minor population of cells that exhibit abluminal cell or transitional features.[333]

Overexpression of bcl-2 protein has been demonstrated consistently in PLGA. In keeping with the low mitotic count observed under light microscope, the proliferative index of PLGA is low (mean Ki67 index 1.56–7%),[49,50,313] which can be

helpful for distinction from adenoid cystic carcinoma (mean Ki67 index >20%, range 11–57%).[50] The low mitotic count, coupled with overexpression of bcl-2, appears to suggest that faulty apoptosis may play a role in tumorigenesis.[49]

Differential diagnosis

Pleomorphic adenoma and adenoid cystic carcinoma are the most important differential diagnoses.

Pleomorphic adenoma can be distinguished from PLGA by the following features:

1. Non-infiltrative
2. Dual luminal and abluminal cell differentiation
3. Chondroid matrix, if present
4. Plasmacytoid hyaline cells, if present
5. "Melting" of myoepithelial layer into surrounding stroma
6. Positive staining for GFAP in a mesenchymal-like cell population adjacent to epithelial nests is a feature commonly observed in pleomorphic adenoma but not in PLGA[328]

Adenoid cystic carcinoma can be distinguished from PLGA by the following features:

1. The tumor cells show a high nuclear-to-cytoplasmic ratio and more hyperchromatic nuclei
2. Prominent abluminal cell component
3. Cribriform structures much more common
4. EMA staining is confined to the glandular lumina rather than diffuse; S-100 protein staining is often patchy and less intense; and proliferative index is higher[49,50,313]
5. p63 immunostaining highlights the peripherally located cells of the tumor islands in "regimented" pattern, in contrast to the haphazardly distributed positive cells in PLGA

Cribriform adenocarcinoma of the tongue

In the World Health Organization classification, cribriform adenocarcinoma of the tongue is considered a possible variant of PLGA due to their similar morphology, immunophenotype, and clinical behavior.[334,335] However, in contrast to the latter, this tumor occurs exclusively in the base of tongue and all patients have cervical lymph node metastasis at presentation. Histologically, the infiltrative tumor shows diverse growth patterns including solid, microcystic, follicular, cribriform, and papillary. The tumor cells are bland-looking and possess uniform, often overlapping, nuclei with vesicular or "ground-glass" chromatin reminiscent of papillary thyroid carcinoma. There is no significant mitotic activity, necrosis, or hemorrhage. The tumor cells express cytokeratin and variably S-100 protein. Myoepithelial markers are either negative or only focally positive.

Epithelial-myoepithelial carcinoma

Definition

Epithelial-myoepithelial carcinoma is a malignant tumor composed of ductal structures lined by a single layer of ductal cells which are surrounded by a single or multiple layers of clear myoepithelial cells. The counterpart in the breast is adenomyoepithelioma.[114,336,337]

Clinical features

The peak incidence is in the sixth and seventh decades, with a slight female predominance. Approximately 60% of cases occur within the parotid gland, while submandibular gland and intraoral minor salivary gland are responsible for the rest. Most patients present with an asymptomatic mass, and a minority of patients have pain and facial weakness. The tumor has also been reported to occur in lacrimal gland, lung, bronchus, trachea, nasal cavity, nasopharynx, and liver.[338–345]

Epithelial-myoepithelial carcinoma is a relatively low-grade malignancy. Recurrence is reported in 30–40% of cases, which may occur as long as 28 years after initial surgery.[346–350] Regional lymph node metastasis occurs in 10–20% of cases, but distant metastasis (lung, kidney, and brain) is uncommon (9%).[346] Tumor-associated mortality is low (0–9%).[346,347]

Fonseca & Soares reported that tumors with more than 20% of cells showing nuclear atypia are associated with a poorer prognosis.[351]

Macroscopic and microscopic appearances

Grossly, the tumor is typically multinodular and circumscribed. The cut surface is tan-colored and firm. Histologically, the tumor invades the surrounding parenchyma in broad fronts, resulting in multiple tumor nodules separated by sclerotic stroma (Fig. 7.114). Perineural and vascular invasion are sometimes seen. Within the tumor nodules, the stroma can be scanty, loose, myxoid, hyalinized, or fibrous.

The prototypic bicellular architecture consists of a tubular structure lined by ductal cells, surrounded by one or several layers of clear cells, which are further enveloped on the outside by a well-defined basement membrane (Fig. 7.115). The tubular luminal cells are cuboidal, with round, bland-looking nuclei and a moderate amount of pink cytoplasm, reminiscent of intercalated duct cells. Rarely, there can be squamous differentiation. The clear cells are polygonal, considerably larger in size, and have abundant water-clear cytoplasm. The cytoplasmic clearing is due to accumulation of glycogen. These cells exhibit a myoepithelial immunophenotype and ultrastructural features.

In some tumors, discrete tubules give way to coalesced tubules, complex glandular structures, papillary-cystic structures, trabeculae, and large sheets of clear cells delineated by thick basement membrane (Figs 7.114B and 7.115B). In clear cell-predominant areas, the small ductal cells can be difficult to find, hence distinction from clear cell carcinoma can be problematic (Fig. 7.115C).[65,346] Rarely, fascicles of spindly clear (myoepithelial) cells can be formed.

In most cases, cytologic atypia is mild, and the mitotic count is low (Fig. 7.115). However, rare cases may show transition to areas with a greater degree of nuclear atypia, more solid growth, and frequent mitoses, suggesting that the tumor can evolve to a higher-grade epithelial-myoepithelial carcinoma. This phenomenon is apparently associated with

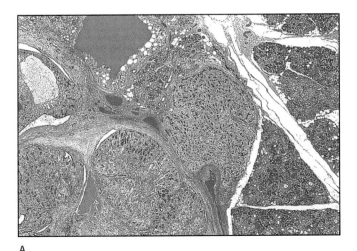

A

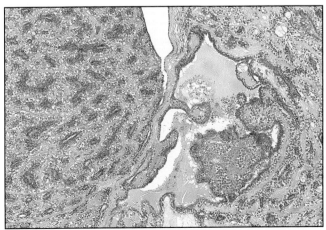

B

Fig. 7.114 • Epithelial-myoepithelial carcinoma. **(A)** The tumor characteristically invades in broad fronts (normal salivary gland tissue seen in right field). A fibrotic stroma is seen between the tumor nodules. **(B)** Some glandular structures have dilated lumens or are thrown into papillary folds (right field). This feature is practically never seen in adenoid cystic carcinoma.

more aggressive behavior.[65,342,349,350] Rare cases of dedifferentiation to poorly differentiated carcinoma no longer recognizable as epithelial-myoepithelial carcinoma have also been reported.[352–354]

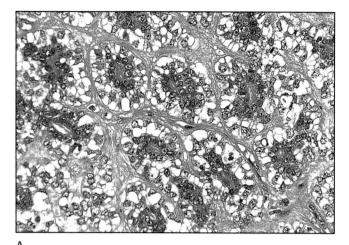

A

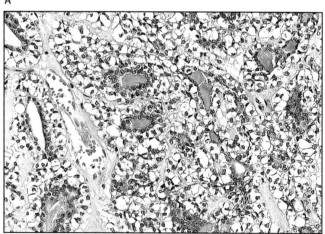

B

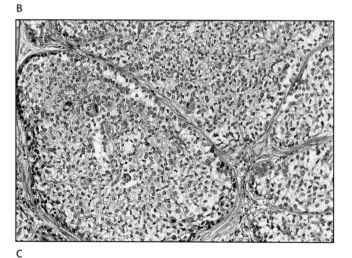

C

Fig. 7.115 • Epithelial-myoepithelial carcinoma. **(A)** The basic neoplastic unit comprises discrete tubules lined by an inner layer of ductal cells with eosinophilic cytoplasm, and an outer layer of large clear myoepithelial cells. The tubules are separated by hyalinized stroma. **(B)** The tubules can be surrounded by thicker mantles of clear cells, which coalesce to form larger cellular islands. **(C)** A more extreme degree of coalescence results in the formation of large islands composed mainly of clear cells. There are few interspersed tubular structures lined by cells with eosinophilic cytoplasm.

Immunohistochemistry and special studies

The ductal cells are strongly positive for pan-cytokeratin and variably positive for S-100 protein, but are negative for myoepithelial markers. The clear cells are positive for pan-cytokeratin (often weakly), high-molecular-weight cytokeratin, p63, S-100 protein, calponin, and actin (Fig. 7.116). The proliferation (Ki67) index is low: <1% for ductal cells, and <3% for myoepithelial clear cells.[349,352] Ploidy analysis shows that most tumors (>80%) are diploid.[349]

Major differential diagnosis

This tumor has to be distinguished from other clear cell tumors, especially for cases showing coalescent islands and sheets of clear cells (Table 7.5). Careful scrutiny and extensive sampling may be required to detect the diagnostic bicellular architecture. The clear cells in epithelial-myoepithelial carcinoma exhibit myoepithelial differentiation, whereas those of clear cell carcinoma do not.

Both epithelial-myoepithelial carcinoma and adenoid cystic carcinoma are infiltrative neoplasms with dual ductal–myoepithelial differentiation. The following features favor the former diagnosis over the latter:

1. The abluminal cells are much larger, with clear cytoplasm and pale nuclei (clear cells, if present in adenoid cystic carcinoma, are very focal)
2. Rarity of cribriform structures (Fig. 7.117)
3. Rarity of lightly basophilic mucosubstance in microcystic spaces
4. Irregular branching glandular lumens, if present
5. Lower proliferative (Ki67) index

Salivary duct carcinoma

Definition

Salivary duct carcinoma is an aggressive malignant tumor morphologically reminiscent of ductal carcinoma of the breast. It can occur *de novo* or as the malignant component in carcinoma *ex* pleomorphic adenoma.[346,355–359]

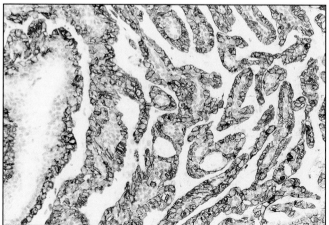

Fig. 7.116 • Epithelial-myoepithelial carcinoma. The clear myoepithelial cells are immunoreactive for actin.

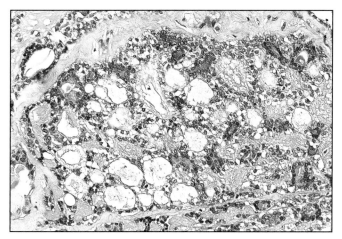

Fig. 7.117 • Epithelial-myoepithelial carcinoma. Rarely, coalescence of the tubules results in the formation of cribriform structures, mimicking adenoid cystic carcinoma.

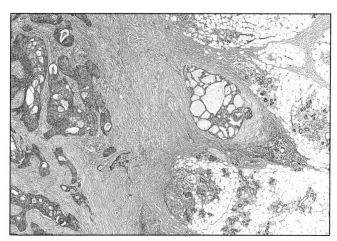

Fig. 7.118 • Salivary duct carcinoma. The tumor (left field) infiltrates the parotid parenchyma (right field), and is accompanied by a desmoplastic stroma. This tumor exhibits a cribriform growth pattern.

Clinical features

Salivary duct carcinoma most frequently affects the elderly (peak incidence in the sixth and seventh decades), with a male to female ratio of 3–6:1. The parotid gland accounts for 80% of cases, and the rest arise in the submandibular gland, and rarely, minor glands of the oral cavity. The patients commonly present with a rapidly enlarging parotid mass associated with facial nerve palsy (42%), pain (23%), and cervical lymphadenopathy (35%).[356]

This is one of the most aggressive salivary gland carcinomas. The tumor mortality can be as high as 77% at a mean follow-up of 3 years.[356] Local recurrence occurs in 35–66% of patients, lymph node metastasis in 66%, and distant metastasis in 50–70%.[346,356,360] The most frequent sites of distant metastases are the lung, bone, and brain. The recommended treatment includes complete surgical excision, neck dissection, and postoperative radiotherapy.

Pathologic features

The tumor is poorly circumscribed, predominantly solid, and tan-colored. There are often foci of necrosis. Gross extension of tumor beyond the salivary gland is noted in about 70% of cases.[356] Histologically, the infiltrative tumor resembles mammary intraductal carcinoma and invasive ductal carcinoma (Fig. 7.118). The intraductal-like component shows cribriform, papillary-cystic, or solid patterns, often with prominent comedo necrosis (Fig. 7.119). However, most of them are not genuine intraductal proliferations since a myoepithelial layer is lacking and similar structures can be seen in metastatic deposits. The obviously infiltrative component consists of cords, nests, small glands, and single cells (Fig. 7.120). The neoplastic cells in both components have a similar morphology characterized by an apocrine appearance with abundant eosinophilic cytoplasm, large pleomorphic vesicular nuclei, and prominent nucleoli (Fig. 7.121). Cytoplasmic mucin is occasionally present. Mitotic figures are easy to find. The stroma is densely fibrous or desmoplastic. Vascular invasion, perineural invasion, intravascular tumor emboli, and invasion of adjacent structures are common.[357]

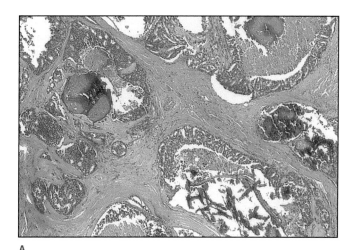

A

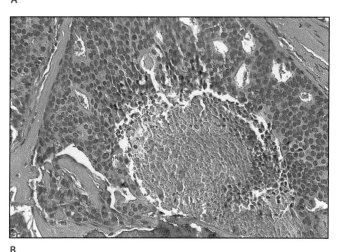

B

Fig. 7.119 • Salivary duct carcinoma. **(A)** Although this is an infiltrative tumor, the large cribriform tumor units with comedo necrosis paradoxically resemble intraductal carcinoma of the breast. **(B)** The cribriform structures comprise moderately pleomorphic cells, and central comedo necrosis is evident.

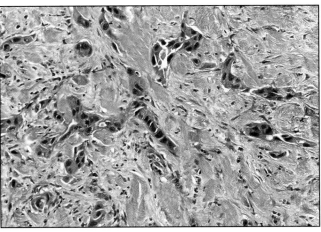

Fig. 7.120 • Salivary duct carcinoma. In areas, the tumor cells infiltrate the fibrous stroma in the form of cords, resembling ordinary infiltrative ductal carcinoma of breast.

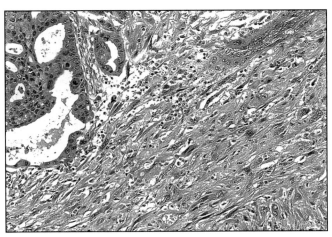

Fig. 7.122 • Salivary duct carcinoma, sarcomatoid (dedifferentiated) variant. The conventional salivary duct carcinoma component is seen in the left upper field. The sarcomatous component is formed by spindly and stellate cells with pleomorphic nuclei.

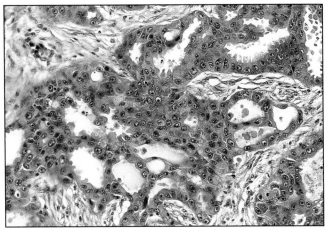

Fig. 7.121 • Salivary duct carcinoma. This example shows a cribriform growth pattern. The constituent cells have an apocrine-like quality and nuclear pleomorphism is significant.

Several histologic variants of salivary duct carcinoma have been described.[361–363] Essentially, they comprise a typical salivary duct carcinoma component and another histologically distinct component. A transitional zone between the two components can often be recognized.

Sarcomatoid variant (dedifferentiated salivary duct carcinoma) The sarcomatoid component comprises anaplastic spindle cells, bizarre multinucleated giant cells, rhabdoid cells, and, rarely, osteosarcomatous cells (Fig. 7.122).[361,364] These cells frequently demonstrate focal immunohistochemical and ultrastructure evidence of epithelial differentiation.[365,366] We consider this variant a form of dedifferentiation of the salivary duct carcinoma.

Mucin-rich variant This variant features areas of mucinous/colloid carcinoma in which clusters of carcinoma cells with or without cytoplasmic mucin float in mucin pools.

Invasive micropapillary variant This subtype is characterized by morule-like tumor cell clusters without fibrovascular cores, surrounded by clear spaces, and is morphologically similar to the micropapillary variant of breast or urothelial carcinoma.

Prognostic factors

Previous studies suggest that tumor size smaller than 3 cm is associated with a more favorable prognosis,[367,368] but this is not confirmed by the Mayo Clinic series.[356] It appears that none of the histologic parameters are of prognostic significance,[356,357,369] although the micropapillary variant may be more aggressive.[363]

Immunohistochemistry

Immunohistochemical and ultrastructural studies confirm the luminal epithelial nature of the tumor cells, with diffuse strong staining for cytokeratin, EMA, and CEA. Almost all cases express androgen receptor, which is a characteristic, although not specific, feature of this salivary gland carcinoma.[370,371] Estrogen and progesterone receptors are usually negative.[372] Most cases overexpress c-erbB2. Tumor cells are usually focally positive for gross cystic disease fluid protein-15 (GCDFP-15 or BRST-2)[373] and typically negative for S-100 protein and myoepithelial markers. Some cases can express prostatic acid phosphatase, prostatic-specific antigen, or CK20.[229,374] Ki67 index is high (mean 21.3%).[375] A single case of salivary duct carcinoma with neuroendocrine differentiation has been described.[376] Staining for myoepithelial markers shows that a genuine in-situ (intraductal) component characterized by a surrounding rim of attenuated myoepithelium is usually minor.

Genetic features

Frequent loss of heterozygosity has been detected in regions of chromosomes 9p21, 6q, 16q, 17p, 17q.[377,378] Mutations and overexpression of the *TP53* gene and protein are frequent.[25,377,379] *HER-2/neu* gene amplification occurs in 36% and protein overexpression in 50–100%[359,380] this has been reported to correlate with more aggressive behaviour.[359] Gene expression profiling shows overexpression of the apoptosis-related genes *CASP10* and *MMP11*.[23] Inactivation of the *CDKN2A/p16* gene is associated with tumor progression.[378]

Major differential diagnosis

In addition to metastatic breast or prostate carcinoma, the major differential diagnoses include high-grade mucoepidermoid carcinoma, oncocytic carcinoma, cystadenocarcinoma, and intraductal carcinoma.

A clinical history of breast carcinoma, positive estrogen/ progesterone receptor, and negative androgen receptor strongly favors a diagnosis of metastatic mammary carcinoma. Immunostaining for GCDFP-15 (BRST-2) is not useful because most salivary duct carcinomas are also positive.[356,373,381]

High-grade mucoepidermoid carcinoma can resemble salivary duct carcinoma, especially in a frozen-section setting. However, the mixture of cell types such as epidermoid cells and goblet cells is not seen in salivary duct carcinoma.

Oncocytic carcinoma is characterized by large tumor cells with granular eosinophilic cytoplasm filled with mitochondria. Both oncocytic carcinoma and cystadenocarcinoma lack the comedo necrosis and intraductal-like pattern typically seen in salivary duct carcinoma.

The rare intraductal carcinoma must not be mistaken for salivary duct carcinoma because of the much better prognosis (see below).

Intraductal carcinoma (so-called low-grade salivary duct carcinoma or low-grade cribriform cystadenocarcinoma)

The concept of intraductal carcinoma of salivary gland and problems in terminology

Intraductal carcinoma, first described by Chen in 1983, is not a recognized entity in the 2005 World Health Organization classification. It is characterized by pure intraductal proliferation of tumor cells, and probably represents the in-situ counterpart of salivary duct carcinoma. The concept of intraductal carcinoma has not gained wide acceptance because some salivary duct carcinomas with an apparently pure intraductal-like growth still pursue an aggressive course, and an intraductal-like component can sometimes be found in the metastases. These observations can be attributable to the indiscriminate use of the term "intraductal" which, by definition, should require the presence of an intact myoepithelial layer, as in mammary intraductal carcinoma. Strictly defined as such, intraductal carcinoma represents a tumor of low malignant potential, with behavior similar to the mammary counterpart.[382]

Intraductal carcinoma has often been reported in the literature under the designation "low-grade salivary duct carcinoma."[383,384] However, the term "intraductal carcinoma" is more appropriate because it emphasizes the fundamental feature and avoids potential confusion with the vastly more aggressive salivary duct carcinoma. The term "low-grade cribriform cystadenocarcinoma" adopted in the new World Health Organization classification is even more confusing.[181]

Clinical features

Similar to salivary duct carcinoma, this tumor most frequently affects the parotid gland of the elderly (mean age 62 years), with a slight female predilection. Minor salivary gland (e.g., tongue, palate, oral cavity) can also be affected.[382] The outcome has been excellent after complete excision, with no metastasis or mortality at follow-up of 2–12 years, irrespective of nuclear grade. Recurrence can occur as a result of incomplete resection.

Pathologic features

The tumor is characterized by multiple smooth-contoured ducts with epithelial cell proliferation forming cribriform, fenestrated, solid-comedo, micropapillary, or Roman-bridge patterns, similar to the architectural patterns observed in atypical ductal hyperplasia or intraductal carcinoma of the breast (Figs 7.123 and 7.124A). The constituent cells generally show low- to intermediate-grade, but sometimes high-grade, cytologic atypia (Fig. 7.124A). Some cells can appear apocrine. The attenuated layer of myoepithelial cells around the cell islands may or may not be evident on light microscopy. The stroma is sclerotic and may exhibit secondary changes such as hemorrhage, a chronic inflammatory infiltrate, and dystrophic calcification.

In occasional cases, there is a microscopic invasive component morphologically identical to salivary duct carcinoma, either at presentation or in a recurrence.[383,385] The clinical significance of microinvasion remains uncertain, but the prognosis appears favorable.

Prerequisites of diagnosis

A diagnosis of intraductal carcinoma can only be confidently made when an invasive component has been ruled out after complete sampling. It is also imperative to perform immunostaining to demonstrate an intact myoepithelial layer around each tumor island (Fig. 7.124B), because it is notoriously difficult to differentiate between in-situ and invasive ductal carcinoma. This precaution in diagnosis is essential because

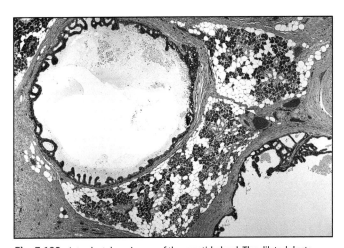

Fig. 7.123 • Intraductal carcinoma of the parotid gland. The dilated ducts show a micropapillary and Roman-bridge pattern of cellular proliferation, similar to mammary intraductal carcinoma.

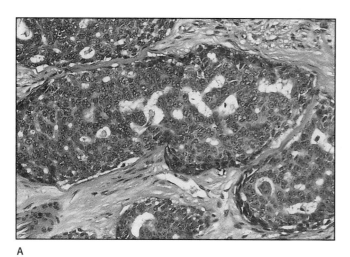
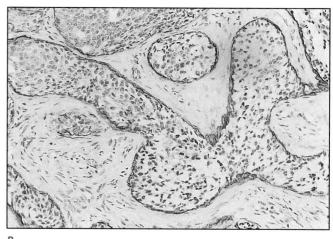

A

B

Fig. 7.124 • Intraductal carcinoma of the oral mucosa. **(A)** The discrete islands of proliferated cells are reminiscent of atypical ductal hyperplasia or intraductal carcinoma of the breast. In this example, cellular atypia is not striking. **(B)** Immunostaining for muscle-specific actin shows intact myoepithelial cells around the cell islands, confirming the in-situ nature of the tumor process.

the alternative interpretation is salivary duct carcinoma, which is a highly aggressive neoplasm.

Clear cell carcinoma, not otherwise specified

Definition

Clear cell carcinoma, NOS, also known as clear cell adeno-carcinoma, is composed of monomorphic epithelial cells with water-clear cytoplasm without evidence of myoepithelial differentiation. It is a diagnosis of exclusion, in that features characteristic of other neoplasms, most notably epithelial-myoepithelial carcinoma, clear cell oncocytoma, muco-epidermoid carcinoma, acinic cell carcinoma, clear-cell myoepithelial tumor, sebaceous carcinoma, and metastatic renal-cell carcinoma, should be absent.[128]

Clinical features

Clear cell carcinoma most frequently occurs in the fifth to seventh decades with no gender predilection. Most reported cases arise from the minor salivary glands of the oral cavity as a painless slow-growing mass, and some may ulcerate or cause fixation to adjacent tissues. It is a low-grade, locally invasive tumor, with a tendency for locoregional recurrence.[386] Cervical lymph node metastasis occurs only rarely, and mortality due to this tumor is exceptional.[65] Wide excision is the treatment of choice; the role of adjuvant radiotherapy remains to be elucidated.

Pathology

The tumor is poorly circumscribed and shows whitish-tan cut surfaces. It is composed of sheets, streaming columns, nests, and cords of large, monomorphic clear cells that show mild variation in size (Fig. 7.115). The cells possess discrete cell membranes and abundant clear cytoplasm due to accumu-lation of glycogen (PAS-positive and diastase-sensitive,

mucicarmine-negative). The nuclei are centrally or eccentrically located, and have finely granular chromatin and inconspicuous nucleoli. Nuclear atypia ranges from mild to moderate. A subpopulation of tumor cells can have eosinophilic cytoplasm (Fig. 7.116). Mitotic figures are rare. There is no duct for-mation. A variable amount of fibrous stroma can be present. See Table 7.5 for differential diagnosis.

Immunohistochemistry and special studies

These tumors are focally to diffusely immunoreactive for cytokeratin. In contrast to metastatic renal-cell carcinoma, the tumor expresses high-molecular-weight cytokeratin and CEA.[387] Myoepithelial markers should be negative. Ultrastructural and immunohistochemical studies have demonstrated only ductal but not myoepithelial differentiation.[65,386]

Variant: hyalinizing clear cell carcinoma

Hyalinizing clear cell carcinoma is a subgroup of clear cell carcinoma described by Milchgrub et al.[388] Most cases originate from minor salivary glands, but major glands can also be affected. The oral cavity, particularly the base of tongue and palate, is the most common site.[388–391] Rare cases have been reported in the larynx, nasopharynx, hypopharynx, mandible, and maxilla.[388,392–394] The tumor usually presents as a slowly growing and painless submucosal mass. The clinical course is indolent. Nonetheless, multiple recurrences over many years can occur in some cases, and cervical lymph node and lung metastasis can rarely occur.[388,392,394] A case reported to show widespread metastasis and death within 1 year showed foci of mitotic activity, necrosis, and anaplasia, and thus can be considered a dedifferentiated hyalinizing clear cell carcinoma.[395] Wide local excision with or without radiotherapy is the treat-ment of choice.

Histologically, the infiltrative tumor comprises uniform clear cells and cells with eosinophilic cytoplasm as described above (Fig. 7.125), forming solid nests, trabeculae, cords, and streaming columns of one to two cell widths.[388,392,396] The stroma is characterized by abundant, thick parallel strands

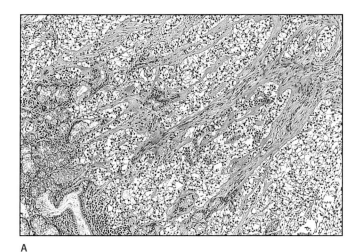 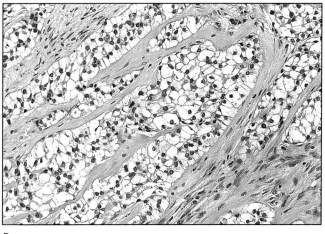

A   B

Fig. 7.125 • Hyalinizing clear cell carcinoma of the palate. **(A)** The tumor is infiltrative, and residual salivary lobules are seen in the left lower field. Note the prominence of clear cells and hyaline material. **(B)** Broad trabeculae of polygonal clear cells are separated by homogeneous eosinophilic hyaline material and cellular desmoplastic stroma.

of fibrous tissue associated with hyalinized and myxoid substance, admixed with cellular fibrous (desmoplastic) tissue. The hyalinized stroma resembles amyloid, but is PAS-positive and congo red-negative.

Immunohistochemical staining reveals diffuse positivity of tumor cells for cytokeratin and EMA and focal positivity for CEA. Myoepithelial markers (S-100 protein, calponin, and smooth muscle actin) are consistently negative. Electron microscopy reveals tonofilaments, well-formed desmosomes, and hemidesmosomes, confirming the pure epithelial nature of the tumor.

Undifferentiated carcinoma

Undifferentiated carcinomas of the salivary glands are uncommon high-grade malignant tumors that are too poorly differentiated by their light microscopic features to be placed in any specific category of carcinoma. Focal isolated gland formation or squamous differentiation does not preclude this diagnosis, nor will ultrastructural evidence of these features. Generally, these tumors are classified into *small cell* and *large-cell* types. Lymphoepithelial carcinoma is a specific subtype of undifferentiated carcinoma with a relatively favorable prognosis.

Small cell carcinoma

Definition Small cell carcinoma is a malignant tumor characterized by small epithelial cells (<30 μm) with scant cytoplasm, fine chromatin, and inconspicuous nucleoli. Based on ultrastructural and immunohistochemical features,[397–399] it can be categorized into:

1. neuroendocrine type
   (a) Merkel cell subtype
   (b) pulmonary subtype
2. ductal type

Clinical features Small cell carcinoma most frequently occurs in the parotid gland and, less commonly, submandibular and sublingual glands. Patients range in age from the fifth to seventh decades (mean 54–56 years), with male predilection. The tumor manifests as a fast-growing mass with or without concomitant cervical lymphadenopathy. Facial nerve palsy is noted in 60% of patients.[14] Pain is only occasionally present.

This is an aggressive malignancy. Local recurrence and distant metastasis have been reported in more than 50% of patients at 2–26 months after diagnosis.[400] The overall survival rate is 40–50%.[397,401–403] This figure is comparable to that of Merkel cell carcinoma of the skin, and much superior to that of small cell carcinoma of the lung or other extrapulmonary sites. A better prognosis has been found to be associated with the Merkel cell subtype, small tumor size (<3–4 cm), and expression of more neuroendocrine markers.[400,404]

Pathologic features Grossly, the tumor is a widely infiltrative mass with firm consistency and white to yellow color. Histologically, the tumor grows in a diffuse or cord-like pattern (Fig. 7.126). The tumor cells are slightly larger than lymphocytes, with finely stippled chromatin and inconspicuous

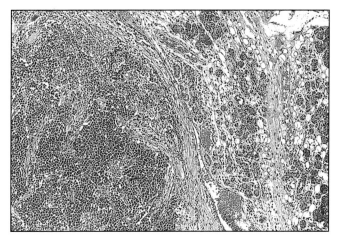

Fig. 7.126 • Small cell carcinoma, Merkel cell type, of the parotid gland. The tumor manifests as an extensive, diffuse, destructive growth in the salivary gland.

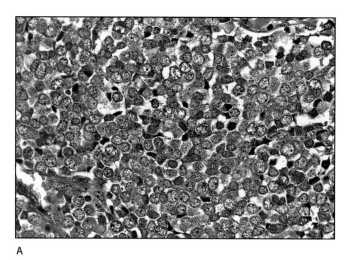

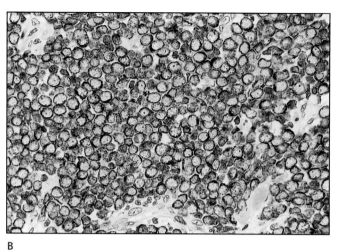

A

B

Fig. 7.127 • Small cell carcinoma, Merkel cell type, of the parotid gland. **(A)** The tumor cells grow in sheets. As characteristic of Merkel cell carcinoma, the nuclei resemble blown-up balloons and have pale "washed-out" chromatin. Nuclear molding is minimal. **(B)** Immunoreactivity for cytokeratin 20 is characteristic.

nucleoli. The nuclei are susceptible to crushing artifact, resulting in deformation and clumping of nuclei as well as diffusion of chromatin material. Necrosis is commonly seen. Vascular and perineural invasion are common. The tumor is often traversed by delicate fibrovascular septa.

In the Merkel cell subtype, the nuclei tend to be round, non-molded, resembling blown-up balloons, with pale and "washed-out" chromatin (Fig. 7.127). In the pulmonary subtype, tumor cells are often short and spindly with nuclear molding; there can be pseudorosette formation (Fig. 7.128).[402] However, the morphologic features of these two subtypes overlap and the distinction may not be made with certainty on histologic examination alone. According to a recent large series,[404] 73% of small cell carcinomas of the salivary gland express CK20 (Merkel cell subtype; Fig. 7.127B); these cases demonstrate a longer overall survival than the CK20-negative group (pulmonary subtype). Both subtypes express neuroendocrine markers such as chromogranin, synaptophysin, and CD56. The Merkel cell subtype also expresses neurofilament, but not thyroid transcription factor-1.[404,405]

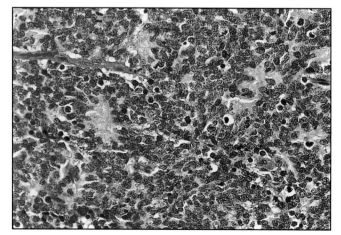

Fig. 7.128 • Small cell carcinoma, pulmonary type, of the parotid gland. In contrast to the Merkel cell type, the nuclei are often more elongated, chromatin-rich, and molded. In this example, pseudorosettes formed by fibrillary cytoplasm are also present.

Isolated ductal differentiation and squamous differentiation with keratinization have been described in rare cases, and these tumors are termed ductal-type small cell carcinoma.[397,406,407]

Differential diagnosis The differential diagnoses include lymphoma, solid-type adenoid cystic carcinoma and metastatic cutaneous Merkel cell carcinoma. It can be difficult to distinguish between small cell carcinoma and malignant lymphoma on histologic grounds. Lymphoma cells grow in a more permeative manner, usually with persistence of residual glandular structures even in areas of extensive involvement. This is in contrast to the extensive destruction and frequently total replacement of glandular structures in small cell carcinoma. Lymphoma cells often possess more irregularly folded nuclei and denser chromatin, and they do not form anastomosing cords or nests. Definitive distinction between the two tumors can easily be achieved by immunostaining (such as leukocyte common antigen and cytokeratin).

Solid-type adenoid cystic carcinoma, with large islands and sheets of isomorphic basaloid cells, may be confused with small cell carcinoma, but cribriform structures can often be found after careful search. Some tumor cells are positive for S-100 protein, actin, and calponin, and focal ductal structures show immunoreactivity for CEA and EMA. Small cell carcinoma is negative for these markers, except EMA.

Metastatic small cell or Merkel cell carcinoma must be excluded before a firm diagnosis of primary salivary gland small cell carcinoma is made. Clinical history, examination, and clinical work-up are essential for this distinction.

Large-cell carcinoma

Definition Large-cell carcinoma is a high-grade malignant tumor comprising large pleomorphic cells with abundant cytoplasm and lacking features of other specific tumor types.

Clinical features Large-cell carcinoma is a rare tumor mainly occurring in the parotid and submandibular glands. The peak incidence is from the seventh to eighth decades, and there is no gender preference. There is no racial predilection or association with EBV.[408]

The patients most commonly present with a rapidly growing firm mass with fixation to adjacent tissues. Cervical lymphadenopathy at presentation is common, i.e., most patients present at an advanced stage (75% stage IV).[408] It is a highly aggressive neoplasm, with 2-year survival of only 36%. Poor prognostic factors include age greater than 50 years, tumor larger than 4 cm and cervical node metastasis.[400,408,409]

Pathologic features Grossly, large-cell carcinomas produce solid, tan-colored infiltrative masses. Morphologically they are similar to anaplastic carcinoma of the lung, thyroid, or pancreas. They consist of sheets and irregular islands of large pleomorphic cells with well-defined cell borders, copious amphophilic to eosinophilic cytoplasm, and large nuclei containing prominent nucleoli (Fig. 7.129). Occasionally multinucleated tumor giant cells are present. Mitoses, tumor necrosis, and lymphatic and vascular invasion are common. The stroma is desmoplastic, and infiltrated by variable numbers of lymphocytes and plasma cells. There can also be interspersed reactive osteoclastic giant cells. Ultrastructural examination may reveal glandular, squamous, or neuroendocrine features which are not evident under the light microscope.

Large-cell neuroendocrine carcinoma

A small subset of large-cell carcinoma demonstrates neuroendocrine features, including rosette-like structures and organoid growth with peripheral palisading. The tumor cells express neuroendocrine markers such as chromogranin and synaptophysin, but not CK20. Pan-cytokeratin and EMA are also expressed. Dense core granules are found on electron microscopy.[400,410,411] Large-cell neuroendocrine carcinoma does not differ from conventional large-cell carcinoma in terms of clinical behavior.

Differential diagnosis Large-cell carcinoma should be distinguished from lymphoepithelial carcinoma, metastatic carcinoma, anaplastic large-cell lymphoma, and malignant melanoma. In addition, metastatic tumor and a dedifferentiated salivary gland tumor have to be considered.

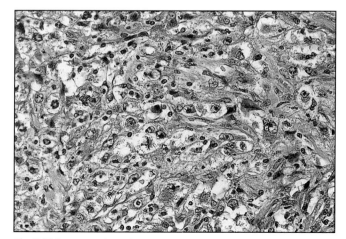

Fig. 7.129 • Large-cell undifferentiated carcinoma. Sheets of large polygonal cells with highly pleomorphic nuclei characterize this tumor cells. There is often a sprinkling of inflammatory cells.

Lymphoepithelial carcinoma

Lymphoepithelial carcinoma, previously known as malignant lymphoepithelial lesion or lymphoepithelioma-like carcinoma, is a rare carcinoma with a much higher prevalence among Eskimos and southern Chinese than Caucasians.[412,413] The tumor is almost invariably associated with EBV in Eskimos, Chinese, and Japanese.[152,414–419] In contrast, EBV is often but not invariably absent in Caucasians.[415,420–422]

Clinical features Usually adults with a mean age of 44.5 years are affected, with no definite or slight female predominance.[408] This tumor most frequently arises from the parotid and submandibular glands as an asymptomatic swelling with or without pain;[413] minor salivary glands can also be affected.[423] There is no association with Sjögren syndrome. Facial nerve palsy is uncommon, but fixation to underlying tissue or skin occurs in advanced cases. Regional lymph node metastasis is seen in approximately 40% of patients at presentation.[416,419,424,425]

Local recurrence and distant metastasis can occur during the course of disease. Lymphoepithelial carcinoma has the best prognosis among the undifferentiated carcinomas.[408] Although previous studies have reported poor outcome (survival as low as 17%), more recent series with patients treated by combined surgery and radiotherapy report survival figures of 75–86%.[408,416,419,425]

Relationship with lymphoepithelial sialadenitis (benign lymphoepithelial lesion) In the past, lymphoepithelial carcinoma was thought to originate through malignant transformation of LESA (see p. 305). This contention is now rejected by most investigators.[413,416,419] Previous reports of benign lymphoepithelial lesion adjacent to lymphoepithelial carcinoma probably represent reactive changes in the residual salivary parenchyma or misinterpretation of the less pleomorphic tumor islands with interspersed amyloid globules as lymphoepithelial lesions (epimyoepithelial islands).

Pathologic features Lymphoepithelial carcinoma of salivary gland is morphologically identical to lymphoepithelial carcinoma occurring elsewhere in the body, especially undifferentiated carcinoma of the nasopharynx. The infiltrative tumor grows in diffuse sheets, anastomosing islands, nests, or cords, separated by desmoplastic stroma (Fig. 7.130). The tumor cells are typically large with eosinophilic cytoplasm and indistinct cell borders. They possess vesicular nuclei and prominent nucleoli. In some cases, the nuclei are smaller and nucleoli are inconspicuous, making recognition of the malignant nature of the lesion difficult. Focal squamous differentiation can occur (Fig. 7.131). The tumor cells can sometimes be spindly.[426] Amyloid globules can occur among the tumor cells.[419] Tumor necrosis and mitotic figures are usually evident. The tumor is characteristically densely infiltrated by lymphocytes and plasma cells, with lymphoid follicle formation. Histiocytes sometimes infiltrate the tumor islands, producing a starry-sky appearance.[413] Non-caseating granulomas with or without multinucleated giant cells are found in some cases.[419] Perineural or lymphovascular invasion can be present (Fig. 7.132).[413]

Immunohistochemistry and special studies The tumor cells are immunoreactive for cytokeratin and EMA. They generally

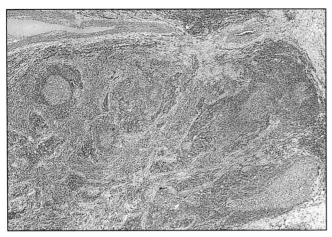

Fig. 7.130 • Lymphoepithelial carcinoma. Large irregular islands of tumor infiltrate a fibrous stroma heavily populated by lymphoid cells. Lymphoid follicles are also present.

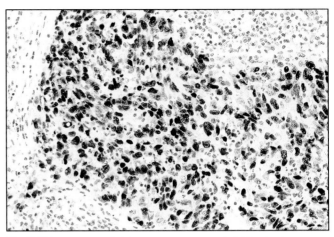

Fig. 7.132 • Lymphoepithelial carcinoma. On in-situ hybridization for Epstein–Barr virus-encoded RNA (EBER), the nuclei of the neoplastic cells are selectively labeled.

exhibit squamous features on ultrastructural examination, such as desmosomes and tonofilaments. In-situ hybridization for EBV is positive in all cases of Eskimo, south-eastern Chinese, and Japanese origin and only rarely in other ethnic groups (Fig. 7.132).[421,427,428]

Differential diagnosis Lymphoepithelial carcinoma is histologically, immunohistochemically, and ultrastructurally indistinguishable from nasopharyngeal undifferentiated carcinoma. Since nasopharyngeal carcinoma is by far commoner, clinical examination as well as endoscopic examination with biopsies should be undertaken to exclude this possibility before a diagnosis of lymphoepithelial carcinoma of salivary gland is made.[425] For prognostic reasons, lymphoepithelial carcinoma should be distinguished from large-cell carcinoma.

The neoplastic islands seen in lymphoepithelial carcinoma differ significantly from the lymphoepithelial lesions of LESA; the latter lack epithelial atypia and are often accompanied by basement membrane-like material. In-situ hybridization for EBV-encoded RNAs (EBER) is consistently negative in the epithelial islands in LESA, except for a few scattered lympho-

cytes,[417] whereas EBV is commonly positive in the epithelial cells in lymphoepithelial carcinoma.

Squamous cell carcinoma

Definition

Primary salivary gland squamous cell carcinoma is a very rare malignant tumor; invasion from an adjacent squamous cell carcinoma or metastasis should always be excluded. This entity is seldom diagnosed with confidence in the minor salivary gland since it is not possible to rule out a mucosal squamous cell carcinoma. In general, metastatic squamous cell carcinomas outnumber primary squamous cell carcinomas of the salivary glands.

Clinical features

This tumor mainly affects elderly males, with a mean age of 64 years. Prior radiation therapy for acne, benign and malignant tumors, enlarged thymus, thyroid gland, and tonsils have

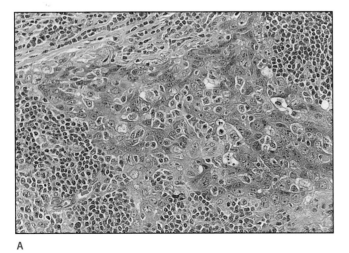

A

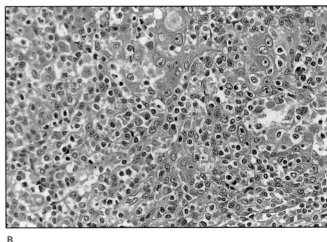

B

Fig. 7.131 • Lymphoepithelial carcinoma. (A) The tumor cells typically have indistinct cell borders and large pale nuclei. Lymphocytes infiltrate into the tumor islands as well as the stroma. (B) Sometimes the intratumoral lymphocytic infiltration is so prominent that the epithelial quality of the tumor is not easily appreciated. In this example, there are isolated cells with eosinophilic cytoplasm consistent with focal squamous differentiation.

been implicated as predisposing factors in some cases.[65] Two-thirds of tumors occur in the parotid gland, and the rest occur in the submandibular gland. Most patients present with a fast-growing, hard, fixed mass. Regional lymph node involvement and facial nerve palsy are common.

Squamous cell carcinoma tends to invade and spread rapidly. Since cervical lymph node metastasis is common, routine radical neck dissection may be advisable. The 5-year survival rate is only around 30%. Ulceration, fixation, advanced patient age, advanced tumor stage, and facial nerve palsy are unfavorable prognostic factors.[429,430]

Pathology

The tumor is most often infiltrative, tan-colored, and hard. It is usually a moderately to well-differentiated squamous cell carcinoma consisting of sheets and islands of squamous cells with readily identifiable keratin formation and intercellular bridges. The stroma is desmoplastic. Although some cells may appear hydropic, intracellular mucin is absent; otherwise the alternative diagnosis of mucoepidermoid carcinoma should be entertained. Occasionally dysplastic squamous epithelium can be seen in a large excretory duct.

Differential diagnosis

Besides high-grade mucoepidermoid carcinoma and metastatic carcinoma, primary salivary gland squamous cell carcinoma has to be distinguished from Warthin tumor, oncocytoma, and pleomorphic adenoma with florid atypical squamous metaplasia related to infarction or inflammation, as well as necrotizing sialometaplasia (see "Analytic approach to diagnosis," p. 310).

Mucinous adenocarcinoma

This tumor represents the histologic equivalent of mucinous or colloid carcinoma of the gastrointestinal tract, breast, and skin. It is characterized by clusters of tumor cells floating in pools of extracellular mucin.[431] Occasionally tumor cells may form ducts, papillae, cysts, and cribriform structures. Only a few cases have been reported in the literature. All affected patients were adults without gender predilection. Mucinous adenocarcinoma appears to be a low-grade tumor, and complete excision is the treatment of choice.

Signet-ring cell (mucin-producing) adenocarcinoma of minor salivary gland

Definition

This is a low-grade malignant tumor of the minor salivary gland characterized by mucin-containing signet ring cells.

Clinical features

The mean age of the patients is 56.4 years with a female predilection of 2.5:1.[432] All reported cases have occurred in the minor salivary glands of the oral cavity, in the form of an exophytic nodule or mass which can be fixed. There was no recurrence or metastasis after excision.

Pathologic features

The infiltrative tumor comprises narrow parallel strands, randomly scattered small nests, or isolated cells. Signet-ring cells are characterized by single or several cytoplasmic mucin vacuoles and eccentric indented nuclei. Admixed with these signet-ring cells are minor populations of tumor cells with eosinophilic or clear cytoplasm. The overall cytologic atypia is very mild with rare or absent mitoses and no necrosis. Extra-cellular mucin pools were seen in only 1 of 7 reported cases.[432] Perineural invasion is not uncommon. The tumor cells strongly express CAM5.2 (low-molecular-weight cytokeratin) and p63, and variably actin, S-100, and GFAP. Calponin is negative.

Adenocarcinoma, not otherwise specified

Definition

Nearly all carcinomas arising from the salivary gland proper are adenocarcinomas. Adenocarcinoma NOS, refers to primary carcinoma of the salivary gland that exhibits glandular differentiation but lacks diagnostic criteria of other defined tumor categories. As more and more neoplastic entities of salivary glands are characterized (such as PLGA), adenocarcinoma NOS becomes a diminishing diagnostic waste-basket (Table 7.10).

Clinical features

Adenocarcinoma NOS most commonly occurs in the elderly, the peak age being between the sixth and eighth decades, with a male predilection.[431,433] The most common locations in descending order are: parotid gland, submandibular gland, palate, and buccal mucosa. The patients present with an asymptomatic or fast-growing painful mass associated with ulceration and fixation to the adjacent structures. Facial nerve palsy is common. According to Spiro et al.,[434] the 15-year survival rates for low-, intermediate-, and high-grade adenocarcinomas are 54%, 31%, and 3% respectively, although grading is not found to be significant according to another study.[435] Stage is also important, in that the 10-year cure rate is 75% for stage I, irrespective of grade. Tumors involving the oral cavity are reported to have more favorable outcome than those of the parotid or submandibular gland.[435,436]

Pathology

Grossly the tumors show irregular infiltrative borders. The cut surface is tan and solid, with areas of hemorrhage or necrosis.

The tumors are characterized by glandular or ductal structures with variable organization (Fig. 7.133). The growth patterns are protean, including glandular, papillary, cystic, cribriform, solid, lobular, nest and strand-like, with the single unifying feature being the lack of recognizable patterns diagnostic of other specific neoplasms (Fig. 7.133).[433] Small areas of the tumor may resemble specific neoplasms such as acinic cell carcinoma or epithelial-myoepithelial carcinoma, but if

Table 7.10	Unifying features of the various adenocarcinomas of the salivary gland grouped by cytologic grade (excluding mucoepidermoid, acinic cell, and adenoid cystic carcinomas)	
	Low-grade adenocarcinoma	**High-grade adenocarcinoma**
Entities included	• Polymorphous low-grade adenocarcinoma • Epithelial-myoepithelial carcinoma • Basal cell adenocarcinoma • Cystadenocarcinoma • Low-grade adenocarcinoma, NOS	• Salivary duct carcinoma • Oncocytic carcinoma • High-grade adenocarcinoma, NOS
Unifying histologic features	• Infiltrative growth • Minimal or mild nuclear atypia • Infrequent mitoses • Coagulative necrosis uncommon	• Infiltrative growth • High nuclear grade • Frequent mitoses • Coagulative necrosis common
Behavior	• Slow-growing and indolent • May recur if incompletely excised • Regional lymph node metastasis 5–15% • Distant metastasis very rare • Favorable prognosis	• Fast-growing • Early and frequent metastasis to lymph nodes and distant sites • Poor prognosis

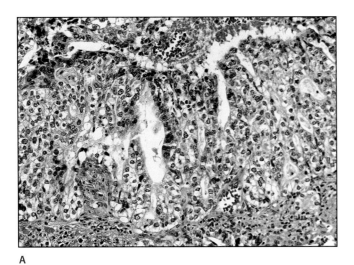
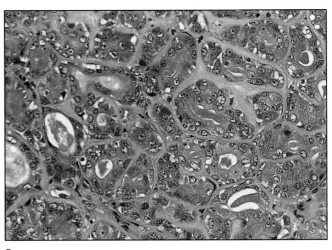

A   B

Fig. 7.133 • Adenocarcinoma, not otherwise specified, intermediate-grade. **(A)** This tumor grows in the form of large islands punctuated by occasional glandular spaces. **(B)** The tumor is composed of nondescript tubules lined by moderately atypical cells, lacking diagnostic patterns of the various known tumor types.

the overall picture is not in keeping with the known repertoire of a given tumor, the diagnosis of adenocarcinoma NOS is still applicable.

The neoplastic cells can be oncocytoid, clear, melanoma-like, mucinous, sebaceous, or plasmacytoid.[433] The glandular structures are formed by one single cell type (luminal cells only) or, rarely, two cell types (luminal and basal/myoepithelial cells). Infiltration of the normal parenchyma, nerves, and blood vessels is common.

Attempts have been made to subclassify adenocarcinoma NOS, but so far no subtypes of prognostic relevance have been delineated. The tubular type shows prominent duct formation.[431] The sclerosing type is characterized by marked fibrous desmoplasia, which may obscure the neoplastic component.[431] Most adenocarcinomas NOS are histologically high-grade, but grading is a relatively subjective assessment without well-defined criteria.

Sialoblastoma

Definition

Sialoblastoma, also known as embryoma,[437] congenital carcinoma,[15] or congenital basal cell adenoma,[438] is a tumor of newborns or infants which is composed of primitive-appearing cells with occasional ductal formation, recapitulating embryonic salivary tissue. Fetal, or dysembryoplastic, salivary gland tissue occasionally found adjacent to sialoblastoma may represent the precursor lesion.[439]

Clinical features

The tumors occur in major salivary glands, most commonly in the parotid. They present at birth or within the first or second years as an asymptomatic mass. Occasional cases can be associated with skin ulceration, facial paralysis, obstruction to delivery, congenital nevi, and concomitant hepatoblastoma.[440–443]

The clinical behavior is highly variable. Approximately one-third of cases develop local recurrence, and 6% develop regional lymph node metastasis.[443] One reported case also developed intracerebral extension and pulmonary metastasis.[444] Increases in anaplasia and proliferative activity have been reported in multiple recurrences.[443] Complete surgical excision is the treatment of choice;[445] adjuvant radiotherapy may be indicated for recurrence or incomplete excision.[443]

Pathology

The tumor can be well circumscribed or infiltrative, and comprises closely packed or loosely scattered islands of cells separated by fibromyxoid stroma. The majority of cells are primitive-looking and basaloid and possess large ovoid vesicular nuclei and a small amount of cytoplasm (Fig. 7.134). They form cellular ductules and solid organoid nests with vague palisading of nuclei at the periphery of the tumor islands. Mild nuclear atypia and variable mitotic activity are present. Focally, ducts lined by larger polygonal to cuboidal cells with eosinophilic cytoplasm can be identified, and the ductal lumens often contain secretory product.[438,442,446] Focally, cribriform structures reminiscent of adenoid cystic carcinoma can be present. Cytologic atypia, necrosis, and neural or vascular invasion vary from case to case, and have been suggested to correlate with the clinical outcome.[446,447] Immunostaining for cytokeratin highlights the ductal structures. The basaloid cells show staining for S-100 protein and actin in the peripherally located cells.

Mesenchymal neoplasms and tumor-like lesions

Mesenchymal tumors comprise about 2–5% of all salivary glands tumors,[11,14,448] with over 95% of cases involving the major salivary glands. Benign tumors outnumber malignant ones, with a ratio varying from 2.4:1 to 18:1 according to different series.[11,14] Hemangioma and lymphangioma are the commonest, accounting for 50% of all mesenchymal tumors in the Hamburg Salivary Gland Tumor Registry (1965–1981),[14] followed by lipomas (19.2%), nerve sheath tumors (neurofibroma, schwannoma: 15.8%), and sarcomas (7.5%). Hemangioma is also the most common salivary gland tumor in childhood.[449] According to a series of 85 cases reviewed by Luna et al., the most frequent types of sarcoma in the salivary gland are rhabdomyosarcoma and so-called malignant fibrous histiocytoma.[450] Mesenchymal tumors share the same histologic features and behavior as those found in other parts of the body (see Chs 3, 24, and 27).

Vascular tumors and tumor-like lesions

Capillary hemangioma

Clinical features Capillary hemangioma, often known as cellular hemangioma, juvenile hemangioendothelioma, or infantile hemangioendothelioma, tends to affect infants of

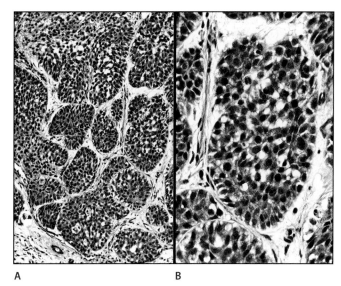

Fig. 7.134 • Sialoblastoma. **(A)** The tumor comprises lobules of basaloid cells. **(B)** In contrast to basal cell adenoma or basal cell adenocarcinoma, the cells have more vesicular or active-looking nuclei, and nuclear palisading in the peripheral portion is not striking.

either gender.[15,65,451,452] Presentation varies from an asymptomatic mass discovered at or shortly after birth to a rapidly enlarging lesion. Most are found in the parotid glands.[65,452] The overlying skin may show bluish discoloration. Pain and facial nerve palsy are absent but rare cases can be complicated by consumptive coagulopathy (Kasabach–Merritt syndrome). Spontaneous regression is expected in 75–90% of cases by the age of 7 years.[65,453] Occasional cases show progressive growth and even perhaps transformation to angiosarcoma.[454,455]

Pathology On gross examination, the tumor is dark red, lobulated, and non-encapsulated, ranging in size from 1 to 8 cm in diameter. Some cases may show extension into surrounding tissues.

In the immature form (cellular hemangioma), the neoplastic endothelial cells are plump, with large regular nuclei and frequent mitoses. The vascular lumina are often inconspicuous, and they are surrounded by collars of spindly cells that represent pericytes (Fig. 7.135). The solid appearance and brisk mitoses may invite a misdiagnosis of sarcoma. As the lesion matures, usually starting from the periphery inwards, the vascular lumens become well formed, and the capillaries are lined by flat endothelial cells (Fig. 7.135). The salivary gland lobular architecture is remarkably well preserved even in areas of involvement, a feature testifying to the non-aggressive nature of the neoplasm (Fig. 7.135A). Residual salivary ducts and acini are "comfortably" interspersed among the proliferating vessels (Fig. 7.135A). Infiltration of nerves can be found occasionally, but does not imply malignancy. Regression of the tumor is correlated with progressive, diffuse interstitial fibrosis.

Cavernous hemangioma

Cavernous hemangioma of the salivary gland is rare, and mostly affects adults.[65] There is no tendency to undergo spontaneous regression. Histologically, the dilated and thin-walled

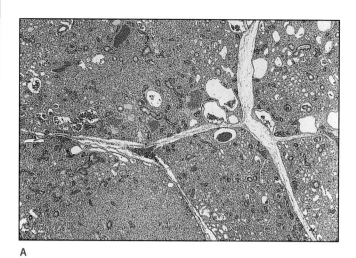

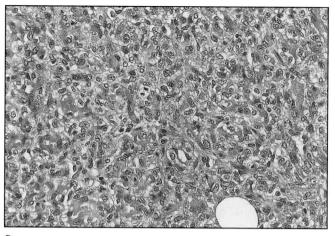

Fig. 7.135 • Cellular hemangioma of the parotid gland. **(A)** The lobular pattern of the salivary gland is characteristically preserved. **(B)** In some lobules, well-formed capillaries are recognizable. Other fields show immature capillaries growing in a solid pattern, which, combined with mild nuclear atypia and scattered miteses, may invite an erroneous interpretation of malignancy.

vascular channels are lined by attenuated endothelial cells. Dystrophic calcification within organized thrombi is frequent.

Epithelioid hemangioma

Epithelioid hemangioma, also known as angiolymphoid hyperplasia with eosinophilia,[456] can rarely involve the parotid glands or other major glands. It can be accompanied by eosinophilia in the peripheral blood. After excision, recurrence develops in approximately one-third of cases.[453]

Epithelioid hemangioma features lobular proliferation of capillary to medium-sized vessels lined by cuboidal or polygonal endothelial cells with abundant eosinophilic, hyaline cytoplasm that is frequently vacuolated (Fig. 7.136). Resemblance to glandular structures can be striking. The vessels are often accompanied by many eosinophils, lymphocytes, mast cells, and plasma cells. The lymphoid component is often denser in the peripheral portion of the lesion.

Malignant vascular tumors

Primary angiosarcoma is exceedingly rare in the salivary glands. It mainly affects the major glands, with peak incidence in the sixth decade.[457] The tumor usually presents as a mass lesion with recent enlargement and bleeding. Morphologically, a high representation of the epithelioid variant (up to one-third of cases) is observed.[457–460] Surgery is the treatment of choice. There is no proven benefit of radiation therapy and chemotherapy.

Epithelioid hemangioendothelioma has also rarely been reported in the parotid gland.[461]

Kimura disease

Clinical features

Kimura disease, which has often been confused with epithelioid hemangioma, represents an entirely unrelated lesion.[462] It is believed to result from an immunologic reaction of allergic or autoimmune nature. Kimura disease typically presents as a subcutaneous mass, lymph node enlargement, and/or swelling of the parotid or submandibular glands in young oriental males, but non-orientals can also be affected. The masses are indurated or rubbery with ill-defined borders, and grow slowly. Peripheral blood eosinophilia is almost invariably found, often accompanied by raised erythrocyte sedimentation rate and serum immunoglobulin E (IgE). The lesion often persists unchanged for years, but new additional lesions may develop. Recurrences after excision are common.

Pathology

The salivary gland is usually involved in a patchy pattern, with a dense inflammatory infiltrate, atrophy, loss of acini, and periductal and interlobular sclerosis. The inflammatory infiltrate comprises lymphocytes, plasma cells, and eosinophils. There are prominent lymphoid follicles, often with germinal center vascularization, necrosis, eosinophil infiltration, or even abscess formation. The interfollicular zone shows vascular proliferation, but these vessels represent high endothelial

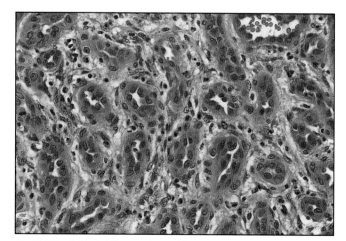

Fig. 7.136 • Epithelioid hemangioma of the parotid gland. Tubules (blood vessels) lined by epithelioid endothelial cells with eosinophilic cytoplasm characterize this tumor, which may be mistaken for an epithelial neoplasm. Some eosinophils are present between the blood vessels.

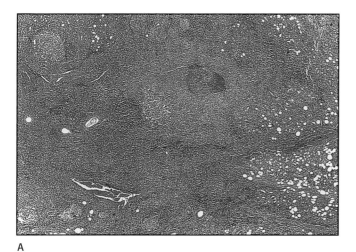
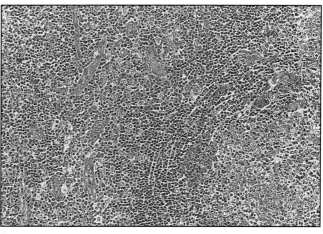

A

B

Fig. 7.137 • Kimura disease involving the parotid gland. (**A**) The lesion has poorly defined borders, featuring lymphoid cell and eosinophil infiltration, accompanied by destruction of salivary parenchyma. Lymphoid follicles are present (left upper field). An eosinophil abscess is also seen (upper middle field). (**B**) A reactive lymphoid follicle with eosinophil precipitate in the germinal center is seen in the right lower field. In the interfollicular zone, there is an increase of eosinophils among the lymphoid cells. The proliferated blood vessels are high endothelial venules.

venules lined by cuboidal to flat endothelium with pale cytoplasm (Fig. 7.137). Thus the proliferated vessels differ from those of epithelioid hemangioma in lacking a hyaline quality and plumpness, as well as lacking cytoplasmic vacuoles.

Solitary fibrous tumor

Solitary fibrous tumor (see Ch. 24) is a fibroblastic or myofibroblastic neoplasm which was initially described in the pleura but is recognized now in almost all sites in the body.[463,464] Some cases have been reported in the major salivary glands.[465–472] The presentation is usually in the form of a firm painless mass. Most cases pursue a benign course.

Solitary fibrous tumor is typically oval or round and well circumscribed. The cut surface is gray-white or whorled. Microscopically, it is characterized by haphazard growth of short spindle or plump cells with scanty cytoplasm that are intimately admixed with variably hyaline collagen. There are typically hypocellular (collagen-rich) areas alternating with hypercellular (tumor cell-rich) areas. Pericytomatous vessels are frequently seen. CD34 is strongly and diffusely expressed in the tumor cells.

Inflammatory pseudotumor

Inflammatory pseudotumor is a reactive fibroinflammatory mass-forming lesion (distinct from inflammatory myofibroblastic tumor) that may affect the salivary gland, especially the parotid gland. It presents as a firm, nodular swelling that has equal distribution in males and females, with a mean age of 70 years.[65,473–476] Excision is curative. Gross examination reveals a circumscribed mass with gray-white, whorled cut surface. The lesion consists of spindle cells (fibroblasts and myofibroblasts) intimately admixed with collagen fibers and variable amounts of plasma cells, lymphocytes, polymorphs, and foamy histiocytes. The spindle cells may form vague fascicles or storiform structures. Multinucleated histiocytic giant cells and calcification are common. Some spindle cells show immunoreactivity for CD68 and actin, but cytokeratin is negative.

Nodular fasciitis

Nodular fasciitis of the salivary gland often presents as a solitary, rapidly growing and painful mass in children or infants.[477,478] It is a self-limiting condition and recurrence is rare.[453] Nodular fasciitis is a circumscribed, non-encapsulated oval mass comprising reactive fibroblasts or myofibroblasts.[479] The spindle cells are arranged in short, broad fascicles with focal storiform pattern. Areas of low cellularity have a myxoid, feathery appearance interspersed with small mucoid pools. The spindly cells possess vesicular nuclei and sometimes prominent nucleoli. Mitotic figures are easily found, but atypical ones are not seen. Sprinkled in the lesions are lymphocytes and extravasated erythrocytes.

Giant cell tumor

Rare examples of giant cell tumor have been reported in the major salivary glands.[480,481] Half of the cases are associated with a carcinoma, usually salivary duct carcinoma and carcinoma *ex* pleomorphic adenoma. The giant cell component comprises uniformly distributed osteoclastic giant cells in a background of mononuclear cells. Although there is morphologic resemblance to giant cell tumor of bone, the mononuclear cells often express epithelial markers and androgen receptor, and show a microsatellite pattern more akin to carcinoma, and a more aggressive behavior.[481] The rare high-grade carcinomas with interspersed osteoclastic giant cells should not be considered a form of giant cell tumor.[482]

Hematolymphoid tumors and tumor-like lesions

Lymphoepithelial sialadenitis

Definition

LESA, previously known as myoepithelial sialadenitis or benign lymphoepithelial lesion,[65,483–486] is characterized by

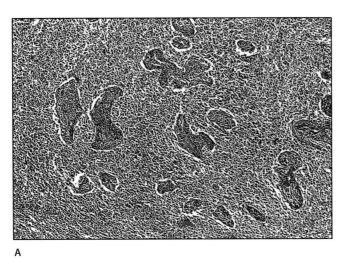

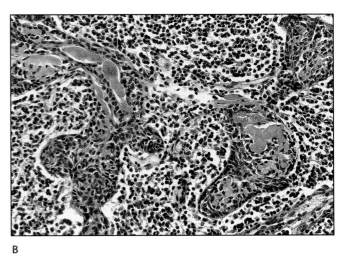

A

B

Fig. 7.138 • Lymphoepithelial sialadenitis. **(A)** Irregular epithelial islands are scattered in the dense lymphoid stroma. **(B)** The lymphoepithelial islands, also known as epimyoepithelial islands, are characterized by epithelial proliferation in a pre-existing duct, often obliterating the original lumen. Intercellular hyaline basement membrane-like material is commonly found. The island is infiltrated by small lymphocytes.

lymphoid infiltration in the salivary gland parenchyma, atrophy of acini, and ductal proliferation with formation of lymphoepithelial lesions (formerly called epimyoepithelial islands). The term "myoepithelial sialadenitis" is misleading because there is no good evidence of myoepithelial participation in the characteristic lymphoepithelial lesions.

Clinical features

LESA mainly affects the parotid (80–85%) and submandibular glands (10–15%),[65,477] and presents as recurrent, diffuse, firm swelling. Twenty percent of patients have bilateral disease, and pain is noted in 40% of cases.[477] A high proportion of affected patients (50–84%) manifest clinical and laboratory evidence of Sjögren syndrome.[487,488] There is female predominance (M:F = 1:3), and the peak age is from the fourth to seventh decades.

LESA is a risk factor for the development of salivary gland lymphoma, especially when associated with Sjögren syndrome or other related connective tissue diseases such as rheumatoid arthritis.[489] The increased risk is estimated to be 44-fold, and 80% of the lymphomas are of extranodal marginal zone B-cell (MALT) type.[486,490–492] Viruses such as EBV, human herpesvirus 8, human lymphotropic virus-1, and hepatitis C have not been found to play a role in the lymphomatous transformation.[493,494] It should be noted that some lesions previously reported as LESA actually represent MALT lymphoma or LESA complicated by MALT lymphoma.[495,496] The incidence of lymphoma in LESA has been reported to range from 20 to 28%.[497,498]

It can be difficult to recognize early lymphomatous change in LESA on morphologic grounds. Some investigators have used the detection of monoclonal B-cell expansion to indicate "prelymphomatous" change or to diagnose lymphoma.[496,499–503] Jordan et al., by combining immunohistochemistry, PCR, and in-situ hybridization, have been able to identify monoclonal populations in 77% of LESA.[504] Although some cases do eventually develop lymphoma,[491] most cases with monoclonal populations pursue an uneventful course.[505] Thus, the significance of clonal populations in LESA in the absence of morphologic evidence of lymphoma is still controversial.[496,502,506–508]

Because of the increased risk for lymphoma and difficulties in ruling out the presence of lymphoma in small biopsies or fine-needle aspirates, parotidectomy appears to be the treatment of choice. Long-term follow-up for the associated autoimmune conditions as well as for development of lymphoproliferative disease is still required after operation.

Pathological features

LESA exhibits discrete or ill-defined borders, but the lobular architecture of the salivary gland is preserved. The lymphoid infiltrate apparently begins in the periductal areas and gradually replaces the lobules. It comprises small lymphocytes and plasma cells with or without germinal center formation. There is marked atrophy or loss of acinar tissue, but proliferation of the residual ductal epithelium and insinuation of lymphocytes into the epithelium result in the characteristic lymphoepithelial lesions (epimyoepithelial islands) (Fig. 7.138).[509–512] Lymphoepithelial lesions comprise round to irregular solid islands of cells, which may be punctuated by small residual ductal lumens. The epithelial cells are plump spindly, polygonal to syncytial, and have uniform oval nuclei with fine chromatin, reminiscent of intraductal epithelial hyperplasia of the breast (Fig. 7.138B). Hyaline basement membrane-like material is often seen among the cells. The proliferated cells have been considered to represent a mixture of ductal and myoepithelial cells, but recent studies have not found evidence of myoepithelial participation.[513] Rarely, squamous metaplasia and keratinization can occur.[506,514,515]

On immunostaining, the epithelial cells in the lymphoepithelial lesions are immunoreactive for cytokeratin. The lymphoid cells in the lymphoepithelial lesions are mostly B cells. The lymphoid cells in between represent a mixture of B and T cells, with the former outnumbering the latter.[484] The features suggestive of lymphoma in LESA are listed in Table 7.11.

Primary lymphoma of salivary gland

Primary lymphomas of the salivary gland are rare, accounting for only 2.4–4.5% of salivary gland tumors,[14,477,516] with most cases occurring in the parotid (50–93%) and submandibular

Table 7.11	Morphologic and immunohistochemical features favoring a diagnosis of mucosa-associated lymphoid tissue (MALT) lymphoma (or MALT lymphoma complicating lymphoepithelial sialadenitis (LESA)) over LESA
Morphologic features	**Immunohistochemical features**
• Presence of collars of clear cells (monocytoid B-cell-like) around the epithelial islands; this is considered by Hyjek et al. (1988)[514] and Diss et al. (1995)[506] to be the earliest evidence of a supervening lymphoma	• Demonstration of light-chain restriction
	• Demonstration of diffuse sheets of B cells
• "Cavitation" of epithelial islands by large clusters of lymphoid cells	• Aberrant immunophenotype of B cells, e.g., coexpression of CD43
• Infiltration of the delicate lobular septa or nerves	

tation. A serum monoclonal component (IgG or IgM) is detected in 25% of cases.[491] The overall prognosis is excellent, with a 5-year survival of 85–90%.[491,492] Local therapy, such as surgery or radiotherapy, appears to be adequate. Poor prognostic factors include transformation to diffuse large B-cell lymphoma (incidence 12%) and advanced age.

Pathology Grossly, the tumor is non-circumscribed, firm, and tan-colored. Interspersed cysts formed by dilatation of the ducts are a common finding (Fig. 7.139). The histologic features are similar to MALT lymphomas occurring elsewhere, often featuring a mixture of cell types (commonly including clear cells reminiscent of monocytoid B cell), reactive lymphoid follicles, and many lymphoepithelial lesions. The involvement of the salivary gland can be extensive and destructive, or can still be accompanied by preserved lobular architecture (Fig. 7.140). As emphasized by Isaacson & Norton,[518] the earliest evidence of *de novo* MALT lymphoma or MALT lymphoma evolving from LESA is the presence of broad collars of

glands.[14,477,517] To qualify for primary salivary gland lymphoma, the main bulk of the disease should be located in the salivary gland. However, it is often difficult to make a distinction between lymphoma arising in the salivary gland proper (primary salivary gland lymphoma) and those in the lymph nodes embedded in the salivary gland (conventional nodal lymphoma) on clinical or histologic grounds. The latter lymphoma types show no difference in morphology and prognosis from those arising in other lymph nodes. The commonest types are Hodgkin lymphoma, follicular lymphoma, and diffuse large B-cell lymphoma, but any nodal lymphoma type can occur.[65,486,497,500]

MALT lymphoma is the commonest primary salivary gland lymphoma, followed by diffuse large B-cell lymphoma and follicular lymphoma.[486,490,518] There is an increased risk for high-grade B-cell lymphomas in patients with acquired immune deficiency syndrome (AIDS), and some of these lymphomas are associated with EBV.[519,520] Rarely, peripheral T-cell lymphoma, anaplastic large-cell lymphoma and natural killer/T cell lymphoma can occur as primary salivary gland lymphomas, and they often pursue an aggressive course.[521]

MALT lymphoma (extranodal marginal zone B-cell lymphoma of MALT type)

The clinical, histologic, and immunogenetic findings of MALT lymphoma are detailed in Chapter 21. Only specific features related to the salivary gland are discussed in this section.

Clinical features The best-known predisposing factors for MALT lymphoma of the salivary gland are LESA or Sjögren syndrome and hepatitis C infection.[490–492] In a series of 33 cases, 46% were associated with LESA and 29% with hepatitis C virus infection.[491] The median age is 61 years (range 55–65 years), with female predominance. The patients usually present with a slow-growing mass in the salivary gland. Cervical lymph node involvement is found in almost 30% of patients at presen-

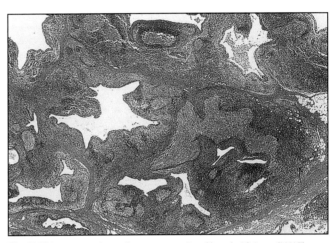

Fig. 7.139 • Low-grade B-cell mucosa-associated lymphoid tissue (MALT) lymphoma. Multiple cysts formed by dilatation of the ducts are not infrequently present. Within the dense lymphoid infiltrate, reactive lymphoid follicles are characteristically present.

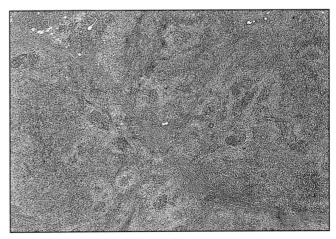

Fig. 7.140 • Low-grade B-cell mucosa-associated lymphoid tissue (MALT) lymphoma. In this dense lymphoid proliferation, the collars of pale cells around the epithelial islands (lymphoepithelial lesions) provide the strongest clue to the diagnosis of MALT lymphoma over benign lymphoepithelial lesion. Many reactive lymphoid follicles are interspersed.

clear cells around the lymphoepithelial lesions (Figs 7.140 and 7.141). Lymphoepithelial lesions are ducts markedly expanded and distorted by neoplastic lymphoid cells, which may produce "abscesses" in the proliferated epithelium. The lymphoid cells within and around the ducts are typically larger than the rest of the tumor cells, with oval to indented nuclei and abundant pale-staining to clear cytoplasm, resembling monocytoid B cells (Fig. 7.141B). Other lymphoid cells resemble small lymphocytes or have folded nuclei (centrocyte-like). Commonly, there are variable numbers of plasma cells, which usually occur in clusters; they may show mild atypia, and may contain Dutcher bodies. Isolated interspersed large lymphoid cells with round nuclei and distinct nucleoli are commonly present (Fig. 7.142). In occasional cases, wreaths of epithelioid histiocytes surround the lymphoepithelial lesions.

On immunostaining, there are dense sheets of B cells (CD20+) (Fig. 7.143), and light-chain restriction can often be demonstrated. CD5, CD10, and cyclin D1 are negative. The B cells may show aberrant coexpression of CD43, a feature that can aid in the diagnosis of lymphoma in difficult cases.

Genetic features Translocation t(14;18) with *IgH/MALT* fusion and trisomies 3 and 18 have been demonstrated in a proportion of cases, whereas t(11;18), the translocation most frequently found in MALT lymphoma of the stomach and lung, is very rare.[522,523]

Diffuse large B-cell lymphoma arising in MALT lymphoma

MALT lymphoma can transform to a diffuse large B-cell lymphoma, when the behavior becomes more aggressive. However, there is no universally accepted minimum criterion on how to define large-cell transformation. A supervening large B-cell lymphoma can certainly be diagnosed when there are dense sheets or sizeable clusters of large cells. The greatest problem is when there is an increase in large cells, which are still intimately intermingled with the small cells. In such circumstances, a designation such as "MALT lymphoma with increased large cells" is justified. There is recent evidence that the presence of more than 5% large cells already confers a

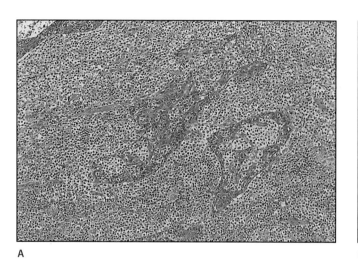
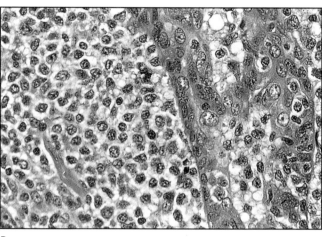

Fig. 7.141 • Low-grade B-cell mucosa-associated lymphoid tissue (MALT) lymphoma. (**A**) The characteristic lymphoepithelial lesions are extensively infiltrated and surrounded by pale cells. (**B**) Higher magnification shows that the pale cells resemble monocytoid B cells. Many such cells also infiltrate into the ductal epithelium (right field) to produce the lymphoepithelial lesion.

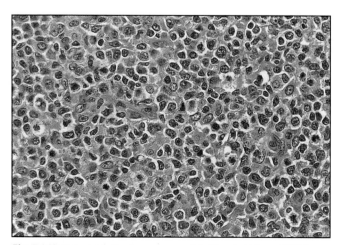

Fig. 7.142 • Low-grade B-cell mucosa-associated lymphoid tissue (MALT) lymphoma. The main lymphoid population comprises small lymphocytes admixed with plasma cells and occasional large activated cells.

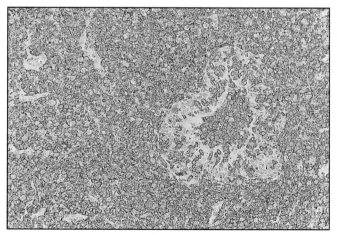

Fig. 7.143 • Low-grade B-cell mucosa-associated lymphoid tissue (MALT) lymphoma. Immunostaining with L26 (CD20) shows diffuse sheets of B cells, a feature strongly supporting a diagnosis of lymphoma. The lymphoid cells that constitute the lymphoepithelial lesion (right field) are also shown to be B cells.

slightly worse outcome compared with conventional MALT lymphoma.[524]

Lymphoepithelial cyst

Lymphoepithelial cyst of the salivary gland is characterized by epithelial-lined cysts with a dense lymphoid stroma in the wall. It has been proposed to arise from cystic proliferation of salivary inclusions in intraparotid lymph node. Its incidence has greatly increased over the past two decades because of the association with human immunodeficiency virus (HIV) infection.[5]

Clinical features

Lymphoepithelial cyst unassociated with HIV typically occurs in adults (average age 45 years) with a male predominance. It usually presents as parotid swelling, and is curable by surgical excision.

HIV-associated lymphoepithelial cyst (also known as cystic lymphoid hyperplasia) commonly presents as bilateral parotid swelling accompanied by cervical lymphadenopathy. The swellings are slow-growing and painless. Males are more frequently affected than females (7:1), with the peak age spanning from the second to fourth decades. The cyst may represent the first clinical manifestation of HIV infection concurrent with persistent generalized lymphadenopathy syndrome. Symptoms of xerostomia or xerophthalmia that are characteristic of Sjögren syndrome are absent. Treatment by parotidectomy, excision, curettage, or radiation is mostly for cosmetic reason, and will not affect the course of HIV infection.[525–527]

Pathology

Lymphoepithelial cyst unassociated with HIV infection is almost always solitary, while that associated with HIV usually comprises multiple variable-sized cysts (Fig. 7.144). The cysts often have an undulating luminal surface, and are lined by stratified squamous epithelium, although the epithelial lining can be of cuboidal, columnar, or respiratory type. Beneath the epithelium, there is a thick band of lymphoid tissue whose base is often well demarcated from the surrounding salivary parenchyma. Lymphoid follicles are frequently present, and small lymphocytes may infiltrate the epithelium.

In HIV-associated lymphoepithelial cyst, the lymphoid tissue exhibits florid lymphoid hyperplasia similar to that found in lymph node of persistent generalized lymphadenopathy (Fig. 7.144). There is explosive follicular hyperplasia, follicle lysis, increased monocytoid B cells, increased vascularity, and a plasma cell infiltrate. Some lymphoepithelial lesions may be found. The main differential diagnosis is MALT lymphoma.

Chronic sclerosing sialadenitis (Kuttner tumor)

Clinical features

Chronic sclerosing sialadenitis is a chronic inflammatory disease believed to result from inspissated secretion, stones, or microliths, and perpetuated by ascending infection.[528–530] The recent demonstration of abundant IgG4-positive plasma cells in the lesion raises a possible relationship with the IgG4-associated sclerosing lymphoplasmacytic pancreatitis/cholangitis syndrome.[531] It affects almost exclusively the submandibular gland, and is called Kuttner tumor in its advanced stage as it presents clinically as a hard swelling indistinguishable from a tumor.[532] The disease can be bilateral. The mean age of the patients is 42–44 years, with slight male predominance.[528–530]

Pathology

The histologic features vary according to stage of evolution and severity of the inflammation.[528,530] The lobular architecture is preserved and the degree of involvement varies from lobule to lobule. In the early stages, lymphoplasmacytic infiltration commences around the salivary ducts, followed by periductal fibrosis (Fig. 7.145). Focal squamous and mucous metaplasia and proliferation of the duct epithelium follow, but lymphoepithelial lesions are absent or rare. The ducts may

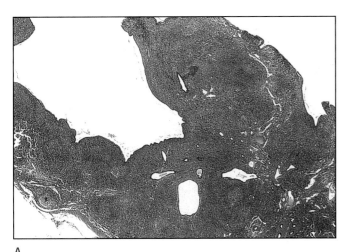

A

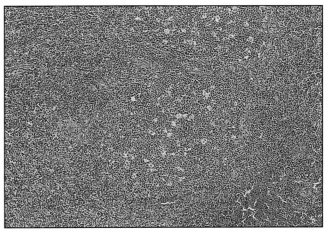

B

Fig. 7.144 • Cystic lymphoid hyperplasia (lymphoepithelial cyst) in human immunodeficiency virus (HIV)-seropositive subject. **(A)** Multiple epithelium-lined cysts are present. The undulating appearance of the lumen is produced by projecting nodules of lymphoid tissue. **(B)** The lymphoid tissue shows "naked" reactive follicles, as commonly observed in HIV-associated explosive follicular hyperplasia of lymph node.

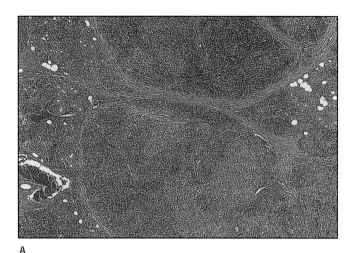
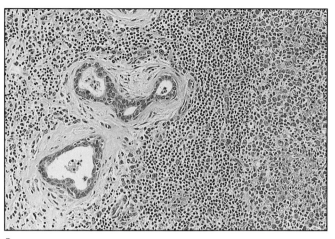

A

B

Fig. 7.145 • Chronic sclerosing sialadenitis of the submandibular gland (Kuttner tumor). **(A)** The lobular architecture is preserved, and the septa show sclerosis. There is lymphoid infiltration with lymphoid follicle formation, accompanied by loss of acini and ducts. **(B)** Periductal sclerosis is a common finding. In contrast to lymphoepithelial sialadenitis, lymphoepithelial lesions are rare.

contain inspissated secretion. The lymphocytic infiltrate and fibrosis intensify and gradually involve the whole lobule associated with atrophy of the acini. Reactive lymphoid follicles are frequently present. In the advanced stage, there is marked fibrosis and loss of parenchyma, resembling liver cirrhosis.[14] On immunostaining, T cells predominate and they show an intimate relationship with ducts and acini. B cells are mostly restricted to the lymphoid follicles.[533]

Kuttner tumor is underrecognized and not uncommonly misdiagnosed as LESA; it can be distinguished from the latter by the scarcity or lack of lymphoepithelial lesions and its usually more prominent sclerosis.[528] On the other hand, sclerosing follicular lymphoma mimicking Kuttner tumor and, rarely, MALT lymphoma complicating Kuttner tumor have been reported.[534,535]

Analytic approach to diagnosis of epithelial tumors of the salivary gland

The diagnostic problem

Warthin tumor often has a stereotyped appearance, and rarely causes problems in diagnosis. Most pleomorphic adenomas do not pose problems in diagnosis either, because of the presence of the characteristic chondromyxoid stroma. However, as is evident from the descriptions of the various types of salivary gland tumor, the histologic spectrum of each tumor entity can be very broad, and there is considerable morphologic overlap among the various entities. For example, although a cribriform pattern is highly characteristic of adenoid cystic carcinoma, this can be seen focally in pleomorphic adenoma, basal cell adenoma, PLGA, salivary duct carcinoma, and epithelial-myoepithelial carcinoma – tumors with very different prognoses (Figs 7.14A, 7.38, 7.91, and 7.117). Adenoid cystic carcinoma may have a minor component of clear cells, focally mimicking epithelial-epimyoepithelial carcinoma.

Therefore, in formulating a diagnosis, one should not rely on isolated microscopic fields of the tumor, but should take

the overall features into consideration, the most important of which are:[131]

1. tumor borders
2. cellular composition
3. architectural arrangement
4. cytologic features
5. stromal components

If the patterns appear non-diagnostic, thorough sampling of the tumor will often prove rewarding because some more diagnostic foci can often be identified. The major pitfalls in diagnosis are listed in Tables 7.12 and 7.13.

Assessment of the malignant potential of basal cell, myoepithelial, and oncocytic neoplasms is particularly problematic. A schematic approach to this problem is shown in Figure 7.46. Table 7.10 shows the unifying features of low-grade and high-grade adenocarcinomas.

Morphologic assessment

Invasive or not?

Assessment of the tumor interface with adjacent tissues, either at the macroscopic or microscopic level, is extremely important. Benign tumors are circumscribed, while malignant tumors have infiltrative borders, with the following exceptions: some acinic cell carcinomas and carcinomas *ex* pleomorphic adenoma may have circumscribed borders, while Warthin tumor complicated by infarction or inflammation can result in a lot of adhesions to surrounding tissue, mimicking a malignant neoplasm clinically or grossly. The pattern of infiltration also differs among different types of carcinomas – this tends to be of pushing type in epithelial-myoepithelial carcinoma, basal cell adenocarcinoma, myoepithelial carcinoma (except high-grade ones), and acinic cell carcinoma (Figs 7.43, 7.51, and 7.98); whereas the other carcinomas usually exhibit irregular tongue-like infiltrative growth (Figs 7.78, 7.108, and 7.118).

The importance of identification of invasion cannot be overemphasized. A presumptive diagnosis of adenoid cystic carcinoma must be wrong if tissue infiltration is not identified;

Table 7.12	Common misdiagnoses (overdiagnosis) in salivary gland epithelial neoplasms	
Overdiagnosis of malignancy		
Benign tumor	**Misdiagnosed as…**	**Clues or features favoring the correct diagnosis**
Warthin tumor or oncocytoma with squamous and/or mucinous metaplasia	Squamous cell carcinoma or mucoepidermoid carcinoma	• Extreme rarity of primary squamous cell carcinoma • Lack of invasive growth • Convoluted cystic architecture of Warthin tumor • Low-grade mucoepidermoid carcinoma never frankly squamous in appearance • Merging of atypical squamous cells with residual oncocytic cells • Prominent reparative features
Pleomorphic adenoma with squamous and mucinous metaplasia (often post fine-needle aspiration)	Mucoepidermoid carcinoma	• Lack of invasive growth • Low-grade mucoepidermoid carcinoma never frankly squamous in appearance or showing keratinization • Presence of thick elastic fibers • Presence of a bicellular ductal-myoepithelial architecture in areas • Plasmacytoid hyaline cells, if present • Chondromyxoid stroma, if present
Pleomorphic adenoma or basal cell adenoma with cribriform architecture	Adenoid cystic carcinoma	• Lack of invasive growth • "Melting" of myoepithelial cells into the stroma at least focally
Clear cell variant of oncocytoma	Clear cell carcinoma or mucoepidermoid carcinoma	• Lack of invasive growth • Presence of typical onocytes at least focally • Positive staining for PTAH and antimitochondrial antibody
Non-sebaceous lymphadenoma	Lymphoepithelial carcinoma	• Lack of significant nuclear atypia (although mild nuclear atypia is acceptable) • Glandular differentiation (morphologic or immunohistochemical) is present at least focally • Epstein–Barr virus-negative

PTAH, phosphotungstic acid hematoxylin.

similarly, this diagnosis should be viewed with some skepticism if extensive sampling of the tumor fails to reveal perineural invasion. Since adenoid cystic carcinoma may overlap morphologically with basal cell adenoma and sometimes pleomorphic adenoma, identification of invasion is one of the most important parameters for making the distinction. For some tumors, the presence of frank invasive features alone automatically moves the designation from the benign to the malignant category even if the tumor is morphologically bland-looking, for example, myoepithelial, basal cell and oncocytic neoplasms (Fig. 7.46). The implication is that the tumor borders must be adequately sampled for examination. In some circumstances, a definitive diagnosis may not be possible without the opportunity to assess the tumor borders, such as in needle or incisional biopsies.

Does the tumor show a dual cellular population or only a single line of differentiation?

Figure 7.7 lists the various salivary gland tumors with dual luminal and abluminal cell differentiation. Identification of this feature greatly narrows down the differential diagnoses. For instance, adenoid cystic carcinoma can be difficult to distinguish from PLGA, but the former shows dual-cell differentiation whereas the latter does not (Fig. 7.146). Canalicular adenoma can be distinguished from basal cell adenoma by the lack of abluminal cell component. In some tumors, careful search and detailed morphologic analysis, sometimes aided by judicious application of immunohistochemistry, are required to identify dual-cell-type differentiation. Adenocarcinoma NOS exceptionally can show dual-cell differentiation, but by definition should lack diagnostic features of adenoid cystic carcinoma and basal cell adenocarcinoma. Some PLGA can also show very focal dual-cell-type differentiation. Although basal cells (abluminal cells) are inconspicuous in oncocytoma at the light microscopic level, they are often evident on immunostaining in the form of attenuated cells.

Architectural arrangement

Some tumors exhibit architectural features that may provide important clues to their diagnosis (Table 7.14). When extravasated mucin is seen in a fibrous stroma with chronic inflammatory cell infiltration, the most likely diagnosis is low-grade mucoepidermoid carcinoma (Fig. 7.147). For any "difficult-to-classify" carcinoma, the possibility of carcinoma *ex* pleomorphic adenoma has to be considered.

Table 7.13   Common misdiagnoses (underdiagnosis) in salivary gland epithelial neoplasms

Underdiagnosis of malignancy		
Malignant tumor	**Misdiagnosed as ...**	**Clues or features favoring the correct diagnosis**
Cystic mucoepidermoid carcinoma	Benign cyst or cystadenoma	• Cells lining the cyst are multilayered in at least some foci • Intraluminal nodules of cells • Multiplicity of cell types • Epithelial islands in fibrous wall or beyond
Mucoepidermoid carcinoma with prominent mucin extravasation	Mucocele	• Presence of pools of extravasated mucin in the major salivary gland mandates careful search for a low-grade mucoepidermoid carcinoma, since extravasation mucocele is extremely rare
Polymorphous low-grade adenocarcinoma	Pleomorphic or basal cell adenoma	• Invasive borders • Neural invasion common • Lack of dual-cell differentiation • Chondromyxoid stroma absent • Diverse growth patterns • Pale nuclei
Adenoid cystic carcinoma in mucosal sites	Pleomorphic or basal cell adenoma	• Invasive growth, if identifiable in the biopsy • Tubules strangulated by hyalinized stroma • Focal cribriform structures
Oncocytic variant of mucoepidermoid carcinoma	Oncocytoma	• Invasive growth • Other cell types (e.g., epidermoid, intermediate, and mucinous cells) present in some foci • Inflamed fibrous stroma
Cystic or papillary-cystic variant of acinic cell carcinoma	Benign cyst	• Hobnailed lining cells • Vacuolated lining cells • Focal cellular tufts projecting into lumen • Acinar-cell differentiation (periodic acid–Schiff-positive granular cytoplasm) in the lining cells • Tumor islands in fibrous wall focally
Epithelial-myoepithelial carcinoma	Pleomorphic or basal cell adenoma	• Invasive growth • Prominent clear cells forming the outer layers of tubules or islands
Lymphoepithelial carcinoma	Lymphadenoma	• Invasive growth often present • Definite nuclear atypia (albeit sometimes mild) • Tumor cells exhibit squamoid/squamous rather than glandular features at the morphologic or immunohistochemical level • Epstein–Barr virus in tumor cells, if present

Some tumors that are commonly partially or completely cystic are Warthin tumor, cystadenoma, cystadenocarcinoma, mucoepidermoid carcinoma, and the papillary-cystic variant of acinic cell carcinoma (Fig. 7.148). A number of reactive cystic lesions can also produce tumor-like mass, such as lymphoepithelial cyst, keratinous cyst, mucocele, salivary duct cyst, polycystic (dysgenetic) disease of parotid glands, and sclerosing polycystic adenosis (Figs 7.72 and 7.74).

Cytologic features

When certain cell types are found in a salivary gland tumor, they may provide important clues to classification (Table 7.15). The presence of vacuolated cells should raise the possibilities of acinic cell carcinoma and sebaceous neoplasms. The fea-

tures that are helpful for distintinguishing clear cells in various tumors are listed in Table 7.5. For practical purposes, the majority of clear cell salivary gland tumors are malignant (Fig. 7.149).

Squamous nests with or without keratinization can be seen in a variety of tumors. Importantly, frank squamous features such as intercellular bridges and keratinization are almost never seen in low- to intermediate-grade mucoepidermoid carcinomas; the correct diagnosis is probably pleomorphic adenoma or Warthin tumor with squamous metaplasia (Figs 7.17 and 7.67). Neoplastic oncocytic cells, such as in Warthin tumor, oncocytoma and oncocytic carcinoma, also tend to undergo squamous metaplasia in response to injury from ischemia or inflammation; such metaplastic squamous cells often exhibit variable degrees of atypia, inviting a misdiagnosis of squamous cell carcinoma (Fig. 7.58; Table 7.12).

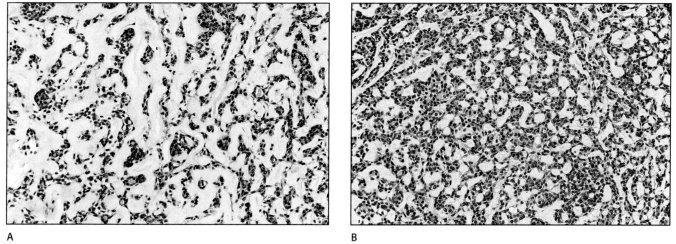

A

B

Fig. 7.146 • Adenoid cystic carcinoma of nasal cavity. **(A)** Strangulation of tubules by myxohyaline material is a common feature. **(B)** With prominent anastomosis of tubules of two-cell-type, distinction from a cellular pleomorphic adenoma or basal cell adenoma is difficult, if not impossible, without identification of definite invasive growth.

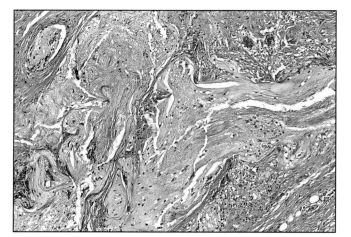

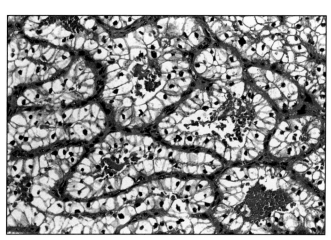

Fig. 7.147 • "Mucocele" in major salivary gland. The presence of extravasated pools of mucus in the stroma in a major salivary gland is practically synonymous with a diagnosis of low-grade mucoepidermoid carcinoma. Careful search in this case does reveal mucoepidermoid carcinoma (not shown).

Fig. 7.149 • Metastatic renal-cell carcinoma in parotid gland. Features favoring this diagnosis over primary clear cell carcinoma of salivary gland include: delicate fibrovascular septa, true gland formation, and intraluminal hemorrhage.

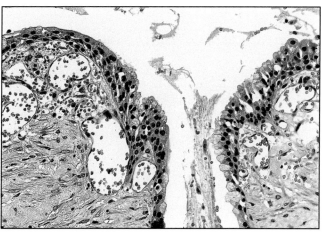

A

B

Fig. 7.148 • Cystic mucoepidermoid carcinoma masquerading as simple cyst. **(A)** The parotid gland harbors a single cyst. Lymphoid follicles are present in the fibrous wall. **(B)** Although the cyst lining is attenuated in many areas, mucoepidermoid epithelium is present at least focally.

Table 7.14 Architectural features providing clues to diagnosis of salivary gland tumors

Architectural pattern	Diagnoses to consider	Remarks
Microcystic	• Acinic cell carcinoma • Polymorphous low-grade adenocarcinoma (focal) • Myoepithelioma (some cases)	Acinic cell carcinoma should be the first consideration whenever microcystic pattern is prominent, especially when accompanied by a lymphoid infiltrate
Cribriform	• Adenoid cystic carcinoma • Salivary duct carcinoma • Intraductal carcinoma • Pleomorphic/basal cell adenoma (focal) • Polymorphous low-grade adenocarcinoma (focal) • Cribriform adenocarcinoma of the tongue	Cribriform structures are highly characteristic, but not diagnostic, of adenoid cystic carcinoma. Most of the spaces in the cribriform plates in adenoid cystic carcinoma are in continuity with the stroma rather than true glandular spaces. The cribriform structures in salivary duct carcinoma and intraductal carcinoma are however true glandular spaces
Tubular	• Adenoid cystic carcinoma • Polymorphous low-grade adenocarcinoma • Epithelial-myoepithelial carcinoma • Adenocarcinoma, NOS • Pleomorphic/basal cell adenoma (focal) • Cystadenoma and cystadenocarcinoma (some cases) • Salivary duct carcinoma (some cases) • Oncocytoma and oncocytic carcinoma (rare cases)	A tubular pattern is common in salivary gland tumors. Assessment of the tumor interface with the surrounding tissues, cellular composition, and differentiation, and the cytomorphology of the tumor cells is helpful in arriving at the diagnosis
Fascicular	• Myoepithelioma and myoepithelial carcinoma • Basal cell adenoma with myoepithelium-derived stroma • Pleomorphic adenoma (focal) • Polymorphous low-grade adenocarcinoma (focal) • Epithelial-myoepithelial carcinoma (focal) • Various mesenchymal tumors	The presence of spindle cells in fascicles, excluding mesenchymal tumors, is usually indicative of the presence of myoepithelial differentiation, except polymorphous low-grade adenocarcinoma
Papillary	• Warthin tumor • Cystadenoma and cystadenocarcinoma • Ductal papillomas • Acinic cell carcinoma, papillary-cystic variant • Adenocarcinoma, NOS (some cases) • Polymorphous low-grade adenocarcinoma (some cases) • Epithelial-myoepithelial carcinoma (very focal)	Analysis of the tumor cells covering the papillae is helpful in diagnosis. Dual-cell differentiation is seen in Warthin tumor and epithelial-myoepithelial carcinoma, sialadenoma papilliferum, and intraductal papilloma
Lattice	• Myoepithelioma and myoepithelial carcinoma • Pleomorphic adenoma (focal) • Adenoid cystic carcinoma (focal, in areas of extensive hyalinization)	The lattice pattern is a prominent feature of some myoepithelial neoplasms, but is rare in other salivary gland tumors. Ectomesenchymal chondromyxoid tumor of the tongue (not a salivary gland tumor) also shows a prominent lattice growth pattern

NOS, not otherwise specified.

Necrotizing sialometaplasia is a reactive lesion that enters into the differential diagnosis of squamous cell carcinoma. It affects almost exclusively the minor glands, and most commonly presents as an ulcerated palatal lesion.[536,537] The lesion most probably has an ischemic etiology, such as vasculitis, atheromatous emboli, and prolonged intubation.[536,538,539] Some cases have been associated with herpes infection,[540] traumatic injury, or prior surgery. The most important histologic feature distinguishing this lesion from carcinoma is the preserved lobular configuration. Partial necrosis of salivary lobules is accompanied by florid squamous metaplasia of the adjacent ducts and acini, similar to the phenomenon seen in the prostate around areas of infarction (Fig. 7.150). An inflammatory infiltrate is often present. The overlying squamous epithelium commonly exhibits pseudoepitheliomatous hyperplasia.

When the following tumors are encountered in the salivary gland, the possibility of metastasis should always be considered before accepting them as primary neoplasms: squamous cell carcinoma, clear cell carcinoma, small cell carcinoma, lymphoepithelial carcinoma, and neuroendocrine carcinoma.

Stromal components

Eosinophilic hyaline or basement membrane-like material generally indicates the presence of myoepithelial or basal cell differentiation (Figs 7.14A, 7.41, 7.47, 7.90, 7.92, and 7.115),

Table 7.15 Special cell types as clues to diagnosis in salivary gland tumors

	Oncocytic cells	Squamous cells	Basaloid cells	Spindle cells	Sebaceous cells	Clear cells	Apocrine or apocrine-like cells
Constituting a prominent component	• Warthin tumor • Oncocytoma • Oncocytic carcinoma • Oncocytic cystadenoma	• Warthin tumor or oncocytic neoplasm with squamous metaplasia • Squamous cell carcinoma (primary, metastasis, or invasion from adjacent sites) • Adenosquamous carcinoma • High-grade mucoepidermoid carcinoma • Keratocystoma	• Basal cell adenoma • Basal cell adenocarcinoma • Pleomorphic adenoma (some cases) • Adenoid cystic carcinoma • Lymphadenoma • Basaloid squamous cell carcinoma • Sialoblastoma	• Myoepithelioma • Myoepithelial carcinoma • Salivary gland anlage tumor • Pleomorphic adenoma (some cases) • Various benign and malignant mesenchymal tumors	• Sebaceous adenoma/lymphadenoma • Sebaceous carcinoma/lymphadenocarcinoma	• Clear cell carcinoma • Epithelial-myoepithelial carcinoma • Clear cell oncocytoma • Sebaceous adenoma or adenocarcinoma • Clear cell myoepithelioma or myoepithelial carcinoma • Mucoepidermoid carcinoma, clear cell variant • Metastatic renal cell carcinoma	• Salivary duct carcinoma • Intraductal carcinoma
Present focally	• Many different tumor types, e.g., pleomorphic adenoma, acinic cell carcinoma, mucoepidermoid carcinoma, cystadenocarcinoma, polymorphous low-grade adenocarcinoma • Adenocarcinoma NOS	• Pleomorphic adenoma • Basal cell adenoma or adenocarcinoma (centers of cell islands) • Sebaceous adenoma or adenocarcinoma • Epithelial-myoepithelial carcinoma	• Epithelial-myoepithelial carcinoma • Polymorphous low-grade adenocarcinoma • Canalicular adenoma	• Basal cell adenoma or adenocarcinoma (some cases) • Epithelial-myoepithelial carcinoma (some cases) • Lymphoepithelial carcinoma (some cases)	• Warthin tumor (rare) • Pleomorphic adenoma (rare) • Mucoepidermoid carcinoma (rare) • Adenoid cystic carcinoma (rare)	• Mucoepidermoid carcinoma • Acinic cell carcinoma • Pleomorphic adenoma (rare) • Squamous cell carcinoma (rare) • Adenoid cystic carcinoma (rare) • Polymorphous low grade adenocarcinoma (rare) • Adenocarcinoma NOS (rare)	• Pleomorphic adenoma (rare) • Carcinoma ex pleomorphic adenoma
Non-neoplastic lesion potentially mistaken for neoplasm	• Oncocytic metaplasia • Oncocytosis • Nodular oncocytic hyperplasia	• Necrotizing sialometaplasia • Keratinous cyst	• Lymphoepithelial sialadenitis	• Inflammatory pseudotumor • Nodular fasciitis	–	• Clear cell oncocytic hyperplasia	• Sclerosing polycystic adenosis

NOS, not otherwise specified.

Analytic approach to diagnosis of epithelial tumors of the salivary gland

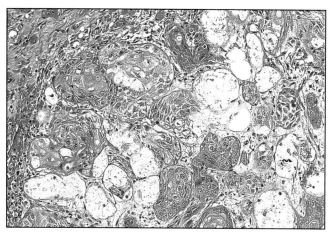

Fig. 7.150 • Necrotizing sialometaplasia of the palate. Some acini have "dropped out," leaving behind rarefied spaces. Other acini are filled up with squamous cells with mildly atypical nuclei. There is often a sprinkling of chronic inflammatory cells. The most important feature distinguishing this lesion from a squamous cell carcinoma is the preserved lobulated pattern (not shown).

with the exception of hyalinizing clear cell carcinoma (which shows pure luminal cell differentiation; Fig. 7.125). In fact, stromal hyaline material can be the first clue to the diagnosis of a salivary gland-type tumor for neoplasms occurring outside the major salivary glands. The hyaline material is found around cell islands, in the pseudoglandular spaces, or interspersed as bands (such as in pleomorphic adenoma and myoepithelioma) or droplets among the tumor cells (such as membranous basal cell adenoma and basal cell adenocarcinoma).

Elastic fibers are often present in abundance in long-standing pleomorphic adenoma, usually in the form of thick or fluffy branching fibers (Fig. 7.23). They can provide a clue to the existence of this tumor in the scenario of carcinoma *ex* pleomorphic adenoma.

Stromal mucin, which appears lightly basophilic in hematoxylin and eosin-stained sections, is such a common finding in salivary gland tumors that it is not of much discriminatory value in tumor classification (Figs 7.21 and 7.110D). Nonetheless, when present in abundance, the most likely candidate is pleomorphic adenoma.

The presence of cartilage in a salivary gland tumor is practically synonymous with a diagnosis of pleomorphic adenoma (Fig. 7.11). Occasionally, it can also be seen in carcinosarcoma and carcinoma *ex* pleomorphic adenoma.

The surgical pathology report on salivary gland tumor excision

The surgical pathology report should provide the following information:[541]

1. Tumor site and diagnosis (and variant if applicable)
2. All prognostic factors, e.g., tumor size, tumor grade, mitotic count, extent of invasion, vascular invasion, nerve invasion, lymph node status
3. Status of resection margins. To avoid distortion of the resection margins, it is preferable to fix the tissue intact before cutting. The resection margins should be appropriately inked

Interpretation of needle or incisional biopsies of salivary gland tumors

A diagnosis of salivary gland tumors from needle or incisional biopsy is sometimes easy. For example, pleomorphic adenoma is readily recognized when the typical chondromyxoid matrix is seen or the characteristic plasmacytoid hyaline cells are present (Fig. 7.20). However, it is not always possible to render a definitive diagnosis; it may even not be possible to tell whether the tumor is benign or malignant. The difficulties stem from the morphologic overlap among the different tumor types, and difficulties in proper assessment of the tumor borders in biopsies. For example, a biopsy showing tubules with dual luminal and abluminal cell differentiation may represent a pleomorphic adenoma, basal cell adenoma, adenoid cystic carcinoma, epithelial-myoepithelial carcinoma, or even adenocarcinoma NOS (Fig. 7.151). In the absence of more definitive diagnostic features, only a descriptive diagnosis of "salivary gland neoplasm" can be made, and complete excision or a larger-size biopsy is required to arrive at a definitive diagnosis.

Fig. 7.151 • Adenoid cystic carcinoma as seen in a needle biopsy of the tongue. In this biopsy, tubules lined by a double layer of luminal–abluminal cells are distributed in a sclerotic stroma. This pattern can be observed in pleomorphic adenoma, basal cell adenoma of the tubular type, and adenoid cystic carcinoma. Invasion of the skeletal muscle fibers (arrows) provides unequivocal support for the interpretation of this tumor as adenoid cystic carcinoma among the differential diagnoses being considered.

1. Kaplan M, Johns M 1993 Malignant neoplasms. In: Cummings C, Fredrickson J, Harker L et al. (eds) Otolaryngology – head and neck surgery, 2nd edn. C V Mosby, St. Louis, p 1043–1078

2. Frommer J 1977 The human accessory parotid gland: its incidence, nature, and significance. Oral Surg Oral Med Oral Pathol 43: 671–676

3. Lin D T, Coppit G L, Burkey B B et al. 2004 Tumors of the accessory lobe of the parotid gland: a 10-year experience. Laryngoscope 114: 1652–1655

4. Harris N 1991 Extranodal lymphoid infiltrates and mucosa-associated lymphoid tissue (MALT). A unifying concept. Am J Surg Pathol 15: 879–884

5. Cleary K R, Batsakis J G 1990 Lymphoepithelial cysts of the parotid region: a new face on an old lesion. Ann Otol Rhnol Laryngol 99:162–164

6. Dardick I 1996 Color atlas/text of salivary gland tumor pathology. Igaku-Shoin, New York

7. Savera A T, Zarbo R J 2004 Defining the role of myoepithelium in salivary gland neoplasia. Adv Anat Pathol 11: 69–85

8. Ihrler S, Zietz C, Sendelhofert A et al. 2002 A morphogenetic concept of salivary duct regeneration and metaplasia. Virchows Arch 440: 519–526

9. Krech R, Zerban H, Bannasch P 1981 Mitochondrial anomalies in renal oncocytes induced in rat by N-nitrosomorpholine. Eur J Cell Biol 25: 331–339

10. Auclair P L, Ellis G L, Gnepp D R et al. 1991 Salivary gland neoplasms: general considerations. In: Ellis G L, Auclair P L, Gnepp D R (eds) Surgical pathology of the salivary glands. Major problems in pathology. W B Saunders, Philadelphia, PA, p 135–164

11. Ellis G L, Auclair P L, Gnepp D R 1991 Surgical pathology of the salivary glands. In: LiVolsi V (ed.) Major problems in pathology. Saunders, Philadelphia, PA

12. Kokemueller H, Swennen G, Brueggemann N et al. 2004 Epithelial malignancies of the salivary glands: clinical experience of a single institution – a review. Int J Oral Maxillofac Surg 33: 423–432

13. Wahlberg P, Anderson H, Biorklund A et al. 2002 Carcinoma of the parotid and submandibular glands – a study of survival in 2465 patients. Oral Oncol 38: 706–713

14. Seifert G, Miehlke A, Haubrich J et al. 1986 Diseases of the salivary glands. Georg Thieme, Stuttgart

15. Lack E E, Upton M P 1988 Histopathologic review of salivary gland tumors in childhood. Arch Otolaryngol Head Neck Surg 114: 898–906

16. da Cruz Perez D E, Pires F R, Alves F A et al. 2004 Salivary gland tumors in children and adolescents: a clinicopathologic and immunohistochemical study of fifty-three cases. Int J Pediatr Otorhinolaryngol 68: 895–902

17. Nagao T, Sugano I, Ishida Y et al. 1998 Basal cell adenocarcinoma of the salivary glands: comparison with basal cell adenoma through assessment of cell proliferation, apoptosis, and expression of p53 and bcl-2. Cancer 82: 439–447

18. Eneroth C M, Hamberger C A 1974 Principles of treatment of different types of parotid tumors. Laryngoscope 84: 1732–1740

19. Maruya S, Kim H W, Weber R S et al. 2004 Gene expression screening of salivary gland neoplasms: molecular markers of potential histogenetic and clinical significance. J Mol Diagn 6: 180–190

20. Francioso F, Carinci F, Tosi L et al. 2002 Identification of differentially expressed genes in human salivary gland tumors by DNA microarrays. Mol Cancer Ther 1: 533–538

21. Frierson H F Jr, El-Naggar A K, Welsh J B et al. 2002 Large scale molecular analysis identifies genes with altered expression in salivary adenoid cystic carcinoma. Am J Pathol 161: 1315–1323

22. Gibbons M D, Manne U, Carroll W R et al. 2001 Molecular differences in mucoepidermoid carcinoma and adenoid cystic carcinoma of the major salivary glands. Laryngoscope 111: 1373–1378

23. Leivo I, Jee K J, Heikinheimo K et al. 2005 Characterization of gene expression in major types of salivary gland carcinomas with epithelial differentiation. Cancer Genet Cytogenet 156: 104–113

24. Seifert G, Donath K 1996 Hybrid tumours of salivary glands. Definition and classification of five rare cases. Eur J Cancer B Oral Oncol 32B: 251–259

25. Nagao T, Sugano I, Ishida Y et al. 2002 Hybrid carcinomas of the salivary glands: report of nine cases with a clinicopathologic, immunohistochemical, and p53 gene alteration analysis. Mod Pathol 15: 724–733

26. Croitoru C M, Suarez P A, Luna M A 1999 Hybrid carcinomas of salivary glands. Report of 4 cases and review of the literature. Arch Pathol Lab Med 123: 698–702

27. Grenko R T, Abendroth C S, Davis A T et al. 1998 Hybrid tumors or salivary gland tumors sharing common differentiation pathways? Reexamining adenoid cystic and epithelial-myoepithelial carcinomas. Oral Surg Oral Med Oral Pathol Oral Radiol Endod 86: 188–195

28. Ruiz-Godoy L M, Mosqueda-Taylor A, Suarez-Roa L et al. 2003 Hybrid tumours of the salivary glands. A report of two cases involving the palate and a review of the literature. Eur Arch Otorhinolaryngol 260: 312–315

29. Chetty R 2000 Intercalated duct hyperplasia: possible relationship to epithelial-myoepithelial carcinoma and hybrid tumours of salivary gland. Histopathology 37: 260–263

30. Zardawi I M 2000 Hybrid carcinoma of the salivary gland. Histopathology 37: 283–284

31. Noguchi S, Aihara T, Yoshino K et al. 1996 Demonstration of monoclonal origin of human parotid gland pleomorphic adenoma. Cancer 77: 431–435

32. Sweeney E C, McDermott M 1996 Pleomorphic adenoma of the bronchus. J Clin Pathol 49: 87–89

33. Badia L, Weir J N, Robinson A C 1996 Heterotopic pleomorphic adenoma of the external nose. J Laryngol Otol 110: 376–378

34. Tyagi S, Abdi U, Tyagi S P et al. Pleomorphic adenoma of skin (chondroid syringoma) involving the eyelid. J Postgrad Med 42: 125–126

35. Kilpatrick S E, Hitchcock M G, Kraus M D et al. Mixed tumors and myoepitheliomas of soft tissue: a clinicopathologic study of 19 cases with a unifying concept. Am J Surg Pathol 21: 13–22

36. Agnantis N J, Maounis N, Priovolou-Papaevangelou M et al. 1992 Pleomorphic adenoma of the human female breast. Pathol Res Pract 188: 235–240; discussion 240–241

37. Hickman R E, Cawson R A, Duffy S W 1984 The prognosis of specific types of salivary gland tumors. Cancer 54: 1620–1654

38. Jackson S R, Roland N J, Clarke R W et al. Recurrent pleomorphic adenoma. J Laryngol Otol 107: 546–549

39. Laskawi R, Schott T, Schroder M 1998 Recurrent pleomorphic adenomas of the parotid gland: clinical evaluation and long-term follow-up. Br J Oral Maxillofac Surg 36: 48–51

40. Henriksson G, Westrin K M, Carlsoo B et al. 1998 Recurrent primary pleomorphic adenomas of salivary gland origin: intrasurgical rupture, histopathologic features, and pseudopodia. Cancer 82: 617–620

41. McGregor A D, Burgoyne M, Tan K C 1988 Recurrent pleomorphic salivary adenoma – the relevance of age at first presentation. Br J Plast Surg 41: 177–181

42. Auclair P L, Ellis G L 1996 Atypical features in salivary gland mixed tumors: their relationship to malignant transformation. Mod Pathol 9: 652–657

43. Lam K H, Wei W I, Ho H C et al. 1990 Whole organ sectioning of mixed parotid tumors. Am J Surg 160: 377–381

44. Lam P W, Chan J K, Sin V C 1997 Nasal pleomorphic adenoma with skeletal muscle differentiation: potential misdiagnosis as rhabdomyosarcoma. Hum Pathol 28: 1299–1302

45. Takeda Y, Satoh M, Nakamura S 2004 Pigmented pleomorphic adenoma, a novel melanin-pigmented benign salivary gland tumor. Virchows Arch 445: 199–202

46. Lee K C, Chan J K, Chong Y W 1992 Ossifying pleomorphic adenoma of the maxillary antrum. J Laryngol Otol 106: 50–52

46a. Haskell H D, Butt K M, Woo S B 2005 Pleomorphic adenoma with extensive lipometaplasia. Report of three cases. Am J Surg Pathol 29: 1389–1393.

47. Chan J K, Tang S K, Tsang W Y et al. 1996 Histologic changes induced by fine-needle aspiration. Adv Anat Pathol 3: 71–90

48. Bilal H, Handra-Luca A, Bertrand J C et al. 2003 p63 is expressed in basal and myoepithelial cells of human normal and tumor salivary gland tissues. J Histochem Cytochem 51: 133–139

49. Vargas H, Sudilovsky D, Kaplan M J et al. 1997 Mixed tumor, polymorphous low grade adenocarcinoma and adenoid cystic carcinoma of the salivary gland: pathogenic implications and differential diagnosis by Ki67 (MIB1), BCL2 and S100 immunohistochemistry. Appl Immunohistochem 5: 8–16

50. Skalova A, Simpson R H, Lehtonen H et al. 1997 Assessment of proliferative activity using the MIB1 antibody help to distinguish polymorphous low grade adenocarcinoma from adenoid cystic carcinoma of salivary glands. Pathol Res Pract 193: 695–703

51. Eveson J W, Kusafuka K, Stenman G et al. 2005 Pleomorphic adenoma. In: Barnes L, Eveson J W, Reichart P et al. (eds) World Health Organization classification of tumours. Pathology and genetics: head and neck tumours. IARC, Lyon, p 254–258

52. Bullerdiek J, Wobst G, Meyer-Bolte K et al. 1993 Cytogenetic subtyping of 220 salivary gland pleomorphic adenomas: correlation to occurrence, histological subtype, and in vitro cellular behavior. Cancer Genet Cytogenet 65: 27–31

53. Voz M L, Agten N S, Van de Ven W J et al. 2000 PLAG1, the main translocation target in pleomorphic adenoma of the salivary glands, is a positive regulator of IGF-II. Cancer Res 60: 106–113

54. Geurts J M, Schoenmakers E F, Roijer E et al. 1998 Identification of NFIB as recurrent translocation partner gene of HMGIC in pleomorphic adenomas. Oncogene 16: 865–872

55. Czader M, Eberhart C G, Bhatti N et al. 2000 Metastasizing mixed tumor of the parotid: initial presentation as a solitary kidney tumor and ultimate carcinomatous transformation at the primary site. Am J Surg Pathol 24: 1159–1164

56. Wenig B M, Hitchcock C L, Ellis G L et al. 1992 Metastasizing mixed tumor of salivary glands. a clinicopathologic and flow cytometric analysis. Am J Surg Pathol 16: 845–858

57. Qureshi A A, Gitelis S, Templeton A A et al. 1994 "Benign" metastasizing pleomorphic adenoma. A case report and review of literature. Clin Orthop Rel Res 308: 192–198

58. Sampson B A, Jarcho J A, Winters G L 1998 Metastasizing mixed tumor of the parotid gland: a rare tumor with unusually rapid progression in a cardiac transplant patient. Mod Pathol 11: 1142–1145

59. Fujimura M, Sugawara T, Seki H et al. 1997 Carcinomatous change in the cranial metastasis from a metastasizing mixed tumor of the salivary gland – case report. Neurol Med Chir (Tokyo) 37: 546–550

60. Hoorweg J J, Hilgers F J, Keus R B et al. 1998 Metastasizing pleomorphic adenoma: a report of three cases. Eur J Surg Oncol 24: 452–455

61. Eneroth C M, Zetterberg A 1974 Malignancy in pleomorphic adenoma. A clinical and microspectrophotometric study. Acta Otolaryngol (Stockh) 77: 426–432

62. Altemani A, Martins M T, Freitas L et al. 2005 Carcinoma ex pleomorphic adenoma (CXPA): immunoprofile of the cells involved in carcinomatous progression. Histopathology 46: 635–641

63. Lewis J E, Olsen K D, Sebo T J 2001 Carcinoma ex pleomorphic adenoma: pathologic analysis of 73 cases. Hum Pathol 32: 596–604

64. Di Palma S, Skalova A, Vanieek T et al. 2005 Non-invasive (intracapsular) carcinoma ex pleomorphic adenoma: recognition of focal carcinoma by HER-2/neu and MIB1 immunohistochemistry. Histopathology 46: 144–152

65. Ellis G L, Auclair P L 1996 Tumors of the salivary glands. Atlas of tumor pathology, 3rd series, fascicle 17. Armed Forces Institute of Pathology, Washington, DC

66. Felix A, Rosa-Santos J, Mendonca M E et al. 2002 Intracapsular carcinoma ex pleomorphic adenoma. Report of a case with unusual metastatic behaviour. Oral Oncol 38: 107–110

67. Tortoledo M E, Luna M A, Batsakis J G 1984 Carcinomas ex pleomorphic adenoma and malignant mixed tumors. Histomorphologic indexes. Arch Otolaryngol 110: 172–176

68. Brandwein M, Huvos A G, Dardick I et al. 1996 Noninvasive and minimally invasive carcinoma ex mixed tumor: a clinicopathologic and ploidy study of 12 patients with major salivary tumors of low (or no?) malignant potential. Oral Surg Oral Med Oral Pathol Oral Radiol Endod 81: 655–664

69. Roijer E, Nordkvist A, Strom A K et al. 2002 Translocation, deletion/amplification, and expression of HMGIC and MDM2 in a carcinoma ex pleomorphic adenoma. Am J Pathol 160: 433–440

70. Sugano S, Mukai K, Tsuda H et al. 1992 Immunohistochemical study of c-erbB-2 oncoprotein overexpression in human major salivary gland carcinoma: an indicator of aggressiveness. Laryngoscope 102: 923–927

71. Muller S, Vigneswaran N, Gansler T et al. 1994 c-erbB-2 oncoprotein expression and amplification in pleomorphic adenoma and carcinoma ex pleomorphic adenoma: relationship to prognosis. Mod Pathol 7: 628–632

72. Rosa J C, Fonseca I, Felix A et al. 1996 Immunohistochemical study of c-erbB-2 expression in carcinoma ex-pleomorphic adenoma. Histopathology 28: 247–252

73. Nordkvist A, Roijer E, Bang G et al. 2000 Expression and mutation patterns of p53 in benign and malignant salivary gland tumors. Int J Oncol 16: 477–483

74. Karja V J, Syrjanen K J, Kurvinen A K et al. 1997 Expression and mutations of p53 in salivary gland tumours. J Oral Pathol Med 1997 26: 217–223

75. Li X, Tsuji T, Wen S et al. 1997 Detection of numeric abnormalities of chromosome 17 and p53 deletions by fluorescence in situ hybridization in pleomorphic adenomas and carcinomas in pleomorphic adenoma. Correlation with p53 expression. Cancer 79: 2314–2319

76. Deguchi H, Hamano H, Hayashi Y 1993 c-myc, ras p21 and p53 expression in pleomorphic adenoma and its malignant form of the human salivary glands. Acta Pathol Jpn 43: 413–422

77. Coleman H, Altini M 1999 Intravascular tumour in intra-oral pleomorphic adenomas: a diagnostic and therapeutic dilemma. Histopathology 35: 439–444

78. Altini M, Coleman H, Kienle F 1997 Intra-vascular tumour in pleomorphic adenomas – a report of four cases. Histopathology 31: 55–59

79. Talmi Y, Halpern M, Finkelstein Y et al. 1990 View from beneath: pathology in focus. True malignant mixed tumour of the parotid gland. J Larngol Otol 104: 360–361

80. Kwon M Y, Gu M 2001 True malignant mixed tumor (carcinosarcoma) of parotid gland with unusual mesenchymal component. A case report and review of the literature. Arch Pathol Lab Med 125: 812–815

81. Gnepp D R 1993 Malignant mixed tumors of the salivary glands: a review. Pathol Annu 28: 279–328

82. Batsakis J G, Luna M A, el-Naggar A K 1991 Basaloid monomorphic adenomas. Ann Otol Rhinol Laryngol 100: 687–690

83. Nagao T, Sugano I, Ishida Y et al. 1997 Carcinoma in basal cell adenoma of the parotid gland. Pathol Res Pract 193: 171–178

84. Gallimore A P, Spraggs P D, Allen J P et al. Basaloid carcinomas of salivary glands. Histopathology 24: 139–144

85. Dardick I, Daley T D, van Nostrand A W 1986 Basal cell adenoma with myoepithelial cell-derived "stroma": a new major salivary gland tumor entity. Head Neck Surg 8: 257–267

86. Biggs P J, Wooster R, Ford D et al. 1995 Familial cylindromatosis (turban tumour syndrome) gene localised to chromosome 16q12-q13: evidence for its role as a tumour suppressor gene. Nat Genet 11: 441–443

87. Choi H R, Batsakis J G, Callender D L et al. 2002 Molecular analysis of chromosome 16q regions in dermal analogue tumors of salivary glands: a genetic link to dermal cylindroma? Am J Surg Pathol 26: 778–783

88. Edwards P C, Bhuiya T, Kelsch R D 2004 Assessment of p63 expression in the salivary gland neoplasms adenoid cystic carcinoma, polymorphous low-grade adenocarcinoma, and basal cell and canalicular adenomas. Oral Surg Oral Med Oral Pathol Oral Radiol Endod 97: 613–619

89. Weber A, Langhanki L, Schutz A et al. 2002 Expression profiles of p53, p63, and p73 in benign salivary gland tumors. Virchows Arch 441: 428–436

90. Seifert G, Sobin L H 1991 Histological typing of salivary gland tumours. World Health Organization international histological classification of tumours, 2nd edn. Springer-Verlag, New York

91. Muller S, Barnes L 1996 Basal cell adenocarcinoma of the salivary glands. Report of seven cases and review of the literature. Cancer 78: 2471–2477

92. Fonseca I, Soares J 1996 Basal cell adenocarcinoma of minor salivary and seromucous glands of the head and neck region. Semin Diagn Pathol 13: 128–137

93. Jayakrishnan A, Elmalah I, Hussain K et al. 2003 Basal cell adenocarcinoma in minor salivary glands. Histopathology 42: 610–614

94. Luna M A, Batsakis J G, Tortoledo M E et al. 1989 Carcinomas ex monomorphic adenoma of salivary glands. J Laryngol Otol 103: 756–759

95. Ellis G L, Wiscovitch J G 1990 Basal cell adenocarcinomas of the major salivary glands. Oral Surg Oral Med Oral Pathol 69: 461–469

96. Atula T, Klemi P J, Donath K et al. 1993 Basal cell adenocarcinoma of the parotid gland: a case report and review of the literature. J Laryngol Otol 107: 862–864

97. Ellis G L, Auclair P L 1991 Basal cell adenocarcinoma. In: Ellis G L, Auclair P L, Gnepp D R (eds): Surgical pathology of the salivary glands. W B Saunders, Philadelphia, PA, p 585–661

98. Murty G, Welch A, Soames JV 1990 Basal cell adenocarcinoma of the parotid gland. J Laryngol Otol 104: 150–151

99. Williams S B, Ellis G L, Auclair P L 1993 Immunohistochemical analysis of basal cell adenocarcinoma. Oral Surg Oral Med Oral Pathol 75: 64–69

100. Quddus M R, Henley J D, Affify A M et al. 1999 Basal cell adenocarcinoma of the salivary gland: an ultrastructural and immunohistochemical study. Oral Surg Oral Med Oral Pathol Oral Radiol Endod 87: 485–492

101. Dardick I, Thomas M J, van Nostrand A W 1989 Myoepithelioma – new concepts of histology and classifiation: a light and electron micropic study. Ultrastruct Pathol 13: 187–224

102. Dardick I, Cavell S, Boivin M et al. 1989 Salivary gland myoepithelioma variants. Histological, ultrastructural, and immunocytological features. Virchows Arch A Pathol Anat Histopathol 416: 25–42

103. Dardick I 1995 Myoepithelioma: definitions and diagnostic criteria. Ultrastruct Pathol 19: 335–345

104. Simpson R H, Jones H, Beasley P 1995 Benign myoepithelioma of the salivary glands: a true entity? Histopathology 27: 1–9

105. Hornick J L, Fletcher C D 2003 Myoepithelial tumors of soft tissue: a clinicopathologic and immunohistochemical study of 101 cases with evaluation of prognostic parameters. Am J Surg Pathol 27: 1183–1196

106. Alos L, Cardesa A, Bombi J et al. 1996 Myoepithelial tumors of salivary glands: a clinicopathologic, immunohistochemical, ultrastructural, and flow-cytometric study. Semin Diagn Pathol 13: 138–147

107. Skalova A, Leivo I, Michal M et al. 1992 Analysis of collagen isotypes in crystalloid structures of salivary gland tumors. Hum Pathol 23: 748–754

108. Franquemont D W, Mills S E 1993 Plasmacytoid monomorphic adenoma of salivary glands. Absence of myogenous differentiation and comparison to spindle cell myoepithelioma. Am J Surg Pathol 17: 146–153

109. Nagao T, Sugano I, Ishida Y et al. 1998 Salivary gland malignant myoepithelioma: a clinicopathologic and immunohistochemical study of ten cases. Cancer 83: 1292–1299

110. Savera A T, Gown A M, Zarbo R J 1997 Immunolocalization of three novel smooth muscle-specific proteins in salivary gland pleomorphic adenoma: assessment of the morphogenetic role of myoepithelium. Mod Pathol 10: 1093–1100

111. Savera A T, Sloman A, Huvos A G et al. 2000 Myoepithelial carcinoma of the salivary glands: a clinicopathologic study of 25 patients. Am J Surg Pathol 24: 761–774

112. Di Palma S, Guzzo M 1993 Malignant myoepithelioma of salivary glands: clinicopathological features of ten cases. Virchows Arch A Pathol Anat Histopathol 423: 389–396

113. Nagao K, Matsuzaki O, Saiga H et al. 1981 Histopathologic studies on carcinoma in pleomorphic adenoma of the parotid gland. Cancer 48: 113–121

114. Tavassoli F A 1991 Myoepithelial lesions of the breast. Myoepitheliosis, adenomyoepithelioma, and myoepithelial carcinoma. Am J Surg Pathol 15: 554–568

115. Lakhani S R, O'Hare M J, Monaghan P et al. 1995 Malignant myoepithelioma (myoepithelial carcinoma) of the breast: a detailed cytokeratin study. J Clin Pathol 48: 164–167

116. Ogawa I, Nishida T, Miyauchi M et al. 2003 Dedifferentiated malignant myoepithelioma of the parotid gland. Pathol Int 53: 704–709

117. Thompson L D, Wenig B M, Ellis G L 1996 Oncocytomas of the submandibular gland. A series of 22 cases and a review of the literature. Cancer 78: 2281–2287

118. Pecorella I, Garner A 1997 Ostensible oncocytoma of accessory lacrimal glands. Histopathology 30: 264–270

119. Takeda Y 1986 Diffuse oncocytosis of the parotid gland. Int J Oral Maxillofac Surg 15: 765–768

120. Palmer T J, Gleeson M J, Eveson J W et al. 1990 Oncocytic adenomas and oncocytic hyperplasia of salivary glands: a clinicopathological study of 26 cases. Histopathology 16: 487–493

121. Hartwick R W, Batsakis J G 1990 Non-Warthin's tumor oncocytic lesions. Ann Otol Rhinol Laryngol 99: 674–677

122. Capone R B, Ha P K, Westra W H et al. 2002 Oncocytic neoplasms of the parotid gland: a 16-year institutional review. Otolaryngol Head Neck Surg 126: 657–662

123. Brandwein M S, Huvos A G 1991 Oncocytic tumors of major salivary glands. A study of 68 cases with follow-up of 44 patients. Am J Surg Pathol 15: 514–528

124. Shintaku M, Honda T 1997 Identification of oncocytic lesions of salivary glands by anti-mitochondrial immunohistochemistry. Histopathology 31: 408–411

125. Prasad A R, Savera A T, Regezi J A et al. 1999 Immunohistochemical demonstration of myoepithelial cell participation in salivary gland basal cell and canalicular adenomas. Mod Pathol 12: 130A (abstract)

126. Gilcrease M Z, Nelson F S, Guzman-Paz M 1998 Tyrosine-rich crystals associated with oncocytic salivary gland neoplasms. Arch Pathol Lab Med 122: 644–649

127. Ellis G L 1988 "Clear cell" oncocytoma of salivary gland. Hum Pathol 19: 862–867

128. Ellis G L 1998 Clear cell neoplasms in salivary glands: clearly a diagnostic challenge. Ann Diagn Pathol 2: 61–78

129. Maiorano E, Altini M, Favia G 1997 Clear cell tumors of the salivary glands, jaws, and oral mucosa. Semin Diagn Pathol 14: 203–212

130. Huvos A G 2005 Oncocytoma. In: Barnes L, Eveson J W, Reichart P et al. (eds) World Health Organization classification of tumours. Pathology and genetics: head and neck tumours. IARC, Lyon, France, p 273

131. Perzin K H 1982 A systematic approach to the diagnosis of salivary gland tumors. In: Fenoglio C M, Wolff M (eds) Progress in surgical pathology. Masson, New York, vol 4, p 137–180

132. Goode R K, Corio R L 1988 Oncocytic adenocarcinoma of salivary glands. Oral Surg Oral Med Oral Pathol 65: 61–66

133. Batsakis J 1979 Tumors of the head and neck. Clinical and pathological considerations, 2nd edn. Williams & Wilkins, Baltimore

134. Sugimoto T, Wakizono S, Uemura T et al. 1993 Malignant oncocytoma of the parotid gland: a case with an immunohistochemical and ultrastructural study. J Laryngol Otol 107: 69–74

135. Rousseau A, Mock D, Dover D G et al. 1999 Multiple canalicular adenomas: a case report and review of the literature. Oral Surg Oral Med Oral Pathol 57: 181–188

136. Suarez P, Hammong H L, Luna M A et al. 1998 Palatal canalicular adenoma: report of 12 cases and review of the literature. Ann Diagn Pathol 2: 224–228

137. Smullin S E, Fielding A F, Sausarla S M et al. 2004 Canalicular adenoma of the palate: case report and literature review. Oral Surg Oral Radiol Endod 98: 32–36

138. Batsakis J 1991 Oral monomorphic adenomas. Ann Otol Rhinol Laryngol 100: 348–350

139. McMillan M D, Smith C J, Smillie A C 1993 Canalicular adenoma: report of five cases with ultrastructural observations. J Oral Pathol Med 22: 368–373

140. Zarbo R J, Prasad A R, Regezi J A et al. 2000 Salivary gland basal cell and canalicular adenomas: immunohistochemical demonstration of myoepithelial cell participation and morphogenetic considerations. Arch Pathol Lab Med 124: 401–405

141. Arida M, Barnes E L, Hunt J L 2005 Molecular assessment of allelic loss in Warthin tumors. Mod Pathol 18: 964–968

142. Honda K, Kashuma K, Daa T et al. 2000 Clonal analysis of the epithelial component of Warthin's tumor. Hum Pathol 31: 1377–1380

143. Teymoortash A, Werner J A 2005 Tissue that has lost its track: Warthin's tumor. Virchows Arch 446: 585–588

144. Eneroth C 1971 Salivary gland tumors in the parotid gland, submandibular gland, and the palate region. Cancer 27: 1415–1418

145. Eveson J W, Cawson R A 1989 Infarcted ('infected') adenolymphomas. A clinicopathological study of 20 cases. Clin Otolaryngol 14: 205–210

146. Spiro R H 1986 Salivary neoplasms: overview of a 35-year experience with 2807 patients. Head Neck Surg 8: 177–184

147. Kotwell C 1992 Smoking as an etiologic factor in the development of Warthin's tumor of the parotid gland. Am J Surg 164: 646–647

148. Monk J J, Church J 1992 Warthin's tumor. A high incidence and no sex predominance on central Pennsylvania. Arch Otolaryngol Head Neck Surg 118: 477–478

149. Yoo G H, Eisele D W, Askin F B et al. 1994 Warthin's tumor: a 40-year experience at the Johns Hopkins Hospital. Laryngoscope 104: 799–803

150. Saku T, Hayashi Y, Takahara O et al. 1997 Salivary gland tumors among atomic bomb survivors, 1950–1987. Cancer 79: 1465–1475

151. Santucci M, Gallo O, Calzolari A et al. 1993 Detection of Epstein–Barr viral genome in tumor cells of Warthin's tumor of parotid gland. Am J Clin Pathol 100: 662–665

152. Chan J K, Yip T T, Tsang W Y et al. 1994 Specific association of Epstein–Barr virus with lymphoepithelial carcinoma among tumors and tumorlike lesions of the salivary gland. Arch Pathol Lab Med 118: 994–997

153. Ogata T, Hongfang Y, Kayano T et al. 1997 No significant role of Epstein–Barr virus in the tumorigenesis of Warthin tumor. J Med Dent Sci 44: 45–52

154. Chapnik J 1983 The controversy of Warthin's tumor. Laryngoscope 93: 695–716

155. Maiorano E, Lo Muzio L, Favia G et al. 2002 Warthin's tumour: a study of 78 cases with emphasis on bilaterality, multifocality and association with other malignancies. Oral Oncol 38: 35–40

156. Gnepp D R 2001 Diagnostic surgical pathology of the head and neck. Saunders, Philadelphia

157. Lam K H, Ho H C, Ho C M et al. 1994 Multifocal nature of adenolymphoma of the parotid. Br J Surg 81: 1612–1614

158. Shikhani A H, Shikhani L T, Kuhajda F P et al. 1993 Warthin's tumor-associated neoplasms: report of two cases and review of the literature. Ear Nose Throat J 72: 264–269, 272–273

159. Lefor A T, Ord R A 1993 Multiple synchronous bilateral Warthin's tumors of the parotid glands with pleomorphic adenoma. Case report and review of the literature. Oral Surg Oral Med Oral Pathol 76: 319–324

160. Dykun R, Deitel M, Borowy Z 1980 Treatment of parotid neoplasms. Can J Surg 23: 14–19

161. Ebbs S, Webb A 1986 Adenolymphoma of the parotid: aetiology, diagnosis and treatment. Br J Surg 73: 627–630

162. Eveson J, Cawson R 1985 Salivary gland tumors. A review of 2410 cases with particular reference to histological types, site, age and sex distribution. J Pathol 146: 51–58

163. Heller K S, Attie J N 1988 Treatment of Warthin's tumor by enucleation. Am J Surg 156: 294–296

164. Seifert G, Bull H G, Donath K 1980 Histologic subclassification of the cystadenolymphoma of the parotid gland. Analysis of 275 cases. Virchows Arch [Pathol Anat] 388: 13–38

165. David R, Buchner A 1978 Corpora amylacea in adenolymphoma (Warthin's tumor). Am J Clin Pathol 69: 173–175

166. Taxy J B 1992 Necrotizing squamous/mucinous metaplasia in oncocytic salivary gland tumors. A potential diagnostic problem. Am J Clin Pathol 97: 40–45

167. Nagao T, Sugano I, Ishida Y et al. 1998 Mucoepidermoid carcinoma arising in Warthin's tumor of the parotid gland: report of two cases with histopathological, ultrastructural and immunohistochemical studies. Histopathology 33: 379–386

168. Kessler E, Koznizky I L, Schinderl J 1977 Malignant Warthin's tumor. Oral Surg Oral Med Oral Pathol 43: 111–115

169. Therkildsen M, Christensen N, Andersen L et al. 1992 Malignant Warthin's tumor: a case study. Histopathology 21: 167–171

170. Bolat F, Kayaselcuk F, Erkan A N et al. 2004 Epidermoid carcinoma arising in Warthin's tumor. Pathol Oncol Res 10: 240–242

171. Foschini M P, Malvi D, Betts C M 2005 Oncocytic carcinoma arising in Warthin tumour. Virchows Arch 446: 88–90

172. Fornelli A, Eusebi V, Pasquinelli G et al. 2001 Merkel cell carcinoma of the parotid gland associated with Warthin tumour: report of two cases. Histopathology 39: 342–346

173. Medeiros L J, Rizzi R, Lardelli P et al. 1990 Malignant lymphoma involving a Warthin's tumor: a case with immunophenotypic and gene rearrangement analysis. Hum Pathol 21: 974–977

174. Bunker M L, Locker J 1989 Warthin's tumor with malignant lymphoma. DNA analysis of paraffin-embedded tissue. Am J Clin Pathol 91: 341–344

175. Melato M, Falconieri G, Fanin R et al. 1986 Hodgkin's disease occurring in a Warthin's tumor: first case report. Pathol Res Pract 181: 615–620

176. Park C K, Manning J T Jr, Battifora H et al. 2000 Follicle center lymphoma and Warthin tumor involving the same anatomic site. Report of two cases and review of the literature. Am J Clin Pathol 113: 113–119

177. Gnepp D R 1983 Sebaceous neoplasms of salivary gland origin: a review. Pathol Annu 18: 71–102

178. Gnepp D R, Brannon R 1984 Sebaceous neoplasms of salivary gland origin. Report of 21 cases. Cancer 53: 2155–2170

179. Ellis G L, Auclair P L, Gnepp D R et al. 1991 Other malignant epithelial neoplasms. In: Ellis G L, Auclair P L, Gnepp D R (eds) Surgical pathology of the salivary glands. W B Saunders, Philadelphia, PA, p 455–488

180. Linhartova A 1974 Sebaceous glands in salivary gland tissue. Arch Pathol 98: 320–324

181. Auclair P L, Ellis G L, Gnepp D R 1991 Other benign epithelial neoplasms. In Ellis G L, Auclair P L, Gnepp D R (eds) Surgical pathology of the salivary glands. Major problems in pathology. Saunders, Philadelphia, PA, p 252–268

182. Michal M, Skalova A, Mukensnabl P 2000 Micropapillary carcinoma of the parotid gland arising in mucinous cystadenoma. Virchows Arch 437: 465–468

183. Foss R D, Ellis G L, Auclair P L 1996 Salivary gland cystadenocarcinomas. A clinicopathologic study of 57 cases. Am J Surg Pathol 20: 1440–1447

184. Brandwein-Genster M, Gnepp D R 2005 Low-grade cribriform cystadenocarcinoma. In: Barnes L, Eveson J W, Reichart P et al. (eds) World Health Organization classification of tumours. Pathology and genetics: head and neck tumours. IARC, Lyon, France, p 241

185. Brannon R B, Sciubba J J, Giulani M 2001 Ductal papillomas of salivary gland origin: a report of 19 cases and a review of the literature. Oral Surg Oral Med Oral Pathol Oral Radiol Endod 92: 68–77

186. Shimoda M, Kameyama K, Morinaga S et al. 2004 Malignant transformation of sialadenoma papilliferum of the palate: a case report. Virchows Arch 445: 641–646

187. Nagao T, Sugano I, Matsuzaki O et al. 2000 Intraductal papillary tumors of the major salivary glands. Case reports of benign and malignant variants. Arch Pathol Lab Med 124: 291–295

188. Seifert G, Donath K, Jautzke G 1999 Unusual choristoma of the parotid gland in a girl. A possible trichoadenoma. Virchows Arch 434: 355–359

189. Nagao T, Serizawa H, Iwaya K et al. 2002 Keratocystoma of the parotid gland: a report of two cases of an unusual pathologic entity. Mod Pathol 15: 1005–1010

190. Dehner L P, Valbuena L, Perez-Atayde A et al. 1994 Salivary gland anlage tumor ("congenital pleomorphic adenoma"). A clinicopathologic, immunohistochemical and ultrastructural study of nine cases. Am J Surg Pathol 18: 25–36

191. Buchino J 1995 Salivary gland anlage tumor: a newly recognized clinicopathologic entity of uncertain histogenesis. Adv Anat Pathol 2: 94–98

192. Cohen E G, Yoder M, Thomas R M et al. 2003 Congenital salivary gland anlage tumor of the nasopharynx. Pediatrics 112: e66–e69

193. Har-El G, Zirkin H Y, Tovi F et al. 1985 Congenital pleomorphic adenoma of the nasopharynx (report of a case). J Laryngol Otol 99: 1281–1287

194. Gnepp D R 2003 Sclerosing polycystic adenosis of the salivary gland: a lesion that may be associated with dysplasia and carcinoma in situ. Adv Anat Pathol 10: 218–222

195. Smith B C, Ellis G L, Slater L J et al. 1996 Sclerosing polycystic adenosis of major salivary glands. A clinicopathologic analysis of nine cases. Am J Surg Pathol 20: 161–170

196. Batsakis J G 1996 Sclerosing polycystic adenosis: newly recognized salivary gland lesion – a form of chronic sialadenitis. Adv Anat Pathol 3: 298–304

197. Donath K, Seifert G 1997 [Sclerosing polycystic sialadenopathy. A rare non-tumorous disease.] Pathologe 18: 368–373

198. Kabani S, Gallagher G 2002 Sclerosing polycystic adenosis (SPCA) of minor salivary glands. Oral Surg Oral Med Oral Pathol Radiol Endod 94: 187

199. Skalova A, Michal M, Simpson R H W et al. 2002 Sclerosing polycystic adenosis of parotid gland with dysplasia and ductal carcinoma in situ. Report of three cases with immunohistochemical and ultrastructural examination. Virchows Arch 440: 29–35

199a. Gnepp D R, Wang L J, Brandwein-Gensler M et al. 2006 Sclerosing polycystic adenosis of the salivary gland: a report of 16 cases. Am J Surg Pathol 30: 154–164

200. Batsakis J G, Bruner J M, Luna M A 1988 Polycystic (dysgenetic) disease of the parotid glands. Arch Otolaryngol Head Neck Surg 114: 1146–1148

201. Dobson C M, Ellis H A 1987 Polycystic disease of the parotid glands: case report of a rare entity and review of the literature. Histopathology 11: 953–961

202. Seifert G, Thomsen S, Donath K 1981 Bilateral dysgenetic polycystic parotid glands. Morphological analysis and differential diagnosis of a rare disease of the salivary glands. Virchows Arch [Pathol Anat] 390: 273–288

203. Auclair P L 1994 Tumor-associated lymphoid proliferation in the parotid gland. A potential diagnostic pitfall. Oral Surg Oral Med Oral Pathol 77: 19–26

204. Ma J, Chan J K, Chow C W et al. 2002 Lymphadenoma: a report of three cases of an uncommon salivary gland neoplasm. Histopathology 41: 342–350

205. Yau K C, Tsang W Y, Chan J K 1997 Lipoadenoma of the parotid gland with probable striated duct differentiation. Mod Pathol 10: 242–246

206. Hirokawa M, Shimizu M, Manabe T et al. 1998 Oncocytic lipoadenoma of the submandibular gland. Hum Pathol 29: 410–412

207. Hornigold R, Morgan P R, Pearce A et al. 2005 Congenital sialolipoma of the parotid gland: first reported case and review of the literature. Int J Pediatr Otorhinolaryngol 69: 429–434

208. Nagao T, Sugano I, Ishida Y et al. 2001 Sialolipoma: a report of seven cases of a new variant of salivary gland lipoma. Histopathology 38: 30–36

209. Loy T, McLaughlin R, Odom L et al. 1989 Mucoepidermoid carcinoma of the parotid as a second malignant neoplasm in children. Cancer 64: 2174–2177

210. Modan B, Chetrit A, Alfandary E et al. 1998 Increased risk of salivary gland tumors after low-dose irradiation. Laryngoscope 108: 1095–1097

211. Nonaka D, Klimstra D, Rosai J 2004 Thymic mucoepidermoid carcinomas: a clinicopathologic study of 10 cases and review of the literature. Am J Surg Pathol 28: 1526–1531

212. Shilo K, Foss R D, Franks T J et al. 2005 Pulmonary mucoepidermoid carcinoma with prominent tumor-associated lymphoid proliferation. Am J Surg Pathol 29: 407–411

213. Riedlinger W F, Hurley M Y, Dehner L P et al. 2005 Mucoepidermoid carcinoma of the skin: a distinct entity from adenosquamous carcinoma: a case study with a review of the literature. Am J Surg Pathol 29: 131–135

214. Simpson R J, Hoang K G, Hyams V J et al. 1988 Mucoepidermoid carcinoma of the maxillary sinus. Otolaryngol Head Neck Surg 99: 419–423

215. Pia-Foschini M, Reis-Filho J S, Eusebi V et al. 2003 Salivary gland-like tumours of the breast: surgical and molecular pathology. J Clin Pathol 56: 497–506

216. Kuo T, Tsang N M 2001 Salivary gland type nasopharyngeal carcinoma: a histologic, immunohistochemical, and Epstein–Barr virus study of 15 cases including a psammomatous mucoepidermoid carcinoma. Am J Surg Pathol 25: 80–86

217. Sekine J, Anami M, Fujita S et al. 2005 A case of mucoepidermoid carcinoma with melanin pigmentation manifested in the palate. Virchows Arch 446: 460–462

218. Donath K, Seifert G, Roser K 1997 The spectrum of giant cells in tumours of the salivary glands: an analysis of 11 cases. J Oral Pathol Med 26: 431–436

219. Ross D, Huaman J, Barsky S 1992 A study of the heterogeneity of the mucoepidermoid tumor and the implication for future therapies. Arch Otol Head Neck Surg 118: 1172–1178

220. Jahan-Parwar B, Huberman R M, Donovan D T et al. 1999 Oncocytic mucoepidermoid carcinoma of the salivary glands. Am J Surg Pathol 23: 523–529

221. Brannon R B, Willard C C 2003 Oncocytic mucoepidermoid carcinoma of parotid gland origin. Oral Surg Oral Med Oral Pathol Oral Radiol Endod 96: 727–733

222. Chan J K, Saw D 1987 Sclerosing mucoepidermoid tumour of the parotid gland: report of a case. Histopathology 11: 203–207

223. Batsakis J G, Luna M A 1990 Histopathologic grading of salivary gland neoplasms: I. Mucoepidermoid carcinomas. Ann Otol Rhinol Laryngol 99: 835–838

224. Muller S, Barnes L, Goodurn W J Jr 1997 Sclerosing mucoepidermoid carcinoma of the parotid. Oral Surg Oral Med Oral Pathol Oral Radiol Endod 83: 685–690

225. Fadare O, Hileeto D, Gruddin Y L et al. 2004 Sclerosing mucoepidermoid carcinoma of the parotid gland. Arch Pathol Lab Med 128: 1046–1049

226. Urano M, Abe M, Horibe Y et al. 2002 Sclerosing mucoepidermoid carcinoma with eosinophilia of the salivary glands. Pathol Res Pract 198: 305–310

227. Baloch Z W, Solomon A C, LiVolsi V A 2000 Primary mucoepidermoid carcinoma and sclerosing mucoepidermoid carcinoma with eosinophilia of the thyroid gland: a report of nine cases. Mod Pathol 13: 802–807

228. Prasad A R, Savera A T, Gown A M et al. 1999 The myoepithelial immunophenotype in 135 benign and malignant salivary gland tumors other than pleomorphic adenoma. Arch Pathol Lab Med 123: 801–806

229. Nikitakis N G, Tosios K I, Papanikolaou V S et al. 2004 Immunohistochemical expression of cytokeratins 7 and 20 in malignant salivary gland tumors. Mod Pathol 17: 407–415

230. Nordkvist A, Gustafsson H, Juberg-Ode M et al. 1994 Recurrent rearrangements of 11q14-22 in mucoepidermoid carcinoma. Cancer Genet Cytogenet 74: 77–83

231. Tonon G, Modi S, Wu L et al. 2003 t(11;19)(q21;p13) translocation in mucoepidermoid carcinoma creates a novel fusion product that disrupts a Notch signaling pathway. Nat Genet 33: 208–213

232. Martins C, Cavaco B, Tonon G et al. 2004 A study of MECT1-MAML2 in mucoepidermoid carcinoma and Warthin's tumor of salivary glands. J Mol Diagn 6: 205–210

233. Bullerdiek J, Haubrich J, Meyer K et al. 1988 Translocation t(11;19)(q21;p13.1) as the sole chromosome abnormality in a cystadenolymphoma (Warthin's tumor) of the parotid gland. Cancer Genet Cytogenet 35: 129–132

234. Mark J, Dahlenfors R, Stenman G et al. 1989 A human adenolymphoma showing the chromosomal aberrations del (7)(p12p14-15) and t(11;19)(q21;p12-13). Anticancer Res 9: 1565–1566

235. Evans H L 1984 Mucoepidermoid carcinoma of salivary glands: a study of 69 cases with special attention to histologic grading. Am J Clin Pathol 81: 696–701

236. Hicks M J, el-Naggar A K, Flaitz C M et al. 1995 Histocytologic grading of mucoepidermoid carcinoma of major salivary glands in prognosis and survival: a clinicopathologic and flow cytometric investigation. Head Neck 17: 89–95

237. Auclair P L, Goode R K, Ellis G L 1992 Mucoepidermoid carcinoma of intraoral salivary glands. Evaluation and application of grading criteria in 143 cases. Cancer 69: 2021–2030

238. Goode R K, Auclair P L, Ellis G L 1998 Mucoepidermoid carcinoma of the major salivary glands: clinical and histopathologic analysis of 234 cases with evaluation of grading criteria. Cancer 82: 1217–1224

239. Fonseca I, Clode A L, Soares J 1993 Mucoepidermoid carcinoma of major and minor salivary glands, a survey of 43 cases with study of prognostic indicators. Int J Surg Pathol 1: 3–12

240. Jensen O J, Poulsen T, Schiodt T 1988 Mucoepidermoid tumors of salivary glands. A long term follow-up study. APMIS 96: 421–427

241. Eversole L R, Rovin S, Sabes W R 1972 Mucoepidermoid carcinoma of minor salivary glands: report of 17 cases with follow-up. J Oral Surg 30: 107–112

242. Guzzo M, Andreola S, Sirizzotti G et al. 2002 Mucoepidermoid carcinoma of the salivary glands: clinicopathologic review of 108 patients treated at the National Cancer Institute of Milan. Ann Surg Oncol 9: 688–695

243. Monoo K, Sageshima M, Ito E et al. 2003 Histopathological grading and clinical features of patients with mucoepidermoid carcinoma of the salivary glands. Nippon Jibiinkoka Gakkai Kaiho 106: 304–308

244. Boahene D K, Olsen K D, Lewis J E et al. 2004 Mucoepidermoid carcinoma of the parotid gland: the Mayo clinic experience. Arch Otolaryngol Head Neck Surg 130: 849–856

245. Skalova A, Lehtonen H, von Boguslawsky K et al. 1994 Prognostic significance of cell proliferation in mucoepidermoid carcinomas of the salivary gland: clinicopathological study using MIB 1 antibody in paraffin sections. Hum Pathol 25: 929–935

246. Kokemueller H, Brueggemann N, Swennen G et al. 2005 Mucoepidermoid carcinoma of the salivary glands – clinical review of 42 cases. Oral Oncol 41: 3–10

247. Pires F R, de Almeida O P, de Araujo V C et al. 2004 Prognostic factors in head and neck mucoepidermoid carcinoma. Arch Otolaryngol Head Neck Surg 130: 174–180

248. Handra-Luca A, Lamas G, Bertrand J C et al. 2005 MUC1, MUC2, MUC4, and MUC5AC expression in salivary gland mucoepidermoid carcinoma: diagnostic and prognostic implications. Am J Surg Pathol 29: 881–889

249. Perzin K H, Gullane P, Clairmont A C 1978 Adenoid cystic carcinomas arising in salivary glands: a correlation of histologic features and clinical course. Cancer 42: 265–282

250. Huvos A G, Strong E W 1973 Epithelial tumors of the lacrimal gland (abstract). Lab Invest 28: 386

251. Hajdu S I, Huvos A G, Goodner J T et al. 1970 Carcinoma of the trachea, a clinicopathologic study of 41 cases. Cancer 25: 1448

252. Nelms D, Luna M 1972 Primary adenocystic carcinoma (cylindromatous carcinoma) of the esophagus. Cancer 29: 440

253. Gray H R, Helwig E B 1963 Epithelioma adenoides cysticum and solitary trichoepithelioma. Arch Dermatol 87: 102

254. Weltzer S 1970 Adenoid cystic carcinoma of the breast. Am Surg 36: 271

255. Lassaletta L, Patron M, Oloriz J et al. 2003 Avoiding misdiagnosis in ceruminous gland tumours. Auris Nasus Larynx 30: 287–290

256. Friedrich R E, Bleckmann V 2003 Adenoid cystic carcinoma of salivary and lacrimal gland origin: localization, classification, clinical pathological correlation, treatment results and long-term follow-up control in 84 patients. Anticancer Res 23: 931–940

257. Chomette G, Auriol M, Tranbaloc P et al. 1982 Adenoid cystic carcinoma of minor salivary glands. Analysis of 86 cases. Clinico-pathological, histoenzymological and ultrastructural studies. Virchows Arch [Pathol Anat] 395: 289–301

258. Conley J, Dingman D L 1974 Adenoid cystic carcinoma in the head and neck (cylindroma). Arch Otolaryngol 100: 81–90

259. Eby L S, Johnson D S, Baker H W 1972 Adenoid cystic carcinoma of the head and neck. Cancer 29: 1160–1168

260. Eneroth C M, Zajicek J 1969 Aspiration biopsy of salivary gland tumors. IV. Morphologic studies on smears and histologic sections from 45 cases of adenoid cystic carcinoma. Acta Cytol 13: 59–63

261. Leafstedt S W, Gaeta J F, Sako K et al. 1971 Adenoid cystic carcinoma of major and minor salivary glands. Am J Surg 122: 756–762

262. Matsuba H M, Simpson J R, Mauney M et al. 1986 Adenoid cystic salivary gland carcinoma: a clinicopathologic correlation. Head Neck Surg 8: 200–204

263. Nascimento A G, Amaral A L, Prado L A et al. 1986 Adenoid cystic carcinoma of salivary glands. A study of 61 cases with clinicopathologic correlation. Cancer 57: 312–319

264. Spiro R H, Huvos A G, Strong E W 1974 Adenoid cystic carcinoma of salivary origin. A clinicopathologic study of 242 cases. Am J Surg 128: 512–520

265. Hamper K, Lazar F, Dietel M et al. 1990 Prognostic factors for adenoid cystic carcinoma of the head and neck: a retrospective evaluation of 96 cases. J Oral Pathol Med 19: 101–107

266. Chilla R, Schroth R, Eysholdt U et al. 1980 Adenoid cystic carcinoma of the head and neck. Controllable and uncontrollable factors in treatment and prognosis. ORL J Otorhinolaryngol Relat Spec 42: 346–367

267. Rapidis A D, Givalos N, Gakiopoulou H et al. 2005 Adenoid cystic carcinoma of the head and neck. Clinicopathological analysis of 23 patients and review of the literature. Oral Oncol 41: 328–335

268. Kokemueller H, Eckardt A, Brachvogel P et al. 2004 Adenoid cystic carcinoma of the head and neck – a 20 years experience. Int J Oral Maxillofac Surg 33: 25–31

269. Batsakis J G, El-Naggar A K 1999 Myoepithelium in salivary and mammary neoplasms is host-friendly. Adv Anat Pathol 6: 218–226

270. Cheuk W, Chan J K C, Ngan R K C 1999 Dedifferentiation in adenoid cystic carcinoma of salivary gland: an uncommon complication associated with an accelerated clinical course. Am J Surg Pathol 23: 465–472

271. Nagao T, Gaffey T A, Serizawa H et al. 2003 Dedifferentiated adenoid cystic carcinoma: a clinicopathologic study of 6 cases. Mod Pathol 16: 1265–1272

272. Chau Y, Hongyo T, Aozasa K et al. 2001 Dedifferentiation of adenoid cystic carcinoma: report of a case implicating p53 gene mutation. Hum Pathol 32: 1403–1407

273. Emanuel P, Wang B, Wu M et al. 2005 p63 immunohistochemistry in the distinction of adenoid cystic carcinoma from basaloid squamous cell carcinoma. Mod Pathol 18: 645–650

274. Edwards P C, Bhuiya T, Kelsch R D 2003 C-kit expression in the salivary gland neoplasms adenoid cystic carcinoma, polymorphous low-grade adenocarcinoma, and monomorphic adenoma. Oral Surg Oral Med Oral Pathol Oral Radiol Endod 95: 586–593

275. Mino M, Pilch B Z, Faquin W C 2003 Expression of KIT (CD117) in neoplasms of the head and neck: an ancillary marker for adenoid cystic carcinoma. Mod Pathol 16: 1224–1231

276. Hotte S J, Winquist E W, Lamont E et al. 2005 Imatinib mesylate in patients with adenoid cystic cancers of the salivary glands expressing c-kit: a Princess Margaret Hospital phase II consortium study. J Clin Oncol 23: 585–590

277. Nordkvist A, Mark J, Gustafsson H et al. 1994 Non-random chromosome rearrangements in adenoid cystic carcinoma of the salivary glands. Genes Chromos Cancer 10: 115–121

278. Sandros J, Mark J, Happonen R P et al. 1988 Specificity of 6q- markers and other recurrent deviations in human malignant salivary gland tumors. Anticancer Res 8: 637–643

279. Jin C, Martins C, Jin Y et al. 2001 Characterization of chromosome aberrations in salivary gland tumors by FISH, including multicolor COBRA-FISH. Genes Chromos Cancer 30: 161–167

280. El-Rifai W, Rutherford S, Knuutila S et al. 2001 Novel DNA copy number losses in chromosome 12q12-q13 in adenoid cystic carcinoma. Neoplasia 3: 173–178

281. Maruya S, Kurotaki H, Shimoyama N et al. 2003 Expression of p16 protein and hypermethylation status of its promoter gene in adenoid cystic carcinoma of the head and neck. ORL J Otorhinolaryngol Relat Spec 65: 26–32

282. Stallmach I, Zenklusen P, Komminoth P et al. 2002 Loss of heterozygosity at chromosome 6q23-25 correlates with clinical and histologic parameters in salivary gland adenoid cystic carcinoma. Virchows Arch 440: 77–84

283. Queimado L, Reis A, Fonseca I et al. 1998 A refined localization of two deleted regions in chromosome 6q associated with salivary gland carcinomas. Oncogene 16: 83–88

284. Batsakis J G, Luna M A, el-Naggar A 1990 Histopathologic grading of salivary gland neoplasms: III. Adenoid cystic carcinomas. Ann Otol Rhinol Laryngol 99: 1007–1009

285. Szanto P A, Luna M A, Tortoledo M E et al. 1984 Histologic grading of adenoid cystic carcinoma of the salivary glands. Cancer 54: 1062–1069

286. Yamamoto Y, Virmani A K, Wistuba I I et al. 1996 Loss of heterozygosity and microsatellite alterations in p53 and RB genes in adenoid cystic carcinoma of the salivary glands. Hum Pathol 27: 1204–1210

287. Enamorado I, Lakhani R, Korkmaz H et al. 2004 Correlation of histopathological variants, cellular DNA content, and clinical outcome in adenoid cystic carcinoma of the salivary glands. Otolaryngol Head Neck Surg 131: 646–650

288. Greiner T C, Robinson R A, Maves M D 1989 Adenoid cystic carcinoma. A clinicopathologic study with flow cytometric analysis. Am J Clin Pathol 92: 711–720

289. Nordgard S, Franzen G, Boysen M et al. 1997 Ki-67 as a prognostic marker in adenoid cystic carcinoma assessed with the monoclonal antibody MIB1 in paraffin sections. Laryngoscope 107: 531–536

290. Gnepp D R, Schroeder W, Heffner D 1989 Synchronous tumors arising in a single major salivary gland. Cancer 63: 1219–1224

291. Von Biberstein S E, Spiro J D, Mancoll W 1999 Acinic cell carcinoma of the nasal cavity. Otolaryngol Head Neck Surg 120: 759–762

292. Crissman J D, Rosenblatt A 1978 Acinous cell carcinoma of the larynx. Arch Pathol Lab Med 102: 233–236

293. Schmitt F C, Ribeiro C A, Alvarenga S et al. 2000 Primary acinic cell-like carcinoma of the breast: a variant with a good prognosis? Histopathology 36: 286–289

294. Lee H Y, Mancer K, Koong H N 2003 Primary acinic cell carcinoma of the lung with lymph node metastasis. Arch Pathol Lab Med 127: e216–e219

295. Ohike N, Kosmahl M, Kloppel G 2004 Mixed acinar-endocrine carcinoma of the pancreas. A clinicopathological study and comparison with acinar-cell carcinoma. Virchows Arch 445: 231–235

296. Colmenero C, Patron M, Sierra I 1991 Acinic cell carcinoma of the salivary glands. A review of 20 new cases. J Craniomaxillofac Surg 19: 260–266

297. Ellis G L, Corio R L 1983 Acinic cell adenocarcinoma. A clinicopathologic analysis of 294 cases. Cancer 52: 542–549

298. Abrams A M, Melrose R J 1978 Acinic cell tumors of minor salivary gland origin. Oral Surg Oral Med Oral Pathol 46: 220–233

299. Abrams A, Cornyn J, Scofield H et al. Acinic cell adenocarcinoma of the major salivary glands: a clinicopathologic study of 77 cases. Cancer 18: 1145–1162

300. Lewis J, Olsen K, Weiland L 1991 Acinic cell carcinoma. Clinicopathological review. Cancer 67: 172–179

301. Chaudhry A, Cutler L, Leifer C et al. 1986 Histogenesis of acinic cell carcinoma of the major and minor salivary glands. An ultrastructural study. J Pathol 148: 307–320

302. Stanley R J, Weiland L H, Olsen K D et al. 1988 Dedifferentiated acinic cell (acinous) carcinoma of the parotid gland. Otolaryngol Head Neck Surg 98: 155–161

303. Henley J D, Geary W A, Jackson C L et al. 1997 Dedifferentiated acinic cell carcinoma of the parotid gland: a distinct rarely described entity. Hum Pathol 28: 869–873

304. Timon C I, Dardick I 2001 The importance of dedifferentiation in recurrent acinic cell carcinoma. J Laryngol Otol 115: 639–644

305. Childers E L, Ellis G L, Auclair P L 1996 An immunohistochemical analysis of anti-amylase antibody reactivity in acinic cell adenocarcinoma. Oral Surg Oral Med Oral Pathol Oral Radiol Endod 81: 691–694

306. Skalova A, Leivo I, Von Boguslawsky K et al. 1994 Cell proliferation correlates with prognosis in acinic cell carcinomas of salivary gland origin. Immunohistochemical study of 30 cases using the MIB 1 antibody in formalin-fixed paraffin sections. J Pathol 173: 13–21

307. Michal M, Skalova A, Simpson RH et al. 1997 Well-differentiated acinic cell carcinoma of salivary glands associated with lymphoid stroma. Hum Pathol 28: 595–600

308. Freedman P D, Lumerman H 1983 Lobular carcinoma of intraoral minor salivary gland origin. Report of twelve cases. Oral Surg Oral Med Oral Pathol 56: 157–166

309. Batsakis J G, Pinkston G R, Luna M A et al. 1983 Adenocarcinomas of the oral cavity: a clinicopathologic study of terminal duct carcinomas. J Laryngol Otol 97: 825–835

310. George M K, Mansour P, Pahor A L 1991 Terminal parotid duct carcinoma. J Laryngol Otol 105: 780–781

311. Ritland F, Lubensky I, LiVolsi V A 1993 Polymorphous low-grade adenocarcinoma of the parotid salivary gland. Arch Pathol Lab Med 117: 1261–1263

312. Nagao T, Gaffey T A, Kay P A et al. 2004 Polymorphous low-grade adenocarcinoma of the major salivary glands: report of three cases in an unusual location. Histopathology 44: 164–171

313. Perez-Ordonez B, Linkov I, Huvos A G 1998 Polymorphous low-grade adenocarcinoma of minor salivary glands: a study of 17 cases with emphasis on cell differentiation. Histopathology 32: 521–529

314. Castle J T, Thompson L D, Frommelt R A et al. 1999 Polymorphous low grade adenocarcinoma: a clinicopathologic study of 164 cases. Cancer 86: 207–219

315. Selva D, Davis G J, Dodd T et al. 2004 Polymorphous low-grade adenocarcinoma of the lacrimal gland. Arch Ophthalmol 122: 915–917

316. Lengyel E, Somogyi A, Godeny M et al. 2000 Polymorphous low-grade adenocarcinoma of the nasopharynx. Case report and review of the literature. Strahlenther Onkol 176: 40–42

317. Young S, Leon M, Talerman A et al. 2003 Polymorphous low-grade adenocarcinoma of the vulva and vagina: a tumor resembling adenoid cystic carcinoma. Int J Surg Pathol 11: 43–49

318. Sato T, Indo H, Takasaki T et al. 2001 A rare case of intraosseous polymorphous low-grade adenocarcinoma (PLGA) of the maxilla. Dentomaxillofac Radiol 30: 184–187

319. Lee V K, McCaughan B C, Scolyer R A 2004 Polymorphous low-grade adenocarcinoma in the lung: a case report. Int J Surg Pathol 12: 287–292

320. Tsang Y W, Tung Y, Chan J K 1991 Polymorphous low grade adenocarcinoma of the palate in a child. J Laryngol Otol 105: 309–311

321. Vincent S D, Hammond H L, Finkelstein M W 1994 Clinical and therapeutic features of polymorphous low-grade adenocarcinoma. Oral Surg Oral Med Oral Pathol 77: 41–47

322. Evans H L, Luna M A 2000 Polymorphous low-grade adenocarcinoma: a study of 40 cases with long-term follow up and an evaluation of the importance of papillary areas. Am J Surg Pathol 24: 1319–1328

323. Fonseca I, Felix A, Soares J 1997 Cell proliferation in salivary gland adenocarcinomas with myoepithelial participation. A study of 78 cases. Virchows Arch 430: 227–232

324. Araujo V, Sousa S, Jaeger M et al. 1999 Characterization of the cellular component of polymorphous low-grade adenocarcinoma by immunohistochemistry and electron microscopy. Oral Oncol 35: 164–172

325. Thompson L D 2004 Polymorphous low-grade adenocarcinoma. Pathol Case Rev 9: 259–263

326. Pelkey T J, Mills S E 1999 Histologic transformation of polymorphous low-grade adenocarcinoma of salivary gland. Am J Clin Pathol 111: 785–791

327. Simpson R H, Pereira E M, Ribeiro A C et al. 2002 Polymorphous low-grade adenocarcinoma of the salivary glands with transformation to high-grade carcinoma. Histopathology 41: 250–259

328. Gnepp D R, el-Mofty S 1997 Polymorphous low-grade adenocarcinoma: glial fibrillary acidic protein staining in the differential diagnosis with cellular mixed tumors. Oral Surg Oral Med Oral Pathol Oral Radiol Endod 83: 691–695

329. Anderson C, Krutchkoff D, Pedersen C et al. 1990 Polymorphous low grade adenocarcinoma of minor salivary gland: a clinicopathologic and comparative immunohistochemical study. Mod Pathol 3: 76–82

330. Regezi J A, Zarbo R J, Stewart J C et al. 1991 Polymorphous low-grade adenocarcinoma of minor salivary gland. A comparative histologic and immunohistochemical study. Oral Surg Oral Med Oral Pathol 71: 469–475

331. Simpson R H, Clarke T J, Sarsfield P T et al. 1991 Polymorphous low-grade adenocarcinoma of the salivary glands: a clinicopathological comparison with adenoid cystic carcinoma. Histopathology 19: 121–129

332. Curran A E, White D K, Damm D D et al. 2001 Polymorphous low-grade adenocarcinoma versus pleomorphic adenoma of minor salivary glands: resolution of a diagnostic dilemma by immunohistochemical analysis with glial fibrillary acidic protein. Oral Surg Oral Med Oral Pathol Oral Radiol Endod 91: 194–199

333. Dardick I, Burford-Mason A P 1994 Pathology of the salivary glands: the contribution of electron microscopy. Microsc Res Tech 27: 46–60

334. Michal M, Skalova A, Simpson R H et al. 1999 Cribriform adenocarcinoma of the tongue: a hitherto unrecognized type of adenocarcinoma characteristically occurring in the tongue. Histopathology 35: 495–501

335. Luna M A, Wenig B M 2005 Polymorphous low-grade adenocarcinoma. In: Barnes L, Eveson J W, Reichart P et al. (eds) World Health Organization classification of tumours. Pathology and genetics: head and neck tumours. IARC, Lyon, p 231–232

336. Seifert G 1998 Are adenomyoepithelioma of the breast and epithelial-myoepithelial carcinoma of the salivary glands identical tumours? Virchows Arch 433: 285–288

337. Loose J H, Patchefsky A S, Hollander I J et al. 1992 Adenomyoepithelioma of the breast. A spectrum of biologic behavior. Am J Surg Pathol 16: 868–876

338. Fulford L G, Kamata Y, Okudera K et al. 2001 Epithelial-myoepithelial carcinomas of the bronchus. Am J Surg Pathol 25: 1508–1514

339. Chan W M, Liu D T, Lam L Y et al. 2004 Primary epithelial-myoepithelial carcinoma of the lacrimal gland. Arch Ophthalmol 122: 1714–1717

340. Ru K, Srivastava A, Tischler A S 2004 Bronchial epithelial-myoepithelial carcinoma. Arch Pathol Lab Med 128: 92–94

341. Doganay L, Bilgi S, Ozdil A et al. 2003 Epithelial-myoepithelial carcinoma of the lung. A case report and review of the literature. Arch Pathol Lab Med 127: e177–e180

342. Lee H M, Kim A R, Lee S H 2000 Epithelial-myoepithelial carcinoma of the nasal cavity. Eur Arch Otorhinolaryngol 257: 376–378

343. Imate Y, Yamashita H, Endo S et al. 2000 Epithelial-myoepithelial carcinoma of the nasopharynx. ORL J Otorhinolaryngol Relat Spec 62: 282–285

344. Horinouchi H, Ishihara T, Kawamura M et al. 1993 Epithelial myoepithelial tumour of the tracheal gland. J Clin Pathol 46: 185–187

345. Tsuneyama K, Hoso M, Kono N et al. 1999 An unusual case of epithelial-myoepithelial carcinoma of the liver. Am J Surg Pathol 23: 349–353

346. Luna M A, Batsakis J G, Ordonez N G et al. 1987 Salivary gland adenocarcinomas: a clinicopathologic analysis of three distinctive types. Semin Diagn Pathol 4: 117–135

347. Hamper K, Brugmann M, Koppermann R et al. 1989 Epithelial-myoepithelial duct carcinoma of salivary glands: a follow-up and cytophotometric study of 21 cases. J Oral Pathol Med 18: 299–304

348. Corio R L, Sciubba J J, Brannon R B et al. 1982 Epithelial-myoepithelial carcinoma of intercalated duct origin. A clinicopathologic and ultrastructural assessment of sixteen cases. Oral Surg Oral Med Oral Pathol 53: 280–287

349. Cho K J, el-Naggar A K, Ordonez N G et al. 1995 Epithelial-myoepithelial carcinoma of salivary glands. A clinicopathologic, DNA flow cytometric, and immunohistochemical study of Ki-67 and HER-2/neu oncogene. Am J Clin Pathol 103: 432–437

350. Fonseca I, Soares J 1993 Proliferating cell nuclear antigen immunohistochemistry in epithelial-myoepithelial carcinoma of the salivary glands. Arch Pathol Lab Med 117: 993–995

351. Fonseca I, Soares J 1993 Epithelial-myoepithelial carcinoma of the salivary glands. A study of 22 cases. Virchows Arch A Pathol Anat Histopathol 422: 389–396

352. Alos L, Carrillo R, Ramos J et al. 1999 High-grade carcinoma component in epithelial-myoepithelial carcinoma of salivary glands: clinicopathological, immunohistochemical and flow-cytometric study of three cases. Virchows Arch 434: 291–299

353. Simpson R H, Clarke T J, Sarsfield P T et al. 1991 Epithelial-myoepithelial carcinoma of salivary glands. J Clin Pathol 44: 419–423

354. Manuel S, Mathews A, Chandramohan K et al. 2002 Carcinosarcoma of the parotid gland with epithelial-myoepithelial carcinoma and pleomorphic sarcoma components. Br J Oral Maxillofac Surg 40: 480–483

355. Delgado R, Vuitch F, Albores-Saavedra J 1993 Salivary duct carcinoma. Cancer 72: 1503–1512

356. Lewis J E, McKinney B C, Weiland L H et al. 1996 Salivary duct carcinoma. Clinicopathologic and immunohistochemical review of 26 cases. Cancer 77: 223–230

357. Barnes L, Rao U, Krause J et al. 1994 Salivary duct carcinoma. Part I. A clinicopathologic evaluation and DNA image analysis of 13 cases with review of the literature. Oral Surg Oral Med Oral Pathol 78: 64–73

358. Barnes L, Rao U, Contis L et al. 1994 Salivary duct carcinoma. Part II. Immunohistochemical evaluation of 13 cases for estrogen and progesterone receptors, cathepsin D, and c-erbB-2 protein. Oral Surg Oral Med Oral Pathol 78: 74–80

359. Jaehne M, Roeser K, Jaekel T et al. 2005 Clinical and immunohistologic typing of salivary duct carcinoma. A report of 50 cases. Cancer 103: 2526–2533

360. Guzzo M, Di Palma S, Grandi C et al. 1997 Salivary duct carcinoma: clinical characteristics and treatment strategies. Head Neck 19: 126–133

361. Nagao T, Gaffey T A, Serizawa H et al. 2004 Sarcomatoid variant of salivary duct carcinoma: clinicopathologic and immunohistochemical study of eight cases with review of the literature. Am J Clin Pathol 122: 222–231

362. Simpson R H, Prasad A R, Lewis J E et al. 2003 Mucin-rich variant of salivary duct carcinoma: a clinicopathologic and immunohistochemical study of four cases. Am J Surg Pathol 27:1070–1079

363. Nagao T, Gaffey T A, Visscher D W et al. 2004 Invasive micropapillary salivary duct carcinoma: a distinct histologic variant with biologic significance. Am J Surg Pathol 28: 319–326

364. Ide F, Mishima K, Saito I 2003 Sarcomatoid salivary duct carcinoma of the oral cavity. Virchows Arch 443: 686–689

365. Henley J D, Seo I S, Dayan D et al. 2000 Sarcomatoid salivary duct carcinoma of the parotid gland. Hum Pathol 31: 208–213

366. Padberg B C, Sasse S, Huber A et al. 2005 Sarcomatoid salivary duct carcinoma. Ann Diagn Pathol 9: 86–92

367. Hui K K, Batsakis J G, Luna M A et al. 1986 Salivary duct adenocarcinoma: a high grade malignancy. J Laryngol Otol 100: 105–114

368. Brandwein M S, Jagirdar J, Patil J et al. 1990 Salivary duct carcinoma (cribriform salivary carcinoma of excretory ducts). A clinicopathologic and immunohistochemical study of 12 cases. Cancer 65: 2307–2314

369. Grenko R T, Gemryd P, Tytor M et al. 1995 Salivary duct carcinoma. Histopathology 26: 261–266

370. Nasser S M, Faquin W C, Dayal Y 2003 Expression of androgen, estrogen, and progesterone receptors in salivary gland tumors. Frequent expression of androgen receptor in a subset of malignant salivary gland tumors. Am J Clin Pathol 119: 801–806

371. Moriki T, Ueta S, Takahashi T et al. 2001 Salivary duct carcinoma: cytologic characteristics and application of androgen receptor immunostaining for diagnosis. Cancer 93: 344–350

372. Fan C Y, Wang J, Barnes E L 2000 Expression of androgen receptor and prostatic specific markers in salivary duct carcinoma: an immunohistochemical analysis of 13 cases and review of the literature. Am J Surg Pathol 24: 579–586

373. Kapadia S B, Barnes L 1998 Expression of androgen receptor, gross cystic disease fluid protein, and CD44 in salivary duct carcinoma. Mod Pathol 11: 1033–1038

374. James G K, Pudek M, Berean K W et al. 1996 Salivary duct carcinoma secreting prostate-specific antigen. Am J Clin Pathol 106: 242–247

375. Martinez-Barba E, Cortes-Guardiola J A, Minguela-Puras A et al. 1997 Salivary duct carcinoma: clinicopathological and immunohistochemical studies. J Craniomaxillofac Surg 25: 328–334

376. Laforga J B 2004 Salivary duct carcinoma with neuroendocrine features. Virchows Arch 444: 473–476

377. Hoang M P, Callender D L, Sola Gallego J J et al. 2001 Molecular and biomarker analyses of salivary duct carcinomas: comparison with mammary duct carcinoma. Int J Oncol 19: 865–871

378. Cerilli L A, Swartzbaugh J R, Saadut R et al. 1999 Analysis of chromosome 9p21 deletion and *p16* gene mutation in salivary gland carcinomas. Hum Pathol 30: 1242–1246

379. Mutoh H, Nagata H, Ohno K et al. 2001 Analysis of the *p53* gene in parotid gland cancers: a relatively high frequency of mutations in low-grade mucoepidermoid carcinomas. Int J Oncol 18: 781–786

380. Skalova A, Starek I, Vanecek T et al. 2003 Expression of HER-2/neu gene and protein in salivary duct carcinomas of parotid gland as revealed by fluorescence in-situ hybridization and immunohistochemistry. Histopathology 42: 348–356

381. Wick M R, Ockner D M, Mills S E et al. 1998 Homologous carcinomas of the breasts, skin, and salivary glands. A histologic and immunohistochemical comparison of ductal mammary carcinoma, ductal sweat gland carcinoma, and salivary duct carcinoma. Am J Clin Pathol 109: 75–84

382. Cheuk W, Miliauskas J R, Chan J K 2004 Intraductal carcinoma of the oral cavity: a case report and a reappraisal of the concept of pure ductal carcinoma in situ in salivary duct carcinoma. Am J Surg Pathol 28: 266–270

383. Delgado R, Klimstra D, Albores-Saavedra J 1996 Low grade salivary duct carcinoma. A distinctive variant with a low grade histology and a predominant intraductal growth pattern. Cancer 78: 958–967

384. Brandwein-Gensler M, Hille J, Wang B Y et al. 2004 Low-grade salivary duct carcinoma. Description of 16 cases. Am J Surg Pathol 28: 1040–1044

385. Anderson C, Muller R, Piorkowski R et al. 1992 Intraductal carcinoma of major salivary gland. Cancer 69: 609–614

386. Wang B, Brandwein M, Gordon R et al. 2002 Primary salivary clear cell tumors – a diagnostic approach: a clinicopathologic and immunohistochemical study of 20 patients with clear cell carcinoma, clear cell myoepithelial carcinoma, and epithelial-myoepithelial carcinoma. Arch Pathol Lab Med 126: 676–685

387. Rezende R B, Drachenberg C B, Kumar D et al. 1999 Differential diagnosis between monomorphic clear cell adenocarcinoma of salivary glands and renal (clear) cell carcinoma. Am J Surg Pathol 23: 1532–1538

388. Milchgrub S, Gnepp D R, Vuitch F et al. 1994 Hyalinizing clear cell carcinoma of salivary gland. Am J Surg Pathol 18: 74–82

389. Urban S D, Keith D A, Goodman M 1996 Hyalinizing clear cell carcinoma: report of a case. J Oral Pathol Med 25: 562–564

390. Balakrishnan R, Nayak D R, Pillai S et al. 2002 Hyalinizing clear cell carcinoma of the base of the tongue. J Laryngol Otol 116: 851–853

391. Chao T K, Tsai C C, Yeh S Y et al. 2004 Hyalinizing clear cell carcinoma of the hard palate. J Laryngol Otol 118: 382–384

392. Tang S K, Wan S K, Chan J K 1995 Hyalinizing clear cell carcinoma of salivary gland: report of a case with multiple recurrences over 12 years. Am J Surg Pathol 19: 240–241

393. Berho M, Huvos A G 1999 Central hyalinizing clear cell carcinoma of the mandible and the maxilla: a clinicopathologic study of two cases with an analysis of the literature. Hum Pathol 30: 101–105

394. Ereno C, Grande J, Alija V et al. 2000 Hyalinizing clear cell carcinoma of the hypopharynx metastasizing to the lung: a case report. Histopathology 37: 89–91

395. O'Regan E, Shandilya M, Gnepp D R et al. 2004 Hyalinizing clear cell carcinoma of salivary gland: an aggressive variant. Oral Oncol 40: 348–352

396. Simpson R H, Sarsfield P T, Clarke T et al. 1990 Clear cell carcinoma of minor salivary glands. Histopathology 17: 433–438

397. Gnepp D R, Wick M R 1990 Small cell carcinoma of the major salivary glands. An immunohistochemical study. Cancer 66: 185–192

398. Toyosawa S, Ohnishi A, Ito R et al. 1999 Small cell undifferentiated carcinoma of the submandibular gland: immunohistochemical evidence of myoepithelial, basal and luminal cell features. Pathol Int 49: 887–892

399. Chan J K, Suster S, Wenig B M et al. 1997 Cytokeratin 20 immunoreactivity distinguishes Merkel cell (primary cutaneous neuroendocrine) carcinomas and salivary gland small cell carcinomas from small cell carcinomas of various sites. Am J Surg Pathol 21: 226–234

400. Hui K K, Luna M A, Batsakis J G et al. 1990 Undifferentiated carcinomas of the major salivary glands. Oral Surg Oral Med Oral Pathol 69: 76–83

401. Gnepp D R, Corio R L, Brannon R B 1986 Small cell carcinoma of the major salivary glands. Cancer 58: 705–714

402. Huntrakoon M 1987 Neuroendocrine carcinoma of the parotid gland: a report of two cases with ultrastructural and immunohistochemical studies. Hum Pathol 18: 1212–1217

403. Kraemer B B, Mackay B, Batsakis J G 1983 Small cell carcinomas of the parotid gland. A clinicopathologic study of three cases. Cancer 52: 2115–2121

404. Nagao T, Gaffey T A, Olsen K D et al. 2004 Small cell carcinoma of the major salivary glands: clinicopathologic study with emphasis on cytokeratin 20 immunoreactivity and clinical outcome. Am J Surg Pathol 28: 762–770

405. Cheuk W, Kwan M Y, Suster S et al. 2001 Immunostaining for thyroid transcription factor 1 and cytokeratin 20 aids the distinction of small cell carcinoma from Merkel cell carcinoma, but not pulmonary from extrapulmonary small cell carcinomas. Arch Pathol Lab Med 125: 228–231

406. Koss L G, Spiro R H, Hajdu S 1972 Small cell (oat cell) carcinoma of minor salivary gland origin. Cancer 30: 737–741

407. Hayashi Y, Nagamine S, Yanagawa T et al. 1987 Small cell undifferentiated carcinoma of the minor salivary gland containing exocrine, neuroendocrine, and squamous cells. Cancer 60: 1583–1588

408. Wang C P, Chang Y L, Ko J Y et al. 2004 Lymphoepithelial carcinoma versus large cell undifferentiated carcinoma of the major salivary glands. Cancer 101: 2020–2027

409. Batsakis J G, Luna M A 1991 Undifferentiated carcinomas of salivary glands. Ann Otol Rhinol Laryngol 100: 82–84

410. Larsson L G, Donner L R 1999 Large cell neuroendocrine carcinoma of the parotid gland: fine needle aspiration, and light microscopic and ultrastructural study. Acta Cytol 43: 534–536

411. Nagao T, Sugano I, Ishida Y et al. 2000 Primary large-cell neuroendocrine carcinoma of the parotid gland: immunohistochemical and molecular analysis of two cases. Mod Pathol 13: 554–561

412. Eversole L R, Gnepp D R, Eversole G M 1991 Undifferentiated carcinoma. In: Ellis G L, Auclair P L, Gnepp D R (eds) Surgical pathology of the salivary glands. W B Saunders, Philadelphia, PA, p 422–440

413. Saw D, Lau W H, Ho J H et al. 1986 Malignant lymphoepithelial lesion of the salivary gland. Hum Pathol 17: 914–923

414. Huang D P, Ng H K, Ho Y H et al. 1988 Epstein–Barr virus (EBV)-associated undifferentiated carcinoma of the parotid gland. Histopathology 13: 509–517

415. Hamilton-Dutoit S J, Therkildsen M H, Neilsen N H et al. 1991 Undifferentiated carcinoma of the salivary gland in Greenlandic Eskimos: demonstration of Epstein–Barr virus DNA by in situ nucleic acid hybridization. Hum Pathol 22: 811–815

416. Tsai C C, Chen C L, Hsu H C et al. 1996 Expression of Epstein–Barr virus in carcinomas of major salivary glands: a strong association with lymphoepithelioma-like carcinoma. Hum Pathol 27: 258–262

417. Nagao T, Ishida Y, Sugano I et al. 1996 Epstein–Barr virus-associated undifferentiated carcinoma with lymphoid stroma of the salivary gland in Japanese patients. Comparison with benign lymphoepithelial lesion. Cancer 78: 695–703

418. Leung S Y, Chung L P, Yuen S T et al. 1995 Lymphoepithelial carcinoma of the salivary gland: in situ detection of Epstein–Barr virus. J Clin Pathol 48: 1022–1027

419. Kuo T, Hsueh C 1997 Lymphoepithelioma-like salivary gland carcinoma in Taiwan: a clinicopathological study of nine cases demonstrating a strong association with Epstein–Barr virus. Histopathology 31: 75–82

420. Gallo O, Santucci M, Calzolari A et al. 1994 Epstein–Barr virus (EBV) infection and undifferentiated carcinoma of the parotid glands in Caucasian patients. Acta Otolaryngol 114: 572–575

421. Kotsianti A, Costopoulos J, Morgello S et al. 1996 Undifferentiated carcinoma of the parotid gland in a white patient: detection of Epstein–Barr virus by in situ hybridization. Hum Pathol 27: 87–90

422. Mrad K, Ben Brahim E, Driss M et al. 2004 Lymphoepithelioma-like carcinoma of the submandibular salivary gland associated with Epstein–Barr virus in a North African woman. Virchows Arch 445: 419–420

423. Worley N K, Daroca P J Jr 1997 Lymphoepithelial carcinoma of the minor salivary gland. Arch Otolaryngol Head Neck Surg 123: 638–640

424. Hanji D, Gohao L 1983 Malignant lymphoepithelial lesions of the salivary glands with anaplastic carcinomatous change. Report of nine cases and review of literature. Cancer 52: 2245–2252

425. Saw D, Ho J H, Lau W H et al. 1986 Parotid swelling as the first manifestation of nasopharyngeal carcinoma: a report of two cases. Eur J Surg Oncol 12: 71–75

426. Christiansen M S, Mourad W A, Hales M L et al. 1995 Spindle cell malignant lymphoepithelial lesion of the parotid gland: clinical, light microscopic, ultrastructural, and in situ hybridization findings in one case. Mod Pathol 8: 711–715

427. Squillaci S, Bertalot G, Vago L et al. 2000 Lymphoepithelioma-like carcinoma of the parotid gland. Description of a case with detection of EBV by in situ hybridization. Pathologica 92: 89–194

428. Bialas M, Sinczak A, Choinska-Stefanska A et al. 2002 EBV-positive lymphoepithelial carcinoma of salivary gland in a woman of a non-endemic area – a case report. Pol J Pathol 53: 235–238

429. Shemen L J, Huvos A G, Spiro R H 1987 Squamous cell carcinoma of salivary gland origin. Head Neck Surg 9: 235–240

430. Gaughan R, Olsen K, Lewis J 1992 Primary squamous cell carcinoma of the parotid gland. Arch Otolaryngol Head Neck Surg 118: 798–801

431. Cawson R A, Gleeson M J, Eveson J W 1997 Carcinomas of salivary glands, pathology and surgery of the salivary glands. ISIS Medical Media, Oxford, p 117–169

432. Ghannoum J E, Freedman P D 2004 Signet-ring cell (mucin-producing) adenocarcinomas of minor salivary glands. Am J Surg Pathol 28: 89–93

433. Li J, Wang B Y, Nelson M et al. 2004 Salivary adenocarcinoma, not otherwise specified: a collection of orphans. Arch Pathol Lab Med 128: 1385–1394

434. Spiro R H, Huvos A G, Strong E W 1982 Adenocarcinoma of salivary origin. Clinicopathologic study of 204 patients. Am J Surg 144: 423–431

435. Matsuba H M, Mauney M, Simpson J R et al. 1988 Adenocarcinomas of major and minor salivary gland origin: a histopathologic review of treatment failure patterns. Laryngoscope 98: 784–788

436. Spiro R H, Koss L G, Hajdu S I et al. 1973 Tumors of minor salivary origin. A clinicopathologic study of 492 cases. Cancer 31: 117–129

437. Vawter G, Tefft M 1966 Congenital tumors of the parotid gland. Arch Pathol 82: 242–245

438. Canalis R F, Mok M W, Fishman S M et al. 1980 Congenital basal cell adenoma of the submandibular gland. Arch Otolaryngol 106: 284–286

439. Ortiz-Hidalgo C, de Leon-Bojorge B, Fernandez-Sobrino G et al. 2001 Sialoblastoma: report of a congenital case with dysembryogenic alterations of the adjacent parotid gland. Histopathology 38: 79–84

440. Simpson P R, Rutledge J C, Schaefer S D et al. 1986 Congenital hybrid basal cell adenoma – adenoid cystic carcinoma of the salivary gland. Pediatr Pathol 6: 199–208

441. Siddiqi S H, Solomon M P, Haller J O 2000 Sialoblastoma and hepatoblastoma in a neonate. Pediatr Radiol 30: 349–351

442. Harris M D, McKeever P, Robertson J M 1990 Congenital tumours of the salivary gland: a case report and review. Histopathology 17: 155–157

443. Brandwein M, Al-Naief N, Manwani D et al. 1999 Sialoblastoma: clinicopathological/immunohistochemical study. Am J Surg Pathol 23: 342–348

444. McKnight H A 1939 Malignant parotid tumor in the newborn. Am J Surg 45: 128–130

445. Hsueh C, Gonzalez-Crussi F 1992 Sialoblastoma: a case report and review of the literature on congenital epithelial tumors of salivary gland origin. Pediatr Pathol 12: 205–214

446. Batsakis J G, Frankenthaler R 1992 Embryoma (sialoblastoma) of salivary glands. Ann Otol Rhinol Laryngol 101: 958–960

447. Batsakis J G, Mackay B, Ryka A F et al. 1988 Perinatal salivary gland tumours (embryomas). J Laryngol Otol 102: 1007–1011

448. Cawson R A, Gleeson M J, Eveson J W 1997 Pathology and surgery of the salivary glands. ISIS Medical Media, Oxford

449. Kane W, McCaffrey T, Olsen K et al. 1991 Primary parotid malignancies. Arch Otolaryngol Head Neck Surg 117: 307–315

450. Luna M, Tortoledo M, Ordonez N et al. 1991 Primary sarcomas of the major salivary glands. Arch Otolaryngol Head Neck Surg 117: 302–306

451. Mantravadi J, Roth L, Kafrawy A 1993 Vascular neoplasms of the parotid gland. Parotid vascular tumors. Oral Surg Oral Med Oral Pathol 75: 70–75

452. Childers E L B, Furlong M A, Fanburg-Smith J C 2002 Hemangioma of the salivary gland: a study of ten cases of a rarely biopsied/excised lesion. Ann Diagn Pathol 6: 339–344

453. Enzinger F M, Weiss S W 1995 Soft tissue tumors, 3rd edn. C V Mosby, St. Louis

454. Robertson J S, Wiegand D A, Schaitkin B M 1991 Life-threatening hemangioma arising from the parotid gland. Otolaryngol Head Neck Surg 104: 858–862

455. Damiani S, Corti B, Neri F et al. 2003 Primary angiosarcoma of the parotid gland arising from benign congenital hemangioma. Oral Surg Oral Med Oral Pathol Oral Radiol Endod 96: 66–69

456. Wells G, Whimster I 1969 Subcutaneous angiolymphoid hyperplasia with eosinophilia. Br J Dermatol 81: 1–14

457. Fanburg-Smith J C, Furlong M A, Childers E L 2003 Oral and salivary gland angiosarcoma: a clinicopathologic study of 29 cases. Mod Pathol 16: 263–271

458. Piscioli F, Leonardi E, Scappini P et al. 1986 Primary angiosarcoma of the gingiva. Case report with immunohistochemical study. Am J Dermatopathol 8: 430–435

459. Tomec R, Ahmad I, Fu Y S et al. Malignant hemangioendothelioma (angiosarcoma) of the salivary gland: an ultrastructural study. Cancer 43: 1664–1671

460. Wesley R K, Mintz S M, Wertheimer F W 1975 Primary malignant hemangioendothelioma of the gingiva. Report of a case and review of the literature. Oral Surg Oral Med Oral Pathol 39: 103–112

461. Falvo L, Marzullo A, Catania A et al. 2004 Epithelioid haemangioendothelioma of the parotid salivary gland: a case report. Chir Ital 56: 457–462

462. Chan J K C, Hui P K, Ng C S et al. 1989 Epithelioid hemangioma and Kimura's disease in Chinese. Histopathology 15: 557–574

463. Chan J K C 1997 Solitary fibrous tumor – everywhere, and a diagnosis in vogue. Histopathology 31: 568–576

464. Nascimento A G 1996 Solitary fibrous tumor: a ubiquitous neoplasm of mesenchymal differentiation. Adv Anat Pathol 3: 388–395

465. Hanau C, Miettinen M 1995 Solitary fibrous tumor: histological and immunohistochemical spectrum of benign and malignant variants presenting at different sites. Hum Pathol 26: 440–449

466. Brunnemann R, Ro J, Ordonez N et al. 1997 Extrathoracic localized fibrous tumor: a clinicopathologic study of 24 cases. Mod Pathol 12: 1034–1042

467. Ferreiro J A, Nascimento A G 1996 Solitary fibrous tumour of the major salivary glands. Histopathology 28: 261–264

468. Guarino M, Giordano F, Pallotti F et al. 1998 Solitary fibrous tumor of the submandibular gland. Histopathology 32: 571–572

469. Gunhan O, Yildiz F R, Celasun B et al. 1994 Solitary fibrous tumour arising from sublingual gland: report of a case. J Laryngol Otol 108: 998–1000

470. Sato J, Asakura K, Yokoyama Y et al. 1998 Solitary fibrous tumor of the parotid gland extending to the parapharyngeal space. Eur Arch Otorhinolaryngol 255: 18–21

471. Hofmann T, Braun H, Kole W et al. 2002 Solitary fibrous tumor of the submandibular gland. Eur Arch Otorhinolaryngol 259: 470–473

472. Ogawa I, Sato S, Kudo Y et al. 2003 Solitary fibrous tumor with malignant potential arising in sublingual gland. Pathol Int 53: 40–45

473. Williams S B, Foss R D, Ellis G L 1992 Inflammatory pseudotumors of the major salivary glands. Clinicopathologic and immunohistochemical analysis of six cases. Am J Surg Pathol 16: 896–902

474. Inui M, Tagawa T, Mori A et al. 1993 Inflammatory pseudotumor in the submandibular region. Oral Surg Oral Med Oral Pathol 76: 333–337

475. Rahimi S, Mafera B, Vigili M G 2004 Inflammatory pseudotumor of the parotid gland: report of a case with fine needle aspiration cytology. Acta Cytol 48: 574–576

476. Kojima M, Nakamura S, Itoh H et al. 2001 Inflammatory pseudotumor of the submandibular gland: report of a case presenting with autoimmune disease-like clinical manifestations. Arch Pathol Lab Med 125: 1095–1097

477. Cawson R, Gleeson M, Eveson J 1997 Mesenchymal, lymphoreticular, metastatic and periglandular tumours and other uncommon types of salivary gland tumours. In: Cawson R, Gleeson M, Eveson J (eds) The pathology and surgery of the salivary glands. ISIS Medical Media, Oxford, p 170–190

478. Carr M M, Fraser R B, Clarke K D 1998 Nodular fasciitis in the parotid gland of a child. Head Neck 20: 645–648

479. Fischer J R, Abdul-Karim F W, Robinson R A 1989 Intraparotid nodular fasciitis. Arch Pathol Lab Med 113: 1276–1278

480. Eusebi V, Martin S A, Govoni E et al. 1984 Giant cell tumor of major salivary glands: report of three cases, one occurring in association with a malignant mixed tumor. Am J Clin Pathol 81: 666–675

481. Tse L L, Finkelstein S D, Siegler R W et al. 2004 Osteoclast-type giant cell neoplasm of salivary gland. A microdissection-based comparative genotyping assay and literature review: extraskeletal "giant cell tumor of bone" or osteoclast-type giant cell "carcinoma"? Am J Surg Pathol 28: 953–961

482. Balogh K, Wolbarsht R, Federman M et al. 1985 Carcinoma of the parotid gland with osteoclast-like giant cells, immunohistochemical and ultrastructural observations. Arch Pathol Lab Med 109: 756–761

483. Kondratowicz G, Smallman L, Morgan D 1988 Clinicopathological study of myoepithelial sialadenitis and chronic sialadenitis (sialolithiasis). J Clin Pathol 41: 403–409

484. Metwaly H, Cheng J, Ida-Yonemochi H et al. 2003 Vascular endothelial cell participation in formation of lymphoepithelial lesions (epi-myoepithelial islands) in lymphoepithelial sialadenitis (benign lymphoepithelial lesion). Virchows Arch 443: 17–27

485. Carbone A, Gloghini A, Ferlito A 2000 Pathological features of lymphoid proliferations of the salivary glands: lymphoepithelial sialadenitis versus low-grade B-cell lymphoma of the MALT type. Ann Otol Rhinol Laryngol 109: 1170–1175

486. Harris N L 1999 Lymphoid proliferation of the salivary glands. Am J Clin Pathol 111: S94–S103

487. Ostberg Y 1983 The clinical picture of benign lympho-epithelial lesion. Clin Otolaryngol 8: 381–390

488. Gleeson M J, Cawson R A, Bennett M H 1986 Benign lymphoepithelial lesion: a less than benign disease. Clin Otolaryngol 11: 47–51

489. Barnes L, Myers E N, Prokopakis E P 1998 Primary malignant lymphomas of the parotid gland. Arch Otolaryngol Head Neck Surg 124: 573–577

490. Dunn P, Kuo T T, Shih L Y et al. 2004 Primary salivary gland lymphoma: a clinicopathologic study of 23 cases in Taiwan. Acta Hematol 112: 203–208

491. Ambrosetti A, Zanotti R, Pattaro C et al. 2004 Most cases of primary salivary mucosa-associated lymphoid tissue are associated with Sjögren syndrome or hepatitis C virus infection. Br J Hematol 126: 43–49

492. Zucca E, Conconi A, Pedrinis E et al. 2003 Nongastric marginal zone B-cell lymphoma of mucosa-associated lymphoid tissue. Blood 101: 2489–2495

493. Royer B, Cazals-Hatem D, Sibilia J et al. 1997 Lymphomas in patients with Sjögren's syndrome are marginal zone B-cell neoplasms, arise in diverse extranodal and nodal sites, and are not associated with viruses. Blood 90: 766–775

494. Mariette X 1999 Lymphomas in patients with Sjögren's syndrome: review of the literature and physiopathologic hypothesis. Leuk Lymphoma 33: 93–99

495. Bridges A J, England D M 1989 Benign lymphoepithelial lesion: relationship to Sjögren's syndrome and evolving malignant lymphoma. Semin Arthritis Rheum 19: 201–208

496. Falzon M, Isaacson P G 1991 The natural history of benign lymphoepithelial lesion of the salivary gland in which there is a monoclonal population of B cells. A report of two cases. Am J Surg Pathol 15: 59–65

497. Gleeson M J, Bennett M H, Cawson R A 1986 Lymphomas of salivary glands. Cancer 58: 699–704

498. Takahashi H, Cheng J, Fujita F et al. 1992 Primary malignant lymphoma of the salivary gland: a tumor of mucosa-associated lymphoid tissue. J Oral Pathol Med 21: 318–325

499. Schmid U, Lennert K, Gloor F 1989 Immunosialadenitis (Sjögren's syndrome) and lymphoproliferation. Clin Exp Rheumatol 7: 175–180

500. Schmid U, Helbron D, Lennert K 1982 Primary malignant lymphomas localized in salivary glands. Histopathology 6: 673–677

501. Fishleder A, Tubbs R, Hesse B et al. Uniform detection of immunoglobulin-gene rearrangement in benign lymphoepithelial lesions. N Engl J Med 316: 1118–1121

502. Freimark B, Fantozzi R, Bone R et al. 1989 Detection of clonally expanded salivary gland lymphocytes in Sjögren's syndrome. Arthritis Rheum 32: 859–869

503. Speight P M, Jordan R, Colloby P et al. 1994 Early detection of lymphomas in Sjögren's syndrome by in situ hybridization for kappa and lambda light chain mRNA in labial salivary glands. Oral Oncol Eur J Cancer 30: 244–247

504. Jordan R, Pringle J, Speight P 1995 High frequency of light chain restriction in labial salivary gland biopsies of Sjögren's syndrome detected by in situ hybridisation. J Pathol 177: 35–40

505. Pablos J L, Carreira P E, Morillas L et al. 1994 Clonally expanded lymphocytes in the minor glands of Sjögren's syndrome patients without lymphoproliferative disease. Arthritis Rheum 37: 1441–1444

506. Diss T C, Wotherspoon A C, Speight P et al. 1995 B-cell monoclonality, Epstein Barr virus, and t(14;18) in myoepithelial sialadenitis and low-grade B-cell MALT lymphoma of the parotid gland. Am J Surg Pathol 19: 531–536

507. Bahler D W, Swerdlow S H 1998 Clonal salivary gland infiltrates associated with myoepithelial sialadenitis (Sjögren's syndrome) begin as nonmalignant antigen-selected expansions. Blood 91: 1864–1872

508. Quintana P G, Kapadia S B, Bahler D W et al. 1997 Salivary gland lymphoid infiltrates associated with lymphoepithelial lesions: a clinicopathologic, immunophenotypic, and genotypic study. Hum Pathol 28: 850–861

509. Palmer R M, Eveson J W, Gusterson B A 1986 'Epimyoepithelial' islands in lymphoepithelial lesions: an immunocytochemical study. Virchows Arch [Pathol Anat] 408: 603–609

510. Chaudhry A P, Cutler L S, Yamane G M et al. 1986 Light and ultrastructural features of lymphoepithelial lesions of the salivary glands in Mikulicz's disease. J Pathol 146: 239–250

511. Caselitz J, Osborn M, Wustrow J et al. 1986 Immunohistochemical investigations on the epimyoepithelial islands in lymphoepithelial lesions. Lab Invest 55: 427–432

512. Dardick I, van Nostrand A W P, Rippstein P et al. 1988 Characterization of epimyoepithelial islands in benign lymphoepithelial lesions of major salivary gland: an immunohistochemical and ultrastructural study. Head Neck Surg 10: 168–178

513. Ihrler S, Zietz C, Sendelhofert A et al. 1999 Lymphoepithelial duct lesions in Sjögren-type sialadenitis. Virchows Arch 434: 315–323

514. Hyjek E, Smith W J, Isaacson P G 1988 Primary B-cell lymphoma of salivary glands and its relationship to myoepithelial sialadenitis. Hum Pathol 19: 766–776

515. Hsi E D, Zukerberg L R, Schnitzer B et al. 1995 Development of extrasalivary gland lymphoma in myoepithelial sialadenitis. Mod Pathol 8: 817–824

516. Abbondanzo S L 2001 Extranodal marginal-zone B-cell lymphoma of the salivary gland. Ann Diagn Pathol 5: 246–254

517. Takahashi H, Tsuda N, Tezuka F et al. 1990 Non-Hodgkin's lymphoma of the major salivary gland: a morphologic and immunohistochemical study of 15 cases. J Oral Pathol Med 19: 306–312

518. Isaacson P G, Norton A J 1994 Extranodal lymphomas. Churchill Livingstone, Edinburgh, p 67–83

519. Egerter D A, Beckstead J H 1988 Malignant lymphomas in the acquired immunodeficiency syndrome. Additional evidence for B-cell origin. Arch Pathol Lab Med 112: 602–608

520. Ioachim H L, Antonescu C, Giancotti F et al. 1998 EBV-associated primary lymphomas in salivary glands of HIV-infected patients. Pathol Res Pract 194: 87–95

521. Chan J K, Tsang W Y, Hui P K et al. 1997 T- and T/natural killer-cell lymphomas of the salivary gland: a clinicopathologic, immunohistochemical and molecular study of six cases. Hum Pathol 28: 238–245

522. Ye H, Liu H, Attygalle A et al. 2003 Variable frequencies of t(11;18)(q21;q21) in MALT lymphomas of different sites: significant association with CagA strains of H. pylori in gastric MALT lymphoma. Blood 102: 1012–1018

523. Streubel B, Simonitsch-Klupp I, Mullauer L et al. 2004 Variable frequencies of MALT lymphoma-associated genetic aberrations in MALT lymphomas of different sites. Leukemia 18: 1722–1726

524. Harris N L, Jaffe E S, Diebold J et al. 1999 World Health Organization classification of neoplastic diseases of the hematopoietic and lymphoid tissues: report of the Clinical Advisory Committee meeting, Airlie House, Virginia, November 1997. J Clin Oncol 17: 3835–3849

525. Ferraro F J, Rush B J, Ruark D et al. 1993 Enucleation of parotid lymphoepithelial cyst in patients who are human immunodeficiency virus positive. Surg Gynecol Obstet 177: 524–526

526. Goldstein J, Rubin J, Silver C et al. 1992 Radiation therapy as a treatment for benign lymphoepithelial parotid cysts in patients infected with human immunodeficiency virus-1. Int J Radiat Oncol Biol Phys 23: 1045–1050

527. Huang R, Pearlman S, Friedman W et al. 1991 Benign cystic vs solid lesions of the parotid gland in HIV patients. Head Neck 13: 522–527

528. Chan J K C 1998 Kuttner tumor (chronic sclerosing sialadenitis) of the submandibular gland: an underrecognized entity. Adv Anat Pathol 5: 239–251

529. Isaacson G, Lundquist P G 1982 Salivary calculi as an aetiological factor in chronic sialadenitis of the submandibular gland. Clin Otolaryngol 7: 231–236

530. Seifert G 1992 Tumour-like lesions of the salivary glands. The new WHO classification. Pathol Res Pract 188: 836–846

531. Kitagawa S, Zen Y, Harada K et al. 2005 Abundant IgG4-positive plasma cell infiltration characterizes chronic sclerosing sialadenitis (Kuttner's tumor). Am J Surg Pathol 29: 783–791

532. Yoshihara T, Kanda T, Yaku Y et al. 1983 Chronic sialadenitis of the submandibular gland (so-called Kuttner tumor). Auris Nasus Larynx 10: 117–123

533. Tiemann M, Teymoortash A, Schrader C et al. 2002 Chronic sclerosing sialadenitis of the submandibular gland is mainly due to a T lymphocyte immune reaction. Mod Pathol 15: 845–852

534. Kojima M, Nakamura S, Itoh H et al. 2003 Sclerosing variant of follicular lymphoma arising from submandibular glands and resembling "Kuttner tumor": a report of 3 patients. Int J Surg Pathol 11: 303–307

535. Ochoa E R, Harris N L, Pilch B Z 2001 Marginal zone B-cell lymphoma of the salivary gland arising in chronic sclerosing sialadenitis (Kuttner tumor). Am J Surg Pathol 25: 1546–1550

536. Brannon R B, Fowler C B, Hartman K S 1991 Necrotizing sialometaplasia, a clinicopathologic study of 69 cases and review of the literature. Oral Surg Oral Med Oral Pathol 72: 317–325

537. Abrams A M, Melrose R J, Howell F V 1973 Necrotizing sialometaplasia. A disease simulating malignancy. Cancer 32: 130–135

538. Walker G, Fehner R, Johns M et al. 1982 Necrotizing sialometaplasia of the larynx secondary to atheromatous embolism. Am J Clin Pathol 77: 221–223

539. Wenig B M 1995 Necrotizing sialometaplasia of the larynx, a report of cases and a review of the literature. Am J Clin Pathol 103: 609–613

540. Ben-Izhak O, Ben-Arieh Y 1993 Necrotizing squamous metaplasia in herpetic tracheitis following prolonged intubation: a lesion similar to necrotizing sialometaplasia. Histopathology 22: 265–269

541. Min K W, Houck J R Jr 1998 Protocol for the examination of specimens removed from patients with carcinomas of the upper aerodigestive tract: carcinomas of the oral cavity including lip and tongue, nasal and paranasal sinuses, pharynx, larynx, salivary glands, hypopharynx, oropharynx, and nasopharynx. Cancer Committee, College of American Pathologists. Arch Pathol Lab Med 122: 222–230

Tumors of the esophagus and stomach

Fiona Campbell   Gregory Y. Lauwers   Geraint T. Williams

8

Esophagus

Epithelial tumors

Squamous cell papilloma and papillomatosis

Clinical features Squamous cell papilloma may occur any-where in the esophagus but is found most commonly in the lower third as a single, well-demarcated sessile intraluminal tumor, usually less than 1.5 cm in size.[1] A giant form has been described[2] and also multiple lesions,[3] sometimes in association with Goltz syndrome (focal dermal hypoplasia), may occur.[4] The etiology of these lesions is not clear, although some are related to chronic irritation[3] and others to human papilloma virus infection.[5,6]

Histologic appearances Histologically, squamous papilloma has a papillary architecture with a core of vascular connective tissue covered by hyperplastic, normally maturing, squamous epithelium (Fig. 8.1). There may be papilloma virus-associated changes, including koilocytosis and multinucleation. The lesion has no recognized malignant potential.

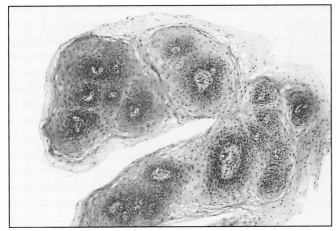

Fig. 8.1 • Benign esophageal squamous papilloma.

Differential diagnosis In biopsy material, squamous papilloma must be differentiated from well-differentiated verrucous squamous cell carcinoma (see below).

Adenoma

Adenoma is a rare, usually polypoid, tumor, which is indistinguishable histologically from gastric adenoma (see p. 340), and usually occurs as a manifestation of raised dysplasia in columnar (Barrett's) esophagus.[7] Multiple adenomatous polyps with synchronous adenocarcinoma have been reported.[8]

Pleomorphic adenoma

A few cases of pleomorphic adenoma of the esophagus, arising from the submucosal mucous glands and comparable to those arising in salivary gland (see Ch. 7), have been described.[9]

Epithelial dysplasia (intraepithelial neoplasia)

Epithelial dysplasia, arising in squamous or columnar epithelium, is considered as a precancerous lesion, i.e., a histologic abnormality that can progress to cancer. Epithelial dysplasia is characterized by cellular atypia, abnormal differentiation and disorganized architecture, all these features being more prominent in severe or high-grade dysplasia. Conversely, these cytologic and architectural abnormalities are less pronounced in mild or low-grade dysplasia. Because high-grade dysplasia may be histologically indistinguishable from intraepithelial or in situ carcinoma, the expression intraepithelial neoplasia is often used synonymously with dysplasia.

Squamous cell dysplasia

In the esophagus, squamous cell dysplasia, morphologically indistinguishable from its counterpart in other squamous mucosae such as the uterine cervix, often precedes or coexists with invasive squamous cell carcinoma. Careful histologic examination of esophagectomy specimens for non-irradiated

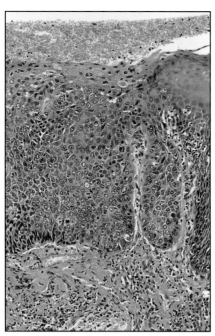

Fig. 8.2 • Severe dysplasia of esophageal squamous epithelium adjacent to an invasive squamous cell carcinoma.

squamous carcinoma discloses squamous dysplastic lesions of all grades in the adjacent background mucosa in a high proportion of cases (Fig. 8.2)[10] and prospective studies have demonstrated the relative risk of malignancy with increasing grades of dysplasia.[11] Endoscopically visible and histologically evident squamous dysplastic lesions frequently occur in the esophagi of high-risk populations, as in Northern China.[12] These findings support the idea of a sequential progression from squamous cell dysplasia to invasive squamous carcinoma. Two histologic variants of squamous cell dysplasia are recognized: basal squamous dysplasia in which the abnormal cells are confined to the basal layer,[13] and pagetoid squamous dysplasia characterized by dysplastic cells occupying the midzone of the epithelium only.[14]

Glandular dysplasia

In the esophagus, glandular dysplasia is considered as a precursor of adenocarcinoma complicating Barrett's esophagus; it may be present extensively or focally, with or without endoscopic abnormality. Glandular dysplasia may also be found in conjunction with obvious adenocarcinoma, adjacent to and away from the tumor area.[15] Glandular dysplasia may be graded like squamous cell dysplasia into low or high grade, based on the degree of architectural or cellular abnormalities.[16]

"Early cancer"

So-called "early cancer" of the esophagus is a clinical concept which, in terms of pathology, corresponds to invasive carcinoma that is strictly confined to the mucosa or submucosa, with or without lymph node spread. It is best referred to as "superficial carcinoma". Most superficial carcinomas of the esophagus are conventional squamous carcinomas,[17] but adenocarcinoma arising in Barrett's esophagus may also present as superficial cancer.[18]

Squamous cell carcinoma

Clinical features Squamous cell carcinoma is the commonest malignant tumor of the esophagus, affecting males more often than females. Its frequency increases with age, with a median age of 65 years. There is a marked geographic variation in its incidence, which is high in central Asia, China and South Africa, and low in Europe and North America. Putative etiologic factors include smoking, alcohol consumption, dietary deficiency, fungal contamination of foodstuffs and lye ingestion; there is also an association with the Paterson–Kelly (Plummer–Vinson) syndrome, achalasia, esophageal diverticula, and celiac disease.[19] In most of these conditions there is a chronic esophagitis, more often than not asymptomatic, but its incidence and histologic diagnosis, particularly in high-risk populations, remain controversial.[20,21] Studies have suggested a role for human papillomaviruses, especially types 16 and 18, in the pathogenesis of some esophageal cancers,[22,23] although this seems to vary according to the geographic incidence of esophageal carcinoma.[24] Apart from the rare occurrence but very high frequency of esophageal carcinoma in autosomally inherited tylosis (non-epidermolytic palmoplantar keratoderma)[25] (Fig. 8.3), there is little evidence that heredity plays a major part. Studies of molecular abnormalities in carcinoma of the esophagus have suggested a role for autocrine stimulation of over-expressed epidermal growth factor receptors by epidermal growth factor and transforming growth factor-alpha, amplification of *cyclin D1*, mutation of *p53* and *MTS1*, allelic loss in the *p53*, *Rb*, and *APC* genes, and loss of heterozygosity (LOH) at loci on chromosomes 3p, 9q, 10p, 17q, 18q, 19q and 21q.[26,27] The LOH on chromosome 17q in about 70 percent of sporadic esophageal squamous carcinomas is of particular interest because it usually involves the locus of the gene for inherited tylosis, suggesting that this acts as a tumor suppressor gene for esophageal cancer.[28]

Squamous cell carcinomas occur usually in the middle or lower third of the esophagus and present clinically with progressive dysphagia, weight loss, anemia or, rarely, esophageal perforation. Tumor spread, locally within the mediastinum or more widely following lymphovascular permeation, is usually advanced at presentation and the overall prognosis is poor.[29,30] However, cases of so-called superficial (early) squamous cell

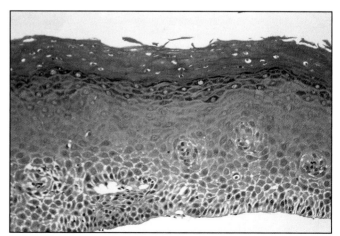

Fig. 8.3 • Esophageal biopsy from a patient with tylosis showing parakeratosis and hypergranulosis of the squamous epithelium.

carcinoma, where the lesion is confined to the mucosa or submucosa, have a much better outlook;[17] unfortunately, most such tumors are asymptomatic and are diagnosed incidentally during endoscopy with or without chromoendoscopy. About 10 percent of patients with esophageal squamous carcinoma, whether advanced or superficial, have synchronous or metachronous squamous cell carcinoma of the oropharyngeal ring.[31]

The uncommon *verrucous variant* of squamous cell carcinoma, although very well differentiated, slowly growing and rarely metastatic, not infrequently proves fatal because of failure to make a diagnosis before extensive local spread has occurred.[32] This is because endoscopic biopsies regularly produce pieces of well-differentiated squamous epithelium, showing minimal atypia, that are misdiagnosed by the pathologist as reactive epithelial hyperplasia, even when the endoscopic appearances are clearly sinister. Correlation between clinical, endoscopic, radiologic and histologic features is therefore particularly important in reaching the correct diagnosis.

Macroscopic appearances Squamous cell carcinomas are usually circumferential, partly exophytic, partly ulcerating lesions that result in esophageal stricture (Fig. 8.4). Early (superficial) tumors are often pale plaque-like nodules which occasionally undergo surface erosion to give an appearance resembling esophagitis, or they may be virtually unrecognizable on gross examination (Fig. 8.5). Well-differentiated verrucous squamous cell carcinomas are usually large, warty lesions (Fig. 8.6) with well-demarcated, pushing margins which can be recognized on the cut surface. On the other hand, some poorly differentiated widely infiltrative lesions can give rise to a diffuse, ill-defined thickening of the esophageal wall, reminiscent of gastric linitis plastica. Post-cricoid carcinomas in the Paterson–Kelly syndrome have no special macroscopic features; their accompanying esophageal webs may be seen as a thin connective tissue diaphragm.

Fig. 8.4 • Advanced ulcerating squamous cell carcinoma. The tumor virtually encircles the lumen of the esophagus.

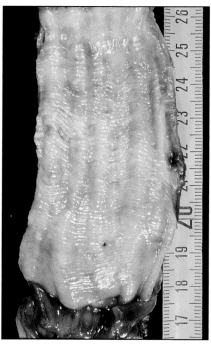

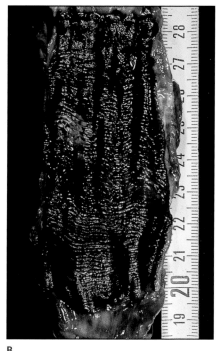

A

B

Fig. 8.5 • Superficial squamous cell carcinoma before (**A**) and after (**B**) applying Lugol's solution. The tumor is inconspicuous in the fresh specimen but is highlighted by its relative lack of iodine staining. (Reproduced with permission from Bogomoletz W V, Molas G, Gayet B et al. 1989 Superficial squamous cell carcinoma of the esophagus. Am J Surg Pathol 13: 535–546.)

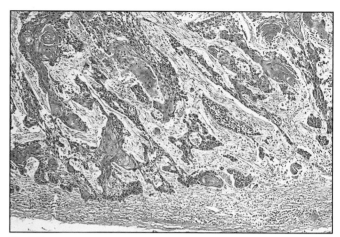

Fig. 8.7 • Invasive well-differentiated keratinizing squamous cell carcinoma of the esophagus.

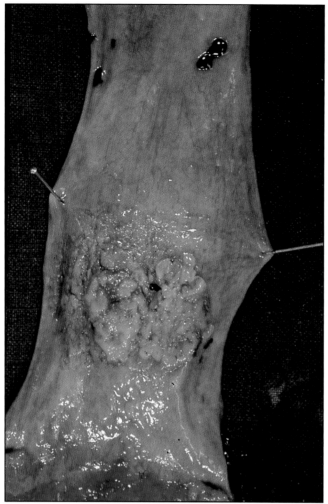

Fig. 8.6 • Early (superficial) squamous cell carcinoma of verrucous type. (Reproduced with permission from Bogomoletz W V, Molas G, Gayet B et al. 1989 Superficial squamous cell carcinoma of the esophagus. Am J Surg Pathol 13: 535–546.)

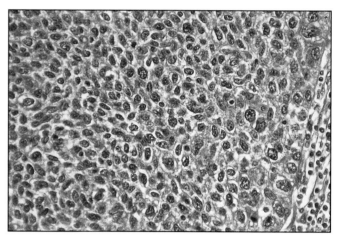

Fig. 8.8 • Poorly differentiated squamous cell carcinoma.

Multicentric esophageal squamous cell carcinomas do occur rarely, but data about their incidence and pathogenesis are conflicting. Multicentricity may be due to synchronous malignant transformation of several coexisting dysplastic lesions[33] or to submucosal spread from a single primary tumor giving rise to satellite nodules.[34] Occult intramural spread of this sort may result in inadequate surgical excision, and histologic examination of resection margins should always be undertaken to check for this.[35]

Microscopic appearances Squamous cell carcinomas of the esophagus show a range of differentiation from abundantly keratinized, well-differentiated lesions (Fig. 8.7) containing prominent intercellular bridges to poorly differentiated, virtually anaplastic, large or small cell tumors in which morphologic evidence of squamous differentiation may only be identified after prolonged searching (Fig. 8.8). Sometimes, this spectrum of appearances may occur within different areas of a single lesion. Occasionally, the squamous cell carcinoma is combined with a second, smaller component, either of adenocarcinoma[36] or small cell carcinoma[37] (see below). Tumors in resection specimens usually demonstrate invasion into, and often through, the muscle coats with infiltration of the extramural

mediastinal tissues to a variable degree; the extent of such local spread is an important prognostic factor.[38] Many cases show widespread infiltration of intramural, especially submucosal, lymphatics and this, along with spread along the ducts of esophageal glands,[39] may lead to extensive proximal and distal spread of tumor within the esophageal wall and the appearance of satellite deposits. The presence of a marked desmoplastic reaction or a pronounced lymphocytic response to the tumor,[40] both favorable prognostic indices,[38] at the advancing margin makes the macroscopic assessment of the extent of invasion difficult, and histologic evaluation of the deep (circumferential) margin is important in assessing adequacy of excision. Other histologic indicators of aggressive behavior include poor differentiation, tumor necrosis and lymphatic or vascular invasion.[38] DNA aneuploidy, as assessed by flow cytometry, is common in squamous carcinoma; it does not appear to be a useful prognostic marker.[41]

Superficial spreading carcinoma is a histologic variant of superficial squamous carcinoma characterized by in situ or invasive carcinoma confined to the mucosa and submucosa that extends over a distance of 20 mm or more.[42] It has been said to be associated with a particularly high incidence of lymphatic invasion, lymph node metastasis and a poor prognosis.

The *verrucous variant* of squamous cell carcinoma[32] is characterized by broad papillae of well-differentiated keratinizing

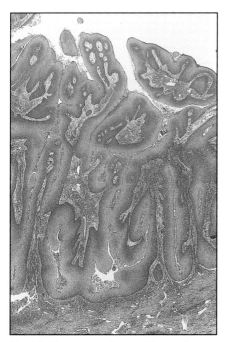

Fig. 8.9 • Verrucous carcinoma of the esophagus.

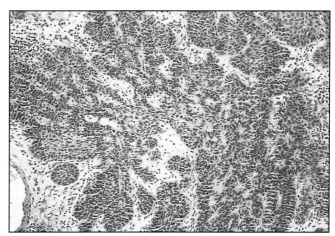

Fig. 8.10 • Basaloid type of squamous cell carcinoma.

squamous epithelium showing minimal cytologic atypia; these invade the underlying tissues over a broad front in the form of well-demarcated bulbous epithelial tongues (Fig. 8.9). Difficulties in its diagnosis have been highlighted above.

Superficial *basal cell carcinomas*, morphologically similar to those of the skin and with an apparently good prognosis, have also been described very rarely.[43] They should be distinguished from another less well-recognized variant, the so-called *basaloid squamous carcinoma* in which typical invasive and/or in situ squamous cell carcinoma is combined with a "basaloid" component comprising solid, discrete nests or lobules of small, mitotically active cells with pale nuclei and small nucleoli (Fig. 8.10), sometimes with microcystic spaces containing basophilic material or central foci of necrosis but without significant peripheral palisading.[44,45,46] Basaloid squamous carcinoma is commonest in elderly males and has an aggressive behavior with high metastatic potential. Some examples

show marked stromal hyalinization, producing an appearance reminiscent of adenoid cystic carcinoma; indeed it has been suggested that many examples in the literature of esophageal adenoid cystic carcinomas which have demonstrated a much more aggressive behavior than their salivary gland counterparts are misdiagnosed basaloid squamous carcinomas.[45]

Differential diagnosis The histologic diagnosis of squamous cell carcinoma of the esophagus is usually straightforward. The major differential diagnosis in biopsy interpretation is from regenerating squamous epithelium at the margin of a benign ulcer, where there may be expansion of the basal proliferative zone and brisk mitotic activity. The most useful features pointing to benign reactive hyperplasia are surface maturation of the epithelial cells and a lack of nuclear pleomorphism or atypical mitoses. Particular difficulty may arise when these epithelial changes are accompanied by bizarre reactive stromal cells in association with granulation tissue (Fig. 8.11), since these may display hyperchromatic, pleomorphic nuclei and large nucleoli which can easily tempt the unwary into a diagnosis of invasive carcinoma.[47,48] Paradoxically, these stromal cells usually show little mitotic activity, and their lack of cohesion betrays their non-epithelial nature. Another source of difficulty is the cytonuclear atypia of squamous epithelial

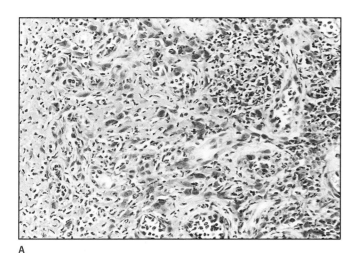

A

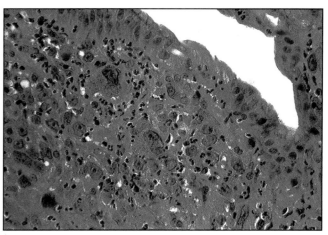

B

Fig. 8.11 • Pleomorphic spindle cells and endothelial cells in granulation tissue (**A**) from a biopsy of a benign lower esophageal ulcer and (**B**) in a small inflammatory polyp at the gastroesophageal junction.

cells that follows irradiation,[10] misinterpretation of which may lead to a false diagnosis of recurrent malignancy after radiotherapy. For pathologists practicing in the West, a definite diagnosis of infiltrating squamous cell carcinoma can only be made when there is unequivocal invasion by cohesive aggregates of neoplastic epithelial cells, but Japanese pathologists are prepared to diagnose carcinoma on the basis of nuclear and architectural changes alone.[49] This may be related to the higher frequency and better prognosis of superficial esophageal squamous carcinoma in Japan. In the case of verrucous carcinoma, unequivocal invasion is seldom demonstrable in superficial biopsies and clinicopathologic correlation is often vital in reaching the correct diagnosis.

Spindle cell (sarcomatoid) carcinoma (syn.: polypoid carcinoma, carcinosarcoma and pseudosarcoma)

Clinical features It is now widely accepted that spindle cell carcinoma, polypoid carcinoma, carcinosarcoma and pseudosarcoma are synonyms for an unusual esophageal epithelial neoplasm with distinctive macroscopic and microscopic features.[50-52] The tumors usually present with a short history of dysphagia and weight loss, most commonly in middle-aged or elderly men. Most reports suggest a better prognosis than for typical squamous cell carcinoma.[53] Not surprisingly, metastasis is related to the extent of invasion into the wall of the esophagus and to the size of the tumor; dissemination is almost invariable in tumors measuring more than 8 cm in diameter, but it occurs in only about 40 percent of smaller lesions.[53]

Macroscopic appearances The tumors are virtually always bulky, polypoid, intraluminal esophageal growths, sometimes with a quite narrow pedicle (Fig. 8.12), situated in the mid or lower third of the esophagus, and measuring up to 15 cm in length.[52]

Microscopic appearances These tumors are characterized by a biphasic pattern with a malignant spindle cell sarcomatoid component and an in situ or invasive carcinoma that is usually of squamous type (Fig. 8.13) but occasionally may show glandular differentiation.[51] The relative proportions of these components vary greatly from case to case, though the sarcomatoid element often predominates. Indeed, the carcinomatous tissue is quite often confined to the most superficial part of the mass where it is prone to destruction by ulceration. The sarcomatoid component usually consists of haphazardly arranged or interlacing bundles of mitotically active spindle cells, admixed with variable numbers of bizarre giant cells and, occasionally, heterologous components including neoplastic bone, cartilage or striated muscle.[54] Interestingly, the sarcoma-like component appears to have a higher proliferation index and is more frequently aneuploid than the epithelial component.[55] The stroma may contain conspicuous amounts of collagen, or have a myxoid appearance. Despite the large size and anaplastic appearance of the tumor, infiltration of the esophageal wall is sometimes only superficial, and a significant number of reported cases have been confined to the mucosa and submucosa. When metastases occur, they may contain the carcinomatous component, the spindle cell element, or both. Although the precise histogenesis of this tumor is not under-

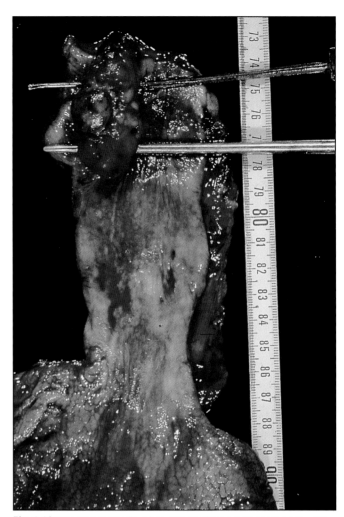

Fig. 8.12 • The typical spindle cell carcinoma of the esophagus is a polypoid tumor on a narrow pedicle.

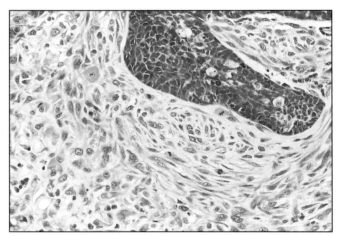

Fig. 8.13 • Spindle cell carcinoma. Both the epithelial and spindle components show cytologic features of malignancy.

stood, the most popular explanation for its sarcomatoid component is spindle cell differentiation or so-called mesenchymal metaplasia within what is essentially an invasive squamous cell carcinoma. In most cases, the spindle cell component retains at least focal keratin positivity and recent LOH studies support this viewpoint.[56] However, its clinical and pathologic features are sufficiently distinctive to warrant its separation as a special entity.

Differential diagnosis Problems may arise when a biopsy, or even a sample from a resection specimen, shows only the spindle cell component of the tumor, when the main differential diagnosis is polypoid leiomyosarcoma. Gastrointestinal stromal tumor (GIST) should also be considered in the differential diagnosis but is rare in the esophagus and typically is cytologically more bland (see below). Usually, a careful search for a carcinomatous component in further sections allows the correct diagnosis to be made. In biopsies this means further levels from the tissue block; in a resection specimen, careful sampling of the non-ulcerated tumor surface, or of the adjacent background mucosa, is most likely to be fruitful but, if this fails, examination of regional lymph nodes may identify metastases showing epithelial differentiation. Unequivocal immunopositivity for keratin in a spindle cell tumor, if present, would support the diagnosis. A positive reaction for desmin and smooth muscle actin would suggest leiomyosarcoma, while KIT immunopositivity suggests a GIST. However, KIT expression has been described in a carcinosarcoma,[57] but this may be an artifact of antigen retrieval. The combination of florid reactive epithelial changes and bizarre stromal cells in granulation tissue at the margin of benign esophageal erosions or ulcers (see above)[47,48] may raise the possibility of spindle cell carcinoma at first sight, but correlation with the endoscopic appearances usually allows the correct diagnosis to be made.

Adenocarcinoma

Clinical features The vast majority of primary esophageal adenocarcinomas arise in the lower esophagus within a background of the glandular (columnar) metaplasia of Barrett's esophagus, and hence, most cases are associated with chronic gastroesophageal reflux.[15] However, the development of carcinoma in Barrett's esophagus is not clearly related to the duration or severity of the esophagitis, although the length of the metaplastic segment may be important.[58] There is increasing evidence of an association between increasing body mass index and adenocarcinoma,[59] and drugs such as anticholinergic agents and beta-blockers that relax the gastroesophageal sphincter may also contribute to an increased risk of malignant transformation.[60] To date it is uncertain whether antireflux surgery reduces the cancer risk. The epidemiology of esophageal adenocarcinoma is very similar to that of carcinoma of the gastric cardia.[61] Men are affected much more frequently than women, there is an association with smoking, alcohol consumption and a diet low in fresh fruit, and there is evidence of an increasing incidence in Western populations.[62] Many genetic alterations have been reported in Barrett's adenocarcinoma. Mutations of the *p53* gene, accompanied by chromosome 17p allelic loss, c-*erb*B-2 overexpression and *p16* loss of heterozygosity and methylation play an important role in the pathogenesis of the tumor[63–65] and have also been described in dysplasia and non-neoplastic metaplastic Barrett's type mucosa.[64] Upregulation of cyclo-oxygenase 2 (COX-2) expression in the metaplasia-dysplasia-carcinoma sequence may be of potential importance with regard to chemoprevention.[66]

Most esophageal adenocarcinomas are diagnosed in patients without a prior clinical diagnosis of Barrett's esophagus and

present at a late stage with progressive dysphagia and weight loss resulting from extensive infiltration through the esophageal wall. The prognosis in these symptomatic patients is poor: in one series only 34 percent of operable cases survived for 2 years, and only 15 percent for 5 years.[67] However, increasing endoscopic surveillance of patients with Barrett's esophagus may lead to the identification of tumors at an early stage, with an improved prognosis.[68]

Esophageal adenocarcinomas occurring in the absence of histologically demonstrable Barrett's esophagus are infrequent and may represent cases where the original metaplastic mucosa has been destroyed by the tumor.[69] Adenocarcinoma may also rarely arise in heterotopic gastric mucosa, such as in the so-called cervical inlet patch in the upper esophagus.[70]

Macroscopic appearances Most adenocarcinomas are flat, ulcerating, infiltrative lesions that lead to stenosis of the esophageal lumen. Some have an exophytic, polypoid component and, in a few cases, the whole tumor is of this type. The background metaplastic Barrett's mucosa, when visible, has a red, finely granular appearance which can be readily distinguished from the paler, smooth esophageal squamous epithelium.

Microscopic appearances Most examples are tubular or papillary adenocarcinomas of "intestinal" pattern and show variable differentiation with a morphologic spectrum that is very similar to adenocarcinomas of the gastric cardia (Fig. 8.14).[71] High-grade dysplasia in the background Barrett's-type metaplastic glandular epithelium is very common (Fig. 8.15).[72] Some tumors have the pattern of mucinous adenocarcinoma, with prominent extracellular mucus production, but the diffuse type of signet-ring carcinoma is very unusual.[73] While neuroendocrine cells are commonly found in Barrett's metaplasia and dysplasia, they are found in only about 20 percent of esophageal adenocarcinomas.[74] However, adenocarcinoma mixed with carcinoid tumor has been described at this site.[71] There are also rare reports of tumors showing areas of squamous differentiation[71] and one of carcinosarcoma in which the epithelial component was adenocarcinomatous.[75] The poor outlook for

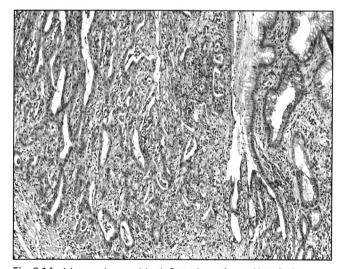

Fig. 8.14 • Adenocarcinoma arising in Barrett's esophagus. Metaplastic intestinal-type epithelium is seen in the right side of the field

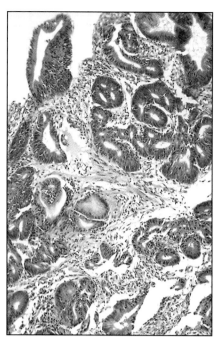

Fig. 8.15 • High-grade dysplasia in metaplastic glandular epithelium of Barrett's esophagus.

symptomatic (non-screened) tumors, even when they are resectable, is explained by the fact that more than 80 percent show infiltration through the esophageal muscular coat, often with conspicuous perineurial invasion; they also often have lymph node metastases, and are aneuploid on DNA flow cytometric analysis – all indices of an adverse prognosis.[15]

Differential diagnosis Difficulties in histologic diagnosis are largely confined to esophageal biopsies and relate to the differentiation between reactive hyperplasia of the glandular epithelium, dysplasia, and indisputable invasive adenocarcinoma. The principles involved are identical to those in the biopsy diagnosis of gastric adenocarcinoma and are considered fully on page 344, in conjunction with the Vienna classification of precancerous lesions (Table 8.2).[16] The often difficult distinction between high-grade dysplasia in Barrett's mucosa and adenocarcinoma in biopsies, based upon the demonstration of unequivocal invasion, is not always critical since about 20 percent of cases with a biopsy diagnosis of high-grade dysplasia have invasive malignancy in a subsequent resection specimen.[76] Some authorities, therefore, recommend surgery for high-grade dysplasia alone, if confidently diagnosed. Other centers use a variety of different local endoscopic therapies, including endoscopic mucosal resection (EMR), photodynamic therapy and argon plasma coagulation, on the basis that lymph node spread is very infrequent in such cases. Careful pathologic examination of EMR specimens is required to evaluate completeness of excision (which in one study was frequently not achieved[77]) and biopsy follow-up following photodynamic therapy may identify residual tumor covered by regenerated squamous epithelium.[78]

Mucoepidermoid and adenoid cystic carcinoma

There is great confusion in the literature regarding the nomenclature, definition and histogenesis of these two esophageal tumors, making evaluation of published reports very difficult. Examples of "classical" mucoepidermoid carcinoma and adenoid cystic carcinoma[79,80] arising from the submucosal glands of the esophagus, as defined strictly by the criteria used for neoplasms of the salivary glands (see Ch. 7), are extremely uncommon. They are usually small, intramural lesions covered by an intact, non-neoplastic, squamous epithelium and are associated with a relatively good prognosis.

Most published cases of esophageal mucoepidermoid or adenoid cystic carcinoma are, however, quite different; they are large, aggressive tumors in which mucoepidermoid[79,81] or adenoid cystic-like[82,83] areas are intermingled with other elements, usually classical squamous cell carcinoma or undifferentiated carcinoma. These tumors frequently metastasize widely and their prognosis is similar to that of pure squamous cell carcinoma. They differ from their classical, salivary-type counterparts in that they often involve the surface epithelium (which sometimes shows typical in situ carcinoma)[83] and show brisk mitotic activity, but apparently little propensity for perineurial invasion. Moreover, the so-called mucoepidermoid elements often show keratinization, not a feature of the classical tumor, and the adenoid cystic areas frequently have necrosis. Some authors have reflected these atypical features in their choice of nomenclature; for example "carcinoma with adenoid cystic differentiation" has been used instead of adenoid cystic carcinoma.[83] Others have emphasized the similarity to the so-called basaloid squamous carcinomas described above, which may contain areas with stromal hyalinization and a microcystic pattern. Moreover, the finding of glandular, mucus-secreting and cribriform elements in as many as 21 percent of esophageal squamous cell carcinomas, usually forming a minority component in the more superficial parts of the tumor,[36] suggests that this whole spectrum of tumors may best be regarded as variants of squamous cell carcinoma showing bidirectional differentiation.

Adenosquamous carcinoma

In addition to the mucoepidermoid and adenoid cystic carcinomas described above, there are a number of reports of so-called adenosquamous carcinoma, a rare tumor made up of invasive adenocarcinoma and squamous cell carcinoma, the latter often keratinized.[84] Most cases have occurred in the lower esophagus, in association with Barrett's esophagus.[71] Adenosquamous carcinoma has also been described intermingled with spindle cell carcinoma.[85]

Small cell carcinoma

Clinical features Both clinically and pathologically, this rare, highly malignant neuroendocrine tumor resembles its counterpart in the lung.[37,86,87] It is somewhat more common in males and usually presents in the middle-aged or elderly with dysphagia and weight loss. Only rarely are there symptoms attributable to ectopic hormone secretion,[88] although occasionally such peptides can be demonstrated in the tumor cells by immunocytochemistry.[89] The prognosis is very poor due to early and widespread metastasis.

Macroscopic appearances Most reported cases are large, exophytic and infiltrative masses (Fig. 8.16A) situated in the

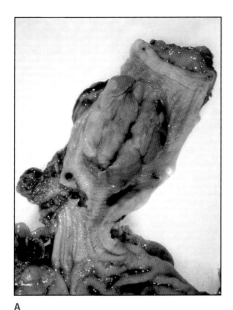

A

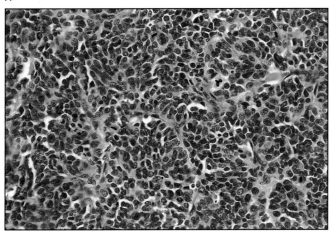

B

Fig. 8.16 • (A,B) Small cell carcinoma of the esophagus. Macroscopically (**A**) this is an exophytic tumor in the lower third of the esophagus.

lower or middle third of the esophagus. Occasionally, multiple tumor foci may be present.

Microscopic appearances The tumor consists of small anaplastic cells with scanty cytoplasm and round to oval hyperchromatic, often molded, nuclei with inconspicuous nucleoli but frequent mitoses (Fig. 8.16B). The cells usually form sheets, often with areas of necrosis; occasionally they are arranged in nests, cords, ribbons or rosettes. Vascular invasion and lymph node metastases are common. Evidence of endocrine differentiation is patchy and variable, both between and within cases, and includes cytoplasmic argyrophilia, immunopositivity for endocrine markers (chromogranin, PGP (protein gene product) 9.5, synaptophysin or Leu-7), or ultrastructural demonstration of neurosecretory granules. There may be endocrine-type amyloid deposition.[37] In a significant proportion of cases, esophageal small cell carcinoma is combined with in situ or invasive squamous cell carcinoma[37,86] and/or adenocarcinoma, reflecting multidirectional differentiation within the tumor.[37,90]

Differential diagnosis Small cell carcinoma of the esophagus should be distinguished from secondary spread from a

primary small cell carcinoma of the lung, poorly differentiated squamous cell carcinoma, basaloid squamous carcinoma and malignant lymphoma. Argyrophil silver stains, immunocytochemistry and electron microscopy each have a potential diagnostic role.

Choriocarcinoma

Choriocarcinoma has been described in the esophagus in pure form,[91] in association with lower esophageal adenocarcinoma,[92] and as a secondary lesion due to direct spread from a mediastinal choriocarcinoma.[93]

Paget's disease

Pagetoid infiltration of the esophageal squamous epithelium from either underlying adenosquamous carcinoma[94] or mucous gland carcinoma[95] has been reported. A similar pattern of spread may occur in esophageal malignant melanoma; mucin histochemistry and immunocytochemistry for carcinoembryonic antigen and S-100 protein should distinguish these lesions in biopsy material.

Pathologic staging of esophageal carcinoma

Esophageal carcinoma, irrespective of its histologic type, is usually staged by the TNM system.[96] This takes into account the depth of direct tumor invasion (pT), the presence or absence of regional lymph node metastases (pN) and the occurrence of distant metastases (pM); it is illustrated in Table 8.1. The pathology report should also include a statement on the completeness of excision at the proximal and distal resection margins, and also at the circumferential resection margin.[97]

The examination and reporting of esophageal resection specimens for carcinoma after preoperative chemotherapy and/or radiotherapy requires special precautions. Indeed, the degree of superficial and deep tumor regression may be such that no naked-eye mucosal lesion is seen. Only examination of

Table 8.1	Pathologic TNM staging of esophageal carcinoma[96]
T — Primary Tumor	
pT1	Tumor invades lamina propria or submucosa
pT2	Tumor invades muscularis propria
pT3	Tumor invades adventitia
pT4	Tumor invades adjacent structures
N — Regional Lymph Nodes	
pN0	No regional lymph node metastasis
pN1	Regional lymph node metastasis present
M — Distant Metastasis[a]	
M0	No distant metastasis
M1	Distant metastasis present

[a]Pathologic staging cannot usually comment on the presence or absence of distant metastasis, unless biopsies of distant organs have been submitted for histologic examination.

the mucosal surface with a hand lens and careful palpation of the esophageal wall may disclose a scarred or thickened area. The latter must then be entirely blocked for histologic study. Systems of grading tumor regression have been proposed, based on a semi-quantitative assessment of residual cancer versus fibrosis.[98] The difficulty with using these is the fact that the degree of tumor-associated fibrosis present before chemoradiotherapy is unknown. More important is the careful pathologic staging of the extent of residual tumor in the post-treatment resection specimen, and this is the best predictor of outcome.[99]

Malignant melanoma

Clinical features Primary esophageal malignant melanoma is a rare but well-documented neoplasm, occurring most frequently in the mid or lower esophagus of middle-aged and elderly individuals. Patients present with dysphagia.[100] The incidence is said to be higher in Japan, especially in women.[101] Rare examples have been reported in younger patients. The prognosis is poor[100,102] and, unlike cutaneous melanoma, does not appear to be related to the thickness of the primary lesion.[101] Secondary spread of melanoma to the esophagus occurs more commonly but is still rare; it was found in 3.2 percent of autopsy cases with disseminated disease.[100]

Macroscopic appearances Most malignant melanomas have macroscopic features that are indistinguishable from those of other primary esophageal malignancies, although many reports describe a polypoid intraluminal growth pattern. Only a minority produce sufficient melanin to be pigmented (Fig. 8.17). As with cutaneous melanoma, the primary tumor may be surrounded by so-called satellite lesions.

Microscopic appearances

There are no special histologic features that distinguish esophageal malignant melanomas from those arising in the skin or at other mucosal surfaces; they show the same range from epithelioid to spindle cell types (Fig. 8.18). Most are amelanotic. While many have an ulcerated, nodular-type growth pattern, some are of superficial spreading type with conspicuous pagetoid or lentiginous (Fig. 8.19) infiltration of the adjacent squamous epithelium by nests of neoplastic melanocytes.[103] Junctional activity in the adjacent epithelium is also common[104] and cases are reported in association with a more widespread focal or diffuse esophageal melanosis (Fig. 8.17) and melanocytic atypia.[105] In contrast, melanocytes are found in only some 4 percent of individuals without esophageal disease,[106] although their numbers may increase with chronic inflammation, a phenomenon that has also been described in association with esophageal carcinoma.[107] The histologic features of primary esophageal melanomas do not predict their behavior.

Differential diagnosis Amelanotic malignant melanomas have to be distinguished from poorly differentiated carcinomas and sarcomas. Immunocytochemistry for S-100 and melanocytic markers (e.g., HMB-45) is invaluable, as is the presence of melanocytic atypia or pagetoid melanomatous infiltration of the adjacent epithelium (after excluding true Paget's disease, see above). The latter features are also useful in distinguishing

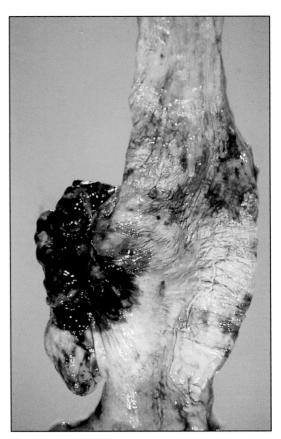

Fig. 8.17 • Pigmented esophageal malignant melanoma with melanosis of the background mucosa. (Reproduced with permission from Bogomoletz W V 1989 Rare and secondary (metastatic) tumors [of esophagus]. In: Whitehead R (ed) Gastrointestinal and esophageal pathology. Churchill Livingstone, Edinburgh, p 701–710.)

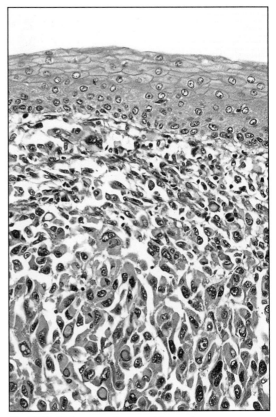

Fig. 8.18 • Malignant melanoma of the esophagus.

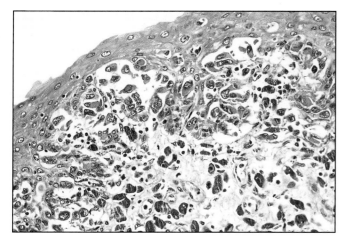

Fig. 8.19 • Lentiginous radial component of malignant melanoma adjacent to the tumor in Figure 8.18.

primary tumors from metastatic melanoma. It is important to be aware that malignant melanomas can sometimes express KIT. Although virtually all esophageal melanocytic neoplasms are malignant melanomas, we are aware of one case report of a benign melanocytic lesion of uncertain histogenesis that was possibly a blue nevus.[108]

Non-epithelial Tumors

Smooth muscle tumors

Clinical features Smooth muscle tumors are uncommon and present most often in middle age with dysphagia or heartburn. Many are asymptomatic and a minority cause bleeding. They are somewhat commoner in men and their frequency increases along the length of the esophagus (i.e., distally).[109,110] Leiomyomas are the most common mesenchymal tumor of the esophagus and greatly outnumber leiomyosarcomas, which tend to occur in an older age group. Both lesions are usually solitary, though multiple leiomyomas are described in patients with multiple endocrine neoplasia type 1,[111] and sometimes in the setting of so-called "diffuse leiomyomatosis of the esophagus" (see p. 339). It is impossible to obtain good prognostic information on esophageal leiomyosarcoma because of its rarity and the fact that some reported cases appear to be misdiagnosed spindle cell carcinomas. Nevertheless, it appears that the clinical behavior is related to the extent of local spread at diagnosis; tumors that are resectable have a favorable outlook and only a minority lead to disseminated blood-borne metastases.[112,113]

Macroscopic appearances Tumors may arise from any of the smooth muscle coats of the esophagus,[109] usually producing large polypoid, intraluminal masses covered by mucosa (Fig. 8.20) that may undergo secondary ulceration; less frequently encountered are well-demarcated, lobulated, extramural mediastinal tumors. Clinically significant tumors that are confined to the wall of the esophagus are rare, though it is not uncommon to find incidental tiny leiomyomas within the muscularis propria or even the muscularis mucosae of the gastroesophageal junction at autopsy or in resection specimens – so-called "seedling leiomyomas".[114] Smooth muscle tumors

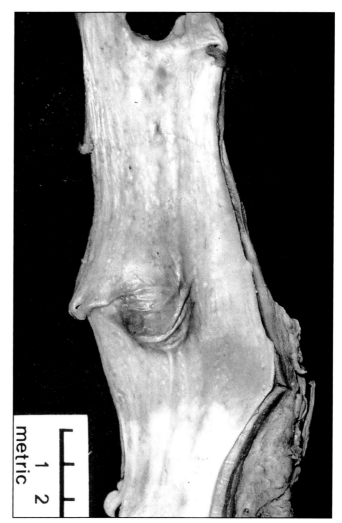

Fig. 8.20 • Polypoid esophageal leiomyoma.

classically show a bulging gray whorled cut surface, sometimes with flecks of calcification, but leiomyosarcomas are often more fleshy, with areas of necrosis and an infiltrative growth pattern (Fig. 8.21).

Microscopic appearances Most esophageal smooth muscle tumors resemble their counterparts elsewhere in the body and are composed of interlacing bundles of smooth muscle cells intermingled with variable amounts of collagen. The cells have blunt-ended, cigar-shaped nuclei and eosinophilic cytoplasm (Fig. 8.22) containing myofibrils that show immunopositivity for desmin or smooth muscle actin, and are negative for KIT and CD34. Leiomyosarcomas may show obviously anaplastic features with marked nuclear pleomorphism, tumor giant cells and abnormal mitotic figures, though more often they are difficult to separate confidently from leiomyomas on the basis of histology alone. Features suggesting malignancy include large size (>5 cm diameter), intratumoral necrosis or hemorrhage, and a mitotic rate in excess of 5 per 10 standard high-power fields.

Differential diagnosis The differential diagnosis includes nerve sheath tumors, GIST, spindle cell carcinoma (see above) and amelanotic malignant melanoma.

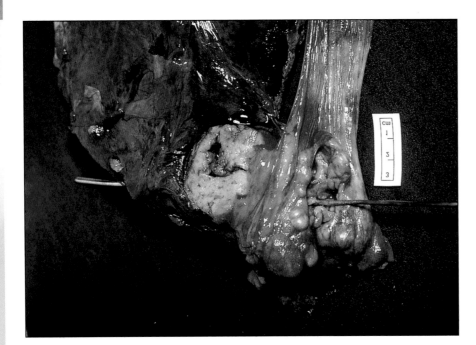

Fig. 8.21 • Leiomyosarcoma of the esophagus invading the mediastinum and adjacent lung.

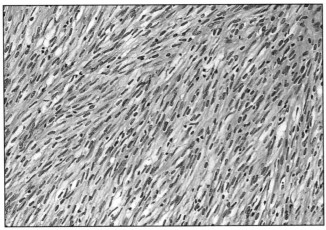

Fig. 8.22 • Cellular leiomyoma of the esophagus.

Gastrointestinal stromal tumor (GIST)

Gastrointestinal stromal tumors (GISTs) are uncommon in the esophagus, but most are clinically malignant and commonly develop liver metastases.[113,115] They occur in older adults, typically presenting with dysphagia. Most are spindle cell tumors and their morphology and immunohistochemical profile is identical to their gastric counterparts (see p. 356).

Granular cell tumor

Though uncommon and usually an incidental finding at autopsy, granular cell tumors occur more frequently in the esophagus than elsewhere in the digestive tract.[116] Most form solitary, circumscribed, 1–2 cm raised, firm, pale-yellow submucosal nodules in the lower third of the esophagus; occasionally they are multiple.[117] Larger tumors may give rise to annular esophageal stenosis and produce symptoms of dysphagia.[118] Histologically, they are indistinguishable from granular cell tumors elsewhere (see Ch. 27) and consist of aggregates of spindle or polygonal cells with regular nuclei and granular

eosinophilic periodic acid–Schiff- (PAS-)positive cytoplasm containing immunoreactive S-100 protein; the overlying squamous epithelium may show pseudoepitheliomatous hyperplasia. Although this is generally a benign tumor, rare cases of malignancy have been reported.[119]

Other connective tissue tumors

Case reports exist of a whole range of benign and malignant connective tissue tumors of the esophagus. Benign lesions include plexiform schwannomas[120] and neurofibromas,[121] rhabdomyomas of the striated muscle of the proximal esophagus,[122] hemangiomas and lymphangiomas,[123,124] glomus tumors,[13] lipomas,[125,126] chondromas and osteochrondromas.[127] Some of these lesions may be hamartomas, rather than true neoplasms.[128]

Reports of primary esophageal sarcomas include embryonal rhabdomyosarcoma in childhood,[129] malignant rhabdoid tumor,[130] Kaposi sarcoma in patients with immunodeficiency,[131] liposarcoma,[132] hemangiopericytoma,[133] malignant mesenchymoma,[134] so-called malignant fibrous histiocytoma,[135] osteosarcoma,[136] and synovial sarcoma.[137] Before making such diagnoses it is vital to sample the tumor extensively to exclude specific sarcomatous differentiation in a spindle cell carcinoma (see above); it is difficult to be sure how comprehensively this was done in many of the published case reports.

Lymphoma and leukemia

Involvement of the esophagus by lymphoma is very uncommon.[138] The tumors may be ulcerated or polypoid and usually present with hemorrhage or dysphagia. Primary Hodgkin[139] and non-Hodgkin lymphomas are recorded, the latter including tumors of T-cell[140] and B-cell[141] phenotypes, with mucosa-associated lymphoid tissue (MALT) lymphoma, diffuse large B-cell lymphoma and mantle cell lymphoma.[141,142] In one case of focal lymphoid hyperplasia of the esophagus, there were some features suggestive of localized Castleman's disease.[143] Extramedullary plasmacytomas[144] of the esophagus have also been reported. Secondary involvement by hemato-lymphoid malignancies is probably more common, and includes direct extension from primary gastric malignant lymphomas,[145] spread from involved mediastinal lymph nodes, or multifocal deposits in the esophageal submucosa as part of a generalized lymphoma or leukemia; the latter may undergo necrosis and ulceration.[146]

Secondary tumors

The esophagus is not a frequent site of metastatic disease. Nevertheless, direct extension from tumors of the stomach, thyroid, hypopharynx, bronchus and lung is well recognized, as is direct invasion from paraesophageal lymph node metastases. Metastatic involvement of the esophagus has been described most frequently from carcinoma of the breast and malignant melanoma, but other primary tumors include carcinomas of the stomach, pancreas, lung, prostate, testis, kidney, cervix and endometrium.

Tumor-like lesions

Fibrovascular (fibrous) polyp

Fibrovascular polyps are most commonly reported in the upper third of the esophagus, at the level of the cricoid cartilage. They are typically solitary, pedunculated lesions, often with long stalks, that may achieve a considerable size and cause dysphagia. Sometimes they may be regurgitated into the mouth, following which impaction in the larynx has been reported to cause death. As the name suggests, fibrovascular polyps are composed of a core of edematous, mucosal or submucosal, fibrous or fibroadipose tissue and blood vessels covered by a thickened or ulcerated squamous epithelium.[147] Their etiology is uncertain but some probably represent an exuberant response to injury or chronic irritation; others may be hamartomas. There are rare cases of squamous cell carcinoma arising within a fibrovascular polyp.[148]

Inflammatory fibroid polyp

Compared with fibrovascular polyps, inflammatory fibroid polyps are commoner in the mid and distal esophagus, are less frequently pedunculated and more frequently ulcerated, and may involve the full thickness of the esophageal wall, sometimes replacing the muscle coats and even apparently "infiltrating" adjacent tissues. They may present with hemorrhage or obstructive symptoms. Like their counterparts elsewhere in the digestive tract (see Ch. 9), they are composed of a loose edematous granulation tissue-like stroma containing variable numbers of mononuclear cells, plasma cells, neutrophils, eosinophils, mast cells and plump spindle-shaped fibroblasts that tend to be arranged concentrically around prominent blood vessels.[149] Controversy remains over whether they represent truly inflammatory lesions or unusual connective tissue neoplasms, but their clinical behavior is always benign.

Cysts

Congenital esophageal cysts are of two types. Unilocular intramural inclusion cysts are found in the lower part of the esophagus (Fig. 8.23).[150] They have a smooth lining of

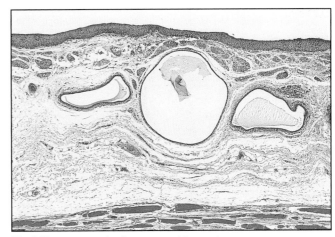

Fig. 8.23 • Submucosal inclusion cysts of the esophagus.

columnar, ciliated columnar or squamous epithelium that may occasionally be thrown into papillary projections. Duplication, bronchogenic and neurenteric cysts result from more complicated developmental abnormalities of the foregut[151] and may involve the wall of the esophagus or lie separately from it in the posterior mediastinum, when they may be accompanied by vertebral anomalies. They are lined by epithelium that is esophageal, bronchial or gastric in type, usually overlying a distinct muscularis propria. They may also contain cartilage or pancreatic tissue.[152] Squamous cell carcinoma arising from an esophageal intramural squamous-lined cyst has been reported.[153]

Acquired retention cysts, sometimes wrongly referred to as pseudodiverticula, are formed by postinflammatory cystic dilatation of the excretory ducts of submucosal esophageal glands. They are usually found in the lower esophagus and may be lined by cuboidal or squamous epithelium.

Amyloid

We know of a single case report of an intramural amyloid tumor of the esophagus.[154] Subclinical non-mass forming involvement by systemic amyloidosis is more frequent.

Glycogenic acanthosis

This lesion, of unknown etiology, is seen most commonly in the lower third of the esophagus and consists of numerous white, discrete, raised mucosal plaques, usually only a few millimeters in size, occurring predominantly on the crests of the longitudinal folds of the esophagus.[155] Microscopically, there is thickening of the superficial layer of the squamous epithelium by glycogen-rich vacuolated cells (Fig. 8.24). The basal layer does not usually show hyperplasia, nor is there any evidence of atypia or hyperkeratosis. The condition has no malignant potential. Diffuse or widespread glycogenic acanthosis is said to be a feature of patients with Cowden's syndrome.[156]

Diffuse leiomyomatosis

In this rare condition of unknown etiology, there is diffuse thickening of the esophageal musculature, sometimes with focal accentuation to form confluent nodules or even overt

Fig. 8.24 • Glycogenic acanthosis.

leiomyomas. Many case reports are of children or young adults presenting with dysphagia, although others are of incidental autopsy findings in the elderly. Microscopically, there is a diffuse hyperplasia of the circular and longitudinal muscle layers with replacement of the normal fiber pattern by disorganized, irregular whorls of interlacing muscle fibers.[157] These may also show degenerative changes with dystrophic calcification,[158] and there may be chronic inflammation and neuronal thickening. Sometimes these abnormalities affect the muscularis mucosae, or they may extend to involve the musculature of the proximal stomach.[158] Although the condition is usually sporadic, autosomal dominant inherited forms of esophageal leiomyomatosis have been associated with clinical features of achalasia,[159] an Alport-like nephropathy,[158] tracheobronchial or female genital (especially vulvar) smooth muscle tumors,[158,160] intestinal leiomyomas and neurofibromas, urticaria pigmentosa and systemic mast cell disease.[159]

Heterotopias

The so-called cervical inlet patch has traditionally been regarded as heterotopic gastric mucosa occurring in the post-cricoid region of the esophagus, where it can be identified endoscopically as one or more well-demarcated pink patches measuring up to 4 cm diameter in an otherwise pale mucosa. The gastric-like glands may replace the normal squamous epithelium or lie in the subepithelial tissue. Most examples are asymptomatic and clinically insignificant lesions discovered incidentally at endoscopy, though there are rare descriptions of both peptic-type ulceration, resulting in an esophagotracheal fistula, and the development of adenocarcinoma.[161] Recently, phenotypic similarity with the mucosa of Barrett's esophagus has challenged the view that all cases represent genuine gastric heterotopia.[162] Heterotopic pancreatic tissue is uncommon; it has been described both in the upper esophagus[163] and in duplication cysts.[152]

Other reported varieties of heterotopia include sebaceous glands within the esophageal submucosa, appearing endoscopically as raised yellow plaques,[164] and respiratory-type ciliated epithelium.[165] Strictly speaking, however, the latter is not a true heterotopia but a developmental remnant, since it is a constituent of normal fetal esophagus.

Hyperplastic polyps at the gastroesophageal junction

Long-standing mucosal injury at the gastroesophageal junction, in association with erosive esophagitis, "junctitis" and ulceration related to gastroesophageal reflux may be associated with inflammation and polypoid hyperplasia of the junctional mucosa.[166] Such inflammatory or hyperplastic polyps usually consist of regenerating cardia-type mucosa, sometimes admixed with squamous epithelium. They may show florid regenerative atypia, either of the epithelium or in stromal cells within granulation tissue (see p. 331 and Fig. 8.11B) that must not be over-interpreted as dysplasia or carcinoma.[48] Having said this, true dysplasia has also been recorded.[166]

Stomach

Epithelial tumors

Adenoma

Clinical features Gastric adenomas usually arise in the context of atrophic gastritis with intestinal metaplasia.[167,168] Most occur as a solitary, large (3–4 cm), sessile or pedunculated polyp[169,170] that is asymptomatic until it bleeds, ulcerates or gives rise to gastric outflow obstruction. These lesions show an increasing incidence with age and may occur in individuals with familial adenomatous polyposis.[171] Since they are preinvasive neoplasms with potential for progression to adenocarcinoma,[168,169,172] they must be treated by local excision, usually endoscopic polypectomy or endoscopic mucosal resection. In addition to being premalignant lesions themselves, they may be accompanied by coexistent carcinoma elsewhere in the stomach; for reasons that are unclear, this association appears to be particularly common in males.[168,173]

Macroscopic appearances Adenomas are sessile or pedunculated mucosal lesions with a velvety lobulated surface (Fig. 8.25). The adjacent gastric mucosa may be smooth and atrophic.

Microscopic appearances Gastric adenomas are, by definition, composed of dysplastic epithelium, which, in view of the fact that they commonly arise within a background of intestinal metaplasia, usually shows some degree of intestinal-type differentiation towards absorptive cells, goblet cells, endocrine cells or even Paneth cells. Many are therefore virtually indistinguishable from colorectal adenomas and show the same range of abnormalities of architecture, differentiation and cell proliferation, allowing them to be subdivided into tubular, tubulovillous and villous types on the basis of architecture, and to show low grade or high grade epithelial dysplasia according to the degree of nuclear crowding, hyperchromasia, stratification, mitotic activity, cytoplasmic differentiation and architectural distortion (Figs 8.26, 8.27).[172,174] However, a minority show morphologic and mucin histochemical characteristics of gastric foveolar or pyloric gland type epithelium[170,175,176] (see type II dysplasia below) and others have both gastric and intestinal type features.[177] Another rare variant is a so-called

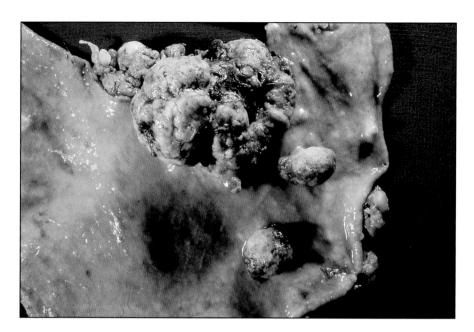

Fig. 8.25 • Part of a gastrectomy specimen containing a large polypoid adenocarcinoma (above) and two smaller pedunculated adenomas (below and right).

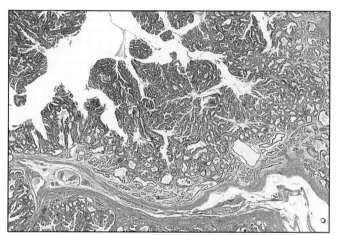

Fig. 8.26 • Sessile tubulovillous adenoma of the stomach.

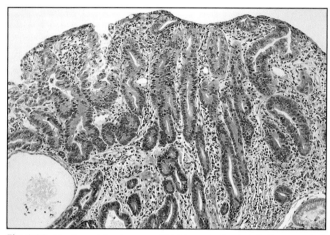

Fig. 8.28 • Sessile gastric adenoma with high-grade dysplasia in the upper half of the mucosa and cystic dilatation of antral glands (bottom left). This type of adenoma has been termed "borderline lesion" in the Japanese literature.

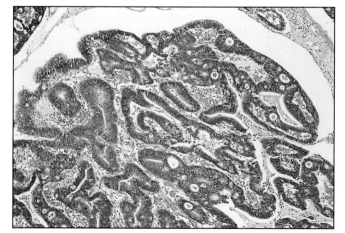

Fig. 8.27 • Tubular adenoma with high-grade dysplasia. The degree of architectural atypia at the top of the field with back-to-back glands amounts to early invasive intramucosal adenocarcinoma.

Paneth cell adenoma,[178] in which Paneth cells are the predominant cell type.

Although most gastric adenomas have an exophytic growth pattern giving rise to an elevated sessile or more rarely pedunculated mass, occasional examples may be "flat" or even depressed below the contour of the surrounding mucosa,[179] supporting the view that adenomas and dysplasia in flat mucosa can be considered as a single entity. In some sessile examples the dysplastic tubular glands, usually of low grade, are confined to the superficial half of the mucosa, with distorted and cystically dilated non-neoplastic glands lined by antral-type mucous cells or intestinal metaplasia occupying the deeper zones (Fig. 8.28).[172]

As with their colonic counterparts, the risk of malignancy in gastric adenomas is related to their size, degree of dysplasia and villosity of growth pattern. Thus, small pedunculated adenomas measuring less than 1 cm in diameter are usually tubular lesions with low-grade dysplasia and a low incidence

Table 8.2	The Vienna classification of gastrointestinal epithelial neoplasia[16]. Reproduced with permission from the BMJ Publishing Group.
Category 1	Negative for neoplasia/dysplasia
Category 2	Indefinite for neoplasia/dysplasia
Category 3	Non-invasive low grade neoplasia (low grade adenoma/dysplasia)
Category 4	Non-invasive high grade neoplasia 4.1 High grade adenoma/dysplasia 4.2 Non-invasive carcinoma (carcinoma in situ)[a] 4.3 Suspicion of invasive carcinoma
Category 5	Invasive neoplasia 5.1 Intramucosal carcinoma[b] 5.2 Submucosal carcinoma or beyond

[a]Non-invasive indicates absence of evident invasion.

[b]Intramucosal indicates invasion into the lamina propria or muscularis mucosae.

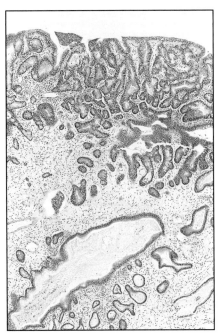

Fig. 8.29 • Well-differentiated intramucosal adenocarcinoma arising in the superficial portion of a hyperplastic (regenerative) polyp.

of carcinoma, as are the sessile variety in which dysplasia is confined to the superficial zones. Larger pedunculated tumors are more frequently villous with high-grade dysplasia, and a significant proportion contain invasive carcinoma; this has been described in 40–50 percent of cases of tumors larger than 2 cm.[177] A diagnosis of intramucosal adenocarcinoma implies the presence of invasion of the neoplastic epithelium into the lamina propria or deeper into the submucosa. Sometimes this can be clearly identified as irregular jagged budding of neoplastic epithelium into the surrounding loose connective tissue. At other times it can only be inferred from severe abnormalities of architecture, such as a solid growth pattern, complex aggregation of back-to-back glands with cribriform or small infiltrative abortive glands without obvious desmoplasia (see Fig. 8.27). Western pathologists usually demand the former (i.e., invasion) for a diagnosis of carcinoma, while Japanese pathologists generally use the latter: this geographic difference in interpretation appears to contribute significantly to the different reported frequencies in gastric cancer between East and West.[180,181] The Vienna classification of precancerous lesions of the gastrointestinal tract[16] (Table 8.2) was conceived in order to reconcile the two approaches. In some respects the distinction between adenoma and adenocarcinoma in a polyp is rather academic because, in practice, the risk of metastatic spread from an intramucosal polypoid adenocarcinoma that has been completely excised by polypectomy is negligible. The primary onus on the pathologist, therefore, is to establish whether or not completeness of excision has been achieved by examining sufficient sections of the lesion.

Differential diagnosis Polypoid gastric adenomas must be distinguished from the commoner types of gastric epithelial polyp, including hyperplastic polyps, fundic gland polyps, hamartomatous polyps, heterotopias and polypoid Ménétrier's disease, all of which are described below.[168,169] The sole criterion for differentiating adenomas from these lesions is the presence or absence of dysplasia, but sometimes this distinction can be

difficult, especially in eroded or inflamed hyperplastic polyps, when regenerative changes in inflamed foveolar epithelium may closely mimic dysplasia. Useful pointers towards dysplasia include lack of surface maturation of the epithelial cells and the presence of intestinal-type differentiation, which is usually inconspicuous in non-neoplastic polyps. On the other hand, an "onion-skin" glandular arrangement (see p. 364) is almost diagnostic of a hyperplastic polyp.

The situation is further complicated by the rare occurrence of true dysplasia or even frank adenocarcinoma developing in large hyperplastic polyps, usually at the tip (Fig. 8.29).[169,182] The terminology of such lesions is open to semantic argument, and they are not generally regarded as adenomas, although similar principles should apply to their clinical management.

Dysplasia in flat gastric mucosa

Clinical features Dysplasia does not always take the form of a visible raised lesion or adenoma in the stomach. Indeed, it is more common to find it in mucosa that is either flat or shows only minimal abnormality of the normal contour.[183] It is unlikely, therefore, that gastric dysplasia *per se* produces symptoms, and the diagnosis is often made in random biopsies of mucosa with only slight endoscopic abnormality. Sometimes the fragile neoplastic epithelium appears to be more susceptible to peptic-type ulceration and the diagnosis is made in biopsies from the margin of a superficial ulcer. Gastric dysplasia is usually a disease of later life; the diagnosis is made most commonly after the sixth decade and usually occurs against a background of long-standing chronic gastritis. Obviously, its main clinical significance is its association with gastric cancer; whenever a diagnosis of dysplasia is made, it is prudent to re-examine the patient endoscopically for an occult established gastric cancer in the vicinity of the original biopsy.

It is now conventional to divide gastric dysplasia into high-grade (previously severe) and low-grade (previously mild and moderate) forms.[16,183–187] For low-grade dysplasia, evidence suggests that progression to carcinoma is relatively uncommon (< 20 percent), slow and indeed may not be inevitable.[188–190] In these cases the recommended management is immediate re-endoscopy with multiple biopsies to exclude concurrent carcinoma, followed by regular (bi-annual) follow-up examinations relaxed to yearly examination after two negative endoscopies.

For high-grade dysplasia the association with concurrent gastric cancer is so strong (at least 70 percent) that many have considered it appropriate to proceed immediately to gastrectomy,[187–189] ideally after mapping out the extent of the lesion by multiple preoperative biopsies to delineate a proximal margin for excision. However, advances in endoscopic techniques, including endoscopic ultrasound, the use of vital dye-spraying and endoscopic mucosal resection can now avoid gastrectomy – meticulous pathologic examination of such resection specimens is required to confirm completeness of excision and to identify adverse prognostic indicators if there is an invasive tumor.[191,192]

Macroscopic appearances "Flat" gastric dysplasia is, by definition, an unimpressive lesion macroscopically. It may be entirely inconspicuous or may take the form of a slightly raised, thickened, congested mucosa, an ill-defined nodularity, or a slightly depressed lesion surrounded by radiating mucosal folds.[193] The use of dye-spraying during endoscopy (chromo-endoscopy) and magnifying endoscopy can highlight the mucosal irregularity. There is a tendency for high-grade dysplasia to be a depressed lesion and low-grade dysplasia to be slightly raised. Some lesions, especially those with high-grade dysplasia, may show superficial erosions or even overt ulceration. Mucosa of the antrum, especially the lesser curve, is more commonly affected than that of the corpus, but sometimes the cardiac mucosa is involved when the lesion may merge with Barrett's esophagus.

Microscopic appearances The essential characteristics of gastric dysplasia, comprising abnormalities of cytology, differentiation and architecture, have already been described in the previous section on adenomas.[174,183–190] These abnormalities may involve the superficial, foveolar and neck zone of the gastric pit (Fig. 8.30), often in association with cystic dilatation of the underlying specialized glands, or the full thickness of the mucosa (Fig. 8.31). Often there is a background of intestinal metaplasia, characteristically the type III sulfomucin-secreting immature variety, and dysplasia arising in this situation often shows intestinal-type differentiation with the appearance of goblet cells, sometimes showing abnormal polarity (Fig. 8.32). Dysplasia of non-metaplastic foveolar epithelium[170] (Fig. 8.30), sometimes called type II dysplasia, is much less common and may be a precursor of diffuse-type gastric carcinoma.[184] Grading of dysplasia is subjective but, in general, low-grade dysplasia is used when the degree of nuclear hyperchromasia, pleomorphism and stratification is limited, atypical mitoses are absent, and there is relative preservation of a glandular architecture. Conversely, high-grade dysplasia shows more cytologic atypia with large irregular nucleoli and an increasingly complex architecture, including back-to-back glands, that merges with carcinoma in situ.[174,183–188] A number of approaches have been attempted to help classify gastric dysplasia and to

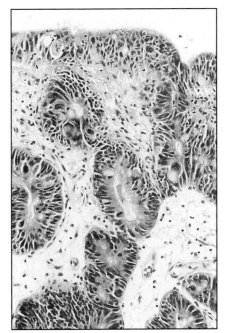

Fig. 8.30 • High-grade dysplasia in non-metaplastic gastric foveolar epithelium.

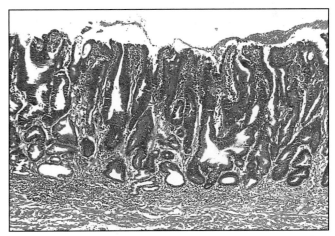

Fig. 8.31 • High-grade dysplasia arising in metaplastic-type epithelium and involving the whole thickness of the mucosa.

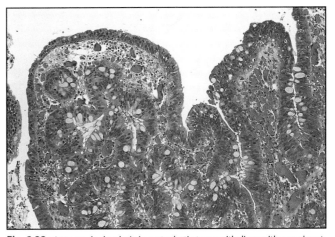

Fig. 8.32 • Low-grade dysplasia in metaplastic-type epithelium with prominent goblet cells, some of which are abnormally polarized or "dystrophic".

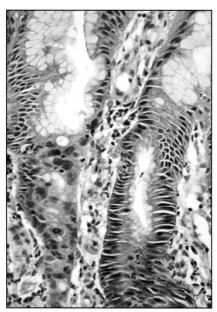

Fig. 8.33 • Regenerative foveolar hyperplasia with atypia in active gastritis – note the prominent intraepithelial neutrophils in the right gland and the epithelial maturation in the upper portion of the left gland.

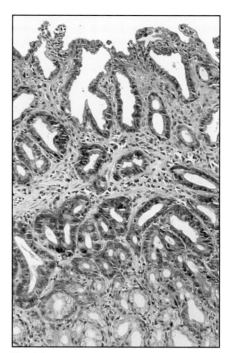

Fig. 8.34 • Reactive gastritis with florid foveolar hyperplasia. Though there is marked epithelial cytonuclear atypia in the central part of the field it is accompanied by cellular maturation in the upper zone of the pit and at the luminal surface – this is not dysplasia.

remove the subjectivity of its grading. These have included mucin histochemistry, immunocytochemistry for markers of differentiation or cell proliferation, oncogene products, and morphometric analysis. Unfortunately none, so far, has shown a clear advantage over conventional morphologic assessment.

Differential diagnosis The principal differential diagnosis of dysplasia is regenerative epithelial hyperplasia/atypia in relation to gastritis, erosion or ulceration. Foveolar hyperplasia is almost inevitable in gastritis, but the degree of accompanying atypia only reaches worrying proportions in a limited number of situations. The first is severe acute inflammation (Fig. 8.33); misdiagnosis here can best be avoided by being extremely wary of diagnosing high-grade dysplasia in the presence of large numbers of intraepithelial neutrophils. The second is reactive (chemical or reflux) gastritis, a condition characterized by edema, vascular ectasia, fibrosis, smooth muscle proliferation and foveolar hyperplasia of the mucosa but relatively few inflammatory cells.[194] Here the apparent atypia of the regenerating epithelium tends to be exaggerated by the paucity of neutrophils, leading to overdiagnosis of dysplasia (Fig. 8.34). In both of these types of gastritis useful pointers to a regenerative, rather than dysplastic change are relative preservation of the glandular architecture and the presence of some degree of maturation of the proliferating epithelium towards the mucosal surface. Furthermore, the nuclei of regenerative hyperplasia, though hyperchromatic, are usually rounder, basally orientated and their nucleoli, though prominent, are small and regular. Thirdly, regenerative hyperplasia, along with swelling and nuclear atypia in degenerating glands, in the vicinity of gastric erosions or ulcers, can give rise to an alarming appearance that may not only suggest dysplasia but even frank carcinoma (Fig. 8.35).[47] A most useful feature here is that the atypical glands are often embedded in eosinophilic fibrin, granulation tissue or ulcer slough rather than in a normal lamina propria. Finally, there is epithelial atypia associated

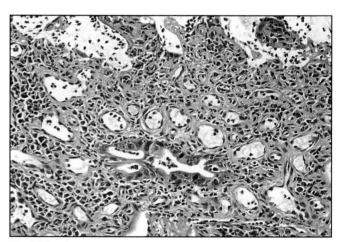

Fig. 8.35 • A bizarre, cytologically atypical gland lying within granulation tissue from the margin of a benign peptic ulcer.

with chemoradiotherapy. Here the degree of atypia may be particularly marked but differs from true dysplasia in that it affects both the foveolar and the deeper, specialized zones of the mucosa and is accompanied by cytoplasmic eosinophilia or vacuolation and sometimes microcystic change of the glands. Unlike true dysplasia, proliferative activity is confined to the deep foveolar zone, atypical mitoses are uncommon, and there is cellular maturation towards the luminal surface.[195]

Adenocarcinoma

Clinical features Adenocarcinoma is the commonest malignant tumor of the stomach. Males are affected more commonly than females, with the male/female ratio varying from 1 in young adults to 2 or more at the age of 60 years. The disease is extremely rare in children and adolescents. There is a higher incidence in Japan, Central and South America, and some parts of northern and eastern Europe,[196] but second generation migrants take on the incidence of the host country. In Northern Europe and the USA, there is a changing distribution of tumors within the stomach: cardia tumors are increasing and distal tumors decreasing. Similarly, there has been a progressive decrease in intestinal-type tumors, while the diffuse type is increasing.[197] Despite an overall declining incidence, gastric adenocarcinoma remains the second most common cause of death from malignant disease worldwide.[196]

From an epidemiologic viewpoint, environmental factors implicated in gastric cancer include low socioeconomic status, a diet with a high intake of salt and dried or pickled foods, smoking and alcohol consumption; vitamin C in fresh fruits and vegetables, carotenoids and green tea are protective.[196] A genetic predisposition is obvious in some cases; germline mutations of the *E-cadherin* gene (*CDH1*) have been described in familial gastric cancer of diffuse histologic type and early onset,[198] while tumors of intestinal histologic type may be seen in other cancer family syndromes, notably hereditary non-polyposis colorectal cancer.[199] Precancerous conditions include chronic gastritis with atrophy and intestinal metaplasia (especially the "incomplete" variety[200]), the postgastrectomy gastric stump, gastric adenomas and Ménétrier's disease.[201] Chronic *Helicobacter pylori* infection of the stomach, particularly by strains harboring the cytotoxin-associated gene (*CagA*), plays a major role in the early stages of the pathogenesis of gastric cancer (except carcinomas of the cardia).[202,203] The host response to this infection is also important, as demonstrated by differing individual susceptibilities to gastric atrophy and carcinoma related to pro-inflammatory interleukin-1 gene polymorphisms.[204] Individuals with *Helicobacter pylori* gastritis that is widespread, mainly affects the corpus, and progresses more rapidly to atrophy, appear to be most at risk; many host and environmental factors appear to be capable of modifying this progression.[205] Carcinomas of the cardia have different epidemiologic characteristics that are similar to those of adenocarcinoma of the lower esophagus. Epstein–Barr virus (EBV) has also been identified in a high proportion of gastric carcinomas with lymphoid stroma (and a small proportion of "ordinary" gastric cancers) by polymerase chain reaction (PCR) and in situ hybridization,[206] but its role in the carcinogenic process is uncertain.

Application of molecular and immunocytochemical techniques has identified a range of abnormalities in gastric cancer, including microsatellite instability, somatic mutation, amplification or altered expression of K-*ras*, K-*sam*, *APC*, c-*met*, c-*erb*B-2, *p53*, TGFα, TGFβ, CD44, *bcl-2*, *cyclin E*, *E-cadherin*, and *nm23*, allele loss of chromosomes 1p, 1q, 3p, 5q (*APC* locus), 7q, 13q, 17p (*p53* locus), 18q (*DCC* locus), and telomerase expression.[27] Some of these appear to be linked with certain histologic patterns of gastric cancer (such as *p53* mutation or microsatellite instability in intestinal-type cancers[207] and K-*sam* amplification in diffuse-type cancers[27]), while others (such as c-*erb*B-2 amplification and 7q deletions) are associated with advanced disease and may have prognostic significance.[27]

Adenocarcinoma commonly arises in the antrum or on the lesser curve, and less frequently in the corpus. An increasing proportion of adenocarcinomas of the cardia (28 percent) have been noted in recent years, mirroring the increase in esophageal adenocarcinoma arising from Barrett's esophagus.[15,61,208] Diffuse involvement of virtually the whole stomach is not uncommon. Clinical symptoms or signs include dyspepsia, anorexia, weight loss, hemorrhage, or obstruction of the gastric inlet or outlet, but these are rarely striking until the tumor is advanced, hence the overall poor prognosis. Nevertheless, early tumors are diagnosed more frequently, usually in individuals with symptoms suggestive of peptic ulcer disease, or by mass screening of asymptomatic populations, as has been pioneered in Japan. Indeed, in that country, early tumors now represent the majority of new diagnoses.

Macroscopic appearances Advanced gastric cancer may take the form of polypoid (see Fig. 8.25), fungating, ulcerated or diffusely infiltrating (Fig. 8.36), so-called linitis plastica types, or may show a combination of these. Ulcerated tumors are most common in the antrum on the lesser curve and classically differ from peptic ulcers by virtue of having more irregular contours with raised, rolled edges. However, it is impossible to make this distinction with certainty and it is essential

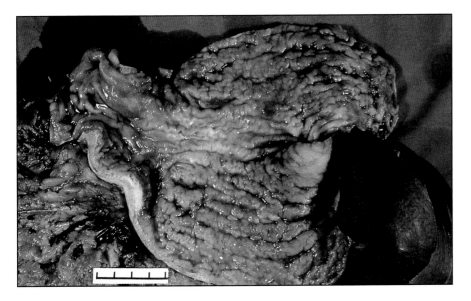

Fig. 8.36 • Diffusely infiltrating gastric adenocarcinoma of linitis plastica type.

that multiple biopsies of the margins of all gastric ulcers are taken before embarking on clinical management. Polypoid and fungating carcinomas are more common in the corpus, often on the greater curve, while the diffusely infiltrating variety may occur as an ill-defined, superficially ulcerating plaque accompanied by conspicuous thickening of the underlying gastric wall or, less commonly as a diffuse thickening of the entire stomach – the "leather bottle stomach". In hereditary diffuse gastric cancer, multiple foci of intramural signet ring cell carcinoma show a predilection for the body/antral transitional zone.[209] A proportion of tumors of all macroscopic types produce sufficient quantities of extracellular mucus to give the gelatinous gross appearance of colloid carcinoma.

Microscopic appearances In general terms, gastric adeno-carcinomas may consist of tubular, acinar or papillary structures, or of poorly cohesive single cells that are widely infiltrative and dissect through the layers of the gastric wall in an insidious way. Cytologically, the tumor cells may show gastric or intestinal-type features, including differentiation towards parietal cells,[210] argyrophil endocrine cells[211,212] or even Paneth cells.[213] They usually produce mucus that gives positive staining with diastase-PAS or alcian blue and which may contain sulfated sialoglycoproteins, and most cases are immunoreactive for carcinoembryonic antigen (CEA) and CA19-9. Carcinoma of the stomach frequently shows considerable variation in histologic pattern and degree of differentiation. A number of histologic classifications have been proposed.

The World Health Organization classification[177] subdivides gastric carcinoma into four predominant patterns – papillary, tubular, mucinous and signet-ring cell adenocarcinomas. Adenocarcinomas may also be graded as well, moderately or poorly differentiated. Papillary adenocarcinoma is characterized by numerous papillary processes with fibrovascular cores (Fig. 8.37); tubular adenocarcinoma is composed predominantly of neoplastic tubules often showing irregular branching and anastomosis (Fig. 8.38); mucinous adeno-carcinoma (colloid or mucoid carcinoma) is characterized by conspicuous amounts of extracellular mucin (more than 50 percent of the tumor) (Fig. 8.39); and signet-ring cell carcinoma consists predominantly of single cells or small clusters of cells

containing intracytoplasmic mucus vacuoles and accounting for more than 50 percent of the tumor (Fig. 8.40). Signet-ring cell carcinoma tends to infiltrate the wall of the stomach diffusely and is often accompanied by marked fibrosis, giving rise to the linitis plastica macroscopic appearance. The tubular, papillary and mucinous patterns are more commonly seen in the localized gastric carcinomas of either polypoid, fungating or ulcerated macroscopic types. An oncocytic variant of tubular adenocarcinoma has been described.[214] Other varieties of gastric carcinoma in the WHO classification include a number of uncommon specific subtypes (described below) and undifferentiated carcinoma, in which no definite glandular structures or any other specific differentiation is present.

The histologic classification of Laurén[215] divides gastric adenocarcinoma into two main types – intestinal and diffuse. The intestinal type shows well-defined glandular structures with papillae, tubules or even solid areas (see Figs 8.37, 8.38). The epithelium lining the neoplastic lumina consists of intestinal-type tall columnar cells, often with a prominent brush border and scattered mucin-secreting goblet cells. However, abundant intracellular mucin production is not a feature. The tumor frequently shows a well-demarcated "pushing" margin and inflammatory infiltration of the stroma is common. The

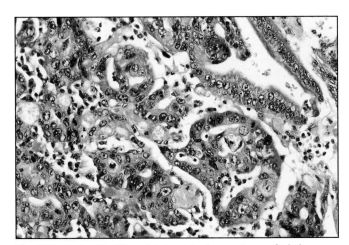

Fig. 8.38 • Moderately differentiated gastric adenocarcinoma of tubular (intestinal) type.

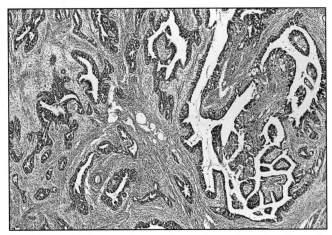

Fig. 8.37 • Well-differentiated gastric adenocarcinoma of mixed papillary and tubular types.

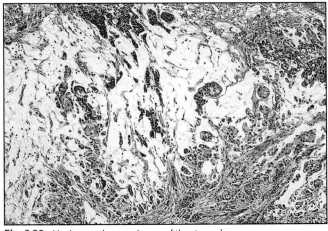

Fig. 8.39 • Mucinous adenocarcinoma of the stomach.

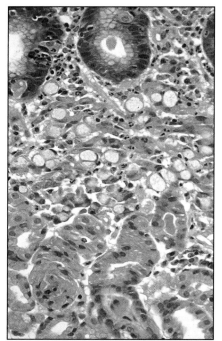

Fig. 8.40 • Early signet-ring cell gastric adenocarcinoma. Tumor cells infiltrating the lamina propria are confined to the zone of epithelial cell proliferation between the foveolar zone (above) and the specialized glandular zone (below).

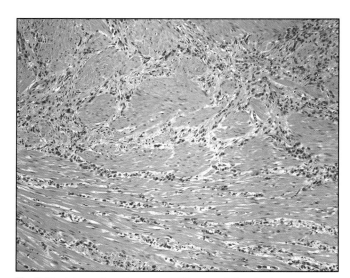

Fig. 8.41 • Advanced gastric cancer of diffuse type infiltrating between intramural smooth muscle fascicles.

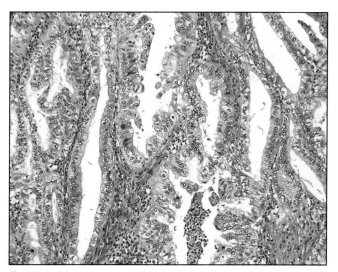

Fig. 8.42 • Pylorocardiac type of gastric adenocarcinoma.

carcinoma cells that invade directly into the lamina propria (see Fig. 8.40), or show pagetoid spread beneath the epithelial lining of local gastric foveolae and glands.[216] A significant proportion of cases (up to 15 percent) show both intestinal and diffuse histologic patterns and are placed in an indeterminate category.

Laurén's classification is useful in that it delineates two broad varieties of tumor that may be fundamentally different in etiology and histogenesis. Intestinal-type tumors are strongly associated with chronic gastritis and intestinal metaplasia and epidemiologically are more closely linked to "environmental" factors; geographic differences in gastric cancer incidence are largely due to variations in intestinal-type cancers. No such factors have been identified in relation to diffuse-type cancers. The pattern of spread of the two types is also different, distal blood-borne spread being usual with intestinal-type carcinomas and widespread peritoneal dissemination being typical of diffuse-type tumors.[217]

The classification of Ming[218] subdivides gastric adenocarcinoma into two types – expanding and infiltrating – while that of Mulligan & Rember[219] expands Laurén's classification by adding a third type – the pylorocardiac gland carcinoma. This arises in the antrum or the cardia, and commonly presents as a well-demarcated fungating growth. Histologically, there is a well-differentiated tubular or papillary pattern and the striking feature is the cytoplasmic clarity and vacuolation of the cells, which resemble the normal cells of the specialized antral or cardiac glands (Fig. 8.42).

The fact that there are numerous histologic classifications of gastric adenocarcinoma suggests that none is entirely satisfactory. Problems of observer reproducibility are considerable and, with the possible exception of Ming's classification,[220] the different subtypes do not allow consistent separation of prognostic groups. Generally speaking, diffuse, infiltrating, signet-ring cell and undifferentiated carcinomas have a worse prognosis in advanced gastric cancer, but paradoxically not in superficial tumors.[221] More recently, two further classifications have been proposed. Goseki et al.[222] divided gastric cancer into four histologic types according to the degree of tubular differentiation and the amount of intracellular mucus. They claimed

adjacent gastric mucosa often shows chronic gastritis with widespread intestinal metaplasia, and may also show dysplasia. The diffuse type, by contrast, consists mainly of scattered individual cells or clusters of cells. Glandular differentiation is uncommon, although it may occur in the more superficial part of the tumor. The majority of the cells are small, uniform and poorly cohesive and some have a signet-ring morphology. The tumor is poorly demarcated and infiltrates widely (Fig. 8.41). Intestinal metaplasia of the adjacent gastric mucosa is conspicuously lacking, as is dysplasia; if dysplasia is present, it is of the gastric foveolar type.[184] Indeed, the neoplastic cells often appear to arise from the proliferative foveolar zones of morphologically normal gastric pits as in situ signet ring that the four types predicted different patterns of tumor spread, either direct, lymphatic or hematogenous. Several independent studies support the utility and reproducibility of this classification.[223] Carneiro et al. proposed a much simpler (and potentially highly reproducible) system in which tumors are divided into (a) isolated cell, (b) glandular, (c) solid, and (d) mixed types.[224] The latter group includes cases with both isolated cell and glandular or solid components (combined glandular and solid tumors are allocated to either the glandular or solid category, depending upon the predominant component). The authors found that mixed type tumors, which formed 38.5 per cent of the cases studied, had a much worse prognosis than the other pure types, and multivariate analysis showed the classification to have independent prognostic significance that was second only to the TNM stage. The worse prognosis of mixed gastric cancers has been confirmed independently and related to molecular differences from the pure types of gastric cancer.[225]

Applications of other potential cellular prognostic markers to gastric carcinoma have met with limited success. Histochemical markers of differentiation, including the presence of endocrine cells,[211] have been disappointing, although there is a suggestion that parietal cell differentiation, in which the tumor cells have abundant eosinophilic granular cytoplasm that is phosphotungstic acid hematoxylin (PTAH) and Luxol fast blue positive, is associated with a better prognosis.[210,226] Studies of cell proliferation[227,228] and DNA ploidy[228–230] have given conflicting results and cannot be recommended at present for routine use. By far the most useful prognostic factor is the clinicopathologic stage of the tumor at diagnosis, though vascular,[223,231] and possibly perineural,[232] invasion have been shown to be of additional independent significance. Interestingly, EBV-positive tumors of intestinal type seem to have a notably better prognosis.[233]

Clinicopathologic staging The TNM staging system,[96] summarized in Table 8.3, is widely used in Western countries; it is the best available predictor of prognosis[231] and is recommended. The pT2 stage has recently been divided into pT2a and pT2b to take into account the much better prognosis (>50 percent 5-year survival) of tumors that have not penetrated the muscle coat of the stomach.[234] The number of lymph nodes involved by tumor is also of strong prognostic significance[235] and it can be seen that allocation of the correct "N" stage requires at least 15 lymph nodes to be examined. Furthermore, examination of lymph nodes using immunohistochemistry to identify occult tumor cells appears to have prognostic significance.[236] Unfortunately, the TNM system is not applied worldwide (the Japanese, for example, have their own system),[237] and this makes international comparison of clinical studies difficult.

Difficulties may also arise in staging tumors occurring at the gastroesophageal junction, because the TNM classifications of esophageal and gastric carcinomas are different (compare Tables 8.1 and 8.3) leading to uncertainty about which to use in an individual case. Siewert et al.[238] have proposed a classification of junctional tumors as follows: type I carcinomas arise in the distal third of the esophagus, usually in a segment of Barrett's and may or may not directly involve the gastroesophageal junction; type II straddle the gastroesophageal junction and appear to arise at the true junction of the stomach and esophagus and type III are sub-cardial gastric cancers

Table 8.3	Pathologic TNM staging of gastric carcinoma[96]

T — Primary Tumor

pT1	Tumor invades lamina propria or submucosa
pT2	Tumor invades muscularis propria or subserosa
	pT2a Tumor invades muscularis propria
	pT2b Tumor invades subserosa
pT3	Tumor penetrates serosa (visceral peritoneum) without invasion of adjacent structures
pT4	Tumor invades adjacent structures

N — Regional Lymph Nodes

pN0	No regional lymph node metastasis
pN1	Metastasis in 1–6 regional lymph nodes
pN2	Metastasis in 7–15 regional lymph nodes
pN3	Metastasis in more than 15 regional lymph nodes

M — Distant Metastasis[a]

M0	No distant metastasis
M1	Distant metastasis present

[a]Pathologic staging cannot usually comment on the presence or absence of distant metastasis, unless biopsies of distant organs have been submitted for histologic examination.

that have grown proximally to invade the gastroesophageal junction. They concluded that the pattern of nodal spread of type II tumors was more similar to gastric cancer and that they should be staged according to gastric cancer rules.

Because of the late clinical presentation of gastric cancer in non-screened Western populations, more than 75 percent of cases have such advanced disease that only palliative surgery is possible.[239] Direct extension into the esophagus is common, infiltration of the duodenum less so. Lymphatic spread is also frequent, with involvement of lymph nodes located along the lesser and greater curvatures or around the celiac axis and abdominal aorta. Supradiaphragmatic and even mediastinal lymph nodes may also contain deposits, though spread to the left supraclavicular nodes by way of the thoracic duct (Virchow's node), despite being well recognized, is uncommon. Hematogenous spread to distant organs may occur in the absence of lymphatic spread. Liver metastases are most frequent, but other sites include the lungs, bones, skin and brain. Massive involvement of both ovaries (Krukenberg tumor) probably results from transperitoneal or blood-borne spread. The prognosis even for patients undergoing "curative" gastrectomy is not good, although the addition of aggressive lymphadenectomy (so-called D2 gastrectomy), with its attendant higher complication rates, has resulted in 50 percent 5-year survival in some studies.[240] Until now, adjuvant chemotherapy has not had a dramatic effect. Despite this gloomy picture, cases of gastric cancer that are confined to the gastric wall at diagnosis have a good prognosis, and these can be divided into two stages – so-called "early" (pT1) gastric cancer and "PM" (pT2a) gastric cancer.

Early gastric cancer Early gastric cancer, also termed surface or superficial gastric cancer, is defined as carcinoma confined to the mucosa or submucosa, irrespective of lymph node status and corresponds to pT1 gastric cancer. The term "early" is not related to tumor size or shape or duration of the disease, but is used to mean gastric cancer at a potentially curable stage. Indeed, surgery for early gastric cancer is followed by an average 5-year survival rate of 80–95 percent.[221,241]

Early gastric cancer is divided into three main macroscopic types. In type I (protruded) the tumor projects into the lumen and may be polypoid, nodular or villous. Type II (superficial) is characterized by an uneven mucosal surface and is subdivided into elevated (IIa) (Fig. 8.43), flat (IIb) and depressed (IIc) (Fig. 8.44) forms. Type III (excavated) presents as an ulcer of variable depth with adenocarcinoma in its margin. Combinations of all three types are commonly encountered.

The microscopic features of early gastric cancer are fundamentally the same as those of advanced gastric cancer and all the various histologic patterns may be found. Types I and IIa tumors are almost invariably well-differentiated tubular or papillary adenocarcinomas (Fig. 8.45), while types IIc and III tumors are more often poorly differentiated or are signet-ring cell adenocarcinomas. Not surprisingly the prognosis in early gastric cancer is related to the depth of spread and most cases with lymph node metastasis show submucosal invasion.[221,241] Paradoxically, raised, well-differentiated intestinal-type tumors that invade the submucosa over a broad front appear to be more aggressive, and the small proportion of early gastric cancers that lead to distant metastases are usually of this type.[242] Such tumors are also more frequently aneuploid.[243,244] About 10 percent of patients with early gastric cancer develop a second gastric cancer, either synchronously or metachronously. It is therefore important to check for a second tumor before undertaking partial gastrectomy for early gastric cancer, and to ensure that there is long-term surveillance of the gastric stump following surgery. The very low frequency (up to 7 percent) of lymph node metastasis in intramucosal early gastric cancer has led to the use of endoscopic mucosal resection as the primary therapy for small, non-ulcerated tumors, especially those that are not poorly differentiated.[192] Meticulous histologic examination of the resection specimen is

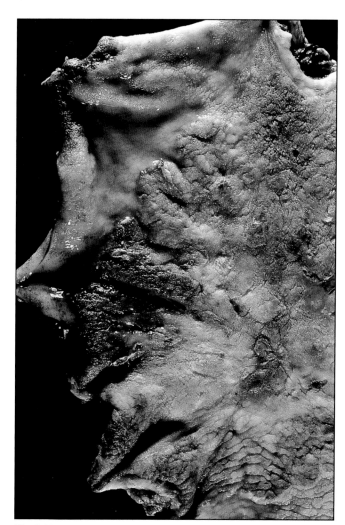

Fig. 8.43 • Elevated type of early (T1) gastric cancer which is virtually involving the whole of the stomach; only a small area of the body (top left) is spared.

Fig. 8.44 • Depressed type of early (T1) gastric cancer surrounded by radiating mucosal folds.

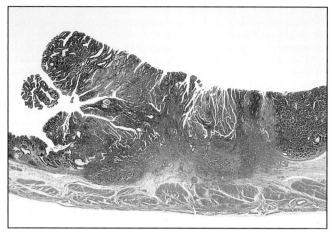

Fig. 8.45 • Well-differentiated early (T1) gastric cancer of tubular and papillary pattern involving mucosa and submucosa.

required to exclude the three indications for further surgery, namely submucosal invasion, incomplete excision, and lymphovascular invasion.[192]

PM gastric cancer This is a term used by Japanese investigators to describe gastric cancer that has invaded into, but not through, the muscularis propria (proper muscle, PM), irrespective of lymph node metastasis,[234] and corresponds to T2a gastric cancer. About 15 percent of resected tumors fall into this category and their prognosis is significantly better than that of more advanced tumors: in most Japanese series and one British study, the 5-year survival was over 60 percent.[228,234] Subdivision of PM gastric cancer into invasion of the superficial muscularis propria compared with deeper invasion into the muscularis propria shows significantly better survival of the former with 5-year survival similar to that of early gastric cancer.[234] There is good reason, therefore, to identify PM tumors as a favorable prognostic group.

Ulcer-cancer

This is defined as adenocarcinoma of the stomach that has arisen in a pre-existing peptic ulcer and which is confined to the edge of the ulcer. This definition implies that ulcer-cancer can only be diagnosed at an early stage, when both inflammatory and neoplastic lesions can still be distinguished histologically. Ulcer-cancer represents about 1 percent of gastric cancers.

Macroscopically, ulcer-cancer tends to be fairly large. The adenocarcinoma is usually represented by a rigid, pale and sloping edge that contrasts with the soft, congested, sharply defined and punched-out margin of a benign peptic ulcer. Microscopically, the carcinomatous component is confined to the mucosa at the edge of the ulcer, and care must be taken to distinguish this from regenerative changes before making the diagnosis. The characteristic features of chronic peptic ulceration are also present, particularly the dense scar tissue with lymphoid aggregates and endarteritis obliterans at the base and fusion of the muscularis mucosae with the muscularis propria at the edge. Despite the fact that it is tempting to regard ulcer-cancers as malignancies arising in a pre-existing peptic ulcer, this is not the only explanation for the appear-

ance. It is well recognized that some intramucosal gastric cancers are slow-growing lesions in which deeper invasion of the gastric wall may not take place for months or years.[245] It is therefore conceivable that ulcer-cancers represent large intramucosal adenocarcinomas within which secondary peptic ulceration has occurred.

Gastric stump carcinoma

Carcinoma in the gastric stump is a well-recognized long-term complication of partial gastrectomy, usually occurring 20 or more years after the original operation. The overall risk has probably been exaggerated in early publications, and more recent, larger series suggest that the risk is about three to five times at 25 years.[246] Macroscopically, stump carcinoma arises on the gastric side of the line of anastomosis, usually close to it. Any of the macroscopic or microscopic variants of gastric cancer may be found.

The pathogenesis of stump carcinoma is uncertain. A number of pathologic lesions have been described in gastric remnants, usually close to the anastomosis, including chronic atrophic gastritis, intestinal metaplasia, dysplasia, adenomatous polyps and inflammatory polyps; the latter may be particularly florid, giving an appearance of so-called "gastritis cystica polyposa" (see below).[247] Great care must be taken in diagnosing dysplasia in biopsies from gastric remnants, however, because the frequent occurrence of reflux of small intestinal contents through the anastomosis often gives rise to a reactive (reflux or chemical) gastritis[194] with accompanying florid foveolar hyperplasia that can mimic dysplasia (see above).

Differential diagnosis Diagnostic difficulties only arise in the interpretation of gastric biopsies where the main danger is overinterpretation of small, distorted fragments, usually derived from a gastric erosion or ulcer, that show florid reactive epithelial hyperplasia, glandular swelling and degeneration, and entrapment of glands within a fibrinous exudate or in granulation tissue (see Fig. 8.35). The problem has been well described by Isaacson.[47] Misdiagnosis of diffuse-type cancer may occur in granulation tissue if reactive fibroblasts and endothelial cells show bizarre appearances with prominent granular cytoplasm, and hyperchromatic or pleomorphic nuclei with prominent nucleoli; such changes, well recognized following irradiation, are not uncommon in peptic ulcers.[47] The true nature of the cells can usually be deduced from their negative reaction with mucin or cytokeratin immunohistochemical stains and the paradoxical lack of mitotic figures despite florid nuclear pleomorphism. A similar change may occur in benign gastric polyps, when there is superficial surface erosion.[248]

Signet-ring and undifferentiated carcinoma cells must be distinguished from lipid- or mucin-containing macrophages within the lamina propria. This is best achieved by carefully assessing the nuclear morphology of the cells; macrophages have rather open vesicular nuclei with one or more small nucleoli and fine heterochromatin, while the nuclei of signet-ring cell carcinoma cells are larger, more hyperchromatic and pleomorphic with coarse, dispersed chromatin and occasional mitoses (Fig. 8.46). A diastase-PAS stain is of limited value in making the distinction, because muciphages and signet-ring cells both show cytoplasmic positivity but, in difficult cases, immunocytochemistry for epithelial and macrophage markers

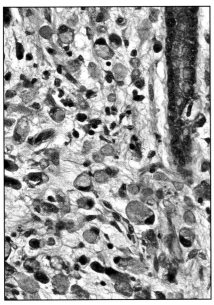

Fig. 8.46 • Poorly differentiated intramucosal adenocarcinoma. Nuclear pleomorphism allows the neoplastic cells to be distinguished from mucin-laden histiocytes.

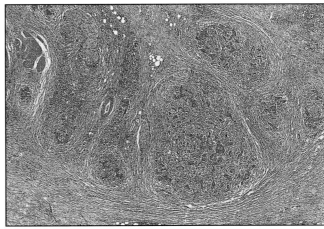

Fig. 8.47 • Gastric medullary carcinoma with lymphoid stroma often has a well-defined advancing growth margin.

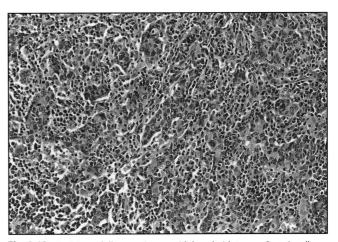

Fig. 8.48 • Gastric medullary carcinoma with lymphoid stroma. Occasionally the lymphoid infiltrate is so dense that immunocytochemistry may be necessary to identify the carcinoma cells with confidence.

may be useful. In practice, muciphages are uncommon in gastric biopsies, unlike colorectal biopsies, and most cases with worrying cells in the lamina propria turn out to have carcinoma on further investigation. Other rare but important mimics are signet-ring change in degenerate epithelial cells in acute erosive gastritis,[249] malignant melanoma and "signet-ring" forms of stromal tumor or malignant lymphoma (see below); appropriate mucin stains and immunohistochemistry usually aid this differential diagnosis. The last, and by no means rare, source of confusion is metastatic lobular carcinoma of the breast, which can be particularly problematic without an appropriate clinical history. Differential cytokeratin staining can be of some help: the majority of lobular breast cancers are CK7+ CK20– while less than 20 percent of gastric cancers have this phenotype. On the other hand, 50–65 percent of diffuse type gastric cancers are CK20+, albeit sometimes focally.[250] Estrogen-receptor positivity, in this specific context, is almost always indicative of spread from a breast primary.[250a]

Uncommon varieties of gastric carcinoma

Gastric carcinoma with lymphoid stroma (medullary carcinoma) This cellular tumor consists mostly of solid nests of large eosinophilic carcinoma cells, with relatively inconspicuous or even absent tubular differentiation, that are admixed with a dense and diffuse infiltrate of mature lymphocytes and plasma cells, sometimes including lymphoid follicles and rare giant cells (Figs 8.47, 8.48).[251, 252] Caution (and, if necessary, immunostaining for cytokeratin and leukocyte markers) must be used to avoid confusion with malignant lymphoma or histiocytic sarcoma. Immunophenotyping usually shows that CD8+ T cells predominate over B cells in the reactive lymphoid component. Reticulin stains show a fine meshwork of reticulin fibers in the stroma but no desmoplastic reaction. The tumor margins are typically well defined (see Fig. 8.47) and the growth pattern expansile. Considerable interest in this tumor has been

generated by the finding that the tumor cells in over 80 percent of cases contain Epstein–Barr virus with intranuclear expression of EBV encoded non-polyadenylated RNA-1 demonstrated by in situ hybridization.[206] Some studies have suggested that this carcinoma has a better prognosis than conventional adenocarcinoma with up to 77 percent survival at 5 years,[251] particularly, in those patients with microsatellite instability – high frequency.[252]

Gastric carcinoma with extensive neutrophilic infiltration Five cases of anaplastic gastric carcinoma composed of highly pleomorphic, discohesive malignant cells with an intense stromal neutrophil infiltrate have recently been described.[253] The authors speculated that the neutrophil infiltrate represented a response to interleukin-8 production by the tumor cells. A subsequent study has suggested an improved prognosis, particularly in women.[254]

Adenosquamous and squamous cell carcinoma Adenosquamous carcinoma of the stomach is a rare tumor in which varying proportions of adenocarcinoma and squamous carcinoma coexist (Fig. 8.49).[255] Most reported cases have

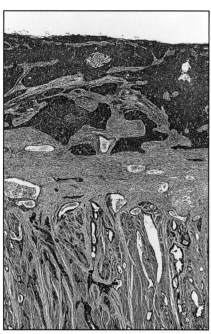

Fig. 8.49 • Adenosquamous carcinoma. In this field the squamous element (above) is well demarcated from the glandular component (below) but in other areas there was more intermingling.

occurred in the antrum, have been diagnosed at a late stage, and have a poor prognosis. The degree of squamous differentiation and keratinization is variable, but sometimes intercellular bridges and keratin pearl formation may be obvious. The tumor results from bidirectional differentiation in a tumor of presumed glandular origin; occasionally ultrastructural evidence of squamous and glandular differentiation may be found within a single tumor cell.[256] Pure gastric squamous carcinomas are extremely rare, and careful histologic sampling of putative examples often discloses the presence of small foci of adenocarcinoma.[257] When pure squamous cell carcinoma is found in the gastric cardia it more likely represents spread from an esophageal primary.

Vimentin-positive gastric carcinoma with rhabdoid features ("malignant rhabdoid tumor") Vimentin immunopositivity is exceptionally uncommon in gastric carcinoma. The rare cases that express this intermediate filament usually have a distinctive morphology, being solid tumors with a diffuse or alveolar growth pattern that are composed of poorly cohesive or non-cohesive, pleomorphic polygonal cells with vesicular nuclei, prominent nucleoli, and abundant deeply eosinophilic cytoplasm.[258] Most cases contain large hyaline, paranuclear, cytoplasmic inclusions; it is within these inclusions that the vimentin positivity is strongest, when the features correspond to so-called "extrarenal malignant rhabdoid tumor", except that the latter is no longer regarded as a distinct entity in adult patients (see Ch. 24). Often the tumor cells also express cytokeratin and neuron-specific enolase, but not carcinoembryonic antigen. This morphologic pattern may exist alone, or in combination with conventional type gastric carcinoma. The prognosis is extremely poor.

Hepatoid and alpha-fetoprotein-producing carcinoma A minority of primary gastric carcinomas contain immuno-reactive alpha-fetoprotein, often accompanied by carcino-embryonic antigen[259] and sometimes by albumin and alpha-1-antichymotrypsin. Some of these have a morphology resembling hepatocellular carcinoma, some have a clear cell tubulopapillary adenocarcinomatous pattern, and others show combinations of the two. These divergent patterns may represent recapitulation of the embryonic endodermal development of the alimentary system towards fetal liver and intestine respectively. One reported case also contained fetal cartilage.[260] The prognosis is poor.

Choriocarcinoma Cells immunoreactive for human chorionic gonadotropin are present in the neck portion of normal gastric glands.[261] It is perhaps not entirely surprising, therefore, that more than 50 cases of gastric choriocarcinoma, without evidence of a primary tumor elsewhere, have been reported.[262] Either sex may be affected. Histologically, most of these tumors are combinations of typical choriocarcinoma (composed of malignant syncytiotrophoblast and cytotrophoblast) and otherwise conventional adenocarcinoma showing a variable degree of differentiation. Occasionally, embryonal carcinoma[263] or yolk sac elements[264] are intermingled. Some cases have been accompanied by raised serum levels of chorionic gonado-tropin, which also can be demonstrated immunohistochemically within the trophoblastic cells. Disseminated hematogenous and lymphatic metastases are common.

Small cell carcinoma Small cell carcinoma of the stomach is best defined as a malignant tumor that shares the morphologic, histochemical and clinical features of small cell carcinoma of the bronchus and is best regarded as a poorly differentiated endocrine cell tumor.[265–267] Less than 1 percent of gastric carcinomas are of this type; occasionally there may be an admixed component of more conventional adeno-carcinoma or carcinoid tumor.

Histologically, the tumor has a solid or sheet-like growth pattern (Fig. 8.50) with occasional acinar or trabecular structures showing basal palisading, and it sometimes merges with a more conventional carcinoid pattern. The stroma is very vascular and necrosis is quite common. The cells may be small or intermediate-sized, round or spindle-shaped, with scanty

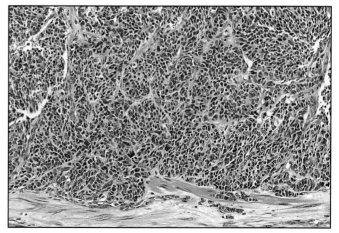

Fig. 8.50 • Small cell carcinoma often has a well-demarcated margin. The cytologic features of the tumor cells are similar to those seen in esophageal tumors (see Fig. 8.16).

cytoplasm and fairly regular nuclei that are hyperchromatic with inconspicuous nucleoli. Mitotic and apoptotic activity is often conspicuous. A proportion of the tumor cells show cytoplasmic argyrophilia, and electron microscopy confirms the presence of occasional neurosecretory granules. Immunocytochemistry usually shows chromogranin A or PGP 9.5 positivity. Rarely, one or more peptide hormones, such as serotonin, peptide YY, somatostatin or gastrin, may be demonstrated, but a clinical syndrome resulting from secretion of such hormones is very unusual. These tumors are frequently diagnosed at an advanced stage and their prognosis is poor, with a mean survival of less than 1 year.

Carcinosarcoma Carcinosarcoma of the stomach is rare.[268,269] Affected individuals, more commonly men, have generally been younger than those with conventional gastric adenocarcinoma. Most of these tumors have occurred at the pylorus; they are usually polypoid, aggressive tumors with a poor prognosis. Histologically, glandular elements of adenocarcinoma are seen in combination with spindle-celled sarcomatoid areas that may show osteosarcomatous, rhabdomyosarcomatous, leiomyosarcomatous[270] or chondrosarcomatous differentiation. We are also aware of a single case report of gastric adenosarcoma, a biphasic tumor that was composed of cytologically benign glandular structures dispersed within a leiomyosarcomatous stromal component.[271]

Carcinoid tumors

Clinical features Carcinoid tumors are uncommon gastric neoplasms that usually present in middle-aged adults as asymptomatic gastric polyps.[265,266,272] The majority occur as multiple asymptomatic lesions of the gastric corpus arising on a background of hypergastrinemia-induced endocrine cell hyperplasia; sporadic tumors unrelated to hypergastrinemia are less common, may occur in the antrum or corpus, and are generally larger, more aggressive lesions that may produce clinical symptoms suggestive of gastric carcinoma.[265,266]

The WHO Classification of gastric endocrine tumors recognizes three types based on clinicopathologic characteristics;[177] in addition a fourth variety has recently been proposed.[273] The salient features of these four are summarized in Table 8.4. The lesions are divided primarily according to their underlying pathogenesis rather than their pathologic appearances; indeed the microscopic features of the four tumor types are generally similar. The great majority are low grade neoplasms of enterochromaffin-like (ECL) cells that normally reside in the gastric corpus and play a role in gastric acid secretion. Proliferation of these ECL cells, and their subsequent neoplastic transformation, is induced by hypergastrinemia, which is the underlying cause of type I, II and IV carcinoids and in these cases multiple tumors can be seen arising in a background of ECL-cell hyperplasia and dysplasia. In type I carcinoids the

Table 8.4	WHO typing of gastric carcinoid tumors (modified after Abraham et al.[273])			
	Type I	**Type II**	**Type III**	**Type IV[a] (provisional)**
Pre-existing condition	Gastritis of corpus (usually autoimmune)	Zollinger–Ellison syndrome (usually with MEN1)	None (sporadic)	Gastric parietal cell acid-secreting dysfunction[a]
Hypergastrinemia	Present	Present	Absent	Present
Carcinoid tumors	Small (<1.5 cm), often multiple, no atypia	Usually small (but 20% >1.5 cm), often multiple, no atypia	Large, solitary, may be cytologically atypical	Small, multiple, no atypia
Distant (liver) metastasis	2–5%	10%	22–75%	Not known[b]
Outcome	Virtually never fatal	Rarely fatal	25% mortality	Not known[b]
ECL-cell hyperplasia/ dysplasia	Present	Present	Absent	Present
Background mucosa	Chronic atrophic gastritis and intestinal metaplasia	Hypertrophic oxyntic glands; hyperplastic parietal cells	Normal	Hypertrophic, distended oxyntic glands; hyperplastic, vacuolated parietal cells
Clinical management	Conservative – endoscopic polypectomy Gastrectomy for rare tumors that are large or overtly malignant	Conservative – endoscopic polypectomy Gastrectomy for rare tumors that are large or overtly malignant	Gastrectomy Polypectomy only for small, completely excised histologically benign tumors	Uncertain[b]

ECL: enterochromaffin-like
[a]Postulated
[b]Insufficient reported cases, but likely to be similar to type I

hypergastrinemia is caused by chronic atrophic gastritis of the corpus, usually due to autoimmune gastritis, and the attendant hypochlorhydria.[272,274,275] In type II carcinoids it is due to the Zollinger–Ellison syndrome, nearly always arising in a context of multiple endocrine neoplasia type I (rather than a sporadic gastrinoma), and is accompanied by hyperchlorhydria.[276] In type IV carcinoids the hypergastrinemia is secondary to achlorhydria that has been postulated to result from a primary defect of gastric acid secretion by parietal cells, which is manifested histologically by florid hyperplasia and vacuolation of parietal cells in the oxyntic mucosa.[272,277] Type III carcinoids are fundamentally different. Although often showing ECL-cell differentiation, they are sporadic, usually solitary neoplasms that do not arise within the context of hypergastrinemia or endocrine cell hyperplasia and are larger, more sinister tumors that usually present with hemorrhage, obstruction or metastasis.[266,272,278] Clinical effects arising from peptide hormone hypersecretion are very uncommon among ECL-cell tumors and generally confined to an atypical carcinoid syndrome.[279] Rare primary gastric carcinoids may show G-cell differentiation with gastrin production (located in the antrum) or ECL-cell differentiation with serotonin production;[265] Cushing's syndrome from ectopic corticotrophin secretion is also recorded.[280]

The majority of gastric carcinoids are small and slowly growing; though locally infiltrative, they are generally of low-grade malignancy. Tumors of less than 1 cm in diameter that are confined to the mucosa and submucosa and show no angioinvasion on microscopy rarely metastasize, but with increasing size, vascular or muscularis propria invasion, cytologic atypia and mitotic activity (so-called atypical carcinoids[265,266,278]) they are more likely to spread, usually to regional lymph nodes and to the liver.[278] The presence of metastases, however, does not preclude long-term survival. Functioning gastric tumors leading to a clinical hypersecretion syndrome are always malignant, but they are exceptionally uncommon. Table 8.5 summarizes the pathologic features that help to predict bio-logic behavior.[278,281] The multiple type I, II and IV carcinoids occurring in the context of hypergastrinemia are usually small (<1 cm) and metastasize uncommonly;[265,266] type II tumors tend to be larger than type I and type IV lesions. Some type I carcinoids appear to regress with time.[282] Clinical management is therefore conservative, aimed at complete removal of visible lesions, either by local excision or endoscopic polypectomy, followed by endoscopic follow-up and extirpation of new lesions as they arise.[283] In the few cases of type I carcinoids that are difficult to control in this way, antrectomy (to remove the antral G-cells that provide the hypergastrinemic drive) may be useful. Only if the tumors are unusually large or numerous, or show clear-cut malignant features, should gastrectomy be considered. Sporadic type III carcinoids, on the other hand, which are usually more mitotically active tumors with cytologic atypia, are potentially aggressive tumors[265,266,272,278] that are best treated by partial or total gastrectomy using the same surgical principles used for gastric carcinoma, unless they are small, amenable to polypectomy, and show the histologic features of a benign lesion in the resected specimen (see Table 8.5).

Macroscopic appearances Most carcinoids occur as small, smooth, firm, well-circumscribed, polypoid elevations of the mucosa and submucosa. Larger tumors may involve the full thickness of the gastric wall, occasionally show central ulceration, and may have a yellow-gray cut surface. The background corpus mucosa may show atrophic changes in type I ECL-cell carcinoids, while in type II and type IV carcinoids it may be hypertrophic with prominent rugae, reflecting parietal cell hyperplasia.

Microscopic appearances Typical gastric carcinoids are composed of small, uniform, polygonal or cuboidal cells with lightly eosinophilic, finely granular cytoplasm and regular, round or oval nuclei, stippled chromatin, very infrequent mitoses and

Table 8.5	Pathologic indicators of clinical behavior in gastric carcinoid tumors (after Capella et al.[281] With kind permission of Springer Science and Business Media.)

Benign

<1 cm, confined to mucosa and submucosa, no angioinvasion

Borderline

Confined to mucosa and submucosa
<1 cm if angioinvasion present
1–2 cm if no angioinvasion

Low-grade malignant

Any functioning tumor
Invasion beyond submucosa
1–2 cm if angioinvasion present
>2 cm if no angioinvasion

High-grade malignant

Atypical carcinoid or small cell carcinoma

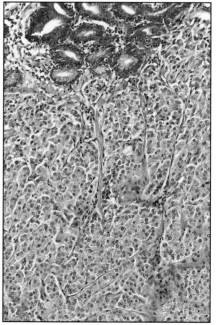

Fig. 8.51 • Gastric carcinoid composed of nests of regular endocrine cells with amphophilic cytoplasm.

minimal nuclear polymorphism (Fig. 8.51). A clear cell variant has been described.[284] Carcinoid cells usually show a mixed growth pattern, with nests or trabeculae of cells separated by a loose connective tissue stroma (Fig. 8.52). Occasionally tumor cells form rosettes, tubules or acinar structures. They arise in the gastric mucosa and commonly infiltrate the submucosa but seldom deeper. Retraction artifact around aggregates of tumor cells may give the impression of lymphovascular invasion. This must be distinguished from true vascular invasion, which is of prognostic significance (see Table 8.5). Perineurial infiltration occurs but is uncommon; its clinical significance is uncertain.

The majority of gastric carcinoids are argyrophilic and react with either the Grimelius (Fig. 8.53) or Sevier–Munger techniques;[272–276] few are argentaffin positive. Immuno-cytochemistry shows consistent positivity for chromogranin A, synaptophysin, Leu-7 and protein gene product (PGP) 9.5, and carcinoembryonic antigen is demonstrable in many.[262] Immuno-staining for vesicular monoamine transporter type 2 (VMAT-2) is a specific marker of ECL-cells[285] and, while the tumors may also contain histamine[286] and histidine decarboxylase, these are difficult to demonstrate in routinely fixed sections. Electron microscopy shows characteristic neurosecretory vesicular and solid granules (Fig. 8.54).[265] Other peptide hormones, such as serotonin, gastrin, somatostatin, pancreatic polypeptide, glucagon, calcitonin and alpha-HCG, may be present as a minority component.[265,272] Sporadic tumors are more likely to contain cells with such endocrine granules.

The background corpus mucosa in type I, II and IV carcinoids shows striking ECL-cell hyperplasia. This takes the form of increased numbers of endocrine cells within the gastric glands, either scattered or forming linear chains, which may extend into the lamina propria and/or muscularis mucosae as nodules or micronests (Fig. 8.55).[274–276,287] As these enlarge further, fuse and begin to invade and induce stroma they are termed dysplastic[288] and when they exceed 0.5 mm or invade the submucosa they are defined as carcinoids. In type I carcinoids there are also changes of chronic atrophic gastritis, often with florid intestinal metaplasia, while in type II carcinoids the corpus mucosa often shows the marked rugal enlargement due to elongation and hypertrophy of the oxyntic glands and hyperplasia of parietal cells that is typical of the Zollinger–Ellison syndrome. Parietal cell hyperplasia and hypertrophy was also described in the two published cases of type IV carcinoids,[272,277] but here the parietal cells were vacuolated, with protrusions of their cytoplasm into distended oxyntic glands containing inspissated eosinophilic material and there was associated bronchiolar (ciliated) metaplasia.

It is important for the histopathologist to separate carcinoids with cytologic atypia from the much more common "typical" tumors, because this has considerable prognostic and therapeutic implications. Such atypical gastric carcinoids[278] are characterized by a more infiltrative growth pattern, which may include obvious vascular invasion, and areas of necrosis.

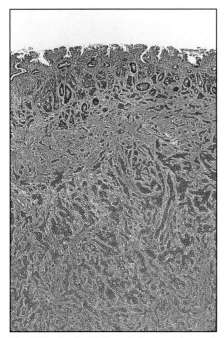

Fig. 8.52 • Carcinoid of gastric fundus with a predominantly trabecular growth pattern infiltrating the mucosa and submucosa. Scattered residual glands showing intestinal metaplasia are a clue to the background of chronic atrophic gastritis which was related to pernicious anemia.

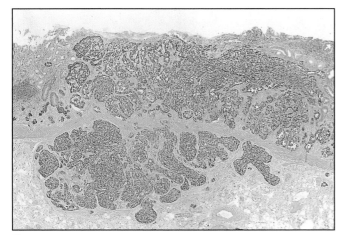

Fig. 8.53 • Argyrophil (Grimelius-positive) gastric carcinoid of enterochromaffin-like cell type in pernicious anemia. Note the micronests of endocrine cells in the background mucosa in the left side of the field (compare with Figure 8.55).

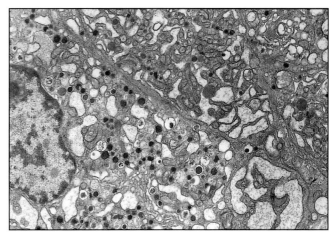

Fig. 8.54 • Ultrastructural appearances of endocrine cell granules of enterochromaffin-like cell type in cells from the tumor shown in Figure 8.53.

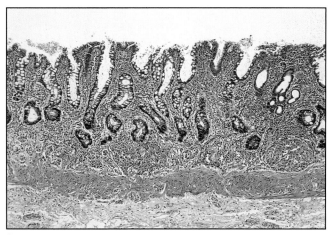

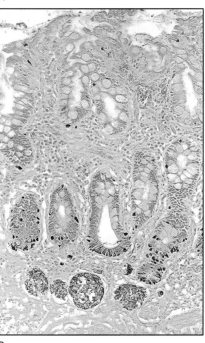

Fig. 8.55 • Enterochromaffin-like cell hyperplasia in chronic atrophic gastritis. Nodular aggregates of endocrine cells are clearly seen in the basal part of the mucosa, immediately above the muscularis mucosae, in a hematoxylin and eosin stained section (**A**). The Grimelius argyrophil reaction (**B**) also allows increased endocrine cells within the gastric glands to be identified.

The cytologic atypia takes the form of nuclear pleomorphism and hyperchromasia, often with prominent nucleoli, mitotic activity greater than 2 per 10 high-power fields[265] and expression of *p53*.[278] Some authors have used the term large cell neuroendocrine carcinoma for tumors when these features are particularly marked;[267] not surprisingly they are associated with a poor prognosis. Features of atypical carcinoid may also coexist with more conventional carcinoid on the one hand, or with more overtly malignant small cell carcinoma (see p. 352) on the other. Rare carcinoids, usually with atypical features, may also coexist with conventional gastric adenocarcinomas, so-called composite tumors, adenocarcinoids, or carcinoid adenocarcinomas.[289] Their prognosis is similar to that of pure adenocarcinomas.

Non-epithelial tumors

Gastrointestinal stromal tumors (GISTs)

It is now established that the great majority of mesenchymal tumors of the stomach are not variants of smooth muscle or nerve sheath neoplasms as had previously been thought, but distinctive tumors that show differentiation characteristics of the interstitial cells of Cajal, the gut pacemaker cells.[290–292] The most notable of these characteristics, immunohistochemical overexpression of the tyrosine kinase growth factor receptor KIT (CD117), also led to the discovery that agents capable of blocking this and analogous receptors, for example imatinib, may have a dramatically beneficial effect on the clinical behavior of GISTs.[293] Accordingly, separation of GISTs from other less common stromal tumors of the stomach has assumed great clinical significance.

Clinical features GISTs may affect any part of the stomach. Most occur in adults aged over 30 years – males and females being equally affected – though examples occurring in childhood are recorded. Recognized predisposing conditions contribute to only a tiny minority of cases and include type 1 neurofibromatosis,[294] two syndromes described by Carney et al.[295,296] in which GISTs coexist with pulmonary chondromas and/or extra-adrenal paragangliomas, and rare inherited germline mutations of growth factor receptor genes that are also implicated in the pathogenesis of sporadic tumors.[297,298]

Small stromal tumors of the stomach are asymptomatic intramural lesions that usually are discovered incidentally at laparotomy for some unrelated condition. Larger tumors often present with hemorrhage or abdominal pain, or occasionally from tumor rupture. Spread, when it occurs, may be by direct extension into adjacent organs, peritoneal dissemination, and by hematogenous spread to the liver and lungs.[299,300]

Macroscopic appearances Gastric stromal tumors may be single or multiple and vary in size from tiny intramural microscopic lesions[301] to bulky tumor masses. Tumors arising in the proximal stomach are commoner, and possibly more aggressive, than those in the antrum.[299] Most neoplasms protrude from the outer surface as exophytic subserosal lesions. Others project into the gastric lumen as an endophytic polypoid submucosal growth and are prone to surface ulceration and bleeding; a few grow in both directions to produce a dumbbell appearance. They are usually well circumscribed, nodular or bosselated masses that lack a true capsule. The cut surface is gray to pink in color with a rubbery or soft consistency (Fig. 8.56). Larger tumors often undergo cystic degeneration, infarction, hemorrhage and necrosis. Apart from obvious invasion of neighboring organs, the only gross feature suggesting malignancy is tumor size; metastasis is relatively infrequent from neoplasms measuring less than 5 cm but occurs in the majority of lesions over 10 cm.[299,302,303]

Microscopic appearances Gastric stromal tumors show a wide range of histologic appearances but, broadly speaking, two basic cell types – spindle and epithelioid – are recognized. Typical spindle cell tumors (Fig. 8.57) are composed of interlacing bundles or whorls of uniform spindle-shaped cells with ovoid or elongated blunt-ended nuclei and fibrillary eosinophilic cytoplasm that may contain a single clear paranuclear

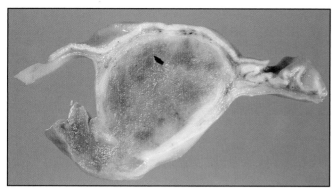

Fig. 8.56 • Cross-section of a predominantly exophytic gastric stromal tumor.

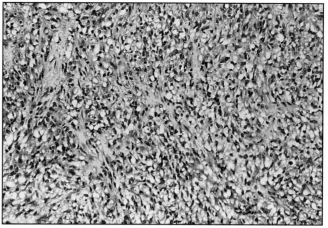

Fig. 8.58 • Epithelioid gastric stromal tumor with prominent cytoplasmic vacuoles.

A

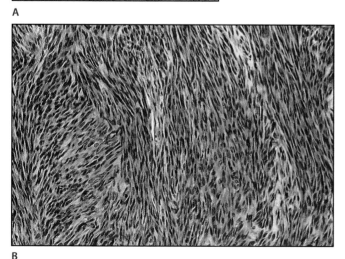

B

Fig. 8.57 • A spindle-celled gastric stromal tumor with a well-demarcated margin (**A**). Some fields are cellular with hyperchromatic nuclei and frequent mitoses (**B**), predictive of a malignant clinical behavior.

vacuole. Some are strikingly vascular, some show features suggestive of neural differentiation including nuclear palisading or a plexiform growth pattern. Occasional cases contain "skeinoid" fibers, which are small, globular or curvilinear, eosinophilic aggregates of filamentous material scattered among the tumor cells.[114] The stroma may be sclerosed, hyalinized, or even calcified, and some examples have an abundant, hyaluronic acid-rich, myxoid connective tissue component, within which round, stellate or multinucleated tumor cells containing "wreath-like" nuclei are widely scattered.[304] The degree of cellularity of gastric spindle celled GISTs varies greatly, both within and between tumors; pleomorphism is uncommon and usually associated with malignant potential, but may occasionally occur in benign tumors in the vicinity of tumor degeneration. Miettinen et al.[299] described a spectrum of morphologies that they termed sclerosing, palisading-vacuolated, hypercellular and sarcomatous that reflected increasing frequency of adverse outcome. Occasionally, clearly malignant spindle cell tumors show foci of liposarcomatous, chondrosarcomatous, or even rhabdomyosarcomatous differentiation,[305] but it is doubtful that these represent true GISTs by modern criteria. Rarely, monophasic tumors with these appearances are encountered (see below).

Epithelioid GISTs, previously termed "leiomyoblastomas" or "bizarre smooth muscle tumors", occur more commonly in the antrum and most often consist of round vacuolated or clear cells, typically arranged in cohesive sheets or nests that impart the epithelioid pattern (Fig. 8.58).[303] The cytoplasmic vacuoles may partly or completely surround the nucleus, occasionally giving rise to "signet-ring" forms;[306] they must not be confused with lipoblasts. Other tumors are composed of cells that are dyscohesive or contain abundant eosinophilic cytoplasm (Fig. 8.59). Occasionally, these can have a striking plasmacytoid appearance.[114] Nuclear characteristics vary from round or ovoid, with finely dispersed chromatin and small nucleoli, to large pleomorphic forms with large eosinophilic nucleoli, the latter sometimes being conspicuous in multinucleated tumor giant cells (Fig. 8.60). Similarly, the mitotic rate also shows considerable variation such that one end of the spectrum consists of overtly sarcomatous histology. Some 10 percent of gastric GISTs show both spindle and epithelioid cell patterns in different areas.[299]

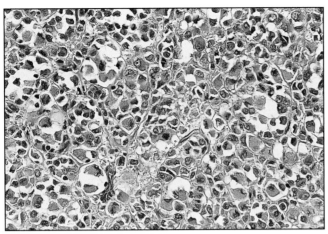

Fig. 8.59 • Malignant epithelioid gastric stromal tumor composed of monomorphic cells with eosinophilic cytoplasm and frequent mitoses.

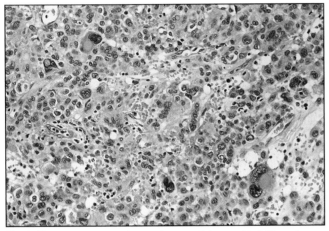

Fig. 8.60 • Marked pleomorphism with giant cells in an epithelioid gastric stromal tumor.

During the 1980s and 1990s, a number of publications described gastric stromal tumors showing features suggestive of enteric nerve plexus differentiation on electron microscopy, so-called gastrointestinal autonomic nerve tumors (GANTs).[307,308] GANTs were said to have greater malignant potential than other gastric stromal tumors, and recurrence or metastasis was especially prone to occur in the abdominal organs or retroperitoneum. More recent studies, however, have indicated that the majority of GANTs share the same light microscopic, immunohistochemical and molecular characteristics as GISTs,[309] especially epithelioid GISTs, and the separation of GANTs as a distinct entity is no longer generally favored.

The most important immunohistochemical marker of GISTs is expression of KIT (CD117), which is found in the vast majority (>90 percent) of GISTs.[115,299,302,310] Staining is usually strong and widespread and may be distributed diffusely in the cytoplasm, localized to a perinuclear dot, or membranous. However, in some cases it can be patchy or weak. Most (>80 percent) gastric GISTs also express CD34, again patchily in some, but smooth muscle actin is demonstrable in about 25 percent, desmin in about 5 percent and S100 protein in <1 percent.[299] Other commonly reported markers of GISTs include vimentin, protein kinase C (theta), nestin, bcl-2 and

heavy caldesmon, while some cases express p53, PGP 9.5, neuron-specific enolase, Leu-7 and synaptophysin.[302,311]

The molecular basis for KIT overexpression in most GISTs is activating mutation of the *KIT* gene,[310] most often in exons 11 or 9, either by deletion or point mutation. Such mutations are commoner in spindle cell GISTs than epithelioid GISTs. There is growing evidence that the site and nature of KIT mutations influence tumor behavior and responsiveness to therapy – tumors with deletions appear to be more aggressive than those with point mutations and those with exon 9 mutations are less responsive to imatinib therapy than those with exon 11 lesions.[312] A smaller number of GISTs, however, have mutations in another growth factor receptor gene, platelet derived growth factor receptor alpha (PDGFRA), instead.[313] These tumors more frequently have epithelioid morphology and may have a good prognosis.[314] While immunohistochemical overexpression of KIT also occurs in many of these PDGFRA mutant tumors,[299] it is by no means universal. Accordingly, some GISTs can be "KIT-negative", despite having typical morphological (and other immunohistochemical) features,[315,316] and, since some of these tumors may respond to tyrosine kinase receptor blocking agents, including imatinib, it is important to realize that KIT immunopositivity is not a *sine qua non* in the diagnosis of GIST. Loss of KIT (and CD34) immunopositivity, along with a change from a spindle cell to an epithelioid phenotype, has also been described in GISTs treated with imatinib, and this can cause diagnostic confusion.[317] Other histologic features associated with imatinib therapy include decreased cellularity, stromal hyalinization or myxoid change and areas of colliquative necrosis with cystic change. However, widespread sampling may also identify pockets of tumor that remain cellular, and these may represent niduses of tumor that have acquired new mutations that are responsible for the development of resistance to therapy.

Predicting behavior The majority of GISTs arising in the stomach appear to follow a benign course.[299] However, pathologic assessment of malignancy in GISTs is notoriously difficult unless invasion of adjacent structures is apparent or there are overt metastases.[318] Conventional histologic pointers to malignancy, such as dense cellularity and nuclear pleomorphism, have been found to be useful in some hands,[318] but disappointing in others, particularly in epithelioid tumors where, paradoxically, nuclear pleomorphism has been said to imply a benign behavior while malignant tumors are deceptively monomorphic.[53,303] Generally speaking, the risk of malignancy is greater in epithelioid tumors than in spindle-celled neoplasms and, while vascular invasion or atypical mitotic figures are good predictors of malignancy, they are uncommon.[305] Clear-cut invasion of the lamina propria, when demonstrable histologically, is highly suggestive of malignancy.[53,299] and coagulation necrosis (but not liquefactive necrosis with cystic change) also correlates with an adverse outcome. However, by far the most consistently useful parameters are the tumor size[302,303,319] and mitotic frequency[13,300,302,305] (or the proliferation fraction as measured by Ki-67 labeling[302,320]). Table 8.6 shows the consensus approach to predicting behavior in GISTs occurring at all gastrointestinal locations.[292] It is reproduced here because it is widely used, both for patient management and clinical research. Since even small, cytologically bland GISTs may metastasize on rare occasions, it avoids labeling

Table 8.6	NIH consensus guidelines for defining risk of aggressive behavior in GISTs at any anatomical site (Fletcher et al.[292])	
	Size (cm) (in greatest dimension)	**Mitotic count (per 50 high power fields)**
Very low risk	<2	<5
Low risk	2–5	≤5
Intermediate risk	≤5	6–10
	5–10	≤5
High risk	>5	>5
	>10	Any mitotic rate
	Any size	>10

any tumor as definitively benign. The findings of a recent large study of 1765 purely gastric GISTs diagnosed before the era of novel therapies, with long-term follow-up,[299] has generally supported the consensus approach, but has also identified some differences. In this study, no case in the "very low risk" category led to tumor-related mortality, and fewer than 3 percent of patients with "low risk" tumors had progressive disease – the authors called such cases benign and "probably benign" respectively. Tumors in the two groups included as "intermediate risk" in the consensus system differed, however. Those measuring 5–10 cm with a low mitotic rate (<5/50 high power field (HPF)) behaved as "low risk" lesions, but tumors measuring 2–5 cm with >5 mitoses/50HPFs were more aggressive with a 12–15 percent tumor-related mortality. Mitotic rate also assumed greater importance than size in tumors assigned to the "high risk" category of the consensus system, such that all tumors measuring more than 5 cm with a mitotic rate of >5/50HPFs had high malignant potential with a 49–86 percent tumor-related mortality, while tumors measuring >10 cm with a lower mitotic rate were considerably less aggressive. The criteria proposed for assessing malignant potential in purely gastric GISTs from this study are summarized in Table 8.7.

A number of studies have attempted to relate DNA ploidy and immunohistochemical expression of differentiation markers to malignant potential. Not surprisingly, aneuploidy

Table 8.7	Proposed guidelines for assessing malignant potential for gastric GISTs (after Miettinen et al.[299])	
	Size (cm) (in greatest dimension)	**Mitotic count (per 50 high power fields)**
Benign	<2	<5
Probably benign	2–10	<5
Uncertain or low malignant potential	<2	>5
Low to moderate malignant potential	2–5	>5
	>10	<5
High malignant potential	>5	>5

correlates strongly with a poor prognosis, despite the fact that a few malignant tumors are diploid.[319,321] Assessment of DNA ploidy may be of particular value in tumors that are of borderline malignancy by other criteria; in one study all such tumors that were aneuploid proved fatal.[318] Another study has suggested that expression of smooth muscle markers in purely spindle-celled lesions that would otherwise be graded as borderline is a favorable prognostic indicator, as was the presence of neural markers exclusively in any type of tumor.[311]

Differential diagnosis Apart from "true" smooth muscle and nerve sheath tumors described below, the differential diagnosis of gastric GIST includes inflammatory fibroid polyp (see p. 366) and a few very rare spindle cell proliferations. These include gastric inflammatory myofibroblastic tumor, a lesion that occurs almost exclusively in children[322] and young adults, solitary fibrous tumor arising from the gastric serosa,[323] so-called calcifying fibrous tumor of the gastric wall,[324] and involvement of the stomach by desmoid fibromatosis (see Ch. 24). Immunostaining for KIT, CD34, desmin, S100, *bcl-2*, CD99, Alk-1 and beta-catenin can help resolve most cases. While it is prudent for the pathologist to consider GIST in the differential diagnosis of any unusual gastric neoplasm, it is important to realize that not all KIT-positive gastric tumors are GISTs – other lesions expressing this marker include myeloid neoplasms, small cell carcinoma, metastatic melanoma, seminoma and breast carcinoma, inflammatory myofibroblastic tumor and, with some commercially available antibodies, fibromatosis.

Smooth muscle tumors

True smooth muscle tumors, morphologically identical to those occurring in the esophagus (see p. 337) do occur rarely in the gastric cardia.[13,291] They demonstrate strong expression of desmin and smooth-muscle actin, but not KIT.

Schwannomas

Some 2 percent of mesenchymal neoplasms of the stomach are benign schwannomas.[325,326] These tumors, which are not associated with neurofibromatosis, are typically nodular or multinodular, polypoid or intramural tumors with little hemorrhage, necrosis or cystic change. They are composed of slender S100 protein-positive cells arranged in bundles in a fibrous background; there may be nuclear pleomorphism but mitoses are very sparse. Verocay bodies, vascular hyalinization, Antoni A and B areas are rarely seen and the appearance is different from soft tissue schwannomas.[326] The tumor margin is characteristically surrounded by a heavy lymphocytic cuff that may have germinal centers. Gastric schwannomas are usually immunopositive for glial fibrillary acidic protein and contain occasional CD34-positive cells. However, they are negative for KIT, desmin and smooth muscle actin.

Vascular tumors

Vascular tumors arising within the wall of the stomach include hemangiomas,[327] lymphangiomas,[328] hemangioendotheliomas,[329] including the epithelioid variety,[330] Kaposi sarcoma, occurring both as a primary gastric tumor in AIDS[331] and as part of systemic disease,[332] and angiosarcomas,[333] including the epithelioid type.[334] Glomus tumors, for which the gastric antrum is the second commonest site after the skin, usually occur as intramural nodules that may undergo ulceration to cause hemorrhage.[335] They are commoner in women and very occasional examples may metastasize. Histologically and immunophenotypically they are identical to their cutaneous counterparts (Fig. 8.61) (see Ch. 3) but, to the unwary, they may be confused with epithelioid GISTs, carcinoids, other vascular tumors, or even malignant lymphoma.

Other connective tissue tumors

Many benign and malignant connective tissue tumors of the stomach have been recorded, often in single case reports. These include rhabdomyomas[336] and rhabdomyosarcomas,[337] lipomas[338] of the submucosa (Fig. 8.62) or subserosa,

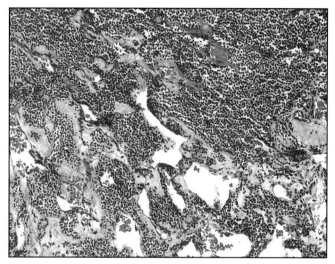

Fig. 8.61 • Gastric glomus tumor.

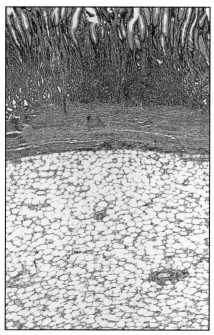

Fig. 8.62 • Submucosal lipoma of the stomach.

angiolipomas,[339] liposarcomas,[340] benign fibrous histiocytoma,[341] synovial sarcoma,[342] clear cell sarcomas,[343] paragangliomas,[344] ganglioneuromas and ganglioneuroblastomas,[345,346] single or multiple granular cell tumors,[116] benign mesenchymomas[347] and teratomas.[348]

Malignant lymphoma of the stomach

Great advances have been made in our understanding of the mucosa-associated lymphoid tissue (MALT) of the gastro-intestinal tract in recent years (see also Ch. 21). This, coupled with careful morphologic, immunohistochemical and molecular biologic studies of cell lineage, has allowed a reappraisal of lymphoid neoplasms of the stomach to be made with the appreciation of distinctive tumor types.[349,350]

Malignant lymphoma of the stomach may be primary, or secondary to systemic lymphoma.[350] Features favoring a primary tumor are concentration of the major tumor bulk within the stomach and/or the regional lymph nodes, without involvement of superficial or mediastinal lymph nodes, the liver, spleen, marrow or peripheral blood. However, this distinction is somewhat artificial in that it fails to recognize occasional cases of disseminated lymphoma with a cellular phenotype that strongly suggests origin from the gastro-intestinal tract.

Immunophenotyping shows that the great majority of primary gastric lymphomas are of B-cell lineage, mostly arising from MALT, with a small number of mantle cell lymphomas.[350] T-cell and null cell tumors are very uncommon and primary Hodgkin lymphoma of the stomach is virtually unknown,[351] although gastric involvement may occur in the context of disseminated disease. With regard to lymphomas that characteristically involve the small intestine, enteropathy-associated T-cell lymphoma does not occur as a primary gastric tumor, while gastric involvement by immunoproliferative small intestinal disease (Mediterranean lymphoma, alpha-chain disease) is very rare; an invasive gastric signet-ring cell lymphoma occurred in one case.[352]

Primary gastric B-cell lymphoma "of MALT"

Clinical features This is by far the commonest type of gastric lymphoma in Western populations. Most patients are middle aged or older and present with features suggesting peptic ulcer or gastric cancer, depending upon the extent of the disease.[353] More than 90 percent of tumors arise in a background of chronic *Helicobacter*-associated gastritis.[354,355] The important role of this organism in the pathogenesis has been shown by epidemiologic studies[350] and confirmed by the fact that eradication of the organism in patients with low-grade gastric MALT lymphoma often leads to regression of the tumor.[356] Some, but not all, high-grade lymphomas with the morphology of diffuse large B-cell lymphoma (DLBCL) arise from trans-formation of such low-grade tumors.[349,354,357] *H. pylori*-negative gastric MALToma has been associated with hepatitis C virus infection and some autoimmune diseases.[355] A few MALT lymphomas have also been described in immunocompromised patients with AIDS or following organ transplantation;[358] high-grade tumors in the latter group may not be *Helicobacter*-related and are frequently associated with Epstein–Barr virus.[359] Synchronous primary gastric adenocarcinoma and MALT lymphoma, though rare, is well recognized.[360]

Fig. 8.63 • Ulcerating high-grade gastric malignant lymphoma.

The prognosis of gastric MALT lymphoma is related to the stage of the disease at presentation and the grade of the tumor.[361] The modified Ann Arbor staging system for extranodal lymphomas is generally used[362] – in the great majority of patients the disease is confined to the stomach or the regional lymph nodes (stages I_E and II_E) at presentation. More recently, the "Paris" staging system, based on the principles of TNM staging, has been proposed as being more clinically useful.[363] Low-grade lymphomas confined to the gastric mucosa and submucosa may be treated in the first instance by *Helicobacter* eradication; those that fail to respond are usually cured by surgery. Patients with more advanced low-grade tumors or high-grade neoplasms are treated by surgery, adjuvant chemotherapy or radiotherapy. In one large series, the overall 5-year survival was 91 percent for low-grade tumors and 56 percent for high-grade tumors.[361] Because the disease is frequently multifocal within the stomach, treated patients require endoscopic follow-up to identify local recurrence.[364] It is notable that some tumors spread preferentially to other MALT-bearing organs, including other regions of the gut, the salivary glands, thyroid and lungs.[365]

Macroscopic features Many gastric B-cell lymphomas simulate gastric carcinomas grossly, being polypoid, fungating or ulcerating tumors (Fig. 8.63), most commonly located in the antrum. Others are indistinguishable from peptic ulcers, and some early low-grade tumors have a relatively unimpressive gross appearance that may be described by the endoscopist as a severe gastritis, sometimes in a nodular, cobblestoned mucosa showing erosions or superficial ulceration.[353] Enlargement of regional lymph nodes may be present.

Microscopic features In low-grade lymphoma of MALT (marginal zone B-cell lymphoma) the gastric mucosa is infiltrated by a heavy, diffuse, often polymorphous population of cells with the immunophenotype of marginal zone B cells (CD20+ CD21+ CD35+ IgM+ IgD–).[349,353,355,361,366,367] Reactive-type follicles with active germinal centers (which probably represent a host reaction to *Helicobacter* infection) are sur-

rounded by sheets of small to medium-sized, irregular, neoplastic lymphoid cells with irregular nuclei (Fig. 8.64), so-called "centrocyte-like cells", that spread diffusely into the surrounding mucosa and characteristically invade the epithelium of the gastric glands to form lymphoepithelial lesions (Fig. 8.65). Florid destruction of such glands often leads to the appearance of isolated, residual eosinophilic epithelial cells in a sea of medium-sized lymphoid cells (Fig. 8.66); occasionally these can acquire signet-ring-like features and care must be taken not to misdiagnose carcinoma.[368] The neoplastic cells do not always resemble centrocytes – sometimes they are more like small lymphocytes or monocytoid B cells with abundant pale-staining

Fig. 8.64 • Primary low-grade gastric B-cell lymphoma. Sheets of small and intermediate-sized lymphoid cells infiltrate the mucosa and submucosa, enveloping reactive mucosal lymphoid follicles and wiping out the specialized mucosal glands.

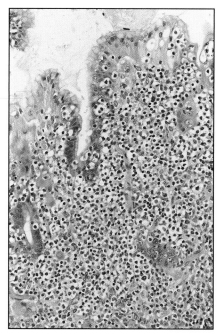

Fig. 8.65 • Lymphoepithelial lesions of primary low-grade B-cell lymphoma. The centrocyte-like cells in the lamina propria of this case have clear cytoplasm and resemble monocytoid B cells.

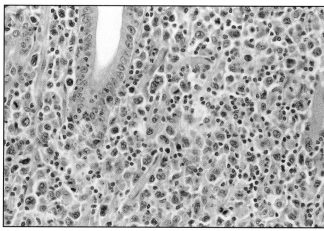

Fig. 8.66 • Primary low-grade B-cell lymphoma. Specialized glands have been virtually destroyed by neoplastic lymphoid cells, leaving only occasional clusters of eosinophilic epithelial cells.

cytoplasm.[366] Scattered blast cells are usually present and often there is striking plasma cell differentiation, especially in the superficial parts of the mucosa, where plasma cells may form a band underneath the surface epithelium.[353] The centrocyte-like cells may invade and "over-run" the reactive B-cell follicles or selectively "colonize" their centers, sparing the mantle zone. When regional lymph nodes are involved they first show the same infiltration around the margin of follicles, resembling so-called "monocytoid B-cell lymphoma" and causing potential confusion with parafollicular infiltration by the entirely different T-zone lymphoma.[367] Immunophenotyping shows tumor cell positivity for B-cell markers (CD20, CD79a), but the cells do not stain for CD5, CD10, CD23, bcl-6 or cyclin D1.[349,350,355] The molecular pathology and cell biology of gastric MALT lymphoma are complex[349,355] and cannot be

reviewed in detail here. However, of particular clinical significance is the finding that tumors bearing the translocation t(11;18)(q21;q21), which leads to expression of a fusion protein AP12-MALT1, and those with nuclear expression of bcl-10, generally fail to respond to H. pylori eradication and are more likely to show dissemination beyond the stomach.[349,369–372]

High-grade B-cell lymphomas of the stomach, or primary gastric DLBCL (Fig. 8.67), are characterized by sheets of transformed blast cells, usually resembling centroblasts but sometimes immunoblasts, which usually wipe-out both the gastric glands and any pre-existing lymphoid follicles. They may be intermingled with polymorphous cells resembling those of low-grade tumors or small reactive T cells; they form lymphoepithelial lesions only rarely.[354] Tumor necrosis may be

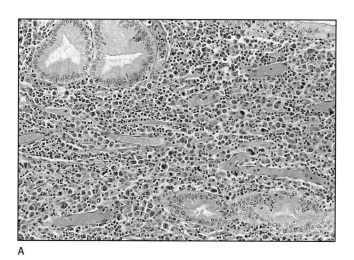

A

B

Fig. 8.67 • (A,B) Primary high-grade gastric B-cell lymphoma. The neoplastic infiltrate is pleomorphic with large numbers of mitotically active blast cells which, in contrast to centrocyte-like cells of low-grade lymphoma, do not form lymphoepithelial lesions.

seen. Careful studies of high-grade lymphomas with widespread sampling have identified a component with typical low-grade features in over 25 percent of cases[357] and there is molecular genetic evidence that this represents high-grade transformation of the latter.[372] High-grade tumors do not regress with *Helicobacter* eradication therapy,[356] and it is important therefore to identify the presence of a high-grade component in endoscopic biopsies by the presence of confluent clusters or sheets of blast cells (diffusely scattered blast cells in small numbers are common in low-grade tumors).[354] A grading system for use in endoscopic biopsies, based on the relative proportion and distribution of blast cells, has claimed clinical utility.[373]

Differential diagnosis It used to be said that the most important differential diagnosis was pseudolymphoma, a reactive lymphoid hyperplasia of mature lymphoid tissue that may affect all layers of the gastric wall, often accompanied by ulceration. However, recent studies, notably using markers of clonality, have indicated that the great majority of pseudolymphomas are, in fact, true lymphomas of low-grade malignancy.[353,367,374,375] Careful study shows the characteristic presence of centrocyte-like cells, lymphoepithelial lesions and light chain restriction. The apparent benign behavior of pseudolymphomas after partial gastrectomy is merely a reflection of the success of surgery in the management of low-grade B-cell lymphomas. It is therefore proposed that the term pseudolymphoma should be abolished. This is not to say that prominent benign lymphoid infiltration of the gastric wall never occurs; it may occasionally be found in inflammatory conditions of the stomach, such as peptic ulcer or Crohn's disease but, in such situations, it usually takes the form of lymphoid aggregates rather than the sheet-like infiltration of centrocyte-like cells in lymphoma.

The main diagnostic difficulty, especially in endoscopic biopsies, is in distinguishing low-grade B-cell lymphoma of MALT from the heavy chronic inflammatory cell infiltrate that sometimes occurs in chronic gastritis. Indeed, this may be impossible, especially in small biopsies, and repeat sampling or careful endoscopic follow-up may be required to clarify the situation. If the lymphoid infiltrate is heavy and diffuse with wipe-out of the gastric glands then the diagnosis of lymphoma is straightforward. On the other hand, if the infiltrate is patchy and does not push the glands apart it is likely to be reactive.[350] The presence of prominent lymphoepithelial lesions, defined as glandular structures expanded *and destroyed* by groups of more than three lymphoid cells,[374] is probably diagnostic of lymphoma; although clusters of intraepithelial B cells are encountered rarely in florid *Helicobacter* gastritis, they are not accompanied by destruction of the epithelial cells with its attendant cytoplasmic eosinophilia.[354] It should be stressed that lymphoepithelial lesions are quite different from the scattered intraepithelial lymphocytosis of lymphocytic gastritis that is usually most prominent in the surface epithelium, virtually never forms clusters, and is composed of T cells.[376] Demonstration of clonal immunoglobulin light chain restriction within the infiltrate on immunostaining, if convincing, supports the diagnosis of malignancy, but interpretation is often difficult because of admixed reactive lymphoid cells and background staining. Investigation of clonal immunoglobulin gene rearrangement by PCR is neither sensitive nor specific; a

positive result is present in only about 75 percent of lymphomas and has been reported in 11 percent of biopsies of chronic *Helicobacter* gastritis.[377]

Low-grade MALT lymphoma must also be distinguished from other, less common varieties of small cell lymphoma affecting the stomach (see below). Apart from morphology, immunostaining with a panel of antibodies that includes CD5, CD23, CD10, *bcl-6* and cyclin D1 helps resolve the diagnosis. High-grade lymphoma may be confused with malignancies of non-lymphoid type. Diffuse-type gastric carcinoma is the most likely mimic, especially when lymphoepithelial destruction of glands leads to isolated epithelial cells with a signet-ring-like morphology[367] (remembering that the two conditions occasionally coexist[360]). Other sources of confusion include myeloid leukemic infiltration (chloroma), gastric sarcomas and metastatic malignant melanoma; one case report[378] has highlighted epithelial infiltration by melanoma cells that closely mimicked lymphoepithelial lesions. Mucin histochemistry and immunocytochemistry are invaluable in reaching the correct diagnosis.

Malignant lymphomatous polyposis Widespread involvement of the gastric mucosa and submucosa sometimes takes the form of multiple polyps or, more frequently, a generalized thickening and pallor of the rugal folds to produce a cerebriform gross appearance. The tumors responsible are not MALT lymphomas, but nearly always mantle cell lymphomas; gastric involvement in such cases is nearly always part of disseminated systemic disease and neoplastic cells can usually be detected in the circulation. Microscopy shows diffuse infiltration by a monotonous population of small lymphoid cells with irregularly folded nuclei that surround, but do not colonize, residual non-neoplastic germinal centers, sometimes interspersed by bands of hyaline collagen.[379] Scattered epithelioid histiocytes are quite frequently present.[350,380] The cells only rarely form lymphoepithelial lesions, unlike B-cell lymphomas of MALT, and show immunopositivity for CD5, IgD and intranuclear cyclin D1, the latter reflecting the t(11:14) translocation that is characteristic of mantle cell lymphoma. The prognosis is poor, with a median survival of 2–3 years.[350]

Although it was once thought that malignant lymphomatous polyposis was characteristic of mantle cell lymphoma, it is now recognized that an identical macroscopic appearance can rarely be found with other types of lymphoma, including follicle center cell lymphoma[350] and T-cell lymphoma.[381]

Other lymphomas Any of the various types of low-grade or high-grade B-cell or T-cell lymphomas that arise in peripheral lymph nodes (see Ch. 21) may occur in the stomach, although, when care is taken to exclude primary B-cell lymphoma of MALT type, they are uncommon and most turn out to be secondary gastric neoplasms.[382] Four (see also Ch. 21) are worthy of mention: follicular lymphoma, the neoplastic follicles of which must be distinguished from reactive follicles colonized by neoplastic centrocyte-like cells that occur in low-grade MALTomas;[350] lymphocytic lymphoma (chronic lymphocytic leukemia), characterized by small round lymphocytes expressing CD5, CD23 without nuclear cyclin D1; Burkitt lymphoma, a tumor usually seen in children and young adults, the histologic appearances of which are identical to those cases arising at other sites; and rare solitary plasmacytomas[383] which must be distinguished from even rarer reactive lesions (plasma cell granuloma[384]) by the demonstration of immunoglobulin light chain restriction.

T-cell tumors of the stomach are rare, aggressive lymphomas that are reported mostly from the Far East where they are frequently associated with HTLV-1 infection.[385,386] They mainly represent gastric involvement with adult T-cell leukemia/lymphoma or peripheral T-cell lymphomas of variable composition, with small, medium or large pleomorphic cells, whose lineage can only be confirmed by immunocytochemistry or by demonstrating clonal T-cell receptor gene rearrangement. Rare examples show evidence of an intraepithelial T-cell phenotype, similar to those seen in the intestine (see p. 384).[387]

Langerhans cell histiocytosis (histiocytosis X)

The stomach may be involved as part of systemic Langerhans cell histiocytosis (see Ch. 21), or may be the site of a localized lesion, sometimes in the form of mucosal nodules or polyposis.[388] Immunocytochemistry and sometimes electron microscopy is required to make a confident distinction from other forms of gastric mononuclear cell infiltration.

Myeloproliferative diseases

Involvement of the gastric wall by myeloid leukemia may give rise to mucosal nodules, plaques or, rarely, polypoid or diffusely infiltrating tumor masses (so-called "granulocytic sarcoma" or "chloroma").[389,390] Myeloid metaplasia has also been reported to cause pyloric obstruction by infiltration of the antral wall.[391] The diagnosis of these myeloproliferative lesions is based on cellular morphology, chloroacetate esterase histochemistry and immunocytochemistry, interpreted in the light of clinical and hematologic findings (see Ch. 22).

Secondary tumors

Tumor metastases to the stomach are rare. Most are asymptomatic, although some cause gastric obstruction, bleeding or perforation. Carcinomas of the lung, pancreas, colon, breast, thyroid and prostate, malignant melanoma and hepatocellular carcinoma are the commonest primaries.[392,393] Metastatic lesions may be solitary or multiple. Metastatic lobular carcinoma of the breast is well recognized for infiltrating the gastric wall diffusely and mimicking linitis plastica (Fig. 8.68).[394]

Tumor-like lesions

Hyperplastic (regenerative or hyperplasiogenous) polyps of the stomach

Clinical features Hyperplastic polyps are the most common type of gastric polyp[168,169,172,182] and can be divided into two types (I and II) according to Nakamura.[172] They are thought to result from excessive regeneration following mucosal damage and, as such, occur in chronic *Helicobacter*-associated gastritis,[395] pernicious anemia, adjacent to ulcers and erosions, or at gastroenterostomy sites, often in a background of atrophic gastritis with intestinal metaplasia.[396] Nakamura type I hyper-

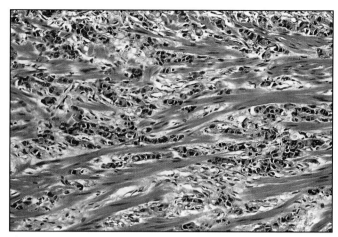

Fig. 8.68 • Metastatic lobular carcinoma of the breast in the wall of the stomach.

plastic polyps are usually solitary and found in the antrum, while type II polyps are usually multiple and distributed in the distal fundic mucosa, often in a row that roughly corresponds to the junction between the body and antrum.

Hyperplastic polyps may increase in number with time or they may regress, either spontaneously or, more frequently, following *Helicobacter* eradication.[396] A small proportion (up to 3 percent), usually those measuring more than 2 cm, show dysplasia or even intramucosal carcinoma (see Fig. 8.29),[182,201] while an association with a synchronous carcinoma elsewhere in the stomach is well described;[169,172,182] careful endoscopic assessment of the background mucosa is therefore important in all patients with hyperplastic polyps. Lesions measuring 2 cm or larger should be completely excised for histologic exclusion of neoplasia.

Macroscopic appearances Hyperplastic polyps are sessile or pedunculated, smooth-surfaced or lobulated, and usually measure less than 2 cm in diameter. Nakamura type II polyps often have a central dimple, corresponding to an infolding of the papillary surface epithelium (Fig. 8.69). Superficial erosion occurs commonly.

Microscopic appearances Histologically, both types of polyp show hyperplasia of the gastric foveolae, leading to elongated tortuous glands showing cystic changes and irregular branching (Fig. 8.70).[397] Additionally, in Nakamura type II polyps, the glands in the central portion of the polyp have a distinctive core-like onion-skin appearance (Fig. 8.71).[172] The glands are lined by a single layer of hyperplastic foveolar-type epithelium, though pyloric-type glands, chief cells, parietal cells and foci of intestinal metaplasia may be found, especially in the deeper zones. The surface of the polyp may be ulcerated and acutely inflamed, showing degenerative and regenerative atypia in the epithelial and stromal cells; this can cause major diagnostic confusion since both true carcinoma (see Fig. 8.29)[182] and pseudo-invasion[248] may be found in hyperplastic polyps (see above). The stroma of the polyp is edematous, infiltrated by plasma cells, lymphocytes (including follicles with germinal centers) and eosinophils, and contains smooth muscle fibers that extend from the muscularis mucosae between the basal gastric glands.

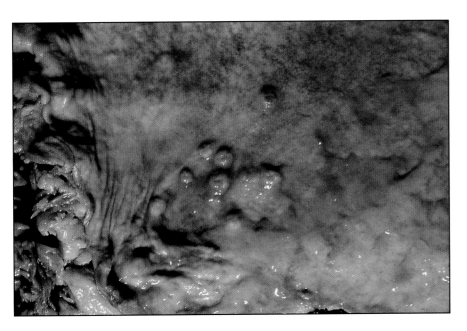

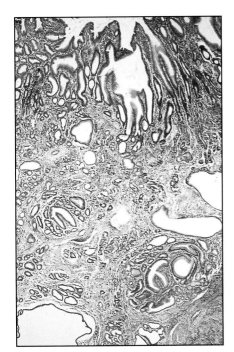

Fig. 8.70 • Gastric hyperplastic polyp.

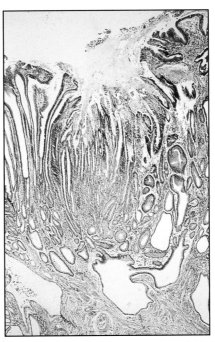

Fig. 8.71 • Onion-skin arrangement of superficial glands at the surface of a hyperplastic gastric polyp. This corresponds to the dimple seen macroscopically (see Fig. 8.69).

Differential diagnosis The differentiation from adenomatous polyps has been discussed on page 342. Hyperplastic polyps may be difficult to distinguish from localized Ménétrier's disease (see p. 368), hamartomatous polyps of juvenile type, or gastric lesions of Cronkhite-Canada syndrome (see below). Consideration of the clinical, endoscopic and macroscopic appearances is usually helpful.

Fundic gland polyps

Fundic gland polyps may occur sporadically,[168,398,399] in patients with familial adenomatous polyposis (FAP)[171] or as a familial condition confined to the stomach.[400] A previously held opinion that they are commoner in patients receiving long-term treatment with proton pump inhibitors[398] has been challenged.[401] Fundic gland polyps are usually multiple and may be found in men and women of any age. Macroscopically, they appear as glassy, transparent, sessile polyps, less than 1 cm in diameter, confined to the body–fundic mucosa. Histologically, they are composed of cystically dilated glands lined by proliferating fundic epithelium, including parietal cells and chief cells, admixed with normal glands (Fig. 8.72).[398] The overlying foveolae are shortened and there is usually no inflammation or evidence of atypia.[402] There may be an irregular and disordered distribution of smooth muscle fibers around the cystic glands.[398] In patients on proton pump inhibitors there is

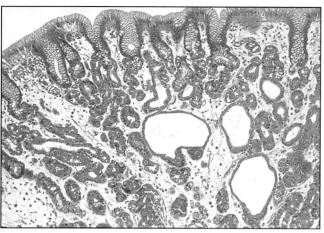

Fig. 8.72 • Fundic gland polyp of the gastric body.

associated hypertrophy and hyperplasia of parietal cells, which protrude into the lumen of the pits, producing a serrated architecture (Fig. 8.73).[403]

More recently, occasional examples of fundic gland polyps with dysplasia have been described, occurring either sporadically or in a background of familial adenomatous polyposis, associated with somatic mutation of the *APC* gene.[404] This, and the finding of beta-catenin mutations in non-dysplastic fundic gland polyps,[405] has raised the possibility that some, if not all, of these lesions may be true neoplasms, rather than hamartomatous or hyperplastic lesions, as previously thought. On the other hand, spontaneous regression has been documented.[399] The implications for patient management are uncertain at present. While a case can be made for endoscopic surveillance of individuals with multiple dysplastic fundic gland polyps, especially in the context of FAP, this is currently not advocated for patients with sporadic, non-dysplastic lesions. However, the finding of fundic gland polyps in a young patient merits consideration of the possibility of underlying FAP.

Inflammatory fibroid polyp

This uncommon benign lesion of unknown etiology is found in male and female adults of all ages, and is associated in some cases with hypo- or achlorhydria.[406,407] It is usually found in the antrum and may occur as an incidental finding or present with gastric hemorrhage or symptoms of gastric outlet obstruction.

Grossly, it is a small, well-circumscribed, solitary, sessile or pedunculated lesion that is often ulcerated (Fig. 8.74), sometimes to a degree that makes confident diagnosis difficult. Histologically, it is usually centered in the submucosa (though purely mucosal lesions are described) and resembles edematous granulation tissue (Fig. 8.75), being composed of small thin-walled blood vessels surrounded by spindle cells with long cytoplasmic processes, which may be arranged in an "onion-skin" pattern around larger vessels. Sometimes "floret"-like multinucleate giant cells with hyperchromatic nuclei are included. There is a chronic inflammatory cell infiltrate which is often dominated by eosinophils but, in contrast to eosinophilic gastritis, which presents with a diffusely thickened and deformed antrum narrowing the pylorus in children and young adults, inflammatory fibroid polyp is not associated with circulating eosinophilia or a history of atopy. The spindle cells show immunopositivity for CD34, fascin and (usually)

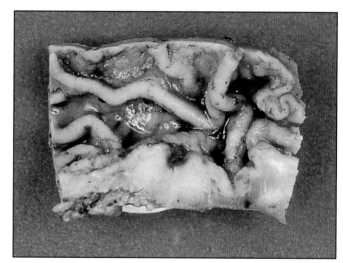

Fig. 8.74 • Cross-section of a gastric inflammatory fibroid polyp with surface ulceration.

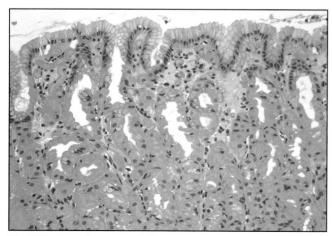

Fig. 8.73 • Hyperplastic parietal cells in the gastric fundus of a patient receiving proton pump inhibitor therapy.

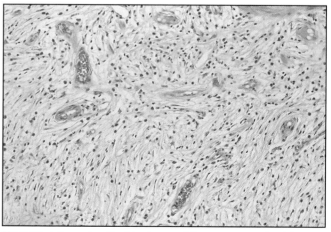

Fig. 8.75 • Inflammatory fibroid polyp containing numerous eosinophils.

calponin, suggesting that they may be of either dendritic cell or myofibroblastic lineage.[407] KIT (and h-caldesmon) staining is consistently negative, which is useful in the differentiation from GIST. Inflammatory fibroid polyps should also be distinguished from rare eosinophilic granulomas associated with parasitic infections.

Other mucosal polyps

The stomach may be involved in *Peutz–Jeghers polyposis*[408] though apparently less frequently than the small intestine or colon. These hamartomatous polyps are composed of hyperplastic glands lined by foveolar-type epithelium, separated by branching cores of smooth muscle, with atrophy of the deep glandular components (Fig. 8.76). Rare reports of gastric carcinoma in association with Peutz–Jeghers polyposis are described,[409] but it is far from clear how often this has arisen within a pre-existing polyp. However, one report has illustrated dysplasia in a gastric Peutz–Jeghers polyp.[410]

Juvenile polyps of the stomach are rare and often occur within the context of juvenile polyposis, either of the stomach alone[411] or of the entire gastrointestinal tract (with or without a family history). They may present at any age, usually with anemia or hypoproteinemia, and are most common in the antrum. Juvenile polyposis is associated with an increased risk of gastrointestinal cancer, particularly in the colorectum, but the stomach may also be at risk – dysplasia and carcinoma have been described in gastric juvenile polyps.[411] Histologically, juvenile polyps of the stomach are composed of edematous and inflamed mucosa with marked elongation, tortuosity and cystic dilatation of the foveolar zones (Fig. 8.77). They are larger than cystic fundic polyps with much more foveolar hyperplasia. They do not show the smooth muscle fibers of Peutz–Jeghers polyps, but they can be confused with hyperplastic polyps.

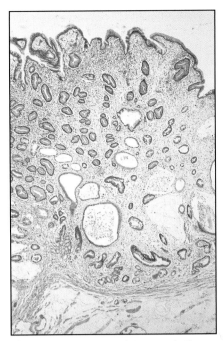

Fig. 8.77 • Juvenile polyp of the stomach. The appearances are indistinguishable from lesions of Cronkhite–Canada syndrome, and may mimic hyperplastic polyps closely.

Gastric polyps may also occur in *Cowden's disease* and may comprise epithelial and/or connective tissue (smooth muscle or neural) components. Published histologic descriptions are sparse, but in one case report the polyps consisted of enlarged, elongated foveolar glands along with more basal, cystically dilated glands that contained papillary infoldings. Smooth muscle fibers were intermingled within the mucosal components and the cystic structures sometimes extended into the submucosa.[412]

Cronkhite-Canada syndrome polyps are well recognized to occur in the stomach,[168] usually in conjunction with lesions in other parts of the gastrointestinal tract. They are indistinguishable histologically from juvenile polyps and the diagnosis can only be made in the presence of clinical evidence of alopecia, nail atrophy or hyperpigmentation.[413,414]

Heterotopias

Pancreatic heterotopia[415] is the most common type of congenital heterotopia in the stomach, presenting as a gastric mass with symptoms of pyloric obstruction or peptic ulcer disease, or incidentally at endoscopy, laparotomy or autopsy. It is usually found in the pylorus or antrum as an intramural hemispherical, conical or short cylindrical mass. The most characteristic feature is a central depression on the mucosal surface, which represents the opening of one or more rudimentary pancreatic ducts. The cut surface resembles normal pancreas. Histologically, the mass is composed of normal pancreatic acini and ducts (Fig. 8.78), many of which are cystically dilated, with occasional islets and Brunner-type glands. When smooth muscle and duct-like structures (with or without Brunner's glands) are the only components (Fig. 8.79) then the term adenomyoma (myoepithelial hamartoma) has been used.[416] Rare cases of adenocarcinoma arising in an adenomyoma[417]

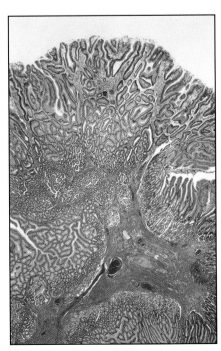

Fig. 8.76 • Gastric Peutz–Jeghers polyp.

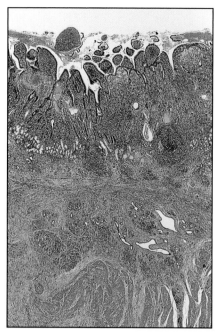

Fig. 8.78 • Pancreatic heterotopia at the gastroduodenal junction. There are both pancreatic acini and ducts in the submucosa, extending deeply into the muscle coat.

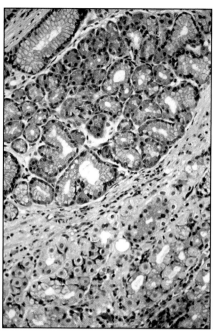

Fig. 8.80 • Pancreatic acinar metaplasia in the cardia.

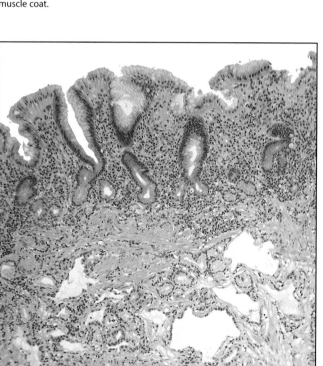

Fig. 8.79 • Biopsy of gastric adenomyoma.

or heterotopic pancreas[418] are recorded. Focal pancreatic-type acini and ducts confined to the mucosa, particularly in the cardia, have been termed pancreatic acinar metaplasia (Fig. 8.80),[419] although this is probably congenital, rather than acquired, in origin.[420]

Other forms of presumed heterotopia in the stomach include localized aggregates of Brunner's glands, which may form a so-called "polypoid mucosal Brunner's adenoma",[421]

intramural cysts lined by ciliated epithelium[422] or accompanied by a dense lymphoid stroma ("lymphoepithelial cyst")[423] and mucosal foci of squamous epithelium. We also know of a single case report of "squamous cell papillomatosis" involving the whole of the posterior wall and lesser curvature of the stomach,[424] in which the gastric mucosa was replaced by mature hyperkeratotic squamous epithelium with no evidence of atypia. Large squamous inclusions were present in the submucosa, and papillomatous squamous epithelium protruded from the serosal surface. It is conceivable that this lesion was metaplastic or even neoplastic in nature.

Ménétrier's disease (hyperplastic or hypertrophic gastropathy, giant rugal hypertrophy)

Clinical features Ménétrier's disease is an uncommon condition of unknown etiology that is rarely familial,[425] shows no regular association with other diseases,[426] has a predilection for males and affects mainly middle-aged adults, though it has been described in children.[427] Patients may be asymptomatic or present with symptoms of peptic ulcer disease, associated with hypochlorhydria, hypoproteinemia and anemia. The disease may regress spontaneously or may progress to chronic atrophic gastritis.[428,429] It is said to be associated with an increased risk of gastric cancer (Fig. 8.81), but the magnitude of this risk is difficult to quantify.[201,426]

Macroscopic appearances Ménétrier's disease is characterized by hypertrophic rugae, measuring 1–3 cm in height, which resemble cerebral convolutions (Fig. 8.81) or, when uneven and nodular, mimic polyposis. It may be localized to the proximal greater curve or generalized in the body and fundus of the stomach. The antrum is rarely involved grossly (although it may show histologic changes), and there is usually an abrupt transition between normal and diseased mucosa.

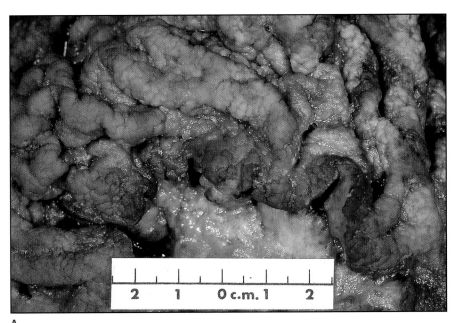

A

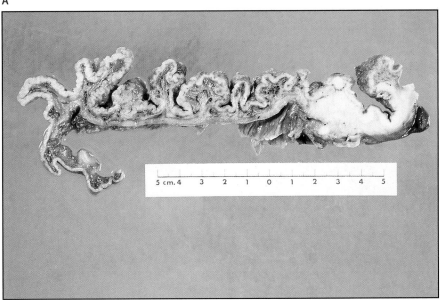

B

Fig. 8.81 • (A,B) Ménétrier's disease complicated by an ulcerating gastric adenocarcinoma. The cerebriform convolutions of the thickened gastric mucosa are obvious.

Microscopic appearances In classical cases there is prominent foveolar hyperplasia with elongated, tortuous, dilated foveolar segments lined by large numbers of engorged mucus-secreting cells, overlying cystically dilated, atrophic, specialized glands, with reduced numbers of parietal and chief cells deep in the mucosa. Sometimes these cystic glands are also lined by mucous cells and they may prolapse into the submucosa. The lamina propria is markedly edematous and may be infiltrated by smooth muscle fibers from the muscularis mucosae. Inflammation is typically sparse, but when present may include prominent eosinophils.[430]

Differential diagnosis The gross appearances may be confused with malignant lymphoma, carcinoma, gastric polyposis or Zollinger–Ellison syndrome (see above). The pathologic lesion of Ménétrier's disease should also be distinguished from état mammelonné, a variant of normal, which is characterized in the empty stomach by prominent longitudinal rugal folds. Histologically, the basic features of Ménétrier's disease resemble those of hyperplastic polyps; a clinical history and macroscopic description are therefore important in making the correct diagnosis. Some cases with macroscopic appearances identical to Ménétrier's disease (and with marked foveolar hyperplasia and cystic glands on microscopy) show heavy mucosal inflammation, relatively little edema, and a marked intraepithelial T-cell lymphocytosis, suggesting that they represent the "hypertrophic" end of the clinicopathologic spectrum of chronic lymphocytic gastritis; it has been proposed that this condition should be separated from true Ménétrier's disease.[430] The same is true for the Ménétrier's-like disease associated with cytomegalovirus infection, which has been observed in pediatric and adult patients with gastro-intestinal protein loss.[431]

Gastritis cystica polyposa or profunda

This lesion is usually found at gastroenterostomy stoma sites,[247,432] although similar changes may occur at margins of

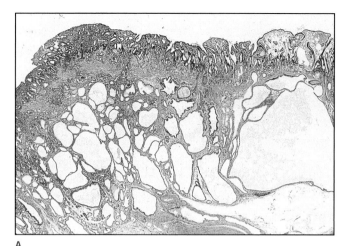

A

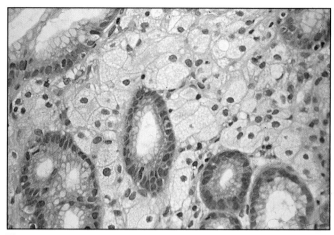

Fig. 8.83 • Gastric xanthelasma.

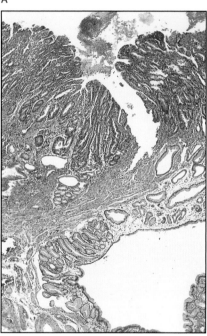

B

Fig. 8.82 • Gastritis cystica polyposa occurring close to a gastroenterostomy site (A). (B) Coexisting intramucosal adenocarcinoma (stump carcinoma) is present.

peptic ulcers.[396] It has also been associated with the development of gastric stump carcinomas (Fig. 8.82).[247] Gastritis cystica polyposa is characterized by multiple sessile, polypoid lesions, which may completely encircle the stoma site. Histologically, they resemble hyperplastic polyps with florid cystic dilatation of the glands but, in contrast to hyperplastic polyps, these dilated glands extend through a thickened and frayed

muscularis mucosae into the submucosa (see Fig. 8.82), where they may be accompanied by mucus extravasation. Intestinal metaplasia may be present and often the overlying mucosa is eroded. The submucosal glands arise by misplacement, due to ischemia and chronic inflammation related to previous surgery, and are bland without cellular atypia, allowing distinction from well-differentiated adenocarcinoma.

Xanthoma/xanthelasma

These clinically insignificant lesions are found with increasing age, in males more than females, and are often associated with chronic gastritis and intestinal metaplasia of the gastric mucosa, as well as with bile reflux gastropathy.[433,434] They are not related to hypercholesterolemia and may be found in association with hyperplastic polyps. Grossly, they are single or multiple, 1–2 mm in diameter, round or oval, well circumscribed, yellow, macular or nodular. These lesions are found most frequently along the lesser curvature. Histologically, they consist of accumulations of mature lipid-laden macrophages, containing cholesterol and neutral fat, within the lamina propria (Fig. 8.83). Their distinction from carcinoma in biopsies has been discussed on page 350. Other differential diagnoses include *Mycobacterium avium-intracellulare* infection, muciphages and granular cell tumors.

Amyloid tumors

Tumor-like masses of amyloid in the stomach mucosa (Fig. 8.84) or wall may occur as part of systemic amyloidosis[435] or as a primary lesion.[436] Rarely they may coexist with primary gastric lymphoma.[437]

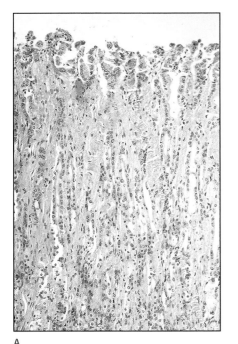

Fig. 8.84 • Gastric mucosal plaque of (A) Amyloid in a patient with long-standing rheumatoid arthritis. (B) Congo red stain/polarized light.

A

B

References

1. Quitadamo M, Benson J 1988 Squamous papilloma of the esophagus: a case report and review of the literature. Am J Gastroenterol 83: 194–201
2. Walker J H 1978 Giant papilloma of the thoracic esophagus. Am J Roentgenol 131: 519–520
3. Parnell S A C, Peppercorn M A, Antonioli D A et al. 1978 Squamous cell papilloma of the esophagus. Report of a case after peptic esophagitis and repeated bougienage with review of the literature. Gastroenterology 74: 910–913
4. Brinson R R, Schuman B M, Mills L R et al. 1987 Multiple squamous papillomas of the esophagus associated with Goltz syndrome. Am J Gastroenterol 82: 1177–1179
5. Odze R, Antonioli D, Shocket D et al. 1993 Esophageal squamous papillomas. A clinicopathologic study of 38 lesions and analysis for human papillomavirus by the polymerase chain reaction. Am J Surg Pathol 17: 803–812
6. Carr N J, Bratthauer G L, Lichy J H et al. 1994 Squamous cell papillomas of the esophagus. A study of 23 lesions for human papillomavirus by in situ hybridization and the polymerase chain reaction. Hum Pathol 25: 536–540
7. Paraf F, Fléjou J-F, Potet F et al. 1992 Adenomas arising in Barrett's esophagus with adenocarcinoma. Report of 3 cases. Pathol Res Pract 188: 1028–1032
8. McDonald G B, Brand D L, Thorning D R 1977 Multiple adenomatous neoplasms arising in columnar lined (Barrett's) esophagus. Gastroenterology 72: 1317–1321
9. Banducci D, Rees R, Bluett M K et al. 1987 Pleomorphic adenoma of the cervical esophagus: a rare tumor. Ann Thorac Surg 44: 653–655
10. Mandard A M, Marnay J, Gignoux M et al. 1984 Cancer of the esophagus and associated lesions: detailed pathologic study of 100 esophagectomy specimens. Hum Pathol 15: 660–669
11. Wang G Q, Abnet C C, Shen Q et al. 2005 Histological precursors of oesophageal squamous cell carcinoma: results from a 13 year prospective follow up study in a high risk population. Gut 54: 187–192
12. Dawsey S M, Wang G Q, Weinstein W M et al. 1993 Squamous dysplasia and early esophageal cancer in the Minxian region of China: distinctive endoscopic lesions. Gastroenterology 105: 1330–1340
13. Lewin K J, Appelman H D 1996 Tumors of the esophagus and stomach. Atlas of tumor pathology. Armed Forces Institute of Pathology, Washington, DC, series 3, fascicle 18
14. Chu P, Stagias J, West B A et al. 1997 Diffuse pagetoid squamous cell carcinoma in situ of the esophagus. A case report. Cancer 79: 1865–1870
15. Potet F, Fléjou J-F, Gervaz H et al. 1991 Adenocarcinoma of the lower esophagus and esophagogastric junction. Semin Diagn Pathol 8: 126–136
16. Schlemper R J, Riddell R H, Kato Y et al. 2000 The Vienna classification of gastrointestinal epithelial neoplasia. Gut 47: 251–255
17. Bogomoletz W V 1994 Early squamous carcinoma of esophagus. Curr Diagn Pathol 1: 212–215
18. De Baecque C, Potet F, Molas G et al. 1990 Superficial adenocarcinoma of the esophagus in Barrett's mucosa with dysplasia: clinicopathologic study of 12 patients. Histopathology 16: 213–220
19. Ribeiro U, Posner M C, Safatle-Ribeiro A V et al. 1996 Risk factors for squamous cell carcinoma of the oesophagus. Br J Surg 83: 1174–1185
20. Chang-Claude J C, Wahrendorf J, Liang Q S et al. 1990 An epidemiologic study of precursor lesions of esophageal cancer among young persons in a high-risk population in Hunxian, China. Cancer Res 50: 2268–2274
21. Dawsey S M, Lewin K J, Liu F S et al. 1994 Esophageal morphology from Linxian, China. Squamous histologic findings in 754 patients. Cancer 73: 2027–2037
22. Togawa K, Jaskiewicz K, Takahashi H et al. 1994 Human papillomavirus DNA sequences in esophagus squamous cell carcinoma. Gastroenterology 107: 128–136
23. Fidalgo P O, Cravo M L, Chaves P P et al. 1995 High prevalence of human papillomavirus in squamous cell carcinoma and matched normal esophageal mucosa. Cancer 76: 1522–1528
24. Poljak M, Cerar A, Seme K 1998 Human papillomavirus infection in esophageal carcinomas. Hum Pathol 29: 266–271
25. Marger R S, Marger D 1993 Carcinoma of the esophagus and tylosis: a lethal genetic combination. Cancer 72: 17–19
26. Stemmermann G, Heffelfinger S C, Noffsinger A et al. 1995 The molecular biology of esophageal and gastric cancer and their precursors: oncogenes, tumor suppressor genes, growth factors. Hum Pathol 25: 968–981
27. Tahara E (ed) 1997 Molecular pathology of gastroenterological cancer. Springer, Tokyo
28. Iwaya T, Maesawa C, Ogasawara S et al. 1998 Tylosis esophageal cancer locus on chromosome 17q25.1 is commonly deleted in sporadic human esophageal cancer. Gastroenterology 114: 1206–1210
29. Earlam R, Cunha-Melo J R 1980 Oesophageal squamous cell carcinoma: I. A critical review of surgery. Br J Surg 67: 381–390
30. Anderson L L, Lad T E 1982 Autopsy findings in squamous cell carcinoma of the esophagus. Cancer 50: 1587–1590
31. Fogel T D, Harrison L B, Son S H 1985 Subsequent aerodigestive malignancies following treatment of esophageal cancer. Cancer 55: 1882–1885
32. Jasim K A, Bateson M C 1990 Verrucous carcinoma of the oesophagus – a diagnostic problem. Histopathology 17: 473–475
33. Morita M, Kuwano H, Yasuda M et al. 1994 The multicentric occurrence of squamous epithelial dysplasia and squamous cell carcinoma in the esophagus. Cancer 74: 2889–2895
34. Pesko P, Rakic S, Milicevic M et al. 1994 Prevalence and clinicopathologic features of multiple squamous cell carcinoma of the esophagus. Cancer 73: 2687–2690
35. Lam K Y, Ma L T, Wong J 1996 Measurement of extent of spread of oesophageal squamous carcinoma by serial sectioning. J Clin Pathol 49: 124–129
36. Kuwano H, Ueo H, Sugimachi K et al. 1985 Glandular or mucus-secreting components in squamous cell carcinoma of the esophagus. Cancer 56: 514–518
37. Briggs J C, Ibrahim N B N 1983 Oat cell carcinoma of the oesophagus: a clinicopathologic study of 23 cases. Histopathology 7: 261–277

38. Edwards J M, Hillier V F, Lawson R A M et al. 1989 Squamous carcinoma of the oesophagus: histologic criteria and their prognostic significance. Br J Cancer 59: 429–433

39. Takubo K, Takai A, Takayama S et al. 1987 Intraductal spread of esophageal squamous cell carcinoma. Cancer 59: 1751–1757

40. Mori M, Matsuda H, Kuwano H et al. 1989 Oesophageal squamous cell carcinoma with lymphoid stroma. A case report. Virchow's Arch [A] 415: 473–479

41. Ruol A, Segalin A, Panozzo M et al. 1990 Flow cytometric DNA analysis of squamous cell carcinoma of the esophagus. Cancer 65: 1185–1188

42. Soga J, Tanaka O, Sasaki K et al. 1982 Superficial spreading carcinoma of the esophagus. Cancer 50: 1641–1645

43. Rubio C A, Liu F S 1990 The histogenesis of the microinvasive basal cell carcinoma of the esophagus. Pathol Res Pract 186: 223–227

44. Abe K, Sasano H, Itakura Y et al. 1996 Basaloid-squamous carcinoma of the esophagus. A clinicopathologic, DNA ploidy, and immunohistochemical study of seven cases. Am J Surg Pathol 20: 453–461

45. Sarbia M, Vereet P, Bittinger F et al. 1997 Basaloid squamous cell carcinoma of the esophagus: diagnosis and prognosis. Cancer 79: 1871–1878

46. Lam K Y, Law S, Luk J M et al. 2001 Oesophageal basaloid squamous cell carcinoma: a unique clinicopathologic entity with telomerase activity as a prognostic indicator. J Pathol 195: 435–442

47. Isaacson P 1982 Biopsy appearances easily mistaken for malignancy in gastrointestinal endoscopy. Histopathology 6: 377–389

48. Gill P, Piris J, Warren B F 2003 Bizarre stromal cells in the oesophagus. Histopathology 42: 88–90

49. Schlemper R J, Dawsey S M, Itabashi M et al. 2000 Differences in diagnostic criteria for esophageal squamous carcinoma between Japanese and Western pathologists. Cancer 88: 996–1006

50. Osamura R Y, Shimamura K, Hata J et al. 1978 Polypoid carcinoma of the esophagus. A unifying concept for "carcinosarcoma" and "pseudosarcoma". Am J Surg Pathol 2: 201–208

51. du Boulay C E H, Isaacson P 1981 Carcinoma of the oesophagus with spindle cell features. Histopathology 5: 403–414

52. Cho S R, Henry D A, Schneider V et al. 1983 Polypoid carcinoma of the esophagus: a distinct radiologic and histopathologic entity. Am J Gastroenterol 78: 476–480

53. Appelman H D (ed) 1984 Stromal tumors of the esophagus, stomach and duodenum. In: Pathology of the esophagus, stomach and duodenum. Churchill Livingstone, Edinburgh, p 195–242

54. Guarino M, Reale D, Micoli G et al. 1993 Carcinosarcoma of the oesophagus with rhabdomyoblastic differentiation. Histopathology 22: 493–498

55. Lauwers G Y, Grant L D, Scott G V et al. 1998 Spindle cell squamous carcinoma of the esophagus: analysis of ploidy and tumor proliferative activity in a series of 13 cases. Hum Pathol 29: 863–868

56. Matsumoto T, Fujii H, Arakawa A et al. 2004 Loss of heterozygosity analysis shows monoclonal evolution with frequent genetic progression and divergence in esophageal carcinosarcoma. Hum Pathol 35: 322–327

57. Martland G T, Goodman A J, Shepherd N A 2004 CD117 expression in esophageal carcinosarcoma: a potential diagnostic pitfall. Histopathology 44: 77–80

58. Iftikhar S Y, James P D, Steele R J C et al. 1992 Length of Barrett's oesophagus: an important factor in the development of dysplasia and adenocarcinoma. Gut 33: 1155–1158

59. Lagergren J, Bergstrom R, Nyren O 1999 Association between body mass and adenocarcinoma of the esophagus and gastric cardia. Ann Intern Med 130: 883–890

60. Lagergren J, Bergstrom R, Adami H O et al. 2000 Association between medications that relax the lower esophageal sphincter and risk for esophageal adenocarcinoma. Ann Intern Med 133: 165–175

61. Wang H H, Antonioli D A, Goldman H 1986 Comparative features of esophageal and gastric adenocarcinomas: recent changes in type and frequency. Hum Pathol 17: 482–487

62. Pera M, Cameron A J, Trastek V F et al. 1993 Increasing incidence of adenocarcinoma of the esophagus and esophagogastric junction. Gastroenterology 104: 510–513

63. Blount P L, Ramel S, Raskind W H et al. 1991 17p allelic deletions and p53 protein overexpression in Barrett's adenocarcinoma. Cancer Res 51: 5482–5486

64. Fléjou J-F, Paraf F, Muzeau F et al. 1994 Expression of c-erbB-2 oncogene product in Barrett's adenocarcinoma: pathologic and prognostic correlations. J Clin Pathol 47: 23–26

65. Klump B, Hsieh C J, Holzmann K 1998 Hypermethylation of the CDKN2/p16 promoter during neoplastic progression in Barrett's esophagus. Gastroenterology 115: 1381–1386

66. Shirvani VN, Ouatu-Lascar R, Kaur B S et al. 2000 Cyclooxygenase 2 expression in Barrett's esophagus and adenocarcinoma: ex vivo induction by bile salts and acid exposure. Gastroenterology 118: 487–496

67. Sanfey H, Hamilton S R, Smith R R L et al. 1985 Carcinoma arising in Barrett's esophagus. Surg Gynecol Obstet 161: 570–574

68. Corley D A, Levin T R, Habel L A et al. 2002 Surveillance and survival in Barrett's adenocarcinomas: a population-based study. Gastroenterology 122: 633–640

69. Cameron A J, Lomboy C T, Pera M et al. 1995 Adenocarcinoma of the esophagogastric junction and Barrett's esophagus. Gastroenterology 109: 1541–1546

70. Chatelain D, de Lajarte-Thirouard AS, Tiret E et al. 2002 Adenocarcinoma of the upper esophagus arising in heterotopic gastric mucosa: common pathogenesis with Barrett's adenocarcinoma? Virchow's Arch 441: 406–411

71. Smith R R L, Hamilton S R, Boitnott J K et al. 1984 The spectrum of carcinoma arising in Barrett's esophagus. A clinicopathologic study of 26 patients. Am J Surg Pathol 8: 563–573

72. Hamilton S R, Smith R R L 1987 The relationship between columnar epithelial dysplasia and invasive adenocarcinoma arising in Barrett's esophagus. Am J Clin Pathol 87: 301–312

73. Chejfec G, Jablokow V R, Gould V E 1983 Linitis plastica carcinoma of the esophagus. Cancer 51: 2139–2143

74. Hamilton K, Chiappori A, Olson S et al. 2000 Prevalence and prognostic significance of neuroendocrine cells in esophageal adenocarcinoma. Mod Pathol 13: 475–481

75. Dworak O, Koerfgen H P 1993 Carcinosarcoma in Barrett's oesophagus: a case report with immunohistologic examination. Virchows Arch [A] 422: 423–426

76. Falk G W 1999 Endoscopic surveillance of Barrett's esophagus: risk stratification and cancer risk. Gastrointest Endosc 49: S29–S34

77. Mino-Kenudson M, Brugge W R, Puricelli W P et al. 2005 Management of superficial Barrett's epithelium-related neoplasms by endoscopic mucosal resection: clinicopathologic analysis of 27 cases. Am J Surg Pathol 29: 680–686

78. Ban S, Mino M, Nishioka N S et al. 2004 Histopathologic aspects of photodynamic therapy for dysplasia and early adenocarcinoma arising in Barrett's esophagus. Am J Surg Pathol 28: 1466–1473

79. Bell-Thomson J, Haggitt R C, Ellis F H Jr 1980 Mucoepidermoid and adenoid cystic carcinomas of the esophagus. J Thorac Cardiovasc Surg 79: 438–446

80. Kabuto T, Taniguchi K, Iwanaga T et al. 1979 Primary adenoid cystic carcinoma of the esophagus. Report of a case. Cancer 43: 2452–2456

81. Woodard B H, Shelburne J D, Vollmer R T et al. 1978 Mucoepidermoid carcinoma of the esophagus: a case report. Hum Pathol 9: 352–354

82. Sweeney E C, Cooney T 1980 Adenoid cystic carcinoma of the esophagus. A light and electron microscopic study. Cancer 45: 1516–1525

83. Epstein J I, Sears D L, Tucker R S et al. 1984 Carcinoma of the esophagus with adenoid cystic differentiation. Cancer 53: 1131–1136

84. Yachida S, Nakanishi Y, Shimoda T et al. 2004 Adenosquamous carcinoma of the esophagus. Clinicopathologic study of 18 cases. Oncology 66: 218–225

85. Orsatti G, Corvalan A H, Sakurai H et al. 1993 Polypoid adenosquamous carcinoma of the esophagus with prominent spindle cells. Report of a case with immunohistochemical and ultrastructural studies. Arch Pathol Lab Med 117: 544–547

86. Mori M, Matsukuma A, Adachi Y 1989 Small cell carcinoma of the esophagus. Cancer 63: 564–573

87. Casas F, Ferrer F, Farrus B et al. 1997 Primary small cell carcinoma of the esophagus. A review of the literature with emphasis on therapy and prognosis. Cancer 80: 1366–1372

88. Watson K J R, Shulkes A, Smallwood R A et al. 1985 Watery diarrhea-hypokalemia-achlorhydria syndrome and carcinoma of the esophagus. Gastroenterology 88: 798–803

89. Johnson F E, Clawson M C, Bashiti H M et al. 1984 Small cell undifferentiated carcinoma of the esophagus. Case report with hormonal studies. Cancer 53: 1746–1751

90. Ho K J, Herrera G A, Jones J M et al. 1984 Small cell carcinoma of the esophagus: evidence for a unified histogenesis. Hum Pathol 15: 460–468

91. Trillo A A, Accettullo L M, Yeiter T L 1979 Choriocarcinoma of the esophagus: histologic and cytologic findings: a case report. Acta Cytol 23: 69–74

92. McKechnie J C, Fechner R E 1971 Choriocarcinoma and adenocarcinoma of the esophagus with gonadotropin secretion. Cancer 27: 694–702

93. Fine G, Smith R W Jr, Pachter M R 1962 Primary extragenital choriocarcinoma in the male subject. Am J Med 32: 776–794

94. Norihisa Y, Kakudo K, Tsutsumi Y et al. 1988 Paget's extension of esophageal carcinoma. Immunohistochemical and mucin histochemical evidence of Paget's cells in the esophageal mucosa. Acta Pathol Jpn 38: 651–658

95. Haleem A, Kfoury H, Al Juboury M et al. 2003 Paget's disease of the esophagus associated with mucous gland carcinoma of the lower esophagus. Histopathology 42: 61–65

96. Sobin L H, Wittekind Ch (eds) 2002 UICC: TNM classification of malignant tumours, 6th edn. John Wiley, New York

97. Dexter S P, Sue-Ling H, McMahon M J et al. 2001 Circumferential resection margin involvement: an independent predictor of survival following surgery for oesophageal cancer. Gut 48: 667–670

98. Mandard A M, Dalibard F, Mandard J C et al. 1994 Pathologic assessment of tumor regression after preoperative chemoradiotherapy of esophageal carcinoma: clinicopathologic correlations. Cancer 73: 2680–2686

99. Chirieac L R, Swisher S G, Ajani J A et al. 2005 Post-therapy pathologic stage predicts survival in patients with esophageal carcinoma receiving preoperative chemoradiation. Cancer 103: 1347–1355

100. Ludwig M E, Shaw R, DeSuto-Nagy G 1981 Primary malignant melanoma of the esophagus. Cancer 48: 2528–2534

101. Kato T, Takematsu H, Tomita Y et al. 1987 Malignant melanoma of mucous membranes. Arch Dermatol 123: 216–220

102. DiCostanzo D P, Urmacher C 1987 Primary malignant melanoma of the esophagus. Am J Surg Pathol 11: 46–52

103. de Mik J I, Kooijman C D, Hoekstra J B L et al. 1992 Primary malignant melanoma of the oesophagus. Histopathology 20: 77–79

104. Raven R W, Dawson I 1964 Malignant melanoma of the oesophagus. Br J Surg 51: 551–555

105. Guzman R P, Wightman R, Ravinsky E et al. 1989 Primary malignant melanoma of the esophagus with diffuse melanocytic atypia and melanoma in situ. Am J Clin Pathol 92: 802–804

106. De La Pava S, Nigogosyan G, Pickren J W et al. 1963 Melanosis of the esophagus. Cancer 16: 48–50

107. Ohashi K, Kato Y, Kanno J et al. 1990 Melanocytes and melanosis of the oesophagus in Japanese subjects – analysis of factors effecting their increase. Virchows Arch [A] 417: 137–143

108. Assor D 1975 A melanocytic tumor of the esophagus. Cancer 35: 1438–1443

109. Seremetis M G, Lyons W S, de Guzman V C et al. 1976 Leiomyomata of the esophagus: an analysis of 838 cases. Cancer 38: 2166–2177

110. Bourque M D, Spigland N, Bensoussan A L et al. 1989 Esophageal leiomyoma in children: two case reports and review of the literature. J Pediatr Surg 24: 1103–1107

111. McKeeby J L, Li X, Zhuang Z et al. 2001 Multiple leiomyomas of the esophagus, lung, and uterus in multiple endocrine neoplasia type 1. Am J Pathol 159: 1121–1127

112. Rocco G, Trastek V F, Deschamps C et al. 1998 Leiomyosarcoma of the esophagus: results of surgical treatment. Ann Thorac Surg 66: 894–896

113. Miettinen M, Sarlomo-Rikala M, Sobin L H et al. 2000 Esophageal stromal tumors: a clinicopathologic, immunohistochemical and molecular genetic study of 17 cases and comparison with esophageal leiomyomas and leiomyosarcomas. Am J Surg Pathol 24: 211–222

114. Takubo K, Nakagawa H, Tsuchiya S et al. 1981 Seedling leiomyoma of the esophagus and esophagogastric junction zone. Hum Pathol 12: 1006–1010

115. Suster S 1996 Gastrointestinal stromal tumors. Semin Diagn Pathol 13: 297–313

116. Johnston J, Helwig E B 1981 Granular cell tumors of the gastrointestinal tract and perianal region. A study of 74 cases. Dig Dis Sci 26: 807–816

117. Goldblum J R, Rice T W, Zuccaro G et al. 1996 Granular cell tumors of the esophagus: a clinical and pathologic study of 13 cases. Ann Thorac Surg 62: 860–865

118. Vuyk H D, Snow G B, Tiwari R M et al. 1985 Granular cell tumor of the proximal esophagus. A rare disease. Cancer 55: 445–449

119. Yoshizawa A, Ota H, Sakaguchi N et al. 2004 Malignant granular cell tumor of the esophagus. Virchow's Arch 444: 304–306

120. Cokelaere K, Sciot R, Geboes K 2000 Esophageal plexiform schwannoma. Int J Surg Pathol 8: 353–357

121. Saitoh K, Nasu M, Kamiyama R et al. 1985 Solitary neurofibroma of the esophagus. Acta Pathol Jpn 35: 527–531

122. Roberts F, Kirk A J, More I A et al. 2000 Oesophageal rhabdomyoma. J Clin Pathol 53: 554–557

123. Gilbert H W, Weston M J, Thompson M H 1990 Cavernous haemangioma of the oesophagus. Br J Surg 77: 106

124. Yoshida Y, Okamura T, Ezaki T et al. 1994 Lymphangioma of the oesophagus: a case report and review of the literature. Thorax 49: 1267–1268

125. Wolf B C, Khettry U, Leonardi H K et al. 1988 Benign lesions mimicking malignant tumors of the esophagus. Hum Pathol 19: 148–154

126. Akiyama S, Kataoka M, Horisawa M et al. 1990 Lipoma of the esophagus – report of a case and review of the literature. Jpn J Surg 20: 458–462

127. Mahour G H, Harrison E G Jr 1967 Osteochondroma (tracheobronchial choristoma) of the esophagus. Report of a case. Cancer 20: 1489–1493

128. Saitoh Y, Inomata Y, Tadaki N et al. 1990 Pedunculated intraluminal osteochondromatous hamartoma of the esophagus. J Otolaryngol 19: 339–342

129. Willen R, Lillo-Gil R, Willen H et al. 1989 Embryonal rhabdomyosarcoma of the oesophagus: case report. Acta Chir Scand 155: 59–64

130. Ng W C, Leong H T, Ma K F et al. 2003 Malignant rhabdoid tumour of the oesophagus: a case report. J Clin Pathol 56: 713–714

131. Laine L, Amerian J, Rarick M et al. 1990 The response of symptomatic gastrointestinal Kaposi's sarcoma to chemotherapy: a prospective evaluation using an endoscopic method of disease quantification. Am J Gastroenterol 85: 959–961

132. Mansour K A, Fritz R C, Jacobs D M et al. 1983 Pedunculated liposarcoma of the esophagus: a first case report. J Thorac Cardiovasc Surg 86: 447–450

133. Burke J S, Ranchod M 1981 Hemangiopericytoma of the esophagus. Hum Pathol 12: 96–100

134. Haratake J, Jimi A, Horie A et al. 1984 Malignant mesenchymoma of the esophagus. Acta Pathol Jpn 34: 925–933

135. Naganuma H, Ohtani H, Sayama J et al. 1996 Malignant fibrous histiocytoma of the esophagus. Pathol Int 46: 462–466

136. McIntyre M, Webb J N, Browning G C P 1982 Osteosarcoma of the esophagus. Hum Pathol 13: 680–682

137. Anton-Pacheco J, Cano I, Cuadros J et al. 1996 Synovial sarcoma of the esophagus. J Ped Surg 31: 1703–1705

138. Okerbloom J A, Armitage J O, Zetterman R et al. 1984 Esophageal involvement by non-Hodgkin's lymphoma. Am J Med 77: 359–361

139. Stein H A, Murray D, Warner H A 1981 Primary Hodgkin's disease of the esophagus. Dig Dis Sci 26: 457–461

140. Bolondi L, de Giorgio R, Santi V et al. 1990 Primary non-Hodgkin's T-cell lymphoma of the esophagus: a case with peculiar endoscopic ultrasonographic pattern. Dig Dis Sci 35: 1426–1430

141. Hosaka S, Nakamura N, Akamatsu T et al. 2002 A case of primary low grade mucosa associated lymphoid tissue (MALT) lymphoma of the esophagus. Gut 51: 281–284

142. Remes-Troche J M, De-Anda J, Ochoa V et al. 2003 A rare case of multiple lymphomatous polyposis with widespread involvement of the gastrointestinal tract. Arch Pathol Lab Med 127: 1028–1030

143. Gervaz E, Potet F, Mahé R et al. 1992 Focal lymphoid hyperplasia of the oesophagus: report of a case. Histopathology 21: 187–189

144. Chetty R, Bramder A, Reddy A D 2003 Primary plasmacytoma of the esophagus. Ann Diagn Pathol 7: 174–179

145. Agha F P, Schnitzer B 1985 Esophageal involvement in lymphoma. Am J Gastroenterol 80: 412–416

146. Thompson B C, Feczko P J, Mezwa D G 1990 Dysphagia caused by acute leukemic infiltration of the esophagus. Am J Roentgenol 155: 654

147. Penagini R, Ranzi T, Velio P et al. 1989 Giant fibrovascular polyp of the oesophagus: report of a case and effects on oesophageal function. Gut 30: 1624–1629

148. Cokelaere K, Geboes K 2001 Squamous cell carcinoma in a giant esophageal fibrovascular polyp. Histopathology 38: 586–589

149. LiVolsi V A, Perzin K H 1975 Inflammatory pseudotumors (inflammatory fibrous polyps) of the esophagus: a clinicopathologic study. Dig Dis 20: 475–481

150. Arbona J L, Fazzi J G F, Mayoral J 1984 Congenital esophageal cysts: case report and review of literature. Am J Gastroenterol 79: 177–182

151. Kirwan W O, Walbaum P R, McCormack R J M 1973 Cystic intrathoracic derivatives of the foregut and their complications. Thorax 28: 424–428

152. Qazi F M, Geisinger K R, Nelson J B et al. 1990 Symptomatic congenital gastroenteric duplication cyst of the esophagus containing exocrine and endocrine pancreatic tissues. Am J Gastroenterol 85: 65–67

153. McGregor D H, Mills G, Boudet R A 1976 Intramural squamous cell carcinoma of the esophagus. Cancer 37: 1556–1561

154. Solanke T F, Olurin E O, Nwakonobi F et al. 1967 Primary amyloid tumour of the oesophagus treated by colon transplant. Br J Surg 54: 943–946

155. Bender M D, Allison J, Cuartas F et al. 1973 Glycogenic acanthosis of the esophagus: a form of benign epithelial hyperplasia. Gastroenterology 65: 373–380

156. Kay P S, Soetikno R M, Mindelzun R et al. 1997 Diffuse esophageal glycogenic acanthosis: an endoscopic marker of Cowden's disease. Am J Gastroenterol 92: 1038–1040

157. Heald J, Moussalli H, Hasleton P S 1986 Diffuse leiomyomatosis of the oesophagus. Histopathology 10: 755–759

158. Lonsdale R N, Roberts P F, Vaughan R et al. 1992 Familial oesophageal leiomyomatosis and nephropathy. Histopathology 20: 127–133

159. Marshall J B, Diaz-Arias A A, Bochna G S et al. 1990 Achalasia due to diffuse esophageal leiomyomatosis and inherited as an autosomal dominant disorder: report of a family study. Gastroenterology 98: 1358–1365

160. Wahlen T, Astedt B 1965 Familial occurrence of coexisting leiomyoma of vulva and oesophagus. Acta Obstet Gynecol Scand 44: 197–203

161. von Rahden BHA, Stein HJ, Becker K et al. 2004 Heterotopic gastric mucosa of the esophagus: literature review and proposal of a clinicopathological classification. Am J Gastroenterology 99: 543–551

162. Lauwers G Y, Mino M, Ban S et al. 2005 Cytokeratins 7 and 20 and mucin core protein expression in esophageal cervical inlet patch. Am J Surg Pathol 29: 437–442

163. Razi M D 1966 Ectopic pancreatic tissue of esophagus with massive upper gastrointestinal bleeding. Arch Surg 92: 101–104

164. Merino M J, Brand M, LiVolsi V A et al. 1982 Sebaceous glands in the esophagus diagnosed in a clinical setting. Arch Pathol Lab Med 106: 47–48

165. Raeburn C 1951 Columnar ciliated epithelium in the adult oesophagus. J Pathol Bacteriol 63: 157–158

166. Abraham S C, Singh V K, Yardley J H et al. 2001 Hyperplastic polyps of the esophagus and esophagogastric junction: histologic and clinicopathologic findings. Am J Surg Pathol 25: 1180–1187

167. Ito H, Hata J, Yokozaki H et al. 1986 Tubular adenoma of the human stomach. An immunohistochemical analysis of gut hormones, serotonin, carcinoembryonic antigen, secretory component and lysozyme. Cancer 58: 2264–2272

168. Oberhuber G, Stolte M 2000 Gastric polyps: an update of their pathology and biological significance. Virchow's Arch 437: 581–590

169. Laxén F, Sipponen P, Ihamäki T et al. 1982 Gastric polyps: their morphologic and endoscopical characteristics and relation to gastric carcinoma. Acta Pathol Microbiol Scand Sect A 90: 221–228

170. Abraham, S C, Park S J, Lee J H et al. 2003 Genetic alterations in gastric adenomas of intestinal and foveolar phenotypes. Hum Pathol 16: 786–795

171. Domizio P, Talbot I C, Spigelman A D et al. 1990 Upper gastrointestinal pathology in familial adenomatous polyposis: results from a prospective study of 102 patients. J Clin Pathol 43: 738–743

172. Nakamura T, Nakano G I 1985 Histopathologic classification and malignant change in gastric polyps. J Clin Pathol 38: 754–764

173. Fieber S S, Boden R E 1977 Polypoid villous adenoma of the stomach. Am J Gastroenterol 68: 286–289

174. Morson B C, Sobin L H, Grundmann E et al. 1980 Pre-cancerous conditions and epithelial dysplasia in the stomach. J Clin Pathol 33: 711–721

175. Kushima R, Muller W, Stolte M et al. 1996 Differential p53 protein expression in stomach adenomas of gastric and intestinal phenotypes: possible sequences of p53 alteration in gastric carcinogenesis. Virchow's Arch 428: 223–227

176. Vieth M, Kushima R, Borchard F et al. 2003 Pyloric gland adenoma: a clinicopathological analysis of 90 cases. Virchow's Arch 442: 317–321

177. Hamilton S R, Aaltonen L A 2000 Pathology and genetics of tumours of the digestive system. World Health Organization Cassification of Tumours. Vol 2. IARC Press, Lyon

178. Rubio C A 1989 Paneth cell adenoma of the stomach. Am J Surg Pathol 13: 325–328

179. Ito H, Yasui W, Yoshida K et al. 1990 Depressed tubular adenoma of the stomach: pathologic and immunohistochemical features. Histopathology 17: 419–426

180. Schlemper R J, Itabashi M, Kato Y et al. 1997 Differences in diagnostic criteria for gastric carcinoma between Japanese and Western pathologists. Lancet 349: 1725–1729

181. Lauwers G Y, Shimizu M, Correa P et al. 1999 Evaluation of gastric biopsies for neoplasia – differences between Japanese and Western pathologists. Am J Surg Path 23: 511–518

182. Hattori T 1985 Morphologic range of hyperplastic polyps and carcinomas arising in hyperplastic polyps of the stomach. J Clin Pathol 38: 622–630

183. Lauwers G Y, Riddell R H 1999 Gastric epithelial dysplasia. Gut 45: 784–790

184. Ghandur-Mnaymneh L, Paz J, Roldan E et al. 1988 Dysplasia of nonmetaplastic gastric mucosa: a proposal for its classification and its possible relationship to diffuse-type gastric carcinoma. Am J Surg Pathol 12: 96–114

185. Tosi P, Baak J P A, Luzi P et al. 1989 Morphometric distinction of low- and high-grade dysplasias in gastric biopsies. Hum Pathol 20: 839–844

186. Lansdown M, Quirke P, Dixon M F et al. 1990 High-grade dysplasia of the gastric mucosa: a marker for gastric carcinoma. Gut 31: 977–983

187. Saraga E-P, Gardiol D, Costa J 1987 Gastric dysplasia: a histologic follow-up study. Am J Surg Pathol 11: 788–796

188. Ming S-C, Bajtai A, Correa P et al. 1984 Gastric dysplasia: significance and pathologic criteria. Cancer 54: 1794–1801

189. Kokkola A, Haapiainen R, Laxén F et al. 1996 Risk of gastric carcinoma in patients with mucosal dysplasia associated with atrophic gastritis: a follow-up study. J Clin Pathol 49: 979–984

190. Rugge M, Cassaro M, Di Mario F et al. 2003 The long term outcome of gastric non-invasive neoplasia. Gut 52: 1111–1116

191. Lauwers G Y, Ban S, Mino M et al. 2004 Endoscopic mucosal resection for gastric epithelial neoplasms: a study of 39 cases with emphasis on the evaluation of specimens and recommendations for optimal pathologic analysis. Mod Pathol 17: 2–8

192. Ono H, Kondo H, Gotoda T et al. 2001 Endoscopic mucosal resection for treatment of early gastric cancer. Gut 48: 225–229

193. Nagayo T 1986 Histopathology of gastric dysplasia. In: Filipe M I, Jass J R (eds) Gastric carcinoma. Churchill Livingstone, Edinburgh, p 116–131

194. Dixon M F, O'Connor H J, Axon A T et al. 1986 Reflux gastritis: a distinct histopathologic entity? J Clin Pathol 39: 524–530

195. Brien T P, Farraye F A, Odze R D 2001 Gastric dysplasia-like epithelial atypia associated with chemoradiotherapy for esophageal cancer: a clinicopathologic and immunohistochemical study of 15 cases. Mod Pathol 14: 389–396

196. Stewart B W, Kleihues P 2003 World Cancer Report. IARC Press, Lyon

197. Henson D E, Dittus C, Younes M et al. 2004 Differential trends in the intestinal and diffuse types of gastric carcinoma in the United States, 1973–2000. Arch Pathol Lab Med 128: 765–770

198. Guildford P, Hopkins J, Grady W et al. 1999 E-cadherin germline mutations define an inherited cancer syndrome dominated by diffuse gastric cancer. Hum Mutat 14: 249–255

199. Aarnio M, Salovaara R, Aaltonen L A et al. 1997 Features of gastric cancer in hereditary non-polyposis colorectal cancer syndrome. Int J Cancer 74: 551–555

200. Cassaro M, Rugge M, Gutierrez O et al. 2000 Topographic patterns of intestinal metaplasia and gastric cancer. Am J Gastroenterol 95: 1431–1438

201. Antonioli D A 1994 Precursors of gastric carcinoma. Hum Pathol 25: 994–1005.

202. Huang J-Q, Sridhar S, Chen Y et al. 1998 Meta-analysis of the relationship between Helicobacter pylori seropositivity and gastric cancer. Gastroenterology 114: 1169–1179

203. Parsonnet J, Friedman G D, Orentreich N et al. 1997 Risk for gastric cancer in people with CagA positive or CagA negative Helicobacter pylori infection. Gut 40: 297–301

204. El-Omar E M, Carrington M, Chow W H et al. 2000 Interleukin-1 polymorphisms associated with increased risk of gastric cancer. Nature 404: 398–402

205. Kuipers E J 1997 Helicobacter pylori and the risk and management of associated diseases: gastritis, ulcer disease, atrophic gastritis and gastric cancer. Aliment Pharmacol Ther 11 (suppl 1): 71–88

206. Oda K, Tamaru J, Takenouchi T et al. 1993 Association of Epstein–Barr virus with gastric carcinoma with lymphoid stroma. Am J Pathol 143: 1063–1071

207. Luinetti O, Fiocca R, Villani L et al. 1998 Genetic pattern, histologic structure and cellular phenotype in early and advanced gastric cancers. Hum Pathol 29: 702–709

208. Locke G R, Talley N J, Carpenter H A et al. 1995 Changes in the site- and histology-specific incidence of gastric cancer during a 50 year period. Gastroenterology 109: 1750–1756

209. Charlton A, Blair V, Shaw D et al. 2004 Hereditary diffuse gastric cancer: predominance of multiple foci of signet-ring cell carcinoma in distal stomach and transitional zone Gut 53: 814–820

210. Capella C, Frigerio B, Cornaggia M et al. 1984 Gastric parietal cell carcinoma – a newly recognized entity: light microscopic and ultrastructural features. Histopathology 8: 813–824

211. Bonar S F, Sweeney E C 1986 The prevalence, prognostic significance and hormonal content of endocrine cells in gastric cancer. Histopathology 10: 53–63

212. Tahara E, Ito H, Nakagami K et al. 1982 Scirrhous argyrophil carcinoma of the stomach with multiple production of polypeptide hormones, amine, CEA, lysozyme, and HCG. Cancer 49: 1904–1915

213. Ooi A, Nakanishi I, Itoh T et al. 1991 Predominant Paneth cell differentiation in an intestinal type gastric cancer. Pathol Res Pract 187: 220–225

214. Takubo K, Honma N, Sawabe M et al. 2002 Oncocytic adenocarcinoma of the stomach: parietal cell carcinoma. Am J Surg Pathol 26: 458–465

215. Laurén P 1965 The two histologic main types of gastric carcinoma: diffuse and so-called intestinal-type carcinoma. Acta Pathol Microbiol Scand 64: 31–49

216. Carneiro F, Huntsman D G, Smyrk T C et al. 2004 Model of the early development of diffuse gastric cancer in E-cadherin mutation carriers and its implications for patient screening. J Pathol 203: 681–687

217. Mori M, Sakaguchi H, Akazawa K et al. 1995 Correlation between metastatic site, histologic type, and serum tumor markers of gastric carcinoma. Hum Pathol 26: 504–508

218. Ming S-C 1977 Gastric carcinoma: a pathobiological classification. Cancer 39: 2475–2485

219. Mulligan R M 1972 Histogenesis and biological behavior of gastric carcinoma. Pathol Annual 7: 349–415

220. Roy P, Piard F, Dusserre-Guion L et al. 1998 Prognostic comparison of the pathological classifications of gastric cancer: a population-based study. Histopathology 33: 304–310

221. Williams G T 1986 Early gastric cancer. In: Filipe MI, Jass JR (eds) Gastric carcinoma. Churchill Livingstone, Edinburgh, p 172–196

222. Goseki N, Takizawa T, Koike M 1992 Differences in the mode of the extension of gastric cancer classified by histologic type: new histologic classification of gastric carcinoma. Gut 33: 606–612

223. McLaren K M, Burnett R A, Goodlad J R et al. 2003 Observer variability in the Goseki grouping of gastric adenocarcinoma in resection and biopsy specimens. Histopathology 42: 472–475

224. Carneiro F, Seixas M, Sobrinho-Simoes M 1995 New elements for an updated classification of the carcinoma of the stomach. Pathol Res Pract 191: 571–584

225. Kozuki T, Yao T, Nakamura S et al. 2002 Differences in p53 and cadherin-catenin complex expression between histological subtypes in diffusely infiltrating gastric carcinoma. Histopathology 41: 56–64

226. Byrne D, Holley M P, Cuschieri A 1988 Parietal cell carcinoma of the stomach: association with long-term survival after curative resection. Br J Cancer 58: 85–87

227. Jain S, Filipe M I, Hall P A et al. 1991 Prognostic value of proliferating cell nuclear antigen in gastric carcinoma. J Clin Pathol 44: 655–659

228. Filipe M I, Rosa J, Sandey A et al. 1991 Is DNA ploidy and proliferative activity of prognostic value in advanced gastric carcinoma? Hum Pathol 22: 373–378

229. Korenaga D, Okamura T, Saito A et al. 1988 DNA ploidy is closely linked to tumor invasion, lymph node metastasis and prognosis in clinical gastric cancer. Cancer 62: 309–313

230. Baretton G, Carstensen O, Schardey M et al. 1991 DNA-ploidy and survival in gastric carcinomas: a flow-cytometric study. Virchow's Arch [A] 418: 301–309

231. Setälä L P, Kosma V-M, Marin S et al. 1996 Prognostic factors in gastric cancer: the value of vascular invasion, mitotic rate and lymphoplasmacytic infiltration. Br J Cancer 74: 766–772

232. Tanaka A, Watanabe T, Okuno K et al. 1994 Perineural invasion as a predictor of recurrence of gastric cancer. Cancer 73: 550–555

233. Van Beek J, zur Hausen A, Kranenbarg E K et al. 2004 EBV-positive gastric adenocarcinomas: a distinct clinicopathologic entity with a low frequency of lymph node involvement. J Clin Oncol 22: 664–670

234. Ishigami S, Natsugoe S, Miyazono F et al. 2004 Clinical merit of subdividing gastric cancer according to invasion of the muscularis propria. Hepatogastroenterology 51: 869–871

235. Wu C W, Hsiech M C, Lo S S et al. 1996 Relation of number of positive lymph nodes to the prognosis of patients with primary gastric adenocarcinoma. Gut 38: 525–527

236. Doekhie F S, Mesker W E, van Krieken J H J M et al. 2005 Clinical relevance of occult tumor cells in lymph nodes from gastric cancer patients. Am J Surg Pathol 29: 1135–1144

237. Japanese Research Society for Gastric Cancer 1995 Japanese classification of gastric carcinoma. Kanehara, Tokyo

238. Siewert R J, Feith M, Werner M et al. 2000 Adenocarcinoma of the esophagogastric junction: results of surgical therapy based on anatomical/topographic classification in 1002 consecutive patients. Ann Surg 232: 353–361

239. Fielding J W L, Roginski C, Ellis D J et al. 1984 Clinicopathologic staging of gastric cancer. Br J Surg 71: 677–680

240. Kappas A M, Fatouros M, Roukos D H 2004 Is it time to change surgical strategy for gastric cancer in the United States? Ann Surg Oncol 11: 727–730

241. Bogomoletz W V 1984 Early gastric cancer. Am J Surg Pathol 8: 381–391

242. Kodama Y, Inokuchi K, Soejima K et al. 1983 Growth patterns and prognosis in early gastric carcinoma: superficially spreading and penetrating growth types. Cancer 51: 320–326

243. Inokuchi K, Kodama Y, Sasaki O et al. 1983 Differentiation of growth patterns of early gastric carcinoma determined by cytophotometric DNA analysis. Cancer 51: 1138–1141

244. Brito M J, Filipe M I, Williams G T et al. 1993 DNA ploidy in early (T1) gastric cancer: a flow cytometric study of 100 European cases. Gut 34: 230–234

245. Eckardt V F, Willems D, Kanzler G et al. 1984 Eighty months persistence of poorly differentiated early gastric cancer. Gastroenterology 87: 719–724

246. Offerhaus G J A, Tersmette A C, Huibregtse K et al. 1988 Mortality caused by stomach cancer after remote partial gastrectomy for benign conditions: 40 years of follow-up of an Amsterdam cohort of 2633 postgastrectomy patients. Gut 29: 1588–1590

247. Bogomoletz W V, Potet F, Barge J et al. 1985 Pathologic features and mucin histochemistry of primary gastric stump carcinoma associated with gastritis cystica polyposa: a study of six cases. Am J Surg Pathol 9: 401–410

248. Dirschmid K, Walser J, Hügel H 1984 Pseudomalignant erosion in hyperplastic gastric polyps. Cancer 54: 2290–2293

249. Dimet S, Lazure T, Bedossa P 2004 Signet-ring cell change in acute erosive gastropathy. Am J Surg Pathol 28: 1111–1112

250. Chu P G, Weiss L M 2002 Keratin expression in human tissues and neoplasms. Histopathology 40: 403–439

250a. van Velthuysen M L, Taal B G, van der Hoeven J J, Peterse J L 2005 Expression of oestrogen receptor and loss of E-cadherin are diagnostic for gastric metastasis of breast carcinoma. Histopathology 46:153–157

251. Minamoto T, Mai M, Watanabe K et al. 1990 Medullary carcinoma with lymphocytic infiltration of the stomach. Cancer 66: 945–952

252. Lu B-J, Lai M, Cheng L et al. 2004 Gastric medullary carcinoma, a distinct entity with microsatellite instability-H, prominent intraepithelial lymphocytes and improved prognosis. Histopathology 45: 485–492

253. Griffiths A P, Rice A, Dixon M F 1998 Anaplastic gastric adenocarcinoma with extensive neutrophilic infiltration. Histopathology 33: 392–393

254. Caruso R A, Bellocco R, Pagano M et al. 2002 Prognostic value of intratumoral neutrophils in advanced gastric carcinoma in a high-risk area in northern Italy. Mod Pathol 15: 831–837

255. Mori M, Iwashita A, Enjoji M 1986 Adenosquamous carcinoma of the stomach: a clinicopathologic analysis of 28 cases. Cancer 57: 333–339

256. Mori M, Kukuda T, Enjoji M 1987 Adenosquamous carcinoma of the stomach: histogenetic and ultrastructural studies. Gastroenterology 92: 1078–1082

257. Volpe C M, Hameer H R, Masetti P et al. 1995 Squamous cell carcinoma of the stomach. Am Surg 61: 1076–1078

258. Ueyama T, Nagai E, Yao T et al. 1993 Vimentin-positive gastric carcinoma with rhabdoid features. Am J Surg Pathol 17: 813–819

259. Petrella T, Montagnon J, Roignot P et al. 1995 Alphafetoprotein-producing gastric adenocarcinoma. Histopathology 26: 171–175

260. Matsunou H, Konishi F, Jala R E A et al. 1994 Alpha-fetoprotein-producing gastric carcinoma with enteroblastic differentiation. Cancer 73: 534–540

261. Yakeishi Y, Mori M, Enjoji M 1990 Distribution of beta human chorionic gonadotrophin positive cells in non-cancerous gastric mucosa and in malignant gastric tumors. Cancer 66: 695–701

262. Ramponi A, Angeli G, Arceci F et al. 1986 Gastric choriocarcinoma: an immunohistochemical study. Pathol Res Pract 181: 390–396

263. Krulewski T, Cohen L B 1988 Choriocarcinoma of the stomach: pathogenesis and clinical characteristics. Am J Gastroenterol 83: 1172–1175

264. Garcia R L, Ghali V S 1985 Gastric choriocarcinoma and yolk sac tumor in a man. Observations about its possible origin. Hum Pathol 16: 955–958

265. Rindi G, Luinetti O, Cornaggia M et al. 1993 Three subtypes of gastric argyrophil carcinoid and the neuroendocrine carcinoma: a clinicopathologic study. Gastroenterology 104: 994–1006

266. Rindi G, Bordi C, Rappel S et al. 1996 Gastric carcinoids and neuroendocrine carcinomas: pathogenesis, pathology, and behavior. World J Surg 20: 168–172

267. Matsui K, Jin X M, Kitagawa M et al. 1998 Clinicopathologic features of neuroendocrine carcinomas of the stomach: appraisal of small cell and large cell variants. Arch Pathol Lab Med 122: 1010–1017

268. Robey-Cafferty S S, Grignon D, Ro J Y et al. 1990 Sarcomatoid carcinoma of the stomach. A report of three cases with immunohistochemical and ultrastructural observations. Cancer 65: 1601–1606

269. Aiba M, Hirayama A, Suzuki T et al. 1991 Carcinosarcoma of the stomach: report of a case with review of the literature of gastrectomized patients. Surg Pathol 4: 75–83

270. Dundas S A C, Slater D N, Wagner B E et al. 1988 Gastric adenocarcinoleiomyosarcoma: a light and electron microscopic and immunohistochemical study. Histopathology 13: 347–350

271. Kallakury B V S, Bui H X, del Rosario A et al. 1993 Primary gastric adenosarcoma. Arch Pathol Lab Med 117: 299–301

272. Thomas R M, Baybick J H, Elsayed A M et al. 1994 Gastric carcinoids: an immunohistochemical and clinicopathologic study of 104 patients. Cancer 73: 2053–2058

273. Abraham S C, Carney J A, Ooi A et al. 2005 Achlorhydria, parietal cell hyperplasia, and multiple gastric carcinoids: a new disorder. Am J Surg Pathol 2: 969–975

274. Carney J A, Go V L W, Fairbanks V F et al. 1983 The syndrome of gastric argyrophil carcinoid tumors and nonantral gastric atrophy. Ann Int Med 99: 761–766

275. Borch K, Renvall H, Kullman E et al. 1987 Gastric carcinoid associated with the syndrome of hypergastrinaemic atrophic gastritis. Am J Surg Pathol 11: 435–444

276. Solcia E, Capella C, Fiocca R et al. 1990 Gastric argyrophil carcinoidosis in patients with Zollinger–Ellison syndrome due to type 1 multiple endocrine neoplasia. Am J Surg Pathol 14: 503–513

277. Ooi A, Ota M, Katsuda S et al. 1995 An unusual case of multiple gastric carcinoids associated with diffuse endocrine cell hyperplasia and parietal cell hypertrophy. Endocr Pathol 3: 229–237

278. Rindi G, Azzoni C, Larosa S et al. 1999 ECL cell tumor and poorly differentiated endocrine carcinoma of the stomach: prognostic evaluation by pathological analysis. Gastroenterology 116: 532–542

279. Christodoulopoulos J B, Klotz A P 1961 Carcinoid syndrome with primary carcinoid tumor of the stomach. Gastroenterology 40: 429–440

280. Marcus F S, Friedman M A, Callen P W et al. 1980 Successful therapy of an ACTH-producing gastric carcinoid APUD tumor: report of a case and review of the literature. Cancer 46: 1263–1269

281. Capella C, Heitz P, Hofler H et al. 1995 Revised classification of neuroendocrine tumours of the lung, pancreas and gut. Virchow's Arch 425: 547–560

282. Harvey R F 1988 Spontaneous resolution of multifocal gastric enterochromaffin-like cell carcinoid tumours. Lancet i: 821

283. Borch K, Ahren B, Ahlman H et al. 2005 Gastric carcinoids: biologic behavior and prognosis after differentiated treatment in relation to type. Ann Surg 242: 64–73

284. Ordonez N, Mackay B, El-Naggar A et al. 1993 Clear cell carcinoid tumour of the stomach. Histopathology 22: 190–193

285. Rindi G, Paolotti D, Fiocca R et al. 2000 Vesicular monoamine transporter 2 as a marker of gastric enterochromaffin-like cell tumors. Virchow's Arch 436: 217–223

286. Sundler F, Eriksson B, Grimelius L et al. 1992 Histamine in gastric carcinoid tumors: immunocytochemical evidence. Endocr Pathol 3: 23–27

287. Müller J, Kirchner T, Müller-Hermelink H K 1987 Gastric endocrine cell hyperplasia and carcinoid tumors in atrophic gastritis type A. Am J Surg Pathol 11: 909–917

288. Solcia E, Fiocca R, Villani L et al. 1995 Hyperplastic, dysplastic and neoplastic enterochromaffin-like cell proliferations of the gastric mucosa: classification and histogenesis. Am J Surg Pathol 19 (suppl 1): S1–S7

289. Ali M H, Davidson A, Azzopardi J G A 1984 Composite gastric carcinoid and adenocarcinoma. Histopathology 8: 529–536

290. Kindblom L-G, Remotti M E, Aldenborg F et al. 1998 Gastrointestinal pacemaker cell tumor (GIPACT): gastrointestinal stromal tumors show phenotypic characteristics of the interstitial cells of Cajal. Am J Pathol 152: 1259–1269

291. Miettinen M, Lasota J 2001 Gastrointestinal stromal tumors – definition, clinical, histological, immunohistochemical, and molecular genetic features and differential diagnosis. Virchow's Arch 438: 1–12

292. Fletcher C D M, Berman J J, Corless C et al. 2002 Diagnosis of gastrointestinal stromal tumors: a consensus approach. Hum Pathol 33: 459–465

293. Verweij J, Casali P G, Zalcberg J et al. 2004 Progression-free survival in gastrointestinal stromal tumours with high-dose imatinib: randomised trial. Lancet 364: 1127–1134

294. Fuller C E, Williams G T 1991 Gastrointestinal manifestations of type I neurofibromatosis (von Recklinghausen's disease). Histopathology 19: 1–11

295. Carney J A 1983 The triad of gastric epithelioid leiomyosarcoma, pulmonary chondroma and functioning extra-adrenal paraganglioma: a 5-year review. Medicine 62: 159–169

296. Carney J A, Stratakis C A 2002 Familial paraganglioma and gastric stromal sarcoma: a new syndrome distinct from the Carney triad. Am J Med Genet 108: 132–139

297. Hirota S, Nishida T, Isozaki K et al. 1998 Familial gastrointestinal stromal tumors with germline mutation of KIT gene. Nat Genet 19: 323–324

298. Chompret A, Kannengiesser C, Barrois M 2004 PDGFRA germline mutation in a family with multiple cases of gastrointestinal stromal tumor. Gastroenterology 126: 318–321

299. Miettinen M, Sobin LH, Lasota J 2005 Gastrointestinal stromal tumors of the stomach: a clinicopathologic, immunohistochemical, and molecular genetic study of 1765 cases with long-term follow-up. Am J Surg Pathol 29: 52–68

300. Evans H L 1985 Smooth muscle tumors of the gastrointestinal tract: a study of 56 cases followed for a minimum of 10 years. Cancer 56: 2242–2250

301. Yamada Y, Kato Y, Yanagisawa A et al. 1988 Microleiomyomas of human stomach. Hum Pathol 19: 569–572

302. Wong N A C S, Young R, Malcomson R D et al. 2003 Prognostic indicators for gastrointestinal stromal tumours: a clinicopathological and immunohistochemical study of 108 resected cases of the stomach. Histopathology 43: 118–126

303. Appelman H D, Helwig E B 1976 Gastric epithelioid leiomyoma and leiomyosarcoma (leiomyoblastoma). Cancer 38: 708–728

304. Suster S, Sorace D, Moran C A 1995 Gastrointestinal stromal tumors with prominent myxoid matrix. Am J Surg Pathol 19: 59–70

305. Appelman H D, Helwig E B 1977 Sarcomas of the stomach. Am J Clin Pathol 67: 2–10

306. Suster S, Fletcher C D M 1996 Gastrointestinal stromal tumors with prominent signet-ring cell forms. Mod Pathol 9: 609–613

307. Lauwers G Y, Erlandson R A, Casper E S et al. 1993 Gastrointestinal autonomic nerve tumors: a clinicopathologic, immunohistochemical, and ultrastructural study of 12 cases. Am J Surg Pathol 17: 887–897

308. Shanks J H, Harris M, Banerjee S S et al. 1996 Gastrointestinal autonomic nerve tumours: a report of nine cases. Histopathology 29: 111–121

309. Lee J R, Joshi V, Griffin J W et al. 2001 Gastrointestinal autonomic nerve tumor: immunohistochemical and molecular identity with gastrointestinal stromal tumor. Am J Surg Pathol 25: 979–987

310. Hirota S, Isozaki K, Moriyama Y et al. 1998 Gain-of-function mutations of c-kit in human gastrointestinal stromal tumors. Science 279: 577–580

311. Newman P L, Wadden C, Fletcher C D M 1991 Gastrointestinal stromal tumours: correlation of immunophenotype with clinicopathologic features. J Pathol 164: 107–117

312. Heinrich M C, Corless C L, Demetri G D et al. 2003 Kinase mutations and imatinib response in patients with metastatic gastrointestinal stromal tumor. J Clin Oncol 21: 4342–4349

313. Heinrich M C, Corless C L, Duensing A et al. 2003 PDGFRA activating mutations in gastrointestinal stromal tumors. Science 299: 708–710

314. Lasota J, Dansonka-Mieszkowska A, Sobin L H et al. 2004 A great majority of GISTs with PDGFRA mutations represent gastric tumors of low or no malignant potential. Lab Invest 84: 874–883

315. Debiec-Rychter M, Wasag B, Stul M et al. 2004 Gastrointestinal stromal tumors (GISTs) negative for KIT (CD117 antigen) immunoreactivity. J Pathol 202: 430–438

316. Medeiros F, Corless C L, Duensing A et al. 2004 KIT-negative gastrointestinal stromal tumors. Am J Surg Pathol 28: 889–894.

317. Pauwels P, Debiec-Rychter M, Stul M et al. 2005 Changing phenotype of gastrointestinal stromal tumours under imatinib mesylate treatment: a potential diagnostic pitfall. Histopathology 47: 41–47

318. Cooper P N, Quirke P, Hardy G J et al. 1992 A flow cytometric, clinical and histologic study of stromal neoplasms of the gastrointestinal tract. Am J Surg Pathol 16: 163–170

319. Trupiano J K, Stewart R E, Misick C et al. 2002 Gastric stromal tumors: a clinicopathologic study of 77 cases with correlation of features with nonaggressive and aggressive clinical behaviors. Am J Surg Pathol 26: 705–714

320. Rudolph P, Gloeckner K, Parwaresch R et al. 1998 Immunophenotype, proliferation, DNA ploidy, and biological behavior of gastrointestinal stromal tumors: a multivariate clinicopathologic study. Hum Pathol 29: 791–800

321. Kiyabu M T, Bishop P C, Parker J W et al. 1988 Smooth muscle tumors of the gastrointestinal tract: flow cytometric quantitation of DNA and nuclear antigen content and correlation with histologic grade. Am J Surg Pathol 12: 954–960

322. Lazure T, Ferlicot S, Gauthier F 2002 Gastric inflammatory myofibroblastic tumors in children: an unpredictable course. J Pediatr Gastroenterol Nutr 34: 319–322

323. Lee W A, Lee M K, Jeen Y M 2004 Solitary fibrous tumor arising in gastric serosa. Pathol Int 54: 436–439

324. Delbecque K, Legrand M, Boniver J et al. 2004 Calcifying fibrous tumour of the gastric wall. Histopathology 44: 399–400

325. Sarlomo-Rikala M, Miettinen M 1995 Gastric schwannoma – a clinicopathologic analysis of six cases. Histopathology 27: 355–360

326. Hou Y, Tan Y, Xu J et al. 2006 Schwannoma of the digestive tract: a clinicopathologic, immunohistochemical and ultrastructural study of 33 cases. Histopathology 48: 536–545

327. Palmer E D 1951 Benign intramural tumors of the stomach: a review with special reference to gross pathology. Medicine 30: 81–181

328. Chodack P, Hurwitz A 1964 Lymphangiectasis of stomach simulating polypoid neoplasm. Arch Intern Med 113: 225–229

329. Sawyer K C, Lubchenco A E 1951 Haemangioendothelioma of the stomach. Surgery 30: 383–387

330. Lee K C, Ng W F, Chan J K C 1988 Epithelioid haemangioendothelioma presenting as a gastric polyp. Histopathology 12: 335–337

331. Lustbader I, Sherman A 1987 Primary gastrointestinal Kaposi's sarcoma in a patient with acquired immune deficiency syndrome. Am J Gastroenterol 82: 894–895

332. Fay D E, Nisbeth H 1990 Massive gastrointestinal hemorrhage in an immunosuppressed man due to gastric Kaposi's sarcoma. Am J Gastroenterol 85: 607–609

333. Taxy J B, Battifora H 1988 Angiosarcoma of the gastrointestinal tract. A report of three cases. Cancer 62: 210–216

334. Amy C, Lazure T, Sales J P et al. 2001 Gastric epithelioid angiosarcoma, a biopsy diagnostic pitfall. Ann Pathol 21: 439–441

335. Miettinen M, Paal E, Lasota J et al. 2002 Gastrointestinal glomus tumors: a clinicopathologic, immunohistochemical, and molecular genetic study of 32 cases. Am J Surg Pathol 26: 301–311

336. Tuazon R 1969 Rhabdomyoma of the stomach. Report of a case. Am J Clin Pathol 52: 37–41

337. Fox K R, Moussa S M, Mitre R J et al. 1990 Clinical and pathologic features of primary gastric rhabdomyosarcoma. Cancer 66: 772–778

338. Maderal F, Hunter F, Fuselier G et al. 1984 Gastric lipomas: an update of clinical presentation, diagnosis and treatment. Am J Gastroenterol 79: 964–967

339. McGregor D H, Kerley S W, McGregor M S 1993 Gastric angiolipoma with chronic hemorrhage and severe anemia. Am J Med Sci 305: 229–235

340. Shokouh-Amiri M H, Hansen C P, Moesgaard F 1986 Liposarcoma of the stomach: a case report. Acta Chir Scand 152: 389–391

341. Alerte F 1963 Xanthofibroma of the stomach. Report of a case with severe secondary hypochromic anemia. Arch Pathol 75: 99–104

342. Billings S D, Meisner L F, Cummings O W et al. 2000 Synovial sarcoma of the upper digestive tract. Mod Pathol 13: 68–76.

343. Pauwels P, Debiec-Rychter M, Sciot R et al. 2002 Clear cell sarcoma of the stomach. Histopathology 41: 526–530

344. Schmid C, Beham A, Steindorfer P et al. 1990 Non functional malignant paraganglioma of the stomach. Virchow's Arch [A] 417: 261–266

345. Pack G T 1964 Unusual tumors of the stomach. Ann NY Acad Sci 114: 985–1011

346. Tapp E 1964 Ganglioneuroblastoma of the stomach. J Pathol Bacteriol 88: 79–82

347. Haqqani M T, Krasner N, Ashworth M 1983 Benign mesenchymoma of the stomach. J Clin Pathol 36: 504–507

348. Matsukuma S, Wada R, Daibou M et al. 1995 Adenocarcinoma arising from gastric immature teratoma. Cancer 75: 2663–2668

349. Isaacson P G, Du M Q 2005 Gastrointestinal lymphoma – where morphology meets molecular biology. J Pathol 205: 255–274

350. Chan J K C 1996 Gastrointestinal lymphomas: an overview with emphasis on new findings and diagnostic problems. Semin Diagn Pathol 13: 260–296

351. Mori N, Yatabe Y, Narita M et al. 1995 Primary gastric Hodgkin's disease: morphologic, immunohistochemical and immunogenetic analyses. Arch Pathol Lab Med 119: 163–166

352. Tungekar M F 1986 Gastric signet-ring cell lymphoma with alpha heavy chains. Histopathology 10: 725–733

353. Isaacson P G, Spencer J, Finn T 1986 Primary B-cell gastric lymphoma. Hum Pathol 17: 72–82

354. Isaacson P G 1996 Recent developments in our understanding of gastric lymphomas. Am J Surg Pathol 20 (suppl 1): S1–S7

355. Farinha P, Gascoyne R D 2005 Helicobacter pylori and MALT lymphoma. Gastroenterology 128: 1579–1605

356. Bayerdörffer E, Neubauer A, Rudolph B et al. 1995 Regression of primary gastric lymphoma of mucosa-associated lymphoid tissue type after cure of Helicobacter pylori infection. Lancet 345: 1591–1594

357. Chan J K C, Ng C S, Isaacson P G 1990 Relationship between high-grade lymphoma and low-grade B-cell mucosa-associated lymphoid tissue lymphoma (MALToma) of the stomach. Am J Pathol 136: 1153–1164

358. Wotherspoon A C, Diss T C, Pan L et al. 1996 Low-grade gastric B-cell lymphoma of mucosa-associated lymphoid tissue in immunocompromised patients. Histopathology 28: 129–134

359. Guettier C, Hamilton-Dutoit S, Guillemain R et al. 1992 Primary gastrointestinal malignant lymphomas associated with Epstein–Barr virus after heart transplantation. Histopathology 20: 21–28

360. Wotherspoon A C, Isaacson P G 1995 Synchronous adenocarcinoma and low-grade B-cell lymphoma of mucosa-associated lymphoid tissue (MALT) of the stomach. Histopathology 27: 325–331

361. Cogliatti S B, Schmid U, Schumacher U et al. 1991 Primary B-cell gastric lymphoma: a clinicopathologic study of 145 patients. Gastroenterology 101: 1159–1170

362. Musshoff K, Schmidt-Vollmer H 1975 Prognosis of non-Hodgkin's lymphomas with special emphasis on the staging classification. Z Krebsforsch 83: 323–341

363. Ruskone-Fourmestraux A, Dragosics B, Morgner A et al. 2003 Paris staging system for primary gastrointestinal lymphomas. Gut 52: 912–913

364. Wotherspoon A C, Doglioni C, Isaacson P G 1992 Low-grade gastric B-cell lymphoma of mucosa-associated lymphoid tissue (MALT): a multifocal disease. Histopathology 20: 29–34

365. Stephen M R, Farquharson M A, Sharp R A et al. 1998 Sequential MALT lymphomas of the stomach, small intestine, and gall bladder. J Clin Pathol 51: 77–79

366. Isaacson P G, Spencer J 1987 Malignant lymphoma of mucosa-associated lymphoid tissue. Histopathology 11: 445–462

367. Isaacson P G 1990 Lymphomas of mucosa-associated lymphoid tissue. Histopathology 16: 617–619

368. Zamboni G, Franzin G, Scarpa A et al. 1996 Carcinoma-like signet-ring cells in gastric mucosa-associated lymphoid tissue (MALT) lymphoma. Am J Surg Pathol 20: 588–598

369. Liu H, Ye H, Dogan A et al. 2001 T(11;18)(q21;q21) is associated with advanced mucosa-associated lymphoid tissue lymphoma that expresses nuclear BCL10. Blood 98: 1182–1187

370. Liu H, Ye H, Ruskone-Fourmestraux A et al. 2002 T(11;18) is a marker for all stage gastric MALT lymphomas that will not respond to H. pylori eradication. Gastroenterology 122: 1286–1294

371. Inagaki H, Nakamura T, Li C et al. 2004 Gastric MALT lymphomas are divided into three groups based on responsiveness to Helicobacter pylori eradication and detection of API2-MALT1 fusion. Am J Surg Pathol 28: 1560–1567

372. Peng H, Du M, Diss T C et al. 1997 Genetic evidence for a clonal link between low and high-grade components in gastric MALT B-cell lymphoma. Histopathology 30: 425–429

373. de Jong D, Boot H, van Heerde P et al. 1997 Histological grading in gastric lymphoma: pretreatment criteria and clinical relevance. Gastroenterology 112: 1466–1474

374. Zukerberg L R, Ferry J A, Southern J F et al. 1990 Lymphoid infiltrates of the stomach. Evaluation of histologic criteria for the diagnosis of low-grade

gastric lymphoma on endoscopic biopsy specimens. Am J Surg Pathol 14: 1087–1099

375. Abbondanzo S L, Sobin L H 1997 Gastric "pseudolymphoma". A retrospective morphologic and immunophenotypic study of 97 cases. Cancer 79: 1656–1663

376. Lynch D A F, Sobala G M, Dixon M F et al. 1995 Lymphocytic gastritis and associated small bowel disease: a diffuse lymphocytic gastroenteropathy? J Clin Pathol 48: 939–945

377. Calvert R J, Evans P A S, Randerson J A et al. 1996 The significance of B-cell clonality in gastric lymphoid infiltrates. J Pathol 180: 26–32

378. Attanoos R, Griffiths D F R 1992 Metastatic small cell melanoma to the stomach mimicking primary gastric lymphoma. Histopathology 21: 173–175

379. Isaacson P G, MacLennan K A, Subbuswamy S G 1984 Multiple lymphomatous polyposis of the gastrointestinal tract. Histopathology 8: 641–656

380. Fraga M, Lloret E, Sanchez-Verde L et al. 1995 Mucosal mantle cell (centrocytic) lymphomas. Histopathology 26: 413–422

381. Hirakawa K, Fuchigami T, Nakamura S et al. 1996 Primary gastrointestinal T-cell lymphoma resembling multiple lymphomatous polyposis. Gastroenterology 111: 778–782

382. Nakamura S, Iida M, Matsui T et al. 1991 Adult T-cell leukemia/lymphoma with gastric lesions. Report of three cases. J Clin Gastroenterol 13: 390–394

383. Nakanishi I, Kajikawa K, Migita S et al. 1982 Gastric plasmacytoma: an immunologic and immunohistochemical study. Cancer 49: 2025–2028

384. Isaacson P G, Buchanan R, Mepham B L 1978 Plasma cell granuloma of the stomach. Hum Pathol 9: 355–358

385. Hatano B, Ohshima K, Katoh A et al. 2002 Non-HTLV-1-associated primary gastric T-cell lymphomas show cytotoxic activity: clinicopathological, immunohistochemical characteristics and TIA-1 expression in 31 cases. Histopathology 41: 421–436

386. Iwamizu-Watanabe S, Yamashita Y, Yatabe Y et al. 2004 Frequent expression of CD30 antigen in the primary gastric non-B, non-Hodgkin lymphomas. Pathol Int 54: 503–509

387. Foss H D, Schmitt G A, Daum S et al. 1999 Origin of primary gastric T-cell lymphomas from intraepithelial T-lymphocytes: report of two cases. Histopathology 34: 9–15

388. Groisman G M, Rosh J R, Harpaz N 1994 Langerhans cell histiocytosis of the stomach: a cause of granulomatous gastritis and gastric polyposis. Arch Pathol Lab Med 118: 1232–1235

389. Brugo E A, Marshall R B, Riberi A M et al. 1977 Preleukemic granulocytic sarcomas of the gastrointestinal tract. Am J Clin Pathol 68: 616–621

390. Wong K F, Yuen R W S, Lok A S F et al. 1989 Granulocytic sarcoma presenting as bleeding gastric polyp. Pathology 21: 63–64

391. Ismail S M, Myers K 1989 Infiltrative myeloid metaplasia: an unusual cause of gastric outlet obstruction. J Clin Pathol 42: 1112–1113

392. Green L K 1990 Hematogenous metastases to the stomach. A review of 67 cases. Cancer 65: 1596–1600

393. Telerman A, Gerard B, van den Heule B et al. 1985 Gastrointestinal metastases from abdominal tumors. Endoscopy 17: 99–101

394. Taal B G, Peterse H, Boot H 2000 Clinical presentation, endoscopic features, and treatment of gastric metastases from breast carcinoma. Cancer 89: 2214–2221

395. Wauters G V, Ferrell L, Ostroff J W et al. 1990 Hyperplastic gastric polyps associated with persistent Helicobacter pylori infection and active gastritis. Am J Gastroenterol 85: 1395–1397

396. Ohkusa T, Takashimizu I, Fujiki K et al. 1998 Disappearance of hyperplastic polyps in the stomach after eradication of Helicobacter pylori. A randomized, clinical trial. Ann Int Med 129: 712–715

397. Muller-Lissner S A, Wiebecke B 1982 Investigations on hyperplasiogenous gastric polyps by partial reconstruction. Pathol Res Pract 174: 368–378

398. Odze R D, Marcial M A, Antonioli D 1996 Gastric fundic polyps: a morphologic study using mucin histochemistry, stereometry, and MIB-1 immunohistochemistry. Hum Pathol 27: 896–903

399. Iida M, Yao T, Watanabe H et al. 1980 Spontaneous disappearance of fundic gland polyposis: report of three cases. Gastroenterology 79: 725–728

400. Tsuchikame N, Ishimaru Y, Ohshima S et al. 1993 Three familial cases of fundic gland polyposis without polyposis coli. Virchow's Arch [A] 422: 337–340

401. Vieth M, Stolte M 2001 Fundic gland polyps are not induced by proton pump inhibitor therapy. Am J Clin Pathol 116: 716–720

402. Lee R G, Burt R W 1986 The histopathology of fundic gland polyps of the stomach. Am J Clin Pathol 86: 498–503

403. Riddell R H 1996 The biopsy diagnosis of gastroesophageal reflux disease, "carditis," and Barrett's esophagus, and sequelae of therapy. Am J Surg Pathol 20 (suppl 1): S31–S51

404. Abraham S C 2002 Sporadic fundic gland polyps with epithelial dysplasia: evidence for preferential targeting for mutations in the adenomatous polyposis coli gene. Am J Pathol 161:1735–1742

405. Torbenson M, Lee J H, Cruz-Correa M et al. 2002 Sporadic fundic gland polyposis: a clinical, histological, and molecular analysis. Mod Pathol 15: 718–23

406. Kolodziejczyk P, Yao T, Tsuneyoshi M 1993 Inflammatory fibroid polyp of the stomach: a special reference to an immunohistochemical profile of 42 cases. Am J Surg Pathol 17: 1159–1168

407. Pantanowitz L, Antonioli D A, Pinkus G S et al. 2004 Inflammatory fibroid polyps of the gastrointestinal tract: evidence for a dendritic cell origin. Am J Surg Pathol 28: 107–114

408. Bartholomew L G, Moore C E, Dahlin D C et al. 1962 Intestinal polyposis associated with mucocutaneous pigmentation. Surg Gynecol Obstet 115: 1–11

409. Shinmura K, Goto M, Tao H et al. 2005 A novel STK11 germline mutation in two siblings with Peutz–Jeghers syndrome complicated by primary gastric cancer. Clin Genet 67: 81–86

410. Cochet B, Carrel J, Desbaillets L et al. 1979 Peutz–Jeghers syndrome associated with gastrointestinal carcinoma. Gut 20: 169–175

411. Hizawa K, Iida M, Yao T et al. 1997 Juvenile polyposis of the stomach: clinicopathologic features and its malignant potential. J Clin Pathol 50: 771–774

412. Weinstock J V, Kawanishi H 1978 Gastrointestinal polyposis with orocutaneous hamartomas (Cowden's disease). Gastroenterology 74: 890–895

413. Kindblom L G, Angervall L, Santesson B et al. 1977 Cronkhite-Canada syndrome. Cancer 39: 2651–2657

414. Lipper S, Kahn L B 1977 Superficial cystic gastritis with alopecia. A forme fruste of the Cronkhite-Canada syndrome. Arch Pathol Lab Med 101: 432–436

415. Barrocas A, Fontenelle L, Williams M J 1973 Gastric heterotopic pancreas: a case report and review of the literature. Am Surg 39: 361–365

416. Yun-Zhong H, Guo Q-X 1990 Adenomyoma of the stomach presenting as an antral polyp. Histopathology 16: 99–101

417. Kneafsey P D, Demetrick D J 1992 Malignant transformation in a pyloric adenomyoma: a case report. Histopathology 20: 433–435

418. Goldfarb W B, Bennett D, Monafo W 1963 Carcinoma in heterotopic gastric pancreas. Ann Surg 158: 56–58

419. Doglioni C, Laurino L, Dei Tos A P et al. 1993 Pancreatic (acinar) metaplasia of the gastric mucosa. Am J Surg Pathol 17: 1134–1143

420. Wang H H, Zeroogian J M, Spechler S J et al. 1996 Prevalence and significance of pancreatic acinar metaplasia at the gastroesophageal junction. Am J Surg Pathol 20: 1507–1510

421. William S A W, Michie W 1957 Adenomatosis of the stomach of Brunner gland type. Br J Surg 45: 259–263

422. Gensler S, Seidenberg B, Rifkin H et al. 1966 Ciliated lined intramural cyst of the stomach: case report and suggested embryogenesis. Ann Surg 163: 954–956

423. Delvaux S, Ectors N, Begoes K et al. 1996 Gastric gland heterotopia with extensive lymphoid stroma: a gastric lymphoepithelial cyst. Am J Gastroenterol 91: 599–601

424. Carr G L, Squires G 1962 Squamous papillomatosis of the stomach. A new pathologic entity: report of a case. Am Surg 28: 790–793

425. Catanzaro C, Weeks C B, Kafka R M 1962 Chronic hypertrophic gastritis. Report of two cases in siblings. Am J Gastroenterol 37: 525–536

426. Scharschmidt B F 1977 The natural history of hypertrophic gastropathy (Ménétrier's disease). Am J Med 63: 644–652

427. Kraut J R, Powell R, Hruby M A et al. 1981 Ménétrier's disease in childhood: report of two cases and a review of the literature. J Pediatr Surg 16: 707–711

428. Frank B W, Kern F Jr 1967 Ménétrier's disease: spontaneous metamorphosis of giant hypertrophy of the gastric mucosa to atrophic gastritis. Gastroenterology 53: 953–960

429. Berenson M M, Sannella J, Freston J W 1976 Ménétrier's disease: serial morphologic, secretory and serological observations. Gastroenterology 70: 257–263

430. Wolfsen H C, Carpenter H A, Talley N J 1993 Menetrier's disease: a form of hypertrophic gastropathy or gastritis? Gastroenterology 1993: 1310–1319

431. Xiao S Y, Hart J 2001 Marked gastric foveolar hyperplasia associated with active cytomegalovirus infection. Am J Gastroenterol 96: 223–226

432. Franzin G, Novelli P 1981 Gastritis cystica profunda. Histopathology 5: 535–547

433. Lin P Y, Brown D B, Deppisch L M 1989 Gastric xanthelasma in hyperplastic gastric polyposis. Arch Pathol Lab Med 113: 428–430

434. Kimura K, Hiramoto T, Buncher C R 1969 Gastric xanthelasma. Arch Pathol 87: 110–117

435. Jensen K, Raynor S, Rose S G et al. 1985 Amyloid tumors of the gastrointestinal tract: a report of two cases and review of the literature. Am J Gastroenterol 80: 784–786

436. Bjornsson S, Johansson J H, Sigurjonsson F 1987 Localised primary amyloidosis of the stomach presenting with gastric haemorrhage. Acta Med Scand 221: 115–119

437. Goteri G, Ranaldi R, Pileri S A et al. 1998 Localised amyloidosis and gastrointestinal lymphoma: a rare association. Histopathology 32: 348–355

Tumors of the small and large intestines (including the anal region)

Jeremy R. Jass

Small intestine

Epithelial tumors

Adenoma

Clinical features

Adenomas of the small intestine are uncommon.[1] The peri-ampullary region is a site of predilection. Patients range in age from 30 to 90 years, with a peak in the seventh decade. Males and females are equally affected. Presentation depends on size and location. Small adenomas are usually asymptomatic, unless they occur in the ampulla, when they may obstruct the biliary flow. Large adenomas are usually of villous type and may present with intestinal obstruction, bleeding, or intussusception. It is likely that most carcinomas of the small bowel arise in pre-existing adenomas. Large villous lesions are more prone to malignant transformation. Multiple duodenal adenomas are a frequent complication of familial adenomatous polyposis (FAP: Fig. 9.1), but usually remain small.[2]

Macroscopic appearances

Adenomas of the small intestine and ampulla have the same gross features as those of the large bowel and are classified similarly as tubular, tubulovillous, and villous (see p. 393). However, compared with the large bowel, a higher proportion of adenomas are sessile and of the villous variety.[3]

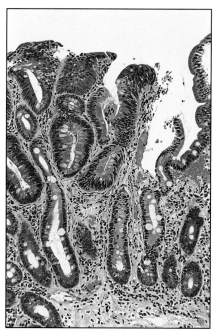

Fig. 9.1 • Tubular adenoma of duodenum in a patient with familial adenomatous polyposis. Crypts in the superficial part of the mucosa are lined by epithelium, showing mild dysplasia with crowding and enlargement of nuclei.

Histologic appearances

The lesions are similar to their counterparts in the large intestine (see p. 393), though absorptive-type columnar cells may be more prominent.

Differential diagnosis

It is important to distinguish between ampullary adenomas and adenomas arising in duodenal mucosa adjacent to the papillary opening. The latter will usually be managed by conservative excision whereas ampullary adenomas (with a high risk of associated malignancy) are treated by radical surgery in selected and symptomatic patients. Inflammatory polyps of the ampulla may mimic neoplasms both clinically and histologically. The demonstration of epithelial dysplasia is a prerequisite for the diagnosis of adenoma. Adenomas showing moderate to severe dysplasia may mimic low-grade adenocarcinoma, but those in the ampulla will often be indicative of an underlying malignancy.

Adenocarcinoma

Clinical features

Adenocarcinomas of the small intestine, which generally affect older adults, are much rarer than carcinomas of the stomach or large bowel.[4,5] Endocrine tumors of the small intestine occur with higher frequency. Obstruction occurs late because of the fluid nature of the small-bowel contents, and tumors are often advanced at the time of diagnosis and associated with a poor prognosis.[6] Most cancers arise within a pre-existing adenoma. The periampullary region of the duodenum is the most common site and patients present with painless jaundice and bleeding. A subset of ampullary carcinomas treated by radical surgery is associated with a good prognosis and is identified by a combination of early stage and low grade.[7] Carcinoma may develop within a background of celiac disease,[8,9] Crohn's disease,[10,11] and hereditary (lynch syndrome) non-polyposis colorectal cancer (HNPCC).[12] Carcinoma arising in the periampullary region is an important complication of FAP.[13]

Macroscopic appearances

Carcinomas of the ampulla present as polypoid or ulcerating tumors; a coexisting adenoma is often seen in the vicinity of low-grade carcinomas.[7] Elsewhere, cancers usually present as annular growths.

Histologic appearances

Most adenocarcinomas are well or moderately differentiated. Mucinous adenocarcinomas occur, but signet-ring cell carcinoma is rare and should be carefully distinguished from secondary spread from other sites, notably the stomach. Ampullary adenocarcinomas are mainly intestinal in type. Reactive or regenerative change in the ampulla and the complex glandular architecture produced by normal ampullary glands should be carefully distinguished from malignancy.

Endocrine tumors

Clinical features

The term carcinoid tumor is used to describe neoplasms composed of endocrine cells. They account for about one-third of small intestinal tumors. Classical carcinoid tumors arise in the duodenum or ileum, usually in the fifth and sixth decades, and are slightly more common in women.[14] A small minority of cases are associated with inflammatory bowel disease.[15] They are slow-growing but invade the bowel wall to produce narrowing. They may metastasize to liver and mesenteric nodes. Patients with multiple carcinoid tumors tend to be younger and to have a poorer outcome.[16] The tumors secrete 5-hydroxytryptamine (5-HT) and other vasoactive amines. When a sufficient volume of tumor is present in the liver, 5-HT is released into the hepatic veins, thus giving rise to the carcinoid syndrome. This has three components: (1) diarrhea; (2) facial flushing; and (3) cardiac lesions, including stenosis of the pulmonary and tricuspid valves. Carcinoid tumors of the duodenum are often smaller and less aggressive than those of the jejunum and ileum, which tend more often to be invasive and metastasize.[17] Carcinoid tumors may produce a variety of polypeptide hormones, including gastrin, somatostatin, cholecystokinin, pancreatic polypeptide, glucagon, bombesin, motilin, and calcitonin. Some endocrine tumors are named after the secreted hormone. For example, gastrinomas lead to gastric hyperacidity and multiple peptic ulcers of the stomach, jejunum, and duodenum (Zollinger–Ellison syndrome). Gastrinomas may occur in the duodenum but are seen more commonly in the pancreas and stomach (see Ch. 8).

Macroscopic appearances

The invasive growth of carcinoid tumors is accompanied by fibrosis and smooth muscle hyperplasia with resultant narrowing of the bowel lumen. These tumors are typically yellow in color following formalin fixation (Fig. 9.2). They are often multiple and may be associated with a synchronous non-endocrine gastrointestinal tract tumor.

Histologic appearances

Carcinoid tumors probably arise from endocrine cell populations within the crypt base and infiltrate the mucosa superficial to the muscularis mucosae before invading the submucosa. The overlying epithelium becomes elevated and may ulcerate. Carcinoid tumors are composed of small cells with uniform,

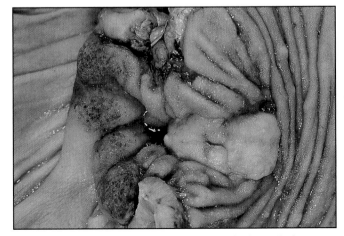

Fig. 9.2 • Carcinoid tumor of terminal ileum close to the ileocecal valve. The nodular tumor is yellow with no associated ulceration.

round nuclei showing very infrequent mitoses. The classical carcinoid consists of cells arranged in islands in which the peripheral cells may show palisading (Fig. 9.3). Conspicuous amongst the peripheral cells are enterochromaffin cells containing brightly eosinophilic subnuclear granules. Other histologic patterns include trabeculae, diffuse sheets, glandular structures, various intermediate forms, and mixtures of all these.[18] Small amounts of mucin may be seen within the central lumen of glandular structures. Histologic features are not useful in determining prognosis. Although regarded as malignant, these tumors are slow-growing and are less aggressive than adenocarcinomas. The more aggressive carcinoid tumors are large and show extensive local spread with ulceration and necrosis. A rare subset of high grade neuroendocrine tumors at this site have small cell carcinoma morphology and are clinically aggressive.[18a] Tumors limited to the intestinal wall are associated with 85% 5-year survival.[19] Five-year survival falls to 5% when there is serosal penetration. Special stains are helpful in demonstrating the enterochromaffin cells. These cells are stained black with the argentaffin reaction, brick red by the diazo method, and blue with lead hematoxylin. Endocrine cells that do not produce 5-HT may be visualized by the argyrophil reaction (e.g., Grimelius) and by immunohistochemistry (see below). Among the less aggressive duodenal carcinoids is a tumor characterized by the presence of periodic acid–Schiff (PAS)-positive psammoma bodies and the production of somatostatin (Fig. 9.4).[20] Such somatostatinomas are relatively more common in the periampullary region.[21]

Immunohistochemistry

Positive reactions for chromogranin, synaptaphysin, neuron-specific enolase, and protein gene product (PGP) 9.5 will assist in the diagnosis of carcinoid tumors. In addition, antibodies to polypeptide hormones allow classification to be achieved at a functional level. Detection of mRNA by in-situ hybridization should increase the sensitivity of functional probing.

Electron microscopy

This will demonstrate the characteristic electron-dense neurosecretory granules, but is rarely required to achieve a diagnosis.

Non-epithelial tumors (mesenchymal and vascular)

Gastrointestinal stromal tumors

Most stromal tumors encountered in the small intestine fall within the category that is now termed gastrointestinal stromal tumor (GIST). As in the stomach, these lesions were originally classified as smooth muscle neoplasms,[22] but are now accepted as tumors that arise from, or show differentiation towards, the interstitial cells of Cajal.[23,24] The latter are pacemaker cells that are intercalated between the autonomic nervous system and the smooth muscle of the bowel wall. Given their association with cells that are intermediate between neurons and smooth muscle cells, the well-documented mixed neural and smooth muscle phenotype based on both immunohistochemistry and electron microscopic examination is understandable. Additionally, 60–70% of GISTs express the ubiquitous mesodermal marker CD34.[25] However, the single most important biomarker is overexpression of the transmembrane tyrosine kinase receptor KIT (CD117).[26,27] This in turn is explained by somatic mutation of the *KIT* gene, which is present in more than 80% of GISTs.[28] As a result of the overexpression of KIT, GISTs may be specifically targeted by the tyrosine kinase inhibitor imatinib (STI-571) or Gleevec, making these previously neglected tumors an important model for targeted solid-tumor chemotherapy.[29]

As compared with GISTs of the stomach, small intestinal GISTs are more likely to show evidence of neural differentiation at the ultrastructural level. For this reason, the literature refers to a subset of stromal tumors of the small intestine, known as plexosarcoma or gastrointestinal autonomic nerve tumor (GANT).[30–34] However, there now seems to be little justification for designating GANTs as entities separate from GISTs since they carry the same *KIT* mutations.[35]

Clinical features

Small tumors may be found incidentally at operation or autopsy, whereas larger lesions may present with bleeding or abdominal discomfort. There is no sex or racial predisposition and adults of all ages may be affected: the mean age at

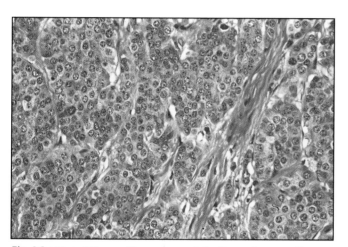

Fig. 9.3 • Carcinoid tumor of ileum composed of uniform cells arranged in nests.

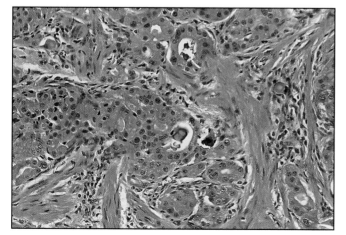

Fig. 9.4 • Somatostatin-secreting carcinoid of duodenum. Tumor cells are arranged in acini, some of which contain psammoma bodies.

diagnosis is around 50 years. GISTs have been described in subjects with neurofibromatosis.[36] About 20% occur in the duodenum, making this the site of predilection given its comparatively limited length.

Macroscopic appearances

Tumors may grow into the lumen, outwards through the serosa, or in both directions, producing a dumbbell growth. They may extend into the mesentery or retroperitoneum.[37] Rarely, they may be multiple.[38] Clinically significant tumors vary in size from 2 to 20 cm. On section they are circumscribed, lack a true capsule, and reveal a pink or gray cut surface with a rubbery consistency. Some may be soft with areas of hemorrhage.[34] Malignant tumors are likely to be larger, with a white cut surface and areas of necrosis. Cystic degeneration characterizes large tumors regardless of malignant potential (Fig. 9.5).

Histologic appearances

Cells may be spindled (Fig. 9.6) and epithelioid with pale to eosinophilic cytoplasm, or occur as a mixture of the two. There may either be infiltration into surrounding normal structures

or pseudoencapsulation. There is often a well-developed micro-vasculature that is prone to focal hemorrhage. A subset is characterized by the presence of eosinophilic skeinoid fibers (Fig. 9.7).[34,37] Nuclear palisading may be conspicuous. A GIST with a marked inflammatory component (simulating inflammatory pseudotumor) has been described.[39]

Immunohistochemistry

The most consistent finding is expression of diffuse cytoplasmic positivity for KIT (CD117), sometimes with a combined dot-like pattern. Non-expression of KIT occurs in approximately 4% of tumors with the clinicopathological features of GISTs. KIT-negativity may be due to technical failure, sampling error, loss through clonal evolution, and a genuine absence in a tumor otherwise indistinguishable from a GIST. KIT-negative GISTs are more likely to have an epithelioid cell morphology, to arise in the omentum/peritoneal surface and to have platelet-derived growth factor receptor-alpha (*PDGFRA*) mutations rather than *KIT* mutations.[40] Some of these KIT-negative GISTs still have mutations in *PDGFRA* or *KIT* that render them sensitive to imatinib.[40]

GISTs stain for CD34 in up to 70% of cases and for smooth muscle actin (SMA) in up to 40% of cases. Unlike genuine smooth muscle tumors, positive staining for desmin is very uncommon. In general only focal positivity is seen for neural markers such as S-100, synaptophysin, and neurofilament protein.[23]

Prognostic markers

The two most usual patterns of relapse are locally within the peritoneal cavity or hepatic metastases. The most important prognostic markers are tumor size and mitotic rate per 50 high-power fields. Features such as cellularity, necrosis, and mucosal invasion have been highlighted in some studies but are difficult to reproduce. Anatomic location within the small bowel has been linked with an adverse outcome. The derivation of four risk categories is shown in Table 9.1. However, even very-low-risk GISTs may relapse at times and some pathologists avoid the term benign GIST, even in the case of very small lesions discovered incidentally.[23] GISTs harboring

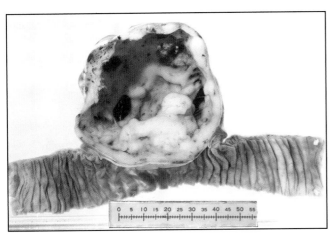

Fig. 9.5 • Gastrointestinal stromal tumor arising in jejunum and showing cystic degeneration. The patient, a male aged 23, presented with melena. The cavity was blood-filled and in communication with an ulcerated surface.

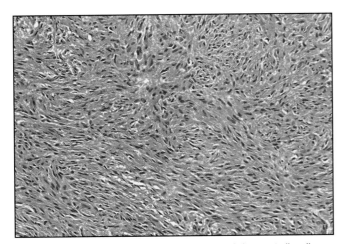

Fig. 9.6 • Gastrointestinal stromal tumor composed of plump spindle cells with pale eosinophilic cytoplasm and arranged in a storiform pattern (same case as in Fig. 9.5).

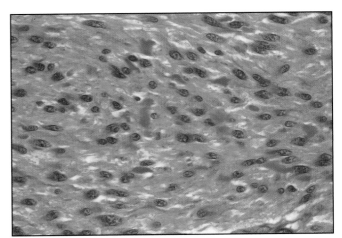

Fig. 9.7 • Gastrointestinal stromal tumor showing eosinophilic skeinoid fibers. The tumor arose in the jejunum of a 66-year-old male and measured $90 \times 80 \times 70$ mm. (Courtesy of Dr D.V. Spagnolo, Western Australia.)

Table 9.1	Risk of aggressive behavior of gastrointestinal stromal tumors (adapted from ref. 23)	
Risk level	**Size (cm)**	**Mitoses/50 hpf**
Very low	<2	≤5
Low	2–5	≤5
Intermediate	≤5	6–10
	>5–10	≤5
High	>5	>5
	>10	Any
	Any	>10

exon 11 *KIT* mutations are more likely to respond to Imatinib than GISTs with exon 9 or no detected mutation.[41]

Lipoma

Lipomas are rare tumors which have an equal sex incidence; most are symptomless.[42] Tumors arising from the submucosa protrude into the bowel lumen and can become pedunculated. Occasionally they may cause obstruction, intussusception, or ulceration with hemorrhage. Their histology is the same as at other sites.

Vascular tumors

Hemangioma

Tumors derived from blood vessels are very uncommon in the small intestine and the majority are benign.[43] Hemangiomas may be asymptomatic but a proportion present with obstruction, intussusception, or, more commonly, bleeding and anemia. Males are more commonly affected and the age incidence varies from 6 months to over 70 years, but with a preponderance of younger subjects.

Macroscopic features

There are five distinct macroscopic types:

1. Diffuse infiltrating cavernous hemangioma is mainly found in the small intestine or rectum.[44] The abnormality involves the entire blood supply, including mesenteric vessels (Fig. 9.8). The mucous membrane has a plum-colored appearance but is usually intact.
2. Circumscribed polypoid cavernous hemangiomas are usually single and develop in the submucosa.
3. Simple capillary hemangiomas are single or multiple lesions.
4. Multiple phlebectasias are small lesions resembling cavernous hemangiomas but they lie in the submucosa and are connected directly with normal vessels. They are usually symptomless.
5. Hemangiomatosis may occur in association with multiple hemangiomas in other sites. The lesions are usually symptomless.

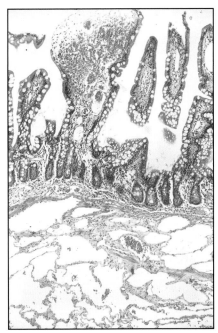

Fig. 9.8 • Hemangioma of small intestine with cavernous vascular spaces replacing submucosa.

Histologic appearances

The picture resembles that of hemangiomas in other tissues (Fig. 9.8; see also Ch. 3).

Differential diagnosis

Capillary hemangiomas should be distinguished from angiodysplasia.[45] The latter occurs mainly in the cecum and ascending colon, affects elderly people, and is regarded as a degenerative vascular abnormality. Glomus tumors of the small bowel are rare.[46]

Angiosarcoma

Angiosarcoma of the gastrointestinal tract is very rare. It is highly aggressive, may be multicentric, and has occasionally been associated with long-term dialysis.[47] When diagnosing angiosarcoma in this location, it is always advisable first to exclude the possibility of metastatic spread, e.g., from the scalp.

Lymphangioma

Lymphangiomas occur very rarely in the intestines and are usually solitary.[48]

Neurogenic tumors

Neurogenic tumors are uncommon and may be difficult to distinguish from smooth muscle tumors, hamartomas, and reactive neural hyperplasia. A group of stromal tumors arising in the muscle coat and showing neuronal differentiation ultrastructurally has been described as gastrointestinal autonomic nerve tumors (see above under gastrointestinal stromal tumors), but is no longer regarded as a distinct entity.

Neurilemmoma (schwannoma)

Neurilemmomas are rarely encountered in the small intestine, though they are well documented in the stomach.[49]

Neurofibroma and neurofibromatosis

Gastrointestinal bleeding in a patient with von Recklinghausen's disease should raise the possibility of intestinal involvement. Neurofibromatosis has been described in association with duodenal carcinoids[50] and gangliocytic paraganglioma of the duodenum[51] (see below). There is a report of gangliocytic paraganglioma coexisting with somatostatin-rich glandular carcinoid in a patient with neurofibromatosis.[52] This could indicate a histogenetic link between the three lesions.

Gangliocytic paraganglioma[53,54]

Most examples of this rare tumor arise in the duodenum. The sexes are affected equally and patients present around the age of 50 years with gastrointestinal bleeding or abdominal pain. The lesion presents as a polyp which may have an ulcerated surface. Histologically, the tumor is composed of endocrine cells, spindle cells expressing S-100 protein, and ganglion cells (Fig. 9.9). It may be mistaken for a carcinoid or a ganglioneuroma if it is inadequately sampled or if a particular component predominates. Reports of solitary ganglioneuroma of the duodenum are probably examples of this condition.

Ganglioneuromatosis

Diffuse intestinal ganglioneuromatosis occurs in association with medullary carcinoma of the thyroid, pheochromocytoma, and multiple neuromas. Together these comprise the inherited syndrome known as multiple endocrine adenomatosis type IIB.[55] Diffuse ganglioneuromatosis involves the nerves of the myenteric and submucosal plexuses. The condition should be distinguished from polypoid ganglioneuromatosis, which occurs in the large bowel and is characterized by neural proliferation within the lamina propria.[56]

Tumors of lymphoid tissue

Lymphoid hyperplasia, lymphoid polyps, and polyposis

Lymphoid hyperplasia occurs in infants and children and presents with right iliac fossa pain, obstruction, and sometimes intussusception.[57] A diffuse pattern of nodular lymphoid hyperplasia complicates about 20% of cases of adult forms of primary hypogammaglobulinemia.[58] These patients are at increased risk of developing intestinal carcinoma and lymphoma.[59]

Lymphoma

Clinical features

Primary lymphomas are uncommon but account for about 30% of small-bowel malignancies.[60] Burkitt's lymphoma often presents in childhood, but most other types occur in adults over the age of 40 years with symptoms that include abdominal pain, obstruction, perforation, intussusception, gastrointestinal bleeding, diarrhea, and a mass in the right iliac fossa. Males are more commonly affected than females. Some lymphomas develop in a background of chronic illness, including the acquired immune deficiency syndrome (AIDS), hypogammaglobulinaemia with lymphoid hyperplasia (see above), alpha-chain disease, and celiac disease.[61] The prognosis is generally poor, but varies with tumor type and extent of spread.[60]

The classification of gastrointestinal and other extranodal lymphomas differs from that of nodal lymphomas (see Chs. 8 and 21). This reflects the special biology of mucosa-associated lymphoid tissue (MALT) and specific etiologic mechanisms that operate exclusively in the gastrointestinal tract. Detailed study of gastrointestinal lymphoma is often hampered by a lack of fresh tissue and poor tissue fixation. Despite these difficulties, gastrointestinal lymphomas can be placed into reasonably distinct groups (Table 9.2). An important subset

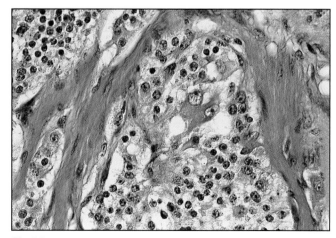

Fig. 9.9 • Gangliocytic paraganglioma. There is a mixture of ganglion cells and endocrine-type cells within this tumor.

Table 9.2	Principal categories of gastrointestinal lymphoma
B-cell	MALToma (more frequent in stomach)
	Immunoproliferative small intestinal disease and Mediterranean lymphoma
	Burkitt's lymphoma
	Mantle-cell lymphoma (not primary)
	Follicular lymphoma (uncommon)
	Plasmacytoma (very uncommon)
	Other B-cell lymphomas (usually high-grade)
T-cell	Celiac disease (enteropathy)-associated
	T-cell lymphoma with tissue eosinophilia
	Other T-cell lymphomas
True histiocytic	Very uncommon
Hodgkin's disease	Exceedingly rare

MALT, mucosa-associated lymphoid tissue.

includes the MALT lymphomas. These are low-grade B-cell lymphomas thought to arise on the basis of chronic antigen exposure. Gastric MALT lymphoma represents the paradigm, developing in a background of *Helicobacter pylori* gastritis (Ch. 8). There is no exact equivalent in the intestinal tract, but chronic antigen exposure is implicated in two types of lymphoma that are peculiar to the small intestine. The first is a B-cell lymphoma encompassing the spectrum of immuno-proliferative small intestinal disease (IPSID) and Mediterranean lymphoma.[62] The second is a T-cell lymphoma associated with celiac disease.[63] The latter is particularly prone to perforation and the prognosis is very poor. Burkitt's lymphoma is a further form of extranodal lymphoma; it consists of B cells resembling lymphoblasts. The ileocecal region is the site of predilection for the sporadic form of Burkitt's lymphoma. Epstein–Barr virus is associated with only 15% of cases (see Ch. 21). Correct diagnosis of this aggressive tumor is important as treatment includes chemotherapy as well as surgery. Other intestinal lymphomas have nodal counterparts, inasmuch as the malignant lymphoid cells and/or architectural patterns are comparable to those of nodal lymphomas. Follicular lymphomas are very uncommon at this site.[64] Diffuse B-cell lymphomas are usually high-grade tumors and form a sizeable, but imperfectly understood subgroup. Although the neoplastic lymphoid cells resemble large-follicle center cells (large centrocytes, centroblasts, or immunoblasts), these lymphomas could arise through transformation of a low-grade MALT lymphoma. Mantle-cell lymphoma differs from the preceding types in the older age at onset (around 65 years) and by the fact that it is a systemic disease associated with leukemic spread. Nevertheless it may present in the gastrointestinal tract, a particular manifestation being that of so-called lymphomatous polyposis. It is discussed under the large intestine (see p. 405) but may present throughout the gastrointestinal tract and cause confusion with MALT lymphoma.

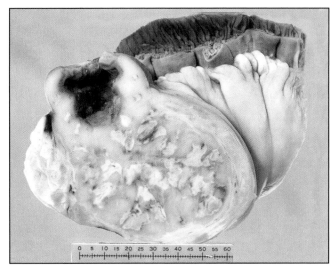

Fig. 9.10 • Bulky, circumscribed and ulcerated lymphoma (B-cell) arising in ileum of a woman aged 61.

Macroscopic features

Large B-cell lymphomas typically protrude into the bowel lumen as bulky, ulcerated masses and occur most frequently in the distal small bowel (Fig. 9.10). Mediterranean lymphoma is more likely to be proximal and is associated with diffuse infiltration of the bowel wall. Burkitt's lymphoma presents as a mass in the ileocecal region, frequently causing intussusception. T-cell lymphomas are often accompanied by multiple ulcers of the proximal bowel, with little evidence of a mass lesion (Fig. 9.11). This disorder was originally termed ulcerative jejunitis and, subsequently, malignant histiocytosis following the demonstration of its neoplastic nature.[65] It should be emphasized that the neoplastic nature of T-cell lymphoma of the small intestine is often not obvious and the correct diagnosis often depends on prior awareness of this entity. The cut surface of most lymphomas is homogeneously white and soft, like fish flesh (Fig. 9.12).

Histologic features

Mediterranean lymphoma develops in a background of alpha-chain disease or immunoproliferative small intestinal disease.[62] In this disorder, the mucosa shows plasma cell and lympho-plasmacytoid cell infiltration associated with wide separation

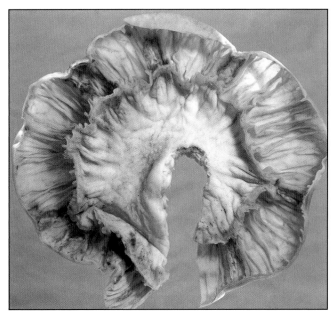

Fig. 9.11 • T-cell lymphoma of jejunum associated with multiple transverse ulcers in a man aged 60 who presented with recurrent bleeding.

of the crypts and broadening and shortening of the villi, leaving the surface epithelium intact (Fig. 9.13). This stage is regarded as early lymphoma, as is supported by the clonal nature of the plasma cell infiltrate.[66] As in gastric MALT lymphomas, treatment with antibiotics at this stage usually leads to regression. Further evolution in untreated cases is associated with transformation to a high-grade B-cell lymphoma.

Burkitt's lymphoma comprises lymphoblast-like cells showing a high mitotic rate and a "starry-sky" pattern, produced by scattered tingible body macrophages containing apoptotic material (Fig. 9.14). The tumor cells are highly infiltrative, dissecting between, rather than destroying, structures and surrounding regional lymph nodes without infiltrating them. Intussusception may be associated with ischemic necrosis, thereby obscuring the lymphoma. However the presence of

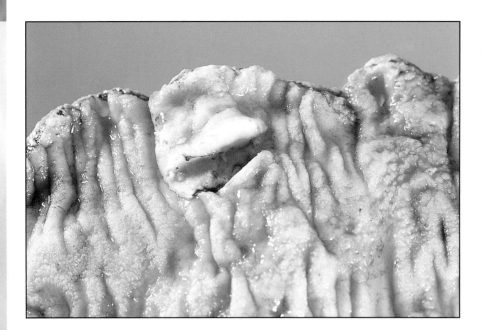

Fig. 9.12 • Plaque-like thickening of small bowel produced by a low-grade B-cell lymphoma. Section reveals pale, homogeneous tumor with a "fish-flesh" consistency.

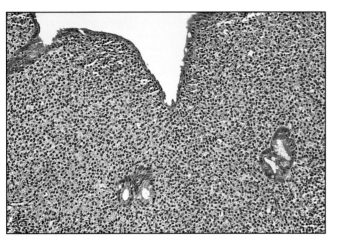

Fig. 9.13 • Immunoproliferative small intestinal disease or alpha-chain disease. There is villous atrophy and the lamina propria is greatly expanded by an infiltrate of lymphoplasmacytoid cells.

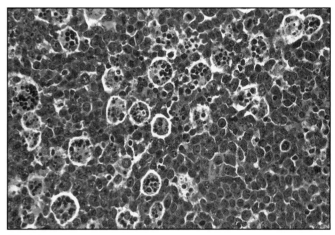

Fig. 9.14 • Burkitt's lymphoma of small intestine. Amongst the neoplastic lymphoid cells are numerous tingible body macrophages giving a "starry-sky" appearance.

lymphoid cells streaming through the muscle coat should facilitate recognition of Burkitt's lymphoma, even in cases showing necrosis. The typical immunophenotype of Burkitt's lymphoma is CD10, CD20 (L26), CD79a, and *bcl-6*-positive but *bcl-2*-negative. Molecular genetic studies show rearrangements of the *c-myc* oncogene.

Other B-cell lymphomas are either low-grade or, more usually, high-grade MALT lymphomas and consist of cells resembling follicle center cells (centrocytes, centroblasts, and immunoblasts; Fig. 9.15). Variable degrees of plasma cell differentiation may be seen. Solitary plasmacytoma is extremely rare. B-cell epitopes demonstrable on paraffin sections include CD10, CD20 (L26), CD79a, kappa or lambda light chains and *bcl-10*. The rare follicular lymphoma expresses CD10, CD20 and *bcl-2*.

An important characteristic of T-cell lymphoma is fissuring ulceration which may mimic that of Crohn's disease. Careful

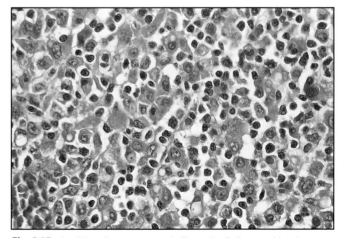

Fig. 9.15 • B-cell lymphoma composed of large B cells (immunoblasts) interspersed with reactive small lymphocytes.

histologic study may be required to identify a population of malignant lymphoid cells which may be scant and obscured by reactive inflammatory cells. This is particularly true for lymphoma complicating celiac disease,[63] which is usually of T-cell type.[67] A rare form of T-cell lymphoma is associated with marked tissue eosinophilia and may occur in the absence of celiac disease.[68] Malignant T cells may vary considerably in their morphology (Fig. 9.16). T-cell epitopes expressed in formalin-fixed tissue include CD3, CD43 and UCHL1 (CD45RO). In T-cell lymphomas that complicate celiac disease, the adjacent mucosa shows villous atrophy and crypt hyperplasia. The crypt epithelium may be infiltrated with T lymphocytes and the appearance of marked epithelial infiltration may represent a prelymphomatous or early lymphomatous state (Fig. 9.17). Alternatively, adult "celiac disease" may in some cases be a secondary manifestation of low-grade lymphoma of intraepithelial T lymphocytes.[69] Regardless of the pre-existence of celiac disease, all T-cell lymphomas are thought to represent the malignant counterpart of the intraepithelial subset of intestinal T cells with the immunophenotype: CD3+, CD4–, CD8+/–, CD103+ (the latter being demonstrable on frozen material only).[70] Four patterns of T-cell lymphoma have been described, according to cell size, distribution of neoplastic cells, presence of ulceration, bulkiness of tumor, and extent of villous atrophy.[70]

Differential diagnosis

It is important to distinguish primary lymphoma from reactive lymphoid hyperplasia, secondary lymphoma, leukemic deposits, small cell carcinoma, and undifferentiated carcinoma. In morphologically difficult cases, demonstration of clonality by gene rearrangement studies or immunohistochemical stains is most often discriminatory. Accumulation of intracytoplasmic immunoglobulin may also confer an appearance mimicking signet-ring cell carcinoma.

Secondary tumors

Secondary tumors are rare, but the small intestine is the main site of metastatic tumor in the gastrointestinal tract.[71,72] Primary sites include bronchus, breast, adrenal, ovary, stomach, large bowel, and cutaneous melanoma. Deposits from the large bowel may invade the mucosa and form a polypoid mass, thereby simulating a primary neoplasm. Diffuse-type adenocarcinoma of the stomach can spread to involve varying lengths of small or large intestine, producing a stricture which can mimic Crohn's disease.[73]

Tumor-like lesions

Brunner gland hamartoma

A sessile mass in the first part of the duodenum consists of proliferated but otherwise normal-appearing Brunner's glands with associated ducts and stroma. The lesion may ulcerate and bleed or may be a cause of obstruction (Figs 9.18 and 9.19).[74]

Peutz–Jeghers polyp and polyposis

Clinical features

The Peutz–Jeghers syndrome is characterized by gastrointestinal polyposis, oral pigmentation, and an autosomal dominant mode of inheritance.[75] Mutation of *LKB1* on chromosome 19p has been demonstrated in most kindreds and appears to be pathogenetically important in tumor development.[76] The small bowel is the most common site for the polyps, which present with abdominal pain and sometimes intussusception. There is an increased risk of malignancy within the gastrointestinal tract and in other sites, including the pancreas and breast.[77,78] A notable association is with ovarian sex cord stromal tumors with annular tubules (see Ch. 13A).[79]

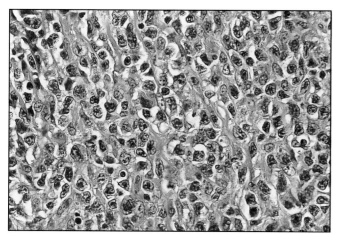

Fig. 9.16 • Pleomorphic T-cell lymphoma of small intestine composed of large lymphoid cells with convoluted, irregularly shaped nuclei and prominent nucleoli.

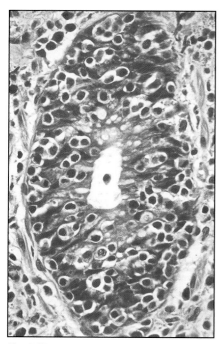

Fig. 9.17 • Intraepithelial lymphocytosis adjacent to T-cell lymphoma.

Fig. 9.18 • Brunner gland hamartoma presenting as submucosal mass in first part of duodenum, just distal to pylorus.

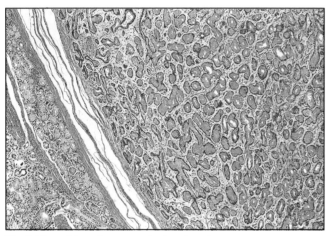

Fig. 9.19 • Proliferated Brunner's glands within a hamartoma.

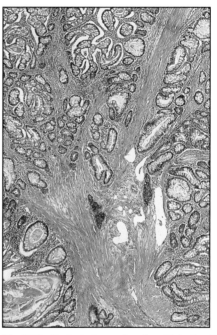

Fig. 9.20 • Peutz–Jeghers polyp of small intestine. The core of this hamartoma contains coarse bands of smooth muscle.

Macroscopic appearances

Peutz–Jeghers polyps may be sessile or pedunculated, though the stalk is short and broad. The head resembles that of an adenoma.

Histologic appearances

The polyps are hamartomas composed of coarse bands of branching smooth muscle covered by normal-appearing glandular epithelium (Fig. 9.20). Displacement of epithelium within the submucosa, muscle coat, and sometimes serosa is not uncommon and may be confused with malignant invasion (Fig. 9.21).[80] Dysplasia and malignant change are very uncommon but may occur. Solitary Peutz–Jeghers-type polyps may occur in the absence of the classical syndrome.

Juvenile polyps and polyposis

See section on large intestine.

Pancreatic heterotopia[81,82]

Pancreatic heterotopia most often occurs in the duodenum and presents as a submucosal or intramural nodule that may include both exocrine and endocrine elements or pancreatic ducts alone. There is an admixture of smooth muscle. Other sites throughout the gastrointestinal tract, including Meckel's diverticulum, are affected occasionally.[82]

Inflammatory fibroid polyp

Clinical features

Inflammatory fibroid polyps occur throughout the gastro-intestinal tract; the small intestine is the site of predilection,

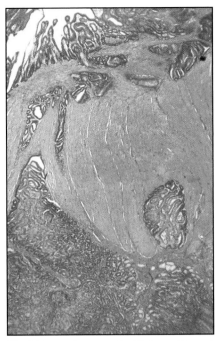

Fig. 9.21 • Displacement of epithelium of Peutz–Jeghers polyp through wall of small intestine.

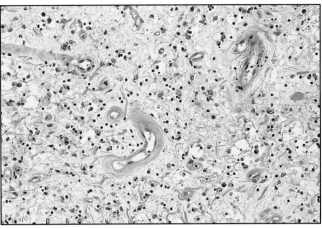

Fig. 9.23 • Inflammatory fibroid polyp of small intestine. The edematous lamina propria contains fibroblasts and inflammatory cells, notably eosinophils. There is an onion-skin-like arrangement of fibroblasts around the small blood vessels.

followed by stomach. They are usually single and affect all ages, though mainly adults. They present with symptoms of obstruction or intussusception (Fig. 9.22).[83]

Macroscopic appearances

The polyps are usually solitary and are sessile at first, but may become pedunculated with increasing size. They are usually between 2 and 5 cm in diameter and often show mucosal ulceration. Penetration through the muscularis propria may lead to the development of a dumbbell-shaped mass.

Histologic appearances

The lesion arises within the submucosa and is composed of loose or more hyalinized fibrous connective tissue that is infiltrated by eosinophils and plasma cells. The ulcerated surface is covered by granulation tissue. Stellate or spindle-shaped fibroblasts within the lesion are characteristically arranged in concentric rings around arterioles (Fig. 9.23). The histogenesis remains uncertain, although dendritic cell origin has most recently been proposed.[84]

Lipohyperplasia of the ileocecal valve

There is an excess of adipose tissue in the submucosa of the ileocecal valve which becomes distorted and protrudes into the cecum.[85]

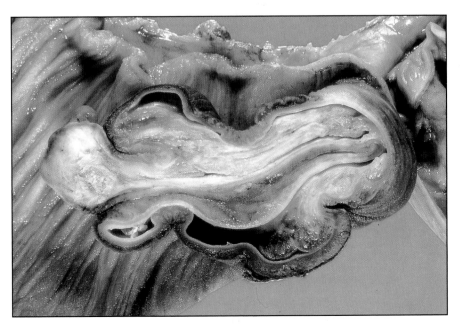

Fig. 9.22 • Intussusception caused by an inflammatory fibroid polyp.

Appendix

Epithelial tumors

Adenoma

Clinical features

Appendiceal adenomas are uncommon. They are usually found incidentally, but mucinous (cyst)adenoma may be complicated by appendicitis.

Macroscopic appearances

Adenomatous change usually affects the mucosa in a diffuse fashion. Secretion of mucus by the neoplastic epithelium within the confined space of the appendiceal lumen may convert the appendix into a large sausage-shaped mass.[86,87] Such tumors are described as mucinous cystadenoma and may sometimes be associated with pseudomyxoma peritonei. Adenomas may also be small and localized. Small tubular adenomas are a not infrequent finding in the appendix of patients with FAP.

Histologic appearances

Small localized adenomas are usually of tubular type (see under large intestine) and show low-grade dysplasia. In mucinous cystadenoma a tubulovillous or villous pattern can usually be discerned and there may be high-grade dysplasia. The latter is more apparent within the basal part of the mucosa. The epithelium overlying the upper parts of the villous fronds is often deceptively bland (Fig. 9.24). Accumulation of mucus

within the lumen, forming a mucocele, may lead to flattening of the epithelium which can hamper the recognition of dysplasia. Such flattening is usually focal, however, and misdiagnosis will be avoided if multiple sections are examined.

Adenomas of the appendix, like adenomas elsewhere in the gastrointestinal tract, are prone to malignant change. True malignant invasion may be mimicked by displacement of adenomatous epithelium and pools of mucus into the wall of the appendix. This may be secondary to the raised intraluminal pressure from accumulated mucus or to episodes of inflammation. Resemblance of the displaced epithelium to the overlying adenoma, the presence of acute inflammation and abscess formation, and the absence of a desmoplastic reaction help to distinguish this complication from malignancy.

Occasionally the epithelium of an appendiceal adenoma is serrated, mimicking the change found in a hyperplastic polyp (Fig. 9.25). The fact that hyperplastic polyps, like adenomas, may involve the mucosa of the appendix in a diffuse fashion may make the distinction particularly difficult. Features that would support the diagnosis of serrated adenoma include branched and back-to-back crypts, superficial mitoses, nuclear enlargement and stratification, and the formation of a mucocele.

Adenocarcinoma

Clinical features

Adenocarcinoma is a rare tumor at this site, and may present either as acute appendicitis or as a mass in the right iliac fossa in a middle-aged or elderly patient. The prognosis is determined by the grade of malignancy and extent of spread. Spread occurs via lymphatics to regional lymph nodes and by the portal vein to the liver. In one series, 5-year survival was 60%, but others have reported a poorer prognosis, particularly for tumors presenting with perforation.[87–90]

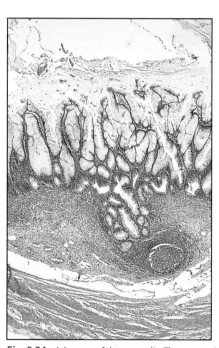

Fig. 9.24 • Adenoma of the appendix. The mucosa is thickened and replaced by villi lined by mucus-secreting cells. The appearance is deceptively bland, with the features of dysplasia present only within the crypt base. There is displacement of epithelium through a breach in the muscularis mucosae in association with a lymphoid follicle. This is to be distinguished from true malignant invasion, which may complicate adenoma.

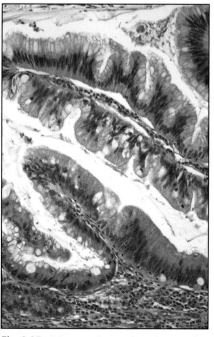

Fig. 9.25 • Adenoma of appendix with serrated pattern.

Mucinous adenocarcinoma of the appendix may be associated with the condition pseudomyxoma peritonei (see also Ch. 15). This is due to the escape of mucus-secreting tumor cells through the wall of the appendix into the peritoneal cavity. The peritoneal involvement is usually extensive, progressive, and ultimately fatal. Spillage of mucus due to displacement of mucus through the wall underlying an adenoma is usually localized and regresses after resection of the lesion.[91]

Macroscopic appearances

The most common type is mucinous adenocarcinoma, in which abundant mucus production often gives rise to a mucocele.

Histologic appearances

Mucinous adenocarcinoma of the appendix is usually well or moderately differentiated. Adenocarcinoma without excessive mucus secretion is mainly moderately differentiated. There is often evidence of an adjacent adenoma. The presence of endocrine cells within an otherwise typical adenocarcinoma does not alter the diagnosis. Microsatellite instability (MSI) appears to be uncommon in these lesions.[92]

Endocrine tumors

Carcinoid tumor

Carcinoid tumor is the most common neoplasm arising in the appendix. Carcinoid tumors occur at all ages but are most common in the third, fourth, and fifth decades. Females are more often affected than males. Most carcinoids are found in appendices removed incidentally at laparotomy for some unrelated condition or in specimens removed for acute appendicitis. The association with appendicitis is usually coincidental. Tumors most often remain small, very rarely metastasize, and therefore do not give rise to the carcinoid syndrome. In rare instances they may behave in a malignant fashion, but this is usually apparent at the time of laparotomy.[93]

Macroscopic appearances

The majority of carcinoids occur close to the tip of the appendix and have a yellow color after formalin fixation. Most measure less than 1 cm in diameter and many are only discovered following microscopic examination. They are typically round and well circumscribed, but diffuse forms can occur.

Histologic appearances

Endocrine cells occur normally both within the crypt base and scattered singly or in small groups in the lamina propria, forming neuroendocrine complexes.[94] It is likely that the endocrine cells in both these locations could give rise to carcinoid tumors, but the majority probably take their origin from neuroendocrine cells in the lamina propria.[95] The classical argentaffin carcinoid is identical to its counterpart in the ileum (p. 380). These tumors spread to involve the muscularis propria and often extend into the mesoappendix. A false impression of

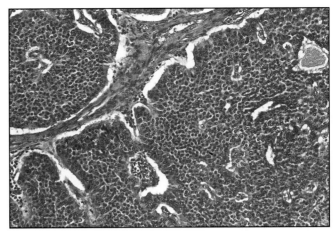

Fig. 9.26 • Carcinoid tumor of appendix showing cells arranged in solid masses with peripheral palisading by eosinophilic cells.

lymphatic invasion is often conveyed by retraction artifact; however, true lymphatic and perineural invasion may be seen. Most argentaffin carcinoids show a pattern of solid cell nests (Fig. 9.26), although the cells may be arranged in cords or ribbons where they penetrate the muscle coat. Some carcinoids have an acinar component which may dominate the histologic picture. In such cases the tumor cells may form solid clusters or small acini containing traces of mucus.

Non-argentaffin carcinoids are usually small and identified on histologic examination as an incidental finding. Their structure resembles that of rectal or hindgut carcinoids (see below), being composed of ribbons or small glandular structures. The cytoplasmic granules are usually argyrophilic.

Immunohistochemistry

Both argentaffin and non-argentaffin carcinoids may secrete one or more polypeptides, including somatostatin, neurotensin, motilin, pancreatic polypeptide, glucagons, and gastrin.

Goblet cell carcinoid

Clinical features

When first described, this neoplasm was thought to behave in a manner similar to conventional carcinoids, but more recent accounts indicate that it is more aggressive.[96–98] Patients are usually in the sixth decade, and the sexes are affected approximately equally. Acute appendicitis or an appendix mass are the most common presentations. Most tumors are confined to the appendix at the time of diagnosis and the prognosis is good. However, the tumor may spread by lymphatics to regional lymph nodes, to the liver by either lymphatic or vascular invasion, and by transcoelomic spread to ovary or peritoneal surfaces. Extension beyond the appendix or incomplete removal is the main indication for further treatment. Extra-appendiceal spread occurs in about 20% of cases.

Macroscopic appearances

Goblet cell carcinoid resembles other carcinoids macroscopically and in its distribution within the appendix.

Histologic appearances

The tumor is composed of clumps, strands, or glandular collections of cells which are distended by mucus, conferring a resemblance to goblet cells or signet-ring cells (Fig. 9.27). Mucus may spill out into the deeper layers of the appendix to form lakes. Endocrine cells are present, but not in the large numbers found in classical carcinoids. Scattered Paneth cells may also be found. The endocrine cells are more often argyrophil than argentaffin-positive (Fig. 9.28). Unlike signet-ring cell carcinoma, the mucous cells form clusters or rosettes and there is usually little nuclear pleomorphism or mitotic activity. In some instances it may not be possible to demonstrate endocrine cells at all, but the designation goblet cell carcinoid still applies.

In the light of the histologic differences from classical carcinoid tumors, other names have been suggested for this neoplasm. These include mucinous carcinoid,[99] adenocarcinoma,[100] and crypt cell carcinoma.[101]

The size of the endocrine cell component usually does not correlate with malignant behavior and, as in conventional carcinoids, perineural and lymphatic spread are unreliable prognostic features. There are reports of aggression being

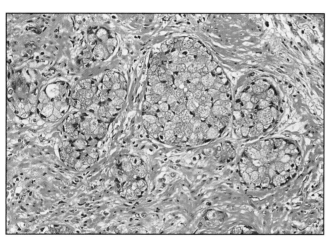

Fig. 9.27 • Goblet cell carcinoid of the appendix. The islands are formed of cells distended with mucus, together with peripheral endocrine cells with granular, eosinophilic cytoplasm.

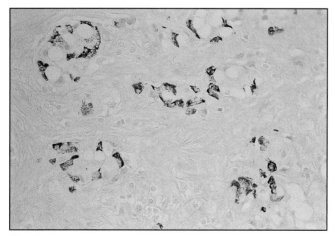

Fig. 9.28 • Goblet cell carcinoid of the appendix showing argyrophilic cells (brown) interspersed with goblet like cells. Grimelius stain.

associated with nuclear pleomorphism and a higher mitotic rate, but this is not accepted by all.[97] Some authors[102] have suggested that the uncommon mixed carcinoid-adenocarcinomas, which have a large carcinomatous component, are more aggressive.

Immunohistochemistry

Most, if not all, goblet cell carcinoids show positive staining with at least one of the markers for endocrine tumors, namely neuron-specific enolase, chromogranin, or PGP 9.5. These endocrine cells do not secrete serotonin but staining has been recorded for somatostatin and pancreatic polypeptide.[97]

Electron microscopy

It is unclear whether endocrine granules and mucin droplets occur within the same cell. This is of histogenetic rather than diagnostic interest.

Differential diagnosis

It is important to distinguish goblet cell carcinoids, particularly those lacking endocrine cells, from the more conventional mucinous adenocarcinoma of the appendix. The latter is more aggressive and requires radical surgery.

Tumor-like lesions

Hamartomas

Both Peutz–Jeghers and juvenile polyps may occur in the appendix. These are described in the sections on small intestine and large intestine respectively.

Hyperplastic polyp

Hyperplastic polyps are described in the section on the large intestine (p. 407). They may occur as discrete lesions within the appendix but, like adenomas at this site, they often present as a diffuse change extending over a wide area of the appendiceal mucosa (Fig. 9.29). The nature of this hyperplastic-like change is unclear. It may be appropriate to designate some of these lesions as mildly dysplastic serrated adenomas. The change may be accompanied by, or merge into, a typical villous adenoma.

Simple (obstructive) mucocele

The term "mucocele" is used in a clinical or macroscopic sense for any process causing dilatation of the appendix due to the accumulation of mucus. When this occurs as a result of a non-neoplastic process, for example as a sequel to inflammation, the mucocele usually remains small.

Nerve sheath proliferations

Neurofibromas usually occur in a background of von Recklinghausen's disease. There is one report of an appendiceal ganglioneuroma.[103] It is not uncommon to find diffuse

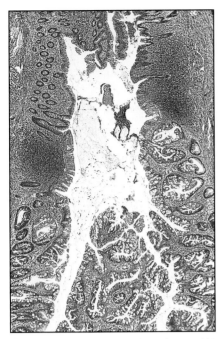

Fig. 9.29 • Diffuse-type hyperplastic change within appendix.

neuromatous proliferation, accompanied by endocrine cells, within appendicectomy specimens, particularly those with fibrous obliteration of the lumen at the tip of the appendix.[104] The frequency increases with age. The histogenesis of this proliferation is uncertain, but it is usually regarded as a hyperplasia secondary to earlier episodes of inflammation.

Endometriosis

The appendix is quite often involved by endometriosis. The endometrial tissue affects the outer layers of the appendix and may mimic adenocarcinoma.

Large intestine

Epithelial tumors

Adenoma

Clinical features

The adenoma is a circumscribed, benign epithelial neoplasm with potential for malignant change. Autopsy studies have shown adenomas to be more prevalent in populations from high-risk areas for colorectal cancer such as North America and Europe.[105,106] Adenomas are more common in males in all regions of the colon and rectum, yet females are at greater risk of cancer of the right colon. The anomaly may be explained by the fact that adenomas in females tend to be larger and more dysplastic.[105,107,108] Thus the prevalence is lower but the conversion rate to carcinoma is higher in females.

Adenomas are uncommon before the age of 40 years but occur with increasing frequency as progressively older cohorts are examined. In high-risk areas the prevalence as determined in autopsy studies may approach 50% in the older age groups. In addition, both size and multiplicity are age-related.[109] Autopsy surveys have also shown that adenomas are relatively evenly distributed along the length of the large intestine. However, adenomas are more likely to occur in the ascending colon with increasing age.[106] The site distribution of adenoma differs from that of carcinoma, which occurs most frequently in the rectum and distal colon. This could again be explained by a higher conversion rate for adenomas in the distal colon and rectum.[106,109] This suggestion is supported by the fact that adenomas of the rectum and distal colon are relatively larger and more dysplastic than those at other sites.[110]

Adenomas are usually asymptomatic. Larger adenomas may bleed and this may be observed either by the patient or through occult blood testing. Rare examples of villous adenoma may produce abundant mucus, leading to severe water and electrolyte depletion.

There is evidence that the tendency to produce adenomas runs in families (apart from the condition FAP) and may be due to an underlying autosomal dominant trait.[111,112] The main clinical importance of adenoma lies in the fact that this lesion serves as the precursor for the majority of colorectal cancers. However, the prevalence of adenoma is approximately 30-fold that of colorectal cancer, indicating that only a very small proportion of adenomas will become malignant.[113]

Macroscopic appearances

Small adenomas are sessile and may be similar in color to the surrounding mucosa. At this stage they may be indistinguishable from hyperplastic polyps. With increasing size, adenomas often become pedunculated; the head darkens and is broken up into lobules, giving it a resemblance to a baby cauliflower (Fig. 9.30). Large adenomas may sometimes be sessile and either slightly elevated, producing a velvety carpet, or more obviously protuberant. Villous adenoma typically presents as a soft, sessile mass with a shaggy surface (Fig. 9.31). Sessile adenomas are often less well circumscribed than their pedunculated counterparts. The blurring of their limits results in their greater tendency to recur following local excision. Flat[114] or even depressed adenomas[115] have been described: the earliest reports, originating from Japan, likely reflect a greater use there of screening endoscopy in the gastrointestinal tract.

Histologic appearances

Adenomas are composed of tubular and/or villous structures lined by dysplastic epithelium. The last is distinguished from normal by the higher proportion of immature cells containing enlarged, hyperchromatic, stratified nuclei. Mitotic activity is not limited to the basal zone and is often accentuated within the upper crypt and surface epithelium. The crypts show architectural irregularities, being coiled, branched, and crowded. Paneth cells and endocrine cells may be scattered haphazardly throughout the epithelium.

Based on their microscopic architecture, adenomas are classified as tubular, tubulovillous, and villous. A tubular adenoma is composed of branching tubules embedded in lamina propria and occupying at least 80% of the neoplasm. Tubular adenomas are usually pedunculated but can be sessile or flat. A villous adenoma is one in which at least 80% of

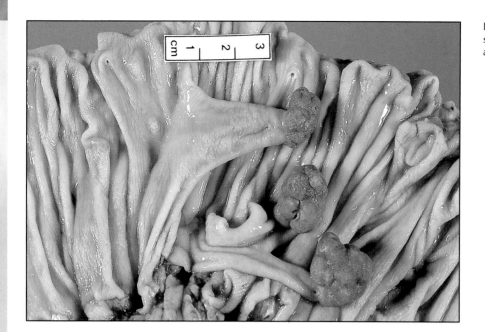

Fig. 9.30 • Three tubular adenomas arising in the sigmoid colon. The elongated stalk is typical of adenomas occurring in this site.

the tumor is composed of leaf-like or finger-like processes of lamina propria covered by epithelium (Fig. 9.32). It is usually sessile and may measure several centimeters in diameter. Tubulovillous adenomas are composed of both tubular and villous structures, each contributing no more than 80% of the tumor mass.

Adenomas are classified according to the grade of evident epithelial dysplasia – mild, moderate, or severe dysplasia.[110] A two-grade system of low (combining mild and moderate) and high grade may be preferred. In mild dysplasia the nuclear-to-cytoplasmic ratio is low and the nuclei are elongated, crowded, and stratified (Fig. 9.33). Mucus secretion is usually preserved,

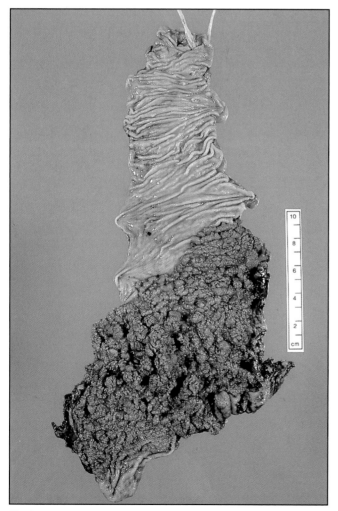

Fig. 9.31 • Large sessile villous adenoma of the rectum. The tumor involves the entire circumference of the upper rectum.

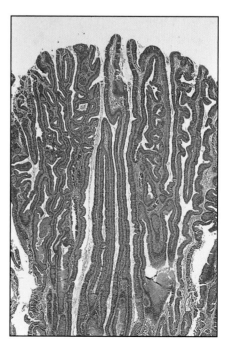

Fig. 9.32 • Villous adenoma of large intestine. Finger-like processes are covered by mildly dysplastic epithelium.

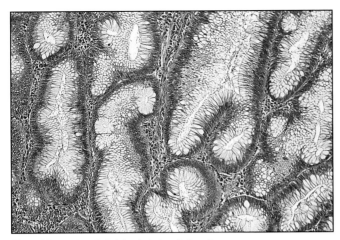

Fig. 9.33 • Mild epithelial dysplasia in tubular adenoma.

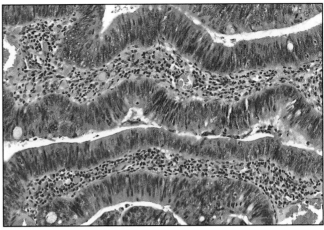

Fig. 9.35 • Adenoma of large intestine showing moderate dysplasia. Nuclei are enlarged, hyperchromatic, and pseudostratified. Few goblet cells are present.

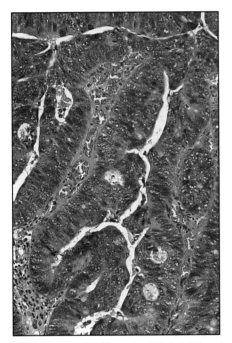

Fig. 9.34 • Severe epithelial dysplasia in tubular adenoma.

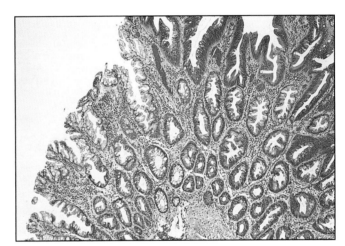

Fig. 9.36 • Mixed hyperplastic polyp–adenoma. The adenomatous component (upper right) has presumably taken origin with the hyperplastic polyp.

but may be reduced or absent in adenomas that include a high proportion of absorptive-type cells within the epithelium. In severe dysplasia the nuclei are enlarged, ovoid, or round, hyperchromatic and often contain prominent nucleoli (Fig. 9.34). The epithelial cells appear undifferentiated and there is considerable architectural irregularity, including crowded, back-to-back glands. Moderate dysplasia shows intermediate appearances (Fig. 9.35). Most adenomas show mild dysplasia, with severe dysplasia being least common. The term carcinoma in situ has been employed when the cytologic and architectural appearances are essentially those of malignancy but invasion across the line of the muscularis mucosae has not occurred. Demonstration of the latter is an important precondition for the diagnosis of invasive cancer. Innocent displacement of epithelium (pseudoinvasion) through the muscularis mucosae into the submucosa must be carefully distinguished from malignant invasion.[116] Features that would support innocent displacement include hemorrhage, deposits

of hemosiderin, retention of lamina propria around the displaced glands, absence of desmoplasia, and similarity of displaced epithelium to the overlying adenomatous epithelium. The risk of malignant change in an adenoma is related to size, presence of villosity, and grade of epithelial dysplasia.[117]

Mixed polyps and serrated adenomas

Traditionally, adenomas or neoplastic polyps have been separated from hyperplastic polyps (p. 407) as fundamentally different lesions.[118] This distinction is blurred by the existence of two types of intermediate polyp. The mixed polyp represents a combination of classic hyperplastic polyp and adenoma (Fig. 9.36), while the serrated adenoma blends the architectural features of epithelial serration with the cytologic changes of adenomatous dysplasia (Fig. 9.37). It has become apparent that serrated adenomas and hyperplastic polyps are related histogenetically. In mixed polyps, the adenomatous component is often serrated and may be clonally related with the hyperplastic component.[119] Additionally hyperplastic polyps and serrated adenomas share certain phenotypic alterations, for example the production of both gastric and intestinal mucin, and have pathogenic genetic alterations in common,

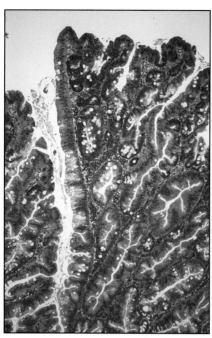

Fig. 9.37 • Serrated adenoma combining serrated architecture with cytologic atypia.

including mutation of K-*ras* or *BRAF* and DNA methylation that may result in silencing of genes such as *hMLH1*.[120]

Serrated adenomas occur throughout the colorectum but appear to differ according to anatomic location.[121] Serrated adenomas in the distal colorectum are often protuberant lesions with a tubulovillous or villous architecture and an epithelium that is deeply eosinophilic. They may be misdiagnosed as adenomas. Unlike most adenomas, the proliferative compartment of serrated adenomas remains basally located, though it may show abnormal extension into the upper crypt.[122] Serrated adenomas in the proximal colon are often sessile, hypermucinous lesions that closely resemble hyperplastic polyps. The distinction between hyperplastic polyp and serrated adenoma may be particularly problematic in the case of right-sided polyps and in the condition hyperplastic polyposis.[123] A new term sessile serrated adenoma has been introduced for subsets of serrated polyps that closely resemble hyperplastic polyps.[124,125] Sessile serrated adenomas are more often proximally located, relatively large and are composed of crypts that are dilated, show exaggerated serration, have an extended proliferative zone, but lack overt adenomatous dysplasia.[124,125a] Serrated polyps of this type have been linked to subsets of sporadic colorectal cancer characterized by DNA methylation, mutation of *BRAF*, and DNA MSI.[125,126]

Familial adenomatous polyposis

Clinical features

In this condition hundreds (if not thousands) of adenomas are present throughout the large bowel[127] (Fig. 9.38). The tendency to form these adenomas is inherited on an autosomal dominant basis and the gene responsible (*APC*) has been located on the long arm of chromosome 5 and cloned.[128–130] A rare autosomal recessive form of polyposis has been linked with the inheritance of two mutated copies of the DNA repair gene *MYH*.[131] In FAP the adenomas usually appear in the second decade, though later development can occur. It has been suggested that the presence of at least 100 adenomas is required for the diagnosis. A smaller number in a young (e.g., preadolescent) at-risk member of a known family would be diagnostic, but it is essential that several polyps are sampled to achieve a tissue diagnosis. Mutations in exons 3 and 4 of the *APC* gene are associated with an attenuated form of the disease with relatively few adenomas that are typically right-sided and flat. Cancer is also right-sided and later in onset than the classical form.[132] Attenuated FAP may be mistaken for HNPCC (see below).

It is now understood that adenomas are not limited to the large bowel but also occur in the duodenum, ileum, and gastric antrum.[2] Adenomas may reach a large size in the periampullary region, where there is a significant risk of malignancy.[133] Various extracolonic lesions are described. The association

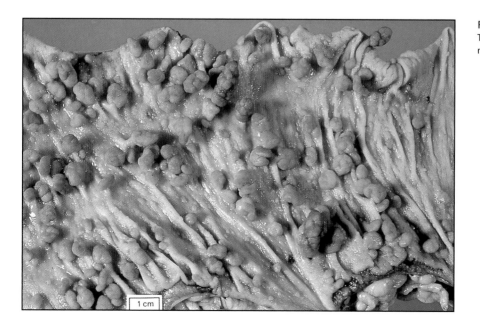

Fig. 9.38 • Familial adenomatous polyposis. The mucosa of the large bowel is studded with numerous tubular adenomas.

with multiple osteomas of the skull and mandible and multiple epidermal cysts of the skin is known as Gardner's syndrome.[134] There is no fundamental or genetic distinction between FAP and Gardner's syndrome except that the *APC* gene mutations in Gardner's patients are typically at the 3′ end of the gene.[135] Other extracolonic lesions include abdominal wall and mesenteric fibromatosis[136] (Figs 9.39 and 9.40), distinctive soft tissue fibromas (see Ch. 24), dental cysts,[137] retinal pigmen-

tation,[138] hepatoblastoma,[139] thyroid carcinoma,[140] and medulloblastoma.[141,142] Cases of Turcot syndrome have turned out to be either FAP or HNPCC (see below).[142] The new mutation rate for the condition is quite high. New mutations (one case in four) usually present with symptoms of advanced cancer and this will also be true for at-risk relatives who are not screened. Cancers, which occur in all affected patients if left untreated, develop earlier than in the general population, usually at around 40 years.

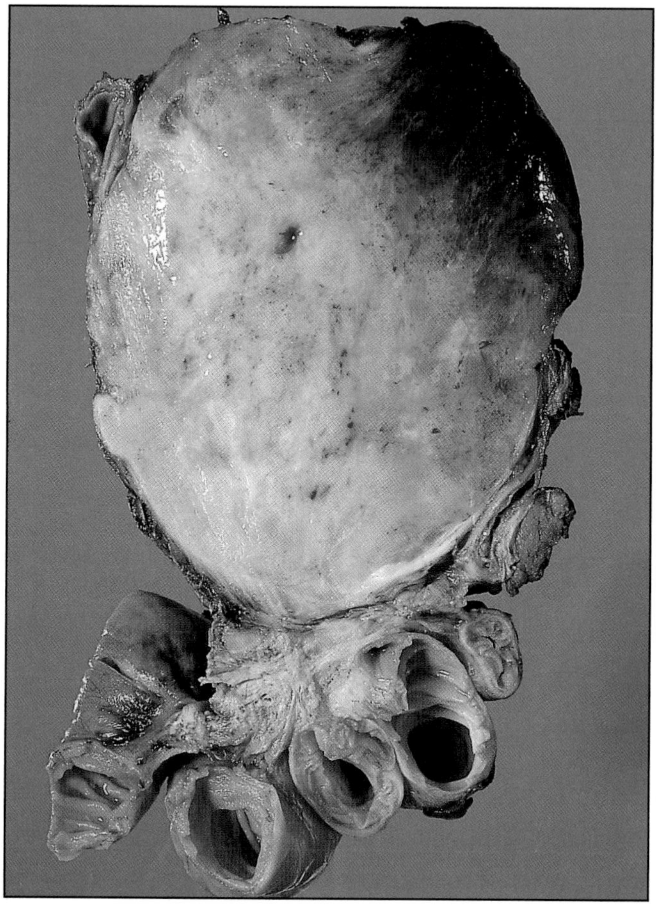

Macroscopic appearances

The size and number of the adenomas will be influenced by the age of the patient and, along with their distribution, may assume a pattern that is characteristic for a particular germline mutation. In addition to the attenuated form of FAP which gives relatively few adenomas (see above), there are particularly severe forms of the disease associated with specific mutations in exon 15 of the *APC* gene.[143]

Histologic appearances

Most adenomas are of the tubular variety, though tubulovillous and villous types may occur. Examination of apparently normal mucosa may reveal the presence of microadenomas comprising one or small numbers of dysplastic crypts (Fig. 9.41).

Carcinoma

Clinical features

Cancer of the colon and rectum is one of the most common forms of malignant disease in north-west Europe, North America, and Australasia. The incidence is low in Africa, Asia, and South America. However, the incidence is rising in countries that are adopting western lifestyles, for example Japan.[144] In areas where rates were initially very high, such as North America, gradual falls in mortality have been noted with time, perhaps due to dietary modifications and screening. Epidemiologic studies indicate that the etiology of sporadic colorectal cancer is closely related to environmental factors, with genetic factors playing an important but less obvious

Fig. 9.39 • Fibromatosis (desmoid tumor) arising in the mesentery of a patient with familial adenomatous polyposis.

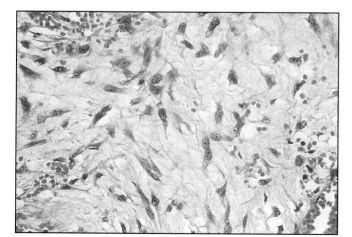

Fig. 9.40 • In intra-abdominal fibromatosis active-looking fibroblasts are set in a mucoid background containing little collagen, mimicking fasciitis.

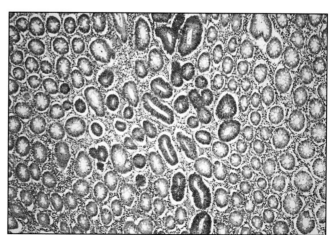

Fig. 9.41 • Horizontal section through microadenoma from a patient with familial adenomatous polyposis.

role.[145] The environmental factors are mainly dietary; there is a close correlation between meat consumption and the incidence of large-bowel cancer, and alcohol is an important risk factor.[145,146] Other foods, notably vegetable fiber, may be protective.[147] The etiology of sporadic colorectal cancer is clearly multifactorial. There is evidence that genetic factors are implicated, giving rise to a propensity for adenoma development.[111] In high-risk countries, the peak age at presentation is around 65 years. Cancer is strongly age-related; the incidence rises progressively with increasing age.

In high-risk areas approximately 8% of patients present under the age of 50 years.[148] The prognosis for young patients differs little from that for more elderly subjects.[149] If there is an increased prevalence of aggressive tumors in the young, this is balanced by improved operative risks.

The incidence of cancer of the large intestine is slightly higher for males than for females. However, a more meaningful picture emerges when the bowel is considered region by region.[148] Cancer of the right colon occurs more frequently in females of all ages. Cancer of the left colon occurs more frequently in females under the age of 50 years and more frequently in males over the age of 70 years. Cancer of the rectum occurs more frequently in males and the sex difference becomes exaggerated with increasing age. In males, 40% occur in the rectum, 30% in the left colon, and 30% in the right colon. In females, 40% occur in the right colon, 30% in the left colon, and 30% in the rectum. This distribution varies with age, with a shift in distribution to the right colon in the elderly of both sexes. The complex interplay of age, sex, and site indicates how the evolution of large-bowel cancer is modified by a variety of factors. For example, there is an excess of cancer in the right colon in individuals aged under 50 years. One likely explanation is the fact that HNPCC occurs in young individuals and shows a predilection for the right colon.[148] In addition, the subset of sporadic cancers with MSI and/or DNA methylation is associated with female gender, proximal location, and age.[150]

There can be no doubt that a large proportion of carcinomas arise within pre-existing adenomas.[151] There are also well-documented descriptions of small ulcerating or non-ulcerating carcinomas in which no residual adenomatous tissue can be identified.[152–154] These have been termed *de novo* carcinomas. It may be more logical to invoke the concept of flat adenomas in the histogenesis of such lesions. Reports from Japan indicate that small, flat adenomas may be of clinical importance because of difficulty in detection and through an increased tendency to transform into carcinoma.[114] Increasingly, subsets of colorectal cancer characterized by DNA methylation and DNA MSI have been linked with serrated precursor lesions, including sessile serrated adenomas,[124,125] mixed polyps, and serrated adenomas.[120,155] Colorectal cancer may evolve within a background of a precancerous condition such as FAP (see above), chronic inflammatory bowel disease encompassing ulcerative colitis,[156] schistosomiasis[157] and Crohn's disease,[158] juvenile polyposis,[159] and following pelvic irradiation.[160] However, the vast majority of cancers do not occur in patients with these conditions. In lynch syndrome or HNPCC, tumors develop at a relatively young age and this tendency is inherited on an autosomal dominant basis.[12] HNPCC is responsible for between 1 and 5% of colorectal cancers[161] and is caused by a germline mutation implicating one of a family of DNA mis-match repair genes – *MSH2*, *MSH6*, *MLH1*, and *PMS2*.[162] Cancers are more likely to develop in the right colon and to be multiple. Malignancies also occur in other sites, notably the uterus, ovary, stomach, small intestine, and brain. Cancers in HNPCC develop in pre-existing adenomas which often include a villous component.[163] The Muir–Torre syndrome (association of cutaneous sebaceous neoplasms with colorectal cancer) is now thought to be synonymous with HNPCC.[164]

The presentation of colorectal cancer is influenced by site. Cancers of the rectum typically present with bleeding or tenesmus. Carcinoma of the left colon leads to alteration in bowel habit and ultimately obstruction. Perforation may occur at the site of the cancer or proximal to an obstructing cancer. Patients with carcinoma of the right colon often present with anemia due to chronic blood loss. Examination may reveal a mass in the right iliac fossa.

Cancer spreads by a direct route through the layers of the bowel wall, by lymphatics to regional lymph nodes, by veins, leading to the risk of hepatic involvement, and trans-coelomically if the serosa is breached. Adequate reporting can only be achieved if relevant clinical information is made available. Surgery that is regarded as non-curative is associated with a very poor prognosis. The pathologist may also identify non-curative cases through the demonstration of tumor transection in the surgical specimen, particularly at the deep or circumferential line of resection.[165–167] This would indicate incomplete removal of the tumor. Unfortunately a favorable outlook is not guaranteed for "curative" cases, the cure rate being 50%. The explanation may lie in the establishment of hepatic micrometastases which elude discovery during the perioperative period.[168] However, examination of the surgical specimen will provide pathologic data that are closely related to prognosis (see below).

Macroscopic appearances

Most cancers of the colon and rectum are ulcerating tumors with a raised, everted edge (Fig. 9.42). Involvement of the bowel circumference may produce stenosis and obstruction (Fig. 9.43). Sometimes this occurs when the mass of the tumor is relatively small. Such annular growths have sometimes been called "string carcinoma" since the appearance is that of a string tied tightly around the bowel. Protuberant types, which are often relatively unaggressive, occur less frequently. The right colon is a common site for protuberant tumors. About 10% of cancers show a mucoid appearance on the cut surface due to secretion of abundant mucus by tumor cells. Surgical specimens should ideally be received fresh, opened, the deep excision margin (of rectal cancers) marked with ink, pinned out on a suitable surface and immersed in a tank containing formalin. They can be unpinned after 24 h but fixation should, if possible, continue for a further 24 h before dissection is attempted. Multiple horizontal sections through the tumor should be made, including the deep line of excision. If these are laid out and examined it is possible to identify the block containing the deepest point of penetration by tumor. Subsequent histologic examination will confirm whether or not there has been surgical transection of tumor. Areas suspicious for serosal penetration should be sampled for histology.[169] Gross examination will also indicate whether the tumor is well circumscribed or growing in a diffusely infiltrative fashion.

All lymph nodes within the fat deep to the tumor must be removed, together with nodes from the high point of vessel ligation and all intervening nodes. Veins should be carefully studied and taken for histology if there is evidence of tumor in the lumen.

The majority of large-bowel cancers are relatively well circumscribed and show little submucosal or intramural spread beyond their gross borders. For this reason it is unusual to find tumor at the distal resection line, even when the margin is close to the tumor. It is unnecessary to sample the distal resection line unless this is within 2 cm of the lower margin of the tumor.[170,171]

Histologic appearances

About 90% of colorectal carcinomas are adenocarcinomas in which tubular differentiation is easily recognized (Fig. 9.44). Scattered Paneth and endocrine cells are not an unusual finding, but the presence of the latter does not alter the diagnosis and is of little prognostic significance. Some tumors have strikingly villous architecture and these apprear to have a good prognosis.[172] About 10% of large-bowel carcinomas secrete abundant mucus. Mucinous adenocarcinoma may be diagnosed when more than 50% of the tumor consists of mucus (Fig. 9.45). Most studies indicate a worse prognosis for

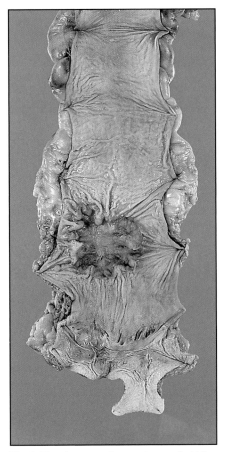

Fig. 9.42 • Ulcerating adenocarcinoma of middle rectum with raised everted edge.

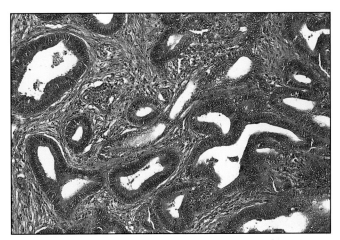

Fig. 9.44 • Well-differentiated adenocarcinoma of large intestine. Glands are well formed and show a distinct resemblance to adenomatous epithelium.

Fig. 9.43 • Stricturing adenocarcinoma of colon arising in patient with long-standing ulcerative colitis. The proximal and distal mucosa is atrophic.

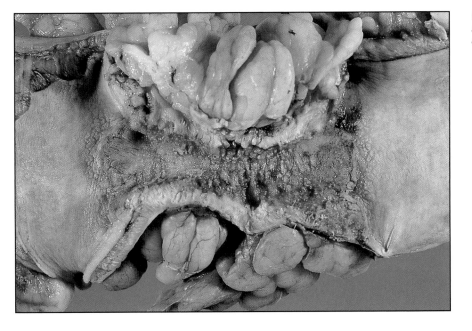

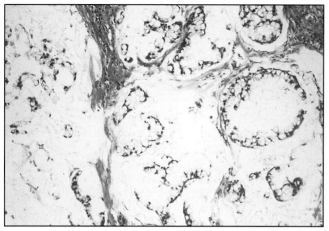

Fig. 9.45 • Moderately differentiated mucinous adenocarcinoma of the large intestine. Mucus-secreting cells are arranged in chains and are surrounded by abundant extracellular mucus.

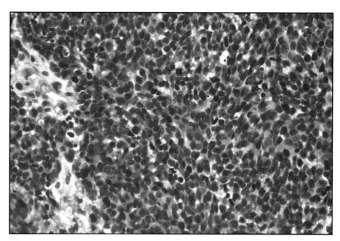

Fig. 9.47 • Small cell carcinoma of rectum.

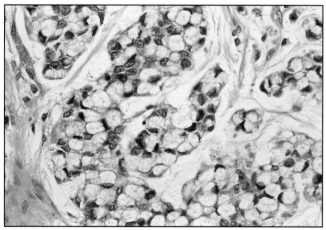

Fig. 9.46 • Signet-ring cell carcinoma of large bowel. The hyperchromatic nuclei are compressed towards the cell periphery by intracytoplasmic mucin.

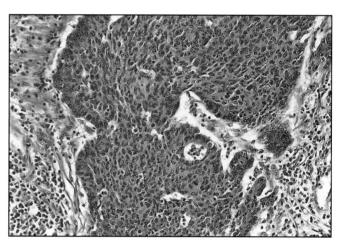

Fig. 9.48 • Undifferentiated ("medullary") carcinoma of the large bowel. The tumor cells form solid aggregates. This type of carcinoma is over-represented among hereditary non-polyposis colorectal cancer and sporadic microsatellite instability-high colorectal cancer.

mucinous adenocarcinoma, but the difference is small and not independent of stage.[173] Signet-ring cell carcinoma has a poor prognosis, but accounts for only 1% of primary large-bowel carcinomas[173] (Fig. 9.46). This is a tumor in which a dominant component (more than 50%) is made up of isolated malignant cells containing intracytoplasmic mucin. The possibility of spread from a gastric primary should be excluded in all cases. Signet-ring cell carcinoma showing exophytic growth has a more favorable prognosis.[174] There is an increased frequency of exophytic or well-circumscribed signet-ring cell carcinoma in association with HNPCC and in sporadic colorectal cancers displaying DNA MSI.[175,176] Squamous cell carcinoma and adenosquamous carcinoma are extremely uncommon. Small cell carcinoma (oat-cell carcinoma) is uncommon and resembles its counterpart in the lung in terms of histology, behaviour, and histochemistry (Fig. 9.47).[177] It is usually widely disseminated at the time of its discovery and surgical treatment is therefore contraindicated. Undifferentiated carcinoma has no glandular structure or other features to indicate the direction of differentiation (Fig. 9.48). It may be relatively uniform, comprising well-circumscribed aggregates of moderate-sized to large cells.

There may be a likeness to medullary carcinoma of the breast, including a dense lymphocytic infiltrate that includes tumor-infiltrating lymphocytes as well as peritumoral inflammation. This type of undifferentiated carcinoma often shows DNA MSI and has a relatively good prognosis.[178–180] It may be mistaken for a classical carcinoid, but the presence of mitoses, nuclear pleomorphism, and absence or sparsity of endocrine cells should lead to the correct diagnosis. Undifferentiated carcinoma may also be highly pleomorphic and infiltrative, when the prognosis is very poor. It should be distinguished from small cell carcinoma, lymphoma, and leukemic deposits and this is facilitated by the use of special stains including immunohistochemistry.

Adenocarcinoma is divided according to the grade of differentiation into well, moderately, or poorly differentiated. Well-differentiated tumors (20%) comprise well-formed glands in which nuclei are uniform in size and shape and retain a basal location (Fig. 9.44). There is often a distinct resemblance to adenomatous epithelium. In moderately differentiated adeno-carcinoma (60%), the glands are less regular but remain easily recognized. The nuclei are large and lack a basal location.

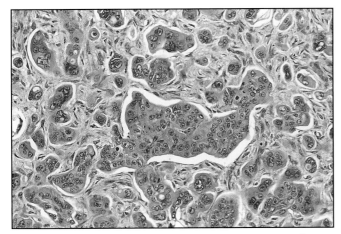

Fig. 9.49 • Poorly differentiated adenocarcinoma of large intestine. Cells are arranged in irregular clusters, with little evidence of glandular differentiation.

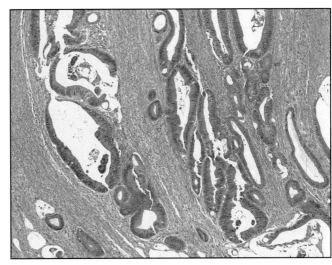

Fig. 9.50 • Pattern of diffuse infiltration by large-bowel adenocarcinoma.

Glands are highly irregular and difficult to discern in poorly differentiated adenocarcinoma (20%) (Fig. 9.49). An adenocarcinoma which shows two or more grades of differentiation is classified according to the worst grade. In mucinous adenocarcinoma the presence of columnar mucus-secreting epithelium indicates a well-differentiated tumor. Where the epithelium comprises chains or irregular clusters of cells surrounded by mucus this may be termed moderately differentiated (Fig. 9.45). Mucinous carcinomas composed of cells in small irregular clusters or containing significant numbers of signet-ring cells are classified as poorly differentiated. Grading is related to prognosis, but is less important than staging and has failed to feature as an independent factor in a number of multivariate studies.[181,182] Recognition of poor differentiation is relevant to the management of early colorectal cancer (see below).

Classification of the advancing margin of the tumor as expanding or infiltrating has been shown to provide prognostic information in multivariate studies.[181–183] The border of infiltrating carcinomas is characterized by widespread dissection of normal tissues by glands or tongues of tumor (Fig. 9.50). The term "infiltrating" does not imply the massive intramural spread seen in diffuse carcinoma of the stomach and occurs in approximately 20–25% of cases. Tumor budding or dedifferentiation at the invasive margin is associated with an infiltrative growth pattern and vascular invasion and has been shown to be an independent adverse prognostic factor (Fig. 9.51).[184] A favorable prognosis is conferred by the presence of lymphocytes, whether within a mantle of inflammatory cells at the growing edge of the tumor, or as tumor-infiltrating (intraepithelial) lymphocytes (Fig. 9.52), or in the form of Crohn's-like aggregates within the submucosa or serosa.[181,183,185] Tumor-infiltrating lymphocytes also serve as a sensitive marker for colorectal cancer with DNA MSI.[186] The presence of a well-marked desmoplastic reaction (tumor stroma composed of fibroblasts and collagen) is associated with a poorer prognosis but is not independent of stage.[181] A desmoplastic stroma is characteristic of malignancy and its presence may be useful in the interpretation of biopsy samples.

Cancers showing extensive DNA MSI are more likely to be mucinous or poorly differentiated adenocarcinomas or undifferentiated carcinomas, yet prognosis appears to be improved

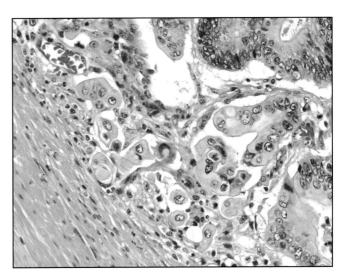

Fig. 9.51 • Tumor budding at the invasive margin of a colorectal cancer. This is characterized by loss of glandular differentiation and cellular discohesion, resulting in single cells or small groups of cells.

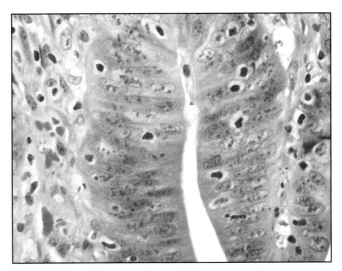

Fig. 9.52 • Tumor-infiltrating or intraepithelial lymphocytes. These represent the most important diagnostic features for hereditary non-polyposis colorectal cancer and sporadic microsatellite instability-high colorectal cancer.

whether these occur in the setting of HNPCC or sporadically.[187] This may be explained in part by the tendency for these cancers to be well circumscribed, to lack tumor budding, and to be associated with tumor-infiltrating lymphocytes.[150,174,175] MSI may be suspected on the basis of site (proximal colon) and histology, and the syndrome HNPCC itself may be suspected when the subject is aged below 60 years.

Spread and staging

Central to histologic examination is the confirmation of extent of spread of tumor:

1. direct spread through the layers of the bowel wall
2. lymph node metastasis
3. note of any vascular or perineural spread

Direct spread is documented and coded by the TNM system as: in situ or limited to mucosa (Tis), invading submucosa (T1), invading muscularis propria (T2), extending beyond muscularis propria (T3), and invading either free (serosal) surface or adjacent organs (T4).[188]

Lymph node involvement is probably the single most important pathologic prognostic indicator. The prospect for cure diminishes with increasing numbers of positive nodes, involved nodes along named vascular trunks,[189] a positive node at the apex of a vascular pedicle,[190] and involvement of nodes by retrograde lymphatic spread. The presence of micrometastases (detected by reverse transcriptase polymerase chain reaction) is also said to be a marker of diminished prognosis.[191] In the TNM system N0 signifies no positive nodes, N1 up to three positive nodes, and N2 four or more positive nodes.

The Dukes classification comprises A cases (tumor invading submucosa or muscularis propria), B cases (tumor extending beyond muscularis propria), C1 cases with positive lymph nodes, and C2 cases with a positive apical node.[190] The 5-year survival for A, B, C1, and C2 cases is approximately 100%, 75%, 50%, and 25%, respectively.[190]

There is growing support for a clinicopathologic approach to staging that includes the absence (M0) or presence (M1) of distant metastasis. The TNM classification is converted into stage as shown in Table 9.3. The presence of residual disease as indicated by the presence of tumor at a resection margin (particularly the circumferential margin) should also be recorded.

It is agreed that the incidence of venous invasion increases with advancing stage and is associated with distant spread of tumor.[192] An independent prognostic effect has been demonstrated by some, but not upheld by others.[181] Nevertheless, the invasion of thick-walled extramural veins by tumor should be recorded. Although lymphatic invasion and perineural spread have been put forward as useful prognostic factors,[193] these observations are probably of greater value in the reporting of early colorectal cancer (see below).

Early colorectal cancer

Neoplastic epithelium that resembles carcinoma histologically (and presumably biologically) may be confined to the mucosa. This may be seen within adenomas and within colitic mucosa. Despite the presence of small vessels within the mucosa, it is a fact that the potential for lymphatic or distant spread does not become realized until the tumor has traversed the line of the muscularis mucosae and invades the submucosa. For this reason, some authorities do not use the term carcinoma in situ but describe such lesions as severe dysplasia or high-grade intraepithelial neoplasia.[117] The term "early colorectal cancer" is reserved for tumors that extend into but not beyond the submucosa. The risk of lymph node spread is low even then – around 4% – provided that the tumor is not poorly differentiated.[194] The pathologic principles for managing early colorectal cancer are the same regardless of whether the cancer is arising in a tubular adenoma (Fig. 9.53) or a large sessile villous adenoma. Local excision is sufficient treatment providing that excision is complete and the tumor is not poorly differentiated.[195] A further proviso is that there should be no invasion of small veins or lymphatics,[196] although one study could demonstrate no prognostic importance for venous invasion.[197] A similar approach has been applied to small, ulcerating cancers of the lower rectum that may be treated by local disk excision even when the tumor has invaded, but is confined to, the muscularis propria.[198]

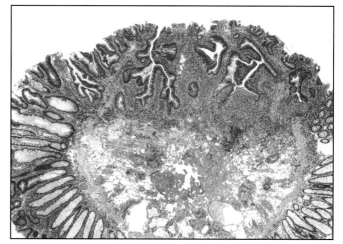

Fig. 9.53 • Tubular adenoma (left) with small focus of well-differentiated adenocarcinoma crossing the muscularis mucosae. The cancer is clear of the line of excision. The cancer is associated with a marked lymphocytic infiltrate and developed in a 43-year-old female with hereditary non-polyposis colorectal cancer (HNPCC: germline mutation in *hMLH1*). The adenoma is minute, with only low-grade dysplasia. However, adenomas are known to be aggressive in HNPCC (high likelihood of rapid and early conversion to cancer).

Table 9.3	System of staging of colorectal cancer using TNM categories		
Stage 0	Tis	N0	M0
Stage I	T1	N0	M0
	T2	N0	M0
Stage II	T3	N0	M0
	T4	N0	M0
Stage III	Any T	N1	M0
	Any T	N2	M0
Stage IV	Any T	Any N	M1

Immunophenotype and molecular pathology

Primary and metastatic colorectal cancer may be distinguished from other epithelial malignancies by the expression of carcinoembryonic antigen, nuclear beta-catenin, and CK20, but not CK7. CDX2 may also be useful in the distinction from non-intestinal adenocarcinomas.[199] Molecular or genetic alterations in colorectal cancer have been studied intensively over the last 20 years and have provided new insights into pathogenesis, classification, diagnosis, and prognosis. The step-wise genetic mutations accompanying the evolution of colorectal adenoma to carcinoma have served as an important paradigm for the pathogenesis of solid tumors. In a well-known molecular model for colorectal neoplasia, alterations in *APC*, K-*ras,* and *TP53* are perceived as key elements in the initiation, progression, and transformation of colorectal adenomas.[200] More recently, however, it has been shown that colorectal cancer does not evolve through a single linear pathway and that only 7% of colorectal cancers are in fact characterized by mutations in *APC*, K-*ras,* and *TP53*.[201]

The recognition of HNPCC as a clinicopathological entity and introduction of colonoscopic surveillance have resulted in improved survival rates. The pathologist may suspect the diagnosis of HNPCC on the basis of histological findings such as tumor-infiltrating lymphocytes.[202] Immunostaining for DNA mismatch repair proteins MLH1, MSH2, MSH6, and PMS2 may indicate loss of expression and pinpoint the gene that is likely to carry a pathogenetic germline mutation.[202] Sporadic examples of colorectal cancer with DNA MSI are mainly explained by methylation of the promoter region of the DNA repair gene *MLH1* that results in gene-silencing.[203] It is likely that sporadic colorectal cancer with MSI has an improved prognosis despite being less responsive to standard chemotherapy.[204] This subset may also serve as a marker for multiple or metachronous neoplasia. Therefore, molecular diagnosis of sporadic MSI colorectal cancer is likely to become increasingly important. It should be noted that sporadic MSI colorectal cancer may not express either CK20 or nuclear beta-catenin. Further exploration of the molecular genetic heterogeneity of colorectal cancer will uncover additional molecular markers for clinically important endpoints in the coming years. In this regard, recent data suggest that tumor karyotype may be prognostic in colorectal carcinomas.[205]

Differential diagnosis

It is essential that displaced and/or dysplastic epithelium is not overdiagnosed as malignancy (see section on adenoma). The criteria for diagnosing cancer are based upon appropriate cytology and architecture, presence of a desmoplastic tumor stroma, and invasion across the line of the muscularis mucosae (Fig. 9.54). Overdiagnosis is to be guarded against, particularly in the case of polypoid lesions. A crushed biopsy from the surface of an adenoma may be mistaken for carcinoma, leading to unnecessary surgery. Displacement of epithelium, which may become cystically dilated, occurs in adenomas, solitary rectal ulcer syndrome, and inflammatory bowel disease. Florid examples of this are sometimes described as colitis cystica profunda[206] and should be distinguished from well-differentiated mucinous adenocarcinoma.

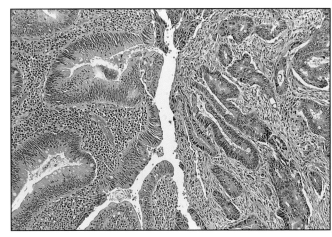

Fig. 9.54 • Sections show contiguous adenoma (left), and adenocarcinoma (right). The adenocarcinomatous glands are smaller, less regular, and embedded with a desmoplastic stroma. Stroma within the adenomatous area resembles normal lamina propria.

Endocrine tumors

Carcinoid tumors are uncommon in the large bowel: the rectum is the commonest site.[207,208] Rectal endocrine tumors usually present incidentally as mucosal nodules less than 1 cm in diameter, but rarely may behave in an aggressive manner, as evidenced by extensive spread, necrosis, nuclear pleomorphism, and high mitotic activity. The apparently high incidence of malignant carcinoids in some reports is due to the inclusion of small cell carcinoma and composite adenocarcinoma-carcinoid. The most frequent histologic pattern of hindgut carcinoids is the ribbon type (Fig. 9.55), followed by the mixed island-tubular form. In one study 28% of rectal carcinoids were argentaffin-positive whereas 55% were argyrophilic.[207] A variety of polypeptide hormones may be secreted. Endocrine cell hyperplasia and neoplasia have been documented in patients with long-standing ulcerative colitis.[209]

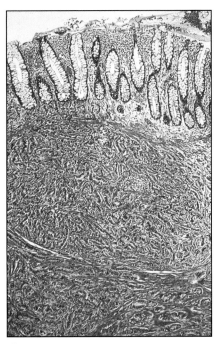

Fig. 9.55 • Carcinoid tumor of large bowel with ribbon pattern.

Non-epithelial tumors

Smooth muscle and stromal tumors

Unlike those in the small intestine, most benign stromal tumors in the large intestine show immunohistochemical evidence of smooth muscle differentiation.[210,211] The rectum is the site of predilection.[212] Small smooth muscle tumors arise from the muscularis mucosae and present as an incidental sessile polyp (Fig. 9.56). The clinical course is benign. Larger tumors arising in the muscularis propria or internal sphincter of the rectum are unpredictable with respect to metastatic behavior. Size, as opposed to mitotic rate, appears to be the best guide to prognosis; tumors greater than 5 cm should be regarded as malignant.[210,213] Among malignant lesions, GIST appears to be more common than leiomyosarcomas.[214]

Lipoma and lipomatosis

Small lipomas are usually an incidental finding, whereas larger lesions may present with bleeding.[215] Intestinal lipomatosis is extremely rare.

Benign vascular tumors

See under section on small intestine.

Nerve sheath tumors

Neurofibromas and neurilemmomas are excessively rare as solitary lesions, but multiple neurofibromas occur in patients with von Recklinghausen's disease. Intestinal perineuriomas have been described recently, most often being identified as small polypoid intramucosal lesions on colonoscopy.[215a]

Ganglioneuroma[216]

Ganglioneuromas are rare and may occur as solitary or multiple lesions.[56] The solitary form may be associated with other pathology, but this is likely to be coincidental.[216] Ganglioneuromatous polyposis has been documented in subjects with juvenile polyposis.[217] Solitary ganglioneuromas occur with equal frequency in males and females, but the multiple form may be more common in males. Adults of all ages are affected. The tumors present as polyps or nodules from a few millimeters to 2 cm in diameter, occurring throughout the large intestine and occasionally in the terminal ileum. Histologically, ganglioneuromas consist of an admixture of ganglion cells staining for neurofilament protein and neuron-specific enolase, nerve fibers, and S-100-positive spindle cells (which usually dominate and represent Schwann cells) (Fig. 9.57). The neural overgrowth may be limited to the mucosa, causing expansion of the lamina propria with crypt distortion (resembling a juvenile polyp at low magnification), or may involve both mucosa and submucosa. Ganglioneuromas are best regarded as choristomas (since ganglion cells are not found in normal mucosa) and have no malignant potential.

Diffuse ganglioneuromatosis[216,218]

Diffuse ganglioneuromatosis appears to be clinically distinct from ganglioneuroma: patients present in infancy, childhood,

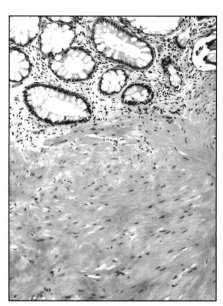

Fig. 9.56 • Benign smooth muscle tumor or leiomyoma arising in muscularis mucosae of rectum.

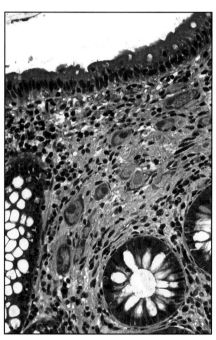

Fig. 9.57 • Solitary ganglioneuroma of rectum. Poorly defined, often polypoid, involvement of the lamina propria is characteristic.

or adulthood. Infants and children often have a history of chronic constipation mimicking Hirschsprung's disease. In adults, there is a well-documented association with multiple endocrine neoplasia (MEN) type IIb[55] and with von Recklinghausen's disease.[218] The macroscopic appearance is of a stricture or nodular mass affecting segments of bowel up to 20 cm in length. The ganglioneuromatous proliferation is centered upon the myenteric plexus and extends into adjacent layers of the bowel wall. The appearance has been described as "neuronal intestinal dysplasia" and represents an abnormal hyperplasia of the enteric nerve plexus. Neuronal hyperplasia in burnt-out Crohn's disease (also described as neuromuscular and vascular hamartoma) is distinguished by the clinical history and additional histologic features of inflammatory bowel disease.[219]

Kaposi's sarcoma and angiosarcoma

The large intestine may be involved as part of generalized Kaposi's sarcoma in patients with AIDS. The lesions are multifocal and involve mucosa and submucosa.[220] Angiosarcoma occasionally presents with metastatic disease in the bowel from a cutaneous primary.

Tumors of lymphoid tissue

Benign lymphoid polyp and polyposis

Benign lymphoid polyps are small submucosal tumors formed of hyperplastic lymphoid tissue which are presumed to have developed in response to local inflammation (Fig. 9.58). Most occur in the region of the lower rectum. Differentiation from low-grade lymphoma is aided by the clinical description of a small, circumscribed lesion. Benign lymphoid polyposis occurs in children following viral infections.[57] The condition may also be familial and has been found in patients with immune deficiency.[58] It should be distinguished from malignant lymphomatous polyposis (see below).

Lymphoma

Primary malignant lymphoma of the large bowel is rare.[221] Localized lymphoma arises mainly in the cecum or rectum. It may complicate ulcerative colitis[222] and AIDS. The great majority of cases are high-grade B-cell tumors. Mantle-cell lymphoma (see Ch. 21) occurs exclusively in adults around the seventh decade and usually presents with diarrhea.[221,223] Other regions of the gut are usually also involved, and this tumor should be distinguished from primary low-grade B-cell lymphoma (MALToma). Surgery is inappropriate for this condition because of the systemic nature of the disorder. The mucosa of the bowel is studded with numerous polyps, hence the earlier designation of *malignant lymphomatous polyposis*. On histology, the mucosa and superficial submucosa are infiltrated by lymphoid cells, giving a distinctly nodular pattern (Fig. 9.59). Higher magnification reveals a diffuse infiltrate formed exclusively of small centrocyte-like cells. Cells are positive for cyclin D1 (*bcl-1*) in over 90% of cases. Additionally, cells are CD20 (L26) and CD79a-positive but negative for CD10 and *bcl-6*. The disease has a slow but relentless course, culminating in generalized lymphadenopathy and bone marrow involvement.

Secondary tumors

Secondary tumors of the large intestine are rare. Occasionally there may be direct spread to the rectum by prostatic carcinoma.

Tumor-like lesions

Peutz–Jeghers polyps and polyposis

See under section on small intestine. Solitary Peutz–Jeghers-type polyps may occur in the large intestine in the absence of the syndrome.

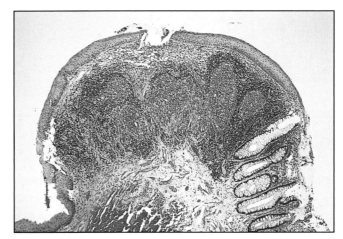

Fig. 9.58 • Benign lymphoid polyp of the anorectal junction.

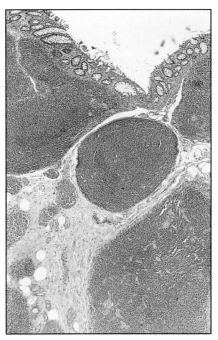

Fig. 9.59 • Malignant lymphomatous polyposis (mantle-cell lymphoma) of the large intestine. The submucosa contains nodular aggregates of centrocytes.

Juvenile polyps and polyposis

Juvenile polyps usually present in childhood with rectal bleeding. They may occur in as many as 1% of children. Although juvenile polyps were in the past regarded as solitary lesions, over half the children in a colonoscopic survey had more than one polyp and the polyps were distributed evenly throughout the large intestine.[224] Juvenile polyps are pedunculated with a spherical head. The head consists of essentially normal epithelium, lining tubules which may become cystically dilated (Fig. 9.60). There is an excess of edematous lamina propria. The surface may become ulcerated and the associated inflammation may produce reactive epithelial hyperplasia that should not be mistaken for dysplasia. Both dysplasia and carcinoma occur extremely infrequently.

Juvenile polyposis is an uncommon condition that presents in two ways. A rare form occurs in infancy and is associated with diarrhea, hemorrhage, protein-losing enteropathy, and

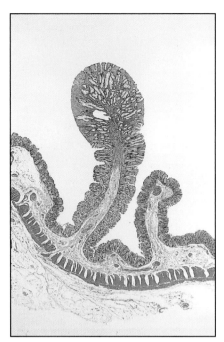

Fig. 9.60 • Small juvenile polyp of the large intestine. The head is spherical and is composed of abundant lamina propria with branched crypts showing cystic change.

intussusception. Death may occur at an early age. No family history is found. The remaining cases vary in their age of onset, but a typical presentation would be rectal bleeding occurring in the second decade. Polyps are either limited to the colorectum (Fig. 9.61) or may be distributed throughout the gastrointestinal tract. There may be a family history indicating an autosomal dominant pattern of inheritance and mutation of *SMAD4/DPC4* on chromosome 18q has been demonstrated in several kindreds.[225] Associated abnormalities of the heart and cranium, cleft palate, polydactyly, and malrotation are described. It is accepted that juvenile polyposis is a precancerous condition with an approximate risk of 20%.[143] The polyps are often multilobated (Fig. 9.62) with a papillary configuration; the excess of lamina propria, so characteristic of solitary polyps, may be less obvious. In addition the epithelium may show dysplastic change.

Hamartomas in Cowden's syndrome

Cowden's syndrome is a rare autosomal dominant condition characterized by tumors of skin, oral mucosa, thyroid, and breast in association with gastrointestinal polyps of a hamartomatous nature.[226] These polyps show distorted crypt architecture and increased mucosal fibrous tissue. Linkage to *PTEN* on chromosome 10q has been demonstrated.[227,228]

Gastric heterotopia[229]

Gastric heterotopia is uncommon and often occurs in association with other gut malformations. It may present with bleeding or as an incidental finding. It appears either as a well-circumscribed area of mucosal granularity or as a polypoid lesion.

Fig. 9.61 • Large bowel showing juvenile polyposis.

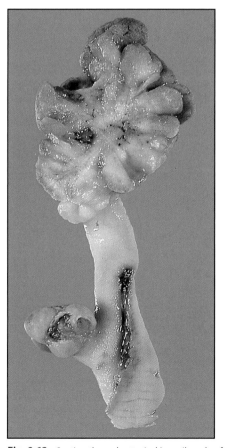

Fig. 9.62 • Section through a typical juvenile polyp from a patient with juvenile polyposis.

Hyperplastic polyp and polyposis

Hyperplastic polyps are small asymptomatic mucosal polyps, found incidentally either on endoscopy or in surgical specimens.[230] The great majority occur in the rectum and distal sigmoid colon. They may be found in large numbers clustering around a carcinoma and there is an association with adenomas.[231] The hyperplastic polyp has traditionally been regarded as neither neoplastic nor preneoplastic, but recent cytogenetic and molecular studies have demonstrated clonal changes in these lesions, implicating neoplasia-associated loci or genes.[232,233] Large hyperplastic polps occurring in the proximal colon have been linked with the subset of colorectal cancer showing DNA methylation and/or DNA MSI.[120] Most remain below 5 mm. Histologic examination reveals elongated crypts showing a serrated pattern (Fig. 9.63). Cells with a cup-like goblet cell appearance are reduced in number but columnar cells are eosinophilic and expanded with apical secretory mucin. Nuclei are round and vesicular with a prominent nucleolus. Mitoses are limited to the crypt base and endocrine cells may be located in the lower crypt. The lamina propria may contain increased numbers of smooth muscle cells whereas lymphocytes and plasma cells are often reduced.[234] Displacement of epithelium through a disrupted muscularis mucosae occurs occasionally (Fig. 9.64) and should not be confused with carcinoma.[235]

There are reports of multiple hyperplastic polyps occurring in relatively young individuals. The polyps are larger than usual and are distributed throughout the large bowel.[236] Serrated adenomas (Fig. 9.37) and polyps with mixed hyperplastic and adenomatous elements may be present (Fig. 9.36) and there is an increased risk of large-bowel carcinoma in such lesions.[237] It has been argued that many cases of hyperplastic polyposis are in reality examples of serrated adenomatous polyposis.[123] However the diagnostic distinction of hyperplastic polyp and serrated adenoma is not always straightforward (see p. 395). Hyperplastic polyposis may be familial and is associated with colorectal cancer.[233]

Cronkhite–Canada syndrome

Cronkhite–Canada syndrome is a diffuse form of gastrointestinal polyposis associated with protein-losing enteropathy, alopecia, nail atrophy, and skin pigmentation. The entire gastrointestinal tract is affected by multiple, sessile, polypoid lesions. Histologic examination reveals cystically dilated glands embedded in edematous lamina propria (Fig. 9.65).[238]

Inflammatory polyp

Inflammatory polyp may complicate inflammatory bowel disease, ureterosigmoidostomy (Fig. 9.66), or mucosal prolapse. The stroma is expanded by edema and inflammatory cell infiltration, and the crypts show branching, dilatation, or regenerative hyperplasia. The surface of the polyp may be ulcerated and covered by granulation tissue.

Lesions secondary to mucosal prolapse

Mucosal prolapse may occur as a result of mechanical dysfunction within various segments of the colon, rectum, and anorectal region. The clinical background includes solitary rectal ulcer syndrome, prolapsing hemorrhoids, complete rectal prolapse, prolapsing ileostomy or colostomy, and diverticular disease.[239] The effects of prolapse may be modified by ischemia, trauma, and inflammation. The resulting lesions differ in their gross and microscopic appearances. In solitary rectal ulcer syndrome there may be a large solitary ulcer or multiple small ulcers. The lamina propria is replaced by a characteristic smooth muscle stroma, the epithelium becomes hyperplastic, and the crypt architecture is distorted (Fig. 9.67).[240] There may be epithelial displacement through the muscularis mucosae

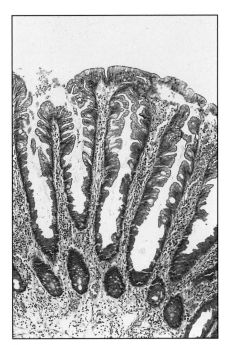

Fig. 9.63 • Hyperplastic polyp of large intestine showing unbranched crypts with a serrated contour.

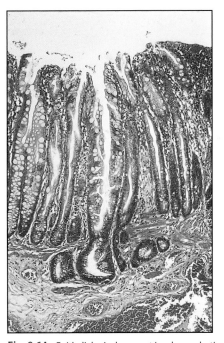

Fig. 9.64 • Epithelial misplacement in a hyperplastic polyp.

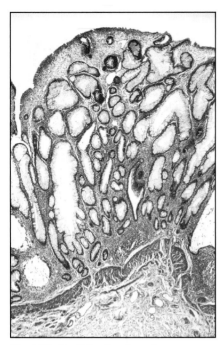

Fig. 9.65 • Cronkhite–Canada syndrome.

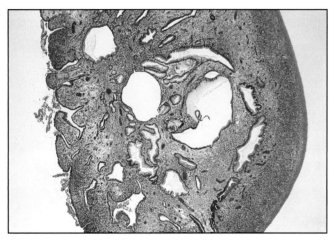

Fig. 9.66 • Inflammatory polyp occurring at site of ureterosigmoidostomy.

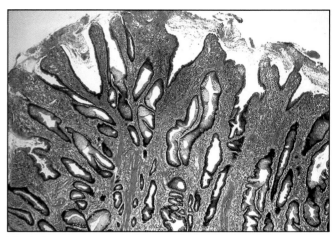

Fig. 9.67 • Solitary rectal ulcer syndrome characterized by hyperplastic crypts separated by bundles of smooth muscle.

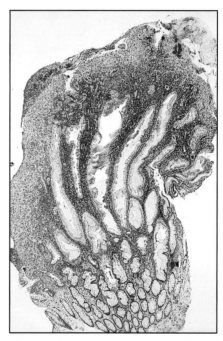

Fig. 9.68 • Inflammatory or "cap" polyp with cap of granulation tissue.

and florid examples of the latter may mimic carcinoma. Other forms of mucosal prolapse may lead to the development of single or multiple inflammatory polyps, the last often having a cap of granulation tissue (Fig. 9.68).[241] Similar lesions have been described as inflammatory myoglandular polyps.[242] A solitary polyp with a papillary surface of hyperplastic epithelium may develop at the anorectal junction. This has been described as inflammatory cloacogenic polyp and it may mimic tubulovillous adenoma[243] or serrated adenoma.

Endometriosis

Involvement of the large bowel may occur but is usually asymptomatic. The sigmoid colon and rectum are the main sites of endometriosis. Extensive involvement may lead to altered bowel habit and thickening and induration of the bowel which may mimic malignancy.[244]

Malakoplakia[245]

The gastrointestinal tract is the second most commonly involved system in malakoplakia (after the urinary tract), the sigmoid colon and rectum being the usual sites. Polypoid or plaque-like lesions are composed histologically of large eosinophilic histiocytes containing the characteristic calcified Michaelis–Gutmann bodies (Fig. 9.69). Malakoplakia may complicate suppurating carcinoma of the large bowel.

Precancerous epithelial lesions

Dysplasia of the large bowel is discussed under adenoma (p. 393). Dysplasia may develop in flat mucosa in patients with chronic ulcerative colitis (Fig. 9.70) and Crohn's disease. Dysplasia may also occur as a raised lesion or mass, often with a papillary surface (Fig. 9.71). There may be difficulty

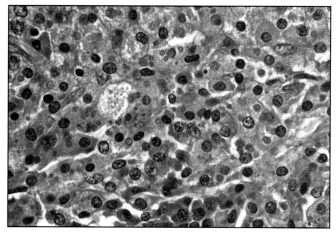

Fig. 9.69 • Malakoplakia of large bowel which occurred in association with an adenocarcinoma (not shown).

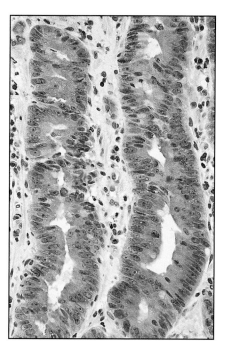

Fig. 9.70 • High-grade epithelial dysplasia in ulcerative colitis. Nuclei are enlarged with prominent nucleoli and there is no cytoplasmic maturation.

in distinguishing between true dysplasia and inflammatory or regenerative change. It is generally unwise to diagnose dysplasia in the presence of active inflammation. It is accepted that assessment and grading are subjective and it is recommended that biopsies be classified as negative, indefinite, or positive for dysplasia.[156] The positive group is further divided into low-grade and high-grade dysplasia, the last approximating to carcinoma in situ. A diagnosis of high-grade dysplasia may lead to proctocolectomy, and it is therefore advisable that two experienced pathologists should be in agreement.

Anal canal

Epithelial tumors

Epithelial tumors of the anal canal are relatively uncommon and benign tumors are very rare indeed.

Squamous cell carcinoma

Clinical features

The incidence of squamous cell carcinoma appears to be increasing, particularly amongst male homosexuals, both with and without AIDS.[246] Human papillomavirus (HPV) types 16 and 18 has been implicated in the etiology.[247] Most carcinomas arise within the transitional zone (epithelium resembling that of the urinary tract) above the dentate line. Direct spread in continuity is preferentially upwards and for this reason most anal canal tumors present as ulcerating growths of the lower rectum.[248]

Fig. 9.71 • Dysplasia-associated lesion or mass in a patient with long-standing ulcerative colitis. The raised, pebbled areas show epithelial dysplasia.

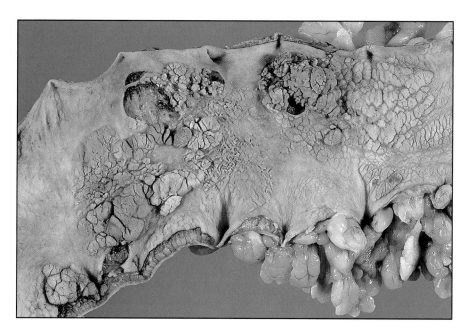

Histologic appearances

Squamous cell carcinoma of the anus is classified as large-cell keratinizing, large-cell non-keratinizing, or basaloid carcinoma (formerly known as cloacogenic carcinoma). The last accounts for about 50% of all squamous cell carcinomas of the anal canal and is composed of solid sheets of small cells, often with peripheral palisading and an abrupt transition to either central eosinophilic necrosis or keratinization (Fig. 9.72). It should be differentiated from basal cell carcinoma of the perianal skin. Grading of squamous cell carcinoma is subjective and is complicated by the variety of tumor types. High-grade carcinomas are composed of cells in small clusters that often show a diffusely infiltrative invasive margin. Nuclei display considerable variation in size and shape and there is conspicuous mitotic activity. There is little keratinization. Squamous cell carcinoma may contain mucus-filled microcysts. Small cell carcinomas are rare tumors of the anal region[249] that should be distinguished from lymphoma and melanoma. Examination of the adjacent squamous epithelium often reveals dysplasia of varying grades up to carcinoma in situ.[250] The histology (Fig. 9.73) is identical to that of intraepithelial neoplasia of the cervix. Squamous cell carcinoma of the anal margin usually arises at the junction between perianal skin and the squamous mucosa of the lower anal canal. The tumor is typically a large-cell keratinizing squamous cell carcinoma that is relatively well differentiated.

The prognosis is influenced by size, depth of invasion, and lymph node spread.[251] Lymph nodes along the superior hemorrhoidal vessels, on the lateral wall of the pelvis, as well as the inguinal glands may be involved. However, radical operative specimens are now seen less frequently as a result of changed management policies. Tumors of 2 cm or less are treated nowadays by local excision (provided that they are not high-grade malignancies), whereas large tumors are generally managed by chemoradiotherapy.[252]

Giant condyloma and verrucous carcinoma[253]

Giant condyloma and verrucous carcinoma lesions are considered as a single entity since they share multiple etiologic, pathologic, and clinical features. Although condyloma acuminatum is mainly limited to the perianal skin, the histologically similar but much rarer giant condyloma often presents as a bulky mass in the anorectal region and shows extensive penetration of the soft tissues around the anus, ischial fossa, perirectal tissues, and even the pelvic cavity. Despite this locally aggressive behavior, there is little propensity for lymphatic invasion. The lesion is identical to the giant condyloma of Buschke & Lowenstein, which affects the male and female genitalia (see Chs 13 and 14).

Adenocarcinoma

Adenocarcinoma that arises in the colorectal-type mucosa of the upper anal canal cannot be distinguished from rectal cancer and is grouped with the latter. A well-differentiated mucinous adenocarcinoma may occasionally develop in association with anorectal fistulae.[254] There may be underlying bowel pathology including duplication of the lower end of the

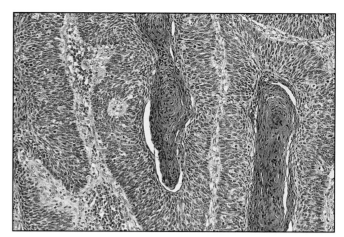

Fig. 9.72 • Squamous cell carcinoma of anal canal of basaloid type. Cells are arranged in aggregates with peripheral palisading and central keratinization.

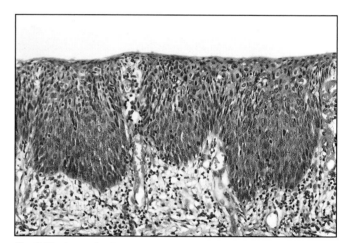

Fig. 9.73 • Severe dysplasia in transitional mucosa of anal canal or anal intraepithelial neoplasia grade III.

hindgut or perianal Crohn's disease. Diagnosis is often delayed until the possibility of carcinoma is considered clinically. Adenocarcinoma may also arise from the anal ducts and glands, although this has been described only very rarely.[255] Evidence for this origin may come from the demonstration of anal gland dysplasia.

Malignant melanoma[256–258]

Malignant melanoma accounts for up to 15% of primary malignant tumors of the anus. It presents as a large protuberant or ulcerating mass which usually extends into the lower rectum. The tumor originates from melanocytes that are normally found in the transitional zone above the dentate line. Malignant melanoma at this site is highly invasive with extensive local spread into perianal and perirectal tissues, involvement of the hemorrhoidal lymph nodes and early hematogenous spread to the liver and lungs. As in melanomas of mucous membranes elsewhere, there are two major histologic subtypes, namely epithelioid and spindle cell melanoma. The main differential diagnosis is from lymphoma, undifferentiated carcinoma of the rectum, and poorly differentiated squamous carcinoma of the anal canal and small cell carcinoma. The tumors often lack abundant pigment but melanin can be found in 50% of cases if searched for carefully. The presence of junctional change in the adjacent mucosa should be sought, but this is often destroyed by ulceration.

Cyst hamartoma[259]

Cyst hamartoma is a retrorectal lesion that may present as an anal tumor in association with recurrent fistula, abscesses, and a history of pain and tenesmus. Two etiologies have been proposed: (1) misplacement of anal gland epithelium following inflammation; and (2) a congenital defect implicating the tailgut. The specimen comprises multilocular cysts lined by squamous, transitional, and columnar epithelium (Fig. 9.74). The differential diagnosis includes simple anal gland cysts, teratoma, dermoid cysts, duplication cysts of the rectum, and well-differentiated adenocarcinoma of anal glands. Malignant change has been reported.[260]

Anal margin

Epidermal and adnexal neoplasms

Cutaneous tumors of the anal margin are essentially the same as other skin tumors (see Ch. 23). However the perianal skin is prone to a variety of growth disorders. This may reflect the general instability of junctional zones, in this instance the junction between squamous mucosa of the anal canal and perianal skin. In addition, several lesions are caused by (or associated to varying degrees with) venereal infection by particular types of HPV.[261] These disorders include condyloma acuminatum, Bowen's disease, bowenoid papulosis, epithelial dysplasia, and squamous cell carcinoma. It should be stressed that the precise relationship between HPV and neoplastic evolution in this site is still unclear. Keratoacanthoma[262] and basal cell carcinoma[263] may occur in the perianal skin. Basaloid carcinoma of the anal canal (see above) should be distinguished from the latter. Hidradenoma papilliferum (Fig. 9.75) is the commonest sweat gland tumor of perianal skin.[264]

A florid and rare form of leukoplakia may affect the anal margin and squamous epithelium of the anal canal.[265] This needs to be distinguished from inflammatory conditions causing simple hyperkeratosis because of its malignant potential. Histologic examination reveals hyperkeratosis, acanthosis, a pronounced saw-tooth contour to the dermoepidermal junction, and a band-like lichenoid chronic inflammatory cell infiltrate (Fig. 9.76).

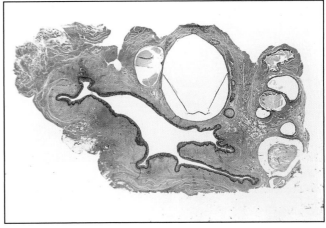

Fig. 9.74 • Retrorectal cyst hamartoma. The lesion is composed of cysts lined by transitional epithelium. The surrounding stroma includes disorganized smooth muscle.

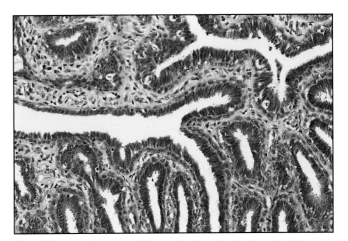

Fig. 9.75 • Hidradenoma papilliferum of anal margin showing glandular structures with a distinct two-cell lining.

Paget's disease may occur in the perianal skin[266] and should be distinguished from downward spread by signet-ring cells (with an associated adenocarcinoma of the anorectal region). As compared with signet-ring cells, Paget cells contain less mucus, have a vesicular nucleus, and are concentrated in the basal portion of the epidermis (Fig. 9.77). The apocrine nature of Paget cells is demonstrated by immunostaining for gross cystic disease fluid protein.[266] Other important differential diagnoses include Bowen's disease and pagetoid spread in malignant melanoma. Perianal Paget's disease is rarely related to an underlying carcinoma, unlike the situation in breast.

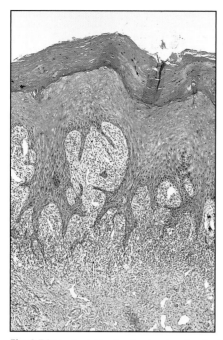

Fig. 9.76 • Leukoplakia of perianal region showing hyperkeratosis, "spiky" acanthosis, and a band-like chronic inflammatory cell infiltrate at the dermal–epidermal interface.

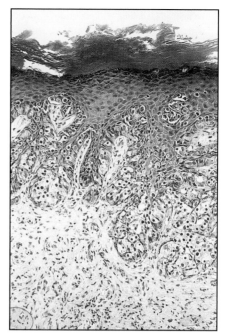

Fig. 9.77 • Perianal Paget's disease. Paget cells with a central round nucleus and clear, mucin-filled cytoplasm infiltrate the basal layer of the squamous epithelium.

References

1. Perzin K H, Bridge M F 1981 Adenomas of the small intestine: a clinicopathologic review of 51 cases and a study of their relationship to carcinoma. Cancer 48: 799–819
2. Domizio P, Talbot I C, Spigelman A D et al. 1990 Upper gastrointestinal pathology in familial adenomatous polyposis: results from a prospective study of 102 patients. J Clin Pathol 43: 738–743
3. Komorowski R A, Cohen E B 1981 Villous tumors of the duodenum: a clinicopathologic study. Cancer 47: 1377–1386
4. Barclay T H, Schapira D V 1983 Malignant tumors of the small intestine. Cancer 51: 878–881
5. Howe J R, Karnell L H, Menck H R et al. 1999 The American College of Surgeons Commission on Cancer and the American Cancer Society. Adenocarcinoma of the small bowel: review of the National Cancer Data Base, 1985–1995. Cancer 86: 2693–2706
6. Dabaja B S, Suki D, Pro B et al. 2004 Adenocarcinoma of the small bowel. Presentation, prognostic factors and outcome of 217 patients. Cancer 101: 518–526
7. Talbot I C, Neoptolemos J P, Shaw D E et al. 1988 The histopathology and staging of carcinoma of the ampulla of Vater. Histopathology 12: 155–165
8. Holmes G K, Dunn G I, Cockel R et al. 1980 Adenocarcinoma of the upper small bowel complicating coeliac disease. Gut 21: 1010–1016
9. Farrell D J, Shrimankar J, Griffin S M 1991 Duodenal adenocarcinoma complicating coeliac disease. Histopathology 19: 285–287
10. Perzin K H, Peterson M, Castiglione C L et al. 1984 Intramucosal carcinoma of the small intestine arising in regional enteritis (Crohn's disease). Report of a case studied for carcinoembryonic antigen and review of the literature. Cancer 54: 151–162
11. Gyde S N, Prior P, Macartney J C et al. 1980 Malignancy in Crohn's disease. Gut 21: 1024–1029
12. Lynch H T, Smyrk T C, Watson P et al. 1993 Genetics, natural history, tumor spectrum, and pathology of hereditary nonpolyposis colorectal cancer: An updated review. Gastroenterology 104: 1535–1549
13. Sugihara K, Muto T, Kamiya J et al. 1982 Gardner's syndrome associated with periampullary carcinoma, duodenal and gastric adenomatosis. Report of a case. Dis Colon Rectum 25: 766–771
14. Godwin JD 2nd. 1975 Carcinoid tumors. An analysis of 2837 cases. Cancer 36: 560–569
15. Sigel J E, Goldblum J R 1998 Neuroendocrine neoplasms arising in inflammatory bowel disease: a report of 14 cases. Mod Pathol 11: 537–542
16. Yantiss R K, Odze R D, Farraye F A et al. 2003 Solitary versus multiple carcinoid tumors of the ileum. A clinical and pathologic review of 68 cases. Am J Surg Pathol 27: 811–817
17. Burke A P, Thomas R M, Elsayed A M et al. 1997 Carcinoids of the jejunum and ileum: an immunohistochemical and clinicopathologic study of 167 cases. Cancer 79: 1086–1093
18. Soga J, Tazawa K 1971 Pathologic analysis of carcinoids. Histologic reevaluation of 62 cases. Cancer 28: 990–998.
18a. Nassar H, Albores-Saavedra J, Klimstra D S 2005 High grade neuroendocrine carcinoma of the ampulla of vater. A clinicopathologic and immunohistochemical analysis of 14 cases. Am J Surg Pathol 29: 588–594
19. Zakariai Y M, Quan S H, Hajdu S I 1975 Carcinoid tumors of the gastrointestinal tract. Cancer 35: 588–591
20. Griffiths D F, Jasani B, Newman G R et al. 1984 Glandular duodenal carcinoid – a somatostatin rich tumour with neuroendocrine associations. J Clin Pathol 37: 163–169
21. Makhlouf H R, Burke A P, Sobin L H 1999 Carcinoid tumors of the ampulla of Vater: a comparison with duodenal carcinoid tumors. Cancer 85: 1241–1249
22. Appelman H D 1986 Smooth muscle tumors of the gastrointestinal tract. What we know now that Stout didn't know. Am J Surg Pathol 10 (suppl. 1): 83–99
23. Fletcher C D, Berman J J, Corless C et al. 2002 Diagnosis of gastrointestinal stromal tumors: a consensus approach. Hum Pathol 33: 459–465
24. Sircar K, Hewlett B R, Huizinga J D et al. 1999 Interstitial cells of Cajal as precursors of gastrointestinal stromal tumors. Am J Surg Pathol 23: 377–389
25. Miettinen M, Virolainen M, Sarlomo-Rikala M 1995 Gastrointestinal stromal tumors – value of CD34 antigen in their identification and separation from true leiomyomas and schwannomas. Am J Surg Pathol 19: 207–216
26. Rubin B P 2006 Gastrointestinal stromal tumors: an update. Histopathology 48: 83–96
27. Miettinen M, Sarlomo-Rikala M, Lasota J 1999 Gastrointestinal stromal tumors: recent advances in understanding of their biology. Hum Pathol 30: 1213–1220
28. Corless C L, Fletcher J A, Heinrich M C 2004 Biology of gastrointestinal stromal tumors. J Clin Oncol 22: 3813–3825
29. Dematteo R P, Heinrich M C, El-Rifai W M et al. 2002 Clinical management of gastrointestinal stromal tumors: before and after STI-571. Hum Pathol 33: 466–477
30. Herrera G A, Pinto de Moraes H, Grizzle W E et al. 1984 Malignant small bowel neoplasm of enteric plexus derivation (plexosarcoma). Light and electron microscopic study confirming the origin of the neoplasm. Dig Dis Sci 29: 275–284
31. Walker P, Dvorak A M 1986 Gastrointestinal autonomic nerve (GAN) tumor. Ultrastructural evidence for a newly recognized entity. Arch Pathol Lab Med 110: 309–316
32. Lauwers G Y, Erlandson R A, Casper E S et al. 1993 Gastrointestinal autonomic nerve tumors. A clinicopathological, immunohistochemical, and ultrastructural study of 12 cases. Am J Surg Pathol 17: 887–897

33. Min K W 1992 Small intestinal stromal tumors with skeinoid fibers. Clinicopathological, immunohistochemical, and ultrastructural investigations. Am J Surg Pathol 16: 145–155

34. Ojanguren I, Ariza A, Navas-Palacios J J 1996 Gastrointestinal autonomic nerve tumor: further observations regarding an ultrastructural and immunohistochemical analysis of six cases. Hum Pathol 27: 1311–1318

35. Lee J R, Joshi V, Griffin J W Jr et al. 2001 Gastrointestinal autonomic nerve tumor: immunohistochemical and molecular identity with gastrointestinal stromal tumor. Am J Surg Pathol 25: 979–987

36. Schaldenbrand J D, Appelman H D 1984 Solitary solid stromal gastrointestinal tumors in von Recklinghausen's disease with minimal smooth muscle differentiation. Hum Pathol 15: 229–232

37. Segal A, Carello S, Caterina P et al. 1994 Gastrointestinal autonomic nerve tumors: a clinicopathological, immunohistochemical and ultrastructural study of 10 cases. Pathology 26: 439–447

38. Gall J A, Chetty R, Kemp A J et al. 1993 Multiple benign stromal cell tumours of the small bowel. J Clin Pathol 46: 869–871

39. Shek T W, Luk I S, Loong F et al. 1996 Inflammatory cell-rich gastrointestinal autonomic nerve tumor. An expansion of its histologic spectrum. Am J Surg Pathol 20: 325–331

40. Medeiros F, Corless C L, Duensing A et al. 2004 KIT-negative gastrointestinal stromal tumors. Proof of concept and therapeutic implications. Am J Surg Pathol 28: 889–894

41. Heinrich M C, Corless C L, Demetri G D et al. 2003 Kinase mutations and Imatinib response in patients with metastatic gastrointestinal stromal tumor. J Clin Oncol 21: 4342–4349

42. Furste W, Solt R Jr, Briggs W 1963 The gastrointestinal submucosal lipoma, a cause of bleeding and pain. Am J Surg 106: 903–909

43. Shepherd J A 1953 Angiomatous conditions of the gastro-intestinal tract. Br J Surg 40: 409–421

44. Parker G W, Murney J A, Kenoyer W L 1960 Cavernous hemangioma of the rectum and rectosigmoid: a case report and review. Dis Colon Rectum 3: 358–363

45. Pounder D J, Rowland R, Pieterse A S et al. 1982 Angiodysplasias of the colon. J Clin Pathol 35: 824–829

46. Geraghty J M, Everitt N J, Blundell J W 1991 Glomus tumour of the small bowel. Histopathology 19: 287–289

47. Usuda H, Naito M 1997 Multicentric angiosarcoma of the gastrointestinal tract. Pathol Int 47: 553–556

48. Elliott R L, Williams R D, Bayles D et al. 1966 Lymphangioma of the duodenum: case report with light and electron microscopic observation. Ann Surg 163: 86–92

49. Sarlomo-Rikala M, Miettinen M 1995 Gastric schwannoma – a clinicopathological analysis of six cases. Histopathology 27: 355–360

50. Arnesjo B, Idvall I, Ihse I et al. 1973 Concomitant occurrence of neurofibromatosis and carcinoid of the intestine. Scand J Gastroenterol 8: 637–643

51. Kheir S M, Halpern N B 1984 Paraganglioma of the duodenum in association with congenital neurofibromatosis. Possible relationship. Cancer 53: 2491–2496

52. Stephens M, Williams G T, Jasani B et al. 1987 Synchronous duodenal neuroendocrine tumours in von Recklinghausen's disease – a case report of co-existing gangliocytic paraganglioma and somatostatin-rich glandular carcinoid. Histopathology 11: 1331–1340

53. Perrone T, Sibley R K, Rosai J 1985 Duodenal gangliocytic paraganglioma. An immunohistochemical and ultrastructural study and a hypothesis concerning its origin. Am J Surg Pathol 9: 31–41

54. Burke A P, Helwig E B 1989 Gangliocytic paraganglioma. Am J Clin Pathol 92: 1–9

55. Williams E D, Pollock D J 1966 Multiple mucosal neuromata with endocrine tumours: a syndrome allied to von Recklinghausen's disease. J Pathol Bacteriol 90: 71–80

56. Weidner N, Flanders D J, Mitros F A 1984 Mucosal ganglioneuromatosis associated with multiple colonic polyps. Am J Surg Pathol 8: 779–786

57. Atwell J D, Burge D, Wright D 1985 Nodular lymphoid hyperplasia of the intestinal tract in infancy and childhood. J Pediatr Surg 20: 25–29

58. Webster A D, Kenwright S, Ballard J et al. 1977 Nodular lymphoid hyperplasia of the bowel in primary hypogammaglobulinaemia: study of in vivo and in vitro lymphocyte function. Gut 18: 364–372

59. Matuchansky C, Touchard G, Lemaire M et al. 1985 Malignant lymphoma of the small bowel associated with diffuse nodular lymphoid hyperplasia. N Engl J Med 313: 166–171

60. Domizio P, Owen R A, Shepherd N A et al. 1993 Primary lymphoma of the small intestine. A clinicopathological study of 119 cases. Am J Surg Pathol 17: 429–442

61. Levison D A, Hall P A, Blackshaw A J 1990 The gut-associated lymphoid tissue and its tumours. Curr Top Pathol 81: 133–175

62. Rambaud C, Galian A, Matuchansky C et al. 1978 Natural history of alpha-chain disease and the so-called Mediterranean lymphoma. Recent Results Cancer Res 64: 271–276

63. Swinson C M, Slavin G, Coles E C et al. 1983 Coeliac disease and malignancy. Lancet 1: 111–115

64. Shia J, Ternya-Feldstein J, Pai D et al. 2002 Primary follicular lymphoma of the gastrointestinal tract. A clinical and pathologic study of 26 cases. Am J Surg Pathol 26: 216–224

65. Isaacson P, Wright D H 1978 Malignant histiocytosis of the intestine. Its relationship to malabsorption and ulcerative jejunitis. Hum Pathol 9: 661–677

66. Smith W J, Price S K, Isaacson P G 1987 Immunoglobulin gene rearrangement in immunoproliferative small intestinal disease (IPSID). J Clin Pathol 40: 1291–1297

67. Isaacson P G, O'Connor N T, Spencer J et al. 1985 Malignant histiocytosis of the intestine: a T-cell lymphoma. Lancet 2(8457): 688–691

68. Shepherd N A, Blackshaw A J, Hall P A et al. 1987 Malignant lymphoma with eosinophilia of the gastrointestinal tract. Histopathology 11: 115–130

69. Wright D H, Jones D B, Clark H et al. 1991 Is adult-onset coeliac disease due to a low-grade lymphoma of intraepithelial T lymphocytes? Lancet 337: 1373–1374

70. Schmitt-Graff A, Hummel M, Zemlin M et al. 1996 Intestinal T-cell lymphoma: a reassessment of cytomorphological and phenotypic features in relation to patterns of small bowel remodelling. Virchows Arch 429: 27–36

71. De Castro C A, Dockerty M B, Mayo C W 1957 Metastatic tumors of the small intestines. Surg Gynecol Obstet 105: 159–165

72. Washington K, McDonagh D 1995 Secondary tumors of the gastrointestinal tract: surgical pathologic findings and comparison with autopsy survey. Mod Pathol 8: 427–433

73. Correia J P, Baptista A S, Antonio J F 1968 Slowly evolving widespread diffuse alimentary tract carcinoma (linitis plastica). Gut 9: 485–488

74. ReMine W H, Brown P W Jr, Gomes M M et al. 1970 Polypoid hamartomas of Brunner's glands. Report of six surgical cases. Arch Surg 100: 313–316

75. Burdick D, Prior J T 1982 Peutz–Jeghers syndrome. A clinicopathologic study of a large family with a 27-year follow-up. Cancer 50: 2139–2146

76. Wang Z J, Ellis I, Zauber P et al. 1999 Allelic imbalance at the LKB1 (STK11) locus in tumours from patients with Peutz–Jeghers' syndrome provides evidence for a hamartoma-(adenoma)-carcinoma sequence. J Pathol 188: 9–13

77. Hsu S D, Zaharopoulos P, May J T et al. 1979 Peutz–Jeghers syndrome with intestinal carcinoma: report of the association in one family. Cancer 44: 1527–1532

78. Riley E, Swift M 1980 A family with Peutz–Jeghers syndrome and bilateral breast cancer. Cancer 46: 815–817

79. Young R H, Welch W R, Dickersin G R et al. 1982 Ovarian sex cord tumor with annular tubules: review of 74 cases including 27 with Peutz–Jeghers syndrome and four with adenoma malignum of the cervix. Cancer 50: 1384–1402

80. Shepherd N A, Bussey H J, Jass J R 1987 Epithelial misplacement in Peutz–Jeghers polyps. A diagnostic pitfall. Am J Surg Pathol 11: 743–749

81. Barbosa J D C, Dockerty M, Waugh J 1946 Pancreatic heterotopia. Surg Gynecol Obstet 82: 527–542

82. Lai E C, Tompkins R K 1986 Heterotopic pancreas. Review of a 26 year experience. Am J Surg 151: 697–700

83. Johnstone J M, Morson B C 1978 Inflammatory fibroid polyp of the gastrointestinal tract. Histopathology 2: 349–361

84. Pantanowitz L, Antonioli D, Pinkus G A et al. 2004 Inflammatory fibroid polyps of the gastrointestinal tract: evidence for a dendritic cell origin. Am J Surg Pathol 28: 107–114

85. Elliott G B, Sandy J T, Elliott K A et al. 1968 Lipohyperplasia of the ileocecal valve. Can J Surg 11: 179–187

86. Qizilbash A H 1975 Mucoceles of the appendix. Their relationship to hyperplastic polyps, mucinous cystadenomas, and cystadenocarcinomas. Arch Pathol 99: 548–555

87. Wolff M, Ahmed N 1976 Epithelial neoplasms of the vermiform appendix (exclusive of carcinoid). II. Cystadenomas, papillary adenomas, and adenomatous polyps of the appendix. Cancer 37: 2511–2522

88. Qizilbash A H 1975 Primary adenocarcinoma of the appendix. A clinicopathological study of 11 cases. Arch Pathol 99: 556–562

89. Gilhome R W, Johnston D H, Clark J et al. 1984 Primary adenocarcinoma of the vermiform appendix: report of a series of ten cases, and review of the literature. Br J Surg 71: 553–555

90. Misdraji J, Yantiss R K, Graeme-Cook F M et al. 2003 Appendiceal mucinous neoplasms. A clinicopathologic analysis of 107 cases. Am J Surg Pathol 27: 1089–1103

91. Ronnett B M, Kurman R J, Zahn C M et al. 1995 Pseudomyxoma peritonei in women: a clinicopathologic analysis of 30 cases with emphasis on site of origin, prognosis, and relationship to ovarian mucinous tumors of low malignant potential. Hum Pathol 26: 509–524

92. Kabbani W, Houlihan P S, Luthra R et al. 2002 Mucinous and nonmucinous appendiceal adenocarcinomas: different clinicopathological features but similar genetic alterations. Mod Pathol 15: 599–605

93. Moertel C G, Weiland L H, Nagorney D M et al. 1987 Carcinoid tumor of the appendix: treatment and prognosis. N Engl J Med 317: 1699–1701

94. Lundqvist M, Wilander E 1987 A study of the histogenesis of carcinoid tumors of the small intestine and appendix. Cancer 60: 201–206

95. Shaw P A 1991 The topographical and age distributions of neuroendocrine cells in the normal human appendix. J Pathol 164: 235–239

96. Park K, Blessing K, Kerr K et al. 1990 Goblet cell carcinoid of the appendix. Gut 31: 322–324.

97. Anderson N H, Somerville J E, Johnston C F et al. 1991 Appendiceal goblet cell carcinoids: a clinicopathological and immunohistochemical study. Histopathology 18: 61–65

98. Berardi R S, Lee S S, Chen H P 1988 Goblet cell carcinoids of the appendix. Surg Gynecol Obstet 167: 81–86

99. Subbuswamy S G, Gibbs N M, Ross C F et al. 1974 Goblet cell carcinoid of the appendix. Cancer 34: 338–344

100. Warkel R L, Cooper P H, Helwig E B 1978 Adenocarcinoid, a mucin-producing carcinoid tumor of the appendix: a study of 39 cases. Cancer 42: 2781–2793

101. Isaacson P 1981 Crypt cell carcinoma of the appendix (so-called adenocarcinoid tumor). Am J Surg Pathol 5: 213–224

102. Burke A P, Sobin L H, Federspiel B H et al. 1990 Goblet cell carcinoids and related tumors of the vermiform appendix. Am J Clin Pathol 94: 27–35

103. Zarabi M, LaBach J P 1982 Ganglioneuroma causing acute appendicitis. Hum Pathol 13: 1143–1146

104. Olsen B S, Holck S 1987 Neurogenous hyperplasia leading to appendiceal obliteration: an immunohistochemical study of 237 cases. Histopathology 11: 843–849

105. Clark J C, Collan Y, Eide T J et al. 1985 Prevalence of polyps in an autopsy series from areas with varying incidence of large-bowel cancer. Int J Cancer 36: 179–186

106. Johannsen L G, Momsen O, Jacobsen N O 1989 Polyps of the large intestine in Aarhus, Denmark. An autopsy study. Scand J Gastroenterol 24: 799–806

107. Hoff G, Foerster A, Vatn M H et al. 1985 Epidemiology of polyps in the rectum and sigmoid colon. Histological examination of resected polyps. Scand J Gastroenterol 20: 677–683

108. Jass J R, Young P J, Robinson E M 1992 Predictors of presence, multiplicity, size and dysplasia of colorectal adenomas. A necropsy study in New Zealand. Gut 33: 1508–1514

109. Williams A R, Balasooriya B A, Day D W 1982 Polyps and cancer of the large bowel: a necropsy study in Liverpool. Gut 23: 835–842

110. Konishi F, Morson B C 1982 Pathology of colorectal adenomas: a colonoscopic survey. J Clin Pathol 35: 830–841

111. Burt R W, Bishop T, Cannon L A et al. 1985 Dominant inheritance of adenomatous colonic polyps and colorectal cancer. N Engl J Med 312: 540

112. Aitken J F, Bain C J, Ward M et al. 1996 Risk of colorectal adenomas in patients with a family history of colorectal cancer: some implications for screening programmes. Gut 39: 105–108

113. Pollock A M, Quirke P 1991 Adenoma screening and colorectal cancer. The need for screening and polypectomy is unproved. Br J Med 303: 3–4

114. Muto T, Kamiya J, Sawada T et al. 1985 Small "flat adenoma" of the large bowel with special reference to its clinicopathologic features. Dis Colon Rectum 28: 847–851

115. Kuramoto S, Ihara O, Sakai S et al. 1990 Depressed adenoma in the large intestine. Endoscopic features. Dis Colon Rectum 33: 108–112

116. Muto T, Bussey H J, Morson B C 1973 Pseudo-carcinomatous invasion in adenomatous polyps of the colon and rectum. J Clin Pathol 26: 25–31

117. Muto T, Bussey H J, Morson B C 1975 The evolution of cancer of the colon and rectum. Cancer 36: 2251–2270

118. Longacre T A, Fenoglio-Preiser C M 1990 Mixed hyperplastic adenomatous polyps/serrated adenomas. A distinct form of colorectal neoplasia. Am J Surg Pathol 14: 524–537

119. Iino H, Jass J R, Simms L A et al. 1999 DNA microsatellite instability in hyperplastic polyps, serrated adenomas, and mixed polyps: a mild mutator pathway for colorectal cancer? J Clin Pathol 52: 5–9

120. Jass J R 2004 Hyperplastic polyps and colorectal cancer: is there a link? Clin Gastroenterol Hepatol 2: 1–8

121. Jass J R 2002 Serrated adenoma of the colorectum. Curr Diagn Pathol 8: 42–49

122. Kang M, Mitomi H, Sada M et al. 1997 Ki-67, p53, and Bcl-2 expression of serrated adenomas of the colon. Am J Surg Pathol 21: 417–423

123. Torlakovic E, Snover D C 1996 Serrated adenomatous polyposis in humans. Gastroenterology 110: 748–755

124. Torlakovic E, Skovlund E, Snover D C et al. 2003 Morphologic reappraisal of serrated colorectal polyps. Am J Surg Pathol 27: 65–81

125. Goldstein N S, Bhanot P, Odish E et al. 2003 Hyperplastic-like colon polyps that preceded microsatellite unstable adenocarcinomas. Am J Clin Pathol 119: 778–796

125a. Higuchi T, Sugihara K, Jass J R 2005 Demographic and pathological characteristics of serrated polyps of colorectum. Histopathology 47: 32–40

126. Kambara T, Simms L A, Whitehall V L J et al. 2004 BRAF mutation and CpG island methylation: an alternative pathway to colorectal cancer. Gut 53: 1137–1144

127. Bussey H J R 1975 Familial polyposis coli. Johns Hopkins Press, Baltimore

128. Bodmer W F, Bailey C J, Bodmer J et al. 1987 Localization of the gene for familial adenomatous polyposis on chromosome 5. Nature 328: 614–616

129. Groden J, Thliveris A, Samowitz W et al. 1991 Identification and characterization of the familial adenomatous polyposis gene. Cell 66: 589–600

130. Nishisho I, Nakamura Y, Miyoshi Y et al. 1991 Mutations of chromosome 5q21 genes in FAP and colorectal cancer patients. Science 253: 665–669

131. Al-Tassan N, Chmiel N H, Maynard J et al. 2002 Inherited variants of MYH associated with somatic G:C – T:A mutations in colorectal tumors. Nature Genet 30: 227–232

132. Spirio L, Olschwang S, Groden J et al. 1993 Alleles of the APC gene: an attenuated form of familial polyposis. Cell 75: 951–957

133. Jagelman D G, DeCosse J J, Bussey H J R 1988 Upper gastrointestinal cancer in familial adenomatous polyposis. Lancet 1: 1149–1151

134. Gardner E J 1962 Follow-up study of a family group exhibiting dominant inheritance for a syndrome including intestinal polyps, osteomas, fibromas and epidermal cysts. Am J Hum Genet 14: 376–390

135. Gebert J F, Dupon C, Kadmon M et al. 1999 Combined molecular and clinical approaches for the identification of families with familial adenomatous polyposis coli. Ann Surg 229: 350–361

136. Simpson R D, Harrison E G Jr, Mayo C W 1964 Mesenteric fibromatosis in familial polyposis. A variant of Gardner's syndrome. Cancer 17: 526–534

137. Utsunomiya J, Nakamura T 1975 The occult osteomatous changes in the mandible in patients with familial polyposis coli. Br J Surg 62: 45–51

138. Heyen F, Jagelman D G, Romania A et al. 1990 Predictive value of congenital hypertrophy of the retinal pigment epithelium as a clinical marker for familial adenomatous polyposis. Dis Colon Rectum 33: 1003–1008

139. Kingston J E, Herbert A, Draper G J et al. 1983 Association between hepatoblastoma and polyposis coli. Arch Dis Child 58: 959–962

140. Thompson J S, Harned R K, Anderson J C et al. 1983 Papillary carcinoma of the thyroid and familial polyposis coli. Dis Colon Rectum 26: 583–585

141. Turcot J, Despré J-P, St Pierre F 1959 Malignant tumors of the central nervous system associated with familial polyposis of the colon: report of two cases. Dis Colon Rectum 2: 465–468

142. Hamilton S R, Liu B, Parsons R E et al. 1995 The molecular basis of Turcot's syndrome. N Engl J Med 332: 839–847

143. Vasen H F A, van der Luijt R B, Slors J F M et al. 1996 Molecular genetic tests as a guide to surgical management of familial adenomatous polyposis. Lancet 348: 433–435

144. Boyle P, Zaridze D G, Smans M 1985 Descriptive epidemiology of colorectal cancer. Int J Cancer 36: 9–18

145. Kune G 1996 Causes and control of colorectal cancer. A model for cancer prevention. Kluwer, Boston

146. Wynder E L, Reddy B S 1974 The epidemiology of cancer of the large bowel. Am J Dig Dis 19: 937–946

147. Burkitt D P 1971 Epidemiology of cancer of the colon and rectum. Cancer 28: 3–13

148. Jass J R 1991 Subsite distribution and incidence of colorectal cancer in New Zealand 1974–1983. Dis Colon Rectum 34: 56–59

149. Isbister W H, Fraser J 1990 Large-bowel cancer in the young: a national survival study. Dis Colon Rectum 33: 363–366

150. Jass J R, Do K-A, Simms L A et al. 1998 Morphology of sporadic colorectal cancer with DNA replication errors. Gut 42: 673–679

151. Jass J R 1989 Do all colorectal carcinomas arise in preexisting adenomas? World J Surg 13: 45–51

152. Lee Y S 1988 Early malignant lesions of the colorectum at autopsy. Dis Colon Rectum 31: 291–297

153. Hunt D R, Cherian M 1990 Endoscopic diagnosis of small flat carcinoma of the colon: report of three cases. Dis Colon Rectum 33: 143–147

154. Shimoda T, Ikegami M, Fujisaki J et al. 1989 Early colorectal carcinoma with special reference to its development de novo. Cancer 64: 1138–1146

155. Jass J R, Whitehall V L J, Young J et al. 2002 Emerging concepts in colorectal neoplasia. Gastroenterology 123: 862–876

156. Riddell R H, Goldman H, Ransohoff D F et al. 1983 Dysplasia in inflammatory bowel disease: standardized classification with provisional clinical applications. Hum Pathol 14: 931–968

157. Ming-Chai C, Chi-Yuan C, Pei-Yu C et al. 1980 Evolution of colorectal cancer in schistosomiasis: transitional mucosal changes adjacent to large intestinal carcinoma in colectomy specimens. Cancer 46: 1661–1675

158. Hamilton S R 1985 Colorectal carcinoma in patients with Crohn's disease. Gastroenterology 89: 398–407

159. Jass J R, Williams C B, Bussey H J R et al. 1988 Juvenile polyposis – a precancerous condition. Histopathology 13: 619–630

160. Qizilbash A H 1974 Radiation-induced carcinoma of the rectum. A late complication of pelvic irradiation. Arch Pathol 98: 118–121

161. Mecklin J-P 1987 Frequency of hereditary colorectal carcinoma. Gastroenterology 93: 1021–1025

162. Kinzler K W, Vogelstein B 1996 Lessons from hereditary colorectal cancer. Cell 87: 159–170

163. Jass J R, Stewart S M 1992 Evolution of hereditary non-polyposis colorectal cancer. Gut 33: 783–786

164. Weitzer M, Pokos V, Jeevaratnam P et al. 1995 Isolated expression of the Muir–Torre phenotype in a member of a family with hereditary non-polyposis colorectal cancer. Histopathology 27: 573–575

165. Quirke P, Durdey P, Dixon M F et al. 1986 Local recurrence of rectal adenocarcinoma due to inadequate surgical resection. Histopathological study of lateral tumour spread and surgical excision. Lancet 2(8514): 996–999

166. Newland R C, Chapuis P H, Smyth E J 1987 The prognostic value of substaging colorectal carcinoma. A prospective study of 1117 cases with standardized pathology. Cancer 60: 852–857

167. Adam I J, Mohamdee M O, Martin I G et al. 1994 Role of circumferential margin involvement in the local recurrence of rectal cancer. Lancet 344: 707–711

168. Finlay I, McArdle C S 1986 Occult hepatic metastases in colorectal carcinoma. Br J Surg 73: 732–735

169. Shepherd N A, Baxter K R, Love S B 1997 The prognostic importance of peritoneal involvement in colonic cancer: a prospective evaluation. Gastroenterology 112: 1096–1102

170. Kirwan W O, Drumm J, Hogan J M et al. 1988 Determining safe margin of resection in low anterior resection for rectal cancer. Br J Surg 75: 720

171. Cross S S, Bull A D, Smith J H 1989 Is there any justification for the routine examination of bowel resection margins in colorectal adenocarcinoma? J Clin Pathol 42: 1040–1042

172. Loy T S, Kaplan P A 2004 Villous adenocarcinoma of the colon and rectum: a clinicopathologic study of 36 cases. Am J Surg Pathol 28: 1460–1465

173. Sasaki P, Atkin W S, Jass J R 1987 Mucinous carcinoma of the rectum. Histopathology 11: 259–272

174. Connelly J H, Robey-Cafferty S S, el-Naggar A K et al. 1991 Exophytic signet-ring cell carcinoma of the colorectum. Arch Pathol Lab Med 115: 134–136

175. Jass J R, Smyrk T C, Stewart S M et al. 1994 Pathology of hereditary non-polyposis colorectal cancer. Anticancer Res 14: 1631–1634

176. Kim H, Jen J, Vogelstein B et al. 1994 Clinical and pathological characteristics of sporadic colorectal carcinomas with DNA replication errors in microsatellite sequences. Am J Pathol 145: 148–156

177. Gaffey M J, Mills S E, Lack E E 1990 Neuroendocrine carcinoma of the colon and rectum. A clinicopathologic, ultrastructural, and immunohistochemical study of 24 cases. Am J Surg Pathol 14: 1010–1023

178. Gibbs N M 1977 Undifferentiated carcinoma of the large intestine. Histopathology 1: 77–84

179. Jessurun J, Romero-Guadarrama M, Manivel J C 1999 Medullary adenocarcinoma of the colon: clinicopathologic study of 11 cases. Hum Pathol 30: 843–848

180. Wick M R, Vitsky J L, Ritter J H et al. 2005 Sporadic medullary carcinoma of the colon. Am J Clin Pathol 123: 56–65

181. Jass J R, Atkin W S, Cuzick J et al. 1986 The grading of rectal cancer: historical perspectives and a multivariate analysis of 447 cases. Histopathology 10: 437–459

182. Quirke P, Dixon M F, Clayden A D et al. 1987 Prognostic significance of DNA aneuploidy and cell proliferation in rectal adenocarcinomas. J Pathol 151: 285–291

183. Jass J R, Ajioka Y, Allen J P et al. 1996 Assessment of invasive growth pattern and lymphocytic infiltration in colorectal cancer. Histopathology 28: 543–548

184. Ueno H, Murphy J, Jass J R et al. 2002 Tumour 'budding' as an index to estimate the potential of aggressiveness in rectal cancer. Histopathology 40: 127–132

185. Halvorsen T B, Seim E 1989 Association between invasiveness, inflammatory reaction, desmoplasia and survival in colorectal cancer. J Clin Pathol 42: 162–166

186. Greenson J K, Bonner J D, Ben-Yzhak O et al. 2003 Phenotype of microsatellite unstable colorectal carcinomas. Am J Surg Pathol 27: 563–570

187. Wright C M, Dent O F, Barker M et al. 2000 The prognostic significance of extensive microsatellite instability in sporadic clinicopathological stage C colorectal cancer. Br J Surg 87: 1197–1202

188. Hermanek P, Sobin L 1987 UICC TNM classification of malignant tulours, 4th edn. Springer-Verlag, Berlin

189. Hermanek P, Gall F P, Altendorf A 1980 Prognostic groups in colorectal carcinoma. J Cancer Res Clin Oncol 98: 185–193

190. Dukes C E, Bussey H J 1958 The spread of rectal cancer and its effect on prognosis. Br J Cancer 12: 309–320

191. Liefers G-J, Cleton-Jansen A-M, van de Velde C J H et al. 1998 Micrometastases and survival in stage II colorectal cancer. N Engl J Med 339: 223–228

192. Talbot I C, Ritchie S, Leighton M et al. 1981 Invasion of veins by carcinoma of rectum: method of detection, histological features and significance. Histopathology 5: 141–163

193. Knudsen J B, Nilsson T, Sprechler M et al. 1983 Venous and nerve invasion as prognostic factors in postoperative survival of patients with resectable cancer of the rectum. Dis Colon Rectum 26: 613–617

194. Morson B C 1966 Factors influencing the prognosis of early cancer of the rectum. Proc R Soc Med 59: 607–608

195. Morson B C, Whiteway J E, Jones E A et al. 1984 Histopathology and prognosis of malignant colorectal polyps treated by endoscopic polypectomy. Gut 25: 437–444

196. Muller S, Chesner I M, Egan M J et al. 1989 Significance of venous and lymphatic invasion in malignant polyps of the colon and rectum. Gut 30: 1385–1391

197. Geraghty J M, Williams C B, Talbot I C 1991 Malignant colorectal polyps: venous invasion and successful treatment by endoscopic polypectomy. Gut 32: 774–778

198. Whiteway J, Nicholls R J, Morson B C 1985 The role of surgical local excision in the treatment of rectal cancer. Br J Surg 72: 694–697

199. Werling R W, Yaziji H, Bacchi C E et al. 2003 CDX2, a highly sensitive and specific marker of adenocarcinomas of intestinal origin: an immunohistochemical survey of 476 primary and metastatic carcinomas. Am J Surg Pathol 27: 303–310

200. Vogelstein B, Fearon E R, Hamilton S R et al. 1988 Genetic alterations during colorectal-tumor development. N Engl J Med 319: 525–532

201. Smith G, Carey F A, Beattie J et al. 2002 Mutations in APC, Kirsten-ras, and p53 – alternative genetic pathways to colorectal cancer. Proc Natl Acad Sci (USA) 99: 9433–9438

202. Young J, Simms L A, Biden K G et al. 2001 Features of colorectal cancers with high-level microsatellite instability occurring in familial and sporadic settings: parallel pathways of tumorigenesis. Am J Pathol 159: 2107–2116

203. Kane M F, Loda M, Gaida G M et al. 1997 Methylation of the hMLH1 promoter correlates with lack of expression of hMLH1 in sporadic colon tumors and mismatch repair-defective human tumor cell lines. Cancer Res 57: 808–811

204. Ribic C M, Sargent D J, Moore M J et al. 2003 Tumor microsatellite instability status as a predictor of benefit from fluorouracil-based adjuvant chemotherapy for colon cancer. N Engl J Med 349: 247–257

205. Bardi G, Fenger C, Johansson B et al. 2004 Tumor karyotype predicts clinical outcome in colorectal cancer patients. J Clin Oncol 22: 2623–2634

206. Epstein S E, Ascari W Q, Ablow R C et al. 1966 Colitis cystica profunda. Am J Clin Pathol 45: 186–201

207. Federspiel B H, Burke A P, Sobin L H et al. 1990 Rectal and colonic carcinoids. A clinicopathologic study of 84 cases. Cancer 65: 135–140

208. Koura A N, Giacco G G, Curley S A et al. 1997 Carcinoid tumors of the rectum: effect of size, histopathology, and surgical treatment on metastasis free survival. Cancer 79: 1294–1298

209. Gledhill A, Hall P A, Cruse J P et al. 1986 Enteroendocrine cell hyperplasia, carcinoid tumours and adenocarcinoma in long-standing ulcerative colitis. Histopathology 10: 501–508

210. Moyana T N, Friesen R, Tan L K 1991 Colorectal smooth muscle tumors. A pathobiologic study with immunohistochemistry and histomorphometry. Arch Pathol Lab Med 115: 1016–1021

211. Tworek J A, Goldblum J R, Weiss S W et al. 1999 Stromal tumors of the abdominal colon: a clinicopathologic study of 20 cases. Am J Surg Pathol 23: 937–945

212. Walsh T H, Mann C V 1984 Smooth muscle neoplasms of the rectum and anal canal. Br J Surg 71: 597–599.

213. Tworek J A, Goldblum J R, Weiss S W et al. 1999 Stromal tumors of the anorectum: a clinicopathologic study of 22 cases. Am J Surg Pathol 23: 946–954

214. Miettinen M, Sarlomo-Rikala M, Sobin L H et al. 2000 Gastrointestinal stromal tumors and leiomyosarcomas in the colon: a clinicopathologic, immunohistochemical and molecular genetic study of 44 cases. Am J Surg Pathol 24: 1339–1352

215. Michowitz M, Lazebnik N, Noy S et al. 1985 Lipoma of the colon. A report of 22 cases. Am Surg 51: 449–454

215a. Hornick J L, Fletcher C D 2005 Intestinal perineuriomas: clinicopathologic definition of a new anatomic subset in a series of 10 cases. Am J Surg Pathol 29: 859–865

216. Shekitka K M, Sobin L H 1994 Ganglioneuromas of the gastrointestinal tract. Relation to Von Recklinghausen disease and other multiple tumor syndromes. Am J Surg Pathol 18: 250–257

217. Mendelsohn G, Diamond M P 1984 Familial ganglioneuromatous polyposis of the large bowel. Report of a family with associated juvenile polyposis. Am J Surg Pathol 8: 515–520

218. d'Amore E S, Manivel J C, Pettinato G et al. 1991 Intestinal ganglioneuromatosis: mucosal and transmural types. A clinicopathologic and immunohistochemical study of six cases. Hum Pathol 22: 276–286

219. Shepherd N A, Jass J R 1987 Neuromuscular and vascular hamartoma of the small intestine: is it Crohn's disease? Gut 28: 1663–1668

220. Friedman S L, Wright T L, Altman D F 1985 Gastrointestinal Kaposi's sarcoma in patients with acquired immunodeficiency syndrome. Endoscopic and autopsy findings. Gastroenterology 89: 102–108

221. Shepherd N A, Hall P A, Coates P J et al. 1988 Primary malignant lymphoma of the colon and rectum. A histopathological and immunohistochemical analysis of 45 cases with clinicopathological correlations. Histopathology 12: 235–252

222. Shepherd N A, Hall P A, Williams G T et al. 1989 Primary malignant lymphoma of the large intestine complicating chronic inflammatory bowel disease. Histopathology 15: 325–337

223. Isaacson P G, MacLennan K A, Subbuswamy S G 1984 Multiple lymphomatous polyposis of the gastrointestinal tract. Histopathology 8: 641–656

224. Mestre J R 1986 The changing pattern of juvenile polyps. Am J Gastroenterol 81: 312–314

225. Roth S, Sistonen P, Salovaara R et al. 1999 SMAD genes in juvenile polyposis. Genes Chromosomes Cancer 26: 54–61

226. Haggitt R C, Reid B J 1986 Hereditary gastrointestinal polyposis syndromes. Am J Surg Pathol 10: 871–887

227. Nelen M R, Padberg G W, Peeters E A J et al. 1996 Localization of the gene for Cowden disease to chromosome 10q22-23. Nature Genet 13: 114–116

228. Eng C 1998 Genetics of Cowden syndrome: through the looking glass of oncology. Int J Oncol 12: 701–710

229. Wolff M 1971 Heterotopic gastric epithelium in the rectum: a report of three new cases with a review of 87 cases of gastric heterotopia in the alimentary canal. Am J Clin Pathol 55: 604–616

230. Arthur J F 1968 Structure and significance of metaplastic nodules in the rectal mucosa. J Clin Pathol 21: 735–743

231. Cappell M S, Forde K A 1989 Spatial clustering of multiple hyperplastic, adenomatous, and malignant colonic polyps in individual patients. Dis Colon Rectum 32: 641–652

232. Williams G T 1997 Metaplastic (hyperplastic) polyps of the large bowel: benign neoplasms after all? Gut 40: 691–692

233. Jeevaratnam P, Cottier D S, Browett P J et al. 1996 Familial giant hyperplastic polyposis predisposing to colorectal cancer: a new hereditary bowel cancer syndrome. J Pathol 179: 20–25

234. Jass J R, Faludy J 1985 Immunohistochemical demonstration of IgA and secretory component in relation to epithelial cell differentiation in normal colorectal mucosa and metaplastic polyp: a semiquantitative study. Histochem J 17: 373–380

235. Sobin L H 1985 Inverted hyperplastic polyps of the colon. Am J Surg Pathol 9: 265–272

236. Williams G T, Arthur J F, Bussey H J R et al. 1980 Metaplastic polyps and polyposis of the colorectum. Histopathology 4: 155–170

237. Bengoechea O, Martinez-Penuela J M, Larrinaga B et al. 1987 Hyperplastic polyposis of the colorectum and adenocarcinoma in a 24 year old man. Am J Surg Pathol 11: 323–327
238. Kindblom L G, Angervall L, Santesson B et al. 1977 Cronkhite–Canada syndrome. Case report. Cancer 39: 2651–2657
239. du Boulay C E, Fairbrother J, Isaacson P G 1983 Mucosal prolapse syndrome – a unifying concept for solitary ulcer syndrome and related disorders. J Clin Pathol 36: 1264–1268
240. Madigan M R, Morson B C 1969 Solitary ulcer of the rectum. Gut 10: 871–881
241. Burke A P, Sobin L H 1990 Eroded polypoid hyperplasia of the rectosigmoid. Am J Gastroenterol 85: 975–980
242. Nakamura S, Kino I, Akagi T 1992 Inflammatory myoglandular polyps of the colon and rectum. A clinicopathological study of 32 pedunculated polyps, distinct from other types of polyps. Am J Surg Pathol 16: 772–779
243. Lobert P F, Appelman H D 1981 Inflammatory cloacogenic polyp. A unique inflammatory lesion of the anal transitional zone. Am J Surg Pathol 5: 761–766
244. Rowland R, Langman J M 1989 Endometriosis of the large bowel: a report of 11 cases. Pathology 21: 259–265
245. Sanusi I D, Tio F O 1974 Gastrointestinal malacoplakia. Report of a case and a review of the literature. Am J Gastroenterol 62: 356–366
246. Croxson T, Chabon A B, Rorat E et al. 1984 Intraepithelial carcinoma of the anus in homosexual men. Dis Colon Rectum 27: 325–330
247. Palmer J G, Shepherd N A, Jass J R et al. 1987 Human papillomavirus type 16 DNA in anal squamous cell carcinoma. Lancet 2(8549): 42
248. Morson B C, Pang L S 1968 Pathology of anal cancer. Proc R Soc Med 61: 623–624
249. Wick M R, Weatherby R P, Weiland L H 1987 Small cell neuroendocrine carcinoma of the colon and rectum: clinical, histologic, and ultrastructural study and immunohistochemical comparison with cloacogenic carcinoma. Hum Pathol 18: 9–21
250. Fenger C, Nielsen V T 1986 Precancerous changes in the anal canal epithelium in resection specimens. Acta Pathol Microbiol Immunol Scand [A] 94: 63–69
251. Shepherd N A, Schofield J H, Love S B et al. 1990 Prognostic factors in anal squamous carcinoma: a multivariate analysis of clinical, pathological and flow cytometric parameters in 235 cases. Histopathology 16: 545–555
252. Boman B M, Moertel C G, O'Connell M J et al. 1984 Carcinoma of the anal canal. A clinical and pathologic study of 188 cases. Cancer 54: 114–125
253. Bogomoletz W V, Potet F, Molas G 1985 Condylomata acuminata, giant condyloma acuminatum (Buschke–Loewenstein tumour) and verrucous squamous carcinoma of the perianal and anorectal region: a continuous precancerous spectrum? Histopathology 9: 155–169
254. Jones E A, Morson B C 1984 Mucinous adenocarcinoma in anorectal fistulae. Histopathology 8: 279–292
255. Hobbs C M, Lowry M A, Owen D et al. 2001 Anal gland carcinoma. Cancer 92: 2045–2049
256. Goldman S, Glimelius B, Pahlman L 1990 Anorectal malignant melanoma in Sweden. Report of 49 patients. Dis Colon Rectum 33: 874–877
257. Brady M S, Kavolius J P, Quan S H 1995 Anorectal melanoma. A 64-year experience at Memorial Sloan-Kettering Cancer Center. Dis Colon Rectum 38: 146–151
258. Ben-Izhak O, Levy R, Weill S et al. 1997 Anorectal malignant melanoma. A clinicopathologic study, including immunohistochemistry and DNA flow cytometry. Cancer 79: 18–25
259. Mills S E, Walker A N, Stallings R G et al. 1984 Retrorectal cystic hamartoma. Report of three cases, including one with a perirenal component. Arch Pathol Lab Med 108: 737–740
260. Marco V, Autonell J, Farre J et al. 1982 Retrorectal cyst-hamartomas. Report of two cases with adenocarcinoma developing in one. Am J Surg Pathol 6: 707–714
261. Ikenberg H, Gissmann L, Gross G et al. 1983 Human papillomavirus type-16-related DNA in genital Bowen's disease and in Bowenoid papulosis. Int J Cancer 32: 563–565
262. Elliott G B, Fisher B K 1967 Perianal keratoacanthoma. Arch Dermatol 95: 81–82
263. Nielsen O V, Jensen S L 1981 Basal cell carcinoma of the anus – a clinical study of 34 cases. Br J Surg 68: 856–857
264. Meeker J H, Neubecker R D, Helwig E B 1962 Hidradenoma papilliferum. Am J Clin Pathol 37: 182–195
265. Donaldson D, Jass J, Mann C 1987 Anal leukoplakia. Gut 28: A1368
266. Armitage N C, Jass J R, Richman P I et al. 1989 Paget's disease of the anus: a clinicopathological study. Br J Surg 76: 60–63

Tumors of the liver, gallbladder, and biliary tree

10

Linda Ferrell   Sanjay Kakar

Benign hepatocellular lesions in non-cirrhotic liver

Hepatic adenoma

Clinical features

Hepatic adenomas (HA) are rare tumors that are seen almost exclusively (95%) in young women during their reproductive years and are only rarely found in men[1,2] or children.[3] HA are solitary lesions that occur in a liver that is histologically normal or nearly normal. Rare instances of "liver cell adenomatosis" have been recorded, with nodules described as "more than 10" or "numerous" and often small.[4–6] It is unclear whether these tumors represent a distinct entity. The lack of a relationship with female gender and synthetic gonadal steroids was suggested in the past,[4] but a later report found that 74% of affected patients were women and 46% had taken oral contraceptives.[7] This study also showed an association with diabetes in all cases of adenomatosis and familial association in 10% of patients.

The clinical presentation is generally that of an abdominal mass, but some patients also have abdominal pain, discomfort, or nausea. Rupture and hemorrhage with hemoperitoneum can occur with larger tumors.[8] Serum alkaline phosphatase may be elevated, but serum alpha-fetoprotein (AFP) levels are generally normal or minimally elevated. HA appears as a hyperdense heterogenous tumor on computed tomography (CT) occasionally with central hemorrhage, and does not show uptake on Tc-scintigraphy. However, precise diagnosis is often not possible even with the combination of new imaging techniques.[9,10]

HAs are thought to result from the use of oral contraceptives: most patients have used them for more than 5 years before diagnosis.[11–13] However, with the low-dose pills now widely used, the incidence may be decreasing. Other related agents like anabolic steroids, clomiphene, danazol, and carbamazepine have also been associated with HA.[14–17] Other risk factors include Klinefelter syndrome and metabolic disorders, especially glycogen storage diseases I and IV, galactosemia, familial diabetes mellitus, and tyrosinemia.[18,19] Other rare associations include severe combined immunodeficiency and familial adenomatous polyposis.[18,20] Two cases of primary liver cell adenoma of the placenta have also been described.[21] The diagnosis of HA should be made with caution in the absence of hormonal or metabolic etiologies, as they may represent well-differentiated hepatocellular carcinoma (HCC). It has been suggested that these patients should be investigated for abnormal secretion of sex steroids.[22] The consensus opinion of the International Working Party is that the diagnosis of adenoma should not be made for a lesion arising in a cirrhotic liver, unless there is evidence of regression when the stimulus is removed or one of the above risk factors is present.[23]

Pathologic features

Gross pathology. HAs tend to bulge on cut section, and are soft and typically lighter in color than the surrounding liver, but the appearance may vary if necrosis or hemorrhage is present. The size can be extremely variable, but most tumors are larger than 10 cm. The tumor may or may not be encapsulated, and if a capsule is present, it is often incomplete, with foci of tumor cells merging with the adjacent parenchyma. HA generally lacks significant fibrosis or nodularity, but rarely, such features may be present.[24] Less commonly, adenomas may be bile-stained or have a slate-gray to black color due to the presence of large amounts of lipofuscin pigment, the so-called black adenoma.[19] All tumors are highly vascular and those associated with anabolic/androgenic steroids may also show macroscopic peliosis. Areas of scarring indicate previous episodes of infarction.

Microscopic features. HA is composed of a uniform population of hepatocytes arranged in 1–3-cell-thick plates (Fig. 10.1). The cell plates are usually more irregular and non-linear than in the normal liver. A key feature is that the reticulin framework of the cell plates is intact and similar to that in normal liver, or only focally decreased. The tumor cells are usually the same size as normal hepatocytes, with normal nuclear-to-cytoplasmic ratio. The cytoplasm may be eosinophilic or clear (Fig. 10.2), and contain fat, bile, or lipofuscin pigment. Periodic acid–Schiff (PAS)-positive diastase-resistant globules, giant mitochondria, and Mallory bodies may be noted, but are not prominent. Other occasional variations in cellular morphology include multinucleation, focal atypia, and nuclear pleomorphism. Regardless of the cellular morphology, mitotic figures are absent or extremely rare. Variations in architecture such as the formation of acini (pseudoglands, or gland-like structures composed of hepatocytes) are common; such acinar structures can contain bile. Alterations in the sinusoids can also be present; they may appear compressed, resulting in a somewhat uniform, solid appearance to the tumor, or alternatively, sinusoidal dilatation or peliosis hepatis may be present. Large vessels are often quite prominent. Areas of infarction and hemorrhage are frequent findings. Organization of these foci can lead to fibrous scars. Kupffer cells may be

seen but tend to be fewer in number than in normal liver. Adenomas associated with anabolic steroids are more likely to show nuclear atypia, prominent nucleoli, peliosis hepatitis, or a prominent acinar (pseudoglandular) pattern.[19,23] By definition, portal zones are absent and the presence of bile ductules rules out the diagnosis of adenoma. The presence of arterioles without accompanying bile ducts and surrounded by scant connective tissue is a characteristic feature of HA ("naked" arterioles).

HA expresses the usual hepatocellular markers, including cytokeratin CAM5.2 and the canalicular marker polyclonal carcinoembryonic antigen (CEA). HA will often show CD34-positivity on the endothelial cells lining the cell plates (Fig. 10.3), similar to that seen in focal nodular hyperplasia (FNH) and HCC. Hence CD34 is not useful in distinguishing these lesions.[25] AFP is negative in HA.

Differential diagnosis

Diagnostic problems most often arise in the differentiation of HA from FNH, well-differentiated HCC, fetal or macrotrabecular hepatoblastoma, and monotypic angiomyolipoma (AML). Compared to HCC, HA shows a relatively uniform cell population resembling normal liver with cell plates three cells or less in thickness, no mitotic activity, and an intact reticulin framework lining the cell plates. History of steroid use and absence of cirrhosis also support HA (Table 10.1). Immunohistochemistry is not helpful in the differential diagnosis. HCC show consistent chromosomal changes, such as gains of 1q, 7q, 8q, and loss of 16q. These changes are observed even in small well-differentiated cases. In contrast, HAs generally lack gross chromosomal abnormalities. Demonstration of these chromosomal gains and losses by comparative genomic hybridization or fluorescence in-situ hybridization can be helpful in differential diagnosis.[26,27] The other differential diagnoses are discussed in later sections.

Prognosis and outcome

Some HAs associated with oral contraceptives regress after withdrawal of the drugs, but the majority do not. Rarely, HCCs have been found arising within HA.[12,24] The risk of HCC

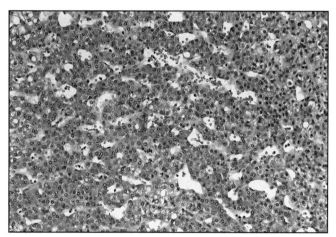

Fig. 10.1 • Hepatic adenoma. Regular plate architecture 1–2 cells thick, low nuclear-to-cytoplasmic ratio, and absence of portal tracts.

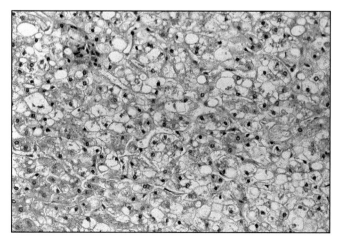

Fig. 10.2 • Hepatic adenoma with clear cell features.

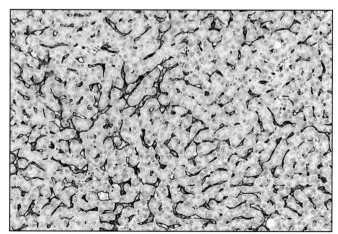

Fig. 10.3 • Hepatic adenoma. CD34 stain shows positive staining along sinusoids.

Table 10.1	Distinction between focal nodular hyperplasia, hepatic adenoma, and hepatocellular carcinoma		
	Focal nodular hyperplasia	Hepatic adenoma	Hepatocellular carcinoma
Clinical features			
Age/gender	All ages; most common in young women	Nearly all women, in their third or fourth decade	More common in men (3×)
Steroid use	Occasional	Almost always	Generally absent
Background liver	Normal	Normal	Cirrhosis (>80%)
Alpha-fetoprotein	Normal	Normal	Often elevated; can be normal in small tumors
Radiology	Homogeneous enhancement on CT and MRI. Normal or increased uptake on scintigraphy. Hypovascular on angiography	Heterogeneous mass on CT and MRI. Decreased uptake on scintigraphy. Hypervascular on angiography	Arterial phase enhancement on CT with contrast. High vascularity on angiography
Morphologic features			
Capsule	Absent	May be present	May be present
Number	Can be multiple	Usually solitary	Solitary or multiple
Central scar	Present	Absent	Absent, except in some fibrolamellar hepatocellular carcinomas
Hemorrhage/necrosis	Rare	Common	Common in larger tumors
Parenchyma	Nodular	Homogeneous	Nodular or homogeneous
Bile	Absent	Can be present	Can be present
Bile ductular proliferation	Present	Absent	Absent
Interlobular bile ducts	Absent	Absent	Absent
Vessels	Aberrant arterioles with myointimal thickening present in fibrous stroma	"Naked" arterioles without bile ducts accompanied by scant stroma	"Naked" arterioles without bile ducts accompanied by scant stroma
Cell plates	1–3 cells thick	1–3 cells thick	Usually >3 cells thick
Kupffer cells	Present	Reduced/absent	Absent
Nuclear atypia	Absent	Absent/minimal	Often present
Nuclear-to-cytoplasmic ratio	Normal	Normal	Increased
Nucleoli	Variable	Variable	Often prominent
Mitoses	Absent	Absent	Often present
Reticulin	Normal	Normal	Often decreased or absent
Immunohistochemistry			
CD34 in sinusoids	Can be positive	Often positive	Positive
Molecular techniques			
Clonality	Polyclonal (some variants can be monoclonal)	Monoclonal	Monoclonal
FISH, CGH	Not known	Normal or minimal abnormalities	Characteristic chromosomal changes (gains of 1q, 7q, 8q; loss of 16q)

CT, computed tomography; MRI, magnetic resonance imaging; FISH, fluorescent in-situ hybridization; CGH, comparative genomic hybridization.

developing in an adenoma may be low,[28] but surgical resection has been advocated in all cases in view of the potentially fatal complication of rupture and hemoperitoneum. Management of adenomatosis can be challenging due to the high risk of hemorrhage, and liver transplantation may be necessary due to the unresectable nature of numerous parenchymal lesions.[7,29]

Focal nodular hyperplasia

Clinical features

FNH is a benign non-neoplastic lesion, most commonly seen in young women in the third and fourth decades.[2,8] Around 5–15% of the lesions occur in males, which is a higher proportion compared to HA. Classic FNH is often noted as an incidental finding at surgery or during radiologic tests for an unrelated disease, but may also present with upper abdominal pain, or rarely with complications like hemorrhage due to large size.[30] Liver function tests are generally normal but some patients may have elevated gamma-glutamyltranspeptidase activity.[30] FNH typically remains static over time, but rapid growth and recurrence have been reported and referred to as the progressive type of FNH.[31]

Classic FNH is usually a solitary lesion; multifocal lesions have been reported in 20–30% of cases.[30,32] FNH has been described adjacent to hemangiomas, the association being more common with multiple FNH. Some patients with the so-called multiple FNH syndrome have at least two FNH lesions associated with one or more lesions such as hepatic hemangioma, systemic arterial structural defects like Klippel–Trenaunay–Weber syndrome and cerebral aneurysms, meningioma, and astrocytoma.[32,33] A rare variant of FNH, the telangiectatic type, is commonly associated with the multiple FNH syndrome.[19]

Unlike HA, FNH is not thought to develop due to the use of oral contraceptives, but many speculate that it may increase in size with their use or regress with their cessation. The currently favored hypothesis is that FNH represents a hyperplastic and altered growth response to changes in blood flow in the parenchyma surrounding a pre-existing arterial malformation.[34] The presence of numerous abnormal muscular vessels and the association with hemangiomas and the Budd–Chiari syndrome lend support to this theory. Aberrant expression of angiopoietin genes occurs in FNH and may play a role in the formation of hyperplastic and dystrophic vessels.[35] The International Working Party has recommended that FNH-like lesions associated with the Budd–Chiari syndrome and Osler–Weber–Rendu disease not be designated as FNH, but rather referred to as regenerative nodules ("FNH-like" nodules).[23] The clonal nature of FNH is controversial, but recent data demonstrate polyclonality in FNH, favoring a reactive process rather than a neoplasm.[36,37]

Pathologic features

Gross pathology. FNH has a nodular appearance (which can suggest the appearance of macronodular cirrhosis), and tends to be lighter brown than the adjacent liver (Fig. 10.4). These lesions are often located near the capsule of the liver and can occasionally be pedunculated. The edges of FNH appear well demarcated from the adjacent normal parenchyma because of the nodularity, but no fibrous capsule is present. Most lesions are small and less than 5 cm, but there is considerable variation in size and an entire lobe can be involved in rare instances. Most of the lesions have a "central fibrous scar," which consists of fibrovascular tissue rather than dense collagen. The central scar may be absent in lesions less than 1 cm.[23] A rare

variant, the telangiectatic type, does not have the central fibrous zone, and can grossly resemble hemangioma or peliosis hepatis.

Microscopic features. The classic type of FNH is composed of normal-appearing hepatocytes arranged in incomplete nodules that are partially separated by fibrous tissue, which tends to extend from the central fibrous zone when it is present. The cell plate architecture has an intact reticulin framework similar to normal liver, but the cell plates are usually wider (2–3 cells thick), as in a regenerative nodule. The hepatocytes may show increased cytoplasmic glycogen, focal steatosis, bile stasis, lipofuscin, iron pigment, copper-associated protein, and Mallory bodies.[23] Foci of atypical hepatocytes with large nuclei, mild nuclear hyperchromasia, and conspicuous nucleoli can be present. Cytologic atypia of the large cell type has been rarely described. An important feature is the variable number of bile ductular structures present within the fibrous stroma at the edge of the nodules (Fig. 10.5). Another important diagnostic feature is the presence of medium to large thick-walled muscular vessels, which often exhibit myointimal myxoid or fibromuscular hyperplastic changes. These vessels are not a component of a portal tract as there is no portal vein or interlobular duct of similar caliber associated with them. Normal portal tracts are not found within the lesion, although a bile duct of intermediate or large caliber can be found in the central fibrous zone in rare cases.[30] Sinusoids can be somewhat dilated and Kupffer cells can be present. Inflammatory cell infiltrates are relatively common, and generally consist of lymphocytes, although neutrophils and eosinophils can be noted, especially around the bile ductular structures. Rarely, granulomas may be seen.

The telangiectatic variant contains dilated blood-filled vascular spaces instead of a central fibrous zone. The arteries in this variant are smaller and more numerous than in typical FNH, and the fibrous septa are less prominent.[23,30] Another rare variant designated as mixed hyperplastic and adenomatous type has features of both FNH and adenoma. This lesion grossly resembles an adenoma and lacks a central fibrous zone. Microscopically, it shows areas resembling adenoma alternating with those showing FNH-like features, often of the

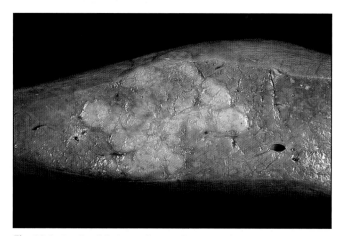

Fig. 10.4 • Focal nodular hyperplasia. Well-circumscribed tumor with nodularity, central scar, and tan to light-brown parenchyma.

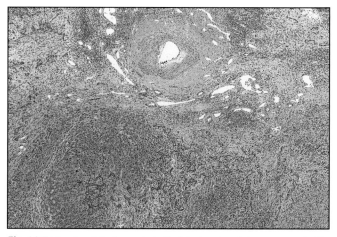

Fig. 10.5 • Focal nodular hyperplasia. Nodular hepatocellular component with thick-walled artery and bile ductular proliferation in the fibrovascular stroma.

telangiectatic type. Bile ductular proliferation is always present, but is focal and inconspicuous.[30] It has been suggested that these telangiectatic lesions should be reclassified as a variant of adenoma, but this issue remains controversial.[37]

As with HA, the hepatocytes in FNH express hepatocellular markers like Hep Par 1, CAM5.2 and polyclonal CEA. CD34 is often positive in the endothelial cells lining the cell plates.[25] AFP is always negative.

Differential diagnosis

FNH needs to be distinguished from normal liver, HA, regenerative nodules and HCC (Table 10.1). FNH shows homogeneous enhancement with a central scar on CT and magnetic resonance imaging (MRI), while adenoma appears as a hyperintense heterogeneous mass. FNH shows normal or increased uptake on Tc-sulfur-colloid scintigraphy, while adenoma appears as a lesion without uptake.[10] Even with the combined use of new imaging techniques, the accuracy of preoperative diagnosis remains only 70–85%.[10] Histologically, the differences between adenoma and FNH can often be subtle and distinction may not always be possible in needle biopsies. The presence of bile ductular structures is the most important distinguishing feature for FNH and will exclude the diagnosis of adenoma, but it is important to remember that normal portal tracts can be trapped within FNH, adenoma, and HCC. Large vessels with abnormal hyperplastic features and surrounded by connective tissue favor FNH, as does the central zone of fibrosis. The larger vessels in adenoma tend to have a more normal configuration and lack significant perivascular connective tissue stroma. Pseudoglandular differentiation in adenomas can be mistaken for bile ductules. Regenerative nodules associated with Budd–Chiari syndrome and vascular malformations resemble FNH, but are not designated as FNH by definition as the surrounding liver is not normal. Both FNH and fibrolamellar HCC have a central scar and can be confused on radiologic studies. The presence of calcification in the scar favors fibrolamellar HCC, although it has occasionally been reported in FNH.[38] Some of the typical features of FNH, such as nodular architecture with fibrosis, bile ductular proliferation, and absence of interlobular bile ducts, can closely resemble chronic ductopenic biliary disease, especially on a limited biopsy. Clinical information of normal liver enzymes and radiologic findings of a focal mass lesion are helpful in the diagnosis of FNH in this setting.

Prognosis and outcome

FNH is a benign lesion and, in contrast to adenomas, the risk of complications such as hemorrhage and malignant transformation is virtually absent. In spite of its rarely reported association with fibrolamellar HCC,[39] there is no real evidence for the progression of FNH to carcinoma. It is speculated that the associated FNH may represent a hyperplastic response in the adjacent parenchyma to the increased vascularity due to the carcinoma. If a confident diagnosis can be made on radiologic grounds, conservative management without resection can be employed. Pathologic diagnosis should be confirmed in all doubtful cases. Since small biopsies may not be helpful in the distinction between adenoma and FNH, it has been advocated that intraoperative biopsies or resection be performed in place of percutaneous biopsy.[10]

Other benign tumors and tumor-like lesions

Focal fatty change (FFC) is a localized zone of hepatocytes, which contain abundant fat. This lesion is often subcapsular, and can be confused grossly or radiographically with a neoplasm. FFC can be associated with diabetes or alcoholic hepatitis.[40]

Pseudolipoma is an encapsulated mass of mature adipose tissue, often necrotic or calcified, that occurs in a subcapsular location.[41] It is thought to be detached peritoneal or pericolic fat that becomes adherent to the liver capsule.

Solitary necrotic nodule is a rare non-neoplastic lesion that consists of a central zone of amorphous, eosinophilic debris rimmed by a hyalinized fibrotic capsule that contains prominent elastic fibers. These lesions may be clinically mistaken for metastatic disease. They probably represent the burnt-out phase of benign disease like a sclerosed hemangioma.[42] Rare instances have been noted in association with parasitic infections.[43]

Nodular regenerative hyperplasia (NRH) is characterized by multiple regenerative nodules throughout the liver in the absence of fibrous septa.[23] NRH is often associated with portal venous obstruction, and can occur in association with polycythemia vera, agnogenic myeloid metaplasia, rheumatoid arthritis, Budd–Chiari syndrome, malignant lymphoma, and a wide variety of other conditions.[2] The nodules are generally 0.1–1.0 cm in diameter, but can occasionally be larger (up to 10 cm) and can mimic a neoplasm. In some cases, the nodules do not involve the entire liver and are localized in the hilar region (partial nodular transformation).[44] Histologically, the nodules are composed of hepatocytes arranged in 2–3-cell-thick plates. The hepatocytes at the periphery of the nodules are atrophic with condensation of the reticulin network, a finding best appreciated on reticulin stain. There are no fibrous septa, but foci of sinusoidal fibrosis are often present. NRH does not have any neoplastic potential. It is seldom confused with a neoplasm, except when the nodules are large and can resemble a HA.

Benign/Premalignant hepatocellular lesions in cirrhotic liver

Large regenerative (macroregenerative) nodule

In cirrhosis, benign nodules that are larger than the typical cirrhotic nodule have been referred to by various names, including large regenerative nodule, macroregenerative nodule, or adenomatous hyperplasia. Similar nodules can occur in the non-cirrhotic liver in the setting of Budd–Chiari syndrome, portal vein thrombosis, or as sequelae of necrosis with regeneration, and are designated as multiacinar regenerative nodules as per the recommendations of the International Working Party.[23] Large regenerative nodules and multiacinar regenerative nodules are thought to be a reactive process rather than a clonal preneoplastic lesion.

Clinical features

Large regenerative nodules occur in the setting of cirrhosis, with few exceptions when they are noted in the setting of chronic liver disease without fully developed cirrhosis.[45] They are often found as incidental findings at autopsy or transplantation, but can be noted on radiographic studies. Serum AFP is normal or within the same range as in chronic liver disease or cirrhosis. These nodules are typically seen in cirrhosis due to hepatitis B, hepatitis C, alcohol, and hemochromatosis, but are uncommon in primary biliary cirrhosis.

Pathologic features

Gross features. Large regenerative nodules are larger than typical cirrhotic nodules. The lower limit for size is generally accepted as 1 cm, and these lesions are almost always less than 3 cm in greatest diameter. The nodules tend to bulge on cut section, the edges are rounded and sharply circumscribed, and they may be bile-stained or pale-yellow to tan compared to other cirrhotic nodules.

Microscopic features. These nodules histologically resemble cirrhotic nodules. They have an intact reticulin framework similar to normal liver, and the cell plates are 1–2 cells thick. The hepatocytes typically have normal cytology, although focal variations in cell size, especially scattered large cell change similar to that seen in the other cirrhotic nodules, can be present. Mallory bodies, bile stasis, clear cell cytoplasmic change, iron or copper deposits, a slight decrease in cell size, and focal or diffuse fatty change may be present.[23,46] Portal tracts are usually present within the nodule and bile ductular proliferation may be prominent (Fig. 10.6), but fibrous septa without the complete triad of duct, vein, and artery may also be present.[47]

Large regenerative nodules tend to have an increased number of arteries that lack the other components of a portal zone, the so-called "unpaired artery." However, staining for vascular markers such as CD34 or CD 31 as a marker for sinusoidal capillarization shows peripheral staining at the edges of the nodule similar to the results seen in cirrhotic nodules.[48,49] The nodules are negative for AFP.[50] Staining patterns with cytokeratin and polyclonal CEA are similar to normal liver.

Differential diagnosis

The size of the nodule differentiates it from other cirrhotic nodules. Rarely, macroregenerative nodules may lack portal zones, but this does not warrant a diagnosis of adenoma in the cirrhotic liver unless one of the risk factors discussed above is present. The features differentiating it from dysplastic nodules and well-differentiated HCC are outlined in Table 10.2.

Significance

These nodules are generally considered benign lesions and are thought to be large regenerative foci without clonal proliferation. Large regenerative nodules have been associated with an increased incidence of HCC.[51] However, these studies defined macroregenerative nodules histologically by the absence of features of high-grade dysplastic nodules or HCC. Since no clonality studies were done to separate macroregenerative nodules and low-grade dysplastic nodules, it is unclear whether the increased risk is associated with polyclonal large regenerative nodules, clonal low-grade dysplastic nodules, or both.

Dysplasia

Two different types of atypical hepatocytes occur in cirrhotic nodules and have been referred to as large cell dysplasia and small cell dysplasia. Since their premalignant potential remains controversial, the International Working Party has recommended that the terms large cell change and small cell change are used.[23] **Large cell change** is characterized by nuclear enlargement, hyperchromasia, prominent nucleoli, but with abundant cytoplasm and hence normal nuclear-to-cytoplasmic ratio (Fig. 10.7). Some cells may be multinucleated. Although large cell change has been significantly associated with the presence of HCC,[52] it is present too frequently in cirrhotic liver to be a premalignant process.[53] Unlike HCC, large cell change shows a normal nuclear-to-cytoplasmic ratio, no mitoses, low proliferation rate, and absence of *p53*

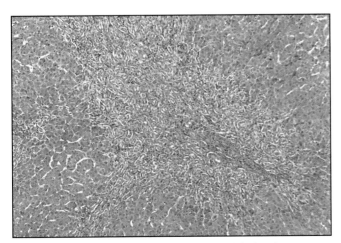

Fig. 10.6 • Large regenerative nodule with prominent bile ductular proliferation.

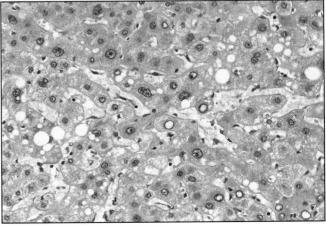

Fig. 10.7 • Large cell change. Atypical large nuclei with normal nuclear-to-cytoplasmic ratio.

Table 10.2 Diagnostic features: large regenerative nodules, dysplastic nodules, and well-differentiated hepatocellular carcinoma (HCC)

Morphology	Large (macro) regenerative nodule	Low-grade dysplastic nodule	High-grade dysplastic nodule	HCC, well-differentiated
Hepatocyte size	Similar to cirrhotic nodules	Uniform hepatocytes with normal cytologic features suggesting a clonal proliferation	Variable, usually close to normal size or slightly smaller	Smaller or larger compared to normal
Small cell change or nuclear density >2× normal	Absent or only scattered cells	Absent or only scattered cells	Occasional small foci, can be diffuse and prominent; may have appearance of nodule within a larger nodule	Commonly present
Large cell change	Scattered cells	Absent	Scattered cells; groups of large cells unlikely unless in dysplastic focus	May be present
Trabeculae with cell plates ≥3 cells thick	Absent	Absent	Occasional plates ≥3 cells thick	Common
Portal tracts	Almost always present; focal bile ductular proliferation	Often present	Often present within larger dysplastic nodules	Absent, unless entrapped at edge of tumor
Periphery of nodule	Well-circumscribed	Well-circumscribed	Some may have irregular edges	Infiltrative edges common
Reticulin framework	Intact; no foci of decreased or absent reticulin	Intact	Focal loss can be present	Usually lost extensively; thickened bands may separate cell plates
Increased iron	Can be present	Not known	Can be present	Almost always absent, even in the setting of siderotic liver

Adapted with permission from Ferrell L D 2004 Benign and malignant tumors of the liver. In: Odze R D, Goldblum J R, Crawford J M et al. (eds) Surgical pathology of the GI tract, liver, biliary tract and pancreas. Saunders, Philadelphia, Table 42-3, p 999–1026.

mutations.[54] According to a recent study, the predictive value of large cell change for HCC is less than 20%.[55] It may instead represent a regenerative or degenerative phenomenon,[56] or a response to prolonged cholestasis.[57] **Small cell change** is characterized by smaller than normal hepatocytes, higher than normal nuclear-to-cytoplasmic ratio, and hyperchromatic nuclei. When small cell change occurs in small expansive foci, it may be more closely associated with HCC than large cell change.[52] High proliferative activity and *p53* overexpression have been described.[54,56] However, poorly defined or diffuse areas of small cell change without nodular configuration may represent a regenerative phenomenon, can occur in chronic biliary disease, and are unlikely to be preneoplastic.[52,56]

The term dysplasia is used to describe a population of cells that display histologic characteristics of abnormal growth caused by presumed genetic alterations without fulfilling definite criteria of malignancy.[23] Since genetic criteria for diagnosis of dysplasia are not established, morphologic features and topographic clustering of abnormal cells are used to diagnose and classify dysplasia. A cluster of dysplastic hepatocytes less than 1 mm in diameter is referred to as dysplastic focus, and 1 mm or larger as dysplastic nodule. Cytologic features are used to classify dysplastic nodules into low- and high-grade categories.

Dysplastic foci have a high prevalence in diseases such as chronic hepatitis B and C, alpha₁-antitrypsin deficiency, and tyrosinemia.[23] The margin is distinct but irregular. The cells are usually uniform and differ from the surrounding hepatocytes in terms of nuclear atypia and cytoplasmic staining. The spectrum of nuclear atypia varies from minimal to severe. Cytoplasmic fat or glycogen may differ in content from the adjacent liver.

Low-grade dysplastic nodule

The low-grade dysplastic nodule in the cirrhotic liver is thought to represent a clonal proliferation of hepatocytes, although the gross and standard microscopic features can be indistinguishable from a large regenerative nodule. Hence it shares the clinical and pathologic features of macroregenerative nodules described above. The low-grade dysplastic nodule would be expected to have a more uniform population of hepatocytes due to its clonal nature, but specific morphologic features of this type of clonal nodule have not been definitively established. In the absence of clonality studies, the terms macroregenerative nodule and low-grade dysplastic nodule have been used interchangeably to describe nodules that lack the cytologic or architectural features of high-grade dysplasia.

High-grade dysplastic nodule

Clinical features. The high-grade dysplastic nodule, also known as borderline nodule, type II macroregenerative nodule, atypical adenomatous hyperplasia, and atypical macroregenerative nodule, almost always occurs in a cirrhotic liver.[23,46,47] Serum AFP is normal or in the range seen in chronic liver disease or cirrhosis. It is recommended that these lesions should be excised or ablated since they are considered to be a premalignant process.

Pathologic features

Gross pathology. These nodules have essentially the same gross appearance as large regenerative and low-grade dysplastic nodules, with the exception that some are not well circumscribed or have irregular edges.

Microscopic features. Dysplastic changes may be present uniformly in the nodule, or noted as one or more dysplastic foci within a nodule (Fig. 10.8). The atypical features are not overtly diagnostic for HCC. The nodule is often recognized by zones of small cell change with increased nuclear-to-cytoplasmic ratio. There is increased nuclear density (estimated number of hepatocyte nuclei per microscopic field) compared to the normal liver (Fig. 10.9).[46] Large cell change is rarely a

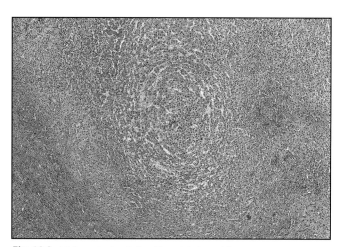

Fig. 10.8 • High-grade dysplasia with nodule in nodule appearance.

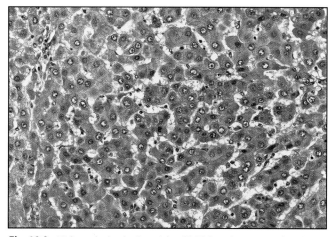

Fig. 10.9 • High-grade dysplastic nodule with high nuclear-to-cytoplasmic ratio and increased nuclear density.

feature of high-grade dysplastic nodules, but if present, the focus must be a discrete zone of atypical cells rather than enlarged nuclei scattered singly in the nodule. Other common features are focal zones of cell plates up to 3 cells thick, focal decrease in the reticulin framework, and mild dilatation of sinusoids. These nodules can also contain foci of acinar (pseudoglandular) architecture, Mallory bodies, fat, clear cell change, cytoplasmic basophilia, bile, and portal tracts. High-grade dysplastic lesions tend to lack iron deposits, in contrast to the regenerative or low-grade dysplastic nodules, in which iron deposits are more common.

Differential diagnosis. Distinction from overt HCC is described in Table 10.2. Features that are probably most helpful for the diagnosis of HCC are the presence of trabeculae with cell plates greater than 3 cells thick, mitotic figures in moderate numbers, nuclear density greater than twice normal, marked reduction in reticulin framework, numerous unpaired arteries, and absence of portal zones.

Dysplasia: genetic changes and outcome

Progressive genetic changes have been demonstrated in large regenerative nodules, dysplastic nodules, and HCC, supporting the multistep progression of carcinogenesis. Allelic imbalance has been documented in 16% of macroregenerative nodules and 50% of low-grade dysplastic nodules.[58] High fractional allelic losses are seen in high-grade dysplastic nodules similar to HCC. Losses of 4q, 8p, and Xq are observed in large regenerative nodules and low-grade dysplastic nodules, while losses of 1p, 13q, 16q, and 17p are seen in high-grade dysplasia.[59]

For current clinical management, large regenerative nodules and low-grade dysplastic nodules can be followed by imaging and serological markers, while high-grade dysplastic nodules are treated more aggressively by surgery or ablative therapy.[46,58]

Other premalignant lesions

Iron-free foci are foci of hepatocytes free of iron or exhibiting much less iron than the surrounding parenchyma. These are frequently found in periportal areas in livers of patients with inherited hemochromatosis complicated by HCC. They have a high proliferative rate and may be preneoplastic.[60] **Foci of altered hepatocytes** are preneoplastic lesions initially described in animal models. These have also been reported in cirrhotic livers in the form of focal hepatic glycogenosis (clear cell foci due to excessive glycogen), foci of amphophilic cells or oncocytic cells (rich in mitochondria), or mixed amphophilic and clear cell foci.[61,62] The exact significance of these foci remains to be determined.

Malignant hepatocellular lesions

Hepatocellular carcinoma and variants
Clinical features

HCC is the most common primary malignant tumor in the liver. It is the fifth most common malignant tumor in men and eighth most common in women worldwide. More than 500 000 cases are reported every year. The incidence varies with geographic area, being 2–7/100 000 in Europe and North America and more than 30/100 000 in Taiwan, south-east China, and sub-Saharan Africa. The incidence of HCC has more than doubled in the USA in the last 25 years.[63] Men are affected three times more often than women.

Most patients are asymptomatic or have abdominal pain; weight loss, malaise, fever, jaundice, and ascites are seen in fewer than 10% of patients at presentation.[64] Increasingly, patients with cirrhosis are being diagnosed by radiologic techniques or elevated AFP detected on screening. A high serum AFP level (>1000 ng/ml) is seen in almost two-thirds of the cases of large tumors;[65] tumors less than 2–3 cm in size are unlikely to have an elevated serum AFP.[45] Elevations of serum AFP up to 500 ng/ml can be seen in many liver disorders and levels between 500 and 1000 ng/ml are suspicious for HCC but not as reliably specific. AFP is also useful for monitoring response to therapy and detection of recurrences. Imaging techniques play a valuable role in diagnosis. Small tumors are hypoechoic on ultrasound, but larger tumors can be hyperechoic. Since HCC receives its principal blood supply from arterial rather than portal blood, it enhances early in the arterial phase while the remaining liver enhances later in the portal phase on CT after contrast. Angiography was formerly used to detect HCC by demonstrating its high vascularity, but has been largely replaced by CT and MRI. The sensitivity and specificity of radiologic techniques are in the range of 70% and 80% respectively, but are much lower for smaller tumors.[66]

A vast majority (>80%) of HCC develop in cirrhotic livers; the following diseases increase the risk for HCC by causing cirrhosis:[67]

1. Hepatitis B virus (HBV): this is the most common underlying cause of HCC worldwide, particularly in areas with a high incidence of HCC. The lifetime risk of developing HCC is 50% in HBV-positive men and 20% in women.[67] HCC in this setting occurs at a young age, often in the third decade. Occasional cases can develop in chronic carriers without cirrhosis.[68]

2. Hepatitis C virus (HCV): this is the principal mechanism underlying HCC in Europe and North America. The risk of HCC in HCV-positive patients is 17-fold compared with negative controls.[69] Nearly all the tumors arise in cirrhosis. Risk factors for developing HCC include older age at HCV acquisition, male gender, obesity, diabetes, heavy alcohol intake, coexistent HBV or human immunodeficiency virus (HIV) and long duration of HCV infection.[68]

3. Alcohol: prolonged intake of alcohol (>50 g/day) can lead to cirrhosis and hence is a risk factor for HCC. The risk is higher with coexistent HBV, HCV, and diabetes.[68]

4. Metabolic disorders: HCC is very common (lifetime risk of 45% in some series) in inherited hemochromatosis. In hereditary tyrosinemia more than one-third of patients who survive till 2 years develop HCC.[67] HCC has also been reported with other metabolic disorders like alpha$_1$-antitrypsin deficiency and Wilson's disease. Although HAs are common in type I glycogen storage disease, development of HCC is rare.[70]

5. Drugs and toxins: exposure to thorotrast (thorium dioxide), aflatoxin, androgenic steroids, and progestational agents has been associated with HCC.[12] Aflatoxin is a fungal toxin of *Aspergillus flavus* and can contaminate food products stored in damp conditions. Exposure to aflatoxin is common in areas endemic for HBV.[67]

Pathologic features

Gross pathology. The background liver shows cirrhosis in the majority of cases. Tumors can be classified as massive when there is a solitary large mass, nodular when there are multiple discrete nodules, and diffuse when there are multiple small indistinct nodules.[65] Tumors less than 2 cm in diameter are referred to as small HCC; these small tumors usually lack gross vascular invasion, necrosis, or hemorrhage. Tumors are generally soft and may be paler than the adjacent liver or bile-stained (Fig. 10.10). Irregular borders and satellite nodules can be present. HCC has a tendency for vascular invasion. Portal and hepatic veins can be involved and the tumor can extend into the inferior vena cava. Bile duct invasion is not common but can occur. Some HCC form a multinodular, macronodular pattern, and can mimic cirrhosis (Fig. 10.11).

Microscopic findings. Several typical histologic patterns of HCC have been described by the World Health Organization.[1,71] The most common is the **trabecular pattern**, also known as the sinusoidal pattern (Fig. 10.12). In this variant, the tumor morphology mimics the plate architecture of normal liver, but the cell plates are 3 cells or greater in thickness, compared to 1–2-cell-thick plates in normal or regenerative liver. The tumor cell plates are lined by endothelial cells similar to normal liver, but the reticulin framework is often absent, markedly decreased, or distorted, with irregular or absent staining of the edges of the trabeculae. The tumor cells often have features of small cell change. Large cell change can also be noted, but is less frequent except in higher-grade tumors. Foci of small or large cell change can be admixed. Kupffer cells are typically absent.

Fig. 10.10 • Hepatocellular carcinoma arising in cirrhotic liver. The tumor is tan-yellow, poorly circumscribed, and shows venous invasion (left of center). The non-neoplastic liver shows cirrhosis and bile staining (left).

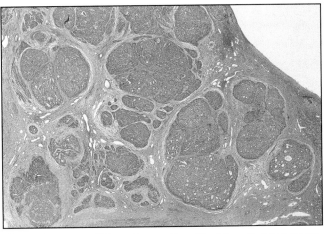

Fig. 10.11 • Hepatocellular carcinoma with multinodular pattern. Low-power appearance can mimic macronodular cirrhosis.

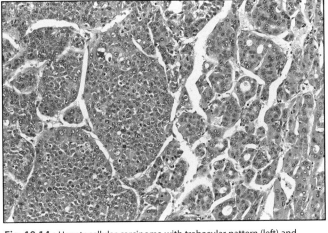

Fig. 10.14 • Hepatocellular carcinoma with trabecular pattern (left) and pseudoglandular pattern (right).

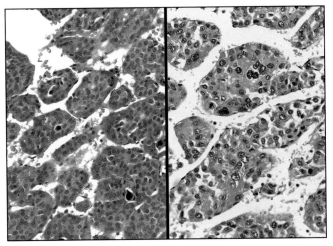

Fig. 10.12 • Hepatocellular carcinoma, trabecular pattern with large cell change (left), and small cell change (right). Note the bile plugs produced by the tumor.

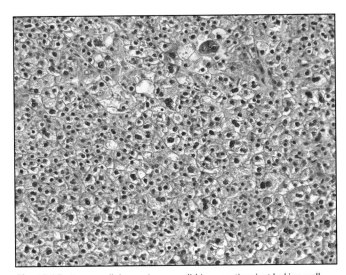

Fig. 10.15 • Hepatocellular carcinoma, solid (compact) variant lacking well-defined cell plates.

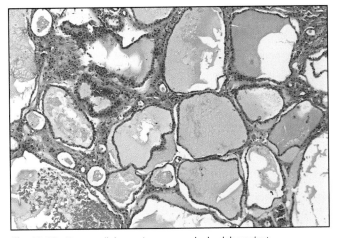

Fig. 10.13 • Hepatocellular carcinoma, pseudoglandular variant.

The **acinar, pseudoglandular, or adenoid pattern** of HCC is less common than the trabecular type. The defining feature in this variant is gland-like spaces, or acini, lined by the hepatocytic tumor cells (Fig. 10.13). These acinar structures are formed by the dilatation or expansion of bile canaliculi and often contain

bile. Less frequently, the spaces are a result of central necrosis and may contain protein, cellular debris, or macrophages. Due to the formation of gland-like spaces, this pattern can be mistaken for adenocarcinoma. The acinar pattern is frequently admixed with the trabecular pattern (Fig. 10.14).

The **solid** or **compact pattern** of HCC is a relatively uncommon variant characterized by dense aggregates of tumor cells that seem to lack the endothelial cell-lined trabeculae or cell plates (Fig. 10.15); however, careful examination with endothelial cell markers will often reveal the presence of compressed trabeculae. Loss of the reticulin framework is typically seen in the solid, crowded zones as well.

The **scirrhous pattern** contains focal or diffuse areas of fibrosis that can be associated with any of the patterns above (Fig. 10.16). It can commonly be confused with cholangiocarcinoma or fibrolamellar carcinoma. Similar fibrotic changes can occur after radiation or chemotherapy and should not be labeled as scirrhous pattern. Sclerosing HCC was used to describe a variant of HCC characterized by hypercalcemia and marked stromal fibrosis.[72] It is thought that it does not represent a distinct entity and that many of these tumors represent intrahepatic cholangiocarcinomas.[65]

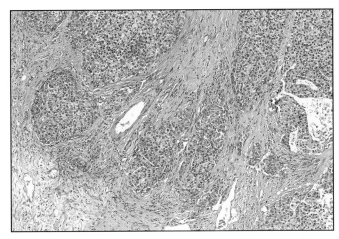

Fig. 10.16 • Hepatocellular carcinoma, scirrhous variant showing prominent stromal fibrosis.

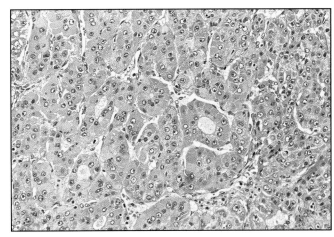

Fig. 10.18 • Hepatocellular carcinoma with prominent granular (oncocytic) cytoplasm.

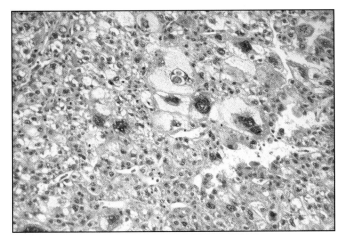

Fig. 10.17 • Hepatocellular carcinoma with a focus of pleomorphic cells.

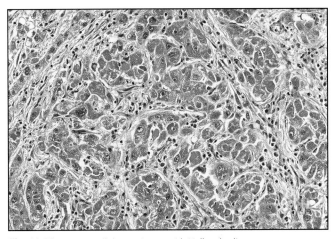

Fig. 10.19 • Hepatocellular carcinoma with Mallory bodies.

The **cytologic features of HCC** within any of these patterns also show great variation. The tumor cells often maintain a polygonal shape and have round vesicular nuclei and prominent nucleoli. Intranuclear vacuoles (representing cytoplasmic invaginations) and glycogenation of nuclei are fairly common findings. Small cell change (as described above) is probably the most common cytologic change, but large cell change and giant and/or pleomorphic cells may be present as a diffuse or focal finding (Fig. 10.17). The amount of cytoplasm may vary, and is often slightly basophilic compared to normal hepatocytes. The cytoplasm may also have a granular or oxyphilic appearance due to the presence of large numbers of mitochondria (Fig. 10.18). Cytoplasmic inclusions such as Mallory bodies (Fig. 10.19) or globular acidophilic bodies (Fig. 10.20), composed of proteins including albumin, fibrinogen, alpha$_1$-antitrypsin or ferritin, may be present. Fat, glycogen, or even water can be prominent, giving the cells a "clear cell" appearance, which has been described as the **clear cell variant** of HCC (Fig. 10.21). If the entire tumor shows this type of clear cell change and occurs in a non-cirrhotic liver, it may be difficult to differentiate from metastatic clear cell tumors like renal cell carcinoma (RCC). Steatosis can be present and is most pronounced in small tumors less than 2 cm (Fig. 10.22). The fat content tends to decrease as the tumor size increases. Pale

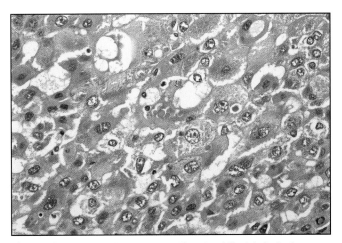

Fig. 10.20 • Hepatocellular carcinoma with eosinophilic globules in the cytoplasm. These often represent alpha$_1$-antitrypsin.

bodies are round to oval, lightly eosinophilic or clear cytoplasmic structures that contain fibrinogen. They are most frequently seen in the fibrolamellar variant (see Fibrolamellar variant of HCC, below), but can be seen in conventional HCC, especially the scirrhous variant. Other less frequent cytoplasmic

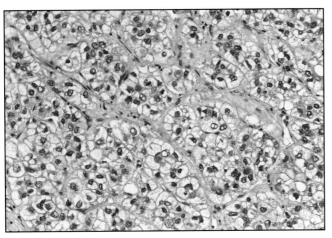

Fig. 10.21 • Hepatocellular carcinoma, clear cell type with abundant cytoplasmic glycogen.

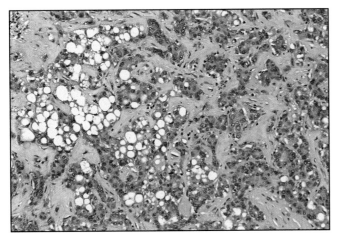

Fig. 10.22 • Hepatocellular carcinoma with fat vacuoles.

changes include ground-glass cells containing hepatitis B surface antigen (HBsAg) that are present in some patients with HBV infections,[73] and may represent entrapped HBsAg hepatocytes rather than tumor cells. Dark-brown to black pigment similar to that seen in the Dubin–Johnson syndrome can be present. Iron is typically not seen in the tumor cells but can be present in stromal mesenchymal cells. Rare forms of HCC include a small cell type and sarcomatoid HCC with a prominent spindle cell component. The latter may be difficult to distinguish from a sarcoma, although transitional areas with typical HCC are often present.

Other special histologic types of HCC include the **encapsulated** HCC, **pedunculated** HCC, **small** HCC, **pelioid** HCC, and **HCC with lymphoid stroma**. Tumor encapsulation has been described in 3–10% of HCC. Encapsulated HCC is usually small, well differentiated, and has a better prognosis after resection.[74] In pedunculated HCC, the tumor is connected to the liver by a pedicle and probably arises from an accessory lobe. These tumors grow slowly and have a better prognosis due to their extrahepatic location.[75] Small HCCs are less than 2 cm by definition. These tumors are often multifocal, well differentiated, and occur in cirrhotic livers. Except for their size, these tumors are similar to other forms of HCC.[65] Large vascular spaces can be seen in HCC mimicking peliosis hepatis, referred to as pelioid HCC. HCC with lymphoid stroma is a

rare variant associated with dense infiltration of lymphocytes and plasma cells, and formation of lymphoid follicles. Most patients are males, AFP is normal, and the lymphocytes outnumber the tumor cells.[76] These patients may have a better prognosis after liver transplantation.

The grading of HCC has traditionally been based on three or four grades, based on the system developed by Edmondson & Steiner in 1954.[77] They originally defined four grades as distinguished by proportional increases in nuclear-to-cytoplasmic ratio, variability in nuclear shape, hyperchromasia, and loss of cell plate architecture from low- to high-grade tumors. These grades are still used with some modifications in the grading of low-grade tumors.[1] Some of Edmondson & Steiner's grade I tumors with minimal cytologic atypia and architectural distortion were only recognized as malignant by their association with areas of higher-grade HCC or by the presence of metastatic lesions.[65,77] With the current criteria established by the International Working Party, some of the grade I lesions will be classified as dysplastic nodules.[23] Grade II tumors are also well differentiated but with increased nuclear size as compared to grade I tumors. Grade II lesions show pseudoacinar or trabecular patterns, and bile can be present. Grade III tumors are moderately differentiated, and have more cytologic and architectural variability than the grade II lesions. Multinucleated and giant tumor cells are often seen focally and, in contrast to grade II lesions, bile is often absent. When trabeculae are present, they are typically wider and more variable in structure than grade II tumors. Grade IV consists of poorly differentiated or anaplastic tumors for which recognition as HCC is difficult without the appropriate clinical setting such as cirrhosis or significantly elevated serum AFP. Grade IV lesions can include sarcomatoid and small cell components as well. An alternate three-grade system is often used, with grade I representing well-differentiated tumors (grade I and II above combined); grade II, the moderately differentiated tumors; and grade III, the poorly differentiated tumors.

Differential diagnosis

1. *Hepatocellular neoplasms*: most of the diagnostic problems arise in differentiating well-differentiated HCC from adenoma or FNH in non-cirrhotic liver and regenerative/dysplastic nodules in cirrhotic liver (Tables 10.1 and 10.2). Reticulin staining can be valuable in the identification of HCC by demonstrating fragmentation and loss of reticulin framework (Fig. 10.23). Occasionally, well-differentiated HCC may have an intact reticulin framework. Immunoperoxidase studies are not helpful to differentiate benign from malignant hepatocellular tumors. CD34 typically stains the endothelial-lined trabeculae in HCC and highlights the increased vascularity, but is often positive in FNH and adenomas as well.[25]

2. *Adenocarcinoma* (cholangiocarcinoma or metastatic adenocarcinoma) (Table 10.3): the presence of cirrhosis, elevated AFP level, and a trabecular pattern of growth favor HCC. Cholangiocarcinoma is less common and metastatic adenocarcinoma is rare in cirrhotic liver. The presence of dense fibrotic stroma favors adenocarcinoma, but sclerosing variants of HCC also occur. An acinar pattern is often seen in HCC, and hence is not diagnostic

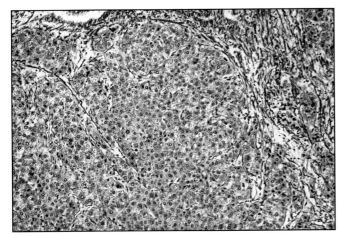

Fig. 10.23 • Hepatocellular carcinoma showing widespread loss of reticulin.

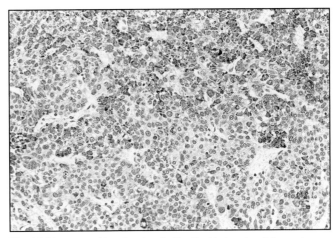

Fig. 10.24 • Immunohistochemistry for Hep Par 1 in hepatocellular carcinoma. The majority of tumors (>80%) show diffuse staining, but expression can be patchy, as shown here.

of adenocarcinoma. Similarly, multiple lesions are more common in metastases, but HCC can be multifocal.

Routine histochemical stains such as mucicarmine or PAS with diastase (PAS-D) can demonstrate mucin in adenocarcinoma. Mucin is absent in HCC, except in combined HCC–cholangiocarcinoma and in some cases of fibrolamellar HCC. Cytoplasmic glycoproteins in HCC can be highlighted by PAS-D staining, leading to potentially false-positive interpretation.

Immunohistochemistry and albumin in-situ hybridization (ISH) are helpful in the differential

diagnosis. **Hep Par 1** has emerged as the most sensitive (>90%) and specific immunohistochemical marker for HCC (Fig. 10.24).[78–82] It can be negative in poorly differentiated and sclerosing HCC. It is usually negative in tumors that commonly enter the differential diagnosis of HCC, including cholangiocarcinoma, endocrine neoplasms, RCC, malignant melanoma, and AML. Adenocarcinomas of the pancreas and colorectum are usually negative. However, gastric, esophageal, and lung adenocarcinomas can show strong positive reactions.[82] **Polyclonal CEA** shows a characteristic canalicular

Table 10.3	Differential diagnosis of hepatocellular carcinoma (HCC) and adenocarcinoma (cholangiocarcinoma or metastatic adenocarcinoma)	
	HCC	Adenocarcinoma
Clinical features		
Cirrhosis	Often present (>80%)	Usually absent
Number	Usually single; multiple nodules can be seen	Often multiple
Alpha-fetoprotein	Elevated; can be normal in tumors <2 cm	Normal
Morphology		
Pattern	Often trabecular; pseudoglandular pattern can be present	Glandular; less often solid or papillary
Fibrosis	Usually not prominent, except in scirrhous or fibrolamellar variants	Often prominent
Mucin	Absent, except for fibrolamellar variant	Can be present
Bile	Often present	Absent
Immunohistochemistry		
Hep Par 1	Highly sensitive and specific; can be negative in poorly differentiated HCC	Negative or weakly positive. Strong reactions can be seen in gastric, esophageal, and lung adenocarcinomas
Polyclonal CEA	Canalicular pattern	Cytoplasmic pattern
Alpha-fetoprotein	Specific, but low sensitivity (30–50%)	Negative
MOC-31	Negative	Strong membrane positive reaction in majority of adenocarcinomas. Excellent marker for clinical use
Cytokeratins	CAM5.2 positive; usually negative for CK19, CK20	CK7/CK20 profile depends on site; cholangiocarcinomas strongly express CK19
Albumin in-situ hybridization	Specific for hepatocellular differentiation; sensitivity >90%	Negative

CEA, carcinoembryonic antigen.

pattern in >90% of HCC as it cross-reacts with biliary glycoprotein (Fig. 10.25).[80,83] HCC is non-reactive with monoclonal CEA. Adenocarcinomas show a cytoplasmic pattern with both polyclonal and monoclonal CEA. The canalicular pattern in HCC can be difficult to interpret; similar patterns have been focally reported in adenocarcinoma. Poorly differentiated HCC may be negative. **CD10** staining yields a canalicular pattern similar to polyclonal CEA in HCC.[80] Even though it is rarely positive in adenocarcinoma, its low sensitivity (around 50%) does not make it a useful substitute for (or addition to) polyclonal CEA. **AFP** is specific for HCC if yolk sac tumor can be excluded. However, staining tends to be patchy and sensitivity is low (30–50%), especially in small, well-differentiated HCC.[79] **Albumin ISH** is specific for hepatocellular differentiation (Fig. 10.26) and has high sensitivity (>90%).[84,85] For reasons that are not clear, weak positive reactions are seen in ovarian clear cell adenocarcinoma.[85] The combination of albumin ISH and Hep Par 1 can yield 100% sensitivity for diagnosis of HCC.[82]

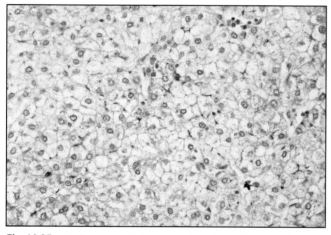

Fig. 10.25 • Canalicular pattern of staining with polyclonal carcinoembryonic antigen in hepatocellular carcinoma.

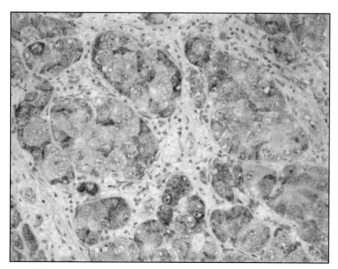

Fig. 10.26 • Albumin in-situ hybridization in hepatocellular carcinoma demonstrating albumin (blue-colored product) in the cytoplasm of tumor cells.

MOC-31, an antibody directed against a cell surface glycoprotein, was initially described for its utility in distinguishing metastatic adenocarcinoma from mesothelioma. Its usefulness in liver tumors has recently become apparent. It consistently (80–100%) stains cholangiocarcinoma and adenocarcinoma from a variety of sites like colorectum, pancreas, stomach, lung, breast, and ovary. It yields a diffuse membranous pattern of staining in adenocarcinoma, which is easy to interpret.[80,83] HCC is almost always negative for MOC 31. **CK7, CK19, and CK20** may be helpful in establishing the diagnosis and origin of metastatic adenocarcinoma.[86–88] CK19 is essentially always positive in cholangiocarcinoma. HCC is usually negative, but can be focally positive in a minority of cases.[87,89] CK8 and 18 (CAM5.2 antibody) are often expressed in HCC. **Leu-M1, B-72.3, and Le^x** tend to be positive in adenocarcinomas and negative in HCC.[90] These can be helpful when used with Hep Par 1 and polyclonal CEA.

Other markers can be used for the diagnosis of metastatic adenocarcinoma depending on the clinical situation, like nuclear TTF-1 for lung and prostate-specific antigen (PSA) for prostate. However, it must be remembered that non-neoplastic hepatocytes, as well as many HCCs, show cytoplasmic positivity for TTF-1.[91] Estrogen receptor (ER) and progesterone receptor (PR) but can be helpful in identifying adenocarcinoma of breast origin in conjunction with other antibodies. However, it must be noted that ER and PR can be positive in HCC.

3. *Neuroendocrine tumors*: HCC can also be difficult to distinguish from a neuroendrocrine neoplasm as both can form acinar or trabecular patterns, and can be composed of relatively large tumor cells with abundant eosinophilic cytoplasm and round nuclei. Features that favor a neuroendocrine tumor are a prominent vascular or capillary network, and/or stromal hyalinization. Neuroendocrine tumors are almost always metastatic, but can rarely arise as a primary lesion in the liver.[65] Focal neuroendocrine differentiation has been noted in HCC, including the fibrolamellar variant, as well as in hepatoblastoma, using various markers such as neuron-specific enolase, protein gene product 9.5, vasoactive intestinal peptide, calcitonin, and S-100.[92–94] However, diffuse staining with chromogranin or synaptophysin would strongly support a neuroendocrine tumor.

4. *Angiomyolipoma (AML)*: the epithelioid variant of AML can be especially difficult to distinguish from well-differentiated HCC. Most AMLs in the liver are not associated with tuberous sclerosis and may often lack a fatty component. The presence of bile or Mallory's hyaline can help in this distinction as these features are not seen in AML. Once the diagnosis is suspected, immunohistochemical confirmation is easy because of their characteristic staining profile. AMLs strongly coexpress smooth muscle markers, such as smooth muscle actin (SMA) or desmin, and melanoma markers like HMB-45, melan A, and microphthalmia-associated factor.[95] Focal S-100 expression can be seen in AML, generally in the epithelioid and fat cells. Hep Par 1 and polyclonal CEA are not expressed.

5. *Other tumors*: clear cell HCC can pose a diagnostic challenge when it occurs in non-cirrhotic liver without significant AFP elevation. The chief differential diagnosis is metastatic clear cell RCC.[96] Hep Par 1 and albumin ISH are consistently positive in clear cell HCC.[82,85] Canalicular pattern of staining with polyclonal CEA will also support HCC. Epithelial membrane antigen (EMA) and vimentin are expressed in RCC but are negative in HCC. Keratin profiles are not helpful as both are positive for CAM5.2, and negative for CK7 and 20.

Melanomas can also mimic HCC, but S-100 and HMB-45 are negative in hepatocellular tumors. Melanomas do not express Hep Par 1 or polyclonal CEA. Rarely, an adrenal cortical tumor may need to be distinguished from a primary hepatocellular tumor. Positive staining for inhibin in adrenal cortical tumors but not in HCC can be helpful.[97] In addition, hepatocyte markers like Hep Par 1 and polyclonal CEA are not expressed in adrenocortical carcinoma.

Molecular genetic features. Low-grade necroinflammatory activity associated with chronic liver disease and cirrhosis produces cytokines and other cytotoxic moieties, like nitric oxide and free oxygen radicals, which lead to DNA damage. The repeated cycles of necrosis and regeneration render the cells susceptible to mutations, and there may be insufficient time to repair DNA damage due to rapid cell turnover.[98] The preoplastic phase is characterized by overexpression of transforming growth factor-α (TGF-α) and insulin-like growth factor-2 (IGF-2), which lead to accelerated hepatocyte proliferation.[99]

Comparative genomic hybridization has revealed a fairly consistent pattern of chromosomal gains and losses in HCC. The most prominent changes are gains of part or entire chromosome arms 8q (49–81%), 1q (60–79%), and 7q (40–64%), and loss of 16q (36–65%).[100–102] Other common abnormalities include overrepresentation at sites Xq and 5p, and losses at 4q, 8p, 13q, 16q, and 17p. Certain clinicopathologic associations have been noted with specific abnormalities. Gains of 8q and 20q are associated with large tumor size.[100] Gain of 8q and loss of 13q are seen more often in HCC arising in non-cirrhotic liver.[100] Chromosome 9p and 6q losses have been reported to be independent predictors of poor outcome.[101]

p53 gene mutations are common in HCC and are reported in 30–50% of cases in most studies.[103,104] The prevalence varies widely between geographic areas, with low or none in Australia to 67% in Senegal.[104] Dietary exposure to aflatoxin is associated with a specific G→T transversion at codon 249 of the *p53* gene.[105] In hepatitis B, the HBx protein encoded by the X region of HBV has been linked to functional inactivation of the p53 protein.[106] Viral proteins encoded by the HCV genome like NS3 and NS5A proteins also interfere with p53 activity.[107,108] Mutations in beta-catenin, a critical component of the *Wnt* signaling pathway, is seen in around 20% of HCCs. The mutation rate may be as high as 40% in HCC associated with hepatitis C.[109] It has been suggested that there are two main pathways of hepatocarcinogenesis: one demonstrating beta-catenin mutations and limited genetic alterations like 8p loss, and the other with widespread allelic losses at multiple chromosomal sites, *p53* mutations, and no beta-catenin mutations.[101] The latter tumors are often poorly differentiated and behave

more aggressively. Abnormalities in cell cycle regulation are common in HCC. Inactivation of p16 by hypermethylation of the promoter region or loss of retinoblastoma protein Rb through gene mutation occurs in around 40% of HCC.[110,111] Reduced expression of inhibitors of cyclin-dependent kinases, p21 and p27, have been reported in 38% and 52% of HCC respectively.[112,113] The core protein produced by HCV can also lead to repression of the p21 promoter.[114]

Many molecular changes have been identified as potential prognostic markers. Tumors with inactivation of *p53*, *Rb*, and *p16* genes and allelic losses of 9p, 6q, and 14q have been reported with adverse outcome.[101,110,111,115] Immunohistochemical expression of p53 in tumor cells is associated with worse prognosis.[116] Beta-catenin mutations and high expression of p27 correlate with better survival,[101,117] while overexpression of cyclin D is a marker for early relapse.[115] High proliferative rate, low E-cadherin expression and nuclear beta-catenin expression are predictive of recurrence after transplantation.[118] However, none of these findings has been shown to be specific enough in large series to be used clinically.

Treatment and prognosis. For patients without cirrhosis and no evidence of vascular invasion or extrahepatic disease, resection is the treatment of choice. Survival in non-cirrhotic patients has been reported to be 40% and 26% at 5 and 10 years respectively.[119] Survival is worse in cirrhotic patients but 5-year survival of 33–44% can be achieved with tumors less than 5 cm, no vascular or extrahepatic involvement and good functional status (Child–Pugh class A). Liver transplantation is the best treatment for HCC in cirrhotic patients. Transplantation is contraindicated with tumors >5 cm, more than 3 tumors, multiple tumors with one of them >3 cm and extrahepatic spread. When these criteria are followed, 5-year survival greater than 75% has been achieved.[120] It has been suggested that the size of eligible solitary tumors should be increased to 6.5 cm.[121] Treatment of HCC using ethanol or radiofrequency ablation can be done under ultrasound or CT guidance. Ablative techniques are often used for small tumors that are considered unresectable due to their location or coexistent advanced liver disease, as well as in patients awaiting transplantation.[122]

The overall prognosis in HCC remains poor, with 5-year survival at 10%. Poor survival is associated with male sex, advanced age, poor differentiation, and presence of cirrhosis.[123–126] Tumors with encapsulation, small size, and a prominent intratumoral inflammatory infiltrate are associated with better outcome.[123,126] The histologic pattern is considered less significant prognostically, although a trabecular pattern has been reported to correlate with aggressive behavior while the pelioid pattern may have a better outcome.[125] Vascular invasion, lymph node metastases, and a positive surgical margin correlate with recurrence after resection.[123,126,127]

Fibrolamellar variant of HCC

Clinical features. The fibrolamellar variant of HCC (FLM) occurs in the non-cirrhotic liver in young adults (mean age 26 years, females > males).[128–130] Clinical presentation may include abdominal pain or swelling, anorexia, weight loss, jaundice, and rarely, hemoperitoneum. No definitive risk factors have been identified. FNH-like nodules have occasionally been seen at the periphery of FLM[131,132] and may be the result of local perfusion abnormalities[133] rather than a benign precursor of FLM.[134] Serum AFP levels are usually normal; rare tumors with high levels have been reported.[128,129]

Pathologic features

Gross features. FLM is a firm, tan-white to brown, well-circumscribed but unencapsulated, lobulated mass that arises in a background of normal liver (Fig. 10.27). Most tumors are large, and can measure up to 17 cm. The larger tumors can shows foci of hemorrhage and necrosis. While 60–70% of tumors are single, multiple tumors, generally in the form of satellite lesions, may be present. Unusually frequent involvement of the left lobe has been noted. A prominent central stellate scar similar to that of FNH can be present.[128] The scar is found in a minority of tumors and can also be seen in lymph node metastases.

Microscopic features. The hallmark features of FLM are large polygonal tumor cells with abundant eosinophilic granular cytoplasm, prominent macronucleoli and lamellar bands of fibrosis (Fig. 10.28). The collagen lamellae consist of plate-like stacks of connective tissue of variable thickness. Collagens I, III, and V are the dominant forms and are produced by

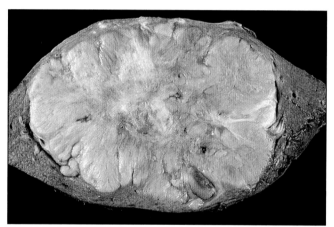

Fig. 10.27 • Fibrolamellar hepatocellular carcinoma. Tan-white to brown unencapsulated lobulated tumor with central scar.

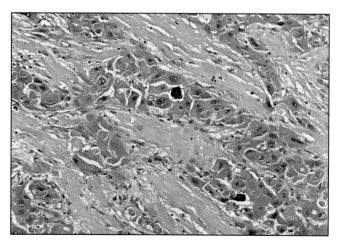

Fig. 10.28 • Fibrolamellar hepatocellular carcinoma showing large polygonal tumor cells with abundant eosinophilic granular cytoplasm, prominent macronucleoli, and lamellar bands of fibrosis.

stromal fibroblasts. The lamellar pattern is not uniformly seen throughout the tumor but often present in half of the tumor in most cases. The tumor cells are typically arranged in cords or nests. In addition to prominent nucleoli, the nuclei show intranuclear cytoplasmic invaginations and margination of chromatin. The cytoplasmic granularity is due to the presence of abundant mitochondria. Other cytoplasmic features include "pale bodies," which may contain fibrinogen and/or albumin. PAS-D-positive bodies, probably representing glycoprotein secretions, can be present. Bile plugs are common, but fat is usually absent. Other features that can occasionally be present are acinar structures, mucin secretion, multinucleated tumor cells, copper, epithelioid granulomas, and peliosis hepatis. Areas resembling trabecular HCC have also been noted;[135] it is not clear whether this represents a variant of FLM or a mixed FLM/conventional HCC.

Immunohistochemically, FLM resembles conventional HCC and expresses Hep Par 1, polyclonal CEA, and low molecular weight keratin. AFP immunoreactivity is uniformly absent. Neuroendocrine markers (see above) have been reported to be focally positive but have no known clinical significance.[94] Albumin ISH is positive in a majority of the cases.[82]

Treatment and prognosis. FLM is an aggressive tumor with 5-year survival of less than 50%. Complete excision of the involved lobe is the current therapy of choice. When the tumor location or extent precludes resection, liver transplantation can be performed, but the outcome is less favorable. Several studies have shown that FLM has a better prognosis than conventional HCC. However, outcome in FLM and conventional HCC arising in non-cirrhotic liver have been shown to be similar.[136,137] The apparently better outcome in FLM may be related to lack of cirrhosis and higher resectability rate rather than due to its unique clinicopathologic features.

Combined hepatocellular–cholangiocarcinoma (HCC-CC)

Clinical features. This is a rare tumor that represents <5% of primary liver tumors. It is more closely related to HCC, as evidenced by its frequent association with HBV or HCV infection and cirrhosis.[138,139] However, this information is largely based on studies in Asia and a large study in the USA revealed that the incidence of positive hepatitis B or C serology and cirrhosis is <15% in combined HCC-CC, which is similar to the rake in cholangiocarcinoma.[140]

Pathologic features. The diagnosis is based on the demonstration of both hepatocellular and glandular differentiation (Fig. 10.29). According to World Health Organization criteria, the hepatocellular component is identified by a trabecular growth pattern, bile production, or intercellular bile canaliculi. The cholangiocellular component is identified by definite gland formation or mucin production. The diagnosis can be confirmed immunohistochemically by demonstrating the HCC component with Hep Par 1, AFP and canalicular polyclonal CEA, and the cholangiocarcinoma component by MOC 31, CK7, and CK19. Areas of transition between HCC and cholangiocarcinoma are often present and both components often show albumin expression by ISH.[141] Some tumors may be composed entirely of cells with features intermediate between

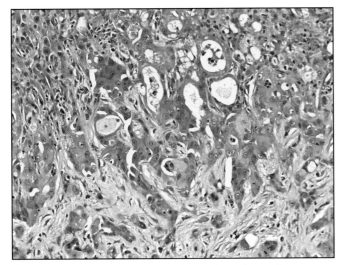

Fig. 10.29 • Combined hepatocellular–cholangiolar carcinoma. The tumor show features of hepatocellular carcinoma-like polygonal cells with abundant cytoplasm and trabecular pattern, but also has gland-like spaces that contain basophilic mucin or bile. Stromal desmoplasia, more typical of cholangiocarcinoma, is also present.

HCC and cholangiocarcinoma, and have been designated as intermediate carcinomas.[142] The histogenesis of combined HCC-CC remains uncertain. It may be an inadvertent collision of HCC and cholangiocarcinoma, or may represent a single tumor with divergent differentiation.[139,143] In the former case, the tumor would presumably be biclonal with no intimate admixture of HCC and cholangiocarcinoma components. The latter would presumably arise from a single clone with HCC or cholangiocarcinoma arising first and then transforming to the other, or origin from intermediate cells with divergent differentiation. Combined HCC-CCs with an intermediate phenotype are often *c-kit*-positive, supporting their origin from progenitor cells.[142] Genetic studies have shown that the majority of combined HCC-CCs arise from the same clone and share abnormalities with conventional HCC such as allelic losses of 4q, 8p, 17p, and 13q.[143]

Prognosis and therapy. The prognosis is poor and the disease is more aggressive than conventional HCC or cholangiocarcinoma. After resection, the 5-year survival is 24%. In unresectable cases, almost all patients die within 2 years.[140]

Hepatoblastoma

Clinical features

Hepatoblastoma is the most common malignant liver tumor in children and comprises approximately 1% of pediatric cancers. Nearly 90% of cases occur between the ages of 6 months and 5 years. This tumor can occasionally arise in older children[144,145] and, very rarely, in adults.[146] The lesion has a male preponderance of almost 2:1, but the sex incidence is similar in older cases. Associations with other congenital conditions such as Beckwith–Wiedemann syndrome,[145] cleft palate, diaphragmatic hernia,[146] Down's syndrome, familial polyposis coli,[148] hemihypertrophy, renal malformations, and other chromosomal abnormalities[149] are noted in one-third of cases. Most patients present with an asymptomatic abdominal mass. Weight loss,

anorexia, and a rapidly enlarging abdominal mass are common presenting symptoms. Less common symptoms include vomiting, diarrhea, or jaundice. Rarely, signs of precocious puberty such as virilization may be the presenting feature, which is associated with production of human chorionic gonadotropin (hCG) by the tumor.[150] Serum AFP is nearly always elevated, and has proven to be a useful marker for tumor recurrence or metastasis after therapy.

Pathologic features

Gross pathology. Hepatoblastoma occurs in the non-cirrhotic liver, typically as a large, single mass. The gross appearance can be variable, but the tumor is often multinodular with foci of hemorrhage and necrosis (Fig. 10.30). Since different nodules or zones within the tumor can represent different histologic components, which in turn may correlate with prognosis, adequate sampling of various areas must be done. After chemotherapy, tumors may be very necrotic and the mesenchymal components, especially osteoid, often appear prominent (Fig. 10.31).[151]

Microscopic features. The two morphologic subtypes of hepatoblastoma are the epithelial (55%) and the mixed epithelial–mesenchymal (45%). The epithelial type may show

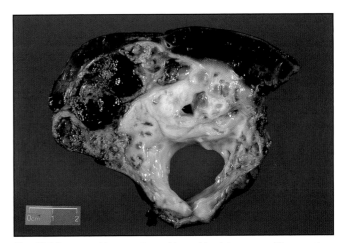

Fig. 10.30 • Hepatoblastoma. Gray-white multinodular tumor with areas of hemorrhage and necrosis.

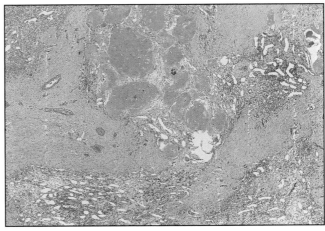

Fig. 10.31 • Hepatoblastoma showing prominent osteoid after chemotherapy.

an embryonal pattern, fetal pattern (Fig. 10.32), or a mixture of the two (Fig. 10.33). The mixed epithelial–mesenchymal subtype is composed of admixed epithelial and mesenchymal components.

The embryonal pattern is the more "immature" form, and consists of small tumor cells arranged in cords, ribbons, rosette-like structures, or tubules. The cells have round, oval, or elongated nuclei and scant basophilic cytoplasm. The fetal pattern is the more "mature" form that closely resembles fetal liver with tumor cell arranged in plates or cords. The tumor cells in the fetal pattern are typically smaller than normal hepatocytes, but are slightly larger than the tumor cells in the embryonal pattern and have moderate amounts of eosinophilic and/or clear cytoplasm. The clear cell change is due to the presence of lipid and/or glycogen. Both eosinophilic and clear cytoplasmic features often occur in the same tumor and result in an alternating pink and white appearance that is quite distinctive. The nuclei in the fetal pattern are typically small and round, similar to normal fetal liver cells. For both patterns, mitotic figures are rare. Extramedullary hematopoiesis is often present, usually associated with the fetal component.

Less common epithelial subtypes of hepatoblastoma include the small cell undifferentiated type and macro-trabecular type, which together account for around 5% of

cases. The small cell type consists of sheets of tumor cells with scant cytoplasm similar to other small blue cell tumors like neuroblastoma, Ewing sarcoma, lymphoma, and embryonal rhabdomyosarcoma. No evidence of hepatocellular differentiation is present. The identification of other typical patterns of hepatoblastoma helps in establishing the diagnosis. The macrotrabecular type forms wide trabeculae greater than 10 cells thick (Fig. 10.34). Fetal and/or embryonal-type tumor cells typically make up these trabeculae, but a less common pattern of large cells with more cytoplasm has rarely been seen, which histologically can mimic HCC. The presence of other patterns of hepatoblastoma and the occurrence in non-cirrhotic liver can help to distinguish this variant of macro-trabecular hepatoblastoma from HCC. A tumor with a limited macrotrabecular component should be classified according to the other predominant patterns.[152]

The epithelial components (embryonal, fetal, or both) are accompanied by a mesenchymal component in nearly half of cases. In 80% of mixed tumors, the mesenchymal component is represented by immature fibrous tissue, osteoid, and/or cartilage. The remaining 20% are mixed hepatoblastoma with teratoid features and show additional tissue types such as intestinal-type glandular elements, squamous epithelium, mucinous epithelium, melanin pigment, skeletal muscle, or neural tissue.

The tumor cells in hepatoblastoma express AFP in the embryonal and fetal components.[153] Hepatocytic markers, including Hep Par 1 and polyclonal CEA, will stain the epithelial component, especially in the fetal subtype.[154] Hepatocytic cytokeratins (8 and 18) and biliary cytokeratins (7 and 19) can be variably positive. Focal staining with chromogranin A has been reported in the embryonal, fetal, and osteoid components.[153]

Differential diagnosis. Pure fetal hepatoblastoma can be histologically similar to adenoma. The tumor cells tend to be smaller in hepatoblastoma than in adenoma and the alternating pink and white cytoplasmic staining pattern of hepatoblastoma is typically not present in adenoma. Clinical parameters can be very helpful in separating the two lesions as HA essentially does not occur before age 5, except in association with a metabolic disorder such as glycogen storage

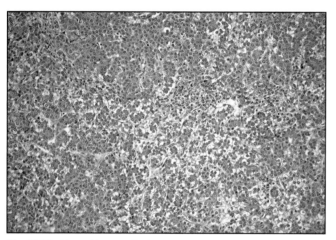

Fig. 10.32 • Hepatoblastoma, fetal pattern.

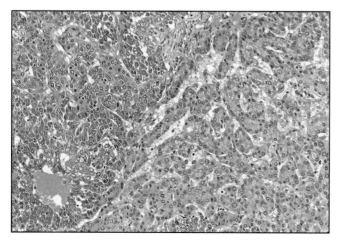

Fig. 10.33 • Hepatoblastoma, embryonal (left) and fetal (right) patterns.

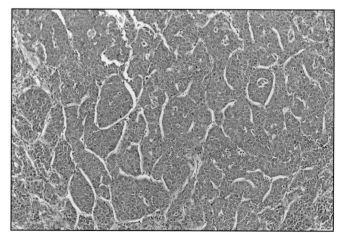

Fig. 10.34 • Hepatoblastoma, macrotrabecular pattern. The trabeculae are more than 10 cells thick.

disease, and serum AFP is not elevated in adenoma. The clinical setting also plays an important role in distinguishing the macrotrabecular variant of hepatoblastoma and HCC, as the latter may occur in this young age group in the presence of a pre-existing liver disease or metabolic disorder, usually in the setting of cirrhosis. The presence of other patterns of hepatoblastoma is helpful in the diagnosis of uncommon patterns like small cell undifferentiated and macrotrabecular. Mixed hepatoblastoma with teratoid features should be distinguished from teratomas. The latter lack the fetal and embryonal epithelial components of hepatoblastoma.

Molecular genetic changes. Hepatoblastoma cells are usually diploid or hyperploid and show limited cytogenetic alterations, often involving chromosomes 1, 2, 8, and 20. The most frequent alterations are trisomies of chromosomes 2 and 20.[155] Rearrangements involving chromosomes 1q and 2q, and gains of chromosome X have also been reported.[156] Loss of heterozygosity (LOH) of maternal 11p15 is seen in one-third of hepatoblastomas. This is characteristic of Beckwith–Wiedemann syndrome patients, who have an increased risk for developing hepatoblastoma. Imprinted genes on 11p15 such as IGF-2 may play an important role in hepatoblastoma.[157] Activation of the *Wnt*/β-catenin signaling pathway may play an important role in the development of hepatoblastoma through stabilizing β-catenin mutations. Abnormal nuclear localization of β-catenin can be demonstrated in the majority of hepatoblastomas by immunohistochemistry. It occurs more frequently in embryonal and undifferentiated hepatoblastoma compared to fetal type and is associated with poor survival in some studies,[157,158] but not in others.[155] *APC* mutations occur in sporadic hepatoblastoma as well as cases associated with familial adenomatous polyposis. Abnormal cell cycle regulation by inactivation of the *p16* gene by hypermethylation has been implicated in the pathogenesis.[159]

Prognosis and therapy. Prognosis is directly related to complete surgical excision and tumor stage.[152] The 5-year survival is around 75%.[157] The treatment of choice is complete surgical resection, but chemotherapy is often used preoperatively to reduce tumor size, as well as for residual and unresectable tumors. Liver transplantation is a treatment option for children with multifocal, bilobar, or recurrent hepatoblastoma without extrahepatic extension.[160,161] Some histologic subtypes, like pure fetal, have a better outcome after complete resection.[144] Other subtypes, such as the small cell and macrotrabecular types, are associated with poor prognosis.[152] Tumor-free margins are important, but vascular invasion does not have a significant impact on survival.[144] Other factors associated with an adverse outcome are age of presentation under 1 year, large tumor size, and involvement of vital structures.

Liver: benign mesenchymal tumors

Cavernous hemangioma

Clinical features

Cavernous hemangioma is the most common primary tumor of the liver. This benign vascular neoplasm is usually noted as an incidental finding at surgery or autopsy, but may come to surgical excision due to hemorrhage or its large size.[162,163] It has been suggested that estrogen therapy may lead to enlargement of the tumors.[162] These tumors can occasionally be multiple in the liver, and can be associated with hemangiomas at other sites as part of von Hippel–Lindau disease or a skeletal/systemic hemangiomatosis syndrome.[164] Small hemangiomas are asymptomatic and do not require therapy. Giant hemangiomas, defined as those 4 cm and greater, can be associated with increased abdominal girth, pain, nausea, jaundice, or hemobilia, and may rarely rupture.[165,166] Large hemangiomas may also lead to thrombocytopenia or consumptive coagulopathy (Kasabach–Merritt syndrome).[163,166]

Pathologic features

Gross pathology. Hemangiomas are well-circumscribed red-brown tumors. They have a spongy texture or honeycombed surface representing the cavernous vascular component, and many undergo thrombosis and sclerosis, resulting in a firm, white to tan appearance (Fig. 10.35).

Microscopic features. The hallmark of this tumor is the cavernous vascular channels lined by a single layer of flattened endothelial cells without cytologic atypia or mitotic activity (Fig. 10.36). The walls of these channels consist of thin fibrous stroma. Dilated vascular channels are often present beyond the confines of the main hemangioma, resembling hemangiomatosis (Fig. 10.37).[167] Vascular thrombosis can occur. Sclerotic zones can be present and when extensive can mimic a localized scar.

Infantile hemangioendothelioma

Clinical features

Infantile hemangioendothelioma (IHE) is the second most common tumor in children under 3 years of age, second only to hepatoblastoma, and almost all the reported cases have occurred in infants less than 6 months old. The tumor is almost twice as common in girls as in boys.[168,169] Hemangiomas in other organs are present in 10–15% of the patients.[163] The

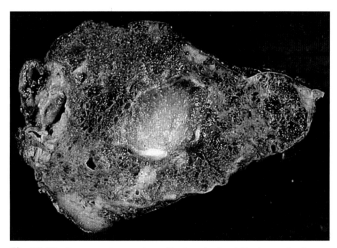

Fig. 10.35 • Cavernous hemangioma. Varying-sized cyst-like hemorrhagic spaces giving a honeycombed appearance. The central tan-white area is the result of thrombosis and organization.

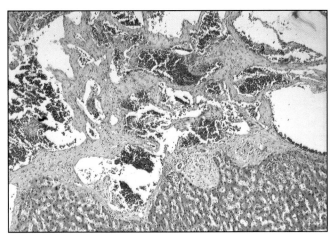

Fig. 10.36 • Cavernous hemangioma. The tumor consists of large vascular channels separated by fibrous bands lined by flattened endothelium.

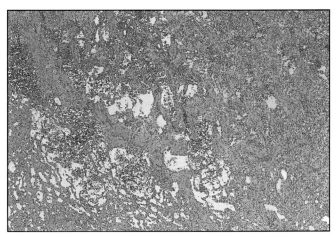

Fig. 10.38 • Infantile hemangioendothelioma, type 1. Irregular varying-size vascular channels lined by uniform endothelial cells embedded in a myxoid stroma.

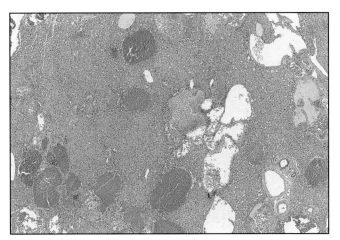

Fig. 10.37 • Cavernous hemangioma. Dilated vascular channels are often present beyond the confines of the main hemangioma, resembling hemangiomatosis.

tumors may also be associated with congenital anomalies such as bilateral renal agenesis, Beckwith–Wiedemann syndrome, trisomy 21, hemihypertrophy, or meningomyelocele.[163,168] Concurrent occurrence of IHE and mesenchymal hamartoma has been reported.[170] The presenting feature may be an abdominal mass or distension, with hepatomegaly, jaundice, diarrhea, constipation, vomiting, congestive heart failure, or failure to thrive.[168] Other less common findings can include thrombocytopenia due to sequestration of platelets within the tumor or rupture with hemoperitoneum.[8] Elevation of AFP, often slight, can occur.[171]

Pathologic features

Gross pathology. IHE is often a poorly circumscribed lesion, and can be solid and cystic, with variably hemorrhagic foci. Nearly half of the tumors are multifocal and vary from less than 1 cm to 15 cm in size.

Microscopic features. Most tumors show a mixture of large numbers of small vascular channels and fewer large, irregularly shaped spaces with a cavernous appearance, embedded in a poorly developed fibromyxomatous stroma containing scattered

collagen or reticulin fibers (Fig. 10.38). The vascular channels are lined by a single layer of endothelial cells. Mitoses can be numerous, but do not appear to influence prognosis. Small bile ducts as well as hepatocytes can be seen in the stroma, often near the periphery of the tumor. Focal necrosis, hemorrhage, fibrosis, and calcification are often present. In a comprehensive review, Dehner & Ishak divided the lesions into two histologic types.[168] The above-mentioned changes corresponded to type 1 lesions. Type 2 lesions contain poorly formed anastamosing channels with papillae and a complex budding or branching pattern. These vascular spaces are lined by atypical endothelial cells with nuclear enlargement and hyperchromasia, irregular nuclear borders, and brisk mitotic activity.[172,173] Type 2 changes can be focal and adequate tumor sampling is recommended. Some studies have shown that there is a low but clear risk of aggressive behavior in tumors with type 2 changes. The clinical outcome is benign in most cases regardless of the presence of type 2 changes. However, all tumors with poor outcomes have type 2 changes. Some authors believe that type 2 changes are a marker for aggressive behavior, but do not equate to a malignant neoplasm. However, other authors consider type 2 IHE as a pediatric angiosarcoma. This view is supported by the presence of solid foci and kaposiform areas in some cases. These are composed of spindle cell fascicles with interspersed PAS-positive diastase-resistant globules. Immunohistochemically, the endothelial cells are positive for CD34, CD31, and factor VIII-related antigen. The stromal cells express alpha-SMA and vimentin, and lack desmin, a profile consistent with pericytes.[174]

Prognosis and therapy

The significance of type 2 changes remains controversial: some regard them as having no impact on outcome,[173] while others consider type 2 IHE as a low-grade angiosarcoma.[163] The overall survival is 70%, with a vast majority of deaths occurring in the first month after diagnosis.[163,173] Mortality is related to local tumor effects and not metastasis, which does not occur. The presence of heart failure, jaundice, multiple nodules, infiltrative borders, and lack of cavernous spaces are poor prognostic features.[172,173] Rare association with true angiosarcoma has been recorded.[175] The tumors can regress spontaneously, or with steroid and alpha-interferon therapy. If medical management fails, resection, liver transplantation, hepatic arterial ligation, or embolization can be considered.[173,176]

Mesenchymal hamartoma

Clinical features

Mesenchymal hamartoma is an uncommon tumor occurring almost exclusively in children, with more than 50% of cases diagnosed in the first year of life.[177] It is the third most common tumor of the liver in this age group, following hepatoblastoma and IHE.[178] Only a few cases have been reported in adults, most often in females.[179] The patients often present with a palpable liver mass, abdominal enlargement or respiratory distress due to compression by the tumor. There is no known risk for malignant transformation.

Pathologic features

Gross pathology. The tumor can be solid or cystic, with solid areas typically being tan in color. When cysts are present, they contain a translucent fluid or a gelatinous material.[145,178] These cysts may form due to the degeneration of the loose mesenchymal tissue of the tumor. Continued accumulation of fluid into these cysts contributes to increase in tumor size.

Microscopic features. Mesenchymal hamartoma shows both epithelial and stromal components. The former consists of relatively normal-appearing hepatocytes and bile ducts, both of which are surrounded by varying amounts of myxoid to fibrous stroma (Fig. 10.39). The hepatocytes are arranged in clusters of varying size with retention of the cell plate architecture, as in the normal liver. The bile duct structures are typically arranged in a branching pattern, and often are associated with an acute inflammatory infiltrate in or adjacent to the duct walls. The cystic spaces, when present, may be lined by flattened to cuboidal epithelial cells, and are surrounded by a loose or dense fibrous tissue. Cysts may also lack any lining cells. The stroma generally contains increased numbers of small vascular structures, spindle cells, and inflammatory cells. No normal portal zones are present. Extramedullary hematopoiesis

is often noted. In adults, the stroma is more fibrotic and densely hyalinized with only focal myxoid areas.[177] In some cases the mesenchymal component may be the predominant feature of the lesion, with sparse ductal elements. Immunohistochemically, the ductal elements express CK7 and lack CK20. The stromal cells are positive for SMA and vimentin. Complex chromosomal translocations between 11, 17, and 19 have been reported.[180]

Prognosis and therapy

Mesenchymal hamartoma is considered a benign tumor with good prognosis if completely resected.[181] Given the histologic similarity between mesenchymal hamartoma and von Meyenburg complexes, it has been proposed that mesenchymal hamartoma represents a developmental anomaly of the ductal plate. However, the presence of cytogenetic abnormalities and occasional aneuploid cases would favor a neoplastic pathogenesis. A link between mesenchymal hamartoma and undifferentiated embryonal sarcoma has been postulated based on overlapping clinicopathologic features, and embryonal sarcoma arising within mesenchymal hamartoma has been reported.[182] Similar genetic abnormalities involving chromosome 19p can occur in mesenchymal hamartoma and embryonal sarcoma.

Angiomyolipoma

Clinical features

AMLs are rare in the liver. The tumor most often presents in the 30–40-year age group with a marked female preponderance.[95,183] Most AMLs in the liver are not associated with tuberous sclerosis.[95,183] Around 10% can occur in the setting of tuberous sclerosis and are usually associated with renal AML. Multiple hepatic AMLs with more than 15 tumors have been reported.[184] The tumor is thought to differentiate towards the so-called perivascular epithelioid cell (PEC), and related lesions in other organs include the clear cell "sugar" tumor and lymphangioleiomyomatosis.[185]

Pathologic features

Gross pathology. AML can present as a large, variably colored tumor due to fat, necrosis, and hemorrhage (Fig. 10.40).[95,183]

Microscopic features. AML is composed of varying proportions of smooth muscle-like cells, blood vessels, and fat, often in association with hematopoietic cells. The smooth muscle-like differentiation is often the most prominent in liver lesions, and consists of epithelioid or spindled cells which often surround or "spin off" vessels (Fig. 10.41). The epithelioid cells are round or polygonal with abundant eosinophilic cytoplasm (Fig. 10.42). The nuclei are typically large with prominent nucleoli, but their appearance can vary. The cytoplasmic contents may be oncocytic, and may be condensed around the nucleus with a clear zone near the cell membrane, giving the appearance of a spider-web.[95] The spindle cells have eosinophilic cytoplasm and small oval nuclei. Trabeculae composed mostly of the epithelioid type of cells have also been noted. The epithelioid or spindle component may predominate to the exclusion of the other. The vascular component is typically

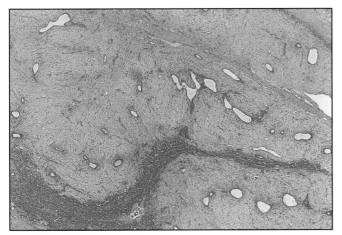

Fig. 10.39 • Mesenchymal hamartoma. Ductular structures embedded in a fibromyxoid stroma.

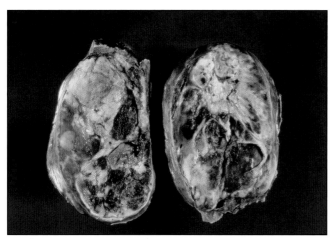

Fig. 10.40 • Angiomyolipoma. The tumor can be large with foci of hemorrhage and necrosis, mimicking a malignant process. (Reproduced with permission from Ferrell L D 2003 Liver. In: Weidner N, Cote R J, Suster S, Weiss L M (eds) Modern surgical pathology. Saunders, Philadelphia, Fig. 27-21, CD, p 919–979.)

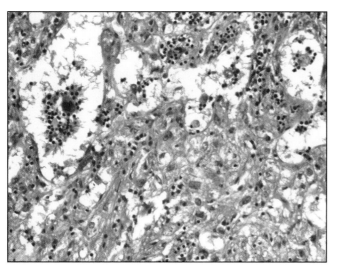

Fig. 10.41 • Angiomyolipoma. Spindle to polygonal myoid tumor cells with prominent vessels and extramedullary hemopoiesis.

made up of thick-walled arterial or venous-like channels admixed with thin-walled venous-like spaces. The fatty tissue consists of mature fat cells scattered throughout the tumor as single, clusters, or sheets of cells. In liver AML, especially the monotypic epithelioid variant with a pure sinusoidal trabecular pattern, the fat component can be scant or absent.[186] Foam cells containing fine droplets of lipid are also often seen. Peliotic spaces closely associated with areas of hemorrhage can be present. These spaces mostly lack an endothelial lining. Prominent dense lymphoid aggregates composed of a mixture of T and B cells can be noted as well. Rarely, the inflammatory cells can be associated with the stromal spindle cell component of the tumor, mimicking inflammatory pseudo-tumor. Hemosiderin and melanin pigment can be present. Variable numbers of hematopoietic elements, including mega-karyocytes, erythroid, and myeloid precursors, are often noted in the stroma.

Most of the diagnostic problems arise in monotypic tumors composed exclusively of epithelioid smooth muscle-like cells as the large round nuclei with prominent nucleoli and abundant eosinophilic cytoplasm mimic HCC, HA, or metastatic melanoma. Epithelioid variants with trabecular pattern often lack fat, furthering the resemblance to a hepatocellular neoplasm. Histologically, the presence of bile and Mallory's hyaline in the tumor points towards HCC. Immunohistochemically, AMLs uniformly express melanocytic markers like HMB-45 (Fig. 10.43), Melan A, tyrosinase, and microphthalmia transcription factor. In addition, SMA is positive in the smooth muscle-like component in >95% of cases. The spindle cells often stain more strongly for SMA and the epithelioid cells for HMB-45.[95] Melanosomes can be demonstrated ultrastructurally in half the cases.[187] Desmin positivity has also been noted in the spindle cells.[95] Stains for cytokeratin and Hep Par 1 are negative. Focal S-100 expression can be seen in AML, generally in the epithelioid and fat cells.[95] Uniform expression of *c-kit* (CD117) has been reported in AML:[188] its significance is uncertain and there are no evident therapeutic implications.

Treatment and prognosis. AML is a benign lesion and resection is curative. To date, recurrences are not known to occur.[189,190]

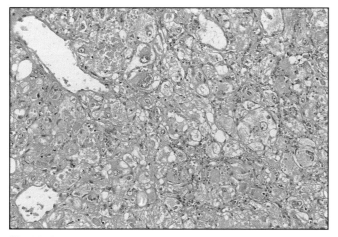

Fig. 10.42 • Monotypic angiomyolipoma with epithelioid tumor cells. This tumor can easily be mistaken for a hepatocellular neoplasm.

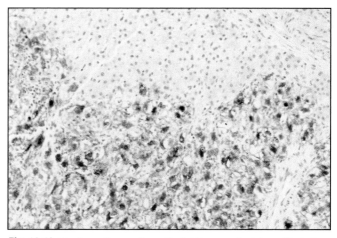

Fig. 10.43 • Angiomyolipoma. The epithelioid tumor cells stain positively for HMB-45 (bottom) while hepatocytes are negative (top).

Inflammatory pseudotumor

Clinical features

Inflammatory pseudotumor is an inflammatory and fibrosing lesion that occurs more frequently in the lungs and mediastinum and rarely in the liver.[191–193] Synonyms for this entity may include inflammatory myofibroblastic tumor and plasma cell granuloma. It accounts for 0.4% of all focal liver lesions.[194] At the present time, it seems likely that lesions grouped under the heading of hepatic inflammatory pseudotumor may be heterogeneous in nature. Patients may present with abdominal pain, fever, chills, jaundice, vomiting, and weight loss. Associations with primary sclerosing cholangitis,[193] inflammatory bowel disease, cholelithiasis, Papillon–Lefevre syndrome in children, Kostmann disease, leukemia, and HIV have been reported.[195] It can be mistaken clinically for cholangiocarcinoma if located in the hilar region. Its pathogenesis is unclear but infections, autoimmunity, and intraparenchymal hemorrhage have been invoked. Evidence of Epstein–Barr virus has been noted in various sites, including the liver.[196] Some have suggested that the latter subset of hepatic lesions are, in fact, follicular dendritic cell (FDC) sarcomas.[196,197]

Pathologic features

Gross pathology. The appearance can vary considerably, especially in the larger lesions, with foci of fibrosis, hemorrhage, and necrosis.[192] The tumor can vary considerably in size, and may be solitary or multiple. Solitary lesions are often large (2–15 cm) and located in the porta hepatis. When multiple, lesions are typically smaller, involve both lobes, and can mimic metastases.[192,198]

Microscopic features. Inflammatory pseudotumor consists of a mixture of inflammatory and fibrous tissue, but the relative degree of these components can be variable (Fig. 10.44). It has been categorized into hyalinized sclerosing, xanthogranuloma, and plasma cell granuloma types, but various patterns can be found in a single lesion, making this categorization less

useful.[199] The inflammatory component of the lesion usually contains a polyclonal population of plasma cells but neutrophils, eosinophils, lymphocytes (predominantly T cells), and macrophages (often xanthomatous) are also often present in varying numbers.[191,193] The spindle cell component is made up of (myo)fibroblasts, often with a fascicular architecture, and sclerotic foci are common. Mitotic figures may be seen but should not be numerous, and abnormal mitotic figures are not present.[192] Occasionally, granulomas or phlebitis may also be identified.[191,193]

The differential diagnosis includes hepatic abscess as well as malignant mesenchymal tumors like angiosarcoma, leiomyosarcoma, and metastatic gastrointestinal stromal sarcoma. These sarcomas show cellular atypia, frequent mitoses, and typically lack numerous inflammatory cells. Immunohistochemistry can be helpful by demonstrating factor VIII-related antigen and other vascular endothelial markers in angiosarcoma, desmin in leiomyosarcoma, and CD117 in metastatic gastrointestinal stromal sarcomas. The differentiation from FDC neoplasms may be more difficult, but the absence of plasma cells, the presence of pleomorphic tumor cells, and expression of specific FDC markers such as CD21, CD35, and R4/23 would favor an FDC neoplasm.[197,199]

Prognosis and treatment

Inflammatory pseudotumors are benign lesions but may require major liver resection based on their location and the inability to distinguish them accurately from malignant lesions before surgery. Most patients show complete recovery after resection, without recurrences. Medical management is often not successful.[200] Multiple smaller lesions appear to involute, and may not require any specific therapy.[198]

Other benign tumors and tumor-like lesions

Benign neoplasms that have also been noted in the liver include chondroma,[201] schwannoma,[202] solitary fibrous tumor,[203] fibroma, leiomyoma, lipoma, lymphangiomatosis, myxoma, and adrenal and pancreatic rests.[163]

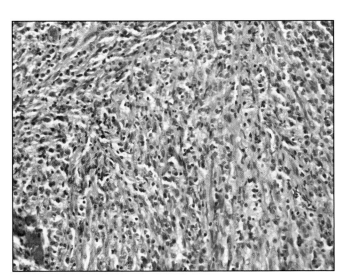

Fig. 10.44 • Inflammatory pseudotumor. Uniform spindle cells with dense infiltrate of lymphocytes and plasma cells.

Liver: malignant mesenchymal tumors

Angiosarcoma

Clinical features

Angiosarcoma is a rare primary malignant tumor constituting 2% of all primary hepatic neoplasms. It is the most common malignant mesenchymal tumor of the liver and usually occurs in middle-aged adults, but has been noted rarely in children,[204] occasionally in the setting of IHE.[173] Risk factors include thorotrast, arsenic, and vinyl chloride exposure.[205] Association with other substances like cyclophosphamide and anabolic steroids has been noted, but more than 75% of cases have no apparent risk factor.[205] The clinical presentation can include hepatomegaly, ascites, jaundice, thrombocytopenia, hemoperitoneum, and liver failure.

Pathologic features

Gross pathology. Angiosarcomas are often large hemorrhagic tumors with indistinct borders and variably solid or cystic areas, the latter usually containing blood (Fig. 10.45). The tumor size usually varies between 4 and 20 cm. Satellite nodules can be present.

Microscopic features. The tumor typically has mixed histology with sinusoidal, solid, papillary, and cavernous growth patterns. The sinusoidal pattern is the most distinctive, with the endothelial cells lining both sides of the hepatic cell plates in a scaffold-like arrangement that dissects the plates, and often results in sinusoidal dilatation (Fig. 10.46). The tumor cells lining the cell plates are more numerous, hyperchromatic, and larger than normal endothelial cells. This sinusoidal pattern is more likely to be noted at the periphery of the tumor and may represent an early growth pattern, which later transforms into the solid or papillary patterns. The solid pattern may have a spindled fascicular or whorled appearance. The papillary pattern consists of nodules of stroma covered by tumor cells that protrude into lumina (Fig. 10.47). The cavernous pattern consists of large blood-filled spaces, and is commonly seen in association with the other patterns. The

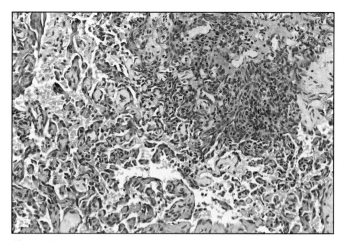

Fig. 10.47 • Angiosarcoma. The tumor shows a papillary pattern with nodular excrescences of fibrous tissue covered by tumor cells.

tumor cells can be spindled or epithelioid. Nuclear pleomorphism, bizarre nuclei, multinucleated cells, and frequent mitoses can be seen. Invasion of the hepatic venules and portal vein branches is common and may account for the hemorrhage and necrosis. Marked periportal and capsular fibrosis can be seen in cases associated with vinyl chloride and thorotrast. Thorotrast deposits can be seen in Kupffer cells, portal connective tissue, and venous walls as granular refractile pink-brown deposits.[206]

The tumor cells express endothelial markers such as factor VIII-related antigen, CD31 and CD34, but all tumor cells may not be uniformly stained. This helps in the differentiation from HCC, metastatic carcinoma, and other mesenchymal tumors.

Genetic changes

Hepatic angiosarcomas are characterized by *p53* mutations, *K-ras-2* mutations and inactivation of *p16* by hypermethylation.[207] Tumors associated with vinyl chloride have a high frequency of G→A transitions in the *K-ras-2* gene and A: T→T: A transversions in the *p53* gene.[206,208]

Prognosis and treatment

Radical resection of the tumor is the best form of treatment, but may not be always feasible due to the extent of the disease. The mean survival after diagnosis is 6 months.[209]

Epithelioid hemangioendothelioma

Clinical features

Epithelioid hemangioendothelioma (EHE) is a rare, low-grade malignancy that primarily affects adults (30–40 years), tends to be more common in women,[210,211] and is rare in children.[212] No risk factors are known, and the reported association with oral contraceptives remains unsubstantiated. Many lesions are discovered as an incidental finding, but presenting symptoms can include an upper abdominal mass or discomfort. The presence of multiple lesions, which is quite common, may mimic metastatic disease. Serum alkaline phosphatase levels may be elevated.

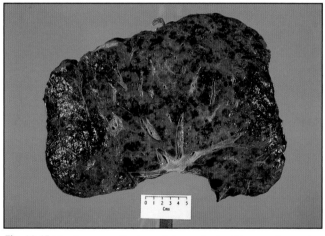

Fig. 10.45 • Angiosarcoma. The tumor is hemorrhagic with zones of necrosis and irregular borders. (Courtesy of Dr. P. Anthony.)

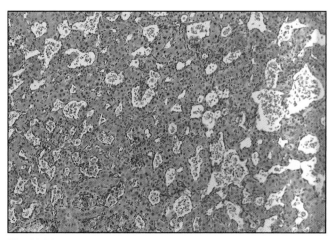

Fig. 10.46 • Angiosarcoma, sinusoidal pattern.

Pathologic features

Gross pathology. EHE is a firm, white to yellow tumor that often has an ill-defined border (Fig. 10.48). Two different forms have been described: a nodular type, representing the early stage of the disease and observed in around 10% of cases at presentation, and the diffuse type, considered as the advanced stage due to coalescence of multiple lesions. The tumor can be multifocal with involvement of both right and left liver lobes. Focal calcification can be present, and cause a somewhat gritty consistency.

Microscopic features. EHE is often fibrotic and paucicellular at the center with cellular areas at the periphery (Fig. 10.49). The tumor tends to grow around and leave intact pre-existing structures such as the portal zones and terminal hepatic venules. The tumor also has a marked predilection for invading vascular structures such as portal and central veins, which can mimic the histologic appearance of vascular thrombosis. Intravascular small papillary projections or tufts can occur

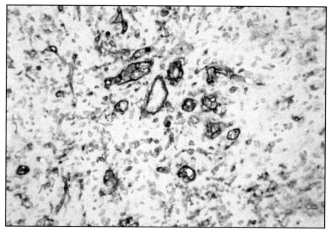

Fig. 10.50 • Epithelioid hemangioendothelioma. CD34 stain highlights endothelial nature of tumor cells.

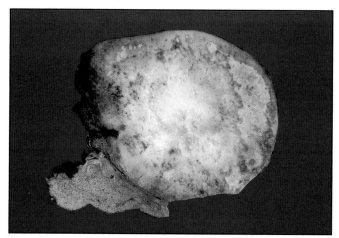

Fig. 10.48 • Epithelioid hemangioendothelioma. The tumor is firm and white. (Reproduced with permission from Ferrell L D 2003 Liver. In: Weidner N, Cote R J, Suster S, Weiss L M (eds) Modern surgical pathology. Saunders, Philadelphia, Fig. 27-25, CD, p 919–979.)

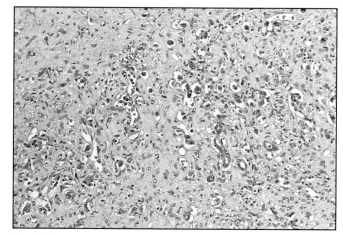

Fig. 10.49 • Epithelioid hemangioendothelioma. Poorly formed vascular structures lined by epithelioid tumor cells and embedded in a fibrous stroma.

within thin-walled vascular spaces. Residual hepatocytes or bile ducts can be present within the tumor, especially near the periphery. The tumor cells can be dendritic or epithelioid in appearance. The former are irregularly shaped, elongated, or stellate cells with branching processes. The cell cytoplasm may contain a vacuole, thought to represent intracellular lumina, which may contain erythrocytes. The epithelioid tumor cells are round with more abundant eosinophilic cytoplasm. Nuclear atypia and mitoses can be seen in the epithelioid cells. Both cell types are surrounded by a myxoid to fibrous stroma. Calcification of the more dense type of stroma may be present. Scattered inflammatory cells such as lymphocytes and neutrophils are often seen.

The main differential diagnosis is with adenocarcinoma (including cholangiocarcinoma), angiosarcoma, and HCC. Features such as young age, multifocal disease, characteristic pattern of tumor infiltration at the lesional periphery and occasional calcification can help in the diagnosis. However, immunohistochemical expression of endothelial markers such as CD34 (Fig. 10.50), CD31, and/or factor VIII-related antigen are required to confirm the diagnosis. Angiosarcoma also expresses endothelial markers, but is more destructive and often has a greater degree of nuclear atypia and mitoses. Focal keratin positivity in the tumor due to entrapped hepatocytes, bile ducts, and also in tumor cells in some cases can be mistaken for carcinoma.[213] Another occasional diagnostic problem can be the differentiation of EHE from venous thrombosis/veno-occlusive disease as the tumor growth within large vessels can mimic an organizing thrombus.

Prognosis and treatment

The natural history of this tumor is extremely variable, with long survival despite no treatment or incomplete resection in some cases, and adverse outcome in others despite adequate resection and adjuvant therapy.[211,214] The primary treatment is hepatic resection. Liver transplantation has been successfully performed in unresectable cases,[215] but data on long-term survival are not available. Extrahepatic disease is not a contraindication for transplantation.[216] Expression of *p53* and decreased expression of vascular endothelial growth factor may be seen in less differentiated tumors.[217] Overall, the prognosis is better than angiosarcoma, even if excision is incomplete or extrahepatic metastases are present. EHE is generally unresponsive to radio- or chemotherapy, although occasional reduction of tumor mass has been reported with interferon 2-alpha and intra-arterial 5-fluorouracil.[218]

Undifferentiated embryonal sarcoma

Clinical features

Embryonal sarcoma is a rare tumor that typically occurs in children 6–10 years old.[219] It is the most common hepatic malignant mesenchymal tumor in children. It has been variously called malignant mesenchymoma, fibromyxosarcoma, and rhabdomyosarcoma of the liver. Abdominal mass and pain are common presenting features.[219,220]

Pathologic features

Gross pathology. Embryonal sarcomas are usually large, soft tumors, with variably cystic and solid areas and a white, shiny or gelatinous or mucoid surface. Areas of necrosis and hemorrhage are often present.

Microscopic features. The tumors may appear well demarcated, but tumor infiltration beyond the pseudocapsule into the liver is common. The tumor comprises a mixture of spindle and stellate cells embedded in a myxoid stroma (Fig. 10.51). The tumor cells have a granular to bubbly, light pink cytoplasm, and may contain cytoplasmic globules of various sizes which are positive with PAS-D. These globules may also be noted in the stroma. Other features include large atypical tumor cells with hyperchromatic nuclei, multinucleated tumor cells, and brisk mitoses. The stroma is usually myxoid but some dense collagen can be present. Extramedullary hematopoiesis is often noted and entrapped hepatocytes and/or ductules can be present at the periphery. Vimentin and *bcl-2* are the only immunohistochemical markers that are consistently expressed, but neither is specific.[221] Focal positive results are often obtained with keratin, desmin, and alpha$_1$-antitrypsin.[220,222] Hep Par 1, S-100, myogenin, and CD34 are negative.[221]

Genetic changes

Multiple chromosomal amplifications and deletions have been reported without any characteristic changes.[223] Translocations involving 19q13 have been found in both embryonal sarcoma and mesenchymal hamartoma.[222] The 19q region is also altered in other mesenchymal tumors such as osteosarcoma and liposarcoma.

Prognosis and therapy

The prognosis is poor with only 20% long-term survival in large series.[219] Complete surgical excision generally offers the best outcome.[220,222] This can be challenging as the tumors are usually large at presentation. Improved outcomes have been reported with the use of adjuvant preoperative and postoperative therapy.[222]

Kaposi sarcoma

Clinical features

Kaposi sarcoma (KS) most often occurs in the liver in the setting of immunosuppression, such as acquired immune deficiency syndrome (AIDS) and liver transplantation. Human herpesvirus-8 is etiologically related to KS in immunosuppressed patients.[224]

Pathologic features

Most of the findings of KS in the liver are similar to those seen at other sites. The tumor is fibrous to hemorrhagic, usually multifocal, and often centered on portal triads. The tumor consists of fascicles of spindle cell with slit-like spaces. As at other sites, cellular pleomorphism and mitotic activity are minimal, and extravasation of erythrocytes, hemosiderin deposits, and small eosinophilic globules are typically present. One pattern that is typically seen only in the liver is the growth of the spindle tumor cells into and along the sinusoidal spaces, usually at the periphery of the tumor nodules (Fig. 10.52).

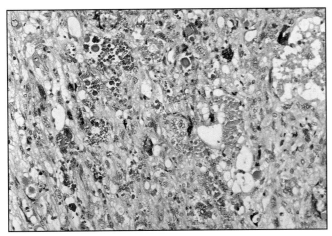

Fig. 10.51 • Undifferentiated embryonal sarcoma with large atypical tumor cells in a myxoid stroma. Note the hyperchromatic nuclei and prominent cytoplasmic globules.

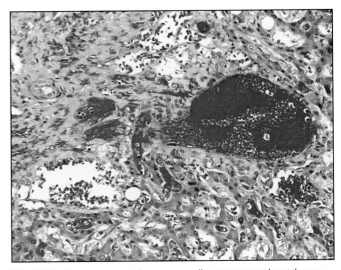

Fig. 10.52 • Kaposi sarcoma. The tumor usually centers around portal zones and extends into the adjacent parenchyma. The tumor cells grow along the sinusoids, causing sinusoidal dilatation and peliosis-like lesions.

This pattern of growth results in dilated channels containing erythrocytes that replace the normal sinusoids, findings that have a peliotic appearance. The tumor also tends to surround or infiltrate the portal zone, often leaving the hepatic artery and interlobular bile duct intact. Immunohistochemically, the tumor cells are positive for endothelial markers CD31 and CD34 as well as for human herpesvirus-8, which can be useful to help differentiate KS from fibroblastic proliferations.

Prognosis and therapy

KS is not known to influence outcome significantly in HIV-positive patients. Fatal disseminated KS has been reported in liver transplant recipients.[225]

Hematopoietic malignancies

All types of leukemia and lymphoma (Hodgkin and non-Hodgkin) may secondarily involve the liver.[225] The **leukemias** typically involve the liver in a diffuse pattern, with infiltration of the sinusoids by leukemic cells, with the exception that chronic lymphocytic and acute lymphoblastic leukemia often involve the portal zones, similar to lymphomatous pattern of infiltrate. Hairy cell leukemia may also be associated with the formation of a peliosis hepatis-like lesion consisting of dilated sinusoids lined by tumor cells.

Hodgkin lymphoma typically involves the liver as nodular masses within the portal zones. Reed–Sternberg cells should be noted in order to make a definitive diagnosis, but the presence of an infiltrate composed of lymphocytes, admixed with plasma cells, eosinophils, and some atypical cells would be consistent with Hodgkin lymphoma if the diagnosis is already well established at another site. Occasionally, epithelioid granulomas may be found in either the parenchyma or in portal zones, but granulomas alone without the other features noted above are not sufficient for the diagnosis. Rarely, intrahepatic cholestasis, occasionally associated with a paucity of bile ducts, can be seen.[226]

Non-Hodgkin lymphomas usually involve the liver as part of disseminated disease by forming nodular masses in the portal tracts. Some lymphomas may show sinusoidal infiltration by the tumor cells similar to that seen in leukemia.[227] Liver involvement is especially common in the peripheral T-cell lymphomas, occurring in as many as 50% of patients.[228] Intrahepatic cholestasis and epithelioid granulomas similar to those seen in Hodgkin lymphoma have also been noted.

Primary hepatic lymphomas are rare and constitute 0.4% of all extranodal lymphomas. Contiguous lymph node involvement and extrahepatic spread may be present but liver involvement is the dominant clinical presentation. Association with AIDS, hepatitis B and C, immunosuppressive therapy, autoimmune diseases, and primary biliary cirrhosis has been noted.[229] These tumors present as solitary or multiple masses, and can occasionally show diffuse infiltration of the liver. Most of the lymphomas are diffuse large B-cell type, but others, like Burkitt lymphoma and low grade B-cell lymphoma of mucosa-associated lymphoid tissue (MALT) type, have been reported. Surgery is an option for resectable tumors, although chemotherapy followed by radiation is currently the treatment of choice in early-stage disease. Recurrence-free 5-year survival of 70% has been achieved.[230] Hepatosplenic T-cell lymphoma originates from cytotoxic gamma delta T cells and commonly involves the liver with sinusoidal infiltration and variable portal involvement.[231] Concomitant involvement of the spleen and bone marrow is common. These tumors are very aggressive, with a mean survival of 1 year.

Other malignant tumors

Carcinoid tumor, fibrosarcoma, so-called malignant fibrous histiocytoma, FDC tumor, leiomyosarcoma, liposarcoma, malignant mesenchymoma, osteosarcoma, pheochromocytoma, plasmacytoma, malignant rhabdoid tumor, rhabdomyosarcoma, malignant schwannoma, squamous cell carcinoma, malignant trophoblastic tumor, teratoma, and yolk sac tumor have all been described as primary malignancies in the liver.[232–240] Malignant tumors with mixed epithelial and stromal elements have been described and probably represent a heterogeneous group of tumors such as mixed hepatoblastoma and sarcomatoid carcinoma. Some of these show ossification and have been referred to as ossifying stromal-epithelial tumor.[232,241]

Among **metastatic tumors**, lung, breast, colon, and pancreas are the most common primary sites, but tumors from any site can spread to the liver. Melanoma and neuroendocrine tumors frequently metastasize to the liver and can be confused with HCC. Diffuse nodular infiltration of the liver resembling cirrhosis can occur, and is most frequently associated with metastatic breast carcinoma.[242] Intrahepatic biliary spread can be seen in metastatic colonic adenocarcinoma and can mimic cholangiocarcinoma.[243] Leiomyosarcomas and gastrointestinal stromal sarcomas are the most common mesenchymal tumors to metastasize to the liver.[232]

Gallbladder: benign neoplasms

Adenoma

Clinical features

Adenoma is infrequent but is nevertheless the most common benign neoplasm of the gallbladder.[244] Adults, with a striking predominance of females, are affected. The symptoms are similar to those of chronic cholecystitis, but there is often no association with inflammation or stones. Adenomas of the gallbladder have been found in association with Gardner's syndrome.[245]

Pathologic features

Gross pathology. Adenomas usually measure 0.5–2 cm in diameter and are multiple in about 30% of cases.[244,246] The tumors are usually pedunculated, but some may be sessile.

Microscopic features. The lesions may be tubular, papillary, or tubulopapillary. The tubular type is the most common and consists of small compact glands separated by a fibrous stroma. The stroma is often scant, but can be more prominent, edematous, or hyalinized. Tubular adenomas can be pyloric or intestinal (Fig. 10.53) in type. Tubular adenomas of the pyloric type are the most common and may be associated with foci of squamoid spindle cell metaplasia.[247] The papillary type

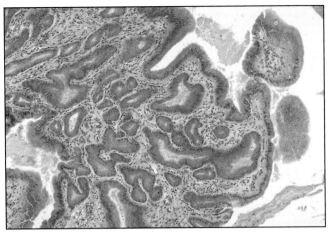

Fig. 10.53 • Gallbladder: tubular adenoma, pyloric type.

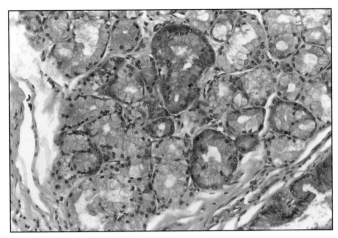

Fig. 10.54 • Gallbladder: metaplasia, pyloric type.

has a branching, tree-like configuration of the fibrovascular connective tissue stalks. The stalks are lined by a single layer of cuboidal to columnar epithelium. Dysplasia is often severe in large lesions and some cases may show foci of carcinoma in situ (CIS).[245]

Treatment and prognosis. Adenomas are benign lesions and are cured by cholecystectomy. Early-stage adenocarcinomas have been reported in 13.7–39% of adenomas.[248] Larger adenomas (>12 mm) are more likely to harbor foci of adenocarcinoma.[249] Patients with symptomatic polyps should undergo cholecystectomy. Surgery should also be considered for asymptomatic patients if the polyps are sessile, multiple, or larger than 1 cm.[250] An adenoma–carcinoma sequence similar to colonic neoplasia has been proposed,[251] but the role of adenomas in gallbladder carcinogenesis remains controversial (see below).

Other rare benign tumors

Granular cell tumors may rarely arise in the gallbladder, but they more commonly occur in the extrahepatic bile ducts. Benign mesenchymal tumors such as lipoma, leiomyoma, hemangioma, and lymphangioma have been reported in the gallbladder. Rarely, paraganglioma can occur in the gallbladder and behaves in a benign fashion.[252]

Gallbladder: metaplasia and dysplasia

The overall pathogenesis of adenocarcinoma is thought to result in evolution from dysplasia (atypical hyperplasia) to carcinoma[253,254] or from adenoma to carcinoma.[251] Metaplastic changes may or may not be premalignant,[253–258] but there is a high incidence of associated metaplasia in gallbladders with adenocarcinoma, especially in those carcinomas with intestinal differentiation.[255,258]

Metaplasia

Metaplastic epithelium in the gallbladder consists of two major types: gastric and intestinal. Both tend to occur in the setting of chronic cholecystitis[258] as well as in association with dysplasia or adenocarcinoma.[259,260]

Gastric metaplasia recapitulates the gastric pyloric or antral mucosa. Focal gastric metaplasia is seen in around 50% of gallbladders with chronic inflammation. The changes appear to begin at the base of the crypt as branches or buds; these glands assume a lobular arrangement, mimicking the architecture of the gastric antrum or pylorus (Fig. 10.54).

Intestinal metaplasia usually consists of foci of goblet cells, but columnar cells with a brush border and Paneth cells may also be seen.[258] The goblet cells tend to occur first in the tips of the villous structures (mucosal folds), rather than in the base of the crypts, as in gastric metaplasia. These changes then progress downwards and can be seen in the Rokitansky–Aschoff sinuses. Endocrine cells, if present, are quite variable in number and randomly distributed.

Squamous metaplasia is rare, tends to be associated with gallstones, and may be associated with dysplasia or squamous cell carcinoma.[258]

Dysplasia and carcinoma in situ

Clinical features

Dysplasia, or atypical hyperplasia, and CIS are thought to be precursor lesions of adenocarcinoma. Dysplasia may be present in 3.3–13.5% and CIS in 1.6–3.5% of resected gallbladders[253,254] and in as many as 40–88% of the gallbladders with adenocarcinoma.[248,261] In a Mexican series, patients with dysplasia were found to be 5 years younger than those with CIS, while those with CIS were 10 years younger than those with invasive adenocarcinoma. The average age at time of diagnosis for invasive carcinoma was in the mid-50s.[253] In another study, the mean age for precursor lesions averaged 69 years, with a similar time span expected for the development of invasive adenocarcinoma.[254] Based on these data, the period for evolution from dysplasia to invasive adenocarcinoma would be around 15 years. These studies also suggest that dysplasia may occur at an earlier age in some populations, and women are more affected than men. It is currently not possible to predict which gallbladders with chronic disease are more likely to contain pre-invasive lesions. Close monitoring of such lesions greatly

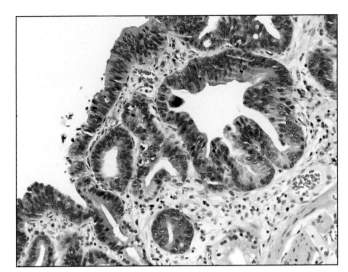

Fig. 10.55 • Gallbladder with high-grade dysplasia/carcinoma in situ. The nuclei are enlarged, crowded, and pseudostratified.

improves the outcome, but if microinvasion is seen, metastases and death may occur.[253,262]

Pathologic features

Dysplasia can be solitary or multifocal, patchy or extensive, and a single random histologic section will detect less than one-third of cases. It has been recommended that more than three longitudinal sections should be taken for routine examination.[248] The histology of dysplasia and CIS has been defined by pseudostratification of the epithelium, nuclear crowding, nuclear atypia, and disorganization of the epithelium with the more severe changes designated as CIS (Fig. 10.55).[253,254] The distinction between severe dysplasia and CIS is not always possible as the criteria do not allow for reproducible discrimination between the lesions. In CIS, the nuclei are larger and the nucleoli are often increased in number and more prominent as compared to dysplasia. Pseudostratification or multilayering is often seen and the changes can appear very similar to adenomatous change in the colon. Giant cells, loss of cell polarity, and atypical mitotic figures are other features that may be present. The cytologic changes in CIS may extend downward into the Rokitansky–Aschoff sinuses. When this occurs, care should be taken not to confuse this with invasive adenocarcinoma.[264] A very rare type of adenocarcinoma in situ is the signet-ring type; squamous CIS is rarely seen.[265]

Gallbladder: malignant neoplasms

Adenocarcinoma

Clinical features

Primary carcinoma of the gallbladder ranks as the fifth most common malignancy of the gastrointestinal tract. Adenocarcinoma accounts for 75–85% of cases. This is a disease of old age, with a peak incidence occurring at 70–79 years of age and a female-to-male predilection of 3:1. The incidence is higher in native Americans, Mexicans, Mexican Americans, Japanese, Central and Eastern Europeans, compared to that

seen in Africans and African-Americans. The incidence is highest in Israel, Chile, and Mexico.[265] The incidence has doubled in some countries from 1975 to 1985, and may be related to a decline in numbers of patients undergoing cholecystectomy.[266] Gallbladder carcinoma usually presents late in its course after the tumor has already metastasized or spread locally. Most lesions have no distinctive presenting features, but often have symptoms resembling those of chronic cholecystitis. Pain is probably the most common presenting symptom; jaundice, right upper-quadrant mass, nausea, vomiting, anorexia, and weight loss can also be present.[267] Laboratory findings are also non-diagnostic, and may include hyperbilirubinemia, elevated serum alkaline phosphatase and elevated serum CEA or CA19-9.[268] The latter are not specific findings for malignancy as they may also be elevated in obstructive biliary disease and with adenocarcinomas arising at other sites.

Gallstones are found in over 80% of patients with gallbladder carcinoma,[268–270] and a true causal relationship is further suggested by the fact that gallbladder carcinoma and stones are both more common in women and native Americans. Chronic irritation of the biliary mucosa by stones is considered the promoter of neoplastic transformation. Diffuse calcification, or porcelain gallbladder, is another condition that has a high association with adenocarcinoma (10–25%).[271] Anomalous pancreaticobiliary ductal junction (APBDJ) occurs more frequently in Japan and China (0.9–8.7%) and is associated with a high incidence of gallbladder carcinoma (12.5–65%).[248] In APBDJ, the common bile duct joins the pancreatic duct outside the duodenal wall, where the normal sphincter mechanism is absent, leading to reflux of pancreatic secretions up the biliary tree. In addition, there is some evidence that chronic *Salmonella typhi* infection of the gallbladder[272] and exposure to chemicals used in the rubber, automotive, textile, and metal-fabricating industries imposes an increased risk for carcinoma.[267] Other putative risk factors include ulcerative colitis/primary sclerosing cholangitis and genetic disorders such as familial adenomatous polyposis and Peutz–Jeghers syndrome.[273,274]

Pathologic features

Gross pathology. Adenocarcinomas usually result in localized thickening of the gallbladder wall, causing it to bulge into the lumen. Less frequently, it may result in a diffuse thickening or an intraluminal papillary growth (Fig. 10.56). Small infiltrative tumors may be overlooked or mistaken for chronic cholecystitis. Gallstones are present in the vast majority of cases. Approximately 90% of carcinomas arise in the body or fundus of the gallbladder; the remainder occur in the neck.[245] Invasion of the adjacent liver parenchyma may occur in as many as 70% of cases. Rarely, carcinoma may arise in the remnants of the gallbladder following partial cholecystectomy.[275] The gallbladder may appear swollen or strictured, depending on the location and extent of the mural invasion by tumor.

Microscopic features. The most common neoplasm is adenocarcinoma, which may be moderately to well differentiated (40–50%), poorly differentiated (30%), papillary (12%), or mucinous (12%). Adenosquamous and squamous variants are infrequent (7%).[267] In well-differentiated tumors, the glands

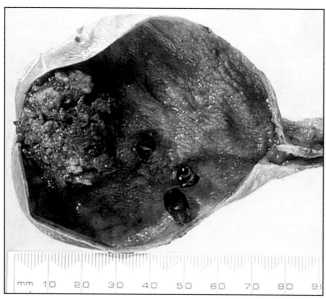

Fig. 10.56 • Gallbladder adenocarcinoma. Exophytic tumor with papillary fronds and bilirubinate-type stones.

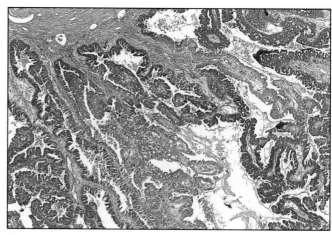

Fig. 10.58 • Gallbladder adenocarcinoma, papillary type. Papillary fronds of adenocarcinoma are covered by atypical columnar cells.

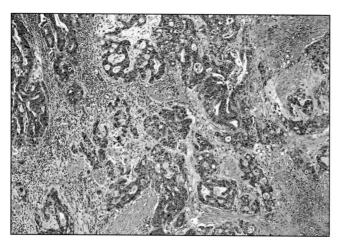

Fig. 10.57 • Gallbladder adenocarcinoma, cribriform pattern. Malignant glands are invading the gallbladder wall in a cribriform pattern.

are lined by columnar to cuboidal tumor cells resembling those of normal gallbladder. The tumor cells are arranged in sheets, cords, glands, or in a cribriform pattern (Fig. 10.57). The nuclei are usually round to oval and are often located basally or centrally. The cytoplasm may be eosinophilic, slightly granular, pale, clear, or mucinous. Occasional goblet, Paneth, or endocrine cells may be seen. The number of mitotic figures is variable. The amount of intraluminal or intracellular mucin may also vary considerably. It may not be possible to find mucin in many malignant glands and overt mucin production is not necessary to make the diagnosis of well-differentiated adenocarcinoma. The amount of desmoplastic stroma surrounding the glands is variable and an inflammatory infiltrate is often present.

The papillary variant of adenocarcinoma is a well-differentiated lesion that grows into the lumen of the gallbladder (Fig. 10.58). The tumor cells proliferate on fibrovascular stalks. These tumors may fill the lumen of the gallbladder prior to invading the wall, and may have a better prognosis.[276] Conversely, once they are invasive then they are very aggressive.[276a] In the mucinous or colloid variant, the gross appearance is often gelatinous and gray, or the gallbladder may be distended due to the accumulation of mucus. The tumor cells are often arranged in small clusters and are surrounded by large pools of basophilic mucin. In order to define an adenocarcinoma as the mucinous variant, the mucin must dominate the histologic picture. The prognosis is comparable to the other, more usual, patterns of well-differentiated adenocarcinoma.

The clear cell variant of carcinoma is composed of sheets, nests, trabeculae, glands, or small papillary structures consisting of tumor cells with clear cytoplasm.[277] The cytoplasm is negative for acidic and neutral mucins and contains PAS-positive material that digests with amylase. On electron microscopy, these cells contain glycogen, prominent rough endoplasmic reticulum, and a moderate number of mitochondria. Most of these tumors represent adenocarcinomas and contain zones of typical adenocarcinoma that account for less than half of the tumor, but rare lesions may represent the clear cell variant of squamous cell carcinoma and, accordingly, may show focal keratinization. The tumor cells are immunohistochemically positive for cytokeratin, EMA, and erythropoiesis-associated antigen; thus, the lesion could easily be mistaken for a metastatic RCC. CEA is only positive in rare cases and neuroendocrine markers are negative.

Other variants of adenocarcinoma include the intestinal, signet-ring, and cribriform types. The intestinal type of adenocarcinoma is characterized by either prominent goblet cell differentiation or an appearance similar to colonic adenocarcinoma.[259] In the colonic type, the glands are lined by tall columnar cells with only a few goblet cells. Signet-ring cell adenocarcinoma is composed predominantly of signet-ring cells. The cribriform type is primarily composed of groups of tumor cells with well-defined punched-out spaces lined by fairly uniform tumor cells with hyperchromatic nuclei. The overall pattern mimics that of cribriform breast carcinoma[264] and possible metastases from a breast primary should be excluded when such a lesion is noted in the gallbladder.

Pleomorphic giant cell carcinoma is a rare variant characterized by variable numbers of multinucleated giant cells as well as polygonal, round, or spindled cells without obvious gland formation or mucin production.[264] Areas of well-differentiated adenocarcinoma are found in about two-thirds of cases, and foci of squamous cell carcinoma may be present in 10–20% of these tumors. This term should be reserved for tumors in which the giant cells comprise a prominent portion of the tumor. Extensive necrosis and mixed inflammatory infiltrates are commonly associated findings. Mucin can sometimes be found in the spindle and giant cells. Approximately 70% of these tumors are focally positive for cytokeratin, 75% for vimentin, and 20% for CEA. Carcinoma with osteoclast-like multinucleated giant cells surrounded by spindle cells mimicking giant cell tumor of bone has also been described.[264] This needs to be distinguished from rare benign histiocytic lesions resembling a giant cell tumor of bone, which may arise in the gallbladder or biliary tree.[277a]

Adenosquamous carcinoma is composed of a mixture of glandular and squamous elements. The histologic differentiation of both elements in these tumors tends to be of a moderate degree, rather than anaplastic or poorly differentiated. Adenosquamous carcinomas with human chorionic gonadotropin production,[278] foci of spindle cells,[279] neuroendocrine,[280] and gastric foveolar type of differentiation[281] have also been described. The squamous portion can be dominant, requiring multiple sections to demonstrate the glandular component. The pure type of squamous cell carcinoma often arises in association with squamous metaplasia.[264]

Small cell (oat cell) carcinoma accounts for less than 3% of carcinomas of the gallbladder.[282] As with adenocarcinoma, the tumor occurs in older individuals (mean age 62.7 years) and is more common in women. The vast majority of cases are associated with gallstones. Rare patients will develop a paraneoplastic syndrome such as Cushing's syndrome due to adrenocorticotropic hormone secretion by the tumor.[264] These tumors are aggressive, metastases are frequent, and mortality is high. Sensitivity to chemotherapeutic agents, including adriamycin, vincristine, cyclophosphamide, and nitrosourea, warrant distinction from other forms of undifferentiated carcinoma. Grossly, the tumor is usually a bulky, gray-white mass with extensive necrosis, mucosal ulceration, and subepithelial spread. The histology is similar to that of the small cell (oat cell) carcinoma of the lung. The tumor cells have irregularly shaped, round to spindle-shaped, hyperchromatic nuclei with inconspicuous nucleoli. The cytoplasm is scant and ill-defined. The tumor cells may be arranged in nests, sheets, or cords. Tubular structures or pseudorosettes are rare. Mixed tumors with areas of adenocarcinoma, squamous carcinoma, atypical carcinoid, and carcinosarcoma have been reported, but these components do not influence the outcome.[264,280,283,284] The majority are positive for neuroendocrine markers such as neuron-specific enolase (75%), synaptophysin (50%), and chromogranin (40%). The vast majority are also positive for keratin.[264] Electron microscopy will usually reveal a few neurosecretory granules.[264,283]

Spindle cell sarcomatoid carcinoma is a rare variant of undifferentiated carcinoma.[285] It often shows small foci of admixed squamous or glandular differentiation, facilitating its distinction from sarcoma.

Genetic changes

Mutation in the *p53* gene is a common event in gallbladder adenocarcinoma. Although a wide range has been reported in the literature (35–92%), most studies show a frequency of greater than 50%.[286,287] Immunohistochemical overexpression of p53 correlates well with the occurrence of point mutations, the majority of which occur in exons 5–8. Overexpression of p53 does not correlate with prognosis.[288] Inactivation of the *CDKN2* gene on 9p21-22 by mutation or allelic loss is a common event in gallbladder adenocarcinoma and occurs in 50–80% of cases. *CDKN2* is a tumor suppressor gene, which encodes for p16, a protein that regulates the cell cycle by inhibiting cyclin-dependent kinase 4.[289,290] Other common genetic changes include loss of 8p22 (44%) and the *DCC* gene locus on 18q21 (31%).[287] In contrast to adenocarcinoma arising in the extrahepatic biliary tree, *K-ras* mutations are uncommon and occur in 5–17% of cases, although some Japanese studies have quoted figures up to 59%.[287] Differences in methodology or geographic variations in the incidence of *K-ras* mutations may be responsible for the discrepancy. In a subset of gallbladder carcinomas arising in the setting of anomalous junction of the pancreaticobiliary duct, *K-ras* mutations are frequent and found in 50–83% of cases.[287] LOH at the *APC* gene locus on 5q and *RB* gene is uncommon in gallbladder cancer. Recent studies have shown the loss of fragile histidine triad *(F-HIT)* gene, a candidate tumor suppressor gene at 3p, as a universal finding that occurs early in gallbladder cancer and may play an important role in its pathogenesis.[291]

Dysplasia and CIS also show allelic loss of 17q13 at the *TP53* gene, 9p21 at the *CDNK* gene, and 18q21 at the *DCC* gene, indicating that these are early events in carcinogenesis.[248] *K-ras* mutations are uncommon in premalignant lesions, except in association with carcinomas arising in the setting of anomalous junction of the pancreaticobiliary duct, where incidences as high as 41–83% have been reported.[248]

The role of adenomas in gallbladder neoplasia is controversial. The adenoma–carcinoma sequence has been invoked by some authors, but others believe that the majority of carcinomas evolve from flat dysplasia/CIS. Adenomas lack the molecular changes frequently detected in dysplasia and invasive carcinoma of the gallbladder. *K-ras* mutations are relatively frequent, while *TP53* mutations in exons 5–8 and LOH at 9p21 were not found in any case in a series of 16 gallbladder adenomas.[292] A low frequency of *p53* mutations has also been reported in carcinomas arising in adenomas (especially of pyloric gland type), suggesting that this subset of adenocarcinomas may have a distinct genetic background.[248]

Prognosis and outcome

The prognosis of gallbladder adenocarcinoma is generally very poor, and correlates well with stage of disease at presentation. Staging of gallbladder carcinoma is determined by the depth of invasion into the gallbladder wall. The extent of tumor at the time of diagnosis is the best indicator for survival. Prognosis is excellent, with nearly 100% survival with CIS (Tis) or tumors confined to the gallbladder wall (T1) that are found incidentally at cholecystectomy, provided that the resection margins are negative.[293] If the tumor infiltrates the serosa (T2), further resection including liver resection and regional lymphadenectomy is indicated. Radical resection in T2 tumors has resulted in 5-year survival of 61–70%.[294,295] Tumors with a polypoid growth pattern have a better survival than infiltrative tumors.[296] Once the tumor spreads beyond the gallbladder

(T3 and T4), prognosis is poor, with 0–28% 5-year survival. The median survival with no residual disease after surgery is 67.2 months, but less than 10 months with gross or microscopic residual disease.[297] Unfortunately, most tumors present at this stage. Presence of regional or distant metastases usually results in a mean survival of only 5.2 months.[245] Nodal status is a powerful predictor of outcome and is the only significant factor in multivariate analysis in some studies.[293] Long-term survival with node-positive disease is rare.[298] Spread to regional lymph nodes is likely to be present in approximately 50% of cases at the time of diagnosis. Involved lymph nodes are usually those near the cystic duct and porta hepatis or pericholedochal lymph nodes, followed later by peripancreatic and para-aortic lymph nodes. Carcinomas tend to spread by direct extension into the liver; they less commonly invade the stomach, duodenum, or colon. Implants of the peritoneal surfaces can lead to intra-abdominal carcinomatosis, and ascites and invasion into an adjacent hollow organ can lead to biliary-enteric fistulas. One of the most serious complications is perforation of the gallbladder, which leads to peritonitis, abscess, or fistula. Bilateral spread to the ovaries, resulting in Krukenberg tumors, may rarely occur.[245]

Carcinoid tumor

Clinical features

Carcinoids of the gallbladder account for less than 1% of gastrointestinal carcinoids, and may be associated with the carcinoid syndrome.[245]

Pathologic features

Gross pathology. The tumors are usually small yellow to gray-white submucosal lesions.

Microscopic features. The tumor cells usually form nests or trabecular structures separated by thin strands of collagen fibers. The tumor cells may form gland-like structures or peripheral palisades.[299] The cells are small with moderate amounts of pale to eosinophilic indistinct cytoplasm. The nuclei are round to oval with inconspicuous nucleoli and stippled chromatin. Some lesions may resemble adeno-carcinoids,[245] signet-ring carcinoids,[300] or be admixed with adenocarcinoma.[301] If mitotic figures (>2 per high-power field) and necrosis are present, a diagnosis of atypical carcinoid should be considered. Most tumor cells will be argyrophilic and will stain for chromogranin A, neuron-specific enolase, somatostatin, serotonin, or lysozyme.[300–302] Argentaffin-positivity may also be seen.

Other malignant tumors

Other malignant tumors that rarely occur in the gallbladder are a broad spectrum of sarcomas, including KS (associated with AIDS), rhabdomyosarcoma, leiomyosarcoma, so-called malignant fibrous histiocytoma, and angiosarcoma. Other rare primaries include carcinosarcoma, melanoma, and non-Hodgkin lymphoma. Metastatic tumors found in the gallbladder include spread from adenocarcinomas arising elsewhere in the gastrointestinal tract, RCC, melanoma, bronchogenic carcinoma, and very rare instances of Hodgkin lymphoma and myeloma.

Tumor-like lesions

Adenomyoma/adenomyomatosis

Clinical features

The most commonly diagnosed form of hyperplasia is adenomyomatosis.[303] It is generally thought to be a reactive process associated with chronic inflammation, but it may occur without this association. It is often an incidental finding during a cholecystectomy for cholecystitis. There is no convincing evidence that the lesion is preneoplastic. The thickened gallbladder wall caused by the lesion may be identified radiographically.

Pathologic features

Gross pathology. There is a thickening of the gallbladder wall in either a diffuse (adenomyomatosis) or localized (adenomyoma) fashion. Most lesions are found in the fundus,[304] and often appear to be limited by the septum known as the Phrygian cap,[305] but some may be ring-like, causing stricture. Cystic spaces within the wall may be grossly visible and stones may be present within the cysts. The cystic spaces often occur in the perimuscular (outer) connective tissue portion of the gallbladder wall.

Microscopic features. The epithelium extends downward as mucosal invaginations into hyperplastic smooth muscle bundles, forming branched ducts, gland-like spaces, or larger cysts (Fig. 10.59). The invaginations are lined by a single layer of tall columnar epithelial cells similar to those seen on the surface of the gallbladder. These spaces may contain bile, calculi, or mucus. Foci of chronic inflammation may be present.

The gross thickening of the wall of the gallbladder could be mistaken for adenocarcinoma, but close examination will often reveal the cystic changes of adenomyoma/adenomyomatosis. The proliferation of the smooth muscle component helps to

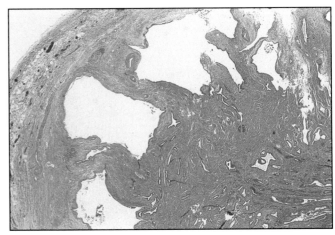

Fig. 10.59 • Adenomyoma. Gland-like structures haphazardly arranged among hyperplastic smooth muscle bundles.

separate these lesions from the Rokitansky–Aschoff sinuses of chronic cholecystitis.

Inflammatory polyp

This is a relatively rare cause of a tumor-like lesion and is generally considered to be an exuberant inflammatory reaction to injury in the setting of chronic cholecystitis.[244,299] The polyps can be single or multiple and range in size from 0.3 to 1.0 cm. Histologically, the polyps consist of inflamed granulation and fibrous tissue. Some polyps may also contain glandular epithelial remnants. Ulceration, chronic inflammatory infiltrates, and hemorrhage are typical.

Cholesterol polyp

Cholesterol polyp is the most common non-neoplastic, polyoid lesion in the gallbladder, probably accounting for 60–90% of intraluminal polyps.[306–308] Some degree of cholesterolosis is usually present. They are usually small, pedunculated lesions measuring less than 1 cm in diameter, and are often multiple. The smaller lesions are bright yellow, but larger lesions may be tan or bile-stained. They are attached to the mucosa by a slender stalk, and may become easily detached. They can also be mistaken for small gallstones adherent to the wall. Histologically, they are characterized by surface villous structures and a connective tissue stalk filled with foamy macrophages similar to cholesterolosis (Fig. 10.60).

Heterotopias

Gastric, pancreatic, liver, adrenal, and thryoid tissues have all been reported to occur in the gallbladder, and can form masses in the gallbladder wall that could clinically be confused with carcinoma. The pancreatic tissue can show both exocrine and endocrine components, and rarely, acute pancreatitis with hemorrhage and fat necrosis can develop.[309,310] Well-developed gastric fundic-type mucosa with parietal and chief cells is required to differentiate gastric heterotopias from gastric antral-type hyperplasia.[299] Gastric heterotopias tend to occur more frequently in the neck and the fundus.[244,311]

Benign biliary tumors

Biliary hamartoma

Clinical features

Biliary hamartoma (BH), or von Meyenburg complex, is thought to represent a ductal plate malformation rather than a neoplasm, and may occur sporadically or as part of polycystic liver disease.

Pathologic features

BH is small (usually <0.5 cm), gray-white, irregular, and commonly multifocal. It is often noticed incidentally in a liver biopsy or at autopsy. BH consists of numerous small to medium-sized irregularly shaped dilated ductules embedded in a dense fibrous stroma (Fig. 10.61). They are located within and at the edge of portal tracts. The ductules are lined by cuboidal to flattened epithelium and may contain eosinophilic debris or inspissated bile but are not connected with the biliary system.

Prognosis

BHs are not considered premalignant, although rare cases of cholangiocarcinoma arising in BH have been reported.[312]

Bile duct adenoma

Clinical features

Bile duct adenoma (BDA) is a less common lesion than BH. The designation of "adenoma" may be a misnomer as it may not represent a true neoplasm, but a localized ductal proliferation at the site of previous injury[313] or peribiliary gland hamartoma.[314] They are usually found incidentally at surgery or autopsy, and may be sent for frozen section to exclude metastasis.

Fig. 10.60 • Cholesterol polyps. The polyp has the appearance of a villous structure expanded by foamy macrophages and stroma. Chronic cholecystitis is also present.

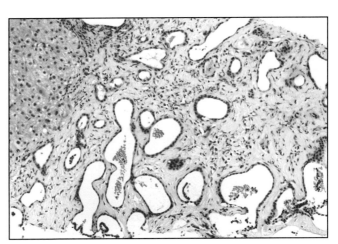

Fig. 10.61 • Biliary hamartoma. Irregularly shaped dilated ductules embedded in a dense fibrous stroma.

Pathologic features

BDA is typically small (<2 cm), firm, gray-white, well circumscribed, often subcapsular, and can be single or multiple. The ducts are uniform in size and with less intervening fibrous stroma compared to hamartomas (Fig. 10.62). The stroma is typically more abundant centrally than peripherally. The lesional ducts have round outlines and are lined by bland cuboidal epithelium without mitotic activity. Bile is not present and the ductules do not communicate with the biliary tree. Mucinous metaplasia, alpha$_1$-antitrypsin droplets, and neuroendocrine differentiation may be seen. The endocrine cell clusters must not be confused with metastatic carcinoid or islet cell tumor.[315] A rare variant with clear cells has been described which can be mistaken for primary or metastatic clear cell carcinoma.[316] Immunohistochemically, BDA expresses both 1F6 and D10 (antigens extracted from bile duct cell cultures), a profile similar to bile ductules and canals of Hering.[314]

Differential diagnosis

The absence of nuclear atypia, mitoses, and vascular invasion distinguishes BDA from adenocarcinoma. The uniform round outlines of glands, relatively less stroma, lack of bile, absence of cystic change, and lack of association with polycystic liver disease separate it from BH. In contrast to BDA, BHs express D10, but not 1F6.[314]

Prognosis. BDA is a benign lesion and malignant change has not been convincingly documented.

Biliary (hepatobiliary) cystadenoma and cystadenocarcinoma

Clinical features

Biliary cystadenomas are rare lesions that occur in the liver, with a higher incidence in women and histologic counterparts in the pancreas and ovary. It can be associated with the development of cystadenocarcinoma, which occurs equally in men and women. The mean age for cystadenocarcinoma (59 years) is higher than cystadenomas (45 years).[317] Rare instances in the extrahepatic bilary tree and gallbladder have been reported.[318] Most patients present with pain, discomfort, or a palpable mass, but jaundice, rupture, or infection can occur. Elevated serum levels of CA19-9 can occur.[319,320]

Pathologic features

Gross pathology. Cystadenomas are 5–15 cm multilocular cysts with a smooth or somewhat trabeculated inner surface. This helps in the differentiation from developmental cysts, which are often unilocular. The cysts are relatively few in number (oligocystic), tend to be large (macrocystic), and contain fluid of variable appearance, including serous, mucinous, gelatinous, occasionally hemorrhagic, or even purulent. There is no communication between the cysts and the biliary tree. The presence of large polypoid projections or solid masses in the cyst wall is characteristic of cystadenocarcinoma.

Microscopic features. The cysts are lined by a single layer of mucinous epithelial cells, and small papillary tufts may be present (Fig. 10.63). The epithelial nuclei are bland and basally located without mitotic activity. In women, the cysts are essentially always associated with a cellular mesenchymal component resembling ovarian stroma. Densely hyalinized stroma often separates the ovarian-like stroma from the adjacent liver. The cyst wall may also be focally lined by macrophages, calcification, or scar-like tissue.

Cystadenocarcinomas arising in this context often have a tubulopapillary, solid, or adenosquamous histology.[317] Features such as marked nuclear pleomorphism, loss of polarity, mitotic figures, and multilayering of the epithelium suggest malignant transformation, and can be designated as in-situ adenocarcinoma, but stromal invasion is necessary for the diagnosis of cystadenocarcinoma.[317] Since malignant change can be focal, extensive sampling is recommended.[321] The presence of a benign epithelial component in up to a third of cystadenocarcinomas supports the view that at least some of them arise from cystadenomas. Immunohistochemically, cystadenomas and cystadenocarcinomas are identical and mark

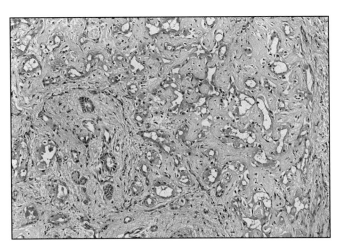

Fig. 10.62 • Bile duct adenoma. Uniform round ducts in a small amount of fibrous stroma.

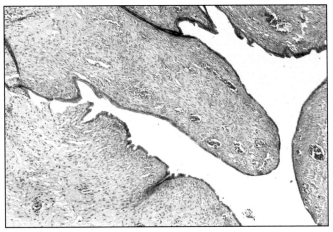

Fig. 10.63 • Mucinous cystadenoma. Multicystic tumor lined by benign columnar to cuboidal mucinous epithelium. The spindle cell stroma is cellular and resembles ovarian stroma.

for cytokeratin, CEA, and EMA. Scattered chromogranin-positive cells can occasionally be present. The mesenchymal stroma immunohistochemically resembles myofibroblasts and appears phenotypically different from ovarian stroma.[322]

Prognosis

Cystadenomas are benign tumors and can be successfully treated by total excision. Cystadenocarcinomas can invade the adjacent viscera and may occasionally spread to the regional lymph nodes, peritoneum, and lung.[323] Cystadenocarcinomas with mesenchymal stroma occur exclusively in women and behave indolently. In men, these tumors lack ovarian-like stroma and behave more aggressively.[317]

Other benign biliary tumors or tumor-like conditions

Biliary adenofibroma is a rare entity, with 3 reported cases in the literature.[324] It consists of tortuous and branching ductular elements with microcystic dilatation, cuboidal to flattened lining epithelium, prominent fibroblastic stroma between the glands, and immunohistochemical expression of D10 but not IF6.[325] Hence it shows a marked resemblance to BH, but is larger and is not associated with any typical von Meyenburg complexes. It differs from BDAs, which usually lack a cystic configuration, have less stroma, and express both 1F6 and D10. Monosomy 22 has been reported in one case.[326] Biliary adenofibroma is considered a benign lesion and malignant transformation has not been observed. However, the large size, and the reported presence of positive *p53* immunostaining and tetraploidy, raise the possibility of a premalignant lesion.

Serous cystadenoma is rare in the liver and is similar to its pancreatic counterpart, consisting of multiple microcysts lined by bland glycogen-rich cuboidal epithelium (Fig. 10.64).[317] The cysts lack the cellular mesenchymal stroma characteristic of mucinous cystadenoma.

Neuromas of the extrahepatic biliary ducts can cause obstructive jaundice. They are often traumatic in origin, typically after cholecystectomy.[327] Histologically, irregular tortuous bundles of nerve fibers, admixed with Schwann cells and fibrous tissue, are scattered in the bile duct submucosa (Fig. 10.65).

Adenomyoma is a hamartomatous lesion that rarely occurs in the extrahepatic biliary tree,[328] being more common in the ampulla. It is characterized by glandular structures with intervening smooth muscle bundles.

Solitary or multiple cysts can be seen around intrahepatic large bile ducts and probably arise from the peribiliary glands.[329] They are lined by columnar or cuboidal epithelium and do not communicate with the biliary tree. Peribiliary cysts can occur in chronic advanced liver disease and normal livers, but are usually not associated with polycystic kidney or liver disease.

Ciliated hepatic foregut cyst is a rare benign solitary cyst that is usually found incidentally on imaging or surgery. It is more common in men and in the medial segment of the left lobe. It is usually unilocular and lined by pseudostratified columnar epithelium, subepithelial connective tissue, smooth muscle, and an outer fibrous capsule.[330] Squamous cell carcinoma has been described in a ciliated hepatic foregut cyst.[331]

Granular cell tumors can involve the extrahepatic biliary tree and are more common in young patients, particularly black women.[332] They can clinically mimic primary sclerosing cholangitis or cholangiocarcinoma. Histologic findings are similar to granular cell tumors at other sites (see Ch. 27) and excision is curative.

Malignant biliary tumors

Cholangiocarcinoma

Cholangiocarcinoma encompasses malignant tumors arising from the intrahepatic bile ducts (intrahepatic, peripheral, or cholangiocellular cholangiocarcinoma) as well as those of perihilar and extrahepatic bile ducts. Recent epidemiologic studies have shown an increase in the incidence of cholangiocarcinoma over time. The reason for this increase is unknown, but does not appear to be entirely explained by greater

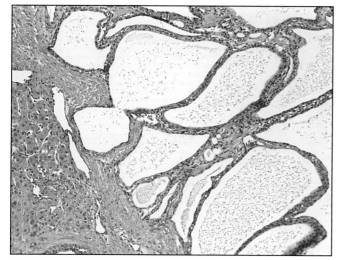

Fig. 10.64 • Serous cystadenoma. Multiple small cysts lined by bland cuboidal epithelium. There is no ovarian-like stroma.

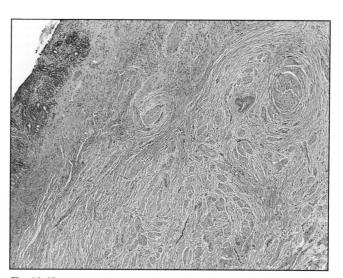

Fig. 10.65 • Neuroma of extrahepatic bile ducts. The tumor is composed of proliferation of nerve bundles.

recognition of the disease.[333] In the USA, the incidence is approximately 8 per million; 20–30% of the cases are intra-hepatic cholangiocarcinoma and the rest occur in an extra-hepatic location.[334] The tumor usually occurs in patients above 65 years of age and both sexes are equally affected.

Intrahepatic cholangiocarcinoma

Clinical features

Patients often remain asymptomatic until the tumor is in a late stage or may have non-specific symptoms like abdominal pain, anorexia, and weight loss. Jaundice is uncommon, although alkaline phosphatase is often elevated. Tumor markers like CA19-9, CEA, and CA-125 can be elevated. However, these markers are non-specific and their role in diagnosis is uncertain. CA19-9 is elevated in up to 85% of patients with cholangiocarcinoma but can also be associated with carcinomas of the stomach and pancreas and in non-neoplastic conditions like obstructive jaundice. Persistent elevation of CA19-9, even after biliary decompression, suggests malignancy and is used as a screening tool in patients with PSC.[335]

Several risk factors for cholangiocarcinoma have been identified:

1. Biliary disease: primary sclerosing cholangitis is the most common known predisposing factor, with a risk of 1.5% per year of the disease.[336–338] Smoking may increase the risk in association with primary sclerosing cholangitis. Hepatolithiasis is uncommon in the west but is endemic in portions of the Far East, where it can be associated with more than 50% of intrahepatic cholangiocarcinomas.[339] Rare cases have been reported with von Meyenburg complexes, choledochal cyst, and Caroli's disease.[340–342]
2. Parasites: cholangiocarcinoma is associated with two species of liver fluke, *Clonorchis sinensis* and *Opisthorchis viverrini*.[342,343] Both are endemic in South-East Asia: *Clonorchis* in Hong Kong, southern China, and Korea, and *Opisthorchis* in Thailand and Laos.
3. Other: thorotrast, a contrast medium, was banned in the 1950s but the associated risk can last for several decades.[344] Cholangiocarcinoma may occur in association with hereditary non-polyposis colon cancer (HNPCC).[345] Smoking and alcohol may act as cofactors.[346] In Japan and the Far East, hepatitis B (around 10%) and hepatitis C (around 25%) frequently coexist with cholangiocarcinoma, raising suspicion of their role in carcinogenesis. Although cholangiocarcinoma typically arises in non-cirrhotic liver, this concept may need to be revisited in view of a Japanese study, which found non-biliary cirrhosis in association with nearly 5% of cholangiocarcinomas.[347]

Pathologic features

Gross pathology. The Liver Cancer Study Group proposes three macroscopic types: mass-forming, periductal-infiltrating, and intraductal.[348] Mass-forming is the most common appearance of intrahepatic cholangiocarcinoma and is characterized by a localized tumor with a distinct border that grows radially

without periductal or intraductal spread (Fig. 10.66). The periductal-infiltrating type infiltrates along the bile duct and is often associated with stricture and involvement of periductal connective tissue. Both these types are usually firm, white-tan lesions due to dense fibrous stroma. Advanced cases can show mixed patterns of growth. Intraductal type is discussed below.

Microscopic features. A vast majority (>95%) of tumors are adenocarcinomas. The well-differentiated tumors show tubular, papillary, and cord-like patterns, and cytologic atypia can be minimal (Fig. 10.67). Intracytoplasmic lumina, focal cribri-form architecture, nuclear stratification, and intraluminal cellular debris favor carcinoma over a benign process. Nucleoli are often less prominent compared to HCC. Mucin can be demonstrated in most cases. A prominent desmoplastic stroma is characteristic of cholangiocarcinoma. Occasionally, the tumor cells form small narrow tubular structures resembling ductules or canals of Hering, a pattern that has been referred to as cholangiocellular carcinoma. Other less common microscopic variants include clear cell, adenosquamous, mucinous, signet-ring, sarcomatous, small cell, and Epstein–Barr virus-associated lymphoepithelioma-like carcinoma.[342]

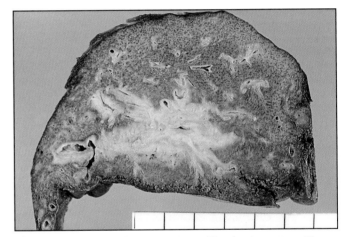

Fig. 10.66 • Intrahepatic cholangiocarcinoma. Mass-forming pattern with radial growth, distinct border, and no periductal or intraductal spread. The non-neoplastic liver shows bile staining. (Courtesy of Dr. P. Anthony.)

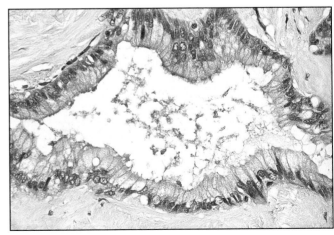

Fig. 10.67 • Cholangiocarcinoma, with well-differentiated mucinous tumor cells. The nuclei are small and basally located.

Differential diagnosis

1. *HCC*: see section on HCC, above.
2. *Metastatic adenocarcinoma*: liver metastasis from primary tumors arising in the pancreas, colon, stomach, lung, and breast can closely mimic cholangiocarcinoma. Distinction from metastatic adenocarcinoma can be difficult on morphologic grounds. The presence of tall columnar cells and luminal necrotic debris favors metastatic colonic carcinoma. Site-specific immunohistochemical markers like TTF-1 for lung, ER and PR for breast, PSA for prostate, and uroplakin for urinary bladder may be helpful. Non-site-specific markers like cytokeratin subsets may yield useful information. Cholangiocarcinoma is generally CK7+/CK20–, while metastatic colorectal adenocarcinoma is CK7–/CK20+ in > 90% of cases.[86,87] It has been suggested that immunohistochemistry for Lewis (x), Leu-M1, and B72.3 can be helpful in distinguishing cholangiocarcinoma from metastatic adenocarcinoma. Lewis (x) shows cytoplasmic and membranous reactivity in cholangiocarcinoma but only cytoplasmic reactivity in metastatic adenocarcinoma. In contrast, Leu-M1 and B72.3 are more likely to show cytoplasmic staining in cholangiocarcinoma and cytoplasmic and membranous staining in metastatic adenocarcinoma.[90] LeuM1, B72.3, or Lewis (x) have not presently been incorporated into our routine practice.

Pathogenesis and genetic abnormalities

The risk factors for cholangiocarcinoma, such as PSC and parasitic infestations, have chronic inflammation and cholestasis as their common link. Chronic inflammation leads to production of cytokines, such as interleukin-1 and 6, and interferon-γ, some of which have potent mitogenic effects on biliary epithelial cells. The proinflammatory cytokines also lead to expression of inducible nitric oxide synthase (iNOS). This in turn leads to generation of nitric oxide and reactive oxygen radicals, which can irreversibly damage the DNA of the epithelial cells. Nitric oxide also inactivates key DNA repair proteins by nitrosylation, leading to accumulation of potentially oncogenic mutations.[335,349] Nitrosylation of caspase proteases can inactivate caspase 9 with inhibition of apoptosis.[350] Bile acids can increase the levels of cyclooxygenase-2 and myeloid cell leukemia protein 1 in cholangiocytes; both these molecules can exert potent antiapoptotic effects.[351] Bile composition is altered in chronic cholestasis and levels of reduced glutathione are reduced. This compromises a key intracellular defense against oxidative injury. Hence chronic inflammation and cholestasis exert strong proliferative and mutagenic influences on the biliary epithelium.

Loss of *p53* and *K-ras* mutations are the most common molecular alterations observed in cholangiocarcinoma. Loss of *p53* is reported in up to 50% of intrahepatic mass-forming tumors, and can occur by mutation, LOH at 17p or *MDM2* gene amplification.[349] Inactivation of *p53* leads to deregulation of *bcl-2*, and potentially causes resistance to apoptosis. Loss of *bcl-2* correlates with lymph node metastasis, vascular invasion, and aberrant *p53* expression.[349] *K-ras* mutations usually affect codon 12 and vary widely with the geographical location and site of tumor. The incidence is up to 100% in England, 50–56%

in Japan, and 0–8% in Thailand, possibly reflecting differences in underlying etiology. *K-ras* mutations are more common in periductal-infiltrative tumors in the extrahepatic biliary tree than in mass-forming intrahepatic cholangiocarcinoma, while *p53* mutations are more common in the latter.[352] Alterations of the *p16* gene are also frequent and promoter hypermethylation may be the most common cause of inactivation in intrahepatic cholangiocarcinoma. Loss of *p16* may be a useful diagnostic test for primary sclerosing cholangitis-associated cancer.[353] Frequent overexpression of human telomerase reverse transcriptase (hTERT) is seen in dysplasia and invasive carcinoma, indicating that it may be an early event in carcinogenesis. The detection of a telomerase ladder in biopsy samples has been shown to be an excellent tool for diagnosis.[354] Hepatocyte growth factor, *c-met*, is overexpressed in cholangiocarcinoma and correlates with tumor differentiation. Other alterations which have been described include mutations of E-cadherin, beta-catenin, and DPC-4 genes, HER-2/neu gene amplification, and microsatellite instability.

Treatment and prognosis

Surgical resection of the involved liver segments offers the only hope of cure but is successful in a minority of cases, with 5-year survival rates of 0–43%.[349,355] The role of adjuvant chemotherapy and radiation is not clearly established for intrahepatic cholangiocarcinoma. Liver transplantation has not been encouraging, with 5-year survival rates less than 20%.[349] Lymph node metastasis and status of surgical margins are the most common factors influencing outcome. Lymph node involvement is seen in more than 50% of patients at presentation.[334] Lymphovascular or perineural invasion, intrahepatic satellite nodules, and bilobar distribution have been shown to predict poor survival.[356] Mass-forming tumors have a better outcome compared to tumors with periductal-infiltrating pattern.[348] Tumors with marked desmoplastic response may have a higher incidence of lymphatic invasion, higher proliferative activity, and poorer survival.[342] Poorly differentiated tumors and variants like signet-ring and sarcomatous carcinoma may behave aggressively.

Carcinoma affecting the extrahepatic biliary tree

Clinical features

Extrahepatic cholangiocarcinoma can be divided into tumors arising close to the hilum of the liver (perihilar cholangiocarcinoma) or in the distal portion of the bile duct (distal cholangiocarcinoma). Perihilar neoplasms (a.k.a. Klatskin tumor) constitute nearly two-thirds of all cholangiocarcinomas. Patients present with obstructive jaundice, repeated attacks of cholangitis and a cholestatic biochemical profile. Persistent elevation of tumor markers like CA19-9 in the absence of cholangitis can be useful for diagnosis.

Pathologic features

The tumors may have an infiltrative (70–80%), nodular (20%), or intraductal (<5%) growth pattern. The infiltrative and

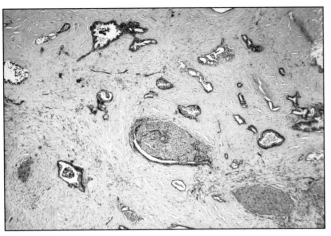

Fig. 10.68 • Cholangiocarcinoma with marked desmoplastic stromal response and perineural invasion.

nodular tumors are often poorly differentiated, tend to spread along the mucosa and submucosa, and are accompanied by a striking desmoplastic response. Encasement of the right or left portal vein is present in one-third of patients and leads to ipsilateral lobar atrophy. Occasionally cases have a papillary growth pattern.[357] Lymph node metastasis is identified in 30–50% of patients at resection; hilar and pericholedochal lymph nodes are the most commonly affected. Tumors arising in the setting of primary sclerosing cholangitis can be multifocal and associated with dysplasia and CIS at multiple sites. Due to the marked stromal desmoplasia (Fig. 10.68), the pathologic diagnosis can often be elusive and multiple endoscopic biopsies and brushings may be required. Pathologic diagnosis may be possible on biopsy in only 40–70% of cases. The use of ancillary techniques, including digital image analysis and fluorescence ISH to detect aneuploid cells in brushings or biopsy samples, has been shown to increase diagnostic sensitivity significantly.[358]

Treatment and prognosis. Surgical treatment of perihilar cholangiocarcinoma often requires partial hepatic resection to achieve negative margins. Since the caudate lobe drains independently, resection of the caudate lobe is also advocated. Distal lesions are treated by Whipple's procedure. The 5-year survival in resectable tumors with negative margins is 20–40% and the operative mortality is 10%.[359] Negative resection margins and T1 disease are major predictors of outcome in resected cases. Tumors with bilateral extension of tumor into segmental biliary radicles, lobar atrophy with portal vein encasement, and metastasis to N2 nodes or distant sites are considered unresectable. Survival in unresectable or advanced-stage disease is less than 1 year. Tumors arising in the setting of PSC have a particularly grim outlook, with 5-year survival of <10%. Some studies have shown the beneficial role of radiation and chemotherapy for palliation and as an adjunct to surgery, but the results are conflicting.[359] Cholangiocarcinoma has been considered to be a contraindication for liver transplantation due to rapid recurrence of the disease. However, recent trials have shown 5-year survival rates of 80% in early-stage disease with neoadjuvant chemotherapy and radiation, and transplantation may be beneficial in selected patients.[335]

Precursor intraductal biliary lesions

Biliary dysplasia (intraepithelial neoplasia/atypical hyperplasia)

Neoplastic transformation to cholangiocarcinoma almost certainly follows the hyperplasia–dysplasia–carcinoma sequence. Biliary dysplasia on liver biopsies is very infrequent but strongly correlates with the presence of cholangiocarcinoma in PSC.[338,360] Histologically, it is characterized by nuclear stratification, micropapillary and cribriform patterns, loss of polarity, nuclear enlargement and hyperchromasia, and irregular nuclear contours (Fig. 10.69). The proliferative activity of the biliary dysplasia is higher than biliary hyperplasia but lower than carcinoma, lending support to the progression sequence. The dysplastic epithelium often expresses CEA, CA19-9, and DUPAN-2, as in cholangiocarcinoma, although the expression can be focal.[361]

Intrahepatic bile ducts with stones or liver flukes often show chronic inflammation, epithelial hyperplasia, hyperplasia of intrahepatic peribiliary glands, and fibrosis. Hyperplasia of mucus acini is common, and pseudopyloric metaplasia may be present. This constellation of findings has been referred to as chronic proliferative cholangitis.[361] In the presence of liver flukes, marked proliferation of intramural glands in the large intrahepatic ducts has been referred to as "adenomatous hyperplasia of the bile duct." Multifocal biliary dysplasia and cholangiocarcinoma can occur in these proliferative lesions.

Intraductal papillary neoplasia

Clinical features

Papillary biliary neoplasms are characterized by intraductal papillary growth with a fine fibrovascular stalk, and include biliary (intraductal) papillomatosis as well as cholangiocarcinoma with an intraductal growth pattern. Intraductal

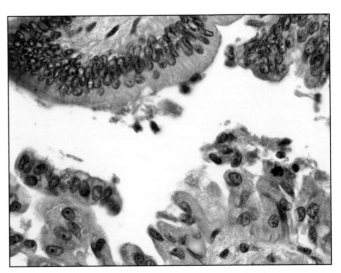

Fig. 10.69 • Biliary dysplasia characterized by cellular and nuclear enlargement, tufting, loss of polarity, and prominent nucleoli. Compare with normal biliary epithelium in the upper portion.

papillomatosis generally involves extensive areas of the intra-hepatic and/or the extrahepatic bile ducts, with predilection for the latter. The patients often present with repeated episodes of acute cholangitis and obstructive jaundice.[362]

Pathologic features

Biliary papillomatosis is a premalignant neoplastic prolifer-ation characterized by multifocal or diffuse papillary prolifer-ations of biliary lining cells without invasion or metastasis. Tumors are composed of delicate papillae covered by tall columnar cells with basal nuclei showing minimal pleo-morphism (Fig. 10.70). Most cases are histologically benign, but foci of biliary epithelial dysplasia can be present. Frank invasion of the stalk and underlying periductular tissues must be seen in order to make a diagnosis of cholangiocarcinoma. Another pattern of intraductal papillary neoplasm of the liver is characterized by mucin hypersecretion and segmental dila-tation of the neoplastic and non-neoplastic biliary tree. The clinical and pathologic features of this type of intraductal biliary neoplasm bear a striking resemblance to intraductal pancreatic mucinous tumor.[342,363,364] The dilated ducts are filled with mucus and papillary excrescences lined by mucinous epithelium. Oncocytic and clear cell change may be seen. Gastric and intestinal metaplasia with goblet cells is also frequent. Involvement of peribiliary glands is common. Epithelial dysplasia or CIS, often multifocal, may be present. The invasive component, when present, may exhibit features of mucinous carcinoma.

Molecular genetic abnormalities

K-ras mutations have been observed in biliary papillomatosis; malignant transformation may be associated with increased expression of MUC1 and Tn antigen.[365] Intraductal papillary mucinous neoplasms often show reduced expression of cytokeratin 7, and aberrant expression of cytokeratin 20, and mucins like MUC2, MUC5AC, and MUC 6.[364] Expression of *p53* occurs in less than one-third of the cases, but is higher in cases with dysplasia and carcinoma.

Prognosis

Although histologically benign in most cases, these lesions are not only premalignant but inherently pernicious due to multicentricity, tendency to recur, and complications such as recurrent bouts of cholangitis and sepsis. However, even in the presence of invasion, the outcome is better than that for more

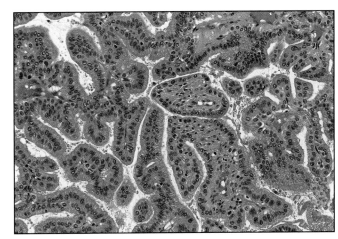

Fig. 10.70 • Intraductal biliary papillomatosis: papillae covered by columnar cells with nuclei showing mild pleomorphism.

typical forms of cholangiocarcinoma.[362,364,366] Lymph node metastasis does not occur in the absence of invasion. Recur-rences are observed in around 10% of intraductal papillary tumors after resection.

Other malignant tumors

Carcinoid tumor,[367] **paraganglioma**,[368] and primary **malignant melanoma**[369] can rarely occur in the extrahepatic bile ducts. The possibility of metastasis from another primary site should be excluded before making a diagnosis of primary malignant melanoma. **Leukemia** and **malignant lymphoma** can involve the extrahepatic bile ducts and may rarely be the initial presen-tation. **Embryonal (botryoid) rhabdomyosarcoma** is a rare neoplasm in the biliary tree but is the most common malignant tumor at this site in children.[370] Rare cases have been reported in adults. Clinically, these tumors present with obstructive jaundice, fever, weight loss, and hepatomegaly. Grossly, the tumor projects into the biliary tree as soft polypoid masses. Microscopically, round to spindle tumor cells are arranged in a variable admixture of hypercellular and loose myxoid areas. The tumor cells are often densely packed below the epithelium (cambium layer). Eosinophilic cytoplasm and cross-striations may be visible as evidence of rhabdomyoblastic differentiation. The diagnosis can be confirmed immunohistochemically with muscle markers like desmin and myogenin. Surgical resection combined with chemoradiation may achieve long-term survival, although the outcome is poor in most cases.[370]

References

1. Ishak K, Anthony P, Sobin L H 1994 Histological typing of tumours of the liver, 2nd edn. Springer-Verlag, Berlin

2. Ishak K G, Goodman Z D, Stocker J T 2001 Tumors of the liver and intrahepatic bile ducts. Armed Forces Institute of Pathology, Washington, DC, p 9–48

3. Wheeler D, Edmondson H, Reynolds T 1986 Spontaneous liver cell adenoma in children. Am J Clin Pathol 85: 6–12

4. Flejou J F, Barge J, Menu Y et al. 1985 Liver adenomatosis: an entity distinct from liver adenoma? Gastroenterology 89: 1132–1138

5. Le Bail B, Jouhanole H, Deugnier Y et al. 1992 Liver adenomatosis in two patients on long-term oral contraceptives. Am J Surg Pathol 16: 982–987

6. Gokhele R, Whitington P F 1996 Hepatic adenomatosis in an adolescent. J Pediatr Gastroenterol Nutr 23: 482–486

7. Chiche L, Dao T, Salame E et al. 2000 Liver adenomatosis: reappraisal, diagnosis, and surgical management: eight new cases and review of the literature. Ann Surg 231: 74–81

8. Ishak K, Rabin L 1975 Benign tumors of the liver. Med Clin North Am 59: 995–1013

9. De Carlis L, Pirotta V, Rondinara G F et al. 1997 Hepatic adenoma and focal nodular hyperplasia: diagnosis and criteria for treatment. Liver Transpl Surg 3: 160–165

10. Herman P, Pugliese V, Machado M A et al. 2000 Hepatic adenoma and focal nodular hyperplasia: differential diagnosis and treatment. World J Surg 24: 372–376

11. Edmondson H A, Henderson B, Benton B 1976 Liver cell adenomas associated with use of oral contraceptives. N Engl J Med 294: 470–472

12. Tao L 1991 Oral contraceptive-associated liver cell adenoma and hepatocellular carcinoma: cytomorphology and mechanism of malignant transformation. Cancer 68: 341–347

13. Lindgren A, Olsson R 1993 Liver damage from low-dose oral contraceptives. J Intern Med 234: 287–292

14. Klava A, Super P, Aldridge M et al. 1994 Body builder's liver. J Roy Soc Med 87: 43–44

15. Carrasco D, Barrachina M, Prieto M et al. 1984 Clomiphene citrate and liver cell adenoma. N Engl J Med 310: 1120–1121

16. Bork K, Pitton M, Harten P et al. 1999 Hepatocellular adenomas in patients taking danazol for hereditary angio-oedema. Lancet 353: 1066–1067

17. Tazawa K, Yasuda M, Ohtani Y et al. 1999 Multiple hepatocellular adenomas associated with long-term carbamezapine. Histopathology 35: 92–94

18. Resnick M B, Kozakewich H P W, Perez-Atayde A R 1995 Hepatic adenoma in the pediatric age group. Am J Surg Pathol 19: 1181–1190

19. Hytiroglou P, Theise N 1998 Differential diagnosis of hepatocellular nodular lesions. Semin Diagn Pathol 15: 285–299

20. Bala S, Wunsch P H, Ballhausen W G 1997 Childhood hepatocellular adenoma in familial adenomatous polyposis: mutations in adenomatous polyposis coli gene and p53. Gastroenterology 112: 919–922

21. Vesoulis Z, Agamanolis D 1998 Benign hepatocellular adenoma of the placenta. Am J Surg Pathol 22: 355–359

22. Grange J D, Guechot J, Legendre C et al. 1987 Liver adenoma and focal nodular hyperplasia in a man with high endogenous sex steroids. Gastroenterology 93: 1409–1413

23. Wanless I, Callea F, Craig J et al. 1995 Terminology of nodular lesions of the liver. Hepatology 25: 983–993

24. Ferrell L 1993 Hepatocellular carcinoma arising in a focus of multilobular adenoma. Am J Surg Pathol 17: 525–529

25. Kong C, Appenzeller M, Ferrell L 2000 Utility of CD34 reactivity in evaluating focal nodular hepatocellular lesions sampled by fine needle aspiration biopsy. Acta Cytol 44: 218–222

26. Wilkens L, Bredt M, Flemming P et al. 2001 Differentiation of liver cell adenomas from well-differentiated hepatocellular carcinomas by comparative genomic hybridization. J Pathol 193: 476–482

27. Wilkens L, Bredt M, Flemming P et al. 2001 Diagnostic impact of fluorescence in situ hybridization in the differentiation of hepatocellular adenoma and well-differentiated hepatocellular carcinoma. J Mol Diagn 3: 68–73

28. Foster J H, Berman M M 1994 The malignant transformation of liver cell adenomas. Arch Surg 129: 712–717

29. Ribeiro A, Burgart L J, Nagorney D M et al. 1998 Management of liver adenomatosis: results with a conservative surgical approach. Liver Transpl Surg 4: 388–398

30. Nguyen B, Flejou J, Terris B et al. 1999 Focal nodular hyperplasia of the liver: a comprehensive pathologic study of 305 lesions and recognition of new histologic forms. Am J Surg Pathol 23: 1441–1454

31. Sadowski D C, Lee S S, Wanless I R et al. 1995 Progressive type of focal nodular hyperplasia characterized by multiple tumors and recurrence. Hepatology 21: 970–975

32. Wanless I R, Albrecht S, Bilbao J et al. 1989 Multiple focal nodular hyperplasia of the liver associated with vascular malformations of various organs and neoplasia of the brain: a new syndrome. Mod Pathol 2: 456–462

33. Haber M, Reuben A, Burrell M et al. 1995 Multiple focal nodular hyperplasia of the liver associated with hemihypertrophy and vascular malformations. Gastroenterology 108: 1256–1262

34. Wanless I, Mawdsley C, Adams R 1985 On the pathogenesis of focal nodular hyperplasia of the liver. Hepatology 5: 1194–1200

35. Paradis V, Bieche I, Dargere D et al. 2003 A quantitative gene expression study suggests a role for angiopoietins in focal nodular hyperplasia. Gastroenterology 124: 651–659

36. Paradis V, Laurent A, Flejou J F et al. 1997 Evidence for the polyclonal nature of focal nodular hyperplasia of the liver by the study of X-chromosome inactivation. Hepatology 26: 891–895

37. Paradis V, Benzekri A, Dargere D et al. 2004 Telangiectatic focal nodular hyperplasia: a variant of hepatocellular adenoma. Gastroenterology 126: 1323–1329

38. Caseiro-Alves F, Zins M, Mahfouz A-E et al. 1996 Calcification in focal nodular hyperplasia: a new problem for differentiation from fibrolamellar hepatocellular carcinoma. Radiology 198: 889–892

39. Berman M M, Libbey N P, Foster J H 1980 Hepatocellular carcinoma. Polygonal cell type with fibrous stroma – an atypical variant with a favorable prognosis. Cancer 46: 1448–1455

40. Kudo M, Ikekubo K, Yamamoto K et al. 1989 Focal fatty infiltration of the liver in acute alcoholic liver injury: hot spots with radiocolloid SPECT scan. Am J Gastroenterol 84: 948–952

41. Sasaki M, Harada K, Nakanuma Y et al. 1994 Pseudolipoma of Glisson's capsule. Report of six cases and review of the literature. J Clin Gastroenterol 19: 75–78

42. Sundaresan M, Lyons B, Akosa A B 1991 'Solitary' necrotic nodules of the liver: an aetiology reaffirmed. Gut 32: 1378–1380

43. Tsui W, Yuen R, Chow L et al. 1992 Solitary necrotic nodule of the liver: parasitic origin? J Clin Pathol 45: 975–978

44. Terayama N, Terada T, Hoso M 1995 Partial nodular transformation of the liver with portal vein thrombosis. J Clin Gastroenterol 20: 71–76

45. Theise N, Lopook J, Thung S 1993 A macroregenerative nodule containing multiple foci of hepatocellular carcinoma in a noncirrhotic liver. Hepatology 17: 993–996

46. Ferrell L, Crawford J, Dhillon A et al. 1993 Proposal for standardized criteria for the diagnosis of benign, borderline, and malignant hepatocellular lesions arising in chronic advanced liver disease. Am J Surg Pathol 17: 1113–1123

47. Ferrell L 1994 Hepatocellular nodules in the cirrhotic liver: diagnostic features and proposed nomenclature. In: Ferrell L (ed) Diagnostic problems in liver pathology. Pathology: state of the art reviews. Hanley & Belfus, Philadelphia, p 105–117

48. Park Y, Yang C-T, Fernandez G et al. 1998 Neoangiogenesis and sinusoidal "capillarization" in dysplastic nodules of the liver. Am J Surg Pathol 22: 656–662

49. Roncalli M, Roz E, Goggi G et al. 1999 The vascular profile of regenerative and dysplastic nodules of the cirrhotic liver: implications for diagnosis and classification. Hepatology 30: 1174–1178

50. Theise N, Fiel I, Hytiroglou P et al. 1995 Macroregenerative nodules in cirrhosis are not associated with elevated serum or stainable tissue alpha-fetoprotein. Liver 15: 30–34

51. Nakanuma Y, Terada T, Ueda K et al. 1993 Adenomatous hyperplasia of the liver as a precancerous lesion. Liver 13: 1–9

52. Le Bail B, Bernard P H, Carles J et al. 1997 Prevalence of liver cell dysplasia and association with HCC in a series of 100 cirrhotic liver explants. J Hepatol 27: 835–842

53. Crawford J 1990 Pathologic assessment of liver cell dysplasia and benign liver tumors: differentiation from malignant tumors. Semin Diagn Pathol 7: 115–128

54. Zhao M, Zhang N X, Laissue J A et al. 1994 Immunohistochemical analysis of p53 protein overexpression in liver cell dysplasia and in hepatocellular carcinoma. Virchows Arch 424: 613–621

55. Lee R G, Tsamandas A C, Demetris A J 1997 Large cell change (liver cell dysplasia) and hepatocellular carcinoma in cirrhosis: matched case-control study, pathological analysis, and pathogenetic hypothesis. Hepatology 26: 1415–1422

56. Su Q, Benner A, Hofmann W J et al. 1997 Human hepatic preneoplasia: phenotypes and proliferation kinetics of foci and nodules of altered hepatocytes and their relationship to liver cell dysplasia. Virchows Arch 431: 391–406

57. Natarajan S, Theise N D, Thung S N et al. 1997 Large-cell change of hepatocytes in cirrhosis may represent a reaction to prolonged cholestasis. Am J Surg Pathol 21: 312–318

58. Maggioni M, Coggi G, Cassani B et al. 2000 Molecular changes in hepatocellular dysplastic nodules on microdissected liver biopsies. Hepatology 32: 942–946

59. Yeh S H, Chen P J, Shau W Y et al. 2001 Chromosomal allelic imbalance evolving from liver cirrhosis to hepatocellular carcinoma. Gastroenterology 121: 699–709

60. Deugnier Y M, Charalambous P, Le Quilleuc D et al. 1993 Preneoplastic significance of hepatic iron-free foci in genetic hemochromatosis: a study of 185 patients. Hepatology 18: 1363–1369

61. Bannasch P, Klimek F, Mayer D 1997 Early bioenergetic changes in hepatocarcinogenesis: preneoplastic phenotypes mimic responses to insulin and thyroid hormone. J Bioenerg Biomembr 29: 303–313

62. Su Q, Benner A, Hofmann W J et al. 1997 Human hepatic preneoplasia: phenotypes and proliferation kinetics of foci and nodules of altered hepatocytes and their relationship to liver cell dysplasia. Virchows Arch 431: 391–406

63. El-Serag H B, Mason A C 1999 Rising incidence of hepatocellular carcinoma in the United States. N Engl J Med 340: 745–750

64. Trevisani F, D'Intino P E, Grazi G L et al. 1996 Clinical and pathologic features of hepatocellular carcinoma in young and older Italian patients. Cancer 77: 2223–2232

65. Ishak K G, Goodman Z D, Stocker J T 2001 Tumors of the liver and intrahepatic bile ducts. Armed Forces Institute of Pathology, Washington, DC, p 199–230

66. Befeler A S, Di Bisceglie A M 2002 Hepatocellular carcinoma: diagnosis and treatment. Gastroenterology 122: 1609–1619

67. Monto A, Wright T L 2001 The epidemiology and prevention of hepatocellular carcinoma. Semin Oncol 28: 441–449

68. El-Serag H B 2002 Hepatocellular carcinoma: an epidemiologic view. J Clin Gastroenterol 35 (5 suppl 2): S72–S78

69. Donato F, Boffetta P, Puoti M 1998 A meta-analysis of epidemiological studies on the combined effect of hepatitis B and C virus infections in causing hepatocellular carcinoma. Int J Cancer 75: 347–354

70. Talente G M, Coleman R A, Alter C et al. 1994 Glycogen storage disease in adults. Ann Intern Med 120: 218–226

71. Hamilton S R, Aaltonen L A 2000 WHO classification of tumors. Pathology and genetics of tumors of the digestive system. IARC Press, Lyon, p 157–202

72. Omata M, Peters R, Tatters D 1981 Sclerosing hepatic carcinoma: relationship to hypercalcemia. Liver 1: 33–49

73. Stromeyer F, Ishak K, Gerber M et al. 1980 Ground-glass cells in hepatocellular carcinoma. Am J Clin Pathol 74: 254–258

74. Okuda K, Musha H, Nakajima Y et al. 1977 Clinicopathologic features of encapsulated hepatocellular carcinoma: a study of 26 cases. Cancer 40: 1240–1245

75. Anthony P P, James K 1987 Pedunculated hepatocellular carcinoma. Is it an entity? Histopathology 11: 403–414

76. Emile J F, Adam R, Sebagh M et al. 2000 Hepatocellular carcinoma with lymphoid stroma: a tumour with good prognosis after liver transplantation. Histopathology 37: 523–529

77. Edmondson H, Steiner P 1954 Primary carcinoma of the liver: a study of 100 cases among 48 900 necropsies. Cancer 1: 462–503

78. Wennerberg A E, Nalesnik M A, Coleman W B 1993 Hepatocyte paraffin 1: a monoclonal antibody that reacts with hepatocytes and can be used for differential diagnosis of hepatic tumors. Am J Pathol 143: 1050–1054

79. Minervini M, Demetris A, Lee R et al. 1997 Utilization of hepatocyte-specific antibody in the immunocytochemical evaluation of liver tumors. Mod Pathol 10: 686–692

80. Morrison C, Marsh W Jr, Frankel W L 2002 A comparison of CD10 to pCEA, MOC-31 and hepatocyte for the distinction of malignant tumors in the liver. Mod Pathol 15: 1279–1287

81. Fan Z, van de Rijn M, Montgomery K et al. 2003 Hep Par 1 antibody stain for the differential diagnosis of hepatocellular carcinoma: 676 tumors tested using tissue microarrays and conventional tissue sections. Mod Pathol 16: 137–144

82. Kakar S, Muir T, Murphy L M et al. 2003 Immunoreactivity of Hep Par 1 in hepatic and extrahepatic tumors and its correlation with albumin in situ hybridization in hepatocellular carcinoma. Am J Clin Pathol 119: 361–366

83. Lau S K, Prakash S, Geller S A et al. 2002 Comparative immunohistochemical profile of hepatocellular carcinoma, cholangiocarcinoma, and metastatic adenocarcinoma. Hum Pathol 33: 1175–1181

84. Krishna M, Lloyd R V, Batts K P 1997 Detection of albumin messenger RNA in hepatic and extrahepatic neoplasms. A marker of hepatocellular differentiation. Am J Surg Pathol 21: 147–152

85. Oliveira A M, Erickson L A, Burgart L J et al. 2000 Differentiation of primary and metastatic clear cell tumors in the liver by in situ hybridization for albumin messenger RNA. Am J Surg Pathol 24: 177–182

86. Maeda T, Kajiyama K, Adachi E et al. 1996 The expression of cytokeratins 7, 19, 20 in primary and metastatic carcinomas of the liver. Mod Pathol 9: 901–909

87. Wang N, Zee S, Zarbo R et al. 1995 Coordinate expression of cytokeratins 7 and 20 defines unique subsets of carcinomas. Appl Immunohistochem 3: 99–107

88. Rullier A, Le Bail B, Fawaz R et al. 2000 Cytokeratin 7 and 20 expression in cholangiocarcinomas varies along the biliary tract but still differs from that in colorectal carcinoma metastases. Am J Surg Pathol 24: 870–876

89. Chu P, Wu E, Weiss L 2000 Cytokeratin 7 and cytokeratin 20 expression in epithelial neoplasms: a survey of 435 cases. Mod Pathol 13: 962–972

90. Fucich L, Cheles M, Thung S et al. 1994 Primary versus metastatic hepatic carcinoma: an immunohistochemical study of 34 cases. Arch Pathol Lab Med 118: 927–930

91. Wieczorek T J, Pinkus J L, Glickman J N et al. 2002 Comparison of thyroid transcription factor-1 and hepatocyte antigen immunohistochemical analysis in the differential diagnosis of hepatocellular carcinoma, metastatic adenocarcinoma, renal cell carcinoma and adrenal cortical carcinoma. Am J Clin Pathol 118: 911–921

92. Garcia de Davila M, Gonzalez-Crussi F, Mangkornkanok M 1987 Fibrolamellar carcinoma of the liver in a child: ultrastructural and immunologic aspects. Pediatr Pathol 7: 319–331

93. Ruck P, Harms D, Kaiserling E 1990 Neuroendocrine differentiation in hepatoblastoma: an immunohistochemical investigation. Am J Surg Pathol 14: 847–855

94. Wang J, Dhillon A, Sankey E et al. 1991 Neuroendocrine differentiation in primary neoplasms of the liver. J Pathol 163: 61–67

95. Tsui W, Colombari R, Bonetti F et al. 1999 Hepatic angiomyolipoma: a clinicopathologic study of 30 cases and delineation of unusual morphological variants. Am J Surg Pathol 23: 34–48

96. Murakata L, Ishak K, Nzeako U 2000 Clear cell carcinoma of the liver: a comparative immunohistochemical study with renal clear cell carcinoma. Mod Pathol 13: 874–881

97. Renshaw A, Granter S 1998 A comparison of A103 and inhibin reactivity in adrenal cortical tumors: distinction from hepatocellular carcinoma and renal tumors. Mod Pathol 11: 1160–1164

98. Idilman R, De Maria N, Colantoni A et al. 1998 Pathogenesis of hepatitis B and C-induced hepatocellular carcinoma. J Viral Hepat 5: 285–299

99. Thorgeirsson S S, Grisham J W 2002 Molecular pathogenesis of human hepatocellular carcinoma. Nat Genet 31: 339–346

100. Wong N, Lai P, Lee S W et al. 1999 Assessment of genetic changes in hepatocellular carcinoma by comparative genomic hybridization analysis: relationship to disease stage, tumor size, and cirrhosis. Am J Pathol 154: 37–43

101. Laurent-Puig P, Legoix P, Bluteau O et al. 2001 Genetic alterations associated with hepatocellular carcinomas define distinct pathways of hepatocarcinogenesis. Gastroenterology 120: 1763–1773

102. Balsara B R, Pei J, De Rienzo A et al. 2001 Human hepatocellular carcinoma is characterized by a highly consistent pattern of genomic imbalances, including frequent loss of 16q23.1-24.1. Genes Chromosomes Cancer 30: 245–253

103. Qin L X, Tang Z Y, Ma Z C et al. 2002 P53 immunohistochemical scoring: an independent prognostic marker for patients after hepatocellular carcinoma resection. World J Gastroenterol 8: 459–463

104. Kazachkov Y, Khaoustov V, Yoffe B et al. 1996 p53 abnormalities in hepatocellular carcinoma from United States patients: analysis of all 11 exons. Carcinogenesis 17: 2207–2212

105. Aguilar F, Hussain S P, Cerutti P 1993 Aflatoxin B1 induces the transversion of G→T in codon 249 of the p53 tumor suppressor gene in human hepatocytes. Proc Natl Acad Sci USA 90: 8586–8590

106. Elmore L W, Hancock A R, Chang S F et al. 1997 Hepatitis B virus X protein and p53 tumor suppressor interactions in the modulation of apoptosis. Proc Natl Acad Sci USA 94: 14707–14712

107. Ishido S, Hotta H 1998 Complex formation of the nonstructural protein 3 of hepatitis C virus with the p53 tumor suppressor. FEBS Lett 438: 258–262

108. Lan K H, Sheu M L, Hwang S J et al. 2002 HCV NS5A interacts with p53 and inhibits p53-mediated apoptosis. Oncogene 21: 4801–4811

109. Huang H, Fujii H, Sankila A et al. 1999 Beta-catenin mutations are frequent in human hepatocellular carcinomas associated with hepatitis C virus infection. Am J Pathol 155: 1795–1801

110. Hui A M, Li X, Makuuchi M et al. 1999 Over-expression and lack of retinoblastoma protein are associated with tumor progression and metastasis in hepatocellular carcinoma. Int J Cancer 84: 604–608

111. Matsuda Y, Ichida T, Matsuzawa J et al. 1999 p16(INK4) is inactivated by extensive CpG methylation in human hepatocellular carcinoma. Gastroenterology 116: 394–400

112. Hui A M, Kanai Y, Sakamoto M et al. 1997 Reduced p21(WAF1/CIP1) expression and p53 mutation in hepatocellular carcinomas. Hepatology 25: 575–579

113. Hui A M, Sun L, Kanai Y et al. 1998 Reduced p27Kip1 expression in hepatocellular carcinomas. Cancer Lett 132: 67–73

114. Lee M N, Jung E Y, Kwun H J et al. 2002 Hepatitis C virus core protein represses the p21 promoter through inhibition of a TGF-beta pathway. J Gen Virol 83: 2145–2151

115. Qin L X, Tang Z Y 2002 The prognostic molecular markers in hepatocellular carcinoma. World J Gastroenterol 8: 385–392

116. Qin L X, Tang Z Y, Ma Z C et al. 2002 P53 immunohistochemical scoring: an independent prognostic marker for patients after hepatocellular carcinoma resection. World J Gastroenterol 8: 459–463

117. Fiorentino M, Altimari A, D'Errico A et al. 2000 Acquired expression of p27 is a favorable prognostic indicator in patients with hepatocellular carcinoma. Clin Cancer Res 6: 3966–3972

118. Fiorentino M, Altimari A, Ravaioli M et al. 2004 Predictive value of biological markers for hepatocellular carcinoma patients treated with orthotopic liver transplantation. Clin Cancer Res 10: 1789–1795

119. Bismuth H, Chiche L, Castaing D 1995 Surgical treatment of hepatocellular carcinomas in noncirrhotic liver: experience with 68 liver resections. World J Surg 19: 35–41

120. Figueras J, Jaurrieta E, Valls C et al. 1997 Survival after liver transplantation in cirrhotic patients with and without hepatocellular carcinoma: a comparative study. Hepatology 25: 1485–1489

121. Yao F Y, Ferrell L, Bass N M et al. 2001 Liver transplantation for hepatocellular carcinoma: expansion of the tumor size limits does not adversely impact survival. Hepatology 33: 1394–1403

122. Befeler A S, Di Bisceglie A M 2002 Hepatocellular carcinoma: diagnosis and treatment. Gastroenterology 122: 1609–1619

123. Ng I O, Lai E C, Fan S T et al. 1995 Prognostic significance of pathologic features of hepatocellular carcinoma. A multivariate analysis of 278 patients. Cancer 76: 2443–2448

124. Nzeako U C, Goodman Z D, Ishak K G 1996 Hepatocellular carcinoma in cirrhotic and noncirrhotic livers. A clinico-histopathologic study of 804 North American patients. Am J Clin Pathol 105: 65–75

125. Chedid A, Ryan L M, Dayal Y et al. 1999 Morphology and other prognostic factors of hepatocellular carcinoma. Arch Pathol Lab Med 123: 524–528

126. Quaglia A, Bhattacharjya S, Dhillon A P 2001 Limitations of the histopathological diagnosis and prognostic assessment of hepatocellular carcinoma. Histopathology 38: 167–174

127. Lauwers G Y, Terris B, Balis U K et al. 2002 Prognostic histologic indicators of curatively resected hepatocellular carcinomas. A multi-institutional analysis of 425 patients with definition of a histologic prognostic index. Am J Surg Pathol 26: 25–34

128. Craig J, Peters R, Edmondson H et al. 1980 Fibrolamellar carcinoma of the liver: a tumor of adolescents and young adults with distinctive clinicopathologic features. Cancer 46: 372–379

129. Berman M, Libbey N, Foster J 1980 Hepatocellular carcinoma: polygonal cell type with fibrous stroma – an atypical variant with a favorable prognosis. Cancer 46: 1448–1455

130. Berman M, Sheahan D 1988 Fibrolamellar carcinoma of the liver: an immunohistochemical study of nineteen cases and a review of the literature. Hum Pathol 19: 784–794

131. Saul S, Titelbaum D, Gansler T et al. 1987 The fibrolamellar variant of hepatocellular carcinoma; its association with focal nodular hyperplasia. Cancer 60: 3049–3055

132. Saxena R, Humphreys S, Williams R et al. 1994 Nodular hyperplasia surrounding fibrolamellar carcinoma: a zone of arterialized liver parenchyma. Histopathology 25: 275–278

133. Hodgson H J 1987 Fibrolamellar cancer of the liver. J Hepatol 5: 241–247

134. Vecchio F M, Fabiano A, Ghirlanda G et al. 1984 Fibrolamellar carcinoma of the liver: the malignant counterpart of focal nodular hyperplasia with oncocytic change. Am J Clin Pathol 81: 521–526

135. Goodman Z, Ishak K, Langloss J et al. 1985 Combined hepatocellular–cholangiocarcinoma: a histologic and immunohistochemical study. Cancer 55: 124–135

136. Nagorney D M, Adson M A, Weiland L H et al. 1985 Fibrolamellar hepatoma. Am J Surg 149: 113–119

137. Kakar S, Burgart L J, Batts K P et al. 2005 Clinicopathologic features and survival in fibrolamellar carcinoma: comparison with conventional hepatocellular carcinoma with and without cirrhosis. Mod Pathol 18: 1417–1423

138. Ng I O, Shek T W, Nicholls J et al. 1998 Combined hepatocellular–cholangiocarcinoma: a clinicopathological study. J Gastroenterol Hepatol 13: 34–40

139. Yano Y, Yamamoto J, Kosuge T et al. 2003 Combined hepatocellular and cholangiocarcinoma: a clinicopathologic study of 26 resected cases. Jpn J Clin Oncol 33: 283–287

140. Jarnagin W R, Weber S, Tickoo S K et al. 2002 Combined hepatocellular and cholangiocarcinoma: demographic, clinical, and prognostic factors. Cancer 94: 2040–2046

141. Tickoo S K, Zee S Y, Obiekwe S et al. 2002 Combined hepatocellular–cholangiocarcinoma, a histopathologic, immunohistochemical and in situ hybridization study. Am J Surg Pathol 26: 989–997

142. Kim H, Park C, Han K H et al. 2004 Primary liver carcinoma of intermediate (hepatocyte–cholangiocyte) phenotype. J Hepatol 40: 298–304

143. Fujii H, Zhu X G, Matsumoto T et al. 2000 Genetic classification of combined hepatocellular–cholangiocarcinoma. Hum Pathol 31: 1011–1017

144. Haas S, Muczynski K, Krailo M et al. 1989 Histopathology and prognosis in childhood hepatoblastoma and hepatocarcinoma. Cancer 64: 1082–1095

145. Weinberg A, Finegold M 1983 Primary hepatic tumors of childhood. Hum Pathol 14: 512–537

146. Altmann H 1992 Epthelial and mixed hepatoblastoma in the adult. Pathol Res Pract 188: 16–26

147. Anthony P 1994 Tumours and tumour-like lesions of the liver and biliary tract. In: MacSween R, Anthony P, Scheuer P et al. (eds) Pathology of the liver, 3rd edn. Churchill Livingstone, Edinburgh, p 635–711

148. Haggitt R, Reid B 1986 Hereditary gastrointestinal polyposis syndromes. Am J Surg Pathol 10: 871–887

149. Stocker J 1994 Hepatoblastoma. Semin Diagn Pathol 11: 136–143

150. Arshad R R, Woo S Y, Abbassi V et al. 1982 Virilizing hepatoblastoma: precocious sexual development and partial response of pulmonary metastases to cis-platinum. CA Cancer J Clin 32: 293–300

151. Saxena R, Leake J, Shafford E et al. 1993 Chemotherapy effects on hepatoblastoma: a histological study. Am J Surg Pathol 17: 1266–1271

152. Conran R, Hitchcock C, Waclawiw M et al. 1992 Hepatoblastoma: the prognostic significance of histologic type. Pediatr Pathol 12: 167–183

153. Ruck P, Kaiserling E 1993 Melanin-containing hepatoblastoma with endocrine differentiation: an immunohistochemical and ultrastructural study. Cancer 72: 361–368

154. Murakata L, Ishak K, Nzeako U 2000 Clear cell carcinoma of the liver: a comparative immunohistochemical study with renal clear cell carcinoma. Mod Pathol 13: 874–881

155. Buendia M A 2002 Genetic alterations in hepatoblastoma and hepatocellular carcinoma: common and distinctive aspects. Med Pediatr Oncol 39: 530–535

156. Terracciano L M, Bernasconi B, Ruck P et al. 2003 Comparative genomic hybridization analysis of hepatoblastoma reveals high frequency of X-chromosome gains and similarities between epithelial and stromal components. Hum Pathol 34: 864–871

157. Schnater J M, Kohler S E, Lamers W H et al. 2003 Where do we stand with hepatoblastoma? Cancer 98: 668–678

158. Park W S, Oh R R, Park J Y et al. 2001 Nuclear localization of beta-catenin is an important prognostic factor in hepatoblastoma. J Pathol 193: 483–490

159. Shim Y H, Park H J, Choi M S et al. 2003 Hypermethylation of the p16 gene and lack of p16 expression in hepatoblastoma. Mod Pathol 16: 430–436

160. Cillo U, Ciarleglio F A, Bassanello M et al. 2003 Liver transplantation for the management of hepatoblastoma. Transplant Proc 35: 2983–2985

161. Otte J B, Pritchard J, Aronson D C et al. 2004 Liver transplantation for hepatoblastoma: results from the International Society of Pediatric Oncology (SIOP) study SIOPEL-1 and review of the world experience. Pediatr Blood Cancer 42: 74–83

162. Hobbs K 1990 Hepatic hemangiomas. World J Surg 14: 468–471

163. Ishak K G, Goodman Z D, Stocker J T 2001 Tumors of the liver and intrahepatic bile ducts. Armed Forces Institute of Pathology, Washington, DC, p 71–146

164. Kane R, Newman A 1973 Diffuse skeletal and hepatic hemangiomatosis. Calif Med 118: 41–44

165. Adam Y G, Huvos A G, Fortner J G 1970 Giant hemangiomas of the liver. Ann Surg 172: 239–245

166. Mikami T, Hirata K, Oikawa I et al. 1998 Hemobilia caused by a giant benign hemangioma of the liver: report of a case. Surg Today 28: 948–952

167. Kim G E, Thung S N, Tsui W M et al. 2003 Cavernous hemangioma: what have we been missing? (abstract) Mod Pathol 16: 279a

168. Dehner L, Ishak K 1971 Vascular tumors of the liver in infants and children: a study of 30 cases and review of the literature. Arch Pathol 92: 101–111

169. Stanley P, Geer G, Miller J et al. 1989 Infantile hepatic hemangiomas: clinical features, radiologic investigations and treatment of 20 patients. Cancer 64: 936–949

170. Bejarano P A, Serrano M F, Casillas J et al. 2003 Concurrent infantile hemangioendothelioma and mesenchymal hamartoma in a developmentally arrested liver of an infant requiring hepatic transplantation. Pediatr Dev Pathol 6: 552–557

171. Han S J, Tsai C C, Tsai H M et al. 1998 Infantile hemangioendothelioma with a highly elevated serum alpha-fetoprotein level. Hepatogastroenterology 45: 459–461

172. Amonkar P, Desai S, Deb R et al. 1999 Infantile hemangioendothelioma of the liver. Med Pediatr Oncol 32: 392–394

173. Selby D M, Stocker J T, Waclawiw M A et al. 1994 Infantile hemangioendothelioma of the liver. Hepatology 20: 39–45

174. Cerar A, Dolenc-Strazar Z, Bartenjev D 1996 Infantile hemangioendothelioma of the liver in a neonate: immunohistochemical observations. Am J Surg Pathol 20: 871–876

175. Selby D, Stocker J, Ishak K 1992 Angiosarcoma of the liver in childhood: a clinicopathologic and follow-up study of 10 cases. Pediatr Pathol 12: 485–498

176. Daller J A, Bueno J, Gutierrez J et al. 1999 Hepatic hemangioendothelioma: clinical experience and management strategy. J Pediatr Surg 34: 98–106

177. Stocker J T 2001 Hepatic tumors in children. Clin Liver Dis 5: 259–281

178. Stocker J, Ishak K 1983 Mesenchymal hamartoma of the liver: report of 30 cases and review of the literature. Pediatr Pathol 1: 245–267

179. Cook J R, Pfeifer J D, Dehner L P 2002 Mesenchymal hamartoma of the liver in the adult: association with distinct clinical features and histological changes. Hum Pathol 33: 893–898

180. Murthi G V, Paterson L, Azmy A 2003 Chromosomal translocation in mesenchymal hamartoma of liver: what is its significance? J Pediatr Surg 2003; 38: 1543–1545

181. Yen J B, Kong M S, Lin J N 2003 Hepatic mesenchymal hamartoma. J Paediatr Child Health 39: 632–634

182. O'Sullivan M J, Swanson P E, Knoll J et al. 2001 Undifferentiated embryonal sarcoma with unusual features arising within mesenchymal hamartoma of the liver: report of a case and review of the literature. Pediatr Dev Pathol 4: 482–489

183. Goodman Z, Ishak K 1984 Angiomyolipomas of the liver. Am J Surg Pathol 8: 745–750

184. Tang L H, Hui P, Garcia-Tsao G et al. 2002 Multiple angiomyolipomata of the liver: a case report. Mod Pathol 15: 167–171

185. Hornick J L, Fletcher C D M 2006 PEComa: what do we know so far? Histopathology 48: 75–82

186. Yamasaki S, Tanaka S, Fujii H et al. 2000 Monotypic epithelioid angiomyolipoma of the liver. Histopathology 36: 451–456

187. Barnard M, Lajoie G 2001 Angiomyolipoma: immunohistochemical and ultrastructural study of 14 cases. Ultrastruct Pathol 25: 21–29

188. Makhlouf H R, Remotti H E, Ishak K G 2002 Expression of KIT (CD117) in angiomyolipoma. Am J Surg Pathol 26: 493–497

189. Ji Y, Zhu X, Xu J et al. 2001 Hepatic angiomyolipoma: a clinicopathologic study of 10 cases. Chin Med J (Engl) 114: 280–285

190. Ren N, Qin L X, Tang Z Y et al. 2003 Diagnosis and treatment of hepatic angiomyolipoma in 26 cases. World J Gastroenterol 9: 1856–1858

191. Anthony P, Telesinghe P 1986 Inflammatory pseudotumor of the liver. J Clin Pathol 39: 761–768

192. Shek T, Ng I, Chan K 1993 Inflammatory pseudotumor of the liver: report of four cases and review of the literature. Am J Surg Pathol 17: 231–238

193. Nakanuma Y, Tsuneyama K, Masuda S et al. 1994 Hepatic inflammatory pseudotumor associated with chronic cholangitis: report of three cases. Hum Pathol 25: 86–91

194. Torzilli G, Inoue K, Midorikawa Y et al. 2001 Inflammatory pseudotumors of the liver: prevalence and clinical impact in surgical patients. Hepatogastroenterology 48: 1118–1123

195. Amankonah T D, Strom C B, Vierling J M et al. 2001 Inflammatory pseudotumor of the liver as the first manifestation of Crohn's disease. Am J Gastroenterol 96: 2520–2522

196. Selves J, Meggetto F, Brousset P et al. 1996 Inflammatory pseudotumor of the liver: evidence for follicular dendritic reticulum cell proliferation associated with clonal Epstein–Barr virus. Am J Surg Pathol 20: 747–753

197. Cheuk W, Chan J K, Shek T W et al. 2001 Inflammatory pseudotumor-like follicular dendritic cell tumor: a distinctive low grade malignant abdominal neoplasm with consistent Epstein–Barr virus association. Am J Surg Pathol 25: 721–731

198. Lee S L, DuBois J J 2001 Hepatic inflammatory pseudotumor: case report, review of the literature, and a proposal for morphologic classification. Pediatr Surg Int 17: 555–559

199. Shek T, Ho F, Ng I et al. 1996 Follicular dendritic tumor of the liver: evidence for an Epstein–Barr virus-related clonal proliferation of follicular dendritic cells. Am J Surg Pathol 20: 313–324

200. Pokorny C S, Painter D M, Waugh R C et al. 1991 Inflammatory pseudotumor of the liver causing biliary obstruction. Treatment by biliary stenting with 5-year follow-up. J Clin Gastroenterol 13: 338–341

201. Fried R, Wardzala A, Willson R et al. 1992 Benign cartilaginous tumor (chondroma) of the liver. Gastroenterology 103: 678–680

202. Hytiroglou P, Linton P, Klion F et al. 1993 Benign schwannoma of the liver. Arch Pathol Lab Med 117: 216–218

203. Moran C A, Ishak K G, Goodman Z D 1998 Solitary fibrous tumor of the liver: a clinicopathologic and immunohistochemical study of nine cases. Ann Diagn Pathol 2: 19–24

204. Awan S, Davenport M, Portmann B et al. 1996 Angiosarcoma of the liver in children. J Pediatr Surg 31: 1729–1732

205. Zocchetti C 2001 Liver angiosarcoma in humans: epidemiologic considerations. Med Lav 92: 39–53

206. Ishak K G, Anthony P P, Niederau C et al. 2000 Mesenchymal tumors of the liver. In: Hamilton S R, Aaltonen L (eds) Tumors of the digestive system. IARC Press, Lyon, p 191–198

207. Tannapfel A, Weihrauch M, Benicke M et al. 2001 p16INK4A-alterations in primary angiosarcoma of the liver. J Hepatol 35: 62–67

208. Weihrauch M, Markwarth A, Lehnert G et al. 2002 Abnormalities of the ARF-p53 pathway in primary angiosarcomas of the liver. Hum Pathol 33: 884–892

209. Timaran C H, Grandas O H, Bell J L 2000 Hepatic angiosarcoma: long-term survival after complete surgical removal. Am Surg 66: 1153–1157

210. Ishak K, Sesterhenn I, Goodman Z et al. 1984 Epithelioid hemangioendothelioma of the liver: a clinicopathologic and follow-up study of 32 cases. Hum Pathol 15: 839–852

211. d'Annibale M, Piovanello P, Carlini P et al. 2002 Epithelioid hemangioendothelioma of the liver: case report and review of the literature. Transplant Proc 34: 1248–1251

212. Taege C, Holzhausen H, Gunter G et al. 1999 Malignant epithelioid hemangioendothelioma of the liver – a very rare tumor in children. Pathologe 20: 345–350

213. Gray M, Rosenberg A, Dickersin G et al. 1990 Cytokeratin expression in epithelioid vascular neoplasms. Hum Pathol 21: 212–217

214. Uchimura K, Nakamuta M, Osoegawa M et al. 2001 Hepatic epithelioid hemangioendothelioma. J Clin Gastroenterol 32: 431–434

215. Madariaga J, Marino I, Karavias D et al. 1995 Long-term results after liver transplantation for primary hepatic epithelioid hemangioendothelioma. Ann Surg Oncol 2: 483–487

216. Ben-Haim M, Roayaie S, Ye M Q et al. 1999 Hepatic epithelioid hemangioendothelioma: resection or transplantation, which and when? Liver Transpl Surg 5: 526–531

217. Theurillat J P, Vavricka S R, Went P et al. 2003 Morphologic changes and altered gene expression in an epithelioid hemangioendothelioma during a ten-year course of disease. Pathol Res Pract 199: 165–170

218. Kayler L K, Merion R M, Arenas J D et al. 2002 Epithelioid hemangioendothelioma of the liver disseminated to the peritoneum treated with liver transplantation and interferon alpha-2B. Transplantation 74: 128–130

219. Stocker J, Ishak K 1978 Undifferentiated (embryonal) sarcoma of the liver: report of 31 cases. Cancer 42: 336–348

220. Lack E, Schloo B, Azumi N et al. 1991 Undifferentiated (embryonal) sarcoma of the liver: Clinical and pathologic study of 16 cases with emphasis on immunohistochemical features. Am J Surg Pathol 15: 1–16

221. Frankel W L, Kiani B, Ferrell L D et al. 2003 Immunohistochemical analysis of embryonal sarcoma of the liver (abstract). Mod Pathol 16: 272a

222. Webber E M, Morrison K B, Pritchard S L et al. 1999 Undifferentiated embryonal sarcoma of the liver: results of clinical management in one center. J Pediatr Surg 34: 1641–1644

223. Sowery R D, Jensen C, Morrison K B et al. 2001 Comparative genomic hybridization detects multiple chromosomal amplifications and deletions in undifferentiated embryonal sarcoma of the liver. Cancer Genet Cytogenet 126: 128–133

224. Noel J C, Hermans P, Andre J et al. 1996 Herpesvirus-like DNA sequences and Kaposi's sarcoma: relationship with epidemiology, clinical spectrum, and histologic features. Cancer 77: 2132–2136

225. Marcelin A G, Roque-Afonso A M, Hurtova M et al. 2004 Fatal disseminated Kaposi's sarcoma following human herpesvirus 8 primary infections in liver-transplant recipients. Liver Transpl 10: 295–300

226. Hubscher S, Lumley M, Elias E 1993 Vanishing bile duct syndrome: a possible mechanism for intrahepatic cholestasis in Hodgkin's lymphoma. Hepatology 17: 70–77

227. Scheimberg I, Pollock D, Collins P et al. 1995 Pathology of the liver in leukaemia and lymphoma. Histopathology 26: 311–321

228. Jaffe E 1987 Malignant lymphomas: pathology of liver involvement. Semin Liver Dis 7: 257–268

229. Santos P, Raez L E, Salvatierra J et al. 2003 Primary hepatic non-Hodgkin's lymphomas: case report and review of the literature. Am J Gastroenterol 98: 2789–2793

230. Page R D, Romaguera J E, Osborne B et al. 2001 Primary hepatic lymphoma: favorable outcome after combination chemotherapy. Cancer 92: 2023–2029

231. Cooke C B, Krenacs L, Stetler-Stevenson M et al. 1996 Hepatosplenic T-cell lymphoma: a distinct clinicopathologic entity of cytotoxic gamma delta T-cell origin. Blood 88: 4265–4274

232. Ishak K G, Goodman Z D, Stocker J T 2001 Tumors of the liver and intrahepatic bile ducts. Armed Forces Institute of Pathology, Washington, DC, p 271–280

233. Shek T, Ho F, Ng I et al. 1996 Follicular dendritic cell tumor of the liver: evidence for an Epstein–Barr virus-related clonal proliferation of follicular dendritic cells. Am J Surg Pathol 20: 313–324

234. Nelson V, Fernandes N F, Woolf G M et al. 2001 Primary liposarcoma of the liver: a case report and review of literature. Arch Pathol Lab Med 125: 410–412

235. Cozzutto C, Bernardi B, Comelli A et al. 1981 Malignant mesenchymoma of the liver in children: a clinicopathologic and ultrastructural study. Hum Pathol 12: 481–485

236. Kawarada Y, Uehara S, Noda M et al. 1985 Nonhepatocytic malignant mixed tumor primary in the liver: report of two cases. Cancer 55: 1790–1798

237. Demirhan B, Sokmensuer C, Karakayali H et al. 1997 Primary extramedullary plasmacytoma of the liver. J Clin Pathol 50: 74–76

238. Parham D, Peiper S, Robicheaux G et al. 1988 Malignant rhabdoid tumor of the liver: evidence for epithelial differentiation. Arch Pathol Lab Med 112: 61–64

239. Gresham G, Rue L 1985 Squamous cell carcinoma of the liver. Hum Pathol 16: 413–416

240. Heaton G, Matthews T, Christopherson W 1986 Malignant trophoblastic tumors with massive hemorrhage presenting as liver primary: a report of two cases. Am J Surg Pathol 10: 342–347

241. Heywood G, Burgart L J, Nagorney D M 2002 Ossifying malignant mixed epithelial and stromal tumor of the liver: a case report of a previously undescribed tumor. Cancer 94: 1018–1022

242. Borja E R, Hori J M, Pugh R P 1975 Metastatic carcinomatosis of the liver mimicking cirrhosis: case report and review of the literature. Cancer 35: 445–449

243. Riopel M A, Klimstra D S, Godellas C V et al. 1997 Intrabiliary growth of metastatic colonic adenocarcinoma: a pattern of intrahepatic spread easily confused with primary neoplasia of the biliary tract. Am J Surg Pathol 21: 1030–1036

244. Christensen A, Ishak K 1970 Benign tumors and pseudotumors of the gallbladder: report of 180 cases. Arch Pathol Lab Med 90: 423–432

245. Albores-Saavedra J, Henson D E, Klimstra D S 2000 Tumors of the gallbladder, extrahepatic bile ducts and ampulla of Vater. Armed Forces Institute of Pathology, Washington, DC, p 21–36

246. Melson G, Reiter F, Evens R 1976 Tumorous conditions of the gallbladder. Semin Roentgenol 11: 260–282

247. Nishihara K, Yamaguchi K, Hashimoto H et al. 1991 Tubular adenoma of the gallbladder with squamoid spindle cell metaplasia. Report of three cases with immunohistochemical study. Acta Pathol Jpn 41: 41–45

248. Sasatomi E, Tokunaga O, Miyazaki K 2000 Precancerous conditions of gallbladder carcinoma: overview of histopathologic characteristics and molecular genetic findings. J Hepatobiliary Pancreat Surg 7: 556–567

249. Kozuka S, Tsubone N, Yasui A et al. 1982 Relation of adenoma to carcinoma in the gallbladder. Cancer 50: 2226–2234

250. Shinkai H, Kimura W, Muto T 1998 Surgical indications for small polypoid lesions of the gallbladder. Am J Surg 175: 114–117

251. Nakajo S, Yamamoto M, Tahara E 1990 Morphometrical analysis of gall-bladder adenoma and adenocarcinoma with reference to histogenesis and adenoma–carcinoma sequence. Virchows Arch A Pathol Anat Histopathol 417: 49–56

252. Miller T, Weber T, Appelman H 1972 Paraganglioma of the gallbladder. Arch Surg 105: 637–639

253. Albores-Saavedra J, Alcantra-Vazquez A, Cruz-Ortiz H et al. 1980 The precursor lesions of invasive gallbladder carcinoma: hyperplasia, atypical hyperplasia and carcinoma. Cancer 45: 919–927

254. Ojeda V, Shilkin K, Walters M 1985 Premalignant epithelial lesions of the gallbladder: a prospective study of 120 cholecystectomy specimens. Pathology 17: 451–454

255. Yamamoto M, Nakajo S, Tahara E 1989 Histogenesis of well-differentiated adenocarcinoma of the gallbladder. Pathol Res Pract 184: 279–286

256. Kijima H, Watanabe H, Iwafuchi M et al. 1989 Histogenesis of gallbladder carcinoma from investigation of early carcinoma and microcarcinoma. Acta Pathol Jpn 39: 235–244

257. Hisatomi K, Haratake J, Horie A et al. 1990 Relation of histopathological features to prognosis of gallbladder cancer. Am J Gastroenterol 85: 567–572

258. Albores-Saavedra J, Nadji M, Henson D et al. 1986 Intestinal metaplasia of the gallbladder; a morphologic and immunocytochemical study. Hum Pathol 17: 614–620

259. Albores-Saavedra J, Nadji M, Henson D 1986 Intestinal-type adenocarcinoma of the gallbladder: a clinicopathologic and immunocytochemical study of seven cases. Am J Surg Pathol 10: 19–25

260. Yamamoto M, Nakajo S, Tahara E 1989 Dysplasia of the gallbladder. Its histogenesis and correlation to gallbladder adenocarcinoma. Pathol Res Pract 185: 454–460

261. Yamagiwa H 1989 Mucosal dysplasia of gallbladder: isolated and adjacent lesions to carcinoma. Jpn J Cancer Res 80: 238–243

262. Bivins B, Meeker W, Weiss D et al. 1975 Carcinoma in situ of the gallbladder: a dilemma. South Med J 68: 297–300

263. Albores-Saavedra J, Shukla D, Carrick K et al. 2001 In situ and invasive adenocarcinomas of the gallbladder extending into or arising from Rokitansky–Aschoff sinuses. Am J Surg Pathol 28: 621–628

264. Albores-Saavedra J, Molberg K, Henson D 1996 Unusual malignant epithelial tumors of the gallbladder. Semin Diagn Pathol 13: 326–338

265. Ligoury C, Canard J M 1983 Tumours of the biliary system. Clin Gastroenterol 12: 269–295

266. Serra I, Calvo A, Maturana M et al. 1990 Biliary tract cancer in Chile. Int J Cancer 46: 965–971

267. Brandt-Rauf P, Pincus M, Adelson S 1982 Cancer of the gallbladder: a review of forty-three cases. Hum Pathol 13: 48–53

268. Strom B L, Iliopoulos D, Atkinson B et al. 1989 Pathophysiology of tumor progression in human gallbladder: flow cytometry, CEA, and CA 19-9 levels in bile and serum in different stages of gallbladder disease. J Natl Cancer Inst 81: 1575–1580

269. Anderson J B, Cooper M J, Williamson R C N 1985 Adenocarcinoma of the extrahepatic biliary tree. Ann R Coll Surg Engl 67: 139–143

270. Kimura W, Shimada H, Kuroda A et al. 1989 Carcinoma of the gallbladder and extrahepatic bile ducts in autopsy cases of the aged, with special reference to its relationship to gallstones. Am J Gastroenterol 84: 386–390

271. Shimizu M, Miura J, Tanaka T et al. 1989 Porcelain gallbladder: relation between its type by ultrasound and incidence of cancer. J Clin Gastroenterol 11: 471–476

272. Welton J, Marr J, Friedman S 1979 Association between hepatobiliary cancer and typhoid carrier state. Lancet 1: 791–794

273. Sameshima Y, Uchimura M, Muto Y et al. 1987 Coexistent carcinoma in congenital dilatation of the bile duct and anomalous arrangement of the pancreatico-bile duct. Carcinogenesis of coexistent gall bladder carcinoma. Cancer 60: 1883–1890

274. Ozmen V, Martin P C, Igci A et al. 1991 Adenocarcinoma of the gallbladder associated with congenital choledochal cyst and anomalous pancreaticobiliary ductal junction. Eur J Surg 157: 549–551

275. Cowley L, Wood V 1964 Carcinoma developing in a remnant of the gallbladder. Ann Surg 159: 466–468

276. Albores-Saavedra J, Henson D E, Klimstra D S 2000 Tumors of the gallbladder, extrahepatic bile ducts and ampulla of Vater. Armed Forces Institute of Pathology, Washington, DC, p 61–104

276a. Albores-Saavedra J, Tuck M, McLaren B K et al. 2005 Papillary carcinomas of the gallbladder: analysis of noninvasive and invasive types. Arch Pathol Lab Med 129: 905–909

277. Vardaman C, Albores-Saavedra J 1995 Clear cell carcinomas of the gallbladder and extrahepatic bile ducts. Am J Surg Pathol 19: 91–99

277a. Albores-Saavedra J, Grider D J, Wu J et al. 2006 Giant cell tumor of the extrahepatic biliary tree: a clinicopathologic study of 4 cases and comparison with anaplastic spindle and giant cell carcinoma with osteoclast-like giant cells. Am J Surg Pathol 30: 495–500

278. Fukuda T, Ohnishi Y 1990 Gallbladder carcinoma producing human chorionic gonadotropin. Am J Gastroenterol 85: 1403–1406

279. Suster S, Huszar M, Herczeg E et al. 1987 Adenosquamous carcinoma of the gallbladder with spindle cell features. A light microscopic and immunocytochemical study of a case. Histopathology 11: 209–214

280. Iida Y, Tsutsumi Y 1992 Small cell (endocrine cell) carcinoma of the gallbladder with squamous and adenocarcinomatous components. Acta Pathol Jpn 42: 119–125

281. Nishihara K, Takashima M, Furuta T et al. 1995 Adenosquamous carcinoma of the gall-bladder with gastric foveolar-type epithelium. Pathol Int 45: 250–256

282. Albores-Saavedra J, Soriano J, Larraza-Hernandez O et al. 1984 Oat cell carcinoma of the gallbladder. Hum Pathol 15: 639–646

283. Cavazzana A, Fassina A, Tollot M et al. 1991 Small-cell carcinoma of the gallbladder. An immunocytochemical and ultrastructural study. Pathol Res Pract 187: 472–476

284. Duan H J, Ishigame H, Ishii Z et al. 1991 Small cell carcinoma of the gallbladder combined with adenocarcinoma. Acta Pathol Jpn 41: 841–846

285. Nishihara K, Tsuneyoshi M 1993 Undifferentiated spindle cell carcinoma of the gallbladder. Hum Pathol 24: 1298–1305

286. Fujii K, Yokozaki H, Yasui W et al. 1996 High frequency of p53 gene mutation in adenocarcinomas of the gallbladder. Cancer Epidemiol Biomarkers Prev 5: 461–466

287. Wistuba I I, Albores-Saavedra J 1999 Genetic abnormalities involved in the pathogenesis of gallbladder carcinoma. J Hepatobiliary Pancreat Surg 6: 237–244

288. Ajiki T, Onoyama H, Yamamoto M et al. 1996 p53 protein expression and prognosis in gallbladder carcinoma and premalignant lesions. Hepatogastroenterology 43: 521–526

289. Wistuba I I, Sugio K, Hung J et al. 1995 Allele-specific mutations involved in the pathogenesis of endemic gallbladder carcinoma in Chile. Cancer Res 55: 2511–2515

290. Yoshida S, Todoroki T, Ichikawa Y et al. 1995 Mutations of p16Ink4/CDKN2 and p15Ink4B/MTS2 genes in biliary tract cancers. Cancer Res 55: 2756–2760

291. Wistuba I I, Ashfaq R, Maitra A et al. 2002 Fragile histidine triad gene abnormalities in the pathogenesis of gallbladder carcinoma. Am J Pathol 160: 2073–2079

292. Wistuba I I, Miquel J F, Gazdar A F et al. 1999 Gallbladder adenomas have molecular abnormalities different from those present in gallbladder carcinomas. Hum Pathol 30: 21–25

293. Arnaud J P, Casa C, Georgeac C et al. 1995 Primary carcinoma of the gallbladder – review of 143 cases. Hepatogastroenterology 42: 811–815

294. Shoup M, Fong Y 2002 Surgical indications and extent of resection in gallbladder cancer. Surg Oncol Clin North Am 11: 985–994

295. Malats N, Porta M, Pinol J L et al. 1995 Ki-ras mutations as a prognostic factor in extrahepatic bile system cancer. J Clin Oncol 13: 1679–1686

296. Ouchi K, Owada Y, Matsuno S et al. 1987 Prognostic factors in the surgical treatment of gallbladder carcinoma. Surgery 101: 731–737

297. North J H Jr, Pack M S, Hong C et al. 1998 Prognostic factors for adenocarcinoma of the gallbladder: an analysis of 162 cases. Am Surg 64: 437–440

298. Bartlett D L, Fong Y, Fortner J G et al. 1996 Long-term results after resection for gallbladder cancer. Implications for staging and management. Ann Surg 224: 639–646

299. Weedon D 1984 Other primary tumors (melanoma, carcinoid). In: Weedon D (ed) Pathology of the gallbladder. Year Book Medical Publishers, Chicago, p 251–254

300. Papotti M, Galliano D, Monga G 1990 Signet-ring cell carcinoid of the gallbladder. Histopathology 17: 255–259

301. Yamamoto M, Nakajo S, Miyoshi N et al. 1989 Endocrine cell carcinoma (carcinoid) of the gallbladder. Am J Surg Pathol 13: 292–302

302. Noda M, Miwa A, Kitagawa M 1989 Carcinoid tumors of the gallbladder with adenocarcinomatous differentiation: a morphologic and immunohistochemical study. Am J Gastroenterol 84: 953–957

303. Bricker D, Halpert B 1963 Adenomyoma of the gallbladder. Surgery 53: 615–620

304. Shepard V, Walters W, Dockerty M 1942 Benign neoplasms of the gallbladder. Arch Surg 45: 1–18

305. Aguirre J, Boher R, Guraieb S 1969 Hyperplastic cholecystoses: a new contribution to the unitarian theory. Am J Roentgenol 107: 1–13

306. Ochsner S 1966 Solitary polypoid lesions of the gallbladder. Radiol Clin North Am 4: 501–510

307. Carrera G, Ochsner S 1958 Polypoid mucosal lesions of the gallbladder. JAMA 166: 888–892

308. MacBeth W 1964 Papillomas of the gallbladder. A technical consideration as illustrated by three cases. Am J Surg 108: 8–12

309. Qizilbash A 1976 Acute pancreatitis occurring in heterotopic pancreatic tissue in the gallbladder. Cancer J Surg 19: 413–414

310. Vidgoff I, Lewis A 1961 Acute hemorrhage from aberrant pancreatic tissue in the gallbladder. Calif Med 94: 317–319

311. Bentivegna S, Hirschl S 1972 Heterotopic gastric mucosa in the gallbladder presenting as a symptom-producing tumor. Am J Gastroenterol 57: 423–428

312. Jain D, Sarode V R, Abdul-Karim F W et al. 2000 Evidence for the neoplastic transformation of Von-Meyenburg complexes. Am J Surg Pathol 24: 1131–1139

313. Allaire G S, Rabin L, Ishak K G et al. 1988 Bile duct adenoma. A study of 152 cases. Am J Surg Pathol 12: 708–715

314. Bhathal P S, Hughes N R, Goodman Z D 1996 The so-called bile duct adenoma is a peribiliary gland hamartoma. Am J Surg Pathol 20: 858–864

315. O'Hara B J, McCue P A, Miettinen M 1992 Bile duct adenomas with endocrine component. Immunohistochemical study and comparison with conventional bile duct adenomas. Am J Surg Pathol 16: 21–25

316. Albores-Saavedra J, Hoang M P, Murakata L A et al. 2001 Atypical bile duct adenoma, clear cell type: a previously undescribed tumor of the liver. Am J Surg Pathol 25: 956–960

317. Devaney K, Goodman Z D, Ishak K G 1994 Hepatobiliary cystadenoma and cystadenocarcinoma. A light microscopic and immunohistochemical study of 70 patients. Am J Surg Pathol 18: 1078–1091

318. Davies W, Chow M, Nagorney D 1995 Extrahepatic biliary cystadenomas and cystadenocarcinoma. Ann Surg 222: 619–625

319. Thomas J A, Scriven M W, Puntis M C A et al. 1992 Elevated serum CA 19-9 levels in hepatobiliary cystadenoma with mesenchymal stroma. Cancer 70: 1841–1846

320. Lee J H, Chen D R, Pang S C et al. 1996 Mucinous biliary cystadenoma with mesenchymal stroma: expression of CA 19-9 and carcinoembryonic antigen in serum and cystic fluid. J Gastroenterol 31: 732–736

321. Shimada M, Kajiyama K, Saitoh A et al. 1996 Cystic neoplasms of the liver: a report of two cases with special reference to cystadenocarcinoma. Hepatogastroenterology 43: 249–254

322. Gourley W K, Kumar D, Bouton M S et al. 1992 Cystadenoma and cystadenocarcinoma with mesenchymal stroma of the liver. Immunohistochemical analysis. Arch Pathol Lab Med 116: 1047–1050

323. Ishak K G, Willis G W, Cummins S D et al. 1977 Biliary cystadenoma and cystadenocarcinoma: report of 14 cases and review of the literature. Cancer 39: 322–338

324. Tsui W M, Loo K T, Chow L T et al. 1993 Biliary adenofibroma. A heretofore unrecognized benign biliary tumor of the liver. Am J Surg Pathol 17: 186–192

325. Varnholt H, Vauthey J N, Cin P D et al. 2003 Biliary adenofibroma: a rare neoplasm of bile duct origin with an indolent behavior. Am J Surg Pathol 27: 693–698

326. Parada L A, Bardi G, Hallen M et al. 1997 Monosomy 22 in a case of biliary adenofibroma. Cancer Genet Cytogenet 93: 183–184

327. Wysocki A, Papla B, Budzynski P 2002 Neuromas of the extrahepatic bile ducts as a cause of obstructive jaundice. Eur J Gastroenterol Hepatol 14: 573–576

328. Ojima H, Takenoshita S, Nagamachi Y 2000 Adenomyoma of the common bile duct: report of a case. Hepatogastroenterology 47: 132–134

329. Nakanuma Y, Kurumaya H, Ohta G 1984 Multiple cysts in the hepatic hilum and their pathogenesis. A suggestion of periductal gland origin. Virchows Arch A Pathol Anat Histopathol 404: 341–350

330. Vick D J, Goodman Z D, Deavers M T et al. 1999 Ciliated hepatic foregut cyst: a study of six cases and review of the literature. Am J Surg Pathol 23: 671–677

331. Vick D J, Goodman Z D, Ishak K G 1999 Squamous cell carcinoma arising in a ciliated hepatic foregut cyst. Arch Pathol Lab Med 123: 1115–1117

332. Eisen R, Kirby W, O'Quinn J 1991 Granular cell tumor of the biliary tree. A report of two cases and a review of the literature. Am J Surg Pathol 15: 460–465

333. Davila J A, El-Serag H B 2002 Cholangiocarcinoma: the "other" liver cancer on the rise. Am J Gastroenterol 97: 3199–3200

334. Khan S A, Davidson B R, Goldin R et al. 2002 Guidelines for the diagnosis and treatment of cholangiocarcinoma: consensus document. Gut 51 (suppl 6): VI1–9

335. Gores G J 2003 Cholangiocarcinoma: current concepts and insights. Hepatology 37: 961–969

336. Wee A, Ludwig J, Coffey R et al. 1985 Hepatobiliary carcinoma associated with primary sclerosing cholangitis and chronic ulcerative colitis. Hum Pathol 16: 719–726

337. Chalasani N, Baluyut A, Ismail A et al. 2000 Cholangiocarcinoma in patients with primary sclerosing cholangitis: a multicenter case-control study. Hepatology 31: 7–11

338. Fleming K A, Boberg K M, Glaumann H et al. 2001 Biliary dysplasia as a marker of cholangiocarcinoma in primary sclerosing cholangitis. J Hepatol 34: 360–365

339. Koga A, Ichimiya H, Yamaguchi K et al. 1985 Hepatolithiasis associated with cholangiocarcinoma. Cancer 55: 2826–2829

340. Chauduri P, Chauduri B, Schuler J et al. 1982 Carcinoma associated with congenital cystic dilatation of bile ducts. Arch Surg 117: 1349–1351

341. Orii T, Ohkohchi N, Sasaki K et al. 2003 Cholangiocarcinoma arising from preexisting biliary hamartoma of liver – report of a case. Hepatogastroenterology 50: 333–336

342. Nakanuma Y, Harada K, Ishikawa A et al. 2003 Anatomic and molecular pathology of intrahepatic cholangiocarcinoma. J Hepatobiliary Pancreat Surg 10: 265–281

343. Okuda K, Nakanuma Y, Miyazaki M 2002 Cholangiocarcinoma: recent progress. Part 1: epidemiology and etiology. J Gastroenterol Hepatol 17: 1049–1055

344. Rubel L, Ishak K 1982 Thorotrast-associated cholangiocarcinoma. Cancer 50: 1408–1415

345. Mecklin J P, Jarvinen H J, Virolainen M 1992 The association between cholangiocarcinoma and hereditary nonpolyposis colorectal cancer. Cancer 69: 1112–1114

346. Altaee M Y, Johnson P J, Farrant J M et al. 1991 Etiologic and clinical characteristics of peripheral and hilar cholangiocarcinoma. Cancer 68: 2051–2055

347. Terada T, Kida T, Nakanuma Y et al. 1994 Intrahepatic cholangiocarcinomas associated with nonbiliary cirrhosis. A clinicopathologic study. J Clin Gastroenterol 18: 335–342

348. Shirabe K, Shimada M, Harimoto N et al. 2002 Intrahepatic cholangiocarcinoma: its mode of spreading and therapeutic modalities. Surgery 131 (1 suppl): S159–S164

349. Okuda K, Nakanuma Y, Miyazaki M 2002 Cholangiocarcinoma: recent progress. Part 2: molecular pathology and treatment. J Gastroenterol Hepatol 17: 1056–1063

350. Torok N J, Higuchi H, Bronk S et al. 2002 Nitric oxide inhibits apoptosis downstream of cytochrome C release by nitrosylating caspase 9. Cancer Res 62: 1648–1653

351. Yoon J H, Werneburg N W, Higuchi H et al. 2002 Bile acids inhibit Mcl-1 protein turnover via an epidermal growth factor receptor/Raf-1-dependent mechanism. Cancer Res 62: 6500–6505

352. Ohashi K, Nakajima Y, Kanehiro H et al. 1995 Ki-ras mutations and p53 protein expressions in intrahepatic cholangiocarcinomas: relation to gross tumor morphology. Gastroenterology 109: 1612–1617

353. Ahrendt S A, Eisenberger C F, Yip L et al. 1999 Chromosome 9p21 loss and p16 inactivation in primary sclerosing cholangitis-associated cholangiocarcinoma. J Surg Res 84: 88–93

354. Niiyama H, Mizumoto K, Kusumoto M et al. 1999 Activation of telomerase and its diagnostic application in biopsy specimens from biliary tract neoplasms. Cancer 85: 2138–2143

355. Hanazaki K, Kajikawa S, Shimozawa N et al. 2002 Prognostic factors of intrahepatic cholangiocarcinoma after hepatic resection: univariate and multivariate analysis. Hepatogastroenterology 49: 311–316

356. Kokudo N, Makuuchi M 2002 Extent of resection and outcome after curative resection for intrahepatic cholangiocarcinoma. Surg Oncol Clin North Am 11: 969–983

357. Hoang M P, Murakata L A, Katabi N et al. 2002 Invasive papillary carcinomas of the extrahepatic bile ducts: a clinicopathologic and immunohistochemical study of 13 cases. Mod Pathol 15: 1251–1258

358. Rumalla A, Baron T H, Leontovich O et al. 2001 Improved diagnostic yield of endoscopic biliary brush cytology by digital image analysis. Mayo Clin Proc 76: 29–33

359. Sarmiento J M, Nagorney D M 2002 Hepatic resection in the treatment of perihilar cholangiocarcinoma. Surg Oncol Clin North Am 11: 893–908

360. Bergquist A, Glaumann H, Stal P et al. 2001 Biliary dysplasia, cell proliferation and nuclear DNA-fragmentation in primary sclerosing cholangitis with and without cholangiocarcinoma. J Intern Med 249: 69–75

361. Shimonishi T, Sasaki M, Nakanuma Y 2000 Precancerous lesions of intrahepatic cholangiocarcinoma. J Hepatobiliary Pancreat Surg 7: 542–550

362. Lee S S, Kin M-H, Lee S K et al. 2004 Clinicopathologic review of 58 patients with biliary papillomatosis. Cancer 100: 783–793

363. Kim H J, Kim M H, Lee S K et al. 2000 Mucin-hypersecreting bile duct tumor characterized by a striking homology with an intraductal papillary mucinous tumor (IPMT) of the pancreas. Endoscopy 32: 389–393

364. Shimonishi T, Zen Y, Chen T C et al. 2002 Increasing expression of gastrointestinal phenotypes and p53 along with histologic progression of intraductal papillary neoplasia of the liver. Hum Pathol 33: 503–511

365. Amaya S, Sasaki M, Watanabe Y et al. 2001 Expression of MUC1 and MUC2 and carbohydrate antigen Tn change during malignant transformation of biliary papillomatosis. Histopathology 38: 550–560

366. Suh K S, Roh H R, Koh Y T et al. 2000 Clinicopathologic features of the intraductal growth type of peripheral cholangiocarcinoma. Hepatology 31: 12–17

367. Maitra A, Krueger J E, Tascilar M et al. 2000 Carcinoid tumors of the extrahepatic bile ducts. A study of seven cases. Am J Surg Pathol 11: 1501–1510

368. Caceres M, Mosquera L F, Shih J A et al. 2001 Paraganglioma of the bile duct. South Med J 94: 515–518

369. Wagner M S, Shoup M, Pickleman J et al. 2000 Primary malignant melanoma of the common bile duct: a case report and review of the literature. Arch Pathol Lab Med 124: 419–422

370. Ruymann F B, Raney R B Jr, Crist W M et al. 1985 Rhabdomyosarcoma of the biliary tree in childhood. A report from the Intergroup Rhabdomyosarcoma Study. Cancer 56: 575–581

Tumors of the exocrine pancreas 11

Günter Klöppel   David S. Klimstra

Classification and general features

The classification and nomenclature used in this chapter are based on a slight modification of the one that is proposed by the World Health Organization (WHO).[1] Its premise is that the cellular phenotype of tumors of the pancreas resembles one of the three main epithelial lineages of this organ: the ductal cell, the acinar cell and the endocrine cell. Most exocrine pancreatic tumors fall into the category of neoplasms showing a ductal cell phenotype and are therefore called ductal adeno-carcinoma. This tumor and its variants, adenosquamous carcinoma, undifferentiated carcinoma, etc., are meant when "pancreatic cancer", "pancreatic carcinoma", or "pancreatic adenocarcinoma" are discussed.[2–7] Ductal adenocarcinoma and its variants are "solid" carcinomas that usually occur in the head of the pancreas. Other "solid" tumors of the pancreas include acinar cell carcinoma, pancreatoblastoma and endocrine tumors. They are much less common and account for only 4 percent (Table 11.1). In contrast to the major group of "solid" neoplasms, the "cystic" group of pancreatic tumors is characterized by a significantly better prognosis, not only of its borderline forms but even of its malignant forms. Serous and mucinous cystic tumors, together with solid pseudo-papillary tumors and intraductal papillary mucinous tumors, represent about 6 percent of all exocrine epithelial tumors (Table 11.1).[4,8,9] Both the mucinous cystic tumors and the intra-ductal papillary mucinous tumors are classified according to their biologic behavior into benign tumors, borderline tumors (or tumors of uncertain malignant potential), and malignant tumors. Primary non-epithelial tumors of the exocrine pancreas, such as sarcomas and malignant lymphomas, are extremely rare. Endocrine tumors of the pancreas are discussed in Chapter 20.

Table 11.1 General features of pancreatic tumors

Type	Frequency (%)	Prognosis
"Solid tumors"		
Ductal adenocarcinoma and variants	90	Unfavorable
Acinar cell carcinoma	1	Unfavorable[a]
Pancreatoblastoma	<1	Unfavorable[a]
Endocrine tumors	2	Intermediate[b]
Non-epithelial tumors	Rare	Intermediate[b]
"Cystic tumors"		
Intraductal papillary-mucinous neoplasm	2	Good
Mucinous cystic neoplasm	1	Good
Serous cystic neoplasm	1	Good
Solid pseudopapillary neoplasm	<1	Good
Other cystic tumors	1	Intermediate[b]
Non-epithelial lesions and tumors	Rare	Intermediate[b]

[a]Improved prognosis with treatment (surgery, chemotherapy) and in pediatric patients
[b]Depending on subtype

Ductal adenocarcinoma

Epidemiology and clinical features

Ductal adenocarcinoma is characterized by its localization in the head of the pancreas and by its infiltrating duct-like and tubular structures embedded in a highly desmoplastic stroma.

Its etiology is largely unknown. Among the few risk factors that have been implicated are smoking, a high intake of dietary fat and chronic pancreatitis, especially hereditary pancreatitis.[10] Familial cases are rare, but pancreatic ductal adenocarcinoma may occur in so-called "cancer families",[11] and, in general, patients with a strong family history of pancreatic carcinoma are at notably increased risk themselves.[12] Recently, *BRCA2* germline mutations were detected in approximately 20 percent of familial ductal adenocarcinomas and a new susceptibility locus for autosomal dominant ductal adenocarcinoma was mapped to chromosome 4q32-34.[13] The pancreatic pathology in kindreds with the latter genetic anomaly showed pre-neoplastic intraductal changes.[14] Other genetic syndromes that are associated with pancreatic carcinoma include familial atypical multiple mole/melanoma syndrome, telangiectatic ataxia and Peutz–Jeghers syndrome.[15]

The age-adjusted annual incidence of ductal adeno-carcinoma in industrialized countries ranges between 3.1 and 20.8 cases per 100 000 people.[15] It affects both sexes almost equally, has its peak incidence in the sixth to seventh decades of life and is extremely rare before the age of 40.[16,17] In about two-thirds of the patients, the tumor involves the head of the pancreas, causing obstruction of the biliary tract and often also of the pancreatic duct. The patients present with jaundice and weight loss and usually also pain because of the early infiltration of nerves in the retroperitoneal tissue. In addition, some patients may have recent-onset diabetes and acute pancreatitis. One-third of the patients have the tumor in the body and/or the tail of the pancreas and a minority in the uncinate process. These patients often present with pain and weight loss or liver metastases from an "occult" primary, because the growth of their carcinomas is hardly hindered by any anatomic border and therefore rapidly involves extra-pancreatic tissues. The tissues that are then involved are the retroperitoneum, peritoneum, stomach, colon, spleen and left adrenal gland.

Macroscopic appearances

Ductal adenocarcinoma, whether in the head or the remaining parts of the gland, is generally a "solid" and poorly demarcated tumor, hard and yellowish-white to gray, usually between 2 and 5 cm in diameter (Fig. 11.1). Hemorrhage, necrosis, cystic changes or a diffuse growth in the entire pancreatic parenchyma are uncommon.[18] In rare cases, ductal adeno-carcinoma may arise in heterotopic pancreatic tissue.[19]

Microscopic appearances

Most ductal adenocarcinomas are well to moderately differentiated adenocarcinomas consisting of tubular and duct-like structures formed by mucus-secreting columnar cells (Fig. 11.2). The neoplastic tubular structures are lined by a single cell layer, varying in height and occasionally showing papillary projections. Occasionally, the tumors show a so-called foamy gland pattern,[20] a large-duct type morphology,[18] a micropapillary structure,[21] or a clear cell phenotype[22] (see also miscellaneous carcinomas – p. 479) (Fig. 11.3). The neoplastic glands infiltrate into the pancreatic parenchyma so that non-neoplastic ducts, acini and islets are interspersed between the carcinomatous structures. This growth is typically

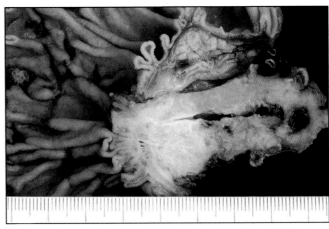
Fig. 11.1 • Gross specimen of ductal adenocarcinoma in the head of the pancreas showing invasion of the ampulla and the duodenal wall with obstruction of the common bile duct and the pancreatic duct.

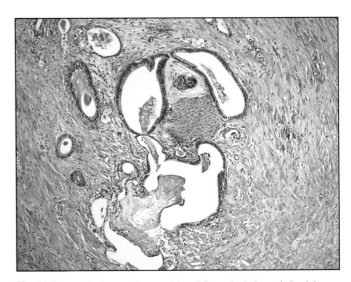
Fig. 11.2 • Ductal adenocarcinoma with well-formed tubular and glandular structures.

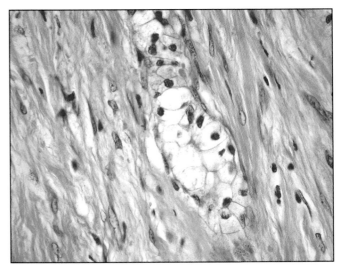
Fig. 11.3 • Ductal adenocarcinoma with a tubular structure formed of clear cells.

associated with a marked desmoplastic reaction. The nuclei of the cells usually are polarized and show a distinct nucleolus.

In the moderately and poorly differentiated tumors, the histologic pattern becomes progressively more irregular, with poorly formed glands and decreased mucus secretion (Fig. 11.4). There is increasing variation in cell and nuclear size. Mitotic figures become conspicuous.

At the time of diagnosis these carcinomas are very rarely still confined to the pancreas. Spread into the peripancreatic fatty tissue combined with perineural invasion is almost the rule. Moreover, there may be invasion of lymphatic vessels and veins. Because of the duct obstructing growth, there is more or less severe obstructive chronic pancreatitis in the peritumorous pancreatic tissue or even in the entire remaining gland.

The medium-sized ducts of the peritumorous tissue frequently show replacement of the duct epithelium by tall columnar mucinous cells, often combined with papillary formations. These lesions are not tumor specific, but are more common in association with ductal adenocarcinoma than without.[23–26] Because of this relationship and the various genetic abnormalities they share with invasive adenocarcinoma, these duct changes are considered to be precursor lesions and are called pancreatic intraepithelial neoplasia, grade 1 to 3 (PanIN-1 to 3, Table 11.2 and Fig. 11.5).[27,28] As for PanIN-3, i.e., carcinoma in situ, it is often difficult to distinguish precisely between a PanIN-3 focus adjacent to, but separate from, the invasive carcinoma and intraductal extension of the tumor ("duct cancerization"). In addition to PanIN lesions there may be squamous metaplasia (Fig. 11.6), the occurrence of which in the pancreas seems to be unrelated to ductal adeno-carcinoma or other tumors, but which may be found after long-term stenting of the main pancreatic duct in chronic pancreatitis.

Pancreatic biopsy and frozen section

Pancreatic biopsy is an invasive diagnostic method that is only performed when all other diagnostic measures for establishing

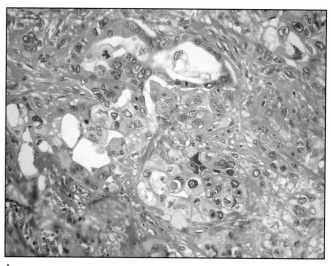

A

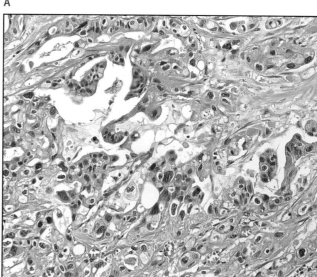

B

Fig. 11.4 • Ductal adenocarcinoma, poorly differentiated (A) showing irregular glands and pleomorphic cells (B).

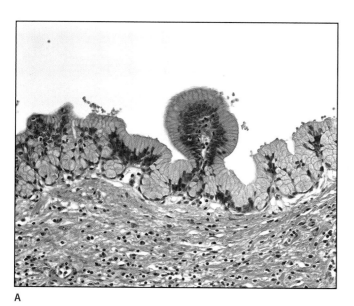

A

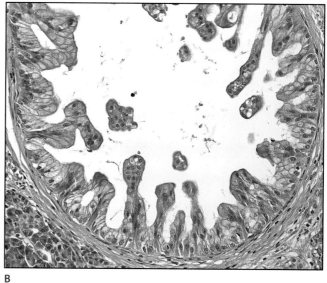

B

Fig. 11.5 • Pancreatic intraepithelial neoplasia, grade 1 (A) and grade 3 (B).

Table 11.2	Pancreatic intraepithelial neoplasia classification

PanIN-1A: (Pancreatic intraepithelial neoplasia 1-A): flat epithelial lesions composed of tall columnar cells with basally located nuclei and abundant supranuclear mucin. Since the neoplastic nature of many cases of PanIn-1A has not been established with certainty, these duct changes may be designated with the modifier term "lesion" ("PanIN/L-1A").

PanIN-1B: (Pancreatic intraepithelial neoplasia 1-B): epithelial lesions that have a papillary, micropapillary or basally pseudostratified architecture, but are otherwise identical to PanIN-1A.

PanIN-2: (Pancreatic intraepithelial neoplasia 2): mucinous epithelial lesions that may be flat but are mostly papillary. By definition, these lesions must have some nuclear abnormalities which, however, fall short of those seen in PanIN-3.

PanIN-3: (Pancreatic intraepithelial neoplasia 3): usually papillary or micropapillary lesions with severe cellular atypia. The lesions resemble carcinoma at the cytonuclear level, but invasion through the basement membrane is absent.

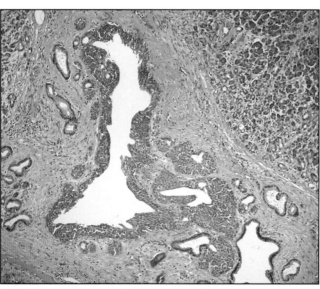

Fig. 11.6 • Pancreatic duct with squamous metaplasia.

the diagnosis of a tumorous lesion of the pancreas have failed. Because of the advances of modern imaging techniques, fine needle biopsy of the pancreas guided by ultrasonography, computer tomography or endosonography has become a reliable method that allows the diagnosis of a ductal adenocarcinoma or any of the other more rare pancreatic tumors with high sensitivity and specificity. Complications are rare, particularly with endosonographically-guided biopsies. A new biopsy indication is the demonstration of certain markers or gene mutations that are needed for the initiation of special treatment, i.e., *EGFR* – Cetuximab. The diagnostic problems that are encountered in biopsy specimens focus on the differential diagnosis of pancreatic carcinoma versus chronic pancreatitis (see differential diagnosis) and on the distinction between the various types of pancreatic tumor (Table 11.3). Intraoperative frozen section assessment of pancreatic lesions also focuses on distinguishing between ductal carcinoma and chronic pancreatitis. Though frozen section diagnosis may remain problematic in a given case, accuracy rates of up to 98 percent have been reported.[29]

Immunohistology

Ductal adenocarcinoma shows positive immunostaining with antibodies to cytokeratins 7, 8, 18 and 19, epithelial membrane antigen (EMA), carcinoembryonic antigen (CEA),[30] as well as CA19-9 or DUPAN-2.[31,32] Moreover, it is positive for the apomucin MUC1 (Fig. 11.7). On the other hand, the tumor generally fails to stain with antibodies against MUC2, pancreatic enzymes (such as trypsin) and neuroendocrine markers (Table 11.4).

Genetics

The majority of ductal adenocarcinomas show an activating mutation of the K-*ras* oncogene and inactivating mutation of the *CDKN2S/p16* tumor suppressor gene. Approximately 50 to 60 percent of the cases have inactivating mutations of the tumor suppressor genes *p53* and *smad4/dpc4*.[15,33,34] Genes that were altered at a much lower frequency include the *MKK4* gene, the gene for the TGF-beta receptors R1 and R2, the *BRCA2* gene and the *KLB/STK11* gene.

Table 11.3	Main indications for diagnostic pancreatic biopsy		
Imaging	\multicolumn{3}{Differential diagnosis}		
	Benign		**Malignant**
Solid mass of uncertain biology	Common:	alcoholic chronic pancreatitis	Ductal adenocarcinoma
	Rare:	autoimmune pancreatitis	Endocrine carcinoma
		Endocrine tumor	Acinar cell carcinoma
			Malignant mesenchymal tumor
			Lymphoma
			Metastasis
Cystic mass	Pseudocyst		Mucinous cystic neoplasm
	Serous cystadenoma		Intraductal papillary-mucinous neoplasm
	Various non-neoplastic cysts		

Table 11.4	Immunohistologic differential diagnosis of the most important pancreatic tumors										
Tumor type	CK7, 19	CK 8, 18	VIM	MUC1	MUC2	TRYP	SYN	CG	NSE	CEA	AFP
Ductal adenocarcinoma	+	+	–	+	–	–	–	–	–	+	–
Intraductal papillary-mucinous neoplasm	+	+	–	+[a]	+[b]	–	(+)	(+)	–	+	
Mucinous cystic neoplasm	+	+	–	(+)	–	–	(+)	(+)	–	+	
Serous cystadenoma	+	+	–	–	–	–	–	–	+	–	–
Acinar cell carcinoma	(+)/	+	–	–	–	+	(+)	(+)	(+)	–	–
Pancreatoblastoma	+	+	–	–	–	+	(+)	(+)	(+)	–	(+)
Solid pseudopapillary tumor	–	–	+	–	–	–	–	–	+	–	–
Endocrine tumor	(+)/–	+	–	–	–	–	+	+	+	–	–

(+) A few cells; + Most cells; CEA, carcinoembryonic antigen; TRYP, trypsin and other pancreatic enzymes; SYN, synaptophysin ; CG, chromogranin A; AFP, alpha-fetoprotein; CK, cytokeratin; VIM, vimentin; NSE, neuron-specific enolase; MUC, MUC core protein.
[a]Pancreatobiliary type
[b]Intestinal type

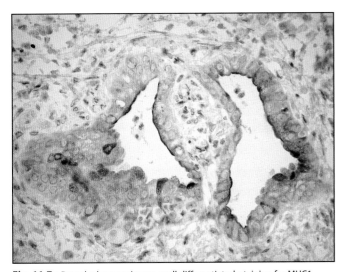

Fig. 11.7 • Ductal adenocarcinoma, well differentiated, staining for MUC1.

Table 11.5	Histopathologic criteria for the differential diagnosis of ductal adenocarcinoma versus chronic pancreatitis	
	Ductal adenocarcinoma	Chronic pancreatitis
Ductal features		
Distribution	Irregular, haphazard	Organized, lobular
Location	Perineural, intravascular, extrapancreatic ("naked ducts" in fat tissue)	Intrapancreatic
Contours	Ruptured	Intact ducts
Contents	Neutrophils, necrotic debris	Calculi, secretory plugs
Cytologic features		
Nucleus	Pleomorphic	Uniform, round-oval
	Mitosis	No mitosis
	Prominent nucleoli	No or small nucleoli
Nuclear polarity	Commonly lost	Retained

Growth factors

Among the various growth factors and their receptors that have been found to be expressed in ductal adenocarcinomas are *EGFR* and *HER2*/neu (*c-erb B2*).[35] Both factors, which have mitogenic and growth factor signal-transduction activity, respectively, are commonly overexpressed in ductal adeno-carcinomas. The angiogenic factor VEGF (vascular endothelial growth factor) is variably expressed in ductal adenocarcinomas.[36]

Differential diagnosis

The main problem is distinguishing well differentiated ductal adenocarcinoma from chronic pancreatitis.[37] Macroscopically, both diseases look very much the same. If, however, calculi are present in the pancreatic ducts, the diagnosis of advanced chronic pancreatitis is most likely. Microscopically, the criteria that are applied are relevant for both biopsy specimens (including frozen sections) and large tissue specimens (Table 11.5). At low power magnification, ductal adenocarcinomas show haphazardly arranged infiltrating tubular and duct-like structures that lack any lobular organization. Some of the neoplastic ducts may be ruptured, show papillary epithelium and are encased by desmoplastic stroma (Fig. 11.8). In chronic pancreatitis, the remaining small ducts, single acini and islets usually show a preserved lobular arrangement. Some ducts may be dilated and contain calculi. At high power magnification, ductal adenocarcinomas show variable epithelial atypia and often mitotic figures. In addition, at least focally, the nuclei are not well polarized and exhibit prominent nucleoli. In chronic pancreatitis, ductal epithelium may be atrophic or occasionally hyperplastic, but atypia and mitoses are usually absent. Immunohistologically, there is no specific marker, but positivity for CEA, MUC1, *p53* and/or MIB1 (Fig. 11.9) is highly suggestive of ductal adenocarcinoma, as is complete loss

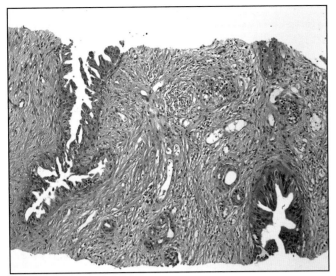

Fig. 11.8 • Needle biopsy specimen from a well differentiated ductal adenocarcinoma showing glands with papillary epithelium.

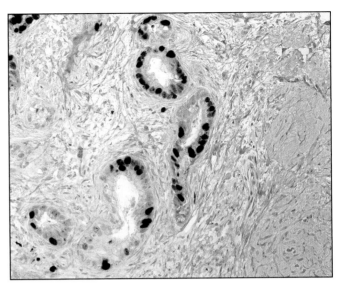

Fig. 11.9 • Ductal adenocarcinoma, well differentiated, with nuclear MIB1 staining.

of expression of *SMAD4/DPC4*. For the differential diagnosis of ductal adenocarcinoma versus other pancreatic tumors, such as intraductal papillary mucinous neoplasms, acinar cell carcinomas, or endocrine tumors, we refer the reader to Table 11.4.

Tumor spread, staging and grading

For standardized processing and accurate staging of resected pancreatic carcinomas, recommendations are available.[38,39] Ductal adenocarcinomas spread early to the retroperitoneal tissues and the various "local" peripancreatic lymph node groups, the precise topography of which depends on the location of the primary growth. Involvement of the "regional" lymph nodes (i.e., in the hepatoduodenal ligament up to the celiac trunk) is found in about 50 percent of cases and involvement of the "juxtaregional," mainly para-aortic lymph nodes in about 10 percent.[40] Hepatic blood-borne metastases are frequent. Metastases to lungs, pleura and bone are seen only in advanced tumor stages, particularly with tumors of the body or tail; cerebral metastases are uncommon.

The currently available grading schemes for ductal adenocarcinomas both follow a three-tiered system (Table 11.6).[15,41] Grading data have shown that the biologically most relevant distinction is that between G1/G2 and G3. Grading appears to be more useful than assessment of proliferative index.[42]

The pathologic staging of ductal adenocarcinoma is based on the TNM classification.[43] It takes into account the size and extent of invasion of the primary tumor (pT1–pT4) and the presence or absence of regional metastatic lymph nodes (pN1a, or pN1b if multiple regional lymph nodes are involved), as well as of distant metastases (pM) (Table 11.7).

Prognosis

Most (80–90 percent) ductal adenocarcinomas are not resectable at the time of diagnosis and the patients rarely live longer than 6 months. Of the patients with resectable tumors, approximately 80–90 percent survive no longer than 3 years. The 5-year survival rate after surgery is approximately 15 percent.[44] However, improved survival data have been reported in some recent series from Japan, the USA and Europe.[45–48] Local tumor recurrence is common after surgical resection and is one of the factors determining survival.

Variants of ductal adenocarcinoma

Pancreatic carcinomas that are closely related to ductal adenocarcinoma are adenosquamous carcinomas, so-called undifferentiated carcinomas (including osteoclast-like giant cell tumor) and mixed ductal-endocrine carcinomas.[15] Mucinous

Table 11.6	Grading scheme for pancreatic ductal adenocarcinoma		
Grade[a]	Glandular structure	Mitoses[b]	Nuclear structure
I	Highly differentiated ductal, tubular	<5	Slight pleomorphism, small nucleolus
II	Combined ductal, tubular and microglandular	6–10	Conspicuous pleomorphism, conspicuous nucleolus
III	Glandular to undifferentiated	>10	Pronounced pleomorphism with enlarged nuclei and prominent nucleoli

[a]If the tumor is heterogeneous the highest tumor grade should be given.
[b]Number of mitotic figures in 10 randomly selected high power fields (×40).

Table 11.7	TNM classification of pancreatic ductal adenocarcinomas

Primary tumor (T)

TX	Primary tumor cannot be assessed
T0	No evidence of primary tumor
Tis	Carcinoma in situ
T1	Tumor limited to the pancreas, 2 cm or less in greatest dimension
T2	Tumor limited to the pancreas, more than 2 cm in greatest dimension
T3	Tumor extends beyond the pancreas but without involvement of the celiac axis or the superior mesenteric artery
T4	Tumor involves the celiac axis or the superior mesenteric artery

Regional lymph nodes (N)

NX	Regional lymph nodes cannot be assessed
N0	No regional lymph node metastasis
N1	Regional lymph node metastasis

Distant metastases (M)

MX	Distant metastasis cannot be assessed
M0	No distant metastasis
MI	Distant metastasis

Stage grouping#

Stage 0	Tis	N0	M0
Stage IA	T1	N0	M0
IB	T2	N0	M0
Stage IIA	T3	N0	M0
IIB	T1,T2,T3	N1	M0
Stage III	T4	any N	M0
Stage IV	any T	any N	M1

pN0 requires regional lymphadenectomy and normally histologic examination of 10 or more lymph nodes
#After tumor resection a R0 stage (no evidence of residual tumor) is distinguished from an R1 or R2 stage (R1 – residual tumor evident microscopically; R2 – residual tumor evident macroscopically). Sobin LH, Wittekind C. International Union Against Cancer (UICC) © 2002 TNM Classification of Malignant Tumors, 6th edition. John Wiley & Sons, Inc., New York, USA. Reprinted with permission of John Wiley & Sons, Inc.

non-cystic (colloid) carcinoma, which has also been considered to be a ductal adenocarcinoma variant,[49] was recently identified as a distinct tumor type associated with intraductal papillary-mucinous neoplasms[50] (see below).

Adenosquamous carcinoma

Adenosquamous carcinoma resembles ductal adenocarcinoma in terms of sex distribution, localization in the pancreas and macroscopic appearance.[15,51] The tumor is characterized by variable admixtures of neoplastic tubuloglandular and squamous elements. The squamous component may be prominent and may almost obliterate the glandular component, a situation which may lead to a diagnosis of "squamous carcinoma". However, even in such cases, extensive tissue sampling usually demonstrates glandular elements. Adeno-

squamous carcinoma may also contain foci composed of anaplastic or spindle cells.[52] In metastases, the adenocarcinoma component often predominates or is even the only component present.

Undifferentiated carcinoma

Undifferentiated carcinomas of the pancreas (synonyms: anaplastic, pleomorphic large cell, pleomorphic giant cell, sarcomatoid carcinoma) account for 2–5 percent of exocrine pancreatic cancers.[2,53,54] They generally have a sex and age distribution similar to that of ductal adenocarcinoma, but clinically they display more aggressive behavior.[54] The tumors are usually large and soft, with conspicuous hemorrhage, necrosis and/or cystic change (Fig. 11.10).

Microscopically, the tumors usually consist of mononuclear pleomorphic cells embedded in a scanty stroma (Fig. 11.11). Occasionally, bizarre multinucleated giant cells or spindle cells with additional squamous components occur. There is no specific architecture and the cells grow either in poorly cohesive sheets or in a sarcoma-like fashion. Mitoses are frequent. Extensive tissue sampling often demonstrates foci of otherwise conventional ductal adenocarcinoma. Undifferentiated carcinomas containing a distinct population of malignant glands

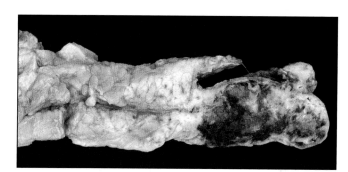

Fig. 11.10 • Undifferentiated carcinoma in the pancreatic tail, showing hemorrhagic necrosis.

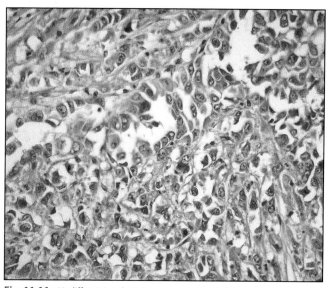

Fig. 11.11 • Undifferentiated carcinoma composed of large pleomorphic cells.

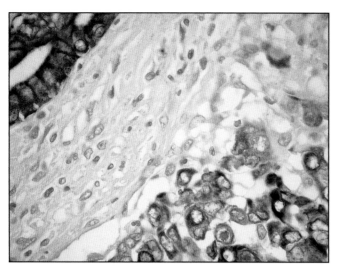

Fig. 11.12 • Undifferentiated carcinoma: pleomorphic cells and adjacent ductal component staining for cytokeratin 7.

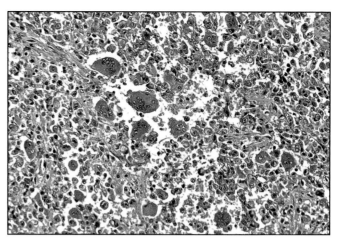

Fig. 11.13 • Undifferentiated carcinoma with pleomorphic mononuclear cells and numerous osteoclast-like multinucleated giant cells.

that result in a biphasic appearance may be designated carcinosarcomas, especially when the spindle cell components display heterologous differentiation with production of chondroid, osteoid, or skeletal muscle elements. The epithelial nature of the pleomorphic or spindle cells is confirmed by positive immunostaining for cytokeratin (Fig. 11.12). The same cells often, however, also stain for vimentin.[55] Undifferentiated carcinoma often shows extensive lymphatic and vascular invasion. The demonstration of *K-ras* mutations provides evidence for its ductal origin.[54,55]

Undifferentiated carcinoma with osteoclast-like giant cells (synonym: giant cell tumor of the osteoclastic type, osteoclast-like giant cell tumor)

Undifferentiated carcinoma with osteoclast-like giant cells is characterized by a dual population of mononuclear pleomorphic spindle and polygonal cells and osteoclast-like multinucleated giant cells. Similar tumors have also been described in other organs, such as the thyroid and lung. The pleomorphic component is identical to that of undifferentiated carcinoma and shows high mitotic activity. The osteoclast-like cells resemble normal osteoclasts in appearance (Fig. 11.13), do not show any mitotic activity, have histiocytic features and are generally thought to represent a peculiar non-neoplastic component, and they lack the *K-ras* mutations that may be detected in the mononuclear component.[56] They are often concentrated near areas of hemorrhage. Glandular and solid structures may be encountered. Positive immunostaining for keratin of the mononuclear pleomorphic cells, although not always present, indicates epithelial origin.[55,57,58] The osteoclast-like cells stain for vimentin, leukocyte common antigen (CD45) and the histiocytic marker CD68. Osteoclast-like giant cell tumor was previously considered to have a better prognosis than ductal adenocarcinoma, but more recent reports have contradicted this view and have suggested that most patients die within one year.[58]

Mixed ductal-endocrine carcinoma

The presence of occasional and most likely non-neoplastic endocrine cells in an otherwise usual ductal carcinoma is not an exceptional situation. This is particularly the case in well differentiated ductal adenocarcinomas.[59] On the other hand, carcinomas with obvious mixed exocrine and endocrine tissues are rare. Such a rare carcinoma type consists of tubulo-glandular structures admixed with endocrine cells which account for at least 30 percent of the total tumor cell population.[59,60]

Signet-ring cell carcinoma

This carcinoma consists almost entirely (at least more than 50 percent of the tumor) of individually arranged signet-ring cells containing intracytoplasmic mucin vacuoles that indent and scallop the nucleus. The neoplastic cells infiltrate in a diffuse fashion. By immunohistology, the tumors cell strongly express CEA. The differential diagnosis includes metastases from diffuse type gastric adenocarcinoma or lobular carcinoma of the breast. The prognosis of signet ring cell carcinoma is at least as poor as that of conventional ductal adenocarcinoma.

Intraductal papillary mucinous neoplasms

Intraductal papillary mucinous neoplasms are grossly visible mucin-producing epithelial tumors that grow within the pancreatic ducts and usually, although not always, have a papillary architecture. Intraductal papillary mucinous neoplasms frequently secrete copious quantities of mucin and are associated with massive dilatation of the ducts, resulting in a cystic radiographic and gross appearance. In some cases mucin spills from the ampulla of Vater. Intraductal papillary mucinous neoplasms affect predominantly males (average age 60). Most tumors arise in the head of the pancreas. Patients tend to have pancreatitis-like symptoms for years. Intraductal papillary mucinous neoplasms account for approximately 3–5 percent of exocrine pancreatic neoplasms, a proportion that is rising with the increased detection of small intraductal papillary mucinous neoplasms due to the greater use of radiologic imaging.[61] Among all types of cystic pancreatic tumors (see Table 11.8), intraductal papillary mucinous neoplasms account for 24 percent, and they now represent the most common cystic tumor type.[61]

In the past, intraductal papillary mucinous neoplasms were described under a variety of names, chiefly depending upon whether papillary proliferations or abundant mucin secretion was the predominant feature: such names have included intraductal papilloma, villous adenoma, intraductal papillary adenocarcinoma, mucin-producing tumor, duct ectatic mucinous cystic neoplasm, mucinous duct ectasia, and intraductal mucin-hypersecreting neoplasm; these names are no longer encouraged. Intraductal papillary mucinous neoplasms can exhibit a range of cytoarchitectural atypia, even within an individual neoplasm. They are graded according to the most atypical area as intraductal papillary mucinous neoplasm with low grade dysplasia (or intraductal papillary mucinous adenoma), intraductal papillary mucinous neoplasm with moderate dysplasia (or intraductal papillary mucinous neoplasm, borderline), or intraductal papillary mucinous neoplasm with high grade dysplasia (or intraductal papillary mucinous carcinoma in situ). Invasive carcinomas are associated with intraductal papillary mucinous neoplasms in about 35 percent of cases, and the size and type of any invasive component should be reported separately. Thus, intraductal papillary mucinous neoplasms provide a model of neoplastic progression from a benign intraductal neoplasm through increasing grades of dysplasia to invasive carcinoma.[62–67]

Macroscopically, intraductal papillary mucinous neoplasms are divided into main duct and branch duct types, depending upon whether they predominantly involve the major pancreatic ducts or the peripheral secondary ducts, respectively. Diffuse involvement of the entire pancreatic duct system including the ampulla of Vater may also occur. The main duct type is preferentially localized in the pancreatic head and often contains viscous mucin (Fig. 11.14). Branch duct intraductal papillary mucinous neoplasms are smaller (Fig. 11.15), less likely to contain invasive carcinoma, and more likely to involve

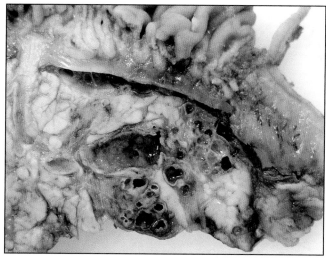

Fig. 11.15 • Resection specimen of intraductal papillary mucinous neoplasm, branch duct type. The resection specimen shows a large and several small cysts in the pancreatic parenchyma (courtesy of Dr. Hartmut Arps, Fulda, Germany).

a localized region of the pancreas than the main duct types.[68] The amount of neoplastic papillary growth, the quantity of mucin secretion and the degree of duct ectasia or cyst formation vary from case to case.

Histologically, intraductal papillary mucinous neoplasms show papillary proliferations of columnar mucus-secreting epithelial cells replacing the normal duct epithelium. Those with low grade dysplasia show relatively simple, uniform papillae or areas with a flat epithelium, and the nuclei are uniform, basally located, and lacking in pleomorphism or mitotic activity. Intraductal papillary mucinous neoplasms with moderate dysplasia show increasingly complex papillae lined by cells with pseudostratified nuclei that have moderate variation in shape and size. High grade dysplasia is characterized by markedly complex papillae and micropapillae with complete loss of polarity, marked nuclear irregularities, and easily identifiable mitoses. Recently, four different morphologic types of papillae have been distinguished: an intestinal type, a pancreatobiliary type, an oncocytic type (also known as intraductal oncocytic papillary neoplasm) and a gastric type.[69,70] The intestinal type shows a villous growth pattern similar to intestinal villous adenomas and produces MUC2 and CDX2, but no MUC1 (Fig. 11.16).[71,72] Associated invasive carcinomas are usually of the colloid (mucinous non-cystic) type variant,[49] a tumor composed at least 80 percent of pools of extracellular mucus containing suspended clumps or strands of neoplastic glandular epithelium or even a small component of signet-ring cells (Fig. 11.17). The pancreatobiliary papillary phenotype shows complex, arborizing papillae (Fig. 11.18) and lacks MUC2 and CDX2 expression, but stains for MUC1. Its invasive components usually resemble a conventional ductal adenocarcinoma. The oncocytic type has complex papillae (Fig. 11.19) lined by large cells with granular eosinophilic cytoplasm and expresses MUC1 or MUC2 inconsistently. The gastric type frequently coexists with other types and exhibits papillary projections lined by mucinous cells resembling gastric foveolar cells. The cells stain for MUC5 (Fig. 11.20), whereas MUC1, MUC2 and CDX2 are not expressed.

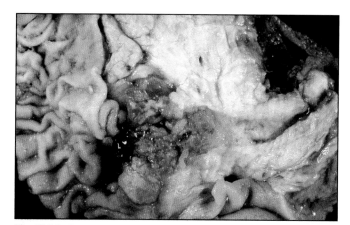

Fig. 11.14 • Resection specimen of intraductal papillary mucinous neoplasm, main duct type. The resection specimen shows a markedly dilated ampulla of Vater and main pancreatic duct, filled with sticky mucin. The remaining pancreatic tissue is severely fibrotic.

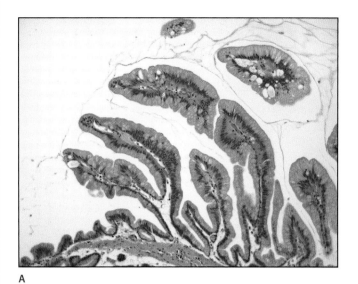

A

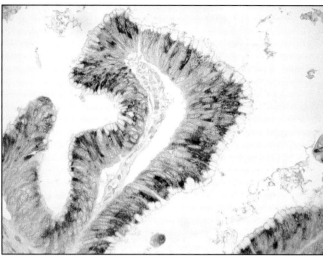

B

Fig. 11.16 • Intraductal papillary mucinous neoplasm, intestinal type, with intraductal papillary proliferation of well-differentiated columnar epithelium (**A**). The tumor cells stain for MUC2 (**B**).

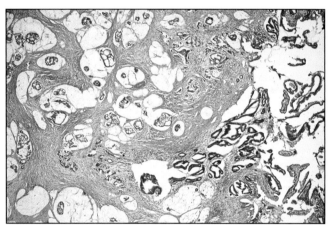

Fig. 11.17 • Intraductal papillary mucinous neoplasm, intestinal type, with intraductal papillary proliferation (right border) and invasion of the surrounding pancreatic tissue (left border). The invasive component shows the features of a colloid (mucinous non-cystic) carcinoma.

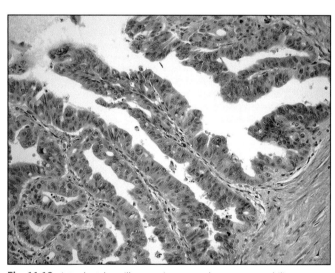

Fig. 11.18 • Intraductal papillary mucinous neoplasm, pancreatobiliary type, with arborizing papillae and cuboidal epithelium.

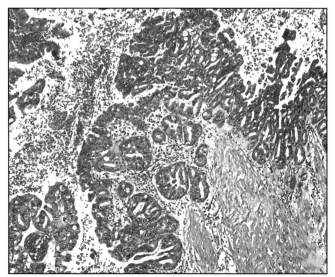

Fig. 11.19 • Intraductal papillary mucinous neoplasm, oncocytic type, with complex papillae and multilayered epithelium.

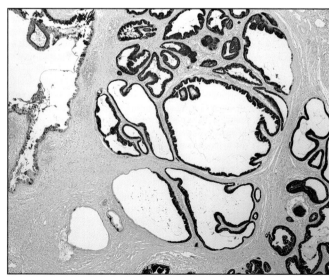

Fig. 11.20 • Intraductal papillary mucinous neoplasm, gastrointestinal type, with immunostaining for MUC5.

All types of intraductal papillary mucinous neoplasm may extend into the smaller ducts in areas of atrophic pancreatitis, a growth pattern that may be difficult to distinguish from invasive carcinoma. Intestinal type intraductal papillary mucinous neoplasms commonly have mucin leakage from the ducts, with accumulation of acellular stromal mucin pools that mimic colloid carcinoma.

The prognosis of intraductal papillary mucinous neoplasms depends largely upon the presence, extent, and histologic type of invasive carcinoma.[67] Completely resected intraductal papillary mucinous neoplasms (even those with high grade dysplasia) are usually cured, although local recurrence within the pancreatic ducts has been reported occasionally. Invasive carcinomas are most likely to occur in association with the pancreatobiliary type, followed by the intestinal type; only rarely is there invasive carcinoma associated with the gastric type. If the invasive component is conventional ductal adenocarcinoma of significant extent, the prognosis is poor, approaching that of other ductal adenocarcinomas. However, colloid carcinomas have a less aggressive course, with a 55 percent 5-year survival after resection.[49]

The differential diagnosis of intraductal papillary mucinous neoplasms includes mucinous cystic neoplasms (Table 11.8) which, in contrast to intraductal papillary mucinous neoplasms, do not show communication with the duct system, occur predominantly in the tail of the pancreas of female patients, and have hypercellular subepithelial "ovarian-like" stroma that is virtually pathognomonic.[73] Small branch duct intraductal papillary mucinous neoplasms with gastric type papillae can resemble ductal retention cysts, but these lack significant mucinous epithelium or papillary formations. The distinction of small intraductal papillary mucinous neoplasms of the gastric type from large foci of pancreatic intraepithelial neoplasia (PanIN) can be nearly impossible, especially for lesions that measure 0.5–1.0 cm. A recent consensus publication attempted to provide some useful criteria.[74]

Recently *intraductal tubular neoplasms* of the pancreas were described, which include intraductal tubular adenoma, pyloric type, and other, so far not well characterized, neoplasms.[75,76] While the intraductal tubular adenoma of pyloric type shows a benign course,[77] other intraductal tubular neoplasms proved to be carcinomas.[75]

Mucinous cystic neoplasms

Mucinous cystic neoplasms of the pancreas comprise a range of lesions that have generally been thought to show differing biologic behaviors. Like intraductal papillary mucinous neoplasms, they are classified based on the degree of cytoarchitectural complexity as mucinous cystic neoplasm with low grade dysplasia (mucinous cystadenoma), mucinous cystic neoplasm with moderate dysplasia (borderline mucinous cystic neoplasm) and mucinous cystic neoplasm with high grade dysplasia (mucinous cystadenocarcinoma in situ).[7–9,73] Invasive carcinomas may also occur, including a wide array of different histologic types. Mucinous cystic neoplasms occur almost exclusively in women (mostly middle-aged), arise in most cases from the tail or body of the pancreas, and most commonly present as a slowly enlarging abdominal mass. Weakness, anorexia and weight loss are features suggesting a component of invasive carcinoma. The majority of patients with mucinous cystic neoplasms lacking an invasive component are cured by complete excision. The prognosis of invasive mucinous cystadenocarcinoma depends on the extent of the invasive carcinoma; those cases with extension of the carcinoma outside of the cyst wall have a poor outcome.[73,78] Interestingly, apparently benign mucinous cystic neoplasms may recur with overtly malignant features if only drained, emphasizing the potential for neoplastic progression in mucinous cystic neoplasms and the need to remove them completely even when benign. Rare cases have been recorded[79] of mucinous cystic tumors associated with gastrin secretion and Zollinger–Ellison syndrome, presumably because of their content of gastrin-producing endocrine cells.

Grossly, mucinous cystic neoplasms are well-circumscribed, encapsulated, unilocular or more often multiloculated cysts, ranging in size from 2 to 30 cm (Fig. 11.21). The individual locules are relatively large (in comparison with serous microcystic adenomas, see below), each measuring 1–10 cm in most cases. The inner surfaces are smooth or show papillary projections and/or mural nodules, particularly in those with high grade dysplasia or invasive carcinoma. The contents are mucoid, occasionally with hemorrhage. The cyst(s) do not communicate with the duct system.

Table 11.8	Most important clinicopathologic features of cystic tumors of the pancreas					
Entity	**Mean age**	**Male (%)**	**Female (%)**	**Size in cm (mean)**	**Localization**	**Duct communication**
IPMN	50–70	60	40	1–13 (5)	Head (80%)	Yes
MCN	40–60	1	99	3–23 (10)	Body-tail (90%)	No
SMA	60–80	10	90	2.5–16 (6)	Body-tail > head	No
SOIA	50–70	60	40	3–14 (7)	Head >body-tail	No
SPN	10–40	5	95	2–17 (7)	Entire pancreas	No
DAC, cystic	50–70	50	50	1–19 (6)	Head (70%)	No
NET, cystic	20–70	30	70	1.2–15 (6)	Entire pancreas	No

IPMN, intraductal papillary-mucinous neoplasm; MCN, mucinous cystic neoplasm; SMA, serous microcystic adenoma; SOIA, serous oligocystic ill-demarcated adenoma; SPN, solid pseudopapillary neoplasm; DAC, ductal adenocarcinoma; NET, neuroendocrine tumor.

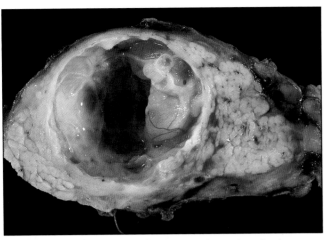

Fig. 11.21 • Resection specimen of mucinous cystic neoplasm showing a multiloculated cut surface and mucoid contents (courtesy of Dr. J. Brenecke, Hannover, Germany).

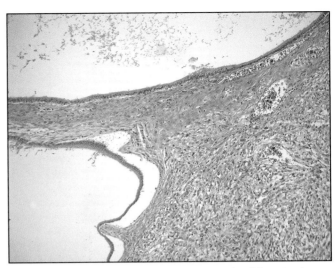

Fig. 11.23 • Mucinous cystic neoplasm with associated undifferentiated (sarcomatoid) pleomorphic carcinoma (bottom right).

Histologically, the cysts are lined by mucus-secreting columnar epithelial cells, occasionally with some endocrine, Paneth or goblet cells. Glycogen is absent. Other more intricate patterns can be seen, such as cellular stratification, papilla or gland formation, and crypt invagination, and greater degrees of atypia correspond to the grades of mucinous cystic neoplasm listed above. Mucinous cystic neoplasms with low grade dysplasia tend to have a simple pattern and bland cytology. Moderate dysplasia is characterized by papillary infolding, cellular pseudostratification, nuclear irregularity and crowding. High grade dysplasia includes severely atypical epithelium. Many mucinous cystic neoplasms have areas with varying grades of dysplasia (Fig. 11.22). Beneath the epithelial lining there is a densely cellular ("ovarian-like") stroma, resembling that seen in mucinous cystic tumors of the ovary or of the biliary tree (Fig. 11.22). These stromal cells express estrogen and progesterone receptors as well as CD10, inhibin,

and A103.[73] Areas of epithelial denudation are common in mucinous cystic neoplasms, and the associated hemorrhage and inflammation simulate the appearance of a pseudocyst. When an invasive component is present, it often resembles conventional ductal adenocarcinoma or one of its variants. Rarely, the cyst wall contains pseudosarcomatous[80] or frankly sarcomatous[81] areas, the latter likely representing a sarcomatoid undifferentiated carcinoma that has lost epithelial differentiation (Fig.11.23). Any mucinous cystic neoplasm may contain highly dysplastic or even invasive areas in addition to more bland areas; extensive if not complete sampling of these lesions is therefore recommended.

Most mucinous cystic tumors show immunoreactivity for epithelial antigens (cytokeratins 7, 8, 18 and 19 and EMA) and CEA. Some tumors show focal positive immunostaining for endocrine markers, particularly for serotonin. When associated pseudosarcomatous or frankly sarcomatous areas are present, the latter show variable immunoreactivity with "mesenchymal" markers (vimentin or smooth muscle actin).

Mucinous cystic tumors have to be distinguished from intraductal papillary mucinous tumors (communication with the duct system, no female preponderance, no ovarian-like stroma); other cystic tumors, including serous cystadenoma, solid pseudopapillary tumor, acinar cell cystadenocarcinoma, cystic endocrine tumor and lymphoepithelial cyst; and pseudocyst (no epithelial lining, association with chronic pancreatitis, male preponderance) (see Table 11.8).

Serous cystic neoplasms

Serous cystic neoplasms are usually benign.[7–9,61,82] They commonly present with the symptoms and signs of an expansile abdominal mass. Jaundice is rare. Asymptomatic cases may be diagnosed incidentally by imaging techniques or at laparotomy.

Serous neoplasms include serous microcystic adenoma (microcystic serous cystadenoma or glycogen-rich adenoma),[83] serous oligocystic and ill-demarcated adenoma (SOIA; or macrocystic serous cystadenoma),[84,85] von Hippel-Lindau

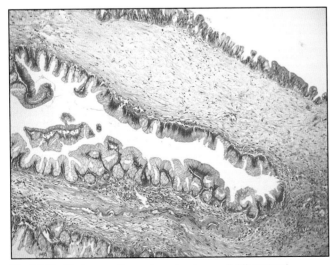

Fig. 11.22 • Mucinous cystic neoplasm showing a well differentiated single-layered mucin-secreting columnar epithelium that is supported by an "ovarian-like" cellular stroma (lower half), next to atypical epithelium (upper half).

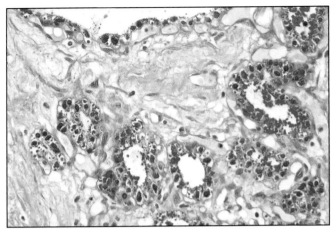

Fig. 11.24 • Serous cystic neoplasm with small cysts lined by cuboidal cells with vacuolated or periodic acid–Schiff- (PAS-)positive cytoplasm.

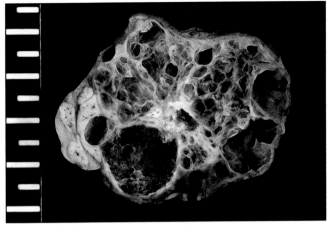

Fig. 11.26 • Resection specimen of a serous microcystic adenoma showing a honeycombed cut surface and a central fibrous scar.

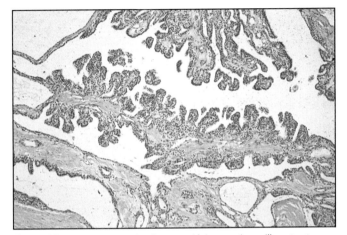

Fig. 11.25 • Serous microcystic adenoma with intracystic papillary structures.

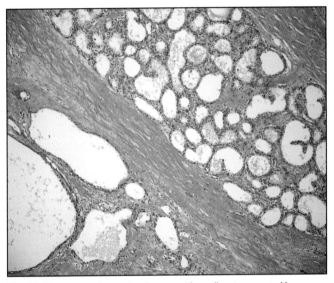

Fig. 11.27 • Serous microcystic adenoma with small cysts separated by hyalinized stroma.

associated cystic neoplasms (VHL-CN), solid serous adenoma (the solid variant of serous cystic adenoma)[86] and serous cystadenocarcinoma. All types are composed of the same cell. It is a flattened or cuboidal cell with a round and regular nucleus, clear cytoplasm due to the presence of periodic acid–Schiff (PAS) positive glycogen (Fig. 11.24), and a ductal immunoprofile. It may form micropapillae, covered by cytologically bland epithelium (Fig. 11.25).[84,87–89] However, despite these cytologic similarities, the serous cystic neoplasms differ in their localization in the pancreas, gross appearance, gender distribution and genetic alterations,[90] suggesting that they represent different entities. The place of the solid serous adenoma[86] and serous cystadenocarcinoma[91] in the spectrum of serous cystic neoplasms is not yet clear, mainly due to the small number of cases that have been reported to date.[84,88,92]

Most common are serous microcystic adenomas, which make up 60 percent of all serous cystic neoplasm.[61] They present as single, well circumscribed, slightly bosselated round tumors, with diameters ranging from 2.5 to 16 cm. Their cut surface shows numerous small (honeycomb-like, only a few millimeters in diameter) cysts arranged around a (para)central stellate scar (Fig. 11.26), which may contain calcifications and from which fine fibrous septa radiate towards the periphery. Between the cysts there is fibrous tissue which is usually hyalinized (Fig. 11.27) and may contain entrapped islets.

About two-thirds of the serous microcystic adenomas arise in the body-tail region and almost all occur in women (median age 66 years). They are usually found incidentally.

SOIAs account for 30 percent of serous cystic neoplasms and are composed of few relatively large cysts (for which reason they have also been described as macrocystic serous cystadenoma)[85] (Fig. 11.28), lack the stellate scar and round shape, and occur predominantly in the head of the pancreas, where they may obstruct the common bile duct and cause jaundice.[84,88] They show no sex predilection.

The VHL-CNs often arise at multiple sites, and in advanced stages of the disease they may merge and involve the entire pancreas.[93,94] Because the VHL-CN may affect the pancreas diffusely, they differ markedly from the gross features of both serous microcystic adenomas and SOIAs. Biologically, it is also important to note that VHL-CN patients, like SOIA patients, are not predominantly female, in contrast to patients with serous microcystic adenoma. This suggests that serous microcystic adenomas differ in their pathogenesis from VHL-CNs and SOIAs. Recently reported molecular data support this assumption. While VHL-CNs were found to be characterized

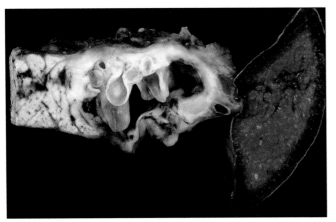

Fig. 11.28 • Serous oligocystic and ill-demarcated adenoma: left sided pancreatectomy specimen with a multilocular cystic tumor between pancreas and spleen.

Fig. 11.29 • Acinar cell carcinoma: resection specimen showing a fleshy hemorrhagic cut surface.

by both LOH at chromosome 3p (which contains the *VHL* gene) and a *VHL* gene germ line mutation, only 40 percent of serous microcystic adenomas had LOH at chromosome 3p and of these tumors only two (22 percent) exhibited a somatic *VHL* gene mutation.[94] Interestingly, more than 50 percent of serous microcystic adenomas showed LOH at 10q. It appears therefore that *VHL*-gene alterations are of minor importance in SMAs, while gene changes at 10q may play a major role. Whether the *VHL* gene is involved in the pathogenesis of SOIAs remains to be elucidated. The same also holds for the extremely rare serous cystadenocarcinomas.[95]

The differential diagnosis of SMAs is primarily with multiloculated mucinous cystic neoplasms (see Table 11.8), although their honeycomb appearance and stellate scar distinguish them quite clearly. SOIAs are more difficult to differentiate from other cystic lesions because of their variegated gross appearance. Immunohistologically, CEA is negative in serous cystic neoplasms, in contrast to mucinous cystic neoplasm, while inhibin is expressed in the serous cystic neoplasms, but not in the epithelial lining of mucinous cystic neoplasms.[73,89]

Solid serous adenoma of the pancreas is an apparently noncystic variant of serous cystic neoplasm.[86] This lesion is formed by tubules of clear cells which are histologically indistinguishable from those occurring in serous cystic neoplasms.

Serous cystadenocarcinoma is an extremely rare malignant tumor; it resembles serous cystadenoma grossly and microscopically, but shows invasion into adjacent structures and vessels or metastases.[95]

Acinar cell carcinoma

Acinar cell carcinoma is a malignant epithelial neoplasm with solid and acinar architectural patterns that demonstrates evidence of enzyme production by the neoplastic cells. Acinar cell carcinoma accounts for about 1–2 percent of pancreatic exocrine tumors. It occurs mostly in adults and predominantly in male patients, although rare cases have been described in children and adolescents.[4,96] In adults, acinar cell carcinoma behaves like ductal adenocarcinoma, with widespread metastases to regional lymph nodes, liver and lungs; however, the clinical course is not as rapidly fatal, with a median

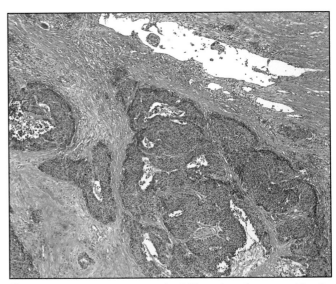

Fig. 11.30 • Acinar cell carcinoma with solid formations of monomorphic cells embedded in fibrous stroma.

survival of 18 months.[96,97] In children, on the other hand, the prognosis of this tumor seems to be more favorable. An association with multifocal fat necrosis (subcutis, bone marrow and abdomen) and polyarthralgia (due to massive secretion of lipase)[96] or non-bacterial thrombotic endocarditis has been described in individual patients.

Grossly, acinar cell carcinomas arise from any portion of the pancreas as large (2–15 cm in diameter), well-demarcated, soft, lobulated masses, with a fleshy to yellow color. Necrosis or hemorrhage may be conspicuous, and cystic degeneration may occur (Fig.11.29). Invasion into adjacent structures (duodenum, stomach or spleen) is often found at surgery.

Microscopically, although the tumor appears well circumscribed, it focally or widely infiltrates surrounding pancreatic tissue. There is marked tumor cellularity, with minimal stroma that is limited to hyalinized fibrous bands between large lobules of tumor (Fig. 11.30). The growth pattern is variable and may be acinar ("microglandular") (Fig. 11.31), solid or mixed; rarely the tumor form is trabecular. There is a rich network of

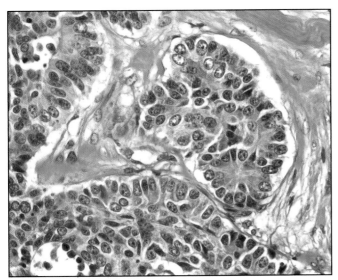

Fig. 11.31 • Acinar cell carcinoma showing acinar and trabecular growth patterns.

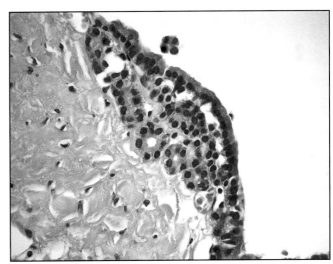

Fig. 11.33 • Acinar cell cystadenoma showing single-layered epithelium that merges with acini.

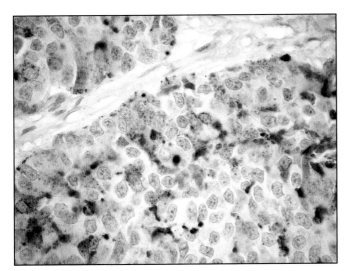

Fig. 11.32 • Acinar cell carcinoma with immunostaining for trypsin.

thin-walled vessels. The best differentiated cells are round and monomorphic and medium to large in size. Their cytoplasm is relatively abundant, eosinophilic and finely granular, containing PAS-positive, diastase-resistant zymogen granules. Nuclei are uniform, round and large with conspicuous nucleoli. Mitoses are frequent. The less well differentiated cells are smaller, have less characteristic nuclei and lack the eosinophilic granularity of the cytoplasm.

Acinar cell carcinoma shows positive immunostaining for lipase, trypsin, and chymotrypsin (Fig. 11.32).[96,98] Paradoxically, stains for amylase are generally negative. Ultrastructurally, zymogen granules are identified in the neoplastic cells. The molecular genetic findings include occasional abnormalities in the APC/β-catenin pathway,[99] but no abnormalities in the genes involved in ductal adenocarcinoma (*p53*, *p16*, K-*ras*, or *smad4/dpc4*).

Stains for chromogranin and synaptophysin are usually negative in acinar cell carcinomas, but 30–40 percent of cases contain scattered individual endocrine cells that are demonstrable by immunohistology. Rarely, a tumor will have signifi-

cant components of more than one line of differentiation. Carcinomas with more than 25 percent of acinar and endocrine cell components (as defined by immunohistology) are regarded as mixed acinar endocrine carcinomas,[59,100] and those with a mixture of acinar and ductal elements (defined by mucin production or immunoexpression of glycoproteins such as CEA or CA19.9) are designated mixed acinar ductal carcinomas. Very rare mixed acinar endocrine ductal carcinomas have significant amounts of all three cell lines.[101] In most cases, these mixed carcinomas consist largely of the acinar component, and the available clinical data suggest that they behave similarly to pure acinar cell carcinomas.

Acinar cell cystadenocarcinoma represents the rare cystic variant of acinar cell carcinoma.[102] Although the individual cysts may be lined by well differentiated acinar epithelium, there are also solid areas and the tumor shows invasion into the peripancreatic tissues. Acinar cell cystadenocarcinomas are just as aggressive as solid acinar cell carcinomas.

Recently, a peculiar acinar cell lesion has been described under the term *acinar cell cystadenoma*.[103] These lesions are extensively cystic, with the individual locules being lined by a continuous layer of mature acinar cells that stain for pancreatic enzymes and usually merge with normal acini (Fig. 11.33). Acinar cell cystadenomas are benign lesions with variably sized cysts that are mixed with the normal pancreatic parenchyma. Some are incidental microscopic findings limited to a few cysts, whereas others measure up to 10 cm and involve the entire gland.

Acinar cell carcinoma should be distinguished from pancreatic endocrine neoplasms, which they can mimic histologically. In general, endocrine tumors show greater cytologic uniformity and are PAS negative. They diffusely express chromogranin and synaptophysin, with staining for pancreatic enzymes being limited to scattered individual cells. Examples of solid acinar cell adenoma have not been recorded convincingly, but acinar cell nodules (focal acinar cell dysplasia) are commonly identified in surgical specimens and autopsies.[104] These circumscribed nodules of cytologically altered acinar cells are likely degenerative in nature in most cases and have not been shown to have preneoplastic significance.

Pancreatoblastoma

Pancreatoblastoma (synonyms: pancreaticoblastoma, infantile pancreatic carcinoma) is a rare malignant tumor occurring almost exclusively in infants and children in the first decade of life.[105] However, a few cases have been reported in older children and adults.[106,107] Pancreatoblastoma occurs more often in boys than girls. The tumor arises in the head or body of the pancreas as a large, soft, circumscribed and (wholly or partly) encapsulated mass, measuring 5–20 cm in diameter. On cut section, there is lobulated tan tissue with hemorrhage, necrosis and occasionally cystic change.

Microscopically, pancreatoblastoma consists mainly of epithelial elements, but in rare cases there is also a mesenchymal component. The epithelial component is characterized by monomorphic polygonal cells, with PAS-positive material in either the cytoplasm or glandular lumina. These cells grow in solid, trabecular or acinar patterns. Mitoses are frequent. Formation of squamoid nests or "corpuscles" is a highly characteristic if not pathognomonic feature (Fig. 11.34). The mesenchymal component, if present, may consist of spindle-shaped cells associated with stromal hyalinization, fibrovascular bands, and myxoid or cartilaginous changes. Pancreatoblastomas are fundamentally acinar neoplasms and show positive immunostaining with lipase, trypsin, and chymotrypsin.[105] In addition, endocrine or α-fetoprotein positive cells can be identified, as can staining for ductal-type glycoproteins (CEA or Ca19.9). Ultrastructurally, the tumor also shows acinar features, with zymogen granules in many of the epithelial cells. Pancreatoblastomas lack the typical genetic abnormalities of ductal adenocarcinomas, instead having abnormalities in the β-catenin/APC pathway.[108] When pancreatoblastoma is localized, complete surgical excision usually results in a fairly good prognosis, at least in pediatric patients; the rarely affected adults more often develop metastatic disease leading to death.[105,106]

Solid pseudopapillary neoplasm

Solid pseudopapillary neoplasm (synonyms: solid cystic or papillary cystic tumor, solid and papillary epithelial neoplasm) is an unusual neoplasm which is often included in the "cystic" group of exocrine tumors of the pancreas. The tumor occurs predominantly in adolescent girls and young women, with a median age of 26 years. About 10 percent of cases occur in men.[109] Patients commonly present with an enlarging and painful abdominal mass, but asymptomatic cases may be found incidentally at laparotomy or by imaging techniques. Some have been discovered after abdominal trauma causing hemorrhage into the neoplasm or the peritoneal cavity. Solid pseudopapillary tumors are considered to be malignant, but with very low grade biology, and most patients are tumor-free many years after complete resection. Approximately 15 percent of cases are associated with metastases that are essentially limited to the liver and peritoneum and are usually present at the time of initial diagnosis.[7,110] Long survival has even been reported in the face of metastatic disease.

The tumor may occur anywhere in the pancreas and presents macroscopically as a round, deceptively well-demarcated lesion, measuring 2–17 cm in diameter (average 8 cm). Sectioning demonstrates a solid mass with cystic areas; and hemorrhage is common (Fig. 11.35).

Microscopically, the solid portions contain sheets, cords and trabeculae of uniform, rather small and fairly round cells; this organoid appearance can mimic an endocrine tumor. The cytoplasm is eosinophilic or vacuolated, containing clustered PAS-positive hyaline globules. Nuclei appear round to oval and have finely dispersed chromatin and inconspicuous nucleoli. Some nuclei contain a groove or indentation. Mitoses are rarely identified. The solid portions are also characterized by a rich and delicate vascular network. Many of the cells farthest from the vessels undergo degeneration, causing the remaining cells around the vessels to form pseudorosette or pseudopapillary patterns (Fig. 11.36). The cystic zones result from more extensive degenerative changes (Fig. 11.37) and there may be conspicuous hemorrhage, with cholesterol granulomas and aggregates of foamy histiocytes. Invasive growth is surprisingly common, and extension into the surrounding pancreas, peripancreatic tissue, or even into vessels can be

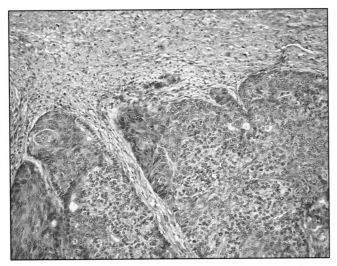

Fig. 11.34 • Pancreatoblastoma with a lobulated solid and acinar growth pattern and a typical squamoid corpuscle at the left border.

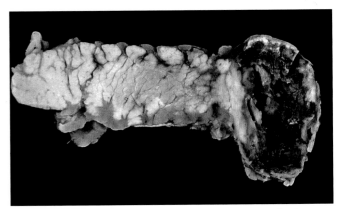

Fig. 11.35 • Resection specimen of solid pseudopapillary tumor showing almost complete hemorrhagic necrosis.

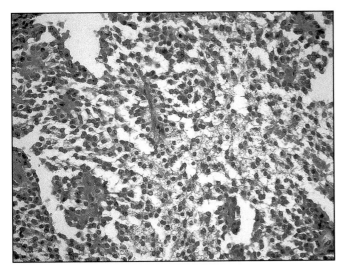

Fig. 11.36 • Solid pseudopapillary tumor consisting of pseudopapillary structures.

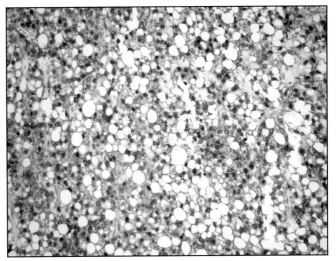

Fig. 11.38 • Solid pseudopapillary tumor with immunostaining for β-catenin; note nuclear positivity.

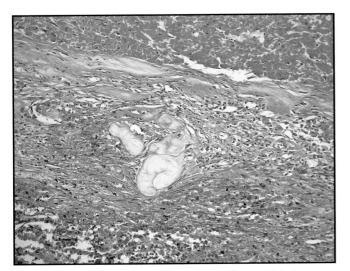

Fig. 11.37 • Solid pseudopapillary tumor with extensive necrosis in the upper half of the picture.

seen. None of these features has demonstrated prognostic significance, however.

Immunohistochemical and electron microscopic studies of solid pseudopapillary neoplasm have produced conflicting results with regard to tumor cell phenotyping.[111–113] The tumors show positive immunostaining for α_1-antitrypsin, neuron-specific enolase, CD56, CD10, progesterone receptor and vimentin, and some express synaptophysin.[114] There is never any staining for chromogranin or pancreatic enzymes, however. Cytokeratins are only rarely expressed. Hence, the line of differentiation of solid pseudopapillary tumor is still debatable. Consistent abnormalities are found in the *β-catenin* gene,[115,116] and the abnormal nuclear localization of β-catenin on immunostaining has been proposed as a diagnostic aid (Fig. 11.38). Interestingly, one case was shown to have a distinctive unbalanced translocation between chromosomes 13 and 17.[117]

Rare cases of solid pseudopapillary neoplasm exhibit a high grade component that consists of diffuse sheets of cells with a high nuclear cytoplasmic ratio, necrosis, and elevated mitotic

activity, suggesting the development of a poorly differentiated carcinoma.[118] These tumors have been associated with a rapidly progressive, fatal clinical course.

Miscellaneous carcinomas

Carcinoma with medullary changes

Quite recently, a medullary type of pancreatic carcinoma has been reported.[119] Like their counterparts in the colorectum, these tumors show morphologic features that set them apart from ductal adenocarcinoma (DAC). They are composed of rather polymorphous cells with a syncytial growth pattern, a high mitotic rate and, occasionally, tumor-infiltrating lymphocytes. It seems that these carcinomas are heterogeneous in nature. Unlike medullary colorectal carcinoma, medullary carcinoma of the pancreas is only occasionally associated with mutations of the mismatch repair genes[120] and is not associated with a significantly better prognosis than DAC.[120] So far, only one case has been reported to be a manifestation of the hereditary non-polyposis colorectal cancer (HNPCC) syndrome.[120]

Carcinoma with lymphoepithelial changes

A lymphoepithelial carcinoma has been described in the body of the pancreas.[121] It expressed genomic components of the Epstein–Barr virus.

Carcinoma with micropapillary changes

This type of carcinoma, first described in the breast, has also been found in the pancreas.[21]

Carcinoma with oncocytic changes

Several cases of oncocytic carcinoma have been reported, arising in the head or tail of the pancreas, often with metastases.[122,123] Microscopically, these carcinomas consisted of sheets or nests of cells with abundant granular eosinophilic cytoplasm. The cytoplasmic granules stained positively with phosphotungstic acid hematoxylin (PTAH), and ultrastructural study disclosed numerous mitochondria in the cytoplasm.[123] There is, as yet, no convincing evidence to support the existence of benign pancreatic oncocytomas.

In addition to such purely oncocytic malignant tumors, focal oncocytic changes may be encountered in otherwise "normal" endocrine tumors. Such change has also been observed in tumors such as solid pseudopapillary tumor[93] and in intraductal papillary mucinous tumor.[69]

Carcinoma with basaloid changes

Recently, a carcinoma composed of solid ("basaloid") nests with small foci of squamous differentiation has been reported.[124]

Carcinoma with clear cell changes

The clear cell carcinomas which have been recorded in the pancreas[22] show cytoplasmic vacuoles that contain glycogen and a variable amount of mucin, but are devoid of fat. One case contained components of an intraductal papillary-mucinous neoplasm (IPMN).[22] Other cases appeared to be variants of DAC.[125] Clear cell carcinoma of the pancreas must be distinguished from metastatic renal cell carcinoma or adrenal cortical carcinoma.

Carcinoma with microglandular changes

Tumors that have been called microglandular adenocarcinomas with small or medium-sized cells had previously been considered to be a variant of ductal adenocarcinoma or a malignant tumor with dual ductal and neuroendocrine differentiation. The tumors described as such were large, showed extensive necrosis, and behaved in an aggressive fashion. More recent immunohistochemical re-evaluation of Cubilla & Fitzgerald's series of microglandular carcinomas[2] has disclosed that these tumors do not constitute an entity of their own, but comprise a group of tumors with heterogeneous histologic features and immunostaining patterns.[126] This group includes some tumors which should be classified with conventional ductal adenocarcinoma and others which have a neuroendocrine, acinar or mixed immunohistochemical phenotype.

Carcinoma with features of small cell carcinoma

The very rare small cell carcinoma of the pancreas was once considered an exocrine tumor of the pancreas and a variant of undifferentiated carcinoma. However, as small cell carcinomas usually stain for neuroendocrine markers such as synaptophysin or CD56 they are now classified as poorly differentiated neuroendocrine carcinomas (see Ch. 20).

Tumors in infants and children

Pancreatic exocrine tumors are rarely encountered in infants and children. In addition to pancreatoblastoma (see p. 478),

acinar cell carcinomas, endocrine tumors and solid pseudo-papillary tumors can occur,[127] while ductal adenocarcinoma is virtually absent.[17] Pancreatoblastomas are the most common neoplasms in infancy and early childhood, while solid-pseudopapillary neoplasms, endocrine tumors and acinar cell carcinomas prevail in older children.[128,129] Pancreatic primitive neuroectodermal tumors (PNETs) also occur in children and young adults.[130] They can be confused with pancreatic endocrine tumors (which often share immunoreactivity for CD99). The diagnosis is confirmed by demonstration of either the t (11; 22)(q24;q12) or a related translocation.

Non-epithelial tumors and secondary tumors

In contrast to the more commonly occurring tumors of epithelial origin, non-epithelial tumors of the pancreas are very rare.[131] The tumors that have been reported include examples of almost all known histologic types of benign and malignant soft tissue tumor. Most frequent are leiomyosarcoma[132,133] and malignant peripheral nerve sheath tumor, followed by liposarcomas and so-called malignant fibrous histiocytomas. At this site, most of the latter likely represent either dedifferentiated liposarcoma or else anaplastic carcinoma. More recently, clear cell "sugar" tumor (or angiomyolipoma),[134,135] desmoplastic small cell tumor,[136] peripheral neuroectodermal tumor,[131] solitary fibrous tumor[137] and gastrointestinal stromal tumor[138] have been described. Contrary to a number of reports describing inflammatory myofibroblastic tumors in the pancreas, it seems that this "tumor" is, in most cases, a pseudotumorous manifestation of autoimmune pancreatitis (see tumor-like lesions). Malignant lymphomas and leukemic infiltrates may occasionally be seen in the pancreas.[139,140] The vast majority of primary pancreatic lymphomas have a B-cell phenotype. Metastases involving the pancreas are uncommon and include metastases from renal cell carcinoma, breast carcinoma, small cell lung carcinoma and melanoma.[141,142]

Tumor-like lesions

Non-neoplastic tumor-like lesions of the pancreas mimic either solid or cystic tumors of the exocrine pancreas. Among the solid non-neoplastic lesions are "inflammatory pseudotumors" and hamartomas;[143] among the cystic lesions are pseudocysts, lymphoepithelial cysts and congenital, retention and parasitic cysts.[61]

Inflammatory pseudotumors that clinically and grossly mimic pancreatic cancer are typically produced by two types of chronic pancreatitis that have only recently been described in detail.[144] These are autoimmune pancreatitis (synonyms: lymphoplasmacytic sclerosing pancreatitis,[145,146] duct destructive chronic pancreatitis) and paraduodenal wall pancreatitis (synonyms: cystic dystrophy of the duodenal wall, parampullary duodenal wall cyst and groove pancreatitis).[147] *Autoimmune pancreatitis* is a chronic inflammatory disease of unknown etiology and pathogenesis. Patients often have serum elevation of IgG4, a finding that may help distinguish the lesion clinically from pancreatic ductal adenocarcinoma.[146] Autoimmune pancreatitis mainly develops in the pancreatic head including the distal bile duct, where it forms an inflammatory mass that usually causes jaundice. Microscopically, it is characterized by a dense lymphoplasmacellular infiltrate that may also contain eosinophils and neutrophils. This infiltrate first appears around medium-sized ducts and later also spreads to the acinar lobules. Extension of the infiltrate into the acinar lobules is associated with the development of intensive fibrosis that may almost replace the acinar tissue and is occasionally associated with numerous myofibroblasts arranged in a storiform pattern. If the latter change prevails, autoimmune pancreatitis resembles inflammatory myofibroblastic tumor (formerly called inflammatory pseudotumor). Obliterative venulitis is another characteristic finding. It seems that a number of cases of autoimmune pancreatitis have been published under this diagnosis in recent years.[148–150] The disease may occur at all ages, but is most common between 50 and 60 years. Men are twice as frequently affected as women. The second type of chronic pancreatitis that clinically is usually misdiagnosed as pancreatic cancer is *paraduodenal wall pancreatitis* (for synonyms see above).[147] Here chronic pancreatitis seems to develop in heterotopic pancreatic tissue[151] in the submucosa of the duodenum in the region of the minor papilla. Typically, there are cystic and/or pseudocystic changes in association with cellular fibrotic tissue that usually extends through the duodenal wall into nearby pancreatic tissue around the bile duct. This may lead to stenosis of the duodenum and/or the bile duct. Most commonly affected are men aged 40 to 60 years who are alcoholics.

Recently, various hamartomas have been found to produce solid or cystic tumor-like lesions in the pancreas.[143,144,152] They were composed of haphazardly arranged mature acinar, ductal and endocrine cells embedded in fibrotic tissue and well demarcated from the surrounding normal pancreatic parenchyma. Some of these lesions were difficult to distinguish clearly from gastrointestinal stromal tumors because of their expression of CD117.[152] Focal lymphoid hyperplasia of the pancreas

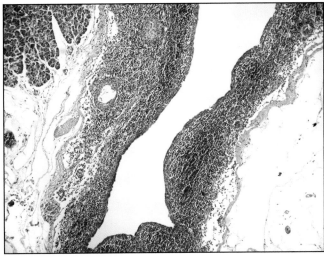

Fig. 11.39 • Lymphoepithelial cyst of the pancreas showing squamous epithelium supported by lymphoid stroma.

(synonym: pseudolymphoma) is characterized by hyperplastic lymphoid follicles with germinal centers and should not be mistaken for nodular malignant lymphoma.[61,153]

Most common among tumor-like cystic lesions are *pseudocysts*. As a *sine qua non* they have to arise in association with pancreatitis,[154] usually of alcoholic, rarely of hereditary origin.[155] Benign lymphoepithelial cyst of the pancreas presents as a unilocular cyst lined by mature squamous epithelium, the latter surrounded by follicular lymphoid tissue (Fig. 11.39).[156,157] In contrast to histologically comparable lesions in salivary gland, there is no evident association with HIV infection. Other cystic non-neoplastic lesions that occasionally have to be considered in the differential diagnosis are mucinous non-neoplastic cysts,[90] some rare congenital cysts such as a ciliated foregut cyst, and finally retention and parasitic cysts.[154]

References

1. Hamilton S R, Aaltonen L A 2000 Pathology and genetics of tumours of the digestive system. WHO classification of tumours. IARC Press, Lyon
2. Cubilla A L, Fitzgerald P J 1984 Tumors of the exocrine pancreas. AFIP Atlas of tumor pathology, series 2, fascicle 19. Armed Forces Institute of Pathology, Washington, DC
3. Solcia E, Capella C, Klöppel G 1997 Tumors of the pancreas. AFIP Atlas of tumor pathology, series 3, fascicle 20. Armed Forces Institute of Pathology, Washington, DC
4. Lack E E 1989 Primary tumors of the exocrine pancreas. Classification, overview, and recent contributions by immunohistochemistry and electron microscopy. Am J Surg Pathol 13, Suppl 1: 66–88
5. Oertel J E, Heffess C S, Oertel Y C 1996 Pancreas. In: Sternberg SS (ed) Diagnostic surgical pathology. Raven Press, New York, p 1419–1457
6. Klöppel G 1997 Pathology and classification of tumours of the exocrine pancreas. In: Trede M, Carter DC (eds) Surgery of the pancreas, 2nd edn. Churchill Livingstone, Edinburgh, p 447–462
7. Klöppel G, Solcia E, Longnecker D S et al. 1996 Histological typing of tumours of the exocrine pancreas, 2nd edn. WHO International Histological Classification of Tumours. Springer, Berlin
8. Albores-Saavedra J, Gould E W, Angeles-Angeles A et al. 1990 Cystic tumors of the pancreas. In: Rosen PP, Fechner RE (eds) Pathology annual. Appleton & Lange, East Norwalk, vol 25, part 2, p 19–50
9. Bogomoletz W V 1991 Cystic tumours of the exocrine pancreas. In: Anthony PP, MacSween RNM (eds) Recent advances in histopathology. Churchill Livingstone, Edinburgh, p 141–155
10. Lowenfels A B, Maisonneuve P, Cavallini G et al. 1993 Pancreatitis and the risk of pancreatic cancer. N Engl J Med 328: 1433–1437
11. Lumadue J A, Griffin C A, Osman M et al. 1995 Familial pancreatic cancer and the genetics of pancreatic cancer. Surg Clin North Am 75: 845–855
12. Klein A P, Brune K A, Petersen G M et al. 2004. Prospective risk of pancreatic cancer in familial pancreatic cancer kindreds. Cancer Res 64: 2634–2638.
13. Eberle M A, Pfützer R, Pogue-Geile K L et al. 2002 A new susceptibility locus for autosomal dominant pancreatic cancer maps to chromosome 4q32–34. Am J Hum Genet 70: 1044–1048
14. Meckler K A, Brentnall T A, Haggitt R C et al. 2001 Familial fibrocystic pancreatic atrophy with endocrine cell hyperplasia and pancreatic carcinoma. Am J Surg Pathol 25: 1047–1053
15. Klöppel G, Hruban R H, Longnecker D S et al. 2000 Ductal adenocarcinoma of the pancreas. In: Hamilton SR, Aaltonen LA (eds) Pathology and genetics of tumours of the digestive system. WHO classification of tumours. IARC Press, Lyon, p 221–230
16. Blackbourne L H, Jones R S, Catalano C J et al. 1997 Pancreatic adenocarcinoma in the pregnant patient: case report and review of the literature. Cancer 79: 1776–1779
17. Lüttges J, Stigge C, Pacena M et al. 2004 Rare ductal adenocarcinoma of the pancreas in patients younger than age 40 years. An analysis of its features and a literature review. Cancer 100: 173–182
18. Kosmahl M, Pauser U, Anlauf M et al. 2005 Pancreatic ductal adenocarcinomas with cystic features: neither rare nor uniform. Mod Pathol 18: 1157–1164
19. Makhlouf H R, Almeida J L, Sobin L H 1999 Carcinoma in jejunal pancreatic heterotopia. Arch Pathol Lab Med 123: 707–711

20. Adsay V, Logani S, Sarkar F et al. 2000 Foamy gland pattern of pancreatic ductal adenocarcinoma. A deceptively benign-appearing variant. Am J Surg Pathol 24: 493–504

21. Nassar H, Pansare V, Zhang H et al. 2004 Pathogenesis of invasive micropapillary carcinoma: role of MUC1 glycoprotein. Mod Pathol 17: 1045–1050

22. Lüttges J, Vogel I, Menke M A O H et al. 1998 Clear cell carcinoma of the pancreas: an adenocarcinoma with ductal phenotype. Histopathology 32: 444–448

23. Cubilla A L, Fitzgerald P J 1976 Morphological lesions associated with human primary invasive nonendocrine pancreas cancer. Cancer Res 36: 2690–2698

24. Klöppel G, Bommer G, Rückert K et al. 1980 Intraductal proliferation in the pancreas and its relationship to human and experimental carcinogenesis. Virchow's Arch [A] Pathol Anat 387: 221–233

25. Lüttges J, Reinecke-Lüthge A, Mööllmann B et al. 1999 Duct changes and K-*ras* mutations in the disease-free pancreas: analysis of type, age relation and spatial distribution. Virchow's Arch 435: 461–468

26. Andea A, Sarkar F, Adsay N V 2003 Clinicopathological correlates of pancreatic intraepithelial neoplasia: a comparative analysis of 82 cases with and 152 cases without pancreatic ductal adenocarcinoma. Mod Pathol 16: 996–1006

27. Brat D J, Lillemoe K D, Yeo C J et al. 1998 Progression of pancreatic intraductal neoplasias to infiltrating adenocarcinoma of the pancreas. Am J Surg Pathol 22: 163–169

28. Hruban R H, Adsay N V, Albores-Saavedra J et al. 2001 Pancreatic intraepithelial neoplasia. A new nomenclature and classification system for pancreatic duct lesions. Am J Surg Pathol 25: 579–586

29. Cioc A M, Ellison E C, Proca D M et al. 2002 Frozen section diagnosis of pancreatic lesions. Arch Pathol Lab Med 126: 1169–1173

30. Bätge B, Bosslet K, Sedlacek H H et al. 1986 Monoclonal antibodies against CEA-related components discriminate between pancreatic duct type carcinomas and nonneoplastic duct lesions as well as nonduct type neoplasias. Virchow's Arch [A] Pathol Anat 408: 361–374

31. Atkinson B F, Ernst C, Herlyn M et al. 1982 Gastrointestinal cancer-associated antigen in immunoperoxidase assay. Cancer Res 42: 4820–4823

32. Takeda S, Nakao A, Ichihara T et al. 1991 Serum concentration and immunohistochemical localization of SPan-1 antigen in pancreatic cancer: A comparison with CA 19-9 antigen. Hepatogastroenterology 38: 143–148

33. Pellegata N S, Sessa F, Renault B et al. 1994 K-*ras* and *p53* gene mutations in pancreatic cancer: ductal and nonductal tumors progress through different genetic lesions. Cancer Res 54: 1556–1560

34. Hruban R H, Iacobuzio-Donahue C, Wilentz R E et al. 2001 Molecular pathology of pancreatic cancer. Cancer J 7: 251–258

35. Wirtz M, Nyarangi J, Köninger J et al. 2005 Molecular basis of pancreatic carcinogenesis: which concepts may be clinically relevant? In: Domínguez-Muñoz JE (ed) Clinical pancreatology for practising gastroenterologists and surgeons. Blackwell, Malden, MA, p 351–358

36. Sipos B, Weber D, Ungefroren H et al. 2002 Vascular endothelial growth factor mediated angiogenic potential of pancreatic ductal carcinomas enhanced by hypoxia: an in vitro and in vivo study. Int J Cancer 102: 592–600

37. Adsay N V, Bandyopadhyay S, Basturk O et al. 2004 Chronic pancreatitis or pancreatic ductal adenocarcinoma? Semin Diagn Pathol 21: 268–276

38. Lüttges J, Zamboni G, Klöppel G 1999 Recommendation for the examination of pancreaticoduodenectomy specimens removed from patients with carcinoma of the exocrine pancreas. A proposal for a standardized pathological staging of pancreaticoduodenectomy specimens including a checklist. Dig Surg 16: 291–296

39. Albores-Saavedra J, Heffess C, Hruban R H et al. 1999 Association of Directors of Anatomic and Surgical Pathology. Recommendations for the reporting of pancreatic specimens containing malignant tumors. Am J Clin Pathol 111: 304–307

40. Lüttges J, Vogel I, Menke M et al. 1998 The retroperitoneal resection margin and vessel involvement are important factors determining survival after pancreaticoduodenectomy for ductal adenocarcinoma of the head of the pancreas. Virchow's Arch 433: 237–242

41. Adsay N V, Basturk O, Bonnett M et al. 2005 A proposal for a new and more practical grading scheme for pancreatic ductal adenocarcinoma. Am J Surg Pathol 29: 724–733

42. Lüttges J, Schemm S, Vogel I et al. 2000 The grade of pancreatic ductal carcinoma is an independent prognostic factor and is superior to the immunohistochemical assessment of proliferation. J Pathol 191: 154–161

43. International Union Against Cancer (UICC) 2002 TNM. Classification of malignant tumours, 6th edn. Wiley-Liss, New York

44. Carpelan-Holmström M, Nordling S, Pukkala E et al. 2005 Does anyone survive pancreatic ductal adenocarcinoma? A nationwide study re-evaluating the data of the Finnish Cancer Registry. Gut 54: 385–387

45. Trede M, Schwall G, Saeger H D 1990 Survival after pancreatoduodenectomy. 118 consecutive resections without an operative mortality. Ann Surg 211: 447–458

46. Nagakawa T, Nagamori M, Futakami F et al. 1996 Results of extensive surgery for pancreatic carcinoma. Cancer 77: 640–645

47. Conlon K C, Klimstra D S, Brennan M F 1996 Long-term survival after curative resection for pancreatic ductal adenocarcinoma. Clinicopathologic analysis of 5-year survivors. Ann Surg 223: 273–279

48. Neoptolemos J P, Stocken D D, Friess H et al. 2004 A randomized trial of chemoradiotherapy and chemotherapy after resection of pancreatic cancer. N Engl J Med 350: 1200–1210

49. Adsay N V, Pierson C, Sarkar F et al. 2001 Colloid (mucinous noncystic) carcinoma of the pancreas. Am J Surg Pathol 25: 26–42

50. Seidel G, Zaharie M, Iacobuzio-Donahue C et al. 2002 Almost all infiltrating colloid carcinomas of the pancreas and periampullary region arise from in situ papillary neoplasms. A study of 39 cases. Am J Surg Pathol 26: 56–63

51. Kardon D E, Thompson L D, Przygodzki R M et al. 2001 Adenosquamous carcinoma of the pancreas: a clinicopathologic series of 25 cases. Mod Pathol 14: 443–451

52. Bralet M P, Terris B, Brégeaud L et al. 1999 Squamous cell carcinoma and lipomatous pseudohypertrophy of the pancreas. Virchow's Arch 434: 569–572

53. Klöppel G 1984 Pancreatic, non-endocrine tumours. In: Klöppel G, Heitz PU (eds). Pancreatic pathology. Churchill Livingstone, Edinburgh, p 79–113

54. Paal E, Thompson L D R, Frommelt R A et al. 2001 A clinicpathologic and immunohistochemical study of 35 anaplastic carcinomas of the pancreas with a review of the literature. Ann Diagn Pathol 5: 129–140

55. Hoorens A, Prenzel K, Lemoine N R et al. 1998 Undifferentiated carcinoma of the pancreas: analysis of intermediate filament profile and Ki-ras mutations provides evidence of a ductal origin. J Pathol 185: 53–60

56. Westra W H, Sturm P, Drillenburg P et al. 1998 K-*ras* oncogene mutations in osteoclast-like giant cell tumors of the pancreas and liver. Genetic evidence to support origin from the duct epithelium. Am J Surg Pathol 22: 1247–1254

57. Newbould M J, Benbow E W, Sene A et al. 1992 Adenocarcinoma of the pancreas with osteoclast-like giant cells: A case report with immunocytochemistry. Pancreas 7: 611–615

58. Molberg K H, Heffess C, Delgado R et al. 1998 Undifferentiated carcinoma with osteoclast-like giant cells of the pancreas and periampullary region. Cancer 82: 1279–1287

59. Ohike N, Kosmahl M, Klöppel G 2004 Mixed acinar-endocrine carcinoma of the pancreas. A clinicopathological study and comparison with acinar-cell carcinoma. Virchow's Arch 445: 231–235

60. Permert J, Mogaki M, Andrén-Sandberg A et al. 1992 Pancreatic mixed ductal-islet tumors. Is this an entity? Int J Pancreatol 11: 23–29

61. Kosmahl M, Pauser U, Peters K et al. 2004 Cystic neoplasms of the pancreas and tumor-like lesions with cystic features: a review of 418 cases and a classification proposal. Virchow's Arch 445: 168–178

62. Sessa F, Solcia E, Capella C et al. 1994 Intraductal papillary-mucinous tumours represent a distinct group of pancreatic neoplasms: an investigation of tumour cell differentiation and K-*ras*, p53, and *c-erb*B-2 abnormalities in 26 patients. Virchow's Arch 425: 357–367

63. Santini D, Campione O, Salerno A et al. 1995 Intraductal papillary-mucinous neoplasm of the pancreas. A clinicopathologic entity. Arch Pathol Lab Med 119: 209–213

64. Nagai E, Ueki T, Chijiiwa K et al. 1995 Intraductal papillary mucinous neoplasms of the pancreas associated with so-called "mucinous ductal ectasia". Histochemical and immunohistochemical analysis of 29 cases. Am J Surg Pathol 19: 576–589

65. Paal E, Thompson L D, Przygodzki R M et al. 1999 A clinicopathologic and immunohistochemical study of 22 intraductal papillary mucinous neoplasms of the pancreas, with a review of the literature. Mod Pathol 12: 518–528

66. Adsay N V, Conlon K C, Zee S Y et al. 2002 Intraductal papillary-mucinous neoplasms of the pancreas. An analysis of in situ and invasive carcinomas in 28 patients. Cancer 94: 62–77

67. D'Angelica M, Brennan M F, Suriawinata A A et al. 2004 Intraductal papillary mucinous neoplasms of the pancreas: an analysis of clinicopathologic features and outcome. Ann Surg 239: 400–408

68. Terris B, Ponsot T, Paye F et al. 2000 Intraductal papillary mucinous tumors of the pancreas confined to secondary ducts show less aggressive pathologic features as compared with those involving the main pancreatic duct. Am J Surg Pathol 24: 1372–1377

69. Adsay N V, Adair C F, Heffess C S et al. 1996 Intraductal oncocytic papillary neoplasms of the pancreas. Am J Surg Pathol 20: 980–994

70. Furukawa T, Klöppel G, Adsay VN et al. 2005 Classification of types of intraductal papillary-mucinous neoplasm of the pancreas: a consensus study. Virchow's Arch 447: 794–799

71. Adsay N V, Merati K, Basturk O et al. 2004 Pathologically and biologically distinct types of epithelium in intraductal papillary mucinous neoplasms. Delineation of an "intestinal" pathway of carcinogenesis in the pancreas. Am J Surg Pathol 28: 839–848

72. Lüttges J, Zamboni G, Longnecker D et al. 2001 The immunohistochemical mucin expression pattern distinguishes different types of intraductal papillary mucinous neoplasms of the pancreas and determines their relationship to mucinous noncystic carcinoma and ductal adenocarcinoma. Am J Surg Pathol 25: 942–948

73. Zamboni G, Scarpa A, Bogina G et al. 1999 Mucinous cystic tumors of the pancreas. Clinicopathological features, prognosis and relationship to other mucinous cystic tumors. Am J Surg Pathol 23: 410–422

74. Hruban R H, Takaori K, Klimstra D S et al. 2004 An illustrated consensus on the classification of pancreatic intraepithelial neoplasia and intraductal papillary mucinous neoplasms. Am J Surg Pathol 28: 977–987

75. Albores-Saavedra J, Sheahan K, O'Riain C et al. 2004 Intraductal tubular adenoma, pyloric type, of the pancreas. Additional observations on a new type of pancreatic neoplasm. Am J Surg Pathol 28: 233–238

76. Tajiri T, Tate G, Inagaki T et al. 2005 Intraductal tubular neoplasms of the pancreas. Histogenesis and differentiation. Pancreas 30: 115–121

77. Nakayama Y, Inoue H, Hamada Y et al. 2005 Intraductal tubular adenoma of the pancreas, pyloric gland type. A clinicopathologic and imunohistochemical study of 6 cases. Am J Surg Pathol 29: 607–616

78. Wilentz R E, Albores-Saavedra J, Zahurak M et al. 1999 Pathologic examination accurately predicts prognosis in mucinous cystic neoplasms of the pancreas. Am J Surg Pathol 23: 1320–1327

79. Margolis R M, Jang N 1984 Zollinger–Ellison syndrome associated with pancreatic cystadenocarcinoma. N Engl J Med 311: 1380–1381

80. Garcia Rego J A, Valbuena Ruvira L, Alvarez Garcia A et al. 1991 Pancreatic mucinous cystadenocarcinoma with pseudosarcomatous mural nodules. A report of a case with immunohistochemical study. Cancer 67: 494–498

81. Wenig B M, Albores-Saavedra J, Buetow P C et al. 1997 Pancreatic mucinous cystic neoplasm with sarcomatous stroma. A report of three cases. Am J Surg Pathol 21: 70–80

82. Alpert L C, Truong L D, Bossart M I et al. 1988 Microcystic adenoma (serous cystadenoma) of the pancreas. A study of 14 cases with immunohistochemical and electron-microscopic correlation. Am J Surg Pathol 12: 251–263

83. Compagno J, Oertel J E 1978 Microcystic adenomas of the pancreas (glycogen-rich cystadenomas): a clinicopathologic study of 34 cases. Am J Clin Pathol 69: 289–298

84. Egawa N, Maillet B, Schröder S et al. 1994 Serous oligocystic and ill-demarcated adenoma of the pancreas: a variant of serous cystic adenoma. Virchow's Arch 424: 13–17

85. Lewandrowski K, Warshaw A, Compton C 1992 Macrocystic serous cystadenoma of the pancreas: a morphologic variant differing from microcystic adenoma. Hum Pathol 23: 871–875

86. Perez-Ordonez B, Naseem A, Lieberman P H et al. 1996 Solid serous adenoma of the pancreas. The solid variant of serous cystadenoma? Am J Surg Pathol 20: 1401–1405

87. Compagno J, Oertel J E 1978 Mucinous cystic neoplasms of the pancreas with overt and latent malignancy (cystadenocarcinoma and cystadenoma). A clinicopathologic study of 41 cases. Am J Clin Pathol 69: 573–580

88. Capella C, Solcia E, Klöppel G et al. 2000 Serous cystic neoplasms of the pancreas. In: Hamilton SR, Aaltonen LA (eds). Pathology and genetics. Tumours of the digestive system. WHO Classification of Tumours. IARC Press, Lyon, p 231–233

89. Kosmahl M, Wagner J, Peters K et al. 2004 Serous cystic neoplasms of the pancreas: an immunohistochemical analysis revealing alpha-inhibin, neuron-specific enolase, and MUC6 as new markers. Am J Surg Pathol 28: 339–346

90. Kosmahl M, Klöppel G 2003 Pancreatic tumours with cystic features. Cesk Patol 39: 155–162

91. George D H, Murphy F, Michalski R et al. 1989 Serous cystadenocarcinoma of the pancreas: a new entity? Am J Surg Pathol 13: 61–66

92. Compton C C 2000 Serous cystic tumors of the pancreas. Semin Diagn Pathol 17: 43–55

93. Lee W Y, Tzeng C C, Jin Y T et al. 1993 Papillary cystic tumor of the pancreas: a case indistinguishable from oncocytic carcinoma. Pancreas 8: 127–132

94. Mohr V H, Vortmeyer A O, Zhuang Z et al. 2000 Histopathology and molecular genetics of multiple cysts and microcystic (serous) adenomas of the pancreas in von Hippel-Lindau patients. Am J Pathol 157: 1615–1621

95. Yoshimi N, Sugie S, Tanaka T et al. 1992 A rare case of serous cystadenocarcinoma of the pancreas. Cancer 69: 2449–2453

96. Klimstra D S, Heffess C S, Oertel J E et al. 1992 Acinar cell carcinoma of the pancreas: a clinicopathologic study of 28 cases. Am J Surg Pathol 16: 815–837

97. Holen K D, Klimstra D S, Hummer A et al. 2002 Clinical characteristics and outcomes from an institutional series of acinar cell carcinomas of the pancreas and related tumors. J Clin Oncol 20: 4673–4678

98. Hoorens A, Lemoine N R, McLellan E et al. 1993 Pancreatic acinar cell carcinoma. An analysis of cell lineage markers, p53 expression, and Ki-ras mutation. Am J Pathol 143: 685–698

99. Abraham S C, Wu T T, Hruban R H et al. 2002 Genetic and immunohistochemical analysis of pancreatic acinar cell carcinoma. Frequent allelic loss on chromosome 11p and alterations in the APC/β-catenin pathway. Am J Pathol 160: 953–962

100. Klimstra D S, Rosai J, Heffess C S 1994 Mixed acinar-endocrine carcinomas of the pancreas. Am J Surg Pathol 18: 765–778

101. Schron D S, Mendelsohn G 1984 Pancreatic carcinoma with duct, endocrine, and acinar differentiation. A histologic, immunocytochemical, and ultrastructural study. Cancer 54: 1766–1770

102. Stamm B, Burger H, Hollinger A 1987 Acinar cell cystadenocarcinoma of the pancreas. Cancer 60: 2542–2547

103. Zamboni G, Terris B, Scarpa A et al. 2002 Acinar cell cystadenoma of the pancreas. A new entity? Am J Surg Pathol 26: 698–704

104. Kishi K, Nakamura K, Yoshimori M et al. 1992 Morphology and pathological significance of focal acinar cell dysplasia of the human pancreas. Pancreas 7: 177–182

105. Klimstra D S, Wenig B M, Adair C F et al. 1995 Pancreatoblastoma. A clinicopathologic study and review of the literature. Am J Surg Pathol 19: 1371–1389

106. Hoorens A, Gebhard F, Kraft K et al. 1994 Pancreatoblastoma in an adult: its separation from acinar cell carcinoma. Virchow's Arch 424: 485–490

107. Dunn J L, Longnecker D S 1995 Pancreatoblastoma in an older adult. Arch Pathol Lab Med 119: 547–551

108. Abraham S C, Wu T T, Klimstra D S et al. 2001 Distinctive molecular genetic alterations in sporadic and familial adenomatous polyposis-associated pancreatoblastomas. Frequent alterations in the APC/β-catenin pathway and chromosome 11p. Am J Pathol 159: 1619–1627

109. Klöppel G, Maurer R, Hofmann E et al. 1991 Solid-cystic (papillary-cystic) tumours within and outside the pancreas in men: report of two patients. Virchow's Arch [A] Pathol Anat 418: 179–183

110. Klimstra D S, Wenig B M, Heffess C S 2000 Solid-pseudopapillary tumor of the pancreas: A typically cystic carcinoma of low malignant potential. Semin Diagn Pathol 17: 66–80

111. Stömmer P, Kraus J, Stolte M et al. 1991 Solid and cystic pancreatic tumors. Clinical, histochemical, and electron microscopic features in ten cases. Cancer 67: 1635–1641

112. Pettinato G, Manivel J C, Ravetto C et al. 1992 Papillary cystic tumor of the pancreas. A clinicopathologic study of 20 cases with cytologic, immunohistochemical, ultrastructural, and flow cytometric observations, and a review of the literature. Am J Clin Pathol 98: 478–488

113. Zamboni G, Bonetti F, Scarpa A et al. 1993 Expression of progesterone receptors in solid-cystic tumour of the pancreas: a clinicopathological and immunohistochemical study of ten cases. Virchow's Arch [A] Pathol Anat 423: 425–431

114. Kosmahl M, Seada L S, Janig U et al. 2000. Solid-pseudopapillary tumour of the pancreas: its origin revisited. Virchow's Arch 436: 473–480

115. Abraham S C, Klimstra D S, Wilentz R E et al. 2002 Solid-pseudopapillary tumors of the pancreas are genetically distinct from pancreatic ductal adenocarcinomas and almost always harbor β-catenin mutations. Am J Pathol 160: 1361–1369

116. Tanaka Y, Kato K, Notohara K et al. 2001 Frequent β-catenin mutation and cytoplasmic/nuclear accumulation in pancreatic solid-pseudopapillary neoplasm. Cancer Res 61: 8401–8404

117. Grant L D, Lauwers G Y, Meloni A M et al. 1996 Unbalanced chromosomal translocation, der(17)t(13;17)(q14;p11) in a solid and cystic papillary epithelial neoplasm of the pancreas. Am J Surg Pathol 20: 339–345

118. Tang L H, Aydin H, Brennan M F et al. 2005 Clinically aggressive solid pseudopapillary tumors of the pancreas. A report of two cases with components of undifferentiated carcinoma and a comparative clinicopathologic analysis of 34 conventional cases. Am J Surg Pathol 29: 512–519

119. Goggins M, Offerhaus G J, Hilgers W et al. 1998 Pancreatic adenocarcinomas with DNA replication errors (RER+) are associated with wild-type K-ras and characteristic histopathology. Poor differentiation, a syncytial growth pattern, and pushing borders suggest RER+. Am J Pathol 152: 1501–1507

120. Wilentz R E, Goggins M, Redston M et al. 2000 Genetic, immunohistochemical, and clinical features of medullary carcinoma of the pancreas: A newly described and characterized entity. Am J Pathol 156: 1641–1651

121. Kekis P B, Murtin C, Künzli B M et al. 2004 Epstein–Barr virus-associated lymphoepithelial carcinoma in the pancreas. Pancreas 28: 98–102

122. Bondeson L, Bondeson A G, Grimelius L et al. 1990 Oncocytic tumor of the pancreas. Report of a case with aspiration cytology. Acta Cytol 34: 425–428

123. Zerbi A, De Nardi P, Braga M et al. 1993 An oncocytic carcinoma of the pancreas with pulmonary and subcutaneous metastases. Pancreas 8: 116–119

124. Marucci G, Betts C M, Liguori L et al. 2005 Basaloid carcinoma of the pancreas. Virchow's Arch 446: 322–324

125. Ray B, New N E, Wedgwood K R 2005 Clear cell carcinoma of exocrine pancreas: a rare tumor with an unusual presentation. Pancreas 30: 184–185

126. Lonardo F, Cubilla A L, Klimstra D S 1996 Microadenocarcinoma of the pancreas – Morphologic pattern or pathologic entity? Am J Surg Pathol 20: 1385–1393

127. Lack E E, Cassady J R, Levey R et al. 1983 Tumors of the exocrine pancreas in children and adolescents. A clinical and pathologic study of eight cases. Am J Surg Pathol 7: 319–327

128. Klöppel G, Kosmahl M, Jänig U et al. 2004 Pancreatoblastoma: one of the rarest among the rare pancreatic neoplasms. Pancreatology 4: 441–453

129. Shorter N A, Glick R D, Klimstra D S et al. 2002 Malignant pancreatic tumors in childhood and adolescence: the Memorial Sloan-Kettering experience, 1967 to present. J Pediatr Surg 37: 887–892

130. Movahedi-Lankarani S, Hruban R H, Westra W H et al. 2002 Primitive neuroectodermal tumors of the pancreas. A report of seven cases of a rare neoplasm. Am J Surg Pathol 26: 1040–1047

131. Lüttges J, Pierré E, Zamboni G et al. 1997 Maligne nicht-epitheliale Tumoren des Pankreas. Pathologe 18: 233–237

132. de Alava E, Torramade J, Vazquez J J 1993 Leiomyosarcoma of the pancreas. Virchow's Arch [A] Pathol Anat 422: 419–422

133. Ishikawa O, Matsui Y, Aoki Y et al. 1981 Leiomyosarcoma of the pancreas. Report of a case and review of the literature. Am J Surg Pathol 5: 597–602

134. Zamboni G, Pea M, Martignoni G et al. 1996 Clear cell "sugar" tumor of the pancreas. A novel member of the family of lesions characterized by the presence of perivascular epithelioid cells. Am J Surg Pathol 20: 722–730

135. Ramuz O, Lelong B, Giovannini M et al. 2005 "Sugar" tumor of the pancreas: a rare entity that is diagnosable on preoperative fine-needle biopsies. Virchow's Arch 446: 555–559

136. Bismar T A, Basturk O, Gerald W L et al. 2004 Desmoplastic small cell tumor in the pancreas. Am J Surg Pathol 28: 808–812

137. Lüttges J, Mentzel T, Hübner G et al. 1999 Solitary fibrous tumour of the pancreas: a new member of the small group of mesenchymal pancreatic tumours. Virchow's Arch 435:37–42

138. Daum O, Klecka J, Ferda J et al. 2005 Gastrointestinal stromal tumor of the pancreas: case report with documentation of KIT gene mutation. Virchow's Arch 446: 470–472

139. Ezzat A, Jamshed A, Khafaga Y et al. 1996 Primary pancreatic non-Hodgkin's lymphomas. J Clin Gastroenterol 23: 109–112

140. Volmar K E, Routbort M J, Jones C K et al. 2004 Primary pancreatic lymphoma evaluated by fine-needle aspiration: findings in 14 cases. Am J Clin Pathol 121: 898–903

141. Thompson L D R, Heffess C S 2000 Renal cell carcinoma to the pancreas in surgical pathology material. A clinicopathologic study of 21 cases with a review of the literature. Cancer 89: 1076–1088

142. Adsay N V, Andea A, Basturk O et al. 2004 Secondary tumors of the pancreas: an analysis of a surgical and autopsy database and review of the literature. Virchow's Arch 444: 527–535

143. Pauser U, Kosmahl M, Kruslin B et al. 2005 Pancreatic solid and cystic hamartoma in adults: characterization of a new tumorous lesion. Am J Surg Pathol 29: 797–800

144. Adsay N V, Basturk O, Klimstra D S et al. 2004 Pancreatic pseudotumors: non-neoplastic solid lesions of the pancreas that clinically mimic pancreas cancer. Semin Diagn Pathol 21: 260–267

145. Notohara K, Burgart L J, Yadav D et al. 2003 Idiopathic chronic pancreatitis with periductal lymphoplasmacytic infiltration: clinicopathologic features of 35 cases. Am J Surg Pathol 27: 1119–1127

146. Klimstra D S, Adsay N V 2004 Lymphoplasmacytic sclerosing (autoimmune) pancreatitis. Semin Diagn Pathol 21: 237–246

147. Adsay N V, Zamboni G 2004 Paraduodenal pancreatitis: A clinico-pathologically distinct entity unifying "cystic dystrophy of heterotopic pancreas", "para-duodenal wall cyst", and "groove pancreatitis". Semin Diagn Pathol 21: 247–254

148. Kroft S H, Stryker S J, Winter J N et al. 1995 Inflammatory pseudotumor of the pancreas. Int J Pancreatol 18: 277–283

149. Klöppel G, Lüttges J, Löhr M et al. 2003 Autoimmune pancreatitis: pathological, clinical, and immunological features. Pancreas 27: 14–19

150. Zamboni G, Lüttges J, Capelli P et al. 2004 Histopathological features of diagnostic and clinical relevance in autoimmune pancreatitis: a study on 53 resection specimens and 9 biopsy specimens. Virchow's Arch 445: 552–563

151. Fléjou J F, Potet F, Molas G et al. 1993 Cystic dystrophy of the gastric and duodenal wall developing in heterotopic pancreas: an unrecognized entity. Gut 34: 343–347

152. Pauser U, da Silva M T S, Placke J et al. 2005 Cellular hamartoma resembling gastrointestinal stromal tumor: a solid tumor of the pancreas expressing c-kit (CD117). Mod Pathol 18: 1211–1216

153. Nakashiro H, Tokunaga O, Watanabe T et al. 1991 Localized lymphoid hyperplasia (pseudolymphoma) of the pancreas presenting with obstructive jaundice. Hum Pathol 22: 724–726

154. Klöppel G 2000 Pseudocysts and other non-neoplastic cysts of the pancreas. Semin Diagn Pathol 17: 7–15

155. Klöppel G 2004 Chronic pancreatitis of alcoholic and nonalcoholic origin. Semin Diagn Pathol 21: 227–236

156. Iacono C, Cracco N, Zamboni G et al. 1996 Lymphoepithelial cyst of the pancreas. Report of two cases and review of the literature. Int J Pancreatol 19: 71–76

157. Adsay N V, Hasteh F, Cheng J D et al. 2002 Lymphoepithelial cysts of the pancreas: a report of 12 cases and a review of the literature. Mod Pathol 15: 492–501

Tumors of the urinary tract

John N. Eble   Robert H. Young

12

Tumors of the kidney

Since the time three decades ago when the two diagnoses of renal cell carcinoma and Wilms' tumor broadly encompassed almost all renal neoplasms, the classification of tumors of the kidney has grown complex.[1] In the following sections on epithelial tumors, mesenchymal tumors, and tumors of children, the diagnostic and prognostic aspects of renal neoplasia are presented with emphasis on the gross pathology and histologic examination, including recently recognized and rare entities. Tumors of the renal pelvis and ureter are discussed in their own section following those of the renal parenchyma.

Epithelial tumors of the kidney

Papillary adenoma

Notwithstanding the historical problems and success of surgery, it is our view that there are data which support the definition of a set of criteria within which the diagnosis of papillary adenoma is safe and justified (Table 12.1). The first criterion indicates that the microscopic morphology of papillary adenoma resembles that of papillary renal cell carcinoma, including lesions with both type 1 and type 2 characteristics (see p. 495).[2] The second criterion defines a group of tumors which appear to be limited in growth potential. This includes more than 95 percent of all papillary neoplasms of the renal tubules.[3] Larger ones are more worrisome because they have

Table 12.1	Diagnostic criteria for papillary adenoma of the kidney

Papillary or tubulopapillary architecture

Diameter ≤5 mm

Does not histologically resemble clear cell, chromophobe, or collecting duct renal cell carcinomas

demonstrated a greater capacity for growth, and may have the potential for metastasis. The third criterion reflects the fact that there is no convincing evidence that very small tumors of those other cell types are not small carcinomas. As early as 1938, Bell[4] recognized that the distinction between papillary neoplasms and those histologically resembling clinically apparent clear cell renal cell carcinoma was important and that among the latter, "the size of the tumor is not a certain criterion as to its malignancy". Subsequent investigations and case reports of small clear cell renal cell carcinomas with metastases have reinforced this conclusion.[5,6] Similar criteria for papillary adenoma were accepted at consensus conferences in Heidelberg, Germany and Rochester, Minnesota and by the most recent WHO Consensus Conference.[1,7]

The frequency of small epithelial tumors in the renal cortex has ranged up to 37 percent in autopsy patients, depending upon the patient population and study methods.[8–12] The frequency of small papillary tumors increases with age to approximately 40 percent of the population over age 65.

Similar lesions frequently develop in patients on long-term hemodialysis and have been reported in up to 33 percent of patients with acquired renal cystic disease.[13] The association between arteriosclerotic renal vascular disease and papillary adenomas has long been recognized.[4] Budin and McDonnell[14] studied autopsy material and found that the prevalence of papillary adenomas not only was much increased in kidneys with arteriosclerotic renal vascular disease, but that this was independent of age. Xipell[9] found a strong correlation between tobacco smoking and the presence of papillary adenomas; this also was observed by Bennington.[15]

That kidneys bearing renal cell carcinoma or oncocytoma are more likely to contain papillary adenomas than normal kidneys has also long been recognized.[16] Occasionally, more than one adenoma will be present adjacent to the carcinoma or oncocytoma, as if some local factor were promoting the development of the adenomas.

Macroscopic appearances Papillary adenomas appear to the naked eye as well circumscribed, yellow to grayish white nodules in the renal cortex. Most occur just below the renal capsule but ones that are invisible from the cortical surface are fairly common. The smallest examples usually are spherical, but larger lesions sometimes are roughly conical with a wedge-shaped appearance in sections cut at right angles to the cortical surface. An association with scars in the renal cortex has been asserted but is controversial.[10,14] In most patients, adenomas are solitary,[10] but occasionally, papillary adenomas are multiple and bilateral, rarely miliary; this latter condition has been called "renal adenomatosis",[17] analogous to renal oncocytomatosis.[18,19]

Histologic appearances Papillary adenomas have tubular, papillary, or tubulopapillary architectures (Fig. 12.1), often corresponding closely to the chromophil-basophil cell type described by Thoenes et al.[20,21] Some are surrounded by a thin fibrous pseudocapsule while others have none. The cells have round to oval nuclei with chromatin which ranges from stippled to clumped, and inconspicuous nucleoli. Nuclear grooves may be present. Mitotic figures usually are absent. In most papillary adenomas, the cytoplasm is scant and pale, amphophilic to basophilic. Occasionally, it is slightly more voluminous and

appears clear or filled with minute vacuoles. Less frequently, the cytoplasm is voluminous and eosinophilic, resembling type 2 papillary renal cell carcinoma.[2] Psammoma bodies often are present, as are foamy macrophages.

Immunohistochemistry, ultrastructure, and special studies Cohen et al.[22] found that almost all papillary adenomas react with antibodies to epithelial membrane antigen and low-molecular-weight cytokeratin, while a majority react with antibody to high-molecular-weight cytokeratin. Neuron-specific enolase and alpha-1-antitrypsin occasionally were present and carcinoembryonic antigen could not be detected.[22] Hiasa et al.[11] studied 65 adenomas ranging from 1 to 5 mm in diameter and found 52 to be positive for peanut agglutinin and epithelial membrane antigen and negative for both Leu M1 and *Lotus tetragonolobus* lectin; a pattern similar to that in the normal distal tubule. Thirteen had the opposite pattern and were similar to the lining cells of the normal proximal tubule.[11]

Renal oncocytoma

Renal oncocytomas are neoplasms of the renal cortex which often are discovered incidentally by radiologic examination of the kidneys for other reasons, but they may also present as a palpable mass or with hematuria.[23,24] In 1976, Klein & Valensi[25] drew attention to renal oncocytoma as a renal tumor previously classified as renal cell carcinoma but distinguishable from it by its pathologic features and benign course. There is a 2:1 preponderance of males to females and almost all cases have occurred in adults, mostly from age 50 to 80. Resection of the tumor is curative. A striking spoke and wheel appearance on radiography was at first thought to be diagnostic of oncocytoma, but greater experience has indicated that this is not specific because renal cell carcinomas may have similar appearances. The tumor cannot reliably be distinguished preoperatively from renal cell carcinoma by imaging or biopsy. Thus, radical nephrectomy is the usual operation. However, a number of patients have had multicentric or bilateral tumors[26] and conservative operations have been successful when performed for these reasons.

Macroscopic appearances The most characteristic feature of renal oncocytoma is its mahogany brown color (Fig. 12.2), which contrasts with the bright yellow color typical of clear cell renal cell carcinomas. Many oncocytomas have central zones of whitish stroma which may connect with the periphery (Fig. 12.3), giving the subcapsular surface a bosselated contour. Occasional tumors exhibit foci of hemorrhage but necrosis is rare, and often can be related to extrinsic factors. Generally, the presence of gross necrosis or hemorrhage suggests extra caution in making the diagnosis of oncocytoma. Bilaterality or unilateral multicentricity occurs in approximately 4 percent of cases and such occurrences are more frequent than with renal cell carcinoma. Rarely, there may be large numbers of small oncocytomas in the cortices of both kidneys, a condition which has been termed *oncocytomatosis* or *oncocytosis*.[18,27]

Histologic appearances The cells usually are arranged either in diffuse sheets or as cellular islands in a background of loose edematous connective tissue (Fig. 12.4). Tubules, often mildly dilated, also are common. Rarely, the groups of cells contain

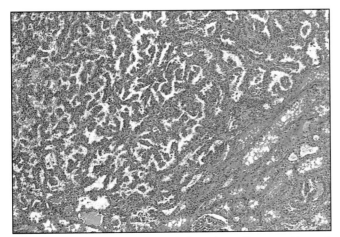

Fig. 12.1 • Papillary adenoma composed of complex papillae covered by small cells.

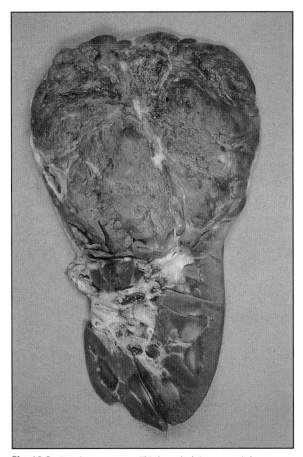

Fig. 12.2 • Renal oncocytoma. This large bulging tumor is homogeneously mahogany brown.

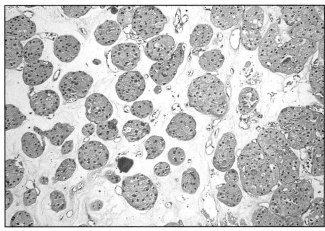

Fig. 12.4 • Renal oncocytoma. Cells with abundant eosinophilic cytoplasm are clustered in islands within an edematous stroma.

hyaline deposits of type IV collagen, giving a cylindromatous appearance.[28] In sections stained with hematoxylin and eosin, the cytoplasm is intensely eosinophilic and finely granular. While the cytoplasmic volume ranges from moderate to abundant, its staining qualities are the same. The nuclei are mainly round with small clumps of chromatin and nucleoli which may be visible with a 10× microscope objective.[29] Occasional bizarre, enlarged nuclei, sometimes containing cytoplasmic invaginations, may be present (Fig. 12.5). Mitotic figures are absent or very rare in oncocytomas. Since they are benign, oncocytomas are not graded. By electron microscopy, the cytoplasm is seen to be filled with mitochondria and other organelles are scant (Fig. 12.6). Microvilli are sparse and completely formed brush borders usually are not present.[30]

Extension into small veins is seen microscopically in a little more than 5 percent of cases and appears to have no adverse prognostic significance. Small extensions into perirenal fat are seen in almost 10 percent of cases and also appear to have no adverse effect.

Differential diagnosis The principal consideration is the eosinophilic variant of chromophobe renal cell carcinoma. In most

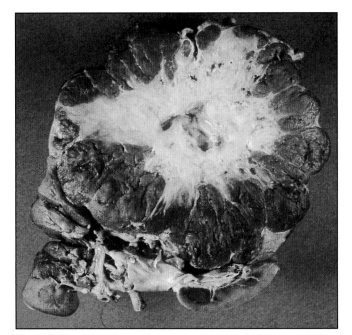

Fig. 12.3 • Renal oncocytoma. These tumors, especially the larger ones, often have central areas of whitish stroma which may undergo cavitary degeneration.

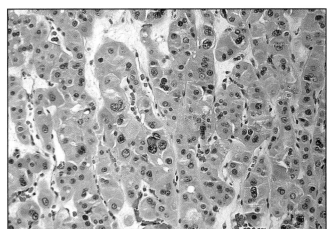

Fig. 12.5 • Renal oncocytoma. Foci in which there are enlarged, degenerate-appearing nuclei, sometimes with cytoplasmic invaginations, are seen in some oncocytomas.

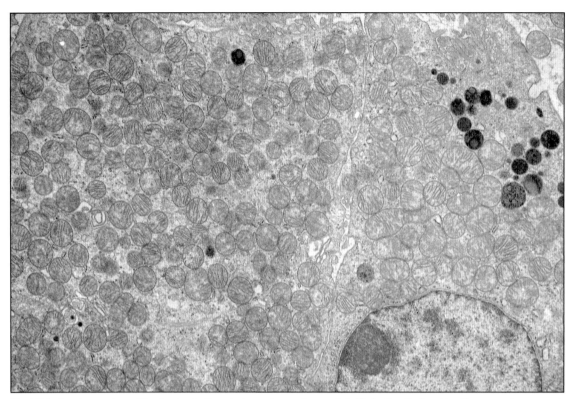

Fig. 12.6 • Renal oncocytoma. Ultrastructurally, the cytoplasm of oncocytoma cells is filled with mitochondria; other organelles are scanty.

cases, strict adherence to the criteria listed in Table 12.2 will enable this distinction. Immunohistochemistry can be helpful since oncocytomas typically express cytokeratin 7 in scattered single cells or small clusters of cells, while chromophobe renal cell carcinomas usually express cytokeratin 7 in almost every cell, with accentuation of the signal at the cell membrane.[31]

Table 12.2	Diagnostic features of renal oncocytoma

Features of renal oncocytoma

Finely granular strongly eosinophilic cytoplasm
Sheet, insular, or tubulocystic architectural patterns
Mitochondria filling cytoplasm with other organelles and microvilli sparse

Features unusual in renal oncocytoma

Microscopic vascular invasion
Microscopic extension into perirenal fat

Features rare or impermissible in renal oncocytoma

Mitotic figures
Papillary architecture
Clear or spindle cells
Positive colloidal iron stain or chromophobe-type vesicles seen by electron microscopy
Gross vascular invasion
Gross extension into perirenal fat

Metanephric adenoma and metanephric adenofibroma

In 1980, Pages and Granier[32] drew attention to a previously unrecognized renal neoplasm which they called "néphrome néphronogene" (nephronogenic nephroma) and which they considered to be a purely epithelial neoplasm arising from persistent blastema. Since that time, more than 100 cases have been described individually or in aggregated studies and the name metanephric adenoma has become accepted.[1,21]

In 1992, Hennigar and Beckwith[33] described 5 cases of a composite neoplasm in which an epithelial component identical to metanephric adenoma was combined with a proliferation of spindle cells; they proposed the name nephrogenic adenofibroma for this tumor. However, Beckwith now favors the name metanephric adenofibroma for these tumors to emphasize their close relationship with metanephric adenoma.

Metanephric adenoma occurs at all ages, most commonly in the fifth and sixth decades and there is a 2:1 female preponderance.[34] Metanephric adenoma is the most common epithelial tumor found in the kidneys of children.[35] Approximately 50 percent are incidental findings, while others present with polycythemia, abdominal or flank pain, mass, or hematuria. Often the polycythemia has resolved after the tumor was removed. Cases reported to date have neither recurred nor metastasized. Four of the 50 patients reported by Davis et al.[34] also had renal cell carcinoma.

Patients with metanephric adenofibroma have ranged in age from 13 months to 36 years (median = 28 months).[36] While the number of cases is small, there does not appear to be any gender predominance. More than 50 percent of the patients have had polycythemia. Other symptoms of metanephric adenofibroma have included hematuria[33] and hypertension.[33] Some have been incidental findings. Three of the five cases reported by Hennigar and Beckwith[33] had separate small papillary epithelial tumors near the renal pelvis which they considered low-grade collecting duct carcinomas.

Macroscopic appearances Metanephric adenomas have ranged widely in size with the largest being 150 mm in diameter; most have been 30 to 60 mm in diameter.[34] Davis et al.[34] found no instance of bilaterality and only two instances of unilateral multifocality in 50 patients. The tumors are typically well circumscribed but, in most instances, are not encapsulated. A thin and discontinuous pseudocapsule is more common than a substantial one. The cut surfaces vary from gray to tan to yellow and may be soft or firm. Calcification is present in approximately 20 percent and a few are densely calcified. Small cysts are present in about 10 percent of tumors and a unique example was entirely cystic.[34] Foci of hemorrhage and necrosis are common.[34,37] Metanephric adenofibromas are typically solitary, firm, bosselated masses without capsules and with indistinct borders.[33,36] The cut surfaces range from gray to tan to yellow and solid with only occasional cysts in some of the tumors.

Histologic appearances Histologically, metanephric adenoma is typically a highly cellular tumor composed of tightly packed small, uniform, round acini (Fig. 12.7). Since the acini and their lumens are so small, at low magnification this pattern may be mistaken for a solid sheet of cells. Long branching and angulated tubular structures also are common. The stroma ranges from inconspicuous to a loose paucicellular edematous stroma. Hyalinized scar or focal osseous metaplasia of the stroma are present in 10–20 percent of tumors.[34] Approximately 50 percent of tumors contain papillary structures, usually consisting of minute cysts into which have grown short blunt papillae reminiscent of immature glomeruli. In most of these papillae no blood vessel is visible. Psammoma bodies are common and may be numerous. The junction with the kidney is usually abrupt and lacks a pseudocapsule.

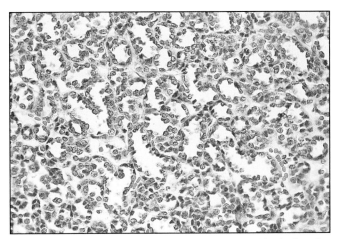

Fig. 12.7 • Metanephric adenoma. Small tubules are lined by bland cells with scant cytoplasm.

The cells of metanephric adenoma have small, uniform nuclei with absent or inconspicuous nucleoli. The nuclei are only slightly larger than lymphocytes and are round or oval and have delicate chromatin. The cytoplasm is scant and pale or light pink. Mitotic figures are absent or rare.

Metanephric adenofibroma is a composite tumor in which nodules of epithelium identical to metanephric adenoma are embedded in sheets of moderately cellular spindle cells. The spindle cell component consists of fibroblast-like cells (Fig. 12.8).[33,36] Their cytoplasm is eosinophilic but pale and the nuclei are oval or fusiform. Nucleoli are inconspicuous and mitotic figures are absent or rare. Variable amounts of hyalinization and myxoid change are present. The relative amounts of the spindle cell and epithelial components vary from predominance of spindle cells to a minor component of spindle cells. The border of the tumor with the kidney is typically irregular and the spindle cell component may entrap renal structures as it advances. The epithelial component consists of small acini, tubules and papillary structures, as described above in metanephric adenoma. Psammoma bodies are common and may be numerous. Neither metanephric

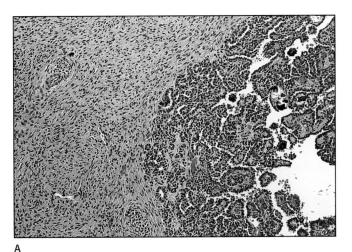

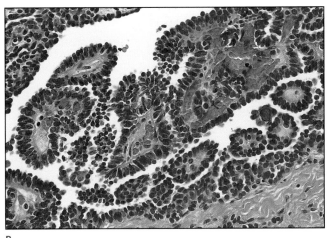

A   B

Fig. 12.8 • Metanephric adenofibroma. Abrupt transition is evident between the fibroma component, consisting of spindle cells with moderate cellularity, and an epithelial nodule with psammoma bodies (**A**). The epithelial component consists of papillary fronds covered by small, uniform cuboidal or columnar cells (**B**). (Courtesy of Dr. B. Beckwith and the National Wilms' Tumor Study Pathology Center.)

adenoma nor metanephric adenofibroma contains blastema, nor is either associated with nephrogenic rests. Lesions composed only of the stromal component, often with a nodular growth pattern and focally more epithelioid morphology, have been termed metanephric stromal tumors.[38]

Immunohistochemistry and lectin histochemistry have given varied results in different laboratories and consequently do not play a large role in the differential diagnosis of metanephric adenoma.[21]

Differential diagnosis At first inspection, metanephric adenoma brings Wilms' tumor to mind because of the dense array of small blue cells and epithelial differentiation. However, the nuclei of metanephric adenoma are smaller and lack the elongation and tapered ends often present in the nuclei of epithelial cells in Wilms' tumor. Further, mitotic figures are rare in metanephric adenoma and blastema is not present. The fibromatous component of metanephric adenofibroma could be mistaken for the stroma of Wilms' tumor but, cytologically, it is benign and its lacks the variety of differentiation often seen in the stroma of Wilms' tumor.

The other major consideration is papillary renal cell carcinoma, type 1. The small cytoplasmic volume, papillary structures, and psammoma bodies bring this to mind. However, most metanephric adenomas are composed mainly of arrays of fairly uniform structures resembling renal tubules in cross-section. This architecture is not typical of papillary renal cell carcinoma. Additionally, metanephric adenomas often have long, pointed, branching channels lined by epithelial cells. These are not found in papillary renal cell carcinoma, nor in Wilms' tumor. The edema of papillary cores and collections of stromal foam cells, which are common in papillary renal cell carcinoma, are not typical of metanephric adenoma. Metanephric adenomas frequently express WT1 which can help to differentiate them from papillary renal cell neoplasms, as can fluorescent in situ hybridization for the chromosomes commonly gained by papillary renal cell neoplasms.[39,40]

Renal cell carcinoma

Presently, renal cell carcinoma is recognized to be a family of carcinomas which arise from the epithelium of the renal tubules.[1] The carcinomas have distinct morphologic features and arise through different constellations of genetic lesions.[7,41–43] The current classification of renal cell carcinoma is presented in Table 12.3.

Since the recognition that renal cell carcinoma comprises a family of diseases arising through different genetic lesions is relatively new, almost all of the clinical and epidemiologic information presently available comes from studies in which all types of renal cell carcinoma were lumped together. This applies to the following generalizations. Renal cell carcinoma is almost exclusively a cancer of adults and approximately 30 000 new cases are diagnosed each year in the USA and its frequency is increasing.[44] Its incidence increases with each decade of life until the sixth and it is two to three times more common in males than in females.[45] Renal cell carcinoma is rare in the first two decades of life, comprising only 2 percent of pediatric renal tumors.[35] Although obesity,[46] smoking,[47] and exposure to industrial chemicals[48] have been implicated as risk factors in the genesis of renal cell carcinomas, in most

Table 12.3	Classification of renal cell neoplasms
Benign	
Papillary adenoma	
Oncocytoma	
Malignant	
Clear cell renal cell carcinoma	
Papillary renal cell carcinoma	
• type 1	
• type 2	
Chromophobe renal cell carcinoma	
• classic	
• eosinophilic	
Collecting duct carcinoma	
• renal medullary carcinoma	
Xp11 translocation carcinomas	
Carcinoma associated with neuroblastoma	
Mucinous tubular and spindle cell carcinoma	
Renal cell carcinoma, unclassified	

cases the pathogenesis is unclear. An association with von Hippel-Lindau disease is seen in occasional cases and from 33 percent to 50 percent of these patients develop renal cell carcinoma.[49,50] Associations also exist with tuberous sclerosis[51,52] and autosomal dominant polycystic kidney disease.[53–55] Acquired renal cystic disease arising in patients with chronic renal failure also is strongly associated with renal cell carcinoma.[56–58] While the localizing findings of hematuria, pain, and a mass in the flank are considered the classic triad of presenting symptoms, many patients with renal cell carcinoma lack any of these and present with systemic symptoms[59] such as fever, malaise, or anemia.[60,61] Paraneoplastic syndromes of hypercalcemia,[62] erythrocytosis,[63] hypertension,[64] and amyloidosis[65] have occasionally been associated with renal cell carcinoma.[63,66,67] Renal cell carcinoma also is notorious for presenting as metastatic carcinoma of unknown primary, sometimes in unusual sites. Multicentricity occurs within the same kidney in from 7 to 13 percent of cases[68] and tumors are present in both kidneys in approximately 1 percent of patients.[69]

The clinical course of renal cell carcinoma is notoriously unpredictable with well-documented cases of spontaneous regression of metastases.[70–72] Recurrences 10 years or more after nephrectomy occur in more than 10 percent of patients who survive that long.[73] There is some evidence that resection of solitary metastases improves survival,[74] while the presence of multiple metastases indicates a worse prognosis.[75] However, the resistance of renal cell carcinoma to radiation and chemotherapy gives most patients with remote metastases extremely poor prognoses.[76] Metastases to bone occur frequently and more than a third of these are to the scapula.[77]

Clear cell renal cell carcinoma

Approximately two-thirds to three-quarters of all renal cell carcinomas are clear cell renal cell carcinoma. This name is given to these tumors because most of them are composed wholly or partially of cells with abundant clear cytoplasm. However, "clear cell renal cell carcinoma" is merely a name, and many of these carcinomas have extensive areas in which the cytoplasm is eosinophilic, and rare examples are composed entirely of cells with eosinophilic cytoplasm.

Clear cell renal cell carcinomas are characterized by loss of genetic material on chromosome 3p. The loss ranges from loss of the whole chromosome to loss of function through hypermethylation.[78–80] Other genetic abnormalities are common and there is some evidence that alterations on chromosomes 14, 8 and 9 affect prognosis.[81,82]

Overall, clear cell renal cell carcinoma has a somewhat worse prognosis than the other common types of renal cell carcinoma.[83,84] Clear cell renal cell carcinoma is resistant to present regimens of chemotherapy and radiation therapy. Immunotherapy has also been disappointing. Since surgery is the main treatment, stage is the principal determinant of prognosis.[85,86] Within individual stage groups, grade adds to the prognostic predictive power. Grading is discussed below.

Macroscopic appearances Clear cell renal cell carcinomas are typically globular masses which may arise anywhere in the renal cortex (Fig. 12.9) and often protrude beyond the normal contour of the kidney. However, they occasionally grow inward or are diffusely infiltrative. The cut surface is usually variegated (Fig. 12.10), being composed of soft bright yellow parenchyma with areas of grayish edematous stroma, hemorrhage, necrosis, and cysts. The cysts are filled with clear straw-colored fluid or with hemorrhage. Clear cell renal cell carcinoma may invade the renal venous system, occasionally filling the renal vein and extending into the vena cava or even the right atrium. Approximately 5 percent of clear cell renal cell carcinomas have areas of sarcomatoid change. These tend to appear grossly as firm solid whitish tissue (Fig. 12.11).

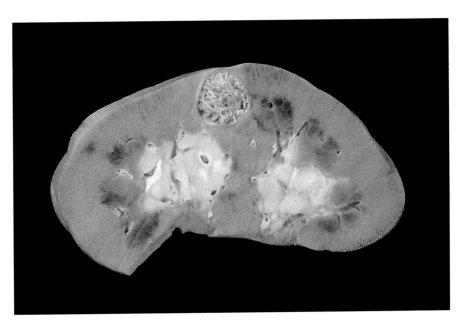

Fig. 12.9 • Clear cell renal cell carcinoma. This 1 cm tumor is yellow, spheroidal, and well circumscribed.

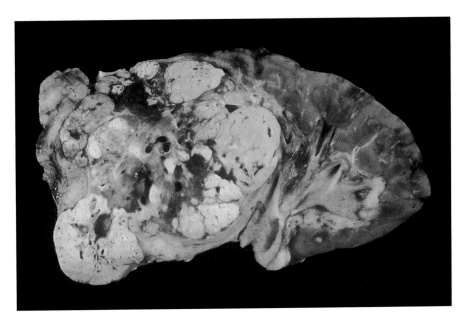

Fig. 12.10 • Clear cell renal cell carcinoma. This large, bulging tumor shows the typical variegation of color, from yellow to tan and brown with dark areas of hemorrhage and whitish areas of stroma.

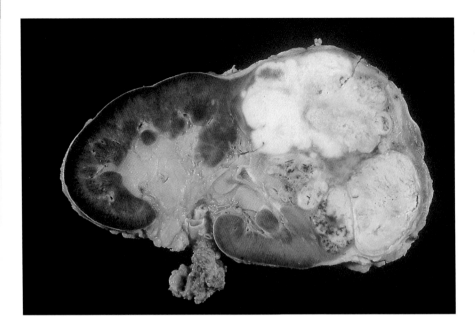

Fig. 12.11 • Clear cell renal cell carcinoma. In this tumor, the white areas were histologically sarcomatoid.

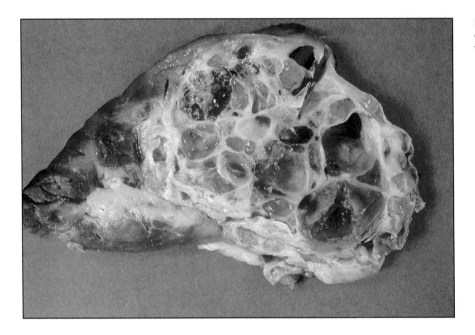

Fig. 12.12 • Multilocular cystic renal cell carcinoma. Numerous thin-walled locules of variable size make up this tumor.

Rarely, cystic masses (Fig. 12.12) grossly resembling cystic nephroma and meeting the criteria listed in Table 12.4 contain aggregates of clear epithelial cells within their septa.[87] These cells almost always have small dark-staining nuclei and are histologically identical to nuclear grade 1 clear cell renal cell carcinoma. Although there is little or no evidence of malignant behavior by such tumors, they should be diagnosed, at least by current convention, as "multilocular cystic clear cell renal cell carcinoma".

Histologic appearances Clear cell renal cell carcinomas typically have a network of small blood vessels which invest alveolar clusters of carcinoma cells (Fig. 12.13). These blood vessels are very delicate and of a uniform small caliber. This vascular pattern is of great help in diagnosis since it is particular to clear cell renal cell carcinoma and not found in other types of renal cell carcinoma.

Table 12.4	Criteria of Eble and Bonsib for multilocular cystic renal cell carcinoma[87]

Expansile mass surrounded by fibrous pseudocapsule

Interior of tumor entirely composed of cysts and septa with no expansile solid nodules

Septa contain aggregates of epithelial cells with clear cytoplasm

While a solid sheet of alveoli is a common pattern of growth, the alveoli often have small central lumens which contain freshly extravasated erythrocytes. Commonly, some of the lumens are larger, forming microscopic cysts of variable size (Fig. 12.14). Among renal cell carcinomas, clear cell renal

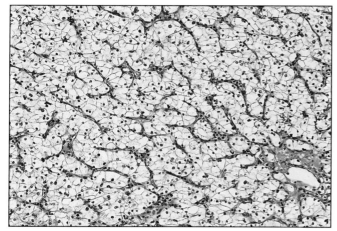

Fig. 12.13 • Clear cell renal cell carcinoma. The prominent delicate vasculature surrounding alveolar clusters of cells is typical of clear cell renal cell carcinoma.

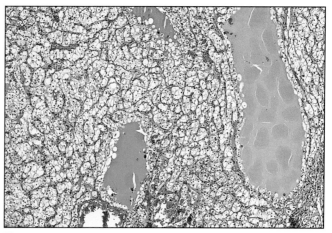

Fig. 12.14 • Clear cell renal cell carcinoma. Tubules and small cysts filled with eosinophilic proteinaceous fluid or fresh hemorrhage are typical of clear cell renal cell carcinoma.

cell carcinoma is the one most prone to the formation of small and large cysts and this is a helpful diagnostic clue.

The cytoplasmic volume of clear cell renal cell carcinoma is variable over a range from moderate to voluminous. However, it is typical that the cells in one area of a tumor are similar in size. This zonal pattern of cellular sizes contrasts with the mosaic pattern characteristic of chromophobe renal cell carcinoma. The clarity of the cytoplasm is caused by the abundant lipid and glycogen which dissolve during tissue processing (Fig. 12.15). Occasional cases show focally rhabdoid features with hyaline cytoplasmic inclusions.[88]

In clear cell renal cell carcinoma, papillary architecture is exceptional, and to some extent controversial. One should think twice before diagnosing a tumor with obvious papillary architecture as clear cell renal cell carcinoma. Psammoma bodies and foamy macrophages, which are common in papillary renal cell carcinoma, are rare in clear cell renal cell carcinoma. Mucin is at most rare in clear cell renal cell carcinoma, and some would categorize tumors containing mucin as renal cell carcinoma, unclassified.

Differential diagnosis The diagnosis of the typical clear cell renal cell carcinoma is usually straightforward. *Sarcomatoid* change occurs in approximately 5 percent of clear cell renal cell carcinomas and may cause difficulty because it very closely mimics a sarcoma.[89,90] This problem is well known however,

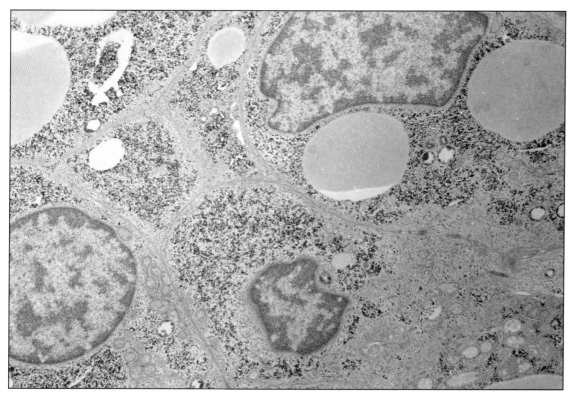

Fig. 12.15 • Clear cell renal cell carcinoma. The cytoplasm contains abundant lipid and glycogen.

and because of the rarity of renal sarcomas, they should be diagnosed with caution. Extensive sampling may be helpful since these tumors frequently have foci, albeit sometimes small, of typical renal cell carcinoma which make the correct diagnosis obvious. Immunohistochemistry for epithelial markers usually demonstrates epithelial features in cells which appear sarcomatous in sections stained with hematoxylin and eosin. Sarcomatoid renal cell carcinomas are generally associated with a poor outcome.[89,90]

In adults, urothelial carcinomas of the renal pelvis may be confused with renal cell carcinomas, especially when the tumors are large and extensively infiltrate the kidney. Microscopically, the diagnosis may be difficult, particularly when the pelvic tumor is predominantly sarcomatoid, as has been described.[91] Extensive sampling may be necessary in order to find small areas of typical transitional cell carcinoma, even in situ, or renal cell carcinoma. Immunohistochemical demonstration of high molecular weight cytokeratin or carcinoembryonic antigen indicate that such a tumor is of transitional cell origin.[92]

Xanthogranulomatous pyelonephritis is an unusual inflammatory disorder which can clinically and pathologically be confused with renal cell carcinoma.[93,94] The presenting symptoms overlap with those of renal cell carcinoma, as most of the patients present with various symptoms including flank pain, fever, malaise, weight loss, and hematuria.[95,96] The preoperative diagnosis is further confused by the frequent finding of a flank mass. The gross appearance also is confusing because the inflammation may produce a tumor-like mass of yellow tissue and infiltrate the perinephric fat (Fig. 12.16). The renal outflow is almost always obstructed, usually by a calculus,

but sometimes by deformity of the ureteropelvic junction.[97] Xanthogranulomatous pyelonephritis may also be confusing microscopically since an infiltrate of foamy histiocytes that may be misconstrued as the clear cells of renal cell carcinoma is usually the predominant element[98] (Fig. 12.17). Close attention to the cytoplasm reveals its foamy character, unlike that of clear cell renal cell carcinoma. The vascular pattern typical of clear cell renal cell carcinomas is absent and the other inflammatory cells, principally lymphocytes and plasma cells, should further assist in its recognition. Malakoplakia is another inflammatory process which may resemble a primary renal tumor.[98] Grossly, large yellowish masses may infiltrate perinephric fat and microscopically, the large eosinophilic histiocytes (von Hansemann cells) characteristic of malakoplakia may be confused with the eosinophilic cells of renal cell carcinoma. The presence of Michaelis–Gutmann bodies is important in establishing the correct diagnosis, as are the lack of cytologic atypia and architectural patterns characteristic of renal cell carcinoma, inconsistent with malakoplakia.

Clinically, occult renal cell carcinomas presenting at distant sites with unknown primaries or recurring years after an apparently successful radical nephrectomy may pose special diagnostic problems. The coexpression of cytokeratin and vimentin, which occurs in a majority of clear cell renal cell carcinomas,[100] is unusual among carcinomas and should be taken as suggestive of a renal primary when found in a metastasis of unknown origin.[92] Ultrastructurally, dense arrays of microvilli at intercellular areas or on lumenal surfaces and prominence of glycogen in the cytoplasm are suggestive of renal cell carcinoma.[101] Solitary metastasis to the contralateral adrenal can resemble primary adrenal cortical carcinoma. In such cases, immunohistochemical staining for epithelial membrane antigen and cytokeratins can be helpful since renal cell carcinomas almost always stain for epithelial membrane antigen or cytokeratin, or both, while adrenal cortical carcinomas do not contain epithelial membrane antigen[102] and stain for cytokeratin only weakly at best. Further immunohistochemistry for inhibin and melanA can also be helpful.[103] Metastasis to the thyroid can mimic clear cell carcinoma of the thyroid;[104] thyroglobulin immunohistochemistry and

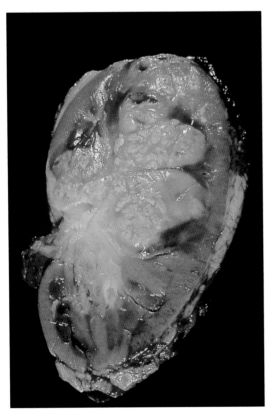

Fig. 12.16 • Xanthogranulomatous pyelonephritis. The aggregates of foamy histiocytes form yellow masses, resembling renal cell carcinoma.

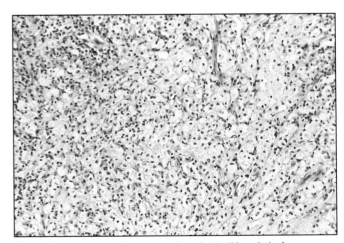

Fig. 12.17 • Xanthogranulomatous pyelonephritis. Although the foamy histiocytes superficially resemble clear cell renal cell carcinoma, the infiltrate of lymphocytes and plasma cells and the lack of the typical vascular pattern clarify the diagnosis.

ultrastructural detection of intracytoplasmic glycogen (which is not found in clear cell carcinomas primary in the thyroid) can be helpful in making the distinction. Metastases to the ovary can be confused with primary ovarian clear cell adenocarcinoma.[105] Capillary hemangioblastoma of the central nervous system may closely resemble clear cell renal cell carcinoma in sections stained with hematoxylin and eosin and poses a particular problem because both neoplasms are associated with von Hippel-Lindau disease. This problem can usually be resolved by staining for epithelial membrane antigen, since capillary hemangioblastomas fail to stain[106] while renal cell carcinomas usually do.

Papillary renal cell carcinoma

Approximately 10–15 percent of renal cell carcinomas in surgical series are papillary renal cell carcinomas.[41,83,84,107] Males predominate in a ratio of approximately 2:1. Ages range from early adulthood to old age, with the mean being between 50 and 55 years. These carcinomas have a much better prognosis than clear cell carcinoma,[83,84] but mortality of at least 16 percent at 10 years[108] and they sometimes present with metastases.[109]

Papillary renal cell carcinoma has a characteristic pattern of genetic abnormalities which differs from those of other renal cell neoplasms. The pattern of lesions is one of chromosomal gains. Most commonly, these are trisomy or tetrasomy of 7 and 17.[110–112] Most papillary renal cell carcinomas in men lose the Y chromosome.[111] These results are consistent and have been corroborated by several laboratories.[79,112–114]

Macroscopic appearances Papillary renal cell carcinomas usually are well-circumscribed, globular tumors with pale tan or brown parenchyma. In about two-thirds of cases, hemorrhage and necrosis are prominent, which may cause the tumor to appear hypovascular radiographically.[107,115] Many of these carcinomas are large. Often the cut surface is friable or granular, a reflection of the papillae seen microscopically. The larger tumors are often surrounded by a rim of dense fibrous tissue.[116] In about one-third of cases, there are calcifications.[107,115]

Histologic appearances The architecture is predominantly papillary or tubulopapillary in more than 90 percent of papillary renal cell carcinomas.[41,117] Tight packing of papillae imparts the appearance of a solid growth pattern in some tumors. The papillae usually have delicate fibrovascular cores covered by a single layer of cells. The form of the papillae varies, ranging from complex branching to long parallel arrays.[118] The cores are sometimes expanded by foamy macrophages (Fig. 12.18) or edema fluid. Psammoma bodies occasionally are present. Rarely, the papillary cores are wide and collagenous.[118] The tubular architecture consists of small tubules lined by a single layer of cells identical to those covering the papillae.

There are two types of papillary renal cell carcinoma, which Delahunt and Eble have designated type 1 and type 2.[2,119] Type 1 is more common than type 2. In type 1, the cells usually are small, with inconspicuous pale cytoplasm (Fig. 12.19). The nuclei are typically uniform, nearly spherical, and small, with nucleoli which are small or invisible. In type 2, the cells are usually larger and often have abundant eosinophilic cytoplasm.

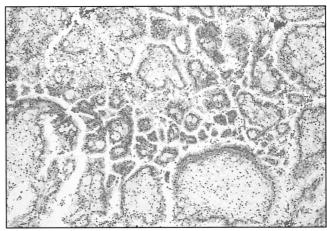

Fig. 12.18 • Papillary renal cell carcinoma. The stromal cores of the papillae are distended by collections of foamy histiocytes.

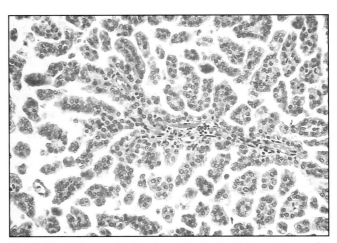

Fig. 12.19 • Papillary renal cell carcinoma. Small cells with inconspicuous pale cytoplasm cover the papillae of type 1 papillary renal cell carcinoma.

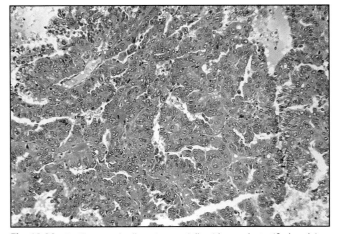

Fig. 12.20 • Papillary renal cell carcinoma. Cells with pseudostratified nuclei and abundant cytoplasm cover the papillae of type 2 papillary renal cell carcinoma.

The nuclei are arranged in a pseudostratified pattern, are large, spherical, and often have prominent nucleoli (Fig. 12.20).

In a series of 39 cases, nuclear morphology correlated with stage and outcome.[109] Thus, the nuclear grading system is recommended.[120]

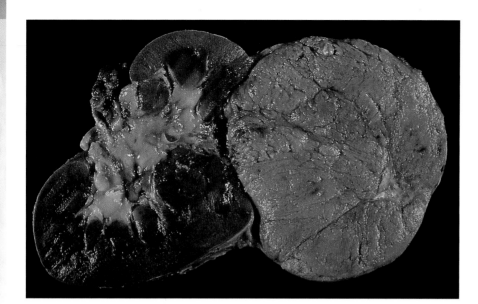

Fig. 12.21 • Chromophobe renal cell carcinoma. This light brown or tan globular tumor is well circumscribed.

Differential diagnosis In children and adolescents, papillary renal cell carcinomas must be distinguished from Wilms' tumors with epithelial predominance. Beckwith[121] has emphasized the similarity of some Wilms' tumors to typical renal cell carcinoma. Thorough sampling of such tumors usually will reveal blastema or differentiated stroma (e.g., skeletal muscle) and the diagnosis of Wilms' tumor will then be made with relative ease. The appearance of the nuclei, elongate with tapered ends in the epithelium of Wilms' tumor and spheroidal in renal cell carcinoma, also may be helpful. The diagnosis of papillary renal cell carcinoma in a young person should be made only after epithelial predominant Wilms' tumor has been excluded.

Chromophobe renal cell carcinoma

In 1985, Thoenes et al.[122] first described and named chromophobe renal cell carcinoma. Since then, it has become apparent that approximately 5 percent of renal cell carcinomas are chromophobe renal cell carcinomas.[84,123–126] The genetic hallmark of chromophobe renal cell carcinoma is the loss of multiple chromosomes.[127–129]

While several deaths have been recorded from chromophobe renal cell carcinoma, it appears that this neoplasm is the least aggressive of the common renal cell carcinomas.[83,84] Sarcomatoid change occurs in chromophobe renal cell carcinoma at about the same frequency as in the other types of renal cell carcinoma and appears to account for a substantial fraction of the deaths.[90,130]

Macroscopic appearances Chromophobe renal cell carcinomas are usually well-circumscribed, globular, solid, tan or brown tumors (Fig. 12.21). Formalin fixation may change their color to a pale off-white. Large cysts are not typical of chromophobe renal cell carcinoma.

Histologic appearances Chromophobe renal cell carcinoma is characterized by the presence of cells with large numbers of minute intracytoplasmic vesicles which impart a pale, reticular or flocculent appearance to the cytoplasm in preparations stained with hematoxylin and eosin (Fig. 12.22). The vesicles are demonstrable by electron microscopy (Fig. 12.23). The Hale's colloidal iron stain colors the cytoplasm blue (Fig. 12.24).[123] The initial description[122] emphasized the well-defined thick cytoplasmic membranes and lightly staining flocculent cytoplasm of what is now called the typical variant of chromophobe renal cell carcinoma. The typical variant also has thick-walled blood vessels. The cells range widely in size and small and large cells are mixed together in a mosaic pattern. Later, the eosinophilic variant of chromophobe cell renal cell carcinoma was recognized.[123] This variant shares the ultrastructural and colloidal iron staining features of the typical variant but, in hematoxylin and eosin-stained slides, often closely resembles renal oncocytoma (Fig. 12.25). For this reason, it is worthwhile routinely to collect specimens for electron microscopy from renal tumors, especially those which do not have the yellow color characteristic of clear cell renal cell carcinoma. It is prudent to perform a colloidal iron stain on any tumor

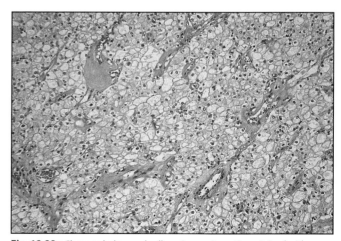

Fig. 12.22 • Chromophobe renal cell carcinoma. In sections stained with hematoxylin and eosin the cytoplasm of typical chromophobe renal cell carcinoma is pale pink and flocculent.

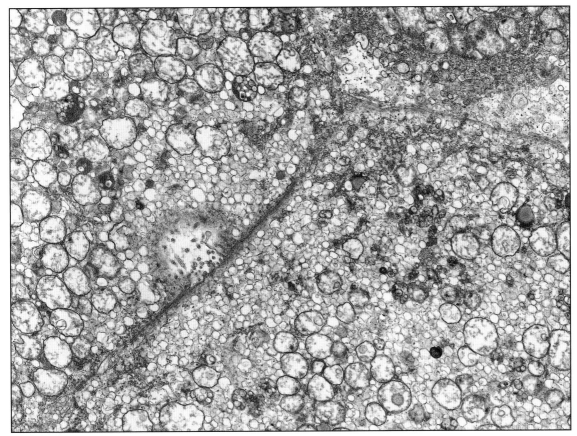

Fig. 12.23 • Chromophobe renal cell carcinoma. Ultrastructurally, the cytoplasm of chromophobe cells is crowded with many small vesicles.

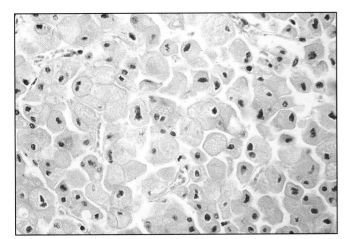

Fig. 12.24 • Chromophobe renal cell carcinoma. The Hale's stain colors the cytoplasm of chromophobe cells blue.

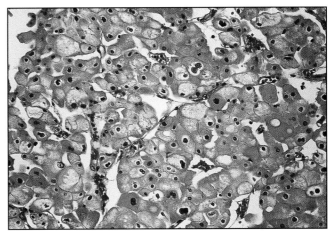

Fig. 12.25 • Chromophobe renal cell carcinoma. The eosinophilic variant of chromophobe carcinoma is composed of cells with deeply eosinophilic, finely granular cytoplasm.

in which the differential diagnosis includes renal oncocytoma and chromophobe cell renal cell carcinoma. The use of immunohistochemical stains to subclassify renal cell carcinomas has turned out to be questionable, since there is considerable phenotypic overlap.[131,132]

Differential diagnosis The vasculature, mosaic pattern of variability of cell size, and cytoplasmic characteristics make the classical form of chromophobe renal cell carcinoma distinctive and the diagnosis can usually be easily achieved in routine sections. The eosinophilic variant is more problematic because of its close resemblance to oncocytoma. In sections stained with hematoxylin and eosin, perinuclear haloes, wrinkled irregular nuclei, and microcystic architecture lend support to the diagnosis of the eosinophilic variant of chromophobe renal cell carcinoma. However, histochemical staining for the Hale's colloidal iron reaction can be helpful and a diffuse cytoplasmic positive reaction is diagnostic of chromophobe renal cell carcinoma, while a negative reaction supports oncocytoma.

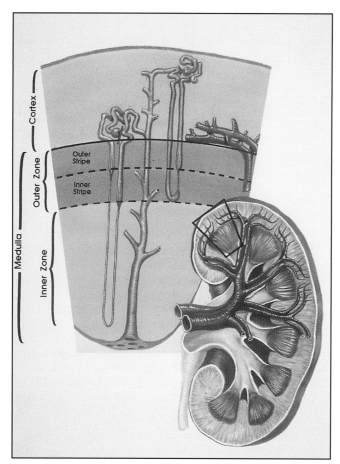

Fig. 12.26 • The collecting ducts of the kidney begin in the outer cortex and become larger by the confluence of connecting tubules as they pass through the cortex and medulla. The terminal segment in the medullary papilla is the duct of Bellini.

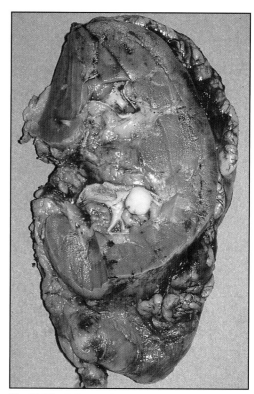

Fig. 12.27 • Collecting duct carcinoma. This small whitish tumor has arisen in the renal medulla. (Courtesy of Dr. Wei-Li Huang.)

Collecting duct carcinoma

The collecting ducts begin in the renal cortex and descend through the medulla to the renal papillae (Fig. 12.26); the short segments just above the papillary orifices are called the ducts of Bellini.[133] There is evidence that the intercalated cells of the collecting duct may be the source of renal oncocytomas[134] and chromophobe renal cell carcinomas.[135] However, the diagnosis of "collecting duct carcinoma" is only applicable to a group of high grade carcinomas thought to arise from the ducts of Bellini in the renal medullary pyramids.[136,137]

In general, the prognosis for collecting duct carcinomas is poor.[137] A variant of collecting duct carcinoma which occurs in young patients with sickle cell trait has been given the name "*medullary carcinoma of the kidney*".[138–140] The prognosis for these patients has been exceptionally bad.

Macroscopic appearances While the collecting ducts are present in the cortex and the medulla, the gross pathologic finding of a tumor arising in the inner medulla (Fig. 12.27), where most other parts of the renal tubular system are absent, can be an important aid to the diagnosis.[141] Unfortunately, precise localization to the medulla is only possible with small tumors and many tumors are too large at the time of resection for the specific site of origin within the kidney to be recognizable. The tumors are usually centered in the medulla, often with extensions into the cortex or hilar tissues.[142,143] Infiltrative borders and white or gray cut surfaces with central necrosis are typical.[144] A connection with the renal pelvis is common.

Histologic appearances Characteristically, these are histopathologically distinctive carcinomas with mixed features of adenocarcinoma and transitional cell carcinoma.[137,144] Microscopic examination shows highly irregular duct-like structures, nests, and cords of cells in an abundant loose, slightly basophilic stroma (Fig. 12.28). The carcinoma cells lining the lumens have small or moderate amounts of cytoplasm and nuclei which are pleomorphic and have thick nuclear membranes. An especially useful feature, rarely found in renal cell

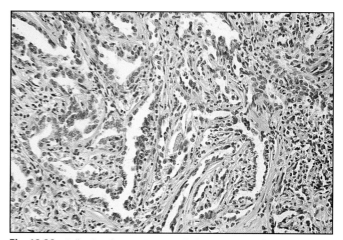

Fig. 12.28 • Collecting duct carcinoma. Tubules with jagged branching lumens embedded in an abundant stroma and lined by cells with small amounts of cytoplasm are typical of collecting duct carcinoma.

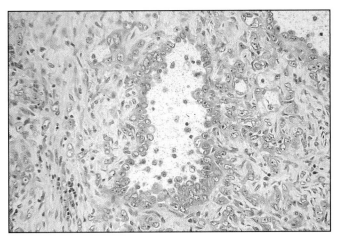

Fig. 12.29 • Collecting duct carcinoma. Slightly basophilic cytoplasm reminiscent of the renal medulla and hobnail cells lining ducts and small cysts are features of collecting duct carcinomas.

carcinoma and not found in transitional cell carcinoma, is the hobnail appearance sometimes seen in the cells lining duct lumens (Fig. 12.29). Atypical epithelium in the medullary tubules adjacent to the carcinoma has been seen in some cases.[143]

Differential diagnosis Awareness of collecting duct carcinoma and appreciation of the differences between the microscopic features described above and those of other renal cancers should establish the diagnosis in most cases. Rumpelt et al.[144] found that collecting duct carcinomas stained strongly positively for cytokeratin 19 and *Ulex europaeus* lectin, but only moderately for vimentin, while failing to stain for cytokeratin 13. Other immunohistochemical studies of collecting duct carcinomas have provided varied results.[145,146] Presently, there is not a well-established specific immunohistochemical profile for collecting duct carcinoma, so it is better to restrict the diagnosis of collecting duct carcinoma to those tumors for which the gross pathologic findings indicate this origin or which have the characteristic histopathologic appearance described above and illustrated in Figures 12.28 and 12.29. Borderline cases should be diagnosed as renal cell carcinoma, unclassified.

Xp11 translocation carcinomas

A family of renal carcinomas which contain a variety of translocations involving chromosome Xp11.2 has been identified in recent years.[147] All of these translocations have resulted in gene fusions involving *TFE3*. This family of carcinomas was classified as Xp11 translocation carcinomas in the 2004 WHO classification.[1] Subsequently, carcinomas with a t(6;11) producing a fusion with *TFEB* have been identified. Since *TFE3* and *TFEB* are members of the *MiTF/TFE* family of transcription factor genes, it appears likely that further carcinomas may be discovered with fusions of other genes in the family.[147] While carcinomas make up less than 5 percent of renal tumors in children, translocation carcinomas appear to make up at least 20 percent of renal carcinomas in children.[35] Translocation carcinomas also occur in adults but their frequency remains unclear. A number of cases have presented at a high stage but have followed surprisingly indolent courses. Due to the small number of cases studied so far, knowledge of

the clinical aspects and outcome of these tumors is sketchy. There may be more female than male patients but that is not conclusive. Some patients have presented with metastases, yet have had prolonged survival. Some patients have had histories of chemotherapy for other conditions.[147a]

Macroscopic appearances Translocation carcinomas usually are solid tan-yellow tumors; foci of hemorrhage and necrosis are common.

Histologic appearances Xp11.2 translocation carcinomas often have large areas of papillary architecture in which the papillae are covered by cells with abundant clear or pale cytoplasm (Fig. 12.30). However, they also have an alveolar or nested architecture and cells with eosinophilic cytoplasm are common. Psammoma bodies are common and may be quite numerous. There are subtle variations in morphology among carcinomas with the different Xp11 translocations.

t(6;11) translocation carcinomas consist of nests and microscopic cysts composed of polygonal cells with pale or eosinophilic cytoplasm. Papillae are uncommon. A distinctive component consists of cells with small amounts of cytoplasm and denser chromatin arranged around nodules of hyaline material in large acini. At low magnification, these resemble rosettes.

Translocation carcinomas with gene fusions involving *TFE3* typically show a positive intranuclear reaction with an antibody to *TFE3*.[148] Carcinoma with gene fusions involving *TFEB* typically show positive intranuclear reactions with an antibody to *TFEB*. Xp11 translocation carcinomas characteristically fail to mark or mark weakly with antibodies to epithelial markers, such as epithelial membrane antigen and cytokeratins. t(6;11) carcinomas are frequently positive for HMB45 and melanA, as well as for *TFEB* protein.[149]

Carcinoma associated with neuroblastoma

Approximately two dozen children and young adults have been diagnosed with renal cell carcinoma after surviving neuroblastoma in the first two years of their lives. In 1999, Medeiros

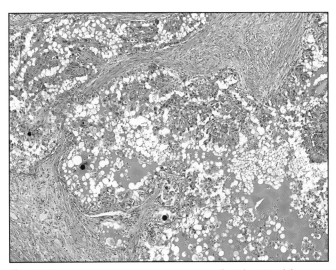

Fig. 12.30 • Xp11 translocation carcinoma. Large cells with eosinophilic cytoplasm and psammoma bodies with papillary and compact architecture.

et al. published an account of 4 survivors of neuroblastoma who had histologically distinctive renal tumors and suggested that they constituted a distinct clinicopathologic entity; later, a second small series was published.[150,151] The 2004 WHO classification included the category of carcinoma associated with neuroblastoma to recognize this entity.[1] All of the patients had neuroblastoma at the usual age; two of them received neither chemotherapy nor radiation therapy. The renal cell carcinomas were diagnosed at ages ranging from 5 to 14 years. In one patient, renal cell carcinoma metastasized to liver and lymph nodes.

Macroscopic appearances The principal tumors have ranged from 35 to 80 mm in diameter; the 20 small tumors in the patient with multiple and bilateral tumors ranged from 1 mm to 24 mm. Two carcinomas invaded the renal capsule, renal vascular system, or peripelvic lymphatics.

Histologic appearances The best-illustrated and best-documented renal carcinomas associated with neuroblastoma contain majority populations of cells with abundant finely granular eosinophilic cytoplasm, growing in papillary and solid patterns. Psammoma bodies are sometimes present, as are small clusters of foamy histiocytes. The nuclei usually are medium-sized and have irregular contours. Nucleoli are easy to find, corresponding to nuclear grade 3. Mitotic figures are usually present in small numbers. All tumors studied have reacted with antibodies to epithelial membrane antigen, vimentin and cytokeratin Cam 5.2.[152]

Mucinous tubular and spindle cell carcinoma

Histologically, distinctive renal neoplasms composed of cuboidal and spindle cells with mucinous extracellular matrix have been described in reports of single cases and in small series since 1998.[152,153] Authors have offered a variety of names for these tumors, often referring to their resemblance to tubules of the lower nephron or loop of Henle and to the remarkably low nuclear grade for a carcinoma with areas of spindle cell morphology. At the WHO consensus conference in December 2002, the diagnostic phrase "mucinous tubular and spindle cell carcinoma" was adopted.[1] All patients have been adults (median age 58 years). There is a roughly 3:1 predominance of women over men. Three of the tumors reported by Hes et al.[154] also had nephrolithiasis. Approximately 50 percent of the tumors have been large (stage pT2); in one patient the tumor invaded perirenal fat and in 2 others there were metastases to lymph nodes. All patients have been treated solely with surgery; no recurrence has been reported.

Macroscopic appearances Mucinous tubular and spindle cell carcinomas have ranged in size from 22 mm to 130 mm in diameter. The cut surfaces are solid and gray to tan brown to pinkish. Foci of hemorrhage or necrosis have been found in a few of the tumors. One small tumor appeared to be centered in the renal medulla. All but one of the tumors have been well-circumscribed and contained within the renal capsule.

Histologic appearances Mucinous tubular and spindle cell carcinomas have a distinctive histologic appearance, consisting

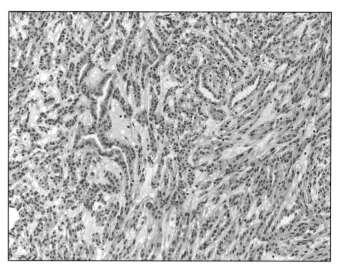

Fig. 12.31 • Mucinous tubular and spindle cell carcinoma. Cuboidal and spindle cells in a mucinous extracellular matrix.

of cuboidal cells arranged in long cords and tubules and making abrupt transitions to spindle cell morphology (Fig. 12.31). These epithelial structures are arrayed against a background of lightly basophilic mucinous or myxoid material. The nuclei usually are spherical or oval, have a few small chromatin clumps and small nucleoli. Mitotic figures are uncommon. The spindle cell component may form sheets. The mucinous background material may focally dominate and then the epithelial elements form small cords in lakes of mucinous material. The mucinous background material has little affinity for mucicarmine but reacts strongly with alcian blue.[155] Plasma cells, mast cells, and clusters of foamy histiocytes are sometimes present.[155,156] The immunohistochemical results obtained in different series have varied.[154,155–157] Positive reactions with antibodies to vimentin and epithelial membrane antigen have been the most frequent findings. Reaction with the cytokeratin cocktail AE1/AE3 was positive in 10 of 14 tumors in two studies.[154,155] The lectin *Ulex europaeus*, which binds to collecting duct epithelium, has consistently failed to bind to the cells of mucinous tubular and spindle cell carcinoma. These tumors lack the cytogenetic aberrations seen in papillary renal cell carcinoma.[157a]

Renal cell carcinoma, unclassified

Renal cell carcinoma, unclassified is a diagnostic category to which renal carcinomas should be assigned when they do not fit readily into one of the other categories.[1] In some surgical series, this group has amounted to approximately 4–5 percent of cases. Since this category must contain tumors with a wide variety of appearances and genetic lesions, it cannot be precisely defined. Features which should prompt assignment of a carcinoma to this category include: apparent composites of recognized types, sarcomatoid carcinoma without recognizable epithelial elements, production of mucin, mixtures of epithelial and stromal elements, and unrecognizable cell types. Since this is a highly heterogeneous group of tumors, it is difficult to make generalizations about them.[158] Interestingly, within this group, it is likely that further distinct subgroups will be identified, since carcinomas arising in the setting of

Table 12.5 Staging of renal cell carcinoma

Robson system[160, 161]	TNM system[162]
Stage 1	T1 Confined by renal capsule & ≤70 mm
Confined within the renal capsule	T1a ≤40 mm
	T1b ≥40 mm but ≤70 mm
	T2 Confined by renal capsule & ≥70 mm
Stage 2	T3a Invasion of adrenal or fat within Gerota's fascia
Confined by Gerota's fascia	T3b Gross extension into veins or vena cava below diaphragm
Stage 3	
A Grossly visible extension into renal vein or vena cava	T3c Intravascular extension above diaphragm or invades wall of cava
B Lymphatic metastasis	N1 Single regional node
	N2 More than one regional node
C Both vascular extension and metastasis to nodes	
Stage 4	
Invasion of adjacent organs (except T4 adrenal)	Extension beyond Gerota's fascia
Hematogenous metastases	M1

acquired cystic disease appear to have unique morphologic features.[158a]

Staging and grading renal cell carcinoma

The extent of spread of renal cell carcinoma is the dominant factor in prognosis.[159] Two staging systems are widely used at present for renal cell carcinoma. The system proposed by Robson et al.[160,161] is compared with the tumor, nodes, metastases (TNM) system[162] in Table 12.5. These schemes are roughly parallel and comparable groupings have been set off by horizontal lines. Surgery is the principal therapy for renal cell carcinoma and, for this reason, both systems include tumors confined within the renal capsule in the most favorable category. The TNM system takes into account the correlation between size and survival by dividing this group according to size. Invasion of the perinephric fat within Gerota's fascia indicates the next stage in both systems. The next group is more complicated and controversial; renal cell carcinoma frequently invades the renal venous system and this is the criterion for stage 3A. The invasive path is frequently through veins in the renal sinus.[163,164] The prognostic significance of venous invasion has been difficult to establish because many tumors with venous invasion have other features of high stage, such as metastases. Medeiros et al.[165,166] compared stage 1 tumors with stage 3 tumors which would have been stage 1 but for venous invasion and found that it was an independent prognostic factor among high grade tumors, but did not affect prognosis in low grade tumors. Invasion of small veins within the main tumor is not sufficient reason to assign stage 3; rather, the invasion must be macroscopically visible or microscopically must occur in large veins with smooth muscle in their walls and must be at the edge or outside of the main tumor. Metastasis to regional lymph nodes without distant metastasis occurs in approximately 10 to 15 percent of cases,[167,168] but more than 50 percent of patients with enlarged regional lymph nodes have only inflammatory or hyperplastic changes.[169] Radical nephrectomy with regional lymph node dissection has been a standard operation for renal cell carcinoma for more than

three decades,[160] but the therapeutic contribution of the lymph node dissection remains controversial.[170,171] Occasionally, metastasis occurs via paraureteral veins or lymphatics[172] and, for this reason, the end of the ureter and its adventitial tissues constitute a relevant surgical margin and should be examined histologically in radical nephrectomy specimens. Improvements in imaging techniques have made it possible to omit resection of the adrenal gland in many cases.[173,174] Partial nephrectomy and laparoscopic nephrectomy have become standard approaches to renal cell carcinoma.[175,176]

Since Hand and Broders[177] introduced grading of renal cell carcinomas in 1932, several different systems have been proposed, with variable success. In addition to nuclear characteristics, cytoplasmic and architectural features have been incorporated, leading to a long controversy and considerable frustration for practicing surgical pathologists. In 1971, Skinner et al.[178] redirected attention to the correlation between nuclear features and survival. These observations were confirmed and refined into a system of practically applicable criteria by Fuhrman et al.[120] The Fuhrman system consists of four grades based on the size, contour, and conspicuousness of nucleoli (Table 12.6). Medeiros et al.[165] showed that the Fuhrman system correlated well with survival in a large population of patients with renal cell carcinoma and in a smaller

Table 12.6 Nuclear grading of renal cell carcinoma

Grade 1 Round, uniform nuclei approximately 10 mm in diameter with minute or absent nucleoli

Grade 2 Slightly irregular nuclear contours and diameters of approximately 15 mm with nucleoli visible at 400×

Grade 3 Moderately to markedly irregular nuclear contours and diameters of approximately 20 mm with large nucleoli visible at 100×

Grade 4 Nuclei similar to those of Grade 3 but also multilobular or multiple nuclei or bizarre nuclei and heavy clumps of chromatin population of patients with stage I tumors. Survival ranged from 86 percent for patients with grade 1 tumors to 24 percent for those with grade 4 tumors. The grade assigned is that of the highest grade found, regardless of extent.[179] Green et al.[180] studied 55 patients with stage I renal cell carcinoma and found a significant decrease in 5-year survival of patients with grade 4 tumors. The importance of nucleolar morphology also has been confirmed by Helpap et al.[181] However, inter-observer and intra-observer variability are less than ideal.[182] Mitotic figures are not a part of this system, but typically are rare in grade 1 and 2 tumors and the finding of more than one mitosis per 10 high power fields has adverse prognostic significance.[179] The grading system also does not include sarcomatoid change or coagulative necrosis, microscopic features which also have adverse prognostic significance.[183]

Neuroendocrine and neuroectodermal neoplasms of the kidney

Neuroendocrine and neuroectodermal neoplasms in the spectrum from carcinoid to small cell carcinoma and primitive neuroectodermal tumor have been found in the kidney.[184-186] Arising equally frequently in males and females, the patients' ages have ranged from adolescence to the ninth decade of life with a mean age of approximately 50 years. A variety of endocrine manifestations have been reported, including cases of the carcinoid syndrome[187] and excess secretion of glucagons.[188] Metastases have been common, even among the cases diagnosed as carcinoid.

While pheochromocytomas arising in the renal sinus and compressing the renal artery appear to be more common than pheochromocytomas within the renal capsule,[189] intrarenal pheochromocytomas also occur[190] and are associated with hypertension. Neuroblastoma rarely arises in the kidneys of adults.[184]

Macroscopic appearances The carcinoids often are well-circumscribed[191-193] and consist of red tan tissue with areas of hemorrhage[194] and necrosis.[195] Two cases have been described in which dysplastic teratoid elements have been associated with renal carcinoid[196,197] and an association with horseshoe kidney has been proposed.[198] Renal small cell carcinomas often are large and infiltrate retroperitoneal soft tissues; regional lymph node metastases are common.[199,200] Renal neuroblastomas are often large, firm tumors with yellowish-red cut surfaces with areas of hemorrhage.[201]

Histological appearances Histopathologically, the tumors fill the spectrum from carcinoid to small cell carcinoma and primitive neuroepithelial tumor.[184] The carcinoids consist of cords or nests of cells with the cytologic features characteristic of carcinoid tumors (Fig. 12.32). At the other end of the spectrum of differentiation, the small cell carcinomas consist of sheets of poorly differentiated cells with darkly staining nuclei and inconspicuous cytoplasm. Necrosis is common and two studies[199,200] noted the Azzopardi phenomenon (deposition of DNA in the walls of blood vessels). Primitive neuroectodermal tumors arising primarily in the kidney are histologically comparable to their counterparts in soft tissue and

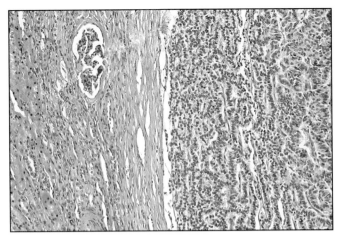

Fig. 12.32 • Renal carcinoid. The cells are arranged in ribbons and the tumor is well circumscribed.

bone[185] (see Chs 25 and 27) and show the same chromosome translocations involving the *EWS* gene. Neuroblastoma is diagnosed using the same criteria applied in the adrenal gland; the presence of neuropil or Homer Wright rosettes is helpful in distinguishing it from small cell carcinoma. Intrarenal pheochromocytomas resemble their adrenal counterparts histologically.

Mesenchymal tumors of the kidney

Angiomyolipoma

These benign neoplasms of the kidney are composed of fat, smooth muscle, and thick-walled blood vessels in varying proportions.[202] In the adult population, angiomyolipoma is approximately as common as renal cell carcinoma.[203] In surgical series, approximately half are associated with tuberous sclerosis and half occur sporadically. In patients with tuberous sclerosis, they are usually asymptomatic, multiple, bilateral, and small (Fig. 12.33), while in the general population they are usually symptomatic, single, and large (Fig. 12.34). They are uncommon in the general population, but more than 50 percent of patients with tuberous sclerosis develop them.[204] Unlike its close relative, epithelioid angiomyolipoma, angiomyolipoma is benign and the evolution of sarcoma from an angiomyolipoma is extremely rare.[205]

Macroscopic appearances Angiomyolipomas range from less than a centimeter to 20 cm or more in diameter. The likelihood of symptoms increases above 4 cm and symptomatic tumors average about 9 cm.[206] These tumors are typically golden yellow but the color varies according to the proportions of smooth muscle and blood vessels. They are not encapsulated and, while generally well demarcated, may be locally infiltrative. The appearance of the cut surface of the tumor may resemble that of a lipoma.

Histologic appearances The histology of these tumors varies according to the relative (and highly variable) proportions of fat, smooth muscle and blood vessels (Fig. 12.35).[207] The smooth muscle component is also variable in appearance. A frequent finding is radial arrays of smooth muscle fibers

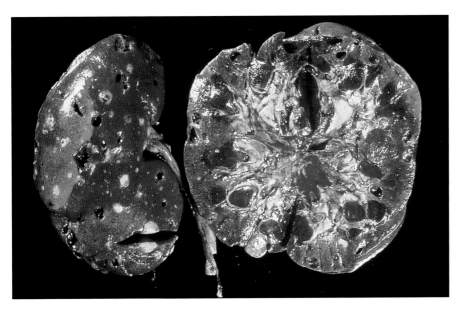

Fig. 12.33 • Angiomyolipoma. The kidneys of a patient with tuberous sclerosis contain multiple small yellowish tumors, typical of angiomyolipomas associated with this disorder.

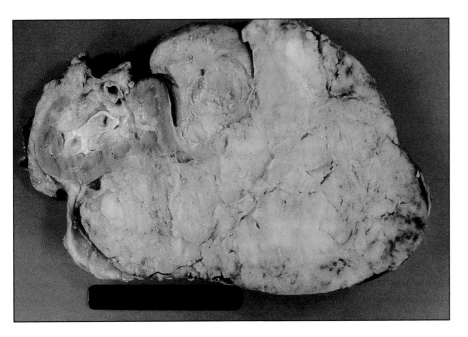

Fig. 12.34 • Angiomyolipoma. A massive solitary tumor composed of lobulated yellowish tissue is typical of sporadic cases of angiomyolipoma.

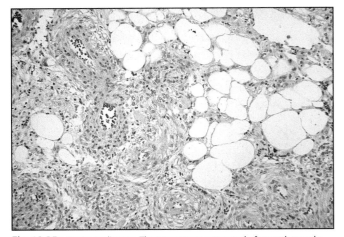

Fig. 12.35 • Angiomyolipoma. The tumors are composed of smooth muscle, fat, and thick-walled blood vessels.

distributed around blood vessels, but smooth muscle is also found in bundles and scattered as individual fibers (Fig. 12.36). The smooth muscle cells are typically spindle-shaped but occasionally they are polygonal or rounded with an epithelioid appearance and have abundant, often rather granular eosinophilic cytoplasm (Fig. 12.37). The blood vessels are often abnormal, with thick walls resembling those of arteries but with eccentrically placed or very small lumens. Nuclear pleomorphism may be pronounced and mitotic figures may be present. The adipocytic component may include cells indistinguishable from lipoblasts. These findings have no adverse prognostic significance in most cases. Rare examples of angiomyolipoma contain prominent cysts, both gross and microscopic, lined by bland epithelium.[207a] In some cases, angiomyolipomatous tissue has been found in regional lymph nodes[208–210] and spleen.[211] This should not be misinterpreted as metastatic sarcoma. Occasionally, angiomyolipoma invades

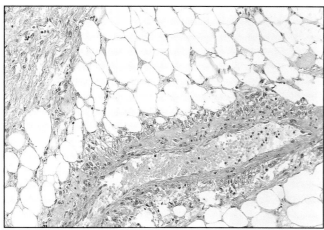

Fig. 12.36 • Angiomyolipoma. Thick-walled blood vessels rimmed by radially oriented smooth muscle fibers are common.

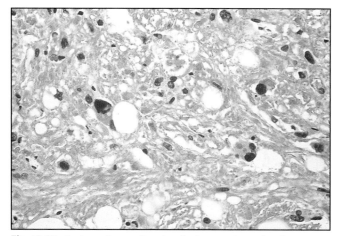

Fig. 12.37 • Angiomyolipoma. Occasionally, the smooth muscle cells are epithelioid and may exhibit nuclear atypia.

the renal vein or vena cava; all of these patients have been cured surgically so this does not indicate malignancy.[202]

A variant of angiomyolipoma, which can easily be mistaken for carcinoma, has recently been recognized and categorized as "*epithelioid angiomyolipoma*".[1,212–214] The tumors are composed of a mixture of large polygonal cells with abundant eosinophilic cytoplasm, some of which superficially resemble ganglion cells, and short spindle cells. Often there is extensive hemorrhage and edema in the tumors. The diagnosis is clinically important because a substantial fraction of these tumors have progressed and been lethal.

Immunohistochemically, both conventional and epithelioid angiomyolipomas show positivity for smooth muscle actin and/or desmin, along with HMB45 and/or Melan-A, in line with other members of the PEComa family. Epithelial markers are negative.

Differential diagnosis In cases with an extreme predominance of fat, angiomyolipoma can be confused with lipoma or even liposarcoma; extensive sampling may be necessary to identify the vascular and smooth muscle components of the tumor. Tumors with scant fat may be confused with other mesenchymal tumors, such as leiomyoma or leiomyosarcoma. Tumors with epithelioid features may mimic epithelial tumors

of the kidney and the possibility should be considered when examining an epithelial-like renal tumor that is hard to classify, particularly if the patient has tuberous sclerosis.

Epithelioid angiomyolipoma is often incorrectly diagnosed as carcinoma at frozen section, in fine needle aspirations or in permanent sections. This diagnosis should be considered when confronted by any unusual renal neoplasm composed of poorly cohesive polygonal cells with eosinophilic cytoplasm.

Hemangioma

Hemangiomas of the kidney have been found mainly in adults and occur equally in men and women.[215,216] Solitary lesions are the most frequent, but more than 10 percent are multiple and bilaterality has been reported. Rarely, they may be associated with the Klippel–Trenaunay and Sturge–Weber syndromes.[217] Many are asymptomatic and found only at autopsy. In symptomatic patients, recurrent hematuria is the usual complaint, frequently associated with anemia.[218]

Macroscopic appearances Most are less than one centimeter in diameter and unimpressive to the naked eye. Larger lesions, up to 18 cm in diameter, occur and have a spongy reddish appearance. While hemangiomas may arise anywhere in the kidney, the medulla and papilla are the sites of the majority of symptomatic lesions.[218]

Histologic appearances Microscopically, these lesions are composed of vascular spaces of variable size, some of which may have smooth muscle and elastic tissue in their walls. Thrombosis and organization are common. While they often have irregular borders and merge with the surrounding renal parenchyma, the lack of endothelial nuclear atypia and multilayering should make recognition of their benign nature easy in most cases. They are distinguished from angiosarcomas using the same criteria applied in soft tissue (see Ch. 3); this also pertains to the other benign mesenchymal tumors discussed here.

Lymphangioma

Renal lymphangiomas are much less common than renal hemangiomas. A few dozen cases have been described in patients ranging in age from infancy[219] to old age, about a third in children and two-thirds in adults.[220] Grossly, most have been solitary, encapsulated masses composed of small cysts containing clear fluid. Microscopic examination shows spaces lined by benign endothelial cells with septa that are generally fibrous but may contain smooth muscle. Lesions in the renal sinus may infiltrate the renal medulla,[221] obstructing the flow of urine.

Leiomyoma

Symptomatic renal leiomyomas are rare;[222] but they may present as large masses as great as 37 kg;[223] small ones are usually found incidentally at autopsy (Fig. 12.38). Most occur in adults.[224] Grossly, they are well-circumscribed solid rubbery masses with whorled cut surfaces. As in the uterus, they consist of bundles of smooth muscle fibers which may focally calcify and show other degenerative changes. The finding of necrosis, nuclear atypia, or more than rare mitotic figures strongly suggests that the tumor is a leiomyosarcoma.

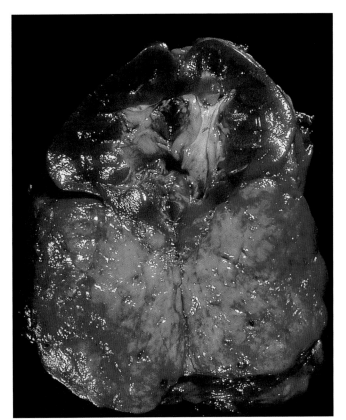

Fig. 12.39 • Renal leiomyosarcoma. The tumor is large and consists of soft tan tissue mottled with hemorrhage. There are small foci of necrosis and cavitary degeneration.

Fig. 12.38 • Renal leiomyoma. The tumor is firm, bulges from the cortical surface, and is composed of whitish tissue.

Lipoma

Symptomatic renal lipomas are rare.[225] The patients usually present with abdominal or flank pain. They occur almost exclusively in middle-aged women. Unlike angiomyolipomas, these tumors are not associated with tuberous sclerosis. Grossly, these are yellow lobulated and encapsulated masses and, histologically, they consist entirely of mature fat. Generous sampling is indicated since, as noted above, angiomyolipomas may consist predominantly of fat and thorough sectioning may be necessary to find the smooth muscle and vascular elements which distinguish them from lipomas. Rarely, renal sinus fat around the renal pelvis may proliferate excessively, mimicking a neoplasm.[226]

Leiomyosarcoma

This is the commonest primary renal sarcoma, more than 100 cases having been reported.[227] While the patients' ages have ranged from childhood to more than 80, most have occurred in patients older than 40, with a peak in the fifth and sixth decades. There have been approximately twice as many women as men. A mass and flank pain are the most common presentation.

Macroscopic appearances The gross appearance of the tumors often resembles that of leiomyomas: firm, solid tumors with well-circumscribed margins and whorled cut surfaces, but necrosis and hemorrhage are more common (Fig. 12.39).[228] Leiomyosarcomas may also arise from the renal capsule[228] and renal vein and the bulk of the tumor may be in the renal sinus.[229] Renal and perirenal infiltration are frequent.

Histologic appearances Microscopically, they are composed of fascicles of eosinophilic spindle-shaped cells with features resembling smooth muscle. The degree of nuclear pleomorphism and the prevalence of mitotic figures vary over a wide range and no clear minimum criteria of malignancy have been established. Necrosis, nuclear pleomorphism, or more than rare mitotic figures should be taken as indications that a renal smooth muscle tumor is probably a leiomyosarcoma. Especially in large smooth muscle tumors, suspicion of leiomyosarcoma should be high because metastasis and death have occasionally been caused by tumors with very low mitotic counts.[230] Staining for HMB45 and Melan-A may be necessary to exclude a smooth muscle-predominant angiomyotipoma.

Liposarcoma

Liposarcoma is common in the retroperitoneal soft tissues, but very rare in the kidney itself.[231,232] Careful gross examination is important to establish the intrarenal origin of the tumors since liposarcomas of the retroperitoneal soft tissues invading or compressing the kidney are far more common than renal liposarcomas invading the retroperitoneal soft tissues.[228] In cases in which the origin is unclear (the larger and more infiltrative ones), the presumption should be in favor of a primary in retroperitoneal soft tissue. Some of the reported cases have, in retrospect, been large solitary angiomyolipomas, giving renal liposarcoma a reputation for a more favorable prognosis than is warranted. Grossly, the tumors are relatively well circumscribed yellow lobulated masses. Histopathologically, renal liposarcomas have shown the usual variety of patterns found elsewhere; 80 percent of the tumors described by Farrow et al.[228] were myxoid.

So-called malignant fibrous histiocytoma

So-called malignant fibrous histiocytomas (MFH) may arise from the renal parenchyma or from the renal capsule.[233,234] Since the retroperitoneal soft tissues are a common site, the recommendations made above for the attribution of primary site for liposarcomas involving the kidney also apply here. Clinically, renal malignant fibrous histiocytomas have mainly occurred in adults and there has been a strong male predominance. For the most part, they have been large infiltrative lesions and histopathologically of the storiform-pleomorphic and inflammatory types. The former may be difficult to distinguish from sarcomatoid renal cell carcinoma and the latter may resemble xanthogranulomatous pyelonephritis. At this anatomic site, however, it is nowadays recognized that most lesions in either of these categories are, in fact, dedifferentiated liposarcomas.

Rhabdomyosarcoma

Rhabdomyosarcomas of the kidney are rare;[235–237] Grignon et al. reviewed the literature and found only eight convincing cases, evenly divided between the genders and occurring in patients from 36 to 70 years old.[238] Four died of the sarcoma within 14 months and the other 4 were reported with less than 12 months of follow-up. Most renal tumors with appearances suggesting rhabdomyosarcoma are something else, so the diagnosis of rhabdomyosarcoma should be made reluctantly. In children, Wilms' tumors may contain elements of skeletal muscle and the existence of rhabdomyosarcoma distinct from Wilms' tumor in children is questionable. Rhabdoid tumor of kidney (see below) may also mimic rhabdomyosarcoma, as may sarcomatoid renal cell carcinoma.

Other sarcomas

Synovial sarcoma occasionally occurs primarily in the kidney and may be extensively cystic.[239,240] Solitary fibrous tumor primary in the kidney is rare[241,242] and subject to the confusion between intrarenal and extrarenal origin discussed in the section on liposarcoma.[223,243] These tumors were often formerly known as hemangiopericytoma.[244–246] The tumors usually are large and cysts and foci of hemorrhage are common. Osteogenic sarcomas arise rarely from the renal parenchyma or pelvis[247,248] and a few chondrosarcomas,[249] and angiosarcomas[250,251] have been reported. Histologically, they show the typical features seen elsewhere.

Juxtaglomerular cell tumor

Juxtaglomerular cell tumors, also known as reninomas, were recognized independently in 1967 by Robertson and associates and Kihara and associates.[252,253] Approximately 100 cases have been reported as single case reports and small series.[254] While almost all of the patients have been hypertensive, Corvol and associates[255] found only seven such tumors in 30 000 new hypertensive patients. Elevation of plasma renin levels is typical of these patients and selective catheterization of the renal veins has been an important guide to the resection of small tumors.[256] Most of the patients have been young adults and adolescents, averaging 27 years old at the time of resection.[254] However, many of the patients have been hypertensive for years before resection. The average age of onset of hypertension is only 22 years. Females exceed males by almost 2:1. Resection has cured the hypertension in most cases and conservative resection has been effective in several cases. One juxtaglomerular cell tumor has metastasized.[257] No instance of local invasion or recurrence, multifocality or bilaterality has been reported.

Macroscopic appearances Most lesions have been smaller than 3 cm and some have not been visible when the renal capsule was stripped. Thus, when a juxtaglomerular cell tumor is suspected, the specimen must be carefully dissected and any abnormal foci submitted for histopathologic examination. The masses are sharply circumscribed and composed of rubbery off-white tissue, sometimes containing small cyst-like smooth-walled cavities (Fig. 12.40).

Histologic appearances The histopathology of these lesions is varied. A common pattern is one of irregular trabeculae of polygonal cells in a loose myxoid stroma (Fig. 12.41). Tubules and cysts often are present. There is frequently prominent vascularity and a lymphocytic infiltrate may be conspicuous (Fig. 12.42). Modified Bowie's stain may reveal intracytoplasmic granules and immunohistochemistry may demonstrate intracytoplasmic renin.[258] Electron microscopy is helpful in demonstrating the typical rhomboid granules of juxtaglomerular cell tumors (Fig. 12.43).[259]

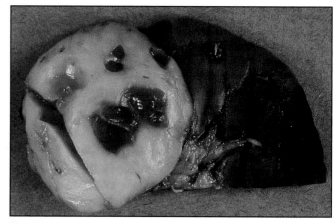

Fig. 12.40 • Juxtaglomerular cell tumor. The tumor is a well-circumscribed spheroidal mass of rubbery, yellow-tan tissue with several smooth-walled cavities and focal hemorrhage.

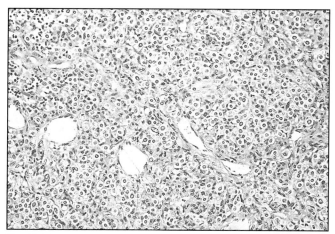

Fig. 12.41 • Juxtaglomerular cell tumor. Polygonal cells with light-staining or clear cytoplasm lie in a richly vascular stroma.

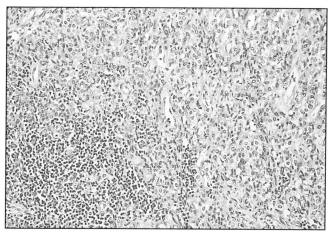

Fig. 12.42 • Juxtaglomerular cell tumor. Sheets of cells with variation in nuclear size and shape and variably eosinophilic cytoplasm are admixed with clusters of lymphocytes.

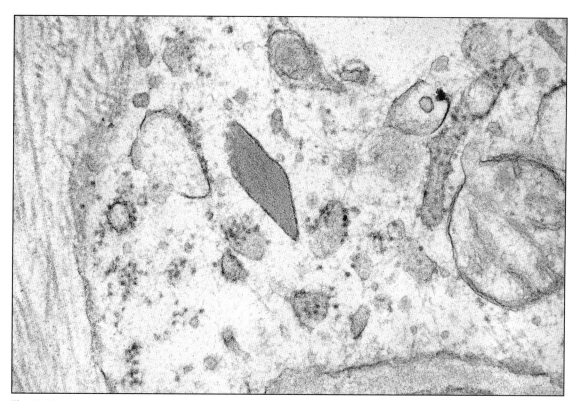

Fig. 12.43 • Juxtaglomerular cell tumor. Ultrastructurally, the renin-containing granules are often strikingly rhomboid.

Differential diagnosis As it is almost invariably discovered in the investigation of hypertension, the nature of the tumor is often suspected preoperatively. The gross finding of a small light-colored rubbery tumor narrows the differential diagnosis and the histologic appearance is distinctive. However, since immunoreactive renin has been found in renal cell carcinomas and Wilms' tumors,[260–262] some of which have caused hypertension, these may rarely cause diagnostic confusion.

Renomedullary interstitial cell tumor

These small tumors of the renal medulla are frequent incidental findings at autopsy and occasionally are seen in surgical pathology specimens.[263] Ultrastructural and other studies have shown that these lesions are composed of the renomedullary interstitial cells which contain vasoactive substances important in the regulation of blood pressure. Whether these are neoplasms or hyperplastic nodules which arise in response to hypertension remains controversial. They are rare in patients younger than 20 years but, in a large series of carefully dissected autopsy kidneys, almost half the patients over 20 had at least one lesion and 57 percent of the patients with renomedullary interstitial cell tumors had more than one.[264]

Since most of these tumors are small, they rarely cause symptoms or diagnostic difficulty in surgical specimens. Most problems have arisen when one is an unexpected finding in a kidney resected for other reasons, such as transplantation (Fig. 12.44). The few symptomatic tumors have usually been pedunculated masses in the renal pelvis, and early reports called them renal pelvic fibromas.[265]

Macroscopic appearances These tumors are white nodules and occur anywhere in the renal medulla (Fig. 12.45). Well-circumscribed and usually spheroidal, most are less than 5 mm in diameter.

Histologic appearances Microscopically, small stellate cells lie in a faintly basophilic loose stroma, reminiscent of the stroma of the renal medulla. Bundles of loose reticulin fibers arranged in an interlacing pattern frequently are present (Fig. 12.46). The stromal matrix often entraps medullary tubules at the periphery of the nodules. The name fibroma is a misnomer

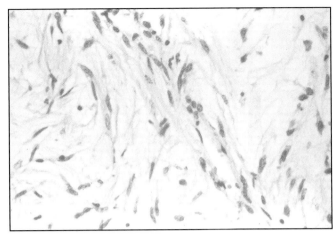

Fig. 12.46 • Renomedullary interstitial cell tumor. These tumors are composed of stellate and spindle cells in a lightly basophilic stroma.

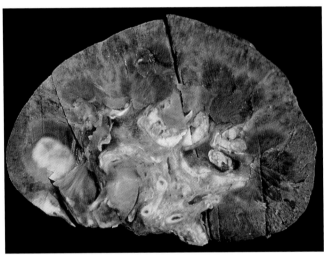

Fig. 12.44 • Renomedullary interstitial cell tumor. This 15 mm light yellow well-circumscribed intramedullary tumor was found in an acutely rejected transplanted kidney.

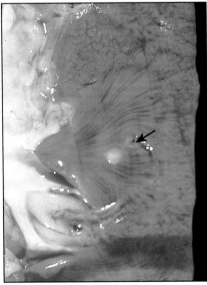

Fig. 12.45 • Renomedullary interstitial cell tumor. A small white intramedullary nodule which bulges slightly above the cut surface of the kidney is the classic appearance of renomedullary interstitial cell tumor.

since most of these lesions contain little collagen. Some do contain amyloid[266] which may be deposited in irregular clumps, obscuring the characteristic delicate stroma.

Cystic nephroma

Cystic nephroma, which has also been called multilocular cyst[267] and multilocular cystic nephroma,[268] is an uncommon benign renal neoplasm which occurs in adults.[87,269] Women predominate over men in a ratio of approximately 7:1. In a few patients, sarcoma has arisen in cystic nephroma.[87] Conservative surgery is generally curative but, in one case, cystic nephroma recurred after incomplete excision.[87,270] The diagnostic criteria for cystic nephroma are listed in Table 12.7.

Macroscopic appearances These lesions are well-circumscribed globular masses surrounded by a fibrous capsule. They are composed of multiple non-communicating cystic locules with smooth inner surfaces. The cysts are filled with clear yellowish fluid (Fig. 12.47). Solid areas are absent and the septa range from paper-thin to a few millimeters thick. Grossly, cystic nephroma is indistinguishable from multilocular cystic renal cell carcinoma and from cystic partially differentiated nephroblastoma.

Histologic appearances Microscopically, the septa are composed of fibrous tissue which may contain foci of calcification.

Table 12.7	Diagnostic criteria of Eble and Bonsib for cystic nephroma[87]

Adult patient

Expansile mass surrounded by fibrous pseudocapsule

Interior entirely composed of cysts and septa with no expansile solid nodules

Cysts lined by flattened, hobnail, or cuboidal epithelium

Septa may contain epithelial structures resembling mature renal tubules

Septa may not contain epithelial cells with clear cytoplasm

Septa may not contain skeletal muscle fibers

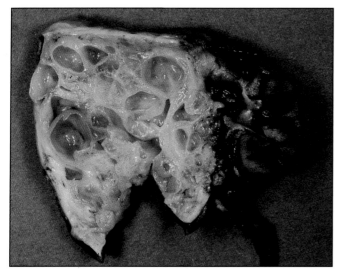

Fig. 12.47 • Cystic nephroma. Multiple smooth-walled locules of variable size make up a mass circumscribed by a fibrous condensation.

The septa may contain structures resembling differentiated renal tubules (as opposed to tubules with the morphology characteristic of Wilms' tumor), inflammatory cells, and reactive fibroblasts (Fig. 12.48).[271] The cellularity of the septa ranges from sparsely cellular hyalinized tissue to highly cellular spindle cell stroma superficially resembling ovarian stroma. The cysts are usually lined by flattened or low cuboidal epithelium with small amounts of cytoplasm; occasionally the lining cells have a hobnail configuration. The cytoplasm ranges from eosinophilic to clear.

Differential diagnosis Cystic Wilms' tumor and cystic renal cell carcinoma are the principal differential diagnostic considerations, clinically, radiographically, and pathologically. The criteria set out in Table 12.7 distinguish cystic nephroma from these tumors. Of critical importance is the absence of blastema and other elements of Wilms' tumor and the lack of collections of epithelial cells with clear cytoplasm within the septa.

Fig. 12.48 • Cystic nephroma. The septa composed of fibrous tissue are of variable thickness and lined by cuboidal or flattened epithelium.

Mixed epithelial and stromal tumor of kidney

A rare and distinctive renal neoplasm apparently composed of a complex mixture of neoplastic stroma and epithelium has been recognized in recent years.[87] A variety of names has been applied to these tumors,[272–274] but the one which most accurately describes them is mixed epithelial and stromal tumor and this has been accepted in the WHO classification.[1,275] To date, virtually all of these appear to have been cured surgically, aside from rare, recently described and somewhat controversial cases with stromal atypia which have metastasized.[276]

Grossly, the tumors typically contain small and large cysts mixed with solid areas.[277] A few have been extensively cystic and have resembled cystic nephroma. They appear to arise from the renal parenchyma, probably the medulla, and a majority have extended into the renal pelvis.

Microscopically, they consist of variably cellular stroma ranging from hyalinized fibrous tissue to smooth muscle.[277] Fat has been present in some. The stroma contains complex epithelial elements forming cysts and tubules. The tubules range from small ones resembling nephrogenic adenoma to long branching tubules. The lining epithelium may be cuboidal, columnar, flattened, or urothelial. Some cases may resemble biphasic synovial sarcoma. Immunohistochemistry almost always confirms smooth muscle differentiation. Estrogen and progesterone receptors can frequently be detected. HMB45 is absent.

Lymphoma

Secondary involvement of the kidney in cases of disseminated malignant lymphoma occurs in as many as 50 percent of cases. However, whether or not lymphomas occur as primary tumors in the kidney is controversial.[278,279] Small numbers of cases of lymphoma which have presented as renal masses have been reported but, in most, extrarenal lymphoma has been discovered shortly thereafter. The symptoms, if any, resemble those of renal cell carcinoma.[280]

Macroscopic appearances The gross appearance of lymphoma in the kidney is variable. Frequently, the mass is parenchymal and well-circumscribed; less frequently, it is diffuse.[281] In the former case, the lesions consist of whitish nodules in the kidney, typically visible on the cortical surface (Fig. 12.49). In the latter case, the renal volume is expanded and the cortex and medulla are pale and their junctions are obscured by the infiltrate (Fig. 12.50). Lymphoma presenting as a renal mass often arises in the renal sinus, surrounding and invading the hilar structures.[281]

Histologic appearances The microscopic appearance varies according to the gross appearance and type of lymphoma. In cases in which the lymphoma consists of circumscribed nodules, the lesions consist almost entirely of lymphoma cells. In examples in which there is diffuse infiltration, the renal interstitium is infiltrated by a monomorphous population of atypical lymphoid cells; there may be sparing of the glomeruli and tubules. Among those presenting as renal primaries, large cell lymphomas are more common than small cell lymphomas[280,281] and Hodgkin's disease is unusual.[281] Plasmacytomas also occur in the kidney.[282,283]

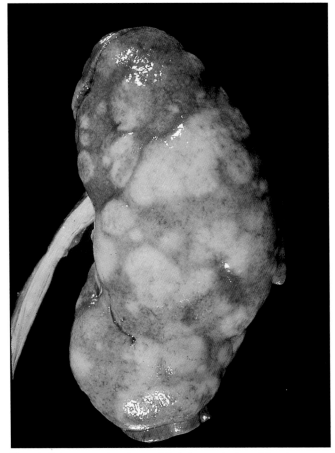

Fig. 12.49 • Malignant lymphoma of the kidney. Multiple nodules of lymphoma replace much of the renal parenchyma.

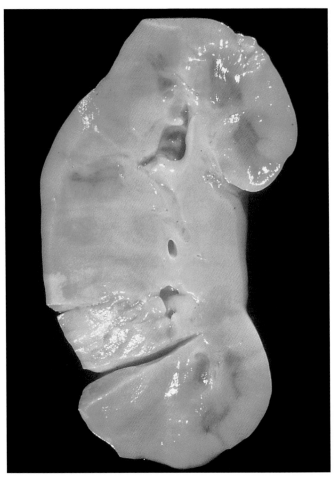

Fig. 12.50 • Malignant lymphoma of the kidney. Lymphoma diffusely infiltrates the kidney, preserving its general shape but enlarging it and obscuring the cortical and medullary landmarks.

Secondary neoplasms of the kidney

In a study of 11 328 autopsies of cancer patients, Bracken et al.[284] found that 7.2 percent of patients had metastases to the kidneys. These findings are supported by other studies.[285–288] Bronchogenic carcinomas are the most frequent sources of metastatic carcinoma.[284,287] Metastases more rarely present as primary renal tumors and may be treated surgically for that mistaken diagnosis.[286] Although solitary metastases may closely mimic primary renal neoplasms grossly, microscopic examination will usually clarify the case when the typical features of a non-renal primary are found. Occasionally, carcinoma metastatic to the kidney is found only as widespread microscopic metastases to the glomeruli (Fig. 12.51),[289] or diffusely within renal lymphatics.[290]

Renal tumors in children

Primary renal neoplasms are uncommon in children; approximately 500 new cases occur in the USA annually. However, they constitute the fifth most common group of pediatric cancers and are the second most frequent abdominal malignancy of children. While not very numerous in absolute terms,

progress in the treatment of Wilms' tumor and the recognition of two highly malignant neoplasms as specific entities distinct from Wilms' tumor, make the correct diagnosis and staging of pediatric renal neoplasms of great clinical importance.[291–293] The variable and overlapping appearances of the tumors, and their rarity, make them an especially challenging group of lesions for the surgical pathologist.

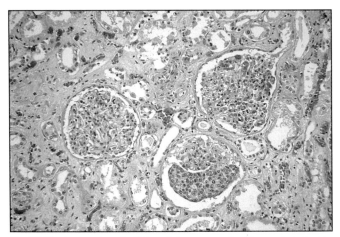

Fig. 12.51 • Metastasis to the kidney. Pulmonary carcinoid has metastasized to a glomerulus.

The most common tumor in this group is Wilms' tumor (nephroblastoma). Important because of their poor response to therapy and consequent morbidity and mortality are clear cell sarcoma and rhabdoid tumor. In children younger than 3 months, mesoblastic nephroma is the most common renal neoplasm and usually has a favorable prognosis. A final rare tumor, the ossifying renal tumor of infancy, will be mentioned briefly in this section. Tumors, such as renal cell carcinoma, lymphoma, sarcomas, neuroendocrine tumors, and angiomyolipoma, which usually are found in adult kidneys, occur rarely in children but do not, in most instances, differ pathologically in this age group from those in adults (see above).

Much of what we know today about the pathology of renal neoplasia in childhood is the result of the work of the National Wilms' Tumor Study (NWTS) and its Pathology Center under the direction of Bruce Beckwith.

Wilms' tumor

Wilms' tumors comprise more than 80 percent of renal tumors of childhood.[294] Most often, they are found in children 2 to 4 years old (median ages for males and females, respectively, are 37 and 43 months);[295] they are relatively uncommon in the first six months of life and in children older than 6 years.[296] Wilms' tumors are rare in the neonatal period.[297] The incidence of Wilms' tumors is about the same in varied populations throughout the world.[298] There is a slight preponderance of females.[295] The tumors are bilateral in 4.4 percent of cases[299] and patients with bilateral tumors are, on average, more than a year younger than patients with unilateral tumors.[295] Associations with congenital anomalies, specifically cryptorchidism, hypospadias, other genital anomalies, hemihypertrophy, and aniridia are well-recognized.[300] As many as 5 percent of patients with Beckwith–Wiedemann syndrome develop Wilms' tumor.[301] Patients with the Drash syndrome also have an increased risk of developing Wilms' tumor.[302] A variety of other malformations are less frequently associated with Wilms' tumor.[296,303] Uncommonly, Wilms' tumors have a familial association.[295] Wilms' tumors are rare in adults and the stage at presentation and frequency of anaplasia are higher than in children and the response to therapy is correspondingly poorer.[304,305]

Nephrogenic rests and nephroblastomatosis Aggregates of cells resembling blastema have been found in pediatric autopsies and in kidneys resected from patients with Wilms' tumors for decades.[306] Bove and McAdams studied 69 kidneys resected for Wilms' tumors and observed microscopic nodules of blastemal cells in a third of the cases.[307] Using these observations, they proposed a classification based on histologic features, including categories of nodular renal blastema, metanephric hamartoma, and others.[307] Subsequently, additional terminology was introduced and the nomenclature became confusing.[294] In 1990, Beckwith et al.[308] proposed a new classification based on the extensive case material of the NWTS; the following discussion is based on that work.

Nephrogenic rests are foci of persistent nephrogenic cells resembling those of the developing kidney (Fig. 12.52). These are divided into two categories: perilobar nephrogenic rests, which are located at the periphery of the renal lobes, and

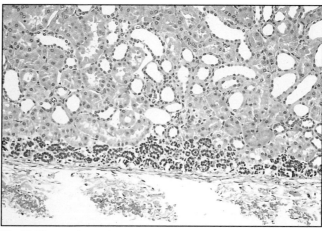

Fig. 12.52 • Perilobar nephrogenic rest. There are small tubular structures composed of cuboidal epithelium with darkly staining nuclei in a linear array deep to the renal capsule. (Courtesy of Dr. B. Beckwith and the National Wilms' Tumor Study Pathology Center.)

cortical surfaces, the centers of the columns of Bertin, and the tissue abutting the renal sinus), and intralobar nephrogenic rests which are located in the cortex or medulla within the renal lobe. In addition to their location, perilobar nephrogenic rests differ from intralobar nephrogenic rests in having well-defined smooth borders, predominance of blastema, and are often numerous or diffuse. Intralobar nephrogenic rests usually are single and mingle irregularly with renal parenchyma; stroma is usually the predominant element. Nephrogenic rests are subclassified according to their histologic appearance as: dormant or nascent; maturing sclerosing, and obsolescent; hyperplastic; and neoplastic. The first are usually composed of blastema, of microscopic size, and exhibit rare mitotic figures. In the maturing, sclerosing and obsolescent types, there are differentiating stromal and epithelial cells with hyalinization of stroma (Fig. 12.53). The hyperplastic rests are macroscopically visible and may contain blastemal, embryonic, or sclerosing areas. Uncommonly, hyperplastic rests may diffusely replace much of the renal parenchyma (Fig. 12.54). Neoplastic rests

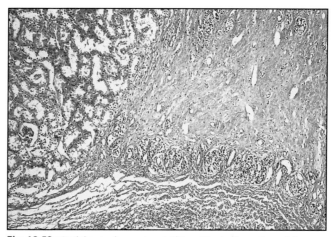

Fig. 12.53 • Perilobar nephrogenic rest. This rest is obsolescent, consisting mainly of fibrous tissue with only a small population of immature tubules. (Courtesy of Dr. B. Beckwith and the National Wilms' Tumor Study Pathology Center.)

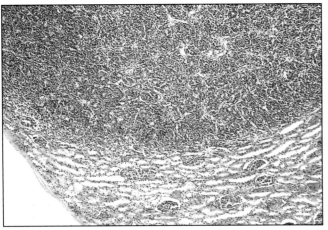

Fig. 12.54 • Perilobar nephrogenic rest. This rest is hyperplastic with a nodular growth pattern and dense cellularity. (Courtesy of Dr. B. Beckwith and the National Wilms' Tumor Study Pathology Center.)

are divided into adenomatous and nephroblastomatous types, based on cellular crowding and the prevalence of mitotic figures. In adenomatous rests, mitotic figures are uncommon, while in nephroblastomatous rests (incipient Wilms' tumors) mitotic figures are common. Typically, neoplastic rests are visibly expansile spherical lesions arising within and compressing a rest. Nephroblastomatosis is defined as the diffuse or multifocal presence of nephrogenic rests, or multicentric or bilateral Wilms' tumors (Fig. 12.55).

Perilobar nephrogenic rests are present in approximately 1 percent of infants younger than 3 months,[69] a frequency much greater than that of Wilms' tumor (1 per 10 000), while intralobar nephrogenic rests are almost never seen except with Wilms' tumor. Nephrogenic rests are extremely rare in adults.[309] In patients with unilateral Wilms' tumor, the NWTS has found that perilobar and intralobar nephrogenic rests occur approximately equally frequently and are present in 41 percent of cases. The situation differs in patients with synchronous or metachronous bilateral tumors in whom nephrogenic rests are present in more than 95 percent of cases. Thus, careful examination of the grossly uninvolved kidney is of importance in cases of Wilms' tumor, for the presence of

nephrogenic rests indicates a greater probability of bilaterality, either synchronously or metachronously.

Macroscopic appearances Wilms' tumors are usually large masses more than 5 cm in diameter and a third or more are larger than 10 cm.[296] Often they weigh more than 500 g. The cut surfaces are typically solid, soft, and grayish or pinkish, resembling brain tissue (Fig. 12.56). Foci of hemorrhage and necrosis are often present and cysts are common. Rarely, the tumors are extensively cystic. The tumors usually are enclosed by a prominent pseudocapsule composed of compressed renal and perirenal tissues; this gives an appearance of circumscription and even true encapsulation (Fig. 12.57). Polypoid growth in the renal pelvic cavity, mimicking sarcoma botryoides, is a

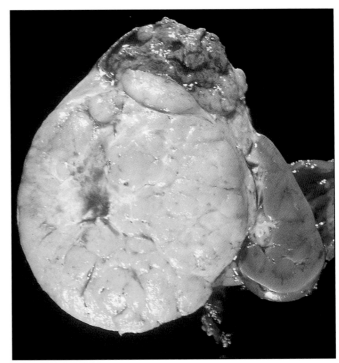

Fig. 12.56 • Wilms' tumor. A large soft tumor, resembling cerebral cortex in color and consistency, dwarfs the kidney in which it has arisen. There is a brown focus of necrosis at the superior end of the tumor.

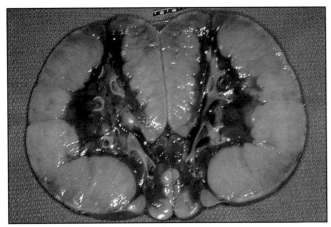

Fig. 12.55 • Nephroblastomatosis. The kidney is diffusely replaced and expanded by soft tan tissue.

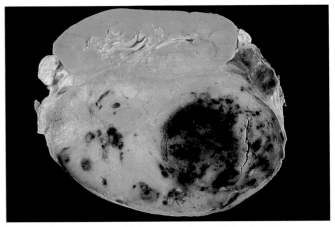

Fig. 12.57 • Wilms' tumor. This large tumor has a well-developed inflammatory pseudo-capsule which contains two nodules of infiltrative tumor.

feature associated with extensive skeletal muscle differentiation[310,311] and could lead to an erroneous diagnosis of rhabdomyosarcoma.

Histologic appearances Wilms' tumors are typically composed of variable mixtures of blastema, epithelium, and stroma, although in some tumors only two and occasionally only one, component is present. Blastema consists of sheets or randomly arranged densely packed small cells with darkly staining nuclei, frequent mitotic figures, and inconspicuous cytoplasm (Fig. 12.58), resembling to some extent, other "small blue cell tumors" of childhood. Blastema is commonly arranged in three patterns, serpentine, nodular, and diffuse. Serpentine and nodular are most common and diagnostically helpful. They consist of anastomosing serpiginous or spheroidal aggregates of blastema sharply circumscribed from the surrounding stromal elements (Fig. 12.59).

The epithelial component usually consists of small tubules or cysts lined by primitive columnar or cuboidal cells (Fig. 12.60). The nuclei of the epithelium are often elongate and wedge-shaped (Fig. 12.61). The epithelium of Wilms' tumor may also form structures resembling glomeruli or may differentiate in extrarenal directions, being mucinous, squamous, neural[312] or endocrine[313] in type.[121] Predominantly cystic Wilms' tumors contain blastemal and other Wilms' tumor tissues in their septa (Fig. 12.62) and have been designated cystic partially differentiated nephroblastoma.

Wilms' tumors' stroma may differentiate along the lines of almost any type of soft tissue. While loose myxoid and fibroblastic spindle cell stroma are most common (Fig. 12.63), smooth muscle, skeletal muscle (Fig. 12.64), fat, cartilage, bone, and neural components also occur.[121] Uncommonly, the differentiation towards more mature soft tissue types is diffuse and predominant and such tumors have sometimes been given special names, such as fetal rhabdomyomatous nephroblastoma[314] and tumors with complex combinations of differentiated epithelium and stroma have been termed teratoid Wilms' tumor.[315,316]

Differential diagnosis Cystic partially differentiated nephroblastomas grossly resemble cystic nephroma and, since the elements typical of Wilms' tumor may be inconspicuous, cystic

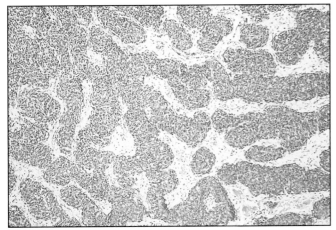

Fig. 12.58 • Wilms' tumor. Blastema consists of sheets of small cells with inconspicuous cytoplasm, hyperchromatic nuclei, and frequent mitotic figures.

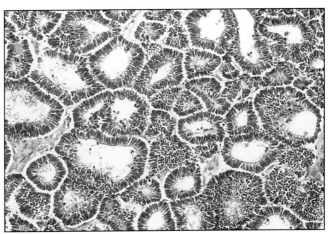

Fig. 12.60 • Wilms' tumor. The epithelium is columnar and forms tubular structures.

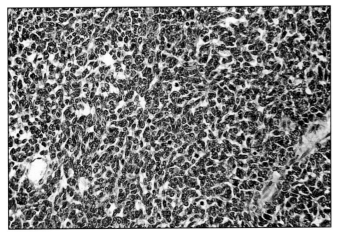

Fig. 12.59 • Wilms' tumor. The blastema is arranged in a serpiginous pattern. (Courtesy of Dr. B. Beckwith and the National Wilms' Tumor Study Pathology Center.)

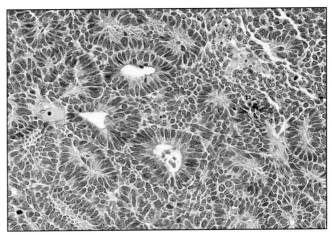

Fig. 12.61 • Wilms' tumor. The nuclei of the epithelium of Wilms' tumors are often elongated, molded, and wedge-shaped.

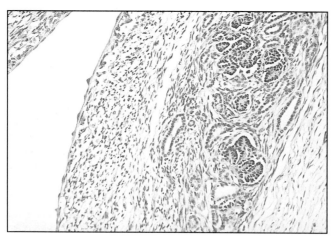

Fig. 12.62 • Wilms' tumor. The septa of cystic, partially differentiated nephroblastomas contain nephroblastic tissues, in this case immature tubules and glomeruloid bodies. The epithelium lining the cysts is flat. (Courtesy of Dr. Beckwith and the National Wilms' Tumor Study Pathology Center.)

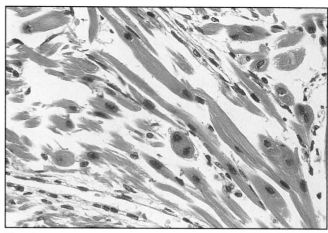

Fig. 12.64 • Wilms' tumor. In some cases, the stroma is predominantly composed of skeletal muscle.

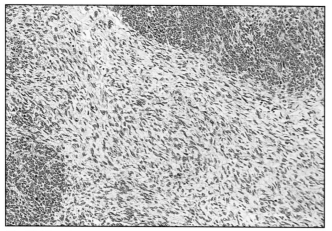

Fig. 12.63 • Wilms' tumor. Although the stroma of Wilms' tumors can differentiate in many directions, most frequently it is composed of spindle cells in an abundant faintly basophilic matrix.

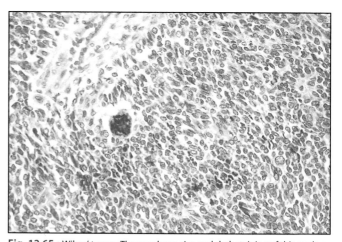

Fig. 12.65 • Wilms' tumor. The very large size and dark staining of this nucleus are necessary for the diagnosis of the unfavorable histologic category of anaplasia. (Courtesy of Dr. B. Beckwith and the National Wilms' Tumor Study Pathology Center.)

renal tumors in children should be sampled extensively before cystic partially differentiated nephroblastoma is excluded.

Fetal rhabdomyomatous nephroblastoma should not be misinterpreted as a rhabdomyosarcoma because the former has a generally favorable prognosis. This tumor contains extensive areas of relatively mature skeletal muscle but lacks the malignant small cells and rhabdomyoblasts found in rhabdomyosarcoma.

Some Wilms' tumors have a monomorphous epithelial appearance and can pose difficult diagnostic problems, especially in adolescents and adults, in their distinction from renal cell carcinoma. Recognition of the nuclear characteristics typical of Wilms' tumor epithelium is usually helpful in distinguishing these Wilms' tumors from renal cell carcinoma. The epithelial nuclei in Wilms' tumor are often elongate or ovoid with molded, sometimes wedged, shapes (see Fig. 12.61), a feature helpful in distinguishing monophasic tubular Wilms' tumor from renal cell carcinomas in which the nuclei are usually spheroidal.

The distinction of Wilms' tumor from rhabdoid tumor and clear cell sarcoma is discussed below.

Grading, staging and prognostic factors in Wilms' tumors

Based on the results of the NWTS, Wilms' tumors are divided into two categories: favorable and unfavorable histologies, based on the absence or presence of anaplasia. Anaplasia is found in approximately 6 percent of Wilms' tumors; it is rare in patients younger than 1 year and more than 80 percent of affected patients are older than two.[317] Early in the NWTS, the presence of anaplasia was recognized to carry a greatly increased risk of treatment failure and death.[318] The significance of anaplasia depends upon its extent; the likelihood of a cure when anaplasia is focal is excellent.[319,320]

Anaplasia has been defined by the NWTS as the combination of cells with very large hyperchromatic nuclei and multipolar mitotic figures. Correct recognition of anaplasia demands good histologic preparations: proper fixation, sectioning, and staining are crucial. The enlarged nuclei must be at least three times as large as typical blastemal nuclei in both axes and their hyperchromasia must be obvious (Fig. 12.65). In addition to the enlarged nuclei, hyperdiploid mitotic figures must be present. Several points should be borne in mind when evaluating a Wilms' tumor for anaplasia. First, enlarged nuclei in skeletal muscle fibers in the stroma of Wilms' tumors are not evidence of anaplasia. Second, the criteria for abnormal hyperdiploid mitotic figures are quite strict, demanding not only structural abnormalities but also enlargement of the mitotic figure as evidence of hyperploidy. Occasionally, mitotic figures of normal ploidy appear multipolar due to artifact but these are much smaller than the hyperploid mitotic figures of anaplasia; comparison with the normal-sized mitotic figures in blastema elsewhere in the tumor facilitates this determination. When anaplasia is present only focally, surgical cure remains likely.[321]

The NWTS has established a staging scheme for Wilms' tumor and other pediatric renal malignancies (Table 12.8).[322] The tabular presentation below, however, does not do justice to the challenges which staging presents to the surgical pathologist. Stage I and stage II require assessment of the renal sinus and capsule. The renal sinus is the space within the kidney extending from the plane defined by the medial-most limits of the cortex laterally to the limits of the space between the medullary pyramids and contains the major branches of the renal artery and vein and the bulk of the renal pelvis. In NWTS 5, vascular invasion in the renal sinus was adopted as evidence of extension requiring upstaging to stage II. Invasion of the soft tissue of the renal sinus is acceptable in stage I unless it involves the margin, in which case stage III is the appropriate

assignment. Stage I also requires evaluation of the renal capsule, but this is often difficult because, as a renal neoplasm grows, it sequentially is surrounded by an intrarenal pseudo-capsule, the renal capsule, a pseudocapsule external to the kidney, Gerota's fascia, and the ultimate limits of the specimen. These layers frequently fuse, confusing the identification of the true renal capsule. In fact, when Wilms' tumor invades perirenal fat, it may destroy the fat cells and a fibrous response may give the appearance of stage I limitation by renal capsule. If the renal capsule can be identified, it is the structure which must be used for staging. When the renal capsule is joined to the soft tissue of Gerota's fascia, this layer must be used for staging. The presence of an inflammatory pseudocapsule beyond the renal capsule is at present not sufficient justification for assigning stage II, but has been shown to be associated with an increase in the rate of relapse.[323] Stages II, and IV are more straightforward as shown in Table 12.8. For stage V, the most advanced individual tumor should be assigned a substage according to the stage it would be assigned if it had occurred alone, for example stage V, substage I.

Clear cell sarcoma of kidney

Originally called bone-metastasizing renal tumor of childhood by Marsden et al.[324] in the UK, clear cell sarcoma[325] is a highly malignant neoplasm resistant to conventional therapy for Wilms' tumor but often responsive to doxorubicin-containing regimens.[326] Thus, it is of considerable therapeutic importance that clear cell sarcomas be correctly diagnosed. Occurring in the same general age range as Wilms' tumor, clear cell sarcomas comprise approximately 6 percent of pediatric renal tumors;[327] most are diagnosed in patients between 12 and 36 months of age. Rarely, clear cell sarcoma occurs in adults.[328] Approximately 66 percent of the patients are male. The propensity for metastasis to bone is marked; it is at least ten times more likely to metastasize to bone than are other pediatric renal cancers. It is important to note that these lesions are in no way related to clear cell sarcoma of soft tissue (see Ch. 27).

Macroscopic appearances The appearance of the cut surfaces of these tumors is variable: they may be homogeneous, grayish and lobular or variegated, including firm grayish whorled tissues and light pink soft areas (Fig. 12.66).[329] Occasionally, the tumor may produce abundant mucin which gives a slimy glistening appearance. Most appear well-circumscribed. Cysts ranging from a few millimeters to centimeters in diameter are present in approximately a third of cases.[330] Often, the tumor weighs more than 500 g.[329] Bilaterality has not been reported.[294]

Histologic appearances Most clear cell sarcomas of kidney consist of a monotonous array of cells with lightly staining or vacuolated cytoplasm and indistinct borders. The nuclei contain finely dispersed chromatin and the nucleoli are small (Fig. 12.67). These nuclear characteristics are helpful in distinguishing clear cell sarcomas from rhabdoid tumors. In the classical pattern, the cells are arranged in sheets supplied with a distinctive branching array of small blood vessels (Fig. 12.68).[330] Another characteristic feature is the infiltrative border between the clear cell sarcoma and the surrounding renal parenchyma; residual renal tubules are frequently

Table 12.8	National Wilms' Tumor Study system for staging pediatric renal tumors[322] With kind permission of Springer Science and Business Media

Stage I Tumor confined to kidney and completely resected

Specific criteria:
The renal capsule is not penetrated by the tumor
Renal sinus veins and lymphatics not invaded
There is no lymph node or hematogenous spread

Stage II Tumor extends locally outside the kidney but is completely resected

Specific criteria:
The renal capsule is penetrated by tumor
Renal sinus veins or lymphatics invaded
The renal vein contains tumor
Local spillage or biopsy involves only the flank
Specimen margins are free of tumor and no residual tumor remains after surgery
No metastases

Stage III There is residual tumor confined to the abdomen without hematogenous spread

Specific criteria:
Grossly visible residual tumor in abdomen
There are tumor implants on the peritoneal surface
The specimen margins contain tumor
Abdominal lymph nodes contain tumor

Stage IV There are blood-borne metastases or spread beyond abdomen

Stage V Tumors are present in both kidneys

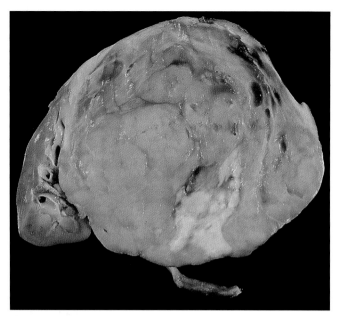

Fig. 12.66 • Clear cell sarcoma of kidney. The gray-tan tumor is large, soft, and focally cystic and necrotic.

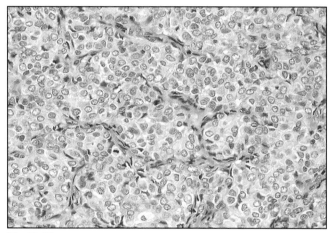

Fig. 12.67 • Clear cell sarcoma of kidney. Nuclei with fine, occasionally vesicular, chromatin patterns and inconspicuous nucleoli are typical of clear cell sarcoma.

Fig. 12.68 • Clear cell sarcoma of kidney. The prominent and branching vascular pattern shown here is characteristic of clear cell sarcoma.

seen surrounded by the sarcoma.[329] Despite their name, the cytoplasm of many clear cell sarcomas is much less clear than that of clear cell renal cell carcinoma and cytoplasmic clarity should not be relied upon to establish the diagnosis. Confusing variations on the classical appearance occur, including spindle cell proliferation, cystic change (Fig. 12.69), hyaline sclerosis, and palisading.[121] The tumors should be sampled generously to find areas in which the vascular pattern and finely dispersed chromatin and small nucleoli in the nuclei indicate the correct diagnosis.

Differential diagnosis In distinguishing clear cell sarcoma of kidney from Wilms' tumor, some pertinent negatives are important: foci of blastema are not seen in clear cell sarcomas; non-renal elements such as cartilage or muscle are not found in clear cell sarcomas; clear cell sarcomas are unilateral and unicentric, and sclerotic stroma is uncommon in Wilms' tumors before therapy. The vascular pattern typical of clear cell sarcoma is often helpful in distinguishing it from Wilms' tumor. The border with the kidney is usually infiltrative, while the border of Wilms' tumor is typically "pushing". Exceptionally, a clear cell sarcoma of kidney may contain foci in which the cells have prominent nucleoli, similar to those of rhabdoid tumor of kidney; other areas with patterns typical of clear cell sarcoma will usually clarify the diagnosis.

Rhabdoid tumor of kidney

The most malignant of the renal neoplasms of childhood, the rhabdoid tumor, usually metastasizes widely and causes the death of the patient within 12 months of diagnosis.[331] The patients usually are very young at the time of diagnosis (NWTS median age 11 months and rare after 3 years) and there is a 1.5:1 predominance of males.[331] Children over the age of 2 have a notably better prognosis.[332] Associations with embryonal tumors of the central nervous system[333] and paraneoplastic hypercalcemia[334] have been reported and a rhabdoid tumor predisposition syndrome has been proposed.[335]

Macroscopic appearances Rhabdoid tumors lack the appearance of encapsulation often seen in cases of Wilms' tumor or

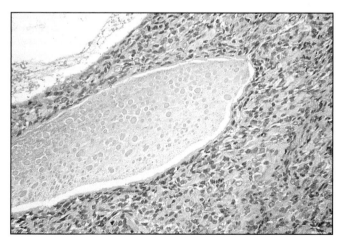

Fig. 12.69 • Clear cell sarcoma of kidney. The cysts are lined by flattened cells and contain proteinaceous and mucoid fluid.

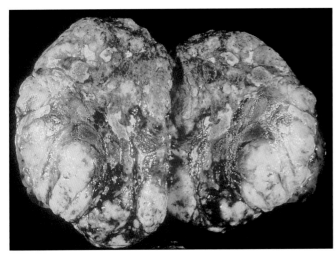

Fig. 12.70 • Rhabdoid tumor of kidney. This is a bulky yellow-brown tumor mottled with hemorrhage and necrosis.

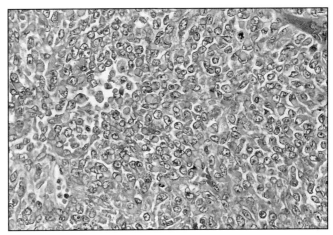

Fig. 12.72 • Rhabdoid tumor of kidney. Globular eosinophilic cytoplasmic inclusions often are present.

clear cell sarcoma. The tumors usually are located medially in the kidney[331] and the renal sinus and pelvis are almost always infiltrated. They are typically yellow-gray or light tan crumbly tumors with indistinct borders (Fig. 12.70). Necrosis and hemorrhage are common.

Histologic appearances Microscopically, the classic pattern of rhabdoid tumor of kidney is a diffuse and monotonous array of medium or large polygonal cells with abundant eosinophilic cytoplasm and spheroidal nuclei with thick nuclear membranes and large nucleoli (Fig. 12.71). It is the resemblance of the cytoplasm of these cells to differentiating rhabdomyoblasts which gave the tumor its name.[325] In fact, the resemblance to skeletal muscle is merely superficial and if definite evidence of differentiation toward skeletal muscle is present, the tumor is not a rhabdoid tumor. Often the cytoplasm contains a large eosinophilic globular inclusion which displaces the nucleus (Fig. 12.72). Electron microscopy has shown that these consist of aggregates of whorled filaments (Fig. 12.73).[336] As more cases have accrued to the NWTS, a wide range of patterns has been appreciated. These include sclerosing, epithelioid,

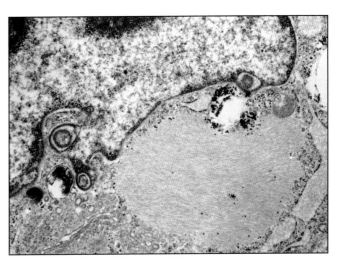

Fig. 12.73 • Rhabdoid tumor of kidney. Ultrastructurally, the cytoplasmic inclusions consist of dense arrays of microfilaments.

spindled, lymphomatoid, vascular, pseudopapillary, and cystic.[331] Typically, these patterns are mixed with the classic pattern and with each other. The characteristic nuclear features of large centrally placed nucleoli and thick nuclear membranes are usually retained. These tumors have a variable immunophenotye, but are most often positive for vimentin and epithelial membrane antigen.

At the molecular level, rhabdoid tumors show loss or deletions of the long arm of chromosome 22 with corresponding loss or deletion of *hSNF5/INI1* gene. This leads to loss of INI1 protein expression, which may serve as a useful immunohistochemical marker.[337]

Differential diagnosis An important problem in the diagnosis of rhabdoid tumor of kidney is the fact that a wide variety of renal and extrarenal tumors may mimic it in hematoxylin and eosin sections. The NWTS has been referred cases of Wilms' tumor, congenital mesoblastic nephroma, renal cell carcinoma, transitional cell carcinoma, collecting duct carcinoma, oncocytoma, rhabdomyosarcoma, neuroendocrine carcinoma, and lymphoma which have been confused with rhabdoid

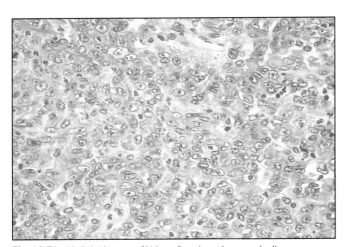

Fig. 12.71 • Rhabdoid tumor of kidney. Prominent large nucleoli are characteristic of rhabdoid tumor of kidney. (Courtesy of Dr. B. Beckwith and the National Wilms' Tumor Study Pathology Center.)

tumor of kidney.[338] Filamentous cytoplasmic inclusions or conspicuous macronucleoli have been the misleading features in most cases. While conventional light microscopy was able to clarify most cases, electron microscopy and immuno-histochemistry were required in some to show characteristic features of the mimics and thus exclude rhabdoid tumor of kidney. While blastemal cells rarely contain inclusions suggestive of rhabdoid tumor, the presence of characteristic aggregates of blastema, such as nodules or serpentine groupings, clarifies the diagnosis.

Congenital mesoblastic nephroma

Although comprising less than 3 percent of primary renal tumors in children, congenital mesoblastic nephroma predominates in the first 3 months of life and is essentially unknown after 24 months.[297,339,340] Polyhydramnios and prematurity have been associated with these tumors.[341,342] In almost all patients, an abdominal mass is the presenting finding. First recognized in 1966,[343] subsequent studies[344] have shown this to be a morphologically distinct and prognostically favorable tumor. The vast majority of patients are cured by surgical resection.[345–347] A few recurrences and adverse outcomes have been recorded, principally in patients older than three months at presentation.[348,349] These tumors are very rare in adults.[350,351] Characteristically, mesoblastic nephromas have infiltrative borders and the surgical pathologist must study these carefully because the risk of recurrence appears related to incomplete resection.[352,353] Cellular mesoblastic nephroma is characterized by the same genetic lesion as infantile fibrosarcoma (See Ch. 24).[354]

Macroscopic appearances Most mesoblastic nephromas are large relative to the infantile kidney. Externally, the surface of the tumor and kidney is smooth and the renal capsule and calyceal systems are stretched over the tumor. The surface may be bosselated. The cut surface resembles that of a leiomyoma: firm, whorled or trabeculated, and light colored (Fig. 12.74). The tumor is not encapsulated and typically interdigitates with the surrounding kidney and may extend into surrounding tissues. Cysts, hemorrhage, and necrosis are present in a

minority of cases, particularly those that are cellular on microscopic examination.[355]

Histologic appearances The pattern described by Bolande et al.[344] was a moderately cellular proliferation of thick interlacing bundles of spindle cells with elongated nuclei and a marked proclivity for infiltration of renal and perirenal tissues (Fig. 12.75). Entrapment of glomeruli and renal tubules is common. Another, and more common pattern was recognized later and consists of a more densely cellular proliferation of polygonal cells with easy-to-find mitotic figures, and this variant often has pushing borders (Fig. 12.76). This pattern has been called cellular mesoblastic nephroma. The two patterns are often mixed in the same tumor. Histologically, cellular lesions are very similar to metanephric stromal tumor, but the latter is much less infiltrative and has a nodular architecture.[38] Some reports have suggested that the cellular pattern is prone to recurrence but, as noted above, age and completeness of resection appear to be the primary risk factors for adverse outcome. In view of the generally favorable outcome for patients with mesoblastic nephroma and the predominance of

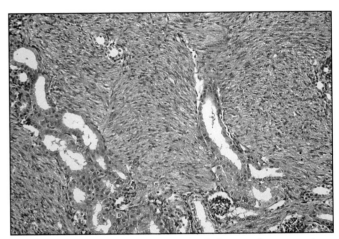

Fig. 12.75 • Mesoblastic nephroma. At the border between the tumor and the kidney, the spindle cells of the tumor infiltrate the interstitium between the renal tubules and glomeruli.

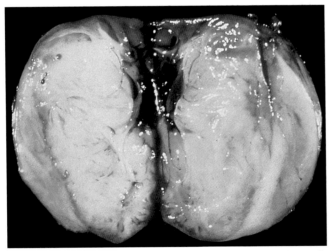

Fig. 12.74 • Mesoblastic nephroma. The tumor is a rubbery lobulated mass of yellow-tan tissue.

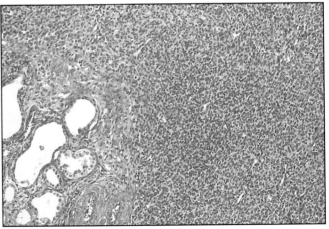

Fig. 12.76 • Mesoblastic nephroma. In the cellular variant, the tumor is more densely cellular and the cells are round rather than spindle-shaped.

lesions containing the cellular pattern, the histologic pattern should not be a primary indication for therapy beyond adequate surgical resection.

Differential diagnosis Mesoblastic nephroma is usually easily diagnosed when the morphology and patient age are considered. Wilms' tumors with stromal predominance may be confused with mesoblastic nephroma, particularly in the case of Wilms' tumors treated preoperatively. This problem can usually be solved by bearing in mind that blastema is not found in mesoblastic nephroma and that Wilms' tumors usually have sharply circumscribed borders, while those of mesoblastic nephromas often are infiltrative. Age assists in making the correct diagnosis and bilaterality favors Wilms' tumor. Although both occur in the same age group, mesoblastic nephroma, even the cellular variant, and rhabdoid tumor are usually easily distinguished.

Ossifying renal tumor of infancy

This rare tumor of uncertain histogenesis has been reported in less than 20 patients, all younger than 6 months.[356] There is a striking predominance of boys and hematuria has been the most common presenting symptom. Radiography often reveals a calcified mass in the collecting system or pelvis. Although there is an irregular infiltrative border, the clinical course has been benign to date.

Grossly, the tumors are typically stone-hard and project into the lumen of the renal pelvis. There are ill-defined margins with the underlying medullary tissue. Microscopically, the bulk of the tumors consists of sparsely cellular calcified osteoid containing nests of cells with small vesicular ovoid nuclei (Fig. 12.77). These plump cells are larger than osteocytes and are more populous at the periphery of the lesion.[357] Mitotic figures are uncommon. Osteoclasts and cartilaginous tissues are absent.

Germ cell neoplasms

Renal teratomas are rare and controversial lesions which may be difficult to distinguish from Wilms' tumors, since they can contain areas of immature renal tissue with primitive glomerulogenesis and tubule formation.[358] The presence of a wide variety of tissue types representing all three germ cell layers is important in the diagnosis. Structures not ordinarily found in Wilms' tumors, such as lymph node or gut-like structures combining epithelium with smooth muscle[359] or hair follicle and sweat glands[360] are most helpful.[359] However, most renal tumors consisting of a variety of epithelial and mesenchymal elements are Wilms' tumors.

Choriocarcinoma has been reported to arise in the kidney.[361] Since differentiation toward choriocarcinoma is seen in some high grade transitional cell carcinomas,[362] a thorough search for recognizable transitional cell carcinoma should be made in all such cases.

Tumors of the renal pelvis and ureter

Given the similarities of these anatomic structures and exposure to urine-borne carcinogens of the renal pelvis, ureter, and urinary bladder, it is not surprising that most of the kinds of tumors that are found in the urinary bladder have also occurred in the segments of the urinary tract above it. The following discussion will focus mainly on those aspects which are particular to the upper urinary tract and for a more general and detailed discussion the reader should look to the sections addressing the same tumors as they occur in the urinary bladder.

Primary tumors of ureters are uncommon, and in a comprehensive review, Abeshouse[363] found that carcinomas were more common than benign tumors.

Benign tumors and tumor-like lesions
Nephrogenic adenoma

Rare in the ureter and much more common in the urinary bladder (see p. 543), nephrogenic adenomas are exophytic lesions which grossly mimic transitional cell carcinoma and microscopically are characterized by benign papillary and tubular proliferations lined by cuboidal or hobnail epithelium.[364,365]

Inverted papilloma

Inverted papillomas are benign transitional cell tumors which occur less commonly in the renal pelvis and ureter than in the urinary bladder (see p. 524).[366,367] They are almost twice as common in the ureter as in the renal pelvis.[368] Males predominate and the mean age of presentation is in the mid-60s.[368] In the upper tract, these are found incidentally by intravenous pyelography[367] or they may cause hematuria.[369,370] These lesions may be multiple and associated with urothelial carcinoma at other sites.[371] Grossly, they are broad-based domed lesions (Fig. 12.78). The tumors consist of trabeculae of histologically typical transitional cell epithelium which, in some cases, forms small glandular structures lined by metaplastic mucinous epithelium.[372] The histologic features of these tumors are discussed in more detail in connection with their occurrence in the urinary bladder (see p. 524). Rarely, transitional cell carcinoma may arise within an inverted papilloma of the ureter.[373,374]

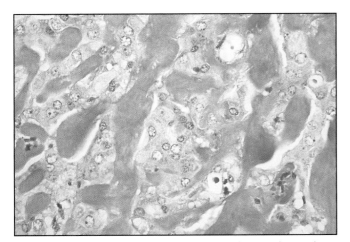

Fig. 12.77 • Ossifying renal tumor of infancy. The cells have regular round to oval nuclei with chromatin clumping and variable amounts of pale cytoplasm and are distributed in a matrix of dense bone. (Courtesy of Dr. B. Beckwith and the National Wilms' Tumor Study Pathology Center.)

Fig. 12.78 • Inverted papilloma of the renal pelvis. The tumor is broad-based, lobulated and tan.

Fibroepithelial polyp

This is an uncommon benign mesenchymal tumor of the renal pelvis[375] and ureter.[376] Most are found in adults of young or middle age, but pediatric[377,378] and geriatric[379] cases have occurred. Macksood et al. concluded that these are the most frequent benign polypoid lesions of the ureters in children.[378] Most (70 percent) of the patients are male.[380] Colicky flank pain and hematuria are the most common symptoms. Grossly, these tumors consist of single or multiple smooth-surfaced slender fronds arising close together from the mucosa (Fig. 12.79). The most common locations are the ureteropelvic junction and upper ureter.[381] The etiology is uncertain.[381] Histopathologically, they consist of a vascular loose edematous stromal core with a

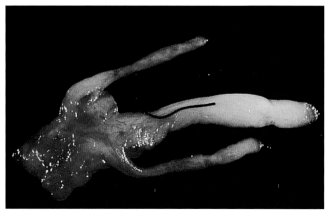

Fig. 12.79 • Fibroepithelial polyp of ureter. Three long fronds arise close to one another on the ureteral mucosa.

variable inflammatory infiltrate, covered by essentially normal urothelium which may show foci of squamous metaplasia or ulceration.

Hemangioma

Hemangiomas of the ureter and renal pelvis are uncommon polypoid tumors consisting of hypervascular fibrous stroma covered by normal transitional cell epithelium.[382,383] Occurring in children and adults, these lesions may be multiple and frequently cause obstruction.

Transitional cell carcinoma

Transitional cell carcinomas (also known as urothelial carcinomas) of the upper tract have epidemiology similar to those of the bladder:[384] male predominance,[385] most common in older individuals, and tobacco use[386] and industrial carcinogen exposure are risk factors. Phenacetin abuse[387,388] is the most important etiologic factor in some populations, accounting for nearly a quarter of renal pelvic tumors and more than 10 percent of ureteral tumors. Balkan nephropathy, and exposure to thorium-containing radiologic contrast material[389] are risk factors for upper tract carcinomas but not for urinary bladder tumors. Tumors of the renal pelvis and calyces are approximately twice as common as tumors of the ureters.[385] Hematuria is the principal symptom but flank pain also is frequent.[390] Multifocality is a significant problem for patients with upper tract tumors.[385,391] Nearly 50 percent have histories of transitional cell carcinoma of the bladder or ureters or later develop additional transitional cell carcinomas.[392,393] In the ureter, the most common location is the distal segment.[394] Grade and stage are the most important prognostic factors in transitional cell carcinomas of the upper tract, while multiplicity of tumors also has an effect.[391] Approximately 75 percent of cases are low grade and stage 1.[395] The grading scheme is identical to that applied in the bladder and the staging system is similar to that used in the bladder. The AJCC staging system is shown in Table 12.9.[396] Tumors which are grade 1 and stage 1 at the time of resection have little effect on survival.[397] Muscle invasion is a critical point in the progression of these tumors and survival decreases markedly when it is present.[393] The lung is the most common site of metastasis.[398] Due to the high rate of recurrence (more than 15 percent) in the ureter distal to the resected tumor, nephroureterectomy with resection of a cuff of urinary bladder is the operation of choice.[399]

Macroscopic appearances The gross appearance of the tumors is similar to that seen in the bladder, except that large papillary tumors frequently fill the pelvic cavity or ureter (Fig. 12.80) and cause obstruction resulting in hydronephrosis (Fig. 12.81). Large tumors of the pelvis may extensively invade the renal parenchyma in an ill-defined infiltrative manner, even extending into the paracortical fat, and they may be very scirrhous (Fig. 12.82). Sometimes, in such tumors, little evidence remains of a mucosal origin in the pelvis and extensive sampling is necessary to demonstrate it.

Histologic appearances The histopathology of upper tract tumors has the same spectrum as do transitional cell carcinomas of the urinary bladder, including squamous and

Table 12.1	Pathologic TNM staging of esophageal carcinoma[96]

Primary Tumor (T)

TX	Primary tumor cannot be assessed
T0	No evidence of primary tumor
Ta	Papillary non-invasive carcinoma
Tis	Carcinoma in situ
T1	Tumor invades subepithelial connective tissue
T2	Tumor invades the muscularis
T3	(For renal pelvis only) Tumors invades beyond muscularis into peripelvic fat or the renal parenchyma
T3	(For ureter only) Tumor invades beyond muscularis into periureteric fat
T4	Tumor invades adjacent organs, or through the kidney into the perinephric fat.

Regional Lymph Nodes (N)*

NX	Regional lymph nodes cannot be assessed
N0	No regional lymph node metastasis
N1	Metastasis in a single lymph node, 2 cm or less in greatest dimension
N2	Metastasis in a single lymph node, more than 2 cm but not more than 5 cm in greatest dimension; or multiple lymph nodes, none more than 5 cm in greatest dimension
N3	Metastasis in a lymph node, more than 5 cm in greatest dimension

*Note: Laterality does not affect the N classification

Distant Metastasis (M)

MX	Distant metastasis cannot be assessed
M0	No distant metastasis
M1	Distant metastasis

STAGE GROUPING

Stage 0a	Ta	N0	M0
Stage 0is	Tis	N0	M0
Stage I	T1	N0	M0
Stage II	T2	N0	M0
Stage III	T3	N0	M0
Stage IV	T4	N0	M0
	Any T	N1	M0
	Any T	N2	M0
	Any T	N3	M0
	Any T	Any N	M1

HISTOPATHOLOGIC TYPE

The histologic types are

Urothelial (transitional cell) carcinoma
Squamous cell carcinoma
Epidermoid carcinioma
Adenocarcinoma

HISTOLOGIC GRADE

GX	Grade cannot be assessed
G1	Well differentiated
G2	Moderately differentiated
G3-4	Poorly differentiated or undifferentiated

Used with permission of the American Joint Committee on Cancer (AJCC®), Chicago, Illinois. The original source for this material is the AJCC® Cancer Staging Manual, 5th Edition (1997) published by Lippincott-Raven Publishers, Philadelphia, Pennsylvania

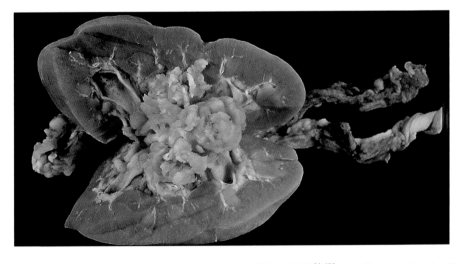

Fig. 12.80 • Transitional cell carcinoma of the renal pelvis. A mass of papillary fronds virtually fills the pelvic cavity.

glandular differentiation and the sarcomatoid (Fig. 12.83)[91,400] and small cell[401] variants. Rare variants, such as trophoblastic differentiation (Fig. 12.84) and tumors with osteoclast-type giant cells[402,402a] have been reported. When the sarcomatoid elements obscure the clearly carcinomatous elements, immunohistochemical studies[91,400] or ultrastructural examination may be of diagnostic help. Mapping studies have shown that virtually all transitional cell carcinomas of the renal pelvis and ureter are associated with changes ranging from hyperplasia to carcinoma in situ in the mucosa elsewhere in the specimen.[403] Thickening of basement membranes around capillaries in the lamina propria of the renal pelvis and ureter has been found to be a histologic marker for analgesic abuse and termed capillarosclerosis.[387]

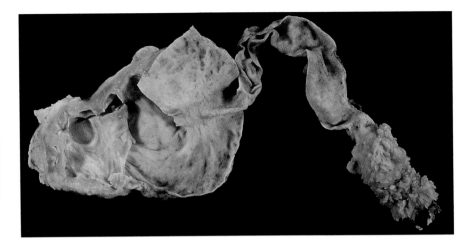

Fig. 12.81 • Transitional cell carcinoma of the ureter. The papillary fronds have obstructed the flow of urine, causing hydroureter and hydronephrosis.

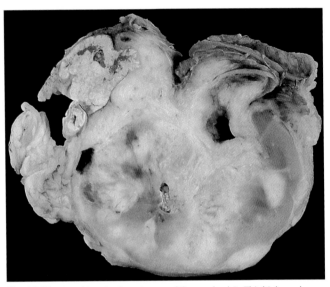

Fig. 12.82 • Transitional cell carcinoma of the renal pelvis. This high-grade carcinoma has extensively infiltrated the renal parenchyma, obscuring its origin in the pelvis.

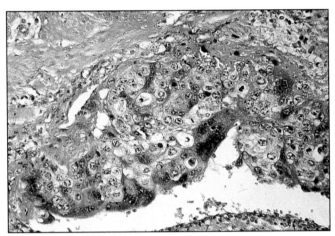

Fig. 12.84 • Transitional cell carcinoma of the renal pelvis. This renal pelvic carcinoma exhibits trophoblastic differentiation. (Courtesy of Dr. D. Grignon.)

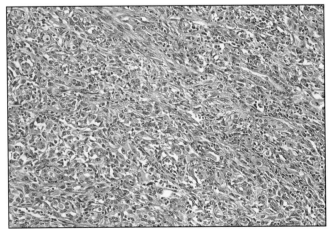

Fig. 12.83 • Transitional cell carcinoma of the renal pelvis. The pleomorphic spindle cells of this sarcomatoid carcinoma infiltrate the kidney, entrapping a few residual renal tubules.

Adenocarcinoma

Primary adenocarcinomas of the upper tract are rare and the reports consist mainly of single cases or small series.[404-409] Most patients are adult but pediatric cases occur.[410] Calculi and chronic inflammation and infection appear to be predisposing conditions. Glandular metaplasia[411,412] may be a precursor lesion and non-invasive carcinoma is sometimes found in the mucosa adjacent to the tumors. A papillary architecture and resemblance to mucinous adenocarcinoma of the colon are common (Fig. 12.85). One tumor had hepatoid areas and contained bile pigment.[408]

Squamous cell carcinoma

Approximately 10 percent of renal pelvic tumors are squamous cell carcinomas[413] and the percentage of ureteral carcinomas which are squamous is even smaller. Calculi and chronic infection are often associated with squamous cell carcinoma. The relationship with squamous metaplasia is more controversial,

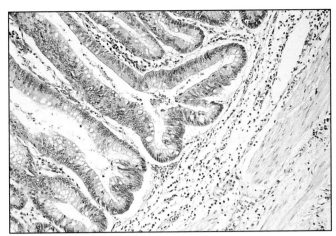

Fig. 12.85 • Adenocarcinoma of the renal pelvis. This tumor consists of columnar cells with atypical nuclei, resembling adenocarcinoma of the colon.

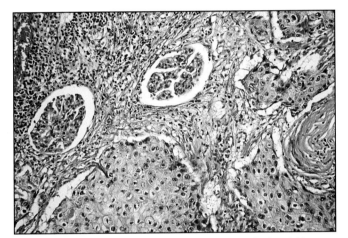

Fig. 12.86 • Squamous cell carcinoma of the renal pelvis. This keratinizing carcinoma invades the renal parenchyma.

some series of tumors finding a strong association[414] while some studies of squamous metaplasia have found little association.[415] This disagreement may be the result of the rarity of squamous cell carcinoma of the upper urinary tract. Prognostically, high stage is common[416] and the outcome is generally unfavorable.[414] The histopathology of these tumors is similar to that of their counterparts in the urinary bladder (Fig. 12.86). Extensive infiltration of the renal parenchyma is very common and survival for 5 years is rare.[414] These tumors should be distinguished from metastatic squamous cell carcinoma, which usually is straightforward when clinical and pathologic features are considered. An exceptional case of adenosquamous carcinoma of the renal pelvis, without transitional cell carcinoma, has been described in association with staghorn calculi.[417]

Other tumors

Smooth muscle neoplasms are the most common mesenchymal tumors of the renal pelvis and ureter; both leiomyomas[418,419] and leiomyosarcomas[420,421] have been reported. Other sarcomas, such as osteogenic sarcoma[422] and malignant peripheral nerve sheath tumor[423] are extremely rare. Malignant melanoma has arisen in the mucosa of the renal pelvis.[424] Obstruction due to secondary infiltration by malignant lymphoma occurs in approximately 16 percent of cases of disseminated lymphoma.[425]

Tumors of the bladder

In the following sections on the urinary bladder and urethra, the approach will be similar to that in the prior section, in that it is oriented primarily to the practical aspects of differential diagnosis as seen in routinely stained sections. Consideration is restricted primarily to neoplasms, but in both the urinary bladder and urethra a wide variety of non-neoplastic lesions are encountered which may mimic neoplasms grossly and/or microscopically;[426] and accordingly some of these are also illustrated. A classification of bladder tumors is presented in Table 12.10.

Benign epithelial tumors

Papillomas

Papillomas of the bladder are divided into typical and inverted types;[427] occasional lesions of one type have a minor component of the second type, and rare examples have a significant component of both types. The term papilloma was widely used in the older literature for what now is usually designated grade 1 papillary transitional cell carcinoma or neoplasm of low malignant potential. A return to the former nomenclature has been advocated[428] because of the good prognosis of most low-grade papillary transitional cell carcinomas, but recent studies[429,430] have more clearly established a distinct microscopic profile for a small subset of benign papillary transitional cell neoplasms and the designation papilloma should be reserved for them.

Typical papilloma

These lesions are rare when strict criteria for their diagnosis are used, and they account for less than 1 percent of papillary urothelial lesions. They affect mainly middle-aged adults with a slight male predominance. Grossly, small excrescences or delicate frond-like lesions are seen. Microscopically, these consist of a single papilla or a cluster of papillae covered by urothelium that closely resembles normal and often has conspicuous umbrella cells (Fig. 12.87).[429,430] The papillae are typically shorter and broader than those of the typical papillary carcinoma however, occasionally, delicate long papillae are seen. The number of cell layers is usually less than seven, cytologic atypia is absent or minimal, and mitotic figures are absent or very rare and confined to the basal layer. The epithelial cells may show a variety of changes such as vacuolation, degenerative atypia and an apocrine-like appearance of the cytoplasm.[430]

Differential diagnosis The papillae in typical papillomas may branch, but the particularly complex branching of many papillary carcinomas is not usually seen. Additionally, the papillae are usually covered by fewer than seven layers of urothelial cells which is less than the urothelium covering the papillae in most papillary carcinomas. When not stratified to more than seven layers, the papillae of papillary carcinomas usually have

Table 12.10 Tumors of the urinary bladder

Benign epithelial tumors
Typical papilloma
Inverted papilloma
Villous adenoma
Mucinous cystadenoma of the urachus
Squamous papilloma

Malignant epithelial tumors
Transitional cell carcinoma

Papillary | Non-papillary
(i) Non-invasive | (i) Transitional cell carcinoma in situ
(ii) Invasive | (ii) Invasive transitional cell carcinoma

Variants:
• with squamous differentiation and/or glandular differentiation
• sarcomatoid carcinoma
• microcystic carcinoma
• with trophoblastic differentiation
• with pseudosarcomatous stroma
• with stromal osseous or cartilaginous metaplasia
• with osteoclast-type giant cells

Squamous cell carcinoma
Variant:
• verrucous carcinoma

Adenocarcinoma
Variants:
• typical intestinal type
• mucinous (including colloid)
• signet-ring cell
• clear cell
• not otherwise specified

Undifferentiated carcinoma
Variants:
• small cell carcinoma
• giant cell carcinoma
• lymphoepithelioma-like carcinoma
• not otherwise specified

Carcinomas of more than one histologic type

Mesenchymal tumors
Benign
Malignant:
• leiomyosarcoma
• rhabdomyosarcoma
• others

Mixed tumors
Adenofibromas and adenosarcomas
Carcinosarcoma

Hematopoietic neoplasms
Lymphoma
Leukemia
Plasmacytoma

Miscellaneous primary tumors
Paraganglioma
Carcinoid
Malignant melanoma
Dermoid cyst
Yolk sac tumor

Metastatic tumors

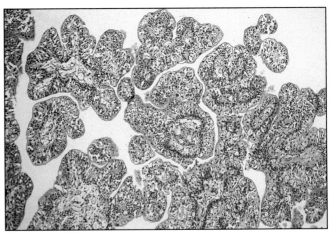

Fig. 12.87 • Typical papilloma of bladder. Numerous small, short papillae are present. There is no appreciable urothelial hyperplasia and many umbrella cells are present.

cells with appreciable cytologic atypia. Umbrella cells are much more common in papillomas than in papillary carcinomas. Finally, although a rare mitotic figure does not necessarily exclude the diagnosis of papilloma, significant mitotic activity strongly favors carcinoma.

Inverted papilloma

Inverted papilloma accounts for approximately 2 percent of all neoplasms of the renal pelves, ureters, bladder, and urethra.[431,432] The great majority occur in the bladder. The male:female ratio is 9:1. The average age of the patients, who typically have obstructive symptoms or hematuria, is about 57 years.[431] Approximately 80 percent of the lesions occur at the trigone or bladder neck. On gross examination they are typically solitary, polypoid, and variably smooth or lobulated. They usually have broad bases but may be pedunculated. Smaller lesions are often nodular rather than polypoid.

On the basis of their microscopic features, inverted papillomas have been divided into trabecular and glandular types.[431] In one series of 40 cases, 25 were glandular and 15 trabecular.[431] However, in our own material, the trabecular type is much more common. These are cellular tumors composed of anastomosing trabeculae and nests of urothelial cells, characteristically covered by normal urothelium (Fig. 12.88). Peripheral palisading often imparts a resemblance to cutaneous basal cell carcinoma (Fig. 12.89). Whorls suggestive of abortive squamous change may be seen, but frank squamous metaplasia with keratinization is rare. The trabeculae and nests are frequently interrupted by cysts (Fig. 12.90) that may contain eosinophilic secretion and are often lined by flattened cells. In contrast, the glandular type is characterized by nests containing spaces lined by mucinous epithelium (Fig. 12.91). Rarely, the urothelium covering an inverted papilloma shows small papillary surface projections representing a component of typical papilloma. Inverted papillomas usually exhibit minimal cytologic atypia and mitotic activity but, in one report, 15 percent had "varying degrees of nuclear abnormalities and increased mitotic activity".[431] In another more recent report, various unusual features were described in some cases: prominent nucleoli; squamous metaplasia, sometimes with dysplasia; dysplasia of transitional cells; and giant cells.[432]

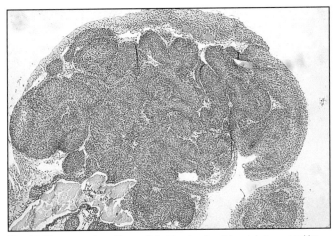

Fig. 12.88 • Inverted papilloma of bladder. A polypoid nodule is covered by normal urothelium, underneath which are anastomosing trabeculae of basaloid-appearing cells.

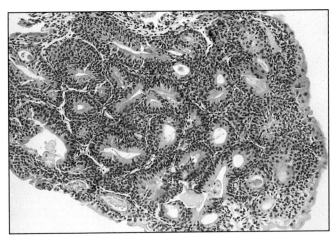

Fig. 12.91 • Inverted papilloma, glandular type.

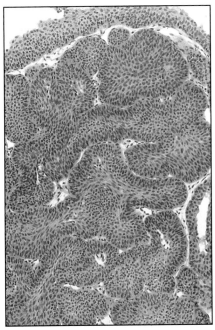

Fig. 12.89 • Inverted papilloma, trabecular type. Peripheral palisading is present.

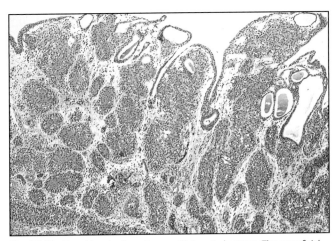

Fig. 12.92 • Transitional cell carcinoma with inverted pattern. The superficial portion of a carcinoma which was irregularly infiltrating in deeper aspects shows relatively regular trabeculae and nests.

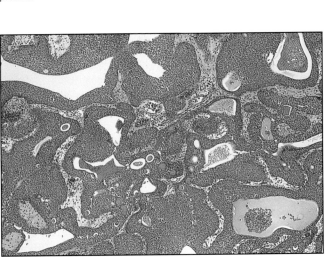

Fig. 12.90 • Inverted papilloma of bladder. Cysts of varying sizes are conspicuous.

Differential diagnosis Inverted papillomas must be distinguished from the relatively rare invasive transitional cell carcinoma that has an inverted pattern (Fig. 12.92).[433] These carcinomas grow in large, well-circumscribed, round to oval aggregates bluntly invading the stroma, rather than as one of the more common irregular or tentacular invasive patterns described below. Carcinomas that mimic inverted papillomas show a degree of cytologic atypia and mitotic activity incompatible with inverted papilloma, and often have areas of more typical invasive carcinoma. As squamous change with keratinization is very rare in inverted papillomas, its presence should suggest that the lesion is a carcinoma. In addition, while inverted papillomas may have a minor exophytic component, a prominent papillary architecture in a tumor with an inverting pattern suggests carcinoma. In one study of 20 cases initially interpreted as inverted papillomas, 2 were reinterpreted on review as low-grade transitional cell carcinomas.[434] A patient also may have both an inverted papilloma and a transitional cell carcinoma, as did 20 percent of the patients in that series. Although it is not an important distinction clinically, it is sometimes difficult to distinguish an exuberant example of von Brunn's nests from a small, developing inverted papilloma.

This distinction is arbitrary but it is helpful to know that a visible mucosal nodule was present before diagnosing inverted papilloma, while recognizing that von Brunn's nests may cause mucosal abnormalities, but usually only very small irregularities. Distinction between polypoid cystitis glandularis and the glandular variant of inverted papilloma is often arbitrary and of no clinical consequence.

Squamous papilloma

Squamous papillomas are rare.[434a] This diagnosis should be made cautiously, as many squamous cell carcinomas of the bladder have areas with slight atypia and papillae, such that misdiagnosis is possible in a small biopsy.

Villous adenoma

As with glandular lesions of the bladder as a whole, villous adenomas of the bladder may be urachal[435] or non-urachal in origin.[436–438] The microscopic picture (Fig. 12.93) is similar to that of villous adenoma of the intestinal tract. The major differential diagnosis of these benign glandular processes is with an adenocarcinoma, with which these lesions may coexist.[437,438] Their orderly architecture, superficial location, and lack of both invasion and malignant nuclear features contrast with adenocarcinoma. We would like to emphasize the extent to which the surface component of papillary adenocarcinoma can simulate a villous adenoma and the latter diagnosis should be made cautiously.

It is difficult to evaluate some reports of benign glandular tumors of the urachus because of the limited information provided. However, some of these lesions have resembled villous adenomas of the intestinal tract.[435] Once the urachal origin is recognized, the presence of glandular elements in the muscularis propria is not alarming, reflecting the course of the urachal canal. Apart from their location at the dome, they do not differ significantly from villous adenomas of non-urachal origin.

Mucinous cystadenoma

Although most multilocular cystic tumors of the urachus are adenocarcinomas, often well-differentiated ones, some mucinous cystadenomas of the urachus have occurred, as reviewed by Eble et al.[435] The diagnosis of mucinous cystadenoma of the urachus should be made cautiously because foci with relatively innocuous features occur in many urachal mucinous cystadenocarcinomas. The diagnosis of cystadenoma should be made only after a lesion has been sampled thoroughly and clearly shows no invasive properties and no significant cytologic atypia. A spectrum of mucinous neoplasia analogous to that seen in the ovary may be encountered in the bladder[439].

Transitional cell carcinoma

Transitional cell carcinoma (also known as urothelial carcinoma) of the bladder is a major cause of morbidity and mortality throughout the world. It is typically seen in patients over 50 years of age, but is occasionally seen in younger adults; it is rare in children. It is approximately three times as common in males as in females. Transitional cell carcinoma has been

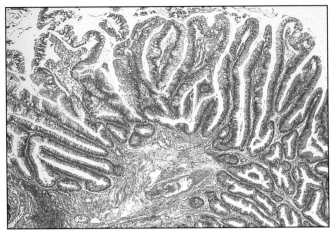

Fig. 12.93 • Villous adenoma of bladder.

of interest epidemiologically because of its association with exposure to aniline dyes[440–442] and an association with cigarette smoking is well substantiated. In contrast to renal cell carcinoma, patients with carcinoma of the bladder only exceptionally have systemic symptoms, paraneoplastic syndromes, or present with metastatic disease. The majority of patients present with hematuria, although dysuria is also quite frequent, tending to be more common in patients with high-grade tumors.[443]

Transitional cell carcinoma is conventionally divided into two types, the papillary and non-papillary (flat-sessile) types. Non-invasive papillary carcinomas account for approximately 25 percent of primary transitional cell tumors of the bladder. From 10 to 20 percent of these patients will, however, subsequently develop an invasive tumor. Looked at from another angle, approximately 20 percent of patients with an invasive bladder cancer have had prior non-invasive papillary lesions.[444–446] In patients with papillary tumors, the disease course may be prolonged and many years may pass before an invasive tumor develops. In the case of papillary tumors that are grade 2, and particularly in the case of the relatively uncommon grade 3 papillary tumors, it is much more common for invasive tumor to be present at the time of presentation.

Papillary transitional cell carcinoma

Macroscopic appearances The appearance of these lesions as seen most commonly at cystoscopy or, less often, in cystectomy specimens, varies greatly (Figs 12.94, 12.95). Some are barely visible small papillary excrescences, whereas others are huge masses of confluent papillary tissue that may have a "cauliflower-like" appearance and may fill, or almost fill, the bladder lumen. They are typically soft, delicate and friable and may be creamy-white, tan, or pink to red. Multiple lesions are often present (see Fig. 12.94). In non-invasive tumors a sharp interface with the underlying normal bladder is apparent on sectioning (see Fig. 12.95).

Histologic appearances Papillary transitional cell carcinomas are characterized by papillae that are usually tall (Fig. 12.96) and often branch. The papillae may be separate from their neighbors or may be adherent to them, particularly near their bases (Fig. 12.97). The papillae are usually covered by more

Fig. 12.94 • Papillary transitional cell carcinoma of bladder. An opened cystectomy specimen shows a large papillary neoplasm at the left and several smaller neoplasms at the top and right.

Fig. 12.95 • Papillary transitional cell carcinoma of bladder. There is a sharp interface between the tumor and underlying tissue.

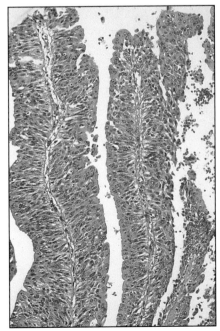

Fig. 12.96 • Papillary transitional cell carcinoma of bladder. Tall, thin, finger-like papillae are characteristic of this neoplasm.

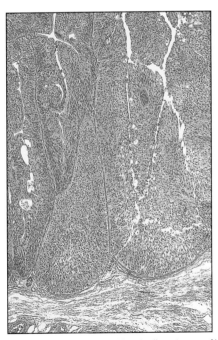

Fig. 12.97 • Papillary transitional cell carcinoma of bladder. At their bases the papillae are adherent to each other.

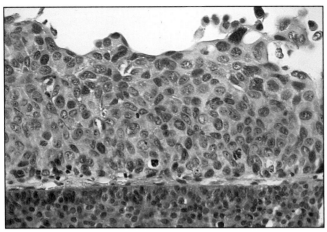

Fig. 12.98 • Papillary transitional cell carcinoma of bladder. The cells in this grade 2/3 neoplasm are moderately atypical and mitotic figures are easy to find.

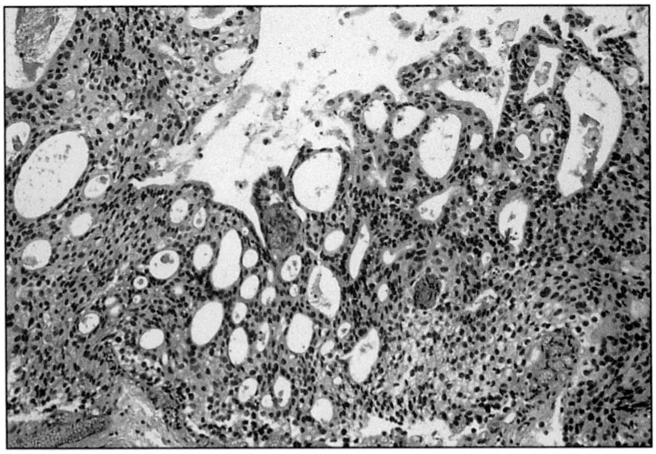

Fig. 12.99 • Papillary transitional cell carcinoma of bladder with glandular differentiation.

than seven layers of cells, which vary from almost normal in appearance to highly atypical (Fig. 12.98). They usually have moderate amounts of pale eosinophilic cytoplasm but sometimes the cytoplasm is more abundant and lightly eosinophilic. Papillary carcinomas are graded using cytologic criteria, and this has major prognostic significance. A system of three grades is in general use. Grade 1 lesions show an increase in the number of layers of urothelial cells and slight cytologic atypia; mitotic figures are rare. Grade 2 lesions show areas of moderate cytologic atypia, and more than occasional mitotic figures. Grade 3 lesions show at least focal high-grade nuclear atypia, and mitotic figures are easy to find. Recently, a proposal has been made to modify the system for classification and grading (Table 12.11).[447] This proposal is intended, in part, to resolve the controversy between those who view low-grade papillary transitional cell neoplasms as benign and those who view them as low-grade carcinomas. Glandular or squamous

differentiation, which occur mainly in moderately to poorly differentiated invasive transitional cell carcinomas, are uncommon in non-invasive papillary carcinoma but, occasionally, produce a striking picture (Fig. 12.99). The grade of the glandular or squamous component usually parallels that of the transitional cell carcinoma. The cores of the papillae are usually slender and moderately vascular, being composed of connective tissue with occasional inflammatory cells. They do not exhibit the range of unusual appearances that may be seen in the stroma of invasive tumors but, occasionally, are edematous to the extent that the lesion appears polypoid rather than papillary. In some cases, the stroma is extensively hyalinized, a change that may be accompanied by hyaline change of blood vessel walls. Rarely the papillae undergo infarction and the necrotic tissue may undergo calcification.

The features of the invasive tumor derived from papillary carcinoma are similar to those seen in non-papillary carcinoma described below. Invasion is very rare in cases of grade 1 papillary carcinoma and should not be diagnosed unless it is unequivocal. Assessment of invasion in cases of papillary carcinoma may be difficult. Tangential sectioning of the bases of papillae may simulate invasion by giving the appearance of detached nests of cells in the lamina propria. The presence of blood vessels within these foci may suggest that they represent the edge of a papilla. Papillary carcinomas may be associated with non-invasive carcinoma in von Brunn's nests, thus mimicking invasion (Fig. 12.100). The well-circumscribed contour of these usually round to oval structures facilitates their distinction from true invasion. Occasionally, the bases of the papillae of papillary carcinoma are bulbous and protrude with a pushing border into the underlying stroma, sometimes compressing the lamina propria such that they abut the muscularis propria. When invasion occurs, it usually is seen at the bases of the papillae but, rarely, invasion from the cores of the papillae is seen.

Differential diagnosis The distinction between papillary carcinoma and urothelial hyperplasia is usually not difficult but, as papillary carcinoma evolves from urothelial hyperplasia,[448,449] it is not surprising that cases occur in which it is debatable whether the diagnosis of papillary urothelial hyperplasia or early papillary carcinoma is most appropriate. Such cases are

Table 12.11	1998 World Health Organization/International Society of Urological Pathology consensus classification of urothelial neoplasms

Normal, including lesions previously diagnosed as mild dysplasia

Hyperplasia, flat and papillary

Flat lesions with atypia

Reactive atypia

Atypia of unknown significance

Dysplasia

Carcinoma in situ, including lesions previously diagnosed as severe
   dysplasia

Papillary neoplasms

Papilloma, typical and inverted

Papillary neoplasm of low malignant potential

Papillary carcinoma, low-grade

Papillary carcinoma, high-grade

Invasive neoplasms

Invasion of lamina propria

Invasion of muscularis propria

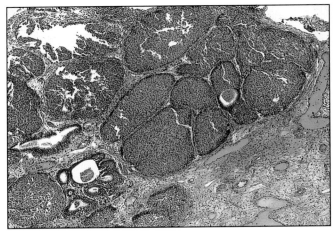

Fig. 12.100 • Low-grade papillary transitional cell carcinoma with extension into von Brunn's nests and expansion of them, mimicking invasion. Note the smooth outline of the expanded von Brunn's nests.

usually encountered in patients with a history of papillary carcinoma; this problem therefore does not generally cause clinical difficulty since these patients will remain under observation. The distinction of papillary carcinoma from papilloma has already been discussed.

It is important to distinguish papillary carcinoma from papillary or polypoid cystitis (Fig. 12.101).[450] The papillae in papillary cystitis are covered by normal urothelium and often have a prominent layer of umbrella cells, a feature which is rare in papillary carcinoma. The frequent branching of small papillae from large papillae seen in papillary carcinoma is not a feature of either papillary or polypoid cystitis. Despite these differences, papillary cystitis and grade 1 papillary carcinoma may be difficult to distinguish from one another. The broad fronds of polypoid cystitis are much thicker than the thin papillae of most papillary carcinomas. The stromal cores of papillary and polypoid cystitis are generally more intensely inflamed and vascular than those of carcinomas; this may give a clue, although it is not diagnostic. The clinical setting – such as the presence of an indwelling catheter or a vesical fistula, both of which may be associated with papillary or polypoid cystitis – is sometimes helpful.[450]

Transitional cell carcinoma (non-papillary)

Transitional cell carcinoma in situ A spectrum of atypical lesions occurs in the bladder urothelium, ranging from the mild cytologic changes of slight dysplasia to urothelium composed of cells with the obviously malignant cytologic characteristics of transitional cell carcinoma in situ. As is the case with premalignant epithelial lesions elsewhere in the body, considerable subjectivity exists in the interpretation of these lesions. From the viewpoint of the surgical pathologist, the most important concern in this area is making sure that high-grade lesions falling in the category of severe dysplasia or transitional cell carcinoma in situ (both of which are usually treated in the same way) are not overlooked. Although mildly and moderately dysplastic lesions should be noted when present, should they be overlooked or incorrectly diagnosed as reactive changes, this is not likely to have major adverse consequences. To be diagnosed as severe dysplasia or transitional cell carcinoma in situ the lesion should contain cells which are comparable to those of a grade 3 invasive tumor. For further reading on premalignant lesions of the urinary bladder the reader is referred to the classic early studies and other more recent studies and reviews[451–462], two of which also discuss early invasive cancer arising from carcinoma in situ.[461,462]

On gross inspection, bladder mucosa involved by transitional cell carcinoma in situ usually is erythematous; it may also be slightly granular, or bulbous due to the frequently associated edema. Microscopically, the abnormal urothelium may vary in thickness – from a single layer of cells, to normal, to hyperplastic. Even when only one layer of cells is present, the diagnosis of carcinoma in situ may be made on the basis of severe cytologic atypia. The cells in this process usually are somewhat pleomorphic but sometimes are relatively uniform. Loss of intercellular cohesion (Fig. 12.102) and adherence to the basement membrane with resultant urothelial denudation frequently occur. This often results in only a single layer of cells being present and, in some cases, considerable areas of the mucosa are denuded completely. When examining biopsies with denudation, one must be careful not to overlook even a small number of highly atypical cells. Deeper sections are often indicated in these cases, as is close correlation with the findings of urine cytology, as malignant cells are often present in cytologic

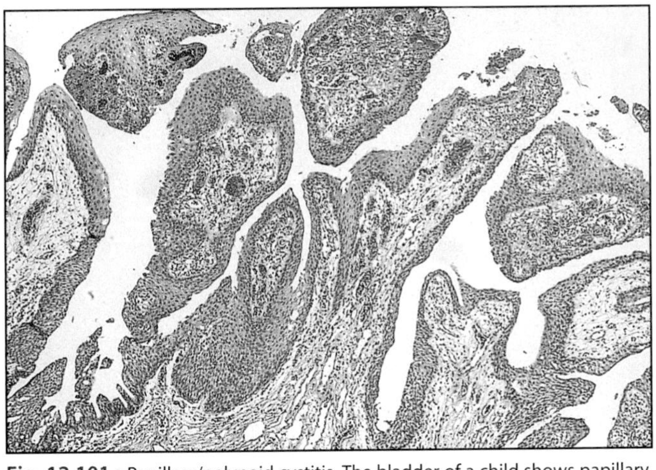

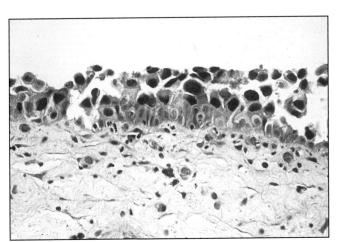

Fig. 12.101 • Papillary/polypoid cystitis. The bladder of a child shows papillary to polypoid structures with marked inflammation and vascularity of their cores.

Fig. 12.102 • Transitional cell carcinoma in situ of bladder. Nuclei are markedly hyperchromatic. Note the loss of intercellular cohesion.

specimens from cases of carcinoma in situ. In the past, patients with carcinoma in situ and marked urothelial denudation have sometimes been followed for long periods of time with the diagnosis of non-specific, denuding or interstitial cystitis.[453,454] In many cases, a low-power clue to the diagnosis of transitional cell carcinoma in situ is a very edematous, inflamed, hypervascular lamina propria. In some cases of transitional cell carcinoma in situ, small polyps of granulation tissue are present and these may be covered by the atypical cells. This process should be distinguished from grade 3 papillary carcinoma. Occasionally, transitional cell carcinoma in situ may show a pagetoid growth pattern.[462,463]

Invasive transitional cell carcinoma

Macroscopic appearances Invasive tumors can arise from both papillary and sessile precursors, thus the gross appearance of invasive transitional cell carcinoma is quite variable (Figs 12.103, 12.104). The tumors may be strikingly papillary or polypoid, sessile and ulcerated or, in some cases, cause only rather subtle abnormalities in the form of a granular or velvety mucosa; rarely a tumor is almost imperceptible when viewing the bladder prior to sectioning of the wall and, indeed, particularly after preoperative therapy, even may be not obviously neoplastic to

the naked eye on sectioning. The size of the lesions is similarly variable, ranging from a few millimeters in diameter to huge masses which may fill the bladder lumen. The tumor tissue is often white but may be tan to red. There may be hemorrhage and necrosis but generally these features are not striking. The appearance of the underlying bladder wall obviously depends upon the extent of invasion and, in deeply invasive neoplasms, the wall is typically replaced by firm, white tumor tissue.

Histologic appearances The microscopic appearance of invasive transitional cell carcinoma is even more variable than its gross appearance. Several specific variants will be described after the usual forms of invasive transitional cell carcinoma are discussed and aspects related to assessing depth of invasion are considered. Most frequently there are sizable irregular aggregates (Fig. 12.105), small clusters (Fig. 12.106), and single neoplastic cells irregularly dispersed in the lamina propria, and in the muscularis propria, if invasion of the latter is present. Essentially, any epithelial pattern of neoplasia may be seen including cords and discrete nests (the latter considered on their own below). The tumor sometimes grows in a more diffuse pattern but, even in these cases, focal nests and clusters are generally present. Rarely, there is a uniformly diffuse pattern.

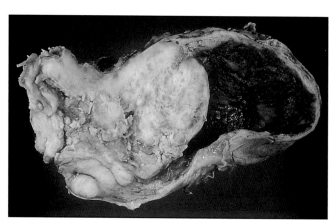

Fig. 12.103 • Transitional cell carcinoma of bladder, non-papillary. A large mass, which is white on its sectioned surface and is focally nodular, protrudes into the bladder lumen.

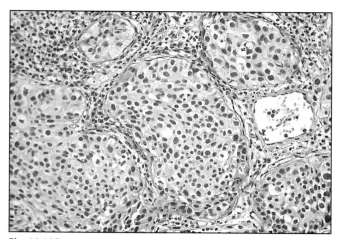

Fig. 12.105 • Transitional cell carcinoma of bladder, grade 2/3. Nests of invasive tumor composed of cells with moderate amounts of lightly eosinophilic cytoplasm and nuclei exhibiting mild to moderate atypia.

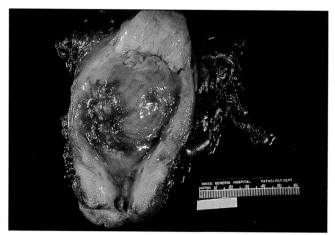

Fig. 12.104 • Transitional cell carcinoma of bladder, non-papillary. A tan mass is elevated slightly above the adjacent mucosa.

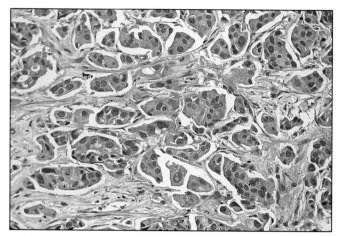

Fig. 12.106 • Transitional cell carcinoma of bladder. The tumor cells are growing in small irregular clusters.

Occasional carcinomas are associated with a pronounced chronic inflammatory cell infiltrate including, in some cases, numerous eosinophils, which sometimes partially obscures the underlying tumor cells which can be highlighted by a cytokeratin stain (Fig. 12.107).

The neoplastic cells in these patterns of transitional cell carcinoma are usually of medium size and have modest amounts of pale to slightly eosinophilic cytoplasm. In some tumors the cytoplasm is more abundant and may be clear or strikingly eosinophilic (Fig. 12.108). At least moderate, and frequently marked, cytologic atypia is present, but occasional tumors are composed of cells showing only mild cytologic atypia. Bizarre, hyperchromatic nuclei may be seen in tumors which have been treated with radiation therapy (Fig. 12.109). The mitotic rate is variable and related to the grade of the tumor. Focal necrosis is common in high-grade tumors; hemorrhage is uncommon.

The pathologist plays a crucial role in the staging of bladder cancer, in assessing not only the presence or absence of invasion, but its depth (Table 12.12). In most cases, the invasive component is quite striking, but invasion is occasionally slight and, indeed, sometimes limited to a few cells (Fig. 12.110) or clusters of cells (Fig. 12.111). Farrow & Utz[461] introduced the term microinvasive transitional cell carcinoma for cases of this type.

They identified small foci of invasion in 24 out of 70 patients with transitional cell carcinoma in situ. They restricted this designation to tumors that did not invade deeper than 5 mm. This depth is too generous for the microinvasive terminology in our opinion and we would reserve the term for cases in

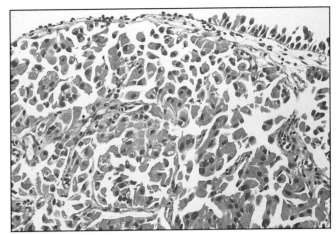

Fig. 12.108 • Transitional cell carcinoma in which cells have abundant eosinophilic cytoplasm.

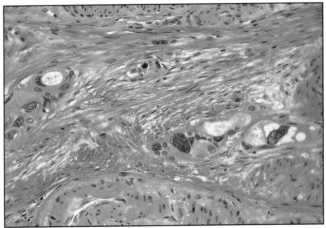

Fig. 12.109 • Transitional cell carcinoma, post irradiation, showing bizarre nuclear features.

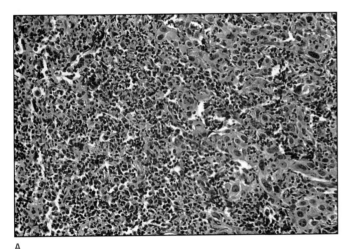

A

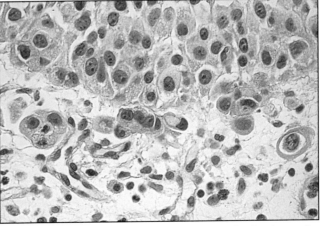

Fig. 12.110 • Microinvasive transitional cell carcinoma. A few tiny clusters of cells and single cells have penetrated into the superficial lamina propria.

Fig. 12.107 • Transitional cell carcinoma of bladder with marked inflammatory infiltrate partially obscuring tumor cells which are seen best at right (**A**). Staining for cytokeratin highlights scattered neoplastic cells (**B**).

B

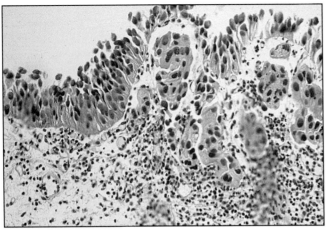

Fig. 12.111 • Microinvasive transitional cell carcinoma. Small clusters of tumor cells are present in the superficial lamina propria.

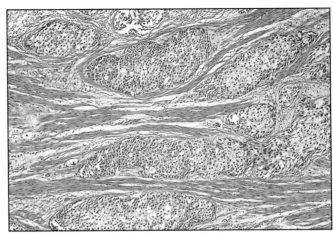

Fig. 12.112 • Transitional cell carcinoma invasive into muscularis propria.

Table 12.12	Staging of bladder cancer	
AJCC–TNM system	**JSM system**	
T0	—	No tumor
Tis	O	Flat carcinoma in situ
Ta	O	Papillary tumor, no invasion
T1	A	Lamina propria invasion
T2	B1	Muscle invasion, superficial
T3a	B2	Muscle invasion, deep
T3b	C	Perivesical fat invasion
T4a	D1	Invasion of contiguous viscera
T4b	D1	Fixed to pelvic or abdominal wall
N0	—	No lymph node involvement
N1	D1	Single, homolateral lymph node involvement
N2	D1	Contralateral, bilateral, or multiple lymph node involvement
N3	D1	Fixed pelvic wall mass separate from primary tumor
N4	D2	Juxtaregional lymph node involvement
M	D2	Distant metastasis

AJC = American Joint Commission on Cancer; JSM = Jewett–Strong (Marshall modification)

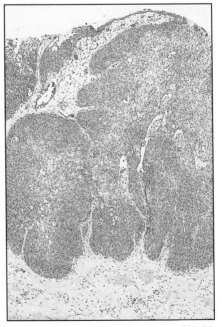

Fig. 12.113 • Transitional cell carcinoma with glandular differentiation invasive into muscle.

which only a few clusters or even single cells invade into the superficial lamina propria.[462] Overt invasion is usually in the form of irregular aggregates that are easily deemed invasive (Figs 12.112, 12.113) but occasionally a more organized inverted growth (Fig. 12.114) presents a diagnostic challenge,[433] as noted earlier in the section on papilloma.

Most crucial to prognosis, overall, is the presence or absence of invasion of the muscularis propria (Figs 12.112, 12.113). Evaluation of this is usually straightforward, although sometimes cautery artifact, marked inflammation, and fragmentation of the specimen may make it difficult. It is important to remember that there is often a muscularis mucosae in the bladder consisting of thin smooth muscle fibers (Fig. 12.115).[464–467] These fibers were scattered in 71 percent, more prominent but discontinuous in 20 percent, formed a discrete layer in 3 percent

Fig. 12.114 • Transitional cell carcinoma of bladder. This invasive tumor is unusual because it is growing in the form of well-circumscribed orderly large aggregates (so-called inverted growth).

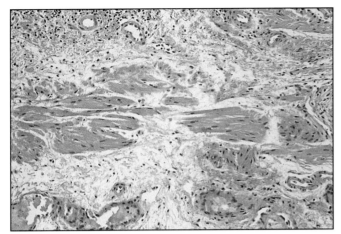

Fig. 12.115 • Thin, interrupted muscle fibers of muscularis mucosae.

and were absent in 6 percent of cases in one series.[464] Another report, however, found a muscularis mucosae in only 35 percent of cases, being much more common in women.[467] These thin muscle fibers contrast with the thick organized bundles of the muscularis propria. In addition, their superficial location and frequent association with blood vessels should enable them to be recognized and their involvement not incorrectly diagnosed as invasion of the muscularis propria, which is the "muscle invasion" of major importance to the urologist. The pathologist should also comment on the presence of vascular or lymphatic invasion (Fig. 12.116) if seen in a case of invasive carcinoma, although this is not found in many high-grade infiltrating carcinomas because of complete effacement of underlying tissue.

Variants of transitional cell carcinoma

With glandular or squamous differentiation Approximately 10 percent of transitional cell carcinomas contain foci of glandular (see Fig. 12.113) or squamous differentiation. The glands are variable in appearance. They range from small and tubular and relatively evenly spaced to closely packed, irregular and of moderate to large size. Intestinal-type adenocarcinomas

and adenocarcinomas of mullerian type, including even clear cell carcinoma (see below), may be mimicked. Glandular differentiation is usually found in moderate to high grade, often deeply invasive, tumors but it is also occasionally seen in well-differentiated, and superficially invasive tumors. The squamous metaplasia has no special features and can vary from high grade to well differentiated with abundant keratin production. By convention the primary diagnosis remains transitional cell carcinoma in these cases, but squamous or glandular differentiation should be recorded, particularly since this may aid in the interpretation of metastases.

Nested carcinoma It has been emphasized, relatively recently, that occasional invasive transitional cell carcinomas grow in quite orderly nests (Figs 12.117–12.119).[468–471] When, as is sometimes the case, there is also bland cytology then these invasive cancers, which are often deeply invasive, can be misconstrued as florid examples of von Brunn's nests.[472]

Microcystic carcinoma

Rarely, spaces develop within nests of transitional cell carcinoma.[471,473–474] The spaces may become cystic and, when these

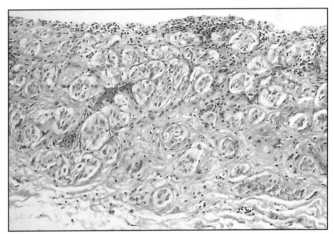

Fig. 12.117 • Transitional cell carcinoma of bladder, grade 1/3. Growth in the form of small nests is prominent.

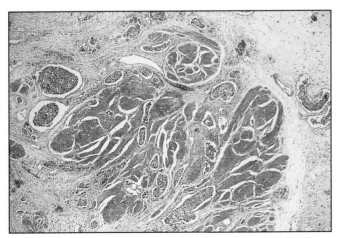

Fig. 12.116 • Transitional cell carcinoma with prominent lymphatic invasion.

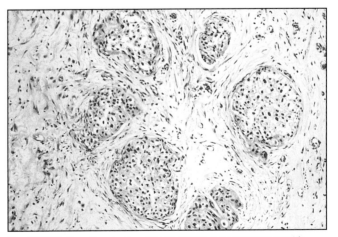

Fig. 12.118 • Transitional cell carcinoma, grade 1/3. Invasive tumors with nests and bland cytologic features are occasionally misinterpreted as benign in superficial biopsies.

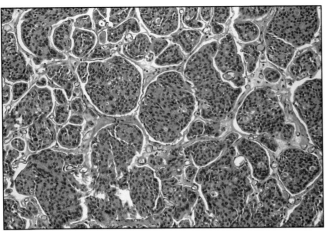

Fig. 12.119 • Transitional cell carcinoma of bladder. The tumor has a relatively regular pattern of round to oval nests. Tumors with this morphology may initially suggest a carcinoid tumor.

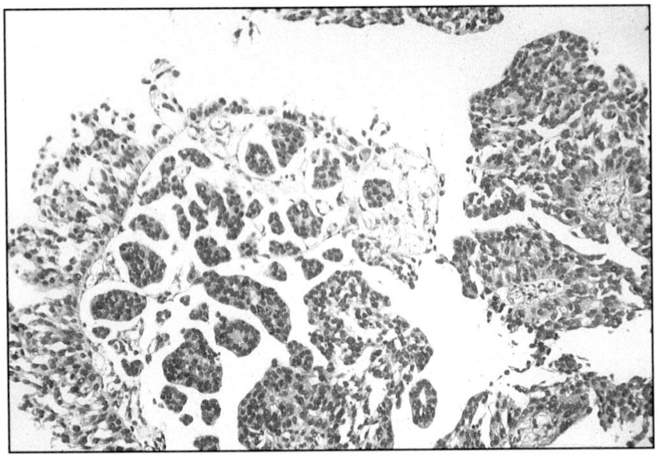

Fig. 12.121 • Transitional cell carcinoma with micropapillary pattern.

are prominent, a striking microcystic appearance may result (Fig. 12.120). These foci are usually scattered among, or adjacent to, foci of typical transitional cell carcinoma, but sometimes almost the entire tumor has this appearance. The cysts are usually round to oval but may be narrow, elongated and branching. In some cases a striking feature is the presence of small cysts, which may contain targetoid eosinophilic secretions, at the periphery of the larger cysts.[471] The center of the cysts is often filled with pale pink mucinous secretions and the lumens may contain detached clusters of cells or necrotic material. The cysts are usually lined by several layers of urothelial cells but may be lined by glandular cells; large cysts may be lined by relatively bland appearing flattened cells and the lining is sometimes completely denuded. In a small biopsy it is possible for these tumors to be misdiagnosed as cystitis glandularis or cystitis cystica. The deep location of the cysts, their irregular disposition and focally significant cytologic atypia differentiate them from cystitis glandularis or cystitis cystica.

Micropapillary carcinoma Rarely, transitional cell carcinoma grows in a micropapillary pattern reminiscent (Fig. 12.121) of papillary serous carcinoma of the ovary.[475-477] This growth pattern persists in invasion of the muscularis propria and in

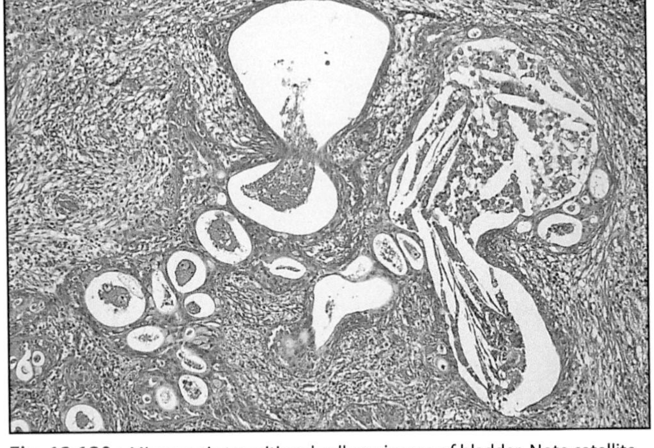

Fig. 12.120 • Microcystic transitional cell carcinoma of bladder. Note satellite cysts at periphery of the largest cyst.

metastases. Although the nuclear atypia may not be great, micropapillary growth is associated with a poor prognosis.

Sarcomatoid carcinoma Some high-grade transitional cell carcinomas contain variably sized areas composed of atypical spindle cells, meriting the descriptive designation sarcomatoid carcinoma.[478-487] These are often bulky, polypoid tumors (Fig. 12.122). The neoplastic cells in these cases may grow in a variety of patterns. Most commonly they are arranged in fascicles which impart a resemblance to leiomyosarcoma (Fig. 12.123). Sometimes there is a storiform pattern reminiscent of that seen in so-called malignant fibrous histiocytoma (Fig. 12.124). A resemblance to rhabdomyosarcoma may result when pleomorphic, round or elongated cells with particularly abundant eosinophilic cytoplasm are present; even angiosarcoma may be simulated.[487] Usually there is moderate to severe nuclear atypia but, occasionally, the nuclei are relatively bland. Mitotic figures are typically frequent but may be inconspicuous in areas. The spindle cells are usually closely packed but, in some cases, they are separated by collagen fibers or lie in a loose, myxoid stroma (Fig. 12.125).[485] The sarcomatoid areas usually merge with either invasive or in situ transitional cell carcinoma (Fig. 12.126) but, sometimes, they merge with a variant such as squamous cell carcinoma. While generous sampling usually reveals the urothelial nature of these tumors, immunohistochemistry is occasionally helpful since the spindle cells may stain immunohistochemically for cytokeratin, epithelial membrane antigen, and vimentin, but are generally negative for desmin and muscle-specific actin.[488] However, we have seen cases of unequivocal sarcomatoid carcinoma based on routine hematoxylin and eosin (H&E) stained slides that have been cytokeratin negative; accordingly, H & E remains the cornerstone of evaluation of these tumors.

Carcinomas with trophoblastic differentiation Immunohistochemical studies have shown human chorionic gonadotropin (hCG) and its beta subunit in the cells of morphologically typical transitional cell carcinomas, invasive or in situ, it having been demonstrated in approximately 30 percent of grade 3 carcinomas.[489] The discovery that hCG production is common in high-grade transitional cell carcinomas (Fig. 12.127) and those well-documented cases in which choriocarcinoma has

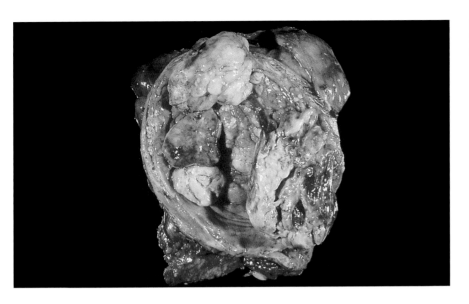

Fig. 12.122 • Sarcomatoid carcinoma of bladder. Multiple nodules of tumor, some of them polypoid, protrude into the bladder lumen.

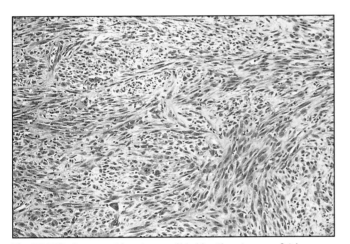

Fig. 12.123 • Sarcomatoid carcinoma of bladder. There is a superficial resemblance to leiomyosarcoma.

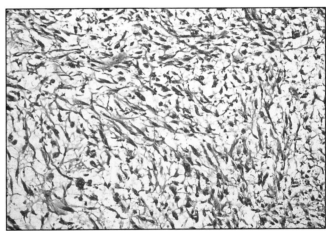

Fig. 12.125 • Sarcomatoid carcinoma of bladder. This tumor focally had a prominent myxoid stroma.

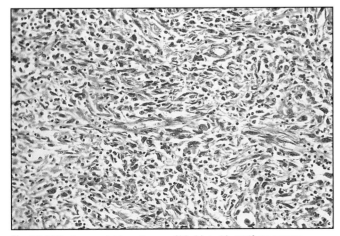

Fig. 12.124 • Sarcomatoid carcinoma of bladder with storiform pattern simulating so-called malignant fibrous histiocytoma.

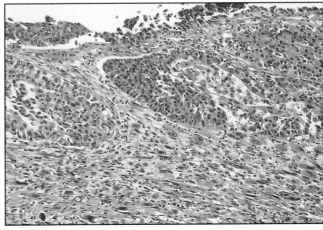

Fig. 12.126 • Sarcomatoid carcinoma (bottom) merges with more typical transitional cell carcinoma superficially.

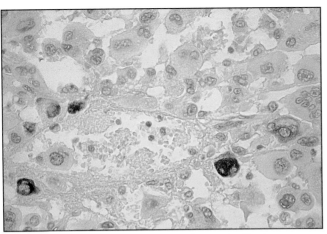

Fig. 12.127 • Transitional cell carcinoma, grade 3/3, stained by the immunohistochemical technique for human chorionic gonadotropin showing a positive reaction in several tumor cells.

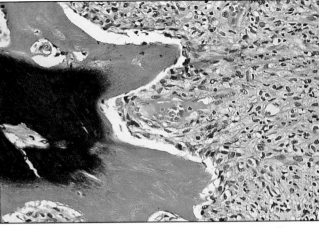

Fig. 12.129 • Transitional cell carcinoma with osseous metaplasia of its stroma.

evolved from, or coexisted with, high-grade urothelial carcinoma suggest that most, if not all, vesical tumors with trophoblastic elements are transitional cell carcinomas in which trophoblastic differentiation has occurred, rather than choriocarcinomas of germ cell origin.[490,491]

Transitional cell carcinomas with unusual stromal changes

The stroma in transitional cell carcinomas may show the range of appearances associated with the stroma of carcinomas in other organs, although it is generally not conspicuous. It may exhibit some degree of desmoplasia but an extremely desmoplastic reaction is unusual. In other cases, the stroma is loose and edematous or, in rare cases, myxoid. The stroma occasionally contains significant numbers of atypical, but benign, mesenchymal cells of the type seen in cases of so-called giant cell cystitis (Fig. 12.128). When adjacent to nests of carcinoma, these cells may be misconstrued as spindle cell forms of carcinoma cells, i.e., sarcomatoid carcinoma. Their degenerative appearance and lack of mitotic activity are a clue to their nature, as is the lack of a transition between them and obvious epithelial cells. Immunohistochemistry may be helpful in problem cases as these cells, in contrast to those of most

sarcomatoid carcinomas, are negative for epithelial markers. These carcinomas with atypical, but non-neoplastic, stromal cells are referred to as transitional cell carcinomas with pseudosarcomatous stroma.[492,493]

The stroma of transitional cell carcinoma may uncommonly undergo osseous metaplasia (Fig. 12.129); cartilaginous metaplasia is also rarely present.[494] The osseous or cartilaginous tissue in these tumors appears cytologically benign; this is important in distinguishing them from carcinosarcoma and osteosarcoma in which malignant bone and cartilage are present.

Transitional cell carcinomas with a prominent component of osteoclast-type giant cells have been reported (Fig. 12.130).[402a,495] This phenomenon may result in a confusing picture if the osteoclast-type giant cells are present in large numbers and obscure the underlying carcinoma. The osteoclast-type giant cells seem to be an unusual component of the stroma of the transitional cell carcinoma in these cases and most likely represent a host response.

Differential diagnosis The usual invasive transitional cell carcinoma generally does not pose much diagnostic difficulty. There is a small subset of cases, less than 5 percent of the total,

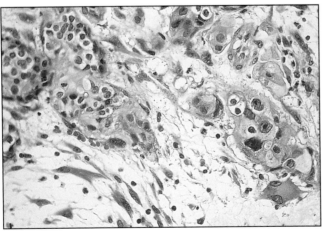

Fig. 12.128 • Transitional cell carcinoma with pseudosarcomatous stroma. Atypical mesenchymal cells are present in the lamina propria adjacent to nests of invasive carcinoma.

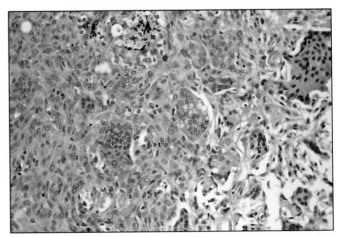

Fig. 12.130 • Transitional cell carcinoma with osteoclast-type giant cells in its stroma.

in which the tumors are grade 1 and these occasionally cause some difficulty in their distinction from von Brunn's nests.[472] It is helpful in these cases of so-called nested carcinoma that nests of well-differentiated carcinoma usually grow in more closely packed aggregates and are more irregular in size and shape than von Brunn's nests, which are much more typically round or oval and generally have an orderly distribution (Fig. 12.131), contrasting with the disorderly architecture of most carcinomas, at least in areas. Additionally, von Brunn's nests often extend to a depth which has an even plane in contrast to the more irregular edge of advancing nested carcinoma.[472] Another differential of nested transitional cell carcinomas, or even non-nested carcinomas is paraganglioma; this issue is discussed in the section on paraganglioma (See p. 549).

Transitional cell carcinomas with squamous and/or glandular differentiation are usually grade 2 or 3 and their distinction from non-neoplastic lesions is usually easy. In rare tumors, the glandular component takes the form of small, relatively regular tubules which may suggest the tubules of a nephrogenic adenoma. The association of the tubules with foci of transitional cell carcinoma usually facilitates the correct diagnosis, although this depends on an adequate sample. The tubules of nephrogenic adenoma are not surrounded by a mantle of transitional cells as is typical of the small tubules in transitional cell carcinoma. Transitional cell carcinomas with squamous or glandular differentiation are distinguished from pure squamous cell or adenocarcinomas by identifying areas of transitional cell carcinoma, however small. This may be crucial in the differential with secondary spread to the bladder.

Grade 3 transitional cell carcinomas often have a relatively nondescript appearance which, viewed in isolation, cannot be distinguished from poorly differentiated carcinomas of other types. A poorly differentiated bladder cancer is considered to be of transitional cell type unless there is good evidence to the contrary. The possibility of prostate carcinoma should be

borne in mind with poorly differentiated tumors in males, particularly if the specimen is obtained from the trigone or bladder neck. Immunohistochemistry may be very helpful in these cases, as most prostate carcinomas will stain for prostate-specific antigen (PSA). Occasional poorly differentiated transitional cell carcinomas without an obvious epithelial pattern may superficially resemble malignant lymphoma,[496] but small foci of epithelial differentiation and high-power scrutiny of the neoplastic cells to recognize that their cytologic features are not typical of lymphoma are usually helpful. Immunohistochemistry for epithelial and lymphoid markers may aid in cases that are difficult to distinguish on the basis of routine stains.

The tumors that enter into the differential diagnosis in cases of sarcomatoid carcinoma are sarcomas (leiomyosarcoma, "malignant fibrous histiocytoma", pleomorphic rhabdomyosarcoma and rarely angiosarcoma), carcinosarcomas, and transitional cell carcinomas with pseudosarcomatous stroma. Although it is occasionally difficult, a distinction between sarcomatoid carcinomas and sarcomas usually can be made by evaluating their features in routinely stained slides. The pathologic feature that is diagnostic of the former tumor is the presence of invasive carcinoma of various types which merges imperceptibly with the sarcomatoid areas. However, a small specimen may contain only the sarcomatoid component.

Sarcomatoid carcinoma differs from carcinosarcoma in that the epithelial component usually merges imperceptibly with the spindle cell component, with the two areas typically being relatively discrete. Carcinosarcomas, on the other hand, are composed of an intimate admixture of more obviously carcinomatous and sarcomatous elements, with the former usually standing out prominently from the background sarcomatous component (see p. 548). Transitions between the two may be found but are not as conspicuous as in a sarcomatoid carcinoma. Carcinosarcomas also often exhibit heterologous differentiation of the sarcomatous component, including skeletal muscle or chondro-osseous tissue, elements that exclude the diagnosis of sarcomatoid carcinoma.

A final tumor that sometimes enters into the differential diagnosis with a sarcomatoid carcinoma is malignant melanoma, either primary or metastatic to the bladder, because of the prominent spindle cell growth that this neoplasm may exhibit. The (occasional) presence of melanin pigment is of obvious importance diagnostically; immunohistochemistry is also of value, particularly reactivity of melanoma for S-100 protein and HMB-45, and its usual non-reactivity for cytokeratin and epithelial membrane antigen.

Transitional cell carcinomas with osteoclast-type giant cells should be distinguished from giant cell carcinomas (see below). The giant cells of the latter carcinoma exhibit much more cytologic atypia than osteoclast-type giant cells; additionally, the latter cells stain for acid phosphatase which is tartrate resistant, whereas tumor giant cells do not. On the other hand, the latter stain for cytokeratin but osteoclast-type giant cells do not.

Squamous cell carcinoma

Squamous cell carcinoma accounts for approximately 5 percent of bladder carcinomas in areas where schistosomiasis is not endemic,[497] although, in some series, higher figures in the range of 10–15 percent have been obtained. However, squamous

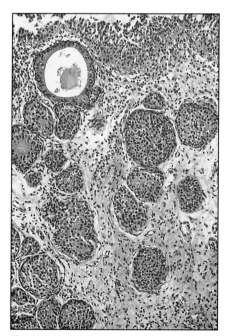

Fig. 12.131 • Von Brunn's nests. Some of the nests are deep in the lamina propria – a feature that occasionally leads to an incorrect diagnosis of carcinoma. Note the very regular round to oval shapes of the nests.

cell carcinomas comprise approximately 75 percent of bladder tumors where schistosomiasis is endemic. The male:female ratio is lower than it is in cases of transitional cell carcinoma but the age distribution is similar. Non-verrucous squamous cell carcinomas have a poor prognosis.[498–506]

Schistosomiasis is the classic condition in which chronic inflammation of the bladder is associated with the development of squamous cell carcinoma, but there are other examples of this association, for example an approximately 15 percent incidence of calculi and a 20 percent frequency of urethral strictures in one report.[502] Additionally, these tumors account for approximately 20 percent of those arising within bladder diverticula, 50 percent of tumors occurring in patients with non-functioning bladders, and 15 percent of tumors in patients who have had renal transplants. The only difference in the manner of presentation in these patients and those with transitional cell carcinoma is a relatively greater frequency of irritative symptoms and the occasional passage of keratinous material in the urine.

One series of 19 verrucous carcinomas of the bladder has been reported.[507] They accounted for 4.6 percent of these tumors in two institutions in Egypt where squamous cell carcinoma is common. They occurred in patients with an average age of 45 years, and the male to female ratio was 6:1. Only 3 cases of verrucous carcinoma of the bladder have been reported from countries where schistosomiasis is not endemic.[508–510] Two patients were elderly men and one a middle-aged woman. One tumor was thought to have arisen from a pre-existent condyloma acuminatum.[508] None of the reported verrucous carcinomas has spread.

Macroscopic and histologic appearances The gross appearance of squamous cell carcinomas varies from sessile and ulcerated, to papillary, polypoid (Fig. 12.132), or nodular. They are usually large and deeply invasive (approximately 90 percent of the cases), even when well differentiated. Their microscopic appearance (Fig. 12.133) is similar to that of squamous cell carcinomas arising elsewhere. Most are moderately or well differentiated and they often are abundantly keratinized. Human papilloma virus type 11 was demonstrated by DNA hybridization techniques within one tumor that arose in a renal transplant patient with condylomata acuminata of the vulva and urethra.[511] Verrucous carcinomas resemble their counterparts elsewhere (see Ch. 4).

Differential diagnosis These tumors often are associated with keratinizing squamous metaplasia (so-called leukoplakia)[434a,512–514] of the adjacent mucosa and are distinguished from it by either their greater degree of atypia and/or the presence of invasion. Many vesical squamous cell carcinomas are well differentiated and have only mild or moderate cytologic atypia. Other benign squamous lesions of the bladder, such as squamous papillomas and condylomas, are rare. These lesions can be distinguished from carcinomas by their lack of cytologic atypia and invasion, and, in condylomas, the presence of koilocytotic cells and other characteristic viral features. However, a condyloma of the bladder may be associated with a squamous cell carcinoma, as is seen more often in the female genital tract.

Verrucous carcinoma of the bladder, like the more common verrucous carcinomas of the male and female genital tract,

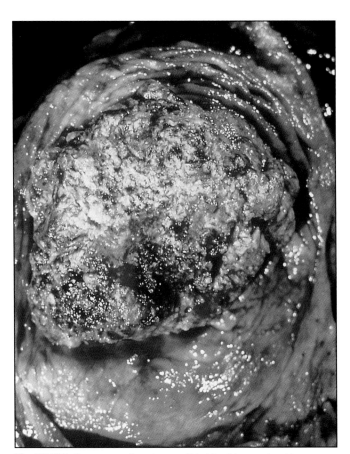

Fig. 12.132 • Squamous cell carcinoma of bladder. A large polypoid mass protrudes into the bladder lumen. This patient had long-standing chronic cystitis and the bladder mucosa adjacent to the tumor showed keratinizing squamous metaplasia.

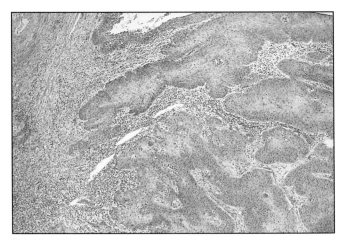

Fig. 12.133 • Squamous cell carcinoma of bladder.

must be distinguished primarily from condyloma acuminatum and invasive squamous cell carcinoma with a focal verrucous pattern (so-called verrucoid carcinoma). The features that help to distinguish typical squamous cell carcinoma from a condyloma are again useful. The diagnosis of verrucous carcinoma should be strictly reserved for tumors that are entirely verrucous. For example, three tumors in the series from Egypt referred to above[507] were partly verrucous but focally were typical infiltrating squamous cell carcinomas, as was another reported example.[515] The diagnosis of verrucous carcinoma can, therefore, be made with certainty only after the entire lesion has been excised and well sampled.

Adenocarcinoma

Adenocarcinoma accounts for 0.5–2 percent of bladder carcinomas.[516-533] It may be of urachal origin,[534] associated with exstrophy,[535] associated with endometriosis,[536,537] or unassociated with any of the aforementioned; the last is the commonest situation. In one large series, one-third of the tumors were urachal.[533]

The age distribution and male:female ratio of adenocarcinoma is similar to that of transitional cell carcinoma, these neoplasms usually arising in male patients over 50 years old. The clinical presentation most often mimics that of transitional cell carcinoma but, occasionally, patients present with mucusuria. Adenocarcinoma, like squamous cell carcinoma, accounts for a greater percentage of bladder cancers in some clinical settings – approximately 15 percent of tumors arising in patients with non-functioning bladders and 85 percent of those associated with exstrophy.[538] Adenocarcinoma of the bladder generally has a poor prognosis with 5-year survival figures varying between 18 percent[527] and 47 percent.[533] The outlook for signet-ring cell carcinoma, which is typically high stage at presentation, is worse than for other types. Urachal tumors have a better prognosis than non-urachal ones, likely because of the low grade cystic nature of many urachal examples.[533]

Macroscopic appearances On gross examination adenocarcinomas vary considerably in appearance according, in part, to whether they are urachal (Fig. 12.134), complicate exstrophy (Fig. 12.135), or have neither association. Tumors of the last type may arise in any part of the mucosa. They vary from papillary or polypoid, to nodular, to sessile and ulcerative. The neoplastic tissue is usually soft and often mucoid (Fig. 12.136); foci of hemorrhage and necrosis are common. In cases of signet-ring cell adenocarcinoma, which accounts for 3–5 percent of vesical adenocarcinomas,[539-541] the mucosa often appears edematous and, in most cases, is ulcerated, but sometimes it is grossly normal.[542] Some cases have the diffuse fibrosis and mural thickening of linitis plastica (Fig. 12.137). About 20 percent of signet-ring cell adenocarcinomas are urachal in origin.[542]

Urachal tumors are typically submucosal masses at the bladder dome and fall into two broad categories: cystic neoplasms with predominantly exophytic growth of the neoplastic tissue[439] and non-cystic neoplasms that are typically more invasive. Some tumors extend in a striking fashion superiorly in the space of Retzius towards the umbilicus. There is usually some degree of overlying mucosal ulceration or mucosal abnormality of some type, but this is variable. On sectioning, the solid tumors often have a gelatinous surface (see Fig. 12.134). Tumors that complicate exstrophy are remarkable primarily for their presence on the anterior abdominal wall (see Fig. 12.135); these neoplasms are now exceedingly rarely seen.

Microscopic appearances Vesical adenocarcinomas are subclassified into the following microscopic groups, the frequency of which in a large series[533] was: adenocarcinoma, not otherwise specified (28 percent); mucinous (24 percent); enteric (19 percent); signet-ring cell (17 percent); and mixed (13 percent).

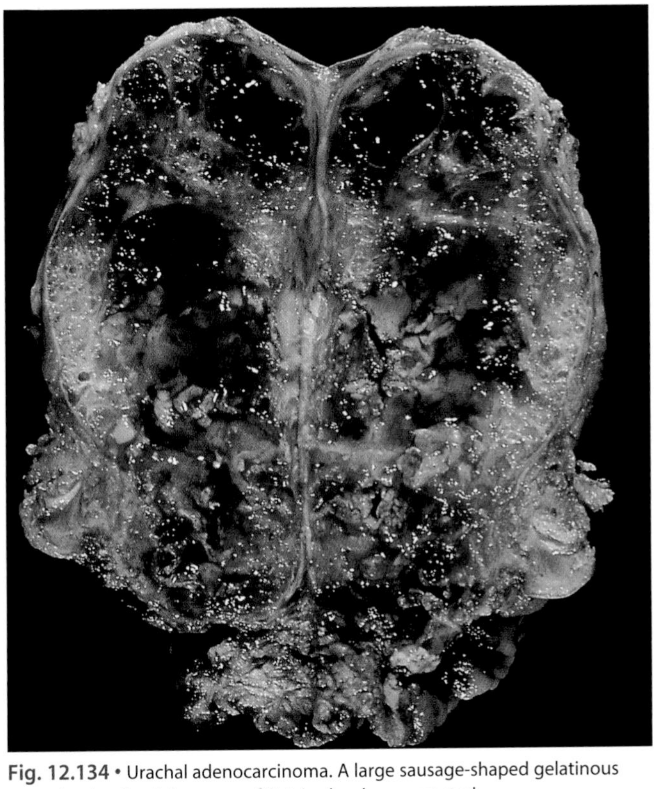

Fig. 12.134 • Urachal adenocarcinoma. A large sausage-shaped gelatinous mass that involved the space of Retzius has been resected.

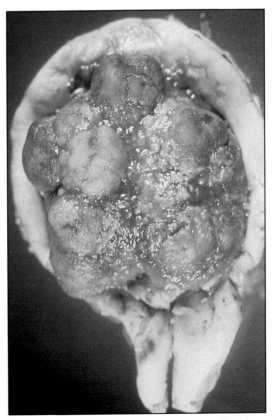

Fig. 12.135 • Adenocarcinoma complicating exstrophy. A large nodular mass is present on the abdominal wall. (Courtesy of Dr. Fred Askin.)

Fig. 12.136 • Adenocarcinoma of bladder in a paraplegic patient. The tumor is papillary and focally gelatinous.

Fig. 12.137 • Signet-ring cell adenocarcinoma of bladder. The bladder wall is diffusely thickened and the lumen is small.

Table 12.13	Frequency (%) of subtypes of adenocarcinoma in urachal and non-urachal tumors (from ref. 533)	
	Urachal	**Non-urachal**
Mucinous	50	10
Enteric	29	15
Mixed	17	10
Signet-ring	4	23
Not otherwise specified	0	42

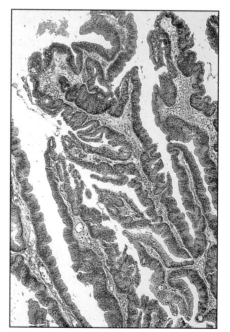

Fig. 12.138 • Papillary adenocarcinoma of bladder.

There are differences in the frequency of these subtypes in urachal and non-urachal tumors (Table 12.13).

Microscopic examination generally shows a predominantly glandular or papillary pattern (Fig. 12.138) although, in poorly differentiated tumors, areas of solid growth may be encountered. The glands may have a non-specific appearance but frequently resemble those of intestinal adenocarcinoma of typical or colloid type (Fig. 12.139). They may contain mucin or necrotic eosinophilic material. Their lining epithelium may have a prominent mucinous character. Paneth cells are rarely present.[531] Focally or exclusively papillary tumors accounted for 8 percent of the tumors in one series.[527] The tumors are associated with

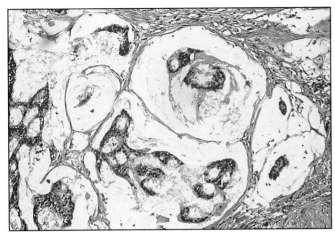

Fig. 12.139 • Colloid adenocarcinoma of bladder.

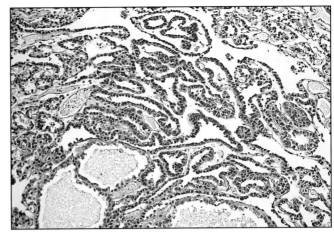

Fig. 12.141 • Clear cell adenocarcinoma of bladder with tubulocystic pattern and hobnail cells.

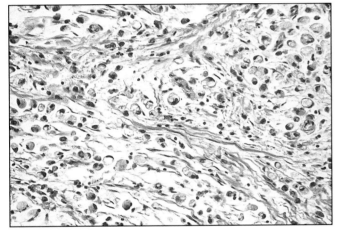

Fig. 12.140 • Signet-ring cell adenocarcinoma of bladder.

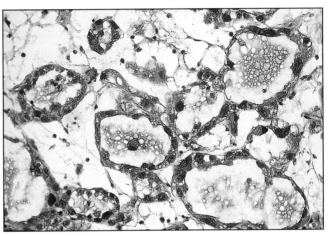

Fig. 12.142 • Clear cell adenocarcinoma of bladder that was associated with endometriosis. Note intraluminal mucin.

cystitis glandularis, usually of the intestinal type, or mucinous metaplasia of the surface urothelium in 14–66 percent of the cases.[518,530] Urachal tumors are more often cystic and may be entirely intracystic or confined to the epithelial lining; they have a spectrum analogous to low grade cystic adenocarcinomas of the ovary.[439]

Signet-ring cell adenocarcinoma of the bladder usually shows the typical features of comparable tumors elsewhere (Fig. 12.140), but the signet-ring cells may be embedded in lakes of extracellular mucus and the tumor is occasionally admixed with a component of adenocarcinoma of another type. Tumors consisting entirely of signet-ring cells have a worse prognosis than those admixed with another component.

Clear cell adenocarcinoma[537] shows tubular glands, cysts, papillae, and diffuse sheets alone or in combination (Figs 12.141, 12.142). In most cases a tubular pattern predominates. Although cells with abundant clear glycogen-rich cytoplasm are common (Fig. 12.143), they are not essential to the diagnosis and some lesions have mainly, or entirely, flattened or hobnail cells. An association with endometriosis indicates a Müllerian origin but, in some cases, there is no such association and the tumors may be the glandular component of a tumor of transitional cell origin.[537] One clear cell adenocarcinoma arising in a Müllerian duct cyst presented as a

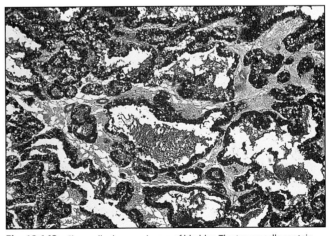

Fig. 12.143 • Clear cell adenocarcinoma of bladder. The tumor cells contain abundant intracytoplasmic glycogen. (Periodic acid-Schiff stain.)

bladder tumor.[543] Most clear cell carcinomas of the bladder are, however, probably not of Müllerian origin.

Differential diagnosis The distinction of adenocarcinoma from primary pure transitional cell carcinoma of the bladder is uncommonly a problem, although, in rare transitional cell carcinomas, necrosis of cells within the center of tumor nests imparts a pseudoglandular appearance. As referred to earlier, some transitional cell carcinomas have prominent areas of glandular differentiation and this is a much greater problem that is hugely dependent on sampling.

The distinction of adenocarcinoma from cystitis glandularis is usually easy because of the superficial location, orderly architecture, and bland cytology of the latter. Some adenocarcinomas are very well differentiated and architectural features may be more helpful than cytologic ones in establishing the diagnosis of carcinoma in these cases. The distinction may be especially difficult in cases of intestinal-type cystitis glandularis;[544] lack of cytologic atypia or muscle invasion is key in this regard. Adenocarcinomas may arise on a background of the intestinal type of cystitis glandularis and, in some cases, there is a spectrum from normal, to atypical, to neoplastic glandular epithelium. Adenocarcinoma should also be distinguished from the rare villous adenoma of the bladder. These lesions lack invasion in contrast to adenocarcinoma, but this feature may not be evident in a superficial biopsy specimen. It is advisable to have a lesion with that differential completely excised so that its invasive properties, or lack of them, can be properly determined.

Adenocarcinoma must also be distinguished from three other non-neoplastic lesions, *endometriosis*,[545] *endocervicosis*,[546] and *endosalpingiosis*.[547] Distinction from endometriosis should be easy in most cases because of the endometrial stroma surrounding the glands. It should be noted, however, that in postmenopausal patients or patients who are being treated with hormones, the stroma may be atrophic and not discernible around every gland. The benign features of the epithelium in endometriosis and endocervicosis are also helpful in the distinction from adenocarcinoma. Endocervicosis may cause particular difficulty because it lacks endometrial stroma and the epithelium is mucinous (Figs 12.144, 12.145). As the glands of endocervicosis often are haphazardly distributed in the muscularis propria of the bladder, lack of familiarity with this entity may suggest the possibility of a deeply invasive, well-differentiated mucinous adenocarcinoma. Endosalpingiosis is cytologically bland and has cilia in contrast to adenocarcinoma.

Primary adenocarcinoma must be distinguished from local or metastatic spread of another adenocarcinoma to the bladder. The most common problem of this type is posed by direct invasion of the bladder by prostatic adenocarcinoma. In most cases, examination of routinely stained sections shows the characteristic small acinar or cribriform appearance of prostatic adenocarcinoma, which differs from that of most adenocarcinomas of the bladder. Nonetheless, in some cases, distinction is difficult or impossible from routinely stained sections; immunoreactivity for both prostate-specific antigen (PSA) and prostatic acid phosphatase (PSAP) will generally establish the correct diagnosis. Even when a prostatic carcinoma has unusual histologic features, it typically stains positively for one of these antigens. It should be remembered that positive PSAP staining has been described in some adenocarcinomas of the bladder.[548] These tumors did not stain for PSA, however, indicating the desirability of obtaining a positive reaction for both PSA and PSAP. In cases of secondary spread from intestinal adenocarcinomas, distinction is often difficult

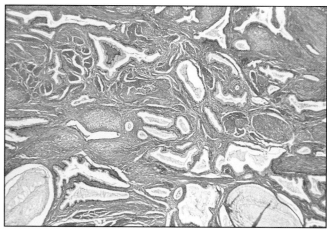

Fig. 12.144 • Endocervicosis of bladder. In this benign lesion glands are often haphazardly disposed in the muscularis propria, raising the concern of carcinoma.

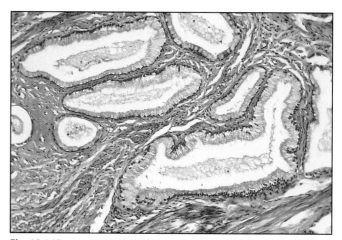

Fig. 12.145 • Endocervicosis of bladder. Glands are lined by benign-appearing columnar mucinous epithelium.

when based on morphologic grounds alone, because many primary adenocarcinomas of the bladder closely resemble intestinal carcinomas. However, the diagnosis of secondary involvement by carcinoma of the intestine or other sites is strongly suggested when the outer portion of the bladder is extensively infiltrated, while the mucosa and lamina propria are relatively spared. In advanced cases of secondary adenocarcinoma, tumor may, however, involve the bladder mucosa, and there are well-documented cases in which bladder involvement by colonic or appendiceal carcinoma has been the presenting feature.[538] Accordingly, the diagnosis of a primary adenocarcinoma of intestinal type is established with certainty only after secondary involvement from the intestinal tract is clinically excluded. We have seen appendiceal adenocarcinoma present with bladder manifestations.

The major lesion in the differential diagnosis with signet-ring cell tumors is metastatic signet-ring cell carcinoma. The distinction is not possible on morphologic grounds and ultimately rests on the exclusion of a tumor elsewhere by clinical evaluation. Distinction between a signet-ring cell carcinoma and a benign process is usually not difficult, although occasional nephrogenic adenomas have tiny tubules which simulate signet-ring cells, rarely leading to confusion with signet-ring cell carcinoma.[549] However, the other distinctive patterns of nephrogenic adenoma (see below) usually facilitate the diagnosis.

The lesion that creates the greatest problem in differential diagnosis with clear cell adenocarcinoma is *nephrogenic adenoma* (Figs 12.146–12.148).[549] The clinical features associated with nephrogenic adenomas typically differ from those of clear cell adenocarcinomas. Many patients with the former lesion have been under 30 years of age (including some children), whereas the youngest patient with clear cell adenocarcinoma of the bladder was 43 years old. Nephrogenic adenoma is usually associated with a history of a genitourinary operation, trauma or calculi, whereas these associations are usually absent in cases of clear cell adenocarcinoma. Large size also favors a diagnosis of clear cell adenocarcinoma over a nephrogenic adenoma; none of them has been an incidental finding on microscopic examination. Nephrogenic adenomas are typically of microscopic size, although lesions up to 7 cm have been described. Histologic distinction is difficult in occasional cases because both these lesions have tubular, cystic, and papillary patterns and some cases of nephrogenic adenoma show cytologic atypia.[550] The cells lining these structures are also similar in both lesions, ranging from columnar to flattened or hobnail (see Fig. 12.147). Several features, however, favor a diagnosis of carcinoma: these include a conspicuously diffuse arrangement of cells with abundant clear cytoplasm, abundant intracytoplasmic glycogen, prominent nucleoli, nuclear pleomorphism, and mitotic activity. Rare clear cell adenocarcinomas, however, may be cytologically bland and difficult to distinguish from a nephrogenic adenoma. In such cases, consideration of the clinical history and the size of the lesion, as well as repeat biopsy may be helpful. Careful clinical follow-up is required whenever a case of presumed nephrogenic adenoma has unusual clinical or pathologic features. It should be remembered that nephrogenic adenomas may recur, so recurrence should not lead to a diagnosis of carcinoma in the absence of convincing microscopic evidence of malignancy. Some have speculated that the clear cell adenocarcinoma is the malignant counterpart of nephrogenic adenoma, but the clinical differences between the two lesions and the rarity of their association argues against such an interpretation. Further, if nephrogenic adenoma were a precursor of clear cell adenocarcinoma, one might expect the latter to be more common in men than women and more common in the bladder than in the urethra, whereas the reverse is true.

The distinctive microscopic features of clear cell adenocarcinoma should allow its differentiation from other primary adenocarcinomas of the bladder. Distinction from a metastatic clear cell carcinoma from the female genital tract or kidney may be more difficult. A young age and a history of perinatal exposure to diethylstilbestrol should bring into consideration a metastasis from the female genital tract, which can be excluded only by clinical evaluation. In practice this problem rarely arises as spread of genital tract adenocarcinoma to the bladder is exceptionally unlikely to antedate the recognition of the primary tumor, but this has happened in one case of uterine papillary serous adenocarcinoma.[551] The diffuse pattern of a clear cell adenocarcinoma of the bladder may be indistinguishable from that of a renal cell carcinoma, but the prominent delicate vascular pattern of many renal cell carcinomas has not been a feature of the admittedly small number of reported

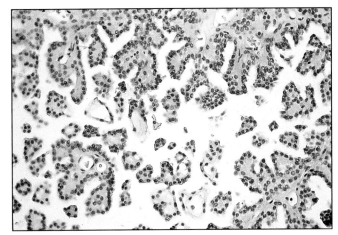

Fig. 12.146 • Nephrogenic adenoma with prominent papillary pattern.

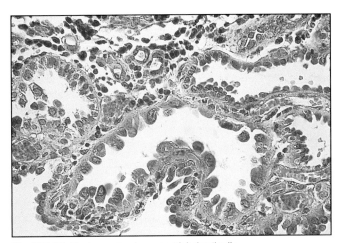

Fig. 12.147 • Nephrogenic adenoma with hobnail cells.

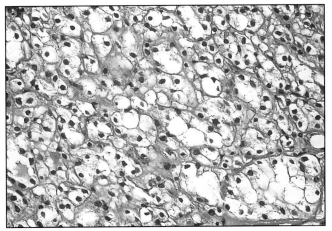

Fig. 12.148 • Nephrogenic adenoma. The cells have abundant clear cytoplasm. This was a small focus in an otherwise more typical nephrogenic adenoma.

vesical clear cell adenocarcinomas. Additionally, hobnail cells and intracytoplasmic mucin are typically absent in the renal tumors in contrast to the bladder tumors. It is also helpful that renal cell carcinoma rarely spreads to the bladder, even in late stages of disease.

Undifferentiated carcinoma

As in the distinction between use of the designation poorly differentiated carcinoma and undifferentiated carcinoma at other sites, usage of the term undifferentiated carcinoma in the bladder is often arbitrary. Truly undifferentiated carcinomas of the bladder are relatively rare and they often have the non-specific features of undifferentiated carcinomas of other sites. Only three specific subtypes, of special importance from the viewpoint of differential diagnosis, will be discussed here.

Small cell carcinoma

Small cell undifferentiated carcinomas that are histologically similar to pulmonary tumors of this type occur occasionally in the bladder.[552–559] In one review they accounted for almost 0.5 percent of malignant tumors of the bladder.[556] Approximately 85 percent of the patients have been male. They are typically elderly, with a mean age of 69 years,[553] and their symptoms are similar to those of other patients with bladder cancer; gross hematuria is the commonest complaint. Hypercalcemia has been present in at least one case[555] and ectopic adrenocorticotropic hormone production in another.[557] Many patients have a history of, or coincident, transitional cell carcinoma. These tumors are often high stage; in one study 16 of 22 patients had stage C or D disease.[553] The prognosis is generally poor but, occasionally, radical cystectomy and aggressive adjuvant chemotherapy has resulted in survival at least for a few years.[558]

Macroscopic and histologic appearances The tumors are typically large, often polypoid, and frequently ulcerated. Histologically, they are composed of sheets of small, oat-shaped cells with hyperchromatic nuclei, as well as slightly larger cells with more variation in nuclear chromatin, comparable to the intermediate cell type of pulmonary small cell carcinoma, or there are mixtures of the two cell types (Fig. 12.149). The tumors may contain small rosette-like structures or, less commonly, malignant giant cells. Other forms of carcinoma, usually either in situ or invasive transitional cell carcinoma, but occasionally squamous cell carcinoma or adenocarcinoma, are often present.

Extensive necrosis is common in these typically deeply invasive tumors. Positive immunohistochemical staining for markers of neuroendocrine differentiation is common. Importantly, a subset of cases are TTF-1 positive,[560] preventing easy distinction from a metastasis from the lung. Dense-core granules with diameters in the range of 150 to 250 nm are present in most cases if electron microscopy is performed.

Differential diagnosis Small cell carcinoma may be confused with lymphoma, particularly in a small biopsy specimen. Immunohistochemical stains for lymphoid and epithelial markers may be helpful in these cases. Primary small cell carcinoma of the bladder should be distinguished from a metastasis. Clinical exclusion of a primary elsewhere (especially the lung) and the finding of associated transitional cell neoplasia, even if only in situ, provide strong evidence for a primary tumor.

Giant cell carcinoma

Occasional undifferentiated carcinomas of the bladder are composed purely or predominantly of large pleomorphic cells with abundant eosinophilic or amphophilic cytoplasm and have a conspicuous component of malignant multinucleate giant cells (Fig. 12.150).[561] These tumors resemble giant cell carcinomas of other organs. They should not be confused with tumors containing osteoclast-type giant cells, as discussed earlier (see p. 536). The two types of giant cell may be present in the same tumor.

Lymphoepithelioma-like carcinoma

Lymphoepithelioma-like carcinomas have been described in recent years.[562–564] Microscopic examination showed small lymphocytes, plasma cells, eosinophils, and larger atypical cells resembling those of large cell lymphoma. Immunohistochemical staining of the atypical cells for keratins is crucial in establishing the epithelial nature of these cells in some. At this anatomic site, there appears to be no association with Epstein–Barr virus infection.[564] The differential diagnosis of this tumor is with malignant lymphoma, as it is in the head and neck. Malignant lymphoma of the bladder should only be diagnosed

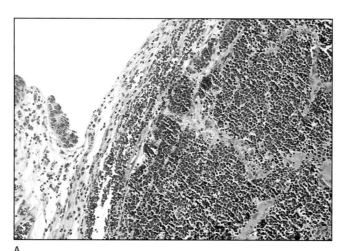

A

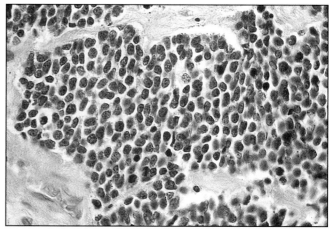

B

Fig. 12.149 • Small cell undifferentiated carcinoma of bladder. A large polypoid tumor occupies most of the bladder lumen.

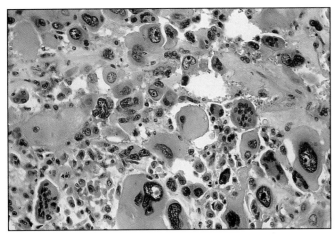

Fig. 12.150 • Giant cell carcinoma of bladder.

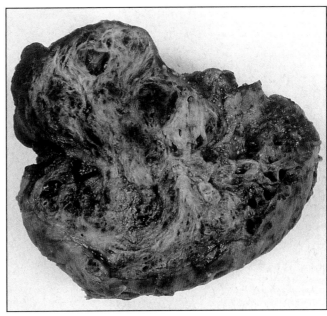

Fig. 12.151 • Hemangioma of bladder. The tumor is cystic and dark blue.

after a lymphoepithelioma-like carcinoma has been excluded. The heterogeneous nature of the infiltrate is a clue to the diagnosis but immunohistochemical stains should be done to confirm or establish the diagnosis.

Carcinomas of more than one histologic type

This category of cases is included in the classification of tumors of the urinary bladder to draw attention to the fact that it is not rare for tumors to contain significant components of two or more of the types discussed above. It is important that each component be mentioned in the diagnosis, or at least in a comment; some of them, such as the presence of a component of small cell carcinoma in an otherwise typical transitional cell carcinoma, have prognostic, and possibly therapeutic, significance.

Mesenchymal tumors

Benign mesenchymal tumors

All benign mesenchymal tumors of the bladder are rare,[565] with leiomyomas accounting for most of the cases.[566-568] Approximately 150 examples of this neoplasm have been reported, many in the older literature under different designations.[569] The reported cases indicate a predilection for females. Their gross appearance varies according to whether they are located predominantly in the lamina propria, in which case they may form a large protuberant mass in the bladder lumen, intramurally, or attached to the serosa. Grossly and microscopically these tumors resemble their more common uterine counterparts. Uncommon subtypes, such as epithelioid leiomyoma, occur but are rare. Similarly, tumors with atypical, but not frankly malignant, features are rare in the bladder. For this reason, the problem of the distinction between a leiomyoma with atypical features and leiomyosarcoma, which is such a problem in the uterus, has rarely arisen in the bladder.

Other benign mesenchymal tumors including hemangiomas (Fig. 12.151), lymphangiomas, neurofibromas, neurilemmomas, granular cell tumors, benign fibrous histiocytomas, and lipomas have been reported;[570-577] although interesting because of their unusual occurrence in this location, they do not appear to have

any features here that differ from those encountered in more common locations. As expected, hemangiomas may present with hematuria. The diagnosis of a neurogenic tumor should be particularly considered when the patient is known to have von Recklinghausen's disease.

Malignant mesenchymal tumors

Leiomyosarcoma Leiomyosarcoma is the most common sarcoma of the urinary bladder in adults.[578-580] Occasional examples have been reported in teenagers, but leiomyosarcoma of the bladder is rare in children. This age distribution contrasts with that of vesical rhabdomyosarcoma, which occurs mainly in children. The clinical presentation of patients with leiomyosarcoma is similar to that of those with transitional cell carcinoma. A few cases have arisen following cyclophosphamide therapy.[581,582] Like leiomyomas, leiomyosarcomas vary in appearance, but most of them appear to have had a significant polypoid component, often forming a large mass protruding into the bladder lumen. The surface of the tumor is often ulcerated. The sectioned surface of the tumors is often soft and white with focal hemorrhage. Some tumors are myxoid on gross inspection. On microscopic examination, these tumors do not differ significantly from their counterparts elsewhere (see Ch. 24). Occasional tumors are myxoid leiomyosarcomas.[583]

Differential diagnosis The differential diagnosis of leiomyosarcoma and sarcomatoid transitional cell carcinoma has been discussed above. Another important distinction is between leiomyosarcoma and two non-neoplastic lesions, the *postoperative spindle cell nodule* (Fig. 12.152)[584] and *pseudosarcomatous reactive myofibroblastic proliferation* (also sometimes known as inflammatory pseudotumor), the latter being most frequent in young adults.[585-590] The clinical history of a recent bladder operation is a key piece of information in making the diagnosis of a postoperative spindle cell nodule, which more closely resembles a leiomyosarcoma than does the spontaneous

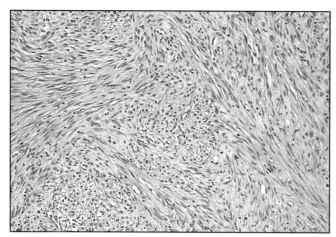

Fig. 12.152 • Postoperative spindle cell nodule of bladder. Note the resemblance to a leiomyosarcoma.

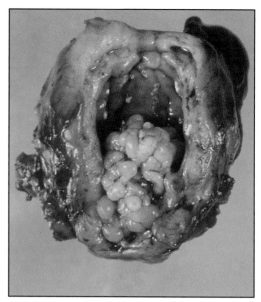

Fig. 12.153 • Embryonal rhabdomyosarcoma (sarcoma botryoides) of bladder of a child. A cluster of edematous polypoid fronds protrudes into the bladder lumen, the classic picture of sarcoma botryoides. (Courtesy of Dr. Glenn Taylor.)

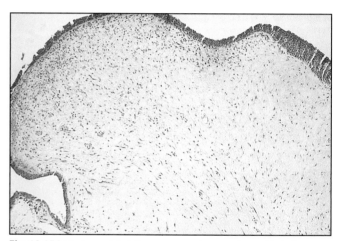

Fig. 12.154 • Embryonal rhabdomyosarcoma (sarcoma botryoides) of bladder. Note the markedly edematous appearance of the neoplasm in this illustration.

reactive myofibroblastic proliferation. A histologic feature which suggests postoperative spindle cell nodule is prominent vascularity, although this is not always present. Postoperative spindle cell nodules may exhibit brisk mitotic activity but they do not show significant cytologic atypia. A major feature that distinguishes the spontaneously occurring reactive myofibroblastic proliferation from leiomyosarcoma is prominent edema in the former. That lesion, which also tends to be seen in younger patients, is also typically quite vascular and, additionally, usually contains many inflammatory cells throughout. Some areas may resemble granulation tissue and the spindle cells often resemble those seen in fasciitis; the absence of nuclear hyperchromasia or significant nuclear atypia are important diagnostic clues. Ultrastructurally, both these non-neoplastic lesions typically contain cells with the features of myofibroblasts and accordingly, this, as opposed to the smooth muscle cells of leiomyosarcomas, may aid in differential diagnosis. Immunohistochemistry is often less helpful since smooth muscle actin, desmin and keratin are all often positive.[589] Some cases also show ALK-1 positivity, but *ALK* gene rearrangements are absent, suggesting that they may be unrelated to inflammatory myofibroblastic tumors.[590]

Rhabdomyosarcoma Rhabdomyosarcoma of the bladder almost always arises in children, with an average age at presentation of about 5 years.[591–596] However, the majority of patients are under 5 years of age, the average age being raised somewhat by the occasional occurrence of this lesion in teenagers.[595] Occasional examples are seen in adults.[597–601] There is a 3:2 male preponderance.[601]

Macroscopic appearances In the typical case, rhabdomyosarcoma is polypoid, resembling a bunch of grapes – the classic gross appearance of sarcoma botryoides (Fig. 12.153). However, other less characteristic gross appearances, which are indistinguishable from those of other malignant neoplasms of the bladder, are encountered.

Histologic appearances Microscopically, rhabdomyosarcomas at this site usually consist of polypoid fronds with hypocellular edematous areas (Fig. 12.154) and cellular areas composed of small hyperchromatic cells, often including a dense layer of such cells immediately beneath the mucosal surface, the well-known cambium layer (see also Ch. 24). In the cellular areas, many of the cells are small and may have relatively non-specific features, but scattered cells with appreciable eosinophilic cytoplasm, including occasional strap cells, almost invariably facilitate the diagnosis. The small cells usually appear obviously malignant but, in some tumors, there may be areas of more mature skeletal muscle cells.

Differential diagnosis It is important to remember that other masses[602–604] in the bladder of a child, such as the rare hamartoma (Figs 12.155, 12.156) may mimic a rhabdomyosarcoma grossly, but bear no resemblance to it microscopically. The major pitfall in the interpretation of this tumor on microscopic examination is to underdiagnose it as a benign process. This usually happens when only a small portion of a neoplasm is obtained in a biopsy specimen; problems rarely arise when the entire lesion is available for examination, although this is

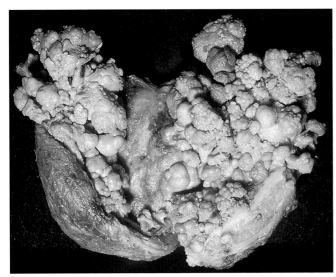

Fig. 12.155 • Hamartoma of bladder from a child. The larger mass, characterized by a prominent polypoid appearance, simulates that of sarcoma botryoides. (Courtesy of Dr. Athanase Billis.)

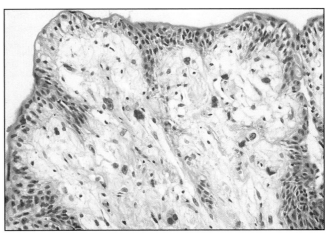

Fig. 12.157 • Fibroepithelial polyp with atypical stromal cells. The atypical cells have hyperchromatic degenerative nuclei and lack mitotic figures. This lesion did not have a cambium layer and occurred in an adult, an unusual age for an embryonal rhabdomyosarcoma, a diagnosis considered in this case.

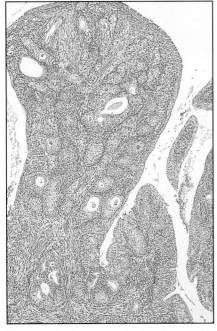

Fig. 12.156 • Hamartoma of bladder from a child. Histologic view of lesion in Figure 12.155 showing polyps comprised of epithelial aggregates similar to those of von Brunn's nests, cystitis glandularis, and cystitis cystica. (Courtesy of Dr. Athanase Billis.)

increasingly less frequent due to the primary role of chemotherapy in treating these tumors. In the setting of a biopsy of a polypoid bladder lesion in a child, there should always be a high index of suspicion for this tumor. An important differential diagnosis is with reactive myofibroblastic proliferations,[605] because the latter have a tendency to occur in young patients, although admittedly, usually somewhat older than the very young age of most patients with rhabdomyosarcoma. The distinction of this lesion from rhabdomyosarcoma should be relatively straightforward because of the uniform spindle-celled morphology and prominent inflammatory component of the former. Although foci in some rhabdomyosarcomas

may be highly differentiated and suggest the diagnosis of a rhabdomyoma, this tumor has not been documented to occur in the bladder. Awareness of the fact that some rhabdomyosarcomas may have more mature skeletal muscle cells should help to avoid this misdiagnosis. One fibroepithelial polyp of the bladder contained atypical stromal cells and brought the diagnosis of rhabdomyosarcoma into consideration,[604] but the lesion was from an adult and lacked mitotic activity (Fig. 12.157).

Other sarcomas Other sarcomas such as fibrosarcoma, so-called malignant fibrous histiocytoma, and osteosarcoma occur rarely in the bladder.[606–609] They resemble their counterparts elsewhere. The first two tumors should be diagnosed only after a sarcomatoid carcinoma has been excluded very carefully. The differential diagnosis of osteosarcoma includes other tumors of the bladder that may contain bone, including carcinosarcoma (see below) and transitional cell carcinomas with osseous metaplasia of the stroma (see above).

Mixed tumors

Benign mixed tumors

One lesion has been reported that falls into the category of benign mixed tumor. The tumor, reported as an "adenofibroma", occurred in a 46-year-old man with hematuria[610] who had a 3 × 2 cm tumor on the posterior bladder wall. On gross examination, the tumor had a cauliflower-like appearance with cysts. Microscopic examination showed duct-like structures within fibromuscular tissue which was focally myxomatous. Papillae projected into some of the lumens, some of which were cystically dilated and contained amorphous pink material.

Low-grade malignant mixed tumors (adenosarcoma)

One adenosarcoma of the bladder has been reported[611] and a tumor reported many years ago as an "adenomyoma"[612] might also represent this entity. The definitive example occurred in a 62-year-old woman with hematuria. The bladder contained a fungating tumor arising from the lateral wall with polypoid projections from its surface. Microscopic examination revealed glands surrounded by a cellular, atypical endometrial-type stroma that invaded through the bladder wall into perivesical fat. The tumor was associated with endometriosis, from which it was presumed to have arisen.

Malignant mixed tumors

Approximately 50 credible vesical carcinosarcomas have been reported.[613-616] Most occur in older patients with an average age of approximately 62 years. Only about 10 percent of the patients have been less than 50 years of age. The symptoms have been the usual ones associated with large bladder tumors, and most of the neoplasms have been bulky and exophytic. On microscopic examination, they show the characteristic admixture of carcinomatous and sarcomatous elements, usually intimately admixed, which are the defining features of this neoplasm (Fig. 12.158). The epithelial component usually resembles high-grade transitional cell carcinoma, but glandular or squamous differentiation is present in approximately one-third of the cases and, occasionally, the carcinomatous component is undifferentiated. The mesenchymal component of the tumor may resemble a high-grade fibrosarcoma, leiomyosarcoma, or non-specific spindle cell sarcoma. Chondrosarcomatous differentiation has been present in one-half of the cases (Fig. 12.159), osseous differentiation in one-third, and skeletal muscle differentiation in one-quarter; one tumor had areas of liposarcoma.[615] The prognosis of carcinosarcoma of the bladder has been poor, despite aggressive therapy, in most cases.

Differential diagnosis The differential diagnosis of carcinosarcoma of the bladder includes sarcomatoid carcinoma, carcinoma with stromal osseous or cartilaginous metaplasia, primary osteosarcoma or chondrosarcoma of the bladder, and carcinoma with a pseudosarcomatous stroma. In sarcomatoid carcinomas, the epithelial portion usually merges imperceptibly with the spindle cell component, which does not have areas of heterologous differentiation, and the spindle cell component

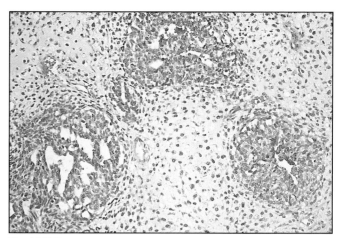

Fig. 12.159 • Carcinosarcoma of bladder. Three islands of malignant epithelium are surrounded by neoplastic stroma showing cartilaginous differentiation.

most often shows at least focal keratin positivity. The epithelial component in carcinosarcomas, in contrast, usually stands out from the sarcomatous background and transitions between the two components are more abrupt than in sarcomatoid carcinomas. In addition, carcinomatous and sarcomatous components are intimately admixed in many areas in a carcinosarcoma, a degree of intermingling which is not common in sarcomatoid carcinomas. Carcinomas with metaplastic bone and cartilage in their stroma differ from carcinosarcomas with osteocartilaginous elements in that the metaplastic elements in the former are histologically benign. Osteosarcomas and chondrosarcomas of the bladder lack the epithelial component necessary for the diagnosis of carcinosarcoma. Finally, the atypical stromal cells in carcinomas with a pseudosarcomatous stroma lack the malignant features characteristic of the spindle cells in carcinosarcomas.

Lymphoma and leukemia

From 10 to 20 percent of patients with non-Hodgkin's lymphoma have infiltration of the bladder at autopsy;[617] Hodgkin's disease involves the bladder in only 4 percent of patients. Only occasional patients with secondary lymphoma of the bladder have vesical symptoms and rarely this accounts for the clinical presentation (Fig. 12.160).[618] Primary non-Hodgkin's lymphoma of the bladder is rare. Most of the literature is represented by case reports with only occasional small series. Most of the tumors have been of low or intermediate grade, but occasionally high-grade lymphomas have been reported.[619-625] Recent data suggest that the most common low-grade lesions are B-cell lesions of MALT type[62] (see Ch. 21). T-cell lymphomas are documented[624] as are diagnostically challenging rare cases with sarcomatoid morphology.[625] The gross appearance of lymphoma of the bladder is variable. In some cases the gross appearance is quite characteristic of this disease, consisting of large fleshy white masses but, occasionally, less characteristic sessile lesions with thickening of the bladder wall are present. The tumors are typically large and are often covered by an intact mucosa, although there may be focal ulceration. Only one credible case of primary Hodgkin's disease of the bladder has been

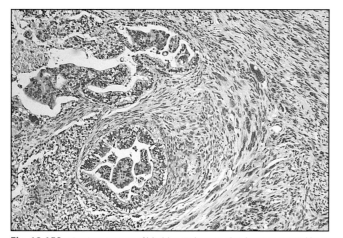

Fig. 12.158 • Carcinosarcoma of bladder. Malignant glands are separated by a sarcomatous stroma.

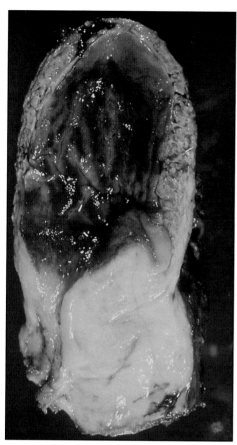

Fig. 12.160 • Malignant lymphoma of bladder. A fleshy white mass occupies a portion of the bladder wall and extends into the surrounding tissue (courtesy of Dr. Fred Askin).

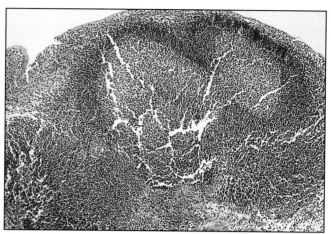

Fig. 12.161 • Follicular cystitis. This lesion may result in small white nodules that are grossly visible. The follicles in this case had the typical appearance of reactive follicles.

reported.[626] It occurred in a 56-year-old woman who had several masses protruding into the bladder lumen at cystoscopy. The tumor was histologically most consistent with the lymphocyte predominant variant.

Bladder involvement may occur in patients with multiple myeloma,[627] but the involvement rarely presents a diagnostic problem in patients known to have this disease. Plasmacytomas without evidence of bone marrow involvement or generalized myeloma have rarely arisen in the bladder.[628] All the patients have been adults. The gross appearances have resembled those of a malignant lymphoma, and microscopic examination has shown the characteristic features of plasmacytoma.

Bladder involvement in patients with leukemia is found at autopsy in approximately 25 percent of patients with acute leukemia and 15 percent of those with chronic leukemia.[629] One granulocytic sarcoma of the bladder has been reported in a 29-year-old woman who presented with dysuria and hematuria and, at the time of diagnosis, had normal peripheral blood and bone marrow. Cystoscopy disclosed an 8 cm polypoid submucosal mass. The patient was alive and well 3 years after presentation.[630]

The differential diagnosis of malignant lymphoma, as elsewhere, is with poorly differentiated carcinomas without any evidence of obvious epithelial differentiation. High-power scrutiny should resolve this problem by showing the distinctive features of lymphoid cells, but immunohistochemistry may be necessary to resolve the situation in rare cases. It should also be remembered that, in cases of the common entity, follicular cystitis (Fig. 12.161), small white nodules may be seen in the bladder mucosa. However, the lymphoid aggregates in this condition, including the germinal centers which may be seen, have the typical features of a reactive lymphoid lesion.

Miscellaneous primary tumors

Paraganglioma

Paragangliomas (see also Ch. 28) represent an important subset of non-transitional cell neoplasms of the urinary bladder and, although uncommon, are not exceptionally rare.[631,632] The tumors have been hormonally active, causing hypertension, in approximately two-thirds of the patients. Almost half the patients have had voiding-associated symptoms of headache, palpitations, hypertension, blurred vision and/or sweating. However, in somewhat more than half the patients, the clinical presentation is hematuria. The tumors have arisen in patients over a wide age range and occur more or less equally in both sexes. Occasional patients have had neurofibromatosis.

Macroscopic and histologic appearances On gross examination the tumors are typically lobulated, solid (Fig. 12.162), submucosal or intramural masses covered by intact urothelium. They have been as large as 10 cm, but most are only a few centimeters in greatest dimension. Microscopic examination usually shows nests of cells in the characteristic Zellballen pattern (Fig. 12.163), but this feature is not always conspicuous and some tumors grow diffusely. Involvement of muscularis propria is often conspicuous (Fig. 12.164). The mitotic activity and degree of nuclear pleomorphism vary from case to case and sometimes within an individual. Approximately 10 percent of the neoplasms are malignant and this is best predicted by depth of invasion into the bladder wall.[632] Sometimes the course is one of local recurrences developing over a period of many years before extravesical spread occurs. Distant metastases are rare.

Differential diagnosis When the Zellballen pattern of this tumor is conspicuous the diagnosis should come to mind; however, as noted above, this pattern is not always prominent.

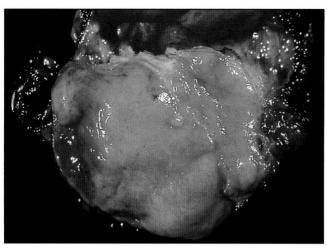

Fig. 12.162 • Paraganglioma of bladder. The tumor is slightly lobulated and brown.

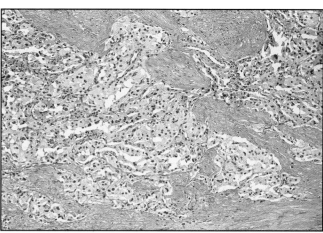

Fig. 12.164 • Paraganglioma of bladder. Involvement of muscularis propria is striking.

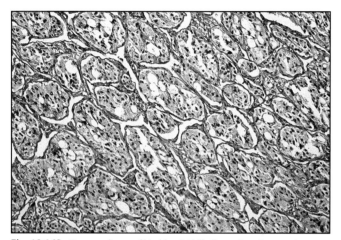

Fig. 12.163 • Paraganglioma of bladder. A Zellballen pattern is present.

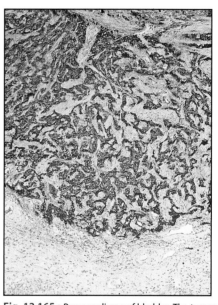

Fig. 12.165 • Paraganglioma of bladder. The tumor cells are strongly positive when stained by the immunohistochemical technique for chromogranin.

Abundant eosinophilic cytoplasm in the cells of a bladder tumor should lead to consideration of this diagnosis and procurement of the appropriate special stains (see Ch. 28) (Fig. 12.165). This consideration may be heightened by the clinical history and the knowledge that the gross appearance is not that of the usual carcinoma of the bladder. The most difficult differential is with transitional cell carcinoma, an issue that has been emphasized in the recent literature,[631] based on a series in which 20 percent of the tumors were initially misdiagnosed as carcinoma. Perhaps the most treacherous facet is the involvement of muscle which, in the context of a nested tumor, may suggest invasive nests of transitional cell carcinoma. The issue can be further confusing because of the artifact that is often present in transurethral resection specimens in which these neoplasms are usually first encountered. When some atypia and mitotic figures are present, it is easy to understand how a misdiagnosis of conventional carcinoma may be made. This is an area in bladder pathology, perhaps more than any other, where immunohistochemical stains may be helpful but these will, of course, only be procured if the index of suspicion of the pathologist is sufficient such that the possibility of paraganglioma comes to mind.

Carcinoid tumors

Carcinoids have been reported in the urinary bladder of adults ranging from 30 to 75 years of age.[633] None of them were associated with the carcinoid syndrome. The tumors ranged up to 5 cm in diameter and were all submucosal. Microscopic examination has shown the characteristic features of carcinoid tumor in three neoplasms but, in one, cytologic atypia was pronounced, suggesting a small cell carcinoma; that neoplasm was clinically malignant.[634]

Differential diagnosis The great rarity of carcinoid of the bladder means that the diagnosis should be made only after other tumors which may simulate carcinoid have been excluded. For example, some transitional cell carcinomas grow in the form of nests which superficially resemble those of a carcinoid. Differences in the cytologic features of transitional cell carcinoma and carcinoid and the performance of silver stains, immunohistochemistry, or electron microscopy should establish the diagnosis.

Malignant melanoma

Malignant melanoma of the bladder is exceptionally rare. In a critical review of the literature in 1984, only 3 reported cases were considered acceptable.[635] An additional case has subsequently been reported.[636] The patients have ranged from 48 to 65 years of age. On gross examination three tumors have had a brown or black color. Their appearances are similar to those of cutaneous melanomas (see Ch. 23).

Differential diagnosis The differential diagnosis with metastatic melanoma may be difficult, because primary cutaneous melanomas may undergo regression. Indeed, it can be argued that it is almost impossible to prove that a melanoma is primary in the bladder. In the differential diagnosis with other tumors, such as sarcomas, the finding of melanin granules and, in amelanotic tumors, immunoreactivity for S-100 protein and HMB-45 may be helpful.

Dermoid cysts

Four dermoid cysts of the bladder have been described in women from 30 to 49 years of age who typically had symptoms of long duration. The lesions were cystic masses containing hair and calcified material.[637,638] It should be remembered that ovarian dermoid cysts may occasionally perforate into the bladder.[637] As ovarian dermoid cysts are much more common than those of the bladder, secondary involvement of the bladder from the ovary must be excluded before a primary dermoid cyst of the bladder is diagnosed.

Choriocarcinoma

As discussed earlier, transitional cell carcinomas may exhibit trophoblastic differentiation and, in some cases, this is so extensive that subtotal sampling may show only choriocarcinoma. In the absence of recognizable transitional cell carcinoma, it is impossible to know whether the tumor originated from somatic cells or represents a true germ cell neoplasm. Even in the reported cases without a component of carcinoma, it is difficult to be sure that the tumors are not of somatic origin. The morphology of choriocarcinoma is distinctive and the tumor should be easily recognized. Other than the distinction of a pure choriocarcinoma of germ cell origin from one of somatic cell origin, problems in diagnosis should not arise.

Yolk sac tumor

One yolk sac tumor of the bladder has been described in a 1-year-old boy with hematuria who had a markedly elevated serum α-fetoprotein level and a polypoid, red-tan, gelatinous, focally hemorrhagic and necrotic tumor.[639] The patient underwent partial cystectomy and chemotherapy and was well 14 months postoperatively. This diagnosis should be entertained when evaluating a bladder tumor from a child if the neoplasm is not obviously of another type and the morphology is consistent with yolk sac tumor.

Secondary tumors of the bladder

The bladder may be invaded by tumors primary in adjacent sites (Figs 12.166, 12.167), usually the genital tract or colon, and, less commonly, is the site of metastases from tumors at distant sites such as breast.[275,640–643] When lymphomas and leukemias were excluded, other secondary tumors accounted for approximately 15 percent of the malignant bladder tumors in one study.[643] The tumors were from the female genital tract (30 percent), the prostate and seminal vesicles (26 percent), the lower intestinal tract (24 percent), and distant sites (20 percent). The great majority of intestinal tumors that involve the bladder are from the rectosigmoid.[645,646] There are also reported cases of appendiceal carcinoma spreading to the bladder.[647]

Differential diagnosis The diagnostic problems posed for the pathologist in cases of secondary involvement vary according to the morphology of the primary neoplasm.[648–653] In most of these cases, knowledge of the history of a primary tumor is helpful if the morphology of the bladder tumor is not sufficiently distinctive to suggest the diagnosis. In some of these cases, however, the primary tumor may have been treated many years previously and the history may not be provided.

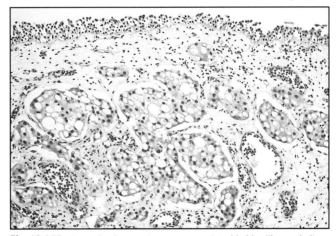

Fig. 12.166 • Prostatic adenocarcinoma metastatic to bladder. The urothelium is seen at the top.

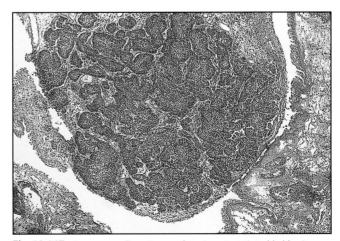

Fig. 12.167 • Squamous cell carcinoma of cervix metastatic to bladder. In some areas this neoplasm grew in rounded aggregates and on low-power examination superficially resembled an inverted papilloma.

Even more troublesome are cases in which the bladder tumor is discovered at the same time as, or before, the primary tumor. In many cases of involvement by female genital tract tumors, the histologic appearance of the primary tumor is distinctive and differs from that of any form of primary bladder cancer. However, in cases of vaginal or cervical squamous cell carcinoma, it is impossible to distinguish the tumor from a primary bladder tumor by morphology alone. Extensive preferential involvement of the outer layers of the bladder and extensive tumor in vessels and lymphatics in the bladder wall should lead to the consideration of metastasis if the morphology of the tumor is not that of a typical bladder carcinoma.

Tumors of the urethra

Benign tumors and tumor-like lesions

By far the most frequent urethral mass is the *caruncle*,[654,655] which accounted for 90 percent of urethral "tumors" in one series.[655] These lesions usually occur in the inferior aspect of the urethral meatus in postmenopausal females. They are typically red, tender, and bleed easily. Perhaps the most important aspect of these lesions is the occasional clinical misdiagnosis of a neoplasm as a caruncle. For example, in one series that included 14 urethral carcinomas, 6 were clinically diagnosed as caruncles.[655] On microscopic examination, there should be no problem distinguishing a caruncle from a neoplasm. Their appearances are variable but always clearly benign. In concert with their red gross appearance is their propensity to be prominently vascular on microscopic examination; some consist almost entirely of inflamed granulation tissue. In others the stroma may be prominently edematous with less intense inflammation. Rarely, the stroma contains atypical cells which appear to be mesenchymal and reactive in nature but can be misconstrued as representing neoplastic cells (Fig. 12.168).[587] Sometimes the surface has a papillary contour, the papillae being covered by hyperplastic urothelium or squamous epithelium.

Fibroepithelial polyps occur in the urethra, but less commonly than in the ureter. Most have been reported in males younger than 10 years, but a few have arisen in

adults.[656,657] They are typically found in the posterior urethra close to the verumontanum, but also have been reported in the anterior urethra.[656] Grossly and microscopically they resemble their ureteral counterparts (see p. 520).

Condylomata acuminata may involve the urethra in cases of genital and perineal condyloma.[658] Typically only the distal urethra is involved,[659] but occasionally there is extension to the proximal urethra; rarely the bladder and ureter are involved.[660,661] Grossly and microscopically, these lesions are similar to those seen on genital mucosae. They should be examined carefully for premalignant changes. At, or close to, the meatus, benign papillary squamous lesions that do not have specific features of human papilloma virus infection are occasionally encountered and in such cases the designation "squamous papilloma" is appropriate.[662]

In a female patient, we have seen one urethral lesion which resembled an adenomatous polyp of the intestinal tract. Three villous adenomas, similar to those seen in the gastrointestinal tract, have been reported in the distal urethra of postmenopausal women.[663–665] One of these was associated with an adenocarcinoma.[663] As adenocarcinomas of the urethra may be papillary, any papillary glandular lesion of the urethra with significant cytologic atypia should be viewed with suspicion and the diagnosis of villous adenoma made with caution. Occasionally, intestinal metaplasia of the urethral mucosa is an incidental microscopic finding[669] and this explains the histogenesis of some urethral adenocarcinomas, although most such tumors probably arise in the periurethral glands.

A benign lesion of the prostatic urethra that has received considerable attention in the literature is the entity that is now most commonly referred to as a *prostatic-type polyp*.[667] These are, as their name suggests, papillary lesions composed of prostatic-type epithelium.[667–675] Most are found in young men who characteristically present with hematuria or hematospermia. In one series of 25 patients, the patients ranged from 18 to 40 years;[673] in another the mean age was 31 years.[667] These lesions also occur in older patients; in one series the age range was 39–70 years.[675] Microscopic examination shows delicate papillae, or occasionally thicker polypoid fronds, covered by cuboidal to low columnar cells similar to those lining prostatic acini (Figs 12.169, 12.170); a component of transitional epithelium may also be present, particularly on the

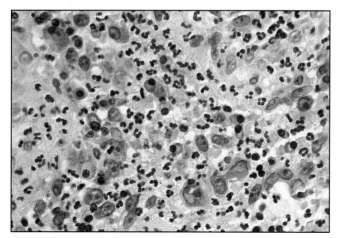

Fig. 12.168 • Atypical cells, presumably of mesenchymal type, in the stroma of a urethral caruncle.

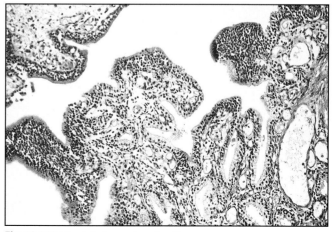

Fig. 12.169 • Prostatic-type polyp of urethra.

surface.[667] Prostatic-type glands may be present in the stroma. The prostatic nature of the epithelium in these cases can be confirmed by immunohistochemical staining for prostate-specific antigen and prostatic acid phosphatase. The differential diagnosis with polypoid protrusion of prostatic adenocarcinoma into the urethra rarely arises when prostatic-type polyps are found in young men, but in older patients this is a possibility, with a similar clinical presentation (Fig. 12.171).[630,671] Thus, the diagnosis of a prostatic-type polyp in an elderly male should be made only after carcinoma has been ruled out. Prostatic-type polyps rarely show atypia but it is possible that some of them may undergo malignant transformation.[674,676]

An important urethral lesion that may mimic a neoplasm is *nephrogenic adenoma*.[677–685] These occur in both sexes but are more common in females. In women, the lesion often occurs within a urethral diverticulum (Fig. 12.172), consistent with the common association of nephrogenic adenoma with chronic irritation. In men, nephrogenic adenoma has been documented to involve the bulbous urethra in some cases and the prostatic urethra in others. The distinctive histologic features of nephrogenic adenoma are present in the urethra, just as in the bladder. The lesion is usually confined to the mucosa (or a relatively narrow zone immediately beneath the mucosa) but, occasionally, the tubules may extend downwards for some distance and, in some male patients, the process has involved the prostate gland and sometimes caused problems in differential diagnosis with prostatic carcinoma.[680,685]

Papillary or polypoid inflammatory lesions that are analogous to papillary or polypoid cystitis may occur in any portion of the urethra.[686]

Urothelial papillomas of both typical and inverted types are much less common in the urethra than in the bladder. In the comprehensive review by Kunze et al.,[431] only 3.5 percent of inverted papillomas occurred in the urethra; all were in the prostatic urethra. A single lesion has been described in the penile urethra.[687] These lesions are diagnosed using the criteria presented above in the section on the bladder (see p. 523). As in that location, one may see papillomas of mixed type (Figs 12.173, 12.174).

Very rarely, benign mesenchymal tumors such as leiomyomas[688,689] occur in the urethra, more commonly in females, but are not known to differ pathologically from those seen elsewhere. One unusual benign tumor of the urethra histologically resembled a fibroadenoma of the breast.[690]

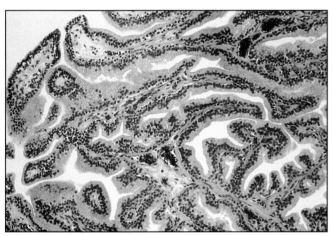

Fig. 12.170 • Prostatic-type polyp of urethra. Note the basal cell layer, bland cytologic features, and stroma between the glands.

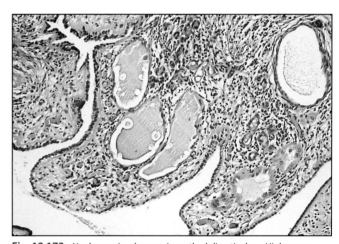

Fig. 12.172 • Nephrogenic adenoma in urethral diverticulum. High-power view showing characteristic small tubules and cysts of nephrogenic adenoma.

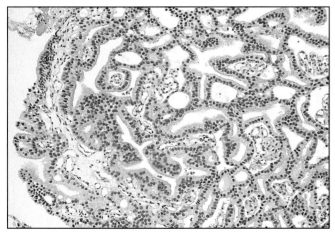

Fig. 12.171 • Adenocarcinoma of prostate forming polypoid intraurethral mass. Note the similarity to the benign lesion in Figures 12.169 and 12.170. Basal cells are absent.

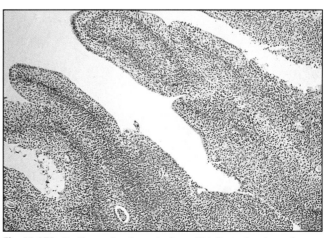

Fig. 12.173 • Papilloma of urethra, mixed type. This illustration shows the exophytic component.

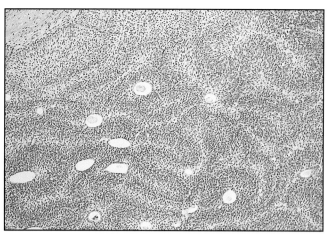

Fig. 12.174 • Papilloma of urethra, mixed type. This illustration shows the inverted component of the lesion illustrated in Figure 12.173.

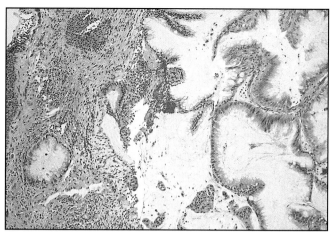

Fig. 12.175 • Low-grade mucinous adenocarcinoma of urethra.

Malignant tumors

Carcinoma

The great majority of malignant urethral tumors are carcinomas.[691–715] As has been shown in many series, in contrast to the situation elsewhere in the urinary tract, urethral carcinomas are much more common in women than men. In one review, slightly more than three times as many cases occurred in females as in males.[692] In both sexes squamous cell carcinomas account for approximately 60–70 percent of the tumors. The remaining neoplasms are transitional cell carcinomas and adenocarcinomas, with occasional undifferentiated carcinomas. In one review of the cases reported in females over a 20-year period, there were twice as many adenocarcinomas as transitional cell carcinomas.[694] In contrast, there were slightly more than twice as many transitional cell carcinomas as adenocarcinomas in a review of tumors in male patients.[715] The relative frequency of bladder carcinoma entails a significant association between transitional cell carcinoma of the urethra, usually the prostatic urethra, and antecedent bladder carcinoma.[716–719] In situ transitional cell carcinoma of the urethra is much more often encountered in a patient with a history of, or concomitant, carcinoma of the bladder than it is as a *de novo* phenomenon. In occasional cases, transitional cell carcinoma involves the urethra in a pagetoid fashion, sometimes involving the periurethral glands, or extending to the meatus.[720,721] Any malignant tumor of the bladder may involve the urethra by direct extension; occasionally, striking cases of urethral recurrence of bladder tumors are seen.

Urethral carcinoma usually occurs in patients in the sixth and seventh decades, although occasional cases have been documented in younger adults and at least one in a teenage male.[715] An association of carcinoma that has been seen in both sexes is with urethral stricture; this was present in approximately one-third of the male patients in one review.[715] Patients of both sexes may have diverse symptoms related to the urethra and, clinically, this condition is well known for the difficulties that may be associated with the establishment of a correct diagnosis. Unusual clinical associations are uncommon but have included hypercalcemia in at least 3 cases,[711,722] disseminated intravascular coagulation in one,[723] and pseudohyperparathyroidism in another.[724] Approximately 40 of the urethral tumors in women have arisen within urethral diverticula.[725,726] Over half of these tumors have been adenocarcinomas, many of them of clear cell type.

Although typically seen in the prostatic urethra, the transitional cell tumors are occasionally encountered in the anterior urethra, including one in the fossa navicularis.[727–729] Human papilloma virus type 6 has been identified in a few low-grade transitional cell carcinomas in males and in one squamous cell carcinoma in a male.[730,731] As in the bladder, some tumors have features of both transitional and squamous cell carcinoma and occasional tumors have had an appearance that has been likened to that of cloacogenic carcinomas of the ano-rectal region.[732,733] Adenosquamous carcinomas, one of which was associated with hypercalcemia, have also been documented.[722]

Adenocarcinomas in both sexes may have a variety of gross and microscopic appearances. Some appear gelatinous grossly but most have non-specific gross features. They frequently have a non-specific glandular architecture, but also commonly have an appearance resembling colonic adenocarcinoma (Fig. 12.175). Some of the latter are of colloid type[734] and rare tumors have had signet-ring cell morphology, either partially or predominantly.[705,706,713] The tumors may be associated with adjacent urethritis glandularis,[700,713] which may show premalignant change.[734] Well-circumscribed intracystic papillary cyst-adenocarcinomas are occasionally seen,[707] presumably arising in periurethral glands.

Clear cell adenocarcinoma is an important subtype of urethral adenocarcinoma (Fig. 12.176).[735] In one report of 22 adenocarcinomas of the urethra in women, 9 were of this type, the remaining 13 being mucinous.[704] The vast majority of clear cell adenocarcinomas of the urethra have occurred in females. This is especially important since the tumor closely resembles the clear cell adenocarcinomas of the female genital tract, and spread to the urethra from such a neoplasm must be excluded. Only 2 tumors of this type have occurred in males.[736,737] An important differential diagnosis of clear cell adenocarcinoma is with nephrogenic adenoma, a problem discussed on page 543. This differential diagnosis may be particularly difficult within a urethral diverticulum, within which approximately a third of these tumors have occurred, but the features outlined in the section on the bladder are again helpful.

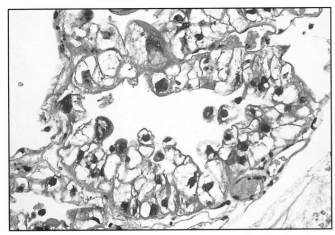

Fig. 12.176 • Clear cell adenocarcinoma of urethra. Note the abundant clear cytoplasm and occasional hobnail cells.

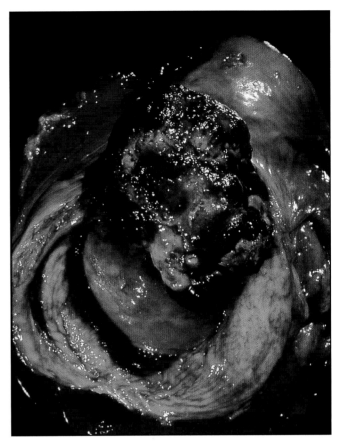

Fig. 12.177 • Malignant melanoma of urethra. The large polypoid tumor is focally black, suggesting the diagnosis.

One unusual urethral adenocarcinoma in a woman histologically resembled a prostatic adenocarcinoma and stained for prostate-specific antigen and prostatic acid phosphatase immunohistochemically.[708] Another adenocarcinoma of the female urethra was unusual because it exhibited focal positive immunohistochemical staining for α-fetoprotein.[709]

The differential diagnosis of a primary versus metastatic carcinoma involving the urethra is often difficult on histologic grounds alone, but the clinical sequence of events and distribution of disease generally aid in these cases. There will, however, be occasional problem cases, such as one in which a carcinoma of the colon recurred in the urethra 6 years after the initial tumor had been treated.[711]

Other rare tumors

When carcinomas are excluded, *malignant melanoma* accounts for the single greatest number of other malignant tumors of the urethra (Fig. 12.177).[635,737–742] Although these tumors are uncommon, they accounted for 4 percent of cancer tumors of the urethra in one series[707] and, when only sites within the genitourinary tract are considered, the urethra is a relatively frequent primary site for melanoma. In a comprehensive literature review published in 1984, Stein & Kendall[635] found 23 primary urethral melanomas in males and 40 in females, and a few additional examples have been reported since that time.[740–742] The tumors almost always occur in patients over 50 years of age. The presenting symptoms are similar to those of other urothelial cancers. The majority of cases in males have involved the fossa navicularis (55 percent), but the prostatic urethra (15 percent), bulbous urethra (10 percent), pendulous urethra (15 percent), and meatus (5 percent) may also be the primary sites. In females, the distal urethra is usually involved. Like melanomas elsewhere, the lesion is frequently noteworthy on gross appearance because of its black color, which obviously suggests the diagnosis (Fig. 12.177). Histologically,

these lesions resemble their counterparts in the skin (see Ch. 23). The melanin content is variable and its absence may make the diagnosis difficult.[742] Similarly, a prominent spindle cell component may cause diagnostic difficulty. In one series of 3 urethral melanomas, one was initially misdiagnosed as a sarcoma and another as a urothelial carcinoma for these reasons.[740] The prognosis of these patients is poor even with aggressive therapy; a few have survived 5 years.[739] Before the diagnosis of primary malignant melanoma is rendered, the possibility of spread to the urethra should be excluded by obtaining a detailed clinical history.

Other malignant tumors of the urethra are uncommon and mainly known through reports of single cases. Non-Hodgkin's lymphoma has rarely presented with manifestations in the urethra, and occasional cases of Hodgkin's disease[697] and plasmacytoma also have been encountered.[743–746] One lymphoma was of T-cell type and was the initial manifestation in a patient with AIDS.[747] Single cases of yolk sac tumor,[748] paraganglioma[749] and carcinoid tumor,[750] all apparently primary in the urethra, have been described and occasional large reviews of urethral neoplasms contain sporadic examples of various forms of sarcoma.

References

1. Eble J N, Sauter G, Epstein J I et al. 2005 World Health Organization classification of tumours. Pathology and genetics of tumours of the urinary system and male genital organs. IARC Press, Lyon
2. Delahunt B, Eble J N 1997 Papillary renal cell carcinoma: a clinicopathologic and immunohistochemical study of 105 tumors. Mod Pathol 10: 537–544
3. Eble J N, Warfel K 1991 Early human renal cortical epithelial neoplasia. Mod Pathol 4: 45A
4. Bell E T 1938 A classification of renal tumors with observations on the frequency of the various types. J Urol 39: 238–243
5. Talamo T S, Shonnard J W 1980 Small renal adenocarcinoma with metastases. J Urol 124: 132–134
6. Eschwege P, Saussine C, Steichen G et al. 1996 Radical nephrectomy for renal cell carcinoma 30 mm or less: long-term followup results. J Urol 155: 1196–1199
7. Störkel S, Eble J N, Adlakha K et al. 1997 Classification of renal cell carcinoma, workgroup 1. Cancer 80: 987–989
8. Newcomb W D 1936 The search for truth, with special reference to the frequency of gastric ulcer-cancer and the origin of Grawitz tumours of the kidney. Proc R Soc Med 30: 113–136
9. Xipell J M 1971 The incidence of benign renal nodules (a clinicopathologic study). J Urol 106: 503–506
10. Reis M, Faria V, Lindoro J et al. 1988 The small cystic and noncystic noninflammatory renal nodules: a postmortem study. J Urol 140: 721–724
11. Hiasa Y, Kitamura M, Nakaoka S et al. 1995 Antigen immunohistochemistry of renal cell adenomas in autopsy cases: relevance to histogenesis. Oncology 52: 97–105
12. Hashine K, Sumiyoshi Y, Kagawa S 1996 A morphological study of renal adenoma and latent renal cell carcinoma in autopsy cases. Nippon Hinyokika Gakkai Zasshi 87: 667–675
13. Hughson M D, Buchwald D, Fox M 1986 Renal neoplasia and acquired cystic kidney disease in patients receiving long-term dialysis. Arch Pathol Lab Med 110: 592–601
14. Budin R E, McDonnell P J 1984 Renal cell neoplasms, their relationship to arteriolonephrosclerosis. Arch Pathol Lab Med 108: 138–140
15. Bennington J L 1973 Cancer of the kidney – etiology, epidemiology, and pathology. Cancer 32: 1017–1029
16. Cristol D S, McDonald J R, Emmett J L 1946 Renal adenomas in hypernephromatous kidneys: a study of their incidence, nature and relationship. J Urol 55: 18–27
17. Syrjänen K J 1979 Renal adenomatosis, report of an autopsy case. Scand J Urol Nephrol 13: 329–334
18. Warfel K A, Eble J N 1982 Renal oncocytomatosis. J Urol 127: 1179–1180
19. Katz D S, Gharagozloo A M, Peebles T R et al. 1996 Renal oncocytomatosis. Am J Kidney Dis 27: 579–582
20. Thoenes W, Störkel S, Rumpelt H-J 1986 Histopathology and classification of renal cell tumors (adenomas, oncocytomas and carcinomas) the basic cytological and histopathological elements and their use for diagnostics. Pathol Res Pract 181: 125–143
21. Grignon D J, Eble J N 1998 Papillary and metanephric adenomas of the kidney. Semin Diagn Pathol 15: 41–53
22. Cohen C, McCue P A, DeRose P B 1995 Immunohistochemistry of renal adenomas and carcinomas. J Urol Pathol 3: 61–71
23. Perez-Ordonez B, Hamed G, Campbell S et al. 1997 Renal oncocytoma: a clinicopathologic study of 70 cases. Am J Surg Pathol 21: 871–883
24. Dechet C B, Bostwick D G, Blute M L et al. 1999 Renal oncocytoma: multifocality, bilateralism, metachronous tumor development and coexistent renal cell carcinoma. J Urol 162: 40–42
25. Klein M J, Valensi Q J 1976 Proximal tubular adenomas of kidney with so-called oncocytic features, a clinicopathologic study of 13 cases of a rarely reported neoplasm. Cancer 38: 906–914
26. Mead G O, Thomas L R Jr, Jackson J G 1990 Renal oncocytoma: report of a case with bilateral multifocal oncocytomas. Clin Imaging 14: 231–234
27. Tickoo S K, Reuter V E, Amin M B et al. 1999 Renal oncocytosis: a morphologic study of fourteen cases. Am J Surg Pathol 23: 1094–1101
28. Kragel P J, Williams J, Emory T S et al. 1990 Renal oncocytoma with cylindromatous changes: pathologic features and histogenetic significance. Mod Pathol 3: 277–281
29. Tickoo S K, Amin M B 1998 Discriminant nuclear features of renal oncocytoma and chromophobe renal cell carcinoma: analysis of their potential utility in the differential diagnosis. Am J Clin Pathol 110: 782–787
30. Eble J N, Hull M T 1984 Morphologic features of renal oncocytoma: a light and electron microscopic study. Hum Pathol 15: 1054–1061
31. Mathers M E, Pollock A M et al. 2002 Cytokeratin 7: a useful adjunct in the diagnosis of chromophobe renal cell carcinoma. Histopathology 40: 563–567
32. Pages A, Granier M 1980 Le néphrome néphronogene. Arch Anat Cytol Pathol 28: 99–103
33. Hennigar R A, Beckwith J B 1992 Nephrogenic adenofibroma, a novel kidney tumor of young people. Am J Surg Pathol 16: 325–334
34. Davis C J Jr, Barton J H, Sesterhenn I A et al. 1995 Metanephric adenoma, clinicopathological study of fifty patients. Am J Surg Pathol 19: 1101–1114
35. Bruder E, Passera O, Harms D et al. 2004 Morphologic and molecular characterization of renal cell carcinoma in children and young adults. Am J Surg Pathol 28: 1117–1132
36. Arroyo M R, Green D M, Perlman E J et al. 2001 The spectrum of metanephric adenofibroma and related lesions: clinicopathologic study of 25 cases from the National Wilms Tumors Study Group Pathology Center. Am J Surg Pathol 25: 433–444
37. Jones E C, Pins M, Dickersin G R et al. 1995 Metanephric adenoma of the kidney, a clinicopathological, immunohistochemical, flow cytometric, cytogenetic, and electron microscopic study of seven cases. Am J Surg Pathol 19: 615–626
38. Argani P, Beckwith J B 2000 Metanephric stromal tumor. Report of 31 cases of a distinctive pediatric renal neoplasm. Am J Surg Pathol 24: 917–926
39. Muir T E, Cheville J C, Lager D J 2001 Metanephric adenoma, nephrogenic rests, and Wilms' tumor: a histologic and immunophenotypic comparison. Am J Surg Pathol 25: 1290–1296
40. Brunelli M, Eble J N, Zhang S et al. 2003 Metanephric adenoma lacks the gains of chromosomes 7 and 17 and loss of Y that are typical of papillary renal cell carcinoma and papillary adenoma. Mod Pathol 16: 1060–1063
41. Thoenes W, Störkel S, Rumpelt H J et al. 1990 Cytomorphological typing of renal cell carcinoma – a new approach. Eur Urol 18 (suppl): 6–9
42. Kovacs G, Akhtar M, Beckwith J B et al. 1997 The Heidelberg classification of renal cell tumours. J Pathol 183: 131–133
43. Linehan W M, Walther M M, Zbar B 2003 The genetic basis of cancer of the kidney. J Urol 170: 2163–2172
44. Hock L M, Lynch J, Balaji K C 2002 Increasing incidence of all stages of kidney cancer in the last 2 decades in the United States: an analysis of surveillance, epidemiology and end results program data. J Urol 167: 57–60
45. Dayal H H, Wilkinson G S 1989 Epidemiology of renal cell cancer. Semin Urol 7: 139–143
46. Maclure M, Willett W 1990 A case-control study of diet and risk of renal adenocarcinoma. Epidemiology 1: 430–440
47. La Vecchia C, Negri E, D'Avanzo B et al. 1990 Smoking and renal cell carcinoma. Cancer Res 50: 5231–5233
48. Sharpe C R, Rochon J E, Adam J M et al. 1989 Case-control study of hydrocarbon exposures in patients with renal cell carcinoma. Can Med Assoc J 140: 1309–1318
49. Solomon D, Schwartz A 1988 Renal pathology in von Hippel-Lindau disease. Hum Pathol 19: 1072–1079
50. Maher E R, Yates J R W, Harries R et al. 1990 Clinical features and natural history of von Hippel-Lindau disease. Q J Med 77: 1151–1163
51. Bernstein J, Robbins T O 1991 Renal involvement in tuberous sclerosis. Ann NY Acad Sci 615: 36–49
52. Washecka R, Hanna M 1991 Malignant renal tumors in tuberous sclerosis. Urology 37: 340–343
53. Gregoire J R, Torres V E, Holley K E et al. 1987 Renal epithelial hyperplastic and neoplastic proliferation in autosomal dominant polycystic kidney disease. Am J Kidney Dis 9: 27–38
54. Bernstein J, Evan A P, Gardner K D Jr 1987 Epithelial hyperplasia in human polycystic kidney diseases, its role in pathogenesis and risk of neoplasia. Am J Pathol 129: 92–101
55. Bonacina R, Di Natale G, Zois G et al. 1986 Adenocarcinoma renale associato a rene policistico (presentazione di un caso e revisone della literatura). Chir Ital 38: 406–411
56. Fallon B, Williams R D 1989 Renal cancer associated with acquired cystic disease of the kidney and chronic renal failure. Semin Urol 7: 228–236
57. Matson M A, Cohen E P 1990 Acquired cystic kidney disease: occurrence, prevalence and renal cancers. Medicine 69: 217–226
58. Ishikawa I 1987 Development of adenocarcinoma and acquired cystic disease of the kidney in hemodialysis patients. Int Symp Princess Takamatsu Cancer Res Fund 18: 77–86
59. Gibbons R P, Montie J E, Correa R J Jr et al. 1976 Manifestations of renal cell carcinoma. Urology 8: 201–206
60. Cronin R E, Kaehny W D, Miller P D et al. 1976 Renal cell carcinoma: unusual systemic manifestations. Medicine 555: 291–311
61. Kiely J M 1966 Hypernephroma – the internist's tumor. Med Clin N Am 50: 1067–1083
62. Fahn H-J, Lee Y-H, Chen M-T et al. 1991 The incidence and prognostic significance of humoral hypercalcemia in renal cell carcinoma. J Urol 145: 248–250
63. Sufrin G, Chasan S, Golio A et al. 1989 Paraneoplastic and serologic syndromes of renal adenocarcinoma. Semin Urol 7: 158–171
64. Moran A 1990 Malignant hypertension due to renal carcinoma. Br J Urol 65: 299–299
65. Somer T P, Törnroth T S 1985 Renal adenocarcinoma and systemic amyloidosis, immunohistochemical and histochemical studies. Arch Pathol Lab Med 109: 571–574
66. Althaffer L F III, Chenault O W Jr 1979 Paraneoplastic endocrinopathies associated with renal tumors. J Urol 122: 573–577
67. Rosenblum S L 1987 Paraneoplastic syndromes associated with renal cell carcinoma. J S C Med Assoc 83: 375–378
68. Cheng W S, Farrow G M, Zincke H 1991 The incidence of multicentricity in renal cell carcinoma. J Urol 146: 1221–1223

69. Bennington J L, Beckwith J B 1975 Tumors of the kidney, renal pelvis, and ureter. Atlas of tumor pathology, series 2, fascicle 12. Armed Forces Institute of Pathology, Bethesda

70. Katz S E, Schapira H E 1982 Spontaneous regression of genitourinary cancer – an update. J Urol 128: 1–4

71. Kavoussi L R, Levine S R, Kadmon D et al. 1986 Regression of metastatic renal cell carcinoma: a case report and literature review. J Urol 135: 1005–1007

72. De Riese W, Goldenberg K, Allhoff E et al. 1991 Metastatic renal cell carcinoma (RCC): spontaneous regression, long-term survival and late recurrence. Int Urol Nephrol 23: 13–25

73. McNichols D W, Segura J W, DeWeerd J H 1981 Renal cell carcinoma: long-term survival and late recurrence. J Urol 126: 17–23

74. Hienert G, Latal D, Rummelhardt S 1988 Urological aspects of surgical management for metastatic renal cell cancer. Semin Surg Oncol 4: 137–138

75. Neves R J, Zincke H, Taylor W F 1988 Metastatic renal cell cancer and radical nephrectomy: identification of prognostic factors and patient survival. J Urol 139: 1173–1176

76. Elson P J, Witte R S, Trump D L 1988 Prognostic factors for survival in patients with recurrent or metastatic renal cell carcinoma. Cancer Res 48: 7310–7313

77. Gurney H, Larcos G, McKay M et al. 1989 Bone metastases in hypernephroma, frequency of scapular involvement. Cancer 64: 1429–1431

78. Gnarra J R, Duan D R, Weng Y et al. 1996 Molecular cloning of the von Hippel-Lindau tumor suppressor gene and its role in renal carcinoma. Biochim Biophys Acta 1242: 201–210

79. van der Hout A H, van den Berg E, van der Vlies P et al. 1993 Loss of heterozygosity at the short arm of chromosome 3 in renal-cell cancer correlates with the cytological tumour type. Int J Cancer 53: 353–357

80. Zbar B, Lerman M 1998 Inherited carcinomas of the kidney: histology. Adv Cancer Res 75: 164–201

81. Schullerus D, Herbers J, Chudek J et al. 1997 Loss of heterozygosity at chromosomes 8p, 9p, and 14q is associated with stage and grade of non-papillary renal cell carcinomas. J Pathol 183: 151–155

82. Presti J C Jr, Wilhelm M, Reuter V et al. 2002 Allelic loss on chromosomes 8 and 9 correlates with clinical outcome in locally advanced clear cell carcinoma of the kidney. J Urol 167: 1464–1468

83. Amin M B, Amin M B, Tamboli P et al. 2002 Prognostic impact of histologic subtyping of adult renal epithelial neoplasms, an experience of 405 cases. Am J Surg Pathol 26: 281–291

84. Cheville J C, Lohse C M, Zincke H et al. 2003 Comparisons of outcome and prognostic features among histologic subtypes of renal cell carcinoma. Am J Surg Pathol 27: 612–624

85. Delahunt B 1998 Histopathologic prognostic indicators for renal cell carcinoma. Semin Diagn Pathol 15: 68–76

86. Leibovich B C, Blute M L, Cheville J C et al. 2003 Prediction of progression after radical nephrectomy for patients with clear cell renal cell carcinoma, a stratification tool for prospective clinical trials. Cancer 97: 1663–1671

87. Eble J N, Bonsib S M 1998 Extensively cystic renal neoplasms: cystic nephroma, cystic partially differentiated nephroblastoma, multilocular cystic renal cell carcinoma, and cystic hamartoma of renal pelvis. Semin Diagn Pathol 15: 2–20

88. Gokden N, Nappi O, Swanson P E et al. 2000 Renal cell carcinoma with rhabdoid features. Am J Surg Pathol 24: 1329–1338.

89. de Peralta-Venturina M, Moch H, Amin M et al. 2001 Sarcomatoid differentiation in renal cell carcinoma; a study of 101 cases. Am J Surg Pathol 25: 275–284

90. Cheville J C, Lohse C M, Zincke H et al. 2004 Sarcomatoid renal cell carcinoma, an examination of underlying histologic subtype and an analysis of associations with patient outcome. Am J Surg Pathol 28: 435–441

91. Wick M R, Perrone T L, Burke B A 1985 Sarcomatoid transitional cell carcinoma of the renal pelvis, an ultrastructural and immunohistochemical study. Arch Pathol Lab Med 109: 55–58

92. Wick M R, Cherwitz D L, Manivel J C et al. 1990 Immunohistochemical findings in tumors of the kidney. In: Eble JN (ed) Tumors and tumor-like conditions of the kidneys and ureters. Churchill Livingstone, New York, p 207–247

93. Kimura I, Takahashi N, Okumura R et al. 1989 Perinephric xanthogranulomatous pyelonephritis simulating a renal or retroperitoneal tumor on x-ray CT and angiography. Radiat Med 7: 111–117

94. Malek R S, Greene L F, DeWeerd J H et al. 1972 Xanthogranulomatous pyelonephritis. Br J Urol 44: 296–308

95. Goodman M, Curry T, Russell T 1979 Xanthogranulomatous pyelonephritis (XGP): a local disease with systemic manifestations, report of 23 patients and review of the literature. Medicine 58: 171–181

96. Rosi P, Selli C, Carini M et al. 1986 Xanthogranulomatous pyelonephritis: clinical experience with 62 cases. Eur Urol 12: 96–100

97. Chuang C-K, Lai M-K, Chang P-L et al. 1992 Xanthogranulomatous pyelonephritis: experience in 36 cases. J Urol 147: 333–336

98. Parsons M A, Harris S C, Longstaff A J et al. 1983 Xanthogranulomatous pyelonephritis: a pathological, clinical and aetiological analysis of 87 cases. Diagn Histopathol 6: 203–219

99. Esparza A R, McKay D B, Cronan J J et al. 1989 Renal parenchymal malakoplakia, histologic spectrum and its relationship to megalocytic interstitial nephritis and xanthogranulomatous pyelonephritis. Am J Surg Pathol 13: 225–236

100. Waldherr R, Schwechheimer K 1985 Co-expression of cytokeratin and vimentin intermediate-sized filaments in renal cell carcinoma, a comparative study of the intermediate-sized filaments in renal cell carcinoma and normal human kidney. Virchow's Arch A Pathol Anat Histopathol 408: 15–27

101. Taxy J B 1981 Renal adenocarcinoma presenting as a solitary metastasis: contribution of electron microscopy to diagnosis. Cancer 48: 2056–2062

102. Wick M R, Cherwitz D L, McGlennen R C et al. 1986 Adrenocortical carcinoma, an immunohistochemical comparison with renal cell carcinoma. Am J Pathol 122: 343–352

103. Renshaw A A, Granter S R 1998 A comparison of A103 and inhibin reactivity in adrenal cortical tumors: distinction from hepatocellular carcinoma and renal tumors. Mod Pathol 11: 1160–1164

104. Green L K, Ro J Y, Mackay B et al. 1989 Renal cell carcinoma metastatic to the thyroid. Cancer 63: 1810–1815

105. Young R H, Hart W R 1992 Renal cell carcinoma metastatic to the ovary: a report of three cases emphasizing possible confusion with ovarian clear cell carcinoma. Int J Gynecol Pathol 11: 96–104

106. Hufnagel T J, Kim J H, True L D et al. 1989 Immunohistochemistry of capillary hemangioblastoma, immunoperoxidase-labeled antibody staining resolves the differential diagnosis with metastatic renal cell carcinoma, but does not explain the histogenesis of the capillary hemangioblastoma. Am J Surg Pathol 13: 207–216

107. Mancilla-Jimenez R, Stanley R J, Blath R A 1976 Papillary renal cell carcinoma, a clinical, radiologic, and pathologic study of 34 cases. Cancer 38: 2469–2480

108. Thoenes W, Störkel S 1991 Die Pathologie der benignen und malignen Nierenzelltumoren. Urologe [A] 30: W41–W50

109. Lager D J, Huston B J, Timmerman T G et al. 1995 Papillary renal tumors, morphologic, cytochemical, and genotypic features. Cancer 76: 669–673

110. Kovacs G 1989 Papillary renal cell carcinoma, a morphologic and cytogenetic study of 11 cases. Am J Pathol 134: 27–34

111. Kovacs G, Fuzesi L, Emanuel A et al. 1991 Cytogenetics of papillary renal cell tumors. Genes Chromosom Cancer 3: 249–255

112. Brunelli M, Eble J N, Zhang S et al. 2003 Gains of chromosomes 7, 17, 12, 16, and 20 and loss of Y occur early in the evolution of papillary renal cell neoplasia: a fluorescence in situ hybridization study. Mod Pathol 16: 1053–1059

113. Presti J C Jr, Rao P H, Chen Q et al. 1991 Histopathological, cytogenetic, and molecular characterization of renal cortical tumors. Cancer Res 51: 1544–1552

114. van den Berg E, van der Hout A H, Oosterhuis J W et al. 1993 Cytogenetic analysis of epithelial renal-cell tumors: relationship with a new histopathological classification. Int J Cancer 55: 223–227

115. Bard R H, Lord B, Fromowitz F 1982 Papillary adenocarcinoma of kidney, II. Radiographic and biologic characteristics. Urology 19: 16–20

116. Reznicek S B, Narayana A S, Culp D A 1985 Cystadenocarcinoma of the kidney: a profile of 13 cases. J Urol 134: 256–259

117. Amin M B, Corless C L, Renshaw A A et al. 1997 Papillary (chromophil) renal cell carcinoma: histomorphologic characteristics and evaluation of conventional pathologic prognostic parameters in 62 cases. Am J Surg Pathol 21: 621–635

118. Renshaw A A, Corless C L 1995 Papillary renal cell carcinoma, histology and immunohistochemistry. Am J Surg Pathol 19: 842–849

119. Delahunt B, Eble J N, McCredie M R E et al. 2001 Morphologic typing of papillary renal cell carcinoma: comparison of growth kinetics and patient survival in 66 cases. Hum Pathol 32: 590–595

120. Fuhrman S A, Lasky L C, Limas C 1982 Prognostic significance of morphologic parameters in renal cell carcinoma. Am J Surg Pathol 6: 655–663

121. Beckwith J B 1983 Wilms' tumor and other renal tumors of childhood: a selective review from the National Wilms' Tumor Study Pathology Center. Hum Pathol 14: 481–492

122. Thoenes W, Störkel S, Rumpelt H-J 1985 Human chromophobe cell renal carcinoma. Virchow's Arch [B] 48: 207–217

123. Thoenes W, Störkel S, Rumpelt H-J et al. 1988 Chromophobe cell renal carcinoma and its variants – a report on 32 cases. J Pathol 155: 277–287

124. Crotty T B, Farrow G M, Lieber M M 1995 Chromophobe renal cell carcinoma: clinicopathologic features of 50 cases. J Urol 154: 964–967

125. Durham J R, Keohane M, Amin M B 1996 Chromophobe renal cell carcinoma. Adv Anat Pathol 3: 336–342

126. Peyromaure M, Misrai V, Thiounn N et al. 2004 Chromophobe renal cell carcinoma, analysis of 61 cases. Cancer 100: 1406–1410

127. Kovacs A, Kovacs G 1992 Low chromosome number in chromophobe renal cell carcinomas. Genes Chromosom Cancer 4: 267–268

128. Bugert P, Gaul C, Weber K et al. 1997 Specific genetic changes of diagnostic importance in chromophobe renal cell carcinoma. Lab Invest 76: 203–208

129. Brunelli M, Eble J N, Zhang S et al. 2005 Eosinophilic and classic chromophobe renal cell carcinomas have similar frequent losses of multiple chromosomes from among chromosomes 1, 2, 6, 10, and 17, and this pattern of genetic abnormality is not present in renal oncocytoma. Mod Pathol 18: 161–169

130. Akhtar M, Tulbah A, Kardar A H et al. 1997 Sarcomatoid renal cell carcinoma: the chromophobe connection. Am J Surg Pathol 21: 1188–1195

131. Pan C-C, Chen P C, Ho D M 2004 The diagnostic utility of MOC31, BerEP4, RCC marker and CD10 in the classification of renal cell carcinoma and renal oncocytoma: an immunohistochemical analysis of 328 cases. Histopathology 45: 452–459

132. Martignoni G, Pea M, Brunelli M et al. 2004 CD10 is expressed in a subset of chromophobe renal cell carcinomas. Mod Pathol 17: 1455–1463

133. Kriz W, Bankir L 1988 A standard nomenclature for structures of the kidney. Kidney Int 33: 1–7

134. Störkel S, Pannen B, Thoenes W et al. 1988 Intercalated cells as a probable source for the development of renal oncocytoma. Virchow's Arch [B] 56: 185–189

135. Störkel S, Steart P V, Drenckhahn D et al. 1989 The human chromophobe cell renal carcinoma: its probable relation to intercalated cells of the collecting duct. Virchow's Arch [B] 56: 237–245

136. Amin M B, Varma M D, Tickoo S K et al. 1997 Collecting duct carcinoma of the kidney. Adv Anat Pathol 4: 85–94

137. Srigley J R, Eble J N 1998 Collecting duct carcinoma of kidney. Semin Diagn Pathol 15: 54–67

138. Davis C J Jr, Mostofi F K, Sesterhenn I A 1995 Renal medullary carcinoma: the seventh sickle cell nephropathy. Am J Surg Pathol 19: 1–11

139. Swartz M, Karth J, Schneider D T et al. 2002 Renal medullary carcinoma: clinical, pathologic, immunohistochemical, and genetic analysis with pathogenetic implications. Urology 60: 1083–1089

140. Simpson L, He X, Pins M et al. 2005 Renal medullary carcinoma and ABL gene amplification. J Urol 173: 1883–1888

141. Aizawa S, Kikuchi Y, Suzuki M et al.1987 Renal cell carcinoma of lower nephron origin. Acta Pathol Jpn 37: 567–574

142. Fleming S, Lewi H J E 1986 Collecting duct carcinoma of the kidney. Histopathology 10: 1131–1141

143. Kennedy S M, Merino M J, Linehan W M et al. 1990 Collecting duct carcinoma of the kidney. Hum Pathol 21: 449–456

144. Rumpelt H J, Störkel S, Moll R et al. 1991 Bellini duct carcinoma: further evidence for this rare variant of renal cell carcinoma. Histopathology 18: 115–122

145. Kuroda N, Naruse K, Miyazaki E et al. 2000 Vinculin: its possible use as a marker of normal collecting ducts and renal neoplasms with collecting duct system phenotype. Mod Pathol 13: 1109–1114

146. Vecchione A, Galetti T P, Gardiman M et al. 2004 Collecting duct carcinoma of the kidney: an immunohistochemical study of 11 cases. BMC Urol 4: 11–12

147. Argani P, Ladanyi M 2005 Translocation carcinomas of the kidney. Clin Lab Med 25: 363–378

147a. Argani P, Lae M, Ballard E T et al. 2006 Translocation carcinomas of the kidney after chemotherapy in childhood. J Clin Oncol 24: 1529–1534

148. Argani P, Lal P, Hutchinson B et al. 2003 Aberrant nuclear immunoreactivity for TFE3 in neoplasm with TFE3 gene fusions, a sensitive and specific immunohistochemical assay. Am J Surg Pathol 27: 750–761

149. Argani P, Lae M, Hutchinson B et al. 2005 Renal carcinomas with the t(6;11)(p21;q12). Clinicopathologic features and demonstration of the specific Alpha-TFEB gene fusion by immunohistochemistry, RT-PCR and DNA PCR. Am J Surg Pathol 29: 230–240

150. Medeiros L J, Palmedo G, Krigman H R et al. 1999 Oncocytoid renal cell carcinoma after neuroblastoma: a report of four cases of a distinct clinicopathologic entity. Am J Surg Pathol 23: 772–780

151. Koyle M A, Hatch D A, Furness P D et al. 2001 Long-term urologic complications in survivors younger than 15 months of advanced stage abdominal neuroblastoma. J Urol 166: 1455–1458

152. Eble J N 2003 Mucinous tubular and spindle cell carcinoma and post-neuroblastoma carcinoma: newly recognised entities in the renal cell carcinoma family. Pathology 35: 499–504

153. Ferlicot S, Allory Y, Compérat E et al. 2005 Mucinous tubular and spindle cell carcinoma, a report of 15 cases with a review of the literature. Virchow's Arch 447: 978–983

154. Hes O, Hora M, Perez-Montiel D M et al 2002 Spindle and cuboidal renal cell carcinoma, a tumour having frequent association with nephrolithiasis: report of 11 cases including a case with hybrid conventional renal cell carcinoma/spindle and cuboidal renal cell carcinoma components. Histopathology 41: 549–555

155. Parwani A V, Husain A N, Epstein J I et al. 2001 Low-grade myxoid renal epithelial neoplasms with distal nephron differentiation. Hum Pathol 32: 506–512

156. Rakozy C, Schmahl G E, Bogner S et al. 2002 Low-grade tubular-mucinous renal neoplasms: morphologic, immunohistochemical, and genetic features. Mod Pathol 15: 1162–1171

157. Srigley J R, Eble J N, Grignon D J et al. 1999 Unusual renal cell carcinoma (RCC) with prominent spindle cell change possibly related to the loop of Henle. Mod Pathol 12: 107A

157a. Cossu-Rocca P, Eble J N, Delahunt B et al. 2006 Renal mucinous tubular and spindle carcinoma lacks the gains of chromosomes 7 and 17 and losses of chromosome Y that are prevalent in papillary renal cell carcinoma. Mod Pathol 19: 488–493

158. Zisman A, Chao D H, Pantuck A J et al. 2002 Unclassified renal cell carcinoma: clinical features and prognostic impact of a new histological subtype. J Urol 168: 950–955

158a. Tickoo S K, dePeralta-Venturina M N, Harik L R et al. 2006 Spectrum of epithelial neoplasms in end-stage renal disease: an experience from 66 tumor-bearing kidneys with emphasis on histologic patterns distinct from those in sporadic adult renal neoplasia. Am J Surg Pathol 30: 141–153

159. Schouman M, Warter A, Roos M et al. 1984 Renal cell carcinoma: statistical study of survival based on pathological criteria. World J Urol 2: 109–113

160. Robson C J 1963 Radical nephrectomy for renal cell carcinoma. J Urol 89: 37–42

161. Robson C J, Churchill B M, Anderson W 1969 The results of radical nephrectomy for renal cell carcinoma. J Urol 101: 297–301

162. American Joint Committee on Cancer 2002 Kidney (sarcomas and adenomas are not included). AJCC Cancer Staging Manual, 6th Ed. Springer, New York, p 323–328

163. Bonsib S M 2004 The renal sinus is the principal invasive pathway, a prospective study of 100 renal cell carcinomas. Am J Surg Pathol 28: 1594–1600

164. Bonsib S M 2005 T2 clear cell renal cell carcinoma is a rare entity: a study of 120 clear cell renal cell carcinomas. J Urol 174: 1199–1202

165. Medeiros L J, Gelb A B, Weiss L M 1988 Renal cell carcinoma, prognostic significance of morphologic parameters in 121 cases. Cancer 61: 1639–1651

166. Medeiros L J, Gelb A B, Weiss L M 1987 Low-grade renal cell carcinoma, a clinicopathologic study of 53 cases. Am J Surg Pathol 11: 633–642

167. Giuliani L, Giberti C, Martorana G et al. 1990 Radical extensive surgery for renal cell carcinoma: long-term results and prognostic factors. J Urol 143: 468–474

168. Herrlinger A, Schrott K M, Sigel A et al. 1984 Results of 381 transabdominal radical nephrectomies for renal cell carcinoma with partial and complete en-bloc lymph-node dissection. World J Urol 2: 114–121

169. Studer U E, Scherz S, Scheidegger J et al. 1990 Enlargement of regional lymph nodes in renal cell carcinoma is often not due to metastases. J Urol 144: 243–245

170. Blute M L, Leibovich B C, Cheville J C et al. 2004 A protocol for performing extended lymph node dissection using primary tumor pathological features for patients treated with radical nephrectomy for clear cell renal cell carcinoma. J Urol 172: 465–469

171. Pantuck A J, Zisman A, Dorey F et al. 2003 Renal cell carcinoma with retroperitoneal lymph nodes, impact on survival and benefits of immunotherapy. Cancer 97: 2995–3002

172. Mitty H A, Droller M J, Dikman S H 1987 Ureteral and renal pelvic metastases from renal cell carcinoma. Urol Radiol 9: 16–20

173. Ito A, Satoh M, Ohyama C et al. 2002 Adrenal metastasis from renal cell carcinoma: significance of adrenalectomy. Int J Urol 9: 125–128

174. Han K R, Bui M H, Pantuck A J et al. 2003 TNM T3a renal cell carcinoma: adrenal gland involvement is not the same as renal fat invasion. J Urol 169: 899–903

175. McKiernan J, Yossepowitch O, Kattan M W et al. 2002 Partial nephrectomy for renal cortical tumors: pathologic findings and impact on outcome. Urology 60: 1003–1009

176. Gill I S, Desai M M, Kaouk J H et al. 2002 Laparoscopic partial nephrectomy for renal tumor: duplicating open surgical techniques. J Urol 167: 469–476

177. Hand J R, Broders A C 1932 Carcinoma of the kidney: the degree of malignancy in relation to factors bearing on prognosis. J Urol 28: 199–216

178. Skinner D G, Colvin R B, Vermillion C D et al. 1971 Diagnosis and management of renal cell carcinoma, a clinical and pathological study of 309 cases. Cancer 28: 1165–1177

179. Grignon D J, Ayala A G, El-Naggar A et al. 1989 Renal cell carcinoma, a clinicopathologic and DNA flow cytometric analysis of 103 cases. Cancer 64: 2133–2140

180. Green L K, Ayala A G, Ro J Y et al. 1989 Role of nuclear grading in stage I renal cell carcinoma. Urology 34: 310–315

181. Helpap B, Knüpffer J, Essmann S 1990 Nucleolar grading of renal cancer, correlation of frequency and localization of nucleoli to histologic and cytologic grading and stage of renal cell carcinomas. Mod Pathol 3: 671–678

182. Al-Aynati M, Chen V, Salama S et al. 2003 Interobserver and intraobserver variability using the Fuhrman grading system for renal cell carcinoma. Arch Pathol Lab Med 127: 593–596

183. Sengupta S, Lohse C M, Frank I et al. 2005 Histologic coagulative necrosis as a prognostic indicator of renal cell carcinoma aggressiveness. Cancer 104: 511–520

184. Parham D M, Roloson G J, Feely M et al. 2001 Primary malignant neuroepithelial tumors of the kidney: a clinicopathologic analysis of 146 adult and pediatric cases from the National Wilms' Tumor Study Group Pathology Center. Am J Surg Pathol 25: 133–146

185. Jimenez R E, Folpe A L, Lapham R L et al. 2002 Primary Ewing's sarcoma/primitive neuroectodermal tumor of the kidney, a clinicopathologic and immunohistochemical analysis of 11 cases. Am J Surg Pathol 26: 320–327

186. Majhail N S, Elson P, Bukowski R M 2003 Therapy and outcome of small cell carcinoma of the kidney, report of two cases and a systematic review of the literature. Cancer 97: 1436–1441

187. Resnick M E, Unterberger H, McLoughlin P T 1966 Renal carcinoid producing the carcinoid syndrome. Med Times 94: 895–896

188. Gleeson M H, Bloom S R, Polak J M et al. 1971 Endocrine tumour in kidney affecting small bowel structure, motility, and absorptive function. Gut 12: 773–782

189. Raghavaiah N V, Singh S M 1976 Extra-adrenal pheochromocytoma producing renal artery stenosis. J Urol 116: 243–245

190. Takahashi M, Yang X J, McWhinney S et al. 2005 cDNA microarray analysis assists in diagnosis of malignant intrarenal pheochromocytoma originally masquerading as a renal cell carcinoma. J Med Genet 42: e48

191. Zak F G, Jindrak K, Capozzi F 1983 Carcinoidal tumor of the kidney. Ultrastruct Pathol 4: 51–59

192. Ghazi M R, Brown J S, Warner R S 1979 Carcinoid tumor of kidney. Urology 14: 610–612

193. Acconcia A, Miracco C, Mattei F M et al. 1988 Primary carcinoid tumor of kidney, light and electron microscopy, and immunohistochemical study. Urology 31: 517–520

194. Cauley J E, Almagro U A, Jacobs S C 1988 Primary renal carcinoid tumor. Urology 32: 564–566

195. Huettner P C, Bird D J, Chang Y C et al. 1991 Carcinoid tumor of the kidney with morphologic and immunohistochemical profile of a hindgut endocrine tumor: report of a case. Ultrastruct Pathol 15: 655–661

196. Kojiro M, Ohishi H, Isobe H 1976 Carcinoid tumor occurring in cystic teratoma of the kidney, a case report. Cancer 38: 1636–1640

197. Fetissof F, Benatre A, Dubois M P et al. 1984 Carcinoid tumor occurring in a teratoid malformation of the kidney, an immunohistochemical study. Cancer 54: 2305–2308

198. Bégin L R, Guy L, Jacobson S A et al. 1998 Renal carcinoid and horseshoe kidney: a frequent association of two rare entities – a case report and review of the literature. J Surg Oncol 68: 113–119

199. Capella C, Eusebi V, Rosai J 1984 Primary oat cell carcinoma of the kidney. Am J Surg Pathol 8: 855–861

200. Tetu B, Ro J Y, Ayala A G et al. 1987 Small cell carcinoma of the kidney, a clinicopathologic, immunohistochemical, and ultrastructural study. Cancer 60: 1809–1814

201. Gohji K, Nakanishi T, Hara I et al. 1987 Two cases of primary neuroblastoma of the kidney in adults. J Urol 137: 966–968

202. Eble J N 1998 Angiomyolipoma of kidney. Semin Diagn Pathol 15: 21–40

203. Filipas D, Spix C, Schulz-Lampel D et al. 2003 Screening for renal cell carcinoma using ultrasonography: a feasibility study. BJU Int 91: 595–599

204. O'Callaghan F J, Noakes M J, Martyns C N et al. 2004 An epidemiological study of renal pathology in tuberous sclerosis complex. BJU Int 94: 853–857

205. Ferry J A, Malt R A, Young R H 1991 Renal angiomyolipoma with sarcomatous transformation and pulmonary metastases. Am J Surg Pathol 15: 1083–1088

206. Oesterling J E, Fishman E K, Goldman S M et al. 1986 The management of renal angiomyolipoma. J Urol 135: 1121–1124

207. L'Hostis H, Deminiere C, Ferriere J-M et al. 1999 Renal angiomyolipoma: a clinicopathologic, immunohistochemical, and follow-up study of 46 cases. Am J Surg Pathol 23: 1011–1020

207a. Davis C J, Barton J H, Sesterhenn I A 2006 Cystic angiomyolipoma of the kidney: a clinicopathologic description of 11 cases. Mod Pathol 19: 669–674

208. Taylor R S, Joseph D B, Kohaut E C et al. 1989 Renal angiomyolipoma associated with lymph node involvement and renal cell carcinoma in patients with tuberous sclerosis. J Urol 141: 930–932

209. McIntosh G S, Hamilton Dutoit S, Chronos N V et al. 1989 Multiple unilateral renal angiomyolipomas with regional lymphangioleiomyomatosis. J Urol 142: 1305–1307

210. Ro J Y, Ayala A G, El-Naggar A et al. 1990 Angiomyolipoma of kidney with lymph node involvement, DNA flow cytometric analysis. Arch Pathol Lab Med 114: 65–67

211. Hulbert J C, Graf R 1983 Involvement of the spleen by renal angiomyolipoma: metastasis or multicentricity. J Urol 130: 328–329

212. Mai K T, Perkins D G, Collins J P 1996 Epithelioid variant of renal angiomyolipoma. Histopathology 28: 277–280

213. Eble J N, Amin M B, Young R H 1997 Epithelioid angiomyolipoma of the kidney, a report of five cases with a prominent and diagnostically confusing epithelioid smooth muscle component. Am J Surg Pathol 21: 1123–1130

214. Pea M, Bonetti F, Martignoni G et al. 1998 Apparent renal cell carcinomas in tuberous sclerosis are heterogeneous: the identification of malignant epithelioid angiomyolipoma. Am J Surg Pathol 22: 180–187

215. Peterson N E, Thompson H T 1971 Renal hemangioma. J Urol 105: 27–31

216. Edward N E, DeWeerd J H, Woolner L B 1962 Renal hemangiomas. Mayo Clin Proc 37: 545–566

217. Schofield D, Zaatari G S, Gay B B 1986 Klippel-Trenaunay and Sturge-Weber syndromes with renal hemangioma and double inferior vena cava. J Urol 136: 442–445

218. Moros Garcia M, Martinez Tello D, Ramon y Cajal Junquera S et al. 1988 Multiple cavernous hemangioma of the kidney. Eur Urol 14: 90–92

219. Caduff R F, Schwöbel M G, Willi U V et al. 1997 Lymphangioma of the right kidney in an infant boy. Pediatr Pathol Lab Med 17: 631–637

220. Honma I, Takagi Y, Shigyo M et al. 2002 Lymphangioma of the kidney. Int J Urol 9: 178–182

221. Pickering S P, Fletcher B D, Bryan P J et al. 1984 Renal lymphangioma: a cause of neonatal nephromegaly. Pediatr Radiol 14: 445–448

222. Di Palma S, Giardini R 1988 Leiomyoma of the kidney. Tumori 74: 489–493

223. Clinton-Thomas C L 1956 A giant leiomyoma of the kidney. Br J Surg 43: 497–501

224. Zollikofer C, Castaneda-Zuniga W, Nath H P et al. 1980 The angiographic appearance of intrarenal leiomyoma. Radiology 136: 47–49

225. Dineen M K, Venable D D, Misra R P 1984 Pure intrarenal lipoma – report of a case and review of the literature. J Urol 132: 104–107

226. Hurwitz R S, Benjamin J A, Cooper J F 1978 Excessive proliferation of peripelvic fat of the kidney. Urology 11: 448–456

227. Deyrup A T, Montgomery E, Fisher C 2004 Leiomyosarcoma of the kidney, a clinicopathologic study. Am J Surg Pathol 28: 178–182

228. Farrow G M, Harrison E G Jr, Utz D C et al. 1968 Sarcomas and sarcomatoid and mixed malignant tumors of the kidney in adults – part I. Cancer 22: 545–550

229. Grignon D J, Ro J Y, Papadopoulos N E et al. 1991 Leiomyosarcoma of renal vein. Urology 38: 255–258

230. Grignon D J, Ayala A G, Ro J Y et al. 1990 Primary sarcomas of the kidney, a clinicopathologic and DNA flow cytometric study of 17 cases. Cancer 65: 1611–1618

231. Mayes D C, Fechner R E, Gillenwater J Y 1990 Renal liposarcoma. Am J Surg Pathol 14: 268–273

232. Cano J Y, D'Altorio R A 1976 Renal liposarcoma: case report. J Urol 115: 747–749

233. Takashi M, Murase T, Kato K et al. 1987 Malignant fibrous histiocytoma arising from the renal capsule: report of a case. Urol Int 42: 227–230

234. Joseph T J, Becker D I, Turton A F 1991 Renal malignant fibrous histiocytoma. Urology 37: 483–489

235. Srinivas V, Sogani P C, Hajdu S I et al. 1984 Sarcomas of the kidney. J Urol 132: 13–16

236. Penchansky L, Gallo G 1979 Rhabdomyosarcoma of the kidney in children. Cancer 44: 285–292

237. Gonzalez-Crussi F, Baum E S 1983 Renal sarcomas of childhood, a clinicopathologic and ultrastructural study. Cancer 51: 898–912

238. Grignon D J, McIsaac G P, Armstrong R F et al. 1988 Primary rhabdomyosarcoma of the kidney, a light microscopic, immunohistochemical, and electron microscopic study. Cancer 62: 2027–2032

239. Argani P, Faria P A, Epstein J I et al. 2000 Primary renal synovial sarcoma: molecular and morphologic delineation of an entity previously included among embryonal sarcomas of the kidney. Am J Surg Pathol 24: 1087–1096

240. Kim D-H, Sohn J H, Lee M C et al. 2000 Primary synovial sarcoma of the kidney. Am J Surg Pathol 24: 1097–1104

241. Magro G, Cavallaro V, Torrisi A et al. 2002 Intrarenal solitary fibrous tumor of the kidney, report of a case with emphasis on the differential diagnosis in the wide spectrum of monomorphous spindle cell tumors of the kidney. Pathol Res Pract 198: 37–43

242. Wang J, Arber D A, Frankel K et al. 2001 Large solitary fibrous tumor of the kidney: report of two cases and review of the literature. Am J Surg Pathol 25: 1194–1199

243. Weiss J P, Pollack H M, McCormick J F et al. 1984 Renal hemangiopericytoma: surgical, radiological and pathological implications. J Urol 132: 337–339

244. Bowers D L, Te A, Hibshoosh H et al. 1995 Renal hemangiopericytoma, case report and review of the literature. Urol Int 55: 162–166

245. Richard G K, Freeborn W A, Zaatari G S 1996 Hemangiopericytoma of the renal capsule. J Urol Pathol 4: 85–98

246. Siniluoto T M J, Päivänsalo M, Hellström P A et al. 1988 Hemangiopericytoma of the kidney: A case with preoperative ethanol embolization. J Urol 140: 137–138

247. O'Malley F P, Grignon D J, Shepherd R R et al. 1991 Primary osteosarcoma of the kidney, report of a case studied by immunohistochemistry, electron microscopy, and DNA flow cytometry. Arch Pathol Lab Med 115: 1262–1265

248. Leventis A K, Stathopoulos G P, Boussiotou A C et al. 1997 Primary osteogenic sarcoma of the kidney, a case report and review of the literature. Acta Oncol 36: 775–777

249. Gomez-Brouchet A, Soulie M, Delisle M B et al. 2001 Mesenchymal chondrosarcoma of the kidney. J Urol 166: 2305–2305

250. Tsuda N, Chowdhury P R, Hayashi T et al. 1997 Primary renal angiosarcoma: a case report and review of the literature. Pathol Int 47: 778–783

251. Cerilli L A, Huffman H T, Anand A 1998 Primary renal angiosarcoma: a case report with immunohistochemical, ultrastructural, and cytogenetic features and review of the literature. Arch Pathol Lab Med 122: 929–935

252. Robertson P W, Klidjian A, Harding L K et al. 1967 Hypertension due to a renin-secreting renal tumour. Am J Med 43: 963–976

253. Kihara I, Kitamura S, Hoshino T et al. 1968 A hitherto unreported vascular tumor of the kidney: a proposal of "juxtaglomerular cell tumor." Acta Pathol Jpn 18: 197–206

254. Martin S A, Mynderse L A, Lager D J et al. 2001 Juxtaglomerular cell tumor, a clinicopathologic study of four cases and review of the literature. Am J Clin Pathol 116: 854–863

255. Corvol P, Pinet F, Galen F X et al. 1988 Seven lessons from seven renin secreting tumors. Kidney Int Suppl 34, Suppl. 25: S-38–S-44

256. Valdés G, Lopez J M, Martinez P et al. 1980 Renin-secreting tumor, case report. Hypertension 2: 714–718

257. Duan X, Bruneval P, Hammadeh R et al. 2004 Metastatic juxtaglomerular cell tumor in a 52-year-old man. Am J Surg Pathol 28: 1098–1102

258. Camilleri J-P, Hinglais N, Bruneval P et al. 1984 Renin storage and cell differentiation in juxtaglomerular cell tumors: an immunohistochemical and ultrastructural study of three cases. Hum Pathol 15: 1069–1079

259. Lindop G B M, Stewart J A, Downie T T 1983 The immunocytochemical demonstration of renin in a juxtaglomerular cell tumour by light and electron microscopy. Histopathology 7: 421–431

260. Lindop G B M, Fleming S 1984 Renin in renal cell carcinoma – an immunocytochemical study using an antibody to pure human renin. J Clin Pathol 37: 27–31

261. Steffens J, Bock R, Braedel H U et al. 1990 Renin-producing renal cell carcinoma. Eur Urol 18: 56–60

262. Lindop G B M, Fleming S, Gibson A A M 1984 Immunocytochemical localisation of renin in nephroblastoma. J Clin Pathol 37: 738–742

263. Horita Y, Tadokoro M, Taura K et al. 2004 Incidental detection of renomedullary interstitial cell tumour in a renal biopsy specimen. Nephrol Dial Transplant 19: 1007–1008

264. Warfel K A, Eble J N 1985 Renomedullary interstitial cell tumors. Am J Clin Pathol 83: 262–262

265. Eble J N 1990 Unusual renal tumors and tumor-like conditions. In: Eble JN (ed) Tumors and tumor-like conditions of the kidneys and ureters. Churchill Livingstone, New York, p 145–176

266. Zimmermann A, Luscieti P, Flury B et al. 1981 Amyloid-containing renal interstitial cell nodules (RICNs) associated with chronic arterial hypertension in older age groups. Am J Pathol 105: 288–294

267. Taxy J B, Marshall F F 1983 Multilocular renal cysts in adults, possible relationship to renal adenocarcinoma. Arch Pathol Lab Med 107: 633–637

268. Boggs L K, Kimmelstiel P 1956 Benign multilocular cystic nephroma: report of two cases of so-called multilocular cyst of the kidney. J Urol 76: 530–541

269. Kanomata N, Halling K, Eble J N 1997 Non-random X chromosome inactivation in cystic nephroma demonstrates its neoplastic nature. J Urol Pathol 7: 81–87

270. Castillo O A, Boyle E T Jr, Kramer S A 1991 Multilocular cysts of kidney, a study of 29 patients and review of the literature. Urology 37: 156–162

271. Joshi V V, Beckwith J B 1989 Multilocular cyst of the kidney (cystic nephroma) and cystic, partially differentiated nephroblastoma, terminology and criteria for diagnosis. Cancer 64: 466–479

272. Pawade J, Soosay G N, Delprado W et al. 1993 Cystic hamartoma of the renal pelvis. Am J Surg Pathol 17: 1169–1175

273. Durham J R, Bostwick D G, Farrow G M et al. 1993 Mesoblastic nephroma of adulthood, report of three cases. Am J Surg Pathol 17: 1029–1038

274. Truong L D, Williams R, Ngo T et al. 1998 Adult mesoblastic nephroma; expansion of the morphologic spectrum and review of the literature. Am J Surg Pathol 22: 827–839

275. Michal M, Syrucek M 1998 Benign mixed epithelial and stromal tumor of the kidney. Pathol Res Pract 194: 445–448

276. Nakagawa T, Kanai Y, Fujimoto H et al. 2004. Malignant mixed epithelial and stromal tumours of the kidney: a report of the first two cases with a fatal clinical outcome. Histopathology 44: 302–304

277. Adsay N V, Eble J N, Srigley J et al. 2000 Mixed epithelial and stromal tumor of the kidney. Am J Surg Pathol 24: 958–970

278. Ferry J A, Harris N L, Papanicolaou N et al. 1995 Lymphoma of the kidney, a report of 11 cases. Am J Surg Pathol 19: 134–144

279. Ferry J A, Young R H 1997 Malignant lymphoma of the genitourinary tract. Curr Diagn Pathol 4: 145–169

280. Osborne B M, Brenner M, Weitzner S et al. 1987 Malignant lymphoma presenting as a renal mass: four cases. Am J Surg Pathol 11: 375–382

281. Farrow G M, Harrison E G Jr, Utz D C 1968 Sarcomas and sarcomatoid and mixed malignant tumors of the kidney in adults – part II. Cancer 22: 551–555

282. Rebelakos A G, Papanastasiou K, Apostolikas N 1995 Renal plasmacytoma. Br J Urol 75: 562–562

283. Igel T C, Engen D E, Banks P M et al. 1991 Renal plasmacytoma: Mayo Clinic experience and review of the literature. Urology 37: 385–389

284. Bracken R B, Chica G, Johnson D E et al. 1979 Secondary renal neoplasms: An autopsy study. South Med J 72: 806–807

285. Klinger M E 1951 Secondary tumors of the genito-urinary tract. J Urol 65: 144–153

286. Payne R A 1960 Metastatic renal tumours. Br J Surg 48: 310–315

287. Wagle D G, Moore R H, Murphy G P 1975 Secondary carcinomas of the kidney. J Urol 114: 30–32

288. Pascal R R 1980 Renal manifestations of extrarenal neoplasms. Hum Pathol 11: 7–17

289. Melato M, Laurino L, Bianchi P et al. 1991 Intraglomerular metastases. A possibly maldiagnosed entity. Zentralbl Allg Pathol 137: 90–92

290. Naryshkin S, Tomaszewski J E 1991 Acute renal failure secondary to carcinomatous lymphatic metastases to kidneys. J Urol 146: 1610–1612

291. Mierau G W, Beckwith J B, Weeks D A 1987 Ultrastructure and histogenesis of the renal tumors of childhood: an overview. Ultrastruct Pathol 11: 313–333

292. Webber B L, Parham D M, Drake L G et al. 1992 Renal tumors in childhood. Pathol Annu 27, part 1: 191–232

293. Beckwith J B 1997 New developments in the pathology of Wilms tumor. Cancer Invest 15: 153–162

294. Sotelo-Avila C 1990 Nephroblastoma and other pediatric renal cancers. In: Eble JN (ed) Tumors and tumor-like conditions of the kidneys and ureters. Churchill Livingstone, New York, p 71–121

295. Breslow N, Beckwith J B, Ciol M et al. 1988 Age distribution of Wilms' tumor: report from the National Wilms' Tumor Study. Cancer Res 48: 1653–1657

296. Lemerle J, Tournade M-F, Gerard-Marchant R et al. 1976 Wilms' tumor: natural history and prognostic factors, a retrospective study of 248 cases treated at the Institut Gustave-Roussy 1952–1967. Cancer 37: 2557–2566

297. Hrabovsky E E, Othersen H B Jr, deLorimier A et al. 1986 Wilms' tumor in the neonate: a report from the National Wilms' Tumor Study. J Pediatr Surg 21: 385–387

298. Innis M D 1973 Nephroblastoma: index cancer of childhood. Med J Aust 2: 322–323

299. Blute M L, Kelalis P P, Offord K P et al. 1987 Bilateral Wilms tumor. J Urol 138: 968–973

300. Breslow N E, Beckwith J B 1982 Epidemiological features of Wilms' tumor: results of the National Wilms' Tumor Study. J Natl Cancer Inst 68: 429–436

301. Sotelo-Avila C, Gonzalez-Crussi F, Fowler J W 1980 Complete and incomplete forms of Beckwith-Wiedemann syndrome: their oncogenic potential. J Pediatr 96: 47–50

302. Heppe R K, Koyle M A, Beckwith J B 1991 Nephrogenic rests in Wilms tumor patients with Drash syndrome. J Urol 145: 1225–1228

303. Miller R W, Fraumeni JF Jr, Manning M D 1964 Association of Wilms's tumor with aniridia, hemihypertrophy and other congenital malformations. N Engl J Med 270: 922–927

304. Huser J, Grignon D J, Ro J Y et al. 1990 Adult Wilms' tumor: a clinicopathologic study of 11 cases. Mod Pathol 3: 321–326

305. Arrigo S, Beckwith J B, Sharples K et al. 1990 Better survival after combined modality care for adults with Wilms' tumor, a report from the National Wilms' Tumor Study. Cancer 66: 827–830

306. Bove K E, Koffler H, McAdams A J 1969 Nodular renal blastema, definition and possible significance. Cancer 24: 323–332

307. Bove K E, McAdams A J 1976 The nephroblastomatosis complex and its relationship to Wilms' tumor: a clinicopathologic treatise. Perspect Pediatr Pathol 3: 185–223

308. Beckwith J B, Kiviat N B, Bonadio J F 1990 Nephrogenic rests, nephroblastomatosis, and the pathogenesis of Wilms' tumor. Pediatr Pathol 10: 1–36

309. Scharfenberg J C, Beckman E N 1984 Persistent renal blastema in an adult. Hum Pathol 15: 791–793

310. Eble J N 1983 Fetal rhabdomyomatous nephroblastoma. J Urol 130: 541–543

311. Gonzalez-Crussi F, Hsueh W, Ugarte N 1981 Rhabdomyogenesis in renal neoplasia of childhood. Am J Surg Pathol 5: 525–532

312. Grimes M M, Wolff M, Wolff J A et al. 1982 Ganglion cells in metastatic Wilms' tumor, review of a histogenetic controversy. Am J Surg Pathol 6: 565–571

313. Cummins G E, Cohen D 1974 Cushing's syndrome secondary to ACTH-secreting Wilms' tumor. J Pediatr Surg 9: 535–539

314. Wigger H J 1976 Fetal rhabdomyomatous nephroblastoma – a variant of Wilms' tumor. Hum Pathol 7: 613–623

315. Fernandes E T, Parham D M, Ribeiro R C et al. 1988 Teratoid Wilms' tumor: The St Jude experience. J Pediatr Surg 23: 1131–1134

316. Variend S, Spicer R D, MacKinnon A E 1984 Teratoid Wilms' tumor. Cancer 53: 1936–1942

317. Bonadio J F, Storer B, Norkool P et al. 1985 Anaplastic Wilms' tumor: clinical and pathologic studies. J Clin Oncol 3: 513–520

318. Breslow N E, Palmer N F, Hill L R et al. 1978 Wilms' tumor: prognostic factors for patients without metastases at diagnosis, results of the National Wilms' Tumor Study. Cancer 41: 1577–1589

319. Beckwith B 1996 Focal versus diffuse anaplasia in nephroblastoma. Arch Anat Cytol Pathol 44: 53–53

320. Vujanic G M, Harms D, Sandstedt B et al. 1999 New definitions of focal and diffuse anaplasia in Wilms tumor: the International Society of Paediatric Oncology (SIOP) experience. Med Pediatr Oncol 32: 317–323

321. Faria P, Beckwith J B, Mishra K et al. 1996 Focal versus diffuse anaplasia in Wilms tumor – new definitions with prognostic significance, a report from the National Wilms Tumor Study Group. Am J Surg Pathol 20: 909–920

322. Perlman E J 2005 Pediatric renal tumors: practical updates for the pathologist. Pediatr Dev Pathol 8: 320–338

323. Weeks D A, Beckwith J B, Luckey D W 1987 Relapse-associated variables in stage I favorable histology Wilms' tumor, a report of the National Wilms' Tumor Study. Cancer 60: 1204–1212

324. Marsden H B, Lawler W 1978 Bone-metastasizing renal tumour of childhood. Br J Cancer 38: 437–441

325. Beckwith J B, Palmer N F 1978 Histopathology and prognosis of Wilms tumor, results from the First National Wilms' Tumor Study. Cancer 41: 1937–1948

326. Argani P, Perlman E J, Breslow N E et al. 2000 Clear cell sarcoma of the kidney, a review of 351 cases from the National Wilms' Tumor Study Group Pathology Center. Am J Surg Pathol 24: 4–18

327. Mierau G W, Weeks D A, Beckwith J B 1989 Anaplastic Wilms' tumor and other clinically aggressive childhood renal neoplasms: Ultrastructural and immunocytochemical features. Ultrastruct Pathol 13: 225–248

328. Amin M B, de Peralta-Venturina M N, Ro J Y et al. 1999 Clear cell sarcoma of kidney in an adolescent and in young adults: a report of four cases with ultrastructural, immunohistochemical, and DNA flow cytometric analysis. Am J Surg Pathol 23: 1455–1463

329. Sotelo-Avila C, Gonzalez-Crussi F, Sadowinski S et al. 1986 Clear cell sarcoma of the kidney: a clinicopathologic study of 21 patients with long-term follow-up evaluation. Hum Pathol 16: 1219–1230

330. Marsden H B, Lawler W 1980 Bone metastasizing renal tumour of childhood, histopathological and clinical review of 38 cases. Virchow's Arch [A] 387: 341–351

331. Weeks D A, Beckwith J B, Mierau G W et al. 1989 Rhabdoid tumor of kidney, a report of 111 cases from the National Wilms' Tumor Study Pathology Center. Am J Surg Pathol 13: 439–458

332. Tomlinson G E, Breslow N E, Dome J et al. 2005. Rhabdoid tumor of the kidney in the National Wilms' Tumor Study: age at diagnosis as a prognostic factor. J Clin Oncol 23: 7641–7645

333. Bonnin J M, Rubinstein L J, Palmer N F et al. 1984 The association of embryonal tumors originating in the kidney and in the brain, a report of seven cases. Cancer 54: 2137–2146

334. Mayes L C, Kasselberg A G, Roloff J S et al. 1984 Hypercalcemia associated with immunoreactive parathyroid hormone in a malignant rhabdoid tumor of the kidney (rhabdoid Wilms' tumor). Cancer 54: 882–884

335. Lee H-Y, Yoon C-S, Sevenet N et al. 2002 Rhabdoid tumor of the kidney is a component of the rhabdoid predisposition syndrome. Pediatr Dev Pathol 5: 395–399

336. Haas J E, Palmer N F, Weinberg A G et al. 1981 Ultrastructure of malignant rhabdoid tumor of the kidney, a distinctive renal tumor of children. Hum Pathol 12: 646–657

337. Hoot A C, Russo P, Judkins A R et al. 2004. Immunohistochemical analysis of hSNF5/INI1 distinguishes renal and extra-renal malignant rhabdoid tumors from other pediatric soft tissue tumors. Am J Surg Pathol 28: 1485–1491

338. Weeks D A, Beckwith J B, Mierau G W et al. 1991 Renal neoplasms mimicking rhabdoid tumor of kidney, a report from the National Wilms' Tumor Study Pathology Center. Am J Surg Pathol 15: 1042–1054

339. Marsden H B, Lawler W 1983 Primary renal tumours in the first year of life. A population based review. Virchow's Arch [A] 399: 1–9

340. Argani P, Beckwith J B 2000 Metanephric stromal tumor, report of 31 cases of a distinctive pediatric renal neoplasm. Am J Surg Pathol 24: 917–926

341. Blank E, Neerhout R C, Burry K A 1978 Congenital mesoblastic nephroma and polyhydramnios. JAMA 240: 1504–1505

342. Favara B E, Johnson W, Ito J 1968 Renal tumors in the neonatal period. Cancer 22: 845–855

343. Kay S, Pratt C B, Salzberg A M 1966 Hamartoma (leiomyomatous type) of the kidney. Cancer 19: 1825–1832

344. Bolande R P 1973 Congenital mesoblastic nephroma of infancy. Perspect Pediatr Pathol 1: 227–250

345. Howell C G, Othersen H B, Kiviat N E et al. 1982 Therapy and outcome in 51 children with mesoblastic nephroma: a report of the National Wilms' Tumor Study. J Pediatr Surg 17: 826–831

346. Chan H S L, Cheng M-Y, Mancer K et al. 1987 Congenital mesoblastic nephroma: a clinicoradiologic study of 17 cases representing the pathologic spectrum of the disease. J Pediatr 111: 64–70

347. Furtwaengler R, Reinhard H, Leuschner I et al. 2006 Mesoblastic nephroma – a report from the Gesellschaft fur Padiatrische Onkologie und Hamatologie (GPOH). Cancer 106: 2275–2283

348. Joshi V V, Kasznica J, Walters T R 1986 Atypical mesoblastic nephroma. Arch Pathol Lab Med 110: 100–106

349. Gonzalez-Crussi F, Sotelo-Avila C, Kidd J M 1980 Malignant mesenchymal nephroma of infancy, report of a case with pulmonary metastases. Am J Surg Pathol 4: 185–190

350. Trillo A A 1990 Adult variant of congenital mesoblastic nephroma. Arch Pathol Lab Med 114: 533–535

351. Van Velden D J J, Schneider J W, Allen F J 1990 A case of adult mesoblastic nephroma: ultrastructure and discussion of histogenesis. J Urol 143: 1216–1219

352. Beckwith J B, Weeks D A 1986 Congenital mesoblastic nephroma, when should we worry? Arch Pathol Lab Med 110: 98–99

353. Gormley T S, Skoog S J, Jones R V et al. 1989 Cellular congenital mesoblastic nephroma: what are the options. J Urol 142: 479–483

354. Rubin B P, Chen C-J, Morgan T W et al 1998 Congenital mesoblastic nephroma t(12;15) is associated with ETV6-NTRK3 gene fusion; cytogenetic and molecular relationship to congenital (infantile) fibrosarcoma. Am J Pathol 153: 1451–1458

355. Pettinato G, Manivel J C, Wick M R et al. 1989 Classical and cellular (atypical) congenital mesoblastic nephroma: a clinicopathologic, ultrastructural, immunohistochemical, and flow cytometric study. Hum Pathol 20: 682–690

356. Sotelo-Avila C, Beckwith J B, Johnson J E 1995 Ossifying renal tumor of infancy: a clinicopathologic study of nine cases. Pediatr Pathol 15: 745–762

357. Chatten J, Cromie W J, Duckett J W 1980 Ossifying tumor of infantile kidney, report of two cases. Cancer 45: 609–612

358. Dehner L P 1973 Intrarenal teratoma occurring in infancy: Report of a case with discussion of extragonadal germ cell tumors in infancy. J Pediatr Surg 8: 369–378

359. Aubert J, Casamayou J, Denis P et al. 1978 Intrarenal teratoma in a newborn child. Eur Urol 4: 306–308

360. Aaronson I A, Sinclair-Smith C 1980 Multiple cystic teratomas of the kidney. Arch Pathol Lab Med 104: 614–614

361. Mihatsch M J, Bleisch A, Six P et al. 1972 Primary choriocarcinoma of the kidney in a 49-year-old woman. J Urol 108: 537–539

362. Young R H, Eble J N 1991 Unusual forms of carcinoma of the urinary bladder. Hum Pathol 22: 948–965

363. Abeshouse B S 1956 Primary benign and malignant tumors of the ureter, a review of the literature and report of one benign and twelve malignant tumors. Am J Surg 91: 237–271

364. Satodate R, Koike H, Sasou S et al. 1984 Nephrogenic adenoma of the ureter. J Urol 131: 332–334

365. Lugo M, Petersen R O, Elfenbein I B et al. 1983 Nephrogenic metaplasia of the ureter. Am J Clin Pathol 80: 92–97

366. Naito S, Minoda M, Hirata H 1983 Inverted papilloma of ureter. Urology 22: 290–291

367. Lausten G S, Anagnostaki L, Thomsen O F 1984 Inverted papilloma of the upper urinary tract. Eur Urol 10: 67–70

368. Kyriakos M, Royce R K 1989 Multiple simultaneous inverted papillomas of the upper urinary tract. A case report with a review of ureteral and renal pelvic inverted papillomas. Cancer 63: 368–380

369. Embon O M, Saghi N, Bechar L 1984 Inverted papilloma of ureter. Eur Urol 10: 139–140

370. Arrufat J M, Vera-Román J M, Casas V et al. 1983 Papiloma invertido de uréter. Actas Urol Esp 7: 225–228

371. Palvio D H B 1985 Inverted papillomas of the urinary tract, a case of multiple, recurring inverted papillomas of the renal pelvis, ureter and bladder associated with malignant change. Scand J Urol Nephrol 19: 299–302

372. Kunze E, Schauer A, Schmitt M 1983 Histology and histogenesis of two different types of inverted urothelial papillomas. Cancer 51: 348–358

373. Kimura G, Tsuboi N, Nakajima H et al. 1987 Inverted papilloma of the ureter with malignant transformation: a case report and review of the literature. Urol Int 42: 30–36

374. Grainger R, Gikas P W, Grossman H B 1990 Urothelial carcinoma occurring within an inverted papilloma of the ureter. J Urol 143: 802–804

375. Wolgel C D, Parris A C, Mitty H A et al. 1982 Fibroepithelial polyp of renal pelvis. Urology 19: 436–439

376. Goldman S M, Bohlman M E, Gatewood O M B 1987 Neoplasms of the renal collecting system. Semin Roentgenol 22: 284–291

377. Bartone F F, Johansson S L, Markin R J et al. 1990 Bilateral fibroepithelial polyps of ureter in a child. Urology 35: 519–522

378. Macksood M J, Roth D R, Chang C-H et al. 1985 Benign fibroepithelial polyps as a cause of intermittent ureteropelvic junction obstruction in a child: a case report and review of the literature. J Urol 134: 951–952

379. van Poppel H, Nuttin B, Oyen R et al. 1986 Fibroepithelial polyps of the ureter, etiology, diagnosis, treatment and pathology. Eur Urol 12: 174–179

380. Williams P R, Feggeter J, Miller R A et al. 1980 The diagnosis and management of benign fibrous ureteric polyps. Br J Urol 52: 253–256

381. Stuppler S A, Kandzari S J 1975 Fibroepithelial polyps of ureter, a benign ureteral tumor. Urology 5: 553–558

382. Uhlir K 1973 Hemangioma of the ureter. J Urol 110: 647–649

383. Jansen T T H, van deWeyer F P H, deVries H R 1982 Angiomatous ureteral polyp. Urology 20: 426–427

384. Kvist E, Lauritzen A F, Bredesen J et al. 1988 A comparative study of transitional cell tumors of the bladder and upper urinary tract. Cancer 61: 2109–2112

385. Mazeman E 1976 Tumours of the upper urinary tract calyces, renal pelvis and ureter. Eur Urol 2: 120–128

386. McLaughlin J K, Blot W J, Mandel J S et al. 1983 Etiology of cancer of the renal pelvis. J Natl Cancer Inst 71: 287–291

387. Palvio D H B, Andersen J C, Falk E 1987 Transitional cell tumors of the renal pelvis and ureter associated with capillarosclerosis indicating analgesic abuse. Cancer 59: 972–976

388. Steffens J, Nagel R 1988 Tumours of the renal pelvis and ureter, observations in 170 patients. Br J Urol 61: 277–283

389. Verhaak R L O M, Harmsen A E, van Unnik A J M 1974 On the frequency of tumor induction in a thorotrast kidney. Cancer 34: 2061–2068

390. Nielsen K, Ostri P 1988 Primary tumors of the renal pelvis: evaluation of clinical and pathological features in a consecutive series of 10 years. J Urol 140: 19–21

391. Corrado F, Ferri C, Mannini D et al. 1991 Transitional cell carcinoma of the upper urinary tract: Evaluation of prognostic factors by histopathology and flow cytometric analysis. J Urol 145: 1159–1163

392. Bonsib S M 1990 Pathology of the renal pelvis and ureter. In: Eble JN (ed) Tumors and tumor-like conditions of the kidneys and ureters. Churchill Livingstone, New York, p 177–205

393. Olgac S, Mazumdar M, Dalbagni G et al. 2004. Urothelial carcinoma of the renal pelvis. A clinicopathologic study of 130 cases. Am J Surg Pathol 28: 1545–1552

394. Anderström C, Johansson S L, Pettersson S et al. 1989 Carcinoma of the ureter: a clinicopathologic study of 49 cases. J Urol 142: 280–283

395. Blute M L, Tsushima K, Farrow G M et al. 1988 Transitional cell carcinoma of the renal pelvis: nuclear deoxyribonucleic acid ploidy studied by flow cytometry. J Urol 140: 944–949

396. American Joint Committee on Cancer 1997 Renal pelvis and ureter. AJCC Cancer Staging Manual. Lippincott-Raven, Philadelphia, p 235–239

397. Murphy D M, Zincke H, Furlow W L 1980 Primary grade 1 transitional cell carcinoma of the renal pelvis and ureter. J Urol 123: 629–631

398. Huben R P, Mounzer A M, Murphy G P 1988 Tumor grade and stage as prognostic variables in upper tract urothelial tumors. Cancer 62: 2016–2020

399. Nocks B N, Heney N M, Daly J J et al. 1982 Transitional cell carcinoma of renal pelvis. Urology 19: 472–477

400. Piscioli F, Bondi A, Scappini P et al. 1984 "True" sarcomatoid carcinoma of the renal pelvis. Eur Urol 10: 350–355

401. Essenfeld H, Manivel J C, Benedetto P et al. 1990 Small cell carcinoma of the renal pelvis: A clinicopathological, morphological and immunohistochemical study of 2 cases. J Urol 144: 344–347

402. Kenney R M, Prat J, Tabernero M 1984 Giant-cell tumor-like proliferation associated with a papillary transitional cell carcinoma of the renal pelvis. Am J Surg Pathol 8: 139–144

402a. Baydar D, Amin M B, Epstein J I 2006 Osteoclast-rich indifferentiated carcinomas of the urinary tract. Mod Pathol 19: 161–171

403. Mahadevia P S, Karwa G L, Koss L G 1983 Mapping of urothelium in carcinomas of the renal pelvis and ureter. Cancer 51: 890–897

404. Martínez García R, Boronat Tormo F, Domínguez Hinarejos C et al. 1989 Adenocarcinoma de pelvis renal. Actas Urol Esp 13: 470–472

405. Takezawa Y, Saruki K, Jinbo S et al. 1990 A case of adenocarcinoma of the renal pelvis. Acta Urol Jpn 36: 841–845

406. Stein A, Sova Y, Lurie M et al. 1988 Adenocarcinoma of the renal pelvis, report of two cases, one with simultaneous transitional cell carcinoma of the bladder. Urol Int 43: 299–301

407. Kim Y I, Yoon D H, Lee S W et al. 1988 Multicentric papillary adenocarcinoma of the renal pelvis and ureter: report of a case with ultrastructural study. Cancer 62: 2402–2407

408. Ishikura H, Ishiguro T, Enatsu C et al. 1991 Hepatoid adenocarcinoma of the renal pelvis producing alpha-fetoprotein of hepatic type and bile pigment. Cancer 67: 3051–3056

409. Brawer M K, Waisman J 1982 Papillary adenocarcinoma of ureter. Urology 19: 205–209

410. Moncino M D, Friedman H S, Kurtzberg J et al. 1990 Papillary adenocarcinoma of the renal pelvis in a child: case report and brief review of the literature. Med Pediatr Oncol 18: 81–86

411. Bullock P S, Thoni D E, Murphy W M 1987 The significance of colonic mucosa (intestinal metaplasia) involving the urinary tract. Cancer 59: 2086–2090

412. Gordon A 1963 Intestinal metaplasia of the urinary tract epithelium. J Pathol Bacteriol 85: 441–444

413. Utz D C, McDonald J R 1957 Squamous cell carcinoma of the kidney. J Urol 78: 540–552

414. Blacher E J, Johnson D E, Abdul-Karim F W et al. 1985 Squamous cell carcinoma of renal pelvis. Urology 25: 124–125

415. Hertle L, Androulakakis P 1982 Keratinizing desquamative squamous metaplasia of the upper urinary tract: leukoplakia-cholesteatoma. J Urol 127: 631–635

416. Strobel S L, Jasper W S, Gogate S A et al. 1984 Primary carcinoma of the renal pelvis and ureter, evaluation of clinical and pathologic features. Arch Pathol Lab Med 108: 697–700

417. Howat A J, Scott E, Mackie B et al. 1983 Adenosquamous carcinoma of the renal pelvis. Am J Clin Pathol 79: 731–733

418. Kao V C T, Graff P W, Rappaport H 1969 Leiomyoma of the ureter, a histologically problematic rare tumor confirmed by immunohistochemical studies. Cancer 24: 535–542

419. Zaitoon M M 1986 Leiomyoma of ureter. Urology 28: 50–51

420. Gislason T, Arnarson O O 1984 Primary ureteral leiomyosarcoma. Scand J Urol Nephrol 18: 253–254

421. Rushton H G, Sens M A, Garvin A J et al. 1983 Primary leiomyosarcoma of the ureter: a case report with electron microscopy. J Urol 129: 1045–1046

422. Eble J N, Young R H, Störkel S et al. 1991 Primary osteosarcoma of the kidney: a report of three cases. J Urogenital Pathol 1: 83–88

423. Fein R L, Hamm F C 1965 Malignant schwannoma of the renal pelvis: A review of the literature and a case report. J Urol 94: 356–361

424. Frasier B L, Wachs B H, Watson L R et al. 1988 Malignant melanoma of the renal pelvis presenting as a primary tumor. J Urol 140: 812–813

425. Scharifker D, Chalasani A 1978 Ureteral involvement by malignant lymphoma, ten years' experience. Arch Pathol Lab Med 102: 541–542

426. Young R H 1989 Non-neoplastic epithelial abnormalities and tumorlike lesions. In: Young RH (ed) Pathology of the urinary bladder. Churchill Livingstone, New York, p 1–63

427. Eble J N, Young R H 1989 Benign and low-grade papillary lesions of the urinary bladder: a review of the papilloma-papillary carcinoma controversy, and a report of five typical papillomas. Semin Diagn Pathol 6: 351–371

428. Jordan A M, Weingarten J, Murphy W M 1987 Transitional cell neoplasms of the urinary bladder, can biological potential be predicted from histologic grading? Cancer 60: 2766–2774

429. McKenney J K, Amin M B, Young R H 2003 Urothelial (transitional cell) papilloma of the urinary bladder: A clinicopathologic study of 26 cases. Mod Pathol 16:623–629

430. Magi-Galluzzi C, Epstein J I 2004 Urothelial papilloma of the bladder. A review of 34 de novo cases. Am J Surg Pathol 28:1615–1620

431. Kunze E, Schauer A, Schmitt M 1983 Histology and histogenesis of two different types of inverted urothelial papillomas. Cancer 51: 348–358

432. Broussard J N, Tan P H, Epstein J I. 2004 Atypia in inverted urothelial papillomas: pathology and prognostic significance. Hum Pathol 35: 1499–1504

433. Amin M B, Gomez J A, Young R H 1997 Urothelial transitional cell carcinoma with endophytic growth patterns. Am J Surg Pathol 21: 1057–1068

434. Mattelaer J, Leonard A, Goddeeris P et al. 1988 Inverted papilloma of bladder: clinical significance. Urology 32: 192–197

434a. Guo C C, Fine S W, Epstein J I 2006 Noninvasive squamous lesions in the urinary bladder: a clinicopathologic analysis of 29 cases. Am J Surg Pathol 30: 883-891

435. Eble J N, Hull M T, Rowland R G et al. 1986 Villous adenoma of the urachus with mucusuria: a light and electron microscopic study. J Urol 135: 1240–1244

436. Adegboyega P A, Adesokan A. 1999 Tubulovillous adenoma of the urinary bladder. Mod Pathol 12:735–738

437. Cheng L, Montironi R, Bostwick D G 1999 Villous adenoma of the urinary tract: a report of 23 cases, including 8 with coexistent adenocarcinoma. Am J Surg Pathol 23: 764–771

438. Seibel J L, Prasad S, Weiss R E et al. 2002 Villous adenoma of the urinary tract: a lesion frequently associated with malignancy. Hum Pathol 33: 236–241

439. Choi W W L, Amin M B, Tamboli P et al. 2005 Glandular neoplasms of the urachus: clinicopathologic and immunohistochemical analysis of 43 cases with special emphasis on low-grade mucinous cystic tumors. Mod Pathol 18 (suppl): 134A

440. Oyasu R, Hopp M L 1974 The etiology of cancer of the bladder. Surg Gynecol Obstet 138: 97–108

441. Morrison A S 1984 Advances in the etiology of urothelial cancer. Urol Clin North Am 11: 557–566

442. Wallace D M A 1988 Occupational urothelial cancer. Br J Urol 61: 175–182

443. Royce R K, Ackerman L V 1951 Carcinoma of the bladder: therapeutic and pathologic aspects of 135 cases. J Urol 65: 66–86

444. Kaye K W, Lange P H 1982 Mode of presentation of invasive bladder cancer: reassessment of the problem. J Urol 128: 31–33

445. Brawn P N 1982 The origin of invasive carcinoma of the bladder. Cancer 50: 515–519

446. Newman L H, Tannenbaum M, Droller M J 1988 Muscle-invasive bladder cancer: Does it arise de novo or from pre-existing superficial disease? Urology 32: 58–62

447. Epstein J I, Amin M B, Reuter V E et al. Bladder Consensus Conference Committee 1998 The World Health Organization/International Society of Urological Pathology consensus classification of urothelial (transitional cell) neoplasms of the urinary bladder. Am J Surg Pathol 22: 1435–1438

448. Sarma K P 1981 Genesis of papillary tumours: histological and microangiographic study. Br J Urol 53: 228–236

449. Taylor D C, Bhagavan B S, Larsen M P et al. 1996 Papillary urothelial hyperplasia. A precursor to papillary neoplasms. Am J Surg Pathol 20:1481–1488

450. Young R H 1988 Papillary and polypoid cystitis, a report of eight cases. Am J Surg Pathol 12: 542–546

451. Melicow M M 1952 Histological study of vesical urothelium intervening between gross neoplasms in total cystectomy. J Urol 68: 261–278

452. Melamed M R, Voutsa N G, Grabstald H 1964 Natural history and clinical behavior of in situ carcinoma of the human urinary bladder. Cancer 17: 1533–1545

453. Elliott G B, Moloney P J, Anderson G H 1973 "Denuding cystitis" and in situ urothelial carcinoma. Arch Pathol 96: 91–94

454. Utz D C, Zincke H 1974 The masquerade of bladder cancer in situ as interstitial cystitis. J Urol 111: 160–161

455. Koss L G, Nakanishi I, Freed S Z 1977 Nonpapillary carcinoma in situ and atypical hyperplasia in cancerous bladders: further studies of surgically-removed bladders by mapping. Urology 9: 442–455

456. Utz D C, Farrow G M, Rife C C et al. 1980 Carcinoma in situ of the bladder. Cancer 45: 1842–1848

457. Prout G R Jr, Griffin P P, Daly J J et al. 1983 Carcinoma in situ of the urinary bladder with and without associated vesical neoplasms. Cancer 52: 524–532

458. Kakizoe T, Matumoto K, Nishio Y et al. 1985 Significance of carcinoma in situ and dysplasia in association with bladder cancer. J Urol 133: 395–398

459. Nagy G K, Frable W J, Murphy W M 1982 Classification of premalignant urothelial abnormalities, a Delphi study of the National Bladder Cancer Collaborative Group A. Pathol Annu 17: 219–233

460. Murphy W M, Soloway M S 1982 Developing carcinoma (dysplasia) of the urinary bladder. Pathol Annu 17 (Pt1): 197–217

461. Farrow G M, Utz D C 1982 Observations on microinvasive transitional cell carcinoma of the urinary bladder. Clin Oncol 1: 609–615

462. McKenney J K, Gomes J A, Desai S et al. 2001 Morphologic expression of urothelial carcinoma in situ. A detailed evaluation of its histologic patterns with emphasis on carcinoma in situ with microinvasion. Am J Surg Pathol 25:356–362

463. Lopez-Beltran A, Luque R J, Moreno A et al. 2002. The pagetoid variant of bladder urothelial carcinoma in situ. A clinicopathological study of 11 cases. Virchow's Arch 441: 148–153

464. Ro J Y, Ayala A G, El-Naggar A 1987 Muscularis mucosa of urinary bladder, importance for staging and treatment. Am J Surg Pathol 11: 668–673

465. Keep J C, Piehl M, Miller A et al. 1989 Invasive carcinomas of the urinary bladder, evaluation of tunica muscularis mucosae involvement. Am J Clin Pathol 91: 575–579

466. Younes M, Sussman J, True L D 1990 The usefulness of the level of the muscularis mucosae in the staging of invasive transitional cell carcinoma of the urinary bladder. Cancer 66: 543–548

467. Weaver M G, Abdul-Karim F W 1990 The prevalence and character of the muscularis mucosae of the human urinary bladder. Histopathology 17: 563–566

468. Talbert M L, Young R H 1989 Carcinomas of the urinary bladder with deceptively benign-appearing foci, a report of three cases. Am J Surg Pathol 13: 374–381

469. Drew P A, Furman J, Civantos F et al. 1996 The nested variant of transitional cell carcinoma: An aggressive neoplasm with innocuous histology. Mod Pathol 9: 989–994

470. Lin O, Cardillo M, Dalbagni G et al. 2003 Nested variant of urothelial carcinoma: A clinicopathologic and immunohistochemical study of 12 cases. Mod Pathol 16: 1289–1298

471. Young R H, Oliva E 1996 Transitional cell carcinomas of the urinary bladder that may be underdiagnosed: a report of four invasive cases exemplifying the homology between neoplastic and non-neoplastic transitional cell lesions. Am J Surg Pathol 20: 1448–1454

472. Volmar K E, Chan T Y, DeMarzo A M et al. 2003 Florid von Brunn nests mimicking urothelial carcinoma. A morphologic and immunohistochemical comparison to the nested variant of urothelial carcinoma. Am J Surg Pathol 27: 1243–1252

473. Young R H, Zukerberg L R 1990 Microcystic transitional cell carcinomas of the urinary bladder, a report of four cases. Am J Clin Pathol 96: 635–639

474. Paz A, Rath-Wolfson L, Lask D et al. 1997 The clinical and histological features of transitional cell carcinoma of the bladder with microcysts: analysis of 12 cases. Br J Urol 79: 772–725

475. Amin M B, Ro J Y, El-Sharkawy T et al. 1994 Micropapillary variant of transitional cell carcinoma of the urinary bladder, histologic pattern resembling ovarian papillary serous carcinoma. Am J Surg Pathol 18: 1224–1232

476. Samaratunga H, Khoo K 2004 Micropapillary variant of urothelial carcinoma of the urinary bladder; a clinicopathological and immunohistochemical study. Histopathology 45: 55–64

477. Alvarado-Cabrero I, Sierra-Santiesteban F I, Mantilla-Morales A et al. 2005 Micropapillary carcinoma of the urothelial tract. A clinicopathologic study of 38 cases. Ann Diag Pathol 9: 1–5

478. Young R H, Wick M R, Mills S E 1988 Sarcomatoid carcinoma of the urinary bladder, a clinicopathologic analysis of 12 cases and review of the literature. Am J Clin Pathol 90: 653–661

479. Pearson J M, Banerjee S S, Haboubi N Y 1989 Two cases of pseudosarcomatous invasive transitional cell carcinoma of the urinary bladder mimicking malignant fibrous histiocytoma. Histopathology 15: 93–99

480. Ro J Y, Wishnow K I, Ayala A G et al. 1988 Sarcomatoid bladder carcinoma: clinicopathologic and immunohistochemical study on 44 cases. Surg Pathol 1: 359–374

481. Ikegami H, Iwasaki H, Ohjimi Y et al. 2000 Sarcomatoid carcinoma of the urinary bladder: A clinicopathologic and immunohistochemical analysis of 14 patients. Hum Pathol 31: 332–340

482. Murata T, Soga T, Tajima K et al. 1994 Sarcomatoid carcinoma of the urinary tract. Pathol Int 44: 138–144

483. Torenbeek R, Blomjous C E M, deBruin P C 1994 Sarcomatoid carcinoma of the urinary bladder. Clinicopathologic analysis of 18 cases with immunohistochemical and electron microscopic findings. Am J Surg Pathol 18:241–249.

484. Serio G, Zampatti C, Ceppi M. 1995 Spindle and giant cell carcinoma of the urinary bladder: a clinicopathological light microscopic and immunohistochemical study. Br J Urol 75: 167–172

485. Jones E C, Young R H 1997 Myxoid and sclerosing sarcomatoid transitional cell carcinoma of the urinary bladder: a clinicopathologic and immunohistochemical study of 25 cases. Mod Pathol 10: 908–916

486. Perret L, Chaubert P, Hessler D et al. 1998 Primary heterologous carcinosarcoma (metaplastic carcinoma) of the urinary bladder. A clinicopathologic, immunohistochemical, and ultrastructural analysis of eight cases and a review of the literature. Cancer 82: 1535–1549.

487. Pitt M A, Morphopoulos G, Wells S et al. 1995 Pseudoangiosarcomatous carcinoma of the genitourinary tract. J Clin Pathol 48: 1059–1061

488. Wick M R, Brown B A, Young R H et al. 1988 Spindle-cell proliferations of the urinary tract: an immunohistochemical study. Am J Surg Pathol 12: 379–389

489. Martin J E, Jenkins B J, Zuk R J et al. 1989 Human chorionic gonadotropin expression and histological findings as predictors of response to radiotherapy in carcinoma of the bladder. Virchow's Arch [A] 414: 273–277

490. Burry A F, Munn S R, Arnold E P et al. 1986 Trophoblastic metaplasia in urothelial carcinoma of the bladder. Br J Urol 58: 143–146

491. Morton K D, Burnett R A 1988 Choriocarcinoma arising in transitional cell carcinoma of the bladder: a case report. Histopathology 12: 325–328

492. Young R H, Wick M R 1988 Transitional cell carcinoma of the urinary bladder with pseudosarcomatous stroma. Am J Clin Pathol 90: 216–219

493. Mahadevia P S, Alexander J E, Rojas-Corona R et al. 1989 Pseudosarcomatous stromal reaction in primary and metastatic urothelial carcinoma, a source of diagnostic difficulty. Am J Surg Pathol 13: 782–790

494. Eble J N, Young R H 1991 Stromal osseous metaplasia in carcinoma of the urinary bladder. J Urol 145: 823–825

495. Zukerberg L R, Armin A-R, Pisharodi L et al. 1990 Transitional cell carcinoma of the urinary bladder with osteoclast-type giant-cells: a report of two cases and review of the literature. Histopathology 17: 407–411

496. Zukerberg L R, Harris N L, Young R H 1991 Carcinomas of the urinary bladder simulating malignant lymphoma: a report of five cases. Am J Surg Pathol 15: 569–576

497. Friedell G H, Bell J R, Burney S W et al. 1976 Histopathology and classification of urinary bladder carcinoma. Urol Clin North Am 3: 53–70

498. Sakkas J L 1966 Clinical pattern and treatment of squamous cell carcinoma of the bladder. Int Surg 45: 71–76

499. Rous S N 1978 Squamous cell carcinoma of the bladder. J Urol 120: 561–562

500. Faysal M H 1981 Squamous cell carcinoma of the bladder. J Urol 120: 598–599

501. Newman D M, Brown J R, Jay A C et al. 1968 Squamous cell carcinoma of the bladder. J Urol 100: 470–473

502. Bessette P L, Abell M R, Herwig K R 1974 A clinicopathologic study of squamous cell carcinoma of the bladder. J Urol 112: 66–67

503. Rundle J S H, Hart A J L, McGeorge A et al. 1982 Squamous cell carcinoma of bladder. A review of 114 patients. Br J Urol 54: 522–526

504. Costello A J, Tiptaft R C, England H R et al. 1984 Squamous cell carcinoma of bladder. Urology 23: 234–236

505. Richie J P, Waisman J, Skinner D G et al. 1976 Squamous carcinoma of the bladder: treatment by radical cystectomy. J Urol 115: 670–672

506. Johnson D E, Schoenwald M B, Ayala A G et al. 1976 Squamous cell carcinoma of the bladder. J Urol 115: 542–544

507. El Sebai I, Sherif M, El Bolkainy M et al. 1974 Verrucose squamous carcinoma of bladder. Urology 4: 407–410

508. Walther M, O'Brien D P, Birch H W 1986 Condyloma acuminata and verrucous carcinoma of the bladder: case report and literature review. J Urol 135: 362–365

509. Wyatt J K, Craig I 1980 Verrucous carcinoma of urinary bladder. Urology 16: 97–99

510. Holck S, Jørgensen L 1983 Verrucous carcinoma of urinary bladder. Urology 22: 435–437

511. Querci Della Rovere G, Oliver R T D, McCance D J et al. 1988 Development of bladder tumour containing HPV type 11 DNA after renal transplantation. Br J Urol 62: 36–38

512. Rabson S M 1936 Leukoplakia and carcinoma of the urinary bladder, report of a case with a review of the literature. J Urol 35: 321–341

513. Connery D B 1953 Leukoplakia of the urinary bladder and its association with carcinoma. J Urol 69: 121–127

514. Benson R C Jr, Swanson S K, Farrow G M 1984 Relationship of leukoplakia to urothelial malignancy. J Urol 131: 507–511

515. Melamed M R, Farrow G M, Haggitt R C 1987 Case 19 in Urologic neoplasms, Proceedings of the 50th Annual Anatomic Slide Seminar of the American Society of Clinical Pathologists. ASCP 98–103

516. Wheeler J D, Hill W T 1954 Adenocarcinoma involving the urinary bladder. Cancer 7: 119–135

517. Mostofi F K, Thomson R V, Dean A L Jr 1955 Mucous adenocarcinoma of the urinary bladder. Cancer 8: 741–758

518. Thomas D G, Ward A M, Williams J L 1971 A study of 52 cases of adenocarcinoma of the bladder. Br J Urol 43: 4–15

519. Johnson D E, Hogan J M, Ayala A G 1972 Primary adenocarcinoma of the urinary bladder. South Med J 65: 527–530

520. Daroca P J Jr, MacKenzie F, Reed R J et al. 1976 Primary adenovillous carcinoma of the bladder. J Urol 115: 41–45

521. Jacobo E, Loening S, Schmidt J D et al. 1977 Primary adenocarcinoma of the bladder: a retrospective study of 20 patients. J Urol 117: 54–56

522. Fuselier H A Jr, Brannan W, Ochsner M G et al. 1978 Adenocarcinoma of the bladder as seen at Ochsner Medical Institutions. South Med J 71: 804–806

523. Kramer S A, Bredael J, Croker B P et al. 1979 Primary non-urachal adenocarcinoma of the bladder. J Urol 121: 278–281

524. Jones W A, Gibbons R P, Correa R J Jr et al. 1980 Primary adenocarcinoma of bladder. Urology 15: 119–121

525. Nocks B N, Heney N M, Daly J J 1983 Primary adenocarcinoma of urinary bladder. Urology 21: 26–29

526. Malek R S, Rosen J S, O'Dea M J 1983 Adenocarcinoma of bladder. Urology 21: 357–359

527. Anderström C, Johansson S, von Schultz L 1983 Primary adenocarcinoma of the urinary bladder, a clinicopathologic and prognostic study. Cancer 52: 1273–1280

528. Bennett J K, Wheatley J K, Walton K N 1984 10-year experience with adenocarcinoma of the bladder. J Urol 131: 262–263

529. O'Brien A M E, Urbanski S J 1985 Papillary adenocarcinoma in situ of bladder. J Urol 134: 544–546

530. Abenoza P, Manivel C, Fraley E E 1987 Primary adenocarcinoma of urinary bladder, clinicopathologic study of 16 cases. Urology 29: 9–14

531. Pallesen G 1981 Neoplastic Paneth cells in adenocarcinoma of the urinary bladder: a first case report. Cancer 47: 1834–1837

532. Young R H, Parkhurst E C 1984 Mucinous adenocarcinoma of bladder. Case associated with extensive intestinal metaplasia of urothelium in patient with nonfunctioning bladder for twelve years. Urology 24: 192–195

533. Grignon D J, Ro J Y, Ayala A G et al. 1991 Primary adenocarcinoma of the urinary bladder: a clinicopathologic analysis of 72 cases. Cancer 67: 2165–2172

534. Sheldon C A, Clayman R V, Gonzalez R et al. 1984 Malignant urachal lesions. J Urol 131: 1–8

535. O'Kane H O J, Megaw J M 1968 Carcinoma in the exstrophic bladder. Br J Surg 55: 631–635

536. Al-Izzi M S, Horton L W L, Kelleher J et al. 1989 Malignant transformation in endometriosis of the urinary bladder. Histopathology 14: 191–198

537. Oliva E, Amin M, Jimenez R et al. 2002 Clear cell carcinoma of the urinary bladder. A report and comparison of four tumors of mullerian origin and nine of probable urothelial origin with discussion of histogenesis and diagnostic problems. Am J Surg Pathol 26:190–197

538. Young R H 1989 Unusual variants of primary bladder carcinoma and secondary tumors of the bladder. In: Young RH (ed) Pathology of the urinary bladder. Churchill Livingstone, New York, p 103–139

539. Saphir O 1955 Signet-ring cell carcinoma of the urinary bladder. Am J Pathol 31: 223–231

540. Rosas-Uribe A, Luna M A 1969 Primary signet ring cell carcinoma of the urinary bladder. Report of two cases. Arch Pathol 88: 294–297

541. Grignon D J, Ro J Y, Ayala A G et al. 1991 Primary signet-ring cell carcinoma of the urinary bladder. Am J Clin Pathol 95: 13–20

542. Torenbeck R, Koot R A C, Blomjous C E M et al 1996 Primary signet-ring cell carcinoma of the urinary bladder. Histopathology 28: 33–40

543. Novak R W, Raines R B, Sollee A N 1981 Clear cell carcinoma in a Müllerian duct cyst. Am J Clin Pathol 76: 339–341

544. Young R H, Bostwick D H 1996 Florid cystitis glandularis of intestinal type with mucin extravasation: a mimic of adenocarcinoma. Am J Surg Pathol 20: 1462–1468

545. Clement P B 1990 Pathology of endometriosis. Pathol Annu 25: 245–295

546. Clement P B, Young R H 1992 Endocervicosis of the urinary bladder, a report of six cases of a benign müllerian lesion that may mimic adenocarcinoma. Am J Surg Pathol 16: 533–542

547. Young R H, Clement P B 1996 Mullerianosis of the urinary bladder. Mod Pathol 9:731–737

548. Epstein J I, Kuhajda F P, Lieberman P H 1986 Prostate-specific acid phosphatase immunoreactivity in adenocarcinomas of the urinary bladder. Hum Pathol 17: 939–942

549. Oliva E, Young R H 1995 Nephrogenic adenoma of the urinary tract: A review of the microscopic appearance of 80 cases with emphasis on unusual features. Mod Pathol 8: 722–730

550. Cheng L, Cheville J C, Selo T J et al. 2000 Atypical nephrogenic metaplasia of the urinary tract. A precursor lesion? Cancer 88: 853–861

551. Young R H, Johnston W H 1990 Serous adenocarcinoma of the uterus metastatic to the urinary bladder mimicking primary bladder neoplasia, a report of a case. Am J Surg Pathol 14: 877–880

552. Mills S E, Wolfe J T III, Weiss M A et al. 1987 Small cell undifferentiated carcinoma of the urinary bladder, a light-microscopic, immunocytochemical, and ultrastructural study of 12 cases. Am J Surg Pathol 11: 606–617

553. Grignon D J, Ro J Y, Ayala A G et al. 1992 Small cell carcinoma of the urinary bladder, a clinicopathologic analysis of 22 cases. Cancer 69: 527–536

554. Abrahams N A, Moran C, Reyes A O et al. 2005 Small cell carcinoma of the bladder: a contemporary clinicopathological study of 51 cases. Histopathology 46: 57–63

555. Reyes C V, Soneru I 1985 Small cell carcinoma of the urinary bladder with hypercalcemia. Cancer 56: 2530–2533

556. Blomjous C E M, Vos W, De Voogt H J et al. 1989 Small cell carcinoma of the urinary bladder, a clinicopathologic, morphometric, immunohistochemical, and ultrastructural study of 18 cases. Cancer 64: 1347–1357

557. Partanen S, Asikainen U 1985 Oat cell carcinoma of the urinary bladder with ectopic adrenocorticotropic hormone production. Hum Pathol 16: 313–315

558. Davis M P, Murthy M S N, Simon J et al. 1989 Successful management of small cell carcinoma of the bladder with cisplatin and etoposide. J Urol 142: 817–818

559. Holmäng S, Borghede G, Johansson S L 1995 Primary small cell carcinoma of the bladder: a report of 25 cases. J Urol 153: 1820–1822

560. Jones T D, Kernek K M, Yang X J et al. 2005 Thyroid transcription factor 1 expression in small cell carcinoma of the urinary bladder: an immunohistochemical profile of 44 cases. Hum Pathol 36: 718–723

561. Komatsu H, Kinoshita K, Mikata N et al. 1985 Spindle and giant cell carcinoma of the bladder: report of 3 cases. Eur Urol 11: 141–144

562. Young R H, Eble J N 1993 Lymphoepithelioma-like carcinoma of the urinary bladder. J Urol Pathol 1: 63–67

563. Amin M B, Ro J Y, Lee K M et al. 1994 Lymphoepithelioma-like carcinoma of the urinary bladder. Am J Surg Pathol 18: 466–473

564. Lopez-Beltran A, Luque R J, Vicioso L et al. 2001. Lymphoepithelioma-like carcinoma of the urinary bladder: a clinicopathologic study of 13 cases. Virchow's Arch 438: 552–557

565. Walker A N, Mills S E, Young R H 1989 Mesenchymal and miscellaneous other primary tumors of the urinary bladder. In: Young RH (ed) Pathology of the urinary bladder. Churchill Livingstone, New York, p 139–178

566. Knoll L D, Segura J W, Scheithauer B W 1986 Leiomyoma of the bladder. J Urol 136: 906–908

567. Belis J A, Post G J, Rochman S C et al. 1979 Genitourinary leiomyomas. Urology 13: 424–429

568. Bramwell S P, Pitts J, Goudie S E et al. 1987 Giant leiomyoma of the bladder. Br J Urol 60: 178

569. Munsie W J, Foster E A 1968 Unsuspected very small foci of carcinoma of the prostate in transurethral resection specimens. Cancer 21: 692–698

570. Cheng L, Nascimento A G, Neumann R M et al. 1999 Hemangioma of the urinary bladder. Cancer 86: 498–504

571. Sarma D P, Weiner M 1983 Hemangioma of the urinary bladder. J Surg Oncol 24: 142–144

572. Bolkier M, Ginesin Y, Lichtig C et al. 1983 Lymphangioma of bladder. J Urol 129: 1049–1050

573. Brooks P T, Scally J K 1985 Case report: bladder neurofibromas causing ureteric obstruction in von Recklinghausen's disease. Clin Radiol 36: 537–538

574. Blum M D, Bahnson R R, Carter M F 1985 Urologic manifestations of von Recklinghausen neurofibromatosis. Urology 26: 209–217

575. Mouradian J A, Coleman J W, McGovern J H et al. 1974 Granular cell tumor (myoblastoma) of the bladder. J Urol 112: 343–345

576. Karol J B, Eason A A, Tanagho E A 1977 Fibrous histiocytoma of bladder. Urology 10: 593–595

577. Cheng L, Scheithauer B W, Leibovich B C et al. 1999 Neurofibroma of the urinary bladder. Cancer 86: 505–513

578. McCrea L E, Post E A 1955 Sarcoma of the bladder. Urol Surv 5: 307–356

579. Sen S E, Malek R S, Farrow G M, Lieber M M 1985 Sarcoma and carcinosarcoma of the bladder in adults. J Urol 133: 29–30

580. Mills S E, Bova G S, Wick M R et al. 1989 Leiomyosarcoma of the urinary bladder, a clinicopathologic and immunohistochemical study of 15 cases. Am J Surg Pathol 13: 480–489

581. Rowland R G, Eble J N 1983 Bladder leiomyosarcoma and pelvic fibroblastic tumor following cyclophosphamide therapy. J Urol 130: 344–346

582. Sigal S H, Tomaszewski J E, Brooks J J et al. 1991 Carcinosarcoma of bladder following long-term cyclophosphamide therapy. Arch Pathol Lab Med 115: 1049–1051

583. Young R H, Proppe K H, Dickersin G R et al. 1987 Myxoid leiomyosarcoma of the urinary bladder. Arch Pathol Lab Med 111: 359–362

584. Proppe K H, Scully R E, Rosai J 1984 Postoperative spindle cell nodules of the genitourinary tract resembling sarcomas, a report of eight cases. Am J Surg Pathol 8: 101–108

585. Nochomovitz L E, Orenstein J M 1985 Inflammatory pseudotumor of the urinary bladder – possible relationship to nodular fasciitis, two case reports, cytologic observations, and ultrastructural observations. Am J Surg Pathol 9: 366–373

586. Ro J Y, Ayala A G, Ordóñez N G et al. 1986 Pseudosarcomatous fibromyxoid tumor of the urinary bladder. Am J Clin Pathol 86: 583–590

587. Young R H, Scully R E 1987 Pseudosarcomatous lesions of the urinary bladder, prostate gland, and urethra, a report of three cases and review of the literature. Arch Pathol Lab Med 111: 354–358

588. Albores-Saavedra J, Manivel J C, Essenfeld H et al. 1990 Pseudosarcomatous myofibroblastic proliferations in the urinary bladder of children. Cancer 66: 1234–1241

589. Lundgren L, Aldenberg F, Angervall L et al. 1994 Pseudomalignant spindle cell proliferations of the urinary bladder. Hum Pathol 25: 181–191

590. Hirsch M S, Dal Cin P, Fletcher C D M 2006 ALK expression in pseudosarcomatous myofibroblastic proliferations of the genitourinary tract. Histopathology 48: 569–578

591. Dehner L P 1989 Pathology of the urinary bladder in children. In: Young RH (ed) Pathology of the urinary bladder. Churchill Livingstone, New York, p 179–211

592. Mostofi F K, Morse W H 1952 Polypoid rhabdomyosarcoma (sarcoma botryoides) of bladder in children. J Urol 67: 681–687

593. Ober W B, Edgcomb J H 1954 Sarcoma botryoides in the female urogenital tract. Cancer 7: 75–91

594. Ghazali S 1973 Embryonic rhabdomyosarcoma of the urogenital tract. Br J Surg 60: 124–128

595. Hays D M, Raney R B Jr, Lawrence W Jr et al. 1982 Bladder and prostatic tumors in the intergroup rhabdomyosarcoma study (IRS-I). Results of therapy. Cancer 50: 1472–1482

596. Williams D I, Schistad G 1964 Lower urinary tract tumours in children. Br J Urol 36: 51–65

597. Hellstrom H R, Fisher E R 1961 Embryonal rhabdomyosarcoma of the bladder in the aged. J Urol 86: 336–339

598. Joshi D P, Wessely Z, Seery W H et al. 1966 Rhabdomyosarcoma of the bladder in an adult: case report and review of the literature. J Urol 96: 214–217

599. Henriksson C, Zetterlund C G, Boiesen P et al. 1986 Large rhabdomyosarcoma of the urinary bladder in an adult: case report. J Urol Nephrol 19: 237–239

600. Tripathi V N P, Dick V S 1969 Primary sarcoma of the urogenital system in adults. J Urol 101: 898–904

601. Narayana A S, Loening S, Weimar G W et al. 1978 Sarcoma of the bladder and prostate. J Urol 119: 72–76

602. Keating M A, Young R H, Lillehei C W et al. 1987 Hamartoma of the bladder in a 4-year-old girl with hamartomatous polyps of the gastrointestinal tract. J Urol 138: 366–369

603. Billis A, Queiroz L S, Oliveira E R et al. 1980 Adenoma of bladder in siblings with renal dysplasia. Urology 16: 299–302

604. Young R H 1986 Fibroepithelial polyp of the bladder with atypical stromal cells. Arch Pathol Lab Med 110: 241–242

605. Hojo H, Newton W A, Hamoudi A B et al. 1995 Pseudosarcomatous myofibroblastic tumors of the urinary bladder in children: a study of 11 cases with a review of the literature. Am J Surg Pathol 19: 1224–1236

606. Keenan R A, Buchanan J D 1979 Fibrosarcoma of bladder exhibiting endocrine characteristics of phaeochromocytoma. J R Soc Med 72: 618–620

607. Harrison G S M 1986 Malignant fibrous histiocytoma of the bladder. Br J Urol 58: 457–458

608. Stroup R M, Chang Y C 1987 Angiosarcoma of the bladder: a case report J Urol 137: 984–985

609. Young R H, Rosenberg A E 1987 Osteosarcoma of the urinary bladder, report of a case and review of the literature. Cancer 59: 174–178

610. Levi M, Soloman C 1953 Adenofibroma of urinary bladder: a case report. J Urol 70: 898–899

611. Vara A R, Ruzics E P, Moussabeck O et al. 1990 Endometrioid adenosarcoma of the bladder arising from endometriosis. J Urol 143: 813–815

612. Judd E S 1921 Adenomyoma presenting as a tumor of the bladder. Surg Clin North Am 1: 1271–1278

613. Young R H 1987 Carcinosarcoma of the urinary bladder. Cancer 59: 1333–1339

614. Cross P A, Eyden B P, Joglekar V M 1989 Carcinosarcoma of the urinary bladder, a light, immunohistochemical, and electron microscopical case report. Virchow's Arch [A] 415: 91–95

615. Bloxham C A, Bennett M K, Robinson M C 1990 Bladder carcinosarcomas: three cases with diverse histogenesis. Histopathology 16: 63–67

616. Vieillefond A, Sinico M, Tighilt M et al. 1988 Carcinosarcomes de vessie, 3 cas avec étude immunohistochimique. Ann Pathol 8: 223–227

617. Sufrin G, Keogh B, Moore R H et al. 1977 Secondary involvement of the bladder in malignant lymphoma. J Urol 118: 251–253

618. Chaitin B, Manning J T, Ordóñez N G 1984 Hematologic neoplasms with initial manifestations in lower urinary tract. Urology 23: 35–42

619. Tremann J A, Norris H T, McRoberts J W 1971 Lymphoproliferative disease of the bladder. J Urol 106: 687–691

620. Siegelbaum M H, Edmonds P, Seidmon E J 1986 Use of immunohistochemistry for identification of primary lymphoma of the bladder. J Urol 136: 1074–1076

621. Aigen A B, Phillips M 1986 Primary malignant lymphoma of urinary bladder. Urology 28: 235–237

622. Forrest J B, Saypol D C, Mills S E et al. 1983 Immunoblastic sarcoma of the bladder. J Urol 130: 350–351

623. Kempton C L, Kurtin P J, Inwards D et al. 1997 Malignant lymphoma of the bladder: evidence from 36 cases that low-grade lymphoma of the MALT-type is the most common primary bladder lymphoma. Am J Surg Pathol 21: 1324–1333

624. Mourad W A, Khalil S, Radwi A et al. 1998 Primary T-cell lymphoma of the urinary bladder. Am J Surg Pathol 22: 373–377

625. Allory Y, Merabet Z, Copie-Bergman et al. 2005 Sarcomatoid variant of anaplastic large cell lymphomas mimics ALK-1-positive inflammatory myofibroblastic tumor in bladder. Am J Surg Pathol 29:838 (Letter to the Editor)

626. Marconis J T 1959 Primary Hodgkin's (paragranulomatous type) disease of the bladder. J Urol 81: 275–281

627. Neal M H, Swearingen M L, Gawronski L et al. 1985 Myeloma cells in the urine. Arch Pathol Lab Med 109: 870–872

628. Yang C, Motteram R, Sanderman T F 1982 Extramedullary plasmacytoma of the bladder. A case report and review of literature. Cancer 50: 146–149

629. Givler R L 1971 Involvement of the bladder in leukemia and lymphoma. J Urol 105: 667–670

630. Meis J M, Butler J J, Osborne B M et al. 1986 Granulocytic sarcoma in nonleukemic patients. Cancer 58: 2697–2709

631. Zhou M, Epstein J I, Young R H 2004 Paraganglioma of the urinary bladder. A lesion that may be misdiagnosed as urothelial carcinoma in transurethral resection specimens. Am J Surg Pathol 28: 94–100

632. Cheng L, Leibovich B C, Cheville J C et al 2000 Paraganglioma of the urinary bladder. Can biologic potential be predicted? Cancer 88: 844–852

633. Colby T V 1980 Carcinoid tumor of the bladder. Arch Pathol Lab Med 104: 199–200

634. Aoyama H, Yoshida K, Kondo T et al. 1978 Primary carcinoid tumor of the urinary bladder (report of a case). Nippon Hinyokika Gakkai Zasshi 69: 124–133

635. Stein B S, Kendall A R 1984 Malignant melanoma of the genitourinary tract. J Urol 132: 859–868

636. Ironside J W, Timperley W R, Madden J W et al. 1985 Primary melanoma of the urinary bladder presenting with intracerebral metastases. Br J Urol 57: 593–594

637. Cauffield E W 1956 Dermoid cysts of the bladder. J Urol 75: 801–804

638. Lazebnik J, Kamhi D 1961 A case of vesical teratoma associated with vesical stones and diverticulum. J Urol 85: 796–799

639. Taylor G, Jordan M, Churchill B et al. 1983 Yolk sac tumor of the bladder. J Urol 129: 591–594

640. Ganem E J, Batal J T 1956 Secondary malignant tumors of the urinary bladder metastatic from primary foci in distant organs. J Urol 75: 965–972

641. Sheehan E E, Greenberg S D, Scott R Jr 1963 Metastatic neoplasms of the bladder. J Urol 90: 281–284

642. Goldstein A G 1967 Metastatic carcinoma to the bladder. J Urol 98: 209–215

643. Bates A W, Baithun S I 2000 Secondary neoplasms of the bladder are histological mimics of nontransitional cell primary tumours: clinicopathological and histological features of 282 cases. Histopathology 36: 32–40

644. Melicow M M 1955 Tumors of the urinary bladder: a clinicopathological analysis of over 2500 specimens and biopsies. J Urol 74: 498–521

645. Majnarich G, Malament M 1958 Urinary tract metastases by cancers of large bowel. Surgery 44: 520–528

646. Hermann H B 1929 Metastatic tumors of the urinary bladder originating from the carcinomata of the gastro-intestinal tract. J Urol 22: 257–273

647. Dalton D P, Dalkin B L, Sener S F et al. 1987 Enterovesical fistula secondary to mucinous adenocarcinoma of appendix. J Urol 138: 617–618

648. Haid M, Ignatoff J, Khandekar J D et al. 1980 Urinary bladder metastases from breast carcinoma. Cancer 46: 229–232

649. Silverstein L I, Plaine L, Davis J E et al. 1987 Breast carcinoma metastatic to bladder. Urology 29: 544–547

650. Coltart R S, Stewart S, Brown C H 1985 Small cell carcinoma of the bronchus: a rare cause of haematuria from a metastasis in the urinary bladder. J R Soc Med 78: 1053–1054

651. Remis R E, Halverstadt D B 1986 Metastatic renal cell carcinoma to the bladder: case report and review of the literature. J Urol 136: 1294–1296

652. Meyer J E 1974 Metastatic melanoma of the urinary bladder. Cancer 34: 1822–1824

653. Edson M, Colmenares E 1983 Transitional cell carcinoma of bladder originating from transitional cell carcinoma of anus. Urology 22: 198–199

654. Palmer J K, Emmett J L, McDonald J R 1948 Urethral caruncle. Surg Gynecol Obstet 87: 611–620

655. Marshall F C, Uson A C, Melicow M M 1960 Neoplasms and caruncles of the female urethra. Surg Gynecol Obstet 110: 723–733

656. Foster R S, Garrett R A 1986 Congenital posterior urethral polyps. J Urol 136: 670–672

657. Tsuzuki T, Epstein J I 2005 Fibroepithelial polyp of the lower urinary tract in adults. Am J Surg Pathol 29: 460–466

658. Debenedictis T J, Marmar J L, Praiss D E 1977 Intraurethral condylomas acuminata: management and review of the literature. J Urol 118: 767–769

659. Gartman E 1956 Intraurethral verruca acuminata in men. J Urol 75: 717–718

660. Bissada N K, Cole A T, Fried F A 1974 Extensive condylomas acuminata of the entire male urethra and the bladder. J Urol 112: 201–203

661. Keating M A, Young R H, Carr C P et al. 1985 Condyloma acuminatum of the bladder and ureter: case report and review of the literature. J Urol 133: 465–467

662. Huvos A G, Grabstald H 1973 Urethral meatal and parameatal tumors in young men: a clinicopathologic and electron microscopic study. J Urol 110: 688–692

663. Powell I, Cartwright H, Jano F 1981 Villous adenoma and adenocarcinoma of female urethra. Urology 18: 612–614

664. Howells M R, Baylis M S, Howell S 1985 Benign urethral villous adenoma. Case report. Br J Obstet Gynaecol 92: 1070–1071

665. Raju G C, Roopnarinesingh A, Woo J 1987 Villous adenoma of female urethra. Urology 29: 446–447

666. Maung R, Kelly J K, Grace D A 1988 Intestinal metaplasia and dysplasia of prostatic urethra secondary to stricture. Urology 32: 361–363

667. Chan J K C, Chow T C, Tsui M S 1987 Prostatic-type polyps of the lower urinary tract: three histogenic types? Histopathology 11: 789–801

668. Nesbit R M 1962 The genesis of benign polyps in the prostatic urethra. J Urol 87: 416–418

669. Butterick J D, Schnitzer B, Abell M R 1971 Ectopic prostatic tissue in urethra: A clinicopathological entity and a significant cause of hematuria. J Urol 105: 97–104

670. Craig J R, Hart W R 1975 Benign polyps with prostatic-type epithelium of the urethra. Am J Clin Pathol 63: 343–347

671. Stein A J, Prioleau P G, Catalona W J 1980 Adenomatous polyps of the prostatic urethra: a cause of hematospermia. J Urol 124: 298–299

672. Walker A N, Mills S E, Fechner R E et al. 1983 Epithelial polyps of the prostatic urethra, a light-microscopic and immunohistochemical study. Am J Surg Pathol 7: 351–356

673. Baroudy A C, O'Connell J P 1984 Papillary adenoma of the prostatic urethra. J Urol 132: 120–122

674. Glancy R J, Gaman A J, Rippey J J 1983 Polyps and papillary lesions of the prostatic urethra. Pathology 15: 153–157

675. Zeid M, Gaeta J F, Asirwatham J E et al. 1986 Papillary adenoma of the prostatic urethra. Prostate 9: 9–14

676. Walker A N, Mills S E, Fechner R E et al. 1982 "Endometrial" adenocarcinoma of the prostatic urethra arising in a villous polyp, a light microscopic and immunoperoxidase study. Arch Pathol Lab Med 106: 624–627

677. Ford T F, Watson G M, Cameron K M 1985 Adenomatous metaplasia (nephrogenic adenoma) of urothelium, an analysis of 70 cases. Br J Urol 57: 427–433

678. Odze R, Bégin L R 1989 Tubular adenomatous metaplasia (nephrogenic adenoma) of the female urethra. Int J Gynecol Pathol 8: 374–380

679. Bhagavan B S, Tiamson E M, Wenk R E et al. 1981 Nephrogenic adenoma of the urinary bladder and urethra. Hum Pathol 12: 907–916

680. Allan C H, Epstein J I 2001 Nephrogenic adenoma of the prostatic urethra. A mimicker of prostatic adenocarcinoma. Am J Surg Pathol 25: 802–808.

681. Peterson L J, Matsumoto L M 1978 Nephrogenic adenoma in urethral diverticulum. Urology 11: 193–195

682. Piazza R, Aragona F, Pizzarella M et al. 1987 Nephrogenic adenoma in urethral diverticulum: an unusual finding. Urol Int 42: 69–70

683. Martin S A, Santa Cruz D J 1981 Adenomatoid metaplasia of the prostatic urethra. Am J Clin Pathol 75: 185–189

684. Medeiros L J, Young R H 1989 Nephrogenic adenoma arising in urethral diverticula, a report of five cases. Arch Pathol Lab Med 113: 125–128

685. Young R H 1992 Nephrogenic adenomas of the urethra involving the prostate gland: a report of two cases of a lesion that may be confused with prostatic adenocarcinoma. Mod Pathol 5: 617–620

686. Schinella R, Thurm J, Feiner H 1974 Papillary pseudotumor of the prostatic urethra: proliferative papillary urethritis. J Urol 111: 38–40

687. Heaton N D, Kadow C, Yates-Bell A J 1990 Inverted papilloma of the penile urethra. Br J Urol 66: 661–662

688. Noto L 1983 Obstructive urethral leiomyoma in a female. Br J Urol 55: 239

689. Saad A G, Kaouk J H, Kaspar H G et al. 2003 Leoimyoma of the urethra: report of 3 cases of a rare entity. Int J Surg Pathol 11: 123–126

690. Bertrand G, Deroide J P, Bidabe M C 1984 Fibroadénome des glandes para-uréthrales: une nouvelle entite tumorale? Ann Pathol 4: 147–150

691. Young R H, Srigley J R, Amin M B et al. 2000 Tumors of the prostate gland, seminal vesicles, male urethra and penis. Atlas of tumor pathology, Series 3, fascicle 28. American Registry of Pathology, Washington, DC

692. Levine R L 1980 Urethral cancer. Cancer 45: 1965–1972

693. Roberts T W, Melicow M M 1977 Pathology and natural history of urethral tumors in females. Urology 10: 583–589

694. Zeigerman J H, Gordon S F 1970 Cancer of the female urethra: a curable disease. Obstet Gynecol 36: 785–788

695. Monaco A P, Murphy G B, Dowling W 1958 Primary cancer of the female urethra. Cancer 11: 1215–1221

696. Grabstald H, Hilaris B, Henschke U et al. 1966 Cancer of the female urethra. JAMA 197: 835–842

697. Turner A G, Hendry W F 1980 Primary carcinoma of the female urethra. Br J Urol 52: 549–554

698. Bracken R B, Johnson D E, Miller L S et al. 1976 Primary carcinoma of the female urethra. J Urol 117: 188–192

699. Desai S, Libertino J A, Zinman L 1973 Primary carcinoma of the female urethra. J Urol 110: 693–695

700. Tiltman A J 1974 Primary adenocarcinoma of the female urethra. J Pathol 117: 97–99

701. Schnitzer B 1964 Primary adenocarcinoma of the female urethra: a review and report of two cases. J Urol 92: 135–139

702. Knoblich R 1960 Primary adenocarcinoma of the female urethra: a review and report of 3 cases. Am J Obstet Gynecol 80: 353–364

703. Ampil F L 1975 Primary malignant neoplasm of the female urethra. Obstet Gynecol 66: 799–804

704. Meis J M, Ayala A G, Johnson D E 1987 Adenocarcinoma of the urethra in women, a clinicopathologic study. Cancer 60: 1038–1052

705. Menville J G, Counseller V S 1935 Mucoid carcinoma of the female urethra. J Urol 33: 76–81

706. Peterson D T, Dockerty M B, Utz D C et al. 1973 The peril of primary carcinoma of the urethra in women. J Urol 110: 72–75

707. Teoh T B 1960 Papillary adenocarcinoma of the female urethra: a case report. Br J Surg 48: 151–152

708. Svanholm H, Andersen O P, Røhl H 1987 Tumour of female paraurethral duct. Immunohistochemical similarity with prostatic carcinoma. Virchow's Arch [A] 411: 395–398

709. Hanai J, Lin M 1990 Primary adenocarcinoma of the female urethra with three histologic patterns and partial AFP positivity. Acta Pathol Jpn 40: 838–844

710. Kreutzmann H A R, Colloff B 1939 Primary carcinoma of the male urethra. Arch Surg 39: 513–529

711. Grabstald H 1973 Tumors of the urethra in men and women. Cancer 32: 1236–1255

712. Melicow M M, Roberts T W 1978 Pathology and natural history of urethral tumors in males, review of 142 cases. Urology 11: 83–89

713. Posso M A, Berg G A, Murphy A I et al. 1961 Mucinous adenocarcinoma of the urethra: report of a case associated with urethritis glandularis. J Urol 85: 944–948

714. Mandler J I, Pool T L 1966 Primary carcinoma of the male urethra. J Urol 96: 67–72

715. Kaplan G W, Bulkley G J, Grayhack J T 1967 Carcinoma of the male urethra. J Urol 98: 365–371

716. Gowing N F C 1960 Urethral carcinoma associated with cancer of the bladder. Br J Urol 32: 428–438

717. Coutts A G, Grigor K M, Fowler J W 1985 Urethral dysplasia and bladder cancer in cystectomy specimens. Br J Urol 57: 535–541

718. Tobisu K-I, Tanaka Y, Mizutani T et al. 1991 Transitional cell carcinoma of the urethra in men following cystectomy for bladder cancer: multivariate analysis for risk factors. J Urol 146: 1551–1554

719. De Paepe M E, André R, Mahadevia P 1990 Urethral involvement in female patients with bladder cancer, a study of 22 cystectomy specimens. Cancer 65: 1237–1241

720. Tomaszewski J E, Korat O C, Livolsi V A et al. 1986 Paget's disease of the urethral meatus following transitional cell carcinoma of the bladder. J Urol 135: 368–370

721. Bégin L R, Deschênes J, Mitmaker B 1991 Pagetoid carcinomatous involvement of the penile urethra in association with high-grade transitional cell carcinoma of the urinary bladder. Arch Pathol Lab Med 115: 632–635

722. Saito R 1982 An adenosquamous carcinoma of the male urethra with hypercalcemia. Hum Pathol 23: 383–385

723. Taylor R N, Lacey C G, Shuman M A 1985 Adenocarcinoma of Skene's duct associated with a systemic coagulopathy. Gynecol Oncol 22: 250–256

724. Colapinto V, Evans D H 1977 Primary carcinoma of the male urethra developing after urethroplasty for stricture. J Urol 118: 581–584

725. Hamilton J D, Leach W B 1951 Adenocarcinoma arising in a diverticulum of the female urethra. Arch Pathol 51: 90–97

726. Gonzalez M O, Harrison M L, Boileau M A 1985 Carcinoma in diverticulum of female urethra. Urology 26: 328–332

727. Maltby C C, Johnston S R 1988 Transitional cell carcinoma of the male anterior urethra. Br J Urol 62: 489

728. Fernando J J R, Wanas T M 1991 Primary transitional cell carcinoma of the anterior urethra: a rare presentation. Genitourin Med 67: 244–246

729. Bans L L, Eble J N, Lingeman J E et al. 1983 Transitional cell carcinoma of the fossa navicularis of the male urethra. J Urol 129: 1055–1056

730. Mevorach R A, Cos L R, di Sant'Agnese P A et al. 1990 Human papillomavirus type 6 in grade I transitional cell carcinoma of the urethra. J Urol 143: 126–128

731. Grussendorf-Conen E-I, Deutz F J, De Villiers E M 1987 Detection of human papillomavirus-6 in primary carcinoma of the urethra in men. Cancer 60: 1832–1835

732. Lucman L, Vadas G 1973 Transitional cloacogenic carcinoma of the urethra. Cancer 31: 1508–1510

733. Díaz-Cano S J, Ríos J J, Rivera-Hueto F et al. 1992 Mixed cloacogenic carcinoma of male urethra. Histopathology 20: 82–84

734. Bostwick D G, Lo R, Stamey T A 1984 Papillary adenocarcinoma of the male urethra, case report and review of the literature. Cancer 54: 2556–2563

735. Oliva E, Young R H 1996 Clear cell adenocarcinoma of the urethra: a clinicopathologic analysis of 19 cases. Mod Pathol 9: 513–520

736. Cantrell B B, Leifer G, DeKlerk D P et al. 1981 Papillary adenocarcinoma of the prostatic urethra with clear-cell appearance. Cancer 48: 2661–2667

737. Ingram E A, DePauw P 1985 Adenocarcinoma of the male urethra with associated nephrogenic metaplasia, case report and review of the literature. Cancer 55: 160–164

738. Gupta T D, Grabstald H 1965 Melanoma of the genitourinary tract. J Urol 93: 607–614

739. Block N L, Hotchkiss R S 1971 Malignant melanoma of the female urethra: report of a case with 5-year survival and review of the literature. J Urol 105: 251–255

740. Oldbring J, Mikulowski P 1987 Malignant melanoma of the penis and male urethra, report of nine cases and review of the literature. Cancer 59: 581–587

741. Manivel J C, Fraley E E 1988 Malignant melanoma of the penis and male urethra: 4 case reports and literature review. J Urol 139: 813–816

742. Oliva E, Quinn T R, Amin M B et al. 2000 Primary malignant melanoma of the urethra. A clinicopathologic analysis of 15 cases. Am J Surg Pathol 24: 785–796

743. Melicow M M, Lattes R, Pierre-Louis C 1972 Lymphoma of the female urethra masquerading as a caruncle. J Urol 108: 748–749

744. Touhami H, Brahimi S, Kubisz P et al. 1987 Non-Hodgkin's lymphoma of the female urethra. J Urol 137: 991–992

745. Nabholtz J M, Friedman S, Tremeaux J C et al. 1989 Non-Hodgkin's lymphoma of the urethra: a rare extranodal entity. Gynecol Oncol 35: 110–111

746. Mark J A, Pais V M, Chong F K 1990 Plasmacytoma of the urethra treated with transurethral resection and radiotherapy. J Urol 143: 1010–1011

747. Kahn D G, Rothman P J, Weisman J D 1991 Urethral T-cell lymphoma as the initial manifestation of the acquired immune deficiency syndrome. Arch Pathol Lab Med 115: 1169–1170

748. Ro J, Dexeus F, Logothetis C et al. 1991 Pure yolk sac tumors in adults: A clinicopathologic study in 18 patients. Mod Pathol 4: 50a (abstract)

749. Cholhan H J, Caglar H, Kremzier J E 1991 Suburethral paraganglioma. Obstet Gynecol 78: 555–558

750. Sylora H O, Diamond H M, Kaufman M et al. 1975 Primary carcinoid tumor of the urethra. J Urol 114: 150–153

Tumors of the female genital tract 13

PART A

Ovary, fallopian tube, and broad and round ligaments

Charles F. Zaloudek

Tumors of the ovary

There are three main categories of primary ovarian tumors. These are:

1 epithelial tumors, which originate from the surface epithelium of the ovary, epithelial inclusions, or endometriosis
2 sex cord-stromal tumors, which arise from the ovarian stroma, from sex cord derivatives, or both
3 germ cell tumors, which originate from germ cells.

In addition, tumors that are not specific to the ovary, such as soft tissue tumors and lymphomas, can arise in the ovary, and tumors from extraovarian primary sites frequently metastasize to the ovaries.

Of the three main groups, epithelial tumors are the most common, comprising about 58 percent of all ovarian tumors (Table 13A.1).[1-5] Serous and mucinous cystadenomas are the most common epithelial tumors, and together account for about 30 percent of ovarian tumors. All types of carcinoma occur with some frequency, but only serous and mucinous borderline tumors are common. Sex cord-stromal tumors of the fibroma–thecoma group account for 9 percent of ovarian tumors. The most common malignant sex cord-stromal tumor, the granulosa cell tumor, accounts for only about 1 percent of ovarian tumors. Other sex cord-stromal tumors are rare. The single most common ovarian tumor is a germ cell tumor, the benign cystic teratoma, which comprises 32 percent of ovarian tumors. All other types of germ cell tumors, including all of the malignant germ cell tumors, are rare.

Table 13A.1	Common ovarian tumors
Tumor	**% of ovarian tumors**
Benign cystic teratoma	32
Serous cystadenoma	16
Mucinous cystadenoma	14
Serous carcinoma	9
Fibroma–thecoma	9
Borderline serous tumor	4
Endometrioid carcinoma	3
Borderline mucinous tumor	1
Clear cell carcinoma	1
Mucinous carcinoma	1

Epithelial tumors of the ovary

Epithelial tumors comprise 58 percent of all ovarian neo-plasms, and more than 90 percent of malignant tumors. Most can be classified according to their predominant pattern of differentiation as serous, mucinous, endometrioid, mixed meso-dermal, clear cell, Brenner/transitional cell, or undifferentiated (Table 13A.2). Mixtures of cell types are common. Minor foci of cell types other than the predominant one can be ignored,

Table 13A.2	Types of epithelial tumor of the ovary
Serous	Brenner/transitional cell
Mucinous	Undifferentiated
Endometrioid	Rare types
Mixed mesodermal	Mixed
Clear cell	Unclassified

Table 13A.3	Categories of epithelial tumor	
Benign	**Intermediate**	**Malignant**
Cystadenoma	Borderline tumor	Carcinoma
Surface papilloma	(also known as: tumor	
Adenofibroma	of low malignant	
Cystadenofibroma	potential, atypically	
(with focal low grade	proliferating tumor)	
proliferation or atypia)		

but when significant amounts (more than 10 percent) of several cell types are present, the tumor is best classified as a mixed epithelial tumor. Rare epithelial tumors cannot be assigned to a specific category and are designated as unclassified.

Epithelial tumors are categorized as benign, malignant, or intermediate, based on their pathologic features (Table 13A.3). A benign epithelial tumor is designated as a cystadenoma, a surface papilloma, a cystadenofibroma, or an adenofibroma, depending on its location in the ovary, the extent of cyst formation and the amount of stroma present. Malignant epithelial tumors are mainly adenocarcinomas, although transitional cell carcinoma and, rarely, squamous cell carcinoma also occur in the ovary. Mixed mesodermal tumors have a malignant epithelial component and behave clinically like a carcinoma, so they are usually classified as epithelial tumors.

Controversy exists over the appropriate nomenclature for tumors in the intermediate group. Such tumors have been called borderline tumors or tumors of low malignant potential (LMP) since those terms were sanctioned by the World Health Organization (WHO) in 1973.[6] They have a favorable prognosis and rarely evolve into carcinoma. It has been proposed that these tumors should be designated atypically proliferating epithelial tumors.[7] However, that terminology has not generally been accepted and, in this chapter, intermediate epithelial tumors are called borderline tumors in accordance with the current WHO classification.[8,9] This term encompasses a spectrum of tumors ranging from grade 1 borderline tumors with a degree of proliferation and atypia equivalent to that seen in simple hyperplasia to grade 3 borderline tumors showing marked proliferation and/or severe cytologic atypia equivalent to in situ carcinoma, but lacking invasion or confluent growth.[10] Borderline epithelial tumors in which there is marked cytologic atypia are designated as borderline tumors with intraepithelial carcinoma. Pathologists should render their diagnoses using terminology that is clearly understood in their community. Other widely used diagnostic terms can be cited as appropriate to ensure that anyone who reads the pathology report will clearly understand the diagnosis.[11]

Clinical features With few exceptions, the clinical presentation, treatment, and results of treatment are similar for all types of epithelial tumors within a given category.

Epithelial tumors occur mainly in adults. They are uncommon in children and teenagers.[12–16] Benign and borderline tumors occur at all ages, but are often detected in premenopausal women.[17] Carcinomas occur chiefly in peri- and postmenopausal women. Ovarian cancer rarely occurs in pregnant women, but when it does the tumor is most likely to be a serous or mucinous carcinoma.[18] More than 70 percent of women with ovarian cancer have extensive extraovarian tumor spread at the time of diagnosis. This is partly because the symptoms caused by epithelial tumors are vague and non-specific and do not prompt early diagnosis. The most common symptoms are pelvic discomfort or pain, a sensation of abdominal fullness or pressure, gastrointestinal disturbances, urinary frequency, and occasionally, menstrual abnormalities.[19] Torsion or rupture of the tumor can result in acute abdominal symptoms. Tumors greater than 15 cm in diameter are too large to fit in the pelvis; they rise into and distend the abdomen, and may be palpated by the patient. Ascites is another cause of abdominal distention in women with ovarian tumors. Rarely caused by benign tumors, ascites is most suggestive of carcinoma. It interferes with gastrointestinal function, leading to nausea and vomiting. Ovarian enlargement of any degree, especially in a woman over 45 years of age, raises the question of ovarian cancer and calls for further evaluation. The identification of a solid or complex mass by sonography or some other imaging technique is particularly worrisome.

The CA-125 monoclonal antibody blood test detects an antigen on a high molecular weight glycoprotein.[20–22] The test is usually positive in women with advanced borderline and malignant epithelial tumors and in some women with localized disease. The CA-125 test is not specific for ovarian cancer, as an increased serum concentration of the antigen is also detected in other cancers, and in association with benign conditions such as pregnancy, endometriosis, pelvic inflammatory disease, leiomyomas, liver disease, and some collagen-vascular disorders.[23]

The treatment of ovarian tumors is primarily surgical. Benign tumors are cured by cystectomy or unilateral salpingo-oophorectomy.

Borderline tumors have a favorable prognosis, even in advanced stages.[24] Tumor is confined to the ovaries in about 80 percent of cases. The remaining 20 percent of patients have pelvic or peritoneal implants. Lymph node involvement is infrequent,[25] as is spread to parenchymal organs or beyond the abdominal cavity.[26] Long-term survival exceeds 90 percent for patients with all stages of disease.[17,24,27–32] Survival approaches 100 percent for patients with tumor confined to the ovaries.[32–35] Tumor-related deaths fall into three main categories:

1 the patient dies of carcinoma
2 the patient develops a fatal complication of a borderline tumor, such as fibrous adhesions with bowel obstruction
3 the patient dies of a complication of treatment.[36]

Conservative therapy appears indicated for borderline tumors, except in a small cohort of women whose tumors exhibit features consistently associated with aggressive behavior or carcinoma. These features include invasive peritoneal implants or recurrence as low grade serous carcinoma.[36]

The standard surgical treatment for a borderline tumor is total abdominal hysterectomy, bilateral salpingo-oophorectomy, omentectomy, and resection of extraovarian tumor implants. Many women with borderline tumors are of reproductive age and wish to retain their childbearing capability. Unilateral salpingo-oophorectomy, or even cystectomy, is therefore considered as a treatment option in some circumstances, although patients treated in this way have about a 25 percent risk of recurrence in the contralateral ovary.[31,35,37–42] Laparoscopic management has been utilized, even in women with small peritoneal implants, in an effort to conserve fertility.[43,44] Conservative surgery to preserve fertility appears possible in some circumstances, even in patients with extraovarian tumor spread.[45] Patients with micropapillary borderline serous tumors appear more likely than those with typical borderline serous tumors to have tumor spread beyond the ovary. When corrected for stage and implant type, however, no difference in survival has been demonstrated.[46] Restaging surgery for women who have been inadequately staged during their initial operation is controversial. The tumor stage is altered in about 15 percent of women who undergo restaging surgery, but the risk of recurrence appears to be similar in women who are restaged and those who are not.[47,48] Restaging is of most value for women with micropapillary borderline serous tumors, since they may have a greater risk of having invasive peritoneal implants.[49] Recurrences are generally detected many years after primary therapy, and recurrent disease can be slowly progressive. Recurrent tumor can be borderline serous tumor, low grade serous carcinoma,[36,50] or rarely, high grade serous carcinoma.[51] Some authors, but not others, have noted an increased rate of disease progression when recurrence is as low grade serous carcinoma.[31] Surgical resection of contralateral or extraovarian tumor deposits is the most effective treatment for women with progressive or recurrent tumors.[36,52] Oncologists are not in complete agreement, but most administer chemotherapy or radiotherapy only in the face of progressive disease that is not amenable to surgical resection.[41,52–55] The survival rate is high, even for women with advanced stage tumors.[56]

Invasive carcinoma of the ovary spreads by direct invasion into adjacent organs or via the peritoneal fluid to the omentum, the peritoneum, the serosal surfaces of the abdominal viscera and the diaphragm. Lymph node metastases are common and distant metastases are occasionally detected in the lungs, pleura, and pericardium. The clinical stage (Table 13A.4) is the most important prognostic factor.

The treatment of ovarian cancer usually includes surgery and chemotherapy.[57,58] The standard surgical treatment is hysterectomy, bilateral salpingo-oophorectomy, omentectomy, pelvic and para-aortic lymph node dissection, and staging biopsies and appendectomy if indicated. Gynecologic oncologists attempt to remove as much extraovarian tumor as possible ("cytoreductive surgery") in order to enhance subsequent chemotherapy or radiotherapy.[59–62] The prognosis is most favorable in early (stage I–II) stage disease.[63] A young woman with a stage IA well differentiated adenocarcinoma can be treated by unilateral salpingo-oophorectomy, omentectomy, and a thorough

| Table 13A.4 | FIGO staging of ovarian cancer. Reprinted from International Journal of Gynecology and obstetrics. Benedet J L, Pecorelli S. Staging classifications and clinical practice guidelines of gynaecologic cancers. p 94, ©2000. With permission from International Federation of Gynecology and Obstetrics. |

Stage	Extent of disease
I	Tumor limited to ovaries
IA	Tumor limited to one ovary; capsule intact; no tumor on surface of ovary; no malignant cells in ascites or peritoneal washings
IB	Tumor limited to both ovaries; capsule intact; no tumor on surface of ovary; no malignant cells in ascites or peritoneal washings
IC	Tumor limited to one or both ovaries with any of the following: rupture of capsule; tumor on surface of ovary; malignant cells in ascites or peritoneal washings
II	Tumor involves one or both ovaries with pelvic extension
IIA	Extension and/or implants on uterus and/or fallopian tube; no malignant cells in ascites or peritoneal washings
IIB	Extension to other pelvic tissues; no malignant cells in ascites or peritoneal washings
IIC	Pelvic extension with malignant cells in ascites or peritoneal washings
III	Tumor involves one or both ovaries with microscopically confirmed peritoneal metastasis outside the pelvis and/or regional lymph node metastasis
IIIA	Microscopic peritoneal metastasis beyond pelvis
IIIB	Macroscopic peritoneal metastasis beyond pelvis ≤2 cm in greatest dimension
IIIC	Peritoneal metastasis beyond pelvis ≥2 cm in greatest dimension and/or regional lymph node metastasis
IV	Distant metastasis

staging procedure if she wishes to retain her fertility.[64,65] Some women with advanced ovarian cancer are treated with chemotherapy prior to surgery to facilitate the subsequent surgical resection.[66] Combination chemotherapy with a platinum-based regimen is ordinarily administered to women with high grade stage IA carcinomas and to those with extraovarian spread or positive peritoneal cytology.[67–75] Chemotherapy results in a partial or complete clinical remission in about 85 percent of women with advanced cancer, but most patients relapse within 2–3 years and the long-term survival rate is less than 20–30 percent.[76] Other types of treatment that are sometimes used for ovarian cancer include intraperitoneal chemotherapy,[77,78] intraperitoneal radiocolloids,[79] and external beam radiotherapy.[80,81]

Serous tumors

Serous tumors constitute about 30 percent of all ovarian tumors, making them the single most common group. They comprise 22 percent of benign and nearly 50 percent of malignant primary tumors of the ovary. Of all serous tumors, 50 percent are benign, 15 percent are borderline, and 35 percent are invasive carcinomas.[5]

Benign serous tumors

Serous cystadenoma may be unilocular or multilocular. It has a thin wall and contains clear fluid. The interior and exterior surfaces are usually smooth, but small papillary excrescences occasionally arise from the cyst lining. Serous adenofibroma is a solid tumor that has a firm white or tan fibrous cut surface. Scattered small cysts may be visible, or the tumor may have a spongy appearance due to the presence of many diminutive cysts. Serous cystadenofibroma is more common than adenofibroma;[82] it is a unilocular or multilocular cystic tumor with solid adenofibromatous areas in its wall. Serous surface papilloma is an uncommon tumor that grows as papillary excrescences on the surface of the ovary. About 20 percent of benign serous tumors are bilateral.

Microscopically, benign serous tumors are lined by ciliated and non-ciliated low columnar cells with bland ovoid basal nuclei (Fig. 13A.1). The epithelium becomes flattened if the cyst is under tension. Abundant fibrous stroma surrounds the glands and cysts in adenofibroma and cystadenofibroma (Fig. 13A.2). In a recent study, only 14 percent of serous cystadenomas, usually the larger ones, were found to be monoclonal.[83] This has led to the proposal that only tumors that exhibit evidence of proliferation of the epithelium, such as cellular stratification or papillations, should be designated as cystadenomas or cystadenofibromas,[84] although this view has not yet been adopted widely. There are small foci of mild to moderate nuclear atypia or branching papillary growth in occasional otherwise benign serous tumors. The behavior of tumors with small foci of borderline-like growth has not been studied adequately,[85] but when these features are observed in only a few low power fields (≤5–10 percent of the tumor), the clinical evolution is generally benign and such tumors are usually classified as a serous cystadenoma, cystadenofibroma, or adenofibroma with focal low-grade atypia or proliferation.[86] In some patients, a borderline serous tumor contains areas with a lesser degree of proliferative activity or the contralateral ovary contains a serous tumor with focal proliferative activity, raising the possibility that serous tumors with focal proliferation may not be entirely inconsequential and that they may rarely progress.[31]

Borderline serous tumors

Borderline serous tumors are large, usually multilocular, cystic neoplasms that are bilateral in 35–40 percent of cases.[42] Coarse papillary excrescences arise from the cyst lining. Papillary growth is focal in some tumors, confluent in others, and present on the external surface of the ovary in 40–50 percent of cases. Areas of solid growth are unusual except in adenofibromatous borderline tumors and zones of hemorrhage or necrosis are seldom seen.[87]

At low magnification, papillae with a hierarchical branching pattern grow from the cyst lining into the lumina (Fig. 13A.3), or from the surface of the ovary.[86] Complex papillary and glandular patterns and secondary cyst formation are typical. The papillae have fibrovascular cores that are conspicuous even in smaller branches, and are surfaced by proliferating columnar cells that are stratified into several layers (Fig. 13A.4). Ciliated cells may be present. Focally, the cells form tufts from which clusters of cells and single cells are detached into the cyst lumen. There is variable, but usually low grade, nuclear atypia and scattered mitotic figures are present. Cells with abundant eosinophilic cytoplasm, the "indifferent" or "metaplastic" cells, are scattered singly or in small clusters among the columnar tumor cells; they tend to be most conspicuous at the tips of the papillae. Plaques or nodules of loose fibrous tissue containing glands and papillae are occasionally seen in borderline serous

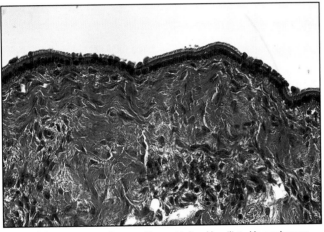

Fig. 13A.1 • Serous cystadenoma. The cyst is lined by ciliated low columnar cells with bland, basal nuclei.

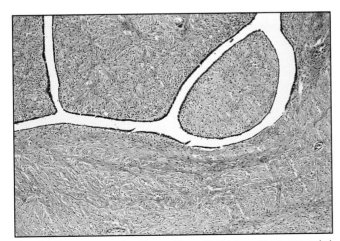

Fig. 13A.2 • Serous cystadenofibroma. The epithelial elements are surrounded by abundant fibrous stroma.

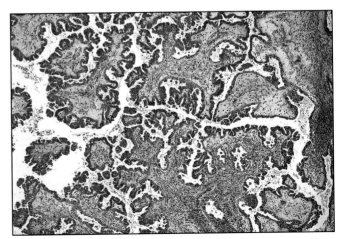

Fig. 13A.3 • Borderline serous tumor. The branching papillae are covered by proliferating columnar cells, some of which are detached into the cyst lumen.

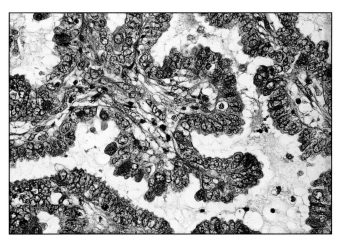

Fig. 13A.4 • Borderline serous tumor. The papillae are covered by columnar cells with large, vesicular nuclei. The nuclear to cytoplasmic ratio is increased relative to that seen in a serous cystadenoma, and there is focal stratification of the nuclei. Note the scattered indifferent cells with conspicuous eosinophilic cytoplasm.

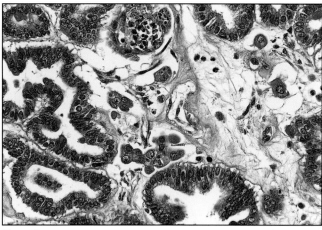

Fig. 13A.5 • Stromal microinvasion in a borderline serous tumor. Single cells and small clumps of cells with abundant eosinophilic cytoplasm are present in the stroma between the glands. The microinvasive cells have enlarged vesicular nuclei, some of which contain nucleoli. Many of the cell groups are surrounded by clear spaces.

tumors. These resemble desmoplastic peritoneal implants (see below) and have been termed "autoimplants". Autoimplants tend to be detected in high stage tumors, but do not appear to have prognostic significance.[31] The wall of a borderline serous tumor is generally thicker than that of a cystadenoma and some tumors have sufficient stroma to be classified as a borderline serous adenofibroma or cystadenofibroma. The microscopic feature that differentiates a serous borderline tumor from a serous carcinoma is the absence of diffuse stromal invasion in the former. In a borderline tumor, papillae and glands that appear to be within the stroma are an artifact resulting from tangential cutting of complicated infoldings of the cyst lining. Such glands are not infiltrative and there is no stromal fibroblastic or inflammatory reaction around them.

Stromal microinvasion is occasionally identified in a borderline serous tumor.[88–90] To qualify as microinvasion, the invasive foci must measure less than 3 mm.[86] Multiple foci of microinvasion are typically present in such cases.[91] Two patterns of microinvasion have been described. First, and most common, is one in which small clusters and cords of cells with eosinophilic cytoplasm, round vesicular nuclei, and prominent nucleoli are haphazardly distributed in the fibrous stroma of the cyst wall or a papilla (Fig. 13A.5). A stromal reaction usually is not seen around these cells. They are found occasionally within lymphatic spaces, but the clinical significance of this finding is unclear.[89] In the second pattern there is stromal invasion by papillae, small glands, cords, or confluent nests of epithelial cells.[89] The tumor cells are surrounded by inflamed or myxoid fibrous stroma or lie within small clear spaces. When this pattern of microinvasion is present, thorough evaluation to exclude more extensive areas of invasion is mandatory. It is difficult to identify stromal microinvasion at low magnification; immunostains for cytokeratin or epithelial membrane antigen can be used to accentuate the microinvasive epithelial cells in the stroma.[91] Most patients whose tumors exhibit stromal microinvasion have an uneventful course and the unfavorable outcome observed in a few patients has been attributed to other factors, such as invasive implants or incomplete staging.[17,33,40,88–93] More recent studies have noted progressive disease in a few patients with microinvasion,[33,94] and microinvasion was a significant adverse finding in a recent large

study of borderline serous tumors.[31] The presence of microinvasion should be noted in the pathology report, although its clinical significance still remains to be fully determined. The epithelium that lines borderline serous tumors includes eosinophilic "metaplastic" or "indifferent" cells. These cells tend to be more numerous in tumors with stromal microinvasion, and are more conspicuous in tumors removed from pregnant patients. In one study, a significant proportion of women with microinvasion were pregnant.[93] Mucin secretion and stromal decidual reactions have also been noted in tumors removed from pregnant women.[89,93] In contrast to borderline serous tumors with small areas of microinvasion, those with larger areas of invasion have an appreciable risk of progression if tumor has spread outside of the ovary.[95]

Peritoneal or omental tumor implants are found in 15–30 percent of women with serous borderline tumors. These are generally small superficial nodular excrescences of only a few millimeters diameter, although larger solid or cystic implants are present occasionally. There is controversy as to whether these represent metastases from the ovarian tumor or sites of synchronous peritoneal neoplasia,[96] although an increasing number of studies show similar genetic profiles in the ovarian and extraovarian tumors.[97–102] Three types of implants occur:

1 a non-invasive epithelial type
2 a non-invasive desmoplastic type
3 an invasive type.[10,86,103]

In the non-invasive epithelial type, papillary serous borderline tumor grows on the surface of the peritoneum or in cystic spaces just beneath it (Fig. 13A.6). The growths are circumscribed and do not invade the underlying stroma. Non-invasive desmoplastic implants are plaques of vascular fibrous stroma that contain a few epithelial cells, small clusters of cells, or scattered small glands lined by bland epithelial cells (Fig. 13A.7). The implants appear plastered on to the peritoneal surface and show no invasion downward into the underlying stroma. Non-invasive papillary growths may overlie these desmoplastic implants. Although patients with non-invasive implants tend to have a favorable prognosis, a few of them develop progressive disease and die of tumor.[31,104–106] Invasive implants are rare

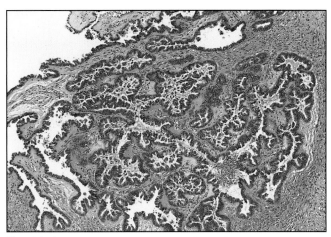

Fig. 13A.6 • Non-invasive papillary implant of borderline serous tumor. This papillary implant resembles the primary ovarian borderline serous tumor. It lies directly on the peritoneal surface. (The peritoneal space is on the left, the peritoneal surface is on the right).

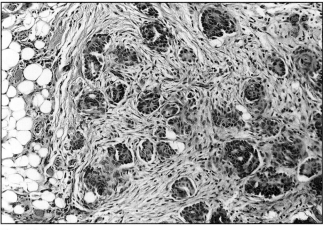

Fig. 13A.8 • Invasive implant of borderline serous tumor. Numerous small nests of epithelium, some surrounded by clefts, invade the fibrous stroma. Note the abundance of epithelium in this invasive implant compared with the paucity of epithelium in the desmoplastic non-invasive implant shown in Figure 13A.7.

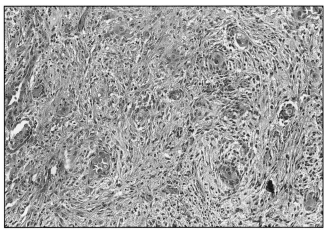

Fig. 13A.7 • Non-invasive desmoplastic implant of borderline serous tumor. Scattered small nests of bland epithelial cells are surrounded by abundant fibrous stroma.

(5–10 percent) but, together with advanced tumor stage, appear to be the most significant adverse prognostic findings in patients with borderline serous tumors.[31–33,46,103,107] Some studies are difficult to evaluate because the authors do not use standard definitions of invasive implants.[108] No invasive implants were found in one hospital-based study of 57 patients that did not include any consultation cases, indicating that practicing pathologists will only rarely see implants of this type.[34] The epithelium is more abundant in an invasive implant than in a desmoplastic implant and there is an infiltrative pattern of growth into the subperitoneal tissues or surrounding omentum (Fig. 13A.8). Expanded criteria for invasive implants have been proposed, but remain controversial.[109] These include a micropapillary pattern of growth, clear spaces or clefts around clusters of tumor cells and infiltrative glands that do not extend into underlying tissues.

Tumor is present in pelvic or para-aortic lymph nodes in up to a third of patients with advanced borderline tumors.[25,110,111,111a] There are two main patterns of lymph node involvement. In one, the tumor grows in a branching papillary pattern similar to that in the primary tumor. In the other, tumor cells are present singly or in small nests in the subcapsular sinuses. Lymph node involvement by hyperplastic mesothelial cells is a rare mimic of the latter pattern.[112] Accompanying peritoneal mesothelial hyperplasia, the appearance of the cells, and positive immunostaining for mesothelial markers such as calretinin, thrombomodulin and cytokeratin 5/6 serve to differentiate hyperplastic mesothelial cells from tumor cells.[113] Tumor is found in extra-abdominal lymph nodes at, or subsequent to, primary surgery in rare patients with borderline serous tumors.[26,114] Epithelial inclusions lined by low columnar cells, many of which are ciliated, are found in the pelvic or para-aortic lymph nodes in 5–25 percent of patients who are operated on for uterine cancers.[115] These inclusions, designated as benign epithelial inclusions or endosalpingiosis, are more frequent in patients with borderline serous tumors.[25,116] It has been proposed that they may represent a type of lymph node involvement by a borderline serous tumor.[116] However, most gynecologic pathologists do not accept this interpretation, and view them as benign inclusions. Some have proposed that lymph node involvement by borderline serous tumors may represent synchronous neoplasia arising in epithelial inclusions rather than metastasis from the ovarian tumor. However, primary extraovarian serous tumors rarely arise in benign epithelial inclusions in the absence of any tumor in the ovaries.[117] Regardless of its origin, lymph node involvement by a borderline serous tumor does not appear to be an adverse prognostic finding in most studies,[25,31,32,118] although recent data have suggested that nodular aggregates of tumor cells >1 mm may be associated with decreased survival.[111a]

The term micropapillary serous carcinoma was proposed for a group of proliferative serous tumors, the morphologic spectrum of which appears to encompass some non-invasive tumors in the high grade borderline category as well as some low grade invasive serous carcinomas.[107,119] Clinical follow-up of patients with micropapillary serous tumors indicates that most patients with stage I tumors are cured by surgery.[49,120] Patients with micropapillary serous tumors appear more likely to have bilateral tumors, surface papillary growth, extra-ovarian disease and, in some studies, invasive implants.[49,104] Survival rates appear to be similar to those for conventional borderline serous tumors, once adjusted for stage and implant type.[31,33,46,49,104,121] Although this is still a somewhat controversial entity, non-invasive micropapillary serous tumors are viewed currently by most gynecologic pathologists as proliferative variants of borderline serous tumors rather than as a type of serous carcinoma.

On gross examination, micropapillary borderline serous tumors are cystic and solid tumors that average 8–9 cm in diameter. They tend to be bilateral, and typically exhibit both intracystic and surface papillary tumor growth. Microscopically, micropapillary borderline serous tumors arise in a background of typical borderline serous tumor and have been defined arbitrarily as having foci of micropapillary growth measuring greater than 0.5 cm.[120] Long tufts of epithelial cells with little or no supporting fibrous stroma sprout from bulbous fibrovascular stromal papillae (Fig. 13A.9), from the cyst wall, or, when tangentially sectioned, are packed together with larger papillae that have more stroma. The papillae are five or more times longer than they are wide.[49] Tumors with foci of cribriform growth along the surfaces of papillae are also classified as micropapillary borderline serous tumors.[49,104] The tumor cells are cuboidal, hobnail-shaped, or columnar, and have uniform nuclei with only mild or moderate atypia (Fig. 13A.10). Mitotic figures are infrequent. Ciliated cells are less frequent in micropapillary serous tumors than in typical borderline serous tumors.

Serous carcinoma

Serous carcinoma is a large, often bilateral neoplasm in which there is a mixture of cystic, papillary, and solid growth patterns. The solid areas are tan or white and contain foci of hemorrhage and necrosis. Carcinoma frequently invades through the ovarian capsule and grows on the surface of the ovary. Serous surface papillary carcinoma grows predominantly on the surface of the ovary, with minimal parenchymal invasion and no intracystic growth.[122–125] When there is extensive extraovarian serous carcinoma with only focal (≤0.5 cm) surface growth on the ovaries, the process can be viewed as primary peritoneal serous carcinoma with involvement of the ovaries[126] (see Ch. 15). Microscopically, serous carcinoma diffusely infiltrates a fibrotic stroma. Papillary growth is usually present, at least focally (Fig. 13A.11). The papillae are lined by stratified low columnar cells. Tumor cells also line glands and grow in solid cords. There are solid nests and sheets of tumor cells in high-grade tumors. Elongated cleft-like glands within foci of solid growth are a characteristic finding in high-grade serous carcinoma. Foci of microcystic growth, sometimes with admixed signet ring type cells, are noted occasionally.[127] The degree of cytologic atypia and mitotic activity varies, but most serous carcinomas are high grade with marked nuclear atypia and frequent mitotic figures (Fig. 13A.12). A limited number of microscopic serous carcinomas have been reported.[128] These tend to be high grade neoplasms despite their small size, suggesting that the typical serous carcinoma originates as a high grade neoplasm.

Immunohistochemical studies reveal that serous carcinoma is cytokeratin 7 positive and cytokeratin 20 negative (Table 13A.5).[129] A majority of high grade serous carcinomas show membrane staining for OC-125,[130,131] and nuclear staining for WT-1[132–136] and p53 protein.[137–142] Staining for WT-1 is helpful in differentiating ovarian serous carcinoma from endometrial

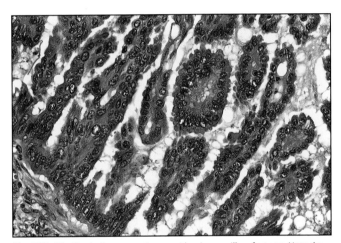

Fig. 13A.10 • Borderline serous tumor with micropapillary features. Note the long micropapillary processes lined by cuboidal or low columnar cells displaying only mild to moderate nuclear atypia.

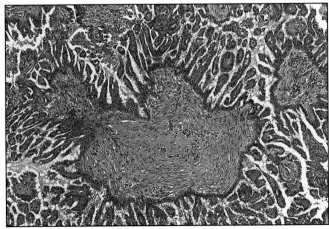

Fig. 13A.9 • Borderline serous tumor with micropapillary features. Long, thin micropapillae, many lacking fibrovascular cores, sprout from the surface of a coarse papillary frond.

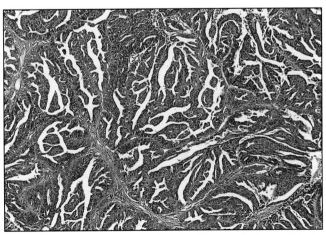

Fig. 13A.11 • Serous carcinoma. Confluent papillary growth, characteristic of serous carcinoma.

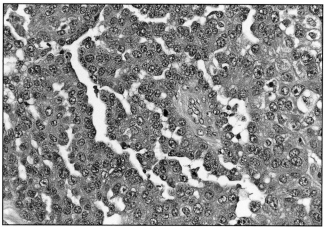

Fig. 13A.12 • Serous carcinoma. The tumor cells cover papillae and grow in sheets. They have large vesicular nuclei with coarse chromatin, and some have prominent nucleoli.

Fig. 13A.13 • Low grade serous carcinoma. Micropapillary fronds, many surrounded by clear spaces, infiltrate the ovarian stroma. Nuclear atypia is low grade and mitotic figures are few in number.

Table 13A.5 Immunohistochemistry of carcinomas of the ovary

	CK7	CK20	WT1	CA125	CEA	CDX2	VIM
Serous	+	–	+	+	–	–	–
TCC	+	–	+	+	–	–	–
Endometrioid	+	–	–	+	–	–	V
Mucinous, intestinal type	+	V	–	–	+	V	-
Clear cell	+	–	–	–	–	–	–
Metastatic colorectal	–	+	–	–	+	+	–

V = variably positive; + = positive; – = negative; CK7 = cytokeratin 7; CK20 = cytokeratin 20; CEA = carcinoembryonic antigen; VIM = vimentin; TCC = transitional cell carcinoma

Table 13A.6 Universal grading system for carcinoma of the ovary

1. Architectural score	
predominantly glandular	1 point
predominantly papillary	2 points
predominantly solid	3 points
2. Nuclear score	
mild atypia	1 point
moderate atypia	2 points
severe atypia	3 points
3. Mitotic score	
0–10 mf/10 hpf	1 point
11–25 mf/10 hpf	2 points
25 mf/10 hpf	3 points
4. Tumor grade	
3–5 points	Grade 1
6–7 points	Grade 2
8–9 points	Grade 3

serous carcinoma, which has a similar microscopic appearance but is less likely to stain for WT-1.[143,144]

A minority of serous carcinomas are low grade carcinomas; these appear to have a different histogenesis than high grade serous carcinoma.[120,145–151] In low grade serous carcinoma, glands, micropapillae, or nests of tumor cells having modest nuclear atypia infiltrate a fibrous stroma (Fig. 13A.13).[120] Clusters of tumor cells or micropapillae are often surrounded by clefts or clear spaces, and zones of invasive carcinoma may be mixed with zones of serous borderline tumor of typical or micropapillary type.[95] Some or all low-grade serous carcinomas may arise by progression from a borderline tumor. Distant metastases from an ovarian low grade serous carcinoma, such as those to lymph nodes, breast or to the mediastinum, can be difficult to diagnose.[152,153]

Grading of ovarian carcinomas has not been standardized, but the "universal" grading system for all types of ovarian carcinomas proposed by Silverberg and colleagues is widely used.[154] With this system, the grade of a serous carcinoma is determined by the degree of nuclear atypia, the frequency of mitotic figures, and the extent to which the tumor cells form papillae or glands (Table 13A.6).[155,156]

Women with *BRCA 1* and *BRCA 2* mutations are at increased risk of developing ovarian cancer. Approximately 10 percent of ovarian carcinomas occur in women with germ-line mutations of *BRCA1* or *BRCA2*. Most of the cancers that develop in women with *BRCA* mutations are of serous type; other common types of ovarian cancer, such as clear cell carcinoma and mucinous carcinoma, are rare in this group of patients.[157] Many patients with *BRCA* mutations or with a family history of ovarian cancer are treated by risk-reducing bilateral salpingo-oophorectomy, which has been shown to lower the patient's risk of developing carcinoma.[158–160] Cancer risk is not eliminated as these patients are still at risk for peritoneal serous carcinoma and for breast cancer.[159,161,162] Microscopic foci of carcinoma in situ or invasive carcinoma and even macroscopic carcinomas are detected in 2–18 percent of asymptomatic women.[158,159,163–166] Most of the carcinomas

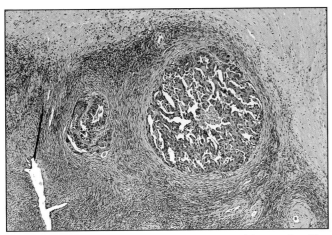

Fig. 13A.14 • Microscopic high grade serous carcinoma of the ovary found in a risk-reducing oophorectomy in a woman with a *BRCA* mutation. The tumor measured less than 1 mm in diameter.

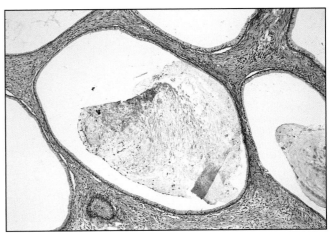

Fig. 13A.15 • Mucinous cystadenoma. This multilocular cystic neoplasm is lined by a single layer of columnar mucinous cells.

found in prophylactic salpingo-oophorectomy specimens are of serous type, measure only a few millimeters in diameter, and are of high grade (Fig. 13A.14).[147,166] The tumors can arise in either the ovary or the fallopian tube or be present in both sites.[164] Thorough sectioning of both ovaries and fallopian tubes is essential to identify small foci of neoplasia.[167,168] Immunohistochemical staining for *p53* protein can facilitate the identification of small foci of neoplasia. Large, clinically detected tumors in *BRCA* mutation carriers are mainly high grade serous carcinomas, although other types occasionally occur.[157,169–171] Patients with *BRCA* mutations also have an increased number of primary fallopian tube carcinomas, mainly of serous type, compared with reference populations.[157]

Psammoma bodies are small laminated calcifications that form around products of cellular degeneration.[172] They are often present in serous tumors, particularly serous carcinomas, and are occasionally numerous. Psammoma bodies may be so numerous in rare low-grade invasive serous carcinomas that they obscure the epithelial elements of the tumor. Such carcinomas, termed serous psammocarcinomas, have a highly favorable prognosis when they can be excised completely.[173–175] Similar tumors can arise as primary neoplasms of the peritoneum.[176] The prognosis for high-grade serous carcinoma with numerous psammoma bodies is unfavorable and they are excluded from the "psammocarcinoma" category. While psammoma bodies are suggestive of a serous tumor, they can also be found in association with such non-neoplastic conditions as epithelial inclusion cysts and endosalpingiosis.

Mucinous tumors

Mucinous cystadenoma is the most common ovarian mucinous tumor; it is about equal in incidence to serous cystadenoma. Borderline and malignant mucinous tumors are less numerous than their serous counterparts, and borderline mucinous tumors outnumber mucinous carcinomas.

Benign mucinous tumors

Mucinous cystadenoma is generally unilateral. The average diameter is about 10 cm, but huge tumors have been reported.[177] The cut surface reveals unilocular or multilocular mucin-filled

cysts of varying size. Mucinous adenofibroma is a predominantly solid, white or tan, fibrous tumor that contains small mucin-filled cysts. Mucinous cystadenofibroma is a cystic tumor that has solid fibrous areas similar to a mucinous adenofibroma.

Microscopically, a layer of columnar cells lines the cysts, papillae, and crypt-like structures that are found in benign mucinous tumors (Fig. 13A.15). A majority of the tumor cells are endocervical-like or gastric-like, with uniform round or oval basal nuclei and clear or amphophilic cytoplasm (Fig. 13A.16). Stains for acid mucins and, to a lesser extent, neutral mucins color the cytoplasm. Intestinal-type epithelium with goblet cells or Paneth cells is present in many mucinous cystadenomas. Histochemical and immunohistochemical studies reveal argyrophilic cells that contain a variety of peptide hormones. Gastric and pancreaticobiliary antigens and mucins are expressed by the columnar cells in most mucinous tumors,[178,179] while expression of intestinal antigens predominates in intestinal-type epithelial cells.[180,181] Peripheral bands of luteinized stromal cells or Leydig cells are noted occasionally around a mucinous cystadenoma.[182] This finding can be associated with clinical evidence of steroid hormone secretion. Mucinous adenofibroma or cystadenofibroma has an abundant

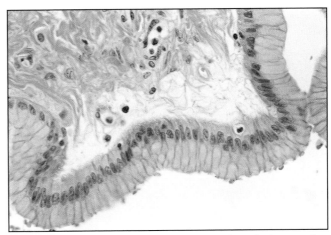

Fig. 13A.16 • Mucinous cystadenoma. The cyst is lined by tall columnar cells with clear cytoplasm and bland basal nuclei.

fibrous stroma that surrounds the glands and dominates the histologic picture.[183,184] An occasional mucinous cystadenoma or adenofibroma has small foci of mild to moderate nuclear atypia or nuclear stratification. When these involve only a few low power fields (≤5–10 percent of the tumor) the clinical evolution is invariably benign. Such tumors are best classified as a mucinous cystadenoma, cystadenofibroma, or adenofibroma with focal low-grade atypia.

Borderline mucinous tumors

Borderline mucinous tumors are usually unilateral.[42,185,186] The 5 percent of borderline mucinous tumors that are bilateral are mainly endocervical-like (also known as müllerian or seromucinous) borderline mucinous tumors.[5] Borderline mucinous tumors are large, with an average diameter of about 15 cm. Most are multilocular, although occasional tumors are unilocular or paucilocular.[185] The cysts are filled with mucin and have a smooth or velvety lining. Intracystic papillae are uncommon in intestinal borderline mucinous tumors, but may be seen in müllerian, or endocervical-like, borderline mucinous tumors. A variable amount of fibrous stroma surrounds the cysts.

Microscopically, two types of borderline mucinous tumors are recognized.[187] Intestinal-type borderline mucinous tumors (IBMT) are by far the most common.[10] The growth pattern tends to be complicated, with crowding of glands and formation of secondary cysts, complex glands, and papillae supported by thin cores of fibrovascular connective tissue (Fig. 13A.17).[188,189] Endocervical-like cells may be present, but goblet cells and cells resembling intestinal absorptive cells are conspicuous (Fig. 13A.18). There is evidence of proliferative activity with focal stratification of the cells into two or three layers.[29,186] The tumor cells have round to oval vesicular nuclei, which usually display mild to moderate atypia.[24] Nucleoli may be prominent, and there are occasional mitotic figures. Non-invasive mucinous tumors with marked nuclear atypia are designated as borderline tumors with intraepithelial carcinoma.[190,191] The risk of recurrence or metastasis is low in a well studied non-invasive mucinous tumor.[190–193] The rare tumors that do metastasize tend to be borderline mucinous tumors with intraepithelial

carcinoma.[191] Metastasis most likely reflects the presence of a small undetected focus of invasive carcinoma in a large predominantly borderline neoplasm.

Foci of stromal microinvasion less than 3 mm in diameter occur in 5–10 percent of IBMT.[90,194] Microinvasive clusters of tumor cells or small complex glands are surrounded by inflamed or edematous stroma, a desmoplastic stromal reaction, or by clear spaces. Most patients with microinvasion have a favorable prognosis,[90,190,191,194] but rare patients develop metastases.[195]

Acellular pseudomyxoma ovarii is a condition in which the cysts or glands rupture, releasing acellular mucin into the surrounding ovarian stroma (Fig. 13A.19). The pools of extravasated mucin are often surrounded by histiocytes and multinucleated foreign body giant cells, and the mucin can organize, with ingrowth of fibroblasts and blood vessels. Cellular pseudomyxoma ovarii, in which the pools of mucin contain clusters and strips of epithelial cells, is found mainly in patients with pseudomyxoma peritonei, and is an unfavorable prognostic finding.[186,196]

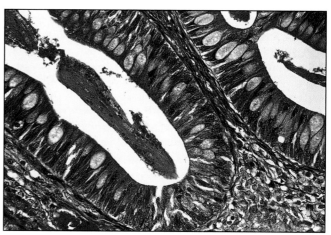

Fig. 13A.18 • Borderline mucinous tumor, intestinal type. Some tumor cells have dense eosinophilic cytoplasm and resemble intestinal absorptive cells, whereas others are goblet cells, with conspicuous cytoplasmic mucin vacuoles. The nuclei are hyperchromatic and are stratified into two to three layers.

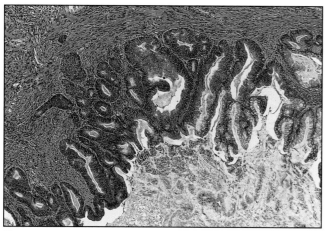

Fig. 13A.17 • Borderline mucinous tumor, intestinal type. Mucinous epithelium lines complicated glands and papillae. Note the absence of stromal invasion.

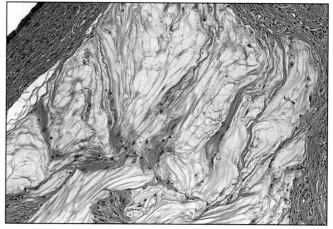

Fig. 13A.19 • Acellular pseudomyxoma ovarii. Pools of acellular mucin are present within the stroma.

Patients with extraovarian spread have an unfavorable prognosis. Rare patients have invasive glandular implants on the peritoneum or omentum, but the typical form of extraovarian tumor is as pseudomyxoma peritonei. Pseudomyxoma peritonei is a progressive condition in which deposits of mucin containing strips of bland epithelium undergo fibrous organization, adhere to and dissect into the omentum and peritoneum, and eventually fill the abdomen. Mucinous tumors having the appearance of IBMT tumors are frequently associated with pseudomyxoma peritonei, but the current view is that nearly all of the ovarian tumors found in this setting are secondary to primary neoplasms of the appendix or colon. Pseudomyxoma peritonei is discussed in more detail in the section on metastatic tumors.

Endocervical-like borderline mucinous tumors (EBMT), also known as müllerian mucinous or seromucinous borderline tumors, comprise 5–15 percent of borderline mucinous tumors.[29,186,197–200] They have a branching papillary growth pattern reminiscent of a borderline serous tumor (Fig. 13A.20).[200,201] The cysts and papillae are lined by columnar mucinous endocervical-like cells and a variable number of cells with eosinophilic cytoplasm (Fig. 13A.21). Foci of endometrioid and serous differentiation are commonly present and tufts of polygonal indifferent cells having abundant eosinophilic cytoplasm are often present at the tips of the papillae, from which clusters of cells detach into the cyst lumen. Neither goblet cells nor intestinal absorptive-type cells are present. Mitotic figures are infrequent in most tumors and there is usually minimal nuclear atypia. There is greater nuclear atypia and mitotic activity in a few EMBT, and these are designated as showing intraepithelial carcinoma.[199–201] Polymorphonuclear leukocytes infiltrate the luminal mucin, the epithelium, and the stroma. Endometriosis is found in the ovary adjacent to the tumor in 30 percent or more of cases.[197] Stromal microinvasion of less than 3 mm in maximum dimension is present occasionally in EBMT.[199–201] Clusters of eosinophilic or pale

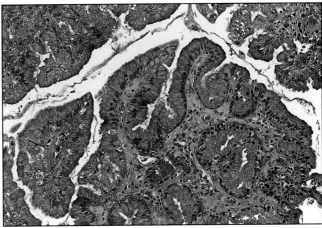

Fig. 13A.21 • Borderline mucinous tumor, endocervical-like. The papillae are covered by columnar cells with basal nuclei and abundant mucin-filled cytoplasm.

cells, usually with little surrounding reaction, are found within the stroma in 15–30 percent of EBMT.[90,194,199,200] EBMT are frequently bilateral and peritoneal implants are present in 20–30 percent of cases. The implants are generally of the non-invasive epithelial type, and frequently are surrounded by desmoplastic stroma. The prognosis is similar to that of a borderline serous tumor, with a benign evolution even when non-invasive extraovarian tumor implants are present.[29,197,201] Neither intraepithelial carcinoma nor stromal microinvasion has been associated with an unfavorable outcome.[199,200]

The immunophenotype of EBMT differs from that of IBMT. Both types of borderline mucinous tumors stain for cytokeratin 7, but only IBMT shows positive staining for cytokeratin 20,[202] and, in about 40 percent of cases, for CDX-2. Immunostains for carcinoembryonic antigen are often strongly and diffusely positive in IBMT. EBMT is less likely to stain, and when it does, often only the eosinophilic cells are reactive.[203] EBMT expresses estrogen and progesterone receptors, which are absent in IBMT.[204] Argyrophilic cells are found in more than 50 percent of intestinal-type borderline mucinous tumors, and immunohistochemical stains reveal peptides such as serotonin, ACTH, synaptophysin, glucagon, gastrin, and chromogranin in them.[178,180,198,205–209]

Mucinous carcinoma

Mucinous carcinoma is a large multilocular cystic tumor averaging 15–20 cm in diameter.[188,210] Firm, fleshy, white or tan solid areas may be present, and foci of hemorrhage or necrosis are often identified, particularly in larger tumors. Bilaterality and surface growth occur in fewer than 10 percent of cases,[185] but rupture of the capsule is frequent because of the large size and mucin content of these tumors. Bilateral or small (≤10 cm) mucinous carcinomas are likely to be metastatic, while large unilateral mucinous carcinomas are likely to be primary.[211]

Microscopically, the glands and cysts are crowded and complex with irregular infoldings and protrusions into the surrounding stroma (Fig. 13A.22). Intestinal-type cells predominate in most mucinous carcinomas. The cells are columnar, have eosinophilic cytoplasm, and tend to stratify into two or more layers (Fig. 13A.23). The nuclei are enlarged and vesicular and have coarse chromatin and prominent nucleoli. Mitotic

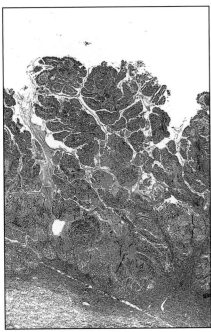

Fig. 13A.20 • Borderline mucinous tumor, endocervical-like. Complex, branching papillae grow into the lumen.

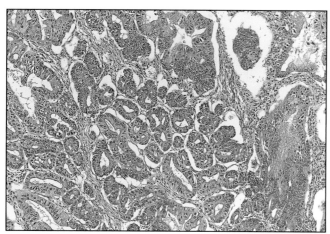

Fig.13A.22 • Mucinous carcinoma. Confluent pattern of growth with back-to-back glands, some surrounded by clear spaces.

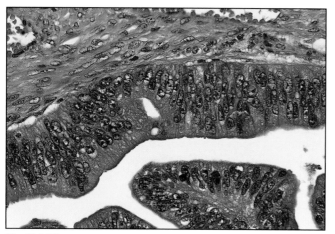

Fig. 13A.23 • Mucinous carcinoma. Most of the cells have dense eosinophilic cytoplasm. The nuclei are stratified, large and vesicular with coarse chromatin, and some contain prominent nucleoli.

figures range from few to many, and atypical mitotic figures are often noted. Goblet cells and argyrophilic cells may be present. Borderline and benign-appearing mucinous epithelia are frequently present in mucinous carcinomas, most often in those that are low grade. Some mucinous carcinomas lack intestinal differentiation and contain a prominent component of endocervical-like cells.[200,201,212] These are malignant counterparts of endocervical-like borderline mucinous tumors. The tumor cells line glands, cysts and papillae. There is a prominent component of columnar cells with mucinous cytoplasm that resemble endocervical cells, although other patterns of differentiation, especially endometrioid, are also commonly present.[212] The immunophenotype is similar to that of endocervical-like borderline mucinous tumors, with strong staining for cytokeratin 7 and for estrogen and progesterone receptors, and absent, or at most weak, staining for cytokeratin 20.[212] These tumors may be less aggressive than those in which intestinal-type cells predominate, although too few examples have been studied to be certain, and deaths due to tumor have been reported.[200,213]

The criteria for diagnosing mucinous carcinoma and for differentiating well-differentiated mucinous carcinoma from a borderline mucinous tumor were controversial in the past, but there is now general agreement that only tumors that show stromal invasion by irregular cords and nests of tumor cells ("destructive stromal invasion") or confluent expansile nodules of back-to-back glands or papillae should be diagnosed as mucinous carcinoma.[8,191] The pathologist should note which type of invasion is present in the pathology report, as the risk of recurrence is greater if destructive stromal invasion is present.[187,190,214] An exclusively confluent pattern of invasion does not, however, guarantee that there will be no recurrence.[195] Destructive stromal invasion can be difficult to identify in complex mucinous tumors, and other criteria have been proposed for the diagnosis of carcinoma in the absence of invasion.[188,215] Features such as cellular stratification into 4 or more layers, limited cribriform growth, papillae without stromal cores, and marked nuclear atypia suggest that a neoplasm may be a carcinoma but are not, by themselves, diagnostic. If such features are present in a tumor in which no invasion is identified then more thorough microscopic evaluation is warranted. At present, stromal invasion is the only criterion for classifying an ovarian mucinous tumor as a carcinoma. Tumors in which invasion is not identified are best classified as borderline tumors, noting when appropriate that they show features of intraepithelial carcinoma. Clinicians should be informed that there is a low risk of recurrence or metastasis in such cases, particularly if the tumor has been sampled inadequately.[29]

Mucinous carcinoma is generally cytokeratin 7 positive,[129,216,217] like other primary ovarian epithelial neoplasms (see Table 13A.5). A majority stain for cytokeratin 20, but staining tends to be patchy and of weak to moderate intensity,[218,219] in contrast with the diffuse strong positive staining seen in metastatic colorectal adenocarcinoma. Mucinous carcinoma can stain for CDX-2,[218] but staining for this antibody is still being evaluated in ovarian mucinous tumors. Some primary mucinous carcinomas do not stain for CDX-2,[220] while others stain less extensively and intensely than metastatic colorectal adenocarcinomas.[216,221,222]

Several unusual variants of mucinous carcinoma have been described. *Mural nodules* of "sarcoma-like" connective tissue, sarcoma, or anaplastic carcinoma occasionally occur in mucinous tumors, usually borderline tumors or carcinomas.[223,224] Reactive mural nodules tend to be circumscribed, measure up to 5 cm, and can be single, or, more often, multiple. They consist of spindle shaped fibroblasts, myofibroblasts, and possibly submesothelial cells, histiocytes, inflammatory cells, and occasional multinucleated cells. Three subtypes have been described: an epulis-like type composed of mononuclear stromal cells and multinucleated giant cells; a pleomorphic type, composed of spindle cells and giant cells; and a histiocytic type.[225] The stroma is typically edematous with foci of hemorrhage and necrosis. Immunostains for vimentin and CD68 are positive. Cytokeratin is expressed in a weak and focal pattern if at all, in contrast to the diffuse strong staining typical of carcinoma.[225–227] Mural nodules of anaplastic carcinoma can be single or multiple, and range from less than 1 cm to more than 10 cm in diameter. The nodules have an infiltrative border and consist of nests and sheets of undifferentiated polygonal epithelial cells or sheets and fascicles of malignant spindle cells (Fig. 13A.24).[190,228–232] Mitotic figures are numerous and may be abnormal. Immunoreactivity for cytokeratin or epithelial membrane antigen is an important diagnostic finding. Rare carcinosarcoma-like nodules have

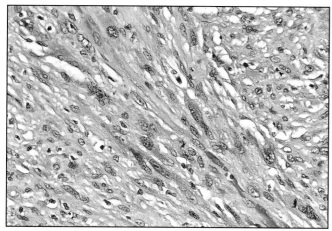

Fig. 13A.24 • Sarcomatoid carcinoma growing as a mural nodule in the wall of a mucinous tumor. This spindle cell neoplasm arose from a mucinous carcinoma. The tumor cells were strongly cytokeratin positive, indicating that this is an area of sarcomatoid carcinoma, not a true sarcoma.

also been reported.[233] Mural nodules of sarcoma are composed of malignant spindle cells, and usually resemble fibrosarcoma or undifferentiated sarcoma.[234,235] The tumor cells are cytokeratin-negative, but positive for vimentin and, depending on the type of sarcoma, may stain for other intermediate filaments such as actin or desmin.

Foci of neuroendocrine carcinoma occasionally evolve within a mucinous tumor, most commonly a mucinous carcinoma.[236–240] The tumor cells may be small, with dark nuclei, fine chromatin, and scanty cytoplasm similar to small cell carcinoma of the lung; or be larger, with dark or vesicular large nuclei, nucleoli, and more abundant cytoplasm similar to pulmonary large cell neuroendocrine carcinoma. Immunohistochemical staining for neuron specific enolase, chromogranin, synaptophysin or other markers of neuroendocrine differentiation can aid in correctly categorizing the small cell component. Electron microscopy can be used to demonstrate neuroendocrine granules in the tumor cell cytoplasm. Individual neuroendocrine cells or microscopic nests of neuroendocrine cells in the glands or stroma of a mucinous tumor may be the site of origin of such neuroendocrine carcinomas.[241] Neuroendocrine carcinoma appears clinically aggressive, based on the few reported cases.

Endometrioid tumors

Endometrioid tumors of the ovary have an epithelial component that resembles proliferative, hyperplastic, or malignant endometrium. Benign and borderline endometrioid tumors are rare. Rare examples of borderline endometrioid tumors have been reported to shed tumor cells into the peritoneal fluid or to spread beyond the ovary, but the clinical outcome has been uniformly favorable.[27,184,242–244] One report made note of a few patients treated by unilateral salpingo-oophorectomy who developed endometrioid carcinomas in the contralateral ovary.[27] Endometrioid carcinoma, which histologically resembles endometrial adenocarcinoma, is the second most common type of ovarian adenocarcinoma, comprising 12–30 percent of all malignant epithelial tumors of the ovary.[5,245,246] Endometrioid carcinoma has a favorable prognosis, relative to other types of adenocarcinoma of the ovary.[245,247] Low grade stage I

endometrioid carcinomas with confluent invasive growth only rarely progress, although those with a destructive pattern of invasion can be more aggressive, as are higher grade tumors.[214,243] Endometrioid carcinoma commonly occurs in women with endometriosis and as many as a third of endometrioid carcinomas arise in, or adjacent to, endometriosis, with possibly a greater risk in patients with atypical endometriosis.[245,248–251] Endometriosis-associated tumors occur in younger women, present at an earlier stage, and may be less aggressive than endometrioid carcinoma of surface epithelial origin.[248,249,252–254]

Benign endometrioid tumors

Benign endometrioid tumors are all adenofibromas and they comprise about 10 percent of ovarian adenofibromas.[184,255] They are solid fibrous tumors that average 8–10 cm in diameter. The cut surfaces are tan or white and contain small cysts ranging from a few millimeters to several centimeters in diameter. Microscopically, tubular or cystic glands are surrounded and separated by fibrous stroma (Fig. 13A.25). The glands are lined by a single layer of endometrial-type cells. These are columnar, with basophilic or amphophilic cytoplasm and uniform round or oval nuclei. The nuclei may be pseudostratified, as in proliferative endometrium, but mitotic figures are usually rare or absent. Squamous metaplasia may be present and, in rare tumors, the glands are lined by ciliated cells.[255,256] In one unusual case, a vaginal recurrence detected six weeks after removal of an ovarian endometrioid adenofibroma was attributed to surgical implantation.[184]

Borderline endometrioid tumors

Various names were used for borderline endometrioid tumors in the past, resulting in a confusing body of literature on this subject. Russell and Roth et al. used the name "proliferating" endometrioid tumors.[27,255] Kao & Norris designated the tumors which they reported "adenofibromas with epithelial atypia".[257] Bell & Scully divided the borderline endometrioid adenofibromas which they studied into two groups, which they called "atypical" and "borderline".[258] Snyder et al. and Norris grouped borderline endometrioid tumors into "proliferative"

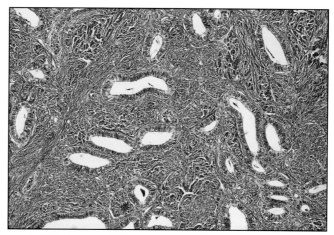

Fig. 13A.25 • Endometrioid adenofibroma. Glands lined by a single layer of benign endometrial-type cells grow in dense fibrous stroma.

and "low malignant potential" categories.[242,259] This author's preference is to include all of these in the category of borderline endometrioid tumors, as has been done in the most recent WHO classification.[8] At the low end of the spectrum of borderline endometrioid tumors are adenofibromas in which the glandular component resembles simple hyperplasia of the endometrium. In the middle are adenofibromas in which glands are more crowded and irregular, as seen in complex hyperplasia of the endometrium. The epithelium in the highest-grade borderline endometrioid tumors exhibits about the same degree of proliferative activity and nuclear atypia as is seen in complex atypical hyperplasia of the endometrium.

Borderline endometrioid tumors are usually unilateral (only 8 percent were bilateral in one recent series) and many are adenofibromas or cystadenofibromas.[243] They are typically predominantly solid, but some, especially higher grade tumors, contain cysts. The average diameter is 6–10 cm and the cut surfaces are tan or white. Papillary excrescences are grossly visible within the cysts in some tumors. Microscopically, low grade borderline endometrioid tumors are adenofibromas with glands of increased density relative to benign endometrioid tumors, showing varied architecture and focal crowding.[260] There may be small foci of cribriform growth or limited areas in which the glands are closely packed. The epithelial cell nuclei are pseudostratified or stratified, there is mild to moderate nuclear atypia, and occasional mitotic figures are present (≤3 per 10 high power fields). Higher grade borderline endometrioid tumors exhibit two main patterns of growth.[27,242,258,260] Some are adenofibromas with increased glandular density; conspicuous areas of glandular crowding (Fig. 13A.26), usually exceeding 5 mm in diameter; foci of cribriform growth; and prominent nuclear atypia, stratification, and mitotic activity. The second pattern is one of papillary growth into cystic spaces. The papillae often have a villoglandular appearance with broad fibrovascular cores. The cells covering the papillae show variable degrees of stratification and atypia. Mitotic activity is usually low (≤3 per 10 high power fields) but, in some tumors, mitotic figures are more frequent. Proliferative activity can be conspicuous in borderline endometrioid tumors but the degree of glandular crowding is usually less than in

endometrioid carcinoma and the proliferative nests have a smooth contour and are surrounded by stroma. Squamous and mucinous metaplasia are common, particularly in adenofibromatous tumors,[243] and rare neoplasms contain numerous ciliated cells.[256] Endometriosis is often present in the involved ovary and elsewhere in the pelvis, and an origin from endometriosis can be demonstrated in occasional cases.[242,243,255] Stromal microinvasion is seen in 5–15 percent of borderline endometrioid tumors, in which small irregular glands infiltrate the stroma or there are foci of confluent glandular growth in an area less than 3 mm in diameter.[242,243,258,260] No patients with microinvasion have had recurrences.

Endometrioid carcinoma

Endometrioid carcinoma is a cystic and solid or completely solid tumor, typically measuring 10–20 cm in diameter.[245,261,262] The solid areas can be firm or soft, and are gray or tan. Areas of hemorrhage and necrosis are common. Only 10–20 percent are bilateral.[5]

Endometrioid carcinoma is a glandular or papillary tumor that resembles adenocarcinoma of the endometrium. The growth pattern is glandular, papillary, or a mixture of the two, and invasion can take the form of haphazard infiltration of the stroma or confluent growth.[243] The glands tend to be small and relatively uniform in size and shape (Fig. 13A.27). The papillae often have a villoglandular appearance, with prominent fibrovascular supporting cores. The glands and papillae are lined by columnar cells with amphophilic to basophilic cytoplasm. The nuclei are basally located, round or oval, and may contain nucleoli (Fig. 13A.28). The degree of atypia, the amount of nuclear stratification and the extent to which the glands coalesce into foci of solid growth increase as the grade increases. Endometrioid carcinoma can be graded using the same criteria as endometrial adenocarcinoma.[263] Grade I tumors grow in a glandular or papillary pattern with less than 5 percent of solid tumor growth. Grade II tumors show 5–50 percent solid growth, and grade III tumors show more than 50 percent solid tumor growth. Areas of squamous or spindle cell differentiation are not counted in the determination

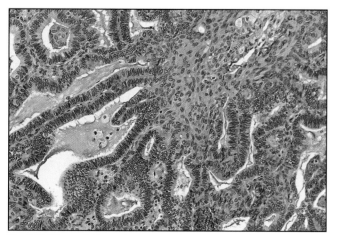

Fig. 13A.26 • Borderline endometrioid tumor. The glandular pattern is similar to that seen in complex hyperplasia of the endometrium. The tumor cell nuclei show only mild atypia. Note the immature squamous metaplasia in the center of the field.

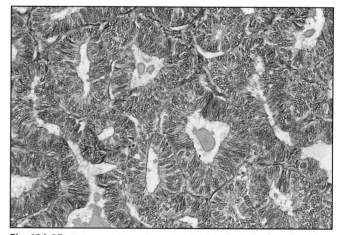

Fig. 13A.27 • Endometrioid carcinoma. The back-to-back glands are lined by columnar cells with stratified hyperchromatic nuclei.

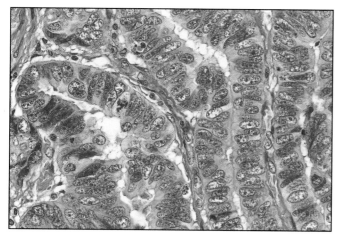

Fig. 13A.28 • Endometrioid carcinoma. The cells lining the glands in this moderately differentiated adenocarcinoma have an increased nuclear to cytoplasmic ratio. The nuclei are round or oval, and have coarse chromatin. Some contain one or more prominent nucleoli. Note the atypical mitotic figure to the left of the center of the field.

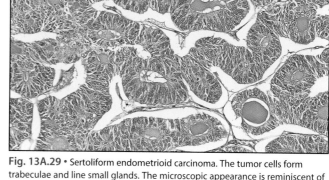

Fig. 13A.29 • Sertoliform endometrioid carcinoma. The tumor cells form trabeculae and line small glands. The microscopic appearance is reminiscent of a Sertoli cell tumor, but the nuclei show greater stratification and atypia than is typical in Sertoli cell tumor.

of percentage of solid growth. If the nuclei are grade III and the growth pattern is grade I or II, the final grade is increased by one level. Endometrioid carcinoma can also be graded using the previously discussed "universal grading system" for ovarian cancer (see Table 13A.6).[154]

Foci of squamous differentiation, which can be either cytologically benign or malignant, are present in 25–50 percent of endometrioid carcinomas. Keratin granulomas, which the surgeon may mistake for tumor implants, are found occasionally on the peritoneum in such patients.[264] Endometrioid carcinomas with a mixed clear cell carcinoma component are reported by some to have a worse prognosis,[261,265] as are endometrioid carcinomas mixed with serous or undifferentiated carcinoma.[266] Consequently, it is important for the pathologist to state whether an endometrioid carcinoma is pure or mixed with other types of surface epithelial tumors.

There are several unusual and potentially confusing variants of endometrioid carcinoma, some of which mimic sex cord-stromal tumors. A *microglandular* pattern is uncommon in endometrioid carcinoma, but when present, the carcinoma can be mistaken for a granulosa cell tumor.[267] *Sertoliform* endometrioid carcinomas have prominent areas in which the tumor cells grow in long, branching, tubular glands or trabeculae (Fig. 13A.29).[267–269] This variant mimics a Sertoli or Sertoli-Leydig cell tumor, particularly when the stroma is abundant and fibrous and luteinized stromal cells are present. The *oxyphilic* variant of endometrioid carcinoma has a prominent component of large polygonal tumor cells with abundant eosinophilic cytoplasm and round central nuclei that contain large nucleoli.[270] The tumor cells grow in nests and sheets or line tubular glands. The *spindle cell* variant has a prominent component of bland spindle cells. The combination of ribbons and cords of tumor cells admixed with lobulated nests of spindle cells can resemble a sex cord-stromal tumor.[271] Clinical, microscopic, and immunohistologic features all serve to differentiate these variants of endometrioid carcinoma from a sex cord-stromal tumor. They occur in peri- or postmenopausal women, and are seldom associated with clinical evidence of steroid hormone production. Grossly, they usually lack the golden or yellow appearance of the cut surface that typifies a

sex cord-stromal tumor, and they may be bilateral. Microscopically, careful search usually reveals foci of typical endometrioid carcinoma, as well as squamous metaplasia or adenofibromatous regions. Endometrioid carcinoma is strongly immunoreactive for cytokeratin (CK) and epithelial membrane antigen (EMA).[272,273] Most are non-reactive for inhibin (I) and calretinin (CR),[269,274] although rare inhibin- or calretinin-positive endometrioid carcinomas have been reported.[275] Sertoli and Sertoli-Leydig cell tumors stain for cytokeratin, as do about one-third of granulosa cell tumors, but sex cord-stromal tumors are almost invariably negative for epithelial membrane antigen and strongly positive for inhibin and calretinin.[274] Thus, the immunophenotype CK$^+$, EMA$^+$, I$^-$, CR$^-$ favors endometrioid carcinoma, while the immunophenotype CK$^+$, EMA$^-$, I$^+$, CR$^+$ favors a sex cord-stromal tumor.

Rare tumors have been described in which there is a mixture of endometrioid carcinoma and yolk sac tumor.[276,277] These occur in the same age group as endometrioid carcinoma, are large, and have an unfavorable prognosis. Immunostains for α-fetoprotein are strongly positive in the yolk sac tumor component and, together with the histologic appearance, serve to identify it.

Endometrioid adenocarcinoma is found in the endometrium in 10–20 percent of women with ovarian endometrioid carcinoma (Fig. 13A.30).[245,248,261,278,279] The endometrial cancer is usually superficial and well-differentiated and the survival rate is high when the carcinomas are confined to the uterus and ovary.[279–283] In this setting, the ovarian and endometrial carcinomas are more compatible with separate, synchronous primary tumors than with advanced endometrial adenocarcinoma with ovarian metastasis or advanced ovarian cancer with endometrial metastasis.[279,280] However, in some patients with simultaneous tumors, the ovarian neoplasm is a metastasis from the endometrial carcinoma. Features that suggest that the ovarian carcinoma might be metastatic include: the endometrial carcinoma is high grade or deeply invasive; there is myometrial or ovarian hilar lymphatic vascular invasion; carcinoma is present within the lumen of the fallopian tube; the ovarian tumor is small; the ovarian tumor is multinodular and solid; the ovarian tumor is bilateral; surface implants are present on the ovary;

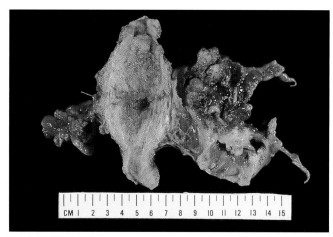

Fig. 13A.30 • Synchronous endometrioid carcinoma of the ovary (right) and endometrial adenocarcinoma.

and extraovarian metastases are present in a distribution characteristic of endometrial adenocarcinoma (i.e., lymph node metastases more likely than peritoneal metastases).[280,284] Molecular diagnostic techniques may provide more definitive information but, at this time, they are not practical for routine clinical use.[285-290] Problems that need to be resolved include discordance of molecular and clinicopathologic findings in some cases and the occasional lack of informative results.

Mixed mesodermal tumor, adenosarcoma, and endometrioid stromal sarcoma

Mixed mesodermal tumor (MMT), or carcinosarcoma, and endometrioid stromal sarcoma arise from endometriosis or by metaplasia. Adenosarcoma can arise directly from ovarian epithelium and stroma, or in endometriosis. The clinical behavior of these tumors is similar to that of their more frequent uterine counterparts.

Mixed mesodermal tumor and adenosarcoma

Mixed mesodermal tumor, also termed carcinosarcoma, occurs predominantly in postmenopausal women of low parity.[291-293] The most common symptoms are pelvic or abdominal pain, abdominal distention, bowel symptoms, and weight loss.[294,295] The serum concentration of CA 125 is usually elevated. Most patients have a palpable adnexal mass and many have ascites. More than 70 percent of MMT have spread beyond the ovaries at diagnosis.[296] The pattern of spread, as in ovarian carcinoma, is primarily to the peritoneum, omentum and regional lymph nodes.[292,294,297,298] Treatment is by hysterectomy, bilateral salpingo-oophorectomy, and excision of as much extraovarian tumor as possible. Patients with disease of limited extent should be thoroughly staged. The prognosis is poor; in studies of more than 400 patients the median survival was only 6–12 months and more than 70 percent of patients were dead at one year.[293,299,300] In most studies there has been a poor response to chemotherapy and a worse prognosis than for comparably staged carcinomas,[300,301] although a few authors have reported a more favorable response to chemotherapy.[302,303] Nearly all patients eventually relapse, and the 5-year survival rate in some studies is less than 10 percent.[295,296,304] The stage

is the most important prognostic factor.[305,306] Histologic parameters, such as the type and grade of the carcinomatous and sarcomatous elements, do not appear to be of prognostic significance.[292,295,296,306] Rare patients present with early stage tumors (stage I–II); they have longer survival and are the most likely to be cured.[291,295,304,306,307]

Mixed mesodermal tumors tend to be large, with an average diameter of 15 cm.[308] They are either cystic and solid or entirely solid tumors. The solid portions are gray or tan, and areas of hemorrhage and necrosis are usually prominent. Microscopically, MMT is a biphasic neoplasm with intermixed epithelial and mesenchymal elements (Fig. 13A.31). The epithelial component can be any type of surface epithelial carcinoma, but serous, endometrioid, and undifferentiated carcinoma are most common.[292] The mesenchymal component is a pure sarcoma or a mixture of various types of sarcoma. Homologous sarcomatous elements include fibrosarcoma, leiomyosarcoma, and undifferentiated sarcoma. Heterologous elements, such as rhabdomyosarcoma, chondrosarcoma, or osteosarcoma, are present in a majority of ovarian MMTs (Fig. 13A.32).[291,308,309] Eosinophilic hyaline globules are often

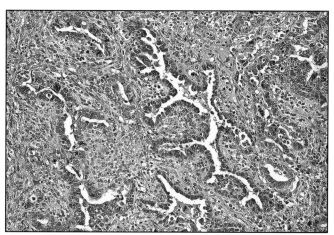

Fig 13A.31 • Mixed mesodermal tumor (carcinosarcoma). Irregular malignant glands are surrounded by sarcomatous stroma.

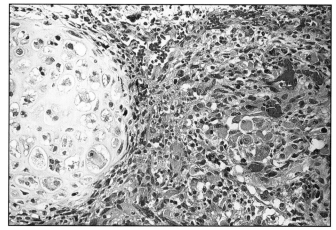

Fig. 13A.32 • Mixed mesodermal tumor (carcinosarcoma). Sarcomatous elements present in this example include chondrosarcoma and rhabdomyosarcoma. Atypical chondroid cells lie in the lacunae of the malignant cartilage on the left, while there are round rhabdomyoblasts with abundant eosinophilic cytoplasm on the right.

present in MMT, scattered among either the epithelial or mesenchymal cells.[292,310] These globules are periodic acid–Schiff- (PAS-) positive and a minority are immunoreactive for α_1-antitrypsin. Singular cases of MMT have been reported to show trophoblastic or neuroectodermal differentiation or to express α-fetoprotein.[311–313] Microscopic study of peritoneal and omental metastases present at diagnosis generally reveals a combination of carcinoma and sarcoma, while lymph node metastases are usually pure carcinoma.[291,298] Late metastases reportedly contain an increased proportion of the sarcomatous component or are entirely sarcomatous.[310,314–316]

Immunohistochemical stains can help differentiate the epithelial and mesenchymal components.[314,317,318] The epithelial components stain for cytokeratin and epithelial membrane antigen, while the mesenchymal components are vimentin-positive.[319,320] Immunostains for desmin and myogenin help in the identification of rhabdomyoblasts.[314,317,318,321]

Adenosarcoma occurs in younger women than MMT, the average age being in the mid-50s.[322] The symptoms are non-specific and most tumors are unilateral. In contrast with mixed mesodermal tumor, a majority of patients present with early stage tumors.[322] Adenosarcoma tends to recur within the pelvis and abdomen, and a majority of patients eventually die of tumor.[322,323] The role of postoperative radiation and chemotherapy has yet to be clearly defined.

Adenosarcoma is a large, partly cystic tumor 10–15 cm in diameter. Microscopically, it is a mixed tumor in which the mesenchymal component is malignant but the epithelium is benign.[322,323] The epithelium lines cysts, covers intracystic papillary or polypoid stromal excrescences, and lines elongated clefts and simple tubular glands in solid portions of the tumor. The epithelium ranges from indifferent cuboidal cells to columnar endometrioid or ciliated tubal-type cells. Foci of squamous or mucinous metaplasia are present in some tumors. The mesenchymal component is usually fibrosarcoma or endometrioid stromal stroma, although heterologous sarcomatous elements, such as rhabdomyosarcoma or chondrosarcoma, are present occasionally. The stroma tends to be hypercellular beneath the cyst lining and around the glands, and less cellular and more collagenous away from them. The degree of nuclear atypia is usually mild or moderate. Mitotic figures are invariably present, and usually number four or more per 10 high power fields. Sex cord-like differentiation is occasionally present within the stroma, and a minority of adenosarcomas exhibit sarcomatous overgrowth, in which epithelium is absent and there is diffuse growth of malignant cellular stroma. Recurrent tumor can be either pure sarcoma or adenosarcoma. Unfavorable prognostic findings include young age at diagnosis, tumor rupture, high grade sarcomatous elements, and sarcomatous overgrowth.[322]

Endometrioid stromal sarcoma

The uterus is the usual primary site for stromal sarcoma, but it can arise in extrauterine sites, including the ovaries.[324] The average patient is 50–55 years old and presents with abdominal distention or pain.[325–328] Extraovarian spread is often present at diagnosis. Women with low grade stromal sarcoma have a relatively favorable short-term prognosis, but a significant percentage of tumors recur, including a substantial number more than 5 years after diagnosis, and some patients die of

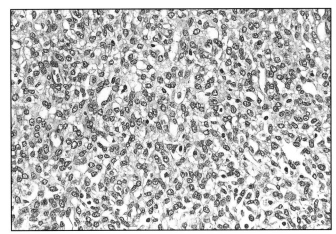

Fig. 13A.33 • Low grade endometrioid stromal sarcoma. The tumor cells have uniform small bland nuclei and indistinct cytoplasmic borders.

tumor.[327,328] Analysis of the clinical evolution is difficult because of limited follow-up. The value of treatment with progesterone, radiotherapy, or chemotherapy is unclear, although there are anecdotal reports of favorable responses to progesterone therapy.[329] High-grade stromal sarcoma appears to pursue a more aggressive clinical course.

Stromal sarcoma averages 11 cm in diameter. Most tumors are solid or solid and cystic and have tan, yellow, or white cut surfaces with foci of hemorrhage or necrosis. Microscopically, low grade stromal sarcoma is composed of small cells that resemble proliferative phase endometrial stromal cells.[326–328,330,331] They have uniform round, oval, or spindled dark nuclei with fine chromatin and inconspicuous nucleoli (Fig. 13A.33). The cytoplasm is scanty and the cell borders are ill defined. Cytologic atypia is minimal, and mitotic figures are infrequent. Foci of epithelioid differentiation are occasionally noted.[328] Nests and cords of tumor cells infiltrate the ovarian parenchyma and lymphatic vascular invasion is prominent once the tumor invades beyond the ovary. An origin in (or association with) ovarian endometriosis can occasionally be demonstrated. High grade stromal sarcoma is composed of cells that are more atypical or that exhibit greater mitotic activity (≥ 10 mitotic figures per 10 high power fields).[327]

The main differential diagnostic considerations are endometrial stromal sarcoma of the uterus metastatic to the ovary and thecoma. Endometrial stromal sarcoma frequently invades the adnexa and extends to the ovary. Any woman with stromal sarcoma of the ovary should have careful evaluation of the uterus, and hysterectomy should be part of the surgical treatment.[327] Low grade stromal sarcoma may contain fibrous areas that mimic thecoma. Thorough histologic evaluation usually reveals areas typical of stromal sarcoma, and an immunohistochemical stain for inhibin, which is usually positive in a thecoma, is negative.

Clear cell tumors

Initially thought to be of mesonephric origin, clear cell tumors were shown by Scully & Barlow to arise from endometriosis or from the surface epithelium.[332] Most clear cell tumors are carcinomas, but benign and borderline clear cell tumors also occur.[27,184,257,333,334] Women with borderline clear cell tumors generally have a favorable prognosis, but exceptional patients develop metastases or die of their tumor.[42,334] More than 90 percent of clear cell tumors are carcinomas. This type of carcinoma comprises 5–10 percent of all ovarian cancers.[261,335–337] Survival rates that are favorable, or at least equivalent to those observed with other malignant epithelial tumors have been found in many studies of clear cell carcinoma, though this may be due to a high proportion of early stage tumors in some series.[261,337–343] The trend in recent reports has been to view clear cell carcinoma as an unfavorable histologic type, with a worse prognosis in advanced stages compared to other common epithelial tumors, and a poor response to platinum-based chemotherapy.[247,344–349] There is some suggestion that the combination of paclitaxel and platinum offers improved prognosis compared with previous platinum-based regimens.[350] Several paraneoplastic syndromes occur in women with clear cell carcinoma.[351] Clear cell carcinoma is more likely than other types of epithelial carcinoma to be associated with hypercalcemia,[344] and women with clear cell carcinoma also are more likely to have thromboembolic events such as deep venous thrombosis and pulmonary emboli.[345,346] In one report of a patient with hypercalcemia caused by metastatic clear cell carcinoma, parathyroid hormone-related protein was detected in the serum, the primary ovarian carcinoma and the metastases, providing a possible explanation for the hypercalcemia.[352]

Benign clear cell tumors

Benign clear cell tumors are unilateral solid tumors 3–15 cm in diameter. Small cysts can usually be identified on close inspection of the white or tan cut surfaces. Microscopically, all benign clear cell tumors are adenofibromas.[184,333,334] Small tubules or cysts are lined by cuboidal or hobnail cells with clear or granular eosinophilic cytoplasm (Fig. 13A.34). The stroma is composed of spindle-shaped fibroblasts and collagen bundles. There is no cytologic atypia or mitotic activity.

Borderline clear cell tumors

Borderline clear cell tumors are unilateral and predominantly solid. They typically measure 10–15 cm in diameter. The cut surface is white, gray, or tan and contains small to medium sized cysts. Microscopically, borderline clear cell tumors are adenofibromas.[27,333,334] Tubules and cysts lined by cuboidal or hobnail cells with clear or eosinophilic cytoplasm are irregularly distributed in a fibrous stroma. Occasionally, the epithelium is stratified or tufted, or grows as small solid circumscribed nests. The presence of mild to moderate nuclear atypia and scattered mitotic figures (usually ≤1 per 10 high power fields) differentiate a borderline clear cell tumor from a benign one. Rare clear cell tumors grow in a parvilocular pattern in which cysts lined by clear cells are surrounded by stroma. Most of these cases exhibit sufficient atypia or mitotic activity to be classified as borderline tumors. The absence of stromal invasion differentiates clear cell adenofibroma from clear cell carcinoma. Non-invasive clear cell adenofibromas with marked nuclear atypia or frequent mitotic figures can be classified as borderline tumors if that category is understood to include tumors with intraepithelial carcinoma. The diagnosis of a benign or borderline clear cell tumor should be made only after thorough histologic study, since bland-appearing areas are often seen in clear cell carcinoma.

Clear cell carcinoma

Most clear cell carcinomas are large tumors, ranging from 10 to 30 cm in diameter. They are solid or, more often, partly cystic, with solid gray-tan nodular areas in their walls. The cut surfaces are soft and tan or gray-white. Tumors that are confined to the ovaries (stage I) are usually unilateral, but when tumors of all stages are considered, about 30 percent are bilateral.

Microscopically, a variety of cell types are present, including clear cells, cells with granular eosinophilic cytoplasm, and hobnail cells with clear or eosinophilic cytoplasm (Fig. 13A.35).[261,332,335,336,338,340] Usually, a mixture of cell types is present. Clear cells are cuboidal, low columnar, or polygonal and have abundant clear cytoplasm, central vesicular nuclei and, usually, conspicuous nucleoli. PAS stains and electron microscopic studies reveal that they contain abundant

Fig. 13A.34 • Clear cell adenofibroma. Tubules and cysts lined by cuboidal to low columnar cells with clear cytoplasm are surrounded by fibrous stroma. Note the "hobnail" nuclei that bulge into the lumens.

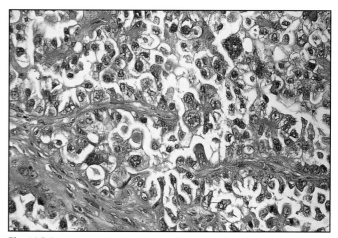

Fig. 13A.35 • Clear cell carcinoma. The tumor cells are cuboidal or columnar. Some have clear cytoplasm, whereas the cytoplasm is amphophilic and granular in others. The nuclei are atypical and pleomorphic. Some cells are "hobnail" cells, with apical nuclei that bulge into the lumen. Note the eosinophilic hyaline globule at left center.

cytoplasmic glycogen. Cells with eosinophilic cytoplasm are similar in size, shape, and nuclear features to the clear cells, but they have granular eosinophilic cytoplasm. Hobnail cells are columnar and have either granular eosinophilic or clear cytoplasm. They have hyperchromatic apical nuclei that bulge into the lumina. Mitotic activity tends to be lower in clear cell carcinoma than in other types of ovarian carcinoma; the low rate of cell proliferation has been proposed as one possible reason for the poor response to chemotherapy.[349] One group found that tumors with a high mitotic rate had a worse prognosis.[338]

The tumor cells grow in a variety of patterns in clear cell carcinoma and most tumors show a mixture of patterns. In some areas, the tumor cells line glands, tubules (Fig. 13A.36), or cysts, or form papillae. Ring-like tubules lined by cuboidal cells with clear cytoplasm and filled with eosinophilic secretions are particularly characteristic. Elsewhere, there are areas of solid growth composed of polygonal cells with clear or eosinophilic cytoplasm (Fig. 13A.37). Eosinophilic hyaline globules are often scattered among the tumor cells,[353] and amorphous eosinophilic hyaline material is a frequent finding in the stroma or the connective tissue cores of the papillae. The hyaline material appears to be basement membrane-like material, based

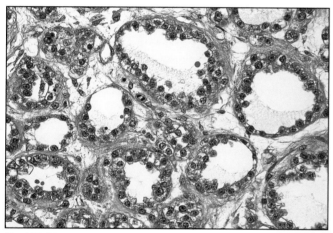

Fig. 13A.36 • Clear cell carcinoma, tubulocystic pattern. Tubules are lined by cuboidal cells with clear cytoplasm and atypical hyperchromatic nuclei.

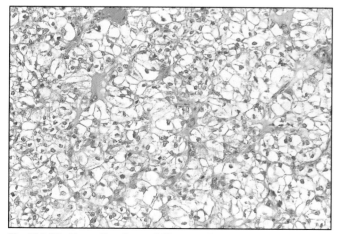

Fig. 13A.37 • Clear cell carcinoma. Diffuse growth of polygonal cells with abundant clear cytoplasm.

on its ultrastructural appearance and immunohistochemical staining for type IV collagen and laminin.[343,354,355] The rare oxyphilic clear cell carcinoma is composed predominantly of large polygonal cells with abundant eosinophilic cytoplasm.[356] Thorough sampling is necessary to reveal areas that are more typical of clear cell carcinoma, thereby establishing the diagnosis. Some clear cell carcinomas contain minor admixtures of endometrioid carcinoma or other types of surface epithelial carcinoma. Clear cell carcinoma can be graded using the universal grading system (see Table 13A.6), but histologic grading has not proven to be of prognostic value in most studies.[357]

Clear cell carcinoma is strongly associated with endometriosis, either within the involved ovary or elsewhere in the pelvis,[253,261,344,346,350] and occasional examples of clear cell carcinoma arise directly from endometriosis.[332,358] The percentage of cases associated with endometriosis, including atypical endometriosis, exceeds 50 percent in some series.[249,359]

Immunohistochemical stains are usually not required to diagnose clear cell carcinoma. Clear cell carcinoma stains for cytokeratin 7 (see Table 13A.5) and high molecular weight keratin, is cytokeratin 20 negative, and may stain for estrogen receptors.[360–362] In comparison, metastatic clear cell renal cell carcinoma is cytokeratin 7 and high molecular weight keratin negative and it is positive for CD10 and renal cell carcinoma antigen, both of which are negative in clear cell carcinoma of the ovary.[360,363] Yolk sac tumor can also occasionally pose differential diagnostic problems, although the clinical setting is usually sufficient to differentiate it from clear cell carcinoma (See p. 605). Yolk sac tumor does not stain for cytokeratin 7 or epithelial membrane antigen (EMA), but it shows patchy, usually weak, staining for alpha-fetoprotein.[364]

Brenner tumor and transitional cell carcinoma

Benign Brenner tumor

The Brenner tumor is a type of adenofibroma in which nests of transitional epithelium grow in a fibrous stroma.[365–371] Brenner tumors comprise around 2 percent of all ovarian tumors.[366] Most are small and are incidental findings.[371] About 20 percent occur together with a mucinous or serous cystadenoma or a benign cystic teratoma or some other form of benign teratoma such as a struma ovarii.[367,372–374]

Grossly, Brenner tumors are circumscribed, firm, pale yellow or gray-white, solid fibrous tumors. Foci of calcification are present in many of them. Occasional Brenner tumors are partly cystic and about 5 percent are bilateral.[371,375] The size ranges from microscopic to more than 10 cm, but they tend to be small; the average tumor measures only 1–2 cm. Microscopically, nests and cords of oval or polygonal epithelial cells resembling urothelial cells of the bladder grow in a fibrous stroma (Fig. 13A.38). The nuclei are round or oval and have small nucleoli. A longitudinal nuclear groove is often present, and is a characteristic feature of the Brenner tumor. The cytoplasm ranges from clear to dense and eosinophilic. Microcysts lined by transitional cells or metaplastic columnar endocervical-like mucinous cells occasionally develop within the cell nests, and there are occasional foci of squamous metaplasia. The stroma is composed of spindle shaped fibroblastic cells and

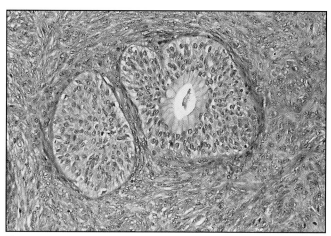

Fig. 13A.38 • Benign Brenner tumor. Nests of transitional epithelial cells are surrounded by fibrous stroma. Metaplastic columnar endocervical-like mucinous cells line a microcyst in the nest on the right.

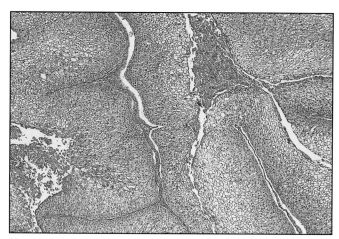

Fig. 13A.39 • Borderline (proliferating) Brenner tumor. Papillae are lined by multilayered transitional epithelium.

collagen in varying proportions. Luteinized cells are present in the stroma in 10–15 percent of Brenner tumors and, in some cases, are associated with evidence of steroid hormone secretion, such as endometrial hyperplasia.[367]

Borderline (proliferating) Brenner tumor

Borderline Brenner tumors have traditionally been referred to as "proliferating" Brenner tumors because of their benign clinical evolution.[376–381] Roth et al. proposed that borderline or intermediate Brenner tumors be subdivided into proliferating and low malignant potential categories, on the basis of greater nuclear atypia in the latter.[377,382] The clinical behavior of all tumors in this group appears to be similar and this author prefers the view that they simply represent low and high grade forms of borderline Brenner tumors.

Borderline Brenner tumors are usually unilateral.[378,381] They are circumscribed white or tan tumors that are considerably larger than benign Brenner tumors. The diameter ranges from 8 to 30 cm, with an average of 14 cm. Most are partially or largely cystic with polyps or friable papillae projecting into the lumen. Microscopically, the epithelium is proliferative and resembles low-grade papillary transitional cell carcinoma of the urinary tract.[377,378,380,381] Much of the cyst lining consists of broad papillae with fibrovascular cores covered by stratified transitional cells (Fig. 13A.39). Similar epithelium lines the non-papillary parts of the cysts. Nests of low-grade transitional cells surrounded by fibrous stroma may be present in the wall of the tumor. The tumor cells have uniform, mildly atypical nuclei with a slightly increased nuclear to cytoplasmic ratio. Mitotic figures are usually not numerous, although they can be frequent in some tumors.[378] Squamous differentiation is seen in some proliferating Brenner tumors.[381] A greater degree of nuclear atypia is the main feature distinguishing high grade borderline Brenner tumors from low grade ones.[377] A diagnosis of intraepithelial carcinoma is warranted if there is significant nuclear atypia and mitotic activity in a non-invasive Brenner tumor.[383] Epithelial proliferation may be remarkable in a borderline Brenner tumor, but it is completely circumscribed and usually intracystic, with no stromal invasion. Foci of benign Brenner tumor are mixed with, or adjacent to, most borderline Brenner tumors.

Malignant Brenner tumor and transitional cell carcinoma

A malignant Brenner tumor is a carcinoma in which features of transitional cell, squamous, or undifferentiated carcinoma are associated with foci of benign or borderline Brenner tumor.[382,384,385] A carcinoma of transitional cell type, but with no associated benign Brenner tumor, is called a transitional cell carcinoma.[382,386,387] It appears important to differentiate between malignant Brenner tumor and transitional cell carcinoma because the latter is more aggressive, but possibly more likely to respond to chemotherapy.[384] There has been a trend in recent years to diagnose transitional cell carcinoma more often. It accounts for 5–10 percent of primary ovarian cancers[388] and, in some studies for an even greater proportion of high stage carcinomas.[386,389] It has been reported that transitional cell carcinoma is more likely to respond to chemotherapy and has better survival than other high grade advanced stage ovarian cancers,[386,388,390,391] but not all authors have been able to confirm this.[389,392]

Malignant Brenner tumor is unilateral and ranges from 5 to 25 cm in diameter. Most are large partly cystic tumors with an average diameter of 15 cm.[378,384] Solid regions are gray, yellow, or tan and frequently contain calcifications. Microscopically, malignant Brenner tumor resembles a high-grade transitional cell carcinoma of the urinary tract.[376,380,384,385,393,394] The tumor cells are polygonal with moderate amounts of amphophilic cytoplasm and pleomorphic, atypical nuclei (Fig. 13A.40). Nuclear grooves are not seen and mitotic figures are numerous. The transitional epithelium lines cysts and broad papillae and invades the stroma in confluent masses or irregular cords and nests of cells. Squamous and glandular differentiation are common.[384] Benign or borderline Brenner tumor must be intermixed with or adjacent to the carcinoma for a diagnosis of malignant Brenner tumor.[385]

Transitional cell carcinoma is a partly cystic tumor that averages 10 cm in diameter and is usually unilateral when confined to the ovary.[386,387] Microscopically, transitional cell carcinoma is similar in appearance to malignant Brenner tumor, except that benign or proliferating Brenner tumor is not identified.[384] Admixtures of other types of surface epithelial tumors, including serous, endometrioid, and undifferentiated

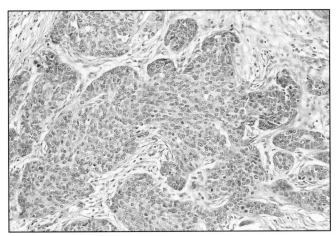

Fig. 13A.40 • Transitional cell carcinoma. Nests and islands of malignant transitional cells infiltrate a desmoplastic stroma. When a benign or proliferating Brenner tumor is found adjacent to transitional cell carcinoma, the tumor is designated as a malignant Brenner tumor.

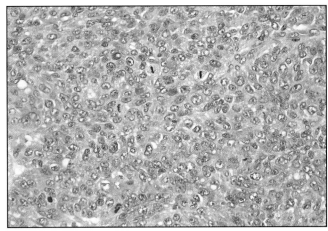

Fig. 13A.41 • Undifferentiated carcinoma. Solid sheet of anaplastic malignant cells with large nuclei, prominent nucleoli, and numerous mitotic figures.

carcinoma, are common,[386] but the transitional cell carcinoma pattern must predominate (i.e., ≥50 percent) to make the diagnosis. Two microscopic patterns have been described. The most common pattern is a papillary one in which thick papillae with conspicuous fibrovascular cores and smooth luminal surfaces grow into cystic spaces.[386,389,390,395] The papillae and cysts are lined by stratified malignant transitional cells that have moderate amounts of eosinophilic cytoplasm and atypical nuclei with one or more nucleoli. Mitotic figures are numerous. Nests and sheets of malignant transitional cells invade the stroma in solid portions of the tumor. Microspaces and slit-like fenestrations are commonly present among the tumor cells, both in papillae and in areas of solid growth. Foci of mucinous and squamous differentiation, spindle cell differentiation, and irregular gland formation can be present. A majority of transitional cell carcinomas are poorly differentiated and foci of necrosis are common. The second, and less common pattern is a "malignant Brenner type" of transitional cell carcinoma in which the growth is more solid, with nests and cords of malignant transitional cells invading a prominent fibrous stroma (see Fig. 13A.40).[382,387] The microscopic appearance of metastatic tumor deposits may be important in transitional cell carcinoma. In one study, patients with metastases resembling transitional cell carcinoma had better survival than those whose metastases resembled other types of ovarian cancer, usually serous carcinoma.[386]

Immunohistochemical study of Brenner tumors and transitional cell carcinoma of the ovary reveals that they are immunoreactive for carcinoembryonic antigen, the CA19-9 antigen, cytokeratin, epithelial membrane antigen, and cytokeratin 7 (see Table 13A.5).[394,396,397] Benign Brenner tumors have a staining pattern that suggests a urothelial line of differentiation, including staining for uroplakin III, thrombomodulin and cytokeratin 20.[398–400] Transitional cell carcinoma, on the other hand, is immunophenotypically similar to other types of surface epithelial carcinoma of the ovary; it does not have a staining pattern that suggests urothelial differentiation. It is negative for uroplakin III, thrombomodulin and cytokeratin 20,[396,401] and it usually exhibits positive staining for estrogen receptors, WT-1, and CA-125.[398,399,402] The immunophenotypic differences between transitional cell carcinomas

of the ovary and bladder can be exploited in those rare cases in which the pathologist is concerned that an ovarian tumor might be metastatic transitional cell carcinoma from the urinary tract.[396,403–405]

Undifferentiated carcinoma

About 5 percent of ovarian cancers are too poorly differentiated to classify, and are designated as "undifferentiated".[262,406] In most cases, undifferentiated carcinoma has spread beyond the ovary by the time of diagnosis and most patients cannot be optimally debulked.[406] Undifferentiated carcinoma has the worst prognosis of any type of surface epithelial carcinoma. In one study, 29 of 35 patients died of tumor in less than 3 years. Of the 6 who survived more than 3 years, 5 eventually died of tumor.[406]

Undifferentiated carcinoma is a large, predominantly solid tumor with foci of hemorrhage and necrosis. Most are bilateral.[406] Microscopically, the carcinoma grows as sheets of pleomorphic epithelial cells with large vesicular nuclei, prominent nucleoli, and variable amounts of cytoplasm (Fig. 13A.41).[262,406] The nuclei are markedly atypical, mitotic figures are numerous and may be abnormal, and bizarre tumor giant cells may be present. Poorly formed glands, areas with vague squamoid or transitional features, or nests and cords of malignant cells are seen in some tumors. Immunohistochemical stains showing reactivity for cytokeratin or epithelial membrane antigen may be needed to prove that the tumor is a carcinoma. Immunostains for B72.3 are positive in most cases, and a stain for OC125 is positive in about 50 percent.[406]

Rare types of carcinoma

Ovarian carcinoma can usually be classified as one of the common types. Unusual kinds of carcinoma that occur only rarely include neuroendocrine carcinoma, squamous cell carcinoma, hepatoid carcinoma, and carcinoma with focal differentiation into a malignant germ cell tumor.

The most common type of ovarian neuroendocrine carcinoma is a *small cell carcinoma* morphologically identical to small cell carcinoma of the lung and other body sites.[237,330,407]

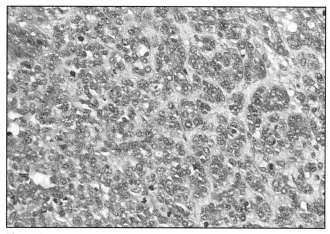

Fig. 13A.42 • Small cell carcinoma of neuroendocrine type. This tumor arose adjacent to a mucinous carcinoma. The tumor cells have scanty cytoplasm, uniform hyperchromatic round nuclei, and there are numerous mitotic figures.

This type of carcinoma is often referred to as small cell carcinoma of "pulmonary" type to differentiate it from the hypercalcemic type of small cell carcinoma that occurs only in the ovary (see p. 616). Neuroendocrine small cell carcinoma is composed of nests and sheets of small to medium sized cells with darkly stained round to oval nuclei, finely granular nuclear chromatin, and inconspicuous or absent nucleoli (Fig. 13A.42). The nuclei of adjacent cells are often molded to each other. The cytoplasm is pale and scanty and the cell borders are ill defined. The immunophenotype is variable. About half of the cases stain for cytokeratin or epithelial membrane antigen. Stains for neuron specific enolase or CD56 are generally positive, but staining for chromogranin or synaptophysin is detected in only a minority of tumors. Neuroendocrine carcinomas composed of larger or more pleomorphic cells also occur in the ovary.[240,407] These are designated as large cell neuroendocrine carcinoma, and are composed of cells with vesicular nuclei, large nucleoli and abundant cytoplasm, or of cells with hyperchromatic nuclei with coarse chromatin, multiple nucleoli, and moderate amounts of amphophilic cytoplasm. The cells grow in nests, sheets, trabeculae, and poorly formed glands. Stains for epithelial and neuroendocrine markers are generally positive in large cell neuroendocrine carcinoma. Most neuroendocrine carcinomas are intimately associated with tumors of surface epithelial type, most typically of either endometrioid or mucinous type, and may arise from neuroendocrine cells within the epithelial tumors.[236–240,408,409] Neuroendocrine carcinoma of the ovary has a clinical presentation and metastatic pattern similar to other types of ovarian cancer, and has a poor prognosis. Patients with neuroendocrine carcinomas of the ovary occasionally develop paraneoplastic syndromes, such as hypercalcemia caused by secretion of parathyroid hormone by the tumor cells.[410] Metastatic neuroendocrine carcinoma from the lung and other sites must be considered in the differential diagnosis.[411–413] Expression of thyroid transcription factor 1 (TTF-1) does not necessarily indicate that a small cell carcinoma is metastatic from the lung, since a significant subset of non-pulmonary small cell carcinomas also express TTF-1.[414–416]

Squamous cell carcinoma occurs infrequently in the ovary. Most examples are secondary neoplasms arising in a benign cystic teratoma; this kind of ovarian squamous cell carcinoma is discussed in the section on teratomas (see p. 612). Squamous cell carcinoma in the ovary can be metastatic from the cervix or another primary site, it can occur in a mixed surface epithelial tumor, in a malignant Brenner tumor, or in an adenosquamous carcinoma of primary or metastatic endometrioid type, so a careful search for other elements is mandatory before a tumor is accepted as a pure primary ovarian squamous cell carcinoma. Non-teratomatous squamous cell carcinoma of the ovary originates in endometriosis, in an epidermoid cyst, or from the surface epithelium.[417,418] It tends to be a predominantly solid tumor with small cysts. The malignant squamous cells grow in solid sheets, infiltrate the stroma, line cysts or papillae and, in some tumors, grow in a spindle cell pattern. The prognosis is most closely correlated with the stage and grade; since a majority of squamous cell carcinomas of the ovary are discovered at an advanced stage, the overall prognosis is poor.

Some rare, apparently primary ovarian carcinomas that occur in older women histologically resemble hepatocellular carcinoma. These tumors, which have been designated as *hepatoid carcinomas*, are composed of polygonal cells with vesicular nuclei and abundant eosinophilic or clear cytoplasm.[419] Additional features of hepatoid differentiation, identified in some or all such tumors, include hyaline globules in the tumor cells and stroma, immunoreactivity with anti-hepatocyte antibody, α-fetoprotein, and albumin, a canalicular pattern of staining with polyclonal carcinoembryonic antigen, and a positive bile stain.[420–423] The main differential diagnostic considerations are the hepatoid variant of yolk sac tumor and metastatic hepatocellular carcinoma.[419,424,425] All of these tumors can be immunoreactive for antihepatocyte antibody and alpha-fetoprotein, so the differential diagnosis must be based on a combination of histologic and clinical findings.[420] The finding of an admixture of other types of surface epithelial carcinoma in some tumors is indicative of ovarian origin.[421]

Surface epithelial carcinomas of the ovary, like adenocarcinomas in other organs, occasionally differentiate focally into malignant germ cell elements. Rare carcinomas secrete human chorionic gonadotropin (HCG) or contain scattered trophoblastic cells,[312,426,427] but only a few *carcinomas with differentiation into choriocarcinoma* have been reported.[428] In addition to the underlying carcinoma, these patients' tumors contain hemorrhagic nodules within which the typical biphasic pattern of choriocarcinoma, with cytotrophoblast and syncytiotrophoblast, is present. There is positive immunohistochemical staining for HCG in the syncytiotrophoblastic cells. Carcinomas with differentiation into choriocarcinoma appear biologically aggressive and capable of the type of hematogenous spread characteristic of choriocarcinoma. A small number of cases of *yolk sac tumor arising from a malignant epithelial tumor*, usually an endometrioid carcinoma, have been reported.[276,277,429] These exhibit typical histologic patterns of yolk sac tumor, are immunoreactive for α-fetoprotein, and secrete α-fetoprotein into the blood. Such tumors appear to have a poor prognosis.

Sex cord-stromal tumors

Tumors derived from the sex cord or ovarian mesenchyme (Table 13A.7) comprise 5–12 percent of all ovarian neoplasms.[1,3]

Table 13A.7	Sex cord-stromal tumors of the ovary

Sex cord-stromal tumors

Granulosa cell tumor
   Adult type
   Juvenile type
Thecoma
   Typical
   Luteinized
Fibrothecoma
Fibroma
   Typical
   Cellular
Fibrosarcoma
Fibroma or thecoma with minor sex cord elements
Sertoli-Leydig cell tumor
   Well differentiated
   Intermediate differentiation
   Poorly differentiated
   Retiform (with heterologous elements)
Sertoli cell tumor
Sex cord tumor with annular tubules (SCTAT)
Leydig cell tumor
Steroid cell tumor (lipid cell tumor)
Gynandroblastoma
Sclerosing stromal tumor
Stromal luteoma
Soft tissue tumor not specific to ovary
Lymphoma and leukemia
Unclassified

Benign tumors in the fibroma–thecoma group are relatively common. Other sex cord-stromal tumors and mesenchymal tumors are rare.

Granulosa cell tumor

Granulosa cell tumor comprises 1–2 percent of all ovarian tumors and is the most common malignant sex cord-stromal tumor.[1,430] There are two types of granulosa cell tumor: an adult type that occurs mainly in postmenopausal women and a juvenile type that occurs mainly in children.

Adult granulosa cell tumor

Clinical findings While most common in postmenopausal women,[431–435] these tumors occur over a wide age range, from teenagers to the elderly. The average age is 50–55 years. Granulosa cell tumors typically secrete estrogens, which stimulate the endometrium to proliferate. The usual presenting symptom is postmenopausal bleeding in older women and menorrhagia, metrorrhagia, or amenorrhea in those who are premenopausal.[436] Endometrial biopsy reveals hyperplasia in 30–40 percent of patients and endometrial adenocarcinoma in 5–10 percent of them.[433,437–441] Rare adult-type granulosa cell tumors, most occurring in young women 15–35 years of age, secrete androgens and induce virilization.[442–446] Typical symptoms include hirsutism, enlargement of the clitoris, deepening

of the voice and amenorrhea.[442] About 25 percent of patients with granulosa cell tumors present with non-specific symptoms such as abdominal distention, pain, or a palpable mass. Rupture or torsion of the tumor and intratumoral hemorrhage can cause acute abdominal symptoms. Rare granulosa cell tumors occur in pregnant women.[447]

Most women with a granulosa cell tumor have a palpable unilateral adnexal mass; bilateral tumors are uncommon. The tumor is confined to the ovary (FIGO stage I) at diagnosis in 80–90 percent of cases.[433,434,437,448] The standard treatment is total abdominal hysterectomy and bilateral salpingo-oophorectomy. Unilateral salpingo-oophorectomy is appropriate treatment for stage IA tumors in young women who wish to conserve their fertility. All granulosa cell tumors have malignant potential, although most do not recur or metastasize. The recurrence rate is 10–15 percent for stage IA tumors and 20–30 percent overall.[432–434,438,439,449,450] Extraovarian spread is to the peritoneum and omentum and occasionally to the liver or lungs.[451,452] When intra-abdominal spread is present at diagnosis (stage III) or the tumor recurs, as many as two-thirds of patients die of tumor.[432,435,439] Granulosa cell tumors grow slowly and metastases are often detected more than 5 years after initial treatment.[433,435,439,441] Disease-free intervals of more than 20 years have been reported.[453] Some patients with advanced or recurrent granulosa cell tumor respond to combination chemotherapy that includes cisplatin,[436,454–456] but responses are seldom durable. The value of radiotherapy is unclear.[436]

Several potential tumor markers have been identified in the sera of women with granulosa cell tumors, including estradiol, müllerian inhibiting substance,[457] follicle regulatory protein,[458] and inhibin.[459] Inhibin has emerged as the most widely used tumor marker, as serum inhibin levels are elevated in nearly all patients with primary or recurrent granulosa cell tumor.[460,461] Inhibin is not specific for granulosa cell tumor, as elevated serum concentrations can be observed in women with other types of ovarian tumor,[462,463] but once the diagnosis has been established it can be used for monitoring treatment and detecting recurrence.

Pathology Granulosa cell tumors range from small, incidentally discovered nodules only a few millimeters in diameter to large tumors more than 30 cm in diameter. The average diameter is about 10 cm. Some are entirely solid, but most are partly cystic. The solid portions are pink, tan, brown, or light yellow and vary from soft to firm in consistency. Rare granulosa cell tumors grow as large cysts with a wall only a few millimeters thick. These are more likely than other granulosa cell tumors to be androgenic.[443,450]

Microscopically, the tumor cells resemble normal granulosa cells. They are small and round, cuboidal, or spindle-shaped with pale cytoplasm and ill-defined cell borders. The nuclei are round or oval with fine chromatin and a single small nucleolus (Fig. 13A.43). Longitudinal folds or grooves are present in many nuclei and are a characteristic feature of adult granulosa cell tumor. Mitotic figures and nuclear pleomorphism and atypia are unusual findings in these tumors, but may be present. Cells with bizarre nuclei are detected in some tumors (Fig. 13A.44), but do not appear adversely to affect the prognosis.[464–466] The tumor cells are extensively luteinized in about 1 percent of adult granulosa cell tumors. Luteinized

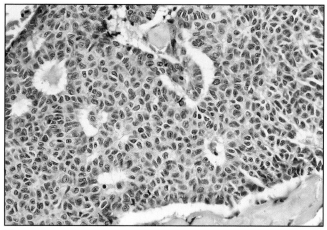

Fig. 13A.43 • Adult granulosa cell tumor. The cells are monotonous with uniform grooved nuclei. Note the Call–Exner bodies. These are microcystic spaces that contain eosinophilic secretions or cellular debris. They are lined by palisaded granulosa cells.

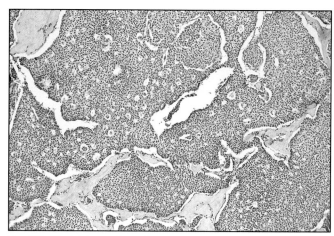

Fig. 13A.45 • Adult granulosa cell tumor. Microfollicular pattern, in which there are numerous Call–Exner bodies within a diffuse proliferation of neoplastic granulosa cells.

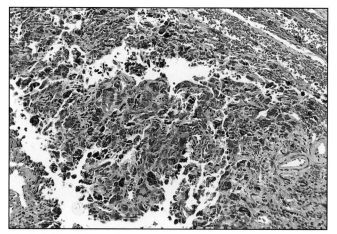

Fig. 13A.44 • Adult granulosa cell tumor. Focus of tumor cells with bizarre nuclei.

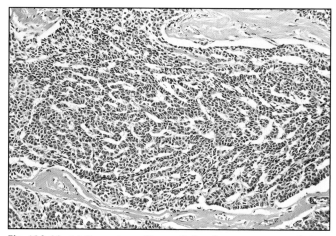

Fig. 13A.46 • Adult granulosa cell tumor. Trabecular pattern composed of ribbons and cords of neoplastic granulosa cells.

granulosa cells have abundant eosinophilic cytoplasm, well-defined cell borders, and central nuclei, and resemble the luteinized granulosa cells of the corpus luteum. Luteinized granulosa cell tumors occur in pregnancy,[447] in patients with androgenic tumors,[442] and as idiopathic findings.[467]

Several histologic patterns have been described. These are often mixed and do not have prognostic significance. The microfollicular pattern is the most characteristic one and consists of nests and sheets of granulosa cells punctuated by small spaces containing eosinophilic secretions and cellular debris (Fig. 13A.45). The spaces resemble the Call–Exner bodies of developing follicles. The macrofollicular pattern is one in which large, often irregularly shaped follicles are lined by stratified granulosa cells. Granulosa cells grow in anastomosing bands, ribbons, and cords in the trabecular pattern (Fig. 13A.46); in irregular undulating ribbons in the gyriform or watered-silk pattern; and in circumscribed nests and islands in the insular pattern. The cells grow in large irregular sheets with no organized substructure in the solid or diffuse pattern. Many granulosa cell tumors contain large cysts lined by one or more layers of granulosa cells. The cysts frequently contain blood and hemosiderin-laden macrophages are often present in the cysts and the lining. Rare cystic granulosa cell tumors grow as large unilocular cysts lined by stratified granulosa cells, among which are microfollicles or areas of trabecular growth.

Granulosa cell tumors contain a variable amount of fibrous or thecomatous stroma. Tumors with a prominent fibro-thecomatous stroma were formerly designated as granulosa-theca cell tumors. In current practice, any tumor in which granulosa cells comprise more than 10 percent of the cellular population is classified as a granulosa cell tumor. Tumors with only a minor granulosa cell component are best classified as a thecoma or fibroma with minor sex cord elements.[468] Rare granulosa cell tumors contain heterologous mucinous epithelium or are composite tumors with mucinous elements.[469–472] A few granulosa cell tumors with focal hepatocellular differentiation have been reported.[473,474]

It is difficult to predict the prognosis of a granulosa cell tumor by pathologic means, although some pathologic findings correlate to a degree with the clinical outcome.[432,433,475] The prognosis is less favorable for large tumors more than 15 cm in diameter, for bilateral tumors, and for those that have ruptured or spread beyond the ovary (i.e., FIGO stage >IA). The stage is the single most powerful prognostic indicator.[476]

Tumors in which there is diffuse moderate or marked nuclear atypia or a high mitotic rate (variably defined as greater than 2 or 4 mitotic figures per 10 high power fields) appear more likely to recur.[434,435,448,449,477] There is no correlation between the microscopic pattern and the clinical outcome.

Small non-neoplastic granulosa cell proliferations, which can mimic small adult granulosa cell tumors, occur occasionally in the ovaries of pregnant or postpartum women.[478] In contrast to a granulosa cell tumor, these granulosa cell proliferations are small, multifocal, and confined to the antra of atretic follicles. They do not have the appearance of a granulosa cell tumor in pregnancy.[447] Strips and clusters of non-neoplastic granulosa cells are observed occasionally within vascular channels, perhaps being misplaced during surgery or at ovulation.[479] These small aggregates of benign granulosa cells, which are often seen within vascular spaces adjacent to follicles, represent an artifact and should not be mistaken for tumor cells.

Immunohistochemical stains are useful in the diagnosis of granulosa cell tumor. Nearly all granulosa cell tumors are vimentin positive.[480,481] The results of keratin stains depend on the antibody used and how the tissue is pretreated. Staining for keratin with polyclonal antibodies usually gives a negative result,[482,483] but immunostains using monoclonal antibodies against low molecular weight cytokeratins 8 and 18 (such as Cam 5.2, AE1/3) stain 30–60 percent of granulosa tumors.[480,484,485] Dot-like or globoid perinuclear staining is particularly suggestive of a granulosa cell tumor, but extensive perinuclear or diffuse cytoplasmic staining is seen in some tumors. Cells throughout the tumor stain in about half of the positive cases, while only occasional cells are reactive in the rest. There is positive staining for smooth muscle actin in most tumors, but granulosa cells generally do not stain for desmin.[485,486] About 50 percent of granulosa cell tumors show positive nuclear or cytoplasmic staining for S-100 protein.[485] There is membrane staining for CD99 (MIC2 gene product) in about 70 percent of granulosa cell tumors.[487,488] The most significant negative staining reaction is for epithelial membrane antigen (EMA), which is uniformly absent in granulosa cell tumors.[482,485,489] The most important positive staining reaction is for inhibin.[490,491] Almost all granulosa cell tumors show cytoplasmic staining for inhibin (Fig. 13A.47).[275,492–498]

Staining is often patchy and of variable intensity, and a positive reaction is not specific for granulosa cell tumor, as other types of sex cord-stromal tumors are also immunoreactive. Most epithelial tumors are inhibin-negative, but focal or diffuse positive staining for inhibin is detected occasionally.[275,496,499] Calretinin is an even more sensitive marker for granulosa cell tumors but, like inhibin, it is not specific as it is positive in other types of sex cord-stromal tumors.[497,500,501] Staining for calretinin is both nuclear and cytoplasmic. As with inhibin, there is occasional staining in epithelial tumors and mesotheliomas are diffusely and strongly positive.[497] An immunohistochemical staining panel used for the diagnosis of granulosa cell tumor should include inhibin, calretinin, cytokeratin (including cytokeratins 8 and 18), EMA, and, in certain circumstances, leukocyte common antigen and chromogranin (Table 13A.8).

Juvenile granulosa cell tumor

Fewer than 5 percent of granulosa cell tumors occur in children and teenagers. Most of those that do have distinctive clinicopathologic features, and have been termed juvenile granulosa cell tumors.[502–506]

Clinical findings Juvenile granulosa cell tumor can occur at any age, from infancy to old age, but most arise in children.[502,503,507,508] The average patient age is 15 years, but in a study limited to children in a pediatric tumor registry, the average age was only 7.1 years.[509]

Symptoms are often caused by estrogens secreted by the tumor.[502,503,507,508,510] Premenarcheal girls often (50–75 percent) have isosexual precocious pseudopuberty, with development of the breasts, growth of pubic and axillary hair, vaginal bleeding, and increased bone age. An estrogen effect is seen in the vaginal smear. Older children and premenopausal women have menstrual abnormalities, including amenorrhea. A third to half of all patients present with non-specific symptoms such as abdominal distention, pain, or a palpable abdominal mass.

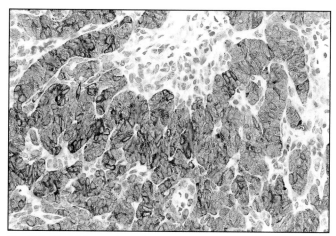

Fig. 13A.47 • Adult granulosa cell tumor. The tumor cells are strongly immunoreactive for inhibin.

Table 13A.8	Immunophenotype of selected ovarian tumors				
Tumor	**Inhibin**	**Cytokeratin**	**EMA**	**LCA**	**Chromogranin**
Granulosa cell tumor	+	–/+	–	–	–
Small cell carcinoma	–	+/–	+/–	–	+/–
Sertoli-Leydig cell tumor	+	+	–	–	–
Carcinoma	–	+	+	–	–
Carcinoid	–	+	+	–	+
Lymphoma	–	–	–	+	–

+ usually positive; – usually negative; +/– can be positive or negative; EMA = epithelial membrane antigen; LCA = leukocyte common antigen

Occasional patients develop acute abdominal symptoms due to torsion or rupture of their tumors. An adnexal mass is palpable in more than 70 percent of patients. With rare exceptions,[509] juvenile granulosa cell tumors are unilateral, and more than 95 percent of them are confined to the ovary (stage I). The prognosis appears to be worse for patients with stage IC tumors, so it is important to collect peritoneal washings for cytologic evaluation. There is an association between juvenile granulosa cell tumor and Ollier's (enchondromatosis) and Mafucci's (enchondromatosis and multiple subcutaneous hemangiomas) syndromes.[502,505,510–513]

Juvenile granulosa cell tumor is typically encapsulated and confined to one ovary at diagnosis (stage IA) and is adequately treated by unilateral salpingo-oophorectomy.[508] Since most patients are young, hysterectomy and bilateral salpingo-oophorectomy should be reserved for the few who have advanced disease (stage II, III, or IV). The long-term survival is good, but patients whose tumors rupture, or who show positive peritoneal cytology or extraovarian tumor spread have a significant risk of recurrence.[502,503,506,514] Recurrence, if it does occur, is usually detected within 3 years of diagnosis. Rare patients with later recurrences have been reported.[515] Some patients with advanced, persistent or recurrent disease respond to platinum-based combination chemotherapy.[516,517] Inhibin and müllerian inhibitory substance are useful as tumor markers for the detection and follow-up of patients with juvenile granulosa cell tumors.[518,519]

Pathology Juvenile granulosa cell tumors vary from 2.5 to 30 cm in diameter, with an average of about 12 cm. Most tumors have a mixed solid-cystic appearance, but some are completely solid and others largely cystic. Solid areas are yellow or tan. Hemorrhage is frequent, but necrosis is uncommon.

Microscopically, the tumors consist of a mixture of cysts and solid lobular or nodular areas (Fig. 13A.48). Macrofollicular, solid, and cystic growth patterns are characteristic of juvenile granulosa cell tumor. In some tumors, the macrofollicles are rounded and relatively uniform in size, while in others, the follicles vary markedly in size and have irregular shapes (Fig. 13A.49). The macrofollicles contain mucinous material, are lined by one or more layers of granulosa cells,

and may be surrounded by a rim of theca cells. Solid areas consist of sheets of granulosa cells with a variable admixture of spindle shaped thecal or fibroblastic stromal cells. Growth patterns that typify adult granulosa cell tumors, such as microfollicular and insular, are usually not seen, although some tumors have foci in which the granulosa cells grow in a trabecular or tubule-like pattern. The granulosa cells in these tumors differ from those seen in adult granulosa cell tumors. They are polygonal to spindled in shape and have a variable, but usually ample, amount of amphophilic or pink cytoplasm. Focal or extensive luteinization is a typical finding. The tumor cell nuclei are large, round, and usually darkly stained (Fig. 13A.50). They lack grooves and may contain conspicuous nucleoli. Some cells have greatly enlarged pleomorphic nuclei and others are multinucleated. Mitotic figures average about 6 per 10 high power fields.

Few immunohistochemical studies have focused on juvenile granulosa cell tumor. The tumor cells are vimentin and inhibin positive, they stain for low molecular weight cytokeratin in about half the cases, and they show nuclear and cytoplasmic staining for calretinin and membrane staining for

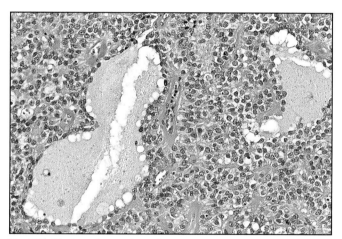

Fig. 13A.49 • Juvenile granulosa cell tumor. Irregular macrofollicles filled with eosinophilic secretions and surrounded by a diffuse proliferation of neoplastic granulosa cells.

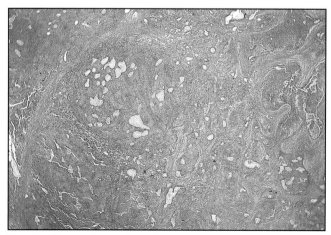

Fig. 13A.48 • Juvenile granulosa cell tumor. Typical multinodular growth pattern with irregular macrofollicular spaces.

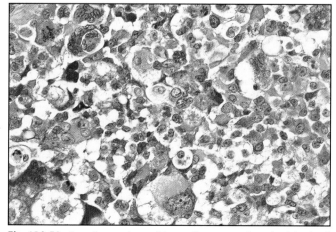

Fig. 13A.50 • Juvenile granulosa cell tumor. The tumor cells are luteinized and have eosinophilic cytoplasm. They have large round nuclei, which in some cells are markedly atypical.

CD99.[274,275,489,492–494,506,509,520] Positive staining for inhibin helps differentiate juvenile granulosa cell tumor from small cell carcinoma of the hypercalcemic type and from yolk sac tumor, both of which are inhibin-negative.[493] The most helpful positive stains are inhibin, calretinin, and CD99, and the most helpful negative stain is EMA.

Thecoma

Thecoma is a gonadal stromal tumor in which the cells resemble those of the theca interna. It is uncommon and comprises 7 percent of sex cord-stromal neoplasms.[2]

Clinical findings Thecomas arise in patients of all ages, but most occur in women who are peri- or postmenopausal. The average patient age is between 50 and 55 years.[2,430,431,437,439] Thecomas only rarely occur in children.[509] The luteinized variant of thecoma occurs at a younger age, with a significant number affecting women in their 20s or 30s.[521] Older patients usually present with postmenopausal bleeding, but as many as 25 percent of them have non-specific symptoms such as pelvic or abdominal pain or abdominal distention. The latter can be caused by a large tumor or be due to ascites. Some patients have a Meigs'-like syndrome, with ascites and hydrothorax. Premenopausal women have either endocrine-associated symptoms, such as irregular bleeding or amenorrhea, or less specific complaints such as pelvic or abdominal pain or abdominal distention. Some patients, usually those with luteinized thecomas, are virilized.[521–523] Estrogens secreted by the tumor cause endometrial hyperplasia in about 15 percent of patients and as many as 30 percent of them have adenocarcinoma of the endometrium.[437,439] Thecoma is almost invariably benign and excision is the appropriate treatment.[439] For all practical purposes extraovarian spread does not occur, but about 5 percent of patients have bilateral tumors.[430,431] Because many thecomas are associated with endometrial hyperplasia or carcinoma, hysterectomy with bilateral salpingo-oophorectomy is the standard treatment. Unilateral salpingo-oophorectomy is adequate treatment for a young woman as long as the endometrium is normal. Rare malignant tumors with unequivocal thecomatous differentiation have been reported.[521,523–525] However, most neoplasms reported as "malignant thecoma" have proven to be sarcomatoid or luteinized granulosa cell tumors, fibrosarcomas, or other types of malignant mesenchymal tumors.

Sclerosing peritonitis occurs rarely in young women who have an unusual form of luteinized thecoma.[526–530] The clinical presentation is with abdominal distention, symptoms of chronic intestinal obstruction, or an acute abdomen. Most patients have ascites and some have hydrothorax. The omentum, mesentery, and the serosa of the small intestine show fibrous thickening and nodularity, often with adhesions and intestinal obstruction. This condition appears to be self-limited and is treated adequately by excision of the ovarian tumor and limited abdominal surgery, including lysis of adhesions, omentectomy, and bowel resections as necessary to relieve obstruction. Despite a high mitotic rate in some cases, no recurrences or metastases have been reported to date, although several patients have died of intestinal obstruction and sepsis related to the peritoneal pathology.[526,527]

Pathology Thecoma is a firm or hard tumor that varies in size from small, incidentally discovered nodules less than 1 cm in diameter to masses more than 20 cm in diameter. The average diameter is about 7 cm. The cut surface is gray or tan, usually with focal to extensive yellow areas. Degenerative changes such as cysts and calcifications may be present.

Microscopically, the tumor is composed of fascicles or sheets of plump, spindled or ovoid stromal cells that resemble the cells of the theca interna (Fig. 13A.51). The stromal cells have pale round or fusiform nuclei with fine, dispersed chromatin. The cytoplasm is amphophilic or lightly eosinophilic. Some cells have clear cytoplasm or contain vacuoles which are best demonstrated with fat stains applied to unfixed frozen sections (Fig. 13A.52). A variable number of fibroblastic cells are intermixed among the theca-like cells. Reticulin stains reveal a network of fibrils surrounding individual tumor cells. Hyalinized connective tissue plaques and microcalcifications are common and extensive calcifications are noted occasionally in thecomas affecting young women.[531] The ovarian cortex adjacent to a thecoma is often hyperplastic.

Electron microscopic studies suggest that fibromas and thecomas are derived from the same cell type and that they differ only in the proportion of collagen-forming and steroid-forming cells.[532,533] It is therefore not surprising to find

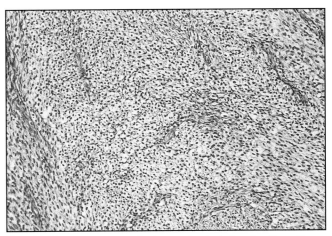

Fig. 13A.51 • Thecoma. Nests of pale, vacuolated spindle cells with small central nuclei.

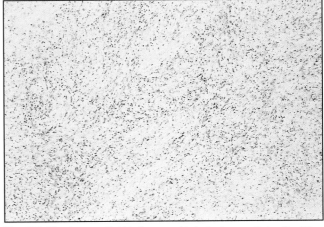

Fig. 13A.52 • Thecoma. Lipid is demonstrable in the tumor cells by oil red O staining.

intermediate forms that are difficult to classify either as thecoma or fibroma. These are designated as fibrothecomas. Fibrothecoma differs from thecoma in that tumor cells with clear cytoplasm or cytoplasmic lipid vacuoles are fewer in number and the tumor is usually non-functional (Fig. 13A.53). In contrast to fibroma, fibrothecoma is more cellular and has less collagen, plumper tumor cells, and at least a few theca cells. From a practical point of view, the diagnosis of thecoma should be restricted to tumors that show evidence of steroid hormone secretion, or that have a conspicuous component of cells with clear or vacuolated cytoplasm, or that contain luteinized cells, as discussed below. A tumor that contains many cells that are immunoreactive for inhibin can also be designated as a thecoma. In daily practice, thecoma is an uncommon diagnosis, while fibroma and fibrothecoma are relatively common.

Clusters, nests, or sheets of luteinized cells are found in some tumors in the thecoma–fibroma group (Fig. 13A.54). Regardless of whether the tumor is a thecoma, a fibro-thecoma, or a fibroma, if luteinized tumor cells are present, it is classified as a luteinized thecoma.[521,522] Luteinized thecomas can be estrogenic (50 percent), androgenic (11 percent), or non-functional (39 percent).[521] Nearly all androgenic thecomas are luteinized thecomas. A luteinized thecoma is differentiated from a stromal Leydig cell tumor only by the presence of cytoplasmic crystalloids of Reinke in the latter.

Rare gonadal stromal tumors that contain theca cells or luteinized cells are clinically malignant. Features that raise the possibility of malignancy include large size, hypercellularity, nuclear atypia and frequent mitotic figures (4 or more mitotic figures/10 high power fields),[521,524,534] but definitive criteria for the histologic diagnosis of malignant thecoma have not been established.

Immunostains for vimentin, inhibin and calretinin are positive in thecoma, while those for cytokeratin are negative.[275,484,492–495,497,500,520,535] A cytogenetic abnormality, trisomy 12, can be detected in some thecomas.[536–539]

Ovarian tumors associated with sclerosing peritonitis appear to fall into two categories. Some patients have large fibromatous or thecomatous neoplasms in which luteinized cells are present (i.e., they are luteinized thecomas).[526,528] These differ from the usual luteinized thecoma in that they tend to be bilateral and the luteinized cells occur in small, ill-defined clusters. Additionally, some cells are only partially luteinized. There is minimal nuclear atypia, but numerous mitotic figures (15–50 mitotic figures per 10 high power fields) are seen in some tumors (Fig. 13A.55). A different, but possibly related, ovarian abnormality is found in other patients who have bilateral nodular cortical spindle cell proliferations that give rise to a polypoid surface contour, but do not form discrete tumor masses.[526,527,540,541] This condition may represent an early form of stromal neoplasia or an unusual type of stromal hyperplasia. Small clusters of partly and completely luteinized cells are scattered among the proliferating stromal cells. No significant nuclear atypia is present, but mitotic figures can be numerous. Despite the worrisome mitotic activity, metastatic spread has not occurred in the limited number of cases with follow-up. Whether the high mitotic rate is an indication of malignant potential is unclear at present. The sclerosing peritonitis involves the omentum, peritoneum, and intestinal serosa. There is serosal thickening with proliferation of fibroblasts and myofibroblasts, deposition of collagen, and focal inflammation, mesothelial hyperplasia, and fibrin deposition.

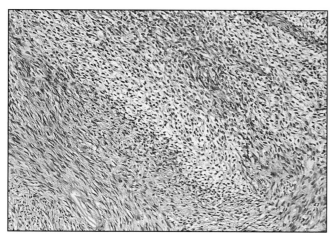

Fig. 13A.53 • Fibrothecoma. Pale lipid-containing theca cells merge with spindle cell areas characteristic of fibroma.

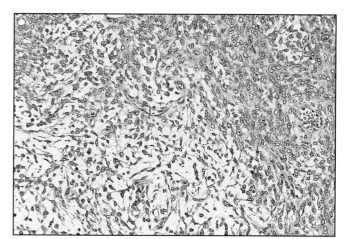

Fig. 13A.54 • Luteinized thecoma. Diffuse sheet of luteinized theca cells with abundant eosinophilic cytoplasm.

Fig. 13A.55 • Thecoma associated with sclerosing peritonitis. There is marked edema. The theca cells are plump, and many have conspicuous pink cytoplasm. Numerous mitotic figures are present.

Fibroma

Ovarian fibroma is a benign tumor composed of fibroblasts and collagen fibers. It is by far the most common sex cord-stromal tumor, accounting for 1–5 percent of all ovarian tumors.[2,542,543] Fibrosarcoma occurs in the ovary, but it is rare.[544]

Clinical findings The clinical presentation is non-specific. Fibromas occur in patients 20–80 years of age, with an average age of 50 or more.[2,543,545] They are often small and asymptomatic and are discovered only when the patient is operated on for some other condition. Large fibromas, cellular fibromas, and fibrosarcomas cause abdominal pain or distention and 30 percent of patients have ascites.[543] Meigs' syndrome is an unusual condition in which an ovarian fibroma is accompanied by ascites and hydrothorax.[546] About 17 percent of patients with the nevoid basal cell carcinoma syndrome (multiple basal cell carcinomas of the skin, odontogenic keratocysts, and other abnormalities) have ovarian fibromas, which can be bilateral.[547]

Fibroma is adequately treated by surgical excision. Cellular fibroma is a tumor of uncertain malignant potential. It is capable of locally aggressive growth if incompletely excised and metastases occasionally occur, indicating that criteria for differentiating between cellular fibroma and fibrosarcoma are imperfect. Fibrosarcoma is a malignant mesenchymal tumor that has a poor prognosis. Treatment is complete resection followed by chemotherapy.[544,548]

Pathology Fibroma is a firm tumor with a smooth, lobulated surface. It ranges from less than 1 cm to more than 10 cm and has a solid white or tan cut surface. It is bilateral in 5–10 percent of cases. Cellular fibroma and fibrosarcoma are large and soft, and may contain areas of hemorrhage and necrosis.

Fibromas are composed of thin spindle cells growing in whorled and anastomosing bundles (Fig. 13A.56). The nuclei are fusiform and uniform from cell to cell. The cytoplasm is scanty and lightly eosinophilic. There is a variable amount of collagenous stroma around the tumor cells.

Small, irregular nests or tubules of sex cord cells are occasionally found in a fibroma. The sex cord cells are polygonal and have uniform nuclei and small amounts of cyto-plasm; they resemble indifferent sex cord cells or granulosa cells. When they comprise less than 10 percent of the tumor, the sex cord cells do not appear to have any prognostic significance. Tumors that contain them are called fibromas with sex cord elements.[468]

Rare fibroblastic tumors are hypercellular with little intercellular collagen. The spindle-shaped tumor cells grow in herringbone, cross-stitch, and storiform patterns. Necrosis may be present and is sometimes extensive. Such tumors are designated as *cellular fibromas* when nuclear atypia is mild to moderate and there are 3 or fewer mitotic figures/10 high power fields (Fig. 13A.57) and as *fibrosarcomas* when there is moderate to marked nuclear atypia and 4 or more mitotic figures/10 high power fields.[544,548] It is difficult to classify accurately tumors with borderline mitotic counts, and occasional tumors classified as a cellular fibroma recur or metastasize. Proliferation indices and in situ hybridization studies (to detect trisomy 8) may help in the classification of these tumors,[548,549] but they are not widely available. It is prudent to report cellular fibromas with more than mild nuclear atypia and 2–3 mitotic figures per 10 high power fields as tumors of uncertain malignant potential. Fibrosarcoma is occasionally associated with another tumor type, such as a benign cystic teratoma, and one example that arose in a fibrothecomatous tumor with minor sex cord elements has been reported.[550,551]

Trisomy 12 is a consistent cytogenetic finding in ovarian fibroma.[536,537,552]

Sertoli-Leydig cell tumor

Sertoli-Leydig cell tumors constitute less than 1 percent of ovarian tumors.[553] There are two main clinicopathologic categories:

1 well differentiated Sertoli-Leydig cell tumors which comprise 10 percent of all such tumors
2 Sertoli-Leydig cell tumors of intermediate and poor differentiation, which make up the remaining 90 percent.

Clinical findings Sertoli-Leydig cell tumors occur mainly in young women, but arise occasionally in children and postmenopausal women.[509] The average age is 24 years and

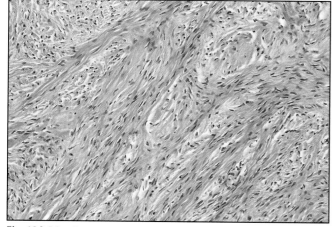

Fig. 13A.56 • Fibroma. Bland spindled fibroblasts are separated by abundant eosinophilic collagen.

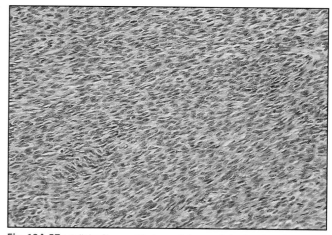

Fig. 13A.57 • Cellular fibroma. The tumor is hypercellular, but there is no nuclear atypia or mitotic activity.

75 percent of patients are under 30 years of age.[554–556] Women with well differentiated Sertoli-Leydig cell tumors average 40 years of age, 10–15 years older than those with intermediate or poorly differentiated tumors.[554–556] Retiform Sertoli-Leydig cell tumors have been reported to occur mainly in younger patients, with an average age of 16 years.[557–559] More recently, however, a series was reported in which the patients had a mean age of 31 years, illustrating that retiform tumors occur in mature and even elderly women as well as in the young.[560]

About 50 percent of Sertoli-Leydig cell tumors secrete steroid hormones in amounts sufficient to cause symptoms and 40 percent of patients are virilized.[554–556] Virilized patients have various combinations of symptoms including amenorrhea, deepening of the voice, hirsutism, temporal alopecia, hypertrophy of the clitoris, and acne. Serum levels of testosterone and urine levels of 17-ketosteroids are increased in virilized patients.

Non-virilized patients present with non-specific symptoms, such as abnormal vaginal bleeding, abdominal distention, an abdominal mass, or abdominal or pelvic pain. Five to 10 percent of patients have acute abdominal symptoms caused by torsion or rupture of the tumor. Occasional Sertoli-Leydig cell tumors are discovered in asymptomatic women.

Sertoli-Leydig cell tumors tend to be unilateral and confined to the ovary (stage IA) at diagnosis. There is extraovarian spread at diagnosis in fewer than 5 percent of cases but, in 5–15 percent of cases, the tumor is ruptured or there are tumor cells in the peritoneal fluid (FIGO stage Ic).[554] Unilateral salpingo-oophorectomy is adequate treatment for most patients. A total abdominal hysterectomy and bilateral salpingo-oophorectomy is appropriate treatment for older patients and can be considered in younger women when there are unfavorable prognostic findings, such as rupture, extraovarian spread, a poorly differentiated neoplasm with frequent stromal cell mitoses, or heterologous mesenchymal differentiation (cartilage or skeletal muscle, or foci of neuroblastoma).[554,555] Regression of virilization and resumption of normal menses follow tumor removal. Rare Sertoli-Leydig cell tumors secrete α-fetoprotein but the precise frequency with which this occurs is unknown, since such testing is not usually performed.[557–559,561–566]

Well-differentiated Sertoli-Leydig cell tumor is a clinically benign tumor that does not recur after complete excision.[555,567] The prognosis is generally favorable for patients with intermediate and poorly differentiated Sertoli-Leydig cell tumors. Only 18 percent of patients had a recurrence in one study,[554] while a 5-year survival rate of 92 percent was found in another.[555] Retiform Sertoli-Leydig cell tumors may have a slightly worse prognosis than the overall group.[557,559] Recurrences are generally detected within the first few years after treatment. Chemotherapy is helpful in about half of the patients who receive it.[454,554,568]

Pathology Well-differentiated Sertoli-Leydig cell tumors are solid, unilateral, encapsulated tumors that range from 1.5 to 10 cm in diameter.[567] The average size is 5 cm. The cut surface is yellow or yellow-tan. Intermediate and poorly differentiated tumors are larger, with an average diameter of 15 cm. Poorly differentiated tumors tend to be larger than those of intermediate differentiation, but there is considerable overlap. Sertoli-Leydig cell tumors are usually partly solid and partly cystic, but tumors that are predominantly solid or cystic are not unusual. Solid areas are firm or soft and gray-pink, yellow or orange in color. Papillae are sometimes visible in tumors with retiform differentiation.

Microscopically, fully developed hollow or closed tubules lined by columnar Sertoli cells are surrounded by fibrous stroma in well-differentiated Sertoli-Leydig cell tumors (Fig. 13A.58). Also present in the stroma are aggregates of Leydig cells with abundant eosinophilic cytoplasm and centrally placed round or oval nuclei. Crystalloids of Reinke are rarely identified within the Leydig cells. One unusual tumor had central ossification.[569] Cytologic atypia and mitotic activity are insignificant, and immature indifferent gonadal stroma, retiform tubules, and heterologous elements are absent.

In intermediate and poorly differentiated Sertoli-Leydig cell tumors, mature and immature Sertoli cells line well formed tubules, ill-defined tubules and trabeculae, and cord-like arrangements reminiscent of the embryonal sex cords (Fig. 13A.59). The tubules have a retiform appearance in 10–25 percent of intermediate and poorly differentiated tumors, and occasionally dominate the histologic picture to the extent that it is difficult to recognize that the neoplasm is a Sertoli-Leydig cell tumor.[560] Retiform tubules are long and branched and may be dilated with prominent areas of papillary growth

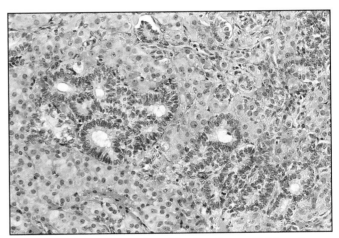

Fig. 13A.58 • Well-differentiated Sertoli-Leydig cell tumor. Well-formed tubules lined by Sertoli cells are surrounded by stroma containing plump Leydig cells with abundant eosinophilic cytoplasm.

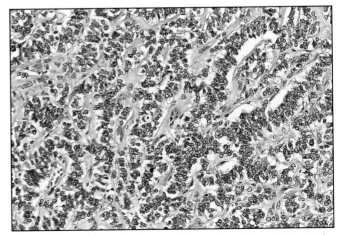

Fig. 13A.59 • Sertoli-Leydig cell tumor of intermediate differentiation. Sertoli cells grow in a trabecular pattern.

(Fig. 13A.60).[570] They are lined by low columnar to cuboidal cells with scanty cytoplasm and oval hyperchromatic nuclei. Mitotic figures are uncommon in Sertoli cells, but numerous mitotic figures are seen occasionally in the cells lining retiform tubules. Sertoli cells with bizarre atypical nuclei are present in some tumors, but this does not appear to be an adverse prognostic finding.[464] The tubules are surrounded by stroma that ranges from fibrous connective tissue to immature mesenchyme with the appearance of indifferent gonadal stroma, as seen in the developing gonad (Fig. 13A.61). The presence of immature Sertoli cells and stroma is the main feature that distinguishes intermediate and poorly differentiated Sertoli-Leydig cell tumors from well differentiated lesions.[555] Stroma is most abundant in poorly differentiated tumors, where it constitutes the bulk of the tumor (Fig. 13A.62).[571] The stromal cells are usually not strikingly atypical, but mitotic figures, which average 4–5 per 10 high power fields, are easy to find. Leydig cells, found singly or in small or medium sized clusters, are present in most tumors. They are often most conspicuous at the periphery of cellular tumor nodules. They are polygonal, with central round nuclei and abundant eosinophilic cyto-

plasm. Evidence has been presented suggesting that the Leydig cells are reactive, and not part of the neoplastic process,[572] but this has not yet been confirmed. There are heterologous elements in 20–25 percent of intermediate and poorly differentiated Sertoli-Leydig cell tumors. The most common of these is mucinous epithelium of intestinal type (Fig. 13A.63), but carcinoid, neuroblasts, cartilage, and rhabdomyoblasts have also been described.[555,573,574] Clusters of polygonal cells with eosinophilic cytoplasm are often present in Sertoli-Leydig cell tumors that secrete α-fetoprotein. Although these were interpreted as Leydig cells by some authors[562,566,575] most now view them as foci of heterologous hepatic differentiation.[560,565,576–578]

Immunohistochemical stains for cytokeratin are positive in most mature and immature Sertoli cells,[579,580] but these cells usually do not stain for epithelial membrane antigen.[520,579] Keratin stains are particularly helpful in confirming the identity of nests and cords of immature Sertoli cells in these tumors. Sertoli cells show membrane staining for CD99,[581] and staining for WT-1 is reported to be present in a majority of tumors, although this may be depend on the antibody that is used.[520]

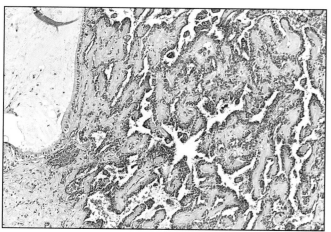

Fig.13A.60 • Sertoli-Leydig cell tumor of intermediate differentiation. Branching retiform tubules with a focal papillary appearance.

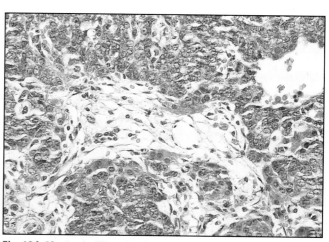

Fig. 13A.62 • Poorly differentiated Sertoli-Leydig cell tumor. Nests of immature stromal cells grow in nests in fibrous stroma. Occasional Leydig cells with eosinophilic cytoplasm grow in small clusters.

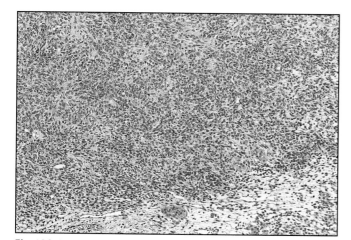

Fig. 13A.61 • Sertoli-Leydig cell tumor of intermediate differentiation. Sheet-like pattern composed of pale Sertoli cells, darkly stained immature stromal cells, and, at the periphery, nests of Leydig cells with conspicuous eosinophilic cytoplasm.

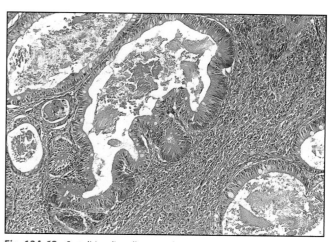

Fig. 13A.63 • Sertoli-Leydig cell tumor of intermediate differentiation with heterologous enteric epithelium. The large glands are lined by intestinal type cells, including goblet cells. Typical features of Sertoli-Leydig cell tumor can be seen in the stroma between the enteric glands.

Stromal cells and Leydig cells are vimentin positive.[483,484] Immunostains for inhibin and calretinin are almost always positive in both Sertoli cells and Leydig cells in Sertoli-Leydig cell tumors.[275,493,495,497,500,520,580] Occasional adenocarcinomas are inhibin or calretinin positive, so, when used in the diagnosis of Sertoli-Leydig cell tumor, inhibin and calretinin should always be part of a panel that includes cytokeratin, epithelial membrane antigen, and, possibly, other antibodies that stain adenocarcinoma, such as carcinoembryonic antigen (CEA). Immunostains for α-fetoprotein reveal positive staining of hepatoid cells in tumors that secrete it as well as in some where the serum α-fetoprotein is not elevated, and immunostains with anti-hepatocyte antibody show positive cytoplasmic staining in hepatoid cells.[562–566,575–578] The gastrointestinal epithelium in heterologous tumors contains argyrophilic cells that stain for chromogranin, serotonin, and other peptides,[582] and heterologous carcinoid elements stain for chromogranin or synaptophysin.[576] Immunoreactivity for P-450 cytochromes in Leydig cells, Sertoli cells, and stromal cells indicates that all are potential sites of steroidogenesis.[583]

Sertoli cell tumor

Sertoli cell tumors are among the rarest sex cord-stromal tumors.[584] They differ from Sertoli-Leydig cell tumors in that they do not contain Leydig cells or immature gonadal stroma.

Clinical features Sertoli cell tumors occur most often in women of reproductive age, but they occasionally arise in children and postmenopausal women. The average patient age is about 30 years.[584,585] Occasionally, a Sertoli cell tumor occurs in a patient with the Peutz–Jeghers syndrome,[584,586,587] although, as discussed below, the sex cord tumor with annular tubules is a more characteristic finding in patients with the Peutz–Jeghers syndrome. Two-thirds of Sertoli cell tumors secrete steroid hormones. Most secrete estrogens but a few secrete androgens. Girls with hormonally active tumors present with precocious pseudopuberty and vaginal bleeding. Older women have irregular bleeding, postmenopausal bleeding, or, rarely, virilization, depending on the type and amount of hormone secreted.[584] Patients with hormonally inactive neoplasms have non-specific symptoms such as pain or abdominal swelling, or their tumors are incidental findings. Sertoli cell tumors are unilateral and most are clinically benign tumors that can be treated by unilateral salpingo-oophorectomy.[585,588] Occasional poorly differentiated or invasive Sertoli cell tumors recur or metastasize, and cause the patient's death.[584] Most of these have spread beyond the ovary at diagnosis, but a few stage Ia Sertoli cell neoplasms have metastasized.

Pathology Sertoli cell tumors are unilateral, encapsulated tumors that average 8 cm in diameter; most are between 4 and 12 cm. The cut surfaces are gray, tan, brown, or yellow and are predominantly solid, although there are small cysts in some tumors.

Microscopically, these are tumors composed of Sertoli cells that grow in mature fibrous or hyalinized stroma. A tubular pattern is characteristic.[584] The tubular pattern tends to be a simple one, consisting of round or oval open glands with a central lumen or long closed cord-like tubules two or three cells thick. Mixed tubular patterns are often present. In some

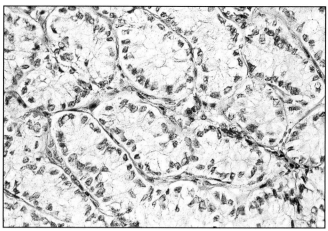

Fig. 13A.64 • Sertoli cell tumor. The tubules are lined by columnar cells with uniform basal nuclei and abundant clear cytoplasm.

tumors, there are cords, trabeculae, or areas of diffuse tumor cell growth.

Sertoli cells are cuboidal or columnar and have round to oval nuclei, which sometimes contain small nucleoli. Bizarre but degenerative nuclei do not appear adversely to affect the prognosis. The cytoplasm varies from clear to eosinophilic (Fig. 13A.64). Uncommon variants of Sertoli cell tumor include a lipid rich type, in which the cells have abundant clear, foamy cytoplasm,[584,585] and an oxyphilic type composed of cells with abundant granular eosinophilic cytoplasm.[586] Most Sertoli cell tumors are well differentiated and have uniform bland nuclei and few mitotic figures. Less than 10 percent of Sertoli cell tumors are clinically malignant. These have a poorly developed pattern of tubules, the Sertoli cells have enlarged atypical nuclei, and there are 5 or more mitotic figures per 10 high power fields.[584,589,590] Sertoli cell tumors that are confined to the ovary at diagnosis and that exhibit no or minimal nuclear atypia and mitotic activity can be viewed as benign.

Sertoli cell tumors tend to be immunoreactive for vimentin and cytokeratin,[579] but not for epithelial membrane antigen, and they stain for inhibin, calretinin, and CD99.[494,500,584] Occasional tumors show focal weak staining for smooth muscle actin, S-100 protein, or neuron specific enolase, but staining for chromogranin is absent.[584]

Sex cord tumor with annular tubules (SCTAT)

The SCTAT is designated as an "unclassified" sex cord-stromal tumor because its histogenesis is controversial. Nevertheless, its microscopic appearance and clinical features are distinctive.[591]

Clinical features The SCTAT occurs in two clinical settings. About a third are detected in women with the Peutz–Jeghers syndrome,[466] a hereditary condition with an autosomal dominant pattern of inheritance in which there is mutation of the *STK11* tumor suppressor gene on chromosome 19.[592–594] Those affected have mucocutaneous melanin pigmentation and hamartomatous intestinal polyps.[595] Palpable ovarian tumors of various types are detected in 10–20 percent of women with the Peutz–Jeghers syndrome,[596] but, if the ovaries are examined microscopically, virtually all contain SCTAT.[597] In this clinical setting, the tumors are generally microscopic in size, multi-centric, and bilateral, and show mutations of *STK11*.[598] SCTAT are almost always an incidental finding in women with the Peutz–Jeghers syndrome since they are too small to palpate and rarely secrete sufficient steroid hormones to cause symptoms. Microscopic SCTAT in women with the Peutz–Jeghers syndrome are clinically benign, and asymptomatic women do not need to have an oophorectomy.[597] A clinically detectable SCTAT in a woman with Peutz–Jeghers syndrome can usually be treated by unilateral salpingo-oophorectomy, although rare patients with bilateral or malignant SCTAT have been reported.[599] A small percentage of women with the Peutz–Jeghers syndrome develop a well differentiated adenocarcinoma of the endocervix, so lifetime surveillance by a gynecologist is appropriate.[596,597,600–602] An extremely rare type of sex cord-stromal tumor of the ovary occurs in children with the Peutz–Jeghers syndrome and causes sexual precocity.[603] Sertoli cell tumors, including unusual variants with oxyphilic or lipidized cytoplasm, also occur rarely in patients with the Peutz–Jeghers syndrome.[584,586]

About two-thirds of SCTAT occur in patients who do not have the Peutz–Jeghers syndrome (non-syndromic SCTAT).[585,597,604–606] Mutations of the *STK11* gene are usually not detected in non-syndromic SCTAT.[598] Non-syndromic SCTAT occur over a wide age range, from 6 to 76 years, with an average age of 36 years.[597] The presenting symptoms depend on the patient's age. Premenarcheal girls often have precocious pseudopuberty.[597,605] Older women may have menstrual dysfunction or postmenopausal bleeding. There is evidence that these tumors are able to produce progesterone as well as estrogen, since the endometrium exhibits a progesterone effect in some patients, and a peritoneal decidual reaction has been observed in others.[585,607,608] A unilateral adnexal mass is palpable in about 50 percent of patients. Increased serum concentrations of antimüllerian hormone (müllerian inhibiting substance) and inhibin have been found in a few women with SCTAT. These substances may prove to be useful tumor markers for the follow-up of patients with SCTAT.[609,610] Young women with localized tumors can be treated by unilateral salpingo-oophorectomy, while older women and those with advanced disease are treated by hysterectomy, bilateral salpingo-oophorectomy, and resection of extraovarian tumor. About 15 percent of non-syndromic SCTAT are clinically malignant.[597,604] Recurrences occur early in some patients,[597] but in many they are detected late, 5 or more years after initial treatment.[604,606,607,610] It is difficult to predict which tumors will metastasize. Combination chemotherapy has been effective, at least in the short term, in some patients,[610] but not in others.[607]

Pathology In patients with the Peutz–Jeghers syndrome, SCTAT are small and are usually not grossly visible. Those that can be seen are solid tan or yellow tumors that may contain calcifications. They tend to be multifocal and bilateral. Non-syndromic SCTAT are generally unilateral and vary in size from microscopic tumors or small nodules less than 1 cm in diameter to large tumors more than 20 cm in diameter. They are mainly solid, although cysts are present in some, and they have fleshy, tan or yellow cut surfaces.

Microscopically, rounded, sometimes coalescent nests of tumor cells growing in simple or complex closed annular tubules enclose cores of eosinophilic hyaline material (Fig. 13A.65). The tumor cells grow in a fibrous stroma and are surrounded by basement membrane-like material that is continuous with the hyaline cores. The cores and the basement membrane-like material are PAS-positive. There is typically a "paired cell" arrangement in the tubules, with the nuclei of the apposed cells located at opposite ends of the cells. The tumor cells are columnar and have clear or foamy cytoplasm and round or oval hyperchromatic nuclei with small nucleoli. Nuclear grooves are occasionally present. Atypia and mitotic figures are uncommon. Large tumors from patients who do not have the Peutz–Jeghers syndrome may contain long closed tubules, coalescent nests of tumor cells, foci of solid growth, cysts, or acellular areas of amorphous hyaline material (Fig. 13A.66). Small areas of granulosa cell or Sertoli cell differentiation are noted occasionally.[597,605,606,611] Metastases from some SCTAT resemble a granulosa cell tumor,[606] while metastases from some granulosa cell tumors resemble a SCTAT,[612] emphasizing the close relationship between these two types of sex cord-stromal tumors. One unique tumor contained areas with endometrioid

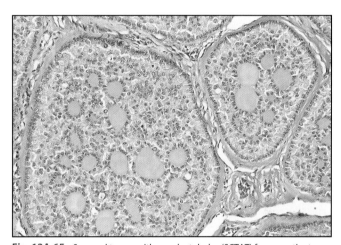

Fig. 13A.65 • Sex cord tumor with annular tubules (SCTAT) from a patient with the Peutz–Jeghers syndrome. Nests of tumor cells are surrounded by fibrous stroma. The complex annular tubules surround hyaline cores of basement membrane material. Note the antipodal arrangement of the tumor cell nuclei.

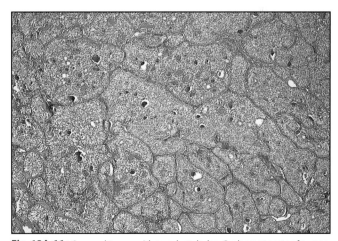

Fig. 13A.66 • Sex cord tumor with annular tubules. Coalescent nests of tumor cells in a large tumor from a patient who did not have the Peutz–Jeghers syndrome.

glandular differentiation.[608] Features associated with aggressive behavior include stromal invasion and increased numbers of mitotic figures.[585,604]

The immunophenotype of the SCTAT is similar to that of a Sertoli cell tumor. It shows positive staining for vimentin, inhibin and calretinin, and it stains for cytokeratin but not for epithelial membrane antigen.[275,520,613] The electron microscopic features of the SCTAT have been studied by numerous investigators with the hope that they might provide a clue to its histogenesis.[514,585,606,611,614–616] Basement membrane material surrounds tumor cell nests and fills the central spaces within the nests, forming the hyaline cores seen by light microscopy. Many tumor cells contain cytoplasmic filaments, which, in some cells, form perinuclear aggregates. These have been interpreted by some as Charcot–Böttcher filaments, leading them to conclude that SCTAT are Sertoli cell tumors.[514,585,611,616] Others have not been able to identify Charcot–Böttcher filaments, and have concluded that the appearance of the tumor cells indicates that SCTAT is a variant of granulosa cell tumor.[606,614,615]

Leydig cell tumor

Most ovarian Leydig cell tumors originate in the hilum, presumably from hilus cells, leading to the occasional designation of hilar Leydig cell tumors as "hilus cell tumors".[617] Less often, Leydig cell tumors arise outside the hilum, from the ovarian stroma. This category includes non-hilar and stromal Leydig cell tumors.[521,618,619]

Clinical findings Leydig cell tumors typically occur in postmenopausal women. The average age is 58 and almost all patients are over 30 years of age.[617] The usual clinical presentation is with hirsutism or signs of virilization such as acne, hair loss, deepening of the voice, a male body contour or hypertrophy of the clitoris. The serum testosterone concentration is elevated in virilized patients, but urinary 17-ketosteroids are generally within normal limits.[617,620] Non-virilized patients have amenorrhea or postmenopausal bleeding, depending on their age. Some Leydig cell tumors are found incidentally during surgery for some other condition. The endometrium can show hyperplasia or even adenocarcinoma,[621] most likely secondary to peripheral conversion of testosterone to estrogen. Symptoms are often present for several years before the diagnosis is made. This is because Leydig cell tumors are usually small and difficult to localize. Non-palpable tumors can be detected by imaging studies in some cases but, in others, it is necessary to measure hormone concentrations in blood obtained by selective catheterization of the ovarian veins.[622,623] Although most Leydig cell tumors are unilateral, rare patients with bilateral tumors have been reported.[624] Virtually all Leydig cell tumors are benign and are cured by surgery.[521,617–619] Signs of virilization usually regress following removal of the tumor. Malignant Leydig cell tumors are very rare; only a few cases have been reported.[617]

Pathology Leydig cell tumors are unilateral small solid brown or yellow-brown tumors located in the hilum of the ovary, or, rarely, in the medulla or cortex. The average diameter is between 3 and 5 cm, but tumors as small as 0.7 cm and as large as 15 cm have been reported.

Microscopically, hilar Leydig cell tumors are circumscribed but not encapsulated. The tumor cells resemble Leydig cells of the testis and the hilus cells normally present around nerves in the hilum of the ovary.[617] They are round or polygonal and have abundant granular eosinophilic cytoplasm (Fig. 13A.67). Many cells contain yellow or brown lipochrome pigment. The nuclei are small and uniform, range from vesicular to hyperchromatic and may contain conspicuous nucleoli. Crystalloids of Reinke are characteristic of Leydig cells, but they are identified in only about 50 percent of hilar Leydig cell tumors. They are intracytoplasmic eosinophilic rods with blunt or tapered ends (Fig. 13A.68). Intracytoplasmic eosinophilic hyaline globules, which are thought to be precursors of Reinke crystals, are often easier to find. Other findings of note include perivascular clustering of nuclei and a peculiar fibrinoid change in the walls of blood vessels within the tumor.[617]

There are two types of non-hilar Leydig cell tumors. Pure non-hilar Leydig cell tumors are circumscribed tumors that are similar to hilar Leydig cell tumors except for their location; they are usually centered in the medulla.[619,625] Stromal Leydig cell tumors are fibromas or thecomas that contain clusters, nests, or sheets of Leydig cells.[521,618,626,627] By definition, crystalloids of Reinke must be identified in the tumor cells in order to diagnose a non-hilar Leydig cell tumor. Since only 50 percent

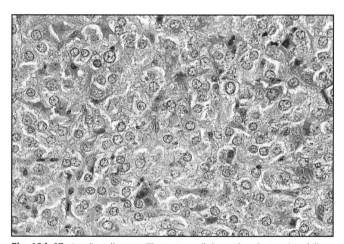

Fig. 13A.67 • Leydig cell tumor. The tumor cells have abundant eosinophilic cytoplasm and uniform round central nuclei.

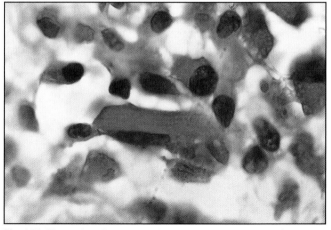

Fig. 13A.68 • Leydig cell tumor. A rod-like eosinophilic crystalloid of Reinke is present in the cell in the center of the field.

of hilar Leydig cell tumors contain crystalloids, some non-hilar Leydig cell tumors are unrecognized and are misdiagnosed as a stromal luteoma[628] or a luteinized thecoma.[521]

Regardless of their site of origin within the ovary, Leydig cell tumors show strong positive staining for inhibin and calretinin.[629]

Steroid cell tumors

This category of ovarian tumors encompasses a somewhat heterogeneous group of stromal neoplasms that cannot be more specifically classified. Tumors of this type are also known as "lipid cell tumors". Cells resembling Leydig cells, but lacking crystalloids of Reinke, and cells resembling adrenal cortical cells are present in variable proportions in most of them.[630,631]

Clinical features Steroid cell tumors occur over a wide age range, from 3 to 80 years. The average patient is a middle-aged woman about 45 years old, but steroid cell tumors occasionally occur in children and in the elderly.[509,632,633] Most steroid cell tumors secrete androgenic steroids in amounts sufficient to cause hirsutism or virilization. Serum testosterone concentrations and urinary 17-ketosteroids are elevated in virilized patients.[630,631] One unusual tumor secreted renin as well as testosterone and was associated with secondary polycythemia.[634] Non-virilized patients present with abdominal distention or pain, menstrual irregularities, or postmenopausal bleeding. Rare steroid cell tumors secrete cortisol and cause Cushing's syndrome.[630,635,636]

Most tumors are confined to the ovaries at diagnosis and bilateral tumors are rare (6 percent).[630] Pelvic, peritoneal or distant metastases are present at diagnosis in 10–20 percent of cases.[630,631] Young patients with stage IA neoplasms can be treated by salpingo-oophorectomy. Older patients and those with advanced tumors are generally treated by hysterectomy and bilateral salpingo-oophorectomy. Hirsutism and signs of virilization regress after removal of the tumor. A significant proportion of steroid cell tumors, 25–43 percent, including a majority of those that cause Cushing's syndrome, are clinically malignant.[630,631,635] Recurrences are generally detected within the first few years after treatment, but about 20 percent are detected more than 5 years later.[630]

Pathology Steroid cell tumors are solid and range from less than 1 cm to more than 20 cm in diameter, with an average of about 7 cm. The cut surface is tan, yellow, or orange, and about 25 percent of them have areas of hemorrhage and necrosis. A few parovarian steroid cell tumors, possibly originating in ectopic ovarian tissue, have been reported.[637–639]

Microscopically, a mixture of Leydig-like and adrenal cortical-like cells is generally present, although one of these may predominate. The Leydig-like cells are round or polygonal and have abundant, sometimes vacuolated eosinophilic cytoplasm (Fig. 13A.69). The nucleus is round, centrally located, and typically contains a small nucleolus. Crystalloids of Reinke are never identified. The adrenal cortical-like cells are also round or polygonal and have abundant pale or clear vacuolated cytoplasm (Fig. 13A.70). The nucleus is vesicular and may contain a small to medium sized but conspicuous nucleolus. Fat stains are positive in adrenal-type cells. In most

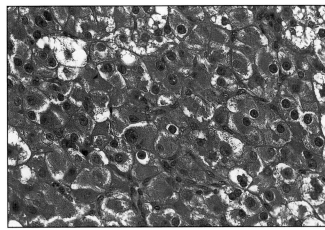

Fig. 13A.69 • Steroid cell tumor. The tumor cells resemble Leydig cells. They have abundant eosinophilic cytoplasm, but crystalloids of Reinke are absent.

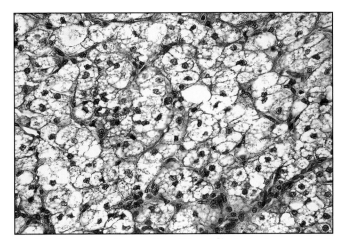

Fig. 13A.70 • Steroid cell tumor. Adrenal-like cells, with abundant vacuolated clear cytoplasm.

cases, mitotic figures are infrequent and nuclear atypia is absent or modest. Pathologic features found in malignant steroid cell tumors include large size, hemorrhage or necrosis, 2 or more mitotic figures/10 high power fields, and moderate or marked nuclear atypia.[630,631]

Immunohistochemical stains for vimentin, inhibin and calretinin are generally positive.[492–494,613,640] Most steroid cell tumors stain for melan-A, but staining for the related marker MART-1 is generally absent.[640,641] Staining for cytokeratin is present in 30–50 percent of tumors, usually focally and sometimes with a perinuclear globoid staining pattern, and stains for smooth muscle actin are positive in about a third of cases.[642]

Other sex cord-stromal tumors

Gynandroblastoma is a rare tumor with substantial areas of both Sertoli or Sertoli-Leydig cell and granulosa cell differentiation (each component ≥10 percent).[643–648] Tumors of this type are placed in the unclassified sex cord-stromal tumor category by some.[649] Patients with a gynandroblastoma are typically virilized, although peripheral conversion of testosterone to estrogen can cause abnormal vaginal bleeding due to endometrial proliferation or hyperplasia.[648] The treatment is surgical excision. All reported examples have had a benign clinical evolution but, given the composition of the tumor, it should probably be viewed as having the same malignant potential as a granulosa cell tumor or intermediate grade Sertoli-Leydig cell tumor. Gynandroblastoma is unilateral and measures 1–18 cm in diameter.[643] It can be solid or partly cystic. Solid areas are white, tan, or yellow. Microscopically, open and closed tubules and cords lined by Sertoli cells are intermixed with nests and sheets of granulosa cells (Fig. 13A.71). Microfollicles and other typical patterns of granulosa cell tumor may be present. The granulosa cell component is usually of the adult type, although in a few cases it has been of the juvenile type.[650–652] The stroma may contain spindle-shaped cells resembling theca cells, luteinized cells, or Leydig cells. Neither significant cytologic atypia nor frequent mitotic figures have been present in reported examples of gynandroblastoma. These tumors express inhibin and calretinin. Vimentin and androgen receptor are preferentially expressed in the granulosa cell component and low molecular weight keratin and CD10 are more likely to be expressed by the Sertoli cell component.[652]

Sclerosing stromal tumor is an uncommon benign tumor that occurs mainly in teenagers and young women in their 20s.[653–657] The usual presentation is with disturbances of menstruation or pelvic pain, although rare examples cause virilization.[658,659] Sclerosing stromal tumor is one of the tumor types that has been associated with Meigs' syndrome.[660] A sclerosing stromal tumor is occasionally detected during pregnancy,[661,662] when it may cause virilization.[663] Sclerosing stromal tumor is benign and, since most examples are found in young women, it is best treated by excision or unilateral salpingo-oophorectomy. Sclerosing stromal tumors range from 1.5 to 17 cm in diameter. Most are solid or predominantly solid with small cysts, but an occasional tumor is predominantly cystic.[654,657] The solid areas are firm, lobulated, and white or yellow. Microscopically, sclerosing stromal tumor has a variegated appearance due to the juxtaposition of cellular nodules and zones of edema or hypocellular fibrous stroma. Blood vessels are prominent and often have a "staghorn" or "hemangiopericytoma-like" appearance. The tumor cells include spindle-shaped fibroblasts, myoid cells, and polygonal theca-like cells with vacuolated eosinophilic cytoplasm (Fig. 13A.72). Immunostains for vimentin, inhibin, calretinin

and melan-A are positive,[494,495,535,641,664] and most tumors contain myoid cells that are immunoreactive for smooth muscle actin or desmin.[535,657,665] Positivity for estrogen or progesterone receptors can often be identified in tumor cell nuclei; staining for progesterone receptors is usually most prominent.[657,666] Recently, vascular endothelial growth factor (VEGF) has been identified in the theca-like cells and its receptor localized to the vascular endothelial cells, suggesting that VEGF may play a role in the vascularity and edema that characterize this tumor.[657]

Stromal luteoma is a rare estrogen-secreting tumor that occurs mainly in postmenopausal women.[628] The most common presentation is with abnormal uterine bleeding, and an endometrial biopsy often reveals hyperplasia. Rarely, stromal luteoma is virilizing. A third of cases are incidental findings at operation or autopsy. It is clinically benign. Stromal luteoma is a small unilateral neoplasm; all reported examples have been less than 3 cm in diameter. The cut surface is gray, white, yellow, or brown. The tumor is located in the ovarian stroma and it is composed of luteinized stromal cells. They are polygonal, with granular eosinophilic cytoplasm and small round centrally placed nuclei. Differentiation from a Leydig cell tumor is based upon the non-hilar location of the stromal luteoma and the absence of cytoplasmic crystalloids of Reinke. Other ovarian abnormalities are typically present, including stromal hyperthecosis, which is often bilateral, and hilus cell hyperplasia.

Tumors that do not fit into any of the named categories are called *unclassified sex cord-stromal tumors*.[8] The clinical presentation tends to be non-specific, with abnormal bleeding, an abdominal mass, or abdominal pain. Sex cord-stromal tumors removed from pregnant women are often difficult to classify, and some must be designated as "unclassified".[447] In most cases, the tumor is confined to the ovary at diagnosis and the prognosis is favorable. A few tumor-related deaths have been reported, so these tumors are viewed as having low malignant potential, along the lines of a granulosa cell or intermediate Sertoli-Leydig cell tumor.[649,667] Unclassified sex cord-stromal tumors consist of variable admixtures of spindle cells, cords and trabeculae of sex cord cells, and vague tubule-like structures.[649,667] They do not show sufficiently distinctive patterns of growth to be classified as granulosa cell or

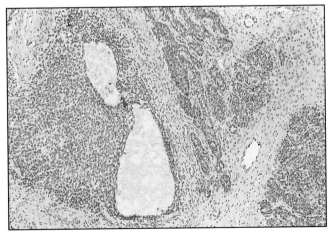

Fig. 13A.71 • Gynandroblastoma. Intimate admixture of granulosa elements containing follicles (left) and Sertoli tubules and Leydig cells (right).

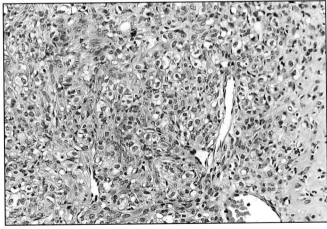

Fig. 13A.72 • Sclerosing stromal tumor. Cellular region composed of plump rounded cells.

Sertoli-Leydig cell tumors, although, as mentioned above, gynandroblastoma is included in this category by some.[649]

Non-specific mesenchymal tumors

Mesenchymal tumors of all types occur in the ovary. The gross and microscopic appearance of these tumors is the same in the ovary as it is in the soft tissues or uterus, as is the clinical behavior. Leiomyomas are the most common mesenchymal tumors of the ovary.[668–671] Lipoleiomyoma is a variant of leiomyoma in which the smooth muscle is mixed with fat.[672,673] Other benign soft tissue tumors that occur in the ovary from time to time are hemangioma[674,675] and myxoma.[676,677] Ovarian myxoma is more cellular and more vascular than soft tissue myxoma. Myxoma has been interpreted by some as a tumor in the fibroma–thecoma group,[678] but the prevailing view is that it is a separate entity.[676]

Primary sarcomas of the ovary are rare.[679] Fibrosarcoma and endometrioid stromal sarcoma, which are discussed above, are the most common ovarian sarcomas. Leiomyosarcoma occurs in the ovary and can be diagnosed by evaluating similar features to those employed for the diagnosis of uterine leiomyosarcoma. Leiomyosarcoma of the ovary exhibits diffuse moderate to severe nuclear atypia, frequent mitotic figures, and tumor cell necrosis. In the largest reported study, it was found that tumors with diffuse significant nuclear atypia and 5 or more mitotic figures per 10 high power fields were likely to behave as leiomyosarcomas; many, but not all, had foci of tumor cell necrosis.[671] Other types of primary ovarian sarcoma are rhabdomyosarcoma,[680] chondrosarcoma,[681] osteosarcoma,[682,683] malignant schwannoma,[684] and angiosarcoma.[685,686]

Malignant lymphoma

Clinical features Lymphoma presents as an ovarian tumor in fewer than 1 percent of cases.[687–689] The clinical presentation in such cases is with pelvic or abdominal pain, abdominal distention, disturbances of menstruation, or lymphoma "B" symptoms of fever, night sweats, or weight loss. On examination, unilateral or bilateral adnexal masses are palpable. Although the clinical presentation is as an ovarian tumor, the lymphoma generally also involves the pelvic or abdominal lymph nodes, the liver or spleen, or other organs, indicating that the ovaries are involved as part of a disseminated disease.[689,690] A few patients treated only by oophorectomy never develop extraovarian lymphoma, indicating that rare lymphomas are primary in the ovary.[687,688,690–692] The Ann Arbor lymphoma stage provides more prognostic information than the FIGO stage.[693] The survival of patients who receive modern combination chemotherapy is greater than 50 percent and is similar to that attained overall in lymphomas of comparable grade and stage.[687,689–691,693]

Pathology Both ovaries are involved in more than 50 percent of cases,[689] although primary lymphomas tend to be unilateral.[692] The size ranges from microscopic to more than 20 cm, with an average diameter of 10–15 cm. Rare ovarian lymphomas are incidental microscopic discoveries in ovaries removed for some other reason.[692] The cut surface is fleshy and pink, tan, or gray. Microscopically, the lymphoma is almost invariably of non-Hodgkin type.[687,688,690,691,694] Burkitt and Burkitt-like lymphomas are most common in children and young women, but can also occur in older women. The tumor cells have uniform, round, small to medium sized nuclei with coarse chromatin and 1–3 nucleoli. Mitotic figures are frequent. The cytoplasm is scanty and basophilic. The cells grow in sheets punctuated by spaces that contain phagocytic histiocytes, producing the "starry sky" appearance typical of Burkitt lymphoma, or in cords.[688] They tend to surround, rather than replace, follicles and other ovarian structures. Large B cell lymphoma is the most common ovarian lymphoma in adults. The tumor cells have round, oval, or cleaved nuclei and scanty to moderate amphophilic cytoplasm (Fig. 13A.73). The nuclei are hyperchromatic with coarse chromatin, or vesicular with a prominent nucleolus. Mitotic figures are numerous. The cells grow in sheets and may focally infiltrate the stroma in cords. Other types of non-Hodgkin lymphoma, including lymphoblastic lymphoma, follicular lymphoma, and T-cell lymphoma occasionally involve the ovary. Vascular invasion and focal stromal sclerosis is common in all types of lymphoma. The most useful immunohistochemical markers are CD45 (leukocyte common antigen), CD20 for B cells, and CD3 for T cells. Other markers of B and T cell differentiation such as CD79a, CD45RA, CD45RO, and CD43, are helpful when the primary markers give an equivocal result, and various additional stains are necessary to immunophenotype unusual types of ovarian lymphoma. Immunohistochemical studies generally reveal a B-cell phenotype.[688,693]

Leukemia

Leukemia frequently involves the ovary, but seldom presents as an ovarian tumor. Granulocytic sarcoma is an extramedullary mass of immature myeloid cells. It is a rare cause of unilateral or bilateral ovarian enlargement.[695,696] The cut surface is lobulated, firm or fleshy, and ranges in color from white or tan to a green color that, although characteristic of granulocytic sarcoma, is rarely seen. Microscopically, granulocytic sarcoma consists of sheets or cords of immature hematopoietic cells with medium-sized round nuclei, fine chromatin, inconspicuous

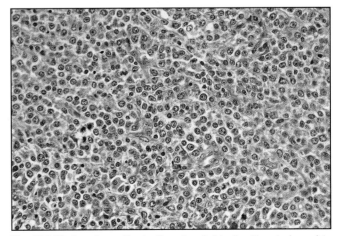

Fig. 13A.73 • Lymphoma. Sheets of large lymphoid cells with vesicular nuclei, coarse chromatin, and scant cytoplasm, consistent with a large cell lymphoma.

nucleoli, and scanty amphophilic cytoplasm. Evidence of myeloid differentiation, such as cytoplasmic eosinophilia or an admixture of eosinophilic myelocytes, is typically inconspicuous and easy to overlook. Histochemical stains for naphthyl chloroacetate esterase are usually positive, although often only focally. A variety of immunohistochemical stains are positive in granulocytic sarcoma and are easier to interpret than histochemical stains. Myeloperoxidase and lysozyme are the most sensitive and specific. Immunostains for markers of B and T lymphocyte differentiation, such as CD20 and CD3, are negative. Leukemia may or may not involve the peripheral blood and bone marrow at the time of diagnosis of granulocytic sarcoma; if leukemia is not present at diagnosis, it generally develops subsequently.

Germ cell tumors

The neoplasms in this group are derived from germ cells (Table 13A.9). Some are composed of undifferentiated cells (dysgerminoma, embryonal carcinoma), while in others there is differentiation towards embryonic (teratoma) or extra-embryonic (choriocarcinoma, yolk sac tumor) structures. Benign cystic teratomas are common, but other types of germ cell tumors, including all the malignant ones, are rare.

Dysgerminoma

Dysgerminoma is the most common malignant germ cell tumor of the ovary,[1,3,4,697] but it accounts for only 1 percent to 2 percent of all malignant ovarian tumors.

Clinical features Dysgerminoma is a tumor of children and young women.[698–702] The average age is 22 years, and 90 percent of patients are under 30 years.[703–705] About 20 percent of malignant ovarian tumors detected during pregnancy are dysger-

Table 13A.9	Germ cell tumors of the ovary
Germ cell tumors	

Dysgerminoma

Yolk sac tumor (endodermal sinus tumor)

Embryonal carcinoma

Polyembryoma

Choriocarcinoma

Teratoma
  Mature teratoma
    Solid
    Cystic (benign cystic teratoma; dermoid cyst)
  Immature teratoma
  Neuroectodermal tumors
Malignant tumor arising in a mature teratoma
Monodermal teratoma
  Struma ovarii
  Carcinoid tumor
Mixed germ cell tumor
Gonadoblastoma
Unclassified germ cell tumor

minomas.[706,707] The typical presentation is with abdominal distention, an abdominal mass, or abdominal pain. Some patients have menstrual abnormalities or gastrointestinal or urinary symptoms. Rare patients have hypercalcemia.[708–711] Serum lactic dehydrogenase (LDH) is frequently elevated, and can serve as a useful tumor marker.[705,712–714] Increased levels of serum α-fetoprotein or human chorionic gonadotropin suggest the presence of other germ cell elements, although rare patients with pure dysgerminoma have increased amounts of these substances in the blood.[714–717] Dysgerminoma is the most common malignant gonadal tumor in patients with gonadal dysgenesis.[704,718,719]

Dysgerminoma is confined to the ovaries (stage I) at diagnosis in 60–80 percent of patients.[698,700,702,712] It is usually unilateral, but both ovaries contain tumor (stage IB) in 5–15 percent of cases.[698–700,702,705] The tumor in the contralateral ovary is microscopic in half of the bilateral cases, leading some oncologists to recommend biopsy of an apparently normal contralateral ovary if treatment is to be by unilateral salpingo-oophorectomy.[698,699,720] Dysgerminoma metastasizes via the lymphatics to the paraaortic lymph nodes, with subsequent spread to the mediastinal lymph nodes, and by transperitoneal spread to the pelvic and abdominal peritoneum.[699,712,719]

Unilateral encapsulated dysgerminoma (FIGO stage Ia) can be treated by salpingo-oophorectomy with a 5-year survival rate of greater than 90 percent.[698–700,702,712,720,721] Postoperative therapy has been advocated for these patients since there are recurrences in 20–35 percent of patients treated by surgery alone.[700,722] Fortunately, recurrences usually are managed successfully and routine adjuvant therapy is often withheld due to its adverse effect on fertility. When dysgerminoma arises in a dysgenetic gonad, the appropriate treatment is bilateral gonadectomy. The standard treatment for advanced disease (stage >IA) is total abdominal hysterectomy, bilateral salpingo-oophorectomy, limited debulking, and postoperative chemotherapy or radiotherapy.[723] If they are not involved by tumor, the uterus and the contralateral ovary may be conserved in advanced cases where preservation of fertility is important.[712,724] Chemotherapy with platinum-based regimens is highly effective against dysgerminoma and is less likely than radiation to cause ovarian failure and infertility.[725–729] Response to chemotherapy approaches 90 percent, and long-term survival rates of more than 80 percent are reported even in patients with advanced or recurrent disease. Any recurrences are usually evident within two years of primary treatment.[701,725,729–731]

Pathology Dysgerminoma is a large solid tumor, usually more than 10 cm in diameter, with a smooth outer surface. On cross-section, it is fleshy, homogeneous or nodular, and gray, tan, or white. Hemorrhage and necrosis are often present in large tumors.

The microscopic appearance of dysgerminoma is the same as that of seminoma of the testis. The tumor cells are polygonal, with distinct cell membranes and abundant granular to clear cytoplasm (Fig. 13A.74). Glycogen can often be demonstrated in the cytoplasm with the PAS stain. The nuclei are central, round, and vesicular, and they contain prominent nucleoli. Mitotic figures are usually numerous. The cells grow in nests, lobules, and trabeculae that are surrounded by fibrous septa. There is occasionally loss of intercellular cohesion with formation of gland-like spaces. Lymphocytes are usually noted

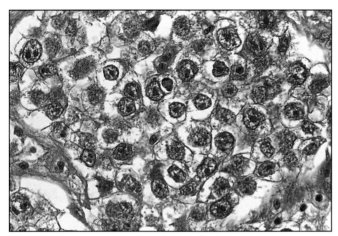

Fig. 13A.74 • Dysgerminoma. The cells have vesicular nuclei with prominent nucleoli, abundant clear cytoplasm, and distinct cell membranes.

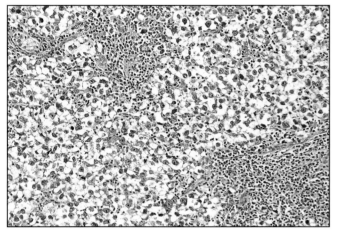

Fig. 13A.75 • Dysgerminoma. Lobules of tumor cells with abundant clear cytoplasm are separated by fibrous septa that contain numerous lymphocytes.

within the fibrous septa, and are occasionally seen among the tumor cells (Fig. 13A.75). Lymphocytes are numerous in some tumors, in which they form sheets or nodules that may contain reactive germinal centers. Epithelioid cells and multinucleated Langhans giant cells are often seen, and some tumors contain sarcoid-like granulomas. A fibrous or granulomatous reaction can be so intense that it obscures the tumor cells. Zones of necrosis are present in some dysgerminomas, especially large ones. Neoplasms with a degree of atypia greater than usual and a high mitotic rate (more than 30 mitotic figures per 10 high power fields) have been termed "anaplastic dysgerminoma". The prognosis in such cases is comparable to that of a typical dysgerminoma.[700,716] About 3 percent of dysgerminomas contain syncytiotrophoblastic giant cells but exhibit no other non-germinomatous differentiation. These tumors are termed dysgerminoma with syncytiotrophoblastic giant cells and have the same prognosis as tumors in which syncytiotrophoblastic giant cells are absent.[716] One example that arose in a dysgenetic gonad has been reported.[732]

Dysgerminoma has an immunophenotype similar to that of seminoma of the testis. The most characteristic findings are positive staining of tumor cells for placental alkaline phosphatase (PLAP), CD117 and OCT4.[733,734] Staining for

PLAP and CD117 is membranous and is generally strong and diffuse. OCT4 is the protein product of a nuclear transcription factor, so staining is nuclear; it is generally strong and diffuse. Monoclonal antibodies against cytokeratin, particularly those against low molecular weight cytokeratins, may be positive in dysgerminoma,[735] but staining is usually focal and can have a dot-like or rim-like appearance. Positive staining for human chorionic gonadotropin is seen in the syncytiotrophoblastic giant cells that are noted occasionally in dysgerminoma,[716,732] and, rarely, in mononuclear tumor cells.[735,736] Immunostains for α-fetoprotein (AFP) are almost invariably negative. Several dysgerminomas with microscopic foci of transformation to yolk sac tumor have been reported to show positive staining for α-fetoprotein and cytokeratin in the foci of yolk sac differentiation, but not in areas of typical dysgerminoma.[717] The tumor-infiltrating lymphocytes in dysgerminoma are T cells, as shown by immunohistochemical staining for various markers of T-cell differentiation.[737]

Yolk sac (endodermal sinus) tumor

Yolk sac tumor is a malignant germ cell tumor in which there is differentiation into yolk sac structures.[738–741] This tumor was formerly known as endodermal sinus tumor. Yolk sac tumor is the second most common malignant germ cell tumor of the ovary and comprises approximately 1 percent of ovarian malignancies.[697]

Clinical features Yolk sac tumor occurs principally in children and young women, although rare examples have been reported in women more than 45 years of age.[742–748] The median age is 19 years.

The most common presenting complaints are abdominal pain, abdominal enlargement, or an abdominal mass.[744,746] About 10 percent of patients have acute abdominal symptoms due to rupture or torsion of the tumor. High levels of α-fetoprotein (AFP) are present in the serum of most patients with yolk sac tumors,[742,749,750] and some have increased levels of CA-125 as well.[749]

Yolk sac tumor appears limited to the ovary at diagnosis in about 50 percent of patients.[742–744] When tumor disseminates beyond the ovary, it spreads to the peritoneum and omentum, the para-aortic lymph nodes, and the liver. Tumor appears confined to the pelvis (stage II) in about 10 percent of cases, while the remaining 40 percent have more widespread metastases (stage III and IV).

The recommended initial surgical treatment for yolk sac tumor is unilateral salpingo-oophorectomy with limited debulking of extraovarian tumor. Bilateral involvement is rare in patients with localized (stage I) tumors, so it is not necessary to biopsy the contralateral ovary.[744] If they are uninvolved, the contralateral ovary and uterus need not be removed in patients with advanced disease. Despite apparently adequate surgery, the prognosis for individuals with yolk sac tumor was dismal prior to the availability of combination chemotherapy.[744,751,752] The clinical course was characterized by rapid development and growth of metastases and high mortality, even when the tumor appeared limited to the ovary at operation. Radiotherapy proved ineffective for treating these tumors.[742,753] The 3-year survival was only 13 percent in one large study of patients treated prior to 1975.[744] The development of VAC

605

(vincristine, dactinomycin, and cyclophosphamide) combination chemotherapy completely changed the outlook for patients with yolk sac tumor. When treated with VAC chemotherapy, about 80 percent of patients with stage I tumors survive, as do about 50 percent of those with advanced disease.[742,754,755] Chemotherapy regimens containing platinum provide even better results in stage I and there is improved survival in patients with advanced disease as well.[731,756–762] The serum AFP level can be used to monitor the response to treatment and to detect tumor recurrence.[749,757] Second look laparotomy appears unnecessary in patients with yolk sac tumor,[763] even though in a few instances, residual tumor has been identified in patients with normal serum AFP levels.[764]

Pathology Yolk sac tumors tend to be large, with an average diameter of 16 cm.[742,744] The cut surface is tan, white, or gray with small cysts and areas of hemorrhage and necrosis.

There are five major patterns of yolk sac tumor growth, as well as a number of rare ones. A mixture of patterns is present in most tumors. The two most common and distinctive patterns are the reticular, or microcystic, pattern and the endodermal sinus pattern.[744] The reticular pattern consists of a loose meshwork of microcystic spaces lined by a single layer of flattened or cuboidal cells (Fig. 13A.76). These have clear or amphophilic cytoplasm and atypical, hyperchromatic nuclei. The endodermal sinus pattern is also known as the festoon or pseudopapillary pattern. It consists of anastomosing glands and papillae lined by columnar cells with clear or amphophilic cytoplasm and fusiform, hyperchromatic nuclei. Schiller–Duval bodies, which consist of fibrovascular papillae covered by columnar tumor cells projecting into glands or cystic spaces lined by cuboidal cells, are a characteristic finding in this pattern (Fig. 13A.77), and are observed in about two-thirds of cases. They are diagnostic of yolk sac tumor. The endodermal sinus pattern often merges into the closely related alveolar-glandular pattern, in which anastomosing tubules or glands are surrounded by a myxoid or spindle cell stroma. The glands are lined by cuboidal or columnar cells that are often stratified into multiple layers or form small papillae. The solid pattern is characterized by nests or sheets of small to medium sized undifferentiated cells with a moderate amount of amphophilic

or clear cytoplasm. In the polyvesicular vitelline pattern, cysts bearing a resemblance to yolk sac vesicles are lined by cuboidal, columnar, or mucinous epithelial cells (Fig. 13A.78). The cysts are surrounded by immature cellular mesenchymal stroma.[765] Rare patterns include a hepatoid pattern composed of sheets or trabeculae of large cells with central vesicular nuclei with prominent nucleoli and abundant granular eosinophilic cytoplasm.[424,741,766,767] These cells are reminiscent of those seen in hepatocellular carcinoma. Although large areas of hepatoid differentiation are present in some yolk sac tumors, this pattern is most often a focal microscopic finding.[768] A glandular pattern, in which there are zones of glands of endometrioid or intestinal type, is a rare but important pattern in yolk sac tumor. In the endometrioid-like variant, which can be mistaken for endometrioid carcinoma, the glands are lined by a single layer of columnar cells which have clear supra- or subnuclear cytoplasmic vacuoles (Fig. 13A.79).[769,770] The intestinal pattern can mimic a primary or metastatic mucinous tumor. It is characterized by aggregates of primitive endodermal glands lined by low columnar cells growing in loose or cellular

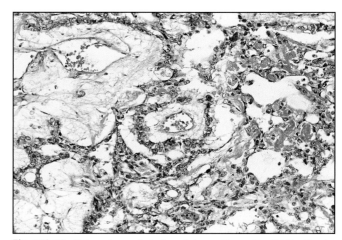

Fig. 13A.77 • Yolk sac tumor. Endodermal sinus pattern with a Schiller-Duval body in the center of the field. A Schiller-Duval body is a papillary structure that grows into a cystic space. The papilla is covered by tumor cells and has a central capillary.

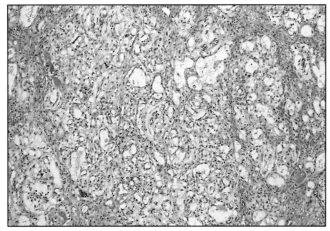

Fig. 13A.76 • Yolk sac tumor. Typical microcystic or reticular pattern.

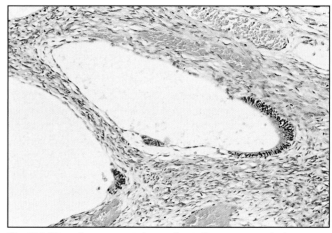

Fig. 13A.78 • Yolk sac tumor. Polyvesicular vitelline pattern in which cysts lined partly by columnar tumor cells and partly by flattened cells are surrounded by immature stroma.

stroma.[771,772] Yolk sac tumor can also contain glands that resemble those seen in fetal lung. These glandular patterns of differentiation in yolk sac tumors of germ cell origin must be differentiated from rare tumors occurring in older women in which a yolk sac tumor arises from, or in association with, an endometrioid or mucinous epithelial tumor.[276,277,429,773]

Eosinophilic, PAS-positive, diastase-resistant hyaline globules are a characteristic finding in yolk sac tumors, and are most often found in the reticular and endodermal sinus patterns (Fig. 13A.80). Reticular and solid areas also typically contain abundant extracellular hyaline PAS-positive material composed of laminin and type IV collagen that resembles basement membrane ultrastructurally.[745,768] This material has been interpreted by some as indicative of parietal yolk sac differentiation.[768] Small, bland, enteric glands lined by columnar and goblet cells are found in 50 percent of yolk sac tumors, and two rare tumors in which yolk sac tumor was admixed with mucinous carcinoid have been described.[774] Myxoid stroma containing spindle or stellate cells that stain with both cytokeratin and vimentin is prominent in 25 percent of yolk sac tumors.[742,775] These stromal cells may differentiate into mesenchymal elements such as cartilage, striated muscle, and bone, which are occasionally seen in yolk sac tumors. Stromal

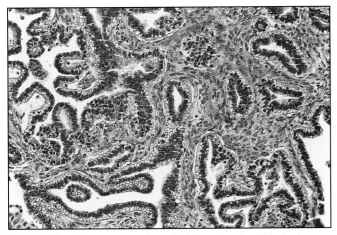

Fig. 13A.79 • Yolk sac tumor. Endometrioid-like variant, in which glands are lined by columnar tumor cells with conspicuous subnuclear vacuoles.

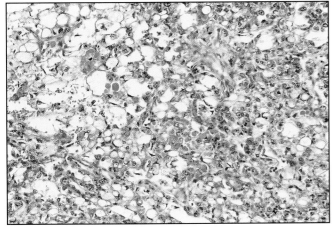

Fig. 13A.80 • Yolk sac tumor. Reticular pattern with numerous eosinophilic hyaline droplets.

cells are luteinized in, or adjacent to, 15–20 percent of yolk sac tumors. Syncytiotrophoblastic giant cells are present in rare cases.[745,746,776]

The most important immunohistochemical finding in yolk sac tumor is positive staining for AFP. Positive staining of tumor cell cytoplasm, secretory material within cysts and glands, and some hyaline bodies is detected in more than 75 percent of yolk sac tumors, but staining is often weak and focal.[364] Immunohistochemical stains for α_1-antitrypsin,[424,777] and placental alkaline phosphatase[778,779] are positive in yolk sac tumor cells and the extracellular hyaline material is laminin-positive.[768] Yolk sac tumor is cytokeratin positive but epithelial membrane antigen negative.[364] There is cytoplasmic staining with cytokeratin AE1/AE3, as opposed to the membrane pattern of staining that is characteristic of embryonal carcinoma. Yolk sac tumor is cytokeratin 7 negative; this result, together with lack of staining for epithelial membrane antigen and positive staining for AFP differentiates yolk sac tumor from clear cell carcinoma.[364] Yolk sac tumor is OCT4 and CD117 negative, which, combined with positive staining for cytokeratin and AFP, differentiates the solid pattern of yolk sac tumor from dysgerminoma. Immunostains for human chorionic gonadotropin are negative except in those rare tumors that contain syncytiotrophoblastic giant cells.[745,746] Small or large zones of hepatoid differentiation in yolk sac tumor stain positively with antihepatocyte antibody, although this is not a specific finding since hepatoid carcinoma and metastatic hepatocellular carcinoma are also positive.[420]

Embryonal carcinoma

Embryonal carcinoma is a rare ovarian neoplasm that is morphologically identical to embryonal carcinoma of the testis.

Clinical features Embryonal carcinoma occurs almost exclusively in children and young women,[745,746,780] though there are some reports of its occurrence in older women.[781] The average age is about 15 years. The typical presentation is with pelvic or abdominal pain or a palpable abdominal mass. Menstrual abnormalities are common in postpubertal patients. Most patients have a positive pregnancy test or an elevated serum β-HCG concentration and about 50 percent of premenarchal patients have precocious pseudopuberty.[780]

Unilateral salpingo-oophorectomy is the appropriate surgical treatment in patients with embryonal carcinoma that is limited to the ovary at diagnosis. Embryonal carcinoma is virtually never bilateral, so biopsy of the contralateral ovary is unnecessary. Advanced tumors (FIGO stage >IA) are treated by total abdominal hysterectomy, bilateral salpingo-oophorectomy, and limited debulking. Patients with embryonal carcinoma are usually young, so treatment by unilateral salpingo-oophorectomy and limited debulking surgery is reasonable if the contralateral ovary and uterus are uninvolved.

Before effective combination chemotherapy was available, embryonal carcinoma was often rapidly fatal, with survival, even in stage I, limited to 50 percent.[780] At present, patients with completely resected embryonal carcinoma are treated with postoperative cisplatin-based adjuvant chemotherapy with nearly complete success.[758] Many patients with residual or recurrent tumors can be cured with combination chemotherapy.[782]

Serum assays for β-HCG and AFP are used to assess treatment efficacy. If serum levels of either or both markers remain elevated after treatment, or if they increase during follow-up, the patient has recurrent or metastatic tumor.

Pathology Embryonal carcinoma is a large solid neoplasm with an average diameter of 15–17 cm. The cut surface is fleshy and tan or gray with small cysts and areas of hemorrhage and necrosis.

The microscopic appearance is similar to that of embryonal carcinoma of the testis. The tumor cells have large vesicular nuclei with coarse chromatin and one or two prominent nucleoli (Fig. 13A.81). The cytoplasm is abundant and amphophilic or clear. The tumor cells grow in nests and sheets, punctuated by occasional clefts, glands, or papillae. Most embryonal carcinomas contain foci of syncytiotrophoblastic giant cells. The stroma is loose and edematous or consists of a cellular proliferation of small, primitive-appearing spindle cells.

Immunostains for cytokeratin and CD30 are positive with a membranous pattern of staining. Embryonal carcinoma shows positive nuclear staining for OCT4, but staining for CD117 and epithelial membrane antigen is negative. Syncytiotrophoblastic giant cells and occasional large mononuclear cells resembling intermediate trophoblasts are immunoreactive for human chorionic gonadotropin.[745,746,780] There is diffuse cytoplasmic staining for AFP in the mononuclear embryonal carcinoma cells in 70 percent of cases.[780]

Polyembryoma is a rare form of malignant germ cell tumor with features intermediate between embryonal carcinoma and more differentiated forms of malignant germ cell tumor; it is usually found as a component of a mixed germ cell tumor.[783–786] Microscopically, polyembryoma is composed of numerous embryoid bodies growing in a primitive embryonal stroma. The embryoid bodies resemble 14–20 week embryos. They contain an embryonic disc composed of tall columnar cells with hyperchromatic nuclei, somewhat similar to the cells that line the clefts and glands in embryonal carcinoma. On one side of the disc is an amnionic cavity and, on the other, a yolk sac lined by α-fetoprotein positive cells.[787] The embryoid bodies are often distorted or incomplete and difficult to recognize.

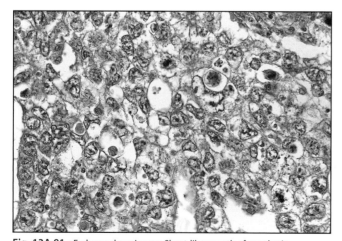

Fig. 13A.81 • Embryonal carcinoma. Sheet-like growth of anaplastic malignant germ cells. Glands and syncytiotrophoblastic giant cells were present elsewhere in the tumor.

Choriocarcinoma

Pure primary ovarian choriocarcinoma of germ cell origin is extremely rare.[697,788–790] In one review of malignant ovarian germ cell tumors, fewer than 1 percent were choriocarcinomas.[697] Choriocarcinoma is seen most frequently as a component of a mixed germ cell tumor.

Clinical features Choriocarcinoma of the ovary occurs in children and young women.[791,792] The clinical presentation is with abdominal pain and abnormal vaginal bleeding. A pregnancy test is positive and the serum β-HCG is elevated.[788,793,794] Premenarchal children may have precocious pseudopuberty.[788] Hemoperitoneum is often found at operation.

Choriocarcinoma of the ovary is unilateral and is treated by salpingo-oophorectomy. Total abdominal hysterectomy and bilateral salpingo-oophorectomy is required only if the contralateral ovary or uterus is involved. Surgery is followed by combination chemotherapy with a platinum-based regimen.[758] Favorable results have been described, even with suboptimal chemotherapy.[788] The chemotherapy and prognosis differ in gestational choriocarcinoma, so it is important to differentiate that entity from choriocarcinoma of germ cell origin. If the patient is premenarchal, the choriocarcinoma is certain to be of germ cell origin. Gestational choriocarcinoma, either metastatic from the uterus or fallopian tube, or primary in the ovary, is as likely to occur in young women of childbearing age as choriocarcinoma of germ cell origin.[789] There are no morphologic differences between gestational choriocarcinoma and choriocarcinoma of germ cell origin, although the presence of a corpus luteum of pregnancy favors the former. The clinical history may help in the differential diagnosis. Choriocarcinoma is of gestational origin if a paternal component can be identified by DNA analysis or HLA typing.[791,795–797]

Pathology Choriocarcinoma is a unilateral soft purple-red tumor with a hemorrhagic and necrotic cut surface. It ranges from 4 to 25 cm in diameter.

Microscopically, much of the tumor is hemorrhagic and necrotic. Viable tumor cells are mainly at the periphery, where cytotrophoblastic cells and syncytiotrophoblastic giant cells grow in a plexiform pattern (Fig. 13A.82). Cytotrophoblastic cells have abundant clear cytoplasm and well defined cell borders. Their nuclei are irregular and vesicular and some contain macronucleoli. Syncytiotrophoblastic giant cells have abundant vacuolated basophilic or amphophilic cytoplasm in which there are multiple hyperchromatic nuclei. All trophoblastic cells are cytokeratin positive, with dense staining of the cytoplasm of the syncytiotrophoblastic giant cells. Immunohistochemical stains for β-HCG mark the cytoplasm of the syncytiotrophoblastic giant cells.[794]

Teratoma

Benign cystic teratoma (dermoid cyst) is the most common ovarian neoplasm, comprising 25 percent or more of all ovarian tumors.[1,3,4] Other types of teratoma are uncommon. Most teratomas have a 46XX karyotype and are thought to develop by parthenogenesis from a single haploid germ cell.[798–801]

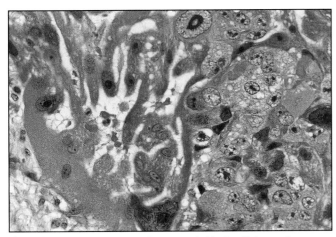

Fig. 13A.82 • Choriocarcinoma. The cytotrophoblastic cells have pale cytoplasm and vesicular nuclei with prominent chromatin clumps. The syncytiotrophoblastic cells have multiple smaller nuclei within a syncytium of basophilic cytoplasm.

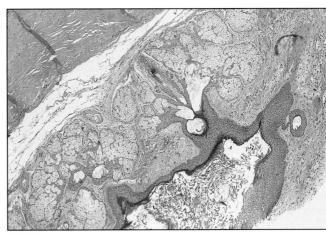

Fig. 13A.83 • Benign cystic teratoma ("dermoid cyst"). The cyst is lined by skin and epidermal appendages. The epithelium is of stratified squamous type and hair shafts and sebaceous glands underlie it. Keratinous debris is present in the cyst lumen.

Mature (benign) teratoma

These are cystic or, rarely, solid tumors that contain various mature tissues derived from one or more of the embryonic germ layers: the ectoderm, mesoderm, and endoderm.

Clinical features Benign teratomas occur in patients of all ages. Most are found in women between 20 and 50 years of age; only about 20 percent are detected in postmenopausal women.[802–805] The peak incidence is between 20 and 29 years.[1,806] Many patients are asymptomatic and the tumors are discovered on routine examination or during evaluation or treatment for some other condition. Symptoms such as pelvic pressure or pain appear when the tumor attains a large size. The most common serious complications are torsion, found in 3–10 percent of cases, and rupture, which occurs in about 1 percent.[806] Torsion causes acute abdominal symptoms. Acute peritonitis or, rarely, chronic granulomatous peritonitis can be a sequela of spontaneous rupture. Mature teratoma is a benign neoplasm that can be treated conservatively. Cystectomy, which can be performed laparoscopically or at laparotomy,[807–810] is adequate treatment, particularly in children and young women.[806] Benign teratoma is bilateral in 10–15 percent of patients.[4,805,806] Peritoneal implants composed of mature glial tissue (grade 0) occur in rare patients with mature teratoma of the ovary.[811,812] Such implants do not adversely affect survival.

Pathology Benign teratomas are nearly always cystic tumors. They range in size from only a few centimeters to large tumors weighing several kilograms; the average diameter is 7–8 cm. The cyst contents are liquid at body temperature but they solidify and are soft or firm at room temperature. On cross-section, there is a unilocular or, less often, a multilocular cyst with a solid protuberance called the dermoid papilla in the wall. The cysts contain hair, grumous material, or oily or serous liquid. Cartilage, bone, or teeth may be found. Foci of soft gray-tan tissue resembling brain and glistening green or brown thyroid tissue are also commonly seen. Dense, solid regions in an otherwise cystic teratoma are unusual; these raise the question of immature teratoma and should be carefully sectioned for histologic study. Rare mature (benign) teratomas are completely solid and can be differentiated from immature teratoma only by microscopic study.[813]

Benign teratomas contain a varied mixture of ectodermal, mesodermal, and endodermal structures distributed in an organized fashion. Tissues from at least two germ layers can be identified in two-thirds of mature teratomas and all three germ layers are represented in about a third of them.[4,803] Ectodermal derivatives such as skin, hair follicles, and sebaceous and sweat glands are the most common and, when they dominate the histologic picture, the tumor is commonly referred to as a "dermoid cyst" (Fig. 13A.83). Other ectodermal elements that are frequently present include brain (usually glia), choroid plexus, peripheral nerve, and dental structures. Common endodermal tissues include digestive tract mucosa, including endocrine cells,[814] respiratory mucosa, renal tissue, and thyroid tissue. The most frequent mesodermal derivatives are adipose tissue, smooth or striated muscle, bone or cartilage, and a loose connective tissue framework that surrounds the other elements. Surprisingly, male tissues such as prostate are occasionally present in a benign teratoma.[815–818] Endodermal and mesodermal derivatives are most likely to be found in sections from the dermal papilla. An individual element is so dominant in some tumors that classification as a monodermal teratoma is appropriate (e.g., struma ovarii). Cystic spaces lined by flattened epithelium or granulation tissue and surrounded by multinucleated giant cells and lipophages are present in some teratomas. The foreign body granulomatous reaction is caused by disruption of the epithelium with liberation of the cyst contents into the surrounding tissue.

Immature teratoma

Immature teratoma is one of most common malignant germ cell tumors of the ovary, representing 20–30 percent of such tumors at major cancer centers.[754,819]

Clinical features Immature teratoma occurs predominantly in children and young women. The average patient age is about 20 years and few patients are younger than 7 or older than 40.[820–826] The clinical presentation is non-specific. Patients complain of pelvic or abdominal pain, abdominal swelling, or a palpable abdominal mass. A few have acute abdominal symptoms caused by torsion or rupture of the tumor.[827] Serum α-fetoprotein can be elevated in patients with pure immature teratoma, and there is often modest elevation of the tumor marker CA-125.[819,827–829] Most (50–80 percent) patients have localized tumors (stage I) at diagnosis. Bilaterality is exceptional, although metastases can involve the contralateral ovary in patients with advanced disease.[821,822,827,830] Immature teratoma spreads mainly by implantation on the pelvic and abdominal peritoneum and the omentum.[831] There is a benign cystic teratoma in the contralateral ovary in 10–15 percent of cases.[821,827,830]

Patients with localized (stage IA) tumors are treated by unilateral salpingo-oophorectomy. A few patients have been treated successfully by cystectomy followed by chemotherapy.[832] More advanced tumors can be treated by unilateral salpingo-oophorectomy and excision of extraovarian tumor.[724,819] If preservation of fertility is not an issue or the contralateral ovary or uterus is involved, the treatment is hysterectomy and bilateral salpingo-oophorectomy. Patients with stage IA grade 1 immature teratoma have an excellent prognosis and are treated by surgery alone.[819] Those who have a stage IA grade 3 immature teratoma or who have advanced disease require post-operative chemotherapy. The issue of adjuvant chemotherapy for patients with stage IA grade 2 tumors is controversial; some authors advocate chemotherapy[758,827,828,833,834] but others do not.[819,820,,824] The prognosis appears to be more favorable in children and is unrelated to tumor grade.[835] In the absence of metastases containing immature tissue or other malignant germ cell elements such as yolk sac tumor, pediatric oncologists frequently withhold chemotherapy regardless of the tumor grade.[836] Cisplatin-containing regimens such as BEP (cisplatin, etoposide, and bleomycin) are highly effective forms of adjuvant chemotherapy for patients with no residual tumor after surgery, with survival rates of 90–100 percent.[758,831] The prognosis is somewhat less favorable for patients with residual gross tumor or recurrent immature teratoma.

In patients with extraovarian tumor spread, the microscopic appearance of the metastases is of prognostic importance. Some peritoneal implants or lymph node metastases contain only mature tissues and do not adversely affect the prognosis.[812,821,822,827,837–840] These grade 0 implants are usually composed partly or completely of mature glia (Fig. 13A.84). Recent molecular studies of glial implants have shown that they are genetically different from the ovarian tumor, but have the same genetic pattern as the patient.[841,842] Presumably, substances produced by the tumor result in metaplastic transformation of peritoneal or subperitoneal tissues into glia. Such an origin provides a plausible explanation for the occasional finding of endometriosis admixed with glial tissues in the implants.[843,844] Second look operations performed after chemotherapy in patients with incompletely resected immature teratoma can reveal residual immature teratoma, no residual tumor, small glial implants, or bulky nodules of mature teratoma.[763] These bulky nodules are resected to avoid adhesions or compression of adjacent organs and to forestall development of the "growing teratoma syndrome".[763,819,845,846] On rare occasions a malignancy may arise in long-standing incompletely resected low-grade teratoma implants.[847]

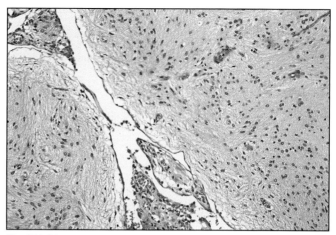

Fig. 13A.84 • Glial implant in the omentum. Nodules of benign-appearing glial tissue are covered by peritoneum in this grade 0 implant.

Pathology Immature teratoma is a predominantly solid unilateral tumor that averages 18 cm in diameter. The solid component is gray or brown and can be soft or hard and gritty. Scattered small cysts are typically seen on the cut surface. In about a quarter of these tumors one or more large cysts contain keratinous debris or hair and resemble a dermoid.[830]

Tissues derived from all three germ cell layers are present and a mixture of mature and immature elements are found in most tumors. These usually have a haphazard distribution and often lack the organized growth patterns seen in benign cystic teratoma. Ectodermal and mesodermal derivatives typically predominate among the immature elements. Immature neuro-ectodermal elements are the easiest immature tissues to recognize and quantitate.[821,822] These include sheets of mitotically active immature neuroepithelial cells, glands and tubules lined by columnar embryonal cells with stratified hyperchromatic nuclei, sheets and nests of neuroblasts containing anuclear fibrillary zones and Homer Wright rosettes, mitotically active immature glia, and primitive retina with melanin pigmentation (Figs 13A.85, 13A.86).[848] Florid benign vascular proliferations are seen occasionally in association with the neural elements of an immature teratoma.[849] Immature mesenchymal stroma is

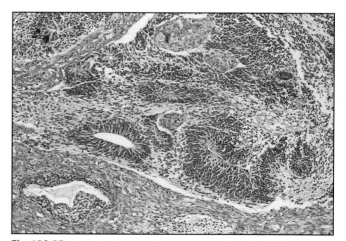

Fig. 13A.85 • Immature teratoma. Immature neural tissue (top) is the easiest immature element to identify and quantitate. Immature endodermal elements are also present in this photograph (lower left).

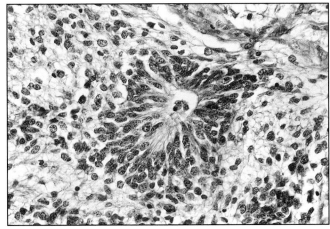

Fig. 13A.86 • Immature teratoma. Immature neural tissue in which small round neuroblasts surround a primitive neural tubule.

Table 13A.10 Histologic grading of immature teratoma

Grade	Immature tissue	Amount of neuroepithelium
0	Absent	None
1	+	Rare, not >1 lpf/slide
2	++	Common, not >3 lpf/slide
3	+++	Prominent, ≥4 lpf/slide

lpf = low power field

hypercellular and composed of small spindle cells with dark nuclei (Fig. 13A.87). Mitotic figures are usually present. Cartilage is often present in immature teratomas and it can be difficult to determine whether it is immature. When there are numerous lacunae containing small chondrocytes and the foci of chondroid differentiation are surrounded by immature small round mesenchymal cells, it is appropriate to interpret the cartilage as an immature mesenchymal element. An unusual, aggressive immature teratoma with a rhabdomyosarcomatous mesenchymal component has been reported.[850] Immature endodermal tissues are less common and are rarely seen in the absence of immature ectodermal derivatives. The types of immature endodermal structures that can be seen include primitive glands lined by columnar cells with subnuclear and supranuclear vacuoles, partially differentiated stratified columnar intestinal epithelium with goblet cells, and islands of fetal liver tissue.[766,851] Immature renal (metanephrogenic) structures such as embryonal-appearing glomeruli are rare constituents of an immature teratoma.[852] Microscopic foci of yolk sac tumor are seen occasionally in an immature teratoma, and as long as there are only a few of them (≤3) and they are less than 3 mm in diameter, they do not appear to affect the prognosis.[822,853] Pediatric pathologists have proposed that fetal-type liver and differentiated glands with subnuclear vacuoles, similar to immature endoderm or fetal lung, represent well differentiated forms of yolk sac tumor,[835] but gynecologic pathologists tend to view limited amounts of these elements as components of the teratoma. Immature teratomas are graded using a system that rates them from grade 0 for a neoplasm composed entirely of mature tissues to grade 3 for a neoplasm containing abundant immature tissue (Table 13A.10).[822] An immature teratoma can give rise to grade 0 metastases, but the primary ovarian tumor must, by definition, be grade 1, 2, or 3. A two grade system in which grade 1 tumors are designated as low grade and grades 2 and 3 as high grade has been proposed but is not in general use.[853]

Rare germ cell tumors contain neuroectodermal cells growing in patterns reminiscent of various tumors of the central nervous system. Tumors of this type also occur in the testis where they are often associated with teratomas. The diagnosis of neuroectodermal tumor of the testis is restricted to those tumors in which the neuroectodermal component measures at least 1 cm in diameter.[854] It seems reasonable to apply this size standard to ovarian tumors as well, although, in ovarian tumors, the neuroectodermal component generally comprises most or all of a large neoplasm. There are three main patterns.[855] *Primitive neuroectodermal tumors* consist of nests and sheets of small cells with hyperchromatic mitotically active nuclei (Fig. 13A.88).[330,820,855,856] Some cells have fibrillary cytoplasm and some tumors contain rosettes with central lumina, neuropil, neuroblastic rosettes, or foci of glial differentiation. Areas

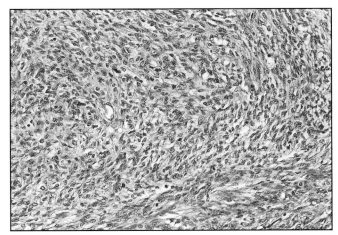

Fig. 13A.87 • Immature teratoma. Immature mesenchymal tissue. This type of immature tissue can be difficult to identify and quantitate.

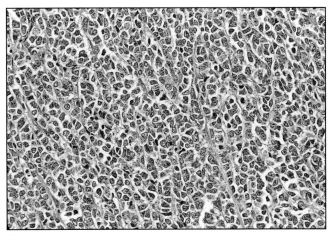

Fig. 13A.88 • Primitive neuroectodermal tumor. Diffuse sheet of small round cells with hyperchromatic nuclei and scanty cytoplasm.

within tumors of this type resemble medulloepithelioma, ependymoblastoma, or neuroblastoma. A second type of neuroectodermal tumor shows extensive glial differentiation and resembles *glioblastoma multiforme*.[855] The third kind of neuroectodermal tumor resembles an *ependymoma*.[855,857–859] Round or columnar cells with fibrillary cytoplasm form perivascular pseudorosettes and true ependymal rosettes with central lumina. In some tumors the ependymal cells line glands, cysts, or papillae, which can result in misdiagnosis as an epithelial tumor. Primitive neuroectodermal tumors and those resembling glioblastoma multiforme often contain teratomatous elements but usually none are found in an ependymoma. Primitive neuroectodermal tumors and malignant glial tumors have an unfavorable prognosis if they have spread beyond the ovary, but ependymoma appears to be an indolent tumor, even when metastases are present. These tumors are generally classified as monodermal teratomas, although they might also be viewed as variants of immature teratoma.

Immunohistochemistry plays a limited role in the diagnosis of immature teratoma. A stain for glial fibrillary acidic protein (GFAP), which stains both glial fibrils and cell bodies, can help identify glial differentiation.[813,860,861] Primitive neuroepithelial cells do not stain with GFAP, although in some tumors they are stained with antibodies for neurofilaments or neuron specific enolase (NSE).[860,861] Intestinal and respiratory epithelia contain argyrophilic cells that react with antibodies to a variety of neurohormonal peptides.[861] AFP stains immature endodermal structures such as isolated yolk sac-like vesicles, immature glandular and intestinal epithelium, and liver.[829,861,862] Immunostains can also help to confirm the presence of certain immature elements. For example, primitive neuroepithelium stains for CD99 and *bcl-2*, and immature cartilage stains for CD34 and *bcl-2*.[862]

Secondary neoplasms in mature (benign cystic) teratoma

Benign or malignant tumors that arise in a benign cystic teratoma are rare. Malignant transformation occurs in only 1–3 percent of benign cystic teratomas.[805,863–866]

Clinical features Secondary malignancies typically occur in postmenopausal women, but they can be found in patients of any age. Presenting complaints are non-specific and include abdominal or pelvic pain, abdominal distention, or a palpable mass. Tumors are confined to the ovary (stage I) in 50–75 percent of patients and these patients have a favorable prognosis.[867] The outcome is unfavorable in women with more advanced tumors.[868] Most do not respond to chemotherapy or radiotherapy and die within a year or two of diagnosis.

Pathology Grossly, a secondary neoplasm may form a nodular or papillary growth in the cyst lining or there may be thickening or induration of the cyst wall. In some instances, the secondary neoplasm is detected only by microscopic examination. Secondary neoplasms are usually unilateral, but the contralateral ovary may contain a benign cystic teratoma. Nevi,[869] sebaceous adenomas and other cutaneous adnexal neoplasms, benign salivary gland type tumors, meningioma,[870] glomus tumor,[871] and hemangiomatous vascular proliferations[849,872] are among the benign neoplasms that arise in

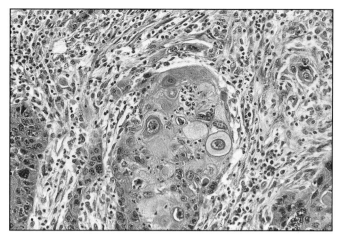

Fig. 13A.89 • Squamous cell carcinoma. This keratinizing squamous cell carcinoma arose as a secondary neoplasm in a benign cystic teratoma.

benign cystic teratoma.[873] In situ malignant tumors that have been reported include squamous cell carcinoma in situ and Paget's disease.[418,874–876] Invasive squamous cell carcinoma comprises about 85 percent of secondary malignancies arising in benign cystic teratoma (Fig. 13A.89).[418,865–868] The remainder are other types of cutaneous carcinomas, such as basal cell carcinoma or sebaceous carcinoma,[877,878] melanoma,[879–882] adenocarcinoma,[864,883–886] various types of sarcoma,[887,888] and other rare tumor types. Rare mucinous epithelial tumors that arise in a teratoma give rise to pseudomyxoma peritonei.[889]

Struma ovarii

Struma ovarii is a teratoma in which thyroid tissue predominates.[890] More than 50 percent of the tumor should consist of thyroid tissue before it is designated as a struma ovarii. Using this definition, struma ovarii comprises 1–3 percent of benign ovarian teratomas.[4,803,891]

Clinical features Struma ovarii occurs mainly in women older than 40 years. It is usually an incidental finding or it is discovered in a patient with non-specific symptoms such as abdominal or pelvic pain or abdominal distention. Rare patients have ascites or ascites and hydrothorax (pseudo-Meigs' syndrome).[892–896] Occasional patients have hormonally mediated symptoms such as abnormal vaginal bleeding.[894] Symptoms of hyperthyroidism occur in fewer than 10 percent of patients with struma ovarii, some of whom have concurrent enlargement of the thyroid gland.[891,893,897] Struma ovarii is benign in most instances, and cystectomy or unilateral salpingo-oophorectomy is adequate treatment. Tumors diagnosed as malignant struma ovarii on histologic grounds are rarely clinically malignant and do not require radical treatment.[891,898–902] Rare malignant strumas metastasize locally to the peritoneum or omentum or to such distant sites as lymph nodes, liver, bone, or lung.[890,903–906] These appear best treated by hysterectomy and bilateral salpingo-oophorectomy, thyroidectomy, and administration of radioactive iodine.[893,904,907]

Pathology Struma ovarii is a circumscribed neoplasm that ranges in size from a small nodule, only 1 or 2 cm in diameter, to a large mass more than 10 cm in diameter. The average size

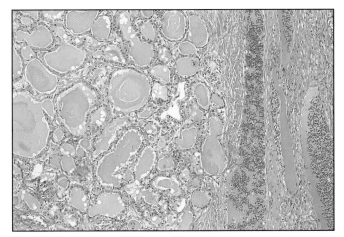

Fig. 13A.90 • Struma ovarii. This type of monodermal teratoma is composed predominantly of mature thyroid follicles.

is 5–10 cm. On cross-section, struma ovarii is red, green, or tan with a glairy, meaty appearance. Small cysts are commonly present and occasional tumors are largely or totally cystic.[908] Microscopically, struma ovarii is composed of follicles filled with eosinophilic colloid and lined by cuboidal or columnar cells with uniform round nuclei (Fig. 13A.90). Degenerative changes such as fibrosis, calcification, and aggregates of hemosiderin-laden macrophages may be present. Cystic variants of struma ovarii may contain few follicles and can be difficult to recognize.[908] Other growth patterns that can cause diagnostic problems include tumors composed of clear, oxy-philic, or signet-ring cells, those with cord-like arrangements of tumor cells, and hypercellular tumors in which the cells grow in microfollicular, trabecular or solid patterns similar to those seen in a follicular adenoma of the thyroid.[891,909] Hyper-cellular variants of struma ovarii can be designated as prolifer-ative struma ovarii.[891] Immunostains for thyroglobulin are positive in the colloid and in the cytoplasm of the follicular cells and immunostains for thyroid transcription factor-1 (TTF-1) are positive in the tumor cell nuclei.[910] These findings confirm the diagnosis in difficult cases. Other teratomatous elements can be found in many cases if they are carefully searched for. Luteinized ovarian stromal cells are present around some examples of struma ovarii.[909] These cells, which are the likely source of the hormones that cause endocrino-logic symptoms in some patients, can be highlighted with an immunostain for inhibin.

Any type of thyroid cancer can arise in struma ovarii. Papil-lary carcinoma is most common and has the same histologic appearance as it does in the thyroid.[891] It grows in an infil-trative manner, usually contains well developed papillae, and is composed of cells with large, crowded, grooved nuclei with small nucleoli.[898,911] Some nuclei are clear and others contain intranuclear cytoplasmic inclusions. The cell cytoplasm is moderate or abundant and appears dense. The colloid within the follicles often has a solid, hypereosinophilic appearance. Follicular variants of papillary carcinoma have been described in struma ovarii, as in the thyroid.[912] Follicular carcinoma is uncommon. It is a hypercellular neoplasm in which the tumor cells grow in a microfollicular, trabecular, or solid pattern. It is difficult to differentiate follicular carcinoma from proliferative struma ovarii, but nuclear atypia, frequent mitotic figures,

and, especially, an invasive growth pattern or vascular invasion favor follicular carcinoma.[891] Rare tumors resembling medul-lary carcinoma have been described. Most cases of malignant struma ovarii have been designated as carcinoma on histologic grounds alone and never spread beyond the ovary. Clinically malignant examples of struma ovarii that have metastasized are, nevertheless, well documented.

Strumosis is a nebulous condition characterized by the find-ing of peritoneal and omental implants of well differentiated thyroid tissue in a patient with benign struma ovarii.[913,914] It is thought to be a consequence of the rupture of a struma. Criteria for distinguishing between strumosis and metastatic malignant struma of the well differentiated follicular carci-noma type are primarily clinical (i.e., lack of progression of the implants) as the histologic features of the implants are similar and the correct diagnosis of the ovarian primary is not always clearcut. Indeed, not all authors accept strumosis as a valid entity.[894]

Carcinoid tumor

Carcinoid tumors are uncommon ovarian neoplasms that are classified as monodermal teratomas, since many are associated with other teratomatous elements.[915] A pure ovarian carcinoid has most likely overgrown the teratoma in which it originated, but other possible sources include neuroendocrine cells in a mucinous tumor or the mucinous component of a heterologous Sertoli-Leydig cell tumor,[573,916,917] ovarian endocrine cells, or non-endocrine ovarian cells by neometaplasia.

Clinical features Most patients are peri- or postmenopausal women who have non-specific symptoms such as pelvic or abdominal pain, abdominal enlargement, menstrual irregu-larities, or abnormal vaginal bleeding. One-quarter to one-third of women with ovarian carcinoid tumors have the carcinoid syndrome.[918] Most of these have large insular carcinoid tumors; the syndrome rarely occurs with other types of carcinoid.[919] Typical symptoms of the carcinoid syndrome include facial flushing, diarrhea, bronchospasm, hypertension, and edema secondary to carcinoid heart disease.[920] Some women with trabecular or strumal carcinoids develop severe chronic con-stipation, caused by tumor secretion of the intestinal hormone peptide YY.[921–923] Rare patients with a strumal carcinoid are hyperthyroid.[924]

Carcinoid tumors are usually unilateral and confined to the ovary at the time of diagnosis.[919] There is a benign cystic teratoma in the contralateral ovary in 10–15 percent of patients. The standard treatment is hysterectomy and bilateral salpingo-oophorectomy, but unilateral salpingo-oophorectomy is adequate treatment for a young woman. Symptoms usually abate rapidly once the tumor is removed, although patients with carcinoid heart disease can have progressive cardiac disease, despite the complete removal of the carcinoid tumor.[918,925] The prognosis is generally favorable. Metastases and tumor-related deaths are rare, and occur mainly in patients with extraovarian spread at diagnosis.[916,918,919,926] Both the strumal and the carcinoid components of strumal carcinoid appear capable of giving rise to metastases.[927]

The ovary is commonly involved by metastases from carcinoids of the gastrointestinal tract, usually the small intestine or the appendix.[928] These can cause the same symptoms as primary ovarian carcinoids, including the carcinoid syndrome. Clues that a carcinoid might be metastatic include bilaterality, multinodularity, and the presence of peritoneal metastases.

Pathology Carcinoid tumors are unilateral, firm, tan or yellow solid tumors. They range from microscopic to 8–10 cm in diameter, and often appear to arise in the wall of a benign cystic teratoma or a mucinous tumor.

All ovarian carcinoids consist either completely or in part of round or cuboidal neuroendocrine cells with uniform round or oval nuclei, coarse chromatin, and small nucleoli (Fig. 13A.91). The cytoplasm is moderate in amount and varies from clear to eosinophilic. The cytoplasm typically appears granular in hematoxylin and eosin stained sections. The granules can usually be stained with argentaffin or argyrophil stains. Four histologic types of carcinoid tumor occur in the ovary; mixtures of these types are seen in some tumors.[407] The *insular* type is the most common one.[919] The cells grow in nests, sheets, or islands, or line small tubular acini. The microscopic appearance is similar to that of a midgut carcinoid. The *trabecular* carcinoid is composed of tall columnar cells with central nuclei and granular eosinophilic cytoplasm.[916,929] The tumor cells grow in cords, ribbons, or trabecula, a pattern reminiscent of that seen in foregut and hindgut carcinoids. The *strumal* carcinoid is a mixed tumor that contains both carcinoid and strumal (thyroid) elements.[924,930–932] The carcinoid component usually has a trabecular pattern, although foci of insular or mucinous growth are also present in some examples.[933] The strumal component consists of thyroid-type follicles filled with colloid and lined by columnar follicular cells. There are calcium oxalate crystals in the colloid in about 50 percent of cases. In the regions where the two elements merge, the carcinoid cells grow between and into the follicles, where they appear to undermine and replace the follicular cells.[932] Thus, some follicles are lined by thyroid cells, some by a mixture of thyroid and carcinoid cells, and some by carcinoid cells.[924,930,934] Amyloid is present in rare examples of strumal carcinoid.[935] Finally, rare cases of primary *mucinous* carcinoid occur in the ovary.[926,936,937] In mucinous carcinoid, round or tubular glands lined by columnar or cuboidal cells and goblet cells infiltrate the stroma or float in pools of mucin. Atypical variants of mucinous carcinoid exhibit a greater degree of glandular crowding with cribriform or microcystic growth and increased nuclear atypia. Mucinous carcinoids can be mixed with carcinoma, and the mixed forms are the type of mucinous carcinoid most likely to spread beyond the ovary.[937] Luteinized stromal cells are noted at the periphery of some carcinoids. Benign teratomatous elements are often detected adjacent to an ovarian carcinoid. Their identification is important evidence that the carcinoid is primary in the ovary. The possibility that an ovarian carcinoid tumor is metastatic should always be considered. Metastatic carcinoid tumors are usually multinodular and bilateral and are not associated with a teratoma.[928,938] An extraovarian primary can often be demonstrated by appropriate clinical studies.

The immunohistochemical stains that are most useful for confirming a diagnosis of carcinoid are chromogranin and synaptophysin. Trabecular and strumal carcinoids typically also stain for prostate specific acid phosphatase (PSAP), as do hindgut carcinoids, but not for prostate specific antigen (PSA).[912,931,932] A variety of peptide hormones can be detected in carcinoid cells by immunohistochemistry, including serotonin, gastrin, pancreatic polypeptide (PP), vasoactive intestinal polypeptide (VIP), insulin, glucagon, substance P, adrenocorticotrophin (ACTH), and somatostatin.[939,940] Trabecular and strumal carcinoids from patients with chronic constipation typically stain for protein YY.[922,923,941] Calcitonin is present in occasional carcinoid tumors, including some strumal carcinoids.[927,935] Despite the association with thyroid-type tissue, strumal carcinoid does not seem to be closely related to medullary carcinoma (of thyroid type). These tumors differ greatly in histologic appearance and clinical behavior. Calcitonin and amyloid are absent from all but rare examples of strumal carcinoid, and immunostains for CEA are negative in strumal carcinoid, while medullary carcinoma is typically positive.[924] The thyroid component of strumal carcinoid stains for thyroglobulin in the colloid and in the cytoplasm of the follicular epithelial cells,[930,932,942,943] and for thyroid transcription factor-1 in the nuclei of the follicular epithelial cells.[912]

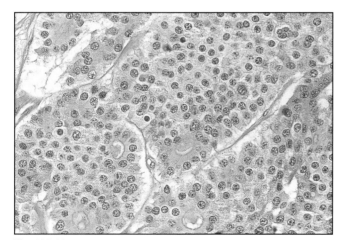

Fig. 13A.91 • Insular carcinoid tumor. The tumor cells form small tubules or grow in circumscribed nests. They have granular eosinophilic or amphophilic cytoplasm and uniform round central nuclei with a distinctive chromatin pattern.

Malignant mixed germ cell tumor

Malignant mixed germ cell tumors contain a mixture of the various pure types of germ cell tumors. They comprise 5–20 percent of all malignant germ cell tumors.[762,944,945] A malignant germ cell tumor that contains benign teratomatous elements does not fall into this category.

Clinical features Mixed germ cell tumors occur in children and young women. The average age is 16 years. The usual presentation is with abdominal pain or swelling or a palpable abdominal mass. A few patients have acute abdominal symptoms. About a third of premenarchal children with mixed germ cell tumors have precocious pseudopuberty, while postmenarchal children and adults often have amenorrhea or abnormal vaginal bleeding.[944] The results of serum marker studies depend on which germ cell elements are present. About 50 percent of patients have a positive pregnancy test or an elevated serum β-HCG. Serum α-fetoprotein is elevated in 50 percent of patients. About two-thirds of patients have stage I tumors at diagnosis.[944,945]

Encapsulated unilateral tumors (stage IA) are treated by salpingo-oophorectomy. More advanced tumors are treated by total abdominal hysterectomy and bilateral salpingo-oophorectomy, or, if conservation of fertility is important and the uterus and contralateral ovary are uninvolved, by unilateral salpingo-oophorectomy and limited debulking. More than half of stage I tumors treated by surgery alone recur.[944–946] Chemotherapy is therefore administered to most patients except those with stage IA tumors that contain only dysgerminoma and grade I immature teratoma. Most stage I patients treated with adjuvant chemotherapy are cured.[758,945] Those with more advanced tumors have a survival rate of about 50 percent.[945,947] In early reports it appeared that the prognosis depended on the size of the tumor, the types and amounts of the various germ cell components present, and the stage.[944,946] Contemporary results indicate that stage is the only significant determinant of prognosis in patients treated with modern combination chemotherapy.[762,945]

Pathology Mixed germ cell tumors tend to be large and average 15 cm in diameter. Their gross appearance depends on which elements are present. Dysgerminoma is fleshy and gray, tan, or white. Yolk sac tumor varies in color, contains small cysts, and often has areas of necrosis. Immature teratoma is white or tan and may contain cysts and firm cartilaginous or bony foci. Areas of choriocarcinoma are hemorrhagic and necrotic. Mixed germ cell tumors are ordinarily unilateral, but when dysgerminoma is present, they can be bilateral.[945]

There are two malignant elements in 80 percent of mixed germ cell tumors (Fig. 13A.92), three in 15 percent of them and four or more in the remainder. The elements can be mixed together or they can grow in separate but contiguous foci. Dysgerminoma is the most frequent element, followed by yolk sac tumor and immature teratoma. Embryonal carcinoma, choriocarcinoma, and polyembryoma are less common.[783,944,945] Choriocarcinoma and polyembryoma are rarely found in the ovary except as a component of a mixed germ cell tumor.

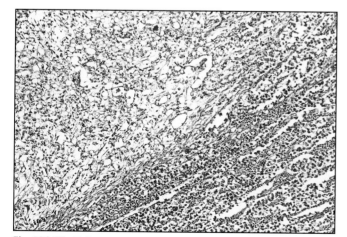

Fig. 13A.92 • Malignant mixed germ cell tumor. This tumor contains two malignant germ cell elements. Yolk sac tumor is present in the upper left part of the field and dysgerminoma in the lower right.

Gonadoblastoma

Gonadoblastoma is a rare tumor that contains an admixture of germ cells and sex cord cells and arises almost exclusively in abnormal gonads.[948–953]

Clinical features Gonadoblastoma is recognized in patients of all ages but it is detected mainly in the young. The average age at diagnosis is 18 years; 80 percent of gonadoblastomas are detected before the age of 20 years,[948] and they may be found in young children.[954] Occasional tumors are incidental findings or are found when adnexal calcifications are seen on abdominal or pelvic x-rays. Most gonadoblastomas are identified when a patient is evaluated for primary or secondary amenorrhea or for an abnormally formed genital tract. Most patients are phenotypic females, but gonadoblastoma also occurs in phenotypic males. Phenotypic females have a normal or short vagina and a small cervix. The uterus is small in 75 percent of patients and the fallopian tubes are small or rudimentary in 35 percent of them. Most patients are mildly virilized.[952] The most common karyotypes are 46 XY and 45X/46XY. A Y chromosome or a Y chromosome fragment is present in more than 90 percent of patients. In some, Y chromosome material cannot be detected by routine karyotypic analysis,[948,955] but can be identified using more sensitive molecular techniques.[956] In situ hybridization studies performed on gonadoblastomas in patients with a mosaic karyotype indicate that the gonadoblastoma is derived from cells with a Y chromosome. Recent studies suggest that there is a region on the long arm of the Y chromosome near the centromere, termed the GBY region (GonadoBlastoma locus on the Y chromosome), that contains a gene that is associated with susceptibility to gonadoblastoma in patients with dysgenetic gonads.[955,957] The most likely candidate gene is thought to be testis specific protein Y-encoded (*TSPY*).[958]

Gonadoblastoma is benign unless it is overgrown by a germinoma or some other type of malignant germ cell tumor. The treatment is gonadectomy since the gonads are abnormal and are not capable of normal reproductive function. Gonadoblastoma is often bilateral, so bilateral gonadectomy is necessary to prevent virilization or evolution of a malignant germ cell tumor.[948,953] The risk that a gonadoblastoma or a malignant germ cell tumor will originate in the abnormal gonads of a patient with a Y-chromosome is about 25 percent.[959] Screening for Y-chromosome material may help identify patients at risk for a gonadal tumor.[960] Most malignant tumors arising in a gonadoblastoma are dysgerminomas,[948,952,961] but about 10 percent are yolk sac tumors or embryonal carcinomas.[948,952,961,962]

Pathology Gonadoblastoma arises in abnormal gonads, including streak gonads, indeterminate gonads, and dysgenetic testes.[952] It is typically small, ranging from microscopic to 2–3 cm in diameter. More than 40 percent are bilateral. The cut surface is tan or white and often contains gritty calcified areas.

Microscopically, nests of germ cells and sex cord cells are surrounded by fibrous stroma (Fig. 13A.93). Two types of germ cells have been described in gonadoblastoma.[963,964] Some are immature, with a high nuclear to cytoplasmic ratio, coarse chromatin, prominent nucleoli in some nuclei and scanty cytoplasm, while others are more mature, with smaller, denser nuclei

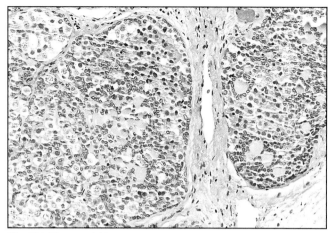

Fig. 13A.93 • Gonadoblastoma. Tumor nests are surrounded by fibrous stroma. The nests contain hyaline basement membrane type material, large germ cells, and small dark sex cord-stromal cells.

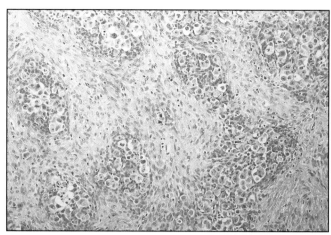

Fig. 13A.94 • Mixed germ cell-sex cord-stromal tumor. This type of tumor occurs in patients with a normal karyotype and contains a mixture of large germ cells and smaller, dark-staining sex cord stromal cells. Note the absence of the nested pattern of growth and hyaline cores that are seen in gonadoblastoma.

and more abundant clear cytoplasm. Sex cord cells surround the germ cells. These are difficult to classify and show overlapping features between granulosa cells and Sertoli cells. They surround germ cells and hyaline cylinders of eosinophilic basement membrane-like material or palisade at the periphery of gonadoblastoma cell nests. The stroma surrounding a gonadoblastoma frequently contains luteinized or Leydig-like cells in postpubertal patients. The stroma may contain micro-calcifications of variable size.

Immunostains for inhibin, vimentin, and cytokeratin are positive in the sex cord elements. The hyaline material reacts with anti-laminin antibodies.[965] The germ cells stain variably for placental alkaline phosphatase, CD117 (c-kit), *OCT-4* and *TSPY*.[963,964,966,967] It has been proposed that cells that coexpress *TSPY* and *OCT-4* are carcinoma in situ cells that can progress to an invasive germ cell tumor, usually a germinoma, in which expression of *TSPY* can be lost.[964] The luteinized cells in the stroma between gonadoblastoma nests stain strongly for inhibin and calretinin.

Rare examples of other types of combined germ cell–sex cord-stromal tumors have been described (Fig. 13A.94),[968] including a neoplasm with an epithelial component.[969] These occur in genotypically normal females and the absence of discrete cell nests containing hyaline cores differentiates them from gonadoblastoma. One gonadoblastoma was associated with a 9 cm sex cord-stromal tumor resembling a Sertoli cell tumor, in addition to a dysgerminoma.[970] Microscopic gonadoblastoma-like lesions occur in fetal and infant ovaries in the absence of genetic abnormalities. They are often found in the walls of follicular cysts. Their relationship with true gonadoblastoma, if any, is unclear.[971,972]

Other rare tumors of the ovary

Small cell carcinoma (of hypercalcemic type)

Small cell carcinoma is a biologically aggressive neoplasm of uncertain histogenesis that occurs predominantly in young women.[330,973–976]

Clinical features Small cell carcinoma has been reported in patients ranging from childhood to 55 years of age,[977] but it is predominantly a tumor of young women, with an average patient age of 24 years.[975,978] Rare cases appear to be familial.[979] The clinical presentation is typically with such non-specific symptoms as abdominal distention, abdominal or pelvic pain, nausea or vomiting, or a palpable abdominal mass. About two-thirds of patients have hypercalcemia, but the hypercalcemia is generally asymptomatic.[351] Serum levels of parathyroid hormone are not elevated. About 50 percent of patients have localized disease at diagnosis. Small cell carcinoma is usually unilateral. Bilateral tumors occur mainly in patients with widespread metastases and probably represent metastatic spread to the contralateral ovary.[975] Small cell carcinoma is aggressive, with a high mortality rate even when the tumor is limited to the ovary at diagnosis.[975,978] Women with localized tumors may have better survival when treated with hysterectomy and bilateral salpingo-oophorectomy, so this is the standard surgical treatment.[975] The role of adjuvant chemotherapy or radiation therapy is unclear, and patients with advanced or recurrent disease have limited responses to radiotherapy or chemotherapy.[980] Occasional patients with a favorable response to treatment have been reported.[981,982] In the largest reported series, 33 percent of patients with stage Ia tumors were alive with no evidence of disease at last follow-up, compared with 10 percent survival in stage Ic and only 6.5 percent survival in stages II, III, and IV.[975]

Pathology Small cell carcinoma is a solid, nodular, grey or tan tumor that ranges from 6 to 27 cm, with an average diameter of 15 cm. On cross-section, small cysts and areas of hemorrhage and necrosis are present in some tumors.

Microscopically, the typical appearance is one of uniform small cells growing in diffuse sheets, occasionally punctuated by irregular follicle-like structures filled with lightly eosinophilic material (Fig. 13A.95).[976] In some tumors, the cells grow in nests and cords. The tumor cells are round or spindled, have scanty cytoplasm, and hyperchromatic round, oval, or fusiform nuclei with finely granular chromatin and inconspicuous or absent nucleoli (Fig. 13A.96). Mitotic figures are numerous

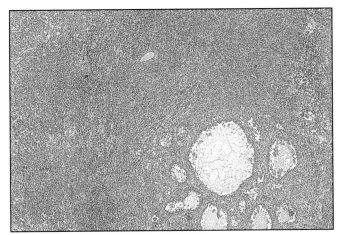

Fig. 13A.95 • Small cell carcinoma. Diffuse pattern of growth with a few follicles filled with eosinophilic material.

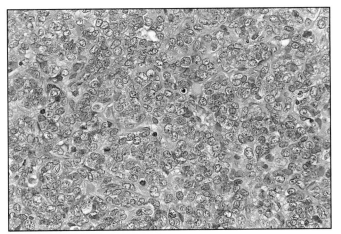

Fig. 13A.96 • Small cell carcinoma. The tumor cells have scanty cytoplasm and monotonous small round or oval nuclei with fine chromatin and inconspicuous nucleoli.

and typically exceed 20 per 10 high power fields. Flow cytometric studies reveal that the tumor cells are DNA diploid.[983] Larger cells with abundant eosinophilic cytoplasm, vesicular nuclei, and prominent nucleoli are present in about 50 percent of cases. When they predominate, the tumor is designated as the "large cell variant" of small cell carcinoma.[351,984] There are glands lined by benign or malignant mucinous epithelium in 12 percent of small cell carcinomas.

Immunostains for low molecular weight cytokeratin generally show patchy positive staining, and a majority of tumors are immunoreactive for epithelial membrane antigen (EMA).[489,984–986] Most small cell carcinomas show positive nuclear staining for *p53* protein, although staining can be moderate and only focal.[978,985] Small cell carcinoma tends to show diffuse strong nuclear staining for WT-1, nuclear and cytoplasmic staining for calretinin and patchy membrane staining for CD10.[985] Only a minority of tumors show staining for neuroendocrine markers such as CD56, chromogranin and synaptophysin, and stains for CD99, desmin, inhibin, and TTF-1 are negative.[493,985,986] Despite the absence of parathyroid hormone in the serum, occasional tumors stain for parathyroid hormone, and immunoreactivity for parathyroid hormone-related protein has been reported.[489,987,988] Negative staining for inhibin, together with positive staining for EMA and WT-1, help in the important

differential diagnosis with juvenile granulosa cell tumor, which is inhibin-positive and EMA-negative. It is important to note that both small cell carcinoma and juvenile granulosa cell tumor can show positive staining for calretinin.

Small cell carcinoma has the ultrastructural features of an epithelial tumor.[973,984,987,989–991] A discontinuous basal lamina surrounds groups of tumor cells and there are desmosome-like junctions between adjacent cells. Rare tubules with lumina are present, lined by cells with a microvillous surface. The most characteristic ultrastructural feature is prominent dilated cisterns of rough endoplasmic reticulum filled with amorphous, moderately electron dense, material. Dense core neurosecretory granules were observed in three of four tumors studied by one group,[987] but have not been detected by others.[973,984,989]

Small cell carcinoma has been designated as a type of sex cord-stromal tumor,[989] a neuroendocrine tumor of germ cell origin,[987] a germ cell tumor related to yolk sac tumor,[984] and an epithelial tumor,[992] but its lineage is currently uncertain. The absence of staining for inhibin, together with immunoreactivity for EMA in some cases, contrasts with the inhibin-positive, EMA-negative immunophenotype typical of sex cord-stromal tumors, and suggests that small cell carcinoma does not fall into that category.

Desmoplastic small round cell tumor

Desmoplastic small round cell tumor (DSRCT) (see also Ch. 15) is a malignant intra-abdominal tumor that occurs mainly in young males.[993–995] However, a distinct minority of these neoplasms occur in females, and rare examples present clinically as primary ovarian tumors.[996–1000] There is invariably extensive intra-abdominal tumor growth at diagnosis and, despite aggressive therapy, most patients die of tumor. Patients treated with multimodality therapy, including surgical resection, chemotherapy, and radiation therapy appear to have the most favorable prognosis, with 3-year survival rates of about 50 percent.[1001,1002] The cell of origin is unknown, but the tumor cells exhibit a translocation t(11;22)(p13;q12) in which the Ewing's sarcoma and Wilms' tumor genes are fused (*EWS-WT1*).[1003–1005]

The tumors are solid and gray, tan, or white, with areas of necrosis. Microscopically, the tumor cells are small, with uniform, round, hyperchromatic nuclei, inconspicuous nucleoli and scanty to modest amounts of cytoplasm.[330,1006] The tumor cells grow in sheets and nests separated by sclerotic fibrous stroma (Fig. 13A.97). DSRCT has a distinctive polyphenotypic pattern of immunoreactivity.[993,996,997] The tumor cells stain for cytokeratin and epithelial membrane antigen, for neuron specific enolase, for desmin, for WT-1, for placental alkaline phosphatase and occasionally for CD99.[995,1007–1009] Stains for other neuroendocrine and muscle markers are usually negative.

Female adnexal tumor of probable Wolffian origin

This distinctive tumor usually occurs in the broad ligament or mesosalpinx (see p. 628),[1010] but rare examples arise in the ovary.[1011–1015] The most likely origin is from mesonephric (Wolffian) remnants. The tumor occurs mainly in middle-aged women. Some are detected incidentally in asymptomatic

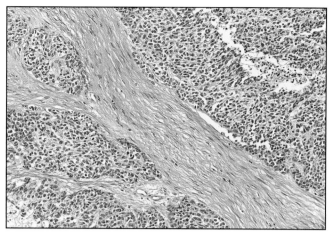

Fig. 13A.97 • Desmoplastic small round cell tumor. Nests and sheets of small round tumor cells are separated by desmoplastic fibrous stroma.

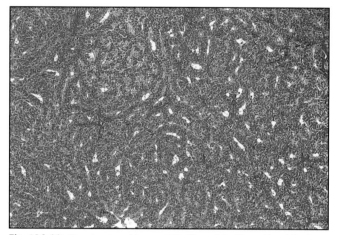

Fig. 13A.98 • Female adnexal tumor of Wolffian origin. The uniform bland tumor cells grow in a mixed diffuse and tubular pattern.

women, but when the tumor is large, the symptoms are those of a pelvic mass. The tumors are solid and gray, tan, or yellow. They range from 2 to 20 cm in diameter, with an average of 11–12 cm. The microscopic picture is one of uniform, small to medium sized, epithelial cells growing in diffuse, trabecular, tubular, and microcystic or sieve-like patterns (Fig. 13A.98). Prominent peritubular basement membranes are characteristic and there is a variable amount of fibrous stroma. The tumor cells are immunoreactive for vimentin, cytokeratin, androgen receptor, inhibin and calretinin, but they are epithelial membrane antigen-negative.[1015,1016] Usually, mitotic figures are rare and there is little cytologic atypia. Most of these neoplasms are benign, but rare malignant examples occur in the ovary or the juxtaovarian region.[1011] The latter exhibit increased mitotic activity or cytologic atypia, overgrowth of spindled cells, or lymphatic invasion.

Adenomatoid tumor

Adenomatoid tumors are most common in the fallopian tube and myometrium, but rare cases have been reported, in or immediately adjacent to, the hilum of the ovary.[1017] Some are microscopic, but others are firm, gray, or tan nodules, typically less than 2 cm in diameter. The microscopic appearance is

similar to that of adenomatoid tumors at other sites (see Ch. 14). They are benign neoplasms of mesothelial derivation and are circumscribed but not encapsulated. They consist of tubules and cysts lined by cuboidal cells surrounded by a variable amount of fibrous or fibromuscular stroma. Immunostains for cytokeratin and calretinin are positive.

Metastatic tumors in the ovary

Metastatic tumors involve the ovaries more often than any other site in the female genital tract.[1018,1019] Ovarian metastases comprise 5–10 percent of all malignant ovarian tumors.[1020–1022] Possible metastatic pathways include retrograde lymphatic spread, transperitoneal dissemination, and hematogenous metastasis.[1023] Based on the pathology of the involved ovaries and on clinical and operative findings, lymphatic and transperitoneal spread account for most ovarian metastases, particularly from primary sites within the abdomen.[1024] Adenocarcinomas of the breast, large intestine, endometrium, and stomach are the most common primary sites, but a wide variety of malignant tumors occasionally give rise to ovarian metastases.[1025] These include cancers of the cervix,[1026,1027] appendix,[1028] pancreas,[1029] bile duct and gallbladder,[1030] liver,[420,425,1031] kidney,[360,404,1032–1034] urinary tract,[404,405] and lung,[412,413] as well as melanoma,[880,1035] malignant lymphoma and various types of soft tissue and gastrointestinal sarcomas.[1036–1039] It is often difficult to differentiate metastatic endometrial adenocarcinoma in the ovary from synchronous primary endometrioid adenocarcinomas of the endometrium and ovary. This problem is discussed in the section on endometrioid adenocarcinoma (see p. 581).

Clinical features Clinically significant ovarian metastases most often occur in women with a history of an extraovarian cancer, usually of the colon or rectum.[1040] The average time between surgery for the primary tumor and detection of the ovarian metastases is about 2 years, but the length of the interval varies and ranges from a few months to more than 5 years.[1041] Some patients have no history of a primary extraovarian tumor.[1018,1042] They present with symptoms of a pelvic tumor, such as pelvic or abdominal pain, gastrointestinal or urinary disturbances, abdominal distention, or abnormal uterine bleeding, and are often thought to have primary ovarian cancer.[1043–1045] In most of these patients, a locally advanced gastrointestinal primary cancer is discovered concurrently with the ovarian metastases but, in rare instances, the primary site is discovered only months or years after the ovarian tumors are removed. When a woman with a history of colorectal cancer develops a new pelvic mass the most likely diagnosis is metastatic adenocarcinoma, but benign or primary malignant ovarian tumors are discovered in a significant percentage of cases (26 percent benign and 17 percent primary ovarian cancers in one study).[1041] Ovarian metastases develop in 2–13 percent of women with colorectal carcinoma,[1046,1047] leading some authors to advocate prophylactic oophorectomy at the time the primary tumor is resected.[1048,1049] Oophorectomy has not been shown to improve survival, however, and, its efficacy is at present unclear.[1050–1053] The prognosis is poor for women with ovarian metastases,[1040,1054,1055] but resection appears to lengthen survival and relieve symptoms. Some investigators have found that ovarian metastases are more likely to develop in premeno-pausal women, but this finding has not been confirmed by others.[1042,1048,1056]

Breast cancer is the most common metastatic tumor of the ovary, but it is rarely clinically significant. Historically, most examples of metastatic breast cancer have been small, some-times even microscopic, foci of tumor cells found in ovaries removed for hormonal therapy of breast cancer.[1018,1057] Adnexal masses in women with a history of breast cancer are more likely to be primary ovarian neoplasms than metastases.[1058] Metastatic breast cancers that present clinically as primary ovarian tumors, prior to discovery of the breast primary, often pose diagnostic problems.[1040,1059]

Pathology Metastatic tumors in the ovary vary in appearance depending on the primary site. Metastatic colorectal cancer is bilateral in 50–70 percent of cases. The ovarian tumors average 10–11 cm in diameter, have a smooth surface, and tend to be cystic or solid and cystic.[1044,1060] In one study, 90 percent of mucinous carcinomas were classified correctly as primary or metastatic by assuming that all bilateral mucinous tumors or mucinous tumors smaller than 10 cm were metastatic, and all unilateral mucinous tumors larger than 10 cm were primary.[211] The cysts are unilocular or multilocular and are filled with mucin. Metastatic stomach cancer usually has the appearance of a Krukenberg tumor. The ovaries tend to retain their shape but are symmetrically or asymmetrically enlarged. They are firm and have areas of nodularity on the surface. The cut surface is gray, tan, or white and is edematous and honeycombed with small mucinous cysts. Most other types of metastatic tumors tend to be solid and grow as multiple nodules in the cortex and medulla, often with implants on the serosa.

General microscopic features that raise the possibility that an ovarian tumor might be metastatic include a bilateral, multi-nodular growth pattern, implants on the surface of the ovary, numerous emboli of metastatic carcinoma in lymphatic spaces, especially in the hilum and mesovarium, and an unusual micro-scopic pattern for a primary ovarian tumor, such as a signet ring cell appearance or an Indian file pattern of invasion.[1061] Luteinization of the stroma occurs around some metastatic tumors,[1044,1060] but it also occurs around primary ovarian tumors and does not necessarily imply that a tumor is metastatic. The luteinized cells occasionally secrete sufficient amounts of estrogen or androgen to cause clinical symptoms.[1062]

Metastatic colorectal adenocarcinoma often simulates a primary adenocarcinoma of the ovary.[1020,1044,1046,1060,1063] The typical colorectal adenocarcinoma, in which absorptive cells predominate and goblet cells are absent or inconspicuous, mimics endometrioid adenocarcinoma (Fig. 13A.99). Metastatic colorectal adenocarcinoma forms large complex glands and cysts that contain necrotic debris. The debris is coarsely granular and contains nuclear fragments and inflammatory cells, resulting in a distinctive appearance, often termed "dirty" necrosis (Fig. 13A.100).[1060] While extensive necrosis is charac-teristic of metastatic colorectal adenocarcinoma, it can also occur in a primary ovarian adenocarcinoma.[1020,1064] The malig-nant cells lining the glands and cysts stratify or grow in cart-wheel, garland, or cribriform patterns with foci of segmental epithelial necrosis (see Fig. 13A.100). The degree of nuclear atypia tends to be greater than is seen in an endometrioid adenocarcinoma of similar architectural grade. Findings that

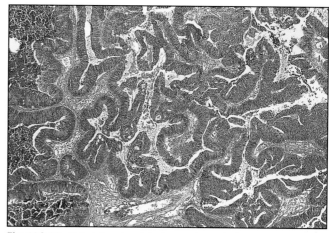

Fig. 13A.99 • Metastatic colorectal adenocarcinoma in the ovary. The tumor glands are lined by columnar cells with dense cytoplasm and goblet cells are inconspicuous. The histologic picture mimics endometrioid carcinoma of the ovary.

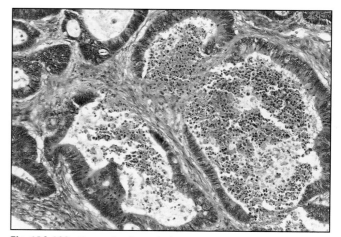

Fig. 13A.100 • Metastatic colorectal adenocarcinoma in the ovary. The malignant glands are filled with mucus and cellular and nuclear debris, so-called "dirty" necrosis. Some of the glands show segmental necrosis.

are typical of primary endometrioid carcinoma, such as squamous metaplasia, a focal adenofibromatous pattern of growth and adjacent endometriosis are generally absent. Metastatic colorectal adenocarcinoma mimics primary mucin-ous carcinoma of the ovary when goblet cells are numerous and there is abundant mucin production.[211] A metastatic adeno-carcinoma from the pancreas or biliary tract can also grow as a mucinous adenocarcinoma and thus enter the differential diagnosis.[1029,1063] Deceptively bland areas that simulate a benign or borderline mucinous tumor are occasionally seen in a metastasis and do not necessarily indicate that a mucinous carcinoma is primary in the ovary. Metastatic mucinous adenocarcinomas exhibit the general microscopic features of metastases, including surface implants and at least focally infiltrative growth,[1061] but it may be necessary to compare the microscopic appearance of the metastasis with that of the primary or to perform immunohistochemical studies in order to arrive at the correct diagnosis.

Several immunohistochemical stains can help in the differ-ential diagnosis between a primary adenocarcinoma of the ovary and metastatic colorectal adenocarcinoma, but no single

Table 13A.11 Immunophenotype of primary and metastatic ovarian adenocarcinomas

Tumor	CK7	CK20	CDX-2	Villin	GCDFP15	CA125	WT-1
Primary ovarian carcinoma							
Serous	+	–	–	–	–	+	+
Endometrioid	+	–	–	–	–	+	–
Mucinous	+	V	V	+	–	NV	–
Metastatic carcinoma							
Colon-rectum	–	+	+	+	–	–	–
Appendix	NV	+	+	V	–	–	–
Stomach	+	V	NV	na	–	–	–
Breast	+	–	–	–	V	NV	–

CK7 = cytokeratin 7; CK20 = cytokeratin 20; GCDFP 15 = gross cystic disease fluid protein 15; na = insufficient data; + usually positive; – usually negative; V can be positive or negative, but often positive; NV, can be positive or negative but most often negative

stain is definitive (Table 13A.11).[733,1023] Immunostains for cytokeratin subtypes are the most useful ones. Primary adenocarcinoma of the ovary is almost invariably strongly reactive for cytokeratin 7, while colorectal adenocarcinoma is usually cytokeratin 7-negative.[219,1064–1067] Immunostains for cytokeratin 20 are usually negative in endometrioid carcinoma.[202,1064] Ovarian mucinous adenocarcinoma may be immunoreactive for cytokeratin 20,[202,1066] but staining is typically weak and focal.[219] In contrast, colorectal adenocarcinoma is diffusely and strongly reactive for cytokeratin 20. Thus, a cytokeratin 7 positive/cytokeratin 20 negative immunophenotype strongly suggests a primary ovarian carcinoma, while a cytokeratin 7 negative/cytokeratin 20 positive immunophenotype strongly favors metastatic adenocarcinoma (see Table 13A.11).[1067–1069] While colonic adenocarcinoma is almost invariably cytokeratin 7 negative, some rectal adenocarcinomas and adenocarcinomas from more proximal portions of the gastrointestinal tract, including the appendix, small intestine, and stomach, can be cytokeratin 7 positive.[1065,1069,1070] Other immunohistochemical stains that may help differentiate between primary and metastatic neoplasms include CDX-2,[216,218,220,221,1071,1072] which shows positive nuclear staining in colorectal carcinoma, is usually negative in endometrioid carcinoma, and stains only a minority of mucinous carcinomas; beta-catenin,[217,221] which shows positive nuclear staining in some colorectal and endometrioid carcinomas, but which is usually negative in primary mucinous carcinoma; OC 125 (CA 125), which shows positive membrane staining in endometrioid carcinoma, but is usually negative in primary mucinous carcinoma and metastatic colorectal carcinoma;[130,1073–1075] alpha-methylacyl-CoA racemase (also known as P504S),[221] which shows granular cytoplasmic staining in some metastatic colorectal adenocarcinomas and primary mucinous adenocarcinomas, but which tends to be negative in endometrioid adenocarcinomas; and carcinoembryonic antigen (CEA), where negative or weak staining favors an ovarian primary over metastatic colorectal adenocarcinoma.[397,1044,1064,1066,1076]

Metastatic tumors from the appendix are rare and account for only 1 percent of ovarian metastases.[1077] A majority of appendiceal tumors that metastasize to the ovary are signet ring cell adenocarcinomas that arise from the base of the mucosa and infiltrate the wall of the appendix. They contain signet ring cells, tubules, and goblet cells in varying proportions.[1028] Carcinomas with a prominent tubular component lined by goblet cells have been classified as goblet cell or mucinous carcinoids, or as mixed carcinoid-adenocarcinomas in the past.[1077,1078] Such tumors are biologically aggressive and do not always exhibit the typical staining pattern of a carcinoid tumor (argentaffin positive and immunoreactive for chromogranin and/or synaptophysin). If there is ovarian stromal proliferation, the metastases may fulfill criteria for classification as a classical or tubular Krukenberg tumor (see below).[1079,1080] Other metastatic appendiceal adenocarcinomas are glandular adenocarcinomas of colorectal or mucinous intestinal types.[1028,1077,1081] These metastases are usually immunoreactive for cytokeratin 20, but are also cytokeratin 7 positive in about 50 percent of the cases.[1028] The issue of pseudomyxoma peritonei in women with appendix and ovarian neoplasms is discussed below.

Metastatic carcinoid tumors are microscopically identical to primary ovarian carcinoids, but they are not associated with other teratomatous elements.[928] Moreover, they are usually bilateral and multifocal. The most common primary site is in the small intestine.

Metastatic breast cancer is often an incidental finding, but in about one-third of cases the ovaries are enlarged by solid diffuse or nodular metastases.[1057,1059] Microscopically, most metastases resemble infiltrating ductal or lobular carcinoma, and are readily recognized as metastatic from the breast. Uncommon microscopic patterns that may be difficult to differentiate from primary tumors or metastases from other organs include a single cell pattern, a diffuse, solid growth pattern, and a cribriform growth pattern.[1057] Metastatic breast cancer is usually cytokeratin 7 positive, cytokeratin 20 negative, and it may show nuclear staining for estrogen and progesterone receptors, an immunophenotype that overlaps with that of many primary ovarian carcinomas. A positive immunostain for gross cystic disease fluid protein (GCDFP)-15 provides support for a diagnosis of metastatic breast cancer (see Table 13A.11), but personal experience suggests that ovarian metastases are immunoreactive with this antibody less often than is reported in the literature.[1082] Metastases from a signet ring cell type of infiltrating lobular carcinoma can form Krukenberg tumors in the ovary.[1083]

A Krukenberg tumor is a form of metastatic adeno-carcinoma, sometimes found in young women, in which malignant signet ring cells grow in a hypercellular stroma.[1084–1086a] The primary carcinoma is usually in the stomach,[1086–1087] but signet-ring cell carcinomas of the breast,[1083,1087] colon,[1086,1087] gallbladder, and other sites can also give rise to metastases of this type. Krukenberg tumors are relatively rare in the USA and Europe, but are common in populations in which there is a high incidence of gastric carcinoma, such as in Japan and in women of Japanese extraction.[1027,1087] Microscopically, the signet-ring cells grow as single cells, in variably sized nests or cords, or in widely scattered tubules (Fig. 13A.101). The malignant cells contain cytoplasmic mucin globules that compress and flatten the hyperchromatic nucleus against the cell wall. Small polygonal or cuboidal cells with eosinophilic cytoplasm and eccentric nuclei are present in some tumors. Rare Krukenberg tumors contain prominent tubular glands in addition to signet ring cells. These have been designated tubular Krukenberg tumors.[1088,1089] The hilar lymphatics often contain tumor cells, which may be cohesive or form glands. The stroma of a Krukenberg tumor is abundant, hypercellular, and focally edematous, and it may contain pools of mucin. The malignant cells may be obscured by the stroma, but they can easily be identified in sections stained for neutral mucins with PAS or mucicarmine, or with immunohistochemical stains for cytokeratin or epithelial membrane antigen. The tumor cells tend to be cytokeratin 7 positive, but staining for cytokeratin 20 is variable. The reactive stromal cells may show strong staining for inhibin. Rare Krukenberg tumors have been designated as "primary Krukenberg tumors" because an extraovarian primary could not be identified.[1090,1091] Gastro-intestinal primary cancers, particularly those of the stomach, can remain undetected even after painstaking investigation, so it is best to consider all Krukenberg tumors to be metastatic until proven otherwise by clinical follow-up or autopsy. Nevertheless, a rare patient survives long-term after resection of a Krukenberg tumor or no primary site is identified at autopsy, raising the possibility of the existence of a primary type of signet ring Krukenberg tumor.[1085,1086]

Pseudomyxoma peritonei

Pseudomyxoma peritonei (see also Ch. 15) is an uncommon condition in which mucinous ascites causes progressive abdominal distention and gastrointestinal dysfunction.[1092] The mucus is viscous, loculated, yellow-brown or red, and contains foci of fibrous organization that form adhesions to adjacent structures. Pseudomyxoma peritonei in women is often associated with ovarian tumors that resemble borderline mucinous tumors (Fig. 13A.102) or, less often, a mucinous cystadenoma, and it has been proposed as the cause of death of nearly all women who die of borderline mucinous tumors.[1093] It also occurs in patients with tumors of the gastrointestinal tract, particularly those of the appendix, and rarely with tumors of other sites.

Three different microscopic patterns have been described in pseudomyxoma peritonei.[191,1094,1095] In the first, the mucin is superficial. It lies on the surface of the ovaries, on the peritoneal surfaces or on the omentum and may contain inflammatory cells, macrophages, fibroblasts and an ingrowth of capillaries. In some cases no epithelium is present, while in others there is

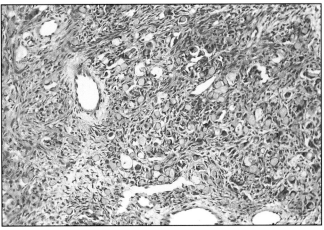

Fig. 13A.101 • Krukenberg tumor. Signet ring cells with cytoplasmic mucin vacuoles infiltrate a hyperplastic ovarian stroma.

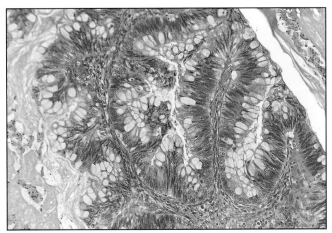

Fig. 13A.102 • Ovarian mucinous tumor in a woman with pseudomyxoma peritonei. This tumor resembles a borderline mucinous tumor. The patient had bilateral ovarian tumors, pseudomyxoma peritonei, and a primary adenocarcinoma of the transverse colon.

a small amount of low grade mucinous epithelium. This has been termed the "acellular" or "superficial organizing" pattern of pseudomyxoma peritonei, depending on whether on not epithelium is present. Second, and most common, is a pattern in which the mucus appears to dissect through the involved tissue. It is surrounded by bands of fibrous tissue and there is organization, with ingrowth of fibroblasts and capillaries. Occasional strips of low grade mucinous epithelium are present in the mucus or in or adjacent to the fibrous bands (Fig. 13A.103).[1096] This pattern, designated as disseminated peritoneal adenomucinosis (DPAM) by some authors,[1095] is found in women with benign or borderline-appearing mucinous tumors of the ovary. In the third pattern, the mucus contains more epithelial cells and the cells exhibit high-grade nuclear atypia or there are clear-cut features of mucinous adeno-carcinoma, such as proliferative malignant glands, solid growth, or signet ring cells. This pattern can be designated as metastatic mucinous carcinoma or peritoneal mucinous carcinomatosis. The prognosis is related to the type of peritoneal mucinous lesion present. Patients with acellular or superficial organizing mucin have the best prognosis.[191,1094] A diagnosis of "acellular mucin" requires careful study, since epithelial cells are usually

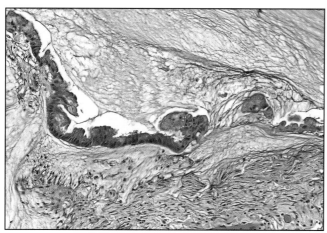

Fig. 13A.103 • Pseudomyxoma peritonei. Organizing dissecting mucin and bland mucinous epithelium in the omentum. This histologic pattern is designated as "disseminated peritoneal adenomucinosis" by some.

found if numerous slides are studied. Patients with so-called DPAM have an intermediate prognosis with a high rate of recurrence, a protracted clinical course and, in some cases, eventual death due to complications of pseudomyxoma peritonei.[1094,1097–1099] Patients with markedly atypical or malignant cells in the mucus have an unfavorable prognosis, and usually die of carcinomatosis within a few years of diagnosis.[1095,1099,1100] Radical forms of therapy for pseudomyxoma peritonei involving peritonectomy and intra-abdominal chemotherapy have been developed in recent years and appear to have some therapeutic benefit.[1101–1104]

The histogenesis of the ovarian tumors that occur in women with pseudomyxoma peritonei has been a source of controversy. Recent clinicopathologic studies have shown that nearly all women with pseudomyxoma peritonei have a tumor in the appendix or, in a few cases, elsewhere in the gastrointestinal tract. These studies have led most authors to conclude that the ovarian tumors are secondary, with the primary site usually being the appendix.[1094,1105,1106] Findings that favor this hypothesis include: the tumors in the ovary and appendix are usually synchronous; the tumors in the ovary and appendix are histologically similar; the ovarian tumors are frequently bilateral, a finding that is more in keeping with a secondary neoplasm than with a primary borderline mucinous tumor; when unilateral, the ovarian tumors are most often right sided, near the appendix; implants are present on the surfaces of the ovaries, a finding characteristic of metastases; the gross and microscopic appearance is not exactly typical of a primary mucinous tumor; the ovarian involvement may be superficial; pseudomyxoma ovarii is almost always present, and frequently contains epithelial cells with an appearance identical to those in the abdominal mucin; immunostains for cytokeratin 7 are negative in some ovarian tumors;[1107,1108] the ovarian and appendiceal tumors show immunohistochemical staining and molecular marking for MUC2, a marker of intestinal neoplasms, while primary ovarian mucinous tumors express MUC5AC but not MUC2;[1109,1110] and there are molecular similarities between the ovarian and appendiceal tumors in some cases.[1111–1113] Not all pathologists and gynecologists agree that the ovarian tumors are secondary; some regard some or all of the ovarian tumors as primary neoplasms and, potentially, as the source of the mucinous epithelium that causes

pseudomyxoma peritonei.[1093,1114] Some of these authors find the concept of ovarian metastases from benign or hyperplastic lesions of the appendix difficult to accept.[1093] Features that favor the interpretation that the tumors of the ovaries and appendix are simultaneous primaries include: the ovarian tumors are large compared to the tumors in the appendix; the ovarian tumors often contain benign-appearing mucinous epithelium, usually with transition to a borderline mucinous tumor; it is impossible to identify a site of rupture of the appendix in a substantial percentage of cases; there are no organ metastases in sites other than the ovaries (although splenic involvement has now been documented);[1115] the appendiceal tumor is sometimes discovered after the ovarian tumor; pseudomyxoma peritonei occasionally occurs in a patient who had an appendectomy years before the onset of pseudomyxoma peritonei, or who had a histologically normal appendix removed at operation for pseudomyxoma peritonei;[1093] isolated patients with pseudomyxoma peritonei and ovarian tumors are cured despite failure to remove the appendix;[1093] and, there are molecular differences between the ovarian and appendiceal tumors in some patients.[1111]

The overall current consensus is that the ovarian tumors in women with pseudomyxoma peritonei are secondary to a gastrointestinal neoplasm, usually one located in the appendix, in almost all cases.[1096,1116,1117] The pathologist should keep in mind that the appendix tends to be abnormal in patients with pseudomyxoma peritonei, even when it is grossly unremarkable and ovarian tumors are present. If possible, the appendix should be removed and processed in its entirety for histologic study. The type of tumor present in the appendix, if any, and the histologic appearance of the tumor cells in the peritoneal mucin are important prognostic factors in pseudomyxoma peritonei, and should be described in the pathology report. In most patients, the appendiceal tumor is a low grade mucinous neoplasm, sometimes associated with a diverticulum,[1118] although in a minority of patients it is an adenocarcinoma.[1119,1120] In a small minority of patients, no extraovarian primary tumor can be identified. In some of these patients, the explanation for the pseudomyxoma peritonei appears to be that an intestinal mucinous type tumor arising in a benign cystic teratoma has spread to the peritoneum and given rise to pseudomyxoma peritonei.[889] Such tumors have the immunophenotype of intestinal (cytokeratin 7 negative, cytokeratin 20 positive, CDX-2 positive), not ovarian (cytokeratin 7 positive, cytokeratin 20 and CDX-2 variable) mucinous tumors. In a few patients, the derivation of the pseudomyxoma peritonei is difficult to reconcile with current concepts of the disease and, in such cases, the pseudomyxoma peritonei may arise from an ovarian mucinous tumor or from an occult primary mucinous tumor in some other organ.

Benign tumor-like conditions of the ovary

Hyperreactio luteinalis (multiple bilateral theca lutein cysts)

Hyperreactio luteinalis is a pregnancy-related form of massive ovarian enlargement. It is caused by numerous large theca lutein cysts and is usually bilateral.

Clinical features Hyperreactio luteinalis is an uncommon cause of ovarian enlargement that occurs in women with an increased serum concentration of human chorionic gonadotropin (HCG).[1121,1122] It is found in about 25 percent of women with gestational trophoblastic disease,[1123] and it occurs occasionally in women with fetal hydrops or multiple gestations.[1124,1125] It is rare in women with singleton gestations.[1126,1126–1128] It can occur in any trimester of pregnancy and is usually asymptomatic and detected by ultrasound. Patients with intracystic hemorrhage may have abdominal pain, and those with ovarian torsion or rupture have acute abdominal symptoms.[1129] Maternal virilization is rare in women with gestational trophoblastic disease, but occurs in about 25 percent of the remaining patients. Female infants are not virilized. The cysts regress following delivery so treatment should be as conservative as possible.

Pathology The ovaries are congested and enlarged, sometimes massively, by numerous cysts measuring up to 3–4 cm in diameter. Microscopically, the cysts are theca lutein cysts. They are lined by several layers of granulosa cells which show varying degrees of luteinization, and are surrounded by a rim of luteinized theca cells (Fig. 13A.104). The luteinized cells are large and polygonal with abundant eosinophilic cytoplasm and central round nuclei. The stroma around the cysts is edematous.

Luteoma of pregnancy

Luteoma of pregnancy is a nodular hyperplasia of gonadal stromal cells that appears during the third trimester of pregnancy and regresses after delivery.[1121,1123,1130,1131] It develops under the influence of human chorionic gonadotropin (HCG) but, in contrast to hyperreactio luteinalis, there is usually not an abnormally high level of HCG.[1130]

Clinical features Luteoma occurs primarily in multiparous pregnant women, a majority of whom are black, at an average age of 27–28 years. Luteoma is often impalpable and is often discovered unexpectedly using ultrasound or during caesarian section or tubal ligation.[1130,1132,1133] About a third of patients become virilized during the third trimester,[1130] and more than

50 percent of the female infants born to virilized mothers are masculinized.[1121,1130,1134] Treatment should be as conservative as possible, since untreated luteoma involutes spontaneously, with degenerative changes becoming apparent within the first 5 days after delivery.[1131] The optimal management is biopsy to confirm the diagnosis, with no additional surgery if the pathologist can confirm the diagnosis by frozen section, and there are no other complicating factors, such as rupture or necrosis secondary to torsion.

Pathology Luteoma of pregnancy presents as nodular enlargement of one (two-thirds of cases) or both ovaries. On cut section, there are one or more soft tan, brown, or yellow nodules in the cortex or medulla. The nodules average 6–10 cm and may contain foci of hemorrhage or necrosis. Small or large cysts are often present.

Microscopically, luteoma of pregnancy consists of sheets and nests of luteinized cells. These have abundant granular eosinophilic cytoplasm and round vesicular nuclei (Fig. 13A.105). There is no nuclear atypia, but mitotic figures (1–2 per 10 high power fields) are easily identified. No crystalloids of Reinke are identified. Theca lutein cysts are often present in the adjacent ovary, and there may be hyperplastic nodules of luteinized cells in the stroma or in the walls of cystic or atretic follicles.

Microscopic granulosa cell proliferations in pregnancy

Microscopic foci of granulosa cell proliferation that mimic small granulosa cell tumors are detected occasionally in the ovaries of pregnant women.[478,1135,1136] The proliferating cells grow in trabecular, insular, diffuse, or microfollicular patterns. These granulosa cell proliferations may occur in an ovary that also harbors a luteoma of pregnancy or hyperreactio luteinalis. They are thought to be benign proliferative responses to HCG rather than small granulosa cell tumors because they occur during pregnancy, are multifocal, are confined to the centers of atretic follicles, and do not show the morphologic changes (luteinization, edema, etc.) that occur in granulosa cell tumors in pregnant women. No recurrences have been reported.

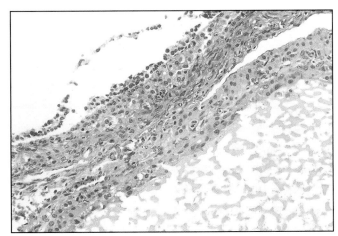

Fig. 13A.104 • Hyperreactio luteinalis. The cyst at the top is lined by granulosa cells overlying luteinized theca cells. Both the granulosa cells and the theca cells lining the cyst at the bottom are luteinized.

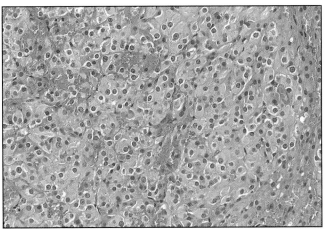

Fig. 13A.105 • Luteoma of pregnancy. The luteoma is composed of round to polygonal cells with abundant eosinophilic cytoplasm and central round nuclei.

Massive edema and fibromatosis

Massive edema is a rare cause of unilateral ovarian enlargement in young women and is thought to be caused by intermittent torsion of the ovary, with obstruction of the lymphatics and veins in the pedicle.[1137-1141] Rare cases of massive edema in older women have been caused by obstruction of the hilar lymphatics by metastatic carcinoma.[1142,1143] The clinical presentation is with acute abdominal symptoms and a solid adnexal mass. The involved ovary has an edematous pink-yellow cut surface and averages 11.5 cm in diameter.[1140] Microscopically, stromal edema is the main finding. Aggregates of luteinized cells are present in some cases. The blood vessels are dilated and congested, suggesting that partial or intermittent torsion may be the cause of the edema. Ovarian fibromatosis is a possibly related condition in which the ovary is enlarged by proliferation of small fibroblasts that surround and separate normal ovarian structures.[1140] Collagen deposition is variable, and edema may be present. The histologic picture is reminiscent of a fibroma, but the fibroblastic proliferation is multifocal and diffuse rather than circumscribed.

Tumors of the fallopian tube

Primary neoplasms of the fallopian tubes are uncommon relative to those in the ovaries and uterus. Many of the same tumor types that occur in the ovaries also arise in the fallopian tubes (Table 13A.12). Several benign tumors that can involve the ovaries, such as adenomatoid tumors and female adnexal tumors of wolffian origin (FATWO), are more common in the tube and paratubal region. Carcinomas of various types are the most common tumors of the tubes. It is important to differentiate primary tumors of the tube from secondary involvement by carcinomas arising elsewhere in the female genital tract, especially the ovaries, or from an extragenital site.

Benign tumors of the fallopian tube

Adenomatoid tumor

Adenomatoid tumor is of mesothelial origin and is the most common benign tumor of the fallopian tube.[1144-1146] Most are discovered incidentally in middle aged or elderly women who are operated on for some other reason, but large tumors can cause symptoms. Adenomatoid tumors are small, with an average diameter of 1–2 cm. They are gray-white or yellow, well-circumscribed nodules that are located just beneath the serosal surface.

Microscopically, the tumor consists of gland-like cystic or microcystic spaces lined by flattened cells or cords and tubules lined by cuboidal cells with abundant eosinophilic cytoplasm (Fig. 13A.106). Some tumors contain cells with prominent cytoplasmic vacuoles that mimic signet ring cells. The vacuoles and gland-like spaces contain Alcian blue-positive material rich in hyaluronic acid, typical of a mesothelial neoplasm. The infiltrative microscopic appearance sometimes raises the question of adenocarcinoma. However, adenomatoid tumors are grossly circumscribed, the cytology is bland and there are no mitotic figures. Adenomatoid tumors occasionally infarct

Table 13A.12	Classification of the most common tumors of the fallopian tube

Malignant epithelial tumors
  Serous adenocarcinoma
  Endometrioid adenocarcinoma
  Transitional cell carcinoma
  Others

Borderline epithelial tumors
  Borderline serous tumor
  Borderline endometrioid tumor
  Others

Carcinoma in situ

Benign epithelial tumors
  Papilloma (specify type)
  Cystadenoma (specify type)
  Adenofibroma (specify type)
  Cystadenofibroma (specify type)
  Metaplastic papillary polyp
  Endometrioid polyp
  Others

Tumor-like epithelial lesions
  Tubal epithelial hyperplasia
  Salpingitis isthmica nodosa
  Endosalpingiosis

Mixed epithelial-mesenchymal tumors
  Malignant mixed müllerian tumor (carcinosarcoma)
  Adenosarcoma

Soft tissue tumors
  Leiomyosarcoma
  Leiomyoma
  Others

Mesothelial tumors
  Adenomatoid tumor

Germ cell tumors
  Mature teratoma
  Immature teratoma
  Others

Trophoblastic disease
  Choriocarcinoma
  Placental site trophoblastic tumor
  Epithelioid trophoblastic tumor
  Hydatidiform mole
  Placental site nodule
  Other

Lymphoid and hematopoietic tumors
  Lymphoma
  Leukemia

Secondary tumors

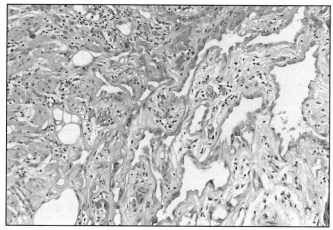

Fig. 13A.106 • Adenomatoid tumor of the fallopian tube. Tubules (right) and microcystic spaces (left) are lined by cuboidal to flattened mesothelial cells with bland nuclei.

and can be difficult to diagnose unless there are residual viable areas or vestiges of the typical histologic pattern can be recognized in the infarcted zones.[1147] An immunostain for cytokeratin often highlights the typical architecture of an adenomatoid tumor even in largely infarcted specimens. Immunohistochemical stains for cytokeratin and the mesothelial markers calretinin and cytokeratin 5/6 are positive.[1148] Adenomatoid tumors also show positive nuclear staining for WT-1, similar to other mesothelial neoplasms.[1149] Stains for the adenocarcinoma markers Ber-EP4, CEA, and B72.3 are negative, or at most, weakly and focally positive.[1150] The immunophenotype supports the mesothelial derivation of adenomatoid tumors, and helps to differentiate them from adenocarcinoma.

Benign epithelial tumors

Cystadenomas, adenofibromas and cystadenofibromas of serous or endometrioid types occur rarely in the tube.[1151–1155] A few borderline serous and endometrioid tumors have also been reported.[1151,1156] Benign and borderline mucinous tumors have been reported, but the possibility that some were metastatic could not be completely excluded.[1157]

Leiomyomas and other mesenchymal tumors

Leiomyomas are the most common mesenchymal tumors of the fallopian tube.[1158,1159] Usually small and solitary, they are often discovered incidentally. The gross and histologic appearance is similar to that of a leiomyoma of the uterus. Microscopically, the tumor is composed of interlacing fascicles of spindle shaped smooth muscle cells with bland fusiform nuclei and fibrillary eosinophilic cytoplasm. The same types of degenerative change that occur in uterine leiomyomas may also occur in tubal leiomyomas, including hydropic change, hyalinization and fibrosis.

Other benign soft tissue tumors that have been reported in the tube include lipoma, angiomyolipoma,[1160] hemangioma,[1161–1163] angiomyofibroblastoma,[1164] solitary fibrous tumor,[1165] neurilemoma,[1166,1167] ganglioneuroma,[1168] and chondroma.[1169,1170]

Teratoma

Teratomas of the fallopian tube are rare and most are benign cystic teratomas.[1171–1173] A few solid mature[1174,1175] and immature teratomas have also been reported.[1176,1177] Patients with tubal teratomas range from 21 to 60 years of age.[1171] Most teratomas are pedunculated masses that grow in the lumen of the isthmus or ampulla, although intramural and serosal tumors have been described. Microscopically, benign teratomas contain a mixture of mature ectodermal, mesodermal and endodermal tissue while immature elements are present in the immature teratomas. Monodermal teratomas can occur in the tube. A mature teratoma composed entirely of thyroid tissue was designated as a "struma salpingis" and was associated with an ipsilateral struma ovarii.[1178] In another case a carcinoid tumor arose in a mature teratoma.[1179] Finally, immature teratoma can be a component of a mixed germ cell tumor of the tube.[1180]

Malignant tumors of the fallopian tube

Adenocarcinoma

Primary adenocarcinoma of the fallopian tube accounts for approximately 1 percent of all female genital tract malignancies.[1181] It has an average annual incidence of 3.6 per million women per year in the USA. Most likely, its incidence is underestimated because advanced tumors that have spread to the ovaries are often diagnosed as ovarian cancers.

Clinical findings Tubal carcinoma occurs mainly in upper middle-aged women. The average patient age is 55 years, but fallopian tube cancer occurs over a wide age range, from 20 to more than 80 years of age.[1182,1183] The usual clinical presentation is with abnormal vaginal bleeding or discharge, abdominal pain, or a pelvic or abdominal mass.[1184] Occasional patients present with signs and symptoms suggestive of pelvic inflammatory disease.[1185] The diagnosis is seldom made preoperatively because the signs and symptoms are not specific and it is difficult to localize an adnexal mass to the tube. Chronic salpingitis has been suggested as a predisposing factor.[1186] About 15 percent of patients with fallopian tube carcinoma have germline *BRCA1* or *BRCA2* mutations.[1187–1189] Evaluation of prophylactic salpingo-oophorectomy specimens from women with *BRCA1* or *BRCA2* mutations or a family history of breast or ovarian cancer has revealed an increased incidence of epithelial dysplasia/carcinoma in situ and occult invasive adenocarcinomas of the fallopian tube.[166–168,1190–1192] Occult carcinomas have been found in 2.5 percent to 17 percent of patients undergoing risk-reducing bilateral salpingo-oophorectomy procedures.[165,166,1193,1194] Epithelial abnormalities are equally or even more frequent in the fallopian tubes than in the ovaries,[164,167] and some high risk patients thought to have developed primary peritoneal serous carcinomas after bilateral oophorectomy may, in fact, have developed peritoneal spread from an occult tubal carcinoma.[1193] It is essential for the pathologist to section the fallopian tubes serially and submit all of the tissue for microscopic examination.[168] Treatment of small carcinomas is determined by standard parameters such as the tumor's location, grade, and stage.

The treatment of fallopian tube cancer is similar to that of ovarian cancer. The primary treatment is surgical excision of the tumor, usually by total abdominal hysterectomy, and bilateral salpingo-oophorectomy. Optimal surgery includes complete surgical staging, including omentectomy, pelvic and para-aortic lymph node dissection, and peritoneal biopsies. Patients with early stage tumors who are at high risk of recurrence based on tumor grade, location, depth of invasion or rupture are usually treated with adjuvant chemotherapy. Women with advanced stage tumors undergo cytoreductive surgery followed by platinum-based chemotherapy.[1195–1198] The stage (Table 13A.13) is the most important prognostic variable. Five-year survival rates in reported series have ranged from 32 to 80 percent in stage I, 16 to 58 percent in stage II, and 0 to 29 percent in stages III–IV.[1184,1195,1199–1203] Survival rates appeared to be more favorable in a study of patients in a SEER database, with 95 percent survival in stage I, 75 percent in stage II, 69 percent in stage III and 45 percent in stage IV.[1204] In stage I, adverse prognostic factors include deep invasion into the tubal wall and rupture.[1199] Tumors in the fimbriae have a worse prognosis than ampullary or isthmic tumors with the same depth of invasion.[1182] Pretreatment serum CA125 levels correlate with the tumor stage and CA 125 levels can be used to monitor the response to treatment.[1199,1205]

Pathology On gross examination, the tube is swollen and has a smooth or granular hemorrhagic serosal surface, depending on the depth of invasion. The surgeon or pathologist may initially suspect a hydrosalpinx, hematosalpinx or pyosalpinx,

rather than a neoplasm. Small tumors in the fimbria, which appears to be the most frequent location,[1205a] can easily be overlooked. Bilaterality ranges from 3 percent to 30 percent in reported series, with an average of about 20 percent. The cut surface reveals a tan to yellow, solid or papillary tumor that partly or completely fills the lumen. Large tumors generally contain zones of hemorrhage and necrosis.

Two categories of intraepithelial atypia of the fallopian tube have been described: carcinoma in situ and hyperplasia. In carcinoma in situ, the epithelial cells have enlarged, hyperchromatic, cytologically malignant nuclei (Fig. 13A.107). Some nuclei contain nucleoli and mitotic figures, which are sometimes abnormal, can be identified. The abnormal cells are low columnar with eosinophilic or amphophilic cytoplasm and the nuclear to cytoplasmic ratio is typically increased. The abnormal cells are usually stratified, with loss of polarity and occasional tufting. Ciliated cells are absent or decreased in number. Immunostains for *p53* protein are frequently strongly positive in areas of carcinoma in situ (Fig. 13A.108), facilitating their recognition and at the same time supporting the diagnosis. Carcinoma in situ is the only accepted precursor

Table 13A.13	FIGO staging of fallopian tube cancer. Reprinted from International Journal of Gynecology and Obstetrics. Benedet J L, Pecorelli S. Staging Classifications and Clinical Practice guidelines of gynaecologic cancers. p 81, ©2000. With permission from International Federation of Gynecology and Obstetrics.
Stage 0	Carcinoma in situ
Stage I	Tumor limited to the fallopian tubes
IA	Tumor limited to one tube, without penetrating the serosal surface and no ascites
IB	Tumor limited to both tubes, without penetrating the serosal surface and no ascites
IC	Tumor limited to one or both tubes with extension onto or through the serosa or with malignant cells in ascites or peritoneal washings
Stage II	Tumor involves one or both fallopian tubes with pelvic extension
IIA	Extension or metastasis to the uterus or ovaries
IIB	Extension to other pelvic structures
IIC	Pelvic extension with malignant cells in ascites or peritoneal washings
Stage III	Tumor involves one or both fallopian tubes with peritoneal implants outside the pelvis
IIIA	Microscopic peritoneal metastasis outside the pelvis
IIIB	Macroscopic peritoneal metastasis outside the pelvis 2 cm or less in diameter
IIIC	Peritoneal metastasis ≥2 cm in diameter
Stage IV	Distant metastasis

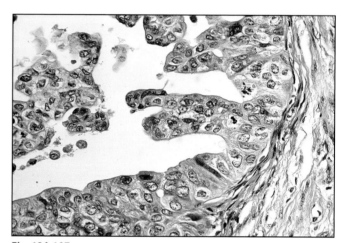

Fig. 13A.107 • Adenocarcinoma in situ of the fallopian tube. The tube is lined by stratified atypical columnar cells that show loss of polarity. The nuclei are atypical, the nuclear to cytoplasmic ratio is increased, and mitotic figures are present.

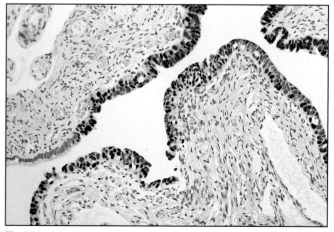

Fig. 13A.108 • Immunostain for *p53* in adenocarcinoma in situ. There is strong positive nuclear staining in the adenocarcinoma in situ, but the residual normal tubal epithelium (lower left) is negative.

of adenocarcinoma of the fallopian tube. It is one of the abnormalities that can be found in prophylactic salpingo-oophorectomy specimens in women with a *BRCA* mutation or a family history of breast or ovarian cancer.[166,1191] A wide range of less atypical hyperplastic proliferations of the tubal epithelium have been reported. The most abnormal have been designated as atypical hyperplasia, and are characterized by cellular crowding, stratification, loss of polarity, and at least moderate nuclear atypia. The degree of nuclear atypia is less than in carcinoma in situ and mitotic activity is either absent or very sparse. The clinical significance of hyperplasia is unclear. It is usually *p53* negative and has not been shown to be a precursor of carcinoma in situ or invasive adenocarcinoma.[1191,1206]

The same types of carcinoma that occur in the ovary also occur in the fallopian tube. Serous carcinoma is the most common type of tubal carcinoma. Occult serous carcinomas detected in risk-reducing salpingo-oophorectomy specimens are typically microscopic (1–2 mm or less) and can occur in the mucosa, within a fimbria, or on the serosa. These small carcinomas are usually detected only on histologic examination and it is necessary to cross-section the fallopian tubes serially and submit all of the tissue for microscopic examination in order to detect them.[166] Endometrioid carcinoma is the second most common, followed by transitional cell carcinoma and undifferentiated carcinoma. Some types of carcinoma that are common in the ovary, such as clear cell and mucinous carcinoma, occur only occasionally in the tube. In one large study of tubal carcinoma 50 percent were serous, 25 percent endometrioid, 11 percent transitional, 8 percent undifferentiated, 4 percent mixed cell types, and 2 percent clear cell.[1182] The percentage of serous carcinomas has been higher in other studies.[1183,1199,1207] Serous carcinoma of the tube has the same microscopic appearance as serous carcinoma of the ovary (Fig. 13A.109). Endometrioid adenocarcinoma tends to grow into the lumen with little or no invasion of the wall of the tube, so the prognosis can be relatively favorable. Endometrioid carcinoma exhibits several patterns of growth in the fallopian tube. The most common pattern is one in which confluent or back-to-back glands are lined by stratified columnar cells (Fig. 13A.110). Squamous differentiation is present in some cases.[1208] A second pattern mimics a female adnexal tumor of

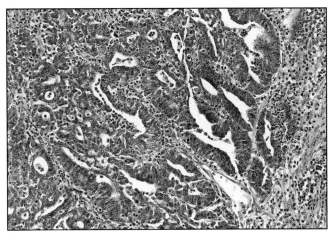

Fig. 13A.110 • Endometrioid carcinoma of the fallopian tube. Endometrioid carcinoma tends to grow as a predominantly glandular tumor. The tumor cells are columnar, with atypical hyperchromatic nuclei. Mitotic figures are present.

probable wolffian origin (FATWO), see below.[1208–1211] It consists of sheets of small polygonal or spindle cells with a focal whorled pattern suggestive of squamous differentiation. The sheets of cells are punctuated by small glands, cysts or sieve-like spaces that contain PAS-positive eosinophilic material. This form of endometrioid carcinoma differs from a FATWO in that it contains foci of recognizable squamous differentiation and exhibits a greater degree of nuclear atypia and mitotic activity. Types of carcinoma that are unusual in the fallopian tube include clear cell carcinoma,[1212–1214] squamous cell carcinoma,[1215] mucinous carcinoma,[1216] glassy cell carcinoma,[1217] hepatoid carcinoma,[1218] neuroendocrine carcinoma,[1219] and lymphoepithelioma-like carcinoma.[1182]

The immunophenotype of adenocarcinoma of the fallopian tube is similar to that of ovarian carcinoma of the same histologic type. Primary tubal carcinomas are generally cytokeratin 7 positive and cytokeratin 20 negative. Serous carcinoma of the fallopian tube shows diffuse strong positive nuclear staining for WT-1.[133]

Tumor stage is the most important prognostic factor. The pathologist should note whether the tumor is ruptured and if it extends to the serosa of the tube. The site of origin within the tube (fimbriated end versus other sites) and the depth of invasion through the tube wall are of prognostic significance in stage I tumors.[1199,1220] There is little correlation between the histologic grade and survival.[1182,1199]

Adenosarcoma and carcinosarcoma

Adenosarcoma is a biphasic tumor in which benign epithelial glands are admixed with malignant mesenchymal elements, usually a non-specific spindle cell sarcoma. Rare examples of primary adenosarcoma of the fallopian tube have been reported.[1221,1222]

Carcinosarcoma, also known as malignant mixed müllerian tumor (MMMT), is a biphasic tumor in which there is an admixture of malignant epithelial and mesenchymal elements. The epithelial component is generally serous or endometrioid carcinoma. The mesenchymal component is a round or spindle cell sarcoma which can contain heterologous elements such as rhabdomyosarcoma or chondrosarcoma. A few primary carcinosarcomas of the fallopian tube have been reported.[1223–1231]

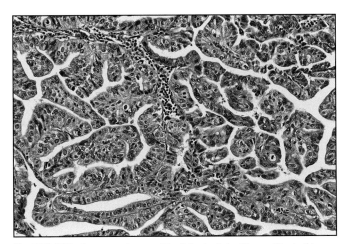

Fig. 13A.109 • Serous carcinoma of the fallopian tube. The papillae in this carcinoma are lined by low columnar cells with enlarged atypical nuclei.

The presence of carcinoma in situ in the tubal mucosa adjacent to the carcinosarcoma supports tubal origin.[1232] Carcinosarcoma must be distinguished from an endometrioid carcinoma with a spindle cell pattern. Carcinosarcoma of the tube occurs mainly in postmenopausal women and tends to be clinically aggressive, but patients with early stage disease can be cured.[1223–1225,1233]

Malignant mesenchymal tumors

Sarcomas of the fallopian tube are rare, but a few examples have been reported, including examples of leiomyosarcoma,[1234,1235] endometrioid stromal sarcoma,[328] embryonal rhabdomyosarcoma,[1236] and so-called malignant fibrous histiocytoma.[1237] Lymphoma generally involves the fallopian tube as part of systemic disease. The lymphoma tends to involve the ipsilateral ovary as well as the tube. Primary lymphoma of the fallopian tube is exceptionally rare.[1238–1240]

Gestational trophoblastic disease

Gestational trophoblastic disease of the fallopian tube is uncommon and overlaps in its clinical presentation with tubal pregnancy. Both partial and complete hydatiform moles occur in the fallopian tube,[1241–1245] as does choriocarcinoma.[1241,1246,1246–1248] They are histologically similar to their counterparts in the uterus (see Ch 13 Part C). Tubal moles are rare and it is important to apply strict criteria for their diagnosis; in one study, a majority of cases referred with a diagnosis of tubal hydatidiform mole proved to be examples of early placentation or hydropic abortion.[1245] Placental site trophoblastic tumor (PSTT) and epithelioid trophoblastic tumor (ETT), two uncommon neoplasms of intermediate trophoblastic cells, rarely occur in the fallopian tube or in the adjacent broad ligament.[1249–1252] A few examples of post-ectopic pregnancy placental site nodule have also been reported in the tube.[1250,1253–1255] These are benign nodules composed of fibrin, connective tissue, and non-proliferative intermediate trophoblastic cells.

Metastatic tumors

Metastatic tumors are more common in the fallopian tube than primary tubal neoplasms. Most examples represent spread of an ovarian or endometrial adenocarcinoma along the peritoneal surface or through the lumen. Metastases can also involve the tubal lymphatics or blood vessels. Metastases from extragenital primary sites involve the fallopian tube only infrequently.

Tumors of the broad and round ligaments

Many tumors that occur in the ovary also occur in the broad ligament (Table 13A.14), arising in accessory ovarian tissue, in endometriosis, or from the peritoneum. All types of mesenchymal tumors also arise occasionally in the broad ligament. These tend to be identical to their ovarian or soft tissue counterparts, and are not discussed further here. This discussion is

Table 13A.14	Tumors of the broad and round ligaments

Epithelial tumors of müllerian type
  Serous adenocarcinoma
  Endometrioid adenocarcinoma
  Mucinous adenocarcinoma
  Clear cell adenocarcinoma
  Borderline tumor (specify type)
  Adenoma and cystadenoma (specify type)

Miscellaneous tumors
  Wolffian adnexal tumor (FATWO)
  Ependymoma
  Papillary cystadenoma associated with von Hippel-Lindau disease
  Uterus-like mass
  Adenosarcoma
  Adrenal rest
  Others

Mesenchymal tumors
  Leiomyosarcoma
  Leiomyoma
  Others

Secondary tumors

focused on tumors and tumor-like lesions that are more common in the broad and round ligaments than in the ovary or fallopian tube.

Adrenal cortical rests and tumors

Nodules of adrenal cortical tissue are noted occasionally in routine sections of the broad ligament, but thorough study reveals that they are relatively common, being present in more than 20 percent of women.[1256] They are small yellow nodules usually measuring only a few millimeters in maximum dimension. They are located beneath the peritoneum and can be either unilateral or bilateral. Microscopically, adrenal rests are composed exclusively of adrenocortical type cells. These are polygonal and have abundant clear vacuolated cytoplasm and small vesicular nuclei (Fig. 13A.111). Hyperplastic adrenal rests can be found in the broad ligament in patients whose adrenals have been destroyed by a disease, such as tuberculosis, or removed. Several patients with Nelson's syndrome (development of an ACTH-secreting pituitary tumor following bilateral adrenalectomy for Cushing's syndrome) have been reported to have virilizing hyperplastic adrenal rests.[1257,1258] A few extraovarian steroid cell tumors have been reported in the broad ligament.[637,1259,1260] As in the ovary, they consist of adrenocortical or Leydig-like cells, or most often, a mixture of the two. Rare examples of other types of sex cord-stromal tumors have been reported in the broad ligament, including a thecoma and a granulosa cell tumor.[1261–1263]

Female adnexal tumor of Wolffian origin (FATWO)

The FATWO arises in the broad ligament or, less often, in the ovary and other pelvic sites.[1010–1012] It is thought to arise from

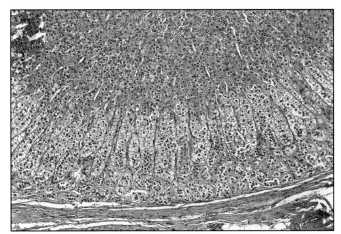

Fig. 13A.111 • Adrenal rest in broad ligament. There is a zonal pattern with cells having foamy clear cytoplasm at the periphery and cells with dense eosinophilic cytoplasm centrally.

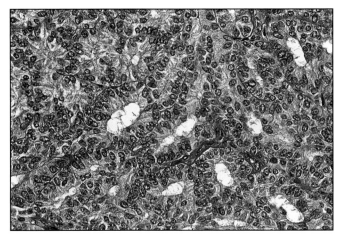

Fig. 13A.112 • Wolffian tumor of the broad ligament. There is a mixed tubular and trabecular growth pattern. The tumor cells have uniform, hyperchromatic basal nuclei, and the apical cytoplasm is amphophilic. No mitotic figures are seen.

mesonephric remnants, which are common in the broad ligament. Most patients are middle aged with a median age of around 50, but there is a wide age range from 15 to 83 years.[1264] The clinical presentation is non-specific, and small tumors are often incidental findings. The tumor is solid with a white or gray cut surface and ranges from 2 to 20 cm in diameter. Microscopically, polygonal or spindled epithelial cells grow in diffuse sheets, or in a trabecular, tubular, retiform, microcystic or sieve-like pattern (Fig. 13A.112). Mixtures of the various patterns are typically present, although one or another can predominate. The tumor cell nuclei are generally hyperchromatic and uniform. Significant nuclear atypia or mitotic activity is unusual and raises the possibility of malignancy. The FATWO is usually benign, although about 15 percent are clinically malignant.[1264–1266] Microscopic findings that are suggestive of malignancy include increased mitotic activity, significant nuclear atypia, overgrowth of spindle cells, and lymphovascular space invasion; if the patient presents with, or develops, metastases then the tumor is obviously malignant, regardless of its histologic appearance.[1266–1270] Malignant FATWOs tend to be slowly progressive, and the median time to recurrence is about 4 years.

The location and distinctive microscopic appearance usually permit the pathologist to make a confident diagnosis of a FATWO. The differential diagnosis includes a variant of endometrioid carcinoma of the fallopian tube that mimics a FATWO, which is discussed above in the section on adenocarcinoma of the fallopian tube,[1209,1211,1271] and a sex cord-stromal tumor, such as a granulosa cell tumor or a Sertoli cell tumor. The FATWO has an immunophenotype that overlaps between an epithelial tumor and a sex cord-stromal tumor, so immunohistochemical studies are not always helpful; the immunophenotype is similar to that of the rete ovarii.[1015] The FATWO shows positive staining for vimentin, cytokeratin, cytokeratin 7, cytokeratin CAM 5.2, and cytokeratin 19, but most are epithelial membrane antigen (EMA) negative.[1015,1016,1272] Immunostains for inhibin, calretinin and melan-A are frequently positive.[613,1015,1273] The FATWO is CD10 positive, which helps to differentiate it from some other diagnostic considerations.[363]

Epithelial cysts and tumors of the broad ligament

Benign cysts of müllerian, mesonephric, or mesothelial origin occasionally develop in the broad ligament. Müllerian and mesonephric cysts are the most common. Müllerian cysts are lined by ciliated or non-ciliated columnar cells and mesonephric cysts are lined by flattened epithelial cells.[1274] Primary epithelial tumors of the broad ligament are uncommon, but benign,[1275] borderline,[1276] and malignant[1277] epithelial tumors that are histologically identical to their ovarian counterparts occur in the broad ligament. Most benign and borderline epithelial tumors are serous tumors,[1276,1278] although a Brenner tumor has also been reported.[1279] A variety of types of adenocarcinoma have been reported in the broad ligament, including endometrioid, clear cell, mucinous, serous and unclassified carcinoma.[1277,1280–1282] The prognosis is favorable for patients with benign and borderline tumors,[1276] but broad ligament adenocarcinomas can be aggressive and are treated like carcinomas of the ovary and fallopian tube.[1277]

von Hippel-Lindau disease is an autosomal dominant hereditary syndrome associated with a mutation of the *VHL* tumor suppressor gene on the short arm of chromosome 13.[1283] Individuals affected by the disease have a tendency to develop tumors, including retinal angiomas, cerebellar hemangioblastomas, pheochromocytomas, and renal cell carcinomas.[1284] Some male patients with von Hippel-Lindau disease develop *clear cell papillary cystadenoma* of the epididymis, which is particularly highly correlated with the syndrome when the tumors are bilateral.[1285] A few female patients with von Hippel-Lindau disease have developed similar papillary tumors in the broad ligament.[1285–1289] The broad ligament tumors are multicystic, and papillae with prominent fibrovascular or hyaline stromal cores grow into the cysts. The papillae are covered by a single layer of cuboidal to columnar cells that have bland, round nuclei and moderate amounts of clear or eosinophilic cytoplasm. Occasionally, the histologic pattern can resemble metastatic clear cell renal cell carcinoma, a serious concern in a patient with von Hippel-Lindau disease. Immunohistochemistry can be used to differentiate a benign broad ligament papillary tumor from metastatic renal cell carcinoma, since papillary tumors are cytokeratin 7 positive and CD10 and renal cell carcinoma antigen negative,[1285] while metastatic renal cell carcinoma shows the opposite staining pattern.

Mesenchymal tumors of the broad ligament and round ligament

Leiomyomas are the most common mesenchymal tumors of the broad and round ligaments.[1290] They are firm, white or tan round nodules with a whorled cut surface. Microscopically, broad and round ligament leiomyomas resemble uterine leiomyomas. Variants of leiomyoma, such as lipoleiomyoma, occur in the broad ligament.[1291] Clear cell epithelioid leiomyoma and the potentially related tumors, perivascular epithelioid cell tumor (PEComa) and angiomyolipoma, have also been reported in the broad and round ligaments.[1292–1294] Primary ligamentary smooth muscle tumors must be differentiated from uterine smooth muscle tumors growing into the broad ligament, including leiomyomas, variants of leiomyoma such as dissecting and cotyledonoid leiomyoma,[1295,1296] and intravenous leiomyomatosis.[1297] Leiomyosarcoma only rarely occurs in the broad ligament.[1298,1299] "Uterus-like" masses have been described in the adnexae and at a glance they may resemble a leiomyoma. However, they have a zonal pattern of growth with endometrial tissue centrally, surrounded by smooth muscle.[1300] Any type of soft tissue tumor can theoretically arise in the broad ligament. Some that have been reported are paraganglioma,[1301] so-called malignant fibrous histiocytoma,[1302] hyalinizing spindle cell tumor with giant rosettes,[1303] and alveolar soft part sarcoma.[1304]

Ependymoma

Ependymoma is rare outside of the central nervous system, but a few examples have been reported in the broad ligament[1305–1307] and the ovary.[855,858,1308,1309] Ligamentary tumors have ranged from 1 to more than 15 cm in diameter, and usually have both solid and cystic areas. Microscopically, adnexal ependymoma resembles ependymoma of the central nervous system and is identical to ependymoma of the ovary (see p. 612). The tumor cells are cuboidal to columnar with eosinophilic cytoplasm and uniform round or oval nuclei. The cells grow in sheets, form ependymal rosettes and tubules, perivascular pseudorosettes, and line papillae. Papillary growth often leads to a mistaken diagnosis of an epithelial tumor. However, the tumor cells are GFAP positive.[1305] Ependymoma of the broad ligament is indolent, but capable of metastatic spread. Ependymoma of the ovary might be of teratomatous origin, but the origin of broad ligament ependymomas is unclear.[1306]

References

1. Koonings P P, Campbell K, Mishell D R Jr et al. 1989 Relative frequency of primary ovarian neoplasms: a 10-year review. Obstet Gynecol 74: 921–926
2. Gee D C, Russell P 1981 The pathological assessment of ovarian neoplasms. IV: The sex cord-stromal tumours. Pathology 13: 235–255
3. Katsube Y, Berg J W, Silverberg S G 1982 Epidemiologic pathology of ovarian tumors: a histopathologic review of primary ovarian neoplasms diagnosed in the Denver Standard Metropolitan Statistical Area, 1 July–31 December 1969 and 1 July–31 December 1979. Int J Gynecol Pathol 1: 3–16
4. Russell P, Painter D M 1982 The pathological assessment of ovarian neoplasms. V. The germ cell tumours. Pathology14: 47–72
5. Russell P 1979 The pathological assessment of ovarian neoplasms. I. Introduction to the common "epithelial" tumours and analysis of benign "epithelial" tumours. Pathology 11: 5–26
6. Serov S F, Scully R E, Sobin L H 1973 Histological typing of ovarian tumours. World Health Organization, Geneva
7. Seidman J D, Russell P, Kurman R J 2002 Surface epithelial tumors of the ovary. In: Kurman RJ (ed) Blaustein's pathology of the female genital tract 5th edn. Springer-Verlag, New York, p 791–904
8. Tavassoli F A, Devilee P 2003. World Health Organization. Pathology and genetics of tumours of the breast and female genital organs. International Agency for Research on Cancer, Lyon
9. Prat J 2003 Serous tumors of the ovary (borderline tumors and carcinomas) with and without micropapillary features. Int J Gynecol Pathol 22: 25–28
10. Hart W R 2005 Borderline epithelial tumors of the ovary. Mod Pathol 18 Suppl 2: S33–S50
11. Lawrence W D 1995 The borderland between benign and malignant surface epithelial ovarian tumors. Current controversy over the nature and nomenclature of "borderline" ovarian tumors. Cancer 76: 2138–2142
12. Diamond M P, Baxter J W, Peerman C G Jr et al. 1988 Occurrence of ovarian malignancy in childhood and adolescence: a community-wide evaluation. Obstet Gynecol 71: 858–860
13. Schultz K A, Sencer S F, Messinger Y et al. 2005 Pediatric ovarian tumors: a review of 67 cases. Pediatr Blood Cancer 44: 167–173
14. Menczer J, Sadetzki S, Murad H et al. 1999 Childhood and adolescent ovarian malignant tumors in Israel. A nationwide study. Acta Obstet Gynecol Scand 78: 813–817
15. Hassan E, Creatsas G, Deligeorolgou E et al. 1999 Ovarian tumors during childhood and adolescence. A clinicopathological study. Eur J Gynaecol Oncol 20: 124–126
16. Morowitz M, Huff D, Von Allmen D 2003 Epithelial ovarian tumors in children: A retrospective analysis. J Pediatr Surg 38: 331–335
17. Kennedy A W, Hart W R 1996 Ovarian papillary serous tumors of low malignant potential (serous borderline tumors) – A long term follow-up study, including patients with microinvasion, lymph node metastasis, and transformation to invasive serous carcinoma. Cancer 78: 278–286
18. Sayedur R M, Al-Sibai M H, Rahman J et al. 2002 Ovarian carcinoma associated with pregnancy. A review of 9 cases. Acta Obstet Gynecol Scand 81: 260–264
19. Webb P M, Purdie D M, Grover S et al. 2004 Symptoms and diagnosis of borderline, early and advanced epithelial ovarian cancer. Gynecol Oncol 92: 232–239
20. McLemore M R, Aouizerat B 2005 Introducing the MUC16 gene: implications for prevention and early detection in epithelial ovarian cancer. Biol Res Nurs 6: 262–267
21. Verheijen R H, Von Mensdorff-Pouilly S, van Kamp G J 1999 CA 125: fundamental and clinical aspects. Semin Cancer Biol 9: 117–124
22. Yin B W T, Dnistrian A, Lloyd K O 2002 Ovarian cancer antigen CA125 is encoded by the MUC16 mucin gene. Int J Cancer 98: 737–740
23. Moss E L, Hollingworth J, Reynolds T M 2005 The role of CA125 in clinical practice. J Clin Pathol 58: 308–312
24. Kaern J, Tropé C G, Abeler V M 1993 A retrospective study of 370 borderline tumors of the ovary treated at the Norwegian Radium Hospital from 1970 to 1982: A review of clinicopathologic features and treatment modalities. Cancer 71: 1810–1820
25. Camatte S, Morice P, Atallah D et al. 2002 Lymph node disorders and prognostic value of nodal involvement in patients treated for a borderline ovarian tumor: An analysis of a series of 42 lymphadenectomies. J Am Coll Surg 195: 332–338
26. Malpica A, Deavers M T, Gershenson D et al. 2001 Serous tumors involving extra-abdominal/extra-pelvic sites after the diagnosis of an ovarian serous neoplasm of low malignant potential. Am J Surg Pathol 25: 988–996
27. Russell P, Merkur H. 1979 Proliferating ovarian "epithelial" tumours: a clinicopathological analysis of 144 cases. Aust NZ J Obstet Gynaecol 19: 45–51
28. Kurman R J, Trimble C L 1993 The behavior of serous tumors of low malignant potential: are they ever malignant? Int J Gynecol Pathol 12: 120–127
29. Siriaunkgul S, Robbins K M, McGowan L et al. 1995 Ovarian mucinous tumors of low malignant potential: a clinicopathologic study of 54 tumors of intestinal and mullerian type. Int J Gynecol Pathol 14: 198–208
30. Kehoe S, Powell J 1996 Long-term follow-up of women with borderline ovarian tumors. Int J Gynaecol Obstet 53: 139–143
31. Longacre T A, McKenney J K, Tazelaar H D et al. 2005 Ovarian serous tumors of low malignant potential (borderline tumors): outcome-based study of 276 patients with long-term (≥5-year) follow-up. Am J Surg Pathol 29: 707–723

32. Seidman J D, Kurman R J 2000 Ovarian serous borderline tumors: A critical review of the literature with emphasis on prognostic indicators. Hum Pathol 31: 539–557

33. Prat J, De Nictolis M 2002 Serous borderline tumors of the ovary: a long-term follow-up study of 137 cases, including 18 with a micropapillary pattern and 20 with microinvasion. Am J Surg Pathol 26: 1111–1128

34. Slomovitz B M, Caputo T A, Gretz H F III et al. 2002 A comparative analysis of 57 serous borderline tumors with and without a non-invasive micropapillary component. Am J Surg Pathol 26: 592–600

35. Zanetta G, Rota S, Chiari S et al. 2001 Behavior of borderline tumors with particular interest to persistence, recurrence, and progression to invasive carcinoma: A prospective study. J Clin Oncol 19: 658–664

36. Crispens M, Bodurka D, Deavers M et al. 2002 Response and survival in patients with progressive or recurrent serous ovarian tumors of low malignant potential. Obstet Gynecol 99: 3–10

37. Morris R T, Gershenson D M, Silva E G et al. 2000 Outcome and reproductive function after conservative surgery for borderline ovarian tumors. Obstet Gynecol 95: 541–547

38. Lim-Tan S K, Cajigas H E, Scully R E 1988 Ovarian cystectomy for serous borderline tumors: a follow-up study of 35 cases. Obstet Gynecol 72: 775–781

39. Rice L W, Berkowitz R S, Mark S D et al. 1990 Epithelial ovarian tumors of borderline malignancy. Gynecol Oncol 39: 195–198

40. Casey A C, Bell D A, Lage J M et al. 1993 Epithelial ovarian tumors of borderline malignancy: long-term follow-up. Gynecol Oncol 50: 316–322

41. Barnhill D, Kurman R, Brady M et al. 1995 Preliminary analysis of the behavior of stage I ovarian serous tumors of low malignant potential: A Gynecologic Oncology Group study. J Clin Oncol 13: 2752–2756

42. Ji H, Yliskoski M, Anttila M et al. 1996 Management of stage-I borderline ovarian tumors. Int J Gynaecol Obstet 54: 37–44

43. Deffieux X, Morice P, Camatte S et al. 2005 Results after laparoscopic management of serous borderline tumor of the ovary with peritoneal implants. Gynecol Oncol 97: 84–89

44. Maneo A, Vignali M, Chiari S et al. 2004 Are borderline tumors of the ovary safely treated by laparoscopy? Gynecol Oncol 94: 387–392

45. Camatte S, Morice P, Pautier P et al. 2002 Fertility results after conservative treatment of advanced stage serous borderline tumour of the ovary. BJOG 109: 376–380

46. Gilks C B, Alkushi A, Yue J J et al. 2003 Advanced-stage serous borderline tumors of the ovary: a clinicopathological study of 49 cases. Int J Gynecol Pathol 22: 29–36

47. Fauvet R, Boccara J, Dufournet C et al. 2004 Restaging surgery for women with borderline ovarian tumors: results of a French multicenter study. Cancer 100: 1145–1151

48. Winter W E III, Kucera P R, Rodgers W et al. 2002 Surgical staging in patients with ovarian tumors of low malignant potential. Obstet Gynecol 100: 671–676

49. Eichhorn J H, Bell D A, Young R H et al. 1999 Ovarian serous borderline tumors with micropapillary and cribriform patterns – A study of 40 cases and comparison with 44 cases without these patterns. Am J Surg Pathol 23: 397–409

50. Silva E G, Tornos C, Zhuang Z et al. 1998 Tumor recurrence in stage I ovarian serous neoplasms of low malignant potential. Int J Gynecol Pathol 17: 1–6

51. Parker R L, Clement P B, Chercover D J et al. 2004 Early recurrence of ovarian serous borderline tumor as high-grade carcinoma: a report of two cases. Int J Gynecol Pathol 23: 265–272

52. Lackman F, Carey M S, Kirk M E et al. 2003 Surgery as sole treatment for serous borderline tumors of the ovary with non-invasive implants. Gynecol Oncol 90: 407–412

53. Trope C, Kaern J, Vergote I B et al. 1993 Are borderline tumors of the ovary overtreated both surgically and systemically? A review of four prospective randomized trials including 253 patients with borderline tumors. Gynecol Oncol 51: 236–243

54. Barakat R R, Benjamin I, Lewis J L Jr et al. 1995 Platinum-based chemotherapy for advanced-stage serous ovarian carcinoma of low malignant potential. Gynecol Oncol 59: 390–393

55. Link C J J, Reed E, Sarosy G et al. 1996 Borderline ovarian tumors. Am J Med 101: 217–225

56. Sherman M E, Mink P J, Curtis R et al. 2004 Survival among women with borderline ovarian tumors and ovarian carcinoma: a population-based analysis. Cancer 100: 1045–1052

57. Awada A, Klastersky J 2004 Ovarian cancer: state of the art and future directions. Eur J Gynaecol Oncol 25: 673–676

58. Cannistra S A 2004 Cancer of the ovary. N Engl J Med 351: 2519–2529

59. Averette H E, Donato D M 1990 Ovarian carcinoma. Advances in diagnosis, staging, and treatment. Cancer 65: 703–708

60. Baker T R, Piver M S, Hempling R E 1994 Long term survival by cytoreductive surgery to less than 1 cm, induction weekly cisplatin and monthly cisplatin, doxorubicin, and cyclophosphamide therapy in advanced ovarian adenocarcinoma. Cancer 74: 656–663

61. Le T, Krepart G V, Lotocki R J et al. 1997 Does debulking surgery improve survival in biologically aggressive ovarian carcinoma? Gynecol Oncol 67: 208–214

62. Bristow R E, Montz F J, Lagasse L D et al. 1999 Survival impact of surgical cytoreduction in stage IV epithelial ovarian cancer. Gynecol Oncol 72: 278–287

63. Leitao M M Jr, Boyd J, Hummer A et al. 2004 Clinicopathologic analysis of early-stage sporadic ovarian carcinoma. Am J Surg Pathol 28: 147–159

64. Schilder J M, Thompson A M, DePriest P D et al. 2002 Outcome of reproductive age women with stage IA or IC invasive epithelial ovarian cancer treated with fertility-sparing therapy. Gynecol Oncol 87: 1–7

65. Ayhan A, Celik H, Taskiran C et al. 2003 Oncologic and reproductive outcome after fertility-saving surgery in ovarian cancer. Eur J Gynaecol Oncol 24: 223–232

66. Pectasides D, Farmakis D, Koumarianou A 2005 The role of neoadjuvant chemotherapy in the treatment of advanced ovarian cancer. Oncology 68: 64–70

67. Johnston S R 2004 Ovarian cancer: review of the National Institute for Clinical Excellence (NICE) guidance recommendations. Cancer Invest 22: 730–742

68. Muggia F M 2004 Recent updates in the clinical use of platinum compounds for the treatment of gynecologic cancers. Semin Oncol 31(Suppl 14): 17–24

69. Bookman M A, Greer B E, Ozols R F 2003 Optimal therapy of advanced ovarian cancer: carboplatin and paclitaxel vs. cisplatin and paclitaxel (GOG 158) and an update on GOG0 182-ICON5. Int J Gynecol Cancer 13: 735–740

70. NIH Consensus Dev Panel Ovarian Cancer 1995 Ovarian cancer: Screening, treatment, and follow-up. JAMA 273: 491–497

71. Hoskins P J 1995 Treatment of advanced epithelial ovarian cancer: Past, present and future. Crit Rev Oncol Hematol 20: 41–59

72. Ozols R F 1995 Current status of chemotherapy for ovarian cancer. Semin Oncol 22 Suppl. 12: 61–66

73. McGuire W P, Hoskins W J, Brady M F et al. 1996 Cyclophosphamide and cisplatin compared with paclitaxel and cisplatin in patients with stage III and stage IV ovarian cancer. N Engl J Med 334: 1–6

74. Partridge E E, Phillips J L, Menck H R 1996 The National Cancer Data Base report on ovarian cancer treatment in United States hospitals. Cancer 78: 2236–2246

75. Ozols R F, Vermorken J B 1997 Chemotherapy of advanced ovarian cancer: Current status and future directions. Semin Oncol 24: S1–S9

76. Lambert H E, Gregory W M, Nelstrop A E et al. 2004 Long-term survival in 463 women treated with platinum analogs for advanced epithelial carcinoma of the ovary: life expectancy compared to women of an age-matched normal population. Int J Gynecol Cancer 14: 772–778

77. Fujiwara K, Sakuragi N, Suzuki S et al. 2003 First-line intraperitoneal carboplatin-based chemotherapy for 165 patients with epithelial ovarian carcinoma: results of long-term follow-up. Gynecol Oncol 90: 637–643

78. Rothenberg M L, Liu P Y, Braly P S et al. 2003 Combined intraperitoneal and intravenous chemotherapy for women with optimally debulked ovarian cancer: Results from an intergroup phase II trial. J Clin Oncol 21: 1313–1319

79. Soper J T, Berchuck A, Dodge R et al. 1992 Adjuvant therapy with intraperitoneal chromic phosphate (^{32}P) in women with early ovarian carcinoma after comprehensive surgical staging. Obstet Gynecol 79: 993–997

80. Mychalczak B R, Fuks Z 1992 The current role of radiotherapy in the management of ovarian cancer. Hematol Oncol Clin North Am 6: 895–913

81. Einhorn N. 1996 Ovarian cancer. Acta Oncol 35: 86–92

82. Randrianjafisamindrakotroka N S, Gasser B, Philippe E 1993 [The malignant potential of adenofibroma and cystadenofibroma of the ovary and mesovarium. 118 cases including 13 proliferative and 5 carcinomatous.] J Gynecol Obstet Biol Reprod (Paris) 22: 33–38

83. Cheng E J, Kurman R J, Wang M et al. 2004 Molecular genetic analysis of ovarian serous cystadenomas. Lab Invest 84: 778–784

84. Seidman J D, Mehrotra A 2005 Benign ovarian serous tumors: a re-evaluation and proposed reclassification of serous "cystadenomas" and "cystadenofibromas". Gynecol Oncol 96: 395–401

85. Silverberg S G, Bell D A, Kurman R J et al. 2004 Borderline ovarian tumors: key points and workshop summary. Hum Pathol 35: 910–917

86. Seidman J D, Soslow R A, Vang R et al. 2004 Borderline ovarian tumors: diverse contemporary viewpoints on terminology and diagnostic criteria with illustrative images. Hum Pathol 35: 918–933

87. De Nictolis M, Montironi R, Tommasoni S et al. 1992 Serous borderline tumors of the ovary: A clinicopathologic, immunohistochemical, and quantitative study of 44 cases. Cancer 70: 152–160

88. Tavassoli F A 1988 Serous tumor of low malignant potential with early stromal invasion (serous LMP with microinvasion). Mod Pathol 1: 407–414

89. Bell D A, Scully R E 1990 Ovarian serous borderline tumors with stromal microinvasion: a report of 21 cases. Hum Pathol 21: 397–403

90. Nayar R, Siriaunkgul S, Robbins K M et al. 1996 Microinvasion in low malignant potential tumors of the ovary. Hum Pathol 27: 521–527

91. Hanselaar A G J M, Vooijs G P, Mayall B et al. 1993 Epithelial markers to detect occult microinvasion in serous ovarian tumors. Int J Gynecol Pathol 12: 20–27

92. Katzenstein A L, Mazur M T, Morgan T et al. 1978 Proliferative serous tumors of the ovary. Histologic features and prognosis. Am J Surg Pathol 2: 339–355

93. Mooney J, Silva E, Tornos et al. 1997 Unusual features of serous neoplasms of low malignant potential during pregnancy. Gynecol Oncol 65: 30–35

94. Buttin B M, Herzog T J, Powell M A et al. 2002 Epithelial ovarian tumors of low malignant potential: the role of microinvasion. Obstet Gynecol 99: 11–17

95. Silva E G, Tornos C S, Malpica A et al. 1997 Ovarian serous neoplasms of low malignant potential associated with focal areas of serous carcinoma. Mod Pathol 10: 663–667

96. Segal G H, Hart W R 1992 Ovarian serous tumors of low malignant potential (serous borderline tumors): The relationship of exophytic surface tumor to peritoneal "implants". Am J Surg Pathol 16: 577–583

97. Diebold J, Seemueller F, Loehrs U. 2003 K-RAS mutations in ovarian and extraovarian lesions of serous tumors of borderline malignancy. Lab Invest 83: 251–258

98. Sieben N L G, Kolkman-Uljee S M, Flanagan A M et al. 2003 Molecular genetic evidence for monoclonal origin of bilateral ovarian serous borderline tumors. Am J Pathol 162: 1095–1101

99. Ortiz B H, Ailawadi M, Colitti C et al. 2001 Second primary or recurrence? Comparative patterns of p53 and K-ras mutations suggest that serous borderline ovarian tumors and subsequent serous carcinomas are unrelated tumors. Cancer Res 61: 7264–7267

100. Krishnamurti U, Sasatomi E, Swalsky P A et al. 2005 Microdissection-based mutational genotyping of serous borderline tumors of the ovary. Int J Gynecol Pathol 24: 56–61

101. Gu J, Roth L M, Younger C et al. 2001 Molecular evidence for the independent origin of extra-ovarian papillary serous tumors of low malignant potential. J Natl Cancer Inst 93: 1147–1152

102. Lu K H, Bell D A, Welch W R et al. 1998 Evidence for the multifocal origin of bilateral and advanced human serous borderline ovarian tumors. Cancer Res 58: 2328–2330

103. Bell D A, Weinstock M A, Scully R E 1988 Peritoneal implants of ovarian serous borderline tumors. Histologic features and prognosis. Cancer 62: 2212–2222

104. Deavers M T, Gershenson D M, Tortolero-Luna G et al. 2002 Micropapillary and cribriform patterns in ovarian serous tumors of low malignant potential: a study of 99 advanced stage cases. Am J Surg Pathol 26: 1129–1141

105. Lee K R, Castrillon D H, Nucci M R 2001 Pathologic findings in eight cases of ovarian serous borderline tumors, three with foci of serous carcinoma, that preceded death or morbidity from invasive carcinoma. Int J Gynecol Pathol 20: 329–334

106. Gershenson D M, Silva E G, Tortolero-Luna G et al. 1998 Serous borderline tumors of the ovary with non-invasive peritoneal implants. Cancer 83: 2157–2163

107. Seidman J D, Kurman R J 1996 Subclassification of serous borderline tumors of the ovary into benign and malignant types: a clinicopathologic study of 65 advanced stage cases. Am J Surg Pathol 20: 1331–1345

108. Gershenson D M, Silva E G, Levy L et al. 1998 Ovarian serous borderline tumors with invasive peritoneal implants. Cancer 82: 1096–1103

109. Bell K A, Sehdev A E S, Kurman R J 2001 Refined diagnostic criteria for implants associated with ovarian atypical proliferative serous tumors (borderline) and micropapillary serous carcinomas. Am J Surg Pathol 25: 419–432

110. Rota S M, Zanetta G, Ieda N et al. 1999 Clinical relevance of retroperitoneal involvement from epithelial ovarian tumors of borderline malignancy. Int J Gynecol Cancer 9: 477–480

111. Leake J F, Rader J S, Woodruff J D et al. 1991 Retroperitoneal lymphatic involvement with epithelial ovarian tumors of low malignant potential. Gynecol Oncol 42: 124–130

111a. McKenny J K, Balzer B L, Longacre T A 2006 Lymph node involvement in ovarian serous tumors of low malignant potential (borderline tumors): pathology, prognosis, and proposed classification. Am J Surg Pathol 30: 614–624

112. Clement P B, Young R H, Oliva E et al. 1996 Hyperplastic mesothelial cells within abdominal lymph nodes: mimic of metastatic ovarian carcinoma and serous borderline tumor – a report of two cases associated with ovarian neoplasms. Mod Pathol 9: 879–886

113. Ordonez N G 1998 Role of immunohistochemistry in distinguishing epithelial peritoneal mesotheliomas from peritoneal and ovarian serous carcinomas. Am J Surg Pathol 22: 1203–1214

114. Chamberlin M D, Eltabbakh G H, Mount S L et al. 2001 Metastatic serous borderline ovarian tumor in an internal mammary lymph node: a case report and review of the literature. Gynecol Oncol 82: 212–215

115. Reich O, Tamussino K, Haas J et al. 2000 Benign mullerian inclusions in pelvic and paraaortic lymph nodes. Gynecol Oncol 78: 242–244

116. Moore W F, Bentley R C, Berchuck A 2000 Some mullerian inclusion cysts in lymph nodes may sometimes be metastases from serous borderline tumors of the ovary. Am J Surg Pathol 24: 710–718

117. Prade M, Spatz A, Bentley R et al. 1995 Borderline and malignant serous tumor arising in pelvic lymph nodes: evidence of origin in benign glandular inclusions. Int J Gynecol Pathol 14: 87–91

118. Tan L K, Flynn S D, Carcangiu M L 1994 Ovarian serous borderline tumors with lymph node involvement: clinicopathologic and DNA content study of seven cases and review of the literature. Am J Surg Pathol 18: 904–912

119. Burks R T, Sherman M E, Kurman R J 1996 Micropapillary serous carcinoma of the ovary – a distinctive low-grade carcinoma related to serous borderline tumors. Am J Surg Pathol 20: 1319–1330

120. Smith Sehdev A E, Sehdev P S, Kurman R J 2003 Non-invasive and invasive micropapillary (low-grade) serous carcinoma of the ovary: a clinicopathologic analysis of 135 cases. Am J Surg Pathol 27: 725–736

121. Goldstein N S, Ceniza N 2000 Ovarian micropapillary serous borderline tumors – clinicopathologic features and outcome of seven surgically staged patients. Am J Clin Pathol 114: 380–386

122. Mills S E, Andersen W A, Fechner R E et al. 1988 Serous surface papillary carcinoma. A clinicopathologic study of 10 cases and comparison with stage III–IV ovarian serous carcinoma. Am J Surg Pathol 12: 827–834

123. White P F, Merino M J, Barwick K W 1985 Serous surface papillary carcinoma of the ovary: a clinical, pathologic, ultrastructural, and immunohistochemical study of 11 cases. Pathol Annu 20 Pt 1: 403–418

124. Rutledge M L, Silva E G, McLemore D et al. 1989 Serous surface carcinoma of the ovary and peritoneum. A flow cytometric study. Pathol Annu 24 Pt 2: 227–235

125. Gooneratne S, Sassone M, Blaustein A et al. 1982 Serous surface papillary carcinoma of the ovary: a clinicopathologic study of 16 cases. Int J Gynecol Pathol 1: 258–269

126. Mulhollan T J, Silva E G, Tornos C et al. 1994 Ovarian involvement by serous surface papillary carcinoma. Int J Gynecol Pathol 13: 120–126

127. Che M, Tornos C, Deavers M T et al. 2001 Ovarian mixed-epithelial carcinomas with a microcystic pattern and signet-ring cells. Int J Gynecol Pathol 20: 323–328

128. Bell D A, Scully R E 1994 Early de novo ovarian carcinoma: a study of fourteen cases. Cancer 73: 1859–1864

129. Cathro H P, Stoler M H 2002 Expression of cytokeratins 7 and 20 in ovarian neoplasia. Am J Clin Pathol 117: 944–951

130. Keen C E, Szakacs S, Okon E et al. 1999 CA125 and thyroglobulin staining in papillary carcinomas of thyroid and ovarian origin is not completely specific for site of origin. Histopathology 34: 113–117

131. Multhaupt H A, Renas-Elliott C P, Warhol M J 1999 Comparison of glycoprotein expression between ovarian and colon adenocarcinomas. Arch Pathol Lab Med 123: 909–916

132. Hwang H, Quenneville L, Yaziji H et al. 2004 Wilms tumor gene product: sensitive and contextually specific marker of serous carcinomas of ovarian surface epithelial origin. Appl Immunohistochem Mol Morphol 12: 122–126

133. Hashi A, Yuminamochi T, Murata S et al. 2003 Wilms tumor gene immunoreactivity in primary serous carcinomas of the fallopian tube, ovary, endometrium, and peritoneum. Int J Gynecol Pathol 22: 374–377

134. Goldstein N S, Bassi D, Uzieblo A 2001 WT1 is an integral component of an antibody panel to distinguish pancreaticobiliary and some ovarian epithelial neoplasms. Am J Clin Pathol 116: 246–252

135. Goldstein N S, Uzieblo A 2002 WT1 immunoreactivity in uterine papillary serous carcinomas is different from ovarian serous carcinomas. Am J Clin Pathol 117: 541–545

136. Shimizu M, Toki T, Takagi Y et al. 2000 Immunohistochemical detection of the Wilms' tumor gene (WT1) in epithelial ovarian tumors. Int J Gynecol Pathol 19: 158–163

137. Otis C N, Krebs P A, Quezado M M et al. 2000 Loss of heterozygosity in P53, BRCA1, and estrogen receptor genes and correlation to expression of p53 protein in ovarian epithelial tumors of different cell types and biological behavior. Hum Pathol 31: 233–238

138. Anttila M A, Ji H, Juhola M T, Saarikoski S V et al. 1999 The prognostic significance of p53 expression quantitated by computerized image analysis in epithelial ovarian cancer. Int J Gynecol Pathol 18: 42–51

139. Wen W H, Reles A, Runnebaum I B et al. 1999 p53 mutations and expression in ovarian cancers: correlation with overall survival. Int J Gynecol Pathol 18: 29–41

140. Eltabbakh G H, Belinson J L, Kennedy A W et al. 1997 p53 overexpression is not an independent prognostic factor for patients with primary ovarian epithelial cancer. Cancer 80: 892–898

141. Diebold J, Suchy B, Baretton GB et al. 1996 DNA ploidy and MYC DNA amplification in ovarian carcinomas – Correlation with p53 and bcl-2 expression, proliferative activity and prognosis. Virchow' Arch 429: 221–227

142. Klemi PJ, Pylkkänen L, Kiilholma P et al. 1995 P53 protein detected by immunohistochemistry as a prognostic factor in patients with epithelial ovarian carcinoma. Cancer 76: 1201–1208

143. Acs G, Pasha T, Zhang P J 2004 WT1 is differentially expressed in serous, endometrioid, clear cell, and mucinous carcinomas of the peritoneum, fallopian tube, ovary, and endometrium. Int J Gynecol Pathol 23: 110–118

144. Al Hussaini M, Stockman A, Foster H et al. 2004 WT-1 assists in distinguishing ovarian from uterine serous carcinoma and in distinguishing between serous and endometrioid ovarian carcinoma. Histopathology 44: 109–115

145. Singer G, Shih I, Truskinovsky A et al. 2003 Mutational analysis of K-ras segregates ovarian serous carcinomas into two types: invasive MPSC (low-grade tumor) and conventional serous carcinoma (high-grade tumor). Int J Gynecol Pathol 22: 37–41

146. Haas C J, Diebold J, Hirschmann A et al. 1999 In serous ovarian neoplasms the frequency of Ki-ras mutations correlates with their malignant potential. Virchow's Arch 434: 117–120

147. Bell D A 2005 Origins and molecular pathology of ovarian cancer. Mod Pathol 18 Suppl 2: S19–S32

148. Meinhold-Heerlein I, Bauerschlag D, Hilpert F et al. 2005 Molecular and prognostic distinction between serous ovarian carcinomas of varying grade and malignant potential. Oncogene 24: 1053–1065

149. Singer G, Stohr R, Cope L et al. 2005 Patterns of p53 mutations separate ovarian serous borderline tumors and low- and high-grade carcinomas and provide support for a new model of ovarian carcinogenesis: a mutational analysis with immunohistochemical correlation. Am J Surg Pathol 29: 218–224

150. Bristow R E, Gossett D R, Shook DR et al. 2002 Micropapillary serous ovarian carcinoma: surgical management and clinical outcome. Gynecol Oncol 86: 163–170

151. Sieben N L, Macropoulos P, Roemen G M et al. 2004 In ovarian neoplasms, BRAF, but not KRAS, mutations are restricted to low-grade serous tumours. J Pathol 202: 336–340

152. Moran C A, Suster S, Silva E G 2005 Low-grade serous carcinoma of the ovary metastatic to the anterior mediastinum simulating multilocular thymic cysts: a clinicopathologic and immunohistochemical study of 3 cases. Am J Surg Pathol 29: 496–499

153. Recine M A, Deavers M T, Middleton L P et al. 2004 Serous carcinoma of the ovary and peritoneum with metastases to the breast and axillary lymph nodes: a potential pitfall. Am J Surg Pathol 28: 1646–1651

154. Silverberg S G 2000 Histopathologic grading of ovarian carcinoma: a review and proposal. Int J Gynecol Pathol 19: 7–15

155. Shimizu Y, Kamoi S, Amada S et al. 1998 Toward the development of a universal grading system for ovarian epithelial carcinoma – Testing of a proposed system in a series of 461 patients with uniform treatment and follow-up. Cancer 82: 893–901

156. Shimizu Y, Kamoi S, Amada S et al. 1998 Toward the development of a universal grading system for ovarian epithelial carcinoma. I. Prognostic significance of histopathologic features – problems involved in the architectural grading system. Gynecol Oncol 70: 2–12

157. Piek J M, Torrenga B, Hermsen B et al. 2003 Histopathological characteristics of BRCA1- and BRCA2-associated intraperitoneal cancer: a clinic-based study. Fam Cancer 2: 7–8

158. Kauff N D, Satagopan J M, Robson M E et al. 2002 Risk-reducing salpingo-oophorectomy in women with a BRCA1 or BRCA2 mutation. N Engl J Med 346: 1609–1615

159. Rebbeck T R, Lynch H T, Neuhausen S L et al. 2002 Prophylactic oophorectomy in carriers of BRCA1 or BRCA2 mutations. N Engl J Med 346: 1616–1622

160. Rutter J L, Wacholder S, Chetrit A et al. 2003 Gynecologic surgeries and risk of ovarian cancer in women with BRCA1 and BRCA2 Ashkenazi founder mutations: an Israeli population-based case-control study. J Natl Cancer Inst 95: 1072–1078

161. Casey M J, Synder C, Bewtra C et al. 2005 Intra-abdominal carcinomatosis after prophylactic oophorectomy in women of hereditary breast ovarian cancer syndrome kindreds associated with BRCA1 and BRCA2 mutations. Gynecol Oncol 97: 457–467

162. Piver M S, Jishi M F, Tsukada Y et al. 1993 Primary peritoneal carcinoma after prophylactic oophorectomy in women with a family history of ovarian cancer: A report of the Gilda Radner Familial Ovarian Cancer Registry. Cancer 71: 2751–2755

163. Lu K H, Garber J E, Cramer D W et al. 2000 Occult ovarian tumors in women with BRCA1 or BRCA2 mutations undergoing prophylactic oophorectomy. J Clin Oncol 18: 2728–2732

164. Colgan T J, Murphy J, Cole D E C et al. 2001 Occult carcinoma in prophylactic oophorectomy specimens – Prevalence and association with BRCA germline mutation status. Am J Surg Pathol 25: 1283–1289

165. Powell C B, Kenley E, Chen L M et al. 2005 Risk-reducing salpingo-oophorectomy in BRCA mutation carriers: role of serial sectioning in the detection of occult malignancy. J Clin Oncol 23: 127–132

166. Leeper K, Garcia R, Swisher E et al. 2002 Pathologic findings in prophylactic oophorectomy specimens in high-risk women. Gynecol Oncol 87: 52–56

167. Agoff S N, Mendelin J E, Grieco V S et al. 2002 Unexpected gynecologic neoplasms in patients with proven or suspected BRCA-1 or -2 mutations: implications for gross examination, cytology, and clinical follow-up. Am J Surg Pathol 26: 171–178

168. Colgan T J 2003 Challenges in the early diagnosis and staging of fallopian-tube carcinomas associated with BRCA mutations. Int J Gynecol Pathol 22: 109–120

169. Lakhani S R, Manek S, Penault-Llorca F et al. 2004 Pathology of ovarian cancers in BRCA1 and BRCA2 carriers. Clin Cancer Res 10: 2473–2481

170. Shaw P A, McLaughlin J R, Zweemer R P et al. 2002 Histopathologic features of genetically determined ovarian cancer. Int J Gynecol Pathol 21: 407–411

171. Werness B A, Ramus S J, DiCioccio R A et al. 2004 Histopathology, FIGO stage, and BRCA mutation status of ovarian cancers from the Gilda Radner Familial Ovarian Cancer Registry. Int J Gynecol Pathol 23: 29–34

172. Ferenczy A, Talens A, Zoghby et al. 1977 Ultrastructural studies on the morphogenesis of psammoma bodies in ovarian serous neoplasia. Cancer 39: 2451–2459

173. Gilks C B, Bell D A, Scully R E 1990 Serous psammocarcinoma of the ovary and peritoneum. Int J Gynecol Pathol 9: 110–121

174. Powell J L, McDonald T J, White W C 1998 Serous psammocarcinoma of the ovary. South Med J 91: 477–480

175. Giordano G, Gnetti L, Milione M 2005 Serous psammocarcinoma of the ovary: a case report and review of literature. Gynecol Oncol 96: 259–262

176. Weir M M, Bell D A, Young R H 1998 Grade 1 peritoneal serous carcinomas – A report of 14 cases and comparison with 7 peritoneal serous psammocarcinomas and 19 peritoneal serous borderline tumors. Am J Surg Pathol 22: 849–862

177. Chao A, Chao A, Yen Y S et al. 2004 Abdominal compartment syndrome secondary to ovarian mucinous cystadenoma. Obstet Gynecol 104: 1180–1182

178. Tenti P, Aguzzi A, Riva C et al. 1992 Ovarian mucinous tumors frequently express markers of gastric, intestinal, and pancreatobiliary epithelial cells. Cancer 69: 2131–2142

179. Shiohara S, Shiozawa T, Shimizu M et al. 1997 Histochemical analysis of estrogen and progesterone receptors and gastric-type mucin in mucinous ovarian tumors with reference to their pathogenesis. Cancer 80: 908–916

180. Ball N J, Robertson D I, Duggan M A et al. 1990 Intestinal differentiation in ovarian mucinous tumours. Virchow's Arch [A] 417: 197–201

181. Klemi P J 1978 Pathology of mucinous ovarian cystadenomas. I. Argyrophil and argentaffin cells and epithelial mucosubstances. Acta Pathol Microbiol Scand [A] 86: 465–470

182. Ishikura H, Sasano H 1998 Histopathologic and immunohistochemical study of steroidogenic cells in the stroma of ovarian tumors. Int J Gynecol Pathol 17: 261–265

183. Bell D A 1991 Mucinous adenofibromas of the ovary. A report of 10 cases. Am J Surg Pathol 15: 227–232

184. Kao G F, Norris H J 1979 Unusual cystadenofibromas: endometrioid, mucinous, and clear cell type. Obstet Gynecol 54: 729–736

185. De Nictolis M, Montironi R, Tommasoni S et al. 1994 Benign, borderline, and well-differentiated malignant intestinal mucinous tumors of the ovary: a clinicopathologic, histochemical, immunohistochemical, and nuclear quantitative study of 57 cases. Int J Gynecol Pathol 13: 10–21

186. Guerrieri C, Högberg T, Wingren S et al. 1994 Mucinous borderline and malignant tumors of the ovary: A clinicopathologic and DNA ploidy study of 92 cases. Cancer 74: 2329–2340

187. Hart W R 2005 Mucinous tumors of the ovary: a review. Int J Gynecol Pathol 24: 4–25

188. Hart W R, Norris H J 1973 Borderline and malignant mucinous tumors of the ovary: Histologic criteria and clinical behavior. Cancer 31: 1031–1045

189. Ronnett B M, Kajdacsy-Balla A, Gilks C B et al. 2004 Mucinous borderline ovarian tumors: points of general agreement and persistent controversies regarding nomenclature, diagnostic criteria, and behavior. Hum Pathol 35: 949–960

190. Rodriguez I M, Prat J 2002 Mucinous tumors of the ovary: a clinicopathologic analysis of 75 borderline tumors (of intestinal type) and carcinomas. Am J Surg Pathol 26: 139–152

191. Lee K R, Scully R 2000 Mucinous tumors of the ovary: a clinicopathologic study of 196 borderline tumors (of intestinal type) and carcinomas, including an evaluation of 11 cases with "pseudomyxoma peritonei". Am J Surg Pathol 24: 1447–1464

192. Nomura K, Aizawa S, Hano H 2004 Ovarian mucinous borderline tumors of intestinal type without intraepithelial carcinoma: are they still tumors of low malignant potential? Pathol Int 54: 420–424

193. Nomura K, Aizawa S 2000 Non-invasive, microinvasive, and invasive mucinous carcinomas of the ovary – A clinicopathologic analysis of 40 cases. Cancer 89: 1541–1546

194. Khunamornpong S, Russell P, Dalrymple J C 1999 Proliferating (LMP) mucinous tumors of the ovaries with microinvasion: morphologic assessment of 13 cases. Int J Gynecol Pathol 18: 238–246

195. Ludwick C, Gilks C B, Miller D et al. 2005 Aggressive behavior of stage I ovarian mucinous tumors lacking extensive infiltrative invasion: a report of four cases and review of the literature. Int J Gynecol Pathol 24: 205–217

196. Michael H, Sutton G, Roth L M 1987 Ovarian carcinoma with extracellular mucin production: reassessment of "pseudomyxoma ovarii et peritonei". Int J Gynecol Pathol 6: 298–312

197. Rutgers J L, Scully R E 1988 Ovarian mullerian mucinous papillary cystadenomas of borderline malignancy. A clinicopathologic analysis. Cancer 61: 340–348

198. Nomura K, Aizawa S 1996 Clinicopathologic and mucin histochemical analyses of 90 cases of ovarian mucinous borderline tumors of intestinal and mullerian types. Pathol Int 46: 575–580

199. Rodriguez I M, Irving J A, Prat J 2004 Endocervical-like mucinous borderline tumors of the ovary: a clinicopathologic analysis of 31 cases. Am J Surg Pathol 28: 1311–1318

200. Shappell H W, Riopel M A, Smith Sehdev A E et al. 2002 Diagnostic criteria and behavior of ovarian seromucinous (endocervical-type mucinous and mixed cell-type) tumors: atypical proliferative (borderline) tumors, intraepithelial, microinvasive, and invasive carcinomas. Am J Surg Pathol 26: 1529–1541

201. Dube V, Roy M, Plante M et al. 2005 Mucinous ovarian tumors of Mullerian-type: an analysis of 17 cases including borderline tumors and intraepithelial, microinvasive, and invasive carcinomas. Int J Gynecol Pathol 24: 138–146

202. Miettinen M 1995 Keratin 20: immunohistochemical marker for gastrointestinal, urothelial, and Merkel cell carcinomas. Mod Pathol 8: 384–388

203. Rutgers J L, Bell D A 1992 Immunohistochemical characterization of ovarian borderline tumors of intestinal and mullerian types. Mod Pathol 5: 367–371

204. Abu-Jawdeh G M, Jacobs T W, Niloff J et al. 1996 Estrogen receptor expression is a common feature of ovarian borderline tumors. Gynecol Oncol 60: 301–307

205. Sasaki E, Sasano N, Kimura N et al. 1989 Demonstration of neuroendocrine cells in ovarian mucinous tumors. Int J Gynecol Pathol 8: 189–200

206. Aguirre P, Scully R E, Dayal et al. 1984 Mucinous tumors of the ovary with argyrophil cells: an immunohistochemical study. Am J Surg Pathol 8: 345–356

207. DeBoer W G, Ma J, Nayman J 1981 Intestine-associated antigens in ovarian tumours: an immunohistochemical study. Pathology 13: 547–555

208. Louwerens J K, Schaberg A, Bosman F T 1983 Neuroendocrine cells in cystic mucinous tumours of the ovary. Histopathology 7: 389–398

209. Sporrong B, Alumets J, Clase L et al. 1981 Neurohormonal peptide immunoreactive cells in mucinous cystadenomas and cystadenocarcinomas of the ovary. Virchow's Arch [A] 392: 271–280

210. Watkin W, Silva E G, Gershenson D M 1992 Mucinous carcinoma of the ovary: pathologic prognostic factors. Cancer 69: 208–212

211. Seidman J D, Kurman R J, Ronnett B M 2003 Primary and metastatic mucinous adenocarcinomas in the ovaries: incidence in routine practice with a new approach to improve intraoperative diagnosis. Am J Surg Pathol 27: 985–993

212. Lee K R, Nucci M R 2003 Ovarian mucinous and mixed epithelial carcinomas of mullerian (endocervical-like) type: a clinicopathologic analysis of four cases of an uncommon variant associated with endometriosis. Int J Gynecol Pathol 22: 42–51

213. Kikkawa F, Kawai M, Tamakoshi K et al. 1996 Mucinous carcinoma of the ovary – Clinicopathologic analysis. Oncology (Basel) 53: 303–307

214. Chen S, Leitao M M, Tornos C et al. 2005 Invasion patterns in stage I endometrioid and mucinous ovarian carcinomas: a clinicopathologic analysis emphasizing favorable outcomes in carcinomas without destructive stromal invasion and the occasional malignant course of carcinomas with limited destructive stromal invasion. Mod Pathol 18: 903–911

215. Hart W R 1977 Ovarian epithelial tumors of borderline malignancy (carcinomas of low malignant potential). Hum Pathol 8: 541–549

216. Raspollini M R, Amunni G, Villanucci A et al. 2004 Utility of CDX-2 in distinguishing between primary and secondary (intestinal) mucinous ovarian carcinoma: an immunohistochemical comparison of 43 cases. Appl Immunohistochem Mol Morphol 12: 127–131

217. Chou Y Y, Jeng Y M, Kao H L et al. 2003 Differentiation of ovarian mucinous carcinoma and metastatic colorectal adenocarcinoma by immunostaining with beta-catenin. Histopathology 43: 151–156

218. Groisman G M, Meir A, Sabo E 2004 The value of Cdx2 immunostaining in differentiating primary ovarian carcinomas from colonic carcinomas metastatic to the ovaries. Int J Gynecol Pathol 23: 52–57

219. Ji H, Isacson C, Seidman J D et al. 2002 Cytokeratins 7 and 20, Dpc4, and MUC5AC in the distinction of metastatic mucinous carcinomas in the ovary from primary ovarian mucinous tumors: Dpc4 assists in identifying metastatic pancreatic carcinomas. Int J Gynecol Pathol 21: 391–400

220. Tornillo L, Moch H, Diener P A et al. 2004 CDX-2 immunostaining in primary and secondary ovarian carcinomas. J Clin Pathol 57: 641–643

221. Logani S, Oliva E, Arnell P M et al. 2005 Use of novel immunohistochemical markers expressed in colonic adenocarcinoma to distinguish primary ovarian tumors from metastatic colorectal carcinoma. Mod Pathol 18: 19–25

222. Moskaluk C A, Zhang H, Powell S M et al. 2003 Cdx2 protein expression in normal and malignant human tissues: an immunohistochemical survey using tissue microarrays. Mod Pathol 16: 913–919

223. Prat J, Scully R E 1979 Ovarian mucinous tumors with sarcoma-like mural nodules. A report of seven cases. Cancer 44: 1332–1344

224. Baergen R N, Rutgers J L 1995 Classification of mural nodules in common epithelial tumors of the ovary. Adv Anat Pathol 2: 346–351

225. Bague S, Rodriguez I M, Prat J 2002 Sarcoma-like mural nodules in mucinous cystic tumors of the ovary revisited – A clinicopathologic analysis of 10 additional cases. Am J Surg Pathol 26: 1467–1476

226. Matias-Guiu X, Aranda I, Prat J 1991 Immunohistochemical study of sarcoma-like mural nodules in a mucinous cystadenocarcinoma of the ovary. Virchow's Arch A Pathol Anat Histopathol 419: 89–92

227. Hamada T, Sasaguri T, Tanimoto A et al. 1995 Ovarian mucinous cystadenocarcinoma with sarcoma-like mural nodules. J Surg Oncol 58: 201–207

228. Sondergaard G, Kaspersen P 1991 Ovarian and extraovarian mucinous tumors with solid mural nodules. Int J Gynecol Pathol 10: 145–155

229. Czernobilsky B, Dgani R, Roth L M 1983 Ovarian mucinous cystadenocarcinoma with mural nodule of carcinomatous derivation: a light and electron microscopic study. Cancer 51: 141–148

230. Prat J, Young R, Scully R 1982 Ovarian mucinous tumors with foci of anaplastic carcinoma. Cancer 50: 300–304

231. Nichols G E, Mills S E, Ulbright T M et al. 1991 Spindle cell mural nodules in cystic ovarian mucinous tumors: A clinicopathologic and immunohistochemical study of five cases. Am J Surg Pathol 15: 1055–1062

232. Baergen R N, Rutgers J L 1994 Mural nodules in common epithelial tumors of the ovary. Int J Gynecol Pathol 13: 62–71

233. Chang W C, Sheu B C, Lin M C et al. 2005 Carcinosarcoma-like mural nodule in intestinal-type mucinous ovarian tumor of borderline malignancy: a case report. Int J Gynecol Cancer 15: 549–553

234. Prat J, Scully R E 1979 Sarcomas in ovarian mucinous tumors. A report of two cases. Cancer 44: 1327–1331

235. Bruijn J A, Smit V T, Que D G et al. 1987 Immunohistology of a sarcomatous mural nodule in an ovarian mucinous cystadenocarcinoma. Int J Gynecol Pathol 6: 287–293

236. Collins R J, Cheung A, Ngan H Y et al. 1991 Primary mixed neuroendocrine and mucinous carcinoma of the ovary. Arch Gynecol Obstet 248: 139–143

237. Eichhorn J H, Young R H, Scully R E 1992 Primary ovarian small cell carcinoma of pulmonary type: a clinicopathologic, immunohistologic, and flow cytometric analysis of 11 cases. Am J Surg Pathol 16: 926–938

238. Khurana K K, Tornos C, Silva E G 1994 Ovarian neuroendocrine carcinoma associated with a mucinous neoplasm. Arch Pathol Lab Med 118: 1032–1034

239. Jones K, Diaz J A, Donner L R 1996 Neuroendocrine carcinoma arising in an ovarian mucinous cystadenoma. Int J Gynecol Pathol 15: 167–170.

240. Eichhorn J H, Lawrence W D, Young R H et al. 1996 Ovarian neuroendocrine carcinomas of non-small-cell type associated with surface epithelial adenocarcinomas. A study of five cases and review of the literature. Int J Gynecol Pathol 15: 303–314

241. Ishikura H, Shibata M, Yoshiki T 1999 Endocrine cell micronests in an ovarian mucinous cystadenofibroma: a mimic of microinvasion. Int J Gynecol Pathol 18: 392–395

242. Snyder R R, Norris H J, Tavassoli F 1988 Endometrioid proliferative and low malignant potential tumors of the ovary. A clinicopathologic study of 46 cases. Am J Surg Pathol 12: 661–671

243. Bell K A, Kurman R J 2000 A clinicopathologic analysis of atypical proliferative (borderline) tumors and well-differentiated endometrioid adenocarcinomas of the ovary. Am J Surg Pathol 24: 1465–1479

244. Gaing A A, Kimble C C, Belmonte A H et al. 1988 Invasive ovarian endometrioid adenofibroma with omental implants and collision with endometrial adenocarcinoma. Obstet Gynecol 71: 440–444

245. Kline R C, Wharton J T, Atkinson E N et al. 1990 Endometrioid carcinoma of the ovary: retrospective review of 145 cases. Gynecol Oncol 39: 337–346

246. Aure J C, Hoeg K, Kolstad P 1971 Clinical and histologic studies of ovarian carcinoma. Long-term follow-up of 990 cases. Obstet Gynecol 37: 1–9

247. Makar A P, Baekelandt M, Trope C G et al. 1995 The prognostic significance of residual disease, FIGO substage, tumor histology, and grade in patients with FIGO stage III ovarian cancer. Gynecol Oncol 56: 175–180

248. McMeekin D S, Burger R A, Manetta A et al. 1995 Endometrioid adenocarcinoma of the ovary and its relationship to endometriosis. Gynecol Oncol 59: 81–86

249. Fukunaga M, Nomura K, Ishikawa E et al. 1997 Ovarian atypical endometriosis: its close association with malignant epithelial tumours. Histopathology 30: 249–255

250. DePriest P D, Banks E R, Powell D E et al. 1992 Endometrioid carcinoma of the ovary and endometriosis: the association in postmenopausal women. Gynecol Oncol 47: 71–75

251. Stern R C, Dash R, Bentley R C et al. 2001 Malignancy in endometriosis: frequency and comparison of ovarian and extraovarian types. Int J Gynecol Pathol 20: 133–139

252. Heaps J M, Nieberg R K, Berek J S 1990 Malignant neoplasms arising in endometriosis. Obstet Gynecol 75: 1023–1028

253. Modesitt S C, Tortoler-Luna G, Robinson J B et al. 2002 Ovarian and extraovarian endometriosis-associated cancer. Obstet Gynecol 100: 788–795

254. Erzen M, Rakar S, Klancar B et al. 2001 Endometriosis-associated ovarian carcinoma (eaoc): an entity distinct from other ovarian carcinomas as suggested by a nested case-control study. Gynecol Oncol 83: 100–108

255. Roth L M, Czernobilsky B, Langley F A 1981 Ovarian endometrioid adenofibromatous and cystadenofibromatous tumors: benign, proliferating, and malignant. Cancer 48: 1838–1845

256. Eichhorn J H, Scully R E 1996 Endometrioid ciliated-cell tumors of the ovary: a report of five cases. Int J Gynecol Pathol 15: 248–256

257. Kao G F, Norris H J 1978 Cystadenofibromas of the ovary with epithelial atypia. Am J Surg Pathol 2: 357–363

258. Bell D A, Scully R E 1985 Atypical and borderline endometrioid adenofibromas of the ovary: a report of 27 cases. Am J Surg Pathol 9: 205–214

259. Norris H J 1993 Proliferative endometrioid tumors and endometrioid tumors of low malignant potential of the ovary. Int J Gynecol Pathol 12: 134–141

260. Roth L M, Emerson R E, Ulbright T M 2003 Ovarian endometrioid tumors of low malignant potential: a clinicopathologic study of 30 cases with comparison to well-differentiated endometrioid adenocarcinoma. Am J Surg Pathol 27: 1253–1259

261. Brescia R J, Dubin N, Demopoulos R I 1989 Endometrioid and clear cell carcinoma of the ovary. Factors affecting survival. Int J Gynecol Pathol 8: 132–138

262. Russell P 1979 The pathological assessment of ovarian neoplasms. III. The malignant "epithelial" tumours. Pathology 11: 493–532

263. Zaino R J, Kurman R J, Diana K L et al. 1995 The utility of the revised International Federation of Gynecology and Obstetrics histologic grading of endometrial adenocarcinoma using a defined nuclear grading system: A Gynecologic Oncology Group study. Cancer 75: 81–86

264. Kim K R, Scully R E 1990 Peritoneal keratin granulomas with carcinomas of endometrium and ovary and atypical polypoid adenomyoma of endometrium. A clinicopathological analysis of 22 cases. Am J Surg Pathol 14: 925–932

265. Kurman R J, Craig J M 1972 Endometrioid and clear cell carcinoma of the ovary. Cancer 29: 1653–1664

266. Tornos C, Silva E G, Khorana S M et al. 1994 High-stage endometrioid carcinoma of the ovary: Prognostic significance of pure versus mixed histologic types. Am J Surg Pathol 18: 687–693

267. Young R H, Prat J, Scully R E 1982 Ovarian endometrioid carcinomas resembling sex cord-stromal tumors. A clinicopathologic analysis of 13 cases. Am J Surg Pathol 6: 513–522

268. Roth L M, Liban E, Czernobilsky B 1982 Ovarian endometrioid tumors mimicking Sertoli and Sertoli-Leydig cell tumors: Sertoliform variant of endometrioid carcinoma. Cancer 50: 1322–1331

269. Ordi J, Schammel D P, Rasekh L et al. 1999 Sertoliform endometrioid carcinomas of the ovary: a clinicopathologic and immunohistochemical study of 13 cases. Mod Pathol 12: 933–940

270. Pitman M B, Young R H, Clement P B et al. 1994 Endometrioid carcinoma of the ovary and endometrium, oxyphilic cell type: a report of nine cases. Int J Gynecol Pathol 13: 290–301

271. Tornos C, Silva E G, Ordonez N G 1995 Endometrioid carcinoma of the ovary with a prominent spindle-cell component, a source of diagnostic confusion – A report of 14 cases. Am J Surg Pathol 19:1343–1353

272. Dabbs D J, Sturtz K, Zaino R J 1996 The immunohistochemical discrimination of endometrioid adenocarcinomas. Hum Pathol 27: 172–177

273. Guerrieri C, Franlund B, Malmstrom H et al. 1998 Ovarian endometrioid carcinomas simulating sex cord-stromal tumors: a study using inhibin and cytokeratin 7. Int J Gynecol Pathol 17: 266–271

274. Matias-Guiu X, Pons C, Prat J 1998 Mullerian inhibiting substance, alpha-inhibin, and CD99 expression in sex cord-stromal tumors and endometrioid ovarian carcinomas resembling sex cord-stromal tumors. Hum Pathol 29: 840–845

275. Hildebrandt R H, Rouse R V, Longacre T A 1997 Value of inhibin in the identification of granulosa cell tumors of the ovary. Hum Pathol 28: 1387–1395

276. Nogales F F, Bergeron C, Carvia R E et al. 1996 Ovarian endometrioid tumors with yolk sac tumor component, an unusual form of ovarian neoplasm – Analysis of six cases. Am J Surg Pathol 20: 1056–1066

277. Lopez J M, Malpica A, Deavers M T et al. 2003 Ovarian yolk sac tumor associated with endometrioid carcinoma and mucinous cystadenoma of the ovary. Ann Diagn Pathol 7: 300–305

278. Sheu B C, Lin H H, Chen C K et al. 1995 Synchronous primary carcinomas of the endometrium and ovary. Int J Gynaecol Obstet 51: 141–146

279. Falkenberry S S, Steinhoff M M, Gordinier M et al. 1996 Synchronous endometrioid tumors of the ovary and endometrium – A clinicopathologic study of 22 cases. J Reprod Med 41: 713–718

280. Eifel P, Hendrickson M, Ross J et al. 1982 Simultaneous presentation of carcinoma involving the ovary and the uterine corpus. Cancer 50: 163–170

281. Pearl M L, Johnston C M, Frank T S et al. 1993 Synchronous dual primary ovarian and endometrial carcinomas. Int J Gynaecol Obstet 43: 305–312

282. Soliman P T, Slomovitz B M, Broaddus R et al. 2004 Synchronous primary cancers of the endometrium and ovary: a single institution review of 84 cases. Gynecol Oncol 94: 456–462

283. Zaino R, Whitney C, Brady M F et al. 2001 Simultaneously detected endometrial and ovarian carcinomas – a prospective clinicopathologic study of 74 cases: a gynecologic oncology group study. Gynecol Oncol 83: 355–362

284. Ulbright T M, Roth L M 1985 Metastatic and independent cancers of the endometrium and ovary: a clinicopathologic study of 34 cases. Hum Pathol 16: 28–34

285. Shenson D L, Gallion H H, Powell D E et al. 1995 Loss of heterozygosity and genomic instability in synchronous endometrioid tumors of the ovary and endometrium. Cancer 76: 650–657

286. Fujita M, Enomoto T, Wada et al. 1996 Application of clonal analysis – Differential diagnosis for synchronous primary ovarian and endometrial cancers and metastatic cancer. Am J Clin Pathol 105: 350–359

287. Emmert-Buck M R, Chuaqui R, Zhuang Z et al. 1997 Molecular analysis of synchronous uterine and ovarian endometrioid tumors. Int J Gynecol Pathol 16: 143–148

288. Ricci R, Komminoth P, Bannwart F et al. 2003 PTEN as a molecular marker to distinguish metastatic from primary synchronous endometrioid carcinomas of the ovary and uterus. Diagn Mol Pathol 12: 71–78

289. Fujii H, Matsumoto T, Yoshida M et al. 2002 Genetics of synchronous uterine and ovarian endometrioid carcinoma: Combined analyses of loss of heterozygosity, PTEN mutation, and microsatellite instability. Hum Pathol 33: 421–428

290. Irving J A, Catasus L, Gallardo A et al. 2005 Synchronous endometrioid carcinomas of the uterine corpus and ovary: alterations in the beta-catenin (CTNNB1) pathway are associated with independent primary tumors and favorable prognosis. Hum Pathol 36 605–619

291. Barakat R R, Rubin S C, Wong G et al. 1992 Mixed mesodermal tumor of the ovary: analysis of prognostic factors in 31 cases. Obstet Gynecol 80: 660–664

292. Boucher D, Tetu B 1994 Morphologic prognostic factors of malignant mixed mullerian tumors of the ovary: a clinicopathologic study of 15 cases. Int J Gynecol Pathol 13: 22–28

293. Brown E, Stewart M, Rye T et al. 2004 Carcinosarcoma of the ovary: 19 years of prospective data from a single center. Cancer 100: 2148–2153

294. Bicher A, Levenback C, Silva E G et al. 1995 Ovarian malignant mixed Müllerian tumors treated with platinum-based chemotherapy. Obstet Gynecol 85: 735–739

295. Chang J, Sharpe J C, A'Hern R P et al. 1995 Carcinosarcoma of the ovary: incidence, prognosis, treatment and survival of patients. Ann Oncol 6: 755–758

296. Harris M A, Delap L M, Sengupta P S et al. 2003 Carcinosarcoma of the ovary. Br J Cancer 88: 654–657

297. Pfeiffer P, Hardt-Madsen M, Rex S et al. 1991 Malignant mixed Müllerian tumors of the ovary: report of 13 cases. Acta Obstet Gynecol Scand 70: 79–84

298. Sreenan J J, Hart W R 1995 Carcinosarcomas of the female genital tract: a pathologic study of 29 metastatic tumors: Further evidence for the dominant role of the epithelial component and the conversion theory of histogenesis. Am J Surg Pathol 19: 666–674

299. DiSilvestro P A, Gajewski W H, Ludwig M E et al. 1995 Malignant mixed mesodermal tumors of the ovary. Obstet Gynecol 86: 780–782

300. Tate T J, Blessing J A, DeGeest K et al. 2004 Cisplatin as initial chemotherapy in ovarian carcinosarcomas: a Gynecologic Oncology Group study. Gynecol Oncol 93: 336–339

301. Barnholtz-Sloan J S, Morris R, Malone J M Jr et al. 2004 Survival of women diagnosed with malignant, mixed mullerian tumors of the ovary (OMMMT). Gynecol Oncol 93: 506–512

302. Duska L R, Garrett A, Eltabbakh G H et al. 2002 Paclitaxel and platinum chemotherapy for malignant mixed mullerian tumors of the ovary. Gynecol Oncol 85: 459–463

303. Sit A S, Price F V, Kelley J L et al. 2000 Chemotherapy for malignant mixed Mullerian tumors of the ovary. Gynecol Oncol 79: 196–200

304. Muntz H G, Jones M A, Goff B A et al. 1995 Malignant mixed Mullerian tumors of the ovary – Experience with surgical cytoreduction and combination chemotherapy. Cancer 76: 1209–1213

305. Le T, Krepart G V, Lotocki R J et al. 1997 Malignant mixed mesodermal ovarian tumor treatment and prognosis: a 20-year experience. Gynecol Oncol 65: 237–240

306. Ariyoshi K, Kawauchi S, Kaku T et al. 2000 Prognostic factors in ovarian carcinosarcoma: a clinicopathological and immunohistochemical analysis of 23 cases. Histopathology 37: 427–43.

307. Hellstrom A C, Tegerstedt G, Silfversward C et al. 1999 Malignant mixed mullerian tumors of the ovary: histopathologic and clinical review of 36 cases. Int J Gynecol Cancer 9: 312–316

308. Dehner L P, Norris H J, Taylor H B 1971 Carcinosarcomas and mixed mesodermal tumors of the ovary. Cancer 27: 207–216

309. Barwick K W, Livolsi V A 1980 Malignant mixed mesodermal tumors of the ovary: a clinicopathologic assessment of 12 cases. Am J Surg Pathol 4: 37–42

310. Terada K Y, Johnson T L, Hopkins M et al. 1989 Clinicopathologic features of ovarian mixed mesodermal tumors and carcinosarcomas. Gynecol Oncol 32: 228–232

311. Ehrmann R L, Weidner N, Welch W R et al. 1990 Malignant mixed mullerian tumor of the ovary with prominent neuroectodermal differentiation (teratoid carcinosarcoma). Int J Gynecol Pathol 9: 272–282

312. Barua R, Richmond D 1988 Trophoblastic differentiation in a malignant mixed mesodermal tumor of the ovary. Hum Pathol 19: 1235–1236

313. Rebischung C, Pautier P, Morice P et al. 2000 Alpha-fetoprotein production by a malignant mixed mullerian tumor of the ovary. Gynecol Oncol 77: 203–205

314. Deligdisch L, Plaxe S, Cohen C J 1988 Extrauterine pelvic malignant mixed mesodermal tumors. A study of 10 cases with immunohistochemistry. Int J Gynecol Pathol 7: 361–372

315. Plaxe S C, Dottino P R, Goodman H M et al. 1990 Clinical features of advanced ovarian mixed mesodermal tumors and treatment with doxorubicin- and cis-platinum-based chemotherapy. Gynecol Oncol 37: 244–249

316. Amant F, Vloeberghs V, Woestenborghs H et al. 2003 Transition of epithelial toward mesenchymal differentiation during ovarian carcinosarcoma tumorigenesis. Gynecol Oncol 90: 372–377

317. Sahin A, Benda J A 1988 An immunohistochemical study of primary ovarian sarcoma. An evaluation of nine tumors. Int J Gynecol Pathol 7: 268–279

318. Costa M J, Khan R, Judd R 1991 Carcinosarcoma (malignant mixed mullerian [mesodermal] tumor) of the uterus and ovary. Correlation of clinical, pathologic, and immunohistochemical features in 29 cases. Arch Pathol Lab Med 115: 583–590

319. Clarke T J 1990 Histogenesis of ovarian malignant mixed mesodermal tumours. J Clin Pathol 43: 287–290

320. Dellers E A, Valente P T, Edmonds P R et al. 1991 Extrauterine mixed mesodermal tumors: an immunohistochemical study. Arch Pathol Lab Med 115: 918–920

321. Mukai K, Varela-Duran J, Nochomovitz L E 1980 The rhabdomyoblast in mixed Mullerian tumors of the uterus and ovary. An immunohistochemical study of myoglobin in 25 cases. Am J Clin Pathol 74: 101–104

322. Eichhorn J H, Young R H, Clement P B 2002 Mesodermal (mullerian) adenosarcoma of the ovary: a clinicopathologic analysis of 40 cases and a review of the literature. Am J Surg Pathol 26: 1243–1258

323. Fukunaga M, Nomura K, Endo Y et al. 1997 Ovarian adenosarcoma. Histopathology 30: 283–287

324. Oliva E, Clement P B, Young R H 2000 Endometrial stromal tumors: an update on a group of tumors with a protean phenotype. Adv Anat Pathol 7: 257–281

325. Baiocchi G, Kavanagh J J, Wharton J T 1990 Endometrioid stromal sarcomas arising from ovarian and extraovarian endometriosis: report of two cases and review of the literature. Gynecol Oncol 36: 147–151

326. Silverberg S G, Nogales F F 1981 Endolymphatic stromal myosis of the ovary: a report of three cases and literature review. Gynecol Oncol 12: 129–138

327. Young R H, Prat J, Scully R E 1984 Endometrioid stromal sarcomas of the ovary. A clinicopathologic analysis of 23 cases. Cancer 53: 1143–1155

328. Chang K L, Crabtree G S, Lim-Tan S K et al. 1993 Primary extrauterine endometrial stromal neoplasms: a clinicopathologic study of 20 cases and a review of the literature. Int J Gynecol Pathol 12: 282–296

329. Geas F L, Tewari D S, Rutgers J K et al. 2004 Surgical cytoreduction and hormone therapy of an advanced endometrial stromal sarcoma of the ovary. Obstet Gynecol 103: 1051–1054

330. McCluggage W G 2004 Ovarian neoplasms composed of small round cells: a review. Adv Anat Pathol 11: 288–296

331. Fukunaga M, Ishihara A, Ushigome S 1998 Extrauterine low-grade endometrial stromal sarcoma: report of three cases. Pathol Int 48: 297–302

332. Scully R E, Barlow J F 1967 "Mesonephroma" of ovary: tumor of Mullerian nature related to endometrioid carcinoma. Cancer 20: 1405–1417

333. Roth L M, Langley F A, Fox H et al. 1984 Ovarian clear cell adenofibromatous tumors: benign, low malignant potential, and associated with invasive clear cell carcinoma. Cancer 53: 1156–1163

334. Bell D A, Scully R E 1985 Benign and borderline clear cell adenofibromas of the ovary. Cancer 56: 2922–2931

335. Montag A G, Jenison E L, Griffiths C et al. 1989 Ovarian clear cell carcinoma. A clinicopathologic analysis of 44 cases. Int J Gynecol Pathol 8: 85–96

336. Kennedy A W, Biscotti C V, Hart W R et al. 1989 Ovarian clear cell adenocarcinoma. Gynecol Oncol 32: 342–349

337. Aure J C, Hoeg K, Kolstad P 1971 Mesonephroid tumors of the ovary. Clinical and histopathologic studies. Obstet Gynecol 37: 860–867

338. Crozier M A, Copeland L J, Silva E G et al. 1989 Clear cell carcinoma of the ovary: a study of 59 cases. Gynecol Oncol 35: 199–203

339. Doshi N, Tobon H 1977 Primary clear cell carcinoma of the ovary. An analysis of 15 cases with review of the literature. Cancer 39: 2658–2664

340. Norris H J, Rabinowitz M 1971 Ovarian adenocarcinoma of mesonephric type. Cancer 28: 1074–1081

341. Rogers L W, Julian C G, Woodruff J D 1972 Mesonephroid carcinoma of the ovary: a study of 95 cases from the Emil Novak Ovarian Tumor Registry. Gynecol Oncol 1: 76–89

342. Shevchuk M M, Winkler-Monsanto B, Fenoglio C M et al. 1981 Clear cell carcinoma of the ovary: a clinicopathologic study with review of the literature. Cancer 47: 1344–1351

343. Klemi P J, Meurman L, Gronroos M et al. 1982 Clear cell (mesonephroid) tumors of the ovary with characteristics resembling endodermal sinus tumor. Int J Gynecol Pathol 1: 95–100

344. Kennedy A W, Biscotti C V, Hart W R et al. 1993 Histologic correlates of progression-free interval and survival in ovarian clear cell adenocarcinoma. Gynecol Oncol 50: 334–338

345. Recio F, Piver M S, Hempling R E et al. 1996 Lack of improved survival plus increase in thromboembolic complications in patients with clear cell carcinoma of the ovary treated with platinum versus nonplatinum-based chemotherapy. Cancer 78: 2157–2163

346. Goff B, Sainz de la Cuesta R, Muntz H et al. 1996 Clear cell carcinoma of the ovary: a distinct histologic type with poor prognosis and resistance to platinum-based chemotherapy in stage III disease. Gynecol Oncol 60: 412–417

347. Sugiyama T, Kamura T, Kigawa J et al. 2000 Clinical characteristics of clear cell carcinoma of the ovary – A distinct histologic type with poor prognosis and resistance to platinum-based chemotherapy. Cancer 88: 2584–2589

348. Omura G A, Brady M F, Homesley H D et al. 1991 Long-term follow-up and prognostic factor analysis in advanced ovarian carcinoma: the Gynecologic Oncology Group experience. J Clin Oncol 9: 1138–1150

349. Itamochi H, Kigawa J, Sugiyama T et al. 2002 Low proliferation activity may be associated with chemoresistance in clear cell carcinoma of the ovary. Obstet Gynecol 100: 281–287

350. Ho C M, Huang Y J, Chen T C et al. 2004 Pure-type clear cell carcinoma of the ovary as a distinct histological type and improved survival in patients treated with paclitaxel-platinum-based chemotherapy in pure-type advanced disease. Gynecol Oncol 94: 197–203

351. Clement P B, Young R H, Scully R E 1991 Clinical syndromes associated with tumors of the female genital tract. Semin Diagn Pathol 8: 204–233

352. Kitazawa R, Kitazawa S, Matui T et al. 1997 In situ detection of parathyroid hormone-related protein in ovarian clear cell carcinoma. Hum Pathol 28: 379–382

353. Al-Nafussi A I, Hughes D E, Williams A R 1993 Hyaline globules in ovarian tumours. Histopathology 23: 563–566

354. Kwon T J, Ro J Y, Tornos C et al. 1996 Reduplicated basal lamina in clear-cell carcinoma of the ovary: An immunohistochemical and electron microscopic study. Ultrastruct Pathol 20: 529–536

355. Mikami Y, Hata S, Melamed J et al. 1999 Basement membrane material in ovarian clear cell carcinoma: correlation with growth pattern and nuclear grade. Int J Gynecol Pathol 18: 52–57

356. Young R H, Scully R E 1987 Oxyphilic clear cell carcinoma of the ovary. A report of nine cases. Am J Surg Pathol 11: 661–667

357. Sato Y, Shimamoto T, Amada et al. 2003 Prognostic value of histologic grading of ovarian carcinomas. Int J Gynecol Pathol 22: 52–56

358. Ohkawa K, Amasaki H, Terashima Y et al. 1977 Clear cell carcinoma of the ovary: light and electron microscopic studies. Cancer 40: 3019–3029

359. Jenison E L, Montag A G, Griffiths CT et al. 1989 Clear cell adenocarcinoma of the ovary: a clinical analysis and comparison with serous carcinoma. Gynecol Oncol 32: 65–71

360. Cameron R I, Ashe P, O'Rourke D M et al 2003 A panel of immunohistochemical stains assists in the distinction between ovarian and renal clear cell carcinoma. Int J Gynecol Pathol 22: 272–276

361. Nolan L P, Heatley M K 2001 The value of immunocytochemistry in distinguishing between clear cell carcinoma of the kidney and ovary. Int J Gynecol Pathol 20: 155–159

362. Vang R, Whitaker B P, Farhood A I et al. 2001 Immunohistochemical analysis of clear cell carcinoma of the gynecologic tract. Int J Gynecol Pathol 20: 252–259

363. Ordi J, Romagosa C, Tavassoli F A et al. 2003 CD10 expression in epithelial tissues and tumors of the gynecologic tract: a useful marker in the diagnosis of mesonephric, trophoblastic, and clear cell tumors. Am J Surg Pathol 27: 178–186

364. Ramalingam P, Malpica A, Silva E G et al. 2004 The use of Cytokeratin 7 and EMA in differentiating ovarian yolk sac tumors from endometrioid and clear cell carcinomas. Am J Surg Pathol 28: 1499–1505

365. Yoonessi M, Abell M R 1979 Brenner tumors of the ovary. Obstet Gynecol 54: 90–96

366. Balasa R W, Adcock L L, Prem K A et al. 1977 The Brenner tumor: a clinicopathologic review. Obstet Gynecol 50: 120–128

367. Fox H, Agrawal K, Langley F A 1972 The Brenner tumour of the ovary. A clinicopathological study of 54 cases. J Obstet Gynaecol Br Commonw 79: 661–665

368. Silverberg S G 1971 Brenner tumor of the ovary. A clinicopathologic study of 60 tumors in 54 women. Cancer 28: 588–596

369. Jorgensen E O, Dockerty M B, Wilson R B et al. 1970 Clinicopathologic study of 53 cases of Brenner's tumors of the ovary. Am J Obstet Gynecol 108: 122–127

370. Carpen E 1976 Brenner tumours of the ovary. A clinicopathological study. Acta Obstet Gynecol Scand 50 Suppl: 1–41

371. Ehrlich C E, Roth L M 1971 The Brenner tumor. A clinicopathologic study of 57 cases. Cancer 27: 332–342

372. Waxman M 1979 Pure and mixed Brenner tumors of the ovary: clinicopathologic and histogenetic observations. Cancer 43: 1830–1839

373. Yoshida M, Obayashi C, Tachibana M et al. 2004 Coexisting Brenner tumor and struma ovarii in the right ovary: case report and review of the literature. Pathol Int 54: 793–797

374. Burg J, Kommoss F, Bittinger F et al. 2002 Mature cystic teratoma of the ovary with struma and benign Brenner tumor: a case report with immunohistochemical characterization. Int J Gynecol Pathol 21: 74–77

375. Lamping J D, Blythe J G 1977 Bilateral Brenner tumors: a case report and review of the literature. Hum Pathol 8: 583–585

376. Trebeck C E, Friedlander M L, Russell P et al. 1987 Brenner tumours of the ovary: a study of the histology, immunochemistry and cellular DNA content in benign, borderline and malignant ovarian tumors. Pathology 19: 241–246

377. Roth L M, Dallenbach-Hellweg G, Czernobilsky B 1985 Ovarian Brenner tumors: I. Metaplastic, proliferating, and low malignant potential. Cancer 562: 582–591

378. Hallgrimsson J, Scully R E 1972 Borderline and malignant Brenner tumours of the ovary. A report of 15 cases. Acta Pathol Microbiol Scand [A] 80 Suppl: 233: 56–66

379. Roth L M, Sternberg W H 1971 Proliferating Brenner tumors. Cancer 27: 687–693

380. Woodruff J D, Dietrich D, Genadry R et al. 1981 Proliferative and malignant Brenner tumors. Review of 47 cases. Am J Obstet Gynecol 141: 118–125

381. Miles P A, Norris H J 1972 Proliferative and malignant Brenner tumors of the ovary. Cancer 30: 174–186

382. Roth L M, Gersell D J, Ulbright T M 1993 Ovarian Brenner tumors and transitional cell carcinoma: recent developments. Int J Gynecol Pathol 12: 128–133

383. Baker P M, Young R H 2003 Brenner tumor of the ovary with striking microcystic change. Int J Gynecol Pathol 22: 185–188

384. Austin R M, Norris H J 1987 Malignant Brenner tumor and transitional cell carcinoma of the ovary: a comparison. Int J Gynecol Pathol 6: 29–39

385. Roth L M, Czernobilsky B 1985 Ovarian Brenner tumors. II. Malignant. Cancer 56: 592–601

386. Silva E G, Robey-Cafferty S S, Smith T L et al. 1990 Ovarian carcinomas with transitional cell carcinoma pattern. Am J Clin Pathol 93: 457–465

387. Eichhorn J H, Young R H 2004 Transitional cell carcinoma of the ovary: a morphologic study of 100 cases with emphasis on differential diagnosis. Am J Surg Pathol 28: 453–463

388. Kommoss F, Kommoss S, Schmidt D et al. 2005 Survival benefit for patients with advanced-stage transitional cell carcinomas vs. other subtypes of ovarian carcinoma after chemotherapy with platinum and paclitaxel. Gynecol Oncol 97: 195–199

389. Hollingsworth H C, Steinberg S M, Silverberg S G et al. 1996 Advanced stage transitional cell carcinoma of the ovary. Hum Pathol 27: 1267–1272

390. Robey S S, Silva E G, Gershenson D M et al. 1989 Transitional cell carcinoma in high-grade high-stage ovarian carcinoma. An indicator of favorable response to chemotherapy. Cancer 63: 839–847

391. Gershenson D M, Silva E G, Mitchell M F et al. 1993 Transitional cell carcinoma of the ovary: a matched control study of advanced-stage patients treated with cisplatin-based chemotherapy. Am J Obstet Gynecol 168: 1178–1187

392. Costa M J, Hansen C, Dickerman A et al. 1998 Clinicopathologic significance of transitional cell carcinoma pattern in nonlocalized ovarian epithelial tumors (stages 2–4). Am J Clin Pathol 109: 173–180

393. Seldenrijk C A, Willig A P, Baak J P et al. 1986 Malignant Brenner tumor. A histologic, morphometrical, immunohistochemical, and ultrastructural study. Cancer 58: 754–760

394. Santini D, Gelli M C, Mazzoleni G et al. 1989 Brenner tumor of the ovary: a correlative histologic, histochemical, immunohistochemical, and ultrastructural investigation. Hum Pathol 20: 787–795

395. Prat J 2005 Ovarian carcinomas, including secondary tumors: diagnostically challenging areas. Mod Pathol 18 Suppl 2: S99–111

396. Soslow R A, Rouse R V, Hendrickson M R et al. 1996 Transitional cell neoplasms of the ovary and urinary bladder: a comparative immunohistochemical analysis. Int J Gynecol Pathol 15: 257–265

397. Charpin C, Bhan A K, Zurawski V R J et al. 1982 Carcinoembryonic antigen (CEA) and carbohydrate determinant 19-9 (CA 19-9) localization in 121 primary and metastatic ovarian tumors: an immunohistochemical study with the use of monoclonal antibodies. Int J Gynecol Pathol 1: 231–245

398. Logani S, Oliva E, Amin M B et al. 2003 Immunoprofile of ovarian tumors with putative transitional cell (urothelial) differentiation using novel urothelial markers: histogenetic and diagnostic implications. Am J Surg Pathol 27: 1434–1441

399. Riedel I, Czernobilsky B, Lifschitz-Mercer B et al. 2001 Brenner tumors but not transitional cell carcinomas of the ovary show urothelial differentiation: immunohistochemical staining of urothelial markers, including cytokeratins and uroplakins. Virchow's Arch 438: 181–191

400. Ogawa K, Johansson S L, Cohen S M 1999 Immunohistochemical analysis of uroplakins, urothelial specific proteins, in ovarian Brenner tumors, normal tissues, and benign and neoplastic lesions of the female genital tract. Am J Pathol 155: 1047–1050

401. Ordonez N G 2000 Transitional cell carcinomas of the ovary and bladder are immunophenotypically different. Histopathology 36: 433–438

402. Croft P R, Lathrop S L, Feddersen R M et al. 2005 Estrogen receptor expression in papillary urothelial carcinoma of the bladder and ovarian transitional cell carcinoma. Arch Pathol Lab Med 129:94–199

403. Young R H, Scully R E 1988 Urothelial and ovarian carcinomas of identical cell types: problems in interpretation. A report of three cases and review of the literature. Int J Gynecol Pathol 7: 197–211

404. Oliva E, Musulen E, Prat J et al. 1995 Transitional cell carcinoma of the renal pelvis with symptomatic ovarian metastases. Int J Surg Pathol 2: 231–236

405. Groutz A, Gillon G, Shimonov M et al. 1996 Late, isolated, secondary ovarian transitional cell carcinoma: An unusual course of bladder malignancy. Br J Urol 78(5): 795–796

406. Silva E G, Tornos C, Bailey M A et al. 1991 Undifferentiated carcinoma of the ovary. Arch Pathol Lab Med 115: 377–381

407. Eichhorn J H, Young R H 2001 Neuroendocrine tumors of the genital tract. Am J Clin Pathol 115 Suppl: S94–112

408. Fukunaga M, Endo Y, Miyazawa Y et al. 1997 Small cell neuroendocrine carcinoma of the ovary. Virchow's Arch 430: 343–348

409. Chen K T 2000 Composite large-cell neuroendocrine carcinoma and surface epithelial-stromal neoplasm of the ovary. Int J Surg Pathol 8: 169–174

410. Ohira S, Itoh K, Shiozawa T et al. 2004 Ovarian non-small cell neuroendocrine carcinoma with paraneoplastic parathyroid hormone-related hypercalcemia. Int J Gynecol Pathol 23: 393–397

411. Eichhorn J H, Young R H, Scully R E 1993 Nonpulmonary small cell carcinomas of extragenital origin metastatic to the ovary. Cancer 71: 177–186

412. Young R H, Scully R E 1985 Ovarian metastases from cancer of the lung: problems in interpretation. A report of seven cases. Gynecol Oncol 21: 337–350

413. Irving J A, Young R H 2005 Lung carcinoma metastatic to the ovary: a clinicopathologic study of 32 cases emphasizing their morphologic spectrum and problems in differential diagnosis. Am J Surg Pathol 29: 997–1006

414. Agoff S N, Lamps L W, Philip A T et al. 2000 Thyroid transcription factor-1 is expressed in extrapulmonary small cell carcinomas but not in other extrapulmonary neuroendocrine tumors. Mod Pathol 13: 238–242

415. Kaufmann O, Dietel M 2000 Expression of thyroid transcription factor-1 in pulmonary and extrapulmonary small cell carcinomas and other neuroendocrine carcinomas of various primary sites. Histopathology 36: 415–420

416. Ordonez N G 2000 Value of thyroid transcription factor-1 immunostaining in distinguishing small cell lung carcinomas from other small cell carcinomas. Am J Surg Pathol 24: 1217–1223

417. Tetu B, Silva E G, Gershenson D M 1987 Squamous cell carcinoma of the ovary. Arch Pathol Lab Med 111: 864–866

418. Pins M R, Young R H, Daly W J et al. 1996 Primary squamous cell carcinoma of the ovary. Report of 37 cases. Am J Surg Pathol 20: 823–833

419. Ishikura H, Scully R E 1987 Hepatoid carcinoma of the ovary. A newly described tumor. Cancer 60: 2775–2784

420. Pitman M B, Triratanachat S, Young R H et al. 2004 Hepatocyte paraffin 1 antibody does not distinguish primary ovarian tumors with hepatoid differentiation from metastatic hepatocellular carcinoma. Int J Gynecol Pathol 23: 58–64

421. Tochigi N, Kishimoto T, Supriatna Y et al. 2003 Hepatoid carcinoma of the ovary: a report of three cases admixed with a common surface epithelial carcinoma. Int J Gynecol Pathol 22: 266–271

422. Senzaki H, Kiyozuka Y, Mizuoka H et al. 1999 An autopsy case of hepatoid carcinoma of the ovary with PIVKA-II production: immunohistochemical study and literature review. Pathol Int 49: 164–169

423. Tsung J S, Yang P S 2004 Hepatoid carcinoma of the ovary: characteristics of its immunoreactivity. A case report. Eur J Gynaecol Oncol 25: 745–748

424. Prat J, Bhan A K, Dickersin G R et al. 1982 Hepatoid yolk sac tumor of the ovary (endodermal sinus tumor with hepatoid differentiation): a light microscopic, ultrastructural and immunohistochemical study of seven cases. Cancer 50: 2355–2368

425. Young R H, Gersell D J, Clement P B et al. 1992 Hepatocellular carcinoma metastatic to the ovary: A report of three cases discovered during life with discussion of the differential diagnosis of hepatoid tumors of the ovary. Hum Pathol 23: 574–580

426. Civantos F, Rywlin A M 1972 Carcinomas with trophoblastic differentiation and secretion of chorionic gonadotrophins. Cancer 29: 789–798

427. Matias-Guiu X, Prat J 1990 Ovarian tumors with functioning stroma. An immunohistochemical study of 100 cases with human chorionic gonadotropin immunoreactivity and polyclonal antibodies. Cancer 65: 2001–2005

428. Oliva E, Andrada E, Pezzica E et al. 1993 Ovarian carcinomas with choriocarcinomatous differentiation. Cancer 72: 2441–2446

429. Rutgers J L, Young R H, Scully R E 1987 Ovarian yolk sac tumor arising from an endometrioid carcinoma. Hum Pathol 18: 1296–1299

430. Stage A H, Grafton W D 1977 Thecomas and granulosa-theca cell tumors of the ovary: an analysis of 51 tumors. Obstet Gynecol 50: 21–27

431. Anikwue C, Dawood M Y, Kramer E 1978 Granulosa and theca cell tumors. Obstet Gynecol 51: 214–220

432. Bjorkholm E, Silfversward C 1981 Prognostic factors in granulosa-cell tumors. Gynecol Oncol 11: 261–274

433. Stenwig J T, Hazekamp J T, Beecham J B 1979 Granulosa cell tumors of the ovary. A clinicopathological study of 118 cases with long-term follow-up. Gynecol Oncol 7: 136–152

434. Malmstrom H, Hogberg T, Risberg B et al. 1994 Granulosa cell tumors of the ovary: prognostic factors and outcome. Gynecol Oncol 52: 50–55

435. King L A, Okagaki T, Gallup D G et al. 1996 Mitotic count, nuclear atypia, and immunohistochemical determination of Ki-67, c-myc, p21-ras, c-erbB2, and p53 expression in granulosa cell tumors of the ovary: mitotic count and Ki-67 are indicators of poor prognosis. Gynecol Oncol 61: 227–232

436. Segal R, DePetrillo A D, Thomas G 1995 Clinical review of adult granulosa cell tumors of the ovary. Gynecol Oncol 56: 338–344

437. Bjorkholm E, Pettersson F 1980 Granulosa cell and theca cell tumors. The clinical picture and long term outcome for the Radiumhemmet series. Acta Obstet Gynecol Scand 59: 361–365

438. Fox H, Agrawal K, Langley F A 1975 A clinicopathologic study of 92 cases of granulosa cell tumor of the ovary with special reference to the factors influencing prognosis. Cancer 35: 231–241

439. Evans A T I, Gaffey T A, Malkasian G D Jr et al. 1980 Clinicopathologic review of 118 granulosa and 82 theca cell tumors. Obstet Gynecol 55: 231–238

440. Aboud E 1997 A review of granulosa cell tumours and thecomas of the ovary. Arch Gynecol Obstet 259: 161–165

441. Pautier P, Lhomme C, Culine S et al. 1997 Adult granulosa-cell tumor of the ovary: A retrospective study of 45 cases. Int J Gynecol Cancer 7: 58–65

442. Nakashima N, Young R H, Scully R E 1984 Androgenic granulosa cell tumors of the ovary. A clinicopathological analysis of 17 cases and review of the literature. Arch Pathol Lab Med 108: 786–791

443. Norris H J, Taylor H B 1969 Virilization associated with cystic granulosa tumors. Obstet Gynecol 34: 629–635

444. Martinez L, Salmeron M, Carvia R E et al. 1997 Androgen producing luteinized granulosa cell tumor. Acta Obstet Gynecol Scand 76: 285–286

445. Castro C V, Malpica A, Hearne R H et al. 2000 Androgenic adult granulosa cell tumor in a 13-year-old prepubertal patient: a case report and review of the literature. Int J Gynecol Pathol 19: 266–271

446. Sayegh R A, DeLellis R, Alroy et al. 1999 Masculinizing granulosa cell tumor of the ovary in a postmenopausal woman – A case report. J Reprod Med 44: 821–825

447. Young R H, Dudley A G, Scully R E 1984 Granulosa cell, Sertoli-Leydig cell, and unclassified sex cord-stromal tumors associated with pregnancy: a clinicopathological analysis of thirty-six cases. Gynecol Oncol 18: 181–205

448. Sehouli J, Drescher F S, Mustea A et al. 2004 Granulosa cell tumor of the ovary: 10 years follow-up data of 65 patients. Anticancer Res 24: 1223–1229

449. Miller B E, Barron B A, Wan J Y et al. 1997 Prognostic factors in adult granulosa cell tumor of the ovary. Cancer 79: 1951–1955

450. Lauszus F F, Petersen A C, Greisen J et al. 2001 Granulosa cell tumor of the ovary: a population-based study of 37 women with stage I disease. Gynecol Oncol 81: 456–460

451. Ali S Z 1998 Metastatic granulosa-cell tumor in the liver: cytopathologic findings and staining with inhibin. Diagn Cytopathol 19: 293–297

452. Duhig E E, Riha R L, Clarke B E 2002 Test and teach. An unusual tumour presenting in the lungs. Metastatic adult granulosa cell tumour of the ovary, microfollicular patttterns. Pathology 34: 78–81

453. Hines J F, Khalifa M A, Moore J L et al. 1996 Recurrent granulosa cell tumor of the ovary 37 years after initial diagnosis: a case report and review of the literature. Gynecol Oncol 60: 484–488

454. Gershenson D M, Morris M, Burke T W et al. 1996 Treatment of poor-prognosis sex cord-stromal tumors of the ovary with the combination of bleomycin, etoposide, and cisplatin. Obstet Gynecol 87: 527–531

455. Chiara S, Merlini L, Campora E et al. 1993 Cisplatin-based chemotherapy in recurrent or high risk ovarian granulosa-cell tumor patients. Eur J Gynaecol Oncol 14: 314–317

456. Pecorelli S, Wagenaar H C, Vergote I B et al. 1999 Cisplatin (P), vinblastine (V) and bleomycin (B) combination chemotherapy in recurrent or advanced granulosa(-theca) cell tumours of the ovary. An EORTC gynaecological cancer cooperative group study. Eur J Cancer [A] 35: 1331–1337

457. Lane A H, Lee M M, Fuller AF Jr et al. 1999 Diagnostic utility of Mullerian inhibiting substance determination in patients with primary and recurrent granulosa cell tumors. Gynecol Oncol 73: 51–55

458. Rodgers K E, Marks J F, Ellefson D D et al. 1990 Follicle regulatory protein: a novel marker for granulosa cell cancer patients. Gynecol Oncol. 37: 381–387

459. Lappohn R E, Burger H G, Bonma J et al. 1989 Inhibin as a marker for granulosa cell tumors. N Engl J Med 321: 790–793

460. Jobling T, Mamers P, Healy D et al. 1994 A prospective study of inhibin in granulosa cell tumors of the ovary. Gynecol Oncol 55: 285–289

461. Boggess J F, Soules M R, Goff B A et al. 1997 Serum inhibin and disease status in women with ovarian granulosa cell tumors. Gynecol Oncol 64: 64–69

462. Healy D L, Burger H G, Mamers P et al. 1993 Elevated serum inhibin concentrations in postmenopausal women with ovarian tumors. N Engl J Med 329: 1539–1542

463. Burger H G, Robertson D M, Cahir N et al. 1996 Characterization of inhibin immunoreactivity in post-menopausal women with ovarian tumours. Clin Endocrinol (Oxf) 44: 413–418

464. Young R H, Scully R E 1983 Ovarian sex cord-stromal tumors with bizarre nuclei: A clinicopathologic analysis of 17 cases. Int J Gynecol Pathol 1: 325–335

465. Gaffey M J, Frierson H F J, Iezzoni J C et al. 1996 Ovarian granulosa cell tumors with bizarre nuclei: an immunohistochemical analysis. Mod Pathol 9: 308–315

466. Young R H 2005 Sex cord-stromal tumors of the ovary and testis: their similarities and differences with consideration of selected problems. Mod Pathol 18 Suppl 2: S81–S98

467. Young R H, Oliva E, Scully R E 1994 Luteinized adult granulosa cell tumors of the ovary: a report of four cases. Int J Gynecol Pathol 13: 302–310

468. Young R H, Scully R E 1983 Ovarian stromal tumors with minor sex cord elements: a report of seven cases. Int J Gynecol Pathol 2: 227–234

469. Price A, Russell P, Elliott et al. 1990 Composite mucinous and granulosa-cell tumor of ovary: case report of a unique neoplasm. Int J Gynecol Pathol 9: 372–378

470. Doussis-Anagnostopoulou I A, Remadi S, Czernobilsky B 1996 Mucinous elements in Sertoli-Leydig and granulosa cell tumours: A revaluation. Histopathology 28: 372–375

471. Chandran R, Rahman J, Gebbie D 1993 Composite mucinous and granulosa-theca-cell tumour of the ovary: an unusual neoplasm. Aust NZ J Obstet Gynaecol 33: 437–439

472. McKenna M, Kenny B, Dorman G et al. 2005 Combined adult granulosa cell tumor and mucinous cystadenoma of the ovary: granulosa cell tumor with heterologous mucinous elements. Int J Gynecol Pathol 24: 224–227

473. Nogales F F, Concha A, Plata C et al. 1993 Granulosa cell tumor of the ovary with diffuse true hepatic differentiation simulating stromal luteinization. Am J Surg Pathol 17: 85–90

474. Ahmed E, Young R H, Scully R E 1999 Adult granulosa cell tumor of the ovary with foci of hepatic cell differentiation: a report of four cases and comparison with two cases of granulosa cell tumor with Leydig cells. Am J Surg Pathol 23: 1089–1093

475. Fox H 2003 Pathologic prognostic factors in early stage adult-type granulosa cell tumors of the ovary. Int J Gynecol Cancer 13: 1–4

476. Schumer S T, Cannistra S A 2003 Granulosa cell tumor of the ovary. J Clin Oncol 21: 1180–1189

477. Fujimoto T, Sakuragi N, Okuyama K et al. 2001 Histopathological prognostic factors of adult granulosa cell tumors of the ovary. Acta Obstet Gynecol Scand 80: 1069–1074

478. Clement P B, Young R H, Scully R E 1988 Ovarian granulosa cell proliferations of pregnancy: a report of nine cases. Hum Pathol 19: 657–662

479. McCluggage W G, Young R H 2004 Non-neoplastic granulosa cells within ovarian vascular channels: a rare potential diagnostic pitfall. J Clin Pathol 57: 151–154

480. Otis C N, Powell J L, Barbuto D et al. 1992 Intermediate filamentous proteins in adult granulosa cell tumors: An immunohistochemical study of 25 cases. Am J Surg Pathol 16: 962–968

481. Park S H, Kim I 1994 Histogenetic consideration of ovarian sex cord-stromal tumors analyzed by expression pattern of cytokeratins, vimentin, and laminin. Correlation studies with human gonads. Pathol Res Pract 190: 449–456

482. Chada S, van der Kwast T H 1989 Immunohistochemistry of ovarian granulosa cell tumours. The value of tissue specific proteins and tumour markers. Virchow's Arch A Pathol Anat Histopathol 414: 439–445

483. Miettinen M, Wahlstrom T, Virtanen I et al. 1985 Cellular differentiation in ovarian sex-cord-stromal and germ-cell tumors studied with antibodies to intermediate-filament proteins. Am J Surg Pathol 9: 640–651

484. Benjamin E, Law S, Bobrow L G 1987 Intermediate filaments cytokeratin and vimentin in ovarian sex cord-stromal tumours with correlative studies in adult and fetal ovaries. J Pathol 152: 253–263

485. Costa M J, DeRose P B, Roth L M et al. 1994 Immunohistochemical phenotype of ovarian granulosa cell tumors: Absence of epithelial membrane antigen has diagnostic value. Hum Pathol 25: 60–66

486. Santini D, Ceccarelli C, Leone O et al. 1995 Smooth muscle differentiation in normal human ovaries, ovarian stromal hyperplasia and ovarian granulosa-stromal cells tumors. Mod Pathol 8: 25–30

487. Loo K T, Leung A K F, Chan J K C 1995 Immunohistochemical staining of ovarian granulosa cell tumours with MIC2 antibody. Histopathology 27: 388–390

488. Choi Y L, Kim H S, Ahn G 2000 Immunoexpression of inhibin alpha subunit, inhibin/activin betaA subunit and CD99 in ovarian tumors. Arch Pathol Lab Med 124: 563–569

489. Aguirre P, Thor A D, Scully R E 1989 Ovarian small cell carcinoma. Histogenetic considerations based on immunohistochemical and other findings. Am J Clin Pathol 92: 140–149

490. McCluggage W G 2001 Value of inhibin staining in gynecological pathology. Int J Gynecol Pathol 20: 79–85

491. Zheng W, Senturk B Z, Parkash V 2003 Inhibin immunohistochemical staining: a practical approach for the surgical pathologist in the diagnoses of ovarian sex cord-stromal tumors. Adv Anat Pathol 10: 27–38

492. Flemming P, Grothe W, Maschek H et al. 1996 The site of inhibin production in ovarian neoplasms. Histopathology 29: 465–468

493. Rishi M, Howard L N, Bratthauer G L et al. 1997 Use of monoclonal antibody against human inhibin as a marker for sex cord stromal tumors of the ovary. Am J Surg Pathol 21: 583–589

494. Stewart C J R, Jeffers M D, Kennedy A 1997 Diagnostic value of inhibin immunoreactivity in ovarian gonadal stromal tumours and their histological mimics. Histopathology 31: 67–74

495. Costa M J, Ames P F, Walls J et al. 1997 Inhibin immunohistochemistry applied to ovarian neoplasms: A novel, effective, diagnostic tool. Hum Pathol 28: 1247–1254

496. Yao D X, Soslow R A, Hedvat C V et al. 2003 Melan-A (A103) and inhibin expression in ovarian neoplasms. Appl Immunohistochem Mol Morphol 11: 244–249

497. Cathro H P, Stoler M H 2005 The utility of calretinin, inhibin, and WT1 immunohistochemical staining in the differential diagnosis of ovarian tumors. Hum Pathol 36: 195–201

498. Shah V I, Freites N O, Maxwell P et al. 2003 Inhibin is more specific than calretinin as an immunohistochemical marker for differentiating sarcomatoid granulosa cell tumour of the ovary from other spindle cell neoplasms. J Clin Pathol 56: 221–224

499. Gurusinghe C J, Healy D L, Jobling T et al. 1995 Inhibin and activin are demonstrable by immunohistochemistry in ovarian tumor tissue. Gynecol Oncol 57: 27–32

500. Movahedi-Lankarani S, Kurman R J 2002 Calretinin, a more sensitive but less specific marker than alpha-inhibin for ovarian sex cord-stromal neoplasms – An immunohistochemical study of 215 cases. Am J Surg Pathol 26: 1477–1483

501. McCluggage W G, Maxwell P 2001 Immunohistochemical staining for calretinin is useful in the diagnosis of ovarian sex cord-stromal tumours. Histopathology 38(5): 403–408

502. Young R H, Dickersin G R, Scully R E 1984 Juvenile granulosa cell tumor of the ovary. A clinicopathological analysis of 125 cases. Am J Surg Pathol 8: 575–596

503. Zaloudek C J, Norris H J 1982 Granulosa tumors of the ovary in children: a clinical and pathologic study of 32 cases. Am J Surg Pathol 6: 503–512

504. Lack E E, Perez-Atayde A R, Murthy A S K et al. 1981 Granulosa-theca cell tumors in premenarchal girls: A clinical and pathologic study of ten cases. Cancer 48: 1846–1854

505. Vassal G, Flamant F, Caillaud J M et al. 1988 Juvenile granulosa cell tumor of the ovary in children: A clinical study of 15 cases. J Clin Oncol 6: 990–995

506. Biscotti C V, Hart W R 1989 Juvenile granulosa cell tumors of the ovary. Arch Pathol Lab Med 113: 40–46

507. Bouffet E, Basset T, Chetail N et al. 1997 Juvenile granulosa cell tumor of the ovary in infants: A clinicopathologic study of three cases and review of the literature. J Pediatr Surg 32: 762–765

508. Calaminus G, Wessalowski R, Harms D et al. 1997 Juvenile granulosa cell tumors of the ovary in children and adolescents: results from 33 patients registered in a prospective cooperative study. Gynecol Oncol 65: 447–452

509. Schneider D T, Janig U, Calaminus G et al. 2003 Ovarian sex cord-stromal tumors – a clinicopathological study of 72 cases from the Kiel Pediatric Tumor Registry. Virchow's Arch 443: 549–560

510. Plantaz D, Flamant F, Vassal G et al. 1992 [Granulosa cell tumors of the ovary in children and adolescents. Multicenter retrospective study in 40 patients aged 7 months to 22 years.] Arch Fr Pediatr 49: 793–798

511. Velasco-Oses A, Alouso-Alvaro A, Blanco-Pozo A et al. 1988 Ollier's disease associated with ovarian juvenile granulosa cell tumor. Cancer 62: 222–225

512. Tamimi H K, Bolen J W 1984 Enchondromatosis (Ollier's disease) and ovarian juvenile granulosa cell tumor: A case report and review of the literature. Cancer 53: 1605–1608

513. Tanaka Y, Sasaki Y, Nishihira H et al. 1992 Ovarian juvenile granulosa cell tumor associated with Maffucci's syndrome. Am J Clin Pathol 97: 523–527

514. Nomura K, Furusato M, Nikaido T et al. 1991 Ovarian sex cord tumor with annular tubules. Report of a case. Acta Pathol Jpn 41: 701–706

515. Frausto S D, Geisler J P, Fletcher M S et al. 2004 Late recurrence of juvenile granulosa cell tumor of the ovary. Am J Obstet Gynecol 191: 366–367

516. Powell J L, Otis C N 1997 Management of advanced juvenile granulosa cell tumor of the ovary. Gynecol Oncol 64: 282–284

517. Schneider D T, Calaminus G, Wessalowski R et al. 2002 Therapy of advanced ovarian juvenile granulosa cell tumors. Klin Padiatr 214: 173–178

518. Silverman L A, Gitelman S E 1996 Immunoreactive inhibin, mullerian inhibitory substance, and activin as biochemical markers for juvenile granulosa cell tumors. J Pediatr 129: 918–921

519. Nishida M, Jimi S, Haji M et al. 1991 Juvenile granulosa cell tumor in association with a high serum inhibin level. Gynecol Oncol 40: 90–94

520. Deavers M T, Malpica A, Liu J et al. 2003 Ovarian sex cord-stromal tumors: an immunohistochemical study including a comparison of calretinin and inhibin. Mod Pathol 16: 584–590

521. Zhang J, Young R H, Arseneau J et al. 1982 Ovarian stromal tumors containing lutein or Leydig cells (luteinized thecomas and stromal Leydig tumors) – a clinicopathological analysis of 50 cases. Int J Gynecol Pathol 1: 270–285

522. Roth LM, Sternberg W H 1983 Partly luteinized theca cell tumor of the ovary. Cancer 51: 1697–1704

523. Norris H J, Taylor H B 1968 Prognosis of granulosa-theca tumors of the ovary. Cancer 21: 255–263

524. Waxman M, Vuletin J C, Ureuyo R et al. 1979 Ovarian low-grade stromal sarcoma with thecomatous features: a critical reappraisal of the so-called "malignant thecoma". Cancer 44: 2206–2217

525. Karck U, Kommoss F, Henne K et al. 1991 [Recurrent theca cell tumor.] Geburtshilfe Frauenheilkd 51: 577–579

526. Clement P B, Young R H, Hanna W et al. 1994 Sclerosing peritonitis associated with luteinized thecomas of the ovary: a clinicopathological analysis of six cases. Am J Surg Pathol 18: 1–13

527. Werness B A 1996 Luteinized thecoma with sclerosing peritonitis. Arch Pathol Lab Med 120: 303–306

528. Spiegel G W, Swiger F K 1996 Luteinized thecoma with sclerosing peritonitis presenting as an acute abdomen. Gynecol Oncol 61: 275–281

529. Iwasa Y, Minamiguchi S, Konishi I et al. 1996 Sclerosing peritonitis associated with luteinized thecoma of the ovary. Pathol Int 46: 510–514

530. Reginella R F, Sumkin J H 1996 Sclerosing peritonitis associated with luteinized thecomas. Am J Roentgenol 167: 512–513

531. Young R H, Clement P B, Scully R E 1988 Calcified thecomas in young women. A report of four cases. Int J Gynecol Pathol 7: 343–350

532. Klemi P J, Gronroos M 1979 An ultrastructural and clinical study of theca and granulosa cell tumors. Int J Gynaecol Obstet 17: 219–225

533. Amin H K, Okagaki T, Richart R M 1971 Classification of fibroma and thecoma of the ovary. An ultrastructural study. Cancer 27: 438–446

534. McCluggage W G, Sloan J M, Boyle D D et al. 1998 Malignant fibrothecomatous tumour of the ovary: diagnostic value of anti-inhibin immunostaining. J Clin Pathol 51: 868–871

535. Tiltman A J, Haffajee Z 1999 Sclerosing stromal tumors, thecomas, and fibromas of the ovary: an immunohistochemical profile. Int J Gynecol Pathol 18: 254–258

536. Fletcher J A, Gibas Z, Donovan K et al. 1991 Ovarian granulosa-stromal cell tumors are characterized by trisomy 12. Am J Pathol 138: 515–520

537. Pejovic T, Heim S, Mandahl N et al. 1990 Trisomy 12 is a consistent chromosomal aberration in benign ovarian tumors. Genes Chromosom Cancer 2: 48–52

538. Mrózek K, Nedoszytko B, Babinska M et al. 1990 Trisomy of chromosome 12 in a case of thecoma of the ovary. Gynecol Oncol 36: 413–416

539. Shashi V, Golden W L, von Kap-Herr C et al. 1994 Interphase fluorescence in situ hybridization for trisomy 12 on archival ovarian sex cord-stromal tumors. Gynecol Oncol 55: 349–354

540. Scurry J, Allen D, Dobson P 1996 Ovarian fibromatosis, ascites and omental fibrosis. Histopathology 28: 81–84

541. Frigerio L, Taccagni G L, Mariani A et al. 1997 Idiopathic sclerosing peritonitis associated with florid mesothelial hyperplasia, ovarian fibromatosis, and endometriosis: a new disorder of abdominal mass. Am J Obstet Gynecol 176: 721–722

542. Sivanesaratnam V, Dutta R, Jayalakshmi P 1990 Ovarian fibroma – clinical and histopathological characteristics. Int J Gynaecol Obstet 33: 243–247

543. Dockerty M B, Masson J C 1944 Ovarian fibromas: a clinical and pathologic study of 283 cases. Am J Obstet Gynecol 47: 741–752

544. Prat J, Scully R E 1981 Cellular fibromas and fibrosarcomas of the ovary. A comparative clinicopathologic analysis of seventeen cases. Cancer 47: 2663–2670

545. Gargano G, De Lena M, Zito F et al. 2003 Ovarian fibroma: our experience of 34 cases. Eur J Gynaecol Oncol 24: 429–432

546. Lurie S 2000 Meigs' syndrome: the history of the eponym. Eur J Obstet Gynecol Reprod Biol 92: 199–204

547. Kimonis V E, Goldstein A M, Pastakia B et al. 1997 Clinical manifestations in 105 persons with nevoid basal cell carcinoma syndrome. Am J Med Genet 69: 299–308

548. Tsuji T, Kawauchi S, Utsunomiya T et al. 1997 Fibrosarcoma versus cellular fibroma of the ovary – A comparative study of their proliferative activity and chromosome aberrations using MIB-1 immunostaining, DNA flow cytometry, and fluorescence in situ hybridization. Am J Surg Pathol 21: 52–59

549. Dal Cin P, Pauwels P, Van den Berghe H 1998 Fibrosarcoma versus cellular fibroma of the ovary. Am J Surg Pathol 22: 508–510

550. Lee H Y, Ahmed Q 2003 Fibrosarcoma of the ovary arising in a fibrothecomatous tumor with minor sex cord elements. A case report and review of the literature. Arch Pathol Lab Med 127: 81–4

551. Kruger S, Schmidt H, Kupker W et al. 2002 Fibrosarcoma associated with a benign cystic teratoma of the ovary. Gynecol Oncol 84: 150–154

552. Leung W Y, Schwartz P E, Ng H T et al. 1990 Trisomy 12 in benign fibroma and granulosa cell tumor of the ovary. Gynecol Oncol 38: 28–31

553. Ayhan A, Tuncer Z S, Hakverdi A U et al. 1996 Sertoli-Leydig cell tumor of the ovary: a clinicopathologic study of 10 cases. Eur J Gynaecol Oncol 17: 75–78

554. Young R H, Scully R E 1985 Ovarian Sertoli-Leydig cell tumors. A clinicopathological analysis of 207 cases. Am J Surg Pathol 9: 543–569

555. Zaloudek C, Norris H J 1984 Sertoli-Leydig tumors of the ovary. A clinicopathologic study of 64 intermediate and poorly differentiated neoplasms. Am J Surg Pathol 8: 405–418

556. Roth L M, Anderson M C, Govan A D T et al. 1981 Sertoli-Leydig cell tumors: a clinicopathologic study of 34 cases. Cancer 48: 187–197

557. Talerman A 1987 Ovarian Sertoli-Leydig cell tumor (androblastoma) with retiform pattern. A clinicopathologic study. Cancer 60: 3056–3064

558. Roth L M, Slayton R E, Brady L W et al. 1985 Retiform differentiation in ovarian Sertoli-Leydig cell tumors: a clinicopathologic study of six cases from a Gynecologic Oncology Group study. Cancer 55: 1093–1098

559. Young R H, Scully R E 1983 Ovarian Sertoli-Leydig cell tumors with a retiform pattern – A problem in diagnosis: a report of 25 cases. Am J Surg Pathol 7: 755–771

560. Mooney E E, Nogales F F, Bergeron C et al. 2002 Retiform Sertoli-Leydig cell tumours: clinical, morphological and immunohistochemical findings. Histopathology 41: 110–117

561. Talerman A, Haije W G 1985 Ovarian Sertoli cell tumor with retiform and heterologous elements (letter). Am J Surg Pathol 9: 459–460

562. Tiltman A, Dehaeck K, Soeters R et al. 1986 Ovarian Sertoli-Leydig cell tumour with raised serum alpha fetoprotein. A case report. Virchow's Arch [A] 410: 107–112

563. Tetu B, Ordóñez N G, Silva E G 1986 Sertoli-Leydig cell tumor of the ovary with alpha-fetoprotein production. Arch Pathol Lab Med 110: 65–68

564. Mann W J, Chumas J, Rosenwaks Z et al. 1986 Elevated serum alpha-fetoprotein associated with Sertoli-Leydig cell tumors of the ovary. Obstet Gynecol 67: 141–144

565. Young R H, Perez-Atayde A R, Scully R E 1984 Ovarian Sertoli-Leydig cell tumor with retiform and heterologous components. Report of a case with hepatocytic differentiation and elevated serum alpha-fetoprotein. Am J Surg Pathol 8: 709–718

566. Gagnon S, Tètu B, Silva E G et al. 1989 Frequency of alpha-fetoprotein production by Sertoli-Leydig cell tumors of the ovary: an immunohistochemical study of eight cases. Mod Pathol 2: 63–67

567. Young R H, Scully R E 1984 Well-differentiated ovarian Sertoli-Leydig cell tumors: a clinicopathological analysis of 23 tumors. Int J Gynecol Pathol 3: 277–290

568. Gershenson D M, Copeland L J, Kavanagh J J et al. 1987 Treatment of metastatic stromal tumors of the ovary with cisplatin, doxorubicin, and cyclophosphamide. Obstet Gynecol 70: 765–769

569. Mooney E E, Vaidya K P, Tavassoli F A 2000 Ossifying well-differentiated Sertoli-Leydig cell tumor of the ovary. Ann Diagn Pathol 4: 34–38

570. Omeroglu A, Husain A N, Siziopikou K 2002 Pathologic quiz case – A papillary ovarian tumor in a 4-year-old girl – Pathologic diagnosis: Sertoli-Leydig cell tumor, retiform type. Arch Pathol Lab Med 126: 377–378

571. Ching B, Klink A, Wang L 2004 Pathologic quiz case: a 22-year-old woman with a large right adnexal mass. Poorly differentiated Sertoli-Leydig cell tumor of the right ovary with retiform differentiation and heterologous elements (mucinous components). Arch Pathol Lab Med 128: e93–e95

572. Mooney E E, Man Y G, Bratthauer G L et al. 1999 Evidence that Leydig cells in Sertoli-Leydig cell tumors have a reactive rather than a neoplastic profile. Cancer 86: 2312–2319

573. Young R H, Prat J, Scully R E 1982 Ovarian Sertoli-Leydig cell tumors with heterologous elements. I. Gastrointestinal epithelium and carcinoid: A clinicopathologic analysis of 36 cases. Cancer 50: 2448–2456

574. Prat J, Young R H, Scully R E 1982 Ovarian Sertoli-Leydig cell tumors with heterologous elements. II. Cartilage and skeletal muscle. A clinicopathologic analysis of twelve cases. Cancer 50: 2465–2475

575. Chumas J C, Rosenwaks Z, Mann W J et al. 1984 Sertoli-Leydig cell tumor of the ovary producing alpha-fetoprotein. Int J Gynecol Pathol 3: 213–219

576. Hammad A, Jasnosz K M, Olson P R 1995 Expression of alpha-fetoprotein by ovarian Sertoli-Leydig cell tumors – Case report and review of the literature. Arch Pathol Lab Med 119: 1075–1079

577. Chadha S, Honnebier W J, Schaberg A 1987 Raised serum alpha-fetoprotein in Sertoli-Leydig cell tumor (androblastoma) of ovary: report of two cases. Int J Gynecol Pathol 6: 82–88

578. Mooney E E, Nogales F F, Tavassoli F A 1999 Hepatocytic differentiation in retiform Sertoli-Leydig cell tumors: distinguishing a heterologous element from Leydig cells. Hum Pathol 30: 611–617

579. Costa M J, Morris R J, Wilson R et al. 1992 Utility of immunohistochemistry in distinguishing ovarian Sertoli-stromal cell tumors from carcinosarcomas. Hum Pathol 23: 787–797

580. Kato N, Fukase M, Ono I et al. 2001 Sertoli-stromal cell tumor of the ovary: Immunohistochemical, ultrastructural, and genetic studies. Hum Pathol 32: 796–802

581. Gordon M D, Corless C, Renshaw A A et al. 1998 CD99, keratin, and vimentin staining of sex cord-stromal tumors, normal ovary, and testis. Mod Pathol 11: 769–773

582. Aguirre P, Scully R E, DeLellis R A 1986 Ovarian heterologous Sertoli-Leydig cell tumors with gastrointestinal-type epithelium. An immunohistochemical analysis. Arch Pathol Lab Med 110: 528–533

583. Sasano H, Okamoto M, Mason J I et al. 1989 Immunohistochemical studies of steroidogenic enzymes (aromatase, 17α-hydroxylase and cholesterol side-chain cleavage cytochromes P-450) in sex cord-stromal tumors of the ovary. Hum Pathol 20: 452–457

584. Oliva E, Alvarez T, Young R H 2005 Sertoli cell tumors of the ovary: a clinicopathologic and immunohistochemical study of 54 cases. Am J Surg Pathol 29: 143–156

585. Tavassoli F A, Norris H J 1980 Sertoli tumors of the ovary. A clinicopathologic study of 28 cases with ultrastructural observations. Cancer 46: 2281–2297

586. Ferry J A, Young R H, Engel G et al. 1994 Oxyphilic Sertoli cell tumor of the ovary: a report of three cases, two in patients with the Peutz-Jeghers syndrome. Int J Gynecol Pathol 13: 259–266

587. Zung A, Shoham Z, Open M et al. 1998 Sertoli cell tumor causing precocious puberty in a girl with Peutz-Jeghers syndrome. Gynecol Oncol 70: 421–424

588. Young R H, Scully R E 1984 Ovarian Sertoli cell tumors. A report of 10 cases. Int J Gynecol Pathol 2: 349–363

589. Watson B, Siegel C L, Ylagan L R 2003 Metastatic ovarian Sertoli-cell tumor: FNA findings with immunohistochemistry. Diagn Cytopathol 29: 283–286

590. Phadke D M, Weisenberg E, Engel G et al. 1999 Malignant Sertoli cell tumor of the ovary metastatic to the lung mimicking neuroendocrine carcinoma: report of a case. Ann Diagn Pathol 3: 213–219

591. Scully R E 2000 The prolonged gestation, birth, and early life of the sex cord tumor with annular tubules and how it joined a syndrome. Int J Surg Pathol 8: 233–238

592. Papageorgiou T, Stratakis C A 2002 Ovarian tumors associated with multiple endocrine neoplasias and related syndromes (Carney complex, Peutz-Jeghers syndrome, von Hippel-Lindau disease, Cowden's disease). Int J Gynecol Cancer 12: 337–347

593. Hemminki A 1999 The molecular basis and clinical aspects of Peutz-Jeghers syndrome. Cell Mol Life Sci 55: 735–750

594. Jenne D E, Reimann H, Nezu J et al. 1998 Peutz-Jeghers syndrome is caused by mutations in a novel serine threonine kinase. Nat Genet 18: 38–43

595. Westerman A M, Wilson J H 1999 Peutz-Jeghers syndrome: risks of a hereditary condition. Scand J Gastroenterol Suppl 230: 64–70

596. Srivatsa P J, Keeney G L, Podratz K C 1994 Disseminated cervical adenoma malignum and bilateral ovarian sex cord tumors with annular tubules associated with Peutz-Jeghers syndrome. Gynecol Oncol 53: 256–264

597. Young R H, Welch W R, Dickersin G R et al. 1982 Ovarian sex cord tumor with annular tubules. Review of 74 cases including 27 with Peutz-Jeghers syndrome and four with adenoma malignum of the cervix. Cancer 50: 1384–1402

598. Connolly D C, Katabuchi H, Cliby W A et al. 2000 Somatic mutations in the STK11/LKB1 gene are uncommon in rare gynecological tumor types associated with Peutz-Jegher's syndrome. Am J Pathol 156: 339–345

599. Lele S M, Sawh R N, Zaharopoulos P et al. 2000 Malignant ovarian sex cord tumor with annular tubules in a patient with Peutz-Jeghers syndrome: a case report. Mod Pathol 13: 466–470

600. Chen K T 1986 Female genital tract tumors in Peutz-Jeghers syndrome. Hum Pathol 17: 858–861

601. Podczaski E, Kaminski P F, Pees R C et al. 1991 Peutz-Jeghers syndrome with ovarian sex cord tumor with annular tubules and cervical adenoma malignum. Gynecol Oncol 42: 74–78

602. Mangili G, Taccagni G, Garavaglia E et al. 2004 An unusual admixture of neoplastic and metaplastic lesions of the female genital tract in the Peutz-Jeghers syndrome. Gynecol Oncol 92: 337–342

603. Young R H, Dickersin G R, Scully R E 1983 A distinctive ovarian sex cord-stromal tumor causing sexual precocity in the Peutz-Jeghers syndrome. Am J Surg Pathol 7: 233–243

604. Gloor E 1979 Ovarian sex cord tumor with annular tubules. Clinicopathologic report of two benign and one malignant cases with long follow-ups. Virchow's Arch [A] 384: 185–193

605. Anderson M C, Govan A D T, Langley F A et al. 1980 Ovarian sex cord tumours with annular tubules. Histopathology 4: 137–145

606. Hart W R, Kumar N, Crissman J D 1980 Ovarian neoplasms resembling sex cord tumors with annular tubules. Cancer 45: 2352–2363

607. Shen K, Wu P-C, Lang J-H et al. 1993 Ovarian sex cord tumor with annular tubules: a report of six cases. Gynecol Oncol 48: 180–184

608. Czernobilsky B, Gaedcke G, Dallenbach-Hellweg G 1985 Endometrioid differentiation in ovarian sex cord tumor with annular tubules accompanied by gestagenic effect. Cancer 55: 738–744

609. Gustafson M L, Lee M M, Scully R E et al. 1992 Müllerian inhibiting substance as a marker for ovarian sex-cord tumor. N Engl J Med 326: 466–471

610. Puls L E, Hamous J, Morrow M S et al. 1994 Recurrent ovarian sex cord tumor with annular tubules: tumor marker and chemotherapy experience. Gynecol Oncol 54: 396–401

611. Ahn G H, Chi J G, Lee S K 1986 Ovarian sex cord tumor with annular tubules. Cancer 57: 1066–1073

612. Matamala M F, Nogales F F, Lardelli P et al. 1987 Metastatic granulosa cell tumor with pattern of sex cord tumor with annular tubules. Int J Gynecol Pathol 6: 185–193

613. Kommoss F, Oliva E, Bhan A K et al. 1998 Inhibin expression in ovarian tumors and tumor-like lesions: an immunohistochemical study. Mod Pathol 11: 656–664

614. Kalifat R, de Brux J 1987 Ovarian sex cord tumor with annular tubules: an ultrastructural study. Int J Gynecol Pathol 6: 380–388

615. Crissman J D, Hart W R 1981 Ovarian sex cord tumor with annular tubules. An ultrastructural study of three cases. Am J Clin Pathol 75: 11–17

616. Astengo-Osuna C 1984 Ovarian sex cord-stromal tumor with annular tubules: case report with ultrastructural findings. Cancer 54: 1070–1075

617. Paraskevas M, Scully R E 1989 Hilus cell tumor of the ovary. A clinicopathological analysis of 12 Reinke crystal-positive cases and nine crystal-negative cases. Int J Gynecol Pathol 8: 299–310

618. Sternberg W H, Roth L M 1973 Ovarian stromal tumors containing Leydig cells. I. Stromal-Leydig tumor and non-neoplastic transformation of ovarian stroma to Leydig cells. Cancer 32: 940–951

619. Roth L M, Sternberg W H 1973 Ovarian stromal tumors containing Leydig cells. II. Pure Leydig cell tumors, non-hilar type. Cancer 32: 952–960

620. Baiocchi G, Manci N, Angeletti G et al. 1997 Pure Leydig cell tumour (Hilus cell) of the ovary: a rare cause of virilization after menopause. Gynecol Obstet Invest 44: 141–144

621. Ichinohasama R, Teshima S, Kishi K et al. 1989 Leydig cell tumor of the ovary associated with endometrial carcinoma and containing 17 beta-hydroxysteroid dehydrogenase. Int J Gynecol Pathol 8: 64–71

622. Regnier C, Bennet A, Malet D et al. 2002 Intraoperative testosterone assay for virilizing ovarian tumor topographic assessment: report of a Leydig cell tumor of the ovary in a premenopausal woman with an adrenal incidentaloma. J Clin Endocrinol Metab 87: 3074–3077

623. Gorgojo J J, Almodovar F, Lopez E et al. 2003 Coincidental diagnosis of an occult hilar steroid cell tumor of the ovary and a cortisol-secreting adrenal adenoma in a 49-year-old woman with severe hyperandrogenism. Fertil Steril 80: 1504–1507

624. Duun S 1994 Bilateral virilizing hilus (Leydig) cell tumors of the ovary. Acta Obstet Gynecol Scand 73: 76–77

625. Oler A, Singh M, Ural S H 1999 Bilateral ovarian stromal hyperplasia concealing a nonhilar, pure stromal-Leydig cell tumor. A case report. J Reprod Med 44: 563–566

626. Paoletti M, Pridjian G, Okagaki T et al. 1987 A stromal Leydig cell tumor of the ovary occurring in a pregnant 15-year-old girl. Ultrastructural findings. Cancer 60: 2806–2810

627. Takeuchi S, Ishihara N, Ohbayashi C et al. 1999 Stromal Leydig cell tumor of the ovary. Case report and literature review. Int J Gynecol Pathol 18: 178–182

628. Hayes M C, Scully R E 1987 Stromal luteoma of the ovary: a clinicopathological analysis of 25 cases. Int J Gynecol Pathol 6: 313–321

629. Cao Q J, Jones J G, Li M 2001 Expression of calretinin in human ovary, testis, and ovarian sex cord-stromal tumors. Int J Gynecol Pathol 20: 346–352

630. Hayes M C, Scully R E 1987 Ovarian steroid cell tumors (not otherwise specified). A clinicopathological analysis of 63 cases. Am J Surg Pathol 11: 835–845

631. Taylor H B, Norris H J 1967 Lipid cell tumors of the ovary. Cancer 20: 1953–1962

632. Lin C J, Jorge A A L, Latronico A C et al. 2000 Origin of an ovarian steroid cell tumor causing isosexual pseudoprecocious puberty demonstrated by the expression of adrenal steroidogenic enzymes and adrenocorticotropin receptor. J Clin Endocrinol Metab 85: 1211–1214

633. Powell J L, Dulaney D P, Shiro B C 2000 Androgen-secreting steroid cell tumor of the ovary. South Med J 93: 1201–1204

634. Stephen M R, Lindop G B M 1998 A renin secreting ovarian steroid cell tumour associated with secondary polycythaemia. J Clin Pathol 51: 75–77

635. Young R H, Scully R E 1987 Ovarian steroid cell tumors associated with Cushing's syndrome: a report of three cases. Int J Gynecol Pathol 6: 40–48

636. Elhadd T A, Connolly V, Cruickshank D et al. 1996 An ovarian lipid cell tumour causing virilization and Cushing's syndrome. Clin Endocrinol (Oxf) 44: 723–725

637. Roth L M, Davis M M, Sutton G P 1996 Steroid cell tumor of the broad ligament arising in an accessory ovary. Arch Pathol Lab Med 120: 405–409

638. Dumic M, Simunic V, Ilic-Forko J et al. 2001 Extraovarian steroid cell tumor "not otherwise specified" as a rare cause of virilization in twelve-year-old girl. Horm Res 55: 254–257

639. Liu A X, Sun J, Shao W Q et al. 2005 Steroid cell tumors, not otherwise specified (NOS), in an accessory ovary: a case report and literature review. Gynecol Oncol 97: 260–262

640. Deavers M T, Malpica A, Ordonez N G et al. 2003 Ovarian steroid cell tumors: an immunohistochemical study including a comparison of calretinin with inhibin. Int J Gynecol Pathol 22: 162–167

641. Stewart C J, Nandini C L, Richmond J A 2000 Value of A103 (melan-A) immunostaining in the differential diagnosis of ovarian sex cord stromal tumours. J Clin Pathol 53: 206–211

642. Seidman J D, Abbondanzo S L, Bratthauer G L 1995 Lipid cell (steroid cell) tumor of the ovary: immunophenotype with analysis of potential pitfall due to endogenous biotin-like activity. Int J Gynecol Pathol 14: 331–338

643. Jaworski R C, Fryatt J J, Turner T B et al. 1986 Gynandroblastoma of the ovary. Pathology 18: 348–351

644. Anderson M C, Rees D A 1975 Gynandroblastoma of the ovary. Br J Obstet Gynaecol 82: 68–73

645. Chalvardjian A, Derzko C 1982 Gynandroblastoma: its ultrastructure. Cancer 31: 664–670

646. Guo L, Liu T 1995 Gynandroblastoma of the ovary: review of the literature and report of a case. Int J Surg Pathol 3: 137–140

647. Fukunaga M, Endo Y, Ushigome S 1997 Gynandroblastoma of the ovary: A case report with an immunohistochemical and ultrastructural study. Virchow's Arch 430: 77–82

648. Yamada Y, Ohmi K, Tsunematu R et al. 1991 Gynandroblastoma of the ovary having a typical morphological appearance: a case study. Jpn J Clin Oncol 21: 62–68

649. Seidman J D 1996 Unclassified ovarian gonadal stromal tumors – A clinicopathologic study of 32 cases. Am J Surg Pathol 20: 699–706

650. McCluggage W G, Sloan J M, Murnaghan M et al. 1996 Gynandroblastoma of ovary with juvenile granulosa cell component and heterologous intestinal type glands. Histopathology 29: 253–257

651. Broshears J R, Roth L M 1997 Gynandroblastoma with elements resembling juvenile granulosa cell tumor. Int J Gynecol Pathol 16: 387–391

652. Vang R, Herrmann M E, Tavassoli F A 2004 Comparative immunohistochemical analysis of granulosa and sertoli components in ovarian sex cord-stromal tumors with mixed differentiation: potential implications for derivation of sertoli differentiation in ovarian tumors. Int J Gynecol Pathol 23: 151–161

653. Chalvardjian A, Scully R E 1973 Sclerosing stromal tumors of the ovary. Cancer 31: 664–670

654. Tiltman A J 1985 Sclerosing stromal tumor of the ovary. Int J Gynecol Pathol 4: 362–369

655. Gee D C, Russell P 1979 Sclerosing stromal tumours of the ovary. Histopathology 3: 367–376

656. Lam R M, Geittmann P 1988 Sclerosing stromal tumor of the ovary. A light, electron microscopic and enzyme histochemical study. Int J Gynecol Pathol 7: 280–290

657. Kawauchi S, Tsuji T, Kaku T et al. 1998 Sclerosing stromal tumor of the ovary. A clinicopathologic, immunohistochemical, ultrastructural, and cytogenetic analysis with special reference to its vasculature. Am J Surg Pathol 22: 83–92

658. Cashell A W, Cohen M L 1991 Masculinizing sclerosing stromal tumor of the ovary during pregnancy. Gynecol Oncol 43: 281–285

659. Ismail S M, Walker S M 1990 Bilateral virilizing sclerosing stromal tumours of the ovary in a pregnant woman with Gorlin's syndrome: implications for pathogenesis of ovarian stromal neoplasms. Histopathology 17: 159–163

660. Bildirici K, Yalcin O T, Ozalp S S et al. 2004 Sclerosing stromal tumor of the ovary associated with Meigs' syndrome: a case report. Eur J Gynaecol Oncol 25: 528–529

661. Gurbuz A, Karateke A, Kabaca C et al. 2004 Sclerosing stromal cell tumor of the ovary in pregnancy: a case report. Eur J Gynaecol Oncol 25: 534–535

662. Calabrese M, Zandrino F, Giasotto V et al. 2004 Sclerosing stromal tumor of the ovary in pregnancy: clinical, ultrasonography, and magnetic resonance imaging findings. Acta Radiol 45: 189–192

663. Duska L R, Flynn C, Goodman A 1998 Masculinizing sclerosing stromal cell tumor in pregnancy: report of a case and review of the literature. Eur J Gynaecol Oncol 19: 441–443

664. Kostopoulou E, Moulla A, Giakoustidis D et al. 2004 Sclerosing stromal tumors of the ovary: a clinicopathologic, immunohistochemical and cytogenetic analysis of three cases. Eur J Gynaecol Oncol 25: 257–260

665. Saitoh A, Tsutsumi Y, Osamura R Y et al. 1989 Sclerosing stromal tumor of the ovary. Immunohistochemical and electron microscopic demonstration of smooth-muscle differentiation. Arch Pathol Lab Med 113: 372–376

666. Lifschitz-Mercer B, Open M, Kushnir I et al. 1995 Hyaline globules and progesterone receptors in an ovarian sclerosing stromal tumour. Histopathology 27: 195–197

667. Simpson J L, Michael H, Roth L M 1998 Unclassified sex cord-stromal tumors of the ovary – A report of eight cases. Arch Pathol Lab Med 122: 52–55

668. Matamala M F, Nogales F F, Aneiros J et al. 1988 Leiomyomas of the ovary. Int J Gynecol Pathol 7: 190–196

669. Prayson R A, Hart W R 1992 Primary smooth-muscle tumors of the ovary: A clinicopathologic study of four leiomyomas and two mitotically active leiomyomas. Arch Pathol Lab Med 116: 1068–1071

670. Doss B J, Wanek S M, Jacques S M et al. 1999 Ovarian leiomyomas: clinicopathologic features in fifteen cases. Int J Gynecol Pathol 18: 63–68

671. Lerwill M F, Sung R, Oliva E et al. 2004 Smooth muscle tumors of the ovary: a clinicopathologic study of 54 cases emphasizing prognostic criteria, histologic variants, and differential diagnosis. Am J Surg Pathol 28: 1436–1451

672. Mira J L 1991 Lipoleiomyoma of the ovary: report of a case and review of the English literature. Int J Gynecol Pathol 10: 198–202

673. Dodd G D, Lancaster K T, Moulton J S 1989 Ovarian lipoleiomyoma: a fat-containing mass in the female pelvis. Am J Roentgenol 153: 1007–1008

674. Alvarez M, Cerezo L 1986 Ovarian cavernous hemangioma. Arch Pathol Lab Med 110: 77–78

675. Gucer F, Ozyilmaz F, Balkanli-Kaplan P et al. 2004 Ovarian hemangioma presenting with hyperandrogenism and endometrial cancer: a case report. Gynecol Oncol 94: 821–824

676. Eichhorn J H, Scully R E 1991 Ovarian myxoma: clinicopathologic and immunocytologic analysis of five cases and review of the literature. Int J Gynecol Pathol 10: 156–169

677. Tetu B, Bonenfant J L 1991 Ovarian myxoma. A study of two cases with long-term follow-up. Am J Clin Pathol 95: 340–346

678. Costa M J, Morris R, DeRose P B et al. 1993 Histologic and immunohistochemical evidence for considering ovarian myxoma as a variant of the thecoma-fibroma group of ovarian stromal tumors. Arch Pathol Lab Med 117: 802–808

679. Shakfeh S M, Woodruff J D 1987 Primary ovarian sarcomas: report of 46 cases and review of the literature. Obstet Gynecol Surv 42: 331–349

680. Nielsen G P, Oliva E, Young R H et al. 1998 Primary ovarian rhabdomyosarcoma: a report of 13 cases. Int J Gynecol Pathol 17: 113–119

681. Talerman A, Auerback W M, Van Meurs A J 1981 Primary chondrosarcoma of the ovary. Histopathology 5: 319–324

682. Hines J F, Compton D M, Stacy C C et al. 1990 Pure primary osteosarcoma of the ovary presenting as an extensively calcified adnexal mass: a case report and review of the literature. Gynecol Oncol 39: 259–263

683. Sakata H, Hirahara T, Ryu A et al. 1991 Primary osteosarcoma of the ovary. A case report. Acta Pathol Jpn 41: 311–317

684. Stone G C, Bell D A, Fuller A et al. 1986 Malignant schwannoma of the ovary. Report of a case. Cancer 58: 1575–1582

685. Nucci M R, Krausz T, Lifschitz-Mercer B et al. 1998 Angiosarcoma of the ovary – Clinicopathologic and immunohistochemical analysis of four cases with a broad morphologic spectrum. Am J Surg Pathol 22: 620–630

686. Nielsen G P, Young R H, Prat J et al. 1997 Primary angiosarcoma of the ovary: a report of seven cases and review of the literature. Int J Gynecol Pathol 16: 378–382

687. Osborne B M, Robboy S J 1983 Lymphomas or leukemia presenting as ovarian tumors: an analysis of 42 cases. Cancer 52: 1933–1943

688. Monterroso V, Jaffe E S, Merino M J et al. 1993 Malignant lymphomas of the ovary. A clinicopathologic analysis of 39 cases. Am J Surg Pathol 17: 154–170

689. Dimopoulos M A, Daliani D, Pugh W et al. 1997 Primary ovarian non-Hodgkin's lymphoma: outcome after treatment with combination chemotherapy. Gynecol Oncol 64: 446–450

690. Fox H, Langley F A, Govan A D et al. 1988 Malignant lymphoma presenting as an ovarian tumour: a clinicopathological analysis of 34 cases. Br J Obstet Gynaecol 95: 386–390

691. Paladugu R R, Bearman R M, Rappaport H 1980 Malignant lymphoma with primary manifestation in the gonad: a clinicopathologic study of 38 patients. Cancer 45: 561–571

692. Vang R, Medeiros L J, Warnke R et al. 2001 Ovarian non-Hodgkin's lymphoma: a clinicopathologic study of eight primary cases. Mod Pathol 14: 1093–1099

693. Vang R, Medeiros L J, Fuller G N et al. 2001 Non-Hodgkin's lymphoma involving the gynecologic tract: a review of 88 cases. Adv Anat Pathol 8: 200–217

694. Chorlton I, Norris H J, King F M 1974 Malignant reticuloendothelial disease involving the ovary as a primary manifestation: a series of 19 lymphomas and 1 granulocytic sarcoma. Cancer 34: 397–407

695. Oliva E, Ferry J A, Young R H et al. 1997 Granulocytic sarcoma of the female genital tract: A clinicopathologic study of 11 cases. Am J Surg Pathol 21: 1156–116.

696. Pressler H, Horny H P, Wolf A et al. 1992 Isolated granulocytic sarcoma of the ovary: histologic, electron microscopic, and immunohistochemical findings. Int J Gynecol Pathol 11: 68–74

697. Kurman R J, Norris H J 1977 Malignant germ cell tumors of the ovary. Hum Pathol 8: 551–564

698. Asadourian L A, Taylor H B 1969 Dysgerminoma. An analysis of 105 cases. Obstet Gynecol 33: 370–379

699. DePalo G, Pilotti S, Kenda R et al. 1982 Natural history of dysgerminoma. Am J Obstet Gynecol 143: 799–807

700. Bjorkholm E, Lundell M, Gyftodimos A et al. 1990 Dysgerminoma. The Radiumhemmet Series 1927–1984. Cancer 65: 38–44

701. Buskirk S J, Schray M F, Podratz K C et al. 1987 Ovarian dysgerminoma: A retrospective analysis of results of treatment, sites of treatment failure, and radiosensitivity. Mayo Clin Proc 62:1149–1157

702. Gordon A, Lipton D, Woodruff J D 1981 Dysgerminoma: a review of 158 cases from the Emil Novak Ovarian Tumor Registry. Obstet Gynecol 58: 497–504

703. Susnerwala S S, Pande S C, Shrivastava S K et al. 1991 Dysgerminoma of the ovary: review of 27 cases. J Surg Oncol 46: 43–47

704. Talerman A, Huyzinga W T, Kuipers T 1973 Dysgerminoma: clinicopathologic study of 22 cases. Obstet Gynecol 41: 137–147

705. Casey A C, Bhodauria S, Shapter A et al. 1996 Dysgerminoma: the role of conservative surgery. Gynecol Oncol 63: 352–357

706. Karlen J R, Akbari A, Cook W A 1979 Dysgerminoma associated with pregnancy. Obstet Gynecol 53: 330–335

707. Buller R E, Darrow V, Manetta A et al. 1992 Conservative surgical management of dysgerminoma concomitant wiht pregnancy. Obstet Gynecol 79: 887–890

708. Fleischhacker D S, Young R H 1994 Dysgerminoma of the ovary associated with hypercalcemia. Gynecol Oncol 52: 87–90

709. Inoue H, Kikuchi Y, Hirata J et al. 1995 Dysgerminoma of the ovary with hypercalcemia associated with elevated parathyroid hormone-related protein. Jpn J Clin Oncol 25: 113–117

710. Okoye B O, Harmston C, Buick R G 2001 Dysgerminoma associated with hypercalcemia: A case report. J Pediatr Surg 36: E10

711. Evans K N, Taylor H, Zehnder D et al. 2004 Increased expression of 25-hydroxyvitamin D-1alpha-hydroxylase in dysgerminomas: a novel form of humoral hypercalcemia of malignancy. Am J Pathol 165: 807–813

712. Thomas G M, Dembo A J, Hacker N F et al. 1987 Current therapy for dysgerminoma of the ovary. Obstet Gynecol 70: 268–275

713. Schwartz P E, Morris J M 1988 Serum lactic dehydrogenase: a tumor marker for dysgerminoma. Obstet Gynecol 72: 511–515

714. Hamm W, Bolte A 1995 Treatment of pure dysgerminomas of the ovary with preservation of fertility. Onkologie 18: 126–129

715. Kapp D S, Kohorn E I, Merino M J et al. 1985 Pure dysgerminoma of the ovary with elevated serum human chorionic gonadotropin: Diagnostic and therapeutic considerations. Gynecol Oncol 20: 234–244

716. Zaloudek C J, Tavassoli F A, Norris H J 1981 Dysgerminoma with syncytiotrophoblastic giant cells: a histologically and clinically distinctive subtype of dysgerminoma. Am J Surg Pathol 5: 361–367

717. Parkash V, Carcangiu ML 1995 Transformation of ovarian dysgerminoma to yolk sac tumor: evidence for a histogenetic continuum. Mod Pathol 8: 881–887

718. Burkons D M, Hart W R 1978 Ovarian germinomas (dysgerminomas). Obstet Gynecol 51: 221–224

719. Gallion H H, van Nagell J R Jr, Donaldson E S et al. 1988 Ovarian dysgerminoma: report of seven cases and review of the literature. Am J Obstet Gynecol 158: 591–595

720. LaPolla J P, Benda J, Vigliotti A P et al. 1987 Dysgerminoma of the ovary. Obstet Gynecol 69: 859–864

721. Ayhan A, Bildirici I, Gunalp S et al. 2000 Pure dysgerminoma of the ovary: a review of 45 well staged cases. Eur J Gynaecol Oncol 21: 98–101

722. Santoni R, Cionini L, D'Elia F et al. 1987 Dysgerminoma of the ovary: A report on 29 patients. Clin Radiol 38: 203–206

723. Zaghloul M S, Khattab T Y 1992 Dysgerminoma of the ovary: Good prognosis even in advanced stages. Int J Radiat Oncol Biol Phys 24: 161–165

724. Low J J H, Perrin L C, Crandon A J et al. 2000 Conservative surgery to preserve ovarian function in patients with malignant ovarian germ cell tumors – A review of 74 cases. Cancer 89: 391–398.

725. Williams S D, Blessing J A, Hatch K D et al. 1991 Chemotherapy of advanced dysgerminoma: trials of the Gynecologic Oncology Group. J Clin Oncol 9: 1950–1955

726. Mitchell M F, Gershenson D M, Soeters R P et al. 1991 The long-term effects of radiation therapy on patients with ovarian dysgerminoma. Cancer 67: 1084–1090

727. Culine S, Lhomme C, Kattan J et al. 1995 Cisplatin-based chemotherapy in dysgerminoma of the ovary: thirteen-year experience at the Institut Gustave Roussy. Gynecol Oncol 58: 344–348

728. Williams S D, Kauderer J, Burnett A F et al. 2004 Adjuvant therapy of completely resected dysgerminoma with carboplatin and etoposide: a trial of the Gynecologic Oncology Group. Gynecol Oncol 95: 496–499

729. Brewer M, Gershenson D M, Herzog C E et al. 1999 Outcome and reproductive function after chemotherapy for ovarian dysgerminoma. J Clin Oncol 17: 2670–2675

730. Freel J H, Cassir J F, Pierve V K et al. 1979 Dysgerminoma of the ovary. Cancer 43: 798–805

731. Segelov E, Campbell J, Ng M et al. 1994 Cisplatin-based chemotherapy for ovarian germ cell malignancies: The Australian experience. J Clin Oncol 12: 378–384

732. Morimura Y, Nishiyama H, Yanagida K et al. 1998 Dysgerminoma with syncytiotrophoblastic giant cells arising from 46,xx pure gonadal dysgenesis. Obstet Gynecol 92: 654–656

733. Baker P, Oliva E 2005 Immunohistochemistry as a tool in the differential diagnosis of ovarian tumors: an update. Int J Gynecol Pathol 24: 39–55

734. Cheng L, Thomas A, Roth L M et al. 2004 OCT4: A novel biomarker for dysgerminoma of the ovary. Am J Surg Pathol 28: 1341–1346

735. Lifschitz-Mercer B, Walt H, Kushnir I et al. 1995 Differentiation potential of ovarian dysgerminoma: an immunohistochemical study of 15 cases. Hum Pathol 26: 62–66

736. Mullin T J, Lankerani M R 1986 Ovarian dysgerminoma: immunocytochemical localization of human chorionic gonadotropin in the germinoma cell cytoplasm. Obstet Gynecol 68: 80S–83S

737. Dietl J, Horny H-P, Ruck P et al. 1993 Dysgerminoma of the ovary: An immunohistochemical study of tumor-infiltrating lymphoreticular cells and tumor cells. Cancer 71: 2562–2568

738. Gonzalez-Crussi F 1979 The human yolk sac and yolk sac (endodermal sinus) tumors. A review. Perspect Pediatr Pathol 5: 179–215

739. Teilum G 1959 Endodermal sinus tumors of the ovary and testis: comparative morphogenesis of the so-called mesonephroma ovarii (Schiller) and extraembryonic (yolk sac-allantoic) structures of the rat's placenta. Cancer 12: 1092–1105

740. Nogales F F 1993 Embryologic clues to human yolk sac tumors: a review. Int J Gynecol Pathol 12: 101–107

741. Sasaki H, Furusato M, Teshima S et al. 1994 Prognostic significance of histopathological subtypes in stage I pure yolk sac tumour of the ovary. Br J Cancer 69: 529–536

742. Gershenson D M, del Junco G, Herson J et al. 1983 Endodermal sinus tumor of the ovary: the M.D. Anderson experience. Obstet Gynecol 61: 194–202

743. Kawai M, Kano T, Furuhashi Y et al. 1991 Prognostic factors in yolk sac tumors of the ovary. A clinicopathologic analysis of 29 cases. Cancer 67: 184–192

744. Kurman R J, Norris H J 1976 Endodermal sinus tumor of the ovary. A clinical and pathologic analysis of 71 cases. Cancer 38: 2404–2419

745. Langley F A, Govan A D T, Anderson M C et al. 1981 Yolk sac and allied tumours of the ovary. Histopathology 5: 389–401

746. Morris H H, La Vecchia C, Draper G J 1985 Endodermal sinus tumor and embryonal carcinoma of the ovary in children. Gynecol Oncol 21: 7–17

747. Kinoshita K 1990 A 62 year old woman with endodermal sinus tumor of the ovary. Am J Obstet Gynecol 162: 760–761

748. Oh C, Kendler A, Hernandez E 2001 Ovarian endodermal sinus tumor in a postmenopausal woman. Gynecol Oncol 82: 392–394

749. Kawai M, Furuhashi Y, Kano T et al. 1990 Alpha-fetoprotein in malignant germ cell tumors of the ovary. Gynecol Oncol 39: 160–166

750. Pliskow S 1993 Endodermal sinus tumor of the ovary: review of 10 cases. South Med J 86: 187–189

751. Jimerson G K, Woodruff J D 1977 Ovarian extraembryonal teratoma. I. Endodermal sinus tumor. Am J Obstet Gynecol 127: 73–79

752. Huntington R W J, Bullock W K 1970 Yolk sac tumors of the ovary. Cancer 25: 1357–1367

753. Ungerleider R S, Donaldson S S, Warnke R A et al. 1978 Endodermal sinus tumor: the Stanford experience and the first reported case arising in the vulva. Cancer 41: 1627–1634

754. Gershenson D M, Copeland L J, Kavanagh J J et al. 1985 Treatment of malignant nondysgerminomatous germcell tumors of the ovary with vincristine, dactinomycin, and cyclophosphamide. Cancer 56: 2756–2761

755. Slayton R E, Hreschyshyn M M, Silverberg S G et al. 1978 Treatment of malignant ovarian germ cell tumors: response to vincristine, dactinomycin, and cyclophosphamide (preliminary report). Cancer 42: 390–398

756. Gershenson D M, Kavanagh J J, Copeland L J et al. 1986 Treatment of malignant nondysgerminomatous germ cell tumors of the ovary by vinblastine, bleomycin, and cisplatin. Cancer 57: 1731–1737

757. Sessa C, Bonazzi C, Landoni F et al. 1987 Cisplatin, vinblastine, and bleomycin combination chemotherapy in endodermal sinus tumor of the ovary. Obstet Gynecol 70: 220–224

758. Williams S D, Blessing J A, Liao S-Y et al. 1994 Adjuvant therapy of ovarian germ cell tumors with cisplatin, etoposide, and bleomycin: a trial of the Gynecologic Oncology Group. J Clin Oncol 12: 701–706

759. Peccatori F, Bonazzi C, Chiari S et al. 1995 Surgical management of malignant ovarian germ-cell tumors: 10 years' experience of 129 patients. Obstet Gynecol 86: 367–372

760. Zalel Y, Piura B, Elchalal U et al. 1996 Diagnosis and management of malignant germ cell ovarian tumors in young females. Int J Gynaecol Obstet 55: 1–10

761. Nawa A, Obata N, Kikkawa F et al. 2001 Prognostic factors of patients with yolk sac tumors of the ovary. Am J Obstet Gynecol 184: 1182–1188

762. Tewari K, Cappuccini F, DiSaia P J et al. 2000 Malignant germ cell tumors of the ovary. Obstet Gynecol 95: 128–133

763. Williams S D, Blessing J A, DiSaia P J et al. 1994 Second-look laparotomy in ovarian germ cell tumors: the gynecologic oncology group experience. Gynecol Oncol 52: 287–291

764. Curtin J P, Rubin S C, Hoskins W J et al. 1989 Second-look laparotomy in endodermal sinus tumor: a report of two patients with normal levels of alpha-fetoprotein and residual tumor at reexploration. Obstet Gynecol 74: 683–685

765. Nogales F F, Matilla A, Nogales-Ortiz F et al. 1978 Yolk sac tumors with pure and mixed polyvesicular vitelline patterns. Hum Pathol 9: 553–566

766. Nakashima N, Fukatsu T, Nagasaka T et al. 1987 The frequency and histology of hepatic tissue in germ cell tumors. Am J Surg Pathol 11: 682–692

767. Devouassoux-Shisheboran M, Schammel D P, Tavassoli F A 1999 Ovarian hepatoid yolk sac tumours: morphological, immunohistochemical and ultrastructural features. Histopathology 34: 462–469

768. Ulbright T M, Roth L M, Brodhecker C A 1986 Yolk sac differentiation in germ cell tumors. A morphologic study of 50 cases with emphasis on hepatic, enteric, and parietal yolk sac features. Am J Surg Pathol 10: 151–164

769. Clement P B, Young R H, Scully R E 1987 Endometrioid-like variant of ovarian yolk sac tumor. A clinicopathological analysis of eight cases. Am J Surg Pathol 11: 767–778

770. Kommoss F, Schmidt M, Merz E et al. 1999 Ovarian endometrioid-like yolk sac tumor treated by surgery alone, with recurrence at 12 years. Gynecol Oncol 72: 421–424

771. Cohen M B, Mulchahey K M, Molnar J J 1986 Ovarian endodermal sinus tumor with intestinal differentiation. Cancer 57: 1580–1583

772. Kim C R, Hsiu J G, Given F T 1989 Intestinal variant of ovarian endodermal sinus tumor. Gynecol Oncol 33: 379–381

773. Mazur M T, Talbot W H Jr, Talerman A 1988 Endodermal sinus tumor and mucinous cystadenofibroma of the ovary. Occurrence in an 82-year old woman. Cancer 62: 2011–2015

774. Nogales F F, Buritica C, Regauer S et al. 2005 Mucinous carcinoid as an unusual manifestation of endodermal differentiation in ovarian yolk sac tumors. Am J Surg Pathol 29: 1247–1251

775. Michael H, Ulbright T M, Brodhecker C A 1989 The pluripotential nature of the mesenchyme-like component of yolk sac tumor. Arch Pathol Lab Med 113: 1115–1119

776. Harms D, Janig U 1986 Germ cell tumours of childhood. Report of 170 cases including 59 pure and partial yolk-sac tumours. Virchow's Arch [A] 409: 223–239

777. Beilby J O W, Horne C H W, Milne G D et al. 1979 Alpha-fetoprotein, alpha-1-antitrypsin and transferrin in gonadal yolk sac tumours. J Clin Pathol 32: 455–461

778. Manivel J C, Jessurun J, Wick M R et al. 1987 Placental alkaline phosphatase immunoreactivity in testicular germ cell neoplasms. Am J Surg Pathol 11: 21–29

779. Bailey D, Marks A, Stratis M et al. 1991 Immunohistochemical staining of germ cell tumors and intratubular malignant germ cells of the testis using antibody to placental alkaline phosphatase and a monoclonal anti-seminoma antibody. Mod Pathol 4: 167–171

780. Kurman R J, Norris H J 1976 Embryonal carcinoma of the ovary: a clinicopathologic entity distinct from endodermal sinus tumor resembling embryonal carcinoma of the adult testis. Cancer 38: 2420–2433

781. Kammerer-Doak D, Baurick K, Black W et al. 1996 Endodermal sinus tumor and embryonal carcinoma of the ovary in a 53-year-old woman. Gynecol Oncol 63: 133–137

782. Williams S D, Blessing J A, Moore D H et al. 1989 Cisplatin, vinblastine, and bleomycin in advanced and recurrent ovarian germ-cell tumors. A trial of the Gynecologic Oncology Group. Ann Intern Med 111: 22–27

783. King M E, Hubbell M J, Talerman A 1991 Mixed germ cell tumor of the ovary with a prominent polyembryoma component. Int J Gynecol Pathol 10: 88–95

784. Chapman D C, Grover R, Schwartz P E 1994 Conservative management of an ovarian polyembryoma. Obstet Gynecol 83 Suppl.: 879–882

785. Jondle D M, Shahin M S, Sorosky J et al. 2002 Ovarian mixed germ cell tumor with predominance of polyembryoma: a case report with literature review. Int J Gynecol Pathol 21: 78–81

786. Nishida T, Oda T, Sugiyama T et al. 1998 Ovarian mixed germ cell tumor comprising polyembryoma and choriocarcinoma. Eur J Obstet Gynecol Reprod Biol 78: 95–97

787. Takemori M, Nishimura R, Yamasaki M et al. 1998 Ovarian mixed germ cell tumor composed of polyembryoma and immature teratoma. Gynecol Oncol 69: 260–263

788. Axe S R, Klein V R, Woodruff J D 1985 Choriocarcinoma of the ovary. Obstet Gynecol 66: 111–114

789. Jacobs A J, Newland J R, Green R K 1982 Pure choriocarcinoma of the ovary. Obstet Gynecol Surv 37: 603–609

790. Corakci A, Ozeren S, Ozkan S et al. 2005 Pure nongestational choriocarcinoma of ovary. Arch Gynecol Obstet 271: 176–177

791. Tsujioka H, Hamada H, Miyakawa T et al. 2003 A pure nongestational choriocarcinoma of the ovary diagnosed with DNA polymorphism analysis. Gynecol Oncol 89: 540–542

792. Goswami D, Sharma K, Zutshi V et al. 2001 Nongestational pure ovarian choriocarcinoma with contralateral teratoma. Gynecol Oncol 80: 262–266

793. Wheeler C A, Davis S, Degefu S et al. 1990 Ovarian choriocarcinoma: a difficult diagnosis of an unusual tumor and a review of the hook effect. Obstet Gynecol 75: 547–549

794. Vance R P, Geisinger K R 1985 Pure nongestational choriocarcinoma of the ovary. Report of a case. Cancer 56: 2321–2325

795. Grover V, Grover R K, Usha R et al. 1990 Primary pure choriocarcinoma of the ovary. Gynecol Obstet Invest 30: 61–63

796. Fisher R A, Newlands E S, Jeffreys A J et al. 1992 Gestational and nongestational trophoblastic tumors distinguished by DNA analysis. Cancer 69: 839–845

797. Shigematsu T, Kamura T, Arima T et al. 2000 DNA polymorphism analysis of a pure non-gestational choriocarcinoma of the ovary: case report. Eur J Gynaecol Oncol 21: 153–154

798. Dahl N, Gustavson K H, Rune C et al. 1990 Benign ovarian teratomas. An analysis of their cellular origin. Cancer Genet Cytogenet 46: 115–123

799. Linder D, McCaw B K, Hecht F 1975 Parthenogenetic origin of benign ovarian teratoma. N Engl J Med 292: 63–66

800. Surti U, Hoffner L, Chakravarti A et al. 1990 Genetics and biology of human ovarian teratomas. I. Cytogenetic analysis and mechanism of origin. Am J Hum Genet 47: 635–643

801. Vortmeyer A O, Devouassoux-Shisheboran M, Li G et al. 1999 Microdissection-based analysis of mature ovarian teratoma. Am J Pathol 154: 987–991

802. Gordon A, Rosenshein N, Parmley T et al. 1980 Benign cystic teratomas in postmenopausal women. Am J Obstet Gynecol 138: 1120–1123

803. Caruso P A, Marsh M R, Minkowitz S et al. 1971 An intense clinicopathologic study of 305 teratomas of the ovary. Cancer 27: 343–348

804. Wei F, Jiang Z, Yan C 2001 Analysis of 20 mature ovarian cystic teratoma cases in postmenopausal women. Chin Med J (Engl)114: 137–138

805. Ayhan A, Bukulmez O, Genc C et al. 2000 Mature cystic teratomas of the ovary: case series from one institution over 34 years. Eur J Obstet Gynecol Reprod Biol 88: 153–157

806. Comerci J T Jr, Licciardi F, Bergh P A et al. 1994 Mature cystic teratoma: a clinicopathologic evaluation of 517 cases and review of the literature. Obstet Gynecol 84: 22–28

807. Lin P, Falcone T, Tulandi T 1995 Excision of ovarian dermoid cyst by laparoscopy and by laparotomy. Am J Obstet Gynecol 173: 769–771

808. Albini S M, Benadiva C A, Haverly K et al. 1994 Management of benign ovarian cystic teratomas: laparoscopy compared with laparotomy. J Am Assoc Gynecol Laparosc 1: 219–222

809. Mecke H, Savvas V 2001 Laparoscopic surgery of dermoid cysts – intraoperative spillage and complications. Eur J Obstet Gynecol Reprod Biol 96: 80–84

810. Templeman C L, Fallat M E, Lam A M et al. 2000 Managing mature cystic teratomas of the ovary. Obstet Gynecol Surv 55: 738–745

811. Fanning J, Bates J 1986 Mature solid teratoma associated with gliomatosis peritonei. Am J Obstet Gynecol 155: 661–662

812. Robboy S J, Scully R E 1970 Ovarian teratoma with glial implants on the peritoneum. An analysis of 12 cases. Hum Pathol 1: 643–653

813. Steeper T A, Mukai K 1984 Solid ovarian teratomas: an immunocytochemical study of thirteen cases with clinicopathologic correlation. Pathol Annu 19: 81–92

814. Bosman F T, Louwerens J W K 1981 APUD cells in teratomas. Am J Pathol 104: 174–180

815. Nogales F F, Vergara E, Medina M T 1995 Prostate in ovarian mature cystic teratoma. Histopathology 26: 373–375

816. Vadmal M, Hajdu S I 1996 Prostatic tissue in benign cystic ovarian teratomas. Hum Pathol 27: 428–429

817. McLachlin C M, Srigley J R 1992 Prostatic tissue in mature cystic teratomas of the ovary. Am J Surg Pathol 16: 780–784

818. Halabi M, Oliva E, Mazal P R et al. 2002 Prostatic tissue in mature cystic teratomas of the ovary: a report of four cases, including one with features of prostatic adenocarcinoma, and cytogenetic studies. Int J Gynecol Pathol 21: 261–267

819. Bonazzi C, Peccatori F, Colombo N et al. 1994 Pure ovarian immature teratoma, a unique and curable disease: 10 years' experience of 32 prospectively treated patients. Obstet Gynecol 84:98–604

820. Nielsen S N, Gaffey T A, Malkasian G D Jr 1986 Immature ovarian teratoma: a review of 14 cases. Mayo Clin Proc 61: 110–115

821. Nogales F F, Favera B E, Major F J et al. 1976 Immature teratoma of the ovary with a neural component ("solid" teratoma). A clinicopathologic study of 20 cases. Hum Pathol 7: 625–642

822. Norris H J, Zirkin H J, Benson W L 1976 Immature (malignant) teratoma of the ovary. A clinical and pathologic study of 58 cases. Cancer 37: 2359–2372

823. Harms D, Janig U 1985 Immature teratomas of childhood. Report of 21 cases. Pathol Res Pract 179: 388–400

824. Koulos J P, Hoffman J S, Steinhoff M M 1989 Immature teratoma of the ovary. Gynecol Oncol 34: 46–49

825. Sen D K, Sivanesaratnam V, Sivanathan R et al. 1988 Immature teratoma of the ovary. Gynecol Oncol 30: 321–328

826. Doss B J, Jacques S M, Qureshi F et al. 1999 Immature teratomas of the genital tract in older women. Gynecol Oncol 73: 433–438

827. Gershenson D M, del Junco G, Silva E G et al. 1986 Immature teratoma of the ovary. Obstet Gynecol 68: 624–629

828. Kawai M, Kano T, Furuhashi Y et al. 1991 Immature teratoma of the ovary. Gynecol Oncol 40: 133–137

829. Perrone T, Steeper T A, Dehner L P 1987 Alpha-fetoprotein localization in pure ovarian teratoma. An immunohistochemical study of 12 cases. Am J Clin Pathol 88: 713–717

830. Yanai-Inbar I, Scully R E 1987 Relation of ovarian dermoid cysts and immature teratomas: an analysis of 350 cases of immature teratoma and 10 cases of dermoid cyst with microscopic foci of immature tissue. Int J Gynecol Pathol 6: 203–212

831. Li H, Hong W, Zhang R et al. 2002 Retrospective analysis of 67 consecutive cases of pure ovarian immature teratoma. Chin Med J (Engl) 115: 1496–1500

832. Beiner M E, Gotlieb W H, Korach Y et al. 2004 Cystectomy for immature teratoma of the ovary. Gynecol Oncol 93(2): 381–384

833. Vergote I B, Abeler V M, Kjrstad K E et al. 1990 Management of malignant ovarian immature teratoma. Role of adriamycin. Cancer 66: 882–886

834. Micha J P, Kucera P R, Berman M L et al. 1985 Malignant ovarian germ cell tumors: a review of thirty-six cases. Am J Obstet Gynecol 152: 842–846

835. Heifetz S A, Cushing B, Giller R et al. 1998 Immature teratomas in children: Pathologic considerations – A report from the combined Pediatric Oncology Group Children's Cancer Group. Am J Surg Pathol 22: 1115–1124

836. Marina N M, Cushing B, Giller R et al. 1999 Complete surgical excision is effective treatment for children with immature teratomas with or without malignant elements: A Pediatric Oncology Group/Children's Cancer Group Intergroup Study. J Clin Oncol 17: 2137–2143

837. Perrone T, Steiner M, Dehner L P 1986 Nodal gliomatosis and alpha-fetoprotein production. Two unusual facets of grade I ovarian teratoma. Arch Pathol Lab Med 110: 975–977

838. Harms D, Janig U, Göbel U 1989 Gliomatosis peritonei in childhood and adolescence. Clinicopathological study of 13 cases including immunohistochemical findings. Pathol Res Pract 184: 422–430

839. Nielsen S N J, Scheithauer B W, Gaffey T A 1985 Gliomatosis peritonei. Cancer 56: 2499–2503

840. El Shafie M, Furay R W, Chablani L V 1984 Ovarian teratoma with peritoneal and lymph node metastases of mature glial tissue: a benign condition. J Surg Oncol 27: 18–22

841. Ferguson A, Katabuchi H, Ronnett B M et al. 2001 Glial implants in gliomatosis peritonei arise from normal tissue, not from the associated teratoma. Am J Pathol 159: 51–55

842. Kwan M Y, Kalle W, Lau G T et al. 2004 Is gliomatosis peritonei derived from the associated ovarian teratoma? Hum Pathol 35: 685–688

843. Calder C J, Light A M, Rollason T P 1994 Immature ovarian teratoma with mature peritoneal metastatic deposits showing glial, epithelial, and endometrioid differentiation: a case report and review of the literature. Int J Gynecol Pathol 13: 279–282

844. Muller A M, Sondgen D, Strunz R et al. 2002 Gliomatosis peritonei: a report of two cases and review of the literature. Eur J Obstet Gynecol Reprod Biol 100: 213–222

845. Kattan J, Droz J P, Culine S et al. 1993 The growing teratoma syndrome: a woman with nonseminomatous germ cell tumor of the ovary. Gynecol Oncol 49: 395–399

846. Amsalem H, Nadjari M, Prus D et al. 2004 Growing teratoma syndrome vs chemotherapeutic retroconversion: case report and review of the literature. Gynecol Oncol 92: 357–360

847. Dadmanesh F, Miller D M, Swenerton K D et al. 1997 Gliomatosis peritonei with malignant transformation. Mod Pathol 10: 597–601

848. Ulbright T M 2005 Germ cell tumors of the gonads: a selective review emphasizing problems in differential diagnosis, newly appreciated, and controversial issues. Mod Pathol 18 Suppl 2: S61–S79

849. Baker P M, Rosai J, Young R H 2002 Ovarian teratomas with florid benign vascular proliferation: a distinctive finding associated with the neural component of teratomas that may be confused with a vascular neoplasm. Int J Gynecol Pathol 21: 16–21

850. Yanai H, Matsuura H, Kawasaki M et al. 2002 Immature teratoma of the ovary with a minor rhabdomyosarcomatous component and fatal rhabdomyosarcomatous metastases: the first case in a child. Int J Gynecol Pathol 21: 82–85

851. Nogales F F, Avila I R, Concha A et al. 1993 Immature endodermal teratoma of the ovary: Embryologic correlations and immunohistochemistry. Hum Pathol 24: 364–370

852. Nogales F F, Ortega I, Rivera F et al. 1980 Metanephrogenic tissue in immature ovarian teratoma. Am J Surg Pathol 4: 297–299

853. O'Connor D M, Norris H J 1994 The influence of grade on the outcome of stage I ovarian immature (malignant) teratomas and the reproducibility of grading. Int J Gynecol Pathol 13: 283–289

854. Michael H, Hull M T, Ulbright T M et al. 1997 Primitive neuroectodermal tumors arising in testicular germ cell neoplasms. Am J Surg Pathol 21: 896–904

855. Kleinman G M, Young R H, Scully R E 1993 Primary neuroectodermal tumors of the ovary: a report of 25 cases. Am J Surg Pathol 17: 764–778

856. Block M, Gilbert E, Davis C 1984 Metastatic neuroblastoma arising in an ovarian teratoma with long-term survival. Case report and review of the literature. Cancer 54: 590–595

857. Dekmezian R H, Sneige N, Ordóñez N G 1986 Ovarian and omental ependymomas in peritoneal washings: cytologic and immunocytochemical features. Diagn Cytopathol 2: 62–68

858. Guerrieri C, Jarlsfelt I 1993 Ependymoma of the ovary: A case report with immunohistochemical, ultrastructural, and DNA cytometric findings, as well as histogenetic considerations. Am J Surg Pathol 17: 623–632

859. Carr K A, Roberts J A, Frank T S 1992 Progesterone receptors in bilateral ovarian ependymoma presenting in pregnancy. Hum Pathol 23: 962–965

860. Vance R P, Geisinger K R, Randall M B et al. 1988 Immature neural elements in immature teratomas. An immunohistochemical and ultrastructural study. Am J Clin Pathol 90: 397–411

861. Calame J J, Schaberg A 1989 Solid teratomas and mixed Mullerian tumors of the ovary: a clinical, histological, and immunocytochemical comparative study. Gynecol Oncol 33: 212–221

862. Cho N H, Kim Y T, Lee J H et al. 2005 Diagnostic challenge of fetal ontogeny and its application on the ovarian teratomas. Int J Gynecol Pathol 24: 173–182

863. Genadry R, Parmley T, Woodruff J D 1979 Secondary malignancies in benign cystic teratomas. Gynecol Oncol 8: 246–251

864. Stamp G W H, McConnell E M 1983 Malignancy arising in cystic ovarian teratomas. A report of 24 cases. Br J Obstet Gynaecol 90: 671–675

865. Hirakawa T, Tsuneyoshi M, Enjoji M 1989 Squamous cell carcinoma arising in mature cystic teratoma of the ovary. Clinicopathologic and topographic analysis. Am J Surg Pathol 13: 397–405

866. Peterson W F 1957 Malignant degeneration of benign cystic teratomas of the ovary. A collective review of the literature. Obstet Gynecol Surv 12: 793–830

867. Tseng C J, Chou H H, Huang K G et al. 1996 Squamous cell carcinoma arising in mature cystic teratoma of the ovary. Gynecol Oncol 63: 364–370

868. Kikkawa F, Ishikawa H, Tamakoshi K et al. 1997 Squamous cell carcinoma arising from mature cystic teratoma of the ovary: a clinicopathologic analysis. Obstet Gynecol 89: 1017–1022

869. Kuroda N, Hirano K, Inui Y et al. 2001 Compound melanocytic nevus arising in a mature cystic teratoma of the ovary. Pathol Int 51: 902–904

870. Takeshima Y, Kaneko M, Furonaka O et al. 2004 Meningioma in mature cystic teratoma of the ovary. Pathol Int 54: 543–548

871. Silver S A, Tavassoli F A 2000 Glomus tumor arising in a mature teratoma of the ovary – Report of a case simulating a metastasis from cervical squamous carcinoma. Arch Pathol Lab Med 124: 1373–1375

872. Itoh H, Wada T, Michikata K et al. 2004 Ovarian teratoma showing a predominant hemangiomatous element with stromal luteinization: report of a case and review of the literature. Pathol Int 54: 279–283

873. Chumas J C, Scully R E 1991 Sebaceous tumors arising in ovarian dermoid cysts. Int J Gynecol Pathol 10: 356–363

874. Tobon H, Surti U, Naus G J et al. 1991 Squamous cell carcinoma in situ arising in an ovarian mature cystic teratoma. Report of one case with histopathologic, cytogenetic, and flow cytometric DNA content analysis. Arch Pathol Lab Med 115: 172–174

875. Shimizu S, Kobayashi H, Suchi T et al. 1991 Extramammary Paget's disease arising in mature cystic teratoma of the ovary. Am J Surg Pathol 15: 1002–1006

876. Monteagudo C, Torres J V, Llombart-Bosch A 1999 Extramammary Paget's disease arising in a mature cystic teratoma of the ovary. Histopathology 35: 582–584

877. Vartanian R K, McRae B, Hessler R B 2002 Sebaceous carcinoma arising in a mature cystic teratoma of the ovary. Int J Gynecol Pathol 21: 418–421

878. Ribeiro-Silva A, Chang D, Bisson F W et al. 2003 Clinicopathological and immunohistochemical features of a sebaceous carcinoma arising within a benign dermoid cyst of the ovary. Virchow's Arch 443: 574–578

879. Davis G L 1996 Malignant melanoma arising in mature ovarian cystic teratoma (dermoid cyst). Report of two cases and literature analysis. Int J Gynecol Pathol 15: 356–362

880. Gupta D, Deavers M T, Silva E G et al. 2004 Malignant melanoma involving the ovary: a clinicopathologic and immunohistochemical study of 23 cases. Am J Surg Pathol 28: 771–780

881. Vimla N, Kumar L, Thulkar S et al. 2001 Primary malignant melanoma in ovarian cystic teratoma. Gynecol Oncol 82: 380–383

882. Watanabe Y, Ueda H, Nakajima H et al. 2001 Amelanotic malignant melanoma arising in an ovarian cystic teratoma – A case report. Acta Cytol 45: 756–760

883. Fujiwara K, Ginzan S, Silverberg S G 1995 Mature cystic teratomas of the ovary with intestinal wall structures harboring intestinal-type epithelial neoplasms. Gynecol Oncol 56: 97–101

884. Cobellis L, Schurfeld K, Ignacchiti E et al. 2004 An ovarian mucinous adenocarcinoma arising from mature cystic teratoma associated with respiratory type tissue: a case report. Tumori 90: 521–524

885. Kushima M 2004 Adenocarcinoma arising from mature cystic teratoma of the ovary. Pathol Int 54: 139–143

886. Levine D A, Villella J A, Poynor E A et al. 2004 Gastrointestinal adenocarcinoma arising in a mature cystic teratoma of the ovary. Gynecol Oncol 94: 597–599

887. Climie A R, Heath L P 1968 Malignant degeneration of benign cystic teratomas of the ovary. Review of the literature and report of a chondrosarcoma and carcinoid tumor. Cancer 22: 824–832

888. Aygun B, Kimpo M, Lee T et al. 2003 An adolescent with ovarian osteosarcoma arising in a cystic teratoma. J Pediatr Hematol Oncol 25: 410–413

889. Ronnett B M, Seidman J D 2003 Mucinous tumors arising in ovarian mature cystic teratomas: relationship to the clinical syndrome of pseudomyxoma peritonei. Am J Surg Pathol 27: 650–657

890. Hasleton P S, Kelehan P, Whittaker J S et al. 1978 Benign and malignant struma ovarii. Arch Pathol Lab Med 102: 180–184

891. Devaney K, Snyder R, Norris H J et al. 1993 Proliferative and histologically malignant struma ovarii: a clinicopathologic study of 54 cases. Int J Gynecol Pathol 12: 333–343

892. Amr S S, Hassan A A 1994 Struma ovarii with pseudo-Meigs' syndrome: report of a case and review of the literature. Eur J Obstet Gynecol Reprod Biol 55: 205–208

893. Kempers R D, Dockerty M B, Hoffman D L et al. 1970 Struma ovarii – ascitic, hyperthyroid, and asymptomatic syndromes. Ann Intern Med 72: 883–893

894. Willemse P H, Oosterhuis J W, Aalders J G et al. 1987 Malignant struma ovarii treated by ovariectomy, thyroidectomy, and 131I administration. Cancer 60: 178–182

895. Huh J J, Montz F J, Bristow R E 2002 Struma ovarii associated with pseudo-Meigs' syndrome and elevated serum CA 125. Gynecol Oncol 86: 231–234

896. Loizzi V, Cormio G, Resta L et al. 2005 Pseudo-Meigs syndrome and elevated CA125 associated with struma ovarii. Gynecol Oncol 97: 282–284

897. Matsuda K, Maehama T, Kanazawa K 2001 Malignant struma ovarii with thyrotoxicosis. Gynecol Oncol 82: 575–577

898. Berghella V, Ngadiman S, Rosenberg H et al. 1997 Malignant struma ovarii – A case report and review of the literature. Gynecol Obstet Invest 43: 68–72

899. Makani S, Kim W, Gaba A R 2004 Struma ovarii with a focus of papillary thyroid cancer: a case report and review of the literature. Gynecol Oncol 94: 835–839

901. Nahn P A, Robinson E, Strassman M 2002 Conservative therapy for malignant struma ovarii – A case report. J Reprod Med 47: 943–945

902. Bolat F, Erkanli S, Kayaselcuk F et al. 2005 Malignant struma ovarii: a case report. Pathol Res Pract 201: 409–412

903. Pardo-Mindan F J, Vazquez J J 1983 Malignant struma ovarii. Light and electron microscopic study. Cancer 51: 337–343

904. McDougall I R, Krasne D, Hanbery J W et al. 1989 Metastatic malignant struma ovarii presenting as paraparesis from a spinal metastasis. J Nucl Med 30: 407–411

905. Ribeiro-Silva A, Bezerra A M, Serafini L N 2002 Malignant struma ovarii: an autopsy report of a clinically unsuspected tumor. Gynecol Oncol 87: 213–215

906. Dardik R B, Dardik M, Westra W et al. 1999 Malignant struma ovarii: two case reports and a review of the literature. Gynecol Oncol 73: 447–451

907. DeSimone C P, Lele S M, Modesitt S C 2003 Malignant struma ovarii: a case report and analysis of cases reported in the literature with focus on survival and I131 therapy. Gynecol Oncol 89: 543–548

908. Szyfelbein W M, Young R H, Scully R E 1994 Cystic struma ovarii: a frequently unrecognized tumor. A report of 20 cases. Am J Surg Pathol 18: 785–788

909. Szyfelbein W M, Young R H, Scully R E 1995 Struma ovarii simulating ovarian tumors of other types. A report of 30 cases. Am J Surg Pathol 19: 21–29

910. Hamazaki S, Okino T, Tsukayama C et al. 2002 Expression of thyroid transcription factor-1 in strumal carcinoid and struma ovarii: an immunohistochemical study. Pathol Int 52: 458–462

911. Rosenblum N G, Livolsi V A, Edmonds P R et al. 1989 Malignant struma ovarii. Gynecol Oncol 32: 224–227

912. Brunskill P J, Rollason T P, Nicholson H O 1990 Malignant follicular variant of papillary struma ovarii. Histopathology 17: 574–576

913. Balasch J, Pahisa J, Márquez M et al. 1993 Metastatic ovarian strumosis in an in-vitro fertilization patient. Hum Reprod 8: 2075–2079

914. Karseladze A I, Kulinitch S I 1994 Peritoneal strumosis. Pathol Res Pract 190: 1082–1085

915. Soga J, Osaka M, Yakuwa Y 2000 Carcinoids of the ovary: an analysis of 329 reported cases. J Exp Clin Cancer Res 19: 271–280

916. Robboy S J, Scully R E, Norris H J 1977 Primary trabecular carcinoid of the ovary. Obstet Gynecol 49: 202–207

917. Robboy S J 1984 Insular carcinoid of ovary associated with malignant mucinous tumors. Cancer 54: 2273–2276

918. Davis K P, Hartmann L K, Keeney G L et al. 1996 Primary ovarian carcinoid tumors. Gynecol Oncol 61: 259–265

919. Robboy S J, Norris H J, Scully R E 1975 Insular carcinoid primary in the ovary. A clinicopathologic analysis of 48 cases. Cancer 36: 404–418

920. Chaowalit N, Connolly H M, Schaff H V et al. 2004 Carcinoid heart disease associated with primary ovarian carcinoid tumor. Am J Cardiol 93: 1314–1315

921. Yaegashi N, Tsuiki A, Shimizu T et al. 1995 Ovarian carcinoid with severe constipation due to peptide YY production. Gynecol Oncol 56: 302–306

922. Motoyama T, Katayama Y, Watanabe H et al. 1992 Functioning ovarian carcinoids induce severe constipation. Cancer 70: 513–518

923. Shigeta H, Taga M, Kurogi K et al. 1999 Ovarian strumal carcinoid with severe constipation: immunohistochemical and mRNA analyses of peptide YY. Hum Pathol 30: 242–246

924. Robboy S J, Scully R E 1980 Strumal carcinoid of the ovary. An analysis of 50 cases of a distinctive tumor composed of thyroid tissue and carcinoid. Cancer 46: 2019–2034

925. Wilkowske M A, Hartmann L C, Mullany C J et al. 1994 Progressive carcinoid heart disease after resection of primary ovarian carcinoid. Cancer 73: 1889–1891

926. Alenghat E, Okagaki T, Talerman A 1986 Primary mucinous carcinoid tumor of the ovary. Cancer 58: 777–783

927. Armes J E, Ostor A G 1993 A case of malignant strumal carcinoid. Gynecol Oncol 51: 419–423

928. Robboy S J, Scully R E, Norris H J 1974 Carcinoid metastatic to the ovary. A clinicopathologic analysis of 35 cases. Cancer 33: 798–811

929. Talerman A, Evans M I 1982 Primary trabecular carcinoid tumor of the ovary. Cancer 50: 1403–1407

930. Snyder R R, Tavassoli F A 1986 Ovarian strumal carcinoid: immunohistochemical, ultrastructural, and clinicopathologic analysis. Int J Gynecol Pathol 5: 187–201

931. Sidhu J, Sánchez R L 1993 Prostatic acid phosphatase in strumal carcinoids of the ovary: An immunohistochemical study. Cancer 72: 1673–1678

932. Stagno P A, Petras R E, Hart W R 1987 Strumal carcinoids of the ovary. An immunohistologic and ultrastructural study. Arch Pathol Lab Med 111: 440–446

933. Matias-Guiu X, Forteza J, Prat J 1995 Mixed strumal and mucinous carcinoid tumor of the ovary. Int J Gynecol Pathol 14: 179–183

934. Ulbright T M, Roth L M, Ehrlich C E 1982 Ovarian strumal carcinoid. An immunocytochemical and ultrastructural study of two cases. Am J Clin Pathol 77: 622–631

935. Dayal Y, Tashjian A J Jr, Wolfe H J 1979 Immunocytochemical localization of calcitonin-producing cells in a strumal carcinoid with amyloid stroma. Cancer 43: 1331–1338

936. Wolpert H R, Fuller A F, Bell D A 1989 Primary mucinous carcinoid tumor of the ovary. A case report. Int J Gynecol Pathol 8: 156–162

937. Baker P M, Oliva E, Young R H et al. 2001 Ovarian mucinous carcinoids including some with a carcinomatous component – A report of 17 cases. Am J Surg Pathol 25: 557–568

938. Serratoni F T, Robboy S J 1975 Ultrastructure of primary and metastatic ovarian carcinoids: analysis of 11 cases. Cancer 36: 157–160

939. Sporrong B, Falkmer S, Robboy S J et al. 1982 Neurohormonal peptides in ovarian carcinoids: an immunohistochemical study of 81 primary carcinoids and of intraovarian metastases from six mid-gut carcinoids. Cancer 49: 68–74

940. Braunschweig R, Hurlimann J, Gloor E et al. 1994 [Ovarian carcinoid tumors: immunohistochemical and ultrastructural study of 8 cases.] Ann Pathol 14: 155–162

941. Matsuda K, Maehama T, Kanazawa K 2002 Strumal carcinoid tumor of the ovary: a case exhibiting severe constipation associated with PYY. Gynecol Oncol 87: 143–145

942. Greco M A, Livolsi V A, Pertschuk L P et al. 1979 Strumal carcinoid of the ovary: an analysis of its components. Cancer; 43: 1380–1388.

943. Senterman M K, Cassidy P N, Fenoglio C M et al. 1984 Histology, ultrastructure, and immunohistochemistry of strumal carcinoid: a case report. Int J Gynecol Pathol 3: 232–240

944. Kurman R J, Norris H J 1976 Malignant mixed germ cell tumors of the ovary. A clinical and pathologic analysis of 30 cases. Obstet Gynecol 48: 579–589

945. Gershenson D M, del Junco G, Copeland L J et al. 1984 Mixed germ cell tumors of the ovary. Obstet Gynecol 64: 200–207

946. Jimerson G K, Woodruff J D 1977 Ovarian extraembryonal teratoma. II. Endodermal sinus tumor mixed with other germ cell tumors. Am J Obstet Gynecol 127: 302–305

947. De Palo G, Zambetti M, Pilotti S et al. 1992 Nondysgerminomatous tumors of the ovary treated with cisplatin, vinblastine, and bleomycin: long-term results. Gynecol Oncol 47: 239–246

948. Troche V, Hernandez E 1986 Neoplasia arising in dysgenetic gonads. Obstet Gynecol Surv 41: 74–79

949. Garvin A J, Pratt-Thomas H R, Spector M et al. 1976 Gonadoblastoma: histologic, ultrastructural, and histochemical observations in five cases. Am J Obstet Gynecol 125: 459–471

950. Govan A D, Woodcock A S, Gowing N F et al. 1977 A clinico-pathological study of gonadoblastoma. Br J Obstet Gynaecol 84: 222–228

951. Woodcock A S, Govan A D, Gowing N F et al. 1979 A report of the histological features in 12 cases of gonadoblastoma. Tumori 65: 181–189

952. Scully R E 1970 Gonadoblastoma: a review of 74 cases. Cancer 25: 1340–1356

953. Deligdisch L, Richards C J, Reyniak V J 1988 Pure gonadal dysgenesis and gonadal tumors: report of three cases and review of literature. Mt Sinai J Med 55: 313–317

954. Pena-Alonso R, Nieto K, Alvarez R et al. 2005 Distribution of Y-chromosome-bearing cells in gonadoblastoma and dysgenetic testis in 45,X/46,XY infants. Mod Pathol 18: 439–445

955. Tsuchiya K, Reijo R, Page D C et al. 1995 Gonadoblastoma: molecular definition of the susceptibility region on the Y chromosome. Am J Hum Genet 57: 1400–1407

956. Mancilla E E, Poggi H, Repetto G et al. 2003 Y chromosome sequences in Turner's syndrome: association with virilization and gonadoblastoma. J Pediatr Endocrinol Metab 16: 1157–1163

957. Salo P, Kaariainen H, Petrovic V et al. 1995 Molecular mapping of the putative gonadoblastoma locus on the Y chromosome. Genes Chromosomes Cancer 14: 210–214

958. Lau Y, Chou P, Iezzoni J et al. 2000 Expression of a candidate gene for the gonadoblastoma locus in gonadoblastoma and testicular seminoma. Cytogenet Cell Genet 91: 160–164

959. Schellhas H F 1974 Malignant potential of the dysgenetic gonad. Part I. Obstet Gynecol 44: 298–309

960. Horn L C, Limbach A, Hoepffner W et al. 2005 Histologic analysis of gonadal tissue in patients with Ullrich-Turner syndrome and derivative Y chromosomes. Pediatr Dev Pathol 8: 197–203

961. Hart W R, Burkons D M 1979 Germ cell neoplasms arising in gonadoblastomas. Cancer 43: 669–678

962. Talerman A 1974 Gonadoblastoma associated with embryonal carcinoma. Obstet Gynecol 43: 138–142

963. Jorgensen N, Müller J, Jaubert F et al. 1997 Heterogeneity of gonadoblastoma germ cells: Similarities with immature germ cells, spermatogonia and testicular carcinoma in situ cells. Histopathology 30: 177–186

964. Kersemaekers A M, Honecker F, Stoop H et al. 2005 Identification of germ cells at risk for neoplastic transformation in gonadoblastoma: an immunohistochemical study for OCT3/4 and TSPY. Hum Pathol 36: 512–52.

965. Roth L M, Eglen D E 1989 Gonadoblastoma. Immunohistochemical and ultrastructural observations. Int J Gynecol Pathol 8: 72–81

966. Rajpert-De M E, Hanstein R, Jorgensen N et al. 2004 Developmental expression of POU5F1 (OCT-3/4) in normal and dysgenetic human gonads. Hum Reprod 19: 1338–1344

967. Hildenbrand R, Schröder W, Brude E et al. 1999 Detection of *TSPY* protein in a unilateral microscopic gonadoblastoma of a Turner mosaic patient with a Y-derived marker chromosome. J Pathol 189: 623–626

968. Talerman A 1972 A distinctive gonadal neoplasm related to gonadoblastoma. Cancer 30: 1219–1224

969. Tavassoli F A 1983 A combined germ cell-gonadal stromal-epithelial tumor of the ovary. Am J Surg Pathol 7: 73–84

970. Nomura K, Matsui T, Aizawa S 1999 Gonadoblastoma with proliferation resembling Sertoli cell tumor. Int J Gynecol Pathol 18: 91–93

971. Kedzia H 1983 Gonadoblastoma: structures and background of development. Am J Obstet Gynecol 147: 81–85

972. Safneck J R, deSa D J 1986 Structures mimicking sex cord-stromal tumours and gonadoblastomas in the ovaries of normal infants and children. Histopathology 10: 909–920

973. Dickersin G R, Kline I W, Scully R E 1982 Small cell carcinoma of the ovary with hypercalcemia: a report of eleven cases. Cancer 49: 188–197

974. Scully R E 1993 Small cell carcinoma of hypercalcemic type. Int J Gynecol Pathol 12: 148–152

975. Young R H, Oliva E, Scully R E 1994 Small cell carcinoma of the ovary, hypercalcemic type: a clinicopathological analysis of 150 cases. Am J Surg Pathol 18: 1102–1116

976. Clement P B 2005 Selected miscellaneous ovarian lesions: small cell carcinomas, mesothelial lesions, mesenchymal and mixed neoplasms, and non-neoplastic lesions. Mod Pathol 18 Suppl 2: S113–S129

977. Schleef J, Wagner A, Kleta R et al. 1999 Small-cell carcinoma of the ovary of the hypercalcemic type in an 8-year-old girl. Pediatr Surg Int 15: 431–434

978. Seidman J D 1995 Small cell carcinoma of the ovary of the hypercalcemic type: p53 protein accumulation and clinicopathologic features. Gynecol Oncol 59: 283–287

979. Longy M, Toulouse C, Mage P et al. 1996 Familial cluster of ovarian small cell carcinoma: a new mendelian entity? J Med Genet 33: 333–335

980. Tewari K, Brewer C, Cappuccini F et al. 1997 Advanced-stage small cell carcinoma of the ovary in pregnancy: long-term survival after surgical debulking and multiagent chemotherapy. Gynecol Oncol 66: 531–534

981. Sholler G L, Luks F, Mangray S et al. 2005 Advanced small cell carcinoma of the ovary in a pediatric patient with long-term survival and review of the literature. J Pediatr Hematol Oncol 27: 169–172

982. Rana S, Warren B K, Yamada S D 2004 Stage IIIC small cell carcinoma of the ovary: survival with conservative surgery and chemotherapy. Obstet Gynecol 103: 1120–1123

983. Eichhorn J H, Bell D A, Young RH et al. 1992 DNA content and proliferative activity in ovarian small cell carcinomas of the hypercalcemic type: Implications for diagnosis, prognosis, and histogenesis. Am J Clin Pathol 98: 579–586

984. Ulbright T M, Roth L M, Stehman F B et al. 1987 Poorly differentiated (small cell) carcinoma of the ovary in young women: evidence supporting a germ cell origin. Hum Pathol 18: 175–184

985. McCluggage W G, Oliva E, Connolly L E et al. 2004 An immunohistochemical analysis of ovarian small cell carcinoma of hypercalcemic type. Int J Gynecol Pathol 23: 330–336

986. Riopel M A, Perlman E J, Seidman J D et al. 1998 Inhibin and epithelial membrane antigen immunohistochemistry assist in the diagnosis of sex cord-stromal tumors and provide clues to the histogenesis of hypercalcemic small cell carcinomas. Int J Gynecol Pathol 17: 46–53

987. Abeler V, Kjrstad K E, Nesland J M 1988 Small cell carcinoma of the ovary. A report of six cases. Int J Gynecol Pathol 7: 315–329

988. Matias-Guiu X, Prat J, Young R H et al. 1994 Human parathyroid hormone-related protein in ovarian small cell carcinoma: an immunohistochemical study. Cancer 73: 1878–1881

989. McMahon J T, Hart W R 1988 Ultrastructural analysis of small cell carcinoma of the ovary. Am J Clin Pathol 90: 523–529

990. Dickersin G R, Scully R E 1993 An update on the electron microscopy of small cell carcinoma of the ovary with hypercalcemia. Ultrastruct Pathol 17: 411–422

991. Dickersin G R, Scully R E 1998 Ovarian small cell tumors: an electron microscopic review. Ultrastruct Pathol 22: 199–226

992. Idei Y, Kitazawa S, Fujimori T et al. 1996 Ovarian small cell carcinoma with K-*ras* mutation: a case report with genetic analysis. Hum Pathol 27: 77–79

993. Gerald W L, Miller H K, Battifora H et al. 1991 Intra-abdominal desmoplastic small round-cell tumor. Report of 19 cases of a distinctive type of high-grade polyphenotypic malignancy affecting young individuals. Am J Surg Pathol 15: 499–513

994. Hassan I, Shyyan R, Donohue J H et al. 2005 Intraabdominal desmoplastic small round cell tumors. Cancer 104: 1264–1270

995. Lae M E, Roche P C, Jin L et al. 2002 Desmoplastic small round cell tumor – A clinicopathologic, immunohistochemical, and molecular study of 32 tumors. Am J Surg Pathol 26: 823–835

996. Young R H, Eichhorn J H, Dickersin G R et al. 1992 Ovarian involvement by the intra-abdominal desmoplastic small round cell tumor with divergent differentiation: a report of three cases. Hum Pathol 23: 454–464

997. Zaloudek C, Miller T R, Stern J L 1995 Desmoplastic small cell tumor of the ovary: a unique polyphenotypic tumor with an unfavorable prognosis. Int J Gynecol Pathol 14: 260–265

998. Elhajj M, Mazurka J, Daya D 2002 Desmoplastic small round cell tumor presenting in the ovaries: report of a case and review of the literature. Int J Gynecol Cancer 12: 760–763

999. Parker L P, Duong J L, Wharton J T et al. 2002 Desmoplastic small round cell tumor: report of a case presenting as a primary ovarian neoplasm. Eur J Gynaecol Oncol 23: 199–202

1000. Slomovitz B M, Girotra M, Aledo A et al. 2000 Desmoplastic small round cell tumor with primary ovarian involvement: case report and review. Gynecol Oncol 79: 124–128

1001. Lal D R, Su W T, Wolden S L et al. 2005 Results of multimodal treatment for desmoplastic small round cell tumors. J Pediatr Surg 40: 251–255

1002. Goodman K A, Wolden S L, La Quaglia M P et al. 2002 Whole abdominopelvic radiotherapy for desmoplastic small round-cell tumor. Int J Radiat Oncol Biol Phys 54: 170–176

1003. Ladanyi M, Gerald W 1994 Fusion of the EWS and WT1 genes in the desmoplastic small round cell tumor. Cancer Res 54: 2837–2840

1004. Gerald W L, Haber D A 2005 The EWS-WT1 gene fusion in desmoplastic small round cell tumor. Semin Cancer Biol 15: 197–205

1005. Sandberg A A, Bridge J A 2002 Updates on the cytogenetics and molecular genetics of bone and soft tissue tumors. Desmoplastic small round-cell tumors. Cancer Genet Cytogenet 138: 1–10

1006. Ordonez N G 1998 Desmoplastic small round cell tumor I: a histopathologic study of 39 cases with emphasis on unusual histological patterns. Am J Surg Pathol 22: 1303–1313

1007. Sebire N J, Gibson S, Rampling D et al. 2005 Immunohistochemical findings in embryonal small round cell tumors with molecular diagnostic confirmation. Appl Immunohistochem Mol Morphol 13: 1–5

1008. Zhang P J, Goldblum J R, Pawel B R et al. 2003 Immunophenotype of desmoplastic small round cell tumors as detected in cases with EWS-WT1 gene fusion product. Mod Pathol 16: 229–235

1009. Ordonez N G 1998 Desmoplastic small round cell tumor II: An ultrastructural and immunohistochemical study with emphasis on new immunohistochemical markers. Am J Surg Pathol 22: 1314–1327

1010. Kariminejad M H, Scully R E. 1973 Female adnexal tumor of probable Wolffian origin: a distinctive pathologic entity. Cancer 31: 671–677.

1011. Young R H, Scully R E 1983 Ovarian tumors of probable Wolffian origin: a report of 11 cases. Am J Surg Pathol 7: 125–136

1012. Tavassoli F A, Andrade R, Merino M 1990 Retiform wolffian adenoma. In: Fenoglio-Preiser CM, Wolffe M, Rilke F (eds) Progress in surgical pathology. Field and Wood Medical Publishers, Inc, New York, vol. XI, p 121–136

1013. Inoue H, Kikuchi Y, Hori T et al. 1995 An ovarian tumor of probable Wolffian origin with hormonal function. Gynecol Oncol 59: 304–308

1014. Delaloye J F, Ruzicka J, De Grandi P 1993 An ovarian tumor of probable Wolffian origin. Acta Obstet Gynecol Scand 72: 314–316

1015. Devouassoux-Shisheboran M, Silver S A, Tavassoli F A 1999 Wolffian adnexal tumor, so-called female adnexal tumor of probable Wolffian origin (FATWO): immunohistochemical evidence in support of a Wolffian origin. Hum Pathol 30: 856–863

1016. Rahilly M A, Williams A R W, Krausz T et al. 1995 Female adnexal tumour of probable Wolffian origin: a clinicopathological and immunohistochemical study of three cases. Histopathology 26: 69–74

1017. Young R H, Silva E G, Scully R E 1991 Ovarian and juxtaovarian adenomatoid tumors: a report of six cases. Int J Gynecol Pathol 10: 364–372

1018. Mazur M T, Hsueh S, Gersell D J 1984 Metastases to the female genital tract. Analysis of 325 cases. Cancer 53: 1978–1984

1019. Abu-Rustum N R, Barakat R R, Curtin J P 1997 Ovarian and uterine disease in women with colorectal cancer. Obstet Gynecol 89: 85–87

1020. Ulbright T M, Roth L M, Stehman F B 1984 Secondary ovarian neoplasia. A clinicopathologic study of 35 cases. Cancer 53: 1164–1174

1021. Young R H, Scully R E 1991 Metastatic tumors in the ovary: a problem-oriented approach and review of the recent literature. Semin Diagn Pathol 8: 250–276

1022. Powari M, Dey P, Gupta S K et al. 2003 Metastatic tumours of the ovary: a clinico-pathological study. Indian J Pathol Microbiol 46: 412–415

1023. McCluggage W G, Wilkinson N 2005 Metastatic neoplasms involving the ovary: a review with an emphasis on morphological and immunohistochemical features. Histopathology 47: 231–247

1024. Chang T C, Changchien C C, Tseng C W et al. 1997 Retrograde lymphatic spread: a likely route for metastatic ovarian cancers of gastrointestinal origin. Gynecol Oncol 66: 372–377

1025. Moore R G, Chung M, Granai C O et al. 2004 Incidence of metastasis to the ovaries from nongenital tract primary tumors. Gynecol Oncol 93: 87–91

1026. Elishaev E, Gilks C B, Miller D et al. 2005 Synchronous and metachronous endocervical and ovarian neoplasms: evidence supporting interpretation of the ovarian neoplasms as metastatic endocervical adenocarcinomas simulating primary ovarian surface epithelial neoplasms. Am J Surg Pathol 29: 281–294

1027. Yada-Hashimoto N, Yamamoto T, Kamiura S et al. 2003 Metastatic ovarian tumors: a review of 64 cases. Gynecol Oncol 89: 314–317

1028. Ronnett B M, Kurman R J, Shmookler B M et al. 1997 The morphologic spectrum of ovarian metastases of appendiceal adenocarcinomas –

A clinicopathologic and immunohistochemical analysis of tumors often misinterpreted as primary ovarian tumors or metastatic tumors from other gastrointestinal sites. Am J Surg Pathol 21: 1144–1155

1029. Young R H, Hart W R 1989 Metastases from carcinomas of the pancreas simulating primary mucinous tumors of the ovary. A report of seven cases. Am J Surg Pathol 13: 748–756

1030. Young R H, Scully R E 1990 Ovarian metastases from carcinoma of the gallbladder and extrahepatic bile ducts simulating primary tumors of the ovary. A report of six cases. Int J Gynecol Pathol 9: 60–72

1031. De Groot M E, Dukel L, Chadha-Ajwani S et al. 2000 Massive solitary metastasis of hepatocellular carcinoma in the ovary two years after liver transplantation. Eur J Obstet Gynecol Reprod Biol 90: 109–111

1032. Young R H, Hart W R 1992 Renal cell carcinoma metastatic to the ovary: a report of three cases emphasizing possible confusion with ovarian clear cell adenocarcinoma. Int J Gynecol Pathol 11: 96–104

1033. Hammock L, Ghorab Z, Gomez-Fernandez C R 2003 Metastatic renal cell carcinoma to the ovary: a case report and discussion of differential diagnoses. Arch Pathol Lab Med 127: e123–e126

1034. Insabato L, De Rosa G, Franco R et al. 2003 Ovarian metastasis from renal cell carcinoma: a report of three cases. Int J Surg Pathol 11: 309–312

1035. Young R H, Scully R E 1991 Malignant melanoma metastatic to the ovary: a clinicopathologic analysis of 20 cases. Am J Surg Pathol 15: 849–860

1036. Young R H, Scully R E 1990 Sarcomas metastatic to the ovary: a report of 21 cases. Int J Gynecol Pathol 9: 231–252

1037. Young R H, Scully R E 1989 Alveolar rhabdomyosarcoma metastatic to the ovary. A report of two cases and a discussion of the differential diagnosis of small cell malignant tumors of the ovary. Cancer 64: 899–904

1038. Eltabbakh G H, Belinson J L, Biscotti C V 1997 Osteosarcoma metastatic to the ovary: a case report and review of the literature. Int J Gynecol Pathol 16: 76–78

1039. Irving J A, Lerwill M F, Young R H 2005 Gastrointestinal stromal tumors metastatic to the ovary: a report of five cases. Am J Surg Pathol 29: 920–926

1040. Demopoulos R I, Touger L, Dubin N 1987 Secondary ovarian carcinoma: a clinical and pathological evaluation. Int J Gynecol Pathol 6: 166–175

1041. Abu-Rustum N, Barakat R R, Curtin J P 1997 Ovarian and uterine disease in women with colorectal cancer. Obstet Gynecol 89: 85–87

1042. Miller B E, Pittman B, Wan J Y et al. 1997 Colon cancer with metastasis to the ovary at time of initial diagnosis. Gynecol Oncol 66: 368–371

1043. Herrera-Ornelas L, Natarajan N, Tsukada Y et al. 1983 Adenocarcinoma of the colon masquerading as primary ovarian neoplasia. An analysis of ten cases. Dis Colon Rectum 26: 377–380

1044. Daya D, Nazerali L, Frank G L 1992 Metastatic ovarian carcinoma of large intestinal origin simulating primary ovarian carcinoma: a clinicopathologic study of 25 cases. Am J Clin Pathol 97: 751–758

1045. Petru E, Pickel H, Heydarfadai M et al. 1992 Nongenital cancers metastatic to the ovary. Gynecol Oncol 44: 83–86

1046. Birnkrant A, Sampson J, Sugarbaker P H 1986 Ovarian metastasis from colorectal cancer. Dis Colon Rectum 29: 767–771

1047. Blamey S L, McDermott F T, Pihl E et al. 1981 Resected ovarian recurrence from colorectal adenocarcinoma: a study of 13 cases. Dis Colon Rectum 24: 272–275

1048. MacKeigan J M, Ferguson J A 1979 Prophylactic oophorectomy and colorectal cancer in premenopausal patients. Dis Colon Rectum 22: 401–405

1049. Graffner H O, Alm P O, Oscarson J E 1983 Prophylactic oophorectomy in colorectal carcinoma. Am J Surg 146: 233–235

1050. Ballantyne G H, Reigel M M, Wolff B G et al. 1985 Oophorectomy and colon cancer. Impact on survival. Ann Surg 202: 209–214

1051. Sielezneff I, Salle E, Antoine K et al. 1997 Simultaneous bilateral oophorectomy does not improve prognosis of postmenopausal women undergoing colorectal resection for cancer. Dis Colon Rectum 40: 1299–1302

1052. Banerjee S, Kapur S, Moran B J 2005 The role of prophylactic oophorectomy in women undergoing surgery for colorectal cancer. Colorectal Dis 7: 214–217

1053. Tentes A, Markakidis S, Mirelis C et al. 2004 Oophorectomy during surgery for colorectal carcinoma. Tech Coloproctol 8 Suppl 1: s214–s216

1054. Blamey S, McDermott F, Pihl E et al. 1981 Ovarian involvement in adenocarcinoma of the colon and rectum. Surg Gynecol Obstet 153: 42–44

1055. Ayhan A, Guvenal T, Coskun F et al. 2003 Survival and prognostic factors in patients with synchronous ovarian and endometrial cancers and endometrial cancers metastatic to the ovaries. Eur J Gynaecol Oncol 24: 171–174

1056. Taylor A E, Nicolson V M C, Cunningham D 1995 Ovarian metastases from primary gastrointestinal malignancies: The Royal Marsden Hospital experience and implications for adjuvant treatment. Br J Cancer 71: 92–96

1057. Gagnon Y, Têtu B 1989 Ovarian metastases of breast carcinoma. A clinicopathologic study of 59 cases. Cancer 64: 892–898

1058. Simpkins F, Zahurak M, Armstrong D et al. 2005 Ovarian malignancy in breast cancer patients with an adnexal mass. Obstet Gynecol 105: 507–513

1059. Young R H, Carey R W, Robboy S J 1981 Breast carcinoma masquerading as primary ovarian neoplasm. Cancer 48: 210–212

1060. Lash R H, Hart W R 1987 Intestinal adenocarcinomas metastatic to the ovaries. A clinicopathologic evaluation of 22 cases. Am J Surg Pathol 11: 114–121

1061. Lee K R, Young R H 2003 The distinction between primary and metastatic mucinous carcinomas of the ovary: gross and histologic findings in 50 cases. Am J Surg Pathol 27: 281–292

1062. Scully R E, Richardson G S 1961 Luteinization of the stroma of metastatic cancer involving the ovary and its endocrine significance. Cancer 14: 827–840

1063. Hart W R 2005 Diagnostic challenge of secondary (metastatic) ovarian tumors simulating primary endometrioid and mucinous neoplasms. Pathol Int 55: 231–243

1064. DeCostanzo D C, Elias J M, Chumas J C 1997 Necrosis in 84 ovarian carcinomas: a morphologic study of primary versus metastatic colonic carcinoma with a selective immunohistochemical analysis of cytokeratin subtypes and carcinoembryonic antigen. Int J Gynecol Pathol 16: 245–249

1065. Ueda G, Sawada M, Ogawa H et al. 1993 Immunohistochemical study of cytokeratin 7 for the differential diagnosis of adenocarcinomas in the ovary. Gynecol Oncol 51: 219–223

1066. Berezowski K, Stastny J F, Kornstein M J 1996 Cytokeratins 7 and 20 and carcinoembryonic antigen in ovarian and colonic carcinoma. Mod Pathol 9: 426–429

1067. Loy T S, Calaluce R D, Keeney G L 1996 Cytokeratin immunostaining in differentiating primary ovarian carcinoma from metastatic colonic adenocarcinoma. Mod Pathol 9: 1040–1044

1068. Wauters C C A P, Smedts F, Gerrits L G M et al. 1995 Keratins 7 and 20 as diagnostic markers of carcinomas metastatic to the ovary. Hum Pathol 26: 852–855

1069. Wang N P, Zee S, Zarbo R J et al. 1995 Coordinate expression of cytokeratins 7 and 20 defines unique subsets of carcinomas. Appl Immunohistochem 3: 99–107

1070. Park S Y, Kim H S, Hong E K et al. 2002 Expression of cytokeratins 7 and 20 in primary carcinomas of the stomach and colorectum and their value in the differential diagnosis of metastatic carcinomas to the ovary. Hum Pathol 33: 1078–1085

1071. Werling R W, Yaziji H, Bacchi C E et al. 2003 CDX2, a highly sensitive and specific marker of adenocarcinomas of intestinal origin: an immunohistochemical survey of 476 primary and metastatic carcinomas. Am J Surg Pathol 27: 303–310

1072. Fraggetta F, Pelosi G, Cafici A et al. 2003 CDX2 immunoreactivity in primary and metastatic ovarian mucinous tumours. Virchow's Arch 443: 782–786

1073. Loy T S, Quesenberry J T, Sharp S C 1992 Distribution of CA 125 in adenocarcinomas: An immunohistochemical study of 481 cases. Am J Clin Pathol 98: 175–179

1074. Koelma I A, Nap M, Rodenburg C et al. 1987 The value of tumour marker CA 125 in surgical pathology. Histopathology 11: 287–294

1075. Leake J, Woolas R P, Daniel J et al. 1994 Immunocytochemical and serological expression of CA 125: A clinicopathological study of 40 malignant ovarian epithelial tumours. Histopathology 24: 57–64

1076. Fleuren G J, Nap M 1988 Carcinoembryonic antigen in primary and metastatic ovarian tumors. Gynecol Oncol 30: 407–415

1077. Merino M J, Edmonds P, LiVolsi V 1985 Appendiceal carcinoma metastatic to the ovaries and mimicking primary ovarian tumors. Int J Gynecol Pathol 4: 110–120

1078. Burke A P, Sobin L H, Federspiel B H et al. 1990 Goblet cell carcinoids and related tumors of the vermiform appendix. Am J Clin Pathol 94: 27–35

1079. Klein E A, Rosen M H 1996 Bilateral Krukenberg tumors due to appendiceal mucinous carcinoid. Int J Gynecol Pathol 15: 85–88

1080. Mandai M, Konishi I, Tsuruta Y et al. 2001 Krukenberg tumor from an occult appendiceal adenocarcinoid: a case report and review of the literature. Eur J Obstet Gynecol Reprod Biol 97: 90–95

1081. McBroom J W, Parker M F, Krivak T C et al. 2000 Primary appendiceal malignancy mimicking advanced stage ovarian carcinoma: a case series. Gynecol Oncol 78: 388–390

1082. Monteagudo C, Merino M J, LaPorte N et al. 1991 Value of gross cystic disease fluid protein-15 in distinguishing metastatic breast carcinomas among poorly differentiated neoplasms involving the ovary. Hum Pathol 22: 368–372

1083. Le Bouëdec G, De Latour M, Levrel O et al. 1997 Ovarian carcinoma mucocellular (Krukenberg's tumor): ten cases of breast cancer metastasis. Presse Med 26: 454–457

1084. Yakushiji M, Tazaki T, Nishimura H et al. 1987 Krukenberg tumors of the ovary: a clinicopathologic analysis of 112 cases. Nippon Sanka Fujinka Gakkai Zasshi 39: 479–485

1085. Wong P C, Ferenczy A, Fan L D et al. 1986 Krukenberg tumors of the ovary. Ultrastructural, histochemical and immunohistochemical studies of 15 cases. Cancer 57: 751–760

1086. Holtz F, Hart W R 1982 Krukenberg tumors of the ovary. A clinicopathologic analysis of 27 cases. Cancer 50: 2438–2447

1086a. Kiyokawa T, Young R H, Scully R E 2006 Krukenberg tumors of the ovary: a clinicopathologic analysis of 120 cases with emphasis on their variable pathologic manifestatations. Am J Surg Pathol 30: 277–299

1087. Hale R W 1968 Krukenberg tumor of the ovaries. A review of 81 records. Obstet Gynecol 32: 221–225

1088. Bullon A, Arseneau J, Prat J et al. 1981 Tubular Krukenberg tumor: a problem in histopathologic diagnosis. Am J Surg Pathol 5: 225–232

1089. Fung M F, Vadas G, Lotocki R et al. 1991 Tubular Krukenberg tumor in pregnancy with virilization. Gynecol Oncol 41: 81–84

1090. Joshi V V 1968 Primary Krukenberg tumor of ovary. Review of literature and case report. Cancer 22: 1199–1207

1091. Woodruff J D, Novak E R 1960 The Krukenberg tumor: Study of 48 cases from the Ovarian Tumor Registry. Obstet Gynecol 15: 351–360

1092. Galani E, Marx G M, Steer C B et al. 2003 Pseudomyxoma peritonei: the "controversial" disease. Int J Gynecol Cancer 13: 413–418

1093. Kahn M A, Demopoulos R I 1992 Mucinous ovarian tumors with pseudomyxoma peritonei: a clinicopathological study. Int J Gynecol Pathol 11: 15–23

1094. Prayson R A, Hart W R, Petras R E 1994 Pseudomyxoma peritonei: a clinicopathologic study of 19 cases with emphasis on site of origin and nature of associated ovarian tumors. Am J Surg Pathol 18: 591–603

1095. Ronnett B M, Zahn C M, Kurman R J et al. 1995 Disseminated peritoneal adenomucinosis and peritoneal mucinous carcinomatosis – A clinicopathologic analysis of 109 cases with emphasis on distinguishing pathologic features, site of origin, prognosis, and relationship to "Pseudomyxoma peritonei". Am J Surg Pathol 19: 1390–1408

1096. Young R H 2004 Pseudomyxoma peritonei and selected other aspects of the spread of appendiceal neoplasms. Semin Diagn Pathol 21: 134–150

1097. Gough D B, Donohue J H, Schutt A J et al. 1994 Pseudomyxoma peritonei: Long-term patient survival with an aggressive regional approach. Ann Surg 219: 112–119

1098. Miner T J, Shia J, Jaques D P et al. 2005 Long-term survival following treatment of pseudomyxoma peritonei: an analysis of surgical therapy. Ann Surg 241: 300–308

1099. Ronnett B M, Yan H, Kurman R J et al. 2001 Patients with pseudomyxoma peritonei associated with disseminated peritoneal adenomucinosis have a significantly more favorable prognosis than patients with peritoneal mucinous carcinomatosis. Cancer 92: 85–91

1100. Yan H, Pestieau S R, Shmookler B M et al. 2001 Histopathologic analysis in 46 patients with pseudomyxoma peritonei syndrome: failure versus success with a second-look operation. Mod Pathol 14: 164–171

1101. Bryant J, Clegg A J, Sidhu M K et al. 2005 Systematic review of the Sugarbaker procedure for pseudomyxoma peritonei. Br J Surg 92: 153–158

1102. Guner Z, Schmidt U, Dahlke M H et al. 2005 Cytoreductive surgery and intraperitoneal chemotherapy for pseudomyxoma peritonei. Int J Colorectal Dis 20: 155–160

1103. Deraco M, Baratti D, Inglese M G et al. 2004 Peritonectomy and intraperitoneal hyperthermic perfusion (IPHP): a strategy that has confirmed its efficacy in patients with pseudomyxoma peritonei. Ann Surg Oncol 11: 393–398

1104. Glehen O, Mohamed F, Gilly F N 2004 Peritoneal carcinomatosis from digestive tract cancer: new management by cytoreductive surgery and intraperitoneal chemohyperthermia. Lancet Oncol 5: 219–228

1105. Young R H, Gilks C B, Scully R E 1991 Mucinous tumors of the appendix associated with mucinous tumors of the ovary and pseudomyxoma peritonei. A clinicopathological analysis of 22 cases supporting an origin in the appendix. Am J Surg Pathol 15: 415–429

1106. Ronnett B M, Kurman R J, Zahn C M et al. 1995 Pseudomyxoma peritonei in women: a clinicopathologic analysis of 30 cases with emphasis on site of origin, prognosis, and relationship to ovarian mucinous tumors of low malignant potential. Hum Pathol 26: 509–524

1107. Guerrieri C, Franlund B, Boeryd B 1995 Expression of cytokeratin 7 in simultaneous mucinous tumors of the ovary and appendix. Mod Pathol 8: 573–576

1108. Ronnett B M, Shmookler B M, Diener-West M et al. 1997 Immunohistochemical evidence supporting the appendiceal origin of pseudomyxoma peritonei in women. Int J Gynecol Pathol 16: 1–9

1109. O'Connell J T, Hacker C M, Barsky S H 2002 MUC2 is a molecular marker for pseudomyxoma peritonei. Mod Pathol 15: 958–972

1110. O'Connell J T, Tomlinson J S, Roberts A A et al. 2002 Pseudomyxoma peritonei is a disease of MUC2-expressing goblet cells. Am J Pathol 161: 551–564

1111. Chuaqui R F, Zhuang Z P, Emmert-Buck M R et al. 1996 Genetic analysis of synchronous mucinous tumors of the ovary and appendix. Hum Pathol 27: 165–171

1112. Cuatrecasas M, Matias-Guiu X, Prat J 1996 Synchronous mucinous tumors of the appendix and the ovary associated with pseudomyxoma peritonei – A clinicopathologic study of six cases with comparative analysis of c-Ki-ras mutations. Am J Surg Pathol 20: 739–746

1113. Szych C, Staebler A, Connolly D C et al. 1999 Molecular genetic evidence supporting the clonality and appendiceal origin of Pseudomyxoma peritonei in women. Am J Pathol 154: 1849–1855

1114. Seidman J D, Elsayed A M, Sobin L H et al. 1993 Association of mucinous tumors of the ovary and appendix: A clinicopathologic study of 25 cases. Am J Surg Pathol 17: 22–34

1115. Du Plessis D G, Louw J A, Wranz B 1999 Mucinous epithelial cysts of the spleen associated with pseudomyxoma peritonei. Histopathology 35: 551–557

1116. Misdraji J, Young R H 2004 Primary epithelial neoplasms and other epithelial lesions of the appendix (excluding carcinoid tumors). Semin Diagn Pathol 21: 120–133

1117. Mukherjee A, Parvaiz A, Cecil T D et al. 2004 Pseudomyxoma peritonei usually originates from the appendix: a review of the evidence. Eur J Gynaecol Oncol 25: 411–414

1118. Lamps L W, Gray G F Jr, Dilday B R et al. 2000 The coexistence of low-grade mucinous neoplasms of the appendix and appendiceal diverticula: a possible role in the pathogenesis of pseudomyxoma peritonei. Mod Pathol 13: 495–501

1119. Misdraji J, Yantiss R K, Graeme-Cook F M et al. 2003 Appendiceal mucinous neoplasms: a clinicopathologic analysis of 107 cases. Am J Surg Pathol 27: 1089–1103

1120. Kabbani W, Houlihan P S, Luthra R et al. 2002 Mucinous and nonmucinous appendiceal adenocarcinomas: different clinicopathological features but similar genetic alterations. Mod Pathol 15: 599–605

1121. Clement P B 1993 Tumor-like lesions of the ovary associated with pregnancy. Int J Gynecol Pathol 12: 108–115

1122. Scully R E, Young R H, Clement P B 1998 Tumors of the ovary, maldeveloped gonads, fallopian tube, and broad ligament. Armed Forces Institute of Pathology, Washington, DC

1123. Clement P B, Young R H, Scully R E 1989 Nontrophoblastic pathology of the female genital tract and peritoneum associated with pregnancy. Semin Diagn Pathol 6: 372–406

1124. Hatjis C G 1985 Nonimmunologic fetal hydrops associated with hyperreactio luteinalis. Obstet Gynecol 65: 11S–3S

1125. Reubinoff B E, Mor-Yosef S, Shushan A et al. 1994 Hyperreactio luteinalis associated with non-immune hydrops fetalis – the role of pituitary hormones. Eur J Obstet Gynecol Reprod Biol 53: 144–146

1126. Schnorr J A Jr, Miller H, Davis J R et al. 1996 Hyperreactio luteinalis associated with pregnancy: a case report and review of the literature. Am J Perinatol 13: 95–97

1127. Bidus M A, Ries A, Magann E F et al. 2002 Markedly elevated beta-hCG levels in a normal singleton gestation with hyperreactio luteinalis. Obstet Gynecol 99: 958–961

1128. Csapo Z, Szabo I, Toth M et al. 1999 Hyperreactio luteinalis in a normal singleton pregnancy – A case report. J Reprod Med 44: 53–56

1129. Upadhyaya G, Goswami A, Babu S 2004 Bilateral theca lutein cysts: a rare cause of acute abdomen in pregnancy. Emerg Med Australas 16: 476–477

1130. Garcia-Bunuel R, Berek J S, Woodruff J D 1975 Luteomas of pregnancy. Obstet Gynecol 45: 407–414

1131. Norris H J, Taylor H B 1967 Nodular theca-lutein hyperplasia of pregnancy (so-called "pregnancy luteoma"). A clinical and pathologic study of 15 cases. Am J Clin Pathol 47: 557–566

1132. Sternberg W H, Barclay D L 1966 Luteoma of pregnancy. Am J Obstet Gynecol 95: 165–184

1133. Choi J R, Levine D, Finberg H 2000 Luteoma of pregnancy: sonographic findings in two cases. J Ultrasound Med 19: 877–881

1134. Hensleigh P A, Woodruff J D 1978 Differential maternal-fetal response to androgenizing luteoma or hyperreactio luteinalis. Obstet Gynecol Surv 33: 262–271

1135. Satyanarayana S, Bohre J K 2001 Ovarian granulosa cell "tumorlet" and mature follicles with ectopic decidua in pregnancy – a case report. Indian J Pathol Microbiol 44: 149–150

1136. Piana S, Nogales F F, Corrado S et al. 1999 Pregnancy luteoma with granulosa cell proliferation: an unusual hyperplastic lesion arising in pregnancy and mimicking an ovarian neoplasia. Pathol Res Pract 195: 859–863

1137. Chervenak F A, Castadot M, Wiederman J et al. 1980 Massive ovarian edema: a review of world's literature and report of two cases. Obstet Gynecol Surv 35: 677–684

1138. Kanbour A I, Salazar H, Tobon H 1979 Massive ovarian edema. A non-neoplastic pelvic mass of young women. Arch Pathol Lab Med 103: 42–45

1139. Roth L M, Deaton R L, Sternberg W H 1979 Massive ovarian edema. A clinicopathologic study of five cases including ultrastructural observations and review of the literature. Am J Surg Pathol 3: 11–21

1140. Young R H, Scully R E 1984 Fibromatosis and massive edema of the ovary, possibly related entities: a report of 14 cases of fibromatosis and 11 cases of massive edema. Int J Gynecol Pathol 3: 153–178

1141. Lara-Torre E, Geist R R, Rabinowitz R et al. 2005 Massive edema of the ovary: a case report and review of the pertinent literature. J Pediatr Adolesc Gynecol 18: 281–284

1142. Krasevic M, Haller H, Rupcic S et al. 2004 Massive edema of the ovary: a report of two cases due to lymphatic permeation by metastatic carcinoma from the uterine cervix. Gynecol Oncol 93: 564–567

1143. Bazot M, Detchev R, Cortez A et al. 2003 Massive ovarian edema revealing gastric carcinoma: a case report. Gynecol Oncol 91: 648–650

1144. Youngs L A, Taylor H B 1967 Adenomatoid tumors of the uterus and fallopian tube. Am J Clin Pathol 48: 537–545

1145. Stephenson T J, Mills P M 1986 Adenomatoid tumours: an immunohistochemical and ultrastructural appraisal of their histogenesis. J Pathol 148: 327–335

1146. Salazar H, Kanbour A, Burgess F 1972 Ultrastructure and observations on the histogenesis of mesotheliomas, "adenomatoid tumors", of the female genital tract. Cancer 29: 141–152

1147. Skinnider B F, Young R H 2004 Infarcted adenomatoid tumor: a report of five cases of a facet of a benign neoplasm that may cause diagnostic difficulty. Am J Surg Pathol 28: 77–83

1148. Nogales F F, Isaac M A, Hardisson D et al. 2002 Adenomatoid tumors of the uterus: an analysis of 60 cases. Int J Gynecol Pathol 21: 34–40

1149. Schwartz E J, Longacre T A 2004 Adenomatoid tumors of the female and male genital tracts express WT1. Int J Gynecol Pathol 23: 123–128

1150. Delahunt B, Eble J N, King D et al. 2000 Immunohistochemical evidence for mesothelial origin of paratesticular adenomatoid tumour. Histopathology 36: 109–115

1151. Alvarado-Cabrero I, Navani S S, Young R H et al. 1997 Tumors of the fimbriated end of the fallopian tube: a clinicopathologic analysis of 20 cases, including nine carcinomas. Int J Gynecol Pathol 16: 189–196

1152. De la Fuente A A 1982 Benign mixed Mullerian tumour–adenofibroma of the fallopian tube. Histopathology 6: 661–666

1153. Chen K T 1981 Bilateral papillary adenofibroma of the fallopian tube. Am J Clin Pathol 75: 229–231

1154. Kayaalp E, Heller D S, Majmudar B 2000 Serous tumor of low malignant potential of the fallopian tube. Int J Gynecol Pathol 19: 398–400

1155. Gurbuz Y, Ozkara S K 2003 Immunohistochemical profile of serous papillary cystadenofibroma of the fallopian tube: a clue of paramesonephritic origin. Appl Immunohistochem Mol Morphol 11: 153–155

1156. Zheng W X, Wolf S, Kramer E E et al. 1996 Borderline papillary serous tumor of the Fallopian tube. Am J Surg Pathol 20: 30–35

1157. Seidman J D 1994 Mucinous lesions of the Fallopian tube: A report of seven cases. Am J Surg Pathol 18: 1205–1212

1158. Honore L H, Dunnett I P 1976 Leiomyoma of the Fallopian tube. A case report and review of the literature. Arch Gynakol 221: 47–50

1159. Moore O A, Waxman M, Udoffia C 1979 Leiomyoma of the fallopian tube: a cause of tubal pregnancy. Am J Obstet Gynecol 134: 101–102

1160. Katz D A, Thom D, Bogard P et al. 1984 Angiomyolipoma of the fallopian tube. Am J Obstet Gynecol 148: 341–343

1161. Talerman A 1969 Haemangioma of the Fallopian tube. J Obstet Gynaecol Br Commonw 76: 559–560

1162. Ebrahimi T, Okagaki T 1973 Hemangioma of the Fallopian tube. Am J Obstet Gynecol 115: 864–865

1163. Joglekar V M 1979 Haemangioma of the fallopian tube. Case report. Br J Obstet Gynaecol 86: 823–825

1164. Kobayashi T, Suzuki K, Arai T et al. 1999 Angiomyofibroblastoma arising from the fallopian tube. Obstet Gynecol 94: 833–834

1165. Berzal-Cantalejo F, Montesinos-Carbonell M, Montesinos-Carbonell M L et al. 2005 Solitary fibrous tumor arising in the fallopian tube. Gynecol Oncol 96: 880–882

1166. Okagaki T, Richart R M 1970 Neurilemoma of the fallopian tube. Am J Obstet Gynecol 106: 929

1167. Duran B, Guvenal T, Yildiz E et al. 2004 An unusual cause of adnexal mass: fallopian tube schwannoma. Gynecol Oncol 92: 343–346

1168. Weber D L, Fazzini E 1970 Ganglioneuroma of the fallopian tube. A heretofore unreported finding. Acta Neuropathol 16: 173–175

1169. Spanta R, Lawrence W D 1995 Soft tissue chondroma of the fallopian tube. Differential diagnosis and histogenetic considerations. Pathol Res Pract 191: 174–176

1170. Han J Y, Han H S, Kim Y B et al. 2002 Extraskeletal chondroma of the fallopian tube. J Korean Med Sci 17: 276–278

1171. Mazzarella P, Okagaki T, Richart R M 1972 Teratoma of the uterine tube. A case report and review of the literature. Obstet Gynecol 39: 381–388

1172. Hurd J K Jr 1978 Benign cystic teratoma of the fallopian tube. Obstet Gynecol 52: 362–364

1173. Kutteh W H, Albert T 1991 Mature cystic teratoma of the fallopian tube associated with an ectopic pregnancy. Obstet Gynecol 78: 984–986

1174. Yoshioka T, Tanaka T 2000 Mature solid teratoma of the fallopian tube: case report. Eur J Obstet Gynecol Reprod Biol 89: 205–206

1175. Alenghat E, Sassone M, Talerman A 1982 Mature, solid teratoma of the fallopian tube. J Reprod Med 27: 484–486

1176. Baginski L, Yazigi R, Sandstad J 1989 Immature (malignant) teratoma of the fallopian tube. Am J Obstet Gynecol 160: 671–672

1177. Sweet R L, Selinger H E, McKay D G 1975 Malignant teratoma of the uterine tube. Obstet Gynecol 45: 553–556

1178. Hoda S A, Huvos A G 1993 Struma salpingis associated with struma ovarii. Am J Surg Pathol 17: 1187–1189

1179. Astall E C, Brewster J A, Lonsdale R 2000 Malignant carcinoid tumour arising in a mature teratoma of the fallopian tube. Histopathology 36: 282–283

1180. Li S, Zimmerman R L, Livolsi V A 1999 Mixed malignant germ cell tumor of the fallopian tube. Int J Gynecol Pathol 18: 183–185

1181. Ajithkumar T V, Minimole A L, John M M et al. 2005 Primary fallopian tube carcinoma. Obstet Gynecol Surv 60: 247–252

1182. Alvarado-Cabrero I, Young R H, Vamvakas E C et al. 1999 Carcinoma of the fallopian tube: a clinicopathological study of 105 cases with observations on staging and prognostic factors. Gynecol Oncol 72: 367–379

1183. Piura B, Rabinovich A 2000 Primary carcinoma of the fallopian tube: study of 11 cases. Eur J Obstet Gynecol Reprod Biol 91: 169–175

1184. Obermair A, Taylor K H, Janda M et al. 2001 Primary fallopian tube carcinoma: the Queensland experience. Int J Gynecol Cancer 11: 69–72

1185. Romagosa C, Torne A, Iglesias X et al. 2003 Carcinoma of the fallopian tube presenting as acute pelvic inflammatory disease. Gynecol Oncol 89: 181–184

1186. Demopoulos R I, Aronov R, Mesia A 2001 Clues to the pathogenesis of fallopian tube carcinoma: a morphological and immunohistochemical case control study. Int J Gynecol Pathol 20: 128–132

1187. Aziz S, Kuperstein G, Rosen B et al. 2001 A genetic epidemiological study of carcinoma of the fallopian tube. Gynecol Oncol 80: 341–345

1188. Zweemer R P, Van Diest P J, Verheijen R H et al. 2000 Molecular evidence linking primary cancer of the fallopian tube to BRCA1 germline mutations. Gynecol Oncol 76: 45–50

1189. Levine D A, Argenta P A, Yee C J et al. 2003 Fallopian tube and primary peritoneal carcinomas associated with BRCA mutations. J Clin Oncol 21: 4222–4227

1190. Paley P J, Swisher E M, Garcia R L et al. 2001 Occult cancer of the fallopian tube in BRCA-1 germline mutation carriers at prophylactic oophorectomy: a case for recommending hysterectomy at surgical prophylaxis. Gynecol Oncol 80: 176–180

1191. Carcangiu M L, Radice P, Manoukian S et al. 2004 Atypical epithelial proliferation in fallopian tubes in prophylactic salpingo-oophorectomy specimens from BRCA1 and BRCA2 germline mutation carriers. Int J Gynecol Pathol 23: 35–40

1192. Piek J M J, Van Diest P J, Zweemer R P et al. 2001 Dysplastic changes in prophylactically removed Fallopian tubes of women predisposed to developing ovarian cancer. J Pathol 195: 451–456

1193. Olivier R I, van B M, Lubsen M A et al. 2004 Clinical outcome of prophylactic oophorectomy in BRCA1/BRCA2 mutation carriers and events during follow-up. Br J Cancer 90: 1492–1497

1194. Scheuer L, Kauff N, Robson M et al. 2002 Outcome of preventive surgery and screening for breast and ovarian cancer in BRCA mutation carriers. J Clin Oncol 20: 1260–1268

1195. Gadducci A 2002 Current management of fallopian tube carcinoma. Curr Opin Obstet Gynecol 14: 27–32

1196. Takeshima N, Hasumi K 2000 Treatment of fallopian tube cancer. Review of the literature. Arch Gynecol Obstet 264: 13–19

1197. Cormio G, Maneo A, Gabriele A et al. 1996 Primary carcinoma of the fallopian tube. A retrospective analysis of 47 patients. Ann Oncol 7: 271–275

1198. Gemignani M L, Hensley M L, Cohen R et al. 2001 Paclitaxel-based chemotherapy in carcinoma of the fallopian tube. Gynecol Oncol 80: 16–20

1199. Baekelandt M, Nesbakken A J, Kristensen G B et al. 2000 Carcinoma of the fallopian tube – Clinicopathologic study of 151 patients treated at the Norwegian Radium Hospital. Cancer 89: 2076–2084

1200. Schneider C, Wight E, Perucchini D et al. 2000 Primary carcinoma of the fallopian tube. A report of 19 cases with literature review. Eur J Gynaecol Oncol 21: 578–582

1201. Rosen A C, Klein M, Hafner E et al. 1999 Management and prognosis of primary fallopian tube carcinoma. Austrian Cooperative Study Group for Fallopian Tube Carcinoma. Gynecol Obstet Invest 47: 45–51

1202. Peters W A III, Andersen W A, Hopkins M P 1989 Results of chemotherapy in advanced carcinoma of the fallopian tube. Cancer 63: 836–838

1203. Tulunay G, Arvas M, Demir B et al. 2004 Primary fallopian tube carcinoma: a retrospective multicenter study. Eur J Gynaecol Oncol 25: 611–614

1204. Kosary C, Trimble E L 2002 Treatment and survival for women with Fallopian tube carcinoma: a population-based study. Gynecol Oncol 86: 190–191

1205. Hefler L A, Rosen A G, Graf A H et al. 2000 The clinical value of serum concentrations of cancer antigen 125 in patients with primary fallopian tube carcinoma – A multicenter study. Cancer 89: 1555–1560

1205a. Medeiros F, Muto M G, Lee Y et al. 2006 The tubal fimbria is a preferred site for early adenocarcinoma in women with familial ovarian cancer syndrome. Am J Surg Pathol 30: 230–236

1206. Yanai-Inbar I, Silverberg S G 2000 Mucosal epithelial proliferation of the fallopian tube: prevalence, clinical associations, and optimal strategy for histopathologic assessment. Int J Gynecol Pathol 19: 139–144

1207. di Re E, Grosso G, Raspagliesi F et al. 1996 Fallopian tube cancer: incidence and role of lymphatic spread. Gynecol Oncol 62: 199–202

1208. Navani S S, Alvarado-Cabrero I, Young R H et al. 1996 Endometrioid carcinoma of the fallopian tube: a clinicopathologic analysis of 26 cases. Gynecol Oncol 63: 371–378

1209. Daya D, Young R H, Scully R E 1992 Endometrioid carcinoma of the fallopian tube resembling an adnexal tumor of probable Wolffian origin: a report of six cases. Int J Gynecol Pathol 11: 122–130

1210. Williamson J M S, Armour A 1993 Microcystic endometrioid carcinoma of the Fallopian tube simulating an adnexal tumour of probable Wolffian origin. Histopathology 23: 578–580

1211. Fukunaga M, Bisceglia M, Dimitri L 2004 Endometrioid carcinoma of the fallopian tube resembling a female adnexal tumor of probable wolffian origin. Adv Anat Pathol 11: 269–272

1212. Barakat R R, Rubin S C, Saigo P E et al. 1991 Cisplatin-based combination chemotherapy in carcinoma of the fallopian tube. Gynecol Oncol 42: 156–160

1213. Hartley A, Rollason T, Spooner D 2000 Clear cell carcinoma of the fimbria of the fallopian tube in a BRCA1 carrier undergoing prophylactic surgery. Clin Oncol (R Coll Radiol) 12: 58–59

1214. Voet R L, Lifshitz S 1982 Primary clear cell adenocarcinoma of the fallopian tube: light microscopic and ultrastructural findings. Int J Gynecol Pathol 1: 292–298

1215. Cheung A N, So K F, Ngan H Y et al. 1994 Primary squamous cell carcinoma of fallopian tube. Int J Gynecol Pathol 13: 92–95

1216. Jackson-York G L, Ramzy I 1992 Synchronous papillary mucinous adenocarcinoma of the endocervix and fallopian tubes. Int J Gynecol Pathol 11: 63–67

1217. Herbold D R, Axelrod J H, Bobowski S J et al. 1988 Glassy cell carcinoma of the fallopian tube. A case report. Int J Gynecol Pathol 7: 384–390

1218. Aoyama T, Mizuno T, Andoh K et al. 1996 alpha-Fetoprotein-producing (hepatoid) carcinoma of the fallopian tube. Gynecol Oncol 63: 261–266

1219. Dursun P, Salman M C, Taskiran C et al. 2004 Primary neuroendocrine carcinoma of the fallopian tube: a case report. Am J Obstet Gynecol 190: 568–571

1220. Peters W A III, Andersen W A, Hopkins M P et al. 1988 Prognostic features of carcinoma of the fallopian tube. Obstet Gynecol 71: 757–762

1221. Benda J A, Veronezi-Gurwell A, Wilcox M et al. 1994 An unusual extrauterine variant of adenosarcoma with multiple recurrences over 16 years. Gynecol Oncol 53: 131–137

1222. Gollard R, Kosty M, Bordin G et al. 1995 Two unusual presentations of mullerian adenosarcoma: case reports, literature review, and treatment considerations. Gynecol Oncol 59: 412–422

1223. Carlson J A Jr, Ackerman B L, Wheeler J E 1993 Malignant mixed Müllerian tumor of the fallopian tube. Cancer 71: 187–192

1224. Weber A M, Hewett W F, Gajewski W H et al. 1993 Malignant mixed mullerian tumors of the fallopian tube. Gynecol Oncol 50: 239–243

1225. Horn L C, Werschnik C, Bilek K et al. 1996 Diagnosis and clinical management in malignant Müllerian tumors of the fallopian tube. A report of four cases and review of recent literature. Arch Gynecol Obstet 258: 47–53

1226. Imachi M, Tsukamoto N, Shigematsu T et al. 1992 Malignant mixed Müllerian tumor of the fallopian tube: report of two cases and review of literature. Gynecol Oncol 47: 114–124

1227. Muntz H G, Rutgers J L, Tarraza H et al. 1989 Carcinosarcomas and mixed Mullerian tumors of the fallopian tube. Gynecol Oncol 34: 109–115

1228. Buchino J J, Buchino J J 1987 Malignant mixed mullerian tumor of the fallopian tube. Arch Pathol Lab Med 111: 386–387

1229. Lim B J, Kim J W, Yang W I et al. 2004 Malignant mixed mullerian tumor of fallopian tube with multiple distinct heterologous components. Int J Gynecol Cancer 14: 690–693

1230. Manes J L, Taylor H B 1976 Carcinosarcoma and mixed mullerian tumors of the fallopian tube: report of four cases. Cancer 38: 1687–1693

1231. van Dijk C M, Kooijman C D, van Lindert A C 1990 Malignant mixed mullerian tumour of the fallopian tube. Histopathology 16: 300–302

1232. Gagner J P, Mittal K 2005 Malignant mixed Mullerian tumor of the fimbriated end of the fallopian tube: origin as an intraepithelial carcinoma. Gynecol Oncol 97: 219–222

1233. Ebert A D, Perez-Canto A, Schaller G et al. 1998 Stage I primary malignant mixed mullerian tumor of the fallopian tube. Report of a case with five-year survival after minimal surgery without adjuvant treatment. J Reprod Med 43: 598–600

1234. Jacoby A F, Fuller A F J, Thor A D et al. 1993 Primary leiomyosarcoma of the fallopian tube. Gynecol Oncol 51: 404–407

1235. Ebert A, Goetze B, Herbst H et al. 1995 Primary leiomyosarcoma of the fallopian tube. Ann Oncol 6: 618–619

1236. Buchwalter C L, Jenison E L, Fromm M et al. 1997 Pure embryonal rhabdomyosarcoma of the fallopian tube. Gynecol Oncol 67: 95–101

1237. Halligan A W, McGuinness E P 1990 Malignant fibrous histiocytoma of the fallopian tube. Br J Obstet Gynaecol 97: 275–276

1238. Noack F, Lange K, Lehmann V et al. 2002 Primary extranodal marginal zone B-cell lymphoma of the fallopian tube. Gynecol Oncol 86: 384–386

1239. Gaffan J, Herbertson R, Davis P et al. 2004 Bilateral peripheral T-cell lymphoma of the fallopian tubes. Gynecol Oncol 95: 736–738

1240. Goodlad J R, MacPherson S, Jackson R et al. 2004 Extranodal follicular lymphoma: a clinicopathological and genetic analysis of 15 cases arising at non-cutaneous extranodal sites. Histopathology 44: 268–276

1241. Muto M G, Lage J M, Berkowitz R S et al. 1991 Gestational trophoblastic disease of the fallopian tube. J Reprod Med 36: 57–60

1242. Newcomer J R 1998 Ampullary tubal hydatidiform mole treated with linear salpingotomy. A case report. J Reprod Med 43: 913–915

1243. Terada S, Suzuki N, Uchide K et al. 1993 Partial hydatidiform mole in the fallopian tube. Gynecol Obstet Invest 35: 240–242

1244. Montgomery E A, Roberts E F, Conran R M et al. 1993 Triploid abortus presenting as an ectopic pregnancy. Arch Pathol Lab Med 117: 652–653

1245. Burton J L, Lidbury E A, Gillespie A M et al. 2001 Over-diagnosis of hydatidiform mole in early tubal ectopic pregnancy. Histopathology 38: 409–417

1246. Dekel A, Van Iddekinge B, Isaacson C et al. 1986 Primary choriocarcinoma of the fallopian tube. Report of a case with survival and postoperative delivery. Review of the literature. Obstet Gynecol Surv 41: 142–148

1247. Lee S M, Kang J H, Oh S Y et al. 2005 A successfully treated case of primary tubal choriocarcinoma coexistent with viable intrauterine pregnancy. Gynecol Oncol 97: 671–673

1248. Bakri Y N, Amri A, Mulla J 1992 Gestational choriocarcinoma in a tubal ectopic pregnancy. Acta Obstet Gynecol Scand 71: 67–68

1249. Su Y N, Cheng W F, Chen C A et al. 1999 Pregnancy with primary tubal placental site trophoblastic tumor – A case report and literature review. Gynecol Oncol 73: 322–325

1250. Baergen R N, Rutgers J, Young R H 2003 Extrauterine lesions of intermediate trophoblast. Int J Gynecol Pathol 22: 362–367

1251. Parker A, Lee V, Dalrymple C et al. 2003 Epithelioid trophoblastic tumour: report of a case in the fallopian tube. Pathology 35: 136–140

1252. Kuo K T, Chen M J, Lin M C 2004 Epithelioid trophoblastic tumor of the broad ligament: a case report and review of the literature. Am J Surg Pathol 28: 405–409

1253. Campello T R, Fittipaldi H, O'Valle F et al. 1998 Extrauterine (tubal) placental site nodule. Histopathology 32: 562–565

1254. Kouvidou C, Karayianni M, Liapi-Avgeri G et al. 2000 Old ectopic pregnancy remnants with morphological features of placental site nodule occurring in fallopian tube and broad ligament. Pathol Res Pract 196: 329–332

1255. Nayar R, Snell J, Silverberg S G et al. 1996 Placental site nodule occurring in a fallopian tube. Hum Pathol 27: 1243–1245

1256. Falls J L 1955 Accessory adrenal cortex in the broad ligament. Incidence and functional significance. Cancer 8: 142–150

1257. Wild R A, Albert R D, Zaino R J et al. 1988 Virilizing paraovarian tumors: a consequence of Nelson's syndrome? Obstet Gynecol 71: 1053–1056

1258. Verdonk C, Guerin C, Lufkin E et al. 1982 Activation of virilizing adrenal rest tissues by excessive ACTH production. An unusual presentation of Nelson's syndrome. Am J Med 73: 455–459

1259. van Ingen G, Schoemaker J, Baak J P 1991 A testosterone-producing tumour in the mesovarium. Pathol Res Pract 187: 362–370

1260. Sasano H, Sato S, Yajima A et al. 1997 Adrenal rest tumor of the broad ligament: case report with immunohistochemical study of steroidogenic enzymes. Pathol Int 47: 493–496

1261. Keitoku M, Konishi I, Nanbu K et al. 1997 Extraovarian sex cord-stromal tumor: case report and review of the literature. Int J Gynecol Pathol 16: 180–185

1262. Lin H H, Chen Y P, Lee T Y 1987 A hormone-producing thecoma of broad ligament. Acta Obstet Gynecol Scand 66: 725–727

1263. Shone N, Duggan M A, Ghatage P 2003 Granulosa cell tumour of the broad ligament. Pathology 35: 265–267

1264. Steed H, Oza A, Chapman W B et al. 2004 Female adnexal tumor of probable wolffian origin: a clinicopathological case report and a possible new treatment. Int J Gynecol Cancer 14: 546–550

1265. Atallah D, Rouzier R, Voutsadakis I et al. 2004 Malignant female adnexal tumor of probable wolffian origin relapsing after pregnancy. Gynecol Oncol 95: 402–404

1266. Ramirez P T, Wolf J K, Malpica A et al. 2002 Wolffian duct tumors: case reports and review of the literature. Gynecol Oncol 86: 225–230

1267. Prasad C J, Ray J A, Kessler S 1992 Female adnexal tumor of wolffian origin. Arch Pathol Lab Med 116: 189–191

1268. Brescia R J, Cardoso de Almeida P C, Fuller A F J et al. 1985 Female adnexal tumor of probable Wolffian origin with multiple recurrences over 16 years. Cancer 56: 1456–1461

1269. Daya D 1994 Malignant female adnexal tumor of probable wolffian origin with review of the literature. Arch Pathol Lab Med 118: 310–312

1270. Sheyn I, Mira J L, Bejarano P A et al. 2000 Metastatic female adnexal tumor of probable wolffian origin – A case report and review of the literature. Arch Pathol Lab Med 124: 431–434

1271. Karpuz V, Berger S D, Burkhardt K et al. 1999 A case of endometrioid carcinoma of the fallopian tube mimicking an adnexal tumor of probable Wolffian origin. APMIS 107: 550–554

1272. Tiltman A J, Allard U 2001 Female adnexal tumours of probable Wolffian origin: an immunohistochemical study comparing tumours, mesonephric remnants and paramesonephric derivatives. Histopathology 38: 237–242

1273. Stewart G J R, Nandini C L, Richmond J A 2000 Value of A103 (melan-A) immunostaining in the differential diagnosis of ovarian sex cord stromal tumours. J Clin Pathol 53: 206–211

1274. Genadry R, Parmley T, Woodruff J D 1977 The origin and clinical behavior of the paraovarian tumor. Am J Obstet Gynecol 15 129: 873–880

1275. Honore L H, O'Hara K E 1980 Serous papillary neoplasms arising in paramesonephric parovarian cysts. A report of eight cases. Acta Obstet Gynecol Scand 59: 525–528

1276. Aslani M, Ahn G H, Scully R E 1988 Serous papillary cystadenoma of borderline malignancy of broad ligament. A report of 25 cases. Int J Gynecol Pathol 7: 131–138

1277. Aslani M, Scully R E 1989 Primary carcinoma of the broad ligament. Report of four cases and review of the literature. Cancer 64: 1540–1545

1278. d'Ablaing G III, Klatt E C, DiRocco G et al. 1983 Broad ligament serous tumor of low malignant potential. Int J Gynecol Pathol 2: 93–99

1279. Hampton H L, Huffman H T, Meeks G R 1992 Extraovarian Brenner tumor. Obstet Gynecol 79: 844–846

1280. Kobayashi Y, Yamazaki K, Shinohara M et al. 1996 Undifferentiated carcinoma of the broad ligament in a 28-year-old woman – a case report and results of immunohistochemical and electron-microscopic studies. Gynecol Oncol 63: 382–387

1281. Altaras M M, Jaffe R, Corduba M et al. 1990 Primary paraovarian cystadenocarcinoma: clinical and management aspects and literature review. Gynecol Oncol 38: 268–272

1282. Mrad K, Driss M, Abdelmoula S et al. 2005 Primary broad ligament cystadenocarcinoma with mucinous component: a case report with immunohistochemical study. Arch Pathol Lab Med 129: 244–246

1283. Lonser R R, Glenn G M, Walther M et al. 2003 von Hippel-Lindau disease. Lancet 361: 2059–2067

1284. Friedrich C A 1999 Von Hippel-Lindau syndrome – A pleomorphic condition. Cancer 86: 1658–1662

1285. Aydin H, Young R H, Ronnett B M et al. 2005 Clear cell papillary cystadenoma of the epididymis and mesosalpinx: immunohistochemical differentiation from metastatic clear cell renal cell carcinoma. Am J Surg Pathol 29: 520–523

1286. Gersell D J, King T C 1988 Papillary cystadenoma of the mesosalpinx in von Hippel-Lindau disease. Am J Surg Pathol 12: 145–149

1287. Korn W T, Schatzki S C, DiSciullo A J et al. 1990 Papillary cystadenoma of the broad ligament in von Hippel-Lindau disease. Am J Obstet Gynecol 163: 596–598

1288. Werness B A, Guccion J G 1997 Tumor of the broad ligament in von Hippel-Lindau disease of probable mullerian origin. Int J Gynecol Pathol 16: 282–285

1289. Gaffey M J, Mills S E, Boyd J C 1994 Aggressive papillary tumor of middle ear/temporal bone and adnexal papillary cystadenoma: manifestations of von Hippel-Lindau disease. Am J Surg Pathol 18: 1254–1260

1290. Breen J L, Neubecker R D 1962 Tumors of the round ligament. A review of the literature and a report of 25 cases. Obstet Gynecol 19: 771–780

1291. Sonobe H, Ohtsuki Y, Iwata J et al. 1995 Myolipoma of the round ligament: report of a case with a review of the English literature. Virchow's Arch 427: 455–458

1292. Fink D, Marsden D E, Edwards L et al. 2004 Malignant perivascular epithelioid cell tumor (PEComa) arising in the broad ligament. Int J Gynecol Cancer 14: 1036–1039

1293. Chopra R, Al Mulhim A R, Hashish H 2003 Parametrial angiomyolipoma with multicystic change. Gynecol Oncol 90: 220–223

1294. Bakotic B W, Cabello-Inchausti B, Willis I H et al. 1999 Clear-cell epithelioid leiomyoma of the round ligament. Mod Pathol 12: 912–918

1295. Roth L M, Reed R J, Sternberg W H 1996 Cotyledonoid dissecting leiomyoma of the uterus – The Sternberg tumor. Am J Surg Pathol 20: 1455–1461

1296. Roth L M, Reed R J 2000 Cotyledonoid leiomyoma of the uterus: report of a case. Int J Gynecol Pathol 19: 272–275

1297. Mulvany N J, Slavin J L, Ostor A G et al. 1994 Intravenous leiomyomatosis of the uterus: a clinicopathologic study of 22 cases. Int J Gynecol Pathol 13: 1–9

1298. Cheng W F, Lin H H, Chen C K et al. 1995 Leiomyosarcoma of the broad ligament: a case report and literature review. Gynecol Oncol 56: 85–89

1299. Shah A, Finn C, Light A 2003 Leiomyosarcoma of the broad ligament: a case report and literature review. Gynecol Oncol 90: 450–452

1300. Ahmed A A, Swan R W, Owen A et al. 1997 Uterus-like mass arising in the broad ligament: a metaplasia or mullerian duct anomaly? Int J Gynecol Pathol 16: 279–281

1301. Al Jafari M S, Panton H M, Gradwell E 1985 Phaeochromocytoma of the broad ligament. Case report. Br J Obstet Gynaecol 92: 649–651

1302. Dieste M C, Lynch G R, Gordon A et al. 1987 Malignant fibrous histiocytoma of the broad ligament: a case report and literature review. Gynecol Oncol 28: 225–229

1303. Fras A P, Frkovic-Grazio S 2001 Hyalinizing spindle cell tumor with giant rosettes of the broad ligament. Gynecol Oncol 83: 405–408

1304. Nielsen G P, Oliva E, Young R H et al. 1995 Alveolar soft-part sarcoma of the female genital tract: a report of nine cases and review of the literature. Int J Gynecol Pathol 14: 283–292

1305. Duggan M A, Hugh J, Nation J G et al. 1989 Ependymoma of the uterosacral ligament. Cancer 64: 2565–2571

1306. Bell D A, Woodruff J M, Scully R E 1984 Ependymoma of the broad ligament. A report of two cases. Am J Surg Pathol 8: 203–209

1307. Grody W W, Nieberg R K, Bhuta S 1985 Ependymoma-like tumor of the mesovarium. Arch Pathol Lab Med 109(3): 291–293

1308. Komuro Y, Mikami M, Sakaiya N et al. 2001 Tumor imprint cytology of ovarian ependymoma – A case report. Cancer 92: 3165–3169

1309. Kleinman G M, Young R H, Scully R E 1984 Ependymoma of the ovary: report of three cases. Hum Pathol 15: 632–638

PART B

Endometrium

George L. Mutter   Tan A. Ince

Endometrial glandular neoplasia

Incidence and pathogenesis

Endometrial carcinoma, which has a variety of histologic sub-types (Table 13B.1), is the commonest invasive cancer of the female genital tract and accounts for 7% of all invasive cancers in women, excluding skin cancer. At one time, it was far less common than cancer of the cervix, but earlier detection and eradication of cervical squamous intraepithelial lesions (SILs) and an increase in endometrial carcinomas in younger age groups have reversed this ratio. In the USA there are now 40 100 new endometrial cancers per year, compared with 12 200 new invasive cervical cancers.[1] Despite their high frequency, endometrial cancers usually arise in postmenopausal women and cause abnormal (postmenopausal) bleeding. This generally permits early detection and cure at an early stage.[2]

Carcinoma of the endometrium is uncommon in women younger than 40 years of age. The peak incidence is in the 55–65-year-old age group. A higher frequency of this form of neoplasia is seen with obesity, diabetes (abnormal glucose tolerance is found in more than 60% of patients), hyper-

tension, and infertility. Women who develop cancer of the endometrium tend to be nulliparous and to give a history of functional menstrual irregularities consistent with anovulatory cycles. Infrequently, both endometrial and breast carcinomas arise in the same patient.[3]

In terms of potential pathogenesis, two general groups of endometrial cancer can be identified: type I and type II.[4] The first and the most well-studied subset (type I) develops on a background of prolonged estrogen stimulation and is often preceded by a premalignant stage characterized by a diagnostic lesion (endometrial intraepithelial neoplasia (EIN), or *atypical endometrial hyperplasia*). In type I neoplasia, both conditions (precancers and cancer) appear to be related to obesity and anovulatory cycles that expose the endometrium to unopposed estrogen stimulation. Additional evidence that implicates a hormonal pathophysiology includes the following:

1. Women with ovarian estrogen-secreting tumors have a higher risk of developing endometrial cancer.
2. Endometrial cancer is extremely rare in women with ovarian agenesis and in those castrated early in life.
3. Estrogen replacement therapy, when unopposed by progestins, is associated with increased risk in women, and prolonged administration of diethylstilbestrol (DES) to laboratory animals may produce endometrial polyps, hyperplasia, and carcinoma.
4. In postmenopausal women, there is greater synthesis of estrogens in body fats from adrenal and ovarian androgen precursors, a finding that may partly explain why there is an increased risk of endometrial cancer with age and obesity.

Endometrial carcinomas that are associated with the afore-mentioned risk factors tend to be well differentiated and mimic normal endometrial glands (*endometrioid*) in histologic appearance. Secretory, squamous, mucinous, and eosinophilic-tubal differentiation may also be a component of tumors in the endometrioid, or type I, group. This group of tumors is generally associated with a more favorable prognosis, as described below.

One must exercise caution, however, to avoid interpreting the epidemiologic association between estrogen exposure and

---

Table 13B.1 Classification and grading of endometrial carcinoma

Endometrioid carcinoma
(grades 1–3 based on architecture, increase in grade by one based on marked nuclear atypia)

* with secretory differentiation
* with ciliated differentiation
* with squamous differentiation

Serous adenocarcinoma (grade 3 by definition)
Clear-cell carcinoma (grade 3 by definition)
Mucinous adenocarcinoma (technically endometrioid, grades 1–3)
Squamous cell carcinoma
Mixed carcinomas
Undifferentiated carcinoma
Other rare types, e.g., transitional cell carcinoma

endometrial carcinoma as evidence that all endometrial changes referable to an unopposed estrogen effect are low-risk precancers. It is normal for perimenopausal women to experience repeated anovulatory menstrual cycles in the years immediately preceding the peak incidence of endometrial cancer in the sixth to seventh decades, during which type I cancers increase in incidence. An unknown number of such patients have had hysterectomies for endometrial pathology referable to anovulatory cycles.

A second and not insignificant subset of patients with endometrial cancer acquire the disease at a somewhat older age without prior association with hyperestrinism or antecedent EIN precursor. In this group (type II), tumors are generally more poorly differentiated, including tumors that resemble subtypes of ovarian carcinomas (*papillary serous carcinomas*). These tumors overall have a poorer prognosis than endometrioid tumors, and the factors predisposing to their development are obscure.[4]

Molecular studies have confirmed that endometrioid and serous subtypes of endometrial adenocarcinoma have a divergent pathogenesis. Inactivation of the *PTEN* tumor suppressor gene in the 10q23 region has been associated with endometrioid tumors, whereas recent studies suggest that losses at 1p may occur preferentially in serous tumors.[5,6] Loss of *p53* function (seen as aberrant protein accumulation on immunohistochemistry) is also more commonly seen in the serous subtype than in endometrioid lesions,[7] while clear cell carcinoma shows an intermediate frequency.[8] Microsatellite instability is more commonly observed in endometrioid tumors than in serous types.[9]

Phases of endometrioid endometrial carcinogenesis

A dynamic model of endometrial tumorigenesis based on mutation-driven sequential clonal selection during tumor evolution (Fig. 13B.1) resembles those proposed for several other tumor systems.[10–13] Each sequential clonal selection occurs through successful competition with elements of the parent field.

Clonal proliferation of a specific cell lineage occurs in limited circumstances in mammals, for example in creation of B-cell clones capable of producing large quantities of particular antibodies. Otherwise, most somatic tissues are polyclonal unless there is a significant growth advantage within a subset of cells which proliferate at the expense of surrounding tissues. As such, clonal proliferation in tissues like the endometrium may be viewed as evidence of the creation of a cell or group of cells with a growth advantage – a characteristic of neoplastic processes.

Presumptive identification of the earliest stages of endometrioid endometrial (type I) precancers has now been accomplished using a variety of molecular marker systems derived from this model. These include lineage continuity (forward carryover) of mutations of genes such as *PTEN* and K-*ras*, between premalignant and malignant carcinogenesis phases in individual patients,[17–19] and demonstration of monoclonal growth of premalignant tissues.[14–16] Molecular characterization of histomorphologically confirmed premalignant endometrial lesions has permitted *de novo* description of histopathologic features of precancers.[20,21] These lesions, referred to as EIN, constitute a biologically more homogenous group

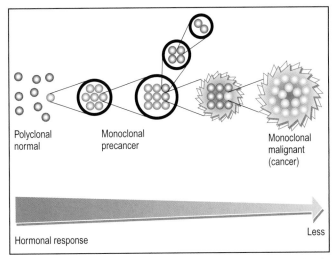

Fig. 13B.1 • Model of endometrial tumorigenesis. Precancers are monoclonal neoplasms that are initiated from a polyclonal normal field by mutations that confer small increases in growth potential under the mitogenic influence of unopposed estrogen. Precancerous clones develop and progress through mutation and selection, eventually reaching a stage where hormonal support is no longer required for survival. Malignant transformation of these precancers occurs by accumulation of sufficient genetic damage to permit invasion of adjacent stromal tissues.

of high-cancer-risk endometria than have been identified previously using the World Health Organization (WHO) hyperplasia schema.

Changing landscape of endometrial precancer criteria and terminology

The postulate that precursor lesions for endometrioid endometrial cancer exist has long been supported by prospective studies showing a high risk for the subsequent development of cancer following the appearance of distinctive histopathologic lesions subdiagnostic of carcinoma itself. Women with atypical endometrial hyperplasia had the highest cancer risk amongst the subtypes of endometrial hyperplasia, which have traditionally been divided by the WHO into four groups based upon presence or absence of cytologic atypia and an architectural pattern which was simple or complex.[22–24] Among these four groups, women with atypical adenomatous hyperplasia had a 25% frequency of concurrent adenocarcinoma at hysterectomy,[24,25] and a 14-fold elevated prospective risk for future adenocarcinoma.[22] This led to the notion that, when atypical hyperplasia is diagnosed, the lesion has traversed a risk threshold that justifies ablational intervention either by surgery or hormonal therapy with progestins. In contrast, non-atypical hyperplasia in this diagnostic scheme presents a significant management challenge as they have a lower, yet still significant, risk for cancer.

Poor reproducibility of endometrial WHO hyperplasia subgroup diagnoses has plagued pathologists, with recent studies reporting that half or fewer than half of diagnoses of atypical endometrial hyperplasia are confirmed by a second pathologist on review.[14,26–28] Perhaps most importantly, cancer outcomes, which occur at elevated frequency amongst the non-atypical hyperplasia patients, diminish the negative predictive value of that approach. In summary, it has been difficult to separate the hyperplasias into benign and precancerous groups based solely on morphology-driven previous approaches. For these reasons, we present here an alternative strategy for diagnosis of endometrial precancers which incorporates substantial new advances in understanding of this disease which have emerged in the last decade.

EIN, a precursor to endometrioid (type I) endometrial adenocarcinoma

Computerized morphometric analysis performed on hematoxylin and eosin-stained slides has shown that these precancers consistently have a surface area of glands which exceeds that of stroma.[15,20] The notion that glandular architectural features should play a major role in identifying precancers is a substantial divergence from long-standing emphasis on nuclear cytology that has characterized the WHO endometrial hyperplasia classification system. It is the impetus behind a newly developed diagnostic paradigm in which precancers, designated as EIN, are diagnosed using combined architectural and cytologic criteria that are fundamentally different from those applied previously to stratify hyperplasias.[15,16] Although discovery of this architectural feature was accomplished with the aid of image analysis, it has led to diagnostic criteria which do not require specialized equipment.

The molecular, clinical, and histologic features of EIN are sufficiently developed so as to provide a crisp overview of the early stages of endometrial carcinogenesis.[29,30] Mutations of the PTEN tumor suppressor gene precede acquisition of any histopathologic changes apparent by routine light microscopy.[31] It is thought that (as yet unspecified) additional genetic changes produce an expansile localizing subclone of morphologically altered endometrial glands with a crowded architecture (gland area exceeds that of stroma) and altered cytology.[20,32] EIN lesions always have a cytology different than the background normal endometrium from which they have emerged, and in the early stages this is readily seen by comparison of epithelial cytology between those crowded glands that define a lesion under low power, and the regular field of less packed normal endometrium. The ultimate cytologic appearance of EIN lesions is highly variable between patients, and may encompass changes in cytoplasmic differentiation (tubal, mucinous, eosinophilic, papillary) or nuclear size, texture, and shape. The combined morphometric and molecular analysis revealed that not all EIN lesions demonstrate the round nuclei and prominent nucleoli classically emphasized as stigmata of nuclear atypia. Rather, the shape may differ from background by being more elongated, or of different size. The critical element is coordinate change in cytology amongst that cohort of glands which grow in an altered architectural pattern.

Clinical cancer outcome prediction using EIN criteria is superior to that seen previously for WHO hyperplasias.[33] Detailed morphometric evaluation of endometria from 477 patients with long-term follow-up shows that, once a lesion of at least 1 mm maximum dimension, with altered cytology and gland-packing meeting EIN criteria, is present, the patient has a 45-fold increased risk of prospectively (at least 1 year later) developing endometrial carcinoma.[34] The risk of concurrent carcinoma is also high – 27%.[35] The negative predictive value of absence of EIN is correspondingly high, on the order of 99%.[34] These compare to a maximum cancer outcome odds ratio for atypical endometrial hyperplasia of 7–27-fold and a negative predictive value of 98%.[22,33,34] Subjective application by pathologists of the EIN schema to a routine hospital-based series of 97 endometrial "hyperplasias" showed excellent EIN diagnostic reproducibility, with intraobserver kappa values of 0.73–0.90, and 75% unanimous agreement amongst a panel of three pathologists. All 8 cancer outcomes (100%) were diagnosed as EIN, whereas these had previously been split between atypical (n = 5) and non-atypical (n = 3) hyperplasia categories.[36]

Diagnosis of EIN

Nomenclature

Tables 13B.2 and 13.B3 show diagnostic classes within the EIN schema, each of which confers differing therapeutic responses.[37] There may be substantial regional differences in therapeutic strategies relevant to impressions of which diagnostic boundaries are most important to distinguish. For example, in the USA, the future reproductive plans of a woman with premalignant disease are often considered in selection between ablation through hormonal treatment with progestins compared to hysterectomy. It is necessary to distinguish clearly between EIN and adenocarcinoma because the latter is routinely managed surgically. This therapeutic distinction between precancerous and cancerous endometrial disease is less relevant in some European settings, where hysterectomy may be the practice standard for both diagnoses. A European proposal, based upon this practical aspect of management, to merge well-differentiated carcinoma with its precursor lesions into a single diagnostic category, has received little support in the USA.[27]

The EIN diagnostic schema is designed to replace, not supplement, older hyperplasia terminology. It should be remembered that the accurate application of this or any other classification depends on the careful consideration of the full constellation of findings in each sample. Individual elements

Table 13B.2	Endometrial intraepithelial neoplasia (EIN): diagnostic schema			
EIN nomenclature		Topography	Functional category	Treatment
Endometrium with architectural changes of unopposed estrogen (disordered proliferative, benign endometrial hyperplasia)		Diffuse	Estrogen effect	Hormonal therapy
EIN		Focal progressing to diffuse	Precancer	Hormonal or surgical
Carcinoma		Focal progressing to diffuse	Cancer	Surgical stage-based

Table 13B.3	Endometrial intraepithelial neoplasia (EIN): diagnostic criteria (all must be met)
EIN criterion	**Comments**
Architecture	Area of glands > stroma (VPS <55%)
Cytology	Cytology differs between architecturally crowded focus and background
Size >1 mm	Maximum linear dimension exceeds 1 mm
Exclude mimics	Benign conditions with overlapping criteria: basal endometrium, secretory, polyps, repair, etc.
Exclude cancer	Carcinoma if maze-like glands, solid areas, or significant cribriforming

VPS, volume percentage stroma.

of altered glandular architecture or cytology that overlap with those of EIN may be seen in a variety of unrelated conditions, and it is the distinction between these endometria and EIN which is the greatest diagnostic challenge.

Endometrial intraepithelial neoplasia

General approach to diagnosis within the EIN schema

Premalignant lesions with a high risk of progression to endometrial adenocarcinoma, EIN, must be distinguished from benign hormonal effects, adenocarcinoma, and a wide variety of mimics, of which the histopathologic appearance partially overlaps with that of EIN. The latter is especially difficult to describe concisely, as accurate resolution of EIN mimics requires recognition of a variety of unrelated entities which should be specifically diagnosed. Benign endometrial polyps, isolated fragments of basal endometrium and lower uterine segment, and tangentially sectioned secretory endometrium are all examples of specific entities susceptible to misdiagnosis as "hyperplasia" or EIN.

Endometria with non-endometrioid differentiation, so-called metaplasias, present special problems. A primary diagnosis of metaplasia without an accompanying benign, premalignant, or malignant diagnosis is rarely indicated, as non-endometrioid differentiation of endometrial glands is generally seen as a feature of benign, premalignant, and malignant processes.[38] Rather, the pathologist should use primary diagnostic terms that clearly indicate a benign (degenerative, hormonal), premalignant (EIN), or malignant (adenocarcinoma) process, and secondarily append a description of non-endometrioid differentiation. For example, tubal differentiation may be part of an anovulatory endometrium with scattered tubal change, an EIN with tubal differentiation, or adenocarcinoma with tubal differentiation. Criteria for resolving benign, premalignant, and malignant subgroups of metaplastic lesions are differentiation-state specific. The topographic distribution of non-endometrioid glands should be carefully examined. Changes secondary to systemic hormonal effects tend to be scattered randomly throughout the

endometrial compartment, and those caused by degeneration are most prominent in areas of breakdown, or inflammation. Premalignant EIN lesions with non-endometrioid differentiation tend to have a more localizing, geographic, expansile quality early in their course.

The best diagnostic criteria are no panacea for a poor specimen. Fragmentation, sample adequacy, local context (e.g., within polyp or lower uterine segment) and patient hormonal state are common confounders of endometrial biopsy and curettage interpretation. The reality is that there will always be a group of specimens which defy diagnosis, and, in those examples, the pathologist should clearly indicate the source of the problem to guide clinical strategies for what is an incomplete diagnostic process and, when appropriate, recommend follow up and repeat sampling of the endometrium.

Endometrium with architectural changes of unopposed estrogens

These endometria are characterized by a homogeneous field effect throughout the endometrial compartment caused by an abnormally long estrogenic interval, typically exceeding the 12–14-day-long follicular phase of the normal menstrual cycle. Protracted estrogen exposures may be secondary to anovulation or exogenous hormone administration. The endometrial field is composed of mitotically active glands, with an architecture that changes as a function of the duration and dose of estrogen exposure (Fig. 13B.2). Initially, architectural changes may be subtle, consisting of rare scattered cysts ("disordered proliferative," Fig. 13B.2A), but, with longer-duration exposures, cysts become more prominent, gland distribution more irregular, and tubular glands may develop branch points (benign endometrial hyperplasia). Although the irregular gland architecture may produce random foci of gland clusters in proximity to one another, this has the appearance of a regularly irregular pattern. These randomly converged glands can readily be distinguished from EIN by having a cytology that is similar to the less crowded areas. Tubal changes, evident as ciliated glands with pink cytoplasm, also occur in a random distribution throughout the field, and may involve cystic or non-cystic glands. Formation of fibrin vascular thrombi within fragile small vessels produces microinfarcts seen histologically as deep scattered areas of stromal breakdown and experienced by the patient as menometrorrhagia (Fig. 13B.2B). Collapse of intervening stroma creates artifactual opposition of displaced degenerating glands that must not be misinterpreted as a localizing EIN lesion. Endometrial breakdown during or following an anovulatory cycle is a common setting in which EIN or atypical endometrial hyperplasia is overdiagnosed.

Endometrial intraepithelial neoplasia

Table 13B.4 lists criteria for diagnosis of EIN, all of which must be met. EIN arises as localized lesions, evident under low magnification as a crowded focus of glands (Fig. 13B.3). In a specimen with many tissue fragments, overview screening of the entire specimen and subsequent selection of individual fields for closer scrutiny based upon architectural pattern are key steps in making the correct diagnosis. Closer examination

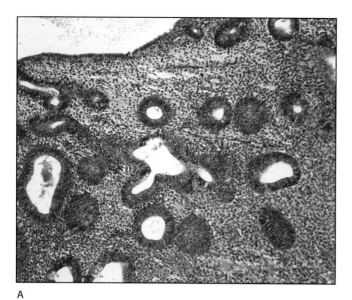

A

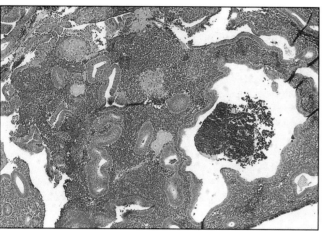

B

Fig. 13B.2 • Disordered proliferative endometrium (anovulatory endometrium). Multiple stigmata of protracted estrogen exposure are readily seen in these biopsies, including tubal metaplasia, and scattered cystically dilated glands in a proliferative setting. Cytology in crowded gland areas is similar to that elsewhere (**A**), and when tubal changes occur they randomly involve tubular and cystically dilated glands. Longer exposures may lead to increased gland-to-stroma ratio, known as benign endometrial hyperplasia, with fibrin thrombi and microinfarcts with stromal breakdown (**B**) that cause menorrhagia.

Table 13B.4	Staging of endometrial carcinoma (FIGO)
Stage	**Extent**
I	Carcinoma is confined to the corpus uteri
Ia	The tumor is confined to the endometrium
Ib	The tumor invades the inner half of the myometrium
Ic	The tumor invades the outer half of the myometrium
II	The tumor involves the corpus and the cervix
IIa	The tumor involves endocervical glands
IIb	The tumor invades cervical stroma
III	The tumor extends outside the uterus but not outside the true pelvis
IIIa	The tumor invades through the serosa to the adnexa, or is associated with positive peritoneal washings
IIIb	The tumor involves the vagina
IIIc	The tumor involves pelvic or peritoneal lymph nodes
IV	Carcinoma has extended outside the true pelvis or has obviously involved the mucosa of the bladder or the rectum
IVa	The tumor involves bladder or bowel mucosa
IVb	The tumor has metastasized to distant sites, including intra-abdominal or inguinal lymph nodes

Adapted from International Journal of Gynecology and Obstetrics. Benedet J L, Pecorelli S. Staging classifications and clinical practice guidelines of gynaecologic cancers, P60, ©2000. With permission from International Federation of Gynecology and Obstetrics.

will show the crowded glands to have a different cytology than that of the uncrowded background. Coordinate changes in both cytology and architecture are critical elements of an EIN lesion, although the exact character of these alterations is evaluated using an approach quite different from that previously applied in the segregation of hyperplasias.

The crowded architecture of EIN can simply be stated as having a surface area of glands (combined epithelium and lumens) that exceeds that of stroma. In precise quantitative terms this can be described as having a volume percentage stroma (VPS) >55%, but with some practice it is possible to recognize this threshold accurately visually. Non-EIN settings where glands may reach this density include secretory endometrium, basalis, and cystically altered endometrium.

Changes in cytology are a cardinal feature of EIN, the presence of which provides reassurance that the crowded area is not just a focus of artificially displaced normal glands. Herein lies a major shift from the old hyperplasia paradigm.[33]

Cytologic changes of EIN are seen in those glands with an abnormal architecture, and may include both nuclear and cytoplasmic alterations, sometimes even non-endometrioid differentiation into mucinous, tubal, or micropapillary cytologies. The altered cytologic appearance within an EIN lesion is thus defined in relative terms by comparison of lesional with non-lesional glands within the same specimen (Fig. 13B.4). There is no fixed cytologic appearance shared by all examples of EIN lesions, and those with non-endometrioid differentiation, elongated nuclei, or predominant cytoplasmic changes are not "atypical" in a classic sense (Fig. 13B.5).

EIN lesions may eventually expand to occupy the entire endometrial compartment, compromising comparison of background with lesional cytology. Usually in these cases there are some residual "overrun" glands, perhaps few in number, which can serve as a suitable reference for comparison (Fig. 13B.4). By the time EIN has occupied the entire endometrial compartment, the cytology is usually sufficiently abnormal that this is not a difficult judgment.

Dimensions of the crowded cytologically altered gland cluster must measure at least 1 mm. Typically this requires dozens (or more) of glands. This threshold size identifies those lesions that have previously been shown by morphometric study to confer a 45-fold increased cancer risk.[34] Most specimens, Pipelle biopsies included, yield fragment sizes well above this threshold so that tissue fragmentation does not preclude application of minimum size criteria at the 1-mm level. Tiny jaw-style hysteroscopic biopsies are the exception. This format, which is often accompanied by crush artifact and disallows examination of the interface between lesion and background, is not suited for evaluation of the possibility of premalignant

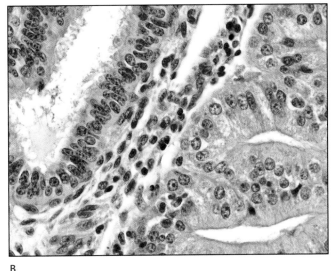
A

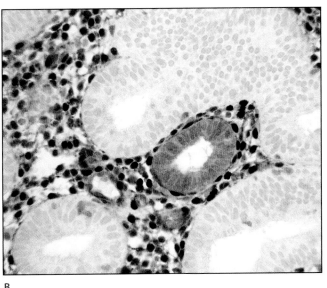
B

Fig. 13B.3 • Endometrial intraepithelial neoplasia (EIN). Localizing EIN. Low magnification shows a circumscribed cluster of crowded glands in which gland area exceeds that of stroma (**A**). Coordinate with this architectural change is a change in cytology, in which lesional glands have abundant cytoplasm and rounded nuclei (**B**, lower right), in contrast to background glands (**B**, upper left). EIN lesions comprise a grouping of individual, occasionally branching, glands without substantial cribriform or solid architecture.

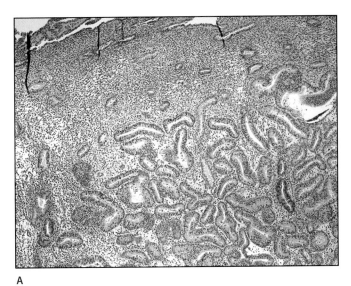
A

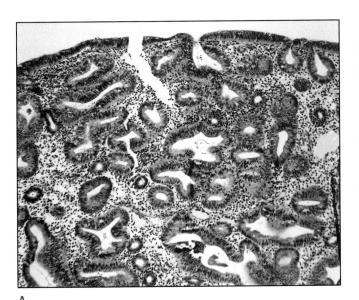
B

Fig. 13B.4 • Endometrial intraepithelial neoplasia (EIN). (**A**) EIN lesion replacing the entire endometrial compartment. It is difficult to identify a perimeter to this premalignant EIN lesion which has permeated the endometrium, having overrun smaller-diameter, round, normal background glands. PTEN protein (antibody 6h2.1) is evident in dark-brown staining of the normal glands (**B**), but absent in this genetically altered EIN lesion.

endometrial disease. Diagnosis of clusters of crowded (gland area > stroma area) cytologically altered glands less than 1 mm in dimension depends on the fragment context. If such a focus appears within a much larger fragment, it may simply be described without making an EIN diagnosis. On the other hand, if multiple very small fragments, all < 1 mm in size, contain crowded glands with a cytology offset from other pieces, it may represent pieces of a fragmented EIN. This should also be diagnosed descriptively, with a caveat that EIN cannot be excluded and re-evaluation is recommended.

Although benign polyps must be discriminated from EIN, these are not always mutually exclusive findings. Approximately 15% of EIN lesions will present within the confines of a polyp. In these cases all EIN diagnostic criteria should be met in their entirety, with the caveat that the comparison background for interpretation of cytology should be the polyp itself, rather than native functional endometrium. Polyps with large gland areas composed of grossly dilated glands lined by bland epithelium should not be misdiagnosed as EIN.

Excluding endometrial adenocarcinoma

Cancers may be identified by the presence of solid areas of neoplastic epithelium or maze-like rambling or molded lumens, uninterrupted by intervening stroma which indicate disruption of the normal gland–stroma relationships (Fig. 13B.6). Poorly differentiated and serous carcinomas may be identified by their distinctive cytologic appearance (see below).

Carcinoma should be distinguished from EIN, as the former must be surgically, not hormonally, ablated. If the

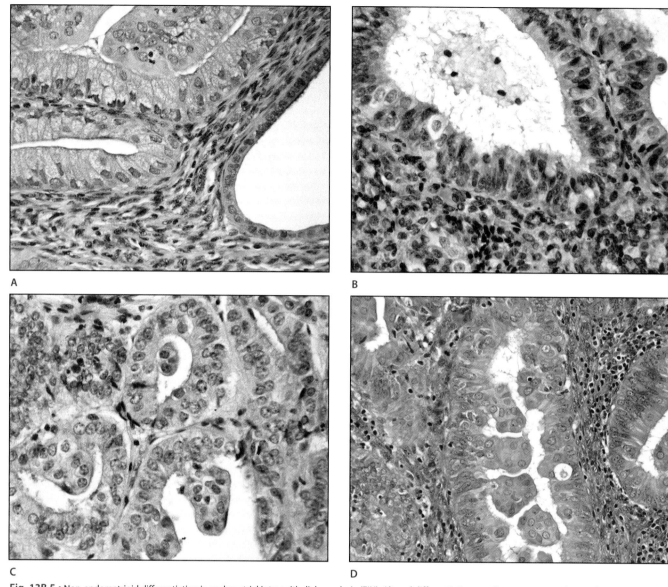

Fig. 13B.5 • Non-endometrioid differentiation in endometrial intraepithelial neoplasia (EIN). Altered differentiation may be seen as part of a neoplastic process, and involve cytoplasmic as well as nuclear changes. Degeneration or hormonal effect may mimic changes in differentiation state. Four examples of EIN with non-endometrioid differentiation are shown: (**A**) mucinous; (**B**) tubal; (**C**) papillary; and (**D**) eosinophilic. All occur as a cohesive region of abnormal architecture with a high gland density that facilitates recognition of an abnormal growth pattern. Note the absence of stromal breakdown, which may in some instances cause secondary papillary or eosinophilic change. Use of the diagnostic term "metaplasia" in these cases may be misleading.

neoplastic epithelium is detached from its stroma, or only present in very small tissue fragments, it may at times be impossible to resolve this differential diagnosis. In these instances, a clear diagnosis of "EIN, cannot exclude carcinoma" will alert the clinician to the problem. Lastly, it is important to emphasize that surgical treatment of endometrial cancers may be modified by the distribution of the lesion. The surgical management of a cancer completely contained within an excised polyp may be very different from that of a well-differentiated cancer which extends to involve the lower uterine segment.

Therapy for EIN

Therapy of EIN is directed towards ablation of the lesion. The preferred management is hysterectomy; however, younger women wishing to retain fertility and patients who are poor surgical risks may not be candidates for surgery. Most endometria with estrogen-induced changes, and some EIN lesions, respond to progesterone therapy.[39–42] Women with anovulatory-type endometria may gain symptomatic relief from longer-term hormonal manipulation, such as placement on oral contraceptives. Endometrial surveillance by a regimen of regular biopsies (usually every 6 months) can provide assurance to the patient with ongoing unopposed estrogen exposures that an emergent neoplastic process will be detected early. Progestin management of women with EIN lesions is controversial, and must take into account the patient's situation and the clinical judgment of the attending physician. Follow-up biopsies should always be performed after a withdrawal bleed to avoid the confounding effects of progesterone on nuclear morphology (Fig. 13B.7). Patients with EIN lesions documented to be refractory to progesterone therapy should be re-evaluated as candidates for surgical intervention.

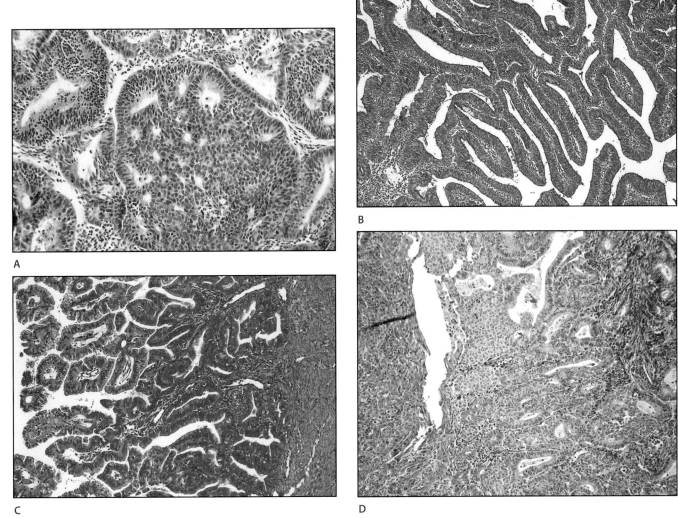

A

B

C

D

Fig. 13B.6 • Well-differentiated adenocarcinomas are distinguished from endometrial intraepithelial neoplasia by displaying one of the following features: (**A**) a cribriform pattern with loss of normal gland outlines; (**B**) irregular maze-like glands; (**C**) villoglandular architecture; or (**D**) solid epithelium or myoinvasion (not shown).

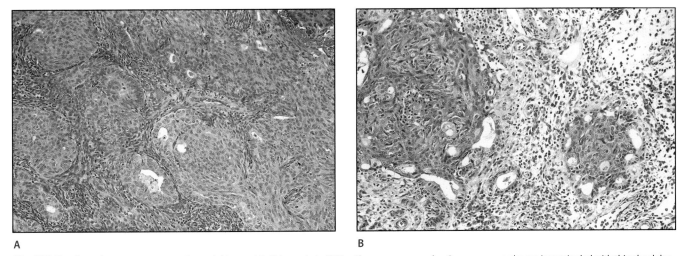

A

B

Fig. 13B.7 • Effect of progesterone on endometrial intraepithelial neoplasia (EIN) with squamous morules. Squamous morules are intermingled with this glandular endometrial lesion which demonstrates dramatic changes in nuclear cytology before (**A**), compared to after (**B**) 6 months of Megace therapy. Morular change is common in EIN. Progesterone exposure has made the nuclei of glandular cells smaller, and the glandular epithelium less lush. Caution should be exercised in interpretation of endometria still under the active influence of therapeutic progestins, as cytology becomes blander and the architecture is altered by an expanded stromal compartment. One strategy is to encourage completion of a withdrawal bleed following progesterone therapy before obtaining a follow-up biopsy.

Precursors to papillary serous adenocarcinoma

Serous endometrial intraepithelial carcinoma ("serous EIC") is an in-situ pattern of papillary serous-type endometrial adenocarcinoma which more commonly accompanies, rather than precedes, invasive papillary serous endometrial adeno-carcinoma.[7,43] Serous EIC should not be confused with the similarly abbreviated EIN, the precursor of endometrioid-type adenocarcinoma (as discussed above). Serous EIC demonstrates very-high-grade nuclear atypia, exfoliative or hobnail cytomorphology, and aberrant *p53* staining indicative of inactivation (Fig. 13B.8). Serous EIC behaves as an adenocarcinoma which happens to be growing along a surface, including the capability for metastasis to peritoneal sites. Diagnosis of serous EIC, especially when it occurs as an isolated finding, should be followed by careful clinical staging to rule out this possibility.

Very rarely, *p53*-mutant endometrial epithelial cells may be seen with a cytology intermediate between normal and serous EIC.[44] These may have *p53* abnormalities and deletions of chromosomes 17p and 1p which persist in more classic areas of serous EIC or papillary serous adenocarcinoma in the same patient.[45] It has been suggested that these "endometrial glandular dysplasias" may represent a *bona fide* premalignant state, but their long-term natural history, and prospective cancer risk, have not yet been fully documented.

Endometrial adenocarcinomas

Gross pathology

Endometrial carcinoma presents either as a localized polypoid tumor or as a diffuse tumor involving the entire endometrial surface (Fig. 13B.9). Spread generally occurs via direct myometrial invasion, with eventual extension to contiguous periuterine structures. Spread into the broad ligaments may create a clinically palpable mass. Eventually, dissemination to regional lymph nodes occurs; in the later stages, tumor may be borne hematogenously to the lungs, liver, bones, and other organs. In certain types, specifically papillary serous carcinoma, relatively superficial endometrial involvement may be associated with extensive peritoneal disease, suggesting spread via peritoneal seeding.[46]

Prognostic factors in endometrial carcinomas

Several authors have proposed criteria for predicting increased mortality for women with endometrial adenocarcinoma. These risk factors fall into several categories, including stage, grade, histologic subtype, and other features.

The staging system for endometrial cancer is summarized in Table 13B.4. Grading of endometrial carcinomas is a complex and controversial issue.[47] Put simply, grading is based on growth pattern, degree of nuclear atypia, and tumor type.

For adenocarcinomas of endometrioid type without marked nuclear atypia or other stigmata of serous carcinoma, tumors can be subdivided into the following categories:

- G1: well-differentiated adenocarcinoma, displaying less than 5% solid growth in the glandular component (excludes squamous areas)
- G2: moderately differentiated adenocarcinoma, displaying between 5 and 50% solid growth
- G3: poorly differentiated adenocarcinoma, demonstrating greater than 50% solid growth

For this group of tumors, some exceptions exist. In the presence of pronounced nuclear atypia, the tumor may be assessed one grade higher than indicated by architecture alone (i.e., G2 rather than G1). Another exception is the frankly biphasic tumor, in which two separate and distinct components, both

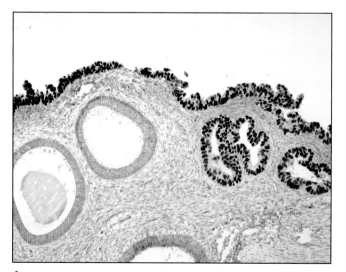

A

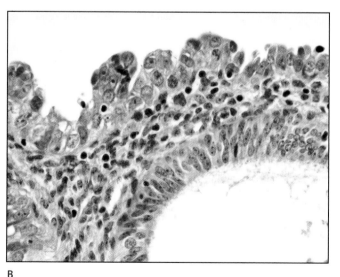

B

Fig. 13B.8 • Serous endometrial intraepithelial carcinoma (EIC). **(A)** *p53* mutant (immunohistochemically stained) cells involve superficial endometrial glands and luminal surface of the uterine cavity. **(B)** These have a papillary serous cytology. This case is typical in that the non-invasive pattern of serous EIC accompanies an adjacent invasive papillary serous carcinoma; however, serous EIC may rarely be seen as an isolated finding.

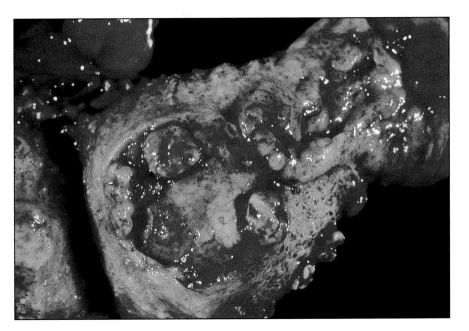

Fig. 13B.9 • Endometrial adenocarcinoma, presenting as a diffuse irregular nodularity on the uterine surface.

13

Tumors of the female genital tract

well and very poorly differentiated, are juxtaposed. In such instances, it is prudent to include both grades in the pathology report.[2]

For the remainder of endometrial carcinomas, specifically *papillary serous adenocarcinomas* and *clear cell carcinomas*, grading the tumor is of virtually no value. Both diagnoses denote a tumor of high risk, and the diagnosis of papillary serous carcinoma demands management with attention to potential peritoneal disease.[46]

Additional prognostic factors, other than grade and cell type, include depth of myometrial invasion, vascular space invasion, status of peritoneal washings, and age.[48]

Endometrioid adenocarcinoma

Endometrioid adenocarcinomas may be subdivided into several morphologic subsets, each of which may vary in their degree of differentiation. Three important parameters to keep in mind when evaluating tumors in this category are: (1) glandular pattern and architecture; (2) degree of nuclear atypia; and (3) pattern of cellular differentiation (or metaplasia). The grading system according to the WHO is summarized on page 660.

Most endometrioid carcinomas are characterized histologically by well-defined glands lined by cytologically malignant stratified columnar epithelial cells. They are classically defined as well-differentiated (grade 1), with easily recognizable glandular patterns (Fig. 13B.10, left); moderately differentiated (grade 2), showing well-formed glands mixed with solid sheets of malignant cells; or poorly differentiated (grade 3), characterized by solid sheets of cells with barely recognizable glands and a greater degree of nuclear atypia and mitotic activity (Fig. 13B.10, right). Between 5 and 10% of cases have a papillary (villoglandular) architecture.[49] In essence, the conventional grading scheme is based on assessment of the *macroglandular* growth pattern. However, a second subset of endometrial carcinomas exhibit a *microglandular* growth pattern, which

differs in appearance from the conventional large branching glands associated with endometrial hyperplasia. These microglandular patterns are characterized by small tubular or cribriform gland arrangements which may vary from extremely well-differentiated to moderately differentiated. The former may be confused with endocervical epithelium when mucinous metaplasia is present[50–52] (Fig. 13B.11). Occasional cases may show cords of cells in a hyaline stroma, producing a sex cord-like appearance.[53] Poorly differentiated tumors with a prominent lymphocytic infiltrate may raise the possibility of association with hereditary non-polyposis colorectal cancer.[54]

Generally, endometrioid tumors exhibit enlarged, stratified nuclei, but the degree of nuclear pleomorphism is mild. Division of endometrioid carcinomas into morphologic subsets is primarily based on the type of differentiation, which may be squamous, mucinous, tubal, or secretory.

Squamous differentiation is observed in 2–20% of endometrioid carcinomas. Squamous elements most commonly are histologically benign in appearance (called "adenocarcinoma

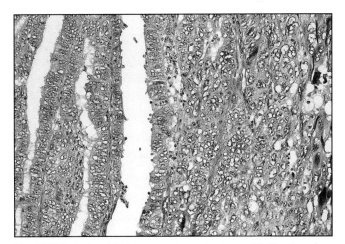

Fig. 13B.10 • Endometrioid adenocarcinoma, showing well (left) and poorly differentiated (right) components within a single tumor.

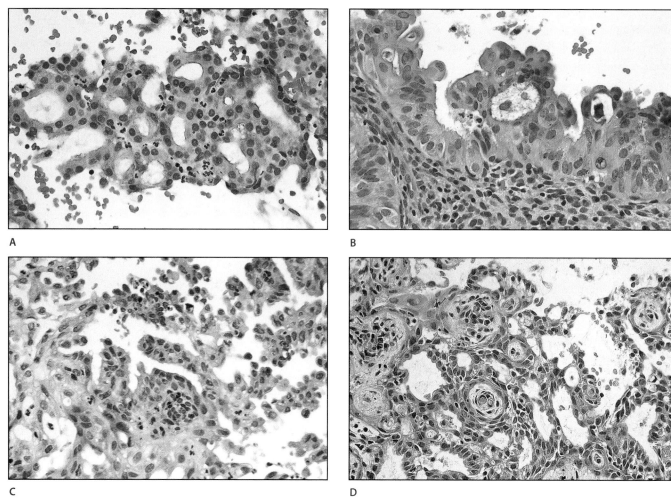

Fig. 13B.11 • (A) Microglandular variant of endometrial carcinoma displays interlacing tubular glands with minimal cytologic atypia. In comparison, (B) uncomplicated mucinous metaplasia in larger glands is not accompanied by microglandular architecture, although micropapillae may be present; (C) papillary syncytial "metaplasia" exhibits a surface growth pattern devoid of tubular architecture. For comparison, (D) microglandular change of the endocervix.

with squamous metaplasia" or, more traditionally, "adeno-acanthoma" when associated with well-differentiated adenocarcinoma). Less commonly, moderately or poorly differentiated endometrioid carcinomas contain squamous elements that appear frankly malignant. Such tumors were previously termed "adenosquamous carcinomas." However, the clinical significance of squamous differentiation has been the subject of debate in the past, with disagreement over whether the term "adenosquamous" was necessary. Ultimately, it was decided that the degree of *glandular* differentiation should govern the grading of these tumors, and the term "squamous metaplasia" be replaced with "squamous differentiation" (e.g., moderately differentiated adenocarcinoma, endometrioid-type, with squamous differentiation).[55] In rare cases with squamous differentiation, coexistent *transitional cell carcinoma* may also be identified.[56]

Like endometrioid carcinomas with squamous differentiation, tumors with *mucinous differentiation* exhibit a spectrum of atypia. The most subtle presentation is a microglandular neoplasm with minimal nuclear atypia, which may mimic endocervix. In contrast to endocervix, there is no squamous differentiation and the cells are arranged in stiff-appearing, cribriform arrays of neoplastic cells with variable mucin production. More easily distinguished are the growth patterns showing

prominent atypia, necrosis, and papillary architecture. In general, lesions with mild atypia tend to be exophytic and minimally invasive, but about half are associated with a more classic endometrioid component which may also invade[50–52] (Fig. 13B.11A).

Tubal and secretory differentiation are two other, albeit uncommon, patterns observed in endometrial cancers. Both are associated with areas of well-differentiated epithelium, and usually portend a good prognosis.[57] Tubal (ciliated) differentiation may be observed in macroglandular and microglandular growth patterns. Complex endometrial growth patterns should generally be viewed with suspicion, irrespective of the degree to which epithelial differentiation is preserved. Very rare examples of endometrioid adenocarcinoma may show sertoliform features.[58]

Papillary serous and clear cell carcinomas

Although classification as a poorly differentiated adenocarcinoma typically requires loss of glandular differentiation and the presence of solid growth, two histologic patterns behave as if poorly differentiated, regardless of their degree of differentiation, and these are *papillary serous carcinomas* and *clear cell carcinomas*. Serous carcinomas in particular are a highly aggressive form of uterine cancer, first properly distinguished from endometrioid carcinomas in 1982.[59] Additional studies have extensively confirmed these original observations while expanding the spectrum of serous tumors, thereby including two specific additional subsets: (1) mixed serous and endometrioid carcinomas; and (2) serous carcinomas arising in endometrial polyps. The latter are most deceptive as the bulk of tumor may be small while there is a strong tendency to spread over the endometrial and peritoneal surfaces.

Pure serous carcinomas are rather rare, comprising only 1.1% of endometrial carcinomas in one study.[60] The authors reported an unusually poor survival with 5- and 10-year survival rates of 27 and 14%. Carcangiu & Chambers analyzed three parameters: (1) tumors apparently confined to polyps; (2) tumors associated with endometrioid components; and (3) tumors coexisting with ovarian carcinomas of similar morphology.[61] The outcome of all three groups was poor, with endometrioid components having no beneficial impact on survival. Tumors confined to polyps behaved as aggressively as those of similar stage with myometrial invasion, and tumors associated with ovarian involvement behaved as high-stage carcinomas – observations also shared by Silva & Jenkins and Gallion et al.[62,63] Goff et al. came to similar conclusions, noting that tumor grade and extent of myometrial invasion had little relationship to the risk of positive peritoneal washings and outcome.[46] There is a negative correlation between survival and capillary lymphatic space invasion. A proportion of patients with small uterine tumors survive and, in subsequent studies, Grice and colleagues found that tumors confined to the uterus following careful staging had a favorable outcome,[64] as also did Carcangiu et al. in stage Ia lesions.[65] Most recently, Hui et al. showed that any such tumor confined to the endometrium (whether or not in a polyp) generally has an excellent prognosis.[66]

When the pathologist is confronted with a serous carcinoma, complete sampling of submitted tubes and ovaries is important, as is liberal sampling of the peritoneum and attention to the presence of capillary lymphatic space invasion.

All serous tumors, including those arising in combination with endometrioid tumors, have one feature in common – that of marked nuclear atypia with macronuclei and prominent nucleoli (Fig. 13B.12). Some tumors are overtly papillary, usually with a broad base and irregular papillae from which numerous individual tumor cells exfoliate. Others exhibit small tubular or slit-like glands with the same nuclear features, or regular glands with one or two layers of atypical cells protruding into the lumen in a "hobnail" fashion. Common features are micropapillary arrangements of neoplastic cells and small, loosely cohesive clusters of cells devoid of stromal support.

Clear-cell carcinomas of the endometrium differ slightly from serous tumors by the presence of two features, one of which is the presence of glands or papillae lined by a single layer of polyhedral cells with uniform nuclei and prominent nucleoli (Fig. 13B.13). Second, in contrast to serous carcinomas, prominent exfoliation is not present. When the tumor cells are arranged in sheets, the preservation of distinct cell borders is maintained, although there may be marked nuclear atypia, as in serous carcinomas. Tubular variants of clear cell carcinoma may also display an eosinophilic periodic acid–Schiff-positive acellular matrix between the neoplastic glands. Clear cell carcinomas should be distinguished from poorly differentiated endometrioid tumors with occasional cells exhibiting clear cytoplasm. Secretory vacuoles, likewise, should not be confused with clear cell carcinoma, the latter requiring high-grade nuclei and the characteristic glandular growth pattern with minimal nuclear stratification.[67]

Like the serous variety, clear cell carcinomas cannot be readily "graded" and such grading is probably not important for the sake of management. Clear cell carcinomas of the uterus generally have a poorer prognosis than endometrioid tumors but do not share the propensity to involve peritoneal surfaces. Abeler and colleagues[68,69] reported crude 5- and 10-year survival rates of 42 and 39% respectively. Capillary lymphatic space invasion, when present, correlated with a 15% 5-year survival in patients with deep myometrial invasion.[68]

Tumors showing mixed differentiation

Carcinosarcomas (includes malignant mixed müllerian tumors)

Carcinosarcomas consist of endometrial adenocarcinomas coexisting with a malignant mesenchymal (stromal) component. The latter may include endometrial stroma, smooth muscle (leiomyosarcoma), skeletal muscle (rhabdomyosarcoma), cartilage (chondrosarcoma), and even osteoid (osteosarcoma). The monoclonal character of epithelial and mesenchymal elements suggests that they are derived from a common stem cell, a concept supported by the fact that the stromal cells often stain positively with epithelial cell markers. The concept of these tumors as "metaplastic carcinomas" is further supported on both immunohistochemical and clinical grounds; prognosis correlates strongly with serous or clear cell glandular histology, as well as other parameters such as myometrial invasion, capillary lymphatic space invasion, and cervical involvement. In contrast, the degree of differentiation of the mesenchymal component does not influence prognosis, and metastases are usually composed of epithelial rather than mesenchymal tissues, implying that the sarcomatous differentiation is a marker for aggressiveness rather than the more aggressive component of the tumor.[70,71] The pattern of metastasis is usually via lymphatics, a behavior more akin to epithelial tumors than the hematogenous spread which characterizes primary sarcomas.

Grossly, carcinosarcomas are more fleshy in appearance than adenocarcinomas, may be bulky and polypoid, and sometimes protrude through the cervical os (Fig. 13B.14). On histology, the tumors usually consist of adenocarcinoma admixed with the stromal (sarcomatous) elements; alternatively, the tumor may comprise two distinct and separate epithelial and mesenchymal components resembling a "collision tumor" (Fig. 13B.15). The adenocarcinomatous component is most often endometrioid in type. Carcinosarcomas were traditionally divided into homologous and heterologous malignant mixed müllerian tumors according to whether the mesenchymal component expressed differentiation that was intrinsic (stromal or leiomyosarcoma) or extrinsic (rhabdomyosarcoma, chondrosarcoma, etc.) to the uterus. This separation was based on

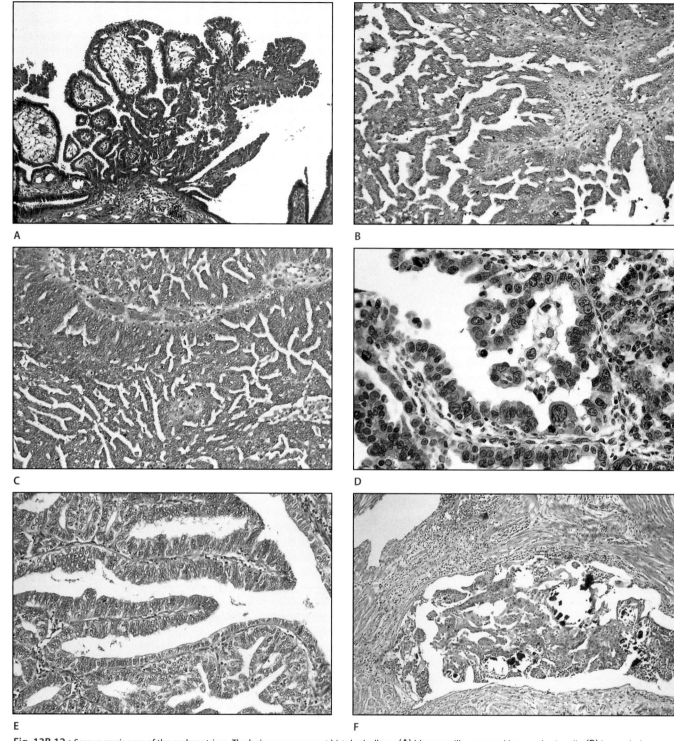

Fig. 13B.12 • Serous carcinoma of the endometrium. The lesions may present histologically as: (**A**) blunt papillae covered by neoplastic cells; (**B**) less orderly micropapillary arrays of interdigitating neoplastic epithelium; and (**C**) irregular small slit-like glands lined by cells (**D**) with conspicuously enlarged hyperchromatic nuclei. The combination of micropapillary architecture and macronuclei is characteristic of serous carcinomas. Occasionally, endometrioid (**E**) and serous (**F**) histology may coexist in the same case.

reports suggesting a more ominous prognosis for the heterologous tumors. However, the prognosis for both forms is currently considered equally poor and all tumors are now termed "carcinosarcomas."[70,71]

Carcinosarcomas occur almost exclusively in postmenopausal patients (most often over the age of 60), some of whom have a history of prior pelvic irradiation. These are aggressive neoplasms and have a 5-year survival rate of 25–30%, with major adverse prognostic factors being adnexal spread, nodal metastases, and the histologic type of carcinoma.[70,72] Adjunctive therapy may provide local control but is unproven for advanced disease.

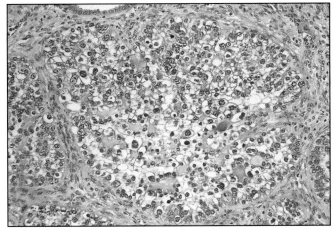

Fig. 13B.13 • Clear cell carcinoma, displaying characteristic clear cells with distinct cell borders and focal eosinophilic stromal cores.

Adenosarcomas

Like carcinosarcomas, müllerian adenosarcomas consist of both epithelial and stromal elements. However, these tumors differ by the presence of generally benign epithelium within a sarcomatous stroma. The prognosis for adenosarcomas is much more favorable than that of carcinosarcomas, but their distinction from endometrial polyps, adenofibromas, and adenomyomas may be important for the purposes of management.[73]

Adenosarcomas, like carcinosarcoma, are most common in postmenopausal women, although the overall age range at onset is wide. They typically present as large bulky tumors filling the endometrial cavity and, less commonly, arising from the endocervix. The important histologic features which distinguish

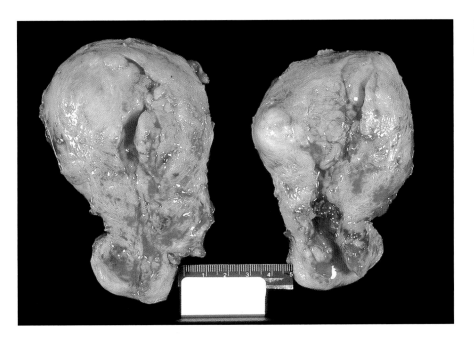

Fig. 13B.14 • Carcinosarcoma. This bivalved uterus displays both anterior and posterior surfaces covered with a glistening homogeneous tumor.

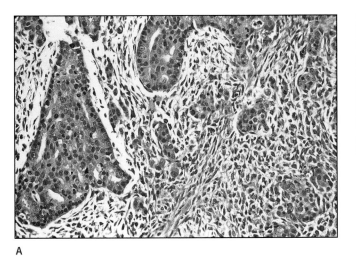

A

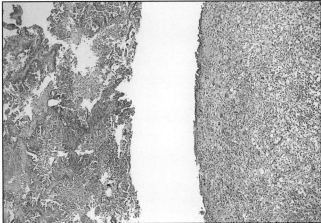

B

Fig. 13B.15 • Two growth patterns of carcinosarcoma include: (A) a subtle blending of epithelial and stromal components; and (B) the juxtaposition of separate epithelial (left) and mesenchymal (right) tumors.

adenosarcoma include irregular glandular architecture with slit- or leaf-like infolding glands, stromal epithelial papillae, and intraglandular polypoid projections. The epithelial cells may vary from pseudostratified to ciliated to hobnail patterns resembling reactive endocervical epithelium. Occasionally glandular atypia is present. The stroma is typically cellular, with periglandular stromal cuffing, a feature which distinguishes these tumors from endometrial or adenomyomatous polyps. The stromal component may exhibit a wide range of differentiation, including homologous and heterologous differentiation (Fig. 13B.16), and some cases show sex cord-like components.[74]

Adenosarcomas generally behave in a benign fashion but do present a local recurrence risk. Clement & Scully reported 23 recurrences in 100 cases, one-third of which developed after 5 years and most of which were local, occurring in the vagina, pelvis, or abdomen.[73] Distant metastases are rare, but the potential risk of malignant behavior dictates caution in distinguishing these tumors from benign polyps. In the distinction from adenofibroma, adenosarcoma usually demonstrates: 1 or more stromal mitoses/10 high-power fields; marked stromal cellularity; and more than mild atypia in the stromal cells.[74]

This liberal diagnostic strategy obviously stems from experience with these tumors, some of which may recur even when bland in appearance, or may easily be confused with endometrial polyps. With the above criteria, a diagnosis of adenofibroma will rarely be made.[73]

An important related clinical decision is whether or not to remove the ovaries in young women with a diagnosis of adenosarcoma. This procedure is often considered standard in cases of adenosarcoma, and the diagnosis of adenosarcoma in young women with unusual endometrial polyps should therefore be made with care.

Other stromal-epithelial tumors include *adenomyomatous polyps* and *atypical polypoid adenomyomas* (APA).[75-78] The latter, which mainly occur in premenopausal patients, will not be confused with adenosarcomas because the stroma is typically myomatous. However, APAs may have abnormal glandular epithelium with squamous morules and occasionally coexist with areas indistinguishable from EIN or adenocarcinoma (Fig. 13B.17). The risk of coexisting invasive carcinoma is low, but these tumors should be managed with attention to excluding carcinoma by careful follow-up or hysterectomy.

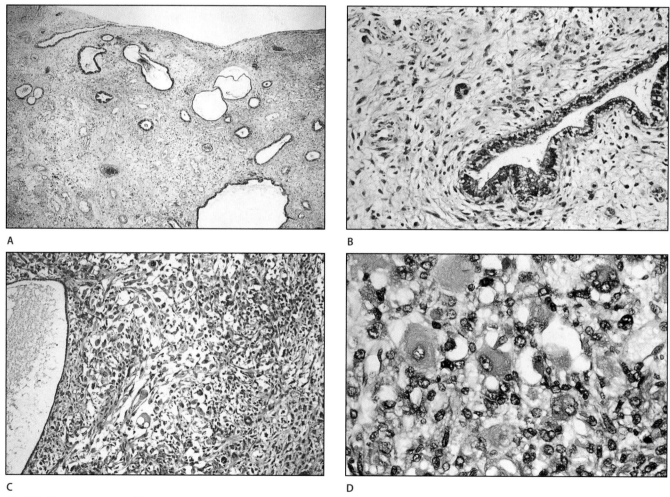

A

B

C

D

Fig. 13B.16 • Adenosarcoma. **(A)** At low power, a mixture of gland sizes coexists with a cellular stroma. **(B)** At higher magnification, an adenosarcoma displays a benign-appearing gland with adjacent sarcomatous stroma. **(C and D)** Stromal cell differentiation may include heterologous differentiation with rhabdomyoblasts. Note the benign-appearing gland in **(C)**.

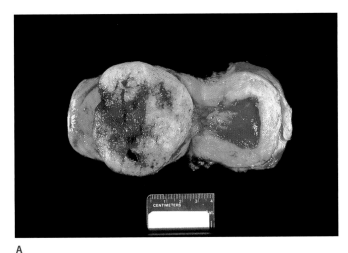

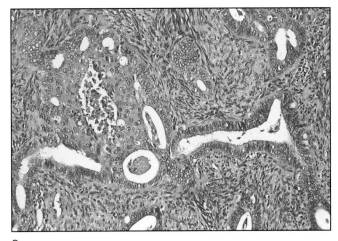

A   B

Fig. 13B.17 • Atypical polypoid adenomyoma. **(A)** This tumor presents as a discrete tumor mass in the lower uterine segment. **(B)** Histologically these tumors comprise a mixture of myomatous stroma with interdigitating endometrioid glands and, often, squamous morules.

Endometrial stromal tumors

The endometrial stroma occasionally gives rise to neoplasms which may closely or more remotely resemble normal stromal cells. Similar to most neoplasms, they may be well or poorly differentiated. Stromal neoplasms are divided into three categories: (1) benign endometrial stromal nodules; (2) low-grade endometrial stromal sarcoma (so-called endolymphatic stromal myosis); and (3) undifferentiated endometrial sarcoma. All may have high mitotic rates, a feature which previously received much attention but is now understood to be of little value in discriminating between these neoplasms.[79]

Clinical features

Endometrial stromal tumors generally occur in younger patients than those with carcinosarcoma: peak incidence is in the fourth and fifth decades. Stromal nodules are benign; both Tavassoli & Norris[80] and Chang et al.[81] reported 100% 5-year survival for these tumors, and this has been confirmed by others more recently.[82] The prognosis for low-grade endometrial stromal sarcoma is guarded, but in general they have a favorable prognosis. About one-third of low-grade stromal sarcomas recur within 10–15 years; distant metastases and death from metastatic tumor occur in about 15% of cases,[81] but may be long delayed. Undifferentiated sarcomas of the endometrium have a high mortality rate, and poor prognosis.

Pathologic features

Stromal nodule is a well-circumscribed neoplasm that on initial inspection may be mistaken for a smooth muscle tumor; however, stromal nodules typically are softer and are yellow. Most examples measure <10 cm. Histologically they are composed of endometrial stromal cells that have a discrete and well-demarcated interface between the tumor and surrounding myometrium, although slight focal interdigitation between the two may be present (Fig. 13B.18A), but this should not exceed 3 mm in depth. The stromal cells are arranged around numerous vessels resembling spiral arteroles. Stromal nodules do not demonstrate capillary lymphatic space invasion.

Low-grade endometrial stromal sarcomas may grossly appear as an intramyometrial, polypoid, or diffusely infiltrative mass. Histologically, they consist of well-differentiated endometrial stromal cells with a plexiform capillary network. Unlike stromal nodules, low-grade endometrial stromal sarcomas invade in a tongue-like fashion between myometrial muscle bundles, and may involve lymphatic channels, hence the outdated term *endolymphatic stromal myosis*. It is important to emphasize that low-grade stromal sarcomas are virtually indistinguishable from stromal nodules on cytologic or mitotic activity grounds, the critical feature being invasion of the surrounding myometrium or vascular structures[81] (Fig. 13B.18B). At the molecular genetic level, most cases of low-grade endometrial stromal sarcoma are characterized by a reciprocal chromosome translocation, $t(7;17)(p15;q21)$;[83] which generates a *JAZF1–JJAZ1* fusion gene product.[84] The same genetic aberration is present in stromal nodules.

Mitotic activity confers little additional prognostic value as a stratifier within the class of low-grade stromal sarcoma. While high surgical stage and mitotic index were associated with poor outcome in univariate analysis, mitotic index does not independently predict outcome in stage I tumors. This is the reason to classify endometrial stromal sarcomas in a single group. While 45% of stage I tumors exhibit minimal cytologic atypia and low mitotic index, 45% of these patients had one or more relapses. This emphasizes the difficulty in assigning recurrence risk in stromal sarcomas based on degree of differentiation, atypia, and mitotic activity. Many low-grade stromal sarcomas may exhibit other forms of differentiation, including smooth muscle[85,86] and sex cord[87] differentiation. The latter may closely resemble granulosa cell or other sex cord-stromal tumors of the ovary, with small uniform oval nuclei and a regular growth pattern. Such tumors may also stain for inhibin,[88] similar to their ovarian counterparts. Distinction of low-grade endometrial stromal sarcoma from a smooth muscle neoplasm may sometimes be difficult but can be aided by immunohistochemistry. While smooth muscle actin (SMA) and desmin may be positive in both tumor types, as also may CD10, nevertheless SMA and desmin staining are usually only focal in stromal sarcoma, CD10 staining is generally stronger and more definite in stromal sarcoma, and caldesmon staining

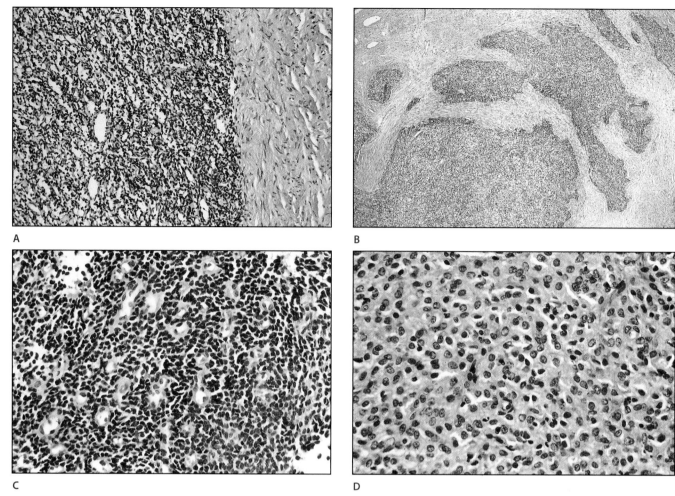

A

B

C

D

Fig. 13B.18 • Endometrial stromal tumors. (**A**) A diagnosis of stromal nodule requires the presence of a sharply demarcated tumor–myometrial interface with minimal interdigitation of tumor and myometrium. (**B**) Low-grade endometrial stromal sarcomas display irregular tongues of neoplastic stroma invading the myometrium. At higher power cells may be arranged in a perivascular pattern (**C**) or in cord-like arrangements resembling sex cord-stromal tumors (**D**).

is positive in most uterine smooth muscle neoplasms, but negative in stromal sarcoma.

Undifferentiated endometrial sarcomas (formerly high-grade stromal sarcomas) bear little resemblance to endometrial stroma. These tumors are characterized by a high mitotic rate, extreme cytologic atypia, loss of progesterone receptors, and frequent necrosis. Evans split this group from those that closely resemble endometrial stroma morphologically (low-grade endometrial stromal sarcomas) based upon severe anaplasia or pleomorphism[89] (Fig. 13B.19). These latter are well described as "undifferentiated" and are now believed to be unrelated to low-grade stromal sarcomas. Because undifferentiated endometrial sarcoma occurs in older women and has a prognosis akin to carcinosarcomas, Chang et al.[81] have recommended excluding this subset of tumors from the category of stromal sarcoma, a proposal recently endorsed by the WHO.[79]

In summary, diagnosis of stromal tumors is based upon their degree of resemblance to endometrial stroma and the nature of the interface with adjacent normal tissues. The distinction of benign stromal nodule from low-grade endometrial stromal sarcoma is based on a uniform stromal–myometrial interface; thus a firm diagnosis may not be possible on curettings. Low-grade endometrial stromal sarcomas invade the myometrium and may exhibit sex cord-like, epithelioid and

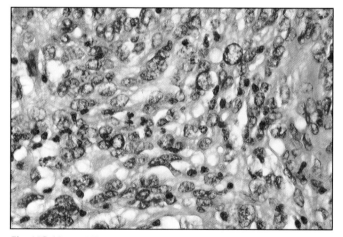

Fig. 13B.19 • Undifferentiated stromal sarcoma. This anaplastic lesion does not resemble conventional (low-grade) endometrial stromal sarcoma.

glandular differentiation. Other features helpful in the diagnosis include an arborizing vascular pattern, foam cells with necrosis, and "ropey" collagen. The oncologist should be aware that relapse rates are high for low-grade endometrial stromal sarcoma and cannot be predicted reliably on an individual case basis. Undifferentiated endometrial sarcoma bears little histologic or antigenic resemblance to endometrial stroma, and often has prominent necrosis.

Endometrial neoplasia and tamoxifen therapy

In recent years, the use of tamoxifen for women with breast cancer has been associated with a wide spectrum of endometrial pathology, including benign polyps, mucinous carcinomas, papillary serous carcinomas, adenosarcomas, and leiomyomas.[90–94] Unfortunately, the majority of studies have reported either individual cases or those obtained via referral. Moreover, risk assessment has been confounded by the inherently higher risk of endometrial neoplasia for women who have previously had a breast neoplasm. It is currently assumed that tamoxifen imparts an increased risk of endometrial neoplasia. The most common complication is the development of endometrial polyps. The weak estrogenic effect of tamoxifen may predispose patients to carcinoma but determining whether these women are at increased risk for all of the tumors reported will require further long-term study.

Non-Müllerian neoplasms

Not all the tumors listed in this section necessarily arise in the endometrium, though all can, on occasion, develop in this site rather than in myometrium; however, it is often impossible to define their precise origin within the uterus.

Vascular tumors

Benign hemangiomas involving endometrium are extremely rare.[95] So-called "hemangiopericytomas" of the uterus can arise at any age, and some form polypoid masses within the uterine cavity.[96–99] The histologic appearance of these neoplasms is the same as that seen elsewhere (see Ch. 3), although the precise nature of such tumors is controversial. A uterine hemangiopericytoma may closely resemble an endometrial stromal sarcoma, from which (arguably but perhaps unconvincingly) it can be distinguished by its content of irregular sinusoidal vessels, particularly those showing a branching, "staghorn" pattern.

Angiosarcomas of the uterus[100–102] are rare but aggressive neoplasms which do not differ histologically from those occurring in skin and soft tissue (see Ch. 3).

Neuroectodermal tumors

Benign nerve sheath tumors have very rarely been described to involve the endometrium.[103] Both primitive neuroectodermal[104–106] and gliomatous[107] neoplasms of the uterus may occur, although their histogenesis is poorly understood. The primitive neuroectodermal tumors tend to show predominantly a neuroblastomatous or medulloblastomatous pattern with focal glial or neuronal differentiation. The only reported pure gliomatous endometrial neoplasm resembled a low-grade fibrillary astrocytoma.[107] There are also exceptional reports of paraganglioma arising in the endometrium.[108,109]

Miscellaneous rare tumors

So-called "malignant fibrous histiocytoma,"[110,111] giant cell tumor,[112,113] malignant rhabdoid tumor,[114–116] alveolar soft-part sarcoma,[117–119] Brenner tumor,[120] mature cystic teratoma,[121] immature teratoma,[122] yolk sac tumor,[123] Wilms tumor,[124,125] and retinal anlage tumor[126] can, on rare occasions, occur in the uterus.

Lymphoma and leukemia

Infiltration of the endometrium by lymphomatous or leukemic cells is not uncommon in women suffering from the advanced stages of these diseases. On rare occasions, however, lymphomas present initially as an endometrial lesion, some of these being confined to, and apparently having arisen primarily at, this site.[127–129] Lymphomas presenting in this fashion are usually of non-Hodgkin's type, although one instance of endometrial Hodgkin's disease has been noted.[130] Most examples show B-cell differentiation and the grade is variable.[131,132] Granulocytic sarcoma may also occur in the endometrium,[133] as may myeloma;[134] very exceptionally, chronic lymphatic leukemia may also present at this site.[135]

Metastatic tumors

Uterine metastases from extragenital tumors are uncommon.[136–138] The primary tumors metastasizing to the uterus are, in descending order of incidence, carcinomas of the breast, stomach, colon, and pancreas: less commonly, metastases from carcinomas of the kidney, urinary bladder, gallbladder, or thyroid are identified, while malignant melanomas may also metastasize to the uterus.[139,140]

References

1. American Cancer Society 2004 American Cancer Society facts and figures. American Cancer Society, Atlanta, Georgia
2. Curry S, Kelly S 1990 Cancer of the female genital tract: overview. In: Osteen R (ed) Cancer manual. American Cancer Society, Boston, p. 253
3. Rose P G 1996 Endometrial carcinoma. N Engl J Med 335: 640–649
4. Deligdisch L, Holinka C 1987 Endometrial carcinoma: two diseases? Cancer Detect Prev 10: 237–246
5. Peiffer S, Herzog T J, Tribune D et al. 1995 Allelic loss of sequences from the long arm of chromosome 10 and replication errors in endometrial cancers. Cancer Res 55: 1922–1926
6. Arlt M F, Herzog T J, Mutch D G et al. 1996 Frequent deletion of chromosome 1p sequences in an aggressive histologic subtype of endometrial cancer. Hum Mol Genet 5: 1017–1021
7. Sherman M E, Bur M E, Kurman R J 1995 *P53* in endometrial cancer and its putative precursors: evidence for diverse pathways of tumorigenesis. Hum Pathol 26: 1268–1274
8. Lax S F, Pizer E S, Ronnett B M et al. 1998 Clear cell carcinoma of the endometrium is characterized by a distinctive profile of p53, Ki-67, estrogen and progesterone receptor expression. Hum Pathol 29: 551–558
9. Faquin W C, Fitzgerald J T, Lin M C et al. 2000 Sporadic microsatellite instability is specific to neoplastic and preneoplastic endometrial tissues. Am J Clin Pathol 113: 576–582
10. Shibata D, Navidi W, Salovaara R et al. 1996 Somatic microsatellite mutations as molecular tumor clocks. Nature Med 2: 676–681
11. Hopkin K 1996 Tumor evolution: survival of the fittest cells. J NIH Res 8: 37–41
12. Califano J, Van der Riet P, Westra W et al. 1996 Genetic progression model for head and neck cancer: implications for field cancerization. Cancer Res 56: 2488–2492

13. Rubin H 1985 Cancer as a dynamic developmental disorder. Cancer Res 45: 2935–2942

14. Zaino R J, Kauderer J, Trimble C L et al. 2006 Reproducibility of the diagnosis of atypical endometrial hyperplasia: a Gynecologic Oncology Group study. Cancer 106: 804–811

15. Mutter G L 2000 Endometrial precancer type collection. Available online at http:www.endometrium.org

16. Mutter G L 2000 Endometrial intraepithelial neoplasia (EIN): will it bring order to chaos? The Endometrial Collaborative Group. Gynecol Oncol 76: 287–290

17. Mutter G L, Boynton K A, Faquin W C et al. 1996 Allelotype mapping of unstable microsatellites establishes direct lineage continuity between endometrial precancers and cancer. Cancer Res 56: 4483–4486

18. Jovanovic A S, Boynton K A, Mutter G L 1996 Uteri of women with endometrial carcinoma contain a histopathologic spectrum of monoclonal putative precancers, some with microsatellite instability. Cancer Res 56: 1917–1921

19. Mutter G L, Chaponot M, Fletcher J 1995 A PCR assay for non-random X chromosome inactivation identifies monoclonal endometrial cancers and precancers. Am J Pathol 146: 501–508

20. Mutter G L, Baak J P A, Crum C et al. 2000 Endometrial precancer diagnosis by histopathology, clonal analysis and computerized morphometry. J Pathol 190: 462–469

21. Mutter G L 2000 Histopathology of genetically defined endometrial precancers. Int J Gynecol Pathol 19: 301–309.

22. Kurman R, Kaminski P, Norris H 1985 The behavior of endometrial hyperplasia: a long term study of "untreated" hyperplasia in 170 patients. Cancer 56: 403–412

23. Sherman A, Brown S 1979 The precursors of endometrial carcinoma. Am J Obstet Gynecol 135: 947–956

24. Tavassoli F, Kraus F 1978 Endometrial lesions in uteri resected for atypical endometrial hyperplasia. Am J Clin Pathol 70: 770–779

25. Colgan T J, Norris H J, Foster W et al. 1983 Predicting the outcome of endometrial hyperplasia by quantitative analysis of nuclear features using a linear discriminant function. Int J Gynecol Pathol 1: 347–352

26. Winkler B, Alvarez S, Richart R et al. 1984 Pitfalls in the diagnosis of endometrial neoplasia. Obstet Gynecol 64: 185–194

27. Bergeron C, Nogales F, Masseroli M et al. 1999 A multicentric European study testing the reproducibility of the WHO classification of endometrial hyperplasia with a proposal of a simplified working classification for biopsy and curettage specimens. Am J Surg Pathol 23: 1102–1108

28. Kendall B S, Ronnett B M, Isacson C et al. 1998 Reproducibility of the diagnosis of endometrial hyperplasia, atypical hyperplasia, and well-differentiated carcinoma. Am J Surg Pathol 22: 1012–1019

29. Mutter G L, Ince T A 2003 Molecular pathogenesis of endometrial cancer. In: Fuller A, Seiden M V, Young R (eds) Uterine cancer: American Cancer Society atlas of clinical oncology. B C Decker, Hamilton, Ontario, Canada, p.10–21

30. Mutter G L 2002 Diagnosis of premalignant endometrial disease. J Clin Pathol 55: 326–331

31. Mutter G L, Ince T A, Baak J P A et al. 2001 Molecular identification of latent precancers in histologically normal endometrium. Cancer Res 61: 4311–4314

32. Mutter G L 2001 Endometrial intraepithelial neoplasia: a new standard for precancer diagnosis. Cont Ob Gyn 46: 92–98

33. Baak J P A, Mutter G L 2005 Endometrial intraepithelial neoplasia (EIN) and the WHO 94 classification of endometrial hyperplasia. J Clin Pathol 58: 1–6

34. Baak J P A, Mutter G L, Robboy S et al. 2005 The molecular genetics and morphometry-based intraepithelial neoplasia classification system predicts disease progression in endometrial hyperplasia more accurately than the 1994 World Health Organization classification system. Cancer 103: 2304–2312

35. Dunton C, Baak J, Palazzo J et al. 1996 Use of computerized morphometric analyses of endometrial hyperplasias in the prediction of coexistent cancer. Am J Obstet Gynecol 174: 1518–1521

36. Hecht J L, Ince T A, Baak J P A et al. 2005 Prediction of endometrial carcinoma by subjective EIN diagnosis. Mod Pathol 18: 324–330

37. Silverberg S G, Mutter G L, Kurman R J et al. 2003 Tumors of the uterine corpus: epithelial tumors and related lesions. In: Tavassoli F A, Stratton M R (eds) WHO classification of tumors: pathology and genetics of tumors of the breast and female genital organs. IARC Press, Lyon, France, p 221–232

38. Nucci M, Crum C, Prasad C et al. 2000 Mucinous endometrial epithelial proliferations: a morphologic spectrum of changes with diverse clinical significance. Mod Pathol 12: 1137–1142

39. Amezcua C A, Lu J J, Felix J C et al. 2000 Apoptosis may be an early event of progestin therapy for endometrial hyperplasia. Gynecol Oncol 79: 169–176

40. Lindahl B, Alm P, Ferno M et al. 1990 Endometrial hyperplasia: a prospective randomized study of histopathology, tissue steroid receptors and plasma steroids after abrasion, with or without high dose gestagen treatment. Anticancer Res 10: 725–730

41. Randall T C, Kurman R J 1997 Progestin treatment of atypical hyperplasia and well-differentiated carcinoma of the endometrium in women under age 40. Obstet Gynecol 90: 434–440

42. Zheng W, Baker H E, Mutter G 2004 Involution of PTEN-null endometrial glands with progestin therapy. Gynecol Oncol 92: 1008–1013

43. Ambros R A, Sherman M E, Zahn C M et al. 1995 Endometrial intraepithelial carcinoma: a distinctive lesion specifically associated with tumors displaying serous differentiation. Hum Pathol 26: 1260–1267

44. Zheng W, Liang S X, Yu H et al. 2004 Endometrial glandular dysplasia: a newly defined precursor lesion of uterine papillary serous carcinoma. Part I: morphologic features. Int J Surg Pathol 12: 207–223

45. Liang S X, Chambers S K, Cheng L et al. 2004 Endometrial glandular dysplasia: a putative precursor lesion of uterine papillary serous carcinoma. Part II: molecular features. Int J Surg Pathol 12: 319–331

46. Goff B A, Kato D, Schmidt R A et al. 1994 Uterine papillary serous carcinoma: patterns of metastatic spread. Gynecol Oncol 54: 264–268

47. Zaino R J, Kurman R J, Diana K L et al. 1995 The utility of the revised International Federation of Gynecology and Obstetrics histologic grading of endometrial adenocarcinoma using a defined nuclear grading system, a Gynecologic Oncology Group study. Cancer 75: 81–86

48. Zaino R J, Kurman R J, Diana K L et al. 1996 Pathologic models to predict outcome for women with endometrial adenocarcinoma. The importance of the distinction between surgical stage and clinical stage. A Gynecologic Oncology Group study. Cancer 77: 1115–1121

49. Zaino R J, Kurman R J, Brunetto V L et al. 1998 Villoglandular adenocarcinoma of the endometrium: a clinicopathologic study of 61 cases. A Gynecologic Oncology Group study. Am J Surg Pathol 22: 1379–1385

50. Ross J C, Eifel P J, Cox R S et al. 1983 Primary mucinous adenocarcinoma of the endometrium. A clinicopathologic and histochemical study. Am J Surg Pathol 7: 715–729

51. Young R H, Scully R E 1992 Uterine carcinomas simulating microglandular hyperplasia: a report of six cases. Am J Surg Pathol 16: 1092–1097

52. Chumas J C, Nelson B, Mann W J et al. 1985 Microglandular hyperplasia of the uterine cervix. Obstet Gynecol 66: 406–409

53. Murray S K, Clement P B, Young R H 2005 Endometrioid carcinomas of the uterine corpus with sex cord-like formations, hyalinization, and other unusual morphologic features: a report of 31 cases of a neoplasm that may be confused with carcinosarcoma and other uterine neoplasms. Am J Surg Pathol 29: 157–166

54. van den Bos M, van den Hoven M, Jongejan E et al. 2004 More differences between HNPCC-related and sporadic carcinomas from the endometrium as compared to the colon. Am J Surg Pathol 28: 706–711

55. Zaino R J, Kurman R J 1988 Squamous differentiation in carcinoma of the endometrium: a critical appraisal of adenoacanthoma and adenosquamous carcinoma. Semin Diagn Pathol 5: 154–171

56. Lininger R A, Ashfaq R, Albores-Saavedra J et al. 1997 Transitional cell carcinoma of the endometrium and endometrial carcinoma with transitional cell differentiation. Cancer 79: 1933–1943

57. Hendrickson M R, Kempson R L 1983 Ciliated carcinoma – a variant of endometrial adenocarcinoma: a report of 10 cases. Int J Gynecol Pathol 2: 13–27

58. Eichhorn J H, Young R H, Clement P B 1996 Sertoliform endometrial adenocarcinoma: a study of four cases. Int J Gynecol Pathol 15: 119–126

59. Hendrickson M, Ross J, Eifel P et al. 1982 Uterine papillary serous carcinoma: a highly malignant form of endometrial adenocarcinoma. Am J Surg Pathol 6: 93–108

60. Abeler V M, Kjorstrad K E 1990 Serous papillary carcinoma of the endometrium: a histopathological study of 22 cases. Gynecol Oncol 39: 266–271

61. Carcangiu M L, Chambers J T 1992 Uterine papillary serous carcinoma: a study on 108 cases with emphasis on the prognostic significance of associated endometrioid carcinoma, absence of invasion, and concomitant ovarian carcinoma. Gynecol Oncol 47: 298–305

62. Silva E G, Jenkins R 1990 Serous carcinoma in endometrial polyps. Mod Pathol 3: 120–128

63. Gallion H H, van Nagell J R Jr, Powell D F et al. 1989 Stage I serous papillary carcinoma of the endometrium. Cancer 63: 2224–2228

64. Grice J, Ek M, Greer B et al. 1998 Uterine papillary serous carcinoma: evaluation of long-term survival in surgically staged patients. Gynecol Oncol 69: 69–73

65. Carcangiu M L, Tan L K, Chambers J T 1997 Stage Ia uterine serous carcinoma. A study of 13 cases. Am J Surg Pathol 21: 1507–1514

66. Hui P, Kelly M, O'Malley D M et al. 2005. Minimal uterine serous carcinoma: a clinicopathological study of 40 cases. Mod Pathol 18: 75–82

67. Kurman R J, Scully R E 1976 Clear cell carcinoma of the endometrium. An analysis of 21 cases. Cancer 37: 872–882

68. Abeler V M, Kjrstad K E 1991 Clear cell carcinoma of the endometrium: a histopathological and clinical study of 97 cases. Gynecol Oncol 40: 207–217

69. Abeler V M, Vergote I B, Kjorstad K E et al. 1996 Clear cell carcinoma of the endometrium. Cancer 78: 1740–1747

70. Silverberg S G, Major F J, Blessing J A et al. 1990 Carcinosarcoma (malignant mixed mesodermal tumor) of the uterus. A Gynecologic Oncology Group pathologic study of 203 cases. Int J Gynecol Pathol 9: 110

71. Bitterman P, Chun B, Kurman R J 1990 The significance of epithelial differentiation in mixed mesodermal tumors of the uterus. A clinicopathologic and immunohistochemical study. Am J Surg Pathol 14: 317–328

72. Major F J, Blessing J A, Silverberg S G et al. 1993 Prognostic factors in early-stage uterine sarcoma: a Gynecologic Oncology Group study. Cancer 71 (4 suppl.): 1702–1709

73. Clement P B, Scully R E 1990 Mullerian adenosarcoma of the uterus: a clinicopathologic analysis of 100 cases with a review of the literature. Hum Pathol 21: 363–381

74. Clement P B, Scully R E 1989 Mullerian adenosarcomas of the uterus with sex cord-like elements. A clinicopathologic analysis of eight cases. Am J Clin Pathol 91: 664–672

75. McCluggage W G, Haller U, Kurman R J et al. 2003 Tumors of the uterine corpus: mixed epithelial and mesenchymal lesions. In: Tavassoli F A, Devilee P (eds) WHO classification of tumors: pathology and genetics of tumors of the breast and female genital organs. IARC Press, Lyon, France, p 245–249

76. Mazur M T 1981 Atypical polypoid adenomyomas of the endometrium. Am J Surg Pathol 5: 473–482

77. Young R H, Treger T, Scully R E 1986 Atypical polypoid adenomyoma of the uterus: a report of 27 cases. Am J Clin Pathol 86: 139–145

78. Longacre T A, Chung M H, Rouse R V et al. 1996 Atypical polypoid adenomyofibromas (atypical polypoid adenomyomas) of the uterus. A clinicopathologic study of 55 cases. Am J Surg Pathol 20: 1–20

79. Hendrickson M R, Tavassoli F A, Kempson R L et al. 2003 Tumors of the uterine corpus: mesenchymal tumors and related lesions. In: Tavassoli F A, Devilee P (eds) WHO classification of tumors: tumors of the breast and female genital organs. IARC Press, Lyon, France, p 233–244

80. Tavassoli F A, Norris H J 1981 Mesenchymal tumors of the uterus. VII. A clinicopathological study of 60 endometrial stromal nodules. Histopathology 5: 1–10

81. Chang K L, Crabtree G S, Lim-Tan S K et al. 1990 Primary uterine endometrial stromal neoplasms. A clinicopathologic study of 117 cases. Am J Surg Pathol 14: 415–438

82. Dionigi A, Oliva E, Clement P B et al. 2002 Endometrial stromal nodules and endometrial stromal tumors with limited infiltration: a clinicopathologic study of 50 cases. Am J Surg Pathol 26: 567–581

83. Micci F, Walter C U, Teixeira M R et al. 2003 Cytogenetic and molecular genetic analyses of endometrial stroma sarcoma: nonrandom involvement of chromosome arms 6p and 7p and confirmation of JAZF1/JJAZ1 gene fusion in t(7;17). Cancer Genet Cytogenet 144: 119–124

84. Koontz J I, Soreng A L, Nucci M et al. 2001 Frequent fusion of the JAZF1 and JJAZ1 genes in endometrial stromal tumors. Proc Natl Acad Sci USA 98: 6348–6353

85. Oliva E, Clement P B, Young R H et al. 1998 Mixed endometrial stromal and smooth muscle tumors of the uterus. A clinicopathologic study of 15 cases. Am J Clin Pathol 22: 997–1005

86. Yilmaz A, Rush D S, Soslow R A 2002 Endometrial stromal sarcomas with unusual histological features: a report of 24 primary and metastatic tumors emphasizing fibroblastic and smooth muscle differentiation. Am J Surg Pathol 26: 1142–1150

87. Clement P B, Scully R E 1976 Uterine tumors resembling ovarian sex-cord tumors. A clinicopathological analysis of 14 cases. Am J Clin Pathol 66: 512–525

88. Baker R J, Hildebrandt R H, Rouse R V et al. 1999 Inhibin and CD99 (MIC2) expression in uterine stromal neoplasms with sex-cord-like elements. Hum Pathol 30: 671–679

89. Evans H L 1982 Endometrial stromal sarcoma and poorly differentiated endometrial sarcoma. Cancer 50: 2170–2182

90. Cohen I, Rosen D J, Shapira J et al. 1994 Endometrial changes with tamoxifen: comparison between tamoxifen-treated and non-treated asymptomatic postmenopausal breast cancer patients. Gynecol Oncol 52: 185–190

91. Dallenbach-Hellweg G, Hahn U 1995 Mucinous and clear cell adenocarcinomas of the endometrium in patients receiving antiestrogens (tamoxifen) and gestagens. Int J Gynecol Pathol 14: 7–15

92. Silva E G, Tornos C S, Follen-Mitchell M 1994 Malignant neoplasms of the uterine corpus in patients treated for breast carcinoma: the effect of tamoxifen. Int J Gynecol Pathol 13: 248–258

93. Clement P B, Oliva E, Young R H 1996 Mullerian adenosarcoma of the uterine corpus associated with tamoxifen therapy: a report of six cases and a review of tamoxifen-associated endometrial lesions. Int J Gynecol Pathol 15: 222–229

94. Assikis V J, Jordan V C 1995 A realistic assessment of the association between tamoxifen and endometrial cancer. Endocr Rel Ca 2: 235–241

95. Shanberge J N 1994 Hemangioma of the uterus associated with heredity hemorrhagic telangiectasia. Obstet Gynecol 84: 708–710

96. Silverberg S G, Wilson M A, Board J A 1971 Hemangiopericytoma of the uterus: an ultrastructural study. Am J Obstet Gynecol 110: 397–404

97. Sooriyaarachchi G S, Ramirez G, Roley G L 1978 Hemangiopericytomas of the uterus: report of a case with a comprehensive review of the literature. J Surg Oncol 10: 399–408

98. Buscema J, Klein V, Rotmensch J et al. 1987 Uterine hemangiopericytoma. Obstet Gynecol 69: 104–108

99. Munoz A K, Berek J S, Fu Y S et al. 1990 Pelvic hemangiopericytomas: a report of five cases and literature review. Gynecol Oncol 36: 380–382

100. Ongkasuwan C, Taylor J E, Tang C K et al. 1982 Angiosarcomas of the uterus and ovary. Cancer 49: 1469–1475

101. Witkin G B, Askin F B, Geratz J D et al. 1987 Angiosarcoma of the uterus: a light microscopic, immunohistochemical and ultrastructural study. Int J Gynecol Pathol 6: 176–184

102. Milne D S, Hinshaw K, Malcolm A J et al. 1990 Primary angiosarcoma of the uterus: a case report. Histopathology 16: 203–205

103. Gordon M D, Weilert M, Ireland K 1996 Plexiform neurofibromatosis involving the uterine cervix, endometrium, myometrium and ovary. Obstet Gynecol 88: 699–701

104. Hendrickson M R, Scheithauer B W 1986 Primitive neuroectodermal tumor of the endometrium: report of two cases, one with electron microscopic observations. Int J Gynecol Pathol 5: 249–259

105. Rose P G, O'Toole R V, Keyhani-Rofhaga S et al. 1987 Malignant peripheral primitive neuroectodermal tumor of the uterus. J Surg Oncol 35: 165–167

106. Daya D, Lukka H, Clement P B 1992 Primitive neuroectodermal tumors of the uterus: a report of four cases. Hum Pathol 23: 1120–1129

107. Young R H, Kleinman G W, Scully R E 1981 Glioma of the uterus: report of a case with comments on histogenesis. Am J Surg Pathol 5: 695–699

108. Young T W, Thrasher T V 1982 Non-chromaffin paraganglioma of the uterus: a case report. Arch Pathol Lab Med 106: 608–609

109. Tavassoli F A 1986 Melanotic paraganglioma of the uterus. Cancer 58: 942–948

110. Chou S T, Fortune D, Beischer N A et al. 1985 Primary malignant fibrous histiocytoma of the uterus – ultrasound and immunocytochemical studies of two cases. Pathology 17: 36–40

111. Fujii S, Kanzaki H, Konishi I et al. 1987 Malignant fibrous histiocytoma of the uterus. Gynecol Oncol 26: 319–330

112. Kindblom L G, Seidal T 1981 Malignant giant cell tumour of the uterus. Acta Pathol Microbiol Scand Sect A 89: 179–184

113. Kawai K, Senba M, Tagawa H et al. 1989 Osteoclast-like giant cell tumour of the endometrium. Zentralb Allg Pathol 135: 743–749

114. Cho K R, Rosenhein N B, Epstein J I 1989 Malignant rhabdoid tumor of the uterus. Int J Gynecol Pathol 8: 381–387

115. Fitko R, Brainer J, Schink J C et al. 1990 Endometrioid stromal sarcoma with rhabdoid differentiation. Int J Gynecol Pathol 9: 379–383

116. Niemann T 1997 Malignant rhabdoid tumor of the uterine corpus. Gynecol Oncol 64: 181–182

117. Gray D G, Glick A D, Kurtin P J et al. 1986 Alveolar soft part sarcoma of the uterus. Hum Pathol 17: 297–300

118. Nolan N P M, Gaffney E F 1990 Alveolar soft part sarcoma of the uterus. Histopathology 16: 97–99

119. Guillou L, Lamoureux E, Masse S et al. 1991 Alveolar soft-part sarcoma of the uterine corpus: histological, immunocytochemical and ultrastructural study of a case. Virchow's Arch [A] Pathol Anat Histopathol 418: 467–471

120. Arhleger R E, Bogian J J 1976 Brenner tumor of the uterus. Cancer 38: 1741–1743

121. Martin E, Scholes J, Richart R M et al. 1979 Benign cystic teratoma of the uterus. Am J Obstet Gynecol 135: 429–431

122. Ansah-Boateng Y, Wells M, Poole D R 1985 Coexistent immature teratoma of the uterus and endometrial adenocarcinoma complicated by gliomatosis peritoneii. Gynecol Oncol 21: 106–110

123. Joseph M G, Fellows F G, Hearn S A 1990 Primary endodermal sinus tumor of the endometrium: a clinicopathologic, immunocytochemical and ultrastructural study. Cancer 65: 297–302

124. Bittencourt A L, Britto J F, Fonseca L E 1981 Wilm's tumor of the uterus: the first report in the literature. Cancer 47: 2496–2499

125. Benatar B, Wright C, Freinkel A L et al. 1998 Primary extrarenal Wilms' tumor of the uterus presenting as a cervical polyp. Int J Gynecol Pathol 17: 277–280

126. Schultz D M 1957 A malignant melanotic neoplasm of the uterus, resembling the "retinal anlage" tumour. Am J Clin Pathol 28: 524–533

127. Fox H, More J R S 1965 Primary malignant lymphoma of the uterus. J Clin Pathol 18: 724–728

128. Harris N L, Scully R E 1984 Malignant lymphoma and granulocytic sarcoma of the uterus and vagina: a clinicopathologic analysis of 27 cases. Cancer 53: 2530–2545

129. Benjamin E, Isaacson P G 1996 Lymphoproliferative disease of the ovaries and female genital tract. In: Fox H, Wells M (eds) Haines and Taylor: obstetrical and gynaecological pathology, 4th edn. Churchill Livingstone, Edinburgh, p 1015–1041

130. Hung L H, Kurtz D M 1985 Hodgkin's disease of the endometrium. Arch Pathol Lab Med 109: 762–764

131. Van de Rijn M, Kamel O W, Chang P P et al. 1997 Primary low-grade endometrial B cell lymphoma. Am J Surg Pathol 21: 187–194

132. Vang R, Medeiros L J, Ha C S et al. 2000 Non-Hodgkin's lymphomas involving the uterus: a clinicopathologic analysis of 26 cases. Mod Pathol 13: 19–28

133. Garcia M G, Deavers M T, Knoblock R J et al. 2006 Myeloid sarcoma involving the gynecologic tract. A report of 11 cases and review of the literature. Am J Clin Pathol 125: 783–790

134. Smith N L, Baird D B, Strausbauch P M 1997 Endometrial involvement by multiple myeloma. Int J Gynecol Pathol 61: 173–175

135. Lucia S P, Mills H, Lowenhaupt E et al. 1952 Visceral involvement in primary neoplastic diseases of the reticuloendothelial system. Cancer 5: 1193–1200

136. Kaier W, Holm-Jensen S 1972 Metastases to the uterus. Acta Pathol Microbiol Scand 80: 835–840

137. Kumar N B, Hart W R 1982 Metastases to the uterine corpus from extragenital cancers: a clinicopathologic study of 63 cases. Cancer 50: 2163–2169

138. Kumar A, Schneider V 1983 Metastases to the uterus from extrapelvic primary tumors. Int J Gynecol Pathol 2: 134–140

139. Bauer R D, McCoy C P, Roberts D K et al. 1984 Malignant melanoma metastatic to the endometrium. Obstet Gynecol 63: 264–267

140. Luxman D, Jossiphov J, Cohen J R et al. 1997 Uterine metastasis from vulvar malignant melanoma. A case report. J Reprod Med 42: 244–246

Tumors of the placenta and gestational trophoblastic disease

Christopher P. Crum   Yonghee Lee   David R. Genest

Introduction

Tumors of the placenta can be divided into three categories. The first consists of benign lesions of the placental parenchyma, including chorangioma; the second are tumors of maternal or fetal origin manifesting in either the maternal vascular spaces (both benign lesions and metastatic malignancies) or fetal vessels (fetal leukemias or other neoplasms); the third are trophoblastic neoplasms.

Placental chorangioma

The chorangioma (hemangioma or so-called angiomyxoma of the placenta) is a benign neoplasm present in approximately 1% of placentas.[1] Most chorangiomas are solitary, firm, solid nodules, up to several centimeters in diameter, located in the superficial placental parenchyma near the fetal surface.[1-3] Cut section reveals a smooth myxoid consistency and a tan, dark red or variegated appearance (Fig. 13C1).

The tumor is composed histologically of numerous thin-walled fetal vessels of capillary or sinusoidal caliber, with scant intervening stroma which may be fibrotic, calcified, or myxoid in appearance; peripherally, chorangiomas have a well-circumscribed border (Fig. 13C.2).

Small, solitary chorangiomas are usually clinically insignificant, but multiple chorangiomas may be associated with fetal hemangiomas. Large chorangiomas (particularly those exceeding 5 cm in diameter) can cause fetal hydrops, congestive heart failure, and thrombocytopenia.[4,5]

Other rare, benign placental tumors

In comparison with the relatively common placental chorangiomas, other benign placental tumors have been reported only rarely; these include teratomas,[6-10] hepatic adenomas,[11] and adrenocortical adenomas or rests.[12-14] All have been incidental pathologic findings, unassociated with significant maternal or fetal morbidity. Placental teratomas are usually small, solid nodules attached to the fetal surface of the placenta, composed of disorganized but mature tissues from

Fig. 13C.1 • Gross appearance of chorangioma.

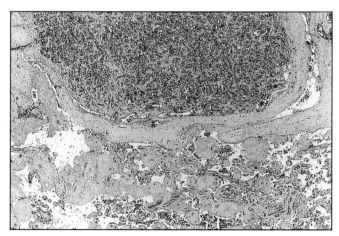

Fig. 13C.2 • Benign chorangioma of term placenta: an enlarged stem villus involved by a fetal fascular proliferation resembling a capillary hemangioma.

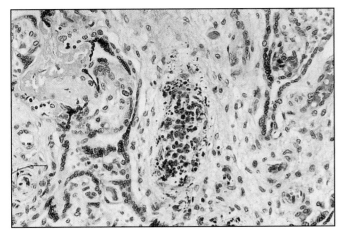

Fig. 13C.3 • Congenital adrenal neuroblastoma widely disseminated throughout the fetal vessels of a term placenta; this picture may mimic erythroblastosis fetalis.

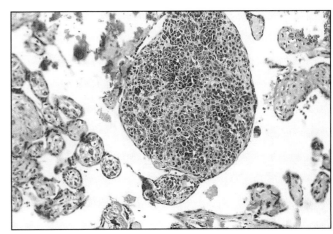

Fig. 13C.4 • Focal involvement of a single, expanded terminal villus by melanocytes; the infant had a giant congenital melanocytic nevus of her trunk and is completely well at 4 years of age.

all three germ layers; in most instances, intestinal and cutaneous differentiation predominate.

Fetal malignancies identified in the placenta

Congenital neuroblastoma, the most common malignant tumor in the fetus, occasionally metastasizes to the placenta.[15–18] Characteristically, numerous small tumor cells disseminate throughout fetal vessels, closely mimicking erythroblastosis fetalis (Fig. 13C.3); placental hydrops and villous edema may further enhance this mimicry.[15] In most instances, tumor cells are confined to the fetal vessels, but invasion of the villous stroma has been described.[16] Another malignancy that may be identified in this setting is fetal leukemia, which has been associated with Down's syndrome. This neoplasm manifests with fetal myeloblasts in the stem and terminal villous vessels, as well as aggregates of malignant cells in the villous parenchyma.

Fetal melanocytic lesions which rarely involve the placenta include malignant melanoma[19] and benign congenital melanocytic nevi.[20–22] The latter are usually small, solitary nodules of pigmented nevus cells located within the villous stroma (Fig. 13C.4); all reported cases have had a benign follow-up, consistent with aberrant neuroectodermal migration rather than metastasis.

Maternal metastatic tumors in the placenta

Metastasis from a maternal malignancy to the placenta is an unusual event; fewer than 100 cases have been reported.[23–31] The four tumors that most commonly metastasize to the placenta are: (1) melanoma; (2) lymphoma/leukemia; (3) breast cancer; and (4) lung cancer.[23–25,27,29–31] Maternal metastatic tumor in the placenta is characteristically confined to the maternal intervillous vascular space, without invasion of the villous stroma (Fig. 13C.5). The differential diagnosis includes benign

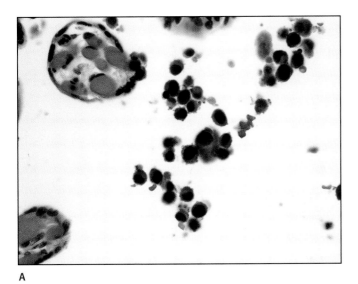

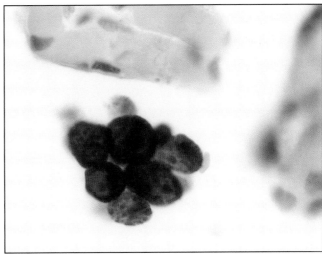

A   B

Fig. 13C.5 • (A) Unattached circulating malignant cells from a maternal melanoma in the intervillous space. **(B)** The tumor is strongly positive for HMB-45.

trophoblastic proliferation within intraplacental fibrin, and intraplacental choriocarcinoma (see below).

Gestational trophoblastic disease

Introduction

The World Health Organization classification of gestational trophoblastic disease organizes trophoblastic neoplasia into the following categories, including malignant tumors (gestational choriocarcinoma and placental site trophoblastic tumor (PSTT)) and tumor-like conditions, including hydatidiform mole (complete, partial, invasive, and metastatic), exaggerated placental site (known in the past as syncytial endometritis), and placental site nodule or plaque.[32,33] However, the absolute distinction of a tumor from a tumor-like condition is dependent on definition. For the purposes of this discussion, hydatidiform moles are viewed as neoplasms with "precursor" properties, i.e. they have a variable risk of progressing to malignancy (choriocarcinoma).

Trophoblastic origins

The trophoblast evolves during gestation, beginning as a relatively homogeneous extraembryonic proliferation (previllous trophoblast) followed by progressive organization and compartmentalization into various differentiation pathways. The latter process begins during embryogenesis and persists throughout life. Early on, trophoblast condenses around the mesenchyme to form villi, a process that defines the villous cytotrophoblast, which exhibits strong *p63* and proliferative (MIB-1) immunostaining (Fig. 13C.6). These qualities distinguish the cytotrophoblast from the more peripheral (*p63*-, MIB-1-) extravillous trophoblast. In the placenta the cytotrophoblast differentiates abruptly into villous syncytiotrophoblast (*p63*–, MIB-1–, inhibin +), and mature extravillous trophoblast, both near the maternal surface and between the chorionic villi. The development of the latter entails an intermediate stage consisting of extravillous cells with a small amount of clear cytoplasm (*p63*+/inhibin+), followed by complete maturation with development of amphophilic cytoplasm (*p63*–/inhibin+). The clear cell phenotype is also prominent in the placental membranes, comprising the chorionic trophoblast (Fig. 13C.6). Ultimately, the cytotrophoblast is viewed as a proliferating stem-cell compartment that matures along these various differentiation pathways. Complete moles and choriocarcinoma are characterized by proliferating cytotrophoblast, partial moles by syncytiotrophoblast only, and PSTTs by extravillous basal trophoblast. A subset of PSTTs contain epithelioid trophoblast that is strongly *p63*-positive, presumably reflecting neoplastic transformation of the cells that are intermediate in differentiation between cytotrophoblast and mature extravillous trophoblast. Some authors propose an origin of these tumors from the membranous trophoblastic cells.

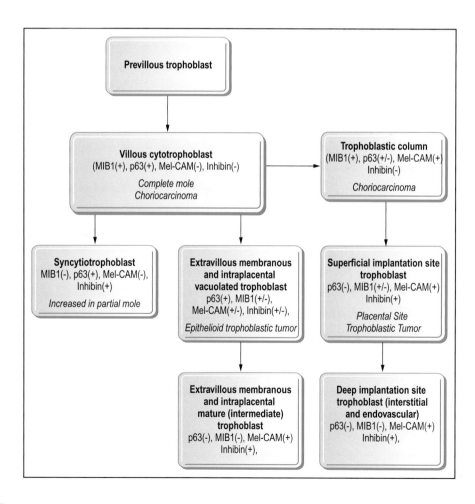

Fig. 13C.6 • Trophoblastic lineages and their neoplasms.

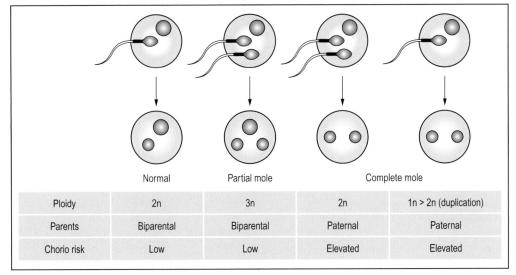

Fig. 13C.7 • Schematic of the genetic basis for hydatidiform mole.

	Normal	Partial mole	Complete mole	
Ploidy	2n	3n	2n	1n > 2n (duplication)
Parents	Biparental	Biparental	Paternal	Paternal
Chorio risk	Low	Low	Elevated	Elevated

However, inasmuch as all trophoblastic cells are formed in a continuum of differentiation, these tumors could conceivably arise from intraplacental extravillous trophoblast.

Complete and partial hydatidiform mole

Hydatidiform mole is an abnormal placentation with hydropic swelling of chorionic villi and trophoblastic proliferation. All molar pregnancies result from abnormal fertilization. In complete hydatidiform mole, an "empty egg" devoid of maternal chromosomes is fertilized either by a single spermatozoon (90% of cases), which duplicates its chromosomal complement to become 46XX, or by two spermatozoa (10% of cases) resulting in a dispermic 46XX or 46XY mole.[34–36] In contrast, a partial hydatidiform mole is triploid, resulting from the addition of two copies of the paternal (diandric) genome, resulting in triploidy (70% 69XXY; 27% 69XXX; 3% 69XYY) (Fig. 13C.7).[37–39] Digynic (two maternal alleles) triploid gestations are non-molar. In addition to these cytogenetic differences, complete and partial moles differ in their clinical presentations, behaviors, and pathologic features.[40–42]

Complete hydatidiform mole is most common in women at the two ends of the reproductive age spectrum, and in women with a prior mole. The prevalence of hydatidiform mole varies considerably in different parts of the world, with the highest frequencies in Asia, Latin America, and the Middle East (up to 1:500 pregnancies). By contrast, the prevalences in an Irish population of complete mole (1:2000 pregnancies) and partial mole (1:700 pregnancies) were notably lower.[43]

Complete moles typically present in the late first trimester or early second trimester with vaginal bleeding, absent fetal heart beat, inappropriately enlarged uterus, markedly elevated βhCG level and characteristic ultrasound findings; the clinical diagnosis of mole is usually evident. In recent years, this classic presentation of complete mole has been significantly modified by the widespread use of sonography, which has permitted earlier recognition and interruption of abnormal gestations. Prior to 1980, complete moles were evacuated at a mean

gestational age of 16 weeks; currently, most complete moles are terminated at 8–12 weeks of gestational age – these frequently are not clinically suspected to be moles.[44] Partial moles are also usually not suspected clinically, but present as missed abortions with late first-trimester bleeding and a small uterus.

Regarding clinical behavior, the incidence of persistent gestational trophoblastic tumor following complete mole is approximately 20–30%,[45,46] and following partial moles is 1–5%.[41,47] Persistent trophoblastic tumor is a clinical diagnosis made on the basis of failure of spontaneous βhCG gonadotropin remission. Persistent trophoblastic tumor pathologically may represent residual intrauterine molar villi, invasive mole, metastatic mole, choriocarcinoma, or PSTT. Tissue for precise pathologic diagnosis is frequently unavailable. Postmolar choriocarcinoma follows approximately 2% of complete moles,[46] but rarely occurs after partial moles, with only three well-documented reports.[48]

Gross specimens of complete hydatidiform moles are usually bulky with numerous transparent, grape-like swollen villi (vesicles) measuring up to 2 cm in diameter. No gestational sac, amnion, umbilical cord, or fetal tissue is found (except in rare instances of twinning) (Fig. 13C.8). Histologically, there is diffuse villous hydrops with numerous well-developed

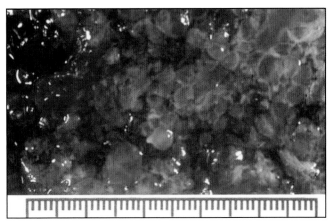

Fig. 13C.8 • Gross appearance of hydropic villi in a complete mole.

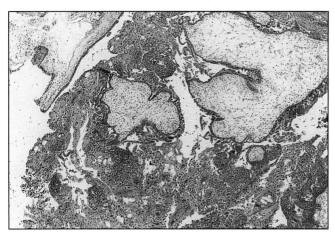

Fig. 13C.9 • Early complete hydatidiform mole (8 weeks' gestational age at evacuation) with only mild villous edema and minimal cavitation. However, marked atypia and hyperplasia of biphasic trophoblast are present, and the villi have a blue, hypercellular stroma with rounded, bulbous protrusions.

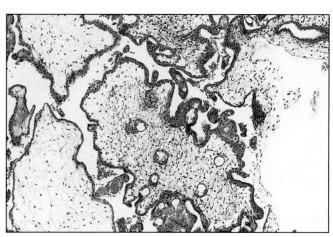

Fig. 13C.10 • Partial hydatidiform mole with minimal trophoblastic hyperplasia; edematous villi have an irregular "scalloped" border with numerous trophoblastic invaginations and "inclusions."

cisterns; the stroma may contain primitive endothelial-lined vascular spaces but fetal blood cells are absent. Trophoblastic proliferation and atypia are invariably present, involving cyto-trophoblast, extravillous trophoblast, and syncytiotrophoblast. Mitotic activity, striking nucleomegaly, and marked hyper-chromasia are common. Proliferating trophoblast is arranged haphazardly and circumferentially around villi (in contrast to the "polar" trophoblast proliferation of normal early placentas). Implantation site trophoblast also commonly shows marked cytologic atypia, with large, bizarre hyperchromatic nuclei; this atypia is prominent in the great majority of complete moles but uncommon in partial moles.[49]

The foregoing pathologic features are most characteristic of complete moles of advanced gestational age (>12 weeks); earlier complete moles (<12 weeks) usually have more subtle, diagnostically challenging pathologic features.[44] On gross examination, cisterns may be absent or inconspicuous in early complete moles. Histologically, although villous cavitation may be inconspicuous, biphasic trophoblastic hyperplasia and atypia are evident (Fig. 13C.9). Additional useful clues suggest-ing the pathologic diagnosis of early complete mole include: marked atypia of implantation site trophoblast, an unusual primitive villous stroma, with tiny stellate mesenchymal cells, stromal hypercellularity and prominent karyorrhexis, and unusually shaped villi with complex bulbous protrusions ("cauliflower-like" villi).[44,50–52] Histologic grading of complete moles (based on the extent of trophoblastic cytologic atypia and hyperplasia) does not correlate with clinical behavior.[45,53]

The partial molar specimen is less bulky than that of the complete mole. It consists of normal-appearing immature placental tissue admixed with occasional molar vesicles; in addition, amnion, cord, and embryonic/fetal tissue are often present. Histologically, partial moles are an admixture of two populations of villi: (1) small, fibrotic "normal" villi; and (2) large, irregular, hydropic villi with multifocal mild to moderate trophoblastic hyperplasia. Some enlarged villi have central cisterns; other enlarged villi have a geographic, scalloped border, with irregular trophoblastic invaginations and inclusions (Fig. 13C.10). The trophoblastic hyperplasia in partial moles is generally focal and mild and comprises

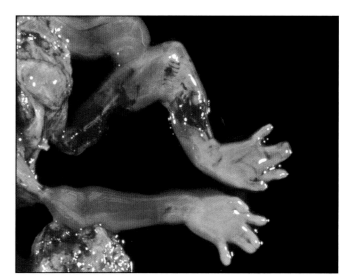

Fig. 13C.11 • Syndactyly associated with partial mole and triploid gestation.

predominantly syncytiotrophoblast, consisting of numerous tiny perivillous tags, or "sprouts," of haphazardly arranged syncytiotrophoblast, or large perivillous aggregates of syncytio-trophoblast with prominent cytoplasmic lacunae, resulting in a "lacy" or "moth-eaten" appearance. Stromal blood vessels often contain nucleated fetal red blood cells; in addition, other histologic evidence of advanced fetal development is common, including chorionic plate, amnion, cord, and embryonic/fetal tissue. When fetal tissue is grossly evident, malformations are almost always found, particularly syndactyly (fusion of adjacent fingers and toes) (Fig. 13C.11).[54,55]

The differential diagnosis of hydatidiform mole includes: complete versus partial mole; hydropic abortus versus hydatidi-form mole; specific fetal syndromes which mimic moles, including trisomy 18, Beckwith–Wiedemann syndrome,[56–58] and placental angiomatous malformation;[59] partial mole versus hydatidiform mole with coexisting twin (Fig. 13C.12).[60–62]

Regarding the distinction between complete and partial mole, several prior studies have employed DNA flow cytometry on the premise that triploidy will segregate the partial

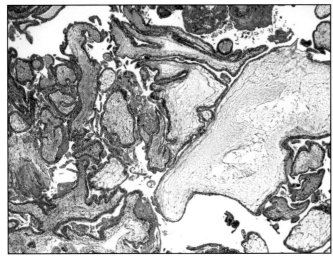

Fig. 13C.12 • Twin complete mole (right) and normal gestational villi (left).

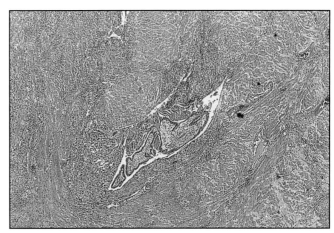

Fig. 13C.14 • Invasive mole in hysterectomy specimen; complete molar villi are present within venous spaces deep within the myometrium.

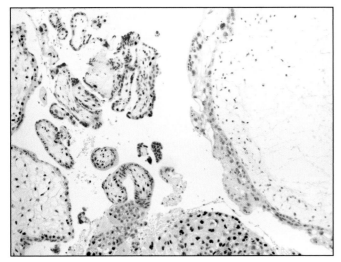

Fig. 13C.13 • Twin complete/normal gestation seen in Figure 13C.12 following *p57* staining. Staining is negative in the cytotrophoblast and stromal cells of the complete molar villi (right) and present in the normal villi (left). The extravillous trophoblast (bottom) stains in both entities and serves as a positive control.

moles.[52,63–68] However, a series of publications in the past few years have established immunohistochemical localization of gene products from imprinted genes as the "gold standard" in the distinction of both partial from complete mole and complete mole from hydropic abortus.[69–73] The most studied is *p57KIP2*, which is expressed from the maternal-derived allele. Because of this epigenetic regulatory mechanism, *p57* is not expressed in the cytotrophoblast and villous stromal cells of complete moles, in contrast to partial moles and hydropic abortuses (Fig. 13C.13). Interestingly, it is expressed in extravillous trophoblast from all gestations, which serve as a useful positive control for staining. With rare exceptions,[74] complete moles will score negatively with this marker. Given the variations in interobserver reproducibility in the distinction of complete moles from either partial mole or hydropic gestation, immunostaining for *p57KIP2* and similar markers should be strongly considered if any question arises concerning the nature of a hydropic gestation.[75]

Invasive and metastatic mole

Invasive mole is a hydatidiform mole (partial or complete), the villi of which are present within the myometrium or uterine vasculature. Following vascular invasion, villi can embolize to distant sites, including the vagina, lung, and brain (metastatic mole). When persistent gestational trophoblastic tumor develops, invasive mole may be suspected clinically if the endometrial cavity contains scant tissue (as determined by curettage or ultrasound examination). Invasive mole cannot be confirmed pathologically from curettage specimens, and requires surgical resection (i.e., hysterectomy, lung biopsy); because major surgery is used infrequently for treatment of gestational trophoblastic tumor, the pathologic diagnoses of invasive and metastatic mole are rendered rarely at the present time.

The gross appearance of an invasive mole is that of an intramyometrial hemorrhagic nodule, often without identifiable villi. Histologically, hydropic villi with atypical, hyperplastic trophoblast are found within the myometrium or blood vessels (Fig. 13C.14). Although invasive and metastatic mole are usually cured by chemotherapy, significant morbidity or mortality may result from local hemorrhage, such as intraperitoneal bleeding with transmural invasive mole, or pulmonary hemorrhage with metastatic mole.

Gestational choriocarcinoma

Gestational choriocarcinoma may occur subsequent to a molar pregnancy (50% of instances), an abortion (25%), an ectopic pregnancy (2.5%), or a normal gestation (22.5%).[76] Choriocarcinoma usually follows a recognized pregnancy (molar or other) by an interval of several months; however, prolonged intervals following gestation (up to 14 years) have been reported.[77] In rare cases, an intraplacental choriocarcinoma is diagnosed immediately after pregnancy, from placental pathologic examination.[78,79] Exceptionally, maternal choriocarcinoma gives rise to metastases in the newborn infant.[80,81]

Most postgestational choriocarcinomas present with abnormal uterine bleeding due to endometrial involvement by tumor; presenting signs may also reflect metastasis, as in hemoptysis and neurologic abnormalities. In patients with metastasis, the lung is most frequently involved (90%), followed by brain and liver (50%).[82] Postmolar choriocarcinomas may have a better prognosis than tumors with non-molar antecedents, possibly reflecting early diagnosis due to close surveillance following hydatidiform mole.[83]

Choriocarcinoma grossly presents as well-circumscribed hemorrhagic nodules (Fig. 13C.15). Histologically, because viable tumor may be found only at the periphery of a hemorrhagic nodule, wide sampling may be necessary. The tumor consists of an admixture of syncytiotrophoblast, cytotrophoblast, and extravillous trophoblast, with prominent hemorrhage, necrosis, and vascular invasion (Fig. 13C.16). Choriocarcinoma does not provoke a stromal response or host neovascularization. The malignant trophoblast shows marked cytologic atypia and biphasic differentiation, with small nests of cytotrophoblast (with distinct cell boundaries and clear cytoplasm) rimmed by multinucleated syncytiotrophoblast (with bubbly purple cytoplasm). Syncytiotrophoblast is strongly immunoreactive for hCG and weakly immunoreactive for human placental lactogen (hPL); mature extravillous (intermediate) trophoblast shows the opposite immunoprofile. All trophoblastic cell types are strongly immunoreactive for cytokeratins. Choriocarcinoma is not graded histologically because this is not clinically useful; however, studies have suggested that tumors with either abundant syncytiotrophoblastic differentiation or marked chronic inflammation may have an improved prognosis.[84] Several tumors have been studied by flow cytometry and reported to be diploid, including some fatal cases.[85]

Choriocarcinoma is often diagnosed from endometrial curettings which reveal abundant blood and necrosis with large sheets of biphasic, markedly atypical, mitotically active trophoblast without chorionic villi (Fig. 13C.17).[86,87] The differential diagnosis of choriocarcinoma includes previllous trophoblast from an early gestation, persistent molar tissue following hydatidiform mole, PSTT, and undifferentiated

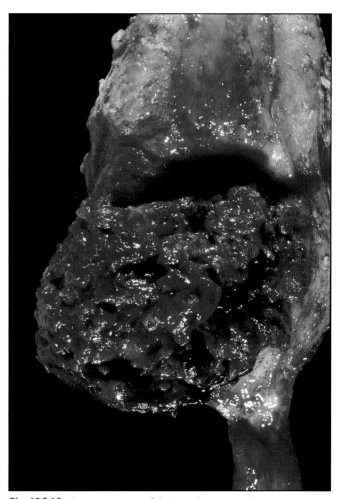

Fig. 13C.15 • Gross appearance of choriocarcinoma, seen here as a hemorrhagic mass in the endometrium.

carcinoma. Regarding previllous trophoblast, scant trophoblast lacking marked cytologic atypia and the absence of hemorrhage or necrosis should suggest an early gestation. In postmolar curettings, scattered microscopic foci of atypical, nonvillous trophoblast may be seen; although this is suggestive of

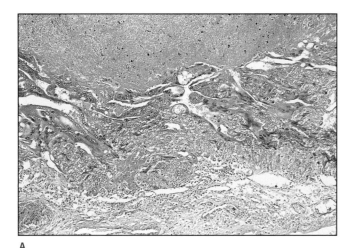

A

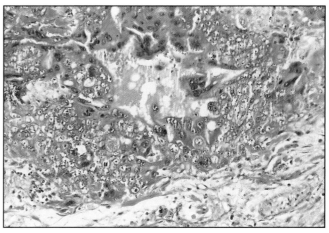

B

Fig. 13C.16 • Choriocarcinoma showing extensive hemorrhage (A), as is common. The tumor shows a biphasic pattern of cytotrophoblast and multinucleated syncytiotrophoblast (B), the appearances mimicking those of normal-implanting blastocyst. It is unusual for a choriocarcinoma to show this degree of viability, as most are extensively necrotic.

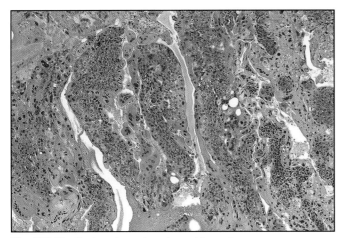

Fig. 13C.17 • Choriocarcinoma in endometrial curettings.

choriocarcinoma, the possibility of trophoblast from an invasive mole should be considered. PSTTs do not contain substantial amounts of syncytiotrophoblast, but are monomorphic intermediate trophoblastic neoplasms. Immunohistochemical studies for hPL and hCG may favor PSTT over choriocarcinoma (if hPL staining predominates). Some PSTTs are strongly hCG positive, although serum levels will be low.

Intraplacental choriocarcinoma

Most gestational choriocarcinomas present weeks to months postpartum. In rare instances, choriocarcinoma contemporaneous with pregnancy has been documented.[78,79,88–91] Intraplacental choriocarcinomas have been diagnosed antenatally (because of metastases) or at delivery (as fortuitous discoveries during placental examination). Choriocarcinoma in a placenta at term usually presents grossly as a solitary "infarct" up to several centimeters in size; in one case, multiple, widely dispersed, 5-mm small white nodules were reported.[90] Histologically, an atypical, biphasic, solid trophoblastic proliferation is located in the maternal intervillous space, multifocally adhering to villous stroma (Fig. 13C.18). Hyperchromatic, mitotically active, primitive-appearing cytotrophoblast is

admixed with syncytiotrophoblast, the latter having numerous cytoplasmic lacunae.

The differential diagnosis of intraplacental choriocarcinoma includes maternal tumors metastatic to the placenta and benign intraplacental intermediate trophoblastic proliferations. The latter are clusters of intermediate trophoblastic cells, individually surrounded by fibrin, with eosinophilic cytoplasm, hyperchromatic, irregular nuclei, occasional intranuclear inclusions, and no mitoses.

Placental site trophoblastic tumor (PSTT)

PSTT is a rare tumor: approximately 150 cases have been reported in the literature.[92–107] Several clinical distinctions can be drawn between choriocarcinoma and PSTT:

1. Although 50% of choriocarcinomas follow molar gestations, only rarely has this been reported for PSTTs and most cases follow a normal pregnancy.
2. Most choriocarcinomas follow an antecedent pregnancy by weeks or months, but PSTTs are frequently recognized years after an antecedent gestation.
3. Choriocarcinoma is highly malignant but very sensitive to chemotherapy and radiation therapy; in contrast, a minority of PSTTs display malignant behavior, but these are typically resistant to chemotherapy and radiation therapy.

Most patients with PSTT present with irregular bleeding and a low-positive βhCG. Some patients have presented with amenorrhea, infertility, or nephrotic syndrome.

Grossly, PSTTs are tan to red solid nodules with variable necrosis and hemorrhage, which typically involve the endometrium and myometrium. Histologically, PSTTs are monophasic proliferations of intermediate trophoblast or cytotrophoblast, without significant amounts of syncytiotrophoblast. Intermediate trophoblastic cells are medium to large-sized mononuclear or multinucleated cells with marked nuclear atypia (Fig. 13C.19), prominent nucleoli, eosinophilic to clear cytoplasm, scattered mitoses, and occasional intranuclear inclusions. Tumor cells characteristically permeate throughout the myometrium (Fig. 13C.20), with prominent

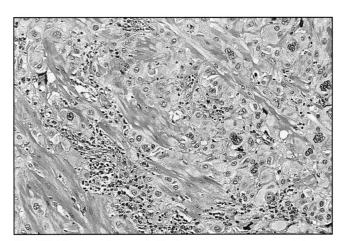

Fig. 13C.18 • Intraplacental choriocarcinoma incidentally discovered in term placenta; a highly atypical proliferation of biphasic trophoblast is present within the maternal intervillous blood space, adherent to villous stroma.

Fig. 13C.19 • Placental site trophoblastic tumor. Note scattered atypical and multinucleated cells.

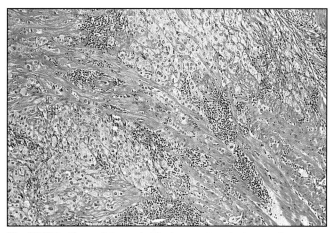

Fig. 13C.20 • Placental site trophoblastic tumor. Neoplastic extravillous cytotrophoblastic cells are infiltrating the myometrium; they are splitting the myometrial fibers with no evidence of hemorrhage or necrosis.

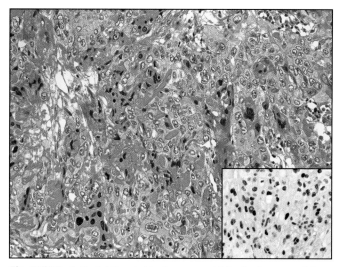

Fig. 13C.21 • Epithelioid trophoblastic tumor and following immunostaining for *p63* (insert).

vasocentric proliferation and intravascular spread. High mitotic activity (>4 mitoses/10 hpf) may indicate a poor prognosis.[103] Flow cytometric evaluation in small numbers of PSTTs has been reported: 8 were diploid (including 3 fatal cases) and 1 was tetraploid.[85,101,107]

Epithelioid trophoblastic tumor (ETT) is a recently described variant of PSTT.[108,109] Its clinical characteristics appear to resemble closely those of PSTT. It is composed of a monomorphic intermediate trophoblastic cell proliferation which differs from PSTT in several respects (Fig. 13C.21):

1. The intermediate trophoblastic tumor cells of ETT are smaller with less pleomorphism.
2. Rather than infiltrating as single cells, ETT grows in a nodular fashion, sometimes replacing the endocervical surface epithelium, closely mimicking carcinoma.[109a]
3. ETTs are focally immunoreactive for hPL, but strongly and diffusely immunoreactive for E-cadherin and epidermal growth factor receptor. Moreover, as

mentioned previously, the tumor cells have an immunophenotype that parallels the vacuolated intervillous trophoblast and membraneous trophoblast.

The differential diagnosis of PSTT includes placental site nodule or plaque, exaggerated implantation site, epithelioid leiomyosarcoma, and poorly differentiated carcinoma. Extensive sampling and immunohistochemistry for keratin, hCG, and hPL are helpful in differentiating a PSTT from non-trophoblastic malignancies. The placental site nodule or plaque[110,111] is a well-circumscribed lesion with abundant hyalinized stroma infiltrated by scattered, degenerate-appearing intermediate trophoblastic cells; these cells show no significant cytologic atypia, but rare mitoses may be present.[107] Placental site nodules occur months to years after an antecedent pregnancy. In contrast, exaggerated implantation site is temporally closely associated with a pregnancy. This diagnosis represents a non-neoplastic exaggeration of the normal implantation process, usually found concurrently with immature villi.

References

1. Wallenburg H C S 1971 Choriangioma of the placenta: thirteen new cases and a review of the literature from 1939 to 1970 with special reference to the clinical complications. Obstet Gynecol Surv 26: 411–425
2. Fox H 1967 Vascular tumors of the placenta. Obstet Gynecol Surv 22: 697–711
3. Majlessi H F, Wagner K M, Brooks J J 1983 Atypical cellular choriangioma of the placenta. Int J Gynecol Pathol 1: 403–408
4. Arodi J, Auskender R, Atad J et al. 1985 Case report: giant choriangioma of the placenta. Acta Obstet Gynecol Scand 64: 91–92
5. Eldar-Geva T, Hochner-Celnikier D, Ariel I et al. 1988 Fetal high output cardiac failure and acute hydramnios caused by large placental choriangioma: case report. Br J Obstet Gynecol 95: 1200–1203
6. Smith L A, Pounder D J 1982 A teratoma-like lesion of the placenta: a case report. Pathology 14: 85–87
7. Sironi M, Declich P, Isimbaldi G et al. 1994 Placental teratoma with three-germ layer differentiation. Teratology 50: 165–167
8. Smith D, Majmudar B 1985 Teratoma of the umbilical cord. Hum Pathol 16: 190–193
9. Unger J L 1989 Placental teratoma. Am J Clin Pathol 92: 371–373
10. Block D, Cruikshank S, Kelly K et al. 1991 Placental teratoma. Int J Obstet Gynecol 34: 377–380
11. Chen K T K, Ma C K, Kassel S H 1986 Hepatocellular adenoma of the placenta. Am J Surg Pathol 10: 436–440
12. Cox J N, Chavier F 1980 Heterotopic adrenocortical tissue within a placenta. Placenta 1: 131–133
13. Labarrere C A, Caccamo D, Telenta M et al. 1984 A nodule of adrenocortical tissue within a human placenta: light microscopic and immunohistochemical findings. Placenta 5: 139–144
14. Qureshi F, Jacques S M 1995 Adrenocortical heterotopia in the placenta. Pediatr Pathol Lab Med 15: 51–56
15. Anders D, Kindermann G, Pfeifer U 1973 Metastasizing fetal neuroblastoma with involvement of the placenta simulating fetal erythroblastosis. J Pediatr 80: 50–53
16. Perkins D G, Kopp C M, Haust M D 1980 Placental infiltration in congenital neuroblastoma: a case study with ultrastructure. Histopathology 4: 383–389
17. Smith C R, Chan H S L, DeSa D J 1981 Placental involvement in congenital neuroblastoma. J Clin Pathol 34: 785–789
18. Strauss L, Driscoll S G 1964 Congenital neuroblastoma involving the placenta: reports of two cases. Pediatrics 34: 23–31
19. Schneidermann H, Yu-Yuan A, Campbell W A et al. 1987 Congenital melanoma with multiple prenatal metastases. Cancer 60: 1371–1377
20. Holaday W J, Castrow F F 1968 Placental metastasis from fetal giant pigmented nevus. Arch Dermatol 98: 486–488
21. Demian S D E, Donnelly W H, Frias J L et al. 1974 Placental lesions in congenital giant pigmented nevi. Am J Clin Pathol 61: 438–442

22. Jauniaux E, de Meeus M, Verellen G et al. 1993 Giant congenital melanocytic nevus with placental involvement: long-term follow-up of a case and review of the literature. Pediatr Pathol 13: 717–721

23. Potter J F, Schoeneman M 1970 Metastasis of maternal cancer to the placenta and fetus. Cancer 25: 380–388

24. Dildy G A, Moise K J, Carpenter R J et al. 1989 Maternal malignancy metastatic to the products of conception. Obstet Gynecol Surv 44: 535–540

25. Salamon M A, Sherer D M, Saller D N et al. 1994 Placental metastases in a patient with recurrent breast carcinoma. Am J Obstet Gynecol 171: 573–574

26. O'Day M P, Nielsen P, Al-Bozom I et al. 1994 Orbital rhabdomyosarcoma metastatic to the placenta. Am J Obstet Gynecol 171: 1382–1383

27. Pollack R N, Sklarin N T, Rao S et al. 1993 Metastatic placental lymphoma associated with maternal human immunodeficiency virus infection. Obstet Gynecol 81: 856–857

28. Pollack R N, Pollack M, Rochon L 1993 Pregnancy complicated by medulloblastoma with metastases to the placenta. Obstet Gynecol 81: 858–859

29. Tsujimura T, Matsumoto K, Aozasa K 1993 Placental involvement by maternal non-Hodgkin's lymphoma. Arch Pathol Lab Med 117: 325–327

30. Delrive C, Locquet E, Mallart A et al. 1989 Placental metastasis from maternal bronchial oat cell carcinoma. Arch Pathol Lab Med 1123: 556–558

31. Read E J, Playzer P B 1981 Placental metastasis from maternal carcinoma of the lung. Obstet Gynecol 58: 387–391

32. Mazur M T, Kurman R J 1995 Gestational trophoblastic disease. In: Kurman R J (ed.) Blaustein's pathology of the female genital tract, 4th edn. Springer Verlag, New York, p 1049–1093

33. Silverberg S G, Kurman R J 1991 Gestational trophoblastic disease. In: Silverberg S G, Kurman R J (eds) Atlas of tumor pathology, 3rd series. Tumors of the uterine corpus and gestational trophoblastic disease. Armed Forces Institute of Pathology, Washington, DC, p 219–287

34. Azuma C, Saji F, Tokugawa Y et al. 1991 Application of gene amplification by polymerase chain reaction to genetic analysis of molar mitochondrial DNA: the genetic analysis of anuclear empty ovum as the cause of complete mole. Gynecol Oncol 40: 29–33

35. Kajii T, Ohama K 1977 Androgenetic origin of hydatidiform mole. Nature 268: 633–634

36. Ohama K, Kajii T, Okamoto E et al. 1981 Dispermic origin of XY hydatidiform moles. Nature 292: 551–552

37. Szulman A E, Surti U 1978 The syndromes of hydatidiform mole. II. Morphologic evolution of the complete and partial hydatidiform mole. Am J Obstet Gynecol 132: 20–27

38. Jacobs P A, Szulman A E, Funkhouser J et al. 1982 Human triploidy: relationship between parental origin of the additional haploid complement and development of partial hydatidiform mole. Ann Hum Genet 46: 223–231

39. Lawler S D, Fisher R A, Dent J 1991 A prospective genetic study of complete and partial hydatidiform moles. Am J Obstet Gynecol 164: 1270–1277

40. Szulman A E, Surti U 1978 The syndromes of hydatidiform mole. I. Cytogenetic and morphologic correlations. Am J Obstet Gynecol 131: 665–671

41. Berkowitz R S, Goldstein D P, Bernstein M R 1985 Natural history of partial molar pregnancy. Obstet Gynecol 66: 677–681

42. Vassilakos P, Riotton G, Kajii T 1977 Hydatidiform mole: two entities. Am J Obstet Gynecol 127: 167–170

43. Jeffers M D, O'Dwyer P, Curran B et al. 1993 Partial hydatidiform mole: a common but underdiagnosed condition. Int J Gynecol Pathol 12: 315–323

44. Mosher R, Goldstein D P, Berkowitz R et al. 1998 Complete hydatidiform mole: comparison of clinicopathologic features, current and past. J Reprod Med 43: 21–27

45. Genest D R, Laborde O, Berkowitz R S et al. 1991 A clinico-pathologic study of 153 cases of complete hydatidiform mole (1980–1990): histologic grade lacks prognostic significance. Obstet Gynecol 78: 402–409

46. Lurain J R, Brewer J I, Torok E E et al. 1983 Natural history of hydatidiform mole after primary evacuation. Am J Obstet Gynecol 145: 591–595

47. Rice L W, Berkowitz R S, Lage J M et al. 1990 Persistent gestational trophoblastic tumor after partial hydatidiform mole. Gynecol Oncol 36: 358–362

48. Bagshawe K D, Lawler S D, Paradinas F J et al. 1990 Gestational trophoblastic tumors following initial diagnosis of partial hydatidiform mole. Lancet 335: 1074–1076

49. Montes M, Roberts D, Berkowitz R S et al. 1996 Prevalence and significance of implantation site trophoblastic atypia in hydatidiform moles and spontaneous abortions. Am J Clin Pathol 105: 411–416

50. Keep D, Zaragoza M V, Hassold T et al. 1996 Very early complete hydatidiform mole. Hum Pathol 27: 708–713

51. Zaragoza M V, Keep D, Genest D R et al. 1997 Early complete hydatidiform moles contain inner cell mass derivatives. Am J Med Genet 70: 273–277

52. Paradinas F J, Browne P, Fisher R A et al. 1996 A clinical, histopathological and flow cytometric study of 149 complete moles, 146 partial moles and 107 non-molar abortions. Histopathology 28: 101–109

53. Elston C W, Bagshawe K D 1972 The value of histologic grading in the management of hydatidiform mole. J Obstet Gynaecol Br Commonw 79: 717–724

54. Doshi N, Surti U, Szulman A E 1983 Morphologic anomalies in triploid liveborn fetuses. Hum Pathol 14: 716–723

55. McFadden D E, Kalousek D K 1991 Two different phenotypes of fetuses with chromosomal triploidy: correlation with parental origin of the extra haploid set. Am J Med Genet 38: 535–538

56. Hillstrom M M, Brown D L, Wilkins-Haug L et al. 1995 Sonographic appearance of placental villous hydrops associated with Beckwith–Wiedemann syndrome. J Ultrasound Med 14: 61–64

57. McCowan L M E, Becroft D M O 1994 Beckwith–Wiedemann syndrome, placental abnormalities and gestational proteinuric hypertension. Obstet Gynecol 83: 813–817

58. Lage J M 1991 Placentomegaly with massive hydrops of placental stem villi, diploid DNA content, and fetal omphaloceles: possible association with Beckwith–Wiedemann syndrome. Hum Pathol 22: 591–597

59. Sander C M 1993 Angiomatous malformation of placental chorionic stem vessels and pseudo-partial molar placentas: report of five cases. Pediatr Pathol 13: 621–633

60. Choi-Hong S R, Genest D R, Crum C et al. 1995 Twin pregnancy with complete hydatidiform mole and coexisting fetus: utilization of fluorescent in situ hybridization to evaluate placental X- and Y-chromosomal content. Hum Pathol 26: 1175–1180

61. Steller M A, Genest D R, Bernstein M R et al. 1994 Natural history of twin pregnancy with complete hydatidiform mole and coexisting fetus. Obstet Gynecol 84: 35–42

62. Steller M A, Genest D R, Bernstein M R et al. 1994 Clinical features of multiple conception with partial or complete molar pregnancy and coexisting fetuses. J Reprod Med 39: 147–154

63. Koenig C, Demopoulos R I, Vamvakas E C et al. 1993 Flow cytometric DNA ploidy and quantitative histopathology in partial moles. Int J Gynecol Pathol 12: 235–240

64. Lage J M, Bagg A 1996 Hydatidiform moles: DNA flow cytometry, image analysis and selected topics in molecular biology. Histopathology 28: 379–382

65. Lage J M, Berkowitz R S, Rice L W et al. 1991 Flow cytometric analysis of DNA content in partial hydatidiform moles with persistent gestational trophoblastic tumor. Obstet Gynecol 77: 111–115

66. Lage J M, Driscoll S G, Yavner D L et al. 1988 Hydatidiform moles. Application of flow cytometry in diagnosis. Am J Clin Pathol 89: 596–600

67. Lage J M, Mark S D, Roberts D J et al. 1992 A flow cytometric study of 137 fresh hydropic placentas: correlation between types of hydatidiform moles and nuclear DNA ploidy. Obstet Gynecol 79: 403–410

68. Lage J M, Weinberg D S, Yavner D L et al. 1989 The biology of tetraploid hydatidiform moles: histopathology, cytogenetics, and flow cytometry. Hum Pathol 20: 419–425

69. Castrillon D H, Sun D, Weremowicz S et al. 2001 Discrimination of complete hydatidiform mole from its mimics by immunohistochemistry of the paternally imprinted gene product p57KIP2. Am J Surg Pathol 25: 1225–1230

70. Chilosi M, Piazzola E, Lestani M et al. 1998 Differential expression of p57kip2, a maternally imprinted cdk inhibitor, in normal human placenta and gestational trophoblastic disease. Lab Invest 78: 269–276

71. Genest D R, Dorfman D M, Castrillon D H 2002 Ploidy and imprinting in hydatidiform moles. Complementary use of flow cytometry and immunohistochemistry of the imprinted gene product p57KIP2 to assist molar classification. J Reprod Med 47: 342–346

72. Fisher R A, Hodges M D, Rees H C et al. 2002 The maternally transcribed gene p57 (KIP2) (CDNK1C) is abnormally expressed in both androgenetic and biparental complete hydatidiform moles. Hum Mol Genet 11: 3267–3272

73. Thaker H M, Berlin A, Tycko B et al. 2004 Immunohistochemistry for the imprinted gene product IPL/PHLDA2 for facilitating the differential diagnosis of complete hydatidiform mole. J Reprod Med 49: 630–636

74. Fisher R A, Nucci M R, Thaker H M et al. 2004 Complete hydatidiform mole retaining a chromosome 11 of maternal origin: molecular genetic analysis of a case. Mod Pathol 17: 1155–1160

75. Fukunaga M, Katabuchi H, Nagasaka T et al. 2005 Interobserver and intraobserver variability in the diagnosis of hydatidiform mole. Am J Surg Pathol 29: 942–947

76. Hertig A T, Mansell H 1956 Tumors of the female sex organs. Part I. Hydatidiform mole and choriocarcinoma. Atlas of tumor pathology, section 9, series I, fascicle 33. Armed Forces Institute of Pathology, Washington, DC

77. Lathrop J C, Watchel T J, Meissner G F 1978 Uterine choriocarcinoma fourteen years following bilateral tubal ligation. Obstet Gynecol 51: 477–478

78. Brewer J I, Mazur M T 1981 Gestational choriocarcinoma. Its origin in the placenta during seemingly normal pregnancy. Am J Surg Pathol 5: 267–277

79. Driscoll S G 1963 Choriocarcinoma. An "incidental finding" within a term placenta. Obstet Gynecol 21: 96–101

80. Aozasa K, Ito H, Kohro T et al. 1981 Choriocarcinoma in infant and mother. Acta Pathol Jpn 31: 317–322

81. Daamen C B, Bloem G W, Westerbeek A J 1961 Chorionepithelioma in mother and child. J Obstet Gynecol Br Commonw 68: 144–149

82. Mazur M T, Lurain J R, Brewer J I 1982 Fatal gestational choriocarcinoma. Cancer 50: 1833–1846

83. Soper J T, Evans A C, Conaway M R et al. 1994 Evaluation of prognostic factors and staging in gestational trophoblastic tumor. Obstet Gynecol 84: 969–973

84. Deligdish L, Driscoll S G, Goldstein D P 1978 Gestational trophoblastic neoplasms: morphologic correlates of therapeutic response. Am J Obstet Gynecol 130: 801–806

85. Elston C W, Bagshawe K D 1972 The diagnosis of trophoblastic tumors from uterine curettings. J Clin Pathol 25: 111–118

86. Fukunaga M, Ushigome S 1993 Malignant trophoblastic tumors: immunohistochemical and flow cytometric comparison of choriocarcinoma and placental site trophoblastic tumors. Hum Pathol 24: 1098–1106

87. Elston C W 1976 The histopathology of trophoblastic tumors. J Clin Pathol (suppl.) (R Coll Pathol) 29: 111–131

88. Mosher R, Genest D R 1996 Primary intraplacental choriocarcinoma: clinical and pathological features of seven cases (1967–1996) and discussion of the differential diagnosis. J Surg Pathol 2: 1–15

89. Fox H, Laurini R N 1988 Intraplacental choriocarcinoma: a report of two cases. J Clin Pathol 41: 1085–1088

90. Lage J M, Roberts D J 1993 Choriocarcinoma in a term placenta. Pathologic diagnosis of a tumor in an asymptomatic patient with metastatic disease. Int J Gynecol Pathol 12: 80–85

91. Olive D L, Lurain J R, Brewer J I 1984 Choriocarcinoma associated with term gestation. Am J Obstet Gynecol 148: 711–716

92. Kurman R J, Scully R E, Norris H J 1976 Trophoblastic pseudotumor of the uterus: an exaggerated form of "syncytial endometritis" simulating a malignant tumor. Cancer 38: 1214–1226

93. Duncan D A, Mazur M T 1989 Trophoblastic tumors: ultrastructural comparison of choriocarcinoma and placental-site trophoblastic tumor. Hum Pathol 20: 370–381

94. Eckstein R P, Paradinas F J, Bagshawe K D 1982 Placental site trophoblastic tumor (trophoblastic pseudotumor). Histopathology 16: 211–226

95. Eckstein R P, Russell P, Friedlander M L et al. 1985 Metastasizing placental site trophoblastic tumor: a case study. Hum Pathol 16: 632–636

96. Finkler N J, Berkowitz R S, Driscoll S G et al. 1988 Clinical experience with placental site trophoblastic tumors at the New England Trophoblastic Disease Center. Obstet Gynecol 71: 854–875

97. Gloor E, Dialdas J, Hurlimann J et al. 1983 Placental site trophoblastic tumor (trophoblastic pseudotumor) of the uterus with metastasis and fatal outcome. Clinical and autopsy outcome of a case. Am J Surg Pathol 7: 483–486

98. Gloor E, Hurlimann J 1981 Trophoblastic pseudotumor of the uterus: clinicopathologic report with immunohistochemical and ultrastructural studies. Am J Surg Pathol 5: 5–13

99. Heintz A P M, Schaberg A, Englesman E et al. 1985 Placental site trophoblastic tumor: diagnosis, treatment and biologic behavior. Int J Gynecol Pathol 4: 75–82

100. Hopkins M, Nunez C, Murphy J R et al. 1985 Malignant placental site trophoblastic tumor. Obstet Gynecol 66 (suppl.): 95S–100S

101. Kotylo P K, Michael H, Davis T E et al. 1992 Flow cytometric DNA analysis of placental-site trophoblastic tumors. Int J Gynecol Pathol 11: 245–255

102. Kurman R J, Young R H, Norris H J et al. 1984 Immunocytochemical localization of placental lactogen and chorionic gonadotropin in the normal placenta and trophoblastic tumors, with emphasis on intermediate trophoblast and the placental site trophoblastic tumor. Int J Gynecol Pathol 3: 101–121

103. Lathrop J C, Lauchlan S, Nayak R et al. 1988 Clinical characteristics of placental site trophoblastic tumor (PSTT). Gynecol Oncol 31: 32–42

104. Twiggs L B, Okagaki T, Phillips G L et al. 1981 Trophoblastic pseudotumor – evidence of malignant disease potential. Gynecol Oncol 12: 238–248

105. Young R H, Kurman R J, Scully R E 1988 Proliferations and tumors of intermediate trophoblast of the placental site. Semin Diagn Pathol 5: 223–237

106. Young R H, Scully R E, McCluskey R T 1985 A distinctive glomerular lesion complicating placental site trophoblastic tumor. Hum Pathol 16: 35–42

107. Fukunaga M, Ushigome S 1993 Metastasizing placental site trophoblastic tumor. An immunohistochemical and flow cytometric study of two cases. Am J Surg Pathol 17: 1003–1010

108. Shih I M, Kurman R J 1998 Epithelioid trophoblastic tumour. A neoplasm distinct from choriocarcinoma and placental site trophoblastic tumor simulating carcinoma. Am J Surg Pathol 22: 1393–1403

109. Shih I M, Kurman R J 2004 *p63* expression is useful in the distinction of epithelioid trophoblastic and placental site trophoblastic tumors by profiling trophoblastic subpopulations. Am J Surg Pathol 28: 1177–1183

109a. Fadare O, Parkash V, Carcangiu M L, Hui P 2006 Epithelioid trophoblastic tumor: clinicopathological features with an emphasis on uterine cervical involvement. Mod Pathol 19: 75–82

110. Huettner P C, Gersell D J 1994 Placental site nodule: a clinicopathologic study of 38 cases. Int J Gynecol Pathol 13: 191–199

111. Young R H, Kurman R J, Scully R E 1990 Placental site nodules and plaques. A clinicopathologic analysis of 20 cases. Am J Surg Pathol 14: 1001–1009

PART D

Myometrium

Marisa R. Nucci

Introduction

The overwhelming majority of myometrial neoplasms are composed of smooth muscle cells. Uterine smooth muscle neoplasia is both challenging diagnostically as well as fascinating scientifically, principally because it encompasses a wide variety of histopathologically diverse benign, malignant, and biologically indeterminate tumors. This section covers principally the histopathologic variants of benign leiomyomata and leiomyosarcoma and discusses those entities that are difficult to classify or exhibit biologic behavior intermediate between a benign and frankly malignant smooth muscle tumor.

Benign smooth muscle neoplasms

Clinical features

Uterine leiomyomata (fibroids, myomata), which most commonly occur in reproductive-aged women, are benign neoplasms arising from the smooth muscle of the uterine wall. They are remarkably common, with estimates of their frequency in hysterectomy specimens following careful histopathologic examination as high as 77% (regardless of the reason for surgery).[1] Although frequent, leiomyomata only result in clinically apparent (and significantly morbid) symptomology in up to 25% of women.[2] Associated clinical symptoms, which correlate with both tumor size and location within the uterine wall, include abnormal uterine bleeding, pelvic pain and pressure, and infertility.

Risk factors for the development of tumors include race and parity, with black and nulliparous women more likely to be affected.[2] There is also abundant evidence supporting the concept that leiomyomata are hormonally responsive and dependent tumors: (1) they are extremely rare before puberty; (2) they tend to regress following menopause; (3) they may exhibit rapid growth with exposure to an altered hormonal state such as pregnancy, clomiphene or progestin therapy; (4) they exhibit increased mitotic activity during the secretory phase of the menstrual cycle; and (5) tumor cells express estrogen and progesterone receptors. Genetic predisposition may also be a factor in tumor formation as leiomyomata are more common in black women, and also occur as part of Reed syndrome, an autosomal dominant genetic disorder characterized by multiple cutaneous and uterine leiomyomata, which has been mapped to the fumarate hydratase gene on chromosome 1.[3–5]

Molecular genetics

Leiomyomata, which represent separate clonal neoplasms that arise independently within the uterus,[6] exhibit simple chromosomal aberrations in 40% of tumors, of which the most common are deletion of 7q, translocation between 12q15 and 14q24, trisomy 12 and rearrangements of 6p, 10q22, or 13q.[7] Although the wide variety of chromosomal aberrations that may occur implies that there are multiple different pathogenetic mechanisms for tumor formation, the t(12;14)(q15;q24) involves the *HMGA2* gene (which encodes a transcriptional regulatory protein) on chromosome 12, whereas rearrangements of 6p have been shown to affect a related gene, *HMGA1*, suggesting that tumors with these two different aberrations may share a common pathogenetic pathway.[8–11]

Pathologic features

Leiomyomata are typically well-circumscribed, white tumors with a firm, rubbery consistency. Prominent bulging of cut surfaces when incised, secondary to release of intratumoral pressure, is characteristic. A variety of histologic variants of leiomyoma are recognized.

Leiomyoma, usual type. These tumors exhibit the classic features of smooth muscle differentiation, being composed of intersecting fascicles of spindled cells with eosinophilic cytoplasm and bland, elongated nuclei with blunt ends (so-called box-car or cigar-shaped appearance; Fig. 13D.1). Mitotic activity may be variable, and is often increased during the secretory phase of the menstrual cycle, but is usually fewer than 5 mitoses per 10 high-power fields. Those tumors with a higher mitotic count that are otherwise morphologically benign are discussed under mitotically active leiomyoma (see below).

Cellular leiomyoma. The threshold for considering a leiomyoma to be cellular is not precisely defined and is rather subjective. As defined by the World Health Organization, cellular leiomyomas are "significantly" more cellular than myometrium and leiomyomas of the usual type (Fig. 13D.2). Similar to leiomyomas of the usual type, cellular leiomyomas are well

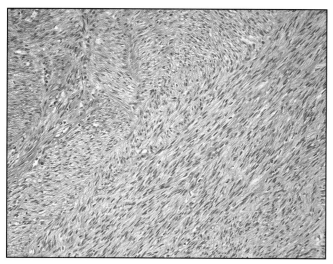

Fig. 13D.1 • Leiomyoma, usual type. Intersecting fascicles of bland spindle cells.

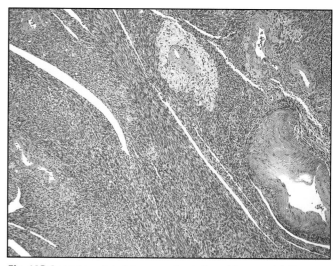

Fig. 13D.3 • Highly cellular leiomyoma. Fascicular architecture, cleft-like spaces, and large thick-walled blood vessels are characteristic.

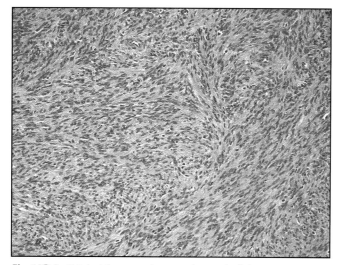

Fig. 13D.2 • Cellular leiomyoma. A greater degree of cellularity is apparent in comparison to the usual type of leiomyoma.

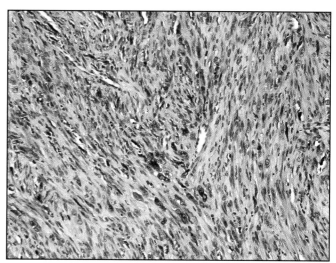

Fig. 13D.4 • Atypical leiomyoma. Enlarged, pleomorphic nuclei are diffusely present throughout the tumor.

circumscribed; however, they may appear tan/brown or yellow on gross examination and have a softer consistency. Cellular leiomyomas have uniformly bland cytomorphologic features and mitotic activity is typically less than 5 per 10 high-power fields. Mitotic activity in excess of this should prompt additional sampling of the tissue and careful assessment for the presence of other histologic features associated with malignancy.

Highly cellular leiomyoma.[12] This variant is defined as a leiomyoma in which the cellularity exceeds or is comparable to the cellularity of an endometrial stromal neoplasm. These tumors are typically well-circumscribed, tan/yellow nodules that tend to have a softer consistency than the usual type of leiomyoma. Histologically, they often have an irregular border, which, in combination with their marked cellularity and morphologic overlap with endometrial stroma, may mimic a low-grade endometrial stromal sarcoma. However, they can be recognized by their following characteristic features: (1) the presence of fascicular areas characteristic of smooth muscle neoplasia at least focally in most cases; (2) large thick-walled

blood vessels; (3) cleft-like spaces; and 4) desmin-positive/h-caldesmon-positive immunoprofile (Fig. 13D.3).

Mitotically active leiomyoma.[13–16] This variant corresponds to leiomyomas with mitotic activity greater than 5 mitoses per 10 high-power fields but which exhibit otherwise typical features of usual leiomyomas, particularly bland cytomorphologic features, circumscribed margins, and the absence of (coagulative tumor cell) necrosis. These tumors may occur over a wide age range but, in contrast to leiomyosarcoma, are typically seen during the reproductive years, with a mean age in the fifth decade. The increased mitotic activity may be secondary to hormonal influences, as these tumors are commonly seen in association with pregnancy, the secretory phase of the menstrual cycle, or in patients on hormonal therapy. Most tumors have fewer than 15 mitoses per 10 high-power fields, and the biologic behavior of histologically banal tumors that cross this mitotic threshold is not clear.

Atypical leiomyoma.[15,17] Also known as symplastic, bizarre, or pleomorphic leiomyoma (but defined as atypical leiomyoma in the most recent World Health Organization classification), this variant is characterized by the presence of cells with enlarged, pleomorphic, often multiple nuclei, which may be unifocal, multifocal, or diffuse in their distribution (Fig. 13D.4). These pleomorphic cells, which are always discernible upon low-power examination, may also have abundant eosinophilic cytoplasm, nuclear pseudoinclusions, and coarse chromatin. Most atypical leiomyomas have a similar gross appearance to leiomyomas of the usual type, but a subset may have a more yellow appearance and a softer consistency. Most of these tumors measure less than 5.5 cm and typically occur in reproductive-aged women with a mean age of 40 years. In addition to the presence of significant nuclear atypia, a defining histologic feature is a mitotic count that numbers fewer than 7 mitoses per 10 high-power fields, particularly in tumors with diffuse nuclear atypia. This threshold is based on the series of Downes & Hart,[17] in which tumors that met these criteria had a benign follow-up (mean 11 years), with most patients in this series being treated by hysterectomy. It is important to note that very few patients who have been treated by myomectomy alone have had long-term follow-up; therefore these tumors, particularly those with diffuse nuclear atypia treated by myomectomy alone, should be diagnosed with care. As a case in point, one example of such a tumor (with fewer than 2 mitoses per 10 high-power fields), treated by myomectomy alone, recurred at the surgical site within the myometrium 3 years after initial excision (personal observation). Moreover, in the series by Bell et al.,[15] one patient with a tumor that had diffuse nuclear atypia and a mitotic count of less than 2 per 10 high-power fields suffered intra-abdominal and pelvic recurrence 24 months following hysterectomy. The size of the original tumor in their series was not known and only 4 hematoxylin and eosin slides were evaluated, which, in this instance, raises the possibility of an undersampled leiomyosarcoma but more importantly underscores the requirement of extensive sampling in all tumors with nuclear atypia. Following adequate sampling (minimum of one section per centimeter, including the interface with normal myometrium), atypical leiomyomas, particularly those with diffuse nuclear atypia, are distinguished from leiomyosarcoma by the absence of coagulative tumor cell necrosis and a mitotic count of fewer than 7 figures per 10 high-power fields; those tumors with mitotic counts between 7 and 10 mitotic figures per 10 high-power fields are best considered as tumors of uncertain malignant potential. For practical purposes, following a diagnosis of atypical leiomyoma in patients treated by myomectomy alone, careful follow-up or hysterectomy should be considered.

Leiomyoma with secondary hormonal changes.[18–24]
Leiomyomata in patients who are pregnant, on oral contraceptive therapy, or being treated by gonadotropin-releasing hormone analogues may show a constellation of secondary degenerative histologic features. Also known as apoplectic or hemorrhagic cellular leiomyomata, these tumors, which typically occur in pregnant patients or women using oral contraceptives, are characterized on gross examination by multiple hemorrhagic foci which correspond histologically to stellate zones of recent hemorrhage and edema surrounded by a rim of hypercellular but banal smooth muscle; mitotic activity is usually sparse. Leiomyomata in patients treated with gonadotropin-releasing hormone analogues may show increased areas of hyalinization,

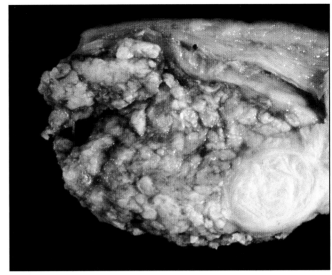

Fig. 13D.5 • Hydropic leiomyoma. Separation of muscle bundles by accumulation of edema fluid produces a multinodular appearance.

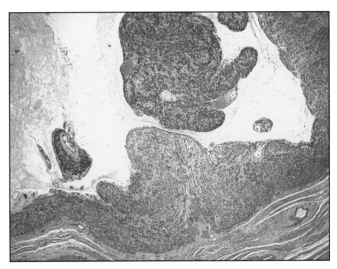

Fig. 13D.6 • Hydropic leiomyoma. Perinodular distribution of edema is characteristic.

alterations in cellularity, and intratumoral vascular changes, including luminal narrowing and arteriosclerotic changes.

Leiomyoma with hydropic degeneration.[25] Accumulation of edema fluid (hydropic change) may occur focally or more diffusely within an otherwise banal leiomyoma. With extensive hydropic change, the gross appearance of the leiomyoma may mimic either a myxoid smooth muscle tumor, due to its glistening cut surface, or intravenous leiomyomatosis, due to protrusion of muscle bundles separated by edema fluid into adjacent areas of cavitation (Fig. 13D.5). Histologically, the intercellular accumulation of edema fluid often has a paler, more eosinophilic appearance than myxoid change and usually results in a characteristic perinodular distribution of deposition (Fig. 13D.6). In some instances the degree of hydropic change is so extensive as to obscure the smooth muscle nature of the tumor (requiring confirmatory immunohistochemistry with smooth muscle markers). The hydropic change may extend beyond the perimeter of the leiomyoma, suggesting infiltration by a myxoid neoplasm; however, these areas typically do not stain for acidic mucins. Its generally well-circumscribed nature and absence of smooth muscle bundle protrusion into endothelial-lined spaces (which may require confirmation by immunohistochemistry) help distinguish a leiomyoma with extensive hydropic degeneration from intravascular leiomyomatosis (see p. 692).

Plexiform leiomyoma.[26–28] Considered a variant of epithelioid leiomyoma due to its pseudoepithelioid appearance on histologic examination, this benign smooth muscle tumor, also known as a plexiform tumorlet, is most commonly an incidental finding in hysterectomy specimens at the time of histologic examination. These tumors, which may be solitary or multiple, typically measure less than 1 cm and are characterized histologically by ribbons or nests of polygonal cells with scant cytoplasm and vesicular nuclei separated by abundant extracellular matrix. Accumulation of the latter causes loss of the typical spindled appearance to the cells and imparts an epithelioid appearance (Fig. 13D.7); mitotic activity is typically sparse. Immunohistochemical and ultrastructural analysis have shown that these tumors show features of smooth muscle rather than epithelial differentiation.

Epithelioid leiomyoma.[29–37] The World Health Organization defines epithelioid leiomyoma as a tumor that is composed of cells with an epithelioid appearance. These tumors have also been described in the literature as leiomyoblastoma (with some suggesting that the neoplastic cells exhibit immature smooth muscle cell differentiation mimicking fetal uterine myocytes) and clear cell leiomyoma (because some tumors have clear cytoplasm secondary to vacuolation of mitochondria or lysosomes). Patients with the epithelioid variant of leiomyoma do not differ in their clinical presentation from those with the usual type of leiomyoma, being most often affected during the reproductive years. On gross examination, some tumors may appear different from the usual type of leiomyoma, having a softer consistency and/or a tan/yellow appearance. Microscopically, these tumors are characterized by a proliferation of rounded cells with abundant clear or eosinophilic cytoplasm arranged in sheets but also sometimes in nests and cords (Fig. 13D.8). The nuclei may be located centrally within the

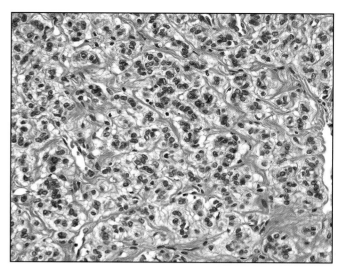

Fig. 13D.8 • Epithelioid leiomyoma. Ribbons and cords of rounded neoplastic cells with eosinophilic cytoplasm.

cytoplasm or at the periphery, which may impart a signet-ring cell appearance.

The validation of diagnostic criteria for reliable prediction of the behavior of smooth muscle tumors with epithelioid differentiation is limited by the rarity of this tumor subtype. Only a limited number of series have been published and, even with these studies, classification and prognostication continue to be problematic. Based on the published literature, and reflecting a conservative approach to these tumors, a diagnosis of a benign epithelioid leiomyoma should only be considered in those tumors in which necrosis is absent, there is no to minimal nuclear atypia, and the mitotic count is less than 3 mitoses per 10 high-power fields. Other features that have correlated with benign behavior include a well-circumscribed margin and tumor size less than 6 cm. Only a few epithelioid leiomyomata have been cytogenetically analyzed and most have shown abnormalities similar to that seen in conventional-type leiomyomata, including del(7)(q21.1q31.2),[33] suggesting that they share similar pathogenetic mechanisms.

Myxoid leiomyoma.[38] This extraordinarily uncommon variant of leiomyoma is characterized by the presence of extracellular matrix deposition composed of acid mucin. Gross examination typically reveals a well-circumscribed tumor that may appear gray and gelatinous depending on the extent of myxoid change within the tumor. Histologically, an abundant pale-blue myxoid matrix, that is typically positive for alcian blue, separates the muscle bundle fibers (Fig. 13D.9). Due to the rarity of this tumor, diagnostic criteria separating benign myxoid leiomyoma from leiomyosarcoma are not well established. For practical purposes, based on limited experience, lack of tumor cell necrosis, no to minimal nuclear atypia, lack of infiltration, and a mitotic count of less than 2 per 10 high-power fields favor a benign myxoid leiomyoma.

Lipoleiomyoma.[39–41] This unusual variant of leiomyoma is characterized by the presence of variable numbers of adipocytes admixed with the smooth muscle cells, which, when numerous, will result in a yellow coloration discernible on gross examination (Figs 13D.10 and 13D.11). Most patients with this variant are postmenopausal, raising the possibility that this

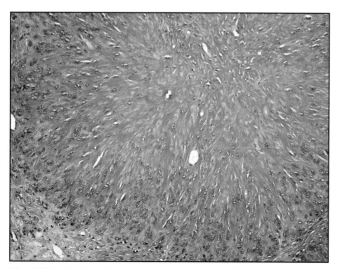

Fig. 13D.7 • Plexiform leiomyoma. Deposition of abundant extracellular matrix separates the tumor cells and imparts an epithelioid appearance.

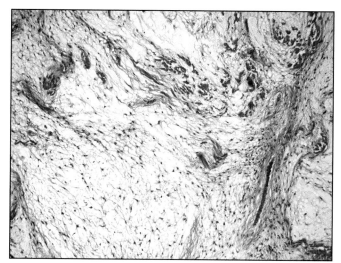

Fig. 13D.9 • Myxoid leiomyoma. Separation of muscle bundle fibers by abundant pale blue myxoid matrix.

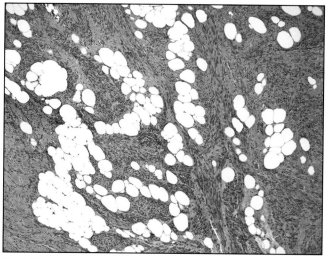

Fig. 13D.11 • Lipoleiomyoma. Admixture of adipocytes in an otherwise typical-appearing leiomyoma.

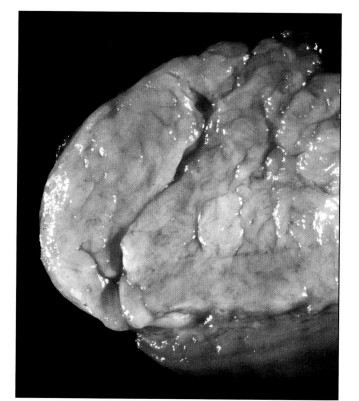

Fig. 13D.10 • Lipoleiomyoma. The presence of a prominent adipocytic component often results in yellow coloration of the leiomyoma on gross examination.

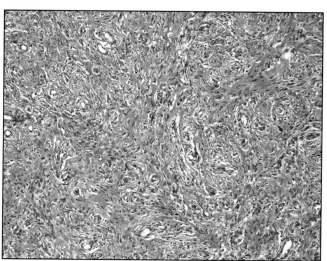

Fig. 13D.12 • Vascular leiomyoma. Increased number of blood vessels characterizes this unusual variant of leiomyoma.

alternative form of differentiation is possibly degenerative in nature; however, cytogenetic analysis of a small number of cases has shown rearrangement of 12q15(40, 41), which is the location of the gene *HMGA2*. Involvement of this area with aberrant expression of *HMGA2* is also seen in lipomas (see Ch. 24).

Vascular leiomyoma.[42] Also termed angiomyoma or angio-leiomyoma, this unusual and somewhat subjective morphologic variant of benign leiomyoma is characterized by a prominent component of blood vessels (Fig. 13D.12).

Leiomyoma with hematopoietic elements.[43–49] Occasionally otherwise morphologically ordinary leiomyomas may be infiltrated by variable, sometimes extensive amounts, of hematopoietic cells including lymphocytes, mast cells, eosinophils, and/or histiocytes. Massive infiltration by lymphocytes, which may be associated with gonadotropin-releasing hormone agonist therapy, can simulate lymphoma but can be recognized as a benign process by: (1) limitation of the inflammatory cells to the leiomyoma; and (2) the polymorphous nature of the infiltrate.

Neurilemmoma (schwannoma)-like leiomyoma.[50,51] This histologic variant of leiomyoma is characterized by palisading of tumor cell nuclei such that the lesion resembles a benign nerve sheath tumor (Fig. 13D.13). Although the resemblance may be uncanny, these tumors do not show ultrastructural evidence of schwannian differentiation.

Adenomyoma.[52] Although considered here as a variant of leiomyoma, whether adenomyomas represent a tumorous mass

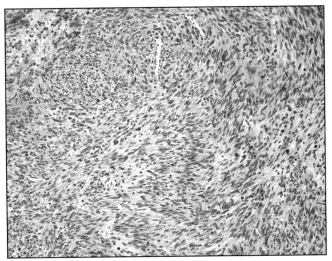

Fig. 13D.13 • Neurilemmoma-like leiomyoma. Palisading of tumor cell nuclei may mimic a benign nerve sheath tumor.

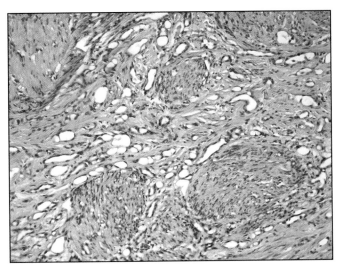

Fig. 13D.15 • Adenomatoid tumor. Pseudovascular spaces lined by bland cuboidal to attenuated epithelium are surrounded by a proliferation of smooth muscle.

as opposed to a circumscribed variant of adenomyosis is not clear and this has not been studied pathogenetically. Similar to leiomyomas, these lesions typically occur during the reproductive years and patients usually present with abnormal uterine bleeding. They are most often submucosal lesions (alternative terms used to describe them in this location include adenomyomatous polyp, polypoid adenomyoma, and pedunculated adenomyoma), but they may be located intramurally or involve the serosal surface. On gross examination, the lesions are typically well demarcated from the surrounding myometrium and often contain small cysts that may appear hemorrhagic. When located submucosally, they may mimic an endometrial polyp but usually have a firmer consistency and a myomatous appearance on the cut surface. Histologically, these lesions are composed of nests and islands of endometrial stroma and well-spaced, sometimes cystic, benign-appearing endometrioid glands that are surrounded by a proliferation of smooth muscle, with the latter component typically predominating (Fig. 13D.14). Distinction from adenomyosis may sometimes

be arbitrary but, in general, adenomyosis tends to be a diffuse process that has indistinct borders with the myometrium. More important is the distinction from atypical polypoid adenomyoma (see Ch. 13B), which, similar to adenomyoma, is characterized by a myomatous stroma but differs in having a more complex proliferation of glands (that in some instances is indistinguishable from well-differentiated endometrioid adenocarcinoma) and which commonly shows squamous morular metaplasia.

Adenomatoid tumor.[53–56] These tumors, which are usually incidental findings in hysterectomy or myomectomy specimens from reproductive-aged women, are not variants of leiomyoma per se but do represent a benign tumorous mass of presumed mesothelial origin with a prominent smooth muscle component that may mimic a leiomyoma on gross and histologic examination. They are most commonly located in the subserosal area, may appear tan, white, or yellow, and are generally more poorly demarcated from the surrounding myometrium than leiomyomas. Most tumors measure less than 5 cm; however, occasionally they may be larger, with many such cases having a prominent cystic component. Histologically, pseudovascular spaces lined by cuboidal to attenuated epithelial cells with bland nuclei are separated by bands of smooth muscle (Fig. 13D.15). A mesothelial origin for these tumors is supported by their phenotype, with the epithelial cell component expressing calretinin, HMBE-1, and WT-1.[56]

Malignant smooth muscle neoplasms

Clinical features

Uterine leiomyosarcoma is uncommon, representing fewer than 2% of all uterine malignancies, with an annual incidence estimated to be 0.64 cases per 100 000 women; however, it does represent the most common uterine sarcoma, accounting for approximately 25% of malignant mesenchymal tumors of the uterus.[57,58] The frequency of leiomyosarcoma in hysterectomy specimens removed for the preoperative diagnosis of benign

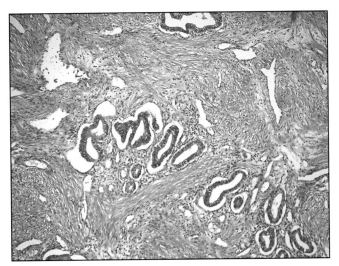

Fig. 13D.14 • Adenomyoma. Benign-appearing endometrial glands and stroma set within a myomatous stroma.

leiomyoma is also uncommon and has been estimated to be 0.49%.[59] There does appear to be a racial difference in the incidence of uterine leiomyosarcoma, with black women being at greater risk for the development of disease; other potential risk factors include oral contraceptive use and tamoxifen.[58,60] The median age of patients diagnosed with leiomyosarcoma is usually in the fifth to sixth decade and the most common presenting symptoms are dysfunctional uterine bleeding and/or pelvic pain.[57,57,59,61–64] While clinical examination typically reveals an enlarged uterus, many leiomyosarcomas are unsuspected and presumed to be enlarged leiomyomata. If the tumor does not involve the endometrial cavity, preoperative endometrial sampling may not be informative; nevertheless, in a postmenopausal patient, the clinical impression of a large or rapidly enlarging fibroid should raise the suspicion for malignancy.

Uterine leiomyosarcoma is an aggressive tumor that has a tendency to recur locally and/or metastasize, most commonly to liver and lung. Regional lymph node involvement is not common and is typically only seen in patients with advanced-stage disease; therefore, lymph node dissection is usually only performed in patients with clinically suspicious nodes.[65,66] Estimates of overall 5-year survival rates have varied widely, which is likely the result of small case numbers in some series, differences in the number of patients with early-stage disease, and shifting criteria for the diagnosis of leiomyosarcoma; however, many studies have estimated an overall 5-year survival rate between 45 and 65%.[57,60–62,64,67–69] Despite differences in survival rates, it is clear that stage is a significant prognostic factor related to outcome.[60–63,68–73] Standard treatment is total abdominal hysterectomy and bilateral salpingo-oophorectomy; however, although controversial, case-controlled studies have suggested that ovarian preservation in premenopausal women does not adversely affect survival.[63] The effect of adjuvant therapy on survival is controversial.[62–64,69,72]

Molecular genetics

In contrast to leiomyomas, leiomyosarcomas are characterized cytogenetically by complex numerical and structural abnormalities, which may vary from one tumor cell to the next within the same malignancy, suggesting that there is a high degree of genomic instability.[74–76] This has been supported by other investigative methods, such as comparative genomic hybridization, which most commonly has shown loss of heterozygosity for the long arms of chromosomes 10 and 13.[77] Transcriptional profiling has shown differences between leiomyosarcoma (which typically shows downregulation of gene expression) and leiomyomata, supporting different pathogenetic pathways for the development of these tumors.[78]

Pathologic features

Leiomyosarcomas are typically a solitary or dominant mass within the uterus, are most commonly intramural but may be submucosal or subserosal, and have a mean diameter of 9 cm.[62,63] Although some may grossly resemble a leiomyoma, most have a distinctly different appearance, being less well circumscribed – some with obvious myometrial infiltration – with a softer consistency, gray to cream color, and variable amounts of randomly distributed geographic hemorrhage and

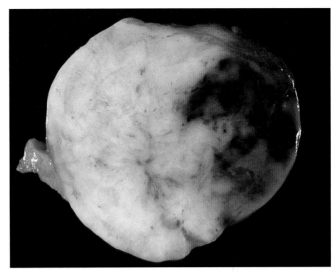

Fig. 13D.16 • Leiomyosarcoma. A more homogeneous, "fish-flesh" appearance with geographic areas of hemorrhage and necrosis is typical.

necrosis, the latter often appearing yellow or green on gross examination (Fig. 13D.16). Although any of these unusual gross features may raise the possibility of malignancy (and should prompt extensive sampling), the diagnosis of leiomyosarcoma is based solely on the histologic appearance of the tumor. The vast majority of leiomyosarcomas are of the spindle cell type; however, epithelioid and myxoid variants occur, with each of these variants having different criteria for the diagnosis of malignancy (Table 13D.1).

Spindle cell leiomyosarcoma

The spindle cell variant of leiomyosarcoma is so called because it morphologically mimics benign leiomyomata, being composed of fascicles of spindled cells with varying amounts of eosinophilic cytoplasm (Fig. 13D.17). Over time it has become apparent that no single histologic feature, perhaps with the exception of tumor cell necrosis (which may be difficult to

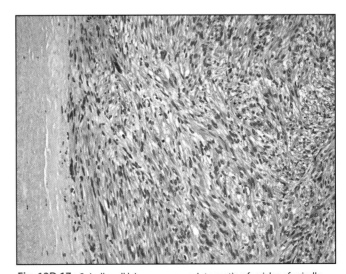

Fig. 13D.17 • Spindle cell leiomyosarcoma. Intersecting fascicles of spindle cells with eosinophilic cytoplasm. Note the nuclear atypia and tumor cell necrosis (left).

Table 13D.1	Diagnostic criteria for smooth muscle tumors

Spindle cell smooth muscle tumors with significant nuclear atypia

Diffuse or multifocal moderate-severe nuclear atypia + no tumor cell necrosis + ≥ 10 mitoses/10 high-power fields = **leiomyosarcoma**

Diffuse, multifocal, or focal moderate-severe nuclear atypia + tumor cell necrosis + ≥ 1 mitosis per 10 high-power fields = **leiomyosarcoma**

Diffuse, multifocal, or focal moderate-severe nuclear atypia + no tumor cell necrosis + < 7 mitoses per 10 high-power fields = **atypical leiomyoma**

Diffuse or multifocal moderate-severe nuclear atypia + no tumor cell necrosis + mitoses > 7 but < 10 per 10 high-power fields = **smooth muscle tumor of uncertain malignant potential**

Spindle cell smooth muscle tumors without significant nuclear atypia

No or minimal nuclear atypia + tumor cell necrosis + ≥ 10 mitoses/10 high-power fields = **leiomyosarcoma**

No or minimal nuclear atypia + tumor cell necrosis + < 10 mitoses/10 high-power fields = **smooth muscle tumor of uncertain malignant potential**

No or minimal nuclear atypia + no tumor cell necrosis + > 5 mitoses but < 15 per 10 high-power fields = **mitotically active leiomyoma**

No or minimal nuclear atypia + no tumor cell necrosis + > 15 per 10 high-power fields = **mitotically active leiomyoma (uncertain behavior)**

Myxoid smooth muscle tumors

<2 mitoses/10 high-power fields + no tumor cell necrosis + no to minimal nuclear atypia + no infiltration of myometrium = **myxoid leiomyoma**

>2 mitoses/10 high-power fields or tumor cell necrosis or moderate-severe nuclear atypia or infiltration of myometrium = **myxoid leiomyosarcoma**

Epithelioid smooth muscle tumors

<3 mitoses/10 high-power fields + no tumor cell necrosis + no to minimal nuclear atypia + no vascular invasion + well-circumscribed margin = **consider epithelioid leiomyoma**

>3 mitoses/10 high-power fields or tumor cell necrosis or moderate-severe nuclear atypia or vascular invasion or infiltrative margin = **epithelioid leiomyosarcoma**

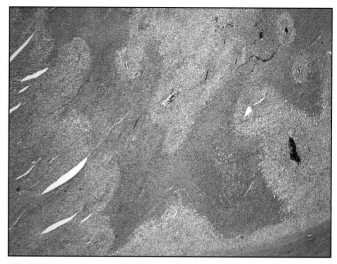

Fig. 13D.18 • Leiomyosarcoma with tumor cell necrosis. Note the irregular, angulated borders of the necrosis ("geographic" necrosis).

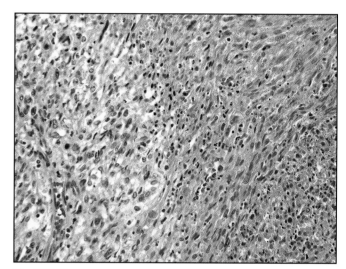

Fig. 13D.19 • Leiomyosarcoma with tumor cell necrosis. A sharp interface between viable and necrotic cells with nuclear debris is characteristic.

recognize in isolation), is diagnostic of malignancy. Rather, the diagnosis of leiomyosarcoma is based on data from a landmark study by Bell et al.,[15] in which a combination of histologic features is assessed. These features include: (1) the presence and extent of significant nuclear atypia (practically defined as atypia notable at low power, i.e. with the 10× objective); (2) the mitotic rate; and (3) the presence or absence of coagulative necrosis. A diagnosis of leiomyosarcoma is made when: (1) there is diffuse moderate to severe nuclear atypia **and** the mitotic count measures 10 or more per 10 high-power fields; or (2) there is diffuse or multifocal moderate to severe nuclear atypia **and** tumor cell necrosis **and** any degree of mitotic activity greater than 1 per 10 high-power fields; or (3) there is no to minimal nuclear atypia **and** there is tumor cell necrosis **and** the mitotic count measures greater than 10 mitoses per 10 high-power fields. This latter scenario is very uncommon and raises the significant diagnostic problem of what constitutes proper tumor cell necrosis versus benign degenerative changes. Coagulative tumor cell necrosis is characterized by: (1) an irregular, angulated border ("geographic" appearance); (2) a sharp interface between the viable and necrotic cells (as opposed to a transition zone composed of granulation or hyalinized tissue characteristic of ischemia); (3) the presence of apoptotic/nuclear debris at the interface; and (4) atypical ghost cells (for those tumors with nuclear atypia) within the necrotic areas (Figs 13D.18 and 13D.19). In those cases in which the necrosis is ambiguous and there is minimal to no cytologic atypia, classification of the tumor as that with uncertain malignant potential should be considered (see section on Smooth muscle tumors of uncertain malignant potential, below).

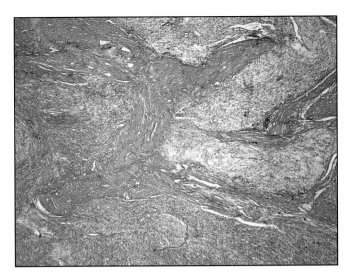

Fig. 13D.20 • Myxoid leiomyosarcoma. Abundant extracellular matrix deposition separates the tumor cells. Note infiltration of myometrium.

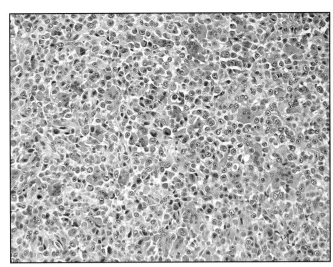

Fig. 13D.22 • Epithelioid leiomyosarcoma. Rounded tumor cells with abundant eosinophilic cytoplasm.

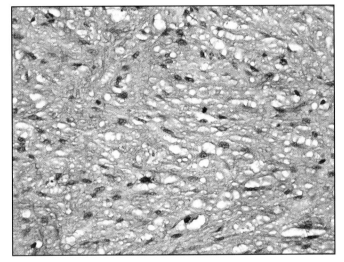

Fig. 13D.21 • Myxoid leiomyosarcoma. Although many of the tumor cells may appear bland, most cases exhibit at least a moderate degree of nuclear atypia.

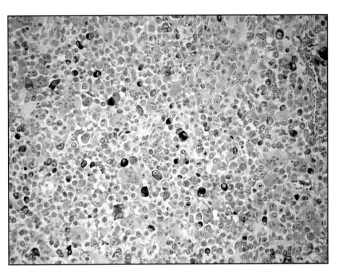

Fig. 13D.23 • Epithelioid leiomyosarcoma. Tumor cells are positive for desmin.

Myxoid leiomyosarcoma[38,79–82]

Similar to the spindle cell variant, myxoid leiomyosarcoma also typically occurs in women in their sixth decade who present with abnormal bleeding, pelvic pain, and/or a pelvic mass. In contrast, however, the gross appearance will have a more gelatinous appearance with a glistening cut surface, which may vary in extent depending on the amount of extracellular myxoid matrix deposition. Histologically, these tumors are characterized by abundant, pale blue, extracellular myxoid matrix that is alcian blue-positive. The tumor cells may be spindled or stellate and the degree of extracellular matrix deposition may obscure the tumors' fascicular architecture (Fig. 13D.20). Tumor cells typically exhibit at least focal moderate atypia, although much of the tumor may have a bland cytomorphologic appearance (Fig. 13D.21). Due to the rarity of this tumor, diagnostic criteria separating myxoid leiomyosarcoma from myxoid leiomyoma are not well established. Atkins et al. have suggested that a rate in excess of 2 mitotic figures per 10 high-power fields, regardless of the presence or absence of either

atypia or necrosis, will separate benign from malignant myxoid tumors.[38] For practical purposes, the diagnosis of myxoid leiomyosarcoma should be considered if any of the following is present: (1) there is moderate to marked cytologic atypia; (2) there is coagulative tumor cell necrosis; (3) mitotic activity exceeds 2 per 10 high-power fields; or (4) there is destructive infiltration of the surrounding myometrium.

Epithelioid leiomyosarcoma[29,34,36,37]

A predominance of rounded tumor cells with abundant eosinophilic or clear cytoplasm characterizes this subtype of leiomyosarcoma (Figs 13D.22 and 13.23). Similar to myxoid leiomyosarcoma, the validation of diagnostic criteria used to predict reliably the behavior of epithelioid smooth muscle tumors is limited by the rarity of this tumor subtype and the limited number of series that have been published. In the largest series of epithelioid smooth muscle tumors published (80 cases; in abstract form[37]), malignant behavior was associated with the presence of tumor cell necrosis, vascular invasion, moderate to severe nuclear atypia, and a mitotic count greater than 3 per 10 high-power fields. Infiltrative margins have also correlated with malignant behavior.

Smooth muscle tumors of uncertain malignant potential

Despite numerous clinicopathologic studies addressing the diagnostic criteria for malignancy of uterine smooth muscle tumors, there remains a subset of these lesions that are difficult to classify. For some, such as epithelioid and myxoid smooth muscle tumors, uncertainty remains because of their rarity and thus inherent difficulty in establishing and validating diagnostic criteria that would predict malignant behavior. Other tumors are best considered in this category because they approach, but fall short of, the diagnostic threshold for malignancy or the presence of tumor cell necrosis is ambiguous and cannot be distinguished from a benign process with certainty. In addition, those features defined by Bell et al.[15] as indicating a tumor with uncertain or low malignant potential are outlined in Table 13D.1. In practice, only a minority of smooth muscle tumors falls within this category.

Smooth muscle proliferations with unusual features

Leiomyoma with vascular invasion[83]

Leiomyoma with vascular invasion is a term applied to the uncommon finding of microscopic intravascular extension of tumor within the confines of an otherwise ordinary leiomyoma. Although there are no reported series of these tumors with long-term follow-up, they are generally considered benign without risk of recurrence. This lesion is distinguished from intravenous leiomyomatosis by its lack of vascular invasion beyond the confines of the leiomyoma.

Intravenous (intravascular) leiomyomatosis[83–85]

Intravenous leiomyomatosis, which typically occurs during the later reproductive years with a mean age at presentation in the fifth decade, is an unusual entity characterized by the intravascular proliferation of benign-appearing smooth muscle. Patients typically present with abnormal uterine bleeding, pelvic pain, and/or a pelvic mass, and clinical examination usually reveals an enlarged uterus. Gross examination, in which multiple myometrial masses are typically present, may also show worm-like plugs of tumor within parametrial vessels (Fig. 13D.24). On rare occasions, extension into the inferior vena cava and its tributaries may occur, including involvement of the heart. Usually a component of conventional leiomyoma is also present within the uterus; however in some cases the entire tumor is present within vascular spaces, which may not be appreciated initially on gross examination. Histologically, the intravascular tumor, which often has a lobulated or clefted contour, resembles a typical uterine leiomyoma, although in many cases it may also exhibit extensive hydropic or hyaline

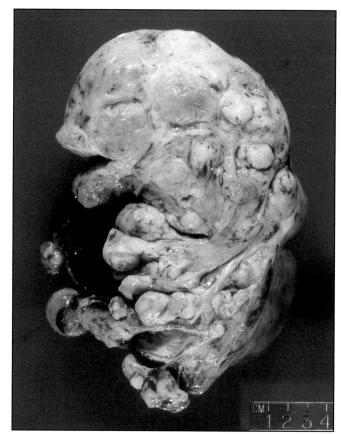

Fig. 13D.24 • Intravenous leiomyomatosis. Multiple tumor nodules fill intramyometrial vascular spaces. (Courtesy of Dr. Christopher Otis, Baystate Medical Center, Springfield, MA.)

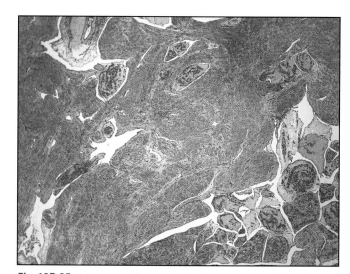

Fig. 13D.25 • Intravenous leiomyomatosis. Multiple tumor nodules within vascular spaces exhibiting a clefted contour are characteristic.

change (Figs 13D.25 and 13D.26). Other histologic variants may occur, including cases in which the intravascular component is cellular, myxoid, epithelioid, or contains a component of adipocytes (lipoleiomyoma-like). While vascular smooth muscle origin has been proposed, cytogenetic analysis of two cases has shown the presence of a derivative chromosome – der(14)t(12;14)(q15;q24) –frequently found in uterine leiomyomata, supporting uterine origin.[86] Intravenous leiomyomatosis

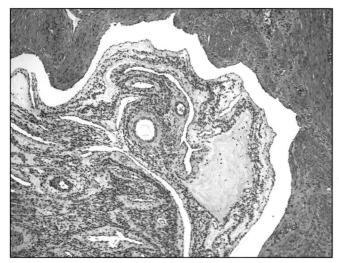

Fig. 13D.26 • Intravenous leiomyomatosis. Tumor nodule within a vascular space with hydropic change.

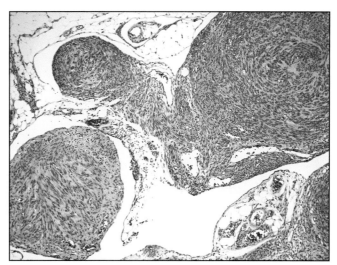

Fig. 13D.28 • Disseminated peritoneal leiomyomatosis. Histologically banal smooth muscle tumorlets involving the omentum.

is considered to have a good prognosis, particularly if resectable, despite the presence of extensive vascular involvement. Most cases pursue a benign clinical course with a low risk of pelvic recurrence or distant metastasis, most commonly to the lung. The principal differential diagnostic consideration is distinction of intravenous leiomyomatosis, particularly the cellular variant, from endometrial stromal sarcoma. The latter lacks the clefted contour of the intravascular component as well as thick-walled blood vessels; in difficult cases, the lack of muscle marker positivity, particularly h-caldesmon, is characteristic of endometrial stromal tumors.

Disseminated peritoneal leiomyomatosis[87–90]

Disseminated peritoneal leiomyomatosis (leiomyomatosis peritonealis disseminata) is a rare disorder that typically occurs in women of reproductive age and is characterized by numerous histologically benign, leiomyomatous tumorlets with minimal mitotic activity that stud the peritoneal and omental surfaces (Figs 13D.27 and 13D.28). The number and size of the tumorlets vary and range from a few to innumerable

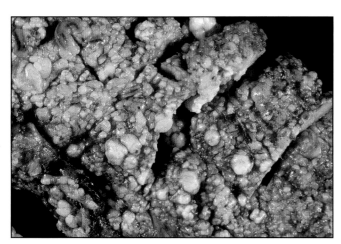

Fig. 13D.27 • Disseminated peritoneal leiomyomatosis. Numerous tumor nodules stud the omentum, mimicking metastatic carcinoma.

nodules and from microscopic to usually less than 3 cm. Extensive disease often clinically simulates a disseminated malignancy. There is an association, although not invariably, with concurrent pregnancy or exogenous hormonal therapy. Although these associations suggest that hormonal influence plays a role in the pathogenesis, clonality studies indicate that the nodules of disseminated peritoneal leiomyomatosis are clonal and have an identical pattern of X-chromosome inactivation,[90] suggesting that they all arose from a single transformation event and are all derived from the same parent nodule (i.e. are "metastatic"). Despite this intriguing finding, patients with this disease generally pursue a benign clinical course and conservative treatment with long-term follow-up is typically recommended.

Intrauterine diffuse leiomyomatosis[91–93]

Diffuse leiomyomatosis is a rare benign disorder characterized by diffuse, symmetric enlargement of the uterus by numerous, variably sized, confluent, often ill-defined leiomyomata. It typically affects women less than 40 years of age who most commonly present with abnormal uterine bleeding. Gross examination reveals an enlarged uterus, which may exceed 1 kg, in which the myometrium is almost entirely replaced by numerous leiomyomata, which may appear confluent and not as well demarcated from each other as in a uterus otherwise involved by the usual type of leiomyomata (Fig. 13D.29). Histologically, the leiomyomatous nodules, many more of which are appreciated on microscopic examination, are composed of bland, typically cellular smooth muscle. Although some may be well demarcated, usually the leiomyomatous nodules are poorly defined and often appear to merge together (Fig. 13D.30). Clonality analysis of a case of diffuse leiomyomatosis revealed a different, but non-random, X-chromosome inactivation pattern in eight separate leiomyomatous nodules, supporting the hypothesis that the tumorous nodules arose from independent transformation events.[93] This finding is similar to that in typical uterine leiomyomata, suggesting that patients with diffuse leiomyomatosis are particularly prone to the formation of leiomyomatous nodules.

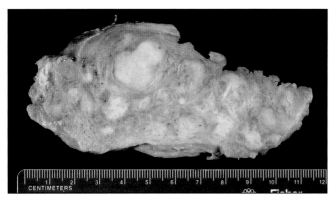

Fig. 13D.29 • Intrauterine diffuse leiomyomatosis. The myometrium is diffusely involved by somewhat ill-defined leiomyomatous nodules.

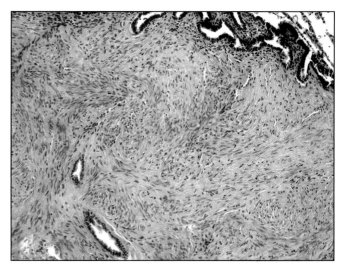

Fig. 13D.31 • Benign metastasizing leiomyoma. Banal smooth muscle proliferation involving lung parenchyma in a patient with benign uterine leiomymata.

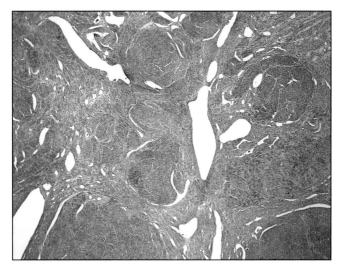

Fig. 13D.30 • Intrauterine diffuse leiomyomatosis. Numerous, somewhat confluent leiomyomata diffusely involve the myometrium.

Benign metastasizing leiomyoma[94–97]

So-called benign metastasizing leiomyoma is a term used to describe the presence of cytologically bland, mitotically inactive smooth muscle proliferations occurring in the lung or lymph nodes of patients with similar-appearing uterine smooth muscle tumors. This terminology is based on the premise that the origin of these tumors is from the spread of histologically benign-appearing uterine smooth muscle tumors (leiomyoma) that cannot, based upon morphologic criteria alone, be recognized as a tumor with metastatic potential (leiomyosarcoma). However, it is not clear whether lesions classified as such represent biologically distinct clinico-pathological entities, or whether this diagnostic entity is composed of lesions that are histologically similar, but biologically unrelated. Patients with this disease usually have had a history (often many years prior) of hysterectomy/myomectomy for uterine leiomyomata or have concurrent leiomyomata at the time of presentation. Histologically, the "metastatic" deposits are composed of a proliferation of bland-appearing smooth muscle cells, which show no evidence of nuclear pleomorphism, necrosis, or significant mitotic activity (Fig. 13D.31). The clinical course is variable, with some cases being indolent, while others lead to progressive (and even fatal) pulmonary involvement.

Rare and unusual neoplasms

Rhabdomyosarcoma[98–100]

Pure rhabdomyosarcomas of the uterus are extremely uncommon and should only be considered once sarcomatous overgrowth of a carcinosarcoma or adenosarcoma have been excluded with extensive sampling. When pure, uterine rhabdomyosarcomas are most commonly of the pleomorphic subtype; however; the spindle and alveolar subtypes have also been described. In the largest series, patients with pure pleomorphic uterine rhabdomyosarcoma presented with vaginal bleeding, uterine enlargement, or an acute abdomen and the mean age at presentation was 65 years.[98] Tumors were either polypoid endometrial or intramyometrial masses and histologically were similar to pleomorphic rhabdomyosarcoma of soft tissue. The prognosis is poor, with most patients succumbing to disease in under 2 years.

Uterine perivascular epithelioid cell tumor[101–104]

Perivascular epithelioid cell tumors (PEComas) are tumors composed of epithelioid or polygonal cells with abundant clear to granular cytoplasm that have a tendency to exhibit a perivascular growth pattern and which are positive for HMB-45 and desmin. Uterine perivascular epithelioid cell tumors are members of a family of tumors that include epithelioid angiomyolipoma, clear cell "sugar" tumor, clear cell myomelanocytic of the ligamentum teres/falciform ligament, abdominopelvic sarcoma of perivascular epithelioid cells, and lymphangioleiomyomatosis, which are related by their similar morphology and immunophenotype (see also Ch. 24). Two histologic patterns in those lesions that occur in the uterus have been described. One subtype exhibits a growth pattern similar to low-grade endometrial stromal sarcoma, with finger-like permeation of the uterine wall, and is composed of cells with abundant eosinophilic, clear, or granular cytoplasm; these tumors exhibit diffuse HMB-45 expression with only focal muscle marker positivity.[101] The other subtype is composed of epithelioid cells with less abundant clear cytoplasm, less HMB-45 expression, and more extensive muscle marker positivity.[101,102] The relationship of uterine perivascular epithelioid tumor to epithelioid smooth muscle tumors is therefore unclear; however, it appears that they may be part of a morphologic spectrum. Uterine perivascular epithelioid cell tumors are best considered tumors of uncertain malignant potential as recurrences and late metastases may occasionally occur. Due to the small number of reported cases, identification and validation of histologic criteria that may predict the behavior of these tumors remain to be achieved.

References

1. Cramer S F, Patel A 1990 The frequency of uterine leiomyomas. Am J Clin Pathol 94: 435–438
2. Stewart E A 2001 Uterine fibroids. Lancet 357: 293–298
3. Alam N A, Bevan S, Churchman M et al. 2001 Localization of a gene (MCUL1) for multiple cutaneous leiomyomata and uterine fibroids to chromosome 1q42.3-q43. Am J Hum Genet 68: 1264–1269
4. Tomlinson I P, Alam N A, Rowan A J et al. 2002 Germline mutations in FH predispose to dominantly inherited uterine fibroids, skin leiomyomata and papillary renal cell cancer. Nat Genet 30: 406–410
5. Toro J R, Nickerson M L, Wei M H et al. 2003 Mutations in the fumarate hydratase gene cause hereditary leiomyomatosis and renal cell cancer in families in North America. Am J Hum Genet 73: 95–106
6. Mashal R D, Fejzo M L, Friedman A J et al. 1994 Analysis of androgen receptor DNA reveals the independent clonal origins of uterine leiomyomata and the secondary nature of cytogenetic aberrations in the development of leiomyomata. Genes Chromos Cancer 11: 1–6
7. Nilbert M, Heim S 1990 Uterine leiomyoma cytogenetics. Genes Chromos Cancer 2: 3–13
8. Schoenmakers E F, Wanschura S, Mols R et al. 1995 Recurrent rearrangements in the high mobility group protein gene, HMGI-C, in benign mesenchymal tumours. Nat Genet 10: 436–444
9. Gattas G J, Quade B J, Nowak R A et al. 1999 HMGIC expression in human adult and fetal tissues and in uterine leiomyomata. Genes Chromos Cancer 25: 316–322
10. Kazmierczak B, Dal Cin P, Wanschura S et al. 1998 HMGIY is the target of 6p21.3 rearrangements in various benign mesenchymal tumors. Genes Chromos Cancer 23: 279–285
11. Klotzbucher M, Wasserfall A, Fuhrmann U 1999 Misexpression of wild-type and truncated isoforms of the high-mobility group I proteins HMGI-C and HMGI(Y) in uterine leiomyomas. Am J Pathol 155: 1535–1542
12. Oliva E, Young R H, Clement P B et al. 1995 Cellular benign mesenchymal tumors of the uterus. A comparative morphologic and immunohistochemical analysis of 33 highly cellular leiomyomas and six endometrial stromal nodules, two frequently confused tumors. Am J Surg Pathol 19: 757–768
13. O'Connor D M, Norris H J 1990 Mitotically active leiomyomas of the uterus. Hum Pathol 21: 223–227
14. Prayson R A, Hart W R 1992 Mitotically active leiomyomas of the uterus. Am J Clin Pathol 97: 14–20
15. Bell S W, Kempson R L, Hendrickson M R 1994 Problematic uterine smooth muscle neoplasms. A clinicopathologic study of 213 cases. Am J Surg Pathol 18: 535–558
16. Dgani R, Piura B, Ben Baruch G et al. 1998 Clinical–pathological study of uterine leiomyomas with high mitotic activity. Acta Obstet Gynecol Scand 77: 74–77
17. Downes K A, Hart W R 1997 Bizarre leiomyomas of the uterus: a comprehensive pathologic study of 24 cases with long-term follow-up. Am J Surg Pathol 21: 1261–1270
18. Myles J L, Hart W R 1985 Apoplectic leiomyomas of the uterus. A clinicopathologic study of five distinctive hemorrhagic leiomyomas associated with oral contraceptive usage. Am J Surg Pathol 9: 798–805
19. Norris H J, Hilliard G D, Irey N S 1988 Hemorrhagic cellular leiomyomas ("apoplectic leiomyoma") of the uterus associated with pregnancy and oral contraceptives. Int J Gynecol Pathol 7: 212–224
20. Colgan T J, Pendergast S, LeBlanc M 1993 The histopathology of uterine leiomyomas following treatment with gonadotropin-releasing hormone analogues. Hum Pathol 24: 1073–1077
21. Rutgers J L, Spong C Y, Sinow R et al. 1995 Leuprolide acetate treatment and myoma arterial size. Obstet Gynecol 86: 386–388
22. Deligdisch L, Hirschmann S, Altchek A 1997 Pathologic changes in gonadotropin releasing hormone agonist analogue treated uterine leiomyomata. Fertil Steril 67: 837–841
23. Demopoulos R I, Jones K Y, Mittal K R et al. 1997 Histology of leiomyomata in patients treated with leuprolide acetate. Int J Gynecol Pathol 16: 131–137
24. Sreenan J J, Prayson R A, Biscotti C V et al. 1996 Histopathologic findings in 107 uterine leiomyomas treated with leuprolide acetate compared with 126 controls. Am J Surg Pathol 20: 427–432
25. Clement P B, Young R H, Scully R E 1992 Diffuse, perinodular, and other patterns of hydropic degeneration within and adjacent to uterine leiomyomas. Problems in differential diagnosis. Am J Surg Pathol 16: 26–32
26. Kaminski P F, Tavassoli F A 1984 Plexiform tumorlet: a clinical and pathologic study of 15 cases with ultrastructural observations. Int J Gynecol Pathol 3: 124–134
27. Seidman J D, Thomas R M 1993 Multiple plexiform tumorlets of the uterus. Arch Pathol Lab Med 117: 1255–1256
28. Nagel H, Brinck U, Luthje D et al. 1999 Plexiform leiomyoma of the uterus in a patient with breast carcinoma: case report and review of the literature. Pathology 31: 292–294
29. Kurman R J, Norris H J 1976 Mesenchymal tumors of the uterus. VI. Epithelioid smooth muscle tumors including leiomyoblastoma and clear-cell leiomyoma: a clinical and pathologic analysis of 26 cases. Cancer 37: 1853–1865
30. Mazur M T, Priest J B 1986 Clear cell leiomyoma (leiomyoblastoma) of the uterus: ultrastructural observations. Ultrastruct Pathol 10: 249–255
31. Hyde K E, Geisinger K R, Marshall R B et al. 1989 The clear-cell variant of uterine epithelioid leiomyoma. An immunohistologic and ultrastructural study. Arch Pathol Lab Med 113: 551–553
32. Kyriazis A P, Kyriazis A A 1992 Uterine leiomyoblastoma (epithelioid leiomyoma) neoplasm of low-grade malignancy. A histopathologic study. Arch Pathol Lab Med 116: 1189–1191
33. Karaiskos C, Pandis N, Bardi G et al. 1995 Cytogenetic findings in uterine epithelioid leiomyomas. Cancer Genet Cytogenet 80: 103–106
34. Prayson R A, Goldblum J R, Hart W R 1997 Epithelioid smooth-muscle tumors of the uterus: a clinicopathologic study of 18 patients. Am J Surg Pathol 21: 383–391
35. Watanabe K, Ogura G, Suzuki T 2003 Leiomyoblastoma of the uterus: an immunohistochemical and electron microscopic study of distinctive tumours with immature smooth muscle cell differentiation mimicking fetal uterine myocytes. Histopathology 42: 379–386
36. Atkins K, Bell S, Kempson R L et al. 2002 Epithelioid smooth muscle tumors of the uterus [abstract]. Mod Pathol 14: 132A
37. Oliva E, Nielsen G P, Clement P B et al. 1997 Epithelioid smooth muscle tumors of the uterus. A clinicopathologic analysis of 80 cases [abstract]. Lab Invest 76: 107A
38. Atkins K, Bell S, Kempson R L et al. 2002 Myxoid smooth muscle tumors of the uterus [abstract]. Mod Pathol 14: 132A
39. Shintaku M 1996 Lipoleiomyomatous tumors of the uterus: a heterogeneous group? Histopathological study of five cases. Pathol Int 46: 498–502
40. Hu J, Surti U, Tobon H 1992 Cytogenetic analysis of a uterine lipoleiomyoma. Cancer Genet Cytogenet 62: 200–202
41. Pedeutour F, Quade B J, Sornberger K et al. 2000 Dysregulation of HMGIC in a uterine lipoleiomyoma with a complex rearrangement including chromosomes 7, 12, and 14. Genes Chromos Cancer 27: 209–215
42. Hsieh C H, Lui C C, Huang S C et al. 2003 Multiple uterine angioleiomyomas in a woman presenting with severe menorrhagia. Gynecol Oncol 90: 348–352
43. Ferry J A, Harris N L, Scully R E 1989 Uterine leiomyomas with lymphoid infiltration simulating lymphoma. A report of seven cases. Int J Gynecol Pathol 8: 263–270
44. Bardsley V, Cooper P, Peat D S 1998 Massive lymphocytic infiltration of uterine leiomyomas associated with GnRH agonist treatment. Histopathology 33: 80–82
45. McClean G, McCluggage W G 2003 Unusual morphologic features of uterine leiomyomas treated with gonadotropin-releasing hormone agonists: massive lymphoid infiltration and vasculitis. Int J Surg Pathol 11: 339–344
46. Vang R, Medeiros L J, Samoszuk M et al. 2001 Uterine leiomyomas with eosinophils: a clinicopathologic study of 3 cases. Int J Gynecol Pathol 20: 239–243
47. Maluf H M, Gersell D J 1994 Uterine leiomyomas with high content of mast cells. Arch Pathol Lab Med 118: 712–714
48. Orii A, Mori A, Zhai Y L et al. 1998 Mast cells in smooth muscle tumors of the uterus. Int J Gynecol Pathol 17: 336–342
49. Adany R, Fodor F, Molnar P et al. 1990 Increased density of histiocytes in uterine leiomyomas. Int J Gynecol Pathol 9: 137–144
50. Gisser S D, Young I 1977 Neurilemoma-like uterine myomas: an ultrastructural reaffirmation of their non-Schwannian nature. Am J Obstet Gynecol 129: 389–392
51. Evans H L, Chawla S P, Simpson C et al. 1988 Smooth muscle neoplasms of the uterus other than ordinary leiomyoma. A study of 46 cases, with emphasis on diagnostic criteria and prognostic factors. Cancer 62: 2239–2247

52. Gilks C B, Clement P B, Hart W R et al. 2000 Uterine adenomyomas excluding atypical polypoid adenomyomas and adenomyomas of endocervical type: a clinicopathologic study of 30 cases of an underemphasized lesion that may cause diagnostic problems with brief consideration of adenomyomas of other female genital tract sites. Int J Gynecol Pathol 19: 195–205

53. Nogales F F, Isaac M A, Hardisson D et al. 2002 Adenomatoid tumors of the uterus: an analysis of 60 cases. Int J Gynecol Pathol 21: 34–40

54. Palacios J, Suarez M A, Ruiz V A et al. 1991 Cystic adenomatoid tumor of the uterus. Int J Gynecol Pathol 10: 296–301

55. De Rosa G, Boscaino A, Terracciano L M et al. 1992 Giant adenomatoid tumors of the uterus. Int J Gynecol Pathol 11: 156–160

56. Schwartz E J, Longacre T A 2004 Adenomatoid tumors of the female and male genital tracts express WT1. Int J Gynecol Pathol 23: 123–128

57. Friedrich M, Villena-Heinsen C, Mink D et al. 1998 Leiomyosarcomas of the female genital tract: a clinical and histopathological study. Eur J Gynaecol Oncol 19: 470–475

58. Harlow B L, Weiss N S, Lofton S 1986 The epidemiology of sarcomas of the uterus. J Natl Cancer Inst 76: 399–402

59. Leibsohn S, D'ablaing G, Mishell D R Jr et al. 1990 Leiomyosarcoma in a series of hysterectomies performed for presumed uterine leiomyomas. Am J Obstet Gynecol 162: 968–974

60. Brooks S E, Zhan M, Cote T et al. 2004 Surveillance, epidemiology, and end results analysis of 2677 cases of uterine sarcoma 1989–1999. Gynecol Oncol 93: 204–208

61. Mayerhofer K, Obermair A, Windbichler G et al. 1999 Leiomyosarcoma of the uterus: a clinicopathologic multicenter study of 71 cases. Gynecol Oncol 74: 196–201

62. Hsieh C H, Lin H, Huang C C et al. 2003 Leiomyosarcoma of the uterus: a clinicopathologic study of 21 cases. Acta Obstet Gynecol Scand 82: 74–81

63. Giuntoli R L, Metzinger D S, DiMarco C S et al. 2003 Retrospective review of 208 patients with leiomyosarcoma of the uterus: prognostic indicators, surgical management, and adjuvant therapy. Gynecol Oncol 89: 460–469

64. Dinh T A, Oliva E A, Fuller A F Jr et al. 2004 The treatment of uterine leiomyosarcoma. Results from a 10-year experience (1990–1999) at the Massachusetts General Hospital. Gynecol Oncol 92: 648–652

65. Leitao M M, Sonoda Y, Brennan M F et al. 2003 Incidence of lymph node and ovarian metastases in leiomyosarcoma of the uterus. Gynecol Oncol 91: 209–212

66. Goff B A, Rice L W, Fleischhacker D et al. 1993 Uterine leiomyosarcoma and endometrial stromal sarcoma: lymph node metastases and sites of recurrence. Gynecol Oncol 50: 105–109

67. Kahanpaa K V, Wahlstrom T, Grohn P et al. 1986 Sarcomas of the uterus: a clinicopathologic study of 119 patients. Obstet Gynecol 67: 417–424

68. Nordal R R, Thoresen S O 1997 Uterine sarcomas in Norway 1956–1992: incidence, survival and mortality. Eur J Cancer 33: 907–911

69. Chauveinc L, Deniaud E, Plancher C et al. 1999 Uterine sarcomas: the Curie Institut experience. Prognosis factors and adjuvant treatments. Gynecol Oncol 72: 232–237

70. Larson B, Silfversward C, Nilsson B et al. 1990 Prognostic factors in uterine leiomyosarcoma. A clinical and histopathological study of 143 cases. The Radiumhemmet series 1936–1981. Acta Oncol 29: 185–191

71. Gadducci A, Sartori E, Landoni F et al. 2002 The prognostic relevance of histological type in uterine sarcomas: a Cooperation Task Force (CTF) multivariate analysis of 249 cases. Eur J Gynaecol Oncol 23: 295–299

72. Bodner K, Bodner-Adler B, Kimberger O et al. 2003 Evaluating prognostic parameters in women with uterine leiomyosarcoma. A clinicopathologic study. J Reprod Med 48: 95–100

73. Pautier P, Genestie C, Rey A et al. 2000 Analysis of clinicopathologic prognostic factors for 157 uterine sarcomas and evaluation of a grading score validated for soft tissue sarcoma. Cancer 88: 1425–1431

74. Fletcher J A, Morton C C, Pavelka K et al. 1990 Chromosome aberrations in uterine smooth muscle tumors: potential diagnostic relevance of cytogenetic instability. Cancer Res 50: 4092–4097

75. Nilbert M, Mandahl N, Heim S et al. 1990 Complex karyotypic changes, including rearrangements of 12q13 and 14q24, in two leiomyosarcomas. Cancer Genet Cytogenet 48: 217–223

76. Sreekantaiah C, Davis J R, Sandberg A A 1993 Chromosomal abnormalities in leiomyosarcomas. Am J Pathol 142: 293–305

77. Quade B J, Pinto A P, Howard D R et al. 1999 Frequent loss of heterozygosity for chromosome 10 in uterine leiomyosarcoma in contrast to leiomyoma. Am J Pathol 154: 945–950

78. Quade B J, Wang T Y, Sornberger K et al. 2004 Molecular pathogenesis of uterine smooth muscle tumors from transcriptional profiling. Genes Chromos Cancer 40: 97–108

79. King M E, Dickersin G R, Scully R E 1982 Myxoid leiomyosarcoma of the uterus. A report of six cases. Am J Surg Pathol 6: 589–598

80. Kunzel K E, Mills N Z, Muderspach L I et al. 1993 Myxoid leiomyosarcoma of the uterus. Gynecol Oncol 48: 277–280

81. Chang E, Shim S I 1998 Myxoid leiomyosarcoma of the uterus: a case report and review of the literature. J Korean Med Sci 13: 559–562

82. Vigone A, Giana M, Surico D et al. 2005 Massive myxoid leiomyosarcoma of the uterus. Int J Gynecol Cancer 15: 564–567

83. Norris H J, Parmley T 1975 Mesenchymal tumors of the uterus. V. Intravenous leiomyomatosis. A clinical and pathologic study of 14 cases. Cancer 36: 2164–2178

84. Clement P B, Young R H, Scully R E 1988 Intravenous leiomyomatosis of the uterus. A clinicopathological analysis of 16 cases with unusual histologic features. Am J Surg Pathol 12: 932–945

85. Mulvany N J, Slavin J L, Ostor A G et al. 1994 Intravenous leiomyomatosis of the uterus: a clinicopathologic study of 22 cases. Int J Gynecol Pathol 13: 1–9

86. Dal Cin P, Quade B J, Neskey D M et al. 2003 Intravenous leiomyomatosis is characterized by a der(14)t(12;14)(q15;q24). Genes Chromos Cancer 36: 205–206

87. Tavassoli F A, Norris H J 1982 Peritoneal leiomyomatosis (leiomyomatosis peritonealis disseminata): a clinicopathologic study of 20 cases with ultrastructural observations. Int J Gynecol Pathol 1: 59–74

88. Valente P T 1984 Leiomyomatosis peritonealis disseminata. A report of two cases and review of the literature. Arch Pathol Lab Med 108: 669–672

89. Hardman W J III, Majmudar B 1996 Leiomyomatosis peritonealis disseminata: clinicopathologic analysis of five cases. South Med J 89: 291–294

90. Quade B J, McLachlin C M, Soto-Wright V et al. 1997 Disseminated peritoneal leiomyomatosis. Clonality analysis by X chromosome inactivation and cytogenetics of a clinically benign smooth muscle proliferation. Am J Pathol 150: 2153–2166

91. Clement P B, Young R H 1987 Diffuse leiomyomatosis of the uterus: a report of four cases. Int J Gynecol Pathol 6: 322–330

92. Mulvany N J, Ostor A G, Ross I 1995 Diffuse leiomyomatosis of the uterus. Histopathology 27: 175–179

93. Baschinsky D Y, Isa A, Niemann T H et al. 2000 Diffuse leiomyomatosis of the uterus: a case report with clonality analysis. Hum Pathol 31: 1429–1432

94. Abell M R, Littler E R 1975 Benign metastasizing uterine leiomyoma. Multiple lymph nodal metastases. Cancer 36: 2206–2213

95. Wolff M, Silva F, Kaye G 1979 Pulmonary metastases (with admixed epithelial elements) from smooth muscle neoplasms. Report of nine cases, including three males. Am J Surg Pathol 3: 325–342

96. Gal A A, Brooks J S, Pietra G G 1989 Leiomyomatous neoplasms of the lung: a clinical, histologic, and immunohistochemical study. Mod Pathol 2: 209–216

97. Esteban J M, Allen W M, Schaerf R H 1999 Benign metastasizing leiomyoma of the uterus: histologic and immunohistochemical characterization of primary and metastatic lesions. Arch Pathol Lab Med 123: 960–962

98. Ordi J, Stamatakos M D, Tavassoli F A 1997 Pure pleomorphic rhabdomyosarcomas of the uterus. Int J Gynecol Pathol 16: 369–377

99. Chiarle R, Godio L, Fusi D et al. 1997 Pure alveolar rhabdomyosarcoma of the corpus uteri: description of a case with increased serum level of CA-125. Gynecol Oncol 66: 320–323

100. McCluggage W G, Lioe T F, McClelland H R et al. 2002 Rhabdomyosarcoma of the uterus: report of two cases, including one of the spindle cell variant. Int J Gynecol Cancer 12: 128–132

101. Vang R, Kempson R L 2002 Perivascular epithelioid cell tumor ('PEComa') of the uterus: a subset of HMB-45-positive epithelioid mesenchymal neoplasms with an uncertain relationship to pure smooth muscle tumors. Am J Surg Pathol 26: 1–13

102. Silva E G, Deavers M T, Bodurka D C et al. 2004 Uterine epithelioid leiomyosarcomas with clear cells: reactivity with HMB-45 and the concept of PEComa. Am J Surg Pathol 28: 244–249

103. Greene L A, Mount S L, Schned A R et al. 2003 Recurrent perivascular epithelioid cell tumor of the uterus (PEComa): an immunohistochemical study and review of the literature. Gynecol Oncol 90: 677–681

104. Dimmler A, Seitz G, Hohenberger W et al. 2003 Late pulmonary metastasis in uterine PEComa. J Clin Pathol 56: 627–628

PART E

Cervix

Marisa R. Nucci   Kenneth R. Lee   Christopher P. Crum

Introduction

This chapter covers the range of neoplastic conditions of the cervix that arise at or near the cervical transformation zone. It is separated into sections on precancerous intraepithelial neoplasia, epithelial malignancies (including squamous neoplasia, glandular neoplasia, mixed-type carcinoma, and neuroendocrine carcinoma), mixed epithelial and mesenchymal tumors, mesenchymal tumors, melanocytic tumors, and miscellaneous rare malignancies.

Precancerous disease

Squamous intraepithelial neoplasia (squamous intraepithelial lesions; cervical intraepithelial neoplasia (CIN))

Introduction

Cervical squamous intraepithelial neoplasia refers to all squamous alterations that occur in or near the transformation zone in association with human papillomavirus (HPV) infection, thereby encompassing the terms condyloma, CIN, dysplasia, and squamous intraepithelial lesions. Since it has become apparent that HPV infection can result in a morphologic continuum of squamous alterations, all of these entities will be presented within the single classification system of squamous intraepithelial lesions. In this classification, low-grade squamous intraepithelial lesions encompass flat and exophytic, immature and mature condylomata, as well as lesions graded as I in the CIN classification scheme. High-grade squamous intraepithelial lesions correspond to CIN II and III.

Clinical features

Squamous intraepithelial neoplasia may be identified at any age following the onset of sexual activity. It is now well established that HPV infection is causally related to cervical neoplasia, both preinvasive and invasive disease. HPV infection is ubiquitous in young, sexually active women with a peak frequency of infection in this age group; while infections are usually transient without any associated morphologic abnormality, persistent infection with a single HPV type is highly associated with cervical neoplasia, either concurrently or subsequently.[1–5] Numerous HPV types are known to infect the genital tract, particularly the cervix, and they have been separated into low- and high-risk groups based upon their association with invasive cervical carcinoma. HPV 6 and 11 are the prototypic low-risk viruses since they are not associated with cervical carcinoma or high-grade squamous precancers. In contrast, HPV type 16 is considered high-risk as this virus is associated with 50% of invasive squamous cell carcinomas and high-grade squamous precancers.[6] Besides HPV infection, other risk factors for cervical squamous intraepithelial neoplasia include: (1) age (with young, sexually active women at greatest risk for preinvasive cervical disease); (2) defects in immunity, such as human immunodeficiency virus (HIV) infection or therapeutic immunosuppression; and (3) tobacco use.[7–13]

Squamous intraepithelial lesion, low-grade

Low-grade squamous intraepithelial lesions can be divided into three morphologic subsets: (1) condyloma acuminatum (exophytic condyloma); (2) immature condyloma (squamous papilloma, papillary immature metaplasia); and (3) flat condyloma (CIN I). **Exophytic condyloma** (Fig. 13E.1) is characterized by a verruciform growth pattern with blunt-shaped papillae, acanthosis, and superficial koilocytotic atypia (nuclear hyperchromasia, karyomegaly, binucleation, irregular nuclear contour). These exophytic lesions, which are highly associated with HPV types 6 and 11, are relatively uncommon in the cervix. **Immature condyloma** (Fig. 13E.2) is characterized by slender, filiform papillae, which are lined by squamous epithelium that shows little keratinocyte maturation (mimicking squamous metaplasia) but exhibits slight nuclear crowding, and mild superficial koilocytotic atypia. This relative lack of koilocytotic atypia likely reflects the dependence of viral cytopathic effect on maturation, which is limited in these lesions. Similar to exophytic condyloma, immature condylomas harbor HPV types 6 and 11, which supports their inclusion in the condyloma category. Papillary immature metaplasia and

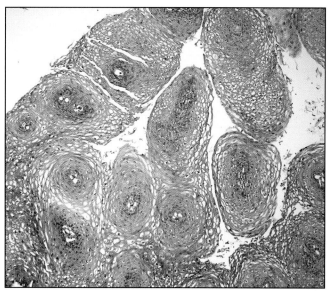

Fig. 13E.1 • Exophytic condyloma. Verruciform growth pattern with superficial koilocytotic atypia.

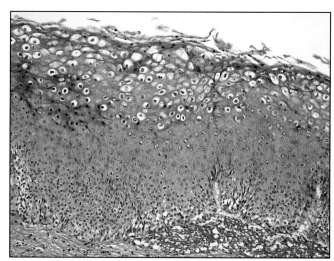

Fig. 13E.3 • Flat condyloma. Koilocytotic atypia is confined to the upper portions of the epithelium.

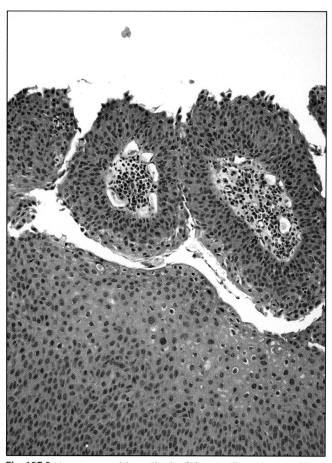

Fig. 13E.2 • Immature condyloma. Slender, filiform papillae with minimal superficial atypia.

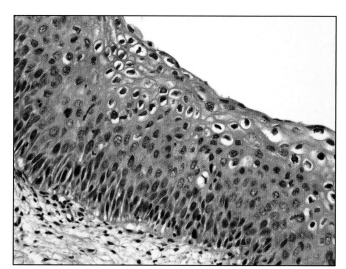

Fig. 13E.4 • High-grade squamous intraepithelial lesion (cervical intraepithelial neoplasia II). Note surface koilocytotic change.

squamous papillomas are histologically identical to immature condyloma and also contain HPV types 6 and 11, hence their inclusion in this category.[14,15] **Flat condyloma** exhibits morphologic features similar to condyloma acuminatum but lacks an exophytic growth pattern (Fig. 13E.3). The amount of koilocytotic atypia may vary; however, the atypia is confined to the upper third of the epithelium with minimal basal and parabasal nuclear atypia. These lesions are usually associated with HPV types that confer an intermediate risk.[6] Expression of cell proliferation markers such as Ki-67 in low-grade squamous intraepithelial lesions can help distinguish them from reactive changes in difficult cases (its main differential diagnosis), as positivity in the upper cell layers is characteristic of HPV-infected epithelium, whereas this marker is typically confined to the lower layers in normal mucosa.[16–18]

Squamous intraepithelial lesion, high-grade

High-grade squamous intraepithelial lesions are characterized by nuclear atypia in all levels of the epithelium with a variable degree of surface maturation. Lesions that exhibit surface koilocytotic change and epithelial maturation correspond to CIN II (Fig. 13E.4), whereas those with little to no maturation correspond to CIN III (Fig. 13E.5). These lesions are distinguished from low-grade squamous intraepithelial lesions

Fig. 13E.5 • High-grade squamous intraepithelial lesion (cervical intraepithelial neoplasia III). Full-thickness nuclear atypia with minimal maturation.

by: (1) the presence of nuclear atypia in the lower layers; (2) increased mitotic index with mitoses in the upper half of the epithelium; (3) loss of cell polarity; (4) abnormal mitotic figures; and, in some cases, (5) the presence of markedly atypical, bizarre cells. These lesions are associated with high-risk HPV types, particularly type 16. p16[ink4], a cyclin-dependent kinase inhibitor, appears to be a surrogate marker of HPV infection, being strongly expressed in lesions associated with intermediate- and high-risk HPV. As intermediate- and high-risk HPVs may be associated with low- and high-grade squamous intraepithelial lesions, this marker cannot distinguish between the two; however, it may be useful in supporting the diagnosis of a squamous intraepithelial lesion.[19]

Glandular intraepithelial neoplasia

Introduction

It is now well accepted that adenocarcinoma in situ is the precursor to most invasive cervical adenocarcinomas. This conclusion is based upon: (1) the similar cytomorphologic appearance between in-situ carcinoma and invasive carcinoma; (2) the close spatial association between in-situ carcinoma and early invasive adenocarcinoma;[20–22] (3) the similar frequency of association with high-risk HPV types (primarily types 16 and 18);[23] (4) the mean age at diagnosis for adenocarcinoma in situ predates that for invasive adenocarcinoma;[22] and (5) rare examples of progression from in-situ carcinoma to invasive adenocarcinoma have been documented.[24–27]

Clinical features

Adenocarcinoma in situ typically occurs in young women in their reproductive years with an average age at presentation of 38 years.[22] As associated symptoms are quite uncommon (though if present, the most common is abnormal vaginal bleeding[28,29]), adenocarcinoma in situ is usually identified via routine Papanicolaou smear examination or else is discovered during tissue sampling, most commonly for treatment of squamous precursor lesions or in follow-up to the identification of atypical glandular cells in a smear. In comparison to

squamous precancers, Papanicolaou smear examination has a lower sensitivity for detecting both adenocarcinoma in situ and invasive adenocarcinoma, which is probably related to incomplete sampling of the endocervix as well as inherent difficulty in distinguishing benign from neoplastic glandular epithelium in cytologic preparations.[30–32] Since many women with adenocarcinoma in situ are young and wish to maintain their fertility, excision by cervical conization is the most widely recommended treatment if hysterectomy is not performed. Patients opting for conservative treatment need to undergo close clinical follow-up as a cone biopsy with clear margins does not guarantee freedom from recurrent in-situ or invasive carcinoma.[33–42]

Pathologic features

Adenocarcinoma in situ almost always arises at the squamo-columnar junction (transformation zone) as a spatially continuous lesion, although rarely it may develop in the upper endocervix or be multifocal.[43,44] Lesional extent may vary from focal to diffuse circumferential cervical involvement; on rare occasions, extension into the lower uterine segment and endometrial cavity can occur. In 30–50% of cases, adenocarcinoma in situ is associated with a squamous intraepithelial lesion.[42,43,45] Histologically, normal cervical glandular architecture is preserved, with the glands being lined by crowded cells with enlarged, hyperchromatic, stratified or pseudostratified nuclei (Fig. 13E.6); an abrupt transition from normal to neoplastic within a gland is characteristic. Nucleoli are usually small and inconspicuous, but occasionally may be prominent. The presence of mitotic figures is essential to the diagnosis and they are typically located on the luminal side, having a "suspended" appearance. Basally located apoptotic bodies are common, and are present in up to 70% of cases.[46,47] Adenocarcinoma in situ may sometimes have a more complex growth pattern, with intraluminal papillary infolding or cribriform growth (Fig. 13E.7); however, the overall benign glandular architecture is maintained.

A number of histologic subtypes may occur,[33,43,48–50] which are often mixed within a single case. Although the subtypes are not associated with differences in biologic behavior or

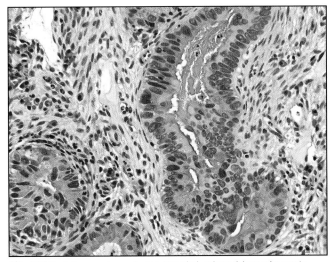

Fig. 13E.6 • Adenocarcinoma in situ. Crowded, enlarged, hyperchromatic nuclei.

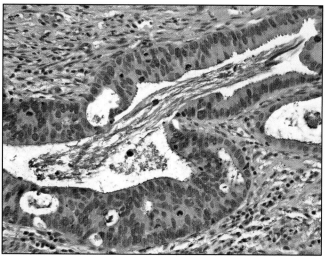

Fig. 13E.7 • Adenocarcinoma in situ. Note complex cribriform growth pattern.

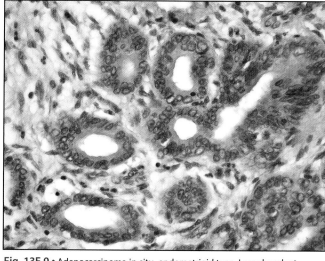

Fig. 13E.9 • Adenocarcinoma in situ, endometrioid type. Less abundant cytoplasm mimics endometrioid glands.

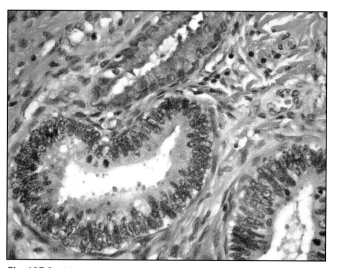

Fig. 13E.8 • Adenocarcinoma in situ, endocervical type. Apical mucinous cytoplasm mimics the appearance of normal endocervical differentiation.

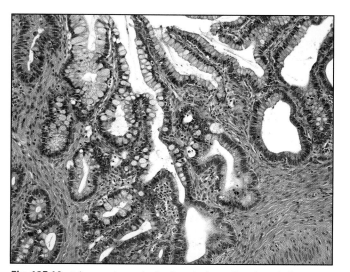

Fig. 13E.10 • Adenocarcinoma in situ, intestinal type. Note intestinal-type goblet cells.

progression, awareness of the morphologic diversity of adenocarcinoma in situ is important in its recognition.

Endocervical. This subtype is the most common, having an appearance that closely resembles normal endocervical cells with columnar mucinous cytoplasm (Fig. 13E.8).

Endometrioid. Less cytoplasm and greater nuclear stratification in this subtype mimic neoplastic endometrioid glands (Fig. 13E.9).

Intestinal. This subtype, which often exhibits less nuclear crowding and hyperchromasia, contains varying proportions of intestinal-type goblet cells (Fig. 13E.10). The presence of goblet cells should strongly raise the possibility that the process is neoplastic, as benign goblet cell metaplasia of the cervix is extremely uncommon.

Stratified/squamomucinous. Stratified neoplastic cells that exhibit both a glandular and squamous histologic appearance characterize this unusual subtype of adenocarcinoma in situ.

Similar to a high-grade squamous intraepithelial lesion, the neoplastic cells are stratified; however, they also contain mucin as discrete cytoplasmic vacuoles or in a characteristic "honeycomb" pattern (Fig. 13E.11).

Ciliated. Ciliated cells with marked cytologic atypia and mitotic activity characterize this rare subtype. It is almost invariably associated with the more typical endocervical adenocarcinoma in situ, which helps in its recognition and distinction from benign tubal metaplasia.

A comparison of adenocarcinoma in situ and its most common benign mimics is outlined in Table 13.1.

Early invasive squamous cell carcinoma

Early-stage invasive squamous cell carcinoma (stage IA) is defined as ≤3.0 mm in depth by 7.0 mm in length without capillary lymphatic space invasion, and, unlike patients with higher-stage tumors, patients with stage IA invasive squamous cell carcinoma are amenable to conservative (excision only) therapy without lymph node dissection. Assessing the presence

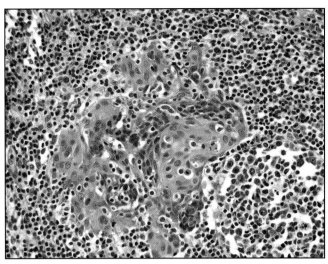

Fig. 13E.12 • Early invasive squamous cell carcinoma. Note blurring of the epithelial stromal interface, loss of polarity, and conspicuous maturation.

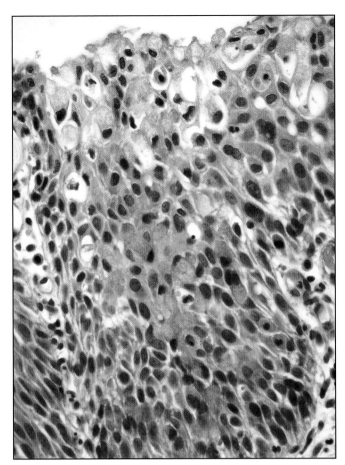

Fig. 13E.11 • Adenocarcinoma in situ, squamomucinous (stratified) type. Stratified neoplastic cells containing intracytoplasmic mucin.

of early stromal invasion, in which tumor cells have breached the basement membrane and there is <3 mm of stromal invasion, is difficult. The most common criteria for the diagnosis of early invasion include: (1) a desmoplastic response in the adjacent stroma; (2) focal conspicuous maturation of the neoplastic squamous epithelium; (3) blurring of the epithelial–stromal interface; and (4) loss of polarity of the nuclei at the epithelial–stromal border (Fig. 13E.12). The most important mimics of early stromal invasion include: (1) tangential sectioning of endocervical glands involved by a high-grade squamous intraepithelial lesion; (2) site of prior biopsy which may be associated with epithelial displacement and an inflammatory reaction; (3) artifactual changes secondary to crush or cautery; (4) an intense inflammatory response to a high-grade squamous intraepithelial lesion obscuring the epithelial–stromal

Table 13E.1	Comparison of adenocarcinoma in situ (ACIS) and its mimics					
	ACIS	**Tubal/tuboendometrioid metaplasia**	**Endometriosis**	**Arias-Stella reaction**	**Radiation effect**	**Cervicitis**
Location	Transformation zone; superficial or deep glands	Usually upper endocervical canal; deep > superficial glands	Superficial or deep glands	Superficial > deep glands; usually focal	Superficial or deep glands	Transformation zone
Partial gland involvement	Characteristic	Occasional	Unusual	Characteristic	Unusual	Unusual
Nuclear stratification	Present	Less pronounced	Present	Present	Absent	Less pronounced
Hyperchromasia	Present	Less pronounced	Present	Present	Present	Less pronounced
Nuclear enlargement	Present	Less pronounced	Uncommon	Present	Present	Present
Nucleoli	Rare	May be present	May be present	Present	Present	Present
Mitotic activity	Present	Uncommon	Present	Rare	Rare	Present
Apoptosis	Present	Rare/absent	Uncommon	Absent	Absent	May be present
Cilia	May be present	Present	Occasional	Absent	Absent	Absent
Complex architecture	May be present	Absent	Uncommon	Uncommon	Absent	Absent
Mib-1 proliferation index	High	Low	Variable	Low	Low	Variable

interface; and (5) misinterpretation of a cervical placental implantation site.

Invasive squamous cell carcinoma

Worldwide, cervical carcinoma is the most common malignancy of the female genital tract and represents the second most common malignancy in women following breast cancer (and excluding skin cancer).[51] In the USA, cervical carcinoma is much less frequent, representing the third most common malignancy of the female genital tract after cancer of the uterine corpus and ovary respectively.[52] Worldwide, there are approximately 470 000 cases of cervical carcinoma per year and 233 000 deaths from this disease, whereas in the USA, there are approximately 13 000 new cervical cancer cases per year and 4800 cancer deaths.[51,52] Overall, the international incidence of cervical squamous cell carcinoma in developed countries has been declining over the past few decades, which in part seems attributable to cervical cancer screening.[53] While formerly regarded as a disease of older patients, cervical carcinoma is nowadays often encountered in the third to fifth decades. It is now well established, through an abundance of experimental, molecular, and clinical data, that the development of invasive squamous cell carcinoma of the cervix is causally related to HPV infection. Approximately 25 different HPVs have been isolated from the genital tract, among which there is a spectrum of risk of developing cancer, with HPV type 16 conferring the greatest risk.

Patients with invasive squamous cell carcinoma of the cervix most commonly present with abnormal vaginal bleeding or an abnormal Papanicolaou smear.[54] Patients presenting with an abnormal Papanicolaou smear (in comparison with clinical symptoms such as vaginal bleeding or discharge) may have a better outcome, presumably as a result of earlier detection. Early invasive tumors may only exhibit changes similar to high-grade precancers of the cervix on clinical examination; more advanced tumors may be polypoid, fungating, or cause diffuse enlargement of the cervix. A number of histologic variants of invasive squamous cell carcinoma are recognized.

Keratinizing. This tumor type shows conspicuous evidence of keratinization in the form of keratin pearls, keratohyaline granules, individual keratinized cells, and nests of squamous cells with central keratinization (Fig. 13E.13). These tumors are usually classified as well differentiated and often have a pushing border of invasion.

Large cell non-keratinizing. This tumor is composed of histologically recognizable squamous cells, which are large and polygonal with eosinophilic cytoplasm and cellular bridges, but which lack keratin pearl formation, keratohyaline granules, or nests of squamous cells with central keratinization (Fig. 13E.14). A greater degree of nuclear pleomorphism and an infiltrative border with associated inflammation are often present and most tumors are usually classified as moderately differentiated.

Small cell (poorly differentiated) non-keratinizing. This tumor type is composed of tumor cells with a high nuclear-to-cytoplasmic ratio with minimal evidence of histologically

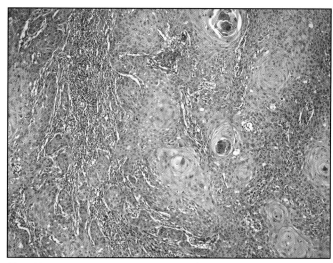

Fig. 13E.13 • Invasive squamous cell carcinoma, keratinizing type. Prominent keratin pearls and nests of tumor cells with central keratinization.

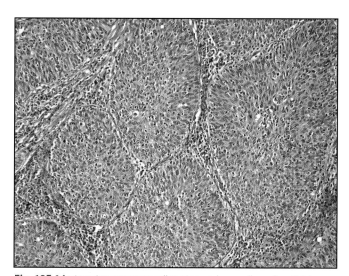

Fig. 13E.14 • Invasive squamous cell carcinoma, large cell non-keratinizing type. Lack of conspicuous keratin pearl formation or central keratinization of tumor nests.

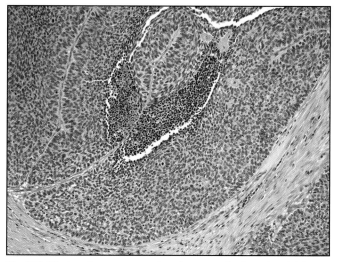

Fig. 13E.15 • Invasive squamous cell carcinoma, small cell non-keratinizing type. Mimimal recognizable squamous differentiation.

recognizable squamous differentiation (Fig. 13E.15). These tumors are generally classified as poorly differentiated. Use of the term small cell is discouraged in routine practice (with classification of these tumors as a poorly differentiated non-keratinizing squamous cell carcinoma instead), to prevent confusion with small cell neuroendocrine carcinoma.

Basaloid. Some invasive squamous cell carcinomas have a basaloid appearance with nests of tumor cells having less abundant eosinophilic cytoplasm and peripheral palisading of nuclei with variable amounts of squamous differentiation (Fig. 13E.16). Tumors of this type should be diagnosed as invasive squamous cell carcinoma with basaloid features to avoid confusion with adenoid basal carcinoma.

Verrucous. This extremely rare subtype of cervical carcinoma is characteristically exophytic and composed of broad-based papillae lined by squamous epithelium with little to no cyto-logic atypia (Fig. 13E.17). These tumors show a pushing margin

of invasion with a uniform epithelial–stromal interface. Strict application of diagnostic criteria is mandatory and these tumors should be diagnosed with caution (so as not to under-diagnose a well-differentiated squamous cell carcinoma, which, unlike verrucous carcinoma, is associated with the risk of regional lymph node metastasis).[55]

Warty (condylomatous). This subtype refers to exophytic squamous cell carcinomas that have koilocytotic surface epithelial changes characteristic of HPV infection.

Papillary. Papillary carcinomas of the cervix are characterized by a papillary growth pattern and may be subdivided into three histologic subtypes:[56] (1) papillary undifferentiated carcinoma, in which the tumor cells lining the papillae do not show any histologic evidence of a specific type of differentiation; (2) papillary transitional cell carcinoma, which has a similar histologic appearance to lesions that occur in the urinary tract; and (3) papillary squamotransitional carcinoma, which has a combination of transitional and squamous features (Fig. 13E.18). The clinical importance of histologic separation of the latter two types is unclear.

Lymphoepithelial-like. This subtype consists of poorly defined aggregates of non-keratinizing tumor cells with large vesicular nuclei, prominent nucleoli, and moderate amounts of eosinophilic cytoplasm with indistinct cytoplasmic borders, imparting

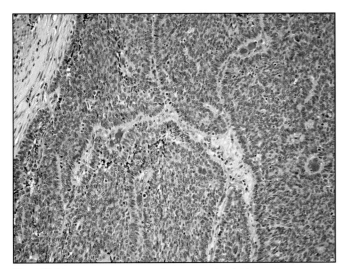

Fig. 13E.16 • Invasive squamous cell carcinoma, basaloid type. Note peripheral palisading of nuclei.

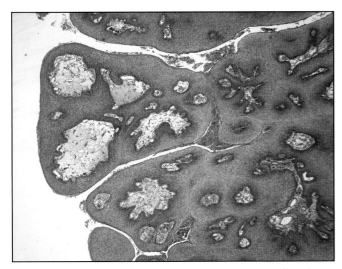

Fig. 13E.17 • Verrucous carcinoma. Exophytic tumor comprised of broad-based papillae with minimal cytologic atypia.

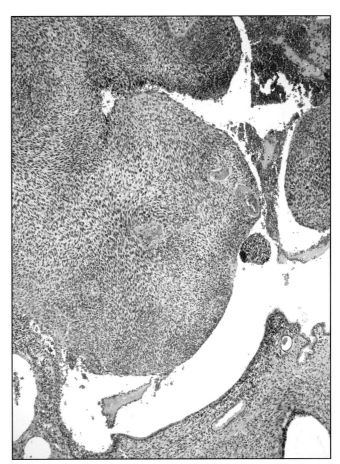

Fig. 13E.18 • Papillary squamotransitional cell carcinoma. Exophytic papillae lined by neoplastic cells that have a combination of squamous and transitional features.

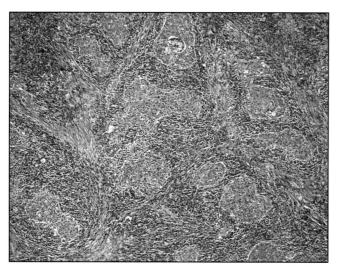

Fig. 13E.19 • Lymphoepithelial-like carcinoma. Poorly defined aggregates of non-keratinizing tumor cells admixed and surrounded by numerous lymphocytes.

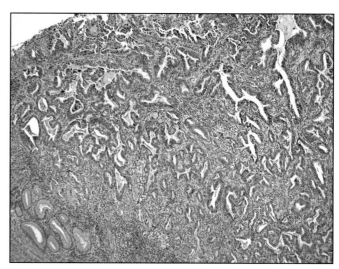

Fig. 13E.20 • Early invasive adenocarcinoma. Note small irregularly shaped glands within a desmoplastic stroma.

a syncytial appearance. Characteristically, the tumor cells are intermixed with numerous lymphocytes, similar to their morphologic counterpart in the nasopharynx, from which terminology for this tumor type is borrowed (Fig. 13E.19).

Early invasive adenocarcinoma[20,21,22,33,57–68]

There are many descriptions of the histopathology and biologic behavior of early invasive adenocarcinoma of the cervix. Unfortunately, there is no generally accepted consensus for the definition of microinvasive adenocarcinoma; therefore, this terminology should not be used in diagnostic reports as its meaning is not standardized. Use of the term superficially invasive adenocarcinoma is recommended and should always be accompanied by a measurement of the depth of invasion. Assessing early invasion is difficult since adenocarcinoma in situ may have a complex architecture and some early invasive adenocarcinomas maintain an in-situ architectural appearance. The possibility of invasion should be considered if any of the following histologic features are present: (1) atypical glands deeper than normal; (2) small, irregularly shaped glands; (3) individual glands; (4) an inflammatory or desmoplastic stroma; (5) exuberant glandular budding; (6) confluent foci of back-to-back glands; or (7) a complex papillary pattern (Fig. 13E.20). Outcome is closely linked to depth of invasion, with an increasing probability of metastasis or recurrence with increasing depth; however, the exact depth at which metastatic potential is acquired is not known. If strictly defined, it seems that lymph node metastasis from early invasive lesions is very infrequent.[68,68a]

Invasive adenocarcinoma

There has been an apparent increase in both the relative and absolute frequency of invasive cervical adenocarcinoma, particularly in Caucasian women under 35 years of age.[69,70] Currently invasive adenocarcinoma comprises 20–25% of all invasive cervical carcinomas. Possible explanations for this increase, which is in contrast to the declining incidence of invasive squamous cell carcinoma, is the apparently increased frequency of adenocarcinoma in situ and the relative ineffectiveness of Papanicolaou smear screening in identifying this type of lesion, in contrast to squamous precancers.

The usual endocervical (mucinous) and adenosquamous types are closely associated with HPV infection.[71] There is some debate over the histopathologic classification of invasive cervical adenocarcinoma with regard to the distinction between the endocervical type of adenocarcinoma and mucinous adenocarcinoma. Some maintain that the endocervical type should be classified under the category of mucinous adenocarcinoma (which also includes minimal-deviation adenocarcinoma, villoglandular adenocarcinoma, and intestinal adenocarcinoma), while others argue that this most common type of cervical adenocarcinoma is not obviously mucinous on hematoxylin and eosin (H&E) examination and therefore should be considered in a separate category. This controversy is largely semantic as this distinction does not appear to have any clinical relevance. For the purposes of this chapter, each subtype of mucinous adenocarcinoma will be discussed separately. Adenocarcinomas in which a second type of adenocarcinoma is present, comprising more than 10% of a tumor, are designated mixed epithelial types and the relative amount of each component is specified.

Endocervical adenocarcinoma (adenocarcinoma, usual endocervical type)

Clinical features

This is the most common type, representing approximately 80% of cervical adenocarcinomas.[72] The most common presenting symptom is vaginal bleeding and, in most women, a clinically evident cervical mass is present, which is usually polypoid and exophytic but may be indurated and ulcerated.[73] Occasionally, the cervix is circumferentially enlarged (so-called barrel cervix). The vast majority of these tumors are associated with high-risk HPV, particularly types 16 and 18.[74] Overall 5-year survival for invasive lesions is in the range of 50–60% with seemingly better survival in younger white women.

Pathologic features

Histologically, the neoplastic cells simulate, at least to some degree, endocervical epithelium, particularly in-situ neoplastic endocervical cells, hence the designation of this type of adenocarcinoma as endocervical. The tumor cells have varying amounts of cytoplasm, which may be mucinous, eosinophilic, or a combination of both (Fig. 13E.21). The nuclei are enlarged and hyperchromatic and, similar to adenocarcinoma in situ, which may be present adjacent to the invasive component, apoptotic bodies and mitotic figures are often numerous. Tumors can have a variety of growth patterns. Glands can vary in size from small to large, with some tumors having a striking microcystic component. The glands can be closely packed, simulating microglandular hyperplasia (Fig. 13E.22), or be more widely spaced. The stroma between the neoplastic glands often, but not always, shows a desmoplastic or inflammatory response.

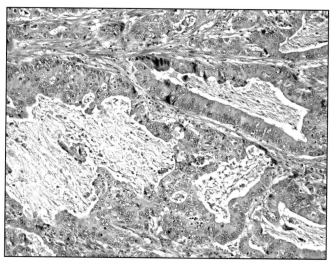

Fig. 13E.21 • Endocervical adenocarcinoma. Tumor cells with abundant mucinous cytoplasm resemble normal endocervical glands.

Minimal-deviation adenocarcinoma (adenoma malignum)[75–80]

Clinical features

Minimal-deviation adenocarcinoma is a rare, extremely well-differentiated mucinous tumor that represents approximately 1–2% of cervical adenocarcinomas. It occurs in reproductive-aged women (mean age 42 years) and the most common symptoms, if present, are menometrorrhagia, vaginal (often mucoid) discharge or abnormal bleeding. Approximately 10–15% of patients with adenoma malignum have Peutz–Jeghers syndrome. Mutations of the tumor suppressor *STK11*, a serine threonine kinase gene, responsible for Peutz–Jeghers syndrome, have also been identified in sporadic cases of minimal-deviation adenocarcinoma.[81,82] The cervix is usually clinically abnormal, being enlarged and/or indurated. Patients with adenoma malignum tend to present at high stage and appear to fare worse than patients with conventional endocervical adenocarcinoma with an overall survival rate of 28% for all stages and a survival rate of 50% for stage 1 tumors. Adenoma malignum may be associated with mucinous ovarian carcinoma, which in most cases likely represents metastatic spread.[83–85]

Pathologic features

Minimal-deviation adenocarcinoma is characterized histologically by the presence of deeply infiltrative, irregularly shaped glands, some of which may have bulbous or finger-like protrusions that usually extend into the outer third of the cervical wall (Fig. 13E.23). Although bland mucinous epithelial cells with small, basally located nuclei and pale columnar cytoplasm line many of the glands, many cells have enlarged nuclei with nucleoli in comparison to normal endocervical glands; malignant cytologic features and an inflammatory, edematous or desmoplastic stromal response are usually present at least focally. Immunohistochemically, minimal-deviation adenocarcinoma may be positive for carcinoembryonic antigen; however, the staining may be focal, which limits its diagnostic use. The glands of minimal-deviation adenocarcinoma contain

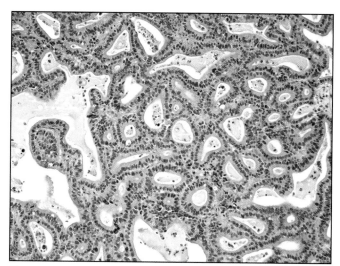

Fig. 13E.22 • Endocervical adenocarcinoma. Numerous small glands mimic microglandular hyperplasia.

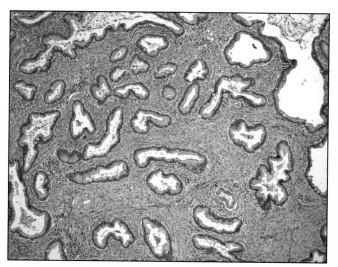

Fig. 13E.23 • Minimal-deviation adenocarcinoma. Irregularly shaped glands extend deep into the cervical wall.

predominantly neutral mucin, similar to that in gastric mucous glands (rather than equal amounts of neutral and acidic mucin characteristic of non-neoplastic mucinous endocervical epithelium), which may be useful diagnostically.[86,87] Only rarely has HPV been associated with this tumor type.[74]

The differential diagnosis of minimal-deviation adenocarcinoma includes a variety of non-neoplastic conditions, the distinction from which is outlined in Table 13E.2. These conditions are much more common and should always be excluded prior to diagnosing minimal-deviation adenocarcinoma.

Villoglandular adenocarcinoma (well-differentiated villoglandular adenocarcinoma; well-differentiated villoglandular papillary adenocarcinoma)[88–92]

This uncommon variant of adenocarcinoma typically occurs in women in their fourth decade, with abnormal vaginal bleeding being the most common presenting symptom. Tumors usually are clinically evident, often having an exophytic polypoid or papillary appearance. The histologic hallmark of this tumor is the presence of a surface papillary component composed of fine finger-like papillae with a distinctive fibrous spindled stroma. The papillae often blend with an underlying invasive component, which is composed of interlacing branching glands that typically have a broad, pushing interface with the underlying stroma (Fig. 13E.24). Stratified, columnar cells showing mild to moderate nuclear atypia and usually without conspicuous mucinous cytoplasm line the papillae. This variant is associated with high-risk HPV types 16 and 18 and is also

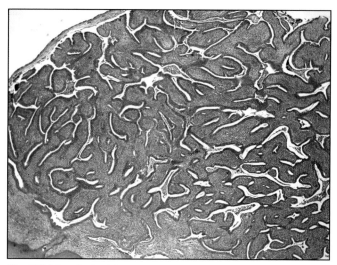

Fig. 13E.24 • Villoglandular adenocarcinoma. Note complex interlacing glands and the cellular fibrous stroma.

often associated with adjacent adenocarcinoma in situ. Since some more conventional invasive adenocarcinomas have a papillary villoglandular component, a diagnosis of villoglandular adenocarcinoma should only be reserved for cases which are well differentiated and in which no other type of invasive carcinoma is present. Often this may only be determined with certainty in a cone biopsy or hysterectomy specimen. Although initial studies suggested an indolent biologic behavior, some cases are associated with local nodal involvement; therefore consideration of conservative therapy, similar to conventional invasive adenocarcinoma, should take into account factors such as lymphatic/vascular invasion and depth of invasion.

Table 13E.2	Comparison of minimal-deviation adenocarcinoma and its most common mimics					
	Minimal-deviation adenocarcinoma	Deep nabothian glands/cysts	Tunnel clusters	Adenomyoma, endocervical type	Endocervicosis	Lobular endocervical glandular hyperplasia
Location in cervix	Usually extends to outer half of wall/ transmural	May be present in outer half of wall	Usually inner third of wall; rarely involves outer half	Mural-based mass	Typically only involves outer half of wall and paracervical soft tissue	Usually inner half of wall
Abnormal appearance of cervix	Common	Unusual	Unusual	Common	Unusual	Unusual
Lobular growth pattern	Rare	Uncommon	Characteristic	Frequent	Absent	Characteristic
Leaf-like glands	Present	Absent	Absent	Present	Absent	Present
Cytologic atypia	Present, usually only focal	Absent	Uncommon	Uncommon	Uncommon	Uncommon
Mitotic activity	Present	Uncommon	Uncommon	Uncommon	Uncommon	Uncommon
Desmoplasia	Present, usually only focal	Absent	Absent	Absent	Absent	Absent
Myomatous stroma	Absent	Absent	Absent	Present	Absent	Absent

Enteric adenocarcinoma[93–96]

Usual-type endocervical adenocarcinoma (and some adeno-squamous carcinomas) may exhibit foci of intestinal differentiation in the form of goblet cells, Paneth cells, argentaffin cells, or signet-ring cells. Extremely rarely, this pattern may predominate. When these patterns are present, the possibility of metastatic gastrointestinal adenocarcinoma should be excluded.

Endometrioid adenocarcinoma

This tumor bears a close resemblance to endometrioid adenocarcinoma of the endometrium, having cells with non-mucinous cytoplasm that are more crowded and stratified than those in the endocervical type of adenocarcinoma (Fig. 13E.25); occasionally squamous metaplasia is present, but this occurs much less commonly than in endometrial primaries. The distinction of endometrioid adenocarcinoma from the endocervical type is somewhat subjective; therefore the reported frequency of this subtype has varied.[97,98] Similar to the endocervical subtype, endometrioid adenocarcinoma is associated with high-risk HPV and adenocarcinoma in situ, supporting a shared pathogenesis.[22] The behavior and prognosis of endometrioid adenocarcinoma appear to parallel that of the usual endocervical type. The main differential diagnosis is its distinction from an endometrial primary, which may be problematic in biopsy/curettage specimens. Features that favor an endocervical primary include: (1) the presence of a cervical mass; (2) the majority of the tumor is present in the endocervical (in comparison with endometrial) sampling; (3) cervical adenocarcinoma in situ is present; (4) the patient is <40 years old; (5) the carcinoma is negative for vimentin, estrogen receptor and progesterone receptor; and (6) the carcinoma is HPV positive. Features that favor an endometrial primary include: (1) the patient has an enlarged uterus, thickened endometrial stripe, or abnormal menses; (2) the majority of the tumor is present in the endometrial sampling; (3) endometrial intra-epithelial neoplasia is present; (4) the tumor contains foamy

stromal cells; (5) the patient is >50 years old; (6) the tumor is positive for vimentin, estrogen receptor, and progesterone receptor; and (7) the tumor is HPV-negative.

Minimal-deviation endometrioid adenocarcinoma[78,99,100]

A subset of endometrioid cervical adenocarcinomas are extremely well differentiated, and are similar in their growth pattern and bland appearance to minimal-deviation endo-cervical adenocarcinoma, except that the cells lining the invasive glands appear endometrioid as opposed to mucinous (Fig. 13E.26). This subtype of endometrioid adenocarcinoma is distinguished from endometriosis or tuboendometrioid metaplasia by its infiltrative architectural pattern and presence, at least focally, of malignant cytologic features and/or a desmoplastic stroma.

Clear cell adenocarcinoma[101–105]

Clear cell adenocarcinoma of the cervix is a rare malignancy, which may occur sporadically or be associated with diethyl-stilbesterol exposure *in utero*. In either case, there appears to be a bimodal age distribution with two peaks, one at a young age (mean third decade) and one at an older age (mean eighth decade).[103] Patients usually present with abnormal vaginal bleeding or dyspareunia and have a clinically evident cervical mass. Histologically, these tumors are similar in appearance to clear cell carcinomas that occur at other sites in the female genital tract, being composed of glycogen-rich tumor cells with hyperchromatic, irregularly shaped nuclei that are arranged in tubulocystic, solid, and/or papillary growth patterns. Patients with clear cell carcinoma appear to have a greater tendency for sometimes late, local, or distant relapse in comparison to other histologic types.

The differential diagnosis includes two pseudoneoplastic lesions of the cervix, microglandular hyperplasia, and the Arias–Stella reaction. Features that distinguish microglandular hyperplasia from clear cell carcinoma include: (1) only focal

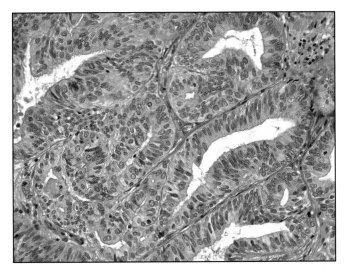

Fig. 13E.25 • Endometrioid adenocarcinoma. Neoplastic glands lined by cells with stratified nuclei and less conspicuous apical cytoplasm mimic an endometrial primary.

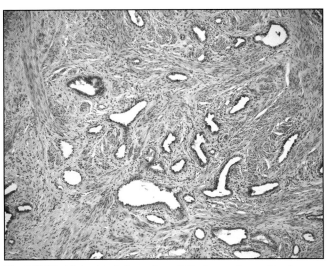

Fig. 13E.26 • Minimal-deviation endometrioid adenocarcinoma. Deeply invasive glands lack apical mucinous cytoplasm and thus appear endometrioid.

nuclear atypia; (2) the presence of subnuclear vacuoles and intracytoplasmic mucin; (3) lack of glycogen; (4) lack of an infiltrative pattern; and (5) the presence of reserve cell hyperplasia/squamous metaplasia. Features that distinguish Arias–Stella reaction from clear cell carcinoma include: (1) no associated mass lesion; (2) its usually focal nature; and (3) the nuclei exhibit a spectrum of cytologic atypia.

Papillary serous adenocarcinoma[106]

Primary papillary serous adenocarcinoma of the cervix is extremely uncommon. In the largest series of 17 patients,[106] there was a bimodal age distribution with patients being either younger than 45 years of age or older than 65. The most common presenting symptom is abnormal vaginal bleeding or discharge and most patients have a clinically detectable exophytic or polypoid mass. These tumors are histologically similar to conventional papillary serous adenocarcinoma that occurs elsewhere in the female genital tract, having complex branching papillae lined by cells with moderate to severe cytologic atypia. Cellular tufting, micropapillae, and slit-like spaces are common; mitoses are usually numerous. Almost half of the tumors have been associated with another histologic subtype of adenocarcinoma, most commonly the villoglandular type, suggesting a possible common etiology. Based on personal experience, cervical serous adenocarcinomas in younger women are typically positive for HPV, which is similar to villoglandular adenocarcinoma. A diagnosis of primary papillary serous adenocarcinoma of the cervix should only be rendered following exclusion of secondary spread from the endometrium or ovary, particularly in older patients. Outcome of patients with stage I papillary serous adenocarcinoma of the cervix does not appear to be different from those with conventional adenocarcinoma.

Mesonephric adenocarcinoma[107–109]

Mesonephric adenocarcinoma is a rare malignancy of the uterus that most commonly occurs in the cervix. Most references to mesonephric carcinoma in the older literature represent clear cell carcinoma, which was originally considered to be mesonephric in origin. True mesonephric carcinoma presumably arises from mesonephric remnants, the vestigial elements of the mesonephric ducts which, in men, develop into the efferent ducts of the testis, epididymis, vasa deferentia, seminal vesicles, and ejaculatory ducts; however, in women, the ducts usually regress but can persist as small foci in the broad ligament, cervix, and vagina. Mesonephric carcinoma occurs over a wide age range (34–73 years), with a mean age in the sixth decade. The most common presenting symptom is abnormal vaginal bleeding and most patients have a cervical abnormality, most commonly an exophytic polypoid mass; however, the tumor may also be nodular, ulcerated, or cause diffuse enlargement of the cervix ("barrel cervix"). The prognosis for mesonephric carcinoma is uncertain, although it has been suggested to have relatively indolent behavior. Local or intra-abdominal relapse occurs in patients with early-, as well as late-, stage disease, but may do so over an extended period of time.

Mesonephric carcinoma usually involves the full thickness of the cervical wall, has an infiltrative margin, and extends up to and sometimes erodes the overlying cervical mucosa. A component of mesonephric hyperplasia is commonly, but not invariably, present. Mesonephric carcinoma exhibits a wide variety of histologic patterns (Figs 13E.27 and 13E.28), the most common being ductal, which resembles endometrioid glandular neoplasia, and tubular, which is composed of closely apposed, variably sized, usually small round cysts and/or tubules which often contain brightly eosinophilic intraluminal material (similar to mesonephric remnants). Retiform, solid, sex-cord-like and spindled patterns may also occur. Spindled patterns commonly resemble endometrial stromal sarcoma or a non-specific spindle cell sarcoma; for this reason, the term malignant mixed mesonephric tumor has been proposed to describe tumors with this component. As these spindled foci are usually positive for epithelial markers, they most likely represent spindle cell carcinoma. Mesonephric carcinoma is positive for cytokeratin 7 and epithelial membrane antigen,

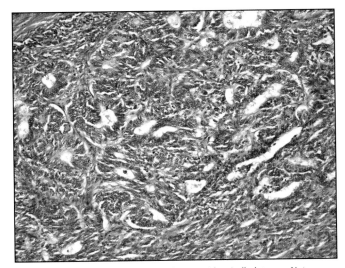

Fig. 13E.27 • Mesonephric adenocarcinoma with spindled stroma. Note ductal differentiation merging with a cellular spindled stroma.

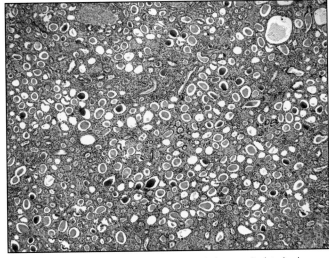

Fig. 13E.28 • Mesonephric adenocarcinoma, tubular type. Back-to-back tubules without intervening stroma are indicative of invasion.

and may also be positive for calretinin and CD10 (in an apical staining pattern).

The differential diagnosis of mesonephric carcinoma includes mesonephric hyperplasia (for the tubular variant) and endometrioid carcinoma (for the ductal variant). Features that distinguish mesonephric carcinoma from mesonephric hyperplasia include: (1) irregular, disorderly invasion; (2) back-to-back glandular crowding; (3) mitotic activity; (4) nuclear atypia; (5) lymphatic/vascular/perineural invasion; and (6) the presence of other histologic patterns. Distinction of the ductal variant of mesonephric carcinoma from endometrioid carcinoma is afforded by finding the characteristic eosinophilic intraluminal material and associated mesonephric hyperplasia in the former.

Mixed-type carcinomas

Adenosquamous carcinoma

If strictly defined as a tumor that clearly exhibits recognizable squamous and glandular elements by H&E examination (Fig. 13E.29), then adenosquamous carcinoma probably accounts for approximately one-third of cervical carcinomas with a glandular component.[97] Adenosquamous terminology should not be applied to poorly differentiated tumors that have intracytoplasmic mucin but do not show clear evidence of squamous differentiation. Similarly, invasive squamous cell carcinomas with histochemically identified intracytoplasmic mucin should also be excluded from this category. The prognosis of patients with adenosquamous carcinoma in comparison to adenocarcinoma is not clear; some studies suggest a worse prognosis, while others do not.[97,110,111] In addition to a mixture of clearly recognizable neoplastic glandular and squamous elements exhibiting the typical morphologic appearance of squamous cell carcinoma and adenocarcinoma, two histologic variants of adenosquamous carcinoma are recognized: glassy cell carcinoma and clear cell adenosquamous carcinoma.

Glassy cell carcinoma[112–116]

This rare tumor is considered a variant of adenosquamous carcinoma because some examples may exhibit focal squamous or glandular differentiation by microscopic examination, while others have demonstrated a biphasic appearance by electron microscopy. This tumor can occur over a wide age range but does appear to occur in a younger age group than cervical adenocarcinoma in general. Patients usually present with vaginal bleeding and have a large, bulky fungating mass on clinical examination. Diffuse sheets and nests of large cells with abundant eosinophilic to granular cytoplasm imparting a ground glass appearance, large round to oval nuclei with prominent nucleoli and distinct cell borders characterize this tumor histologically (Fig. 13E.30). In addition, numerous mitoses and a prominent inflammatory stromal infiltrate, often composed of eosinophils and plasma cells, are present. As some otherwise typical adenocarcinomas and large cell non-keratinizing squamous cell carcinomas may exhibit focal glassy cell features, the diagnosis of glassy cell carcinoma should be reserved for those tumors that show these distinctive histologic features in pure form. Although this tumor is recognized as a variant of adenosquamous carcinoma, controversy exists as to whether it might represent the non-specific growth pattern of a poorly differentiated carcinoma, as some recurrent adenocarcinomas and adenosquamous carcinomas treated by radiation therapy may exhibit morphologic features of glassy cell carcinoma. Overall, it appears that patients with glassy cell carcinoma may have a worse prognosis, although survival data are limited due to the rarity of this tumor type.

Clear cell adenosquamous carcinoma[117]

This rare variant of adenosquamous carcinoma is characterized histologically by the presence of an admixture of glandular and squamous elements, the latter containing abundant glycogen-rich cytoplasm imparting a pronounced clear cell appearance (Fig. 13E.31). This tumor is highly associated with HPV type 18 and appears to have a poor prognosis.

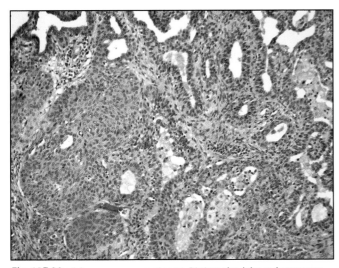

Fig. 13E.29 • Adenosquamous carcinoma. Distinct glandular and squamous differentiation is present.

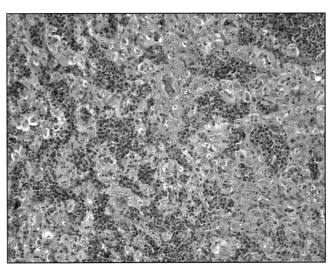

Fig. 13E.30 • Glassy cell carcinoma. Nests and aggregates of tumor cells with abundant eosinophilic cytoplasm admixed with numerous inflammatory cells.

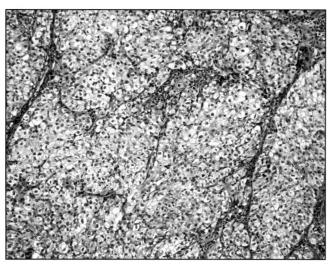

Fig. 13E.31 • Clear cell adenosquamous carcinoma. Note abundant clear cytoplasm.

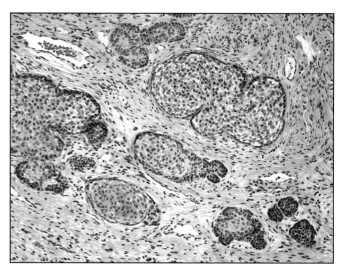

Fig. 13E.32 • Adenoid basal carcinoma. Note peripheral nuclear palisading and central atypical squamous differentiation.

Adenoid basal carcinoma (adenoid basal epithelioma)[118–128]

Clinical features

Adenoid basal carcinoma is an uncommon tumor, representing less than 5% of cervical carcinomas. Typically there is no clinically detectable cervical abnormality and it is usually discovered incidentally in cone biopsy or hysterectomy specimens in postmenopausal, usually black, women with high-grade squamous intraepithelial lesions. The prognosis is excellent, with no metastases or recurrences in patients who have tumors that exhibit classic or pure histopathologic features. Occasionally, though, adenoid basal carcinoma may occur in association with other tumor types, particularly basaloid squamous cell carcinoma, adenosquamous carcinoma, adenoid cystic carcinoma, or carcinosarcoma; the prognosis of these combined tumors correlates with the more aggressive component. Because of its excellent prognosis, the term adenoid basal epithelioma[121] has been proposed to replace adenoid basal carcinoma; however, this morphology does not always signify a predictable biologic behavior. There appears to be a histogenetic relationship between adenoid basal carcinoma and adenoid cystic carcinoma[120] since both tumors occur in postmenopausal women, have the capacity for divergent differentiation, and are associated with high-risk HPV types. In addition, rare tumors with features of both adenoid cystic and adenoid basal cell carcinoma may occur, suggesting that they may be part of a morphologic spectrum.

Pathologic features

In the majority of cases, an overlying high-grade squamous intraepithelial lesion (CIN) is present, beneath which three patterns of differentiation of the invasive tumor may occur: (1) discrete rounded nests and islands of variably atypical squamous epithelium with prominent peripheral nuclear palisading; (2) nests of basaloid cells with scant cytoplasm; and (3) basaloid nests admixed with small acini indicative of glandular differentiation (Fig. 13E.32). Typically, there is no associated stromal reaction.

Adenoid cystic carcinoma[120,124,125,128,129]

Clinical features

Adenoid cystic carcinoma is an extremely rare tumor (representing <1% of cervical carcinomas) that typically occurs in postmenopausal, usually black, women with a mean age of 70 years. Patients usually present with postmenopausal bleeding and have a friable polypoid or ulcerated cervical mass on clinical examination. Patients have an unfavorable prognosis, as adenoid cystic carcinoma is frequently associated with local recurrence or metastatic spread. Based on differences in biologic behavior, this tumor should be distinguished from adenoid basal carcinoma; however, it appears that these two tumors share a close histogenetic relationship, as they both occur in postmenopausal women and are associated with high-risk HPV (usually type 16). In addition, both tumors may exhibit areas with morphologic features of the other and rare examples of hybrid tumors may occur.

Pathologic features

Histologically, cervical adenoid cystic carcinoma has a similar appearance to those of the salivary gland, consisting of nests, islands, cords, and trabeculae of crowded cells with little cytoplasm and hyperchromatic nuclei. Characteristically, the cellular nests have a cribriform pattern with palisading nuclei, surrounding rounded spaces filled with eosinophilic hyaline or mucinous material (Fig. 13E.33). Cellular pleomorphism, numerous mitoses, necrosis, and a desmoplastic stromal response are common. Adenoid cystic carcinoma is often positive for S-100 protein and may also be positive for muscle-specific actin (HHF35), suggesting myoepithelial differentiation.

Neuroendocrine carcinoma

Tumors that fall within the spectrum of cervical neuroendocrine carcinoma, which have been defined by a consensus workshop as carcinoid, atypical carcinoid, small cell carcinoma, and large cell neuroendocrine carcinoma, are uncommon.[130]

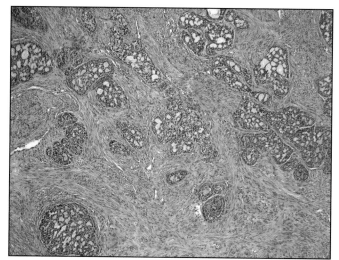

Fig. 13E.33 • Adenoid cystic carcinoma. Note cribriform growth pattern and central rounded spaces filled with mucinous material similar to tumors of salivary gland origin.

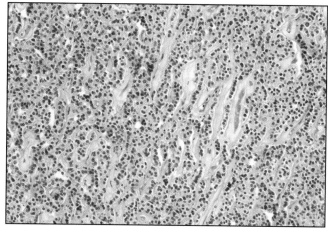

Fig. 13E.34 • Carcinoid tumor. Cord-like growth pattern.

These tumors have no defined precursor lesion but may coexist with more common subtypes of cervical squamous and glandular carcinoma and are also highly associated with HPV type 18, suggesting a shared origin.[131] Separation into the different subtypes is based on morphologic differences alone; however, different patterns may coexist and diagnostic reproducibility between these categories is not known. Therefore, differences in biologic behavior are not easily assessed and, in clinical terms, most of these tumors are managed similarly. In addition, these different morphologic categories have similar molecular abnormalities, the most common being loss of heterozygosity at 9p21 and localized 3p deletions, suggesting a common pathogenesis.[132] Overall, the outcome for cervical neuroendocrine carcinoma, regardless of morphologic subtype, is poor.[133–136]

Carcinoid

Carcinoid tumors of the cervix, similar to carcinoid tumors elsewhere, are composed of cells having modest amounts of amphophilic to eosinophilic granular cytoplasm with small to medium-sized round to oval nuclei having finely granular chromatin. Tumor cells are typically arranged in a trabecular, organoid, nested, microacinar, or cord-like growth pattern (Fig. 13E.34). Necrosis is absent and mitoses number fewer than 5 per 10 high-power fields.

Atypical carcinoid

Atypical carcinoid has the same architectural features as carcinoid but differs in having necrosis, cytologic atypia, and mitotic activity between 5 and 10 mitotic figures per 10 high-power fields.

Small cell carcinoma[131,137]

Similar to small cell carcinoma of the lung, cervical small cell carcinoma is typically composed of a dense population of small cells with hyperchromatic nuclei and little cytoplasm resulting in a high nuclear-to-cytoplasmic ratio (Fig. 13E.35).

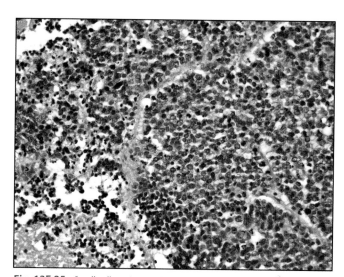

Fig. 13E.35 • Small cell carcinoma. Dense population of small cells with hyperchromatic nuclei, little cytoplasm, and numerous mitoses. Note necrosis in lower left portion of image.

The tumor cells are arranged in sheets, irregular aggregates, or nests with little cohesion, although occasional rosettes or poorly defined acini may be present. Nuclear molding is characteristic and necrosis is commonly present. These lesions are typically aggressive.

Large cell neuroendocrine carcinoma

Large cell neuroendocrine carcinoma has a trabecular, nested, or insular growth pattern and is composed of cells with moderate to abundant amounts of eosinophilic cytoplasm and large nuclei with vesicular chromatin and prominent nucleoli (Fig. 13E.36). Numerous mitoses and necrosis are characteristic.[138]

Mixed epithelial and mesenchymal tumors

Müllerian papilloma[139,140]

Müllerian papilloma is a rare benign papillary lesion that more commonly occurs in the vagina (see p. 725) but may also

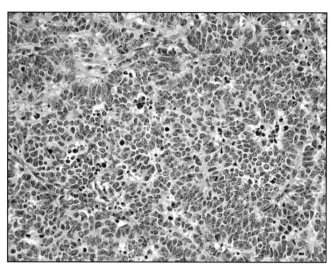

Fig. 13E.36 • Large cell neuroendocrine carcinoma. Tumor cell nuclei are larger and have vesicular chromatin with conspicuous nucleoli.

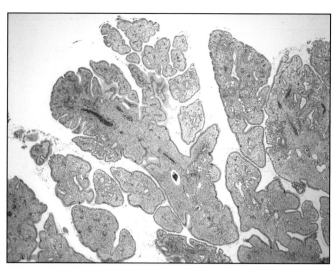

Fig. 13E.37 • Endocervical polyp. Exophytic papillae with fibrous cores.

occasionally occur in the cervix. They typically develop in children in their first decade of life and the most common presenting symptom is vaginal bleeding or discharge. Histologically, the lesion is composed of complex branching papillae lined by non-ciliated cuboidal or columnar bland-appearing epithelium without mitotic activity. The fibrous stromal cores may contain varying amounts of inflammatory cells. These lesions are treated by local excision and occasionally may recur.

Endocervical polyp

Endocervical polyps typically are incidental findings in women in their fifth decade; those that present with symptoms most commonly cause abnormal vaginal bleeding or discharge.[141,142] They most commonly arise in or adjacent to the cervical os, although they may occur anywhere along the cervical canal. In postmenopausal women, cervical polyps are highly associated with the presence of endometrial polyps and consideration of endometrial sampling as an explanation for clinical symptomatology (and to exclude coexistent neoplasia) is recommended.[143] Histologically, these lesions are polypoid with stromal cores covered by benign-appearing endocervical epithelium (Fig. 13E.37). The amount of stroma in relation to glandular epithelium may vary, with some examples showing a predominance of epithelium in the form of microglandular change. The principal differential diagnostic consideration is the exclusion of adenosarcoma. Cervical adenosarcoma differs from endocervical polyps in: (1) usually, but not always, having a leaf-like or phyllodes appearance to the gland outlines; as well as (2) periglandular cuffing; (3) stromal mitotic activity greater than 2 mitoses per 10 high-power fields; and, in some cases, (4) atypical stromal cells. Sarcomatous overgrowth and heterologous stromal differentiation may also be seen in adenosarcoma. Some endocervical polyps exhibit selected features of adenosarcoma but do not fulfill diagnostic criteria for the latter (e.g., a polyp with a phyllodes architecture but without periglandular cuffing or stromal mitotic activity); in these situations, we recommend the diagnosis of "endocervical polyp with unusual histologic features," a descriptive note, and

suggest clinical follow-up with prompt removal of any recurrent lesion.

Adenofibroma[144]

Cervical adenofibroma is a mixed epithelial and mesenchymal tumor in which both the epithelial component and the fibrous stromal component are benign. These are exceedingly rare and there is some controversy as to their existence, although they are recognized in the World Health Organization classification of cervical tumors. Histologically, these lesions are composed of papillary fronds with a fibrous core, which are lined by bland cuboidal or columnar epithelium that may be mucinous, ciliated, or nondescript. Distinction from adenosarcoma is afforded by the absence of periglandular cuffing, stromal mitotic activity, or stromal atypia in adenofibroma. These lesions are benign, but, similar to benign cervical polyps, have the potential to recur. Local excision is the treatment of choice.

Adenomyoma, endocervical type[145]

Endocervical-type adenomyoma is a rare mixed epithelial–mesenchymal tumor of the cervix that presents most commonly as an asymptomatic mass in women with a mean age of 40 years. Tumor size has ranged up to 23 cm, with most examples measuring less than 8 cm. Tumors typically arise in the endocervical canal into which they usually protrude and occasionally prolapse through the os; intramural tumors may also occur. This lesion is characteristically a well-circumscribed, gray/white mass that may contain multiple mucinous cysts. Histologically it is composed of irregularly shaped glands, some of which may exhibit papillary infoldings, and a leaf-like architecture surrounded by smaller rounded glands imparting a lobular appearance. The glands are usually lined by bland, tall columnar, endocervical-type mucinous epithelium (occasionally focal tubal differentiation and endometrioid-type glands are present) and mitotic activity is uncommon. Surrounding and separating the glands is a proliferation of bland smooth muscle, arranged in intersecting fascicles reminiscent of leiomyoma (Fig. 13E.38). These tumors are

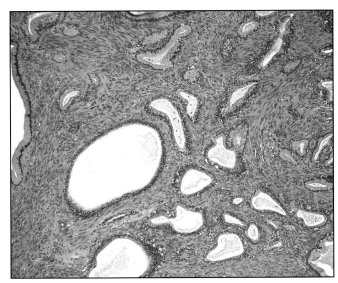

Fig. 13E.38 • Adenomyoma, endocervical type. The glands are separated by a myomatous stroma.

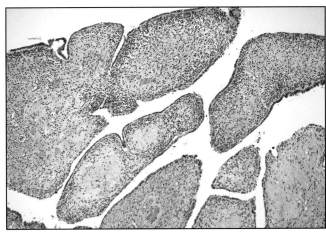

Fig. 13E.39 • Müllerian adenosarcoma. Polypoid frond-like growth pattern with subepithelial and periglandular cellular spindled stroma.

considered benign; residual tumor may be present in patients treated by hysterectomy and regrowth (in comparison with recurrence) may occur in patients treated by local excision alone. Endocervical-type adenomyoma is distinguished from minimal-deviation adenocarcinoma, its principal differential diagnostic consideration, by: (1) its well-circumscribed nature; (2) its lobular glandular arrangement (which would be unusual for minimal-deviation adenocarcinoma); (3) the presence of a smooth muscle component and lack of desmoplastic stroma; and (4) uniform bland cytomorphologic features.

Endometrial-type adenomyomas and atypical polypoid adenomyomas may occasionally involve the cervix, but more commonly occur in the uterine corpus (see Ch. 13B).

Adenosarcoma (Müllerian adenosarcoma)

Müllerian adenosarcoma is a biphasic tumor composed of a malignant stromal component admixed with a benign epithelial component. This tumor occurs most commonly in the uterine corpus (see Ch. 13B) but also occurs, in order of descending frequency, as a primary lesion in the ovary, pelvis, and cervix, the latter representing 2% of cases in one series.[146] The average age of women with primary cervical tumors is in the fourth decade (with a range from the second to seventh decades) and patients usually present with either recurrent polyps or abnormal vaginal bleeding.[147,148] Tumors are characteristically polypoid or papillary and protrude through the cervical os on clinical examination. Histologically, the tumors are polypoid and composed of complex irregular, branching glands with a phyllodes or leaf-like appearance lined by mucinous, ciliated, or endometrioid-type epithelium (Fig. 13E.39). Periglandular cuffing by cellular spindled stroma, which may show a range of nuclear atypia, is characteristic. Mitoses should number at least 2 per 10 high-power fields, although in most cases the mitotic index exceeds 4. Similar to endometrial adenosarcoma, these tumors may show sarcomatous overgrowth and heterologous differentiation.[149,150] Prognostic factors and outcome of patients with cervical adenosarcoma are not well defined as this tumor is uncommon

at this site; in the largest series of 12 patients, two had unfavorable outcomes – one died of disease 1 year after initial diagnosis and one developed a recurrence.[147] In the latter study, similar to endometrial adenosarcoma, prognosis appeared to be related to the presence of deep invasion.

Carcinosarcoma (malignant Müllerian mixed tumor)[151–155]

Carcinosarcoma, which is composed of malignant epithelial and mesenchymal components, is more common in the uterine corpus. Cervical primaries are rare and typically occur in postmenopausal, usually black patients, with the majority being older than 60 years of age. Tumors are typically polypoid or pedunculated and sizes range from 1 to 10 cm in the largest series[151] but tumors as large as 17 cm have been the subject of case reports. Unlike their counterparts in the uterine corpus, cervical carcinosarcoma is associated with HPV infection, particularly type 16. This association may be related to the presence of (cervical-type) glandular or squamous epithelial components in cervical primaries as opposed to uterine primaries – basaloid squamous cell carcinoma, adenoid cystic carcinoma, adenoid basal carcinoma, and undifferentiated carcinoma (as opposed to endometrioid or papillary serous carcinoma) are more commonly seen in association with cervical primaries (Fig. 13E.40). The mesenchymal component tends to show homologous differentiation with a fibrosarcomatous or endometrioid stromal sarcomatous pattern. Cervical carcinosarcomas appear more likely to be confined to the uterus than their endometrial counterparts and may therefore have a better prognosis.[151] The differential diagnosis includes mesonephric carcinoma with a spindled component and Wilms tumor, both of which occur in a younger age group.

Mesenchymal tumors

Leiomyoma

Leiomyomata of the uterine cervix are uncommon, being present in fewer than 1% of hysterectomy specimens removed

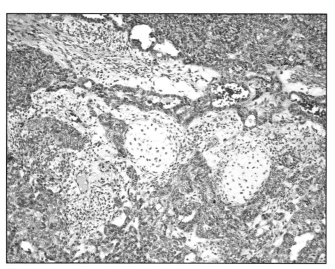

Fig. 13E.40 • Carcinosarcoma. Note that the carcinomatous component is glandular.

either for symptomatic uterine corpus fibroids or for other reasons.[156] In most instances, cervical leiomyomata are incidental and do not represent clinically significant lesions.

Genital rhabdomyoma

Genital rhabdomyoma is a benign tumor composed of mature rhabdomyoblasts, which may occasionally involve the cervix but more commonly occurs in the vagina (see p. 723).

Embryonal rhabdomyosarcoma[157-160]

The sarcoma botryoides variant of embryonal rhabdomyosarcoma more frequently involves the vagina but may also rarely involve the cervix. The peak incidence of cervical sarcoma botryoides typically is in the second or third decade, although occasional cases have occurred in infants and in women in their fifth decade. This incidence differs from those tumors that arise in the vagina, which typically affect infants and young children. Similar to tumors of vaginal origin, cervical sarcoma botryoides is often polypoid or has a "cluster of grapes" gross appearance. The most common presenting symptoms include vaginal bleeding and the sensation of a mass in the introitus. Histologically, tumors of cervical origin have the same morphologic appearance as those that occur in the vagina (see p. 724). Notably, however, areas of cartilaginous differentiation may be present in some cases.[158] Some studies have shown that patients with cervical (in comparison with vaginal) primaries have a much more favorable outcome[158] and that these patients can be treated with conservative fertility-sparing treatment with local excision followed by chemotherapy.

Leiomyosarcoma[161-164]

Primary leiomyosarcoma of the cervix is exceedingly rare. Patients are typically perimenopausal, with a median age in the fifth decade, and the most common presenting symptom is abnormal vaginal bleeding. Criteria for malignancy are those that are used for smooth muscle tumors of the uterine corpus (see p. 690).

Endometrioid stromal sarcoma, low-grade

Tumors that morphologically resemble low-grade endometrial stromal sarcoma may rarely occur as a primary tumor of the cervix, either in pure form or as a component of a malignant mixed tumor or adenosarcoma.[151,165] The principal differential diagnostic consideration, particularly for pure tumors, is separation from endometriosis, which can also present with abnormal vaginal bleeding. Typically cervical endometriosis is well circumscribed and does not exhibit the characteristic growth pattern of a stromal sarcoma.[166]

Alveolar soft part sarcoma[167,168]

Alveolar soft part sarcoma more commonly arises in the limbs of young adults but may rarely occur in the female genital tract, including the vagina, uterine cervix, and corpus. Patients are usually less than 40 years of age and present with abnormal vaginal bleeding. Primary cervical tumors have the same characteristic morphologic appearance and immunophenotypic profile as their counterparts in soft tissue (see Ch. 24).

Malignant peripheral nerve sheath tumor (malignant schwannoma)[169]

Malignant peripheral nerve sheath tumor of the cervix is extremely uncommon, with the largest series of cases amounting to only three patients.[169] In this study, the patients were 25, 65, and 73 years of age and two presented with abnormal vaginal bleeding. Two tumors were polypoid and one was ulcerated and they measured 1.3, 4.4, and 5.0 cm in dimension. Histologically, the tumors were composed of hypercellular and hypocellular zones of fascicular spindle cells, similar to malignant peripheral nerve sheath tumors arising in soft tissue (see Ch. 27). All tumors were mitotically active and were positive for S-100 protein and negative for muscle markers. Follow-up in two patients showed no evidence of disease at 15 months and multiple abdominal metastases 2 years posthysterectomy respectively.

Melanocytic tumors

Blue nevus

Cervical blue nevi, similar to their cutaneous counterparts, are composed of a proliferation of dendritic, often heavily pigmented, melanocytes located in the cervical stroma near the epithelial interface. They most often involve the posterior endocervical canal and are usually discovered incidentally in hysterectomy specimens in middle-aged women. These lesions are usually not detectable by clinical examination, but can have a blue-black gross appearance. Foci of stromal melanocytes have been identified in up to 29% of cervix uteri in which step sections were examined, suggesting that stromal dendritic melanocytes are more common in this location than initially appreciated. It is postulated that malignant melanoma of the cervix may arise from these foci.

Malignant melanoma[170,171]

Primary malignant melanoma of the cervix is extremely rare with approximately 30 cases reported in the literature, some of which are not well documented. The mean patient age is in the sixth decade and they usually present with abnormal vaginal bleeding. Clinical examination generally reveals an exophytic friable mass that may be pigmented in appearance, having a gray, blue, or black coloration, or may be amelanotic. Tumors have a similar histologic appearance to melanoma elsewhere, having a spindled and/or epithelioid appearance; clear cell variants mimicking clear cell carcinoma may also occur. Positivity for melanoma markers (S-100, HMB-45, Mart-1, and Melan-A) aids in the distinction of this tumor from potential mimics. Most patients present with stage I or II disease; however, the prognosis is poor, with most succumbing to tumor within 2 years.

Miscellaneous rare tumors

Extrarenal Wilms tumor[172–177]

Extrarenal Wilms tumor is rare at this site, with only six reports in the literature of this tumor occurring in the uterus. The patient's ages were 2, 11, 13, 13, 14, and 22. In two cases, the tumor originated in the cervix, with the remainder arising in the uterine corpus. All patients had polypoid masses, ranging in size from 2.2 to 17 cm. Histologically, these tumors show the characteristic appearance of Wilms tumor. One patient died of disease, one patient had extensive intra-abdominal recurrence 7 months post-resection, and three had no evidence of disease 2, 5.6, and 9.6 years later.

Yolk sac tumor (endodermal sinus tumor)[178]

Yolk sac tumor may rarely involve the lower genital tract, being more common in the vagina than the cervix . Tumors are typically polypoid and patients usually present with abnormal vaginal bleeding. Cervical yolk sac tumors have a similar histologic appearance to those that occur in the ovary (see p. 605).

Mature cystic teratoma

Rare examples of mature teratoma have been described to occur in the cervix, typically presenting as a polypoid mass that histologically is composed of endodermal, mesodermal, and ectodermal components.[179–181]

Hematopoietic tumors

Non-Hodgkin's lymphoma may rarely involve the female genital tract as a primary lesion or as evidence of systemic spread. The most common type is diffuse large B-cell lymphoma.[182]

Granulocytic sarcoma[183–185] (acute myelocytic leukemia involving soft tissue/organs) rarely presents initially as a primary cervical neoplasm, and even more rarely this presentation will precede overt leukemia by more than a few weeks or months. Patients usually present with abnormal bleeding (menometrorrhagia, postcoital, or postmenopausal bleeding) and the tumors tend to attenuate or ulcerate the overlying mucosa. Granulocytic sarcoma involving the female genital tract has the same morphologic characteristics and immunophenotypic profile as its counterpart in extramedullary tissues elsewhere (see Ch. 21).

References

1. Rosenfeld W D, Rose E, Vermund S H et al. 1992 Follow-up evaluation of cervicovaginal human papillomavirus infection in adolescents. J Pediatr 121: 307–311
2. Melkert P W, Hopman E, van den Brule A J et al. 1993 Prevalence of HPV in cytomorphologically normal cervical smears, as determined by the polymerase chain reaction, is age-dependent. Int J Cancer 53: 919–923
3. Moscicki A B 1998 Genital infections with human papillomavirus (HPV). Pediatr Infect Dis J 17: 651–652
4. Moscicki A B, Shiboski S, Broering J et al. 1998 The natural history of human papillomavirus infection as measured by repeated DNA testing in adolescent and young women. J Pediatr 132: 277–284
5. Levert M, Clavel C, Graesslin O et al. 2000 [Human papillomavirus typing in routine cervical smears. Results from a series of 3778 patients.] Gynecol Obstet Fertil 28: 722–728
6. Lorincz A T, Reid R, Jenson A B et al. 1992 Human papillomavirus infection of the cervix: relative risk associations of 15 common anogenital types. Obstet Gynecol 79: 328–337
7. Koutsky L A, Holmes K K, Critchlow C W et al. 1992 A cohort study of the risk of cervical intraepithelial neoplasia grade 2 or 3 in relation to papillomavirus infection. N Engl J Med 327: 1272–1278
8. Brown M R, Noffsinger A, First M R et al. 2000 HPV subtype analysis in lower genital tract neoplasms of female renal transplant recipients. Gynecol Oncol 79: 220–224
9. Alloub M I, Barr B B, McLaren K M et al. 1989 Human papillomavirus infection and cervical intraepithelial neoplasia in women with renal allografts. BMJ 298: 153–156
10. Halpert R, Fruchter R G, Sedlis A et al. 1986 Human papillomavirus and lower genital neoplasia in renal transplant patients. Obstet Gynecol 68: 251–258
11. Wright T C Jr, Sun X W 1996 Anogenital papillomavirus infection and neoplasia in immunodeficient women. Obstet Gynecol Clin North Am 23: 861–893
12. Moscicki A B, Ellenberg J H, Vermund S H et al. 2000 Prevalence of and risks for cervical human papillomavirus infection and squamous intraepithelial lesions in adolescent girls: impact of infection with human immunodeficiency virus. Arch Pediatr Adolesc Med 154: 127–134
13. La Ruche G, You B, Mensah-Ado I et al. 1998 Human papillomavirus and human immunodeficiency virus infections: relation with cervical dysplasia-neoplasia in African women. Int J Cancer 76: 480–486
14. Trivijitsilp P, Mosher R, Sheets E E et al. 1998 Papillary immature metaplasia (immature condyloma) of the cervix: a clinicopathologic analysis and comparison with papillary squamous carcinoma. Hum Pathol 29: 641–648
15. Ward B E, Saleh A M, Williams J V et al. 1992 Papillary immature metaplasia of the cervix: a distinct subset of exophytic cervical condyloma associated with HPV-6/11 nucleic acids. Mod Pathol 5: 391–395
16. Resnick M, Lester S, Tate J E et al. 1996 Viral and histopathologic correlates of MN and MIB-1 expression in cervical intraepithelial neoplasia. Hum Pathol 27: 234–239
17. Mittal K 1999 Utility of proliferation-associated marker MIB-1 in evaluating lesions of the uterine cervix. Adv Anat Pathol 6: 177–185
18. Mittal K, Palazzo J 1998 Cervical condylomas show higher proliferation than do inflamed or metaplastic cervical squamous epithelium. Mod Pathol 11: 780–783
19. Keating J T, Cviko A, Riethdorf S et al. 2001 Ki-67, cyclin E, and p16INK4 are complimentary surrogate biomarkers for human papilloma virus-related cervical neoplasia. Am J Surg Pathol 25: 884–891
20. Kaku T, Kamura T, Sakai K et al. 1997 Early adenocarcinoma of the uterine cervix. Gynecol Oncol 65: 281–285
21. Ostor A, Rome R, Quinn M 1997 Microinvasive adenocarcinoma of the cervix: a clinicopathologic study of 77 women. Obstet Gynecol 89: 88–93
22. Lee K R, Flynn C E 2000 Early invasive adenocarcinoma of the cervix. Cancer 89: 1048–1055
23. Tase T, Okagaki T, Clark B A et al. 1989 Human papillomavirus DNA in adenocarcinoma in situ, microinvasive adenocarcinoma of the uterine cervix, and coexisting cervical squamous intraepithelial neoplasia. Int J Gynecol Pathol 8: 8–17
24. Boon M E, Baak J P, Kurver P J et al. 1981 Adenocarcinoma in situ of the cervix: an underdiagnosed lesion. Cancer 48: 768–773

25. Kashimura M, Shinohara M, Oikawa K et al. 1990 An adenocarcinoma in situ of the uterine cervix that developed into invasive adenocarcinoma after 5 years. Gynecol Oncol 36: 128–133

26. Boddington M M, Spriggs A I, Cowdell R H 1976 Adenocarcinoma of the uterine cervix: cytological evidence of a long preclinical evolution. Br J Obstet Gynaecol 83: 900–903

27. Hocking G R, Hayman J A, Ostor A G 1996 Adenocarcinoma in situ of the uterine cervix progressing to invasive adenocarcinoma. Aust NZ J Obstet Gynaecol 36: 218–220

28. Andersen E S, Arffmann E 1989 Adenocarcinoma in situ of the uterine cervix: a clinico-pathologic study of 36 cases. Gynecol Oncol 35: 1–7

29. Tobon H, Dave H 1988 Adenocarcinoma in situ of the cervix. Clinicopathologic observations of 11 cases. Int J Gynecol Pathol 7: 139–151

30. Krane J F, Granter S R, Trask C E et al. 2001 Papanicolaou smear sensitivity for the detection of adenocarcinoma of the cervix: a study of 49 cases. Cancer 93: 8–15

31. Schoolland M, Segal A, Allpress S et al. 2002 Adenocarcinoma in situ of the cervix. Cancer 96: 330–337

32. Lee K R, Minter L J, Granter S R 1997 Papanicolaou smear sensitivity for adenocarcinoma in situ of the cervix. A study of 34 cases. Am J Clin Pathol 107: 30–35

33. Ostor A G, Duncan A, Quinn M et al. 2000 Adenocarcinoma in situ of the uterine cervix: an experience with 100 cases. Gynecol Oncol 79: 207–210

34. Andersen E S, Nielsen K 2002 Adenocarcinoma in situ of the cervix: a prospective study of conization as definitive treatment. Gynecol Oncol 86: 365–369

35. Im D D, Duska L R, Rosenshein N B 1995 Adequacy of conization margins in adenocarcinoma in situ of the cervix as a predictor of residual disease. Gynecol Oncol 59: 179–182

36. Wolf J K, Levenback C, Malpica A et al. 1996 Adenocarcinoma in situ of the cervix: significance of cone biopsy margins. Obstet Gynecol 88: 82–86

37. Denehy T R, Gregori C A, Breen J L 1997 Endocervical curettage, cone margins, and residual adenocarcinoma in situ of the cervix. Obstet Gynecol 90: 1–6

38. Goldstein N S, Mani A 1998 The status and distance of cone biopsy margins as a predictor of excision adequacy for endocervical adenocarcinoma in situ. Am J Clin Pathol 109: 727–732

39. Azodi M, Chambers S K, Rutherford T J et al. 1999 Adenocarcinoma in situ of the cervix: management and outcome. Gynecol Oncol 73: 348–353

40. Poynor E A, Barakat R R, Hoskins W J 1995 Management and follow-up of patients with adenocarcinoma in situ of the uterine cervix. Gynecol Oncol 57: 158–164

41. Kennedy A W, Biscotti C V 2002 Further study of the management of cervical adenocarcinoma in situ. Gynecol Oncol 86: 361–364

42. Shin C H, Schorge J O, Lee K R et al. 2000 Conservative management of adenocarcinoma in situ of the cervix. Gynecol Oncol 79: 6–10

43. Jaworski R C, Pacey N F, Greenberg M L et al. 1988 The histologic diagnosis of adenocarcinoma in situ and related lesions of the cervix uteri. Adenocarcinoma in situ. Cancer 61: 1171–1181

44. Bertrand M, Lickrish G M, Colgan T J 1987 The anatomic distribution of cervical adenocarcinoma in situ: implications for treatment. Am J Obstet Gynecol 157: 21–25

45. Weisbrot I M, Stabinsky C, Davis A M 1972 Adenocarcinoma in situ of the uterine cervix. Cancer 29: 1179–1187

46. Biscotti C V, Hart W R 1998 Apoptotic bodies: a consistent morphologic feature of endocervical adenocarcinoma in situ. Am J Surg Pathol 22: 434–439

47. Moritani S, Ioffe O B, Sagae S et al. 2002 Mitotic activity and apoptosis in endocervical glandular lesions. Int J Gynecol Pathol 21: 125–133

48. Schlesinger C, Silverberg S G 1999 Endocervical adenocarcinoma in situ of tubal type and its relation to atypical tubal metaplasia. Int J Gynecol Pathol 18: 1–4

49. Willett G D, Kurman R J, Reid R et al. 1989 Correlation of the histologic appearance of intraepithelial neoplasia of the cervix with human papillomavirus types. Emphasis on low grade lesions including so-called flat condyloma. Int J Gynecol Pathol 8: 18–25

50. Park J J, Sun D, Quade B J et al. 2000 Stratified mucin-producing intraepithelial lesions of the cervix: adenosquamous or columnar cell neoplasia? Am J Surg Pathol 24: 1414–1419

51. Parkin D M, Bray F, Ferlay J et al. 2001 Estimating the world cancer burden: Globocan 2000. Int J Cancer 94: 153–156

52. Landis S H, Murray T, Bolden S et al. 1999 Cancer statistics, 1999. CA Cancer J Clin 49: 8–31

53. Vizcaino A P, Moreno V, Bosch F X et al. 2000 International trends in incidence of cervical cancer: II. Squamous-cell carcinoma. Int J Cancer 86: 429–435

54. Pretorius R, Semrad N, Watring W et al. 1991 Presentation of cervical cancer. Gynecol Oncol 42: 48–53

55. Wong W S, Ng S, Lee C K 1990 Verrucous carcinoma of the cervix. Arch Gynecol Obstet 247: 47–51

56. Koenig C, Turnicky R P, Kankam C F et al. 1997 Papillary squamotransitional cell carcinoma of the cervix: a report of 32 cases. Am J Surg Pathol 21: 915–921

57. Qizilbash A H 1975 In-situ and microinvasive adenocarcinoma of the uterine cervix. A clinical, cytologic and histologic study of 14 cases. Am J Clin Pathol 64: 155–170

58. Christopherson W M, Nealon N, Gray L A Sr 1979 Noninvasive precursor lesions of adenocarcinoma and mixed adenosquamous carcinoma of the cervix uteri. Cancer 44: 975–983

59. Yeh I T, LiVolsi V A, Noumoff J S 1991 Endocervical carcinoma. Pathol Res Pract 187: 129–144

60. Noda K, Kimura K, Ikeda M et al. 1983 Studies on the histogenesis of cervical adenocarcinoma. Int J Gynecol Pathol 1: 336–346

61. Burghardt E 1984 Microinvasive carcinoma in gynaecological pathology. Clin Obstet Gynaecol 11: 239–257

62. Buscema J, Woodruff J D 1984 Significance of neoplastic atypicalities in endocervical epithelium. Gynecol Oncol 17: 356–362

63. Schorge J O, Lee K R, Flynn C E et al. 1999 Stage IA1 cervical adenocarcinoma: definition and treatment. Obstet Gynecol 93: 219–222

64. Webb J C, Key C R, Qualls C R et al. 2001 Population-based study of microinvasive adenocarcinoma of the uterine cervix. Obstet Gynecol 97: 701–706

65. Kaspar H G, Dinh T V, Doherty M G et al. 1993 Clinical implications of tumor volume measurement in stage I adenocarcinoma of the cervix. Obstet Gynecol 81: 296–300

66. Berek J S, Hacker N F, Fu Y S et al. 1985 Adenocarcinoma of the uterine cervix: histologic variables associated with lymph node metastasis and survival. Obstet Gynecol 65: 46–52

67. Teshima S, Shimosato Y, Kishi K et al. 1985 Early stage adenocarcinoma of the uterine cervix. Histopathologic analysis with consideration of histogenesis. Cancer 56: 167–172

68. Smith H O, Qualls C R, Romero A A et al. 2002 Is there a difference in survival for IA1 and IA2 adenocarcinoma of the uterine cervix? Gynecol Oncol 85: 229–241

68a. Ceballos K M, Shaw D, Daya D 2006 Microinvasive cervical adenocarcinoma (FIGO stage 1A tumors): results of surgical staging and outcome analysis. Am J Surg Pathol 30: 370–374

69. Peters R K, Chao A, Mack T M et al. 1986 Increased frequency of adenocarcinoma of the uterine cervix in young women in Los Angeles County. J Natl Cancer Inst 76: 423–428

70. Smith H O, Tiffany M F, Qualls C R et al. 2000 The rising incidence of adenocarcinoma relative to squamous cell carcinoma of the uterine cervix in the United States – a 24-year population-based study. Gynecol Oncol 78: 97–105

71. Pirog E C, Kleter B, Olgac S et al. 2000 Prevalence of human papilloma virus DNA in different histological subtypes of cervical adenocarcinoma. Am J Pathol 157: 1055–1062

72. Young R H, Clement P B 2002 Endocervical adenocarcinoma and its variants: their morphology and differential diagnosis. Histopathology 41: 185–207

73. Miller B E, Flax S D, Arheart K et al. 1993 The presentation of adenocarcinoma of the uterine cervix. Cancer 72: 1281–1285

74. An H J, Kim K R, Kim I S et al. 2005 Prevalence of human papillomavirus DNA in various histological subtypes of cervical adenocarcinoma: a population-based study. Mod Pathol 18: 528–534

75. McKelvey J L, Goodlin R R 1963 Adenoma malignum of the cervix. Cancer 16: 549–557

76. Silverberg S G, Hurt W G 1975 Minimal deviation adenocarcinoma ("adenoma malignum") of the cervix: a reappraisal. Am J Obstet Gynecol 121: 971–975

77. Kaku T, Enjoji M 1983 Extremely well-differentiated adenocarcinoma ("adenoma malignum") of the cervix. Int J Gynecol Pathol 2: 28–41

78. Kaminski P F, Norris H J 1983 Minimal deviation carcinoma (adenoma malignum) of the cervix. Int J Gynecol Pathol 2: 141–152

79. Gilks C B, Young R H, Aguirre P et al. 1989 Adenoma malignum (minimal deviation adenocarcinoma) of the uterine cervix. A clinicopathological and immunohistochemical analysis of 26 cases. Am J Surg Pathol 13: 717–729

80. Michael H, Grawe L, Kraus F T 1984 Minimal deviation endocervical adenocarcinoma: clinical and histologic features, immunohistochemical staining for carcinoembryonic antigen, and differentiation from confusing benign lesions. Int J Gynecol Pathol 3: 261–276

81. Lee J Y, Dong S M, Kim H S et al. 1998 A distinct region of chromosome 19p13.3 associated with the sporadic form of adenoma malignum of the uterine cervix. Cancer Res 58: 1140–1143

82. Kuragaki C, Enomoto T, Ueno Y et al. 2003 Mutations in the STK11 gene characterize minimal deviation adenocarcinoma of the uterine cervix. Lab Invest 83: 35–45

83. LiVolsi V A, Merino M J, Schwartz P E 1983 Coexistent endocervical adenocarcinoma and mucinous adenocarcinoma of ovary: a clinicopathologic study of four cases. Int J Gynecol Pathol 1: 391–402

84. Kaminski P F, Norris H J 1984 Coexistence of ovarian neoplasms and endocervical adenocarcinoma. Obstet Gynecol 64: 553–556

85. Young R H, Scully R E 1988 Mucinous ovarian tumors associated with mucinous adenocarcinomas of the cervix. A clinicopathological analysis of 16 cases. Int J Gynecol Pathol 7: 99–111

86. Hayashi I, Tsuda H, Shimoda T 2000 Reappraisal of orthodox histochemistry for the diagnosis of minimal deviation adenocarcinoma of the cervix. Am J Surg Pathol 24: 559–562

87. Utsugi K, Hirai Y, Takeshima N et al. 1999 Utility of the monoclonal antibody HIK1083 in the diagnosis of adenoma malignum of the uterine cervix. Gynecol Oncol 75: 345–348

88. Young R H, Scully R E 1989 Villoglandular papillary adenocarcinoma of the uterine cervix. A clinicopathologic analysis of 13 cases. Cancer 63: 1773–1779

89. Hopson L, Jones M A, Boyce C R et al. 1990 Papillary villoglandular carcinoma of the cervix. Gynecol Oncol 39: 221–224

90. Jones M W, Silverberg S G, Kurman R J 1993 Well-differentiated villoglandular adenocarcinoma of the uterine cervix: a clinicopathological study of 24 cases. Int J Gynecol Pathol 12: 1–7

91. Kaku T, Kamura T, Shigematsu T et al. 1997 Adenocarcinoma of the uterine cervix with predominantly villogladular papillary growth pattern. Gynecol Oncol 64: 147–152

92. Jones M W, Kounelis S, Papadaki H et al. 2000 Well-differentiated villoglandular adenocarcinoma of the uterine cervix: oncogene/tumor suppressor gene alterations and human papillomavirus genotyping. Int J Gynecol Pathol 19: 110–117

93. Mayorga M, Garcia-Valtuille A, Fernandez F et al. 1997 Adenocarcinoma of the uterine cervix with massive signet ring cell differentiation. Int J Surg Pathol 5: 95–100

94. Haswani P, Arseneau J, Ferenczy A 1998 Primary signet ring cell carcinoma of the uterine cervix: a clinicopathologic study of two cases with review of the literature. Int J Gynecol Cancer 8: 374–379

95. Fox H, Wells M, Harris M et al. 1988 Enteric tumours of the lower female genital tract: a report of three cases. Histopathology 12: 167–176

96. Lee K R, Trainer T D 1990 Adenocarcinoma of the uterine cervix of small intestinal type containing numerous Paneth cells. Arch Pathol Lab Med 114: 731–733

97. Schorge J O, Lee K R, Lee S J et al. 1999 Early cervical adenocarcinoma: selection criteria for radical surgery. Obstet Gynecol 94: 386–390

98. Zaino R J 2002 The fruits of our labors: distinguishing endometrial from endocervical adenocarcinoma. Int J Gynecol Pathol 21: 1–3

99. Young R H, Scully R E 1993 Minimal-deviation endometrioid adenocarcinoma of the uterine cervix. A report of five cases of a distinctive neoplasm that may be misinterpreted as benign. Am J Surg Pathol 17: 660–665

100. Rahilly M A, Williams A R, Al Nafussi A 1992 Minimal deviation endometrioid adenocarcinoma of cervix: a clinicopathological and immunohistochemical study of two cases. Histopathology 20: 351–354

101. Nordqvist S R, Fidler W J Jr, Woodruff J M et al. 1976 Clear cell adenocarcinoma of the cervix and vagina. A clinicopathologic study of 21 cases with and without a history of maternal ingestion of estrogens. Cancer 37: 858–871

102. Herbst A L, Cole P, Colton T et al. 1977 Age-incidence and risk of diethylstilbestrol-related clear cell adenocarcinoma of the vagina and cervix. Am J Obstet Gynecol 128: 43–50

103. Hanselaar A, van Loosbroek M, Schuurbiers O et al. 1997 Clear cell adenocarcinoma of the vagina and cervix. An update of the central Netherlands registry showing twin age incidence peaks. Cancer 79: 2229–2236

104. Reich O, Tamussino K, Lahousen M et al. 2000 Clear cell carcinoma of the uterine cervix: pathology and prognosis in surgically treated stage IB–IIB disease in women not exposed in utero to diethylstilbestrol. Gynecol Oncol 76: 331–335

105. Jones W B, Tan L K, Lewis J L Jr 1993 Late recurrence of clear cell adenocarcinoma of the vagina and cervix: a report of three cases. Gynecol Oncol 51: 266–271

106. Zhou C, Gilks C B, Hayes M et al. 1998 Papillary serous carcinoma of the uterine cervix: a clinicopathologic study of 17 cases. Am J Surg Pathol 22: 113–120

107. Ferry J A, Scully R E 1990 Mesonephric remnants, hyperplasia, and neoplasia in the uterine cervix. A study of 49 cases. Am J Surg Pathol 14: 1100–1111

108. Clement P B, Young R H, Keh P et al. 1995 Malignant mesonephric neoplasms of the uterine cervix. A report of eight cases, including four with a malignant spindle cell component. Am J Surg Pathol 19: 1158–1171

109. Silver S A, Devouassoux-Shisheboran M, Mezzetti T P et al. 2001 Mesonephric adenocarcinomas of the uterine cervix: a study of 11 cases with immunohistochemical findings. Am J Surg Pathol 25: 379–387

110. Look K Y, Brunetto V L, Clarke-Pearson D L et al. 1996 An analysis of cell type in patients with surgically staged stage IB carcinoma of the cervix: a Gynecologic Oncology Group study. Gynecol Oncol 63: 304–311

111. Alfsen G C, Kristensen G B, Skovlund E et al. 2001 Histologic subtype has minor importance for overall survival in patients with adenocarcinoma of the uterine cervix: a population-based study of prognostic factors in 505 patients with nonsquamous cell carcinomas of the cervix. Cancer 92: 2471–2483

112. Ulbright T M, Gersell D J 1983 Glassy cell carcinoma of the uterine cervix. A light and electron microscopic study of five cases. Cancer 51: 2255–2263

113. Littman P, Clement P B, Henriksen B et al. 1976 Glassy cell carcinoma of the cervix. Cancer 37: 2238–2246

114. Costa M J, Kenny M B, Hewan-Lowe K et al. 1991 Glassy cell features in adenosquamous carcinoma of the uterine cervix. Histologic, ultrastructural, immunohistochemical, and clinical findings. Am J Clin Pathol 96: 520–528

115. Pak H Y, Yokota S B, Paladugu R R et al. 1983 Glassy cell carcinoma of the cervix. Cytologic and clinicopathologic analysis. Cancer 52: 307–312

116. Cherry C P, Glucksmann A 1956 Incidence, histology, and response to radiation of mixed carcinomas (adenoacanthomas) of the uterine cervix. Cancer 9: 971–979

117. Fujiwara H, Mitchell M F, Arseneau J et al. 1995 Clear cell adenosquamous carcinoma of the cervix. An aggressive tumor associated with human papillomavirus-18. Cancer 76: 1591–1600

118. Baggish M S, Woodruff J D 1966 Adenoid-basal carcinoma of the cervix. Obstet Gynecol 28: 213–218

119. Cviko A, Briem B, Granter S R et al. 2000 Adenoid basal carcinomas of the cervix: a unique morphological evolution with cell cycle correlates. Hum Pathol 31: 740–744

120. Grayson W, Taylor L F, Cooper K 1999 Adenoid cystic and adenoid basal carcinoma of the uterine cervix: comparative morphologic, mucin, and immunohistochemical profile of two rare neoplasms of putative 'reserve cell' origin. Am J Surg Pathol 23: 448–458

121. Brainard J A, Hart W R 1998 Adenoid basal epitheliomas of the uterine cervix: a reevaluation of distinctive cervical basaloid lesions currently classified as adenoid basal carcinoma and adenoid basal hyperplasia. Am J Surg Pathol 22: 965–975

122. Grayson W, Taylor L F, Cooper K 1997 Adenoid basal carcinoma of the uterine cervix: detection of integrated human papillomavirus in a rare tumor of putative "reserve cell" origin. Int J Gynecol Pathol 16: 307–312

123. Jones M W, Kounelis S, Papadaki H et al. 1997 The origin and molecular characterization of adenoid basal carcinoma of the uterine cervix. Int J Gynecol Pathol 16: 301–306

124. Ferry J A, Scully R E 1988 "Adenoid cystic" carcinoma and adenoid basal carcinoma of the uterine cervix. A study of 28 cases. Am J Surg Pathol 12: 134–144

125. van Dinh T, Woodruff J D 1985 Adenoid cystic and adenoid basal carcinomas of the cervix. Obstet Gynecol 65: 705–709

126. Daroca P J Jr, Dhurandhar H N 1980 Basaloid carcinoma of uterine cervix. Am J Surg Pathol 4: 235–239

127. Grayson W, Cooper K 2000 Adenoid basal epithelioma versus adenoid basal carcinoma. Am J Surg Pathol 24: 313–314

128. Grayson W, Cooper K 2002 A reappraisal of "basaloid carcinoma" of the cervix, and the differential diagnosis of basaloid cervical neoplasms. Adv Anat Pathol 9: 290–300

129. Albores-Saavedra J, Manivel C, Mora A et al. 1992 The solid variant of adenoid cystic carcinoma of the cervix. Int J Gynecol Pathol 11: 2–10

130. Albores-Saavedra J, Gersell D, Gilks CB et al. 1997 Terminology of endocrine tumors of the uterine cervix: results of a workshop sponsored by the College of American Pathologists and the National Cancer Institute. Arch Pathol Lab Med 121: 34–39

131. Stoler M H, Mills S E, Gersell D J et al. 1991 Small-cell neuroendocrine carcinoma of the cervix. A human papillomavirus type 18-associated cancer. Am J Surg Pathol 15: 28–32

132. Wistuba I I, Thomas B, Behrens C et al. 1999 Molecular abnormalities associated with endocrine tumors of the uterine cervix. Gynecol Oncol 72: 3–9

133. Delaloge S, Pautier P, Kerbrat P et al. 2000 Neuroendocrine small cell carcinoma of the uterine cervix: what disease? What treatment? Report of ten cases and a review of the literature. Clin Oncol (R Coll Radiol) 12: 357–362

134. Weed J C Jr, Graff A T, Shoup B et al. 2003 Small cell undifferentiated (neuroendocrine) carcinoma of the uterine cervix. J Am Coll Surg 197: 44–51

135. Boruta D M, Schorge J O, Duska L A et al. 2001 Multimodality therapy in early-stage neuroendocrine carcinoma of the uterine cervix. Gynecol Oncol 81: 82–87

136. Walker A N, Mills S E, Taylor P T 1988 Cervical neuroendocrine carcinoma: a clinical and light microscopic study of 14 cases. Int J Gynecol Pathol 7: 64–74

137. Connor M G, Richter H, Moran C A et al. 2002 Small cell carinoma of the cervix: a clinicopathologic and immunohistochemical study of 23 cases. Ann Diagn Pathol 6: 345–348

138. Gilks C B, Young R H, Gersell D J et al. 1997 Large cell neuroendocrine carcinoma of the uterine cervix: a clinicopathologic study of 12 cases. Am J Surg Pathol 21: 905–914

139. Schmedding A, Zense M, Fuchs J et al. 1997 Benign papilloma of the cervix in childhood: immunohistochemical findings and review of the literature. Eur J Pediatr 156: 320–322

140. Smith Y R, Quint E H, Hinton E L 1998 Recurrent benign Müllerian papilloma of the cervix. J Pediatr Adolesc Gynecol 11: 29–31

141. Caroti S, Siliotti F 1988 Cervical polyps: a colpo-cyto-histological study. Clin Exp Obstet Gynecol 15: 108–115

142. Golan A, Ber A, Wolman I et al. 1994 Cervical polyp: evaluation of current treatment. Gynecol Obstet Invest 37: 56–58

143. Vilodre L C, Bertat R, Petters R et al. 1997 Cervical polyp as risk factor for hysteroscopically diagnosed endometrial polyps. Gynecol Obstet Invest 44: 191–195

144. Zaloudek C J, Norris H J 1981 Adenofibroma and adenosarcoma of the uterus: a clinicopathologic study of 35 cases. Cancer 48: 354–366

145. Gilks C B, Young R H, Clement P B et al. 1996 Adenomyomas of the uterine cervix of endocervical type: a report of ten cases of a benign cervical tumor that may be confused with adenoma malignum. Mod Pathol 9: 220–224

146. Verschraegen C F, Vasuratna A, Edwards C et al. 1998 Clinicopathologic analysis of Müllerian adenosarcoma: the M.D. Anderson Cancer Center experience. Oncol Rep 5: 939–944

147. Jones M W, Lefkowitz M 1995 Adenosarcoma of the uterine cervix: a clinicopathological study of 12 cases. Int J Gynecol Pathol 14: 223–229

148. Kerner H, Lichtig C 1993 Müllerian adenosarcoma presenting as cervical polyps: a report of seven cases and review of the literature. Obstet Gynecol 81: 655–659

149. Ramos P, Ruiz A, Carabias E et al. 2002 Müllerian adenosarcoma of the cervix with heterologous elements: report of a case and review of the literature. Gynecol Oncol 84: 161–166

150. Park H M, Park M H, Kim Y J et al. 2004 Müllerian adenosarcoma with sarcomatous overgrowth of the cervix presenting as cervical polyp: a case report and review of the literature. Int J Gynecol Cancer 14: 1024–1029

151. Clement P B, Zubovits J T, Young R H et al. 1998 Malignant Müllerian mixed tumors of the uterine cervix: a report of nine cases of a neoplasm with morphology often different from its counterpart in the corpus. Int J Gynecol Pathol 17: 211–222

152. Grayson W, Taylor L F, Cooper K 2001 Carcinosarcoma of the uterine cervix: a report of eight cases with immunohistochemical analysis and evaluation of human papillomavirus status. Am J Surg Pathol 25: 338–347

153. Manhoff D T, Schiffman R, Haupt H M 1995 Adenoid cystic carcinoma of the uterine cervix with malignant stroma. An unusual variant of carcinosarcoma? Am J Surg Pathol 19: 229–233

154. Yannacou N, Gerolymatos A, Parissi-Mathiou P et al. 2000 Carcinosarcoma of the uterine cervix composed of an adenoid cystic carcinoma and an homologous stromal sarcoma. A case report. Eur J Gynaecol Oncol 21: 292–294

155. Takeshima Y, Amatya V J, Nakayori F et al. 2002 Co-existent carcinosarcoma and adenoid basal carcinoma of the uterine cervix and correlation with human papillomavirus infection. Int J Gynecol Pathol 21: 186–190

156. Tiltman A J 1998 Leiomyomas of the uterine cervix: a study of frequency. Int J Gynecol Pathol 17: 231–234

157. Brand E, Berek J S, Nieberg R K et al. 1987 Rhabdomyosarcoma of the uterine cervix. Sarcoma botryoides. Cancer 60: 1552–1560

158. Daya D A, Scully R E 1988 Sarcoma botryoides of the uterine cervix in young women: a clinicopathological study of 13 cases. Gynecol Oncol 29: 290–304

159. Bernal K L, Fahmy L, Remmenga S et al. 2004 Embryonal rhabdomyosarcoma (sarcoma botryoides) of the cervix presenting as a cervical polyp treated with fertility-sparing surgery and adjuvant chemotherapy. Gynecol Oncol 95: 243–246

160. Miyamoto T, Shiozawa T, Nakamura T et al. 2004 Sarcoma botryoides of the uterine cervix in a 46-year-old woman: case report and literature review. Int J Gynecol Pathol 23: 78–82

161. Kasamatsu T, Shiromizu K, Takahashi M et al. 1998 Leiomyosarcoma of the uterine cervix. Gynecol Oncol 69: 169–171

162. Grayson W, Fourie J, Tiltman A J 1998 Xanthomatous leiomyosarcoma of the uterine cervix. Int J Gynecol Pathol 17: 89–90

163. Gotoh T, Kikuchi Y, Takano M et al. 2001 Epithelioid leiomyosarcoma of the uterine cervix. Gynecol Oncol 82: 400–405

164. Irvin W, Presley A, Andersen W et al. 2003 Leiomyosarcoma of the cervix. Gynecol Oncol 91: 636–642

165. Boardman C H, Webb M J, Jefferies J A 2000 Low-grade endometrial stromal sarcoma of the ectocervix after therapy for breast cancer. Gynecol Oncol 79: 120–123

166. Clement P B, Young R H, Scully R E 1990 Stromal endometriosis of the uterine cervix. A variant of endometriosis that may simulate a sarcoma. Am J Surg Pathol 14: 449–455

167. Nielsen G P, Oliva E, Young R H et al. 1995 Alveolar soft-part sarcoma of the female genital tract: a report of nine cases and review of the literature. Int J Gynecol Pathol 14: 283–292

168. Sahin A A, Silva E G, Ordonez N G 1989 Alveolar soft part sarcoma of the uterine cervix. Mod Pathol 2: 676–680

169. Keel S B, Clement P B, Prat J et al. 1998 Malignant schwannoma of the uterine cervix: a study of three cases. Int J Gynecol Pathol 17: 223–230

170. Cantuaria G, Angioli R, Nahmias J et al. 1999 Primary malignant melanoma of the uterine cervix: case report and review of the literature. Gynecol Oncol 75: 170–174

171. Furuya M, Shimizu M, Nishihara H et al. 2001 Clear cell variant of malignant melanoma of the uterine cervix: a case report and review of the literature. Gynecol Oncol 80: 409–412

172. Bittencourt A L, Britto J F, Fonseca L E Jr 1981 Wilms' tumor of the uterus: the first report of the literature. Cancer 47: 2496–2499

173. Bell D A, Shimm D S, Gang D L 1985 Wilms' tumor of the endocervix. Arch Pathol Lab Med 109: 371–373

174. Comerci J T Jr, Denehy T, Gregori C A et al. 1993 Wilms' tumor of the uterus. A case report. J Reprod Med 38: 829–832

175. Benatar B, Wright C, Freinkel A L et al. 1998 Primary extrarenal Wilms' tumor of the uterus presenting as a cervical polyp. Int J Gynecol Pathol 17: 277–280

176. Babin E A, Davis J R, Hatch K D et al. 2000 Wilms' tumor of the cervix: a case report and review of the literature. Gynecol Oncol 76: 107–111

177. Massarelli G, Bosincu L, Costanzi G et al. 1999 Uterine Wilms' tumor. Int J Gynecol Pathol 18: 402–403

178. Copeland L J, Sneige N, Ordonez N G et al. 1985 Endodermal sinus tumor of the vagina and cervix. Cancer 55: 2558–2565

179. Iwanaga S, Ishii H, Nagano H et al. 1990 Mature cystic teratoma of the uterine cervix. Asia Oceania J Obstet Gynaecol 16: 363–366

180. Lim S C, Kim Y S, Lee Y H et al. 2003 Mature teratoma of the uterine cervix with lymphoid hyperplasia. Pathol Int 53: 327–331

181. Khoor A, Fleming M V, Purcell C A et al. 1995 Mature teratoma of the uterine cervix with pulmonary differentiation. Arch Pathol Lab Med 119: 848–850

182. Vang R, Medeiros L J, Ha C S et al. 2000 Non-Hodgkin's lymphomas involving the uterus: a clinicopathologic analysis of 26 cases. Mod Pathol 13: 19–28

183. Friedman H D, Adelson M D, Elder R C et al. 1992 Granulocytic sarcoma of the uterine cervix – literature review of granulocytic sarcoma of the female genital tract. Gynecol Oncol 46: 128–137

184. Kapadia S B, Krause J R, Kanbour A I et al. 1978 Granulocytic sarcoma of the uterus. Cancer 41: 687–691

185. Seo I S, Hull M T, Pak H Y 1977 Granulocytic sarcoma of the cervix as a primary manifestation: case without overt leukemic features for 26 months. Cancer 40: 3030–3037

Vagina

Marisa R. Nucci

Introduction

The vast majority of precancerous and malignant disease affecting the vagina is of the squamous subtype (vaginal squamous intraepithelial neoplasia and invasive squamous cell carcinoma). Less commonly, glandular neoplasms, mixed epithelial-mesenchymal tumors, mesenchymal tumors, and melanocytic neoplasms may also occur. One exception among this list of rare tumors at this site is embryonal rhabdomyosarcoma, which represents the most common vaginal malignancy of childhood.

Epithelial tumors

Squamous neoplasia

The risk factors for the development of squamous neoplasia of the vagina parallel those for the cervix and include: (1) age at first sexual intercourse; (2) number of sexual partners; (3) conditions associated with immunosuppression; and (4) tobacco use.[1] Vaginal squamous neoplasia is also similarly highly associated with human papillomavirus (HPV) infection.[1,2] Comparable to the terminology used for HPV-related cervical squamous lesions, the term vaginal intraepithelial lesion (VAIL) comprises lesions classified as condyloma (low-grade VAIL; vaginal intraepithelial neoplasia (VAIN) I) and lesions classified as VAIN (high-grade VAIL; VAIN II and III).

Squamous intraepithelial neoplasia (vaginal intraepithelial lesion; vaginal intraepithelial neoplasia)

Clinical features

VAIN is much less common than its counterpart in the cervix, which may be related to the greater degree of susceptibility of the cervical transformation zone to HPV infection; however, similar to the cervix, the range of HPV types that can affect this area is greater than those that occur in the vulva.[2] Patients with VAIN most commonly present with an abnormal Papanicolaou smear in their fifth and sixth decades without associated clinical symptoms.[3–5] High-grade lesions tend to occur in an older age group, with a mean age 15 years older than that for low-grade lesions.[6,7] Clinical/colposcopic examination usually reveals multifocal involvement, manifest by white epithelium or white epithelium in association with spots (punctation), most commonly involving the upper third of the vagina.[3,5,7–11] Multicentric disease involving the cervix and/or vulva as well as the vagina is common.[3,10] Studies of the natural history of VAIN suggest a low risk of progression to invasion (particularly for low-grade lesions), with most lesions regressing and only a subset persisting.[5,10,12] Patients at greater risk for progression include those with high-grade, multifocal, and/or multicentric disease and those who are immunosuppressed.[1] Risk factors for initial development of the disease include HPV infection, immunosuppression, diethylstilbestrol (DES) exposure (although this is controversial), radiation therapy, and squamous neoplasia elsewhere in the female genital tract (cervix, vulva).[1,13–16] Management of patients with this disease depends on the patient's age and the morphology (low versus high grade) of the lesion. Young patients with low-grade lesions may be treated conservatively by observation alone as the majority of these lesions usually regress spontaneously; other options for both high- and low-grade lesions include topical treatments, laser ablation, or excision.

Pathologic features

Vaginal intraepithelial neoplasia I (low-grade vaginal intraepithelial lesion). The histologic appearance of low-grade VAILs parallels that of the cervix and includes exophytic and flat condyloma (VAIN I). Exophytic condyloma, which is highly associated with HPV types 6 and 11, is characterized histologically by a verrucopapillary growth pattern with blunt-shaped papillae, acanthosis, and superficial koilocytotic atypia manifest as nuclear hyperchromasia, nucleomegaly, binucleation, and irregular nuclear contours (Fig. 13F.1). Flat condyloma has a similar morphologic appearance but lacks the papillary architecture (Fig. 13F.2).

Vaginal intraepithelial neoplasia II–III (high-grade vaginal intraepithelial lesion). High-grade VAILs are characterized by

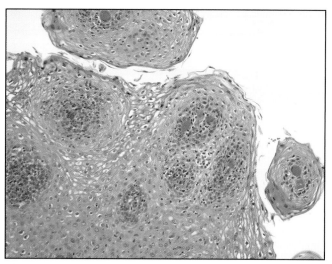

Fig. 13F.1 • Exophytic condyloma. Verrucopapillary growth and superficial koilocytotic atypia.

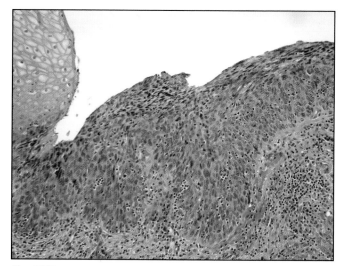

Fig. 13F.3 • Vaginal intraepithelial neoplasia III. Full-thickness nuclear atypia without surface maturation.

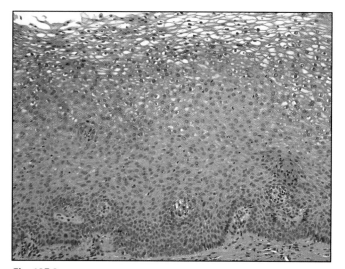

Fig. 13F.2 • Flat condyloma. Atypia is limited to the upper portions of the epithelium.

nuclear atypia in all levels of the epithelium, with a varying degree of surface maturation. Lesions that exhibit surface koilocytotic change and epithelial maturation correspond to VAIN II, whereas those with little to no maturation correspond to VAIN III (Fig. 13F.3).

Squamous cell carcinoma

In contrast to cervical and vulvar primaries, invasive squamous cell carcinoma of the vagina is uncommon. It represents approximately 2% of all tumors of the female genital tract and less than 0.2% of all new cancer cases diagnosed in 2005.[17,18] These figures may underestimate the actual frequency of primary vaginal squamous cell carcinoma, as tumors that involve both the cervix and the vagina are considered cervical primaries by convention.[17] Of note, invasive squamous cell carcinoma that occurs in the vagina within 5 years of a prior invasive cervical squamous cell carcinoma is considered a recurrence of the cervical primary. Risk factors for the development of vaginal invasive squamous cell carcinoma are similar to in-situ squamous neoplasia, and include HPV infection,

tobacco use, immunosuppression, and squamous neoplasia elsewhere in the female genital tract.[1]

Invasive squamous cell carcinoma of the vagina may occur over a wide age range; however, patients are typically postmenopausal, with a mean age at diagnosis in the seventh or eighth decade.[17,19,20] Symptoms at presentation may include vaginal bleeding, discharge, and/or symptoms related to a mass lesion. In advanced cases, involvement of adjacent structures may lead to urinary obstruction. Similar to in-situ squamous neoplasia, these tumors are most commonly located in the upper third of the vagina, and may have a varied clinical appearance, ranging from flat ulcerated lesions to exophytic, polypoid, or fungating masses. Histologically, the types and range of differentiation are similar to those seen in the cervix (see p. 702). Treatment usually consists of surgery and radiation therapy and survival is related to stage of disease, with a 5-year relative survival rate (based on the National Cancer Center Data Base) of 96% for stage I (confined to vagina), 73% for stage II (invasion of paravaginal tissues but not pelvic wall), and 36% for stage III (extension to pelvic wall) and IV (invasion of bladder or rectal mucosa and/or extends beyond pelvis) disease.[17]

Glandular neoplasia

Clear cell adenocarcinoma[13,21–27]

Clear cell adenocarcinoma of the vagina is a rare malignancy, which may occur sporadically or be associated with DES exposure *in utero*. Based on data from the Central Netherlands Registry, there appears to be a bimodal age distribution with two peaks, one at a young age (mean third decade) and one at an older age (mean eighth decade), occurring in patients with or without exposure to DES. In patients exposed to DES *in utero*, the risk of developing carcinoma is low (approximately 1:1000 women), with increased risk associated with exposure during early gestation and the frequency of exposure. Given the low risk associated with DES exposure, suggesting that other factors are involved in the development of clear cell carcinoma in this population, additional potential risk factors

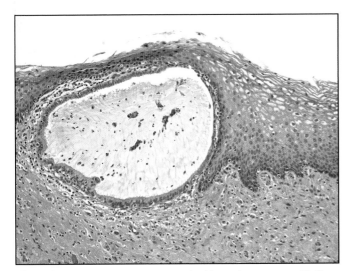

Fig. 13F.4 • Vaginal adenosis. Mucinous gland beneath squamous epithelium.

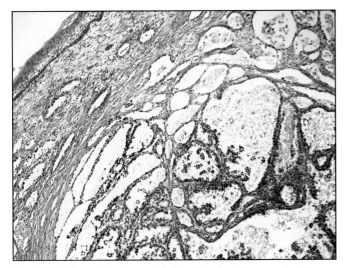

Fig. 13F.5 • Clear cell carcinoma. Tubulocystic and papillary growth pattern.

identified include a prior history of miscarriage and premature birth. DES exposure also commonly results in a number of non-malignant changes in the cervix and vagina, such as cervical ectropion/eversion and vaginal adenosis (Fig. 13F.4), the latter often seen in association with or adjacent to vaginal clear cell carcinoma.

Patients with vaginal clear cell carcinoma usually present with abnormal vaginal bleeding or dyspareunia and have a clinically evident nodular or polypoid mass; however, smaller tumors without associated clinical symptoms may be discovered in known DES-exposed patients undergoing routine clinical surveillance. Overall outcome for patients with clear cell carcinoma of the vagina and cervix is very good, with 5- and 10-year survival rates of 91 and 85% respectively. Stage at presentation is the best predictor of outcome, although a more favorable prognosis has also been linked to age >19 years at diagnosis and a predominant tubulocystic histologic pattern.

Histologically, these tumors are similar in appearance to clear cell carcinomas that occur elsewhere in the female genital tract, being composed of glycogen-rich tumor cells with hyperchromatic, irregularly shaped nuclei that are arranged in tubulocystic, solid, and/or papillary growth patterns (Fig. 13F.5). The

differential diagnosis includes two pseudoneoplastic lesions which may occasionally occur in vaginal adenosis: microglandular hyperplasia and the Arias–Stella reaction. Features that distinguish microglandular hyperplasia from clear cell carcinoma include: (1) only focal nuclear atypia; (2) presence of subnuclear vacuoles and intracytoplasmic mucin; (3) lack of glycogen; (4) lack of an infiltrative pattern; and (5) the presence of reserve cell hyperplasia/squamous metaplasia. Features that distinguish Arias–Stella reaction from clear cell carcinoma include: (1) no associated mass lesion; (2) its usual focal nature; and (3) the nuclei exhibit a spectrum of cytologic atypia.

Rare types of epithelial neoplasia

Endometrioid, mucinous, and intestinal-type adenocarcinoma

Metastatic upper genital tract or colorectal tumors involving the vagina represent the most likely source of adenocarcinoma at this site; however, there are rare examples of primary vaginal adenocarcinomas, which may show endometrioid, mucinous, or intestinal-type differentiation, or combinations of these morphologies.[28–35] Presumably these tumors arise from foci of endometriosis, endocervicosis, or an intestinal-type adenoma (Fig. 13F.6) and, in some instances, these latter lesions may be seen adjacent to or intimately admixed with the neoplastic component (Fig. 13F.7). The finding of endometriosis or endocervicosis in the vagina is not surprising; however, the presence of intestinal-type tissue is more puzzling, with possible etiologies including intestinal metaplasia, heterotopia, or cloacogenic remnants. The presence of these potential precursors favors a vaginal primary; however, exclusion of spread from another site should always be considered prior to diagnosing a primary vaginal adenocarcinoma.

Other rare epithelial malignancies

Rare examples of a variety of carcinomas have been described in the vagina, including adenosquamous carcinoma,[36,37] malignant mixed mesonephric tumor,[38] and small cell neuroendocrine carcinoma,[39] among others. Of these rare tumors, the most common is primary small cell neuroendocrine carcinoma of the vagina, which occurs in patients with a mean

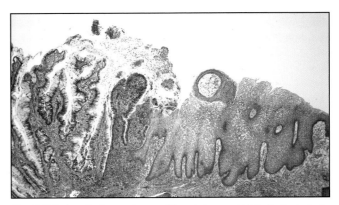

Fig. 13F.6 • Intestinal-type adenoma. These lesions are histologically similar to those that occur in the colon.

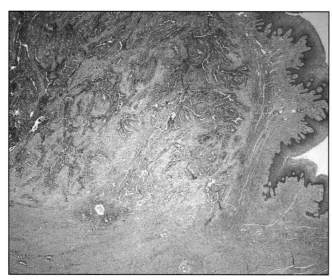

Fig. 13F.7 • Endometrioid adenocarcinoma. The tumor is arising in association with endometriosis located at periphery of main tumor mass.

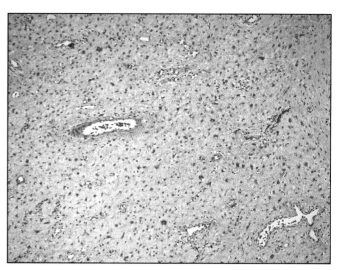

Fig. 13F.8 • Fibroepithelial stromal polyp. Pseudosarcomatous stromal changes with increased cellularity and enlarged atypical stromal cells.

age in the sixth decade, is usually <5 cm and is similar histologically to pulmonary small cell carcinoma.[39] Given the rarity of this tumor, the possibility of a metastasis from the lung should always be considered.

Mesenchymal neoplasia and tumor-like conditions

Fibroepithelial stromal polyp[40–51]

Fibroepithelial stromal polyps may occur at any age but are most frequent during the reproductive years and are rare before puberty. These lesions most commonly arise in the vagina but may also involve the vulva (see p. 739) and occasionally the cervix. Although usually solitary, multiple polyps may occur, a feature more commonly associated with pregnancy. These lesions may be sessile, polypoid, or filiform and may be of varying sizes but are usually <5 cm. Histologically, they are characteristically polypoid lesions covered by squamous epithelium with a central fibrovascular core. The stroma is the most distinctive and morphologically variable component, ranging from hypocellular to hypercellular and containing cells that range from bland spindle-shaped cells with indistinct cytoplasm to cells with markedly enlarged hyperchromatic nuclei and abundant eosinophilic cytoplasm[51] (Fig. 13F.8). These latter pseudosarcomatous changes, which most commonly occur in patients who are pregnant, have prompted the use of the term pseudosarcoma botryoides by some.[41,44] Stellate and multinucleate cells, which typically are located superficially, as well as the lack of any clear margin between the lesional stromal cells and the overlying epithelium, are also characteristic histologic features (Fig. 13F.9). The stromal cells are usually desmin, vimentin, estrogen receptor and progesterone receptor-positive; actin is less commonly positive. These lesions may rarely recur locally, particularly if incompletely excised or if there is continued hormonal stimulation (e.g., pregnancy/hormone replacement therapy).

The pathogenesis of these lesions is not clear, although they likely represent a reactive hyperplastic process, probably arising

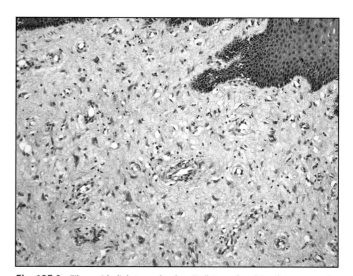

Fig. 13F.9 • Fibroepithelial stromal polyp. Stellate and multinucleate stromal cells are characteristically located near the epithelial–stromal interface.

from the distinctive subepithelial myxoid stroma of the distal female genital tract, rather than representing a neoplastic process. The expression of hormone receptors, their occurrence in pregnancy, during which they can be multiple and after which they can spontaneously regress, and their association with hormone replacement therapy in postmenopausal women support the notion that these are reactive lesions in which hormonal influences play a role in their pathogenesis.

The principal differential diagnostic considerations are aggressive angiomyxoma (for those polyps that are hypocellular and edematous), sarcoma (for those that exhibit pseudosarcomatous features), and embryonal rhabdomyosarcoma (more from a historical than practical viewpoint). Aggressive angiomyxoma is located more deeply, is more infiltrative, rarely polypoid, and exhibits a more prominent and regularly spaced vascular component than fibroepithelial stromal polyps. Pseudosarcomatous stromal polyps, unlike sarcoma, lack an identifiable lesional margin, with extension of atypical stromal cells to the stromal–epithelial interface, and often exhibit multinucleate cells near the stromal–epithelial interface, characteristic of this lesion. Unlike botryoid embryonal rhabdomyosarcoma, fibroepithelial stromal polyps are rare before puberty, lack the subepithelial hypercellular cambium layer, lack rhabdomyoblasts, and lack skeletal muscle-specific marker expression.

Leiomyoma[52]

Vaginal leiomyoma is a rare, usually submucosal, typically solitary lesion, which more commonly involves the lateral vaginal wall, although it may occur at any site. It occurs during the reproductive age range (similar to its uterine counterpart) and usually measures less than 5 cm. Although typically small and asymptomatic, larger tumors may cause abnormal vaginal bleeding, dyspareunia, pain, or dystocia. Histologically, vaginal leiomyoma is similar to its uterine counterpart, being well circumscribed, without evidence of infiltration and being composed of intersecting fascicles of bland, spindle-shaped cells with eosinophilic cytoplasm. Tumors that do not show evidence of infiltration or significant cytologic atypia and have a low mitotic index (<5 mitoses/10 high-power fields) are considered benign leiomyomata (see section on leiomyosarcoma, below, for criteria for malignancy).

Genital rhabdomyoma[53–55]

Genital rhabdomyoma is a benign tumor showing well-formed skeletal muscle differentiation that most commonly occurs in the vagina; however, it may also arise in the vulva and occasionally the cervix. This tumor, which typically occurs in middle-aged women, is usually polypoid and symptoms are generally related to a mass lesion and include dyspareunia and bleeding. Histologically, it is characterized by a submucosal, somewhat fascicular proliferation of spindle- or strap-shaped rhabdomyoblasts with abundant eosinophilic cytoplasm and easily identifiable cross-striations within the cytoplasm (Figs 13F.10 and 13F.11); mitotic activity is uncommon and nuclear pleomorphism is absent. Although usually not necessary diagnostically, tumor cells are positive for skeletal muscle markers. Genital rhabdomyoma is distinguished from embryonal rhabdomyosarcoma, its chief differential diagnostic consideration, by its lack of nuclear atypia/hyperchromasia, lack of significant mitotic activity, and lack of a cambium layer; in addition, genital rhabdomyoma occurs in an older age population.

Postoperative spindle cell nodule[56–58] (pseudosarcomatous myofibroblastic proliferation)

Postoperative spindle cell nodule was first described in the genitourinary tract, particularly the bladder, but may occasionally occur in the female genital tract, including the vagina. Although originally described to occur following surgical instrumentation (hence the term), these lesions may arise in the absence of surgery or any other history of trauma. They typically form a polypoid mass or nodule, characterized histologically by intersecting fascicles of plump spindle cells with round to oval nuclei and bipolar palely eosinophilic cyto-

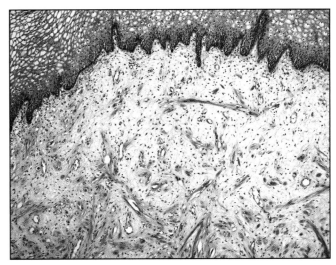

Fig. 13F.10 • Genital rhabdomyoma. Submucosal proliferation of strap-shaped cells with abundant eosinophilic cytoplasm.

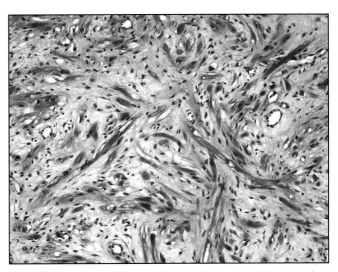

Fig. 13F.11 • Genital rhabdomyoma. Tumor cells are arranged in a somewhat fascicular pattern.

plasmic processes. These myofibroblastic cells may be immunopositive for actin, desmin, and/or cytokeratin. Interspersed chronic inflammatory cells, extravasated red blood cells and hemosiderin deposition may be present. The principal differential diagnostic consideration is exclusion of sarcoma, which postoperative spindle cell nodule may mimic due to the common presence in the latter of numerous mitoses and its relatively poor circumscription. Lack of significant nuclear atypia, nuclear hyperchromasia, the presence of stromal inflammation and, if known, the association with a prior procedure helps in this distinction. These lesions are benign and typically do not recur even after incomplete excision.

Angiomyofibroblastoma

Angiomyofibroblastoma is a benign, non-recurring, mesenchymal neoplasm that may occur in the vagina but more commonly occurs in the vulva of reproductive-aged women (see p. 740).

Deep (aggressive) angiomyxoma

Deep angiomyxoma is a non-metastasizing, locally infiltrative neoplasm that commonly involves the perineum and/or pelvic soft tissue of women with a median age in the fourth decade (see p. 742).

Embryonal rhabdomyosarcoma[17,59,60]

Rhabdomyosarcoma (see also Ch. 24) is the most common mesenchymal malignancy of childhood, of which embryonal rhabdomyosarcoma represents the most common histologic subtype. When embryonal rhabdomyosarcoma involves mucosal sites, as it does in the vagina, it tends to grow in a characteristic exophytic, grape-like configuration, garnering the term sarcoma botryoides; therefore, in essence, sarcoma botryoides simply represents a macroscopically distinct subset of embryonal rhabdomyosarcoma with a characteristic clinical appearance, presumably due to unrestricted growth into a cavitary space. The vast majority of children with vaginal embryonal rhabdomyosarcoma are less than 5 years old and most present with vaginal bleeding; in some patients, the first indication may be tumor prolapsing through the vaginal opening. Clinically, soft, friable, and edematous polypoid projections are present and may fill the vagina.

Histologically, embryonal rhabdomyosarcoma is a polypoid proliferation composed of round, spindled, or strap-shaped cells, some of which have brightly eosinophilic cytoplasm, within a loose myxoid stroma beneath squamous epithelium (Fig. 13F.12); cytoplasmic cross-striations may be apparent on hematoxylin and eosin examination. A characteristic, but not invariably present, histologic feature of the botryoides subtype is the condensation of neoplastic cells, which appear relatively undifferentiated, beneath the mucosal surface (so-called cambium layer; Fig. 13F.13). Tumor cells are typically positive for markers of skeletal muscle differentiation, including MyoD1 and myogenin (myf 4), which are antibodies directed against skeletal muscle-specific nuclear transcription factors. Outcome for patients with embryonal rhabdomyosarcoma in this

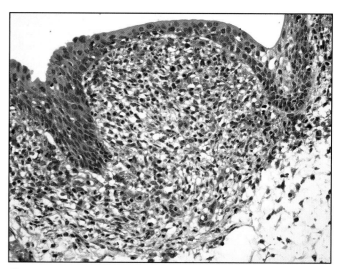

Fig. 13F.13 • Embryonal rhabdomyosarcoma. Condensation of neoplastic cells underneath the surface epithelium, forming the so-called cambium layer.

location, particularly the botryoid subtype, is excellent, with a greater than 90% 10-year survival rate. Treatment usually consists of surgery and chemotherapy, of which the latter may cause dramatic differentiation and maturation of tumor cells. The differential diagnosis includes: (1) fibroepithelial stromal polyp, which, in contrast to embryonal rhabdomyosarcoma, rarely occurs before puberty, lacks a cambium layer, and is negative for specific markers of skeletal muscle differentiation; (2) genital rhabdomyoma, which occurs in adults and lacks nuclear atypia/hyperchromasia, significant mitotic activity, and a cambium layer; and (3) müllerian papilloma (see below), which may be exophytic and polypoid, but lacks the characteristic histologic features of embryonal rhabdomyosarcoma, as described above.

Leiomyosarcoma[17,52,61]

Although leiomyosarcoma of the vagina is rare, with fewer than 100 cases reported in the literature, it represents the most common vaginal sarcoma to affect adults. Vaginal leiomyosarcoma can occur over a wide age range, from the third to the ninth decades, with most patients being over 40 years of age. These tumors most commonly involve the posterior or lateral wall of the vagina and typically present with vaginal bleeding/discharge or symptoms related to a mass. Because this tumor is uncommon, criteria for malignancy are difficult to establish and validate; nevertheless, tumors that are greater than 3 cm, have significant cytologic atypia, and have greater than 5 mitoses per 10 high-power fields should be considered malignant; coagulative tumor cell necrosis and infiltrative margins are also associated with malignant behavior (Fig. 13F.14). Treatment is primarily surgical excision and prognosis is related to stage, with an overall survival rate of approximately 43%.

Other rare sarcomas[62–64]

Endometrioid stromal sarcoma primary in the vagina may occur rarely and presumably arises in foci of endometriosis. Even in the presence of endometriosis, spread from a uterine

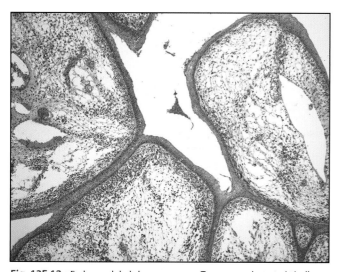

Fig. 13F.12 • Embryonal rhabdomyosarcoma. Tumors are characteristically polypoid and composed of round and spindled cells within a loose myxoid stroma beneath the surface epithelium.

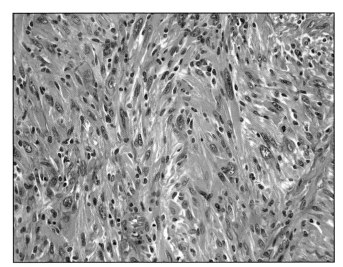

Fig. 13F.14 • Leiomyosarcoma. Diffuse cytologic atypia is one of the criteria for malignancy.

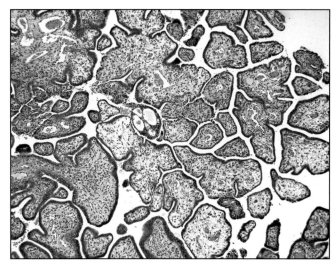

Fig. 13F.15 • Müllerian papilloma. Complex, arborizing papillary projections are characteristic.

primary should always be excluded. Rarely, Ewing's sarcoma, proximal-type epithelioid sarcoma, and epithelioid angiosarcoma may present as a vaginal primary; these tumors have the same histologic and immunophenotypic appearance as those that occur elsewhere (see Ch. 24).

Mixed epithelial-mesenchymal neoplasia

Müllerian papilloma[65–71]

Müllerian papilloma is a rare benign neoplasm that occurs in the vagina and cervix of children usually <5 years of age. Previously described in the literature as mesonephric papillomas, they are now considered to be of müllerian origin based on their morphology, immunophenotype, and ultrastructural features. These benign, predominantly mucosal-based, exophytic papillary growths most commonly present with vaginal bleeding and are characterized histologically by complex, arborizing papillary projections lined by bland-appearing, low columnar to cuboidal epithelium (Figs 13F.15 and 13F.16). Recurrences and rare examples of malignant transformation have been described.

Spindle cell epithelioma (benign mixed tumor)[72–74]

Spindle cell epithelioma is a benign tumor that most commonly occurs in the distal portion of the vagina near the hymenal ring as a well-circumscribed, painless submucosal mass that is usually less than 5 cm. The mean age at presentation is in the fourth decade and these lesions, which are usually discovered during routine gynecologic examination, are most commonly thought clinically to represent a cyst or polyp.

Histologically these tumors are well-circumscribed unencapsulated masses located near, but unconnected to, the epithelial surface and are composed of a proliferation of bland palely eosinophilic spindle-shaped cells that may be variably cellular, with paler hypocellular zones containing fibroblastic-type cells

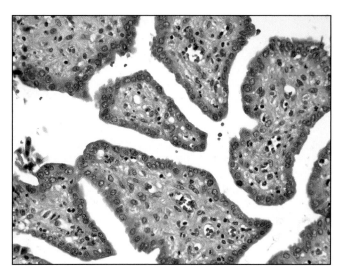

Fig. 13F.16 • Müllerian papilloma. The papillae are typically lined by cuboidal to low columnar epithelium with eosinophilic cytoplasm.

separating the more cellular areas into nests and interconnecting islands (Fig. 13F.17). Small foci of epithelial differentiation, most commonly in the form of nests and interlacing strands of squamous epithelium, which may have a vacuolated or glycogenated appearance, are usually present (Fig. 13F.18). Eosinophilic hyaline globules, which represent condensation of the stromal matrix, are characteristic (Fig. 13F.19). Immunohistochemically, the spindle cells are positive for keratin (Fig. 13F.20) and smooth muscle actin, and may be positive for CD10 and hormone receptors, but are negative for S-100 protein and glial fibrillary acidic protein. While the coexpression of keratin and smooth muscle actin suggested the possibility of myoepithelial differentiation and led to the former designation of these lesions as mixed tumors (terminology used to describe myoepithelial tumors at other sites), it is now evident based on immunohistochemical and ultrastructural evidence that these tumors do not show true myoepithelial differentiation and the term spindle cell epithelioma was introduced.[72] These lesions are benign and local excision appears curative; one case with

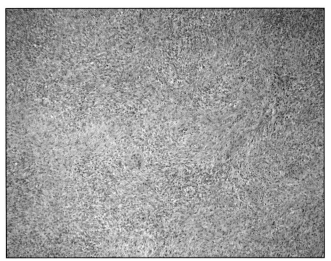

Fig. 13F.17 • Spindle cell epithelioma. Variably cellular spindle cell proliferation with paler hypocellular zones separating more cellular areas into vague nests.

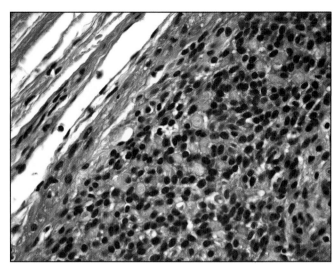

Fig. 13F.19 • Spindle cell epithelioma. Condensation of the extracellular matrix in the form of eosinophilic hyaline globules is characteristic.

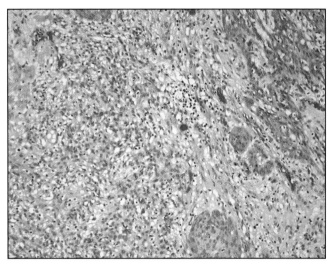

Fig. 13F.18 • Spindle cell epithelioma. Epithelial differentiation in the form of squamous epithelial nests and interlacing cords is usually present.

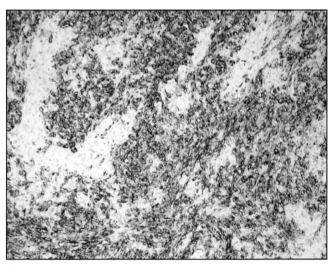

Fig. 13F.20 • Spindle cell epithelioma. The cellular spindle cell areas are diffusely positive for keratin.

recurrence has been documented 8 years after initial excision.[73] The differential diagnosis includes malignant mixed tumor of the vagina, which contains a malignant epithelial and stromal component and lacks the bland biphasic appearance of spindle cell epithelioma.

Adenosarcoma[75–77]

Extrauterine adenosarcoma most commonly involves the ovary or peritoneum; however, three examples of extrauterine adenosarcoma have been described in the vagina arising in the setting of endometriosis. The patients' ages were 42, 45, and 56 and all had a history of extensive endometriosis involving pelvic organs or soft tissue that predated the diagnosis of adenosarcoma by up to 5 years. The tumor sizes were large (6, 10, and 16 cm), with the largest tumor presenting as a prolapsing mass through the vaginal opening. Histologically, they were similar to adenosarcoma arising in the uterus (see p. 663).

Carcinosarcoma[78,79]

Primary carcinosarcoma (malignant mixed müllerian tumor) of the vagina is rare and spread from a uterine primary should always be considered prior to making this diagnosis. Similar to uterine carcinosarcoma, patients with vaginal primaries are typically postmenopausal, usually in their seventh decade, and the tumors show a similar range of histologic appearances (see p. 661). Although the number of cases is limited, overall prognosis appears to be poor, with most succumbing to disease within 2 years of diagnosis.

Melanocytic lesions

Blue nevus[80,81]

Blue nevus rarely involves the vagina as a blue-black macule or plaque that clinically may mimic malignant melanoma.

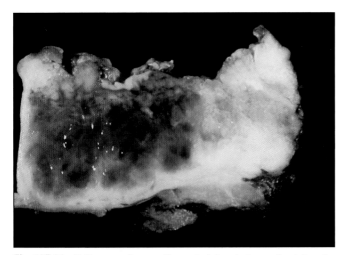

Fig. 13F.21 • Malignant melanoma. Pigmented ulcerated mass deeply invades vaginal wall.

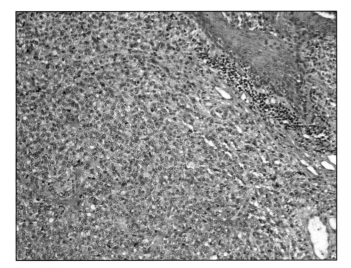

Fig. 13F.22 • Malignant melanoma. Sheets of epithelioid tumor cells with eosinophilic cytoplasm are characteristic.

Histologically, these lesions are similar to blue nevi occurring elsewhere, being composed of pigmented dendritic melanocytes within the submucosa (see Ch. 23).

Malignant melanoma[82–86]

Primary malignant melanoma of the vagina is extremely uncommon, representing fewer than 3% of malignant tumors that occur at this site. These tumors may occur over a wide age range; however, most patients are postmenopausal with a mean age in the seventh decade. Most patients present with vaginal bleeding or symptoms related to a mass. Clinical examination typically reveals a polypoid or nodular mass that may be pigmented or ulcerated and which more commonly involves the anterior or lateral vaginal wall (Fig. 13F.21). Tumors have a similar histologic appearance to melanoma elsewhere, having an epithelioid, spindled, or mixed morphologic appearance (Fig. 13F.22). Positivity for melanoma

markers (S-100, HMB-45, Mart-1, and Melan-A) aids in the distinction of this tumor from potential mimics, particularly the distinction of amelanotic or spindled melanoma from invasive squamous cell carcinoma or leiomyosarcoma. The prognosis for vaginal melanoma is uniformly poor, with a less than 20% overall 5-year survival; stage is the most important prognostic factor.

Lymphoid and hematopoietic tumors

Lymphoma

Extranodal non-Hodgkin's lymphoma most commonly involves the skin and gastrointestinal tract; however, it may occasionally be primary in the vagina. In the largest series studied,[87] patients' ages ranged from 26 to 66 years (mean 42 years), the most common presenting symptom was vaginal bleeding, and histologically all tumors were diffuse large B-cell lymphomas. Most patients were alive without evidence of disease at last follow-up (range 1.8–18 years).

Leukemia[88]

Granulocytic sarcoma rarely involves the female genital tract, where it may represent either the first clinical manifestation of the disease or relapse of acute myeloid leukemia. The ovary is the most common site of involvement; however, the vagina and, less commonly, the cervix may also be involved. These tumors have a similar histologic appearance to granulocytic sarcoma elsewhere (see Ch. 22) and are typically positive for chloroacetate esterase, lysozyme, myeloperoxidase, CD68, and CD43. The principal differential diagnostic consideration is the distinction from non-Hodgkin's lymphoma and poorly differentiated carcinoma, which can usually be established by immunohistochemical staining.

Other rare tumors

Endodermal sinus (yolk sac) tumor[89,90]

Endodermal sinus tumor of the vagina characteristically occurs in young infants and children under 5 years of age. Patients usually present with vaginal bleeding and clinical examination typically reveals a polypoid, friable mass that may mimic sarcoma botryoides. Histologically, these tumors are similar to those that occur more commonly in the ovary (see p. 605).

Metastatic tumors

The vagina is a frequent site of metastasis from both genital and non-genital primaries. Prior to the diagnosis of a primary epithelial malignancy, the possibility of spread from the cervix, uterus, and ovary should be considered. The most common site of origin of a metastasis from a non-genital primary was the colorectum based on a large series examining the frequency and patterns of metastasis to the female genital tract.[91]

References

1. Daling J R, Madeleine M M, Schwartz S M et al. 2002 A population-based study of squamous cell vaginal cancer: HPV and cofactors. Gynecol Oncol 84: 263–270
2. Sugase M, Matsukura T 1997 Distinct manifestations of human papillomaviruses in the vagina. Int J Cancer 72: 412–415
3. Lenehan P M, Meffe F, Lickrish G M 1986 Vaginal intraepithelial neoplasia: biologic aspects and management. Obstet Gynecol 68: 333–337
4. Mao C C, Chao K C, Lian Y C et al. 1990 Vaginal intraepithelial neoplasia: diagnosis and management. Zhonghua Yi Xue Za Zhi (Taipei) 46: 35–42
5. Aho M, Vesterinen E, Meyer B et al. 1991 Natural history of vaginal intraepithelial neoplasia. Cancer 68: 195–197
6. Audet-Lapointe P, Body G, Vauclair R et al. 1990 Vaginal intraepithelial neoplasia. Gynecol Oncol 36: 232–239
7. Diakomanolis E, Stefanidis K, Rodolakis A et al. 2002 Vaginal intraepithelial neoplasia: report of 102 cases. Eur J Gynaecol Oncol 23: 457–459
8. Petrilli E S, Townsend D E, Morrow C P et al. 1980 Vaginal intraepithelial neoplasia: biologic aspects and treatment with topical 5-fluorouracil and the carbon dioxide laser. Am J Obstet Gynecol 138: 321–328
9. Rome R M, England P G 2000 Management of vaginal intraepithelial neoplasia: a series of 132 cases with long-term follow-up. Int J Gynecol Cancer 10: 382–390
10. Dodge J A, Eltabbakh G H, Mount S L et al. 2001 Clinical features and risk of recurrence among patients with vaginal intraepithelial neoplasia. Gynecol Oncol 83: 363–369
11. Cardosi R J, Bomalaski J J, Hoffman M S 2001 Diagnosis and management of vulvar and vaginal intraepithelial neoplasia. Obstet Gynecol Clin North Am 28: 685–702
12. Sillman F H, Fruchter R G, Chen Y S et al. 1997 Vaginal intraepithelial neoplasia: risk factors for persistence, recurrence, and invasion and its management. Am J Obstet Gynecol 176: 93–99
13. Hatch E, Herbst A, Hoover R et al. 2000 Incidence of squamous neoplasia of the cervix and vagina in DES-exposed daughters. Ann Epidemiol 10: 467
14. Barzon L, Pizzighella S, Corti L et al. 2002 Vaginal dysplastic lesions in women with hysterectomy and receiving radiotherapy are linked to high-risk human papillomavirus. J Med Virol 67: 401–405
15. Fujimura M, Ostrow R S, Okagaki T 1991 Implication of human papillomavirus in postirradiation dysplasia. Cancer 68: 2181–2185
16. Robboy S J, Truslow G Y, Anton J et al. 1981 Role of hormones including diethylstilbestrol (DES) in the pathogenesis of cervical and vaginal intraepithelial neoplasia. Gynecol Oncol 12: S98–S110
17. Creasman W T, Phillips J L, Menck H R 1998 The National Cancer Data Base report on cancer of the vagina. Cancer 83: 1033–1040
18. Jemal A, Murray T, Ward E et al. 2005 Cancer statistics, 2005. CA Cancer J Clin 55: 10–30
19. Hellman K, Silfversward C, Nilsson B et al. 2004 Primary carcinoma of the vagina: factors influencing the age at diagnosis. The Radiumhemmet series 1956–96. Int J Gynecol Cancer 14: 491–501
20. Diakomanolis E, Rodolakis A, Stefanidis K et al. 2002 Primary invasive vaginal cancer. Report of 12 cases. Eur J Gynaecol Oncol 23: 573–574
21. Herbst A L, Ulfelder H, Poskanzer D C 1971 Adenocarcinoma of the vagina. Association of maternal stilbestrol therapy with tumor appearance in young women. N Engl J Med 284: 878–881
22. Herbst A L, Cole P, Colton T et al. 1977 Age-incidence and risk of diethylstilbestrol-related clear cell adenocarcinoma of the vagina and cervix. Am J Obstet Gynecol 128: 43–50
23. Herbst A L, Cole P, Norusis M J et al. 1979 Epidemiologic aspects and factors related to survival in 384 registry cases of clear cell adenocarcinoma of the vagina and cervix. Am J Obstet Gynecol 135: 876–886
24. Melnick S, Cole P, Anderson D et al. 1987 Rates and risks of diethylstilbestrol-related clear-cell adenocarcinoma of the vagina and cervix. An update. N Engl J Med 316: 514–516
25. Herbst A L 1981 The current status of the DES-exposed population. Obstet Gynecol Annu 10: 267–278
26. Herbst A L, Anderson D 1990 Clear cell adenocarcinoma of the vagina and cervix secondary to intrauterine exposure to diethylstilbestrol. Semin Surg Oncol 6: 343–346
27. Hanselaar A, van Loosbroek M, Schuurbiers O et al. 1997 Clear cell adenocarcinoma of the vagina and cervix. An update of the central Netherlands registry showing twin age incidence peaks. Cancer 79: 2229–2236
28. Kapp D S, Merino M, LiVolsi V 1982 Adenocarcinoma of the vagina arising in endometriosis: long-term survival following radiation therapy. Gynecol Oncol 14: 271–278
29. Haskel S, Chen S S, Spiegel G 1989 Vaginal endometrioid adenocarcinoma arising in vaginal endometriosis: a case report and literature review. Gynecol Oncol 34: 232–236
30. Mikami M, Nakamura M, Kurahashi T et al. 2003 A case of pT4 vaginal adenocarcinoma in which surgery prolonged disease-free interval. Arch Gynecol Obstet 268: 214–216
31. DeMars L R, Van Le L, Huang I et al. 1995 Primary non-clear-cell adenocarcinomas of the vagina in older DES-exposed women. Gynecol Oncol 58: 389–3192
32. Ebrahim S, Daponte A, Smith T H et al. 2001 Primary mucinous adenocarcinoma of the vagina. Gynecol Oncol 80: 89–92
33. Fox H, Wells M, Harris M et al. 1988 Enteric tumours of the lower female genital tract: a report of three cases. Histopathology 12: 167–176
34. Yaghsezian H, Palazzo J P, Finkel G C et al. 1992 Primary vaginal adenocarcinoma of the intestinal type associated with adenosis. Gynecol Oncol 45: 62–65
35. Mudhar H S, Smith J H, Tidy J 2001 Primary vaginal adenocarcinoma of intestinal type arising from an adenoma: case report and review of the literature. Int J Gynecol Pathol 20: 204–209
36. Rhatigan R M, Mojadidi Q 1973 Adenosquamous carcinomas of the vulva and vagina. Am J Clin Pathol 60: 208–217
37. Sulak P, Barnhill D, Heller P et al. 1988 Nonsquamous cancer of the vagina. Gynecol Oncol 29: 309–320
38. Bague S, Rodriguez I M, Prat J 2004 Malignant mesonephric tumors of the female genital tract: a clinicopathologic study of 9 cases. Am J Surg Pathol 28: 601–607
39. Bing Z, Levine L, Lucci J A et al. 2004 Primary small cell neuroendocrine carcinoma of the vagina: a clinicopathologic study. Arch Pathol Lab Med 128: 857–862
40. Norris H J, Taylor H B 1966 Polyps of the vagina. A benign lesion resembling sarcoma botryoides. Cancer 19: 227–232
41. Elliott G B, Reynolds H A, Fidler H K 1967 Pseudo-sarcoma botryoides of cervix and vagina in pregnancy. J Obstet Gynaecol Br Commonw 74: 728–733
42. Burt R L, Prichard R W, Kim B S 1976 Fibroepithelial polyp of the vagina. A report of five cases. Obstet Gynecol 47: 52S–54S
43. Chirayil S J, Tobon H 1981 Polyps of the vagina: a clinicopathologic study of 18 cases. Cancer 47: 2904–2907
44. O'Quinn A G, Edwards C L, Gallager H S 1982 Pseudosarcoma botryoides of the vagina in pregnancy. Gynecol Oncol 13: 237–241
45. Miettinen M, Wahlstrom T, Vesterinen E et al. 1983 Vaginal polyps with pseudosarcomatous features. A clinicopathologic study of seven cases. Cancer 51: 1148–1151
46. Maenpaa J, Soderstrom K O, Salmi T et al. 1988 Large atypical polyps of the vagina during pregnancy with concomitant human papilloma virus infection. Eur J Obstet Gynecol Reprod Biol 27: 65–69
47. Ostor A G, Fortune D W, Riley C B 1988 Fibroepithelial polyps with atypical stromal cells (pseudosarcoma botryoides) of vulva and vagina. A report of 13 cases. Int J Gynecol Pathol 7: 351–360
48. Hartmann C A, Sperling M, Stein H 1990 So-called fibroepithelial polyps of the vagina exhibiting an unusual but uniform antigen profile characterized by expression of desmin and steroid hormone receptors but no muscle-specific actin or macrophage markers. Am J Clin Pathol 93: 604–608
49. Mucitelli D R, Charles E Z, Kraus F T 1990 Vulvovaginal polyps. Histologic appearance, ultrastructure, immunocytochemical characteristics, and clinicopathologic correlations. Int J Gynecol Pathol 9: 20–40
50. Nucci M R, Fletcher C D 1998 Fibroepithelial stromal polyps of vulvovaginal tissue: From the banal to the bizarre. Pathol Case Rev 3: 151–157
51. Nucci M R, Young R H, Fletcher C D 2000 Cellular pseudosarcomatous fibroepithelial stromal polyps of the lower female genital tract: an underrecognized lesion often misdiagnosed as sarcoma. Am J Surg Pathol 24: 231–240
52. Tavassoli F A, Norris H J 1979 Smooth muscle tumors of the vagina. Obstet Gynecol 53: 689–693
53. Chabrel C M, Beilby J O 1980 Vaginal rhabdomyoma. Histopathology 4: 645–651
54. Hanski W, Hagel-Lewicka E, Daniszewski K 1991 Rhabdomyomas of female genital tract. Report on two cases. Zentralbl Pathol 137: 439–442
55. Iversen U M 1996 Two cases of benign vaginal rhabdomyoma. Case reports. APMIS 104: 575–578
56. Guillou L, Gloor E, De Grandi P et al. 1989 Post-operative pseudosarcoma of the vagina. A case report. Pathol Res Pract 185: 245–248
57. Proppe K H, Scully R E, Rosai J 1984 Postoperative spindle cell nodules of genitourinary tract resembling sarcomas. A report of eight cases. Am J Surg Pathol 8: 101–108
58. Young R H, Scully R E 1987 Pseudosarcomatous lesions of the urinary bladder, prostate gland, and urethra. A report of three cases and review of the literature. Arch Pathol Lab Med 111: 354–358
59. Leuschner I, Harms D, Mattke A et al. 2001 Rhabdomyosarcoma of the urinary bladder and vagina: a clinicopathologic study with emphasis on recurrent disease: a report from the Kiel pediatric tumor registry and the German CWS study. Am J Surg Pathol 25: 856–864
60. Andrassy R J, Hays D M, Raney R B et al. 1995 Conservative surgical management of vaginal and vulvar pediatric rhabdomyosarcoma: a report from the Intergroup Rhabdomyosarcoma Study III. J Pediatr Surg 30: 1034–1036
61. Ciaravino G, Kapp D S, Vela A M et al. 2000 Primary leiomyosarcoma of the vagina. A case report and literature review. Int J Gynecol Cancer 10: 340–347
62. Chang Y C, Wang T Y, Tzen C Y 2000 Endometrial stromal sarcoma of the vagina. Zhonghua Yi Xue Za Zhi (Taipei) 63: 714–719
63. Liao X, Xin X, Lu X 2004 Primary Ewing's sarcoma – primitive neuroectodermal tumor of the vagina. Gynecol Oncol 92: 684–688
64. McAdam J A, Stewart F, Reid R 1998 Vaginal epithelioid angiosarcoma. J Clin Pathol 51: 928–930
65. Ulbright T M, Alexander R W, Kraus F T 1981 Intramural papilloma of the vagina: evidence of Mullerian histogenesis. Cancer 48: 2260–2266

66. Luttges J E, Lubke M 1994 Recurrent benign Mullerian papilloma of the vagina. Immunohistological findings and histogenesis. Arch Gynecol Obstet 255: 157–160

67. Cohen M, Pedemonte L, Drut R 2001 Pigmented mullerian papilloma of the vagina. Histopathology 39: 541–543

68. Dobbs S P, Shaw P A, Brown L J et al. 1998 Borderline malignant change in recurrent mullerian papilloma of the vagina. J Clin Pathol 51: 875–877

69. Abu J, Nunns D, Ireland D et al. 2003 Malignant progression through borderline changes in recurrent Mullerian papilloma of the vagina. Histopathology 42: 510–511

70. Arbo E, dos Reis R, Uchoa D et al. 2004 Vaginal Mullerian papilloma in a 2-year-old child. Gynecol Obstet Invest 58: 55–56

71. McCluggage W G, Nirmala V, Radhakumari K 1999 Intramural mullerian papilloma of the vagina. Int J Gynecol Pathol 18: 94–95

72. Branton P A, Tavassoli F A 1993 Spindle cell epithelioma, the so-called mixed tumor of the vagina. A clinicopathologic, immunohistochemical, and ultrastructural analysis of 28 cases. Am J Surg Pathol 17: 509–515

73. Wright R G, Buntine D W, Forbes K L 1991 Recurrent benign mixed tumor of the vagina. Gynecol Oncol 40: 84–86

74. Murdoch F, Sharma R, Al Nafussi A 2003 Benign mixed tumor of the vagina: case report with expanded immunohistochemical profile. Int J Gynecol Cancer 13: 543–547

75. Judson P L, Temple A M, Fowler W C Jr et al. 2000 Vaginal adenosarcoma arising from endometriosis. Gynecol Oncol 76: 123–125

76. Anderson J, Behbakht K, De Geest K et al. 2001 Adenosarcoma in a patient with vaginal endometriosis. Obstet Gynecol 98: 964–966

77. Liu L, Davidson S, Singh M 2003 Mullerian adenosarcoma of vagina arising in persistent endometriosis: report of a case and review of the literature. Gynecol Oncol 90: 486–490

78. Neesham D, Kerdemelidis P, Scurry J 1998 Primary malignant mixed Mullerian tumor of the vagina. Gynecol Oncol 70: 303–307

79. Shibata R, Umezawa A, Takehara K et al. 2003 Primary carcinosarcoma of the vagina. Pathol Int 53: 106–110

80. Tobon H, Murphy A I 1977 Benign blue nevus of the vagina. Cancer 40: 3174–3176

81. Heim K, Hopfl R, Muller-Holzner E et al. 2000 Multiple blue nevi of the vagina. A case report. J Reprod Med 45: 42–44

82. Chung A F, Casey M J, Flannery J T et al. 1980 Malignant melanoma of the vagina – report of 19 cases. Obstet Gynecol 55: 720–727

83. Weinstock M A 1994 Malignant melanoma of the vulva and vagina in the United States: patterns of incidence and population-based estimates of survival. Am J Obstet Gynecol 171: 1225–1230

84. DeMatos P, Tyler D, Seigler H F 1998 Mucosal melanoma of the female genitalia: a clinicopathologic study of forty-three cases at Duke University Medical Center. Surgery 124: 38–48

85. Gupta D, Malpica A, Deavers M T et al. 2002 Vaginal melanoma: a clinicopathologic and immunohistochemical study of 26 cases. Am J Surg Pathol 26: 1450–1457

86. Ragnarsson-Olding B, Johansson H, Rutqvist L E et al. 1993 Malignant melanoma of the vulva and vagina. Trends in incidence, age distribution, and long-term survival among 245 consecutive cases in Sweden 1960–1984. Cancer 71: 1893–1897

87. Vang R, Medeiros L J, Silva E G et al. 2000 Non-Hodgkin's lymphoma involving the vagina: a clinicopathologic analysis of 14 patients. Am J Surg Pathol 24: 719–725

88. Oliva E, Ferry J A, Young R H et al. 1997 Granulocytic sarcoma of the female genital tract: a clinicopathologic study of 11 cases. Am J Surg Pathol 21: 1156–1165

89. Young R H, Scully R E 1984 Endodermal sinus tumor of the vagina: a report of nine cases and review of the literature. Gynecol Oncol 18: 380–392

90. Copeland L J, Sneige N, Ordonez N G et al. 1985 Endodermal sinus tumor of the vagina and cervix. Cancer 55: 2558–2565

91. Mazur M T, Hsueh S, Gersell D J 1984 Metastases to the female genital tract. Analysis of 325 cases. Cancer 53: 1978–1984

Vulva

Marisa R. Nucci

Introduction

Much the most frequent vulvar specimens that are submitted for pathologic review are biopsies, partial excisions, or radical resections for squamous neoplasia, which is the subject of the first section of this chapter. Glandular neoplasia, melanocytic neoplasms, and mesenchymal neoplasia, which are much less common, comprise the remainder.

Squamous neoplasia

Introduction

By far the most common types of pre-neoplastic and neoplastic tumors that occur in the vulva are of the squamous subtype. For many of these lesions, the primary etiologic agent is the human papillomavirus (HPV). In contrast to the cervix, only certain HPV subtypes (namely types 6, 11, and 16) predominate in their association with vulvar squamous neoplasia. However, not all types of squamous neoplasia are associated with HPV infection, as a subset of benign and malignant squamous lesions have other etiologies.

Benign neoplasms

Vestibular papilloma (synonyms: vestibular papillomatosis, micropapillomatosis labialis, physiologic papillomatosis)

Clinical features

Vestibular vaginal papillae are a common and normal finding around the introitus on external exam; however, in a patient with an abnormal Papanicolaou smear, their appearance may prompt a biopsy to exclude the possibility of an HPV-related lesion, most commonly condyloma acuminatum. These finger-like papillary projections are typically small (usually <5 mm), soft, and are often arranged in a linear distribution around the vaginal opening. Symptoms, if present, include pruritus or pain. Their etiology is not known; they do not appear to be associated with HPV infection.[1–3]

Pathologic features

Squamous papillomas are typically small, narrow-based, finger-like papillae that are covered by glistening mucosa. Histologically, there is a central fibrous core covered by stratified squamous, typically well-glycogenated epithelium, without evidence of acanthosis or viral cytopathic atypia (Fig. 13G.1). The principal differential diagnostic consideration is with condyloma acuminatum; however, the lack of acanthosis and cytologic atypia excludes that possibility.

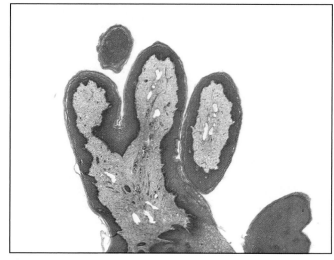

Fig. 13G.1 • Squamous papilloma. The stratified squamous epithelium does not exhibit acanthosis or viral cytopathic effect.

Seborrheic keratosis

Clinical features

Seborrheic keratosis is a benign epidermal proliferation that more commonly occurs in the trunk and head and neck region (see Ch. 23) but does occasionally involve vulvar skin. Most appear as a raised, well-demarcated lesion with a waxy appearance; pigmentation is not uncommon. HPV, particularly type 6, has been detected in genital seborrheic keratoses and may have a role in their pathogenesis at this site.[4-6]

Pathologic features

The morphology of these lesions is similar to those that occur outside the genital area (see Ch. 23). They typically are an exophytic proliferation of squamous epithelium, with acanthotic, hyperkeratotic, verrucous, or reticular subtypes of growth. Although viral cytopathic changes are not typically identified, genital seborrheic keratoses may exhibit hyperkeratosis, papillomatosis, and acanthosis, which are features shared with condyloma acuminatum. Given the frequent association of HPV with these genital lesions, in combination with their morphologic overlap, they appear to be a histologic variant of condyloma acuminatum or, at the very least, an alternative morphologic manifestation of vulvar HPV infection, which should be considered in the context of patient management.

Condyloma acuminatum

Clinical features

Condyloma acuminatum, being a lesion related to infection by HPV (most commonly types 6 and 11 in the vulva), typically occurs in an age range associated with sexual activity, although it can occasionally occur in prepubertal children, raising the possibility of sexual abuse.[7] The lesions may be solitary but more typically are multiple, sometimes forming larger, confluent masses. Widespread vulvar involvement, as well as an increased prevalence, is associated with immunosuppression.[8] Condylomata acuminata are grey/pink/tan papillary or verruciform proliferations that can involve the labial, perineal, and perianal skin or mucosa. Symptoms, if any, include local irritation and pruritus. Treatment options include local ablative therapy, excision, or systemic therapy (interferon). Recurrences are not uncommon, particularly in patients who are immuno-suppressed, diabetic, or pregnant;[9] spontaneous regression following pregnancy may occur.

Pathologic features

The papillary or verrucous excrescences of condyloma acuminata, evident on gross examination, correlate histologically to papillary fronds covered by squamous epithelium and containing fibrovascular cores. Acanthosis, hyperkeratosis, and parakeratosis are common; however, unlike cervical/vaginal condylomata, koilocytotic atypia may be subtle or only focal (Fig. 13G.2). Lack of koilocytotic atypia does not exclude the possibility of a condyloma, as lesions which exhibit acanthosis and papillomatosis but which lack clear histologic evidence of viral cytopathic changes are strongly associated with HPV types 6 and 11 (Table 13G.1).[7] In these situations diagnosis of a squamous papilloma, with a comment that these lesions are often associated with HPV, is recommended; molecular-based HPV testing may also be considered. Fibroepithelial polyps and flat squamous hyperplasias that lack koilocytotic atypia are not associated with HPV infection. Condylomata acuminata are distinguished histologically from high-grade vulvar intraepithelial neoplasia (VIN II–III) by the presence

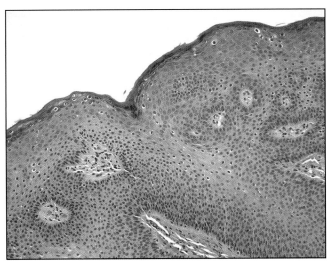

Fig. 13G.2 • Condyloma acuminatum. Koilocytotic atypia may be subtle.

Table 13G.1	Comparison of histologic features of squamous vulvar lesions			
	Papillomatosis	**Acanthosis**	**Koilocytosis**	**Basal atypia**
Fibroepithelial stromal polyp	+	–	–	–
Squamous papilloma	+	+	–	–
Condyloma acuminatum	+	+	+	–
Bowenoid papulosis (VIN II–III)	+	+	±	+
Differentiated VIN	–	±	–	+

VIN, vulvar intraepithelial neoplasia.

Table 13G.2 Differential diagnosis of human papillomavirus (HPV)-related squamous intraepithelial lesions		
	Condyloma acuminatum	High-grade VIN
Clinical appearance	Verrucopapillary	Variable (flat or papillary)
Nuclear features	Koilocytotic atypia Hyperchromasia Irregular contour	Koilocytotic atypia Hyperchromasia Irregular contour
Location of atypia	Mid to superficial	Basal to full-thickness
Associated features	Acanthosis Papillomatosis Parakeratosis	Abnormal maturation Atypical mitoses
HPV type	6, 11	16

VIN, vulvar intraepithelial neoplasia.

in the latter of full-thickness (or near-full-thickness) atypia, characterized by nuclear enlargement, irregular nuclear contour, and nuclear hyperchromasia; mitotic activity at all levels of the epithelial thickness as well as abnormal forms are present in VIN (Table 13G.2).

Premalignant neoplasia

Vulvar intraepithelial neoplasia

The diagnostic category of VIN refers to precancerous change of the squamous type; other terms that are synonymous (and more historical in their usage) include squamous dysplasia, Bowen's disease, and squamous cell carcinoma in situ. Bowenoid papulosis is a term used to describe a *clinical* scenario of raised pigmented lesions, usually occurring in young women, that often regress spontaneously; this term should not be used as a histopathologic diagnosis. There are two generally accepted and quite distinct pathways (with regard to clinical, morphologic, and viral-associated parameters) for the development of invasive squamous cell carcinoma of the vulva: (1) the HPV-related pathway associated with VIN of the classic type; and (2) the non-HPV related pathway associated with VIN of the differentiated (simplex) type, lichen sclerosus, and/or vulvar hyperplasia.

Vulvar intraepithelial neoplasia, classic type

Clinical features

The incidence of the classic type of VIN has increased in the past few decades, particularly in young reproductive-aged women.[10,11] This may be related to increased exposure to HPV, particularly high-risk types 16, 18, and 33, which is highly associated with this type of VIN. Other risk factors include cigarette smoking and human immunodeficiency virus (HIV) infection.[12,13] Patients with the classic type of VIN may complain of vulvar burning, itching, or soreness. Clinical appear-

ance is variable, with changes ranging from flat erythematous areas to deeply pigmented or white-appearing plaques, papules, or verrucous lesions; combinations of these appearances may also be present. Multifocal involvement of the vulva is common; approximately 30% of women will also have HPV-related disease of the cervix and/or vaginal mucosa.[14,15] Treatment options include laser ablation and, more commonly, wide local excision. As VIN can be multifocal with subclinically evident disease, recurrences are not uncommon. There is also an increased risk of recurrence with incomplete excision in HIV-positive patients and in those who smoke heavily. Margins of at least 1 cm are optimal; however, wide or negative margins may not always be achievable in order to maintain sexual function. Invasive squamous cell carcinoma is identified following histopathologic examination in up to 20% of cases in which only VIN was suspected clinically; in most cases the carcinoma is superficially invasive.[16,17]

Pathologic features

The gross appearance of VIN is identical to its clinical appearance, as described above. Histologically, it is characterized by full-thickness or near-full-thickness atypia. Typical findings include nuclear enlargement, nuclear hyperchromasia, apoptosis, and increased mitotic activity, with mitotic figures (including abnormal forms) being present in the upper portion of the epithelium (Fig. 13G.3). Varying degrees of maturation and koilocytotic atypia may be present; hyperkeratosis and atypical parakeratosis may be prominent, correlating to the white appearance visualized clinically. Similarly, pigmentation of the epithelium and melanin deposition in the stroma and within stromal macrophages may be pronounced, corresponding to clinically apparent pigmented areas. Extension into skin appendages, which is not uncommon, should not be misinterpreted as invasion.

Analogous to precursor lesions of the cervix, there are three grades of VIN: I, II, and III. VIN II and III correspond to high-grade precursor lesions, distinction between which for the most part is irrelevant, inasmuch as they should be managed

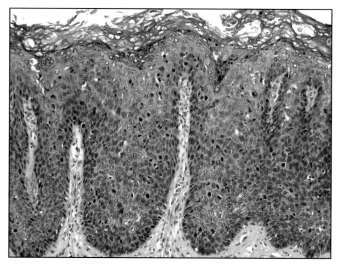

Fig. 13G.3 • Vulvar intraepithelial neoplasia, classic type. Nuclear enlargement, nuclear hyperchromasia, apoptosis, and mitotic activity are present in all levels of the epithelium.

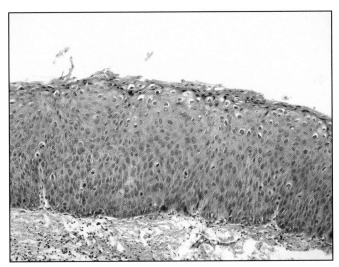

Fig. 13G.4 • Vulvar intraepithelial neoplasia II. Surface maturation with koilocytotic atypia.

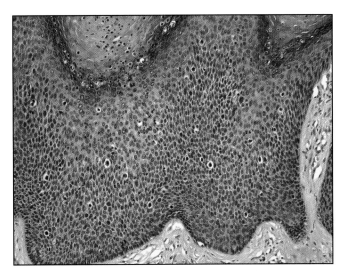

Fig. 13G.5 • Vulvar intraepithelial neoplasia III. Minimal surface maturation.

clinically in a similar fashion. In general, VIN II corresponds to lesions that show maturation, with surface keratinization and koilocytotic atypia (Fig. 13G.4); VIN III exhibits minimal maturation (Fig. 13G.5). Unlike its counterpart in the cervix, VIN I does not correspond to an exophytic or flat condyloma, and histologic changes akin to these low-grade precursor lesions should be termed condyloma (acuminatum). By definition, VIN I corresponds to atypia confined to the lower layers; however, a variety of non-neoplastic inflammatory disorders, as well as the differentiated variant of VIN (see below) may show atypia in the lower layers, and these changes may not necessarily correspond to a low-risk/low-grade lesion. For these reasons, use of the term VIN I is discouraged.

The differential diagnosis of VIN includes pigmented seborrheic keratoses, particularly those that are inflamed and show a modest degree of nuclear enlargement; nevertheless, these lesions lack the nuclear crowding, hyperchromasia, and atypia characteristic of VIN. Multinucleation associated with reactive changes (so-called multinucleated atypia of the vulva) may mimic VIN; however, the nuclei of the affected cells are not hyperchromatic or enlarged, and the surrounding epithelium appears normal.[18]

Vulvar intraepithelial neoplasia, differentiated (simplex) type

Clinical features

VIN of the differentiated (simplex) type occurs in a slightly older age population than the classic form of VIN. In addition, it is less commonly multifocal and has a lower risk of association with precancerous disease of the cervix/vagina, presumably because of its lack of association with HPV. Clinically, differentiated VIN does not have a distinctive appearance; it is often associated with lichen sclerosus or other vulvar inflammatory disorders and may only be appreciated on histologic examination. It is not uncommon for this variant of VIN to be first diagnosed adjacent to a clinically apparent invasive squamous cell carcinoma. For these reasons, it is very difficult to manage patients diagnosed with differentiated VIN

identified in a biopsy for another reason (mainly lichen sclerosus). In general, complete excision of the lesion with close clinical follow-up and a low-threshold for biopsy of clinically apparent lesions to exclude invasion is recommended.

Pathologic features

In differentiated VIN, unlike the classic type, the atypia is confined to the lower layers of the epithelium, and may be subtle (Fig. 13G.6). Typically there is acanthosis, abnormal keratinocyte maturation, and basal nuclear crowding, with nuclear hyperchromasia and paradoxically prominent nucleoli (the latter classically thought to be present in reactive lesions). Acantholysis may occasionally be prominent. Associated changes of lichen sclerosus, with homogenization of the dermal collagen and a band-like infiltrate of lymphocytes beneath this sclerotic zone, may also be present.

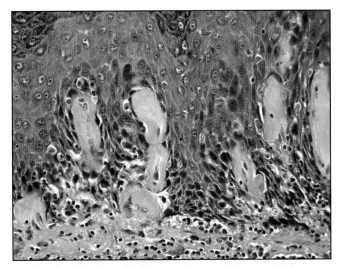

Fig. 13G.6 • Vulvar intraepithelial neoplasia, differentiated type. Nuclear atypia is confined to the basal portion of the epithelium.

Malignant squamous neoplasms

Squamous cell carcinoma

Invasive squamous cell carcinoma represents the most common malignant tumor of the vulva. Incidence rates vary from 1:100 000 to 20:100 000, with an increase in the rate as a function of age and a peak in the eighth decade.[11,19] Recent studies have identified two distinct pathways for the pathogenesis of vulvar squamous cell carcinoma: (1) carcinomas arising in association with HPV infection and VIN of the classic type; and (2) carcinomas arising in the absence of HPV infection and in association with either VIN of the differentiated type, lichen sclerosus (with or without squamous hyperplasia), or no appreciable premalignant lesion.[19] Carcinomas arising in association with classic VIN and HPV infection tend to occur in a relatively younger age group than women whose cancers arise as a result of non-viral factors; cigarette smoking is also a risk factor in this group.[20]

Clinical features

Invasive squamous cell carcinoma tends to present as a solitary tumor, which may be exophytic (nodular, verrucous, fungating), endophytic (ulcerated with raised firm borders), or a more subtle area of mucosal thickening. Symptoms include local discomfort, pain, itching, and burning, the latter two possibly related to superimposed infection, which is not uncommon. Staging is by FIGO classification and outcome is correlated with stage of disease; in a Gynecologic Oncology Group study, 5-year survivals of 98%, 85%, 74%, and 31% for stages I–IV disease respectively have been reported.[21] Surgery is the mainstay of treatment. Patients with greater than FIGO stage IA disease (carcinoma <2 cm in diameter with <1 mm stromal invasion) are treated by excision (wide local, partial/total vulvectomy) with inguinal lymph node sampling. For FIGO stage IA disease, wide local excision with 1 cm margins is adequate; lymph node dissection is not necessary. Radiation therapy is considered: (1) in patients considered to be a poor surgical risk; (2) as adjuvant therapy in patients with tumors that have a poor prognosis; and (3) in patients with recurrent or metastatic disease who are not surgical candidates;[22] radiation therapy may also play a role in preventing regional lymph node recurrences.[23] Risk factors for groin node metastasis include: (1) higher tumor grade; (2) clinically suspicious nodes (e.g., fixed, ulcerated); (3) presence of capillary lymphatic space invasion; (4) older patient age; and (5) greater depth of invasion; tumor size and location do not appear to be independent risk factors.[24] Factors for risk of tumor recurrence with regard to lymph node status include number of lymph nodes involved by metastatic disease and presence of extracapsular spread; HPV DNA status does not appear to be prognostically significant.[25]

Pathologic features

A number of morphologic subtypes of invasive squamous cell carcinoma have been described, including keratinizing, non-keratinizing, basaloid, warty, spindle, and verrucous. With the exception of verrucous carcinoma, which, when strictly defined, has little or no metastatic potential, morphologic subdivision of these cancers into keratinizing, non-keratinizing, basaloid, and warty subsets has no clinical implications. Keratinizing tumors have appreciable keratin pearl formation, whereas non-keratinizing carcinomas do not, although focal keratinization with dyskeratotic cells may be present (Fig. 13G.7). The basaloid and warty variants are the subtypes often associated with HPV infection (particularly type 16); basaloid tumors have a histologic appearance similar to VIN and are often referred to as the intraepithelial type of invasive squamous cell carcinoma (Fig. 13G.8), whereas the warty variant has surface koilocytotic atypia. Some invasive squamous cell carcinomas, particularly in older patients, may have prominent spindled tumor cells (Fig. 13G.9). Such an appearance often raises the possibility of sarcoma; however, a spindled squamous carcinoma is much more common at this site and (along with melanoma) should first be excluded prior to consideration of sarcoma. In addition, acantholytic lesions may mimic angiosarcoma. It is important to note that some spindle cell squamous cell carcinomas may be only focally positive for keratin and a wide panel of keratins may have to be employed;

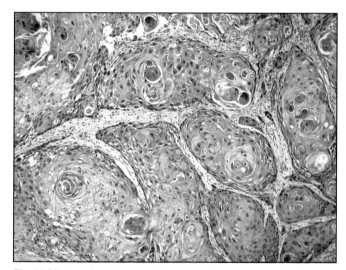

Fig. 13G.7 • Invasive squamous cell carcinoma, keratinizing type. Prominent keratin pearl formation and central whorls of keratinization.

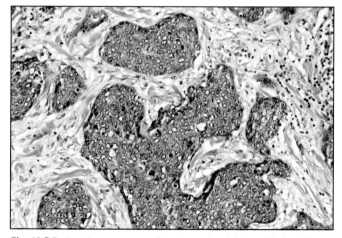

Fig. 13G.8 • Invasive squamous cell carcinoma, basaloid type. The invasive nests of tumor show minimal maturation.

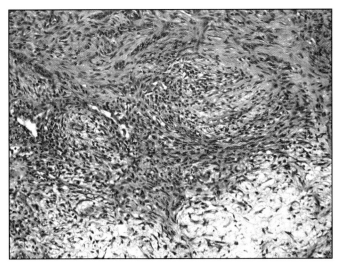

Fig. 13G.9 • Invasive squamous cell carcinoma, spindle cell type. Prominent spindling of tumor cells mimic a sarcoma. Note the presence of nests of tumor cells in the upper portion of the image, which belies the true nature of the tumor.

adjacent in-situ carcinoma may suggest (and help support) the diagnosis.

Verrucous carcinoma

Verrucous carcinoma is a rare variant of invasive squamous cell carcinoma that typically occurs in older women, usually in their ninth decade. It is characterized clinically by its excellent prognosis (with little or no metastatic potential) and histologically by its extremely well-differentiated appearance with minimal cytologic atypia (Fig. 13G.10) and a blunt invasive margin. The pathogenesis of verrucous carcinoma is unclear and, in some studies, does not appear to be associated with HPV infection.[26] In some cases, the adjacent vulvar mucosa may show varying degrees of acanthosis, verruciform architecture, loss of the granular cell layer, superficial epithelial cell pallor, and parakeratosis; these changes have been termed vulvar acanthosis with altered differentiation and they may be a precursor to (or risk factor for) this tumor.[26]

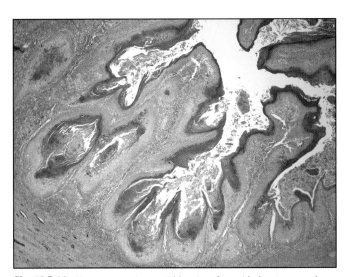

Fig. 13G.10 • Verrucous carcinoma. A blunt interface with the stroma and minimal to no cytologic atypia is characteristic.

Basal cell carcinoma

Basal cell carcinoma of the vulva[27–31] is an uncommon tumor, representing less than 2–5% of malignant tumors at this site. It occurs predominantly in postmenopausal women, with a peak incidence in the eighth decade. Symptoms most commonly include pruritus, soreness, and/or irritation and may be of varied duration, from months to years. The clinical appearance is variable, being that of a polypoid lesion, nodule, or plaque with or without ulceration; hyper- or hypopigmentation may also occur. Tumors are usually located on the labium majus and typically measure less than 2 cm, although larger tumors and multifocal disease can occur. Histologically, vulvar basal cell carcinoma is similar in appearance to basal cell carcinomas that occur in chronically sun-exposed skin. Vulvar basal cell carcinoma may be locally aggressive but only occasionally metastasizes; therefore, wide local excision without regional lymph node sampling is standard treatment unless there is a clinical suspicion of local nodal involvement.

Glandular neoplasia

Introduction

Glandular neoplasia of the vulva may arise from cutaneous adnexal structures, specialized anogenital mammary-type glands, major (Bartholin's) and minor vestibular glands, Skene's glands, or it may have an uncertain origin.

Benign neoplasms

Bartholin's gland adenoma (adenomyoma)

Bartholin's gland adenoma[32] is an extremely rare neoplasm that averages 2–3 cm in diameter, is solid, and often is believed to be a cyst on clinical examination. It is characterized by an irregular proliferation of ducts and acini lined by mucus-secreting epithelium that may be separated by myomatous stroma. The distinction between an adenoma and nodular hyperplasia is presumptively based on the retention of a normal duct-to-acinar relationship in the latter, although whether lesions classified as adenomas are truly neoplastic is controversial. Rarely, a salivary gland-like carcinoma may arise in association with an adenoma.[32,33]

Papillary hidradenoma

Clinical features

Papillary hidradenoma[34,35] is a benign adnexal (sweat gland) neoplasm that arises almost exclusively in the anogenital region of Caucasian women. It may occur over a wide age range, affecting both reproductive-aged and postmenopausal women. Papillary hidradenomas typically measure less than 3.0 cm and are solitary, dermal-based, dome-shaped nodules located on the labium majus; occasionally multiple tumors (usually <3) may occur. Symptoms, if present, may include pain or bleeding. Occasionally, patients notice fluctuations in lesional size associated with their menstrual cycle. Rarely, patients have an exophytic or ulcerating lesion that clinically mimics a malignancy.

Pathologic features

Papillary hidradenomas are well-circumscribed, dermal-based, solid or solid-and-cystic lesions, which have a histologic appearance similar to intraductal papillomas of the breast (Fig. 13G.11). They are non-encapsulated but often have a pseudocapsule, comprised of a surrounding rim of compressed stroma. The tumors contain varying combinations of a complex proliferation of glandular acini, tubules, papillae, and/or cysts. Two cell layers line these structures: an outer basal layer (akin to the myoepithelial layer in mammary intraductal papillomas) and an inner secretory cell layer, which exhibits features of apocrine differentiation, having granular eosinophilic cytoplasm with apical snouts and basally located, round nuclei.

Adenoma of minor vestibular glands

Minor vestibular gland adenoma[36,37] is a rare benign neoplasm that most commonly is an incidental finding in patients who have undergone minor vestibular adnexectomy for the treatment of persistent dyspareunia and/or pain (vulvar vestibulitis). Tumors are usually <2.0 cm and are comprised of a proliferation of glands and ducts lined by cuboidal to columnar cells containing apical mucinous cytoplasm.

Mixed tumor (pleomorphic adenoma, chondroid syringoma)

Salivary gland-type mixed tumors (pleomorphic adenomas),[38,39] which are believed to arise from Bartholin's glands, minor vestibular glands, or cutaneous sweat glands, rarely occur in the vulva. Soft tissue myoepitheliomas, which fall into the spectrum of mixed tumors, also may rarely involve the groin/inguinal area.[40] The most common presentation is that of a well-circumscribed, subcutaneous nodule. Histologic features

are similar to their salivary gland counterparts. Rare cases of malignant mixed tumor, and myoepithelial carcinoma, characterized by malignant cytomorphologic features, may occur. Nearly all mixed tumors and myoepitheliomas express keratin, and the majority also express S-100, calponin, and epithelial membrane antigen. Expression of glial fibrillary acidic protein, smooth muscle actin, p63, and desmin may also be present, but less consistently.[40]

Other benign skin appendage neoplasms

Syringoma is a benign tumor of eccrine sweat glands that has a predilection for the face, neck, and trunk but also may occur on the vulva, where it typically presents as multiple bilateral flesh-colored papules.[41–43] It may occur over a wide age range, with an average age at presentation in the third decade. Symptoms, if present, most commonly include pruritus. Histologically, vulvar syringomas appear identical to those that occur at more conventional sites (see Ch. 23).

Other skin appendage neoplasms, which may rarely involve the vulva, include trichilemmal (pilar) cysts, apocrine cystadenoma, trichoblastic fibroma, and trichoepithelioma.[44–48]

Malignant glandular neoplasms

Vulvar Paget's disease

Clinical features

Extramammary Paget's disease[49–55] is a rare neoplasm that may solely involve the epidermis (with or without associated dermal invasion) or be derived from spread of an underlying malignancy. The most common site of involvement is the vulva, but even at this site it is a rare neoplasm, representing less than 1–2% of all vulvar malignancies. Unlike Paget's disease of the breast, vulvar Paget's disease is not as commonly associated with an underlying malignancy, being related to a regional (most commonly skin appendage) carcinoma in the minority of cases (usually less than 10–15%).[49–55] This is in contrast to perianal Paget's disease (in which the neoplastic intraepidermal process mainly involves perianal mucosa) which is very often associated with an underlying rectal adenocarcinoma.[56] Invasive Paget's disease, in which tumor cells invade past the basement membrane into the dermis, occurs in approximately 15–20% of cases.[49–55] Patients with <1 mm of invasion appear to have an outcome similar to those with non-invasive Paget's disease,[49,50] although occasional cases have been associated with local nodal metastasis.[57,58] Patient's with >1 mm of invasion or who have an underlying carcinoma have a worse prognosis and greater risk for regional and distant metastasis.[49–51,54] There is an approximately 30% overall recurrence rate, the rate being highest with lesions that are incompletely excised.[49–52,54,55]

Vulvar Paget's disease typically occurs in the seventh decade, is more common in Caucasians, and most frequently presents as pruritus.[54] Clinical examination typically reveals a red, excoriated, irregularly surfaced and well-demarcated process that may be mistaken for an eczematous inflammatory lesion. Vulvar Paget's disease characteristically involves the labia, not uncommonly bilaterally, and may extend to involve

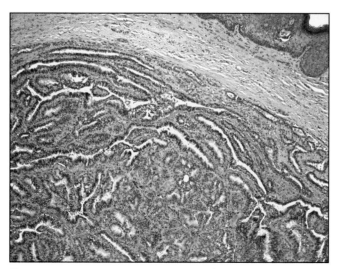

Fig. 13G.11 • Papillary hidradenoma. Complex proliferation of tubules and acini resembles intraductal papilloma of the breast.

the perianal region. The disease process can extend farther than the clinical appearance suggests; therefore, biopsy mapping of disease extent is often performed to help guide surgical management.

Pathologic features

Vulvar Paget's disease is characterized by an intraepidermal proliferation of large, epithelioid cells with abundant granular or vacuolated pale cytoplasm, and round nuclei with prominent nucleoli. The cells are present singly or in clusters within the epidermis, most often in the parabasal area but with some cells approaching the upper layers (Fig. 13G.12). The presence of single cells or clusters of cells beneath the basement membrane signifies invasion into the dermis (invasive Paget's disease). The immunoprofile of vulvar Paget's disease in comparison to other intraepithelial malignancies is summarized in Table 13G.3. Tumor cells are typically positive for intracytoplasmic mucin, cytokeratin 7, epithelial membrane antigen, carcinoembryonic antigen (CEA), and gross cystic disease fluid protein (GCDFP); rare cases may also coexpress cytokeratin 20.[49,50] The finding of a cytokeratin 7-negative, cytokeratin 20-positive, GCDFP-negative example of Paget's disease should strongly raise the possibility of spread from an

occult gastrointestinal (rectal) primary.[50,56] The principal differential diagnosis is with malignant melanoma in situ, which can readily be distinguished by its expression of melanoma markers (S-100, HMB45, MART-1) and its lack of positivity for keratins, CEA, and GCDFP.

Bartholin's gland carcinoma

Malignancy of Bartholin's gland (major vestibular gland) is uncommon, representing 2–7% of all vulvar malignancies.[59–62] Most examples occur as a painless vulvar mass in postmenopausal women in their sixth decade. Tumors are considered to be a primary Bartholin's gland neoplasm if: (1) transition from benign Bartholin's gland to the neoplastic process is identified; (2) a primary is not identified elsewhere; and (3) the histology of the tumor is consistent with origin from Bartholin's gland. A number of different types of carcinoma may arise from Bartholin's glands, the most common being squamous cell carcinoma, adenocarcinoma (mucinous, papillary, or colloid subtypes) and adenoid cystic carcinoma; adenosquamous carcinoma, transitional cell carcinoma, and small cell carcinoma may also occur rarely.[63–67]

Mammary-type adenocarcinoma

Mammary-type adenocarcinoma[68–77] is an extremely uncommon malignancy believed to arise from benign glandular tissue in the vulva that morphologically resembles mammary gland. Although originally considered "ectopic" breast tissue, these glands, which have features of eccrine and apocrine differentiation, may represent a mammary-like anogenital variant of cutaneous sweat glands.[78] These tumors typically arise in postmenopausal women in the sixth to eighth decades and usually measure <4.0 cm. Similar to primary breast carcinoma, they may show ductal, lobular, or apocrine differentiation on histologic examination. Associated in-situ carcinoma may occur; rarely, ductal carcinoma in situ without invasion may be seen.[79,80] Not surprisingly, tumors may be positive for estrogen receptor, progesterone receptor, and GCDFP.

Skene's gland adenocarcinoma

Skene's glands are located adjacent to the urethral meatus bilaterally and are comprised of mucinous glands that open into ducts lined by transitional epithelium. Based upon their

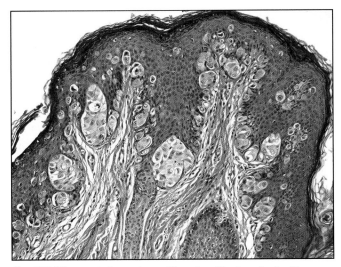

Fig. 13G.12 • Paget's disease. Intraepidermal proliferation of cells with abundant eosinophilic cytoplasm and round nuclei with prominent nucleoli.

Table 13G.3	Comparison of immunohistochemical findings in various types of Vulvar intraepithelial malignancy								
	CK7	CAM5.2	CK20	EMA	CEA	GCDFP	S-100	HMB45	Uroplakin
Paget's disease	+	+	– (rare +)	+	+	+	–	–	–
Melanoma in situ	–	–	–	–	–	–	+	+	–
Pagetoid squamous cell carcinoma	+	–	–	–	–	–	–	–	–
Pagetoid rectal adenocarcinoma	–	–	+	–	+	–	–	–	–
Pagetoid transitional cell carcinoma	±	+	±	+	+	–	–	–	+

EMA, epithelial membrane antigen; CEA, carcinoembryonic antigen; GCDFP, gross cystic disease fluid protein.

morphology and expression of prostate markers, these glands are thought to represent the female counterpart (or developmental homologue) of the male prostate gland. Rarely, adenocarcinomas originating from these glands may occur.[81-83] Histologically, these tumors share features with prostatic adenocarcinoma, with well-differentiated tumors being composed of small glandular structures composed of cells with uniform nuclei, prominent nucleoli, and moderate amounts of eosinophilic or granular cytoplasm. Similar to benign Skene's glands, tumor cells are positive for prostate-specific antigen.

Other rare types of adenocarcinoma

Villoglandular (cloacogenic) adenocarcinoma is an extremely rare, intestinal-type neoplasm that presumably arises from vulvar cloacogenic rests.[84-88] Very few cases have been reported, but tumors usually occur in women >40 years of age, measure <2.0 cm, and have a red nodular or polypoid appearance on clinical examination. Histologically, tumors may appear to be in direct continuity with the epidermis and appear morphologically similar to an enteric adenocarcinoma. Tubulovillous adenomas of the vulva are also extremely uncommon, from which invasive adenocarcinoma may also arise.[87,89,90]

Adenocarcinoma arising in association with endometriosis may rarely occur in the vulva; similar to malignant transformation of endometriosis elsewhere, most cases have endometrioid morphology but clear cell adenocarcinoma has also been reported to occur.[91-93]

Primary sweat gland carcinomas not associated with Paget's disease may very uncommonly be encountered in the vulva; these include eccrine adenocarcinoma, eccrine porocarcinoma, clear cell hidradenocarcinoma, and microcystic adnexal carcinoma.[94-96]

Melanocytic lesions and neoplasms

Lentigo

A variety of terms have been used to describe benign pigmented macules in the genital area, including vulvar melanosis and vulvar lentigo (genital lentiginosis). The former term applies to those pigmented lesions in the vulva that have increased basal pigmentation of keratinocytes without associated melanocytic hyperplasia. As very few pigmented macules of the vulva are not associated with at least some degree of melanocytic hyperplasia, the term lentigo is more often and more appropriately used. Vulvar lentigo is usually a solitary, uniformly homogeneous pigmented macule measuring <5 mm; however, sometimes genital lentigo may be clinically worrisome, exhibiting a more mottled appearance with irregular pigmentation and achieving a larger than usual size.[97] Vulvar lentigines may occur in association with the LAMB syndrome (mucocutaneous lentigenes, atrial myxoma, and blue nevi) or multiple lentigines syndrome (lentigines and hypertrophic cardiomyopathy).[98,99] Vulvar lentigo does not appear to represent a significant precursor lesion to melanoma in situ or malignant melanoma. Histologically, these lesions show varying degrees of acanthosis, melanocytic hyperplasia, and hyperpigmentation of the basal epithelium (Fig. 13G.13);

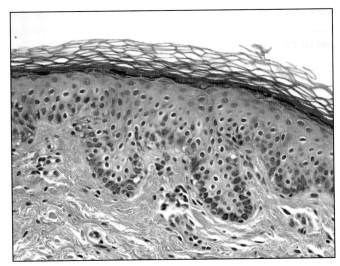

Fig. 13G.13 • Lentigo. Note the melanocytic hyperplasia and hyperpigmentation of the basal epithelium.

pigmentary incontinence may be a prominent feature. No melanocytic atypia should be present.

Genital-type nevi

The usual variants of melanocytic nevi, including acquired dermal, junctional, and compound nevi, dysplastic nevi, and blue nevi, may occur in the vulva. These subtypes of vulvar nevi are analogous to those seen at extragenital sites and are further discussed in Chapter 23. Genital-type nevi, however, do appear to have distinctive histopathologic features.[100,101] These nevi are also termed flexural nevi because they can occur at any site characterized by redundant skin. Genital-type nevi are often larger than usual-type nevi and exhibit a more irregular pigmentation pattern; however, they are usually symmetrical and well circumscribed. Histologically, they exhibit larger junctional nests with architectural variation, including variations in nest size, shape, and position as well as confluence (Fig. 13G.14). In addition, there is often an

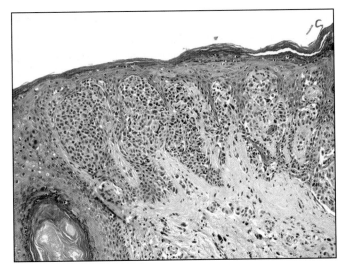

Fig. 13G.14 • Genital-type nevus. Note the large junctional nests with variation in nest size, shape, and position.

associated lentiginous melanocytic proliferation, as well as intraepidermal nests of melanocytes. Pagetoid spread is unusual and its presence should strongly raise concern for melanoma. Although nevus cells commonly exhibit cytologic atypia, usually it is only present in a subset of cells; diffuse cytologic atypia should also raise concern for melanoma. In cases with features raising the possibility of melanoma, the age of the patient should be considered, as vulvar melanoma is typically a tumor of elderly women. While genital-type nevi share some histologic overlap with dysplastic nevi, the latter tend to exhibit a more prominent lentiginous growth pattern and show greater elongation of the rete ridges. In addition, stromal fibrosis and an associated chronic inflammatory infiltrate are more commonly associated with dysplastic nevi.

Malignant melanoma[102–117]

Malignant melanoma uncommonly involves the vulva but is the second most frequent vulvar malignancy after squamous cell carcinoma. In contrast to extragenital melanoma, which has a peak incidence in patients around the fourth decade, vulvar melanoma typically occurs in older women, with most patients being in their sixth to eighth decades. Patients usually present with symptoms related to a mass; pain, bleeding, or pruritus are also common complaints. Tumors more commonly involve vulvar mucosa than skin and are usually deeply pigmented; however, amelanotic tumors are not uncommon, representing 30% of vulvar melanoma in one large series.[107] The pathogenesis of vulvar melanoma is poorly understood; sun exposure, genetic factors, and parity do not appear to play a role. Increasing tumor thickness is associated with a worse prognosis; however, overall prognosis for vulvar melanoma is generally poor, as most patients present with late-stage disease, in comparison to extragenital melanoma. Five-year survival rates of up to 54% have been reported;[105,108–110] in a large series of 219 patients, the rate was 47%.[107] Histologically, vulvar melanoma commonly has an appearance similar to acral lentiginous melanoma, followed by nodular melanoma and least commonly superficial spreading melanoma. A detailed histopathologic description of these types of melanoma may be found in Chapter 23. Microstaging is performed as for cutaneous melanoma; however, since the papillary and reticular dermis is not present in vulvar mucosa, Clark-level determination is not possible. It is our practice to report Breslow thickness only for mucosal melanomas. A modification of Clark levels, as described by Chung, may also be used.[114]

Mesenchymal neoplasia and tumor-like conditions

Reactive lesions

Fibroepithelial stromal polyp

Clinical features

Fibroepithelial stromal polyps[118–129] are hormonally responsive lesions that arise from cells residing in the distinctive subepithelial zone of the distal female genital tract. They occur in reproductive-aged women, generally developing during pregnancy, but may also be associated with hormonal replacement therapy.[119,124,125] These lesions vary in size (but are generally <5 cm), are typically polypoid or pedunculated, and are usually solitary, although pregnant women may develop multiple polyps.[122,124] Following pregnancy, the polyps will often regress, lending support to the notion that they represent benign reactive proliferations responding to an altered hormonal environment. These lesions have the potential to recur locally, particularly if incompletely excised or if there is continued hormonal stimulation (e.g., pregnancy), but this is relatively infrequent.[118,125,129]

Pathologic features

Fibroepithelial stromal polyps are polypoid lesions that are characterized by: (1) a central fibrovascular core; (2) a variably cellular stroma; (3) stellate and multinucleate stromal cells, most commonly present near the epithelial–stromal interface or adjacent to the prominent central vasculature; and (4) overlying squamous epithelium, which may exhibit varying degrees of hyperplasia. These lesions have no defined margin, extending right up to the mucosal–submucosal interface, consistent with hyperplastic expansion of submucosal tissue. A greater degree of stromal cellularity, nuclear pleomorphism, and mitotic activity may be seen in polyps occurring during pregnancy, which has led to the use of the term pseudosarcoma botryoides in the past. These worrisome histologic findings are not limited to pregnancy-associated polyps, and their presence may raise the possibility of malignancy;[129] however, even in the most florid examples, these lesions share morphologic overlap with their more banal-appearing counterparts, including: (1) lack of an identifiable lesional margin; (2) extension of atypical stromal cells to the stromal–epithelial interface; and (3) the frequent presence of multinucleate cells near the stromal–epithelial interface so common in usual polyps at this site (Fig. 13G.15). Similar to normal vulval mesenchyme, the stromal cells of these lesions may be positive for desmin,

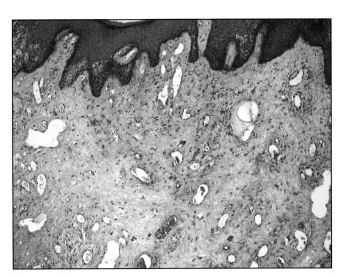

Fig. 13G.15 • Fibroepithelial stromal polyp. Stellate and multinucleate stromal cells are characteristically present near the stromal–epithelial interface.

actin, vimentin, estrogen receptor, and progesterone receptor. Although often discussed, these lesions are readily distinguished from sarcoma botryoides; fibroepithelial stromal polyps are rare before puberty, lack the subepithelial hypercellular cambium layer, lack rhabdomyoblasts, and lack skeletal muscle marker expression.

Nodular fasciitis

Nodular fasciitis is a reactive myofibroblastic proliferation that more typically involves the extremities; however, it may occur in a wide range of locations, including the vulva on rare occasions.[130–132] Awareness of its occurrence at this unusual site is essential in not misinterpreting this process as a malignant neoplasm. Vulvar nodular fasciitis is usually <3 cm in size and is identical histologically to cases that occur elsewhere (see Ch. 24), being comprised of a relatively well-circumscribed proliferation of loosely arranged spindle cells with bipolar cytoplasmic processes, often likened to tissue culture fibroblasts. Scattered inflammatory cells and extravasated erythrocytes are common; mitotic activity is commonly brisk.

Benign neoplasms

Angiomyofibroblastoma

Clinical features

Angiomyofibroblastoma[133–138] is a benign neoplasm that occurs almost exclusively in the vulvovaginal region of reproductive-aged women; similar tumors also occur more rarely in postmenopausal women and in the inguinal/scrotal region in men. Tumors are typically small (<5 cm), well circumscribed, and may be mistaken for a cyst on clinical examination. These tumors have no potential for recurrence; therefore, local excision with clear margins is adequate treatment. Exceptionally they have been said to undergo sarcomatous transformation.[139]

Pathologic features

Angiomyofibroblastoma is a well-demarcated neoplasm comprised of an admixture of numerous delicate thin-walled capillary-sized vessels and plump round to spindle shaped cells, which are typically clustered around the prominent vasculature (Fig. 13G.16). The stromal cells are set within a variably edematous to collagenous matrix with alternating zones of cellularity, and often appear somewhat epithelioid (except in postmenopausal patients, in whom they are more often spindled), having moderate amounts of eosinophilic cytoplasm and nuclei with fine chromatin and inconspicuous nucleoli. There are typically few mitoses. Occasionally intralesional adipose tissue may be present. The stromal cells are typically desmin-positive and show variable positivity for actin, although they are usually negative for this marker. The principal differential diagnostic consideration is aggressive angiomyxoma, from which it must be distinguished due to differences in biologic behavior (see below); however, they are quite distinct histologically. Aggressive angiomyxoma is uniformly less cellular, has an infiltrative margin, and tends to

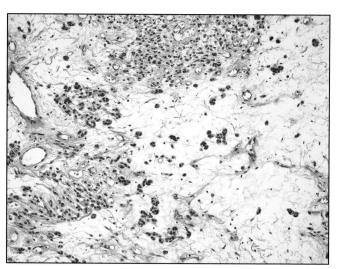

Fig. 13G.16 • Angiomyofibroblastoma. Note the numerous capillary-sized vessels and the alternating cellularity.

have larger, thicker-walled vessels. Table 13G.4 summarizes the clinical and histologic differences between the common vulvar mesenchymal lesions.

Cellular angiofibroma

Clinical features

Cellular angiofibroma[140–142] is a benign mesenchymal neoplasm, which most commonly occurs in the vulvovaginal region. Although initially thought to occur exclusively in women, it is now well documented that these tumors occur as commonly in the inguinoscrotal region of men, as well as occasionally in extragenital sites. In women, they average 2.7 cm, occur over a wide age range (mean 53.5 years), and most commonly present as a well-circumscribed, painless, subcutaneous mass.[142] If completely excised, recurrence seems very rare; a single report of a recurrent cellular angiofibroma most likely represents continued growth of residual tumor.[143] Local conservative excision with negative margins appears to be adequate treatment.

Pathologic features

Cellular angiofibroma typically has a firm, rubbery consistency and is gray/white in appearance. The majority of cases have a well-circumscribed margin histologically; however, a small subset may be poorly marginated and infiltrate surrounding normal tissue. It is a cellular neoplasm consisting of: (1) short, intersecting fascicles of bland spindle-shaped cells with short ovoid to fusiform nuclei and scant, pale-staining cytoplasm with ill-defined borders; (2) numerous small to medium-sized, thick-walled, and often hyalinized blood vessels; and (3) wispy collagen bundles (Fig. 13G.17). Many also contain intralesional adipose tissue. Mitoses are typically infrequent and significant nuclear pleomorphism absent, although degenerative nuclear atypia is an occasional feature. Hyalinized or edematous areas may contribute to variations in cellularity. Approximately 60% of cases will show positivity for CD34 in the stromal component; smooth muscle actin and desmin are

Table 13G.4	Common entities in the differential diagnosis of vulvar mesenchymal lesions				
	Aggressive angiomyxoma	**Angiomyofibroblastoma**	**Cellular angiofibroma**	**Fibroepithelial stromal polyp**	**Superficial angiomyxoma**
Age at presentation	Reproductive age	Reproductive age	Reproductive age	Reproductive age	Reproductive age
Location/ configuration	Deep-seated, not polypoid	Subcutaneous	Subcutaneous	Usually polypoid, exophytic	Superficial, subcutaneous, or polypoid
Size	Variable	Usually <5 cm	Usually <3 cm	Variable	Usually <3 cm
Margins	Infiltrative	Well circumscribed	Usually well circumscribed	Merges with normal	Lobulated, distinct
Cellularity	Paucicellular	Alternating hyper- and hypocellular	Cellular	Variable	Hypocellular
Vessels	Medium to large, thick-walled	Delicate, capillary-sized, numerous	Small to medium, thick-walled, often hyalinized	Variable, usually large, thick-walled, and located in central core	Delicate, thin-walled, elongated
Mitotic index	Rare	Usually uncommon	Variable, may be brisk	Variable	Usually uncommon
Biomarkers	Desmin-positive	Desmin-positive	Desmin-variable	Desmin-positive	Desmin-negative
Clinical course	30% local recurrence, may be destructive	Benign, no recurrent potential	Benign, recurrence very rare	Benign, rare recurrences (e.g., during pregnancy)	30% local non-destructive recurrence

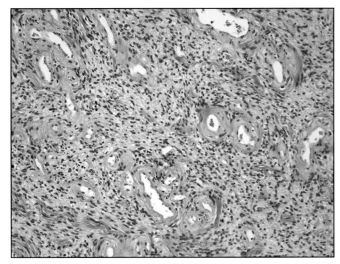

Fig. 13G.17 • Cellular angiofibroma. Short intersecting fascicles of bland spindle cells, wispy collagen bundles, and thick-walled vessels are characteristic.

less commonly positive, present in approximately 20% and 8% of cases respectively.[142]

Dermatofibroma (fibrous histiocytoma)

Dermatofibroma is a benign tumor of dermal stroma that most commonly occurs in adults on the limbs and trunk (see Ch. 23) but may also occasionally involve vulvar skin.[144] The clinical appearance varies, with most cases presenting as flesh-colored or pigmented plaques, nodules, or papules. Dimpling of the tumor by applying external pressure to either side of the

lesion is a characteristic clinical sign. The classic histologic appearance, which is most common in the vulva, is that of a relatively well circumscribed storiform proliferation of spindle or histiocytoid cells with entrapment of hyaline dermal collagen, which is birefringent under polarized light. Not uncommonly, the epithelium overlying the tumor exhibits hyperplasia. No further treatment or consideration of re-excision is usually necessary for tumors with this classic cytomorphologic appearance.

Granular cell tumor

Granular cell tumor (see Ch. 27) is an uncommon neoplasm that typically occurs in the head and neck area; however, approximately 5–15% of these tumors occur in the vulva, usually on the labium majus.[145–147] They are more frequent in black women, with a mean age at presentation of 50 years; rarely they may occur in children.[148,149] They typically present as a slowly growing, solitary, asymptomatic nodule, which is often discovered incidentally during routine examination. If present, pain, increased growth, and pruritus are the most common symptoms. Rarely, as elsewhere, multiple granular cell tumors of the vulva may occur.[150] Tumors rarely recur, even if incompletely excised;[145] however, complete excision is typically the usual treatment of choice. Malignant granular cell tumors are extremely rare, but have been reported in the vulva.[151]

Leiomyoma

Although genital smooth muscle tumors were originally considered within the category of superficial smooth muscle

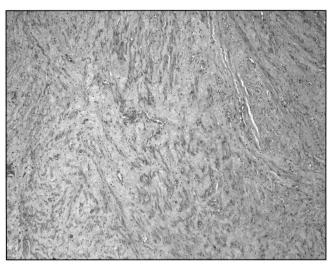

Fig. 13G.18 • Leiomyoma. Note the prominent myxohyaline change characteristic of smooth muscle tumors arising in the distal female genital tract.

tumors, it is now well established that smooth muscle tumors of the distal female genital tract differ from cutaneous (pilar) smooth muscle tumors and should not be considered or classified as such.[152] In comparison to uterine smooth muscle tumors, vulvar leiomyoma is distinctly uncommon. It occurs over a wide age range, but predominantly in the fourth and fifth decades, typically presenting as a painless, well-circumscribed subcutaneous mass that is usually <3 cm.[152–154] Similar to uterine leiomyoma, tumors may have a spindled (usual) appearance or (rarely) be epithelioid. Common to the vulva, the spindled smooth muscle cells may be separated by variable amounts of myxohyaline material, which imparts a lacy or plexiform appearance (Fig. 13G.18); occasionally, prominent mucin pooling may be present, masking the smooth muscle nature of the neoplasm.[154] Although a combination of size, circumscription, atypia, and mitotic count has been proposed to identify those smooth muscle tumors with malignant potential, currently established criteria probably underdiagnose smooth muscle tumors that have recurrent potential.[152–154] Based on personal experience, if a smooth muscle tumor at this site has any mitotic activity, nuclear pleomorphism, or evidence of an infiltrative margin, it has the potential for local recurrence, often decades after initial excision.[155]

Angiokeratoma

Angiokeratoma involving the vulva typically presents before the sixth decade as a papular, sometimes warty-appearing lesion that may be solitary or multiple, usually measures <1 cm and varies in color from red to purple.[156] Multiple lesions should raise the possibility of Fabry's disease, a rare X-linked chromosomal lipid disorder (deficiency of lysosomal alpha-galactosidase). Lesions are usually asymptomatic; symptoms, when present, may include bleeding, pain, or pruritus. Histologically, angiokeratoma is characterized by the presence of closely apposed dilated, blood-filled vascular spaces in the papillary dermis. The vascular spaces are typically partially surrounded by the overlying epithelium, which may exhibit acanthosis, hyperkeratosis, and sometimes papillomatosis.

Lymphangioma circumscriptum

Lymphangioma circumscriptum, a lesion of lymphatic channels that may be either congenital or acquired (secondary to lymphatic damage), more commonly affects the skin and subcutaneous tissue of the trunk, thigh, and buttock (see Ch. 3), but may also involve the vulva.[157] Numerous small vesicles filled with clear fluid are characteristic, and symptoms may include swelling, pain, and infection secondary to excoriation. Histologically, numerous dilated or cystic lymphatic channels are present, some of which are closely apposed to the overlying epithelium, resulting in the clinical impression of a vesicle.

Other rare neoplasms

Leiomyomatosis of the vulva is a rare condition characterized by ill-defined submucosal multinodular proliferations of smooth muscle. Patients with vulval leiomyomatosis can have synchronous or metachronous esophageal lesions (esophageal leiomyomatosis).[158] Possible pathogenetic mechanisms include altered hormonal responsiveness and familial factors, including an association with Alport's syndrome.[155,158]

Lipoblastoma-like tumor of the vulva is a rare mesenchymal tumor that is histologically similar to lipoblastomatosis (see Ch. 24) but which differs clinically, occurring in young women, as opposed to the trunk and extremities of young boys (<5 years old).[159]

Genital rhabdomyoma, a benign tumor composed of mature rhabdomyoblasts, more commonly occurs in the vagina (see p. 723).

A variety of other benign mesenchymal neoplasms, which more commonly occur in the skin and subcutaneous tissue outside the genital region, may also, on occasion, involve the vulva, but have no particular predilection for this site. They have similar clinical and histologic features to those that occur in more conventional locations. These include lipoma, neurofibroma, schwannoma, capillary hemangioma, and cavernous hemangioma. Rarely, neurofibromatosis involves the female genital tract and may present as clitoromegaly.[160,161]

Locally recurrent mesenchymal neoplasms

Deep (aggressive) angiomxyoma

Clinical features

Deep angiomyxoma is a locally infiltrative, non-metastasizing neoplasm that typically occurs in the pelvis and perineum of women, with a median age in the fourth decade, but it may also arise in the inguinoscrotal region of men.[162–167] Similar to other soft tissue neoplasms at this site, this tumor may be mistaken for a labial cyst, most commonly a Bartholin's gland cyst. Tumors can be of varying size, but are often relatively large (>10 cm) and may be disfiguring. Deep angiomyxoma has the propensity for local recurrence, which occurs in approximately 30% of cases, sometimes many years (often decades) after the initial excision. Destructive recurrence may occur, rarely, but it is nowadays appreciated that more than

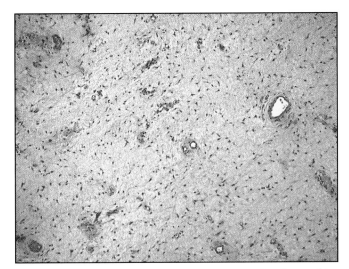

Fig. 13G.19 • Deep (aggressive) angiomyxoma. Bland spindle cells set within a myxoid matrix. Note the large thick-walled vessels.

one recurrence is very uncommon. Wide local excision with 1 cm margins is considered optimal.

Pathologic features

Aggressive angiomyxoma is characteristically a soft, gelatinous tumor with ill-defined margins. Histologically, it is a pauci-cellular neoplasm comprised of spindle-shaped cells with delicate cytoplasmic processes set within a copious myxoid stroma that is interspersed with medium to large-sized vessels that are often thick-walled and hyalinized (Fig. 13G.19). Loose fibrillary collagen and collections of smooth muscle cells (so-called myoid bundles) are typically arranged in either loose clusters or tight whorls adjacent to blood vessels. This tumor has deceptively infiltrative borders, which accounts for the difficulty, both surgically and pathologically, in defining its borders; this uncertainty regarding margin status is likely associated with its propensity to recur. The lesional stromal cells of aggressive angiomyxoma are often positive for desmin as well as actin, particularly in the myoid bundles. Cytogenetic analysis of a case of deep angiomyxoma revealed a t(8;12), and reverse transcriptase polymerase chain reaction confirmed aberrant expression of HMGA2, a DNA architectural factor important in transcriptional regulation, which is also aberrantly expressed in other tumors (e.g., uterine leiomyoma, lipoma) with similar translocations.[168] Although it is unclear how expression of HMGA2 results in tumor development, altered transcription of target genes is a possibility.

Superficial angiomyxoma

Clinical features

Superficial angiomyxoma only occasionally occurs in the genital area, being more common in the head and neck region and trunk (see Ch. 24); however, since it is a myxoid neoplasm that may be mistaken for aggressive angiomyxoma, a discussion is also included in this chapter. This tumor most commonly occurs in the fourth decade, and typically presents as a slowly growing, painless, polypoid tumor that usually measures <5 cm.[169–171] Although this association is less clear for super-

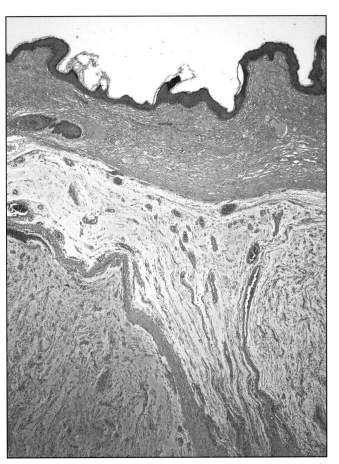

Fig. 13G.20 • Superficial angiomyxoma. Multinodular myxoid proliferation of bland spindle cells. Note the superficial dermal location.

ficial angiomyxomas occurring in the genital area, the presence of multiple cutaneous lesions elsewhere is highly associated with Carney's complex.[170]

Pathologic features

Histologically, this tumor is a well-demarcated (but unencapsulated), multilobulated, myxoid nodular proliferation that is superficially located in the dermis and subcutis (Fig. 13G.20). The myxoid nodules are composed of slender spindle and stellate-shaped cells, inflammatory cells (particularly polymorphonuclear leukocytes), and thin-walled vessels. An epithelial component, usually in the form of a squamous epithelial-lined cyst or basaloid epithelial nests and strands and likely derived from skin appendages, is present in about a third of cases. These tumors have the potential for local nondestructive recurrence in approximately 30% of cases; complete excision with clear margins should be performed. In contrast to aggressive angiomyxoma, superficial angiomyxoma typically involves the dermis and subcutis, lacks significantly infiltrative borders or thick-walled vessels, and has lesional stromal cells that are desmin-negative.

Dermatofibrosarcoma protuberans

Clinical features

Dermatofibrosarcoma protuberans is a fibroblastic tumor that only occasionally arises in the vulva,[172–181] being more commonly located on the trunk (see Ch. 23). Its clinical appearance can vary from a flesh-colored to variably pigmented plaque or nodules to an exophytic, multinodular growth. This tumor has a high propensity for local recurrence, therefore wide local excision is recommended. Metastasis in typical cases is extremely rare; however, those that show fibrosarcomatous change have a higher risk of metastasis (15% in one series).[181]

Pathologic features

Dermatofibrosarcoma protuberans is a poorly circumscribed, monomorphous storiform proliferation of spindle cells that typically infiltrates subcutaneous adipose tissue in a characteristic lacy or honeycomb pattern. Separation from the overlying normal-appearing or atrophic epidermis (Grenz zone), entrapment of adnexal structures, and lack of polarizable collagen are also characteristic. A subset of these tumors, including cases in the vulva, exhibit higher-grade fibrosarcomatous change, which is most often characterized by a herringbone pattern of growth in combination with increased cellularity and mitoses.[172,181] Dermatofibrosarcoma protuberans is typically diffusely positive for CD34 and negative for factor XIIIa.

These tumors generally harbor a translocation between chromosomes 17 and 22 (which often appears as a supernumerary ring chromosome) that results in the fusion of two genes, collagen type I alpha 1 (COL1A1) and platelet-derived growth factor B-chain (PDGFB).[182] Those that occur in the vulva may also contain COL1A1-PDGFB chimeric fusion transcripts.[173,174]

Dermatofibrosarcoma protuberans is distinguished from dermatofibroma by its tendency to infiltrate subcutaneous tissue in a characteristic lacy pattern, lack of overlying epidermal hyperplasia, lack of birefringent collagen when viewed under polarized light, tendency to infiltrate around and surround adnexal structures, which can often be found within the substance of the tumor, and typically diffuse positivity for CD34 and lack of positivity for factor XIIIa (although there can be overlap in staining for these markers in these two entities).

Malignant mesenchymal neoplasms

Leiomyosarcoma

Leiomyosarcoma is the most common vulvar sarcoma.[183–185] Patients are typically in their fourth or fifth decades and present with a mass that is usually >5 cm, although these tumors can be of varying size. Morphologically, these tumors are most commonly of the usual spindle cell type, although myxoid variants may also occur. Because of the relative infrequency of smooth muscle tumors at this site and the limited series of cases with long-term follow-up, reliable identification of those tumors with metastatic potential is difficult. Nevertheless, use of the criteria proposed by Tavassoli & Norris (which has been validated in other studies) is recommended.[152–154] Tumors with three or more of the following criteria should be classified as a sarcoma: (1) >5 cm in size; (2) infiltrative margins; (3) >5 mitoses/10 high-power fields; and (4) moderate to severe cytologic

atypia. Although necrosis is not listed as a criterion, its presence should strongly raise the possibility of sarcoma.

Rhabdomyosarcoma

In the distal female genital tract, rhabdomyosarcoma, particularly the sarcoma botryoides variant of embryonal rhabdomyosarcoma, more commonly occurs in the vagina (see p. 724). However, any subtype of rhabdomyosarcoma may also rarely involve the vulva.[186–188] Similar to, but not as commonly seen in comparison to its counterpart in the vagina, embryonal rhabdomyosarcoma may present as a polypoid, grape-like mass (sarcoma botryoides) with similar characteristic clinical and histopathologic features. Pure alveolar rhabdomyosarcoma may also occur, characterized histologically by a nested pattern of loosely cohesive cells, but mixtures of embryonal, alveolar, and even pleomorphic rhabdomyosarcoma may also be seen. The presence of an alveolar pattern connotes a worse prognosis.

Liposarcoma

Liposarcoma of the vulva arises in predominantly middle-aged women (median age 52), is of variable size, and is most commonly of the well-differentiated histologic subtype.[189–193] Most cases have the usual appearance of well-differentiated liposarcoma (atypical lipomatous tumor) with variation in adipocyte size, adipocytic nuclear atypia, and cellular fibrous septa containing atypical stromal cells. Some, however, can exhibit a different histologic appearance with the presence of an admixture of bland spindle cells, variable-sized adipocytes, and numerous bivacuolated lipoblasts (Fig. 13G.21).

Proximal-type epithelioid sarcoma

Proximal-type epithelioid sarcoma[194] is a large cell variant of epithelioid sarcoma that occurs more commonly in a proximal/axial location with a predilection for the genital and perineal regions (see Ch. 24). For patients with vulvar primaries, the median age is in the fourth decade, tumors are

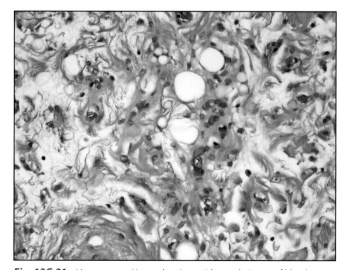

Fig. 13G.21 • Liposarcoma. Unusual variant with an admixture of bland spindle cells, variably sized adipocytes, and bivacuolated lipoblasts.

usually <6 cm, and development of a mass is the main presenting symptom. This tumor is characterized histologically in most cases by a multinodular or sheet-like proliferation of markedly enlarged cells with abundant eosinophilic cytoplasm (imparting an epithelioid appearance), large nuclei with vesicular nuclei and prominent nucleoli; rhabdoid features are commonly present, the number of cells with this appearance being variable. These tumors express epithelial markers (keratin, epithelial membrane antigen), commonly express CD34, and may also express desmin or smooth muscle actin.

Other rare sarcomas

Alveolar soft part sarcoma has been described in a 62-year-old woman who presented with a 4 cm asymptomatic tumor of the right labium majus.[195] Histologically, this tumor appears identical to tumors of this type occurring in the extremities, its more common location, being comprised of large polygonal cells with abundant granular cytoplasm arranged in a nested, alveolar pattern separated by delicate sinusoidal vessels.

Extraskeletal mesenchymal chondrosarcoma has been described in a 40-year-old woman who presented with a mass of the left labium which progressively increased in size to 9 cm over the course of 1 year.[196] Histologically, the tumor showed characteristic histologic features, being comprised of a poorly differentiated spindle-to-round cell sarcoma with pericytoma-like vessels, abruptly merging into areas with cartilaginous differentiation.

Synovial sarcoma, one of the more common soft tissue sarcomas in the extremities, may also rarely arise in the vulva.[197] Two cases have been reported, occurring in a 30- and 37-year-old woman, with both tumors measuring <2 cm and having a biphasic pattern.

Angiosarcoma may rarely involve the vulva, having typical growth patterns and cytomorphology to those tumors that arise in more conventional locations.[184,185]

Kaposi's sarcoma may also rarely involve the vulva, and in some instances may be a manifestation of HIV infection and acquired immune deficiency syndrome (AIDS).[198,199]

Other rare neoplasms

Non-Hodgkin's lymphoma may rarely involve the vulva, either as a primary at this site or as secondary involvement, where they usually present as a mass, are most often of the diffuse large B-cell type, and are clinically aggressive.[200,201]

Endodermal sinus tumor most commonly occurs in the ovary (in pure form or as a component of a mixed germ cell tumor) and the vagina (see p. 605). Rarely this tumor may arise in the vulva.[202] These tumors have occurred in infants but have also been described in young women in their third decade. Patients present with a painless mass of varying size (up to 7 cm) of relatively short duration.

Merkel cell carcinoma, itself an uncommon neoplasm, may, on very rare occasions, occur in the vulva.[203] Patients are usually >40 years of age, and tumor size is <4 cm. Vulvar Merkel cell carcinoma exhibits typical cytomorphologic and immunophenotypic findings similar to those tumors that occur more commonly elsewhere (see Ch. 23). Prognosis is uniformly poor.

Sebaceous carcinoma typically occurs in the head and neck region, particularly on the face, but may occur anywhere that pilosebaceous units occur, including the vulva, albeit rarely.[204,205]

Metastatic tumors[206] are infrequent in the vulva. Approximately 50% represent spread from a gynecologic primary, particularly from the cervix. Among the wide range of other possible primary sites, spread from gastrointestinal carcinomas appears most common.

References

1. Pao C C, Hor J J, Fu Y L 1994 Genital human papillomavirus infections in young women with vulvar and vestibular papillomatosis. Eur J Clin Microbiol Infect Dis 13: 433–436
2. Gentile G, Formelli G, Pelusi G et al. 1997 Is vestibular micropapillomatosis associated with human papillomavirus infection? Eur J Gynaecol Oncol 18: 523–525
3. Moyal-Barracco M, Leibowitch M, Orth G 1990 Vestibular papillae of the vulva. Lack of evidence for human papillomavirus etiology. Arch Dermatol 126: 1594–1598
4. Zhu W Y, Leonardi C, Penneys N S 1992 Detection of human papillomavirus DNA in seborrheic keratosis by polymerase chain reaction. J Dermatol Sci 4: 166–171
5. Gushi A, Kanekura T, Kanzaki T et al. 2003 Detection and sequences of human papillomavirus DNA in nongenital seborrhoeic keratosis of immunopotent individuals. J Dermatol Sci 31: 143–149
6. Bai H, Cviko A, Granter S et al. 2003 Immunophenotypic and viral (human papillomavirus) correlates of vulvar seborrheic keratosis. Hum Pathol 34: 559–564
7. McLachlin C M, Kozakewich H, Craighill M et al. 1994 Histologic correlates of vulvar human papillomavirus infection in children and young adults. Am J Surg Pathol 18: 728–735
8. Chiasson M A, Ellerbrock T V, Bush T J et al. 1997 Increased prevalence of vulvovaginal condyloma and vulvar intraepithelial neoplasia in women infected with the human immunodeficiency virus. Obstet Gynecol 89: 690–694
9. Marshburn P B, Trofatter K F Jr 1988 Recurrent condyloma acuminatum in women over age 40: association with immunosuppression and malignant disease. Am J Obstet Gynecol 159: 429–433
10. Iversen T, Tretli S 1998 Intraepithelial and invasive squamous cell neoplasia of the vulva: trends in incidence, recurrence, and survival rate in Norway. Obstet Gynecol 91: 969–972
11. Sturgeon S R, Brinton L A, Devesa S S et al. 1992 In situ and invasive vulvar cancer incidence trends (1973 to 1987). Am J Obstet Gynecol 166: 1482–1485
12. Crum C P, McLachlin C M, Tate J E et al. 1997 Pathobiology of vulvar squamous neoplasia. Curr Opin Obstet Gynecol 9: 63–69
13. Spitzer M 1999 Lower genital tract intraepithelial neoplasia in HIV-infected women: guidelines for evaluation and management. Obstet Gynecol Surv 54: 131–137
14. Hording U, Daugaard S, Junge J et al. 1996 Human papillomaviruses and multifocal genital neoplasia. Int J Gynecol Pathol 15: 230–234
15. Sherman K J, Daling J R, Chu J et al. 1988 Multiple primary tumours in women with vulvar neoplasms: a case-control study. Br J Cancer 57: 423–427
16. Chafe W, Richards A, Morgan L et al. 1988 Unrecognized invasive carcinoma in vulvar intraepithelial neoplasia (VIN). Gynecol Oncol 31: 154–165
17. Husseinzadeh N, Recinto C 1999 Frequency of invasive cancer in surgically excised vulvar lesions with intraepithelial neoplasia (VIN 3). Gynecol Oncol 73: 119–120
18. McLachlin C M, Mutter G L, Crum C P 1994 Multinucleated atypia of the vulva. Report of a distinct entity not associated with human papillomavirus. Am J Surg Pathol 18: 1233–1239
19. Crum C P 1992 Carcinoma of the vulva: epidemiology and pathogenesis. Obstet Gynecol 79: 448–454
20. Haefner H K, Tate J E, McLachlin C M et al. 1995 Vulvar intraepithelial neoplasia: age, morphological phenotype, papillomavirus DNA, and coexisting invasive carcinoma. Hum Pathol 26: 147–154

21. Homesley H D, Bundy B N, Sedlis A et al. 1991 Assessment of current International Federation of Gynecology and Obstetrics staging of vulvar carcinoma relative to prognostic factors for survival (a Gynecologic Oncology Group study). Am J Obstet Gynecol 164: 997–1003

22. Blake P 2003 Radiotherapy and chemoradiotherapy for carcinoma of the vulva. Best Pract Res Clin Obstet Gynaecol 17: 649–661

23. Katz A, Eifel P J, Jhingran A et al. 2003 The role of radiation therapy in preventing regional recurrences of invasive squamous cell carcinoma of the vulva. Int J Radiat Oncol Biol Phys 57: 409–418

24. Homesley H D, Bundy B N, Sedlis A et al. 1993 Prognostic factors for groin node metastasis in squamous cell carcinoma of the vulva (a Gynecologic Oncology Group study). Gynecol Oncol 49: 279–283

25. Pinto A P, Schlecht N F, Pintos J et al. 2004 Prognostic significance of lymph node variables and human papillomavirus DNA in invasive vulvar carcinoma. Gynecol Oncol 92: 856–865

26. Nascimento A F, Granter S R, Cviko A et al. 2004 Vulvar acanthosis with altered differentiation: a precursor to verrucous carcinoma? Am J Surg Pathol 28: 638–643

27. Copas P R, Spann C O Jr, Majmudar B et al. 1996 Basal cell carcinoma of the vulva. A report of four cases. J Reprod Med 41: 283–286

28. Feakins R M, Lowe D G 1997 Basal cell carcinoma of the vulva: a clinicopathologic study of 45 cases. Int J Gynecol Pathol 16: 319–324

29. Benedet J L, Miller D M, Ehlen T G et al. 1997 Basal cell carcinoma of the vulva: clinical features and treatment results in 28 patients. Obstet Gynecol 90: 765–768

30. Gibson G E, Ahmed I 2001 Perianal and genital basal cell carcinoma: a clinicopathologic review of 51 cases. J Am Acad Dermatol 45: 68–71

31. Piura B, Rabinovich A, Dgani R 1999 Basal cell carcinoma of the vulva. J Surg Oncol 70: 172–176

32. Koenig C, Tavassoli F A 1998 Nodular hyperplasia, adenoma, and adenomyoma of Bartholin's gland. Int J Gynecol Pathol 17: 289–294

33. Padmanabhan V, Cooper K 2000 Concomitant adenoma and hybrid carcinoma of salivary gland type arising in Bartholin's gland. Int J Gynecol Pathol 19: 377–380

34. Woodworth H Jr, Dockerty M B, Wilson R B et al. 1971 Papillary hidradenoma of the vulva: a clinicopathologic study of 69 cases. Am J Obstet Gynecol 110: 501–508

35. Meeker J H, Neubecker R D, Helwig E B 1962 Hidradenoma papilliferum. Am J Clin Pathol 37: 182–195

36. Axe S, Parmley T, Woodruff J D et al. 1986 Adenomas in minor vestibular glands. Obstet Gynecol 68: 16–18

37. Punia R P, Bal A, Jain P et al. 2003 Minor vestibular gland adenoma: a case report. Aust NZ J Obstet Gynaecol 43: 322–323

38. Rorat E, Wallach R C 1984 Mixed tumors of the vulva: clinical outcome and pathology. Int J Gynecol Pathol 3: 323–328

39. Ordonez N G, Manning J T, Luna M A 1981 Mixed tumor of the vulva: a report of two cases probably arising in Bartholin's gland. Cancer 48: 181–186

40. Hornick J L, Fletcher C D M 2003 Myoepithelial tumors of soft tissue: a clinicopathologic and immunohistochemical study of 101 cases with evaluation of prognostic parameters. Am J Surg Pathol 27: 1183–1196

41. Huang Y H, Chuang Y H, Kuo T T et al. 2003 Vulvar syringoma: a clinicopathologic and immunohistologic study of 18 patients and results of treatment. J Am Acad Dermatol 48: 735–739

42. Isaacson D, Turner M L 1979 Localized vulvar syringomas. J Am Acad Dermatol 1: 352–356

43. Tay Y K, Tham S N, Teo R 1996 Localized vulvar syringomas – an unusual cause of pruritus vulvae. Dermatology 192: 62–63

44. Buchler D A, Sun F, Chuprevich T 1978 A pilar tumor of the vulva. Gynecol Oncol 6: 479–486

45. Avinoach I, Zirkin H J, Glezerman M 1989 Proliferating trichilemmal tumor of the vulva. Case report and review of the literature. Int J Gynecol Pathol 8: 163–168

46. Glusac E J, Hendrickson M S, Smoller B R 1994 Apocrine cystadenoma of the vulva. J Am Acad Dermatol 31: 498–489

47. Gilks C B, Clement P B, Wood W S 1989 Trichoblastic fibroma. A clinicopathologic study of three cases. Am J Dermatopathol 11: 397–402

48. Cho D, Woodruff J D 1988 Trichoepithelioma of the vulva. A report of two cases. J Reprod Med 33: 317–319

49. Crawford D, Nimmo M, Clement P B et al. 1999 Prognostic factors in Paget's disease of the vulva: a study of 21 cases. Int J Gynecol Pathol 18: 351–359

50. Goldblum J R, Hart W R 1997 Vulvar Paget's disease: a clinicopathologic and immunohistochemical study of 19 cases. Am J Surg Pathol 21: 1178–1187

51. Kodama S, Kaneko T, Saito M et al. 1995 A clinicopathologic study of 30 patients with Paget's disease of the vulva. Gynecol Oncol 56: 63–70

52. Fanning J, Lambert H C, Hale T M et al. 1999 Paget's disease of the vulva: prevalence of associated vulvar adenocarcinoma, invasive Paget's disease, and recurrence after surgical excision. Am J Obstet Gynecol 180: 24–27

53. Piura B, Rabinovich A, Dgani R 1999 Extramammary Paget's disease of the vulva: report of five cases and review of the literature. Eur J Gynaecol Oncol 20: 98–101

54. Parker L P, Parker J R, Bodurka-Bevers D et al. 2000 Paget's disease of the vulva: pathology, pattern of involvement, and prognosis. Gynecol Oncol 77: 183–189

55. Zollo J D, Zeitouni N C 2000 The Roswell Park Cancer Institute experience with extramammary Paget's disease. Br J Dermatol 142: 59–65

56. Goldblum J R, Hart W R 1998 Perianal Paget's disease: a histologic and immunohistochemical study of 11 cases with and without associated rectal adenocarcinoma. Am J Surg Pathol 22: 170–179

57. Fine B A, Fowler L J, Valente P T et al. 1995 Minimally invasive Paget's disease of the vulva with extensive lymph node metastases. Gynecol Oncol 57: 262–265

58. Feuer G A, Shevchuk M, Calanog A 1990 Vulvar Paget's disease: the need to exclude an invasive lesion. Gynecol Oncol 38: 81–89

59. Chamlian D L, Taylor H B 1972 Primary carcinoma of Bartholin's gland. A report of 24 patients. Obstet Gynecol 39: 489–494

60. Leuchter R S, Hacker N F, Voet R L et al. 1982 Primary carcinoma of the Bartholin gland: a report of 14 cases and review of the literature. Obstet Gynecol 60: 361–368

61. DePasquale S E, McGuinness T B, Mangan C E et al. 1996 Adenoid cystic carcinoma of Bartholin's gland: a review of the literature and report of a patient. Gynecol Oncol 61: 122–125

62. Cardosi R J, Speights A, Fiorica J V et al. 2001 Bartholin's gland carcinoma: a 15-year experience. Gynecol Oncol 82: 247–251

63. Rosenberg P, Simonsen E, Risberg B 1989 Adenoid cystic carcinoma of Bartholin's gland: a report of five new cases treated with surgery and radiotherapy. Gynecol Oncol 34: 145–147

64. Jones M A, Mann E W, Caldwell C L et al. 1990 Small cell neuroendocrine carcinoma of Bartholin's gland. Am J Clin Pathol 94: 439–442

65. Felix J C, Cote R J, Kramer E E et al. 1993 Carcinomas of Bartholin's gland. Histogenesis and the etiological role of human papillomavirus. Am J Pathol 142: 925–933

66. Milchgrub S, Wiley E L, Vuitch F et al. 1994 The tubular variant of adenoid cystic carcinoma of the Bartholin's gland. Am J Clin Pathol 101: 204–208

67. Obermair A, Koller S, Crandon A J et al. 2001 Primary Bartholin gland carcinoma: a report of seven cases. Aust NZ J Obstet Gynaecol 41: 78–81

68. Hendrix R C, Behrman S J 1956 Adenocarcinoma arising in a supernumerary mammary gland in the vulva. Obstet Gynecol 8: 238–241

69. Guerry R L, Pratt-Thomas H R 1976 Carcinoma of supernumerary breast of vulva with bilateral mammary cancer. Cancer 38: 2570–2574

70. Guercio E, Cesone P, Saracino A et al. 1984 [Adenocarcinoma occurring in an aberrant mammary gland located in the vulva.] Minerva Ginecol 36: 315–319

71. Cho D, Buscema J, Rosenshein N B et al. 1985 Primary breast cancer of the vulva. Obstet Gynecol 66: 79S–81S

72. Simon K E, Dutcher J P, Runowicz C D et al. 1988 Adenocarcinoma arising in vulvar breast tissue. Cancer 62: 2234–2238

73. Rose P G, Roman L D, Reale F R et al. 1990 Primary adenocarcinoma of the breast arising in the vulva. Obstet Gynecol 76: 537–539

74. Di Bonito L, Patriarca S, Falconieri G 1992 Aggressive "breast-like" adenocarcinoma of vulva. Pathol Res Pract 188: 211–214

75. Bailey C L, Sankey H Z, Donovan J T et al. 1993 Primary breast cancer of the vulva. Gynecol Oncol 50: 379–383

76. Levin M, Pakarakas R M, Chang H A et al. 1995 Primary breast carcinoma of the vulva: a case report and review of the literature. Gynecol Oncol 56: 448–451

77. Kennedy D A, Hermina M S, Xanos E T et al. 1997 Infiltrating ductal carcinoma of the vulva. Pathol Res Pract 193: 723–726

78. van der Putte S C, van Gorp L H 1994 Adenocarcinoma of the mammary-like glands of the vulva: a concept unifying sweat gland carcinoma of the vulva, carcinoma of supernumerary mammary glands and extramammary Paget's disease. J Cutan Pathol 21: 157–163

79. Pelosi G, Martignoni G, Bonetti F 1991 Intraductal carcinoma of mammary-type apocrine epithelium arising within a papillary hydradenoma of the vulva. Report of a case and review of the literature. Arch Pathol Lab Med 115: 1249–1254

80. Castro C Y, Deavers M 2001 Ductal carcinoma in-situ arising in mammary-like glands of the vulva. Int J Gynecol Pathol 20: 277–283

81. Pongtippan A, Malpica A, Levenback C et al. 2004 Skene's gland adenocarcinoma resembling prostatic adenocarcinoma. Int J Gynecol Pathol 23: 71–74

82. Dodson M K, Cliby W A, Keeney G L et al. 1994 Skene's gland adenocarcinoma with increased serum level of prostate-specific antigen. Gynecol Oncol 55: 304–307

83. Sloboda J, Zaviacic M, Jakubovsky J et al. 1998 Metastasizing adenocarcinoma of the female prostate (Skene's paraurethral glands). Histological and immunohistochemical prostate markers studies and first ultrastructural observation. Pathol Res Pract 194: 129–136

84. Kennedy J C, Majmudar B 1993 Primary adenocarcinoma of the vulva, possibly cloacogenic. A report of two cases. J Reprod Med 38: 113–116

85. Willen R, Bekassy Z, Carlen B et al. 1999 Cloacogenic adenocarcinoma of the vulva. Gynecol Oncol 74: 298–301

86. Zaidi S N, Conner M G 2001 Primary vulvar adenocarcinoma of cloacogenic origin. South Med J 94: 744–746

87. Rodriguez A, Isaac M A, Hidalgo E et al. 2001 Villoglandular adenocarcinoma of the vulva. Gynecol Oncol 83: 409–411

88. Dube V, Veilleux C, Plante M et al. 2004 Primary villoglandular adenocarcinoma of cloacogenic origin of the vulva. Hum Pathol 35: 377–379

89. Vitrey D, Frachon S, Balme B et al. 2003 Tubulovillous adenoma of the vulva. Obstet Gynecol 102: 1160–1163

90. Ghamande S A, Kasznica J, Griffiths C T et al. 1995 Mucinous adenocarcinomas of the vulva. Gynecol Oncol 57: 117–120

91. Mesko J D, Gates H, McDonald T W et al. 1988 Clear cell ("mesonephroid") adenocarcinoma of the vulva arising in endometriosis: a case report. Gynecol Oncol 29: 385–391

92. Hitti I F, Glasberg S S, Lubicz S 1990 Clear cell carcinoma arising in extraovarian endometriosis: report of three cases and review of the literature. Gynecol Oncol 39: 314–320

93. Bolis G B, Maccio T 2000 Clear cell adenocarcinoma of the vulva arising in endometriosis. A case report. Eur J Gynaecol Oncol 21: 416–417

94. Wick M R, Goellner J R, Wolfe J T III et al. 1985 Vulvar sweat gland carcinomas. Arch Pathol Lab Med 109: 43–47

95. Messing M J, Richardson M S, Smith M T et al. 1993 Metastatic clear-cell hidradenocarcinoma of the vulva. Gynecol Oncol 48: 264–268

96. Buhl A, Landow S, Lee Y C et al. 2001 Microcystic adnexal carcinoma of the vulva. Gynecol Oncol 82: 571–574

97. Barnhill R L, Albert L S, Shama S K et al. 1990 Genital lentiginosis: a clinical and histopathologic study. J Am Acad Dermatol 22: 453–460

98. Rhodes A R, Silverman R A, Harrist T J et al. 1984 Mucocutaneous lentigines, cardiomucocutaneous myxomas, and multiple blue nevi: the "LAMB" syndrome. J Am Acad Dermatol 10: 72–82

99. Voron D A, Hatfield H H, Kalkhoff R K 1976 Multiple lentigines syndrome. Case report and review of the literature. Am J Med 60: 447–456

100. Christensen W N, Friedman K J, Woodruff J D et al. 1987 Histologic characteristics of vulvar nevocellular nevi. J Cutan Pathol 14: 87–91

101. Rongioletti F, Ball R A, Marcus R et al. 2000 Histopathological features of flexural melanocytic nevi: a study of 40 cases. J Cutan Pathol 27: 215–217

102. Creasman W T, Phillips J L, Menck H R 1999 A survey of hospital management practices for vulvar melanoma. J Am Coll Surg 188: 670–675

103. Irvin W P Jr, Legallo R L, Stoler M H et al. 2001 Vulvar melanoma: a retrospective analysis and literature review. Gynecol Oncol 83: 457–465

104. Heller D S, Moomjy M, Koulos J et al. 1994 Vulvar and vaginal melanoma. A clinicopathologic study. J Reprod Med 39: 945–948

105. DeMatos P, Tyler D, Seigler H F 1998 Mucosal melanoma of the female genitalia: a clinicopathologic study of forty-three cases at Duke University Medical Center. Surgery 124: 38–48

106. Ragnarsson-Olding B K, Nilsson B R, Kanter-Lewensohn L R et al. 1999 Malignant melanoma of the vulva in a nationwide, 25-year study of 219 Swedish females: predictors of survival. Cancer 86: 1285–1293

107. Ragnarsson-Olding B K, Kanter-Lewensohn L R, Lagerlof B et al. 1999 Malignant melanoma of the vulva in a nationwide, 25-year study of 219 Swedish females: clinical observations and histopathologic features. Cancer 86: 1273–1284

108. Verschraegen C F, Benjapibal M, Supakarapongkul W et al. 2001 Vulvar melanoma at the M D Anderson Cancer Center: 25 years later. Int J Gynecol Cancer 11: 359–364

109. Raber G, Mempel V, Jackisch C et al. 1996 Malignant melanoma of the vulva. Report of 89 patients. Cancer 78: 2353–2358

110. Bradgate M G, Rollason T P, McConkey C C et al. 1990 Malignant melanoma of the vulva: a clinicopathological study of 50 women. Br J Obstet Gynaecol 97: 124–133

111. Khoo U S, Collins R J, Ngan H Y 1991 Malignant melanoma of the female genital tract. A report of nine cases in the Chinese of Hong Kong. Pathology 23: 312–317

112. Piura B, Rabinovich A, Dgani R 1999 Malignant melanoma of the vulva: report of six cases and review of the literature. Eur J Gynaecol Oncol 20: 182–186

113. Neven P, Shepherd J H, Masotina A et al. 1994 Malignant melanoma of the vulva and vagina: a report of 23 cases presenting in a 10-year period. Int J Gynecol Cancer 4: 379–383

114. Chung A F, Woodruff J M, Lewis J L Jr 1975 Malignant melanoma of the vulva: A report of 44 cases. Obstet Gynecol 45: 638–646

115. Trimble E L, Lewis J L Jr, Williams L L et al. 1992 Management of vulvar melanoma. Gynecol Oncol 45: 254–258

116. Johnson T L, Kumar N B, White C D et al. 1986 Prognostic features of vulvar melanoma: a clinicopathologic analysis. Int J Gynecol Pathol 5: 110–118

117. Wechter M E, Gruber S B, Haefner H K et al. 2004 Vulvar melanoma: a report of 20 cases and review of the literature. J Am Acad Dermatol 50: 554–562

118. Norris H J, Taylor H B 1966 Polyps of the vagina. A benign lesion resembling sarcoma botryoides. Cancer 19: 227–232

119. Elliott G B, Reynolds H A, Fidler H K 1967 Pseudo-sarcoma botryoides of cervix and vagina in pregnancy. J Obstet Gynaecol Br Commonw 74: 728–733

120. Burt R L, Prichard R W, Kim B S 1976 Fibroepithelial polyp of the vagina. A report of five cases. Obstet Gynecol 47: 52S–54S

121. Chirayil S J, Tobon H 1981 Polyps of the vagina: a clinicopathologic study of 18 cases. Cancer 47: 2904–2907

122. O'Quinn A G, Edwards C L, Gallager H S 1982 Pseudosarcoma botryoides of the vagina in pregnancy. Gynecol Oncol 13: 237–241

123. Miettinen M, Wahlstrom T, Vesterinen E et al. 1983 Vaginal polyps with pseudosarcomatous features. A clinicopathologic study of seven cases. Cancer 51: 1148–1151

124. Maenpaa J, Soderstrom K O, Salmi T et al. 1988 Large atypical polyps of the vagina during pregnancy with concomitant human papilloma virus infection. Eur J Obstet Gynecol Reprod Biol 27: 65–69

125. Ostor A G, Fortune D W, Riley C J 1988 Fibroepithelial polyps with atypical stromal cells (pseudosarcoma botryoides) of vulva and vagina. A report of 13 cases. Int J Gynecol Pathol 7: 351–360

126. Hartmann C A, Sperling M, Stein H 1990 So-called fibroepithelial polyps of the vagina exhibiting an unusual but uniform antigen profile characterized by expression of desmin and steroid hormone receptors but no muscle-specific actin or macrophage markers. Am J Clin Pathol 93: 604–608

127. Mucitelli D R, Charles E Z, Kraus F T 1990 Vulvovaginal polyps. Histologic appearance, ultrastructure, immunohistochemical characteristics, and clinicopathologic correlations. Int J Gynecol Pathol 9: 20–40

128. Nucci M R, Fletcher C D M 1998 Fibroepithelial stromal polyps of vulvovaginal tissue: from the banal to the bizarre. Pathol Case Rev 3: 151–157

129. Nucci M R, Young R H, Fletcher C D M 2000 Cellular pseudosarcomatous fibroepithelial stromal polyps of the lower female genital tract: an underrecognized lesion often misdiagnosed as sarcoma. Am J Surg Pathol 24: 231–240

130. LiVolsi V A, Brooks J J 1987 Nodular fasciitis of the vulva: a report of two cases. Obstet Gynecol 69: 513–516

131. Roberts W, Daly J W 1981 Pseudosarcomatous fasciitis of the vulva. Gynecol Oncol 11: 383–386

132. Gaffney E F, Majmudar B, Bryan J A 1982 Nodular fasciitis (pseudosarcomatous fasciitis) of the vulva. Int J Gynecol Pathol 1: 307–312

133. Fletcher C D M, Tsang W Y, Fisher C et al. 1992 Angiomyofibroblastoma of the vulva. A benign neoplasm distinct from aggressive angiomyxoma. Am J Surg Pathol 16: 373–382

134. Nielsen G P, Rosenberg A E, Young R H et al. 1996 Angiomyofibroblastoma of the vulva and vagina. Mod Pathol 9: 284–291

135. Ockner D M, Sayadi H, Swanson P E et al. 1997 Genital angiomyofibroblastoma. Comparison with aggressive angiomyxoma and other myxoid neoplasms of skin and soft tissue. Am J Clin Pathol 107: 36–44

136. Fukunaga M, Nomura K, Matsumoto K et al. 1997 Vulval angiomyofibroblastoma. Clinicopathologic analysis of six cases. Am J Clin Pathol 107: 45–51

137. Laskin W B, Fetsch J F, Tavassoli F A 1997 Angiomyofibroblastoma of the female genital tract: analysis of 17 cases including a lipomatous variant. Hum Pathol 28: 1046–1055

138. Hisaoka M, Kouho H, Aoki T et al. 1995 Angiomyofibroblastoma of the vulva: a clinicopathologic study of seven cases. Pathol Int 45: 487–492

139. Nielsen G P, Young R H, Dickersin G R et al. 1997 Angiomyofibroblastoma of the vulva with sarcomatous transformation ("angiomyofibrosarcoma"). Am J Surg Pathol 21: 1104–1108

140. Nucci M R, Granter S R, Fletcher C D M 1997 Cellular angiofibroma: a benign neoplasm distinct from angiomyofibroblastoma and spindle cell lipoma. Am J Surg Pathol 21: 636–644

141. Laskin W B, Fetsch J F, Mostofi F K 1998 Angiomyofibroblastomalike tumor of the male genital tract: analysis of 11 cases with comparison to female angiomyofibroblastoma and spindle cell lipoma. Am J Surg Pathol 22: 6–16

142. Iwasa Y, Fletcher C D M 2004 Cellular angiofibroma: clinicopathologic and immunohistochemical analysis of 51 cases. Am J Surg Pathol 28: 1426–1435

143. McCluggage W G, Perenyei M, Irwin S T 2002 Recurrent cellular angiofibroma of the vulva. J Clin Pathol 55: 477–479

144. Gonzalez S, Duarte I 1982 Benign fibrous histiocytoma of the skin. A morphologic study of 290 cases. Pathol Res Pract 174: 379–391

145. Lack E E, Worsham G F, Callihan M D et al. 1980 Granular cell tumor: a clinicopathologic study of 110 patients. J Surg Oncol 13: 301–316

146. Horowitz I R, Copas P, Majmudar B 1995 Granular cell tumors of the vulva. Am J Obstet Gynecol 173: 1710–1713

147. Haley J C, Mirowski G W, Hood A F 1998 Benign vulvar tumors. Semin Cutan Med Surg 17: 196–204

148. Cohen Z, Kapuller V, Maor E et al. 1999 Granular cell tumor (myoblastoma) of the labia major: a rare benign tumor in childhood. J Pediatr Adolesc Gynecol 12: 155–156

149. Guenther L, Shum D 1993 Granular cell tumor of the vulva. Pediatr Dermatol 10: 153–155

150. Majmudar B, Castellano P Z, Wilson R W et al. 1990 Granular cell tumors of the vulva. J Reprod Med 35: 1008–1014

151. Robertson A J, McIntosh W, Lamont P et al. 1981 Malignant granular cell tumour (myoblastoma) of the vulva: report of a case and review of the literature. Histopathology 5: 69–79

152. Newman P L, Fletcher C D M 1991 Smooth muscle tumours of the external genitalia: clinicopathological analysis of a series. Histopathology 18: 523–529

153. Tavassoli F A, Norris H J 1979 Smooth muscle tumors of the vulva. Obstet Gynecol 53: 213–217

154. Nielsen G P, Rosenberg A E, Koerner F C et al. 1996 Smooth-muscle tumors of the vulva. A clinicopathological study of 25 cases and review of the literature. Am J Surg Pathol 20: 779–93

155. Nucci M R, Fletcher C D M 2000 Vulvovaginal soft tissue tumours: update and review. Histopathology 36: 97–108

156. Cohen P R, Young A W Jr, Tovell H M 1989 Angiokeratoma of the vulva: diagnosis and review of the literature. Obstet Gynecol Surv 44: 339–346

157. Vlastos A T, Malpica A, Follen M 2003 Lymphangioma circumscriptum of the vulva: a review of the literature. Obstet Gynecol 101: 946–954

158. Faber K, Jones M A, Spratt D et al. 1991 Vulvar leiomyomatosis in a patient with esophagogastric leiomyomatosis: review of the syndrome. Gynecol Oncol 41: 92–94

159. Lae M E, Pereira P F, Keeney G L et al. 2002 Lipoblastoma-like tumour of the vulva: report of three cases of a distinctive mesenchymal neoplasm of adipocytic differentiation. Histopathology 40: 505–509

160. Sutphen R, Galan-Gomez E, Kousseff B G 1995 Clitoromegaly in neurofibromatosis. Am J Med Genet 55: 325–330

161. Gersell D J, Fulling K H 1989 Localized neurofibromatosis of the female genitourinary tract. Am J Surg Pathol 13: 873–878

162. Steeper T A, Rosai J 1983 Aggressive angiomyxoma of the female pelvis and perineum. Report of nine cases of a distinctive type of gynecologic soft-tissue neoplasm. Am J Surg Pathol 7: 463–475

163. Begin L R, Clement P B, Kirk M E et al. 1985 Aggressive angiomyxoma of pelvic soft parts: a clinicopathologic study of nine cases. Hum Pathol 16: 621–628

164. Fetsch J F, Laskin W B, Lefkowitz M et al. 1996 Aggressive angiomyxoma: a clinicopathologic study of 29 female patients. Cancer 78: 79–90

165. Granter S R, Nucci M R, Fletcher C D M 1997 Aggressive angiomyxoma: reappraisal of its relationship to angiomyofibroblastoma in a series of 16 cases. Histopathology 30: 3–10

166. Tsang W Y, Chan J K, Lee K C et al. 1992 Aggressive angiomyxoma. A report of four cases occurring in men. Am J Surg Pathol 16: 1059–1065

167. Iezzoni J C, Fechner R E, Wong L S et al. 1995 Aggressive angiomyxoma in males. A report of four cases. Am J Clin Pathol 104: 391–396

168. Nucci M R, Weremowicz S, Neskey D M et al. 2001 Chromosomal translocation t(8;12) induces aberrant HMGIC expression in aggressive angiomyxoma of the vulva. Genes Chromos Cancer 32: 172–176

169. Allen P W, Dymock R B, MacCormac L B 1988 Superficial angiomyxomas with and without epithelial components. Report of 30 tumors in 28 patients. Am J Surg Pathol 12: 519–530

170. Fetsch J F, Laskin W B, Tavassoli F A 1997 Superficial angiomyxoma (cutaneous myxoma): a clinicopathologic study of 17 cases arising in the genital region. Int J Gynecol Pathol 16: 325–334

171. Calonje E, Guerin D, McCormick D 1999 Superficial angiomyxoma: clinicopathologic analysis of a series of distinctive but poorly recognized cutaneous tumors with tendency for recurrence. Am J Surg Pathol 23: 910–917

172. Ghorbani R P, Malpica A, Ayala A G 1999 Dermatofibrosarcoma protuberans of the vulva: clinicopathologic and immunohistochemical analysis of four cases, one with fibrosarcomatous change, and review of the literature. Int J Gynecol Pathol 18: 366–373

173. Gokden N, Dehner L P, Zhu X et al. 2003 Dermatofibrosarcoma protuberans of the vulva and groin: detection of COL1A1-PDGFB fusion transcripts by RT-PCR. J Cutan Pathol 30: 190–195

174. Vanni R, Faa G, Dettori T et al. 2000 A case of dermatofibrosarcoma protuberans of the vulva with a COL1A1/PDGFB fusion identical to a case of giant cell fibroblastoma. Virchows Arch 437: 95–100

175. Moodley M, Moodley J 2000 Dermatofibrosarcoma protuberans of the vulva: a case report and review of the literature. Gynecol Oncol 78: 74–75

176. Soergel T M, Doering D L, O'Connor D 1998 Metastatic dermatofibrosarcoma protuberans of the vulva. Gynecol Oncol 71: 320–324

177. Davos I, Abell M R 1976 Soft tissue sarcomas of vulva. Gynecol Oncol 4: 70–86

178. Leake J F, Buscema J, Cho K R et al. 1991 Dermatofibrosarcoma protuberans of the vulva. Gynecol Oncol 41: 245–249

179. Barnhill D R, Boling R, Nobles W et al. 1988 Vulvar dermatofibrosarcoma protuberans. Gynecol Oncol 30: 149–152

180. Bock J E, Andreasson B, Thorn A et al. 1985 Dermatofibrosarcoma protuberans of the vulva. Gynecol Oncol 20: 129–135

181. Mentzel T, Beham A, Katenkamp D et al. 1998 Fibrosarcomatous ("high-grade") dermatofibrosarcoma protuberans: clinicopathologic and immunohistochemical study of a series of 41 cases with emphasis on prognostic significance. Am J Surg Pathol 22: 576–587

182. Naeem R, Lux M L, Huang S F et al. 1995 Ring chromosomes in dermatofibrosarcoma protuberans are composed of interspersed sequences from chromosomes 17 and 22. Am J Pathol 147: 1553–1558

183. DiSaia P J, Rutledge F, Smith J P 1971 Sarcoma of the vulva. Report of 12 patients. Obstet Gynecol 38: 180–184

184. Nirenberg A, Ostor A G, Slavin J et al. 1995 Primary vulvar sarcomas. Int J Gynecol Pathol 14: 55–62

185. Curtin J P, Saigo P, Slucher B et al. 1995 Soft-tissue sarcoma of the vagina and vulva: a clinicopathologic study. Obstet Gynecol 86: 269–272

186. Copeland L J, Gershenson D M, Saul P B et al. 1985 Sarcoma botryoides of the female genital tract. Obstet Gynecol 66: 262–266

187. Copeland L J, Sneige N, Stringer C A et al. 1985 Alveolar rhabdomyosarcoma of the female genitalia. Cancer 56: 849–855

188. Imachi M, Tsukamoto N, Kamura T et al. 1991 Alveolar rhabdomyosarcoma of the vulva. Report of two cases. Acta Cytol 35: 345–349

189. Nucci M R, Fletcher C D M 1998 Liposarcoma (atypical lipomatous tumors) of the vulva: a clinicopathologic study of six cases. Int J Gynecol Pathol 17: 17–23

190. Brooks J J, LiVolsi V A 1987 Liposarcoma presenting on the vulva. Am J Obstet Gynecol 156: 73–75

191. Gondos B, Casey M J 1982 Liposarcoma of the perineum. Gynecol Oncol 14: 133–140

192. Genton C Y, Maroni E S 1987 Vulval liposarcoma. Arch Gynecol 240: 63–66

193. Vecchione A, Palazzetti P 1967 [Anatomoclinical considerations on a case of liposarcoma with vulvar localization.] Riv Anat Patol Oncol 31: 177–193

194. Guillou L, Wadden C, Coindre J M et al. 1997 "Proximal-type" epithelioid sarcoma, a distinctive aggressive neoplasm showing rhabdoid features. Clinicopathologic, immunohistochemical, and ultrastructural study of a series. Am J Surg Pathol 21: 130–146

195. Shen J T, D'ablaing G, Morrow C P 1982 Alveolar soft part sarcoma of the vulva: report of first case and review of literature. Gynecol Oncol 13: 120–128

196. Lin J, Yip K M, Maffulli N et al. 1996 Extraskeletal mesenchymal chondrosarcoma of the labium majus. Gynecol Oncol 60: 492–493

197. Nielsen G P, Shaw P A, Rosenberg A E et al. 1996 Synovial sarcoma of the vulva: a report of two cases. Mod Pathol 9: 970–974

198. Hall D J, Burns J C, Goplerud D R 1979 Kaposi's sarcoma of the vulva: a case report and brief review. Obstet Gynecol 54: 478–483

199. Macasaet M A, Duerr A, Thelmo W et al. 1995 Kaposi sarcoma presenting as a vulvar mass. Obstet Gynecol 86: 695–697

200. Vang R, Medeiros L J, Malpica A et al. 2000 Non-Hodgkin's lymphoma involving the vulva. Int J Gynecol Pathol 19: 236–242

201. Vang R, Medeiros L J, Fuller G N et al. 2001 Non-Hodgkin's lymphoma involving the gynecologic tract: a review of 88 cases. Adv Anat Pathol 8: 200–217

202. Dudley A G, Young R H, Lawrence W D et al. 1983 Endodermal sinus tumor of the vulva in an infant. Obstet Gynecol 61: 76S–79S

203. Gil-Moreno A, Garcia-Jimenez A, Gonzalez-Bosquet J et al. 1997 Merkel cell carcinoma of the vulva. Gynecol Oncol 64: 526–532

204. Carlson J W, McGlennen R C, Gomez R et al. 1996 Sebaceous carcinoma of the vulva: a case report and review of the literature. Gynecol Oncol 60: 489–491

205. Rulon D B, Helwig E B 1974 Cutaneous sebaceous neoplasms. Cancer 33: 82–102

206. Neto A G, Deavers M T, Silvio E G et al. 2003 Metastatic tumors of the vulva. A clinicopathologic study of 66 cases. Am J Surg Pathol 27: 798–804

Tumors of the male genital tract 14

PART A

Prostate and seminal vesicles

Jae Y. Ro   Mahul B. Amin   Kyu-Rae Kim   Alberto G. Ayala

Prostate

Prostatic carcinoma and benign prostatic hyperplasia (BPH) are the two principal conditions to involve the prostate; they account for more than 90% of all prostatic disease. Prostate cancer is the most common cancer and third leading cause of cancer deaths in men in the USA,[1] and early detection of cancer and better understanding of the premalignant conditions offer practical methods of reducing morbidity and mortality. Over 90% of malignant epithelial tumors of the prostate are common acinar-type carcinomas, whereas about 10% of carcinomas differ from the conventional histology and are regarded as variants.

In general, the morphologic diagnosis of prostatic lesions, particularly separating benign from malignant lesions, is relatively straightforward. However, there are several benign proliferations and normal histoanatomic structures of the prostate, which exhibit a small glandular pattern with or without cytologic atypia, and they may easily be mistaken for malignancy if one is not aware of their morphologic nuances. Most of the benign lesions mimicking cancer occur in the same age group as prostatic carcinoma. They do not have specific clinical manifestations, and most are encountered during examination of prostatic samples from patients in whom the clinical diagnosis is BPH or they are seen in needle biopsies within the spectrum of senescent and hormone-influenced changes occurring in the gland. The classification of prostatic tumors, tumor-like lesions and prostatic hyperplasia, as proposed in the recent World Health Organization (WHO) classification[2] is outlined in Table 14A1. Benign prostatic lesions can be divided into epithelial and stromal lesions. Epithelial lesions include the usual type of BPH, basal cell hyperplasia (BCH), clear cell cribriform hyperplasia (CCCH), atrophy and postatrophic hyperplasia (PAH), sclerosing adenosis (SA), hyperplasia of mesonephric remnants, verumontanum mucosal gland hyperplasia (VMGH), and nephrogenic adenoma (NA).[3]

The most common stromal lesion is stromal hyperplasia; rare lesions include leiomyoma, atypical stromal hyperplasia and the closely related atypical leiomyoma (also known as bizarre or symplastic leiomyoma), phyllodes-type atypical hyperplasia, postoperative spindle cell nodule, and pseudo-sarcomatous fibromyxoid tumor. Stromal sarcoma and other sarcomas of the prostate occur in adults and are relatively rare; rhabdomyosarcoma is the commonest pediatric tumor.

Premalignant lesions of the prostate

Although two putative premalignant lesions of the prostate have been described: prostatic intraepithelial neoplasia (PIN) (synonyms: intraductal dysplasia, primary atypical hyperplasia, large acinar dysplasia, and acinar-ductal dysplasia)[4–9] and atypical adenomatous hyperplasia (AAH) (synonyms: adenosis,

Table 14A.1 World Health Organization histological classification of tumors of the prostate[a]

Epithelial tumors		Hemangioma	9120/0
Glandular neoplasms		Chondroma	9200/0
Adenocarcinoma (acinar)	8140/3	Leiomyoma	8890/0
Atrophic		Granular cell tumor	9580/0
Pseudohyperplastic		Hemangiopericytoma	8150/1
Foamy		Solitary fibrous tumor	8815/0
Colloid	8480/3		
Signet-ring	8490/3	**Hematolymphoid tumors**	
Oncocytic	8290/3	Lymphoma	
Lymphoepithelioma-like	8082/3	Leukemia	
Carcinoma with spindle cell differentiation			
(carcinosarcoma, sarcomatoid carcinoma)	8572/3	**Miscellaneous tumors**	
		Cystadenoma	8440/0
Prostatic intraepithelial neoplasia (PIN)		Nephroblastoma (Wilms tumor)	8960/3
Prostatic intraepithelial neoplasia, grade III (PIN III)	8148/2	Rhabdoid tumor	8963/3
		Germ cell tumors	
Ductal adenocarcinoma	8500/3	Yolk sac tumor	9071/3
Cribriform	8201/3	Seminoma	9061/3
Papillary	8260/3	Embryonal carcinoma and teratoma	9081/3
Solid	8230/3	Choriocarcinoma	9100/3
		Clear cell adenocarcinoma	8130/3
Urothelial tumors		Melanoma	8720/3
Urothelial carcinoma	8120/3		
		Metastatic tumors	
Squamous tumors			
Adenosquamous carcinoma	8560/3	**Tumors of the seminal vesicles**	
Squamous cell carcinoma	8070/3		
		Epithelial tumors	
Basal cell tumors		Adenocarcinoma	8140/3
Basal cell adenoma	8147/0	Cystadenoma	8440/0
Basal cell carcinoma	8147/3		
		Mixed epithelial and stromal tumors	
Neuroendocrine tumors		Malignant	
Endocrine differentiation within adenocarcinoma	8574/3	Benign	
Carcinoid tumor	8240/3		
Small cell carcinoma	8041/3	**Mesenchymal tumors**	
Paraganglioma	8680/1	Leiomyosarcoma	8890/3
Neuroblastoma	9500/3	Angiosarcoma	9120/3
		Liposarcoma	8850/3
Prostatic stromal tumors		Malignant fibrous histiocytoma	8830/3
Stromal tumor of uncertain malignant potential	8935/1	Solitary fibrous tumor	8815/0
Stromal sarcoma	8935/3	Hemangiopericytoma	9150/1
		Leiomyoma	8890/0
Mesenchymal tumors			
Leiomyosarcoma	8890/3	**Miscellaneous tumors**	
Rhabdomyosarcoma	8900/3	Choriocarcinoma	9100/3
Chondrosarcoma	9220/3	Male adnexal tumor of probable wolffian origin	
Angiosarcoma	9120/3		
Malignant fibrous histiocytoma	8830/3	**Metastatic tumors**	
Malignant peripheral nerve sheath tumors	9540/3		

[a]Morphology code of the International Classification of Diseases for Oncology (ICDO) and the Systematized Nomenclature of Medicine (http://snomed.org). Behavior is coded /0 for benign tumors, /2 for in-situ carcinomas and grade III intraepithelial neoplasia, /3 for malignant tumors, and /1 for borderline or uncertain behavior.

small gland hyperplasia), the latter has not been proved to be a premalignant lesion. The first is characterized by cytologic atypia although the architecture is maintained, whereas the second shows architectural atypia characterized by a neoacinar (small gland) proliferation without significant cytologic atypia. This is discussed under Carcinoma mimics (see p. 778).

Prostatic intraepithelial neoplasia

McNeal described this premalignant lesion as early as 1965[10] and in subsequent years,[11,12] but his concept of preneoplasia was not fully embraced until the mid-1980s. In 1986 McNeal & Bostwick provided further evidence of the premalignant nature of PIN (originally termed intraductal dysplasia) and

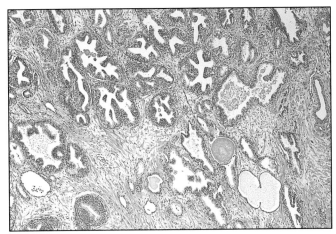

Fig. 14A.1 • Prostatic intraepithelial neoplasia (PIN). The glandular structures of PIN have a complex architecture featuring epithelial proliferation and nuclear stratification. The affected glands that make up the thickened cellular walls stand out over the normal or atrophic glands.

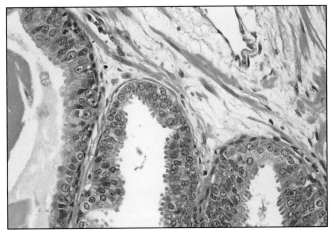

Fig. 14A.2 • Under higher magnification, prostatic intraepithelial neoplasia shows increased number of cells, anisonucleosis, hyperchromasia, and prominent nucleoli.

introduced a grading system.[4] A workshop on premalignant lesions of the prostate was held at Bethesda, Maryland, in March 1989, and at this meeting the term prostatic intra-epithelial neoplasia (PIN) was adopted as the preferred term.[13]

Histologic features of PIN

Microscopically, PIN is easily distinguished from normal or hyperplastic glandular epithelium on low-power magnification, as the affected glands or ducts most often depict striking hyperchromasia and nuclear stratification (Fig. 14A.1). On high-power examination, nucleomegaly and hyperchromasia are seen (Fig. 14A.2). Depending on the severity of nuclear changes, PIN is subdivided into low and high grades.[8,9]

Although the consensus meeting at Bethesda, Maryland[13] agreed upon only two types of PIN, low-grade and high-grade, nevertheless, for the purposes of understanding PIN, the histo-logic description provided here is according to the grading system proposed by McNeal & Bostwick.[4] Low-grade PIN (grade 1) is characterized by a slight increase in cellularity, some variation in nuclear size, hyperchromasia, and the presence of small nucleoli. Grade 2 PIN shows nuclear stratification with some nuclear enlargement and presence of nucleoli. These changes are generally focal, especially the nucleoli, which are not present in all of the cells. Many times it is very difficult to differentiate low-grade PIN (grade 1) from grade 2 PIN. In contrast, the epithelial cells of high-grade PIN (grade 3) look cytologically malignant as any carcinoma in situ would look. Thus, this grade is characterized by a marked increase in cellularity with nuclear stratification, and hyperchromasia. The nuclei are enlarged, a feature that is easily confirmed when one compares the epithelial cells of PIN with those of the adjacent normal epithelial cells and stromal tissue; however, some cases do not exhibit this feature owing to fixation or preparation artifact, or simply because there is no nuclear enlargement. The hallmark of high-grade PIN is the presence of large nucleoli (few in PIN grade 2, numerous in PIN grade 3), which are larger than 1 μm; often a halo is present around these large nucleoli. Mitotic figures are uncommon in PIN, but can be seen (Table 14A.2).

Table 14A.2	Diagnostic criteria of prostatic intraepithelial neoplasia (PIN)	
	Low-grade PIN (PIN 1)	**High-grade (PIN 2 and 3)**
Architecture	Crowding, stratification, irregular spacing	More changes with four patterns: tufting, micropapillary, cribriform, and flat
Nuclei	Slightly increased with more size variation (anisonucleosis)	Markedly enlarged with less size variation
Chromatin	Normal	Increased
Nucleoli	Rarely prominent	Occasional to frequently large and prominent

PIN distribution

PIN is found predominantly in the peripheral zone of the prostate (75–80%), rarely in the transition zone (10–15%), and extremely rarely in the central zone (<5%), and this distri-bution parallels the frequency of the zonal predilection for prostatic carcinoma.[4,5,14] The frequency of high-grade PIN in needle biopsy series ranges from 5% to 16% and in trans-urethral resection of the prostate (TURP) specimens between 2.3% and 4.2%.[15–17]

It may involve part of the lumen of the acinus or the entire unit. At the onset, the epithelial proliferation of PIN is mani-fest by increased cellularity and pseudostratification, but as the process progresses, intraluminal papillary formations develop. PIN exhibits a variety of architectural patterns: tufting, micropapillary, cribriform, or flat.[8,18] The most common are the papillary and tufting patterns, and less frequently the cribriform pattern; the rarest form is the flat pattern.[8,18] Other uncommon patterns include those with mucinous cyto-plasm, signet-ring forms, small cell undifferentiated features,[19] and foamy gland type (Fig. 14A.3) and inverted (hobnail) PIN features.[8,20,21] Except for the foamy gland type, these

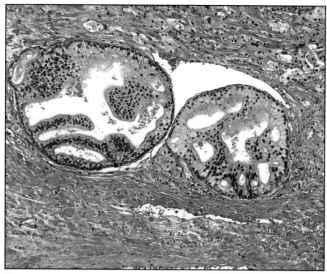

Fig. 14A.3 • Foamy high-grade prostatic intraepithelial neoplasia (PIN): PIN cells have abundant foamy cytoplasm which is better depicted on the upper aspect of the glands.

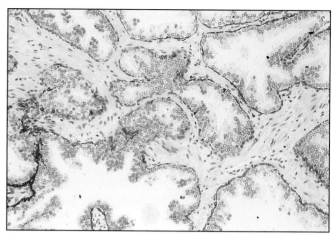

Fig. 14A.4 • The basal cell layer is usually retained in a lower-grade prostatic intraepithelial neoplasia. 34βE12 immunostaining.

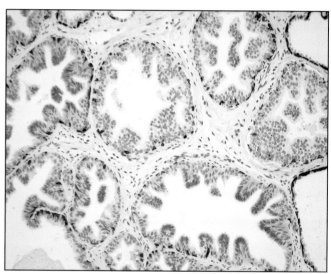

Fig. 14A.5 • High-grade prostatic intraepithelial neoplasia (PIN) glands frequently show partial loss of basal cells. Note skipped nuclear staining. Compare this illustration with the complete basal cell stain of low-grade PIN in Figure 14A.4.

architectural patterns are more commonly seen in high-grade than in low-grade lesions.[18]

Multifocality of PIN and precursor of malignancy

In 1969 McNeal [12] mentioned the multifocality of this process; this observation has since been corroborated by others.[4,5,22] In a study of whole organ sections of the prostate gland obtained from patients undergoing cystoprostatectomy for bladder cancer, Troncoso et al.[14] found PIN in 89 of 100 prostates. Most often PIN was multifocal, and prostates with carcinoma had a greater number of foci of PIN than prostates without cancer. Thus, more than 10 foci of PIN were found in 71% of the prostates with carcinoma; moreover, a significant proportion displayed more than 20 foci of PIN.

In 1986, McNeal & Bostwick,[4] studying 100 serially blocked prostate adenocarcinomas and 100 benign prostates obtained at autopsy, provided strong evidence supporting the contention that high-grade PIN (referred to then as intraductal dysplasia) was a precursor of invasive carcinoma. They reported that high-grade lesions (grade 3) were more common in prostates with carcinoma (33%) than in those without carcinoma (4%) and concluded that, in the majority of prostate cancers, PIN may be the antecedent lesion.[4] This finding was confirmed by the study of Troncoso et al.[14] in which high-grade PIN (grade 3) was found in 44 of 61 (72.1%) prostates with carcinoma and in only 17.9% without carcinoma; since high-grade PIN was closely associated with carcinoma, it had a predictive value for the latter. On occasion, carcinoma may be seen to arise directly from an area of high-grade PIN.[18,23,24]

The basal cell layer is retained in low- and high-grade PIN (Figs 14A.4 and 14A.5), although it may be absent focally in high-grade PIN (Fig. 14A.5). Bostwick & Brawer,[5] using high-molecular-weight cytokeratin specific for basal cells (clone 34βE12) in a series of PIN and carcinoma, found that the basal cell layer was present in PIN but variably lost in higher grades, especially in acini adjacent to adenocarcinoma. These findings led these authors to postulate that early invasion of

prostate cancer occurs commonly in association with high-grade PIN and that early invasion is characterized by disruption of the basal cell layer. McNeal et al. have coined the term transitive glands for these glands.[23] In high-grade PIN with adjacent small atypical glands, the issue is whether the small glands represent budding or tangentially sectioned glands from adjacent high-grade PIN or invasive cancer next to high-grade PIN. Kronz et al.[25] reported that PIN with adjacent small atypical glands appears to be a greater risk factor than high-grade PIN alone in predicting the presence of cancer on rebiopsy. Although age and predominant pattern of associated high-grade PIN may be helpful in predicting which men with this lesion will have cancer on rebiopsy, they cannot be used reliably; therefore, all men with PIN with adjacent small atypical glands should undergo repeat biopsy.

Immunohistochemistry

The basal cell markers are the most commonly utilized markers in the diagnosis of PIN, i.e., high-molecular-weight cytokeratin

(34βE12), p63, and cytokeratin 5/6. However, a whole body of immunohistochemistry studies have been undertaken to correlate the relationship between high-grade PIN and invasive carcinoma. For instance, a monoclonal antikeratin antibody, KA4,[26] and the *Ulex europaeus* lectin (UEA-I) stained over 90% of cases of PIN and invasive carcinoma,[26,27] whereas only 4% of BPHs were immunoreactive for KA4 and not reactive for UEA-I; in contrast, lectin binding was reported to be decreased in foci of dysplasia in a different study.[28] Vimentin is present in the majority of luminal cells of BPH and in 15% of PIN cases, but is absent in invasive adenocarcinoma.[26] Other studies, including argyrophilic nucleolar organizer regions (AgNOR) and static DNA flow cytometry, suggest that high-grade PIN and carcinoma have similar proliferative activity and DNA content and hence high-grade PIN is the most likely precursor of cancer.[29–32] Additional support for the precursor potential of PIN comes from numerous studies, including immunostaining for prostate-specific antigen (PSA), prostatic acid phosphatase (PrAP), CD57, collagen IV, collagenase, metalloproteinase and matrilysin expression, epidermal growth factor receptor, proliferating cell nuclear antigen, Ki-67, MIB1 proliferative activity, p53 tumor suppressor gene protein, c-*myc* gene expression, bcl-2 oncoprotein, etc.[22,33–37] Similar cytogenetic abnormalities (involving 7q, 8q, 10q, 16q) and numerical chromosomal changes are noted in high-grade PIN and cancer.[38–41] A recent study[42] demonstrated that a significantly higher alpha-methylacyl-CoA-racemase (AMACR)/P504S-positive rate (56.0%) was found in isolated high-grade PIN glands adjacent to cancer (distance less than 5 mm) compared with those away from cancer (distance more than 5 mm; 14%, $P < 0.0001$). Glands with high-grade PIN adjacent to cancer also showed a higher ($P < 0.0004$) AMACR/P504S intensity than did those away from cancer. These data indicated that PIN strongly positive for AMACR/P504S might be more closely associated with cancer than PIN negative or weakly positive for AMACR/P504S, and this study provides additional evidence to link high-grade PIN as a precursor lesion to prostatic adenocarcinoma.[42]

Differential diagnosis

The most critical differential diagnosis, for the benign/low-grade lesions, includes differentiation of grade 1 PIN (low-grade PIN) versus grade 2 (regarded as high-grade PIN), and the histologic pattern of the central zone. For high-grade lesions, the differential diagnosis of high-grade PIN includes ductal-endometrioid carcinoma, cribriform carcinoma, and transitional cell carcinoma (TCC) involving prostatic ducts. There are other processes that also enter in the differential diagnosis, but these are more easily ruled out. They are discussed briefly below.

High-grade PIN versus low-grade PIN. The distinguishing features between low-grade PIN and high-grade PIN are listed in Table 14A.2. However, unfortunately, there are no clear-cut histologic criteria to differentiate grade 1 PIN (low-grade PIN) and grade 2 PIN. Hence, the differentiation is subjective and pathologists may wrongly call a lesion high-grade PIN simply because there is hyperchromasia or presence of some nucleoli. In an interesting study by Sakar et al., the authors submitted 30 prostate needle biopsy slides containing glands with variable

degrees of architectural atypia, including 22 cases that had been diagnosed as high-grade PIN, to 11 urologic pathologists. After receiving variable answers for many of the cases, the authors concluded that: "While the morphologic criteria used by urologic pathologists to diagnose HGPIN [high-grade PIN] were similar, the application of criteria in borderline cases varied considerably. This accounts in part for the differing prevalence rates of HGPIN in the literature and has significant clinical implications for individual patients."[43]

High-grade PIN versus central zone and transitional metaplasia. The central zone, often included in the biopsy directed to the base of the prostate, shows changes that may easily be confused with high-grade PIN.[44] The central zone is characterized by the presence of far more stroma between glands than in the peripheral or transition zones. Often there is nuclear stratification, making the ducts appear abnormal as if containing high-grade PIN. However, the nuclei of the epithelial cells are monotonously round without atypia, although occasionally one may see a nucleolus. Small glandular structures simulating so-called Roman arches and/or forming a cribriform pattern are not uncommon in the central zone. In addition, intraglandular papillations may occur, but these contain a central fibrovascular core, and no atypical epithelial features. In contrast the papillations of high-grade PIN do not have a central fibrovascular core.[44]

Transitional metaplasia generally occurs in the central large ducts close to the urethra, but may be seen in the peripheral zone where it may be confused with low-grade PIN. The presence of oval to slightly elongated nuclei, often with nuclear grooves, is characteristic of transitional cell metaplasia.[45]

High-grade PIN versus high-grade tumors. Of the high-grade tumors, TCC of the prostatic ducts and lesions with an intraductal cribriform pattern are the main differential diagnoses.

TCC involving ducts is generally a high-grade carcinoma that may show central, comedo-type necrosis, a feature that is not seen in high-grade PIN. The cells of TCC show significant nuclear anaplasia manifest by considerable variation in size and shape of the cells, hyperchromasia, and often brisk mitotic activity. These cells do not react to PSA, PrAP, or AMACR/P504S.[46–48]

Lesions that share an intraductal cribriform pattern include high-grade PIN, cribriform carcinoma, ductal-endometrioid carcinoma, and intraductal carcinoma in situ. The boundaries between the last three entities are not clear-cut. Cribriform carcinoma is similar to ductal endometrioid carcinoma and, when the patterns overlap, it is difficult to separate them. As a general rule the cells of ductal-endometrioid carcinoma are cuboidal to tall columnar with obvious anaplasia, while those of cribriform carcinoma are monotonously round and high-grade.

Ductal-endometrioid carcinoma simulates high-grade PIN, and distinction may not always be possible in needle biopsy specimens. Ductal-endometrioid carcinoma frequently involves the transition zone around the verumontanum area, and displays a back-to-back complex glandular architecture. It exhibits true papillae, frequent necrosis, and marked nuclear anaplasia, including frequent mitoses.[49,50] The presence of comedo necrosis rules out high-grade PIN.

High-grade PIN generally expands the duct without significant irregularities of its outline. When the cribriform proliferation is florid with marked expansion of the ductal/ acinar unit involved, the lack of a basal cell layer favors a cribriform or ductal endometrioid carcinoma rather than high-grade PIN. Thus, the presence of basal cells would support a diagnosis of high-grade PIN, but caution should be exercised because retrograde extension of a ductal-endometrioid or cribriform carcinoma into a duct/acinus may occur.[49] Therefore, the presence of the basal cell layer should be interpreted with caution.

The term carcinoma in situ has been utilized when ductal/ acinar units are replaced by cribriform carcinoma. McNeal & Yemoto[49] believe that ductal involvement in prostate carcinoma is a common entity that is usually present within the tumor, but is rare away from the invasive aspect of it. In this context they have utilized the term intraductal carcinoma and suggested that the lesions were part of the evolution of prostate cancer rather than precursors.

Using the above criteria for intraductal carcinoma (defined as high-grade PIN with cribriform, solid, or comedo patterns), Wilcox et al.[51] studied whole-mount sections from 252 patients with pT3N0 prostate carcinoma for the presence of intraductal carcinoma and correlated the presence or absence of intraductal carcinoma with Gleason score, total tumor volume, surgical margin status, seminal vesicle involvement, and disease progression. Patients with intraductal carcinoma had a higher Gleason score and total tumor volume and were more likely to show seminal vesicle involvement and disease progression than those patients without intraductal carcinoma. Therefore, the presence of so-called intraductal carcinoma in situ is generally associated with invasive prostate carcinoma and rarely poses a diagnostic problem.

The differential diagnosis of high-grade PIN and infiltrating cribriform carcinoma involving ducts was also discussed by Kronz et al.[52] They reported four clinicopathologic findings (two clinical and two histologic) to be helpful in differentiating cribriform high-grade PIN from infiltrating cribriform carcinoma: positive digital rectal examination ($P = 0.02$); positive transrectal ultrasound ($P = 0.02$); bilateral atypical cribriform glands ($P = 0.02$), and detached cribriform glands ($P = 0.04$). Other findings, including number of cribriform glands, largest size of cribriform glands, necrosis, and stromal fibrosis, failed to show a difference between PIN and carcinoma.

High-grade PIN versus normal structures. Normal structures such as seminal vesicles and ejaculatory ducts may mimic PIN.[53-55] Ejaculatory duct/seminal vesicle epithelium usually shows scattered large pleomorphic nuclei, often with intranuclear inclusions and cytoplasmic lipofuscin pigment, although PIN epithelium may also show pigment which is usually fine and less conspicuous.[56] Pleomorphism is unusual in high-grade PIN. The diagnosis of high-grade PIN should be made with caution if infarction or inflammation (particularly acute) is present in the vicinity, as the nuclear atypia induced by reactive conditions may mimic PIN; the range of architectural features of PIN is usually not present in reactive prostatic epithelium.

Clinical significance of high-grade PIN

There is general agreement that high-grade PIN is associated with invasive carcinoma in about one-third of the patients

(30–35%) so diagnosed, and thus repeat prostatic biopsies are generally performed following this diagnosis. Unfortunately, two-thirds of the patients do not show invasive carcinoma on rebiopsy, and some of these patients undergo yearly repeated biopsies. Urologists and pathologists are becoming aware of this problem. Although there is good interobserver reproducibility for the recognition of high-grade PIN,[57] it is not so for the recognition of low-grade PIN.[58] Thus, some cases of low-grade PIN (grade 1) are probably wrongly diagnosed as high-grade PIN. Numerous recent articles on high-grade PIN have addressed other concomitant factors that may help to select patients at higher risk of having invasive carcinoma.

Kronz et al.[25] analyzed 245 men in whom the only abnormal finding on the initial biopsy was high-grade PIN (Fig. 14A.6) and who had at least one follow-up biopsy. Repeat biopsy identified cancer in 32.2% of men. The only independent histologic predictor for the presence of cancer was the number of cores with high-grade PIN; risk of cancer: 30.2% with 1 or 2 positive cores, 40% with 3 cores, and 75% with >3 cores. The following did not predict cancer: number of high-grade PIN glands, maximum percentage of core involved by high-grade PIN, nucleolar prominence, percentage of cells with prominent nucleoli, pattern of high-grade PIN (flat, tufting, micropapillary, cribriform), marked pleomorphism, digital rectal examination, transrectal ultrasound findings, family history of prostate cancer, serum PSA at time of high-grade PIN diagnosis, and rate of change of serum PSA. If cancer is not found on the first two follow-up biopsies, it will probably not be found. Although clinical findings at the time of diagnosis of high-grade PIN are not useful to predict who might have cancer, histologic findings may help identify who needs additional biopsies.

Bishara et al.[59] reported that histologic subtype analysis revealed a higher risk of carcinoma with the tufting/flat category of PIN (31.9%) as compared with the micropapillary/ cribriform category (22.0%), yet this difference was not near statistical significance. This finding differed from another study that indicated a higher risk associated with micropapillary and cribriform high-grade PIN.[25] Bishara et al.[59] also mentioned that the number of core biopsies involved by high-grade PIN

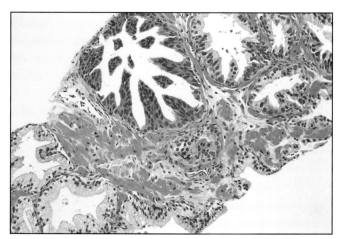

Fig. 14A.6 • Prostatic intraepithelial neoplasia in needle biopsy. Compare the enlarged nuclei of prostatic intraepithelial neoplasia with those of the adjacent benign glands.

was predictive of a subset of men who were at higher risk of having invasive carcinoma on follow-up biopsies.

Is the diagnosis of high-grade PIN becoming obsolete? Probably not! However, the rules of the game might be changing with the introduction of the extended biopsies. These are also called "saturation" biopsies, which target 10 or more sites, in contrast to traditional six-site sextant biopsies. These biopsies allow for extensive mapping of the prostate in such a way that the chances of finding an invasive carcinoma are very high.[60,61] In a recent study of high-grade PIN diagnosed with a 12-site biopsy of 31 patients who were followed for 3 years before a repeat biopsy was done, the authors reported that 8 patients (28.8%) had invasive carcinoma on rebiopsy, 11 (35.5%) showed high-grade PIN, and 12 (38.7%) showed no disease.[62] The authors concluded that high-grade PIN is a precursor to prostate carcinoma and that repeat biopsies at delayed intervals are recommended regardless of changes in the PSA level.[62] Other authors believe that patients diagnosed with high-grade PIN on extended biopsies should be followed on a clinical basis and rebiopsy should only be done if there are clinical indications for it.[63,64] The final decision to perform a rebiopsy or not, on a patient with high-grade PIN diagnosed with 10 or more biopsy sites, should be agreed conjointly between the patient and urologist.

Adenocarcinoma of the prostate

Adenocarcinoma is by far the most common malignancy of the prostate gland and one of the leading causes of cancer-related death in males. The American Cancer Society estimated that, in the USA, 234 460 males would be diagnosed with prostate cancer in 2006, and 27 350 would die of their disease.[167] Prostate cancer is the most common cancer in men, accounting for 33% of all malignant tumors in men, and accounts for 9% of cancer deaths, the third highest in men after lung and colorectal cancers.[1] Both incidence and mortality have decreased in the past few years.[65]

The incidence of prostate cancer is quite variable among races, being very high in the USA, Australia, and Scandinavian countries (probably due to screening). Within the USA, the black population has the highest incidence as well as high mortality rates. Incidence rates in Europe are variable with a higher incidence in the countries of northern and western Europe and lower in the countries of eastern and southern Europe. Prostate cancers are relatively rare in Asian populations. In addition to geographic, ethnic, and racial differences in incidence, genetic polymorphism factors are also likely responsible for the different incidence.[2] Important questions remain about the cause and prevention of prostate cancer, but significant advances have occurred in the understanding of premalignant epithelial lesions as well as new clinical techniques, enhancing early detection of cancer, such as transrectal ultrasound, and serum levels of PSA.[66,67] Detection of tumors likely to cause morbidity and mortality remains the main problem: 20–40% of patients have high-stage tumors at the time of diagnosis. The great clinical paradox, in spite of the high incidence of prostate cancer, is that more men with prostate cancer will die with the disease than of the disease itself.

Conventional adenocarcinoma of the prostate represents over 90% of the epithelial malignancies in this organ. The majority of cases exhibit an acinar or acinar/ductal growth pattern.[2,68,69] The remaining 10% comprise the variants of prostatic carcinoma, which will be discussed separately.

Carcinomas may arise in any zone of the prostate, but the relative distribution is different in each zone: 68% of the carcinomas arise in the peripheral zone, 24% in the transition zone, and 8% in the central zone.[70] The various patterns of growth have been well described by Mostofi & Price[71] and Gleason;[72] they include acinar, fused acinar, cribriform, papillary, trabecular, and solid.

The majority of prostatic adenocarcinomas are not difficult to diagnose; however, certain problem areas exist. First is the separation of well-differentiated adenocarcinoma from the vast number of benign or atypical small gland proliferations. Second is the threshold for recognizing extremely small foci of cancer in needle biopsies. Finally, at the extreme of the histologic spectrum depending on the morphology, a very poorly differentiated adenocarcinoma of the prostate may be difficult to distinguish from inflammatory infiltrates, metastatic carcinoma, and TCC involving the prostate.

The criteria for diagnosis of well-differentiated adenocarcinoma include a small gland proliferation recognized as being discrete or focally infiltrative on low-power examination, the presence of a single cell lining with complete absence of the basal cell layer, nucleomegaly, and presence of large nucleoli.[73–75] The small gland proliferation usually exhibits well-formed acinar structures with acini arranged in a back-to-back fashion (Fig. 14A.7) and a circumscribed or focally infiltrative margin. The size of the nucleoli is critical; in carcinoma, nucleoli must be at least 1 μm in diameter (Fig. 14A.8). We usually do not measure nucleolar size, but one can rely on the presence of prominent nucleoli with a distinct cherry-red color. The number of nucleoli varies from one to several per nucleus. When nucleoli are multiple, they are generally small. A single cell lining (i.e., lack of basal cell layer) is also a requisite for the diagnosis of well-differentiated adenocarcinoma of the prostate.[76] Intraluminal crystalloids (Fig. 14A.9), blue mucin (Fig. 14A.10), glomerulations (Fig. 14A.11), mucinous fibroplasia (collagenous micronodules) (Fig. 14A.12), and perineural invasion (Fig. 14A.13) are also helpful findings that should alert the pathologist to suspect a diagnosis of carcinoma. Intraluminal crystalloids and blue mucin are not pathognomonic,

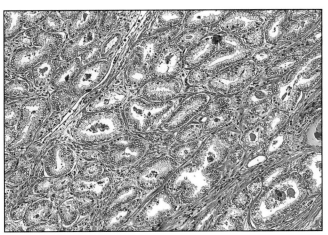

Fig. 14A.7 • Well-differentiated adenocarcinoma. Well-formed small acini are arranged in a back-to-back fashion.

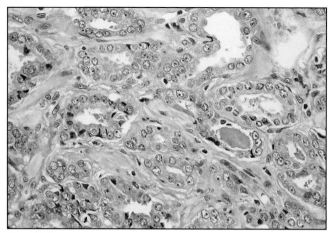

Fig. 14A.8 • The main differences between atypical small gland proliferation and adenocarcinoma of prostate are the presence of prominent nucleoli and absence of the basal cell layer in the latter.

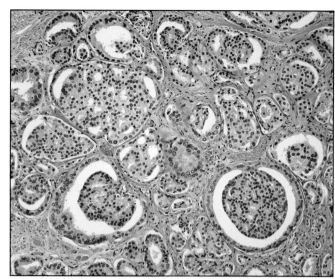

Fig. 14A.11 • Prostate cancer with glomerulations. Glomeruloid structures are characterized by dilated glands containing an intraluminal cribriform proliferation of malignant epithelium, which is attached to only one edge of the gland.

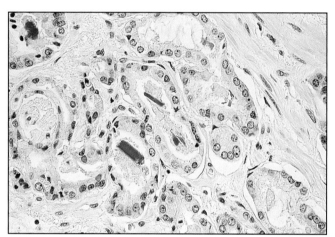

Fig. 14A.9 • Rod-shaped crystalloids in the glandular lumina of a well-differentiated adenocarcinoma.

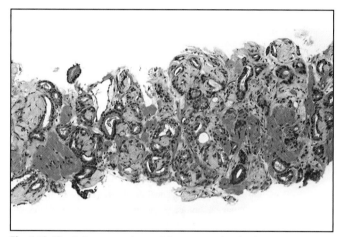

Fig. 14A.12 • Collagenous micronodules associated with adenocarcinoma of prostate.

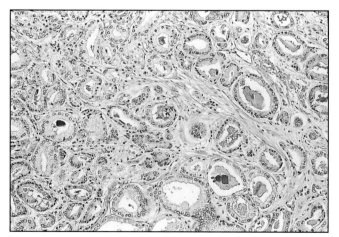

Fig. 14A.10 • Alcian blue staining reveals intraluminal acid mucin. Intraluminal crystalloids are also present.

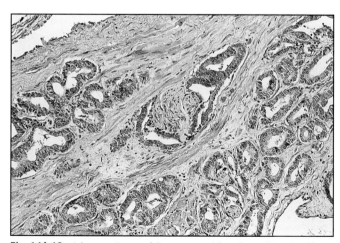

Fig. 14A.13 • Adenocarcinoma of the prostate with perineural invasion. The gland encircles the entire nerve, and its cytologic features fulfill the criteria for a carcinoma.

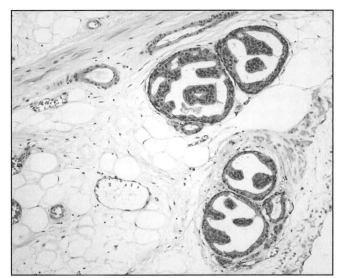

Fig. 14A.14 • The presence of malignant glands in adipose tissue indicates extraprostatic extension of carcinoma.

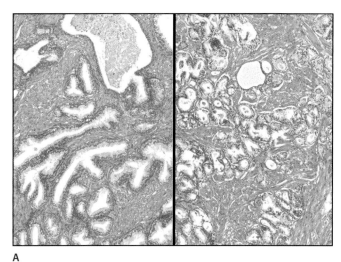

A

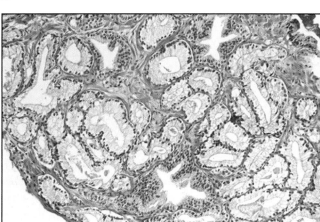

B

Fig. 14A.15 • (A) The illustration on the left shows normal prostate glands, while the illustration on the right side depicts glands suspicious for cancer: they are small (too small) and show back-to-back arrangement (too crowded). (B) In addition to small and crowded glands, the small glands exhibit clear cytoplasm (too clear).

but they are frequently associated with carcinoma. However, mucinous fibroplasia, glomerulation, circumferential involvement of nerve, and glands in fat tissue (Fig. 14A.14) are believed to be pathognomonic and allow an unequivocal diagnosis of prostate cancer.[77] For screening of prostate cancer in biopsy or TURP specimens, the rule of "three toos" (too small glands, too crowded glands with back-to-back arrangement, and too clear glands) is very useful (Fig. 14A.15). To confirm the diagnosis of carcinoma, three diagnostic criteria – nuclear enlargement, prominent nucleolus, and lack of basal cells – should be present (Fig. 14A.16).

Crystalloids

Crystalloids may be found within the lumina of the malignant acini, in the lumina of the glands adjacent to the carcinoma (usually glandular structures exhibiting PIN or AAH and rarely in benign glands), and in SA of the prostate.[78–81] They are generally elongated, may be rhomboid or needle-like, and stain brightly eosinophilic with the usual hematoxylin and eosin (H&E) stain (see Fig. 14A.9). By electron microscopy they are made up of electron-dense material that lacks the parallel periodicity of true crystals, and so they are referred to as crystalloids.[80,82] They have been observed in up to 72.5% of carcinomas, predominantly in the well-differentiated type within neoplastic acini, or in adjacent benign glands, but they have also been observed in cribriform carcinomas and, rarely, in poorly differentiated carcinomas.[80,81] In needle biopsies in which crystalloids are present in benign glands, the likelihood of finding cancer on subsequent biopsies is low.[83,84]

Mucin

Intraluminal mucin also occurs in well and moderately differentiated adenocarcinomas of the prostate.[75,85] Neutral mucin may be found in normal glands, but acid mucins are present predominantly in prostatic adenocarcinoma. The mucin in carcinoma is present in the lumina of the glands, where it may be stained with mucicarmine or alcian blue stains (Fig. 14A.10);

the intraluminal mucin appears to be wispy and basophilic with H&E stain. The cytoplasm of the neoplastic cells usually does not stain; this parameter may be helpful when trying to rule out a metastatic adenocarcinoma. However, intracytoplasmic acid mucin may be found in hyperplastic glands. SA, PIN, and AAH also show intraluminal acid mucin, and the finding of intraluminal acid mucin alone is not diagnostic of carcinoma. Hence, there is little utility in performing histochemical stains for acid mucin in routine diagnostic practice, but the observation of blue mucin in H&E-stained sections should alert the pathologist to rule out prostate carcinoma.

Perineural invasion, mucinous fibroplasia (collagenous micronodules), or glomerulation

Perineural invasion (Fig. 14A.13), mucinous fibroplasia/collagenous micronodules (rounded, dense, hyaline material within and adjacent to neoplastic acini; Fig. 14A.12), and glomerulation (cribriform formations; Fig. 14A.11) are reported to be specific diagnostic features, in addition to

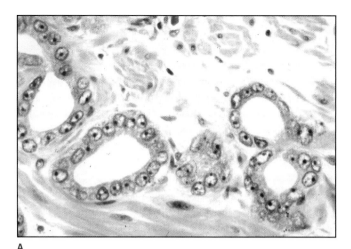

A

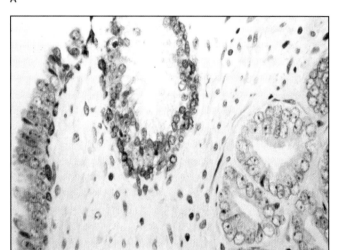

B

Fig. 14A.16 • **(A)** To confirm the diagnosis of prostate cancer, the cells in the suspicious glands must show nuclear enlargement with prominent nucleoli and absence of basal cells. **(B)** This illustration depicts small glands of carcinoma with no basal cells, while the adjacent high-grade prostatic intraepithelial neoplasia reveals prominent basal cells.

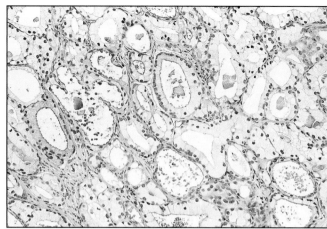

Fig. 14A.17 • Clear cell ("transition-zone") carcinoma. Small to medium back-to-back glands are lined by a single row of epithelial cells that are usually tall, columnar, and have clear cytoplasm.

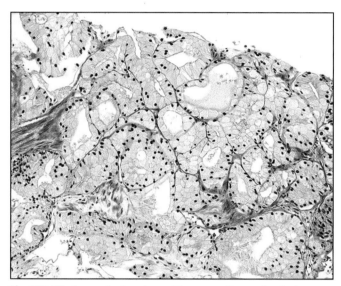

Fig. 14A.18 • Foamy gland carcinoma. The tumor cells are tall and columnar, displaying a clear-foamy cytoplasm and basally located hyperchromatic nuclei.

glands in adipose tissue (Fig 14A.14), for malignancy since they have not been described in benign prostatic glands. Corpora amylacea in the prostate are a frequent finding in benign acini, but are only rarely observed in adenocarcinoma (0.4% incidence). Christian et al.[86] indicated that the incidence of corpora amylacea in adenocarcinoma is low (0.4% incidence), but the presence of such inclusions cannot be used to exclude malignancy.

Transition-zone cancer

Clear cell (tall columnar) carcinoma of the prostate is an interesting variation of the morphology of well-differentiated adenocarcinoma.[70] It has recently been emphasized that this pattern of cancer may mimic BPH, and it has been referred to as the "pseudohyperplastic pattern" of adenocarcinoma.[87,88] The majority of cases arise from the transition zone, but not infrequently this pattern is present in core needle biopsies. It is, then, a pattern likely to be seen in transurethral resectates. This tumor is made up of small to medium-sized glands that are

lined by a single row of epithelial cells. The cells are generally tall columnar but may be cuboidal in shape and characteristically have clear or amphophilic cytoplasm (Fig. 14A.17). When the glands present greater variation in size and some of them are cystically dilated, the resulting configuration of the lesion may be confused with BPH. A similar often well-differentiated lesion is the so-called foamy gland carcinoma,[89] which usually consists of small glands with foamy cytoplasm and pink luminal secretions (Fig. 14A.18). Foamy gland carcinoma is a distinctive histologic variant of prostatic adenocarcinoma and is often associated with aggressive behavior, despite its deceivingly benign histologic appearance.[90] Prostatic adenocarcinoma resembling benign hyperplastic glands architecturally (pseudohyperplastic prostatic adenocarcinoma) is a recently recognized entity (Fig. 14A.19).[88] Benign-appearing features include papillary infoldings, large glands, branching, and corpora amylacea. Within the pseudohyperplastic foci, features helpful in establishing a malignant diagnosis are nuclear enlargement, pink amorphous secretions, occasional to frequent nucleoli, and crystalloids. Other features associated

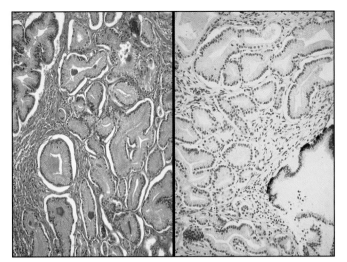

Fig. 14A.19 • Pseudohyperplastic carcinoma: The branching and papillary growth pattern mimic benign hyperplastic glands (left). In the illustration on the right, the high-molecular-weight stain (34βE12) demonstrates lack of basal cells in the pseudohyperplastic carcinoma in contrast to the presence of basal cells in the adjacent benign gland.

with malignancy (mitoses, blue-tinged mucin, adjacent high-grade PIN, and perineural invasion) can be seen infrequently. Immunohistochemical stains for high-molecular-weight keratin, CK5/6, and p63 show an absence of basal cells in the pseudohyperplastic areas, supporting the diagnosis of cancer. It is critical to recognize pseudohyperplastic prostatic adenocarcinoma and the features needed to establish a malignant diagnosis so that these carcinomas are not misdiagnosed as benign.[88]

Differential diagnosis

An important differential diagnosis of well-differentiated adenocarcinoma includes the small gland proliferations of the transition zone. These are: adenomatous hyperplasia (adenosis), SA, BCH, and CCCH of the prostate. A common denominator among these benign small gland proliferations is

the presence of basal cells which are not present in carcinoma of the prostate, and which can be demonstrated by using immuno-histochemical stains for high-molecular-weight cytokeratin (clone 34βE12), CK5/6, and p63. There are also other lesions such as NA, mesonephric and verumontanum hyperplasia and normal anatomic structures, such as atrophy, ejaculatory ducts/seminal vesicle epithelium, and Cowper's glands, that may simulate prostate carcinoma. These entities are discussed under the heading of "carcinoma mimics."[3,73,91,92]

Recently emphasis has been placed on adenocarcinoma with an atrophic pattern (atrophic variant of adenocarcinoma) that may be misdiagnosed as benign (Fig. 14A.20).[93–95] Although this type of carcinoma must be kept in mind when atrophic-like changes are present, the atrophic pattern of this variant is usually accompanied by conventional acinar adeno-carcinoma. In difficult cases, using a panel of immunostains including AMACR, 34βE12, and P63 (positive AMACR immunostaining along with negative basal cell markers in atrophic carcinoma) is recommended in the differentiation of atrophic prostatic cancer and benign atrophy.[96] When carci-noma of the prostate is a high-grade malignant tumor, TCC of the bladder (involving the prostate) or a primary TCC of the prostatic ducts and acini enters the differential diagnosis.[46,47,97,98] The most common situation is that of a patient with a history of treated prostate carcinoma who has been stable for several years, but becomes obstructed. Poorly differentiated adeno-carcinoma of the prostate generally retains the monotonous appearance of its cells, and not infrequently a faint acinar pattern; the nuclei, although variable in size, do not show extreme variation, the chromatin is finely dispersed, and the nucleoli are prominent in most cells (Fig. 14A.21). Mitoses are rare. On the other hand, TCC is likely to exhibit significant nuclear pleomorphism and a variable distribution of chromatin, including numerous hyperchromatic cells and frequent mitoses (Fig. 14A.22). Immunohistochemistry is very valuable in the differential diagnosis with TCC.[99,100] PSA and PrAP staining must be done, but it is important to remember that PSA may be negative when the patient has been treated previously with hormonal manipulation. PrAP is generally positive, but the reaction may be focal (Fig. 14A.23). Such reaction is good

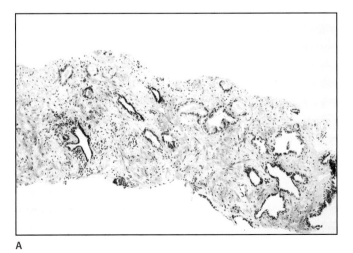

A

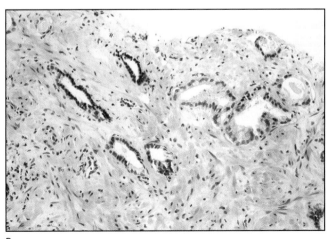

B

Fig. 14A.20 • (A) Adenocarcinoma with atrophic pattern. Although many of the glands have scant cytoplasm, the non-lobular and infiltrative appearance on low power is a feature of carcinoma. (B) High power shows some glands with abundant cytoplasm and other glands with scant cytoplasm ("atrophic") but with an infiltrative architecture.

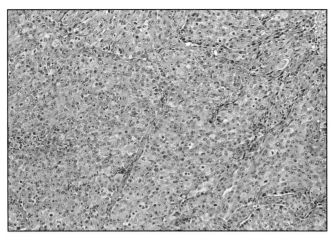

Fig. 14A.21 • High-grade solid prostatic adenocarcinoma. A high-grade prostatic adenocarcinoma may be confused with transitional cell carcinoma, but prostate carcinoma usually shows a monotonous appearance of the tumor cells.

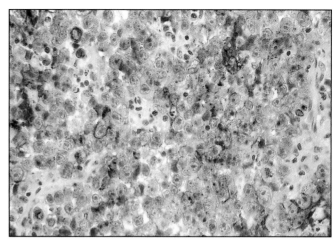

Fig. 14A.23 • Even in solid high-grade prostatic adenocarcinoma, prostate-specific antigen and prostatic acid phosphatase immunostaining are usually positive, as seen here.

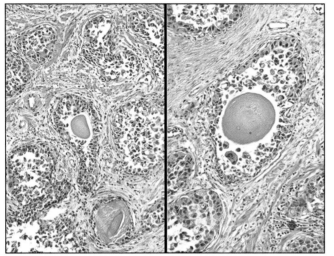

Fig. 14A.22 • Transitional cell carcinoma involving prostatic ducts. In these illustrations the acinar structures are expanded by a proliferation of high-grade malignant pleomorphic cells. Note the presence of corpora amylacea within the lumina of the acinar structures. The tumor cells are far more pleomorphic and mitotically active than expected for a high-grade adenocarcinoma of the prostate.

enough to confirm the diagnosis of adenocarcinoma of the prostate. Thrombomodulin and uroplakin, urothelial markers, are generally disappointing, possibly because high-grade TCC loses all antigenicity.[100]

The surgical pathologist's nightmare in the 1990s has been the accurate recognition of cancer and its separation from mimics in the contemporary 18-gauge needle biopsy, as well as deciding the threshold for diagnosing cancer in the context of extremely small numbers of atypical glands. While criteria for the diagnosis of prostate cancer can be defined eloquently on paper, it is often difficult to apply such criteria when only a small number of atypical glands are present.[101] A meticulous systematic approach is necessary. The process involves appreciating: (1) architectural features; (2) cytologic features; and (3) clues that may assist in the diagnosis.

Architecturally, a small discrete cluster of closely packed, round, rigid glands should draw attention while scanning at low and medium power. The glands may vary in size and have an infiltrative appearance. They must be lined only by secretory cells. Cytologically, the cells are cuboidal to columnar and have eosinophilic, clear, or amphophilic cytoplasm and round nuclei, which are enlarged and distinctly larger than the nuclei of surrounding benign glands. A key feature is the presence of prominent cherry-red nucleoli. Other clues to the diagnosis of cancer include intraluminal blue mucin, crystalloids, collagenous micronodules, glomerulation, mitoses, perineural or intraneural invasion, and the presence of associated high-grade PIN.[102–104] Caution is warranted if there is marked inflammation, budding from apparent benign glands, and artifacts of crushing or thick sections.

Immunohistochemistry

In difficult cases, immunohistochemistry is of great help. A high-molecular-weight cytokeratin (clone 34βE12), CK5/6 or p63 stain for the presence of basal cell layer as well as AMACR (P505S) staining, may be performed. Since the focus in question may be small and may be lost on deeper sections, some institutions prospectively store an intermediate level on gelatinized slides for possible immunostains. The high-molecular-weight cytokeratin, CK5/6, or p63 immunostaining must be interpreted judiciously, in conjunction with morphology, and one must insist on a good internal control and absolute lack of staining in the entire focus in question. Both 34βE12 and p63 are highly specific for basal cells and are negative in areas of prostate carcinoma. p63 is more sensitive than 34βE12 in staining benign basal cells, particularly for TURP specimens, offering a slight advantage over 34βE12 in diagnostically challenging cases.[105] However, basal cell cocktail (34βE12 and p63) not only increases the sensitivity of basal cell detection, but also reduces the staining variability and therefore renders the basal cell immunostaining more consistent.[106] When these steps are systematically followed one may be able to render a more confident diagnosis of cancer in small foci.

A recently discovered tumor marker for prostate cancer, AMACR, monoclonal (P504S) or polyclonal (AMACR-p), is being used increasingly in conjunction with H&E histology and basal cell markers in the work-up of difficult prostate needle biopsies.[107] However, it is not known how often positive AMACR staining is used merely to support a malignant diagnosis that could otherwise be established based on routine H&E histology and negative basal cell staining. Recently, Zhou et al.[108] tested the diagnostic utility of AMACR on 307 prostate needle biopsies that were sent to them for consultation diagnosed as "atypical" by contributing pathologists. A total of 215 cases had a final diagnosis of cancer following evaluation of the H&E-stained section, basal cell markers, and AMACR. Of these 215 cases, 176 (81.9%) were positive and 39 (18.1%) were negative for AMACR staining. Of 81 cases with a final diagnosis of atypical following review of all material, 42 (51.9%) were positive and 39 (48.1%) were negative for AMACR staining. When AMACR staining was negative, in no case was the initial cancer, atypical, or benign diagnosis (based on routine histology and negative basal cell markers) changed based on AMACR stain results. Of 115 cases called atypical after expert review, 76 were positive for AMACR; of these 76 cases, 34 (44.7%) were changed to a final diagnosis of cancer. Of these 34 cases, 11 underwent radical prostatectomy, and cancer was found in all cases. Three additional patients underwent repeat biopsy, and cancer was present in the repeat biopsy in 2 patients. The cases in which the diagnosis was changed from "atypical" to cancer on expert review were all highly suspicious for cancer based on H&E and negative basal cell markers, yet a definitive cancer diagnosis could not be established because of small size, insufficient cytologic atypia, or biopsy artifact. Therefore, when AMACR is used in conjunction with careful histologic examination and basal cell markers, it has great diagnostic utility. However, interpretation of AMACR staining should be undertaken with caution, because a negative AMACR stain can be seen in approximately 20% of cases considered to be cancer based on H&E stain combined with negative basal cell markers. In addition, benign prostatic lesions, such as NA, AAH, and PIN, as well as non-prostatic tumors can be positive with AMACR.[109,110]

To improve the sensitivity and specificity of the diagnosis of prostate cancer, a cocktail of two antibodies (p63/p504s) has been used.[111] With the p504s/p63 cocktail, 89% of the ambiguous lesions were classified versus 53% for CK 5/6. Combined use of the two antibodies, one (p504s) as a positive marker and the other (p63) as a negative marker, with a simple immunostaining procedure, may improve diagnostic performance, sensitivity, and specificity, leading to a reduction in the risk of false negatives; this technique in cases of atypical small acinar proliferation should reduce both the percentage of residual ambiguous lesions as well as the need for additional biopsies (Fig. 14A.24).[48,111]

Magi-Galluzzi et al.[112] reported that the sensitivity of AMACR staining may vary in specimens from different pathology laboratories, possibly related to differences in fixation and processing. Therefore, it is important to optimize the staining technique for each laboratory and recognize that some small cancers on needle biopsy may be AMACR-negative. AMACR is a useful diagnostic marker for foamy gland (Fig. 14.A25) and pseudohyperplastic prostate cancer, although the positivity is lower than that of usual small gland adenocarcinoma.[113] However, when the pathologist favors the diagnosis of any of these variants of cancer on H&E-stained

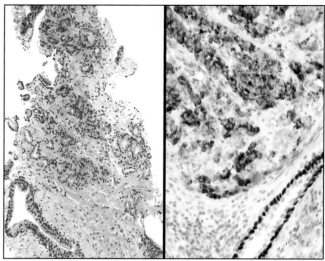

Fig. 14A.24 • Stains with alpha-methylacyl-CoA-racemase (AMACR) and p63 cocktail. The left side shows a hematoxylin and eosin-stained tissue depicting a microacinar carcinoma. The right side, stained with AMACR/p63 cocktail, exhibits nuclear staining of the basal cells with p63, while the microacinar carcinoma, negative for basal cells, is positive for AMACR.

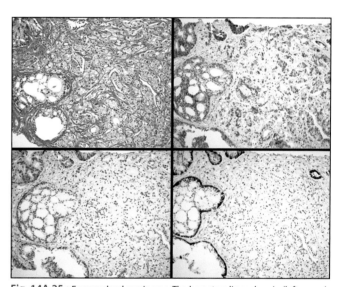

Fig. 14A.25 • Foamy gland carcinoma. The hematoxylin and eosin (left upper) displays a foamy gland carcinoma with a focus of high-grade cribriform prostatic intraepithelial neoplasia (PIN) on the left side, and an invasive carcinoma with tall columnar cells with foamy cytoplasm on the right side of this illustration. Alpha-methylacyl-CoA-racemase (right upper) stains the cytoplasm of the cells of the carcinoma as well as high-grade PIN. p63 (left lower) and high-molecular-weight cytokeratin (right lower) stain the basal cells in the high-grade PIN. Note there is no basal cell staining in the invasive carcinoma.

sections and negative stains for basal cells, but there is still doubt concerning the diagnosis of cancer, because of the deceptively benign appearance, positive staining for AMACR may provide the additional confidence to establish a definitive malignant diagnosis.

However, caution is also required because other malignant tumors may express AMACR. AMACR protein overexpression has been reported in colorectal, ovarian, breast, bladder, lung, and renal cell carcinomas; as well as in lymphoma, and melanoma. Greatest overexpression was seen in colorectal and prostate cancer with positive staining in 92% and 83% of cases,

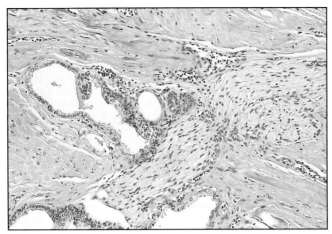

Fig. 14A.26 • A benign prostatic gland can be seen around a nerve. Although a benign gland may impinge upon a nerve, it never completely surrounds it or invades it.

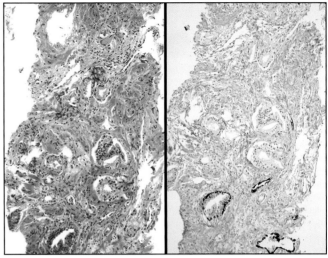

Fig. 14A.27 • Atypical small acinar proliferation. These illustrations demonstrate small gland proliferations that are suspicious for carcinoma. Architecturally, the small glands on the left side are good for carcinoma, but cytologic detail is not clear. Although there is lack of a basal cell layer in the small glands (right side, 34βE12), the overall morphologic features are not distinctive enough to render an unequivocal diagnosis of carcinoma. Therefore, this lesion is considered an atypical small gland proliferation suspicious, but not diagnostic, of malignancy.

respectively. AMACR overexpression was present in 44% of breast cancer cases. AMACR is also overexpressed in 64% of high-grade PIN and in 75% of colonic adenomas.[114]

Nerve invasion

Circumferential perineural invasion is diagnostic for prostatic carcinoma (Fig. 14A.26), although perineural indentation by benign prostatic glands can be seen. The glands in the latter cases appear totally benign and are present at only one edge of the nerve (Fig. 14A.26). Neural cell adhesion molecule (N-CAM), one of the well-known members of the immuno-globulin superfamily of adhesion molecules, has been implicated in perineural invasion and metastasis in prostate cancer. Li et al.[115] studied N-CAM expression in prostate cancers. N-CAM was upregulated in 73% (31 of 42) of the nerves with perineural invasion compared with nerves without perineural invasion ($P > 0.001$). The results suggested that N-CAM is probably involved in perineural invasion in prostate cancer. It is conceivable that cancer cells, through a yet-to-be-established paracrine loop, signal the nerve to increase N-CAM production and increase adhesion. N-CAM upregulation in nerves may also facilitate cancer cells to migrate toward nerves and promote the process of perineural spread.[115]

Atypical glands suspicious for malignancy (atypical small acinar proliferation, ASAP)

There are glandular proliferations that do not reach one's threshold to be diagnosed unequivocally as cancer. If a diagnosis of cancer cannot be made, one should not hesitate in diagnosing the glands as "atypical glands suspicious for malignancy" (AGSM) or "atypical small acinar proliferation (ASAP)." This term is increasingly being utilized to denote some glandular proliferations that suggest adenocarcinoma, but because of different factors, i.e., lack of nucleoli, lack of nuclear enlargement, artifactual distortion, too few glands to be sure, depletion of tissue and inability to do basal cell stains, a definitive diagnosis cannot be made (Fig. 14A.27).[116–119] This diagnosis does not imply an entity, but only implies that the glandular changes are suspicious for malignancy. Chan &

Epstein,[117] studying 144 cases of AGSM (or ASAP) found that 48.9% showed invasive carcinoma on rebiopsy. These authors also stated that if the AGSM (or ASAP) were qualified as "favors malignancy," as opposed to "favors benign," the percentage of invasive carcinoma on rebiopsy rose to 61%. They recommended that patients with this diagnosis should undergo rebiopsy regardless of the PSA level in the serum. Other authors have also found a similar or higher percentage of invasive carcinoma on rebiopsy.[116,118,119] Since the chances of finding an invasive carcinoma are high within the area of suspicion, it is recommended that two or more biopsies be taken from the suspicious area, as well as multiple additional biopsies of other sites in the prostate.[116,119]

Distinguishing benign prostate glands from malignant ones, based on morphology alone, in prostatic core needle biopsy specimens, may prove difficult, particularly if the suspicious focus is small (ASAP). Basal cell cocktail (34βE12 and p63) in combination with AMACR is recommended in diagnostically difficult cases to improve diagnostic accuracy. In small lesions, however, combining AMACR and the basal cell cocktail on a single slide would be superior to using either marker separately because there is a high chance for loss of relevant tissue in the small lesions.[120]

Staging systems

The Whitmore & Jewett staging system (categories: A, B, C, and D), which was commonly used in the past, has largely been replaced[121,122] by the TNM system which utilizes more parameters (Tables 14A.3 and 14A.4). Stage A/T1 disease is an unsuspected carcinoma found in a prostatectomy specimen examined for clinically benign disease. A1/T1a disease comprises those cancers which involve up to 5% of the total TURP specimen; A2/T1b disease includes cancers involving more than 5% of the resected tissue. For TURP specimens, we

Table 14A.3	The North American (Whitmore-Jewett) staging system for prostate cancer

Stage	Definition of criteria for inclusion
A	No palpable tumor; incidental finding in operative specimen
	A1 Cancer involving = 3 chips
	A2 Cancer involving > 3 chips
B	Palpable tumor confined to the prostate
	B1 Prostatic nodule = 2 cm confined to one lobe
	B2 Prostatic nodule > 2 cm but confined to one lobe
	B3 Prostatic nodule involving both lobes
C	Extension beyond the prostatic capsule but without evident metastasis
	C1 Tumor < 6 cm in diameter
	C2 Tumor = 6 cm in diameter
D	Metastatic disease
	D1 Pelvic lymph node metastases or urethral obstruction causing hydronephrosis
	D2 Bone or distant lymph node or organ or soft tissue metastases

recommend reporting both the number of microscopic foci of carcinoma and the percentage of carcinomatous involvement. With regard to the amount of prostatic chips to be examined in any TURP performed for benign disease, we follow the suggestion of Murphy et al.[123] of submitting up to 12 g of any given specimen, which is enough to detect the majority of the incidental carcinomas, and then submitting one additional cassette for each additional 10 g. If cancer is found in less than 5% of the prostatic chips, the remainder of the prostate resectate should be processed for histologic examination.

In the clinical T1 stage, the TNM system includes a third category, T1c, which is assigned to patients with clinically inapparent carcinoma (non-palpable, non-visible) detected by prostatic biopsy because of an elevated PSA.

Palpable carcinoma or carcinoma visible on ultrasound which is confined to the prostate is designated stage B/T2. Since radical prostatectomy for stage B/T2 is performed with the intention of cure, the role of the pathologist is to confirm the diagnosis of carcinoma, grade the tumor, provide the pathologic stage, estimate the tumor volume, and evaluate the seminal vesicles and the surgical margins, including the apex and the bladder cuff. Organ-confined tumors, pathologic stage T2 tumors, are subdivided into pT2a, and T2b, and T2c depending on the extent of involvement (one-half of one lobe or less, more than one-half of one lobe but not both lobes, and both lobes, respectively).[124–126] However, the existence of true pT2b tumors has been questioned.[127] If tumor is found beyond the confines of the prostate (e.g., in the seminal vesicles, or periprostatic connective tissue), the lesion is pathologically upstaged to stage C/T3 disease. Further management depends largely on the pathologic findings in the radical prostatectomy specimen.

Stage C/T3 or T4 (Tables 14A.3 and 14A.4) disease refers to carcinoma extending outside the prostatic capsule to involve the seminal vesicles, bladder, rectum, or pelvic wall. Patients with clinical stage C/T3 or T4 disease, in the past, were generally treated with definitive radiation to the pelvis, which yielded a 5-year survival rate of 60–65%.[128] Currently, the clinician decides whether radiation alone or in combination with hormonal manipulation is the best management. Surgery is usually limited to TURP if the patient becomes obstructed. Toxic chemotherapy is generally reserved for cases unresponsive to hormone treatment.

Stage D/N or M disease is when metastatic disease is present. This stage is also subdivided in both staging systems and is subdivided according to the metastatic sites (Tables 14A.3 and 14A.4). Management essentially comprises hormonal management with blocking agents, orchiectomy, or both, thereby ablating any androgen activity. Tumor histology and expression of PSA and chromogranin A are heterogeneous in metastatic prostatic carcinoma to the bone. Gleason grade of the primary tumor does not predict the histological pattern of the metastases. Although >70% of tumor cells express PSA, the fraction of PSA-positive cells varies widely in separate metastases in some patients. Likewise, the fraction of neuroendocrine tumor cells in different metastases varies widely.[129]

Among 19 316 routine autopsies on men older than 40 years of age, there were 1589 cases (8.2%) with prostate cancer.[130] Metastases were present in 35% of 1589 patients with prostate cancer, with the most frequent sites of involvement being bone (90%), lung (46%), liver (25%), pleura (21%), and adrenals (13%). Based on this autopsy study, the authors demonstrated several important findings: first, there was an inverse relationship between spine and lung metastases, suggesting that metastasis to the spine is independent of lung metastasis. Second, the maximum frequency of spine involvement occurred in smaller tumors (4–6 cm) as compared with the maximum spread to lung (6–8 cm) and liver (>8 cm), suggesting that spine metastases precede lung and liver metastases in many prostate cancers. Third, there was a gradual decrease in spine involvement from the lumbar to the cervical level (97% versus 38%), which is consistent with a subsequent upward metastatic spread along spinal veins after initial lumbar metastasis. The results of this study show that bone, lung, and liver are the most frequent sites of distant prostate cancer metastases. Besides the large vein-type of metastasis through the lungs, there are strong arguments for the existence and clinical significance of backward venous spread to the spine, which is likely to occur early in the metastatic process.[130] Loss of heterozygosity in at least 1 marker was more frequently identified in lymph node-positive than lymph node-negative prostate cancers, and 10q23.3 could be a marker for metastatic progression.[130]

Grading systems

Although numerous grading systems for prostatic carcinoma have been proposed in the literature, only the Gleason system has prevailed. Since the Gaeta's and Mostofi systems[72,131–134] are no longer utilized at the M. D. Anderson Cancer Center, they are not discussed in this chapter.

Gleason system. The Gleason system[72] has been accepted by the majority of urologists and radiotherapists within the USA and many other countries and it is the system upon which management decisions are based. Gleason designed this system to accommodate the fact that carcinoma of the prostate has different patterns of growth, that each may range from well

Table 14A.4 2002 TNM staging of prostate cancer

Primary Tumor (T)

Clinical

TX	Primary tumor cannot be assessed
T0	No evidence of primary tumor
T1	Clinically inapparent tumor neither palpable nor visible by imaging

	T1a	Tumor incidental histologic finding in 5% or less of tissue resected
	T1b	Tumor incidental histologic finding in more than 5% of tissue resected
	T1c	Tumor identified by needle biopsy (e.g., because of elevated PSA)

T2	Tumor confined within prostate*

	T2a	Tumor involves one-half of one lobe or less
	T2b	Tumor involves more then one-half of one lobe but not both lobes
	T2c	Tumor involves both lobes

T3	Tumor extends through the prostate capsule**

	T3a	Extracapsular extension (unilateral or bilateral)
	T3b	Tumor invades seminal vesicle(s)

T4	Tumor is fixed or invades adjacent structures other than seminal vesicles: bladder neck, external sphincter, rectum, levator muscles, and/or pelvic wall

*Note: Tumor found in one or both lobes by needle biopsy, but not palpable or reliably visible by imaging, is classified as T1c

**Note: Invasion into the prostatic apex or into (but not beyond) the prostatic capsule is classified not as T3 but as T2.

Pathologic (pT)

pT2*	Organ confined

	pT2a	Unilateral, involving one-half of one lobe or less
	pT2b	Unilateral, involving more than one-half of one lobe but not both lobes
	pT2c	Bilateral disease

pT3	Extraprostatic extension

	pT3a	Extraprostatic extension**
	pT3b	Seminal vesicle invasion

pT4	Invasion of bladder, rectum

*Note: There is no pathologic T1 classification.

**Note: Positive surgical margin should be indicated by an R1 descriptor (residual microscopic disease).

Regional Lymph Nodes (N)

Clinical

NX	Regional lymph nodes were not assessed
N0	No regional lymph node metastasis
N1	Metastasis in regional lymph node(s)

Pathologic

pNX	Regional nodes not sampled
pN0	No positive regional nodes
pN1	Metastases in regional node(s)

Distant Metastasis (M)*

MX	Distant metastasis cannot be assessed (not evaluated by any modality)
M0	No distant metastasis
M1	Distant metastasis

	M1a	Non-regional lymph node(s)
	M1b	Bone(s)
	M1c	Other site(s) with our without bone disease

*Note: When more than one site of metastasis is present, the most advanced category is used. pM1c is most advanced.

Stage Grouping

Stage I	T1a	N0	M0	G1
Stage II	T1a	N0	M0	G2, 3–4
	T1b	N0	M0	Any G
	T1c	N0	M0	Any G
	T1	N0	M0	Any G
	T2	N0	M0	Any G
Stage III	T3	N0	M0	Any G
Stage IV	T4	N0	M0	Any G
	Any T	N1	M0	Any G
	Any T	Any N	M1	Any G

Used with permission of the American Joint Committee on Cancer (AJCC), Chicago, Illinois. The original source for this material is the AJCC Cancer Staging Manual, Sixth Edition (2002) published by Springer-Verlag New York, www.springeronline.com

differentiated to poorly differentiated, and that usually more than one pattern coexists in any prostatic carcinoma. In the Gleason system the two predominant patterns (primary and secondary) are recorded. The sum of these patterns constitutes a score which ranges from 2 to 10.[132–134] However, a major recent consensus meeting recommended that high-grade tumor of any quantity on needle biopsy should be used as part of the Gleason score, even if another second pattern was greater in extent.[134a]

Pattern 1 is closely packed, single, and separate, round uniform glands with a well-defined margin. The tumors of pattern 1 are characterized by: (1) a well-defined nodule;

(2) relatively uniform gland size and shape; and (3) back-to-back arrangement of glands with minimal intervening stroma (Fig. 14A.28). Unlike BPH or normal secretory cells, cells of pattern 1 cancer are uniformly large with even, straight borders laterally and luminally. Nuclei sometimes appear benign but are arranged in a basal row, dissimilar to the uneven distribution in BPH or normal glands. Immunostaining for glutathione-S transferase is negative in pattern 1 cancer but slightly positive in BPH-secretory cells. These cytologic findings are proposed to be useful as diagnostic clues, especially in small-needle biopsy samples, in which architecture may be difficult to interpret.[135]

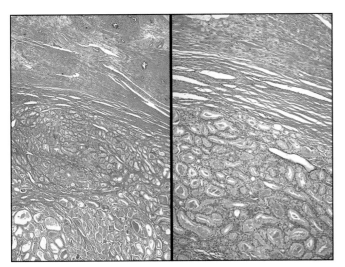

Fig. 14A.28 • Gleason pattern 1 carcinoma. A well-demarcated nodule with glands of similar size and shape that are evenly spaced from each other characterizes this pattern.

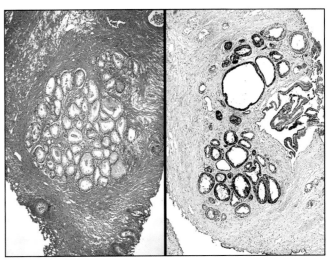

Fig. 14A.29 • These illustrations demonstrate Gleason pattern 2. The nodule of carcinoma on the left side is relatively well circumscribed but some glands are outside the nodule, and there is some variation in size and shape of the individual glands. In the right illustration, the alpha-methylacyl-CoA-racemase stains the small glands, supporting the diagnosis of carcinoma.

Pattern 2 is similar to pattern 1, but: (1) nodular margins are less well defined than in pattern 1; (2) the glands are less uniform than in pattern 1; and (3) intervening stroma of pattern 2 is more obvious than pattern 1, but less than pattern 3 (less than one gland diameter) (Fig. 14A.29). Patterns 1 and 2 are rare in the 18-gauge needle biopsy specimens. It is common knowledge that Dr. Gleason acknowledged that his patterns 1 and 2 could possibly represent AAH (adenosis). When he described his system, there were no basal cell staining markers available. The recent consensus meeting recommended that Gleason score 4 or lower on needle biopsy should not be made by general pathologists without expert consultation.[134a]

In pattern 3, the size of the glands is variable: both small and large glands and a papillary or cribriform pattern appear. The margin is poorly defined. This is the most prevalent pattern

in needle biopsy specimens and is most commonly apparent as foci of small neoplastic glands with an obviously infiltrative pattern or appearing between benign glands (suggesting infiltrative growth).

There are three subgroups of pattern 3. Pattern 3A is characterized by the presence of small to medium-sized glands that are irregular, angulated, pear or teardrop-shaped, and which are separated by a collagenous stroma. The 3A pattern differs from pattern 2 in that the neoplastic glands infiltrate between benign glands, there is more stroma than in pattern 2 (more than one gland diameter), and there are more irregular glands with angulation (Fig. 14A.30) than in pattern 2. The 3B pattern consists of small irregular glands, generally smaller than the glands in pattern 3A, but some of these glands form cords or are elongated, giving the impression of having lost

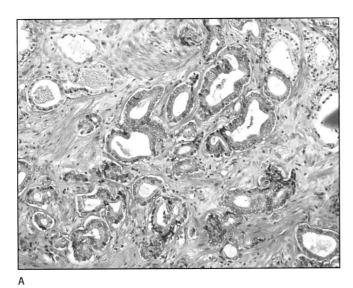

A

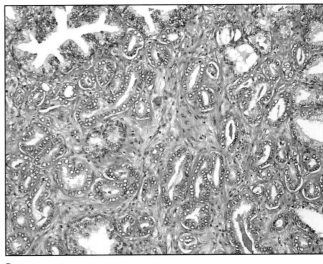

B

Fig. 14A.30 • (A) Gleason pattern 3A, large gland type. This pattern is characterized by small to medium-sized glands that show angulations, elongation, oval shapes, irregularities in their contour, and some variation in their size. They tend to infiltrate between normal glands and have an ill-defined infiltrative border. (B) Gleason pattern 3A, large gland type. This is also a pattern 3A and consists of small angulated and irregular glands separated by variable collagenous connective tissue. Note high-grade prostatic intraepithelial neoplasia in the left upper corner.

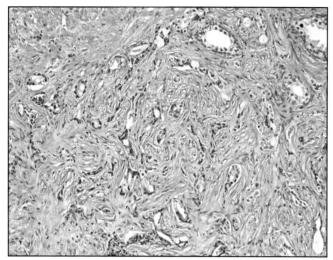

Fig. 14A.31 • Gleason pattern 3B, small gland type. This pattern is characterized by the presence of glands that have lost their lumina and give the false impression of "fusion." In order to rule out true fusion, as seen in pattern 4, deeper sections generally depict the lumina of the glands. In this illustration there are some glands with open lumina, but there are others forming cords, seemingly with collapsed lumina. As a general rule this pattern is difficult to separate from a pattern 4.

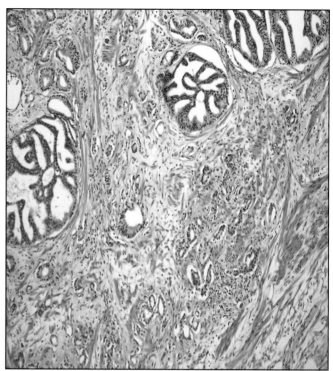

Fig. 14A.32 • Gleason pattern 3C, cribriform type. Gleason pattern 3C refers to tumors that show focal papillary/cribriform pattern. Currently this subtype of pattern is controversial as some pathologists, including us, would not accept it as a pattern 3, but would consider it as pattern 4. Therefore, the illustration herein depicted does show some papillary/cribriform arrangement, but such growth is most likely papillary/cribriform high-grade prostatic intraepithelial neoplasia. In the background, there is Gleason pattern 3B adenocarcinoma.

their lumina. Small nests of cells with inconspicuous lumina are frequently observed in this pattern, but one can draw a line around the cell nests (Fig. 14A.31). This pattern is similar to that of pattern 4, but there is no true glandular fusion or chain of glands. The 3C pattern is similar to pattern 3A but shows focal cribriform/papillary formations (Fig. 14A.32). It is speculated that this pattern included cases with papillary/cribriform types of high-grade PIN. Currently, many pathologists accept only a few ducts with cribriform/papillary pattern as pattern 3C, but if the change is diffuse, it is more likely to be interpreted as a pattern 4.

Pattern 4 contains small fused glands and infiltrating cords; the glandular proliferation may display large papillary or cribriform architecture with ill-defined boundaries or confluent growth (type 4A; Fig. 14A.33), and the cytoplasm of the tumor cells may be clear (hypernephroid; type 4B; Fig. 14A.34). Mucinous adenocarcinoma of the prostate is automatically pattern 4.

In pattern 5 the majority of the tumor is solid, with only a few discernible glands. This pattern includes the undifferentiated small cell carcinoma and any carcinoma exhibiting necrosis, although the recent consensus conference suggested not to assign a Gleason grade to small cell carcinoma.[134a] The prototype tumor with comedo necrosis is ductal-endometrioid carcinoma (5A; Fig. 14A.35). However, poorly differentiated prostate cancers may grow in a solid fashion, infiltrating the stroma as single cells or as ill-defined cords (5B; Fig. 14A.36).

In recent years, this pattern has emerged to be of prognostic significance: tumors with Gleason score 7 or more, i.e., having at least Gleason pattern 4 as primary or secondary pattern, behave worse than tumors with Gleason score 6 or less.[136] Several investigators have analyzed whether primary and secondary Gleason patterns are important prognostically within Gleason score 7 prostate cancers. One study[137] analyzed 823 whole-mount radical prostatectomy specimens with Gleason score 7, tumors with either 3 + 4 or 4 + 3. A total of 643 patients with 3 + 4 tumors and 180 patients with 4 + 3

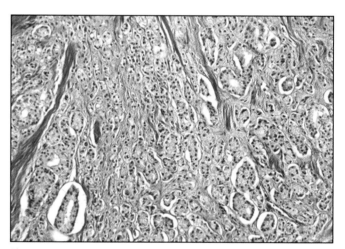

Fig. 14A.33 • Gleason pattern 4A with glandular fusion. This illustration displays numerous irregular and fused glands, some of which merge into each other.

tumors were studied. Statistical analysis using the log-rank test showed a significant difference in recurrence-free survival between patients with primary Gleason pattern 4 and those with primary Gleason pattern 3 ($P < 0.0001$). However, in multivariate analysis with preoperative PSA, total tumor volume, surgical margin status, and the presence or absence of seminal vesicle involvement, extraprostatic extension, and lymph node metastasis, the primary Gleason pattern did not retain independent significance ($P = 0.0557$). Gleason score 7 prostate carcinoma is a heterogeneous group of tumors. In

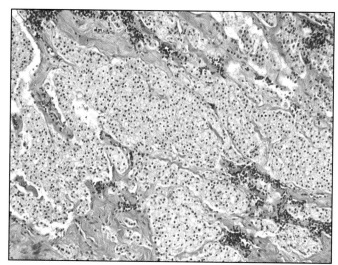

Fig. 14A.34 • Gleason pattern 4B. This is a cellular proliferation of monotonous cells with a distinct acinar pattern, but without intersecting connective tissue between the glands. The cells show clear and amphophilic cytoplasm, superficially resembling clear cell renal cell carcinoma (hypernephroid pattern).

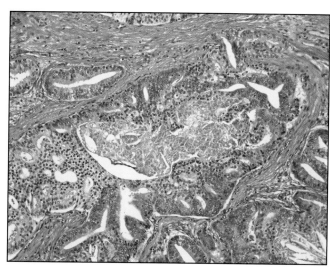

Fig. 14A.35 • Gleason pattern 5A. This illustration shows an irregularly contoured expanded duct/acinus exhibiting a cribriform-papillary pattern with central comedonecrosis. Necrosis always indicates a pattern 5.

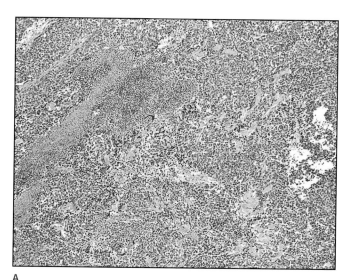

A

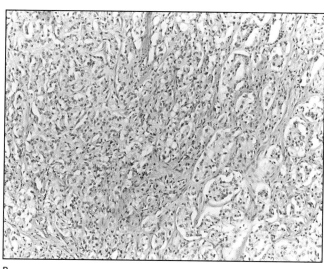

B

Fig. 14A.36 • (A) Gleason pattern 5B with solid small cell proliferation and areas of necrosis. (B) Gleason pattern 5B. A solid growth with a faint acinar pattern.

this cohort of men with Gleason score 7 tumors treated by radical retropubic prostatectomy, primary Gleason pattern showed a significant correlation with other histologic and clinical predictors of disease progression; however, it was not independently predictive of disease progression in multivariate analysis ($P = 0.76$).

Gleason score can easily be assigned to each tissue microarray spot of a 0.6-mm-diameter prostate cancer sample and tissue microarray spot images may be a good approach for teaching the Gleason grading system due to the small areas of tissue examined.[138]

In the USA, the Gleason system has become the gold standard for clinical reporting and correlates with extra-prostatic extension, seminal vesicle invasion, and regional lymph node metastases.[136,139–141] Furthermore, studies of the DNA content of prostate carcinomas have been compared to Gleason score.[142] Gleason scores of up to 5 are usually associated with diploid tumors, whereas high-grade carcinomas

(score 9–10) are generally aneuploid. Tumors with an intermediate grade (score 6–8) have both diploid and aneuploid patterns.

Pathology report and communication with clinicians

Recent trends in prostate needle biopsy reporting have resulted in the inclusion of more information and new diagnostic categories. Rubin et al.[143] designed a study to survey surgical Members of the Society of Urologic Oncology to determine what information academic urologists consider important in the management of their prostate cancer patients. They developed a questionnaire to investigate several areas of prostate cancer biopsy reporting, which vary from institution to institution. Urologists were sent questionnaires and asked to return anonymous responses; 42 questionnaires were completely evaluated, with a response rate of 76% (42 of 55). The urologists targeted for this survey were highly experienced, with an average of 22 years in clinical practice (range, 6–35 years). More than 90% of the participants have their patient's biopsy reviewed prior to definitive surgery: more than half of the responders required the primary and secondary Gleason patterns. In biopsies with multiple positive cores from separate locations, more than 80% of the responders used the highest Gleason score, regardless of the overall percentage of involvement, to determine their treatment plan. Other pathology parameters requested by the responders in descending order included: percentage involvement of the core by cancer (67%), the presence or absence of perineural invasion (38%), the number of cores with cancer (33%), and the length of core involvement (29%). Only a minority of responders (24%) used perineural invasion status to guide nerve-sparing surgery. The more radical prostatectomies performed by a surgeon, the greater the likelihood that they considered perineural invasion clinically important (Mann–Whitney, two-tailed, $P = 0.015$). The term ASAP was uniformly considered sufficient as an indication for rebiopsy by 98% of the urologists.

The ability of perineural invasion by carcinoma to predict independently pathologic stage in radical prostatectomy tissues remains uncertain. In many studies utilizing univariate analysis, the finding of perineural invasion in core biopsies has been related to extraprostatic extension of tumor on examination of the entire prostate gland in radical prostatectomy specimens. However, when multivariate analysis has been applied, only few studies have shown that perineural invasion possesses a significant capacity to predict extraprostatic extension.[144,145] Despite the controversy, it is recommended that the presence or absence of perineural invasion be reported routinely in needle biopsies of the prostate.

Maru et al.[146] reported that the perineural invasion diameter was an independent predictor of prognosis (perineural invasion >0.25 mm versus <0.25 mm), and that the measurement of the perineural invasion diameter, easily recorded from prostatectomy specimens, could add important information to the prognosis of prostate cancer patients. They concluded that controversy regarding the significance of perineural invasion may result from the lack of quantitative assessment of perineural invasion in previous studies.

Also important is the presence or absence of lymphovascular invasion. Herman et al.[147] demonstrated that lymphovascular invasion was found to be a significant predictor of disease progression in univariate analysis ($P < 0.0001$) and was significantly related to Gleason sum ($P < 0.001$), extraprostatic extension (focal versus established; $P = 0.033$), and seminal vesicle involvement ($P < 0.001$). Furthermore, in multivariate analysis, lymphovascular invasion was a significant independent predictor of disease progression as well ($P = 0.0014$).

Minimal tumor on biopsy is defined as less than 1 mm or 5% involvement of one biopsy core; excluded from this definition are biopsies where two Gleason patterns could be identified and/or tumor is seen on more than one biopsy core. Rubin et al.'s study[148] was to determine if a Gleason score assigned to a minimal focus of adenocarcinoma had predictive value. In cases with minimal carcinoma, pretreatment PSA was the only independent predictor of higher tumor stage and Gleason score was not found to predict higher tumor stage significantly. The results of this study confirm that biopsy Gleason score in most cases predicts the score in the prostatec-

tomy and tumor stage. However, for cases with minimal tumor on biopsy, the assigned Gleason score did not predict tumor stage. To convey this uncertainty to clinicians properly, a cautionary note should accompany Gleason scores derived from a minimal focus of carcinoma. If multiple biopsy cores contain prostate cancer with differing Gleason scores, each core should be assigned a separate Gleason score rather than overall Gleason score, especially in cases with a high Gleason score cancer on at least one core.[134a,149]

Pathologists frequently sign out benign prostate needle biopsies as showing "benign prostatic hyperplasia (BPH)," when there are no histologic findings on biopsy specific for BPH. While, occasionally, a stromal nodule, indicative of the transition zone, may be found in a core biopsy, glandular hyperplasia is a very difficult diagnosis to make on a core biopsy. Thus benign prostate biopsies should not be signed out as displaying BPH unless a stromal nodule is present.[150]

Treatment effect

Radiation treatment for prostate cancers is the most common cause of reactive atypia in the prostate. Cytologic atypia of non-neoplastic glands, including enlarged and hyperchromatic nuclei with prominent nucleoli (Fig. 14A.37), have been reported in approximately three-quarters of radiated prostates.[151] However, the architecture of the glands remains relatively normal, a helpful feature in excluding carcinoma. Other radiation-induced changes include a decrease in the ratio of glands to stroma, atrophy, squamous metaplasia and BCH, stromal fibrosis with atypical fibroblasts, foreign-body giant cells, intimal proliferation of arteries, and foam cells in vessel walls. Types of radiation affect the histologic changes. There is both more cytologic atypia and stromal fibrosis in cases treated with interstitial radiotherapy (brachytherapy)/combined interstitial and external-beam radiotherapy than with external-beam radiation alone. However, there is no correlation between the type of treatment and the effect on vessels. There is no change over time in the degree of epithelial atypia in men treated with interstitial radiotherapy (brachytherapy)/combined interstitial and external-beam radiotherapy. With external-beam radiation, there is less epithelial atypia in cases biopsied >48 months after treatment compared with those with a shorter interval between biopsy and treatment. Radiation atypia in benign prostate glands may persist for a long time after the initial treatment, resulting in a significant pitfall in evaluating prostate biopsies, because prominent radiation effect can be detected for up to 72 months in patients treated with interstitial radiotherapy (brachytherapy).[152] Radiation can induce tumor necrosis and fibrosis, but in many instances, residual viable tumor is identified after completion of treatment. When cribriform structures, fused glands, solid sheets, and cords are identified, the diagnosis can usually be made with confidence. In needle biopsies, distinguishing small acini with atypia induced by radiation from microacinar carcinoma can be a difficult diagnostic challenge. An irregular distribution of acini in the stroma should increase the suspicion of cancer. The absence of basal cells is helpful, but at times the presence or absence of basal cells is difficult to judge because of acinar shrinkage and distortion. The application of a high-molecular-weight cytokeratin stain, CK5/6, p63, or basal cell cocktail ($34\beta E12$ and p63) may be useful to identify residual

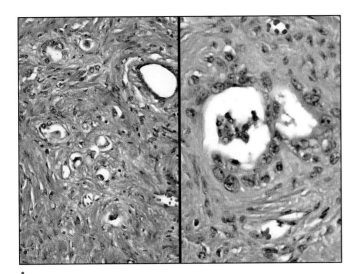

A

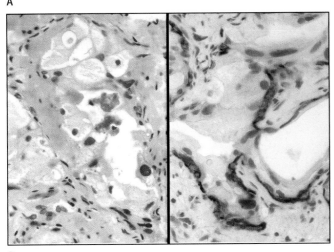

B

Fig. 14A.37 • (A) Radiation treatment effect in benign glands. On the left side, there are distorted glands and isolated cells with cytologic atypia. On the right side there is an atypical gland depicting large, irregular, and distinctly atypical cells, indicative of a radiation-induced epithelial atypia. **(B)** Radiation treatment effect in benign glands. On the left side there is a gland seemingly without basal cells, that is lined by very atypical cells; the cells depict abnormal nuclei and clear cytoplasm resembling foamy gland carcinoma. However, in the right illustration, basal cells are prominent (34βE12), indicating radiation-induced changes in normal glands.

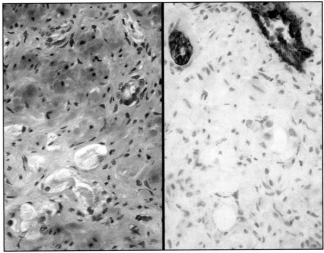

Fig. 14A.38 • Radiation treatment effect in prostate cancer. The left side shows two or three glands lined by hyperchromatic nuclei, and several distorted small glands. The illustration in the right side shows absence of basal cells in the carcinomatous area, in contrast to basal cell-lined benign glands (upper) that are highlighted by the high-molecular-weight cytokeratin.

and loss of nucleoli. Irregular "empty" spaces representing remnants of shrunken neoplastic glands may be seen, similar to the changes seen with androgen deprivation therapy. Recent studies have analyzed the effects of antiandrogen neoadjuvant therapy, including total androgen blockade using drugs such as luteinizing hormone-releasing hormone agonists, flutamide, and cyproterone acetate. The effects of finasteride, a 5-alpha-reductase inhibitor commonly used to treat hyperplastic and carcinomatous tissue, have recently been described.[154] Finasteride produces less pronounced morphologic changes than other androgen deprivation strategies. In radical prostatectomy specimens, neoadjuvant therapy leads to a reduction in tumor volume, reduced margin positivity, and an apparent down-staging effect, although the latter may be spurious.

Androgen deprivation has significant effects on both non-neoplastic and carcinomatous tissue. In non-neoplastic areas, there is pronounced glandular atrophy with shrinkage of the secretory cell compartment and basal cell prominence (Fig.14A.39). Foci of BCH are common, and squamous and transitional cell metaplasia may also be seen. The frequency of high-grade PIN is significantly reduced in prostates treated with neoadjuvant hormonal therapy compared with surgery alone.[155]

Carcinomatous glands exhibit reduction in cytoplasmic quantity, cytoplasmic vacuolation, nuclear pyknosis, reduced gland diameter, and mucinous breakdown (Fig. 14A.40). In many cases there is prominence of collagenous stroma, obscuring malignant glands.[155] At times, there is a complete disappearance of the neoplastic acini leaving spaces, some of which may contain a mucosubstance, which is highlighted with the alcian blue stain. This appearance has been likened to that of pseudomyxoma ovarii (Fig. 14A.41). Collagenous micro-nodules are often present and likely represent organization of extravasated mucin. Stromal proliferation, resulting in a hemangiopericytoma-like appearance, may be seen. Nuclear changes include nucleolysis, nuclear pyknosis, and fragmentation. Paneth cell-like change is sometimes prominent in treated carcinoma, and this correlates with increased numbers

basal cells, thus excluding carcinoma (Fig. 14A.38). The nuclear atypia associated with radiation can mimic that of carcinoma, although the spotty distribution of the atypia may be a clue in addition to the history. Radiation may induce pleomorphism that often exceeds that of cancer. Immunostains for PSA help identify residual single or vacuolated tumor cells in the stroma that by routine light microscopy may mimic stromal cells with vacuolar change. It has been suggested that needle biopsy evaluation is of little value in the 12 months after radiation therapy because of the delayed manifestation of tumor cell death. Similar radiation changes in benign and malignant glands after three-dimensional conformal external-beam radiation therapy have been reported.[153]

The morphologic effects induced by estrogen compounds such as diethylstilbestrol have been known for more than 50 years. There may be squamous metaplasia and individual tumor cells may display prominent cytoplasm, nuclear pyknosis,

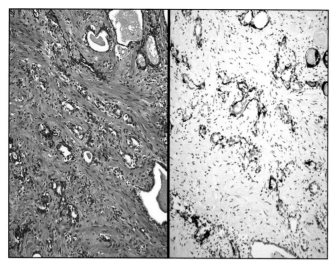

Fig. 14A.39 • Benign glands with atrophy and basal cell hyperplasia induced by hormonal management. In these illustrations there are prominent atrophic glands characterized by the presence of low cuboidal/flattened cells (basal cells) with little cytoplasm and hyperchromatic nuclei (left side). High-molecular-weight cytokeratin stain (34βE12) highlights the presence of basal cells (right).

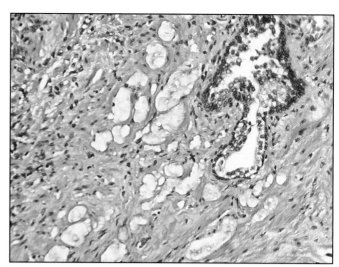

Fig. 14A.41 • Hormone-treated prostate cancer. Adjacent to the large benign gland with prominent basal cells there are distorted and dilated glandular structures lined by a flattened epithelium and filled with mucinous material. There are also extravasated mucin pools in the stroma that closely mimic pseudomyxoma ovarii. In addition, isolated small clusters of tumor cells are present infiltrating diffusely in the stroma.

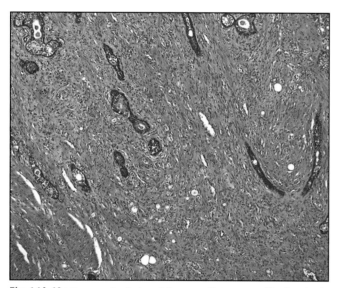

Fig. 14A.40 • Hormone-treated prostate cancer. Note scattered benign glands on a background of distorted cords of hyperchromatic neoplastic cells. Carcinomatous glands exhibit reduction in cytoplasmic quantity, cytoplasmic vacuolation, nuclear pyknosis, and reduced gland diameter.

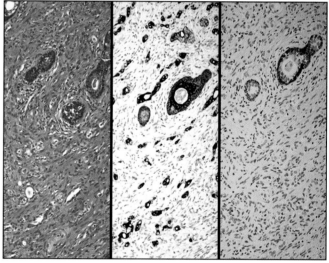

Fig. 14A.42 • Immunostaining in hormone-treated prostate cancer. A high-power picture of Figure 14A.40 on the extreme left shows isolated and small clusters of tumor cells which in the middle illustration are positive for pancytokeratin, but are negative for high-molecular-weight cytokeratin (far right). Note positively stained basal cells in atrophic normal glands.

of neuroendocrine cells. The architectural changes associated with androgen deprivation therapy lead to an apparent worsening of the Gleason score when compared to the preoperative biopsy results. This change is likely spurious and related in large part to the cytoplasmic shrinkage and loss of lumina noted with the therapy. Studies utilizing DNA content and proliferating cell nuclear antigen have shown less proliferative activity in areas of apparently poor differentiation than in non-treated carcinomas with similar patterns, suggesting that the "upgrading" is artifactual. From a practical viewpoint, cases showing marked treatment effect should not be graded. In some situations, the neoadjuvant hormones have relatively little effect on tumor pattern, and in these situations a grade can be rendered, remembering not to overinterpret areas

that superficially resemble Gleason grade 5 tumor. Some authors[155,156] have advocated adjusting the Gleason score to compensate for treatment effect, but this approach is not recommended since, in our opinion, some pseudo-grades 4 and 5 tumors in treated prostates cannot be reproducibly separated from *de novo* grades 4 and 5. In some cases, residual carcinoma is very difficult to appreciate in the treated prostate tissue, and immunohistochemical stains for pancytokeratin and PSA are necessary to look for carcinoma cells (Fig. 14A.42). Stromal reactions, including a histiocytic infiltrate, may also mimic residual carcinoma cells, sometimes necessitating the use of both macrophage and prostatic epithelial markers.

In a number of centers, cryotherapy is being used to treat locally advanced tumors. Postcryotherapy biopsies show a variety of histologic changes depending on the timing of the biopsy with respect to treatment. Acute injury is manifest by necrosis, hemorrhage, and acute inflammation. Chronic changes include fibrosis, hyalinization, calcification, hemosiderin deposition, granulomatous inflammation, BCH, and transitional and squamous metaplasia.[157,158] Residual carcinoma is sometimes present, and it generally retains its original morphology and grade. Pathologic analysis of salvage prostatectomies performed after failed cryotherapy has revealed viable carcinoma in areas thought to be destroyed on intraoperative transrectal ultrasound.

There is a morphologic study of in-situ gene therapy effects in patients with prostate cancer using the herpes simplex virus thymidine kinase (HSV-tk) gene, followed by ganciclovir.[159] Prostatectomy specimens showed the following morphologic changes: (1) various degrees of necrosis were seen in cancer foci; (2) cytopathic changes were seen across the whole spectrum of Gleason grades; (3) the normal prostate was rarely affected by necrosis, but contained an intense mononuclear infiltrate; (4) loss of nuclear detail was a common finding. Volumetric studies showed that only parts of the tumor show morphologic effects and demonstrated an inverse relationship between percentage of affected tumor and prostate and tumor size. An inflammatory response was observed, with predominance of CD20-positive cells in normal prostate tissue, CD8 (cytotoxic T cells) in the tumor, and macrophages in all areas of the treated prostates.[159]

Variants of adenocarcinoma

Variants of prostatic adenocarcinoma account for 5–10% of cases. Their recognition is important because many have a poor prognosis, and their differential diagnosis often differs from that of conventional microacinar carcinomas. The Gleason grading can often be applied to these variants, which are almost always grade 3 or higher.[160,161]

Mucinous adenocarcinoma

Since Boyd first reported a case of prostatic mucinous adenocarcinoma in 1882,[162] approximately 100 cases of primary mucinous adenocarcinoma have been reported.[50,163–165] The criteria for primary mucinous adenocarcinoma of the prostate are: (1) at least 25% of the resected tumor must be composed of lakes of extracellular mucin; (2) non-dilated glands containing mucinous material do not qualify as mucinous carcinoma; (3) spread from extraprostatic tumor sites should be excluded, or tumor cells should be positive for PSA and PrAP immunostaining. Using these criteria, Epstein & Lieberman[164] and Ro et al.[163] reported that the incidence of mucinous adenocarcinoma was approximately 0.4% of all prostatic adenocarcinomas.

In the past, mucinous adenocarcinoma of the prostate was believed to be less aggressive than usual prostatic adenocarcinoma,[166–169] unlikely to metastasize to bone,[167,168,170–172] not to be associated with an elevated serum PSA level,[166,167,170,173] and to arise from the "female" portion of the gland.[166,169,171–173] Recent studies, however, have found that clinical symptoms, metastatic pattern, level of serum PSA, and response to hormonal treatment were similar to those of patients with the usual type of prostatic adenocarcinoma.[163,164] Common metas-

tatic sites include lymph nodes, bone, and lung; interestingly, one case showed an endobronchial metastasis that was initially confused with a primary bronchogenic carcinoma.[174]

Histologically, primary mucinous adenocarcinoma of the prostate is associated with the usual types of prostatic adenocarcinoma (Fig. 14A.43); no pure cases of mucinous adenocarcinoma of the prostate have been reported. The mucinous component is manifest as extracellular mucin lakes, often containing gyriform masses of tumor cells with occasional acini or well-formed glandular structures (Fig. 14A.44). The pattern of the non-mucinous component varies between specimens and from area to area within the same tumor. The pattern is predominantly microglandular, but cribriform, comedo, solid, and hypernephroid types can also be seen. One distinctive feature is that tumor cells floating within mucin lakes have a non-papillary growth pattern reminiscent of breast colloid carcinoma.[163]

Before a diagnosis of primary mucinous adenocarcinoma of the prostate is made, metastasis from another site or direct extension of a mucinous carcinoma of the colon, bladder, prostatic urethra, or Cowper's gland should be excluded.[163–166,175,176] Several features of primary prostatic mucinous adenocarcinomas help in differentiating them from non-prostatic

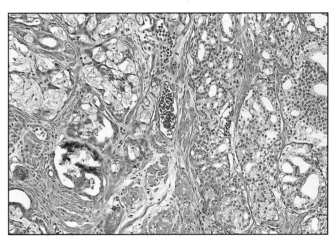

Fig. 14A.43 • Mucinous adenocarcinoma. The mucinous carcinoma is seen on the left and a usual adenocarcinoma on the right. In the mucinous carcinoma area, the tumor cells are floating in mucin lakes.

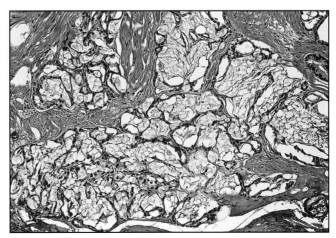

Fig. 14A.44 • Tumor cells forming gyriform masses are associated with abundant extracellular mucin.

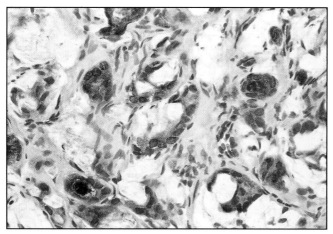

Fig. 14A.45 • Tumor cells of mucinous adenocarcinoma are immunopositive for prostate-specific antigen and prostatic acid phosphatase.

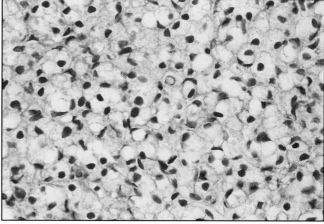

Fig. 14A.46 • Signet-ring cell carcinoma. These tumor cells are characterized by clear cytoplasm and peripherally displaced nuclei.

mucinous adenocarcinomas. The most characteristic feature is the almost invariable association with "usual-type" prostatic adenocarcinoma. Furthermore, the primary mucinous adeno-carcinomas of the prostate, unlike those of the intestine or urinary bladder, do not usually contain columnar cells or goblet cells, or signet-ring cells,[163–165,175] although exceptions are reported.[165,177]

Mucinous adenocarcinoma shows positive immunostaining for PSA and PrAP (Fig. 14A.45), but does not stain with carcinoembryonic antigen (CEA).[163] Because more than two-thirds of usual prostatic adenocarcinomas contain intra-luminal mucin,[75,85,178–180] a tumor that has mucin confined within glandular lumina should not be classified as a mucinous carcinoma.

Signet-ring cell carcinoma of prostate

Primary signet-ring cell carcinoma (SRCC) of the prostate is extremely rare; about two dozen cases have been reported in the literature.[50,164,181–187] The age of the patients reported ranges from 50 to 80 years (mean 67.5 years), and the symptoms and signs are no different from those of usual prostatic carcinoma. Patients with SRCCs of the prostate frequently present with advanced-stage disease, either stage pT3 or T4 with or without metastases (C or stage D).[181]

SRCC grows as focal or diffuse sheets of undifferentiated cells with signet-ring cell morphology, and as such this tumor is considered a Gleason pattern 5. The signet-ring cells are characterized by nuclear displacement and clear cytoplasm (Fig. 14A.46). Although a few cases of prostatic SRCCs have been reported to contain intracytoplasmic mucin, the majority do not.[181–183,185] The tumor cells diffusely infiltrate the prostatic stroma (Fig. 14A.47) in a pattern similar to that of SRCCs at other sites, such as stomach, colon, and breast. All SRCCs of the prostate are associated with other forms of high-grade prostatic carcinoma, including solid, comedo, and cribriform types.[181] Pure SRCC has not been reported in the literature. Unlike SRCC of other sites, SRCC of the prostate is usually not associated with mucinous adenocarcinoma.[75,163,164,175,177,181–183,185–187]

The signet-ring cells are positive for prostatic markers, including PrAP and PSA,[177,181] but CEA is usually negative.

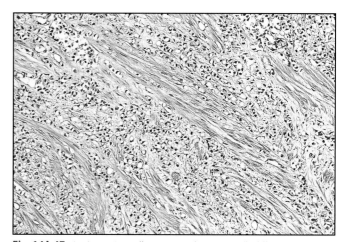

Fig. 14A.47 • In signet-ring cell carcinoma the tumor cells diffusely infiltrate the prostatic stroma.

Electron microscopically, signet-ring cells display intra-cytoplasmic lumina and cytoplasmic vacuoles. Mucin or fat vacuoles are not usually present.[182]

The differential diagnosis of SRCC of the prostate should include other similar-appearing tumors or cells with a signet-ring cell appearance. Vacuolated signet-ring-appearing cells that are distorted lymphocytes present within areas of chronic inflammation may mimic SRCC because they may appear to infiltrate fibromuscular stroma.[188,189] However, the absence of immunoreactivity for PSA and PrAP and positivity for leukocyte common antigen help to rule out carcinoma.[188] Before a diagnosis of primary SRCC of the prostate is made, metastatic SRCC from other sites, including direct extension of a SRCC of the urinary bladder, should be excluded.[181] SRCCs of the urinary bladder or other organs produce mucin and can be identified with routine mucin stains. Another finding that is helpful in establishing a diagnosis of primary prostatic SRCC is its association with other histologic patterns of prostatic adenocarcinoma. Hormonal treatment can also lead to the formation of signet-ring-type tumor cells, but the frequent association of squamous metaplasia of uninvolved glands and pyknosis of tumor nuclei provide clues to such treatment (Fig. 14A.48).[181,190]

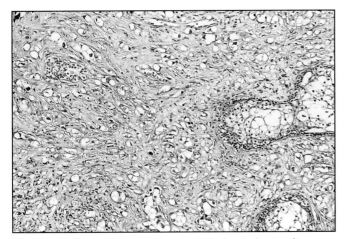

Fig. 14A.48 • Hormonal treatment can cause cytoplasmic clearing of tumor cells that may resemble signet-ring cell carcinoma. Note the squamous metaplasia in the benign prostatic glands.

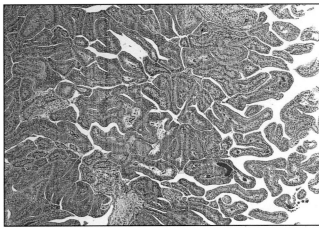

Fig. 14A.49 • Ductal endometrioid carcinoma. Type A pattern shows exuberant papillary growth with central fibrovascular stalks.

In general, the survival rate of patients with SRCC of the prostate is poor. Most patients die of tumor between 32 and 60 months after diagnosis. These survival data are comparable with those of patients with high-grade prostatic adeno-carcinoma. The clinical symptoms, metastatic pattern, and level of serum PrAP and PSA are also similar to those of patients with usual high-grade adenocarcinoma of prostate.[181,183–187]

Ductal-endometrioid carcinoma

Endometrioid adenocarcinoma of the prostate, arising in or near the prostatic verumontanum, was first described in 1967 by Melicow & Pachter.[191] They believed that the histologic pattern was similar to that of adenocarcinoma of the uterus and suggested that this tumor originated in the prostatic utricle, a structure homologous to the female uterus and vagina.[191] Although there is still some controversy regarding the histogenesis of this lesion, on the basis of histochemical and ultrastructural findings, this tumor is believed to be a ductal variant of prostatic adenocarcinoma.[50,192–195]

Ductal endometrioid carcinoma shows two distinct histo-logic patterns of growth.[192] Type A pattern shows exuberant papillary growth characterized by papillary fronds; the tumor cells lining a central fibrovascular stalk range from a single layer to a stratified tall columnar epithelium (Fig. 14A.49). They have basally located nuclei and contain large prominent nucleoli and abundant eosinophilic cytoplasm (Fig. 14A.50). Mitoses are common (more than 10 mitoses per 10 high-power fields) in some cases, but rare cases may have fairly bland cytologic features. Subnuclear vacuoles and secretory activity, manifest by prominent intraluminal apocrine snouts, are often observed. Type A tumors are frequently seen when the tumor grows into the prostatic urethra or within centrally located large ducts. Type B is characterized by intraductal papillary growth associated with complex glandular, solid, and comedo carcinomatous patterns (Fig. 14A.51). This type of tumor is usually located deep in the prostate, beneath an intact or partially denuded urothelium. The tumor cells are similar to those seen in type A tumors. The two growth patterns (type A and B) coexist in approximately half of the cases and the two

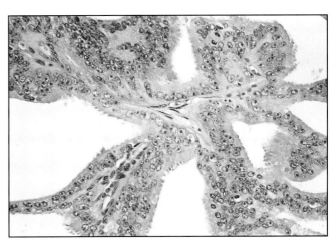

Fig. 14A.50 • The tumor cells are tall and columnar with abundant eosinophilic cytoplasm. They have basally located nuclei with large prominent nucleoli.

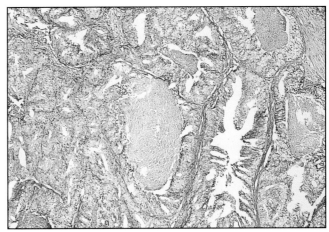

Fig. 14A.51 • Type B ductal endometrioid carcinoma is characterized by an intraductal papillary growth associated with ramifying glands and glands with comedo necrosis.

components tend to merge into each other. Microacinar carcinoma is frequently associated with endometrioid carcinoma, but it is usually focal and low-grade. There has been controversy whether ductal carcinoma of the prostate is a distinct entity.[196] In our opinion, when this histology is seen as pure or predominant (greater than 80%), such a diagnosis is appropriate. In needle biopsy specimens, ductal carcinoma histology may not be representative of the tumor within the prostate gland and hence, if the ductal-endometrioid carcinoma pattern is present, the diagnosis may be worded as adenocarcinoma of prostate with ductal-endometrioid histology. All ductal-endometrioid carcinomas show immunoreactivity for PSA and PrAP.[192–195,197] CEA can be positive in endometrioid carcinoma, but it is weak and focal.[192]

The reported patients who have developed this tumor range in age from 50 to 86 years (mean 65 years). Like usual adenocarcinoma of the prostate, the presenting symptoms are urinary obstruction and hematuria. Serum levels of PrAP and PSA are frequently normal but can be elevated. Metastatic sites include pelvic lymph nodes, lung, and bone. However, the tumor is more likely to metastasize to viscera before it goes to bone. Bone metastases are usually osteoblastic but may be mixed lytic–osteoblastic. Some objective responses to hormonal therapy (defined as relief of obstructive symptoms, decrease in tumor size, decreased serum PrAP and PSA levels, relief of bone pain, and a halt in the progression of new bone metastasis) have been observed, further supporting the contention that this tumor is a variant of prostatic adenocarcinoma.[192–195]

Melicow et al.[191,198] originally believed that this tumor usually presented as a low-stage lesion and behaved less aggressively than conventional prostatic adenocarcinomas. Subsequent reports also stated that, owing possibly to its central, periurethral location and to its propensity to produce early symptoms, most patients presented with disease limited to the prostate.[199–202] Recently, however, several large studies have demonstrated that these tumors present at a more advanced stage (T3/C or D) than was previously believed.[192–195]

The 5-year survival rate of 30% and median survival time of 46.3 months in our series[192] were comparable with the survival data from the literature. Bostwick et al.[194] reported that the mean survival of their 10 patients was 37 months and the crude 5-year survival rate was 15%; Dube et al.[203,204] reported a 5-year survival rate of 42.8%. Christensen et al.[205] reported the results of radical surgical treatment of prostatic duct adenocarcinoma. This study demonstrated that prostatic duct adenocarcinoma presented at a more advanced pathologic stage than clinically suspected, and with a higher rate of recurrence after radical prostatectomy when compared to stage-matched microacinar carcinomas. Another study confirmed that prostatic ductal adenocarcinoma seen on needle biopsy implies more advanced cancer with a shortened time to progression.[206]

The differential diagnoses include papillary adenoma of the urethra, prostatic-type urethral polyp, PIN, and TCC of the prostatic duct.[46,47,97,98,192,207–212] High-grade PIN lacks the confluent growth, comedo necrosis, mitotic activity, and degree of nuclear atypia associated with ductal carcinoma. TCC involving the prostatic ducts and acini should be differentiated from the solid form (type B pattern) of prostatic duct adenocarcinoma. Prostatic ductal-endometrioid adenocarcinoma is positive for PSA and PrAP, and these stains would resolve

this differential.[192–195] Some ductal-endometrioid carcinomas exhibit a bland cytologic appearance and may resemble a benign papillary adenoma of the utricle. In these cases clinicopathologic correlation may give the clue as to the true nature of the lesion. The cells of prostatic-type urethral polyp are extremely bland and the glands show two cell layers.

Other types of prostatic carcinoma

Small cell carcinoma of the prostate

Primary small cell carcinoma of the prostate is rare. It has been reported to be a highly aggressive neoplasm,[213–218] and some cases have demonstrated neuroendocrine differentiation.[216–222] The age of most affected patients is over 50 years (median 67 years), but a few patients are younger. The symptoms and signs are those of usual prostatic adenocarcinoma, but rare cases have been reported to be associated with a paraneoplastic syndrome, including Cushing syndrome,[214,221,222] Eaton–Lambert syndrome,[220] and hyperglucagonemia syndrome associated with inappropriate antidiuretic hormone secretion, malignant hypercalcemia, and thyrotoxicosis.[50,216] In some patients, adenocarcinoma of the prostate precedes the recognition of the small cell carcinoma, whereas in other patients the small cell carcinoma presents as a *de novo* tumor.[213,214] Those presenting initially with a conventional microacinar adenocarcinoma have survived between 7 months and 9 years (median 24 months). After recognition of the small cell carcinoma component, regardless of a history of adenocarcinoma, death followed within 1.5 years (median 5 months).[213] However, newly developed chemotherapeutic regimens similar to those used for small cell carcinoma of the lung promise prolonged survival, particularly in patients with only regional lymph node spread.[50,213,217,218,223]

The histologic features of small cell carcinoma of the prostate are similar to those seen in the lung and at other extrapulmonary sites.[213–217,219–222] The small cells are of either oat or intermediate types (Fig. 14A.52). Small cell carcinoma of the prostate is most frequently associated with conventional adenocarcinoma (more than 50% of cases) (Fig. 14A.53) and

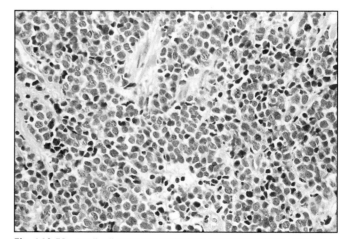

Fig. 14A.52 • Small cell carcinoma under high-power magnification the tumor cells show hyperchromatic nuclei and prominent nuclear molding, which are characteristic features of small cell carcinoma in general.

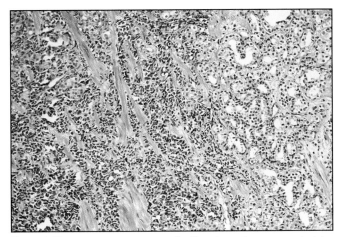

Fig. 14A.53 • Small cell carcinoma. Small cell carcinoma is present on the left and a usual adenocarcinoma on the right.

rarely may be associated with sarcomatoid and squamous carcinoma components.[213] Immunohistochemical and electron microscopic studies demonstrate that the cells of small cell carcinoma of the prostate are heterogeneous, like those of pulmonary or extrapulmonary small cell carcinomas.[214,216,219] The cells of some tumors contain dense-core neurosecretory granules and show positive immunohistochemical staining for neuroendocrine markers (Fig. 14A.54), whereas others are poorly differentiated adenocarcinomas or possibly carcinomas arising from basal (reserve) cells.[214,216,219,219a] Its frequent association with other prostatic carcinomas and its immuno-histochemical and ultrastructural heterogeneity have led to the belief that small cell carcinoma of the prostate arises from multipotential prostatic epithelium; it is also believed that it does not originate from specific neuroendocrine cells.[214,216,219]

The levels of both PSA and PrAP are useful clinical markers of disseminated adenocarcinoma of the prostate, but small cell carcinoma of the prostate is often not accompanied by significant elevation of these markers. Small cell carci-nomas of the prostate have a tendency to metastasize early to the pelvic lymph nodes, lung, and liver. Unusual metastatic locations such as the omentum, vocal cord, temporal bone,

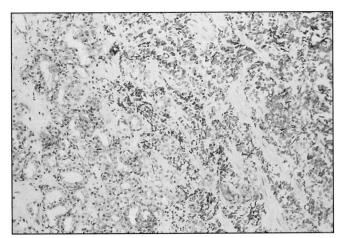

Fig. 14A.54 • Immunostaining for prostate-specific antigen and prostatic acid phosphatase is positive in the adenocarcinoma component, but it is usually negative in the small cell carcinoma component.

axillary lymph node, and peripheral soft tissue have also been cited.[223]

Metastatic small cell carcinoma of the lung to the prostate must be considered in the differential diagnosis of primary small cell carcinoma of the prostate. Metastatic tumors in the prostate are found in approximately 0.5–2.2% of autopsies, and they represent 1.2% of all malignant diseases of the prostate.[224,225] Only a few cases of metastatic oat cell carcinoma of the lung to the prostate have been reported.[224-226] Since there is no morphologic difference between small cell carcinoma of the prostate and extraprostatic small cell carcinoma, careful clinicopathologic correlation is mandatory.[213] Although TTF-1 is not a specific marker for small cell carcinoma of the lung, it may assist in distinguishing small cell carcinoma of the lung from some non-pulmonary small cell carcinomas.[227] Another finding helpful in making a diagnosis of primary small cell carcinoma of the prostate is the intimate association with adenocarcinoma of the prostate; such an association has been noted in many cases.[50,213] Lymphoma involving the prostate is rare but may mimic small cell carcinoma of prostate. Immuno-staining for leukocyte common antigen and keratin is helpful in the differential diagnosis. Embryonal rhabdomyosarcoma of the prostate has "round blue cell histology" but occurs in the pediatric population in the overwhelming majority of cases. Recently, Paneth cell-like change has been described in prostatic adenocarcinoma and probably represents a form of neuroendocrine differentiation.[228,229]

Squamous cell and adenosquamous carcinoma of prostate

Squamous carcinoma of the prostate is rare; it constitutes 0.2% of malignant tumors of the prostate.[230-237] Fewer than 70 cases have been reported in the literature. They are either pure squamous carcinoma or squamous carcinoma admixed with adenocarcinoma (adenosquamous carcinoma). In addition, TCC and sarcomatoid carcinoma have been reported to be associated with squamous and adenosquamous carcinoma.[237] Clinically, primary squamous carcinoma and adenosquamous carcinoma cannot be distinguished from adenocarcinoma of the prostate. Criteria for the diagnosis of pure squamous carcinoma are: (1) a clearly malignant neoplasm with dis-ordered growth, cellular anaplasia, and invasion; (2) definite squamous features with evidence of keratinization, squamous pearl formation, and intercellular bridges; (3) lack of any glandular or acinar component; (4) absence of primary squamous carcinoma elsewhere, particularly in the bladder.[238] Most patients do not have a history of prior radiation or hormonal treatment, but some may have a history of prior treatment.[237] The histogenesis of pure squamous carcinoma remains unclear; prostatic urethral epithelium, transitional epithelium of the periurethral duct, basal (reserve) cells of the prostatic acini, and common acinar cells have all been specu-lated to be the cells of origin. However, it is difficult to accept any single pathogenetic mechanism because of the rarity of this tumor.[230–232,233–235,237–241] Occurrence in a patient with *Schistosoma haematobium* infection has been reported.[242]

Adenosquamous carcinoma (Fig. 14A.55), with rare exceptions, usually develops several years after radiation or hormone therapy for an ordinary adenocarcinoma of the prostate.[231–233,237,241,243] Bennett & Edgerton[234] offered two

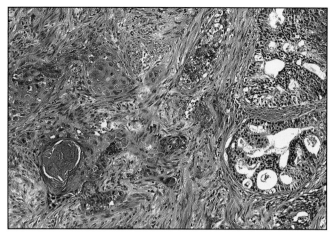

Fig. 14A.55 • Adenosquamous carcinoma of the prostate. Squamous carcinoma (right) is associated with adenocarcinoma (left).

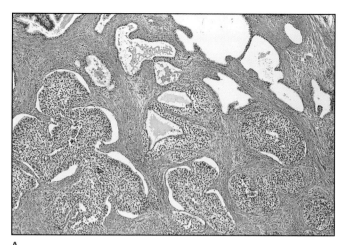

A

B

Fig. 14A.56 • **(A)** Transitional cell carcinoma (TCC) involving prostatic ducts and acini. TCC involves the luminal surface of ducts and acini. There is no stromal invasion. **(B)** Under high-power magnification, the tumor cells are revealed between basal lamina and prostatic epithelial cells.

hypotheses for its occurrence: (1) the influence of hormone and/or radiation therapy alters the nature of prostatic cancer to a mixed cell type; or (2) a second adenocarcinoma involving periurethral ducts, concomitant with the prostatic adenocarcinoma, develops a squamous component under the influence of radiation or hormonal therapy.

Even with metastatic disease, the serum PrAP and PSA levels are usually not elevated in squamous carcinoma.[238,244,245] The bone metastases are usually osteolytic, whereas they are osteoblastic in most prostatic adenocarcinomas.[238,245] Squamous carcinoma of the prostate is a highly aggressive tumor.[237] Various therapeutic modalities have not been very effective in controlling this cancer. Estrogen therapy is usually unhelpful.[230–235,238–241] Squamous metaplasia of prostatic ducts and acini is a well-documented lesion that forms in response to infarction and estrogen treatment.[233] This lesion can usually be differentiated from squamous carcinoma by the lack of invasion and cellular anaplasia. Bladder and urethral TCCs may show squamous and glandular differentiation and may mimic a squamous and/or adenosquamous carcinoma. Extension from a squamous carcinoma of the anal canal or metastasis from distant sites, e.g., lung, should also be ruled out.

Transitional cell carcinoma of prostate

The incidence of TCC of the prostate varies from 1% to 5% of all prostatic carcinomas, depending on the series.[246] Despite the low percentage, it is a very important lesion since its biologic behavior is significantly different from that of conventional prostatic adenocarcinoma. The prognosis of TCC is unfavorable; TCC does not respond to hormonal therapy.[46,47,97,98,246] Although TCC may arise *de novo* in the prostate, most cases represent secondary involvement from a TCC of the urinary bladder.[50,246–249] When TCC of the urinary bladder involves the prostate, there are two patterns of involvement: (1) mucosal pagetoid spread through the prostatic urethra, prostatic ducts, and acini with or without stromal invasion (Fig. 14A.56), and (2) direct invasion through the bladder wall (Fig. 14A.57).[247,250–255]

In primary TCC of the prostate, the periurethral glands and ducts are affected initially.[46,47,256] The TCC may spread along the ducts and acini and frequently invades the fibromuscular

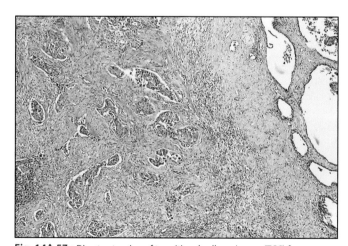

Fig. 14A.57 • Direct extension of transitional cell carcinoma (TCC) from a bladder cancer. Prostatic stroma is involved by TCC. Note the normal prostatic glands on the right.

stroma. In secondary TCC, a deeply invasive bladder carcinoma located at the bladder neck invades the prostate directly. In patients who have (or had) a long-standing history of bladder TCC, pagetoid spread along the prostatic urethra and ducts is another mechanism of prostatic involvement. Just as

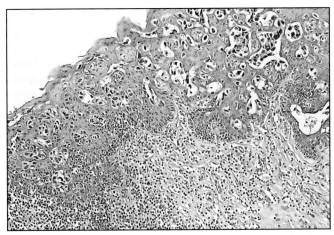

Fig. 14A.58 • Transitional cell carcinoma extends intraepithelially within the squamous epithelium of the urethral meatus.

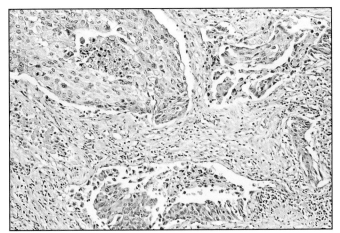

Fig. 14A.59 • Transitional cell carcinoma usually shows a solid growth pattern with frequent tumor necrosis, a high number of mitoses, and nuclear pleomorphism.

in primary TCC of the prostate, the tumor grows initially as malignant pagetoid cells, progresses to carcinoma in situ confined within the ducts or acini, and eventually may invade the stroma. TCC may spread intraepithelially to the ejaculatory duct, seminal vesicle, and urethral meatus (Fig. 14A.58).[247,256,257] The mechanism of TCC secondarily involving the prostate in patients with a long history of bladder cancer is that intravesical therapy is successful in overcoming the bladder disease, but the prostatic urethra and periurethral ducts and acini involved by transitional carcinoma escape the influence of topical therapy, resulting in urothelial carcinoma within the prostate gland.

TCC of the prostate typically shows a solid growth pattern. Furthermore, peritumoral inflammation, prominent nuclear pleomorphism, solid cell nests containing a high mitotic count, and tumor necrosis are important criteria for the diagnosis of TCC (Fig. 14A.59) over that of adenocarcinoma of the prostate.[47,246]

In TCC of the prostate, invasion into the stroma is a very important prognostic factor. Those patients who have TCC confined to the ducts or acini at prostatectomy or cysto-prostatectomy have a relatively good prognosis, but most patients with TCC invading the stroma develop metastatic disease.[248,251,253,254]

Since TCC of the prostate is hormonally resistant, distinction of the solid form of usual prostatic adenocarcinoma and ductal adenocarcinoma from TCC of the prostate is clinically important in terms of management. Clinical history, careful microscopic evaluation, and immunohistochemical stains are helpful in differentiating TCC from the usual prostatic adenocarcinoma and its ductal variant. TCC is negative for PrAP and PSA immunostaining, whereas CEA, uroplakin, and thrombomodulin are often positive.[99,246,258] Because some prostate cancers are CK7+, CK20+ and some urothelial carcinomas are CK7–, CK20–, these markers are of no help in making the differential diagnosis.[258]

Transitional metaplasia can easily be differentiated from TCC of the prostate since TCC of the prostate is cytologically anaplastic and the cells of transitional cell metaplasia appear bland, with prominent nuclear grooves.[45]

Sarcomatoid carcinoma

Sarcomatoid carcinoma of the prostate, a biphasic tumor containing carcinoma and a spindle or pleomorphic sarcomatoid component (Fig. 14A.60), is another uncommon variant of prostatic carcinoma. It can be difficult to differentiate from true sarcomas when either the conventional microacinar carcinoma histology is minimal or the tissue sample is limited. The terms carcinosarcoma, malignant mixed mesodermal tumor, spindle cell carcinoma, and carcinoma with pseudosarcomatous stroma have been used in the literature to describe this lesion. Strictly speaking, carcinosarcoma has traditionally been defined as a biphasic tumor with heterologous sarcomatous components. We use the term sarcomatoid carcinoma to describe all tumors showing biphasic growth with carcinoma and sarcomatous components, regardless of the presence or absence of heterologous elements.[259–263]

Several cases of sarcomatoid carcinoma of the prostate have been reported in the literature; they often present with obstructive symptoms and hence are frequently diagnosed in TURP specimens.[259,262–266] The ages of the patients with these tumors range from 58 to 85 years (mean 71 years). In our experience, these tumors are always associated with a high-grade prostatic adenocarcinoma that occurred either previously to, or simultaneously with, the sarcomatoid component. The majority of patients have metastatic disease at the time of diagnosis and 50% have a history of prostate cancer treated with radiation or hormonal therapy.[266] The sarcomatoid areas are composed of spindle cells with large, pleomorphic, hyperchromatic nuclei. The pattern is that of high-grade sarcoma (in most cases, similar to that of so-called malignant fibrous histiocytoma) (Fig. 14A.61). The sarcomatoid component may also resemble fibrosarcoma or leiomyosarcoma. A heterologous sarcomatoid component (osteosarcomatous, chondrosarcomatous, or rhabdomyosarcomatous) can be observed in up to one-third of cases.[259,264,265] Immunohistochemical studies using antibodies against keratin, PrAP, and PSA can be helpful in proving the epithelial nature of this neoplasm.[99,259,264] The spindle cell components seldom express keratin reactivity, and approximately one-third of the cases show focal reactivity for PSA, PrAP, or both.[99,259,264]

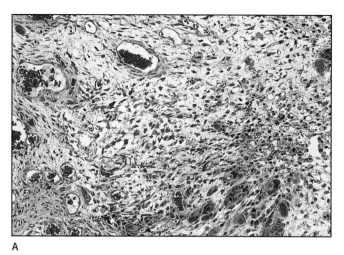

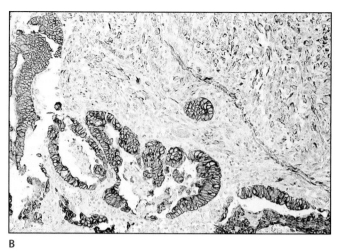

Fig. 14A.60 • (A) Sarcomatoid carcinoma. A biphasic tumor with carcinomatous and spindle sarcomatoid components; the latter is usually of a malignant fibrous histiocytoma-like pattern, but is often of an unclassified myxoid pattern, as seen in this example. **(B)** Immunostaining for keratin is positive in both the carcinomatous and sarcomatoid components.

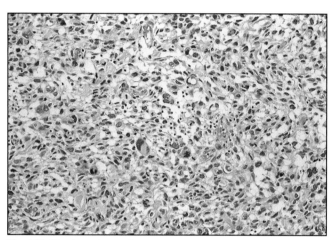

Fig. 14A.61 • The malignant fibrous histiocytoma-like pattern is the most frequent form of the sarcomatoid component.

Sarcomatoid carcinoma has a poor prognosis. All 9 patients in the series reported by Shannon et al.[259] for whom follow-up data were available died of their disease between 3 and 48 months (median 12 months) after diagnosis. The clinical course was characterized by aggressive local recurrence. Dundore et al.[262] reported a 41% 5-year and 14% 7-year cancer specific survival; 86% of patients died of disease (median 9.5 months).

The differential diagnosis of sarcomatoid carcinoma includes a variety of primary prostatic sarcomas. Distinction from sarcomatoid carcinoma lies in the absence of epithelial components (after extensive sampling) and usually the absence of a history of adenocarcinoma. Postoperative spindle cell nodule, phyllodes tumor, and pseudosarcomatous fibromyxoid tumor should also be considered in the differential diagnosis. In those conditions, the spindle cells lack pleomorphism or atypical mitoses.

Miscellaneous carcinomas

Lymphoepithelioma-like carcinoma,[267] oncocytic carcinoma,[268] giant cell carcinoma, renal-type clear cell carcinoma,[50,269] and

tubulocystic clear cell adenocarcinoma, simulating the tumor seen in the female genital tract rather than a typical prostatic adenocarcinoma,[270] have been reported.

Carcinoma mimics

Although most acinar proliferations simulating carcinoma are from the transition zone, and are consequently most commonly seen in TURP or suprapubic/retropubic prostatectomies for benign disease, not infrequently such changes are seen on needle biopsies. The targeting by core biopsies of the transition zone, as well as the inclusion of transition zone in the core biopsy directed to the peripheral zone when the prostate gland is too small or too large, leads to biopsies of benign small acinar proliferations of the transition zone. Therefore it is important to be familiar with these lesions.

Acinar proliferations of the transition zone: atypical adenomatous hyperplasia (adenosis)

AAH, or adenosis of the prostate is difficult to distinguish from well-differentiated adenocarcinoma of the prostate. Although McNeal referred to this lesion as a possible premalignant proliferation, to date a convincing argument for it being a precursor lesion has not been made by most studies.[23,271–274] In 1982, Brawn[92] provided the only large study with clinical follow-up on patients with adenosis. One hundred and eight patients with AAH (adenosis) were followed for 5–15 years (average 7.7 years), and 7 developed carcinoma (6.5%); carcinoma developed in 84 of 2263 patients with hyperplasia (3.7%) who had been followed for a similar period of time. It is, however, argued by many experts that some of the cases of AAH as illustrated by Brawn may represent well-differentiated carcinoma. Lopez-Beltran et al.[275] investigated three-dimensional nuclear volume in AAH, nodular hyperplasia, and well-differentiated prostate adenocarcinoma. Significant differences were found between prostate cancer and AAH or nodular hyperplasia, but the difference between AAH and benign hyperplasia was not significant, suggesting that AAH is probably a histologic variant of BPH. However, genetic alterations in AAH lesions were found to be variable.[276,277] It is uncommon in needle biopsies as it is a lesion of the transition zone and is therefore not biopsied unless there is marked BPH or the biopsy is specifically targeted to sample this zone. AAH may be multifocal; its incidence in TURP specimens is 1.5–19.6% and up to 33% in radical prostatectomies.[278–280]

AAH is a proliferation of small to medium-sized glands that are seemingly lined by a single row of epithelial cells with monotonous round nuclei and fine but dark chromatin pattern, showing neither nuclear atypia nor prominent nucleoli (Fig. 14A.62).[3,8,272] The basal cell layer is usually inconspicuous and attenuated, or obscured, and one may have to resort to high-molecular-weight cytokeratin staining (clone 34βE12), p63, or cytokeratin 5/6 to confirm the presence of basal cells and prove the benignity of the lesion (Fig. 14A.63). AAH may have intraluminal crystalloids, blue mucin, and a focally

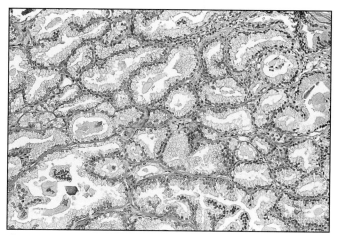

Fig. 14A.62 • Atypical adenomatous hyperplasia (small gland hyperplasia). A proliferation of small glands with back-to-back arrangement. Prominent nucleoli are not seen.

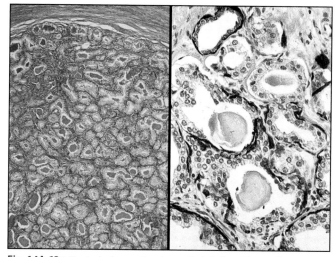

Fig. 14A.63 • Atypical adenomatous hyperplasia (adenosis). A well-demarcated nodule (left side) contains small glands with minimal intervening stroma; this pattern superficially resembles Gleason 1 or 2 patterns of prostate cancer, but the glands of adenosis retain the basal cell layer (34βE12, right).

infiltrative pattern, making distinction from cancer even more treacherous.

The differential diagnosis of AAH includes well-differentiated adenocarcinoma and all other lesions with small glandular proliferations. AAH may show focal P504S staining, but most cases are negative for this marker. In contrast the majority of prostate carcinomas show diffuse staining.[109–111] Yang et al.[281] studied P504S expression in 40 cases of AAH to understand the significance of a precursor lesion of prostatic adenocarcinoma. The 34βE12 stain confirmed the presence of patchy basal cells in all 40 cases of AAH. P504S was undetectable in the majority of AAHs (33 of 40, 82.5%), focally expressed in 4 of 40 (10.0%), or diffusely positive only in 3 of 40 (7.5%) cases of AAH. Interestingly, 2 of 7 P504S-positive AAHs were found adjacent to adenocarcinoma. In contrast, all BPHs (20 of 20, 100%) were negative for P504S, and all 20 cases of prostatic carcinomas (100%) showed diffuse P504S staining pattern. These findings suggest that AAH is a heterogeneous entity.

Basal cell hyperplasia

BCH of the prostate gland is a relatively common lesion in hyperplastic prostates being examined in TURP specimens,[3,282–285] but is uncommon in needle biopsies.[286] It is usually seen in the setting of BPH, and hence occurs in the same age group as BPH (range 63–80 years, mean 74 years); it may present with urinary obstruction, although in most instances it is seen coincidentally with BPH-related histologic features.[283–287] The other clinically significant association is with antiandrogen therapy.[157]

Microscopically, the degree of proliferation varies in extent: most foci of BCH show only individual or small groups of acini with proliferating basal cells, but lobular or diffuse areas of BCH are rather uncommon.[3,282–284] BCH has a distinctive microscopic appearance. Its recognition is not difficult in most cases, but it may mimic adenocarcinoma of small acinar pattern, particularly if one is not familiar with this histologic entity[3,73,282,283,288,289] and when the case shows prominent nucleoli.[3,290] This lesion has also been described as "fetalization" of the prostate simply because, on light microscopy, it resembles fetal prostate.[291] BCH is characterized by a nodular growth of nests, tubules, and cords filled with proliferating, small, darkly staining basal cells. Most of the nests of BCH show vertical palisading of basal cells toward the periphery. The basal cells have scanty cytoplasm and oval to short-spindled hyperchromatic nuclei. Nucleoli are usually absent or, if present, small and inconspicuous (Fig. 14A.64). Nuclear grooves are not present. Mitoses are absent or extremely rare, and there is no necrosis. The margin of the nodule is not encapsulated but is well demarcated in most cases.[3,73,91,288,282–284,290] BCH frequently merges into hyperplastic or normal prostatic glands. It has been reported to be associated with SA[292] and CCCH,[293] which are two other benign hyperplastic lesions of the prostate. For the sake of understanding the morphology, BCH can be classified as complete or incomplete on the basis of whether central lumina are absent or present.[91,284,288] Complete BCH is characterized by solid nests of basal cells without luminal differentiation (Fig. 14A.65), whereas incomplete BCH often shows significant central glandular differentiation with cuboidal or columnar secretory cells (Fig. 14A.66); the lumina may contain both neutral and acid mucin positive for PAS and

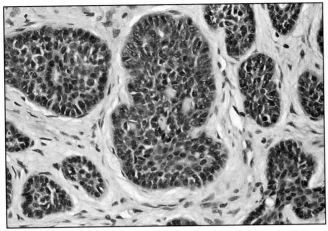

Fig. 14A.64 • Basal cell hyperplasia. Solid proliferation of basal cells with peripheral palisading that superficially resembles basal cell carcinoma of the skin is seen.

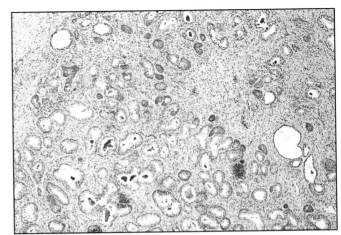

Fig. 14A.66 • Incomplete basal cell hyperplasia (BCH). This example shows the presence of lumina in most basal cell nests, a characteristic of incomplete BCH.

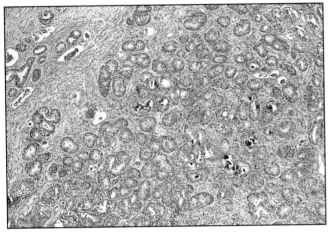

Fig. 14A.65 • Complete basal cell hyperplasia (BCH). Although some nests have lumina, most are solid. Scattered calcification is frequently seen in BCH.

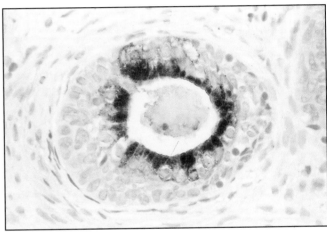

Fig. 14A.67 • Incomplete basal cell hyperplasia showing prostate-specific antigen (PSA) immunoreactivity in the luminal secretory cells. Note the absence of PSA staining in the basal cells.

alcian blue stains.[284] Scattered microcalcifications and corpora amylacea in the lumina are frequently seen.[91,283,284,288,294] The stroma of BCH is usually more cellular than that of nearby normal prostate of BPH and shows proliferation of fibroblasts/myofibroblasts. BCH is often found at the margin of infarcts, where it presumably represents a reaction to ischemia.[74,91,295]

The basaloid cells of BCH show positive immunoreactivity for high-molecular-weight cytokeratin (clone 34βE12), p63,[105,296] and cytokeratin 5/6,[296] but are negative for PSA, PrAP, and AMACR.[68,105,284,296,297] Neither basaloid nor secretory cells show immunoreactivity for S-100 protein, muscle-specific actin, or vimentin. In the areas of luminal differentiation (incomplete BCH), the luminal secretory cells are positive for PSA and PrAP (Fig. 14A.67).[284] The incomplete variant of BCH is more likely to be confused with carcinoma, because some cases show a small acinar pattern with minimal basal cell proliferation. However, acini of incomplete BCH are composed of two cell types – the inner luminal layer of cuboidal to columnar cells and the outer layer of basaloid cells – whereas prostatic adenocarcinoma by definition does not contain a basal cell layer.[73,74,297] The well-circumscribed

growth pattern of BCH on low-power examination is the best clue in this differential, as most prostatic carcinomas have an infiltrative growth pattern.[91,283,284,288] In addition, carcinoma shows nucleomegaly and prominent nucleoli.[68,298–302] The basal cells of BCH may have nucleoli, but, as mentioned above, they are generally small and inconspicuous.[283,284,303,304] However, an atypical variant of BCH characterized by nucleomegaly, pleomorphism, mitoses, or large prominent nucleoli (mean diameter 1.96 μm) has been described.[305,306] The designation of atypical BCH has no clinical relevance or premalignant connotations and the changes may in part be due to associated inflammation.[306]

TCC involving the prostate is easily differentiated from BCH, since TCC shows significant cellular pleomorphism, frequent mitoses, and necrosis. In addition, most patients with TCC have a previous history of TCC of the urinary bladder.[246,307]

Other benign lesions, such as squamous or transitional cell metaplasia, can also mimic BCH and, although their distinction from BCH is not clinically meaningful, they can readily be separated in most instances because of fairly characteristic

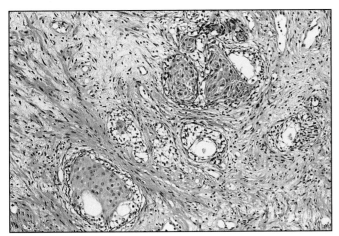

Fig. 14A.68 • Squamous metaplasia. The cells of squamous metaplasia have abundant eosinophilic cytoplasm and distinct cell borders. Squamous metaplasia is usually associated with hormonal treatment or infarction.

histology. Squamous metaplasia (Fig. 14A.68) is usually seen in areas adjacent to an infarct or in patients who have received estrogen therapy.[230–233,239] The cells of squamous metaplasia tend to have more cytoplasm and more distinct cell borders than basal cells in BCH. Transitional cell metaplasia (Fig. 14A.69) is quite common in the transition zone around the prostatic urethra, although it may be fairly prominent and involve the peripheral zone; in a review of 103 consecutive biopsies it was seen in 34% of specimens.[45] The cells of transitional cell metaplasia are much larger and have more cytoplasm than the basal cells of BCH. The nuclear chromatin is diffusely and evenly dispersed in transitional cell metaplasia and more clumped in BCH, and the nuclei of transitional cell metaplasia have prominent nuclear grooves, not seen in the basal cells of BCH.[304]

Rioux-Leclercq & Epstein[294] described 25 cases of BCH with unusual features and identified four distinct groups: (1) BCH with intracytoplasmic globules (5 cases); (2) BCH with calcifications (8 cases), including one with globules; (3) BCH with squamous features (3 cases); and (4) cribriform BCH (9 cases), including two cases with globules. A total of 5 cases

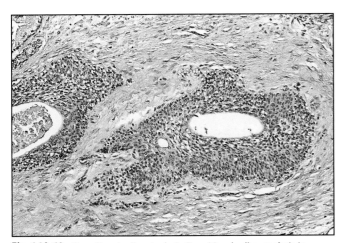

Fig. 14A.69 • Transitional cell metaplasia. Transitional cell metaplasia is usually seen in the periurethral areas of the prostate. The cells of transitional cell metaplasia are larger and have more cytoplasm than those of basal cell hyperplasia.

contained prominent nucleoli and/or cytologic atypia. Hyaline cytoplasmic globules have not been described in any other prostatic entity and appear diagnostic of BCH. Calcifications observed in BCH were psammomatous, differing from the finely stippled calcifications occasionally seen in areas of comedo necrosis within high-grade prostatic carcinoma. BCH with squamous features differed from squamous differentiation in carcinomas (adenosquamous carcinoma) and from benign foci of squamous differentiation seen associated with either prostatic infarcts or with hormonal therapy. Whereas cribriform PIN and cribriform cancer glands represent a single glandular unit with punched-out lumina, many of the glands within a focus of cribriform BCH appeared as fused individual BCH glands. The use of cytokeratin 34βE12, CK5/6, or p63 can help in difficult cases. In cribriform BCH high-molecular-weight cytokeratin, CK5/6 or p63 shows multilayered staining of the basal cells in some of the glands and a continuous layer of immunoreactivity. Cribriform PIN demonstrates an interrupted immunoreactive single-cell layer of basal cells. Recognition of the architectural and cytologic features of unusual morphologies in BCH can be used to facilitate its diagnosis and differentiation from prostatic carcinoma and high-grade PIN.

BCH in the peripheral zone can occur and is present in a significant minority of prostate needle biopsy samples (10.2%) and whole prostate glands (23%).[290] The presence of prominent nucleoli in BCH may cause diagnostic concern for a neoplastic proliferation. The increase in cell number in BCH appears to be due to a coordinate increase in proliferation index coupled with a diminished apoptotic index. The presence of inflammation in the majority of BCH foci suggests that peripheral-zone BCH in untreated patients may represent a stereotyped response to injury.[290]

Adenoid basal cell tumor (ABT)

This is an accentuated form of BCH, characterized by larger and confluent nodules of proliferating basal cells ranging up to 1 cm in diameter.[284,308] The cells of ABT often contain nuclei two to three times larger than those of BCH and show some variation in size and shape. The chromatin is finely dispersed and these nuclei contain occasional small nucleoli. The nests of ABT reveal areas of luminal differentiation with an occasional cribriform arrangement (Fig. 14A.70). Individual nests are often invested by a thick basement membrane. Immunohistochemical findings in ABT are similar to those of BCH, suggesting that they have a common origin from the basal cells of the prostate. ABT is considered a locally aggressive lesion, but some lesions merge, in histology, with adenoid cystic/basaloid carcinoma.

Adenoid cystic carcinoma (ACC)/ basaloid carcinoma

This tumor is very rare in the prostate and its occurrence has been challenged by some investigators because these lesions do not show infiltrative growth, or typical perineural invasion, and they often contain typical BCH. Patients do not die from this disease and it is argued that the reported cases are probably ABT[308] or adenoid cystic-like tumor.[309] The tumor has been considered to have indolent biologic potential. However,

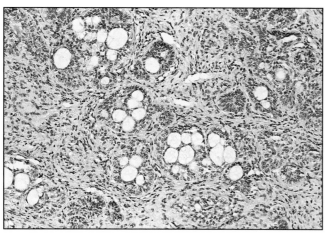

Fig. 14A.70 • Adenoid basal cell tumor. Solid nests and nests with single or multiple lumina are present in a cellular stroma.

a more recent study of 19 patients has shown extraprostatic extension (26%), perineural invasion (26%) (Fig. 14A.71), and distant metastasis (21%).[310] These authors claimed that ACC/basal cell carcinoma of the prostate is a potentially aggressive neoplasm requiring ablative therapy.

Bcl-2 expression ($P < 0.0001$) and Ki-67 index ($P = 0.005$) were elevated in basaloid carcinoma compared with typical BCH or BCH with nucleoli, whereas there was no significant difference between typical BCH and BCH with nucleoli. p53 was not discriminatory in separating benign from malignant basal cell lesions of the prostate. Therefore, elevated expression of bcl-2 and higher Ki-67 index may aid in the diagnosis of basal cell proliferative lesions of the prostate.[311]

Since basaloid tumors are frequently positive for p63, CK5/6, and 34βE12,[284,310] it has been proposed that there is a relationship between the basal cells of the normal prostate gland, BCH, ABT, and ACC, representing a continuum in the progression of hyperplasia to benign and then malignant neoplasia.[284]

McKenney et al.[312] recently reported cases with basaloid proliferations of the prostate showing morphologic patterns other than usual BCH. Most florid basaloid proliferations of

the prostate fall into one of two categories. In the first, there is a clear association with nodular hyperplasia (adenoid cystic-like hyperplasia) and, although cytologic atypia and mitoses may be seen, they are present within a lesion that retains an orderly, vaguely nodular (non-infiltrative) pattern. The second group of cases (ACC and basaloid carcinoma) shows a widespread, haphazard infiltrative growth pattern. ACCs are biologically indolent following prostatectomy but have a low risk of distant metastasis.

Clear cell cribriform hyperplasia

CCCH of prostate is a rare form of BPH.[293,313] It was recognized by the WHO in 1980,[69] and Gleason described it as florid benign papillary-cribriform hyperplasia of prostate in 1985.[74] CCCH has a nodular growth pattern, as does BPH. It is characterized by a complex papillary-cribriform hyperplasia of clear cells involving acini of BPH. In most of the cases, gradual transition from the usual type of benign hyperplasia to CCCH can be demonstrated.[74,69,293] Its appropriate recognition as a benign condition is primarily important to avoid confusing it with malignant or premalignant lesions of the prostate, especially those with a cribriform-papillary pattern. The clinical features of CCCH are essentially those of BPH. Patients' ages range from 58 to 88 years (mean 68 years).[290] The clinical diagnosis is almost always BPH with a presenting symptom of urinary obstruction; the diagnosis is made during the examination of TURP or prostatectomy specimens.[293,313]

On histologic examination, CCCH may be focal or florid, involving part of one or several prostatic chips. On low-power examination, it has a nodular growth pattern. The acinar unit in CCCH is distended by a proliferation of bland-looking clear cells which have a papillary-cribriform arrangement (Fig. 14A.72).[293] A distinct basal cell layer occurs at the periphery of the dilated acini and consists of flat cells in close contact with the basement membrane. The proliferating cells are round, cuboidal to tall columnar with a varying, but usually abundant amount of cytoplasm which is most often clear (Fig. 14A.73). They have uniform, small, round to oval nuclei, which are usually the same size as the nuclei of epithelial cells in adjacent hyperplastic acini. The nuclei at the periphery are

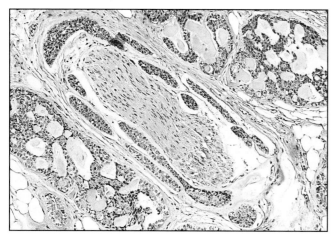

Fig. 14A.71 • Adenoid cystic carcinoma. A cribriform pattern of adenoid cystic carcinoma with perineural invasion is seen.

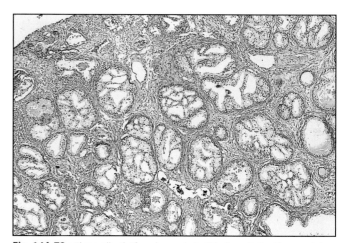

Fig. 14A.72 • Clear cell cribriform hyperplasia. It is characterized by a nodular growth pattern of distended acini with a complex papillary-cribriform architecture.

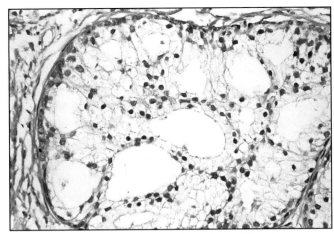

Fig. 14A.73 • Clear cell cribriform hyperplasia. A basal cell layer is present at the periphery of the acini. The clear cells range in shape from cuboidal to tall and columnar, and nucleoli are absent or inconspicuous.

slightly larger than those at the center of the proliferation, suggesting cellular maturation toward the center. Nucleoli are rarely seen but, if present, they are small and inconspicuous. Mitotic figures are absent. The cribriform spaces are devoid of acid mucins or crystalloids. Scant glycogen may be present, but mucin typically is not found in the cytoplasm. The surrounding stroma of CCCH is not different from that of BPH or of a normal prostate and lacks evidence of desmoplasia. CCCH may be associated with BCH; BCH can be present in an area distant from CCCH or can occur in the same nodule as CCCH. Some areas display transition between the two components.[293] Immunoperoxidase studies demonstrate that the clear cells of CCCH show strong immunoreactivity for PSA and PrAP. High-molecular-weight cytokeratin (clone 34βE12), CK5/6, and p63 stain the basal cell layer in a continuous fashion (Fig. 14A.74); although occasionally the staining is focal in nature, it is never absent or questionably present.[98,304,313]

It is important that CCCH should not be mistaken for a carcinoma or preneoplastic condition of the prostate with a papillary-cribriform pattern. Cribriform adenocarcinoma and high-grade PIN are the two main lesions in the differential

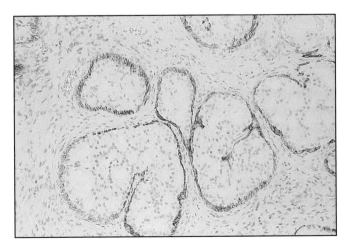

Fig. 14A.74 • Basal cells of clear cell cribriform hyperplasia react to antibody for 34βE12 (K-903) while the clear cells remain unstained.

diagnosis of CCCH.[271,314] The cribriform variant of prostatic adenocarcinoma, although less common, is well recognized.[314] Gleason in his grading system recognized it as pattern 3 when necrosis is not present. When necrosis is present it is pattern 5.[72] Predominance of this pattern has been reported to be associated with large-volume disease and a poor prognosis, making the differential diagnosis from CCCH of paramount importance. The key to the diagnosis of CCCH is the combination of bland cytologic features and architectural uniformity. Its expansile nodular growth pattern, with a well-demarcated margin, and retention of two cell types are also important features in its recognition, along with uniformity of the clear cells and the lack of prominent cytologic atypia or nucleoli.[293] The presence of the basal cell layer in CCCH is easily recognized by routine H&E stain, but its recognition may be facilitated by high-molecular-weight cytokeratin, CK5/6, and p63 immunostains which would be uniformly negative in carcinoma. Cribriform adenocarcinoma, on the other hand, is characterized by a diffuse growth pattern, nucleomegaly, prominent nucleoli, and occasional necrosis. PIN may show intraluminal papillary projections of secretory cells and may have a cribriform pattern in high-grade cases. High-grade PIN usually shows a spectrum of architectural patterns, including micropapillary, tufting, cribriform, and flat, and on high-power examination has nucleomegaly and prominent nucleoli.[4,5,271] DNA flow cytometry may also be helpful sometimes to separate CCCH from cribriform carcinoma and high-grade PIN, although realistically this is not necessary. CCCH invariably shows diploid DNA content, whereas cribriform carcinoma and high-grade PIN may show aneuploid DNA content.[313]

Sclerosing adenosis

SA of the prostate has been reported under a number of different names (adenomatoid tumor, fibroepithelial nodule, and pseudoadenomatoid tumor).[78,315–321] Chen & Schiff[315] first reported this lesion, noticing the morphologic resemblance to adenomatoid tumor, and named it adenomatoid prostatic tumor. Hulman[316] reported a similar lesion of the prostate, which he compared with typical adenomatoid tumors using histochemical and immunohistochemical methods; he concluded that the lesion was of prostatic origin, proposing the term pseudoadenomatoid tumor. Sesterhenn & Mostofi[317] presented data on 25 cases of SA, which they termed fibroepithelial nodule of the prostate in abstract form. The term SA was introduced by Young & Clement[318] on the basis of the histologic resemblance to SA of the breast. SA is a rare lesion characterized by proliferation of variably sized, but usually small glands in a cellular stroma. It is of both practical and academic importance, because of its remarkable resemblance to adenocarcinoma on histologic examination and because of its myoepithelial cell differentiation[78,79,309,318] (normal prostatic basal cells show absent myoepithelial features, as has been elegantly demonstrated by Srigley[91]). Sakamoto et al.[319] reviewed sections of the prostate from 263 patients and found 5 cases of SA, with an incidence of 1.9%.

SA is not a premalignant condition. The lesion is usually small, ranging from 1.5 to 11.0 mm (mean 4.2 mm). It is seen in TURP or prostatectomy specimens (rarely being seen in prostatic biopsies)[320] and is localized to the transition zone, as are other proliferative benign lesions.[78] SA is for the most part well circumscribed, but it is non-encapsulated. In certain cases, minor infiltration can be observed at the periphery.

On microscopic examination, SA is characterized by an ill-defined nodule containing irregular, small acini and nests or clusters of cells embedded in a cellular stroma (Fig. 14A.75).[78,315–318] Some of these glands are slightly dilated while others have a microacinar pattern. Assessment of the nature of the lining cells is frequently difficult. The basal cells are for the most part obscured or compressed, but in all cases some glands clearly show the presence of a basal cell layer (Fig. 14A.76). The luminal cells are larger and have clear to eosinophilic cytoplasm and basally located nuclei. The basally located cells tend to be flat to cuboidal, and their nuclei are oriented parallel to the basement membrane. An intensely eosinophilic, thick, basement membrane-like material surrounds some of the glands. The lumina of the glands may have alcian blue-positive acid mucin and crystalloids.[78] The stroma is an integral component of this lesion and is typically very cellular, often myxoid,[320,321] and made up of plump fibroblasts/ myofibroblasts and smooth muscle cells.

An immunohistochemical and ultrastructural analysis of examples of SA revealed that cells within the glandular component demonstrated positivity for pan-cytokeratin, high-molecular-weight keratin (clone 34βE12), CK5/6, and p63, indicating prostatic basal cell origin. In addition, a distinct population of cells reacting for muscle-specific actin and S-100 protein was identified within the glandular element and the stroma, suggesting myoepithelial differentiation.[319–321] Ultrastructural evidence of myoepithelial differentiation in SA was also demonstrated and it was concluded that myoepithelial cell participation in SA most likely results from metaplastic alteration process of the prostatic basal cells.[78] These findings have been confirmed by others.[3,319,320]

Small acinar adenocarcinoma of the prostate is the main differential diagnosis. Unlike adenocarcinoma of the prostate, SA is characterized by a proliferation of both glandular and stromal elements. The small, closely packed acini with an infiltrative pattern in SA may be confused with neoplastic glands, and the proliferating stroma may be misinterpreted as a desmoplastic reaction. SA is a lobular proliferation at low power in which the acini typically show variation in size and shape, and at least some of the glands have a clearly visible double cell layer. The presence of basal cells may be highlighted by staining for high-molecular-weight cytokeratin (clone 34βE12), CK5/6, or p63 and this is a critical feature for excluding a diagnosis of adenocarcinoma.[99,292,295] The basal cell staining for high-molecular-weight cytokeratin (clone 34βE12), CK5/6, or p63, however, may be focal. In contrast to SA, small acinar adenocarcinoma more often tends to infiltrate into the surrounding prostatic stroma.[73,74] The nucleoli in carcinoma are usually prominent. The glands and compressed tubules of SA may be surrounded by a thick hyaline basement membrane-like material, which is not seen in carcinoma. The stroma in SA is hypercellular and composed of plump spindle cells, whereas infiltrating adenocarcinoma often does not elicit a stromal response or induces a hyalinized, hypocellular desmoplastic response. Demonstration of intraluminal acid mucin and crystalloids is not helpful in differential diagnosis between SA and carcinoma since both SA and carcinoma have these characteristics.[75,78–81]

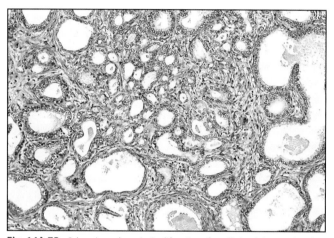

Fig. 14A.75 • Sclerosing adenosis. Proliferation of small glands is associated with a cellular stroma.

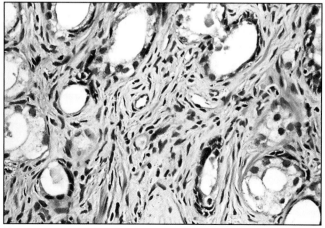

Fig. 14A.76 • Sclerosing adenosis. At least some small glands have basal cells. Note the prominent cellular stroma.

Miscellaneous lesions that mimic carcinoma

Hyperplasia of mesonephric remnants

Hyperplasia of mesonephric remnants is a rare, yet important, small glandular proliferation within the prostate gland, the severity of the diagnostic pitfall being exemplified by a case misdiagnosed as cancer which resulted in a radical prostatectomy that did not show evidence of cancer.[322] Recently Bostwick et al.[323] indicated that mesonephric remnants are present in <1% of transurethral resections and are rarely identified in needle biopsies. The acini are lobular or infiltrative and may be architecturally mistaken for adenocarcinoma. This cytologically innocuous finding is probably underreported and interpreted as benign prostatic acini, but this is of no apparent clinical consequence.[323] The lesion is asymptomatic, discovered incidentally, and hence has no distinctive gross attributes. Microscopically, it is characterized by a lobular proliferation of small tubular structures lined by a single layer of epithelium or by infiltrating glands between

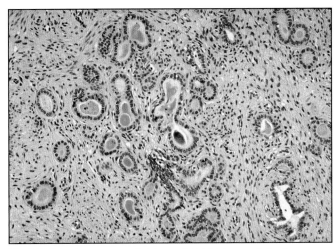

Fig. 14A.77 • Classic mesonephric hyperplasia. This is a small gland proliferation with small and larger glands lined by hyperchromatic nuclei. Pink secretions are present and the stroma is reactive.

muscle bundles and prostatic acini without a stromal desmoplastic response.[323] There is variation in the size of the tubules, with occasional cyst formation, intratubular papillary proliferation, and eosinophilic secretions within dilated glands (Fig. 14A.77).[322–325] The cells are cuboidal with minimal cytoplasm and hence appear "atrophic." The non-prostatic lineage of the lesional cells can be confirmed by negativity for PSA and PrAP; the lesional cells themselves are positive for high-molecular-weight cytokeratin clone 34βE12.[323] The nuclei are bland without prominent nucleoli. Confusion with cancer is compounded by the potential of mesonephric remnants to be associated with ganglia and nerves, simulating perineural invasion.[322,324]

A previously unrecognized mesonephric hyperplastic lesion was described by Ayala et al.[326] The lesion consists of tubular structures that are slightly larger than normal ducts, lined by a hyperplastic and hyperchromatic proliferation of elongated-fusiform epithelial cells; these are negative for PSA, PrAP, p63, or high-molecular weight cytokeratin. The nuclei of this lesion are elongated or fusiform and so intensely hyperchromatic that there is no visible intranuclear detail (Fig. 14A.78). This lesion resembles epididymis and, consequently, in core biopsies of the prostate may be confused with high-grade PIN.

Verumontanum mucosal gland hyperplasia

VMGH was noted as a small gland proliferation in the verumontanum found in 14–29% of radical prostatectomies.[327,328] Subsequently it has been documented to occur in needle biopsies where it has the potential to be misdiagnosed as carcinoma.[329] VMGH has an expansile circumscribed growth pattern with glands of small caliber arranged in a back-to-back fashion. Distinction from cancer is usually not a problem when one pays attention to the cytologic features at higher power. The glands readily show a basal cell layer and contain corpora amylacea or orange-brown secretions, and the nuclei lack nucleomegaly or prominent nucleoli (Fig. 14A.79). Besides cancer, the differential diagnosis includes NA, hyperplasia of mesonephric remnants, and AAH. The glands are positive for PSA and PrAP and the basal cells stain for high-molecular-weight cytokeratin (clone 34βE12), cytokeratin 5/6, and P63. The distinction of VMGH from normal verumontanum glands is relatively arbitrary and the chief reason for awareness of this process is its potential to be misdiagnosed as cancer.[328] One study reported that there was a significant association between the presence of VMGH and AAH ($P < 0.001$, Fisher exact test) and concluded that AAH and VMGH occur more commonly in prostates when the other is also present.[328]

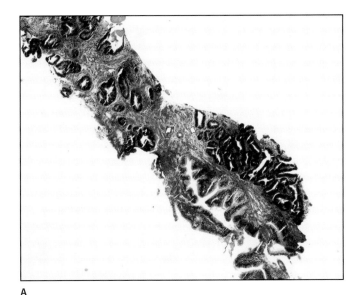

A

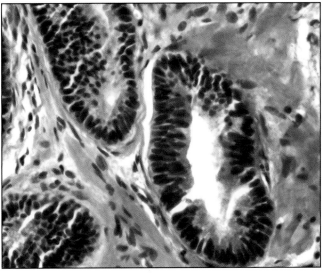

B

Fig. 14A.78 • **(A)** Mesonephric hyperplasia, epididymal type, simulating high-grade prostatic intraepithelial neoplasia (PIN). The lesion consists of tubular structures that are slightly larger than normal ducts and are lined by stratified proliferation of elongated fusiform epithelial cells. **(B)** Mesonephric hyperplasia, epididymal type, simulating high-grade PIN. On high power, the nuclei of the glands are characteristically hyperchromatic, obscuring any nuclear detail, and the cells are situated perpendicular to the basal membrane. This lesion closely resembles a cross-section of epididymis and in core biopsies of the prostate may be confused with high-grade PIN.

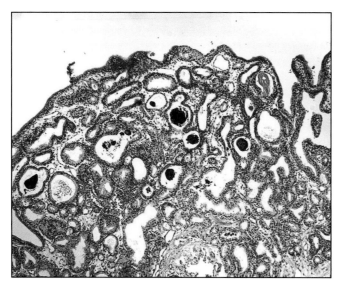

Fig. 14A.79 • Verumontanum mucosal gland hyperplasia. This is a proliferation of small to medium-size glands with inconspicuous basal cells. There is also a golden-brown type of intraluminal secretion.

Nephrogenic adenoma

NA is a benign lesion of the urothelial-lined organs from the renal pelvis to the urethra (see also Ch. 12); it was first described in 1949 by Davis,[330] who designated it as a hamartoma of the urinary bladder, but Friedman & Kuhlenbeck,[331] shortly thereafter, assigned its present name on the basis of its striking resemblance to the developing renal tubules and its possible neoplastic potential. Although NA occurs primarily in the bladder, the urethra is involved in 10–15% of cases as also, less frequently, is the ureter[332] and renal pelvis.[288,333] In the urethra, NA occurs in the bulbous or prostatic portion and may also occur in a urethral diverticulum.[332–334] Although there is a strong male predominance among adults, there is a 3:1 female predominance of NA among children.[288,333,335,336] The patients range in age from 4 to 83 years (mean 41 years). The most common associated conditions include previous surgery or trauma, infection, calculi, or a history of renal transplant.[288,333] The lesion is usually solitary, but can be multifocal;[333] it is usually small (0.5–2.0 cm), but much larger lesions involving even the entire bladder surface have been reported.[337] The lesion is discovered at the time of cystoscopy or is an incidental microscopic finding in about 20% of patients. The signs and symptoms in the remainder of the patients are non-specific, and include hematuria, dysuria, frequency, urgency, and suprapubic or flank pain.[333]

NA may be observed in TURP specimens as urethral mucosa and suburethral tissue may be sampled during the TURP procedure. Rarely it may be seen in prostatic needle biopsy specimens. When NA is present in the prostatic urethra and involves suburethral tissue and seemingly infiltrates the prostatic parenchyma proper, it may potentially be confused with a prostatic adenocarcinoma since the common histologic manifestation of NA is a proliferation of closely packed small glands.[288,338,339]

Grossly, two-thirds of NA are papillary; the rest are polypoid or sessile.[288] Microscopically, NA is characterized by closely packed small tubular structures (endophytic component)

associated with an edematous lamina propria, and seemingly infiltration between prostatic ducts, compounding the diagnostic overlap with cancer. The tubules show considerable variation in size and shape, sometimes being cystically dilated. They are usually small and round to oval but may be convoluted, resembling collecting ducts or convoluted tubules of the kidney (Fig. 14A.80). Papillary projections may be seen, either on the surface (exophytic component) or within the dilated tubules.[340] The tubules, cysts, and papillae are lined predominantly by cuboidal or columnar cells. The cytoplasm is usually scant but occasionally a moderate to large amount of eosinophilic or clear cytoplasm may be seen. The nuclei are round and small or pyknotic and usually lack nucleoli, although the latter may sometimes be conspicuous. In some areas the nuclei may have a "hobnail" appearance (Fig. 14A.81). In rare cases, a diffuse proliferation of solid tubules or small tubules lined by single cells, the nuclei of which are compressed by intracytoplasmic lumina, resembling signet-ring adenocarcinoma, has been described.[288,333] Glycogen and mucin can be found in the cytoplasm in some cases. Despite the fact that NA may be seen between prostatic ducts, it must be remembered that NA is not an invasive lesion. In the prostatic urethra there are submucosal glands, but also prostatic ducts emptying their

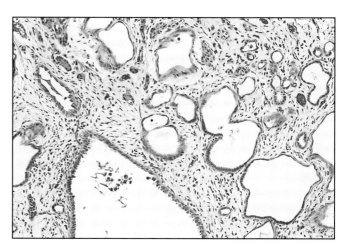

Fig. 14A.80 • Nephrogenic adenoma. The proliferating, small, dilated glands resemble kidney tubules.

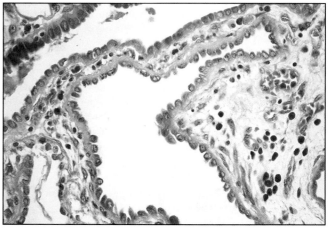

Fig. 14A.81 • Nephrogenic adenoma. The tubules are lined predominantly by cuboidal cells with eosinophilic cytoplasm. Some have a "hobnail" appearance.

products into the urethral lumen. Thus, NA may be in contact with prostatic ducts, giving a false impression of prostatic invasion.

Ultrastructural and lectin-binding studies reveal some similarities between embryonic renal tubules and NA;[341] however, an embryonic origin remains unproven. Most investigators currently favor a metaplastic origin based on the wide age range, site distribution, close association with trauma or inflammation, and evidence of transition from urothelium to NA.[333,338,342] Some investigators have suggested that NA is a precursor or a benign counterpart of clear cell carcinoma of the genitourinary tract. Although there have been a few reported cases of NA coexisting with a clear cell adenocarcinoma, a direct relationship between the two has not been proven. NA can recur following conservative therapy, but in no case has it been associated with unequivocal malignant change. The current consensus is that NA is not a premalignant lesion.[288,333,342–344]

The main differential diagnoses of NA when it involves the prostatic urethra include prostatic adenocarcinoma and clear cell adenocarcinoma of the urethra.[288,333,338,339,344] The differentiation of NA from clear cell adenocarcinoma is generally not difficult, as the latter has a more diffuse growth pattern and more appreciable cytologic atypia; occurrence of clear cell carcinoma in the male urethra is also very rare, with only 3 reported cases (Fig. 14A.82).[68,345] The small, closely packed tubules of NA can closely mimic prostate cancer when they show the presence of tubules, cords, and signet-ring-like tubules, prominent nucleoli, underlying fibromuscular involvement, blue-tinged mucinous secretion, focal PSA and PrAP positivity and negative staining (in some cases) for 34βE12.[346,347] However, features useful in the diagnosis of NA include: (1) the usual lack of nuclear atypia or nucleoli; (2) variation in tubular size; (3) the typically edematous or inflammatory stroma; (4) distinctive nephrogenic patterns, such as papillary and "vascular;" (5) adjacent urothelium; (6) thyroidization; (7) peritubular sheaths; (8) negativity for PrAP and PSA; and (9) positivity for cytokeratin 7 and, in some cases, 34βE12 in difficult cases.[288,338,339,346,347] Intracytoplasmic mucin positivity suggests NA, since the mucin in prostatic adenocarcinoma tends to be intraluminal.[75]

AMACR (P504S), a recently identified prostate cancer marker, demonstrated strong cytoplasmic positivity in NA, indicating that NA is not only a morphologic mimic but immunohistochemical mimic as well.[346,348] It encodes for AMACR, a protein involved in the beta-oxidation of branched-chain fatty acids. Awareness of NA as a significant pitfall in the differential diagnosis of prostatic adenocarcinoma and careful examination of H&E-stained sections remains the key to the correct diagnosis, which can be supported by a negative PSA stain.[348]

Prostatic-type urethral polyp

Polypoid lesions containing prostatic tissue are occasionally found in the prostatic urethra, especially in the region of the verumontanum, and rarely in the membranous urethra, ureteric orifices, and trigonal area of the bladder (see also Ch. 12).[207–212,349] Patients with these lesions are usually young, in the third or fourth decade of life, and present with hematospermia or hematuria closely associated with ejaculation.[207–212,349] These lesions are considered to be the most common cause of hematuria in young men. They have been termed adenomatous polyp of prostatic urethra,[210] prostatic urethral polyp,[211] papillary adenoma of prostatic urethra,[212,350] and prostatic caruncle.[349] The pathogenesis is still uncertain, although ectopia secondary to developmental anomalies,[209,212,349,351–354] prolapse of prostatic ducts,[349] hyperplastic processes,[211,355] mucosal redundancy,[355] metaplasia,[208] and neoplasia[356] have been suggested.

These lesions are composed of papillary and glandular histologic patterns (Fig. 14A.83). They are covered by columnar prostatic epithelium or by a mixture of prostatic and transitional epithelium. Varying numbers of glandular structures are seen within the stroma of the polyps. They are morphologically identical to prostatic glands and typically are lined by two cell layers, composed of tall columnar epithelial cells with basally located nuclei and a surrounding layer of flattened basal cells. Occasionally, corpora amylacea are seen within the lumina. No cellular pleomorphism, necrosis, increased mitoses, or prominent nucleoli are seen (Fig. 14A.84). Immunohistochemical staining for PSA and PrAP is strongly positive,

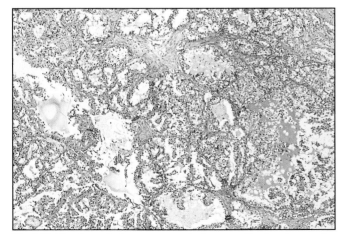

Fig. 14A.82 • Clear cell adenocarcinoma. This low-magnification photograph shows a cellular tumor with tubular and papillary configuration.

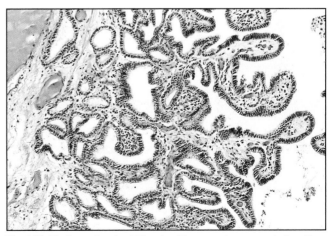

Fig. 14A.83 • Prostatic polyp. This polypoid structure is composed of papillary and glandular structures.

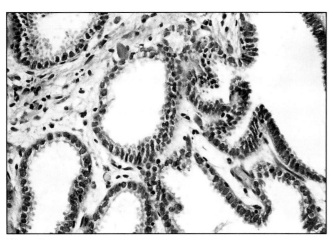

Fig. 14A.84 • Prostatic polyp. The lining cells are uniform without nuclear pleomorphism, increased mitoses, or prominent nucleoli.

confirming the prostatic origin of these lesions.[207–212,349,351–356] All of these lesions behave in a benign fashion and they are not considered preneoplastic lesions. The main differential diagnosis includes ductal endometrioid carcinoma of the prostate. In contrast to the prostatic polyps, ductal endometrioid carcinoma usually exhibits nuclear anaplasia, prominent nucleoli, mitoses, and tumor necrosis.[192]

Normal histoanatomic structures and non-neoplastic lesions that may simulate adenocarcinoma of the prostate

Ejaculatory ducts and seminal vesicle tissue

Tissue fragments derived from seminal vesicles and ejaculatory ducts are occasionally observed during examination of TURP or prostatic needle biopsy specimens, with a reported frequency of between 3% and 23% in two studies.[357,358] The histologic features of the seminal vesicle and ejaculatory duct are quite similar and sometimes it is difficult to tell them apart in needle biopsy or TURP specimens. Both have tubuloalveolar glands as well as closely packed small acini, which are lined by pseudostratified, tall columnar secretory cells and a layer of small basal cells. [53,54,357,358] When these structures are found in biopsies, usually from the central zone, they are more often ejaculatory ducts rather than seminal vesicles. Unless the seminal vesicle is specifically targeted under ultrasound it is usually too deeply seated to be readily sampled by either random needle biopsy or TURP procedures. Epithelium of ejaculatory duct and seminal vesicle characteristically contains coarsely granular, yellow-brown lipofuscin pigment.[53] The epithelial cells in the seminal vesicle and ejaculatory duct often have large atypical nuclei; these are hyperchromatic, but nuclear detail is often not discernible because of a smudged chromatin pattern (Fig. 14A.85). Neither nucleoli nor mitoses are readily apparent.[53,55,288] Kuo & Gomez[53] demonstrated monstrous epithelial cells in 24 of 32 (75%) seminal vesicles they examined. Since these structures often show small glandular structures arranged in a back-to-back pattern, they may be confused with a small acinar carcinoma of the prostate.[53,55,73,282,288] The three cardinal features for the recognition of seminal vesicle and ejaculatory duct epithelium are marked nuclear irregularity including monstrous cells, intranuclear inclusions, and golden-brown, coarse, refractile pigment in the cytoplasm.[53,54,73,282,288] It must be remembered, however, that prostatic adenocarcinoma also rarely contains intracytoplasmic lipofuscin pigment. The pigment tends to be more fine and less refractile than seminal vesicle pigment.[56] The presence of regular, monotonous nuclei with prominent nucleoli and the absence of a basal cell layer support a diagnosis of carcinoma. Seminal vesicle secretions are fairly common and, when fluid-like, are composed of acid mucopolysaccharides. Inspissation of secretions appears to be associated with loss of acidity, presumably resulting in dense plate-like secretions and crystallization. Awareness of both the crystalloid morphology in seminal vesicle tissue and the distinguishing features from prostatic crystalloids may be important when interpreting prostate needle biopsies in which seminal vesicle epithelium may be confused with prostate carcinoma because of a small acinar morphology with accompanying cytologic atypia and crystalloid morphology.[359]

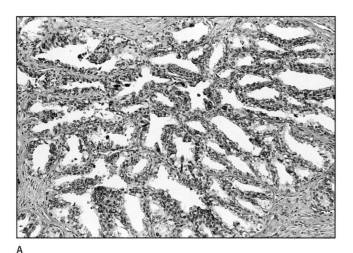
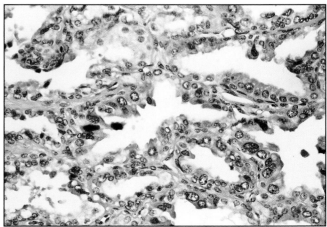

A B

Fig. 14A.85 • (A) A seminal vesicle with a small acinar configuration. The main characteristics of seminal vesicles include scattered pleomorphic nuclei (monster cells) and golden-brown lipofuscin pigment in the cytoplasm. **(B)** Higher magnification reveals monster cells and golden-brown lipofuscin pigment.

Seminal vesicle/ejaculatory duct epithelium is negative for PSA and PrAP, but is positive for MUC6, which is a helpful staining to differentiate seminal vesicle/ejaculatory duct epithelium from prostatic adenocarcinoma (MUC6-negative).[360]

Cowper's glands and paraganglionic tissue

Tissue from bulbourethral Cowper's glands may occasionally be included in TURP or needle biopsy specimens.[361,362] Cowper's glands are paired structures located in the urogenital diaphragm near the apex of the prostate, and composed of lobules of mucinous acini arranged in a back-to-back arrangement (Fig. 14A.86). They are associated with an excretory duct and are frequently surrounded by skeletal muscle. Cowper's gland may be confused with a well-differentiated adenocarcinoma of the prostate; however, the superficial resemblance of Cowper's gland to minor salivary glands, the bland nuclear features, lack of prominent nucleoli, associated skeletal muscle, abundant intracytoplasmic mucin, and negative immunoreactivity for PSA and PrAP point to the appropriate diagnosis.[91,73,282,361–363]

Mucous gland metaplasia of the prostate (Fig. 14A.87) has been described and may resemble Cowper's gland. The lesion, however, is located randomly within the prostate; it may be focal within an acinus or involve groups of acini, but is usually small.[364,365]

Another normal structure that may be present in prostate specimens and which can be confused with carcinoma is paraganglionic tissue.[91,282,366,367] Typically, paraganglionic tissue is present in periprostatic fat adjacent to lateral neurovascular bundles and, rarely, in lateral prostatic stroma. It consists of clusters of clear cells with a sinusoidal vascular pattern, and "Zellballen" appearance, bland oval nuclear features, and clear cytoplasm, which is often abundant, and a close association with nerve fibers that allow the correct recognition of this structure (Fig. 14A.88). Occasionally, larger cells with larger nuclei were present. If there is any doubt regarding its true nature, negative immunostaining for prostatic (PSA and PrAP) and epithelial (keratin and epithelial membrane antigen) markers and positive staining for neuroendocrine markers such as neuron-specific enolase (NSE), chromogranin and

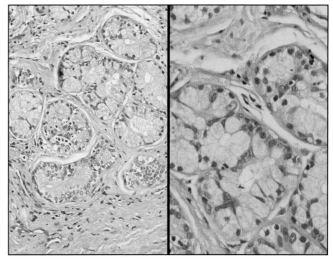

A

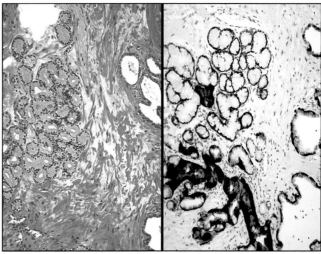

B

Fig. 14A.87 • (A) Mucinous metaplasia. The right and left illustrations depict round glands characterized by the presence of mucus-secreting cells with goblet-like vacuoles, superficially resembling Cowper's glands. (B) Mucinous metaplasia. In the left illustration there are small glands resembling Gleason pattern 1 or 2 carcinoma, but on the right side the basal cell layer is highlighted by the high-molecular-weight cytokeratin.

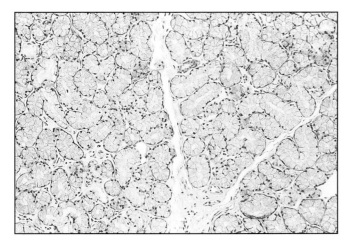

Fig. 14A.86 • Cowper's gland. Lobules of mucinous acini are arranged back to back. The bland nuclear morphology without prominent nucleoli and abundant mucinous cytoplasm are key features in the recognition of Cowper's glands.

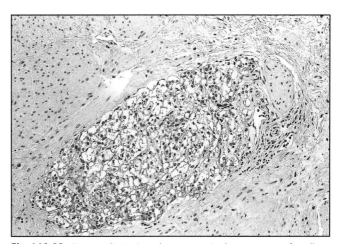

Fig. 14A.88 • Paraganglionic tissue has an organized arrangement of small cells with clear cytoplasm in close proximity to small nerves and vessels.

synaptophysin, should resolve the diagnostic problem.[363] Several cases of paraganglioma involving prostate have been reported.[368]

Atrophy

Prostatic atrophy is a relatively common lesion in an aged man but also has been noted in adults as young as 20 years.[3,73,369–372] Atrophy may coexist with hyperplasia, even within the same microscopic fields.[373] It is usually located in the peripheral zone but may be present in the transition and central zones.[91,295] In the vast majority of cases, the cause of atrophy is unknown but it has been postulated to be a physiological and age-related phenomenon.[370] Inflammation,[373] nutritional deficiency, local ischemia,[374] and compression are thought to play important roles in the pathogenesis of atrophy.[11,372,375] Most patients with atrophy are asymptomatic, and atrophy is found incidentally during the examination of needle biopsies or TURP specimens performed for other reasons.

On microscopic examination, atrophy may be diffuse, or it can be focal. On the basis of histologic appearance it can be classified as simple lobular, cystic, or sclerotic atrophy.[373] Simple lobular atrophy is characterized by a collection of closely packed small acinar glands, usually situated around a central duct, with preservation of normal lobular architecture (Fig. 14A.89). In cystic atrophy, the peripheral acini become cystic (Fig. 14A.90). In sclerotic atrophy, the lobular architecture may or may not be preserved. Atrophic acini are variably separated and compressed by sclerotic stromal elements, resulting in elongated and distorted glands separated by proliferating periacinar fibrocollagenous tissue (Fig. 14A.91). This type of atrophy is usually seen at a later age than simple lobular atrophy.[73,91,282,288,295] Elastosis of the prostatic stroma is frequently associated with atrophy.[376]

Gardner & Culberson[369] described another pattern of atrophy giving the overall appearance of hypoplasia. They believed that it was not a true atrophy but was actually the post-pubertal persistence of glands that retained the unstimulated appearance of neonatal or prepubertal prostate. Regardless of the pattern of atrophy, atrophic glands are lined by hyper-

chromatic, low cuboidal to flattened cells with scanty amounts of cytoplasm and bland nuclei (Fig. 14A.92). Of particular note is the absence of prominent nucleoli in most cases; when nucleoli are present, they are invariably small and inconspicuous. Double-cell layering of basal and secretory cells is

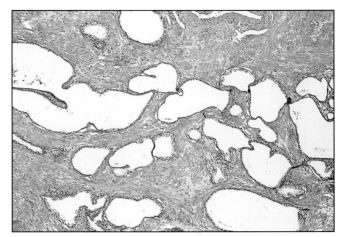

Fig. 14A.90 • Cystic atrophy. Dilated acini are lined by flattened atrophic cells.

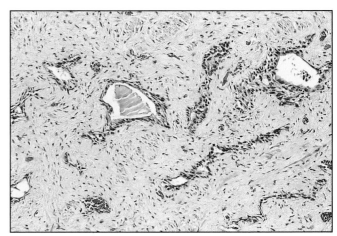

Fig. 14A.91 • Sclerotic atrophy. Irregularly distorted slit-like acini are lined by atrophic epithelial cells lying in broad bands of sclerotic stroma.

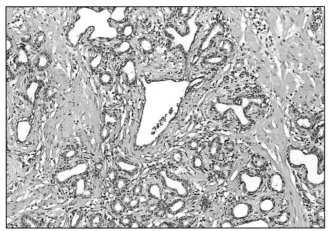

Fig. 14A.89 • Simple lobular atrophy. Small glandular proliferation around a central dilated duct that retains its lobular architecture is the characteristic feature.

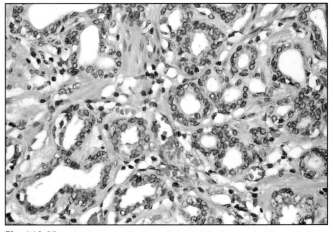

Fig. 14A.92 • A higher magnification of simple lobular atrophy. The atrophic glands are lined by uniform cells with hyperchromatic nuclei. Nucleoli are usually absent or inconspicuous.

generally present, but, since the secretory cells lack abundant cytoplasm, they appear similar to basal cells, making it difficult to recognize the two cell types.[73,91,282,288,295,371–373] If any doubt exists, high-molecular-weight keratin (clone 34βE12), cytokeratin 5/6, or p63 staining should be performed to confirm the presence of basal cells and thus rule out carcinoma (Fig. 14A.93).[297,377,378] Atrophy is sometimes accompanied by inflammation and periglandular fibrosis, and often there are scattered inflammatory cells in the adjacent stroma.[295,373] When atrophy is seen in TURP or prostatectomy specimens, there is little difficulty in making the diagnosis; however, in needle biopsy specimens it may be difficult to differentiate it from adenocarcinoma. Sclerotic atrophy may cause the most diagnostic difficulty, especially if the stromal reaction is interpreted as tumor-induced desmoplasia.[91,288] The low-power architecture, double-cell layer, and bland cytology point in the direction of a benign process. A particularly challenging situation is the separation of atrophy from carcinoma with "atrophic" features. Appreciation of an infiltrative pattern and judicious use of immunohistochemistry (high-molecular-weight cytokeratin, clone 34βE12, cytokeratin 5/6, p63) are helpful.[93–95,379] Atrophic acini may, on occasion, be associated with secondary proliferative changes of the epithelium; this has been referred to by some researchers as PAH.[371,372,380–382]

Postatrophic hyperplasia

PAH may occur in a background of either simple lobular or sclerotic atrophy: lobular hyperplasia develops from simple lobular atrophy and postsclerotic hyperplasia from sclerotic atrophy. When lobular atrophy undergoes a secondary proliferative change, the entire lobule is usually involved, and tightly packed new acini bud off from the small atrophic glands. When secondary hyperplasia occurs in a background of sclerotic atrophy, small acini bud off from the atrophic ducts, proliferating and penetrating into the adjacent dense sclerotic stroma.

PAH may closely mimic carcinoma in needle biopsy specimens, where it is seen in 2–3% of cases.[380] Since PAH is a combination of two processes, atrophy and hyperplasia, the glands may be small and closely packed with scant cytoplasm

as with conventional atrophy, or may show a neoacinar pattern with proliferating acini with appreciable clear cytoplasm. A clue to the diagnosis is the variation in size and shape of the glands and the cytoplasmic content.[380,381] Bland cytology without prominent nucleoli, the absence of overtly infiltrative growth or gland fusion, and the presence, at least focally, of a basal cell layer, will help avoid a misdiagnosis of carcinoma. A high-molecular-weight cytokeratin (clone 34βE12), CK5/6, or p63 immunostain will help accentuate the basal cells and confirm the benign diagnosis.[380]

Correlation of PAH and prostatic adenocarcinoma has been controversial. Anton et al.[382] insisted that there was no association between the two lesions based on a systematic topographic study. However, Franks[371] and Liavag[372] postulated that PAH that followed sclerotic atrophy was a forerunner of small acinar carcinoma, based on the observations that the two conditions can occur together in the peripheral zone and that small acinar proliferation (regeneration) was frequently observed near the atrophy[371,372] (Fig. 14A.94). In contrast, McNeal reported that carcinoma of the prostate arises in glands with active epithelium that have never undergone any atrophy.[10,12,375,383,384] Recent studies have demonstrated that the frequency of p53 mutation in PAH was similar to that of high-grade PIN[385] and that proliferative activity, defined by MIB-1 labeling, and gain of chromosome 8 were significantly higher than BPH or simple atrophy, suggesting a possible association between PAH and prostate adenocarcinoma.[385–387] Anton et al.[382], however, failed to demonstrate any association between PAH and prostate cancer. The frequency of PAH in cystoprostatectomy specimens and its relationship to incidental prostate carcinoma were not significantly different from that of radical prostatectomy specimens. PAH is a relatively common lesion, most often seen in the peripheral zone of the apical third of the gland.

Skeletal muscle within prostate gland and benign glands in perineural space

Traditionally, textbooks have stated that there is no skeletal muscle present in the prostate;[288,388–391] thus the finding of prostatic glands interspersed with skeletal muscle bundles in a

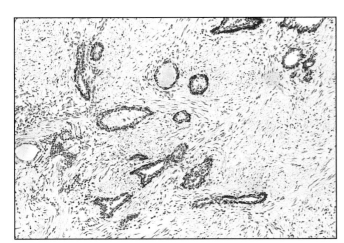

Fig. 14A.93 • Basal cell-specific keratin 34βE12 (K-903) immunostaining shows the preservation of basal cells in the atrophic glands.

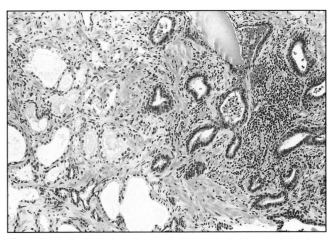

Fig. 14A.94 • Small gland proliferation (left) associated with a simple lobular atrophy (right). The small glands are lined with cells with abundant clear cytoplasm and occasional nucleoli.

biopsy or a TURP specimen may raise the possibility of an adenocarcinoma extending beyond the prostate. However, in reality, in a normal human prostate gland, the skeletal muscle from the pelvic floor is anchored to the prostate. The muscle fibers penetrate the apex anteriorly and laterally, extending upwards toward the superior aspect of the prostate or base of the prostate, but are not present in the posterior aspect at all. Skeletal muscle fibers are, thus, commonly seen from the apex, anteriorly and laterally, up towards the base of the prostate.[288,295,388] In these locations the skeletal muscle fibers not uncommonly intermix with the normal glandular tissue of the prostate. Therefore, prostate samples taken from the anterior or anterolateral areas may have scattered skeletal muscle bundles among prostatic glands. Manley[390] has reported the presence of skeletal muscle fibers in 30.2% of prostatic specimens obtained by TURP. This finding can be a diagnostic problem to one who is not familiar with this normal anatomy, but the absence of cytologic criteria for carcinoma and the presence of the basal cell layer in the glands are sufficient evidence for benignity to avoid the erroneous diagnosis of carcinoma (Fig. 14A.95). Awareness of the presence of skeletal muscle fibers is also important to stage the tumor correctly. Thus the presence of carcinoma involving striated muscle does not necessarily indicate extraprostatic extension of the tumor.[391]

As indicated earlier, several papers have reported the presence of benign prostatic glands around nerves (Fig. 14A.26), emphasizing the potential hazard of using perineural invasion as a single criterion for the diagnosis of adenocarcinoma of the prostate.[392–394] McIntire & Franzini[392] reported that benign glands were demonstrated in perineural spaces in 6 of 26 prostates. However, when benign prostatic glands are found in the perineural spaces, the glands never completely surround the nerve or invade it. In contrast, carcinomas of the prostate often encircle the entire nerve and penetrate it (Fig. 14A.26). Non-neoplastic benign glands do not really invade the perineural space, but they simply appose the nerve, giving the impression of invasion.[288] In addition, the non-neoplastic glands in perineural spaces do not meet morphologic criteria for carcinoma. The double-cell layer of the benign glands is easily recognized and the cells do not contain prominent nucleoli.

Rare benign epithelial lesions of the prostate

Cystadenoma (giant multilocular cystadenoma)

Multilocular cystadenoma of the prostate is the only *bona fide* benign epithelial neoplasm of the prostate with less than two dozen cases being reported.[395,396] It occurs most often in patients 20–80 years old (mean age of 64.5 years) with symptoms of urinary obstruction with or without a palpable abdominal mass. The size has ranged from 7.5 to 45 cm in greatest dimension. Imaging studies are useful to determine the extent and invasiveness of the lesion. In all reported cases the diagnosis was made following surgical resection but the anatomical relationship of the mass to the native prostate varied. The masses are well circumscribed and partially adherent to adjacent organs. They are large, bosselated, multilocular, and cystic (Fig. 14A.96). The cysts range from a few millimeters to about 4 cm and contain yellowish-brown or gray, semi-solid to inspissated material. Microscopically they are composed of glands and cysts lined by cuboidal to low columnar epithelial cells with basally located nuclei (Fig. 14A.97). Metaplastic squamous and transitional epithelium may be seen. Immunohistochemical staining of the epithelial cells is positive for PSA and PrAP. Complete surgical excision with preservation of normal pelvic structures is the treatment of choice.[395,396]

Stromal lesions of the prostate

Benign stromal lesions of the prostate

The most common stromal lesion of the prostate is benign stromal hyperplasia, which is easily recognized since it is usually associated with areas of glandular hyperplasia and seen in TURP specimens removed for clinical BPH. Other stromal lesions occur much more rarely in the prostate and include blue nevus, leiomyoma, and phyllodes-type tumor.

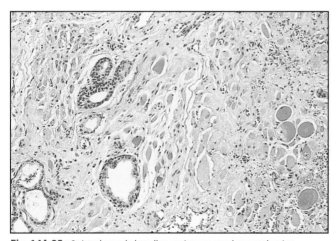

Fig. 14A.95 • Striated muscle bundles are interspersed among benign prostatic glands. This should not be misinterpreted as prostatic carcinoma invading skeletal muscle.

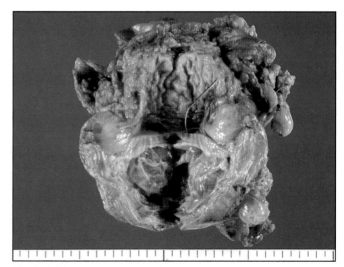

Fig. 14A.96 • Cystadenoma. In this radical cystoprostatectomy a multiloculated cystic lesion replaces the entire prostate.

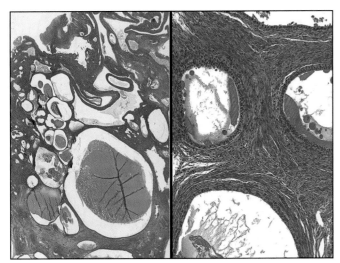

Fig. 14A.97 • Cystadenoma. The lesion is characterized by numerous varying-sized cysts and a cellular stroma. On high power, flattened or cuboidal epithelial cells line the cysts, and the stroma is very cellular.

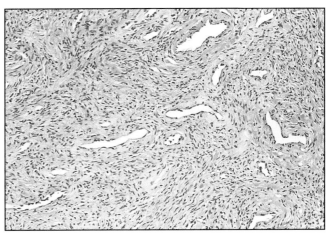

Fig. 14A.98 • A stromal nodule is characterized by vascular and spindle cell proliferation. The spindle cells are arranged in a whorled pattern around blood vessels.

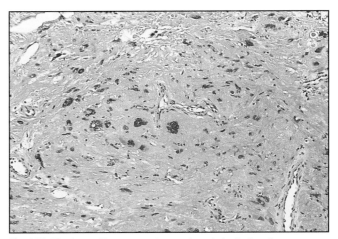

Fig. 14A.99 • Atypical leiomyoma. Scattered atypical spindle cells are present in the background of an otherwise typical leiomyoma.

Two pseudosarcomatous lesions of the prostate – post-operative spindle cell nodule and pseudosarcomatous fibromyxoid tumor (inflammatory myofibroblastic tumor) – have been increasingly recognized. These lesions mimic sarcomas because of their cellularity, cellular pleomorphism, and/or mitotic activity and they may erroneously be diagnosed as such. The great differences in clinical behavior and management mean that proper recognition of these entities is very important.

Stromal hyperplasia

Stromal hyperplasia (stromal nodule) occurs most often in the setting of BPH. It is usually microscopic in size and seldom, if ever, is confused with a malignant spindle cell lesion but may be confused with a leiomyoma.[397–401] Stromal hyperplasia is characterized by a bland spindle cell proliferation devoid of glandular elements. The lesion is well demarcated from the surrounding prostatic tissue, but is not encapsulated. The spindle cells are arranged in a fascicular or whorled pattern simulating leiomyoma. These lesions frequently contain small, thick-walled blood vessels surrounded by the spindle cellular component (Fig. 14A.98). Although myxoid change in the stroma can be seen and may be prominent,[402] nuclear atypia or mitoses are not features of usual stromal hyperplasia. The distinction between a stromal nodule and a leiomyoma is somewhat arbitrary; leiomyomas are defined as lesions greater than 1 cm in diameter which are usually encapsulated.[403–405]

Atypical stromal hyperplasia

There are several reports of rare smooth muscle proliferations characterized by the presence of large atypical cells with hyperchromatic smudged nuclei.[406] Two types of proliferation occur: in one the atypical cells infiltrate between normal glandular structures of the prostate, and in the other the proliferative change forms a single nodule. The former type is known as atypical stromal proliferation, while the second is known as atypical (bizarre or symplastic) leiomyoma.[399,407–412] These lesions, whether they form a nodule or infiltrate between the normal glands, are characterized by large "bizarre" cells haphazardly arranged in a background of a stromal leiomyomatous proliferation (Fig. 14A.99). The bizarre cells vary in size and shape, have hyperchromatic nuclei, and often exhibit multinucleated forms; mitoses are rare or non-existent and necrosis is not present.

The reported patients' ages ranged from 49 to 69 years (median 53 years). All patients presented with obstructive symptoms caused by prostatic enlargement, and treatment consisted of either a TURP or a suprapubic prostatectomy. One patient was initially diagnosed as having leiomyosarcoma and received chemotherapy.[413] Subsequent TURP and suprapubic prostatectomy were done, and the patient is alive and well without evidence of disease at 36 months. Follow-up in 6 of the 7 reported cases disclosed no evidence of disease at 14–96 months, but 1 patient died 16 months after surgery. There was no evidence of prostatic disease at autopsy. Although the clinical behavior of these lesions appears to be benign, the number of reported cases is very small, such that investigators consider these lesions as lesions of uncertain malignant potential.[399,409,411,412] In our own experience (unpublished data) no patient has developed signs of malignancy, although one patient has shown recurrence of his disease, which was successfully managed with conservative surgery (TURP).

If a symplastic lesion is found in a needle biopsy, the diagnosis should be made with caution in as much as degenerate-appearing "symplastic" cells may indicate a stromal tumor of at least low malignant potential on surgical excision.[414] The main differential diagnoses include stromal sarcomas and sarcomatoid carcinoma. Stromal sarcomas usually show high mitotic activity and tumor necrosis in addition to cellular pleomorphism.[415,416] The sarcomatoid component in sarcomatoid carcinoma is typically pleomorphic and fairly active mitotically. The most important clue is the demonstration of the associated carcinomatous component.[259]

Leiomyoma

Leiomyoma is defined as a solitary, circumscribed, encapsulated mass of smooth muscle proliferation measuring at least 1 cm in diameter.[403–405] Prostatic leiomyoma has not been accepted universally as a distinct entity: some researchers regard the majority, if not all, of the reported cases to be stromal nodules of a hyperplastic nature.[343,397] Fewer than 70 cases of solitary leiomyoma of the prostate have been reported.[405,409,413,417,418] Most cases occurred in men older than 48 years of age, but a few patients were under 40 years of age. The cases presenting in relatively young patients can be considered as true neoplastic lesions, rather than hyperplastic, but there is no histologic criterion that defines the lesion as being neoplastic.[343] The tumors have measured up to 12 cm and have a firm, whorled, white cut surface. Prostatic leiomyoma is histologically identical to leiomyoma occurring at other sites and is composed of eosinophilic spindle cells separated by variable amounts of collagen. The tumor cells are arranged in an orderly pattern of intersecting fascicles. The individual cells have blunt-ended nuclei with evenly distributed nuclear chromatin.

Since the number of reported cases of prostatic smooth muscle tumors is few, there are no reliable histologic criteria to distinguish a leiomyoma from a leiomyosarcoma of the prostate. However, infiltrative growth, cellularity, nuclear atypia, tumor necrosis, and increased mitotic activity appear to be of the utmost importance, and the diagnosis of sarcoma should be made if at least two or more of these features are present.[398,409]

Blue nevus, melanosis and prostatic epithelial pigment

Pigmented lesions in the prostate are rare and include blue nevus and melanosis.[419,420] In the prostate, the term "blue nevus" has been used when melanin is confined to the melanocytes in the stroma (Fig. 14A.100) and the term "melanosis" has been applied variably for a grossly apparent lesion and/or microscopically conspicuous melanin pigment, found both in the glandular epithelium and within histiocytes in the stroma (Fig. 14A.101).[419,421–423] There have been about 30 reported cases of prostatic blue nevus and/or melanosis since the report by Nigogosyan et al.[424] of the first case of a pigmented lesion in the prostate in 1963. About two-thirds of the pigmented lesions are blue nevi and one-third melanosis. The histogenesis of melanin-containing lesions in the prostate is unknown.[419,425–431] Most investigators believe that melanin is produced by migrating melanocytes in the stroma, which is then transferred to the glandular epithelium.[419,427,431]

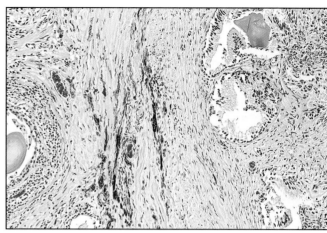

Fig. 14A.100 • Blue nevus. Pigment-containing spindle cells are present in the prostatic stroma.

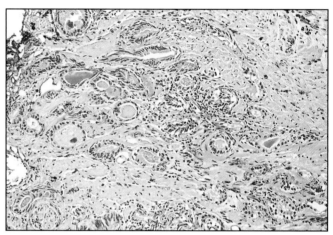

Fig. 14A.101 • Melanosis. Brown-black pigment is present in both the stromal spindle cells and the glandular epithelial cells.

The age of recorded patients with blue nevus or melanosis ranged from 20 to 80 years (mean 68 years) and the finding was usually incidental, the most common clinical presentation being urinary tract obstruction; the usual clinical diagnosis was BPH. Occasionally, malignant melanoma was suspected intraoperatively because of diffuse dark staining of the prostate. Black to brown discoloration was visible in some lesions on gross examination.[419,424,427,429,431–434] Microscopically, pigmented spindle cells with long dendritic processes are found scattered in the stroma, close to the prostatic acini. The cytoplasm of the spindle cells contains finely granular, brown or black pigment. The pigment is Masson–Fontana-positive, consistent with melanin. On ultrastructural analysis, the spindle cells contain different stages of melanosomes in white men and only mature type IV melanosomes in black men.[410] Although Das Gupta et al.[435] have stated that no satisfactory instance of primary malignant melanoma of the prostate has been reported, a possible case was described by Berry & Reese.[436]

More recently, attention has been focused on pigment that is frequently noted in prostatic epithelium upon closer scrutiny. This pigment, characterized as lipofuscin by virtue of its positivity for Masson–Fontana, Ziehl–Nielsen stain, Luxol fast blue, and oil red O, is present in 10–100% of the prostate glands. The incidence of pigment was greater if the entire gland was examined or if special stains were used for detection. This lipofuscin pigment is present in all zones of the prostate, in normal prostate, and in several pathologic conditions, including high-grade PIN and cancer.[56,422] The pigment is usually fine, golden-yellow, intranuclear, or occurring throughout the cytoplasm; when it is conspicuous it may appear to be golden-brown or blue. It is more fine and less refractile than seminal vesicle lipofuscin pigment. The pigment in the prostate is thought to represent "wear and tear" and "aging pigment" due to accumulation of endogenous byproducts within the cell. Awareness of this pigment in prostate is critical, particularly in scant biopsies. Glands with nuclear atypia and pigment should not automatically be interpreted as seminal vesicle/ejaculatory duct epithelium and the possibility of PIN or cancer should be considered.

Fibroadenoma-like lesion and phyllodes-type tumor

Prostatic lesions with morphology similar to fibroadenomas of the breast are encountered infrequently. Kafandaris & Polyzonis[437] reported a dozen prostatic lesions characterized by stromal and glandular hyperplasia without cytologic atypia, reminiscent of pericanalicular and intracanalicular fibroadenoma. Cox & Dawson[438] reported a prostatic lesion characterized by a hypercellular fibromuscular stroma without atypia, surrounding irregularly shaped hyperplastic glands which they designated as cystadenoma-leiomyofibroma (giant fibroadenoma). Lesions with increased cellularity and nuclear atypia of the stroma have been referred to as phyllodes-type atypical prostatic hyperplasias or cystosarcoma phyllodes of the prostate, because they are considered to be analogous to phyllodes tumors of the breast.[409,413,438–445] These tumors occurred in adults between the ages of 22 and 78 years (mean 52 years) and generally caused urinary retention along with prostatic enlargement, hematuria, and dysuria; most of the patients were clinically diagnosed as having BPH. These lesions may grow to be up to 58 cm in greatest dimension.[441,446,447]

The phyllodes-type tumor is histologically reminiscent of cellular fibroadenoma and cystosarcoma phyllodes of the breast. Since the phyllodes architecture may not always be present, some authors have preferred to designate these tumors as mixed epithelial-stromal tumor of the prostate.[68] There is a biphasic growth pattern with epithelial and stromal cell elements displaying a varying degree of stromal cellularity and cytologic atypia (Fig. 14A.102). The epithelial cells are cuboidal to columnar and have a well-formed basal cell layer; they are arranged in glands, slit-like spaces, or cysts, which are frequently compressed and distorted by hyperplastic stroma. Exuberant epithelial proliferation with leaf-like papillary projections may also be seen. The stromal cells are spindle-shaped, often in a myxoid matrix, and are more striking than the glandular component. Focal pure stromal hyperplasia devoid of glands is occasionally observed. The atypical stromal cells are present predominantly around the glands. Heterologous rhabdomyoblastic differentiation has been noted occasionally.[448]

Bostwick et al.[449] studied a large series of phyllodes tumors to define the relationship between histologic features and clinical outcome. They classified 23 such tumors as low-grade (14), intermediate grade (7), and high-grade phyllodes tumors

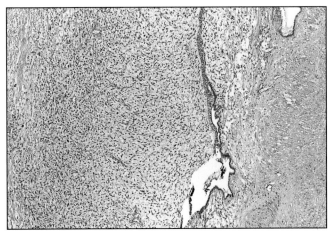

Fig. 14A.102 • Phyllodes tumor. A biphasic pattern with glandular and stromal proliferation characterizes this lesion.

(2) according to the cellularity (scale of 1–3), cytologic atypia (scale of 1–3), the number of mitotic figures per 10 high-power fields, the stroma-to-epithelium ratio (low or high) and necrosis (present or absent). Recurrence was seen in 7 of 14 low-grade tumors (50%) and in 1 patient low-grade sarcoma emerged with subsequent distant metastases 14 years after initial diagnosis following 5 recurrences. Recurrence was seen in 6 of 7 intermediate-grade tumors and low-grade sarcoma emerged with subsequent abdominal wall metastases in 1 patient 11 years after initial diagnosis following 3 recurrences.

In addition to Bostwick et al.'s cases of malignant phyllodes tumors there have been reports of phyllodes tumors with histologic evidence of malignancy; these were characterized by stromal overgrowth, nuclear pleomorphism, frequent mitotic figures[446,448,450–458] and, rarely, rhabdomyoblastic[448,454] or leiomyosarcomatous differentiation.[459] These tumors exhibited aggressive clinical behavior because they grew rapidly, recurred after initial therapy, invaded into the adjacent organs, or metastasized to the distant organs, such as pelvic lymph nodes, lung, and liver, [446,450,451,455] and at least 2 patients died of disease.[450,451]

The pathogenesis of this lesion is uncertain. Attah et al.[407,441] suggested a relation to estrogen based upon the location of the tumor (the verumontanum); however, the relationship between hormonal imbalance and development of prostatic phyllodes tumor has not been examined carefully.

Phyllodes-type tumor is distinguished from malignant phyllodes tumor and prostatic sarcomas by the virtual absence of mitotic figures in stromal cells, lack of stromal overgrowth, and tumor necrosis.[442] Sarcomatoid carcinoma of the prostate should also be considered in the differential diagnosis because of its biphasic nature. Although the spindle stromal component of sarcomatoid carcinoma may mimic phyllodes tumor, the glandular component in sarcomatoid carcinoma is clearly malignant.[259]

All reported cases of phyllodes-type tumors have been treated surgically;[438–445] most investigators advocate surgical treatment similar to that for nodular hyperplasia. Chemotherapy and radiation therapy have been tried and partial remission could be obtained.[454,455]

The qualifier "tumor of uncertain malignant potential" may be used for lesions in which histologic malignancy is not clearly evident.[414]

Postoperative spindle cell nodule

Postoperative spindle cell nodule is a reactive fibroproliferative process histologically resembling sarcoma. In 1984, Proppe et al.[460] first described 8 patients with postoperative spindle cell lesions in the genitourinary tract. These authors stated that most of these lesions had initially been interpreted as sarcomas or the diagnosis of sarcoma had been strongly considered in the differential diagnosis, but follow-up indicated a benign course. The lesions occurred in the urinary bladder, prostate gland, and prostatic urethra 5 weeks to 3 months after a cystoscopic procedure for another disease, such as BPH, prostatic adenocarcinoma, or TCC.[460–462]

The lesion is rare, considering the high number of lower urinary tract procedures performed each year. Patient ages have ranged from 29 to 79 years (median 60 years). Most were asymptomatic, but hematuria and urinary obstruction could be presenting symptoms. A postoperative spindle cell nodule may recur locally, necessitating re-excision, but there is no reported case of distant metastasis.

The postoperative spindle cell nodule is usually a small lesion ranging from 5 to 9 mm in greatest dimension, but it can be large (up to 4 cm in diameter).[460,462] It is composed of intersecting fascicles of plump spindle cells, interspersed blood vessels, and a slight to moderate number of inflammatory cells. The nuclei of the spindle cells are uniform without atypia or pleomorphism. Mitotic figures range from 1 to 25 per 10 high-power fields in the reported cases (Fig. 14A.103). Abnormal mitoses are not found. Nucleoli may be seen but they are small or inconspicuous. The background may be edematous and focally hyalinized, depending upon the interval between surgical manipulation and the discovery of the lesion. In general, the margins of the lesion are ill defined and frequently show infiltrative growth, replacing collagenous stroma and destroying surrounding smooth muscle.[460–462]

Immunostaining has demonstrated positivity for vimentin, smooth muscle actin, and desmin.[461,462] Interestingly, cytokeratin may also be positive in these lesions.[461] On ultrastructural analysis, these spindle cells show fibroblastic/myofibroblastic differentiation.[460–463] Many benign and malignant neoplasms may simulate a postoperative spindle cell nodule histologically.

The most important differential diagnosis is with sarcoma of the prostate.[460–462] Mitotic count is not useful in differentiating leiomyosarcoma from postoperative spindle cell nodule, since the latter may have up to 25 mitoses per 10 high-power fields.[460–462] Furthermore, leiomyosarcoma may not show significant cytologic atypia. The key feature in recognizing a postoperative spindle cell nodule is the clinical history of surgery or instrumentation within the previous few months.[460,462]

Other benign spindle cell lesions that may be confused with a postoperative spindle cell nodule include pseudosarcomatous fibromyxoid tumor[410,464–466] and stromal nodule.[407,409] Unlike postoperative spindle cell nodules, these lesions arise *de novo* without a history of previous urologic manipulation. They are benign and therefore should not result in therapeutic mismanagement.

The differential diagnosis also includes malignant spindle cell tumors other than leiomyosarcoma: stromal sarcomas, rhabdomyosarcoma, neurofibrosarcoma, and fibrosarcoma.[414,461] So-called malignant fibrous histiocytoma has also been

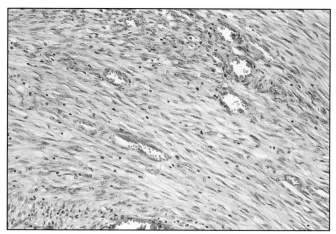

Fig. 14A.103 • Postoperative spindle cell nodule (PSCN). Mitoses are frequently seen, but proliferating cells of PSCN are relatively uniform, and their nuclei lack the features of malignancy.

described in the prostate.[467] These sarcomas are sufficiently cytologically pleomorphic that differentiation from postoperative spindle cell nodule is usually not a problem. Another differential diagnosis is sarcomatoid carcinoma.[259,264,468] When this tumor is made up of the sarcomatoid component only, such as in a limited sampling of a needle biopsy or TURP, the differential diagnosis with postoperative spindle cell nodule may be considered. The spindle cell component of sarcomatoid carcinoma, however, is typically pleomorphic, contains atypical mitoses, and may stain positively with cytokeratin in some cases and rarely with PSA and PrAP.[259,264,468] Close cooperation between the clinician and the pathologist is essential to diagnose this lesion appropriately and to avoid unnecessarily radical treatment. The clinician should raise the possibility of a postoperative spindle cell nodule when sarcoma is diagnosed in a patient who has undergone a recent operation for another disease.

Pseudosarcomatous fibromyxoid tumor

A pseudosarcomatous spindle cell proliferation similar to postoperative spindle cell nodule may occur without a prior history of surgical manipulation in the genitourinary tract. This lesion has been variously designated as inflammatory pseudotumor, pseudosarcoma, and inflammatory myofibroblastic tumor.[410,464–466,469,470] It is rare and poses considerable difficulty in diagnosis. It may occur anywhere along the urinary tract, especially in the urinary bladder (see Ch. 12) and prostate gland. Since it was first described by Roth in 1980[470] in the urinary bladder, approximately 50 cases in the bladder and prostate have been reported in the literature;[410,465,466,469–476] the prostate has been the site of involvement in only 6 of the reported cases.[410,465,466,476]

The exact histogenesis of pseudosarcomatous fibromyxoid tumor is not clear, but the histologic features, including the presence of granulation tissue-type vasculature and a prominent inflammatory cell component, along with a benign clinical course observed in the reported cases, strongly suggest a reactive/pseudoneoplastic process. It is histologically similar to nodular fasciitis,[477] and Nochomovitz & Orenstein[469] indeed reported that this lesion represented a visceral form of nodular fasciitis.

Histologic examination reveals a myxoid lesion characterized by an atypical fibroblastic/myofibroblastic proliferation associated with a prominent inflammatory component and granulation tissue-type vasculature (Fig. 14A.104). It has an ill-defined infiltrative pattern and may extend into the surrounding structures. The spindle cells may appear bizarre, including strap- or tadpole-shaped cells with eosinophilic cytoplasm and prominent nucleoli (Fig. 14A.105). Mitotic activity may be present but is not prominent, and abnormal mitoses are not a feature of this process.[410,464–466,469–476] The most important differential diagnoses are various myxoid lesions (Table 14A.5). Other malignant neoplasms such as sarcomatoid carcinoma, malignant peripheral nerve sheath tumor, fibrosarcoma, inflammatory fibrosarcoma,[478] and so-called malignant fibrous histiocytoma[467] should also be considered in the differential diagnosis. However, these lesions usually have sufficient cytologic atypia and mitotic activity, including atypical forms, to prevent their confusion with benign lesions.

Although pseudosarcomatous fibromyxoid tumors are apparently rare, their correct diagnosis is of paramount importance in avoiding unnecessary radical treatment. As they have only recently been recognized and the few reports of this entity have limited follow-up, there is no universal agreement on treatment. No patient has developed metastases or died of the disease.[410,464–466,469–476]

Given this experience, our general recommendation is conservative management with close follow-up. When pathologists find this type of lesion in the genitourinary tract, clinico-pathologic correlation is mandatory.

Other benign stromal lesions

A few cases of pheochromocytoma,[479,480] several cases of hemangiopericytoma,[481] solitary fibrous tumor,[482] para-ganglioma,[368] and approximately 30 cases of malakoplakia have been reported in the prostate.[483] Some of the cases of hemangiopericytomas, in our opinion, may represent stromal sarcomas and others may be solitary fibrous tumors of the prostate.[484] Their morphologic features are similar to those arising in their more usual sites. Rare cases of prostatic xanthoma which may mimic clear cell adenocarcinoma have been described.[485]

Non-specific granulomatous prostatitis, usually associated with BPH, can clinically and, rarely, pathologically mimic prostatic carcinoma. Specific granulomatous inflammation may result from infectious agents (histoplasmosis, cryptococcosis, tuberculosis), following TURP (Fig. 14A.106) or bacillus Calmette-Guérin (BCG) treatment for superficial bladder cancer (Fig. 14A.107).[486–488] Granuloma formation with destruction of ducts and acini and a chronic inflammatory reaction is the typical finding in granulomatous prostatitis; however, a lesion with a predominance of histiocytes and a paucity of other inflammatory elements can be confused histologically with a solid, high-grade prostatic carcinoma.[489–491] Careful histologic evaluation with the aid of immuno-histochemical staining (negative staining with keratin, PSA, and PrAP, and positive reaction with lysozyme or KP-1) may help to establish the correct diagnosis.

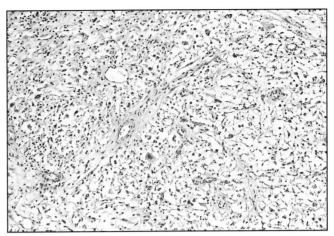

Fig. 14A.104 • Pseudosarcomatous fibromyxoid tumor. The myxoid stroma contains spindle cells, small, slit-like blood vessels, and inflammatory cells, mainly lymphocytes and plasma cells.

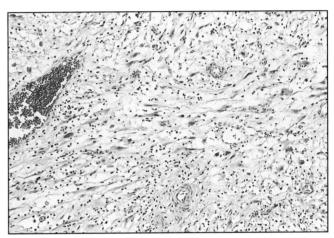

Fig. 14A.105 • Pseudosarcomatous fibromyxoid tumor. Some bizarre cells with one or two large nuclei and dense eosinophilic cytoplasm are present.

Table 14A.5 Distinguishing features between pseudosarcomatous fibromyxoid tumor (PSFMT) and other myxoid lesions

Features	PSFMT	PSCN	ML	MR
Cellularity	+/++	+++	+/++	+/++
Growth pattern	ND	Fascicles	ND	Cambium
Pleomorphism	+	–	±	+
Mitoses per 10 hpf	1–2	1–25	1→10	1→10
Vessels	Slit	ND	ND	ND
Keratin	±	±	±	±
SMA	±	±	+	–
Desmin	±	±	+	+
Myogenin	–	–	-	+
EM	F/MF	F/MF	SM	STM
Clinical course	I	I	R/M	R/M

PSCN, postoperative spindle cell nodule; ML, myxoid leiomyosarcoma; MR, myxoid rhabdomyosarcoma; ND, nondescript; SMA, smooth muscle actin; EM, electron microscopic findings; F, fibroblast; MF, myofibroblast; SM, smooth muscle; STM, striated muscle; I, indolent; R/M, recurrent/malignant.

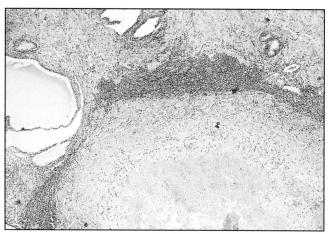

Fig. 14A.106 • An ovoid, large, well-circumscribed granuloma. A dense band of palisading histiocytes surrounds a necrotic center. At the periphery is a dense zone of inflammatory cells comprising predominantly lymphocytes and plasma cells.

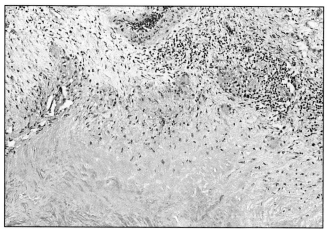

Fig. 14A.107 • Bacillus Calmette-Guérin (BCG) granulomatous inflammation. A central amorphous area of necrosis is surrounded by histiocytes and Langhans giant cells. An acid-fast bacillus stain may demonstrate acid-fast organisms.

Malignant soft tissue tumors

Sarcomas of the prostate are rare, comprising fewer than 0.1% of all primary prostatic neoplasms. Most of the sarcomas of the prostate are sarcomas of specialized prostatic stroma, leiomyosarcomas, or rhabdomyosarcomas.[414–416,492–502] Rhabdomyosarcoma, the most common sarcoma of the prostate, occurs frequently in infants, children, and young adults, whereas leiomyosarcoma, the second most common sarcoma of the prostate, occurs more commonly in older age groups. In fact, sarcomas of the prostate are known to have a bimodal age distribution: (1) patients older than 60 years; and (2) infants, children, and young adults.

Rhabdomyosarcoma

Rhabdomyosarcoma (see also Ch. 24) is the most frequent sarcoma in the prostate. While at least 18 cases of rhabdo-myosarcoma have been reported in adults older than 50 years of age,[494,503–509] it typically occurs in persons less than 20 years old. The genitourinary system, including the prostate, accounts for 21% of rhabdomyosarcomas in children, and is second in frequency after head and neck locations.[510]

More than 80% are embryonal rhabdomyosarcomas, including the botryoid and spindle cell subtypes, and the remainder are the alveolar subtype. The alveolar type tends to occur in a somewhat older age group (median 22 years).[499,511–514] Pleomorphic rhabdomyosarcoma has also been reported in the prostate but is extremely rare.[415,512]

When the tumor is composed predominantly of round cells, additional studies such as electron microscopy and immuno-histochemistry may be necessary to confirm the diagnosis. Antibodies to muscle antigens, including MyoD1, myogenin, desmin and muscle actin, are most commonly used in the diagnosis of rhabdomyosarcoma.[99]

More recently chromosomal analysis has been applied to make a diagnosis in difficult cases, using t(2;13) or t(1;13) in the alveolar subtype or gains of chromosomes 2, 8, and 13 in the embryonal type.[515]

Small cell carcinoma of the prostate[213,219] and lymphoma[516] may be difficult to differentiate from rhabdomyosarcoma on morphologic grounds alone in the adult population. Clinical presentation, as well as immunohistochemical and electron microscopic analysis of the tumor, will usually establish a definitive diagnosis. A pseudosarcomatous fibromyxoid tumor is another consideration in differential diagnosis. It may have strap cells or tadpole-like cells which are set in a myxoid background, as in embryonal rhabdomyosarcoma; however, pseudosarcomatous fibromyxoid tumor does not have the cambium layer or the cells with cross-striations, and does not stain with MyoD1 or myogenin, as do the spindle cells of embryonal rhabdomyosarcoma.[410,464,465]

Bladder–prostate rhabdomyosarcomas are discovered relatively early because they produce symptoms and signs referable to the urinary tract, which lead to prompt medical attention. Rhabdomyosarcoma may be small and apparently limited to the prostate at the time of diagnosis, but may grow rapidly, invading adjacent soft tissue and bladder. In contrast, extraprostatic pelvic tumors are often large and infiltrative when they are first detected.[415,503–510,512–514] Therefore, rhabdo-myosarcomas of the bladder–prostate region are said to have a better prognosis than those of the soft tissue of the retro-peritoneum–pelvis outside the prostate.[512,517] According to the results from Intergroup Rhabdomyosarcoma Study IV, which included 54 rhabdomyosarcomas in bladder–prostate gland, the factors associated with the best outcome were: age 1–9 years at diagnosis; non-invasive tumors; tumor size <5 cm; uninvolved lymph nodes; stage I or II disease; primary site in the orbit or head and neck; and embryonal histologic features ($P = 0.001$ for all factors) in the univariate analysis, and the multivariate analysis identified only age, clinical nodal status, and stage as independent prognostic factors.[517,518]

The prognosis of rhabdomyosarcoma has improved considerably with the introduction of combination therapy (multidrug chemotherapy, surgery, and complementary radiation) therapy leading, at least in younger patients, to a 5-year disease-free survival rate of 70% and overall survival rate of 75%.[518] Metastases are less frequent since the advent of combination therapy.[511,512,517,518]

Leiomyosarcoma

Leiomyosarcoma is the most common sarcoma of the prostate in adults[508,521] and the second most common sarcoma after rhabdomyosarcoma among all prostatic sarcomas.[415,493,508] It accounts for 25% of prostatic sarcomas. Although most patients are in their fifth to eighth decades (median age 58 years),[415,493,496,500,520] leiomyosarcoma may affect patients over a wide age range, including patients younger than 10 years.[501]

Leiomyosarcoma typically tends to be large, up to 21 cm (mean 9 cm), with macroscopic findings similar to its soft tissue counterpart. It diffusely infiltrates the prostate and periprostatic soft tissue. Prostatic enlargement is readily detectable and the clinical diagnosis is usually BPH or prostatitis.[501,519–521]

Microscopically, it is similar to leiomyosarcoma of soft tissue or viscera (see Ch. 24) and consists of interlacing fascicles of spindle cells with blunt-ended nuclei and fibrillar eosinophilic cytoplasm. Nuclear atypia and mitoses are variable in extent but are always present (Fig. 14A.108). Tumor necrosis and hemorrhage are frequently observed.[415,511,522] Although the smooth muscle nature of leiomyosarcoma is usually appreciated by routine light microscopic examination, immunohistochemistry or electron microscopy may help to confirm this.[492,519] Most tumors are intermediate- to high-grade. At the low end of atypia there are no established criteria to distinguish leiomyosarcoma from a cellular or symplastic leiomyoma. We suggest making a diagnosis of leiomyosarcoma when the tumor has at least two of the following adverse histologic parameters: cellularity, pleomorphism, nuclear atypia, necrosis, infiltrative pattern, and mitotic activity. However, there are scant data on reliable pathologic features for assessing biologic behavior of prostatic smooth muscle tumors because of their rarity and insufficient follow-up of the reported cases.[492,501,522] It is also difficult to differentiate gastrointestinal stromal tumor of rectum from leiomyosarcoma of prostate in case of contact with the prostate. In this situation, *c-kit* and CD34 immunostaining help in their differentiation.

The reported 5-year survival rate for patients with leiomyosarcoma has been 50–60%;[416,521] however, the prognosis of leiomyosarcoma is encouraging, with aggressive combination treatment involving radical surgery, preoperative and postoperative combination chemotherapy, and radiation therapy in selected patients. Ahlering et al.[522] reported a 90% survival rate with the above-mentioned regimens at a mean follow-up of 5 years. Local recurrence and visceral metastasis complicate half the cases.[519,522]

Stromal sarcoma (sarcoma of specialized prostatic stroma)

Within the relatively rare category of adult soft tissue sarcomas that occur in the prostate, there is a group of sarcomas that are different from leiomyosarcoma and are thought to arise from specialized prostatic stroma, the latter assertion being based on positivity for progesterone and/or estrogen receptors.[414] Like phyllodes tumors of the prostate, they represent a spectrum. Gaudin et al.[414] have proposed the term prostatic stromal proliferation of uncertain malignant potential for lesions defying unequivocal characterization as sarcoma, and prostatic stromal sarcoma for tumors with stromal overgrowth, mitoses, and necrosis. Local recurrence resulting in death of the patient and/or metastasis, usually to the lung, is known to occur. Even the relatively bland lesions of uncertain malignant potential may recur, sometimes repeatedly, and may require radical prostatectomy. Histologically, the tumor is composed of primitive round, oval, or spindle cells, occasionally with a herringbone pattern, diffusely infiltrating the prostatic stroma (Fig. 14A.109). The tumors are positive for CD34 (stem cell marker) and hormone receptors (progesterone and/or estrogen), and stain variably (usually negatively in overt sarcomas) for muscle markers (smooth muscle actin, HHF-35, and desmin).[414]

Other sarcomas

Fibrosarcoma in the prostate has been mentioned by Tannenbaum[493] but there is no detailed description of this lesion in the literature. Two cases of osteosarcoma of the prostate have been reported in the literature.[523,524] Both cases were

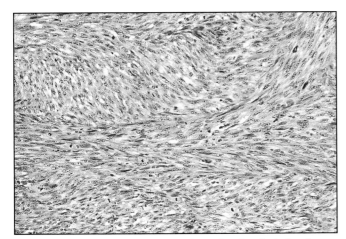

Fig. 14A.108 • Leiomyosarcoma with interlacing fascicles of spindle cells.

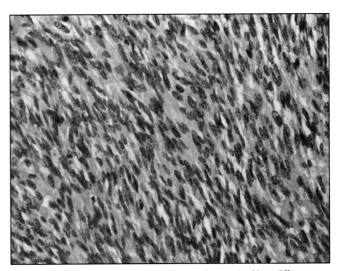

Fig. 14A.109 • Stromal sarcoma. This lesion is characterized by a diffuse proliferation of tightly packed spindle cells with indistinct cytoplasm and mitotic activity.

associated with adenocarcinoma of the prostate: one patient developed osteosarcoma *de novo*[523] and the other developed osteosarcoma after radiation therapy for carcinoma.[524] These cases may be classified as sarcomatoid carcinoma by our definition rather than as primary osteosarcoma of the prostate. We encountered one patient among a series of 12 sarcomatoid carcinomas with osteosarcoma as a sarcomatoid component.[259]

A few cases of so-called malignant fibrous histiocytoma of the prostate have been reported.[467,525,526] Unlike comparable lesions in soft tissue, this tumor displayed only moderate pleomorphism with rare mitoses. Although the degree of malignancy is difficult to evaluate from the case reports and the follow-up is too short, the prognosis appears to be poor.

Several cases of angiosarcoma, including postradiation angiosarcoma, have been described in the literature with adequate histologic description.[527,528] The patients' ages ranged from 2 to 60 years (mean 34.5 years) and the tumor occurred 10 years after therapeutic irradiation for prostatic adenocarcinoma in 1 patient. The prognosis appears to be dismal because 3 of them died within 6 months after the diagnosis.[527] The tumors were poorly differentiated; immunostaining for vascular markers may be useful in differentiating angiosarcoma from poorly differentiated sarcomas.[527,528] One case of radiation-induced prostatic sarcoma has been reported by Scully et al.[529] Chondrosarcoma, malignant peripheral nerve sheath tumor, neuroblastoma, primitive peripheral neuroectodermal tumor, malignant perivascular epithelioid cell tumor, and rhabdoid tumor have been reported to occur in the prostate.[68,530,531]

Rare malignant tumors involving the prostate

Malignant lymphoma, leukaemia, and plasmacytoma

Malignant lymphoma of the prostate, either as a primary tumor or as a tumor secondary to systemic involvement, is rare. Over 150 well-documented cases have been reported.[516,532–535] Patients ranged in age from 14 to 86 years (mean 61 years). There are no specific symptoms or signs for lymphoma. Urinary obstructive symptoms, hematuria, or both are usual presenting symptoms. The clinical diagnosis is almost always BPH, prostatitis, or carcinoma, even in patients with a previous diagnosis of lymphoma.[516,536–540]

Reported series include the entire spectrum of malignant lymphomas seen at other sites; the predominant types are large cell, mixed cell, and small cleaved cell lymphomas.[516] There are only a few reported cases of nodular, T-cell, undifferentiated Burkitt's, and non-Burkitt's lymphomas.[516,537] Hodgkin lymphoma, lymphomatoid granulomatosis, and angiotropic lymphoma have also been reported in the prostate.[415,541–543] Bostwick et al.[539] reported the largest series (62 cases) of malignant lymphoma involving the prostate: 35% were primarily extranodal of the following types: B-cell small lymphocytic (4), follicle center cell, follicular, grade I (small cell) (1), follicle center cell, follicular, grade II (mixed small and large) (1), follicle center cell, diffuse, small cell (2), diffuse large B-cell

lymphoma (12), high-grade B-cell lymphoma, Burkitt-like (2). Forty-eight percent with previously documented lymphoma at other sites developed prostatic involvement, including B-cell chronic lymphocytic leukemia (8), follicle center, follicular, grade I (small cell) (1), follicle center cell, follicular, grade II (mixed small and large cell) (1), follicle center cell, diffuse, small cell (2), diffuse large cell B-cell lymphoma (11), peripheral T-cell lymphoma (2), high-grade B-cell lymphoma, Burkitt-like (1), Burkitt's lymphoma (1), Hodgkin's lymphoma (2, nodular sclerosis, 1, mixed cellularity, 1); 17% were unclassifiable as primary or secondary lymphoma.[539]

The criteria for primary lymphoma of the prostate set by King & Cox[534] include limitation of tumor to the prostate and adjacent tissues and absence of lymph node involvement. In addition to the above criteria, Bostwick & Mann[516] required that the major presenting symptoms be limited to the prostate and that there be a disease-free interval of at least 1 month to allow completion of staging procedures.

The prognosis of lymphoma involving the prostate is poor regardless of the patient's age, the tumor stage, or histologic type, or treatment regimens used.[532–537] Twenty-seven patients in the series of 62 cases reported by Bostwick et al.[539] died of malignant lymphoma, 18 were alive 12–120 months after diagnosis (8 primary and 10 secondary), 12 died of other or unknown causes, and 5 were lost to follow-up. There was no statistical difference in mean survival following diagnosis of prostatic involvement between primary and secondary lymphoma (9.8 months versus 12.7 months).

About 20% of patients with leukemia have evidence of prostatic involvement at autopsy, but fewer than 1% have clinical manifestations of prostatic symptoms as a direct result of the leukemic process.[541,544,545] Chronic lymphocytic leukemia is the most common type.[541,544,545] Three cases of prostatic granulocytic sarcoma have been reported.[546–548]

Plasmacytoma is extremely rare in the prostate and the involvement is recognized after the diagnosis of systemic disease or is made at autopsy. There has been a reported case with a moderately enlarged, non-tender, irregular gland mimicking a primary prostatic carcinoma. On microscopic examination, sheets of neoplastic plasma cells diffusely infiltrate the prostatic stroma.[549] Rarely Hodgkin lymphoma and mucosa-associated lymphoid tissue lymphoma have been reported in the prostate.[550]

The main differential diagnoses include prostatitis (particularly for small lymphocytic lymphoma[535]) and prostatic carcinoma, particularly small cell carcinoma and rhabdomyosarcoma. Clinical history and a careful microscopic evaluation with ancillary methods including immunohistochemistry and electron microscopy are essential to differentiate these lesions from lymphoma or leukemia.[99,219,497,516,551–553]

Germ cell tumors

A few germ cell tumors involving the prostate have been reported. Some are possibly primary, but most others represent secondary involvement from the retroperitoneum or retrovesical space. These tumors occur in young to middle-aged men. The pathogenesis of primary germ cell tumor of the prostate is unclear, but sequestration of germ cells, neoplastic transformation of uncommitted stem cells into germ cells, or metastasis from an occult testicular primary are possible explanations. The diagnosis of a primary prostatic germ cell tumor should be made after a testicular primary is excluded. Seminomas and non-seminomatous germ cell tumors, including yolk sac tumor, choriocarcinoma, and mixed germ cell tumors have been reported. A case of yolk sac tumor mixed with a small focus of seminoma has been reported. The prognosis is favorable in patients with seminoma, but less favorable in those with non-seminomatous germ cell tumors.[554]

Metastatic solid tumors to the prostate

The prostate gland is infrequently involved by metastatic tumors when lymphoma, leukemia, and cases of contiguous spread from the bladder and colon are excluded. Johnson et al.[224] found the prostate to be involved in metastatic disease in 0.5% of male patients dying of malignant tumors. In similar studies, Zein et al.[225] and Bates[555] reported incidences of 2.2% and 0.2% respectively. Combining these series,[224,225] the most common tumor secondarily involving the prostate is bronchogenic carcinoma, followed by melanoma. Other frequent primary sites include the gastrointestinal tract, including pancreas and kidney.[556,557] A metastatic testicular germ cell tumor and thyroid, penile, and laryngeal carcinoma have also been reported.[558]

Tumors and tumorous conditions of seminal vesicles

Cysts of the seminal vesicle

Cysts of the seminal vesicle are uncommon: fewer than 100 cases have been reported. This number does not reflect the real frequency, however. Correct clinical diagnosis of these lesions has been uncommon in the past because of difficulty in imaging the seminal vesicles. Cysts of seminal vesicles are frequently associated with ipsilateral renal agenesis.[559–561] In some cases, postinfection fibrosis has been suggested as the etiologic factor.[556] Acquired cysts are usually associated with obstruction of the ejaculatory duct because of urinary tract infection, usually ascending from the lumen of prostatic urethra into the seminal vesicles.[559] Compression of the ejaculatory duct by prostatic adenomatous nodules explains the association with BPH. The cyst is usually unilocular and can be hemorrhagic. Unilaterality is the rule but a few cases are bilateral.[559–562] Sometimes cysts of the seminal vesicles are associated with an absent testis; a few have been associated with an anomaly of the vas deferens. The differential diagnoses include abscesses, hydatid cysts, solid and cystic tumors of seminal vesicle or prostate, and diverticulum of the ejaculatory duct.[559,562,563]

Seminal vesicle cysts occur most commonly in the third decade of life (range 18–59 years), and most are asymptomatic.[559–563] When a cyst is symptomatic, the initial signs in the majority of cases are lower urinary tract symptoms such as burning, urgency, and increased frequency of urination. Epididymitis, abdominal pain, and perineal discomfort after ejaculation are not infrequent. Most reported cases have lacked

any histologic description. A few reports describe a cyst lined by a uniform layer of columnar to cuboidal epithelium with no mesenchymal component except for a fibrous wall.[564–566]

Amyloid deposition in seminal vesicle

Localized amyloidosis in the seminal vesicles, which is considered as senile process, has been reported occasionally in autopsies and in surgical specimens, with its incidence being about 9–16%.[567] Amyloid deposition in the vas deferens as well as ejaculatory ducts has also been reported in the literature. Jun et al.[568] recently reported amyloid deposition in the seminal vesicle mimicking extension of carcinoma. Grossly the seminal vesicle may be thickened with reduced or absent lumina. Microscopically, amyloid deposition tends to be nodular. The seminal vesicle is frequently distorted by the deposition of fine fibrillar eosinophilic material in a subepithelial location (Fig. 14A.110). Involvement of vessel walls is not seen. Positive staining and apple-green birefringence with Congo red staining confirm the amyloid nature of the eosinophilic material.

Other benign neoplasms

Leiomyomas of seminal vesicles are extremely rare; only a few cases have been reported.[569] They appear to arise from the wall of the seminal vesicle and present as a pelvic mass. Mesonephric hamartoma is another rare tumor which is known to develop in the vas deferens or seminal vesicle.[570,571]

Other benign neoplasms include cystomyoma,[572] cystadenoma,[573–577] neurilemmoma, angioendothelioma, and mesenchymoma.[577,578] Mazur et al.[579] reported an unusual epithelial-stromal tumor of the seminal vesicle with cytologic atypia. They designated this lesion as a cystic epithelial-stromal tumor with uncertain biologic potential.

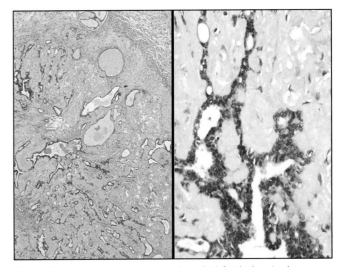

Fig. 14A.110 • Amyloid in seminal vesicle. In the left side there is a low-power view of the seminal vesicle. Amyloid can be already noticed, but on the high-power illustration on the right side, the amyloid is better appreciated. The typical amorphous/fibrillar eosinophilic material replaces the lamina propria. Also notice lipofuscin pigment in the seminal vesicle epithelium. Involvement of vessel walls by amyloid is not seen.

Malignant neoplasms

Adenocarcinoma of seminal vesicle

Primary adenocarcinoma of the seminal vesicle is a rare tumor: about 50 cases have been reported in the literature.[580–586] The age of the patients ranged from 19 to 88 years. Most of the patients presented after the age of 50 years. It is usually difficult to establish a diagnosis of primary carcinoma of the seminal vesicle before surgery or antemortem, and differential diagnoses should include invasion of the seminal vesicle by prostatic carcinoma, colonic carcinoma, or bladder carcinoma. In order for a diagnosis of primary seminal vesicle carcinoma to be made, the tumor should be localized to the seminal vesicle and be negative for PSA and PrAP, and there should be no other primary neoplasms.[580–583]

Adenocarcinomas and normal prostate structures have been reported to be negative for MUC6 (MUC6 belongs to the family of human mucin genes). In contrast, all seminal vesicles and ejaculatory ducts are diffusely immunostained with the MUC6 antibody. Although there are no studies of seminal vesicle adenocarcinoma utilizing MUC6, this marker is potentially valuable for the differential diagnosis with prostate adenocarcinoma.[360]

Microscopically, all tumors are adenocarcinomas; they frequently show papillary growth or they may be poorly differentiated with solid, nested, and cord-like growth (Fig. 14A.111). The tumor cells are usually tall, columnar, or cuboidal. Carcinoma in situ is frequently noted in the adjacent normal seminal vesicular epithelium. The tumors are positive for mucin, CA125, and CEA.

The differential diagnosis includes carcinoma extending from the urinary bladder, prostate, or rectum. TCC of the urinary bladder can involve the seminal vesicle in two different patterns – mucosal spread and direct tumor extension[247] (Fig. 14A.112). When the tumor involves the mucosal side, carcinoma in situ change can usually be identified. Therefore, carcinoma in situ change is not necessarily *bona fide* evidence

of primary carcinoma. Prostatic adenocarcinoma also frequently involves the seminal vesicle (Fig. 14A.113).[587] Sometimes primary adenocarcinoma of the seminal vesicle cannot be differentiated from carcinoma extending from the prostate,

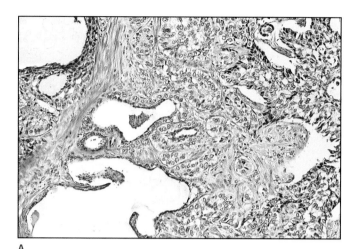

A

B

Fig. 14A.112 • (A, B) Transitional cell carcinoma of bladder with mucosal spread to a seminal vesicle. Clusters of tumor cells infiltrate in a pagetoid manner between epithelial cells of the seminal vesicle and basal lamina.

Fig. 14A.111 • Adenocarcinoma of seminal vesicle. On the left side, the low-power view displays a pattern of irregular glandular arrangement. On higher power, the malignant character of this lesion is seen characterized by nuclear anaplasia, prominent nucleoli, and multiple mitoses.

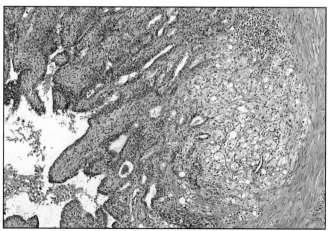

Fig. 14A.113 • Prostate carcinoma invades the seminal vesicle.

based solely on histologic evaluation. Immunohistochemical studies for prostatic markers are therefore mandatory.

Ormsby et al.'s more recent study[586] has shown that the CK7-positive, CK20-negative, CA-125-positive, PSA/PrAP-negative immunophenotype of seminal vesicle adenocarcinoma is unique and can be used in conjunction with histomorphology to distinguish it from other tumors that enter the differential diagnosis, including prostatic adenocarcinoma (CA-125-negative, PSA/PrAP-positive), bladder TCC (CK20-positive, CA-125-negative), rectal adenocarcinoma (CA-125-negative, CK7-negative, CK20-positive), bladder adenocarcinoma (CA-125-negative), and adenocarcinoma arising in a müllerian duct cyst (CA-125-negative).

The prognosis for adenocarcinoma of the seminal vesicles is poor. Radical surgical treatment has been attempted, with dismal results. There have been few long-term survivors among those patients treated with radiation therapy, orchiectomy, or estrogen therapy.[580–583]

Other malignant neoplasms

A case of male adnexal tumor of probable wolffian origin has been reported in the seminal vesicle in a 29-year-old man.[588] Sarcomas of the seminal vesicle are extremely rare. Leiomyosarcoma,[589–591] rhabdomyosarcoma,[592,593] angiosarcoma,[589,594–596] fibrosarcoma, liposarcoma, and cystosarcoma phyllodes[597] "of the seminal vesicle" have been reported in the literature. There is a tendency for these tumors to invade neighboring structures widely, often obscuring the actual site of origin. In recognition of this difficulty, some authors believe that all sarcomas occurring behind the bladder and prostate should simply be categorized collectively as retrovesical sarcomas.[589,594,595,598] Recommendations for therapy are limited because of the paucity of experience with these tumors. Surgical excision, combined external and implant radiation therapy, and hormonal manipulation have been used.

References

1. Jemal A, Siegel R, Ward E et al. 2006 Cancer statistics, 2006. CA Cancer J Clin 56: 106–130
2. Eble J N, Sauter G, Epstein J I et al. 2004 Pathology and genetics: Tumours of the urinary system and male genital organs. WHO classification of tumors. IARC Press, Lyon, p 160–215.
3. Srigley J R 2004 Benign mimickers of prostatic adenocarcinoma. Mod Pathol 17: 328–348
4. McNeal J E, Bostwick D G 1986 Intraductal dysplasia: a premalignant lesion of the prostate. Hum Pathol 17: 64–71
5. Bostwick D G, Brawer M K 1987 Prostatic intraepithelial neoplasia and early invasion in prostate cancer. Cancer 59: 788–794
6. Kastendieck H, Altenahr E, Husselmann H et al. 1976 Carcinoma and dysplastic lesions of the prostate. Z Krebsforsch 88: 33–54
7. Helpap B 1980 The biological significance of atypical hyperplasia of the prostate. Virchow's Arch [A] 387: 307–317
8. Amin M B, Ro J Y, Ayala A G 1993 Ideas in pathology. Putative precursor lesions of prostatic adenocarcinoma: fact or fiction? Mod Pathol 6: 476–483
9. Amin M B, Ro J Y, Ayala A G 1994 Prostatic intraepithelial neoplasia: relationship to adenocarcinoma of prostate. Pathol Annu 29: 1–30
10. McNeal J E 1965 Morphogenesis of prostate carcinoma. Cancer 18: 1659–1666
11. McNeal J E 1968 Regional morphology and pathology of the prostate. Am J Clin Pathol 49: 347–357
12. McNeal J E 1969 Origin and development of carcinoma in the prostate. Cancer 23: 24–34
13. Drago J R, Mostofi F K, Lee F 1989 Introductory remarks and workshop summary. Urology 34: 2–3
14. Troncoso P, Babaian R J, Ro J Y 1989 Prostatic intraepithelial neoplasia and invasive prostatic adenocarcinomas in cystoprostatectomy specimens. Urology 34: 52–56
15. Gaudin P B, Sesterhenn I A, Wojno K J et al. 1997 Incidence and clinical significance of high grade prostatic intraepithelial neoplasia in TURP specimens. Urology 49: 558–563
16. Pacelli A, Bostwick D G 1997 Clinical significance of high-grade prostatic intraepithelial neoplasia in transurethral resection specimens. Urology 50: 355–359
17. Bostwick D G, Qian J, Frankel K 1995 The incidence of high-grade prostatic intraepithelial neoplasia in needle biopsies. J Urol 154: 1791–1794
18. Bostwick D G, Amin M B, Dundore P 1993 Architectural patterns of high-grade prostatic intraepithelial neoplasia. Hum Pathol 24: 298–310
19. Reyes A O, Swanson P E, Carbone J M et al. 1997 Unusual histologic types of high-grade prostatic intraepithelial neoplasia. Am J Surg Pathol 21: 1215–1222
20. Argani P, Epstein J I 2001 Inverted (hobnail) high-grade prostatic intraepithelial neoplasia (PIN): report of 15 cases of a previously undescribed pattern of high-grade PIN. Am J Surg Pathol 25: 1534–1539
21. Berman D M, Yang J, Epstein J I 2000 Foamy gland high-grade prostatic intraepithelial neoplasia. Am J Surg Pathol 24: 140–144
22. Qian J, Jenkins R B, Bostwick D G 1997 Detection of chromosomal anomalies and c-myc gene amplification in the cribriform pattern of prostatic intraepithelial neoplasia and carcinoma by fluorescence in situ hybridization. Mod Pathol 10: 1113–1119
23. McNeal J E, Villers A, Redwine E A 1991 Microcarcinoma in the prostate: its association with duct-acinar dysplasia. Hum Pathol 22: 644–652
24. Bostwick D G 1995 High-grade prostatic intraepithelial neoplasia: the most likely precursor of prostate cancer. Cancer 75: 1823–1836
25. Kronz J D, Allan C H, Shaikh A A et al. 2001 Predicting cancer following a diagnosis of high-grade prostatic intraepithelial neoplasia on needle biopsy: data on men with more than one follow-up biopsy. Am J Surg Pathol 25: 1079–1085
26. Nagle R B, Brawer M K, Kittelson J 1991 Phenotypic relationships of prostatic intraepithelial neoplasia to invasive prostatic carcinoma. Am J Pathol 138: 119–128
27. Perlman E J, Epstein J I 1990 Blood group antigen expression in dysplasia and adenocarcinoma of the prostate. Am J Surg Pathol 14: 810–818
28. McNeal J E, Leav I, Alroy J 1988 Differential lectin staining of central and peripheral zones of the prostate and alterations in dysplasia. Am J Clin Pathol 89: 41–48
29. Deschenes J, Weidner N 1990 Nucleolar organizer regions (NOR) in hyperplastic and neoplastic prostate disease. Am J Surg Pathol 14: 1148–1155
30. Sesterhenn I A, Becker R L, Avallone F A 1991 Image analysis of nucleoli and nucleolar organizer regions in prostatic hyperplasia, intraepithelial neoplasia, and prostatic carcinoma. J Urogen Pathol 1: 61–74
31. Amin M B, Schultz D S, Zarbo R J 1994 Computerized static DNA ploidy analysis of prostatic intraepithelial neoplasia. Arch Pathol Lab Med 118: 260–264
32. Weinberg D S, Weidner N 1993 Concordance of DNA content between prostatic intraepithelial neoplasia and concomitant invasive carcinoma. Evidence that prostatic intraepithelial neoplasia is a precursor of invasive prostatic carcinoma. Arch Pathol Lab Med 117: 1132–1137
33. McNeal J E, Alroy J, Leav I et al. 1988 Immunohistochemical evidence for impaired cell differentiation in the premalignant phase of prostate carcinogenesis. Am J Clin Pathol 90: 23–32
34. Tamboli P, Amin M B, Xu H J et al. 1998 Immunohistochemical expression of retinoblastoma and p53 tumor suppressor genes in prostatic intraepithelial neoplasia: comparison with prostatic adenocarcinoma and benign prostate. Mod Pathol 11: 247–252
35. Tamboli P, Amin M B, Schultz D S et al. 1996 Comparative analysis of nuclear proliferative index (Ki-67) in benign prostate, prostatic intraepithelial neoplasia and prostatic carcinoma. Mod Pathol 9: 1015–1019
36. Zeng L, Rowland R G, Lele S M et al. 2004 Apoptosis incidence and protein expression of p53, TGF-beta receptor II, p27Kip1, and Smad4 in benign, premalignant, and malignant human prostate. Hum Pathol 35: 290–297
37. Zhang P J, Driscoll D L, Lee H K et al. 1999 Decreased immunoexpression of prostate inhibin peptide in prostatic carcinoma: a study with monoclonal antibody. Hum Pathol 30: 168–172
38. Emmert-Buck M R, Vocke C D, Pozzatt R O et al. 1995 Allelic loss of chromosome 8p12-21 in microdissected prostatic intraepithelial neoplasia. Cancer Res 55: 2959–2962
39. Macoska J A, Trybus T M, Benson P D et al. 1995 Evidence for three tumor suppressor gene loci on chromosome 8p in human prostate cancer. Cancer Res 55: 5390–5395
40. Qian J, Jenkins R B, Bostwick D G 1999 Genetic and chromosomal alterations in prostatic intraepithelial neoplasia and carcinoma detected by fluorescence in situ hybridization. Eur Urol 35: 479–483

41. Al-Maghrabi J, Vorobyova L, Toi A et al. 2002 Identification of numerical chromosomal changes detected by interphase fluorescence in situ hybridization in high-grade prostate intraepithelial neoplasia as a predictor of carcinoma. Arch Pathol Lab Med 126: 165–169

42. Wu C L, Yang X J, Tretiakova M et al. 2004 Analysis of alpha-methylacyl-CoA racemase (P504S) expression in high-grade prostatic intraepithelial neoplasia. Hum Pathol 35: 1008–1013

43. Sakar W A, Srigley J R, Dey J et al. 2001 What features do urologic pathologists emphasize in diagnosing intraepithelial neoplasia (PIN)? A study of morphologic criteria and reproducibility. Mod Pathol 14: 122A (abstract)

44. Srodon M, Epstein J I 2002 Central zone histology of the prostate: a mimicker of high-grade prostatic intraepithelial neoplasia. Hum Pathol 33: 518–523

45. Yantiss R K, Young R H 1997 Transitional cell "metaplasia" in the prostate gland. A survey of its frequency and features based on 103 consecutive prostatic biopsy specimens. J Urol Pathol 7: 71–80

46. Greene L F, O'Dea M J, Dockerty M B 1976 Primary transitional cell carcinoma of the prostate. J Urol 116: 761–763

47. Rubenstein A B, Rubnitz M E 1969 Transitional cell carcinoma of the prostate. Cancer 24: 543–546

48. Molinie V, Fromont G, Sibony M et al. 2004 Diagnostic utility of a p63/alpha-methyl-CoA-racemase (p504s) cocktail in atypical foci in the prostate. Mod Pathol 17: 1180–1190

49. McNeal J E, Yemoto C E 1996 Spread of adenocarcinoma within prostatic ducts and acini. Morphologic and clinical correlations. Am J Surg Pathol 20: 802–814

50. Randolph T, Amin M B, Ro J Y 1997 Histologic variants of the prostatic adenocarcinoma and other carcinomas of the prostate. Mod Pathol 10: 612–629

51. Wilcox G, Soh S, Chakraborty S et al. 1998 Patterns of high-grade prostatic intraepithelial neoplasia associated with clinically aggressive prostate cancer. Hum Pathol 29: 1119–1123

52. Kronz J D, Shaikh A A, Epstein J I 2001 Atypical cribriform lesions on prostate biopsy. Am J Surg Pathol 25: 147–155

53. Kuo T, Gomez L G 1981 Monstrous epithelial cells in human epididymis and seminal vesicles: a pseudomalignant change. Am J Surg Pathol 5: 483–490

54. Arias-Stella J, Takano-Moron J 1958 Atypical epithelial changes in the seminal vesicles. Arch Pathol 66: 761–766

55. Coyne J D, Kealy W T, Annis P 1987 Seminal vesicle epithelium in prostatic needle biopsy specimens (letter). J Clin Pathol 40: 932

56. Amin M B, Bostwick D G 1996 Pigment in prostatic epithelium and adenocarcinoma: a potential source of diagnostic confusion with seminal vesicular epithelium. Mod Pathol 9: 791–795

57. Epstein J I, Grignon D J, Humphrey P A et al. 1995 Interobserver reproducibility in the diagnosis of prostatic intraepithelial neoplasia. Am J Surg Pathol 19: 873–886

58. Allam C K, Bostwick D G, Hayes J A et al. 1996 Interobserver variability in the diagnosis of high grade prostatic intraepithelial neoplasia and adenocarcinoma. Mod Pathol 9: 742–751

59. Bishara T, Ramnani D M, Epstein J I 2004 High-grade prostatic intraepithelial neoplasia on needle biopsy: risk of cancer on repeat biopsy related to number of involved cores and morphologic pattern. Am J Surg Pathol 28: 629–633

60. Eskew L A, Bare R L, McCullough D L 1997 Systematic 5 region prostate biopsy is superior to sextant method for diagnosing carcinoma of the prostate. J Urol 157: 199–202

61. Chen M E, Troncoso P, Johnston D A et al. 1997 Optimization of prostate biopsy strategy using computer based analysis. J Urol 158: 2168–2175

62. Lefkowitz G K, Taneja S S, Brown J et al. 2002 Followup interval prostate biopsy 3 years after diagnosis of high grade prostatic intraepithelial neoplasia is associated with high likelihood of prostate cancer, independent of change in prostate specific antigen levels. J Urol 168: 1415–1418

63. Babaian R J, Toi A, Kamoi K et al. 2000 A comparative analysis of sextant and an extended 11-core multisite directed biopsy strategy. J Urol 163: 152–157

64. San Francisco I F, Olumi A F, Kao J et al. 2003 Clinical management of prostatic intraepithelial neoplasia as diagnosed by extended needle biopsies. Br J Urol Int 91: 350–354

65. Hankey B F, Feuer E J, Clegg L X 1999 Cancer surveillance series: interpreting trends in prostate cancer – part I: evidence of the effects of screening in recent prostate cancer incidence, mortality, and survival rates. J Natl Cancer Inst 91: 1017–1024

66. Cooner W H, Mosley B R, Rutherford C L J 1988 Clinical application of transrectal ultrasonography and prostate specific antigen in the search for prostatic cancer. J Urol 139: 758–761

67. Lee F, Siders D B, Torp-Pedersen S T 1991 Prostate cancer: transrectal ultrasound and pathology comparison. A preliminary study of outer gland (peripheral and central zones) and inner gland (transition zone) cancer. Cancer 67: 1132–1142

68. Young R H, Srigley J R, Amin M B et al. 2000 Tumors of the prostate gland, seminal vesicles, male urethra, and penis. Atlas of tumor pathology, 3rd series. AFIP, Washington, DC

69. Mostofi F K, Sesterhenn I, Sobin L H (eds) 1980 Histological typing of prostate tumours. International histological classification of tumours. World Health Organization, Geneva, p 17–23

70. McNeal J E, Redwine E A, Freiha F S 1988 Zonal distribution of prostatic adenocarcinoma. Correlation with histologic pattern and direction of spread. Am J Surg Pathol 12: 897–906

71. Mostofi F K, Price E B J 1973 Tumors of the male genital system. Atlas of tumor pathology, 2nd series. Armed Forces Institute of Pathology, Washington, DC

72. Gleason D F 1977 Histologic grading and clinical staging of prostate carcinoma. In: Tannenbaum M (ed) Urologic pathology: the prostate. Lea & Febiger, Philadelphia, p 171–198

73. Kovi J 1985 Microscopic differential diagnosis of small acinar adenocarcinoma of prostate. Pathol Annu 20: 157–196

74. Gleason D F 1985 Atypical hyperplasia, benign hyperplasia and well differentiated adenocarcinoma of the prostate. Am J Surg Pathol 9 (suppl): 53–67

75. Ro J Y, Grignon D J, Troncoso P 1988 Mucin in prostatic adenocarcinoma. Semin Diagn Pathol 5: 273–283

76. Kramer C E, Epstein J I 1993 Nucleoli in low-grade prostate adenocarcinoma and adenosis. Hum Pathol 24: 618–623

77. Varma M, Lee M W, Tamboli P et al. 2002 Morphologic criteria for the diagnosis of prostatic adenocarcinoma in needle biopsy specimens. A study of 250 consecutive cases in a routine surgical pathology practice. Arch Pathol Lab Med 126: 554–561

78. Grignon D G, Ro J Y, Srigley J R 1992 Sclerosing adenosis of the prostate gland: a lesion showing myoepithelial differentiation. Am J Surg Pathol 16: 383–391

79. Holmes E J 1977 Crystalloids of prostatic carcinoma: relationship to Bence–Jones crystals. Cancer 39: 2073–2080

80. Ro J Y, Ayala A G, Ordonez N G et al. 1986 Intraluminal crystalloids in prostatic adenocarcinoma: immunohistochemical, electron microscopic and x-ray microanalytic studies. Cancer 57: 2397–2407

81. Ro J Y, Grignon D J, Troncoso P 1988 Intraluminal crystalloids in whole organ sections of prostate. Prostate 13: 233–239

82. Ohtsuki Y, Furihata M, Inoue K 1992 Immunohistochemical and ultrastructural studies of intraluminal crystalloids in human prostatic carcinomas. Virchow's Arch [A] 421: 421–425

83. Anton R C, Chakraborty S, Wheeler T M 1998 The significance of intraluminal prostatic crystalloids in benign needle biopsies. Am J Surg Pathol 22: 446–449

84. Henneberry J M, Kahane H, Humphrey P A et al. 1997 The significance of intraluminal crystalloids in benign prostatic glands on needle biopsy. Am J Surg Pathol 21: 725–728

85. Hukill P B, Vidone R A 1967 Histochemistry of mucus and other polysaccharides in tumors: carcinoma of the prostate. Lab Invest 16: 395–406

86. Christian J D, Lamm T C, Morrow J F et al. 2005 Corpora amylacea in adenocarcinoma of the prostate: incidence and histology within needle core biopsies. Mod Pathol 18: 36–39

87. Humphrey P A, Kaleem Z, Swanson P E et al. 1998 Pseudohyperplastic prostatic adenocarcinoma. Am J Surg Pathol 22: 1239–1246

88. Levi A W, Epstein J I 2000 Pseudohyperplastic prostatic adenocarcinoma on needle biopsy and simple prostatectomy. Am J Surg Pathol 24: 1039–1046

89. Nelson R S, Epstein J I 1996 Prostatic carcinoma with abundant xanthomatous cytoplasm. Foamy gland carcinoma. Am J Surg Pathol 20: 419–426

90. Tran T T, Sengupta E, Yang X J 2001 Prostatic foamy gland carcinoma with aggressive behavior: clinicopathologic, immunohistochemical, and ultrastructural analysis. Am J Surg Pathol 25: 618–623

91. Srigley J R 1988 Small-acinar patterns in the prostate gland with emphasis on atypical adenomatous hyperplasia and small-acinar carcinoma. Semin Diagn Pathol 5: 254–272

92. Brawn P N 1982 Adenosis of the prostate: a dysplastic lesion that can be confused with prostate adenocarcinoma. Cancer 49: 826–833

93. Egan A J, Lopez-Beltran A, Bostwick D G 1997 Prostatic adenocarcinoma with atrophic features: malignancy mimicking a benign process. Am J Surg Pathol 21: 931–935

94. Kaleem Z, Swanson P E, Vollmer R T et al. 1998 Prostatic adenocarcinoma with atrophic features: a study of 202 consecutive completely embedded radical prostatectomy specimens. Am J Clin Pathol 109: 695–703

95. Cina S J, Epstein J I 1997 Adenocarcinoma of the prostate with atrophic features. Am J Surg Pathol 21: 289–295

96. Farinola M A, Epstein J I 2004 Utility of immunohistochemistry for alpha-methylacyl-CoA racemase in distinguishing atrophic prostate cancer from benign atrophy. Hum Pathol 35: 1272–1278

97. Johnson D E, Hogan J M, Ayala A G 1972 Transitional cell carcinoma of the prostate. Cancer 29: 287–293

98. Rhamy R K, Buchanan R D, Spalding M J 1973 Intraductal carcinoma of the prostate gland. J Urol 109: 457–460

99. Ordonez N G, Ro J Y, Ayala A G 1990 Application of immunocytochemistry in the pathology of the prostate, In: Bostwick D G (ed) Pathology of the prostate. Churchill Livingstone, New York, p 137–160

100. Huang Q, Chu P G, Lau S K et al. 2004 Urothelial carcinoma of the urinary bladder with a component of acinar/tubular type differentiation simulating prostatic adenocarcinoma. Hum Pathol 35: 769–773

101. Epstein J I 2004 Diagnosis and reporting of limited adenocarcinoma of the prostate on needle biopsy. Mod Pathol 17: 307–315

102. Blaire B L, Kahane H, Epstein J I 1999 Perineural invasion, mucinous fibroplasia, and glomerulations. Diagnostic features of limited cancer on prostate needle biopsy. Am J Surg Pathol 23: 918–924

103. Bostwick D G, Wollan P, Adlakha K 1995 Collagenous micronodules in prostate cancer. A specific but infrequent finding. Arch Pathol Lab Med 119: 444–447

104. Pacelli A, Lopez-Beltran A, Egan A J et al. 1998 Prostatic adenocarcinoma with glomeruloid features. Hum Pathol 28: 543–546

105. Shah R B, Zhou M, LeBlanc M et al. 2004 Comparison of the basal cell-specific markers, 34betaE12 and p63, in the diagnosis of prostate cancer. Am J Surg Pathol 26: 1161–1168

106. Zhou M, Shah R, Shen R et al. 2003 Basal cell cocktail (34betaE12 + p63) improves the detection of prostate basal cells. Am J Surg Pathol 27: 365–371

107. Jiang Z, Wu C L, Woda B A et al. 2002 P504S/alpha-methylacyl-CoA racemase: a useful marker for diagnosis of small foci of prostatic carcinoma on needle biopsy. Am J Surg Pathol 26: 1169–1174

108. Zhou M, Aydin H, Kanane H et al. 2004 How often does alpha-methylacyl-CoA-racemase contribute to resolving an atypical diagnosis on prostate needle biopsy beyond that provided by basal cell markers? Am J Surg Pathol 28: 239–243

109. Beach R, Gown A M, De Peralta-Venturina M N et al. 2002 P504S immunohistochemical detection in 405 prostatic specimens including 376 18-gauge needle biopsies. Am J Surg Pathol 26: 1588–1596

110. Jiang Z, Fanger G R, Woda B A et al. 2003 Expression of alpha-methylacyl-CoA racemase (P504s) in various malignant neoplasms and normal tissues: a study of 761 cases. Hum Pathol 34: 792–796

111. Sanderson S O, Sebo T J, Murphy L M et al. 2004 An analysis of the p63/alpha-methylacyl coenzyme A racemase immunohistochemical cocktail stain in prostate needle biopsy specimens and tissue microarrays. Am J Clin Pathol 121: 220–225

112. Magi-Galluzzi C, Luo J, Isaacs W B et al. 2003 Alpha-methylacyl-CoA racemase: a variably sensitive immunohistochemical marker for the diagnosis of small prostate cancer foci on needle biopsy. Am J Surg Pathol 27: 1128–1133

113. Zhou M, Jiang Z, Epstein J I 2003 Expression and diagnostic utility of alpha-methylacyl-CoA-racemase (P504S) in foamy gland and pseudohyperplastic prostate cancer. Am J Surg Pathol 27: 772–778

114. Zhou M, Chinnaiyan A M, Kleer C G et al. 2002 Alpha-methylacyl-CoA racemase: a novel tumor marker over-expressed in several human cancers and their precursor lesions. Am J Surg Pathol 26: 926–931

115. Li R, Wheeler T, Dai H et al. 2003 Neural cell adhesion molecule is upregulated in nerves with prostate cancer invasion. Hum Pathol 34: 457–461

116. Allen E A, Kahane H, Epstein J I 1998 Repeat biopsy strategies for men with atypical diagnoses on initial prostate needle biopsy. Urology 52: 803–807

117. Chan T Y, Epstein J I 1999 Follow-up of atypical prostate needle biopsies. Urology 53: 351–355

118. Thorson P, Vollmer R T, Arcangeli C et al. 1998 Minimal carcinoma in prostate needle biopsy specimens: diagnostic features and radical prostatectomy follow-up. Mod Pathol 11: 543–551

119. Fadare O, Wang S, Mariappan M R 2004 Practice patterns of clinicians following isolated diagnoses of atypical small acinar proliferation on prostate biopsy specimens. Arch Pathol Lab Med 128: 557–560

120. Browne T J, Hirsch M S, Brodsky G et al. 2004 Prospective evaluation of AMACR (P504S) and basal cell markers in the assessment of routine prostate needle biopsy specimens. Hum Pathol 35: 1462–1468

121. Catalona W J 1984 Prostate cancer. Grune & Stratton, New York

122. Greene F L, Page D L, Fleming I D et al. 2002 AJCC cancer staging manual. Springer, New York, p 309–316

123. Murphy W M, Dean P J, Brasfield J A 1986 Incidental carcinoma of the prostate. How much sampling is adequate? Am J Surg Pathol: 170–174

124. Epstein J I 1991 The evaluation of radical prostatectomy specimens. Therapeutic and prognostic implications. Pathol Annu 26: 159–210

125. Mills S E, Bostwick D G, Murphy W M 1990 A symposium on the surgical pathology of the prostate. Pathol Annu 25: 109–158

126. Bastacky S I, Walsh P C, Epstein J I 1993 Relationship between perineural tumor invasion on needle biopsy and radical prostatectomy capsular penetration in clinical stage B adenocarcinoma of the prostate. Am J Surg Pathol 17: 336–341

127. Eichelberger L E, Cheng L 2004 Does pT2b prostate carcinoma exist? Critical appraisal of the 2002 TNM classification of prostate carcinoma. Cancer 100: 2573–2576

128. Brawn P N, Ayala A G, von Eschenbach A C 1982 Histologic grading study of prostate adenocarcinoma: the development of a new system and comparison with other methods – a preliminary study. Cancer 49: 525–532

129. Roudier M P, True L D, Higano C S et al. 2003 Phenotypic heterogeneity of end-stage prostate carcinoma metastatic to bone. Hum Pathol 34: 646–653

130. Bubendorf L, Schopfer A, Wagner U et al. 2000 Metastatic patterns of prostate cancer: an autopsy study of 1589 patients. Hum Pathol 31: 578–583

131. Mostofi F K 1975 Grading of prostatic carcinoma. Cancer Chemother Rep 59: 111–117

132. Humphrey P A 2004 Gleason grading and prognostic factors in carcinoma of the prostate. Mod Pathol 17: 292–306

133. Gaeta J F, Asirwatham J E, Miller G et al. 1980 Histologic grading of primary prostatic cancer: a new approach to an old problem. J Urol 123: 689–693

134. Amin M B, Grignon D J, Humphrey P A et al. 2004 Gleason grading of prostate cancer. A contemporary approach. Lippincott, Williams and Wilkins, Philadelphia

134a. Epstein J I, Allsbrook W C Jr, Amin M B et al. 2005 The 2005 International Society of Urologic Pathology (ISUP) consensus conference on Gleason grading of prostatic carcinoma. Am J Surg Pathol 29: 1228–1242

135. McNeal J E, Cohen R J, Brooks J D 2004 Role of cytologic criteria in the histologic diagnosis of Gleason grade 1 prostatic adenocarcinoma. Hum Pathol 32: 441–446

136. Epstein J I, Pound C R, Partin A W et al. 1998 Progression following radical prostatectomy in men with Gleason score 7 tumor. J Urol 160: 97–101

137. Herman C M, Kattan M W, Ohori M et al. 2001 Primary Gleason pattern as a predictor of disease progression in Gleason score 7 prostate cancer: a multivariate analysis of 823 men treated with radical prostatectomy. Am J Surg Pathol 25: 657–660

138. De la Taille A, Viellefond A, Berger N et al. 2003 Evaluation of the interobserver reproducibility of Gleason grading of prostatic adenocarcinoma using tissue microarrays. Hum Pathol 34: 444–449

139. Bostwick D G 1994 Gleason grading of prostatic needle biopsies. Correlation with grade in 316 matched prostatectomies. Am J Surg Pathol 18: 796–803

140. Stamey T A, McNeal J E, Yemoto C M et al. 1999 Biological determinants of cancer progression in men with prostate cancer. JAMA 281: 1395–1400

141. Carlson G D, Calvanese C B, Kahane H et al. 1998 Accuracy of biopsy Gleason scores from a large uropathology laboratory: use of a diagnostic protocol to minimize observer variability. Urology 51: 525–529

142. Dejter S W, Cunningham R E, Noguchi P D 1989 Prognostic significance of DNA ploidy in carcinoma of prostate. Urology 33: 361–366

143. Rubin M A, Bismar T A, Curtis S et al. 2004 Prostate needle biopsy reporting: how are the surgical members of the Society of Urologic Oncology using pathology reports to guide treatment of prostate cancer patients? Am J Surg Pathol 28: 946–952

144. Bismar T A, Lewis J S J, Vollmer R T et al. 2003 Multiple measures of carcinoma extent versus perineural invasion in prostate needle biopsy tissue in prediction of pathologic stage in a screening population. Am J Surg Pathol 27: 432–440

145. Rubin M A, Bassily N, Sanda M et al. 2000 Relationship and significance of greatest percentage of tumor and perineural invasion on needle biopsy in prostatic adenocarcinoma. Am J Surg Pathol 24: 183–189

146. Maru N, Ohori M, Kattan M W et al. 2001 Prognostic significance of the diameter of perineural invasion in radical prostatectomy specimens. Hum Pathol 32: 828–833

147. Herman C M, Wilcox G E, Kattan M W et al. 2000 Lymphovascular invasion as a predictor of disease progression in prostate cancer. Am J Surg Pathol 24: 859–863

148. Rubin M A, Dunn R, Kambham N et al. 2000 Should a Gleason score be assigned to a minute focus of carcinoma on prostate biopsy? . Am J Surg Pathol 24: 1634–1640

149. Kunz G M J, Epstein J I 2003 Should each core with prostate cancer be assigned a separate Gleason score? Hum Pathol 34: 911–914

150. Viglione M P, Potter S, Partin A W et al. 2002 Should the diagnosis of benign prostatic hyperplasia be made on prostate needle biopsy? Hum Pathol 33: 796–800

151. Cheng L, Cheville J C, Bostwick D G 1999 Diagnosis of prostate cancer in needle biopsies after radiation therapy. Am J Surg Pathol 23: 1173–1183

152. Magi-Galluzzi C, Sanderson H, Epstein J I 2003 Atypia in nonneoplastic prostate glands after radiotherapy for prostate cancer: duration of atypia and relation to type of radiotherapy. Am J Surg Pathol 27: 206–212

153. Gaudin P B, Zelefsky M J, Leibel S A et al. 1999 Histopathologic effects of three-dimensional conformal external beam radiation therapy on benign and malignant prostate tissues. Am J Surg Pathol 23: 1021–1031

154. Bostwick D G, Qian J, Civantos F et al. 2004 Does finasteride alter the pathology of the prostate and cancer grading? Clin Prostate Cancer 2: 228–235

155. Bullock M J, Srigley J R, Klotz L H et al. 2002 Pathologic effects of neoadjuvant cyproterone acetate on nonneoplastic prostate, prostatic intraepithelial neoplasia, and adenocarcinoma: a detailed analysis of radical prostatectomy specimens from a randomized trial. Am J Surg Pathol 26: 1400–1413

156. Bentley G, Dey J, Sakr W A et al. 2000 Significance of the Gleason scoring system after neoadjuvant hormonal therapy. Mol Urol 4: 125–131

157. Shabaik A, Wilson S, Bidair M et al. 1995 Pathologic changes in prostate biopsies following cryoablation therapy of prostate carcinoma. J Urol Pathol 3: 183–193

158. Bahn D K, Lee F, Solomon M H et al. 1995 Prostate cancer: US-guided percutaneous cryoablation. Radiology 194: 551–556

159. Ayala A G, Wheeler T M, Shalev M et al. 2000 Cytopathic effect of in situ gene therapy in prostate cancer. Hum Pathol 31: 866–870

160. Grignon D J 2004 Unusual subtypes of prostate cancer. Mod Pathol 17: 316–327

161. Ro J Y, Grignon D J, Amin M B et al. 1997 Atlas of surgical pathology of the male reproductive tract. W B Saunders, Philadelphia

162. Boyd S 1882 A case of colloid scirrhus of the prostate. Trans Pathol Soc Lond 33: 200–203

163. Ro J Y, Grignon D J, Ayala A G 1990 Mucinous adenocarcinoma of the prostate: histochemical and immunohistochemical studies. Hum Pathol 21: 593–600

164. Epstein J I, Lieberman P H 1985 Mucinous adenocarcinoma of the prostate gland. Am J Surg Pathol 9: 299–308

165. Saito S, Iwaki H 1999 Mucin-producing carcinoma of the prostate: review of 88 cases. Urology 54: 141–144

166. Proia A D, McCarty K S, Woodard B H 1981 Prostatic mucinous adenocarcinoma: a Cowper gland carcinoma mimicker. Am J Surg Pathol 5: 701–706

167. Cricco R P, Kassis J 1979 Mucinous adenocarcinoma of prostate. Urology 14: 276–278

168. Alfthan O, Koivuniemi A 1970 Mucinous carcinoma of the prostate: case report. Scand J Urol Nephrol 4: 78–80

169. Sika J V, Buckley J J 1977 Mucus-forming adenocarcinoma of prostate. J Urol 118: 124–125

170. Elbadawi A, Craig W, Linke C A et al. 1979 Prostate mucinous carcinoma. Urology 13: 658–666

171. Patel R C, Dias R, Fernandes M et al. 1981 Adenocarcinoma of the prostate. Mucin secreting. NY State J Med 81: 936–937

172. Chica G, Johnson D E, Ayala A G 1977 Mucinous adenocarcinoma of the prostate. J Urol 118: 124–125

173. Lightbourn G A, Abrams M, Seymour L 1969 Primary mucoid adenocarcinoma of the prostate gland with bladder invasion. J Urol 101: 78–80

174. Lee D W, Ro J Y, Sahin A A 1990 Mucinous adenocarcinoma of the prostate with endobronchial metastasis. Am J Clin Pathol 94: 641–645

175. Odom D G, Donatucci C F, Deshon G E 1986 Mucinous adenocarcinoma of the prostate. Hum Pathol 17: 863–865

176. Manne R K, Haddad F S 1989 Mucinous adenocarcinoma of prostate. Urology 33: 247–249

177. Uchijima Y, Ito H, Takahashi M et al. 1990 Prostate mucinous adenocarcinoma with signet ring cells. Urology 36: 267–268

178. Franks L M, O'Shea J D, Thomson A E R 1964 Mucin in the prostate: a histochemical study in normal glands, latent, clinical, and colloid cancers. Cancer 17: 983–991

179. Pinder S E, McMahon R F T 1990 Mucins in prostatic carcinoma. Histopathology 16: 43–46

180. Nagakura K, Hayakawa M, Mukai K et al. 1986 Mucinous denocarcinoma of prostate: a case report and review of the literature. J Urol 135: 1025–1028

181. Ro J Y, El-Naggar A, Ayala A G 1988 Signet-ring-cell carcinoma of the prostate: electron-microscopic and immunohistochemical studies of eight cases. Am J Surg Pathol 12: 453–460

182. Hejka A G, England D M 1989 Signet ring cell carcinoma of prostate: immunohistochemical and ultrastructural study of a case. Urology 34: 155–158

183. Remmele W, Weber A, Harding P 1988 Primary signet ring cell carcinoma of the prostate. Hum Pathol 19: 478–480

184. Giltman L I 1981 Signet-ring adenocarcinoma of the prostate. J Urol 126: 134–135

185. Kums J J, van Helsdingen P J 1985 Signet-ring-cell carcinoma of the bladder and prostate. Urol Int 40: 116–119

186. Leong F J, Leong A S, Swift J 1996 Signet-ring cell carcinoma of the prostate. Pathol Res Pract 192: 1232–1238

187. Torbenson M, Dhir R, Nangia A et al. 1998 Prostatic carcinoma with signet ring cells: a clinicopathologic and immunohistochemical analysis of 12 cases, with review of the literature. Mod Pathol 11: 552–559

188. Alguacil-Garcia A 1986 Artifactual changes mimicking signet-ring-cell carcinoma of transurethral prostatectomy specimens. Am J Surg Pathol 10: 795–800

189. Schned A R 1987 Artifactual signet-ring cells (letter). Am J Surg Pathol 11: 736–737

190. Fergusson J D, Frank L M 1953 The response of prostatic carcinoma to estrogen treatment. Br J Surg 40: 422–428

191. Melicow M M, Pachter M R 1967 Endometrial carcinoma of prostate utricle (uterus masculinus). Cancer 20: 1715–1722

192. Ro J Y, Ayala A G, Wishnow K I 1988 Prostatic duct adenocarcinoma with endometrioid features: immunohistochemical and electron microscopic study. Semin Diagn Pathol 5: 301–311

193. Zaloudek C, Williams J W, Kempson R L 1976 "Endometrial" adenocarcinoma of the prostate: a distinctive tumor of prostatic duct origin. Cancer 37: 2255–2262

194. Bostwick D G, Kindrachuk R W, Rouse R V 1985 Prostatic adenocarcinoma with endometrioid features: clinical, pathologic, and ultrastructural findings. Am J Surg Pathol 9: 595–609

195. Epstein J I, Woodruff J M 1986 Adenocarcinoma of the prostate with endometrioid features: a light microscopic and immunohistochemical study of ten cases. Cancer 57: 111–119

196. Bock B J, Bostwick D G 1999 Does prostatic ductal adenocarcinoma exist? Am J Surg Pathol 23: 781–785

197. Lee S S 1994 Endometrioid adenocarcinoma of the prostate: a clinicopathologic and immunohistochemical study. J Surg Oncol 55: 235–238

198. Melicow M M, Tannenbaum M 1971 Endometrial carcinoma of uterus masculinus (prostatic utricle): report of 6 cases. J Urol 106: 892–902

199. Young B W, Lagios M D 1973 Endometrial (papillary) carcinoma of the prostatic utricle: response to orchiectomy. A case report. Cancer 32: 1293–1300

200. Sufrin G, Gaeta J, Staubitz W J 1986 Endometrial carcinoma of prostate. Urology 27: 18–29

201. Merchant R F, Graham A R, Bucher W C J 1976 Endometrial carcinoma of prostatic utricle with osseous metastases. Urology 8: 169–173

202. Rotterdam H Z, Melicow M M 1975 Double primary prostatic adenocarcinoma. Urology 6: 245–248

203. Dube V E, Farrow G M, Greene L F 1973 Prostatic adenocarcinoma of ductal origin. Cancer 32: 402–409

204. Dube V E, Joyce G T, Kennedy E 1972 Papillary primary duct adenocarcinoma of the prostate. J Urol 107: 825–826

205. Christensen W N, Steinberg C, Walsh P C et al. 1991 Prostatic duct adenocarcinoma: findings at radical prostatectomy. Cancer 67: 2118–2124

206. Brinker D A, Potter S R, Epstein J I 1999 Ductal adenocarcinoma of the prostate diagnosed on needle biopsy: correlation with clinical and radical prostatectomy findings and progression. Am J Surg Pathol 23: 1471–1479

207. Chan J K, Chow T C, Tsui M S 1987 Prostatic-type polyps of the lower urinary tract: three histogenetic types? Histopathology 11: 789–801

208. Remick D G, Kumar N B 1984 Benign polyps with prostatic-type epithelium of the urethra and the urinary bladder: a suggestion of histogenesis based on histologic and immunohistochemical studies. Am J Surg Pathol 8: 833–839

209. Butterick J D, Schnitzer B, Abell M R 1971 Ectopic prostatic tissue in urethra: a clinicopathological entity and a significant cause of hematuria. J Urol 105: 97–104

210. Stein A J, Prioleau P G, Catalona W J 1980 Adenomatous polyps of the prostatic urethra: a cause of hematospermia. J Urol 124: 298–299

211. Goldstein A M, Bragin S D, Terry R et al. 1981 Prostatic urethral polyps in adults: histopathologic variations and clinical manifestations. J Urol 126: 129–131

212. Baroudy A C, O'Connell J P 1984 Papillary adenoma of the prostatic urethra. J Urol 132: 120–122

213. Tetu B, Ro J Y, Ayala A G 1987 Small cell carcinoma of the prostate. Part 1: a clinicopathologic study of 20 cases. Cancer 59: 1803–1809

214. Schron D S, Gipson T, Mendelsohn G 1984 The histogenesis of small cell carcinoma of the prostate: an immunohistochemical study. Cancer 53: 2478–2480

215. Sarma D P, Weilbaecher T G 1989 Small-cell carcinoma of prostate. Urology 33: 332–335

216. Hagood P G, Johnson F E, Bedrossian C W 1991 Small cell carcinoma of the prostate. Cancer 67: 1046–1050

217. Amato R J, Logothetis C J, Hallinan R 1992 Chemotherapy for small cell carcinoma of prostatic origin. J Urol 147: 935–937

218. Oesterling J E, Hauzeur C G, Farrow G M 1992 Small cell anaplastic carcinoma of the prostate: a clinical, pathologic and immunohistological study of 27 patients. J Urol 147: 804–807

219. Ro J Y, Tetu B, Ayala A G 1987 Small cell carcinoma of the prostate. II. Immunohistochemical and electron microscopic study of 18 cases. Cancer 59: 977–982

219a. Yao J L, Madeb R, Bourne P et al. 2006 Small cell carcinoma of the prostate: an immunohistochemical study. Am J Surg Pathol 30: 705–712

220. Tetu B, Ro J Y, Ayala A G 1989 Small cell carcinoma of prostate associated with myasthenic (Eaton–Lambert) syndrome. Urology 33: 148–152

221. Wenk R E, Bhagavan B S, Levy R 1977 Ectopic ACTH, prostatic oat cell carcinoma and marked hypernatremia. Cancer 40: 773–778

222. Ghali V S, Garcia R L 1984 Prostatic adenocarcinoma with carcinoidal features producing adrenocorticotropic syndrome: immunohistochemical study and review of the literature. Cancer 54: 1043–1048

223. Hindson D A, Knight L L, Ocker J M 1985 Small cell carcinoma of prostate: transient complete remission with chemotherapy. Urology 26: 182–184

224. Johnson D E, Chalbaud R, Ayala A G 1974 Secondary tumors of the prostate. J Urol 112: 507–508

225. Zein T A, Huben R, Lane W 1985 Secondary tumors of the prostate. J Urol 133: 615–616

226. Smedley H M, Brown C, Turner A 1983 Ectopic ACTH-producing lung cancer presenting with prostatic metastasis. Postgrad Med J 59: 371–372

227. Ordonez N G 2000 Value of thyroid transcription factor-1 immunostaining in distinguishing small cell lung carcinomas from other small cell carcinomas. Am J Surg Pathol 24: 1217–1223

228. Weaver M G, Abdul-Karim F W, Srigley J R 1992 Paneth cell-like change of the prostate gland. A histological, immunohistochemical, and electron microscopic study. Am J Surg Pathol 16: 62–68

229. Adlakha H, Bostwick D G 1994 Paneth cell-like change in prostatic adenocarcinoma represents neuroendocrine differentiation: report of 30 cases. Hum Pathol 25: 135–139

230. Accetta P A, Gardner W A 1982 Squamous metastases from prostatic adenocarcinoma. Lab Invest 46: 2A

231. Moyana T N 1987 Adenosquamous carcinoma of the prostate. Am J Surg Pathol 11: 403–407

232. Saito R, Davis B K, Ollapally E P 1984 Adenosquamous carcinoma of the prostate. Hum Pathol 15: 87–89

233. Lager D J, Goeken J A, Kemp J D 1988 Squamous metaplasia of the prostate: an immunohistochemical study. Am J Clin Pathol 90: 597–601

234. Bennett R S, Edgerton E O 1973 Mixed prostatic carcinoma. J Urol 110: 561–563

235. Gray G F, Marshall V F 1975 Squamous carcinoma of the prostate. J Urol 113: 736–738

236. Mai K T, Leahy C F 1996 Squamous cell carcinoma occurring as a circumscribed nodule in the transition zone of the prostate. J Urol Pathol 5: 85–92

237. Parwani A V, Kronz J D, Genega E M et al. 2004 Prostate carcinoma with squamous differentiation: an analysis of 33 cases. Am J Surg Pathol 28: 651–657

238. Mott L J 1979 Squamous cell carcinoma of the prostate: report of 2 cases and review of the literature. J Urol 121: 833–835

239. Sieracki J C 1955 Epidermoid carcinoma of the human prostate: report of three cases. Lab Invest 4: 232–240

240. Sarma D P, Weilbaecher T G, Moon T D 1991 Squamous cell carcinoma of prostate. Urology 37: 260–262
241. Wernert N, Goebbels R, Bonkhoff H 1990 Squamous cell carcinoma of the prostate. Histopathology 17: 339–344
242. Al Adnani M S 1985 Schistosomiasis, metaplasia and squamous cell carcinoma of the prostate: histogenesis of the squamous cells determined by localization of specific markers. Neoplasma 32: 613–622
243. Gattuso P, Carson H J, Candel A et al. 1995 Adenosquamous carcinoma of the prostate. Hum Pathol 26: 123–126
244. Corder M P, Cicmil G A 1976 Effective treatment of metastatic squamous cell carcinoma of the prostate with adriamycin. J Urol 115: 222
245. Thompson G J, Albers D D, Broders A C 1953 Unusual carcinomas involving the prostate gland. J Urol 69: 416–425
246. Goebbels R, Amberger L, Wernert N l 1985 Urothelial carcinoma of the prostate. Appl Pathol 3: 242–254
247. Ro J Y, Ayala A G, El-Naggar A 1987 Seminal vesicle involvement by in situ and invasive transitional cell carcinoma of the bladder. Am J Surg Pathol 11: 951–958
248. Wishnow K I, Ro J Y 1988 Importance of early treatment of transitional cell carcinoma of prostatic ducts. Urology 32: 11–12
249. Terris M K, Villers A, Freiha F S 1990 Transrectal ultrasound appearance of transitional cell carcinoma involving the prostate. J Urol 143: 952–956
250. Kirk D, Savage A, Makepeace M A et al. 1981 Transitional cell carcinoma involving the prostate – an unfavorable prognostic sign in the management of bladder cancer? Br J Urol 53: 610–612
251. Mahadevia P S, Koss L G, Tar I J 1986 Prostatic involvement in bladder cancer. Prostate mapping in 20 cystoprostatectomy specimens. Cancer 58: 2096–2102
252. Schellhammer P F, Bean M A, Whitmore W F J 1977 Prostatic involvement by transitional cell carcinoma: pathogenesis, patterns and prognosis. J Urol 118: 399–403
253. Amin M B, Murphy W M, Reuter V E 1997 Controversies in the pathology of transitional cell carcinoma of the urinary bladder, part II. In: Fechner F E, Rosen P P (eds) ASCP reviews in pathology, vol. 1. ASCP Press, Chicago, p 1–38
254. Cheville J C, Dundore P A, Bostwick D G 1998 Transitional cell carcinoma of the prostate. Clinical, pathological study of 50 cases. Cancer 82: 703–707
255. Wendelken J R, Schellhammer P F, Ladaga L E et al. 1979 Transitional cell carcinoma: cause of refractory cancer of the prostate. Urology 13: 557–560
256. Tomaszewski J E, Korat O C, LiVolsi V A 1986 Paget's disease of urethral meatus following transitional cell carcinoma of the bladder. J Urol 135: 368–370
257. Wood D P J, Montie J E, Pontes J E 1989 Transitional cell carcinoma of the prostate in cystoprostatectomy specimens removed for bladder cancer. J Urol 141: 346–349
258. Mhawech P, Uchida T, Pelte M F 2002 Immunohistochemical profile of high-grade urothelial bladder carcinoma and prostate adenocarcinoma. Hum Pathol 33: 1136–1140
259. Shannon R L, Ro J Y, Grignon D J 1992 Sarcomatoid carcinoma of the prostate: a clinicopathologic study of 12 patients. Cancer 69: 2676–2682
260. Ro J Y, Ayala A G, Sella A 1987 Sarcomatoid renal cell carcinoma: a clinicopathologic study of 42 cases. Cancer 59: 516–526
261. Ro J Y, Ayala A G, Wishnow K I 1988 Sarcomatoid bladder carcinoma: clinicopathologic and immunohistochemical study of 44 cases. Surg Pathol 2: 359–374
262. Dundore P A, Chevill J C, Nascimento A G et al. 1995 Carcinosarcoma of prostate. Report of 21 cases. Cancer 76: 1035–1042
263. Ohtsuki Y, Ro J Y, Ordonez N G 1996 Sarcomatoid carcinoma of the prostate with rhabdomyosarcomatous differentiation. J Urol Pathol 5: 157–163
264. Wick M R, Young R H, Malvesta R 1989 Prostatic carcinosarcomas. Clinical, histologic, and immunohistochemical data on two cases, with a review of the literature. Am J Clin Pathol 92: 131–139
265. Ogawa K, Kim Y C, Nakashima Y 1987 Expression of epithelial markers in sarcomatoid carcinoma: an immunohistochemical study. Histopathology 11: 511–522
266. Lauwers G Y, Schevchuk M, Armenakas N 1993 Carcinosarcoma of the prostate. Am J Surg Pathol 17: 342–349
267. Montironi R, Alexander E, Bostwick D G 1997 Prostate pathology case study seminar. Virchows Arch 430: 83–94
268. Ordonez N G, Ro J Y, Ayala A G 1992 Metastatic prostatic carcinoma presenting as an oncocytic tumor. Am J Surg Pathol 16: 1007–1012
269. Singh H, Flores-Sandoval N, Abrams J 2003 Renal-type clear cell carcinoma occurring in the prostate. Am J Surg Pathol 27: 407–410
270. Pan C C, Chiang H, Chang Y H et al. 2000 Tubulocystic clear cell adenocarcinoma arising within the prostate. Am J Surg Pathol 24: 1433–1436
271. Bostwick D G 1988 Premalignant lesions of the prostate. Semin Diagn Pathol 5: 240–253
272. Bostwick D G, Srigley J, Grignon D 1993 Atypical adenomatous hyperplasia of the prostate: morphologic criteria for its distinction from well-differentiated carcinoma. Hum Pathol 24: 819–832
273. Bostwick D G, Algaba F, Ayala A G 1994 Consensus statement on terminology: recommendation to use atypical adenomatous hyperplasia in place of adenosis of the prostate. Am J Surg Pathol 18: 1069–1071
274. Gaudin P B, Epstein J I 1994 Adenosis of the prostate: histologic features in transurethral resection specimens. Am J Surg Pathol 18: 863–870
275. Lopez-Beltran A, Artacho-Perula E, Luque-Barona R J et al. 2000 Nuclear volume estimates in prostatic atypical adenomatous hyperplasia. Anal Quant Cytol Histol 22: 438–444
276. Doll J A, Zhu X, Furman J et al. 1999 Genetic analysis of prostatic atypical adenomatous hyperplasia (adenosis). Am J Pathol 155: 967–971
277. Cheng L, Shan A, Cheville J C et al. 1998 Atypical adenomatous hyperplasia of the prostate: a premalignant lesion? Cancer Res 58: 389–391
278. Bostwick D G, Qian J 1995 Atypical adenomatous hyperplasia of the prostate. Relationship with carcinoma in 217 whole-mount radical prostatectomies. Am J Surg Pathol 19: 506–518
279. Mittal B V, Amin M B, Kinare S G 1989 Spectrum of histologic lesions in 185 consecutive prostatic specimens. J Postgrad Med 35: 157–161
280. Srigley J R, Toth P, Hartwick R W 1989 Atypical histologic patterns in cases of benign prostatic hyperplasia [abstract]. Lab Invest 60: 90A
281. Yang X J, Wu C L, Woda B A et al. 2002 Expression of alpha-methylacyl-CoA racemase (P504S) in atypical adenomatous hyperplasia of the prostate. Am J Surg Pathol 26: 921–925
282. Young R H 1988 Pseudoneoplastic lesions of the prostate gland. Pathol Annu 23: 105–128
283. Cleary K R, Choi H Y, Ayala A G 1983 Basal cell hyperplasia of the prostate. Am J Clin Pathol 80: 850–854
284. Grignon D J, Ro J Y, Ordonez N G et al. 1988 Basal cell hyperplasia, adenoid basal cell tumor, and adenoid cystic carcinoma of the prostate gland: an immunohistochemical study. Hum Pathol 19: 1425–1433
285. Sesterhenn I, Mostofi F K, Davis C J 1987 Basal cell hyperplasia and basal cell carcinoma. Lab Invest 56: 71A (abstract)
286. Hosler G A, Epstein J I 2005 Basal cell hyperplasia: an unusual diagnostic dilemma on prostate needle biopsies. Hum Pathol 36: 480–485
287. Van de Voorde W, Baldewijns M, Lauweryns J 1994 Florid basal cell hyperplasia of the prostate. Histopathology 24: 341–348
288. Sahin A A, Ro J Y, Troncoso P et al. 1990 Benign prostatic lesions with small acinar pattern mimicking adenocarcinoma. In: Damjanov I, Mills S E, Cohen A H et al. (eds) Progress in reproductive and urinary tract pathology. Field and Wood, Philadelphia, p 69–86
289. Yang X J, Tretiakova M S, Sengupta E et al. 2003 Florid basal cell hyperplasia of the prostate: a histological, ultrastructural, and immunohistochemical analysis. Hum Pathol 34: 462070
290. Thorson P, Swanson P E, Vollmer R T et al. 2003 Basal cell hyperplasia in the peripheral zone of the prostate. Mod Pathol 16: 598–606
291. Vales-Depena A 1979 Prostate, Histology of the fetus and newborn. W B Saunders, Philadelphia, p 415–429
292. Ronnett B M, Epstein J I 1989 A case showing sclerosing adenosis and an unusual form of basal cell hyperplasia of the prostate. Am J Surg Pathol 13: 866–872
293. Ayala A G, Srigley J R, Ro J Y 1986 Clear cell cribriform hyperplasia of prostate: report of 10 cases. Am J Surg Pathol 10: 665–671
294. Rioux-Leclercq N C, Epstein J I 2002 Unusual morphologic patterns of basal cell hyperplasia of the prostate. Am J Surg Pathol 26: 237–243
295. McNeal J E 1988 Normal histology of the prostate. Am J Surg Pathol 12: 619–633
296. Molinie V, Herve J M, Lebret T 2004 Value of the antibody cocktail anti p63 + anti p504s for the diagnosis of prostatic cancer. Ann Pathol 24: 6–16
297. Hendrick L, Epstein J I 1989 Use of keratin 903 as an adjunct in the diagnosis of prostate carcinoma. Am J Surg Pathol 13: 389–396
298. Tannenbaum M, Becker S W 1977 Histopathology of the prostate gland. In: Tannenbaum M (ed) Urologic pathology: the prostate. Lea & Febiger, Philadelphia, p 303–397
299. Totten R S, Heinemann M W, Hudson P B et al. 1953 Microscopic differential diagnosis of latent carcinoma of prostate. Arch Pathol 55: 131–141
300. Harade M, Mostofi F K, Corle D K et al. 1977 Preliminary studies on histologic prognostic significance in cancer of the prostate. Cancer Treat Rep 61: 223–225
301. Myers R P, Neves R J, Farrow G M et al. 1982 Nucleolar grading of prostatic adenocarcinoma: light microscopic correlation with disease progression. Prostate 3: 423–432
302. Tannenbaum M, Tannenbaum S, DeSanctis P N et al. 1982 Prognostic significance of nucleolar surface area in prostate cancer. Urology 19: 546–551
303. Derme G B 1978 Basal cell proliferation in benign prostatic hyperplasia. Cancer 41: 1857–1862
304. Lin J I, Cohen E L, Villacin A B 1978 Basal cell adenoma of prostate. Urology 11: 409–410
305. Devaraj L T, Bostwick D G 1993 Atypical basal cell hyperplasia of the prostate: immunohistochemical profile and proposed classification of basal cell proliferations. Am J Surg Pathol 17: 645–659
306. Epstein J I, Armas O A 1992 Atypical basal cell hyperplasia of the prostate. Am J Surg Pathol 16: 1205–1214
307. Ayala A G, Ro J Y 1989 Premalignant lesions of the urothelium and transitional cell tumors. In: Young R H (ed) Pathology of the urinary bladder. Churchill Livingstone, New York, p 65–101
308. Reed R J 1984 Consultation case: prostate (prostatectomy) – adenoid basal cell tumor-multifocal basal cell hyperplasia. Am J Surg Pathol 8: 699–704
309. Young R H, Frierson H F, Mills S E 1988 Adenoid cystic-like tumor of the prostate gland. A report of two cases and review of the literature on "adenoid cystic carcinoma" of the prostate. Am J Clin Pathol 89: 49–56
310. Iczkowski K A, Ferguson K L, Grier D D et al. 2003 Adenoid cystic/basal cell carcinoma of the prostate: clinicopathologic findings in 19 cases. Am J Surg Pathol 27: 1523–1529

311. Yang X J, McEntee M, Epstein J I 1998 Distinction of basaloid carcinoma of the prostate from benign basal cell lesions by using immunohistochemistry for bcl-2 and Ki-67. Hum Pathol 29: 1447–1450
312. McKenney J K, Amin M B, Srigley J R 2004 Basal cell proliferations of the prostate other than usual basal cell hyperplasia: a clinicopathologic study of 23 cases, including four carcinomas, with a proposed classification. Am J Surg Pathol 28: 1289–1298
313. Frauenhoffer E E, Ro J Y, El-Naggar A K 1991 Clear cell cribriform hyperplasia of the prostate: immunohistochemical and DNA flow cytometric study. Am J Clin Pathol 95: 446–453
314. McNeal J E, Reese J H, Redwine E A 1986 Cribriform adenocarcinoma of the prostate. Cancer 58: 1714–1719
315. Chen K T, Schiff J J 1983 Adenomatoid prostatic tumor. Urology 21: 88–89
316. Hulman G 1989 "Pseudoadenomatoid" tumor of prostate. Histopathology 14: 317–319
317. Sesterhenn I A, Mostofi F K 1988 Fibroepithelial nodules of the prostate simulating carcinoma. Lab Invest 58: 83A
318. Young R H, Clement P B 1987 Sclerosing adenosis of the prostate. Arch Pathol Lab Med 111: 363–366
319. Sakamoto N, Tsuneyoshi M, Enjoji M 1991 Sclerosing adenosis of the prostate. Histopathologic and immunohistochemical analysis. Am J Surg Pathol 15: 660–667
320. Luque R J, Lopez-Beltran A, Perez-Seoane C et al. 2003 Sclerosing adenosis of the prostate. Histologic features in needle biopsy specimens. Arch Pathol Lab Med 127: e14–16
321. Jones E C, Clement P B, Young R H 1991 Sclerosing adenosis of the prostate gland. A clinicopathological and immunohistochemical study of 11 cases. Am J Surg Pathol 15: 1171–1180
322. Gikas P W, Del Buono E A, Epstein J I 1993 Florid hyperplasia of mesonephric remnants involving prostate and periprostatic tissue. Possible confusion with adenocarcinoma. Am J Surg Pathol 17: 454–460
323. Bostwick D G, Qian J, Ma J et al. 2003 Mesonephric remnants of the prostate: incidence and histologic spectrum. Mod Pathol 16: 630–635
324. Amin M B, Tamboli P, Varma M et al. 1995 Florid hyperplasia of mesonephric remnants: yet another differential diagnostic consideration under "small acinar proliferations of the prostate." Adv Anat Pathol 2: 108–113
325. Jimenez R E, Raval M F, Spanta R et al. 1998 Mesonephric remnants hyperplasia. Pitfall in the diagnosis of prostatic adenocarcinoma. J Urol Pathol 9: 83–92
326. Ayala A G, Tibbs R F, Tamboli P et al. 2004 High-grade prostatic intraepithelial neoplasia (PIN)-like lesion; a possible embryologic remnant mimicking carcinoma. Mod Pathol 17: 138A (abstract)
327. Gaudin P B, Wheeler T M, Epstein J I 1995 Verumontanum mucosal gland hyperplasia (VMGH) in prostatic needle biopsy specimens: a mimic of low-grade prostatic adenocarcinoma. Am J Clin Pathol 104: 620–626
328. Muezzinoglu B, Erdamar S, Chakraborty S et al. 2001 Verumontanum mucosal gland hyperplasia is associated with atypical adenomatous hyperplasia of the prostate. Arch Pathol Lab Med 125: 358–360
329. Gagucas R J, Brown R W, Wheeler T M 1995 Verumontanum mucosal gland hyperplasia. Am J Surg Pathol 19: 30–36
330. Davis T A 1949 Hamartoma of the urinary bladder. Northwest Med 48: 182–185
331. Friedman N B, Kuhlenbeck H 1950 Adenomatoid tumors of the bladder reproducing renal structures (nephrogenic adenomas). J Urol 64: 657–670
332. Peterson L J, Matsumoto L M 1978 Nephrogenic adenoma in urethral diverticulum. Urology 11: 193–195
333. Young R H, Scully R E 1986 Nephrogenic adenoma. A report of 15 cases, review of the literature, and comparison with clear cell adenocarcinoma of the urinary tract. Am J Surg Pathol 10: 268–275
334. Bhagavan B S, Tiamson E M, Wenk R E 1981 Nephrogenic adenoma of the urinary bladder and urethra. Hum Pathol 12: 907–916
335. Navarre R J J, Loening S A, Platz C 1982 Nephrogenic adenoma: a report of 9 cases and review of the literature. J Urol 127: 775–779
336. Rubin P, Murphy W M, Driver C 1985 Nephrogenic adenoma. Urology 25: 190–193
337. Newman J, Antonakopoulos G N 1985 Widespread mucous metaplasia of the urinary bladder with nephrogenic adenoma. Arch Pathol Lab Med 109: 560–563
338. McIntire T L, Soloway M S, Murphy W M 1987 Nephrogenic adenoma. Urology 29: 237–241
339. Malpica A, Ro J Y, Troncoso P 1994 Nephrogenic adenoma of prostatic urethra involving the prostate gland: a clinicopathologic and immunohistochemical study of eight cases. Hum Pathol 25: 390–395
340. Oliva E, Young R H 1995 Nephrogenic adenoma of the urinary tract: a review of the microscopic appearance of 80 cases with emphasis on unusual features. Mod Pathol 8: 722–730
341. Devine P, Ucci A A, Krain H 1984 Nephrogenic adenoma and embryonic kidney tubules share PNA receptor sites. Am J Clin Pathol 81: 728–732
342. Murphy W M 1989 Diseases of the urinary bladder, urethra, ureters, and renal pelvis. In: Murphy W M (ed) Urological pathology. W B Saunders, Philadelphia, p 34–146
343. Peterson R O 1986 Urologic pathology. J B Lippincott, Philadelphia
344. Amin M B, Young R H 1997 Primary carcinoma of the urethra. Semin Diagn Pathol 14: 147–160
345. Drew P A, Murphy W M, Civantos F et al. 1996 The histogenesis of clear cell adenocarcinoma of the lower urinary tract. Case series and review of the literature. Hum Pathol 27: 248–252
346. Gupta A, Wang H L, Policarpio-Nicolas M L et al. 2004 Expression of alpha-methylacyl-coenzyme A racemase in nephrogenic adenoma. Am J Surg Pathol 28: 1224–1229
347. Allan C H, Epstein J I 2001 Nephrogenic adenoma of the prostatic urethra: a mimicker of prostate adenocarcinoma. Am J Surg Pathol 25: 802–808
348. Skinnider B F, Oliva E, Young R H et al. 2004 Expression of alpha-methylacyl-CoA racemase (P504S) in nephrogenic adenoma: a significant immunohistochemical pitfall compounding the differential diagnosis with prostatic adenocarcinoma. Am J Surg Pathol 28: 701–705
349. Hara S, Horie A 1977 Prostatic caruncle: a urethral papillary tumor derived from prolapse of the prostatic ducts. J Urol 117: 303–305
350. Mugler K C, Woods J E 2003 Pathologic quiz case: urethral mass in a 62-year-old man. Prostatic-type polyp of verumontanum. Arch Pathol Lab Med 127: e351–e352
351. Nesbit R M 1962 The genesis of benign polyps in the prostatic urethra. J Urol 87: 416–418
352. Walker A N, Mills S E, Fechner R E 1983 Epithelial polyps of the prostatic urethra. Am J Surg Pathol 7: 351–356
353. Craig J R, Hart W R 1975 Benign polyps with prostatic type epithelium of the urethra. Am J Clin Pathol 63: 343–347
354. Klein H Z, Rosenberg M L 1984 Ectopic prostatic tissue in bladder trigone: distinctive cause of hematuria. Urology 23: 81–82
355. Mostofi F K, Davis C J 1985 Male reproductive system and prostate. In: Kissane J M (ed) Anderson's pathology. C V Mosby, St. Louis, p 791–831
356. Eglen D E, Pontius E E 1984 Benign prostatic epithelial polyp of the urethra. J Urol 131: 120–122
357. Jensen K M, Sonneland P, Madsen P O 1983 Seminal vesicle tissue in "resectate" of transurethral resection of prostate. Urology 22: 20–23
358. Tsuang M T, Weiss M A, Evans A T 1981 Transurethral resection of the prostate with partial resection of the seminal vesicle. J Urol 126: 615–617
359. Shah R B, Lee M W, Giraldo A A et al. 2001 Histologic and histochemical characterization of seminal vesicle intraluminal secretions. Arch Pathol Lab Med 125: 141–145
360. Leroy X, Ballereau C, Villers A et al. 2003 MUC6 is a marker of seminal vesicle-ejaculatory duct epithelium and is useful for the differential diagnosis with prostate adenocarcinoma. Am J Surg Pathol 27: 519–521
361. Melcher M P 1986 Bulbourethral glands of Cowper. Arch Pathol Lab Med 110: 991 (letter)
362. Saboorian M H, Huffman H, Ashfaq R et al. 1997 Distinguishing Cowper's glands from neoplastic and pseudoneoplastic lesions of prostate. Immunohistochemical and ultrastructural studies. Am J Surg Pathol 21: 1069–1074
363. Cina S J, Silberman M A, Kahane H et al. 1997 Diagnosis of Cowper's glands on prostate needle biopsy. Am J Surg Pathol 21: 550–555
364. Shiraishi T, Kusano I, Watanabe M 1993 Mucous gland metaplasia of the prostate. Am J Surg Pathol 17: 618–622
365. Grignon D J, O'Malley F P 1993 Mucinous metaplasia in the prostate gland. Am J Surg Pathol 17: 287–290
366. Rode J, Bentley A, Parkinson C 1990 Paraganglial cells of urinary bladder and prostate: potential diagnostic problem. J Clin Pathol 43: 13–16
367. Ostrowski M L, Wheeler T M 1994 Paraganglia of the prostate; location, frequency, and differentiation from prostatic adenocarcinoma. Am J Surg Pathol 18: 412–420
368. Parwani A V, Cao D, Epstein J I 2004 Pathologic quiz case: a 35-year old man with hematuria. Paraganglioma involving the prostate. Arch Pathol Lab Med 128: e104–e106
369. Gardner W A J, Culberson D E 1987 Atrophy and proliferation in the young adult prostate. J Urol 137: 53–56
370. Moore R A 1936 The evolution and involution of the prostate gland. Am J Pathol 12: 599–624
371. Franks L M 1954 Atrophy and hyperplasia in the prostate proper. J Pathol Bacteriol 68: 617–621
372. Liavag I 1968 Atrophy and regeneration in the pathogenesis of prostate carcinoma. Acta Pathol Microbiol Scand 73: 338–350
373. Billis A, Magna L A 2003 Inflammatory atrophy of the prostate. Prevalence and significance. Arch Pathol Lab Med 127: 840–844
374. Meirelles L R, Billis A, Cotta A C et al. 2002 Prostatic atrophy: evidence for a possible role of local ischemia in its pathogenesis. Int Urol Nephrol 34: 345–350
375. McNeal J E 1983 The prostate gland: morphology and pathology. Monogr Urol 4: 3–33
376. Billis A, Magna L A 2000 Prostate elastosis: a microscopic feature useful for the diagnosis of postatrophic hyperplasia. Arch Pathol Lab Med 124: 1306–1309
377. O'Malley F P, Grignon D J, Shum D T 1990 Usefulness of immunoperoxidase staining with high molecular weight cytokeratin in the differential diagnosis of small acinar lesions of the prostate gland. Virchows Arch [A] 417: 191–196
378. Brawer M K, Nagle R B, Pitts W et al. 1989 Keratin immunoreactivity as an aid to the diagnosis of persistent adenocarcinoma in irradiated human prostates. Cancer 63: 454–460
379. Abrahams N A, Bostwick D G, Ormsby A H et al. 2003 Distinguishing atrophy and high-grade prostatic intraepithelial neoplasia from prostatic adenocarcinoma with and without previous adjuvant hormone therapy with the aid of cytokeratin 5/6. Am J Clin Pathol 120: 368–376
380. Amin M B, Tamboli P, Varma M et al. 1999 Postatrophic hyperplasia of the prostate gland: a detailed analysis of its morphology in needle biopsy specimens. Am J Surg Pathol 8: 925–931

381. Cheville J C, Bostwick D G 1995 Post-atrophic hyperplasia of the prostate. A histologic mimic of prostatic adenocarcinoma. Am J Surg Pathol 19: 1068–1076

382. Anton R C, Kattan M W, Chakraborty S et al. 1999 Postatrophic hyperplasia of the prostate: lack of association with prostate cancer. Am J Surg Pathol 23: 932–936

383. McNeal J E 1979 The origin and evolution of prostatic cancer. Cancer Detect Prev 2: 565–577

384. McNeal J E 1981 Normal and pathologic anatomy of prostate. Urology 17: 11–16

385. Tsujimoto Y, Takayama H, Nonomura N et al. 2002 Postatrophic hyperplasia of the prostate in Japan: histologic and immunohistochemical features and p53 gene mutation analysis. Prostate 52: 279–287

386. Ruska K M, Sauvageot J, Epstein J I 1998 Histology and cellular kinetics of prostatic atrophy. Am J Surg Pathol 22: 1073–1077

387. Shah R, Mucci N R, Amin A et al. 2001 Postatrophic hyperplasia of the prostate gland: neoplastic precursor or innocent bystander? Am J Pathol 158: 1767–1773

388. Ayala A G, Ro J Y, Babaian R 1989 The prostate capsule: does it exist? Am J Surg Pathol 13: 21–27

389. Graversen P H, England D M, Madsen P O 1988 Significance of striated muscle in curettings of the prostate. J Urol 139: 751–753

390. Manley C B 1966 The striated muscle of the prostate. J Urol 95: 234–240

391. Hasui Y, Shinkawa T, Osada Y 1989 Striated muscle in the biopsy specimen of the prostate. Prostate 14: 65–69

392. McIntire T L, Franzini D A 1986 The presence of benign prostatic glands in perineural spaces. J Urol 135: 507–509

393. Cramer S F 1981 Benign glandular inclusion in prostatic nerve. Am J Clin Pathol 75: 854–855

394. Carstens P H 1980 Perineural glands in normal and hyperplastic prostates. J Urol 123: 686–688

395. Choi Y H, Namkung S, Ryu B Y et al. 2000 Giant multilocular prostatic cystadenoma. J Urol 163: 246–247

396. Sung C O, Seo J, Song S Y 2004 Giant multilocular cystadenoma of the prostate. Kor J Pathol 38: 106–108

397. Franks L M 1954 Benign nodular hyperplasia of the prostate: a review. Ann R Coll Surg 14: 92–106

398. Regan J B, Barrett D M, Wold L E 1987 Giant leiomyoma of the prostate. Arch Pathol Lab Med 11: 381–382

399. Rosen Y, Ambiavagar P C, Vuletin J C 1980 Atypical leiomyoma of prostate. Urology 15: 183–185

400. Patch F S, Rhea L J 1935 Leiomyoma of the prostate gland. Br J Urol 7: 213–228

401. Michaels M M, Brown H E, Favino C J 1974 Leiomyoma of the prostate. Urology 3: 617–620

402. Begin L R 1993 Mucosubstance-rich myxoid stromal nodule of the prostate. Arch Pathol Lab Med 117: 318–320

403. Belis J A, Post G J, Rochman S C 1979 Genitourinary leiomyomas. Urology 13: 424–429

404. Kaufman J J, Berneike R R 1951 Leiomyoma of the prostate. J Urol 65: 297–310

405. Leonard A, Baert L, Van Praet F 1989 Solitary leiomyoma of the prostate. Br J Urol 60: 184–185

406. Wang X, Bostwick D G 1997 Prostatic stromal hyperplasia with atypia; a study of 11 cases. J Urol Pathol 6: 15–25

407. Attah E B, Powell M E 1977 Atypical stromal hyperplasia of the prostate gland. Am J Clin Pathol 67: 324–327

408. Leong S S, Vogt P J, Yu G S 1988 Atypical stromal smooth muscle hyperplasia of prostate. Urology 31: 163–167

409. Tetu B, Srigley J R, Bostwick D G 1990 Soft tissue tumors. In: Bostwick D G (ed) Pathology of the prostate. Churchill Livingstone, New York, p 117–135

410. Young R H, Scully R E 1987 Pseudosarcomatous lesions of the urinary bladder, prostate gland, and urethra; a report of three cases and review of the literature. Arch Pathol Lab Med 111: 354–358

411. Karolyi P, Endes P, Krasznai G 1988 Bizarre leiomyoma of the prostate. Virchow's Arch [A] 412: 383–386

412. Persaud V, Douglas L L 1982 Bizarre (atypical) leiomyoma of the prostate gland. West Ind Med J 31: 217–220

413. Tetu B, Ro J Y, Ayala A G 1988 Atypical spindle cell lesions of the prostate. Semin Diagn Pathol 5: 284–293

414. Gaudin P B, Rosai J, Epstein J J 1998 Sarcomas and related proliferative lesions of specialized prostatic stroma: a clinicopathologic study of 22 cases. Am J Surg Pathol 58: 43–50

415. Smith B H, Dehner L P 1972 Sarcoma of the prostate gland. Am J Clin Pathol 58: 43–50

416. Mottola A, Selli C, Carini M 1985 Leiomyosarcoma of the prostate. Eur Urol 11: 131–133

417. Muzafer M H 1987 Large leiomyoma of prostate. Br J Urol 5: 284–293

418. Vassilakis G B 1978 Pure leiomyoma of prostate. Urology 11: 93–94

419. Ro J Y, Grignon D J, Ayala A G 1988 Blue nevus and melanosis of the prostate: electron-microscopic and immunohistochemical studies. Am J Clin Pathol 90: 530–535

420. Lew S, Richter S, Jelin N 1991 A blue naevus of the prostate: a light microscopic study including an investigation of S-100 protein positive cells in the normal and in the diseased gland. Histopathology 18: 443–448

421. Langley J W, Weitzner S 1974 Blue nevus and melanosis of prostate. J Urol 112: 359–361

422. Brennick J B, O'Connell J X, Dickersin G R 1994 Lipofuscin pigmentation (so-called melanosis) of the prostate. Am J Surg Pathol 18: 446–454

423. Farid M K, Gahukamble L D 1995 Melanosis of the prostate in an elderly patient – a case report. Central Afr J Med 41: 101–102

424. Nigogosyan G, de la Pava S, Pickren J W 1963 Blue nevus of the prostate gland. Cancer 16: 1097–1099

425. Goldman R L 1968 Melanogenic epithelium in the prostate gland. Am J Clin Pathol 49: 75–78

426. Tannenbaum M 1974 Differential diagnosis in uropathology. III. Melanotic lesions of the prostate: blue nevus and prostatic epithelial melanosis. Urology 4: 617–621

427. Aguilar M, Gaffney E F, Finnerty D P 1982 Prostatic melanosis with involvement of benign and malignant epithelium. J Urol 128: 825–827

428. Block N L, Weber D, Schinella R 1972 Blue nevi and other melanotic lesions of the prostate: report of 3 cases and review of the literature. J Urol 107: 85–87

429. Gardner W A J, Spitz W U 1971 Melanosis of the prostate gland. Am J Clin Pathol 56: 762–764

430. Guillan R A, Zelman S 1970 The incidence and possible origin of melanin in the prostate. J Urol 104: 151–153

431. Rios C N, Wright J R 1976 Melanosis of the prostate gland: report of a case with neoplastic epithelium involvement. J Urol 115: 616–617

432. Jao W, Fretzin D F, Christ M L 1971 Blue nevus of the prostate gland. Arch Pathol Lab Med 91: 187–191

433. Kovi J, Jackson A G, Jackson M A 1977 Blue nevus of the prostate: ultrastructural study. Urology 9: 576–578

434. Martinez Marinez C J, Garcia Gonzalez R, Castaneda Casanova A L 1992 Blue nevus of the prostate: report of two new cases with immunohistochemical and electron-microscopic studies. Eur Urol 22: 339–342

435. Das Gupta T K, Brasfield R D, Paglia M A 1969 Primary melanomas in unusual sites. Surg Gynecol Obstet 128: 841–848

436. Berry N E, Reese L 1953 Malignant melanoma which had its first clinical manifestations in the prostate gland. J Urol 69: 286–290

437. Kafandaris P M, Polyzonis M B 1983 Fibroadenoma-like foci in human prostatic nodular hyperplasia. Prostate 4: 33–36

438. Cox R, Dawson M P 1960 A curious prostatic tumour: probably a true mixed tumour (cystadenoleiomyofibroma). Br J Urol 32: 306–311

439. Manivel C, Shenoy B V, Wick M R 1986 Cystosarcoma phyllodes of the prostate. Arch Pathol Lab Med 110: 534–538

440. Kirkland K L, Bale P M 1967 A cystic adenoma of the prostate. J Urol 97: 324–327

441. Attah E B, Nkposong E O 1976 Phyllodes type of atypical prostatic hyperplasia. J Urol 115: 762–764

442. Reese J H, Lombard C M, Krone K 1987 Phyllodes type of atypical prostatic hyperplasia: a report of 3 new cases. J Urol 138: 623–626

443. Ito H, Ito M, Mitsuhata N 1989 Phyllodes tumor of the prostate: a case report. Jpn J Clin Oncol 19: 299–304

444. Kendall A R, Stein B S, Shea F J 1986 Cystic pelvic mass: phyllodes-type variant of prostatic hyperplasia. J Urol 135: 550–553

445. Cummine H G, Johnson A S 1949 Report of a case of retrovesical polycystic tumour of probable prostatic origin. Aust NZ J Surg 19: 91–92

446. Lopez-Beltran A, Gaeta J F, Huben R et al. 1990 Malignant phyllodes tumor of prostate. Urology 35: 164–167

447. Kerley S W, Pierce P, Thomas J 1992 Giant cystosarcoma phyllodes of the prostate associated with adenocarcinoma. Arch Pathol Lab Med 116: 195–197

448. Yokota T, Yamashita Y, Okuzono Y 1984 Malignant cystosarcoma phyllodes of prostate. Acta Pathol Jpn 34: 663–668

449. Bostwick D G, Hossain D, Qian J et al. 2004 Phyllodes tumor of the prostate: long-term followup study of 23 cases. J Urol 172: 894–899

450. Agrawal V, Sharma D, Wadhwa N 2003 Case report: malignant phyllodes tumor of prostate. Int Urol Nephrol 35: 37–39

451. Watanabe M, Yamada Y, Kato H 2002 Malignant phyllodes tumor of the prostate: retrospective review of specimens obtained by sequential transurethral resection. Pathol Int 52: 777–783

452. Lam K C, Yeo W 2002 Chemotherapy induced complete remission in malignant phyllodes tumor of the prostate metastasizing to the lung. J Urol 168: 1104–1105

453. Probert J L, O'Rourke J S, Farrow R et al. 2000 Stromal sarcoma of the prostate. Eur J Surg Oncol 26: 100–101

454. De Raeve H, Jeuris W, Wyndaele J J et al. 2001 Cystosarcoma phyllodes of the prostate with rhabdomyoblastic differentiation. Pathol Res Pract 197: 657–662

455. Yamamoto S, Ito T, Miki M et al. 2000 Malignant phyllodes tumor of the prostate. Int J Urol 7: 378–381

456. De Siati M, Busolo A, Contin F et al. 1999 High grade phyllodes tumour of the prostate. Arch Ital Urol Androl 71: 225–227

457. Young J F, Jensen P E, Wiley C A 1992 Malignant phyllodes tumor of the prostate. A case report with immunohistochemical and ultrastructural studies. Arch Pathol Lab Med 116: 296–299

458. Gueft B, Walsh M A 1975 Malignant prostatic cystosarcoma phyllodes. NY State J Med 75: 2226–2228

459. Yum M, Miller J C, Agrawal B L 1991 Leiomyosarcoma arising in atypical fibromuscular hyperplasia (phyllodes tumor) of the prostate with distant metastasis. Cancer 68: 910–915

460. Proppe K H, Scully R E, Rosai J 1984 Postoperative spindle cell nodules of genitourinary tract resembling sarcomas. A report of 8 cases. Am J Surg Pathol 8: 101–108

461. Wick M R, Brown B A, Young R H 1988 Spindle-cell proliferations of the urinary tract: an immunohistochemical study. Am J Surg Pathol 12: 379–389

462. Huang W L, Ro J Y, Grignon D J 1990 Postoperative spindle cell nodule of the prostate and bladder. J Urol 143: 824–826

463. Young R H 1989 Non-neoplastic epithelial abnormalities and tumor-like lesions. In: Young R H (ed) Pathology of the urinary bladder. Churchill Livingstone, New York, p 44–49

464. Ro J Y, Ayala A G, Ordonez N G 1986 Pseudosarcomatous fibromyxoid tumor of the urinary bladder. Am J Clin Pathol 86: 583–590

465. Sahin A A, Ro J Y, El-Naggar A K et al. 1991 Pseudosarcomatous fibromyxoid tumor of the prostate; a case report with immunohistochemical, electron microscopic, and DNA flow cytometric analysis. Am J Clin Pathol 96: 253–258

466. Hafiz M A, Toker C, Sutula M 1984 An atypical fibromyxoid tumor of the prostate. Cancer 54: 2500–2504

467. Bain G O, Danyluk J M, Shnitka T K 1985 Malignant fibrous histiocytoma of prostate gland. Urology 26: 89–91

468. Ordonez N G, Ayala A G, von Eschenbach A C et al. 1982 Immunoperoxidase localization of prostatic acid phosphatase in prostatic carcinoma with sarcomatoid changes. Urology 19: 210–214

469. Nochomovitz L E, Orenstein J M 1985 Inflammatory pseudotumor of the urinary bladder – possible relationship to nodular fasciitis. Am J Surg Pathol 9: 366–373

470. Roth J A 1980 Reactive pseudosarcomatous response in urinary bladder. Urology 15: 635–637

471. Olsen S 1984 Tumors of the kidney and urinary tract. Color atlas and textbook. W B Saunders, Philadelphia, p 203–205

472. Hughes D F, Biggart J D, Hayes D 1991 Pseudosarcomatous lesions of the urinary bladder. Histopathology 18: 67–71

473. Coyne J D, Wilson G, Sandhu D 1991 Inflammatory pseudotumor of the urinary bladder. Histopathology 18: 261–264

474. Jones E C, Clement P B, Young R H 1993 Inflammatory pseudotumor of the urinary bladder: a clinicopathological, immunohistochemical, ultrastructural, and flow cytometric study of 13 cases. Am J Surg Pathol 17: 264–274

475. Ro J Y, El-Naggar A K, Amin M B 1993 Pseudosarcomatous fibromyxoid tumor of the urinary bladder and prostate: immunohistochemical, ultrastructural and DNA flow cytometric analysis of nine cases. Hum Pathol 24: 1203–1210

476. Jensen J B, Langkilde N C, Lundbeck F et al. 2003 Pseudosarcomatous fibromyxoid tumor of the prostate. Scand J Urol Nephrol 37: 85–87

477. Das S, Upton J D, Amar A D 1988 Nodular fasciitis of the bladder. J Urol 140: 1532–1533

478. Meis J M, Enzinger F M 1991 Inflammatory fibrosarcoma of the mesentery and retroperitoneum. A tumor closely simulating inflammatory pseudotumor. Am J Surg Pathol 15: 1146–1156

479. Voges G E, Wippermann F, Duber C et al. 1990 Pheochromocytoma in the pediatric age group: the prostate – an unusual location. J Urol 144: 1219–1221

480. Dennis P J, Lewandowski A E, Rohner T J J 1989 Pheochromocytoma of the prostate: an unusual location. J Urol 141: 130–132

481. Chen K T, Schiff J J 1987 Hemangiopericytoma of the prostate. J Surg Oncol 35: 42–43

482. Pins M R, Campbell S C, Laskin W B et al. 2001 Solitary fibrous tumor of the prostate a report of 2 cases and review of the literature. Arch Pathol Lab Med 125: 274–277

483. Sujka S K, Malin B T, Asirwatham J E 1989 Prostatic malakoplakia associated with prostatic adenocarcinoma and multiple prostatic abscesses. Urology 34: 159–161

484. Takeshima Y, Yoneda K, Sanda N et al. 1997 Solitary fibrous tumor of the prostate. Pathol Int 47: 713–717

485. Sebo T J, Bostwick D G, Farrow G M et al. 1994 Prostatic xanthoma. A mimic of prostatic adenocarcinoma. Hum Pathol 25: 386–389

486. Mies C, Balogh K, Stadecker M 1984 Palisading prostatic granulomas following surgery. Am J Surg Pathol 8: 217–221

487. Oates R D, Stilmant M M, Freedlund M C et al. 1988 Granulomatous prostatitis following bacillus Calmette–Guerin immunotherapy of bladder cancer. J Urol 140: 751–754

488. Dhundee J, Maciver A G 1991 An immunohistological study of granulomatous prostatitis. Histopathology 18: 435–441

489. Presti B, Weidner N 1991 Granulomatous prostatitis and poorly differentiated prostate carcinoma. Their distinction with the use of immunohistochemical methods. Am J Clin Pathol 95: 330–334

490. Helpap B 1994 Histological and immunohistochemical study of chronic prostatic inflammation with and without benign prostatic hyperplasia. J Urol Pathol 2: 49–64

491. Oppenheimer J R, Kahane H, Epstein J I 1997 Granulomatous prostatitis on needle biopsy. Arch Pathol Lab Med 121: 724–729

492. Carmel M, Masse S R, Lehoux J G 1983 Leiomyosarcoma of prostate. Urology 22: 190–193

493. Tannenbaum M 1975 Sarcomas of the prostate gland. Urology 5: 810–814

494. Narayana A S, Loening S, Weimar G W 1978 Sarcoma of the bladder and prostate. J Urol 119: 72–76

495. Rogers P C, Howards S S, Komp D M 1976 Urogenital rhabdomyosarcoma in childhood. J Urol 115: 738–739

496. Schmidt J D, Welch M J 1976 Sarcoma of the prostate. Cancer 37: 1908–1912

497. Tungekar M F, Al Adnani M S 1986 Sarcomas of the bladder and prostate: the role of immunohistochemistry and ultrastructure in diagnosis. Eur Urol 12: 180–183

498. Hays D M, Raney R B, Lawrence W J 1982 Bladder and prostatic tumors in the intergroup rhabdomyosarcoma study (IRS-1). Results of therapy. Cancer 50: 1472–1482

499. McDougal W S, Persky L 1980 Rhabdomyosarcoma of the bladder and prostate in children. J Urol 123: 882–885

500. Camuzzi F A, Block N L, Charyulu K 1981 Leiomyosarcoma of prostate gland. Urology 18: 295–297

501. Christoffersen J 1973 Leiomyosarcoma of the prostate. Acta Chir Scand 433: 75–84

502. Muller H-A, Wunsch P H 1981 Features of prostatic sarcomas in combined aspiration and punch biopsies. Acta Cytol 25: 480–484

503. Miettinen M 1988 Rhabdomyosarcoma in patients older than 40 years of age. Cancer 62: 2060–2065

504. King D G, Finney R P 1977 Embryonal rhabdomyosarcoma of the prostate. J Urol 117: 88–90

505. Waring P M, Newland R C 1992 Prostatic embryonal rhabdomyosarcoma in adults. A clinicopathologic review. Cancer 69: 755–762

506. Keenan D J, Graham W H 1985 Embryonal rhabdomyosarcoma of the prostatic urethral region in an adult. Br J Urol 57: 241

507. Nabi G, Dinda A K, Dogra P N 2002–2003 Primary embryonal rhabdomyosarcoma of prostate in adults: diagnosis and management. Int Urol Nephrol 34: 531–534

508. Sexton W J, Lance R E, Reyes A O et al. 2001 Adult prostate sarcoma: the M D Anderson Cancer Center Experience. J Urol 166: 521–525

509. Dalal D D, Tongaonkar H B, Krishnamurthy S et al. 2000 Embryonal rhabdomyosarcoma of prostate in an adult – a diagnostic dilemma. Ind J Cancer 37: 50–53

510. Newton W A J, Soule E H, Hamoudi A B 1988 Histopathology of childhood sarcomas, Intergroup Rhabdomyosarcoma studies I and II. Clinicopathologic correlation. J Clin Oncol 6: 67–75

511. Ghavimi F, Herr H, Jereb B 1984 Treatment of genitourinary rhabdomyosarcoma in children. J Urol 132: 313–319

512. Raney B J, Carey A, Snyder H M 1986 Primary site as a prognostic variable for children with pelvic soft tissue sarcomas. J Urol 136: 874–878

513. Fleischmann J, Perinetti E P, Catalona W J 1981 Embryonal rhabdomyosarcoma of the genitourinary organs. J Urol 126: 389–392

514. Kaplan W E, Firlit C F, Berger R M 1983 Genitourinary rhabdomyosarcoma. J Urol 130: 116–119

515. Gordon R, McManus A, Anderson J et al. 2001. Cytogenetic abnormalities in 42 rhabdomyosarcomas: a United Kingdom Cancer Cytogenetics Group study. Med Pediatr Oncol 36: 259–267

516. Bostwick D G, Mann R B 1985 Malignant lymphomas involving the prostate. A study of 13 cases. Cancer 56: 2932–2938

517. Raney R B, Anderson J R, Barr F G et al. 2001 Rhabdomyosarcoma and undifferentiated sarcoma in the first two decades of life: a selective review of intergroup rhabdomyosarcoma study group experience and rationale for Intergroup Rhabdomyosarcoma Study V. J Pediatr Hematol Oncol 23: 215–220

518. Donaldson S S, Meza J, Breneman J C et al. 2001 Results from the IRS-IV randomized trial of hyperfractionated radiotherapy in children with rhabdomyosarcoma – a report from the IRSG. Int J Radiat Oncol Biol Phys 51: 718–728

519. Aragona F, Serretta V, Marconi A 1985 Leiomyosarcoma of the prostate in adults. Ann Chir Gynaecol 74: 191–194

520. Cheville J C, Dundore P A, Nascimento A G 1995 Leiomyosarcoma of the prostate. Report of 23 cases. Cancer 76: 1422–1427

521. Fitzpatrick T J, Stump G 1960 Leiomyosarcoma of the prostate: case report and review of the literature. J Urol 83: 80–83

522. Ahlering T E, Weintraub P, Skinner D G 1988 Management of adult sarcomas of the bladder and prostate. J Urol 140: 1397–1399

522a. Herawi M, Epstein J I 2006 Specialized stromal tumors of the prostate: a clinicopathologic study of 50 cases. Am J Surg Pathol 30: 694–704

523. Meeter U L, Richards J N 1960 Osteogenic sarcoma of the prostate. J Urol 84: 654–657

524. Locke J R, Soloway M S, Evans J 1986 Osteogenic differentiation associated with x-ray therapy for adenocarcinoma of the prostate gland. Am J Clin Pathol 85: 375–378

525. Chin W, Fay R, Ortega P 1986 Malignant fibrous histiocytoma of prostate. Urology 27: 363–365

526. Oesterling J E, Epstein J I, Brendler C B 1990 Myxoid malignant fibrous histiocytoma of the bladder. Cancer 66: 1836–1842

527. Chandan V S, Wolsh L 2003 Postirradiation angiosarcoma of the prostate. Arch Pathol Lab Med 127: 876–878

528. Smith D M, Manivel C, Kapps D 1986 Angiosarcoma of the prostate: report of 2 cases and review of the literature. J Urol 135: 382–384

529. Scully J M, Uno J M, McIntyre M et al. 1990 Radiation-induced prostatic sarcoma: a case report. J Urol 144: 746–748

530. Colecchia M, Dagrada G, Poliani P L et al. 2003 Primary primitive peripheral neuroectodermal tumor of the prostate. Arch Pathol Lab Med 127: e190–e193

531. Pan C C, Yang A H, Chiang H 2003 Malignant perivascular epithelioid cell tumor involving the prostate. Arch Pathol Lab Med 127: E96–E98

532. Kerbl K, Pauer W 1988 Primary non-Hodgkin lymphoma of prostate. Urology 32: 347–349

533. Patel D R, Gomez G A, Henderson E S 1988 Primary prostatic involvement in non-Hodgkin lymphoma. Urology 32: 96–98

534. King L S, Cox T R 1951 Lymphosarcoma of the prostate. Am J Pathol 27: 801–823

535. Chu P G, Huang Q, Weiss L M 2005 Incidental and concurrent malignant lymphomas discovered at the time of prostatectomy and prostate biopsy. A study of 29 cases. Am J Surg Pathol 29: 693–699

536. Boe S, Nielsen H, Ryttov N 1981 Burkitt's lymphoma mimicking prostatitis. J Urol 125: 891–892

537. Cos L R, Rashid H A 1984 Primary non-Hodgkin lymphoma of prostate presenting as benign prostatic hyperplasia. Urology 23: 176–179

538. Doll D C, Weiss R B, Shah S 1978 Lymphoma of the prostate presenting as benign prostatic hypertrophy. South Med J 71: 1170–1171

539. Bostwick D G, Iczkowski K A, Amin M B et al. 1998 Malignant lymphoma involving the prostate: report of 62 cases. Cancer 83: 732–738

540. Ferry J A, Young R H 1997 Malignant lymphoma of the genitourinary tract. Curr Diagn Pathol 4: 145–169

541. Sridhar K N, Woodhouse C R J 1983 Prostatic infiltration in leukaemia and lymphoma. Eur Urol 19: 153–156

542. Banerjee S S, Harris M 1988 Angiotropic lymphoma presenting in the prostate. Histopathology 12: 667–670

543. Feinberg S M, Leslie K O, Colby T V 1987 Bladder outlet obstruction by so-called lymphomatoid granulomatosis (angiocentric lymphoma). J Urol 137: 989–990

544. Lewi H J E, White A, Cassidy M et al. 1984 Lymphocytic infiltration of the prostate. Br J Urol 56: 301–303

545. Cachia P G, McIntyre M A, Dewar A E et al. 1987 Prostatic infiltration in chronic lymphatic leukaemia. J Clin Pathol 40: 342–345

546. Garcia-Gonzalez R, Bellas-Mendez C, Llorente-Abarca C 1964 Leukemic infiltration of the prostate causing acute urinary retention. Eur Urol 10: 356–357

547. Chan Y F 1990 Granulocytic sarcoma (chloroma) of the kidney and prostate. Br J Urol 65: 655–656

548. Frame R, Head D, Lee R 1987 Granulocytic sarcoma of the prostate: two cases causing urinary obstruction. Cancer 59: 142–146

549. Hollenberg G M 1978 Extraosseous multiple myeloma simulating primary prostatic neoplasm. J Urol 119: 292–294

550. Jhavar S, Agarwal J P, Naresh K N et al. 2001 Primary extranodal mucosa associated lymphoid tissue (MALT) lymphoma of the prostate. Leuk Lymphoma 41: 445–449

551. Yao J C T, Wang W C C, Tseng H H et al. 1988 Primary rhabdomyosarcoma of the prostate: diagnosis by needle biopsy and immunocytochemistry. Acta Cytol 32: 509–512

552. Henkes D N, Stein N 1987 Fine-needle aspiration cytology of prostatic embryonal rhabdomyosarcoma: a case report. Diagn Cytol 3: 163–165

553. Kodet R, Kasthuri N, Marsden H B et al. 1986 Gangliorhabdomyosarcoma: a histopathological and immunohistochemical study of three cases. Histopathology 10: 181–193

554. Han G, Miura K, Takayama T et al. 2003 Primary prostatic endodermal sinus tumor (yolk sac tumor) combined with a small focal seminoma. Am J Surg Pathol 27: 554–559

555. Bates A W, Baithun S I 2002 Secondary solid neoplasms of the prostate: clinicopathological series of 51 cases. Virchows Arch 440: 392–396

556. Green L K 1990 Metastatic neoplasms to the prostate: a review of 43 cases. Am J Clin Pathol 94: 509

557. Leung C S, Srigley J R, Robertson A R 1997 Metastatic renal cell carcinoma presenting as solitary bleeding prostatic metastasis. J Urol Pathol 7: 1–6

558. Motley R C, Utz D C, Farrow G M 1986 Testicular seminoma metastatic to the prostate. J Urol 135: 801–802

559. Gevenois P A, Van Sinoy M L, Sintzoff S A 1990 Cysts of the prostate and seminal vesicles: MR imaging findings in 11 cases. AJR 155: 1021–1024

560. Ejeckam G C, Govatsos S, Lewis A S 1984 Cyst of seminal vesicle associated with ipsilateral renal agenesis. Urology 24: 372–374

561. Haeney J A, Pfister R C, Maeres E M J 1987 Giant cysts of the seminal vesicles with renal agenesis. AJR 149: 139–140

562. Kenney P J, Leeson M D 1983 Congenital anomalies of the seminal vesicles: spectrum of computed tomographic findings. Radiology 149: 247–251

563. Shabsigh R, Lerner S, Fishman I J 1989 The role of transrectal ultrasonography in the diagnosis and management of prostatic and seminal vesicle cysts. J Urol 141: 1206–1209

564. Ornstein M H, Kershaw D R 1985 Cysts of the seminal vesicle are Mullerian in origin. J R Soc Med 78: 1050–1051

565. Stenos J, Pavlakis A, Rebelakos A 1985 Cysts of the seminal vesicle. A case report and review of the literature. Acta Urol Belg 53: 718–723

566. Van Lerberghe E, Beeckman P, Roelens J et al. 1987 Seminal vesicle cyst: report of a case. J Belg Radiol 70: 137–139

567. Coyne J D, Kealy W F 1993 Seminal vesicle amyloidosis. Histopathology 22: 173–176

568. Jun S Y, Kim K R, Cho K S et al. 2003 Localized amyloidosis of seminal vesicle and vas deferens: report of two cases. J Kor Med Sci 18: 447–451

569. Bahn D K, Brown R K J, Shei K Y 1990 Sonographic findings of leiomyoma of seminal vesicle. J Clin Ultrasound 18: 517–519

570. Kinas H, Kuhn M J 1987 Mesonephric hamartoma of the seminal vesicle: a rare cause of a retrovesical mass. NY State J Med 87: 48–49

571. Tamayo J L, Ruffolo E H 1967 Spermatic cord tumor. Mesonephric hamartoma of the vas deferens. Arch Surg 94: 430–431

572. Plaut A L, Standard S 1944 Cystomyoma of seminal vesicle. Ann Surg 119: 253–261

573. Lundhus E, Bundgaard N, Sorensen F B 1984 Cystadenoma of the seminal vesicle. Scand J Urol Nephrol 18: 341–342

574. Bullock K N 1988 Cystadenoma of the seminal vesicle. J R Soc Med 81: 294–295

575. Damjanov I, Apic R 1974 Cystadenoma of the seminal vesicles. J Urol 111: 808–809

576. Peker K R, Hellman B H J, McCammon K A et al. 1997 Cystadenoma of the seminal vesicle: a case report and review of the literature. J Urol Pathol 6: 213–221

577. Kan D V 1963 Benign tumors of the seminal vesicles. Urologia 28: 27–30

578. Islam M 1979 Benign mesenchymoma of seminal vesicles. Urology 13: 203–205

579. Mazur M T, Myers J L, Maddox W A 1987 Cystic epithelial-stromal tumor of the seminal vesicle. Am J Surg Pathol 11: 210–217

580. Kawahara M, Matsuhashi M, Tajima M 1988 Primary carcinoma of seminal vesicle. Diagnosis assisted by sonography. Urology 32: 269–272

581. Davis N S, Merguerian P A, Dimarco P L 1988 Primary adenocarcinoma of seminal vesicle presenting as bladder tumor. Urology 32: 466–468

582. Benson R C, Clark W R, Farrow G M 1984 Carcinoma of the seminal vesicle. J Urol 132: 483–485

583. Oguchi K, Takeuchi T, Kuriyama M 1988 Primary carcinoma of the seminal vesicle (cross-imaging diagnosis). Br J Urol 62: 383–384

584. Chinoy R F, Kulkarni J N 1993 Primary papillary adenocarcinoma of the seminal vesicle. Ind J Cancer 30: 82–84

585. Ohmori T, Okada K, Tabei R 1994 CA 125-producing adenocarcinoma of the seminal vesicle. Pathol Int 44: 333–337

586. Ormsby A H, Haskell R, Jones D et al. 2000 Primary seminal vesicle carcinoma: an immunohistochemical analysis of four cases. Mod Pathol 13: 46–51

587. Jun S Y, Kim K R, Ro J Y 2003 Mucosal spread of prostate adenocarcinoma to seminal vesicle. Pathol Case Rev 8: 78–81

588. Middleton L P, Merino M J, Popok S M et al. 1998 Male adnexal tumour of probable Wolffian origin occurring in a seminal vesicle. Histopathology 33: 269–274

589. Schned A R, Ledbetter J S, Selikowitz S M 1986 Primary leiomyosarcoma of the seminal vesicle. Cancer 57: 2202–2206

590. Muentener M, Hailemariam S, Dubs M et al. 2000 Primary leiomyosarcoma of the seminal vesicle. J Urol 164: 2027

591. Amirkhan R H, Molberg K H, Wiley E L et al. 1994 Primary leiomyosarcoma of the seminal vesicle. Urology 44: 132–135

592. Berger A P, Bartsch G, Horninger W 2002 Primary rhabdomyosarcoma of the seminal vesicle. J Urol 168: 643

593. Sanghvi D A, Purandare N C, Jambhekar N A et al. 2004 Primary rhabdomyosarcoma of the seminal vesicle. Br J Radiol 77: 159–160

594. Chiou R K, Limas C, Lance P H 1985 Hemangiosarcoma of the seminal vesicle: case report and literature review. J Urol 134: 371–373

595. Panageas E, Kuligowska E, Dunlop R 1990 Angiosarcoma of the seminal vesicle: early detection using transrectal ultrasound-guided biopsy. J Clin Ultrasound 18: 666–670

596. Lamont J S, Hesketh P J, de las Morenas A et al. 1991 Primary angiosarcoma of the seminal vesicle. J Urol 146: 165–167

597. Fain J S, Cosnow I, King B F et al. 1993 Cystosarcoma phyllodes of the seminal vesicle. Cancer 71: 2055–2061

598. Lazarus J A 1946 Primary malignant tumors of the seminal vesicles: report of a case of retrovesical sarcoma. J Urol 55: 190–205

PART B

Testis and paratesticular tissues

Jae Y. Ro   Mahul B. Amin   Kyu-Rae Kim   Alberto G. Ayala

Testicular neoplasms constitute approximately 1% of all cancers in males.[1] The American Cancer Society estimated that in the year 2006, 8250 patients developed testicular cancer, and 370 of these will die of their disease.[2] Tumors of germ cell origin account for 94–96% of all testicular neoplasms, and those of sex cord-stromal origin constitute 4–6%. The remaining testicular neoplasms of diverse histologic derivations are rare, and account for approximately 1% of all testicular neoplasms. Table 14B.1 lists the classification of testicular and paratesticular tumors and tumor-like lesions, as published in the recent World Health Organization (WHO) book.[3]

The pathologist plays a key role in the management of patients with testicular tumors by accurately classifying the tumor, by providing the appropriate pathologic stage, and by identifying prognostic parameters, which may be useful in making the decision between surveillance and further treatment (Table 14B.2). Therefore, evaluation of a testicular tumor must include a careful gross examination to document tumor size, to determine if the tumor extends into the spermatic cord and tunica, to note the presence of variations in gross appearance including necrosis and hemorrhage, and to direct adequate sampling for microscopic examination (in general, one section per 1 cm tumor diameter, including areas with differing appearances). Microscopic examination must identify the histologic type (i.e., germ cell or non-germ cell tumor, seminoma or non-seminomatous, or mixed germ cell tumors (MGCTs), including the different components and their relative percentages), determine the involvement of the spermatic cord and tunica albuginea, and confirm the presence or absence of vascular or lymphatic invasion. Other features that may be included in the report are tumor necrosis, mitoses, fibrosis, syncytiotrophoblastic giant cells, lymphoplasmacytic infiltrate, a granulomatous reaction, and the status of the background testis, including intratubular germ cell neoplasia (ITGCN).[4-8]

Germ cell neoplasms

The diverse views on the histogenesis of germ cell neoplasms and the wide range of their histologic appearances are reflected in various classifications that have been proposed (Table 14B.3).[3,9] For the purposes of treatment, however, the tumors are conventionally divided into two major categories: seminoma and non-seminomatous germ cell tumor (NSGCT).[4-6]

If the tumor is non-seminomatous, it must be further classified as a pure or mixed tumor. For MGCTs, all components present in the tumor should be reported along with the approximate volume of each. Tumors containing both seminomatous and non-seminomatous elements are regarded as NSGCTs for treatment purposes.[4-6]

Intratubular germ cell neoplasia

ITGCN is widely believed to be the precursor of most invasive germ cell tumors. Although Wilms[10] in 1896 described the presence of atypical intratubular cells adjacent to an invasive carcinoma, it was Skakkebaek[11] who, in 1972, first reported that the atypical germ cells within the seminiferous tubules actually represented the precursor of the invasive testicular germ cell neoplasm. This in-situ phase of germ cell tumor occurs in 0.5–1% of infertile patients with severe oligospermia, 2–8% of those with cryptorchidism, and 5% of patients with a history of testicular cancer.[12-23] There is a 15–20% risk for development of ITGCN in the remaining (contralateral) testis in patients with a history of undescended testis and testicular carcinoma.[16,24] Patients with dysgenetic gonads and testicular feminization syndrome also have an increased incidence of

Table 14B.1   World Health Organization histological classification of testis tumors[a]

Germ cell tumors			**Sex cord/gonadal stromal tumors:**	
Intratubular germ cell neoplasia, unclassified	9064/2		Incompletely differentiated	8591/1
Other types			Sex cord/gonadal stromal tumors, mixed forms	8592/1
			Malignant sex cord/gonadal stromal tumors	8590/3
Tumors of one histological type (pure forms)			Tumors containing both germ cell and sex cord/	
Seminoma	9061/3		gonadal stromal elements	
Seminoma with syncytiotrophoblastic cells			Gonadoblastoma	9073/1
Spermatocytic seminoma	9063/3		Germ cell-sex cord/gonadal stromal tumor, unclassified	
Spermatocytic seminoma with sarcoma			**Miscellaneous tumors of testis**	
Embryonal carcinoma	9070/3		Carcinoid tumor	8240/3
Yolk sac tumors	9071/3		Tumors of ovarian epithelial types	
Trophoblastic tumors			Serous tumor of borderline malignancy	8442/1
Choriocarcinoma	9100/3		Serous carcinoma	8441/3
Trophoblastic neoplasms other than choriocarcinoma			Well-differentiated endometrioid carcinoma	8380/3
Monophasic choriocarcinoma			Mucinous cystadenoma	8470/0
Placental-site trophoblastic tumors	9104/1		Mucinous cystadenocarcinoma	8470/3
Teratoma	9080/3		Brenner tumor	9000/0
Dermoid cyst	9084/0		Nephroblastoma	8960/3
Monodermal teratoma			Paraganglioma	8680/1
Teratoma with somatic-type malignancies	9084/3			
			Hematopoietic tumors	
Tumors of more than one histological type (mixed forms)				
Mixed embryonal carcinoma and teratoma	9081/3		**Tumors of collecting ducts and rete**	8140/0
Mixed teratoma and seminoma	9085/3		Adenoma	8140/3
Choriocarcinoma and teratoma/embryonal carcinoma	9101/3		Carcinoma	
Others				
			Tumors of paratesticular structures	9054/0
Sex cord/gonadal stromal tumors			Adenomatoid tumor	9050/3
Pure forms			Malignant mesothelioma	
Leydig cell tumors	8650/1		Benign mesothelioma	9052/0
Malignant Leydig cell tumor	8650/3		Well-differentiated papillary mesothelioma	9055/0
Sertoli cell tumors	8640/1		Cystic mesothelioma	8140/3
Sertoli cell tumor lipid-rich variant	8641/0		Adenocarcinoma of epididymis	8450/0
Sclerosing Sertoli cell tumor			Papillary cystadenoma of epididymis	9363/0
Large cell calcifying Sertoli cell tumor	8642/1		Melanotic neuroectodermal tumor	8806/3
Malignant Sertoli cell tumor	8640/3		Desmoplastic small round cell tumor	
Granulosa cell tumor	8620/1			
Adult-type granulose cell tumor	8620/1		**Mesenchymal tumors of spermatic cord and testicular adnexa**	
Juvenile-type granulose cell tumor	8622/1			
Tumors of the thecoma/fibroma group			**Secondary tumors of testis**	
Thecoma	8600/0			
Fibroma	8810/0			

[a]Morphology code of the International Classification of Diseases for Oncology (ICDO) and the Systematized Nomenclature of Medicine (http://snomed.org). Behavior is coded /0 for benign tumors, /2 for in-situ carcinomas and grade III intraepithelial neoplasia, /3 for malignant tumors, and /1 for borderline or uncertain behavior.

ITGCN.[25–27] Approximately 50% of patients with ITGCN will progress to invasive carcinoma within 5 years, and 90% or more if orchiectomy is not performed.[13,16,20] Most patients with ITGCN develop seminoma, and, in fact, the terms seminoma in situ and carcinoma in situ (or gonocytoma in situ) have been used interchangeably for ITGCN. The term seminoma in situ is considered unsuitable because seminiferous tubules are not entirely replaced by atypical cells, and follow-up studies have shown that even non-seminomatous tumors may develop if orchiectomy is not performed. The term carcinoma in situ is not recommended either, because germ cells are not epithelial

and their malignant potential has not been well established in all cases. Nevertheless, it is recognized that the presentation and behavior of this lesion are that of a preinvasive process clearly analogous to carcinoma in situ in other sites.[13,28]

Pathologic features

On gross examination there are no abnormal findings produced by ITGCN, other than conditions that may harbor it. Microscopically, the seminiferous tubules show decreased diameters and thickened tubular walls. In the early stages there

Table 14B.2 TNM classification of germ cell tumors of the testis

Primary Tumor (T)

The extent of primary tumor is usually classified after radical orchiectomy, and for this reason, a *pathologic* stage is assigned.

*pTX	Primary tumor cannot be assessed
pT0	No evidence of primary tumor (e.g., histologic scar in testis)
PTis	Intratubular germ cell neoplasia (carcinoma *in situ*)
PT1	Tumor limited to the testis and epididymis without vascular/lymphatic invasion; tumor may invade into the tunica albuginea but not the tunica vaginalis
pT2	Tumor limited to the testis and epididymis with vascular/lymphatic invasion, or tumor extending through the tunica albuginea with involvement of the tunica vaginalis
PT3	Tumor invades the spermatic cord with or without vascular/lymphatic invasion
pT4	Tumor invades the scrotum with or without vascular/lymphatic invasion

Note: Except for pTis and pT4, extent of primary tumor is classified by radical orchiectomy. TX may be used for other categories in the absence of radical orchiectomy.

Regional Lymph Nodes (N)

Clinical

NX	Regional lymph nodes cannot be assessed
N0	No regional lymph node metastasis
N1	Metastasis with a lymph node mass 2 cm or less in greatest dimension; or multiple lymph nodes, none more then 2 cm in greatest dimension
N2	Metastasis with a lymph node mass more than 2 cm but not more than 5 cm in greatest dimension; or multiple lymph nodes, any one mass greater than 2 cm but not more than 5 cm in greatest dimension
N3	Metastasis with a lymph node mass more then 5 cm in greatest dimension

Pathologic (pN)

pNX	Regional lymph nodes cannot be assessed
pN0	No regional lymph node metastasis
pN1	Metastasis with a lymph node mass 2 cm or less in greatest dimension and less than or equal to 5 nodes positive, none more then 2 cm in greatest dimension
pN2	Metastasis with a lymph node mass more than 2 cm but not more then 5 cm in greatest dimension; or more then 5 nodes positive, none more than 5 cm; or evidence of extranodal extension of tumor
pN3	Metastasis with a lymph node mass more then 5 cm in greatest dimension

Distant Metastasis (M)

MX	Distant metastasis cannot be assessed
M0	No distant metastasis
M1	Distant metastasis
	M1a Non-regional nodal or pulmonary metastasis
	M1b Distant metastasis other than to non-regional lymph nodes and lungs

Serum Tumor Markers (S)

SX	Marker studies not available or not performed
S0	Marker study levels within normal limits
S1	LDH $<1.5 \times$ N* **AND** hCG (mIu/ml) <5000 **AND** AFP (ng/ml) <1000
S2	LDH $1.5-10 \times$ N **OR** hCG (mIu/ml) $5000-50,000$ **OR** AFP (ng/ml) $1000-10,000$
S3	LDH $>10 \times$ N **OR** hCG (mIu/ml) $>50,000$ **OR** AFP (ng/ml) $>10,000$

*N indicates the upper limit of normal for the LDH assay.

Stage Grouping				
Stage 0	pTis	N0	M0	S0
Stage I	pT1–4	N0	M0	SX
Stage IA	pT1	N0	M0	S0
Stage IB	pT2	N0	M0	S0
	pT3	N0	M0	S0
	pT4	N0	M0	S0
Stage IS	Any pT/Tx	N0	M0	S1–3
Stage II	Any pT/Tx	N1–3	M0	SX
Stage IIA	Any pT/Tx	N1	M0	S0
	Any pT/Tx	N1	M0	S1
Stage IIB	Any pT/Tx	N2	M0	S0
	Any pT/Tx	N2	M0	S1
Stage IIC	Any pT/Tx	N3	M0	S0
	Any pT/Tx	N3	M0	S1
Stage III	Any pT/Tx	Any N	M1	SX
Stage IIIA	Any pT/Tx	Any N	M1a	S0
	Any pT/Tx	Any N	M1a	S1
Stage IIIB	Any pT/Tx	N1–3	M0	S2
	Any pT/Tx	Any N	M1a	S2
Stage IIIC	Any pT/Tx	N1–3	M0	S3
	Any pT/Tx	Any N	M1a	S3
	Any pT/Tx	Any N	M1b	Any S

Used with permission of the American Joint Committee on Cancer (AJCC), Chicago, Illinois. The original source for this material is the AJCC Cancer Staging Manual, Sixth Edition (2002) published by Springer-Verlag New York, www.springeronline.com

are scattered large atypical cells (twice the size of normal germ cells) with prominent nucleoli and abundant clear cytoplasm (Fig. 14B.1A), situated between other cells exhibiting an apparently normal maturation sequence. In the later stages, the atypical cells (Fig. 14B.1B) frequently align themselves circumferentially along the basement membrane, and as the process progresses, the number of abnormal cells increases to the point of entirely packing the seminiferous tubule. High-magnification demonstrates large prominent cells imparting a pagetoid appearance; these cells display large nuclei with a coarse chromatin pattern and large, prominent, and irregular nucleoli. Mitotic figures, including abnormal forms, are present, and there is abundant clear cytoplasm, that contains lipids and glycogen.

Table 14B.3	Comparison of various classifications of testicular germ cell tumors			
AFIP (1999)	WHO (1977)	Dixon & Moore (1952)	Mostofi (1980)[4]	British Testicular Tumour Panel (Pugh 1976)
Seminoma	Seminoma	Group I seminoma	Seminoma	Seminoma
Spermatocytic seminoma	Spermatocytic seminoma	Not listed	Spermatocytic seminoma	Spermatocytic seminoma
Embryonal carcinoma	Embryonal carcinoma	Group II embryonal carcinoma	Embryonal carcinoma adult-type	Malignant teratoma undifferentiated
Yolk sac tumor	Yolk sac tumor (endodermal sinus tumor)	Not listed	Infantile embryonal carcinoma	Yolk sac tumor in children (orchioblastoma)
Polyembryoma	Polyembryoma	Not listed	Polyembryoma	Not listed
Choriocarcinoma Placental-site trophoblastic tumor	Choriocarcinoma, pure	Group V choriocarcinoma	Choriocarcinoma, pure	Malignant teratoma, trophoblastic
Teratoma: • mature • immature • monodermal	Teratoma: • mature • immature	Group III teratoma • pure ± seminoma	Teratoma: • mature • immature	Teratoma, differentiated
Teratoma with secondary malignant component (specify)	Teratoma with malignant transformation	Group IV teratoma, with EC and/or C ± seminoma	Teratoma with malignant areas other than S, EC, C	Malignant teratoma, intermediate
Mixed germ cell tumor (specify components)	Embryonal carcinoma and teratoma (teratocarcinoma) Choriocarcinoma and other type Other combinations	Group IV teratoma with EC and/or C ± S Group V choriocarcinoma with S and/or EC Not listed	Embryonal carcinoma and teratoma (teratocarcinoma) Specify tumor type Specify tumor type	Malignant teratoma, intermediate Malignant teratoma trophoblastic Combination tumors

AFIP, Armed Forces Institute of Pathology; WHO, World Health Organization; EC, embryonal carcinoma; C, choriocarcinoma; S, seminoma.

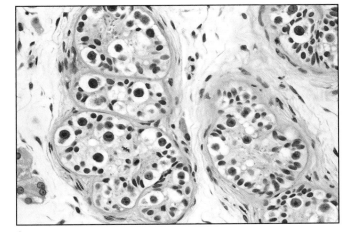
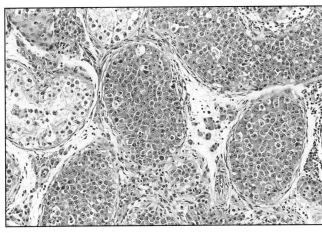

Fig. 14B.1 • Intratubular germ cell neoplasia. (**A**) Note the large atypical cells with abundant clear cytoplasm scattered along the basement membrane of the seminiferous tubules. (**B**) Large atypical cells completely fill the seminiferous tubules (seminoma in situ).

The atypical germ cells have the ultrastructural characteristics of spermatogenic precursor cells or malignant seminomatous cells. The DNA content of these cells demonstrates an aneuploid pattern.[14,29] Periodic acid–Schiff (PAS) stains, with and without diastase, show abundant glycogen in the cytoplasm (Fig. 14B.2).

Immunohistochemistry

Placental alkaline phosphatase (PLAP) has been the most utilized diagnostic antibody, but other markers, including CD117 (*c-kit*), p53, neuron-specific enolase (NSE), ferritin, monoclonal antibody M2A (D2-40), and 43-9F are positive in

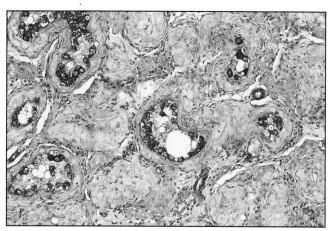

Fig. 14B.2 • Intratubular atypical germ cells contain abundant glycogen (periodic acid–Schiff (PAS) staining). Only the atypical germ cells are stained with PAS.

the atypical intratubular germ cells.[30–37] Most recently OCT4, a transcription factor identified in neoplastic germ cells with pluripotent potential, is gaining considerable popularity.[38]

Giwercman et al.[37] reported that the cells of ITGCN reacted with 43-9F antibody, whereas normal germ cells, Sertoli cells, Leydig cells, and endothelial cells did not.

The loss of FHIT expression (FHIT gene, located at human chromosome 3p14.2) is a consistent characteristic of ITGCN, which suggests a potential role in a maturation/differentiation defect early in the development of testicular germ cell tumors. Likewise, the lack of its expression in seminomas is supportive of this view. However, re-expression of FHIT in well-differentiated glandular epithelium of the teratomatous component of MGCTs suggests that there is no loss of FHIT gene in this subset of tumors, but rather that FHIT protein expression is differentially regulated through the phases of germ cell tumor progression.[39] Cytokeratin, α-fetoprotein (AFP), and human chorionic gonadotropin (hCG) are usually negative. However, intratubular embryonal carcinoma is immunoreactive for CD30, cytokeratin (AE1/AE3), cytokeratin 7 focally, and p53, but negative for cytokeratin 20, p21, and AFP.[40] Karyotypic analyses have demonstrated the common occurrence of a marker chromosome, isochromosome (12p), in ITGCN and seminomatous and NSGCTs.[41,42]

RNA-binding motif (RBM) protein is a novel marker consistently expressed in normal male germ cells but not in malignant germ cells tumors or ITGCN. Thus, the absence of RBM expression in germ cells provides a new diagnostic tool of preinvasive malignancy of the testis.[43]

In 75–99% of cases, ITGCN is seen in tubules adjacent to invasive germ cell tumors; it is associated more frequently with NSGCTs than with seminomas.[32,44–46] In most cases, the intratubular neoplastic cells lack evidence of further differentiation; therefore, specific histologic subtypes can only be determined after extratubular extension occurs. Whether all invasive germ cell tumors develop from an intratubular phase or some develop *de novo* remains to be determined, but the frequent finding of abnormal germ cells in the tubules adjacent to invasive lesions suggests that the former is more likely.

Commonly seen intratubular neoplasms include intra-tubular seminoma and intratubular embryonal carcinoma;[40]

other forms include intratubular spermatocytic seminoma and, rarely, intratubular forms of yolk sac tumors or trophoblastic neoplasia.[47] Direct evidence that ITGCN is a precursor of pediatric yolk sac tumors and teratoma, and of the adult spermatocytic seminoma, is lacking.[48,49] However, recent reports have described ITGCN in children and adolescents.[50–53]

Management

There is controversy as to whether ITGCN should be treated. Some investigators advocate low-dose radiation, while others advocate surveillance on the basis that, if a new primary develops, it would be easy to detect by the patient's self-examination, physical examination, or elevation of serum markers. Furthermore, if a tumor develops, modern management is very effective.

Seminomatous tumors

There are two types of seminoma: classic seminoma and spermatocytic type.

Classic seminoma

Seminoma is the most common testicular neoplasm and comprises 40–50% of all testicular germ cell tumors;[54–56] 85–90% of seminomas are of the typical or classic type, and the remainder consist of rare variants such as anaplastic seminoma, and seminoma with syncytiotrophoblastic giant cells.[54,57,58] Seminoma is the most frequent germ cell tumor in patients with bilateral germ cell tumors (2%) and frequently occurs in undescended testes (5–8%).[59–64]

Clinical presentation

Seminoma occurs most commonly in patients 35–45 years old, is relatively uncommon in men over 50 years of age, and is rare in children. This age group is a decade higher than that of patients with non-seminomatous tumors. The clinical presentation includes testicular enlargement, with or without pain, in more than 70% of all affected patients, and 10% present with symptoms of metastases. Some patients with seminoma are asymptomatic. Gynecomastia, exophthalmos, and infertility are rare presenting symptoms. Elevated serum PLAP and hCG are seen in 40% and 10% of patients respectively; the latter is the cause of gynecomastia. Approximately 75% of seminomas are confined to the testis at the time of presentation (extension to the spermatic cord or epididymis is seen in 5–8%); in contrast, 50–70% of NSGCTs are metastatic by the time they are diagnosed.[54]

Pathologic features

On gross examination, the tumor is usually a well-demarcated, homogeneous, firm mass, frequently white-gray, coarsely lobulated, and bulging (Fig. 14B.3). Hemorrhage and necrosis are uncommon but may be seen in large tumors. The tumors average 5 cm in size, with rare cases exceeding 10 cm; in a series of stage I seminomas, 61% measured 2–6 cm.[65]

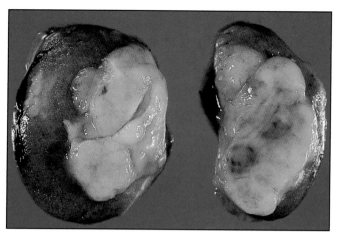

Fig. 14B.3 • Grossly, seminoma has a well-demarcated, cream-colored, homogeneous, and coarsely lobulated appearance.

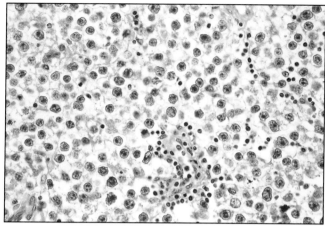

Fig. 14B.5 • On closer view, the cells in seminoma are uniformly large and contain abundant clear cytoplasm. The tumor cells have a distinct cell membrane and are evenly spaced.

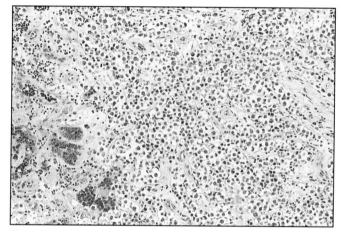

Fig. 14B.4 • Seminoma consists of a monotonous cell population divided into lobules by thin bands of fibrovascular stroma. Scattered syncytiotrophoblastic cells are also seen.

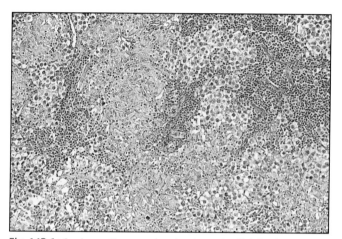

Fig. 14B.6 • Seminoma. Numerous lymphocytes and an ill-defined granulomatous reaction with epithelioid histiocytes are seen in this seminoma.

Microscopic examination shows a diffuse proliferation of large cells arranged in sheets, nests, or cords (Fig. 14B.4). Tubular, reticular, cystic, microcystic, and cribriform patterns have also been reported; the descriptive term tubular seminoma has often been used for such pseudoglandular variations.[66–70] Areas of typical seminoma are always present in tumors with such variations. Usually seminoma destroys seminiferous tubules as it grows, but seminiferous tubules may be found entrapped between the tumor cells, at the periphery of the mass. Rarely there may even be predominantly intertubular growth.[71]

The tumor cells are evenly spaced, are relatively large but uniform, and have a distinct cell membrane (Fig. 14B.5). They contain a centrally located, large, round nucleus which has a sharp nuclear membrane, traversed by thin bands of chromatin, with one or two prominent nucleoli. The cytoplasm is abundant and usually clear, but may be eosinophilic or amphophilic. Mitotic figures are common.

A discrete or diffuse granulomatous reaction, with or without multinucleate giant cells, often occurs in seminoma (50–60% cases). In metastatic disease, the granulomatous inflammation may predominate, making diagnosis extremely difficult. Immunohistochemistry with PLAP is very helpful in this situation.

Scattered syncytiotrophoblastic giant cells are present in 10–20% of cases.[57,72] Other forms of giant cells that may be present in seminoma include mulberry cells[73] and the previously mentioned Langhans-type giant cells associated with granulomata. Extensive calcification and ossification may occur in seminoma (ossifying seminoma).[74] The tumor is separated into lobules by a supporting stroma, which contains a variable number of lymphocytes (Fig. 14B.6). The extent of lymphocytic infiltration (predominantly T lymphocytes)[75] varies from tumor to tumor as well as within different parts of the same tumor. The stroma also varies in amount from scanty to abundant, and varies in appearance from a fine fibro-vascular network to large fibrous bands or septa, which may be hyalinized. In some tumors the amount of connective tissue may be abundant to such an extent that the cells are difficult to discern. Up to a third of seminomas may show an intertubular pattern of growth, away from the main mass, and this appears to be associated with rete testis invasion.[75a] In rare instances, the seminoma cells are no longer present, but the whole tumor is replaced by a mass of hyalinized fibrotic, occasionally calcified tissue, which, in the proper circumstances, would suggest a burnt-out seminoma. The presence of ITGCN strongly supports the diagnosis of burnt-out seminoma.

The pattern of seminoma cells involving rete testis epithelium is indistinguishable from the pattern of ITGCN. When pagetoid involvement of the rete testis occurs, the resulting tubuloglandular architecture may be confused with embryonal carcinoma.[76,77] This pagetoid extension has no prognostic significance.

Seminomas may infarct completely, resulting in a mass containing "ghost" cells suspicious for a neoplasm. When architectural distortion is present in a neoplasm suspicious for seminoma, special stains may help. Florentine et al.[78] reported that a Masson trichrome stain greatly improved nuclear and cytologic detail, confirming the suspicion of a neoplasm. PLAP revealed specific membrane staining of the neoplastic cells and established a diagnosis of seminoma. Thus, Masson-trichrome stain plus selected immunostains offer a promising approach to the diagnosis of certain necrotic neoplasms.

The controversial *anaplastic variant* constitutes 5–15% of seminomas.[58,72] There is no gross difference between anaplastic seminoma and the classic seminoma. On microscopic examination, anaplastic seminoma is characterized by increased mitotic activity (3 or more mitoses per 1 high-power field) and nuclear pleomorphism. Kademian et al.[72] reporting on 8 cases of anaplastic seminoma, concluded that this variant is more aggressive than classic seminoma, even when the two are compared stage by stage; Bobba et al.[79] reported similar results, stating that there was a difference in survival and relapse rate between classic and anaplastic seminomas. Other authors, however, have contended that, although the overall survival rate of patients with anaplastic seminoma is lower than that recorded for patients with classic seminoma, this difference disappears when equivalent stages are compared. A higher percentage of anaplastic seminomas have already metastasized at presentation, in contrast to classic seminomas that are usually confined to the testis. This undoubtedly contributes to the lower overall survival rate for patients with anaplastic seminoma.[58,80] More recently, Tickoo et al., in describing seminomas with atypia, found that tumors of larger size and with a higher mitotic rate behaved more aggressively.[81]

Histochemistry and immunohistochemistry

Staining by PAS, with and without diastase, demonstrates glycogen in the cytoplasm of the tumor cells. Immunostaining for PLAP, D2-40 and NSE is diffusely positive in these cells (Fig. 14B.7).[82,83] OCT4 (POU5F1) is a transcription factor expressed in embryonic stem and germ cells and is positive in seminoma cell nuclei.[84,85] Vimentin can be positive, but epithelial membrane antigen (EMA), AFP, and Ki-1 (Ber-H2; CD30) are negative in most seminomas.[86–88] Most seminomas are KIT (CD117) positive, although ITGCN is not.[88a] Cytokeratin may be focally positive in up to 40% of the tumor cells.[88] The syncytiotrophoblastic giant cells are positive for cytokeratin and hCG, findings that should not be misinterpreted as indicating carcinomatous differentiation. A recent study demonstrated that a somatic isoform of angiotensin I-converting enzyme (CD143) is an appropriate marker for seminomatous differentiated tumors, since spermatocytic seminoma and NSGCTs are negative for this marker.[36]

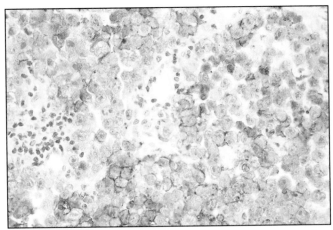

Fig. 14B.7 • Seminoma. Placental alkaline phosphatase immunostaining of seminoma shows diffuse membranous immunoreactivity in the tumor cells.

hCG and α-fetoprotein in seminoma

Between 5% and 60% of patients with pure seminoma have mildly elevated serum levels of hCG because of the presence of syncytiotrophoblastic giant cells,[89–93] but these levels normalize after orchiectomy. An elevated hCG level does not appear to have an adverse effect on the prognosis of patients. Persistently elevated levels of hCG following orchiectomy indicate a hidden focus of choriocarcinoma.

An elevated serum AFP level virtually excludes a diagnosis of pure seminoma, even though microscopic evaluation may show only the seminomatous component without evidence of any other non-seminomatous germ cell elements; these patients should be treated on a non-seminoma protocol.[94–96] However, minor elevations of serum AFP (<16 ng/ml) may be acceptable.[96] The differences in management between seminoma and non-seminomatous tumors and the potentially focal nature of the non-seminomatous component make it imperative that multiple tumor sections be examined before the tumor is diagnosed as a seminoma. Another marker that may be useful in monitoring patients with seminoma is the serum level of NSE.[97] Increased serum NSE was found in 8 of 11 patients (73%) with metastatic seminoma, whereas serum NSE level was normal in 53 of 54 seminoma patients with no evidence of metastasis. Furthermore, serum NSE level returns to normal following chemotherapy. Based on these findings, Kuzmits et al.[97] reported that NSE measurement is clinically valuable for monitoring the results of chemotherapy in patients with metastatic seminoma.

Cytogenetic findings

The most common structural cytogenetic abnormality in seminoma is the presence of isochromosome 12p. Some tumors lack the isochromosome 12p but have other structural chromosomal abnormalities.[98]

The *hiwi* gene[99] maps to the long arm of chromosome 12, band 12q24.33, a genomic region that displays linkage to the development of testicular germ cell tumors, seminomas, and non-seminomas, in adolescents and adults. In normal human testes, *hiwi* is specifically expressed in germ cells, with its expression detectable in spermatocytes and round spermatids during spermatogenesis. No expression was observed in testicular tumors of somatic origin, such as Sertoli cell and Leydig cell tumors (LCTs). Qiao et al.[99] reported that enhanced expression was found in 12 of 19 sampled testicular seminomatous tumors, but no enhanced expression was detected in 10 non-seminomatous testicular tumors that originated from the same precursor cells as seminomas, yet had lost their germ cell characteristics. Finally, no enhanced expression was detected in four spermatocytic seminomatous tumors.

Loss of growth hormone variant (*GH-V*) gene expression in testicular germ cell tumors compared with normal testis and loss (seminoma) or mutation (NSGCT) of placental lactogen-like (*PLL*) gene products might have significance in terms of the relationship between these tumors and for testicular germ cell tumor development.[100] A recent study reported that MAGE-1 antigen (member of the melanoma antigen-encoding gene family) was identified in 16.6% of seminomas. No embryonal carcinomas, yolk sac tumors, or teratomas contained MAGE-1 protein. MAGE-3 antigen was identified in 41.8% of seminomas, and this protein was not identified in embryonal carcinomas, yolk sac tumors, or teratoma. In seminoma, the presence of MAGE-1 and MAGE-3 antigens did not correlate with tumor size, tumor stage, the presence of a lymphoid infiltrate, or patient outcome. The low frequency of MAGE-specific human leukocyte antigen (HLA) alleles in the population, the loss of the HLA class I antigens in neoplastic germ cells, and the finding that the majority of seminomas and all NSGCTs lacked MAGE-1 and MAGE-3 antigenic peptides indicate that immunotherapy directed towards MAGE-1 and MAGE-3 antigen is not a likely treatment option for seminoma and NSGCTs.[101] Zeeman et al.[102] detected *VASA* mRNA (by quantitative reverse transcriptase polymerase chain reaction) and protein (by immunohistochemical staining) in normal spermatogenesis, seminoma (both classic and spermatocytic), carcinoma in situ (the precursor of classic seminoma and non-seminoma), dysgerminoma, and gonadoblastoma.

Differential diagnosis

The main differential diagnosis includes malignant lymphoma, embryonal carcinoma, and endodermal sinus tumor. Other lesions may also enter in the differential diagnosis and these include choriocarcinoma, granulomatous orchitis, Sertoli cell tumor, and spermatocytic seminoma. Large cell lymphoma, either primary or metastatic, is relatively easy to rule out. Characteristically, large cell lymphoma shows interstitial infiltration of tumor cells between the seminiferous tubules. There is absence of a malignant intratubular germ cell proliferation and usually there is no fibrosis or granulomatous reaction. Lymphoma more frequently involves the tunica, epididymis, and spermatic cord than does seminoma. PLAP, CD20, CD3, and leukocyte common antigen (LCA) immunostains are helpful.

Embryonal carcinoma is usually seen in the third decade of life; it shows greater cellular and nuclear pleomorphism and more brisk mitotic activity than seminoma. It may also show areas of papillary and pseudoglandular patterns and a syncytial arrangement of the cells. Embryonal carcinoma is positive for cytokeratin and Ki-1 (CD30) antigen, in contrast to seminomas (Table 14B.4). Pure endodermal sinus tumor is usually seen in children and is more likely to be arranged in reticular, myxoid, and microcystic patterns. The deposition of basement membrane-like material between tumor cells (parietal yolk sac differentiation) is a characteristic feature. Cytokeratin and AFP immunostaining are helpful in differentiating this tumor from seminoma.

Spermatocytic seminoma occurs in patients over 50 years of age and generally consists of round cells with marked polymorphism due to the presence of three cell types, including the very characteristic giant cells. It is usually not associated with fibrovascular septa, lymphocytic infiltration, or granulomatous reaction. Seminomas with numerous syncytiotrophoblastic giant cells differ from choriocarcinoma in that the former lack the typical biphasic appearance, abortive villous architecture, and tumor necrosis and hemorrhage.

A marked granulomatous reaction in seminoma, which masks neoplastic cells, may mimic granulomatous orchitis. The presence of ITGCN at the periphery of the lesion, a careful search under high-power examination for tumor cells, and immunostains for PLAP are helpful to resolve the diagnostic difficulty.

Finally, the tubular and pseudoglandular architecture in seminomas ("tubular seminoma") and pagetoid spread into the rete testis may mimic Sertoli cell tumor. The former is invariably associated with more typical areas of classic seminoma. PLAP immunostaining is also helpful as it is negative in Sertoli cell tumors.

Table 14B.4	Immunohistochemical findings in malignant germ cell tumors										
Component	No. of cases	PLAP	AFP	NSE	VIM	K	CEA	Leu-M1	EMA	hCG	Ki-1
Sem	(7)	6	–	7	–	–	–	–	–	–	–
EC	(33)	24	±	30	11	22	–	–	–	–	23
EST	(18)	±	15	3	–	18	–	–	–	–	1
IT	(23)	–	–	21	21	7	–	–	–	–	–
MT	(30)	±	–	24	14	30	22	22	21	18	–

Sem, seminoma; EC, embryonal carcinoma; EST, endodermal sinus tumor; IT, immature teratoma; MT, mature teratoma; PLAP, placental alkaline phosphatase; AFP, α-fetoprotein; NSE, neuron-specific enolase; VIM, vimentin; K, cytokeratin; CEA, carcinoembryonic antigen; EMA, epithelial membrane antigen; hCG, human chorionic gonadotropin.

Management of seminoma

Management of patients with classic seminoma depends largely on the stage of the disease.[103,104] Stage I disease (localized tumor to testis without metastasis) may be treated with a surveillance protocol or with radiotherapy after radical orchiectomy. The recommended treatment after orchiectomy is low-dose radiotherapy, which would cure 99% of cases. Pathologic parameters, including intensity of lympho-plasmacytic infiltrations, the degree of granulomatous reaction, tumor necrosis, fibrosis, invasion, and interstitial cell hyperplasia, do not correlate with survival.[105] Therefore, these tumor characterisitics are not of clinical significance when low-dose radiotherapy is utilized for stage I classic seminoma. Although vascular-lymphatic invasion does have an impact on prognosis, its presence makes the patient ineligible for "surveillance-only" protocols.[106]

In surveillance protocols, studies have shown that the size of the primary tumor and invasion of the rete testis are independent prognostic factors.[65,106,107] Lesions less than 3 cm, 3–6 cm, and larger than 6 cm have shown relapse-free survival rates of 94%, 82%, and 64% respectively at 4 years.[65,107] A tumor size greater than 6.0 cm has been correlated with a higher rate of relapse.[108] Therefore, for surveillance protocols, these factors are very important.

Stage II disease is generally treated according to the size of the lesion, low-volume (<5 cm) or high-volume disease (>6 in the retroperitoneum). The former receive radiotherapy, while larger lesions receive chemotherapy. Stage III disease is treated with chemotherapy.

The most important prognostic factor for seminoma is the clinical stage at presentation.[103] Five-year survival rates according to stage of disease are 99%, 89%, and 70–85% for stages I, II, and III, respectively.[109,110]

Spermatocytic seminoma

Spermatocytic seminoma is an uncommon tumor comprising 3–7% of all seminomas.[109,110] It was first described as a separate histologic variant of seminoma by Masson in 1946.[111] He postulated that the classic seminoma originated from undifferentiated germ cells and that spermatocytic seminoma was derived from cells undergoing spermatogenesis and hence represented a more differentiated type of germ cell neoplasm.[111]

Proteins which are highly expressed in spermatocytes and spermatogonia, such as Chk2,[112] MAGE-A4,[112] NSE,[112] SSX,[113] and NY-ESO-1,[114] are also expressed in spermatocytic seminoma, but p19[INK4d], which may be associated with the transition from mitotic to meiotic cell cycle are not expressed.[112] Based on these results it has been proposed that the pattern of expression is consistent with the origin of spermatocytic seminoma from a premeiotic germ cell, spermatogonia, or primary spermatocytes of the adult testis, which have lost embryonic traits and have committed to the spermatogenic lineage but have not yet passed the meiotic checkpoint.[112,114]

Clinical features

Spermatocytic seminoma is a germ cell neoplasm unique to the testis and is almost always seen in pure form, although rare cases have been associated with sarcomatous dedifferentiation.[115,116] It is prevalent in men older than 50 years of age (median 55 years) who present with painless testicular enlargement, but rarely may occur at a much younger age, as young as 23 years.[117–119] It has an indolent clinical behavior.[109,110,116,120–122] Of over 150 reported cases there is only one *bona fide* case of a pure tumor with distant metastasis. In contrast, 5 of 9 cases of spermatocytic seminoma with sarcomatoid dedifferentiation have died of metastasis.[110,115,116,122–124] This tumor is not associated with either cryptorchidism or ITGCN. It is more often bilateral (10%) than is classic seminoma (2%).

Pathologic features

The size of the tumors varies from 3 to 15 cm.[110] On gross examination they are yellow-gray, soft, and gelatinous, and form a well-circumscribed mass with cystic change and hemorrhage. They are yellower, softer, and more mucoid than[111] classic seminomas (Fig. 14B.8). In cases with sarcomatous dedifferentiation the tumor may appear more solid and dull-gray.

On low-magnification microscopy, spermatocytic seminoma shows a diffuse proliferation of polymorphic cells, usually of three types, with focal microcysts and intratubular and interstitial growth patterns. There is lack of a prominent fibrovascular stroma, and minimal or no lymphocytic infiltrate or granulomas are seen. The cytoplasm usually does not contain glycogen. No other germ cell components are associated with this tumor.

On high magnification, there are three cell types, and each has distinctive morphology (Fig. 14B.9). The large cells (50–100 mm) are the least common and are uninucleated or multinucleated. The cytoplasm of the tumor cells is abundant and eosinophilic. The tumor cells have uniform, round nuclei but vary markedly in size. The nuclei contain "spireme" chromatin similar to primary spermatocytes in meiotic prophase. The intermediate cells (10–20 mm) have perfectly round nuclei with evenly dispersed granular chromatin or, rarely, spireme chromatin and eosinophilic cytoplasm. The small cells are lymphocyte-like (6–8 mm) and have uniformly hyperchromatic nuclei and scant cytoplasm. The spireme character of the nucleus in the intermediate and large cells

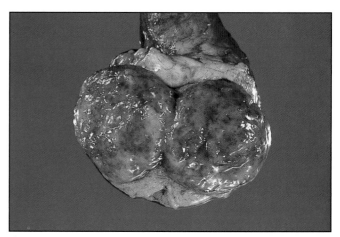

Fig. 14B.8 • Grossly, spermatocytic seminoma is similar to the classic seminoma, but is yellower, more gelatinous, and softer.

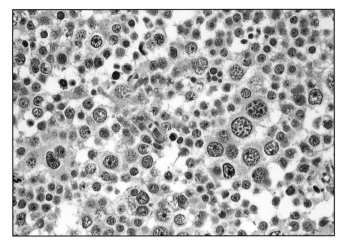

Fig. 14B.9 • Spermatocytic seminoma shows three cell types: large cells, medium-sized cells, and small lymphocyte-like cells.

differentiates this tumor from the classic seminoma. Numerous mitoses may be evident.

Although spermatocytic seminomas are not associated with other germ cell components, in about 6% of cases they are associated with a high-grade sarcoma such as fibrosarcoma, rhabdomyosarcoma, or undifferentiated sarcoma (Fig. 14B.10).[116,122,124] True et al.[122] proposed that this is an expression of anaplastic transformation of the spermatocytic seminoma, analogous to that seen in tumors in other organs. The presence of the sarcomatous elements transforms the usually innocuous spermatocytic seminoma into a highly aggressive neoplasm.[116,122,124] In 5 of 9 reported patients with sarcomatous transformation who died of metastatic disease, death occurred within 2 years after orchiectomy, and only the sarcomatous elements metastasized. This type of spermatocytic seminoma is reported to be resistant to chemotherapy.[116,122]

An "anaplastic" variant of spermatocytic seminoma has been described; it is characterized by a marked predominance of monomorphous cells with prominent nucleoli, which may be potentially mistaken for an embryonal carcinoma or seminoma.[119] There is no apparent prognostic significance to the diagnosis of "anaplastic" spermatocytic seminoma.

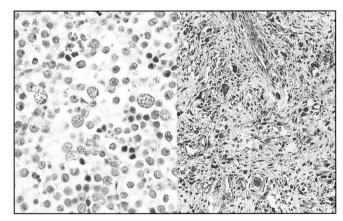

Fig. 14B.10 • Spermatocytic seminoma (left) is associated with a sarcomatoid component (right). The sarcomatoid component in this picture is rhabdomyosarcoma.

Immunohistochemistry

Various tumor markers, including the intermediate filaments, OCT4, and PLAP that are demonstrated in other types of germ cell tumor, have not been detected in spermatocytic seminoma.[115,125,126] Consistent expression of *c-kit* and *VASA* has been described in spermatocytic seminoma.[102,126] Dot-like expression may be found with cytokeratin 18.[115] Proteins highly expressed in gonocytes and spermatogonia, such as Chk2, MAGE-A4, and NSE, are consistently present in spermatocytic seminoma.[112] Antigens expressed in embryonic germ cells but not in the normal adult testis, e.g. TRA-1-60, are undetectable, with the exception of p53 protein, which is demonstrated in 80% of cases. A proto-oncogene p19^{INK4d}, which is involved in the transition from mitotic to meiotic division in germ cells, is not detected in spermatocytic seminoma. The pattern of expression is highly consistent with origin of spermatocytic seminoma from a premeiotic germ cell, which has lost embryonic traits and has committed to the spermatogenic lineage but has not yet passed the meiotic checkpoint, most probably from the spermatogonium of the adult testis.[112] The *NY-ESO-1* gene is the most recently identified member of the cancer/testis family and its product is one of the most immunogenic tumor antigens. Satie et al.[114] reported that NY-ESO-1 was not expressed in the Sertoli cells, Leydig cells, classical seminomas, or non-seminomatous germ cells in the 59 testicular tumors. In contrast, NY-ESO-1 was expressed both in carcinomas in situ, which are the earliest stage of testicular tumors (7 of 15 cases), and in spermatocytic seminomas, which are believed to be derived from spermatogonia or primary spermatocytes (8 of 16 cases). NY-ESO-1 is a marker that can be used to follow the early progression of testicular tumorigenesis, when the tumors present a similar pattern of expression to the cells from which they originated, although the later tumors cease to express NY-ESO-1.

Differential diagnosis

The differential diagnosis of spermatocytic seminoma includes classic seminoma, malignant lymphoma, and solid embryonal carcinoma. In classic seminoma, tumor cells are large and are of only one type, with abundant clear or eosinophilic cytoplasm; the nuclei are more vesicular and have one or two prominent nucleoli. The tumor cells are evenly spaced with distinct cell borders, and fibrovascular septa divide the tumor cells into lobules, imparting a mosaic appearance. There is an associated lymphoplasmacytic infiltrate and granulomatous response in the stroma and uninvolved seminiferous tubules.

Malignant lymphoma is characterized by a higher frequency of bilaterality. The large cell lymphoma consists of oval to round lymphoid cells with cellular and nuclear pleomorphism, and the growth pattern is predominantly interstitial with destruction of seminiferous tubules. LCA staining is very useful.

Embryonal carcinoma is usually seen in the third decade of life. This tumor shows more nuclear pleomorphism than spermatocytic seminoma, and has a brisker mitotic rate and syncytial arrangement of tumor cells. It usually displays other growth patterns, including papillary, solid, and pseudoglandular components.

Management

Radical orchiectomy is the treatment of choice and there is no role for retroperitoneal lymphadenectomy. Most patients receive low-dose radiation to the lower abdomen, but the utility of postoperative radiation remains uncertain and needs to be addressed with a randomized study in the future.[117]

Non-seminomatous germ cell tumors

Tumors designated NSGCT include embryonal carcinomas, immature or mature teratomas, choriocarcinomas, and other rare trophoblastic tumors, endodermal sinus tumors (yolk sac carcinomas), diffuse embryomas, and polyembryomas; these may be found alone or in various combinations. Tumors containing both seminomatous and non-seminomatous components, and tumors with histologically pure seminoma but with a significantly elevated serum AFP level, are regarded as NSGCTs for treatment purposes. Mild elevation of AFP (less than 18 ng/ml) has been reported in several cases of pure seminoma.[96]

Multidisciplinary diagnostic and staging procedures, including computed tomography (CT), tumor marker assays, and retroperitoneal lymph node dissection (RPLND), have proven that the stage of disease at initial presentation is an important prognostic determinant. Recent reports indicate that the presence of embryonal carcinoma accounting for more than 80% of total tumor volume in the primary tumor and the presence of vascular (Fig. 14B.11) or lymphatic invasion are adverse prognostic factors of primary importance in stage I NSGCT for selection of appropriate therapy after orchiectomy.[63,127–131] Tumor size and other histologic parameters do not appear prognostically significant, although other investigators have found that increased pathologic tumor stage (tumor invades beyond tunica albuginea or into epididymis), primary scrotal surgery, and presence of teratoma in less than 50% of the tumor all have adverse prognostic influence.[130,131] In some series where multiple regression analyses were employed, only the embryonal carcinoma cell component and vascular invasion emerged as independent variables; the others were interrelated.[132]

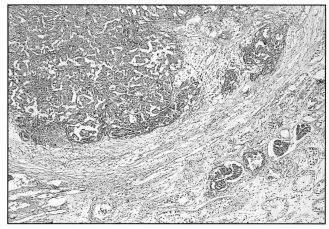

Fig. 14B.11 • Embryonal carcinoma with vascular invasion. The tumor cells conform to the shape of the vessel, indicating true vascular invasion.

Embryonal carcinoma

Embryonal carcinoma, the second most common pure testicular germ cell neoplasm, comprises 15–30% of these tumors.[133–135] It occurs most frequently in the third decade of life between 25 and 35 years of age, with an average of 32 years. It is not found in infants or children and is very rare after the fifth decade[130,136] Patients generally present with painless testicular enlargement, mostly unilateral; one-third of patients present with metastasis to the para-aortic lymph nodes, lungs, or liver.[134] The tumor is occasionally associated with gynecomastia, and serum AFP and/or hCG may be elevated.[137,138]

In an immunohistochemical re-evaluation of the WHO material, which showed a 20% incidence of embryonal carcinoma, Mostofi et al.[139] classified only 3.1% of these embryonal carcinoma cases as "pure" when yolk sac differentiation, based on AFP immunoreactivity, was not permitted in the pure category. The current trend is to recognize the presence of AFP, either in the cells or in the serum, as evidence of yolk sac differentiation, regardless of the cytologic appearance of the neoplasm;[140,141] however, this recognition does not in itself alter the diagnosis unless tissue patterns characteristic of yolk sac tumor can be identified by light microscopy.

Pathologic features

Grossly, embryonal carcinoma may be the smallest germ cell tumor (in pure form), measuring on average 2.5 cm, but may also be very large; it has a variegated, gray-white, granular or smooth, bulging cut surface which is poorly demarcated and has areas of hemorrhage and necrosis (Fig. 14B.12). Twenty percent of embryonal carcinomas have invaded the adjacent epididymis or tunica albuginea at the time of excision.

On low-power microscopic examination, embryonal carcinoma exhibits an acinar, tubular, papillary, or solid pattern with syncytial growth and areas of necrosis, hemorrhage, and fibrosis (Fig. 14B.13). Intratubular embryonal carcinoma is seen within, and at the periphery of the tumor. The involved seminiferous tubules contain anaplastic tumor cells, frequently with central necrosis with or without calcification.

At high magnification, there is marked cellular pleomorphism, with large, prominent, irregular, somewhat vesicular nuclei and abundant, finely granular eosinophilic to amphophilic cytoplasm with indistinct cellular borders (Fig. 14B.14). Giant and bizarre tumor cells are not uncommon, as are darkly staining degenerate-appearing smudged cells. Chromatin is coarse with a distinct nuclear membrane and prominent nucleoli, and there is high mitotic activity with frequent atypical forms. Lymphocytic infiltration and a granulomatous reaction in the stroma are infrequent. Peritumoral vascular lymphatic invasion occurs commonly, and is an important feature to document.

Immunohistochemistry

Immunohistochemically, cytokeratin cocktail, PLAP, Ki-1 (CD 30), and OCT4 are most commonly positive (Fig. 14B.15). OCT4 is consistently positive in the tumor cell nuclei of embryonal carcinoma.[83,85] AFP may be positive in the tumor cells. hCG immunostaining is only seen within syncytiotrophoblastic giant cells, not in embryonal carcinoma tumor

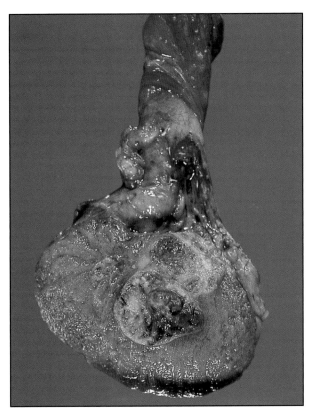

Fig. 14B.12 • Embryonal carcinoma. An ill-defined tumor with a variegated, gray-white, and granular surface. Note also areas of tumor necrosis and hemorrhage.

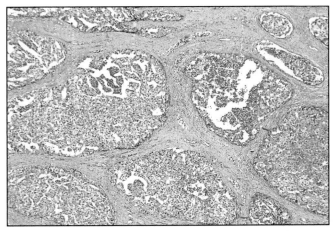

Fig. 14B.13 • Embryonal carcinoma with tubular, papillary, and solid patterns.

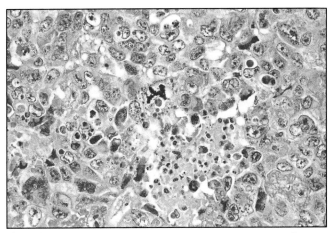

Fig. 14B.14 • Embryonal carcinoma with a solid pattern. The tumor cells are large and pleomorphic. They contain large vesicular nuclei and prominent nucleoli. The cell borders are indistinct and there is frequent nuclear overlapping, forming a syncytial growth. Mitoses are frequent with occasional atypical forms.

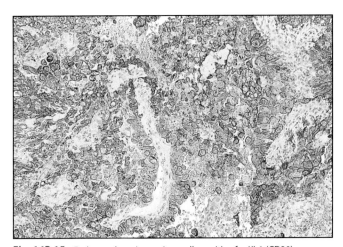

Fig. 14B.15 • Embryonal carcinoma is usually positive for Ki-1 (CD30) immunostaining.

cells. CK20, high-molecular-weight cytokeratin, carcino-embryonic antigen (CEA), and Leu-M1 are usually negative.[86,88,90,125,142–148]

Berney et al.[148] reported that loss of CD30 expression occurs frequently in metastatic embryonal carcinomas after chemotherapy. This finding has implications in the use of CD30 in the diagnosis of metastatic NSGCTs and suggests that chemotherapy may alter the immunophenotype of embryonal carcinoma, even while retaining its characteristic histological appearances.

Ploidy analysis has shown a mean index of 1.43× diploid control, less than that obtained for seminomas (1.66× diploid control).[149] The data have supported the hypothesis that embryonal carcinomas arise from seminomas secondary to the loss of tumor suppressor genes. Cytogenetic analysis has confirmed the presence of isochromosome 12p in many cases.[98,150]

Differential diagnosis

The differential diagnosis includes seminoma, malignant lymphoma, endodermal sinus tumor, and metastatic carcinoma. Although the majority of the embryonal carcinomas are easily differentiated from seminoma, on some occasions it is a very difficult problem as the histologic features of both of these tumors merge. In such cases the utilization of CD30 (Ki-1) is handy, as it is a marker that is often positive in embryonal carcinomas but is negative in seminomas. Cytokeratin cocktail may be of help, but both tumors may be positive. Seminoma tends to show positivity in single cells, and this process may be focal but rarely may be diffuse. The presence of clusters of cells positive for Ki-1 would favor an embryonal carcinoma.

Large cell lymphoma is seen in older patients and is frequently bilateral. There is more commonly epididymal involvement. The papillary, cystic, tubular, and acinar patterns seen in embryonal carcinoma are not present in lymphoma. CD20, CD3, CD5, and LCA may show the lymphoid lineage of the tumor, while cytokeratin is negative. Immunoblastic lymphomas and Ki-1 lymphomas are the most problematic; the diagnostic dilemma with the latter is compounded by Ki-1-positivity in both tumors. PLAP immunostaining is helpful.[86,151] In metastatic carcinoma, there is almost always a clinical history of previous cancer, and involvement is usually bilateral with a predominantly interstitial pattern of infiltration. Vascular invasion is more frequent in metastatic carcinoma. The metastatic tumor may be multifocal and/or bilateral.

Yolk sac tumor may have cytologic and architectural features similar to those of embryonal carcinoma, but it is generally less pleomorphic and shows more architectural diversity. Yolk sac tumor frequently shows intracytoplasmic and extracellular hyaline droplets and basement membrane-like material deposition between the cells (parietal yolk sac differentiation). AFP immunostaining is more diffusely and frequently positive in yolk sac tumor, and it is Ki-1 (CD30)-negative. Embryonal carcinoma contains larger and more pleomorphic nuclei with prominent nucleoli with high mitotic rates and frequently has a solid growth pattern.

Yolk sac tumor (endodermal sinus tumor)

Yolk sac tumor is a tumor of infants and young children (birth to 5 years),[152–160] and, in this age group, it is almost always seen in pure form. It accounts for 75–80% of all childhood testicular neoplasms, most commonly occurring in children between 1 and 2 years of age (range newborn to 8 years). In adults, the pure form is extremely rare and it is invariably admixed with other neoplastic germ cell elements.[140,161,162] Patients present with rapid testicular enlargement and an elevated serum AFP. There seems to be no convincing relationship to cryptorchidism in the pediatric tumors.

Pathologic features

On gross examination, the enlarged testis contains a poorly defined, lobulated, white-gray or gray-yellow tumor ranging in size from 2 to 6 cm in diameter. It may be focally cystic, or a solid mass with variable consistency, and hemorrhage and necrosis may be present. The cut surface often has a mucinous texture.

Microscopically, the key to the recognition of yolk sac tumor is the simultaneous presence of myriad histologic patterns. The reticular-microcystic pattern is most common, occurring in 80% of patients, and consists of irregular loose spaces and anastomosing thin cords and tubules lined by flat or cuboidal cells (Fig. 14B.16); the microcystic pattern is characterized by prominent cytoplasmic vacuoles (resembling lipoblasts) or small cystic spaces with papillary clusters of cells projecting into the lumen (Fig. 14B.17). The stroma is usually myxoid (Fig. 14B.18), and reticular/microcystic areas may show transition into spindled, solid, or macrocystic areas. The most distinctive pattern is the one forming Schiller–Duval bodies (Fig. 14B.19), in which a central fibrovascular core is sur-

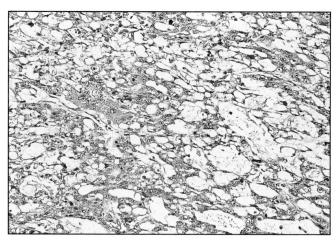

Fig. 14B.16 • Endodermal sinus tumor with a reticular pattern that consists of irregular anastomosing channels, forming loose cystic spaces containing myxoid material.

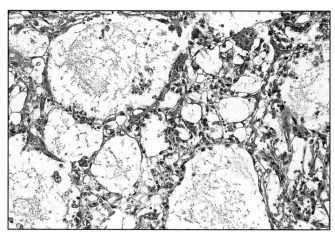

Fig. 14B.17 • Endodermal sinus tumor with micro- and macrocystic patterns. The spaces are lined by flat or cuboidal cells.

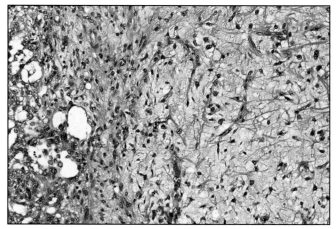

Fig. 14B.18 • Myxoid and spindle cell pattern of endodermal sinus tumor. The spindled neoplastic cells are separated by abundant myxoid stroma.

rounded by malignant cuboidal to columnar epithelioid cells, and the structure is recessed into a cystic space that is in turn lined by flattened cells. The polyvesicular vitelline pattern, seen in another 10% of these tumors, contains irregular tubules with eccentric constrictions resembling the yolk sac vesicles.

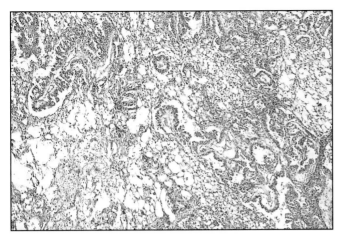

Fig. 14B.19 • Endodermal sinus tumor with cross- and longitudinal sections of Schiller–Duval bodies on a reticular background.

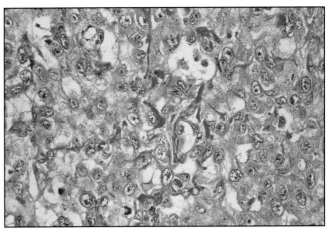

Fig. 14B.21 • Endodermal sinus tumor with a solid growth pattern. Also note the presence of abundant extracellular basement membrane material (parietal yolk sac differentiation).

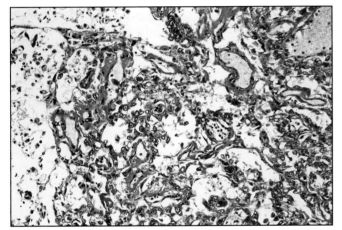

Fig. 14B.20 • Parietal pattern of endodermal sinus tumor. Note the production of the abundant eosinophilic basement membrane-like material associated with the neoplastic cells.

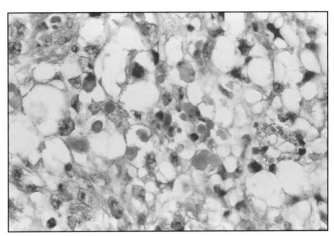

Fig. 14B.22 • Endodermal sinus tumor with extracellular eosinophilic hyaline bodies.

Parietal yolk sac differentiation is rather frequent and is characterized by the presence of abundant extracellular hyaline material corresponding to basement membrane material (Fig. 14B.20).[163] Other variations include solid (5%) (Fig. 14B.21), papillary (5%), spindle cell, enteric (glandular-alveolar pattern), and hepatoid patterns.[164–167] The cells lining the anastomosing tubules are usually flat or columnar and can be deceptively benign in appearance. Intracellular and extracellular hyaline globules are characteristic of yolk sac differentiation and occur in 85% of cases (Fig. 14B.22). These bodies react with PAS, are resistant to digestion with diastase, and contain AFP or α-antitrypsin. The tumor cells are positive for AFP, cytokeratin, and PLAP, and negative for Ki-1 and hCG.[90,140,142,144,146,147,168–170] The basement membrane material of the parietal pattern is usually negative for AFP. Rare pediatric tumors are associated with ITGCN; in contrast, almost all adult tumors with yolk sac tumor occurring as a component of MGCTs have ITGCN.[171,172]

Patients less than 2 years old have the best prognosis.[173] In adults with yolk sac differentiation as a part of NSGCT, the prognosis varies with the stage of disease, but its presence does not appear to affect outcome adversely when current therapeutic modalities are used. Since pure yolk sac tumor in adults is very rare, little is known about its behavior at this time.

Polyembryoma

Polyembryoma in its pure form is an extremely rare neoplasm composed exclusively of embryoid bodies in which embryonal carcinoma and yolk sac tumor components, sometimes additionally with teratoma, are arranged in a pattern resembling the presomite embryo, prior to day 18 of development. It is more often, however, associated with other germ cell tumor components, especially yolk sac tumor and teratoma. The serum AFP levels may be substantially elevated. It exhibits the same malignant behavior as other NSGCTs and most experts would regard it as a non-seminomatous (mixed) germ cell tumor.[174–176] The tumor is solid, soft, and somewhat edematous; cystic areas suggest an associated teratomatous component. At low magnification there are numerous embryoid bodies surrounded by loose myxomatous mesenchymal tissue. Embryoid bodies consist of an embryonic disk lined by cuboidal cells on one side, a dorsal amnion-like

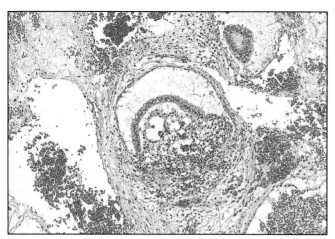

Fig. 14B.23 • Polyembryoma with an embryoid body. It consists of an amniotic cavity, an embryonic disk, a yolk sac, and myxoid extraembryonic mesenchyme.

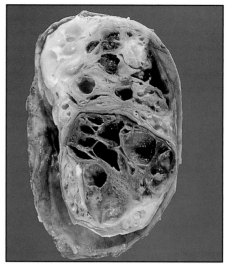

Fig. 14B.24 • Teratoma with solid and multicystic areas.

cavity lined by flattened epithelium, and a ventral yolk sac-like vesicle composed of reticular and myxomatous yolk sac tumor (Fig. 14B.23).[174–176]

In embryoid bodies, AFP and cytokeratin are usually positive, and PLAP may be positive. Vimentin is positive in the surrounding mesenchyme and myxomatous stroma. hCG and CEA are negative.

Teratoma, mature

Mature teratoma is a common component of MGCTs. Its pure form is rare, however, and constitutes only 2–3% of all testicular germ cell tumors. It occurs most commonly in the first and second decades of life. Mature teratoma is the second most common tumor of infancy and childhood; mean age at diagnosis is 20 months.[133,177–179] Patients present with gradual testicular swelling with or without pain. Although mature teratoma is almost always benign in prepubertal patients, it can pursue an aggressive clinical course after puberty, when metastases that develop in these patients may contain non-teratomatous malignant germ cell tumor components. It is seen in approximately 50% of adult non-seminomatous tumors.[133,177,180–184]

Pathologic features

On gross examination, the tumor is well demarcated from the surrounding uninvolved testis and may be solid or multicystic (Fig. 14B.24). Cysts may be filled with clear, keratinous, gelatinous, or mucinous material. Cartilage, spicules of bone, patches of pigmented tissue, or brain tissue may be discernible.

At low magnification, there is an admixture of ectoderm, endoderm, and mesoderm, assembled in either a disorganized or an organized pattern (Fig. 14B.25). The ectodermal components usually consist of epidermis and neural tissue, the endoderm of gastrointestinal and respiratory mucosa and other mucous glands, and the mesoderm of bone, cartilage, and muscle. Other mature somatic components may be present. The most common components are nerve, cartilage, and different types of epithelium.[181] Pigmented retinal-type epithelium,

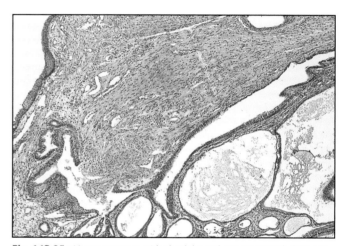

Fig. 14B.25 • Mature teratoma with glandular and squamous epithelium and smooth muscle fibers.

kidney, liver, prostate, choroid plexus, pancreatic tissue, and salivary gland tissue may occur, though very infrequently. Granulomas containing Langhans-type multinucleate giant cells occur in about 8% of the teratomas, and they may also be a response to keratin leakage into the stroma.[185]

It is controversial if the rare *dermoid cyst* of the testis should be classified as a variant of mature teratoma or separately. The spectrum of morphologic findings is also ill defined, as is the relationship of dermoid cyst to ITGCN of the unclassified type (IGCNU). Ulbright & Srigley[186] reported their findings in five testicular dermoid cysts that occurred in 5 patients, 17–42 years of age, who presented with testicular masses. Four lesions consisted of a keratin-filled cyst with a thickened wall, whereas one had islands of "shadow" squamous epithelial cells with superimposed calcification and ossification (pilomatrixoma-like variant). Hair was identified grossly in two cases. On microscopic examination, four tumors had hair follicles with sebaceous glands showing a typical, cutaneous-type orientation to an epidermal surface, although no hair shafts were present in two. In addition, the fibrous wall contained smooth muscle bundles (all tumors) and eccrine or apocrine sweat glands (four tumors). In some cases there were also glands lined by ciliated epithelium (four tumors, including the pilomatrixoma-like variant), intestinal mucosa (one tumor), and bone (two tumors). There was no cytologic atypia or apparent mitotic activity, and no case had IGCNU in the seminiferous tubules. All patients were clinical stage I and were treated by orchiectomy without adjuvant therapy. All were well on follow-up from 1.5 to 9.5 years later. This study supports that dermoid cyst may have non-cutaneous teratomatous elements and that an important criterion for its diagnosis is the absence of IGCNU. It also supports that it should be categorized separately from mature testicular teratoma because of the malignant nature of the latter in postpubertal patients. These observations suggest that there are at least two pathways for testicular teratomas in postpubertal patients: the more common being through IGCNU by differentiation from an invasive malignant germ cell tumor and the less common one, taken by dermoid cyst, by direct transformation from a non-malignant germ cell. Therefore distinction of teratoma from dermoid cyst is critical as metastasis from a dermoid cyst has not been reported.[186]

Epidermoid cyst (see p. 843) is not considered to be a teratoma and it is histologically composed of a cyst lined at least in part by keratinizing squamous epithelium.[187] There may be features of rupture accompanied by ulceration, foreign-body granulomatous reaction, and fibrosis. Uninvolved testicular tissue should be extensively sampled, as the presence of ITGCN argues against a diagnosis of an epidermoid cyst.

Recently a case of mucinous cystadenoma with intestinal differentiation of the testis has been reported. The authors claimed that this seems to be the first published case of benign mucinous cystadenoma occurring within the testis. This intra-testicular tumor with intestinal differentiation may represent a benign monodermal teratoma.[188]

Teratoma, immature

Immature teratoma is a common component of NSGCTs, but its pure form is extremely rare.[189,190] Painless swelling of the testis is the most frequent symptom. The size of the tumor varies from 2 to 4 cm. It frequently occurs in patients between birth and 7 years of age (median 13 months).[191] The immaturity of teratomatous components has not been shown to be an indicator of poor biologic behavior in the primary tumor. Aggressive behavior in testicular teratomas is more directly related to the age of the patient than to the histologic type.

Immaturity in a teratoma is defined as tissues that cannot be recognized as normal elements and those that resemble embryonic or fetal tissue. Thus, the immature teratomatous elements are mostly cellular spindle mesenchymal components, but immature neural and epithelial elements can be seen (Fig. 14B.26). The spindle cells show frequent mitoses. Other forms of immature elements include neuroepithelium resembling neural tube and embryonic nervous system, and blastomatous tissue resembling embryonic kidney or lung.[192] Embryonic rhabdomyoblastic tissue as well as more mature-appearing skeletal muscle may be present.[193] Minor foci resembling primitive neuroectodermal tumor (PNET) may be present.[192] Frank overgrowth of sarcomatous elements (greater than 1 low-power field) and PNET should be documented,

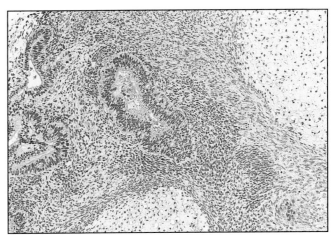

Fig. 14B.26 • Immature teratoma showing a cellular primitive mesenchyme, glandular epithelium, and cartilaginous tissue.

although the prognostic implications of such observations are not entirely clear.

Teratomas with malignant transformation are rare in the testis. They generally contain a malignant tumor typically encountered in other organs and tissues such as squamous carcinoma, adenocarcinoma, or sarcomas (e.g., rhabdo-myosarcoma, angiosarcoma); the prognosis for patients with sarcomatous elements is generally poor.[194,195]

Also included within the category of teratomas of the testis are monodermal and highly specialized tumors, including carcinoid tumor (see p. 841) and PNET of testis.[193]

Choriocarcinoma

In its pure form, choriocarcinoma is extremely rare and accounts for fewer than 1% of all testicular germ cell neoplasms.[3,196] It is more commonly found as a component of NSGCT in approximately 8–10% of tumors. The pure chorio-carcinoma occurs in the second and third decades as a highly malignant testicular tumor. Patients may present with hormonal symptoms, such as gynecomastia (10%), symptoms of distant metastases, and an elevated serum hCG. Patients may present with choriocarcinoma syndrome dominated by visceral hemorrhage due to widespread metastasis. The testis is usually small or normal in size, but may be enlarged and firm, depending on the extent of hemorrhage. The tumor typically shows extensive hemorrhage and necrosis with grayish-white viable tissue at the periphery. Occasionally a hemosiderin-laden scar may be the only stigma in the testis in the presence of widespread metastatic tumor. As a rule the tumor is composed of two cellular components, syncytiotrophoblasts and cytotrophoblasts, arranged in solid nests or sheets, occasionally in a villus-like arrangement (Fig. 14B.27). The syncytio-trophoblasts are large, vacuolated, multinucleated giant cells with dark eosinophilic cytoplasm. The cytotrophoblasts are uniform, medium-sized, polygonal cells with abundant clear cytoplasm and distinct cytoplasmic borders. Cytotrophoblasts are histologically nondescript and cannot always be differentiated reliably from seminoma or embryonal carcinoma cells except by their juxtaposition to the syncytiotrophoblasts. The

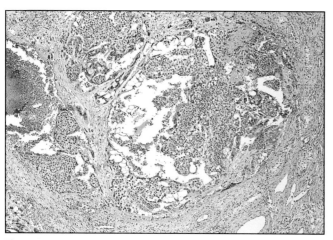

Fig. 14B.27 • Choriocarcinoma. The tumor is characterized by a villous-like arrangement with peripheral syncytiotrophoblasts and central cytotrophoblasts. Hemorrhage and necrosis are frequently observed.

syncytiotrophoblastic giant cells typically "cap" or wrap the cytotrophoblastic cells, resulting in a villous configuration. Very uncommonly, syncytiotrophoblastic cells are rare, creating a "monophasic appearance." Many of the cells in these cases resemble intermediate trophoblasts, having large single or double nuclei with abundant cytoplasm.[197,198]

Ulbright & Loehrer[199] have described two interesting lesions which they named choriocarcinoma-like lesions (CCLL) in 9 patients with testicular germ cell neoplasms. One variant was felt to represent an unusual proliferation of teratomatous epithelium and was termed teratomatous CCLL (5 cases). The second variant was believed to represent a non-biphasic and cystic form of choriocarcinoma similar to the atypical choriocarcinoma described by Mazur et al.[200] All but one patient received chemotherapy before the excision of CCLL. Follow-up was too short (average 1.9 years) to determine clinical significance, but all patients were alive and well following surgical excision. Placental-site trophoblastic tumor (PSTT) is a well-defined entity in the female genital tract. In the male genital tract, two cases of PSTT in the testis have been reported.[198,201] Despite its very rare occurrence, PSTT of the testis has been incorporated in the latest WHO classification of tumors of the male genital tract. The first case was a 16-month-old boy with testicular tumor containing mononucleated intermediate trophoblastic cells positive for human placental lactogen and an uneventful course during the 8-year available follow-up (Fig. 14B.28).[198] The second case was detected as a late retroperitoneal recurrence of a testicular NSGCT in an adult male patient. The tumor was discovered due to an elevated serum level of β-hCG 4 years after chemotherapy. Upon review of the primary testicular tumor, small foci of intermediate trophoblastic tumor cells were discerned. The second case illustrates that tumor cells resembling intermediate trophoblastic cells may metastasize to regional retroperitoneal lymph nodes.

Immunohistochemistry

hCG is positive in syncytiotrophoblasts and in transitional cells between syncytiotrophoblasts and cytotrophoblasts. Human placental lactogen is also positive but usually less pronounced; cytokeratin is positive in both cytotrophoblasts and syncytiotrophoblasts. Vimentin is negative and CEA may be positive.[202] Inhibin is positive in syncytiotrophoblasts and the intermediate form of trophoblastic cells but negative in cytotrophoblasts.[203] Collections of syncytiotrophoblastic giant cells without cytotrophoblasts are often found in other germ cell tumors, but they do not represent choriocarcinoma. Pure choriocarcinoma has a worse prognosis because of its propensity for widespread dissemination. When the choriocarcinoma is a component of NSGCTs, the term NSGCT with choriocarcinomatous component is more appropriate than choriocarcinoma. Choriocarcinoma is a germ cell tumor component frequently found in brain metastases. Higher hCG levels, a greater amount of choriocarcinoma, and choriocarcinoma syndrome are associated with an adverse outcome; however the threshold of choriocarcinoma component below which progression does not occur is not determined.[204–206]

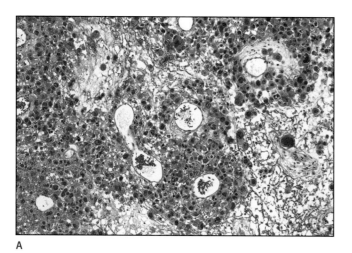

A

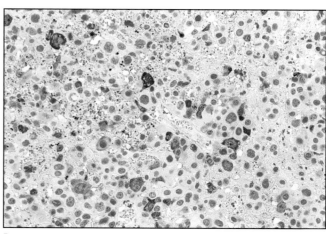

B

Fig. 14B.28 • Placental-site trophoblastic tumor of testis. The tumor cells have abundant dense eosinophilic cytoplasm and enlarged nuclei with clefted and multinucleated appearance similar to placental-site trophoblastic tumor of the uterus. **(A)** Hematoxylin and eosin stain; **(B)** immunostain for human placental lactogen. (Courtesy of Dr. Robert H. Young, Massachusetts General Hospital, Harvard Medical School.)

Mixed germ cell tumors

MGCTs are the second most common testicular germ cell tumor following seminoma and account for 40–45% of all primary testicular germ cell tumors.[3,4,207] Combinations include teratoma and embryonal carcinoma (25%), embryonal carcinoma and seminoma (15%), teratoma and embryonal carcinoma and seminoma (15%), and, rarely, seminoma and yolk sac tumor. Foci of yolk sac tumor are identified in 40% of MGCTs. The term teratocarcinoma was used to indicate a clinical group of patients with germ cell tumors; it was not meant to designate a histologic subtype of MGCTs. Unfortunately, this term has been used for several combinations of germ cell neoplasms, including embryonal carcinoma and teratoma, yolk sac tumor and teratoma, embryonal carcinoma with yolk sac tumor and teratoma, and embryonal carcinoma with seminoma and teratoma. In view of present knowledge of the histopathology of testicular neoplasms and within the scope of current management and treatment, this term has little value. Therefore, we recommend using the names and relative proportions of different germ cell tumor components. We believe this approach provides accurate information necessary for the prediction of prognosis and for appropriate treatment selection. MGCTs are seen most frequently during the third and fourth decades of life. Testicular enlargement is the most common symptom.

Pathologic features

Grossly, the testis is often entirely replaced by the tumor, which typically shows a variegated appearance with cystic and solid areas and areas of hemorrhage and necrosis (Fig. 14B.29). The different components cannot be distinguished on gross examination, except that the presence of hemorrhage and necrosis suggests either embryonal carcinoma or chorio-

carcinoma, and macrocystic and cartilaginous or bony areas suggest teratomatous components. On microscopic examination the lesion can be cystic or solid. Multiple different germ cell components are readily identifiable on low-power examination by their architectural patterns.

Embryonal carcinoma, immature and mature teratoma, yolk sac tumor, and choriocarcinoma are present in different proportions in different tumors or in different areas of the same tumor (Fig. 14B.30). These components are distributed haphazardly throughout the tumor in most cases. Rarely yolk sac tumor cells wrap diffusely around embryonal carcinoma, forming the distinctive "diffuse embryoma" pattern (Fig. 14B.31).[208,209]

A case of microcystic variant of meningioma arising in an MGCT of the testis, composed predominantly of mature and immature teratoma with elements of seminoma and embryonal carcinoma, has been reported.[210] Recognition of a non-germ cell tumor arising in the setting of a teratoma in the testis may be prognostically important depending on the nature of the non-germ cell component and whether it has spread beyond the testis.

Immunohistochemical staining reflects the differentiation of the germ cell component. AFP is usually positive in yolk sac

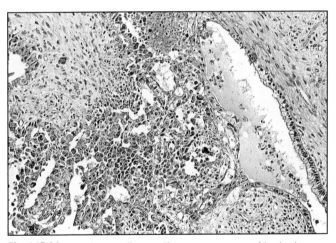

Fig. 14B.30 • Mixed germ cell tumor. The most common combination is embryonal carcinoma and teratoma.

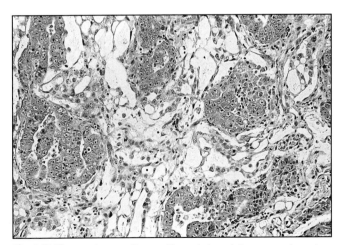

Fig. 14B.31 • Mixed germ cell tumor. The endodermal sinus tumor elements wrap around the embryonal carcinoma and this combination has been referred to as diffuse embryoma.

Fig. 14B.29 • Mixed germ cell tumor. This tumor is mixed embryonal carcinoma and teratoma. The necrotic central part is embryonal carcinoma and the peripheral mucoid areas are mature and immature teratoma.

tumor areas, and hCG is negative in embryonal carcinoma and seminoma cells but positive in syncytiotrophoblastic giant cells; PLAP is usually positive in all germ cell tumor components, although variably. Cytokeratin is positive in embryonal carcinoma, epithelial components of teratoma, yolk sac tumor, and choriocarcinoma but usually negative in seminoma; Ki-1 is positive in an embryonal carcinoma component. Stains for CEA and Leu-M1 are negative (Table 14B.4).[211]

Tezel et al.[212] reported that RET finger protein (RFP), which belongs to the large B-box RING finger protein family, was seen uniformly and specifically in 12 of the 13 pure seminomas examined. It was also detected in seminomatous components of MGCTs, whereas pure NSGCT were negative for RFP expression. The expression of RFP in male germ cells and seminomas together with the lack of its expression observed in highly aggressive NSGCT suggested that RFP could be associated with the regulation of germ cell proliferation and/or histologic type of germ cell tumors. Recently Jones et al.[84] reported that immunostaining with antibodies to OCT4 is a useful diagnostic tool in the identification of primary testicular embryonal carcinomas and "usual," but not spermatocytic, seminoma. OCT4 immunostaining has comparable sensitivity but greater consistency compared with CD30 in the diagnosis of embryonal carcinoma. The other germ cell tumor components (yolk sac tumor, mature teratoma, immature teratoma, and choriocarcinoma) showed no staining. Syncytiotrophoblastic cells were also completely negative, as were all spermatocytic seminomas. The non-germ cell tumors of the testis were all immunohistochemically negative for OCT4.[83,85]

Mixed germ cell and sex cord tumors

Gonadoblastoma

Gonadoblastoma, first described by Scully in 1953 in an 8-year-old girl,[213] is almost always seen in dysgenetic gonads or in an undescended testis,[214–218] but rarely may occur in a normal gonad.[219,220] Among affected individuals, 80% are of phenotypic females and 20% are of phenotypic males. The majority of patients are negative for sex chromatin, with karyotypes of 46XY or mosaicism of 45XO/46XY.[221] Patients usually have abnormal gonads with cryptorchidism, hypospadias, and internal female secondary sex organs, which are in an inguinal or intra-abdominal location.

Gonadoblastomas are usually incidental findings on histologic examination of gonads excised for other reasons.[214] The tumor is bilateral in one-third of cases, and the majority of patients are younger than 20 years. Gonadoblastomas, per se, are clinically benign neoplasms, but many consider them as a form of "in-situ" germ cell tumor as 10–50% are accompanied by foci of malignant germ cell neoplasms, mostly seminoma, but sometimes embryonal carcinoma, yolk sac tumor, choriocarcinoma, or teratoma.[214–220] The extent of the associated germ cell neoplasm ranges from in-situ to invasive carcinoma.[218]

The tumor is gray to yellow-brown, ranging in size from microscopic foci (25%) to several centimeters (up to 8 cm) in diameter. It can be soft and fleshy, firm, or resemble cartilage,

flecked with granules of calcification, or be almost totally calcified. Larger tumors are usually superimposed by other malignant germ cell tumor elements.

On low magnification the tumor shows nests composed of large, round germ cells with vacuolated clear cytoplasm (resembling seminoma cells), closely admixed with and frequently surrounded by smaller cells of sex cord derivation surrounded by connective tissue stroma (Fig. 14B.32). Sertoli and granulosa cells line the periphery of the nests and surround individual germ cells (follicles). They may surround circular spaces containing amorphous, eosinophilic, PAS-positive, hyaline material (Call–Exner bodies). Numerous Call–Exner bodies and calcifications may be present within the cell nests. The germ cells may show mitotic figures, but mitoses are not found in the sex cord-stromal elements. The overgrowth of other neoplastic germ cells, usually seminoma, may lead to distortion and obliteration of the gonadoblastomatous foci. Coarse calcifications in an invasive germ cell tumor raise the possibility of origin from a gonadoblastoma. The seminoma-like cells are positive for PLAP, and inhibin marks the sex cord-stromal cells.[222,223] The prognosis for patients with gonadoblastoma is variable and seems to be dependent on the presence and extent of other germ cell components.[3,218] The prognosis is excellent in patients with pure gonadoblastoma. The prognosis of gonadoblastoma associated with seminoma is fair, but is poor in patients who have gonadoblastoma with other malignant germ cell elements. Gonadectomy is the treatment of choice for gonadoblastoma. Further treatment with radiation or chemotherapy is dependent on the presence and type of other germ cell components. Bilateral gonadectomy has been recommended when the contralateral gonad is abnormal or undescended, because of the high incidence of bilaterality of gonadoblastoma in dysgenetic gonads.

Unclassified mixed germ cell and sex cord-stromal tumor

This tumor occurs in the normally descended testes of phenotypically, anatomically, and genetically normal adult males, usually 30–60 years of age.[217,224–228] Patients present with a gradual, painless testicular enlargement not associated with

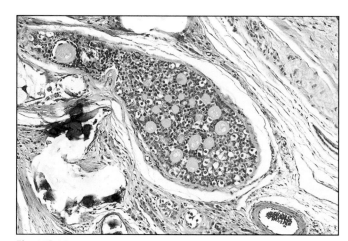

Fig. 14B.32 • Gonadoblastoma. A nest is composed of large germ cells with clear cytoplasm and oval round cells of sex cord derivation. Hyalinized bodies and scattered calcifications are also present.

endocrine abnormalities. The tumor is confined to the gonad in the pure form and is not seen in extragonadal locations or the contralateral testis.[217] ITGCN is rarely seen. The tumor is not associated with metastatic disease, and patients have an excellent prognosis after radical resection of the affected gonad. The contralateral gonad in every case is a normal testis.

This tumor is often large, up to 12 cm in diameter; it is a well-circumscribed, solid, and firm nodule whose cut surface is gray-white. The testis is usually entirely replaced by the tumor, without hemorrhage or necrosis. The testicular tissue surrounding the tumor is normal but compressed.

Two cell types constitute the tumor – germ cells and sex cord derivatives (Fig. 14B.33). The germ cell elements form cellular aggregates, clusters, and trabecula, which are surrounded and intersected by fibrous septa. The sex cord derivatives most commonly demonstrate trabecular, solid, tubular, and cord-like patterns; a follicular pattern with numerous Call–Exner bodies or an absence of any specific pattern may also be seen in sex cord derivatives. The degree of cellularity varies from densely cellular areas to hyalinized fibrous tissue.

At high magnification, large germ cells with clear cytoplasm and round, pale nuclei with prominent nucleoli are seen. The sex cord-derived tumor cells have indistinct cell boundaries, denser cytoplasm, and elongated or short spindle-shaped nuclei with dispersed granular chromatin, occasional nuclear grooves, and a centrally located, often indistinct, single nucleolus.

The germ cells are usually PLAP-positive, but AFP, hCG, Ki-1, CEA, and Leu-M1 are usually negative. Cytokeratin may be negative in large cells of germ cell derivation but, along with vimentin and inhibin, may be positive in sex cord-stromal components. Caution is warranted in interpreting this tumor type as it is extraordinarily rare; a frequent pitfall is the presence of entrapped non-neoplastic germ cells at the periphery, but occasionally in the center, of sex cord-stromal tumors. One paper suggested that some tumors of the testis with features that initially suggest unclassified mixed germ cell and sex cord-stromal tumor are sex cord-stromal tumors with entrapped germ cells.[229]

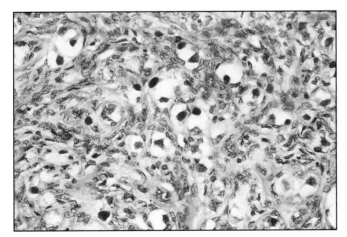

Fig. 14B.33 • Unclassified mixed germ cell and sex cord-stromal tumor. It shows two cell types: germ cells and cells of sex cord derivation. The germ cells have a large round nucleus and abundant clear cytoplasm. The cells of sex cord derivation are spindled and have scanty cytoplasm. The nuclei may show longitudinal nuclear grooves.

Management of NSGCT

Management of germ cell tumors of the testis varies to some degree at the major institutions. The following is a brief and superficial discussion of management strategies and its intent is to be informative and to highlight some of the important pathologic features of clinical significance.

Stage I NSGCT. Conventional management strategies for stage I NSGCT after orchiectomy include retroperitoneal lymph node dissection (RPLND), surveillance, chemotherapy for high-risk patients, and retroperitoneal radiotherapy.

RPLND remains the treatment of choice. Classic RPLND was associated with significant morbidity and a high incidence of sterility as the sympathetic and parasympathetic nerves and ganglia were removed. The current RPLND is less aggressive, attempting to remove all lymph nodes but preserving the sympathetic and parasympathetic ganglia – so-called "nerve-sparing" lymph node dissection.

Most investigators generally agree that predominance of embryonal carcinoma (>80%) and presence of lymphovascular invasion in the primary tumor are high-risk histologic factors for distant metastasis. At M. D. Anderson Cancer Center the presence of >80 ng/ml of AFP in the serum is also considered a high-risk factor for metastasis.[127] The presence or absence of these factors stratifies patients into low- and high-risk for the development of metastasis. Surveillance protocols, in existence since 1981, may be utilized for low-risk patients.[6,127–132] Surveillance protocols are expensive and require full cooperation from patients. They consist of close clinical monitoring with frequent serum marker determinations (LDH, hCG, and AFP), chest radiographs, and abdominal CT scans; furthermore, the surveillance is for 2 years as 95% of failures occur during the first year, and 5% in the second year. If patients are placed on surveillance, their chance of relapse is approximately 27%.

Amato et al.[230] evaluated whether two courses of chemotherapy after orchiectomy in patients with clinical stage I non-seminomatous germ cell testicular tumor at high risk of relapse would avoid additional chemotherapy or surgery for these patients. They found that two courses of postorchiectomy adjuvant chemotherapy were safe and well tolerated and markedly decreased the relapse rate in high-risk patients with clinical stage I non-seminomatous germ cell testicular tumor without additional surgery or more protracted chemotherapy. This approach is strictly investigational as there is still a fear that chemotherapy may induce another neoplasm after a long-term period. Radiotherapy to the retroperitoneoum for stage I disease is not utilized.

Stage II NSGCT. Patients with clinical stage II disease have either retroperitoneal metastasis, as determined by radiologic imaging, or they have elevated serum markers after orchiectomy without radiographic evidence of nodal metastasis.

For patients with stage II low-volume disease (metastases less than 5 cm in maximum diameter), standard current treatment options include: (1) RPLND followed by expectant observation, or chemotherapy;[231] and (2) chemotherapy followed by selective retroperitoneal lymphadenectomy for those patients with a persistent mass.[232]

The preferred treatment is RPLND, especially if the primary shows a component of teratoma. The rationale is that surgery will remove any teratomatous elements in the retroperitoneal lymph nodes. Chemotherapy, on the other hand, would destroy the high-grade tumor but would not affect the low-grade teratomatous components, and these will continue to grow (growing teratoma syndrome). RPLND for teratomatous elements following chemotherapy is far more difficult than for patients who have not undergone chemotherapy.

For patients with stage II low-volume disease who received chemotherapy, the frequency of radiographically identified retroperitoneal abnormalities that require surgery is directly proportional to the initial bulk of disease and the histologic type of the primary tumor (8–26% for embryonal carcinoma, 36–51% for teratocarcinoma). Interestingly, for 50 patients who received chemotherapy, surgery was not subsequently required if the pretreatment serum level of AFP was normal.

The pathologic findings in the metastatic foci may differ from those of the primary tumor. Moreover, in up to 15%, teratoma is present in metastases when it was absent in the primary tumor.[233–237]

Stage III NSGCT. The prognostic factors for advanced testicular NSGCTs include tumor volume, sites of metastasis, total number of metastases, and levels of serum markers (AFP, hCG, and lactate dehydrogenase).[63,204,232,238–240]

Chemotherapy is the treatment of choice for patients with bulky stage II and stage III NSGCTs; currently 60–90% of patients with these stages are cured of their disease by chemotherapy.[204,241,242] The most frequently used chemotherapy protocol for advanced-stage NSGCTs is the combination of bleomycin, cisplatin, and either vinblastine or etoposide. Treatment with this protocol leads to residual masses requiring surgery in 30% of cases; of these, residual viable carcinoma is found in 15–20%, teratoma in 36–50%, and necrosis or fibrosis in 36–40%.[242] The frequency of viable carcinoma can be further reduced up to 4% by a more aggressive chemotherapy protocol;[243] furthermore, most of the patients with residual masses can survive with further surgery.[232] Viable carcinoma after chemotherapy generally implies a guarded prognosis; approximately 33–75% of affected patients die of their disease despite postoperative chemotherapy.[244,245]

Investigators generally agree that, if radiographic abnormalities are absent, the relapse rate after chemotherapy without subsequent RPLND is relatively small (4–20%).[204,241,246] Fossa et al.[247] have challenged this notion, reporting that 30% of patients in their study had microscopic mature teratoma (and one patient had viable carcinoma) despite normal serum markers and negative radiologic findings.

In some patients, macroscopic teratoma remaining after chemotherapy implies relapse. Investigators at the University of Indiana reported a 40% rate of relapse of either carcinoma or teratoma (20% each).[248] Relapses in that study were related to initial tumor volume and the presence of immature teratoma along with non-germ cell elements. Resection was advised for all areas of visible disease remaining after chemotherapy. In the series reported from the Royal Marsden Hospital, relapse occurred in 7 of 12 patients whose teratoma or fibrosis had been incompletely resected.[249] Dexeus et al.[250] have also seen relapses in 3 of 6 patients with incompletely resected teratoma.

Despite its benign histologic appearance, mature teratoma has displayed aneuploid DNA content on flow cytometry and structural chromosome aberrations documented by cytogenetic analysis.[251,252] These results support the malignant potential of mature teratoma; the concept is strengthened by the frequent relapses of patients in whom teratoma has been incompletely resected. In the series of Roth et al.,[241] all late-relapsing patients (after 3–6 years) had evidence of prior teratoma.

The most important function of surgery is to resect residual mature teratoma that would indicate when chemotherapy for patients with residual radiographic masses can cease. Complete surgical excision of teratoma remains the most effective treatment. Thereafter, continued close follow-up is recommended, especially for high-risk patients who have immature teratoma with non-germ cell elements, patients with a large tumor burden, and patients who have primary mediastinal tumors with resectable teratoma.[248]

Non-germ cell malignancies following chemotherapy

During the past several years, investigators have described the development of non-germ cell malignancies following chemotherapy for a germ cell tumor.[253–255] They attributed the development of these new malignancies either to partial differentiation of totipotential germ cells to somatic tissues with concomitant malignant transformation or to malignant transformation of pre-existing teratomatous elements. The prognosis of these patients depends on the nature of the non-germ cell malignancies. Ulbright and colleagues from Indiana University encountered several types of non-germ cell malignancies, including various forms of sarcoma, carcinomas of teratomatous origin, nephroblastomas, PNET, and glioblastoma multiforme.[192,193,253,254,256,257] The prognosis was worst for patients who developed rhabdomyosarcomas. Other forms of sarcoma, carcinomas of teratomatous origin, and nephroblastoma did not appear to affect the prognosis any more adversely than did teratoma alone.[253,254] The effectiveness of chemotherapy directed against the sarcomatous elements is speculative at this time. The diagnostic dilemma that one must realize, however, is that no postoperative evaluation can reliably exclude the presence of viable carcinoma following chemotherapy. The morphologic spectrum after chemotherapy includes necrosis, fibrosis, teratoma, and residual viable germ cell tumor. The presence of persistent germ cell tumor such as seminoma, embryonal carcinoma, yolk sac tumor, or choriocarcinoma is an indication that additional chemotherapy is needed, whereas for persistent teratoma, necrosis and fibrosis are not regarded as indicative of a need for additional treatment. The prognosis is good for patients whose postchemotherapy resections contain necrosis, fibrosis, or teratoma. Therefore, proper recognition of residual malignant germ cell elements is important. Although choriocarcinoma has the highest metastatic potential among germ cell tumors, it rarely presents as stage II disease.

Pathologic evaluation of resected metastatic disease

Teratomatous metastases that were completely resected after chemotherapy sometimes display cellular atypia in the epithelial or mesenchymal components, but these changes did not influence subsequent biologic behavior. The most important histologic parameter in teratomatous metastasis is the recognition of frank malignant transformation by the teratomatous element rather than by the presence of high-grade cytologic atypia. Identification of such malignant transformation is relatively easy for epithelial elements that are represented by a carcinoma. Malignancy of mesenchymal elements is based on the amounts of the pure mesenchymal elements; thus, a field area in excess of that viewed with a ×4 objective is cause for concern (Fig. 14B.34). With these findings, the Indiana University Group concluded that cytologic atypia in mesenchymal and epithelial elements, in the absence of frank malignant transformation, was not sufficient justification for altering the usual therapeutic strategy for patients with teratomatous metastases.[258]

Chong et al.[259] reviewed the records of 16 patients with advanced NSGCTs who underwent initial chemotherapy followed by delayed orchiectomy; 13 patients had achieved a complete remission and 3 had a partial remission at the time of the delayed orchiectomy. Three of the 13 patients (23%) had persistent viable tumor in the testis. One of the 3 patients with a partial remission had residual tumor in the testis, and his disease progressed despite further therapy. No tumor was evident in the testes of the other 2 patients. These data indicate that germ cell tumors in primary and metastatic sites respond differently.

In summary, since pathologic findings are important to the clinician treating patients with testicular germ cell tumors, pathology reports should include the following information: (1) gross features, including tumor size, extension beyond the tunica, invasion into the spermatic cord including cord margin, and tumor necrosis; (2) histologic classification: seminoma versus non-seminoma (NSGCT); (3) for NSGCT, a statement as to whether the tumor is pure or mixed and the relative amount of each component in a mixed tumor; (4) a statement as to whether vascular or lymphatic invasion is present; (5) a statement as to whether viable carcinoma or teratoma elements containing non-germ components are present in the resected specimen after chemotherapy. Proper interpretation of per-sistent masses after chemotherapy is important in determining the future treatment of these patients. It is apparent that modifications of tumor growth patterns after chemotherapy are not uncommon and that additional experience and review of these specimens will lead to the discovery of further modification of classic patterns.[260]

Sex cord-stromal tumors

Leydig (interstitial) cell tumor

LCTs comprise 1–3% of all testicular neoplasms and may occur at any age, but are most commonly seen between the second and sixth decades of life.[3,261–264] Approximately 20% are detected in the prepubertal age group. The tumors are usually unilateral; only 3% occur bilaterally.[261] Testicular swelling, decreased libido (20%), and gynecomastia (15%) are common symptoms in adults. Pseudoprecocity is usually seen in children. Malignant clinical behavior occurs in approximately 10% and metastasis is the sole criterion for malignancy. A malignant outcome has not been reported in children, or in tumors manifesting with endocrine abnormalities.

The tumor is a sharply circumscribed, solid mass, 3–5 cm in diameter, with a homogeneous and soft consistency. The color is usually yellow to mahogany-brown but may rarely be gray-white (Fig. 14B.35). Focal hemorrhage and/or necrosis are present in one-quarter of cases, and extraparenchymal tumor extension can be seen in 10–15% of cases. Rare cases of extra-testicular LCT have been reported.[263]

The diffuse and nodular patterns are most common; however, trabecular, tubular, and pseudofollicular patterns occur.[261] Sheets or broad cords of tumor cells are separated by a fibrous stroma which is typically inconspicuous but may rarely be hyalinized, edematous, or myxoid. There are numerous thin-walled blood vessels (Fig. 14B.36). Rarely, there may be a microcystic growth pattern that mimics yolk sac tumor.[264] Tumor cells are large and polygonal with round nuclei and abundant eosinophilic or vacuolated cytoplasm, the latter type reflecting abundant lipid within the cytoplasm

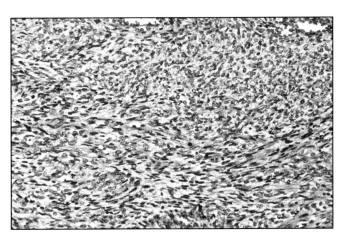

Fig. 14B.34 • Immature teratoma with sarcomatoid overgrowth from a patient treated for a mixed germ cell tumor of the testis. The lesion, from the retroperitoneum, displays a diffuse spindle cell proliferation indistinguishable from any other spindle cell sarcoma of soft tissue.

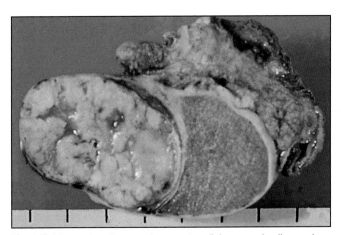

Fig. 14B.35 • Leydig cell tumor. The tumor is well demarcated, yellow, and has focal fibrous scarring.

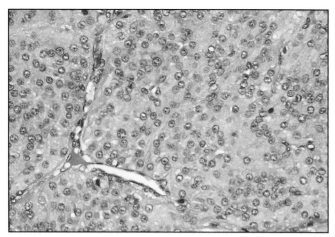

Fig. 14B.36 • Leydig cell tumor. The tumor cells are arranged in diffuse fashion and separated by thin-walled vessels.

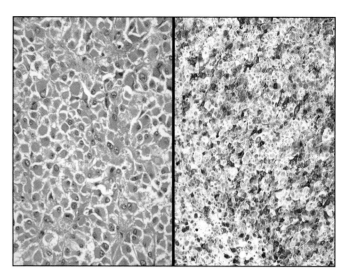

Fig. 14B.38 • Leydig cell tumor with rhabdoid cells (left) and positive staining in the tumor cells by inhibin stain (right).

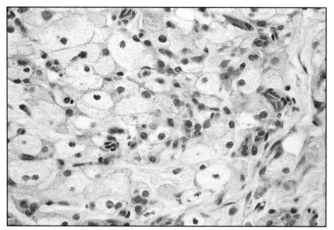

Fig. 14B.37 • Leydig cell tumor. Tumor cells are large and polygonal. The cytoplasm is abundant and eosinophilic, and can be clear due to abundant intracytoplasmic lipids.

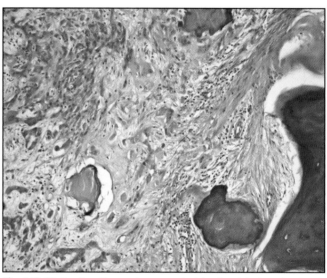

Fig. 14B.39 • Leydig cell tumor is seen on the left side, while the right side shows mature bone formation.

(Fig. 14B.37). Spindle-shaped cells with abundant eosinophilic cytoplasm may predominate in rare cases. The nuclei are typically round with a single prominent nucleolus, and there may be rare nuclear grooves, mimicking the nuclei of granulosa cells. We recently observed a case of LCT with abundant rhabdoid tumor cells (Fig. 14B.38). Mitoses are rare or absent, although they may be frequent in occasional cases.[261] Nuclear pleomorphism may be striking in some cases. Pathognomonic crystalloids of Reinke are seen in 25–40% of cases, and lipofuscin pigment is present in 10–15%.[261] Psammoma bodies and ossification are rarely observed.[265,266] Various steroid hormones can be detected by immunohistochemistry.[267]

Recently Ulbright et al.[268] reported 19 LCTs of the testis with unusual features, including adipose differentiation, calcification with ossification (Fig. 14B.39), and spindle-shaped tumor cells. Awareness of these unusual patterns in LCTs is important to prevent misinterpretation of fat admixed with neoplastic Leydig cells, as evidence of extratesticular growth (a criterion for malignant LCT) may help avoid misdiagnosis

of a LCT as a "testicular tumor of the adrenogenital syndrome" (which may contain fat) and may prevent misdiagnosis of an LCT with spindle cells as a sarcoma or unclassified sex cord-stromal tumor, and LCT with calcification and ossification as large cell calcifying Sertoli cell tumors (LCCSCT).

The majority of these tumors are benign, but malignancy may be present in 10–20% of cases.[261,269,270] Unfortunately, there is no single criterion to separate benign and malignant tumors on the basis of morphology. Tumors with a malignant outcome tend to be large in size and show infiltrative margins, vascular invasion, nuclear atypia, necrosis, high mitotic rate, and lack of lipofuscin pigment; a single feature is not diagnostic for malignancy and usually tumors with a malignant outcome show more than three of these features.[261]

Hekimgil et al.[271] reported that a panel of antibodies, including Ki-67, p53, and bcl-2, used for immunohistochemical analysis could be of diagnostic value in the identification of malignant and borderline cases of LCT. Tumor cells are positive for inhibin, calretinin, and vimentin, but immunostaining for keratin and S-100 protein is negative or focally positive.[271–276] The differential diagnosis of an LCT includes Leydig cell hyperplasia, LCCSCT, tumor of adrenogenital syndrome (TTAGS), malignant melanoma, lymphoma, plasmacytoma, metastatic carcinoma, hepatoid yolk sac tumor, and malakoplakia. Leydig cell hyperplasia is suspected by the absence of a discrete mass on gross examination, the proliferating cells occurring in an interstitial location in a background of testicular atrophy.

TTAGS are bilateral, multifocal, and occur in patients with adrenogenital syndrome. Microscopically, the cells that resemble Leydig cells are often present in an interstitial location. Abundant lipofuscin pigment, the presence of seminiferous tubules between the cellular proliferation, and the clinical history are helpful features.

LCCSCT are frequently bilateral and multifocal and may show intratubular growth at the periphery. The hallmark of the tumor is prominent calcifications, usually distributed throughout the tumor. The cells of LCCSCT otherwise have a marked cytologic resemblance to LCTs. An inflammatory component and trabecular, small cluster, or solid tubular configurations are helpful features, along with calcification and intratubular growth, to distinguish LCCSCT from LCT. However, LCT may show prominent calcification in the stroma, which requires special attention not to misinterpret as LCCSCT.

Metastatic malignant melanoma is usually bilateral with a predominantly interstitial pattern of infiltration. The cells are pleomorphic, with numerous mitoses, and often have golden-brown melanin pigment. Malignant melanoma is usually positive for S-100 protein and HMB-45.

Malignant lymphoma is frequently bilateral; invasion of the epididymis and spermatic cord is common. The tumor cells show an interstitial pattern of infiltration and also invade seminiferous tubules. LCA is usually positive in lymphoma cells. Metastatic carcinoma is usually bilateral or multifocal with frequent vascular invasion and an interstitial pattern of infiltration. Cytokeratin is strongly positive in most metastatic carcinomas.

Hepatoid yolk sac tumor may mimic an LCT because of prominent cytoplasmic eosinophilia. Hepatoid yolk sac tumors invariably exhibit other patterns of yolk sac tumor, making discrimination from LCT fairly straightforward. Malakoplakia contains histiocytes admixed with other inflammatory cells, with characteristic Michaelis–Gutmann bodies.

Sertoli cell tumor

Fewer than 1% of all testicular neoplasms are Sertoli cell tumors.[3,277–280] They occur at all ages but 30% occur in the first decade of life.[279] Patients present with a scrotal mass which is usually unilateral, but bilateral cases have been reported.[3,278,279] Approximately 20% of patients have gynecomastia,[3,278] which is more commonly associated with malignant forms, and the tumor can be seen in patients with undescended testes,[279] Peutz–Jeghers syndrome,[281,282] and testicular feminization syndrome.[283] The majority of Sertoli cell tumors are benign, but approximately 10% are malignant. Malignant tumors most commonly metastasize to iliac and para-aortic lymph nodes and rarely to lung.[284–286] Two variants, LCCSCT (see below) and sclerosing Sertoli cell tumor, have been described. No tumors of the sclerosing variant have metastasized.

Pathologic features

Gross examination shows a small (mean diameter 3.5 cm), well-delineated, usually homogeneous, sometimes lobulated, yellow-gray, or tan-white mass that is rarely cystic. Hemorrhage, necrosis, and extension beyond the testis are unusual.[3,278,279] Bilaterality is distinctly rare, except in LCCSCT.

The conventional type of Sertoli cell tumor consists of uniform cells arranged in tubules, solid nests, cords with or without lumina, and a retiform pattern; a delicate fibrous stroma surrounds the tumor nests (Fig. 14B.40). Sclerosing Sertoli cell tumors have prominent stromal sclerosis and hyalinization but otherwise have architectural patterns similar to the conventional form (Fig. 14B.41).[280] The tubules of sclerosing tumors occasionally have a well-developed basement membrane. When a malignant spindle cell component predominates, the term sarcomatoid Sertoli cell tumor has been used.[287] The tubules are lined by uniform cuboidal or columnar cells with abundant clear or eosinophilic cytoplasm in well-differentiated tumors, but pleomorphism is a feature in less differentiated forms.[3,278–280] The tumor cells have large vesicular nuclei with prominent and centrally located nucleoli.

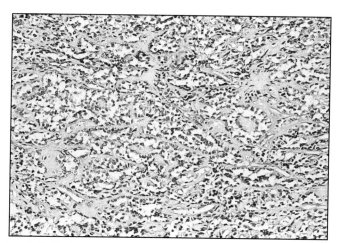

Fig. 14B.40 • Sertoli cell tumor. The uniform cells are arranged in tubules within a fibrous stroma.

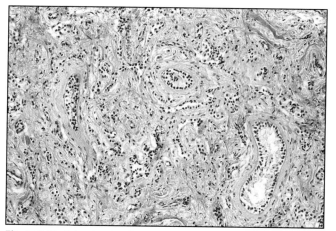

Fig. 14B.41 • Sclerosing Sertoli cell tumor. There are scattered, small, anastomosing tubules and cords of tumor cells typical of this lesion in a densely collagenized stroma.

Occasional cases show more sheet-like growth with less obvious tubules and may mimic seminoma.[288] Large size (5 cm or more), vascular invasion, increased mitotic activity (greater than 5 mitoses per 10 high-power fields), necrosis, pleomorphism, solid architecture, and spindle cell differentiation are features which are more commonly seen in tumors with a malignant outcome.[289]

Immunohistochemistry

Cytokeratin is usually positive in well-differentiated tumors; vimentin is positive in most cases.[267,290] Inhibin and calretinin staining is variable.[272,274] Sertoli cells as well as granulosa cells produce anti-müllerian hormone (AMH). Therefore, AMH can be used as a specific marker of human granulosa or Sertoli cell origin in gonadal tumors, to distinguish them from other primary or metastatic neoplasms, using immuno-histochemistry.[291] CD99, a marker for MIC-2, reacts with Sertoli cell tumors and granulosa cell tumors that might aid in distinguishing Sertoli cell tumors and granulosa cell tumors from carcinomas.[292]

Differential diagnosis

Primary carcinoma of the rete testis and metastatic carcinoma of the testis should be differentiated from Sertoli cell tumors. Metastatic carcinoma usually exhibits a mixture of small and large glands with significant nuclear atypia and frequent mitoses. Mucin is frequently demonstrated in metastatic carcinoma, and CEA immunostaining is usually positive in tumor cells. In contrast, Sertoli cell tumors show relatively uniform glandular size, solid tubular structures, and a mixture of glandular, trabecular, and sarcomatoid growth patterns. Mucin and CEA are negative in tumor cells. The epicenter of rete testis carcinoma is in the region of the rete. Transition from normal rete epithelium to hyperplastic and neoplastic epithelium is confirmatory. Non-neoplastic clusters, which are usually focal and seen in cryptorchidism, Sertoli cell nodules (Pick's adenoma), and adenomatoid tumor may also mimic Sertoli cell tumor. A seminoma with abundant clear cells and with a "tubular" pattern may also simulate a predominantly solid Sertoli cell tumor; PLAP and cytokeratin immunostains are helpful.

Large cell calcifying Sertoli cell tumor

The LCCSCT, a subtype of Sertoli cell tumor, is most commonly seen in the second decade of life (range 2–51 years, average 21 years).[293–295] Patients with this tumor have a testicular mass, frequently bilateral (40%) and multifocal (60%).[293] These tumors are usually associated with gynecomastia, sexual precocity, acromegaly, sudden death, and Peutz–Jeghers syndrome.[293] In up to 50% of cases, features of Carney syndrome, including pituitary adenoma, cardiac myxoma, nodular hyperplasia of adrenal cortex, and pigmentation of skin, can be found.[293,296] Less than 10 of approximately 50 reported cases of LCCSCT have had a clinically malignant course.[296,297] Malignant tumors usually occur in non-pubertal patients and in patients without a syndrome (Carney or Peutz–Jeghers). Such cases are frequently solitary, of large size, and with necrosis and extension beyond the testis.[297]

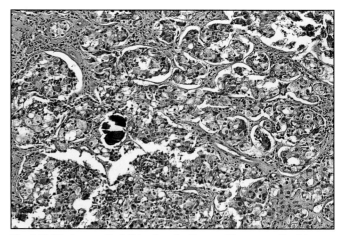

Fig. 14B.42 • Large cell calcifying Sertoli cell tumor. The tumor cells with abundant eosinophilic cytoplasm are arranged in nests and clusters. A laminated calcific body is also seen.

Macroscopically LCCSCT are usually less than 4 cm in diameter, firm, yellow-tan, and well circumscribed.[294,295,298,299] On microscopic examination, large neoplastic cells (15–35 mm) with abundant eosinophilic cytoplasm are arranged in diffuse sheets or nests, trabeculae, cords, tubules, or clusters separated by fibrous stroma (Fig. 14B.42).[294] There is calcification which is usually conspicuous and forms large, basophilic, laminated calcific bodies.[294] Foci of intratubular tumor growth with hyalinization of basement membranes are seen in 50% of the cases. The bilateral and multicentric character of intratubular Sertoli cell proliferations and their association with LCCSCTs and Peutz–Jeghers syndrome suggest that they represent either proliferative lesions with tumorigenic potential or the intra-epithelial stage in the evolution of some testicular Sertoli cell tumors.[300]

Tumor cells are usually round, occasionally cuboidal or columnar, and rarely spindle-shaped. The nuclei are round or oval with stippled chromatin and small nucleoli. The cytoplasm is eosinophilic, ground-glass, finely granular, or vacuolated. Mitoses are rare. On ultrastructural analysis the tumor cells show features of Sertoli cells.[295,298,299,301,302]

The differential diagnosis includes LCT and TTAGS.[303] LCTs are usually solitary and unilateral with a lack of intra-tubular growth and laminated calcific bodies. Reinke crystal-loids and lipofuscin pigment may be seen in the LCTs. A recent study demonstrated that both S-100-alpha and S-100-beta immunopositivity can potentially be used as immuno-histochemical markers for LCCSCT, especially when differen-tiating it from LCT, which may mimic LCCSCT on routine histopathology and expresses only S-100-alpha with negative staining for S-100-beta.[304] TTAGSs are seen in patients with the salt-losing form of adrenocortical disease (see below). Laboratory examination reveals the typical findings of adrenogenital syndrome. The tumor has a large amount of lipofuscin pigment, but lacks crystalloids of Reinke.

Granulosa cell tumor

Granulosa cell tumors, like their ovarian counterparts, have two distinctive types: juvenile and adult. The juvenile form is seen predominantly in infants and is the most common non-germ cell neoplasm of the neonatal testis. It may be associated

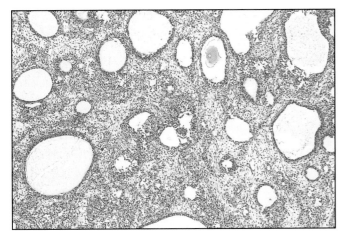

Fig. 14B.43 • Juvenile granulosa cell tumor. Most of the tumor cells are arranged diffusely, but also form follicular structures containing basophilic mucinous fluid which is positive for mucicarmine stain.

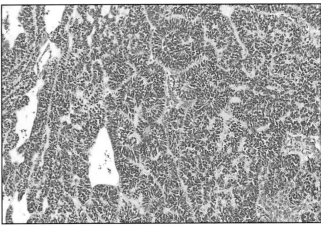

Fig. 14B.44 • Adult granulosa cell tumor. The tumor is arranged in a diffuse solid pattern and forms small follicular structures (Call–Exner bodies).

with undescended testes or gonadal dysgenesis. Patients present with a scrotal mass. Malignant behavior has never been reported in juvenile tumors.[305–310]

Four patients with adult granulosa cell tumors have had a malignant outcome with metastasis, usually to retroperitoneal lymph nodes.[311,312]

The juvenile form is usually 6–8 cm in diameter and mostly cystic, or partially solid, with a thin cystic wall and intracystic viscid fluid.[305,313] Microscopically, the juvenile form shows a follicular, solid, or mixed pattern with variably sized follicles, which may be quite large (Fig. 14B.43); there is often prominent hyalinization. The follicles contain basophilic or eosinophilic fluid which is mucicarmine and PAS-positive.[305] The tumor consists of round to polyhedral cells with hyperchromatic nuclei and usually abundant to moderate eosinophilic cytoplasm. Mitotic activity may be prominent.

The adult form is the least common type of sex cord-stromal tumor of the testis. Fewer than a dozen cases have been reported in the literature.[3,278,311,312,314–317] The patients' ages ranged from 20 to 53 years. The adult form can be associated with gynecomastia.[314,315,317] The tumor is a yellow-tan, firm, lobulated mass, which may vary in size from 1 to 10 cm. On microscopic examination, it shows a microfollicular pattern with Call–Exner bodies or a solid pattern (Fig. 14B.44). Typically the nuclei are oval to round and show characteristic grooves. Focal cytologic atypia may be present.

Special stains and differential diagnosis

Mucicarmine and PAS stains are negative in the adult type, in contrast to the juvenile type. Cytokeratin is usually negative or focally positive in granulosa cell tumors of the testis. Vimentin, inhibin, and calretinin are usually positive. The differential diagnosis of adult granulosa cell tumors includes carcinoid tumor, LCT, and Sertoli cell tumor. The carcinoid tumor has oval to round nuclei without nuclear grooves, and has a "salt-and-pepper" (finely granular) chromatin pattern. There is a solid or insular growth pattern with tubules, trabeculae, and cords. These tumors are positive for synaptophysin, NSE, and chromogranin, and negative for inhibin and calretinin.

LCTs and Sertoli cell tumors are fairly distinctive and different enough from granulosa cell tumors that they usually pose minimal problems in the differential diagnosis. The differential diagnosis of juvenile granulosa cell tumors includes yolk sac tumor, which is separable by the absence of prominent follicles, lack of conspicuous basophilic or eosinophilic secretions, and the frequent presence of other tumor patterns. Embryonal rhabdomyosarcoma and malignant lymphoma are other possibilities, although the former does not occur within the testis, and the latter is positive for LCA.

Tumors in the fibroma-thecoma group

Tumors in the fibroma-thecoma category are distinctly rare and resemble their ovarian counterparts. The mean age is 30 years, and patients typically present with a testicular mass. The follow-up is uneventful.[3,318–321]

The tumors vary from less than 1 cm to up to 7 cm. The cut section is usually firm and tan-white to yellow. The microscopic features are identical to their ovarian counterparts (see Ch. 13A). Cellular tumors may show mitotic activity up to two mitotic figures per 10 high-power fields. One recent report stated that the neoplastic cells of the fibroma were positive for vimentin and smooth muscle actin, but not for cytokeratin, S-100 protein, desmin, CD99/MIC2 (a protein expressed by Sertoli cells and granulosa cells), and CD34.[321]

Mixed or unclassified gonadal stromal tumor

Some testicular sex cord-stromal tumors have two or more patterns of the above-discussed histologic subtypes and hence are considered mixed. When these tumors are admixed with a spindle cell component, or are predominantly composed of an otherwise unclassifiable spindle cell component, the term unclassified gonadal stromal tumor is used. For this discussion both are grouped together as they have similar clinico-pathologic features and it is not possible accurately to separate the mixed from the unclassified tumors that have been reported in the literature. Although these tumors can occur at all ages, they are most common in children (30% of patients are

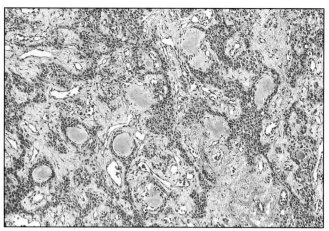

Fig. 14B.45 • Unclassified sex cord-stromal tumor. The tumor cells are arranged in trabeculae and nests separated by fibrous stroma.

Fig. 14B.46 • Unclassified sex cord-stromal tumor. In this field, the neoplastic cells have a spindle cell appearance with occasional mitotic activity.

younger than 1 year old).[3,278] Painless testicular enlargement is the most common presenting symptom, and gynecomastia or other hormone-related symptoms may be present. The behavior is mostly benign in prepubertal children (10 years of age or younger), but these tumors have the potential to pursue a malignant clinical course in older individuals.[278,322–324] The frequency of gynecomastia is higher in malignant tumors than in benign tumors.

The tumor is grossly characterized by a well-circumscribed, lobulated, white-yellow mass of variable size that may replace the entire testis. Cystic areas can be seen, but hemorrhage and necrosis are uncommon.

At low magnification various patterns are evident dependent on histologic differentiation. Most commonly, epithelioid and stromal components are seen in varying proportions (Fig. 14B.45). The epithelioid component consists of well-formed, solid, or hollow tubules or cords (Sertoli cell elements) in well-differentiated tumors and irregular aggregates or anastomosing trabeculae of sex cord-type cells embedded in a fibrous stroma in less differentiated tumors. The stromal component may be hypercellular or fibrous. An arrangement of cells, which are smaller with scant cytoplasm, may be similar to that of Call–Exner bodies (granulosa cell elements).

The cells of the epithelioid component usually have eosinophilic, amphophilic, or vacuolated cytoplasm that may contain abundant lipid. They generally have round to oval vesicular nuclei and may have prominent nucleoli. Mitotic figures are rare or absent.[278] The stromal component consists of spindle cells, which may show nuclear grooves and pleomorphism depending on the degree of differentiation (Fig. 14B.46). Mitotic figures can be frequent in the stromal component. Immunostains generally show positivity for S-100 protein and smooth muscle actin.[318] Mixed Sertoli-LCTs are distinctly uncommon in the testis.[325]

The important parameters affecting the prognosis include the age of the patient, the size of the tumor, invasion beyond the testis, necrosis, pleomorphism, and mitotic activity. Approximately 25% of tumors in adults have pursued a malignant course. Benign sex cord-stromal tumors are treated by inguinal orchiectomy. If the clinical and pathologic features suggest the possibility of malignancy, a careful staging work-up, including CT scan and retroperitoneal lymphangiogram

with close follow-up and/or retroperitoneal lymphadenectomy, should be considered. The high frequency of lymph node metastases in malignant sex cord-stromal tumors justifies this approach.

Differential diagnosis includes interdigitating dendritic cell tumor, which is an extremely rare neoplasm mainly occurring in lymph nodes. Luk et al.[326] reported an example of such a tumor in the testis. Microscopically, it was formed by whorls and fascicles of spindle cells intermingling with small lymphocytes. Such a histologic appearance can, however, mimic a wide variety of other tumors and tumor-like lesions, among which sex cord-stromal tumor, mesenchymal sarcoma, spindle cell carcinoma, follicular dendritic cell tumor, and inflammatory pseudotumor are the main differential diagnoses. A pathologist should be aware of such an entity and consider it in the list of differential diagnoses for unusual spindle cell lesions with a significant background population of small lymphocytes. However, because of its non-specific histologic appearance, additional immunohistochemical and electron microscopic studies are generally required for definitive diagnosis. This tumor is positive for S-100 protein and vimentin and focally positive for CD68 and CD4, but negative for inhibin, calretinin, and melan-A, which are markers for sex cord stromal tumors.

Tumor of adrenogenital syndrome

TTAGS are commonly bilateral and seen in patients with the salt-losing form of adrenogenital syndrome (21-hydroxylase deficiency). The masses become evident in childhood or early adult life. They are well circumscribed, dark brown, lobulated, and traversed by fibrous septa. Lesions may be multifocal or single and may be as large as 10 cm; they most commonly originate in the hilar region.[327]

At low magnification, there is a diffuse proliferation of large cells, with broad cords of tumor cells separated by thin fibrovascular septa (Fig. 14B.47).[327] The large cells resemble Leydig cells, with abundant eosinophilic cytoplasm containing lipofuscin pigment and central nuclei with prominent nucleoli.[327–329]

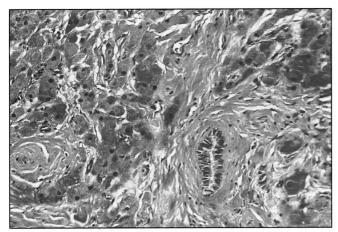

Fig. 14B.47 • Tumor of adrenogenital syndrome. There is a diffuse proliferation of large cells with abundant eosinophilic cytoplasm separated by fibrovascular septa.

Lymphoreticular neoplasms

Lymphoma

Primary malignant lymphoma of the testis is rare.[331–333] Testicular involvement is more commonly seen as a late manifestation of disseminated disease, occurring in about 20% of all lymphomas.[331–336] Malignant lymphoma of the testis constitutes about 5% of all testicular neoplasms.[331,332] It is the most common malignant tumor of the testis in patients over 60 years of age[337] and the second most frequent malignant neoplasm of testis.[331] Patients have testicular enlargement that is usually painless. The median age at diagnosis of diffuse large B-cell lymphoma was 66 years (range, 19–91 years).[338] Ninety percent of lymphomas are of B-cell lineage.[332,335,339] There is a propensity for testicular lymphomas to be associated with skin, central nervous system, and Waldeyer's ring involvement. The incidence of bilaterality varies from 6% to 38% (average 20%).[331–333,335,340]

Pathologic features

Part or all of the testicular parenchyma is replaced by a mass or multiple confluent nodules.[331–333] The nodules are firm or soft, fleshy and homogeneous, with a cream, tan, or slightly pink color, closely resembling seminoma (Fig. 14B.48).[331,332] Necrosis is uncommon. Up to 50% of these tumors spread to the spermatic cord or epididymis.[331–335] The tumor growth pattern is characterized predominantly by interstitial infiltration of neoplastic cells with relative sparing of seminiferous tubules, although the seminiferous tubules may be filled up or effaced (Fig. 14B.49). Vascular invasion is seen in up to two-thirds of cases.[332,333]

High-power magnification allows for subtyping of most lymphomas. In the largest study, approximately 80% were diffuse large cell, and 9% were small non-cleaved cell using the Working Formulation classification; 62% were centroblastic, 14% were immunoblastic, and 9% were Burkitt's lymphoma

Fibrosis can be prominent. Seminiferous tubules may be present within the tumor. Focal nuclear atypia and mitotic figures can be found. They lack crystalloids of Reinke.[327] Bilaterality, multifocality, the presence of intralesional seminiferous tubules, and response to medical therapy suggest that these tumorous lesions may not be truly neoplastic but may be hyperplastic. One exceptional case occurring in a patient with adrenogenital syndrome and interpreted as LCT was reported to show malignant behavior; hence one must exercise caution against the consideration that all these tumors are benign or "hyperplastic."[330] These tumors are responsive to adrenocorticotropic hormone (ACTH) suppression, and orchiectomy is not required except for cosmetic reasons.

The differential diagnosis includes LCTs and LCCSTs. Clinical information alone should be sufficient in most cases to differentiate this tumor from the LCTs and LCCSTs, although patients may present with the testicular lesion before seeking attention for other symptoms of the syndrome.

Fig. 14B.48 • Lymphoma. Testicular parenchyma is diffusely replaced by a soft, homogeneous, tan-colored nodule closely resembling seminoma.

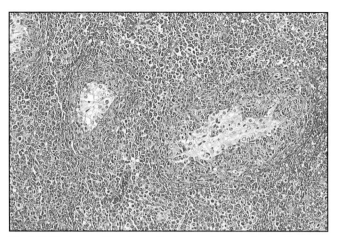

Fig. 14B.49 • Large cell lymphoma. The tumor cells are predominantly infiltrating the interstitium of the testis, but seminiferous tubules may be involved.

using the Kiel classification.[333] Cases of anaplastic Ki-1 lymphoma, lymphoma of T/natural killer cell origin, and Hodgkin's disease have also been reported.[151,341–348] T-cell lymphomas, lymphoblastic type, are more common in children and young adults.[349] Cytokeratin and PLAP are negative in the tumor cells, and LCA is usually positive, as mentioned.

Primary pediatric follicular lymphoma of the testis (PPFLT) has been described, but pathologic findings and clinical features suggest that it may represent a unique subset of follicular lymphoma with a different pathogenesis and a better prognosis compared with adult follicular lymphoma.[340,348] Molecular analysis supports the follicular origin, by revealing monoclonal immunoglobulin heavy-chain gene rearrangement and *BCL-6* mutations, in the absence of *BCL-2* major break-point and *BCL-2* minor cluster region rearrangements, *p53* mutations, and death-associated protein kinase gene hypermethylation.[340,348,350]

Survival

Overall survival is 15–30% at 2 years.[351] In a large series the actuarial 5-year disease-free survival was 35%, and the 10-year overall survival rate was 32%; the median overall survival was 4.4 years.[337,352] Of 84 patients, disease was classified as stage I in 42 cases, stage II in 19, and stage III–IV in 23. Median overall survival was 32 months for the entire population, 52 months for stage I, 32 months for stage II, and 12 months for stage III–IV cases ($P < 0.0001$).[337] Within the entire cohort, adverse prognostic factors for treatment failure were serum albumin ≤ 3.5 g/dl ($P = 0.02$), advanced age, advanced stage, and lack of anthracycline-containing chemotherapy (each $P \leq 0.3$).[340,352] The outcome of the patients with diffuse large B-cell lymphoma seemed worse than that reported for diffuse large B-cell lymphoma at other sites, even in cases with stage I disease and favorable international prognostic index score.[338] At a median follow-up of 7.6 years, 195 patients (52%) had relapsed. Relapses in the central nervous system were detected in 56 patients (15%) up to 10 years after presentation. Testicular diffuse large cell lymphoma is characterized by a particularly high risk of extranodal relapse, even in cases with localized disease at diagnosis. Anthracycline-based chemotherapy, central nervous system prophylaxis (because the most frequent

site of relapse was the central nervous system),[338,353,354] and contralateral testicular irradiation seem to improve the outcome.[338,353,354]

Leukemic infiltration

Leukemia involves the testis when the disease is widely disseminated. At autopsy, leukemic infiltration of the testis has been reported in up to 65% of patients with acute leukemia and in 30% with chronic leukemia.[355–357] It is seen most commonly, in contemporary times, in biopsies of patients with acute lymphoblastic leukemia to detect relapse after treatment. The majority of patients who have testicular involvement also have leukemic infiltration in other organs, which supports the view that testicular infiltration is indicative of widespread disease. Leukemic infiltration is invariably bilateral but usually asymmetrical, and may also involve the epididymis.

Symptomatic testicular enlargement is rare; it is seen in only 4.5% of cases. On gross examination, there is a bulging cut surface above the tunica albuginea. Leukemic infiltration is more often a microscopic finding.[358] The incidence of testicular involvement has increased as longer remissions from bone marrow and meningeal disease have been achieved.[358–362] Testicular infiltration is a harbinger of systemic relapse, and is especially common among children with lymphoblastic leukemia.

Leukemic cells have an interstitial pattern of infiltration, with rare tubular invasion. There may be vessel wall infiltration. Depending on the type of leukemia, primitive lymphoid cells and immature myeloid cells comprise the infiltrate.[363]

Plasmacytoma (multiple myeloma)

Extramedullary plasmacytoma is rare at this site. It may represent an early manifestation of multiple myeloma or it may be discovered at autopsy of patients with multiple myeloma. Only a few primary testicular tumors with no evidence of bone marrow involvement have been reported.[364–368] Testicular enlargement may be present alone[364,365] or in association with systemic manifestations of multiple myeloma.[369–374] A case of primary extramedullary plasmacytoma of the testis in a patient with acquired immunodeficiency syndrome (AIDS) has been reported.[368] It occurs primarily (75%) in the fifth to seventh decades of life, and is bilateral in 20–30% of cases.

The gross appearance is that of a pink-tan, lobulated, firm, ill-defined, or discrete nodule. The tumor may be a fleshy mass up to 8 cm, and generally there is no hemorrhage, necrosis, or cyst formation. Involvement of adnexa is less frequent than in lymphoma.

There is a predominantly interstitial infiltrative growth pattern of immature plasma cells, with frequent invasion of seminiferous tubules, blood vessels, and tunica albuginea (Fig. 14B.50). The tumor cell population is homogeneous and is composed of cytologically immature plasma cells. There are no associated histiocytes, lymphocytes, or neutrophils.

Metastatic neoplasms

Tumors metastatic to the testis are relatively rare and accounted for only 3.6% of testicular tumors at one institution.[375] They

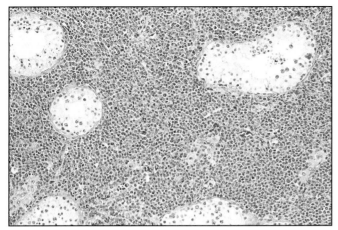

Fig. 14B.50 • Plasmacytoma. Immature plasma cells are infiltrating the interstitial tissue of the testis, separating seminiferous tubules.

affect men mainly over the age of 50 years (mean 55 years), who present with testicular enlargement associated with intra-testicular nodules or masses.[375–380] The incidence of bilaterality is 15%.[375,376] Testicular metastases occur in 2.5% of men with malignant tumors, and the most common primary sites include prostate, lung, skin (malignant melanoma), colon, and kidney (together constituting 80% of these tumors). Rare tumors include neuroblastoma, Wilms tumor, retinoblastoma, mesothelioma, and Merkel cell tumor.[375–377,381,382] Although the majority of patients have a history of a primary tumor elsewhere, in rare cases (up to 6%) the initial presenting manifestation can be a testicular mass.[375–377]

Metastases usually occur as single or multiple discrete nodules. Rarely, diffuse effacement of the entire parenchyma may be seen.[375–377,383] Low-power examination shows single or multiple nodules with areas of necrosis or hemorrhage. There is a desmoplastic reaction around tumor nests. High magnification shows predominantly interstitial localization of metastatic tumor nests with relative sparing of seminiferous tubules (Fig. 14B.51). There may be frequent lymphatic and blood vessel invasion.[375,376] The histologic character of the metastatic tumor is similar to that of the primary tumor.[375]

Rare tumors and tumor-like conditions of the testis

Carcinoid tumor

The majority of carcinoid tumors are seen in patients between 40 and 60 years of age.[384,385] The patients present with painful or asymptomatic testicular enlargement, which is nearly always unilateral. Fewer than 15% of patients have been reported to have symptoms of carcinoid syndrome.[386] Undescended testis is not usually associated with carcinoid tumor, but there is one reported case.[387] Carcinoid tumors in the testis are usually primary, but, to establish this, a primary lesion elsewhere should be excluded.

Carcinoid tumors are mostly seen in pure form (approximately 75%), but there have been a few cases arising in testicular teratomas.[385,387–390] Berdjis & Mostofi[384] reported 12 primary carcinoid tumors occurring among 7000 testicular tumors, of which two arose in teratomas.

Pathologic features

The tumors measure between 3 and 5 cm in diameter, are gray-tan to yellow, solid and lobulated, and usually devoid of necrosis and hemorrhage. Typical gross features of the teratoma are present when the carcinoid tumor is associated with a teratoma. Low magnification shows an insular, acinar, or trabecular pattern, with cords, nests, or aggregates of uniform tumor cells separated by fine or wide fibrous strands (Fig. 14B.52). At high power, the tumor cells show uniformly round nuclei containing finely dispersed chromatin (salt-and-pepper pattern). They have acidophilic, finely granular cytoplasm.

With rare exceptions, primary testicular carcinoid tumors have shown a positive argentaffin reaction.

Fontana–Masson and Grimelius stains are usually positive. Cytokeratin, NSE, synaptophysin, and chromogranin immunostain are positive in the tumor cells (Fig. 14B.53).

The behavior cannot be reliably predicted from histologic pattern alone, and all testicular carcinoid tumors must be considered at least low-grade malignant tumors. The majority

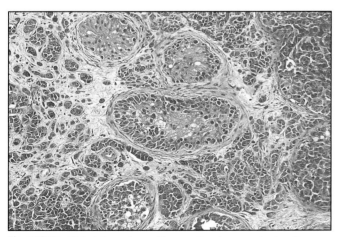

Fig. 14B.51 • Metastatic carcinoma. Tumor cell nests are predominantly located in the interstitium with relative sparing of seminiferous tubules.

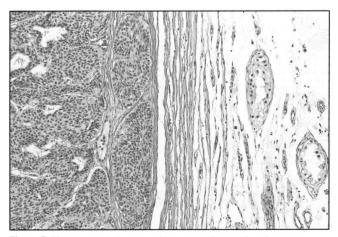

Fig. 14B.52 • Carcinoid. The tumor shows an insular or trabecular pattern arranged in cords, nests, or aggregates of monotonous cells.

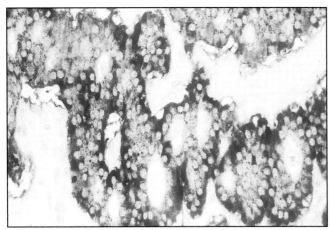

Fig. 14B.53 • Carcinoid tumor. Immunostaining for chromogranin is strongly positive in the tumor cells.

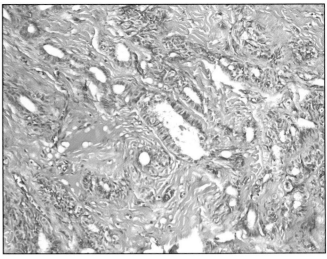

Fig. 14B.54 • Rete testis showing adenomatous hyperplasia.

of pure carcinoid tumors have a benign clinical course,[391] but distant metastases have been described in up to 20% in one study[385,386,392–394] and the tumors that metastasized were larger than those that did not.

Reyes et al.[391] recently reported 10 additional cases of primary testicular carcinoid tumors and graded the tumors into low and intermediate grades based on the WHO criteria for classification of carcinoid tumors in the lung.[395] There were nine low-grade tumors and one intermediate grade tumor. All patients with low-grade carcinoid tumors were alive and well, but the one patient with intermediate grade died of tumor. Based on this group's findings, they proposed replacing the term testicular carcinoid with neuroendocrine carcinoma, which better reflects the nature of these neoplasms. Primary carcinoid tumors are assumed either to arise as a monodermal teratoma or to originate from argentaffin or enterochromaffin cells present in the gonad.[390,396,397]

Kato et al.[386] recently reported that testicular carcinoid tumors did not show a significant numerical abnormality of the X chromosome, which is common in testicular germ cell tumors. Therefore, the genetic background of pure carcinoids might be different from that of common germ cell tumors.

Adenomatous hyperplasia of rete testis

Adenomatous hyperplasia of the rete testis is an uncommon lesion that has been described by Hartwick et al. and others.[398–402] Hartwick et al. reported nine cases of adenomatous hyperplasia identified in two institutions (M. D. Anderson Cancer Center, Houston, Texas, and Sunnybrook Medical Center, Toronto, Canada).[398] Their ages ranged from 30 to 74 years (mean, 59 years; median, 66 years). Although some patients presented with a grossly identifiable solid or cystic testicular hilar mass, most were an incidental microscopic finding.

Microscopically, hyperplasia consisted of a tubulopapillary epithelial proliferation of rete testis. The lining cells are cuboidal to low columnar and lack nuclear pleomorphism or mitotic figures (Fig. 14B.54). The involvement of the rete testis is predominantly diffuse. The surrounding seminiferous

tubules show atrophic changes. Ultrastructural and immuno-histochemical (keratin, EMA: positive; vimentin, muscle-specific actin, desmin, and S-100 protein: negative) studies show similar features to those of non-hyperplastic rete testis epithelium. No patients with adenomatous hyperplasia show local recurrence or metastasis. The authors reported that the possible pathogeneses include hormonal imbalance or an unidentified stimulatory influence.[398–401]

Ulbright & Gersell,[399] reporting on three patients with germ cell tumors, described the association of rete testis hyperplasia exhibiting eosinophilic hyaline globules. In the florid examples, this proliferation formed a solid and microcystic pattern that mimicked a yolk sac tumor component. However, the bland cytologic features of the cells and conformation with the configuration of the rete testis were keys to its reactive nature. In the same article they reported the subsequent review of 48 additional testicular specimens, among which they found hyaline globule formation in the rete testis or tubuli recti in 16 of 27 germ cell tumors, one of five other testicular tumors (four stromal tumors and one plasmacytoma), and in none of 16 non-neoplastic cases. Many of the cases that had hyaline globules also showed epithelial hyperplasia. Immunostains supported the non-neoplastic nature of the proliferative lesions and indicated that the globules represented various proteins that had been absorbed from the lumen of the rete testis by the epithelial-lining cells but not successfully secreted. Ulbright & Gersell[399] concluded that this pseudoneoplastic reaction developed secondary to invasion of the rete testis by tumor.

Microlithiasis of rete testis and epididymis

Testicular microlithiasis is a well-defined clinical and patho-logic entity easily diagnosed through testicular echography; however, its association with cancer and infertility is now under debate. Many efforts have been made in recent years to clarify the spectrum of lesions observed in testicular micro-lithiasis, but no published data as to the existence of a possible microlithiasis of the epididymis and the rete testis have been found.

Nistal et al.[401] have observed microlithiasis of the epididymis and the rete testis in surgical (8 epididymis and 6 testis) and autopsy specimens (12 cases). In decreased order of frequency, microliths of the proximal spermatic pathway were seen in rete testis, epididymal duct, and efferent ducts. Intraluminal, subepithelial, and interstitial microliths were localized along these segments of the ductal system. Subepithelial microliths were the most frequently found. A granulomatous reaction around the interstitial epididymal microliths, mimicking malakoplakia, was observed in one case. The differential diagnosis of microliths includes corpora amylacea, Michaelis–Gutmann bodies, calcium deposits, hyaline globules, and parasites, like the giant kidney worm *Dioctophyme renale*. In infants and young adults, microlithiasis of the epididymis and the rete testis is frequently associated with alterations in the development of the proximal ductal system. In elderly adults, it is related to ischemia and obstruction of the ductal system.

Adenocarcinoma of rete testis

Adenocarcinoma of the rete testis is rare and only about 50 cases have been reported. It occurs most often in men over the age of 60 years (range 20–90 years).[403–407] Twenty-five percent are associated with a hydrocele.[403,404] A painful scrotal mass is the most common symptom.[403,404] The outcome is usually poor, with approximately 40% disease-free survival.[404–406,408] Five criteria must ideally be met before a tumor is diagnosed as a rete testis carcinoma: (1) absence of histologically similar tumor at other sites; (2) tumor centered in the region of the hilus; (3) morphology incompatible with any other type of testicular or paratesticular tumor; (4) a transition from unaffected rete testis to tumor; and (5) a predominantly solid appearance with tubular, papillary, and cribriform growth patterns.[409]

Pathologic features

Adenocarcinoma of the rete testis is usually solid but may occasionally be cystic.[403,404] Histologic patterns include tubular, papillary, cribriform, and solid (Fig. 14B.55). The stroma may be prominent, extensively desmoplastic, or extensively hyalinized. A single case with a spindled sarcomatoid component has been reported.[410] The tumor cells are columnar to cuboidal with a moderate amount of acidophilic or amphophilic cytoplasm, and there is nuclear stratification and moderate nuclear pleomorphism. There is frequent mitotic activity.

PAS with diastase treatment, alcian blue, mucicarmine, and immunostaining for keratin, CEA, and EMA are usually positive. Markers for germ cell tumors, including AFP, hCG, and PLAP, are negative.

Metastatic carcinoma should be differentiated from a rete testis adenocarcinoma; however, in most cases, differentiation from metastatic carcinoma cannot be made reliably on the histology alone. Malignant mesothelioma and serous carcinomas are other important differential diagnostic considerations.

Epidermoid cyst

Epidermoid cysts comprise 1% of testicular masses.[187,411–413] They are benign lesions, seen at all ages but most commonly in the second to fourth decades of life.[411–413] By definition, no other germ cell components are present. Epidermoid cysts are round to oval, averaging 2 cm in diameter, but they may measure up to 10 cm.[411,412] They consist of a soft and well-demarcated cystic mass containing laminated cheesy material within a thin, fibrous cystic wall (Fig. 14B.56).

Microscopic examination shows a discrete squamous cell-lined cyst within the testis containing keratin and necrotic material (Fig. 14B.57). There are no associated skin appendages; there may, however, be focal ulceration and a foreign-body giant cell reaction.

Epidermoid cysts can be differentiated from dermoid cyst by their lack of skin adnexal structures, and from a mature cystic teratoma by the absence of other adult tissue elements and of ITGCN. A recent study demonstrated that some epidermoid cysts harbor allelic loss at some of the same loci identified in malignant testicular germ cell tumors. These findings suggest that some examples of epidermoid cysts are neoplastic, although their low frequency of loss of heterozygosity

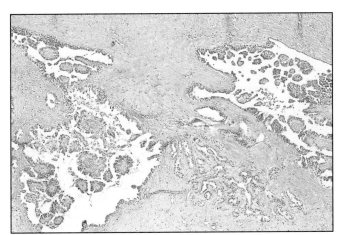

Fig. 14B.55 • Adenocarcinoma of rete testis. Portions of rete testis are occupied by a papillary and trabecular neoplastic epithelial cell proliferation.

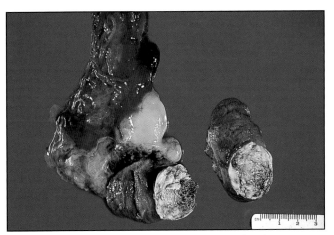

Fig. 14B.56 • Epidermoid cyst. A soft and well-demarcated cystic mass containing laminated cheesy material.

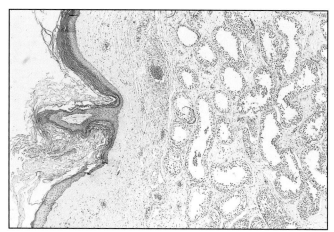

Fig. 14B.57 • Epidermoid cyst. A discrete squamous cell-lined cyst contains keratinous material devoid of skin appendages.

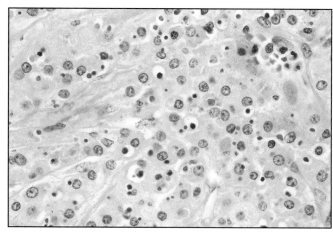

Fig. 14B.58 • Malakoplakia. It is characterized by a diffuse proliferation of large histiocytes with abundant granular eosinophilic cytoplasm. Some cells contain intracytoplasmic basophilic inclusions with a clear halo around them.

also supports that they are genetically different from malignant germ cell tumors.[414]

Malakoplakia

Malakoplakia may involve the testis, epididymis, or both. Testicular malakoplakia is associated with epididymal involvement in about one-third of cases; 6 of 12 cases of epididymal malakoplakia had concurrent involvement of the testis.[415,416] Although malakoplakia can be seen at any age, 75% of reported cases occurred in patients between 40 and 69 years of age.[415,416] It is almost always unilateral and more commonly involves the right testis. Patients usually present with a painful or painless swelling of the testis which is fixed to the scrotal wall because of fibrous adhesions to surrounding tissues.[415–417] It may cause testicular infarction without torsion.[418] Urine cultures in these patients may be positive for bacteria, most commonly *Escherichia coli*.[415] On gross examination, there is replacement of testicular parenchyma by a yellow, tan, or brown, soft to firm nodular mass. Fibrosis can be prominent and there may be areas of necrosis.[415–417]

Malakoplakia is a destructive inflammatory lesion with one or more abscesses in the testicular parenchyma[419] and reactive inflammatory changes in the tunica albuginea. The tubules and interstitial tissue are replaced by large histiocytes with abundant granular eosinophilic cytoplasm (von Hansemann cells), some of which may contain intracytoplasmic, targetoid, basophilic inclusions (Michaelis–Gutmann bodies) (Fig. 14B.58).[415–417] Acute and chronic inflammatory cells, granulation tissue, and fibrosis are seen in the background. By electron microscopy, these inclusions represent phagolysosomes that have ingested the breakdown products of bacteria such as *Escherichia coli*.[415] Michaelis–Gutmann bodies are positive for von Kossa, PAS, and iron stains.[419,420] The differential diagnosis includes sclerosing lipogranuloma, sperm granuloma, and granulomatous orchitis. Sclerosing lipogranulomas consist of a foreign-body inflammatory response to exogenous or endogenous oil droplets. Michaelis–Gutmann bodies are absent. Sperm granulomas are confined to the epididymis and spermatic cord with phagocytosis of sperm fragments; Michaelis–Gutmann bodies are absent. Non-specific granulomatous orchitis

involves the seminiferous tubules, which are replaced by an inflammatory infiltrate consisting of lymphocytes, plasma cells, and epithelioid macrophages. Sperm fragments are rarely observed.

Tumors and tumorous conditions of paratesticular tissues

Benign tumors of paratesticular area

Adrenal rests

Adrenal rests are defined as an ectopic adrenocortical tissue seen anywhere along the route of descent of the testis from abdomen to scrotum; they can occur in the spermatic cord, rete testis, epididymis, and tunica albuginea and are found incidentally in 3.8% of male infants undergoing surgery for either undescended testis or hernia.[421–423] The rests consist of small yellow-orange nodules (usually less than 1 cm in diameter) that are usually encapsulated. Czaplicki et al.[424] have reported a rare case of adrenal rest in the spermatic cord presenting as a mass in a 34-year-old man. Cut section may show the zones of the normal adrenal gland.

On microscopic examination, the lesion is characterized by encapsulated solid sheets and nests of polygonal cells with abundant cytoplasm and bland nuclear features (Fig. 14B.59), similar to normal adrenal cortical tissue, predominantly the zona fasciculata. Rarely, the lesions are not encapsulated. Adrenal medullary tissue has not been reported in paratesticular adrenal rests.

Splenic–gonadal fusion

Splenic–gonadal fusion is a rare condition usually involving the left testis. Fewer than 100 cases have been reported in the literature.[425–431] Splenic–gonadal fusion occurs in two forms: continuous and discontinuous.[432,433] In the continuous variant, a cord connects the abdominal spleen and the scrotal ectopic splenic tissue; the cord may be pure splenic tissue, fibrous

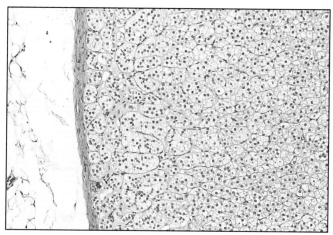

Fig. 14B.59 • Adrenal rest. The nodule shows the histologic features typical of normal adrenal cortical tissue.

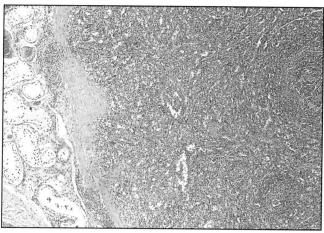

Fig. 14B.60 • Splenic–gonadal fusion. Testicular tissue is connected to the splenic tissue by tunica albuginea.

tissue, or both. In the discontinuous form there is no connection between abdominal spleen and scrotal accessory splenic tissue. Splenic–gonadal fusion is believed to be a developmental anomaly that occurs between 5 and 8 weeks of fetal life when the splenic and gonadal anlages are topographically close together. It is significant that splenic–gonadal fusion is frequently associated with a high incidence of congenital anomalies such as micrognathia and peromelia (severe defect of the extremities).

In the reported cases the age of the patients ranged from infancy to 69 years; most patients were children or teenagers. Splenic–gonadal fusion is found predominantly in Caucasian subjects. Although it may present with a scrotal or inguinal mass, or scrotal tenderness, it is usually an incidental finding. Approximately 25% of the cases reported to date have been associated with cryptorchid testes.

Splenic–gonadal fusion is characterized grossly by a discrete, usually small mass (but which may be as large as 12 cm), which is almost always fused to the upper pole of the testis or to the head of the epididymis. The gross and microscopic appearance is that of normal splenic tissue separated from testicular tissue by bands of fibrous tissue (Fig. 14B.60); areas of fibrosis, calcification, hemosiderin deposition, and trabecular thickening have been reported.[429] Splenic–gonadal fusion can be differentiated from a mature teratoma because it lacks other forms of somatic tissues. A few cases of NSGCT have been reported in a testicle involved by splenogonadal fusion.[431]

Sperm granuloma

Sperm granulomas almost always involve the epididymis or vas deferens. They occur in patients aged 18–74 years; 50% occur within the third decade of life.[434–436] They present as painful, firm to hard nodules.[434–436] Fifteen to 40% of patients give a history of vasectomy, trauma, or epididymitis; 1–5% of men undergoing vasectomy have sperm granuloma. Ninety percent of sperm granulomas associated with vasectomy are located in the vas deferens, and the remainder are in the epididymis.[435,437] Vasitis nodosa is associated with sperm granulomas in 30% of all cases.[435] Sperm granulomas have occasionally been mistaken for testicular tumors and treated by orchiectomy.[438]

Typically the lesions are firm, well-demarcated nodules measuring 2–3 mm with small, soft yellow to white-cream foci on sectioning. They can measure up to 3 cm.[434] In the early stage, neutrophils predominate; these are gradually replaced by epithelioid histiocytes with granuloma formation. The later stage shows progressive fibrosis and hyalinization with prominent deposition of lipochrome pigment. The ducts show an intense inflammatory infiltrate with ulceration and necrosis. The inflammatory infiltrate consists of neutrophils, lymphocytes, histiocytes, and giant cells. Phagocytosis of sperm by the histiocytes is usually evident (Fig. 14B.61). Occasionally there is squamous metaplasia of the ductal epithelium. Multinucleated giant cells are rare.[434–436] The detection of sperm fragments may be facilitated by an acid-fast stain that stains the lipid component of sperm.[439]

Sclerosing lipogranuloma

This distinctive, granulomatous reaction, most commonly occurring in response to exogenous lipids, paraffin, or trauma, and rarely to a laparoscopic herniorrhaphy and varicocelectomy,[440] is seen mostly in adults younger than 40 years of age, commonly in a paratesticular location but occasionally also within the

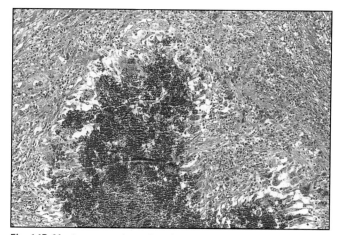

Fig. 14B.61 • Sperm granuloma. Granulomatous inflammation with histiocytes, plasma cells, lymphocytes, and collections of sperm.

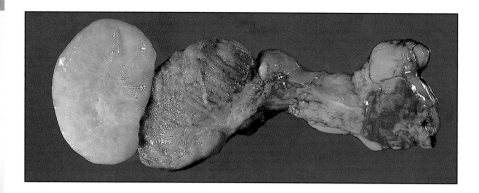

Fig. 14B.62 • Fibrous pseudotumor. A round mass is attached to the tunica albuginea showing a firm and white cut surface.

testis. Primary sclerosing lipogranulomas without any particular history have been identified.[441] The patients present with a palpable hard mass, clinically suspicious for neoplasm. It is usually caused by injections of exogenous material into the genitalia to enhance their size; rarely is the lesion ascribed as being causally related to cold and trauma.[442–446] The lesion is also known as a paraffinoma of the genital area.[443] The mass is ill defined, firm, and oily. Lipid vacuoles of varying size are present, surrounded by foreign-body giant cells, chronic inflammation, fat necrosis, and fibrosis.

Fibrous periorchitis (fibrous pseudotumor)

Fibrous periorchitis is a diffuse or localized, reactive, fibromatous proliferation involving the tunicae, epididymis, and spermatic cord. In reported cases, the patients' ages ranged from 7 to 95 years; the peak incidence was in the third decade of life.[320,447–459]

The terms fibroma, non-specific peritesticular fibrosis, nodular fibrous periorchitis, chronic proliferative periorchitis, proliferative funiculitis, nodular fibropseudotumor, inflammatory pseudotumor, reactive periorchitis, pseudofibrous periorchitis, peritesticular fibromatosis, and fibrous mesothelioma have been used for this lesion.[320,447,455] The consensus in the literature is that this is a reactive non-neoplastic lesion that may clinically mimic testicular or paratesticular neoplasms.[454,455,459] Some have restricted the use of "pseudotumor" to mass-forming lesions and have used "fibrous periorchitis" for more diffuse lesions.

The lesion shows a firm, white cut surface. In the diffuse form there is diffuse thickening and band-like myofibroblastic proliferation that encases the testis, termed fibromatous periorchitis. The localized form consists of single or multiple nodules; the size of the nodules ranges from 0.2 mm to 9.5 cm in diameter (Fig. 14B.62). The lesion shows variable histology; some cases contain spindle cells with a whorled appearance and hyalinized collagen. Focal calcification and ossification may be seen, representing burnt-out lesions. The histology may be more cellular, with granulation tissue-type fibrous proliferation with markedly reactive stromal cells,[456] and there may be an inflammatory component, including lymphocytes, plasma cells, histiocytes, and scattered eosinophils (Fig. 14B.63).

Pseudotumors should be differentiated from sarcomas. Sarcomas are generally more cellular and more pleomorphic, with a high mitotic rate and fewer inflammatory cells.

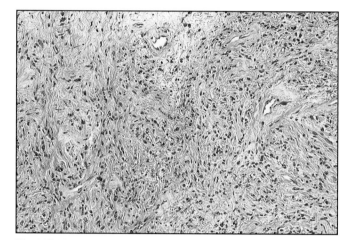

Fig. 14B.63 • Fibrous pseudotumor. The lesion is characterized by a spindle cell proliferation in association with inflammatory cell components.

Adenomatoid tumor

Adenomatoid tumor is the most common benign neoplasm of the paratesticular tissues.[460–470] It is almost always a unilateral, solitary mass which does not transilluminate.[461] Pain may or may not be present. It can be seen in all age groups but is most common in the third to fifth decades of life. The typical location is the epididymis, most commonly in the lower pole, but it can be found in the tunica albuginea, spermatic cord, ejaculatory ducts, prostate, and suprarenal recess.[460–470] Local extension into testicular parenchyma can occur.[463] The clinical behavior is uniformly benign.

Pathologic features

The tumor is usually less than 5 cm in diameter (the majority are less than 2 cm) and is typically a single, gray-white, well-demarcated, firm nodule. Rarely a plaque-like lesion may be formed. The cut surface may resemble seminoma when the testis is involved. The tumor is composed of two major elements: epithelial-like cells and fibrous stroma. The epithelial-like cells are arranged in a network of tubules (round, oval, or slit-like), numerous irregular cysts, or small cords and clusters.[464,465] The fibrous stroma may sometimes be hyalinized and may contain smooth muscle. The tumor can have infiltrative borders. When the tumor shows extensive necrosis, presumably due to infarction, it causes diagnostic difficulty.[466]

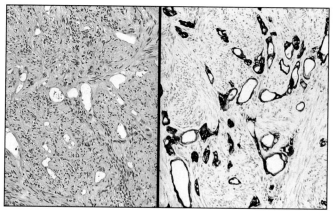

Fig. 14B.64 • Adenomatoid tumor. Irregular slit-like or glandular spaces are present within the fibrous stroma (left). The cells lining the spaces are positive for cytokeratin (right).

The tubules are lined by flat to cuboidal or low columnar cells with round or oval nuclei and abundant dense cytoplasm (Fig. 14B.64). The cytoplasm may contain large intracytoplasmic vacuoles with overall features resembling signet-ring cells. Lymphoid aggregates may be prominent throughout the tumor or at its periphery. Recently four adenomatoid tumors (three epididymal tumors and one intratesticular) with extensive necrosis, presumably due to infarction, have been reported.[466] Two of the men presented with acute scrotal pain simulating epididymitis, and two with a palpable mass. Microscopically, they were all characterized by central necrosis with pale mummified adenomatoid tumor identified at least focally but often overshadowed by nondescript necrotic tissue. Viable adenomatoid tumor was identified in all cases but was minor in amount. A florid reactive process of fibroblasts and myofibroblasts that had plump nuclei (often with prominent nucleoli and occasional mitoses) surrounded the necrotic areas. Two of the epididymal cases had adjacent rete testis showing epithelial hyperplasia with hyaline globule formation. The microscopic appearance often suggested the possibility of a malignant neoplasm because of: (1) blurring of the normally identifiable junction between adenomatoid tumor and adjacent tissue; (2) irregular pseudoinfiltration of fat by reactive tissue and adenomatoid tumor; (3) paucity of typical adenomatoid tumor due to the infarction and the fact that viable tumor usually showed a solid pattern; and (4) atypia of the associated reactive cells. The authors concluded that this unemphasized feature of adenomatoid tumors may potentially lead to more aggressive therapy than warranted if not correctly interpreted.

Electron microscopy demonstrates numerous microvilli on the luminal surface and well-developed desmosomes on the lateral cell surface.[467] PAS with diastase and mucicarmine are negative. Alcian blue can be positive but is hyaluronidase-sensitive. All tumors express cytokeratin AE1/AE3 (Fig. 14B.64), EMA, and vimentin, with weak expression of cytokeratin 34βE12 in some tumors.[468] CEA, Leu-M1, factor VIII, and *Ulex europaeus* agglutinin I are negative.[468–470] Thrombomodulin, HBME-1, CK5/6, OC125, and calretinin are positive, indicating the mesothelial nature of the lesion.[468]

The differential diagnosis includes metastatic carcinoma (including signet-ring cell carcinoma), carcinoma of the rete testis, malignant mesothelioma, sclerosing lipogranuloma, para-

testicular yolk sac tumor, and the rare histiocytoid hemangioma of testis. In metastatic carcinoma, there is generally a clinical history of a prior cancer. It is most common in the fifth to seventh decades and is usually bilateral. The cells are usually frankly malignant. Mucin stains may show hyaluronidase-resistant positivity in the cytoplasm and lumina. Carcinoma of the rete testis occurs in a tubulopapillary pattern with cytologically malignant cuboidal or columnar cells that are CEA-positive and mucin-positive with hyaluronidase resistance. Malignant mesothelioma shows greater cellularity and pleomorphism with high mitotic activity. The vacuoles of sclerosing lipogranuloma stain with lipid stains and the cells are negative for cytokeratin. Histiocytoid hemangioma is positive for vascular immunostains and contains many eosinophils.[471]

Papillary cystadenoma of epididymis

Papillary cystadenoma is a rare benign tumor.[472,473] It occurs in males between 16 and 81 years of age with a mean of 35 years. The most frequent presentation is a scrotal mass. About two-thirds of cases occur in patients with von Hippel–Lindau (VHL) syndrome, particularly in cases with bilateral involvement. Overall, bilateral involvement is about 40%. The tumor is solid and cystic, occurring in the head of epididymis and measuring up to 6 cm in greatest dimension.

Microscopically, the tumor consists of dilated cysts and tubules lined by papillae with a single or double layer of cuboidal to low columnar cells. The cytoplasm is abundant and clear, containing glycogen (Fig. 14B.65). Cilia can be seen at the surface of the lining cells. The nuclei are small, oval-round and smooth with no or inconspicuous nucleoli. Mitoses are absent. Eosinophilic colloid-like secretion is frequently seen in the dilated cystic or tubular spaces. In-situ hybridization revealed high levels of vascular endothelial growth factor (VEGF) mRNA in the clear cells of the epididymal papillary cystadenoma in VHL syndrome. This lends support to the notion that upregulation of VEGF is caused by loss of the wild-type VHL protein, and postulates that the elevated VEGF levels may account for the cyst formation and vascularized stroma present in these VHL-associated tumors.[474]

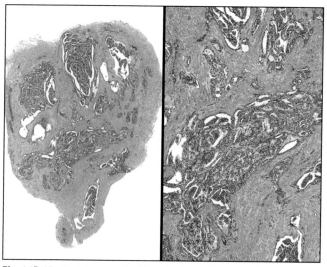

Fig. 14B.65 • Cystadenoma of epididymis with papillary growth (low power) and clear cell component (high power).

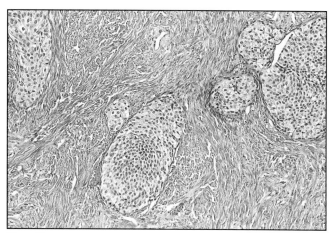

Fig. 14B.66 • Brenner tumor. Epithelial cell nests are scattered in a collagenous stroma.

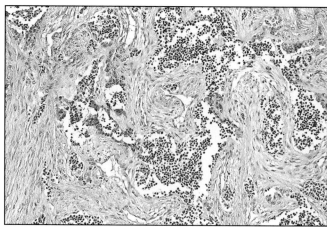

Fig. 14B.67 • Retinal anlage tumor. The tumor is characterized by the two cell types: small cells and large columnar to cuboidal epithelial-like cells.

Differential diagnoses include metastatic renal cell carcinoma, papillary serous tumor of müllerian origin, mesothelioma, and rete testis or epididymal adenocarcinomas. Prostate gland-like epithelium may occur in the epididymis and can be confused with papillary cystadenoma.[472]

Brenner tumor

A Brenner tumor is very rare in this location,[475–478] but even rarer is its association to an adenomatoid tumor.[479] It probably arises from the Walthard nests of the tunica vaginalis. Small (6 mm to 2.7 cm) nodules may be seen in paratesticular tissues, tunica albuginea, or tunica vaginalis.

These tumors are characterized by well-defined nests, mostly solid and occasionally cystic, comprised of polygonal cells (transitional cell type) that possess characteristic longitudinal nuclear grooves.[475] A collagenous stroma in the background separates the epithelial nests (Fig. 14B.66). Brenner tumors are benign and of no clinical significance, but an exceptional malignant Brenner tumor of the testis and epididymis has been reported.[480]

Retinal anlage tumor of epididymis or testis

Retinal anlage tumor has also been called melanotic neuroectodermal tumor, melanotic progonoma, or melanotic hamartoma (see also Ch. 27). Fewer than 10 cases of retinal anlage tumor of the epididymis or testis have been reported.[471–491] Most cases occur at 10 months of age or younger.[481,482] There is rarely testicular involvement. The most common presenting symptom is scrotal enlargement. These tumors are usually benign but one case with malignant behavior has been reported with metastatic tumor in inguinal and retroperitoneal lymph nodes.[481]

The tumor is a pigmented, well-circumscribed, round to oval, solid nodule, usually less than 4 cm in diameter. It is closely apposed to the testis, but rarely invades the parenchyma. The cut surface is typically brown, black, or gray with areas of dark pigmentation; one case was exclusively cream-colored.[492]

Under low power, irregularly shaped nests, cords, and, in places, cleft-like or glomeruloid-like spaces are composed of,

or lined by, two types of cell – melanin-containing pigmented epithelioid cells and neuroblastoma-like small cells (Fig. 14B.67). There is typically a prominent fibrous and hyalinized stroma.[481,482]

The two cell types can be distinguished under high magnification.[481,482,485] Small, undifferentiated, round to oval, dark staining cells with small hyperchromatic nuclei and scant cytoplasm resemble the cells of a neuroblastoma. Mitotic activity may be present, but Homer Wright rosettes are absent. The second cell type is large columnar or cuboidal epithelial-like, with abundant eosinophilic cytoplasm, and contains melanin pigment. The cells have large vesicular nuclei with small nucleoli. Vascular invasion may be present in malignant tumors. Both small and large cells are positive for NSE, synaptophysin, and HMB-45. S-100 protein staining may be present in the large cells. Large cells are positive for cytokeratin and occasional small cells are positive for cytokeratin and vimentin.[487]

Tumors of Müllerian type

Testicular and paratesticular tumors resembling ovarian tumors of common epithelial type are rare.[478,493–500] The age of the patients ranges from 11 to 68 years with an average of 46 years. Most ovarian-type epithelial tumors resemble a serous tumor of borderline malignancy, with lesser numbers of invasive serous carcinomas. Serous borderline tumor of the paratestis is morphologically and immunophenotypically identical to ovarian serous borderline tumor. To date, no serous borderline tumor of the paratestis reported in the literature has recurred or metastasized after resection.[501]

There is little information on mucinous tumors.[478,495] Ulbright & Young[499] recently reported nine cases of mucinous tumors with the same criteria and terminology used in the ovary. The patients were 44–69 years of age (median 64 years) and presented with masses in the testis (four) or paratestis (five). Eight tumors were cystic (median size, 3.5 cm) and contained gelatinous material; one (a paratesticular carcinoma) appeared as thickening of the tunica vaginalis. Two were classified as mucinous cystadenomas (both paratesticular), six as purely or predominantly borderline tumors (four, testis; two, paratestis; one had intraepithelial carcinoma and one microinvasive carcinoma) and one (paratestis) as mucinous carcinoma. The cystadenomas were composed of endocervical-like cells, but intestinal-like cells typified the borderline tumors and carcinomas. Cyst rupture with mucin dissection into the stroma, inflammation, and dystrophic calcification with ossification were common. No tumor was associated with ITGCN or with teratomatous elements. One patient with carcinoma died shortly after presentation with peritoneal spread; autopsy disclosed no other potential primary site. The follow-up (1.8–12 years) in all other cases was uneventful. Mucinous tumors of the testis and paratestis resemble their ovarian counterparts, exhibiting the same morphologic spectrum, from benign to borderline to malignant, and having both endocervical-like and intestinal features. Clinical features are important to exclude metastasis, particularly in cases of carcinoma and, to a lesser extent, in tumors of borderline type.

Other rare types include endometrioid adenocarcinoma,[478] and clear cell adenocarcinoma.[478,498] Fewer than 10 cases of each category have been described.[493]

A variety of germ cell tumors of the testis have been reported in association with persistent müllerian duct syndrome (which is characterized by the persistence of müllerian derivatives in otherwise normally virilized males). However, malignant change of the persistent müllerian duct structures has rarely been reported. A case of clear cell adenocarcinoma has been reported in a patient who had persistent müllerian duct structures in müllerian duct syndrome.[500] These tumors may derive from mesothelium by the process of müllerian neometaplasia, from müllerian remnants, or from the mucinous epithelium of a teratoma.[494,499]

Histologically, the müllerian-type tumors are similar to those seen in the female genital tract (see Ch. 13). Therefore, the diagnosis of these tumors usually does not pose a problem, but their unusual location and rarity may cause erroneous interpretation. The diagnosis of invasive carcinoma has prognostic significance, and invasion, even if focal, must be recognized.

The differential diagnosis includes rete testis adenocarcinoma, epididymal adenocarcinoma, malignant mesothelioma, and metastatic carcinoma. Rete testis carcinoma is located in the hilum of the testis, shows transition from normal epithelial cells to neoplastic cells, and has slit-like tubules and solid areas as well as a papillary growth. Adenocarcinoma of the epididymis is exceptionally rare,[502] and has a tubular or tubulopapillary appearance, often with clear cell features. Unlike mesothelioma, müllerian tumors do not have a biphasic histologic pattern or a history of asbestos exposure and have more numerous psammoma bodies. Immunostaining for CEA and CA125 is positive in tumor cells of müllerian (ovarian)-type tumors, and CK5/6, thrombomodulin, and calretinin are usually positive in mesotheliomas.

Benign soft tissue tumors

A wide range of soft tissue neoplasms, encompassing almost the entire spectrum present in tumors of soft tissues at other sites (see Ch. 3, 24 and 27), may involve the paratesticular soft tissue.[503] These include leiomyomas, lipomas, rhabdomyomas,[504,505] fibromas, hemangiomas, schwannoma, and neurofibroma.[455] The more distinctive soft tissue tumors at this site include histiocytoid hemangioma,[471] aggressive

angiomyxoma,[506,507] angiomyofibroblastoma, and cellular angiofibroma (also known as angiomyofibroblastoma-like tumor).[508,509,510] A non-neoplastic excess of native smooth muscle in the paratestis or spermatic cord growing between or around vessels or efferent ducts has also been described.[511,512] This lesion may be confused clinically and pathologically with a true neoplasm, particularly leiomyoma. The lesion consists of fascicles of smooth muscle, growing in a periductal, perivascular, interstitial, or mixed pattern. The cohesive, interlacing growth pattern of a leiomyoma was missing in all cases, a diagnostic feature separable from leiomyoma. The cause of this lesion is not known, although microscopic epididymal or vas deferens duct ectasia in some cases suggests a possible obstructive etiology. In any case, these are benign lesions without clinical significance after excision and correct diagnosis.

Malignant tumors of paratesticular region

Adenocarcinoma of epididymis

Primary epididymal neoplasms are rare and are usually benign, with adenomatoid tumor and leiomyoma being most common, followed by papillary cystadenoma and a variety of benign soft tissue tumors.

Primary epididymal carcinoma is extremely rare and has been the subject of only sporadic case reports; the validity of some of the reported tumors is questionable. Some of them are probably other forms of primary or metastatic cancer. Less than a dozen cases of epididymal adenocarcinoma have been reported in the literature.[502] Patients' ages range from 27 to 82 years, with a mean age of 60 years. All of them presented with scrotal masses, pain, or both, and small hydroceles in some. Unlike papillary cystadenoma of epididymis, none had a history of VHL disease. Grossly, all of the tumors are centered in the epididymis. Some tumors invaded the periepididymal soft tissue, spermatic cord, and the adjacent testis. The tumors ranged in size from 2.0 to 7.0 cm in greatest dimension with foci of hemorrhage and necrosis.

Pathologic features

Microscopically, most of the tumors are adenocarcinomas with simple tubules or more complex tubulocystic or tubulopapillary formations lined by cuboidal or columnar, predominantly clear, cells that infiltrate the epididymal smooth muscle wall, periepididymal soft tissue, or both (Fig. 14B.68). Tumor necrosis is frequently seen. Carcinomas with undifferentiated, sheet-like growth and squamous carcinomas have been reported.[502,513] Unlike benign papillary cystadenoma, cilia are absent in epididymal carcinomas. Immunohistochemical staining demonstrates strong positivity for cytokeratins (AE1/3, Cam 5.2) and EMA (luminal only), but CEA, Leu-M1, B72.3, and Ber-EP4 are reported to be negative. Most patients with follow-up data died of disease.

The differential diagnosis of epididymal adenocarcinoma includes papillary cystadenoma of epididymis, adenomatoid tumor, malignant mesothelioma, serous papillary carcinoma of müllerian type, carcinoma of rete testis, and finally

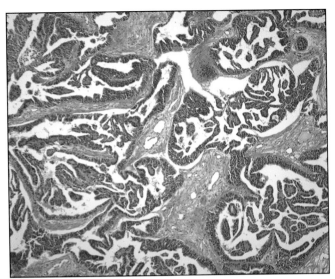

Fig. 14B.68 • Adenocarcinoma of epididymis. There is an irregular, and anatomizing glandular proliferation with intraluminal papillary infolding and cellular atypia.

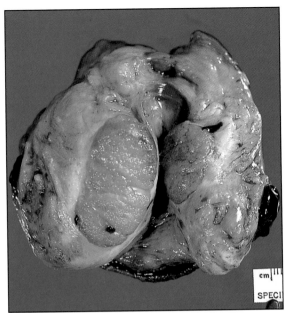

Fig. 14B.69 • Mesothelioma. The tunica vaginalis is diffusely thickened by a solid mass which coats the tunica vaginalis and invades tunica albuginea and epididymis.

metastatic carcinoma. Distinction from metastasis may be difficult and may depend largely on careful clinical evaluation. Finally, to avoid unnecessary overdiagnosis as epididymal carcinoma it should be remembered that normal epididymis often shows a cribriform pattern with atypical cells.[514]

Mesothelioma of tunica vaginalis

Malignant mesothelioma of the tunica vaginalis testis is an aggressive tumor characterized by local recurrence and distant metastases. It has a strong relationship with occupational exposure to asbestos, having a history of asbestos exposure in 40% of cases.[478,515] The tumor may present with long-lasting hydrocele, which most often recurs after tapping, but may form a firm mass.[515–523] It occurs between 20 and 75 years of age, with bimodal peaks in the third and fourth and sixth and eighth decades of life, although cases in the pediatric age group have been reported.[478,520–522,524–527] Mesothelioma is a solid or partly cystic tumor measuring 0.6–6.0 cm in diameter. The tumor forms multiple shaggy or papillary nodules on the surface of the tunica vaginalis and may coat the entire surface of tunica vaginalis with infiltration of the adjacent soft tissues of the spermatic cord, testis, or epididymis (Fig. 14B.69).[520–522,524–528]

Epithelial, sarcomatoid, or biphasic (epithelial and sarcomatoid) patterns may be present. Epithelial mesotheliomas are more common, account for 75% of tumors, and may be papillary, glandular (tubuloalveolar), or solid.[515,528,529] Sarcomatoid mesotheliomas consist of poorly defined fascicles of spindle cells. Biphasic mesotheliomas show both epithelial and spindled patterns. The neoplastic cells in epithelial mesotheliomas are typically cuboidal with oval, vesicular nuclei and moderate amounts of eosinophilic cytoplasm. Psammoma bodies may be seen in pure papillary mesotheliomas. A high mitotic rate, significant nuclear atypia, prominent nucleoli, and invasion of adjacent structures are also seen.[515,520,522] In sarcomatoid

mesotheliomas, spindle cells are arranged in poorly defined fascicles or sheets. Marked cellular pleomorphism and bizarre cells can be present.[523,528]

Well-differentiated papillary mesothelioma is an unusual variant of epithelial mesothelioma considered to be of low malignant potential. The majority of cases have been reported in the peritoneum in women of reproductive age, but it can occur in the tunica vaginalis of men.[530] Half of the patients have a history of occupational asbestos exposure. These lesions must be carefully separated from malignant mesotheliomas with a focally exophytic papillary growth pattern. The tumor does not exhibit stromal invasion or shows only limited invasion of the submesothelial layer.[531]

Electron microscopy demonstrates the presence of long, slender microvilli, glycogen, tonofilaments, desmosomes, and the perinuclear location of mitochondria.[515,526] Mucin stains (PAS and mucicarmine) and immunostaining for CEA, Leu-M1, B72.3, MOC.31, and factor VIII are negative in the tumor cells. Alcian blue is positive but hyaluronidase-sensitive. Cytokeratin, CK 5/6, EMA, and calretinin are positive, although CK5/6 staining is more variable than in pleural mesotheliomas.[531a] The overall prognosis of mesothelioma is poor. Of patients with follow-up of over 2 years, 45% died of disease, 17% were alive with disease, and 38% were apparently free of disease.[528]

Small papillary mesothelial projections are commonly seen in hernia sacs (see Ch. 15). These lesions must be differentiated from mesotheliomas. They are usually microscopic and single. Histologic features favoring a reactive process include focality, associated inflammatory changes, minimal cytologic atypia, and lack of necrosis. Adenocarcinoma, either metastatic or primary, should also be differentiated from mesothelioma. In metastatic tumors, there is generally a clinical history of a prior cancer and they are positive for CEA, MOC.31, and Leu-M1. Carcinoma of the rete testis is an important differential diagnosis.

Rhabdomyosarcoma

Rhabdomyosarcoma is the most common sarcoma in children (see also Ch. 24). It occurs between 7 and 36 years of age (mean age 6.6 years); 60% occur in the first two decades of life.[532–536] Most of the patients present with a mass in the scrotum;[533–536] lumbar pain, weight loss, hypercalcemia, and thrombocytopenia have been reported to occur in adult patients.[537] The tumor is common in the spermatic cord and paratesticular tissue, but testicular parenchyma may rarely be involved.[538]

The tumors have a lobulated, smooth, gray-white, glistening appearance and usually displace the testicle without replacing it (Fig. 14B.70).[533,534] The size ranges from 1.5 to 20 cm in greatest dimension. Embryonal rhabdomyosarcoma is the most frequent (90%) histologic type.[533–535] Strap cells, with or without cross-striations, as well as bizarre "tadpole" cells, may be seen under high magnification. The cells are of the primitive myoblast-type, some with intensely eosinophilic cytoplasm, set in a myxoid stroma (Fig. 14B.71). A spindle cell variant of embryonal rhabdomyosarcoma has been recognized at this location and is usually associated with more limited disease and a significantly better prognosis than the classical type.[539,540] Approximately 6% of paratesticular rhabdomyosarcomas are of the alveolar subtype. Desmin, muscle-specific actin,

myogenin, myoD1, and vimentin are positive. Cytokeratin is generally negative.

The prognosis depends largely on the tumor invasiveness, size, resectability, nodal involvement, and age in patients with localized tumor.[541] The outcome for patients with localized disease is excellent, despite the chemotherapy with reduced intensity and duration for low-risk patients. Five-year survival was 85.5% for the series as a whole, 94.6% for patients with localized disease, and 22.2% for metastatic cases.[541] Retroperitoneal nodal recurrence was the major cause of treatment failure. The tumors in adult patients show more aggressive behavior compared with those in the children. The 5-year survival is 80% for embryonal rhabdomyosarcoma and 95% for patients with the spindle cell variant.[542] However, the alveolar subtype does not appear to have an adverse prognostic influence in the paratesticular area, showing a distinctly better clinical behavior compared with same type of tumors at other sites.[543] The prognosis is poor for patients with stage III or IV disease, although a few long-term survivors have been reported.[544,545]

Other soft tissue sarcomas

Leiomyosarcoma is a relatively common sarcoma of the paratesticular area, especially in adults.[455,546–551] Patients' ages ranged from 15 to 84 years (mean 58 years). Leiomyosarcoma arises from soft tissue of the spermatic cord, epididymis (in a ratio of 5:1, spermatic cord versus epididymis), tunica vaginalis, scrotal subcutis, and dartos muscles.[549] The histologic features are similar to those of tumors seen elsewhere, and the tumors may demonstrate a spectrum of differentiation from well differentiated to poorly differentiated. The criteria for separation from leiomyoma are not well defined, although the threshold for the diagnosis of sarcoma should be low at this site. Any mitotic activity, especially if accompanied by increased cellularity, necrosis, or infiltrative growth should be regarded as a sign of malignancy. The majority of the tumors in this site are histologically low-grade and tumors with high-grade lesions behave more aggressively.[549]

More than 100 cases of liposarcoma of the paratesticular soft tissue, ranging in age presentation from 16 to 90 years (mean 56 years) have been reported in the literature,[455,551–555] although this number significantly underestimates the relative frequency of this occurrence. The tumor involves the spermatic cord, testicular tunics, and epididymis and the size ranges from 3 to 30 cm (mean 11.7 cm; median 10 cm).[552] Montgomery & Fisher[552] reported 30 patients with paratesticular liposarcoma. Nineteen were well differentiated, 10 were dedifferentiated (five with high-grade and five with low-grade dedifferentiation), and one was a myxoid-round cell liposarcoma.

Grossly, the tumors are bulky, lobulated, and resemble a lipoma. Histologically, most are well differentiated (lipoma-like or sclerosing type; also known as atypical lipomatous tumor) or dedifferentiated.[552] Myxoid liposarcomas, round cell (cellular myxoid) liposarcoma, and the pleomorphic variant may also occur, but these are rare. Paratesticular well-differentiated liposarcoma has a prolonged course with recurrences in more than half the cases, sometimes late, and the overall prognosis is good. However, dedifferentiated liposarcoma frequently recurs and may develop metastases with poor prognosis.[552] The chief differential diagnosis for

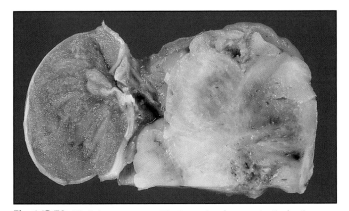

Fig. 14B.70 • Rhabdomyosarcoma. The tumor involves paratesticular tissue and is lobulated, smooth, and gray-white.

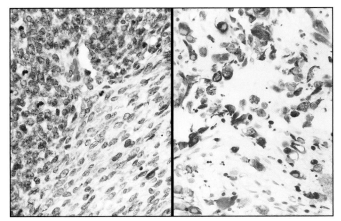

Fig. 14B.71 • Rhabdomyosarcoma. Embryonal rhabdomyosarcoma with cellular and myxoid areas (left). The tumor cells are strongly positive with desmin immunostaining (right).

the well-differentiated form includes large lipomas and lipogranulomas.

Other soft tissue sarcomas reported to occur in the para-testicular area include fibrosarcoma, angiosarcoma, Kaposi's sarcoma,[551] so-called malignant fibrous histiocytoma,[551] malignant solitary fibrous tumor,[556] and malignant rhabdoid tumor.[557,558] Their gross and microscopic features are similar to those observed in more common sites (see Ch. 24).

References

1. Krain L S 1973 Testicular cancer in California from 1942 to 1969: the California Tumor Registry experience. Oncology 27: 45–51
2. Jemal A, Siegel R, Ward E et al. 2006 Cancer statistics, 2006. CA Cancer J Clin 56: 106–130
3. Eble J N, Sauter G, Epstein J I et al. 2004 Pathology and genetics: tumours of the urinary system and male genital organs. WHO classification of tumors. IARC, Lyon
4. Mostofi F K 1980 Pathology of germ cell tumors of testis. A progress report. Cancer 45: 1735–1754
5. Risdon R A 1973 Germ cell tumours of the testis. J Pathol Bacteriol 141: 355–361
6. Ro J Y, Dexeus F H, El-Naggar A 1991 Testicular germ cell tumors: clinically relevant pathologic findings. Pathol Annu 26: 59–87
7. Dry S M, Renshaw A A 1999 Extratesticular extension of germ cell tumors preferentially occurs at the hilum. Am J Clin Pathol 111: 534–538
8. Nazeer T, Ro J Y, Kee K H et al. 1996 Spermatic cord contamination in testicular cancer. Mod Pathol 9: 762–766
9. Damjanov I 1989 Tumors of the testis and epididymis, In: Murphy W M (ed) Urologic pathology. W B Saunders, Philadelphia, p 314–379
10. Wilms M 1896 Die teratoiden Geschwulste des Hoden mit Einschluss der sog: Cystoide und enchondrome. Beitr Pathol Anat Allg Pathol 19: 233–366
11. Skakkebaek N E 1972 Possible carcinoma-in-situ of the testis. Lancet 2: 516–517
12. Dorman S, Trainer T D, Lefke D 1979 Incipient germ cell tumor in a cryptorchid testis. Cancer 44: 1357–1362
13. Gondos B, Migliozzi J A 1987 Intratubular germ cell neoplasia. Semin Diagn Pathol 4: 292–303
14. Nistal M, Codesal J, Paniagua R 1989 Carcinoma in situ of the testis in infertile men: a histological, immunocytochemical, and cytophotometric study of DNA content. J Pathol Bacteriol 159: 205–210
15. Pryor J P, Cameron K M, Chilton C P 1983 Carcinoma in situ in testicular biopsies from men presenting with infertility. Br J Urol 55: 780–784
16. Skakkebaek N E, Berthelsen J G, Muller J 1982 Carcinoma-in-situ of the undescended testis. Urol Clin North Am 9: 377–385
17. Skakkebaek N E 1978 Carcinoma-in-situ of the testis: frequency and relationship to invasive germ cell tumours in infertile men. Histopathology 2: 157–170
18. Von der Maase H, Giwercman A, Muller J 1987 Management of carcinoma-in-situ of the testis. Int J Androl 10: 209–220
19. Von der Maase H, Rorth M, Walbom-Jorgensen S 1986 Carcinoma-in-situ of contralateral testis in patients with testicular germ cell cancer: study of 27 cases in 500 patients. Br Med J 293: 1398–1401
20. Von Eyben F E, Mikulowski P, Busch C 1981 Microinvasive germ cell tumors of the testis. J Urol 126: 842–844
21. Berthelsen J G, Skakkebaek N E, Mogensen P 1979 Incidence of carcinoma in-situ of germ cells in contralateral testes of men with testicular tumors. Br Med J 2: 363–364
22. Skakkebaek N E, Berthelsen J G 1978 Carcinoma-in-situ of testis and orchiectomy. Lancet 2: 204–205
23. Berthelsen J G, Skakkebaek N E, von der Maase H 1982 Screening for carcinoma in-situ of the contralateral testis in patients with germinal testicular cancer. Br Med J 285: 1683–1686
24. Dieckmann K P, Loy V 1998 The value of the biopsy of the contralateral testis in patients with testicular germ cell cancer: the recent German experience. APMIS 106: 12–23
25. Muller J, Skakkebaek N E, Ritzen M 1985 Carcinoma in-situ of the testis in children with 45, X/46, XY gonadal dysgenesis. J Pediatr 106: 431–436
26. Nogales F F, Toro M, Ortega J 1981 Bilateral incipient germ cell tumours of the testis in the incomplete testicular feminization syndrome. Histopathology 5: 511–515
27. Muller J, Skakkebaek N E 1984 Testicular carcinoma in-situ in children with the androgen insensitivity (testicular feminization) syndrome. Br Med J 288: 1419–1420
28. Gondos B, Berthelsen J G, Skakkebaek N E 1983 Intratubular germ cell neoplasia (carcinoma in-situ): a preinvasive lesion of the testis. Ann Clin Lab Sci 13: 185–192
29. Giwercman A, Clausen O P F, Skakkebaek N E 1988 Carcinoma in-situ of the testis: aneuploid cells in semen. Br Med J 296: 1762–1764
30. Burke A P, Mostofi F K 1988 Placental alkaline phosphatase immunohistochemistry of intratubular malignant germ cells and associated testicular germ cell tumors. Hum Pathol 19: 663–670
31. Burke A P, Mostofi F K 1988 Intratubular malignant germ cells in testicular biopsies: clinical course and identification by staining for placental alkaline phosphatase. Mod Pathol 1: 475–479
32. Coffin C M, Ewing S, Dehner L P 1985 Frequency of intratubular germ cell neoplasia with invasive testicular germ cell tumors. Histologic and immunohistochemical features. Arch Pathol Lab Med 109: 555–559
33. Giwercman A, Marks A, Bailey D 1988 A monoclonal antibody as a marker for carcinoma in situ germ cells of the human adult testis. APMIS 96: 667–670
34. Jacobsen G K, Jacobsen M 1983 Ferritin (FER) in testicular germ cell tumours: an immunohistochemical study. Acta Pathol Microbiol Immunol Scand 91: 177–181
35. Bailey D, Marks A, Stratis M et al. 1991 Immunohistochemical staining of germ cell tumors and intratubular malignant germ cells of the testis using antibody to placental alkaline phosphatase and a monoclonal antiseminoma antibody. Mod Pathol 4: 167–171
36. Franke F E, Pauls K, Kerkman L et al. 2000 Somatic isoform of angiotensin I-converting enzyme in the pathology of testicular germ cell tumors. Hum Pathol 31: 1466–1476
37. Giwercman A, Lindenberg S, Kimber S J 1990 Monoclonal antibody 43-9F as a sensitive immunohistochemical marker of carcinoma in situ of human testis. Cancer 65: 1135–1142
38. Jones T D, Ulbright T M, Eble J N et al. 2004 OCT4: a sensitive and specific biomarker for intratubular germ cell neoplasia of the testis. Clin Cancer Res 10: 8544–8547
39. Eyzaguirre E, Gatalica Z 2002 Loss of Fhit expression in testicular germ cell tumors and intratubular germ cell neoplasia. Mod Pathol 15: 1068–1072
40. Rakheja D, Hoang M P, Sharma S et al. 2002 Intratubular embryonal carcinoma. Arch Pathol Lab Med 126: 487–490
41. van Echten J, van Gurp R J, Stoepker M et al. 1995 Cytogenetic evidence that carcinoma in situ is the precursor lesion for invasive testicular germ cell tumors. Cancer Genet Cytogenet 85: 133–137
42. Looijenga L H, Zafarana G, Grygalewicz B et al. 2003 Role of gain of 12p in germ cell tumour development. APMIS 111: 161–171
43. Lifschitz-Mercer B, Elliott D J, Leider-Trejo L et al. 2000 Absence of RBM expression as a marker of intratubular (in situ) germ cell neoplasia of the testis. Hum Pathol 31: 1116–1120
44. Jacobsen G K, Henriksen O B, Van der Maase H 1981 Carcinoma in situ of testicular tissue adjacent to malignant germ-cell tumors: a study of 105 cases. Cancer 47: 2660–2662
45. Reinberg Y, Manivel J C, Fraley E E 1989 Carcinoma in situ of the testis. J Urol 142: 243–247
46. Scully R E 1986 Testis. In: Hedson D E, Albores-Saavedra J (ed) The pathology of incipient neoplasia. W B Saunders, Philadelphia, p 329–343
47. Christensen T B, Daugaard G, Geertsen P F et al. 1998 Effect of chemotherapy on carcinoma in situ of the testis. Ann Oncol 9: 657–660
48. Manivel J C, Simonton S, Wold L E 1988 Absence of intratubular germ cell neoplasia in testicular yolk sac tumors in children: a histochemical and immunohistochemical study. Arch Pathol Lab Med 112: 641–645
49. Hartwick W, Ro J Y, Ordonez N 1990 Testicular germ cell tumors under age 5. Does intratubular germ cell neoplasia exist? Mod Pathol 3: 43A
50. Hu L M, Phillipson J, Barsky S H 1992 Intratubular germ cell neoplasia in infantile yolk sac tumor. Verification of tandem repeat sequence by in situ hybridization. Diagn Mol Pathol 1: 118–128
51. Ramani P, Yeung C K, Habeebu S S 1993 Testicular intratubular germ cell neoplasia in children and adolescents with intersex. Am J Surg Pathol 17: 1124–1133
52. Parkinson M C, Ramani P 1993 Intratubular germ cell neoplasia in an infantile testis. Histopathology 23: 99–100
53. Renedo D E, Trainer T D 1994 Intratubular germ cell neoplasia (ITGCN) with p53 and PCNA expression and adjacent mature teratoma in an infant testis. An immunohistochemical and morphologic study with a review of the literature. Am J Surg Pathol 18: 947–952
54. Jacobsen G K, Barlebo H, Oslen J 1984 Testicular germ cell tumors in Denmark 1976–1980: pathology of 1058 consecutive cases. Acta Radiol Oncol 23: 239–247
55. Ulbright T M, Roth L M 1987 Recent developments in the pathology of germ cell tumors. Semin Diagn Pathol 4: 304–319
56. Ulbright T M 1993 Germ cell neoplasms of the testis. Am J Surg Pathol 17: 1075–1091
57. Hedinger C, von Hochstetter A R, Egloff B 1979 Seminoma with syncytiotrophoblastic giant cells: a special form of seminoma. Virchow's Arch [A] 383: 59–67
58. Cockburn A G, Vugrin D, Batata M 1984 Poorly differentiated (anaplastic) seminoma of the testis. Cancer 53: 1991–1994
59. Giwercman A, Grindsted J, Hansen B 1987 Testicular cancer risk in boys with maldescended testis: a cohort study. J Urol 138: 1214–1216

60. Sokal M, Peckham M J, Hendry W F 1980 Bilateral germ cell tumours of the testis. Br J Urol 52: 158–162
61. Che M, Tamboli P, Ro J Y et al. 2002 Bilateral testicular germ cell tumors. Twenty-year experience at M D Anderson cancer Center. Cancer 95: 1228–1233
62. Fraley E E, Lange P H, Kennedy B J 1979 Germ-cell testicular cancer in adults. N Engl J Med 301: 1370–1377, 1420–1426
63. Javadpour N, Young J D J 1986 Prognostic factors in non-seminomatous testicular cancer. J Urol 135: 497–499
64. Scheiber K, Ackermann D, Studer U E 1987 Bilateral testicular germ cell tumors: a report of 20 cases. J Urol 138: 73–76
65. Jacobsen G K, von der Maase H, Specht L 1995 Histopathological features in stage I seminoma treated with orchiectomy only. J Urol Pathol 3: 85–94
66. Young R H, Finlayson N, Scully R E 1989 Tubular seminoma: report of a case. Arch Pathol Lab Med 113: 414–416
67. Damjanov I, Niejadlik D C, Rabuffo J V 1980 Cribriform and sclerosing seminoma devoid of lymphoid infiltrates. Arch Pathol Lab Med 104: 527–530
68. Zavala-Pompa A, Ro J Y, El-Naggar A K 1994 Tubular seminoma: an immunohistochemical and DNA flow-cytometric study of four cases. Am J Clin Pathol 102: 397–401
69. Takeshima Y, Sanda N, Yoneda K et al. 1999 Tubular seminoma of the testis. Pathol Int 49: 676–679
70. Ulbright T M, Young R H 2005 Seminoma with tubular, microcystic and related patterns. A study of 28 cases of unusual morphologic variants that often cause confusion with yolk sac tumor. Am J Surg Pathol 29: 500–505
71. Henley J D, Young R H, Wade C L et al. 2004 Seminomas with exclusive intertubular growth. A report of 12 clinically and grossly inconspicuous tumors. Am J Surg Pathol 28: 1163–1168
72. Kademian M, Bosch A, Caldwell W L 1977 Anaplastic seminoma. Cancer 40: 3082–3086
73. Thackray A C, Crane W A J 1976 Seminoma. In: Pugh R C P (ed) Pathology of the testis. Blackwell, Oxford, p 164–198
74. Kahn D G 1993 Ossifying seminoma of the testis. Arch Pathol Lab Med 117: 321–322
75. Bell D A, Flotte T J, Bhan A K 1987 Immunohistochemical characterization of seminoma and its inflammatory cell infiltrate. Hum Pathol 18: 511–520
75a. Browne T J, Richie J P, Gilligan T D, Rubin M A 2005 Intertubular growth in pure seminomas: associations with poor prognostic parameters. Hum Pathol 36: 640–645
76. Perry A, Wiley E L, Albores-Saavedra J 1994 Pagetoid spread of intratubular germ cell neoplasia into rete testis: a morphologic and immunohistochemical study of 100 orchiectomy specimens with invasive germ cell tumors. Hum Pathol 25: 235–239
77. Mai K T, Yazdi H M, Rippstein P 2001 Light and electron microscopy of the pagetoid spread of germ cell carcinoma in the rete testis: morphologic evidence suggestive of field effect as a mechanism of tumor spread. Appl Immunohistochem Mol Morphol 9: 335–339
78. Florentine B D, Roscher A A, Garrett J et al. 2002 Necrotic seminoma of the testis: establishing the diagnosis with Masson trichrome stain and immunostains. Arch Pathol Lab Med 126: 205–206
79. Bobba V S, Mittal B B, Hoover S V 1988 Classical and anaplastic seminoma: difference in survival. Radiology 167: 849–852
80. Johnson D E, Gomez J J, Ayala A G 1975 Anaplastic seminoma. J Urol 114: 80–82
81. Tickoo S K, Hutchinson B, Bacik J et al. 2002. Testicular seminoma: a clinicopathologic and immunohistochemical study of 105 cases with special reference to seminomas with atypical features. Int J Surg Pathol 10: 23–32
82. Manivel J C, Jessurun J, Wick M R 1987 Placental alkaline phosphatase immunoreactivity in testicular germ-cell neoplasms. Am J Surg Pathol 11: 21–29
83. Mostofi F K, Sesterhenn I A, Davis C J J 1987 Immunopathology of germ cell tumors of the testis. Semin Diagn Pathol 4: 320–341
84. Jones T D, Ulbright T M, Eble J N et al. 2004 OCT4 staining in testicular tumors: a sensitive and specific marker for seminoma and embryonal carcinoma. Am J Surg Pathol 28: 935–940
85. Looijenga L H, Stoop H, de Leeuw H P 2003 POU5F1 (OCT3/4) identifies cells with pluripotent potential in human germ cell tumors. Cancer Res 63: 2244–2250
86. Ferreiro J A 1994 Ber-H2 expression in testicular germ cell tumors. Hum Pathol 25: 522–524
87. Hittmair A, Rogatsch H, Hobisch A et al. 1996 CD30 expression in seminoma. Hum Pathol 27: 1166–1171
88. Cheville J C, Rao S, Iczkowski K A et al. 2000 Cytokeratin expression in seminoma of the human testis. Am J Clin Pathol 113: 583–588
88a. McIntyre A, Summersgill B, Grygalewicz B et al. 2005 Amplification and overexpression of the KIT gene is associated with progression in the seminoma subtype of testicular germ cell tumors of adolescents and adults. Cancer Res 65: 8085–8089
89. Butcher D N, Gregory W M, Gunter P A 1985 The biological significance of HCG-containing cells in seminoma. Br J Cancer 51: 473–478
90. Jacobsen G K 1983 Alpha-fetoprotein (AFP) and human chorionic gonadotropin (HCG) in testicular germ cell tumors. A comparison of histologic and serologic occurrence of tumor markers. Acta Pathol Microbiol Scand Sect A 91: 183–190
91. Paus E, Fossa S D, Risberg T 1987 The diagnostic value of human chorionic gonadotrophin in patients with testicular seminoma. Br J Urol 59: 572–577
92. Javadpour N 1980 Management of seminoma based on tumor markers. Urol Clin North Am 7: 773–781
93. Javadpour N 1984 Human chorionic gonadotropin in seminoma. J Urol 131: 407
94. Javadpour N 1980 Significance of elevated serum alphafetoprotein (AFP) in seminoma. Cancer 45: 2166–2168
95. Raghavan D, Vogelzang N J, Bosl G L 1982 Tumor classification and size in germ-cell testicular cancer. Influence on the occurrence of metastases. Cancer 50: 1591–1595
96. Nazeer T, Ro J Y, Amato B et al. 1998 Histologically pure seminoma with elevated alpha-fetoprotein (AFP): a clinicopathologic study of ten cases. Oncol Rep 5: 1425–1429
97. Kuzmits R, Schernthaner G, Krisch K 1987 Serum neuron-specific enolase: a marker for response to therapy in seminoma. Cancer 60: 1017–1021
98. Smolarek T A, Blough R I, Foster R S 1999 Cytogenetic analyses of 85 testicular germ cell tumors: comparison of postchemotherapy and untreated tumors. Cancer Genet Cytogenet 108: 57–69
99. Qiao D, Zeeman A M, Deng W et al. 2002 Molecular characterization of hiwi, a human member of the piwi gene family whose overexpression is correlated to seminomas. Oncogene 21: 3988–3999
100. Berger P, Untergasser G, Hermann M et al. 1999 The testis-specific expression pattern of the growth hormone/placental lactogen (GH/PL) gene cluster changes with malignancy. Hum Pathol 30: 1201–1206
101. Cheville J C, Roche P C 1999 MAGE-1 and MAGE-3 tumor rejection antigens in human germ cell tumors. Mod Pathol 12: 974–978
102. Zeeman A M, Stoop H, Boter M et al. 2002 VASA is a specific marker for both normal and malignant germ cells. Lab Invest 82: 159–166
103. Babaian R J, Zagars G K 1988 Testicular seminoma: the MD Anderson experience. An analysis of pathological and patient characteristics and treatment recommendations. J Urol 139: 311–315
104. Zagars G K, Babaian R J 1987 The role of radiation in stage II testicular seminoma. Int J Radiat Oncol Biol Phys 13: 163–170
105. Johnson D E, Gomez J J, Ayala A G 1976 Histologic factors affecting prognosis of pure seminoma of the testis. South Med J 69: 1173–1174
106. Marks L B, Rutgers J L, Shipley W U 1990 Testicular seminoma: clinical and pathological features that may predict para-aortic lymph node metastases. J Urol 143: 524–527
107. Warde P, Specht L, Horwich A et al. 2002 Prognostic factors for relapse in stage I seminoma managed by surveillance: a pooled analysis. J Clin Oncol 20: 4448–4452
108. Warde P, Gospodarowicz M K, Banerjee D 1997 Prognostic factors for relapse in stage I testicular seminoma treated with surveillance. J Urol 157: 1705–1709
109. Farivari A, Mostofi F K 1984 Spermatocytic seminoma. J Urol 131: 226A
110. Talerman A 1980 Spermatocytic seminoma: clinicopathological study of 22 cases. Cancer 45: 2169–2176
111. Masson P 1946 Etude sur le seminome. Rev Can Biol 5: 361
112. Rajpert-De Meyts E, Jacobsen G K, Bartkova J et al. 2003 The immunohistochemical expression pattern of Chk2, p53, p19INK4d, MAGE-A4 and other selected antigens provides new evidence for the premeiotic origin of spermatocytic seminoma. Histopathology 42: 217–226
113. Stoop H, van Gurp R et al. 2001 Reactivity of germ cell maturation stage-specific markers in spermatocytic seminoma: diagnostic and etiological implications. Lab Invest 81: 919–928
114. Satie A P, Rajpert-De Meyts E, Spagnoli G C et al. 2002 The cancer-testis gene, NY-ESO-1, is expressed in normal fetal and adult testes and in spermatocytic seminomas and testicular carcinoma in situ. Lab Invest 82: 775–780
115. Cummings O W, Ulbright T M, Eble J N et al. 1994 Spermatocytic seminoma: an immunohistochemical study. Hum Pathol 25: 54–59
116. Floyd C, Ayala A G, Logothetis C J 1988 Spermatocytic seminoma of testis with associated sarcoma of the testis. Cancer 61: 409–414
117. Chung P W, Bayley A J, Sweet J et al. 2004 Spermatocytic seminoma: a review. Eur Urol 45: 495–498
118. Burke A P, Mostofi F K 1993 Spermatocytic seminoma: a clinicopathologic study of 79 cases. J Urol Pathol 1: 21–32
119. Albores-Saavedra J, Huffman H, Alvarado-Cabrero I et al. 1996 Anaplastic variant of spermatocytic seminoma. Hum Pathol 27: 650–655
120. Rosai J, Siber I, Khodadoust K 1969 Spermatocytic seminoma: clinicopathologic study of six cases and review of the literature. Cancer 24: 92–102
121. Talerman A, Fu Y S, Okagaki T 1984 Spermatocytic seminoma: ultrastructural and microspectrophotometric observations. Lab Invest 51: 343–349
122. True L D, Otis C N, Delprado W 1988 Spermatocytic seminoma of testis with sarcomatous transformation. A report of five cases. Am J Surg Pathol 12: 75–82
123. Matoska J, Ondrus D, Hornak M 1988 Metastatic spermatocytic seminoma: a case report with light microscopic, ultrastructural and immunohistochemical findings. Cancer 62: 1197–1201
124. Matoska J, Talerman A 1990 Spermatocytic seminoma associated with rhabdomyosarcoma. Am J Clin Pathol 94: 89–95
125. Miettinen M, Virtanen I, Talerman A 1985 Intermediate filament proteins in human testis and testicular germ-cell tumors. Am J Pathol 120: 402–410
126. Decaussin M, Borda A, Bouvier R et al. 2004 Spermatocytic seminoma. A clinicopathological and immunohistochemical study of 7 cases. Ann Pathol 24: 161–166

127. Dunphy C H, Ayala A G, Swanson D A 1986 Clinical stage I non-seminomatous and mixed germ cell tumors of the testis: a clinicopathologic study of 93 patients on a surveillance protocol after orchiectomy alone. Cancer 62: 1202–1206

128. Dewar J M, Spagnolo D V, Jamrozik K D 1987 Predicting relapse in stage I non-seminomatous germ cell tumours of the testis. Lancet 1: 454

129. Koops H S, Sleijfer D T, Oosterhuis J W 1986 Wait-and-see policy in clinical stage I non-seminomatous germ cell tumors of the testis. Eur J Surg Oncol 12: 283–287

130. Rodriquez P N, Hafez G R, Messing E M 1986 Non-seminomatous germ cell tumor of the testicle: does extensive staging of the primary tumor predict the likelihood of metastatic disease? J Urol 136: 604–608

131. Fung C Y, Kalish L A, Brodsky G L 1988 Stage I non-seminomatous germ cell testicular tumour: prediction of metastatic potential by primary histopathology. J Clin Oncol 6: 1467–1473

132. Hoskin P, Dilly S, Easton D 1986 Prognostic factors in stage I non-seminomatous germ-cell testicular tumors managed by orchiectomy and surveillance: implicators for adjuvant chemotherapy. J Clin Oncol 4: 1031–1036

133. Nochomovitz L E, DeLa Torre F E, Rosai J 1977 Pathology of germ cell tumors of the testis. Urol Clin North Am 4: 359–378

134. Vugrin D, Chen A, Feigl P 1988 Embryonal carcinoma of the testis. Cancer 61: 2348–2352

135. Pierce G B J, Abell M R 1970 Embryonal carcinoma of the testis. Pathol Annu 5: 27–60

136. Tuttle J P J, Pratt-Thomas H R, Thomason W B 1977 Embryonal carcinoma of the testis in elderly men. J Urol 118: 1070–1072

137. Bosl G J, Lange P H, Nochomovitz L E 1981 Tumor markers in advanced non-seminomatous testicular cancer. Cancer 47: 572–576

138. Morinaga S, Ojima M, Sasano N 1983 Human chorionic gonadotropin and alpha-fetoprotein in testicular germ tumors: an immunohistochemical study in comparison with tissue concentrations. Cancer 52: 1281–1289

139. Mostofi F K, Sesterhenn I A, Davis C J J 1988 Developments in histopathology of testicular germ cell tumors. Semin Urol 6: 171–188

140. Talerman A, Haije W G, Baggerman L 1980 Serum alphafetoprotein (AFP) in patients with germ cell tumors of the gonads and extragonadal sites: correlation between endodermal sinus (yolk sac) tumor and raised serum AFP. Cancer 46: 380–385

141. Talerman A 1980 Endodermal sinus (yolk sac) tumor elements in testicular germ-cell tumors in adults: comparison of prospective and retrospective studies. Cancer 46: 1213–1217

142. Jacobsen G K, Jacobsen M, Clausen P P 1981 Distribution of tumor-associated antigens in the various histologic components of germ cell tumors of the testis. Am J Surg Pathol 5: 257–266

143. Battifora H, Sheibani K, Tubbs R R 1984 Antikeratin antibodies in tumor diagnosis. Distinction between seminoma and embryonal carcinoma. Cancer 54: 843–848

144. Jacobson G K 1986 Histogenetic considerations concerning germ cell tumours. Morphological and immunohistochemical comparative investigation of human embryo and testicular germ cell tumours. Virchow's Arch [A] 408: 509–525

145. Pallesen G, Hamilton-Dutoit S J 1988 Ki-1 (CD30) antigen is regularly expressed by tumor cells of embryonal carcinoma. Am J Pathol 133: 446–450

146. Shah V I, Amin M B, Linden M D et al. 1998 Utility of a selective immunohistochemical (IHC) panel in the detection of components of mixed germ cell tumors (GCT) of testis. Mod Pathol 11: 95A (abstract)

147. Shah V I, Amin M B, Linden M D et al. 1998 Immunohistologic profile of spindle cell elements in non-seminomatous germ cell tumors (NSGCT): histogenetic implications. Mod Pathol 11: 96A (abstract)

148. Berney D M, Shamash J, Pieroni K et al. 2001 Loss of CD30 expression in metastatic embryonal carcinoma: the effects of chemotherapy? Histopathology 39: 382–385

149. Oosterhuis J W, Castedo S M, de Jong B 1989 Ploidy of primary germ cell tumors of the testis. Pathogenetic and clinical relevance. Lab Invest 60: 14–21

150. Motzer R J, Rodriguez E, Reuter V E 1991 Genetic analysis as an aid in diagnosis for patients with midline carcinomas of uncertain histologies. J Natl Cancer Inst 83: 341–346

151. Ferry J A, Ulbright T M, Young R H 1997 Anaplastic large cell lymphoma presenting in the testis. J Urol Pathol 5: 139–147

152. Green D M 1983 The diagnosis and treatment of yolk sac tumors in infants and children. Cancer Treat Rev 10: 265–288

153. Harms D, Janig U 1986 Germ cell tumours of childhood: Report of 170 cases, including 59 pure and partial yolk-sac tumours. Virchows Arch [A] 409: 223–239

154. Griffin G C, Raney R B J, Snyder H M 1967 Yolk sac carcinoma of the testis in children. J Urol 137: 954–957

155. Gonzalez-Crussi F 1979 The human yolk sac and yolk sac (endodermal sinus) tumors: a review. Perspect Pediatr Pathol 5: 179–215

156. Kaplan G W, Cromie W C, Kelalis P P 1988 Prepubertal yolk sac testicular tumors: Report of the Testicular Tumor Registry. J Urol 140: 1109–1112

157. Kramer S A, Wold L E, Gilchrist G S 1984 Yolk sac carcinoma: an immunohistochemical and clinicopathologic review. J Urol 131: 315–318

158. Olsen M M, Raffensperger J G, Gonzalez-Crussi F 1982 Endodermal sinus tumor: a clinical and pathological correlation. J Pediatr Surg 17: 832–840

159. Pierce G B J, Bullock W K, Huntington R W J 1970 Yolk sac tumors of the testis. Cancer: 644–658

160. Wold L E, Kramer S A, Farrow G M 1984 Testicular yolk sac and embryonal carcinomas in pediatric patients: comparative immunohistochemical and clinicopathologic study. Am J Clin Pathol 81: 427–435

161. Logothetis C J, Samuels M L, Trindade A 1984 The prognostic significance of endodermal sinus tumor histology among patients treated for stage III non-seminomatous germ cell tumors of the testes. Cancer 53: 122–128

162. Talerman A 1975 The incidence of yolk sac tumor (endodermal sinus tumor) elements in germ cell tumors of the testis in adults. Cancer 36: 211–215

163. Ulbright T M, Roth L M, Broadhecker C A 1986 Yolk sac differentiation in germ cell tumors: a morphologic study of 50 cases with emphasis on hepatic, enteric, and parietal yolk sac features. Am J Surg Pathol 10: 151–164

164. Cohen M B, Friend D S, McInar J J 1987 Gonadal endodermal sinus (yolk sac) tumor with pure intestinal differentiation: a new histologic type. Pathol Res Pract 182: 609–616

165. Jacobsen G K, Jacobsen M 1983 Possible liver cell differentiation in testicular germ cell tumours. Histopathology 7: 537–548

166. Nakashima N, Fukatsu T, Nagasaka T 1987 The frequency and histology of hepatic tissue in germ cell tumors. Am J Surg Pathol 11: 682–692

167. Horie Y, Kato M 2000 Hepatoid variant of yolk sac tumor of the testis. Pathol Int 50: 754–758

168. Eglen D E, Ulbright T M 1987 The differential diagnosis of yolk sac tumor and seminoma: usefulness of cytokeratin, alpha-fetoprotein, and alpha-1-antitrypsin immunoperoxidase reactions. Am J Clin Pathol 88: 328–332

169. Noorgaard-Pedersen B, Albrechtsen R, Teilum G 1975 Serum alpha-fetoprotein as a marker for endodermal sinus tumour (yolk sac tumour) or a vitelline component of "teratocarcinoma." Acta Pathol Microbiol Scand [A] 83: 573–589

170. Tsuchida Y, Kaneko M, Yokomori K 1978 Alpha-fetoprotein, prealbumin, albumin, alpha-1-antitrypsin and transferrin as diagnostic and therapeutic markers for endodermal sinus tumors. J Pediatr Surg 13: 25–29

171. Koide O, Iwai S, Baba K et al. 1987 Identification of testicular atypical germ cells by an immunohistochemical technique for placental alkaline phosphatase. Cancer 60: 1325–1330

172. Ro J Y, Grignon- D J, Amin M B et al. 1997 Atlas of surgical pathology of the male reproductive tract. W B Saunders, Philadelphia

173. Grady R W, Ross J H, Kay R 1995 Patterns of metastatic spread in prepubertal yolk sac tumor of the testis. J Urol 153: 1259–1261

174. Gaillard J A 1972 Yolk sac tumour patterns and entoblastic structures in polyembryomas. Acta Pathol Microbiol Scand [A] 233: 18–25

175. Marin-Padilla M 1965 Origin, nature and significance of the "embryoids" of human teratomas. Virchow's Arch [A] 340: 105–121

176. Nakashima N, Murakami S, Fukatsu T 1988 Characteristics of "embryoid body" in human gonadal germ cell tumors. Hum Pathol 19: 1144–1154

177. Colodny A H, Hopkins T B 1977 Testicular tumors in infants and children. Urol Clin North Am 4: 347–358

178. Fraley E E, Ketcham A S 1968 Teratoma of testis in an infant. J Urol 100: 659–660

179. Hawkins E P 1990 Pathology of germ cell tumors in children. Crit Rev Oncol Hematol 10: 165–179

180. Leibovitch I, Foster R S, Ulbright T M et al. 1995 Adult primary pure teratoma of the testis. The Indiana experience. Cancer 75: 2244–2250

181. Pugh R C B, Smith J P 1964 Teratoma. Br J Urol 36: 28–44

182. Mahour G H, Wooley M M, Trivedi S N 1974 Teratomas in infancy and childhood: experience with 81 cases. Surgery 76: 309–318

183. Mosli H A, Carpenter B, Schillinger J F 1985 Teratoma of the testis in a pubertal child. J Urol 133: 105–106

184. Tapper D, Lack E E 1983 Teratomas in infancy and childhood: a 54 year experience at the Children's Hospital Medical Center. Ann Surg 198: 398–410

185. Tiltman A J 1974 Granulomatous reaction in testicular teratomas. S Afr Med J 48: 1231

186. Ulbright T M, Srigley J R 2001 Dermoid cyst of the testis: a study of five postpubertal cases, including a pilomatrixoma-like variant, with evidence supporting its separate classification from mature testicular teratoma. Am J Surg Pathol 25: 788–793

187. Dieckmann K P, Loy V 1994 Epidermoid cyst of the testis: a review of clinical and histogenetic considerations. Br J Urol 73: 436–441

188. Nokubi M, Kawai T, Mitsu S et al. 2002 Mucinous cystadenoma of the testis. Pathol Int 52: 648–652

189. Collins D H, Pugh R C P 1964 Classification and frequency of testicular tumours. Br J Urol 36: 1–11

190. Harms D, Janig U 1985 Immature teratomas of childhood. Report of 21 cases. Pathol Res Pract 179: 388–400

191. Kooijman C D 1988 Immature teratomas in children. Histopathology 12: 491–502

192. Michael H, Hull M T, Ulbright T M et al. 1997 Primitive neuroectodermal tumors arising in testicular germ cell neoplasms. Am J Surg Pathol 21: 896–904

193. Ulbright T M 1999 Testis risk and prognostic factors. The pathologist's perspective. Urol Clin North Am 26: 611–626

194. Comiter C V, Kibel A S, Richie J P et al. 1998 Prognostic features of teratomas with malignant transformation: a clinicopathologic study of 21 cases. J Urol 159: 359–363

195. Michael H 1998 Non-germ cell tumors arising in patients with testicular germ cell tumors. J Urol Pathol 9: 39–60

196. Cajal S R Y, Pinango L, Barat A 1987 Metastatic pure choriocarcinoma of the testis in an elderly man. J Urol 137: 516–519

197. Manivel J C, Niehans G, Wick M R et al. 1987 Intermediate trophoblast in germ cell neoplasms. Am J Surg Pathol 11: 693–701

198. Ulbright T M, Young R H, Scully R E 1997 Trophoblastic tumors of the testis other than classic choriocarcinoma: "monophasic" choriocarcinoma and placental site trophoblastic tumor: a report of two cases. Am J Surg Pathol 21: 282–288

199. Ulbright T M, Loehrer P J 1988 Choriocarcinoma-like lesions in patients with testicular germ cell tumors. Two histologic variants. Am J Surg Pathol 12: 531–541

200. Mazur M T, Lurain J R, Brewer J I 1982 Fatal gestational choriocarcinoma. Clinicopathologic study of patients treated at a trophoblastic disease center. Cancer 50: 1833–1846

201. Suurmeijer A J, Gietema J A, Hoekstra H J 2004 Placental site trophoblastic tumor in a late recurrence of a non-seminomatous germ cell tumor of the testis. Am J Surg Pathol 28: 830–833

202. Lind H M, Haghighi P 1986 Carcinoembryonic antigen staining in choriocarcinoma. Am J Clin Pathol 86: 538–540

203. Shih I M, Kurman R J 1999 Immunohistochemical localization of inhibin-alpha in the placental and gestational trophoblastic lesions. Int J Gynecol Pathol 18: 144–150

204. Logothetis C J, Samuels M L, Selig D E 1986 Cyclic chemotherapy with cyclophosphamide, doxorubicin, and cisplatin plus vinblastine and bleomycin in advanced germinal tumors: results with 100 patients. Am J Med 81: 219–228

205. Vaeth M, Schultz H P, von der Maase H 1984 Prognostic factors in testicular germ cell tumours: experiences with 1058 consecutive cases. Acta Radiol Oncol 23: 271–285

206. Stoter G, Sylvester R, Sleijfer D T 1988 A multivariate analysis of prognostic factors in disseminated non-seminomatous testicular cancer. Prog Clin Biol Res 269: 381–393

207. Pugh R C B, Thackray A C 1964 Combined tumour. Br J Urol 36: 45–51

208. De Almeida P C C, Scully R E 1983 Diffuse embryoma of the testis: a distinctive form of mixed germ cell tumor. Am J Surg Pathol 7: 633–642

209. de Peralta-Venturina M N, Ro J Y, Ordonez N G et al. 1994 Diffuse embryoma of the testis: an immunohistochemical study of two cases. Am J Clin Pathol 102: 402–405

210. Allen E A, Burger P C, Epstein J I 1999 Microcystic meningioma arising in a mixed germ cell tumor of the testis: a case report. Am J Surg Pathol 23: 1131–1135

211. Ro J Y, Han W, Ordonez N 1991 Non-seminomatous germ cell tumors of the testis: an immunohistochemical study of 46 cases. Lab Invest 64: 50A

212. Tezel G, Nagasaka T, Shimono Y et al. 2002 Differential expression of RET finger protein in testicular germ cell tumors. Pathol Int 52: 623–627

213. Scully R E 1953 Gonadoblastoma: a gonadal tumor related to the dysgerminoma (seminoma) and capable of sex-hormone production. Cancer 6: 455–463

214. Scully R E 1970 Gonadoblastoma: a review of 74 cases. Cancer 25: 1340–1356

215. Hughesdon P E, Kumarasamy T 1970 Mixed germ cell tumours (gonadoblastomas) in normal and dysgenetic gonads. Virchow's Arch [A] 349: 258–280

216. Ishida T, Tagatz G E, Okagaki T 1976 Gonadoblastoma: ultrastructural evidence for testicular origin. Cancer 37: 1770–1781

217. Talerman A 1980 The pathology of gonadal neoplasms composed of germ cells and sex cord stroma derivatives. Pathol Res Pract 170: 24–38

218. Hart W R, Burkons D M 1979 Germ cell neoplasms arising in gonadoblastomas. Cancer 43: 669–678

219. Chapman W H H, Plymyer M R, Dresner M L 1990 Gonadoblastoma in an anatomically normal man: a case report and literature review. J Urol 144: 1472–1474

220. Talerman A, Delemarre J F 1975 Gonadoblastoma associated with embryonal carcinoma in an anatomically normal man. J Urol 113: 355–359

221. Iezzoni J C, von Kap-Herr C, Golden W L et al. 1997 Gonadoblastomas in 45,X/46,XY mosaicism: analysis of Y-chromosome distribution by fluorescence in situ hybridization. Am J Clin Pathol 108: 197–201

222. Kommoss F, Oliva E, Bhan A et al. 1998 Inhibin expression in ovarian tumors and tumor-like lesions: an immunohistochemical study. Mod Pathol 11: 656–664

223. Jorgensen N, Muller J, Jaubert F et al. 1997 Heterogeneity of gonadoblastoma germ cells: similarities with immature germ cells, spermatogonia and testicular carcinoma in-situ cells. Histopathology 30: 177–186

224. Bolen J V 1981 Mixed germ cell–sex cord stromal tumor: a gonadal tumor distinct from gonadoblastoma. Am J Clin Pathol 75: 565–573

225. Matoska J, Talerman A 1989 Mixed germ cell–sex cord stromal tumor of the testis. Cancer 64: 2146–2153

226. Talerman A 1972 A distinctive gonadal neoplasm related to gonadoblastoma. Cancer 30: 1219–1224

227. Talerman A 1987 Tumors composed of germ cells and sex cord stromal derivatives. In: Talerman A, Roth L M (ed) Pathology of the testis and its adnexa. Churchill Livingstone, New York, p 59–62

228. Rames R A, Richardson M, Swiger F et al. 1995 Mixed germ cell–sex cord stromal tumor of the testis: the incidental finding of a rare testicular neoplasm. J Urol 54: 1479

229. Ulbright T M, Srigley J R, Reuter V E et al. 2000 Sex cord stromal tumors of the testis with entrapped germ cells: a lesion mimicking unclassified mixed germ cell sex cord stromal tumors. Am J Surg Pathol 24: 535–542

230. Amato R J, Ro J Y, Ayala A G et al. 2004 Risk-adapted treatment for patients with clinical stage I non-seminomatous germ cell tumor of the testis. Urology 63: 144–148

231. Johnson D E 1987 Improved survival results from early detection and diagnosis of testicular cancer. Oncology 32: 1

232. Logothetis C J, Swanson D A, Dexeus F 1987 Primary chemotherapy for clinical stage II non-seminomatous germ cell tumors of the testis: a follow-up of 50 patients. J Clin Oncol 5: 906–911

233. Pizzocaro G, Zanon-i F, Milani A 1984 Retroperitoneal lymphadenectomy and aggressive chemotherapy in non-bulky clinical stage II non-seminomatous germinal testis tumors. Cancer 53: 1363–1368

234. Pizzocaro G, Monfardini S 1984 No adjuvant chemotherapy in selected patients with pathologic stage II non-seminomatous germ cell tumors of the testis. J Urol 131: 677–680

235. Williams S D, Stablein D M, Einhorn L H 1987 Immediate adjuvant chemotherapy versus observation with treatment at relapse in pathological stage II testicular cancer. N Engl J Med 317: 1433–1438

236. Vugrin D, Whitemore W F, Cvitkovic E 1981 Adjuvant chemotherapy combination of vinblastine, actinomycin D, bleomycin, and chlorambucil following retroperitoneal lymph node dissection for stage II testis tumor. Cancer 47: 840–844

237. Moran C A, Travis W D, Carter D 1993 Metastatic mature teratoma in lung following testicular embryonal carcinoma and teratocarcinoma. Arch Pathol Lab Med 117: 641–644

238. Samuels M L, Johnson D E 1980 Adjuvant therapy of testis cancer: the role of vinblastine and bleomycin. J Urol 124: 369–371

239. Blacken R B, Johnson D E, Frazier O H 1983 The role of surgery following chemotherapy in stage III germ cell neoplasms. J Urol 129: 39–43

240. Peckham M J, Oliver R T D, Bagshawe K D 1985 Prognostic factors in advanced non-seminomatous germ-cell testicular tumours: results of a multicentre study. Report from the Medical Research Council Working Party on Testicular Tumours. Lancet 1: 8–11

241. Roth B J, Greist A, Kubilis P S 1988 Cisplatin-based combination chemotherapy for disseminated germ cell tumors: long-term follow-up. J Clin Oncol 6: 1239–1247

242. Williams S D, Birch R, Einhorn L H 1987 Treatment of disseminated germ-cell tumors with cisplatin, bleomycin, and either vinblastine or etoposide. N Engl J Med 316: 1435–1440

243. Lo R K, Friha F S, Torti F M 1989 Chemotherapy for advanced germ cell tumors of the testis: the Stanford experience. In: Johnson D E, Logothetis C J, von Eschenbach A C (eds) Systemic therapy for genitourinary cancers. Year Book, Chicago, p 338–341

244. Logothetis C J, Samuels M L 1984 Surgery in the management of stage III germinal cell tumors: observation in the MD Anderson Hospital experience, 1971–1979. Cancer Treat Rev 11: 27–37

245. Geller N L, Bosl G J, Chan E Y M 1989 Prognostic factors for relapse after complete response in patients with metastatic germ cell tumors. Cancer 63: 440–445

246. Peckham M J, Hendry W F 1985 Clinical stage II non-seminomatous germ cell testicular tumours: results of management by primary chemotherapy. Br J Urol 57: 763–768

247. Fossa S D, Ous S, Lien H H 1989 Post-chemotherapy lymph node histology in radiologically normal patients with metastatic non-seminomatous testicular cancer. J Urol 141: 557–559

248. Loehrer P J S, Hui S, Clark S 1986 Teratoma following cisplatin-based combination chemotherapy for non-seminomatous germ cell tumors: a clinicopathological correlation. J Urol 135: 1183–1189

249. Tait D, Peckham M J, Hendry W F 1984 Post-chemotherapy surgery in advanced non-seminomatous germ-cell testicular tumours: the significance of histology with particular reference to differentiated (mature) teratoma. Br J Cancer 50: 601–609

250. Dexeus F M, Shirkhoda A, Logothetis C J 1989 Clinical and radiological correlation of retroperitoneal metastasis from non-seminomatous testicular cancer treated with chemotherapy. Eur J Cancer Clin Oncol 25: 35–43

251. Castedo S M M J, de Jong B, Oosterhuis J W 1989 Chromosomal changes in mature residual teratomas following polychemotherapy. Cancer Res 49: 672–676

252. Sella A, El-Naggar A, Ro J Y et al. 1991 Evidence of malignant features in histologically mature teratoma. J Urol 146: 1025–1028

253. Ulbright T M, Loehrer P J, Roth L M 1984 The development of non-germ-cell malignancies within germ cell tumors. A clinicopathologic study of 11 cases. Cancer 54: 1824–1833

254. Ulbright T M, Goheen M P, Roth L M 1986 The differentiation of carcinomas of teratomatous origin from embryonal carcinoma: a light and electron microscopic study. Cancer 57: 257–263

255. Ahlgren A D, Simrell C R, Triche T J 1984 Sarcoma arising in a residual testicular teratoma after cytoreductive chemotherapy. Cancer 54: 2015–2018

256. Michael H, Hull M T, Foster R S et al. 1998 Nephroblastoma-like tumors in patients with testicular germ cell tumors. Am J Surg Pathol 22: 1107–1114

257. Sahoo S, Ryan C W, Recant W M et al. 2003 Angiosarcoma masquerading as embryonal carcinoma in the metastasis from a mature testicular teratoma. Arch Pathol Lab Med 127: 360–363

258. Davey D D, Ulbright T M, Loehrer P J 1987 The significance of atypia within teratomatous metastases after chemotherapy for malignant germ cell tumors. Cancer 49: 533–539

259. Chong C, Logothetis C J, von Eschenbach A 1986 Orchiectomy in advanced germ cell cancer following intensive chemotherapy: a comparison of systemic to testicular response. J Urol 136: 1221–1223

260. Ro J Y, Amato R J, Ayala A G 1996 What does the pathology report really mean? Semin Urol Oncol 14: 2–7

261. Kim I, Young R H, Scully R E 1985 Leydig cell tumors of the testis. A clinicopathological analysis of 40 cases and review of the literature. Am J Surg Pathol 9: 177–192

262. Caldamone A A, Altebarmakian V, Frank I N 1979 Leydig cell tumor of testis. Urology 14: 39–43

263. Mauer R, Taylor C, Schmucki O 1980 Extratesticular gonadal stromal tumor of the pelvis. A case report with immunoperoxidase findings. Cancer 45: 985–990

264. Billings S D, Roth L M, Ulbright T M 1999 Microcystic Leydig cell tumors mimicking yolk sac tumor. A report of four cases. Am J Surg Pathol 23: 546–551

265. Minkowitz S, Soloway H, Soscia J 1965 Ossifying interstitial cell tumor of the testis. J Urol 94: 592–595

266. Balsitis M, Sokol M 1990 Ossifying malignant Leydig (interstitial) cell tumour of the testis. Histopathology 16: 597–601

267. Kurman R J, Andrade D, Goebelsmann U 1978 An immunohistological study of steroid localization in Sertoli–Leydig tumors of the ovary and testis. Cancer 42: 1772–1783

268. Ulbright T M, Srigley J R, Hatzianastassiou D K et al. 2002 Leydig cell tumors of the testis with unusual features: adipose differentiation, calcification with ossification, and spindle-shaped tumor cells. Am J Surg Pathol 26: 1424–1433

269. Cheville J C, Sebo T J, Lager D J et al. 1998 Leydig cell tumor of the testis: a clinicopathologic, DNA content and MIB-1 comparison of non-metastasizing and metastasizing tumors. Am J Surg Pathol 22: 1361–1367

270. Gulbahce H E, Lindeland A T, Engel W et al. 1999 Metastatic Leydig cell tumor with sarcomatoid differentiation. Arch Pathol Lab Med 123: 1104–1107

271. Hekimgil M, Altay B, Yakut B D et al. 2001 Leydig cell tumor of the testis: comparison of histopathological and immunohistochemical features of three azoospermic cases and one malignant case. Pathol Int 51: 792–796

272. Amin M B, Young R H, Scully R E 1998 Immunohistochemical profile of Sertoli and Leydig cell tumors of the testis [abstract]. Mod Pathol 11: 76A

273. Iczkowski K A, Bostwick D G, Cheville J C 1998 Inhibin is a sensitive and specific marker for testicular sex cord–stromal tumors. Mod Pathol 11: 774–779

274. McCluggage W G, Shanks J H, Whiteside C et al. 1998 Immunohistochemical study of testicular sex cord–stromal tumors, including staining with anti-inhibin antibody. Am J Surg Pathol 22: 615–619

275. Lugli A, Forster Y, Haas P et al. 2003 Calretinin expression in human normal and neoplastic tissues: a tissue microarray analysis on 5233 tissue samples. Hum Pathol 34: 994–1000

276. McCluggage W G, Maxwell P 2001 Immunohistochemical staining for calretinin is useful in the diagnosis of ovarian sex cord–stromal tumours. Histopathology 38: 403–408

277. Collins D H, Symington T 1964 Sertoli-cell tumor. Br J Urol 36: 52–61

278. Lawrence W D, Young R H, Scully R E 1986 Sex cord-stromal tumor. In: Talerman A, Roth L M (ed) Pathology of the testis and its adnexa. Churchill Livingstone, New York, p 67–92

279. Kaplan G W, Cromie W J, Kelalis P P 1986 Gonadal stromal tumors: a report of the prepubertal testicular tumor registry. J Urol 136: 300–302

280. Zukerberg L R, Young R H, Scully R E 1991 Sclerosing Sertoli cell tumor of the testis: a report of 10 cases. Am J Surg Pathol 15: 829–834

281. Dubois R S, Hoffman W H, Krishnan T H 1982 Feminizing sex cord tumor with annular tubules in a boy with Peutz–Jeghers syndrome. J Pediatr 101: 568–571

282. Wilson D M, Pitts W C, Hintz R L 1986 Testicular tumors with Peutz–Jeghers syndrome. Cancer 57: 2238–2240

283. Gabrilove J L, Freiberg E K, Leiter E 1980 Feminizing and non-feminizing Sertoli cell tumors. J Urol 124: 757–767

284. Talerman A 1971 Malignant Sertoli cell tumor of the testis. Cancer 28: 446–455

285. Rosvoll R V, Woodard J R 1968 Malignant Sertoli cell tumor of the testis. Cancer 22: 8–13

286. Godec C R 1985 Malignant Sertoli cell tumor of testicle. Urology 26: 185–188

287. Gilcrease M Z, Delgado R, Albores-Saavedra J 1998 Testicular Sertoli cell tumor with a heterologous sarcomatous component: immunohistochemical assessment of Sertoli cell differentiation. Arch Pathol Lab Med 122: 907–911

288. Henley J D, Young R H, Ulbright T M 2002 Malignant Sertoli cell tumors of the testis. A study of 13 examples of a neoplasm frequently misinterpreted as seminoma. Am J Surg Pathol 26: 541–550

289. Young R H, Koelliker D D, Scully R E 1998 Sertoli cell tumors of the testis, not otherwise specified. A clinicopathologic analysis of 60 cases. Am J Surg Pathol 22: 709–721

290. Nielsen K, Jacobsen G K 1988 Malignant Sertoli cell tumor of the testis: an immunohistochemical study and a review of the literature. APMIS 96: 755–760

291. Rey R, Sabourin J C, Venara M et al. 2000 Anti-Mullerian hormone is a specific marker of Sertoli- and granulosa-cell origin in gonadal tumors. Hum Pathol 31: 1202–1208

292. Gordon M D, Corless C, Renshaw A A et al. 1998 CD99, keratin, and vimentin staining of sex cord–stromal tumors, normal ovary, and testis. Mod Pathol 11: 769–773

293. Proppe K H, Scully R E 1980 Large-cell calcifying Sertoli cell tumor of the testis. Am J Clin Pathol 74: 607–619

294. Tetu B, Ro J Y, Ayala A G 1991 Large cell calcifying Sertoli cell tumor of the testis: a clinicopathologic, immunohistochemical and ultrastructural study of two cases. Am J Clin Pathol 96: 717–722

295. Chang B, Borer J G, Tan P E 1998 Large cell calcifying Sertoli cell tumor of the testis: case report and review of the literature. Urology 52: 520–522

296. De Raeve H, Schoonooghe P, Wibowo R et al. 2003 Malignant large cell calcifying Sertoli cell tumor of the testis. Pathol Res Pract 199: 113–117

297. Kratzer S S, Ulbright T M, Talerman A 1997 Large cell calcifying Sertoli cell tumor of the testis: contrasting features of six malignant and six benign tumors and a review of the literature. Am J Surg Pathol 21: 1271–1280

298. Waxman M, Damjanov I, Khapra A 1984 Large cell calcifying Sertoli tumor of testis: light microscopic and ultrastructural study. Cancer 54: 1574–1581

299. Proppe K H, Dickersin G R 1982 Large-cell calcifying Sertoli cell tumor of the testis: light microscopic and ultrastructural study. Hum Pathol 13: 1109–1114

300. Venara M, Rey R, Bergada I et al. 2001 Sertoli cell proliferations of the infantile testis: an intratubular form of Sertoli cell tumor? Am J Surg Pathol 125: 1237–1244

301. Horn T, Jao W, Keh P C 1983 Large-cell calcifying Sertoli cell tumor of the testis: a case report with ultrastructural study. Ultrastruct Pathol 4: 359–364

302. Perez-Atayde A R, Nunez A E, Carroll W L 1983 Large-cell calcifying Sertoli cell tumor of the testis: an ultrastructural, immunocytochemical, and biochemical study. Cancer 51: 2287–2292

303. Adesokan A, Adegboyega P A, Cowan D F et al. 1997 Testicular "tumor" of the adrenogenital syndrome: a case report of an unusual association with myelolipoma and seminoma in cryptorchidism. Cancer 80: 2117–2120

304. Tanaka Y, Carney J A, Ijiri R et al. 2002 Utility of immunostaining for S-100 protein subunits in gonadal sex cord–stromal tumors, with emphasis on the large-cell calcifying Sertoli cell tumor of the testis. Hum Pathol 33: 285–289

305. Lawrence W D, Young R H, Scully R E 1985 Juvenile granulosa cell tumor of the infantile testis: a report of 14 cases. Am J Surg Pathol 9: 87–94

306. Raju U, Fine G, Warrier R 1986 Congenital testicular juvenile granulosa cell tumor in a neonate with X/XY mosaicism. Am J Surg Pathol 10: 577–583

307. Crump W D 1983 Juvenile granulosa cell (sex-cord–stromal) tumor of fetal testis. J Urol 129: 1057–1058

308. Mostofi F K, Theiss E A, Ashley D J B 1959 Tumors of specialized gonadal stroma in human male subjects. Cancer 12: 944–957

309. Young R H, Lawrence W D, Scully R E 1985 Juvenile granulosa cell tumor: another neoplasm associated with abnormal chromosomes and ambiguous genitalia: a report of three cases. Am J Surg Pathol 9: 737–743

310. Harms D, Kock L R 1997 Testicular juvenile granulosa cell and Sertoli cell tumours: a clinicopathologic study of 29 cases from the Kiel Paediatric Tumor Registry. Virchows Arch 430: 301–309

311. Jimenez-Quintero L P, Ro J Y, Zavala-Pompa A 1993 Granulosa cell tumor of the adult testis: a clinicopathologic study of seven cases and a review of the literature. Hum Pathol 24: 1120–1125

312. Matoska J, Ondrus D, Talerman A 1992 Malignant granulosa cell tumor of the testis associated with gynecomastia and long survival. Cancer 69: 1769–1772

313. Groisman F M, Dische M R, Fine E M et al. 1993 Juvenile granulosa cell tumor of the testis: a comparative immunohistochemical study with normal infantile gonads. Pediatr Pathol 13: 389–400

314. Talerman A 1985 Pure granulosa cell tumour of the testis: report of a case and review of the literature. Appl Pathol 3: 117–122

315. Gaylis F D, August C, Yeldandi A 1989 Granulosa cell tumor of the adult testis: ultrastructural and ultrasonographic characteristics. J Urol 141: 126–127

316. Nistal M, Lazaro R, Garcia J et al. 1992 Testicular granulosa cell tumor of the adult type. Arch Pathol Lab Med 115: 284–287

317. Al-Bozom I A, El-Faqih S R, Hassan S H et al. 2000 Granulosa cell tumor of the adult type: a case report and review of the literature of a very rare testicular tumor. Arch Pathol Lab Med 124: 1525–1528

318. Renshaw A A, Gordon M, Corless C L 1997 Immunohistochemistry of unclassified sex cord-stromal tumors of the testis with a predominance of spindle cells. Mod Pathol 10: 693–700

319. Nistal M, Puras A, Perna C et al. 1996 Fusocellular gonadal stromal tumour of the testis with epithelial and myoid differentiation. Histopathology 29: 259–264

320. Jones M A, Young R H, Scully R E 1997 Benign fibromatous tumors of the testis and paratesticular region: a report of 9 cases with proposed classification of fibromatous tumors and tumor-like lesions. Am J Surg Pathol 21: 296–305

321. Deveci M S, Deveci G, Onguru O et al. 2002 Testicular (gonadal stromal) fibroma: case report and review of the literature. Pathol Int 52: 326–330

322. Gohji K, Higuchi A, Fujii A et al. 1994 Malignant gonadal stromal tumor. Urology 43: 244–247

323. Eble J N, Hull M T, Warfel K A et al. 1984 Malignant sex cord–stromal tumor of testis. J Urol 131: 546–550

324. Campbell C M, Middleton A W J 1981 Malignant gonadal stromal tumor: case report and review of the literature. J Urol 125: 257–259

325. Oosterhuis J W, Castedo S M, de Jong B 1989 A malignant mixed gonadal stromal tumor of the testis with heterologous components and i (12p) in one of its metastases. Cancer Genet Cytogenet 41: 105–114

326. Luk I S, Shek T W, Tang V W et al. 1999 Interdigitating dendritic cell tumor of the testis: a novel testicular spindle cell neoplasm. Am J Surg Pathol 23: 1141–1148

327. Rutgers J L, Young R H, Scully R E 1988 The testicular "tumor" of the adrenogenital syndrome: a report of six cases and review of the literature on testicular masses in patients with adrenocortical disorders. Am J Surg Pathol 12: 503–513

328. Fore W W, Bledsoe T, Weber D M et al. 1972 Cortisol production by testicular tumors in adrenogenital syndrome. Arch Intern Med 130: 59–63

329. Kirkland R T, Kirkland J L, Keenan B S et al. 1977 Bilateral testicular tumors in congenital adrenal hyperplasia. J Clin Endocrinol Metab 44: 369–378

330. Davis J M, Woodroof J, Sadasivan R et al. 1995 Case report: congenital adrenal hyperplasia and malignant Leydig cell tumor. Am J Med Sci 309: 63–65

331. Sussman E B, Hajdu S I, Lieberman P H 1977 Malignant lymphoma of the testis: a clinicopathologic study of 37 cases. J Urol 118: 1004–1007

332. Talerman A 1977 Primary malignant lymphoma of the testis. J Urol 118: 783–786

333. Ferry J A, Harris N L, Young R H 1994 Malignant lymphoma of the testis, epididymis, and spermatic cord. A clinicopathologic study of 69 cases with immunophenotypic analysis. Am J Surg Pathol 18: 376–390

334. Baldetorp L A, Brunkvall J, Cavallin-Stahl E 1984 Malignant lymphoma of the testis. Br J Urol 56: 525–530

335. Wilkins B S, Williamson J M, O'Brien C J 1989 Morphological and immunohistological study of testicular lymphomas. Histopathology 15: 147–156

336. Paladugu R R, Bearman R M, Rappaport H 1980 Malignant lymphoma with primary manifestation in the gonad. A clinicopathologic study of 38 patients. Cancer 45: 561–571

337. Lagrange J L, Ramaioli A, Theodore C H 2001 Non-Hodgkin's lymphoma of the testis: a retrospective study of 84 patients treated in the French anticancer centres. Ann Oncol 12: 1313–1319

338. Zucca E, Conconi A, Mughal T I 2003 Patterns of outcome and prognostic factors in primary large-cell lymphoma of the testis in a survey by the International Extranodal Lymphoma Study Group. J Clin Oncol 21: 20–27

339. Visco C, Medeiros L J, Mesina O M et al. 2001 Non-Hodgkin's lymphoma affecting the testis: is it curable with doxorubicin-based therapy? Clin Lymphoma 2: 40–46

340. Pileri S A, Sabattini E, Rosito P 2002 Primary follicular lymphoma of the testis in childhood: an entity with peculiar clinical and molecular characteristics. J Clin Pathol 55: 684–688

341. Akhtar M, Al-Dayel F, Siegrist K et al. 1996 Neutrophil-rich Ki-1 positive anaplastic large cell lymphoma presenting as a testicular mass. Mod Pathol 9: 812–815

342. Chan J K, Tsang W Y, Lau W H 1996 Aggressive T/natural killer cell lymphoma presenting as testicular tumor. Cancer 77: 1198–1205

343. Ng S B, Lai K W, Murugaya S et al. 2004 Nasal-type extranodal natural killer/T-cell lymphomas: a clinicopathologic and genotypic study of 42 cases in Singapore. Mod Pathol 17: 1097–1107

344. Ko Y H, Cho E Y, Kim J E et al. 2004 NK and NK-like T-cell lymphoma in extranasal sites: a comparative clinicopathological study according to site and EBV status. Histopathology 44: 480–489

345. Heller K N, Teruya-Feldstein J, La Quaglia M P et al. 2004 Primary follicular lymphoma of the testis: excellent outcome following surgical resection without adjuvant chemotherapy. Pediatr Hematol Oncol 26: 104–107

346. Kim Y B, Chang S K, Yang W I et al. 2003 Primary NK/T cell lymphoma of the testis. A case report and review of the literature. Acta Haematol 109: 95–100

347. van Droogenbroeck J, Altintas S, Pollefliet C et al. 2001 Intravascular large B-cell lymphoma or intravascular lymphomatosis: report of a case diagnosed by testicle biopsy. Ann Hematol 80: 316–318

348. Pakzad K, MacLennan G T, Elder J S et al. 2002 Follicular large cell lymphoma localized to the testis in children. J Urol 168: 225–258

349. Moller M B, d'Amore F, Christensen B E 1994 Testicular lymphoma: a population-based study of incidence, clinicopathological correlations and prognosis. The Danish Lymphoma Study Group. LYFO. Eur J Cancer 30A: 1760–1764

350. Lu D, Medeiros L J, Eskenazi A E et al. 2001 Primary follicular large cell lymphoma of the testis in a child. Arch Pathol Lab Med 125: 551–554

351. Doll D C, Weiss R B 1986 Malignant lymphoma of the testis. Am J Med 81: 515–524

352. Pectides D, Economopoulos T, Kouvatseas G 2000 Anthracycline-based chemotherapy of primary non-Hodgkin's lymphoma of the testis: the Hellenic Cooperative oncology group experience. Oncology 58: 286–292

353. Seymour J F, Solomon B, Wolf M M et al. 2001 Primary large-cell non-Hodgkin's lymphoma of the testis: a retrospective analysis of patterns of failure and prognostic factors. Clin Lymphoma 2: 109–115

354. Lagrange J L, Ramaioli A, Theodore C H et al. 2001 Radiation Therapy Group and the Genito-Urinary Group of the French Federation of Cancer Centres. Non-Hodgkin's lymphoma of the testis: a retrospective study of 84 patients treated in the French anticancer centres. Ann Oncol 12: 1313–1319

355. Givler R L 1969 Testicular involvement in leukemia and lymphoma. Cancer 23: 1290–1295

356. Reid H, Marsden H B 1980 Gonadal infiltration in children with leukemia and lymphoma. J Clin Pathol 33: 722–729

357. Miyoshi I, Saito T, Taguchi H et al. 2004 Granulocytic sarcoma of the testis. Br J Haematol 124: 695

358. Askin F B, Land V J, Sullivan M P 1981 Occult testicular leukemia: testicular biopsy at three years continuous complete remission of childhood leukemia. A Southwest Oncology Group Study. Cancer 47: 470–475

359. Eden O B, Hardisty R M, Innes E M 1978 Testicular disease in acute lymphoblastic leukemia in childhood. Report on behalf of the Medical Research Council's working party on leukemia in childhood. Br Med J 1: 334–338

360. Stoffel T J, Nesbit M E, Levitt S H 1975 Extramedullary involvement of the testes in childhood leukemia. Cancer 35: 1203–1211

361. Nesbit M E, Robinson L L, Ortega J A 1980 Testicular relapse in childhood acute lymphoblastic leukemia: association with pretreatment patient characteristics and treatment. Cancer 45: 2009–2016

362. Layfield L J, Hilborne L H, Ljung B M 1988 Use of fine needle aspiration cytology for the diagnosis of testicular relapse in patients with acute lymphoblastic leukemia. J Urol 139: 1020–1022

363. Ferry J A, Srigley J R, Young R H 1997 Granulocytic sarcoma of the testis. A report of two cases of a neoplasm prone to misinterpretation. Mod Pathol 10: 320–325

364. Terzian N, Blumenfrucht M J, Yook C R 1987 Plasmacytoma of the testis. J Urol 137: 745–746

365. Ferry J A, Ulbright T M, Young R H 1996 Anaplastic large cell lymphoma of the testis: a lesion that may be confused with embryonal carcinoma. J Urol Pathol 5: 139–147

366. Levin H S, Mostofi F K 1970 Symptomatic plasmacytoma of the testis. Cancer 25: 1193–1203

367. Suzuki K, Shioji Y, Morita T et al. 2001 Primary testicular plasmacytoma with hydrocele of the testis. Int J Urol 8: 139–140

368. Ramadan A, Naab T, Frederick W et al. 2000 Testicular plasmacytoma in a patient with the acquired immunodeficiency syndrome. Tumori 86: 480–482

369. Anghel G, Petti N, Remotti D et al. 2002 Testicular plasmacytoma: report of a case and review of the literature. Am J Hematol 71: 98–104

370. Cavanna L, Fornari F, Civardi G 1990 Extramedullary plasmacytoma of the testicle: sonographic appearance and ultrasonically guided biopsy. Blut 60: 328–330

371. Chica G, Johnson D E, Ayala A G 1978 Plasmacytoma of testis presenting as primary testicular tumor. Urology 11: 90–92

372. Weitzner S 1969 Metastatic plasma cell myeloma in testis. Report of a case and review of the literature. Rocky Mt Med J 66: 48–50

373. Soumerai S, Gleason E A 1980 Asynchronous plasmacytoma of the stomach and testis. Cancer 45: 396–400

374. Scully R E, Parham A R 1948 Testicular tumors. II. Interstitial cell and miscellaneous neoplasms. Arch Pathol 46: 229–242

375. Haupt H M, Mann R B, Trump D L 1984 Metastatic carcinoma involving the testis: clinical and pathologic distinction from primary testicular neoplasms. Cancer 54: 709–714

376. Tiltman A J 1979 Metastatic tumors in the testis. Histopathology 3: 31–37

377. Almagro U A 1988 Metastatic tumors involving testis. Urology 32: 357–360

378. Meares E M J, Ho T L 1973 Metastatic carcinomas involving the testis: a review. J Urol 109: 653–655

379. Young R H, van Patter H T, Scully R E 1987 Hepatocellular carcinoma metastatic to the testis. Am J Clin Pathol 87: 117–120

380. Ro J Y, Sahin A A, Ayala A G 1990 Lung carcinoma with metastasis to testicular seminoma. Cancer 66: 347–353

381. Salesi N, Fabi A, Di Cocco B et al. 2004 Testis metastasis as an initial manifestation of an occult gastrointestinal cancer. Anticancer Res 24: 1093–1096

382. Ro J Y, Ayala A G, Tetu B 1990 Merkel cell carcinoma metastatic to the testis. Am J Clin Pathol 94: 384–389

383. Dutt N, Bates A W, Baithun S I 2000 Secondary neoplasms of the male genital tract with different patterns of involvement in adults and children. Histopathology 37: 323–331

384. Berdjis C C, Mostofi F K 1977 Carcinoid tumors of the testis. J Urol 118: 777–782

385. Zavala-Pompa A, Ro J Y, El-Naggar A 1993 Primary carcinoid tumor of testis: immunohistochemical, ultrastructural, and DNA flow cytometric study of three cases with a review of the literature. Cancer 72: 1726–1732

386. Kato N, Motoyama T, Kameda N 2003 Primary carcinoid tumor of the testis: immunohistochemical, ultrastructural and FISH analysis with review of the literature. Pathol Int 53: 680–685

387. Finci R, Gunhan O, Celasun B 1987 Carcinoid tumor of undescended testis. J Urol 137: 301–302

388. Mason J C, Belville W D 1986 Primary carcinoid of the testis. Milit Med 151: 497–498

389. Ordonez N G, Ayala A G, Sneige N 1982 Immunohistochemical demonstration of multiple neurohormonal polypeptides in a case of pure testicular carcinoid. Am J Clin Pathol 78: 860–864

390. Wurster K, Brodner O, Rossner J A 1976 A carcinoid occurring in the testis. Virchow's Arch [A] 370: 185–192

391. Reyes A, Moran C A, Suster S et al. 2003 Neuroendocrine carcinomas (carcinoid tumor) of the testis. A clinicopathologic and immunohistochemical study of ten cases. Am J Clin Pathol 120: 182–187

392. Hosking D H, Bowman D M, McMorris S L 1981 Primary carcinoid tumor of the testis with metastases. J Urol 125: 255–256

393. Kaufman J J, Waisman J 1985 Primary carcinoid tumor of testis with metastasis. Urology 25: 534–536

394. Sullivan J L, Packer J T, Bryant M 1981 Primary malignant carcinoid of the testis. Arch Pathol Lab Med 105: 515–517

395. Travis W D, Colby T V, Corrin B 1999 Histological typing of lung and pleural tumours, 3rd edn. Berlin, Germany: Springer-Verlag

396. Bates R J, Perrone T L, Parkhurst E C 1981 Insular carcinoid arising in a mature teratoma of the testis. J Urol 126: 55–56

397. Talerman A, Gratama S, Miranda S 1978 Primary carcinoid tumor of the testis: case report, ultrastructure and review of the literature. Cancer 42: 2696–2706

398. Hartwick R W, Ro J Y, Srigley J R et al. 1991 Adenomatous hyperplasia of the rete testis: a clinicopathologic study of nine cases. Am J Surg Pathol 15: 350–357

399. Ulbright T M, Gersell D J 1991 Rete testis hyperplasia with hyaline globule formation. A lesion simulating yolk sac tumor. Am J Surg Pathol 15: 66–74

400. Nistal M, Garcia-Cabezas M A, Regadera J et al. 2004 Microlithiasis of the epididymis and the rete testis. Am J Surg Pathol 28: 514–522

401. Nistal M, Castillo M C, Regadera J et al. 2003 Adenomatous hyperplasia of the rete testis. A review and report of new cases. Histopathology 18: 741–752

402. Uguz A, Gonlusen G, Ergin M et al. 2002 Adenomatous hyperplasia of the rete testis: report of two cases. Int Urol Nephrol 34: 87–89

403. Haas G P, Ohorodnik J M, Farah R N 1987 Cystadenocarcinoma of the rete testis. J Urol 137: 1232–1233

404. Crisp-Lindgren N, Travers H, Wells M M 1988 Papillary adenocarcinoma of rete testis: autopsy findings, histochemistry, immunohistochemistry, ultrastructure, and clinical correlations. Am J Surg Pathol 12: 492–501

405. Sarma D P, Weilbaecher T G 1985 Adenocarcinoma of the rete testis. J Surg Oncol 30: 67–71

406. Nochomovitz L E, Orenstein J M 1984 Adenocarcinoma of the rete testis: case report, ultrastructural observations, and clinicopathologic correlates. Am J Surg Pathol 8: 625–634

407. Ballotta M R, Borghi L, Barucchello G 2000 Adenocarcinoma of the rete testis. Report of two cases. Adv Clin Pathol 4: 169–173

408. Gruber H, Ratschek M, Pummer K et al. 1997 Adenocarcinoma of the rete testis: report of a case with surgical history of adenomatous hyperplasia of the rete testis. J Urol 158: 1525–1526

409. Nochomovitz L E, Orenstein J M 1994 Adenocarcinoma of the rete testis: consolidation and analysis of 31 reported cases with a review of the literature. J Urol Pathol 2: 1–37

410. Visscher D W, Talerman A, Rivera L R 1989 Adenocarcinoma of the rete testis with a spindle cell component: a possible metaplastic carcinoma. Cancer 64: 770–775

411. Shah K H, Maxted W C, Chun B 1981 Epidermoid cysts of the testis: a report of three cases and analysis of 141 cases from the world literature. Cancer 47: 577–582

412. Price E B 1969 Epidermoid cysts of the testis: a clinical and pathologic analysis of 69 cases from the testicular tumor registry. J Urol 102: 708–713

413. Malek R S, Rosen J S, Farrow G M 1986 Epidermoid cyst of the testis: a critical analysis. Br J Urol 58: 55–59

414. Younger C, Ulbright T M, Zhang S et al. 2003 Molecular evidence supporting the neoplastic nature of some epidermoid cysts of the testis. Arch Pathol Lab Med 127: 858–860

415. McClure J 1980 Malakoplakia of the testis and its relationship to granulomatous orchitis. J Clin Pathol 33: 670–678

416. Diaz Gonzalez R, Levina O, Navas Palacias J J 1982 Testicular malakoplakia. J Urol 127: 325–328

417. Paquin F, Schick E, Parent C 1983 Malakoplakia of testis. Urology 21: 194–198

418. Grove J D, Harnden P, Clark P B 1993 Malakoplakia of epididymis associated with testicular infarction. Br J Urol 72: 656–657

419. Damjanov I, Katz S M 1981 Malakoplakia. Pathol Annu 16: 103–126

420. McClure J 1983 Malakoplakia. J Pathol Bacteriol 140: 275–330

421. Dahl E V, Bahn R C 1962 Aberrant adrenal cortical tissue near the testis in human infants. Am J Pathol 40: 587–598

422. Mares A J, Shkolnik A, Sacks M 1980 Aberrant (ectopic) adrenocortical issue along the spermatic cord. J Pediatr Surg 15: 289–292

423. Nelson A A 1939 Accessory adrenal cortical tissue. Arch Pathol 27: 955–965

424. Czaplicki M, Bablock L, Kuzaka B 1985 Heterotopic adrenal tissue. Int Urol Nephrol 17: 177–181

425. Andrews R W, Copeland D D, Fried F A 1985 Splenogonadal fusion. J Urol 133: 1052–1053

426. Ceccacci L, Tosi S 1981 Splenic–gonadal fusion: case report and review of the literature. J Urol 126: 558–559

427. Mendez R, Morrow J W 1969 Ectopic spleen simulating testicular tumor. J Urol 102: 598–601

428. Gouw A S, Elema J D, Bink-Boelkens M T et al. 1985 The spectrum of splenogonadal fusion: case report and review of 84 reported cases. Eur J Pediatr 144: 316–323

429. Pendse A K, Mathur P N, Sharma M M 1975 Splenic–gonadal fusion. Br J Surg 62: 624–628

430. Knorr P A, Borden T A 1994 Splenogonadal fusion. Urology 44: 136–138

431. Imperial S L, Sidhu J S 2002 Non-seminomatous germ cell tumor arising in splenogonadal fusion. Arch Pathol Lab Med 126: 1222–1225

432. Putschar W G, Manion W C 1956 Splenic–gonadal fusion. Am J Pathol 32: 15–34

433. McPherson F, Frias J L, Spicer D et al. 2003 Splenogonadal fusion–limb defect "syndrome" and associated malformations. Am J Med Genet 1: 518–522

434. Glassy F J, Mostofi F K 1956 Spermatic granulomas of the epididymis. Am J Clin Pathol 26: 1303–1313

435. Schmidt S S, Morris R R 1973 Spermatic granuloma: the complication of vasectomy. Fertil Steril 24: 941–947

436. Schmidt S S 1979 Spermatic granuloma: an often painful lesion. Fertil Steril 31: 178–181

437. Boorjian S, Lipkin M, Goldstein M 2004 The impact of obstructive interval and sperm granuloma on outcome of vasectomy reversal. J Urol 171: 304–306

438. Dunner P S, Lipsit E R, Nochomovitz L E 1982 Epididymal sperm granuloma simulating a testicular neoplasm. J Clin Ultrasound 10: 353–355

439. Berg J W 1954 An acid-fast lipid from spermatozoa. Arch Pathol 57: 115–120

440. Baladas H G, Ng B K 1997 Sclerosing lipogranuloma of the scrotum following a laparoscopic hernioraphy and varicocelectomy – a case report. Ann Acad Med Singapore 26: 238–240

441. Bussey L A, Norman R W, Gupta R 2002 Sclerosing lipogranuloma: an unusual scrotal mass. Can J Urol 9: 1464–1469

442. Oertel Y C, Johnson F B 1977 Sclerosing lipogranuloma of male genitalia: review of 23 cases. Arch Pathol Lab Med 101: 321–326

443. Brown A F, Joergenson E J 1974 Genital mammary paraffin oil granulomas in the male. Ann West Med Surg 1: 301–305

444. Smetana H F, Bernhard W 1950 Sclerosing lipogranuloma. Arch Pathol 50: 296–325

445. Marcil-Rojas R A, Colon J E, Figueroa J J 1956 Sclerosing lipogranulomas of the male genitalia: report of one case and review of the literature. J Urol 75: 334–338

446. Ricchiuti V S, Richman M B, Haas C A et al. 2002 Sclerosing lipogranuloma of the testis. Urology 60: 515

447. Benisch B, Peison B, Sobel H J 1981 Fibrous mesotheliomas (pseudofibroma) of the scrotal sac: a light and ultrastructural study. Cancer 47: 731–735

448. Gilchrist K W, Benson R C 1979 Multifocal fibrous pseudotumor of testicular tunics: possible clinical dilemma. Urology 14: 285–287

449. Nistal M, Paniagua R, Torres A 1986 Idiopathic peritesticular fibrosis associated with retroperitoneal fibrosis. Eur Urol 12: 64–68

450. Sarlis I, Yakoymakis S, Rebelakos A G 1980 Fibrous pseudotumor of the scrotum. J Urol 124: 742–743

451. Strom G W 1977 Pseudotumor of testicular tunic. J Urol 118: 340

452. Turner W R J, Derrick F C, Sanders P I 1977 Benign lesions of the tunica albuginea. J Urol 117: 602–604

453. Young R H, Scully R E 1986 Miscellaneous neoplasms and non-neoplastic lesions. In: Talerman A, Roth L M (ed) Pathology of the testis. Churchill Livingstone, New York, p 93–130

454. Thompson J E, van der Walt J D 1986 Nodular fibrous proliferation (fibrous pseudotumor) of the tunica vaginalis testis. A light, electron microscopic and immunocytochemical study of a case and review of the literature. Histopathology 10: 741–748

455. Srigley J R, Hartwick R W 1990 Tumors and cysts of the paratesticular region. Pathol Annu 25: 51–108

456. Hollowood K, Fletcher C D M 1992 Pseudosarcomatous myofibroblastic proliferations of the spermatic cord ("proliferative funiculitis"). Histologic and immunohistochemical analysis of a distinctive entity. Am J Surg Pathol 16: 448–454

457. Fetsch J F, Montgomery E A, Meis J M 1993 Calcifying fibrous pseudotumor. Am J Surg Pathol 17: 502–508

458. Seethala R R, Tirkes A T, Weinstein S et al. 2003 Diffuse fibrous pseudotumor of the testicular tunics associated with an inflamed hydrocele. Arch Pathol Lab Med 127: 742–744

459. Oliva E, Young R H 2000 Paratesticular tumor-like lesions. Semin Diagn Pathol 17: 340–358

460. De Klerk D P, Nime F 1975 Adenomatoid tumors (mesothelioma) of testicular and paratesticular tissue. Urology 6: 635–641

461. Viprakasit D, Tannenbaum M, Smith A M 1974 Adenomatoid tumor of the male genital tract. Urology 4: 325–327

462. Williams S B, Han M, Jones R et al. 2004 Adenomatoid tumor of the testes. Urology 63: 779–781

463. Keily E A, Flanagan A, Williams G 1987 Intrascrotal adenomatoid tumors. Br J Urol 60: 255–257

464. Taxy J B, Battifora H, Oyasu R 1974 Adenomatoid tumors. A light microscopic, histochemical, and ultrastructural study. Cancer 34: 306–316

465. Yasuma T, Saito S 1980 Adenomatoid tumor of the male genital tract. A pathological study of eight cases and review of the literature. Acta Pathol Jpn 30: 883–906

466. Skinnider B F, Young R H 2004 Infarcted adenomatoid tumor: a report of five cases of a facet of a benign neoplasm that may cause diagnostic difficulty. Am J Surg Pathol 28: 77–83

467. Mackay B, Bennington J L, Skoglund R W 1971 The adenomatoid tumor. Fine structural evidence for a mesothelial differentiation. Cancer 27: 109–115

468. Delahunt B, Eble J N, King D G et al. 2000 Immunohistochemical evidence for mesothelial origin of paratesticular adenomatoid tumour. Histopathology 36: 109–115

469. Mucientes F, Govindarajan S, Burotto S 1985 Immunoperoxidase study on adenomatoid tumor of the epididymis using anti-mesothelial cell serum. Cancer 55: 363–365

470. Barwick K W, Madri J A 1982 An immunohistochemical study of adenomatoid tumor. Implications for histogenesis. Cancer 50: 931–938

471. Banks E R, Mills S E 1990 Histiocytoid (epithelioid) hemangioma of the testis. The so-called vascular variant of "adenomatoid tumor." Am J Surg Pathol 14: 584–589

472. Calder C J, Gregory J 1993 Papillary cystadenoma of the epididymis: a report of two cases with an immunohistochemical study. Histopathology 23: 89–91

473. Kragel P J, Pestaner J, Travis W D 1993 Papillary cystadenoma of the epididymis: a report of three cases with lectin histochemistry. Arch Pathol Lab Med 114: 672–675

474. Leung S Y, Chan A S, Wong M P et al. 1998 Expression of vascular endothelial growth factor in von Hippel–Lindau syndrome-associated papillary cystadenoma of the epididymis. Hum Pathol 29: 1322–1328

475. Goldman R L 1970 A Brenner tumor of the testis. Cancer 26: 853–856

476. Ross L 1968 Paratesticular Brenner-like tumor. Cancer 21: 722–726

477. Uzoaru I, Ray V H, Nadimpalli V 1995 Brenner tumor of the testis. Immunohistochemical comparison with its ovarian counterparts. J Urol Pathol 3: 249–253

478. Young R H, Scully R E 1986 Testicular and paratesticular tumors and tumor-like lesions of ovarian common epithelial and Mullerian types. Am J Clin Pathol 86: 146–152

479. Nogales F F J, Matilla A, Ortega I 1979 Mixed Brenner and adenomatoid tumor of the testis. An ultrastructural study and histogenetic considerations. Cancer 43: 539–543

480. Caccamo D, Socias M, Truchet C 1991 Malignant Brenner tumor of the testis and epididymis. Arch Pathol Lab Med 115: 524–527

481. Johnson R E, Scheithauer B W, Dahlin D C 1983 Melanocytic neuroectodermal tumor of infancy. A review of seven cases. Cancer 52: 661–666

482. Ricketts R R, Majmudar B 1985 Epididymal melanotic neuroectodermal tumor of infancy. Hum Pathol 16: 416–420

483. Frank G L, Koten J W 1967 Melanotic hamartoma ("retinal anlage tumor") of the epididymis. J Pathol Bacteriol 93: 549–554

484. Eaton W L, Ferguson J P 1956 Retinoblastic teratoma of the epididymis. Case report. Cancer 9: 718–720

485. Cutler L S, Chaudhry A P, Topazian R 1981 Melanotic neuroectodermal tumor of infancy. An ultrastructural study, literature review and reevaluation. Cancer 48: 257–270

486. Zone R M 1970 Retinal anlage tumor of the epididymis. A case report. J Urol 103: 106–107

487. Pettinato G, Manivel J C, d'Amore E S 1991 Melanotic neuroectodermal tumor of infancy. A reevaluation of a histogenetic problem based on immunohistochemical, flow cytometric, and ultrastructural study of 10 cases. Am J Surg Pathol 15: 233–345

488. Henley J D, Ferry J, Ulbright T M 2000 Miscellaneous rare paratesticular tumors. Semin Diagn Pathol 17: 319–339

489. Toda T, Sadi A M, Kiyuna M et al. 1998 Pigmented neuroectodermal tumor of infancy in the epididymis. A case report. Acta Cytol 42: 775–780

490. Kobayashi T, Kunimi K, Imao T et al. 1996 Melanotic neuroectodermal tumor of infancy in the epididymis. Case report and literature review. Urol Int 57: 262–265

491. Calabrese F, Danieli D, Valente M 1995 Melanotic neuroectodermal tumor of the epididymis in infancy: case report and review of the literature. Urology 46: 415–418

492. Diamond D A, Breitfeld P P, Bur M et al. 1992 Melanotic neuroectodermal tumor of infancy; an important mimicker of paratesticular rhabdomyosarcoma. J Urol 147: 673–675

493. Jones M, Young R H, Srigley J R et al. 1995 Paratesticular serous papillary carcinoma. A report of six cases. Am J Surg Pathol 19: 1359–1366

494. Kernohan N M, Coutts A G, Best P V 1990 Cystadenocarcinoma of the appendix testis. Histopathology 17: 147–154

495. Remmele W, Kaiserling E, Zerban U 1992 Serous papillary cystic tumor of borderline malignancy with focal carcinoma arising in testis: case report with immunohistochemical and ultrastructural observations. Hum Pathol 23: 75–79

496. Axiotis C A 1988 Intratesticular serous papillary cystadenoma of low malignant potential: an ultrastructural and immunohistochemical study suggesting Mullerian differentiation. Am J Surg Pathol 12: 56–63

497. Blumberg H M, Hendrix L E 1991 Serous papillary adenocarcinoma of the tunica vaginalis of the testis with metastasis. Cancer 67: 1450–1453

498. Tulunay O, Gogus C, Baltaci S et al. 2004 Clear cell adenocarcinoma of the tunica vaginalis of the testis with an adjacent uterus-like tissue. Pathol Int 54: 641–647

499. Ulbright T M, Young R H 2003 Primary mucinous tumors of the testis and paratestis: a report of nine cases. Am J Surg Pathol 27: 1221–1228

500. Shinmura Y, Yokoi T, Tsutsui Y 2002 A case of clear cell adenocarcinoma of the mullerian duct in persistent mullerian duct syndrome: the first reported case. Am J Surg Pathol 126: 1231–1234

501. McClure R F, Keeney G L, Sebo T J et al. 2001 Serous borderline tumor of the paratestis: a report of seven cases. Am J Surg Pathol 25: 373–378

502. Jones M A, Young R H, Scully R E 1997 Adenocarcinoma of the epididymis. A report of four cases and review of the literature. Am J Surg Pathol 21: 1474–1480

503. Folpe A L, Weiss S W 2000 Paratesticular soft tissue neoplasms. Semin Diagn Pathol 17: 307–318

504. Tanda F, Rocca P C, Bosincu L et al. 1997 Rhabdomyoma of the tunica vaginalis of the testis: a histologic, immunohistochemical, and ultrastructural study. Mod Pathol 10: 608–611

505. Wehner M S, Humphreys J L, Sharkey F E 2000 Epididymal rhabdomyoma: report of a case, including histologic and immunohistochemical findings. Arch Pathol Lab Med 124: 1518–1519

506. Iezzoni J C, Fechner R E, Wong L S et al. 1995 Aggressive angiomyxoma in males. A report of four cases. Am J Clin Pathol 104: 391–396

507. Tsang W Y, Chan J K, Lee K C et al. 1992 Aggressive angiomyxoma. A report of four cases occurring in men. Am J Surg Pathol 16: 1059–1065

508. Laskin W B, Fetsch J F, Mostofi F K 1998 Angiomyofibroblastoma-like tumor of the male genital tract: analysis of 11 cases with comparison to female angiomyofibroblastoma and spindle cell lipoma. Am J Surg Pathol 22: 6–16

509. Ockner D M, Sayadi H, Swanson P E et al. 1997 Genital angiomyofibroblastoma. Comparison with aggressive angiomyxoma and other myxoid neoplasms of skin and soft tissue. Am J Clin Pathol 107: 36–44

510. Iwasa Y, Fletcher C D M 2004 Cellular angiofibroma: clinicopathologic and immunohistochmical analysis of 51 cases. Am J Surg Pathol 28: 1426–1435

511. Barton J H, Davis C J J, Sesterhenn I A et al. 1999 Smooth muscle hyperplasia of the testicular adnexa clinically mimicking neoplasia: clinicopathologic study of sixteen cases. Am J Surg Pathol 23: 903–909

512. Kikugawa T, Tanji N, Kurihara K et al. 2003 Smooth muscle hyperplasia of the epididymis: a case report. Pathology 35: 454–455

513. Rowlands R D, Nicholson G W 1909 A case of primary squamous-celled epithelioma of the epididymis. Lancet 1: 304–306

514. Shah V I, Ro J Y, Amin M B et al. 1998 Histologic variations in the epididymis: findings in 167 orchiectomy specimens. Am J Surg Pathol 22: 990–996

515. Grove A, Jensen M L, Donna A 1989 Mesotheliomas of the tunica vaginalis testis and hernial sacs. Virchows Arch [A] 415: 283–292

516. Antman K, Cohen S, Dimitrov N V 1984 Malignant mesothelioma of the tunica vaginalis testis. J Clin Oncol 2: 447–451

517. Carp N Z, Peterson R O, Kusiak J F 1990 Malignant mesothelioma of the tunica vaginalis testis. J Urol 144: 1475–1478

518. McDonald R E, Sago A L, Novicki D E 1983 Paratesticular mesotheliomas. J Urol 130: 360–361

519. Nistal M, Revestido R, Paniagua R 1992 Bilateral mucinous cystadenocarcinoma of the testis and epididymis. Arch Pathol Lab Med 116: 1160–1163

520. Chen K T, Arhelger R B, Flam M S 1982 Malignant mesothelioma of tunica vaginalis testis. Urology 20: 316–319

521. Eimoto T, Inoue I 1977 Malignant fibrous mesothelioma of the tunica vaginalis. A histologic and ultrastructural study. Cancer 39: 2059–2066

522. Fitzmaurice H, Hotiana M Z, Crucioli V 1987 Malignant mesothelioma of the tunica vaginalis testis. Br J Urol 60: 184

523. Abe K, Kato N, Miki K et al. 2002 Malignant mesothelioma of testicular tunica vaginalis. Int J Urol 9: 602–603

524. Khan M A, Puri P, Devaney D 1997 Mesothelioma of tunica vaginalis testis in a child. J Urol 158: 198–199

525. Fligiel Z, Kaneko M 1976 Malignant mesothelioma of the tunica vaginalis propria testis in a patient with asbestos exposure. A case report. Cancer 37: 1478–1484

526. Kamiya M, Eimoto T 1990 Malignant mesothelioma of the tunica vaginalis. Pathol Res Pract 186: 680–684

527. Linn R, Moskovitz B, Bolkier M 1988 Paratesticular papillary mesothelioma. Urol Int 43: 60–61

528. Jones M A, Young R H, Scully R E 1995 Malignant mesothelioma of the tunica vaginalis. A clinicopathologic analysis of 11 cases with review of the literature. Am J Surg Pathol 19: 815–825

529. Sawada K, Inoue K, Ishihara T et al. 2004 Multicystic malignant mesothelioma of the tunica vaginalis with an unusually indolent clinical course. Hinyokika Kiyo 50: 511–513

530. Galateau-Salle F, Vignaud J M, Burke L et al. 2004 Well-differentiated papillary mesothelioma of the pleura: a series of 24 cases. Am J Surg Pathol 28: 534–540

531. Churg A 2003 Paratesticular mesothelial proliferations. Semin Diagn Pathol 20: 272–278

531a. Winstanley A M, Landon G, Berney D et al. 2006 The immunohistochemical profile of malignant mesotheliomas of the tunica vaginalis: a study of 20 cases. Am J Surg Pathol 30: 1–6

532. Arlen M, Grabstald H, Whitmore W F J 1969 Malignant tumors of the spermatic cord. Cancer 23: 525–532

533. Loughlin K R, Retik A B, Weinstein H J 1989 Genitourinary rhabdomyosarcoma in children. Cancer 63: 1600–1606

534. Cecchetto G, Grotto G, De Bernardi P 1988 Paratesticular rhabdomyosarcoma in childhood: experience of the Italian Cooperative Study. Tumori 74: 645–647

535. Fortune A, Bolton B R 1981 Rhabdomyosarcoma of the paratesticular tissues. J Urol 126: 563–564

536. Arean V M, Kreager J A 1965 Paratesticular rhabdomyosarcoma. Am J Clin Pathol 43: 418–427
537. Kattan J, Culine S, Terrier-Lacombe M J et al. 1993 Paratesticular rhabdomyosarcoma in adult patients: 16-year experience at Institut Gustave-Roussy. Ann Oncol 4: 871–875
538. Kumar P V, Khezri A A 1987 Pure testicular rhabdomyosarcoma. Br J Urol 59: 282
539. Leuschner I, Newton W A, Schmidt D 1993 Spindle cell variant of embryonal rhabdomyosarcoma in the paratesticular region: a report of the Intergroup Rhabdomyosarcoma Study. Am J Surg Pathol 17: 221–230
540. Cavazzana A O, Schmidt D, Ninfo V 1992 Spindle cell rhabdomyosarcoma. A prognostically favorable variant of rhabdomyosarcoma. Am J Surg Pathol 16: 229–235
541. Ferrari A, Bisogno G, Casanova M et al. 2002 Paratesticular rhabdomyosarcoma: report from the Italian and German Cooperative Group. J Clin Oncol 20: 449–455
542. Ferrari A, Casanova M, Massimino M et al. 1998 The management of paratesticular rhabdomyosarcoma: a single institutional experience with 44 consecutive children. J Urol 159: 1031–1034
543. Ferrari A, Bisogno G, Casanova M et al. 2004 Is alveolar histotype a prognostic factor in paratesticular rhabdomyosarcoma? The experience of Italian and German Soft Tissue Sarcoma Cooperative Group. Pediatr Blood Cancer 42: 134–138
544. Fleischmann J, Perinetti E P, Catalona W J 1981 Embryonal rhabdomyosarcoma of the genitourinary organs. J Urol 126: 389–392
545. Olive D, Flamat F, Zucker J M 1984 Paraaortic lymphadenectomy is not necessary in the treatment of localized paratesticular rhabdomyosarcoma. Cancer 54: 1283–1287
546. Kinjo M, Hokamura K, Tanaka K 1986 Leiomyosarcoma of the spermatic cord. A case report and review of the literature. Acta Pathol Jpn 36: 929–934
547. Soosay G N, Parkinson M C, Paradinas J et al. 1996 Paratesticular sarcomas revisited: a review of cases in the British Testicular Tumour Registry. Br J Urol 77: 143–146
548. Yashia P, Ausleaender L 1989 Primary leiomyosarcoma of the testis. J Urol 141: 955–956
549. Fisher C, Goldblum J R, Epstein J I et al. 2001 Leiomyosarcoma of the paratesticular region: a clinicopathologic study. Am J Surg Pathol 25: 1143–1149
550. Ptochos A, Iosifidis N, Papazafiriou G et al. 2003 Primary paratesticular epithelioid leiomyosarcoma. Urol Int 70: 321–323
551. Berkmen F, Celebioglu A S 1997 Adult genitourinary sarcomas: a report of seventeen cases and review of the literature. J Exp Clin Cancer Res 16: 45–48
552. Montgomery E, Fisher C 2003 Paratesticular liposarcoma: a clinicopathologic study. Am J Surg Pathol 27: 40–47
553. Ozkara H, Ozkan B, Alici B et al. 2004 Recurrent paratesticular myxoid liposarcoma in a young man. J Urol 171: 343
554. Kalyvas K D, Kotakidou R, Trantos A et al. 2004 Paratesticular well-differentiated, adipocytic type liposarcoma presenting as inguinal hernia. Urol Int 72: 264–268
555. Schwartz S L, Swierzewski S Jr, Sondak V K et al. 1995 Liposarcoma of the spermatic cord: report of 6 cases and review of the literature. J Urol 153: 154–157
556. Vallat-Decouvelaere W, Dry S M, Fletcher C D M 1998 Atypical and malignant solitary fibrous tumors in extrathoracic locations. Am J Surg Pathol 22: 1501–1511
557. Salamanca J, Rodriguez-Peralto J L, Azorin D et al. 2004 Paratesticular congenital malignant rhabdoid tumor diagnosed by fine-needle aspiration cytology. A case report. Diagn Cytopathol 30: 46–50
558. Kawanishi Y, Tamura M, Akiyama K 1989 Rhabdoid tumors of the spermatic cord. Br J Urol 63: 439–440

Penis and scrotum

Jae Y. Ro   Mahul B. Amin   Kyu-Rae Kim   Alberto G. Ayala

Miscellaneous benign lesions

Condyloma

The most common tumorous lesion of the penis is condyloma, which is caused by human papillomavirus (HPV). Condylomas are usually seen in young adults, among whom HPV infections have reached epidemic proportions during the last two decades.[1,2] The incidence of condylomas is reported to be around 5% among adults aged 20–40 years.[3,4] The great majority of these lesions are sexually transmitted. Men whose partners have HPV-related cervical lesions have a higher than average incidence of penile condyloma.[5] When genital condyloma is seen in children, sexual abuse should be suspected.[6] After the initial infection, autoinfections are common. The incubation period for penile condyloma varies from several weeks to months, or even years.[7]

These lesions are most often located on the corona of the glans, fossa navicularis, or penile meatus, but involvement of the scrotal skin or perineum is also seen (Fig. 14C.1).[7] Grossly, the lesions appear as either flat or papillary cauliflower-like lesions. Microscopically, they are essentially squamous papillomas characterized by a proliferation of squamous epithelium showing orderly maturation. Hyperkeratosis, parakeratosis, and koilocytosis are common associated findings (Fig. 14C.2).[8] Cytologic atypia in the common penile condyloma is minimal and mitoses are confined to the basal layers. In the past it was believed that treatment of these lesions with podophyllin or laser could cause bizarre morphologic changes that raise the question of malignancy.[9] However, current opinion of different types of HPV species, especially the carcinogenic types, indicates that the atypical changes are most likely due to the type of virus rather than to treatment. HPV can be demonstrated by in-situ hybridization or by immunohistochemical methods.[10–13] HPV types 6 and 11 are the most commonly involved in non-dysplastic genital warts, whereas HPV types 16 and 18 are frequently associated with dysplastic condylomas.[10–12] Although spontaneous regression of these lesions can

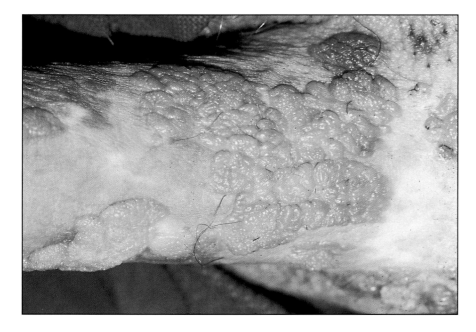

Fig. 14C.1 • Condyloma. Multiple tan-white papillary lesions on the penile shaft.

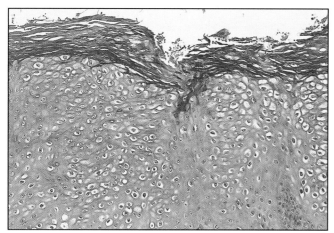

Fig. 14C.2 • Condyloma. High magnification shows koilocytosis and hyperkeratosis. Note the lack of significant cytologic atypia and mitotic activity.

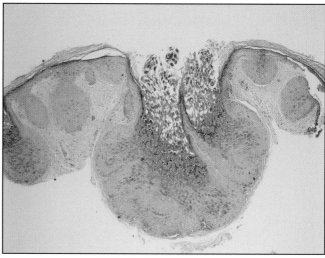

Fig. 14C.3 • Molluscum contagiosum with numerous spherical molluscum bodies (inset).

occur, they persist in approximately 50% of affected patients. The lesions are usually treated with topical podophyllin or laser and, in the great majority of cases, they respond to treatment.[13]

Molluscum contagiosum

Molluscum contagiosum is a fairly common pseudotumoral condition that is caused by the molluscum contagiosum virus, a large brick-shaped DNA poxvirus. Lymphangioma circumscriptum of the penis, which is rare at this site, with only five cases being reported, may clinically mimic molluscum contagiosum.[14]

Molluscum contagiosum usually occurs in children, adolescents, young adults, and in immunocompromised patients (including acquired immunodeficiency syndrome (AIDS) patients). In immunocompromised patients, there may be hundreds of lesions, which fail to involute.

Histologically, the characteristic low-power picture is of a cup-shaped invagination of acanthotic epidermis into the dermis (Fig. 14C.3).[15] The basal layer is uninvolved, but the cells of the stratum malpighii acquire cytoplasmic inclusions that progressively enlarge as they reach the surface. The inclusions, known as molluscum bodies (Henderson–Patterson bodies), contain viral particles. The inclusions are initially eosinophilic but gradually acquire basophilia and granularity as they enlarge and displace the nucleus. The stratum corneum ultimately ruptures, releasing the molluscum bodies through a central crater. The underlying dermis usually lacks significant inflammation, unless the molluscum bodies and epidermal contents rupture into it.

Most lesions regress spontaneously within 6–12 months, but treatment is necessary to prevent autoinoculation and transmission to others. Treatment consists of curettage, with application of podophyllin or silver nitrate, or laser vaporization.

Fibroepithelial polyps

Fibroepithelial polyp is very rare on the penis and usually presents as a polypoid or cauliflower-like mass or masses involving glans penis or prepuce.[16,17] It ranges in size from less than 1 cm to 7.5 cm in greatest dimension, is strongly associated with long-term condom catheter use and, on rare occasions, may develop in association with phimosis. The age of the patients ranges from 4 to 58 years (median age, 40 years) at the time of initial surgical resection and the preoperative duration of the lesions varies from 6 months to 10 years. The majority of lesions affect the ventral surface of the glans, near the urethral meatus.

Histologically, the lesions have a polypoid configuration and a keratinizing squamous epithelial surface. The underlying stroma is notably edematous, with telangiectasia of pre-existing vessels, and in many instances, there is focal mild small vessel proliferation. The stroma exhibits mildly to moderately increased cellularity with mononuclear and multinucleate mesenchymal cells. A mild inflammatory infiltrate is often present. Immunohistochemically, the stromal cells demonstrate limited immunoreactivity for muscle-specific actin, α-smooth muscle actin, and desmin and show no reactivity for S-100 protein or CD34. Surgical intervention should be local excision in all instances. Although these lesions may recur, the recurrences can also be managed by local excision.[16]

Hirsutoid papillomas

Hirsutoid papillomas, also called pearly penile papules, are common penile lesions without clinical significance that are present in approximately 20–30% of normal males.[18] These papillomas most likely represent embryologic remnants of a copulative organ that is well developed in other mammals. The characteristic lesions are yellow-white papules (1–3 mm in diameter) usually located on the corona or, rarely, on the frenulum of the penis.[19] The individual lesions are dome-like, resembling hair follicles, and usually arranged in a row.

Histologically, they show epithelial thickening associated with a central fibrovascular core (angiofibroma).[20] As they are associated with no infectious agents and have no potential for malignant transformation, they require no treatment.

Penile cysts

Among penile cysts, epidermal inclusion cyst is common and is usually found on the penile shaft; the size of the cyst usually varies from 1 mm to 1 cm in diameter, although, infrequently, large cysts are reported.[21,22] Mucoid cysts of the penis arise from ectopic urethral mucosa.[23] These cysts contain mucoid material and are lined by stratified columnar epithelium associated with mucous cells. Usually located on the prepuce or glans, these cysts tend to be unilocular, ranging in size from 2 mm to 2 cm across.

Median raphe cysts represent developmental defects in the embryogenesis of the genital tract and are most likely caused by incomplete closure of the genital fold. Histologically, these cysts are lined by pseudostratified columnar epithelium. They can be uni- or multilocular.[21,24,25]

Peyronie's disease

Peyronie's disease (also called *plastic induration of the penis*, *fibrous sclerosis of the penis*, and *fibrous cavernositis*) presents with painful erection accompanied by distortion, bending, or constriction of the erect penis. Although this lesion has been recognized since 1743, its etiology is still unknown.[26] Some authors suggest that Peyronie's disease may be related to fibromatosis, based upon its association, in approximately 10% of patients, with other types of fibromatoses such as Dupuytren's contracture or palmar or plantar fibromatoses.[26] Others postulate that this disease may be caused by an inflammatory/fibrosing reaction secondary to urethritis. Other contributing factors in the development of Peyronie's disease include repeated mechanical trauma, hypertension, diabetes, and immune reactions.[27–30] Although earlier studies suggested a possible relationship between specific human leukocyte antigen (HLA) types and development of Peyronie's disease, later studies did not show such a correlation.[30] Bivens et al., reporting 6 patients who had Peyronie's disease associated with carcinoid syndrome, suggested a possible role for elevated serotonin levels in the development of the disease.[31] In one study, Guerneri et al.[32] found structural chromosome aberrations, most frequently loss of chromosome Y, in 9 of 14 cases of Peyronie's disease.

The disease, which affects middle-aged or older men and is rare among those under 40 years old, is generally characterized by the development of circumscribed fibrous tissue between the corpora cavernosa and the tunica albuginea.[26,33] The lesion is often palpated as a firm plaque or nodule on the dorsal surface of the erect penile shaft. In rare cases, multiple plaques are formed or the disease process may be diffuse. The inelasticity of the fibrous tissue leads the plaques to cause penile curvature and pain during erection.[34] Histologically, fibrosis is the main finding.[26] Depending on the stage of development of the lesion, slight variations can be seen.[35] An inflammatory cell component is usually present in the early-stage lesions. Hyalinization with areas of bone and cartilage formation is usually seen in advanced lesions.[26,36] The clinical course of Peyronie's disease is variable.[37] The lesion may resolve spontaneously in a third of patients. Radiotherapy, steroid injections, or surgical resection can alleviate the symptoms.

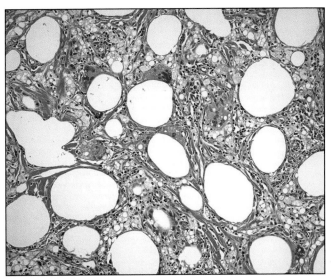

Fig. 14C.4 • Lipogranuloma with various-sized empty spaces and occasional giant cells.

Lipogranulomas (paraffinomas)

Lipogranulomas almost always result from the injection of foreign substances such as paraffin, wax, silicone, or oil to enlarge the penis.[38–42] Rare idiopathic cases have been reported, however.[43] Clinically, the lesions present as localized areas of induration with no surface changes. If the patient denies that foreign material has been injected, the diagnosis may be difficult to establish and may require biopsy. Microscopic examination reveals a typical foreign-body-type granulomatous inflammatory reaction with lipid vacuoles that are variable in size and embedded in dense fibrous tissue (Fig. 14C.4). The presence of lipids can be demonstrated by oil red O stain. Adenomatoid tumor, liposarcoma, metastatic carcinoma, and lymphangioma enter the differential diagnosis. In the Far East, glass spheres may be implanted into the penis to increase sexual stimulation of the partner. These foreign objects also cause a granulomatous reaction and resultant mass (Tancho's nodule).[44]

Balanitis xerotica obliterans (penile lichen sclerosus)

Balanitis xerotica obliterans is a chronic and atrophic mucocutaneous disorder of unknown etiology, affecting epidermis and dermal connective tissue, that most commonly involves the genital and perianal skin of both males and females. Extragenital lesions may accompany genital lesions, although they may also occur in isolation. Lichen sclerosus is a term used as a synonym for balanitis xerotica obliterans of the glans penis and prepuce. This lesion has been found to be associated with penile carcinomas and it has been postulated to be a preneoplastic condition for at least some types of penile cancers, particularly in non-HPV variants of squamous cell carcinoma (SCC).[45–50]

Balanitis xerotica obliterans is commonly encountered in preputial resectates for phimosis in older men. In contrast, the prepubertal incidence in a series of 117 cases was only 4%.[51]

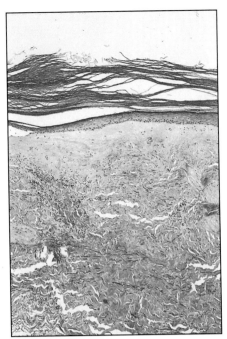

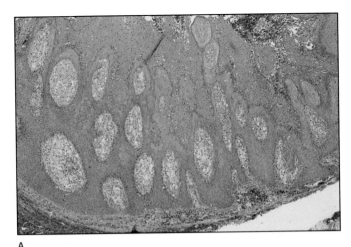

A

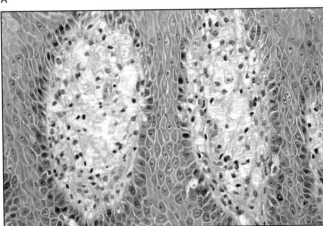

B

Fig. 14C.5 • Balanitis xerotica obliterans shows thin epidermis with blunting and loss of rete ridges and hyperkeratosis. The subepithelial layer is collagenized. Scattered lymphocytes are present.

The idiopathic form of balanitis xerotica obliterans is not associated with phimosis and presents with the classic clinical and pathologic features. The cause of this classic form is unknown, but an autoimmune mechanism has been suggested.[51] Patients with lichen sclerosus may have increased organ-specific antibodies (thyroid microsomal and parietal cell antibodies in women and smooth muscle and parietal cell antibodies in men). Association with autoimmune diseases, including vitiligo and alopecia areata, further supports the premise that autoimmune pathogenetic mechanisms may play an important role in these lesions.

Clinically, white papules or plaques involving foreskin and glans penis characterize the lesion and it may result in phimosis, narrowing of the preputial orifice, meatal stenosis, or fissure formation. Histologically, the lesion shows similar features to those seen in lichen sclerosus of the vulva, including epidermal atrophy, interface dermatitis, and dermal edema and fibrosis (Fig. 14C.5).

Verruciform xanthoma

Verruciform xanthoma is a warty lesion characterized by acanthosis, hyperkeratosis, and parakeratosis with long rete ridges, associated with a neutrophilic infiltrate. A variable (often prominent) xanthomatous infiltrate occupies the dermis between the rete ridges (Fig. 14C.6). This lesion is usually solitary and encountered in the oral cavity, and only a few genital lesions have been described (in scrotal, penile, and vulvar areas). Despite the architectural resemblance of verruciform xanthoma to other verruciform mucocutaneous lesions of the penis related to HPV infection, this lesion is most likely not an HPV-associated penile lesion. The xanthoma cells have been reported to be weakly and focally positive for cytokeratin, KP1, Mac 387, and factor XIIIa, but negative for S-100

Fig. 14C.6 • (A) Verruciform xanthoma. This illustration shows a thickened squamous epithelium with papillae of dermal connective tissue. (B) On high-power view, within the papillary cores there are numerous xanthoma cells.

protein and HPV immunostainings. Mohsin et al.[52] postulated that the xanthoma (foam) cells, a histologic hallmark of the lesion, are possibly derived from dermal dendritic cells.

Pseudoepitheliomatous keratotic and micaceous balanitis

This is a rare lesion that appears as hyperkeratotic, micaceous growths on the glans penis.[53] It was first described by Lortat-Jacob & Civatte[54] as a rare, scaling, raised lesion of the glans penis characterized by acanthosis, hyperkeratosis, and pseudo-epitheliomatous hyperplasia. Pseudoepitheliomatous keratotic and micaceous balanitis often recurs and may be a precursor of verrucous carcinoma (VC).

Neoplastic lesions

Premalignant lesions

One of the major controversies concerning penile lesions is the terminology of the premalignant intraepithelial lesions.

Three terms – erythroplasia of Queyrat (EQ), Bowen's disease (BD), and bowenoid papulosis (BP) – have been used to describe lesions that are histologically similar but have different clinical presentations and biologic behaviors.[55–59] Some have recommended that these three diseases may be replaced by terms such as high-grade penile intraepithelial lesions.[56–58,60] Lesions with a lesser degree of cytologic atypia (squamous hyperplasia or dysplasia) may or may not manifest clinically, but are often seen at the periphery of squamous carcinomas, bearing testimony to their premalignant potential.[61]

EQ was first described by Queyrat in 1911 as a distinct entity involving the glans penis and prepuce.[62] EQ has been reported in patients over a wide age range but usually occurs in the fifth and sixth decades of life. In the 100 cases reported by Graham & Helwig, the median patient age was 51 years.[63] Circumcision confers a protective effect against the development of EQ, as it also does against invasive squamous carcinoma of penis (see detailed discussion on the etiology of invasive carcinoma, p. 867).

Clinically, EQ presents as a shiny, elevated, reddish, velvety, erythematous plaque located on the glans penis or the prepuce.[57,58,63,64] Sometimes lesions also involve the urethral meatus, frenulum, or neck of the penis. In more than half of patients, EQ presents as a solitary lesion; however, multiple lesions can also occur.[63] Histologically, EQ is characterized by a full-thickness dysplastic alteration of the squamous epithelium with loss of polarity, proliferation of large hyperchromatic cells, dyskeratosis, multinucleate cells, and numerous typical and atypical mitoses (Fig. 14C.7). The underlying stroma shows band-like chronic inflammatory cell infiltration and vascular proliferation. About 10% of patients with EQ develop invasive squamous carcinoma and 2% of patients with EQ-associated carcinoma develop distant metastases.[63]

The cause of EQ is largely unknown. HPV type 16 DNA has previously been detected only in very few distinctly characterized patients. Recently, however, Wieland et al.[65] reported that HPV DNA was detected in all eight EQ patients and in none of the controls with inflammatory penile lesions. Although HPV types 8, 16, 39 and 51 were detected in these patients, HPV type 8 was not detected in cervical or vulvar precancerous and cancerous lesions, nor in BD lesions that carried genital HPV types. These data suggest that in EQ, in contrast to other genital neoplasias, a coinfection with HPV type 8 and carcinogenic genital HPV types occurs. The presence or absence of HPV type 8 might help to distinguish between penile EQ and BDs.

A number of different diseases may produce penile lesions that are clinically similar to EQ. These include Zoon's balanitis, other inflammatory processes, and penile manifestations of benign dermatoses such as drug eruption, psoriasis, and lichen planus.[66]

Bowen's disease

The term BD is used to denote a lesion histologically similar to EQ (squamous carcinoma in situ) when it involves the shaft of the penis, or when the lesion is not red grossly, as EQ is.[57,58,67,68] BD most often occurs in the fourth and fifth decades of life, one decade earlier than EQ.[68] Typically, it presents as crusted, sharply demarcated scaly plaques. Rarely BD forms papillomatous lesions.[69] Histologically, BD shows features virtually identical to those of EQ (Fig. 14C.8). Although some authors have pointed out minor differences, these are mainly the result of differing anatomic locations.[55] BD shows hyperkeratosis, whereas EQ does not. Involvement of pilosebaceous units is common in BD, but involvement of pilosebaceous units is not a feature of EQ since it involves the mucocutaneous epithelium.[70]

The incidence of progression into invasive carcinoma is similar (approximately 5–10%) for both lesions. The main reason for separating these two lesions has been the differences in their natural histories. Thus it has been stated that a third of patients with BD develop cutaneous or extracutaneous malignancies,[63] whereas patients with EQ do not have the same propensity for the development of systemic malignancy.[63,71–73] However, newer studies of BD have raised questions regarding the development of internal malignancies.

Bowenoid papulosis

The term BP was first used by Wade et al.[74] in 1978 to describe a lesion involving the penile shaft or perineum in young males.

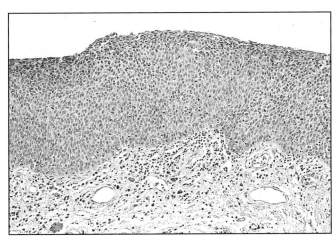

Fig. 14C.7 • Microscopic appearance of erythroplasia of Queyrat. The full thickness of the epithelium is composed of dysplastic cells with large hyperchromatic nuclei and scant cytoplasm. Frequent mitoses are present.

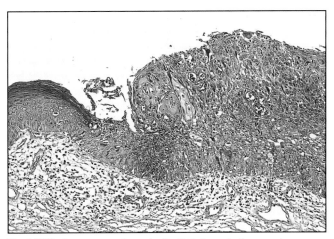

Fig. 14C.8 • Squamous carcinoma in situ. Both Bowen's disease and erythroplasia of Queyrat show full-thickness dysmaturation of the epithelium with marked cytologic atypia.

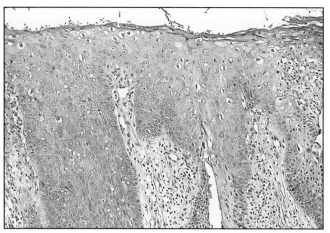

Fig. 14C.9 • Bowenoid papulosis. Histologically, bowenoid papulosis is essentially identical to carcinoma in situ (Bowen's disease and erythroplasia of Queyrat). Although there is full-thickness dysplastic change, there are architectural and cytologic changes resembling condyloma.

demonstrated in several cases of BP.[77] Viral, immunologic, and chemical irritation factors have all been speculated to be causative.[70] There is growing evidence that BP is related to HPV. In several cases, HPV DNA has been demonstrated in BP lesions.[78-80] However, hormonal and immunologic factors may also play important roles in its etiology.[70]

Follow-up data from the reported cases indicate that the behavior of BP differs significantly from that of BD or EQ. Spontaneous regression of the lesions has been reported in a number of cases. Neither progression to invasive carcinoma nor the development of systemic malignancies has been observed in any of the cases.[81] A recent study stated that there were significant differences in the morphometric evaluation between BD and BP. The nuclei were larger, more oval, with more irregular margins in BD than BP.[82] However, the minor histologic differences between BP and carcinoma in situ (BD/EQ) do not allow for a correct clinicopathologic diagnosis based on histology alone; rather, the diagnosis of BP should be based on clinical presentation and gross appearance as well as on histologic features (Table 14C.1).

The lesion histologically resembles squamous carcinoma in situ; however, it is multicentric and has an indolent clinical course.[59,70,75] In all reported cases, the lesions either respond to conservative treatment (local excision, topical or laser treatment) or regress spontaneously.[70,76]

BP usually occurs in young adults. In Patterson et al.'s series of 51 cases of BP in men,[70] the mean age was 29.5 years and the lesions were most commonly located on the penile shaft; they were usually multicentric and characterized by papules ranging in size from 2 to 10 mm. Sometimes the papules coalesced to form plaques that resembled condylomata acuminata.

Histologically, BP is characterized by varying degrees of hyperkeratosis, parakeratosis, irregular acanthosis, and papillomatosis (Fig. 14C.9).[70] Although scattered atypical keratinocytes and mitoses may be seen, even at the top layers of the epithelium, usually more maturation of keratinocytes is observed in BP than is apparent in BD or EQ. Patterson et al.[70] pointed out that the atypical keratinocytes in BP involve the upper parts of the sweat gland whereas pilosebaceous units are usually spared. This pattern is reversed in BD.

The etiology of BP is unknown, but viral, immunologic, and chemical causes have been suggested. HPV DNA has been

Benign tumors

Benign epithelial tumors are rare and squamous papillomas have been reported. Benign soft tissue neoplasms such as leiomyoma, hemangioma (including the epithelioid variant),[83] schwannoma, neurofibroma, lymphangioma, glomus tumor, fibrous histiocytoma, and granular cell tumor have been reported in the penis.[83,84] According to the experience of the US Armed Forces Institute of Pathology, benign soft tissue tumors were seen most often on the glans and malignant tumors in the shaft.[83,84]

Angiokeratoma is a distinctive benign vascular lesion, but is not considered to be a true neoplasm. This lesion characteristically involves the scrotum, but it may involve the penis. Morphologically, this lesion reveals superficial vascular ectasia with overlying warty epidermal changes (Fig. 14C.10). There are four clinical types: (1) angiokeratoma corporis diffusum in association with Fabry's disease, in which multiple angiokeratomas appear late in childhood; (2) angiokeratoma of Mibelli, in which bilateral angiokeratomas are found on the dorsum of fingers and toes; (3) angiokeratoma of Fordyce, in

Table 14C.1	Distinguishing features of three different dysplastic conditions		
Features	Erythroplasia of Queyrat	Bowen's disease	Bowenoid papulosis
Site	Glans, prepuce	Penile shaft	Penile shaft
Age	Fifth and sixth decades	Fourth and fifth decades	Third and fourth decades
Lesion	Erythematous plaque	Scaly plaque	Plaques
Hyperkeratosis	–	+	+
Maturation	–	–	+
Sweat gland involvement	–	–	+
Pilosebaceous involvement	–	+	–
Progress to carcinoma	5–10%	5–10%	–
Association with internal cancer	–	10%	–
Spontaneous regression	–	–	+

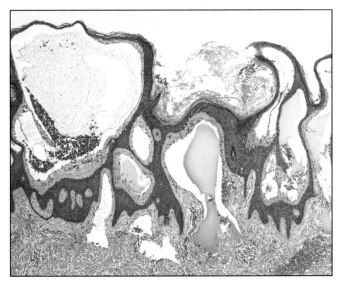

Fig. 14C.10 • Angiokeratoma characterized by large dilated vascular channels and warty epidermal changes.

which angiokeratoma characteristically occurs on the scrotum; and (4) solitary angiokeratoma.

Another recently described lesion is *myointimoma* (myointimal proliferation), involving the corpus spongiosum of the glans penis.[85] Patients ranged in age from 2 to 61 years old (mean age, 29 years) and presented with a mass that varied in size from 0.5 to 1.9 cm in greatest dimension. The lesions were present from 4 days to more than 6 months before surgical intervention. Microscopically there was a prominent, often occlusive, fibrointimal proliferation with plexiform architecture involving the vasculature of the corpus spongiosum. The proliferation consisted of stellate-shaped and spindled cells embedded in abundant fibromyxoid matrix (Fig. 14C.11). Occasional lesional cells had well-developed myoid characteristics with moderately abundant eosinophilic cytoplasm, blunt-ended nuclei, and juxtanuclear vacuoles, leading to considerable morphologic overlap with myofibroma. Foci with degenerative changes, including ghost cell morphology, were also present. The myointimal process was extensively immuno-

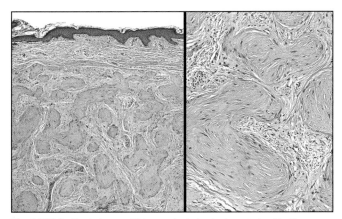

Fig. 14C.11 • Myointimoma. This vascular lesion is characterized by the presence of anastomosing cords of spindle cells seemingly arising from intima of vessels. On the high-power illustration (right side) the plexiform architecture of vessels exhibits the myointimal proliferation.

reactive for smooth muscle actin, muscle-specific actin (HHF-35), and calponin, but it was minimally reactive for desmin. The myointimal cells were non-reactive for CD34, S-100 protein, and keratin. Factor VIIIrAg, CD31, and CD34 highlighted intact endothelial cells lining suboccluded vessels, scattered capillaries that penetrated the proliferation, and the normal uninvolved vasculature. Follow-up data demonstrated that the lesions were benign without evidence of metastasis. Myofibroma, late-stage intravascular (nodular) fasciitis, vascular leiomyoma, and plexiform fibrohistiocytic tumor can be potential differential diagnoses.

Benign melanocytic lesions, such as melanocytic nevi, melanosis, and lentiginous melanosis, also occur on the penis. These lesions may pre-exist or coexist with penile melanoma.

Malignant neoplasms

In general, the incidence of malignant neoplasms of the penis is quite low (approximately 1 in 100 000), accounting for less than 0.5% of all male neoplasms in western countries and 3.0% of all genitourinary cancers.[86] The American Cancer Society has estimated that, in the year 2006, 1530 patients will have developed penile cancer, and 280 of these will die of the disease.[87] In certain countries such as Uganda, Brazil, Jamaica, Mexico, and Haiti, however, penile cancer is far more common, representing 10–12% of all malignancies in those countries.[86,88–90] Despite these statistics, the incidence of penile cancer has been declining in many countries, partly because of increased attention to personal hygiene.[91] The most frequently occurring type of malignant neoplasm is carcinoma, and squamous carcinoma is by far the most common type of penile carcinoma (Table 14C.2).[92]

Squamous carcinoma

A variety of factors, including lack of circumcision, poor hygiene, phimosis, and viruses, have been speculated to be associated with an increased risk of developing SCC of the penis.[86,88–90,93–96] SCC is extremely unusual among individuals who were circumcised in infancy. An extremely low incidence of SCC is observed in Jews, who practice circumcision at birth.[97] Later circumcision, performed during late childhood or adolescence, seems to confer some, but not full, protection.[94–96] Thus, a higher incidence of SCC among Muslims, who are circumcised later in childhood, has been reported.[97] In India, more than 95% of penile carcinomas occur among Hindus, who do not undergo circumcision; only 5% of the cases in India are seen in the Muslim population.[95] Although circumcision at birth provides excellent protection against penile cancer, most authors believe that equally low incidence rates can be achieved in uncircumcised males through good hygienic practices. The very low rate of penile carcinoma in northern European countries, where males are not routinely circumcised but where good hygiene is practiced, supports this view.[98]

Phimosis has been reported as a coexisting abnormality in almost half the patients with penile carcinoma.[99] Experimental evidence suggests that smegma (desquamated epithelial debris) may play an important role in penile carcinogenesis.[86]

Table 14C.2 World Health Organization histological classification of tumors of the penis[a]

Malignant epithelial tumors of the penis		Precursor lesions	
Squamous cell carcinoma	8070/3	Intraepithelial neoplasia grade III	8077/2
Basaloid carcinoma	8083/3	Bowen disease	8081/2
Warty (condylomatous) carcinoma	8051/3	Erythroplasia of Queyrat	8080/2
Verrucous carcinoma	8051/3	Paget disease	8542/3
Papillary carcinoma, not otherwise specified	8050/3		
Sarcomatous carcinoma	8074/3	**Melanocytic tumors**	
Mixed carcinomas	8060/3	Melanocytic nevi	8720/0
Adenosquamous carcinoma	8247/3	Melanoma	8720/3
Merkel cell carcinoma	8041/3		
Small cell carcinoma of neuroendocrine type	8410/3	**Mesenchymal tumors**	
Sebaceous carcinoma	8310/3	**Hematopoietic tumors**	
Clear cell carcinoma	8090/3		
Basal cell carcinoma		**Secondary tumors**	

[a]Morphology code of the International Classification of Diseases for Oncology (ICD-O) and the Systematized Nomenclature of Medicine (http://snomed.org). Behavior is coded /0 for benign tumors, /2 for in-situ carcinomas and grade III intraepithelial neoplasia, and /3 for malignant tumors.

Retention of smegma or its derivatives is thought to have an irritating effect on penile epithelium. In the uncircumcised and phimotic penis, this effect may be exacerbated.[86]

A viral etiology for penile carcinoma has also been suggested.[100–105] HPV types 16 and 18 have been demonstrated in approximately half the cases of penile carcinoma.[102–104] Some studies have suggested an increase in the incidence of cervical cancer among wives of men who had penile carcinoma, and thus have supported the hypothesis that a sexually transmitted agent plays a causative role.[106,107] However, other studies showed that wives of men with penile cancer did not incur a significant risk of genital cancer.[108] HPV infections may play a role in the development of penile cancer, but it is most likely that these lesions have a multifactorial etiology; other rare factors implicated include tobacco, radiation, psoralens and ultraviolet A (PUVA) therapy, and association with verruciform xanthomas.[109–111]

Penile carcinoma is generally a disease of older men.[112–117] Patient ages at diagnosis range from 20 to 90 years, but SCC is rare among men under age 40 years.[118] The patients usually present with an exophytic or ulcerated mass. Penile pain, discharge, difficulty in voiding, or lymphadenopathy can also be presenting symptoms.[86] The majority of the lesions develop on the glans or prepuce,[86] but lesions can also arise from the preputial sac or coronal sulcus. The penile shaft and urethral meatus are rare sites for carcinoma.[114–119]

The majority of penile carcinomas originate in the squamous epithelium of the mucosa covering the glans, followed in decreasing order of frequency by those involving the foreskin, coronal sulcus, and skin of the shaft.[120] The growth pattern may be superficial-spreading (flat tumor growing horizontally with minimal superficial invasion), vertical growth (vertical growth with deep penetration),[86] or verruciform growth (verrucous/papillary exophytic growth which microscopically correlates with VC, warty carcinoma, or papillary carcinoma, not otherwise specified (NOS) histology).[120,121] Mixed growth and multicentric growth (Fig. 14C.12) patterns may occur.

Fig. 14C.12 • Squamous cell carcinoma of penis. The tumor forms a large, broad-based, polypoid mass.

Tumors with a superficial spreading pattern have a favorable prognosis if the surgical margins of excision are negative, but tumors with vertical growth do more poorly, often being associated with lymph node metastases.[122–125]

Histologically, the majority of SCCs of the penis are similar to their counterparts in other organs, exhibiting a range from good to moderate to poor differentiation (Figs 14C.13 and 14C.14). Among the histologic variants (see below), VC has a better prognosis than warty or papillary carcinoma NOS. Basaloid carcinoma and sarcomatoid carcinoma have a poorer outcome.[121]

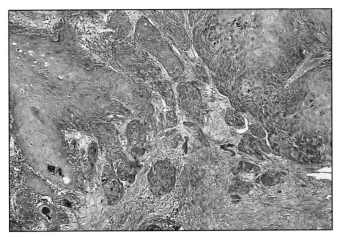

Fig. 14C.13 • Well-differentiated invasive squamous carcinoma. Although the papillary type of proliferation resembles verrucous carcinoma, the infiltrative invasion pattern negates this diagnosis.

Fig. 14C.15 • Verrucous carcinoma involving penis and penile urethra.

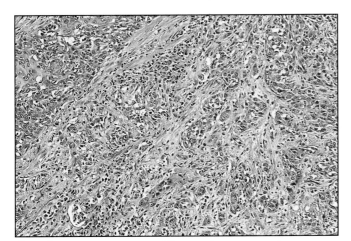

Fig. 14C.14 • Invasive moderately differentiated squamous carcinoma.

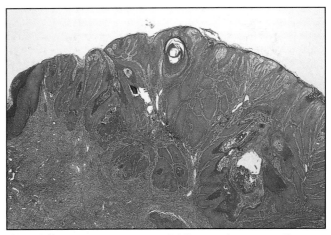

Fig. 14C.16 • Verrucous carcinoma. Well-differentiated squamous cells arranged in fern-like papillae. The tumor characteristically shows a broad-based infiltration pattern.

Variants of squamous cell carcinoma

Verrucous carcinoma

Since its first description in the oral cavity, VC has been recognized in a variety of organs, including the larynx, vulva, vagina, anus, and penis. VC of the penis accounts for 5–16% of penile malignancies.[126] It is most commonly seen in middle-aged patients.[126–131] Typically, it is a large, fungating, frequently ulcerated warty lesion that burrows through the normal tissues. Most of these lesions start on the coronal sulcus and spread to the glans and preputial skin (Fig. 14C.15).

Microscopically, VC is a well-differentiated squamous carcinoma with an exophytic and endophytic papillary growth pattern (Fig. 14C.16). Characteristically, the tumor shows a pattern of broad-based bulbous infiltration (Fig. 14C.17). Cytologic atypia is minimal, and mitoses are very rare, usually being confined to the deeper portion of the tumor. These tumors tend to grow locally and they do not metastasize. If VC is not treated adequately, multiple recurrences can occur. The main differential diagnoses include condyloma acuminatum, particularly large (giant) condyloma, warty (condylomatous) carcinoma, and the usual type of keratinizing squamous

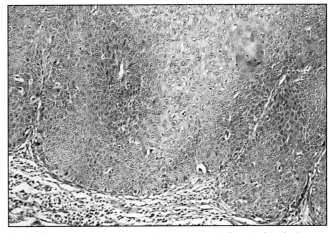

Fig. 14C.17 • This pushing-type infiltration pattern is the main histologic criterion to differentiate verrucous carcinoma from well-differentiated invasive squamous carcinoma. It is not unusual to encounter hybrid tumors showing a predominantly pushing border of invasion with foci of classic invasive carcinoma.

carcinoma. When a lesion is small, it is only of academic interest to differentiate condyloma from VC as the management of both lesions is conservative. When the lesion is large, giant condyloma of Buschke–Lowenstein enters the differential diagnosis. Many authorities consider these lesions to be the same entity,[126,127] but the two lesions are readily separable histologically, with HPV-induced changes being evident in giant condyloma and rare to absent in VC. Whether or not one decides to separate them, the management is essentially similar. However, warty and usual squamous carcinoma must be differentiated from VC because the behavior is different and the management often requires sentinel node biopsy or radical inguinal lymphadenectomy in the former. The lack of significant cytologic atypia, mitoses, and an infiltrative growth pattern are helpful in differentiating VC from the usual type of SCC. Warty carcinoma shows HPV-associated changes in addition to cytologic atypia and destructive invasion.[121] The demonstration of HPV DNA (types 6 and 11), as well as pre-existing condyloma acuminatum, in some cases of VC, has suggested a viral etiology for these lesions.[101,130]

Mixed carcinomas

Verrucous/squamous carcinoma (hybrid)

About 25% of cases of penile VC show microscopic foci of cellular anaplasia, higher mitotic activity, and ruptured basement membranes.[126,131] These tumors have been called *hybrid squamous–VC* and similar tumors have been described in the oral cavity. Hybrid squamous–VC and VC are similar with regard to patient age, location, and outcome after similar treatments, although the data on hybrid squamous–VC are limited.[126,131] DNA ploidy and cell cycle analysis done by Masih et al.[131]showed that both VC and hybrid squamous–

VC have diploid cell populations with similar proliferative indices.

Other mixed carcinomas include warty-basaloid carcinoma, adenocarcinoma and basaloid carcinoma (adenobasaloid carcinoma), and squamous carcinoma and neuroendocrine carcinoma.

Warty (condylomatous) carcinoma

The warty carcinoma is a morphologically distinct verruciform neoplasm, which has similar histologic features to the vulvar neoplasm of the same name. The tumor may involve multiple anatomic sites such as glans, coronal sulcus and foreskin, or a single site of the penis.[121]

Grossly, it is characterized by exophytic, cauliflower-like, white gray, firm masses. Histologically, the lesion is papillomatous with acanthosis, hyperkeratosis, and horny cysts, which may be visible at low-power magnification. The long papillae with central fibrovascular cores show cytologic features of HPV infection as well as architectural features of invasion. Obvious nuclear atypia with koilocytosis and binucleation is evident even in clearly invasive carcinomatous foci (Fig. 14C.18).[121] The advancing borders are infiltrative, pushing, or mixed.[132] Warty (condylomatous) carcinoma is frequently associated with HPV DNA in the range of 25–45% of cases, far more than found in conventional squamous carcinoma.[132]

The differential diagnosis includes other verruciform neoplasms, such as VC, giant condyloma, and papillary squamous carcinoma, NOS.

Warty carcinoma has a preferential association with HPV compared to other types of penile cancer such as typical squamous, papillary, verrucous, or anaplastic; it has been suggested to be the malignant counterpart of giant condyloma.[132] The tumor has a definite risk for regional lymph node metastasis, although less than that for typical squamous carcinoma.[132] Therefore, this tumor should be distinguished from VC or other types of verruciform carcinoma.[132,133]

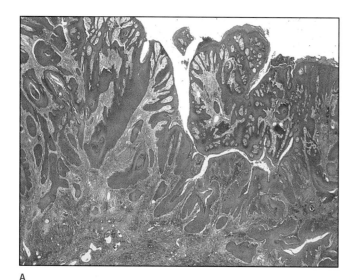

A

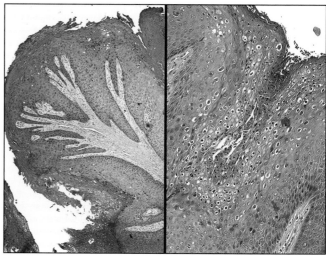

B

Fig. 14C.18 • (A) Warty carcinoma. The low-power view shows a papillary growth pattern. **(B)** Warty carcinoma with papillary growth on the left and atypical koilocytotic changes of the epithelial cells on the right side.

Papillary carcinoma, NOS

Papillary carcinoma NOS is an exophytic squamous carcinoma grossly similar to warty carcinoma. The tumor is composed of atypical cells without HPV-related features and shows infiltrative borders. This variant occurs most commonly in the fifth and sixth decades. Microscopically, this variant is a well-differentiated, hyperkeratotic lesion with irregular, complex papillae, with or without fibrovascular cores. Unlike VC, the interface with the underlying stroma is infiltrative and irregular. Although this type of tumor can invade corpus spongiosum or cavernosum, regional lymph node metastases are exceptionally rare and therefore the prognosis is excellent.

Basaloid carcinoma

This tumor presents primarily with a vertical growth phase and is deeply penetrating. Histologically, the tumor is poorly differentiated, with nests of basaloid cells (Fig. 14C.19) showing comedo necrosis, numerous mitoses, and only rare keratinization.[134] The absence of retraction artifact or peripheral palisading, as well as the high nuclear grade, help to distinguish this tumor from the rare basal cell carcinoma (BCC) involving the penis.

Pseudohyperplastic non-verruciform squamous cell carcinoma

Cubilla et al.[135] presented 10 cases of well-differentiated squamous carcinoma of the penis with pseudohyperplastic features which they termed pseudohyperplastic non-verruciform SCC. At presentation, the median age was 69 years. Seven of the tumors were multicentric, and the majority preferentially involved the inner mucosal surface of the foreskin. Grossly the tumors were typically flat or slightly elevated,

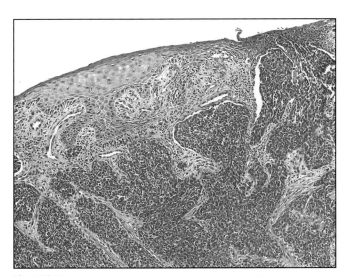

Fig. 14C.19 • Basaloid carcinoma. The tumor shows nests of hyperchromatic basaloid cells. (Courtesy of Dr G. Ayala, Baylor College of Medicine, Houston, TX)

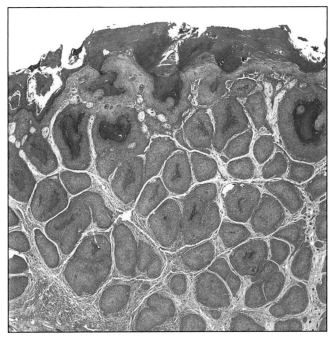

Fig. 14C.20 • Pseudohyperplastic non-verruciform carcinoma. The tumor shows downward proliferation of well-differentiated carcinoma with nests of variable sizes and minimal atypia, superficially mimicking pseudoepitheliomatous hyperplasia.

white, and granular, and measured approximately 2 cm. Histologically, the salient features included keratinizing nests of squamous cells with minimal atypia surrounded by a reactive fibrous stroma (Fig. 14C.20). In biopsies or individual areas of resected specimens, the differential diagnosis with pseudo-epitheliomatous hyperplasia was difficult, but when samples of adequate size were available, obvious evidence of infiltration was present. The adjacent squamous epithelium typically showed changes that are known to be associated with squamous carcinoma, ranging from squamous hyperplasia to low-grade, and in a few cases high-grade, squamous intraepithelial lesions. Well-developed lichen sclerosus was seen in all cases. Patients were treated by circumcision or partial penectomy. With the exception of one patient who developed recurrence in the glans 2 years after initial circumcision, follow-up after the initial surgical procedure was uneventful. These cases indicate that a subset of non-verruciform, often multicentric tumors with a high degree of differentiation and pseudohyperplastic features occur and preferentially involve the foreskin.[135]

Sarcomatoid carcinoma (spindle cell squamous carcinoma)

Although spindle cell squamous carcinomas are common in the oral cavity, upper respiratory tract, and esophagus, only a few cases have been reported to occur on the penis.[136–139] In these reported cases, the lesions showed a tendency to form polypoid masses. Histologically, the tumors are composed predominantly of spindle cells with focal areas of squamous differentiation (Fig. 14C.21). Marked nuclear pleomorphism and increased mitoses are common in the spindle component. An acantholytic, pseudovascular pattern may also be seen.

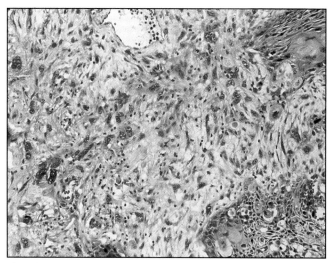

Fig. 14C.21 • Sarcomatoid carcinoma. This is a biphasic tumor with squamous carcinoma and spindle sarcomatoid components.

Some authors have reported that spindle cell squamous carcinomas grow locally and have a favorable prognosis; however, Velazquez et al.[138] and Lont et al.[140] reported cases that had a very aggressive clinical course. Since the number of reported cases is limited, the prognostic significance of this variant remains unclear. The association with radiation therapy is also unclear, although sarcomatoid transformation in VCs treated with radiation has been reported.[136]

Adenosquamous carcinoma and other rare carcinomas

Tumors showing both glandular and squamous differentiation (adenosquamous carcinoma) have been reported on the glans and coronal sulcus.[141] The tumors are usually deeply invasive.[142,143] Rare cases of adenocarcinomas and mucoepidermoid carcinoma of the penis have also been reported.[143,144] Other rarely reported tumors include small cell carcinoma,[145] Merkel cell carcinoma,[146] clear cell carcinoma,[147] and sebaceous carcinoma.[148]

Prognosis

Prognostic factors that help to predict regional or systemic metastasis are size, site of primary tumor, morphologic pattern of presentation, histologic grade, tumor stage (Table 14C.3), depth of invasion, and histologic types.[120,125,149–154] Slaton et al.[155] recently reported that pathologic stage of the penile tumor, vascular invasion, and greater than 50% of the tumor being poorly differentiated were independent prognostic factors for inguinal lymph node metastasis. Therefore, prophylactic lymphadenectomy in compliant patients with pT1 lesions without vascular invasion and 50% or less poorly differentiated tumor does not appear warranted.

The chief problem with tumors that have a superficial spreading growth pattern lies in obtaining negative surgical margins; if achieved, these portend a favorable prognosis.

Table 14C.3	TNM classification of carcinomas of the penis[a]

Primary Tumor (T)

TX	Primary tumor cannot be assessed
T0	No evidence of primary tumor
Tis	Carcinoma *in situ*
Ta	Non-invasive verrucous carcinoma
T1	Tumor invades subepithelial connective tissue
T2	Tumor invades corpis spongiosum or cavernosum
T3	Tumor invades urethra or prostate
T4	Tumor invades other adjacent structures

Regional Lymph Nodes (N)

NX	Regional lymph nodes cannot be assessed
N0	No regional lymph node metastasis
N1	Metastasis in a single superficial, inguinal lymph node
N2	Metastasis in multiple or bilateral superficial inguinal lymph nodes
N3	Metastasis in deep inguinal or pelvic lymph node(s) unilateral or bilateral

Distant Metastasis (M)

MX	Distant metastasis cannot be assessed
M0	No distant metastasis
M1	Distant metastasis

Additional Descriptor

The **m suffix** indicates the presence of multiple primary tumors and is recorded in parentheses – e.g., pTa(m)N0M0.

Stage grouping

Stage	T	N	M
Stage 0	Tis	N0	M0
	Ta	N0	M0
Stage I	T1	N0	M0
Stage II	T1	N1	M0
	T2	N0	M0
	T2	N1	M0
Stage III	T1	N2	M0
	T2	N2	M0
	T3	N0	M0
	T3	N1	M0
	T3	N2	M0
Stage IV	T4	Any N	M0
	Any T	N3	M0
	Any T	Any N	M1

Used with permission of the American Joint Committee on Cancer (AJCC), Chicago, Illinois. The original source for this material is the AJCC Cancer Staging Manual, Sixth Edition (2002) published by Springer-Verlag New York, www.springeronline.com

The ulcerating type of tumor (vertical growth) shows a higher incidence of lymph node metastases. Penile cancer initially spreads locally, destroying the prepuce and penile shaft. Urethral involvement usually occurs secondary to fistula formation. Buck's fascia, which has rich elastic fibers, forms an initial barrier against tumor invasion. However, with progressive tumor growth, penetration of Buck's fascia and the corpus cavernosum occurs. Distant metastasis most commonly occurs via lymphatic spread; the inguinal lymph nodes are generally

Table 14C.4	Low- and high-risk penile cancers	
Low-risk group	**High-risk group**
Tis	T2 and T3 tumors with grade 3 tumors
Verrucous carcinoma	Tumors with vascular invasion
T1 with grade 1 or 2 tumors	Basaloid carcinoma
Tumor without vascular invasion	Sarcomatoid carcinoma

the first to be involved. The lymphatics of the penis form richly anastomosing channels that cross the midline along the shaft and at the penile base; therefore, cross-inguinal lymph node metastasis may occur.[156] The presence and number of lymph nodes involved by metastatic tumor correlate with prognosis.[122–125] However, infection of the primary tumor can cause inguinal lymph node enlargement without tumor metastases; for this reason, sentinel node biopsy is commonly performed to stage the tumor correctly. Hematogenous dissemination is rare. Fewer than 2% of patients with penile carcinoma show distant visceral metastases at the time of diagnosis; however, hepatic, pulmonary, and osseous metastases can occur in untreated cases.

VC has a better prognosis than warty and papillary carcinoma NOS. Basaloid carcinoma and sarcomatoid carcinoma have a poor outcome. The high- and low-risk groups are listed in Table 14C.4.

Basal cell carcinoma

BCC is the most common malignant skin tumor seen in other regions of the body (see Ch. 23), but it is very uncommon in penile or scrotal skin.[115,116] The lesion may involve the glans, prepuce, or shaft. Typically, it forms a small, irregular, ulcerated mass. Histologically, it shows nests of small, uniform basaloid cells having peripheral palisading (Fig. 14C.22). In general, the clinical course of BCC tends to be indolent.[157,158]

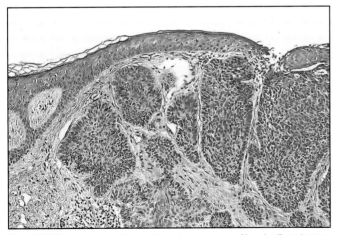

Fig. 14C.22 • Basal cell carcinoma. Typical appearance of basal cell carcinoma with well-demarcated nests of uniform basaloid cells.

Malignant melanoma

Primary melanomas of the penis are rare, with fewer than 150 cases having been reported in the literature.[159–167] Most of the reported cases occurred in patients in their fifth and sixth decades.[168] In the majority of cases, the melanomas were located on the glans. Occasional lesions were reported to occur on the prepuce and shaft. The identified risk factors for the development of penile melanoma are melanosis and pre-existing nevus. The histologic findings in penile melanomas are similar to those of malignant melanomas arising in any other mucosal or skin site (see Ch. 23).[68] Different histologic types of malignant melanoma, including nodular, superficial spreading, and lentiginous types, have been reported.[163–165,168,169]

Malignant melanoma of soft parts (clear cell sarcoma) is an uncommon neoplasm occurring most frequently in the tendons and aponeuroses of the extremities. This type of lesion has also been reported to occur in the penis.[170]

The prognosis of penile malignant melanomas is very poor.[68] Half of the patients show lymph node metastases at the time of diagnosis.[68] Possible reasons for poor survival include unusual manifestations of the disease, or non-specific symptoms resulting in late discovery and delay in treatment. Furthermore, anatomical constraints precluding surgery with generous margins, rich vascularity, and multiple lymphatic drainage pathways facilitate early dissemination.[166]

Sarcoma

Sarcomas of the penis are the second most common type of penile cancer, but are much rarer than carcinomas. Vascular tumors, particularly epithelioid hemangioendothelioma, angiosarcoma, and Kaposi's sarcoma, are the most common types of penile sarcoma.[171,172] Sarcomas of myogenic (leiomyosarcoma and rhabdomyosarcoma), neurogenic, chondroid, osteoid, and fibrous types, as well as so-called malignant fibrous histiocytoma and epithelioid sarcoma, can also occur.[84,173–180] The histologic features of these lesions are similar to those arising at any other location (see Ch. 24).

Metastatic tumors

The penis has a rich and complex vascular circulation interconnected to the pelvic organs, but metastases to the penis are rare. In 1985, Powell et al.[181] reviewed the literature and found only 219 cases. In a 1989 review, Perez-Mesa & Oxenhandler reported only 6 additional cases.[182] In all reported series, the most common primary site of origin was the prostate, followed by the rectosigmoid colon, bladder, and kidney.[181–186] Less common primary sites include the testis, ureter, and non-pelvic organs such as the lung, pancreas, nasopharynx, and bone.[181–185,187–189] A recent report from Tu et al.[190] stated that, among prostate carcinomas, the ductal-endometrioid variant was more prone to develop penile metastasis.

The most common location of the metastatic tumors is the corpus cavernosum.[183] Clinically, the disease usually presents as multiple, palpable, painless nodules. These nodules may involve the skin and ulcerate, mimicking a syphilitic chancre.

In half the patients, diffuse involvement of the corpus cavernosum occurs, causing priapism.[183] Hematuria and dysuria can occur. In the great majority of cases, penile metastases develop in the later stages of a known primary tumor and do not pose any diagnostic difficulty. In some cases, however, the penis can be the first site of metastases.[191,192]

Tumors and tumorous conditions of scrotum

Non-neoplastic lesions

Epidermal inclusion cysts

Epidermal inclusion cysts (keratinous cysts) are common scrotal lesions. They present as single or multiple rubbery-firm subdermal or intradermal nodules. They typically contain gray-white cheesy material.[68] Histologically, they are lined by keratinizing squamous epithelium.

Idiopathic scrotal calcinosis

Idiopathic calcinosis is a rare condition of the scrotal skin.[193,194] It occurs in two settings: calcification of pre-existing epidermal or pilar cysts and calcification of dermal connective tissue in the absence of cysts (idiopathic scrotal calcinosis).[195,196] A hypothesis for the latter form favors origin from eccrine duct milia because of immunohistochemical positivity for carcinoembryonic antigen (CEA), a marker for eccrine sweat glands.[196]

Patients are usually young men, but children and older men have also been affected. They usually have multiple (up to 50) long-standing firm-to-hard nodules varying in size from a few millimeters up to 3 cm. The overlying skin is usually intact but may ulcerate, releasing cheesy material. Occasionally, a single hard nodule may be present.

Histologically, the lesions lie within the dermis and contain granules and globules of hematoxylinophilic calcific material. They may or may not be accompanied by giant cell granulomatous inflammation and include a recognizable cyst wall (Fig. 14C.23). It is plausible that idiopathic scrotal calcinosis represents an end-stage phenomenon of numerous "old" epidermal cysts that, over time, have lost their cyst walls.[197–199] Treatment may be unnecessary for asymptomatic lesions, but surgery may be necessary for infected, recurrent, or extensive lesions.

Sclerosing lipogranuloma

This lesion can also involve the scrotum.[39,40] Its clinical presentation and histologic findings are identical to those of penile and paratesticular sclerosing lipogranulomas (see pp. 863 and 845).

Fat necrosis

This lesion most commonly occurs in children and adolescents.[200] The patient presents with firm nodules in the lower portion of the scrotal wall. Two-thirds of the patients have

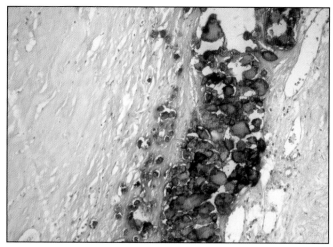

Fig. 14C.23 • Calcinosis characterized by extensive calcium phosphate deposition in a dense collagenous stroma.

bilateral nodules.[200] It has been suggested that the lesion develops when the scrotal fat crystallizes following exposure to cold.

Neoplastic lesions

Both benign and malignant neoplasms of scrotum are rare. Most neoplastic lesions arise from the skin and adnexal structures.[201] Hemangiomas, both cavernous and capillary, lymphangiomas, leiomyomas,[202] and angiokeratomas are the most common benign scrotal neoplasms.[201] Squamous carcinoma (see below) is the most common malignant scrotal neoplasm. Condyloma accuminatum and verruciform xanthoma are two lesions that clinically present as warts on the scrotal skin; rarely, squamous carcinoma can mimic a condyloma. Verruciform xanthoma occurs more commonly as a lesion in the oral mucosa, but has a second predilection for genital (scrotal and penile) skin. On low power, the lesion mimics a condyloma by virtue of acanthosis, papillomatosis, and parakeratosis, but is distinguished by the presence of foamy macrophages which occupy the papillary dermis and the tips of elongated rete ridges (Fig. 14C.6).[52]

A hamartomatous lesion with angioleiomyomatous features (angioleiomyomatous hyperplasia) has been rarely reported in the scrotum and may occasionally simulate malignancy. This lesion has not been properly characterized as it has been poorly described and labeled under various terms, including hamartoma,[203] muscular hyperplasia, leiomyoma, and vascular leiomyoma.[204] Chronic scrotal lymphedema may induce hyperplasia of the dartos muscle, resulting in a histologic appearance of smooth muscle hamartoma. Smooth muscle hyperplasia due to scrotal lymphedema is reactive rather than hamartomatous in nature and, therefore, clinicopathologic correlation may be required to differentiate true hamartomas from reactive smooth muscle hyperplasia.[205] A rare case of atypical fibrous histiocytoma has been reported in the scrotum. The tumor showed large hyperchromatic irregular nuclei, bizarre multinucleated cells (monster cells), and xanthomatous cells with large prominent nuclei set in a background of classic fibrous histiocytoma. Rare mitotic figures were identified.[206]

Squamous carcinoma

The incidence of squamous carcinoma of the scrotum is much lower than that of penile carcinoma.[207–211] The tumor, which occurs primarily during the sixth and seventh decades of life,[207,208] usually begins as a solitary, small nodule that often ulcerates. Scrotal carcinomas tend to grow locally and invade deeply. Inguinal lymph node metastases occur in half of the patients. The prognosis is poor and related to stage. The staging system currently used is Lowe's modification of the Ray & Whitmore system.[207] Histologically, the majority of cases are well or moderately differentiated squamous carcinomas.

Scrotal carcinoma was the first well-documented malignancy to be recognized as being associated with an occupational exposure. In the eighteenth century, Sir Percival Pott noted that persons exposed to soot and dust (e.g., chimney sweeps and cotton factory workers) had a higher than average incidence of scrotal carcinoma. Later, 3',4'-benzpyrene was discovered to be the causative agent.[212] Over the past two centuries, numerous industrial and occupational carcinogens have been associated with scrotal carcinoma. Other risk factors include HPV infection and the combination of psoralens and ultraviolet radiation.[109,213–215]

Some authors have suggested that scrotal cancer is uncommon among blacks; however, because of the small number of cases in each reported series, a racial predilection has not been well established.[200]

Basal cell carcinoma

BCC occurring on non-sun-exposed sites, especially the perianal and genital regions, is very rare. BCCs of the scrotum account for fewer than 5% of all scrotal malignancies.[216] Of all non-nevoid BCC syndrome cases, 51 BCCs (0.27%) were located within the perianal and genital regions.[217] They present as painless, ulcerated nodules.[218,219] The histology is similar to that of cutaneous tumors and elsewhere the entire range of histologic subtypes, including fibroepithelioma of Pinkus, is known to occur. HPV was not detected in the specimens tested. The prognosis is relatively good for BCC. Of 30 patients with 5 years' follow-up or longer, one recurrence was noted 7 years after wide excision. There were no metastases.[217]

Paget's disease

Extramammary Paget's disease involving the penis or scrotal skin is a rare occurrence.[220–226] Association with an underlying carcinoma (either adnexal or visceral) has been demonstrated in the majority of cases. Bladder, prostate, and urethral carcinomas have been reported to be associated with the development of Paget's disease. Penile and/or scrotal Paget's disease most often occurs during the sixth and seventh decades of life. Paget's disease usually presents as a scaly, eczematous lesion. Histologically, it is characterized by an intraepithelial proliferation of atypical cells with vacuolated cytoplasm and large vesicular nuclei (Fig. 14C.24). The atypical cells tend to cluster at the tips of the rete ridges. Hyperkeratosis, parakeratosis, and papillomatosis are commonly seen. The intraepithelial neoplastic cells contain intracytoplasmic neutral and acid mucopolysaccharides, which can be demonstrated by periodic acid–Schiff, mucicarmine, alcian blue, and aldehyde

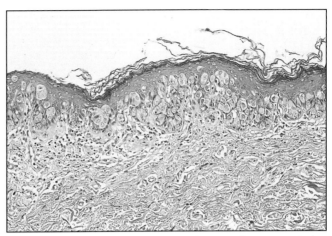

Fig. 14C.24 • Paget's disease of penis. Nests of Paget's cells are present in the mucosa. The individual cells have large hyperchromatic nuclei and pale, occasionally vacuolated cytoplasm.

fuchsin stains. Paget cells from cases of extramammary Paget's disease express a uniform phenotype of mucin (MUC1 + MUC2 − MUC5AC+) which is different from that of mammary Paget's disease (MUC1 + MUC2 − MUC5AC−).[227]

The differential diagnosis includes squamous carcinoma in situ, pagetoid BD, and malignant melanoma. Intracytoplasmic mucin is not a feature of melanoma or squamous carcinoma in situ; therefore mucin stains are helpful in establishing the diagnosis. Immunoperoxidase staining for CEA is also helpful, as Paget's cells show strong positivity for CEA, whereas melanoma cells do not.[228] In pagetoid BD, the affected epidermis contains a proliferation of neoplastic epithelial cells with a nested pagetoid distribution and the nested cells are devoid of mucin. They are non-immunoreactive with gross cystic disease fluid protein (GCDFP-15), CEA, CAM5.2 and c-erbB2. Stains for cytokeratin (CK) 20, S-100 protein, and Melan A are also negative.[229] Although CK7 has been thought to be a sensitive marker for Paget's cells, unexpected CK7 positivity is identified in pagetoid BD.[229] Williamson et al.[230] reported two cases of pagetoid BD, one in a 65-year-old man with a thigh lesion and the other in a 25-year-old man with a lesion in the penile/scrotal region. Neither patient had clinical evidence of an internal malignant neoplasm. In both cases, the neoplastic cells were positive for CK7 and CK19 and were negative for CK18, CK20, CEA, GCDFP-15, c-erbB2, S-100, and HMB-45. In aggregate, these findings support the diagnosis of pagetoid BD. Previously, others have shown that CK7 is an almost invariable marker of Paget disease. These two cases illustrated that CK7 can be expressed by pagetoid BD and should not be a cause of confusion in the differential diagnosis.[230]

Coexistence of extramammary Paget's disease with SCC in-situ in an adjacent area has also been described.[231] The outcome of patients depends on the extent of local disease and evolution of the associated malignancy.

Sarcoma

Sarcoma of the scrotum, excluding extension of sarcoma from the spermatic cord, is extremely rare. The most common type is leiomyosarcoma (Fig. 14C.25), which arises from the dartos

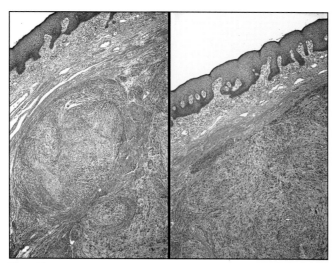

Fig. 14C.25 • Scrotal leiomyosarcoma. Beneath the skin, there is spindle cell proliferation that is depicting the same features as seen in a leiomyosarcoma of the usual sites.

muscle; fewer than 30 cases have been reported.[203,232–234] The age at presentation ranges from 35 to 89 years. A case of radiation-induced leiomyosarcoma was reported in the scrotum.[233] Only five patients have a long-term follow-up, and four of the five eventually developed distant metastases.[229] Scrotal leiomyosarcoma appears to behave similarly to subcutaneous leiomyosarcoma. Lymphatic metastases are rare, but long-term follow-up is necessary because of the possibility of late visceral metastases or recurrence. A case with combined features of liposarcoma and leiomyosarcoma was also reported in the scrotum.[235] Cases of liposarcoma, so-called malignant fibrous histiocytoma, epithelioid sarcoma, and synovial sarcoma arising from the scrotal wall have also been reported.[236–239] Other malignant tumors are extremely rare and include malignant lymphoma, and melanoma. Posttraumatic spindle nodules can mimic sarcoma and have been described in the scrotum.[240] To avoid misdiagnosis, careful clinicopathologic evaluation is required.

References

1. Rosenberg S K, Reid R 1987 Sexually transmitted papilloma viral infections in the male. I: Anatomic distribution and clinical features. Urology 29: 488–492
2. Chuang T Y 1987 Condyloma acuminata (genital warts). An epidemiologic view. J Am Acad Dermatol 16: 376–384
3. Chuang T Y, Perry H O, Kurland L T 1984 Condyloma acuminatum in Rochester, Minn, 1950–1978. I: Epidemiology and clinical features. Arch Dermatol 120: 469–475
4. Syrjanen K, Syrjanen S 1990 Epidemiology of human papilloma virus infections and genital neoplasia. Scand J Infect Dis Suppl 69: 7–17
5. Barrasso R, De Brux J, Croissant O 1987 High prevalence of papilloma virus-associated penile intraepithelial neoplasia in sexual partners of women with cervical intraepithelial neoplasia. N Engl J Med: 916–923
6. Schackner L, Hankin D E 1985 Assessing child abuse in childhood condyloma acuminatum. J Am Acad Dermatol 123: 157–160
7. Oriel J D 1971 Natural history of genital warts. Br J Vener Dis 47: 1–13
8. Margolis S 1984 Genital warts and molluscum contagiosum. Urol Clin North Am 11: 163–170
9. Goette D K 1976 Review of erythroplasia of Queyrat and its treatment. Urology 8: 311–315
10. Del Mistro A, Braunstein J D, Halwer M 1987 Identification of human papilloma virus types in male urethral condylomata acuminata by in situ hybridization. Hum Pathol 18: 936–940
11. O'Brien W M, Jenson A B, Lancaster W D 1989 Human papilloma virus typing of penile condyloma. J Urol 141: 863–865
12. Nuovo G J, Hochman H A, Eliezri H A 1990 Detection of human papilloma virus DNA in penile lesions histologically negative for condylomata. Analysis by in-situ hybridization and the polymerase chain reaction. Am J Surg Pathol 14: 829–836
13. Weaver M G, Abdul-Karim F M, Dale G 1989 Detection and localization of human papilloma virus in penile condylomas and squamous cell carcinomas using in-situ hybridization with biotinylated DNA viral probes. Mod Pathol 2: 94–100
14. Gupta S, Radotra B D, Javaheri S M et al. 2003 Lymphangioma circumscriptum of the penis mimicking venereal lesions. J Eur Acad Dermatol Venereol 17: 598–600
15. Epstein W L 1992 Molluscum contagiosum. Semin Dermatol 11: 184–189
16. Fetsch J F, Davis C J J, Hallman J R et al. 2004 Lymphedematous fibroepithelial polyps of the glans penis and prepuce: a clinicopathologic study of 7 cases demonstrating a strong association with chronic condom catheter use. Hum Pathol 35: 190–195
17. Yildirim I, Irkilata C, Sumer F et al. 2004 Fibroepithelial polyp originating from the glans penis in a child. Int J Urol 11: 187–188
18. Glicksman J M, Freeman R G 1966 Pearly penile papules. A statistical study of incidence. Arch Dermatol 93: 56–59
19. Johnson B L, Baxter D L 1964 Pearly penile papules. Arch Dermatol 90: 166–167
20. Tannenbaum M H, Becker S W 1965 Papillae of the corona of the glans penis. J Urol 93: 391–395
21. Elder D, Elenitsas R, Ragsdale B D 1997 Tumors of the epidermal appendages. In: Elder D, Elenitsas R, Jaworsky C et al. (ed) Lever's histopathology of the skin. Lippincott-Raven, Philadelphia. p 747–803
22. Rattan J, Rattan S, Gupta D K 1997 Epidermoid cyst of the penis with extension into the pelvis. J Urol 158: 593
23. Cole L A, Helwig E B 1976 Mucoid cysts of the penile skin. J Urol 115: 397–400
24. Golitz L E, Robin M 1981 Median raphe canals of the penis. Cutis 27: 170–172
25. Asarch R G, Golitz L E, Sausker W F 1979 Median raphe cysts of the penis. Arch Dermatol 115: 1084–1086
26. Enzinger F M, Weiss S W 2001 Fibromatoses. In: Enzinger F M, Weiss S W (ed) Soft tissue tumors. Mosby, St. Louis. p 309–346
27. Smith B H 1969 Subclinical Peyronie's disease. Am J Clin Pathol 52: 385–390
28. Nyberg L M, Bias W B, Hochberg M C 1982 Identification of an inherited form of Peyronie's disease with autosomal dominant inheritance and association with Dupuytren's contracture and histocompatibility B7 cross reacting antigens. J Urol 128: 48–51
29. Vande Berg J S, Devine C J, Horton C E 1981 Peyronie's disease: an electron microscopic study. J Urol 126: 333–336
30. Hinman F J 1980 Etiologic factors in Peyronie's disease. Urol Int 35: 407–413
31. Bivens C H, Marecek R L, Feldman J M 1973 Peyronie's disease – a presenting complaint of the carcinoid syndrome. N Engl J Med 289: 844–846
32. Guerneri S, Stioui S, Mantovani F et al. 1991 Multiple clonal chromosome abnormalities in Peyronie's disease. Cancer Genet Cytogenet 52: 181–185
33. Brock G, Hsu G L, Nunes L et al. 1997 The anatomy of the tunica albuginea in the normal penis and Peyronie's disease. J Urol 157: 276–281
34. McRoberts J W 1969 Peyronie's disease. Surg Gynecol Obstet 129: 1291–1294
35. Smith B H 1966 Peyronie's disease. Am J Clin Pathol 45: 670–678
36. Guileyardo J M, Sarma D P 1982 Human penile ossification. Urology 20: 428–429
37. Williams J L, Thomas G G 1970 The natural history of Peyronie's disease. J Urol 103: 75–76
38. Smetana H F, Bernhard W 1950 Sclerosing lipogranuloma. Arch Pathol 50: 296–325
39. Oertel Y C, Johnson F B 1977 Sclerosing lipogranuloma of male genitalia: review of 23 cases. Arch Pathol Lab Med 101: 321–326
40. Matsushima M, Tajima M, Maki A 1988 Primary lipogranuloma of the male genitalia. Urology 31: 75–77
41. Steward R C, Beason E S, Hayes C W 1979 Granulomas of the penis from self-injection with oils. Plast Reconstr Surg 64: 108–111
42. Lee T, Choi H R, Lee Y T et al. 1994 Paraffinoma of the penis. Yonsei Med J 35: 3440–3448
43. Matsuda T, Shichiri Y, Hida S 1988 Eosinophilic sclerosing lipogranuloma of the male genitalia not caused by exogenous lipids. J Urol 140: 1021–1024
44. Serour F 1993 Artificial nodules of the penis. Report of six cases among Russian immigrants in Israel. Sex Transm Dis 20: 192–193
45. Velazquez E F, Cubilla A L 2003 Lichen sclerosus in 68 patients with squamous cell carcinoma of the penis: frequent atypias and correlation with special carcinoma variants suggests a precancerous role. Am J Surg Pathol 27: 1448–1453

46. Powell J, Robson A, Cranston D 2001 High incidence of lichen sclerosus in patients with squamous cell carcinoma of the penis. Br J Dermatol 145: 85–89

47. Powell J, Robson A, Cranston D et al. 2003 High incidence of lichen sclerosus in patients with squamous cell carcinoma of the penis. Br J Dermatol 148: 1083–1084

48. Bouyssou-Gauthier M L, Boulinguez S, Dumas J P et al. 1999 Penile lichen sclerosus: follow-up study. Ann Dermatol Venereol 126

49. Nasca M R, Innocenzi D, Micali G 1999 Penile cancer among patients with genital lichen sclerosus. J Am Acad Dermatol 41: 911–914

50. Kumaran M S, Kanwar A J 2004 Squamous cell carcinoma in untreated lichen sclerosus of the penis: a rare complication. J Dermatol 31: 239–241

51. Campus G V, Alia F, Bosincu L 1992 Squamous cell carcinoma and lichen sclerosus et atrophicus of the prepuce. Plast Reconstr Surg 89: 692–694

52. Mohsin S K, Lee M W, Amin M B et al. 1998 Cutaneous verruciform xanthoma: a report of five cases investigating the etiology and nature of xanthomatous cells. Am J Surg Pathol 22: 479–487

53. Gray M R, Ansell I D 1990 Pseudo-epitheliomatous hyperkeratotic and micaceous balanitis: evidence for regarding it as pre-malignant. Br J Urol 66: 103–104

54. Lortat-Jacob E, Civatte J 1961 Balanite pseudoepithéliomateuse kératosique et micacée. Bull Soc Franc Dermatol Syph 68: 164–167

55. Rosai J 2004 Penis and scrotum. In: Rosai J (ed) Rosai and Ackerman's surgical pathology, 9th edn. Mosby, Edinburgh. p 1466–1482

56. Gerber G S 1994 Carcinoma in situ of the penis. J Urol 151: 829–833

57. Aynaud O, Lonesco M, Barrasso R 1994 Penile intraepithelial neoplasia. Specific clinical features correlate with histologic and virologic findings. Cancer 74: 1762–1767

58. Kaye V, Zhang G, Dehner L P et al. 1990 Carcinoma in situ of penis. Is distinction between erythroplasia of Queyrat and Bowen's disease relevant? Urology 36: 479–482

59. Su C K, Shipley W U 1997 Bowenoid papulosis: a benign lesion of the shaft of the penis misdiagnosed as squamous carcinoma. J Urol 157: 1361–1362

60. Cubilla A L, Meijer C J, Young R H 2000 Morphological features of epithelial abnormalities and precancerous lesions of the penis. Scand J Urol Nephrol Suppl 205: 215–219

61. Cubilla A L, Velazquez, E F, Young R H 2004 Epithelial lesions associated with invasive penile squamous cell carcinoma: a pathologic study of 288 cases. Int J Surg Pathol 12: 351–364

62. Queyrat L 1911 Erytroplasie du gland. Bull Soc Fr Dermatol Syphil 22: 378–382

63. Graham J H, Helwig E B 1973 Erythroplasia of Queyrat. A clinicopathologic and histochemical study. Cancer 32: 1396–1414

64. Anderson L, Johnson G, Brehmer-Anderson E 1967 Erythroplasia of Queyrat – carcinoma in situ. Scand J Urol Nephrol 1: 303–306

65. Wieland U, Jurk S, Weissenborn S 2000 Erythroplasia of Queyrat: coinfection with cutaneous carcinogenic human papillomavirus type 8 and genital papillomaviruses in a carcinoma in situ. J Invest Dermatol 115: 396–401

66. Davis-Daneshfar A, Trueb R M 2000 Bowen's disease of the glans penis. Cutis 65: 395–398

67. Hewan-Lowe L, Moreland A, Finnerty D P et al. 1990 Penis and scrotum, tumors and related disorders. In: Someren A (ed) Urologic pathology with clinical and radiologic correlations. Macmillan, New York, p 640–659

68. Young R H, Srigley J R, Amin M B et al. 2000 Tumors of the prostate gland, seminal vesicles, male urethra, and penis. Atlas of tumor pathology, series 3, fascicle 28. AFIP, Washington, DC

69. Haneke E 1982 Skin diseases and tumors of the penis. Urol Int 37: 172–182

70. Patterson J W, Kao G F, Graham J H 1986 Bowenoid papulosis. A clinicopathologic study with ultrastructural observations. Cancer 57: 823–836

71. Graham J H, Helwig E B 1961 Bowen's disease and its relationship to systemic cancer. Arch Dermatol 83: 738–758

72. Chuang T Y, Tse J, Reizner G T 1990 Bowen's disease (squamous cell carcinoma in-situ) as a skin marker for internal malignancy. A case control study. Am J Prev Med 6: 238–243

73. Callen J P, Headington J T 1980 Bowen's and non-Bowen's squamous intraepithelial neoplasia of the skin: relationship to internal malignancy. Arch Dermatol 116: 422–426

74. Wade T R, Kopf A W, Ackerman A B 1978 Bowenoid papulosis of the penis. Cancer 42: 1890–1903

75. Taylor D R J, South D A 1981 Bowenoid papulosis: a review. Cutis 27: 92–98

76. Eisen R F, Bhawan J, Cahn T H 1983 Spontaneous regression of bowenoid papulosis of the penis. Cutis 32: 269–272

77. Endo M, Yamashita T, Jin H Y et al. 2003 Detection of human papillomavirus type 16 in bowenoid papulosis and nonbowenoid tissues. Int J Dermatol 42: 474–476

78. Reyes A, Moran C A, Suster S et al. 2003 Neuroendocrine carcinomas (carcinoid tumor) of the testis. A clinicopathologic and immunohistochemical study of ten cases. Am J Clin Pathol 120: 182–187

79. Zachow K R, Ostrow R S, Bender M 1982 Detection of human papilloma virus DNA in anogenital neoplasias. Nature 300: 771–773

80. Zelickson A S, Prawer S E 1980 Bowenoid papulosis of the penis, demonstration of intranuclear viral-like particles. Am J Dermatopathol 2: 305–308

81. Barnes R D, Sarembock L A, Abratt R P 1989 Carcinoma of penis. J R Coll Surg Edinb 34: 44–46

82. Yu D S, Kim G, Song H J et al. 2004 Morphometric assessment of nuclei in Bowen's disease and bowenoid papulosis. Skin Res Technol 10: 67–70

83. Fetsch J F, Sesterhenn I A, Miettinen M et al. 2004 Epithelioid hemangioma of the penis: a clinicopathologic and immunohistochemical analysis of 19 cases, with special reference to exuberant examples often confused with epithelioid hemangioendothelioma and epithelioid angiosarcoma. Am J Surg Pathol 28: 523–533

84. Dehner L P, Smith B H 1970 Soft tissue tumors of the penis. A clinicopathologic study of 46 cases. Cancer 25: 1431–1447

85. Fetsch J F, Brinsko R W, Davis C J J et al. 2000 A distinctive myointimal proliferation ('myointimoma') involving the corpus spongiosum of the glans penis: a clinicopathologic and immunohistochemical analysis of 10 cases. Am J Surg Pathol 24: 1524–1530

86. Sufrin G, Huben R 1987 Benign and malignant lesions of the penis. In: Gillenwater J Y, Grayhack J T, Howards S S et al. (ed) Adult and pediatric urology. Year Book, Chicago, p 1448–1483

87. Jemal A, Siegel R, Ward E et al. 2006 Cancer statistics, 2006. CA Cancer J Clin 56: 106–130

88. Persky L, deKernion J 1986 Carcinoma of the penis. CA Cancer J Clin 36: 258–273

89. Dodge O G, Linsell C A 1963 Carcinoma of the penis in Uganda and Kenya Africans. Cancer 16: 1255–1263

90. Riveros M, Lebron R 1963 Geographic pathology of cancer of penis. Cancer 16: 798–811

91. Razdan S, Gomella L G 2005 Cancer of the genitourinary system. In: Devita V T, Hellman S, Rosenberg S A (ed) Cancer principles and practice of oncology. Lippincott, Williams and Wilkins, Philadelphia, p 1260–1267

92. Eble J N, Sauter G, Epstein J I et al. 2004 Pathology and genetics: tumours of the urinary system and male genital organs. WHO classification of tumors. IARC Press, Lyons, France

93. Brinton L A, Li J Y, Rong S D 1991 Risk factors for penile cancer: results from a case-control study in China. Int J Cancer 47: 504–509

94. Leiter E, Lefkovits A M 1975 Circumcision and penile cancer. NY State J Med 75: 1520–1525

95. Dagher R, Selzer M L, Lapides J 1980 Carcinoma of the penis and the anti-circumcision crusade. J Urol 110: 79–80

96. Apt A 1965 Circumcision and penile cancer. Acta Med Scand 174: 493–504

97. Bissada N K, Morcos R R, El-Senoussi M 1986 Post-circumcision carcinoma of the penis. Clinical aspects. J Urol 135: 283–285

98. Jensen M S 1977 Cancer of the penis in Denmark 1942 to 1962 (511 cases). Dan Med Bull 24: 66–72

99. Reddy C R R M, Devendranath V, Pratap S 1984 Carcinoma of penis – role of phimosis. Urology 24: 85–88

100. Koutsky L A, Wolner-Hanssen P 1989 Genital papillomavirus infections: current knowledge and future prospects. Obstet Gynecol Clin North Am 16: 541–564

101. Loning T, Riviere A, Henke R P 1988 Penile/anal condylomas and squamous cell cancer. A HPV DNA hybridization study. Virchow's Arch [A] 413: 491–498

102. McCance D J, Kalache A, Ashdown K 1986 Human papillomavirus types 16 and 18 in carcinomas of penis from Brazil. Int J Cancer 37: 55–59

103. Cupp M R, Malek R S, Goellner J R 1995 The detection of human papillomavirus deoxyribonucleic acid in intraepithelial, in-situ, verrucous and invasive carcinoma of the penis. J Urol 154: 1024–1029

104. Masih A S, Stoler M H, Farrow G M 1993 Human papillomavirus in penile squamous cell lesions: a comparison of an isotopic RNA and two commercial nonisotopic DNA in situ hybridization methods. Arch Pathol Lab Med 117: 302–307

105. Gregoire L, Cubilla A L, Reuter V E et al. 1995 Preferential association of virus with high grade histologic variants of penile-invasive squamous cell carcinoma. J Natl Cancer Inst 87: 1705–1709

106. Graham S, Priore R, Graham M 1979 Genital cancer in wives of penile cancer patients. Cancer 44: 1870–1874

107. Iversen T, Tretli S, Johansen A et al. 1997 Squamous cell carcinoma of the penis and of the cervix, vulva and vagina in spouses: is there any relationship? An epidemiological study from Norway 1960–92. Br J Cancer 76: 658–660

108. Mainche A G, Pyrhonen S 1990 Risk of cervical cancer among wives of men with carcinoma of the penis. Acta Oncol 29: 569–571

109. Stern R S 1990 Genital tumors among men with psoriasis exposed to psoralens and ultraviolet A radiation (PUVA) and ultraviolet B radiation. The photochemotherapy follow up study. N Engl J Med 322: 1149–1151

110. Ravi R 1995 Radiation-induced carcinoma of the penis. Urol Int 54: 147–149

111. Takiwaki H, Yokota M, Ahsan K et al. 1996 Squamous cell carcinoma associated with verruciform xanthomas of the penis. Am J Dermatopathol 18: 551–554

112. Droller M J 1980 Carcinoma of penis: an overview. Urol Clin North Am 7: 783–784

113. Fraley E E, Zhang G, Sazama R 1985 Cancer of the penis. Prognosis and treatment plans. Cancer 55: 1618–1624

114. Jones W G, Hamers H, van den Bogaert W 1989 Penis cancer. A review by the joint radiotherapy committee of the European Organization for Research and Treatment of Cancer (EORTC) genitourinary and radiotherapy groups. J Surg Oncol 40: 227–231

115. Fossa S D, Hall K S, Johannessen N B 1987 Cancer of the penis. Eur Urol 13: 372–377

116. Narayana A S, Olney L E, Loening S A 1982 Carcinoma of the penis. Cancer 49: 2185–2191

117. Merrin C E 1980 Cancer of the penis. Cancer 45: 1973–1979

118. Derrick F C J, Lynch K M J, Kretkowski R C 1973 Epidermoid carcinoma of the penis: computer analysis of 87 cases. J Urol 110: 303–305

119. Hanash K A, Furlow W L, Utz D C et al. 1970 Carcinoma of the penis: a clinicopathologic study. J Urol 104: 291–297

120. Cubilla A L, Barreto J E, Caballero C et al. 1993 Pathologic features of epidermoid carcinomas of the penis. A prospective study of 66 cases. Am J Surg Pathol 17: 753–763

121. Cubilla A L, Velazques E F, Reuter V E et al. 2000 Warty (condylomatous) squamous cell carcinoma of the penis. A report of 11 cases and proposed classification of "verruciform" penile tumors. Am J Surg Pathol 24: 505–512

122. Johnson D E, Lo R K 1984 Management of regional lymph nodes in penile carcinoma. Five year results following therapeutic groin dissections. Urology 24: 308–311

123. Pow-Sang J E, Benavente V, Pow-Sang J M 1990 Bilateral inguinal lymph node dissection in the management of cancer of the penis. Semin Surg Oncol 6: 241–242

124. Ayyappan K, Anathakrishnan N, Sankaran V 1994 Can regional lymph node involvement be predicted in patients with carcinoma of the penis? Br J Urol 73: 549–553

125. Horenblas S, van Tinteren H 1994 Squamous cell carcinoma of the penis. IV. Prognostic factors of survival: analysis of tumor, nodes and metastasis classification system. J Urol 151: 1239–1243

126. Johnson D E, Lo R K, Srigley J 1985 Verrucous carcinoma of the penis. J Urol 133: 216–218

127. McKee P H, Lowe D, Haigh R J 1983 Penile verrucous carcinoma. Histopathology 7: 897–906

128. Kraus F T, Perez-Mesa C 1966 Verrucous carcinoma. Clinical and pathologic study of 105 cases involving oral cavity, larynx, and genitalia. Cancer 19: 26–38

129. Yeager J K, Findlay R F, McAleer I M 1990 Penile verrucous carcinoma. Arch Dermatol 126: 1208–1210

130. Blessing K, McLaren K, Lessells A 1986 Viral etiology for verrucous carcinoma. Histopathology 10: 1101–1102

131. Masih A S, Stoler M H, Farrow G M 1992 Penile verrucous carcinoma: a clinicopathologic, human papillomavirus typing and flow cytometric analysis. Mod Pathol 5: 48–55

132. Bezerra A L, Lopes A, Landman G et al. 2001 Clinicopathologic features and human papillomavirus DNA prevalence of warty and squamous cell carcinoma of the penis. Am J Surg Pathol 25: 673–678

133. Rubin M A, Kleter B, Zhou M et al. 2001 Detection and typing of human papillomavirus DNA in penile carcinoma: evidence for multiple independent pathways of penile carcinogenesis. Am J Pathol 159: 1211–1218

134. Cubilla A L, Reuter V, Ayala G et al. 1998 Basaloid squamous cell carcinoma of the penis: a distinctive human papilloma virus-related penile neoplasm. Am J Surg Pathol 22: 755–761

135. Cubilla A L, Velazquez E F, Young R H 2004 Pseudohyperplastic squamous cell carcinoma of the penis associated with lichen sclerosus. An extremely well-differentiated, nonverruciform neoplasm that preferentially affects the foreskin and is frequently misdiagnosed: a report of 10 cases of a distinctive clinicopathologic entity. Am J Surg Pathol 28: 895–900

136. Fukunaga M, Yokoi K, Miyazawa Y et al. 1994 Penile verrucous carcinoma with anaplastic transformation following radiotherapy. A case report with human papillomavirus typing and flow cytometric DNA studies. Am J Surg Pathol 18: 501–505

137. Morinaga S, Nakamura S, Moro K et al. 1995 Carcinosarcoma (carcinoma with sarcomatous metaplasia) of the penis. J Urol Pathol 3: 369–376

138. Velazquez E F, Melamed J, Barreto J E 2005 Sarcomatoid carcinoma of the penis. A clinicopathologic study of 15 cases. Am J Surg Pathol 29: 1152–1158

139. Wood E W, Gardner W A J, Brown F M 1972 Spindle cell squamous carcinoma of the penis. J Urol 107: 990–991

140. Lont A P, Gallee M P, Snijders P et al. 2004 Sarcomatoid squamous cell carcinoma of the penis: a clinical and pathological study of 5 cases. J Urol 172: 932–935

141. Lenowitz H, Graham A P 1946 Carcinoma of the penis. J Urol 56: 458–484

142. Cubilla A L, Ayala M T, Barreto J E et al. 1996 Surface adenosquamous carcinoma of the penis. A report of three cases. Am J Surg Pathol 20: 156–160

143. Masera A, Ovcak Z, Volavsek M et al. 1997 Adenosquamous carcinoma of the penis. J Urol 157: 2261

144. Layfield L J, Liu K 2000 Mucoepidermoid carcinoma arising in the glans penis. Arch Pathol Lab Med 124: 148–151

145. Galanis E, Frytak S, Lloyd R V 1997 Extrapulmonary small cell carcinoma. Cancer 79: 1729–1736

146. Tomic S, Warner T F, Messing E et al. 1995 Penile Merkel cell carcinoma. Urology 45: 1062–1065

147. Liegl B, Regauer S 2004 Penile clear cell carcinoma. A report of 5 cases of a distinct entity. Am J Surg Pathol 28: 1513–1517

148. Oppenheim A R 1981 Sebaceous carcinoma of the penis. Arch Dermatol 117: 306–307

149. Adeyoju A B, Thornhill J, Corr J et al. 1997 Prognostic factors in squamous cell carcinoma of the penis and implications for management. Br J Urol 80: 937–939

150. Heyns C F, van Vollenhoven P, Steenkamp J W et al. 1997 Cancer of the penis – a review of 50 patients. S Afr J Surg 35: 120–124

151. McDougal W S 1995 Carcinoma of the penis: improved survival by early regional lymphadenectomy based on the histologic grade and depth of invasion of the primary lesion. J Urol 154: 1364–1366

152. Ornellas A A, Seixas A L, Marota A et al. 1994 Surgical treatment of invasive squamous cell carcinoma of the penis: retrospective analysis of 350 cases. J Urol 151: 1244–1249

153. Soria J C, Fizazi K, Piron D 1997 Squamous cell carcinoma of the penis: multivariate analysis of prognostic factors and natural history in a monocentric study with a conservative policy. Ann Oncol 8: 1089–1098

154. Denkow T 1999 The treatment of penile carcinoma: experience in 64 cases. Int Urol Nephrol 31: 525–531

155. Slaton J W, Morgenstern N, Levy D A et al. 2001 Tumor stage, vascular invasion and the percentage of poorly differentiated cancer: independent prognosticators for inguinal lymph node metastasis in penile squamous cancer. J Urol 165: 1138–1142

156. Velazquez E F, Soskin A, Bock A 2004 Positive resection margins in partial penectomies: sites of involvement and proposal of local routes of spread of penile squamous cell carcinoma. Am J Surg Pathol 28: 384–389

157. Ladocsi L T, Siebert C F J, Rickert R R et al. 1998 Basal cell carcinoma of the penis. Cutis 61: 25–27

158. Kim E D, Kroft S, Dalton D P 1994 Basal cell carcinoma of the penis: case report and review of the literature. J Urol 152: 1557–1559

159. Stillwell T J, Zincke H, Gaffey T A 1988 Malignant melanoma of the penis. J Urol 140: 72–75

160. Oldbring J, Mikulowski P 1987 Malignant melanoma of the penis and male urethra. Report of nine cases and review of the literature. Cancer 59: 581–587

161. Begun F P, Grossman H B, Diokno A C 1984 Malignant melanoma of the penis and male urethra. J Urol 132: 123–125

162. Manivel J C, Fraley E E 1988 Malignant melanoma of the penis and male urethra: 4 case reports and literature review. J Urol 139: 813–816

163. Johnson D E, Ayala A G 1973 Primary melanoma of the penis. Urology 2: 174–177

164. Rashid A M, Williams R M, Horton L W 1993 Malignant melanoma of penis and male urethra. Is it a difficult tumor to diagnose? Urology 41: 470–471

165. de Bree E, Sanidas E, Tzardi M et al. 1997 Malignant melanoma of the penis. Eur J Surg Oncol 23: 277–279

166. Larsson K B, Shaw H M, Thompson J F et al. 1999 Primary mucosal and glans penis melanomas: the Sydney Melanoma Unit experience. Aust NZ J Surg 69: 121–126

167. Orlandini V, Kolb F, Spatz A et al. 2004 [Melanoma of the penis: 6 cases.] Ann Dermatol Venereol 131: 541–544

168. Konigsberg H A, Gray G F 1976 Benign melanosis and malignant melanoma of penis and male urethra. Urology 7: 323–326

169. aeger N, Wirtler H, Tschubel K 1982 Acral lentiginous melanoma of penis. Eur Urol 8: 182–184

170. Saw D, Tse C H, Chan J K C 1986 Clear cell sarcoma of the penis. Hum Pathol 17: 423–425

171. Waguespack R L, Fair K P, Svetec D A et al. 1996 Glomangioma of the penile and scrotal median raphe. J Urol 156: 179

172. Pacifico A, Piccolo D, Fargnoli M C et al. 2003 Kaposi's sarcoma of the glans penis in an immunocompetent patient. Eur J Dermatol 13: 582–583

173. Calonje E, Fletcher C D M, Wilson-Jones E et al. 1994 Retiform hemangioendothelioma. A distinctive form of low-grade angiosarcoma delineated in a series of 15 cases. Am J Surg Pathol 18: 115–125

174. Pow-Sang M R, Orihuela E 1994 Leiomyosarcoma of the penis. J Urol 151: 1643–1645

175. Ormsby A H, Liou L S, Oriba H A 2000 Epithelioid sarcoma of the penis: report of an unusual case and review of the literature. Ann Diagn Pathol 4: 88–94

176. Amin M B, Srigley J R, Ro J Y 1997 Leiomyosarcoma of the penis: a study of 7 cases. Mod Pathol 10: 68A (abstract)

177. Blasius S, Brinkschmidt C, Bier B 1995 Extraskeletal myxoid chondrosarcoma of the penis. J Urol Pathol 3: 73–80

178. Yantiss R K, Althausen A F, Young R H 1998 Malignant fibrous histiocytoma of the penis. Report of a case and review of the literature. J Urol Pathol 9: 171–180

179. Lowentrit B, Parsons J K, Argani P et al. 2004 Pediatric epithelioid sarcoma of the penis. J Urol 172: 296–297

180. Dominici A, Delle Rose A, Stomaci N et al. 2004 A rare case of leiomyosarcoma of the penis with a reappraisal of the literature. Int J Urol 11: 440–444

181. Powell B L, Craig J B, Muss H B 1985 Secondary malignancies of the penis and epididymis: a case report and review of the literature. J Clin Oncol 3: 110–116

182. Perez-Mesa C, Oxenhandler R 1989 Metastatic tumors of the penis. J Surg Oncol 42: 11–15

183. Haddad F S 1984 Penile metastases secondary to bladder cancer. Review of the literature. Urol Int 39: 125–142

184. Robey E L, Schellhammer P F 1984 Four cases of metastases to the penis and review of the literature. J Urol 132: 992–994

185. Khubchandani M 1986 Metachronous metastasis to the penis from carcinoma of the rectum. Report of a case. Dis Colon Rectum 29: 52–54

186. Philip A T, Amin M B, Cubilla A L et al. 1999 Secondary tumors of the penis: a study of 16 cases. Mod Pathol 12: 104A (abstract)

187. Hashimoto H, Saga Y, Watabe Y 1989 Case report: secondary penile carcinoma. Urol Int 44: 56–57

188. Ordonez N G, Ayala A G, Bracken R B 1982 Renal cell carcinoma metastatic to penis. Urology 19: 417–419

189. Perez L M, Shumway R A, Carson C C 1992 Penile metastasis secondary to supraglottic squamous cell carcinoma: review of the literature. J Urol 147: 157–160

190. Tu S M, Reyes A, Maa A 2002 Prostate carcinoma with testicular or penile metastases. Clinical, pathologic, and immunohistochemical features. Cancer 94: 2610–2617

191. Adjiman S, Flam T A, Zerbib M 1989 Delayed nonurothelial metastatic lesions to the penis. A report of two cases. Eur Urol 16: 391–392

192. Powell F C, Venencie P Y, Winkelmann R K 1984 Metastatic prostate carcinoma manifesting as penile nodules. Arch Dermatol 20: 1604–1606

193. Malcolm A 1982 Idiopathic calcinosis of the scrotum. Br J Urol 54: 190

194. Cecchi R, Giomi A 1999 Idiopathic calcinosis cutis of the penis. Dermatology 198: 174–175

195. Swinehart J M, Golitz L E 1982 Scrotal calcinosis. Dystrophic calcification of epidermoid cysts. Arch Dermatol 118: 985–988

196. Dare A J, Axelsen R A 1988 Scrotal calcinosis: origin from dystrophic calcification of eccrine duct milia. J Cutan Pathol 15: 142–149

197. Kaskas M, Dabrowski A, Sabbah M 1991 Idiopathic calcinosis of the scrotum. Apropos of a case. A review of the literature. J Urol (Paris) 97: 287–290

198. Song D H, Lee K H, Kang W H 1988 Idiopathic calcinosis of the scrotum: histopathologic observations of fifty-one nodules. J Am Acad Dermatol 97: 287–290

199. Akosa A B, Gilliland E A, Ali M H 1989 Idiopathic scrotal calcinosis: a possible aetiology reaffirmed. Br J Plast Surg 42: 324–327

200. Hollander J B, Begun F P, Lee R D 1985 Scrotal fat necrosis. J Urol 134: 150–151

201. Ulbright T M, Amin M B, Young R H 1999 Tumors of the testis, adnexa, spermatic cord, and scrotum, 3rd series. Atlas of tumor pathology. Armed Forces Institute of Pathology, Washington, D C

202. Newman P L, Fletcher C D M 1991 Smooth muscle tumours of the external genitalia: clinicopathological analysis of a series. Histopathology 18: 523–529

203. Quinn T R, Young R H 1997 Smooth muscle hamartoma of the tunica dartos of the scrotum: report of a case. J Cutan Pathol 24: 322–324

204. Nuciforo P G, Roncalli M 2003 Pathologic quiz case: a scrotal sac mass incidentally discovered during autopsy. Paratesticular hamartoma with angioleiomyomatous features (angioleiomyomatous hyperplasia). Arch Pathol Lab Med 127: 239–240

205. van Kooten E O, Hage J J, Meinhardt W et al. 2004 Acquired smooth-muscle hamartoma of the scrotum: a histological simulator? J Cutan Pathol 31: 388–392

206. Huan Y, Vapnek J, Unger P D 2003 Atypical fibrous histiocytoma of the scrotum. Ann Diagn Pathol 7: 370–373

207. Lowe F C 1983 Squamous cell carcinoma of the scrotum. J Urol 130: 423–427

208. McDonald M W 1982 Carcinoma of scrotum. Urology 19: 269–274

209. Ray B, Whitmore W F 1977 Experience with carcinoma of the scrotum. J Urol 117: 741–745

210. Gerber W L 1985 Scrotal malignancies: the University of Iowa experience and review of the literature. Urology 26: 337–342

211. Andrews P E, Farrow G M, Oesterling J E 1991 Squamous cell carcinoma of the scrotum: long-term follow-up of 14 patients. J Urol 146: 1299–1304

212. Waldron H A 1983 On the history of scrotal cancer. Ann R Coll Surg 65: 420–422

213. Oesterling J E, Lowe F C 1990 Squamous cell carcinoma of the scrotum. Am Urol Assoc Update Series 9: 178–183

214. Orihuela E, Tyring S K, Pow-Sang M 1995 Development of human papillomavirus type 16 associated squamous cell carcinoma of the scrotum in a patient with Darier's disease treated with systemic isotretinoin. J Urol 153: 1940–1943

215. de la Brassinne M, Richert B 1992 Genital squamous cell carcinoma after PUVA therapy. Dermatology 185: 316–318

216. Grossman H B, Sogani P C 1981 Basal cell carcinoma of scrotum. Urology 17: 241–242

217. Gibson G E, Ahmed I 2001 Perianal and genital basal cell carcinoma: a clinicopathologic review of 51 cases. J Am Acad Dermatol 45: 68–71

218. Greider H E, Vernon S D 1982 Basal cell carcinoma of the scrotum. A case report and literature review. J Urol 127: 145–146

219. Ho W S, King W W, Chan W Y 1995 Basal cell carcinoma of the scrotum. N Med J Ind 8: 195

220. Hoch W H 1984 Adenocarcinoma of the scrotum (extramammary Paget's disease). A case report and review of the literature. J Urol 132: 137–139

221. Mitsudo S, Nakanishi I, Koss L 1981 Paget's disease of the penis and adjacent skin. Its association with fatal sweat gland carcinoma. Arch Pathol Lab Med 105: 518–520

222. Helwig E B, Graham J H 1963 Anogenital extramammary Paget's disease. A clinicopathological study. Cancer 16: 387–403

223. Perez M A, Larossa D D, Tomaszewski J E 1989 Paget's disease primarily involving the scrotum. Cancer 63: 970–975

224. Takahashi Y, Komeda H, Horie M 1988 Paget's disease of the scrotum. Acta Urol Jpn 34: 1069–1072

225. Smith D J, Handy F C, Evans J W 1994 Paget's disease of the glans penis: an unusual urological malignancy. Eur Urol 25: 316–319

226. Koh K B, Nazarina A R 1995 Paget's disease of the scrotum: report of a case with underlying carcinoma of the prostate. Br J Dermatol 133: 306–307

227. Kuan S F, Montag A G, Hart J et al. 2001 Differential expression of mucin genes in mammary and extramammary Paget's disease. Am J Surg Pathol 25: 1469–1477

228. Ordonez N G, Awalt H, Mackay B 1987 Mammary and extramammary Paget's disease: an immunohistochemical and ultrastructural study. Cancer 59: 1173–1183

229. Raju R R, Goldblum J R, Hart W R 2003 Pagetoid squamous cell carcinoma in situ (pagetoid Bowen's disease) of the external genitalia. Int J Gynecol Pathol 22: 127–135

230. Williamson J D, Maria I, Colome M I et al. 2000 Pagetoid Bowen disease: a report of 2 cases that express cytokeratin 7. Arch Pathol Lab Med 124: 427–430

231. Quinn A M, Sienko A, Basrawala Z et al. 2004 Extramammary Paget disease of the scrotum with features of Bowen disease. Arch Pathol Lab Med 128: 84–86

232. Moon T D, Sarma D P 1989 Leiomyosarcoma of the scrotum. J Am Acad Dermatol 20: 290–292

233. Dalton D P, Rushovich A M, Victor T A et al. 1988 Leiomyosarcoma of the scrotum in a man who had received scrotal irradiation as a child. J Urol 139: 136–138

234. Desai S R, Angarkar N N 2003 Leiomyosarcoma of the scrotum. Ind J Pathol Microbiol 46: 212–213

235. Suster S, Wong T Y, Moran C A 1993 Sarcoma with combined features of liposarcoma and leiomyosarcoma. Study of two cases of an unusual soft-tissue tumor showing dual lineage differentiation. Am J Surg Pathol 17: 905–911

236. Watanabe K, Ogawa A, Komatsu H 1988 Malignant fibrous histiocytoma of the scrotal wall: a case report. J Urol 140: 151–152

237. Chan J A, McMenamin M E, Fletcher C D M 2003 Synovial sarcoma in older patients: clinicopathological analysis of 32 cases with emphasis on unusual histological fetures. Histopathology 43: 72–83

238. Bajaj P, Aiyer H, Sinha B K et al. 2001 Pitfalls in the diagnosis of epithelioid sarcoma presenting in an unusual site: a case report. Diagn Cytopathol 24: 36–38

239. Kochman A, Jablecki J, Rabczynski J 1999 Recurrent primary well-differentiated intrascrotal liposarcoma: case report and review of the literature. Tumori 85: 135–136

240. Papadimitrious J C, Drachenberg C B 1994 Posttraumatic spindle cell nodules. Immunohistochemical and ultrastructural study of two scrotal lesions. Arch Pathol Lab Med 118: 709–711

Tumors of the peritoneum 15

Philip B. Clement

In this chapter, peritoneal lesions are reviewed under the following headings: tumor-like lesions, mesothelial neoplasms, miscellaneous primary tumors, metastatic tumors, and lesions derived from the so-called secondary müllerian system. Disorders of the retroperitoneum, except those of peritoneal origin, are not included.

Tumor-like lesions

Mesothelial hyperplasia

Mesothelial hyperplasia is a common response to acute and chronic inflammation and chronic effusions (Figs 15.1–15.4).[1–4] Hyperplastic lesions may be observed at operation as solitary or multiple, typically small, nodules or plaques, but more commonly are incidental findings on microscopic examination. Mesothelial hyperplasia often occurs in the adnexa of women with chronic salpingitis and endometriosis,[2] and is often encountered in these and other areas (particularly the omentum) in patients with ovarian neoplasms.[3] Additionally, mesothelial hyperplasia on the surface of the ovary or within the superficial ovarian stroma overlying a borderline epithelial tumor may be misinterpreted as invasive tumor (Fig. 15.5).[3] Mesothelial hyperplasia may also involve a hernia sac, in some cases due to trauma or incarceration (Fig. 15.2).[4]

In florid examples of mesothelial hyperplasia, solid, trabecular, tubular, papillary, or tubulopapillary patterns

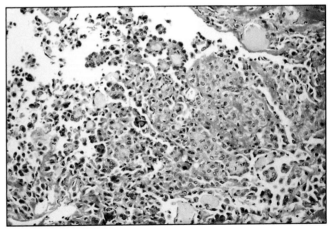

Fig. 15.2 • Florid papillary mesothelial hyperplasia involving a hernia sac.

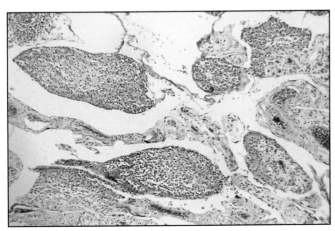

Fig. 15.1 • Nodular mesothelial hyperplasia involving omentum.

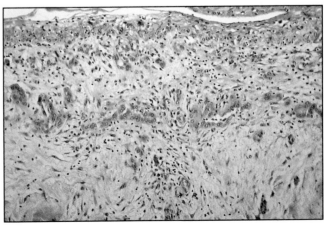

Fig. 15.3 • Mesothelial hyperplasia. Note the linear arrangement of the mesothelial cells within inflamed fibrous tissue.

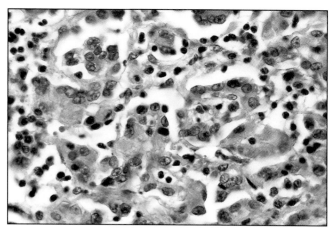

Fig. 15.4 • Periovarian papillary mesothelial hyperplasia. Note mild nuclear atypia and admixed inflammatory cells.

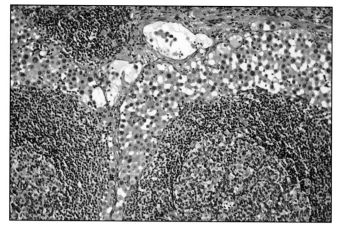

Fig. 15.6 • Hyperplastic mesothelial cells within pelvic lymph node. The mesothelial cells fill the subcapsular lymphatics and sinusoids. There was associated mesothelial hyperplasia of the peritoneum.

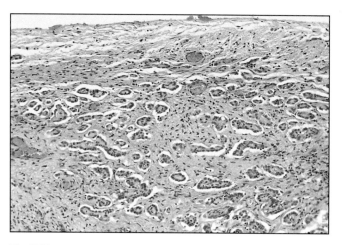

Fig. 15.5 • Nests of hyperplastic mesothelial cells within ovarian stroma (the spaces surrounding the nests are retraction artifact). The hyperplastic mesothelial cells were adjacent to a mucinous borderline tumor and were misinterpreted as foci of invasion.

(Figs 15.1–15.5) may occur, in some cases being accompanied by superficial extension of the mesothelial cells into the underlying tissues (Figs 15.3 and 15.5). The cells focally may be arranged in linear, occasionally parallel, thin layers, separated by fibrin or fibrous tissue (Fig. 15.3). The mesothelial cells may contain cytoplasmic vacuoles filled with acid mucin (predominantly hyaluronic acid) or, less commonly, may exhibit marked clearing of their cytoplasm. Mild to moderate nuclear atypia, mitotic figures, and, occasionally, multinucleated cells may be present. Psammoma bodies and, in rare cases, eosinophilic strap-shaped cells resembling rhabdomyoblasts have been encountered.[4] In some cases of mesothelial hyperplasia, variable numbers of histiocytes may be admixed with the mesothelial cells ("nodular histiocytic/mesothelial hyperplasia"), and in a subset, histiocytes are the dominant component.[5,6] The distinction of these two types of cells, although unlikely to be clinically important, may require immunohistochemistry.

Hyperplastic mesothelial cells may rarely involve intra-abdominal lymph nodes, a finding that has been associated with, and in such cases is presumably secondary to, mesothelial hyperplasia of the peritoneum.[7] The hyperplastic mesothelial cells can prominently expand the subcapsular lymphatics and the intranodal sinusoids (Fig. 15.6), potentially mimicking sinus histiocytosis, nodal involvement by an ovarian serous borderline tumor, metastatic carcinoma, or metastatic mesothelioma. Cytokeratin staining in such cases may reveal more extensive involvement of the lymph node by the mesothelial cells than is appreciable with routinely stained sections.

The major differential diagnosis of mesothelial hyperplasia is malignant mesothelioma. The presence of grossly visible nodules, necrosis, conspicuous large cytoplasmic vacuoles, severe nuclear atypia, and deep infiltration favors mesothelioma over mesothelial hyperplasia.[1] Some of these features, however, are not always present or may be present only focally within a mesothelioma. Although immunoreactivity for epithelial membrane antigen (EMA) and p53 is more typical of malignant mesothelioma and desmin immunoreactivity is more typical of mesothelial hyperplasia,[8] these markers cannot be relied upon in individual cases.[1] Sometimes the distinction between a hyperplastic mesothelial lesion and a mesothelioma may be difficult or impossible, especially in a small biopsy specimen.

In addition to mesothelioma, the differential diagnosis of peritoneal or intranodal mesothelial hyperplasia includes serous borderline tumors, either in the form of spread from an ovarian serous borderline tumor or a primary peritoneal or intranodal serous borderline tumor (see p. 894). Grossly visible ovarian or peritoneal tumor nodules, columnar cells that may bear cilia, the presence of intracellular or extracellular neutral mucin, and numerous psammoma bodies favor a serous borderline tumor. Immunoreactivity for "epithelial" antigens (see section on malignant mesothelioma, below) is also useful in the differential diagnosis.

Peritoneal inclusion cysts

Peritoneal inclusion cysts usually occur in women of reproductive age,[9–27] but the same lesions rarely occur in males or have involved the pleura.[16–18] Some cysts are discovered incidentally at laparotomy as single or multiple, small, thin-walled, translucent, unilocular cysts attached or lying free in the peritoneal cavity (Fig. 15.7). They occasionally involve the round ligament, potentially mimicking an inguinal hernia. Some cysts are an incidental serosal finding in appendectomy specimens. Rare cases have been retroperitoneal.[25] Pathologic examination of these cysts typically reveals a smooth lining, yellow and watery to gelatinous contents, and a single layer of flattened, benign-appearing mesothelial cells. Mature stratified squamous epithelium may be seen in some cases. Most unilocular mesothelial cysts are probably reactive in origin, although developmental origin has been suggested for at least some of those cases involving the mesocolon, mesentery of the small intestine, retroperitoneum, and splenic capsule.

Multilocular cystic masses as large as 20 cm in diameter (Fig. 15.8) and lined by mesothelial cells have been referred to as *multilocular peritoneal inclusion cysts* (MPICs), *benign cystic mesotheliomas*, inflammatory cysts of the peritoneum, or postoperative peritoneal cysts.[9–15,26] MPICs often cause clinical manifestations – usually lower abdominal pain, a palpable mass, or both. Typically they are adherent to pelvic viscera and may mimic a cystic ovarian tumor clinically, intraoperatively,[13] or on pathologic examination; the upper peritoneal cavity, the spleen,[19] the liver,[23] the retroperitoneum, the inguinal region,[24] and hernia sacs can also be involved. The septa and walls of MPICs may contain considerable amounts of fibrous tissue, and their contents may resemble those of the unilocular cysts or they may be serosanguineous or frankly bloody.

Microscopic examination reveals that MPICs are usually lined by a single layer of flat to cuboidal, rarely hobnail-shaped, mesothelial cells that typically have benign nuclear features, although some reactive atypia is not uncommon (Figs 15.9 and 15.10). The mesothelial cells may proliferate into the cyst lumina as small papillae or in cribriform patterns, and occasionally they may undergo squamous metaplasia.[14,15] Mural proliferations of typical or atypical mesothelial cells disposed singly, as glands or nests (Fig. 15.11), or in patterns mimicking an adenomatoid tumor, may occur, resulting in infiltrative patterns that may suggest a cancer.[13–15] In some cases, vacuolated mesothelial cells in the stroma may raise the possibility of a signet-ring carcinoma.[15] The cyst walls and

Fig. 15.7 • Unilocular peritoneal inclusion cysts.

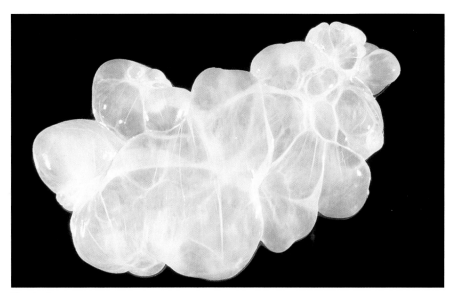

Fig. 15.8 • Multilocular peritoneal inclusion cyst.

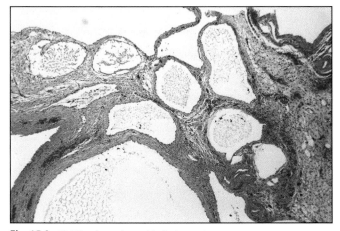

Fig. 15.9 • Multilocular peritoneal inclusion cyst.

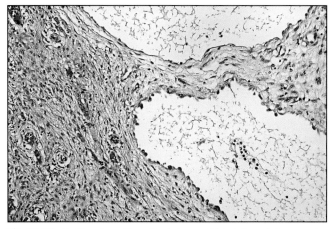

Fig. 15.10 • Multilocular peritoneal inclusion cyst. Note inflamed stroma and occasional hobnail-like mesothelial cells lining the cysts.

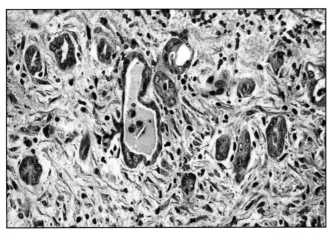

Fig. 15.11 • Multilocular peritoneal inclusion cyst with mural mesothelial cells.

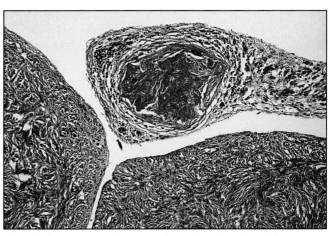

Fig. 15.12 • Keratin granuloma on ovarian surface. The patient had an endometrial adenocarcinoma with extensive squamous metaplasia.

septa are usually composed of fibrovascular connective tissue with a sparse inflammatory infiltrate, but in other cases, severe acute and chronic inflammation (that may include foamy histiocytes), fibrin, granulation tissue, and hemorrhage are encountered.

A history of one or more factors – an abdominal surgical procedure, pelvic inflammatory disease, or endometriosis – was present in 84% of patients in one study,[15] indicating a likely role for inflammation in the pathogenesis of MPICs. The occurrence of cases in which the distinction between florid adhesions and an MPIC may be difficult is also consistent with an inflammatory etiology. Only rare cases[18] have been associated with asbestos exposure. Occasional MPICs have been immunoreactive for estrogen and/or progesterone receptors[26] or have diminished in size following treatment with a gonadotropin-releasing hormone (GnRH) agonist,[27] suggesting that hormonal factors may play a role in some cases.

Follow-up of cases that we consider to be MPICs has shown no evidence of malignant behavior, but as many as 50% of the lesions have recurred locally, in some cases several times, months to years after their removal.[15] At least some of these "recurrences," however, are probably due to newly formed postoperative adhesions. We therefore prefer the designation multilocular peritoneal inclusion cyst to benign cystic mesothelioma for these lesions.

MPICs may be confused on both gross and microscopic examination with multilocular cystic lymphangiomas.[9] Unlike MPICs, the latter usually occur in children, typically boys, and are usually extrapelvic, being localized in most cases to the small bowel mesentery, the omentum, the mesocolon, or the retroperitoneum. In contrast to MPICs, their contents are often chylous; mural lymphoid aggregates and smooth muscle are usually found on microscopic examination and the lining cells stain positively with endothelial markers rather than keratin. Similarly, MPICs within the spleen have been confused with splenic lymphangiomas.[19] Immunohistochemical stains to distinguish between endothelial and mesothelial cells are diagnostic in problematic cases. The differential diagnosis of MPICs also includes the rare cystic adenomatoid tumor.[28] This tumor, in contrast to MPICs, usually occurs in the uterus, contains foci of typical adenomatoid tumor, and lacks a prominent inflammatory cell infiltrate.

Peritoneal keratin granulomas

Infectious and non-infectious peritoneal granulomas are almost always readily distinguishable from a neoplasm on microscopic examination.[29] In contrast, peritoneal granulomas secondary to implants of keratin originating from neoplasms of the female reproductive tract may be confused with metastatic tumor.[30] The tumors are usually endometrial (or, less commonly, ovarian) endometrioid carcinomas with squamous differentiation; additionally, squamous cell carcinomas of the cervix and atypical polypoid adenomyomas of the uterus have rarely been the source of the keratin.[30] The granulomas consist of laminated keratin deposits, in some cases accompanied by necrotic squamous cells, surrounded by foreign-body giant cells and fibrous tissue (Fig. 15.12).

Although follow-up data have shown that these granulomas have had no effect on the prognosis, the prognostic significance of these lesions has not been established with complete certainty because of the short follow-up interval in some cases, and because some of the patients have received postoperative radiation therapy, chemotherapy, or both. Keratin granulomas, if visible, should be sampled extensively by the surgeon and assiduously examined microscopically by the pathologist to exclude the additional presence of any viable carcinoma cells. The differential diagnosis includes peritoneal granulomas in response to keratin derived from other sources, including amniotic fluid and ovarian dermoid cysts. In the latter situation, cyst rupture releases sebaceous material and keratin that typically evoke an intense granulomatous, lipogranulomatous, and fibrosing peritoneal inflammatory reaction that may mimic a neoplasm at operation.[29]

Peritoneal fibrosis, sclerosing peritonitis, and sclerosing mesenteritis

Reactive peritoneal fibrosis (including fibrous adhesions), a common sequela of peritoneal inflammation and abdominal operations, is rarely a diagnostic problem. A reactive peritoneal fibrotic lesion may contain "multipotential subserosal cells"[31] that take the form of plump, often fasciitis-like spindle cells that immunoreact for vimentin, smooth muscle actin, and cytokeratin.

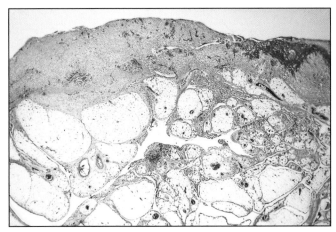

Fig. 15.13 • Sclerosing peritonitis that was associated with a luteinized thecoma of the ovary. There is fibrotic thickening of the omental surface and its interlobular septa (Masson trichrome stain).

Sclerosing peritonitis is a rare disorder characterized by fibrous peritoneal thickening that can encase the small bowel ("abdominal cocoon"), causing bowel obstruction. Although it may be idiopathic (such cases typically occur in adolescent girls), common etiologic associations include practolol therapy, chronic ambulatory peritoneal dialysis, the use of a peritoneovenous (LeVeen) shunt, and fibrothecomatous proliferations of the ovary (typically, luteinized thecoma) (Fig. 15.13).[32] With respect to the last association, the intraoperative appearance may mimic that of a malignant ovarian tumor with peritoneal spread, and the microscopic appearance of the peritoneal process in several of the cases was initially misinterpreted as metastatic thecoma (Fig. 15.13). The etiology of the sclerosing peritonitis in these cases is unknown.

Sclerosing mesenteritis (retractile mesenteritis, mesenteric panniculitis, mesenteric lipodystrophy) is an idiopathic disorder characterized by varying degrees of fat necrosis, chronic inflammation, and fibrosis, usually involving the mesentery of the small bowel. In the largest study,[33] the patients ranged in age from 23 to 87 (mean, 60) years; the most common clinical manifestations were abdominal pain or an abdominal mass. Gross examination of the mesentery most commonly revealed a solitary mass; less commonly there are multiple masses or diffuse mesenteric thickening. The differential diagnosis includes a variety of benign lesions as well as sarcoma.[33] Mesenteric fibromatosis (intraabdominal desmoid tumor), in contrast to sclerosing mesenteritis, infiltrates the bowel wall, has a fascicular architecture, and is devoid of inflammation and fat necrosis. Retroperitoneal fibrosis can histologically mimic sclerosing mesenteritis, and indeed may be a related disorder, but the two processes are usually distinguishable by their different clinical presentation, location, and intraoperative appearance. Inflammatory pseudotumor (plasma cell granuloma), unlike sclerosing mesenteritis, is characterized by an intense plasma cellular infiltrate as well as leukocytosis, an elevated erythrocyte sedimentation rate, and anemia. Sarcomas (principally liposarcoma) involving the mesentery will almost always exhibit more cellularity, stromal or adipocytic nuclear atypia, and mitotic activity than are present in sclerosing mesenteritis.

In occasional cases, reactive fibrous lesions of the peritoneum may be difficult to differentiate from a desmoplastic mesothelioma, particularly in a small biopsy specimen. Features favoring a diagnosis of mesothelioma include nuclear atypia, necrosis, the presence of organized patterns of collagen deposition (fascicular, storiform), and infiltration of adjacent tissues.[34]

Calcifying fibrous (pseudo) tumor

This is a rare lesion that is typically an incidental finding involving the visceral peritoneum of the small bowel and stomach in adults.[35–37] Rare cases have been familial.[36] The process, which can be misinterpreted intraoperatively as metastatic carcinoma, forms a well-circumscribed solid mass, usually less than 10 cm in diameter that may have a gritty sectioned surface. Histologic examination reveals dense hyalinized collagen, often in concentric whorls, usually sparsely to occasionally cellular areas of benign-appearing fibroblasts, as well as lymphocytes, plasma cells (that may form perivascular aggregates), and psammoma bodies. The relationship of these lesions (which had been presumed to be reactive) to similarly named masses arising in soft tissue, which appear to be neoplastic (see Ch. 24), is uncertain, but increasing evidence suggests that all of these tumors may be potentially recurrent.[37]

Splenosis

Splenosis, or the implantation of splenic tissue, is usually discovered incidentally during an abdominal operation performed months to years after splenectomy for traumatic splenic rupture.[38,39] Several to numerous red-blue, peritoneal nodules, from barely visible to 7 cm in diameter, are scattered throughout the abdominal, and in some cases the pelvic, cavities (Fig. 15.14). The intraoperative appearance may resemble peritoneal involvement by endometriosis, benign or malignant vascular tumors, or metastatic cancer.

"Melanosis"

Seven cases of brownish pigmentation of the peritoneum (peritoneal "melanosis") have been associated with ovarian dermoid cysts; in two cases, there had been preoperative

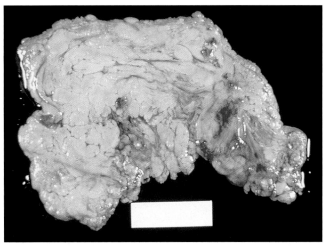

Fig. 15.14 • Splenosis of omentum.

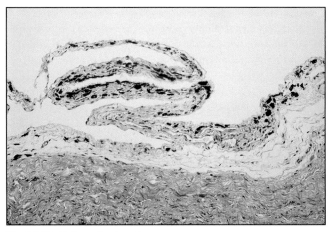

Fig. 15.15 • Peritoneal melanosis.

rupture of the cysts.[40] Focal or diffuse, tan to black, peritoneal staining or pigmented tumor-like nodules are encountered within the pelvis and in the omentum at laparotomy. Some locules within the dermoid cysts have had pigmentation of their contents and lining. On microscopic examination, the ovarian and peritoneal lesions consist of pigment-laden histiocytes within a fibrous stroma (Fig. 15.15). In at least half of the reported cases, gastric mucosa was prominent within the dermoid cyst, sometimes associated with ulceration, necrosis, and hemorrhage. One study found that the pigment was neither melanin nor hemosiderin, but contained a high concentration of iron; a relation to peptic ulceration and hemorrhage within the dermoid cyst was suggested.[40] Distinction of peritoneal "melanosis" from metastatic malignant melanoma is straightforward because of the bland nuclear features and mitotic inactivity of the pigmented histiocytes.

Infarcted appendix epiploica

Torsion and infarction of appendices epiploicae, in some cases with subsequent calcification, can result in a hard tumor-like mass that may be found attached or loose within the peritoneal cavity.[41,42] When examined microscopically, these structures are typically composed of layers of hyalinized fibrous tissue surrounding a central necrotic and calcified zone of infarcted adipose tissue (Fig. 15.16).

Cartilaginous nodules

Two cases of cartilaginous differentiation of the peritoneum have been reported, both in postmenopausal women.[43] The heterotopic peritoneal lesions were incidental intraoperative findings. In one case, multiple nodules ranged up to 7 mm in maximal dimension, whereas in the other case there was a single 2 cm nodule. In both cases the nodules consisted of mature hyaline cartilage surrounded by fibrous tissue. The authors speculated that the nodules could represent metaplastic lesions of the secondary müllerian system or chondromas derived from submesothelial tissues.

Mesothelial neoplasms

Solitary fibrous tumor

Solitary (or localized) fibrous tumors of the type that more frequently involve the pleura (see Ch. 5) or soft tissue (see Ch. 24) are rare in the peritoneal cavity (Fig. 15.17).[44–46] Although these tumors have been referred to as "fibrous mesotheliomas," they are now considered to be derived from submesothelial fibroblasts. Their clinical and pathologic features, including strong immunoreactivity for vimentin and CD34 and negativity for cytokeratin, are similar to those encountered in the pleura and other sites and help distinguish these tumors from desmoplastic mesotheliomas.[44–48] Occasional otherwise typical tumors with foci of high cellularity, marked nuclear pleomorphism, or a high mitotic rate have been interpreted as malignant.[47,48]

Adenomatoid tumor

This benign tumor of mesothelial origin rarely arises from extragenital peritoneum, such as the omentum[49] or mesentery,[50] but is more commonly encountered within the male and female genital tracts, and is discussed in Chapters 13 and 14.

Well-differentiated papillary mesothelioma

Well-differentiated papillary mesotheliomas (WDPMs) of the peritoneum are uncommon; approximately 50 cases have

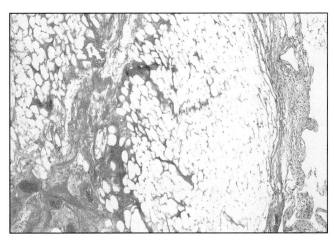

Fig. 15.16 • Infarcted appendix epiploica.

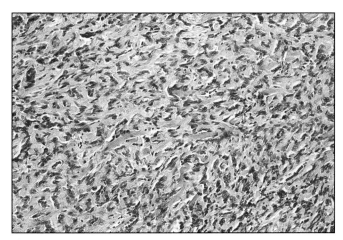

Fig. 15.17 • Solitary fibrous tumor ("fibrous mesothelioma") of peritoneum.

been reported in detail,[51–56] including a series of 22 cases.[52] Approximately 75% of the tumors have occurred in females, who are usually of reproductive age, but occasionally, post-menopausal.[51,52] WDPMs are usually an incidental finding at laparotomy but rare tumors have been associated with abdominal pain or ascites. The presence of symptoms and/or ascites, however, is much more common in malignant mesothelioma.[54] Occasional patients have a history of asbestos exposure.[55]

At laparotomy, and on gross examination, WDPMs can be solitary or multiple, and take the form of gray to white, firm, papillary or nodular lesions usually less than 2 cm in diameter. The omental and pelvic peritoneum is typically involved;[52,54] several tumors have arisen from the gastric, intestinal, or mesenteric peritoneum.[51]

On microscopic examination, fibrous papillae are covered by a single layer of flattened to cuboidal mesothelial cells (Figs 15.18 and 15.19) that may contain occasional basal vacuoles; the nuclear features are benign and mitotic figures are sparse or absent. Other patterns encountered less commonly include tubulopapillary (Fig. 15.18), branching cords, and solid sheets. The stroma of some tumors is extensively fibrotic or occasionally myxoid; psammoma bodies are encountered in occasional cases.

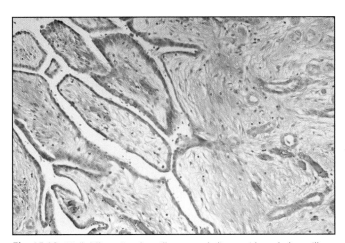

Fig. 15.18 • Well-differentiated papillary mesothelioma with a tubulopapillary pattern.

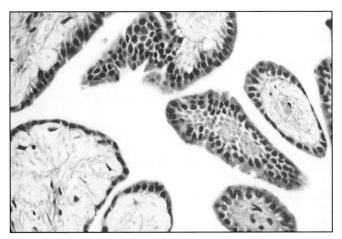

Fig. 15.19 • Well-differentiated papillary mesothelioma.

Solitary WDPMs are clinically benign in most, if not all, cases, although rarely the tumors may persist for decades.[52] When multiple lesions are present, the clinical course is less certain. Each lesion should be sampled for microscopic examination to exclude malignant mesothelioma, as Goldblum & Hart[54] found that all of their peritoneal mesotheliomas with involvement of more than one site had, at least focally, malignant histologic features. Only those lesions that were localized and had uniformly benign histologic features had a predictably benign clinical course. The series of WDPMs reported by Butnor et al.[55] included a patient with a multifocal WDPM who died of disease after 3 years of follow-up, although it was not clear how thoroughly the tumor had been sampled to exclude a malignant component.

Malignant mesothelioma

Clinical features

Peritoneal malignant mesotheliomas (PMMs) are much less common than their pleural counterparts (see Ch. 5), accounting for only 10–20% of all malignant mesotheliomas.[54,57–64] PMMs are particularly uncommon in women, a population in whom most malignant papillary peritoneal neoplasms are extraovarian papillary serous carcinomas (see section on tumors and tumor-like lesions of the secondary müllerian system, below).

The male:female ratio is approximately 2:1. The patients are usually middle-aged or elderly, but occasional cases of PMM occur in young adults or children.[65–69] Patients usually present with non-specific manifestations, most commonly abdominal discomfort and distension, digestive disturbances, and weight loss. Rare patients have had an elevated serum level of CA125.[70] Ascites is present in the majority of cases, and cytologic examination of the ascitic fluid is occasionally diagnostic.[61] Diagnosis, however, usually requires laparotomy, or laparoscopy and biopsy. PMMs rarely present within a hernia or hydrocele sac, as a localized retroperitoneal, hepatic, umbilical, intestinal, pelvic, or ovarian tumor,[61,64,71–74] or as cervical or inguinal lymphadenopathy.[75] Some cases have presented as an inflammatory mass mimicking appendicitis or cholecystitis.[76]

The majority of males with PMMs reported in the literature have had a history of asbestos exposure, although such a history is rare in females.[54,62–64] Genetic factors, irradiation, chronic inflammation, exposure to organic chemicals, and non-asbestos mineral fibers may also play an etiologic role in some cases.[77–79] In most series, in which most or all of the patients have been male, the survival has usually been less than 2 years after diagnosis, although there have been occasional long-term survivors.[60,61,80,81] In contrast, Kerrigan et al.,[62] in a study of PMMs confined to women, found that 40% of the patients survived 4 years or longer – some for over a decade. Younger patients with minimal or no residual disease after surgery show improved survival.[82]

Pathologic features

The visceral and parietal peritoneum is diffusely thickened or extensively studded by nodules and plaques (Fig. 15.20), and the viscera are often encased (and may be invaded) by tumor,

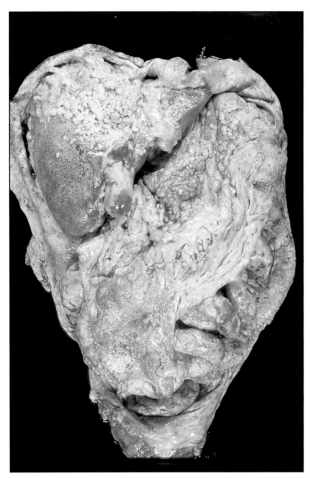

Fig. 15.20 • Diffuse malignant mesothelioma of peritoneum.

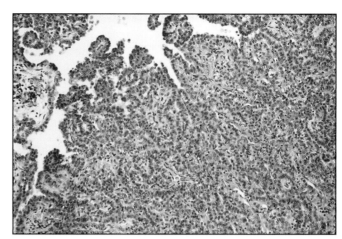

Fig. 15.21 • Diffuse malignant mesothelioma.

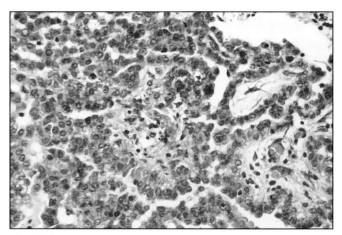

Fig. 15.22 • Diffuse malignant mesothelioma.

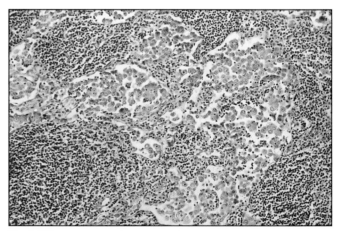

Fig. 15.23 • Metastatic malignant mesothelioma in an abdominal lymph node.

although invasion of viscera and metastases to lymph nodes, liver, lungs, and pleura is less frequent than in carcinomas with comparable degrees of peritoneal involvement. Significant invasion and metastatic involvement of abdominal organs, however, may be encountered at autopsy.

The microscopic features (Figs 15.21–15.23) are generally similar to those of pleural mesotheliomas (see Ch. 5), except for a notably lower frequency of sarcomatoid and biphasic tumors. Occasional sarcomatoid and biphasic peritoneal PMMs do occur, and one biphasic tumor in which the sarcomatous component contained rhabdoid cells has been reported.[74] A prominent inflammatory response occurs in occasional tumors, including dense lymphocytic infiltrates[69] and numerous foamy, lipid-rich histiocytes.[83] Psammoma bodies may occur but are more common and often more numerous in serous carcinomas. The immunohistochemical (see section on differential diagnosis, below) and ultrastructural features of PMMs do not differ significantly from those of their pleural counterparts.

Rare PMMs are characterized by an exclusively sheet-like pattern composed of polygonal cells with abundant eosinophilic cytoplasm (Fig. 15.24).[66–68] The designation "deciduoid mesothelioma" has been applied to such tumors to emphasize their resemblance to ectopic decidua (see section on tumors and tumor-like lesions of the secondary müllerian system, below). Although first thought to be more common in young females, there is only a slight female predominance and the age range is wide.[68] These tumors are usually rapidly fatal. A variety of features, including prominent eosinophilic nucleoli, mitotic activity, and immunohistochemical and ultrastructural findings typical for mesothelioma (see below), facilitate the diagnosis.

Differential diagnosis

The differential diagnosis of DMM with mesothelial hyperplasia is discussed elsewhere (see section on mesothelial

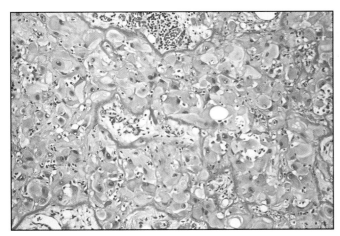

Fig. 15.24 • "Deciduoid" malignant mesothelioma.

hyperplasia, above). WDPMs (discussed above), in contrast to PMMs, are characterized by uniformly benign histologic features, although PMMs may be focally well differentiated with areas resembling WDPM.[54] PMMs must also be distinguished from malignant vascular tumors of serous membranes (see p. 891 and Ch. 5) and adenocarcinomas with diffuse peritoneal involvement, including metastatic adenocarcinomas and, in women, adenocarcinomas of peritoneal origin (see section on tumors and tumor-like lesions of the secondary müllerian system, below). The diagnosis of PMM should always be considered in tumors with a tubulopapillary pattern and lesional cells that are polygonal with a moderate amount of eosinophilic cytoplasm. In contrast, the presence of columnar cells favors a diagnosis of adenocarcinoma. Most primary peritoneal adenocarcinomas are papillary serous carcinomas that are indistinguishable from those arising in the ovary, including, in contrast to PMMs, the usual presence of cells with high-grade or even bizarre nuclear features and numerous psammoma bodies. Similar features facilitate the distinction of rare primary peritoneal malignant mixed mesodermal tumors from rare biphasic PMMs.

Histochemical, immunohistochemical, and ultrastructural methods can facilitate the differential diagnosis of PMM with adenocarcinoma.[84–90] In contrast to adenocarcinomas, PMMs (like their pleural counterparts) are characterized by the usual absence of neutral mucins and the presence of acid mucin (predominantly hyaluronic acid), appreciable as alcian blue-positive, diastase periodic acid–Schiff (D-PAS)-negative, hyaluronidase-sensitive material within cytoplasmic vacuoles. Rarely, however, the hyaluronic acid may leach into the formalin, resulting in false-negative staining, or there is intra- or extracellular D-PAS-positivity that is reduced by hyaluronidase predigestion. Most malignant mesotheliomas, including PMMs, are immunoreactive for cytokeratin 5/6 and calretinin and lack reactivity for a variety of "epithelial" antigens, the most useful of which are carcinoembryonic antigen (CEA), B72.3, Leu-M1, Ber-EP4, S-100, and placental alkaline phosphatase (PLAP). In the differential diagnosis between PMMs and serous adenocarcinomas, immunoreactivity for Ber-EP4, B72.3, Leu-M1 (CD15), MOC-31, and CA19-9 favors serous carcinoma, whereas immunoreactivity for thrombomodulin, D2-40 (or podoplanin) and calretinin favors PMM.[89,90] No single immunohistochemical stain, however, is

diagnostic in the separation of PMM from adenocarcinoma, and the results of a panel of antibodies should be interpreted along with the hematoxylin and eosin and mucin stains.

Miscellaneous primary tumors

Intra-abdominal desmoplastic small round cell tumor

Clinical features

The desmoplastic small round cell tumor (DSRCT) is of uncertain histogenesis.[91–105] Its predilection for serosal involvement (including rare examples involving the pleura) suggests the possibility of a primitive tumor of mesothelial origin,[91] although their exceptional occurrence at non-serosal locations suggests a non-mesothelial origin in at least some cases. Unique to DSRCTs is the fusion of the Ewing's sarcoma (*EWS*) gene on chromosome 22 and the Wilms tumor gene (*WT1*) on chromosome 11, resulting from the chromosomal translocation t(11;22)(p13;q12).[94,96,101]

The DSRCT is much more common in males (M:F ratio 4:1) and typically occurs in adolescents and young adults (mean age of 22 years in the largest series). Abdominal distension, pain, and a palpable abdominal, pelvic, or scrotal mass, sometimes in association with ascites, are the usual clinical manifestations. Some patients have had an elevated serum level of neuron-specific enolase.[95] At laparotomy, a variably sized but usually large, intra-abdominal mass associated with numerous smaller peritoneal "implants" may involve any portion of the peritoneal cavity or, occasionally, the retroperitoneum; rare tumors have been pleurally based.[101] In females, the tumor is frequently confined to the pelvis, and in such cases there may be prominent ovarian involvement, potentially mimicking a primary ovarian tumor.[92] In males, the paratesticular region may be involved.[99]

DSRCTs are highly aggressive, with over 90% of patients dying from tumor progression within just a few years. Typically, an initial partial response to tumor debulking and chemotherapy is followed by uncontrollable tumor relapse. Even in advanced stages, most of the tumor remains within the peritoneal cavity; extra-abdominal metastases, however, occur in occasional patients and rare cases may present primarily with lymph node metastasis.

Pathologic features

On gross examination, the tumors may reach 40 cm in diameter. Their outer surface is smooth or bossellated and their sectioned surfaces are firm to hard and gray-white, with focal myxoid change and necrosis (Fig. 15.25). Direct invasion of intra-abdominal or pelvic viscera has occurred in occasional cases. On microscopic examination, tumor cells are arranged in well-defined basaloid nests and trabeculae of varying size and shape which are delimited by a cellular desmoplastic stroma (Figs 15.26 and 15.27). The relative proportions of the cellular and stromal components may vary considerably. Peripheral palisading in some of the nests is a common feature, and central necrosis with or without calcification may

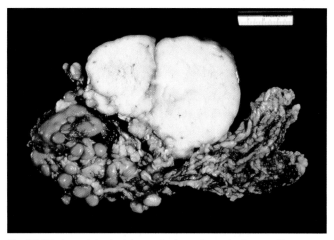

Fig. 15.25 • Intra-abdominal desmoplastic small round cell tumor. The sectioned surface of a fleshy white mass that involves the omentum is shown. A number of smaller satellite nodules of tumor are also seen.

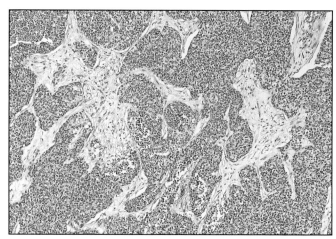

Fig. 15.26 • Intra-abdominal desmoplastic small round cell tumor.

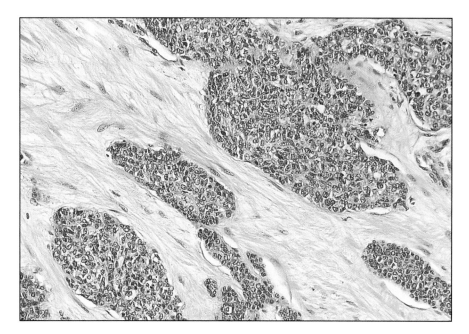

Fig. 15.27 • Intra-abdominal desmoplastic small round cell tumor.

be present in some of the larger islands. Rosette-like spaces have been encountered in occasional cases.[91,99] The tumor cells are uniform, with scanty cytoplasm, indistinct cell borders, and small to medium-sized, round to oval, hyperchromatic nuclei; nucleoli are usually indistinct. Mitotic figures and single necrotic cells are numerous. In many cases, some of the tumor cells are characterized by eosinophilic cytoplasmic "inclusions" and an eccentric nucleus, resulting in a rhabdoid appearance (Fig. 15.28). Invasion of vascular spaces, especially lymphatics, is common. The desmoplastic stroma consists of fibroblasts and myofibroblasts (without cytologic atypia) set in a collagenous matrix. Uncommon features[102] include tubular or glandular differentiation (sometimes with luminal mucin), papillae, vacuolated signet-ring-like cells, minor foci of pleomorphic tumor cells, larger cells with moderate amounts of cytoplasm, and only a scanty desmoplastic stroma.

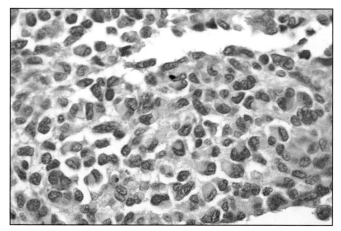

Fig. 15.28 • Intra-abdominal desmoplastic small round cell tumor. Note rhabdoid inclusions.

Special techniques indicate a multidirectional phenotype, including immunoreactivity for epithelial (low-molecular-weight cytokeratins (such as CAM 5.2), EMA), neural/neuroendocrine (NSE, Leu-7), and muscle (desmin) markers, as well as vimentin. Desmin and vimentin positivity is typically paranuclear and globular. Focal myoglobin immunoreactivity (of uncertain significance) was found in almost 30% of cases in one recent study.[105] Nuclear immunoreactivity for the C-terminal region of the Wilms tumor protein (WT1) is present in most cases.[104,105] There is variable reactivity for CD99. Ultrastructural examination typically reveals paranuclear cytoplasmic filaments of intermediate size, cell junctions of various types, and basal lamina surrounding the tumor nests. Microvillus-like structures projecting into spaces, polar cell processes, microtubules, lipid droplets, glycogen, and dense-core granules have also been encountered in occasional cases.[91] Detection of *EWS/WT1* gene fusion by reverse transcriptase-polymerase chain reaction is diagnostic and especially useful when the histologic features are not typical.

Malignant vascular tumors

Malignant vascular tumors of the peritoneum have been described recently, specifically two epithelioid hemangio-endotheliomas (EHE) and two epithelioid angiosarcomas (EA) that were diagnosed in male and female patients who were 34–51 years of age.[106,107] Such tumors appear distinct from angiosarcomas that arise in the mesentery or retro-peritoneum[108] and involve the peritoneum secondarily. The four tumors in the studies just cited above were fatal. They had diffuse sheet-like and nested patterns with variable degrees of vascular differentiation, principally in the form of cytoplasmic lumina. Features resulting in an initial impression of PMM in some of the tumors included a diffuse distribution, a tubulopapillary pattern, spindle cells (both reactive and neoplastic) creating a biphasic pattern, and immunoreactivity for vimentin and variable reactivity for cytokeratin. The correct diagnosis was facilitated by immunoreactivity of the tumor cells for at least two endothelial markers, a finding absent in a control group of PMMs.

Inflammatory myofibroblastic tumor

In 1986 Day et al. initially reported seven cases of abdominal "inflammatory pseudotumor,"[109] synonymously referred to as "plasma cell granuloma" or "inflammatory myofibroblastic tumor."[110] Subsequently, much larger series have been published[111,112] and the possibility that such examples might be better regarded as inflammatory fibrosarcoma was suggested.[109] These tumors are discussed more fully in Chapter 24. The abdominal lesions usually occur in the first two decades of life in patients who present with a mass, fever, growth failure or weight loss, hypochromic anemia, thrombocytosis, and polyclonal hypergammaglobulinemia.[109] A solid mesenteric mass is found at operation that on microscopic examination consists of myofibroblastic spindle cells, mature plasma cells, and small lymphocytes (Fig. 15.29). On follow-up, most patients have had an uneventful postoperative course, but perhaps 20–25% develop local recurrence and very rare cases behave in a truly malignant fashion.[113]

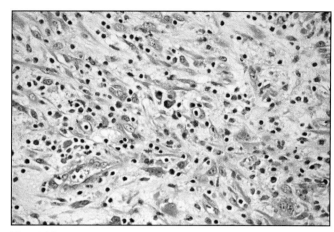

Fig. 15.29 • Intra-abdominal inflammatory myofibroblastic tumor.

Omental-mesenteric myxoid hamartoma

The term "omental-mesenteric myxoid hamartoma" was applied by Gonzalez-Crussi et al.[114] to a lesion occurring in infants characterized by multiple omental and mesenteric nodules composed of plump mesenchymal cells in a myxoid, vascularized stroma. Although a diagnosis of sarcoma was initially considered in some of the cases, the follow-up was uneventful. With the passage of time, it seems that these lesions fall within the spectrum of inflammatory myofibroblastic tumor (see above).

Metastatic tumors

Metastatic involvement of the peritoneum is usually due to seeding from a primary tumor arising within the abdomen or pelvis, most commonly the female genital system, especially the ovary (peritoneal involvement by ovarian tumors is discussed in Ch. 13), but also occasionally from the endometrium or fallopian tube. The differential diagnosis of serous carcinomas metastatic to the peritoneum from these sites includes primary peritoneal serous carcinomas (PSCs: see section on tumors and tumor-like lesions of the secondary müllerian system, below). Other tumors that can spread to the peritoneum are carcinomas of the breast (the metastases from which may appear many years after treatment of the primary tumor),[115,116] gastrointestinal tract (especially the colon and stomach), and the pancreas. The metastatic tumor in some of these cases may be a signet-ring carcinoma in which the tumor cells are widely scattered in a fibrous stroma (Figs 15.30 and 15.31). The sparseness of the signet-ring cells and their relatively bland nuclear features in some cases can result in a deceptively benign appearance.

Pseudomyxoma peritonei

Peritoneal involvement by a mucinous neoplasm may be accompanied by extensive collections of intra-abdominal mucus (Fig. 15.32), so-called "pseudomyxoma peritonei" (PP).[117–123a] The microscopic appearance of lesions designated PP in the literature has included: free mucin in the abdominal cavity (mucinous ascites); small or large deposits of mucin adherent to peritoneal surfaces, containing inflammatory and

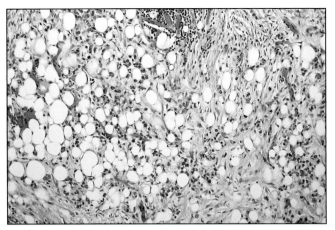

Fig. 15.30 • Metastatic gastric adenocarcinoma to omentum. The tumor cells have relatively uniform nuclei and at this magnification could be mistaken for inflammatory cells.

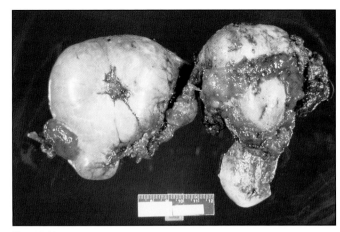

Fig. 15.32 • Pseudomyxoma peritonei. Mucinous material involves the serosa of an ovarian mucinous tumor and the uterus. (Courtesy of Dr. W. Dwayne Lawrence.)

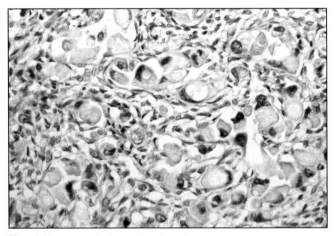

Fig. 15.31 • Metastatic signet-ring cell carcinoma to omentum.

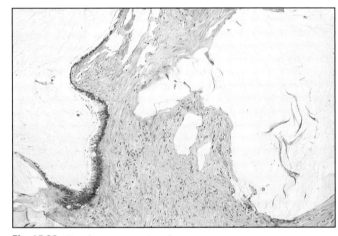

Fig. 15.33 • Pseudomyxoma peritonei.

mesothelial cells and sometimes organizing capillaries and fibroblasts, but usually lacking neoplastic epithelial cells; and pools of mucin, which may or may not contain neoplastic cells (Figs 15.27 and 15.28), surrounded by dense collagenous tissue (dissecting mucin) (Fig. 15.33). If neoplastic cells are present in PP, they are usually well-differentiated mucinous columnar cells of intestinal type (Fig. 15.33). There is currently no consensus on whether all or only some of these collections of intra-abdominal mucus warrant the designation of PP.

The primary tumor in the vast majority of cases of PP is a low-grade mucinous tumor of the appendix, which may be visible only microscopically. An appendectomy should thus be performed in all cases of PP and the entire appendix should be submitted for histologic examination if there is no grossly visible lesion. In this context both the appendiceal tumors and associated PP show consistent overexpression of MUC2.[124] Cases of PP not associated with an appendiceal tumor may be due to metastases from mucinous tumors elsewhere in the gastrointestinal and pancreaticobiliary tracts, from mucinous tumors of the ovary (especially those arising within an ovarian teratoma),[125,126] and rarely from mucinous tumors in other sites. In such cases, one or typically both ovaries may be replaced by low-grade mucinous cystic tumors that are also

considered metastatic from the appendiceal tumor. Acellular mucin dissecting through the ovarian stroma ("pseudomyxoma ovarii") is often also present.[117,118]

The term pseudomyxoma peritonei, which is a clinical and surgical designation, should not appear as a pathologic diagnosis in the pathology report. The report should contain:

• an appraisal of the tumors (appendiceal, ovarian, or other) as benign, borderline, or malignant, with a notation of the presence or absence of rupture
• assessment of the peritoneal lesions as mucinous ascites (free fluid in abdomen), organizing mucinous fluid, or mucin dissection with fibrosis
• a notation as to the presence or absence of neoplastic epithelial cells and whether they appear benign, borderline (atypical), or malignant. Cell-free peritoneal deposits in PP are associated with a better prognosis than deposits containing well-differentiated mucinous epithelium, whereas peritoneal deposits composed of obviously carcinomatous cells are associated with a much poorer prognosis and shorter survival than those composed of well-differentiated mucinous epithelium.[121,123,123a]

Tumors and tumor-like lesions of the secondary müllerian system

This section considers the variety of tumors and tumor-like lesions (excluding endometriosis and tumors arising from endometriosis [see Ch.13]) that share origin from the so-called secondary müllerian system, that is, the pelvic and lower abdominal mesothelium and the subjacent mesenchyme of females.[127–129] The müllerian potential of these tissues is consistent with their close embryonic relation to the müllerian ducts that arise by invagination of the coelomic epithelium. Secondary müllerian lesions include those containing serous, endometrioid, and mucinous epithelium, mimicking normal or neoplastic tubal, endometrial, and endocervical epithelium. The metaplastic potential of the pelvic peritoneum also includes possible differentiation into transitional (urothelial) and squamous epithelium. Proliferation of the subjacent mesenchyme may accompany the epithelial lesions or may give rise to a variety of purely mesenchymal lesions composed of endometrial stromal-type cells, decidua, or smooth muscle.

Peritoneal serous lesions

A variety of serous lesions may involve the peritoneal surfaces (and in some cases the retroperitoneal lymph nodes) with minimal or absent ovarian involvement, a pattern that suggests multifocal origin from the peritoneum. Not considered here are serous neoplasms that take the form of localized unilocular cystic masses within the broad ligament or retroperitoneum.

Endosalpingiosis

Endosalpingiosis is defined as the presence of glands lined by benign tubal-type epithelium involving the peritoneum or pelvic or para-aortic lymph nodes.[130–140] A secondary müllerian origin is favored by most investigators, but the association of endosalpingiosis with tubal damage (chronic salpingitis, hydrosalpinx, prior tubal pregnancies, salpingitis isthmica nodosa, tubal lavage) implicates implantation of tubal epithelium as another histogenetic mechanism. Endosalpingiosis is a benign lesion with an uneventful clinical course, but it is commonly associated with serous tumors of the ovary or peritoneum, which are often of borderline type.[141,142]

Endosalpingiosis occurs almost exclusively in females, typically during the reproductive era, although occasional patients are postmenopausal. This age distribution and the presence of estrogen receptors within endosalpingiotic epithelium suggest that the process is estrogen-dependent. As the lesion is usually an incidental microscopic finding, its reported frequency varies with the extent of histologic sampling. Zinsser & Wheeler,[130] for example, found endosalpingiotic glands in 12.5% of omenta examined retrospectively, but this figure doubled when omenta were examined more thoroughly in a prospective study. Similarly, nodal involvement has varied from 2% to 41% of patients undergoing lymphadenectomy.[134–137] In one study, in which six slides were taken from each lymph node in patients undergoing lymphadenectomy for pelvic cancer, inclusions were found in at least one node in 15.4% of cases.[137] Uncommon clinical manifestations of endosalpingiosis have included peritoneal cystic masses;[143] lymphadenopathy;

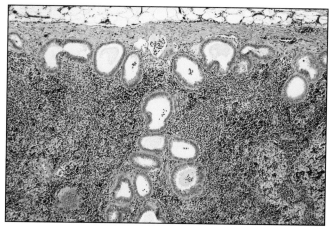

Fig. 15.34 • Endosalpingiosis involving intra-abdominal lymph node. Note the intracapsular location of most of the glands.

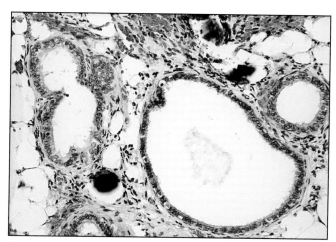

Fig. 15.35 • Endosalpingiosis of omentum. Note psammoma bodies.

uterine enlargement;[143] an inguinal mass (which represented endosalpingiosis and a serous borderline tumor likely arising from it);[144] radiologically visible pelvic calcifications; and psammoma bodies within cul-de-sac fluid, peritoneal washings,[132] or cervical Papanicolaou smears.

On microscopic examination, endosalpingiotic glands typically lie within the submesothelial stroma or within the capsule or superficial cortical parenchyma of lymph nodes (Figs 15.34 and 15.35). In occasional cases, the glands extend more deeply, involving, for example, the wall of the bowel,[140] uterus,[143] or urinary bladder,[145] or the medullary region of lymph nodes.[134] Endosalpingiotic glands, which may be cystic and contain occasional intraluminal stromal papillae, are usually lined by a single layer of ciliated columnar cells or an admixture of cell types (ciliated cells, non-ciliated secretory cells, peg cells) resembling those lining the fallopian tube (Fig. 15.36). The cells usually have bland nuclear features and lack mitotic activity. Psammoma bodies are frequently present within the lumina or in the adjacent stroma (Fig. 15.35), and occasionally are numerous. Endosalpingiosis may be admixed with other benign müllerian glands (so-called müllerianosis)[145,146] or contain metaplastic squamous epithelium.[138]

The term atypical endosalpingiosis has been applied to endosalpingiotic lesions in which there is cellular stratification, including cellular buds, cribriform patterns, and varying degrees of cellular atypia, occurring in the absence of an ovarian serous

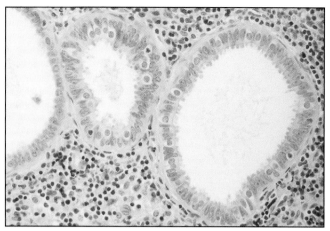

Fig. 15.36 • Endosalpingiosis of lymph node. Note admixture of cell types, including ciliated cells.

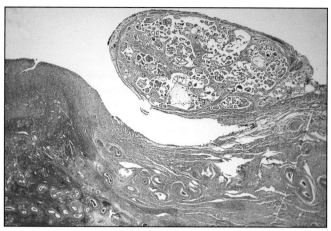

Fig. 15.38 • Peritoneal serous borderline tumor. A nodule of tumor on the mesovarium is adjacent to the ovary (extreme left), which was unremarkable.

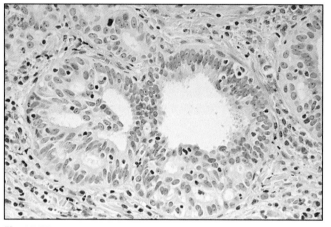

Fig. 15.37 • Atypical endosalpingiosis of lymph node. Note cellular stratification and luminal bridges. The cells, however, have bland nuclear features.

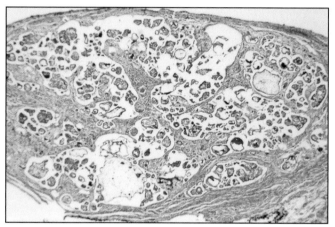

Fig. 15.39 • Peritoneal serous borderline tumor.

tumor of borderline malignancy (Fig. 15.37).[141] Atypical endosalpingiosis has rarely abutted, and in such cases has likely been the origin of, intranodal serous neoplasms.[147] In other cases, intranodal endosalpingiosis may be associated with an ovarian serous borderline tumor, and it has been suggested that, in some such cases, the former represents metastatic serous borderline tumor that has undergone maturation.[142] Atypical endosalpingiosis should be distinguished on microscopic examination from intranodal and peritoneal serous borderline tumors (see below), but there are no uniformly accepted criteria for this distinction. Bell & Scully use the term serous borderline tumor if the "lesions composed of tubal-type epithelium exhibit papillarity, tufting, or detachment of cell clusters ... even when they arise on a background of endosalpingiosis."[141,148] Involvement of the lymph node capsule (rather than the sinusoids), an association of the atypical glands with typical endosalpingiotic glands, and bland nuclear features facilitate distinction of endosalpingiosis and atypical endosalpingiosis from metastatic adenocarcinoma.

Peritoneal serous tumors of borderline malignancy (PSBT)

PSBTs are histologically identical to the non-invasive peritoneal implants of ovarian serous borderline tumors

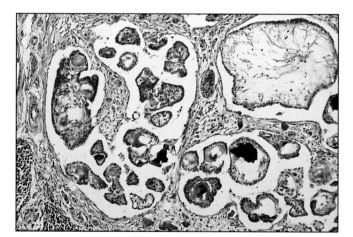

Fig. 15.40 • Peritoneal serous borderline tumor.

(Figs 15.38–15.40) and are diagnosed only when the ovaries are uninvolved, have only minimal surface involvement by similar tumor, or harbor a serous cystadenoma.[148,149] Coexistent endosalpingiosis is found in most cases. The lesions occur in young adult women who present with abdominal pain or infertility; in some cases, the peritoneal lesions are an incidental finding at laparotomy. The typical intraoperative findings are adhesions or granularity of the peritoneal surfaces; masses are only rarely encountered. In most cases, only the pelvic peritoneum is involved, but occasionally the upper abdominal peritoneum is also affected.

Among the 39 patients on whom follow-up data were available,[148,149] four patients were well after resection of persistent or recurrent borderline tumor, one developed an invasive low-grade serous carcinoma of the peritoneum, and one died of disseminated serous tumor; the remaining patients had an uneventful follow-up. These data indicate that most PSBTs have a good prognosis, similar to that of patients with comparable ovarian lesions with non-invasive implants, even when the patients are treated conservatively in order to preserve fertility.

High-grade peritoneal serous carcinomas

Peritoneal serous carcinomas have a clinical presentation similar to that of patients with stage III ovarian carcinoma.[84,150–164] Some peritoneal serous carcinomas have occurred in women who have undergone a prior prophylactic oophorectomy for familial ovarian cancer[150] and some have occurred in patients with documented *BRCA-1* mutations.[161,165] In the latter group, the tumors show a distinctively higher incidence of *p53* mutations when compared to sporadic cases.[162] At operation, the presence of peritoneal carcinomatosis and ovaries of normal size and shape can suggest the diagnosis of diffuse malignant mesothelioma or carcinomatosis from an occult primary tumor. In at least some cases, inspection of the ovaries reveals varying degrees of involvement of their surfaces (Fig. 15.41) as part of multifocal peritoneal involvement by the peritoneal serous carcinoma. These tumors, which are usually high-grade, resemble typical ovarian serous carcinomas (Figs 15.42 and 15.43), including the frequent presence of psammoma bodies. In most studies, the behavior of peritoneal serous carcinomas has been similar to or worse than that of stage III ovarian serous carcinomas when matched for stage, grade, and volume of residual tumor.

Low-grade peritoneal serous carcinomas, including psammocarcinomas

Rare peritoneal serous carcinomas are characterized by low-grade nuclei resembling those seen in serous borderline tumors (see above) but, in contrast to the latter, visceral and lymphovascular invasion is present.[166] A subset of low-grade peritoneal serous carcinomas are the peritoneal psammo-carcinomas,[166–168] which are characterized by psammoma bodies in at least 75% of the papillae or nests (Figs 15.44–15.46). Low-grade peritoneal serous carcinomas are, like serous borderline

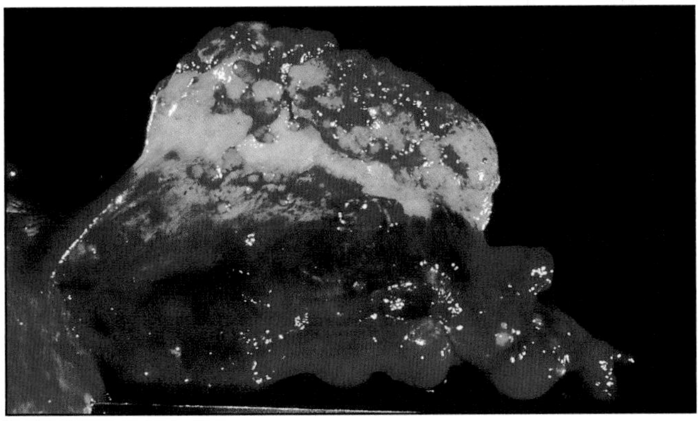

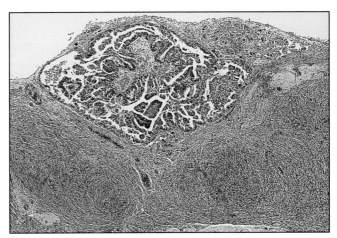

Fig. 15.42 • Peritoneal serous carcinoma involving ovary. Most of the tumor was extraovarian and the ovarian involvement is confined to the surface of the ovary.

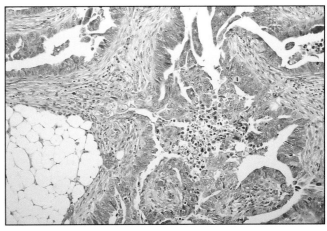

Fig. 15.43 • Serous surface papillary carcinoma involving omentum.

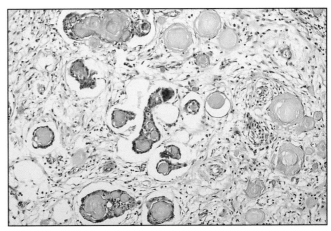

Fig. 15.44 • Peritoneal psammocarcinoma.

Fig. 15.41 • Peritoneal serous carcinoma involving serosa of ovary and fallopian tube. The tumor was widespread with bulky omental disease. Note small excrescences on serosa of ovary and fallopian tube.

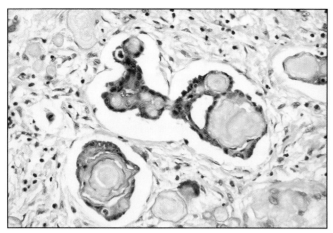

Fig. 15.45 • Peritoneal psammocarcinoma.

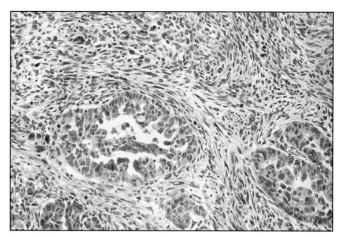

Fig. 15.47 • Peritoneal malignant müllerian mixed tumor (carcinosarcoma). The ovaries and uterus in this patient were unremarkable.

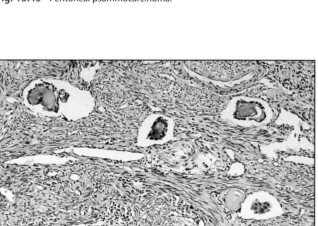

Fig. 15.46 • Peritoneal psammocarcinoma involving myometrial lymphatics.

tumors, usually indolent tumors with a good prognosis, although occasional tumors recur, persist, or are fatal. The microscopic features of serous borderline tumors and low-grade peritoneal serous carcinomas overlap, and adequate sampling is therefore required for their correct diagnosis.

Peritoneal endometrioid tumors

A variety of endometrioid neoplasms have been encountered in the pelvis or retroperitoneum in women with no evidence of similar tumor involving their ovaries or uterus, and no evidence of endometriosis. Although it is possible that some of these tumors arose from, and then obliterated, a focus of endometriosis, it is likely that others have arisen directly from the mesothelium or submesothelial stroma. These tumors have included examples of endometrioid cystadenofibroma[169] and cystadenocarcinoma,[170] endometrioid stromal sarcoma (ESS),[171] homologous and heterologous types of malignant mesodermal mixed tumor (Fig. 15.47),[172–174] and mesodermal adenosarcoma.[175,176] These tumors generally resemble, both clinically and pathologically, their counterparts in the uterine corpus and ovary. Primary extrauterine ESSs, however, behave more like high-stage, rather than low-stage, primary uterine ESSs.[171]

Peritoneal mucinous lesions

Benign glands of endocervical type involving the peritoneum ("endocervicosis") are rare, but examples involving the posterior uterine serosa and cul de sac have been documented;[127] similar benign glands have been found in abdominopelvic lymph nodes.[177] In one such case, some of the intranodal mucinous epithelium was papillary, and the intranodal lesion was associated with mucinous metaplasia of the endometrium and bilateral mucinous borderline tumors of the ovary.[177] Endocervicosis may also occur as a tumor-like mass within the posterior wall or posterior dome of the urinary bladder,[178,179] the outer wall of the uterine cervix,[180] the apex of the vagina,[181] and within the wall of the bowel.[182] In such cases, the infiltrative pattern of the glands within smooth muscle, mild focal epithelial atypia, and a reactive periglandular stroma, alone or in combination, may suggest a minimal-deviation adenocarcinoma. The presence of a mixture of benign müllerian-type glands (endosalpingiotic, endometrioid so-called "mullerianosis,"[145,146]), endometriotic stroma,[178] or both, can facilitate the correct diagnosis.

Mucinous neoplasms similar to those of ovarian origin have been described in extraovarian sites, usually the mesentery and retroperitoneum; a single case has been described in the inguinal region.[183–187] These tumors typically form large cystic masses (Fig. 15.48) that microscopically have resembled ovarian mucinous cystadenomas, borderline tumors (Fig. 15.49), or cystadenocarcinomas. Rare tumors have contained mural nodules of anaplastic tumor.[187] Although the behavior of these tumors generally has not differed from their ovarian counterparts (see Ch. 13), one otherwise typical borderline tumor metastasized 4 years after its removal.[183]

Other peritoneal epithelial lesions

Walthard nests of transitional (urothelial) epithelium are commonly present on the pelvic peritoneum in women of all ages, typically involving the serosal surfaces of the fallopian tubes, mesosalpinx, and mesovarium (Fig. 15.50).[188–190] Although Walthard nests may occasionally be composed of cells with a squamoid appearance, true squamous metaplasia of the peritoneum is very rare.[191] Rare examples of extraovarian

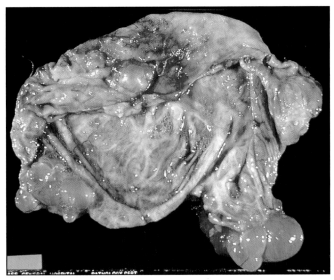

Fig. 15.48 • Extraovarian (retroperitoneal) mucinous cystadenoma. The ovaries were unremarkable in this patient.

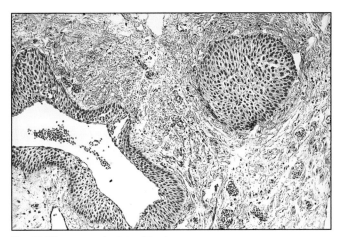

Fig. 15.50 • Cystic and solid Walthard nests.

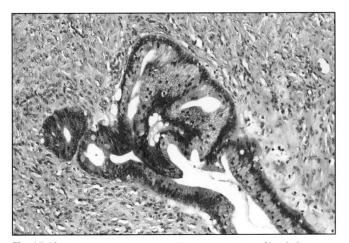

Fig. 15.49 • Extraovarian (retroperitoneal) mucinous tumor of borderline malignancy.

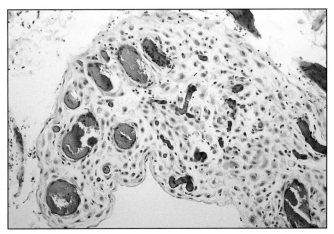

Fig. 15.51 • Ectopic decidua in a periovarian adhesion. Note numerous small blood vessels.

Brenner tumor have been reported in women, usually in the broad ligament or, rarely, in the uterus.[192] An origin from the pelvic peritoneum, a derivation similar to that postulated for most ovarian Brenner tumors, has generally been favored.

Almost all extragenital clear cell carcinomas of müllerian type encountered in the pelvis have arisen within foci of endometriosis and are not considered further here. In addition, two clear cell carcinomas apparently not associated with endometriosis and of probable peritoneal origin have been encountered. One was a localized mass within the sigmoid mesocolon and the other diffusely involved the peritoneum.[193,194]

Ectopic decidua

In pregnant women, ectopic decidua is a common finding within the submesothelial stroma of the pelvic peritoneum and omentum and, less commonly, within the superficial cortex of abdominopelvic lymph nodes.[135,138,195–198] The ectopic decidua is typically an incidental microscopic finding, but florid peritoneal lesions may be visible at the time of cesarean section or postpartum tubal ligation as multiple, gray to white,

focally hemorrhagic nodules or plaques studding the peritoneal surfaces and simulating a malignant tumor. Several cases have been associated with massive, occasionally fatal, hemoperitoneum during the third trimester, labor, or the puerperium. One florid case of peritoneal decidual reaction was associated with obstruction of labor.[199] Ectopic decidua usually involutes by the sixth postpartum week.

On microscopic examination, the ectopic decidual cells are disposed individually or arranged in nodules or plaques and typically resemble eutopic decidua (Figs 15.51–15.53). Smooth muscle cells, probably derived from submesothelial myofibroblasts, may be admixed. The decidual foci are often vascular (Fig. 15.51) and may contain a sprinkling of lymphocytes. Focal hemorrhagic necrosis and varying degrees of nuclear pleomorphism and hyperchromasia of the decidual cells may rarely suggest a malignant tumor, but the bland appearance of most of the cells and an absence of mitotic figures point to the correct diagnosis. It should be noted, however, that occasionally ectopic decidua and metastatic squamous cell carcinoma can involve the same lymph node.[197] Ectopic decidual cells, like their eutopic counterparts, occasionally contain an eccentric nucleus and cytoplasmic

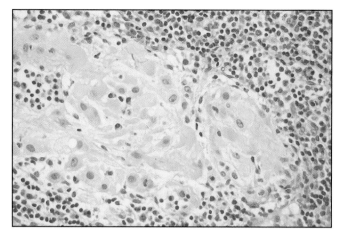

Fig. 15.52 • Ectopic decidua in a pelvic lymph node.

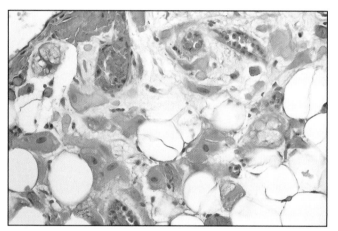

Fig. 15.53 • Ectopic decidua in omentum. Some of the cells have intracytoplasmic vacuoles containing basophilic mucin.

vacuoles with basophilic mucin (Fig. 15.53). In such cases, some of the cells can resemble the signet-ring cells of a carcinoma but, in contrast to the latter, special stains show the presence of only acidic mucin within the vacuoles.

Peritoneal leiomyomatosis

Peritoneal leiomyomatosis (synonyms: disseminated peritoneal leiomyomatosis, leiomyomatosis peritonealis disseminata) is characterized by the presence of multiple peritoneal nodules composed predominantly or exclusively of benign-appearing smooth muscle cells.[200–204] Approximately 60 examples of this disorder have been reported, mostly in women of reproductive age (mean, 37 years), but occasionally in postmenopausal patients. Forty percent of the reported cases have occurred in black women. The patients fall into three groups: (1) pregnant or puerperal women (43%); (2) oral contraceptive users (27%); and (3) women in neither of those categories (30%); a single case has been associated with a granulosa cell tumor. In pregnant women, the disorder is usually an incidental finding during the course of a cesarean section or postpartum tubal ligation. Symptoms in non-pregnant women and in some symptomatic pregnant women are usually related to the coexistence of uterine leiomyomas; in other cases, a diagnostic laparotomy was prompted by palpation of pelvic nodules.

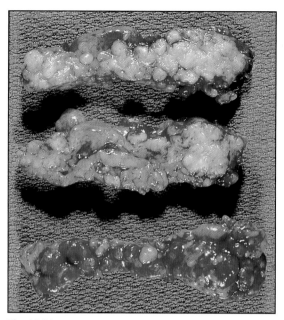

Fig. 15.54 • Peritoneal leiomyomatosis involving omentum, sectioned surface. Note multiple nodules.

Several to innumerable, firm, discrete, solid, round nodules are scattered over the parietal pelvic peritoneum and omentum, producing a matted nodularity or an ill-defined sheet-like thickening that can simulate metastatic tumor (Fig. 15.54). The nodules range in size from microscopic to 10 cm in diameter, although most are less than 0.5 cm. Similar nodules also frequently involve the serosa of the uterus, ovary, bowel, and mesentery; less commonly, the upper abdominal peritoneum is affected. One case with simultaneous pelvic lymph node involvement has also been reported.[201]

On microscopic examination, the nodules usually have the appearance of a typical leiomyoma or, less commonly, a cellular leiomyoma (Fig. 15.55). The smooth muscle cells usually exhibit no significant nuclear pleomorphism or mitotic activity; occasionally, however, they may contain up to 3 mitoses per 10 high-power fields.[200] Sex-cord-like patterns were noted in the recurrent nodules in one case.[204] In pregnant patients, decidual cells and cells intermediate in appearance between muscle and decidual cells may be admixed with the smooth

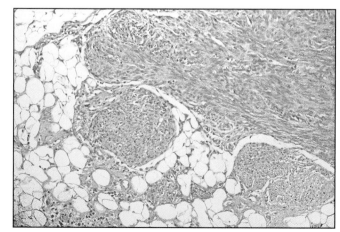

Fig. 15.55 • Peritoneal leiomyomatosis involving omentum.

muscle cells (Fig. 15.56). Foci of endometriosis or endosalpingiosis have been identified in continuity with the nodules in 10% of the cases. Ultrastructural studies have confirmed the presence of smooth muscle cells, sometimes admixed with myofibroblasts, fibroblasts, and, in pregnant patients, decidual cells.[200]

With the exceptions noted below, there have been no reports of progressive disease on follow-up examination, despite incomplete excision. In several pregnant patients who had a second-look procedure when they were no longer pregnant, the nodules had completely or partially regressed. After frozen section confirmation of the diagnosis, conservative therapy is indicated, although the disorder may recur in subsequent pregnancies. Occasional cases of persistent peritoneal leiomyomatosis have been successfully treated with GnRH agonists.[202,203]

Five cases of leiomyosarcomatous transformation of peritoneal leiomyomatosis have been reported.[205] In each case, rapidly growing intra-abdominal tumor (and metastatic tumor in one) with the histologic appearance of leiomyosarcoma appeared within a year of a diagnosis of typical peritoneal leiomyomatosis. Four of the women died of disease within 2 years of their initial presentation.

Peritoneal leiomyomatosis is considered to be a result of metaplastic transformation of submesothelial mesenchymal cells into smooth muscle cells. The submesothelial location of the nodules and the occasional juxtaposition to other metaplastic lesions (ectopic decidua, endometriosis, endosalpingiosis) support this interpretation. A hormonal background for this disorder is suggested by the association with pregnancy or hormone administration in 70% of cases; the

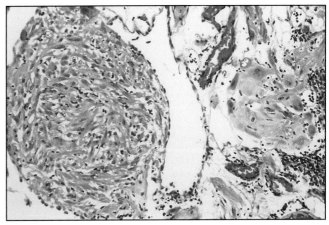

Fig. 15.56 • Nodule of peritoneal leiomyomatosis (left) adjacent to focus of ectopic decidua (right).

presence of estrogen and progesterone receptors within the lesional cells;[206] the reduction in size of the tumors after pregnancy, surgical castration, or treatment with GnRH-agonists;[202,203] and the production in guinea pigs of similar uterine and submesothelial nodules by the administration of estrogen alone or in combination with progesterone.[207] In a study of four cases in which X-chromosome inactivation in this disorder was analyzed,[208] the same parental X chromosome was non-randomly inactivated in all of the nodules examined in each case, consistent with a unicentric clonal neoplasm or selection for an X-linked allele in clonal multicentric lesions.

References

1. Churg A, Colby T V, Cagle P et al. 2000 The separation of benign and malignant mesothelial proliferations. Am J Surg Pathol 24: 1183–1200
2. Kerner H, Gaton E, Czernobilsky B 1981 Unusual ovarian, tubal and pelvic mesothelial inclusions in patients with endometriosis. Histopathology 5: 277–282
3. Clement P B, Young R H 1993 Florid mesothelial hyperplasia associated with ovarian tumors: a potential source of error in tumor diagnosis and staging. Int J Gynecol Pathol 12: 51–58
4. Rosai J, Dehner L P 1975 Nodular mesothelial hyperplasia in hernia sacs. A benign reactive condition stimulating a neoplastic process. Cancer 35: 165–175
5. Ordonez N G, Ayala A G 1998 Lesions described as nodular mesothelial hyperplasia are primarily composed of histiocytes. Am J Surg Pathol 22: 285–292
6. Chikkamuniyappa S, Herrick J, Jagirdar J S 2004 Nodular histiocytic/mesothelial hyperplasia: a potential pitfall. Ann Diagn Pathol 8: 115–120
7. Clement P B, Young R H, Oliva E et al. 1996 Hyperplastic mesothelial cells within abdominal lymph nodes: a mimic of metastatic ovarian carcinoma and serous borderline tumor. A report of two cases associated with ovarian neoplasms. Mod Pathol 9: 879–886
8. Attanoos R L, Griffin A, Gibbs A R 2003 The use of immunohistochemistry in distinguishing reactive from neoplastic epithelium. A novel use for desmin and comparative evaluation with epithelial membrane antigen, p53, platelet-derived growth factor, P-glycoprotein, and bcl-2. Histopathology 43: 231–238
9. Carpenter H A, Lancaster J R, Lee R A 1982 Multilocular cysts of the peritoneum. Mayo Clin Proc 57: 634–638
10. Schneider V, Partridge J R, Gutierrez F et al. 1983 Benign cystic mesothelioma involving the female genital tract: report of four cases. Am J Obstet Gynecol 145: 355–359
11. Katsube Y, Mukai K, Silverberg S G 1982 Cystic mesothelioma of the peritoneum. A report of five cases and review of the literature. Cancer 50: 1615–1622
12. Moore J H Jr, Crum C P, Chandler J G et al. 1980 Benign cystic mesothelioma. Cancer 45: 2395–2399
13. McFadden D E, Clement P B 1986 Peritoneal inclusion cysts with mural mesothelial proliferation. A clinicopathological analysis of six cases. Am J Surg Pathol 10: 844–854
14. Weiss S W, Tavassoli F A 1988 Multicystic mesothelioma. An analysis of pathologic findings and biologic behavior in 37 cases. Am J Surg Pathol 12: 737–746
15. Ross M J, Welch W R, Scully R E 1989 Multilocular peritoneal inclusion cysts (so-called cystic mesotheliomas). Cancer 64: 1336–1346
16. Blumberg N A, Murray J F 1981 Multicystic peritoneal mesothelioma. S Afr Med J 59: 85–86
17. Sienkowski I, Russell A J, Dilly S A et al. 1986 Peritoneal cystic mesothelioma: an electron microscopic and immunohistochemical study of two male patients. J Clin Pathol 39: 440–445
18. Kjellevold K, Nesland J M, Holm R et al. 1986 Multicystic peritoneal mesothelioma. Pathol Res Pract 181: 767–771
19. Arber D A, Strickler J G, Weiss L M 1997 Splenic mesothelial cysts mimicking lymphangiomas. Am J Surg Pathol 21: 334–338
20. Harper G B Jr, Awbrey B J, Thomas C G Jr et al. 1986 Mesothelial cysts of the round ligament simulating inguinal hernia. Report of four cases and review of the literature. Am J Surg 151: 515–517
21. Demopoulos R I, Kahn M A, Feiner H D 1986 Epidemiology of cystic mesotheliomas. Int J Gynecol Pathol 5: 379–381
22. Gussman D, Thickman D, Wheeler J E 1986 Postoperative peritoneal cysts. Obstet Gynecol 68 53S–55S
23. Flemming P, Becker T, Klempnauer J et al. 2002 Benign cystic mesothelioma of the liver. Am J Surg Pathol 26: 1523–1527
24. Chen K T K 1998 Multicystic mesothelioma. Int J Surg Pathol 6: 43–48
25. Smith V C, Edwards R A, Jorgensen J L et al. 2000 Unilocular retroperitoneal cyst of mesothelial origin presenting as a renal mass. A report of 2 cases. Arch Pathol Lab Med 124: 766–769
26. Sawh R, Malpica A, Deavers M T et al. 2003 Benign cystic mesothelioma of the peritoneum: a clinicopathologic study of 17 cases and immunohistochemical analysis of estrogen and progesterone receptor status. Hum Pathol 34: 369–374
27. Letterie G S, Yon J L 1995 Use of a long-acting GnRH agonist for benign cystic mesothelioma. Obstet Gynecol 85: 901–903

28. Bisset D L, Morris J A, Fox H 1988 Giant cystic adenomatoid tumor (mesothelioma) of the uterus. Histopathology 12: 555–558
29. Clement P B 1995 Reactive tumor-like lesions of the peritoneum. Editorial. Am J Clin Pathol 103: 673–676
30. Kim K, Scully R E 1990 Peritoneal keratin granulomas with carcinomas of endometrium and ovary and atypical polypoid adenomyoma of endometrium. Am J Surg Pathol 14: 925–932
31. Bolen J W, Hammar S P, McNutt M A 1986 Reactive and neoplastic serosal tissue. A light microscopic, ultrastructural and immunohistochemical study. Am J Surg Pathol 10: 34–47
32. Clement P B, Young R H, Hanna W et al. 1994 Sclerosing peritonitis associated with luteinized thecomas of the ovary: a clinicopathological analysis of six cases. Am J Surg Pathol 18: 1–13
33. Emory T S, Monihan J M, Carr N J et al. 1997 Sclerosing mesenteritis, mesenteric panniculitis and mesenteric lipodystrophy: a single entity? Am J Surg Pathol 21: 392–398
34. McCaughey W T E, Al-Jabi M 1986 Differentiation of serosal hyperplasia and neoplasia in biopsies. Pathol Annu 21: 271–292
35. Kocova L, Michal M, Sulc M et al. 1997 Calcifying fibrous pseudotumor of visceral peritoneum. Histopathology 31: 182–184
36. Chen K T K 2003 Familial peritoneal multifocal calcifying fibrous tumor. Am J Clin Pathol 119: 811–815
37. Nascimento A F, Ruiz R, Hornick J L et al. 2002 Calcifying fibrous pseudotumor: clinicopathologic study of 15 cases and analysis of its relationship to inflammatory myofibroblastic tumor. Int J Surg Pathol 10: 189–196
38. Auerbach R D, Kohorn E I, Cornelius E A 1985 Splenosis: a complicating factor in total abdominal hysterectomy. Obstet Gynecol 65: 65S–68S
39. Matonis L M, Luciano A A 1995 A case of splenosis masquerading as endometriosis. Am J Obstet Gynecol 173: 971–973
40. Jaworski R C, Boadle R, Greg J et al. 2001 Peritoneal "melanosis" associated with a ruptured ovarian dermoid cyst: report of a case with electron-probe energy dispersive X-ray analysis. Int J Gynecol Pathol 20: 386–389
41. Elliott G B, Freigang B 1962 Aseptic necrosis, calcification and separation of appendices epiploicae. Ann Surg 155: 501–505
42. Vuong P N, Guyot H, Moulin G et al. 1990 Pseudotumoral organization of a twisted epiploic fringe or "hard-boiled egg" in the peritoneal cavity. Arch Pathol Lab Med 114: 531–533
43. Fadare O, Bifulco C, Carter D et al. 2002 Cartilaginous differentiation in peritoneal tissues: a report of two cases and a review of the literature. Mod Pathol 15: 777–780
44. Young R H, Clement P B, McCaughey W T E 1990 Solitary fibrous tumors ("fibrous mesotheliomas") of the peritoneum: a report of three cases. Arch Pathol Lab Med 114: 493–495
45. Flint A, Weiss S W 1995 CD-34 and keratin expression distinguishes solitary fibrous tumor (fibrous mesothelioma) of pleura from desmoplastic mesothelioma. Hum Pathol 26: 428–431
46. Fukunaga M, Naganuma H, Nikaido T et al. 1997 Extrapleural solitary fibrous tumor: a report of seven cases. Mod Pathol 10: 443–450
47. Hanau C A, Miettinen M 1995 Solitary fibrous tumor: histological and immunohistochemical spectrum of benign and malignant variants presenting at different sites. Hum Pathol 26: 440–449
48. Fukunaga M, Naganuma H, Ushigome S et al. 1996 Malignant solitary fibrous tumour of the peritoneum. Histopathology 28: 463–466
49. Hanrahan J B 1963 A combined papillary mesothelioma and adenomatoid tumor of the omentum. Report of a case. Cancer 16: 1497–1500
50. Craig J R, Hart W R 1979 Extragenital adenomatoid tumor. Evidence for the mesothelial theory of origin. Cancer 43: 1678–1679
51. Goepel J R 1981 Benign papillary mesothelioma of peritoneum: a histological, histochemical and ultrastructural study of six cases. Histopathology 5: 21–30
52. Daya D, McCaughey W T E 1990 Well-differentiated papillary mesothelioma of the peritoneum. A clinicopathologic study of 22 cases. Cancer 65: 292–296
53. Burrig K, Pfitzer P, Hart W 1990 Well-differentiated papillary mesothelioma of the peritoneum: a borderline mesothelioma. Virchow's Arch [Pathol Anat] 417: 443–447
54. Goldblum J, Hart W R 1995 Localized and diffuse mesotheliomas of the genital tract and peritoneum in women. A clinicopathologic study of nineteen true mesothelial neoplasms, other than adenomatoid tumors, multicystic mesotheliomas, and localized fibrous tumors. Am J Surg Pathol 19: 1124–1137
55. Butnor K J, Sporn T A, Hammar S P et al. 2001 Well-differentiated papillary mesothelioma. Am J Surg Pathol 25: 1304–1309
56. Diaz L K, Okronkwo A, Solans E P et al. 2002 Extensive myxoid change in well-differentiated papillary mesothelioma of the pelvic peritoneum. Ann Diagn Pathol 6: 164–167
57. Kannerstein M, Churg J 1977 Peritoneal mesothelioma. Hum Pathol 8: 83–94
58. Jones D E C, Silver D 1979 Peritoneal mesotheliomas. Surgery 86: 556–560
59. Plaus W J 1988 Peritoneal mesothelioma. Arch Surg 123: 763–766
60. Piccigallo E, Jeffers L J, Reddy R et al. 1988 Malignant peritoneal mesothelioma. A clinical and laparoscopic study of ten cases. Dig Dis Sci 33: 633–639
61. Asensio J A, Goldblatt P, Thomford N R 1990 Primary malignant peritoneal mesothelioma. A report of seven cases and a review of the literature. Arch Surg 125: 1477–1481
62. Kerrigan S A J, Turnnir R T, Clement P B et al. 2002 Diffuse malignant epithelial mesotheliomas of the peritoneum in women. A clinicopathologic study of 25 patients. Cancer 94: 378–385
63. Baker P M, Clement P B, Young R H 2005 Malignant peritoneal mesothelioma in women. A study of 75 cases with emphasis on their morphologic spectrum and differential diagnosis. Am J Clin Pathol 123: 724–737
64. Clement P B, Young R H, Scully R E 1996 Malignant mesotheliomas presenting as ovarian masses. A report of nine cases, including two primary ovarian mesotheliomas. Am J Surg Pathol 20: 1067–1080
65. Kane M J, Chahinian A P, Holland J F 1990 Malignant mesothelioma in young adults. Cancer 65: 1449–1455
66. Nascimento A G, Keeney G L, Fletcher C D M 1994 Deciduoid peritoneal mesothelioma. An unusual phenotype affecting young females. Am J Surg Pathol 18: 439–445
67. Shanks J H, Harris M, Banerjee S S et al. 2000 Mesotheliomas with deciduoid morphology. A morphologic spectrum and a variant not confined to young females. Am J Surg Pathol 24: 285–294
68. Shia J, Erlandson R A, Klimstra D S 2002 Deciduoid mesothelioma: a report of 5 cases and literature review. Ultrastruct Pathol 26: 355–363
69. Berry P J, Favara B E, Odom L F 1986 Malignant peritoneal mesothelioma in a child. Pediatr Pathol 5: 397–409
70. Almudevar Bercero E, Garcia-Rostan Y, Perez G M A et al. 1997 Prognostic value of high serum levels of CA-125 in malignant secretory peritoneal mesotheliomas affecting young women. A case report with differential diagnosis and review of the literature. Histopathology 31: 267–273
71. Chen K T K 1991 Malignant peritoneal mesothelioma presenting as Sister Joseph's nodule. Am J Dermatopathol 13: 300–303
72. Mayall F G, Gibbs A R 1991 Malignant peritoneal mesothelioma giving rise to multiple intestinal polyps. Histopathology 18: 480–482
73. Fukayama M, Takizawa T, Koike M et al. 1987 Malignant peritoneal mesothelioma as a pelvic mass. Acta Pathol Jpn 37: 1149–1156
74. Matsukuma S, Aida S, Hata Y et al. 1996 Localized malignant peritoneal mesothelioma containing rhabdoid cells. Pathol Int 46: 389–391
75. Sussman J, Rosai J 1990 Lymph node metastasis as the initial manifestation of malignant mesothelioma. Report of six cases. Am J Surg Pathol 14: 818–828
76. Kerrigan S A J, Cagle P, Churg A 2003 Malignant mesothelioma of the peritoneum presenting as an inflammatory lesion. Am J Surg Pathol 27: 248–253
77. Gilks B, Hegedus C, Freeman H et al. 1988 Malignant peritoneal mesothelioma after remote abdominal radiation. Cancer 61: 2019–2021
78. Peterson J T Jr, Greenberg S D, Buffler P A 1984 Non-asbestos-related malignant mesothelioma. A review. Cancer 54: 951–960
79. Huncharek M 1995 Genetic factors in the aetiology of malignant mesothelioma. Eur J Cancer 31A: 1741–1747
80. Brenner J, Sordillo P P, Magill G B 1981 Seventeen year survival in a patient with malignant peritoneal mesothelioma. Clin Oncol 7: 249–251
81. Norman P E, Whitaker D 1989 Nine-year survival in a case of untreated peritoneal mesothelioma. Med J Aust 150: 43–44
82. Feldman A L, Libutt S K, Pingpark J F et al. 2003 Analysis of factors associated with outcome in patients with malignant peritoneal mesothelioma undergoing surgical debulking and intraperitoneal chemotherapy. J Clin Oncol 21: 4560–4567
83. Kitazawa M, Kaneko H, Toshima M et al. 1984 Malignant peritoneal mesothelioma with massive foamy cells. Acta Pathol Jpn 34: 687–692
84. Bollinger D J, Wick M R, Dehner L P et al. 1989 Peritoneal malignant mesothelioma versus serous papillary adenocarcinoma. A histochemical and immunohistochemical comparison. Am J Surg Pathol 13: 659–670
85. Wick M R, Mills S E, Swanson P E 1990 Expression of "myelomonocytic" antigens in mesotheliomas and adenocarcinomas involving the serosal surfaces. Am J Clin Pathol 94: 18–26
86. McCaughey W T E, Colby T V, Battifora H et al. 1991 Diagnosis of diffuse malignant mesothelioma: experience of a US/Canadian mesothelioma panel. Mod Pathol 4: 342–353
87. Sheibani K, Esteban J M, Bailey A et al. 1992 Immunopathologic and molecular studies as an aid in the diagnosis of malignant mesothelioma. Hum Pathol 23: 107–116
88. Sheibani K, Stroup R M 1996 Immunopathology of malignant mesothelioma. Pathology 4: 191–212
89. Ordonez N G 2006 The diagnostic utility of immunohistochemistry and electron microscopy in distinguishing between peritoneal mesotheliomas and serous carcinomas: a comparative study. Mod Pathol 19: 34–48
90. Attanoos R L, Webb R, Dojcinov S D et al. 2002 Value of mesothelial and epithelial antibodies in distinguishing diffuse peritoneal mesothelioma in females from serous papillary carcinoma of the ovary and peritoneum. Histopathology 40: 237–244
91. Gerald W L, Miller H K, Battifora H et al. 1991 Intra-abdominal desmoplastic small round cell tumor. Am J Surg Pathol 15: 499–513
92. Young R H, Eichhorn J H, Dickersin G R et al. 1992 Ovarian involvement by the intra-abdominal desmoplastic small round cell tumor with divergent differentiation: a report of three cases. Hum Pathol 23: 454–464
93. Ordonez N G, El-Naggar A, Ro J Y et al. 1993 Intra-abdominal desmoplastic small cell tumor: a light microscopic, immunocytochemical, ultrastructural, and flow cytometric study. Hum Pathol 24: 850–865
94. Brodie S G, Stocker S J, Wardlaw J C et al. 1995 EWS and WT-1 gene fusion in desmoplastic small round cell tumor of the abdomen. Hum Pathol 26: 1370–1374

95. Schroder S, Padberg B 1993 Desmoplastic small-cell tumor of the peritoneum with divergent differentiation: immunocytochemical and biochemical findings (letter). Am J Clin Pathol 99: 353–354

96. Argatoff L H, O'Connell J X, Mathers J A et al. 1996 Detection of the EWS/WT1 gene fusion by reverse transcriptase-polymerase chain reaction in the diagnosis of intra-abdominal desmoplastic small round cell tumor. Am J Surg Pathol 20: 406–412

97. Dorsey B V, Benjamin L E, Rauscher F III et al. 1996 Intra-abdominal desmoplastic small round-cell tumor: expansion of the pathologic profile. Mod Pathol 9: 703–709

98. Amato R J, Ellerhorst J A, Ayala A G 1996 Intraabdominal desmoplastic small cell tumor. Report and discussion of five cases. Cancer 78: 845–851

99. Cummings O W, Ulbright T M, Young R H et al. 1997 Desmoplastic small round cell tumors of the paratesticular region. A report of six cases. Am J Surg Pathol 21: 219–225

100. Charles A K, Moore I E, Berry P J 1998 Immunohistochemical detection of the Wilms' tumour gene WT1 in desmoplastic small round cell tumour. Histopathology 30: 312–314

101. Gerald W, Ladanyi M, de Alava E et al. 1998 Clinical, pathologic and molecular spectrum of tumors associated with t(11;22)(p13;q12): desmoplastic small round-cell tumor and its variants. J Clin Oncol 16: 3028–3036

102. Ordonez N G 1998 Desmoplastic small round cell tumor. I. A histopathologic study of 39 cases with emphasis on unusual histologic patterns. Am J Surg Pathol 22: 1303–1313

103. Lae M E, Roche P C, Jin L et al. 2002 Desmoplastic small round cell tumor. A clinicopathologic, immunohistochemical, and molecular study of 32 tumors. Am J Surg Pathol 26: 823–835

104. Ordonez N G 1998 Desmoplastic small round cell tumor. II. An ultrastructural and immunohistochemical study with emphasis on new immunohistochemical markers. Am J Surg Pathol 22: 1314–1327

105. Zhang P J, Goldblum J R, Pawel B R et al. 2003 Immunophenotype of desmoplastic small round cell tumors as detected in cases with EWS-WT1 gene fusion product. Mod Pathol 16: 229–235

106. Lin B T, Colby T, Gown A M et al. 1996 Malignant vascular tumors of the serous membranes mimicking mesothelioma. A report of 14 cases. Am J Surg Pathol 20: 1431–1439

107. Attanoos R L, Dallimore N S, Gibbs A R 1997 Primary epithelioid haemangioendothelioma of the peritoneum: an unusual mimic of diffuse malignant mesothelioma. Histopathology 30: 375–377

108. Meis-Kindblom J M, Kindblom L-G 1998 Angiosarcoma of soft tissue. A study of 80 cases. Am J Surg Pathol 22: 683–697

109. Day D L, Sane S, Dehner L P 1986 Inflammatory pseudotumor of the mesentery and small intestine. Pediatr Radiol 16: 210–215

110. Pettinato G, Manivel J C, De Rosa N et al. 1990 Inflammatory myofibroblastic tumor (plasma cell granuloma). Clinicopathologic study of 20 cases with immunohistochemical and ultrastructural observations. Am J Clin Pathol 94: 538–546

111. Meis J M, Enzinger F M 1991 Inflammatory fibrosarcoma of the mesentery and retroperitoneum. Am J Surg Pathol 15: 1146–1156

112. Coffin C M, Watterson J, Priest J R et al. 1995 Extrapulmonary inflammatory myofibroblastic tumor (inflammatory pseudotumor): a clinicopathologic and immunohistochemical study of 84 cases. Am J Surg Pathol 19: 859–872

113. Coffin C M, Humphrey P A, Dehner L P 1998 Extrapulmonary inflammatory myofibroblastic tumor: a clinical and pathological survey. Semin Diagn Pathol 15: 85–101

114. Gonzalez-Crussi F, deMello D E, Sotelo-Avila C 1983 Omental-mesenteric myxoid hamartomas. Am J Surg Pathol 7: 567–578

115. Merino M J, Livolsi V A 1981 Signet ring carcinoma of the female breast: a clinicopathologic analysis of 24 cases. Cancer 48: 1830–1837

116. Abu-Rustum N R, Aghajanian C A, Venkatraman E S et al. 1997 Metastatic breast carcinoma to the abdomen and pelvis. Gynecol Oncol 66: 41–44

117. Young R H, Gilks C B, Scully R E 1991 Mucinous tumors of the appendix associated with mucinous tumors of the ovary and pseudomyxoma peritonei. A clinicopathological analysis of 22 cases supporting an origin in the appendix. Am J Surg Pathol 15: 415–429

118. Michael H, Sutton G, Roth L M 1987 Ovarian carcinoma with extracellular mucin production: reassessment of "pseudomyxoma ovarii et peritonei." Int J Gynecol Pathol 6: 298–312

119. Seidman J D, Elsayed A M, Sobin L H et al. 1993 Association of mucinous tumors of the ovary and appendix. A clinicopathologic study of 25 cases. Am J Surg Pathol 17: 22–34

120. Costa M J 1994 Pseudomyxoma peritonei. Histologic predictors of patient survival. Arch Pathol Lab Med 118: 1215–1219

121. Prayson R A, Hart W R, Petras R E 1994 Pseudomyxoma peritonei. A clinicopathologic study of 19 cases with emphasis on site of origin and nature of associated ovarian tumors. Am J Surg Pathol 18: 591–603

122. Ronnett B M, Kurman R J, Zahn C M et al. 1995 Pseudomyxoma peritonei in women: a clinicopathologic analysis of 30 cases with emphasis on site of origin, prognosis, and relationship to ovarian mucinous tumors of low malignant potential. Hum Pathol 56: 509–524

123. Ronnett B M, Zahn C M, Kurman R J et al. 1995 Disseminated peritoneal adenomucinosis and peritoneal mucinous carcinomatosis. A clinicopathologic analysis of 109 cases with emphasis on distinguishing pathologic features, site of origin, prognosis, and relationship to "pseudomyxoma peritonei." Am J Surg Pathol 19: 1390–1408

123a. Bradley R F, Stewart J H 4th, Russell G B et al. 2006 Pseudomyxoma peritonei of appendiceal origin: a clinicopathologic analysis of 101 patients uniformly treated at a single institution, with literature review. Am J Surg Pathol 30: 551–559

124. O'Connell J T, Hacker C M, Barsky S H 2002 MUC2 is a molecular marker for pseudomyxoma peritonei. Mod Pathol 15: 958–972

125. Ronnett B M, Seidman J D 2003 Mucinous tumors arising in ovarian mature cystic teratomas. Relationship to the clinical syndrome of pseudomyxoma peritonei. Am J Surg Pathol 27: 650–657

126. McKenney J K, Soslow R A, Longacre T A 2004 Mucinous neoplasms arising in mature teratomas: a clinicopathologic study of ovarian and sacrococcygeal tumors. Mod Pathol 17: 206A (abstract)

127. Lauchlan S C 1972 The secondary mullerian system. Obstet Gynecol Surv 27: 133–146

128. Ober W B, Black M B 1955 Neoplasms of the subcoelomic mesenchyme. Arch Pathol Lab Med 59: 698–705

129. Clement P B 2002 Endometriosis, lesions of the secondary mullerian system, and pelvic mesothelial proliferations. In: Kurman R J (ed) Blaustein's pathology of the female genital tract, 5th edn. Springer Verlag, New York, p 729–789

130. Zinsser K R, Wheeler J E 1982 Endosalpingiosis in the omentum. A study of autopsy and surgical material. Am J Surg Pathol 6: 109–117

131. McCaughey W T E, Kirk M E, Lester W et al. 1984 Peritoneal epithelial lesions associated with proliferative serous tumours of the ovary. Histopathology 8: 195–208

132. Sidaway M K, Silverberg S G 1987 Endosalpingiosis in female peritoneal washings: a diagnostic pitfall. Int J Gynecol Pathol 6: 340–346

133. Copeland L J, Silva E G, Gershenson D M et al. 1988 The significance of mullerian inclusions found at second-look laparotomy in patients with epithelial ovarian neoplasms. Obstet Gynecol 71: 763–770

134. Kheir S M, Mann W J, Wilkerson J A 1981 Glandular inclusions in lymph nodes. The problem of extensive involvement and relationship to salpingitis. Am J Surg Pathol 5: 353–359

135. Yoonessi M, Satchindanand S K, Ortinez C G et al. 1982 Benign glandular elements and decidual reaction in retroperitoneal lymph nodes. J Surg Oncol 19: 81–86

136. Horn L-C, Bilek K 1995 Frequency and histogenesis of pelvic retroperitoneal lymph node inclusions of the female genital tract. Pathol Res Pract 191: 991–996

137. Maaben V, Hiller K 1994 Glandular inclusions in lymph nodes: pattern of distribution and metaplastic formation. Arch Gynecol Obstet 255: 1–8

138. Mills S E 1983 Decidua and squamous metaplasia in abdominopelvic lymph nodes. Int J Gynecol Pathol 2: 209–215

139. Reich O, Tamussino K, Haas J et al. 2000 Benign mullerian inclusions in pelvic and paraaortic lymph nodes. Gynecol Oncol 78: 242–244

140. McCluggage W G, Clements W D B 2001 Endosalpingiosis of the colon and appendix. Histopathology 39: 639–650

141. Bell D A, Scully R E 1989 Benign and borderline serous lesions of the peritoneum in women. Pathol Annu 24: 1–25

142. Moore W F, Bentley R C, Berchuk A et al. 2000 Some mullerian inclusion cysts in lymph nodes may sometimes be metastases from serous borderline tumors of the ovary. Int J Gynecol Pathol 24: 710–718

143. Clement P B, Young R H 1999 Tumor-like manifestations of florid cystic endosalpingiosis: a report of four cases including the first reported cases of mural endosalpingiosis of the uterus. Am J Surg Pathol 23: 166–175

144. Carrick K S, Mivenan J S, Albores-Saavedra J 2003 Serous tumor of low malignant potential arising in inguinal endosalpingiosis: report of a case. Int J Gynecol Pathol 22: 412–415

145. Young R H, Clement P B 1996 Mullerianosis of the urinary bladder. Mod Pathol 9: 731–737

146. Lim S, Kim J Y, Park K et al. 2003 Mullerianosis of the mesosalpinx: a case report. Int J Gynecol Pathol 22: 209–212

147. Prade M, Spatz A, Bentley R et al. 1995 Borderline and malignant serous tumor arising in pelvic lymph nodes: evidence of origin in benign glandular inclusions. Int J Gynecol Pathol 14: 87–91

148. Bell D A, Scully R E 1990 Serous borderline tumors of the peritoneum. Am J Surg Pathol 14: 230–239

149. Biscotti C V, Hart W R 1992 Peritoneal serous micropapillomatosis of low malignant potential (serous borderline tumors of the peritoneum). Am J Surg Pathol 16: 467–475

150. Tobacman J K, Tucker M A, Kase R et al. 1982 Intra-abdominal carcinomatosis after prophylactic oophorectomy in ovarian-cancer-prone families. Lancet 2: 795–797

151. White P F, Merino M J, Barwick K W 1985 Serous surface papillary carcinoma of the ovary: a clinical, pathologic, ultrastructural, and immunohistochemical study of 11 cases. Pathol Annu 20: 403–418

152. Chen K T K, Flam M S 1986 Peritoneal papillary serous carcinoma with long-term survival. Cancer 58: 1371–1373

153. Lele S B, Piver M S, Matharu J et al. 1988 Peritoneal papillary carcinoma. Gynecol Oncol 31: 315–320

154. Mills S E, Andersen W A, Fechner R E et al. 1988 Serous surface papillary carcinoma. A clinicopathologic study of 10 cases and comparison with stage III–IV ovarian serous carcinoma. Am J Surg Pathol 12: 827–834

155. Dalrymple J C, Bannatyne P, Russell P et al. 1989 Extraovarian peritoneal serous papillary carcinoma. A clinicopathologic study of 31 cases. Cancer 64: 110–115

156. Raju U, Fine G, Greenawald K A et al. 1989 Primary papillary serous neoplasia of the peritoneum: a clinicopathologic and ultrastructural study of eight cases. Hum Pathol 20: 426–436

157. Wick M R, Mills S E, Dehner L P et al. 1989 Serous papillary carcinomas arising from the peritoneum and ovaries. A clinicopathologic and immunohistochemical comparison. Int J Gynecol Pathol 8: 179–188

158. Fromm G, Gershenson D M, Silva E G 1990 Papillary serous carcinoma of the peritoneum. Obstet Gynecol 75: 89–95

159. Ransom D T, Shreyaskumar R P, Keeney G L et al. 1990 Papillary serous carcinoma of the peritoneum. A review of 33 cases treated with platin-based chemotherapy. Cancer 66: 1091–1094

160. Truong L D, Maccato M L, Awalt H et al. Serous surface carcinoma of the peritoneum: a clinicopathologic study of 22 cases. Hum Pathol 1990; 21: 99–110

161. Bandera C A, Muto M G, Schorge J O et al. 1998 BRCA1 gene mutations in women with papillary serous carcinoma of the peritoneum. Obstet Gynecol 92: 596–600

162. Schorge J O, Muto M G, Lee S J et al. 2000 BRCAI-related papillary serous carcinoma of the peritoneum has a unique molecular pathogenesis. Cancer Res 60: 1361–1364

163. Halperin R, Zehavi S, Langer R et al. 2001 Primary peritoneal serous papillary carcinoma: a new epidemiologic trend? Int J Gynecol Cancer 11: 403–408

164. Halperin R, Zehavi S, Hadas E et al. 2001 Immunohistochemical comparison of primary peritoneal and primary ovarian serous papillary carcinoma. Int J Gynecol Pathol 20: 341–345

165. Barda G, Menczer J, Chetrit A et al. 2004 Comparison between primary peritoneal and epithelial ovarian carcinoma: a population-based study. Am J Obstet Gynecol 190: 1039–1045

166. Weir M M, Bell D A, Young R H 1998 Grade 1 peritoneal serous carcinomas: a report of 14 cases and comparison with 7 peritoneal serous psammomatous and 19 peritoneal serous borderline tumors. Am J Surg Pathol 22: 849–862

167. McCaughey W T E, Schryer M J P, Lin X et al. 1986 Extraovarian pelvic serous tumor with marked calcification. Arch Pathol Lab Med 110: 78–80

168. Gilks C B, Bell D A, Scully R E 1990 Serous psammocarcinoma of the ovary and peritoneum. Int J Gynecol Pathol 9: 110–121

169. Hafiz M A, Toker C 1986 Multicentric ovarian and extraovarian cystadenofibroma. Obstet Gynecol 68: 94S–98S

170. Clark J E, Wood H, Jaffurs W J et al. 1979 Endometrioid-type cystadenocarcinoma arising in the mesosalpinx. Obstet Gynecol 54: 656–658

171. Chang K L, Crabtree G S, Lim-Tan S K et al. 1993 Primary extrauterine endometrial stromal neoplasms: a clinicopathologic study of 20 cases and a review of the literature. Int J Gynecol Pathol 12: 282–296

172. Mira J L, Fenoglio-Preiser C M, Husseinzadeh N 1995 Malignant mixed mullerian tumor of the extraovarian secondary mullerian system. Report of two cases and review of the English literature. Arch Pathol Lab Med 119: 1044–1049

173. Shen D, Khoo U, Xue W et al. 2001 Primary peritoneal malignant mixed mullerian tumors. A clinicopathologic, immunohistochemical, and genetic study. Cancer 91: 1052–1060

174. Sumathi V P, Murnaghan M, Dobbs S P et al. 2002 Extragenital mullerian carcinosarcoma arising from the peritoneum: report of two cases. Int J Gynecol Cancer 12: 764–767

175. Visvalingam S, Jaworski R, Blumenthal N et al. 2001 Primary peritoneal mesodermal adenosarcoma: report of a case and review of the literature. Gynecol Oncol 81: 500–505

176. Dincer A D, Timmins P, Fisher H et al. 2001 Primary peritoneal mullerian adenosarcoma with sarcomatous transformation. Int J Gynecol Pathol 21: 65–68

177. Baird D B, Reddick R L 1991 Extraovarian mucinous metaplasia in a patient with bilateral mucinous borderline ovarian tumors: a case report. Int J Gynecol Pathol 10: 96–103

178. Clement P B, Young R H 1992 Endocervicosis of the urinary bladder: a report of six cases of a benign mullerian lesion that may mimic adenocarcinoma. Am J Surg Pathol 16: 533–542

179. Nazeer T, Ro J Y, Tornos C et al. 1996 Endocervical-type glands in the urinary bladder: a clinocopathologic study of six cases. Hum Pathol 27: 816–820

180. Young R H, Clement P B 2000 Endocervicosis involving the uterine cervix: a report of four cases of a benign process that may be confused with deeply invasive endocervical adenocarcinoma. Int J Gynecol Pathol 19: 322–328

181. Martinka M, Allaire C, Clement P B 1999 Endocervicosis presenting as a painful vaginal mass: a case report. Int J Gynecol Pathol 18: 274–276

182. Chen K T K 2002 Endocervicosis of the small intestine. Int J Surg Pathol 10: 65–67

183. Banerjee R, Gough J 1988 Cystic mucinous tumours of the mesentery and retroperitoneum: report of three cases. Histopathology 12: 527–532

184. Pennell T C, Gusdon J P Jr 1989 Retroperitoneal mucinous cystadenoma. Am J Obstet Gynecol 160: 1229–1231

185. Pearl M L, Valea F, Chumas J et al. 1996 Primary retroperitoneal mucinous cystadenocarcinoma of low malignant potential: a case report and literature review. Gynecol Oncol 61: 150–152

186. Lee I, Ching K, Pang M et al. 1996 Two cases of primary retroperitoneal mucinous cystadenocarcinoma. Gynecol Oncol 63: 145–150

187. Mikami M, Tei C, Takehara K et al. 2003 Retroperitoneal primary mucinous adenocarcinoma with a mural nodule of anaplastic tumor: a case report and literature review. Int J Gynecol Pathol 22: 205–208

188. Bransilver B R, Ferenczy A, Richart R M 1974 Brenner tumors and Walthard cell nests. Arch Pathol Lab Med 98: 76–86

189. Roth L M 1974 The Brenner tumor and the Walthard cell nest. An electron microscopic study. Lab Invest 31: 15–23

190. Teoh T B 1953 The structure and development of Walthard nests. J Pathol 66: 433–439

191. Schatz J E, Colgan T J 1991 Squamous metaplasia of the peritoneum. Arch Pathol Lab Med 115: 397–398

192. Hampton H L, Huffman H T, Meeks G R 1992 Extraovarian Brenner tumor. Obstet Gynecol 79: 844–846

193. Evans H, Yates W A, Palmer W E et al. 1990 Clear cell carcinoma of the sigmoid mesocolon: a tumor of the secondary mullerian system. Am J Obstet Gynecol 162: 161–163

194. Lee K R, Verma U, Belinson J 1991 Primary clear cell carcinoma of the peritoneum. Gynecol Oncol 41: 259–262

195. Burnett R A, Millan D 1986 Decidual change in pelvic lymph nodes: a source of possible diagnostic error. Histopathology 10: 1089–1092

196. Zaytsev P, Taxy J B 1987 Pregnancy-associated ectopic decidua. Am J Surg Pathol 11: 526–530

197. Cobb C J 1988 Ectopic decidua and metastatic squamous carcinoma: presentation in a single pelvic lymph node. J Surg Oncol 38: 126–129

198. Buttner A, Bassler R, Theele C 1993 Pregnancy-associated ectopic decidua (deciduosis) of the greater omentum. An analysis of 60 biopsies with cases of fibrosing deciduosis and leiomyomatosis peritonealis disseminata. Pathol Res Pract 189: 352–359

199. Malpica A, Deavers M T, Shahab I 2002 Gross deciduosis peritonei obstructing labor: a case report and review of the literature. Int J Gynecol Pathol 21: 273–275

200. Tavassoli F A, Norris H J 1982 Peritoneal leiomyomatosis (leiomyomatosis peritonealis disseminata): a clinicopathologic study of 20 cases with ultrastructural observations. Int J Gynecol Pathol 1: 59–74

201. Hsu Y K, Rosenshein N B, Parmley T H et al. 1981 Leiomyomatosis in pelvic lymph nodes. Obstet Gynecol 57: 91S–93S

202. Clavero P A, Nogales F F, Ruiz-Avila I et al. 1992 Regression of peritoneal leiomyomatosis after treatment with gonadotropin releasing hormone analogue. Int J Gynecol Cancer 2: 52–54

203. Hales H A, Peterson C M, Jones K P et al. 1992 Leiomyomatosis peritonealis disseminata treated with a gonadotropin-releasing hormone agonist. Am J Obstet Gynecol 167: 515–516

204. Ma K F, Chow L T C 1992 Sex cord-like pattern leiomyomatosis peritonealis disseminata: a hitherto undescribed feature. Histopathology 21: 389–391

205. Raspagliesi F, Quattrone P, Grosso G et al. 1996 Malignant degeneration in leiomyomatosis peritonealis disseminata. Gynecol Oncol 61 272–274

206. Due W, Pickartz H 1989 Immunohistologic detection of estrogen and progesterone receptors in disseminated peritoneal leiomyomatosis. Int J Gynecol Pathol 8: 46–53

207. Lipschutz A, Vargas L Jr 1941 Structure and origin of uterine and extragenital fibroids induced experimentally in the guinea pig by prolonged administration of estrogen. Cancer Res 1: 236–243

208. Quade B J, McLachlin C M, Soto-Wright V et al. 1997 Disseminated peritoneal leiomyomatosis. Clonality analysis by X chromosome inactivation and cytogenetics of a clinically benign smooth muscle proliferation. Am J Pathol 150: 2153–2166

Tumors of the breast 16

Ian O. Ellis   Sarah E. Pinder   Andrew H.S. Lee

Classification of breast disease

In general, there is now consistency in the terminology, definitions and systems used for the pathologic and clinical classification of breast disease. The WHO,[1] American Society of Pathology,[2] Royal College of Pathologists,[3–5] and European Commission[6] have produced guidelines on reporting breast disease. These propose virtually identical systems of classification of benign conditions which pathologists are encouraged to adopt.[2–4,6] The Royal College and European Commission have also produced guidelines on classification of breast carcinoma and assessment of prognostic factors.[3–6]

In this chapter we use and endorse these classifications. Benign breast tumors are presented according to the major accepted groupings of fibrocystic change, fibroadenoma and variants, sclerosing lesions, papilloma and proliferative breast disease and malignant epithelial tumors according to type, with relevant descriptions of prognostic and predictive factor assessment.

Fibrocystic change and associated conditions

Fibrocystic change

Fibrocystic change is the preferred term used by pathologists to note combinations of breast changes including cyst formation, apocrine metaplasia, columnar cell change (blunt duct adenosis) and various other forms of adenosis. Minor changes, including fibrosis, microcyst formation, lobular involution and minor degrees of sclerosing adenosis or columnar cell change, should be regarded as variants of normality and classified as minimal alteration or aberrations of normal development and involution.[7]

The use of an umbrella category such as fibrocystic change, which covers a variety of alterations in the breast which may have differences in etiology or clinical relevance, is only acceptable when a dominant and distinct histologic process is absent.

Following publication of retrospective studies of breast cancer risk related to pre-existing benign breast disease, the importance of the presence of epithelial proliferation in association with fibrocystic change and other benign conditions, such as papilloma, has increasingly become recognized. The presence or absence of epithelial hyperplasia and its character is now regarded as a mandatory form of subclassification of fibrocystic change[2,3] (see proliferative breast disease, p. 919).

Clinical features

In symptomatic breast practice, fibrocystic change usually presents as a mass of variable size with variably defined margins. Ultrasound and imaging investigations may reveal cyst formation and microcalcification. The entity is rare before the age of 25 and most patients present clinically between the ages of 35 and 50. Cyst formation occurs rarely after the menopause.[8]

Macroscopic appearances

There are no characteristic gross appearances of fibrocystic change. In general, areas of breast involved by this process are ill defined and contain areas of firm fibro-fatty tissue and multiple cysts of varying size.

Histologic appearances

As defined above, fibrocystic change characteristically is a mixture of a number of benign entities which are dealt with individually below or elsewhere in this chapter.

Cysts

Clinical features

Cysts are believed to arise from a process of lobular "involution",[9,10] with microcyst formation within lobular acini and progression, through expansion or coalescence, into macroscopic cysts.

Cysts are very common, occurring in 19 percent of the general population[11] and being palpable in 7 percent.[8] Management is usually by aspiration. The cyst fluid can be examined cytologically, although this is not regarded as worthwhile unless the fluid is bloodstained or a residual mass is present, as the incidence of intracystic carcinoma is very low in comparison to the frequency of symptomatic cysts. There is no known association between single cysts and breast cancer.

Macroscopic appearances

Cysts may be single or multiple. They are rarely removed, exceptions being recurrent large cysts, multiple cysts causing disfigurement or discomfort, or the presence of an intracystic lesion. Cysts may be found in approximately 77 percent of cancer-bearing breasts as a chance finding.[12] They vary in size, are rounded and contain a range of fluid types from thin clear straw colored fluid to thick opaque green or brown material.

Histologic appearances

Two main forms of cyst are recognized, those lined by a single layer of cuboidal (Fig. 16.1) or flattened attenuated epithelium and, more commonly, those lined by apocrine-type epithelium (Fig. 16.1). This type of epithelium resembles normal apocrine sweat gland epithelium, the cells being large and columnar with abundant granular eosinophilic cytoplasm and basally positioned nuclei. The cytoplasm may protrude into the lumen in the form of apical snouts. The granules show Sudan black and periodic acid–Schiff (PAS) diastase-resistant positivity.[10] The apocrine epithelial layer is usually single, but hyperplasia resulting in a papillary architecture structure can occur. The significance of papillary apocrine change and apocrine metaplasia is dealt with below.

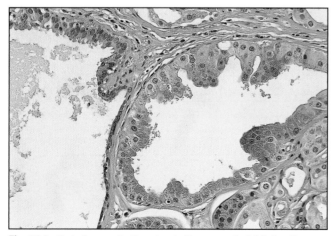

Fig. 16.1 • Cysts. Two small adjacent cysts. The one on the left is lined by cuboidal epithelium; the one on the right is lined by apocrine epithelium.

The distinction of two principal cyst types is supported by biochemical studies of cyst fluid. Cysts with a high pH and a low sodium:potassium ratio (similar to intracellular fluid) are more frequently recurrent and usually of apocrine type, in contrast with those with a lower pH and higher sodium:potassium ratio (corresponding to plasma) which are less likely to recur and are lined by a cuboidal or attenuated epithelial layer.[13,14]

Apocrine metaplasia

Apocrine metaplasia is a frequent finding in the breast and is associated with cyst formation (see above). In its usual form, regular columnar cells are arranged in a single layer above a normal myoepithelial layer. Apocrine proliferation may be more florid and take on a papillary configuration; usually these are well structured with fine fibrovascular cores. More rarely, complex patterns of apocrine hyperplasia may be found in the form of sheets or complex architectural patterns with multiple irregular luminal spaces.

In addition to its usual association with cysts, apocrine metaplasia can involve other benign processes, including sclerosing adenosis, papillomas and fibroadenomas. No particular significance is attributed to this phenomenon.

Although usually regular in nuclear and cytologic morphology, DNA tetraploidy has been identified in apocrine metaplasia.[15] This is believed to be the explanation for forms of "apocrine atypia", in which nuclear enlargement and variation in size with prominence of nucleoli can be observed. The relevance of apocrine atypia is at present poorly understood. Some authorities[16] believe this to be a purely benign phenomenon, while others have suggested it may be a precursor lesion of some forms of carcinoma such as apocrine carcinoma or medullary carcinoma.[8] Pure apocrine change is currently regarded as carrying a low, but significantly increased, risk of subsequent development of breast cancer.[2]

Differential diagnosis

Apocrine metaplasia is generally easily recognized and distinguishable from other epithelial proliferative lesions. Apocrine atypia may occur with apocrine metaplasia in areas of sclerosing adenosis. This has been classified as apocrine adenosis.[17] The combination of large cells with atypical features in a pseudoinfiltrative process, such as sclerosing adenosis, may be mistaken for invasive adenocarcinoma. The presence of a myoepithelial component and the apocrine nature of the cells should be used to differentiate these conditions.

Columnar cell change (blunt duct adenosis)

Columnar cell change (blunt duct adenosis) is retained in this section which deals with common lesions forming the spectrum of fibrocystic change. Columnar cell lesions associated with proliferative changes are described on p. 917.

Clinical features

Columnar cell change is an extremely common benign change in the breast. Some authors dismiss it as a normal phenomenon.[8] It rarely presents as a distinct clinical entity and, instead, is either a chance finding or is associated with other changes in an area of fibrocystic change. It has no recognized association with breast cancer.

Macroscopic appearances

Columnar cell change is not usually discernible to the naked eye, but it may rarely be seen as ill defined areas of microcyst formation.

Histologic appearances

Individual terminal duct lobular units show replacement of the normal luminal epithelial layer by a single layer of taller columnar epithelial cells which have basally placed nuclei and cytoplasmic apical snouts. The normal rounded acinar configuration is changed to larger irregular branching blind-ended duct-like structures (Fig. 16.2). There is an accompanying mild stromal proliferation. The myoepithelial layer and basement membrane are easily visible.

Differential diagnosis

Columnar cell change is rarely mistaken for other breast conditions. Forms of epithelial proliferation may occur in association with blunt duct adenosis, particularly gynecomastoid epithelial hyperplasia.[18] Rarely secretory or lactational changes may be observed.

Inflammatory disorders

Most inflammatory disorders of the breast are straightforward to diagnose pathologically, but sclerosing lymphocytic lobulitis can be mistaken for malignancy both clinically and histologically.

Sclerosing lymphocytic lobulitis

Sclerosing lymphocytic lobulitis, also known as lymphocytic mastopathy, is a recently recognized inflammatory disorder of the breast.[19,20] There is evidence that supports an autoimmune pathogenesis. There is a strong association with autoimmune diseases, particularly with long-standing insulin-dependent diabetes mellitus and thyroiditis. The pattern of inflammation and expression of HLA class II by breast epithelium is similar to that seen in autoimmune disorders such as Hashimoto's thyroiditis.

Clinical features

Sclerosing lymphocytic lobulitis usually presents as a mass, and can mimic carcinoma. The masses can be multiple or bilateral. Thus, by recognizing this condition, unnecessary surgery may be avoided. It can be seen in women from about 20 to 65 years old, but is most common in women in their 30s. It has also been described in men.

Macroscopic features

Typically there is a poorly defined firm grey-white mass, but sometimes the appearance resembles normal fibrous breast tissue.

Histologic appearances

The characteristic feature is circumscribed clusters of lymphocytes in and around lobules and ducts, and around blood vessels (Fig. 16.3). Typically the lymphocytes are predominantly B cells. Germinal centers may be present. Frequently, there is associated lobular atrophy. Fibrosis is usually present between lobules and sometimes within lobules. Epithelioid fibroblasts may be present,[21] but are not specific for this disorder. Patients with sclerosing lymphocytic lobulitis who have had a series of biopsies often show progression from dense inflammation to increasing lobular atrophy and fibrosis and decreasing inflammation.[20] The changes seen later in the disease (lobular atrophy and fibrosis with little inflammation) are not specific to this disorder. The pathologic features in patients with and without diabetes mellitus are similar. Thus a general *pathologic* designation such as sclerosing lymphocytic lobulitis or lymphocytic mastopathy is preferable to diabetic mastopathy.

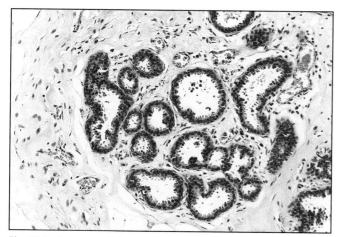

Fig. 16.2 • Columnar cell change. Columnar cells replace the normal acinar lining cells and the normal configuration of the terminal duct lobular unit is changed to a group of variably dilated duct-like structures.

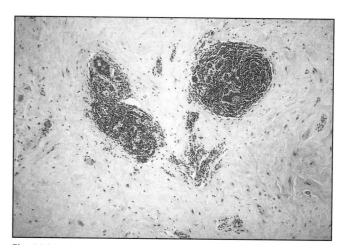

Fig. 16.3 • Sclerosing lymphocytic lobulitis showing circumscribed infiltration of the specialized terminal duct lobular stroma by small mature lymphocytes.

Differential diagnosis

The diagnosis of sclerosing lymphocytic lobulitis is usually straightforward. It may be confused with lymphoma, but lymphoma typically has a different architecture, composed of sheets of cells, and the cytology often of centroblastic type. An association between lymphoma and sclerosing lymphocytic lobulitis has been described in Japan,[22] but was not seen in recent European[23] or American series.[24] A pattern of inflammation like sclerosing lymphocytic lobulitis may be seen in association with carcinomas, particularly invasive lobular carcinoma,[25] and if marked, the inflammation may obscure the carcinoma.

Fibroadenoma, variants and related conditions

Fibroadenoma

Although fibroadenomas are still designated as benign tumors in many standard textbooks,[8,26–28] it is now believed that they are not true neoplasms[29] but may arise as a result of hyperplasia of normal lobules. This view is based on morphologic,[30] morphometric[31] and chromosomal[32] studies. In the latter, restriction fragment length polymorphism (RFLP) of the X-linked phosphoglycerokinase gene was used to demonstrate that both epithelial and stromal cells are polyclonal. The etiology is unknown, although most studies support the concept that fibroadenomas are due to the proliferation of hormone responsive tissue in the presence of a relative excess of circulating estradiol over progesterone.[33] They are included here because they produce palpable breast lumps which may be indistinguishable clinically from carcinomas.

Clinical features

Fibroadenoma is one of the most common causes of a benign lump in the breast. These lesions may occur at any age after puberty but are most frequent in the third decade. They may be single or multiple and unilateral or bilateral. Clinically, they present as firm or rubbery, mobile, well defined masses which are painless. Most measure between 1 and 2 cm in diameter but fibroadenomas measuring up to 4 cm are not uncommon. Following the advent of screening programs for breast cancer, impalpable fibroadenomas are being detected increasingly by mammography. The great majority of fibroadenomas behave in a benign way clinically and do not recur following adequate resection. Since they may be multiple it is not unusual for new lesions to become apparent, even close to the site of a previous biopsy.

There is an increasing trend for surgeons to adopt a more conservative approach to the management of women with suspected fibroadenoma using the triple approach of clinical examination, imaging and fine needle aspiration cytology (FNAC) or needle core biopsy.[34–36] Provided that all the criteria for benignity are satisfied, surgery may safely be avoided unless the patient specifically requests removal.

Malignant change is exceedingly uncommon, and to date only about 120 cases of in situ or invasive carcinoma associated with fibroadenoma have been reported.[37] The majority, about 50 percent, are lobular carcinoma in situ. In less than 40 percent the tumor is invasive and the rest are ductal carcinomas in situ. In a substantial proportion of cases, tumor is present in the adjacent tissues and it may be difficult to establish whether or not involvement of the fibroadenoma is merely coincidental. Epidemiologic studies have shown a very slight increase in relative risk for *subsequent* invasive carcinoma of approximately twofold in patients with fibroadenoma.[38,39] This risk is increased to threefold for fibroadenomas with a "complex" morphologic pattern (see below) and to fourfold for patients with a family history of breast cancer.[38] However, the absolute risk for uncomplicated fibroadenomas remains very low at 4 percent.

Macroscopic appearances

The gross appearances of a fibroadenoma are distinctive (Fig. 16.4). They are sharply circumscribed, spherical or ovoid nodules, gray white in color and clearly separate from the adjacent breast tissue. The cut surface is usually slightly lobulated and often has a glistening myxoid appearance. Most lesions are firm to the touch, but in older women they may be hard and sclerotic, even calcified.

Histologic appearances

The dominant element is a proliferation of loose cellular stromal connective tissue, which surrounds a variable number of ductular structures (Figs 16.5A,B, 16.6). The stromal nuclei are spindle shaped and normally exhibit little pleomorphism with infrequent mitoses. The quality of the stromal matrix can vary markedly, some fibroadenomas having a definite myxoid background while in others hyalinization is apparent. The ductules also vary in configuration, and two classical patterns are described – *intracanalicular* when they are compressed by the stroma into clefts (Fig. 16.5B) and *pericanalicular* when the

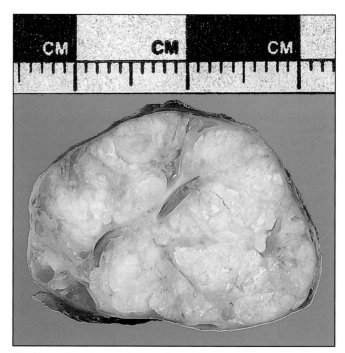

Fig. 16.4 • Fibroadenoma. The lesion has a lobulated cut surface.

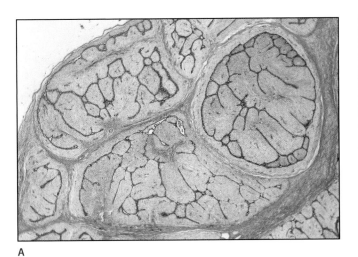

A

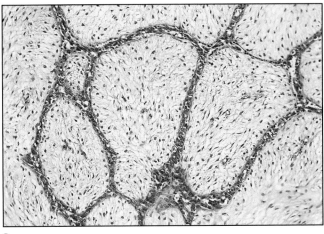

B

Fig. 16.5 • Fibroadenoma. This lesion demonstrates a typical intracanalicular pattern. The nodular structure is evident in (**A**), while the characteristic combination of epithelial clefts and cellular intralobular stroma is seen in (**B**).

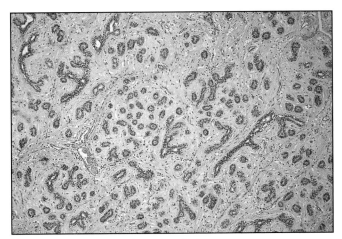

Fig. 16.6 • Fibroadenoma with a pericanalicular pattern.

stroma appears to surround ductules in a circumferential fashion (Fig. 16.6). In fact, both patterns may be seen in the same lesion and the differences in appearance are probably related to the plane in which the section is taken. These terms have no practical or prognostic significance and are purely descriptive. In about 20 percent of cases, cysts (greater than 3 mm in diameter), sclerosing adenosis, epithelial calcifications and papillary apocrine change are seen, either alone or in combination; such lesions have been termed complex fibroadenoma by Page and colleagues.[38] Epithelial hyperplasia is common and although tangential sectioning may produce worrying patterns, true atypical hyperplasia is not seen.[27]

In older patients, especially after the menopause, the stroma of fibroadenomas becomes less cellular and hyalinized. Dystrophic calcification may ensue and, in the elderly, some fibroadenomas become completely calcified.

Differential diagnosis

The most important lesion to consider in the differential diagnosis is phyllodes tumor (see p. 909). Although the latter is more often seen in an older age group, difficulties may be experienced with large fibroadenomas having a cellular stroma and numerous epithelial clefts. The distinction between fibro-

adenoma and benign phyllodes tumor may indeed be impossible to establish, but relative uniformity of stromal nuclei and lack of mitoses would favor the former. Although we disagree with use of the term fibroadenoma phyllodes,[40] it may be necessary to issue an equivocal report. Complete excision of such cases is advisable to avoid the risk of local recurrence.

The distinction of fibroadenoma from mammary hamartoma is discussed on p. 909.

Fibromatosis[41] is a rare cause of a breast lump, and the fibroblastic proliferation around ductular structures may resemble a fibroadenoma. The infiltrative edge, cellularity of stroma and relatively scanty epithelial component are all points in favor of a fibromatosis (see p. 959).

Juvenile fibroadenoma

Much confusion has been produced by inconsistent use of the terms juvenile and giant fibroadenoma. Indeed, the latter has been used to describe both large fibroadenomas and, incorrectly, benign phyllodes tumor. In practice, all juvenile fibroadenomas are large and the term is best reserved for those fibroadenomas which occur in adolescents and have a very rapid growth rate. They are well circumscribed lobulated masses which may reach 15–20 cm in diameter, stretching the skin and distorting the nipple.[42,43] Morphologically, they have an identical structure to the more typical fibroadenoma. The basic peri- and intracanalicular growth patterns are seen, but the stroma is likely to be cellular rather than hyalinized (Fig. 16.7) and may show features of pseudoangiomatous stromal hyperplasia. Epithelial proliferation is usually present and often florid[43] and Rosen has emphasized the variety of patterns which may be encountered;[28,42] care must be taken not to misinterpret the appearances as atypical ductal hyperplasia. Juvenile fibroadenomas are entirely benign and do not recur after complete local excision.

Tubular adenoma

Although most authorities have now accepted the entity of a pure mammary adenoma,[27,40,44] Rosen considers tubular adenoma to be an unusual type of fibroadenoma.[28] It is true

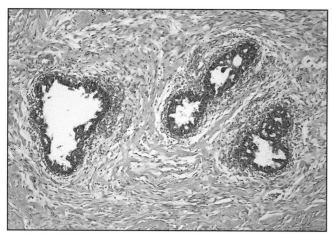

Fig. 16.7 • Juvenile fibroadenoma. Note the cellular stroma. There is also mild epithelial proliferation.

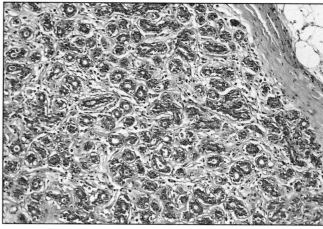

Fig. 16.8 • Tubular adenoma. Numerous small tubular structures, composed mainly of secretory epithelial cells but with less obvious myoepithelial cells, are set in a fine cellular stroma.

that some fibroadenomas contain focal areas with a tubular structure, but we exclude such cases by following the strict morphologic criteria laid down by Hertel and colleagues.[45] They emphasized the well circumscribed nature of the lesion composed of closely-packed tubules with very little associated stroma. The nature of the so-called pregnancy or lactating adenoma is also dubious. The great majority of lesions given this label are simply nodules of physiologic lobular proliferation which become more prominent than the adjacent breast tissue and may appear clinically to be a distinct mass.[46] Very rarely they may indeed be true tubular adenomas which undergo hyperplasia as a result of the hormonal stimulation of pregnancy.[47]

Clinical features

The clinical features of tubular adenoma are similar to fibroadenoma.

A variety of benign non-inflammatory mass lesions may present during pregnancy. In a consecutive series of 28 patients with an age range of 16 to 48 years (mean 23 years), three types of lesions were identified.[47] Adenomas in the form of fibroadenoma (16 cases) and tubular adenoma (two cases) were the most common lesions and usually showed lactational changes with "lactational adenoma" (10 cases) being less frequent. The lesions presented either during pregnancy or within a few months postpartum, usually as non-tender masses.

Macroscopic appearances

Tubular adenomas are well circumscribed nodules measuring between 1 and 4 cm in diameter, the majority being no greater than 2 cm. The cut surface is finely nodular.[48]

Histologic appearances

The lesions are sharply demarcated from adjacent breast tissue, but lack a true capsule. They consist of closely packed tubular structures of approximately the same size as the acini within a normal lobule (Fig. 16.8). The tubules are lined by a single layer of secretory cells, but scanty flattened myoepithelial

cells may also be present. There is no nuclear atypia and mitoses are usually infrequent. A small amount of fine connective tissue stroma is seen between the tubules.

In the "lactational adenomas", large dilated acini are present showing the typical alveolar pattern of lactating breast tissue. Luminal secretion is usually present.

Differential diagnosis

The only lesions to be considered are the fibroadenoma and tubular carcinoma. In the former, the stroma is much more prominent and the tubular structures present are arranged in lobules. A clearly two layered epithelium is seen in the tubules. Tubular adenoma should not be mistaken for tubular carcinoma. The latter has a characteristic stellate configuration with central fibrosis and elastosis with radiating tubules. The tubules are lined by a single layer of epithelial cells and infiltrate into stroma and adipose tissue at the periphery.

Mammary hamartoma

Mammary clinical features

Hamartomas are relatively uncommon lesions which occur predominantly in the peri-menopausal age group.[49–53] They may present as a large palpable mass but, surprisingly, they are often impalpable and detectable only mammographically. Clinically, they may be confused with both fibroadenoma and phyllodes tumor. Radiologically, they are large well circumscribed mass lesions with a characteristic central lucency. Although they may cause marked distortion of the breast, hamartomas are entirely benign, and do not recur after adequate local excision.

Macroscopic appearances

The lesions vary considerably in size from 1 to 15 cm, although the majority measure between 2 and 5 cm. They form well circumscribed oval masses which have a firm fleshy consistency; the lobulated structure characteristic of a fibroadenoma is not seen.

Histologic appearances

Microscopically, mammary hamartomas lack a true capsule, although they separate easily from adjacent breast tissue. They are composed of a variable mixture of connective tissue stroma and breast lobules (Fig. 16.9). The latter usually have a normal configuration. Occasional ectatic ducts are present and these may become cystic. Epithelial hyperplasia is not a feature. Islands of adipose tissue are found frequently, often in the center of the lesion (Fig. 16.10); the term adenolipoma may be applied to such lesions.[28,50] In some cases pseudoangiomatous hyperplasia is present in the stroma.[52]

Differential diagnosis

For palpable masses the differential diagnosis includes fibro-adenoma for smaller lesions and "juvenile" fibroadenoma, pseudoangiomatous stromal hyperplasia (PASH) and phyllodes tumor for larger lesions. At the microscopic level, the presence of more extensive stroma with relatively scanty lobules distinguishes fibroadenoma, and the cellular stroma surrounding characteristic leaf-like epithelial clefts is indicative of phyllodes tumor. Although pseudoangiomatous hyperplasia

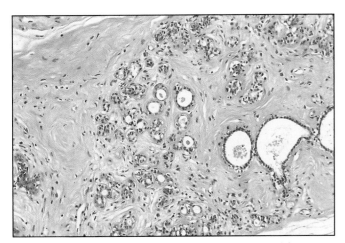

Fig. 16.9 • Hamartoma of breast. Ill-defined lobular structures and ducts are situated within a hyalinized connective tissue stroma.

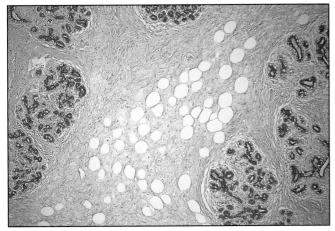

Fig. 16.10 • Hamartoma. This section was taken from the center of a large mass lesion and shows a combination of lobular structures, stroma, and adipose tissue.

is described as a component of some hamartomas,[52,53] it is usually a relatively minor component and should not be confused with the mass forming lesion of PASH,[54] in which the stromal component predominates. Mammographically, hamartoma may be mistaken for *adenolipoma*. These lesions are well circumscribed nodules of mature adipose tissue in which scanty breast lobules are scattered, with little associated stroma.[27,55]

Phyllodes tumor

These uncommon tumors of the breast were first recognized by Müller,[56] who used the term "cystosarcoma phyllodes" to describe a large breast tumor with a leaf-like cut surface on macroscopic examination (*phyllos* = leaf, Greek). Since most cases are benign, this nomenclature is misleading, as too is the designation giant fibroadenoma when some are undoubtedly malignant. For these reasons we agree with the WHO (World Health Organization) classification[57] which suggested use of the broad term phyllodes tumor, qualified as "benign" or "malignant" according to the histologic appearances.[58]

Clinical features

Phyllodes tumors occur predominantly in middle-aged or elderly women and are relatively rare below the age of 40 years. They form lobulated firm masses which may grow rapidly and cause unilateral breast enlargement or even ulceration of overlying skin. Traditionally, phyllodes tumors were said to be very large but, perhaps due to greater breast awareness, many patients now present with tumors of 2 cm or less in diameter.

Macroscopic appearances

Phyllodes tumor forms a firm lobulated mass, varying in size from about 2 cm up to 10 cm in diameter, with an average size of 5 cm.[58–60] It is usually well circumscribed, often with a bosselated contour. The cut surface shows a characteristic whorled pattern, resembling a compressed leaf bud, with visible clefts. Larger tumors frequently exhibit cystic spaces and foci of hemorrhage and necrosis are not unusual.

Histologic appearances

Microscopically, phyllodes tumors are composed of two major elements, clefts lined by epithelial cells and an associated cellular stroma (Fig. 16.11). The epithelial element consists of the usual two layers of myoepithelial and secretory epithelial cells. Focal epithelial hyperplasia is not uncommon and, although this may occasionally be florid, malignant change is extremely rare. Both lobular neoplasia and ductal carcinoma in situ have been recorded;[8,61,62] associated invasive carcinoma is an even greater rarity.[63,64]

The appearances of the stromal element vary considerably from case to case. In the majority the features are those of a benign process. Although the stroma is more cellular than in a fibroadenoma, the spindle cells do not exhibit pleomorphism and mitoses are infrequent. The presence of occasional bizarre giant cells (Fig. 16.12A) does not indicate malignant change. At the other end of the spectrum, a minority of tumors will show frankly sarcomatous features, characterized by stromal

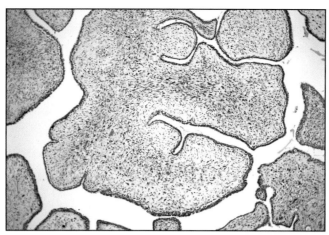

Fig. 16.11 • Phyllodes tumor. Large leaf-like structures form clefts lined by epithelial cells. There is an associated cellular stroma.

overgrowth and hypercellularity, nuclear atypia and an increased mitotic count (Fig. 16.12B). In particular, specific patterns, such as rhabdomyosarcoma, chondrosarcoma and osteosarcoma, are clear indicators of malignancy. There remains an intermediate group of tumors with appearances which pose problems for both the pathologist and clinician in predicting the likelihood of local recurrence and metastatic potential.

A number of studies[59,65–70] have addressed the question of prognostication since Norris and Taylor[71] first suggested that an infiltrative rather than pushing margin, cellular atypia, increased mitotic count and large size all favored malignancy. No coherent pattern emerges from these studies because of the small number of cases assessed, the varied database (most series being derived from secondary or tertiary referral centers), and the division into two groups, benign and malignant, by some and three groups, benign, borderline and malignant, by others. However, the majority of studies have confirmed the importance of the criteria proposed by Norris and Taylor[71] and refined by Pietruszka and Barnes.[59] In one of the few studies based on a community population rather than referred cases,[58] and using semiquantitative criteria derived from those

proposed by Pietruszka and Barnes[59] and Ward and Evans,[67] we divided phyllodes tumor into three groups – benign, borderline and malignant. In benign tumors (22 cases, 68 percent) the margins were pushing, there was minimal stromal overgrowth, cellularity and pleomorphism, and mitotic counts were less than 10 per 10 fields (field area 0.152 mm). Malignant tumors (5 cases, 16 percent) had infiltrative margins, marked stromal overgrowth, cellularity and pleomorphism, with mitotic counts greater than 10 per 10 fields. A further five cases with intermediate features were classified as borderline. We found that none of these factors was useful in predicting local recurrence which was strongly related to completeness of local excision. All recurrences in benign tumors (4 cases) occurred in patients treated initially by local excision and were controlled by complete local re-excision or mastectomy. In our small series, there were no recurrences or metastases in malignant tumors treated initially by mastectomy, but uncontrolled chest wall recurrences occurred in one patient treated by local excision.

In summary, the histopathologic criteria described above should be used to categorize phyllodes tumors as benign or malignant. Benign tumors may be managed by local conservation surgery provided that complete excision can be obtained. Malignant tumors should be managed by mastectomy. Metastasis by phyllodes tumors is very uncommon, but undoubtedly occurs.

Differential diagnosis

The differential diagnosis has been considered previously in the section on fibroadenoma (p. 907). In most cases, the distinction from fibroadenoma is straightforward, but difficulties may be encountered with small lesions. A leaf-like pattern and hypercellular stroma favor a diagnosis of phyllodes tumor, but size alone cannot be used as a distinguishing feature. Another important consideration is that some phyllodes tumours show intralesional heterogeneity including bland areas resembling fibroadenoma. Fibromatosis, primary sarcoma and metaplastic carcinoma of the breast, although very rare, must be distinguished from malignant phyllodes tumors. Again, the mixture of elements, with the leaf-like epithelial clefts are

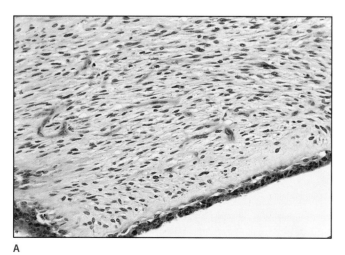

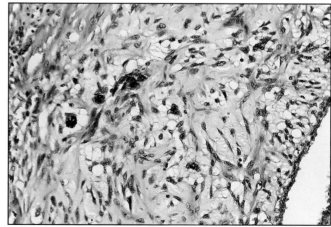

A   B

Fig. 16.12 • Phyllodes tumor **(A)** In this example of a benign lesion there is little nuclear pleomorphism. **(B)** Marked nuclear atypia is seen in the stromal cells of this malignant lesion with an abnormal mitosis.

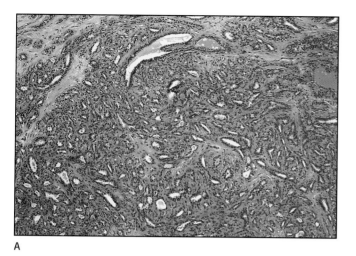

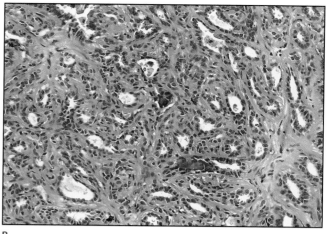

A

B

Fig. 16.13 • Sclerosing adenosis. (A) Low-power view showing a nodular disorganized proliferation of epithelial glands and intralobular stroma. (B) Foci of microcalcification are present within microtubular structures.

features of phyllodes tumor not seen in the other lesions. Metaplastic carcinoma may be distinguished by positive immunostaining of the spindle cells with keratin antibodies such as AE1/AE3, MNF 116 and CAM 5.2. Most phyllodes tumours express CD34 in the stromal component, whereas spindle cell carcinoma is typically negative.[72]

Sclerosing lesions

This broad heading covers those entities in which the combination of epithelial proliferation and stromal fibrosis and sclerosis forms a mass lesion which may be mistaken clinically, mammographically and histologically for carcinoma. The specific lesions concerned are sclerosing adenosis, microglandular adenosis, radial scar and complex sclerosing lesion.

Sclerosing adenosis

The terms adenosis and fibroadenosis, implying general disorders of glandular tissue, are so non-specific, and are so frequently applied by pathologists to breast tissue in which, in truth, there is no discernible abnormality, that their use should be abandoned. Sclerosing adenosis, however, denotes a more specific proliferative lesion arising from the terminal duct lobular unit. It is found frequently as a microscopic component of fibrocystic change but, more rarely, as a mass lesion which may be palpable.[73] This latter form has been termed adenosis tumor.[74,75] Tumor is used here in its broadest sense, with no implication of neoplasia intended, and this seems to have gained general acceptance, although "nodular sclerosing adenosis" would perhaps be a preferable designation.

Clinical features

The majority of patients who present with a clinically palpable mass are pre- or peri-menopausal but the age range varies from 20 to 70 years. The mass is usually ill defined, but skin and deep fascial fixation do not occur. In contrast with carcinoma of the breast, associated pain and tenderness are not uncommon. Following the advent of screening programs for breast cancer, sclerosing adenosis is being detected with

increasing frequency by mammography, due to the presence of microcalcifications (see below).

Macroscopic appearances

In the diffuse, microscopic form, there are, of course, no distinctive gross appearances. The nodular or tumor-type forms an ill defined, firm or hard mass varying in size from 0.5 cm to 3 cm, with an average of 1.5 cm. No specific coloration is seen.

Histologic appearances

Histologically, the normal configuration of a group of lobules is distorted by a disorderly proliferation of acini and intralobular stromal cells (Fig. 16.13) which gives an overall whorled appearance. Compressed microtubular structures may be seen, but acinar lumina are frequently obliterated. A two-layered structure is usually visible, at least in part, but epithelial and myoepithelial cells may proliferate separately. Identification of the myoepithelial component is facilitated by the use of immunostaining with anti-smooth muscle actin (Fig. 16.14) or smooth muscle myosin heavy chain. Nuclei are small and regular, usually without atypia, and mitoses are infrequent.

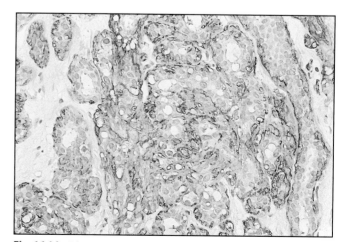

Fig. 16.14 • Sclerosing adenosis. The myoepithelial component is clearly identified by immunostaining for anti-smooth muscle actin.

Fine speckled microcalcification is found frequently in the luminal spaces of microtubular structures (Fig. 16.13B).

In the diffuse form, several small discrete lobular collections may be seen, often admixed with other features of fibrocystic change. In the nodular form the distorted lobules are fused together in an "organoid" configuration to form a definite mass lesion.

Differential diagnosis

If the nodular form produces a large enough mass it will become palpable, and may be indistinguishable clinically from a carcinoma. Mammographically, it is often impossible to distinguish the microcalcifications which are found from those seen in the cribriform type of ductal carcinoma in situ.[76] Histologically, the main differential diagnoses are a complex sclerosing lesion and invasive carcinoma. Central elastosis with entrapped tubules, an important diagnostic feature of complex sclerosing lesions, is also occasionally seen in sclerosing adenosis.[73] Conversely, foci of sclerosing adenosis are found not infrequently in complex sclerosing lesions. This suggests that the two lesions may represent ends of a spectrum of proliferative changes and, in attempting to separate them, one is indulging in a somewhat semantic argument. For the present, it is probably most practical to decide which pattern predominates and use that as the diagnostic category.

The distinction from invasive carcinoma, especially the tubular type, is the more important differential diagnosis. In a very small proportion of cases of sclerosing adenosis, extension into perineural spaces and blood vessels can be demonstrated.[77–79] Areas of apocrine change may also be present, with cytologic atypia;[80,81] in the absence of confirmatory evidence neither feature should be taken as evidence of malignancy. The main distinguishing features from invasive tubular carcinoma are the lobulocentric configuration, the disorderly proliferation of microtubules lined by two-layered epithelium and the lack of separate tubular structures with clear lumina, set in a desmoplastic stroma.

Although the risk for subsequent invasive carcinoma appears to be low,[82] both ductal carcinoma in situ and lobular neoplasia have been recorded in association with the nodular form of sclerosing adenosis.[73,83] The diagnosis of ductal carcinoma in situ should pose little problem, since benign ductal epithelial hyperplasia is rarely seen in sclerosing adenosis. Lobular proliferations require a more cautious approach, and a diagnosis of lobular carcinoma in situ should not be made unless all the criteria are fully satisfied (see p. 923).[60]

Microglandular adenosis

Microglandular adenosis is a rare, benign proliferation of small ductular or acinar structures which may be mistaken for invasive carcinoma, particularly the tubular type.[84–87]

Clinical features

Presentation of microglandular adenosis is usually in the form of a palpable mass with relatively sharp definition which may be up to several centimeters in diameter. Smaller foci can be identified as a chance finding in breast tissue excised for other reasons. Age at presentation varies widely from the mid-20s to over 80, with the majority of patients presenting between the ages of 45 and 60. Mammographic features are not specific, but may be suspicious for malignancy.[87]

Most authorities regard microglandular adenosis in its pure form as an entirely benign condition which carries no associated risk for the development of breast cancer.[88] However, a number of authors have reported the coexistence of epithelial proliferative lesions including atypical hyperplasia, in situ and invasive carcinoma.[89,90] Others believe that there is no definite evidence to support such an association.[86] Some have proposed a relationship between microglandular adenosis and acinic cell carcinoma (see p. 954), based on morphologic and immunophenotypic overlap, but this is controversial.

Macroscopic appearances

The cut surface of involved breast tissue shows an ill defined area of nondescript fibrofatty tissue. The density and appearance varies, reflecting the nature of the underlying breast stroma.

Histologic appearances

Microglandular adenosis is defined as a proliferation of small round acinar structures which are not lobulocentric but haphazardly arranged and appear to infiltrate fibrous stromal tissue and adipose tissue. These glands are typically formed by a single layer of uniform cuboidal epithelial cells which have clear or eosinophilic cytoplasm and lack apical snouts (Fig. 16.15). Mitoses are absent or very rare. Importantly, a basal myoepithelial cell component is usually absent.[84] No associated stromal reaction is seen and occasionally hyalinization can occur. There is a periglandular distribution of reticulin fibers and glands may contain PAS-positive secretions. In cases associated with epithelial proliferation the glands may vary in size. The glands are S-100 protein-positive, but are negative for EMA, ER, PR and HER2/neu.

Differential diagnosis

The principal differential diagnosis of microglandular adenosis is invasive adenocarcinoma of pure tubular type, particularly

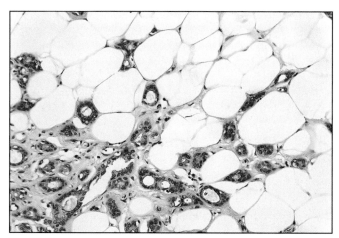

Fig. 16.15 • Microglandular adenosis. Small, rounded acinar structures are present in an irregular distribution within fibrous and adipose tissue.

the sclerosing variant.[91] In both conditions there is abnormal placement of glandular structures in mammary stroma and adipose tissue. Distinction can be made using the following criteria: tubular carcinomas usually have a distinctive stellate configuration with central elastosis and fibrosis. They excite a characteristic metachromatic stromal reaction which is not found in microglandular adenosis. The glandular structures in tubular carcinoma contain a high proportion of irregular shapes and elongated tubular forms, with some showing branching. Cytologically, the cells in tubular carcinoma are larger with more abundant eosinophilic cytoplasm, often forming characteristic apical snouts. Secretion is rare in tubular carcinoma. Although most studies have emphasized that microglandular adenosis is characterized by a single layer of epithelial cells,[84,86,87] some authors have reported the presence of myoepithelial cells in a minority of cases (Figs 16.16).[92–94] In such cases the use of immunostaining with anti-smooth muscle actin is of additional value in distinguishing microglandular adenosis from tubular carcinoma. Furthermore, tubular carcinomas usually express EMA and hormone receptors.

Sclerosing adenosis can be distinguished from microglandular adenosis by its lobulocentric configuration and the presence of a more distinct layer of myoepithelial cells.

The rare form of adenomyoepithelioma described by Eusebi and Kiaer[95] may have components indistinguishable from microglandular adenosis but typically has a dual myoepithelial and epithelial component. Its features are described in more detail in a later section (p. 952).

Radial scar/complex sclerosing lesion

These distinctive stellate lesions, characterized by a fibroelastotic center, have acquired a varied and confusing terminology including rosette-like lesions,[96] sclerosing papillary proliferation,[97] benign sclerosing ductal proliferation,[98] and infiltrating epitheliosis.[10] The latter is perhaps the least appropriate, and radial scar (RS) a translation of Hamper's "Strahlige Narben",[99] has become the most widely used.[60,100,101] The lesions vary in size, and larger examples are more likely to have a more complex structure, including epithelial hyperplasia. For this reason, Page and Anderson[60] have suggested that those lesions which measure 1–9 mm be designated radial scar and those which are 10 mm or more should be termed complex sclerosing lesions (CSL).

Clinical features

RS/CSL are reported to occur in women from 15 to 80 years of age, but are most frequent in the pre- and perimenopausal era. They were initially thought to be uncommon, perhaps because they do not usually present as a palpable mass. However, studies of surgical mastectomy specimens and breast tissue from autopsies have shown them to be common, multiple and frequently bilateral.[101–104] They are detected with increasing frequency in breast screening programs because it is virtually impossible to distinguish them from small invasive carcinomas mammographically.[100,101,105] For this reason all stellate lesions detected mammographically should be excised.

Macroscopic appearances

The gross appearances of small radial scars are unremarkable, and lesions which measure less than 3–4 mm may only become apparent on histologic examination. The larger radial scars, together with complex sclerosing lesions, form firm white stellate nodules with a dense center of variable size and fine radiating spicules of fibrous tissue. Central elastosis may be visible to the naked eye as pale yellow flecks.

Histologic appearances

The microscopic features depend on the stage of evolution of the lesion. Small early radial scars are composed of a group of radiating ductules surrounded by cellular connective tissue, with minimal elastosis (Fig. 16.17). In larger lesions, there is an accumulation of dense sclerotic fibrous tissue in the center of the lesion and elastic tissue is more evident (Fig. 16.18). The central tubules become compressed, but the normal two-layered epithelium is preserved (Fig. 16.19). Tubular structures are also present within the radiating arms, and cystic change is frequently observed (Fig. 16.17). A variable degree of

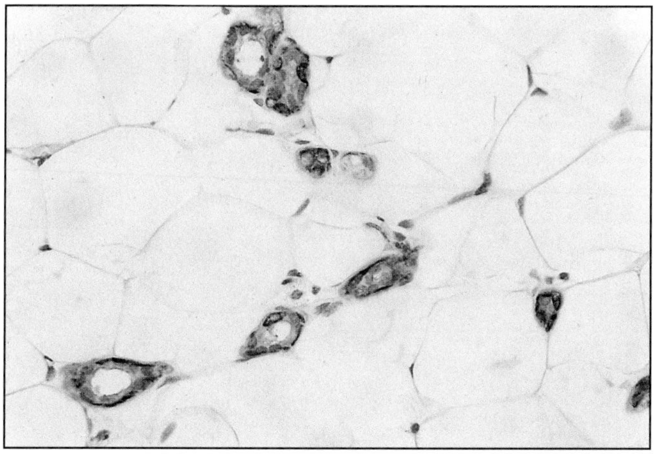

Fig. 16.16 • In this case a definite myoepithelial cell layer is demonstrated by immunostaining for anti-smooth muscle actin, indicating that this is most probably a form of sclerosing adenosis rather than microglandular adenosis.

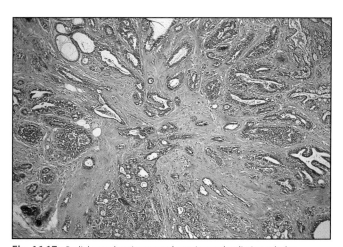

Fig. 16.17 • Radial scar showing central scarring and radiating tubular structures.

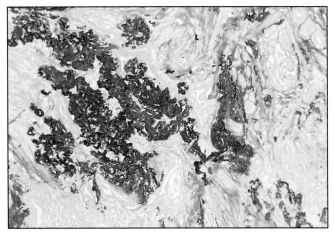

Fig. 16.18 • Complex sclerosing lesion, stained with elastic van Gieson to demonstrate the marked central elastosis.

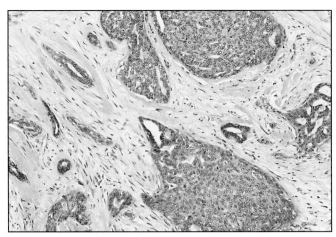

Fig. 16.20 • Epithelial hyperplasia of usual type, merging with entrapped tubules, is seen within this complex sclerosing lesion.

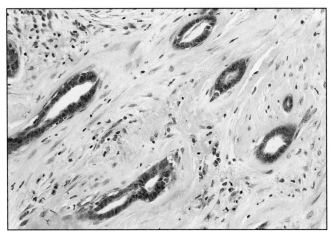

Fig. 16.19 • Fibrous and elastic tissue in the center of this complex sclerosing lesion surround entrapped tubules in which two layers of epithelium can be distinguished.

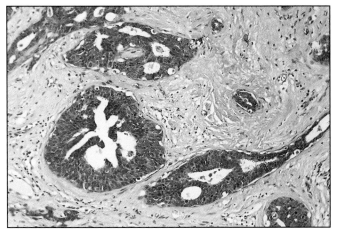

Fig. 16.21 • Atypical ductal hyperplasia in a radial scar, with adjacent elastosis and an entrapped tubule.

epithelial hyperplasia may be seen; this is most frequently of usual type (Fig. 16.20), but careful evaluation for the presence of atypical features, both ductal and lobular, is important (Fig. 16.21).

Apart from their larger size, complex sclerosing lesions, as the name implies, exhibit a wider variety of morphologic patterns. All the basic histologic features of a radial scar are present but, in addition, there may be foci of sclerosing adenosis and papilloma formation, with more florid epithelial hyperplasia. Multiple blocks of a lesion may be required in order to obtain a full appreciation of the structures present.

Differential diagnosis

Histologically, RS/CSL must be distinguished from the nodular form of sclerosing adenosis and from tubular carcinomas. The former has been discussed previously (p. 911) and this section will concentrate on the distinction from tubular carcinoma. It is the presence of entrapped tubules within the central fibro-elastotic core which poses the greatest problem. In RS/CSL the tubular structures are lined by two layers of epithelial cells in contrast with the single layer of the neoplastic tubules of a tubular carcinoma (compare Figure 16.19 with Figure 16.56). Smooth muscle actin immunostaining is useful in confirming

the difference. The entrapped tubules of RS/CSL are flattened and elongated, while those of a tubular carcinoma are rounded or oval. The nature of the associated connective tissue stroma also provides a useful contrast, being dense and relatively acellular in RS/CSL but desmoplastic in tubular carcinoma.

As noted above there is a variable degree of epithelial proliferation in RS/CSLs, ranging from usual hyperplasia to atypical hyperplasia of both ductal and lobular types. The latter needs to be distinguished from in situ carcinoma, but it is quite clear that both in situ (Fig. 16.22) and invasive carcinoma may arise in association with RS/CSLs.[101,106] As long as the diagnostic criteria for malignancy are met, the appropriate designation should be recorded.

Duct papilloma and related conditions

Duct papilloma

Papillomas are thought to be hyperplastic lesions of ducts. They occur predominantly in women between the ages of 35 and 55 years. Most patients present with single duct nipple discharge, which is often bloodstained, while in a minority

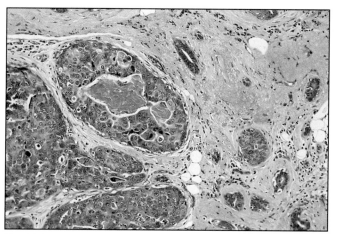

Fig. 16.22 • Complex sclerosing lesion. Elastosis surrounds entrapped tubules on the right, and ductal carcinoma in situ (DCIS) of comedo type is present on the left.

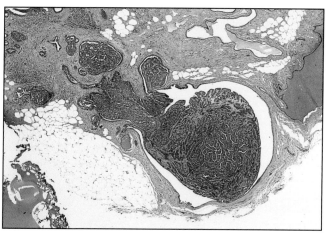

Fig. 16.23 • Duct papilloma. A large duct papilloma distends and fills a duct space.

there may be a palpable mass, usually close to the areola. Duct papillomas can be divided into two main subgroups, central, which arise from the main ducts and are usually single, and peripheral, which are associated with terminal duct lobular units and are multiple.[8,107–109]

All the available evidence suggests that the finding of a solitary central benign duct papilloma carries no increased risk of subsequent carcinoma, while multiple papillomas have an association both with concurrent ductal carcinoma in situ and an increased risk of subsequent carcinoma.[8,107–109]

Macroscopic appearances

In the great majority of cases, duct papillomas measure less than 2–3 mm in diameter and are therefore difficult to visualize by the naked-eye. The site of a papilloma within a dilated duct may be indicated by adjacent amorphous debris, including blood clot but, in most cases, the pathologist receives a specimen of fibro-fatty tissue in which there is no discernible gross abnormality. Multiple blocks may be required in order to identify the site of the lesion. Larger papillomas, up to 1–2 cm, may become encysted.

Histologic appearances

Microscopically, papillomas consist of a fronded fibrovascular core attached by a stalk to the duct wall (Fig. 16.23). Multiple fronds from the same lesion may extend into several adjacent duct spaces. Occasionally the base may be sessile. The fronds are covered by two types of epithelium (Fig. 16.24), an outer cuboidal or columnar secretory cell layer and an inner, myoepithelial cell layer. Any doubts concerning the presence of two cell types may be resolved by use of myoepithelial markers such as anti-smooth muscle actin, smooth muscle myosin or p63 immunostaining. The myoepithelial cell layer may be incomplete but, in rare cases, it forms a major part of the epithelial proliferation. In the case of single, central duct papillomas, the adjacent duct structures are usually unremarkable, although they may be dilated and contain hemorrhagic debris. Apocrine change is common and is usually focal. Infarction and hemorrhage are less common.

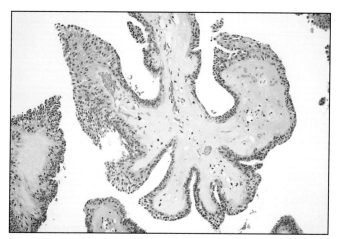

Fig. 16.24 • Duct papilloma. The papillary fronds have a fibrovascular core and are covered by a bilayer of myoepithelium and epithelium.

Multiple papillomas are usually found in smaller peripheral ducts, frequently as part of a focal or more diffuse epithelial proliferative process. They may, therefore, be accompanied by almost any type of epithelial lesion, including usual type hyperplasia, atypical ductal hyperplasia, lobular neoplasia and ductal carcinoma in situ.

Differential diagnosis

Papillary lesions can be categorized into three main groups; both morphology and immunohistochemistry for myoepithelial markers (smooth muscle actin, p63 and smooth muscle myosin heavy chain) and basal keratins (cytokeratin 5 and cytokeratin 14) are useful in separating them. Intraductal papillomas have a myoepithelial layer and any associated epithelial hyperplasia of usual type shows patchy expression of basal keratins. Papillary carcinoma in situ shows an absent myoepithelial layer and the epithelium is usually negative for basal keratins. The third and least common category of benign papilloma with involvement by ductal carcinoma in situ or atypical ductal hyperplasia shows a retained myoepithelial layer and negativity for basal keratins in the atypical areas.

Sclerosed papillomas may contain entrapped epithelial structures. Care must be taken to interpret these correctly to avoid overdiagnosis of malignancy (see p. 929). Retention of a myoepithelial layer using immunohistochemistry may be helpful. Smooth muscle myosin heavy chain and/or p63 are the markers of choice as they are expressed by myoepithelium, but not by myofibroblasts; smooth muscle actin is expressed by both cell types so cannot distinguish fibrosis from myoepithelium.

If a papillary lesion is completely infarcted then definite categorization is usually not possible.

Adenoma of nipple

This term does not delineate a specific entity but has been used in the past to describe any mass lesion of the nipple which is benign. However, the main entity is composed of an exuberant proliferation of epithelial structures which exhibit both papillary and adenomatous patterns. Because of the variability of the histologic appearances there has been disagreement concerning the appropriate nomenclature, some preferring the term florid papillomatosis of the nipple (or subareolar duct papillomatosis),[110–113] while others use nipple adenoma[60,114,115] or papillary adenoma.[8,116]

Adenomas of the nipple may occur at any age after puberty, with a peak in the perimenopausal era. They present clinically as nipple discharge or as a small firm nodule beneath the nipple epithelium. The latter may be reddened and even crusted, mimicking the appearances of Paget's disease.

Macroscopic appearances

The pathologist usually receives all or part of the nipple and areola, depending on the size of the lesion, which rarely measures more than 1 to 1.5 cm. The nodule is ill defined and firm, but has no specific distinguishing features.

Histologic appearances

The microscopic features are variable but consist principally of a diffuse papillary ductular epithelial proliferation, often intermingled with adenomatous areas (Fig. 16.25). The epithelium is two-layered with a variable degree of secretory epithelial hyperplasia, mainly of usual type (Fig. 16.26). Normal ductular and lobular structures may be included within the lesion. A cellular stroma accompanies the proliferative process and, at the periphery, a pseudo-infiltrative pattern of entrapped tubules may be seen. This, together with a tendency towards nuclear hyperchromasia may lead the unwary into a mistaken diagnosis of malignancy.

Differential diagnosis

Adenoma of the nipple must be distinguished from the rare entity of *syringomatous adenoma* of nipple.[85] In this lesion there is an infiltrate of tubular structures between lactiferous ducts, in contrast to the intraductal papillary proliferation of nipple adenoma (Fig. 16.27). As indicated above, the pseudo-infiltrative pattern in nipple adenoma may raise the possibility of a malignant process. The regularity of the epithelial structures throughout the lesion and absence of the characteristic features of ductal carcinoma in situ favor a benign process, as does the presence of a two-layered epithelium. Careful sampling is important, however, and although the risk is low, there are some reports of an association with carcinoma.[113,117]

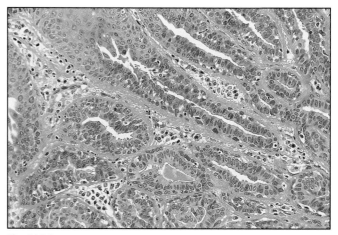

Fig. 16.26 • Nipple adenoma. The glands are lined by a bilayer of epithelial and myoepithelial cells. Epithelial hyperplasia is often seen.

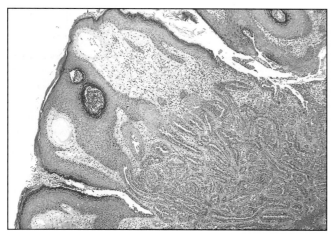

Fig. 16.25 • Nipple adenoma. There is a proliferation of glandular structures arising from the nipple ducts close to the skin surface.

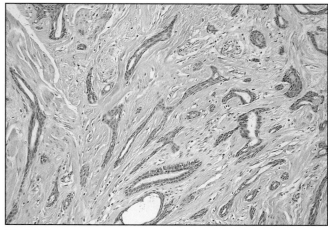

Fig. 16.27 • Syringomatous adenoma of nipple. Infiltrating glandular structures, which are often elongated or oval, are surrounded by distinctive cellular stroma.

Ductal adenoma

This term was introduced by Azzopardi and Salm to describe a solid benign lesion, usually occurring in association with one of the main breast ducts,[118] with a sclerosing adenomatous or papillary structure. As more cases have been described, it has become clear that there is considerable overlap in the morphologic appearances with sclerosing duct papilloma, sclerosing adenosis and complex sclerosing lesions,[60,119] but the central location in the breast is a distinguishing feature in most cases. The majority are thought to evolve by sclerosis of duct papillomas.[119]

Ductal adenoma is uncommon and can occur at any age after puberty, but the majority have been found in women over the age of 45. Most present as a solitary palpable mass close to the nipple, although some lesions may be peripheral.

Macroscopic appearances

Grossly, most ductal adenomas appear as well defined pale brown or grey nodules measuring up to 3 cm in diameter. In some cases, a clear association with a duct lumen or a cystic structure can be identified.

Histologic appearances

The microscopic appearances are varied, depending in large measure on the amount of associated fibrosis. Single or multiple adenomatous nodules are seen, composed of two-layered epithelium, luminal secretory cells and basal myoepithelium (Fig. 16.28). This structure can be confirmed by immunostaining for myoepithelial cells.[119,120] In some cases, the epithelial proliferation has a papillary configuration. The lesion is surrounded by dense fibrosis which often contains fragmented elastic tissue, presumably derived from the original duct, parts of which may be discernible. A minority of duct adenomas have a central stellate sclerosing appearance. Apocrine change is frequently seen within the epithelial component and this component may show nuclear atypia.

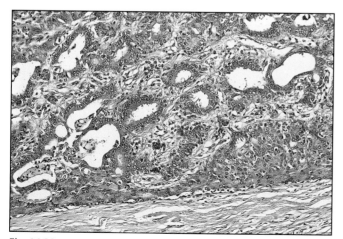

Fig. 16.28 • Ductal adenoma. A distended duct space filled with a complex mixture of epithelial-lined glandular structures, myoepithelial cells, and stromal tissue.

Differential diagnosis

Ductal adenomas are benign lesions and care must be taken not to overdiagnose malignancy. This is particularly the case if entrapped tubules are found and where there is apparent epithelial atypia. As noted above, there is considerable overlap in the morphologic features with sclerosing adenosis and complex sclerosing lesions and, in some cases, it may be impossible to make a firm distinction.[60]

Columnar cell lesions

Clinical features

This entity has previously been known under a variety of names and the nomenclature still requires consensus agreement.[121] Previous names and terms used by other groups include blunt duct adenosis, columnar alteration with prominent apical snouts and secretions (CAPSS),[122] atypical cystic lobules,[123] cancerization of small ectatic ducts of the breast by ductal carcinoma in situ cells with apocrine snouts,[124] hypersecretory hyperplasia, mammary ductal intraepithelial neoplasia-flat type, clinging ductal carcinoma in situ of monomorphic type, hyperplastic unfolded lobules, and enlarged lobular units with columnar alteration (ELUCA). We, however, use the purely descriptive term, columnar cell lesions, for this spectrum of processes.

The apparent increase in incidence in columnar cell lesions is due both to the increased recognition of the entity by pathologists and to the increasing number of core biopsy specimens received from mammographically detected lesions with microcalcifications. Indeed, one of the first descriptions of columnar cell lesions found that microcalcification was present in almost three-quarters of cases of CAPSS.[122]

The significance of these lesions is not, however, clear. While columnar cell change is considered a benign change with no further clinical implications, cytologic atypia may be present (see below). Particularly in a core biopsy sample, this causes concern and a subsequent surgical biopsy is regarded as prudent in such cases. The proportion of such cases that will have an associated in situ or invasive carcinoma has been reported to be as high as 25–33 percent.[125] Columnar cell atypia may be seen in association with ductal carcinoma in situ (DCIS) and invasive carcinoma, the latter often of tubular type[124] and genetic similarities between such processes when coexisting suggest that at least in some cases, columnar cell atypia may behave as a precursor lesion.[121,126]

Histologic appearances

Columnar cell change arises in the terminal duct lobular unit (TDLU) and the low power view demonstrates the lobulocentric nature of the process (Fig. 16.29). At higher power one can identify the columnar cell morphology of the epithelial cells lining these TDLUs, the structures often being mildly dilated and bearing secretions, which may be calcified. The columnar cells are one or two cells in depth, are arranged perpendicular to the basement membrane and are cytologically bland (Fig. 16.30). Apical snouts are often present and can be noted as "blebs" on the luminal surface of the cells. The nuclei are uniform, oval in shape. Mitotic figures are very rare.

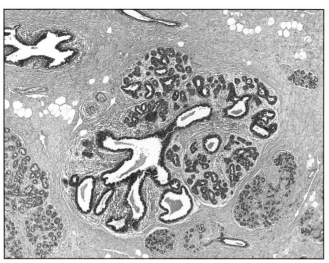

Fig. 16.29 • An example of columnar cell alteration resulting in expansion of a terminal duct unit.

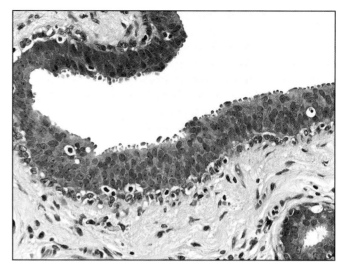

Fig. 16.31 • An example of columnar cell hyperplasia with atypia which falls within the spectrum of flat epithelial atypia. The cells are arranged in a stratified manner and show low grade atypia with rounded monotonous nuclei. Apical cytoplasmic snouts are retained.

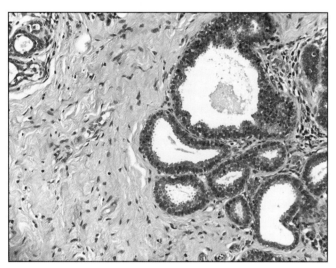

Fig. 16.30 • An example of columnar cell change. The columnar cells lining the expanded terminal duct unit are orientated to the basement membrane, have apical cytoplasmic snouts and relatively regular ovoid nuclei.

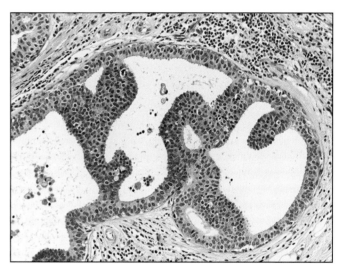

Fig. 16.32 • An example of flat epithelial atypia with focal hyperplasia of identical cells arranged in complex architectural patterns which should be classified as atypical ductal hyperplasia.

Columnar cell hyperplasia is formed from cells with the same appearance but which are more than 2 cells thick and which are often arranged in tufts or hummocks. There may be more crowding and overlapping of nuclei, but the cytonuclear features are essentially the same as the non-hyperplastic form. Apical snouts may be more obvious with a somewhat hobnail appearance and intraluminal secretions with microcalcification of psammomatous type may be prominent. It is important to note that if true micropapillae, bridges or a cribriform architecture are seen, then a diagnosis of atypical ductal hyperplasia or ductal carcinoma should be considered rather than columnar cell hyperplasia.

Columnar cell change and columnar cell hyperplasia may show cytologic atypia. Such lesions are also known as flat epithelial atypia.[127,128] This may be identified in either columnar cell change or in columnar cell hyperplasia.

In flat epithelial atypia, the TDLUs are, on low power, often darker than typically seen in columnar cell change. The lobules are often mildly to moderately dilated, as in the less cytologically worrisome process. The cells lining the TDLUs are formed from one or more layers of monotonous cuboidal cells akin to those seen in atypical ductal hyperplasia/low grade ductal carcinoma in situ. In some cases, more columnar morphology is seen and the cells remain perpendicularly arranged to the basement membrane but cytologically atypical features, such as clumped chromatin, prominent nucleoli or pleomorphism, are present (Fig. 16.31). Mitotic figures are very uncommon.

If marked pleomorphism is present, or there are features of high grade atypia, then the lesion should not be classified as flat epithelial atypia, but as flat high grade ductal carcinoma in situ (just as there is no entity of high grade atypical ductal hyperplasia). Similarly, if there is significant architectural atypia in the form of more solid bridges or well-defined micropapillary structures then the diagnosis of atypical ductal hyperplasia/low grade ductal carcinoma should be considered (Fig. 16.32).

Differential diagnosis

Columnar cell lesions arise within the TDLU and recognition of the topography of the process and the columnar cell morphology of the cells enables the correct diagnosis to be made in the majority of cases. Apocrine change may mimic columnar cell change and also arises in the TDLU. In problematic cases, estrogen receptor assessment can be performed; columnar cell lesions strongly express luminal cytokeratins (CK19), estrogen receptor and progesterone receptor, while apocrine cells express estrogen receptor weakly or are negative.

Proliferative breast disease/ epithelial hyperplasia

Clinical features

Evidence of an association between epithelial hyperplasia and carcinoma was demonstrated in the publication in 1985 of a retrospective study by Page and Dupont. These authors presented a very large series of women who had undergone biopsy for benign breast disease.[129,130] Page had earlier defined prognostic categories of epithelial hyperplasia.[131] This study stimulated a conference among pathology groups in the USA. The proceedings were published as a consensus statement[2,132] that summarized the understanding of benign conditions having a significant risk of the subsequent development of cancer by giving appropriate magnitudes of risk for each diagnostic category.

The risks attributable to these lesions[129,130,133–135] can be summarized as follows. Approximately 70 percent of women undergoing breast biopsy for benign disease have no significant histologically evident epithelial hyperplasia. Regardless of the other forms of pathology present, this group of women has no increased risk for development of carcinoma over a 15-year period compared with the general population. Twenty five percent of benign biopsies show epithelial hyperplasia of usual type and approximately 4 percent of these women develop breast cancer within 15 years, which is a twofold increase in risk. The group of women who have atypical ductal hyperplasia is small, approximately 2 percent of biopsies, 10 percent of whom develop breast cancer during 15 year follow up, a fivefold increased risk. It should be noted that the risk associated with atypical ductal hyperplasia is doubled in the very small group of women who have a family history of breast carcinoma in addition to atypical ductal hyperplasia. Similar magnitudes of risk are identified with atypical lobular hyperplasia. The subsequent tumors associated with these risks were originally described to occur with equal frequency in the ipsilateral and contralateral breast.

Proliferative breast disease usually coexists with other benign conditions such as fibrocystic change, papilloma or a sclerosing lesion and, in general, does not itself have distinctive clinical features.

Macroscopic appearances

Epithelial hyperplasia is generally a microscopic abnormality that is invisible to the naked eye. It commonly occurs in association with fibrocystic change or other benign conditions and the overall appearance of involved breast shows the features of these benign conditions as described above.

Histologic appearances

The histologic appearances and differential diagnoses of usual-type epithelial hyperplasia (proliferative disease without atypia) and atypical ductal hyperplasia (proliferative disease with atypia) are described separately below.

Usual-type epithelial hyperplasia – proliferative disease without atypia

Histologic appearances

Any increase in cell numbers above the normal bilayer of normal luminal epithelial cell and myoepithelial cell is regarded as epithelial hyperplasia, but this is usually recognized as significant if the epithelium is 4 cells or more in depth (i.e., of moderate degree, see below). The detailed histologic features are described below in differential diagnosis (Figs 16.33–16.35). Further classification is based on the degree and nature of the hyperplastic process.

The term mild epithelial ductal hyperplasia (which has no significant attributable increased risk of breast cancer) is used to note an increase of no more than 4 cells thick extending upwards from the basement membrane. Moderate hyperplasia describes an increase more than 4 cells thick in which there may be bridging of the luminal space (Fig. 16.33). In florid hyperplasia, the lumen is distended and may be obliterated (Fig. 16.34). The distinction between moderate and florid epithelial hyperplasia of usual type is relatively subjective; clearly, this is a continuous spectrum of changes. Pragmatically, there is little necessity recognized at present to sharpen the distinction between the categories of moderate and florid usual epithelial hyperplasia, as they are generally grouped together to form a single category for the purpose of risk assessment.

Epithelial hyperplasia can occur in the terminal ducts, peripheral small ducts or large ducts and may involve areas of columnar cell change, papillomas or other benign conditions.

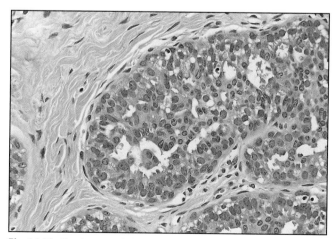

Fig. 16.33 • Usual type epithelial hyperplasia. An example of mild epithelial hyperplasia. There is an increase in the number of epithelial cells above the basement membrane with preservation of the myoepithelial layer. Epithelial cells form bridges which cross the luminal space. The residual spaces are irregular in shape and size and have a typical slit-like appearance.

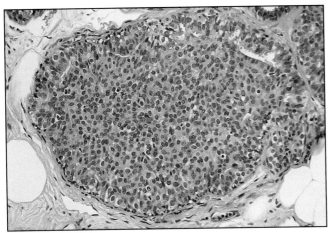

Fig. 16.34 • Usual epithelial hyperplasia. The process is far more florid than in Figure 16.33, with virtual obliteration of the lumen. Residual peripheral slit-like luminal spaces are preserved and are a useful diagnostic feature. The cells are arranged in a haphazard fashion with indistinct cell boundaries.

The site and association with other processes has no known additional significance.

Differential diagnosis

Ductal hyperplasia of usual type can be distinguished from atypical ductal hyperplasia and carcinoma in situ by its architectural low power and microscopic high power features. The population of cells is mixed. Epithelial cells predominate, but myoepithelial cells, basal/intermediate epithelial cells and lymphocytes may also be present (Fig. 16.35). In contrast to luminal epithelial cells (CK8, 18, 19+ve) seen in ADH and DCIS, basal/intermediate epithelial cells can be highlighted by molecular weight cytokeratin (CK5/6, 14) positivity.[141,142] The epithelial cells are, in general, ovoid and small but show variation in size and morphology (Figs 16.34, 16.35). As a hyperplastic process, the cells have a haphazard and irregular arrangement (Fig. 16.34) as swirling sheets, irregular, often micropapillary, projections and bridges that are often somewhat ragged in outline. A streaming character may be seen in sheets or when cells are arranged parallel to the line of papillary or bridge formations. The luminal spaces formed or remaining are irregular, not sharply defined and often slit-like (Fig. 16.35). A particular diagnostic feature is the preservation of a peripheral ring or partial ring of narrow slit-like luminal spaces (Fig. 16.35). The arrangement of cells within usual epithelial hyperplasia is uneven and varying in density from duct space to duct space and within a given duct space. Intra-luminal necrosis and hemorrhage and surrounding stromal changes may occur but are very rare and usually confined to the most florid examples. Microcalcification can occur and does not help in distinguishing between this condition and atypical hyperplasia or ductal carcinoma in situ.

Atypical ductal hyperplasia – proliferative disease with atypia

Histologic appearances

Page's broad criteria for atypical ductal hyperplasia (ADH) were accepted by the Consensus Conference in the USA and by the Royal College of Pathologists[2,5,132] as defining a process with a recognized risk of breast carcinoma.

The condition was modeled on low grade/small cell variants of ductal carcinoma in situ of cribriform and micropapillary subtypes. Lesions with some, but not all, of the features of DCIS are classified as ADH. Microscopic low power (architectural) and high power (cytologic) features are both required in order to make a confident diagnosis (Figs 16.36–16.38).

The criteria Page used[135] to identify DCIS and on which to model atypical ductal hyperplasia are:

1. a uniform population of cells.
2. smooth geometric spaces between cells or micropapillary formations with even cellular placement
3. hyperchromatic nuclei.

Separation from ductal carcinoma in situ requires strict adherence to criteria. Page and colleagues[135,136] stated that the full features of ductal carcinoma in situ should be present in at least two duct spaces for diagnosis of low grade ductal carcinoma in situ. Any lesion falling short of this is classified as atypical ductal hyperplasia. This definition provides some

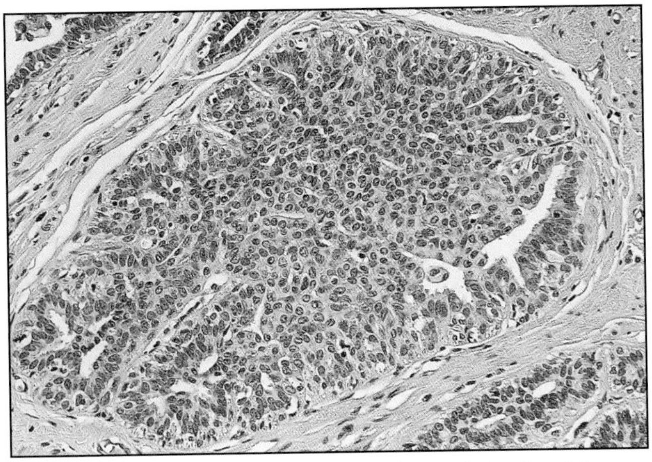

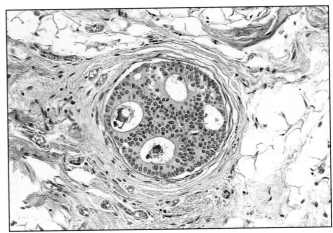

Fig. 16.35 • Usual epithelial hyperplasia. A good example showing all the cardinal features. Although epithelial cells predominate, some myoepithelial and lymphoid cells are present.

Fig. 16.36 • Atypical ductal hyperplasia. A relatively uniform single population of epithelial cells that have formed distinctive punched-out luminal spaces fills this small duct space. Myoepithelial cells appear absent around the periphery and there is some polarization of the cells around the luminal spaces.

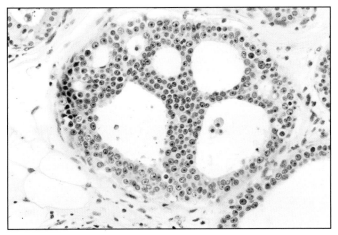

Fig. 16.37 • Atypical ductal hyperplasia. A dilated ductal space containing a proliferation of regular epithelial cells forming relatively regular luminal holes.

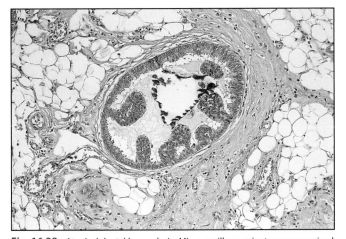

Fig. 16.38 • Atypical ductal hyperplasia. Micropapillary variants are recognized where clusters of uniform epithelial cells protrude from the population of duct-lining cells into the lumen.

objectivity to distinguish these two clinically significant entities. Other groups have used a measure of size. Tavassoli and colleagues[137] require definite features of ductal carcinoma in situ extending over an area at least 2 mm in maximum dimension for diagnosis of ductal carcinoma in situ, while smaller lesions are classified as atypical intraductal hyperplasia.

We would advise caution when attempting to make this diagnosis. Useful rules of thumb are that these lesions (ADH) are small (at least <5 mm) and localized. These are usually cases in which the diagnosis of carcinoma in situ is seriously considered but in which the features are not sufficiently developed for a confident diagnosis. Very minor changes amounting to mild atypical hyperplasia appear to be irrelevant with regard to risk and are best disregarded in a background of florid or moderate epithelial hyperplasia. When an epithelial proliferative lesion is more extensive (>1 cm) and involves otherwise normal breast parenchymal structures a diagnosis of DCIS should be made.

Differential diagnosis

Atypical ductal hyperplasia falls in the borderland or grey area of epithelial proliferative lesions of the breast. Some studies using standardized criteria have described a satisfactory inter-

observer concordance among groups of expert pathologists,[125] but reproducibility in separating atypical hyperplasia from low grade ductal carcinoma in situ in other studies appears poor.[138,139]

Another useful rule for separating atypical hyperplasia from regular hyperplasia is to recognize that atypical hyperplasia is a clonal, autonomous population of cells[140] which are relatively identical one to another (see Fig. 16.36), in contrast to usual epithelial hyperplasia where the cells are polyclonal and vary in size and shape (see Figs 16.33–16.35). Aside from the regularity in shape, the architectural arrangement takes on a structured rather than haphazard arrangement in atypical ductal hyperplasia, with evenly spaced cells forming distinctive cribriform spaces or micropapillary structures (see Figs 16.36–16.38). The mixed population of cells seen in hyperplasia is lost and replaced by a single uniform epithelial cell population (see Figs 16.36–16.38).

The clonality of ADH (or low grade DCIS) can be demonstrated by uniform homogeneous lack of expression of basal cytokeratin markers such as CK5/6 and CK14 in the epithelial cells of the proliferation, along with uniform positivity with luminal cytokeratin markers such as CK19.[141,142] Conversely, in usual epithelial hyperplasia, heterogeneous expression of luminal and basal markers is seen. The presence of mitoses, necrosis, hemorrhage and calcification are not usually useful in discriminating ADH from usual hyperplasia, or indeed from low grade DCIS. It should be noted that immunohistochemical examination of intraductal epithelial proliferations with basal and luminal markers is not of much assistance in distinguishing hyperplasia from higher grade clonal proliferations which may express basal markers, although low grade lesions express luminal cytokeratins only.

The distinction of ADH from low grade DCIS may be difficult. ADH, like low grade DCIS, is usually uniformly and strongly estrogen receptor positive and, as noted above, expresses luminal cytokeratins but is *HER2*, *p53* and basal cytokeratin negative. The cytogenetic features of low grade DCIS and ADH are also essentially similar.[140,141] In essence, distinguishing the two processes is based on assessment of extent within an individual duct, as well as the number of ducts that bear the proliferation in a pure form.

We can only emphasize the need to apply Page's or others' criteria strictly at this borderline. Diagnosis of DCIS requires a full set of all the diagnostic features listed above and the process must involve at least two duct spaces. ADH lacks one or more of these features (see Figs 16.36–16.38).

If ADH is diagnosed at the edge of a biopsy or in a needle core, the adjacent tissue may harbor in situ (or invasive) carcinoma, so re-excision should be performed.[143] It has been reported that approximately 50 percent of such cases will show ductal carcinoma in situ or invasive carcinoma in the subsequent surgical specimen following core biopsy.[143,144] This is particularly the case if smaller width core biopsy samples (e.g., 16-gauge) are examined; "up-staging" is less common with extensive sampling with larger 11-gauge core biopsy specimens.[145]

A further group of atypical hyperplastic lesions is recognized by some authorities,[88] where specific architectural patterns are absent but cytologically abnormal cells with high nuclear to cytoplasmic ratios, pleomorphism and hyperchromasia are present. In the absence of long-term follow-up studies of this type of lesion there is no clear evidence of an association with an increased risk of breast carcinoma. In some lesions of this type, the cells appear to have apocrine morphology. Their classification as atypical hyperplasia has not been accepted by some authorities,[146] although this view is relaxing[147,148] (see also Apocrine DCIS, p. 927). We currently restrict the use of atypical ductal hyperplasia to lesions that have been demonstrated to carry a long-term increased risk for the development of breast carcinoma, requiring the presence of both architectural and cytologic characteristics of low grade ductal carcinoma in situ. Any high grade cytologic atypia should not be classified as atypical ductal hyperplasia.

Lobular neoplasia

Clinical features

We share the view of Haagensen[8,149] and others[146] that this distinctive epithelial process, which occurs in the TDLU, represents a spectrum from mild atypical lobular hyperplasia (ALH) through to florid lobular carcinoma in situ (LCIS); this is, by some, classified as a single entity "lobular neoplasia". Those who regard the spectrum of ALH through to LCIS as one entity would argue that the cell type in both forms of the process is morphologically identical (Figs 16.39–16.41), the distinction being made mainly on the extent and degree of TDLU involvement with consequent issues of reproducibility of categorization. The genetic changes throughout this spectrum of lobular neoplasia are essentially similar; greater genetic and immunohistological abnormalities have not been identified in LCIS when compared to ALH. The term lobular carcinoma in situ is something of a misnomer and this is not at present regarded as an obligate precursor of invasive carcinoma. The nature of the risk associated with LCIS has resulted in the currently prevailing view that this lesion should be regarded (and managed) as a risk factor rather than as established carcinoma.

Lobular neoplasia of either form (ALH or LCIS) is a relatively uncommon lesion, occurring in approximately 1 percent of biopsies. It rarely produces a significant clinical abnormality, nor is it visible to the naked eye on macroscopic examination of resected tissue. The incidence of lobular neoplasia has increased with mammographic screening, but the changes of lobular neoplasia are generally a chance finding rather than the specific cause of the mammographic abnormality.[88] However, lobular neoplasia may rarely be identified as a result of associated microcalcification that has been noted radiologically. The frequency of detection is very dependent on the volume of tissue resected by a surgeon and the extent of histologic examination carried out by pathologists. The more tissue removed and the greater volume examined then the higher is the frequency of detection.

The magnitude of risk of subsequent carcinoma for ALH and LCIS is comparable to ADH and DCIS, i.e., a fourfold increased risk for ALH and a tenfold risk for LCIS.[130,133–135,150] However, the clinical course of LCIS appears to be more indolent than that of DCIS.[151] These lesions are most commonly identified in the perimenopausal age range with a decreasing incidence with advancing age. There is also a similar interaction with a family history of breast cancer; the combination of ALH and a first degree relative (mother, sister

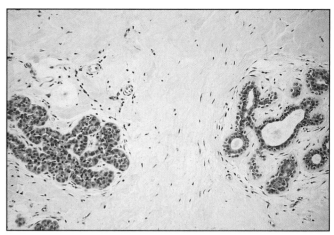

Fig. 16.39 • Lobular neoplasia. Atypical lobular hyperplasia. Two adjacent terminal duct lobular units. On the right, the acini are lined by the normal bilayer of cells and on the left, there is a population of cells resembling the normal lining cells, representing mild atypical lobular hyperplasia.

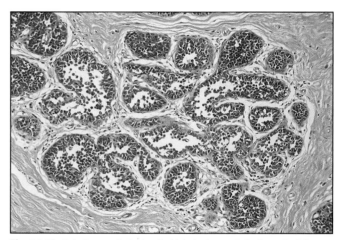

Fig. 16.40 • Lobular neoplasia. Atypical lobular hyperplasia. A terminal duct lobular unit showing proliferation of a population of uniform small cells. Some of the acini are filled but the majority show residual luminal spaces.

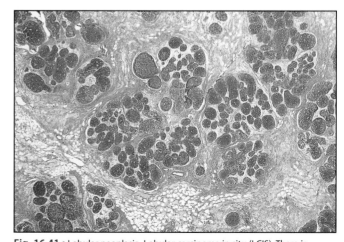

Fig. 16.41 • Lobular neoplasia. Lobular carcinoma in situ (LCIS). There is complete filling and marked distension of the terminal duct lobular units by a population of small cells resembling the normal acinar lining cells.

or daughter) with a history of breast cancer doubles the risk to nine- to tenfold. Pagetoid extension of ALH to involve adjacent ducts (see below) increases the risk to approximately sevenfold.[134] Subsequent carcinomas can occur in either breast, but more recent analyses demonstrate that ipsilateral carcinoma is three times more frequent than contralateral disease[126] and experts have described that ALH has a role "intermediate between a local precursor and a generalized risk for both breasts".[152] Tumors can arise shortly after diagnosis of LCIS, but the majority occur sporadically over the next 15–20 years.[149,153]

Lobular neoplasia appears to be a truly multifocal phenomenon, with many cases having separate lesions in other quadrants of the breast and disease in the opposite breast as identified by mirror image biopsy (see review[154]). Thus, approximately one-third of patients will have contralateral disease and over 50 percent will have additional multiple foci of disease in the ipsilateral breast.

Macroscopic appearances

Except for very rare circumstances in which there is florid localized lobular carcinoma in situ forming an indistinct mass lesion, both ALH and LCIS are invisible to the naked eye. As discussed above, lobular neoplasia is usually identified as a chance finding in tissue resected for another reason.

Histologic appearances

Lobular neoplasia is defined as a uniform population of characteristic cells within the acini of TDLUs (Figs 16.39–16.41). Loss of heterozygosity studies show that lobular neoplasia is a clonal process.[155] This clonal proliferation can fill, distend and distort the TDLU in LCIS. It may extend to involve adjacent ducts in a Pagetoid fashion beneath the luminal epithelial cells or replace the normal duct epithelial layer.

The cells have a characteristic appearance resembling the acinar epithelial cell, being small with a regular rounded lightly-stained nucleus and a surrounding thin rim of cytoplasm. Nucleoli are indistinct or small. The small size, uniformity and roundness of the cell population are its hallmarks. The cells are discohesive and cell membranes are indistinct. Occasional cells may contain intracytoplasmic lumina. These are mucin-filled vacuoles formed by microvillous apical membrane. They may be identified using epithelial membrane immunoreactivity or, more traditionally, a combined alcian blue periodic acid-Schiff (PAS) stain.

As noted above, lobular neoplasia can extend to involve ducts, typically in a Pagetoid fashion; the neoplastic lobular cells extend singly or in groups beneath a preserved luminal epithelial layer. More rarely, with greater involvement, the luminal layer may be replaced, a process which may extend to complete filling of a duct space and leads to difficulty in differentiation from low grade solid ductal carcinoma in situ (see below).

Minor forms of lobular proliferation are variously regarded as mild ALH, although some have classified this as "typical lobular hyperplasia".[88] Page found no significantly increased risk of subsequent development of carcinoma in this group and we have tended to ignore minor degrees of lobular epithelial proliferation.[146] The large NSABP P1 trial demonstrated, however, a 56 percent reduction in subsequent development of invasive carcinoma in patients with LCIS who received tamoxifen as a preventative agent, highlighting the importance of histologic recognition of lobular neoplasia.[156]

A form of pleomorphic lobular in situ neoplasia is also described.[157] This process has the same architectural appearances as more classical forms of the disease including the lobulo-centric low power appearance. The cells are discohesive but are larger and more pleomorphic with abundant eosinophilic cytoplasm and large nuclei. These often have prominent nucleoli. Mitoses may be more conspicuous and immunohistochemical assays show a higher proliferation rate and more frequent *HER2* membrane reactivity, but the typical chromosomal changes of lobular neoplasia including loss of 16q and gain of 1q are consistently present.[158] As this form of the disease shows more aggressive morphology and a worrisome immunophenotype, there is a view that this form of the disease should be regarded as more akin to DCIS clinically, but the behaviour is poorly understood; further studies are required to address the behaviour and management of this subtype of lobular neoplasia. Other variants of LCIS are recognized, including clear cell and signet ring types. Apocrine metaplasia may also coexist with lobular carcinoma in situ.[159]

Lobular neoplasia may be identified within the confines of benign lesions such as fibroadenomas, radial scars and sclerosing adenosis. In some of these situations, it may be difficult to use the criteria laid down by Page to distinguish between ALH and LCIS, but judgment and distinction can often only be subjective based on the degree of involvement. The risk attributable to ALH or LCIS involving such lesions is currently regarded as similar to that involving distinct TDLUs.[146]

Distinction between atypical lobular hyperplasia and LCIS

The risks currently attributed to ALH, ALH with duct involvement and LCIS are largely based on Page and Dupont's work.[133,150] Page has reported consistency in the diagnosis of LCIS[146] by using the following criteria:

1 the characteristic and uniform cells described above must comprise the entire population of cells in a lobular unit
2 there must be filling (no interspersed intercellular spaces between cells) of all the acini (of the terminal duct lobular unit)
3 there must be expansion or distention of at least one half of the acini in the lobular unit.

The above criteria are used in the same manner to identify ALH, i.e., when the features present fail to achieve the criteria for LCIS. Some groups would regard "expansion" to require a population of 8 or more cells across the acinus. In ALH, in addition, the cell population may be mixed with accompanying myoepithelial cells, leukocytes and residual acinar epithelial cells.

Differential diagnosis

The most common diagnostic problem with lobular carcinoma in situ is distinction from lobular involvement by ductal carcinoma in situ, particularly when the latter is of a low grade solid type. All forms of ductal carcinoma in situ can extend to involve the acinar units of the TDLU, although this is most common with high grade disease, which causes less diagnostic difficulty. A diagnosis of ductal carcinoma in situ rests on the presence of characteristic histology in duct spaces that may be mirrored in the TDLU. LCIS and ALH usually appear lobulocentric and, when extending into adjacent ducts, typically do so in a Pagetoid fashion.

Lobular neoplasia is typically discohesive, with weak or complete loss of E-cadherin. This is a calcium dependent cell–cell adhesion molecule that can be demonstrated immunohistochemically. E-cadherin has been proposed to be a specific marker of lobular lesions and, indeed, in some borderline lesions, E-cadherin immunohistochemistry may prove extremely helpful; weak or absent membrane E-cadherin staining is seen in more than 95 percent of cases of lobular neoplasia. However, rarely, one can see a solid, regular, small cell proliferation filling and distorting ducts and also involving terminal duct lobular units (Fig. 16.42). In some instances it may be impossible to separate small cell solid DCIS and LCIS. There are also relatively unusual lesions which show features of DCIS but with a coexisting, lobulocentric, morphologically different process with histologic features of LCIS. In such cases of low grade solid epithelial proliferation, in which the differential diagnosis lies between LCIS and DCIS, a borderline pattern of E-cadherin staining may be seen.[160] There is thus a group of borderline lesions that show a mixed pattern on both routine haematoxylin and eosin stains and with E-cadherin immunostaining and which cannot be definitively categorized as LCIS or DCIS. It is our policy to report both these types of lesion (i.e., indeterminate lesions and proliferations with features of both processes) as combined DCIS and LCIS. The logic of this approach is to imply to the clinicians the risk attributable to DCIS, relating largely to the ipsilateral breast, as well as the bilateral risk attributable to LCIS.

As noted above, extension of high grade variants of ductal carcinoma in situ into the lobules tends to present no great difficulty in differentiation from lobular carcinoma in situ[161] as the cellular characteristics are typically malignant with a high

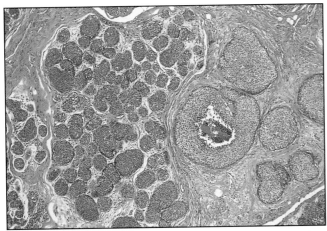

Fig. 16.42 • Lobular neoplasia with solid duct involvement. A florid example of LCIS which shows extension to adjacent ducts in a solid non-pagetoid manner. In these ducts the process is indistinguishable from small cell solid DCIS and, in this example, there is also comedo central necrosis.

nuclear to cytoplasmic ratio, large cell size, frequent mitotic figures, and necrosis. Where the differential diagnosis is pleomorphic LCIS, the architectural pattern, presence of disease predominantly in ducts and positive E-cadherin membrane reactivity favors high grade DCIS.

Malignant tumors

Carcinoma

Carcinoma of the breast is the most frequent solid epithelial malignant tumor in women, although in some countries it is now equalled by carcinoma of the bronchus. It can occur at any age, but is rare in patients younger than 25 years and over 80 years; the peak incidence is 45–60 years. The incidence and mortality are high in most developed countries, especially the UK and USA. The frequency is increasing, especially in younger age groups, and this is not due entirely to an increase in the "at risk" population. The lifetime risk for women in the western hemisphere is 1:10. Breast carcinoma is more than 200 times more common in women than men. Affected males tend to be somewhat older.[162]

It is conventional to subdivide carcinoma of the breast into two main pathologic categories – in situ carcinoma and invasive carcinoma.

In situ carcinoma
Ductal carcinoma in situ
Clinical features

Ductal carcinoma in situ (DCIS) is defined as a proliferation of malignant epithelial cells within parenchymal structures of the breast and is distinguished from invasive adenocarcinoma by the absence of microscopic stromal invasion across the limiting basement membrane.

Historically, DCIS was treated by mastectomy, following the experience of studies carried out in the 1930s and 1940s, the most widely quoted demonstrating a 50 percent rate of progression to invasive carcinoma after three years when DCIS was treated by biopsy alone.[163,164] However, it should be borne in mind that only the large cell/comedo subtypes of DCIS were recognized at that time. Initial reviews of the natural history of lesions originally classified as benign and treated by biopsy alone[165,166] showed lower frequencies of recurrence and progression to invasive carcinoma, with approximately 20–30 percent of patients developing invasive cancer over a period of 15–20 years. More recent updates of such series have suggested that the progression into invasive carcinoma continues with longer follow-up, with 40 percent of women with low grade (largely previously missed) DCIS developing invasive lesions by up to 30 years subsequently.[167]

The prognosis and optimal management of DCIS treated by wide local excision alone (with or without radiotherapy) without mastectomy remains unclear, although there are differences related to grade and biology. Further evidence of a difference in the long-term behavior of forms of DCIS has emerged from trials of conservation therapy of localized DCIS, usually detected by mammography. An increased risk of recurrent DCIS for patients who have undergone conservative surgery is associated with younger age as well as histologic features such as involved margins and high grade disease, necrosis or growth pattern.[168-173] Recurrence of in situ cancer is usually at, or close to, the original biopsy site and shows a similar genetic profile, indicating that this is residual disease.[174] Several large studies have shown that radiotherapy to the breast reduces the risk of local recurrence, but margin status in several of these series has proven problematic to quantify.[175,176] Subsequent invasive tumors also develop in the same breast, close to the biopsy site. This, together with three-dimensional reconstruction studies,[177] demonstrates that, in contrast to LCIS, DCIS appears to be a focal disease process.[178]

The pattern of presentation of DCIS has changed considerably in recent years. Historically, DCIS presented as a palpable mass or with nipple discharge, often blood stained. The propensity of all types of DCIS to undergo microcalcification, either in the center of the duct space in association with comedo type necrosis, or in inspissated secretions in cribriform acinar spaces allows detection as coarse or fine particulate densities, respectively, by mammography. This ability to detect DCIS via microcalcification has led to a substantial increase in its prevalence following the introduction of mammographic breast cancer screening. Prior to the widespread use of mammographic detection programs, DCIS constituted 5 percent or less of cases of breast cancer. In mammographic screening programs its frequency rises to 20–25 percent.[179-181]

In the past, in symptomatic practice, comedo DCIS often presented as a large clinically palpable abnormality and, in at least some series,[165,182] low grade/small cell types of DCIS were focal at presentation leading to misdiagnosis as benign breast disease. This polarized view in terms of biology and extent is less helpful in screening practice, where high grade comedo DCIS that calcifies early in a prominent coarse fashion, is often picked up as a localized small lesion. In contrast, low grade, non-necrotic types of DCIS, which tend to calcify later in their evolution and in a finely particulate fashion, are less easy to identify mammographically; in particular the extent of disease may be underestimated by over 50 percent.[178] Low grade micropapillary and cribriform, non-necrotic types of DCIS are often extensive at presentation and, for this reason, may potentially be less suitable for conservation therapy.[178,183]

Axillary nodal involvement is described in symptomatic series of DCIS at frequencies of around 1–2 percent. This usually occurs in association with extensive disease and presumably small foci of invasive carcinoma have been missed due to the logistics of sampling such large areas of disease. Smaller foci of DCIS are generally detected in mammographic breast screening. In such lesions, thorough microscopic sampling is less problematic with respect to resources and, to our knowledge, axillary node involvement has not been described. For this reason, prior to the widespread use of sentinel lymph node biopsy techniques, axillary surgery was not indicated in the management of localized DCIS.[184] However, when pure high grade DCIS is diagnosed in core biopsy samples, when associated with very extensive radiologic calcification (>40 flecks), there is an unsuspected invasive focus in approximately 50 percent of cases[185] and, in such lesions, axillary node sampling or sentinel lymph node biopsy may be appropriate.

Macroscopic features

Cases presenting symptomatically as a mass lesion may show an ill-defined area of firm fibrous tissue but often without the demarcation and solidity seen in many invasive carcinomas. DCIS with associated comedo-like necrosis, particularly if the duct spaces are dilated, may be visible to the naked eye as soft cheese-like necrotic debris which can be expressed from a cut surface.

Mammographically detected disease is frequently invisible to the naked eye. Examination of tissues requires the use of specimen radiography to select appropriate areas for histologic examination and often more extensive sampling is necessary than for invasive tumors.[5]

Classification of DCIS

Historically, DCIS was divided into different architectural patterns. Advantages of recognizing these different patterns are that it facilitates the diagnosis of DCIS and that the architecture of DCIS is often related to extent of disease.[183] However, there is often more than one architectural pattern present in an individual lesion, making this classification difficult to use reproducibly.

There is robust evidence that cytologically high grade DCIS is more likely to recur, and to progress to invasive carcinoma.[169,170,172,183] In the mid 1990s there was increasing interest in the classification of DCIS and several systems were proposed. The systems most favoured are techniques based on grade, such as that recommended in the UK,[5] U.S., Europe[6] and by the WHO[1] or on grade and architecture/differentiation,[186] or assessment of a combination of grade and necrosis.[169,170] The optimum system is not globally agreed[187] and questions remain regarding reproducibility.[188]

The validity of grading of DCIS is reinforced by studies of biologic markers. High grade DCIS is often positive for HER2 and p53, tends to be negative for estrogen receptors, progesterone receptors and bcl-2, with a high proliferation rate, while low grade DCIS is typically negative for HER2 and p53, positive for estrogen receptors, progesterone receptors and bcl-2, and has a low proliferation rate.[189-192] This is similar to the relationships between these markers and grade in invasive carcinomas.

There are also genetic differences between different grades of DCIS,[193] suggesting that these are truly different pathways to the progression of invasive carcinoma. In invasive carcinomas, the grade of the in situ and invasive components correlate.[194] Indeed, there tends to be consistency of cytonuclear grade between DCIS and invasive tumor or indeed between recurrent carcinoma and subsequent metastatic disease.[195,196]

The majority of DCIS grading systems are primarily based on nuclear grade and use three categories; there is some overlap between most classifications. The Van Nuys system uses a combination of nuclear grade and necrosis.[169] High grade is defined by the nuclear grade. The remainder are divided into non-high grade with necrosis and non-high grade without necrosis. The European Pathologists' Working Group[186] have proposed using a combination of nuclear grade and cell polarization/differentiation. The National Health Service Breast Screening Programme of the UK and the WHO[1] recommends using nuclear grade alone.[5] This is the method we use, and which we describe below.

High nuclear grade DCIS

This is composed of large pleomorphic cells with high nuclear cytoplasmic ratio. The chromatin is typically coarse and large nucleoli are common. Mitoses are often frequent, and may be atypical. Necrosis is often seen. A common pattern is central necrosis in a duct distended by a solid pattern of neoplastic cells, previously known as comedo DCIS (Fig. 16.43). The necrosis may undergo dystrophic calcification which, mammographically, is seen as a branching or linear pattern. Periductal fibrosis and adjacent perivascular clusters of inflammatory cells are often present. In addition to the solid type with central comedo-type necrosis, high grade DCIS may have a cribriform or micropapillary architecture or, less commonly, be solid without necrosis (Fig. 16.44).

Low nuclear grade DCIS

This is composed of evenly spaced cells with small regular nuclei. Nucleoli, if present, are indistinct. Cribriform (Fig. 16.45) and micropapillary (Fig. 16.46) architectures are more common than a solid growth pattern. The neoplastic cells form geometric punched-out spaces or bulbous projections around which the cells are polarized. Mitoses are infrequent and necrosis is uncommon. Calcification has a different mechanism from high grade DCIS. The calcification is found in luminal secretions and has a circumscribed edge and laminated appearance. Mammographically, this is typically seen as clusters of finely granular microcalcification.

Intermediate nuclear grade DCIS

The nuclei in intermediate nuclear grade DCIS show less pleomorphism than in high grade disease, and lack the uniformity of the low grade type. Nucleoli may be present but are usually not large. Necrosis may be present, but is not extensive. There may be some cell polarization. The architectural pattern may be solid, cribriform or micropapillary.

Rare variants of DCIS

There is a variety of rarer variants of DCIS, which may occur in pure forms or as a mixed form coexisting with the more common subtypes.

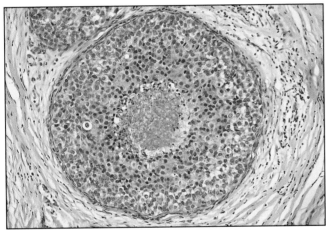

Fig. 16.43 • Comedo DCIS. The tumor cell population exhibits all the cytologic hallmarks of high-grade malignancy including large nuclear size, pleomorphism, and frequent mitosis. This subtype derives its name from necrosis of tumor cells in the central duct space.

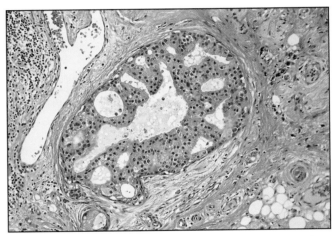

Fig. 16.45 • Low grade cribriform DCIS. A uniform single population of cells forms distinctive punched-out luminal spaces. The cells have distinct cell borders and are evenly placed.

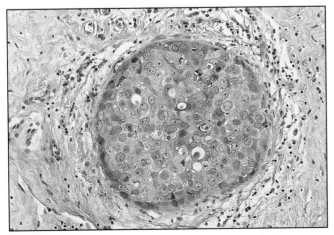

Fig. 16.44 • Large cell solid DCIS. An identical tumor cell population to comedo DCIS (Fig. 16.43) but without central comedo necrosis.

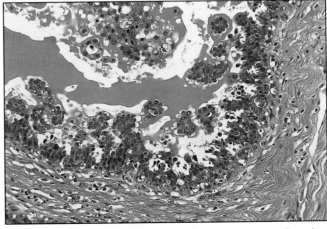

Fig. 16.46 • Low grade micropapillary DCIS. The tumor cells are small, regular, and arranged in micropapillary clusters.

Small cell solid DCIS

In this process, the duct spaces are filled by a uniform population of cells, which resemble the cells found in low grade DCIS but without their structured architectural arrangement. This condition, if it extends to involve terminal duct lobules, may be indistinguishable from lobular carcinoma in situ (see p. 922).

Apocrine DCIS

Overtly malignant apocrine lesions with marked nuclear pleomorphism, very often accompanied by necrosis, are easy to diagnose as high grade apocrine DCIS. Criteria to classify apocrine lesions with less atypia have been proposed based on nuclear pattern and extent of lesion,[147] or on nuclear pattern, necrosis, architecture and extent of the lesion.[148,197] In essence, caution should be used in diagnosing low grade apocrine DCIS; we only make this diagnosis if the lesion involves at least a few ducts as well as having architectural abnormalities, often in the form of punched-out cribriform spaces or, less commonly, micropapillary structures, as are seen in the non-apocrine form of low grade DCIS. Apocrine proliferations that do not show marked cytologic atypia and which are small or microfocal should be diagnosed with care and can be classified as apocrine atypia.

Neuroendocrine DCIS

This variant of grade DCIS with neuroendocrine features[198] is usually seen in women over 60 years. Because of a lack of microcalcification, these lesions tend to present symptomatically, often as a mass or nipple discharge. The ducts are filled by small polygonal or spindle cells, often with fibrovascular cores seen at least focally, but often merging with architecturally solid areas of DCIS. Mucin may be present. Neuroendocrine differentiation may be shown immunohistochemically and neuroendocrine DCIS very often expresses homogeneously high levels of oestrogen receptor which may be of assistance in differential diagnosis, as this lesion can mimic usual epithelial hyperplasia focally.

Signet ring cell DCIS

Mixed forms of DCIS with a signet ring cell component are well recognized; although pure forms are described, these are very rare.[199] The significance of this histologic variant is unclear.

Cystic hypersecretory DCIS

This rare form of DCIS[200,201] is distinctive through its formation of large distended cystic spaces filled with mucinous material. Some spaces may contain eosinophilic material resembling thyroid colloid. The lining epithelium may be attenuated to a large extent, making identification of the diagnostic secretory tumor cell population difficult. Where present, these cells are usually arranged in short papillary structures resembling more typical micropapillary DCIS. Cytologically, the cells have more abundant cytoplasm than the latter but show secretory changes. Distinction from cystic hypersecretory hyperplasia may be difficult.

Prognostic factors

Traditionally, DCIS was treated by mastectomy with a 98 to 99 percent cure rate. More conservative surgery is now used for DCIS less than about 3 to 4 cm in extent, the only proviso now being the cosmetic result that can be achieved with removal of, sometimes large, portions of the breast.

Initial clinical studies showed that breast conserving surgery was associated with a higher rate of recurrence than mastectomy and, as a result, a great deal of interest arose with regard to factors of value in predicting such recurrence. As noted above, high grade DCIS is more likely to recur after local excision.[169,170,172] Some studies have suggested that more extensive DCIS is more likely to recur.[170] The growth pattern[173] and the presence of necrosis[169,171] have also been recorded to be of clinical significance.

However, the most important predictor of recurrence is almost certainly completeness of excision. The greater the margin of excision, the less the risk of recurrence.[170] DCIS is typically monofocal and skip lesions with a gap of more than 10 mm are uncommon.[202] This implies that, if complete excision with an adequate margin of normal tissue can be achieved, the disease should be eradicated in most cases.

There is, however, no agreement regarding the optimum margin width of clear tissue that should be sought around a focus of DCIS. Some centers desire a 20 mm margin of uninvolved tissue, others only a 1 or 2 mm margin. In Nottingham, excision alone of DCIS with a 10 mm margin resulted in a 6 percent local recurrence rate after median follow up of 58 months[203] and other authorities similarly recommend this wide a margin.[204] Others have achieved comparable local recurrence rates with narrower margins and radiotherapy.[175] Detailed assessment of margins requires taking more sections than is usual, but the above results suggest that this is worthwhile. The role of hormone therapy in the management of DCIS is less clear.[205,206]

Differential diagnosis

The distinction between small cell DCIS and atypical ductal hyperplasia is discussed above, but rests on the presence of all of the hallmarks of DCIS (typically cribriform or micropapillary) completely involving at least two duct spaces.

DCIS may extend to involve TDLUs, so-called "cancerization of lobules".[161] Cytologic features of the cells are identical to those present in adjacent ducts and there is little difficulty in distinguishing this high grade DCIS from lobular carcinoma in situ.

High grade DCIS commonly excites a lymphocytic reaction with periductal fibrosis. These associated features are responsible for the formation of a mass in symptomatic DCIS and may mislead experienced radiologists to suggest that an invasive carcinoma is present in an area of DCIS. This fibrous reaction can also present problems in classification and can mimic invasive breast carcinoma as a result of distortion of peripheral duct structures, particularly if there is cancerization of lobules (Fig. 16.47). It is largely this phenomenon that has led to wide variation in the reported frequency of microinvasive carcinoma and early invasion between series of DCIS.

Most authorities require conclusive evidence of invasion in order to diagnose microinvasion, with the presence of

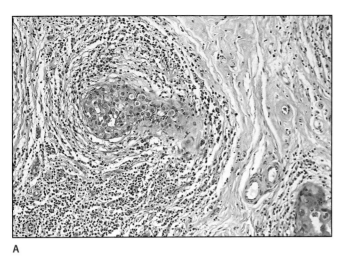
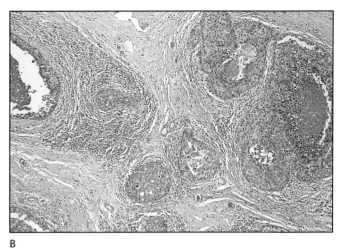

A   **B**

Fig. 16.47 • Pseudo-invasion by large cell comedo DCIS. A phenomenon which is difficult to illustrate. In this example there is an irregular focus of tumor that on high magnification (**A**) could represent invasion. The focus is, however, surrounded by specialized lobular stroma which contains an infiltrate of lymphoid cells (A,B). No tumor is seen in extralobular stroma (**B**).

unequivocally invasive foci measuring <1 mm within adipose or stromal tissue. In particular, this should extend beyond the confines of the lobulocentric and organoid configuration which is usually retained in DCIS, with or without cancerization of lobules.[146] Lesions >1 mm should be classified as established invasive carcinoma.

Paget's disease of the nipple

Clinical features

Paget's disease of the nipple is a manifestation of high grade DCIS which, when involving subareolar ducts, can extend within the confines of the duct into the epidermis. This view is supported by the fact that high grade DCIS is virtually always identified, if sufficiently thoroughly sought, in at least one subareolar nipple duct. In earlier reports, between 35 percent and 50 percent of patients had associated invasive adenocarcinoma.[8] Paget's disease occurs in around 2 percent of patients with breast cancer, presenting clinically as an erythematous or eczematous rash of the nipple.[8] The clinical features may be indistinguishable clinically from eczema or other chronic forms of dermatitis. For this reason, any nipple lesion with such features, particularly if it fails to heal rapidly, should be regarded as suspicious for Paget's disease and biopsied.

Macroscopic features

The skin of the nipple area bears a moist erythematous eczematous eruption, which may be encrusted or scaly.

Histologic features

The epidermis contains an infiltrate of single or small groups of large pleomorphic DCIS cells, usually having abundant clear staining cytoplasm, which may be vacuolated (Fig. 16.48). Some larger groups of cells may occasionally form acinar structures. There is often an accompanying infiltrate of small mature lymphoid cells that extends to involve the epidermal

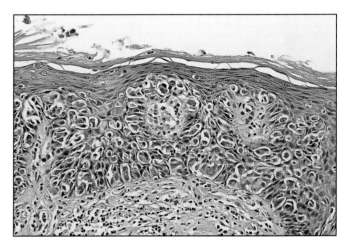

Fig. 16.48 • Paget's disease of the nipple. The epidermis of the nipple is infiltrated by large pleomorphic cells identical to those seen in large cell comedo DCIS.

layers; acute inflammatory cells may also be present. The epidermis may be hyperplastic and show parakeratosis.

The tumor cell population may show positive staining for PAS-positive diastase resistant mucins, but immunohistochemistry is often a more valuable method for confirmation of diagnosis[207] (see below).

Differential diagnosis

In a severely inflamed nipple it may be difficult to identify the infiltrate of neoplastic cells. These cells may also prove difficult to distinguish from melanocytes and, in cases where the cytoplasm is not particularly vacuolated or clear, they may resemble atypical keratinocytes such as those seen in other forms of chronic dermatitis. The use of mucin stains is an unreliable special technique in difficult cases. Immunocytochemistry using antibodies to low molecular weight cytokeratins CK8, 18, 19 (e.g., CAM5.2), which are not expressed in normal keratinocytes, and *HER2*, which is identified in over 90 percent of mammary Paget's disease, are invaluable in difficult cases.[207]

Papillary carcinoma in situ and encysted papillary carcinoma

Clinical features

Papillary carcinoma in situ is defined as an in situ malignant epithelial process occurring in a lesion with the underlying structure of a papilloma. Such lesions are circumscribed and, in the form described as "encysted", have a well-defined zone of surrounding collagenous fibrous tissue. This lesion is typically seen in older women and presents as a symptomatic mass or an ill-defined mass on mammography. The prognosis following conservation therapy is extremely good if there is no extension of DCIS beyond the fibrous capsule and so long as there is no DCIS in the adjacent breast tissue.[208]

Macroscopic features

Papillary carcinoma in situ can often be seen as a well circumscribed tumor mass. Cystic areas may be visible, containing fluid that is often brown or blood-stained. Size at presentation may vary but is usually between 1 and 3 cm.

Histologic features

Tumors are usually very well-defined, circumscribed round masses and often have a surrounding collagen-rich fibrous capsule of varying thickness. An underlying papillary structure is evident with fibrovascular cores. The fibrovascular cores are covered at least in part by the normal bilayer of myoepithelium and luminal epithelium or hyperplastic epithelial tissue. In some cases, a more solid epithelial proliferation surrounds the fibrovascular cores.[209]

Classically, the neoplastic cells in papillary carcinoma in situ are tall and columnar, arranged perpendicular to the papillary stalk (Fig. 16.49). They are closely packed and have basally-placed oval, pale or hyperchromatic nuclei. Loss of nuclear polarization and nuclear pleomorphism may occur in some cases. These cells replace the normal bilayer of epithelium, i.e., the myoepithelial layer is absent, at least focally.

Other forms of DCIS, particularly micropapillary and cribriform DCIS, may be present in isolation or in combination with some of the above features. Papillomas with foci of associated, more classical, cribriform or solid DCIS are also categorized as papillary carcinoma in situ. Thus the classic description of papillary carcinomas by Kraus and Neubecker[210] includes micropapillary and cribriform DCIS within the definition.

In many cases, particularly large examples, there is extensive hyalinization or fibrosis of fibrovascular fronds. Examination of adjacent tissue for extension of the in-situ process into adjacent ducts is important as local recurrence after conservation therapy is more frequent when DCIS is present in the adjacent breast tissue.

Differential diagnosis

The associated fibrous tissue component, particularly in the surrounding zone of breast tissue, can lead to entrapped epithelial structures containing in situ carcinoma. These may take on an angulated contour, resembling infiltrative carcinoma. We would dismiss such foci within the capsule and only report associated invasive carcinoma if there is clear extension of an invasive process into the surrounding, otherwise normal, breast tissue.

Invasive carcinoma

Clinical features

In the absence of mammographic breast screening, the great majority of invasive carcinomas are detected because of the presence of a palpable lump. This is almost invariably the case in the rare lesions arising in men. These vary in size from one to several centimeters in diameter, are firm or hard and the edge may be well or poorly defined. Overlying skin dimpling may be present and, in advanced cases, fixity to deep fascia is observed. The mass may be found anywhere in the breast, but the outer upper quadrant is the most frequent site. Approximately 2 percent of patients present with synchronous bilateral

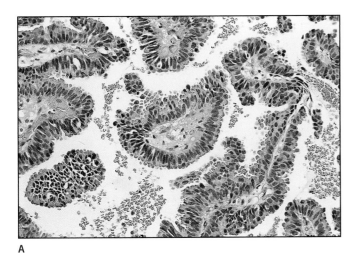

A

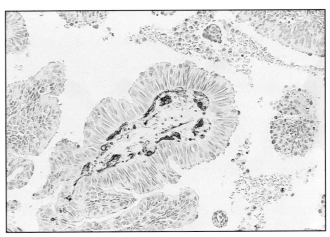

B

Fig. 16.49 • Papillary carcinoma in situ. The tumor cells typically are tall, columnar and arranged perpendicular to the basement membrane (**A**). Myoepithelial cells are absent, as shown in (**B**) using smooth muscle actin immunostaining.

invasive tumors.[211] Nipple discharge is an infrequent presenting sign and breast pain is very rarely a manifestation of malignancy. The introduction of a mammographic breast screening has altered the pattern of presentation and, in the target age group, many cases are now detected because of an impalpable mammographic abnormality.

Although there is a tendency for clinicians to regard invasive carcinoma of the breast as a single entity, pathologists have recognized an increasing number of morphologic subtypes.[1,212–214] The importance of histologic type, and its contribution to prognosis is discussed below. A description of each main category follows. Grading of invasive carcinoma is discussed separately on p. 942.

The current classification methods are descriptive and relatively subjective, with reliance on assessment by experienced histopathologists. Furthermore, the histologic appearance of the tumours cannot fully reveal the underlying complex genetic alterations and the biologic events involved in their development and progression. Intuitively, this will require development of a new classification based on key molecular events involved in the process of carcinogenesis, thereby providing a molecular explanation for the different morphologic phenotypes and behavior. The cellular and molecular heterogeneity in breast cancer and the large number of molecular events involved in controlling cell growth, differentiation, proliferation, invasion and metastasis emphasize the importance of studying multiple molecular alterations in concert. Recent high-throughput genomic studies have offered the opportunity to challenge the molecular complexity of breast cancer and have provided evidence for an alternative method for classifying breast cancer into biologically and clinically distinct groups based on gene expression patterns.[215–219] Such new molecular taxonomies have identified many genes, some of which are being proposed as candidate genes for subgrouping breast cancer. Such studies have been applied on a relatively small number of tumors and require validation in large series and comparison with traditional classification systems prior to acceptance in clinical practice. This has partly been achieved using high throughput tissue screening tissue microarray (TMA) technology. These studies have examined expression of proteins (gene products) known to be of relevance in breast cancer and have resulted in recognition of classes of breast cancer broadly similar to those identified by gene expression studies. Of note is the recognition of the importance of luminal or basal epithelial differentiation, as well as hormone receptor and *HER-2* expression. Basal epithelial differentiation or *HER-2* expression are associated with an adverse outcome when compared to tumors showing luminal epithelial differentiation and hormone receptor expression.[215,216] The concept of a basal type of breast cancer has emerged recently and is described below.

Aside from recognition of such new types of breast cancer, other recent studies have also challenged the relevance of some accepted subtypes. Medullary breast cancer has been subject to concerns regarding diagnostic reproducibility and prognostic relevance. The observation that tumours having medullary carcinoma-like features occur at high frequency in *BRCA1* gene mutation carriers[220] has been considered by some groups to merit relaxation in the definition of medullary cancer and use of the alternative term medullary-like carcinoma to distinguish such tumours.[5]

Invasive carcinoma of no special type (ductal NST)

This group contains those carcinomas which do not satisfy the criteria required to qualify for any of the other categories. It should therefore not be considered to be a distinct type of breast carcinoma. It is the most common "type" of invasive carcinoma, comprising between 47 and 75 percent in published series.[212,213,221–223] It is also the commonest type in males.[224] A variety of terms has been used to describe such tumors, including ductal carcinoma, carcinoma not otherwise specified (NOS) and invasive carcinoma of no special type (NST). The term ductal carcinoma perpetuates the idea that these tumors develop from ductal rather than lobular epithelial cells. Although this view is no longer rigidly held, the term is in common usage and has been maintained by the WHO.[1] For the present time, therefore, our preferred nomenclature is ductal no special type (ductal NST).

Macroscopic appearances

Because ductal NST is a diagnosis of exclusion there are no specific morphologic features and a variety of appearances may be seen. Tumors vary considerably in size with a range from 0.5 cm up to 10 cm or more in advanced cases. The majority are firm or hard in consistency, hence the former designation "scirrhous" carcinoma, and they may feel "gritty" on incision. They frequently have an irregular stellate outline and are moderately or ill defined.

Histologic appearances

There is considerable variation in the histologic appearances, depending in part on the interplay between the epithelial and stromal components and it is not possible to be prescriptive about the features used for its classification. The carcinoma cells may be arranged in syncytial sheets, cords or be diffusely infiltrative (Fig. 16.50). Nuclei may be highly pleomorphic or regular and glandular structures extensive or absent. In most cases foci of associated DCIS will be present and some authorities recognize a subtype with an extensive in situ component; this is discussed further on p. 946. Occasionally, areas of squamous metaplasia are encountered. Around

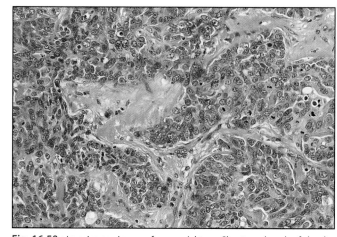

Fig. 16.50 • Invasive carcinoma of no special type. Sheets and cords of closely packed carcinoma cells invade adjacent fibrous tissue.

10 percent of cases may show immunohistochemical evidence of neuroendocrine differentiation but this has no convincing clinical or prognostic relevance.[225] To be typed as ductal NST, 90 percent must be composed of that type, after careful examination of several representative sections. If the ductal NST pattern comprises between 50 and 90 percent of a tumor and the rest is of a recognized special type then it will be classified as one of the mixed types described below.[1,5] It is interesting to note that estrogen receptor-negative examples of ductal NST are typically high grade with a prominent lymphoid stroma and pushing margins.[226]

Infiltrating lobular carcinoma

The classical form of infiltrating lobular carcinoma was first described by Foote and Stewart.[227] This terminology was used because of the association between the particular pattern of diffuse single file infiltrating carcinoma and lobular carcinoma in situ[228] in over 60 percent of cases. Whether all such carcinomas are indeed derived exclusively from lobular cells remains unproven. The criteria for the diagnosis of the classical type have been fully reviewed[229,230] and several variants have subsequently been recognized.[1] These are termed solid lobular,[231] alveolar lobular,[232] tubulo-lobular,[233] and pleomorphic lobular carcinoma.[234,235] The reported frequency of infiltrating lobular carcinoma varies widely, from 2 percent up to 15 percent,[212,213,223,231] and this probably reflects variations in the application of diagnostic criteria rather than true differences in incidence.

Both invasive lobular carcinoma and lobular neoplasia (LCIS and ALH) are associated with a high frequency of loss of E-cadherin protein expression.[83,236] There is currently a debate centered on whether E-cadherin protein loss should be considered to be a diagnostic characteristic feature of lobular lesions. There is considerable evidence favouring its use as a supporting feature and to help in classification of equivocal lesions, but it should be borne in mind that loss may also occur in other forms of invasive carcinoma.[237]

Macroscopic appearances

There is a common misconception that, because of the diffuse nature of the tumor cell infiltrate, lobular carcinoma always forms an ill defined impalpable mass. In our experience, the majority of lobular carcinomas form a scirrhous mass indistinguishable from ductal NST tumors, and only rarely do they present as ill defined areas of induration. It is the latter which may be difficult to detect clinically by palpation and which may not produce an abnormal pattern on imaging, although we have found no significant difference in mammographic features between infiltrating lobular and ductal NST carcinomas.[238]

Histologic appearances

The following histologic variants are recognized:

a Classical The classical subtype accounts for approximately 40 percent of infiltrating lobular carcinomas.[213,230] It is composed of small round or ovoid cells with little cytoplasm; the nuclei are often eccentrically placed, exhibit little pleo-

morphism and mitoses are infrequent. Although intracytoplasmic lumina are seen in all types of breast carcinoma, they are most frequent in infiltrating lobular carcinoma and may be prominent.[239] They are best visualized histochemically with periodic acid-Schiff/Alcian blue or by immunostaining for epithelial membrane antigen.[239] The tumor cells infiltrate in a diffuse manner and form characteristic files between bundles of collagen (Fig. 16.51A). Where normal ductular structures are preserved, these single cords of tumor cells infiltrate in a concentric fashion giving a "targetoid" pattern (Fig. 16.51B).

b Alveolar This is an uncommon pattern seen in only 4–5 percent of lobular carcinomas.[213,230] The cells have the same microscopic features as those in the classical type but are clustered in rounded aggregates of 20 or more cells (Fig. 16.52).

c Solid Approximately 10 percent of lobular carcinomas are of this type.[213,230] The tumor is composed of typical lobular cells, but they infiltrate diffusely in sheets rather than single cords, with little intervening stroma (Fig. 16.53).

d Tubulolobular This is another uncommon variant, accounting for 5 percent of lobular carcinomas.[213] The overall infiltrative pattern is reminiscent of classical lobular carcinoma but, to a

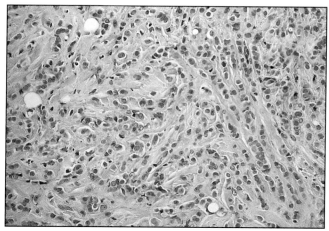

A

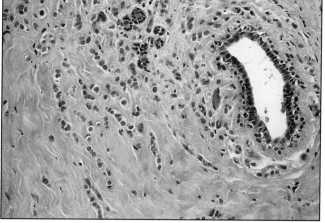

B

Fig. 16.51 • Infiltrating lobular carcinoma, classical type. Single files of tumor cells infiltrate the breast stroma (**A**). Note the "targetoid" pattern around a normal ductular structure in (**B**).

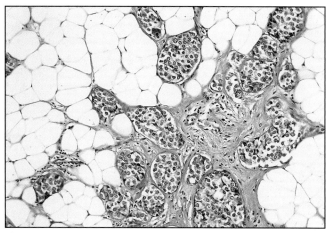

Fig. 16.52 • Alveolar type of infiltrating lobular carcinoma. The tumor is composed of rounded clusters of cells with the characteristic lobular morphology.

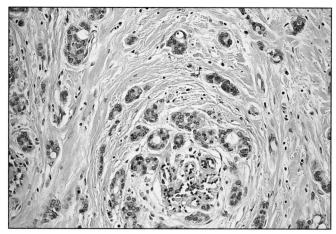

Fig. 16.54 • Tubulolobular carcinoma. A single file "targetoid" lobular infiltration is present but in places the tumor cells form definite microtubular structures.

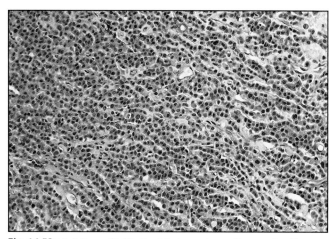

Fig. 16.53 • Solid type of infiltrating lobular carcinoma. Tumor cells with lobular cytology infiltrate in broad sheets within connective tissue stroma.

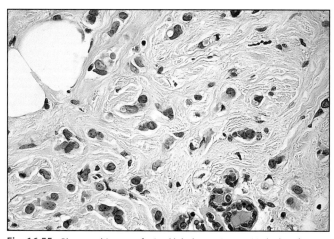

Fig. 16.55 • Pleomorphic type of mixed lobular carcinoma. Marked nuclear atypia is present in these tumor cells which otherwise exhibit typical lobular morphology.

variable degree, the cells in some cords form distinct microtubules (Fig. 16.54). These are much smaller than the tubules found in tubular carcinoma (compare Figure 16.54 with Figure 16.56), but also consist of a single layer of epithelial cells. In situ carcinoma, usually of cribriform or micropapillary type, is often present. To fulfil the criteria for tubulolobular carcinoma, at least 90 percent of the area must show the appropriate pattern.

The nature or derivation of tubulolobular carcinoma, specifically whether these tumours should be regarded as a variant of lobular carcinoma or of tubular carcinoma, remains an issue and, to some degree, relates to differences in diagnostic criteria used. One recent study has shown a high frequency of E-cadherin expression in tubulolobular carcinomas, indicating that they may not share this phenomenon with other types of lobular carcinoma and this further questions their inclusion in the group of lobular carcinoma subtypes.[240] They do appear to share a similar good prognosis with tubular carcinoma, although they are more often multifocal.[241]

e Pleomorphic Cases with a classical lobular infiltrative pattern but with cells exhibiting cellular atypia, particularly nuclear pleomorphism (Fig. 16.55)[230] are recognized as the pleomorphic variant of infiltrating lobular carcinoma.[1,157] The cells in this variant are often larger than usual, with more cytoplasm, often eosinophilic, than seen in the classical type. Emphasis has been placed on apocrine differentiation which can be seen in this variant.[234,235,242] They appear to share molecular genetic and immunophenotypic characteristics with other forms of lobular carcinoma,[158,243,244] although they appear to have an increased frequency of adverse prognostic characteristics such as higher grade and higher frequency of *HER-2* gene amplification.[1,245]

f Mixed Cases are only placed in a specific subtype if there is a dominant single pattern, e.g., classical. All other cases can be included in the mixed group, which makes up 40 percent of cases of infiltrating lobular carcinoma.[213]

In tumors which are composed of both lobular and ductal NST elements, more than 90 percent must be of lobular type (or mixed lobular pattern) to be included in this category. Those cases with a true biphasic pattern with less than 90 percent and more than 50 percent lobular component are classified as lobular and ductal NST mixed carcinomas (see below).

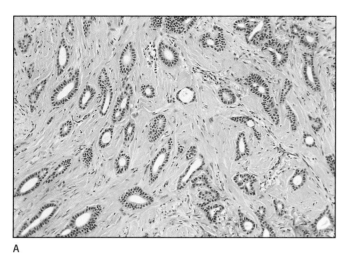 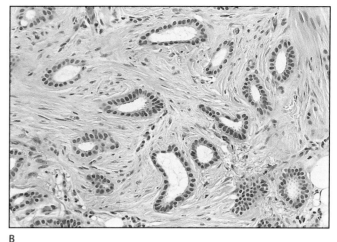

A B

Fig. 16.56 • Tubular carcinoma. **(A)** Low-power view showing tubular structures with central lumina infiltrating within a desmoplastic stroma. **(B)** High-power view of same case; the tubules are lined by a single layer of small regular nuclei with little nuclear pleomorphism.

Tubular carcinoma

In symptomatic practice, tubular carcinoma is uncommon, with a frequency of 1–3 percent.[212,213,221,222] However, a much higher frequency (between 9 and 19 percent) is found in cases detected by mammographic breast screening.[246–249] This is, of course, due to the radiologic detection of small impalpable lesions. Tubular carcinoma is widely recognized to have an excellent prognosis.[213,250,251]

Macroscopic appearances

It is usually impossible to distinguish a tubular carcinoma from the more common ductal NST or mixed types, save in the overall size of the tumor. Tubular carcinomas usually measure between 2 mm and 1.5 cm in diameter; most are 1 cm or less but, rarely, examples of 2 cm or above are encountered. Two main morphologic subtypes are recognized, the "pure" type in which the stellate nature is pronounced, with central yellow elastosis and radiating arms, and the "sclerosing" type characterized by a more diffuse, ill defined structure.[91,252]

Histologic appearances

In the *pure* type, there is central fibrosis and elastosis containing scanty tubular structures which radiate outwards and are more abundant peripherally. The *sclerosing* type has less obvious central elastosis, with a more diffuse and haphazard infiltration of tubules within connective and adipose tissue. In both types the tubules have oval or rounded lumina and are lined by a single layer of epithelial cells (Fig. 16.56A). The latter are small and regular with little nuclear pleomorphism (Fig. 16.56B). Apical snouts are frequent, but not pathognomonic. Mitoses are rare. The accompanying connective tissue stroma is cellular and desmoplastic in appearance but, at the periphery of the tumor, tubules may infiltrate into adjacent adipose tissue without an associated stroma. Ductal carcinoma in situ (usually of low grade, cribriform type) is often present.

For a tumor to be confirmed as tubular, it must exhibit clearly tubular morphology in over 90 percent of its area.[91,103,212,213,252] If a tumor contains less than 90 percent of tubules, it enters the tubular mixed, ductal and special type or

miscellaneous category. The only exception to this is the combination of pure tubular and pure cribriform elements; a tumor is typed as tubular if that pattern forms over 50 percent of the tumor area.

Tubular mixed carcinoma

Although there is now general agreement concerning the 90 percent cut off point referred to above, some authors have proposed that tumors should be classified as tubular carcinomas if they are composed of a minimum of 75 percent tubular structures.[101,253,254] Yet others have used the terms tubular mixed[91] or tubular variant carcinoma,[246,255] for those cases in which tubules occupy between 75 and 90 percent of the area. Such definitions exclude a significant number of tumors in which the tubular component amounts to less than 75 percent, and which are therefore lost within the general category of ductal NST. Since this may result in loss of potentially useful prognostic information, we have proposed a broader definition for our category of tubular mixed carcinoma.[213] This identifies approximately 14 percent of carcinomas in a symptomatic series and such cases appear to carry an improved prognosis (see p. 942). In terms of routine practice we have now adopted the standard convention of between 50 percent and 90 percent special tumour type content for classification of all mixed carcinoma types.[5]

Macroscopic appearances

Since they form a group intermediate between tubular and ductal NST carcinoma, the gross features are similar to these types. Tumors generally measure between 1.5 and 3 cm with an average size of about 2 cm. They are firm or hard in consistency, with a stellate structure and are moderately or ill defined.

Histologic appearances

To be included in the tubular mixed category, a tumor must have a stellate configuration with central fibrosis enclosing tubular structures and an infiltrating border of variable thickness composed of cords or sheets of cells with the features of

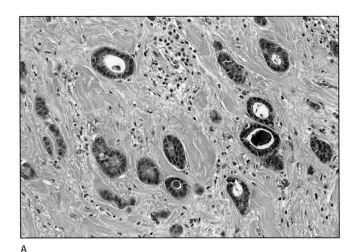

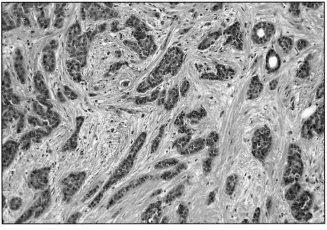

A   B

Fig. 16.57 • Tubular mixed carcinoma. (**A**) Central area, showing well-formed tubular structures. (**B**) Periphery, where tubules merge into solid cords having the pattern of ductal NST carcinoma.

ductal NST carcinoma (Fig. 16.57). There is usually central elastosis. The two types of pattern merge one into the other, there being a gradual progression from well differentiated central tubular carcinoma to less differentiated ductal NST carcinoma at the periphery. A minimum cut off point for tubule formation of 50 percent is now used in routine practice, although we have observed that, even if the number of tubules is very small, provided that the characteristic distribution of tubular and ductal NST carcinoma is seen, then the tumor may be typed as tubular mixed carcinoma.

Invasive cribriform carcinoma

These tumors are recognized as a special type of breast carcinoma related closely to tubular carcinoma.[10,213,256,257] They have been separated off from the ductal NST group because of their distinctive morphologic pattern and excellent prognosis. They are uncommon in symptomatic practice, forming less than 1 percent of cases,[213] but are encountered more frequently following mammographic screening.[246,248,249]

Macroscopic appearances

There are no specific gross features. The tumors form a firm mass, often with a stellate configuration, measuring between 1 and 3 cm in diameter.

Histologic appearances

The term invasive cribriform carcinoma has been applied to this tumor because it is composed of cords and islands of small regular epithelial cells similar to those found in DCIS of cribriform type. The nuclei are dense, with little pleomorphism and infrequent mitoses. Within the invasive islands, arches of cells form well defined, punched out spaces (Fig. 16.58); "apical snouting" of the epithelial cells is commonly present. In some cases, well formed tubular structures are seen, similar to those in a tubular carcinoma, while in others there may be more solid cords of ductal NST appearance. For a tumor to be included in the cribriform group this pattern must form at least 90 percent of the lesion, with the exception that a tumor

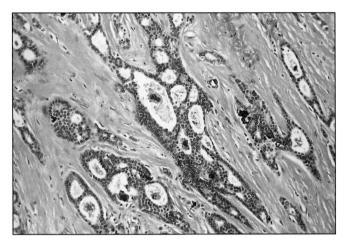

Fig. 16.58 • Invasive cribriform carcinoma. The tumor is composed of infiltrating tubular structures in which there is a prominent cribriform pattern.

with 50 percent or more can be accepted if the rest of the lesion is composed of pure tubular carcinoma.[212] A rare but distinct variant of invasive cribriform carcinoma has been described in which the stroma contains osteoclast-like giant cells.[258–260] The giant cells have been shown to be histiocytic in origin by immunohistochemistry and their presence appears to have no prognostic significance.

Mucinous carcinoma

This type is also referred to as mucoid or colloid carcinoma and, as the names imply, these are tumors in which the mucin content is apparent to the naked eye. They are relatively uncommon, accounting for between 1 and 4 percent of cases in a symptomatic series.[212,213,221–223] The frequency is not increased in breast screening.[246]

Macroscopic appearances

Characteristically, mucinous carcinomas form well, usually sharply, defined tumor masses which have a soft consistency and a glistening gelatinous cut surface. These tumors may measure between 1 and 4 cm in diameter.

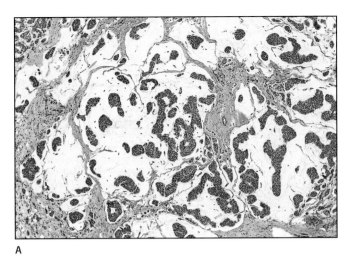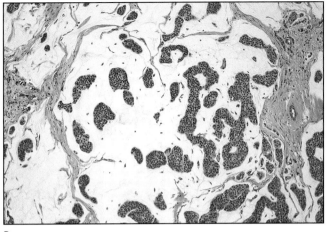

A

B

Fig. 16.59 • Mucinous carcinoma. **(A)** Clumps of carcinoma cells form islands within large lakes of mucin. **(B)** The cells are small with regular, darkly staining nuclei.

Histologic appearances

Microscopically, the tumors consist of small islands or clusters of regular epithelial cells (10–20 cells) set within extensive lakes of extracellular mucin (Fig. 16.59A) with MUC2 and MUC6 content.[261] The islands may form a cribriform or papillary pattern. The cells are small, with darkly staining nuclei which exhibit little nuclear pleomorphism; mitoses are infrequent (Fig. 16.59B). At the lesional periphery, the islands of tumor cells may be embedded in a loose fibrous stroma. Necrosis and vascular invasion are rare. Some tumors are composed of a mixture of mucinous carcinoma and ductal NST carcinoma and, in the past, there has been a lack of agreement as to how such cases should be classified. There is now general acceptance of the rule that the term mucinous carcinoma should be applied only to tumors in which at least 90 percent of the structure is of pure mucinous appearance.[212,213,262–264] We place cases with more than between 10 and 50 percent of a ductal NST element in the mixed ductal and special type carcinoma category.

Neuroendocrine differentiation can be identified in mucinous carcinomas using silver stains or immunocytochemistry for neuroendocrine markers.[10,265–267] and may be associated with an improved prognosis.[267]

Medullary carcinoma

Ever since this specific type of invasive carcinoma was described, controversy has surrounded both its diagnostic criteria and the correlation with prognosis. Medullary carcinoma was first established as a separate entity because of its apparently favourable prognosis[268] and, while some studies have supported this view,[269–272] others have not.[213,273–275] Several reproducibility studies have shown unacceptable inter- and intra-observer variability in diagnosis[276–278] and the lack of specificity of the diagnostic criteria is highlighted by the wide variation in the reported frequency of this tumor type, which ranges from 2 to 10 percent.[213,221–223] The observations that tumors having broader medullary carcinoma-like features, rather than absolutely pure morphology, are seen in tumors developing in *BRCA1* gene mutation carriers[220] has been considered by some groups to relax the definition of medullary

cancer and promote the use of the alternative term "medullary like carcinoma" to distinguish such tumors.[5] There are also recent data emerging to indicate that these tumors are associated with a basal cytokeratin phenotype[279] and may form part of the broader spectrum of tumors of basal type recognized in gene expression and other studies.[216,280]

Macroscopic appearances

Grossly, the typical medullary carcinoma is well circumscribed, with a soft and uniform consistency, measuring between 1 and 4 cm in diameter.

Histologic appearances

It is generally accepted that there are three main morphologic criteria for the diagnosis of medullary carcinoma (Fig. 16.60):

1 The epithelial cells are arranged in interconnecting sheets, forming a syncytial network. They are large and pleomorphic with a proportion of bizarre nuclei and a high mitotic count, i.e., poorly differentiated. This pattern should comprise at least 75 percent of the tumor area.

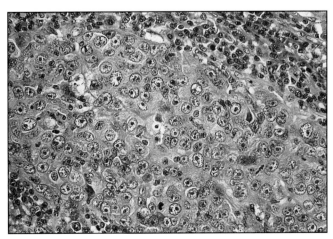

Fig. 16.60 • Medullary carcinoma. High-power view to demonstrate tumor circumscription, syncytial growth pattern, high-grade morphology, and intense lymphoplasmacytic infiltrate.

2 The intervening stroma contains a moderate or severe lymphoplasmacytic infiltrate which does not intervene extensively between individual tumor cells.

3 In keeping with the grossly evident circumscription, the border of the tumor is pushing rather than infiltrative.

The presence of associated in situ carcinoma does not preclude a diagnosis of medullary carcinoma, but it should only be present to a limited degree. Tumor necrosis is also minimal.

Tumors bearing some but not all the features of medullary carcinoma have been designated as atypical medullary carcinoma,[221,269] although it should be noted that Lidang Jensen and colleagues have not found this to be a prognostically useful group.[272] There may be a lesser degree of lymphoid infiltrate, microscopic infiltration beyond the main border or areas of dense fibrosis. A tumor may also be classified as atypical medullary if up to 25 percent is composed of ductal NST and the rest is classical medullary carcinoma. More recently, the term medullary-like carcinoma has been promoted.[5] Tumors with medullary-like carcinoma features have been identified to occur at increased frequency in *BRCA 1* gene mutation carriers (see Familial breast carcinoma section, p. 937).

Invasive papillary carcinoma

Invasive papillary carcinoma must be distinguished clearly from in situ papillary carcinoma.[242,281,282] It is a rare tumor, accounting for less than 1 percent of cases in most symptomatic series,[213,222,255] although it is possibly more frequent in the elderly.[281]

Macroscopic appearances

The gross features are varied, but many papillary carcinomas are well demarcated. They may feel soft or be indistinguishable from ductal NST carcinoma. Tumors usually measure between 1 and 3 cm in diameter.

Histologic appearances

The characteristic feature is the presence of papillary structures with associated fibrovascular cores (Fig. 16.61). Mucin secretion is frequently seen, but we distinguish such cases from mucinous carcinoma. Cytologic appearances are varied and nuclear pleomorphism and increased numbers of mitoses may be seen. In most cases, micropapillary or cribriform ductal carcinoma in situ is present in adjacent ducts. Invasive papillary carcinomas are rarely "pure" and there is often an admixture with other types such as ductal NST, mucinous and invasive cribriform carcinoma.

Invasive micropapillary carcinoma

As noted above, by definition, papillary carcinomas have a fronded structure with supportive fibrovascular cores *within* the papillary processes. The term invasive micropapillary carcinoma has now been applied to an uncommon and unusual variant of invasive breast carcinoma in which epithelial tufts forming micropapillae *without* a fibrovascular core are located

within clear spaces (Fig. 16.62).[283–285] In fact this tumor was first described formally by Peterse as an invasive carcinoma with an unexpected "inside out" growth pattern,[286] best seen using immunocytochemical staining or epithelial membrane antigen (EMA) (Fig. 16.63). All observers have noted the

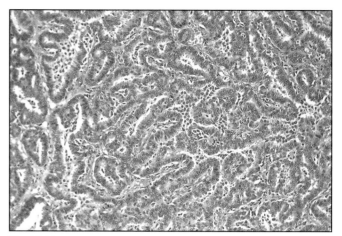

Fig. 16.61 • Invasive papillary carcinoma. Although solid, the tumor consists of papillary structures with central fibrovascular cores.

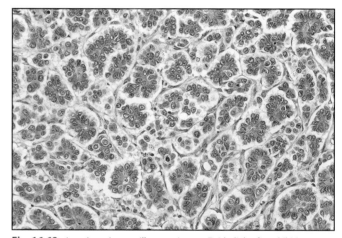

Fig. 16.62 • Invasive micropapillary carcinoma. Epithelial tufts exhibiting "reverse polarity" are seen within clear spaces.

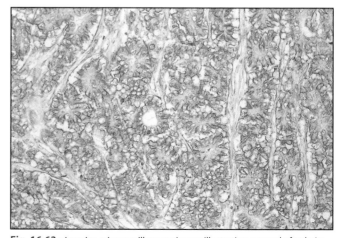

Fig. 16.63 • Invasive micropapillary carcinoma illustrating reversal of polarity (inside out) immunocytochemical staining for epithelial membrane antigen.

association with peritumoral vascular invasion and lymph node metastasis, and the prognosis is generally poor.[284,285] This may at least in part be related to a high incidence of *HER-2/ neu* overexpression.[287]

Mixed types

Excluding tubular mixed carcinoma, which is regarded as a specific tumor type closely allied to tubular carcinoma, we recognize two mixed types with a biphasic pattern.

In mixed ductal and lobular carcinoma, there are distinct ductal NST and infiltrating lobular elements, the former amounting to between 10 and 90 percent of the tumor. Such tumors are distinguished from infiltrating lobular carcinomas with a mixed pattern.

The mixed ductal and special type carcinomas include any tumors composed of a mixture of tubulolobular, tubular, invasive cribriform or mucinous carcinoma with ductal NST carcinoma in which the latter forms over 10 percent of the tumor mass.

Familial breast cancer

The histopathologic and immunohistochemical features of breast cancers arising in patients harboring germ line mutations in the *BRCA1*, *BRCA2* genes and *non-BRCA 1* or 2 genes have been studied in detail by the Breast Cancer Linkage Consortium group.[220,288–291] Breast cancers arising in patients with *BRCA1* mutations have a higher histologic grade, higher mitotic counts, a greater degree of nuclear pleomorphism, and less tubule formation than sporadic cancers. They are more likely to be steroid receptor and *HER-2* negative and harbor mutations in the *p53* gene than age-matched sporadic breast cancers unselected for family history. Breast cancers arising in patients with *BRCA2* mutations are also of a higher overall grade due to less tubule formation. They were not found to be significantly different from controls with respect to mitoses, pleomorphism, steroid receptor expression, or mutation in *p53*. *non-BRCA1/2* familial breast cancers differ histologically from both *BRCA1* and *BRCA2* breast cancers and are overall of lower grade.[220]

Attempts have been made to predict the probability of familial gene mutation association using histologic assessment of a primary breast cancer. Assessment of morphologic features alone are insufficient to give clinically useful accuracy. However, a very recent study[289] does indicate that combined use of morphologic features and immunophenotypic characteristics can be used to indicate a higher chance of *BRCA1* association. This group have shown that basal cell markers, including cytokeratins CK14, CK5/6, CK17, epidermal growth factor receptor, and osteonectin are commoner in *BRCA1* tumors than in control tumors and, in a multivariate analysis, CK14, CK5/6, and estrogen receptor (ER) remained significant predictors of *BRCA1* carrier status. In contrast, the frequency of basal markers in *BRCA2* tumors did not differ significantly from controls. The authors conclude that combined use of age of diagnosis, family history, basal markers and ER status can considerably enhance our ability to identify patients with *BRCA1* mutations by defining more precisely those subgroups of patients with a high probability of harboring a mutation.

Basal type breast cancer

Breast cancer in general is believed to arise most often from the luminal epithelial cell of the terminal duct lobular unit of the breast. Recent microarray studies have identified a small but significant subpopulation of breast cancers with a basal epithelial cell-like gene expression profile.[215,216,292] Earlier less high profile studies have shown that a proportion (2–18 percent) of cancers have a basal or myoepithelial phenotype as defined by immunohistochemical positivity for intermediate filaments such as CK5 and CK14.[293–295] Although a clear working definition for basal carcinomas is lacking, there are a number of features reported to be associated with this type of tumor. Morphologically, they are usually high grade,[295] and some of them have been reported to contain large central acellular zones comprising necrosis, tissue infarction, collagen, and hyaline material[296–298] (Fig. 16.64). Immunohistochemically, as well as expressing a number of myoepithelial markers, these tumors are often ER, progesterone receptor, and *HER-2* negative,[295,298] an immunophenotype resembling *BRCA1* tumors.[3] Microarray analysis has also shown a similarity

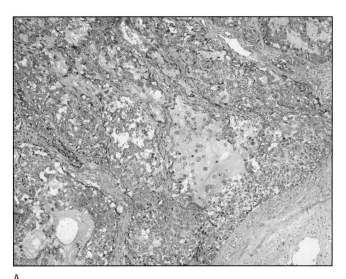

A

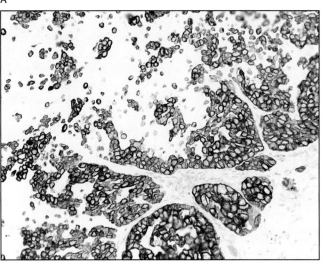

B

Fig. 16.64 • A grade 3 invasive carcinoma of breast exhibiting metaplastic matrix producing characteristics (**A**). This tumor has a basal epithelial phenotype with expression of cytokeratins 5,6 (**B**).

between sporadic, basal-like tumors and those familial tumours harboring a *BRCA1* mutation, based upon their patterns of gene expression.[13,14,216,299] Recent data have also indicated the existance of occasional cases of high grade DCIS with a basal-type phenotype.[299a]

Our group[300] have tried to define classification of basal tumours using 2 groups:

1 tumors with a basal phenotype (expressing one or both basal markers (CK5/6 and/or CK14))
2 tumors with a myoepithelial phenotype (expressing SMA and/or p63).

Group 1 was further subdivided into two subgroups:

A dominant basal pattern (>50 percent of cells are positive)
B basal characteristics (10–50 percent of cells are positive).

Group 1 tumors constituted 18.6 percent (10 percent and 8.6 percent for group 1A and 1B respectively) and group 2 constituted 13.7 percent of the cases. Basal (group 1) expression was strongly associated with both reduced overall survival and reduced disease-free interval and multivariate analysis showed that basal, but not myoepithelial, phenotype had independent value in predicting outcome.

Rare types

In this section brief descriptions are given of a miscellaneous group of uncommon tumor types which, in total, comprise less than 2 percent of invasive carcinomas. It is worth noting that pure *apocrine carcinomas* (as defined morphologically) are very rare,[301] but that apocrine change may be a focal feature in virtually any type of invasive carcinoma. Even more rare are the primary *small cell carcinomas* of breast.[302]

Secretory carcinoma

These tumors were first described in children,[303] but are now also known to occur in adults of all ages.[304,305]

Macroscopically, they are well circumscribed, and usually measure less than 2 cm in diameter. Histologically, the border is well defined, often with peripheral fibrosis. The diagnostic feature is the presence of intra- and extracellular rounded vacuoles giving an overall clear cell pattern. Where present, secretory material within vacuoles stains positively with Alcian blue and PAS with diastase digestion, indicating its mucinous nature. Genetically, they appear to be quite distinct from conventional ductal carcinomas,[306] and are particularly notable for expression of the *ETV6-NTRK3* fusion gene, also identified in infantile fibrosarcoma (see Ch. 24). In children, secretory carcinoma appears to carry an excellent prognosis, but the limited evidence available suggests that in adults the outlook is not so favorable.[307,308]

Squamous cell carcinoma

Pure squamous cell carcinoma of the breast is exceedingly rare,[308] and must be distinguished from cases of ductal NST carcinoma with focal squamous metaplasia and metaplastic carcinoma (see below). Most reported cases of squamous cell carcinoma of the breast have had a cystic element,[309] although some solid tumors have been recorded.[310] Although

relatively few cases have been studied to assess the prognostic significance of this pattern, most lesions are high grade and seem to pursue an aggressive clinical course.[311]

Metaplastic carcinoma

This term is used for those carcinomas which, in addition to epithelial elements, display sarcomatous elements including cartilage, bone, myxoid stroma and spindle cell stroma. Based on ultrastructural studies, most authorities believe that these cases represent a metaplastic alteration of carcinoma cells.[312,313] These tumors are uncommon, and represent about 0.3 percent of invasive carcinomas.[314] Grossly, they usually form large, firm, nodular tumors, often measuring as much as 5 cm in diameter. Fixity to skin or deep fascia is not uncommon.

Microscopically, two main subtypes of metaplastic carcinoma can be recognized and used for purposes of classification: monophasic "sarcomatoid" or spindle cell carcinoma and biphasic "sarcomatoid" carcinoma (which has also been referred to as "carcinosarcoma" or "malignant mixed tumor".[214,315–317] The monophasic pattern may be composed of pure spindle cells or show small cohesive foci of a few cells. The biphasic pattern contains areas of conventional carcinoma, usually invasive carcinoma of no special type or ductal carcinoma in situ.

The spindle cell variant can show a range of appearances, from sheets of pleomorphic cells to bland spindle cells resembling fibromatosis (Fig. 16.65).[315,317–321] The mesenchymal element usually shows no clear line of differentiation; more rarely angiosarcomatous, leiomyosarcomatous, osteosarcomatous, chondrosarcomatous or rhabdomyosarcomatous components may be seen. Wargotz and Norris have described a "matrix forming" pattern with a better prognosis than expected in metaplastic carcinoma.[322] Mitoses are variable in number but are usually plentiful in the tumor cells. The epithelial phenotype of the spindle cells may be established by immunostaining with a panel of markers including 34βE12, CAM5.2, MNF116, CK7, CK19 and CK20 (Fig. 16.66). It is important to use a panel of antibodies as no particular keratin is expressed in all spindle cell carcinomas.[72]

It is difficult to assess the prognosis of metaplastic carcinomas because of their rarity, but available anecdotal

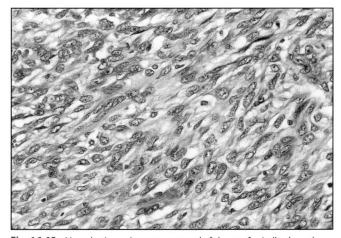

Fig. 16.65 • Metaplastic carcinoma composed of sheets of spindle-shaped cells with no morphologic epithelial differentiation.

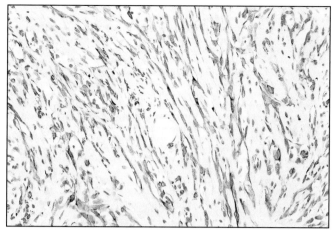

Fig. 16.66 • Metaplastic spindle cell carcinoma showing positive reactivity of tumor cell cytoplasm for cytokeratin (MNF 116).

evidence suggests that the majority behave as highly malignant tumors with early recurrence and poor survival.[314–316,320,321] Metaplastic carcinomas almost always do not express estrogen or progesterone receptors or *HER-2*, thus limiting potential systemic treatments.[314,321] The monophasic spindle cell type rarely involves axillary nodes.

Low-grade adenosquamous carcinoma

A low-grade variant of metaplastic carcinoma, low-grade adenosquamous carcinoma, has been described.[308,323,324] In this rare tumor, syringoma-like glandular elements, some showing squamous differentiation, are surrounded by a rather bland fibromatosis-like cellular spindle cell stroma (Fig. 16.67). In the published literature, low-grade adenosquamous carcinomas range in size between 5 mm and 34 mm and are found in women whose age ranges from 31 to 87 years. They have been described to occur in association with sclerosing papillary lesions, radial scars and complex sclerosing lesions.[323,325,326]

Low-grade adenosquamous carcinomas are composed of small glandular epithelial-lined structures and solid cords of epithelial cells, haphazardly arranged in an infiltrative spindle celled stromal component.[324,326] The proportions of these three

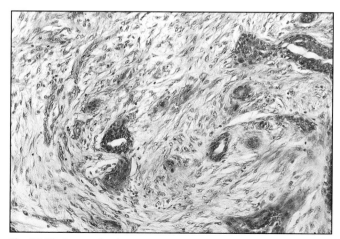

Fig. 16.67 • Low-grade adenosquamous carcinoma composed of glandular structures, some showing squamous differentiation, with surrounding bland spindle cell stroma.

components is variable between cases and the spindle cell component may be dominant. The solid nests of cells may contain squamous cells, squamous pearls or squamous cyst formation and will express high molecular weight cytokeratins. The stroma is described as "fibromatosis-like", being cellular and composed of bland spindle cells. The stromal component can, however, be collagenous, hyalinized or variably cellular, and osteocartilagenous foci can occur rarely. The frequency of ductal carcinoma in situ in association with adenosquamous carcinomas is variable. In similarity with salivary-like tumors of the breast, the epithelial component of these tumors lacks estrogen receptor expression.

The epithelial elements and, in some cases, a proportion of the spindle cell component can be shown to express cytokeratins. In some cases, smooth muscle actin reactivity of the spindle cells has been described. There is a general belief that this form of metaplastic carcinoma should be regarded as low-grade with a risk of local recurrence after incomplete excision but with low metastatic potential.

Prognostic factors in breast cancer

For a number of tumors, the role of histopathology in the provision of prognostic information has been well established for many years (e.g., measurement of tumor thickness in malignant melanoma, assessment of histologic subtype in malignant lymphoma). The main reason for this has been the availability of a range of therapies and the need to stratify patients appropriately. Paradoxically, until comparatively recently, the main role of the diagnostic histopathologist in breast disease lay only in the establishment of a basic diagnosis of breast cancer. Apart from the examination of locoregional lymph nodes for the presence or absence of metastases, it was unusual for any other prognostic information to be supplied, or indeed requested. The treatment of breast cancer was standardized and predominantly surgical, with little attempt to stratify patients for appropriate therapy on an individual basis. However, in the last two decades the treatment of breast cancer has undergone dramatic changes and a much wider range of therapeutic options is now available. Early diagnosis, particularly since the advent of breast screening, is detecting tumors which are likely to have a favorable outcome, and it has become increasingly important to assess prognosis for each patient before a therapeutic plan is agreed.

A wide range of potential prognostic factors has now been studied, some well established, some at the development stage, while others are still research tools. They can be divided broadly into two groups, traditional and molecular. The traditional factors can be assessed during conventional examination and histologic evaluation of tumors. Techniques for assessment of molecular markers are less widely available, but some, such as hormone receptors, are becoming increasingly important in the prediction of therapeutic response. In this chapter we have concentrated on the traditional factors, but we also include a brief description of those molecular markers which may be of value in patient management.

Traditional pathologic factors

A considerable amount of important prognostic information is available from the careful histopathologic examination of routine breast carcinoma specimens. In order to obtain the most accurate data, careful attention must be paid to specimen preparation.[5,327–329] Ideally, specimens should be sliced fresh so that immediate fixation of tumor slices can be achieved. Once optimum fixation has been obtained, a sufficient number of blocks is taken to ensure adequate sampling and routine paraffin embedding is carried out. Standard "thin" sections are then cut (4-μm) and, for most of the parameters described below, staining with H&E (hematoxylin and eosin) is all that is required.

The following pathologic factors, all of which are relatively simple to assess, have been shown to provide clinically useful prognostic information, to a greater or lesser degree.

Tumor size For prognostic purposes, the size of tumors should only be assessed by the pathologist, as clinical measurement is not sufficiently accurate. Measurements of tumor diameter in three planes should be made to the nearest millimeter, initially in the fresh state. The measurements are checked after fixation and the greatest diameter is taken as the tumor size. For small tumors, those measuring 1 cm or less, and for cases in which there is a large in situ component, it may be more accurate to carry out measurements on histologic sections using the stage micrometer.[330]

As a time-dependent factor, tumor size has been shown in numerous studies to correlate with prognosis,[331–334] patients with small tumors having a better survival than those with large tumors. Furthermore, the Nottingham/Tenovus Primary Breast Cancer Study (NTPBCS) has confirmed by multi-variate analysis that tumor size is an important independent variable[335,336] forming an integral component of the Nottingham Prognostic Index (NPI).

Estimation of tumor size has become particularly import-ant in the context of breast cancer screening. Tumors which measure 10 mm or less in diameter, so called minimal invasive carcinomas (MIC),[337–339] are more likely to be of an earlier stage, i.e., lymph node negative, than tumors which measure 15 mm or more.[121,246,333,338,340–343] Interestingly, analysis of size categories in the Nottingham Tenovus study indicates that, for long-term survival, the better cut off point is actually at 1.5 cm. In the UK National Breast Screening Program (NHSBSP) over 50 percent of the invasive cancers detected are expected to measure <15 mm.[344]

Lymph node stage Lymph node staging provides very powerful prognostic information in breast cancer and it is now generally accepted that this should be based on histologic examination of excised nodes rather then clinical examination.

Numerous studies have shown that patients who have histo-logically involved locoregional lymph nodes have a much poorer prognosis than those without nodal involvement.[331,335,345,346] Overall, 10-year survival is reduced from 75 percent for node negative patients to 25–30 percent for node positive patients. Of note, lymph node involvement is significantly more frequent in rarely affected male patients.[162,224] Prognosis is also related to the number and level of locoregional lymph nodes involved. The greater the number of nodes involved the poorer the prognosis[281,347] and, in the USA, the NSABP divides patients into two groups for therapeutic purposes, those with 1–3 positive nodes and those with four or more positive. This approach is recommended by the UICC, AJCC,

EU and UK.[5,348] Similarly, involvement of nodes in the "higher" or more distal levels of the axilla carries a worse prognosis,[8,349] and this is also true for involvement of internal mammary nodes.[350] Our group and others have demonstrated that highly significant prognostic information can be obtained by a lymph node sampling method, which avoids the morbidity inherent with axillary clearance.[335,336,351,352] Debate continues, however, concerning the relative merits of axillary sampling and clearance.[353–357] This is not the place to rehearse the argument and, in practical terms, we believe that a sensible tailoring of treatment should now be employed. The decreasing frequency of lymph node positivity and the increasingly widespread availability of sentinel node biopsy, with or without additional node sampling, is resulting in reduced use of axillary clearance as standard treatment for all in some centers. Internal mammary sampling only provides useful information in medially sited tumors and need not be performed for more lateral tumors. Low axillary clearance, below the inter-costobrachial nerve, produces enough lymph nodes for accu-rate prognostication (usually between 4 and 15), with minimal morbidity. Lymph node stage is divided into three categories as follows:

Stage 1 (TMN N0) – no lymph node involvement
Stage 2 (TMN N1) – up to 3 axillary nodes or a single
  internal mammary node involved
Stage 3 (TMN N2, N3) – 4 or more axillary nodes involved
  (TNM2 = 4–9 involved nodes; TNM3 >10 nodes
  involved).

The UICC, AJCC, UK and EU[5,348] allocate single node involvement by micrometastatic disease (deposit size 0.2–2 mm) the node positive Stage 2, TNM N1mic category and isolated tumor cells (deposit size <0.2 mm) to the node negative Stage 1, TNM N0 category. Although there is no substantive evidence to support these proposals, there will be a practical benefit from the use of consensus criteria for nodal metastasis classification.

These proposals also reflect recent attention focused on the size of lymph node metastases and, in particular, the definition and relevance of so-called occult metastases (missed by convential H&E staining and of any size), micrometastases (with an upper inclusive size of 2 mm) or isolated tumour cells (ITCs, with an upper inclusive size of 0.2 mm), as defined by the TNM classification. There is some evidence that the presence of "micrometastases" measuring 2 mm or less does not affect survival adversely, compared with that of node negative patients.[358–360] The data concerning the detection of tiny deposits, often single cells, by serial sectioning or immuno-histochemical staining are conflicting. Some groups have found a significantly worse prognosis for such patients,[361–364] while others could detect no difference in survival.[359,365,366] Cserni and Dowlatshahi have reviewed the data and the practical issues.[367,368] In most publications before 2002, the range of micrometastases included the current ITC category. Their prognostic relevance remains uncertain and is still debated. Dowlatshahi[367] has identified that only larger studies with substantial follow up have demonstrated a worse prognosis for patients with micrometastases. However, a recent large retrospective study from a single center, in which there was long follow up and which was subjected to multivariate analysis, revealed that the prognosis of patients with occult metastases, many of which would have been called micrometastases historically,[367] was no worse than that for patients without nodal involvement.[360] Aside from problems of prognostic relevance, there are also issues in achieving concordance between pathologists in the classification of small metastatic deposits, implying that more robust criteria are required.[369]

It appears to have been accepted as "received wisdom" that the presence of metastatic carcinoma in the adipose tissue surrounding axillary lymph nodes, so-called extranodal spread or extracapsular metastasis (ECM), is a poor prognostic factor,[370,371] and some radiation oncologists regard its presence as an indication for postoperative axillary irradiation. However, several studies have shown that ECM is not an independent factor, but correlates closely with the number of involved nodes.[372–374] Donegan and colleagues[374] have concluded further that the presence of ECM is not an indicator *per se* for radiation therapy after complete axillary clearance.

Sentinel node biopsy Morton and colleagues, working in the field of melanoma, have defined the sentinel node (first-echelon node) as the first lymph node on a direct drainage pathway from the primary lesion.[375] It is now widely accepted that sentinel lymph nodes (SLNs) are the most likely first site of lymphatic metastatic spread in breast cancer.[376] This has been substantiated by studies involving a similarly detailed histopathologic investigation of both SLNs and non-SLNs.[377–380] This type of approach to SLN biopsy examination leads to upstaging of a proportion of cases when compared to historical series.[381] Most of the metastases revealed by more detailed investigation are small, and often defined as micrometastases or ITCs, using the TNM classification system,[348] but some may be larger.[382] Because most of the prognostic information relating to nodal status stemmed from the assessments of standard single hematoxylin and eosin stained sections of the lymph nodes, it is obvious that most of the metastases identified historically were macrometastases (>2 mm). Such metastases are clearly associated with the worse prognosis attributed to node-positive status.

Methods for the pathologic investigation of SLNs vary considerably; in general, the more rigorous the methods, such as number and distance between step sectioning levels and use of immunocytochemistry, the more ITCs, micrometastases or metastases can be identified.[381–383]

Practical guidance for pathologic examination of lymph nodes Our current policy is to follow UK and EU guidance on lymph node examination.[5] Resected lymph nodes, usually axillary and occasionally internal mammary, are routinely submitted for pathologic examination in patients undergoing surgery for breast carcinoma. These specimens may take the form of axillary clearance specimens, lymph node samples or sentinel lymph node biopsies. Every lymph node identified should be examined histologically. The method used should ensure that the total number of lymph nodes should be assessable which necessitates a minimum examination of at least one tissue block from each node. This minimum standard allows examination of multiple lymph nodes as composite blocks. For sentinel node samples and non-guided node sample specimens (and ideally axillary clearance specimens) we recommend that each lymph node identified should be blocked independently for histologic examination. In this setting, the methodology used

should provide the highest chance of finding metastatic disease by conventional microscopic examination of H&E stained tissue sections. A representative complete section of any grossly involved lymph node is adequate. Lymph nodes over 5 mm in maximum size should be sliced at 2–3 mm intervals perpendicular to the long axis. If these slices are 2 mm or less in thickness then, in theory, all macrometastases (>2 mm) will be detected. Block sampling can therefore provide an alternative to step sectioning. All the tissue blocks prepared should be embedded and examined histologically. In larger lymph nodes this may necessitate examination of more than one paraffin block. Lymph nodes under 5 mm can be bisected and blocked. Alternatively, lymph nodes under 5 mm can be blocked in their entirety and examined at at least 3 levels.

Pathology reports should include the total number of lymph nodes identified and the number of lymph nodes involved with metastatic disease. Specific axillary levels and nodes, i.e., the apical node, may have been identified by the surgeon and can be recorded independently, but they should also be included in the total lymph node figures.

Additional techniques Additional techniques include sectioning at multiple levels, use of immunocytochemistry and molecular technology. These tests may increase the frequency of detection of micrometastatic disease, but at present their significance remains uncertain. Additional resources required for detailed lymph node examination cannot be justified in routine practice at present, until the evidence to support their use becomes more substantive and when there is improved consensus on appropriate methodology. However, should local interest or resources permit, the following could be considered.

The frequency of detection of micrometastatic disease is increased through examination of a greater proportion of the lymph node volume and any method used should aim to increase the area fractional of lymph nodes examined. Methodology can include serial sectioning in some form and the majority of research studies to date have used 3 levels at approximately 100 μm separation. Cserni[368] has reviewed these studies and concluded that steps of 1 mm for macrometastases, or at 200 or 250 μm for micrometastases (depending on the aim of the studies, or on the resources), may obviate the need for further sections at shorter intervals. Increasing the number of levels examined will increase detection but reduce practicality.[368]

Immunocytochemical tests are an adjunct to conventional histology and can facilitate identification of micrometastatic disease through direct labeling of the tumor cell population, thereby enhancing visualization of small foci. Most research studies have used broad spectrum or low molecular weight cytokeratins, i.e., AE1/AE3, MNF116, CAM5.2, CK19.[367,384] Cross-reactivity with some reticulum cells and lymphoid cells may lead to false positive results when using some cytokeratin antibodies. Assessment should be based on immunoreactivity and morphologic correlates. We currently use immunocytochemistry with antibody AE1/AE3 to resolve cases where there is a suspicion of early metastatic spread. We do not currently use immunocytochemistry to screen routinely for micrometastatic disease. The clinical and prognostic significance of detection of micrometastatic disease and ITCs in particular is still uncertain.

Histologic type The favorable prognosis of certain histologic types of invasive carcinoma of the breast is now well recognized. Thus tubular carcinoma,[252,254,385,386] mucinous carcinoma,[262,387] invasive cribriform carcinoma,[256] medullary carcinoma,[269,388] infiltrating lobular carcinoma,[149] and tubulolobular carcinoma,[233] have all been reported to have a more favorable prognosis than invasive carcinomas of no special type (ductal NST). There have been very few comprehensive long-term follow-up studies relating histologic type to survival, but Dawson and colleagues[389] found a relative excess of tubular, mucinous, medullary and infiltrating lobular carcinomas in patients who had survived at least 25 years after mastectomy, compared with those surviving less than 10 years. These findings have been confirmed in a similar study from Edinburgh,[263] with the addition of invasive cribriform carcinoma among the long-term survivors. The Edinburgh group have also shown a relative excess of these "special type" categories in cases of invasive carcinoma detected in the prevalent round of mammographic breast screening[246] and this has been confirmed in our own studies.

Further objective evidence that histologic type can provide powerful prognostic information has been reported from the NTPBCS.[213] In a series comprising over 1500 patients with primary operable invasive carcinoma followed up for a minimum of 10 years, the excellent prognosis of the special types, pure tubular, invasive cribriform and mucinous, was confirmed. The study also showed that patients with both tubular mixed carcinoma and mixed ductal NST and special type carcinoma have a good prognosis, considerably better than ductal NST carcinoma. In previous studies, such mixed types were rarely recognized, and these tumors were included within the general category of ductal NST; since they account for at least 15 percent of a symptomatic series, valuable prognostic information is easily lost.

It has generally been accepted that medullary carcinoma has an excellent or good prognosis,[269,270,272,387,390] despite the fact that a number of groups have been unable to confirm a survival advantage compared with ductal NST carcinoma.[213,274,275] Several of these latter studies, however, found that medullary carcinoma has a better prognosis than ductal NST carcinoma of comparable histologic grade 3.[213,274,275] We feel, therefore, that medullary carcinoma should be regarded as having a moderate prognosis, rather than a good prognosis.[213,391]

Overall, infiltrating lobular carcinoma conveys a better prognosis than ductal NST carcinoma,[8,213] although the 10-year survival of 54 percent clearly implies only a moderate category. However, Dixon and colleagues[230] found significant differences in survival between the morphologic subtypes of lobular carcinoma and this has been confirmed in the NTPBCS.[392] Thus, the classical type carries a good prognosis (60 percent 10-year survival), mixed lobular type an average prognosis (55 percent at 10 years) and the solid type has a poor prognosis (40 percent at 10 years). Tubulolobular carcinoma, which has an excellent prognosis (over 90 percent 10-year survival), is currently considered as a distinct and separate type, because of the lack of agreement concerning its assignment as a tubular or a lobular variant.

More recent studies, based upon cDNA expression array studies and phenotyping studies using basal cytokeratin, have identified that basal type breast cancers have a poor prognosis when compared to other types.[300]

Patients with invasive carcinoma of the breast can therefore be stratified into broad prognostic groups according to histologic type: the *excellent* prognosis group comprises the special types (tubular, cribriform, mucinous) and tubulolobular carcinoma; the *good* group, tubular mixed, mixed ductal NST and special type and classical lobular carcinoma; the *average* group includes mixed lobular, medullary and atypical medullary carcinoma; the *poor* group is composed of ductal NST, mixed ductal and lobular, solid lobular carcinoma and grade 3 basal type carcinoma.

In addition, histologic typing of breast cancer adds to our understanding of the biology of breast cancer. For example, infiltrating lobular carcinomas show estrogen receptor (ER) expression more frequently than do ductal NST carcinomas[393] and they also have a different pattern of metastasis, with a prediction for unusual sites such as the retroperitoneum and serosal surfaces.[394,395] There is now very interesting evidence emerging of a correlation between histologic type and expression of the *BRCA-1* and *BRCA-2* genes. For example, in two important studies there appears to be an excess of high grade (grade 3) carcinomas with medullary features in *BRCA-1* related cases in comparison with *BRCA-2* cases [290,291,396,397] (see section on familial breast cancer above).

Histologic grade One of the most fundamental aspects of oncologic pathology has been the recognition that the morphologic appearances of tumors can be correlated with their degree of malignancy. The first formal study of the grading of histologic differentiation in breast cancer was undertaken by Greenhough[398] and, despite the subjective nature of his method and paucity of clinical data, he showed a good correlation with prognosis. Since then a number of different methods have been devised, but all can be traced back to that originally proposed by Greenhough. The principal methods used currently fall into two groups, the majority which have followed the original concept of using multiple cellular factors,[331,332,399–403] and those which have concentrated on nuclear characteristics.[404–406] It is remarkable, given the diversity of methods employed, that very many studies have demonstrated a significant association between grade and survival, clearly indicating the powerful prognostic information provided; these data have been reviewed in some detail previously.[330,403]

Despite this evidence, and the adoption of one of the methods, the so-called Scarff-Bloom-Richardson method,[399,400,407,408] by the World Health Organization,[1,409] acceptance of histologic grade as a routine practice in diagnostic pathology has been slow. In the past, this was due to lack of clinical demand, as discussed previously. A further reason for the reluctance to rely on histologic grading is the subjective nature of the published methods, and perceived poor consistency and reproducibility,[410,411] despite the fact that several other studies report acceptable levels of inter and intra-observer variability.[221,281,412,413]

These conflicting views highlight the need for grading to be carried out by trained histopathologists who work within an agreed protocol. While recognizing that assessment of histologic differentiation will always have an underlying subjective element, one of the main problems with the reproducibility of many of the methods used in previous studies has been the lack of strictly defined, written morphologic criteria. For this reason the method which we have evolved in Nottingham employs modifications to the original WHO method[399,400,409] in order to introduce greater objectivity.[330,403] This method is now recommended by the WHO.[1]

Three tumor characteristics are assessed: tubule formation as an expression of glandular differentiation, nuclear pleomorphism and mitotic counts (Table 16.1, Figs 16.68–16.70). A numeric scoring system on a scale of 1–3 is used to ensure that each factor is assessed individually. Cut off points of 75 percent and 10 percent are used to estimate the area of tumor composed of tubules with clear central lumina, based on a previous pilot study (Fig. 16.68).[414] Nuclear pleomorphism is evaluated by reference to the appearances of normal epithelial cells in adjacent breast tissue (Fig. 16.69). Increasing irregularity of nuclear outlines and the number and size of nucleoli are useful features in allocating points for pleomorphism, but it must be recognized that this feature retains a subjective element. The most important modification concerns the evaluation of mitotic activity. Care must be taken to count only clearly defined mitotic figures. Hyperchromatic nuclei and pyknotic cells are ignored, since they are more likely to represent apoptosis than proliferation. Quantitatively, a more accurate assessment is required than designations such as "about two or three mitoses per high power field",[400] since the area of a single high power field may vary by as much as six-fold from one microscope to another.[415] However, the most accurate method, the mitotic index (the fraction of mitoses expressed as a percentage of cells counted)[416] is laborious and time consuming and therefore unlikely to be of practical utility in a routine setting. Based on a detailed study of mitosis counting,[417] we have therefore standardized mitotic counts to a fixed field area (Table 16.2, Fig. 16.70). Using this system, any microscope can be calibrated to produce reproducible and comparable data.

The method described above has been fully evaluated in the NTPBCS. The results, based on life table analysis of over 2000 patients followed up for between 3 and 18 years, confirm conclusively the highly significant relationship between histologic grade and prognosis; survival worsens progressively with increasing grade.[213,330] The method has now been shown to have good reproducibility in other centers[418–420] and it has

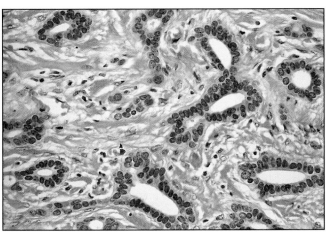

Fig. 16.68 • Assessment of tubule formation in histologic grade. Structures should only be counted if they exhibit clear central lumina, as shown here.

Table 16.1	Summary of semi-quantitative method for assessing histologic grade in breast carcinoma
Tubule formation	
Majority of tumor (>75%) 1 point	
Moderate degree (10–75%) 2 points	
Little or none (<10%) 3 points	
Nuclear pleomorphism	
Small, regular uniform cells 1 point	
Moderate increase in size and variability 2 points	
Marked variation 3 points	
Mitotic counts	
Dependent on microscope field area* 1–3 points	

*See Table 16.2

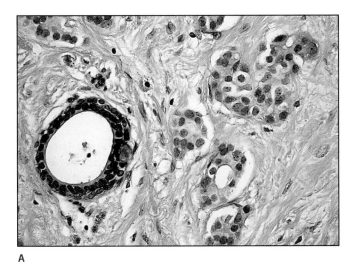

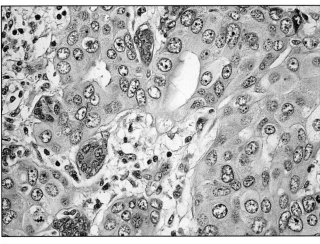

A   B

Fig. 16.69 • Nuclear pleomorphism in histologic grade is assessed by comparison with adjacent normal epithelial cells. **(A)** 1 point is scored in this case; nuclei are slightly larger than the normal epithelial cells but vary little in size and shape. **(B)** In this example the score is 3 points; nuclei are much larger than in the normal epithelium and vary considerably in size and shape.

Table 16.2	Assignment of points for mitotic counts according to the microscope field area		
Field diameter in mm	**Number of mitoses corresponding to**		
	Score 1	Score 2	Score 3
0.40	up to 4	5 to 8	9 or more
0.41	up to 4	5 to 9	10 or more
0.42	up to 4	5 to 9	10 or more
0.43	up to 4	5 to 10	11 or more
0.44	up to 5	6 to 10	11 or more
0.45	up to 5	6 to 11	12 or more
0.46	up to 5	6 to 11	12 or more
0.47	up to 5	6 to 12	13 or more
0.48	up to 6	7 to 12	13 or more
0.49	up to 6	7 to 13	14 or more
0.50	up to 6	7 to 13	14 or more
0.51	up to 6	7 to 14	15 or more
0.52	up to 7	8 to 14	15 or more
0.53	up to 7	8 to 15	16 or more
0.54	up to 7	8 to 16	17 or more
0.55	up to 8	9 to 16	17 or more
0.56	up to 8	9 to 17	18 or more
0.57	up to 8	9 to 17	18 or more
0.58	up to 9	10 to 18	19 or more
0.59	up to 9	10 to 19	20 or more
0.60	up to 9	10 to 19	20 or more
0.61	up to 9	10 to 20	21 or more
0.62	up to 10	11 to 21	22 or more
0.63	up to 10	11 to 21	22 or more
0.64	up to 11	12 to 22	23 or more
0.65	up to 11	12 to 23	24 or more
0.66	up to 11	12 to 24	25 or more
0.67	up to 12	13 to 25	26 or more
0.68	up to 12	13 to 25	26 or more
0.69	up to 12	13 to 26	27 or more
0.70	up to 13	14 to 27	28 or more

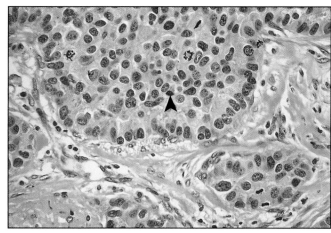

Fig. 16.70 • Quantitative evaluation of mitotic figures in histologic grade. Several clearly defined mitoses are shown; hyperchromatic nuclei (arrowhead) should not be counted.

In Nottingham, we carry out histologic grading in all cases of invasive breast carcinoma, regardless of morphologic type, and this practice has now received general acceptance.[5,6,327,422] This practice has been criticized by some pathologists who feel that grading is not appropriate for the special histologic types. We would argue, however, that grading is actually an integral part of assessing histologic type; e.g., tubular carcinomas are always histologic grade 1, while grading for lobular carcinoma produces appropriate survival curves.[330] Furthermore, we have shown that for some special types, such as mucinous and tubular mixed carcinoma, grading provides a more appropriate estimation of prognosis than histologic type alone.[391]

Vascular invasion Conflicting views have been expressed concerning the prognostic value of estimating vascular invasion in breast cancer.[423] Some studies have found no correlation with clinical outcome,[424,425] while others have shown the presence of vascular invasion to predict for both recurrence[353,426,427] and long-term survival.[425,428–431] A possible explanation for such discrepancies may be the wide variation in the reported frequency of vascular invasion and the related problem of the distinction of true vessels from artefactual soft tissue spaces. The majority of studies have examined specific patient subgroups (e.g., lymph node negative), so that an accurate estimate of the overall frequency is difficult to obtain. The reported incidence of vascular invasion extends from 34 percent to 54 percent.

Although muscular blood vessels may occasionally be involved, tumor emboli are mainly seen in relation to thin walled channels; since it is almost impossible to determine whether such spaces are lymphatics or venules, vascular permeation should be left unspecified and the broad term vascular invasion used. In order to avoid overdiagnosis, care must be taken to avoid misinterpretation of both ductal carcinoma in situ, and cords of invasive carcinoma with associated shrinkage artefact as vessel invasion.[432] These problems can be reduced greatly by obtaining good fixation and by using simple but strict criteria. Determination of vascular invasion should only be made in tissue adjacent to the tumor mass and not within it. Tumor emboli must be seen within spaces having

been adopted for use in the minimum pathologic data set of the UK NHSBSP,[5,327] by the European Breast Screening Pathology Group,[6] the WHO[1] and by the Association of Directors of Anatomic and Surgical Pathology (ADASP) in the USA.[421]

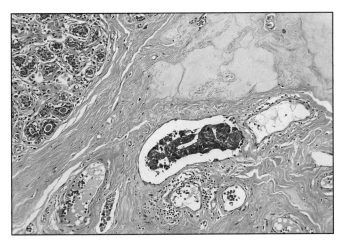

Fig. 16.71 • Definite vascular invasion in breast carcinoma. This field, several millimeters from the main tumor nodule, shows part of a normal breast lobule on the left and, in the center, a vessel, lined by flattened endothelial cells, containing a tumor embolus.

a clear lining of endothelial cells (Fig. 16.71); these spaces are usually located within connective tissue separated from mammary lobular elements by interlobular stroma, and are often in close proximity to small muscular blood vessels. These topographic patterns have been evaluated by Örbo et al.[432] Immunostaining for endothelial markers such as CD31, CD34, laminin, type IV collagen, factor VIII-related antigen and *Ulex europeus* agglutinin I is not helpful in distinguishing vessels from ductal structures but may be useful in excluding shrinkage artefact.[433–437] In routine practice, their use should be confined to the resolution of equivocal cases. Reproducibility of the evaluation of vascular invasion has been shown to be satisfactory in a number of studies[332,427] and, even where this has been questioned,[438] complete agreement was obtained between three observers in nearly 90 percent of cases.

Vascular invasion correlates very closely with locoregional lymph node involvement,[430–432,439] and, possibly because of this association, it has been claimed that it can provide prognostic information as powerful as lymph node stage.[426] There is certainly a correlation between the presence of vascular invasion and early recurrence in lymph node-negative patients[426,427,440,441] and these studies have shown that the adverse prognostic effects are also independent of occult axillary node involvement. In the NTPBCS we have confirmed the prognostic value of vascular invasion in assessing long-term survival, but have also demonstrated in multivariate analysis that this effect is independent of lymph node stage. Finally, the presence of vascular invasion is one of the most important factors in prediction of local recurrence following conservation therapy[353,425,428–430] and flap recurrence following mastectomy.[442]

Necrosis The presence of focal necrosis within invasive breast carcinomas is a relatively common phenomenon, occasionally visible macroscopically as a sharply demarcated area of dullness, usually centrally placed. Microscopically, necrotic tumor is characterized, as in any tissue, by the nuclear changes of karyorrhexis, pyknosis and karyolysis with loss of cytoplasmic detail, generally accompanied by a neutrophil infiltrate. When tumor necrosis has been present for a sufficient length of time it may be accompanied by replacement fibrosis. Necrosis is

almost entirely confined to tumors of no special histologic type (ductal NST), appears to be most common in those of high grade[359,443] and is related to the basal phenotype.[297] Few studies have assessed the actual proportion of invasive carcinomas which exhibit tumor necrosis. Carter et al.[444] gave a figure of 40 percent, compared with 60 percent estimated by Fisher et al.[359] However, the latter figure is an overestimate as areas of necrosis within associated in situ carcinoma were included.

The value of tumor necrosis as a potential prognostic factor has now been evaluated in a number of studies. Carter et al.[444] showed decreased 10-year survival in patients with tumor necrosis and Fisher et al.[332] found that the presence of necrosis was associated with early treatment failure. More recently, Parham and colleagues,[445] in a relatively small morphometric study, found a strong correlation between extensive necrosis and poor survival. Unfortunately, in none of these studies is a precise definition given of terms such as extensive necrosis, which limits their value. Parham and colleagues have subsequently proposed a simplified method for grading breast cancer[446] by combining mitotic counts with tumor necrosis. The authors claim a good correlation with survival, but it has been pointed out that little numeric data were provided, especially concerning the diagnostic criteria used, and for this reason the method lacks practical utility.

In summary, there is some evidence that the presence of necrotic tumor is a poor prognostic sign, but more detailed studies are required to generate reproducible estimates of the extent of necrosis, and its correlation with other prognostic variables, in particular histologic grade.

Stromal features There is considerable variation in the amount of stromal connective tissue within invasive breast carcinomas.[445,447] The prognostic significance of this finding is uncertain, with conflicting published data. Thus, in subjective or semiquantitative studies, stromal fibrosis has been associated variably with a favorable prognosis,[448] poorer survival[449] or has been shown to make no difference in a comparison of short- and long-term survivors.[389] More recently, Parham and colleagues[445] have conducted a morphometric study in a small group of patients and concluded that tumors with a high proportion of tumor cells to stroma carry a better prognosis than those with a low proportion of tumor to stroma. Tumor type is a confounding factor since extensive fibrosis may be found both in low grade tumors, such as tubular carcinoma, and in high grade ductal NST carcinomas. For this reason, it is unlikely that stromal fibrosis will produce useful independent prognostic information.

A further variable component of the stroma of breast carcinomas is elastic tissue. Elastic fibers are distributed in two basic patterns, periductal and diffuse.[450] In the former, the elastic fibers surround obliterated residual ducts in a concentric fashion while, in the latter, there are variable collections of fibrillary fibers, best identified by special stains (e.g., elastic Van Gieson). As is the case with stromal fibrosis, there are conflicting data on the relationship between elastosis and prognosis. Some studies have suggested that the presence of elastosis is associated with a good prognosis,[451,452] but this has not been confirmed by others.[453,454] Giri et al.[455] found that elastosis in the center of the tumor had greater clinical significance, but this was based on a small study with short-term follow-up. Elastosis is particularly associated with tumors of special type (e.g., tubular, tubular mixed, invasive cribriform)[213] which intrinsically have a good prognosis. This suggests that the presence of elastic fibers in a tumor is not an independent prognostic factor.

Extensive in situ component (EIC) The amount of ductal carcinoma in situ (DCIS) associated with invasive carcinomas is extremely variable and the assessment of its extent is highly subjective. Some studies have shown that the presence of prominent DCIS within invasive carcinomas conveys a better prognosis and a decreased frequency of nodal metastases.[456,457] Millis and colleagues[458] have shown, however, that, in the majority of cases, the grades of the in situ and invasive components correspond (e.g., low grade DCIS with a low grade invasive carcinoma) and it is likely that this is a confounding factor in evaluating the independent prognostic value of an EIC. It has been suggested that EIC may be of greater importance in the management of patients undergoing conservation surgery for invasive breast carcinoma. At the European Organisation for Research into the Treatment of Cancer consensus meeting in 1989, it was concluded that "the principal risk factor for breast relapse after breast conserving treatment is large residual burden and the main source of the burden is EIC".[459] This statement was based on data from a number of studies,[178,460-462] but a subsequent publication from the Boston group has cast some doubt on its validity.[463] They found that assessment of completeness of excision was by far the most powerful factor influencing local recurrence rates and that EIC was not a predictive factor if complete excision was obtained. EIC did, however, predict for the *likelihood* that margins would be involved and it therefore has some value in this respect.

Molecular prognostic factors and predictive factors in breast cancer

Prognostic factors, although not specific predictors of response to a therapy, can be used for appropriate treatment selection of patients with malignancies; those patients who have an extremely good prognosis after tumor excision may not warrant noxious adjuvant therapies which themselves carry significant morbidity. Conversely, those with a poor prognosis may benefit from an aggressive adjuvant approach. Identifying the prognostic features of an invasive breast carcinoma for these reasons is particularly important[464] as the disease has a markedly variable course; a group of women with "curable" carcinomas who do not receive significant benefit from adjuvant therapy can be identified,[465] while others will succumb relatively rapidly to the disease. Because of this widely differing clinical outcome and because breast carcinoma is common, prognostic factors and, more recently, predictive factors in this malignant disease are probably among the most widely studied.

The assessment and role of traditional histologic prognostic factors in breast cancer has been presented in the preceding section. Many of the recent studies of possible prognostic factors in primary breast carcinoma have examined novel variables, either morphologically, immunohistochemically or biochemically, which experimentally at least, are associated

with invasion, metastasis, differentiation or growth rate of the tumor. Thus, cell adhesion molecules such as integrins[466] and cadherins, proteases, metalloproteinases, growth factors and their receptors, [467] hormone receptors,[468] tumor suppressor genes such as *p53*[469] and oncogene expression including *c-erbB2* status[470] have been assessed. Others have investigated the tumor cell DNA content and the proliferation index in breast carcinomas. The latter has been examined using immuno-histochemical (IHC) techniques with determination of the proportion of nuclei demonstrating the MIB1/Ki67 antigen either subjectively or by image analysis[471,472] and alternatives such as thymidine and bromodeoxyuridine labelling index can be assessed. Several of these studies have found that, in univariate analysis, these molecular markers show a significant association with prognosis of patients with primary breast cancer. However, as novel treatment strategies directed at specific cellular mechanisms, e.g., growth control or regulation, are being developed, tests recognizing the activation or amplification of such pathways in a specific tumor will be required.

In breast cancer, estrogen receptor (ER) is the best example of a specific test used to predict response to a specific therapy in breast cancer management. It is not in our hands of *independent* significance in predicting prognosis in breast cancer patients due to its close relationship with histologic grade. We nevertheless assess ER status routinely on all patients with invasive breast carcinoma as a *predictive* factor to determine the probability of a response to hormone treatment.[473]

Estrogen receptor

Steroid hormones bind with high specificity and affinity to intracellular receptors. These steroid receptors belong to a "superfamily" of proteins whose function is to control the transcription of a repertoire of other cellular genes.[474] Steroid receptors such as estrogen and progesterone receptor are located in the cell nucleus. Hormone is believed to diffuse or be transported to the nucleus, where a steroid-receptor complex is formed with receptor dimerization. Some of the genes regulated by steroid receptors are involved in controlling cell growth and currently it is believed that these effects are the most relevant in terms of estrogen receptor influences on the behavior and treatment of breast cancer.

Approximately 30 percent of unselected patients with breast cancer will respond to hormone therapy such as oophorectomy (or chemical castration) or tamoxifen treatment. The demonstration that radiolabeled estradiol bound to some breast cancer specimens and that this effect was related to response to hormone ablation[475] led to the development of hormone receptor assays directed at identification of patients suitable for hormone therapy. By assay of estrogen receptor status alone, using the standard radioligand binding assay on tissue cytosol samples, a response is seen in between 50 and 60 percent of patients with estrogen receptor-positive tumors, in contrast to a <10 percent response observed in patients with estrogen receptor-negative tumors.[476] Historically, in studies using biochemical methods prior to the introduction of IHC methods for hormone receptor detection, the threshold for designation of estrogen receptor positivity has been usually 10 fmol/mg cytosol protein. Levels of response are recognized to increase to over 80 percent in patients with tumors having high receptor levels of several hundred or more fmol/mg protein. Prediction of response can be refined further by combining estrogen receptor assay with progesterone receptor assay.[476] Patients with ER-positive PR-positive tumors have a 78 percent response, those with ER-positive PR-negative a 34 percent response, those with ER-negative PR-positive a 45 percent response and ER-negative PR-negative tumors have a 10 percent response.[476] It should be noted that these data relate to ligand binding assay systems and results from combined ER and PR immuno-cytochemical assay may differ.

Assay methods

The cytosol ligand binding assay was, until the late 1980s, the standard assay method but has a number of disadvantages. In particular, it requires a relatively large amount of tissue homogenate and is affected by bound estrogen receptor from high endogenous levels of estradiol in premenopausal women. The development of monoclonal antibodies specific for the receptor protein[477] in the 1980s led the way to both enzyme immunoassay[478] and immunocytochemical assay development.[479,480] More recently, the immunocytochemical methods, despite being less readily quantifiable, have superseded both the ligand binding and enzyme immunobiochemical assays, as they require less tissue, allow formal histologic assessment thereby reducing sampling error,[479,481–490] and may be used on very small samples such as fine needle aspirates.[468,491] Results of all these forms of assay correlate well,[468,482,484,488,490,491] but there is some evidence that there is a closer association with response to hormone therapy using immunocytochemical assay results,[468,481,482] probably because of avoidance of sampling error and lack of influence of tumor cellularity and type.

Immunocytochemical assay

Modern immunocytochemical methods using microwave or pressure cooker antigen retrieval, high sensitivity antibodies and modern IHC visualization systems can be applied successfully to routinely processed formalin fixed tissue.[492–495]

These techniques allow successful use of modern antibodies on tissues routinely processed in any histopathology laboratory,

giving the potential for evaluation of estrogen receptor status as part of the process of histologic assessment of breast carcinoma. In our center, this method[490] has now been adopted for all cases of primary breast carcinoma, allowing inclusion of estrogen receptor status as part of the standard histologic report and this has become part of the Royal College of Pathologists Minimum Dataset for Breast Cancer.[5]

Assessment of ER status using these antibodies, with microwave pre-treatment of tissues, gives comparable results with other means of assessment but has many advantages, particularly its applicability to routine histologic samples,[490] as well as methodologic ease and speed.

Estrogen receptor is a thermolabile unstable nuclear protein which is water soluble and has a short half-life after surgical removal of tumor. Most tissue fixatives can be used to preserve receptor reactivity if microwave predigestion is used. It is essential, however, to ensure that rapid fixation occurs and tumor specimens should be incised immediately after resection to ensure rapid penetration of fixative. Alternatively, needle core biopsy samples, which fix more rapidly, can be used successfully as an alternative to surgical resection tissues.

Controls

Use of control tissue is essential in hormone receptor assays, particularly because of the risk of false negative classification. Positive control tissues should include not only a block of a known strongly positive tissue but also a block of tissue showing weak expression to ensure that sensitivity is maintained; ideally the test block should include normal breast lobules and ducts to provide an internal control population of cells, since a proportion of these should show positive reactivity (see Fig. 16.72). Use of internal control cells in this fashion protects against the effects of poor fixation.

Assessment of staining

Estrogen and progesterone receptor are located in the nucleus of breast epithelial and carcinoma cells (Fig. 16.72). There is currently no internationally accepted scoring system for hormone receptor immunocytochemical assays. The proportion

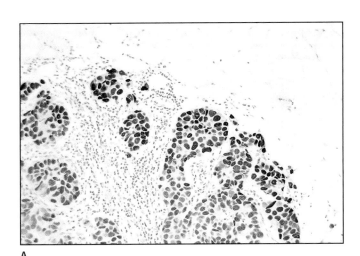

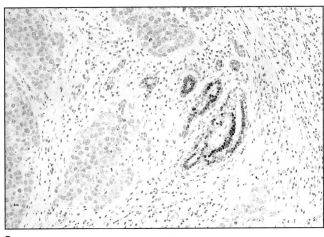

A   B

Fig. 16.72 • Estrogen receptor immunocytochemical reactivity, showing strong nuclear reactivity indicating positivity in one case **(A)** and no nuclear reactivity indicating negativity in the second case **(B)**. Note positivity of adjacent normal mammary epithelium in (B), which provides an internal positive control.

of tumor cells showing positive reactivity, their intensity of reactivity, combinations of both of these (H-score)[480] simple categorical[496] and "Quick Score"[497] systems have all been promoted. Assistance on staining methods is available from the commercial suppliers of the currently available antibodies. Happily, it seems that essentially all scoring methods have prognostic utility.[498]

There are two main scoring systems in use, the H-score and the Quick Score systems, both of which combine intensity and proportion of cells reacting. The H-score is based on a summation of the proportion of tumor cells showing different degrees of reactivity; no reactivity = 0, weak = 1, moderate = 2, strong = 3. This gives a maximum total score of 300 if 100 percent of tumor cells show strong reactivity.

Many laboratories have moved to the simpler Quick Score system. This is based on assessment of the proportion and intensity of staining:

Score for proportion	Score for intensity
0 = no staining	0 = no staining
1 = <1 percent nuclei staining	1 = weak staining
2 = 1–10 percent nuclei staining	2 = moderate staining
3 = 11–33 percent nuclei staining	3 = strong staining
4 = 34–66 percent nuclei staining	
5 = 67–100 percent nuclei staining	

The scores are summed to give a maximum of 8. Patients with tumors scoring 2 or less are regarded as ER negative and have a negligible chance of response. There are several reasons for evaluating the extent of reactivity of a carcinoma:

1 many of the data relate to treatment of metastatic disease in which it has been shown that the higher the level of receptor then the greater the chance of response to endocrine therapy

2 patients whose carcinomas have no evidence of immunopositivity essentially have no chance of responding to endocrine treatment;

3 determination of progesterone receptor as well as estrogen receptor can be of value, e.g., for those patients whose tumor has low estrogen receptor/high progesterone receptor values, endocrine treatment is worthwhile

4 patients whose breast cancers have very low levels of staining (Quick Score of 2) may still benefit from adjuvant endocrine treatment.[497] This emphasizes the need to have sensitive, reproducible techniques that can detect these very low levels of protein expression.

Clinical application

Use of semiquantitative methods, such as the Quick Score or H-score, which produce a numeric score influenced by the intensity of reactivity, have an association with the amount of receptor present as assessed by biochemical methods.[490,487] Informed clinicians are now beginning to use not just a standard result, based on a common cut off point or threshold, but some form of added quantitation of known sensitivity and specificity. It is possible to assess the sensitivity and specificity of an assay at different cut off points, giving an ability to choose differing thresholds for different clinical situations.[490,487] For example, when selecting for adjuvant hormone therapy sensitivity is required, a low threshold may be appropriate; in contrast, elderly patients or patients with advanced tumors being selected for primary/first line hormone treatment require specificity and a higher threshold is needed.

HER-2 (C-erbB2 HER-2/neu)

Studies of the humanized anti-HER-2 neu (c-erbB2) monoclonal antibody trastuzumab (Herceptin) have demonstrated potent inhibitory activity of the antibody against tumor cell lines overexpressing the HER-2 protein. Two large pivotal multicenter trials have reported objective responses in 16 percent of patients (8 percent complete) in a group of patients with c-erbB2 overexpressing tumors who had received prior combination chemotherapy,[499] and improved response rates when combined with other chemotherapeutic agents.[500] Similar impressive results have recently been identified in the adjuvant setting.[501] Patients suitable for this targeted therapy will require selection by demonstration of overexpression of the HER-2 protein by immunocytochemistry (Fig. 16.73) or amplification of the gene by fluorescent in situ hybridization.

HER-2 immunocytochemistry assay Formalin fixed, paraffin embedded tumor tissue samples are appropriate for this assay. Ideally, buffered formalin should be used for fixation, as use of Bouin's fixative will preclude testing by fluorescence in situ based methods. Other methods of tissue fixation can also adversely affect antigen reactivity.

Some countries have recommended that laboratories which provide a testing service should be carrying out a minimum number of assays per year for immunohistochemical detection of HER-2; the UK recommendation is a minimum of 250 cases.[502] There is evidence of higher consistency of assay quality when tests are performed by high volume reference laboratories.[503,504] Such a target level can also ensure continuing expertise of assay providers. Centers with low numbers of cases (<250 per year) requiring this immunohistochemistry (IHC) assay should consider using a reference laboratory service.

Immunohistochemistry (IHC) and fluorescence in situ hybridization (FISH) are the techniques currently recommended for determining HER-2 status.[502] Other available HER-2 testing techniques (chromogenic in situ hybridization (CISH), polymerase chain reaction, enzyme-linked immunosorbent assay, Southern blotting) are available but have not been adopted widely. For both immunohistochemical and FISH-based HER-2 testing, comprehensive standardization of methodology, including monitoring of scoring procedures and the inclusion of validated controls, is mandatory. Participation and satisfactory performance in external quality assessment schemes are important to maintain consistency of performance.[502,505]

There is a very high level of correlation between IHC and FISH assay results in the 0/1+ and 3+ IHC categories, negating the need for dual IHC and FISH-based assays in the majority of cases;[506,507] however, other published studies show higher rates of discordance. It is logical, in the light of such data, to use FISH as a secondary test in the equivocal (2+) IHC category to clarify the HER-2 status of these cases.

Controls The inclusion of controls and their detailed scrutiny are essential to ensure test accuracy. The minimum recommended

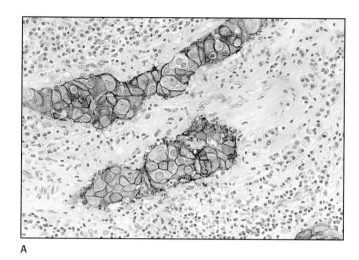

A

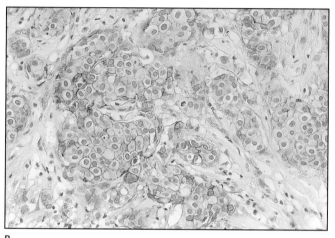

B

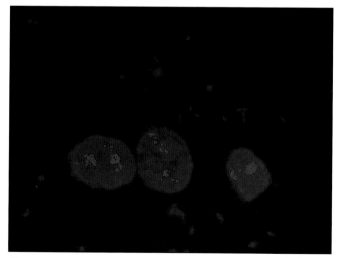

C

Fig. 16.73 • *HER-2* neu immunocytochemical staining of two tumors. One (**A**) shows intense complete tumor cell membrane reactivity that is associated with gene amplification and response to Herceptin therapy. The second tumor (**B**) shows weak focal incomplete membrane reactivity that is not associated with gene amplification and is regarded as a negative result. FISH analysis (**C**) of the case illustrated in (A) demonstrates marked amplification of *HER-2 ERBB2* signal.

is a positive control or controls producing results close to important decision-making points and a negative control. Cell line preparations containing multiple samples of known *HER-2* status characterized by FISH and IHC are useful as controls.[508] Where possible, tissue-based controls, preferably from breast cancers, should also be used in all assay runs. Excessive antigen retrieval can be monitored by evaluation of normal breast epithelial cells as an internal control. Should membrane reactivity be identified in the normal cell population, excessive antigen retrieval may have occurred and retesting of the entire run should be considered.

Scoring of *HER-2* immunohistochemistry assays Only membrane staining of the invasive tumour should be considered when scoring IHC tests. If a commercial kit assay system is used, it is recommended that laboratories adhere strictly to the kit assay protocol and scoring methodology. Local modifications of techniques can lead to false positive and negative assay results. The scoring method recommended is a semi-quantitative system based on the intensity of reaction product and percentage of membrane positive cells, giving a score range of 0–3+ (Table 16.3). Samples scoring 3+ are regarded as unequivocally positive, and those scoring 0/1+ as negative. Borderline scores of 2+ require confirmation using another analysis system, ideally FISH.

HER-2 FISH assay FISH testing for *HER-2* (*ERBB2*) should meet the following criteria:[502]

1 comprehensive standardization of methodology
2 validated controls, including incorporation of a chromosome 17 control to allow for correction of the *HER-2* signal number for chromosome 17 aneusomy (seen in over 50 percent of cases) is considered beneficial by many laboratories
3 validated scoring procedures.

Table 16.3	Recommended *HER-2* immunohistochemistry scoring method	
Score to report	HER-2 protein overexpression assessment	Staining pattern
0	Negative	No staining is observed, or membrane staining in less than 10% of tumor cells
1+	Negative	A faint/barely perceptible membrane staining is detected in more than 10% of tumor cells. The cells are only stained in part of the membrane
2+	Borderline	A weak to moderate complete membrane staining is observed in more than 10% of tumor cells
3+	Positive	A strong complete membrane staining is observed in more than 10% of the tumor cells

Tissue digestion should be standardized to maintain nuclear morphology and should follow strict protocols.[509] Some laboratories find it helpful to evaluate nuclear structure before hybridization and to adjust digestion, where appropriate, to preserve nuclear integrity. This may be particularly valuable with difficult sections, cytology samples, bone biopsies, etc. Hybridization and washing steps should be standardized. Use of automated tissue processors and standardized commercial tissue digestion kits can improve consistency and should be considered. It is recommended that validated commercially available probes or assays are used.

Scoring of *HER-2* FISH assays It is advisable to locate areas of invasive tumour using a serial section stained with hematoxylin and eosin (H&E) and to use this to locate tumour areas to be scored after testing. Care should be taken to avoid areas of ductal carcinoma in situ, which can show amplification even when adjacent invasive tumor cells are negative. With experience, such features can be identified under fluorescence microscopy; however, the use of serial H&E sections is essential should there be any uncertainty.

HER-2 FISH testing results are conventionally expressed as the ratio of *HER-2* signal to chromosome 17 signal. Tumors showing a ratio >2 should be considered as positive. Cut off values for *HER-2* gene amplification when chromosome 17 probes are not used have not been established. The number of chromosome 17 and *HER-2* signals is scored for 20–60 cells, where possible using at least three distinct tumor fields, and the mean *HER-2* to chromosome 17 copy ratio is calculated. In most cases, where either clear amplification is observed or the ratio is below 1.5, scoring of 20 cells is sufficient. In cases where either tumor heterogeneity is seen (1–2 percent of cases) or the ratio is close to 2.0 (ratio of 1.5–2.3), more cells should be scored (up to 60). Samples with >2.0 copies of *HER-2* for each chromosome 17 are considered to be amplified.

Use of prognostic factors

The pathology laboratory has a major role to play in both the diagnosis and the prediction of prognosis of breast cancer patients. At the present time, the most valuable prognostic factors appear to be those which can be assessed on routinely fixed, processed and stained material: histologic grade, lymph node stage, tumor size, vascular invasion and tumor type. The accurate determination of these features requires well prepared H&E sections. Using a combination of histologic features it is possible at this time to predict reliably an individual patient's likelihood of survival. Additional information predicting response to specific therapies can be obtained from immunohistochemically stained sections; in particular ER status can be used to identify those patients who are likely to receive benefit from hormone therapies and, similarly, *HER-2* positivity is a requirement for targeted *HER-2* therapy. In the future, it is to be hoped that other markers of response to specific treatments can be identified, so that patients can be started on the most suitable therapy for their individual tumor without delay.

Nottingham Prognostic Index

Although some individual prognostic factors may be extremely powerful, there is now increasing recognition that combining the results of a range of prognostic variables in the form of an index can give a high level of accuracy in predicting a prognosis which can be used to distinguish groups of patients suitable for different forms of therapy. For example, a patient with extremely good long-term prognosis similar to age-matched control women without breast cancer is unlikely to benefit from adjuvant forms of chemotherapy and is satisfactorily treated with surgical excision alone.

The Nottingham Prognostic Index is the most widely accepted of such indices and uses three prognostic factors, lymph node stage, tumor size and histologic grade.[335,336,510] It was developed through multivariate analysis of a wide range of prognostic variables including time-dependent and biologic variables. The index formula is simple:

Nottingham Prognostic Index (NPI)
= (Size (cm) $\times$ 0.2) + lymph node stage (1–3) + grade (1–3)

In clinical practice, three prognostic groups are identified: a good group with scores of less than 3.4; a moderate prognostic group with scores of 3.4–5.4; a poor group with scores of over 5.4. The respective 15-year survival rates are good – 80 percent, moderate – 42 percent, poor – 13 percent. The 15-year survival of an age-matched control population of women is 83 percent. A major strength of the NPI is the fact that it has been validated prospectively in the NTPBCS.[510] Further confirmation of its utility has been provided by its independent validation in two large multicenter studies.[511,512] The Danish Breast Cancer Cooperative Group study[512] consisted of over 9000 patients and it is pertinent to note that the histologic grading was carried out in 32 separate pathology departments without central review, confirming its robustness as a prognostic factor.

There has been positive critical appraisal of the use and integration of these prognostic factors[513] and the NPI is being used increasingly in breast units for stratification of patients for systemic therapy, especially in the UK.[514] Because it is based on traditional pathologic factors, it can be made available in most pathology departments.

The original outcomes relating to NPI were derived from patients treated in Nottingham between 1973 and 1987. During this time no adjuvant treatment was given routinely. In 1987, we changed our treatment policies in Nottingham, introducing more diligent pathology examination of specimens, improved surgical procedures, review of radiotherapy policies, introduction of adjuvant hormone therapy and adjuvant chemotherapy where deemed appropriate. This major management change appears to have led to an improvement in survival in all prognostic groups, even those to whom we do not currently offer adjuvant hormonal chemotherapy (Table 16.4). We therefore believe that this improvement in survival is due to an overall improvement in our treatment policies rather than any individual factor such as use of adjuvant therapy.

Effects of therapy

Chemotherapy

There are very few descriptions of the effect of multiagent chemotherapy on breast tumors. Kennedy et al. described the histologic features pre- and post-treatment with cyclophosphamide, doxorubicin, premarin, methotrexate, five

Table 16.4	Outcome of patients according to NPI score		
Prognostic group	NPI value	10-year survival (%) 1973–1987 patients	10-year survival (%) 1990–1996 patients
Excellent	≤2.4	94	95
Good	≤3.4	83	91
Moderate I	≤4.4	70	80
Moderate II	≤5.4	51	70
Poor	≤6.4	19	45
V poor	>6.4		33

fluorouracil, tamoxifen and leucovorin rescue.[515] In "normal" breast adjacent to tumors, the common changes observed were essentially those seen following menopausal involution, specifically lobular and stromal involution with adipose tissue replacement. The presence of tumor cell changes showed a strong correlation with clinical response. Few post-therapy changes were observed in patients with little or no response. In patients showing response to chemotherapy, the most frequent observation was a change in tumor cell morphology and arrangement. The tumor cells took on a bland histiocyte-like appearance and were present in the stroma as single cells. Other features observed were nucleomegaly, multinucleation, hyperchromasia, coarse chromatin clumping, and smudging of nuclear outlines. Nucleomegaly and multinucleation were observed in coexisting benign epithelial atypia, but these cells had sharp nuclear membranes, small nucleoli and showed less prominent hyperchromasia. The presence of mixed atypical and normal cells, lack of necrosis and retention of a continuous layer of myoepithelial cells were also found helpful in distinguishing cytologic atypia from residual carcinoma.

Hormone therapy

Again there are few studies describing the histologic effects of hormone therapy. In the same study as that described above,[515] hormone therapy was also used. The authors ascribed a tear-drop appearance and vacuolation of tumor cells, observed in 23 percent of their cases, to hormone therapy (tamoxifen), citing in support evidence of similar changes seen in normal breast during phases of the menstrual cycle or with hypertensive and antipsychotic drugs.[516–518]

Radiotherapy

Schnitt et al.[519] have described the features present following radiotherapy to the breast. Non-neoplastic breast shows similar changes to those seen after chemotherapy, including lobular sclerosis, atrophy and epithelial atypia, as well as those changes commonly associated with radiotherapy in other sites such as atypical stromal fibroblasts and vascular changes. Highly atypical cells can also be found in the TDLU. This may be combined with exaggerated fibrosis of the lobule, conferring a pseudoinfiltrative pattern which may simulate invasive carcinoma. A lobulocentric low power configuration is useful in identifying these benign changes. Despite having large hyper-

chromatic nuclei, their nucleoli are small and there is no evidence of proliferation. Distinction from residual intraduct carcinoma may also be difficult. Features to support a diagnosis of malignancy would be evidence of proliferation, such as cellular stratification, loss of polarity, mitoses, distention of involved ducts or acini and necrosis.[60] The nuclei of tumor cells have more prominent nucleoli and irregular chromatin dispersion.

Rare epithelial tumors

Adenomyoepithelioma

The combined proliferation of epithelial and myoepithelial cells is common within the breast, e.g., in papillomas and sclerosing adenosis. The existence of a rare distinct entity described as adenomyoepithelioma, has been proposed by a number of authors in recent years.[520–523] The myoepithelial proliferation is usually more marked than in other disorders such as papillomas, but there are no agreed diagnostic criteria, and some series have included lesions which others would have classified in more common diagnostic categories, such as ductal adenoma.

Clinical features

Virtually all reported cases of adenomyoepithelioma have presented with a palpable mass, occasionally with an associated serous nipple discharge. There is a wide age range from the third to ninth decades.

Adenomyoepitheliomas usually behave as benign lesions,[524] with recurrences reported in about 10 percent.[520,522] Metastatic spread from malignant variants occur rarely.[525] Metastatic spread from the pure malignant myoepithelial lesions (myoepithelial carcinoma/malignant myoepithelioma) has also been recorded rarely.[526–528]

Macroscopic appearances

Adenomyoepitheliomas are usually nodular, with a well circumscribed margin, have a white or tan cut surface, and are up to 7 cm across.

Histologic appearances

Adenomyoepitheliomas are usually predominantly solid rather than glandular. There are two cell types. Myoepithelium is usually the major component. These cells are polygonal or spindle shaped with clear or eosinophilic cytoplasm, and form the outer layer where glands are present. Immunohistochemistry shows positive staining for actin and S-100 protein.[524] The glandular component is composed of columnar or cuboidal cells that are cytokeratin and epithelial membrane antigen positive. Necrosis can be present.

Classification

Tavassoli[522] has proposed the term myoepitheliosis to describe a process that, in its typical form, is multifocal, involves the peripheral duct system and is characterized by subepithelial proliferation of rounded or spindle-shaped myoepithelial cells. These proliferations may protrude into the duct lumen to form papillary-like processes. Myoepitheliosis has a large overlap with other lesions, such as papillomas, making it of limited value.

Tavassoli and colleagues[521] have also described spindle cell, tubular and lobulated variants of adenomyoepithelioma. In the spindle cell type, the myoepithelial component is dominant and the cells have a spindle cell appearance. The differential distinction from leiomyoma rests on identification of epithelial-lined luminal spaces. The tubular type is virtually indistinguishable from tubular adenoma as it is composed of a circumscribed aggregate of glandular structures formed by a bilayer of myoepithelial and epithelial cells (Fig. 16.74). In the lobulated type, the myoepithelial cells are plumper and often have eosinophilic cytoplasm. They are arranged in clusters which give the lesion its architectural pattern. There is often associated fibrosis, again producing a lobular character. A similar fibrous reaction often surrounds the tumor. Tavassoli suggests that the tubular variant is more likely to recur.[525]

Malignancy in adenomyoepithelioma takes two forms.[525] First, there may be areas of obvious malignancy in an otherwise typical adenomyoepithelioma. Second, there may be an overall appearance of adenomyoepithelioma which, on close inspection, shows foci of cellular atypia and increased numbers of mitoses. The malignant component of either type described above (and any metastases) can be epithelial, myoepithelial or a combination of the two.[521,522,525] Adenomyoepithelioma is also associated with adenosquamous carcinoma.[324]

In malignant myoepithelial lesions (myoepithelial carcinoma/malignant myoepithelioma),[527,528] a spindle cell myoepithelial component predominates. These cells are atypical, showing pleomorphism and frequent mitotic figures. The margin is infiltrative. Immunohistochemistry shows positive staining for actin, cytokeratins and sometimes S-100 protein. A similar morphology and immunophenotype may be seen in spindle cell carcinoma, making differential diagnosis difficult.

Adenomyoepithelioma with apocrine adenosis

Eusebi and Kiaer have used the term adenomyoepithelioma to describe a histologically different lesion with distinctive histologic features.[95,523] The two cases described by Eusebi were in older women, both presenting with breast lumps. The tumors were firm on the cut surfaces, one being circumscribed, the other slightly ill defined. This tumor is composed of nests of cells of two distinct types (Fig. 16.75). The predominant cell is small, uniform with clear cytoplasm and in areas these cells merge to form large sheets. In the center of the nest, the second population of columnar cells of apocrine epithelial morphology are present and these form glandular lumina. The clear cell population shows positive actin immunoreactivity and has ultrastructural features of myoepithelial cells. The glandular cells exhibit low molecular weight cytokeratin immunoreactivity and produce abundant PAS-positive, diastase-resistant material. The ratio of glandular to myoepithelial components may vary between tumors and within different regions of the same tumor. Little follow up information is available from Eusebi's description but the other case described by Kiaer et al.[95] behaved as a low grade malignant tumor, recurring multiple times despite apparent adequate

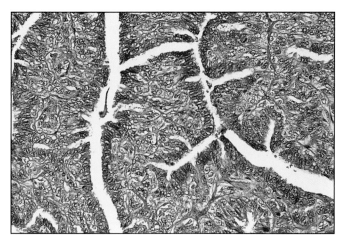

Fig. 16.74 • Adenomyoepithelioma. An intraductal proliferation with a striking myoepithelial cell population.

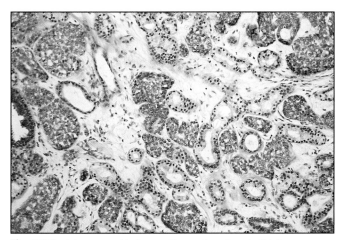

Fig. 16.75 • Adenomyoepithelioma with apocrine adenosis. This is a very unusual tumor with two distinct components. Glandular structures are lined by clear or apocrine epithelial cells with a second group of small cells (myoepithelial) arranged in clusters or sheets.

local excision. The tumor does appear to be locally infiltrative with an ill defined margin.

Differential diagnosis

The wide variety of patterns described in myoepithelial tumors of the breast have led to a number of problems of distinction between other benign entities including papilloma, ductal adenoma, tubular adenoma, sclerosing adenosis and complex sclerosing lesion. Distinction in some cases is arbitrary and rests on subjective opinion and various authorities' viewpoints. It is our practice to restrict the diagnosis of adenomyoepithelioma to cases falling outside the spectrum of these well-recognized and common benign conditions.

Pure spindle cell myoepithelial tumors may resemble spindle cell carcinoma when the tumor cells are large and pleomorphic, leiomyoma or fibromatosis if small and regular. As mentioned above distinction from spindle cell carcinoma is difficult. Fibromatosis has a characteristically infiltrative pattern with uniform spindle cells and interlacing fascicles. Pure spindle cell myoepithelioma cells are usually larger and less uniform than those seen in fibromatosis.

Tumors of salivary gland type

A variety of tumors indistinguishable from those seen in the salivary glands and bronchial tissue may occur in the breast. These include pleomorphic adenomas, adenoid cystic carcinoma and mucoepidermoid carcinoma.

Pleomorphic adenoma (mixed tumor)

Clinical features

These tumors present as discrete palpable masses or suspicious mass lesions on mammography.[529] They have a wide age range of presentation from the fourth to ninth decades, but are more common in the postmenopausal years.

There is still uncertainty whether these represent a true distinct entity or a variant of ductal adenoma or intraduct papilloma showing cartilagenous metaplasia in the stromal component.

Macroscopic appearances

The lesions are single or multifocal, measuring between 1 and 4 cm in diameter. They have a well circumscribed, sometimes lobulated, appearance with a white or yellow homogeneous rubbery cut surface.

Histologic appearances

By definition, pleomorphic adenomas should be composed of a minimum of three elements: epithelial cells, myoepithelial cells, and chondromyxoid tissue (Fig. 16.76). The epithelial components may form acinar or tubular structures and may be arranged in islands or trabeculae. There is minimal cellular atypia and no significant mitotic activity. The myoepithelial component often adjoins the chondromyxoid areas and may dominate areas of the tumor. The chondromyxoid stromal tissue may contain areas of well formed hyaline cartilage and show focal calcification. Bone formation is found in up to 50 percent of cases.[530,531]

The lesions are generally circumscribed and may have a collagen-rich fibrous pseudocapsule. There may be evidence of

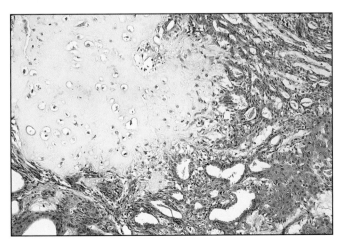

Fig. 16.76 • Pleomorphic adenoma (mixed tumor). There is an intimate admixture of glandular structures, myoepithelial cells, and chondromyxoid stroma.

origin from a papilloma with a residual surrounding luminal space. Non-specific coexisting features may be present, including epithelial hyperplasia, sclerosing adenosis, cystic change and apocrine metaplasia.

Immunocytochemistry

The epithelial component can be distinguished using low molecular weight cytokeratin and the myoepithelial component using S-100 protein or anti-smooth muscle actin antibodies.

Differential diagnosis

These lesions may occur in isolation or be indistinguishable from a complex intraduct papilloma or ductal adenoma. There is no real merit in attempting to differentiate between these conditions. Cartilage formation may be present in a variety of other breast tumors including fibroadenoma and hamartoma, intraduct papilloma and ductal adenoma; it may also be seen in some malignant tumors, including phyllodes tumor and metaplastic carcinoma. The diagnosis of mixed tumor rests strictly on the coexistence of bland epithelial tissue with myoepithelial proliferation and chondromyxoid stroma.

Adenoid cystic carcinoma

Clinical appearances

This is a rare form of breast tumor, usually presenting clinically as a mass lesion, most often in postmenopausal patients.[532] Tumors may vary in size from below 2 cm to over 10 cm. They are recognized to have an extremely good long term prognosis.[532] Metastatic spread, although rare, does occur.[533] Local recurrences do not appear to alter the favorable prognosis.[534,535] They are usually well defined clinically and, on occasion, may be painful.[536]

The existence of this lesion in the breast has been questioned by some authorities in view of its close similarity to invasive cribriform carcinoma.[10] However, immunocytochemical and ultrastructural studies now provide convincing evidence of the existence of true adenoid cystic tumors within the breast.[533,537]

Macroscopic appearances

This is usually well defined tumor with a firm pale cut surface appearance, and most cases are between 1 and 6 cm in size with a mean size of 2.5 cm.[538]

Histologic appearances

The tumor resembles invasive cribriform carcinoma (Fig. 16.77A), although solid areas may be present. The characteristic feature of adenoid cystic carcinoma of the breast is that, like its salivary gland counterpart, it is composed of two cell types. The two cell types are:

1. small basaloid myoepithelial cells arranged in solid, cribriform or tubular growth patterns; and surrounding pseudoglandular spaces containing basement membrane material
2. epithelial cells arranged around true glandular lumina.

953

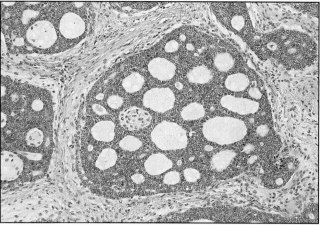

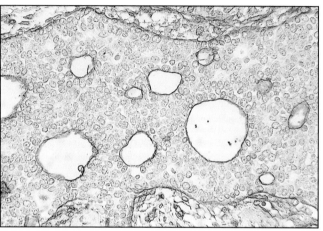

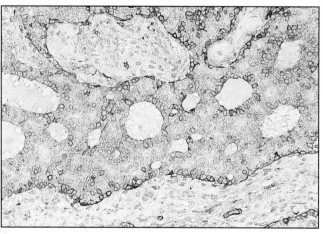

Fig. 16.77 • Adenoid cystic carcinoma. Infiltration of nests of tumor cells with a cribriform architecture. The diagnostic dual cell population may be visible histologically but can often be more easily identified using immunohistology. Basement membrane deposition (laminin) can be seen around tumor nests and in the lumina (**B**). Myoepithelial cells can be highlighted using actin immunostaining (**C**).

These two cell types may be difficult to distinguish histologically. Mucin stains are useful. Alcian blue stains the contents of the pseudoglandular spaces, whereas the true lumina are PAS positive.

Immunohistochemistry

Immunohistochemistry is particularly good at showing the two cell types. The epithelial cells stain with antibodies to cytokeratin, such as CAM5.2, whereas the myoepithelial cells stain with antibodies to smooth muscle actin (Fig. 16.77C) and S-100 protein. In addition, basement membrane material, both around the periphery of the tumor nests and in the pseudocysts, may be shown with antibodies to laminin and collagen IV (Fig. 16.77B). Salivary tumors of this type are also typically negative for ER, PR and HER2/neu.

Ultrastructure

Ultrastructural examination may confirm the biphasic nature of the tumor with the presence of basal lamina and epithelial-lined glandular spaces.[533,538]

Differential diagnosis

The main differential diagnosis is with invasive cribriform carcinoma of the breast. The latter is composed solely of epithelial cells, usually has an admixture of tubular elements typical of invasive tubular carcinoma and may show a characteristic stromal fibrous reaction. The tumor cell groups may show rudimentary basement membrane formation, usually around the periphery of tumor nests, but this is usually minimal. Cribriform carcinoma is typically strongly estrogen receptor positive, whereas most adenoid cystic carcinomas are estrogen receptor negative.[539]

Acinic cell carcinoma

Clinical appearances

Acinic cell carcinoma (see also Ch. 7) is a rare tumor with seven recorded cases.[540–542] It affects women between 35 and 80 years of age (mean 56)[541] and presents as a palpable nodule ranging from 2 to 5 cm size. In two cases, axillary lymph node metastases were found. Treatment varied from neoadjuvant chemotherapy with radical mastectomy to lumpectomy alone. None of the 7 reported patients has died of the tumor, although follow-up was limited (maximum 5 years).

Histologic appearances

Acinic cell carcinoma of the breast resembles similar tumors of the parotid gland and shows acinic cell (serous) differentiation with zymogen-type cytoplasmic granules and the presence of amylase, lysozyme and alpha-1 antichymotrypsin.

The tumors show a combination of solid (dedifferentiated), microcystic and microglandular areas (Fig. 16.78A). Cytologically, the cells have abundant, usually granular, amphophilic to eosinophilic cytoplasm. The granules may be coarse and bright red, reminiscent of those in Paneth cells (Fig. 16.78B). However, clear "hypernephroid" cytoplasm may also be present. The nuclei are irregular, round to ovoid, with a single nucleolus. The mitotic count varies and can be as high as 15 mitoses/10 high power fields.[541]

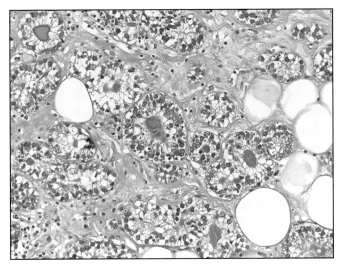

A

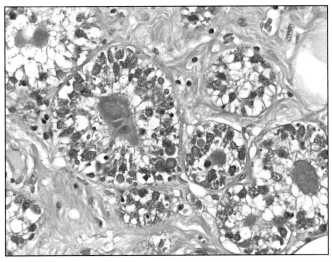

B

Fig. 16.78 • An example of an acinic cell carcinoma of the breast showing diffuse stromal infiltration by glandular structures formed by a single layer of epithelial cells. There is no stromal reaction to the tumor. (**A**) The tumor cells have clear cytoplasm and many contain prominent eosinophilic globules (**B**).

Immunohistochemistry

Most of the cells stain intensely for anti-amylase, lysozyme, chymotrypsin, EMA and S-100 protein.[541] GCDFP-15, the mucoapocrine marker, can also be focally positive.

Ultrastructure

The 3 cases studied were composed of cells with cytoplasm filled by zymogen-like granules measuring from 0.08 cm to 0.9 cm.[541]

Mucoepidermoid carcinoma

Clinical features

The argument for the existence of true mucoepidermoid carcinoma of the breast is perhaps even more controversial than for pleomorphic adenoma and adenoid cystic carcinoma

of the breast. It is also extremely rare.[543] Squamous differentiation or metaplasia is well recognized to occur focally in invasive adenocarcinomas of breast, particularly in elderly women.[10] The close admixture of these two features has led to descriptions of mucoepidermoid carcinoma in the breast. The significance of this tumor as a special type is also questionable. Low grade histologic features are associated with a good long-term prognosis.[544,545] More typically, the coexistence of mucin and squamous differentiation occurs in high grade tumors in which there appears to be no particular prognostic benefit. One group[546] has proposed that true mucoepidermoid tumors of the breast can be distinguished by the presence of a mixture of elements including mucin-secreting cells, squamous, intermediate cells, and myoepithelial cells. Others have suggested the predominance of mucin-secreting cells as a diagnostic feature.[547] Either way, these lesions have a similar age distribution as ductal carcinomas.

Macroscopic appearances

The appearances vary but are generally indistinguishable from conventional invasive adenocarcinoma of the breast.

Histologic appearances

This tumor is invasive and is composed of neoplastic squamous, glandular and intermediate cell elements varying in proportion and often intimately associated with one another.

Immunocytochemistry

The squamous and glandular elements may be distinguished using appropriate low and high molecular weight cytokeratin antibodies. Myoepithelial components can be identified using anti-smooth muscle actin and S-100 protein antibodies. Keratin subtyping reveals similar features to comparable lesions in salivary gland.[543]

Differential diagnosis

The existence of this entity is still argued by some but, apart from exceptionally rare low grade variants, carries no particular prognostic relevance. Metaplastic carcinoma often has a dominant component of undifferentiated sarcomatoid spindle cells with a paucity of differentiated squamous elements. Some forms of adenocarcinoma in the elderly may show very extensive squamous metaplasia and be virtually indistinguishable from pure squamous cell carcinoma.

Stromal tumors

Benign vascular tumors

Benign vascular tumors of the breast are rare and make up about one-third of vascular lesions in the breast. Differentiation from angiosarcoma may present problems as angiosarcomas of all grades, at least focally, may have bland histologic characteristics, especially at their periphery. Rosen's group[548–551] have reviewed their experience of vascular tumors of the breast and have described a range of benign vascular tumors in a series of

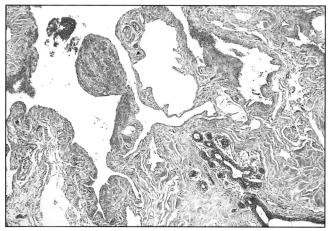

Fig. 16.79 • Venous hemangioma. A benign vascular tumor of the breast composed of large, dilated vascular channels, some having smooth muscle in their walls.

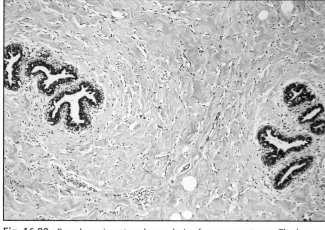

Fig. 16.80 • Pseudoangiomatous hyperplasia of mammary stroma. The breast extralobular stroma appears hypercellular and at high magnification has the appearance of linear slit-like vascular spaces.

articles. This serves as the most comprehensive classification of these lesions to date.

Venous hemangioma

These are rare tumors of intramammary stroma, measuring between 1 and 5 cm in size, composed of large venous channels surrounded by smooth muscle (Fig. 16.79).[548]

Hemangioma or perilobular hemangioma

These are small tumors 2 mm to 2.5 cm in size, approximately half of which are chance findings on microscopy. They are usually relatively circumscribed and are composed of bland vascular channels often surrounded by a spindle cell cuff and frequently having a visible afferent muscular vessel nearby.[549] Many examples are confined to perilobular fibrous stroma. Some may show some endothelial cell atypia and anastomosis of channels making distinction from grade 1 angiosarcoma difficult. As a general rule it is very rare for a vascular tumor of the breast under 2 cm in size to behave in a malignant fashion.

Angiomatosis

These are very rare, sometimes congenital, large lesions (median 9 cm diameter) composed of non-anastomotic dilated blood and lymphatic channels lined by flattened endothelial cells which are present in the interlobular stroma and do not involve terminal duct lobular units.[550]

Pseudoangiomatous stromal hyperplasia

As its name suggests, this phenomenon is not a true vascular lesion. The interlobular stroma contains slit-like spaces which appear to be lined by bland flattened cells (Fig. 16.80).[54,552] This is thought to represent an alteration of the stromal fibroblasts that occurs in association with localized or diffuse parenchymal changes, such as mammary hamartoma[52] and gynecomastia.[553] To the unwary, this lesion could be confused with angiosarcoma. Clues to the diagnosis are the association with other adjacent pathology and immunohistochemistry which shows that the cells are positive for vimentin and CD34,[52] but negative for other endothelial markers (e.g. von Willebrand factor, CD31).

Subcutaneous lesions

A variety of non-parenchymal cutaneous or subcutaneous vascular lesions may be misinterpreted as vascular tumors of the breast. These include hemangiomas, arteriovenous malformations and hamartomas.[551]

Angiosarcoma
Clinical features

Angiosarcoma of the breast is rare, but is the most common pure malignant stromal tumor of the breast. The usual presentation is in the form of a painless mass, but diffuse breast enlargement without a mass, which may appear vascular clinically, is seen in some patients. Bilateral involvement is relatively common.[554] Although angiosarcoma may present over a wide age range, the peak incidence is in the 30s.[554] Overall survival rates are poor with 3-year survival of 38 percent and 5-year survival of 33 percent being recorded.[526,554] Histologic grade appears to be of great importance in predicting prognosis. Grade 1 (40 percent of cases) and grade 2 (19 percent of cases) have a good-to-intermediate prognosis differing in magnitude in various studies; some describe a favorable prognosis,[526] others a poor prognosis.[555] Five-year survival for grade 3 tumors is universally regarded as poor, being at the level of 15 percent.[556] Sites for metastatic spread are widespread but liver, lung, skin and contralateral breast are the most common.

Macroscopic appearances

A wide variation in size is recorded from 2 to over 11 cm. Malignant tumors under 2 cm are rare, but the majority measure between 2 and 5 cm. Low grade tumors tend to have a relatively vascular homogeneous hemangioma-like cut surface, while high grade tumors are more variable, with vascular appearances at the periphery and more solid central areas with necrosis and hemorrhage.

Histologic appearances

The most important feature to emphasize in the microscopic appearances of mammary angiosarcoma is the presence of low grade histologic features resembling hemangioma, especially at the periphery, in a high proportion of tumors. This can lead the unwary to underinterpret and misdiagnose these tumors on biopsy or if a large resection specimen is inadequately sampled.

Grade 1 tumors are composed of anastomosing and inter-communicating vascular channels lined by one or two layers of endothelial cells with very rare or absent mitotic figures (Fig. 16.81A). Focal tufting of endothelial cells and thrombosis may be identified. Dissection between adipocytes is common. Papillary formation, solid anaplastic or spindle cell areas and necrosis are absent. Differentiation from benign hemangioma may be difficult. Features recommended to assist differentiation are:

1 size of the tumor: benign tumors are generally less than 2 cm in size and may be microscopic. Angiosarcomas are generally larger than 2 cm
2 the vascular channels in a benign lesion are non-anastomosing and lined by flat, usually non-proliferative endothelium
3 a non-neoplastic muscular vessel may be identified close to benign hemangiomas in approximately 50 percent of cases[549]
4 smooth muscle may be present around benign vascular structures.

Worryingly, a rare microscopic (<2 mm in size) form of peri-lobular hemangioma has been described[549] in which there is some endothelial cell nuclear atypia and proliferation with some anastomosing channels and a larger (3 mm–2.5 cm) form with endothelial nuclear atypia but non-anastomosing channels.

Grade 2 angiosarcomas (Fig. 16.81B) have a mixed structure with areas showing endothelial tufting with papillary formation and solid spindle cell components. Mitoses are usually visible in the papillary structures. The predominant pattern is, however, of grade 1 histology, particularly at the periphery of the tumor. This variation in pattern further emphasizes the need to sample tumors adequately.

Grade 3 tumors are composed predominantly of solid, often spindle-celled tumor with a paucity of distinctive vascular channels. Hemorrhage, necrosis, cellular pleomorphism and mitotic figures are evident. In these tumors distinction from other spindle cell neoplasms is the main problem.

The use of immunocytochemistry in identification of angiosarcoma is discussed in Chapter 3.

Post-radiation angiosarcoma

Radiation-induced sarcomas are well recognized. Conservative surgery with radiotherapy is increasingly used in the treatment of breast cancer, and it is estimated that about 0.1 percent of such patients will develop angiosarcoma in the radiation field,[557] most often in the skin. The interval between radiation exposure and development of angiosarcoma is usually between two and a half and 10 years, but may sometimes be shorter.[558] The majority of such lesions arise in the skin or subcutaneous fat, with a minority in the breast parenchyma.[558a] Angiosarcoma arising after radiotherapy is more common than *de novo* angiosarcoma, and because it is associated with breast cancer treatment, it is seen in older women. Atypical vascular lesions can also arise after radiotherapy and must be distinguished from well differentiated angiosarcoma.[558]

Lymphangiosarcoma (Stewart-Treves lesion)

This is a rare complication of radical mastectomy developing usually 10 years after surgery in areas of lymphedema induced by the prior operation, typically, the arm (see Ch. 3). Some patients have also had radiotherapy, which may be a contributory factor. The tumor has a very aggressive behavior spreading rapidly through the area of lymphedema and disseminating widely throughout the body.[559,560] The 5-year survival rate is

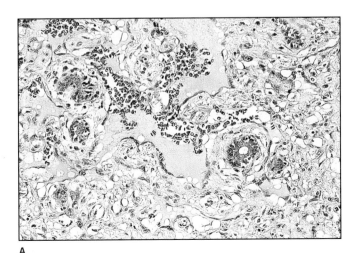
A

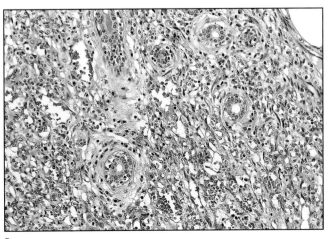
B

Fig. 16.81 • Angiosarcoma. Two photomicrographs from the periphery (A) and center (B) of an angiosarcoma of the breast. Peripherally, the tumor has a low-grade appearance, with large vascular channels lined by endothelial cells. Centrally, the tumor has a grade 2 appearance with spindle cell areas.

dismal. Histologically, the tumor is composed of papillary or solid growth of undifferentiated or epithelioid cells. This morphology has led, in the past, to speculation that they may represent retrograde vascular spread of breast carcinoma cells rather than a true angiosarcoma. Immunohistological and ultrastructural studies confirm that they are vascular in origin[561,562] and best regarded as very high grade lymphangiosarcoma.

Other sarcomas

Most types of sarcoma have been described, at least rarely, in the breast. The diagnostic criteria for tumors not specific to the breast are covered elsewhere in this book. It must be borne in mind that the breast is a rare site for primary presentation of sarcoma (Fig. 16.82). Most cases of apparently pure spindle cell or undifferentiated sarcoma of the breast will, on diligent sampling or else by immunohistochemistry, either show focal evidence of biphasic epithelial and stromal structures characteristic of phyllodes tumor or focal evidence of neoplastic epithelial differentiation and are best regarded as a spindle cell or metaplastic carcinoma (see p. 938). Diagnosis of the latter may be helped by the identification of ductal carcinoma in situ within the tumor or in the surrounding breast.

Myofibroblastoma
Clinical features

This uncommon tumor[563] can present over a wide age range. The initial report found a male predominance,[563] but this is not a consistent finding in later studies.[564] Clinically, the tumor presents with a short history of a mass which, on examination, is firm and freely mobile. Comparable lesions have also been described outside the breast.[565] Follow up after local excision or mastectomy shows no evidence of development of metastatic disease and the tumor is regarded as a benign entity.

Macroscopic features

The tumor most often occurs within the breast parenchyma. The mean size described in the literature is 2.3 cm, range 1–4 cm, although isolated much larger examples may be seen.

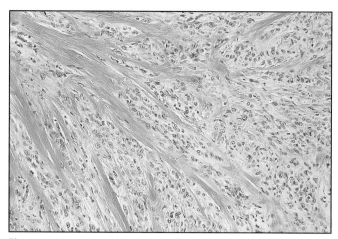

Fig. 16.83 • Myofibroblastoma. Clusters of plump spindle-shaped cells separated by bands of hyaline collagen are the two characteristic features of this tumor.

They are rounded and well circumscribed and have a vague multinodular cut surface appearance.

Histologic features

These tumors are circumscribed and have a false capsule of compressed breast tissue, with usually no entrapped mammary parenchymal structures. They are composed of spindle cells often arranged in short bundles within a collagenous stroma (Fig. 16.83). The collage bundles are often ropey, as in spindle cell lipoma. The nuclei are oval with a slightly irregular outline, small nucleoli and occasional grooves (Fig. 16.84). Variable cellularity is common. Smooth muscle, cartilage and (often) fat may be present.[563,566] Mitoses may be present, but are infrequent. The spindle cells show reactivity for desmin,[567] alpha-smooth muscle actin, and CD34,[568] but not for cytokeratin or S-100. Ultrastructurally, the tumor cells contain bundles of myofilaments with focal densities.

Differential diagnosis

There is some morphologic overlap with solitary fibrous tumor, although the latter has a more patternless architecture (see

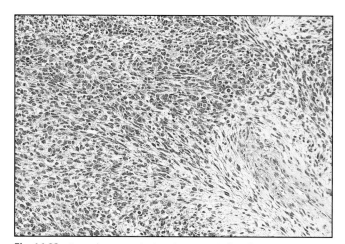

Fig. 16.82 • Stromal sarcoma. An invasive pure spindle cell tumor with a mesenchymal phenotype (vimentin positivity only).

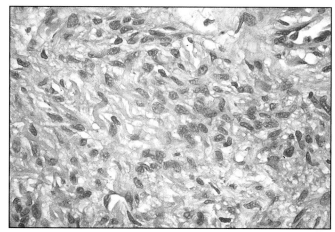

Fig. 16.84 • Myofibroblastoma. The cells are small, spindle-shaped, and have grooved nuclei.

Ch. 24). A recent study[568] suggested that distinguishing features are that solitary fibrous tumors have inconspicuous nucleoli, thick bands of collagen and no staining for desmin or alpha-smooth muscle actin. Furthermore, myofibroblastoma has a karyotype indistinguishable from spindle cell lipoma.

Fibromatosis

Clinical features

Fibromatosis of the breast is an uncommon but well recognized condition, essentially comparable to desmoid fibromatoses elsewhere (See Ch. 24). There have been numerous case reports in the literature and a few series reported.[41,569–571] It occurs almost exclusively in women. The mean age of presentation ranges between 25 and 45 with a wide overall age range from 15 to 80 years. The tumors usually present as a breast mass which, on examination, is firm and variably circumscribed or ill defined. It may be fixed to the deep fascia or to the overlying skin. Mammographically, the lesion is often indistinguishable from breast cancer and is usually seen as an ill-defined dense mass.[572]

Fibromatosis of the breast treated by incomplete excision has a high risk of local recurrence. Excision margins should be examined closely and re-excision carried out promptly if disease is present at margins. The natural behavior of fibromatosis, as at other sites, is poorly understood. Aggressive variants are described, which may extend through the breast into the chest wall and mediastinal tissues. However, in some patients who have recurrence after diagnosis but refuse further surgery, the disease becomes static.

Macroscopic findings

A wide size range at presentation is described, from under 1 cm to over 10 cm, with an average of between 2 and 3 cm. The cut surface shows an ill defined firm area of pale fibrous tissue.

Histologic findings

Fibromatosis may have cellular and collagen-rich hyalinized areas. The diagnosis is based on recognition of a bland infiltrative spindle cell proliferation (Fig. 16.85). Typically, very few or no mitotic figures are identified. Nuclear pleomorphism and atypia should raise doubts about the diagnosis. The cells are arranged in long fascicles and storiform or interlacing patterns may be seen. The tumor extends along fibrous septae and histologic evidence of the disease may be present a considerable distance from the macroscopically visible focus of tumor. The most cellular areas are usually identified at the periphery of the tumor with fibrosis and hyalinization occurring centrally. Additional features include the presence of focal lymphocytic infiltrates in approximately 50 percent of cases.[9,570] Mammary parenchymal ducts and lobules, when surrounded by fibromatosis, may exhibit features of gynecomastoid hyperplasia with micropapillary epithelial proliferation.

Differential diagnosis

Nuclear expression of beta catenin is present in up to 80 percent of fibromatoses of the breast and is also described in fibro-

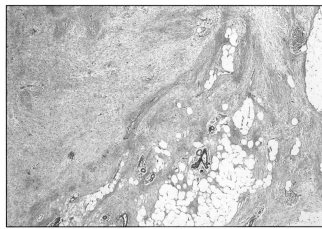

A

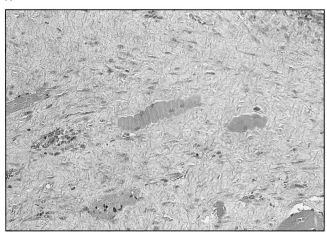

B

Fig. 16.85 • Fibromatosis. An ill-defined infiltrative tumor which surrounds pre-existing mammary structures (**A**). The tumor is composed of bland spindle-shaped cells (**B**).

adenomas and phyllodes tumours. Spindle cell carcinoma needs to be excluded with cytokeratin immunohistochemistry. Further details of immunocytochemical and ultrastructural features of fibromatosis are described in Chapter 24.

Granular cell tumor

Granular cell tumor of the breast is a rare neoplasm that clinically and mammographically may appear malignant, but almost always has a benign behavior.[573,574] The pathology is essentially the same as granular cell tumors at other sites (see Ch. 27). Macroscopically, the edge is irregular. Histology shows typically large polygonal cells with eosinophilic granular cytoplasm. The nuclei are almost always small and bland. Sometimes the stroma shows extensive sclerosis and the granular cells may not be prominent: occasionally, distinction from fibrotic fat necrosis may be difficult, particularly on core biopsy. There may be histologic clues to the very rare granular cell tumors with malignant behavior.[575] Immunohistochemistry shows expression of S-100, CD68, inhibin, PGP9.5 and neurone-specific enolase.[576] Cytokeratins are negative.

Non-intrinsic tumors

Malignant lymphoma

Primary malignant lymphoma of the breast may present as a mass and be indistinguishable clinically from carcinoma. The majority have a B-cell phenotype with the most common being diffuse large B-cell lymphoma, follicle center cell lymphoma and lymphomas of mucosa-associated lymphoid tissue.[23,24,577,578] Histologically, the lymphoid cells may be arranged in linear "Indian files" which may resemble invasive lobular carcinoma of classical type (Fig. 16.86). Lymphomas involving the breast secondarily, as part of disseminated disease, are mostly low grade B-cell neoplasms. Malignant lymphoma is dealt with in Chapter 21.

Metastatic tumors

Spread to the breast from primary tumors at other sites is well recognized and can occur in many different cancers.[579] When faced with an unusual tumor in the breast, it is essential to obtain a full clinical history and to enquire whether there is evidence of a previous tumor elsewhere or of disseminated tumor. Metastatic tumors seen most commonly in the breast are lymphoma/leukemia, melanoma and carcinomas of the lung (particularly small cell), stomach, prostate and ovary.[580]

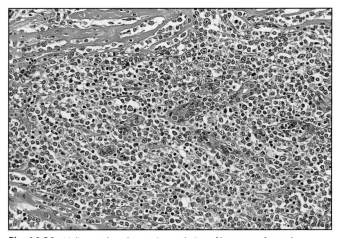

Fig. 16.86 • Malignant lymphoma. A population of large transformed lymphoid cells shows infiltration through a terminal duct lobular unit. Note the preservation of pre-existing structures and similarities to classical invasive lobular carcinoma.

Occasional sarcomas, notably alveolar rhabdomyosarcoma, may also metastasize to the breast. Primary breast adenocarcinoma may also metastasize to the contralateral breast or ipsilateral breast if conservation therapy has been used.

A useful rule to distinguish primary from metastatic carcinomas is the presence of coexistent in situ carcinoma, which would support a primary origin within the breast.

References

1. Tavassoli F, Devilee, P 2003 Pathology and genetics of tumours of the breast and female genital organs. World Health Organisation classification of tumours. IARC Press, Lyon.
2. Hutter R V P 1986 Consensus meeting. Is fibrocystic disease of the breast precancerous? Arch Pathol Lab Med 110: 171–173
3. Royal College of Pathologists Working Group on Breast Screening 1990 Breast cancer screening guidelines for pathologists. NHSBSP Publications
4. Royal College of Pathologists Working Group on Breast Screening 1991 Pathology reporting in breast cancer screening. J Clin Pathol 44: 710–725
5. Pathologists, NBSPa.Rco 2005 Pathology reporting of breast disease 3rd edn. NHSBSP Publication No 58. NHS Cancer Screening Programmes, Sheffield
6. European Commission 1996 European guidelines for quality assurance in mammography screening 2nd edn. de Wolf CJM, Perry NM (eds). Office for Official Publications of the European Communities, Luxembourg
7. Hughes L E, Mansell R E, Webster D J T 1987 Aberrations of normal development and involution (ANDI): a new perspective on pathogenesis and nomenclature of benign breast disorders. Lancet ii: 1316–1319
8. Haagensen C D 1986 Diseases of the breast. WB Saunders, Philadelphia
9. Hayward J L, Parks A G 1958 Alterations in the microanatomy of the breast as a result of changes in the hormonal environment. In: Currie AR (ed) Endocrine aspects of breast cancer. Churchill Livingstone, Edinburgh, p. 133–134
10. Azzopardi J E 1979 Problems in breast pathology. WB Saunders, London
11. Frantz V K, Pickren J W, Melcher G W et al. 1951 Incidence of chronic cystic disease in so called normal breasts. Cancer 4: 762–783
12. Foote F W Jr, Stewart F W 1945 Comparative studies of cancerous versus non-cancerous breasts. Ann Surg 121: 574–585
13. Dixon J M, Scott W N, Miller W R 1985 Natural history of cystic disease: the importance of cyst type. Br J Surg 72: 190–192
14. Hughes L E, Mansel R E, Webster D J T 1989 Benign disorders and diseases of the breast. Baillière Tindall, London, 93–101
15. Izuo M, Okagaki T, Richart R M et al. 1971 DNA content in apocrine metaplasia of fibrocystic disease, complex and breast cancer. Cancer 27: 643–650
16. Page D L, Anderson T J, Johnson R L 1987 Sarcomas of the breast. In: Page DL, Anderson TJ (eds) Diagnostic histopathology of the breast. Churchill Livingstone, Edinburgh
17. Tesluk H, Amott T, Goodnight J E Jr 1986 Apocrine adenoma of the breast. Arch Pathol Lab Med 110: 351–352
18. Tham K T, Dupont W D, Page D L et al. 1989 Micropapillary hyperplasia with atypical features in female breasts, resembling gynecomastia. In Fenoglio-Preiser CM, Wolff M, Rilke F (eds) Progress in surgical pathology. Springer Verlag, Heidelberg
19. Schwartz I S, Strauchen J A 1990 Lymphocytic mastopathy. An autoimmune disease of the breast? Am J Clin Pathol 93: 725–730
20. Lammie G A, Bobrow L G, Staunton M D et al. 1991 Sclerosing lymphocytic lobulitis of the breast – evidence for an autoimmune pathogenesis. Histopathology 19: 13–20
21. Ashton M A, Lefkowitz M, Tavassoli F A 1994 Epithelioid stromal cells in lymphocytic mastitis – a source of confusion with invasive carcinoma. Mod Pathol 7: 49–54
22. Aozasa K, Ohsawa M, Saeki K et al. 1992 Malignant lymphoma of the breast. Immunologic type and association with lymphocytic mastopathy. Am J Clin Pathol 97: 699–704
23. Bobrow L G, Richards M A, Happerfield L C 1993 Breast lymphomas: a clinicopathological review. Hum Pathol 24: 274–278
24. Arber D A, Simpson J F, Weiss L M et al. 1994 Non-Hodgkin's lymphoma involving the breast. Am J Surg Pathol 18: 288–295
25. Lee A H, Happerfield L C, Millis R R et al. 1996 Inflammatory infiltrate in invasive lobular and ductal carcinoma of the breast. Br J Cancer 74: 796–801
26. Sloane J P 1987 Biopsy pathology of the breast. Chapman & Hall, London
27. Fechner R E 1987 Fibroadenoma and related conditions. In: Page DL, Anderson TJ (eds) Diagnostic histopathology of the breast. Churchill Livingstone, Edinburgh. p 72–85
28. Rosen P P (ed) 1996 Fibroepithelial neoplasms. In: Rosen's Breast pathology. Lipincott-Raven, Philadelphia, p 143–175
29. Dent D M 1989 Fibroadenoma. World J Surg 13: 706–710
30. Orcel L, Douvin D 1973 Contribution à l'étude histogénétique des fibro-adénomes mammaires. Ann Anat Pathol Paris 18: 255–276
31. Pesce C, Colacino R 1986 Morphometry of the breast fibroadenoma. Pathol Res Pract 181: 718–720
32. Noguchi S, Motomura K, Inaji H et al. 1993 Clonal analysis of fibroadenoma and phyllodes tumor of the breast by means of polymerase chain reaction. Cancer Res 53: 4071–4074
33. Martin P M, Kuttenn F, Serment H et al. 1979 Progesterone receptors in breast fibroadenomas. J Steroid Biochem 11: 1295–1298
34. Wilkinson S, Anderson T J, Rifkind E et al. 1989 Fibroadenoma of the breast: a follow-up of conservative management. Br J Surg 76: 390–391

35. Galea M H, Dixon A R, Pye G et al. 1993 Non-operative management of discrete breast lumps in women over 35 years of age (abstract). Breast 1: 164

36. Blamey R W 1998 Clinical aspects of benign breast lesions. In: Elston CW, Ellis IO (eds) Systemic pathology. The breast. Churchill Livingstone, London, p 231–238

37. Diaz N M, Palmer J O, McDivitt RW 1991 Carcinoma arising within fibroadenomas of the breast. Am J Clin Pathol 95: 614–622

38. Dupont W D, Page D L, Parl F F et al. 1994 Long term risk of breast cancer in women with fibroadenoma. New Engl J Med 331: 10–15

39. Levi F, Randimbison L, Te V C et al. 1994 Incidence of breast cancer in women with fibroadenoma. Int J Cancer 57: 681–683

40. Tavassoli F A (ed) 1992 Biphasic tumors. In: Pathology of the breast. Norwalk, Appleton and Lange, p. 425–481

41. Wargotz E S, Norris H J, Austin R M et al. 1987 Fibromatosis of the breast. A clinical and pathological study of 28 cases. Am J Surg Pathol 11: 38–45

42. Mies C, Rosen P P 1987 Juvenile fibroadenoma with atypical epithelial hyperplasia. Am J Surg Pathol 11: 184–190

43. Pike A M, Oberman H A 1985 Juvenile (cellular) adenofibromas. A clinicopathologic study. Am J Surg Pathol 9: 730–736

44. Elston C W, Ellis I O (eds) 1998 Fibroadenoma and related conditions. In Systemic pathology. The breast. Churchill Livingstone, London, p 147–186

45. Hertel B G, Zaloudek C, Kempson R L 1976 Breast adenomas. Cancer 37: 2891–2905

46. Slavin J L, Billson V R, Ostor A G 1993 Nodular breast lesions during pregnancy and lactation. Histopathology 22: 481–485

47. O'Hara M F, Page D L 1985 Adenomas of the breast and ectopic breast under lactational influences. Hum Pathol 16: 707–712

48. Moross T, Lang A P, Mahoney L 1983 Tubular adenoma of the breast. Arch Pathol 107: 84–86

49. Arrigoni M G, Dockerty M B, Judd E S 1971 The identification and treatment of mammary hamartoma. Surg Gynec Obstet 132: 259–262

50. Hessler C, Schnyder P, Ozzello L 1979 Hamartoma of the breast: diagnostic observation of 16 cases. Radiology 126: 95–98

51. Linell F, Ostberg G, Soderstrom J et al. 1979 Breast hamartomas. An important entity in mammary pathology. Virchow's Arch (A) Anat Pathol 383: 253–264

52. Fisher C J, Hanby A M, Robinson L et al. 1992 Mammary hamartoma – a review of 35 cases. Histopathology 20: 99–106

53. Daya D, Trus T, D'Souza T J et al. 1995 Hamartoma of the breast, an underrecognized breast lesion. A clinicopathologic and radiographic study of 25 cases. Am J Clin Pathol 103: 685–689

54. Powell C M, Cranor M L, Rosen P P 1995 Pseudoangiomatous stromal hyperplasia (PASH): a mammary stromal tumor with myofibroblastic differentiation. Am J Surg Pathol 19: 270–277

55. Spalding J E 1945 Adenolipoma and lipoma of the breast. Guys Hosp Rep 94: 80–84

56. Müller J 1838 Uber den feinern Bau und die Formen der krankhaften Geschwulste. Reimer, Berlin, p 54–60

57. World Health Organization 1981 International histological classification of tumours. Histologic types of breast tumours. World Health Organization, Geneva

58. Moffat C J, Pinder S E, Dixon A R et al. 1995 Phyllodes tumours of the breast: a clinicopathological review of 32 cases. Histopathology 27: 205–218

59. Pietruska M, Barnes L 1978 Cytosarcoma phyllodes. A clinico-pathologic analysis of 42 cases. Cancer 41: 1974–1983

60. Page D L, Anderson T J (eds) 1987 Radial scars and complex sclerosing lesions. In: Diagnostic pathology of the breast. Churchill Livingstone, Edinburgh, p 89–103

61. Grove A, Kirstensen L D 1986 Intraductal carcinoma within a phyllodes tumour of the breast – a case report. Tumori 72: 187–190

62. Knudsen P J T, Ostergaard J 1987 Cystosarcoma phylloides with lobular and ductal carcinoma in situ. Arch Pathol Lab Med 111: 873–875

63. Leong A S-Y, Meredith D J 1980 Tubular carcinoma developing within a recurring cystosarcoma phyllodes of the breast. Cancer 46: 1863–1867

64. Grimes M M 1992 Cystosarcoma phyllodes of the breast: histologic features, flow cytometry analysis and clinical correlations. Mod Pathol 5: 232–239

65. Hart W R, Bauer R C, Oberman H A 1978 Cystosarcoma phyllodes. A clinicopathologic study of twenty six hypercellular periductal stromal tumours of the breast. Am J Clin Pathol 70: 211–216

66. Hajdu S I, Espinosa M H, Robbins G F 1976 Recurrent cystosarcoma phylloides. A clinicopathologic study of 32 cases. Cancer 38: 1402–1406

67. Ward R M, Evans H L 1986 Cystosarcoma phyllodes. A clinicopathologic study of 26 cases. Cancer 58: 2282–2289

68. Murad T M, Hines J R, Beal J et al. 1988 Histopathological and clinical correlations of cystosarcoma phyllodes. Arch Path Lab Med 112: 752–756

69. Cohn-Cedermark G, Rutqvist L E, Rosendahl I et al. 1991 Prognostic factors in cystosarcoma phyllodes. A clinicopathologic study of 77 patients. Cancer 68: 2017–2022

70. Tan P H, Jayabaskar T, Chuah K L et al. 2005 Phyllodes tumor of the breast: the role of pathologic parameters. Am J Clin Pathol 123: 529–540

71. Norris H J, Taylor H B 1967 Relationship of histologic features to behaviour of cystosarcoma phyllodes. Analysis of ninety four cases. Cancer 20: 2090–2099

72. Dunne B, Lee A H, Pinder S E et al. 2003 An immunohistochemical study of metaplastic spindle cell carcinoma, phyllodes tumor and fibromatosis of the breast. Hum Pathol 34(10): 1009–1015

73. Nielsen B B 1987 Adenosis tumour of the breast – a clinico-pathological investigation of 27 cases. Histopathology 11: 1259–1275

74. Haagensen C D, Lane N, Lattes R 1972 Neoplastic proliferation of the epithelium of the mammary lobules. Surg Clin N Am 52: 497–524

75. Linell F, Ljunberg O 1984 Atlas of breast pathology. Copenhagen, Munksgaard

76. Roebuck E J 1990 Clinical radiology of the breast. Heinemann Medical, Oxford

77. Taylor H B, Norris H J 1967 Epithelial invasion of nerves in benign diseases of the breast. Cancer 20: 2245–2249

78. Davies J D 1973 Neural invasion in benign mammary dysplasia. J Pathol 109: 225–231

79. Eusebi V, Azzopardi J G 1976 Vascular infiltration in benign breast disease. J Pathol 118: 9–16

80. Simpson J F, Page D L, Dupont W D 1990 Apocrine adenosis – a mimic of mammary carcinoma. Surg Pathol 3: 289–299

81. Carter D J, Rosen P P 1991 Atypical apocrine metaplasia in sclerosing lesions of the breast: a study of 51 patients. Mod Pathol 4: 1–5

82. Jensen R A, Page D L, Dupont W D et al. 1989 Invasive breast cancer risk in women with sclerosing adenosis. Cancer 64: 1977–1983

83. Rasbridge S A, Gillett C E, Sampson S A et al. 1993 Epithelial (E-) and placental (P-) cadherin cell adhesion molecule expression in breast carcinoma. J Pathol 169: 245–250

84. Clement P B, Azzopardi J G 1983 Microglandular adenosis of the breast – a lesion simulating tubular carcinoma. Histopathology 7: 169–180

85. Rosen P P 1983 Microglandular adenosis: a benign lesion simulating invasive mammary carcinoma. Am J Surg Pathol 7: 137–144

86. Tavassoli F A, Norris H J 1983 Microglandular adenosis of the breast. A clinicopathologic study of 11 cases with ultrastructural observations. Am J Surg Pathol 7: 731–737

87. Millis R R, Eusebi V 1995 Microglandular adenosis of the breast. Adv Anat Pathol 2: 10–18

88. Fechner R E, Mills S E 1990 Breast pathology. Benign proliferations, atypias and in situ carcinomas. ASCP Press, Chicago

89. Rosenblum M K, Purrazzella R, Rosen P P 1986 Is microglandular adenosis a precancerous disease? A study of carcinoma arising therein. Am J Surg Pathol 10: 237–245

90. James B A, Cranor M L, Rosen P P 1993 Carcinoma of the breast arising in microglandular adenosis. Am J Clin Pathol 100: 507–513

91. Parl F F, Richardson L D 1983 The histologic and biologic spectrum of tubular carcinoma of the breast. Hum Pathol 14: 694–698

92. Kay S 1985 Microglandular adenosis of the female mammary gland: Study of a case with ultrastructural observations. Hum Pathol 16: 637–640

93. Diaz N M, McDevitt R W, Wick M R 1991 Microglandular adenosis of the breast. An immunohistochemical comparison with tubular carcinoma. Arch Pathol Lab Med 115: 578–582

94. Elston C W, Ellis I O, Goulding H 1998 Sclerosing lesions. In Elston CW, Ellis IO (eds) Systemic pathology. The breast. Churchill Livingstone, London, p 501–513

95. Kiaer H, Nielson B, Paulsen S et al. 1984 Adenomyoepithelial adenosis and low grade malignant adenomyoepithelioma of the breast. Virchow's Arch A Pathol Ann 405: 55–67

96. Semb C 1928 Fibroadenomatosis cystic mammae. Acta Chirurg 10: 1–148

97. Fenoglio C, Lattes R 1974 Sclerosing papillary proliferations in the female breast. A benign lesion often mistaken for carcinoma. Cancer 33: 691–700

98. Tremblay G, Buell R H, Seemayer T A 1987 Elastosis in benign sclerosing ductal proliferations of the female breast. Am J Surg Pathol 1: 1155–1158

99. Hamperl H 1975 Strahlige Narben und Obliterierende mastopathie. Beitr pathol histol mamma. XI Virchow's Arch (A) 369: 55–68

100. Andersen J A, Carter D, Linell F 1986 A symposium on sclerosing duct lesions of the breast. Pathol Annu 21: 145–179

101. Linell F, Ljunberg O, Andersson I 1980 Breast carcinoma. Aspects of early stages, progression and related problems. Acta Path Microbiol Scand 272: 1–233

102. Welling S R, Alpers G E 1984 Subgross pathologic features and incidence of radial scars in the breast. Hum Pathol 15: 475–479

103. Nielsen M, Thomson J L, Primdahl S et al. 1987 Breast cancer and atypia among young and middle-aged women: a study of 110 medicolegal autopsies. Br J Cancer 56: 814–819

104. Nielsen M, Christensen L, Andersen J 1987 Radial scars in women with breast cancer. Cancer 59: 1019–1025

105. Ciatto S, Morrone D, Catarzi S et al. 1993 Radial scars of the breast: review of 38 consecutive mammographic diagnoses. Radiology 187(3): 757–760

106. Sloane J P, Mayers M M 1993 Carcinoma and atypical hyperplasia in radial scars and complex sclerosing lesions importance of lesion size and patient age. Histopathology 23: 225–231

107. Carter D 1977 Intraduct papillary tumors of the breast. A study of 78 cases. Cancer 59: 1689–1692

108. Ohuchi N, Abe R, Kasai M 1984 Possible cancerous change of intraductal papillomas of the breast. Cancer 54: 605–611

109. Papotti M, Gugliotta P, Ghiringhello B et al. 1984 Association of breast carcinoma and multiple intraductal papillomas: an histological and immunohistochemical investigation. Histopathology 8: 963–975

110. Jones D B 1955 Florid papillomatosis of the nipple ducts. Cancer 8: 315–319

111. Doctor V M, Sirsat M V 1971 Florid papillomatosis (adenoma) and other benign tumours of the nipple and areola. Br J Cancer 25: 1–9

112. Bhagavan B S, Patchefsy A, Koss L G 1973 Florid subareolar duct papillomatosis (nipple adenoma) and mammary carcinoma: report of three cases. Hum Pathol 4: 289–295

113. Rosen P P, Caicco J A 1986 Florid papillomatosis of the nipple. A study of 51 patients, including nine with mammary carcinoma. Am J Surg Pathol 10: 87–101

114. Handley R S, Thackray A C 1962 Adenoma of the nipple. Br J Cancer 16: 187–194

115. Ahmed A 1992 Diagnostic breast pathology. Churchill Livingstone, Edinburgh

116. Perzin K H, Lattes R 1972 Papillary adenoma of the nipple (florid papillomatosis, adenoma, adenomatosis). A clinico-pathologic study. Cancer 29: 996–1009

117. Gudjonsdottir A, Hagerstrand I, Ostberg G 1971 Adenoma of the nipple with carcinomatous development. Acta Pathol Microbiol Scand (A) 79: 676–680

118. Azzopardi J G, Salm R 1984 Ductal adenoma of the breast: a lesion which can mimic carcinoma. J Pathol 144: 15–23

119. Lammie G A, Millis R R 1989 Ductal adenoma of the breast – a review of fifteen cases. Hum Pathol 20: 903–908

120. Gusterson B A, Sloane J P, Middwood C et al. 1987 Ductal adenoma of the breast – a lesion exhibiting a myoepithelial/epithelial phenotype. Histopathology 11: 103–110

121. Schnitt S J, Vincent-Salomon A 2003 Columnar cell lesions of the breast. Adv Anat Pathol 10: 113–124

122. Fraser J L, Raza S, Chomy K et al. 1998 Columnar alteration with prominent apical snouts and secretions. A spectrum of changes frequently present in breast biopsies performed for microcalcifications. Am J Surg Pathol 22: 1521–1527

123. Oyama T, Maluf H, Koerner F 1999 Atypical cystic lobules: an early stage in the formation of low-grade ductal carcinoma in situ. Virchow's Arch 435: 413–421

124. Goldstein N S, O'Malley B A 1997 Cancerization of small ectatic ducts of the breast by ductal carcinoma in situ cells with apocrine snouts. A lesion associated with tubular carcinoma. Am J Clin Pathol 107: 561–566

125. Schnitt S J, Connolly J L, Tavassoli F A et al. 1992 Interobserver reproducibility in the diagnosis of ductal proliferative breast lesions using standardized criteria. Am J Surg Pathol 16: 1133–1143

126. Simpson P T, Gale T, Fulford L G et al. 2003 Pathology of atypical lobular hyerplasia and lobular carcinoma in situ. Breast Cancer Res 5: 258–262

127. Schnitt S J 2003 Flat epithelial atypia – classification, pathologic features and clinical significance. Breast Cancer Res 5: 263–268

128. Tavassoli F A, Hoefler H, Rosai J et al. 2003 Intraductal proliferative lesions. In: Tavassoli FA, Devilee P (eds) Pathology and genetics of tumours of the breast and female genital organs. IARC Press, Lyon

129. Dupont W D, Page D L 1989 Relative risk of breast cancer varies with time since diagnosis of atypical hyperplasia. Hum Pathol 20: 723–725

130. Page D L 1986 Cancer risk assessment in benign breast biopsies. Hum Pathol 17: 871–874

131. Page D L, Vander Zwaag R, Rogers L W et al. 1978 Relation between component parts of fibrocystic disease complex and breast cancer. J Natl Cancer Inst 61: 1055–1063

132. Hutter R V P 1985 Goodbye to "fibrocystic disease". New Eng J Med 312: 179–181

133. Dupont W D, Page D L 1985 Risk factors for breast cancer in women with proliferative breast disease. New Eng J Med 312: 146–151

134. Page D L, Dupont W E, Rogers L W 1986 Breast cancer risk of lobular-based hyperplasia after biopsy: "ductal" pattern lesions. Cancer Detec Prev 9: 441–448

135. Page D L, Dupont W D, Rogers L W et al. 1985 Atypical hyperplastic lesions of the female breast. A long-term follow-up study. Cancer 55: 2698–2708

136. Page D L, Rogers L W 1992 Combined histologic and cytologic criteria for the diagnosis of mammary atypical hyperplasia. Hum Pathol 23: 1095–1097

137. Tavassoli F A, Norris H J 1990 A comparison of the results of long term follow-up for atypical intraductal hyperplasia and intraductal hyperplasia of the breast. Cancer 65: 518–529

138. Rosai J 1991 Borderline epithelial lesions of the breast. Am J Surg Pathol 15: 209–221

139. Sloane J P, Amendoeira I, Apostolikas N et al. 1999 Consistency achieved by 23 European pathologists from 12 countries in diagnosing breast disease and reporting prognostic features of carcinomas. Virchow's Arch 434(1): 3–10

140. Lakhani S R, Collins N, Stratton M R et al. 1995 Atypical ductal hyperplasia of the breast: clonal proliferation with loss of heterozygosity on chromosomes 16q and 17p. J Clin Pathol 48: 611–615

141. Bocker W, Decker T, Ruhnke M et al. 1997 Ductal hyperplasia and ductal carcinoma in situ. Pathologie 18(1): 3–18

142. Bocker W, Moll R, Poremba C et al. 2002 Common adult stem cells in the human breast give rise to glandular and myoepithelial cell lineages: a new cell biological concept. Lab Invest 82: 737–746

143. Liberman L, Cohen M A, Dershaw D D et al. 1995 Atypical ductal hyperplasia diagnosed at stereotaxic core biopsy of breast lesions: an indication for surgical biopsy. Am J Roentgenol 164: 1111–1113

144. Dahlstrom J E, Jain S, Sutton T et al. 1996 Diagnostic accuracy of stereotactic core biopsy in a mammographic breast cancer screening programme. Histopathology 28: 421–427

145. Darling M L, Smith D N, Lester S C et al. 2000 Atypical ductal hyperplasia and ductal carcinoma in situ as revealed by large-core needle breast biopsy: results of surgical excision. Am J Roentgenol 175: 1341–1346.

146. Page D L, Anderson T J 1987 Diagnostic histopathology of the breast. Churchill Livingstone, Edinburgh

147. O'Malley F P, Page D L, Nelson E H, et al. 1994 Ductal carcinoma in situ of the breast with apocrine cytology: definition of a borderline category. Hum Pathol 25: 164–168

148. Tavassoli F A, Norris H J 1994 Intraductal apocrine carcinoma: a clinicopathologic study of 37 cases. Mod Pathol 7: 813–818

149. Haagensen C D, Lane N, Lattes R et al. 1978 Lobular neoplasia (so called lobular carcinoma in situ) of the breast. Cancer 42: 737–769

150. Page D L, Kidd T E Jr, Dupont W D et al. 1991 Lobular neoplasia of the breast: higher risk for subsequent invasive cancer predicted by more extensive disease. Hum Pathol 22: 1232–1239

151. Fisher E R, Land S R, Fisher B et al. 2004 Pathologic findings from the National Surgical Adjuvant Breast and Bowel Project. Twelve year observations concerning lobular carcinoma in situ. Cancer 100: 238–244

152. Page D L, Schuyler P A, Dupont W D et al. 2003 Atypical lobular hyperplasia as a unilateral predictor of breast cancer risk: a retrospective cohort study. Lancet 361: 125–129

153. Rosen P P, Kosloff C, Leiberman P H et al. 1978 Lobular carcinoma in situ of the breast: detailed analysis of 99 patients with average follow up of 24 years. Am J Surg Pathol 2: 225–251

154. Frykberg E R, Santiago F, Betshill W L Jr et al. 1987 Lobular carcinoma in situ of the breast. Surg Gynecol and Obstet 164: 285–301

155. Lakhani S R, Collins N, Sloane J P et al. 1995 Loss of heterozygosity in lobular carcinoma in-situ of the breast. J Clin Pathol Clin Mol Pathol 48(2): M74–M78

156. Fisher B, Costandino J P, Wickerham D L et al. 1998 Tamoxifen for prevention of breast cancer: report of the national Surgical Adjuvant Breast and Bowel Project P-1 Study. J Natl Cancer Inst 90: 1371–1388

157. Sneige N, Wang J, Baker B A et al. 2002 Clinical, histopathologic, and biologic features of pleomorphic lobular (ductal-lobular) carcinoma in situ of the breast: a report of 24 cases. Mod Pathol 15(10): 1044–1050

158. Reis-Filho J S, Simpson P T, Jones C et al. 2005 Pleomorphic lobular carcinoma of the breast: role of comprehensive molecular pathology in characterization of an entity. J Pathol 207: 1–13.

159. Eusebi V, Betts C, Haagensen D E Jr et al. 1984 Apocrine differentiation in lobular carcinoma of the breast. A morphologic, immunologic and ultrastructural study. Hum Pathol 15: 134–140

160. Jacobs T W, Pliss N, Kouria G et al. 2001 Carcinomas in situ of the breast with indeterminate features: role of E-cadherin staining in categorization. Am J Surg Pathol 25: 229–236

161. Kerner H, Lichtig C 1986 Lobular cancerization: incidence and differential diagnosis with lobular carcinoma in-situ of breast. Histopathology 10: 621–629

162. Donegan W L, Redlich P N, Lang P J et al. 1998 Carcinoma of the breast in males. A multi-institutional survey. Cancer 83: 498–509

163. Geschickter C F, Lewis D 1938 Comedo carcinomas of the breast. Arch Surg 33: 225–244

164. Geschickter C F 1943 Diseases of the breast. Lippincott, Philadelphia, p 502–507

165. Page D L, Dupont W D, Rogers L W et al. 1982 Intraductal carcinoma of the breast: follow up after biopsy alone. Cancer 49: 751–758

166. Rosen P P, Braun D W Jr, Kinne D W 1980 The clinical significance of preinvasive breast carcinoma. Cancer 46: 919–925

167. Page D L, Dupont W D, Rogers L W et al. 1995 Continued local recurrence of carcinoma 15–25 years after a diagnosis of low grade ductal carcinoma in situ of the breast treated by biopsy. Cancer 76: 1197–1200

168. Lagios M D 1990 Duct carcinoma in situ: pathology and treatment. Surg Clin North Am 70: 853–871

169. Silverstein M J, Poller D N, Waisman J R et al. 1995 Prognostic classification of breast ductal carcinoma-in-situ. Lancet 345: 1154–1157

170. Silverstein M J, Lagios M D, Craig P H et al. 1996 A prognostic index for ductal carcinoma in situ of the breast. Cancer 77: 2267–2274

171. Fisher E R, Costandino J, Fisher B et al. 1995 Pathologic findings from the National Surgical Adjuvant Breast Project (NSABP) Protocol B-17. Intraductal carcinoma (ductal carcinoma in situ). The National Surgical Adjuvant Breast and Bowel Project Collaborating Investigators. Cancer 75: 1310–1319

172. Lagios M D, Margolin F R, Westdahl P R et al. 1989 Mammographically detected duct carcinoma in situ. Frequency of local recurrence following tylectomy and prognostic effect of nuclear grade on local recurrence. Cancer 63: 618–624

173. Bijker N, Peterse J L, Duchateau L et al. 2001 Risk factors for recurrence and metastasis after breast-conserving therapy for ductal carcinoma-in-situ: analysis of European Organisation for Research and Treatment of Cancer Trial 10853. J Clin Oncol 19: 2263–2271

174. Waldman F M, DeVries S, Chew K L et al. 2000 Chromosomal alterations in ductal carcinomas in situ and their in situ recurrences. J Natl Cancer Inst 92: 313–320

175. Fisher B, Costandino J, Redmond C et al. 1993 Lumpectomy compared with lumpectomy and radiation therapy for the treatment of intraductal breast cancer. N Engl J Med 328: 1581–1586

176. Ottensen G L, Graversen H P, Blichert-Toft M et al. 2000 Carcinoma in situ of the female breast. 10 year follow-up results of a prospective nationwide study. Breast Cancer Res Treat 62: 197–210.

177. Faverly D, Holland R, Burgers L 1992 Three dimensional imaging of mammary ductal carcinoma in situ. Virchow's Arch (A) Pathol Anat 421: 115–119

178. Holland R, Hendriks J H, Vebeek A L 1990 Extent, distribution, and mammographic/histological correlations of breast ductal carcinoma in situ. Lancet 335: 519–522

179. Smart C, Myers M, Gloecker L 1978 Implications from SEER data on breast cancer management. Cancer 41: 787–789

180. Andersson I, Aspegren K, Janzon L et al. 1988 Mammographic screening and mortality from breast cancer: the Malmo mammographic screening trial. Br Med J 297: 943–948

181. Gibbs N M 1985 Comparative study of the histopathology of breast cancer in a screened and unscreened population investigated by mammography. Histopathology 9: 1307–1318

182. Bettshill W L Jr, Rosen P P, Leiberman P H et al. 1978 Intraductal carcinoma. Long term follow up after treatment by biopsy alone. J Am Med Assoc 239: 1863–1867

183. Bellamy C O, McDonald C, Salter D M et al. 1993 Noninvasive ductal carcinoma of the breast: the relevance of histologic categorization. Hum Pathol 24: 16–23

184. Van Dongen, J A, Holland R, Peterse J L et al. 1992 Ductal carcinoma in situ of the breast – 2nd Eortc Consensus Meeting. Eur J Cancer 28(2–3): 626–629

185. Bagnall M J, Evans A J, Wilson A R et al. 2001 Predicting invasion in mammographically detected microcalcification. Clin Rad 56: 828–832

186. Holland R, Peterse J L, Millis R R et al. 1994 Ductal carcinoma in situ: a proposal for a new classification. Semin Diagn Pathol 11(3): 167–180

187. Badve S, A'Hern R P, Ward A M et al. 1998 A long-term comparative study of the ability of five classifications of ductal carcinoma in situ of breast to predict local recurrence after surgical excision. Hum Pathol 29: 915–923

188. European Commission Working Group on Breast Screening Pathology 1998 Consistency achieved by 23 European pathologists in categorizing ductal carcinoma in situ of the breast using five classifications. Hum Pathol 29: 1056–1062

189. Bobrow L G, Happerfield L C, Gregory W M et al. 1994 The classification of ductal carcinoma in situ and its association with biological markers. Semin Diagn Pathol 11(3): 199–207

190. Poller D N, Roberts E C, Bell J A et al. 1993 p53 protein expression in mammary ductal carcinoma in situ: relationship to immunohistochemical expression of estrogen receptor and c-erbB-2 protein. Hum Pathol 24: 463–468

191. Allred D C, Clark G M, Molina R et al. 1992 Overexpression of HER-2/neu and its relationship with other prognostic factors change during the progression of in situ to invasive breast cancer. Hum Pathol 23: 974–979

192. Gupta S K, Douglas-Jones A G, Johnson R C et al. 1997 Classification of DCIS of the breast in relation to biological markers: p53, E-cadherin and MIB-1 expression. J Pathol 181(SS): A22

193. Buerger H, Otterbach F, Simon R et al. 1999 Comparative genomic hydridization of ductal carcinoma in situ of the breast – evicence of multiple genetic pathways. J Pathol 187: 396–402

194. Lampejo O T, Barnes D M, Smith P et al. 1994 Evaluation of infiltrating ductal carcinoma with a DCIS component: correlation of the histologic type of the in situ component with grade of the infiltrating component. Semin Diagn Pathol 11: 215–222

195. Millis R R, Barnes D M, Lampejo O T et al. 1998 Tumour grade does not change between primary and recurrent mammary carcinoma. Eur J Cancer 34: 548–553

196. Millis R R, Pinder S E, Ryder K et al. 2004 Grade of recurrent in situ and invasive carcinoma following treatment of pure ductal carcinoma in situ of the breast. Br J Cancer 90: 1538–1542

197. Leal C, Henrique R, Monteiro P et al. 2001 Apocrine ductal carcinoma in situ of the breast: histologic classification and expression of biologic markers. Hum Pathol 32: 487–493

198. Cross A S, Azzopardi J G, Krausz T et al. 1985 A morphological and immunocytochemical study of a distinctive variant of ductal carcinoma in-situ of the breast. Histopathology 9: 21–37

199. Fisher E R, Brown R 1985 Intraductal signet ring carcinoma: a hitherto undescribed form of intraductal carcinoma of the breast. Cancer 55: 2533–2537

200. Rosen P P, Scott M 1984 Cystic hypersecretory duct carcinoma of the breast. Am J Surg Pathol 8: 31–41

201. Guerry P, Erlandson R A, Rosen P P 1988 Cystic hypersecretory hyperplasia and cystic hypersecretory duct carcinoma of the breast. Pathology, therapy, and follow-up of 39 patients. Cancer 61: 1611–1620

202. Faverly D R, Burgers L, Bult P et al. 1994 Three dimensional imaging of mammary ductal carcinoma in situ: clinical implications. Semin Diagn Pathol 11: 193–198

203. Sibbering D M, Blamey R W 1997 Nottingham experience. In: Silverstein MJ (ed) Ductal carcinoma in situ of the breast. Williams and Wilkins, Baltimore, p 367–372

204. Silverstein M J, Lagios M D, Groshen S et al. 1999 The influence of margin width on local control of ductal carcinoma in situ of the breast. N Eng J Med 340: 1455–1461

205. Fisher B, Dignam J, Wolmark N 1999 Tamoxifen in the treatment of intraductal breast cancer: national Surgical Adjuvant Breast and Bowel Project B-24 randomised control trial. Lancet 353: 1993–2000

206. UK Coordinating Committee on Cancer Research Ductal Carcinoma in situ Working Party 2003 Radiotherapy and tamoxifen in women with completely excised ductal carcinoma in situ of the breast in the UK, Australia, and New Zealand: randomised controlled trial. Lancet 362: 95–102

207. Hitchcock A, Topham S, Bell J et al. 1992 Routine diagnosis of mammary Paget's disease. A modern approach. Am J Surg Pathol 16: 58–61

208. Carter D, Orr S L, Merino M J 1983 Intracystic papillary carcinoma of the breast. After mastectomy, radiotherapy or excisional biopsy alone. Cancer 52: 14–19

209. Maluf H M, Koerner F C 1995 Solid papillary carcinoma of the breast. Am J Surg Pathol 19: 1237–1244

210. Kraus F T, Neubecker R D 1962 The differential diagnosis of papillary tumours of the breast. Cancer 15: 444–455

211. Intra M, Rotmensz B, Viale G et al. 2004 Clinicopathologic characteristics of 143 patients with synchronous bilateral invasive breast carcinomas treated in a single institution. Cancer 101: 905–912

212. Page D L, Anderson T J, Sakamoto G 1987 Infiltrating carcinoma: major histological types. In: Page DL, Anderson TJ (eds) Diagnostic histopathology of the breast. WB Saunders, London, p 193–235

213. Ellis I O, Galea M, Broughton N et al. 1992 Pathological prognostic factors in breast cancer. II Histological type. Relationships with survival in a large study with long-term follow-up. Histopathology 20: 479–489

214. Pinder S E, Elston C W, Ellis I O 1998 Invasive carcinoma – usual histological types. In: Systemic pathology – the breast. Elston CW, Ellis IO (eds) Churchill Livingstone, London, p 283–338

215. Perou C M, Sorlie T, Eisen M B et al. 2000 Molecular portraits of human breast tumours. Nature 406: 747–752

216. Sorlie T, Tibshirani R, Parker J et al. 2003 Repeated observation of breast tumor subtypes in independent gene expression data sets. Proc Natl Acad Sci USA 100: 8418–8423

217. van't Veer L J, Dai H, van de Vijver M J et al. 2002 Gene expression profiling predicts clinical outcome of breast cancer. Nature 415: 530–536

218. van de Vijver M J, He Y D, van't Veer L J et al. 2002 A gene-expression signature as a predictor of survival in breast cancer. N Engl J Med 347: 1999–2009

219. Wang Y, Klijn J G, Zhang Y, et al. 2005 Gene-expression profiles to predict distant metastasis of lymph-node-negative primary breast cancer. Lancet 365: 671–679

220. Lakhani S R, Gusterson B A, Jacquemier J et al. 2000 The pathology of familial breast cancer: histological features of cancers in families not attributable to mutations in BRCA1 or BRCA2. Clin Cancer Res 6(3): 782–789

221. Fisher E R, Gregorio R M, Fisher B 1975 The pathology of invasive breast cancer. A syllabus derived from findings of the national surgical adjuvant breast cancer project (protocol no. 4). Cancer 36: 1–85

222. Rosen P P 1979 The pathological classification of human mammary carcinoma: past, present and future. Ann Clin Lab Sci 9: 144–156

223. Sakamoto G, Sugano H, Hartmann W H et al (eds) 1981 Comparative pathological study of breast carcinoma among American and Japanese women. Plenum, New York, p 211–231

224. Giordano S H, Cohen D S, Buzdar A. 2004 Breast carcinoma in men. A population-based study. Cancer 101: 51–57

225. Miremadi A, Pinder S E, Lees A H S et al. 2002 Neuroendocrine differentiation and prognosis in breast adenocarcinoma. Histopathology 40: 215–222

226. Putti T C, Abd El Rehim D, Pinder S E et al 2005 Estrogen receptor-negative breast carcinomas: a review of morphology and immunophenotypical analysis. Mod Pathol 46: 26–35

227. Foote F W Jr, Stewart F W 1946 A histologic classification of carcinoma in the breast. Surgery 19: 74–99

228. Foote F W Jr, Stewart F W 1941 Lobular carcinoma in situ. A rare form of mammary cancer. Am J Pathol 7: 491–496

229. Wheeler J E, Enterline H T 1976 Lobular carcinoma of the breast in situ and infiltrating. Pathol Annu 11: 161–188

230. Dixon J M, Anderson T J, Page D L et al. 1982 Infiltrating lobular carcinoma of the breast. Histopathology 6: 149–161

231. Fechner R E 1975 Histological variants of infiltrating lobular carcinoma of the breast. Hum Pathol 6: 373–378

232. Martinez V, Azzopardi J 1979 Invasive carcinoma of the breast: incidence and variants. Histopathology 3: 467–488

233. Fisher E R, Gregorio R M, Redmond C et al. 1977 Tubulolobular invasive breast cancer: a variant of lobular invasive cancer. Hum Pathol 8: 679–683

234. Eusebi V, Magalhaes F, Azzopardi J G 1992 Pleomorphic lobular carcinoma of the breast: an aggressive tumour showing apocrine differentiation. Hum Pathol 23: 655–662

235. Weidner N, Semple J P 1992 Pleomorphic variant of invasive lobular carcinoma of the breast. Hum Pathol 23: 1167–1171

236. Moll R, Mitze M, Frixen U H et al. 1993 Differential loss of E-cadherin expression in infiltrating ductal and lobular breast carcinomas. Am J Pathol 143(6): 1731–1742

237. Rakha E A, Abd El-Rehim D M, Pinder S E et al. 2005 E-cadherin expression in invasive non-lobular carcinoma of the breast and its prognostic significance. Histopathology 46: 685–693

238. Cornford E J, Wilson A R M, Athanassiou E 1995 Mammographic features of invasive lobular and invasive ductal carcinoma of the breast: a comparative analysis. Br J Radiol 68: 450–453

239. Quincey C, Raitt N, Bell J et al. 1991 Intracytoplasmic lumina – a useful diagnostic feature of adenocarcinomas. Histopathology 19: 83–87

240. Wheeler D T, Tai L H, Bratthauer G L et al. 2004 Tubulolobular carcinoma of the breast: an analysis of 27 cases of a tumor with a hybrid morphology and immunoprofile. Am J Surg Pathol 28: 1587–1593

241. Green I, McCormick B, Cranor M et al. 1997 A comparative study of pure tubular and tubulolobular carcinoma of the breast. Am J Surg Pathol 21(6): 653–657

242. Page D L, Anderson T J (eds) 1987 Uncommon types of invasive carcinoma. In: Diagnostic histopathology of the breast. Churchill Livingstone, Edinburgh

243. Wahed A, Connelly J, Reese T 2002 E-cadherin expression in pleomorphic lobular carcinoma: an aid to differentiation from ductal carcinoma. Ann Diagn Pathol 6(6): 349–351

244. Palacios J, Sarrio D, Garcia-Macias M C 2003 Frequent E-cadherin gene inactivation by loss of heterozygosity in pleomorphic lobular carcinoma of the breast. Mod Pathol 16(7): 674–678

245. Middleton L P, Palacios D M, Bryant B R et al. 2000 Pleomorphic lobular carcinoma: morphology, immunohistochemistry and molecular analysis. Am J Surg Pathol 24: 1650–1656

246. Anderson T J, Lamb J, Donnan P et al. 1991 Comparative pathology of breast cancer in a randomised trial of screening. Br J Cancer 64: 108–113

247. Patchefsky A S, Shaber G S, Schwartz G F et al. 1977 The pathology of breast cancer detected by mass population screening. Cancer 40: 1659–1670

248. Rajakariar R, Walker R A 1995 Pathological and biological features of mammographically detected invasive breast carcinomas. Br J Cancer 71: 150–154

249. Cowan W K, Kelly P, Sawan A et al. 1997 The pathological and biological nature of screen-detected breast carcinomas: a morphological and immunohistochemical study. J Pathol 182: 29–35

250. Diab S G, Clark G M, Osborne C K et al. 1999 Tumor characteristics and clinical outcome of tubular and mucinous breast carcinomas. J Clin Oncol 17(5): 1442–1448

251. Sullivan T, Raad R A, Goldberg S et al. 2005 Tubular carcinoma of the breast: a retrospective analysis and review of the literature. Breast Cancer Res Treat 93: 199–205

252. Carstens P H, Huvos A G, Foote F W Jr et al. 1972 Tubular carcinoma of the breast: a clinicopathological study of 35 cases. Am J Clin Pathol 58: 231–238

253. Peters, G N, Wolff M, Haagenson C D 1981 Tubular carcinoma of the breast – clinical pathologic correlations on 100 cases. Ann Surg 193: 138–149

254. McDivitt R W, Boyce W, Gersell G 1982 Tubular carcinoma of the breast. Am J Surg Pathol 6: 401–411

255. Dixon J M, Page D L, Anderson T J et al. 1985 Long term survivors after breast cancer. Br J Surg 72: 445–448

256. Page D L, Dixon J M, Anderson T J et al. 1983 Invasive cribriform carcinoma of the breast. Histopathology 7: 525–536

257. Venable J G, Schwartz A M, Silverberg S G 1990 Infiltrating cribriform carcinoma of the breast: a distinctive clinicopathologic entity. Hum Pathol 21: 333–338

258. Holland R, Van Haelst U J G M 1984 Mammary carcinoma with osteoclast-like giant cells. Cancer 53: 1963–1973

259. Saout L, Leduc M, Suy-Beng P T et al. 1985 Présentation d'un nouveau cas de carcinoma mammaire cribriforme associé à une réaction histiocytaire giganto-cellulaire. Arch Anat Cytol Pathol 33: 58–61

260. Tavassoli F A, Norris H J 1986 Breast carcinoma with osteoclast-like giant cells. Arch Pathol Lab Med 110: 636–639

261. Rakha E A, Boyce R W, Abd El-Rehim D et al. 2005 Expression of mucins (MUC1, MUC2, MUC3, MUC4, MUC5AC and MUC6) and their prognostic significance in human breast cancer. Mod Pathol 18: 1295–1304

262. Clayton F 1986 Pure mucinous carcinomas of the breast: morphologic features and prognostic correlates. Hum Pathol 17: 34–39

263. Rasmussen B B, Rose C, Christensen J B 1987 Prognostic factors in primary mucinous breast carcinoma. Am J Clin Pathol 87: 155–160

264. Komaki K, Sakamoto G, Sugano H et al. 1988 Mucinous carcinoma of the breast in Japan. A prognostic analysis based on morphologic features. Cancer 61: 989–996

265. Maluf H M, Koerner F C 1994 Carcinomas of the breast with endocrine differentiation: a review. Virchow's Arch 425(5): 449–457

266. Sapino A, Righi L, Cassoni P et al. 2000 Expression of the neuroendocrine phenotype in carcinomas of the breast. Semin Diagn Pathol 17(2): 127–137

267. Tse G M, Ma T K, Chu W C et al. 2004 Neuroendocrine differentiation in pure type mammary mucinous carcinoma is associated with favorable histologic and immunohistochemical parameters. Mod Pathol 17(5): 568–572

268. Moore O S, Foote F W Jr 1949 The relatively favourable prognosis of medullary carcinoma of the breast. Cancer 2: 635–642

269. Ridolfi R L, Rosen P P, Port A et al. 1977 Medullary carcinoma of the breast – a clinicopathological study with a ten year follow up. Cancer 40: 1365–1385

270. Rapin V, Contesso G, Mouriesse H et al. 1988 Medullary breast carcinoma. A re-evaluation of 95 cases of breast carcinoma with inflammatory stroma. Cancer 61: 2503–2510

271. Wargotz E S, Silverberg S G 1988 Medullary carcinoma of the breast. A clinicopathologic study with appraisal of current diagnostic criteria. Hum Pathol 19: 1340–1346

272. Jensen M L, Kiaer H, Andersen J et al. 1997 Prognostic comparison of three classifications for medullary carcinomas of the breast. Histopathology 30: 523–532

273. Cutler S J, Black M M, Friedall G H et al. 1966 Prognostic factors in cancer of the female breast. Cancer 19: 75–82

274. Pedersen L, Holck S, Schiodt T 1988 Medullary carcinoma of the breast. Cancer Treat Rev 15: 53–63

275. Fisher E R, Kenny J P, Sass R et al. 1990 Medullary cancer of the breast revisited. Breast Cancer Res Treat 16: 215–229

276. Pederson L, Zedeler K, Holck S et al. 1991 Medullary carcinoma of the breast, proposal for a new simplified histopathological definition. Br J Cancer 63: 591–595

277. Rigaud C, Theobald S, Noël P 1993 Medullary carcinoma of the breast. A multicenter study of its diagnostic consistency. Arch Path Lab Med 117: 1005–1008

278. Gaffey M J, Mills S E, Frierson H F 1995 Medullary carcinoma of the breast: interobserver variability in histopathologic diagnosis. Mod Pathol 8: 31–38

279. Jacquemier J, Padovani L, Rabayrol L et al. 2005 Typical medullary breast carcinomas have a basal/myoepithelial phenotype. J Pathol 207: 260–268

280. Jones C, Ford E, Gillett C et al. 2004 Molecular cytogenetic identification of subgroups of grade III invasive ductal breast carcinomas with different clinical outcomes. Clin Cancer Res 10: 5988–5997

281. Fisher E R, Palekar A S, Redmond C et al. 1980 Pathologic findings from the National Surgical Adjuvant Breast Project (protocol no. 4). VI. Invasive papillary carcinoma. Am J Clin Pathol 73: 313–322

282. Ellis I O, Elston C W, Pinder S E 1998 Papillary lesions. In: Elston CW, Ellis IO (eds) Systemic pathology. The breast. Churchill Livingstone, London, p 133–146

283. Siriaunkgul S, Tavassoli F A 1993 Invasive micropapillary carcinoma of the breast. Mod Pathol 6: 660–662

284. Luna More S, Gonzalez B, Acedo C et al. 1994 Invasive micropapillary carcinoma of the breast. A new special type of invasive mammary carcinoma. Pathol Res Pract 190: 668–674

285. Pettinato G, Manivel C J, Panico L et al. 2004 Invasive micropapillary carcinoma of the breast. Clinicopathologic study of 62 cases of a poorly recognized variant with highly aggressive behavior. Am J Clin Pathol 121: 857–866

286. Peterse J L 1993 Breast carcinomas with an unexpected inside out growth pattern. Rotation of polarisation associated with angio-invasion. Pathol Res Pract 189: 780

287. Varga Z, Zhao J, Ohlschlegel C et al. 2004 Preferential Her-2/neu overexpression and/or amplification in aggressive histological subtypes of invasive breast cancer. Histopathology 44: 332–338

288. Lakhani S R, Jacquemier J, Sloane J P et al. 1998 Multifactorial analysis of differences between sporadic breast cancers and cancers involving BRCA1 and BRCA2 mutations. J Natl Cancer Inst 90(15): 1138–1145

289. Lakhani S R, Reis-Filho J S, Fulford L et al. 2005 Prediction of BRCA1 status in patients with breast cancer using estrogen receptor and basal phenotype. Clin Cancer Res 11(14): 5175–5180

290. Lakhani S R 1999 The pathology of hereditary breast cancer. Dis Markers 15(1-3): 113–114

291. Lakhani S R, Van de Vijver M J, Jacquemier J et al. 2002 The pathology of familial breast cancer: predictive value of immunohistochemical markers estrogen receptor, progesterone receptor, HER-2, and p53 in patients with mutations in BRCA1 and BRCA2. J Clin Oncol 20(9): 2310–2318

292. Sorlie T, Perou C M, Tibshirani R et al. 2001 Gene expression patterns of breast carcinomas distinguish tumor subclasses with clinical implications. Proc Natl Acad Sci USA 98(19): 10869–10874

293. Dairkee S H, Ljung B M, Smith H et al. 1987 Immunolocalization of a human basal epithelium specific keratin in benign and malignant breast disease. Breast Cancer Res Treat 10(1): 11–20

294. Heatley M, Maxwell P, Whiteside C et al. 1995 Cytokeratin intermediate filament expression in benign and malignant breast disease. J Clin Pathol 48(1): 26–32

295. Jones C, Nonni A V, Fulford L et al. 2001 CGH analysis of ductal carcinoma of the breast with basaloid/myoepithelial cell differentiation. Br J Cancer 85(3): 422–427

296. Tsuda H, Takarabe T, Hasegawa T et al. 1999 Myoepithelial differentiation in high-grade invasive ductal carcinomas with large central acellular zones. Hum Pathol 30(10): 1134–1139

297. Tsuda H, Takarabe T, Hasegawa F et al. 2000 Large, central acellular zones indicating myoepithelial tumor differentiation in high-grade invasive ductal carcinomas as markers of predisposition to lung and brain metastases. Am J Surg Pathol 24(2): 197–202

298. Jimenez R E, Wallis T, Visscher D W 2001 Centrally necrotizing carcinomas of the breast: a distinct histologic subtype with aggressive clinical behavior. Am J Surg Pathol 25(3): 331–337

299. Hedenfalk I, Duggan D, Chen Y et al. 2001 Gene-expression profiles in hereditary breast cancer. N Engl J Med 344(8): 539–548

299a. Bryan B B, Schnitt S J, Collins L C 2006 Ductal carcinoma in situ with basal-like phenotype: a possible precursor to invasive basal-like breast cancer. Mod Pathol 19: 617–621

300. Rakha E A, Putti T C, Abd El-Rehim D M et al. 2006 Breast carcinomas with basal and myoepithelial differentiation: a review of morphology and immunophenotypical analysis. J Pathol 208: 495–506

301. Abati A D, Kimmel M, Rosen P P 1990 Apocrine mammary carcinoma. A clinicopathologic study of 72 cases. Am J Clin Pathol 94: 371–377

302. Shin S J, DeLellis R A, Ying L et al. 2000 Small cell carcinoma of the breast. A clinicopathologic and immunohistochemical study of nine patients. Am J Surg Pathol 24: 1231–1238

303. McDivitt R W, Stewart F W 1966 Breast carcinoma in children. J Am Med Assoc 195: 388–390

304. Oberman H A 1980 Secretory carcinoma of the breast in adults. Am J Surg Pathol 4: 465–470

305. Rosen P P, Cranor M L 1991 Secretory carcinoma of the breast. Arch Pathol Lab Med 115: 141–144

306. Diallo R, Schaefer K-L, Bankfalvi A et al. 2003 Secretory carcinoma of the breast: a distinct variant of invasive ductal carcinoma assessed by comparative genomic hybridization and immunohistochemistry. Hum Pathol 34: 1299–1305

307. Tavassoli F A, Norris H J 1980 Secretory carcinoma of the breast. Cancer 45: 2404–2413

308. Eusebi V, Foschini M P 1998 Rare carcinomas of the breast. In: Elston CW, Ellis IO (eds) Systemic pathology. The breast. Churchill Livingstone, London, p. 339–364

309. Hasleton P S, Misch K A, Vasudev K S et al. 1978 Squamous carcinoma of the breast. J Clin Pathol 31: 116–124

310. Eggers J W, McChesney T 1984 Squamous cell carcinoma of the breast: a clinicopathologic analysis of eight cases and review of the literature. Hum Pathol 15: 526–531

311. Hennessy B T, Krishnamurthy S, Giordano S et al. 2005 Squamous cell carcinoma of the breast. J Clin Oncol 23: 7827–7835

312. Kaufman M W, Marti J R, Gallager H S et al. 1984 Carcinoma of the breast with pseudosarcomatous metaplasia. Cancer 53: 1908–1917

313. Tavassoli F A 1992 Classification of metaplastic carcinomas of the breast. Pathol Ann 27: 89–119

314. Khan H N, Wyld L, Dunne B et al. 2003 Spindle cell carcinoma of the breast: a case series of a rare histological subtype. Eur J Surg Oncol 29(7): 600–603

315. Wargotz E S, Deos P H, Norris H J 1989 Metaplastic carcinomas. II. Spindle cell carcinoma. Hum Pathol 20: 732–740

316. Wargotz E S, Norris H J 1989 Metaplastic carcinomas. III. Carcinosarcoma. Cancer 64: 1490–1499

317. Foschini M P, Dina R E, Eusebi V 1993 Sarcomatoid neoplasms of the breast: proposed definitions for biphasic and monophasic sarcomatoid mammary carcinomas. Semin Diagn Pathol 10: 128–136

318. Gobbi H, Simpson J F, Borowsky A et al. 1999 Metaplastic breast tumors with a dominant fibromatosis-like phenotype have a high risk of local recurrence. Cancer 85(10): 2170–2182

319. Sneige N, Yaziji H, Mandavilli S R et al. 2001 Low-grade (fibromatosis-like) spindle cell carcinoma of the breast. Am J Surg Pathol 25(8): 1009–1016

320. Davis W G, Hennessy B, Babiera G et al. 2005 Metaplastic sarcomatoid carcinoma of the breast with absent or minimal overt invasive carcinomatous component. A misnomer. Am J Surg Pathol 29: 1456–1463

321. Carter M R, Hornick J L, Lester S et al. 2006 Spindle cell (sarcomatoid) carcinoma of the breast: a clinicopathologic and immunohistochemical analysis of 29 cases. Am J Surg Pathol 30: 300–309

322. Wargotz E S, Norris H J 1989 Metaplastic carcinomas of the breast. I. Matrix-producing carcinoma. Hum Pathol 20: 628–635

323. Rosen P P, Ernsberger D 1987 Low grade adenosquamous carcinoma. A variant of metaplastic mammary carcinoma. Am J Surg Pathol 11: 351–358

324. Van Hoeven K H, Drudis T, Cranor M L et al. 1993 Low-grade adenosquamous carcinoma. A clinicopathologic study of 32 cases with ultrastructural study. Am J Surg Pathol 17: 248–258

325. Denley H, Pinder S E, Tan P H et al. 2000 Metaplastic carcinoma of the breast arising within complex sclerosing lesion: a report of five cases. Histopathology 36(3): 203–209

326. Rosen P P 2001 Rosen's breast pathology. 2nd edn. Lippincott Williams and Wilkins, Philadelphia

327. National Coordinating Group for Breast Screening Pathology 1995 Pathology Reporting in Breast Cancer Screening. 2 edn. NHS BSP Publications No 3.

328. Davies J D, Bogomoletz W M 1987 Examination of breast specimens. ACP Broadsheet

329. Ellis I O, Elston C W, Evans A J et al. 1998 Diagnostic techniques and examination of pathological specimens. In: Elston CW, Ellis IO (eds) Systemic pathology. The breast. Churchill Livingstone, London, p. 21–46

330. Elston C W, Ellis I O, Goulding H et al. 1998 Role of pathology in the prognosis and management of breast cancer. In: Elston CW, Ellis IO (eds) Systemic pathology. The breast. Churchill Livingstone, London, p. 385–433

331. Elston C W, Gresham G A, Rao G S et al. 1982 The Cancer Research Campaign (Kings/Cambridge) Trial for Early Breast Cancer – pathological aspects. Br J Cancer 45: 655–669

332. Fisher E R, Sass R, Fisher B 1984 Pathologic findings from the National Surgical adjuvant Project for breast cancers (protocol No 4) X Discriminants for tenth year treatment failure. Cancer 53: 712–723

333. Carter C L, Allen C, Henson D E 1989 Relation of tumour size, lymph node status, and survival in 24 270 breast cancer cases. Cancer 63: 181–187

334. Neville A M, Bettelheim R, Gelber R D et al. 1992 Predicting treatment responsiveness and prognosis in node-negative breast cancer. J Clin Oncol 10: 696–705

335. Haybittle J L, Blamey R W, Elston C W et al. 1982 A prognostic index in primary breast cancer. Br J Cancer 45: 361–366

336. Todd J H, Dowle C, Williams M R et al. 1987 Confirmation of a prognostic index in primary breast cancer. Br J Cancer 56: 489–492

337. Gallager H S, Martin J E 1971 An orientation to the concept of minimal carcinoma. Cancer 28: 1505–1507

338. Beahrs O H, Shapiro S, Smart C et al. 1979 Summary report of the Working Group to review the National Cancer Institute – American Cancer Society Breast Cancer Demonstration Detection projects. J Nat Cancer Inst 62: 641–709

339. Hartman W H 1984 Minimal breast cancer: an update. Cancer 53: 681–684

340. Bedwani R, Vana J, Rosner D et al. 1981 Management and survival of female patients with "minimal" breast cancer: as observed in the long-term and short-term surveys of the American College of Surgeons. Cancer 47: 2769–2778

341. Rosen P P, Groshen S 1990 Factors influencing survival and prognosis in early breast carcinoma (TINOMO-TININO). Assessment of 644 patients with median follow up of 19 years. Surg Clin N Am 70: 937–962

342. Tabar L, Duffy S W, Krusemo V B 1987 Detection method tumour size and node metastases in breast cancers diagnosed during a trial of breast cancer screening. Eur J Cancer Clin Oncol 23: 959–962

343. Frisell J, Eklund G, Hellstrom L et al. 1987 Analysis of interval breast carcinomas in a randomised screening trial in Stockholm. Br Cancer Res Treat 9: 219–225

344. Royal College of Radiologists 1997 Quality Assurance Guidelines for Radiologists. Revised January 1997. NHSBSP Publications no 15

345. Fisher B, Slack N H, Katryk D 1975 Ten year follow up results of patients with carcinoma of the breast in a cooperative clinical trial evaluating surgical adjuvant chemotherapy. Surg Gynecol Obstet 140: 528–534

346. Ferguson D J, Meier P, Karrison T et al. 1982 Staging of breast cancer and survival rates: an assessment based on 50 years of experience with radical mastectomy. J Am Med Assoc 248: 1337–1341

347. Nemoto T, Vana J, Bedwani R N 1980 Management and survival of female breast cancer: results of a national survey by the American College of Surgeons. Cancer 45: 2917–2924

348. Sobin L H, Wittekind C 2002 TNM classification of malignant tumors 6th edn. Wiley, New York

349. Schottenfeld D, Nash A G, Robbins G F et al. 1976 Ten year results of the treatment of primary operable breast carcinoma. Cancer 38: 1001–1007

350. Handley R F 1972 Observations and thoughts on carcinoma of the breast. Proc R Soc Med 65: 437–444

351. Blamey R W, Davies C J, Elston C W et al. 1979 Prognostic factors in breast cancer: the formation of a prognostic index. Clin Oncol 5: 227

352. Du Toit R S, Locker A P, Ellis I O et al. 1990 Evaluation of the prognostic value of triple node biopsy. Br J Surg 77: 163–167

353. Locker A P, Ellis I O, Morgan D A et al. 1989 Factors influencing local recurrence after excision and radiotherapy for primary breast cancer. Br J Surg 76: 890–894

354. Steele R J C, Forrest A P M, Gibson T 1985 The efficacy of lower axillary sampling in obtaining lymph node status in breast cancer: a controlled randomized trial. Br J Surg 72: 368–369

355. Chetty U, Jack W, Dillon P et al. 1997 Axillary surgery in patients with breast cancer being treated by breast conservation: a randomised trial of node sampling and axillary clearance. Breast 6: 226

356. O'Dwyer P J 1992 Editorial. Axillary dissection in primary breast cancer; the benefits of node clearance warrant reappraisal. Br Med J 302: 360–361

357. Cabanes P A, Salmon R J, Vilcoq J R et al. 1992 Value of axillary dissection in addition to lumpectomy and radiotherapy in early breast cancer. Lancet 339: 1245–1248

358. Huvos A G, Hutter R V P, Berg J W 1970 Significance of axillary macrometastases and micrometastases in mammary cancer. Ann Surg 173: 44

359. Fisher E R, Palekar A, Rockette H et al. 1978 Pathologic findings from the National Surgical Adjuvant Breast Project (protocol no 4). V. Significance of axillary nodal micro and macro metastases. Cancer 42: 2032–2038

360. Millis R R, Springall R, Lee A H et al. 2002 Occult axillary lymph node metastases are of no prognostic significance in breast cancer. Br J Cancer 86(3): 396–401

361. Trojani M, de Mascarel I, Coindre J M et al. 1987 Micrometastases to axillary lymph nodes from invasive lobular caricnoma of breast: Detection by immunohistochemistry and prognostic significance. Br J Cancer 56: 838–839

362. Wells C A, Heryet A, Brochier J et al. 1984 The immunohistochemical detection of axillary micrometatases in breast cancer. Br J Cancer 50: 193–197

363. Springall R J, Ryina E R C, Millis R R 1990 Incidence and significance of micrometastases in axillary lymph nodes detected by immunohistochemical techniques. J Path 160: 174A

364. International Breast Cancer Study Group 1990 Prognostic importance of occult axillary lymph node micrometastases from breast cancers. Lancet 335: 1565–1568

365. Galea M, Athanassiou E, Bell J et al. 1991 Occult regional lymph node metastases from breast carcinoma: immunohistological detection with antibodies CAM 5.2 and NCRC-11. J Pathol 165: 221–227

366. McGuckin M A, Cummings M C, Walsh M D et al. 1996 Occult axillary node metastases in breast cancer: their detection and prognostic significance. Br J Cancer 73: 88–95

367. Dowlatshahi K, Fan M, Snider H C et al. 1997 Lymph node micrometastases from breast carcinoma: reviewing the dilemma. Cancer 80(7): 1188–1197

368. Cserni G 2004 A model for determining the optimum histology of sentinel lymph nodes in breast cancer. J Clin Pathol 57(5): 467–471

369. Cserni G, Bianchi S, Boecker W et al. 2005 Improving the reproducibility of diagnosing micrometastases and isolated tumor cells. Cancer 103(2): 358–367

370. Mambo N C, Gallager H S 1977 Carcinoma of the breast. The prognostic significance of extranodal extension of axillary disease. Cancer 39: 2280–2285

371. Cascinelli N, Greco M, Bufalino R et al. 1987 Prognosis of breast cancer with axillary node metastases after surgical treatment only. Eur J Cancer Clin Oncol 23: 795–799

372. Fisher E R, Gregorio R M, Redmond C et al. 1976 Pathologic findings from the National Surgical Adjuvant Breast Project (protocol no 4). III. The significance of extranodal extension of axillary metastases. Am J Clin Pathol 65: 439–444

373. Hartveit F 1984 Paranodal tumour in breast cancer: extranodal extension versus vascular spread. J Pathol 144: 253–256

374. Donegan W L, Stine S B, Samter T G 1993 Implications of extracapsular nodal metastases for treatment and prognosis of breast cancer. Cancer 72: 778–782

375. Morton D L, Wen D R, Wong J H et al. 1992 Technical details of intraoperative lymphatic mapping for early stage melanoma. Arch Surg 127(4): 392–399

376. Giuliano A E, Dale P S, Turner R R et al. 1995 Improved axillary staging of breast cancer with sentinel lymphadenectomy. Ann Surg 222(3): 394–399; discussion 399–401

377. Turner R R, Ollila D W, Krasne D L et al. 1997 Histopathologic validation of the sentinel lymph node hypothesis for breast carcinoma. Ann Surg 226(3): 271–276

378. Czerniecki B J, Scheff A M, Callans L S et al. 1999 Immunohistochemistry with pancytokeratins improves the sensitivity of sentinel lymph node biopsy in patients with breast carcinoma. Cancer 85(5): 1098–1103

379. Sabel M S, Zhang P, Barnwell J M et al. 2001 Accuracy of sentinel node biopsy in predicting nodal status in patients with breast carcinoma. J Surg Oncol 77(4): 243–246

380. Stitzenberg K B, Calvo B F, Iacocca M V et al. 2002 Cytokeratin immunohistochemical validation of the sentinel node hypothesis in patients with breast cancer. Am J Clin Pathol 117(5): 729–737

381. Cserni G, Amendoeira I, Apostolikas N et al. 2003 Pathological work-up of sentinel lymph nodes in breast cancer. Review of current data to be considered for the formulation of guidelines. Eur J Cancer 39(12): 1654–1667

382. Cserni G 2002 Complete sectioning of axillary sentinel nodes in patients with breast cancer. Analysis of two different step sectioning and immunohistochemistry protocols in 246 patients. J Clin Pathol 55(12): 926–931

383. Torrenga H, Rahusen F D, Meijer S et al. 2001 Sentinel node investigation in breast cancer: detailed analysis of the yield from step sectioning and immunohistochemistry. J Clin Pathol 54(7): 550–552

384. Dowlatshahi K, Fan M, Anderson J M et al. 2001 Occult metastases in sentinel nodes of 200 patients with operable breast cancer. Ann Surg Oncol 8(8): 675–681

385. Cooper H S, Patchefsky A S, Krall R A 1978 Tubular carcinoma of the breast. Cancer 42: 2334–2342

386. Carstens P H, Greenberg R A, Francis D et al. 1985 Tubular carcinoma of the breast. A long term follow up. Histopathology 9: 271–280

387. Lee B J, Hauser H, Pack G T 1934 Gelatinous carcinoma of the breast. Surg Gynecol Obstet 59: 841–850

388. Bloom H J C, Richardson W W, Fields J R 1970 Host resistance and survival carcinoma of the breast: a study of 104 cases of medullary carcinoma in a series of 1411 cases of breast cancer followed for 20 years. Br Med J 3: 181–188

389. Dawson P, Ferguson D J, Karrison T 1982 The pathologic findings of breast cancer in patients surviving 25 years after radical mastectomy. Cancer 50: 2131–2138

390. Richardson W W 1956 Medullary carcinoma of the breast. A distinctive tumour type with a relatively good prognosis following radical mastectomy. Br J Cancer 10: 415–423

391. Pereira H, Pinder S E, Sibbering D M 1995 Pathological prognostic factors in breast cancer. IV: Should you be a typer or a grader? A comparative study of two histological prognostic features in operable breast carcinoma. Histopathology 27: 219–226

392. Ellis I O 1991 Practical application of determinants of cell behaviour. Br Med Bull 42: 324–342

393. Domagala W, Markiewski M, Kubiak R et al. 1993 Immunohistochemical profile of invasive lobular carcinoma of the breast: predominantly vimentin and p53 protein negative, cathepsin D and oestrogen receptor positive. Virchow's Arch A Pathol Anat Histopathol 423: 497–502

394. Harris M, Khan M K 1984 Phyllodes tumour and stromal sarcoma of the breast: an ultrastructural comparison. Histopathology 8: 315–330

395. Lamovec J, Bracko M 1991 Metastatic pattern of infiltrating lobular carcinoma of the breast: an autopsy study. J Surg Oncol 48: 28–33

396. Breast Cancer Linkage Consortium 1997 Pathology of familial breast cancer: differences between breast cancer in carriers of BRCA1 or BRCA2 mutations and sporadic cases. Lancet 349: 1505–1510

397. Marcus J N, Watson P, Page D L et al. 1996 Hereditary breast cancer. Pathobiology, prognosis and BRCA1 and BRCA2 gene linkage. Cancer 77: 697–709

398. Greenhough R B 1925 Varying degrees of malignancy in cancer of the breast. J Cancer Res 9: 452–463

399. Patey D H, Scarff R W 1928 The position of histology in the prognosis of carcinoma of the breast. Lancet i: 801–804

400. Bloom H J G, Richardson W W 1957 Histological grading and prognosis in breast cancer. Br J Cancer 11: 359–377

401. Elston C W 1987 Grading of invasive carcinoma of the breast. In: Page DL, Anderson T (eds) Diagnostic histopathology of the breast. Churchill Livingstone, Edinburgh, p 300–311

402. Contesso G, Mouriesse H, Friedman S et al. 1987 The importance of histologic grade in long-term prognosis of breast cancer: a study of 1010 patients, uniformly treated at the Institut Gustave-Roussy. J Clin Oncol 5: 1378–1386

403. Elston C W, Ellis I O 1991 Pathological prognostic factors in breast cancer. I. The value of histological grade in breast cancer: experience from a large study with long term follow up. Histopathology 19: 403–410

404. Black M M, Barclay T H C, Hankey B F 1975 Prognosis in breast cancer utilising histologic characteristics of the primary tumour. Cancer 36: 2048–2055

405. Hartveit F 1971 Prognostic typing in breast cancer. Br Med J 4: 253–257

406. Le Doussal V, Tubiana-Hulin M, Friedman S et al. 1989 Prognostic value of histologic grade nuclear components of Scarff Bloom Richardson (SBR). An improved score modification based on a multivariate analysis of 1262 invasive ductal breast carcinomas. Cancer 64: 1914–1921

407. Bloom H J G 1950 Prognosis in carcinoma of the breast. Br J Cancer 4: 259–288

408. Bloom H J G 1950 Further studies on prognosis of breast carcinoma. Br J Cancer 4: 347–367

409. Scarff R W, Torloni H 1968 Histological typing of breast tumours (International histological classification of tumours, no 2). World Health. Organization, Geneva

410. Stenkvist B, Westman-Naeser S, Vegelius J et al. 1979 Analysis of reproducibility of subjective grading systems for breast carcinoma. J Clin Pathol 32: 979–985

411. Gilchrist K W, Kalish L, Gould V E et al. 1985 Interobserver reproducibility of histopathological features in stage II breast cancer. An ECPG study. Breast Cancer Res Treat 5: 3–10

412. Hopton D S, Thorogood J, Clayden A D et al. 1989 Observer variation in histological grading of breast cancer. Eur J Surg Oncol 15: 21–23

413. Theissig F, Kunze K D, Haroske G et al. 1990 Histological grading of breast cancer – interobserver, reproducibility and prognostic significance. Pathol Res Pract 186: 732–736

414. Ellis I O, Broughton N, Elston C W et al 1987 The relationship of histological type to survival and oestrogen receptor status in primary operable breast carcinoma. J Pathol 152: 219A (abstract)

415. Ellis P, Whitehead R 1981 Mitosis counting – a need for reappraisal. Hum Pathol 12: 3–4

416. Quinn C M, Wright N A 1990 The clinical assessment of proliferation and growth in human tumours: evaluation of methods and applications as prognostic variables. J Pathol 160: 93–102

417. Mann R, Elston C W, Hunter S et al. 1985 Evaluation of mitotic activity as a component of histological grade and its contribution to prognosis in primary breast carcinoma. J Pathol 146: 271A

418. Dalton L W, Page D L, Dupont W D 1994 Histologic grading of breast carcinoma: a reproducibility study. Cancer 73: 2765–2770

419. Frierson H F Jr, Wolber R A, Berean K W et al. 1995 Interobserver reproducibility of the Nottingham modification of the Bloom and Richardson histological grading scheme for infiltrating ductal carcinoma. Am J Clin Pathol 103: 195–198

420. Robbins P, Pinder S, de Klerk N et al. 1995 Histological grading of breast carcinomas. A study of interobserver agreement. Hum Pathol 26: 873–879

421. Connolly J L, Fechner R E, Kempson R L et al. 1996 Recommendations for the reporting of breast carcinoma. Hum Pathol 27: 220–224

422. Page D L, Ellis I O, Elston C W 1995 Histologic grading of breast cancer. Let's do it. Am J Clin Pathol 103: 123–124

423. Lee A K, Delellis R A, Silverman M L et al. 1986 Lymphatic and blood vessel invasion in breast carcinoma: a useful prognostic indicator? Hum Pathol 17: 984–987

424. Sears H F, Janus C, Levy W et al. 1982 Breast cancer without axillary metastases. Are there subpopulations. Cancer 50: 1820–1827

425. Dawson P J, Karrison T, Ferguson D J 1986 Histological features associated with long-term survival in breast cancer. Hum Pathol 17: 1015–1021

426. Bettelheim R, Penman H G, Thornton-Jones H et al. 1984 Prognostic significance of peritumoral vascular invasion in breast cancer. Br J Cancer 50: 771–777

427. Roses D F, Bell D A, Flotte T J et al. 1982 Pathologic predictors of recurrence in stage I (TIN0M0) breast cancer. Am J Clin Path 78: 817–820

428. Nime F A, Rosen P P, Thaler H T et al. 1977 Prognostic significance of tumour emboli in intramammary lymphatics in patients with mammary carcinoma. Am J Surg Pathol 1: 25–30

429. Nealon T F Jr, Nkongho A, Grossi C E et al. 1981 Treatment of early cancer of the breast (T1N0M0 and T2N0M0) on the basis of histological characteristics. Surgery 89: 279–289

430. Rosen P P 1983 Tumour emboli in intramammary lymphatics in breast carcinoma: pathological criteria for diagnosis and clinical significance. Pathol Annu 18: 215–232

431. Pinder S E, Ellis I O, Galea M et al. 1994 Pathological prognostic factors in breast cancer. III. Vascular invasion: relationship with recurrence and survival in a large series with long-term follow-up. Histopathology 24: 41–47

432. Örbo A, Stalsberg H, Kunde D 1990 Topographic criteria in the diagnosis of tumor emboli in intramammary lymphatics. Cancer 66: 972–977

433. Bettelheim R, Mitchell D, Gusterson B A 1984 Immunocytochemistry in the identification of vascular invasion in breast cancer. J Clin Pathol 37: 364–366

434. Martin S A, Perez-Reyes N, Mendelsohn G 1987 Angioinvasion in breast carcinoma: an immunohistochemical study of factor VIII-related antigen. Cancer 59: 1918–1922

435. Lee A K C, DeLellis R A, Wolffe H J 1986 Intramammary lymphatic invasion in breast carcinomas. Evaluation using ABH isoantigens as endothelial markers. Am J Surg Pathol 10: 589–594

436. Ordonez N G, Brooks T, Thompson S et al. 1987 Use of *Ulex Europeus* agglutinin I in the identification of lymphatic and blood vessel invasion in previously stained microscopic slides. Am J Surg Pathol 11: 543–550

437. Saigo P E, Rosen P P 1987 The application of immunohistochemical stains to identify endothelial-lined channels in mammary carcinoma. Cancer 59: 51–54

438. Gilchrist K W, Gould V E, Hirschl S et al. 1982 Interobserver variation in the identification of breast carcinoma in intramammary lymphatics. Hum Pathol 13: 170–172

439. Cote R J, Rosen P P 1988 Monoclonal antibodies detect occult breast carcinoma metatases in the bone marrow of patients with early stage disease. Am J Surg Pathol 12: 333–340

440. Rosen P P, Saigo P E, Braun D W Jr et al. 1981 Predictors of recurrence in stage I (T1N0M0) breast carcinoma. Ann Surg 193: 15–25

441. Rosen P P, Saigo P E, Braun D W Jr et al. 1982 Occult axillary lymph node metastases from breast cancers with intramammary lymphatic tumour emboli. Am J Surg Path 6: 639–641

442. O'Rourke S, Galea M H, Morgan D et al. 1994 An audit of local recurrence after simple mastectomy. Br J Surg 81: 386–389

443. Page D L, Anderson T J, Connolly J et al. 1987 Miscellaneous features of carcinoma. In: Page DL, Anderson TJ (eds) Diagnostic histopathology of the breast. Churchill Livingstone, Edinburgh, p 51–61

444. Carter D, Pipkin R D, Shepard R H et al. 1978 Relationship of necrosis and tumour border to lymph node metastases and 10 year survival in carcinoma of the breast. Surg Pathol 2: 39–46

445. Parham D M, Robertson A J, Brown R A 1988 Morphometric analysis of breast carcinoma: association with survival. J Clin Pathol 45: 517–520

446. Parham D M, Hagen N, Brown R A 1992 Simplified method of grading primary carcinomas of the breast. J Clin Pathol 45: 517–520

447. Underwood J C 1972 A morphometric analysis of human breast carcinoma. Br J Cancer 26: 234–237

448. Sistrunk W E, MacCarty W C 1922 Life expectancy following radical amputation for carcinoma of the breast – a clinical and pathological study of 218 cases. Ann Surg 75: 61–69

449. Black M M, Prescott R, Bers K et al. 1983 Tumour cellularity, oestrogen receptors and prognosis in breast cancer. Clin Oncol 9: 311–318

450. Parfrey N A, Doyle C T 1985 Elastosis in benign and malignant breast disease. Hum Pathol 16: 674–676

451. Shivas A A, Douglas J G 1972 The prognostic significance of elastosis in breast carcinoma. J Roy Coll Surg Edinb 17: 315–320

452. Masters J R, Millis R R, King R J et al. 1979 Elastosis and response to endocrine therapy in human breast cancer. Br J Cancer 39: 536–539

453. Robertson A J, Brown R A, Cree I A et al. 1981 Prognostic value of measurement of elastosis in breast carcinoma. J Clin Path 34: 738–743

454. Rasmussen B B, Pedersen B V, Thorpe S M et al. 1985 Elastosis in relation to prognosis in primary breast carcinoma. Cancer Res 45: 1428–1430

455. Giri D D, Lonsdale R N, Dangerfield V J et al. 1987 Clinicopathological significance of intratumoral variations in elastosis grades and the oestrogen receptor status of human breast cacinomas. J Pathol 151: 297–303

456. Silverberg S G, Chitale A R 1973 Assessment of the significance of the proportion of intraductal and infiltrating tumor growth in ductal carcinoma of the breast. Cancer 32: 830–837

457. Matsukuma A, Enjoji M, Toyoshima S 1991 Ductal carcinoma of the breast. An analysis of the proportion of intraductal and invasive components. Pathol Res Prac 187: 62–67

458. Millis R R, Thynne G S J 1975 In situ intraduct carcinoma of the breast: a long-term follow up study. Br J Surg 62: 957–962

459. Van Dongen J A, Fentiman I S, Harris J R et al. 1989 In situ breast cancer: the EORTC consensus meeting. Lancet ii: 25–27

460. Schnitt S J, Connolly J L, Harris J R 1984 Pathologic predictors of early local recurrence in stage I and stage II breast cancer treated by primary radiation therapy. Cancer 53: 1049–1057

461. Fourquet A, Campana F, Zafrani B et al. 1989 Prognostic factors of breast recurrence in the conservation management of early breast cancer: a 25 year follow up. Int J Radiation Oncol Biol Phys 17: 719–725

462. Jacquemier J, Kurtz J M, Amalric R et al. 1990 An assessment of extensive intraductal component as a risk factor for local recurrence after breast-conserving therapy. Br J Cancer 61: 873–876

463. Gage I, Schnitt S J, Nixon A J et al. 1996 Pathologic margin involvement and the risk of recurrence in patients treated with breast-conserving therapy. Cancer 78: 1921–1928

464. Clark G M 1994 Do we really need prognostic factors for breast cancer? Br Cancer Res Treat 30: 117–126

465. Page D L 1991 Prognosis and breast cancer. Recognition of lethal and favorable prognostic types. Am J Surg Pathol 15: 334–349

466. Gui G P, Wells C A, Browne P D et al. 1995 Integrin expression in primary breast cancer and its relation to axillary nodal status. Surgery 117: 102–108

467. Harris A L 1994 What is the biological, prognostic, and therapeutic role of the EGF receptor in human breast cancer? Br Cancer Res Treat 29: 1–2

468. Robertson J F, Bates K, Pearson D et al. 1992 Comparison of two oestrogen receptor assays in the prediction of the clinical course of patients with advanced breast cancer. Br J Cancer 65: 727–730

469. Barbareschi M 1996 Prognostic value of the immunohistochemical expression of p53 in breast carcinomas. A review of the literature involving over 9000 patients. Appl Immunohistochem 4: 106–116

470. Lovekin C, Ellis I O, Locker A et al. 1991 C-erbB-2 oncoprotein in primary and advanced breast cancer. Br J Cancer 63: 439–443

471. Veronese S M, Gambacorta M, Gottardi O et al. 1993 Proliferation index as a prognostic marker in breast cancer. Cancer 71: 3926–3931

472. Pinder S, Wencyk P, Sibbering D M et al. 1995 Assessment of the new proliferation marker MIB1 in breast carcinoma using image analysis: Associations with other prognostic factors and survival. Br J Cancer 71: 146–149

473. Robertson J F, Ellis I O, Pearson D et al. 1994 Biological factors of prognostic significance in locally advanced breast cancer. Br Cancer Res Treat 29: 259–264

474. Parker M G 1991 Nuclear hormone receptors. Academic Press, London

475. Jensen E V, Jacobson H I 1962 Buyers guide to the mechanism of oestrogen action. Recent Prog Horm Res 18: 387

476. NIH consensus development conference on steroid receptors in breast cancer 1980 Cancer 46: 2759–2963

477. Greene G L, Nolan C, Engler J P et al. 1980 Monoclonal antibodies to human estrogen receptor. Proc Natl Acad Sci USA 77: 5115–5119

478. Jensen E V, Greene G L, De Sombre E R 1986 The estrogen-receptor immunoassay in the prognosis and treatment of breast cancer. Lab Manager 24: 25–42

479. King W J, Greene G L 1984 Monoclonal antibodies localise oestrogen receptor in nuclei of target cells. Nature 307: 745–747

480. McCarty K S Jr, Miller L S, Cox E B et al. 1985 Estrogen receptor analyses: correlation of biochemical and immunohistochemical methods using monoclonal antireceptor antibodies. Arch Pathol Lab Med 109: 716–721

481. Pertschuk L P, Eisenberg K B, Carter A C et al. 1985 Immunohistologic localization of estrogen receptors in breast cancer with monoclonal antibodies. Cancer 55: 1513–1518

482. Gaskell D J, Hawkins R A, Tesdale A L et al. 1992 The differing predictive values of oestrogen receptor assays for large breast cancers. Postgrad Med J 68: 900–903

483. McClelland R A, Berger U, Miller L S et al. 1986 Immunocytochemical assay for estrogen receptor in patients with breast cancer. Relationship to biochemical assay and to outcome of therapy. J Clin Oncol 4: 1171–1176

484. Seymour L, Meyer K, Esser J et al. 1990 Estimation of ER and PR by immunocytochemistry in breast cancer. Comparison with radioligand binding methods. Am J Clin Pathol 94: S35–40

485. Anderson J, Orntoft T, Skovgaard Poulson H 1986 Semiquantitive oestrogen receptor assay in formalin-fixed paraffin sections of human breast cancer tissue using monoclonal antibodies. Br J Cancer 53: 691–694

486. De Rosa C M, Ozzello L, Greene G L et al. 1987 Immunostaining of oestrogen receptor in paraffin sections of breast carcinoma using monoclonal antibody D753P: effects of fixation. Am J Surg Pathol 11: 943–950

487. Jackson D P, Payne J, Bell S et al. 1990 Extraction of DNA from exfoliative cytology specimens and its suitability for analysis and the polymerase chain reaction. Cytopathology 1: 87–96

488. Paterson D A, Reid C P, Anderson T J et al. 1990 Assessment of oestrogen receptor content of breast carcinoma by immunohistochemical techniques on fixed and frozen tissue and by chemical ligand binding assay. J Clin Pathol 43: 46–51

489. Snead D J, Bell J A, Dixon A R et al. 1993 Methodology of immunohistochemical detection of oestrogen receptor in human breast carcinoma in formalin fixed paraffin embedded tissue: a comparison with frozen section morphology. Histopathology 23: 233–238

490. Goulding H, Pinder S, Cannon P et al. 1995 A new method for the assessment of oestrogen receptor status on routine formalin-fixed tissue samples. Hum Pathol 26: 291–294

491. Hawkins R A, Sangster K, Tesdale A et al. 1988 The cytochemical detection of oestrogen receptors in fine needle aspirates of breast cancer: correlation with biochemical assay and prediction of response to endocrine therapy. Br J Cancer 58: 77–80

492. Poulson H S, Jensen J, Hermansen C 1981 Human breast cancer: heterogeneity of estrogen binding sites. Cancer 43: 1791

493. Chiu K Y 1987 Use of microwave for rapid immunoperoxidase staining of paraffin sections. Med Lab Sci 44: 3–5

494. Shi S R, Key M E, Kalra K L 1991 Antigen retrieval in formalin-fixed, paraffin embedded tissues: an enhancement method for immunohistochemical staining based on microwave oven heating of tissue sections. J Histochem Cytochem 39: 741–748

495. Cuevas E C, Bateman A C, Wilkins B S et al. 1994 Microwave antigen retrieval in immunocytochemistry: a study of 80 antibodies. J Clin Pathol 47: 448–452

496. Barnes D M, Millis R R 1995 Oestrogen receptors: the history, the relevance and the methods of evaluation. In: Kirkham N, Lemoine NR (eds) Progress in pathology. Churchill Livingstone, Edinburgh, p 89–114

497. Harvey J M, Clark G M, Osborne C K et al. 1999 Estrogen receptor status by immunohistochemistry is superior to the ligand binding assay for predicting response to adjuvant endocrine therapy in breast cancer. J Clin Oncol 17: 1474–1481

498. Fisher E R, Anderson S, Dean S et al. 2005 Solving the dilemma of the immunohistochemical and other methods used for scoring estrogen receptor and progesterone receptor in patients with invasive breast carcinoma. Cancer 103: 164–173

499. Cobleigh M A, Vogel C L, Tripathy D et al. 1998 Efficacy and safety of Herceptin as a single agent in 222 women with HER2 overexpression who relapsed following chemotherapy for metastatic breast cancer. ASCO, Los Angeles

500. Slamon D, Leyland-Jones B, Shak S et al. 2001 Concurrent administration of anti-HER2 monochonal antibody and first-line chemotherapy for HER2-overexpressing metastatic breast cancer. A phase III multinational randomized controlled trial. N Engl J Med 344: 783–792

501. Piccart-Gebhardt M J, Proctor M, Leyland-Jones M et al. 2005 Trastuzumab after adjuvant chemotherapy in HER2-positive breast cancer. N Eng J Med 353: 1659–1672

502. Ellis I O, Bartlett J, Dowsett M et al. 2004 Best practice no 176: updated recommendations for HER2 testing in the UK. J Clin Pathol 57(3): 233–237

503. Paik S, Bryant J, Tan-Chiu E et al. 2002 Real-world performance of HER2 testing – National Surgical Adjuvant Breast and Bowel Project experience. J Natl Cancer Inst 94(11): 852–854

504. Roche P C, Suman V J, Jenkins R B et al. 2002 Concordance between local and central laboratory HER2 testing in the breast intergroup trial N9831. J Natl Cancer Inst 94(11): 855–857

505. Rhodes A, Jasani B, Anderson E et al. 2002 Evaluation of HER-2/neu immunohistochemical assay sensitivity and scoring on formalin-fixed and paraffin-processed cell lines and breast tumors: a comparative study involving results from laboratories in 21 countries. Am J Clin Pathol 118(3): 408–417

506. Dowsett M, Bartlett J, Ellis I O et al. 2003 Correlation between immunohistochemistry (HercepTest) and fluorescence in situ hybridization (FISH) for HER-2 in 426 breast carcinomas from 37 centres. J Pathol 199(4): 418–423

507. Lal P, Salazar P A, Hudis C A et al. 2004 HER-2 testing in breast cancer using immunohistochemical analysis and fluorescence in-situ hybridization. A single institution experience of 2279 cases and comparison of dual-color and single-color scoring. Am J Clin Pathol 121: 631–636

508. Rhodes A, Jasani B, Couturier J et al. 2002 A formalin-fixed, paraffin-processed cell line standard for quality control of immunohistochemical assay of HER-2/neu expression in breast cancer. Am J Clin Pathol 117(1): 81–89

509. Watters A D, Bartlett J M 2002 Fluorescence in situ hybridization in paraffin tissue sections: pretreatment protocol. Mol Biotechnol 21(3): 217–220

510. Galea M H, Blamey R W, Elston C E et al. 1992 The Nottingham Prognostic Index in primary breast cancer. Br Cancer Res Treat 22: 207–219

511. Brown J M, Benson E A, Jones M 1993 Confirmation of a long-term prognostic index in breast cancer. Breast 2: 144–147

512. Balslev I, Axelsson C K, Zedeler K et al. 1994 The Nottingham Prognostic Index applied to 9149 patients from the studies of the Danish Breast Cancer Cooperative Group (DBCG). Br Cancer Res Treat 32: 281–290

513. Clark G M 1992 Integrating prognostic factors. Br Cancer Res Treat 22: 187–191

514. Miller W R, Ellis I O, Sainsbury J R et al. 1994 Prognostic factors. ABC of breast diseases. Br Med J 309: 1573–1576

515. Kennedy S, Merino M J, Swain S M et al. 1990 The effects of hormonal and chemotherapy on tumoral and non neoplastic breast tissue. Hum Pathol 21: 192–198

516. Longacre T A, Bartow S A 1986 A correlative study of human breast and endometrium in the menstrual cycle. Am J Surg Pathol 10: 382–393

517. Vogel P M, Georgiade N G, Fetter B F et al. 1981 The correlation of histologic changes in the human breast with the menstrual cycle. Am J Pathol 104: 23–34

518. Tavassoli F A, Tienyeh I 1987 Lactational and clear cell changes of the breast in non lactating, non pregnant women. Am J Clin Pathol 87: 23–29

519. Schnitt S J, Connolly J L, Harris J R et al. 1984 Radiation-induced changes in the breast. Hum Pathol 15: 545–550

520. Rosen P P 1987 Adenomyoepithelioma of the breast. Hum Pathol 18: 1232–1237

521. Loose J H, Patchefsky A S, Hollander I J et al. 1992 Adenomyoepithelioma of the breast. A spectrum of biologic behaviour. Am J Surg Pathol 16: 868–876

522. Tavassoli F A 1991 Myoepithelial lesions of the breast. Myoepitheliosis, adenomyoepithelioma, and myoepithelial carcinoma. Am J Surg Pathol 15: 554–568

523. Eusebi V, Casadei G P, Bussolati G et al. 1987 Adenomyoepithelioma of the breast with a distinctive type of apocrine adenosis. Histopathology 11: 305–315

524. McLaren B K, Smith J, Shuyler P A et al. 2005 Adenomyoepithelioma. Clinical, histologic and immunohistochemical evaluation of a series of related lesions. Am J Surg Pathol 29: 1294–1299

525. Rasbridge S A, Millis R R 1998 Adenomyoepithelioma of the breast with malignant features. Virchow's Arch 432: 123–130

526. Donnell R M, Rosen P P, Lieberman P H et al. 1981 Angiosarcoma and other vascular tumours of the breast. Pathologic analysis as a guide to prognosis. Am J Surg Path 5: 629–642

527. Schurch W, Seemayer T A 1985 Malignant myoepithelioma (myoepithelial carcinoma) of the breast – an ultrastructural and immunohistochemical study. Ultrastructural Pathol 8: 1–11

528. Thorner P S, Kahn H J, Baumal R et al. 1986 Malignant myoepithelioma of the breast – an immunohistochemical study by light and electron microscopy. Cancer 57: 745–750

529. Moran C A, Suster S, Carter D 1990 Benign mixed tumours (pleomorphic adenomas) of the breast. Am J Surg Pathol 40: 913–921

530. Smith B H, Taylor H B 1968 The occurrence of bone and cartilage in mammary tumours. Am J Clin Pathol 51: 610–618

531. Van der Walt J D, Rohlova B 1982 Pleomorphic adenoma of the human breast. A report of a benign tumour closely mimicking a carcinoma clinically. Clin Oncol 8: 361–365

532. Arpino G, Clark G M, Mohsin S et al. 2002 Adenoid cystic carcinoma of the breast. Molecular markers, treatment and clinical outcome. Cancer 94: 2119–2127

533. Wells C A, Nicoll S, Ferguson D J P 1986 Adenoid cystic carcinoma of the breast: a case with axillary lymph node metastasis. Histopathology 10: 415–424

534. Anthony P P, James P D 1975 Adenoid cystic carcinoma of the breast: prevalence, diagnostic criteria and histogenesis. J Clin Pathol 28: 647–655

535. Quizilbash A H, Patterson M C, Oliveria K F 1977 Adenoid cystic carcinoma of the breast. Arch Pathol Lab Med 101: 302–306

536. Jaworski R C, Kneale K L, Smith R C 1983 Adenoid cystic carcinoma of the breast. Postgrad Med J 59: 48–51

537. Bennett A K, Mills S E, Wick M R 2003 Salivary-type neoplasms of the breast and lung. Semin Diagn Pathol 20: 279–304

538. Ro J Y, Silva E G, Gallager H S 1987 Adenoid cystic carcinoma of the breast. Hum Pathol 18: 1276–1281

539. Kleer C G, Oberman H A 1998 Adenoid cystic carcinoma of the breast. Value of histologic grading and proliferative activity. Am J Surg Pathol 22: 569–575

540. Roncaroli F, Lamovec J, Zidar A et al. 1996 Acinic cell-like carcinoma of the breast. Virchow's Arch 429(1): 69–74

541. Damiani S, Pasquinelli G, Lamovec J et al. 2000 Acinic cell carcinoma of the breast: an immunohistochemical and ultrastructural study. Virchow's Arch 437: 74–81

542. Schmitt F C, Ribiero C A, Alvarenga S et al. 2000 Primary acinic cell-like carcinoma of the breast – a variant with good prognosis? Histopathology 36(3): 286–289

543. Di Tommaso L, Foschini M P, Ragazzini T et al. 2004 Mucoepidermoid carcinoma of the breast. Virchow's Arch 444: 13–19

544. Patchefsky A S, Frauenhoffer C M, Krall R A et al. 1979 Low grade mucoepidermoid carcinoma of the breast. Arch Pathol Lab Med 103: 196–198

545. Fisher E R, Palekar A S, Gregorio R M et al. 1983 Mucoepidermoid and squamous carcinoma of the breast with reference to squamous metaplasia and giant cell tumours. Am J Surg Pathol 7: 15–27

546. Hanna W, Kahn H J 1985 Ultrastructural and immunohistochemical characteristics of mucoepidermoid carcinoma of the breast. Hum Pathol 16: 941–946

547. Covi J, Duong J D, Leffall L D 1981 High grade mucoepidermoid carcinoma of the breast. Arch Pathol Lab Med 105: 612–614

548. Rosen P P, Jozefczyk M A, Boram L H 1985 Vascular tumours of the breast. IV. Venous haemangioma. Am J Surg Path 9: 659–665

549. Josefczyk M A, Rosen P P 1985 Vascular tumours of the breast. II. Perilobular haemangiomas and haemangiomas. Am J Surg Path 9: 491–503

550. Rosen P P 1985 Vascular tumours of the breast. III. Angiomatosis. Am J Surg Pathol 9: 652–658

551. Rosen P P 1985 Vascular tumours of the breast. V. Non parenchymal haemangiomas of mammary subcutaneous tissues. Am J Surg Pathol 9: 723–729

552. Vuitch M F, Rosen P P, Erlandson R 1986 A pseudoangiomatous hyperplasia of mammary stroma. Hum Pathol 17: 185–191

553. Badve S, Sloane J P 1995 Pseudoangiomatous hyperplasia of the male breast. Histopathology 26: 463–466

554. Chen K T, Kirkegaard D D, Bocian J J 1980 Angiosarcoma of the breast. Cancer 46: 368–371

555. Merino M J, Carter D, Berman M 1983 Angiosarcoma of the breast. Am J Surg Pathol 7: 53–60

556. Rosen P P, Kimmel M, Ernsberger D 1988 Mammary angiosarcoma: the prognostic significance of tumour differentiation. Cancer 62: 2145–2152

557. Strobbe L J, Peterse H L, van Tinteren H et al. 1998 Angiosarcoma of the breast after conservation therapy for invasive cancer, the incidence and outcome. An unforeseen sequela. Br Cancer Res Treat 47: 101–109

558. Brenn T, Fletcher C D M 2005 Radiation-associated cutaneous atypical vascular lesions and angiosarcoma: clinicopathologic analysis of 42 cases. Am J Surg Pathol 29: 983–996

558a. Vorburger S A, Xing Y, Hunt K K et al. 2005 Angiosarcoma of the breast. Cancer 104: 2682–2688

559. Stewart R W, Treves N 1948 Lymphangiosarcoma in post mastectomy lymphoedema. A report of six cases in Elephantiasis Chirurgica. Cancer 1: 64–81

560. Martin M B, Kon N D, Kawamoto E H et al. 1984 Post mastectomy angiosarcoma. Am Surg 50(10): 541–545

561. Miettinen M, Lehto V P, Virtanen I 1983 Post mastectomy angiosarcoma (Stewart-Treves syndrome). Light microscopic, immunohistochemical and ultrastructural characteristics of two cases. Am J Surg Path 7: 329–339

562. McWilliam L J, Harris M 1985 Histogenesis of post mastectomy angiosarcoma – an ultrastructural study. Histopathology 9: 331–343

563. Wargotz E S, Weiss S W, Norris H J 1987 Myofibroblastoma of the breast. 16 cases of a distinctive benign mesenchymal tumour. Am J Surg Pathol 11: 493–502

564. McMenamin M E, DeSchryver K, Fletcher C D M 2000 Fibrous lesions of the breast: a review. Int J Surg Pathol 8: 99–108

565. McMenamin M E, Fletcher C D M. 2001 Mammary-type myofibroblastoma of soft tissue: a tumor closely related to spindle cell lipoma. Am J Surg Pathol 25: 1022–1029

566. Magro G, Michal M, Vasquez E, Bisceqlia M 2000 Lipomatous myofibroblastoma: a potential diagnostic pitfall in the spectrum of the spindle cell lesions of the breast. Virchows Arch 437: 540–544

567. Lee A H, Sworn M J, Theaker J M et al. 1993 Myofibroblastoma of the breast: an immunohistochemical study. Histopathology 22: 75–78

568. Salomao D R, Crotty T B, Nascimento A G 1997 Myofibroblastoma and solitary fibrous tumor of the breast: Histopathological and immunohistochemical comparative study. Lab Invest 76: 126

569. Gump F E, Sternschein M J, Wolff M 1981 Fibromatosis of the breast. Surg Gynaecol Obstet 15: 57–60

570. Rosen P P, Ernsberger D 1989 Mammary fibromatosis. A benign spindle cell tumour with significant risk for local recurrence. Cancer 63: 1363–1369

571. Devouassoux-Shisheboran M, Schammel M D, Man Y G et al. 2000 Fibromatosis of the breast: age-correlated morphofunctional features of 33 cases. Arch Pathol Lab Med 124: 276–280

572. Matherne T H, Green A Jr, Tucker J A et al. 2004 Fibromatosis: the breast cancer imitator. South Med J 97: 1100–1103

573. Adeniran A, Al-Ahmadie H, Mahoney M C et al. 2004 Granular cell tumor of the breast: a series of 17 cases and review of the literature. Breast J 10(6): 528–531

574. Gibbons D, Leitch M, Coscia J et al. 2000 Fine needle aspiration cytology and histological findings of granular cell tumor of the breast: review of 19 cases with clinical/radiologic correlation. Breast J 6: 27–30

575. Fanburg-Smith J C, Meis-Kindblom J M, Fante R et al. 1998 Malignant granular cell tumor of soft tissue: diagnostic criteria and clinicopathologic correlation. Am J Surg Pathol 22: 779–794

576. Le B H, Boyer P J, Lewis J E et al. 2004 Granular cell tumor: immunohistochemical assessment of inhibin-a, protein gene product 9.5, S-100 protein, CD68, and Ki-67 proliferative index with clinical correlation. Arch Pathol Lab Med 128: 771–775

577. Mattia A R, Ferry J A, Harris N L 1993 Breast lymphoma. A B-cell spectrum including the low grade B-cell lymphoma of mucosa associated lymphoid tissue. Am J Surg Pathol 17: 574–587

578. Domchek S M, Hecht J L, Fleming M D et al. 2002 Lymphomas of the breast. Primary and secondary involvement. Cancer 94: 6–13

579. Toombs B D, Kalisher L 1997 Metastatic disease in the breast; clinical, pathologic and radiographic features. Am J Roentgenol 129: 673–676

580. Georgiannos S N, Aleong J C, Goode A W 2001 Secondary neoplasms of the breast. A survey of the 20th century. Cancer 92: 2259–2266

Index